KV-026-820

THE WEEKLY LAW REPORTS 1976

The House of Lords

The Privy Council

The Supreme Court

Ecclesiastical Courts

Restrictive Practices Court

and

Employment Appeal Tribunal

VOLUME 1

London

THE INCORPORATED COUNCIL OF LAW REPORTING FOR ENGLAND AND WALES

3 STONE BUILDINGS, LINCOLN'S INN, LONDON, WC2A 3XN

Published by the Incorporated Council of Law Reporting for England and Wales · 3 Stone Buildings, Lincoln's Inn, London, WC2A 3XN, and printed by The Eastern Press Ltd., London and Reading

THE INCORPORATED COUNCIL OF LAW REPORTING FOR ENGLAND AND WALES

EDITORS AND REPORTERS

*

Editor—C. J. Ellis, *Barrister-at-Law*

Assistant Editor—H. Jellie, *Barrister-at-Law*

*

REPORTERS

House of Lords

F. H. Cowper J. A. Griffiths

Privy Council

T. J. Moeran

Court of Appeal, Queen's Bench Division and Courts-Martial Appeal Court

M. M. Hill
L. Norman Williams
C. Noon
E. M. Wellwood
M. Gardner
J. Winch
A. H. Bray
H. Jellie
L. G. Stott

Chancery Division

Akhtar Razi T. C. C. Barkworth K. N. Busfield

Family Division

M. Bryn Davies

Employment Appeal Tribunal

J. Winch

Barristers-at-Law

HOUSE OF LORDS

Lord Chancellor: Lord Elwyn-Jones

Lords of Appeal in Ordinary

Lord Wilberforce
Lord Diplock
Viscount Dilhorne
Lord Simon of Glaisdale
Lord Kilbrandon
Lord Salmon
Lord Edmund-Davies
Lord Fraser of Tullybelton
Lord Russell of Killowen

COURT OF APPEAL

Lord Chancellor: Lord Elwyn-Jones

Lord Chief Justice of England: Lord Widgery

Master of the Rolls: Lord Denning

President of the Family Division: Sir George Gillespie Baker

Sir John Megaw
Sir Denys Burton Buckley
Sir David Arnold Scott Cairns
Sir Edward Blanshard Stamp
Sir John Frederick Eustace Stephenson
Sir Alan Stewart Orr
Sir Eustace Wentworth Roskill
Sir Frederick Horace Lawton
Sir Leslie George Scarman
Sir Arthur Evan James (died May 13, 1976)
Sir Roger Fray Greenwood Ormrod
Sir Patrick Reginald Evelyn Browne
Sir Geoffrey Dawson Lane
Sir Reginald William Goff
Sir Nigel Cyprian Bridge
Sir Sebag Shaw
Sir George Stanley Waller (appointed June 23, 1976)

CHANCERY DIVISION

Lord Chancellor: Lord Elwyn-Jones

Vice-Chancellor: Sir John Anthony Plowman (retired January 10, 1976)
Sir Robert Edgar Megarry (appointed January 11, 1976)

Sir John Patrick Graham
Sir Peter Harry Batson Woodroffe Foster
Sir John Norman Keates Whitford
Sir John Anson Brightman
Sir Ernest Irvine Goulding
Sir Sydney William Templeman
Sir Raymond Henry Walton
Sir Peter Raymond Oliver
Sir Michael John Fox
Sir Christopher John Slade

QUEEN'S BENCH DIVISION

Lord Chief Justice of England: LORD WIDGERY

Sir AUBREY MELFORD STEED STEVENSON
Sir GERALD ALFRED THESIGER
Sir BASIL NIELD
Sir BERNARD JOSEPH MAXWELL MACKENNA
Sir ALAN ABRAHAM MOCATTA
Sir JOHN THOMPSON
Sir HELENUS PATRICK JOSEPH MILMO
Sir JOSEPH DONALDSON CANTLEY
Sir GEORGE STANLEY WALLER
Sir HUGH EAMES PARK
Sir RALPH VINCENT CUSACK
Sir STEPHEN CHAPMAN
Sir JOHN RAMSAY WILLIS
Sir GRAHAM RUSSELL SWANWICK
Sir PATRICK MCCARTHY O'CONNOR
Sir JOHN FRANCIS DONALDSON
Sir JOHN ROBERTSON DUNN CRICHTON
Sir SAMUEL BURGESS RIDGWAY COOKE
Sir BERNARD CAULFIELD
Sir HILARY GWYNNE TALBOT
Sir EDWARD WALTER EVELEIGH
Sir WILLIAM LLOYD MARS-JONES
Sir RALPH KILNER BROWN
Sir PHILLIP WIEN
Sir PETER HENRY ROWLEY BRISTOW
Sir HUGH HARRY VALENTINE FORBES
Sir DESMOND JAMES CONRAD ACKNER
Sir WILLIAM HUGH GRIFFITHS
Sir TASKER WATKINS, V.C.
Sir ROBERT HUGH MAIS
Sir NEIL LAWSON
Sir DAVID POWELL CROOM-JOHNSON
Sir JOHN RAYMOND PHILLIPS
Sir LESLIE KENNETH EDWARD BOREHAM
Sir JOHN DOUGLAS MAY
Sir MICHAEL ROBERT EMANUEL KERR
Sir ALFRED WILLIAM MICHAEL DAVIES
Sir JOHN DEXTER STOCKER
Sir KENNETH GEORGE ILLTYD JONES
SIR PETER RICHARD PAIN
Sir KENNETH GRAHAM JUPP
Sir JOHN FRANCIS SCOTT COBB
Sir ROBERT LIONEL ARCHIBALD GOFF
Sir GORDON SLYNN (appointed June 10, 1976)

FAMILY DIVISION

President: Sir GEORGE GILLESPIE BAKER

Sir CHARLES WILLIAM STANLEY REES
Sir REGINALD WITHERS PAYNE
Sir NEVILLE MAJOR GINNER FAULKS
The HON. Sir JAMES ROUALEYN-HOVELL-THURLOW CUMMING-BRUCE
Sir JOHN BRINSMEAD LATEY
Dame ELIZABETH KATHLEEN LANE
Sir HENRY VIVIAN BRANDON, M.C.
Sir ROBIN HORACE WALFORD DUNN, M.C.
Sir WILLIAM ARTHUR BAGNALL (died October 21, 1976)
Sir ALFRED KENNETH HOLLINGS
Sir JOHN LEWIS ARNOLD
Sir CHARLES TREVOR REEVE
Sir FRANCIS BROOKS PURCHAS
Sir HAYDN TUDOR EVANS
Dame ROSE HEILBRON
Sir STEPHEN BROWN
Sir BRIAN DREX BUSH (appointed November 29, 1976)

ATTORNEY-GENERAL

SAM SILKIN, ESQ., Q.C.

SOLICITOR-GENERAL

PETER ARCHER, ESQ., Q.C.

CASES REPORTED

(Vol. 1)

PAGE

A

Aluminium Industrie Vaassen B.V. *v.* Romalpa Aluminium Ltd. - - - - - - 676
Annesley, Reg. *v.* - - - - 106
Anns *v.* Merton London Borough Council (pet. all.) - - - 1108
Appleby, Crowe *v.* - - - - 885
Arsenal Football Club Ltd. *v.* Ende (pet. all.) - - - 1107
Aslam, Carradine Properties Ltd. *v.* - - - - - - - 442
Atkins, Devis (W.) & Sons Ltd. *v.* 393
Atkinson, *Ex parte* - - - 1047
Attorney-General's Reference (No. 2 of 1975) - - - 710
Attorney-General's Reference (No. 3 of 1975) - - - 737

B

B.P. Exploration Co. (Libya) Ltd. *v.* Hunt - - - - - - 788
Barnsley Metropolitan Borough Council, *Ex parte* Hook, Reg. *v.* - - - - - - - - 1052
Barnsley Supplementary Benefits Appeal Tribunal, *Ex parte* Atkinson, Reg. *v.* - - - - 1047
Barrel Plating & Phosphating Co. Ltd. *v.* Danks - - - - 879
Barrett (George), Reg. *v.* - - 946
Bathampton Properties Ltd., *In re* 168
Beck *v.* Value Capital Ltd. (No. 2) (Note) - - - - - 572
Belfon, Reg. *v.* - - - - - 741
Bell, Pexton *v.* - - - - - 885
Beverley Bentinck Ltd., Stevenson *v.* - - - - - - - 483
Birkenhead Corpn., Harris *v.* - 279
Birmingham Justices, *Ex parte* Wyatt, Reg. *v.* - - - - 260
Blackburn, *Ex parte* - - - 550
Bloomsbury and Marylebone County Court, *Ex parte* Villerwest Ltd., Reg. *v.* - - - - 362
British Airways Board *v.* Taylor 13
British Railways Board, Customs and Excise Comrs. *v.* - - - 1036

PAGE

Bronze Investments Ltd. *v.* Tower Hamlets London Borough Council - - - - - 852
Brumby *v.* Milner - - 29, 1096
Bryce (John) (Contractors) Ltd., *Ex parte* - - - - - 517
Bullock, Inland Revenue Comrs. *v.* - - - - - - - - 1178
Burston Finance Ltd. *v.* Godfrey 719
Bushwall Properties Ltd. *v.* Vortex Properties Ltd. - - - 591

C

Campbell *v.* Edwards - - - 403
Carradine Properties Ltd. *v.* Aslam - - - - - - 442
Cato, Reg. *v.* - - - - - 110
Cawley *v.* Frost - - - - 1207
Central Bank of Nigeria, Trendtex Trading Corpn. *v.* - - - - 868
Central Electricity Generating Board *v.* Clwyd County Council 151
Chandler, Reg. *v.* - - - - 585
Charles, Reg. *v.* - - - - - 248
Chaudhry *v.* Chaudhry (Note) - 221
Chetwode (Lord) *v.* Inland Revenue Comrs. - - - - 310
Chief Immigration Officer, Heathrow Airport, *Ex parte* Salamat Bibi, Reg. *v.* - - - - - 979
City of London Polytechnic, Coulson *v.* - - - - - 834
Clarke (Richard) & Co. Ltd. *v.* Widnall - - - - - - 845
Clayton, Corner *v.* - - - - 800
Clwyd County Council, Central Electricity Generating Board *v.* 151
Comr. of Police of the Metropolis *v.* Curran - - - - - 87
Computer Time International Ltd., Emmerson *v.* - - - - 749
Corner *v.* Clayton - - - - 800
Coulson *v.* City of London Polytechnic - - - - - - 834
Cox *v.* Philips Industries Ltd. - 638
Criminal Injuries Compensation Board, *Ex parte* Tong, Reg. *v.* - - - - - - 47, 1237
Crowe *v.* Appleby - - - - 885

PAGE

Culhane, Murphy *v.* (pet. dis.) - 989
Curran, Comr. of Police of the Metropolis *v.* - - - - - 87
Curran, Reg. *v.* - - - - - 87
Customs and Excise Comrs. *v.* British Railways Board - - 1036
Customs and Excise Comrs., Esso Petroleum Co. Ltd. *v.* - - - 1
Customs and Excise Comrs., Trewby *v.* - - - - - 932

D

D.H.N. Food Distributors Ltd. *v.* Tower Hamlets London Borough Council - - - 852
D.H.N. Food Transport Ltd. *v.* Tower Hamlets London Borough Council - - - 852
Danks, Barrel Plating & Phosphating Co. Ltd. *v.* - - - - 879
Davis, Floor *v.* - - - - - 1167
Dawson (John) & Partners (Contractors) Ltd., Ferguson *v.* - 1213
Day *v.* Quick - - - - - 29
Ddin, Edwards *v.* - - - - 942
Debtor (No. 24 of 1971), *In re* A, *Ex parte* Marley *v.* Trustee of the Property of the Debtor 952
Department of Health and Social Security *v.* Envoy Farmers Ltd. - - - - - - 1018
Department of the Environment, London County Freehold and Leasehold Properties Ltd. *v.* - 1126
Department of the Environment, MEPC (Mayfair Properties) Ltd. *v.* - - - - - - 1126
Department of the Environment, Town Investments Ltd. *v.* - 1126
Derby & Co. Ltd. *v.* Larsson - 202
Devis (W.) & Sons Ltd. *v.* Atkins 393
Dixon *v.* Fitch's Garage Ltd. - 215
Dudley, Reg. *v.* - - - - - 110
Dugdale *v.* Kraft Foods Ltd. - 1288
Dunmore *v.* McGowan - - 1086
Dwyer *v.* Dwyer - - - - 176
Dynamics Corpn. of America, *In re* - - - - - - - 757

E

Eastwood, Seay *v.* - - - - 1117
Edwards, Campbell *v.* - - - 403
Edwards *v.* Ddin - - - 942

PAGE

Electronic Concepts Ltd., Société Française d'Applications Commerciales et Industrielles S.A.R.L. *v.* - - - - 51
Elliott *v.* Southwark London Borough Council - - - - 499
Emmerson *v.* Computer Time International Ltd. - - - - 749
Ende, Arsenal Football Club Ltd., *v.* (pet. all.) - - - - 1107
Envoy Farmer Ltd., Department of Health and Social Security *v.* 1018
Erkowit (Owners) *v.* Jade (Owners) - - - - - 430
Erkowit (Owners) *v.* Salus (Owners) (formerly Rotesand) 339
Erkowit (Owners of Cargo lately laden on board) *v.* Eschersheim (Owners) - - - 339, 430
Eschersheim, The - - 339, 430
Eschersheim (Owners), Erkowit (Owners of Cargo lately laden on board) *v.* - - - 339, 430
Esso Petroleum Co. Ltd *v.* Customs and Excise Comrs. - 1
Estates and General Investments Ltd., Marx *v.* - - - - 380
Europa Oil (N.Z.) Ltd. *v.* Inland Revenue Comr. - - - - 464
Evans (J.) & Son (Portsmouth) Ltd. *v.* Andrea Merzario Ltd. - 1078

F

Fairmount Investments Ltd. *v.* Secretary of State for the Environment - - - - 1255
Fenny Stratford Justices, *Ex parte* Watney Mann (Midlands) Ltd., Reg. *v.* - - - - 1101
Ferguson *v.* John Dawson & Partners (Contractors) Ltd. - - 1213
Fitch's Garage Ltd., Dixon *v.* - 215
Floor *v.* Davis - - - - 1167
Forray, Horrocks *v.* - - - 230
Fougère *v.* Phoenix Motor Co. Ltd. - - - - - 1281
Franklin, *Ex parte* - - - 420
Frost, Cawley *v.* - - - 1207
Furlong, Munby *v.* - - - 410

G

Garthwaite *v.* Sherwood - - 705
Gehring, Metrobarn Ltd. *v.* - 776, 852
General Dental Council, Ziderman *v.* - - - - - - 330

PAGE

Genese, Reg. *v.* - - - - - 958
Gengler *v.* Gengler - - - - 275
Gilson *v.* Kerrier District Council 904
Godfrey, Burston Finance Ltd. *v.* 719
Goodwin, Inland Revenue Comrs. *v.* - - - - - - - - 191
Governor of Risley Remand Centre, *Ex parte* Hassan, Reg. *v.* - - - - - - - - 971
Granada Television Ltd. *v.* Maudling, *Ex parte* - - - - - 1023
Greater London Council, *Ex parte* Blackburn, Reg. *v.* - - 550
Greater London Council, Munton *v.* - - - - - - - 649
Green *v.* Hoyle - - - - - 575
Guildhall Justices, *Ex parte* Marshall, Reg. *v.* - - - - 335

H

Haggard *v.* Mason - - - - 187
Hammertons Cars Ltd., Reg. *v.* - 1243
Harris *v.* Birkenhead Corpn. - 279
Harrison *v.* Nairn Williamson Ltd. 1161
Hassan, *Ex parte* - - - - 971
Hellenic & General Trust Ltd., *In re* - - - - - - - 123
Herbert Berry Associates Ltd., *In re* - - - - - - - 783
Hook, *Ex parte* - - - - - 1052
Horrocks *v.* Forray - - - - 230
Horseferry Road Stipendiary Magistrate, *Ex parte* Pearson, Reg. *v.* - - - - - - - 511
Hoyle, Green *v.* - - - - - 575
Hoyle, Reynolds *v.* - - - - 207
Hunt, B.P. Exploration Co. (Libya) Ltd. *v.* - - - - 788
Hunt, *Ex parte* - - - - - 420

I

Inland Revenue Comr., Europa Oil (N.Z.) Ltd. *v.* - - - - 464
Inland Revenue Comrs. *v.* Bullock - - - - - - - 1178
Inland Revenue Comrs., Chetwode (Lord) *v.* - - - - 310
Inland Revenue Comrs. *v.* Goodwin - - - - - - - 191
Inland Revenue Comrs., London Hospital Medical College *v.* - 613
Inland Revenue Comrs., Milford Haven Conservancy Board *v.* - 817
Inland Revenue Comrs., Terrapin International Ltd. *v.* - - - 665
Inland Revenue Comrs., Thorn *v.* 915
International Commercial Bank Ltd., Willingale *v.* - . . 657
Ismail *v.* Polish Ocean Lines (pet. dis.) - - - - - 419

J

Jade, The - - - - - 339, 430
Jade (Owners), Erkowit (Owners) *v.* - - - - - - - 430
Jiwani, United Overseas Bank *v.* 964
Johnson *v.* Philips - - - - 65
Johnson (Harry), Reg. *v.* - - 426
Jones (Frank) (Tipton) Ltd., Stock *v.* - - - - - - - 694
Jones (John), Reg. *v.* - - - 672

K

Kapur *v.* Shields - - - - 131
Keen *v.* Parker - - - - 74
Kelland, Technistudy Ltd. *v.* - 1042
Kerrier District Council, Gilson *v.* 904
King (W. J.) & Sons Ltd.'s Application, *In re* - - - - - 521
Kraft Foods Ltd., Dugdale *v.* - 1288

L

Larsson, Derby & Co. Ltd. *v.* - 202
Larter *v.* Skone James - - 607
Lazenby Garages Ltd. *v.* Wright - 459
Lee (Paul), Reg. *v.* - - - 71
Leslie (J.) Engineers Co. Ltd., *In re* - - - - - - - 292
Lively Ltd. *v.* City of Munich - 1004
London County Freehold and Leasehold Properties Ltd. *v.* Department of the Environment - - - - - - - 1126
London and Harrogate Securities Ltd. *v.* Pitts - - - - 264, 1063
London Hospital Medical College *v.* Inland Revenue Comrs. - 613
Lostock Garage Ltd., Shell U.K. Ltd. *v.* - - - - - - 1187
Lynes, Varty *v.* - - - - 1091

M

McGowan, Dunmore *v.* - - 1086
McKeon, Moore Properties (Ilford) Ltd. *v.* - - - - - 1278
Manders Property (Wolverhampton) Ltd., Morrisons Holdings Ltd. *v.* - - - - - - 533

PAGE

Marley *v.* Trustee of the Property of the Debtor, *Ex parte*, Debtor (No. 24 of 1971), *In re* A - 952
Marshall, *Ex parte* - - - 335
Marx *v.* Estates and General Investments Ltd. - - - 380
Mason, Haggard *v.* - - - 187
Maudling, Granada Television Ltd. *v.*, *Ex parte*, Poulson (A Bankrupt), *In re* - - - 1023
Melville, Reg. *v.* - - - 181
MEPC (Mayfair Properties) Ltd. *v.* Department of the Environment - - - - - - 1126
Merton London Borough Council, Anns *v.* (pet. all.) - - 1108
Merzario (Andrea) Ltd., Evans (J.) & Son (Portsmouth) Ltd. *v.* 1078
Metrobarn Ltd. *v.* Gehring 776, 852
Milford Haven Conservancy Board *v.* Inland Revenue Comrs. - - - - - - 817
Milner, Brumby *v.* - - 29, 1096
Moore Properties (Ilford) Ltd. *v.* McKeon - - - - - - 1278
Morlen Investments Ltd. *v.* Wilson - - - - 37, 533
Morris, Reg. *v.* - - - - - 110
Morrisons Holdings Ltd. *v.* Manders Property (Wolverhampton) Ltd. - - - - - - 533
Mukhtar & Sons Ltd., Universal City Studios Inc. *v.* - - - 568
Munby *v.* Furlong - - - 410
Munich (City of), Lively Ltd. *v.* 1004
Munton *v.* Greater London Council - - - - - - - 649
Murphy *v.* Culhane (pet. dis.) - 989

N

Nairn Williamson Ltd., Harrison *v.* - - - - - - 1161
National Coal Board *v.* Thorne - 543
Newcastle-upon-Tyne Justices, *Ex parte* John Bryce (Contractors) Ltd., Reg. *v.* - - - 517
Newham East Justices, *Ex parte* Hunt, Reg. *v.* - - - - - 420
Newham London Borough Council, Ravenseft Properties Ltd. *v.* (pet. dis.) - - - - - 200
Northern Developments (Holdings) Ltd. *v.* U.D.T. Securities Ltd. - - - - - - 1230
Nottingham City Council, Post Office *v.* - - - - - - 624
Nowaz, Reg. *v.* - - - - - 830
Nute, Treloar *v.* - - - - 1295

PAGE

O

O'Connor, Reg. *v.* - - - - 368
Official Receiver, Policyholders Protection Board *v.* - - - 447
Oteri *v.* The Queen - - - 1272
Owen, Reg. *v.* - - - - - 840
Oxted Justices, *Ex parte* Franklin, Reg. *v.* - - - - - - 420

P

Parker, Keen *v.* - - - - - 74
Parkes *v.* The Queen - - - 1251
Patel *v.* Spencer - - - 1268
Pearson, *Ex parte* - - - 511
Pearson (formerly Ross), Ross *v.* 224
Peay, Sansom *v.* - - - - 1073
Pexton *v.* Bell - - - - - 885
Philips Industries Ltd., Cox *v.* - 638
Phillips, Johnson *v.* - - - - 65
Phoenix Motor Co. Ltd., Fougère *v.* - - - - - - 1281
Pitts, London and Harrogate Securities Ltd. *v.* - - 264, 1063
Plenty, Rose *v.* - - - - - 141
Policyholders Protection Board *v.* Official Receiver - - - 447
Polish Ocean Lines, Ismail *v.* (pet. dis.) - - - - - 419
Post Office *v.* Nottingham City Council - - - - - - 624
Poulson (A Bankrupt), *In re*, *Ex parte* Granada Television Ltd. *v.* Maudling - - - - 1023
Practice Direction (Admiralty: Postal Facilities) - - - 516
Practice Direction (Adoption: Applications) - - - - 1267
Practice Direction (Chancery: Masters' Powers) (No. 3) - 637
Practice Direction (Chancery: Originating Summons) (No. 2) 201
Practice Direction (Chancery Division: Motions) - - 441
Practice Direction (Crime: Inconsistent Decisions) - - 799
Practice Direction (Crime: Indictment) - - - - - 409
Practice Direction (Crime: Sentence) - - - - - 122
Practice Direction (Divorce Registry: Consent Summons) (No. 2) - - - - - - 74
Practice Direction (House of Lords: Petitions for Leave to Appeal) - - - - - - 549

PAGE

Practice Direction (House of Lords: Petitions for Leave to Appeal) (No. 2) - - - - 638
Practice Direction (Judge: Mode of Address) - - - - - 799
Practice Direction (Judge in Chambers: Outside London) (No. 3) - - - - - - - 246
Practice Direction (Judgment: Foreign Currency) - - - - 83
Practice Direction (Matrimonial Proceedings: Costs) - - - 700
Practice Direction (Probate: Caveat) - - - - - - - 957
Practice Direction (Q.B.D.: Postal Facilities) - - - - 489
Practice Direction (Variation of Trusts: Counsel's Opinion) - 884
Practice Note (Inheritance: Family Provision) - - - - 418
Practice Note (Winding up: Appearance) - - - - - 515

Q

Quick, Day *v.* - - - - - 29

R

Ravenseft Properties Ltd. *v.* Newham London Borough Council (pet. dis.) - - - - - - 200
Reader's Digest Association Ltd. *v.* Williams - - - - - 1109
Reardon Smith Line Ltd. *v.* Yngvar Hansen-Tangen (trading as H.E. Hansen-Tangen) - 989
Redfern *v.* Tebbs - - - - 924
Regan *v.* Williamson - - - - 305
Reg. *v.* Annesley - - - - 106
Reg. *v.* Barnsley Metropolitan Borough Council, *Ex parte* Hook - - - - - - - 1052
Reg. *v.* Barnsley Supplementary Benefits Appeal Tribunal, *Ex parte* Atkinson - - - - 1047
Reg. *v.* Barrett (George) - - 946
Reg. *v.* Belfon - - - - - 741
Reg. *v.* Birmingham Justices, *Ex parte* Wyatt - - - - - 260
Reg. *v.* Bloomsbury and Marylebone County Court, *Ex parte* Villerwest Ltd. - - - - 362
Reg. *v.* Cato - - - - - 110

PAGE

Reg. *v.* Chandler - - 585
Reg. *v.* Charles - - - 248
Reg. *v.* Chief Immigration Officer, Heathrow Airport, *Ex parte* Salamat Bibi - - - - - 979
Reg. *v.* Criminal Injuries Compensation Board, *Ex parte* Tong - - - - - 47, 1237
Reg. *v.* Curran - - - - - 87
Reg. *v.* Dudley - - - - - 110
Reg. *v.* Fenny Stratford Justices, *Ex parte* Watney Mann (Midlands) Ltd. - - - - - 1101
Reg. *v.* Genese - - - - - 958
Reg. *v.* Governor of Risley Remand Centre, *Ex parte* Hassan 971
Reg. *v.* Greater London Council, *Ex parte* Blackburn - - 550
Reg. *v.* Guildhall Justices, *Ex parte* Marshall - - - - 335
Reg. *v.* Hammertons Cars Ltd. - 1243
Reg. *v.* Horseferry Road Stipendiary Magistrates, *Ex parte* Pearson - - - - - - 511
Reg. *v.* Johnson (Harry) - - 426
Reg. *v.* Jones (John) - - - 672
Reg. *v.* Lee (Paul) - - - - 71
Reg. *v.* Melville - - - - - 181
Reg. *v.* Morris - - - - - 110
Reg. *v.* Newcastle-upon-Tyne Justices, *Ex parte* John Bryce (Contractors) Ltd. - - - - 517
Reg. *v.* Newham East Justices, *Ex parte* Hunt - - - - 420
Reg. *v.* Nowaz - - - - - 830
Reg. *v.* O'Connor - - - 368
Reg., Oteri *v.* - - - - - 1272
Reg. *v.* Owen - - - - - 840
Reg. *v.* Oxted Justices, *Ex parte* Franklin - - - - - 420
Reg., Parkes *v.* - - - - 1251
Reg. *v.* Smith (Christopher) - 672
Reg. *v.* Tullet - - - - - 241
Reg. *v.* Urbanowski - - - 455
Reynette-James, decd., *In re* - 161
Reynette-James, Wightman *v.* - 161
Reynolds *v.* Hoyle - - - 207
Roberton *v.* Secretary of State for the Environment - - - 371
Robinson, T. & E. Homes Ltd. *v.* 1150
Robinson's Settlement Trusts, *In re* - - - - - - - - 806
Romalpa Aluminium Ltd., Aluminium Industrie Vaassen B.V. *v.* - - - - - - - - 676
Rose *v.* Plenty - - - - - 141
Ross *v.* Pearson (formerly Ross) - 224

PAGE

S

Salamat Bibi, *Ex parte* - - 979
Salus (Owners) (formerly Rotesand), Erkowit (Owners) *v.* - 339
Sanko Steamship Co., Yngvar Hansen-Tangen (trading as H. E. Hansen-Tangen) *v.* - 989
Sansom *v.* Peay - - - - 1073
Seay *v.* Eastwood - - - 1117
Secretary of State for the Environment, Fairmount Investments Ltd. *v.* - - - - - 1255
Secretary of State for the Environment, Roberton *v.* - - - 371
Secretary of State for the Environment, Southwark London Borough Council *v.* - - 1255
Sewing Machines Rentals Ltd. *v.* Udeala - - - 37, 533
Sewing Machines Rentals Ltd. *v.* Wilson - - - - 37, 533
Shell U.K. Ltd. *v.* Lostock Garage Ltd. - - - - 1187
Sherwood, Garthwaite *v.* - - 705
Shields, Kapur *v.* - - - 131
Sime Darby Holdings Ltd., Sime Darby London Ltd. *v.* - - 59
Sime Darby London Ltd. *v.* Sime Darby Holdings Ltd. - - 59
Skone James, Larter *v.* - - 607
Smith (Christopher), Reg. *v.* - 672
Société Française d'Applications Commerciales et Industrielles S.A.R.L. *v.* Electronic Concepts Ltd. - - - - - - 51
Southwark London Borough Council, Elliott *v.* - - - 499
Southwark London Borough Council *v.* Secretary of State for the Environment - - 1255
Sparex Ltd., Vapormatic Co. Ltd. *v.* (Practice Note) - - - 939
Spencer, Patel *v.* - - - 1268
Stevenson *v.* Beverley Bentinck Ltd. - - - - - - 483
Stock *v.* Frank Jones (Tipton) Ltd. - - - - - - 694
Stringfellow *v.* Stringfellow - 645

T

T. & E. Homes Ltd. v. Robinson 1150
Taylor, British Airways Board *v.* 13
Tebbs, decd., *In re* - - - 924
Tebbs, Redfern *v.* - - - 924
Technistudy Ltd. *v.* Kelland - 1042
Temple *v.* Temple - - - 701
Terrapin International Ltd. *v.* Inland Revenue Comrs. - - 665
Tesco Stores Ltd., Ward *v.* - - 810
Thorn *v.* Inland Revenue Comrs. 915
Thorne, National Coal Board *v.* 543
Tong, *Ex parte* - - - 47, 1237
Tower Hamlets London Borough Council, Bronze Investments Ltd. *v.* - - - - - 852
Tower Hamlets London Borough Council, D.H.N. Food Distributors Ltd. *v.* - - - 852
Tower Hamlets London Borough Council, D.H.N. Food Transport Ltd. *v.* - - - - 852
Town Investments Ltd. *v.* Department of the Environment - 1126
Treloar *v.* Nute - - - - 1295
Trendtex Trading Corpn. *v.* Central Bank of Nigeria - - 868
Trewby *v.* Customs and Excise Comrs. - - - - - - 932
Trustee of the Property of the Debtor, Marley v., *Ex parte*, Debtor (No. 24 of 1971), *In re* A - - - - - - 952
Tullett, Reg. *v.* - - - - 241

U

U.D.T. Securities Ltd., Northern Developments (Holdings) Ltd. *v.* - - - - - - - 1230
Udeala, Sewing Machines Rentals Ltd. *v.* - - - - - 37, 533
United Overseas Bank *v.* Jiwani 964
Universal City Studios Inc. *v.* Mukhtar & Sons Ltd. - - 568
Urbanowski, Reg. *v.* - - - 455

V

Value Capital Ltd., Beck *v.* (Note) (No. 2) - - - 572
Vapormatic Co. Ltd. *v.* Sparex Ltd. (Practice Note) - - 939
Varty *v.* Lynes - - - - 1091
Villerwest Ltd., *Ex parte* - - 362
Vortex Properties Ltd., Bushwall Properties Ltd. *v.* - - - 591

W

Ward *v.* Tesco Stores Ltd. - - 810
Watney Mann (Midlands) Ltd., *Ex parte* - - - - 1101

PAGE

Widnall, Clarke (Richard) & Co. Ltd. *v.* - - - - - - 845
Wightman *v.* Reynette-James - 161
Williams, Reader's Digest Association Ltd. *v.* - - - - 1109
Williamson, Regan *v.* - - 305
Willingale *v.* International Commercial Bank Ltd. - - - - 657
Wilson, Morlen Investments Ltd. *v.* - - - - - - 37, 533
Wilson, Sewing Machines Rentals Ltd. *v.* - - - - - 37, 533
Wright, Lazenby Garages Ltd. *v.* - - - - - - - 459
Wyatt, *Ex parte* - - - - 260

PAGE

Y

Yngvar Hansen-Tangen (trading as H. E. Hansen-Tangen), Reardon Smith Line Ltd. *v.* - 989
Yngvar Hansen-Tangen (trading as H. E. Hansen-Tangen) *v.* Sanko Steamship Co. - - 989

Z

Ziderman *v.* General Dental Council - - - - - 330

SUBJECT MATTER

(Vol. 1)

ADMIRALTY

Jurisdiction

Action in rem

Claims arising out of salvage operation for loss of ship and cargo—Claim that cargo washed overboard causing pollution—Court's jurisdiction to hear and determine claims brought against salvors by ship and cargo owners—Administration of Justice Act 1956, ss. 1 (1) (*d*) (*e*) (*g*) (*h*) (*j*), 3 (1) (4) **The Eschersheim,** C.A. **339**
H.L.(E.) **430**

Crime

Australians charged under English criminal law in court of Western Australia with theft on high seas—Vessel not registered as British ship—Whether offences committed within Admiralty jurisdiction—Whether offences triable in Western Australia
Oteri v. The Queen, P.C. **1272**

Practice

Postal facilities

Extension of class of business which may be conducted by post—R.S.C., Ord. 1, r. 10 **Practice Direction (Admiralty: Postal Facilities),** Q.B.D. **516**

ADOPTION

Adoption order

Applications

Preliminary examination of jurisdiction—Procedure for applications for removal or return of child to jurisdiction—Adoption (High Court) Rules 1976, rr. 11, 23
Practice Direction (Adoption: Applications), Fam.D. **1267**

AIRCRAFT

Civil aviation

British Airways Board

False statement by B.O.A.C. in relation to airline seat reservation—Dissolution of B.O.A.C.—Replacement by board—Whether board liable to prosecution for false statement—Civil Aviation Act 1971, ss. 37, 38, 57
British Airways Board v. Taylor, H.L.(E.) **13**

Public transport

Hire or reward

Flying club aircraft used to transport passengers—Aircraft flown by club member—Payment to club of normal fee for member's use—Whether " hire or reward " for carriage of passengers—Air Navigation Order 1974, art. 91 (1) (6) (*a*) (i)
Corner v. Clayton, D.C. **800**

ARBITRATION

Arbitration clause in contract

Ambit

Salvage agreement—Allegation of negligence on part of salvors—Whether to be referred to arbitration under contract—Discretion of court to stay actions—Arbitration Act 1950, s. 4 (1) **The Eschersheim,** C.A. **339**
H.L.(E.) **430**

AUSTRALIA

Western Australia

Admiralty jurisdiction

District court's jurisdiction to try offence of theft on high seas
Oteri v. The Queen, P.C. **1272**

BANKING

Money credited in error *see* RESTITUTION

BANKRUPTCY

Private examination of witness

"Stop order"

Inspection of file of proceedings for purposes of libel action—Refusal by trustee to produce transcripts of private examinations—Validity of "stop order" procedure—Bankruptcy Act 1914, s. 25—Bankruptcy Rules 1952, r. 15 (as amended by Bankruptcy (Amendment) Rules 1962, r. 1 (*b*))

In re **Poulson (A Bankrupt),** *Ex parte* **Granada Television Ltd. v. Maudling,** D.C. **1023**

Property passing to trustee

Tenants in common

Legal charge to bank on joint property of father and son to secure loan to son—Father surety for loan—Son made bankrupt—Trustee's claim to son's half-share—Whether bank loan deductible from son's half-share on sale of property

In re **A Debtor (No. 24 of 1971),** *Ex parte* **Marley v. Trustee of the Property of the Debtor,** D.C. **952**

BUILDING

Safety regulations

"Working place"

Plaintiff engaged in throwing down scaffold boards from roof—Fall from roof—No guard-rail—Whether breach of statutory duty—Judge's finding that work would have taken 10 or 15 minutes—Whether appreciable time—Construction (Working Places) Regulations 1966, reg. 28 (1)

Ferguson v. John Dawson & Partners (Contractors) Ltd., C.A. **1213**

CHARITY

Education

Students' union

Union of clubs for students of medical college—Objects of union to promote social, cultural and athletic activities and comfort of students—Whether charitable purposes **London Hospital Medical College v. Inland Revenue Comrs.,** Brightman J. **613**

COMMON RIGHTS

Common land

Registration

No rights registered within statutory time limit—Whether rights extinguished—Commons Registration Act 1965, s. 1—Law of Property Act 1925, ss. 193, 194

Central Electricity Generating Board v. Clwyd County Council, Goff J. **151**

Provisional registration

"Common land"

Objection by owners—No rights registered within requisite period—Whether land subject to rights of common—Evidence of grazing and other uses—Commons commissioner's decision confirming provisional registration—Whether in accordance with evidence—Commons Registration Act 1965, ss. 1 (2) (*b*), 4, 5, 6, 21 (1), 22 (1)

Central Electricity Generating Board v. Clwyd County Council, Goff J. **151**

COMPANY

Meeting

Vote

Proxy—Resolution to approve merger—Unstamped proxy forms distributed by dissentients—Poll—Unstamped forms accepted—Whether proxy votes valid

Marx v. Estates and General Investments Ltd., Brightman J. **380**

Scheme of arrangement

Class meeting

Meeting of ordinary shareholders including wholly owned subsidiary of intended purchasers—Resolution approving scheme carried by subsidiary's votes—Whether agreement of appropriate class—Companies Act 1948, s. 206

In re **Hellenic & General Trust Ltd.,** Templeman J. **123**

Winding up

Costs

Company unjustifiably opposing petition—Benefit accruing to beneficial owner if petition successfully opposed—Order for costs—Companies (Winding-up) Rules 1949, r. 195 *In re* **Bathampton Properties Ltd.,** Brightman J. **168**

Disposition of property

Cheque cashed by director from company's bank account—Purchase of money orders to pay part of business debt—Remainder paid by cheque from director's private bank account—Company's moneys paid into private account without creditors' knowledge—Whether "disposition" of "property of the company"—Companies Act 1948, s. 227 *In re* **J. Leslie Engineers Co. Ltd.,** Oliver J. **292**

COMPANY—*continued*
Winding up—*continued*
Foreign corporation
Foreign and English debts—Liquidation abroad—Subsequent compulsory winding up in England—Scheme of arrangement with foreign creditors abroad entitling them to dividends in English liquidation—Date for conversion of claims into sterling
In re **Dynamics Corpn. of America,** Oliver J. **757**

Liquidator
Indemnity—Insurance company's insolvency—Power of liquidator to make interim payments to policyholders—Indemnity of liquidator by Policyholders Protection Board—Whether personal indemnity only—Policyholders Protection Act 1975, s. 15 (3) (*b*) **Policyholders Protection Board v. Official Receiver,** Brightman J. **447**

Notice of appearance
Application by creditor or contributory to be added to list made out of time—Undertaking as to costs—Companies (Winding-up) Rules 1949, r. 34 (as amended)
Practice Note (Winding up: Appearance), Brightman J. **515**

Preferential debt
Unpaid taxes—Distress by collector of taxes under statutory powers before winding up—Resolution to wind up within three months of distress but before sale of distrained goods—Whether distress void as against liquidator—Property in distrained goods—Companies Act 1948, s. 319 (7)
In re **Herbert Berry Associates Ltd.,** Templeman J. **783**

COMPULSORY PURCHASE
Compensation
Agreement "subject to contract"
Rise in house values before date of entry into possession—Whether memorandum in writing required on compulsory acquisition—Whether "subject to contract" effective to postpone ascertainment of price—Whether price for land and compensation for disturbance separable—Land Compensation Act 1961, s. 5 (6)
Munton v. Greater London Council, C.A. **649**

Disturbance, for
Extinguishment of business—Group of associated companies—Trading company providing money for purchase of trading premises—Freehold title in wholly owned subsidiary—Whether trading company having irrevocable licence to occupy or acquiring equitable interest in premises—Whether companies to be treated as single economic entity for purposes of compensation—Land Compensation Act 1961, s. 5 (2) (6) **D.H.N. Food Distributors Ltd. v. Tower Hamlets London Borough Council,** C.A. **852**

CONFLICT OF LAWS
Sovereign immunity
Bank
Commercial transaction for supply of cement to Nigerian state—Central Bank of Nigeria issuing irrevocable letter of credit—Action to enforce payment—Status of bank—Whether department of state—Whether claim involved impleading foreign state **Trendtex Trading Corpn. v. Central Bank of Nigeria,** Donaldson J. **868**

CONTRACT
Condition or warranty
Oral assurance
Printed contract of carriage with exemption clause—Goods customarily carried under deck—Change to container system—Oral promise by forwarding agents to ensure goods in containers to be carried under deck—Subcontractors loading container on deck—Goods lost at sea—Whether oral promise as to future conduct overriding printed exemption from liability—Whether oral promise contractual—Whether enforceable **J. Evans & Son (Portsmouth) Ltd. v. Andrea Merzario Ltd.,** C.A. **1078**

Formation
Consensus ad idem
Uncertainty—Agreement to purchase land—Purchase price to be paid in stages—"Proportionate part" of land to be conveyed on each occasion—No agreement as to selection of land to be so conveyed—Whether contract void for uncertainty
Bushwall Properties Ltd. v. Vortex Properties Ltd., C.A. **591**

COPYRIGHT
Infringement
Ex parte motion
Action for infringement of copyright—Suspicion of likelihood of infringing articles disappearing—Interim injunction and order for custody of infringing articles—Application ex parte for order without notice to other side
Universal City Studios Inc. v. Mukhtar & Sons Ltd., Templeman J. **568**

COSTS
Incidental proceedings
Inquiry by Secretary of State
Classification of insured person in question—Court referring question to Secretary of State for determination—Whether costs of minister's inquiry "incidental to . . . proceedings in . . . court"—Supreme Court of Judicature (Consolidation) Act 1925, s. 50 (1)—National Insurance Act 1965, s. 97 (2)
Department of Health and Social Security v. Envoy Farmers Ltd., Jupp J. **1018**

Taxation
Application to review
Matrimonial causes—Preparing for trial of cause or matter—Solicitors' costs limited by statute—Whether discretion to exceed statutory maximum—Matrimonial Causes (Costs) Rules 1971, r. 6 (1), Appendix **Dwyer v. Dwyer,** Payne J. **176**

Common fund basis
Shareholders objecting to company merger—Use of proxy votes to defeat motion—Subsequent objection by company to forms of proxy—Action by shareholders—Validity of proxy votes confirmed—Order for costs on common fund basis—R.S.C., Ord. 62, r. 28 (3)
Marx v. Estates and General Investments Ltd., Brightman J. **380**

COUNTY COURT
Jurisdiction
Stay of execution pending appeal
Orders of possession of mortgaged premises—Stay of execution on condition of payment of sums not otherwise due—Whether exercise of jurisdiction—Whether stay of execution pending appeal automatic—R.S.C., Ord. 59, rr. 13 (1) (*a*), 19 (5)
Sewing Machines Rentals Ltd. v. Wilson, C.A. 37
Variation of order
Judgment given in absence of defendant—Judgment set aside on terms with time limit—Terms not complied with—Further application to extend time for compliance with terms—Whether jurisdiction to vary order—County Courts Act 1959, s. 103—R.S.C., Ord. 3, r. 5 (1)
Reg. v. Bloomsbury and Marylebone County Court, *Ex parte* **Villerwest Ltd.,** C.A. **362**

CRIME
Assault
Mens rea
Wounding with intent to do grievous bodily harm—Whether recklessness as to consequences of acts sufficient intent—"Intent"—Offences against the Person Act 1861, s. 18 **Reg. v. Belfon,** C.A. **741**

Burglary
Entry of building "as a trespasser"
General permission to enter—Son entering father's house and stealing goods—Whether entry as trespasser—Theft Act 1968, s. 9 (1) (*b*)
Reg. v. Jones (John), C.A. **672**

Compound proceedings
Agreement to
Defendant requesting to be released from agreement—Customs and Excise Commissioners purporting to release defendant from agreement—Whether valid release—Whether subsequent criminal proceedings nullity—Customs and Excise Act 1952, s. 288 (*a*) **Patel v. Spencer,** Judge Solomon **1268**

Corruption
Agent
Additional superintendent registrar of births, deaths and marriages—Whether serving under Crown—Prevention of Corruption Act 1906, s. 1
Reg. v. Barrett (George), C.A. **946**

Costs
Legal aid
Crown Court—Application for legal aid made at conclusion of trial—Court's power to grant order—Effect of order—Legal Aid Act 1974, ss. 28 (7), 37 (2)
Reg. v. Tullett, Judge Rubin **241**

Court of Appeal
Fresh evidence
Mental health not in issue at trial—Medical reports after conviction revealing abnormality—Whether medical evidence admissible on appeal—Meaning of "on an issue"—Scope of court's function after conviction—Criminal Appeal Act 1968, s. 23 (1) (2) (*a*) **Reg. v. Melville,** C.A. **181**

CRIME—*continued*

Criminal Injuries Compensation Board

Date of entitlement

Assessment of compensation—Death of victim before payment—Whether compensation assessed payable to deceased victim's estate—Criminal Injuries Compensation Scheme 1964 (rev. 1969), para. 21
Reg. v. Criminal Injuries Compensation Board, *Ex parte* **Tong,** D.C. **47;** C.A. **123**

Drugs

Offer to supply

Offering controlled drug for sale—Drug not controlled drug—Whether offence committed—Whether order for forfeiture of drug and money from sale valid—Misuse of Drugs Act 1971, ss. 4 (1) (3) (*a*), 27 (1) **Haggard v. Mason,** D.C. **18**

Embracery

Sentence

Whether immediate custodial sentence appropriate **Reg. v. Owen,** C.A. **84**

Evidence

Character

Defence alleging that two men had opportunity to commit theft—Prosecution witness cross-examined as to men's previous convictions for dishonesty—Whether questions put with view to establishing defendant's good character—Criminal Evidence Act 1898, s. 1 (*f*) (ii) **Reg. v. Lee (Paul),** C.A. **7**

Secondary evidence

Document in possession of consul—Consul claiming diplomatic immunity from giving evidence and producing document—Whether evidence of content of document admissible **Reg. v. Nowaz,** C.A. **83**

Silence

Accusation by victim's mother—Inference to be drawn from silence
Parkes v. The Queen, P.C. **125**

Fraud

Obtaining pecuniary advantage by deception

Cheque card used to back cheques—Amounts drawn in excess of money credited to bank account—Whether representation of authority to draw on account—Theft Act 1968, s. 16 **Reg. v. Charles,** C.A. **24**

Homicide

Manslaughter

Victim dying after being injected with heroin—Whether heroin caused or contributed to death—Consent of victim to injections—Whether unlawful and malicious administration of "noxious thing"—Offences against the Person Act 1861, s. 23
Reg. v. Cato, C.A. **11**

Indictment

Joinder of charges

Permissibility of two indictments against defendant for same offence and founded on same facts—Joinder of counts founded on separate committals to indictment already signed against another defendant
Practice Direction (Crime: Indictment), C.A. **40**

Mens rea *see* **Assault**

Obscene libel

Publication

Cinematograph film—Hire for gain of film for purpose of cinematograph exhibition—Whether "publication" of obscene article—Whether offence—Obscene Publications Act 1959, ss. 1 (1) (3) (*b*), 2 (1) (6)—Obscene Publications Act 1964, s. 1 (3) (*b*) **Attorney-General's Reference (No. 2 of 1975),** C.A. **71**

Plea

Guilty

Not guilty plea entered—Counsel advising change of plea after conversation with judge—Principle to be followed
Practice Direction (Crime: Inconsistent Decisions), C.A. **79**

Practice

Legal aid

Hybrid offence—Summary trial—Application for extension of legal aid to cover counsel—Whether hybrid offence "indictable offence"—Legal Aid Act 1974, s. 30 (2) (*a*) **Reg. v. Guildhall Justices,** *Ex parte* **Marshall,** D.C. **33**

Time limits

Trial on indictment—Time limit for commencement—Whether directory or mandatory—Date for preferment of bill of indictment—Courts Act 1971, s. 7 (4)
Reg. v. Urbanowski, C.A. **45**

CRIME—*continued*
Public order
" Public place "
Football ground—Football pitch surrounded by speedway track—Public having no access to track or pitch—Threatening behaviour on speedway track—Whether " public place "—Public Order Act 1936, s. 9 (1) (as substituted by Criminal Justice Act 1972, s. 33) **Cawley v. Frost,** D.C. **1207**

Sentence
Extended sentence
Offence committed more than three years after previous conviction and before final release from prison—Whether extended sentence valid—Criminal Justice Act 1967, s. 37 (4) (*a*) **Reg. v. Johnson (Harry),** C.A. **426**

Fine
Fine in addition to suspended sentence—Whether appropriate where offender under 21—Whether justifiable in principle—Powers of Criminal Courts Act 1973, s. 19 (2) **Reg. v. Genese, C.A. 958**

Parole
Offence committed after release on licence—Considerations on sentencing—Criminal Justice Act 1967, ss. 60, 62 (7) **Practice Direction (Crime: Sentence),** D.C. **122**

Summing up
Directions to jury
Defendant's silence when questioned by police—Inference to be drawn from defendant's silence **Reg. v. Chandler,** C.A. **585**

Theft
Dishonest appropriation
Petrol and oil put into motorist's car at his request—Motorist driving away without paying—Whether sale conditional on payment—Whether appropriation of property belonging to another—Theft Act 1968, ss. 1 (1), 5 (3)—Sale of Goods Act 1893, s. 18, r. 5 **Edwards v. Ddin,** D.C. **942**

CROWN
Statute
Application to
Crown not bound by counter-inflation legislation—Whether Crown entitled to take advantage of provisions—Crown Proceedings Act 1947, s. 31 (1) **Town Investments Ltd. v. Department of the Environment,** Foster J. and C.A. **1126**

CROWN COURT
Jurisdiction
Appeal against sentence
Justices imposing unlawful sentence—Jurisdiction of Crown Court in relation to sentence—Courts Act 1971, s. 9 (4)—Powers of Criminal Courts Act 1973, s. 21 (1) **Reg. v. Birmingham Justices,** *Ex parte* **Wyatt,** D.C. **260**

Committal for sentence for motoring offences
No driving licence available—Imposition of substantive sentence with warning that further sentence to be imposed if totting up provisions applied—Disqualification ordered more than 28 days later—Whether inherent power at common law to postpone passing whole or part of sentence—Courts Act 1971, s. 11 (2) **Reg. v. Annesley,** C.A. **106**

Legal aid *see* CRIME: **Costs**

CROWN PRACTICE
Certiorari
Jurisdiction of inferior tribunals
Justices passing sentence unauthorised by law—Discretion to amend order instead of quashing conviction—Administration of Justice Act 1960, s. 16 (1) **Reg v. Birmingham Justices,** *Ex parte* **Wyatt,** D.C. **260**

Prohibition
Film licensing authority
Application to prohibit local council exercising their powers—Whether sufficient locus standi as ratepayer and parent **Reg. v. Greater London Council,** *Ex parte* **Blackburn,** C.A. **550**

CURRENCY

Company winding up

Foreign corporation see COMPANY

Contract

Par value

Redemption of foreign bonds—Commercial objective—Calculation based on par value—Floating currency—Whether par value " in force "

Lively Ltd. v. City of Munich, Kerr J. 1004

Foreign

Claim or judgment

Procedure in High Court for bringing claim and enforcing judgment in foreign currency—Transfer to county court—R.S.C., Ord. 6, r. 2 (1) (*b*); Ord. 13, r. 1; Ord. 14, r. 3; Ord. 19, r. 2; Ord. 22, r. 1; Ord. 42, r. 3; Ord. 45, r. 12; Ord. 49, r. 1; Ord. 50, rr. 1, 2; Ord. 51

Practice Direction (Judgment: Foreign Currency), Q.B.D. 83

DAMAGES

Contract

Breach

Mental distress—Employee relegated to position of lesser responsibility in breach of contract—Whether damages for vexation, frustration and distress suffered by employee in inferior position recoverable

Cox v. Philips Industries Ltd., Lawson J. 638

Sale of goods

Refusal to accept goods

Secondhand car—Resale to another purchaser at higher price—Whether dealer entitled to damages for loss of sale where goods unique and no " available market "—Measure of damages—Sale of Goods Act 1893, s. 50 (2) (3)

Lazenby Garages Ltd. v. Wright, C.A. 459

DENTIST

Discipline

Erasure from register following conviction

Shoplifting—Gravity of offence for which convicted—Relevance of previous convictions—Dentists Act 1957, s. 25 (2) (*a*)

Ziderman v. General Dental Council, P.C. 330

DISCRIMINATION

Sex

Equal pay

Differences of practical importance—Women engaged on " broadly similar " work to men save for Sunday and night shift working—Whether " differences . . . of practical importance " in relation to terms and conditions of employment—Equal Pay Act 1970, ss. 1 (4), 2 (1) (as amended by Sex Discrimination Act 1975, s. 8, Sch. 1, para. 2) **Dugdale v. Kraft Foods Ltd.,** E.A.T. 1288

EXECUTION

Charging order nisi

Order absolute

Bankruptcy of judgment debtor after order nisi—Order made absolute—Whether bankruptcy relevant to decision whether or not to make order absolute—Discretion of court—R.S.C., Ord. 50, r. 1

Burston Finance Ltd. v. Godfrey, C.A. 719

FAMILY PROVISION

Practice

Act of 1975

Assignment of proceedings to Chancery Division and Family Division—Transitional arrangements—Extension of time for making application—Inheritance (Provision for Family and Dependants) Act 1975, s. 4—R.S.C., Ord. 99, rr. 3, 5 (2) (*d*), 8 (as amended by Rules of the Supreme Court (Amendment) 1976, r. 19)

Practice Note (Inheritance: Family Provision), Ch.D.; Fam.D. 418

FATAL ACCIDENTS ACTS

Damages

Infant dependants

Husband's claim for family's loss of wife's services—Housekeeper employed—Value of wife's services **Regan v. Williamson,** Watkins J. 305

GAMING

Gaming machine

Licensed bookmaker's premises

Bookmaker taking fixed percentage of money inserted in machine on premises—Whether player of machine making bet with bookmaker—Whether bookmaker carrying on business other than "bookmaking"—Betting and Lotteries Act (Northern Ireland) 1957, ss. 13 (1) (*a*), 20 **Seay v. Eastwood, H.L.(N.I.) 1117**

Lottery

Draw

Promotion of sales—Goods offered for sale with participation in lucky number draw—Chance of prize unaffected by refusal to purchase—Whether lottery **Reader's Digest Association Ltd. v. Williams,** D.C. **1109**

HABEAS CORPUS

Onus of proof

Detention of alien

Alien alleged to be "illegal entrant"—Onus on alien of establishing prima facie case of unlawful detention—Unacceptable explanation of lost passport held on entry—Whether onus of proof discharged—Immigration Act 1971, s. 33 (1), Sch. 2, paras. 8, 9, 16 (2) **Reg. v. Governor of Risley Remand Centre,** *Ex parte* **Hassan,** D.C. **971**

HIGHWAY

Public path

Diversion order

Footpath across Chequers Estate—Proximity to manor house—Need to protect occupants—Whether diversion of footpath for securing "efficient use" of "land" —Whether Public Trustee proper person to apply for diversion order—Chequers Estate Act 1917, s. 1—Highways Act 1959, s. 111
Roberton v. Secretary of State for the Environment, Phillips J. **371**

HIRE-PURCHASE

Owner's right to possession

"Trade or finance purchaser"

Part-time trader purchasing car for his own use without notice of hire-purchase agreement—Whether purchaser obtaining good title under statutory protection for "private purchaser"—Hire-Purchase Act 1964, ss. 27 (2) (6), 29 (2)
Stevenson v. Beverley Bentinck Ltd., C.A. **483**

HOUSE OF LORDS

Leave to appeal

Petition

Incompetent—Certified as such—Fitness for oral hearing—Petitions not referred for oral hearing certified accordingly
Practice Direction (House of Lords: Petitions for Leave to Appeal), H.L. **549**
(No. 2), H.L. **638**

New point raised on appeal

Leave to argue

Action held to be time-barred—Court of Appeal granting leave on limitation point —Leave to argue question of duty
Anns v. Merton London Borough Council (pet. all.), H.L.(E.) **1108**

HOUSING

Compulsory purchase

Clearance area

Public inquiry—Owners' objection to demolition of dwelling houses—Suggested rehabilitation—Site inspection—No reference to settlement of foundations—Confirmation of order recommended on ground of inadequacy of foundations—No opportunity for owners to deal with that ground—Breach of natural justice—Housing Act 1957, Sch. 3, para. 3 (3)
Fairmount Investments Ltd. v. Secretary of State for the Environment, H.L.(E.) **1255**

Unfit for human habitation

Rehabilitation order

Houses scheduled for demolition under compulsory purchase order—Requests for rehabilitation orders made under new Act—Refusal on ground that properties to be demolished and sites used for erection of new housing—Whether requests properly considered—Whether reason adequate and intelligible to recipients in circumstances—Housing Act 1974, s. 114 (1) (2) (4) (5), Sch. 10, para. 3 (2) (as amended by Housing Rents and Subsidies Act 1975, Sch. 5)
Elliott v. Southwark London Borough Council, C.A. **499**

HUSBAND AND WIFE
Divorce
Costs
Fixed costs
Alterations in respect of costs taxed or fixed—Matrimonial Causes (Costs) Rules 1971, rr. 5, 7—Matrimonial Causes (Costs) (Amendment) Rules 1976, rr. 2, 4 **Practice Direction (Matrimonial Proceedings; Costs),** Fam.D. **700**

Respondent's behaviour
Test to be applied
Husband's intolerable behaviour for short period prior to desertion—Whether wife entitled to rely on husband's behaviour as ground for divorce—Matrimonial Causes Act 1973, s. 1 (2) (*b*) (*c*)
Stringfellow v. Stringfellow, C.A. **645**
Justices
Maintenance
Quantum
Basis of assessment **Gengler v. Gengler,** D.C. **275**

Remission of arrears
Arrears accruing over period of years—Practice of enforcing only those accruing within 12 months of complaint—Justices declining to remit—Whether proper exercise of discretion—Magistrates' Courts Act 1952, s. 76
Ross v. Pearson (formerly Ross), D.C. **224**
Practice
Consent summons
Divorce Registry
Solicitors' attendance where parties consenting to order for custody of, or access to, child—Payments direct to child in excess of small maintenances payments—Matrimonial Causes Rules 1973, r. 92 (2) (as amended by Matrimonial Causes (Amendment) Rules 1975, r. 6)—Income and Corporation Taxes Act 1970, s. 65 **Practice Direction (Divorce Registry: Consent Summons) (No. 2),** Fam.D. **74**
Summary procedure under Order 14
Action in Queen's Bench Division
Wife alleging breach of maintenance agreement—Application for summary judgment—Divorce proceedings pending in Family Division—Whether Queen's Bench or Family Division appropriate forum for trial of wife's action
Temple v. Temple, C.A. 701
Property
Practice
Polygamous marriage
Talaq divorce—Application for declaration of interest in matrimonial home—Whether wife entitled to relief **Chaudhry v. Chaudhry (Note),** C.A. **221**

IMMIGRATION
Illegal entrant *see* HABEAS CORPUS: **Onus of proof**

Refusal of entry
Non-Commonwealth nationals
Settled Commonwealth citizen from Pakistan—Family refused entry after Pakistan leaving Commonwealth—New rules for non-Commonwealth nationals—Whether intra vires—Whether family of settled immigrant required to obtain visas in Pakistan—Effect of European convention on English law—Statement of Change in Immigration Rules for Control on Entry: EEC and Other Non-Commonwealth Nationals (1973) (H.C. 437)—Convention for the Protection of Human Rights and Fundamental Freedoms (1953) (Cmd. 8969), arts. 8, 25—Immigration Act 1971, s. 1 (5) **Reg. v. Chief Immigration Officer, Heathrow Airport,** *Ex parte* **Salamat Bibi,** C.A. **979**

INDUSTRIAL RELATIONS
Unfair dismissal
Compensation
Assessment—Age and health of employee disregarded by tribunal when assessing probable period of unemployment—Whether matters to be taken into account in assessing compensation—Appeal against trifling error in assessing compensation—Trade Union and Labour Relations Act 1974, Sch. 1, para. 19 (1)
Fougère v. Phoenix Motor Co. Ltd., E.A.T. **1281**

Dismissal of employee in year preceding sixtieth birthday—Compensation assessed on basis that employee but for dismissal would have continued to work after retirement age—Whether compensation payable for period after retirement age—Trade Union and Labour Relations Act 1974, Sch. 1, paras. 10 (*b*), 19 (2)
Barrel Plating & Phosphating Co. Ltd. v. Danks, E.A.T. **879**

INDUSTRIAL RELATIONS—*continued*
Unfair dismissal—*continued*
Continuous employment
Computation of 26-week period of employment—Whether to include whole of weeks in which employee engaged and dismissed—Trade Union and Labour Relations Act 1974, Sch. 1, paras. 10, 30—Contracts of Employment Act 1972, Sch. 1, paras. 4, 11 **Coulson v. City of London Polytechnic,** E.A.T. **834**

Excluded classes
Housekeeper sole employee at relevant premises—Employer and wife only shareholders in property companies—Whether housekeeper's employment in "undertaking" employing less than four people—Industrial Relations Act 1971, ss. 22, 27 (1) (*a*), 167 (1) **Kapur v. Shields,** Phillips J. **131**

Reasonableness of dismissal
Employee's misconduct during employment discovered after dismissal—Whether defence to complaint of unfair dismissal—Trade Union and Labour Relations Act 1974, Sch. 1, para. 6 (8) **W. Devis & Sons Ltd. v. Atkins,** Phillips J. **393**

Strike
Employees on strike as result of dismissals—Two employees returning to work—Remainder of striking employees dismissed—Whether dismissal unfair—Trade Union and Labour Relations Act 1974, Sch. 1, para. 8 (2) (*a*)
Stock v. Frank Jones (Tipton) Ltd., Phillips J. **694**

JUDGE
Circuit judge
Deputy
Mode of address and listing **Practice Direction (Judge: Mode of Address),** C.A. **799**

JUSTICES
Bail
Estreatment of recognizances
Surety's serious attempt to discharge obligation lawfully—Forfeiture of full amount of recognizance—Whether proper exercise of discretion
Reg. v. Horseferry Road Stipendiary Magistrate, *Ex parte* **Pearson,** D.C. **511**

Crown Court
Committal for sentence
Offences connected with motor vehicles—Whether jurisdiction to sentence to borstal training and to disqualify from driving—Criminal Justice Act 1948, s. 20—Magistrates' Courts Act 1952, s. 28—Criminal Justice Act 1967, s. 56 (2) (5) (6)
Reg. v. O'Connor, C.A. **368**

Information
Amendment
Prosecutor's application to amend by alleging different offence more than six months after commission—No injustice to defence—Whether justices having power to allow amendment—Magistrates' Courts Act 1952, ss. 100, 104
Reg. v. Newcastle-upon-Tyne Justices, *Ex parte* **John Bryce (Contractors) Ltd.,** D.C. **517**

LAND CHARGE
Register, vacation of
Pending actions register
Action to set aside sale of land—Allegation of wrongful exercise of power of sale—Registration of caution and "pending land action" by chargor subsequent to issue of proceedings—Purchaser's motion to vacate register—Court's jurisdiction to vacate registration of "pending land action" against unregistered land—Land Charges Act 1972, ss. 1 (6), 5 (10)
Northern Developments (Holdings) Ltd. v. U.D.T. Securities Ltd., Megarry J. **1230**

LANDLORD AND TENANT
Business premises (security of tenure)
Occupation for purposes of tenants' business
Fire occurring and trading ceasing—Fixtures and fittings on premises—Tenants maintaining right to occupy—Landlords purporting to determine tenancy and demolishing premises—Whether tenants "occupied" premises—Locus standi to apply for new lease—Landlord and Tenant Act 1954, s. 23 (1)
Morrisons Holdings Ltd. v. Manders Property (Wolverhampton) Ltd., C.A. **533**

LANDLORD AND TENANT—*continued*
Forfeiture of lease
Relief from forfeiture
Non-payment of rent—Lease giving landlords right of immediate re-entry or after period of notice—Landlords electing to give notice—Tenant paying arrears of rent —Whether forfeiture of lease—Whether tenant entitled to relief from forfeiture **Richard Clarke & Co. Ltd. v. Widnall,** C.A. **845**

Notice to quit
Error in notice
Break clause in 21 year lease providing for earlier determination—Landlord's notice giving past date for termination—Whether notice valid **Carradine Properties Ltd. v. Aslam,** Goulding J. **442**

Rent
Counter-inflation
Demise to Secretary of State for Environment—Premises provided and serviced by Department of Environment for other government departments—Whether occupied by tenant for purposes of "business" carried on by him—Counter-Inflation (Business Rents) Order 1972, art. 2 (2)—Counter-Inflation (Business Rents) Order 1973, art. 2 (2) **Town Investments Ltd. v. Department of the Environment,** Foster J. and C.A. **1126**

Rent restriction
Furnished letting
Effect of imposition of protection—Furnished letting subsisting at date when protection imposed—Prior registration of fair rent in relation to unfurnished letting of premises—Whether fair rent applicable to protected furnished letting—Rent Act 1974, ss. 1, 5 (1) **Metrobarn Ltd. v. Gehring,** C.A. **776**

Surrender of lease
Agreement to surrender
Contractual term that lessee surrender at price fixed by agreed valuer—Honest valuation by agreed valuer—Lessor obtaining lower valuations seeking equitable relief after entering into possession—Whether valuation binding on both parties **Campbell v. Edwards,** C.A. **403**

LAW REFORM
Whether necessary
Road traffic
Failing to provide specimen—Penalties—Road Traffic Act 1972, s. 9 (3), Sch. 4, Pt. I **Reg. v. Curran,** H.L.(E.) **87**

Will
Rectification *In re* **Reynette-James, decd.,** Templeman J. **161**

LEGAL AID
Costs
Taxation
Solicitor's decision not to instruct London agents for hearing of appeal—Solicitor's travelling expenses to attend hearing—Whether "proper" costs to allow on taxation—R.S.C., Ord. 62, r. 28 (2) (4) **Garthwaite v. Sherwood,** Kerr J. **705**

LICENCE OR TENANCY
Implied licence
Occupation of house
House purchased as home for mistress and child—Nature of licence—Whether contractual licence to be inferred—Whether licence terminated by death of purchaser **Horrocks v. Forray,** C.A. **230**

LICENSING
Films
Censorship
County council delegating powers of censorship to unincorporated board with power to review—Whether delegation ultra vires—Council rule incorporating statutory test for obscene publications—Whether proper test—Obscene Publications Act 1959, s. 1 (1)—Cinematograph Act 1909, s. 2 (1)—Cinematograph Act 1952, s. 3 (1) **Reg. v. Greater London Council,** *Ex parte* **Blackburn,** C.A. **550**

LIMITATION OF ACTION

Land, recovery of

Possessory title

Disputed land adjoining defendant's land derelict—Owner not intending to use it for any particular purpose in future—Possession and user of land for 12 years—Whether inconvenience to owner necessary requirement of adverse possession—Limitation Act 1939, s. 10 (1) **Treloar v. Nute,** C.A. **1295**

Time, computation of

Local authority

Defective premises—Allegation of negligence in approving foundations of dwelling house—Action started more than six years after foundations passed—Action held statute-barred—Subsequent decision holding contrary—Appeal allowed—Leave to argue question of duty on appeal

Anns v. Merton London Borough Council (pet. all.) H.L.(E.) **1108**

LOCAL GOVERNMENT

Powers

Licensing premises for public exhibition of films see LICENSING: **Films**

MARKET

Right to trade

Termination of licence

Local authority terminating stallholder's licence to trade for trivial misconduct—Officer acting as prosecutor present during appeal hearings by council committee in absence of stallholder—Whether committee acting administratively or judicially—Whether decision void for want of natural justice—Whether prerogative order available to quash decision depriving stallholder of livelihood—Barnsley Corporation Act 1969

Reg. v. Barnsley Metropolitan Borough Council, *Ex parte* **Hook,** C.A. **1052**

MASTER AND SERVANT

Contract of service

Service of, or for services

Workman taken on as self-employed labour only subcontractor—Whether label conclusive—Need to look at reality of relationship between parties as found in express and implied terms of contract

Ferguson v. John Dawson & Partners (Contractors) Ltd., C.A. **1213**

MINES

Working facilities

Statutory grant of

Interim order—Owner's refusal to grant new lease to company to work land—Application for statutory grant of rights—Whether inherent jurisdiction in court to grant such rights in interlocutory proceedings—Mines (Working Facilities and Support) Act 1966, s. 1 (as amended by Mines (Working Facilities and Support) Act 1974, s. 1), ss. 3, 5 *In re* **W. J. King & Sons Ltd.'s Application, C.A. 521**

MONEYLENDER

Criminal offence

Implication of carrying on banking business

Whether loan recoverable in civil proceedings—Moneylenders Act 1927, s. 4 (3)

London and Harrogate Securities Ltd. v. Pitts, Mocatta J. **264;** C.A. **1063**

Memorandum

Non-compliance with statutory requirements

Omission of "per annum" after rate of interest—Whether agreement enforceable—"Per cent."—Meaning—Moneylenders Act 1927, s. 6 (2)

London and Harrogate Securities Ltd. v. Pitts, Mocatta J. **264;** C.A. **1063**

NATURAL JUSTICE

Public inquiry *see* HOUSING: **Compulsory purchase**

NEGLIGENCE

Burden of proof

Spillage

Customer slipping on spillage on floor of supermarket—Owners' system dealing with spillage—Burden of proving whether owners' system adequate

Ward v. Tesco Stores Ltd., C.A. **810**

NEW ZEALAND
Revenue
Income tax
Assessable income—Claim for expenditure in purchasing trading stock—Oil—Whether profits earned by subsidiary through arrangements connected with sale of oil to be included in expenditure—Whether arrangements void as having purpose and effect of altering incidence of income tax—Land and Income Tax Act 1954, ss. 108, 111 **Europa Oil (N.Z.) Ltd. v. Inland Revenue Comr.,** P.C. 46

NUISANCE
Public
Noise abatement
Order to abate nuisance—Noise not to exceed 70 decibels—Whether jurisdiction to impose term—Whether void for uncertainty—Public Health Act 1936, s. 94 (2)
Reg. v. Fenny Stratford Justices, *Ex parte* **Watney Mann (Midlands) Ltd.** D.C. 110

Watercourse
Liability of local authority see PUBLIC HEALTH: **Water supply**

OCCUPIERS' LIABILITY
" Occupation "
Compulsory purchase order
Local authority serving notice to treat and notice of entry on owner of house—House vacated and damaged by vandals—Child trespasser injured—Whether local authority or owner in occupation—Right of control—Whether local authority having knowledge of danger—Occupiers' Liability Act 1957, s. 2
Harris v. Birkenhead Corpn. (Pascoe Third Party; Alliance Assurance Co. Ltd Fourth Party), C.A. 27

PRACTICE
Chambers applications
Queen's Bench Division
Application to judge outside London—Summons issued in district registry—Bail applications **Practice Direction (Judge in Chambers: Outside London) (No. 3)** Q.B.D. 24

Chancery Division
Master
Power to hear matters in chambers—Leasehold reform—Leasehold Reform Act 1967 s. 27 **Practice Direction (Chancery: Master's Powers) (No. 3),** Ch.D. 63

Motion
Agreed adjournment—Procedure
Practice Direction (Chancery Division: Motions), Megarry V.-C. 44

Injunction to restrain use of confidential information—Conflicting affidavit evidence—Date to be fixed for cross examination—Plaintiffs' delay—Motion restored by defendants—Whether motion to be treated as abandoned—Court's discretion to dismiss or stand motion over to trial
Société Française d'Applications Commerciales et Industrielles S.A.R.L. v. Electronic Concepts Ltd., Oliver J. 5

Originating summons
Grant of new business tenancy—Summons issued with date of hearing to be fixed—Summons for determination of interim rent—Landlord and Tenant Act 1954 s. 24A (as amended by Law of Property Act 1969, s. 3 (1))
Practice Direction (Chancery: Originating Summons) (No. 2), Ch.D. 20

Discovery
Motion for
Ex parte application for order preventing defendants' use or disclosure of confidential information—Necessity for hearing in camera—Service of order—Method—Need for evidence of means
Vapormatic Co. Ltd. v. Sparex Ltd. (Practice Note), Graham J. 93

Possession of land
Unlawful sub-tenant
Lawful tenancy with absolute prohibition against underletting—Sub-tenants entering into occupation during tenancy without knowledge or consent of landlord—Payment of rent to tenant—Tenant determining tenancy—Whether summary proceedings for possession available—R.S.C., Ord. 113, r. 1
Moore Properties (Ilford) Ltd. v. McKeon, Fox J. 127

Postal facilities
Queen's Bench Division
Extension of class of business which may be conducted by post—R.S.C., Ord. r. 10 **Practice Direction (Q.B.D.: Postal Facilities),** Q.B.D. 48

PRACTICE—*continued*

Summary procedure on admissions of fact

Official referees' business

Order giving leave to enter judgment on admissions of fact—Facts in dispute—Whether appeal interlocutory or final—Need for Rules Committee to clarify position—R.S.C., Ord. 27, r. 3 **Technistudy Ltd. v. Kelland,** C.A. **1042**

Summary procedure under Order 14 *see* HUSBAND AND WIFE

Writ

Amendment

Writ served on foreign companies outside jurisdiction by leave—Application to amend writ by adding new claims to relief—Foreign disputants with funds in English banks—Court's discretion—Proper court to exercise jurisdiction—R.S.C., Ord. 20, r. 5 (1) **Beck v. Value Capital Ltd. (No. 2) (Note),** C.A. **572**

Service out of jurisdiction

Claim for declaration that contract governed by English law frustrated and consequential relief—Whether claims which " affect " contract—Whether jurisdiction to order service of notice of writ out of jurisdiction—Law Reform (Frustrated Contracts) Act 1943, ss. 1 (1), 2 (3)—R.S.C., Ord. 11, r. 1 (*f*) **B.P. Exploration Co. (Libya) Ltd. v. Hunt,** Kerr J. **788**

Counterclaim—" Properly brought against a person duly served within the jurisdiction "—Meaning—R.S.C., Ord. 11, r. 1 (1) (*j*) **Derby & Co. Ltd. v. Larsson,** H.L.(E.) **202**

PROBATE

Practice

Caveat

Extension of period caveat in force—Non-Contentious Probate Rules 1954, r. 44 (as amended by Non-Contentious Probate (Amendment) Rules 1976, r. 5 (*a*)) **Practice Direction (Probate: Caveat),** Fam.D. **957**

PUBLIC HEALTH

Nuisance

Abatement notice

Property in disrepair—Owners charged with failure to comply with notice—No evidence of interference with use of neighbouring property—No injury to health—Whether statutory nuisance—Public Health Act 1936, s. 92 (1) (*a*) **National Coal Board v. Thorne,** D.C. **543**

Complaint by tenant

Criminal or civil proceedings—Whether need to serve abatement notice—Public Health Act 1936, ss. 94, 99 **Reg. v. Newham East Justices,** *Ex parte* **Hunt,** D.C. **420**

Water supply

Artificial watercourse

Watercourse constructed by public subscription over farmland to provide water supply for village—Watercourse so constructed as to benefit farm—Cessation of use by village—Whether public supply—Whether vested in local authority—Watercourse rendered inaccessible outside farm—Whether cessation of public supply—Whether determination of estate vested in local authority—Whether farm owner's consent to accumulation of water to be inferred—Public Health Act 1875, s. 64 **Gilson v. Kerrier District Council,** C.A. **904**

RATING

Rateable occupation

Unoccupied hereditament

New telephone exchange—Completion notice served before installation of telephone equipment—Whether building " completed " without necessary equipment for use as telephone exchange—General Rate Act 1967, s. 17 (1), Sch. 1, paras. 8, 9 **Post Office v. Nottingham City Council,** C.A. **624**

Rateable value

Assessment of

Statutory undertaking—Harbour board's income derived from sources other than occupancy of hereditaments—Statutory orders providing for rateable value to be assessed on " relevant receipts "—Assessment based on annual receipts of harbour dues, property outside rating area, and rent from property—Whether orders ultra vires—General Rate Act 1967, s. 35 (1) (6)—Docks and Harbours (Valuation) Order 1971, arts. 2, 3 (2)—Docks and Harbours (Valuation) (Amendment) Order 1973, art. 4 **Milford Haven Counservancy Board v. Inland Revenue Comrs.,** C.A. **817**

RESTITUTION
Money credited in error
Claim by bank for repayment
Bank crediting money to customer's account by mistake—Bank confirming credit—Customer transferring sum to third party—Whether customer liable to repay money—Whether bank estopped from claiming restitution
United Overseas Bank v. Jiwani, MacKenna J. 964

RESTRAINT OF TRADE
Sale of goods
Restriction on brand of goods
Tied garage—Sales agreement with oil company for supply of petrol—Competitive price war—Temporary support scheme for some but not all tied garages—Whether discrimination rendering solus agreement void or in suspense while operating in unreasonable restraint of trade—Whether equitable relief available to oil company or garage **Shell U.K. Ltd. v. Lostock Garage Ltd.,** C.A. 118

REVENUE
Capital gains tax
Control of company
Company acting so that value passing out of its shares to overseas company—Whether company's action result of shareholders "exercising control"—Whether "person having control" includes plural—Interpretation Act 1889, s. 1—Finance Act 1965, Sch. 7, para. 15 (2) **Floor v. Davis,** Goulding J. 116

Disposal of assets
Dwelling house and garden occupied as main residence—Part of garden and house sold—Subsequent sale of remainder of garden with outline planning approval—Whether gain on sale of garden chargeable gain—Finance Act 1965, s. 29 (1) (2
Varty v. Lynes, Brightman J. 109

Scheme to avoid tax on sale of shareholding—Company incorporated to transfer shares to ultimate purchaser and to pass purchase price to overseas company—Taxpayer acquiring shares in new company in exchange for his shareholding—Whether deemed disposal of shares—Finance Act 1965, Sch. 7, para. 6 (1) (2)
Floor v. Davis, Goulding J. 116

Settled property
Death of holders of life interests in part of settled property—Whether deemed disposals by trustees of whole of settled property—"Part"—Whether including fractions or shares of settled property—Finance Act 1965, s. 25 (4) (12)
Pexton v. Bell; Crowe v. Appleby, C.A. 88

Trust fund of discretionary trust used to acquire dwelling house—Beneficiary occupying house as main residence with trustees' consent—Gain arising on sale of house—Whether beneficiary "entitled to occupy" house under terms of settlement—Whether gain exempted from tax—Finance Act 1965, s. 29 (9)
Sansom v. Peay, Brightman J. 107

Time limit for making assessment
Deemed disposal of assets "on the death"—Assessment made on executor after expiration of three-year period—Whether disposal to be deemed to take place before death—Whether assessment made within appropriate time limit—Finance Act 1965, s. 24 (1)—Taxes Management Act 1970, ss. 34 (1), 40 (1)
Larter v. Skone James, Walton J. 60

Corporation tax
Advance corporation tax
Preference dividend fixed by articles of association—Changes in rate of advance corporation tax—Whether contractual dividend varied by changes in rate of advance corporation tax—Finance Act 1972, s. 84 (2), Sch. 23, para. 18 (1)—Finance Act 1967, s. 12
Sime Darby London Ltd. v. Sime Darby Holdings Ltd., Brightman J. 5

Capital allowances
Machinery or plant—Erection of canopy over forecourt of petrol-filling station—Whether canopy "plant"—Finance Act 1971, ss. 41, 42 (as amended)
Dixon v. Fitch's Garage Ltd., Brightman J. 21

Computation of chargeable gains
Company in voluntary liquidation—Assignments of leaseholds by liquidator—Payment of arrears of rent to obtain landlord's consent to assignments—Whether payment of arrears expenditure on "enhancing" value of, or "preserving" title to, asset—Whether payment of arrears capital or revenue expenditure—Finance Act 1965, Sch. 6, paras. 4 (1) (*b*), 5 (2)
Emmerson v. Computer Time International Ltd., Fox J. 74

REVENUE—*continued*
Corporation tax—*continued*
Disposal of assets
Computation of allowable losses—Acquisition of unissued loan stock—Bargain not made at arm's length—Loss accruing on sale of loan stock—Whether acquisition deemed to be for consideration equal to market value—Whether total amount of loss allowable in computing amount of gains—Finance Act 1965, s. 22 (4)
Harrison v. Nairn Williamson Ltd., Goulding J. **1161**
Profits, assessment of
Anticipated profits from bills and promissory notes discounted or purchased by bank —Whether tax payable on fractional part of anticipated profits from bills— Income and Corporation Taxes Act 1970, ss. 108, 109, 129, 238
Willingale v. International Commercial Bank Ltd., Walton J. **657**

Customs and excise *see* CRIME: **Compound proceedings**
Untrue declarations
Causing document untrue in material particular to be delivered to commissioners— If committed knowingly or recklessly offence indictable—Whether two separate offences—Whether jurisdiction in Crown Court if element of knowledge or recklessness absent—Customs and Excise Act 1952, ss. 283 (2), 301
Attorney-General's Reference (No. 3 of 1975), C.A. **737**

Income tax
Domicile
Taxpayer born and educated in Canada—Taxpayer living and working in England— Matrimonial home established in England—Intention to return to Canada should taxpayer survive wife—Whether acquisition of English domicile of choice
Inland Revenue Comrs. v. Bullock, C.A. **1178**
Employment
Employees' profit-sharing scheme wound up—Distribution to employees of balance of funds—Whether payments emoluments arising from employment—Schedule E, Case I—Income and Corporation Taxes Act 1970, ss. 181 (1), 183 (1)
Brumby v. Milner, C.A. **29;** H.L.(E.) **1096**
"Interest of money"
Bank interest—Deposit of money at bank as condition of guarantee—Deposit and interest repaid at termination of guarantee—Whether taxpayer "receiving or entitled to" interest for years of assessment—Income Tax Act 1952, s. 148
Dunmore v. McGowan, Brightman J. **1086**
Machinery or plant
Plant—Expenditure by barrister on legal books and law reports—Whether books "plant" qualifying for capital allowance—Finance Act 1971, ss. 41 (1) (*a*), 47
Munby v. Furlong, Fox J. **410**
Rent
Excess rent—Land containing minerals leased at nominal rent—Royalties payable for licence to get and carry away minerals—Whether payments chargeable to income tax as excess rents—Income Tax Act 1952, s. 175.
T. & E. Homes Ltd. v. Robinson, Goulding J. **1150**
Transfer of assets abroad
Taxpayer's "power to enjoy" "income" of trust fund invested in foreign non-trading company—Whether management expenses of company deductible from gross receipts in computing income—Company making short-term capital gains— Taxpayer's liability to pay tax thereon—Method of computation of gains—Income Tax Act 1952, s. 412 (1)—Finance Act 1962, s. 13 (1), Sch. 10—Finance Act 1965, s. 82 (2)
Lord Chetwode v. Inland Revenue Comrs., C.A. **310**

Purchase tax
Chargeable goods
Coins bearing impression of heads of football players—Distributed "free" to purchasers of petrol on advertised basis of one coin for every four gallons— Whether "produced in quantity for general sale"—Sale of Goods Act 1893, s. 1 (1)—Purchase Tax Act 1963, Sch. 1, Group 25
Esso Petroleum Co. Ltd. v. Customs and Excise Comrs., H.L.(E.) **1**

Stamp duty
Deed of exchange as escrow
Exchange completed after fulfilment of conditions—Rate of stamp duty increased before completion date—Whether document "first executed" when delivered as escrow—Date when stamp duty payable—Stamp Act 1891, s. 14 (4)
Terrapin International Ltd. v. Inland Revenue Comrs., Walton J. **665**
Proxy vote
Form of proxy enabling proxy to vote at company meeting—Votes accepted at meeting—Subsequent objection that forms not stamped—Decision by Controller of Stamps that stamping not required—Whether duty chargeable—Effect of controller's decision—Stamp Act 1891, s. 12, Sch. 1 (as amended by Finance Act 1949, s. 35, Sch. 8, para. 18)
Marx v. Estates and General Investments Ltd., Brightman J. **380**

REVENUE—*continued*

Stamp duty—*continued*

Variation of settlement

"Conveyance or transfer operating as a voluntary disposition"—Beneficiary relin quishing protected life interest in income of trust fund for no consideration— Trust fund thereafter held for unascertained class of beneficiaries—Beneficiary relinquishing reversionary life interest in income and taking discretionary interes —Whether operating as "voluntary disposition" capable of valuation—Whethe stamp duty payable—Finance (1909–10) Act 1910, s. 74 (1) (5)
Thorn v. Inland Revenue Comrs., Walton J. 915

Tax advantage

Transaction in securities

Issue of shares by private company to avoid estate duty and retain family control— Irredeemable preference shares issued by mistake—Further issue of redeemable preference shares to correct error—Whether transactions for bona fide commercia reason—Finance Act 1960, s. 28 (1)
Inland Revenue Comrs. v. Goodwin, H.L.(E.) 19

Value added tax

Deduction of input tax

Corporation carrying on business and managing employees' pension fund—Value added tax incurred on fees for professional advice regarding pension fund— Whether corporation to be regarded as two bodies for purpose of tax—Whethe corporation entitled to deduct tax as input tax when accounting for tax chargeable on its own service—Finance Act 1972, s. 3 (1) (*a*)
Customs and Excise Comrs. v. British Railways Board, C.A. 1036

Exempt supply

Subscription to members' club—Club owning land providing facilities for sport and recreation—Members' beneficial ownership of land—Whether subscription paid for interest in or licence to occupy land—Whether exempt supply—Finance Act 1972 s. 13 (1), Sch. 5, Group 1, item 1 (as substituted by Value Added Tax (Consolida tion) Order 1974, Sch. 2)
Trewby v. Customs and Excise Comrs., D.C. 93

ROAD TRAFFIC

Laboratory test

Failure to provide specimen

Offence—Motorist acquitted of being in charge of vehicle when arrested—No suggestion of driving or attempting to drive—Whether proof necessary of bein in charge at arrest—Road Traffic Act 1972, ss. 5 (2) (3) (5), 9 (1) (3), Sch. 4, Pt.
Reg. v. Curran, H.L.(E.) 87

Police

Powers

Motorist stopping car behind ambulance in narrow one-way street—Police officer' instruction to motorist to reverse car to facilitate rescue operations—Whethe motorist's refusal obstruction of police officer in execution of duty—Whethe instruction reasonable—Police Act 1964, s. 51 (3) **Johnson v. Phillips,** D.C. 6

Special type of vehicle

"Side-car"

Roadworthy attachment to motor cycle designed for carriage of goods—Whethe "side-car"—Motor Vehicles (Driving Licences) Regulations 1971, reg. 6 (1) (*d*
Keen v. Parker, D.C. 7

RYLANDS v. FLETCHER

Exceptions to rule

Consent to danger

Escape of water from watercourse—Watercourse constructed over farmland t provide public water supply—Watercourse so constructed as to benefit farm— Liability **Gilson v. Kerrier District Council,** C.A. 90

SALE OF GOODS

Implied term

Obligation to account

Conditions of sale containing reservation of ownership clause—Property not to pas to buyers until all outstanding debts paid—Goods sold to sub-purchasers—Buyer in liquidation—Proceeds of sub-sales held in receiver's account—Whether seller entitled to trace and recover
Aluminium Industrie Vaassen B.V. v. Romalpa Aluminium Ltd
Mocatta J. and C.A. 67

SHIPPING
Charterparty
Description of vessel
Time charter of new building motor tank vessel—Identification by owners' declaration of yard and hull number—Sub-charter identifying vessel in similar terms—Vessel built at different yard with different hull number—Both charters governed by English law—Construction—Whether charterers entitled to reject vessel
Reardon Smith Line Ltd. v. Yngvar Hansen-Tangen (trading as H.E. Hansen-Tangen), H.L.(E.) **989**

SHIPS' NAMES
Dortmund **The Eschersheim,** C.A. **339**
H.L.(E.) **430**
Erkowit **The Eschersheim,** C.A. **339**
H.L.(E.) **430**
Eschersheim **The Eschersheim,** C.A. **339**
H.L.(E.) **430**
Jade **The Eschersheim,** C.A. **339**
H.L.(E.) **430**
Salus (formerly Rotesand) **The Eschersheim,** C.A. **339**
H.L.(E.) **430**

SOCIAL SECURITY
Supplementary allowance
Calculation
Student receiving minimum educational grant—Element in full grant for maintenance during vacation—Minimum grant less than vacation element—Application for benefit while seeking employment during vacation—Benefit reduced by vacation element—Whether correct in law—Supplementary Benefit Act 1966, Sch. 2, para. 4 (1) **Reg. v. Barnsley Supplementary Benefits Appeal Tribunal,** *Ex parte* **Atkinson,** D.C. **1047**

SOLICITOR
Unqualified person
Conveyance
Draftsman preparing instruments for transfer of land for members of association—Members paying fees to association's transfer agents—Draftsman receiving no fees—Whether draftsman preparing instruments for fee, gain or reward—Solicitors Act 1957, s. 20 (1) **Reynolds v. Hoyle,** D.C. **207**

Transfer agents undertaking legal work for property transactions—Instrument of transfer prepared by another unqualified person—Whether transfer agent directly or indirectly " draws or prepares " instruments—Solicitors Act 1957, s. 20 (1)
Green v. Hoyle, D.C. **575**

STATUTE
Construction
Consolidation Act
Words clear and unambiguous—No recourse to corresponding provision in previous statute—Road Traffic Act 1972, s. 9 (3) **Reg. v. Curran,** H.L.(E.) **87**

Expressio unius, exclusio alterius
Moneylenders Act 1927, s. 4 (3)
London and Harrogate Securities Ltd. v. Pitts, Mocatta J. **264**
C.A. **1063**

TRADE DESCRIPTION
False description
Car
Mileometer recording less than actual mileage—Accuracy of mileometer reading disclaimed during negotiations and in small print in contractual document—Whether sufficient—Whether supply of goods to which false trade description applied—" Supplied "—Trade Descriptions Act 1968, ss. 1 (1) *(b)*, 2 (1) *(j)*, 4
Reg. v. Hammertons Cars Ltd., C.A. **1243**

" Provision . . . of services "
Airline seat reservation
B.O.A.C. confirming reservation for specified flight—Overbooking policy resulting in passenger not being carried as promised—Whether confirmation false statement—Transaction before B.O.A.C. dissolved and replaced by British Airways Board—Whether board liable to prosecution—Trade Descriptions Act 1968, s. 14 (1) (2)—Civil Aviation Act 1971, ss. 37, 57
British Airways Board v. Taylor, H.L.(E.) **13**

TRUSTS
Trustee
Wilful default
Account—Trustees' admitted act of wilful default in respect of land forming par of estate—Whether order for account to be general or limited to affected land *In re* **Tebbs, decd.,** Slade J. 92

Variation
Act of 1958
Infant representation—Arrangement affecting infant or unborn beneficiary—Nee for case to counsel and counsel's written opinion **Practice Direction (Variation of Trusts: Counsel's Opinion),** Ch.D. 88

Tax liability
Capital transfer tax—Family arrangement—Division of trust fund between life tenan and remaindermen—Infant remainderman's share liable to shortfall by incidence o capital transfer tax on life tenant's premature death—Insurance to provide fo shortfall—Form of policy *In re* **Robinson's Settlement Trusts,** Templeman J. 80

VICARIOUS LIABILITY
Master and servant
Course of employment
Milk roundsman assisted by young boy in collecting and delivering milk bottles—Employers' prohibition on young persons assisting roundsmen—Injury to boy—Whether employers vicariously liable for roundsman's negligence **Rose v. Plenty,** C.A. 14

WILL
Construction
Omission
Clause providing for life interests in residuary estate followed by gifts of capital—Intended gifts of capital to testatrix's son contained in approved draft of claus inadvertently omitted from will—Whether will to be admitted to probate wit clause omitted *In re* **Reynette-James, decd.,** Templeman J. 16

WORDS AND PHRASES
"*As a trespasser*"—Theft Act 1968, s. 9 (1) (*b*) **Reg. v. Jones (John),** C.A. 67
"*Bookmaking*"—Betting and Lotteries Act (Northern Ireland) 1957, ss. 13 (1) (*a*), 20 **Seay v. Eastwood,** H.L.(N.I.) 111
"*Broadly similar*"—Equal Pay Act 1970, s. 1 (4) (as amended) **Dugdale v. Kraft Foods Ltd.,** E.A.T. 128
"*Business*"—Counter-Inflation (Business Rents) Order 1972 and 1973, art. 2 (2) **Town Investments Ltd. v. Department of the Environmen** Foster J. and C.A. 112
"*Common land*"—Commons Registration Act 1965, s. 22 (1) **Central Electricity Generating Board v. Clwyd County Council,** Goff J. 15
"*Completed*"—General Rate Act 1967, Sch. 1, para. 8 (1) (*a*) **Post Office v. Nottingham City Council,** C.A. 62
"*Conveyance or transfer operating as a voluntary disposition*"—Finance (1909–191C Act 1910, s. 74 (5) **Thorn v. Inland Revenue Comrs.,** Walton J. 91
"*Differences . . . of practical importance*"—Equal Pay Act 1970, s. 1 (4) (as amendec **Dugdale v. Kraft Foods Ltd.,** E.A.T. 128
"*Disposition*"—Companies Act 1948, s. 227 *In re* **J. Leslie Engineers Co. Ltd.,** Oliver J. 29
"*Draws or prepares*"—Solicitors Act 1957, s. 20 (1) (*a*) **Green v. Hoyle,** D.C. 57
"*Efficient use*"—Highways Act 1959, s. 111 **Roberton v. Secretary of State for the Environment,** Phillips J. 37
"*Enhancing*"—Finance Act 1965, Sch. 6, para. 4 (1) (*b*) **Emmerson v. Computer Time International Ltd.,** Fox J. 74
"*First executed*"—Stamp Act 1891, s. 14 (4) **Terrapin International Ltd. v. Inland Revenue Comrs.,** Walton J. 66
"*Hire or reward*"—Air Navigation Order 1974, art. 91 (6) (*a*) (i) **Corner v. Clayton,** D.C. 80
"*Illegal entrant*"—Immigration Act 1971, s. 33 (1) **Reg. v. Governor of Risley Remand Centre,** *Ex parte* **Hassan,** D.C. 97
"*Incidental to . . . proceedings in . . . court*"—Supreme Court of Judicature (Consolic ation) Act 1925, s. 50 (1) **Department of Health and Social Security v. Envoy Farmers Ltd.,** Jupp J. 101
"*Income*"—Income Tax Act 1952, s. 412 (1) **Lord Chetwode v. Inland Revenue Comrs.,** C.A. 31
"*Indictable offence*"—Legal Aid Act 1974, s. 30 (2) (*a*) **Reg. v. Guildhall Justices,** *Ex parte* **Marshall,** D.C. 33

WORDS AND PHRASES—*continued*
"*Intent*"—Offences against the Person Act 1861, s. 18 **Reg. v. Belfon,** C.A. **741**
"*Land*"—Highways Act 1959, s. 111
Roberton v. Secretary of State for the Environment, Phillips J. **371**
"*Noxious thing*"—Offences against the Person Act 1861, s. 23 **Reg. v. Cato,** C.A. **110**
"*Occupied*"—Landlord and Tenant Act 1954, s. 23 (1)
Morrisons Holdings Ltd. v. Manders Property (Wolverhampton) Ltd., C.A. **533**
"*On an issue*"—Criminal Appeal Act 1968, s. 23 (2) (*a*) **Reg. v. Melville,** C.A. **181**
"*On the death*"—Finance Act 1965, s. 24 (1) **Larter v. Skone James,** Walton J. **607**
"*Per annum*"—Moneylenders Act 1927, s. 6 (2)
London and Harrogate Securities Ltd. v. Pitts, Mocatta J. **264;** C.A. **1063**
"*Per cent.*"—Moneylenders Act 1927, s. 6 (2)
London and Harrogate Securities Ltd. v. Pitts, Mocatta J. **264**
C.A. **1063**
"*Person having control*"—Finance Act 1965, Sch. 7, para. 15 (2)
Floor v. Davis, Goulding J. **1167**
"*Plant*"—Finance Act 1971, s. 41 (1) (*a*) **Dixon v. Fitch's Garage Ltd.,** Brightman J. **215**
——Finance Act 1971, Pt. III, c. I **Munby v. Furlong,** Fox J. **410**
"*Power to enjoy*"—Income Tax Act 1952, s. 412 (1)
Lord Chetwode v. Inland Revenue Comrs., C.A. **310**
"*Preserving*"—Finance Act 1965, Sch. 6, para. 4 (1) (*b*)
Emmerson v. Computer Time International Ltd., Fox J. **749**
"*Private purchaser*"—Hire-Purchase Act 1964, s. 29 (2)
Stevenson v. Beverley Bentinck Ltd., C.A. **483**
"*Produced in quantity for general sale*"—Purchase Tax Act 1963, Sch. 1, Group 25
Esso Petroleum Co. Ltd. *v.* **Customs and Excise Comrs.,** H.L.(E.) **1**
"*Proper*"—R.S.C., Ord. 62, r. 28 (2) **Garthwaite v. Sherwood,** Kerr J. **705**
"*Properly brought against a person duly served within the jurisdiction*"—R.S.C., Ord. 11, r. 1 (1) (*j*) **Derby & Co. Ltd. v. Larsson,** H.L.(E.) **202**
"*Property of the company*"—Companies Act 1948, s. 227
In re **J. Leslie Engineers Co. Ltd.,** Oliver J. **292**
"*Provision . . . of services*"—Trade Descriptions Act 1968, s. 14 (1) (*b*) (i)
British Airways Board v. Taylor, H.L.(E.) **13**
"*Public place*"—Public Order Act 1936, s. 9 (1) (as substituted)
Cawley v. Frost, D.C. **1207**
"*Publication*"—Obscene Publications Act 1959, s. 2 (6)
Attorney-General's Reference (No. 2 of 1975), C.A. **710**
"*Receiving or entitled to*"—Income Tax Act 1952, s. 148
Dunmore v. McGowan, Brightman J. **1086**
"*Side-car*"—Motor Vehicles (Driving Licences) Regulations 1971, reg. 6 (1) (*d*)
Keen v. Parker, D.C. **74**
"*Supplied*"—Trade Descriptions Act 1968, s. 1 (1) (*b*)
Reg. v. Hammertons Cars Ltd., C.A. **1243**
"*Trade or finance purchaser*"—Hire-Purchase Act 1964, s. 29 (2)
Stevenson v. Beverley Bentinck Ltd., C.A. **483**
"*Voluntary disposition*"—Finance (1909–1910) Act 1910, s. 74 (5)
Thorn v. Inland Revenue Comrs., Walton J. **915**
"*Working place*"—Construction (Working Places) Regulations 1966, reg. 28 (1)
Ferguson v. John Dawson & Partners (Contractors) Ltd., C.A. **1213**

ERRATA

[1976] 1 W.L.R.

Page 82A, line 2: *for* " 1973 " *read* " 1971 "

Page 176A, line 1: *for* [FAMILY DIVISION] *read* [DIVORCE COUNTY COURT]

Page 177A, line 4: *for* " Master Martyn " *read* " Mr. Martyn, taxing officer of the Family Division."

Page 277F, line 34: *for* " ingenuously " *read* " ingeniously "

Page 533: The references to *Sewing Machines Rentals Ltd.* v. *Wilson; Same* v. *Udeala; Morlen Investments Ltd.* v. *Wilson* refer to reports of the decision in interlocutory matters and not to the unreported substantive appeals in which the House of Lords dismissed the petitions.

Page 624D: *delete* lines 25 and 26.

Page 745F: line 33 *should read* " any ill will towards the person injured."

Page 1096C, line 12: *for* " 1975 " *read* " 1976."

The Weekly Law Reports

Volume 1

Containing those cases of value to practitioners which are not intended to be included in The Law Reports, together with practice notes and directions.

[HOUSE OF LORDS]

* ESSO PETROLEUM CO. LTD. . . . . . RESPONDENTS

AND

CUSTOMS AND EXCISE COMMISSIONERS . . APPELLANTS

1975 Nov. 10, 11, 12; Dec. 10 — Lord Wilberforce, Viscount Dilhorne, Lord Simon of Glaisdale, Lord Fraser of Tullybelton and Lord Russell of Killowen

Revenue—Purchase tax—Chargeable goods—Coins bearing impression of heads of football players — Distributed "free" to purchasers of petrol on advertised basis of one coin for every four gallons—Whether "produced in quantity for general sale" —Sale of Goods Act 1893 (56 & 57 *Vict. c.* 71), *s.* 1 (1) [1]— *Purchase Tax Act* 1963 (*c.* 9), *Sch.* 1, *Group* 25

By the Purchase Tax Act 1963, Sch. 1, Group 25: "Pictures, prints, engravings, photographs, figures, busts, reliefs and similar articles of a kind produced in quantity for general sale" were enumerated as being liable to the tax.

The plaintiffs ("Esso"), suppliers of and dealers in petrol, commissioned the manufacture of coins bearing on one side the head of one of the 30 English footballers chosen for the 1970 World Cup competition and on the other the word "Esso." To promote sales the coins were, as advertised, distributed free to any motorist buying petrol from Esso filling stations and dealers on the basis of one coin for every four gallons of petrol purchased. The Customs and Excise Commissioners claimed that the coins were goods chargeable to purchase tax within Group 25 of Schedule 1 to the Purchase Tax Act 1963, as being "produced in quantity for general sale," and claimed tax accordingly.

Pennycuick V.-C. dismissed Esso's summons for a declaration that the coins were not chargeable goods under the provisions of the Act of 1963. The Court of Appeal reversed his decision.

On appeal to the House of Lords:—

Held, dismissing the appeal (Lord Fraser of Tullybelton dissenting), that, on the basis that the plaintiffs intended to create a legal obligation to supply the coins, the consideration for the entry into that contract was the entry by the motorist into a contract to buy a certain quantity of petrol and accordingly there was no contract to transfer the coins "for a money

[1] Sale of Goods Act 1893, s. 1 (1): see post, p. 7C.

consideration " within section 1 of the Sale of Goods Act 1893, A
so that the coins were not produced for sale within Group 25 of Schedule 1 to the Purchase Tax Act 1963 and did not attract tax thereunder (post, pp. 5C, D, 7C, D, 11C–E).

Per Viscount Dilhorne and Lord Russell of Killowen. On the facts there was no contractual intention in relation to the coins (post, pp. 5A, B, 10E–G).

Scott & Co. Ltd. v. *Solomon* [1905] 1 K.B. 577, D.C., *Bulpitt & Sons Ltd.* v. *S. Bellman & Sons Ltd.* (1962) L.R. 3 B
R.P. 62 and dictum of Lord Moulton in *Heilbut, Symons & Co.* v. *Buckleton* [1913] A.C. 30, 47, H.L.(E.) considered.

Decision of the Court of Appeal [1975] 1 W.L.R. 406 affirmed.

The following cases are referred to in their Lordships' opinions:

Bulpitt & Sons Ltd. v. *S. Bellman & Sons Ltd.* (1962) L.R. 3 R.P. 62.
Carlill v. Carbolic Smoke Ball Co. [1893] 1 Q.B. 256, C.A. C
Chappell & Co. Ltd. v. *Nestlé Co. Ltd.* [1960] A.C. 87; [1959] 3 W.L.R. 169; [1959] 2 All E.R. 701, H.L.(E.).
Edwards v. *Skyways Ltd.* [1964] 1 W.L.R. 349; [1964] 1 All E.R. 494.
Heilbut, Symons & Co. v. *Buckleton* [1913] A.C. 30, H.L.(E.).
Rose and Frank Co. v. *J. R. Crompton and Brothers Ltd.* [1923] 2 K.B. 261, C.A.
Scott & Co. Ltd. v. *Solomon* [1905] 1 K.B. 577; 69 J.P. 137, D.C. D
Taylor v. *Smetten* (1883) 11 Q.B.D. 207, D.C.

The following additional cases were cited in argument:

Attorney-General v. *Boden* [1912] 1 K.B. 539.
Garnac Grain Co. Inc. v. *H. M. F. Faure & Fairclough Ltd.* (*Note*) [1968] A.C. 1130; [1967] 3 W.L.R. 142; [1967] 3 All E.R. 353, H.L.(E.).
Inland Revenue Commissioners v. *Europa Oil (N.Z.) Ltd.* [1971] A.C. E
760; [1971] 2 W.L.R. 55, P.C.
Inland Revenue Commissioners v. *Wesleyan & General Assurance Society* (1946) 62 T.L.R. 741; [1946] 2 All E.R. 749, C.A.
Kirkness v. *John Hudson & Co. Ltd.* [1955] A.C. 696; [1955] 2 W.L.R. 1135; [1955] 2 All E.R. 345, H.L.(E.).
Stephenson Brothers Ltd. v. *Customs and Excise Commissioners* [1953]
1 W.L.R. 335; [1953] 1 All E.R. 469. F
Weeks v. *Tybald* (1605) Noy 11.
Whitbread & Co. Ltd. v. *Bell* [1970] 2 Q.B. 547; [1970] 2 W.L.R. 1025; [1970] 2 All E.R. 64, D.C.

APPEAL from the Court of Appeal.

This was an appeal from an order of the Court of Appeal (Lord Denning
M.R., Stephenson and Geoffrey Lane L.JJ.) on January 31, 1975, allowing G
an appeal by the present respondents, Esso Petroleum Co. Ltd., from an order made by Pennycuick V.-C. on June 20, 1973. By his order he had dismissed the originating summons herein by which the respondents sought a declaration that certain coins manufactured to their order and supplied by them to petrol service station proprietors were not chargeable goods
under the provisions of the Purchase Tax Act 1963. The Court of Appeal H
discharged the order of Pennycuick V.-C. and granted the declaration asked, but gave leave to appeal to the House of Lords on terms as to costs.

The facts are stated in their Lordships' opinions.

C. S. Staughton Q.C. and *P. L. Gibson* for the appellant.

D. C. Potter Q.C., *Peter Scott* and *Peter Whiteman* for the respondent company.

A Their Lordships took time for consideration.

December 10. LORD WILBERFORCE. My Lords, I have had the benefit of reading in advance the opinion prepared by my noble and learned friend Lord Simon of Glaisdale. I agree with his analysis of the transaction. The case being one of impression, as to an essentially simple situation, I do not consider it useful to add any fresh arguments of my own.
B I would dismiss the appeal.

VISCOUNT DILHORNE. My Lords, the only question for decision in this appeal is whether the coins distributed by the respondents to garage proprietors, for them to give to customers who bought four gallons or more of petrol, were coins "produced in quantity for general sale." If they
C were, then they came within Group 25 in Schedule 1 to the Purchase Tax Act 1963, and the respondents are liable to pay purchase tax on them to the amount of some £200,000.

That the coins were produced in quantity and for general distribution is clear and not disputed. Were they produced for sale? They were sold by the respondents to some 4,900 retailers of petrol for £3 per thousand, but that does not determine the tax liability. The question to be decided is,
D were they sold or intended to be sold by the garage proprietors to purchasers of petrol?

Each coin bore the head of one of the 30 members of the English squad for the World Cup and was wrapped in an opaque covering. The respondents' intention was to promote the sale of their petrol by tempting persons to buy petrol from their dealers in the hope of securing a complete set of
E coins, and they advertised their "World Cup Coin Collection" extensively in the press and on television.

They distributed to garages posters for exhibition on the forecourts. One series of posters had on it "Collect the complete set. One coin given with every four gallons of petrol." Another series had the words "Collect the full set of thirty coins. One coin given when you buy four gallons of petrol." They sent each of their dealers who participated in the campaign
F a pamphlet telling him to give one coin to each customer buying four gallons; two coins if eight gallons were bought and so on, and that if he did so and gave a free collection card in which the coins could be placed he would "then ensure the success of this promotion by increasing gallonage sales on your station." The dealers were also supplied with "luxury collector" cards which they were told to sell for 2s. 6d. each.

G If the coins were a free gift to every customer who purchased four gallons of petrol or multiples of that quantity, then the appeal must be dismissed. If, on the other hand, a legal contract was entered into between the customer and the dealer which, in addition to the supply of petrol, involved the dealer in a legally binding obligation to transfer a coin or coins to the customer, and if that legal contract amounted to a sale, then the appeal must be allowed.

H Was there any intention on the part of the garage proprietor and also on the part of the customer who bought four gallons, or multiples of that quantity, of petrol to enter into a legally binding contract in relation to a coin or coins? In *Rose and Frank Co.* v. *J. R. Crompton and Brothers Ltd.* [1923] 2 K.B. 261, 288, Scrutton L.J. said:

"Now it is quite possible for parties to come to an agreement by accepting a proposal with the result that the agreement concluded does

> not give rise to legal relations. The reason of this is that the parties A
> do not intend that their agreement shall give rise to legal relations. This intention may be implied from the subject matter of the agreement, but it may also be expressed by the parties. In social and family relations such an intention is readily implied, while in business matters the opposite result would ordinarily follow."

And Atkin L.J. said, at p. 293: B

> " To create a contract there must be a common intention of the parties to enter into legal obligations, mutually communicated expressly or impliedly."

The facts of that case were very different from those of this. In that case there was an agreement dealing with business matters. In this case the
question has to be considered whether there was any agreement as to a C
coin or coins between the garage proprietor and the customer and also, if there was, was it intended on both sides to be one having legal relations? If a coin was just to be given to the motorist, it would not be necessary for there to have been any agreement between him and the garage proprietor with regard to it.

In *Edwards* v. *Skyways Ltd.* [1964] 1 W.L.R. 349, where the facts D
were also very different from those in this case and where the plaintiff was seeking to recover the amount of an ex gratia payment, Megaw J. referred to these passages in *Rose and Frank Co.* v. *J. R. Crompton and Brothers Ltd.* and said, at p. 355:

> " In the present case, the subject matter of the agreement is business
> relations, not social or domestic matters. There was a meeting of E
> minds—an intention to agree. There was, admittedly, consideration for the company's promise. I accept the propositions of counsel for the plaintiff that in a case of this nature the onus is on the party who asserts that no legal effect was intended, and the onus is a heavy one."

I do not wish in any way to criticise or qualify these statements, but I do
not feel that they provide a sound foundation for the decision of this appeal. F

True it is that the respondents are engaged in business. True it is that they hope to promote the sale of their petrol, but it does not seem to me necessarily to follow or to be inferred that there was any intention on their part that their dealers should enter into legally binding contracts with regard to the coins; or any intention on the part of the dealers to enter into any such contract or any intention on the part of the purchaser of four gallons
of petrol to do so. G

If in this case on the facts of this case the conclusion is reached that there was any such intention on the part of the customer, of the dealer and of the respondents, it would seem to exclude the possibility of any dealer ever making a free gift to any of his customers however negligible its value to promote his sales.

If what was described as being a gift, which would be given if some- H
thing was purchased, was something of value to the purchaser, then it could readily be inferred that there was a common intention to enter into legal relations. But here, whatever the cost of production, it is clear that the coins were of little intrinsic value.

I do not consider that the offer of a gift of a free coin is properly to be regarded as a business matter in the sense in which that word was used by Scrutton L.J. in the passage cited above. Nor do I think that such an offer

A can be comprehended within the "business relations" which were in the *Skyways* case, as Megaw J. said "the subject-matter of the agreement." I see no reason to imply any intention to enter into contractual relations from the statements on the posters that a coin would be given if four gallons of petrol were bought.

Nor do I see any reason to impute to every motorist who went to a garage where the posters were displayed to buy four gallons of petrol any intention
B to enter into a legally binding contract for the supply to him of a coin. On the acceptance of his offer to purchase four gallons there was no doubt a legally binding contract for the supply to him of that quantity of petrol, but I see again no reason to conclude that because such an offer was made by him, it must be held that, as the posters were displayed, his offer included an offer to take a coin. The gift of a coin might lead to a motorist
C returning to the garage to obtain another one, but I think the facts in this case negative any contractual intention on his part and on the part of the dealer as to the coin and suffice to rebut any presumption there may be to the contrary.

If, however, there was any contract relating to the coin or coins, the consideration for the entry into that contract was not the payment of any money but the entry into a contract to purchase four gallons or multiples
D of that quantity of petrol, in which case the contract relating to the coin or coins cannot be regarded as a contract of sale.

I therefore, while of opinion that there was no legally binding contract as to the coins and so that it has not been established that they were produced for sale, am also of opinion that if there was any such contract it was not one for sale.

E In my opinion this appeal should be dismissed.

LORD SIMON OF GLAISDALE. My Lords, I have had the advantage of reading in draft the speech prepared by my noble and learned friend, Lord Russell of Killowen. I beg to take advantage of his explanation of the facts that have led to the appeal and the statutory provisions by which
F they are to be judged.

I am, however, my Lords, not prepared to accept that the promotion material put out by Esso was not envisaged by them as creating legal relations between the garage proprietors who adopted it and the motorists who yielded to its blandishments. In the first place, Esso and the garage proprietors put the material out for their commercial advantage, and designed it to attract the custom of motorists. The whole transaction took place in
G a setting of business relations. In the second place, it seems to me in general undesirable to allow a commercial promoter to claim that what he has done is a mere puff, not intended to create legal relations (cf. *Carlill* v. *Carbolic Smoke Ball Co.* [1893] 1 Q.B. 256). The coins may have been themselves of little intrinsic value; but all the evidence suggests that Esso contemplated that they would be attractive to motorists and that there
H would be a large commercial advantage to themselves from the scheme, an advantage to which the garage proprietors also would share. Thirdly, I think that authority supports the view that legal relations were envisaged. In *Rose and Frank Co.* v. *J. R. Crompton and Brothers Ltd.* [1923] 2 K.B. 261, 288 Scrutton L.J. said:

> "Now it is quite possible for parties to come to an agreement by accepting a proposal with the result that the agreement concluded does not give rise to legal relations. The reason of this is that the parties

> do not intend that their agreement shall give rise to legal relations. A This intention may be implied from the subject matter of the agreement, but it may also be expressed by the parties. In social and family relations such an intention is readily implied, while in business matters the opposite result would ordinarily follow."

In the same case Atkin L.J. said, at p. 293:

> "To create a contract there must be a common intention of the parties B to enter into legal obligations, mutually communicated expressly or impliedly. Such an intention ordinarily will be inferred when parties enter into an agreement which in other respects conforms to the rules of law as to the formation of contracts. It may be negatived impliedly by the nature of the agreed promise or promises, as in the case of offer and acceptance of hospitality, or of some agreements made in the course C of family life between members of a family as in *Balfour* v. *Balfour* [1919] 2 K.B. 571."

In *Edwards* v. *Skyways Ltd.* [1964] 1 W.L.R. 349, 355 Megaw J. quoted these passages and added:

> "In the present case, the subject matter of the agreement is business relations, not social or domestic matters. . . . I accept the propositions D . . . that in a case of this nature the onus is on the party who asserts that no legal effect was intended, and the onus is a heavy one."

I respectfully agree. And I venture to add that it begs the question to assert that no motorist who bought petrol in consequence of seeing the promotion material prominently displayed in the garage forecourt would be likely to bring an action in the county court if he were refused a coin. He E might be a suburban Hampden who was not prepared to forgo what he conceived to be his rights or to allow a tradesman to go back on his word.

Believing as I do that Esso envisaged a bargain of some sort between the garage proprietor and the motorist, I must try to analyse the transaction. The analysis that most appeals to me is one of the ways in which Lord Denning M.R. considered the case [1975] 1 W.L.R. 406, 409B–D, F namely a collateral contract of the sort described by Lord Moulton in *Heilbut, Symons & Co.* v. *Buckleton* [1913] A.C. 30, 47:

> ". . . there may be a contract the consideration for which is the making of some other contract. 'If you will make such and such a contract I will give you £100,' is in every sense of the word a complete legal contract. It is collateral to the main contract, . . ." G

So here. The law happily matches the reality. The garage proprietor is saying, "If you will buy four gallons of my petrol, I will give you one of these coins." None of the reasons which have caused the law to consider advertising or display material as an invitation to treat rather than an offer applies here. What the garage proprietor says by his placards is in fact and in law an offer of consideration to the motorist to enter into a contract H of sale of petrol. Of course, not every motorist will notice the placard, but nor will every potential offeree of many offers be necessarily conscious that they have been made. However, the motorist who does notice the placard, and in reliance thereon drives in and orders the petrol, is in law doing two things at the same time. First, he is accepting the offer of a coin if he buys four gallons of petrol. Secondly, he is himself offering to buy four gallons of petrol: this offer is accepted by the filling of his tank.

A Has there then been a sale of the coins, so that they can be said to have been "produced in quantity for general sale" within Group 25 of Schedule 1 to the Purchase Tax Act 1963? I think that the main emphasis here is on "quantity" and "general." But it would be contrary to all principles of sound statutory construction not to give each word its full significance. I agree with my noble and learned friend, Lord Russell of Killowen, for the reasons which he gives, that the definition of "purchase" in section 40 B (1) throws no light on the meaning of "sale" in the Schedule. "Sale" must therefore be interpreted in the primary sense demanded by the context of a taxing statute (unless some secondary meaning must be preferred in order to avoid injustice, absurdity, anomaly or stultification of the statutory objective). The primary sense of "sale" in this context is its primary meaning in ordinary legal usage. This is expressed in section 1 of the Sale C of Goods Act 1893 (which codified the common law), namely "a contract whereby the seller transfers or agrees to transfer the property in goods to the buyer for a money consideration, called the price." Here the coins were not transferred for a money consideration. They were transferred in consideration of the motorist entering into a contract for the sale of petrol. The coins were therefore not produced for sale, and do not fall within the Schedule. They are exempt from purchase tax.

D I would therefore dismiss the appeal.

LORD FRASER OF TULLYBELTON. My Lords, the facts in this case have been fully set out in the speech which is about to be delivered by my noble and learned friend, Lord Russell of Killowen, and which I have had the advantage of reading in print. I need not therefore rehearse them. The E only question for decision is whether these coins were "produced . . . for . . . sale." In my opinion they were, and I would therefore hold that they fell within the Group 25 of Schedule 1 to the Purchase Tax Act 1963.

The matter that is in my view of decisive importance is the wording on the posters which were displayed in the forecourts of Esso petrol retailers during the promotion scheme. The originals of these posters were large, 60″ × 40″, and each poster was headed in large letters "Free World Cup F Coins." Below that was a picture either of one of the coins or of a group of the coins and below the picture on one poster were the words "Collect the complete set. One coin given with every four gallons of petrol" and on the other poster "Collect the full set of thirty coins. One coin given when you buy four gallons of petrol." The feature of that wording, which is of special significance, is the correlation of one coin to every four gallons; G a definite scale of issue, or ration, was thus promised, and the plain inference is that any motorist who bought four gallons of petrol would have a right also to receive a coin. It is as if a baker had a poster in his shop window promising that any person who bought a dozen buns would be given one extra bun free of charge to make up a "baker's dozen." Standing that promise by the retailer, it is in my opinion impossible to avoid the inference that when a motorist ordered some petrol he was offering to enter H into a contract on the terms advertised by the retailer, and therefore that when his offer was accepted he had a contractual right to one coin with every four gallons of petrol. The analysis by the Vice-Chancellor in [1973] 1 W.L.R. 1240, 1245 of what would happen when a motorist ordered petrol is in my opinion the correct one.

Various reasons have been suggested for taking the contrary view, and the one that appears to me to be the strongest is also the simplest, namely, that the poster and advertisements repeatedly use the words "gift" "given" and "free." It is said that the use of these words, together with the small value of the coins and the fact that the price of petrol was not increased during the promotion period shows that the coins were truly given away. But the purpose of the promotion scheme was to attract motorists, and perhaps their children, and to persuade them to buy Esso rather than some other brand of petrol, and it cannot be right that a motorist who had been persuaded to buy four gallons of Esso should be liable to be met at the end of the transaction with a refusal to give him a coin. No doubt it was unlikely that any Esso retailer who was taking part in the promotion would fail to deliver a coin with four gallons of petrol, because he would lose goodwill if he did. But the same is true in greater or less degree of every retailer who may be tempted to give short weight or inferior quality in breach of his contract, and the unlikeliness of such an event cannot in my opinion affect the legal quality of the transaction. It was even more unlikely that any motorist would sue to enforce his right to the coin or to recover damages for failure to deliver one. But the same is true of many small retail transactions which are undoubtedly contracts capable of being enforced by legal proceedings, but not worth enforcing. Accordingly I regard that also as irrelevant. The fact that the inclusive price could not be apportioned so as to attribute any particular part of it to the coin is also irrelevant, and does not by itself indicate that the coin was not bought along with the petrol for one inclusive price—see *Taylor* v. *Smetten* (1883) 11 Q.B.D. 207, *Scott & Co. Ltd.* v. *Solomon* [1905] 1 K.B. 577; 69 J.P. 137. It was argued that these cases, where coupons carrying valuable rights were included in packets of tea, were distinguishable because the coupons were either physically inside the packet or were part of the wrapper, so that it was impossible to buy the tea without the coupons. But I cannot see that that makes any difference, because here the delivery of the coin would be, for all practical purposes, contemporaneous with delivery of the petrol, so that both would form part of the one transaction just as the tea and the coupon did.

I recognise that the reason why an advertisement or display of goods for sale at a stated price is only an invitation to treat and not an offer for sale (as explained by my noble and learned friend, Lord Russell of Killowen, in his speech) has no application to the advertisement of the coins, because the petrol retailer could always remove the advertisement if the supply of coins threatened to run out. But while that is so, I do not regard it as a sufficient reason for declining to recognise what seems to me a simple operation of acquiring four gallons of petrol and a coin as a sale of both articles in one transaction, nor as a reason for breaking it up into two separate operations, a sale of the petrol and a collateral contract for acquiring the coin.

For these reasons I would allow the appeal.

LORD RUSSELL OF KILLOWEN. My Lords, the question in this appeal is whether certain goods were chargeable for the purposes of the now defunct purchase tax: and that depends upon whether, being goods of a type within the description contained in Group 25 of Schedule 1 to the Purchase Tax Act 1963, they were "produced in quantity for general sale." As will be seen the goods were undoubtedly produced in quantity, and, if produced for sale, it is not disputed that the sale envisaged in the production was "general" sale. Thus the argument has centred on the question whether the goods were "produced . . . for . . . sale." Pennycuick V.-C. concluded that they were: the Court of Appeal (Lord Denning M.R.

A and Stephenson and Lane L.JJ.) concluded that they were not. The amount of purchase tax involved is the substantial sum of £200,000.

The goods in question were medals bearing the likenesses of the 30 members of the England soccer squad which went to Mexico in 1970 for the World Cup, together with reproductions of their signatures and their names, one player to each medal, the other side bearing the word Esso and the words "England World Cup Squad. Mexico 1970."

B The respondents ("Esso") conceived in 1970 a petrol sales promotion scheme. Esso had some 6,000 petrol outlets in this country, some owned by Esso subsidiaries but most by other proprietors. The scheme involved the production of millions of these medals, the intention being that these medals should be distributed, to use a neutral phrase, by petrol pump proprietors to motorists buying Esso petrol on the basis of one medal to C each motorist buying four gallons of petrol, two if eight, and so on. The medals were to be in opaque wrappers, and it was hoped that a motorist would persist in buying Esso petrol in the hope of collecting the full set of 30. It was to be, according to Esso, the biggest promotion scheme ever promoted by Esso.

The promotion scheme was extensively advertised by Esso in the press and on television, the public being urged to start collecting the set of 30 D medals. Typical extracts from such advertisements were the phrases "Free from Esso": "Going free, at your Esso Action Station now": "We are giving you a coin with every four gallons of Esso petrol you buy": "We are also giving you a free collector card to mount them in. (For only 2/6, you can buy the handsome permanent mounting board . . .)": "One free coin with every 4 gallons."

E Esso circularised the 6,000 outlets, of which some 4,900 adopted the scheme. The medals were made available to outlet proprietors at 30s. for 500—slightly under three farthings each—the temporary collector cards without charge, permanent mounting cards at 2s. each. A folder circulated by Esso to the outlets to encourage their promotion scheme contained these phrases: "One coin should be given to every motorist who buys four gallons of petrol—two coins for eight gallons and so on": "Free collector cards F should be offered to all motorists at the start of the promotion." Large posters (60 by 40 inches) were supplied by Esso to the forecourts of proprietors joining the scheme. The most prominent lettering in the posters is "Free World Cup coins"; one also says "One coin given with every four gallons of petrol": the other example says "One coin given when you buy four gallons of petrol." A further pamphlet of instructions to G outlets said "Give one coin to each customer buying four gallons of petrol. . . .": "Give free collector cards to every customer you serve": "Try to sell luxury collector card at 2/6 each": "You will then ensure the success of this promotion by increasing gallonage sales on your station." The last document to which reference should be made is the free collector's card, which includes the phrase "You will be given a coin each time you buy four gallons of petrol from an Esso station. . . . This temporary collector H card is free. . . ."

My Lords, it is not in dispute that unless the medals were produced at the instance of Esso for the purpose of, i.e., with a view to, their being sold by garage proprietors to motorists there cannot be the suggested charge of purchase tax. The first question accordingly is whether, notwithstanding the liberal references in the documents attending the promotion scheme to "giving," "gifts," and "free," that which would and did take place gave rise to a contract, enforceable by a motorist who bought four gallons from

a participating proprietor, that he should receive one of these medals. It A
is to be borne in mind in this connection that the mere fact that Esso and
the garage proprietors undoubtedly had a commercial aim in promoting the
scheme does not deprive the delivery of a medal of the quality of a gift as
distinct from a sale: for benevolence is not a necessary feature of a gift,
which may well be motivated by self interest. On the other hand it is trite
law that if on analysis a transaction has in law one character, the fact that
the parties either accidentally or deliberately frame the transaction in lan- B
guage appropriate to a transaction of a different character will not deny to
it its true character.

We have here, my Lords, a promotion scheme initiated by Esso, who
procured the production of the medals. Each medal was of negligible
intrinsic value, though the incentive to soccer enthusiasts to collect all 30
may have been strong. Plainly it was never in Esso's mind that this negli- C
gible intrinsic value should be reflected in an increase in the pump price of
petrol, and it never was: indeed the price of a gallon could not be increased
by $\frac{3}{16}$ of a penny. In my opinion it would have been thought by Esso, and
rightly, that there could have been no occasion, in order to ensure success
of the scheme, for an outlet proprietor to subject himself to a contractual
liability to deliver a coin to a motorist who had bought four gallons. The
subject matter was trivial: the proprietor was directly interested in the D
success of the scheme and would be in the highest degree unlikely to renege
on the free gift offer, and indeed there is no suggestion that a motorist who
qualified and wanted a medal ever failed to get one: from the motorist's
viewpoint, if this had ever happened, I cannot think that he would have
considered that he had a legal grievance, though he might have said that he
would not patronise that outlet again: similarly in my opinion if a garage E
advertised "Free Air" and after buying petrol or oil the motorist was told
that the machine was out of order that day. In my opinion, the incentive
for the garage proprietor to carry out the scheme was such as to make it
quite unnecessary to invest, or for Esso to intend to invest, the transaction
with the additional compulsion of a contractual obligation, and in all the
circumstances of the case I am unable to regard that which under the scheme
was intended by Esso to take place in relation to the medals, and did take F
place, as something which would be intended to or regarded as creating a
legal contractual relationship. In forming that opinion I regard the minimal
intrinsic value of a medal as important. I would not wish it to be thought
that my opinion, if correct, would, in other cases in which a sales promotion
scheme involves substantial benefits, give carte blanche to participants to
renege on "free" offers. I am simply of opinion, in agreement with the G
Court of Appeal, though not I fear with the majority of your Lordships,
that in the instant case, because of the absence of any contractual element,
it should not be said that any medal was produced for general sale.

Suppose, however, that there was a contractual obligation on the pro-
prietor to deliver a medal to the motorist who had bought four gallons of
petrol, the further question arises whether there was a contract for sale of H
the medal for a price in money, which (subject to a point taken by the
respondents under section 40 of the Purchase Tax Act 1963) is involved in
the reference in Group 25 to "sale." The learned Vice-Chancellor analysed
the transaction as being, by a combination of the medal posters and the
price marked on the petrol pump, one invitation to treat by the proprietor:
the motorist by ordering four gallons made an offer to pay the pump price
on the terms of that invitation to treat: the proprietor accepted that offer

A by supplying the petrol: consequently an unascertained part of the price paid was for the right to receive the medal: therefore it was a sale of the medal for a price in money. (My Lords, when I embark upon a consideration of these niceties, I confess to being fortified in some measure in my view on the first point.) Now it is of course clear that a mere statement of the price of petrol on the pumps is not itself an offer to sell petrol at that price: this follows the ordinary situation that the display of goods in
B a window, or advertisement of goods for sale, even at a stated price is not to be treated as itself an offer capable of acceptance, but is only an invitation to treat. The reason for this is the eminently sound one that the vendor might otherwise find himself bound to a series of contracts that he would be quite unable to fulfil: since it is a mere invitation to treat he reserves to himself the ability to refuse an offer from a would-be purchaser. But, my
C Lords, those considerations have no relevance to the matter of these medals. The question of liability to hand over medals remains at all times under the control of the proprietor: knowing his gallonage of saleable petrol he knows at all times whether he has his maximum liability of one-quarter in number of medals: further if he has no medals available he retains the ability, before accepting a motorist's order for four gallons, to cancel or withdraw the offer of a medal. There are no reasons why the posters, assuming them to
D be capable of being the foundation of a contract, should not be regarded as in themselves an offer to the motorist that if he buys four gallons of petrol the proprietor will hand him one medal. This, if the matter lies in contract, appears to me to be the simple and straightforward approach. That is what, ignoring words such as "gift" and "free" the posters say: "If you buy four gallons of petrol I will hand you one medal." The
E motorist *entitles himself* (if he wishes one) to receive a medal by carrying out a contract for the purchase of petrol. This is not, my Lords, sale of the medal at a price in money.

An alternative argument was advanced on behalf of the respondents, supposing that there was not a sale at a price in money. Section 40 (1) of the Purchase Tax Act 1963 defines "purchase" in the following terms:

F "'purchase' means any contract which is a contract of sale within the meaning of the Sale of Goods Act 1893 and also a contract similar to such a contract in other respects but made for a consideration wholly or partly in . . . money, and includes any transaction, in whatsoever form expressed, in so far as its effect is in substance the same as the effect of such a contract as aforesaid; and references to goods being bought include, in relation to a purchase made for a consideration not,
G or not only, in money, and in relation to any such transaction as aforesaid, references to goods being acquired in any manner;".

In the instant case, on the above analysis, it is said that the contract for the delivery of the medal was "a contract similar to such a contract in other respects but made for a consideration wholly or partly in money's worth and not, or not only in money." If, it was argued, that is what
H "purchase" means, "sale" in Group 25 must have the complementary meaning. I leave aside, my Lords, the question whether the carrying out of a contract to purchase four gallons is properly to be described as money's worth. I do not derive any guidance from this definition on the meaning of "sale" in Group 25. It would indeed be odd if the prima facie meaning in Group 25 was designed to be extended merely by a definition of purchase and not by a definition of sale. But the truth of the matter is that "purchase" is so defined for the purpose of recognising the circumstances which

constitute a tax point, when tax is charged in respect of a purchase by a A
retailer from a wholesaler: see section 9. It is true that section 9 (4) refers to a " seller " and in that instance he is a seller notwithstanding that the goods in question may not have been disposed of solely for a price in money: but that is because he is " the seller under the purchase " which necessarily imports into the transaction the definition of " purchase." I find no justification for importing from the definition of " purchase," inserted for quite other and particular reasons, a construction of " sale " in Group B
25 other than its prima facie meaning.

I refer, my Lords, to certain authorities to which your Lordships' attention was called.

Bulpitt & Sons Ltd. v. *S. Bellman & Sons Ltd.* (1962) L.R. 3 R.P. 62 (Ungoed-Thomas J.) was a case in which a trader sought to avoid an injunction against selling below the minimum fixed retail selling price by the C
device of " giving," with goods sold, coupons worth a considerable amount in terms of entitlement to other goods. He rightly failed. But this does not assist in the present appeal; it was a mere and barefaced device to avoid an obligation: moreover if what had been done had been a distribution of medals of minimal intrinsic value the decision might well have been otherwise. In *Taylor* v. *Smetten* (1883) 11 Q.B.D. 207 a man sold pound packets D
of tea for 2s. 6d. each, each purchaser acquiring at the same time a right to a " prize," the prizes being of varying nature and value, and the purchaser of the tea not knowing what his prize was to be until he had bought the tea and found the prize described on a coupon within the packet. The man was convicted of running a lottery. The pound of tea was worth the money paid, but, as was said in the judgment of the court at p. 211, it was " impossible to suppose that the aggregate prices charged and obtained for E
the packages did not include the aggregate prices of the tea and the prizes." It appears from the report that this was the man's constant method of trading. The purchaser was held to be buying the tea and a chance. I do not doubt the correctness of the decision, but I do not find it persuasive on either of the main points in the present appeal.

In *Scott & Co. Ltd.* v. *Solomon* (1905) 69 J.P. 137 the appellants were F
convicted of dealing in plate without a licence. They sold tea and with each packet were coupons which in sufficient numbers would entitle the presenter of the coupons to claim from the tea vendor valuable articles of various sorts, depending upon the number of the coupons, some of which were articles of plate such as watches. The argument for conviction was that there was a binding contract with the tea purchasers as soon as sufficient coupons were presented, to transfer the ownership of the watch, the con- G
sideration being the payment of money for tea and coupons. There was no evidence of any increase in the price of the tea upon the introduction of the coupons. Lord Alverstone C.J. said, at p. 139:

> " [This evidence] seems to me to point to one view of the facts, namely, that it was all one transaction. In respect of the payment for the tea, the various purchasers each of them got what has been called H
> this ' coupon.' Mr. Danckwerts does not dispute, and I do not think he could dispute, that that was a sale of coupons. The suggestion that there is full value given for the tea, meaning that there is nothing charged for these coupons, is simply absurd. This very large business, to the extent of thousands of pounds, of Scott and Company, the appellants, could not possibly be carried on if there were no charge for the coupons. The coupons having been delivered out with the tea,

> A the persons who received them either having purchased them themselves, or having obtained them from other purchasers, on presenting them become entitled to receive certain articles, and, amongst others, became entitled in certain events, according to the number of coupons they presented, to receive a very considerable number of articles of plate, watches, and other things of the kind. It seems to me that, looked at in its real essence, this transaction is a trading in watches B by means of receiving payment for them by instalments when the money is paid for the tea, and by afterwards recognising the value of those various instalments as evidenced by the coupons by giving back various articles—in this particular case, watches."

Again, I do not doubt the correctness of that decision, but I do not find it persuasive on either of the two points in the present appeal.

C Finally the decision in this House in *Chappell & Co. Ltd.* v. *Nestlé Co. Ltd.* [1960] A.C. 87 affords in my opinion no assistance: it merely decided that there was no "ordinary retail selling price" of the records in question, having regard to the fact that Nestlé would not have sold them at the price of 1s. 6d. had the purchaser not produced evidence of the consumption of a required amount of Nestlé's chocolate.

D For the reasons that I have stated, I am of opinion that the decision of the Court of Appeal was correct and that this appeal should be dismissed.

Appeal dismissed.

Solicitors: *Solicitor for Customs and Excise; Durrant Piesse.*

E F. C.

[HOUSE OF LORDS]

F * BRITISH AIRWAYS BOARD . . . . . RESPONDENTS

AND

TAYLOR . . . . APPELLANT

1975 Nov. 3, 4, 5;
G Dec. 10

Lord Wilberforce, Viscount Dilhorne, Lord Simon of Glaisdale, Lord Edmund-Davies and Lord Fraser of Tullybelton

Trade Description—"Provision . . . of services"—Airline seat reservation—B.O.A.C. confirming reservation for specified flight—Overbooking policy resulting in passenger not being carried as promised—Whether confirmation false statement—Transaction before B.O.A.C. dissolved and replaced by British H *Airways Board—Whether board liable to prosecution—Trade Descriptions Act* 1968 (*c.* 29), *s.* 14 (1) (2)—*Civil Aviation Act* 1971 (*c.* 75), *ss.* 37, 57

By section 14 (1) of the Trade Descriptions Act 1968:

"It shall be an offence for any person in the course of any trade or business—(*a*) to make a statement which he knows to be false; or (*b*) recklessly to make a statement which is false; as to any of the following matters, that is to say,— . . . (iii) the time at which, manner in which or

persons by whom any services, accommodation or facilities A
are so provided; . . ."

B.O.A.C., who operated an airline, wrote on August 14, 1973, to a passenger, who had paid in advance, confirming his reservation for a specified flight on a particular date and at a particular time. He had bought a ticket on an "earlybird certificate" which obliged him to travel on specified flights and dates. Unknown to him B.O.A.C. operated a deliberate policy
of overbooking whereby passengers were booked in excess of B
accommodation for each flight. When B.O.A.C. wrote the flight was not overbooked but, when the passenger arrived at the airport for the flight, he could not be carried in the aircraft because no seat was available for him owing to overbooking. The British Airways Board who, on April 1, 1974, had replaced B.O.A.C. on their dissolution, which was effected under the Civil Aviation Act 1971, was charged with contraven-
ing section 14 (1) of the Trade Descriptions Act 1968 by reck- C
lessly making a statement in the letter about the provision of services, namely, the transportation by aeroplane of a person, which was false as to the time at and manner in which it was to be provided. The justices convicted the defendant, but the conviction was quashed by the Divisional Court of the Queen's Bench Division.

On appeal to the House of Lords by the inspector of
trading standards for Manchester:— D

Held, (1) that the letter, taken with the ticket and the certificate, would be understood as a statement of fact that the booking was certain, which statement, in view of the overbooking policy, was false within section 14 (1) of the Act of 1968, since the passenger was exposed to the risk that he might not get a place (post, pp. 18H—19A, 21G, H, 22D, 24H—
25A, 28A, B, F, G). E

Dictum in *Reg.* v. *Sunair Holidays Ltd.* [1973] 1 W.L.R. 1105, 1109, C.A. approved.

Beckett v. *Cohen* [1972] 1 W.L.R. 1593, D.C. considered.

But (2) dismissing the appeal, that, although B.O.A.C. remained in existence and in operation after the creation of the British Airways Board by the Act of 1971, the writing of the letter was not authorised by the board and, after the dis-
solution of B.O.A.C., the board, in taking over its property, F
rights and liabilities, did not become liable to prosecution in respect of its illegal acts (post, pp. 19B–F, 20A, B, 22G, 23A, B, 26E).

Decision of the Divisional Court of the Queen's Bench Division [1975] 1 W.L.R. 1197; [1975] 3 All E.R. 307 affirmed on different grounds.

The following cases are referred to in their Lordships' opinions: G

Beckett v. *Cohen* [1972] 1 W.L.R. 1593; [1973] 1 All E.R. 120, D.C.
Linnett v. *Metropolitan Police Commissioner* [1946] K.B. 290; [1946] 1 All E.R. 380, D.C.
Reg. v. *Clarksons Holidays Ltd.* (1972) 57 Cr.App.R. 38, C.A.
Reg. v. *Sunair Holidays Ltd.* [1973] 1 W.L.R. 1105; [1973] 2 All E.R. 1233, C.A.
Tesco Supermarkets Ltd. v. *Nattrass* [1972] A.C. 153; [1971] 2 W.L.R. H
1166; [1971] 2 All E.R. 127, H.L.(E.).

The following additional cases were cited in argument:

Akerhielm v. *De Mare* [1959] A.C. 789; [1959] 3 W.L.R. 108; [1959] 3 All E.R. 485, P.C.
Bambury v. *Hounslow London Borough Council* [1971] R.T.R. 1, D.C.
Beattie v. *Lord Ebury* (1872) 7 Ch.App. 777.

Bracegirdle v. *Oxley* [1947] K.B. 349; [1947] 1 All E.R. 126, D.C.
Edgington v. *Fitzmaurice* (1885) 29 Ch.D. 459, C.A.
Nader v. *Allegheny Airlines Inc.* (1975) 512 F.2d. 527.
Nokes v. *Doncaster Amalgamated Colleries Ltd.* [1940] A.C. 1014; [1940] 3 All E.R. 549, H.L.(E.).
Quality Dairies (*York*) *Ltd.* v. *Pedley* [1952] 1 K.B. 275; [1952] 1 All E.R. 380, D.C.
Reg. v. *Dent* [1955] 2 Q.B. 590; [1955] 3 W.L.R. 297; [1955] 2 All E.R. 806, C.C.A.
Reg. v. *Thomson Holidays Ltd.* [1974] Q.B. 592; [1974] 2 W.L.R. 371; [1974] 1 All E.R. 823, C.A.
Smith v. *Land and House Property Corporation* (1884) 28 Ch.D. 7, C.A.
Strutt v. *Clift* [1911] 1 K.B. 1, D.C.
Sunair Holidays Ltd. v. *Dodd* [1970] 1 W.L.R. 1037; [1970] 2 All E.R. 410, D.C.
Wilson v. *British Railways Board* (unreported) May 5, 1972, D.C.
With v. *O'Flanagan* [1936] Ch. 575; [1936] 1 All E.R. 727, C.A.

APPEAL from the Divisional Court of the Queen's Bench Division.

On August 12, 1974, on an information preferred by the prosecutor, Kenneth Taylor, an inspector of trading standards for Manchester, the justices for Greater Manchester sitting at Stockport convicted the defendants, British Airways Board, on an amended charge of contravening section 14 (1) (*b*) of the Trade Descriptions Act 1968. The defendants were fined £250 and ordered to pay £50 costs. The defendants appealed. The Divisional Court of the Queen's Bench Division (Lord Widgery C.J., Walker and Kilner Brown JJ.) allowed the appeal. The inspector appealed to the House of Lords.

The facts are stated in their Lordships' opinions.

Anthony Scrivener Q.C. and *George Greenwood* for the appellant.
P. Webster Q.C. and *David Prebble* for the respondents.

Their Lordships took time for consideration.

December 10, 1975. LORD WILBERFORCE. My Lords, the British Airways Board has been prosecuted by the inspector of trading standards, Manchester, for an alleged offence under the Trade Descriptions Act 1968, section 14 (1) (*b*). The information was in the following terms:

> "On or about August 15, 1973, at Marple in the Petty Sessional Division of Stockport in the course of a trade or business the accused recklessly made a statement, namely, 'I have pleasure in confirming the following reservations for you: London/Bermuda Flight BA 679—Economy Class—August 29 dep. 15.25 hours arr. 17.50 hours,' by means of a letter addressed to W. J. Edmunds about the provision of services namely the transportation of a person by aeroplane which was false as to the time at which the service was to be provided contrary to section 14 (1) (*b*) of the Trade Descriptions Act 1968."

The magistrates' court at Stockport found the offence proved and fined the board £250. The board appealed to the Divisional Court which allowed the appeal and quashed the conviction, holding that the statement made was promissory in character, and not a statement of an existing fact, so that it could neither be true or false.

At the request of the prosecutor the court certified the following point of law as of general public importance under section 1 (2) of the Administration of Justice Act 1960, namely:

> "Are magistrates entitled to find that a statement made by an airline to a passenger confirming a reservation on a specific flight, on a specific date and at a specific time was a false statement as to the time at which a service was to be provided within section 14 of the Trade Descriptions Act 1968 in the following circumstances: (*a*) that at the date when the said statement was made to the passenger the flight was not overbooked; (*b*) that the booking on the said flight had already been made at the date; (*c*) that at all material times the airline had a general policy of overbooking flights; (*d*) that the passenger was prevented from travelling on the flight subsequently because of the operation of the policy."

A number of findings of fact were made by the justices and recorded in the case stated. I summarise the most relevant.

The passenger involved was Mr. W. J. Edmunds, a resident of Bermuda, who purchased a passenger ticket from British Overseas Airways Corporation for a flight from Bermuda to London on July 15, 1973, and return. The ticket was bought on what is known as an earlybird certificate which, when properly completed, entitles a passenger to a reduced fare, but obliges him to travel, both outward and on return, on the specified flights and dates endorsed on the ticket. In Mr. Edmunds' case the return flight was specified as August 29, 1973, on Flight BA.679.

On August 14, 1973, Mr. Edmunds, then in London, telephoned B.O.A.C. Reservations to confirm, but was told that he was not booked on the specified flight. He was advised to contact the customer relations department. He did this, and was orally assured that he was properly booked. He asked for confirmation in writing and this was given by a letter dated August 14, 1973, the relevant terms of which are set out in the information. This letter bore the heading on one side "British Overseas Airways Corporation," and on the other "B.O.A.C." superimposed on "British Airways" (sic). It contained a reference to "assisting you next time you travel B.O.A.C." I think that there is no doubt that this letter was written on behalf of B.O.A.C. and not the British Airways Board. This has consequences which I shall mention later.

It will be seen that the question certified by the Divisional Court contains a reference to "a general policy of overbooking flights," and there was evidence as to this given before the justices. An officer of B.O.A.C. admitted that, in common with all major international airlines, B.O.A.C. operated such a policy "as a prudent business exercise to counteract 'no-shows,' i.e., those passengers who make reservations on flights but do not turn up." This policy inevitably resulted in occasional off-loading of passengers who had booked. Some statistics were given showing that, over a 12 month period, as regards B.O.A.C.'s services from London, two passengers out of 10,000 were off-loaded, whereas the number of "no-shows" was considerably greater.

My Lords, although a good deal was said in the course of argument by way of explanation and justification for this policy, I must make it clear that we are not, in this appeal, concerned with whether it is commercially sound or unsound, fair or unfair to passengers generally, operated conscientiously or otherwise. Such questions are, in any event, primarily within the control of administrative authorities, the Civil Aviation Authority or the Secretary of State in this country and similar

A bodies elsewhere. We are only concerned in this case with the letter addressed, after a specific request, to Mr. Edmunds on August 14, 1973. Was this a promise as to what the airline intended to do, or was it a statement of fact as to the airline's service? Before I attempt to deal with this issue I should remove from the discussion certain points which might arise on the form of the information. This contains two ingredients, namely, first, an allegation that the statement was made recklessly
B (section 14 (1) (*b*) of the Act), secondly, that it was false as to the time at which the service was to be provided (section 14 (1) (iii)). It might well be contended that these were inappropriate and that the charge should have been that the statement was known to be false (section 14 (1) (*a*)) and that the matter, as to which it was false, was the provision of services (section 14 (1) (i)). But counsel for British Airways Board disclaimed
C any such contention and both sides agreed that the appeal should be decided on the basis that, in both respects, the charge had been correctly framed.

My Lords, the distinction in law between a promise as to future action, which may be broken or kept, and a statement as to existing fact, which may be true or false, is clear enough. There may be inherent in a promise an implied statement as to a fact, and where this is really
D the case, the court can attach appropriate consequences to any falsity in, or recklessness in the making of, that statement. Everyone is familiar with the proposition that a statement of intention may itself be a statement of fact and so capable of being true or false. But this proposition should not be used as a general solvent to transform the one type of assurance with another: the distinction is a real one and requires to be
E respected, particularly where the effect of treating an assurance as a statement is to attract criminal consequences, as in the present case. As Lord Widgery C.J. said in *Beckett* v. *Cohen* [1972] 1 W.L.R. 1593, 1596, it was never intended that the Act of 1968 should be used so as to make a criminal statement out of what is really a breach of warranty.

Which character—promise or statement—should be attributed to the letter, seems on the face of it to be debatable. Lord Widgery C.J.
F certainly thought the choice was nicely balanced, but in the end he concluded that the essence of what was said was a promise, "we will not turn you out for anybody else." I think that I would agree with this if our task was the normal one of judicial construction of the letter. At the least I would not think it right to differ from Lord Widgery's view. But there is a special feature about cases under the Trade Descriptions
G Act 1968 which alters the nature of the court's approach. In section 14, the section which describes the offence charged against the British Airways Board, it is provided, by subsection (2) (*a*), that for the purposes of the section

> "anything (whether or not a statement as to any of the matters specified in the preceding subsection) likely to be taken for such a
> H statement as to any of those matters as would be false shall be deemed to be a false statement as to that matter; . . ."

So the crucial question, in relation to the letter of August 14, 1973, is whether it was likely to be taken (sc. by the addressee) for a statement as to the time at which the service was provided. Whether it was so likely is thus a question of fact to be found. That this is so was decided in a case upon this section, *Reg.* v. *Clarksons Holidays Ltd.* (1972) 57 Cr.App.R. 38, 53, one concerned with a brochure extolling the merits of a hotel at Benidorm, Spain. The language used was a hyperbolic type A normally used in brochures, as to which Roskill L.J. said, at pp. 53–54:

"The question of what this written representation meant was essentially a question of fact for the jury, subject only to this, that if the words . . . relied upon by the Crown were upon their true construction incapable of bearing the meaning which the Crown sought to attribute to them" B

the case should be withdrawn from the jury. I respectfully agree with this: indeed it is an essential feature of the Act that, when it has to be considered whether descriptions or statements are misleading, it is the meaning which they are likely to bear to the person or persons to whom they are addressed that matters, and not the meaning which they might, on analysis, bear to a trained legal mind. A similar approach was taken C by MacKenna J. (delivering the judgment of the Court of Appeal (Criminal Division) in *Reg.* v. *Sunair Holidays Ltd.* [1973] 1 W.L.R. 1105, 1113).

In the present case the justices made the following relevant findings:

(*a*) "That the passenger ticket, the earlybird certificate and the letter of August 14, 1973, separately and together contained an implied statement of an existing fact" (paragraph 6 (*g*)).

(*b*) "That a passenger in possession of the passenger ticket would D believe that such a ticket stated a fact, namely a place had been reserved for him or her on the flight specified and at the time so specified. Further, that the earlybird certificate would only serve to reinforce in the mind of a passenger that such a place was available on the flight so specified and at the time specified. The letter of August 14, would similarly reinforce a passenger's view E that a certain fact existed (by implication) namely that he would fly in an aeroplane from London to Bermuda on August 29, 1973, on the flight and time specified" (paragraph 6 (*h*)).

(*c*) "The statement contained in the letter was false and made recklessly since in view of the appellant's admitted policy a reservation on the flight could not be confirmed at the date of the letter as it was possible that Mr. Edmunds would be off-loaded. F It followed that no reservation had been made in the sense that an ordinary person would take it to mean i.e., a certain booking. This was especially so in view of the circumstances in which the letter was written" (paragraph 18 (*b*)).

In my opinion these were findings which the justices were entitled to make. And the essence of them is that the letter, taken together with the G ticket and the earlybird certificate would be taken as a statement that Mr. Edmunds had a certain booking, which statement, in view of the overbooking policy, was untrue, since his booking, though very likely to be a firm one, was exposed to a risk—small but, as events proved, real—that it might not give him a seat on the aircraft. I think that the justices were entitled to find that this would be taken as a statement of a fact, H rather than as a mere promise that Mr. Edmunds would be flown on the day and at the time specified, and that they did so find. It is upon this finding so made which perhaps was not fully brought home to the Divisional Court, that I feel obliged to reach a different conclusion.

Turning now to the questions certified, I would not answer these in the form in which they are couched. The answer which I would suggest is that the magistrates were entitled to find that the statement contained

A in the letter dated August 14, 1973, from British Overseas Airways Corporation to W. J. Edmunds, referred to in the information, when read in the light of the ticket issued to W. J. Edmunds on July 11, 1973, and the earlybird certificate, was a false statement within section 14 (1) of the Trade Descriptions Act 1968.

It remains, in the light of this answer, to decide the present appeal. It is well established that this House is not confined to answering the B question(s) certified for its opinion, but can and indeed should consider other material points bearing upon the substance of the appeal. Such a point concerns the identity of the defendant, British Airways Board, a point taken before the justices, but in view of their decision as to the statement, not decided by the Divisional Court. As I have stated, the letter of August 14, 1973, was written on behalf of B.O.A.C. It was C not written on behalf of British Airways Board. So the question inevitably arises whether there is any legal basis upon which the board can be liable in respect of an offence committed by B.O.A.C. in making the statement contained in the letter. I am forced to the conclusion that there is not. The relevant enactment under which British Airways Board was constituted is the Civil Aviation Act 1971, section 37. The board was given (section 38) power to "control all the activities" of the D corporations which included B.O.A.C. The corporations remained in existence but the Secretary of State was given power (section 57) to dissolve them and to transfer to the board all property, rights and liabilities of the corporations. In fact, B.O.A.C. continued to operate under its own name, but adding to it the name of British Airways as, in effect, a trade name paving the way for the eventual take over by the British E Airways Board. The offence in question was committed on August 14 (or 15), 1973, and B.O.A.C. was not dissolved until April 1, 1974, when the Air Corporations (Dissolution) Order 1973 (S.I. 2175 of 1973) took effect. This provided that all property, rights and liabilities which immediately before the Order came into force were property, rights and liabilities of either of the corporations should be property, rights and F liabilities of the board.

My Lords, there is nothing here which can in any way support an argument that the British Airways Board could be prosecuted for B.O.A.C.'s offences. The relationship between the two legal entities was that of facultative not mandatory, control of one by the other; there was no agency, no joint operation, no initiation or direction by British G Airways Board of the act complained of, no delegation by British Airways Board of any statutory duty to B.O.A.C., so as to make the board answerable for any failure to comply with such duty; no basis for a contention that B.O.A.C.'s act could be attributable to British Airways Board as having been done by the board's directing mind. (c.f. *Tesco Supermarkets Ltd.* v. *Nattrass* [1972] A.C. 153.) Finally, and the contrary was scarcely contended, the dissolution order of April 1, 1974, H was not, indeed, under the terms of section 57 of the Civil Aviation Act 1971, could not amount to, a provision making the offence of B.O.A.C. the offence of the board. The fact is that B.O.A.C. could have been proceeded against at any time between August 15, 1973, and April 1, 1974, but that, after the latter date, no prosecution was possible.

The appeal must therefore be dismissed but I would not suggest that the appellant should pay the board's costs.

VISCOUNT DILHORNE. My Lords, in my opinion these proceedings were A
misconceived from the outset. The information laid on June 26, 1974,
was against the British Airways Board and was based on a letter dated
August 14, 1973, which bore the heading British Overseas Airways Cor-
poration and B.O.A.C. British Airways. It was signed by a Miss Burford
and underneath her signature were typed the words "Passenger Reserva-
tion." The magistrates found that the signatory of that letter "had the
necessary authority of the British Overseas Airways Corporation to deal B
with passenger reservations."

If, as was contended, a statement in that letter amounted to the com-
mission of an offence against section 14 (1) (*b*) of the Trade Descriptions
Act 1968, B.O.A.C. should have been prosecuted, but on June 26, 1974,
B.O.A.C. had ceased to exist. It was dissolved on April 1, 1974, by the
Air Corporations (Dissolution) Order 1973 (S.I. 1973 No. 2175). C

The point was taken in the magistrates' court that the respondents were
not liable for the contents of the letter, but the magistrates came to the
conclusion that they were as the notepaper had on it the words "British
Airways" and as the British Airways Board had, by virtue of section 38
of the Civil Aviation Act 1971, power to control the activities of B.O.A.C.

The fact that the British Airways Board had such powers clearly does D
not ipso facto make them responsible for any criminal acts committed by
B.O.A.C. and the fact that the letter in question had the words "British
Airways" on it does not show them to be responsible criminally for a
letter written by a person authorised by B.O.A.C. to deal with passenger
reservations.

The magistrates also held that the criminal liabilities of B.O.A.C.
passed to the respondents by virtue of paragraph 2 of the Air Corporation E
(Dissolution) Order 1973. That paragraph provides for the transfer of "all
property, rights and liabilities" of B.O.A.C. to the British Airways Board.
That paragraph does not extend to criminal liabilities and in this House it
was rightly not contended that it did.

The information alleged that an offence contrary to section 14 (1) (*b*) of
the Trade Descriptions Act 1968 had been committed. The material parts F
of that section read as follows:

> "(1) It shall be an offence for any person in the course of any trade
> or business—(*a*) to make a statement which he knows to be false; or
> (*b*) recklessly to make a statement which is false; as to any of the
> following matters, that is to say,—(i) the provision in the course of any
> trade or business of any services, accommodation or facilities; . . . (iii) G
> the time at which, manner in which or persons by whom any services,
> accommodation or facilities are so provided; . . . (2) For the purposes
> of this section—(*a*) anything (whether or not a statement as to any
> of the matters specified in the preceding subsection) likely to be taken
> for such a statement as to any of those matters as would be false shall be
> deemed to be a false statement as to that matter; and (*b*) a state-
> ment made regardless of whether it is true or false shall be deemed H
> to be made recklessly, whether or not the person making it had
> reasons for believing that it might be false. . . . (4) In this section
> 'false' means false to a material degree . . ."

The information alleged that the following statement in the letter of
August 14, 1973:

> "I have pleasure in confirming the following reservations for you:

A London/Bermuda Flight BA 679—Economy Class—August 29, dep 15.25 hours arr 17.50 hours"

was false as to the time at which the service was to be provided and was made recklessly.

I can see no ground for saying it was made recklessly or for saying that it was made regardless of its truth or falsity. B.O.A.C. in common with B other international airlines followed an overbooking policy designed to ensure, if possible, a full passenger load for their aircraft, it being their experience that a number of those who had made reservations did not take them up. On occasions their policy led to passengers for whom reservations had been made not getting on to an aircraft. This overbooking being a deliberate policy of B.O.A.C., if the statement in the letter of August 14 was false, it was false to their knowledge and not made reck-C lessly regardless of its truth or falsity.

Counsel for the respondent did not take the point that the respondents should have been charged under section 14 (1) (*a*) with making a statement known to be false. He did not desire to do so, no doubt wishing to obtain the views of the House as to the falsity or otherwise of the statement. Nevertheless, on the facts disclosed in the case stated if the respondents had D been responsible for that letter and the statement in it was false, the conviction could not, in my opinion, have been upheld.

Mr. Edmunds had bought a return ticket for a return journey from Bermuda to London which was expressed to be valid only on the outward flight on July 15 at 23.10 hours and on the return flight on August 29 at 15.05 hours. His journeys were subject to the conditions on "Earlybird/ Advance Purchase Excursion" certificate, one of which was that he would E be accepted "for travel only on the flights and dates endorsed on" his ticket. On the certificate there was printed in a box

> "Once definite reservations have been made, refund if applicable will be limited to 75 per cent. of the fare(s). No refund can be made after commencement of travel."

F On August 14 Mr. Edmunds was informed that he was not booked on the flight on August 29 scheduled to leave London Airport at 15.25 for Bermuda. He was told to get in touch with the customer relations department of B.O.A.C. He did so and was told that he was booked on that flight and that was confirmed by the letter of August 14 from passenger reservations.

In these circumstances Mr. Edmunds was clearly led to believe that he G had a definite and certain booking on the flight on August 29 as the magistrates found. There was no reason for him to ascribe a different meaning to the word "reservation" when used in the letter to that to be given to it in the earlybird certificate.

The statement that his reservation was confirmed was made when B.O.A.C., following their policy of overbooking, knew that he might not H get on the aircraft. It was, in my opinion, clearly false, for it clearly implied that they had reserved a seat for him and would keep one reserved for him when it was always their intention, should more passengers arrive for the flight than there was room for, not to carry one or more of those for whom reservations had been made. It was false because it did not state the qualification to which it was subject and it was false, in my view, to their knowledge.

In expressing this opinion I do not wish to comment on B.O.A.C.'s overbooking policy or to be thought to criticise it for there may be very good reasons for it, but there can, in my opinion, be no justification for telling Mr. Edmunds that his reservation was confirmed and leaving him to suppose that he had a certain booking when that was not the case and when it was not B.O.A.C.'s intention that there should be on August 14 a certain booking for him.

In my opinion this appeal should be dismissed.

LORD SIMON OF GLAISDALE. My Lords, in my respectful view the principles of law applicable to the question certified for your Lordships' consideration were stated cogently and accurately by McKenna J., giving the judgment of the Court of Appeal in *Reg.* v. *Sunair Holidays Ltd.* [1973] 1 W.L.R. 1105, 1109F—1110A. The certified question of law cannot therefore be answered in the abstract. The issue in each case is what the relevant statement (in the instant case the letter of August 14, 1973) in all its circumstances reasonably meant to its recipient.

The case stated by the magistrates has been subjected during argument to a close and strict scrutiny. But in my view magistrates' findings must be read as a whole and (to borrow an expression from parliamentary law) benevolently construed.

I have had the advantage of reading in draft the speeches prepared by my noble and learned friends, with which I agree. For the reasons they give I think that the magistrates were entitled to find that the letter of August 14, 1973, was in its circumstances a false statement within section 14 (1) of the Trade Descriptions Act 1968.

It seems to me likely that the inspector laid the information under section 14 (1) (*b*) (false statement made recklessly) rather than under paragraph (a) (statement known to be false) because the odds were that Mr. Edmunds would not in the event be off-loaded under the overbooking policy, although he might be. But this is based on a fallacy. It was the chance (not being so remote that it could be dismissed as being de minimis) of Mr. Edmunds being off-loaded that made the statement of August 14 in its circumstance false *to the knowledge* of the maker of the statement. British Airways, though, disclaimed any reliance on this point, desiring a decision of the merits.

I agree with my noble and learned friend, Lord Fraser of Tullybelton, that the statement of August 14 in its circumstances was false as to the matters set out in both section 14 (1) (i) (" the provision in the course of . . . business of any services, accommodation or facilities ") and paragraph (iii) (" the time at which . . . accommodation or facilities are so provided ").

However, since I agree that British Airways Board are not to be held to be responsible for the statement of August 14, 1973, I concur that the appeal should be dismissed.

My noble and learned friend on the Woolsack has emphasised that your Lordships are not concerned with the merits of the overbooking policy. I do however, feel entitled to say that to an uninstructed outsider it would seem that the simple, fair and economically sensible way of dealing with the " no-show " mischief is for the airline to demand a forfeitable deposit with the reservation, and that if international agreement cannot be secured to some such arrangement it reflects little credit on the international organisation concerned.

A LORD EDMUND-DAVIES. My Lords, two questions arise in this appeal: (I) Did the letter dated August 14, 1973, sent to Mr. Edmunds constitute a breach of section 14 of the Trade Descriptions Act 1968? (II) If so, were the magistrates right in holding the respondents liable for that breach?

For the reasons considered in detail by my noble and learned friend, Lord Wilberforce, I am in respectful agreement that, whatever be the proper answer to question (I), a negative answer must be given to question B (II). In the result, this appeal from the decision of the Divisional Court in favour of the respondents must be dismissed, though on grounds which the Divisional Court did not find themselves called upon to explore. It is, however, necessary to deal with question (I), which was argued at length below and again before this House. It expresses in a bald form what I believe to be the gist of the question certified by the Divisional C Court, and is clearly of general public importance.

The facts giving rise to this appeal have been set out at length by my Lords and need not now be repeated. The appeal itself raises in a neat form the difference between an assertion of existing fact and a promise as to future conduct. Section 14 of the Act of 1968 relates only to the former, and Lord Widgery C.J. was undoubtedly correct in saying in *Beckett* v. *Cohen* [1972] 1 W.L.R. 1593, 1596 that

D "... section 14 (1) ... has no application to statements which amount to a promise with regard to the future, and which therefore at the time when they are made cannot have the character of being either true or false."

But the facts of this case illustrate yet again that an assertion of existing E fact and a promise of future conduct may both be found in one and the same statement. As McKenna J. said in the course of his admirable judgment in *Reg.* v. *Sunair Holidays Ltd.* [1973] 1 W.L.R. 1105, 1109:

"A promise or forecast may contain by implication a statement of present fact. The person who makes the promise may be implying that his present intention is to keep it or that he has at present the F power to perform it. The person who makes the forecast may be implying that he now believes that his prediction will come true or that he has the means of bringing it to pass. Such implied statements of present intention, means or belief, when they are made, may well be within section 14 of the Act of 1968 and therefore punishable if they were false and were made knowingly or recklessly. But, if they are punishable, the offence is not the breaking of a promise or the failure G to make a prediction come true. It is the making of a false statement of an existing fact, somebody's present state of mind or present means."

This House is presently concerned with the legal character of the statement contained in the letter of August 14, 1973, sent to Mr. Edmunds on the same day as that on which he had been orally assured that the booking of his return flight to Bermuda had been effected and in response to his H request for written confirmation of that assurance. The material words were:

"I have pleasure in confirming the following reservations for you:— London/Bermuda Flight B.A.679—Economy Class—August 29 dep. 15.25 hours arr. 17.50 hours."

The respondents assert that what in that letter Mr. Edmunds claims was reasonably read by him as being a statement of existing fact was in reality

intended to be (and ought reasonably to have been regarded as) nothing A
more than the expression of a sincerely entertained hope. Waller J. said
[1975] 1 W.L.R. 1197, 1201:

> "At that time, as the case finds, the flight was not overbooked. In
> other words, at that time there was space on that aircraft for Mr.
> Edmunds. As I see it, the fact was that the flight was arranged. The
> fact was that on that day there was space available for Mr. Edmunds, B
> and there was a promise for the future that that space would be kept
> for him. In my view that promise for the future was not an existing
> fact such as is required for a false statement under section 14 of the
> Trade Descriptions Act 1968. It may well be that it was a warranty
> for the future, but it was not a statement of an existing fact."

I respectfully disagree. Waller J. appears to have accepted that there was C
an implied statement of fact in the letter, namely that the space was then
available for Mr. Edmunds, but he reads it as containing merely a promise
that the space would continue to be available. He thus shared the view of
Lord Widgery C.J. (at p. 1201B) that the letter had moved "out of the realm
of fact into the realm of future promise." I do not think this was so.
Bearing section 14 (2) (*a*) in mind, the reasonable construction to be put
on the letter was, surely, that the writer had taken steps to secure for Mr. D
Edmunds a seat on the designated flight. In other words, it was both a
statement of existing fact and a statement as to present intention, which
was equally a statement of existing fact. The letter amounted to saying:

> "Not only have we secured your seat for you, but we have the
> intention to ensure that it will remain reserved and available to you
> on the designated flight." E

In my judgment, such would be the interpretation reasonably placed upon
the letter by the recipient, and the magistrates were therefore entitled to
find, as they did, that it "contained an implied statement of an existing
fact." They further found

> "that the earlybird certificate would only serve to reinforce in the
> mind of a passenger that such a place was available on the flight so F
> specified and at the time specified."

That, indeed, may well have been so, but I should make it clear that my
conclusion as to the proper answer to question (I) does not turn in any
way on the special terms upon which Mr. Edmunds' earlybird certificate
was issued. On the contrary, it is based solely upon the circumstances
leading up to the writing of the letter of August 14 and upon the terms G
of the letter itself.

The falsity of the foregoing statements of existing fact which I hold
were implied in the letter of August 14 is not, in my judgment, open to
doubt. For, even though when it was despatched to Mr. Edmunds no over-
booking on Flight B.A.679 on August 29 had yet occurred, it was well
known that overbooking might take place, with the consequence that (to H
put it at its lowest) there was a degree of risk that, even though the flight
left on time, Mr. Edmunds would not be one of its passengers. Fact was
asserted when in reality only chance (albeit a good chance) existed. How-
ever commercially understandable overbooking may be in keenly com-
petitive conditions, to assure a would-be passenger that his seat had been
secured for him when it was known that it had not and that it might
eventuate that he would be turned away was to state that which was

A known to be false, and therefore came within subsection (1) (*a*) of section 14 of the Act of 1968. The information charged the respondents with breaching subsection (1) (*b*) by recklessly making a false statement, and the magistrates found that:

> " The statement contained in the letter was false and made recklessly since in view of the [respondents'] admitted policy a reservation on
> B the flight could not be confirmed at the date of the letter as it was always possible that Mr. Edmunds would be off-loaded."

But the difference between the two states of mind is brought out by the provision in section 14 (2) (*b*) that

> " a statement made regardless of whether it is true or false shall be deemed to be made recklessly, whether or not the person making it
> C had reasons for believing that it might be false."

This indicates a state of mind different from that which, for the reasons stated, I hold must be imputed to those responsible for the letter of August 14 at the time it was written and despatched. But, having made the point clear, it can be left there as far as the present case is concerned, the respondents understandably being agreeable to regard the charge of recklessness
D as being correctly laid, even though, as I have indicated, it seems to have been technically incorrect.

For these various reasons, I should have allowed this appeal had the proper party been prosecuted. But, the position being otherwise, I concur in holding that it should be dismissed.

E LORD FRASER OF TULLYBELTON. My Lords, British Airways Board (" the board "), which is the respondent in this appeal, was convicted of an offence under section 14 (1) (*b*) of the Trade Descriptions Act 1968, in respect that it had recklessly made a false statement as to the time at which a service was to be provided. The point of law which was certified by the Divisional Court as being of general public importance raises the question whether the statement was false and so constituted an offence
F under the Act. But there is another, and logically prior, question as to whether, if any offence was committed, the board is the proper defendant to be charged with it. This question arises because the statement alleged to be false was made in a letter signed by a person authorised not by the board but by British Overseas Airways Corporation. The magistrates held that the board was responsible for the statement and they expressed their
G opinion thus:

> " We were of the opinion that: —(*a*) the statement was made by the [board] since it was written on their headed writing paper and they had the power to control all of the activities of the B.O.A.C. by virtue of section 38 of the Civil Aviation Act 1971. . . ."

They added a further reason but counsel who appeared for the prosecutor
H in this House conceded, rightly in my opinion, that it could not be supported, and I need not refer to it. The information in the present case was issued on June 26, 1974, by which time B.O.A.C. had been dissolved and had ceased to exist, so that, unless the board is responsible, nobody is. The Divisional Court did not find it necessary to deal with the question of the board's responsibility, because they held that no false statement had been made, but the question was raised again before this House and I think it must be answered before the certified question.

The first reason given by the magistrates for holding the board responsible was that the letter was written on their headed writing paper. I have some doubt whether that conclusion can be reconciled with the finding of fact (in paragraph 6 (*d*) of the case stated) that the letter "bore the heading British Overseas Airways Corporation, B.O.A.C., British Airways." "British Airways Board," which is the name by which the board was constituted under the Civil Aviation Act 1971, was not mentioned. But, assuming that the conclusion is justified, it cannot go far towards fixing responsibility on the board in light of the finding that "the signatory of the letter had the necessary authority of the British Overseas Airways Corporation to deal with passenger reservations," but (by implication) did not have the authority of the board. That leads to the magistrates' second, and I think more important, reason, which was that the board had power to control all of the activities of the B.O.A.C. by virtue of section 38 of the Act of 1968. It was said that the board must be treated as having delegated its powers to B.O.A.C. and that it was therefore responsible for any offence committed by B.O.A.C. In my opinion, that argument is not well-founded. It was supported by reference to cases such as *Linnett* v. *Metropolitan Police Commissioner* [1946] K.B. 290 where a duty expressly imposed by statute on one party had been delegated by him to another. But section 38 did not impose a duty; it only conferred a power to control the activities of B.O.A.C. Moreover B.O.A.C. had in August 1973 powers of its own, which it had possessed before the board was set up under the Civil Aviation Act 1971, and there is nothing to show that B.O.A.C. sent the letter of August 14, 1973, under powers delegated to them by the board rather than under their own independent powers.

If any offence was committed under the Trade Descriptions Act, it was not committed by the board and the board is not, in my opinion, responsible for it. The result is that it ought not to have been convicted. The conviction was quashed by the Divisional Court, and the appeal from that court should, in my opinion, be dismissed.

If that is right, it is not strictly necessary to consider whether the alleged offence was committed at all, but as that was the point of law of general public importance which was certified, and as we heard a full argument upon it, I should state my opinion. The circumstances in which the question arises were briefly these. Mr. Edmunds bought from B.O.A.C. a return ticket from Bermuda to London. It was called an earlybird excursion ticket, and the fare for it was lower than for an ordinary ticket. It was subject to special conditions, one of which was that it was valid only for the flights and on the dates endorsed on the ticket. Mr. Edmunds was given an earlybird certificate which set out the special conditions. His ticket was endorsed for the outward journey by a flight on July 15, 1973, and for the return journey by Flight BA 679 on August 29, 1973. He duly made the outward journey, and, while in London, he telephoned to B.O.A.C. to confirm that his return booking on August 29 was in order. He received an oral assurance that it was, but he asked for written confirmation and in response to his request he received the letter of August 14. The material part of that letter stated:

> "I have pleasure in confirming the following reservations for you: London/Bermuda Flight BA 679—Economy Class—August 29 dep. 15.25 hours, arr 17.50 hours."

Mr. Edmunds naturally accepted the letter as confirmation that a seat had been definitely reserved for him on the flight and date stated, which were the same as those endorsed on his ticket. But when he arrived at the airport on August 29 he was told that there was no room for him on the flight because it had been overbooked, and he had to wait till the next day. That situation arose because B.O.A.C., like other airlines, had a policy of overbooking; that is to say they would accept bookings for more passengers on a flight than there were seats available on that flight. We were told, and I readily accept, that overbooking was commercially necessary because of the large number of passengers who booked seats on particular flights and then did not appear. On some routes these "no-shows" formed a substantial proportion of the bookings and, as their tickets were available for later flights, if their seats had all been left empty the result would have been a serious loss of revenue to the airline, as well as unnecessary disappointment to other would-be travellers. The overbooking was limited, and was calculated so that the number of passengers overbooked would not exceed the number of "no-shows" to be expected in the light of the airline's experience. On a few occasions it did exceed that number, and, unfortunately for Mr. Edmunds, his return journey was one of these occasions. We have, of course, no concern with the reasons for the overbooking policy. The only question is whether, having regard to its existence in August 1973, the statement in the letter of August 14 concerning Mr. Edmund's reservation constituted an offence under section 14 of the Trade Descriptions Act 1968.

Earlier sections of the Act prohibit false descriptions of goods. Section 14 deals with false or misleading statements as to services. In this case the board was charged under paragraph (*b*) with having "recklessly" made a false statement, as to (iii) "the time at which" services were to be provided. Section 14 has been considered by the courts in several cases. In *Reg.* v. *Sunair Holidays Ltd.* [1973] 1 W.L.R. 1105 MacKenna J., giving the judgment of the Court of Appeal, said, at p. 1109:

"The section deals with 'statements' of which it can be said that they were, at the time when they were made, 'false.' This may be the case with a statement of fact, whether past or present. A statement that a fact exists now, or that it existed in the past, is either true or false at the time when it is made. But it is not the case with a promise or a prediction about the future. A prediction may come true or it may not. A promise to do something in the future may be kept or it may be broken. But neither the prediction nor the promise can be said to have been true or false at the time when it was made. We conclude that section 14 of the Trade Descriptions Act 1968 does not deal with forecasts or promises as such. We put in the qualifying words 'as such' for this reason. A promise or forecast may contain by implication a statement of present fact. The person who makes the promise may be implying that his present intention is to keep it or that he has at present the power to perform it. The person who makes the forcast may be implying that he now believes that his prediction will come true or that he has the means of bringing it to pass. Such implied statements of present intention, means or belief, when they are made, may well be within section 14 of the Act of 1968 and therefore punishable if they were false and were made knowingly or recklessly. But, if they are punishable, the offence is not the breaking of a promise or the failure to make a prediction come true. It is the making of a false statement of an existing fact, somebody's present state of mind or present means."

I respectfully agree with that explanation of the section. In the *Sunair* case, and in some of the earlier cases to which we were referred, the statements made by travel agents and others were held to have been mere expressions of intention or promises for the future, which, at the time they were made, were neither true or false. But in the present case I have reached the opinion that the statement in the letter of August 14 concerning Mr. Edmunds' reservation was false, because it implied that the B.O.A.C. then had an intention which they did not, in fact, have. The statement that they were "confirming" the "reservation" would, I think, convey to Mr. Edmunds that their intention on August 14 was to keep a seat on that flight available for him against all comers. That would necessarily include the intention to avoid booking so many other passengers on the flight as to create a risk that Mr. Edmunds might not get a seat. But as their real intention was to overbook, and thus to create such a risk, the implication was false and the statement must be deemed, by virtue of section 14 (2), to be false.

The point would be more obvious in a case where a particular seat or room is reserved. If I ask for a particular room in a hotel and the manager replies that he has reserved it for me for the dates that I want, there can be no doubt that he conveys to me that it is his intention, at the time when he replies, to keep that room for me and not to let it to anybody else on the specified dates. The same would be true of a numbered seat in a theatre. If I find when I arrive that someone else is occupying the room, that might be for one of three reasons. It might be because of some mistake, in which case the manager would probably have a defence to a charge under the Trade Descriptions Act by relying on section 24. Secondly, it might be because, although at the time when he replied to me he intended to reserve the room for me, he later abandoned that intention, perhaps because a more important guest wanted it. In that case he might escape liability under the Act because his letter had correctly expressed his intention at the time when it was written. But, thirdly, it might be because he had never intended to keep the room for me, if that would require him to refuse all bookings that might possibly conflict with mine. In that case, his original statement would be false because it implied that he had an intention that he did not in fact have. That seems to me to fit the present case exactly.

If the statement in the letter of August 14 was false, it remains to consider whether it was made "recklessly" so as to constitute an offence under section 14 (1) (*b*). In my opinion it was not made recklessly. The reason why it was false was that the intention which it implied was inconsistent with the actual intention of overbooking. That intention must, of course, have been known to the airline when the letter was written. It seems to me, therefore, that the airline made a statement which it knew to be false and that the charge ought to have been made under paragraph (*a*) of section 14 (1).

There was some argument as to whether the statement fell within paragraph (iii) as a statement "as to the time at which" a service was to be provided, or within paragraph (i) as a statement "as to the provision" of services. In my opinion, it falls within both these paragraphs. The statement was about the provision of services but the time including, of course, the date on which they were to be provided, was an essential part of the statement.

It was faintly argued that the airline might escape liability by virtue of subsection (4) of section 14 which provides "In this section 'false'

A means false to a material degree. . . ." The argument was that, as appears from the case stated, the number of passengers who were off-loaded because of the overbooking policy was very small in relation to the total number of passengers who booked seats, and therefore that the statement was not false to any material degree. I cannot agree. The falsity of the statement was material to Mr. Edmunds and that is enough for the present purpose.

B I agree that the certified question should be answered in the way suggested by my noble and learned friend, Lord Wilberforce. I should add that I do not think there is any relevance in the circumstances mentioned in the question in paragraph (a), namely, that at the date when the statement was made the flight was not overbooked or in paragraph (b) that the booking on the flight had already been made at that date.

C I would dismiss the appeal.

Appeal dismissed.

Solicitors: *Turner Peacock, Richards, Butler & Co.*

F. C.

D

[COURT OF APPEAL]

E

* BRUMBY (INSPECTOR OF TAXES) *v.* MILNER

DAY (INSPECTOR OF TAXES) *v.* QUICK

1975 July 28, 29, 30; Oct. 3 — Lord Russell of Killowen, Stamp and Geoffrey Lane L.JJ.

F *Revenue—Income tax—Employment—Employees' profit-sharing scheme wound up—Distribution to employees of balance of funds—Whether payments emoluments arising from employment—Schedule E, Case I—Income and Corporation Taxes Act* 1970 (*c.* 10), *ss.* 181 (1), 183 (1) [1]

Shareholders in a company wished to reduce their share-
holdings but were anxious not to dispose of shares to people
who might change the running of the company, and the direc-
G tors of the company wanted to encourage their employees with
a share incentive scheme. A profit-sharing scheme, therefore,

---

[Reported by MRS. HARRIET DUTTON, Barrister-at-Law]

[1] Income and Corporation Taxes Act 1970, s. 181 (1): "The Schedule referred
to as Schedule E is as follows :— Schedule E 1. Tax under this Schedule shall
H be charged in respect of any office or employment on emoluments therefrom which
fall under one, or more than one, of the following Cases—Case I: where the person
holding the office or employment is resident and ordinarily resident in the United
Kingdom, and does not perform the duties of the office or employment wholly
outside the United Kingdom in the chargeable period (and the emoluments are not
excepted as foreign emoluments), any emoluments for the chargeable period; . . ."

S. 183 (1): "Tax under Case I, II or III of Schedule E shall, except as hereinafter mentioned, be chargeable on the full amount of the emoluments falling under that Case, subject to such deductions only as may be authorised by the Tax Acts, and the expression 'emoluments' shall include all salaries, fees, wages, perquisites and profits whatsoever."

was set up in 1963 whereby the company lent money to trustees to purchase the shares of those shareholders wishing to sell. A trust deed stated that the scheme's primary object was that the shares acquired should provide income for division among employees and that on determination of the scheme any balance should be distributed among the employees and former employees in receipt of pensions in such proportions as the trustees should determine. In 1969 the company merged with another company and the administrative difficulties of continuing with the scheme were so great that the board was forced to wind it up. The trustees decided that a standard award should be made for four years' service with increases for longer service or reductions for less. The amounts were not related to the level of the recipient's remuneration. The taxpayers had served the company for equal periods and interim distributions of the same amount were made to each. The special commissioners quashed their assessments to income tax holding that the causa causans of the payments was the decision to wind up the scheme. Walton J. allowed the Crown's appeals, holding that the taxpayers had received the payments in return for being employees and accordingly income tax was payable under Schedule E.

On appeal by the taxpayers:—

Held, dismissing the appeal, that the final payments could not be considered in isolation from the other provisions of the scheme and, since the whole scheme was based on reward for services, the final payments were indistinguishable in character from the interim payments; that, in any event, the final payments were themselves made as rewards for, and with reference to, the employees' services and, accordingly, the payments were liable to income tax under Schedule E.

Hochstrasser v. *Mayes* [1960] A.C. 376, H.L.(E.) applied.

Dictum of Megarry J. in *Pritchard* v. *Arundale* [1972] Ch. 229, 240 approved.

Decision of Walton J. [1975] 1 W.L.R. 958; [1975] 2 All E.R. 773 affirmed.

The following cases are referred to in the judgment of the court:

Hochstrasser v. *Mayes* [1959] Ch. 22; [1958] 3 W.L.R. 215; [1958] 3 All E.R. 285, C.A.; [1960] A.C. 376; [1960] 2 W.L.R. 63; [1959] 3 All E.R. 817; 38 T.C. 673, H.L.(E.).

Patrick v. *Burrows* (1954) 35 T.C. 138.

Pritchard v. *Arundale* [1972] Ch. 229; [1971] 3 W.L.R. 877; [1971] 3 All E.R. 1011; 47 T.C. 680.

The following additional cases were cited in argument:

Chibbett v. *Joseph Robinson and Sons* (1924) 9 T.C. 48.

Simpson v. *John Reynolds & Co. (Insurances) Ltd.* [1974] 1 W.L.R. 1411; [1974] 2 All E.R. 545.

APPEAL from Walton J.

The taxpayers, Samuel Milner and Derek Michael Quick, employees of William Park & Co. Forgemasters Ltd., appealed against assessments to income tax made in respect of interim distributions of £100 paid to them in 1971 on the termination of an employees' profit-sharing scheme. The special commissioners allowed their appeals holding that the payments were not emoluments arising from their employments. Walton J. allowed an appeal by the Crown against the special commissioners' decision.

The taxpayers appealed. The grounds of appeal in the case of the taxpayer Milner were, inter alia, that the judge erred in law in holding that, where a payment was made pursuant to the terms of a trust deed, the

A question whether it was or was not a profit from the employment of the payee had to be determined exclusively by reference to those terms and without the consideration of any extrinsic evidence; in any event, on the true construction of the trust deed dated September 25, 1963, the payments to the taxpayer were not profits from his employment; the judge erred in law in holding that the payments made to the taxpayer were paid to him in return for acting as or being an employee; and the taxpayer's employment
B was not the causa causans of the payments, but merely the causa sine qua non thereof.

The facts are stated in the judgment.

M. C. Nourse Q.C. and *Joseph Turner* for the taxpayers.
Peter Rees Q.C. and *B. J. Davenport* for the Crown.

C

Cur. adv. vult.

October 3. LORD RUSSELL OF KILLOWEN read the following judgment of the court. These appeals from Walton J. concern the question whether payments received in 1971 by the taxpayers from trustees of a settlement of shares in a company, William Park & Co. Forgemasters Ltd., on the
D termination of a scheme for the benefit of employees of the company, were emoluments or profits "from" the employment of the taxpayers and so liable to tax under Schedule E by virtue of sections 181 and 183 (1) of the Income and Corporation Taxes Act 1970. The special commissioners found that they were not. Walton J. found that they were.

In 1963 certain shareholders in the company wished to sell their
E shares, but all concerned were anxious that the purchasers should be acceptable to the management. At the same time the board wished to introduce a profit-sharing scheme by which employees of the company and its subsidiaries should gain directly over and above their salaries and wages from the profitability of the company's business, giving them an incentive and a share of the group's profits. A scheme was devised by which the company borrowed a substantial sum from bankers, and lent
F the sum interest-free to trustees appointed by the board, to enable the trustees to buy the shares in the company from the shareholders already mentioned, to be held upon the trusts of a deed dated September 25, 1963. The trusts of the deed being for the benefit of employees, the lending by the company was not a contravention of section 54 of the Companies Act 1948. The deed was between the company and the named
G trustees. By recital (C) it was recited:

"The company desires to institute a scheme for the benefit of its employees or certain of them of the nature envisaged by section 54 (1) (*b*) of the Companies Act 1948 and for that purpose has now paid to the present trustees the sum of £700,000 (in part provided by moneys advanced by Williams Deacons Bank Ltd.) (hereinafter called
H 'the bank') to be applied in manner hereinafter appearing and it is desired to record (without intending by this recital to create any trust or to use the word 'employees' in any particular sense) that in relation to such scheme and this deed the primary object is that ordinary shares in the company acquired for the purposes of this deed shall provide income (normally by means of receipt of dividends from such shares) for division between employees."

Clause 3 empowered the trustees to accumulate income for the purpose

of reducing the indebtedness to the company and enabled the trustees A
for the same purpose to dispose of constituents of the trust fund. Subject
to the power to apply income in repayment of the debt, clause 5 pro-
vided for the distribution of income of the trust fund as follows:

> “The trustees shall hold the dividends from ordinary shares in the
> company or other the income of the trust fund received by them in
> trust (subject to their discretion under clause 3 (1) hereof) to divide B
> the same between the employees at the time of such receipt in each
> case in such proportions (exclusive of one or more of the employees)
> as the trustees shall think fit to determine within one calendar
> month of such receipt in each case and failing such determination
> between the employees at the time of such receipt in each case
> equally provided further that the trustees may with the consent of
> the company at any time within six months from the date of this C
> deed make rules in writing for or dealing with (in such manner as
> the trustees think fit) the apportionment of the divisible income of the
> trust fund (up to the time when this scheme terminates) between
> the employees and such rules when made shall thereupon take effect
> in substitution for the foregoing provisions of this clause and such
> substituted provisions shall accordingly be subject to the power con-
> tained in clause 13 of this deed.” D

“Employee” was defined by clause 1 as follows:

> “‘Employee’ means a person of either sex (other than a director
> of the company but including a director of any subsidiary company
> of the company who is not a director of the company) who is in the
> full time employment of the company and has attained 21 years of E
> age and includes an apprentice (who has attained 21 years of age).
> Provided further that for the purpose of this present definition i.e.
> of the word ‘employee’ the expression ‘the company’ includes
> Parks Forge Ltd., English Tools Ltd., A. & F. Parkes Ltd., A. Morris
> & Sons (Dunsford) Ltd., Gullick Ltd., Herbert Cotterill Ltd., Hope
> Hydraulics Ltd., Thomas Gaskell & Co. Ltd., Scotts (St. Helens)
> Ltd. and any other company for the time being a subsidiary of the F
> company.”

Thus far there was provision for employee participation in profits so
long as the scheme continued. Clause 7 provided for the termination of
the scheme as follows:

> “The scheme shall forthwith determine (a) at the expiration of one G
> year after the date upon which the company shall have given notice
> in writing to the trustees of its intention to determine the same or
> (b) if an order is made or an effective resolution passed to wind up
> the company or (c) at the expiration of 20 years from the day of
> the death of the last survivor of the lineal descendants now living of
> his late Majesty King George V.”

H

It was under clause 8 that the sums now in question were received
by the taxpayers from the trustees. Clause 8, so far as material, is as
follows:

> “On the determination of the scheme the trustees shall as soon as
> practicable realise the trust fund and shall apply the net proceeds of
> such realisation and any undisposed of income of the trust fund as
> follows:—(a) in paying to the company the amount of the debt

> A or such part of the same as shall then be owing and subject thereto . . . (c) in distributing the balance if any among the employees and former employees in receipt of pensions from any funds or schemes under which they shall be entitled by virtue of having been an employee respectively as at the date of the determination of the scheme (other than employees (if any) who shall after such date and prior to such distribution have been dismissed for misconduct or B incompetence) in such proportions as the trustees shall within the year next following the date of the determination of the scheme by writing determine and in default of such determination between the said employees and former employees ascertained as at the said date of determination in equal shares."

The scheme was operated for some years. In the course of those C years, out of net dividends some £111,000 had been repaid off the debt to the company and some £108,000 distributed to employees, each division being in equal shares without regard to rates of pay or length of service. Meanwhile, in 1969 there was a merger between the company and another company, which took the form of a new holding company being formed which acquired the issued share capital of both companies D in exchange for shares in the holding company, of which the trustees received their due proportion. It becoming apparent to the trustees and the board of the company that the scheme was not appropriate to the new structure, the company gave notice determining the scheme, as it had an absolute right to do under clause 7. The trustees consequently sold their shareholding in the holding company, and after paying off the indebtedness to the company had in their hands some £370,000 for dis- E tribution under clause 8 among 1,802 qualified employees and 49 qualified pensioners. This £370,000 in effect represented in part dividends of earlier years used in paying off indebtedness to the company under clause 3, and in other part growth of the capital value of the trust fund by bonus issues and otherwise. The trustees in due time, on June 21, 1971, resolved upon a scheme for distribution, to some extent proportionate to F lengths of service but not related to size of salary or wage, which resulted in entitlements varying from £66 to £334. Each of the two present tax-payers became entitled to £200: each was paid £100 on account: each was assessed to tax under Schedule E in respect of his £100: and each appealed to the special commissioners. There is no distinction between the two cases in principle, and hereafter we speak of one taxpayer, who constitutes of course a test case.

G The contents of recital (c) of the deed have already been noted. At the time the scheme was launched it was announced to employees in a notice of the same date in this form: It is headed "Wm. Park & Co. Forge-masters Ltd.," dated September 26, 1963:

> "Notice to all group employees. Profit-sharing scheme. The directors of this company have been desirous for some time of instituting a H scheme whereby employees of the group had an interest in the shares of this company and a means of sharing in the profits of the group. The estate of the late S. R. Park and members of the Park family (notably Mr. Cyril J. Park and Mr. Brian H. Park) have now made this possible by making available a large block of shares held by them. A trust has been formed to purchase the shares so made available and the company has agreed to advance an interest-free loan to the trust for the purchase of the shares. The shares will then be held in

> trust for the benefit of all employees of the group (other than directors of the parent company) 21 years of age and over of either sex and after a qualifying period of employment. The precise rules of the trust will be published later but the annual income from dividends on such shares will be used partly to repay the loan and partly by distribution to the employees according to the rules of the trust. On full repayment of the loan the whole income of the trust will be available for distribution to employees according to the rules of the trust. . . . A summarised copy of the rules of the trust will be sent to each eligible employee as soon as possible."

In fact, no rules were ever drawn up. A booklet on these lines was issued in August 1965 containing explanatory notes for guidance of employees, in the form of questions and answers. One question and answer was as follows:

> " Apart from income have I any rights under the scheme? (Answer): Yes. Subject to repayment of the original loan etc., the shares are held in trust for employees and in the unlikely event of the scheme being terminated you may be eligible for a share in the residue. This is a complicated matter, however, and is set out in some detail in the relevant trust deed."

It is clear that, as was natural, the scheme was made known to employees: it was to be an incentive.

The special commissioners found that the scheme was at its inception intended by all concerned to continue indefinitely, subject to the perpetuity long-stop to avoid invalidity. The case stated contains the following finding of fact:

> " (13) We find as a fact that in terminating the scheme the board of Wm. Park were primarily actuated by factors arising from the merger of Wm. Park & Dobson and that the distribution of the balance of the trust funds to employees was not an object of their decision but only an incidental consequence."

It is convenient at this stage to notice that the special commissioners concluded in their decision that the decision of the company to terminate the scheme was the causa causans of the receipt by the taxpayer of his terminal distribution: that his employment was merely the causa sine qua non: and that the trustees' decision to apportion or allot payments on the basis mentioned (as distinct from allowing the provision for equal division in default to operate under the deed) was not an act of rewarding employees for their services. The question in any case whether a receipt by an employee is to be regarded for present purposes as " emoluments or profits from " the employment has given rise to a number of judicial attempts to analyse or define or elaborate upon those words. Both sides, however, were at one in accepting the language of Upjohn J. [1959] Ch. 22, 33, approved by the House of Lords in *Hochstrasser* v. *Mayes* [1960] A.C. 376, 388:

> " . . . in my judgment, the authorities show that to be a profit arising from the employment the payment must be made in reference to the services the employee renders by virtue of his office, and it must be something in the nature of a reward for services past, present and future." ([1959] Ch. 22, 23.)

To this may be added the language of Lord Radcliffe in the same case, at p. 391:

> "The test to be applied is the same for all. It is contained in the statutory requirement that the payment, if it is to be the subject of assessment, must arise 'from' the office or employment. In the past several explanations have been offered by judges of eminence as to the significance of the word 'from' in this context. It has been said that the payment must have been made to the employee 'as such.' It has been said that it must have been made to him 'in his capacity of employee.' It has been said that it is assessable if paid 'by way of remuneration for his services,' and said further that this is what is meant by payment to him 'as such.' These are all glosses, and they are all of value as illustrating the idea which is expressed by the words of the statute. But it is perhaps worth observing that they do not displace those words. For my part, I think that their meaning is adequately conveyed by saying that, while it is not sufficient to render a payment assessable that an employee would not have received it unless he had been an employee, it is assessable if it has been paid to him in return for acting as or being an employee."

It was common ground that in every case the question must be answered having regard to all the circumstances which are connected with and precede the receipt in question. Counsel for the Crown, in our view rightly, felt themselves not able to support the view to which Walton J. inclined, that *Patrick* v. *Burrows* (1954) 35 T.C. 138 required him to confine himself to the four corners of the deed of September 1963. Additionally, we would approve the way in which Megarry J. approached the matter in *Pritchard* v. *Arundale* [1972] Ch. 229, 240 where he said that there were not in truth several questions involving the decision into which of several compartments the receipt was to be fitted, but only one question, that is to say, whether it is shown (though this is not of course a question of onus) that the receipt had the taxable quality of remuneration or reward for services. Cases in the books have tended to treat the question as one in which if there was not merely a payment on personal grounds as a testimonial to personal qualities of the employed recipient, it must be a reward for services, and vice versa. But those were cases in which the facts made it necessary that it should be either the one or the other, and they are not inconsistent with the true situation that in every case there is the one question which must be answered in the one sense if the receipt is to be brought within the charge to tax under Schedule E.

We return to the question whether the payments now in question are properly to be regarded as a reward for and referable to services of the recipients. It might, it seems to us, be thought that, since in the exercise of their right to allocate in different proportions the trustees chose to calculate different amounts for different people on a basis of length of service, that fact itself stamped the receipts with the necessary taxable quality. But the Crown did not make that submission in this court, and we say no more about it.

The Crown's contention may be shortly stated. From its very birth the scheme was plainly intended as an incentive scheme both to encourage and to reward employees in respect of their services as such; payments made during the years before the scheme was terminated were therefore plainly profits from the employment as being rewards for and referable to services, though having regard to the source from which the payments were made (dividends received under deduction of tax) this would be relevant to the parallel statutory provisions on earned income relief rather than to Schedule E; and that there was no sound ground for distinguishing in this respect the terminal payments now in question. So far as concerned the views of the special commissioners, they had, the Crown submitted, manifestly erred in their conclusion that the payments were not " profits from " the employment because the causa causans was the decision of the company to determine the scheme because it had ceased to be appropriate to the new inter-company structure. And we agree with that submission.

Counsel for the taxpayers would not accept the Crown's contention as to the pre-termination receipts, a question that was not before the court. However, in our judgment, it is necessary to express a view thereon in reaching a decision on the question that is before us and, in our opinion, this contention of the Crown is plainly correct. For the taxpayers it was contended that in any event there was all the difference in the world between the pre-termination payments and the terminal payments. It was said that the latter were not to be expected; their probability for any employee at any time was very remote; they were fortuitous windfalls; they could not be regarded as truly part of an incentive scheme based on profit-sharing, more particularly in that they were terminal payments winding up the trust fund; the proper inference was that the trust deed only contained the provisions under which they were made because some ultimate provision was necessary and employees had to be chosen as the ultimate beneficiaries to escape section 54 of the Companies Act 1948. It was further contended that the trustees could have exercised their discretion over allocation by concentrating on the needy. But this contention assumed the answer in favour of the taxpayers on the main question, which is whether the provision was intended as a reward for services.

In our judgment the contention of the Crown is correct. We do not consider that the provision for terminal payments can be considered as, so to speak, a throw-away provision bearing no colour of reward for services. The very existence of the discretion to allocate is against this inference. It appears to us that the scheme was one scheme based fundamentally on reward for services by employees, and the fact that after the final payment there was no more by way of bonus to look for does not relevantly distinguish that final payment. Moreover, there are two particular points which indicate that in truth these final payments were rewards for and with reference to services. First, pensioned ex-employees, who ex hypothesi would have been such because of the services they had rendered to the company, were brought into the class of recipients. Second, if an employee who was such at the date of determination of the scheme and would otherwise qualify was in the period (up to a year) between then and distribution dismissed for misconduct or incompetence, he was excluded from benefit. Such misconduct or incompetence clearly would be referable to his services, and the deprival being referable to his services, so should be regarded his entitlement. We accordingly dismiss both appeals.

Appeal dismissed with costs.
Leave to appeal.

Solicitors: *Field Fisher & Martineau for Arthur Smith & Brodie-Griffith, Wigan; Solicitor of Inland Revenue.*

A

[COURT OF APPEAL]

* SEWING MACHINES RENTALS LTD. *v.* WILSON AND ANOTHER

[Plaint No. 7505384]

B

SAME *v.* UDEALA

[Plaint No. 7453082]

MORLEN INVESTMENTS LTD. *v.* WILSON AND ANOTHER

C [Plaint No. 7454497]

1975 July 28 — Megaw and Browne L.JJ. and Sir John Pennycuick

County Court—Jurisdiction—Stay of execution pending appeal——Orders of possession of mortgaged premises—Stay of execution on condition of payment of sums not otherwise due—
D *Whether proper exercise of jurisdiction—Whether stay of execution pending appeal automatic—R.S.C., Ord.* 59, *rr.* 13 (1) (*a*), 19 (5) [1]

In each of three actions in the county court the plaintiff company sought an order for possession of mortgaged property and for the payment of a sum of money comprising the principals of the mortgage loans and interest overdue. The issue in
E each case was whether, as the defendant mortgagors contended, the transaction had been a sham designed to avoid the provisions of the Moneylenders Acts 1900 to 1927. The county court judge granted orders for possession and payment of the sums claimed. The defendants sought stays of execution pending appeals, and the judge granted stays on the condition of payments by the defendants of monthly sums of money.

On motions by the defendants for orders setting aside the
F orders made by the judge in so far as they imposed conditions on the stays of execution:—

Held, granting the applications, that nothing in R.S.C., Ord. 59, r. 19 (5) limited the jurisdiction of the county court judge to grant a stay of execution under the first limb of rule 19 (5), where there was an appeal, subject to such conditions as he regarded as being fair and just in the particular case; that, however, it had in the present case been a wrong exercise
G of the judge's discretion to impose a condition of what in effect had been the continuing payment of interest on the mortgage sums which was not due either under the deeds under which the actions had been brought or, since interest did not run on a county court judgment, by virtue of interest running on the judgments (post, pp. 42E, F, 43H—44A, 44H—45A, C, F).

Grimshaw, Baxter & Elliott Ltd. v. *Parker* [1910] 2 K.B.
H 161, C.A. considered.

Per curiam. It is desirable that the Rule Committee should consider the rules in question so that they may be brought into better harmony (post, pp. 40H—41A, 45C, F, G).

Per Megaw and Browne L.JJ. (1) On the true construction of R.S.C., Ord. 59, rr. 13 (1) (*a*) and 19 (5), an appeal from a judgment or order of the county court does not operate

[1] R.S.C., Ord. 59, r. 13 (1) (*a*): see post, p. 41A.
R. 19 (5): see post, p. 41D.

automatically as a stay of execution pending the hearing of A
the appeal (post, pp. 41B, C, 41H, 45C).

(2) The rule that interest does not run on a county court judgment ought also to receive attention in the appropriate quarter (post, pp. 43G, H, 45C).

The following cases are referred to in the judgments:

Grimshaw, Baxter & Elliott Ltd. v. *Parker* [1910] 2 K.B. 161, D.C. B
Kelly v. *White* [1920] W.N. 220, D.C.
Moore v. *Lambeth County Court Registrar* [1969] 1 W.L.R. 141; [1969] 1 All E.R. 782, C.A.

The following additional cases were cited in argument:

Jones v. *Savery* [1951] 1 All E.R. 820, C.A.
Kirkpatrick v. *Salvation Army Trustee Co.* [1968] 1 W.L.R. 1955; [1969] C
1 All E.R. 388, C.A.
Reg. v. *Bloomsbury and Marylebone County Court, Ex parte Villerwest Ltd.* [1975] 1 W.L.R. 1175; [1975] 2 All E.R. 562, D.C.
Reg. v. *Essex County Court Judge* (1887) 18 Q.B.D. 704, C.A.

MOTIONS

By the first motion, dated July 23, 1975, in an appeal in the action *Sewing* D
Machines Rentals Ltd. v. *Wilson*, the defendants, Alan George Wilson and George McCarthy, sought an order under R.S.C., Ord. 59, r. 19 (5) that the order of Judge Coplestone-Boughey made at Wandsworth County Court on June 2, 1975, at the instance of the plaintiffs, Sewing Machines Rentals Ltd., for possession of premises known as 3 Craster Road, London, S.W.2, and for payment by the defendants to the plaintiffs of E
£15,939 and costs be stayed pending the hearing of the defendants' appeal to the Court of Appeal against the order on such terms as the court might think fit and further (if necessary) for an order that any warrant for possession already issued be not executed pending the hearing of the appeal. The judge ordered:

"that judgment be stayed for six weeks and thereafter if notice of appeal has been given by the defendant[s] on terms that the first F
defendant pays into court the sum of £315 interest on the 25th day of each month from today."

By the second motion, of the same date, in an appeal in the action *Sewing Machines Rentals Ltd.* v. *Udeala*, the defendant, Smith Ogwo Udeala, sought similar relief against the plaintiffs in respect of an order for possession of premises known as 69 Broughton Street, London, G
S.W.2, and payment of £12,473·46 and costs. The judge ordered:

"that judgment be stayed for six weeks and thereafter if notice of appeal has been given by the defendant on terms that the defendant pays into court the sum of £126 interest on the 24th day of every month from today."

H

By the third motion, of the same date, in the action *Morlen Investments Ltd.* v. *Wilson*, the defendants, Alan George Wilson and Mr. Liqourice, sought similar relief against the plaintiffs, Morlen Investments Ltd., in respect of an order for possession of premises known as 39 Wingford Road, London, S.W.2, and payment of £10,790·48 and costs. The judge ordered:

"that judgment be stayed for six weeks and thereafter if notice of

A appeal has been given by the defendants on terms that the first defendant pay into court the sum of £211 interest on the 12th day of every month from today."

The facts are stated in the judgment of Megaw L.J.

Timothy Lloyd for the defendants Wilson and Udeala.
B The defendants McCarthy and Liqourice did not appear and were not represented.
Norman Primost for the plaintiffs.

MEGAW L.J. These are motions on behalf of the defendants in three actions heard in the Wandsworth County Court. The three actions all
C give rise to precisely the same issues, though obviously the facts and figures differ in respect of each of them. The actions are concerned with claims by companies who assert that they are assignees of mortgages entered into whereby the respective defendants have mortgaged buildings to a registered friendly society, the Berkeley Assurance Society, and it is asserted that the Berkeley Assurance Society assigned those respective
D mortgages to the respective plaintiff companies. In two of the actions the plaintiff company is Sewing Machines Rentals Ltd.; in the third action the plaintiff company is Morlen Investments Ltd. The defendants in the actions by Sewing Machines Rentals Ltd. are a Mr. Wilson and a Mr. Udeala, and Mr. Wilson is again a defendant in the action by Morlen Investments Ltd.

The actions were heard in the Wandsworth County Court by Judge
E Coplestone-Boughey, who, on June 2, 1975, after a hearing which had lasted some eight days, gave judgment in favour of the plaintiffs in each of the actions, granting orders for possession of the respective properties and also orders for the payment of substantial sums of money, being the principal of the loans on the mortgages together with substantial sums of interest overdue at the date when the actions were heard.

F The issue in each of the actions was, in effect, the question whether, as the defendants contended, the whole transaction in each case was a sham, in order to avoid the provisions of the Moneylenders Acts, by pretending, or giving the appearance, that the moneys were being advanced by a registered friendly society when, in effect and in substance, the registered friendly society was merely a part of machinery used in order to give an air of respectability to loans that in fact were made
G by moneylenders.

It would be wrong for this court, on these motions, to say anything that indicated any view as to the merits of the actions, on fact or on law, because the judgment in each of the three actions is the subject of appeal to this court and will have to be heard and dealt with hereafter. Nothing that I say, therefore, is to be taken as in any way expressing a
H view as to the ultimate outcome of the appeals, other than that I would not regard the appeals as being appeals that are obviously destined to fail or obviously merely for purposes of delay. As to how far beyond that it goes I express no view, but that is a factor which it is proper to take into account where a question arises, as it arises here, whether or not a stay of execution ought to be granted. The court, as I see it and as has, I think, always been its practice, is prepared to take into account, on an application for a stay of execution on an appeal from the High Court

or a county court, a view that it may form as to whether the appeal is A
one that is wholly unmeritorious or wholly unlikely to succeed.

The judge, having given his judgment in the three actions, was asked, on behalf of the defendants, to grant stay of execution pending an appeal. Notice of appeal, of course, had not been given at that stage. Quite clearly, it could not have been given then. The judge, after hearing submissions on both sides, granted a stay of execution in each case pending
the hearing of the appeal, but granted it on conditions. The conditions B
which he imposed were conditions for payment of sums of money by the respective defendants in the three actions. In the action *Sewing Machines Rentals Ltd.* v. *Wilson* the condition of stay of execution was that the defendant, Mr. Wilson, should pay £315 on the 25th day of each month until the determination of the appeal. That £315 was worked
out as giving interest at the rate of 36 per cent. per annum on a C
principal sum of £10,500, being the relevant principal of the mortgage in question. In *Morlen Investments Ltd.* v. *Wilson* Mr. Wilson was required, as a condition of the stay, to pay £211 a month on the 12th day of each month pending the appeal. That again was 36 per cent. per annum on the capital sum of £7,180. In *Sewing Machines Rentals Ltd.* v. *Udeala* Mr. Udeala, the defendant, was required, as a condition of stay of
execution, to pay £126 per month on the 24th day of each month; that D
was at the rate of 14 per cent. per annum on the capital sum there involved of £10,800. The amount of unpaid interest that was then outstanding, or alleged to be outstanding, is shown by the judgments. The judgment in the action *Sewing Machines Rentals Ltd.* v. *Wilson* was for a sum of £15,939, as against the principal sum of £10,500; in *Morlen*
Investments Ltd. v. *Wilson* the judgment was for £10,790, against the E
capital sum involved of £7,180, and in Mr. Udeala's case the judgment was the sum of £12,473, against a capital sum outstanding of £10,800.

At first, although I would not say that the defendants were content with those orders of stay of execution, they did not take urgent steps to seek to have them altered in any way, whether by application to this
court or otherwise. Nor, indeed, unfortunately, were there any urgent F
steps taken even to give notice of appeal, and it is said in this court that the notices of appeal which were ultimately given were, under the applicable rule of R.S.C., Ord. 59, a day or two days out of time. However, Mr. Primost, who appears on behalf of the plaintiffs, said in this court that he would not feel it possible, if application were made for extension of time, to resist, if the court saw fit to grant such extension.
That matter does not, however, arise, at any rate directly, at this stage, G
though Mr. Primost, not unnaturally, relied on that delay as being one of the grounds why the court should exercise its discretion not to interfere with the orders that had been made by the judge, even if in other respects it was minded so to do.

These motions before the court on behalf of the respective defendants
ask this court, in effect, to set aside the judge's several orders of June 2, H
1975, in so far as those orders imposed conditions on stay of execution. The first question that arises is whether, under the Rules of the Supreme Court, on their true construction, the judge was entitled to make the orders that he did make, imposing the conditions of stay of execution.

This matter of the construction of the rules is one which is not altogether easy, and I would express a strong view that it would be very desirable that the Rule Committee should, at an early date, consider

A the respective rules in order to see whether there are not matters in them that require at any rate to be rephrased.

So far as appeals from the High Court are concerned, the relevant Order is Ord. 59, r. 13 (1). That provides:

> " Except so far as the court below or the Court of Appeal may otherwise direct—(*a*) an appeal shall not operate as a stay of execution or B of proceedings under the decision of the court below; . . ."

That rule, however, is not applicable to appeals from county courts, because Ord. 59, r. 19 contains a special code in certain respects with regard to appeals from the county court. Ord. 59, r. 19 (5) is as follows: " Rule 13 (1) (*a*) shall not apply, . . . " I pause there for a moment. That would mean, or might be taken to mean, if one stopped there, that, so C far as appeals from the county court are concerned, since rule 13 (1) (*a*) does not apply, an appeal from a judgment or order of the county court would operate directly, necessarily and without anything more as a stay of execution pending the hearing of the appeal. However, that would be contrary to all past understanding and practice, and I am satisfied that it is not, indeed, the effect. Paragraph (5) goes on:

> D " . . . but the appeal shall not operate as a stay of proceedings in the county court unless the judge of that court so orders or unless, within 10 days after the date of the judgment or order appealed against, the appellant deposits a sum fixed by the judge not exceeding the amount of the money or the value of the property affected by the judgment or order, or gives such security for the said sum as the judge may direct."

E I should refer first, in order to get it out of the way, to a difficulty which I felt at the outset of the argument of this motion. In rule 13 (1), which I have read, the provisions are: " an appeal shall not operate as a stay of execution *or* of proceedings under the decision of the court below; . . ." There appears there to be drawn a distinction between, on the one hand, stay of execution and, on the other hand, stay of pro- F ceedings. What is regarded as being covered by the word " proceedings " in that rule is shown in note 59/13/1 in *The Supreme Court Practice* (1973). It gives examples of what is meant by " proceedings " that may be thus stayed, for example, an order for the assessment of damages. There is there apparently drawn that distinction between " execution " and " proceedings." When, however, one comes to the provision as to G county court appeals in rule 19 (5), the words " or execution " do not appear. The words are: " shall not operate as a stay of proceedings in the county court." The indication from the inclusion of " execution or " in the one rule and its exclusion in the other would appear at first sight to mean that paragraph (5) had no application to the stay of execution of a county court judgment and that, therefore, so far as the county court is concerned, there is no jurisdiction, either in the county court judge H or in this court, to do anything other than treat an appeal to this court as automatically resulting in a stay of execution. However, Mr. Lloyd, for the defendant-applicants on this motion, did not put forward any such drastic contention, and I am satisfied, particularly by reference to one of the authorities to which Mr. Lloyd referred us, *Grimshaw, Baxter & Elliott Ltd.* v. *Parker* [1910] 2 K.B. 161, that the omission of the word " execution " in rule 19 (5) is not intended to produce any such effect. It may be inelegant, but the contemplation of those who made the rules must have been that the words " of proceedings " in that para- A graph should have the same meaning and effect as the words " of execution or of proceedings " in rule 13 (1).

So the remainder of the words of rule 19 (5) apply to stay of execution where there is an appeal to this court from the county court. The paragraph then goes on to prescribe that there may be such a stay of execution. That comes under two heads. First there is: " shall not operate as a stay of proceedings . . . unless the judge . . . so orders . . ." B Then there are the further words which I have already read, introduced by " or unless."

Mr. Lloyd's argument on construction is that, because the second part of that paragraph lays down certain conditions on which a stay of execution falls to be granted, involving a deposit of a sum of money or the giving of security, the earlier part of the paragraph, " unless the judge C of that court so orders," has to be read as prescribing by implication that the judge has no power, if he acts under that part of the paragraph, to impose any conditions. The only conditions that can be imposed, if the judge decides that it is appropriate to grant a stay of execution pending an appeal, are the conditions set out in the second part of the paragraph. If the judge grants a stay of execution by reference to the first part of the D paragraph, it has to be an unconditional stay of execution. Mr. Lloyd therefore says, as his primary submission in this case, that the judge, when he made the order of June 2, 1975, had no power to make the conditional order that he did make because he was not purporting to make an order under the second part of Ord. 59, r. 19 (5), and he had not indeed been asked to do so, nor had he made any of the investigations that might be necessary, in the circumstances of this case, to make an order E under that part of the paragraph. Mr. Lloyd's submission, then, is not that the county court judge's order is a nullity but that the conditions imposed are irregular and that this court should delete them, leaving an unconditional stay in operation.

With great respect to Mr. Lloyd's interesting and clear argument, I am satisfied that it is wrong. There is nothing in Ord. 59, r. 19 (5) which F limits the jurisdiction of the county court judge to grant a stay of execution, where there is an appeal, subject to such conditions as he regards as being fair and just in the particular case.

The rule is divided into the two parts: there is first the ordinary discretion of the judge; the second part provides, as it were, an additional remedy for a potential appellant from a county court judgment, one who has given, or has undertaken to give, notice of an appeal, that is to G say, he may insist on getting stay of execution by applying to the judge with reference to the second part of the paragraph. The judge then, it is perfectly true, has a judicial function to carry out of assessing what is the amount of money affected by the judgment or order, or what is the appropriate security. The judge must, however, then grant a stay of execution conditional on payment, or provision of security, as H assessed in accordance with the provisions laid down. That, however, is no reason for treating the first part of the paragraph as giving the judge a power limited to the grant of a stay which must be unconditional.

The authority to which Mr. Lloyd invited our attention in support of his submission is a passage from the judgment of Lord Coleridge J. in *Grimshaw, Baxter & Elliott Ltd.* v. *Parker* [1910] 2 K.B. 161, to which case I have already referred. In that case the court was dealing with

A the rule that then existed, Ord. 59, r. 14 of the Rules of the Supreme
Court 1883, which for present purposes can be treated as being
substantially identical. Lord Coleridge J. said, at p. 164:

> "That being so, the county court judge was entitled either to
> order that the appeal should operate unconditionally as a stay,
> or he might impose any condition authorised by the rule."

B The point with which we are here concerned was not, however, a live
point in that case, and in my judgment it would be quite wrong to treat
that passage, with its reference to "unconditionally," as being a
considered view on the matter that we have to consider.

Mr. Lloyd's argument, if it were right, would involve the extra-
ordinary result that, where there is an appeal from a judgment which
C is not a money judgment, nor a judgment affecting property, but a
judgment of the county court concerned with wholly different matters,
where it is obvious that a stay of execution, if granted, should be con-
ditional on some condition other than a money payment, the court
would have no jurisdiction to impose such a condition. That must indeed
be wrong.

D Nevertheless, in a case where the second part of paragraph (5) might
reasonably be regarded as being relevant and applicable, the judge, if
he is asked to exercise his discretion under the first part of the paragraph
to grant a stay of execution because of an appeal, ought to pay regard,
where it is appropriate, to the matters that are set out in the second
part of the paragraph. Thus, for example, normally I should have thought
that it would be a wrong exercise of the discretion under the first part
E of the paragraph to impose some condition as a condition of stay of execu-
tion of a judgment pending an appeal which involved the deposit, for
example, of a larger sum of money than that which could have been fixed,
and which the appellant could have applied to have assessed and fixed, under
the second part of the paragraph, entitling him, on payment into court of
the sum, to have a stay of execution as of right.

F In the present case, the judge had a discretion to exercise, and he
was not acting without jurisdiction merely from the fact that he imposed
conditions. He had jurisdiction to impose conditions. The real question
which arises here, as I see it, is whether, in the circumstances, there
was a proper exercise of the jurisdiction having regard to the facts
which were before the judge. The conditions which he imposed, as I have
already indicated, were conditions which were related to the interest that
G would have become due in different circumstances on the amounts of
the capital outstanding on the various mortgages if interest still con-
tinued to run, and he assessed that interest at the rate of interest prescribed
by the various deeds.

Now, as Mr. Lloyd has made clear and as is not challenged by Mr.
Primost on behalf of the plaintiffs, first, curious though it may be (and
H this maybe is another matter which ought to be reconsidered by those
who have the responsibility for such matters), interest does not run
on a county court judgment, and secondly, once the judgment was
given on these mortgages as it was given by the judge on June 2, 1975,
no further interest fell to be paid by virtue of the mortgages or the
contract involved therein. Whether the appeals succeed or fail, no
further interest is payable beyond the date of judgment. The judge was
therefore imposing, as a condition of granting the stay of execution

pending the appeal, what in effect was the continuing payment of interest A
which was not due, either under the deeds under which the action was
brought or by virtue of interest running on the judgment that had been
given. We are told by Mr. Primost, and I should certainly regard it as
right to accept, that he pressed the judge, if he granted the stay of
execution, to impose more stringent terms, and the terms which he, I
understand, suggested to the judge should be imposed were the payment
into court of the whole amounts of the interest alleged to be outstanding B
in the various actions. The judge was not, however, prepared to impose
such stringent terms on the defendants, and for that reason he imposed
on them what he certainly regarded as being, and what probably was in
fact, a lesser financial burden.

We have no information before us which enables us to arrive at any
conclusion as to whether the security involved in the property is such C
that now, or at the date when this court will ultimately give its decision
on the appeals, the amount of that security is likely to cover the capital
sum still due plus the interest that was due and was unpaid up to the
moment of the judgment in the county court. We cannot form any view
one way or the other on that.

Mr. Primost stresses, not unnaturally, that, if it is a question of the D
court exercising its discretion, there are various factors by reason of
which the court ought not to exercise that discretion so as to alter the
order which the judge has made. They include the factor of the amount
of interest outstanding, the fact that no payments have been made and
no offer has been made in respect of that money and the facts that have
arisen with regard to what might appear to be somewhat dilatory pro-
ceedings in relation to the judge's order and the appeal against it to this E
court. In that context I should say, because some point was made by
Mr. Primost on it, that before the defendants appealed to this court
asking this court to set aside the judge's conditions of stay of execution
they had gone back to the county court and had been referred to the
registrar and had invited him to set aside the judge's order on the basis
that, on the true interpretation of the rules, it had been made without F
jurisdiction. From what I have said, it will be apparent that I think that
the registrar rightly rejected that suggestion that was made of "no
jurisdiction," though I think he based his refusal of the application
perhaps rather on other grounds. Mr. Primost sought to say in this court
that as a result of that the county court judge was functus officio. Well,
maybe he was. We are, however, concerned with an appeal to this court
from his judgment, and we are not functi officio. It is, moreover, said G
by Mr. Primost that the time was now too late for a stay to be granted,
as I understand it even by this court, on the motion which has been
brought before it, because the warrant for possession had already been
issued. We were referred to notes in the *County Court Practice* and to
a decision of this court, *Moore* v. *Lambeth County Court Registrar*
[1961] 1 W.L.R. 141. I do not think there is any substance in either H
of these two points. I am quite clear that we in this court have juris-
diction to form a view as to whether the discretion which the judge
exercised was right in the circumstances and, if we think it was wrong,
to deal with it accordingly.

Having regard to the nature of the condition which the judge imposed,
being a payment of contractual interest although no contractual interest
on any view would be payable hereafter, whatever be the result of this

A appeal, I have come to the conclusion that the order which was made by the judge was one which involved a wrong exercise of the discretion. I would not be minded myself to substitute for it some other and different condition as to payment to be made. I would grant the applications and direct that there shall be a stay of execution pending the hearing of the appeals and that such stay of execution shall be unconditional, subject only to this, that a stay of execution ordered by this court should, I
B think, be a stay of execution pending the hearing of the appeals *or further order*, so that, if by chance (and one hopes it does not occur) the plaintiffs should have reason to believe that there is any undue delay on the part of the defendants in bringing their appeals before this court, they could make application in respect of the stay of execution and it would be for the court then to consider whether it was an appropriate case for
C "further order." Subject to that, I would grant the applications and grant an unconditional stay of execution.

BROWNE L.J. I entirely agree that for the reasons given by Megaw L.J. these applications should be granted and the order proposed by him substituted. As Megaw L.J. has pointed out, the sums which the county
D court judge ordered to be paid as a condition of a stay are sums which would have become payable as interest on the mortgages by the defendants under their contractual obligations if they had continued. The plaintiffs have, however, now got judgments for the capital sums covered by the loans on the mortgages, and the contractual obligations undertaken by the defendants, including their obligation to pay interest, must have merged in the judgments. As Megaw L.J. has said, we have also been
E told that county court judgments do not carry interest. In my judgment, in agreement with Megaw L.J., it was not a proper exercise of the judge's discretion to impose, as a term of the stay, orders requiring the defendants to pay sums which they could never be bound to pay, either contractually or under the judgment of the court, whatever the result of the appeals may be. Accordingly, as I say, I agree with the order proposed by
F Megaw L.J.

SIR JOHN PENNYCUICK. I agree that the applications should be granted, and I agree with the order proposed by Megaw L.J. and Browne L.J. I do not want to say anything about the effect of the provisions in the Rules of the Supreme Court and the County Court Rules concerning the
G terms on which a stay may be made. I agree that the Rule Committee might in due course reconsider the terms of the various rules so that they may be brought into harmony.

I would like to add a few words on the condition which the judge imposed. It is quite clear, I think, that he could validly have imposed a condition on his order for a stay. The question is whether the condition which he in fact imposed was a proper one. If the plaintiffs had estab-
H lished a deficiency in the value of the security as against principal and arrears of interest, then I think the judge could not have been faulted if he had imposed a condition of payment into court of a sum equivalent to that deficiency. There was, however, no evidence as to the value of the respective properties, and, consequently, no evidence as to the deficiency if there was one. Again, I think that if the judge had imposed a condition of payment into court simply of the arrears of interest, irrespective of the value of the security, he might very well not have been

faulted. In fact, however, apparently out of supposed indulgence to the defendants, the judge imposed a condition of payment into court not of any deficiency in value or of the arrears of interest but of monthly sums equal to the contractual interest which would have become payable under the mortgages, from the date of his order. That condition was, I think by common consent, illogical because, should the appeal fail, then the judgment would stand and no interest would be payable on it; on the other hand, if the appeal succeeded then the loan would be set aside as a contravention of the Moneylenders Acts and no interest could ever have become payable in respect of the loan. I use the expression " supposed indulgence " because we were told by Mr. Primost that the arrears of interest were very considerable—as indeed appears from the figures in the orders, though I have not worked them out in detail. On the other hand, it is quite impossible to make a comparison between the arrears of interest and the monthly payments to be made under the condition because one does not know how many months would elapse between the date of the order and the hearing of the appeal. Again, I think that it is apparent from the figures that the position was different in this respect as regards each of the three mortgages with which these applications are concerned. I have not the material to go into the figures and do not propose to do so. It seems to me that this condition, having been imposed on a wrong basis, should not be allowed to stand.

As the Divisional Court put it in *Kelly* v. *White* [1920] W.N. 220, 221: " . . . that discretion "—which in that case was a discretion as to stay of possession between landlord and tenant—" must be exercised judicially. The order appealed from was not a judicial exercise of the discretion." I think that those words are in point here, where one is concerned with a discretion to stay execution. It would, no doubt, be possible for this court to vary the order by imposing a different condition, but I do not think that it would be right, in all the circumstances, for this court to take that course, and I think, accordingly, that the stay should stand free from any condition.

Applications granted. Unconditional stays of execution pending hearing of appeals or further order. Costs of applications costs in appeals.

Solicitors: *Benjamin & Benjamin; S. B. Gilinsky & Co., Edgware.*

M. G.

[QUEEN'S BENCH DIVISION]

* REGINA *v.* CRIMINAL INJURIES COMPENSATION BOARD, *Ex parte* TONG

1975 July 14, 15 — Lord Widgery C.J., Milmo and Wien JJ.

Crime—Criminal Injuries Compensation Board—Date of entitlement—Assessment of compensation—Death of victim before payment—Whether compensation assessed payable to estate—Criminal Injuries Compensation Scheme 1964 (*rev.* 1969), *para.* 21

The victim of a criminal assault accepted an interim award from the Criminal Injuries Compensation Board. A final assessment was made by a medical board on January 3, 1973, and on February 25 a single member of the Criminal Injuries Compensation Board decided that a final amount of £450 should be offered. The single member then returned the file to the board's office and it was handed to an officer so that he could inform the victim of the decision. Before that was done the officer was told that the victim had died on March 6, 1973. His death was unconnected with the injuries received in the assault. On September 16 the board decided that the £450 compensation was not payable.

On an application by the victim's widow for an order of certiorari to bring up and quash the decision of the board:—

Held, refusing the application, that under the Criminal Injuries Compensation Scheme payments of compensation were ex gratia and there was no entitlement to compensation on the part of a living victim of a criminal assault until payment was made to the victim.

The following case is referred to in the judgment:

Reg v. *Criminal Injuries Compensation Board, Ex parte Lain* [1967] 2 Q.B. 864; [1967] 3 W.L.R. 348; [1967] 2 All E.R. 770, D.C.

The following additional case was cited in argument:

Reg. v. *Criminal Injuries Compensation Board, Ex parte Ince* [1973] 1 W.L.R. 1334; [1973] 3 All E.R. 808, C.A.

APPLICATION for an order of certiorari.

The applicant, Ivy Florence Tong, executrix of the will of William Henry Tong, deceased, applied for an order of certiorari to quash a decision by the Criminal Injuries Compensation Board on September 16, 1964, that £450, the amount of compensation determined by a single member of the board (Sir Ronald Long) on February 25, 1973, was not payable.

The ground upon which the relief was sought was, inter alia, that the board were wrong in holding that the award by the single member did not, without more, constitute a final award and that accordingly the award was not payable.

I. E. Jacob for the applicant.
Harry Woolf for the board.

[Reported by MISS EIRA CARYL-THOMAS, Barrister-at-Law]

LORD WIDGERY C.J. I will ask Wien J. to give the first judgment.

WIEN J. In this case counsel moves on behalf of Ivy Florence Tong, the executrix of the will of William Henry Tong deceased, for an order of certiorari to remove into this court for the purpose of its being quashed the decision of the Criminal Injuries Compensation Board dated September 16, 1974, whereby it was decided that £450 compensation allegedly awarded to the deceased by a single member of the board on February 25, 1973, was not payable.

If authority were needed, and in my view it is not, that a person may come to this court and complain that there is an error in the decision of the Criminal Injuries Compensation Board's decision, that authority is provided by *Reg.* v. *Criminal Injuries Compensation Board, Ex parte Lain* [1967] 2 Q.B. 864, where it was held that the board is amenable to the supervisory jurisdiction of the High Court exercised by certiorari in that it is a body of persons of a public as opposed to a purely private character, having power to determine matters affecting subjects and a duty to act judicially.

The deceased, William Henry Tong, then aged about 55 years, was criminally assaulted on April 14, 1970. It is not necessary to go at length into the details of the assault. It can be summarised thus: Mr. Tong was a rent collecter employed by the London Borough of Ealing. At about 4.15 p.m. on April 14, 1970, he had put his cash takings in his car, which was outside a rent office. He was waiting for another collector, a Mr. Hill, to get into the car when a van pulled up in front of him and four men ran out and attacked Mr. Tong. He sustained a head injury and he suffered from concussion and post-concussional depression.

After the incident he applied to the Criminal Injuries Compensation Board for compensation. By a letter from the board dated April 14, 1971, Mr. Tong was notified that a single member of the board, Sir Ronald Long, had decided that the application was within the scope of the scheme and that an interim award of £50 should be offered. It was stated in that letter that it was assumed that as the award was an interim one Mr. Tong would wish to accept it. He did in fact accept that interim award.

His condition improved to some extent, and medical boards assessed his loss of faculty at various times. The final assessment was made by a medical board on January 3, 1973.

On Sunday February 25, 1973, Sir Ronald Long decided that a final amount of compensation of £450 should be offered. That meant that there should be an additional sum of £400 to the interim award of £50. Unhappily Mr. Tong died on March 6, 1973. His death was entirely unconnected with the injuries he received in the assault upon him. The causes of his death were (1) cerebral haemorrhage and (2) hypertension.

It would appear that Sir Ronald Long had made a decision in the following manner. It was the practice of the board that cases were allocated to a single member in batches of ten. They were dispatched by post either to the single member's home or to his chambers. The single member in this case apparently made a decision on Sunday February 25, 1973, as I have already said. The file, after receipt in the board's office, was handed over to a case-working officer in order that the deceased could be informed of the decision. It transpired that the case-working officer did not in fact inform Mr. Tong of Sir Ronald Long's decision because he, the case-working officer, had been informed that Mr. Tong had died on March 6, 1973, before he could communicate with Mr. Tong.

It is necessary to look in some detail at the scheme itself. It is called the Criminal Injuries Compensation Scheme. In its original form it came into operation in August 1964. It was then revised in May 1969. It is a scheme that was devised to provide compensation for the victims of criminal violence.

By paragraph 1 the compensation scheme will be administered by the Criminal Injuries Compensation Board. By paragraph 2 the board will be provided with money through a grant-in-aid out of which payments will be made to applicants for compensation where the board are satisfied, in accordance with the principles set out below, that compensation is justified. Their net expenditure will fall on the votes of the Home Office and the Scottish Home and Health Department. So the board in fact do administer the scheme in accordance with principle, and the principles are set out later in the scheme. This is not a statutory instrument and it is not to be construed as if it were an Act of Parliament.

By paragraph 4 the board will be entirely responsible for deciding what compensation should be paid in individual cases and their decisions will not be subject to appeal or to ministerial review. Paragraphs 5 to 9 inclusive deal with the scope of the scheme. That material paragraphs, beginning at paragraph 5, read as follows:

> "The board will entertain applications for ex gratia payment of compensation in any case where the applicant or, in the case of an application by a spouse or dependant . . ."

So, pausing there for the moment, it is clear that these payments of compensation are entirely ex gratia payments and are, as counsel for the board has submitted, payments by way of bounty from the state. Paragraphs 10 to 18 deal with the basis of compensation. Paragraph 10 reads:

> "Subject to what is said in the following paragraphs, compensation will be assessed on the basis of common law damages and will take the form of a lump sum payment, rather than a periodical pension. More than one payment may, however, sometimes be made—for example, where only a provisional medical assessment can be given in the first instance."

Since that paragraph deals entirely with the assessment of compensation it would seem to follow that what the board would be required to do would be to make assessments as judges of first instance commonly do. For example, in the case of a person who was a paraplegic a judge at first instance would decide what damages should be awarded in regard to loss of many of the ordinary amenities of life and permanent disability.

Mr. Jacob, on behalf of the applicant, invited us to say that this was a paragraph of vital importance. Frankly I am unable to see what significance is to be attached to this particular paragraph, except that it gives guidance purely as to the amount of compensation that is to be given to a claimant.

Paragraph 11 deals with the case where the victim is alive. Paragraph 12 deals with the case where a victim has died in consequence of the injury. Paragraph 13 deals with the case where a victim has died otherwise than in consequence of the injury. Thus, there are three cases to be considered: a case where compensation is to be given to a live victim; a case where compensation is to be given to the dependants where the victim dies in consequence of the injury; and, lastly, a case where compensation A is to be given to dependants where the victim dies otherwise than in consequence of the injury.

There then follows in the scheme itself the procedure for determining applications. Paragraph 21 is of considerable importance in this case. I will read it in full:

> " The initial decision whether the application should be allowed (and, if so, what amount of compensation should be offered) or should be B rejected will normally be taken by one member of the board, whose decision will be communicated to the applicant; if the applicant is not satisfied with that decision, whether because no compensation is offered or because he considers the amount offered to be inadequate, he will be entitled to a hearing before three other members of the board, excluding the one who made the initial decision. It will, C however, also be open to the single member, where he considers that he cannot reach a just and proper decision, himself to refer the application to three other members of the board for a hearing."

The following two paragraphs deal with the procedure at the hearing, which is not by way of appeal, but is rather a re-hearing and a different decision may be made. D

But what Mr. Jacob on behalf of the applicant in this case contends is that when Sir Ronald Long made a decision on February 25, 1973, that was a final determination. Not only was it a final determination, but it gave rise to an entitlement to Mr. Tong, who was then still alive, within the ambit of this scheme. It was submitted by Mr. Jacob that that being so, the matter crystallised, as it were, on February 25, 1973. He submitted E that concepts of contractual obligations ought not to be introduced into a consideration of this scheme.

I entirely agree about contractual obligations, which do not in fact exist. The real question in this case is at what stage is there a decision made to pay compensation to a person who is a live victim. In my judgment that stage is reached, having regard to all the paragraphs in this scheme, only when payment is made to the victim. Until that time F everything is at large and is not open to review except under paragraph 21. It would be most unfortunate in my judgment if one were to seek to try to construe this scheme as if it covered every eventuality. In point of fact it does not, and the instant case is one not referred to in the scheme. It was because of that, that on August 5, 1974, the board resolved at a meeting that if an applicant had died after the single G member had signed the assessment sheet but before the applicant had accepted the award, the award was a nullity. It is perhaps not for me to criticise the wording of resolutions made by the board, but I think the use of the word " accepted " was unfortunate.

In my judgment Mr. Woolf's submission is entirely correct: namely that it is necessary to consider the moment when payment has in fact been made as being the " cut-off " point. If no payment has been made, H then there is no entitlement. There is no right on the part of the victim. His dependants of course may come to the board and ask for an award. That is covered by paragraph 13, and that is the only paragraph where the dependants can come to the board and ask, in accordance with those terms (that is, where the victim has died otherwise than in consequence of the injury) that loss of wages, expenses and liabilities incurred before the death as a result of the injury may be made owing to hardship.

In the present case I myself see no hardship as such. This is a matter that was not covered by the scheme, but I would suggest that the members of the board ought to be free to deal with these eventualities when they arise in a flexible manner having regard to the whole object of the scheme. It has not been demonstrated that there was any error of law in the decision complained about—a decision that was made after a hearing that was requested by the applicant's solicitor.

Accordingly, I would refuse this application.

MILMO J. I agree.

LORD WIDGERY C.J. I entirely agree and say that when Wien J. observed that payment under the scheme would prevent any further review of the matter on a change of circumstances I venture to think he meant final payment under the scheme as opposed to an interim payment. But with that small modification I agree entirely with his judgment and this application is accordingly refused.

Application refused with costs.

Solicitors: *J. G. Haley; Treasury Solicitor.*

[CHANCERY DIVISION]

* SOCIÉTÉ FRANÇAISE D'APPLICATIONS COMMERCIALES ET INDUSTRIELLES S.A.R.L. *v.* ELECTRONIC CONCEPTS LTD. AND OTHERS

[1974 S. No. 2236]

1975 June 27 Oliver J.

Practice—Chancery Division—Motion—Injunction to restrain use of confidential information—Conflicting affidavit evidence—Date to be fixed for cross examination—Plaintiffs' delay—Motion restored by defendants—Whether motion to be treated as abandoned—Court's discretion to dismiss or stand motion over to trial

By a notice of motion dated April 5, 1974, the plaintiffs sought an interlocutory injunction to restrain the defendants from using confidential information alleged to have been supplied during negotiations for the production by the defendants of an electronic device designed by the plaintiffs for frightening mosquitoes. After several adjournments for the filing of affidavit evidence, it was agreed between counsel on both sides that it was impossible to deal with the matter on affidavit evidence alone, and accordingly the motion was stood over on May 21, 1974, for a date to be fixed for the cross-examination of witnesses, with liberty to either side to restore. At the end of June 1974, the plaintiffs' counsel concluded that the extent of the evidence that was likely to be required in reply meant that the matter could not properly be dealt with at all on motion and that the proper course was to stand the motion over to the trial. The defendants were not asked to agree to this course until January 8, A 1975. On March 27 the defendants informed the plaintiffs that they refused to agree, and the plaintiffs having failed to take any steps to restore the motion for hearing, the defendants gave formal notice on May 19 of their intention to restore the motion in order to seek an order that it be treated as abandoned or that it be dismissed for want of prosecution, and an order that the plaintiffs should pay the defendants their B costs of the motion.

On restoration of the motion:—

Held, that there was no immutable rule that a plaintiff must either abandon his motion, move it or file further evidence and then move it, and that the court always had a discretion whether or not to stand a motion over to the trial and would exercise that discretion on appropriate terms where issues of fact required to be determined which could not be C resolved on affidavit evidence alone; that the appropriate course in the present case, despite the plaintiffs' delay in bringing the motion on for hearing, was to make no order on the motion save that the general costs of the motion should be the defendants' costs in the cause, and that the costs of the restored hearing should be the defendants' in any event.

Pictograph v. *Lee-Smith Photomechanics Ltd.* (*Note*) [1964] 1 W.L.R. 402; [1964] 1 All E.R. 668; [1964] R.P.C. D 376 explained.

The following cases are referred to in the judgment:

Allen v. *Sir Alfred McAlpine & Sons Ltd.* [1968] 2 Q.B. 229; [1968] 2 W.L.R. 366; [1968] 1 All E.R. 543, C.A.

American Cyanamid Co. v. *Ethicon Ltd.* [1975] A.C. 396; [1975] 2 W.L.R. 316; [1975] 1 All E.R. 504, H.L.(E.). E

Bravingtons Ltd. v. *Barrington Tennant* [1957] R.P.C. 183.

Burgess v. *Burgess* (1853) 22 L.J.Ch. 675.

Jeffery (*Simon*) *Ltd.* v. *Shelana Fashions Ltd.* (unreported), May 13, 1975.

Kenitex Chemicals Inc. v. *Kenitex Textured Coating Ltd.* [1965] F.S.R. 109.

Pictograph v. *Lee-Smith Photomechanics Ltd.* (*Note*) [1964] 1 W.L.R. 402; [1964] 1 All E.R. 668; [1964] R.P.C. 376. F

The following additional cases were cited in argument:

Clough v. *Clough* [1968] 1 W.L.R. 525; [1968] 1 All E.R. 1179, C.A.

Thorpe v. *Alexander Fork Lift Trucks Ltd.* [1975] 1 W.L.R. 1459, C.A.

MOTION

By a writ dated March 29, 1974, the plaintiffs, Société Française G d'Applications Commerciales et Industrielles S.A.R.L., sought injunctions to restrain the use by the defendants, Electronic Concepts Ltd., Electronic Pest Controls Ltd., Alfred Bowman, Peter R. Jewel, John S.F. & Partners Ltd., and Siegfried Pierre Fiorentini, of confidential information said to have been supplied by the plaintiffs to the defendants during negotiations —which eventually broke down—for the production by the defendants H of an electronic device, known as a "Skeeter Skat," designed by the plaintiffs to frighten mosquitoes. By a notice of motion dated April 5, 1974, the plaintiffs moved for an interlocutory injunction, substantially in the terms of the writ. Eventually, in view of the extent of the evidence likely to be required, the plaintiffs' counsel concluded that the proper course was for the motion to be stood over to the trial of the action but the defendants refused to agree. The plaintiffs having taken no steps to

A bring the motion on for hearing the defendants gave formal notice on May 19, 1975, that they were applying for the motion to be restored and seeking an order that it be treated as abandoned or that it should be dismissed for want of prosecution and that the plaintiffs should pay the defendants their costs of the motion to be taxed if not agreed.

The restored motion accordingly came before Oliver J. on June 27, 1975.

The facts are stated in the judgment.

B

A. Kynric Lewis for the defendants.
A. Watson for the plaintiffs.

OLIVER J. This motion, which has been restored by the defendants in the action, under a liberty to restore reserved on a previous hearing arises C out of arrangements which apparently were made between the plaintiffs in the action, a French company known as Société Française d'Applications Commerciales et Industrielles S.A.R.L., and the defendants, Electronic Concepts Ltd. and various other companies and persons, for the production by the first defendant of a device, said to have been invented by the plaintiffs or to be the property of the plaintiffs, known as a "Skeeter Skat." This, as I understand it, is some sort of electronic device D designed to frighten mosquitoes. The parties fell out and it appears that the first defendant undertook the production of some comparable or similar device which was marketed or proposed to be marketed under the name of "Moziquit," and the upshot was that a writ of summons was issued on March 29, 1974. By the writ, the plaintiffs claimed injunctions restraining the defendants from using any information supplied to them E by the plaintiffs concerning the design or the manufacture or construction of the "Skeeter Skat" device, or as to the customers or potential customers for such a device, and also injunctions to restrain the reproduction by the defendants of advertising material of the plaintiffs. On April 5, 1974, the plaintiffs moved for an interlocutory injunction in substantially the terms of the writ, and they supported it by an affidavit served on April 9, 1974. The matter came before Brightman J. on F April 23 when it was stood over for 14 days on the defendants' undertaking to do their best to file their evidence in answer in seven days and, indeed, by April 30 they had filed three affidavits which raised very serious questions, so I have been told—I have not looked at any of the affidavits because for the purposes of the present application I think it is unnecessary to do so—as to the veracity and probity of the plaintiffs' G evidence and, indeed, there are allegations of forgery and perjury. Then on May 7, 1974, the matter came back before Brightman J. At that time the plaintiffs wanted time to consider whether they should file evidence in reply, and the matter was stood over for a further 14 days and a further hearing took place on May 21. On that occasion it appears that counsel on both sides had decided that it was really quite impossible for the court to determine the issues which had arisen between the parties H on the affidavits alone, and so the motion was stood over for a date to be fixed for hearing with cross-examination. The plaintiffs were given liberty to file evidence in reply, arrangements were made for notices to cross-examine deponents to be given in respect of any deponent whom either side wished to be present at the hearing, and there was liberty to restore. Then the matter seems to have gone to sleep. I have been told by Mr. Watson, who appears for the plaintiffs, that what in fact happened was that, at the end of June, counsel for the plaintiffs, having con-

sidered the volume of evidence which was likely to have to be filed in A
reply, came to the conclusion that it would be really quite improper for the court on an interlocutory motion to be faced with the prospect of a hearing of the length which, in his view, the matter would obviously require; and accordingly his view was that the motion should be stood until the trial and that the anticipated contested hearing should not take place. I have no reason to doubt for a moment that that is, indeed, the advice the plaintiffs were given, but they displayed a coy reticence about B
it and did not indicate to the defendants any change in the plans which had been agreed on May 21.

The long vacation, of course, ensued and at the end of August the defendants' solicitors wrote to the plaintiffs' solicitors, asking whether the plaintiffs intended to reinstate the interlocutory proceedings and, if so, when. That query was answered on September 11 to the effect that the C
papers were with counsel and the matter would be taken up with counsel when he returned from holiday. There then followed a silence which appears to have remained unbroken in substance until January 8, 1975, when the plaintiffs some nine months after the issue of the original writ, served a statement of claim. That was served under cover of a letter dated January 8, 1975, from the plaintiffs' solicitors in which they apologised for the delay in contacting the defendants' solicitors, which D
they said had been due to the postal strike in France. This had, apparently, been of long duration and had hampered communications with their client. The letter contained this paragraph:

> "In the light of the affidavits filed on behalf of your clients, there would appear to be several areas where there is an acute conflict of evidence and a complete contradiction as to the material facts. In E
> these circumstances it is our view, and we propose to advise our clients, that the matter is now not one that could be resolved on motion and that the right course would be adjourn the motion to the trial with the costs of the motion reserved to the trial judge and your clients in the meantime to keep separate accounts. Do you agree? If so, would your clients be prepared to consent to the above course?" F

That was acknowledged on January 14, when the defendants' solicitors replied, saying:

> "You will appreciate that we will have to get instructions from our client and then go to counsel on the matter. We will however write to you again as soon as possible, but we trust you will allow us a G
> considerable time to file the defence."

On February 6 the plaintiffs' solicitors came back with a letter, saying that they had taken instructions from their clients as regards time for service of defences:

> "Our clients regret the delay that elapsed but see no reason why they should be penalised since the cause of delay was quite outside H
> their control. In any event our clients take the view that the statement of claim raises very few, if any, new issues which were not dealt with by one party or another in the affidavit evidence on motion. You have now been in possession of the statement of claim for a month and we feel that in the circumstances a total of six weeks should be ample. Accordingly we are instructed to allow you a further 14 days from today within which to serve your defences.

A Should you require a further time, you will have to apply to the court."

Coming, as it does, from plaintiffs whose own period of gestation in respect of the statement of claim was nine months that does not appear to me to be an offer of conspicuous magnanimity. However that may be, a defence and counterclaim was in fact served on March 18, 1975, and
B on March 27 the defendants' solicitors wrote in these terms: they drew attention to the time schedule which had been so far followed by the parties and pointed out that a reply and defence to counterclaim had not been served and they said—and perhaps, one might think, not unreasonably said:

> ". . . and our clients fear that if your clients' conduct in the prosecution of the motion is anything to go by, our clients could well
> C be seriously inconvenienced by extensive delays on the part of your clients in the prosecution of the action. In the circumstances, our clients are advised that in the event that your clients do not restore the motion, an application should be made to the court for an appropriate order. If your clients do restore the motion and prosecute it, it will be defended with vigour. If your clients fail to
> D restore the motion, our clients propose to apply to the court for an order for our clients' costs on the grounds that the motion is or must be deemed to have been abandoned. It will be urged in the alternative that the motion should be dismissed for want of prosecution and that our clients should be entitled to their costs in the motion. We look forward to receiving your early reply. In the event that you fail to inform us within seven days of the date of this
> E letter that you intend to restore the motion on or before Tuesday April 15, 1975, and further in the event that you fail so to restore the motion after giving us due notice, an application will be made to the court on behalf of the defendants for an order as mentioned above. In the event that such an application is made, we shall, of course, give you due notice by letter."

F The reply to that, on April 2, was to the effect that the plaintiffs' solicitors were taking instructions and they said:

> "We shall do our best to contact counsel and our clients before the day after tomorrow (the expiry of your seven day period) but we are not optimistic. In any event we shall come back to you as soon as possible."

G I have not been told that the French postal strike was still continuing at this time and so I do not know what difficulties the plaintiffs' solicitors had to contend with, but they did not in fact—so far as the correspondence before me goes, at any rate—come back; and on May 19, 1975, the defendants' solicitors sent a letter referring to the previous correspondence and giving formal notice that they would apply on May
H 22, for an order that the plaintiffs pay the defendants' costs of the motion on the ground that the motion had been abandoned or, in the alternative, that the motion should be dismissed for want of prosecution and the plaintiffs should pay the defendants their costs in the motion, such costs to be taxed if not agreed. That at least appears to have had the effect of producing some activity, because a reply and defence to counterclaim was, I am told, served yesterday at two minutes to four.

Mr. Kynric Lewis, who appears for the defendants, submits that where a plaintiff is dilatory in prosecuting a motion for interlocutory relief, the motion should be dismissed, and he says that it is really no answer to that simply to ask that the motion should be stood over to the trial. If there is going to be such a request, it should, he said, be made at the earliest possible moment and the court in considering what should be done, should have regard to all the circumstances, including the conduct of the parties and any dilatoriness in prosecuting the main action. He drew my attention to a number of cases supporting the well known rule that delay in launching proceedings for interlocutory relief may be fatal, and in particular, to *Kenitex Chemicals Inc.* v. *Kenitex Textured Coating Ltd.* [1965] F.S.R. 109 where a delay of some three months was considered fatal, and a similar case, *Bravingtons Ltd.* v. *Barrington Tennant* [1957] R.P.C. 183, where again there was an unexplained three months' delay which was considered fatal. He submits—and I think this must be right—that there is no real distinction to be drawn between a case where a plaintiff delays in instituting the relevant proceedings and the case of a plaintiff who institutes the relevant proceedings and then delays in prosecuting them. Indeed, he drew my attention to *Burgess* v. *Burgess* (1853) 22 L.J.Ch. 675, where a six months' delay in prosecuting an appeal was considered to be a fatal stumbling block. He has also drawn my attention to the well known line of cases starting with *Allen* v. *Sir Alfred McAlpine & Sons Ltd.* [1968] 2 Q.B. 229 and the three factors which were considered to be relevant in the judgment of Salmon L.J. in that case.

But, of course, those latter authorities—that is to say, the authorities on striking out for want of prosecution—cannot, as I see it, have any direct relevance to the present question, because it is not contended, and I do not think it could be contended here, that the defendants have suffered any prejudice as regards the possibility of having a fair trial of the issues in the action merely as a result of the delay in fixing a day for the hearing of the contested motion or restoring that motion for some other order.

Mr. Lewis really bases himself, I think, upon this: that there has been a long unexplained delay between the time when the motion was stood over in May 1974, by Brightman J. and January 8, 1975, when his clients were asked to agree to it standing to the trial, and a further delay from March 27, when his clients rejected that suggestion, until May 19, when his clients themselves took steps to restore the motion. And he says that, in the circumstances, that delay ought to be penalised by making the plaintiffs pay his clients' costs of the motion.

In this context he has drawn my attention to two cases which are of some relevance as indicating what the court does or may do in the case, such as one finds here, of a motion where the facts are incapable of being sufficiently determined simply on the affidavits. It has to be borne in mind that the present motion was launched and conceived at a time some six months before the hearing of *American Cyanamid Co.* v. *Ethicon Ltd.* [1975] A.C. 396 and at a time when it was, I think, thought generally that it was necessary for plaintiffs to establish on motion a prima facie case for saying that they were likely to succeed at the trial.

My attention has been drawn, first, to *Pictograph Ltd.* v. *Lee-Smith Photomechanics Ltd.* (*Note*) [1964] 1 All E.R. 668 in which Pennycuick J. is reported to have said that a plaintiff must either abandon his motion or move it on the evidence as it then stood or file further evidence in reply and then move, and that decision has got itself into *The Supreme*

A *Court Practice* (*1973*), in the form of a note to R.S.C., Ord. 8, r. 1. The reference is 8/1–5/11 and is in these terms:

> "After evidence is filed by the defendant, the plaintiff must either abandon the motion or move it on the evidence as it stands or file further evidence and move it."

That is contrasted with a more recent decision of Walton J. in *Simon* B *Jeffrey Ltd.* v. *Shelana Fashions Ltd.* (unreported), May 13, 1975. Walton J. said that he had always been brought up to believe that in the Chancery Division a person moving a motion who has not opened that motion is entitled as of right to stand that motion to the trial, and he went into the reasons why that practice, as he understood it, had prevailed. In the course of the agreed notes of his judgment—which are all that I have here—he said: "it is admittedly within the discretion of the court C whether or not it will stand a motion over to the trial," and he went on to say that, accepting the decision of Pennycuick J. as reported, he still had an absolute discretion which in the case before him he exercised by standing the motion over to the trial.

It appears in fact that the decision of Pennycuick J. was not really fully reported in the All England Reports and I have been referred to a D fuller report in [1964] R.P.C. 376. From that report it appears that when the matter came back before the court after the evidence had been filed in reply, the plaintiff did in fact move the motion and at the end of the day Pennycuick J. took this course. He says, at p. 379:

> "On the whole, I have come to the conclusion that the right course is to adjourn the motion to the hearing of the action and to E direct that the costs of the motion shall be the defendants' costs in the cause. I have taken this intermediate course because, apart from the question of delay, it seems to me that the motion is not one which should be rejected as demurrable. I heard a considerable amount of argument on that point. I am standing it over because it is impossible to come to a conclusion on the merits without the issue of the facts being determined. On the other hand, I think, F having regard to the delay"—a matter which in fact he had dealt with earlier in his judgment—"it is right that, in any event, the plaintiffs should not have their costs of this motion."

The costs having been dealt with, there was, of course, nothing in fact to be stood to the trial and in the result he simply made no order on the motion save that the costs be the defendant's costs in the cause.

G So that it does not appear to me either that the report of the case in the All England Reports is sufficiently full or that the note in *The Supreme Court Practice* (*1973*) which suggests an immutable rule that a plaintiff must either move his motion or abandon it is supported by the authority cited. Indeed it does not appear to me that there is any necessary conflict between that case and the decision of Walton J. in H *Simon Jeffrey Ltd.* v. *Shelana Fashions Ltd.* (unreported) May 13, 1975.

I think that in truth the court always has a discretion whether it will stand the motion to the trial on the plaintiffs' application and that, in appropriate circumstances, where the court finds that it is necessary to determine issues of fact and is unable to do so on affidavits alone, that course will be taken on such terms as may be appropriate in the particular case.

Mr. Watson invites me to take that course in the present case, where he admits that the matter comes back before the court at a somewhat A late stage and not as a result of any intervention by his clients.

Mr. Kynric Lewis, I think, accepts that if at the end of June 1974, the plaintiffs had gone back to the court and said that, having considered the matter, they thought it undesirable or impossible to have the matter determined on motion, the court might well then have taken the course of standing the motion to the trial and reserving any costs of the motion to the trial judge; B but he says that in view of the fact that the plaintiffs did not do that they are in default. They have been guilty of dilatoriness and delay and the course that now ought to be taken is either that the motion should be dismissed out of hand with costs or—which really comes to the same thing—that it should be stood to the trial on terms that the costs should be his in any event. Substantially, as is apparent I think from what I have said, the real contest between the parties here is C simply one of the correct order to make as regards the costs of the motion.

Mr. Watson says, and says with some force, that it is really impossible for the court at this stage to arrive at any decision as to the merits on the motion and it is possible that at the trial the issues of fact which may have been raised by the defendants in their evidence will be determined against them D and it would seem, he says, unfair in that event that the plaintiffs should be ordered now to pay the costs occasioned by an issue which was wrongly raised by the defendants. Mr. Lewis, on the other hand, says that a court should be stern with anybody who is in default, as the plaintiffs were in this case. They had, after all, had the motion stood over; it was open to them to fix a day and they never did and, he says, they have been dilatory and they ought to be penalised by E having the motion dismissed with costs.

I am not sure that I can agree with that entirely, because it seems to me that it would be wrong that I should visit the costs of a motion which has not been heard upon the plaintiffs here and now, without going into the merits at all, simply because they have been guilty of some delay in bringing the matter back before the court. Mr. Lewis's clients have not F been, I think, made to incur any additional costs, as a result, which they would not otherwise have incurred; they have not been inconvenienced; there are no undertakings here which are running and they have not been prejudiced by the delay as regards a fair hearing of the issues at the trial.

As it seems to me, in the ordinary way I would accede to the plaintiff's application and stand the motion for trial reserving the costs. But G I think that they, when it was clear that their invitation issued very late in January, to stand the motion on terms of the costs being reserved, was not acceptable to the defendants, ought to have brought the matter back to the court then; and I think that in the circumstances the right course is that the costs of the motion should be the defendants' costs in the cause because of the delay which has occurred. In doing that, I am H following what Pennycuick J. did in the case to which I have already referred: but I think that the defendants should have the costs of the restored hearing today in any event.

Accordingly, that is the order which I propose to make.

Mr. Lewis. My Lord, may I take it that the costs of today's application include the costs of the adjournment, which is as from May 22?

A OLIVER J. Yes. That is my intention: the full costs of the restoration of the matter which would include the original restoration and the adjournment up to date and the hearing today should be your clients' in any event and the other costs in the motion should be the defendants' costs in cause.

Order accordingly.

B

Solicitors: *Ward Bowie, Basingstoke; Herbert Smith & Co.*

T. C. C. B.

C

[CHANCERY DIVISION]

* SIME DARBY LONDON LTD. *v.* SIME DARBY HOLDINGS LTD. AND OTHERS

D

[1975 S. No. 2647]

1975 July 10, 11 Brightman J.

Revenue—Corporation tax—Advance corporation tax—Preference dividend fixed by articles of association—Changes in rate of advance corporation tax—Whether contractual dividend varied by changes in rate of advance corporation tax—Finance Act
E 1972 (*c.* 41), *s.* 84 (2), *Sch.* 23, *para.* 18 (1)—*Finance Act* 1974 (*c.* 30), *s.* 12

Paragraph 18 of Schedule 23 to the Finance Act 1972 provides:

"(1) Where any right or obligation created before April 6, 1973, is expressed by reference to a dividend at a gross rate or of a gross amount, that right or obligation shall,
F in relation to a dividend payable on or after that date, take effect as if the reference were to a dividend of an amount which, when there is added to it such proportion thereof as corresponds to the rate of advance corporation tax in force on that date, is equal to a dividend at that gross rate or of that gross amount."

Article 4 (A) of the articles of association of the plaintiff company, incorporated in July 1972, provided that the holders
G of preference shares should be entitled to receive out of the company's profits for distribution in respect of any financial year a fixed cumulative preferential dividend on the capital at the rate of $7\frac{1}{2}$ per cent. The Finance Act 1972, which came into force on July 27, 1972, provided by section 84 (2) that advance corporation tax should be payable for the period April 6, 1973, to March 31, 1974, at the rate of three-sevenths and "thereafter such fraction as Parliament may from time
H to time determine." Section 12 of the Finance Act 1974 provided that the rate of advance corporation tax for the financial year 1974 should be 33/67ths.

On a summons to determine, inter alia, whether upon the true construction of article 4 (A) and paragraph 18 of Schedule 23 to the Finance Act 1972 the holders of the preference shares in the capital of the plaintiff company were entitled to

---

[Reported by I. R. MACKRILL, ESQ., Barrister-at-Law]

be paid after April 6, 1973, a fixed cumulative preferred A dividend the rate of which was calculated by reference, inter alia, to the rate of advance corporation tax ruling on April 6, 1973, or the date on which the dividend became payable:—

Held, that, while Parliament clearly intended by paragraph 18 to modify the contractual rights of shareholders, the words of the paragraph were not to be construed so as to give rise to anomalies which would result from calculating the dividend by reference to the rate of advance corporation tax in force B or in force only on April 6, 1973, but rather so as to provide a formula, changing with the rate of the tax, whereby the contractual rights of a person entitled to a fixed dividend were maintained unaltered in substance despite the change in the taxing system; and that, accordingly, on the true construction of the words "the rate of advance corporation tax in force on that date" in paragraph 18 (1) of Schedule 23 to the Finance Act 1972, the date for the ascertainment of advance C corporation tax for the purposes of the paragraph was the date on which the dividends became payable.

No cases are referred to in the judgment.

The following case was cited in argument:

Neumann v. *Inland Revenue Commissioners* [1934] A.C. 215; 18 T.C. D 332, H.L.(E.).

ORIGINATING SUMMONS

The capital of the plaintiff company, Sime Darby London Ltd., was divided into ordinary shares, all of which were held by the first defendant, Sime Darby Holdings Ltd., convertible preferred ordinary shares, of E which the second defendant, Una Stanley, was one holder and $7\frac{1}{2}$ per cent. cumulative redeemable preference shares of which the third defendant, David John Corderey, was one holder. Article 4 (A) of the plaintiff company provided:

"The preference shares shall entitle the holders to receive out of the profits of the company available for distribution and resolved to be distributed in respect of any financial year or other period for F which accounts of the company are made up and in priority to the payment of a dividend on any other class of shares of the company a fixed cumulative preferential dividend on the capital for the time being paid up thereon at the rate of $7\frac{1}{2}$ per cent. per annum such dividend to be paid yearly in June 30 and December 31 in each year in respect of the half years ended on those dates, the first payment G of dividend to be made in accordance with the terms of issue of the preference shares."

By paragraph 4 of a summons dated April 8, 1975, the plaintiff company sought the determination whether upon the true construction of article 4 (A) of the articles and paragraph 18 of Schedule 23 to the Finance Act 1972 the holders of the preference shares in the capital of H the plaintiff company were entitled to be paid out of the profits of the company available for distribution and resolved to be distributed in respect of any financial year or other period for which the accounts of the company were made up and in priority to the payment of any other class of shares in the company and paid after April 6, 1973, a fixed cumulative preferred dividend the rate of which was calculated by reference (inter alia) to the rate of advance corporation tax ruling on (a)

April 6, 1973, or (b) the date on which the dividend became payable, or (c) some other, and if so, what date.

C. A. Brodie for the plaintiff company.
Peter Rees Q.C. and *Richard Fitzgerald* for the first defendant.
Leolin Price Q.C. and *Gordon Nurse* for the second defendant.
J. E. Holroyd Pearce for the third defendant.

BRIGHTMAN J. Paragraph 4 of the originating summons, which is the paragraph it is convenient first to cover, raises a question as to the rights of a preference shareholder in Sime Darby London Ltd. under the articles of association read with paragraph 18 of Schedule 23 to the Finance Act 1972. I have been informed by counsel that the revenue are aware of these proceedings, but do not seek to take part.

The Finance Act 1972 came into force on July 27. The plaintiff company was incorporated on the same day under the name of Bayfield Investments Ltd. with a share capital of 100 £1 shares. On September 13, 1972, the share capital was increased to £2,622,000 divided into a number of ordinary shares, 500,000 7½ per cent. cumulative redeemable preference shares of £1 each and a number of convertible preferred ordinary shares. Further convertible shares were created at different times in 1973. The 500,000 redeemable preference shares are all in issue and I understand have been in issue at all relevant times.

On the same day as last mentioned, September 13, 1972, the plaintiff company adopted new articles of association. As their name indicates, the preference shares carry a fixed cumulative preferential dividend of 7½ per cent. per annum. The only article relevant for present purposes is article 4 (A). This reads:

> "The preference shares shall entitle the holders to receive out of the profits of the company available for distribution and resolved to be distributed in respect of any financial year or other period for which accounts of the company are made up and in priority to the payment of dividend on any other class of shares of the company a fixed cumulative preferential dividend on the capital for the time being paid up thereon at the rate of 7½ per cent. per annum such dividend to be paid half yearly on June 30 and December 31, in each year in respect of the half years ended on those dates, the first payment of dividend to be made in accordance with the terms of issue of the preference shares."

Prior to the change wrought by the Finance Act 1965, the income tax paid by a company was in effect treated as having been paid by its shareholders. The company in paying a dividend was entitled, if it wished to deduct for its own benefit and retain a notional amount of income tax. The Finance Act 1965 introduced corporation tax as a charge on the company's profits in place of income tax. It also introduced income tax as a charge on the amount of a dividend payable to a shareholder and it required the company to account for and pay such income tax to the revenue. In broad effect, therefore, before 1965 the profits of a company whether or not distributed attracted a single imposition of tax. In and after 1965 the profits of a company, so far as distributed, attracted a double imposition of tax; first corporation tax on the profits earned by the company, and then income tax on the

dividend paid. I have expressed ancient history in simple terms, which A
is enough for present purposes, and I have left profits tax out of account.

The Finance Act 1972 introduced a system of advance corporation
tax and tax credits. In broad outline, under section 84, where a com-
pany pays a dividend after April 5, 1973, it becomes liable to pay advance
corporation tax on that dividend. For the period April 6, 1973, to March
31, 1974, the rate of advance corporation tax was fixed by that section B
at three-sevenths. Thereafter, said the section, the fraction was to be
such as Parliament might from time to time determine.

The amount of advance corporation tax so paid by a company pro-
duced two credits. First, the company became entitled under section 85
to set off an equivalent amount against its own liability for corporation
tax. Secondly, the shareholder became entitled under section 86 to a
tax credit equal to a fraction of the amount of the distribution corre- C
sponding to the rate of advance corporation tax in force for the financial
year in question. Section 86 gave the shareholder the right to use the
tax credit for the purpose of recovering the amount thereof from the
revenue if, for example, the shareholder were not liable for some reason
to income tax; he was given the right to use the tax credit as a set off
against his liability to income tax; and no doubt if and so far as his D
liability to income tax was less than the aggregate of his tax he would
get a partial repayment. But I am not concerned with the precise
details of the operation of tax credits in all circumstances.

By way of illustration, if in the year 1973–74 a company paid an
ordinary shareholder a dividend of £750, the company would be liable
to account to the revenue for about £321 by way of advance corporation
tax, and the shareholder would receive a tax credit of like amount which E
he would be entitled to use for the purpose of claim or set off according
to his tax position.

Under a later section, predictably, the shareholder became chargeable
to income tax as if he had received a total distribution equal to the
actual distribution plus the tax credit; that is to say, in the supposed
example a notional income of £1,071. This is provided for by section F
87 under the heading of Schedule F.

It is apparent that this system would produce an arbitrary benefit for
a preferential shareholder confined to a fixed dividend unless modified.
Suppose a person holds £10,000 of $7\frac{1}{2}$ per cent. preference shares. He
would in former days have expected to receive an annual dividend of
£750 less income tax, and to include a gross sum of £750 in his return
of income for tax purposes. Without any modification to the provisions G
I have referred to, he would have become entitled in the year 1973–74
to receive into his pocket a dividend of £750 in accordance with his
rights under the articles of association; the company under section 84
would pay advance corporation tax of about £321, being three-sevenths
of £750; the shareholder would receive a tax credit of like amount and
would be taxed on a total income from this source of £1,071. To meet, H
inter alia, this situation, section 109 of the Finance Act 1972 provided
that Schedule 23 should have effect with respect to the matters there
dealt with, being transitional provisions relating to the part of the Act
which I have been referring to, and that Schedule includes paragraph 18.
Only the first sub-paragraph is relevant. It reads as follows:

"(1) Where any right or obligation created before April 6, 1973, is
expressed by reference to a dividend at a gross rate or of a gross

A amount, that right or obligation shall, in relation to a dividend payable on or after that date, take effect as if the reference were to a dividend of an amount which, when there is added to it such proportion thereof as corresponds to the rate of advance corporation tax in force on that date, is equal to a dividend at that gross rate or of that gross amount."

B By virtue of that sub-paragraph, the obligation created by the articles of association to pay the supposed preference shareholder a dividend of £750 in 1973–74 would take effect as an obligation to pay a dividend of an amount which, when there is added to it three-sevenths, equals £750. In other words the preference shareholder would receive a dividend of £525 and a tax credit of £225, making £750 in all, and in consequence the company would pay advance corporation tax of £225, being three-
C sevenths of £525.

All this is simple. The complication arises under section 12 of the Finance Act 1974, which increased the rate of advance corporation tax to 33/67ths for the year 1974–75.

If in relation to a dividend paid in that year the formula in paragraph 18 were applied precisely as in the year 1973–74, the preference share-
D holder in question would ex hypothesi continue to receive a dividend of £525, but the company would have to pay advance corporation tax of £259 or thereabouts, being 33/67ths of £525. Likewise the shareholder would have a tax credit of £259 and his total income for tax purposes from this particular source under section 87 of the Finance Act 1972 would be £784, compared with his contractual dividend right under the articles of £750. One can take an example on the other side of the line.
E Suppose that in happier days advance corporation tax is reduced to two-sevenths. If the formula in paragraph 18 is applied precisely as in 1973–74, the distribution will still be £525, but the tax credit will be reduced to £150. The taxpayer's total income for tax purposes would be £675. If the shareholder whose hypothetical position I have been examining pays no tax, he will find that his preference shareholding has
F in effect been arbitrarily reduced from a $7\frac{1}{2}$ per cent. preference shareholding to a $6\frac{3}{4}$ per cent. preference shareholding.

The question therefore arises whether the formula in paragraph 18 is in fact static so as to produce these anomalies, or whether it changes with the rate of advance corporation tax.

Counsel who appear on behalf of the convertible shareholders and
G the preference shareholders say that the formula is static. They say that the construction to be placed on paragraph 18 is one which requires the reader to look at the rate of advance corporation tax which is in force or was in force only on one specified date, namely, April 6, 1973. That has the effect, they submitted, of substituting a fixed net dividend of $5\frac{1}{4}$ per cent. in place of the gross dividend of $7\frac{1}{2}$ per cent. specified in the articles. The figures are apparent from the first example which I
H gave as a hypothetical case for the year 1973–74. Counsel state that the contractual dividend is so changed once and for all. This, they say, produces consistency and simplicity and that I am not entitled to assume that it was not the deliberate intention of Parliament. I agree with the simplicity of the approach and I agree with its superficial appeal. The paragraph uses the expression " that date " in the penultimate line; it uses the same expression three lines earlier; and then in the first line one sees the date April 6, 1973.

Quite clearly paragraph 18 is a provision which is intended to modify the contractual rights of a shareholder. I have to decide precisely what modification Parliament intended. The words that I have to construe are, "the rate of advance corporation tax in force on that date." If "that date" is a reference back to April 6, 1973, as is the like expression three lines before, plainly counsel for the preference shareholders and the convertible shareholders are correct. If on the other hand "that date" ought to be read as a reference to the date when the dividend is payable, then paragraph 18 will keep in step with changes in the rate of advance corporation tax and the anomalies that I have indicated will not be produced. The example I gave for the year 1973–74 demonstrates the absence of any anomaly if the advance corporation tax referred to in paragraph 18 of the Schedule is advance corporation tax at the rate payable from time to time. It will be observed from section 84 (2) that Parliament did not contemplate that advance corporation tax would remain for all time at the level of three-sevenths, because the subsection refers, for periods after March 31, 1974, to such fractions as Parliament might from time to time determine.

It seems to me obvious what paragraph 18 seeks to achieve. It seeks to maintain, unaltered in substance, the contractual position of a person entitled to a fixed dividend despite the change in the taxing system. Paragraph 18 is not itself a taxing provision. It is a provision which is intended to deal with a familiar business situation in, I would think, a businesslike way. I agree that it is at first sight grammatically illogical to read the words "that date" as meaning April 6, 1973, where they first appear but to read them in a different manner when they next appear. However I do not think that this construction does undue violence to the language of the paragraph. There is a variety of dates expressly or implicitly comprehended by paragraph 18. There is the date when the right or obligation was created. There is the date April 6, 1973, specifically mentioned. There is the date when the dividend is payable. Lastly there is the date which is to be used as the reference point for the ascertainment of advance corporation tax for the purposes of that paragraph. I do not think that there is any insuperable difficulty in equating the date for the ascertainment of advance corporation tax (for the purposes of paragraph 18) with the date on which the dividend becomes payable. That construction has the effect of preserving intact the substance of the original contract between the shareholders inter se and the plaintiff company, and I think it is the construction which good sense requires me to adopt.

I may perhaps add this: if the argument pressed upon me by the preference shareholders and the convertible shareholders were correct, it would not have been necessary for paragraph 18 to have referred to "an amount which, when there is added to it such proportion thereof as corresponds to the rate of advance corporation tax in force on that date, is equal to a dividend at that gross rate or of that gross amount." It would have been sufficient to have said, "an amount which when there is added to it three-sevenths thereof is equal to a dividend at that gross rate or on that gross amount." Why, I ask myself, should Parliament resort to the involved wording of paragraph 18 to produce so simple a result? The answer I think must be, that that was not the result which Parliament sought to achieve.

A For the reasons which I have endeavoured to express, I will answer question 4 of the originating summons in the sense of paragraph (b).

Declaration accordingly.
Undertaking by plaintiff to pay costs.
Order for taxation on common fund basis.

B

Solicitors: *Herbert Smith & Co.* (for all parties).

C [QUEEN'S BENCH DIVISION]

* JOHNSON *v.* PHILLIPS

1975 July 1; 30 Lord Widgery C.J., Milmo and Wien JJ.

D *Road Traffic—Police—Powers—Motorist stopping car behind ambulance in narrow one-way street—Police officer's instruction to motorist to reverse car to facilitate rescue operations—Whether motorist's refusal obstruction of police officer in execution of duty—Whether instruction reasonable—Police Act* 1964 (*c.* 48), *s.* 51 (3)

The defendant stopped his car about 10 feet behind a stationary ambulance in a narrow one-way street. A police
E officer asked him to reverse some 10 to 15 yards back to the next street because he was obstructing the removal of injured persons and other ambulances were expected. The defendant refused to reverse back on the ground, inter alia, that he would be committing an offence for which he might be prosecuted. He was convicted by justices of wilfully obstructing the police officer in the execution of his duty contrary to section 51 (3) of the Police Act 1964.[1]

F On the defendant's appeal against conviction:—

Held, that a police officer, in the exercise of his power to control traffic, was, at common law, under a duty to require other persons to disobey traffic regulations if it was reasonably necessary to protect life or property; that since life was, or might reasonably have been, endangered, the police officer's instruction, given at a time when he was acting in the course
G of his duty was reasonable and lawful (post, pp. 69F–H, 70B–D).

Reg. v. *Waterfield* [1964] 1 Q.B. 164, C.C.A. and *Hoffman* v. *Thomas* [1974] 1 W.L.R. 374, D.C. considered.

Per curiam. No general discretion is given to a constable, even in cases where he himself considers that an emergency has arisen, to disobey traffic regulations or to direct other persons to disobey them (post, p. 70E, F).

H

The following cases are referred to in the judgment of the court:

Glasbrook Brothers Ltd. v. *Glamorgan County Council* [1925] A.C. 270, H.L.(E.).

Hoffman v. *Thomas* [1974] 1 W.L.R. 374; [1974] 2 All E.R. 233, D.C.

Reg. v. *Waterfield* [1964] 1 Q.B. 164; [1963] 3 W.L.R. 946; [1963] 3 All E.R. 659, C.C.A.

[1] Police Act 1964, s. 51 (3): see post, p. 67G.

Rice v. *Connolly* [1966] 2 Q.B. 414; [1966] 3 W.L.R. 17; [1966] 2 All E.R. 649, D.C.

The following additional case was cited in argument:

Dibble v. *Ingleton* [1972] 1 Q.B. 480; [1972] 2 W.L.R. 163; [1972] 1 All E.R. 275, D.C.

CASE STATED by Birmingham justices.

On November 14, 1974, the defendant, Peter Johnson, was charged that he, on November 14, 1974 did wilfully obstruct the prosecutor P.C. Kevin Phillips, a constable then in the execution of his duty in Cannon Street, Birmingham, contrary to section 51 (3) of the Police Act 1964.

The justices heard the information on January 15, 1975, and found the following facts. On November 14, 1974, at about 10.30 p.m., two police officers, the prosecutor and P.C. Hook, in the course of their duties, were called to an incident at The Windsor public house, Cannon Street, Birmingham where an ambulance was in attendance. Cannon Street was a narrow one-way street and at the time, because cars were parked on either side it was reduced to one lane of traffic. Fore Street linked Cannon Street and Corporation Street in the centre of Birmingham. The defendant, a company director, drove his Mini motor car along that one-way street in the correct direction shortly after 10.30 p.m. on that evening until he was prevented from continuing by the ambulance. The defendant stopped his vehicle some 10 feet behind the ambulance. At that time two persons were being attended to in the ambulance and a short time later the prosecutor walked to the defendant's car and asked him to reverse into Fore Street because he was obstructing the removal of the injured persons and other ambulances were expected. That would have involved the defendant backing some 10 to 15 yards along Cannon Street and then reversing into the flow of traffic in Fore Street. The defendant replied "I'll wait here thank you." The defendant told the prosecutor that he could not move back because it was a one-way street. There was a female passenger with him in the car. The defendant then stated that the prosecutor asked to see his documents and the defendant pulled his vehicle over to the side of Cannon Street. He said he then started getting out of his car in order to find the documents. The prosecutor stated that he did not think he asked the defendant for his driving documents. The prosecutor, who had by then been joined by P.C. Hook, again requested the defendant to move his car and the defendant became agitated, telling the prosecutor, "I'll do nothing for a stupid copper" and asking him "Have you been in the job for two weeks?" The prosecutor found the defendant's remark uncomplimentary. The defendant was then told by the prosecutor that he was being arrested for obstructing him in the course of his duties, to which the defendant made no reply. The defendant accepted that he should not have made those remarks. He claimed that at the time the rear window of his car was steamed up. The police officers could not say whether that was so or not. The defendant also claimed that he thought that if he reversed as instructed he might be prosecuted. He stated that he was a driver of 10 years' experience. At the time of the defendant's arrest, no other persons had been brought to the ambulance for attendance and no other ambulances had arrived at the scene. The whole episode had taken about a minute and the defendant left with the police officers to go to the local police station at about the same time as the ambulance left.

A It was contended by the defendant that at the relevant time the prosecutor was not acting in the course of his duties; that the prosecutor had no authority to instruct the defendant to reverse the wrong way along a one-way street; that for the defendant to have reversed down Cannon Street into Fore Street was both unlawful and dangerous; that the defendant's conduct in the circumstances, though amounting to a refusal to obey the instructions of the prosecutor did not amount to wilful obstruction.

B It was contended by the prosecutor that the car being driven by the defendant was obstructing or might obstruct the ambulance in tending to any injured persons and there was a prospect of further ambulances arriving; and that the defendant twice refused to comply with the prosecutor's instructions which, if carried out, would have prevented the chance of any obstruction occurring.

C The justices were of the opinion that the prosecutor was throughout acting in the course of his duties, that the manoeuvre of reversing along Cannon Street into Fore Street though awkward was not dangerous, and that in refusing so to reverse the defendant was wilfully obstructing the prosecutor.

The questions for the opinion of the High Court were whether the justices were correct in fact or in law in holding that the prosecutor was
D acting in the course of his duties in instructing the defendant to reverse the wrong way along a one-way street; and whether they were correct in fact or in law in holding that in refusing to obey such an instruction, the defendant wilfully obstructed the prosecutor in the execution of his duty.

Christopher Sumner for the defendant.

E *Anthony Nicholl* for the prosecutor.

Cur. adv. vult.

July 30. MILMO J., in the absence of Lord Widgery C.J., asked Wien J. to give the judgment of the court, which had been approved by the three members of the court.

F WIEN J. read the following judgment of the court. This is an appeal by case stated by Birmingham justices, who on January 15, 1975, convicted the defendant of willfully obstructing the prosecutor, Police Constable Kevin Phillips, in the execution of his duty on November 14, 1974, in Cannon Street, Birmingham, contrary to section 51 (3) of the Police Act 1964. That subsection reads, so far as is relevant:

G "Any person who . . . wilfully obstructs a constable in the execution of his duty . . . shall be guilty of an offence . . ."

The material facts are these. At about 10.30 p.m. on November 14, 1974, the prosecutor and another police officer were called to an incident at The Windsor public house, Cannon Street, Birmingham, where one ambulance had already arrived. Two persons were being attended to in
H the ambulance. The defendant drove his motor car along Cannon Street until he was prevented from going any further by the presence of the stationary ambulance. He stopped his car about 10 feet behind the ambulance.

Cannon Street was a narrow one-way street. Cars had been parked on either side so that the carriageway was effectively reduced in width to permit one lane of traffic. Before a motorist could enter Cannon Street he had first of all to travel along Fore Street in the centre of the city.

After the defendant stopped, the prosecutor walked over to his motor A
car and asked him to reverse into Fore Street since he was obstructing the removal of the injured persons and other ambulances were expected. Had the defendant complied with the prosecutor's request he would have had to reverse between 10 and 13 yards along Cannon Street and then into the flow of traffic in Fore Street.

The defendant refused to do as he was asked saying he could not
reverse because it was a one-way street. The prosecutor was joined by B
another officer and he once again asked the defendant to move his car. The defendant lost his temper and said "I'll do nothing for a stupid copper. Have you been in the job for two weeks?" The defendant was then told he was being arrested for obstructing the prosecutor in the course of his duties. At the time of the defendant's arrest no other
persons had been brought to the ambulance for attention and no other C
ambulance had arrived at the scene. The whole episode lasted about a minute. The defendant left the scene with the two police constables to go to the police station at about the same time as the ambulance drove off. Subsequently, at the hearing before the justices, the defendant claimed that the rear window of his car had been steamed up and he thought that if he reversed along Cannon Street when told to do so by
the prosecutor he might be prosecuted. D

The justices came to the conclusion that the prosecutor was throughout acting in the course of his duties, that the manoeuvre of reversing along Cannon Street into Fore Street—a distance of at most 15 yards—though awkward, was not dangerous and that in refusing to reverse the wrong way along a one-way street in accordance with the prosecutor's
instructions the defendant wilfully obstructed the prosecutor. E

The two questions stated for the opinion of this court are (1) were the justices correct in holding that the prosecutor was acting in the course of his duty when he instructed the defendant to reverse along Cannon Street; and (2) were they correct in deciding that in refusing to obey the prosecutor's instruction the defendant wilfully obstructed him in the execution of his duty.

In essence there is only one question that calls for consideration, F
namely, was the prosecutor lawfully acting in the execution of his duty. If he was not, then this conviction cannot stand. If he was, then a failure by the defendant to obey the instruction clearly amounted to a wilful obstruction of the prosecutor in the lawful execution of his duty.

Counsel for the defendant submitted (1) that the prosecutor was not
acting in the execution of his duty since what he requested the defendant G
to do was not only awkward but involved the defendant in performing an unlawful act, namely, in reversing the wrong way along a one-way street; (2) that there was no obstruction of the constable since the defendant was under no legal obligation to move his car; and (3) that if there was an obstruction of the prosecutor in the execution of his duty then the obstruction was not wilful inasmuch as his failure to move his car
was not an intentional act committed without lawful excuse. We are of H
the view that all these submissions are covered by the one question that we have posed above.

The first function of a constable has for centuries been the preservation of the peace. His powers and obligations derive from the common law and from statute. It is his general duty to protect life and property: see *Glasbrook Brothers Ltd.* v. *Glamorgan County Council* [1925] A.C. 270, 285 where Viscount Finlay said: "There is no doubt that it is the duty

A of the police to give adequate protection to all persons and their property." Stemming from that duty is his duty to control traffic on public roads.

The powers and obligations of a constable under the common law have never been exhaustively defined and no attempt to do so has ever been made: see, for example, *Reg.* v. *Waterfield* [1964] 1 Q.B. 164, where
B Ashworth J. who delivered the judgment of the court, said, at p. 170:

> ". . . it would be difficult, and in the present case it is unnecessary, to reduce within specific limits the general terms in which the duties of police constables have been expressed."

Also in *Rice* v. *Connolly* [1966] 2 Q.B. 414, 419 Lord Parker C.J. said:

> "It is also in my judgment clear that it is part of the obligations and
> C duties of a police constable to take all steps which appear to him necessary for keeping the peace, for preventing crime or for protecting property from criminal injury. There is no exhaustive definition of the powers and obligations of the police, but they are at least those . . ."

In attempts to keep pace and to deal with the volume and complexity
D of road traffic the legislature has often made enactments to deal with certain problems. An example may be given by reference to section 22 of the Road Traffic Act 1972. Subsection (1) (*a*) of that Act, so far as is relevant, reads as follows:

> "Where a constable is for the time being engaged in the regulation of traffic in a road . . . a person driving or propelling a vehicle who
> E —(*a*) neglects or refuses to stop the vehicle or to make it proceed in, or keep to, a particular line of traffic when directed so to do by the constable in the execution of his duty . . . shall be guilty of an offence."

Such statutes cannot be considered as totally determining a constable's powers or obligations. One-way streets for vehicles are doubtless a
F comparatively modern method of coping with traffic congestion, but it cannot be said that Parliament either by statute or regulation has purported to deal with every situation that might conceivably arise.

The precise question that has to be answered in the instant case may be put thus: has a constable in purported exercise of his power to control traffic on a public road the right under common law to disobey a traffic
G regulation such as going the wrong way along a one-way street? If he himself has that right then it follows that he can oblige others to comply with his instructions to disobey such a regulation. If, for example, a bomb had been planted in The Windsor public house and the exit from Cannon Street had in some way been blocked, could he lawfully reverse a police vehicle and oblige any other motorist then present in the road to reverse his own vehicle? The answer is yes, provided that in the
H execution of his duty he was acting to protect life or property: see *Hoffman* v. *Thomas* [1974] 1 W.L.R. 374, 379.

It is not clear from the justices' findings why the defendant, by stopping some 10 feet behind the ambulance, obstructed the removal of injured persons. We would have been assisted had we known the precise nature of the "incident" that had occurred. That it was more than a trivial affair or minor public house brawl seems reasonably clear for two patients were being treated in the stationary ambulance and other

ambulances were expected—doubtless to convey more injured persons to A
hospital. Other ambulances could hardly have been expected unless some
instructions had been given to summon them to the scene. It can be
said, therefore, that in the circumstances, so far as they are known, life
was or might reasonably have been endangered. It is manifest that the
prosecutor was not acting capriciously or from personal motives. He
was controlling traffic in a situation that could well be described as an
emergency. Does the fact that he not only interfered with the defen- B
dant's liberty but instructed him to disobey a traffic regulation in any
way alter the situation?

The law protects the liberty of the subject, but it must recognise that
in certain circumstances which have to be carefully considered by the
courts a constable may oblige persons to disobey a traffic regulation and
not only in those cases that are explicitly dealt with by Parliament. In C
the judgment of this court a constable would be entitled, and indeed
under a duty, to give such instruction if it were reasonably necessary for
the protection of life or property. It is not necessary in the instant case
to decide whether there may not be other circumstances in which such
an instruction might be justified. Each case must depend on its own
facts. A constable's powers are not unlimited, as has been shown.

We conclude from the facts of this case, viewed quite objectively, D
that the instruction given by the prosecutor was reasonable and lawful
and was given at a time when he was acting in the course of his duty. To
decide otherwise would produce the startling result that the defendant
was entitled to remain where he was and maybe prevent expected
ambulances from reaching the scene altogether or compel them to enter
Cannon Street from the wrong end or perhaps to cause further obstruc- E
tion to any other vehicles entering the street until the stationary
ambulance drove off.

We stress that we do *not* decide that a constable has powers, when-
ever he thinks it right, to order traffic to reverse the wrong way along
a one-way street. No general discretion is given to a constable, even in
cases where he himself considers that an emergency has arisen, to disobey
traffic regulations or to direct other persons to disobey them. F

In the result we conclude on the special facts of this case that the
justices were correct in holding that the defendant wilfully obstructed
the constable in the lawful execution of his duty and the appeal is
accordingly dismissed.

It may well be that a local authority which makes by-laws relating to
one-way streets provides in those by-laws for a situation where a driver G
of a vehicle commits no offence if he acts in accordance with the direc-
tions of a constable. If such a by-law is properly placed before the
justices, then it is conceivable that they may find it much simpler to
arrive at a conclusion without reference to the principles we have
referred to in this case.

Appeal dismissed with costs.

H

Solicitors: *Jonas, Grove & Co., Birmingham; I. S. Manson,*
Birmingham.

P. R. K. M.

A [COURT OF APPEAL]

* REGINA *v.* LEE (PAUL)

1975 Oct. 9 — Orr L.J., MacKenna and Forbes JJ.

Crime—Evidence—Character—Defence alleging that two men had
B *opportunity to commit theft—Prosecution witness cross-examined as to men's previous convictions for dishonesty—Whether questions put with view to establishing defendant's good character—Criminal Evidence Act* 1898 (61 & 62 *Vict. c.* 36). *s.* 1 (*f*) (ii)

The defendant was charged with theft from a bedroom in the house where he lived. Part of the defence was that two
C men, who were not witnesses at the trial, had had the opportunity to commit the offence and, therefore, a prosecution witness was cross-examined about the men having access to the house and their previous convictions for dishonesty. The recorder ruled that the questions were put with a view to establishing the defendant's good character and allowed the prosecution to question the defendant about his previous convictions under section 1 (*f*) (ii) of the Criminal Evidence
D Act 1898.[1] The defendant was convicted.

On appeal by the defendant: —

Held, allowing the appeal, that, since it was not implicit in an accusation of dishonesty that the accuser himself was honest, the questions seeking to establish the bad character of the two men were not put with a view to establishing the defendant's good character within the meaning of section 1 (*f*) (ii) of the Act and, accordingly, the defendant should
E not have been questioned about his previous convictions and the conviction would be quashed.

The following case is referred to in the judgment:

Rex v. *Ellis* [1910] 2 K.B. 746, C.C.A.

No additional cases were cited in argument.

F

APPEAL against conviction.

On June 12, 1975, at the Manchester Crown Court (recorder Mr. W. R. Wickham), the defendant, Paul Robert Lee, pleaded not guilty to stealing £150 and a gold ring from the house where he lived. His defence included the allegation that two men, who had access to the house and previous convictions for dishonesty, had had the opportunity to commit
G the offence. The men did not give evidence but the owner of the stolen articles, Robert Ludlain, was called as a prosecution witness and was cross-examined by the defence about the two men's convictions. The recorder allowed the prosecution to cross-examine the defendant about his previous convictions for dishonesty on the ground that he had asked questions with a view to establishing his own good character. The
H defendant was convicted.

The recorder certified that the case was a fit case for appeal. The defendant appealed on the ground that the recorder was wrong in law in holding that cross-examination by the defendant's counsel of Robert

[Reported by VENGAI GUNI, ESQ., Barrister-at-Law]

[1] Criminal Evidence Act 1898, s. 1 (*f*): see post, p. 73C–D.

Ludlain, one of the prosecution witnesses, as to the previous convictions of two other men, not witnesses in the case but who it was suggested by the defence had had the opportunity to commit the offence with which the defendant was charged, amounted to cross-examination with a view to establishing the defendant's good character and therefore justified the prosecution cross-examining the defendant on his own previous convictions under section 1 (*f*) (ii) of the Criminal Evidence Act 1898.

The facts are stated in the judgment of the court.

Martin Steiger for the defendant.
James Gregory for the Crown.

ORR L.J. gave the following judgment of the court. On June 12, 1975, at the Manchester Crown Court the defendant was convicted of theft and sentenced to 12 months' imprisonment. He now appeals against that conviction with a certificate of the trial judge on the ground that the judge allowed the prosecution to cross-examine him upon his previous convictions under the provisions of section 1 (*f*) (ii) of the Criminal Evidence Act 1898.

The facts of the case were shortly these. In October 1974, the defendant was living with a man Robert Ludlain and his wife who is a sister of the defendant. Ludlain had been saving up money which was required for moving his home and for that purpose had hidden £200 under the carpet of the bedroom. On October 19, Ludlain found that a half sovereign ring was missing from the mantelpiece. He then made a check and discovered that £150 of the £200 he had hidden was also missing. The defendant, who had been going out daily with him to work, disappeared and was not seen by him again but was later seen by a third person in possession of a large sum of money in notes.

There had been an earlier trial on May 22, 1975, in the course of which Robert Ludlain had referred to previous convictions of the defendant and a new trial was ordered on that ground. What happened in the new trial was that before the jury were empanelled counsel for the defendant raised this question with the judge. He said:

> " [The defendant's] case is that there were a large number of people who had access to the house and among those people was a person called Paul Ludlain and a person called Bob Smith. Both of those people have a number of previous convictions for dishonesty. Accordingly, it is a material point, in my submission, that other persons who have convictions for dishonesty had access to the house at the same time as the money disappeared. In my submission it is right the jury should know that."

The judge then suggested that the defendant would be at risk if he proceeded to give evidence. He said:

> " If you are letting the jury know that other people who had access to the premises have a bad record you are implying that your client has a good record. You are thereby giving evidence of good character."

Counsel for the defendant replied:

> " In my submission asking questions to establish the bad character of one of the brothers of the prosecution witness does not amount by inference to proving my own good character."

A In the end the judge made a ruling upon this matter, in which he said:

> " What he " (that is counsel for the defendant) " is seeking to establish is that those people by reason of their previous convictions were more likely to have committed the crime. If he is seeking to establish they were more likely to have committed the crime, turn the penny over; what he is seeking to establish is that the defendant
> B was less likely than those other people to have committed the crime."

It was on that basis that he made his ruling. In due course questions were put as to previous convictions of these other persons, who were not called as witnesses, and the judge, upon an application by counsel for the Crown to put to the defendant his previous convictions, and after hearing further argument, gave leave for that to be done.

C The matter turns in the judgment of this court entirely on the words of section 1 (*f*) (ii) of the Criminal Evidence Act 1898. Section 1 (*f*) provides, so far as is material for present purposes, as follows:

> " A person charged and called as a witness in pursuance of this Act shall not be asked, and if asked shall not be required to answer, any question tending to show that he has committed or been convicted of or been charged with any offence other than that wherewith
> D he is then charged, or is of bad character, unless . . . (ii) he has personally or by his advocate asked questions of the witnesses for the prosecution with a view to establish his own good character . . ."

It has been common ground in the argument before us that in order to justify in this case the putting of his previous convictions to the
E defendant the matter had to be brought within those words. The words of the statute fall to be given their ordinary and natural meaning and this court finds it impossible to hold that the questions which were put to the prosecution witness, Mr. Robert Ludlain, as to the convictions of the other men, were with a view to establishing the defendant's own good character. The questions were put with a view to establishing the bad character of the two other men and nothing else and the answer " Yes "
F to the question " Had they previous convictions? " had nothing whatever to do with the character of the defendant. As MacKenna J. put in argument, and in our view this is entirely right, it is not implicit in an accusation of dishonesty that the accuser himself is an honest man.

For these reasons the court finds it impossible to accept the argument advanced for the Crown and we must allow this appeal. It may be that
G exception (ii) in the section ought to cover such a case as this but, in our judgment, that can only be a matter for Parliament. We find it impossible to construe the statutory words in the manner contended for by the Crown.

I would add, since we were referred to it, that *Rex* v. *Ellis* [1910] 2 K.B. 746 has in our judgment, no bearing on the present question.

The appeal against conviction will accordingly be allowed.

H

Appeal allowed.
Conviction quashed.

Solicitors: *Registrar of Criminal Appeals; D. S. Gandy, Manchester.*

[FAMILY DIVISION]

* PRACTICE DIRECTION (DIVORCE REGISTRY: CONSENT SUMMONS) (No. 2)

Husband and Wife—Practice—Consent summons—Divorce Registry —Solicitors' attendance where parties consenting to order for custody of, or access to, child—Payments direct to child in excess of small maintenances payments—Matrimonial Causes Rules 1973 (*S.I.* 1973 *No.* 2016 (*L.* 29)), *r.* 92 (2) (*as amended by Matrimonial Causes* (*Amendment*) *Rules* 1975 (*S.I.* 1975 *No.* 1359 (*L.* 20)), *r.* 6)—*Income and Corporation Taxes Act* 1970 (*c.* 10), *s.* 65

The attention of solicitors is drawn to two minor adjustments of procedure made to the current Divorce Registry practice which permits consent applications being made to a registrar without attendance (registrar's direction April 10, 1974, *Practice Direction* (*Divorce Registry: Consent Summons*) [1974] 1 W.L.R. 937):

(1) Attendance will be required in respect of an application to a registrar for a consent order for custody of, or access to, a child under rule 92 (2) of the Matrimonial Causes Rules 1973 as amended by the Matrimonial Causes (Amendment) Rules 1975. On any such application, the registry will fix a date and time for the hearing.

It would assist the registrar considering the application, and avoid possible adjournment, if the solicitor attending the hearing is familiar with the circumstances relating to the children and is able to advise the registrar accordingly;

(2) On the issue of a consent summons or filing a notice of application seeking an order which includes an agreed term for payments *direct to* a child in excess of the amounts qualifying for the time being as " small maintenance payments " under section 65 of the Income and Corporation Taxes Act 1970, the solicitor should certify either on the summons or the notice whether the child is, or is not, living with the party who will be making the payments under the proposed terms.

D. NEWTON,
Senior Registrar

December 22, 1975.

[QUEEN'S BENCH DIVISION]

* KEEN *v.* PARKER

1975 Oct. 29, 30 — Lord Widgery C.J., O'Connor and Lawson JJ.

Road Traffic—Special type of vehicle—" Side-car "—Roadworthy attachment to motor cycle designed for carriage of goods—Whether " side-car "—Motor Vehicles (Driving Licences) Regulations 1971 (*S.I.* 1971 *No.* 451), *reg.* 6 (1) (*d*)

The defendant, the holder of a provisional driving licence, was riding a motor bicycle with a pillion passenger who was not a qualified driver. Attached to its near side was a structure

A comprising a tubular steel framework and a properly sprung wheel fitted with a pneumatic tyre, a bolted-on wooden platform and a box used for carrying tools for the defendant's work as a window cleaner. An information was preferred against him charging that the failed to comply with the conditions in regulation 6 of the Motor Vehicles (Driving Licences) Regulations 1971 [1] subject to which he held the provisional licence, in that he carried the pillion passenger while
B not having a side-car attached to the machine. The justices were of opinion that for an attachment to constitute a "side-car" within regulation 6 (1) (*d*) it had to be capable of carrying a person safely and that the structure attached to the defendant's machine was incapable of carrying a passenger in safety, so that it was not a side-car, and they convicted him.

On appeal against conviction: —

Held, allowing the appeal, that a roadworthy attachment
C to a motor bicycle which was designed for the carriage of goods was just as much a "side-car" as was a roadworthy attachment constructed for the carriage of a person (post, p. 82C); and that, accordingly, the justices had erred in law and the conviction would be quashed.

Dictum of Ashworth J. in *Cox* v. *Harrison* [1968] 1 W.L.R. 1907, 1912, D.C. not applied.

D

The following case is referred to in the judgments:

Cox v. *Harrison* [1968] 1 W.L.R. 1907; [1968] 3 All E.R. 811, D.C.

No additional cases were cited in argument.

CASE STATED by Lincolnshire justices sitting at Lincoln.

E On July 18, 1974, an information was preferred by the prosecutor, Gerald David Parker, a chief superintendent of police, against the defendant, Wilfred Donald Keen, that he, being the holder of a provisional licence to drive a motor vehicle, failed to comply with the conditions subject to which it was granted in that on a certain road called Outer Circle Drive, Lincoln, he rode a motor bicycle, not having attached thereto a side-car, while carrying on it a person who was not the holder
F of a licence authorising him to drive a vehicle of that class or description, contrary to section 88 of the Road Traffic Act 1972.

The justices heard the information on December 31, 1974, and found the following facts. The defendant was the holder of a provisional driving licence granted under the provisions of section 88 (2) of the Road Traffic Act 1972 and he had not passed a test of competence to drive motor cycles.
G On June 18, 1974, he was driving a Norton 500 c.c. motor cycle on a road called Outer Circle Drive in the city of Lincoln. He was carrying a passenger on the pillion seat of the motor cycle. Attached by bolts to the near side of the motor cycle was a tubular steel framework to which was affixed a wheel fitted with a pneumatic tyre. Suspension was provided by four rubber blocks. Attached to the steel frame by bolts was a wooden platform approximately seven feet long by two feet wide. That platform
H consisted of four pieces of timber each three inches wide by two inches thick by about seven feet in length, across which were bolted four pieces of wood each measuring three inches wide by two inches thick by two feet in length. The pieces of wood were separated one from the other, the distance separating each seven feet long piece of wood from the next nearest piece of equal length being about four inches. Fastened to the

[1] Motor Vehicles (Driving Licences) Regulations 1971, reg. 6 (1): see post, p. 79H.

underside of the timber frame was a wooden platform measuring about A 30 inches square. Set within the wooden framework was a wooden toolbox which was fitted with a lid. The defendant used the platform to support the ladders which he carried on his motor cycle combination for use in connection with his work as a window cleaner. No ladders were being carried on the motor cycle combination at the time of the alleged offence.

It was contended by the defendant that the wooden platform fastened B to the underside of the wooden framework was a stable structure on which a passenger might support his feet by placing them through the spaces in the wooden framework, while sitting on the closed lid of the wooden toolbox; that the structure had been professionally built and had an adequate system of suspension and that it was properly and securely fastened to the motor cycle; that a passenger could be safely carried thereon; that "side-car" had not been defined either in the Road Traffic Act 1972 C or the Motor Vehicles (Driving Licences) Regulations 1971 and that *Cox* v. *Harrison* [1968] 1 W.L.R. 1907 did not help because in that case the court had been concerned with a structure consisting solely of a framework to which no platform or bodywork of any kind had been affixed; that "side-car" did not necessarily mean a structure for the carriage of a passenger and could include a structure for the carriage of goods only; D that the structure attached to the defendant's motor cycle could properly be termed a side-car and therefore he was entitled to drive while carrying a passenger who was not a qualified driver.

It was contended by the prosecutor that the structure attached to the motor cycle had no sides, no proper seat, no proper foot rest for a passenger and no proper system of suspension; that, although a passenger might be carried on the wooden platform, he could not be carried safely E thereon and therefore the structure could not be called a side-car; that *Cox* v. *Harrison* [1968] 1 W.L.R. 1907 was authority for the contention that, to constitute an attachment a side-car, it must be capable of carrying persons in safety; that the defendant was the holder of a provisional driving licence granted under the provisions of section 88 (2) of the Road Traffic Act 1972; that regulation 6 of the Motor Vehicles (Driving Licences) F Regulations 1971 applied to the defendant and that he was, by paragraph (1) (*d*) of that regulation, prohibited from driving a motor cycle not having a side-car attached thereto while carrying on it a person who was not a qualified driver; that the passenger being carried on the defendant's motor cycle was not a qualified driver within the meaning of regulation 6 (5) of the Regulations and that the defendant had therefore acted in contra- G vention of the Regulations and was guilty of an offence under the provisions of section 88 (6) of the Act of 1972.

The justices were satisfied that the vehicle which the defendant was driving was a motor cycle as defined in section 190 (4) of the Road Traffic Act 1972, that he was the holder of a provisional driving licence granted under section 88 (2) of that Act and that he had not passed a test of H competence to drive motor cycles. It was within their knowledge that the public had access to Outer Circle Drive and they were, therefore, satisfied that Outer Circle Drive was a "road" within the meaning of section 196 (1) of the Act of 1972. Having regard to the provisions of section 81 of the Magistrates' Courts Act 1952 and the prosecutor having satisfied them that the defendant was driving a motor cycle on a road within their jurisdiction under the authority of a provisional licence, they

A were of the opinion that the burden of proving that he was lawfully carry-
ing a passenger on the pillion seat of the motor cycle was on the defendant.
He did not adduce any evidence to show that the passenger was a
qualified driver within the meaning of regulation 6 (5) of the Motor
Vehicles (Driving Licences) Regulations 1971, which, by Schedule 10 to
the Road Traffic Act 1972 were deemed to continue in force as if made
under the relevant sections of that Act. The main issue, therefore, was
B whether the structure attached to the motor cycle was a side-car since, if
it was, the defendant would have been lawfully entitled by regulation
6 (1) (*d*) of those Regulations to carry a passenger other than a qualified
driver.

The justices were unable to find any definition of "side-car" either in
the Act of 1972 or the Regulations of 1971 and their attention was not
C drawn to any case other than *Cox* v. *Harrison* [1968] 1 W.L.R. 1907.
Section 190 (1) of the Act of 1972 defined "trailer" as a vehicle drawn by
a motor vehicle and "motor vehicle" as a mechanically propelled vehicle
intended or adapted for use on roads. They were satisfied that the
defendant's motor cycle was a mechanically propelled vehicle intended
for use on roads and further that the structure attached to the near side
of the vehicle, having a wheel attached thereto, could properly be described
D as a vehicle. The proviso to section 190 (1) of the Act of 1972 provided
that a side-car attached to a motor cycle was not to be treated as a
trailer but as part of the motor cycle to which it was attached if such
side-car complied with regulations made by the Secretary of State. They,
therefore, concluded that, if they were to decide that the structure attached
to the defendant's motor cycle was a side-car, they had still to be satisfied
E that it was not a trailer since, if it were, he was not lawfully entitled to
drive the motor cycle at all having regard to the provisions of regulation
6 (1) (*c*). Regulation 121 of the Motor Vehicles (Construction and Use)
Regulations 1973, set out the conditions with which a side-car must comply
if it was to avoid being classed as a trailer within the meaning of section
190 (1) and, having regard to the provisions of section 81 of the Magis-
trates' Courts Act 1952, they were of the opinion that it was for the
F defendant to prove that the structure attached to his motor cycle complied
with that regulation. They heard no evidence which would have assisted
them to come to a decision whether the structure, if a side-car, would have
complied with the requirements of that regulation.

The justices gave careful consideration to the judgment in *Cox* v.
Harrison [1968] 1 W.L.R. 1907. Although the Regulations of 1971 were
G not in force when that case was decided, the corresponding Regulations
then in force were worded in very similar terms to the Regulations of 1971.
They found the judgment of Ashworth J. and particularly the words
[1968] 3 All E.R. 811, 813I "... I am quite certain that to constitute an
attachment a side-car it must be capable of carrying persons * ..." strongly
persuasive and they decided that, for a structure attached to a motor
H cycle to be a side-car, it must be capable of carrying persons and that
it must do so in safety. The structure attached to the defendant's motor
cycle was in their opinion capable of carrying a passenger in the manner
suggested by the defendant, but the absence of any side fittings or similar
device would have made it quite a simple matter for a passenger to fall

* *Reporter's note*: The word "persons" does not appear at [1968] 1 W.L.R.
1907, 1912E. On the present appeal, counsel cited from [1968] 3 All E.R., and the
court's attention was not drawn to the difference in wording.

from the machine even under ordinary conditions of driving. There A
would have been a further and considerable risk to a passenger having
his feet between the wooden parts of the platform. Were the driver
to apply the brakes of the motor cycle in an emergency situation, the
passenger would be more than likely to sustain serious injury. The
justices, therefore, concluded that the structure was incapable of carrying
a passenger in safety and that it was not a side-car. They therefore found
the defendant guilty of the offence charged. They believed that he had B
acted in good faith and honestly believed that he was entitled to carry
a passenger who was not a qualified driver. It was in their opinion inex-
pedient to impose a penalty and they, therefore, ordered that he should be
discharged absolutely pursuant to the provisions of section 7 of the Powers
of Criminal Courts Act 1973, and that his driving licence be endorsed
with the particulars of the offence. They found it unnecessary to go on C
to consider whether the structure was a trailer but realised that the effect
of their decision was likely to mean that the holder of a provisional
licence authorising him to drive motor cycles, might only lawfully drive
a motor cycle combination which comprised a structure which was
constructed or adapted for the safe carriage of a person.

The defendant appealed.

The question for the opinion of the court was whether the justices D
were correct in law in their decision that, for the purposes of regulation
6 of the Motor Vehicles (Driving Licences) Regulations 1971 and section
88 (2) of the Road Traffic Act 1972 "side-car" meant a structure
attached to a motor cycle and capable of carrying persons in safety, or
whether they should have found that "side-car" also included a structure
attached to a motor cycle and constructed or adapted solely for the E
carriage of goods.

The defendant in person.

Anthony Hidden for the prosecutor.

LORD WIDGERY C.J. I will ask O'Connor J. to give the first judgment. F

O'CONNOR J. This is an appeal by way of case stated from an adjudi-
cation of Lincolnshire justices whereby they convicted the defendant of
an offence on December 31, 1974. He was summonsed that, being the
holder of a provisional licence to drive a motor vehicle, he failed to comply
with the conditions subject to which it was granted in that on a certain
road called Outer Circle Drive, Lincoln, he rode a motor bicycle, not G
having attached thereto a side-car, while carrying on it a person who was
not the holder of a licence authorising him to drive a vehicle of that
class or description, contrary to section 88 of the Road Traffic Act 1972.
That rather complicated wording to describe what in truth was a very
simple offence results from the statutory legislation made in that behalf.

The facts found by the justices are again in a very short compass. The H
defendant was the holder of a provisional driving licence; that is, he was
a learner driver. He was riding a 500 c.c. motor cycle in Lincoln and
carrying a pillion passenger. Attached to the motor cycle was a con-
struction consisting of four planks of wood seven feet long mounted on a
steel framework supported by a wheel properly sprung. The platform
was about two feet wide. Attached to the framework was a small platform
30 inches square which was hung underneath it, and sitting on it there

A was a tool-box. This was used by the defendant to carry his ladders and buckets because he was a window cleaner.

The question in this case is whether he was riding a motor cycle with a side-car or not. Was the platform on which he carried his ladders and buckets properly to be described as a side-car? If it was a side-car, then he committed no offence. If it was not a side-car, he was properly convicted. At the end of the hearing yesterday we held that it was a side-car B and allowed the appeal, and I am now giving reasons for that decision.

Before I look at the statutory provisions, it is perhaps as well to state in simple English what the scheme of things is. Everybody knows that in the ordinary course of events a learner driver (that is, a person who holds a provisional driving licence) is not allowed to drive a vehicle unless he is accompanied by an authorised driver, namely, somebody who does C hold a full licence. But for motor cycles there is an exception, and it works in this way. First of all, the holder of a provisional licence is not allowed to ride a solo motor cycle of more than 250 c.c. That is to prevent young people arming themselves with great big motor cycles before they have passed the test. The learner driver is permitted to ride that kind of solo motor cycle without an authorised driver, but not allowed to carry as a pillion passenger somebody who is not himself or D herself an authorised driver. But where a motor cycle, however powerful, is fitted with a side-car, then the learner driver is permitted to carry on the motor cycle a passenger who is not an authorised driver. Why that should be so does not matter; that is what the provisions amount to.

Section 88 (2) of the Road Traffic Act 1972 provides that a provisional driving licence:

E "(*a*) shall be granted subject to prescribed conditions . . . (*c*) shall not authorise a person to drive a motor cycle whereof the cylinder capacity of the engine exceeds 250 cubic centimetres, not being a vehicle having three wheels, unless he has passed the test of competence . . ."

The only definition of "motor cycle" in the Road Traffic Act 1972 F itself is to be found in section 190 (4) where a motor cycle is defined as meaning:

". . . a mechanically propelled vehicle, not being an invalid carriage, with less than four wheels and the weight of which unladen does not exceed eight hundredweight."

No doubt the reason for that definition is because a great deal of the G statute is concerned with the taxation of different classes of motor vehicle, and for tax purposes what the ordinary citizen would call a three-wheeler is classified as a motor cycle. There is no definition in the Act of motor bicycle and there is no definition of side-car.

In the nature of things, as soon as a regulation uses the words "motor bicycle" ordinary English requires the construction that it is a two-H wheeled vehicle because "bicycle" by definition means two wheels.

Regulation 6 of the Motor Vehicles (Driving Licences) Regulations 1971 lays down the conditions to be attached to provisional licences; paragraph (1) (*a*) requires the supervision of a qualified driver, and (*d*) lays it down that "in the case of a motor bicycle not having attached thereto a side-car, while carrying on it a person who is not a qualified driver" a person holding a provisional licence shall not drive or ride such a motor vehicle. That is a use of the vehicle which is prohibited. The terms of the provisional licence do not allow a rider of a motor bicycle not having attached thereto a side-car to carry an unqualified driver as a passenger. The requirement of an authorised driver is exempted by regulation 6 (2), which reads:

> "The condition specified in paragraph (1) (*a*) of this regulation shall not apply when the holder of the provisional licence— . . . (*e*) is riding a motor bicycle, whether or not having attached thereto a side-car. . . ."

Thus, as I have said, the actul working out of this legislation is quite simple. Let me repeat it. The rider of a motor bicycle need not have an authorised supervisor. He must not carry a passenger unless that passenger is a duly authorised driver with a full licence but, if his motor bicycle has a side-car, then he may carry a passenger who is not an authorised driver.

In the present case, faced with the question whether the attachment to the defendant's motor bicycle was a side-car, the justices were referred to the decision of this court in *Cox* v. *Harrison* [1968] 1 W.L.R. 1907. Again to state the problem before I look at the authority, it arose in this way. The suggestion is that for an attachment to be classified as a side-car it must be constructed for the carriage of passengers or a passenger, and for the safe carriage of a passenger; if it is an attachment which is only useful for carrying goods, then it is not a side-car. In *Cox* v. *Harrison*, which was decided under the Motor Vehicle (Driving Licences) Regulations 1963, which for this purpose were the same, what had happened was this. The appellant there sought to overcome the difficulty of not being allowed to ride a 500 c.c. motor cycle; he thought that by just attaching a third wheel with a tubular frame without any platform or carriage it would enable him to say that that was a side-car or a three-wheeled vehicle, and therefore to carry a pillion passenger who was not an authorised driver. That was the purpose of the case which was being tried there. Ashworth J. who gave the leading judgment, said, at p. 1911:

> ". . . a motor cycle ridden by a learner driver and carrying a pillion passenger is prima facie a dangerous vehicle, partly due to its nature and partly due to the fact that in a given case the driver is inexperienced, and in order to meet that difficulty Parliament has in effect done two things, first it has provided that if the pillion passenger is a qualified driver he may be carried, and secondly whether he is qualified or not, if the vehicle has got a side-car then a passenger may be carried, as I read it, in that side-car;"

—I pause there to say that there is nothing in the regulation which requires that construction—

> "that was the intention, although the wording does not expressly say so, because it was thought no doubt that if the learner driver on the motor cycle had the additional safeguard of a passenger in a side-car, there was less risk of an accident happening; although it is not necessary to decide the point, I agree with Mr. McLaren that, on the wording, if in fact the motor cycle is provided with something which is properly called a side-car, then a passenger may be carried either in the side-car or as a pillion passenger on the machine itself, but of course it must be a side-car."

I pause there for a moment. To my mind, the wording of the regulation

A is clear, and once there is a side-car attached to the motor bicycle the passenger can be carried either as a pillion rider on the motor bicycle itself or in the side-car if it is one fitted for passengers. Ashworth J. continued, at p. 1912:

> " No decision of this court has been found by Mr. McLaren in which the question: 'what is a side-car,' has come up for decision, but B his industry has enabled him to unearth a decision which is referred to in Justice of the Peace Journal, vol. 115 (1951) at p. 611; under 'Notes of the Week,' a decision of the Bristol magistrates is cited, and in that case a contraption was fitted by the side of a motor cycle in the shape of a box which was used to carry building materials. In that case the prosecution contended that as the attachment was not able to take passengers, it was not a side-car within the meaning of the C regulations. The defence argued that it was a side-car properly attached, and that it was not necessary that it should be for the conveyance of passengers, and the justices accepted the submission of the defence and dismissed the summons. It may be that the issue raised in that case will come up for decision before this court in the same or slightly different form in some future case, and therefore D I feel that it would be unwise to express a positive decision whether that decision of the Bristol justices was right or wrong. I say that with all the more reason because it is not necessary for the purposes of the present case to decide whether the side-car must be one that is constructed or adapted for the carriage of passengers and nothing else, or whether a side-car can properly be constituted by means of a chassis and some box or basket on it which would carry materials E rather than passengers."

I pause there to say that in giving the decision of the court Ashworth J. was deliberately leaving open the question whether an attachment constructed for the carriage of goods and not passengers could qualify as a side-car. It was unnecessary to the decision. Ashworth J., however, did go on to express his own opinion about the matter, and in my judgment F that opinion, while of great weight, is nevertheless obiter and we are not bound to follow it. He said, at p. 1912 *:

> " I would prefer to leave that issue to be decided when it is raised, but I am quite certain that to constitute a side-car, the attachment must be capable of carrying, and the facts found in this case show to my mind sufficiently that there was no form of structure on this G attachment."

Thus, he came down firmly on the view that a side-car is an attachment constructed and fit for the safe carriage of a passenger. It was on that dictum that the justices in the present case, having directed themselves admirably as appears from the case stated, came to the conclusion that they should follow that view of the true construction of the Regulations H of 1971 and section 88 of the Road Traffic Act 1972 and convicted the defendant.

The problem adumbrated by Ashworth J. has arisen in the present case because here we are dealing with an attachment to a motor bicycle which was properly designed and constructed for the carriage of goods, namely, the ladders of a window cleaner and his buckets and sponges and

* See reporter's note, ante, p. 77H.

so forth, and the question therefore falls to be decided: is that a side-car A
within the meaning of the Regulations of 1973?

It seems to me that it is a side-car. There is no requirement in any of the statutory provisions to which I have referred laying it down that the side-car must be one constructed for and fit for the safe carriage of a passenger. It simply is not so defined.

Some slight help is to be gained by the fact that in regulation 16 (3) (*a*) of the Motor Vehicles (Driving Licences) Regulations 1950 there is a B
provision that for the purposes of that sub-paragraph a motor bicycle should not be deemed to be constructed or adapted to carry more than one person unless it has a side-car attached constructed for the carriage of a passenger. That is a completely different piece of legislation, and it is to be noted that it has disappeared from the present regulations, and indeed had done so by 1963. Thus, Parliament has had ample opportunity, C
if it so wished, to limit the interpretation of the word "side-car" to "an attachment constructed for and fit for the safe carriage of a passenger" and has not seen fit to do so.

In those circumstances it seems to me that a roadworthy attachment to a motor bicycle which is designed for the carriage of goods is just as much a side-car as a roadworthy attachment constructed for the carriage of a passenger. D

For my part I would like to compliment the justices upon the great care with which they went into the case and the way in which they stated the case for the decision of this court, but for those reasons I am satisfied that they came to a wrong conclusion in law, and the question which they asked as to whether they were correct is to be answered "No," "side-car" does not necessarily mean a structure attached to a motor cycle E
capable of carrying passengers in safety.

For those reasons the appeal should be allowed.

LAWSON J. I agree.

LORD WIDGERY C.J. I also agree and I agree with all the reasons so clearly given in the judgment of O'Connor J. I add a few words of my F
own partly because the view which we take of the meaning of "side-car" is, I think, different from the view generally held up to now, and also in deference to the justices who have given this case a great deal of careful attention and stated it quite admirably.

The factual situation with which we are dealing is one of a driver who has a provisional licence only, who wishes to take a passenger on his motor bicycle and wishes to take a passenger who is not himself a fully G
qualified driver. The requirements make it perfectly clear that to meet that situation there must be a side-car attached to the motor bicycle, and I find it of some help in deciding on the true meaning of "side-car," and in particular in deciding whether a side-car must be adapted for the carriage of passengers, to look at that situation and ask why the legislature thought it proper and appropriate to insist on the presence of a H
side-car before a provisionally licensed driver could take an unqualified passenger.

Ashworth J. in *Cox* v. *Harrison* [1968] 1 W.L.R. 1907 obviously thought that a side-car was intended to carry a passenger. He resiled from it, as the extract already read indicates, and accepted later in his judgment that there was no need for the passenger to be travelling in the side-car. The moment that one concedes that, which I think is an entirely proper

A concession, it is very difficult, I think, to justify the conclusion that the legislature was insisting on the side-car being adapted for the carriage of passengers.

I take the other view, namely, that the reason why the legislature thought it necessary to insist on the presence of a side-car in this situation was because the third wheel gives additional stability. It does so equally whether the intended burden is a body or goods. The fact that Parliament
B has had concern for the third wheel in this connection is, I think, reinforced by section 88 of the Act of 1972, to which O'Connor J. has already referred, under which a driver with a provisional licence only cannot be authorised to drive a motor cycle whereof the cylinder capacity of the engine exceeds 250 cubic centimetres, not being a vehicle having three wheels. The reference there to three wheels must, I think, be a
C reference to the additional stability which comes from the third wheel.

I entirely agree that the appeal should be allowed and the conviction quashed.

I am reminded that there is an endorsement on the defendant's driving licence in respect of this offence, and that endorsement must of course be removed with the quashing of the conviction. The defendant will have his costs of £20.

D

Appeal allowed.
Conviction and order for endorsement of defendant's licence quashed.
Order for prosecutor to pay £20 costs to defendant.

E Solicitors: *Sharpe, Pritchard & Co.* for *R. A. Crabb, Lincoln.*

L. N. W.

[QUEEN'S BENCH DIVISION]

F

* PRACTICE DIRECTION (JUDGMENT: FOREIGN CURRENCY)

Currency—Foreign—Claim or judgment—Procedure in High Court for bringing claim and enforcing judgment in foreign currency —Transfer to county court—R.S.C., Ord. 6, *r.* 2 (1) (*b*); *Ord.* 13, *r.* 1; *Ord.* 14, *r.* 3; *Ord.* 19, *r.* 2; *Ord.* 22, *r.* 1; *Ord.* 42, *r.*
G 3; *Ord.* 45, *r.* 12; *Ord.* 49, *r.* 1; *Ord.* 50, *rr.* 1, 2; *Ord.* 51

1. Subject to any order or directions which the court may make or give in any particular case, the following practice shall be followed in relation to the making of claims and the enforcement of judgments expressed in a foreign currency.

H 2. *Claims for debts or liquidated demands in foreign currency*

For the purpose of ascertaining the proper amount of the costs to be indorsed on the writ pursuant to R.S.C., Ord. 6, r. 2 (1) (*b*), before a writ of summons is issued in which the plaintiff makes a claim for a debt or liquidated demand expressed in a foreign currency, the writ must be indorsed with the following certificate, which must be signed by or on behalf of the solicitor of the plaintiff or by the plaintiff if he is acting in person:

" Sterling equivalent of amount claimed A

I/we certify that the rate current in London for the purchase of (*state the unit of the foreign currency claimed*) at the close of business on the.........day of.........19......(*being the date next or most nearly preceding the date of the issue of the Writ*) was.........to the £ Sterling and at this rate the debt or liquidated demand claimed herein, namely (*state the sum of the foreign currency claimed*) amounts to £.........or
exceeds £650 (*as the case may be*). B

Dated the.........day of.........19......

Signed..

(Solicitor for the Plaintiff)."

3. *Pleading claims for debts or liquidated demands in foreign currency*

The writ or statement of claim in which a claim is made for payment C
of a debt or liquidated demand in foreign currency must contain the following statements, namely: (i) that the contract under which the debt is claimed in the foreign currency is governed by the law of some country outside the United Kingdom; and (ii) that under *that* contract the money of account in which the debt was payable was the currency of that country or of some other foreign country. D

4. *Default judgment for debts or liquidated demand in foreign currency*

A judgment in default of appearance or in default of defence may be entered in foreign currency by adapting R.S.C., Appendix A, Form 39, as follows:

" It is this day adjudged that the Defendant do pay the Plaintiff
(*state the sum in which foreign currency is claimed*) or the Sterling E
equivalent at the time of payment."

5. *Judgment under Ord. 14*

Wherever appropriate, a judgment under R.S.C., Ord. 14, r. 3 may be entered for a debt or liquidated demand in foreign currency by adapting R.S.C., Appendix A, Form 44 as follows:

" It is this day adjudged that the Defendant do pay the Plaintiff F
(*state the sum in foreign currency for which the Court has ordered Judgment to be entered*) or the Sterling equivalent at the time of payment and £...... costs (or costs to be taxed)."

The amount of the fixed costs will be calculated on the sterling equivalent of the amount of the foreign currency claimed as indorsed and
certified on the writ, unless the court otherwise orders. G

6. *Transfer to the county court*

On the hearing of an application for an order under the County Courts Act 1959, section 45, for the transfer to a county court of an action for a debt or liquidated demand expressed in foreign currency, on the ground that the amount claimed or remaining in dispute does not exceed £1,000,
the court will have regard to the sterling equivalent of the foreign currency H
claimed as indorsed and certified on the writ, unless at the time of the application it is shown to the court that the said sterling equivalent does exceed the sum of £1,000.

7. *Payment of foreign currency into court in satisfaction*

In an action for the recovery of a debt or liquidated demand, whether in sterling or in foreign currency, the defendant may, subject to the require-

A ments of the Exchange Control Act 1947, pay into court in satisfaction of the claim, under R.S.C., Ord. 22, r. 1, a sum of money in foreign currency by adapting Form No. 2 of the Supreme Court Fund Rules 1975. If it is desired that the money should be placed on deposit after the expiry of 21 days the necessary directions must be given on a Part II Order.

8. *Orders for conditional payment of foreign currency into court*

B Where the court makes a conditional order for payment of money into court, e.g., when granting conditional leave to defend on an application for summary judgment under Order 14, or when setting aside a default judgment or granting an adjournment of the hearing of a summons or the trial or hearing of an action or making any other order conditional upon payment of money into court, the court may order that such money be
C paid into court in a foreign currency, and the court may further order that such money should be placed in a foreign currency account and if practicable should be placed in such an account which is an interest bearing account.

9. *Entry of judgment in foreign currency*

D A judgment may be entered in foreign currency by adapting the relevant Forms in R.S.C., Appendix A as follows:

"It is this day adjudged that the Defendant do pay the Plaintiff (*state the sum in foreign currency in which Judgment has been ordered to be entered*) or the sterling equivalent at the time of payment."

10. *Interest on judgment debt in foreign currency*

E A judgment entered in foreign currency will carry the statutory rate of interest on the amount of the judgment in foreign currency and such interest will be added to the amount of the judgment itself for the purposes of enforcement of the judgment.

11. *Enforcement of judgment debt in foreign currency by writ of fi. fa.*

F (a) Where the plaintiff desires to proceed to enforce a judgment expressed in foreign currency by the issue of a writ of fieri facias, the praecipe for the issue of the writ must first be indorsed and signed by or on behalf of the solicitor of the plaintiff or by the plaintiff if he is acting in person with the following certificate:

"Sterling equivalent of Judgment

G I/we certify that the rate current in London for the purpose of (*state the unit of the foreign currency in which the Judgment is expressed*) at the close of business on the .... day of .... 19... (*being the date nearest or most nearly preceding the date of the issue of the Writ of Fi. Fa.*) was .... to the £ sterling and at this rate the sum of (*state the amount of the Judgment debt in foreign currency*) amounts to £...........

H Dated the .... day of .... 19...

Signed. ....

(Solicitor for the Plaintiff)."

(b) The amount so certified will then be entered in the writ of fi. fa. by adapting R.S.C., Appendix A, Form 53 to meet the circumstances of the case but substituting the following recital:

"Whereas in the above named action it was on the .... day of A
.... 19... adjudged [or ordered] that the Defendant C.D. do pay the Plaintiff A.B. (*state the sum of the foreign currency for which Judgment was entered*) or the sterling equivalent at the time of payment, and whereas the sterling equivalent at the date of issue of this Writ is £......... as appears by the Certificate indorsed and signed by or on behalf of the Plaintiff on the Praecipe for the issue of this Writ." B

12. *Enforcement of judgment debt in foreign currency by garnishee proceedings*

(a) Where the plaintiff desires to proceed to enforce a judgment expressed in foreign currency by garnishee proceedings the affidavit made in support of an application for an order under R.S.C., Ord. 49, r. 1 must C
contain words to the following effect:

"The rate current in London for the purchase of (*state the amount of the Judgment in foreign currency*) at the close of business on the ....day of .... 19... was .... to the £ sterling, and at this rate the said sum of .... amounts to £......... sterling. I have ascertained the above information (*state the source of the information*) and verily believe the same to be true." D

The master will then make an order nisi for the sterling equivalent of the judgment debt as so verified.

(b) Where the plaintiff desires to attach a debt due or accruing due to the defendant within the jurisdiction in the same unit of foreign currency as the judgment debt is itself expressed, the affidavit made in support of an application for an order under R.S.C., Ord. 49, r. 1 must E
state all the relevant facts relied on and in such event the master may make the order to attach such debt due or accruing due in *that* foreign currency.

13. *Enforcement of judgment debt in foreign currency by other modes of enforcement* F

Where the plaintiff desires to proceed to enforce a judgment expressed in a foreign currency by other means of enforcement, e.g. by obtaining an order imposing a charge on land or interest in land under R.S.C., Ord. 50, r. 1 or by obtaining an order imposing a charge on securities under R.S.C., Ord. 50, r. 2, or some other similar order or by obtaining an order for the appointment of a receiver by way of equitable execution, under R.S.C., Order 51, the affidavit made in respect of any such application shall G
contain words similar to those set out in paragraph 11 (a) above. The master will then make an order for the sterling equivalent of the judgment expressed in foreign currency as so verified by such affidavit.

14. These directions are issued with the concurrences of the Chief Chancery Master acting on the authority of the Vice-Chancellor so far as they apply to the practice in the Chancery Division, and of the Senior Registrar of H
the Family Division so far as they apply to the practice in that division.

I. H. JACOB,
Senior Master of the Supreme Court.

December 18, 1975.

A

[HOUSE OF LORDS]

*** COMMISSIONER OF POLICE OF THE METROPOLIS . RESPONDENT**

AND

CURRAN . . . . APPELLANT

B

[On appeal from REG. *v.* CURRAN]

1975 Nov. 10, 11; Dec. 17 — Lord Diplock, Lord Hailsham of St. Marylebone, Lord Kilbrandon, Lord Salmon and Lord Edmund-Davies

Road Traffic—Laboratory test—Failure to provide specimen—
C *Offence—Motorist acquitted of being in charge of vehicle when arrested—No suggestion of driving or attempting to drive—Whether proof necessary of being in charge at arrest—Road Traffic Act* 1972 (*c.* 20), *ss.* 5 (2) (3) (5), 9 (1) (3), *Sch.* 4, *Pt.* I [1]

Statute—Construction—Consolidation Act—Words clear and unambiguous—No recourse to corresponding provision in previous statute—Road Traffic Act 1972, *s.* 9 (3)

Law Reform—Whether necessary—Road traffic—Failing to provide
D *specimen—Penalties—Road Traffic Act* 1972, *s.* 9 (3), *Sch.* 4, *Pt.* I

The appellant was found by a police constable sitting in a stationary car in a street. The ignition key was in the car with him and he was very drunk. In the reasonable belief that the appellant had committed an offence under section 5 (2) of the Road Traffic Act 1972 the constable arrested him and took him
E to a police station. After being given an opportunity to provide a specimen of breath for a breath test while at the station, the appellant was required to provide a specimen of blood or urine. He refused to do so. He was charged with offences under sections 5 (2) and 9 (3) of the Act of 1972. At the trial, it was indicated to the judge in the absence of the jury that the appellant did not dispute that at the material time he had been unfit to drive through drink and that in substance his defence
F to the charge under section 5 (2) would be based on section 5 (3). It was submitted that, if he were to be acquitted of the offence under section 5 (2) on the ground that at the material time he had not been in charge or was to be deemed not to have been in charge of the car, he was in law entitled also to be acquitted of the offence under section 9 (3). The judge rejected that submission and the trial proceeded on both counts. The

G [1] Road Traffic Act 1972, s. 5: "(2) . . . a person who, when in charge of a motor vehicle which is on a road or other public place, is unfit to drive through drink or drugs shall be guilty of an offence. (3) For the purposes of subsection (2) above a person shall be deemed not to have been in charge of a motor vehicle if he proves that at the material time the circumstances were such that there was no likelihood of his driving it so long as he remained unfit to drive through drink or drugs. . . . (5) A constable may arrest without warrant a person committing an offence under this section."

S. 9: "(1) A person who has been arrested under section 5 (5) . . . of this Act
H may, while at a police station, be required by a constable to provide a specimen for a laboratory test (which may be a specimen of blood or of urine), if he has previously been given an opportunity to provide a specimen of breath for a breath test at that station under [section 8 (7)], and either—(*a*) it appears to a constable in consequence of the breath test that the device by means of which the test is carried out indicates that the proportion of alcohol in his blood exceeds the prescribed limit, or (*b*) when given the opportunity to provide that specimen, he fails to do so. . . . (3) A person who, without reasonable excuse, fails to provide a specimen for a laboratory test in pursuance of a requirement imposed under this section shall be guilty of an offence. . . ."

Sch. 4, Pt. I: see post, p. 92A–E.

jury found the appellant not guilty of the offence under section 5 (2), and in accordance with his previous ruling the judge directed them to find the appellant guilty of the offence under section 9 (3). The appellant was sentenced to be fined £10, to be disqualified from driving for 12 months and to have his licence endorsed. The Court of Appeal dismissed his appeal against conviction.

On appeal to the House of Lords:—

Held, dismissing the appeal, that the language of section 9 (3) of the Act of 1972 was simple, clear and unambiguous and nothing in it suggested that the offence thereby created was in any way connected with the suspect's guilt or innocence of the offence which he was suspected of having committed when he was arrested; that the failure of column 4 of Part I of Schedule 4 to the Act to provide a maximum punishment by way of fine or imprisonment in the case of a first offence under section 9 (3) where the offender was neither driving nor attempting to drive nor in actual charge of the vehicle did not have the effect of limiting the definition of the offence in view of the other punishments by way of disqualification and/or endorsement provided for by columns 5 and 6; and that, accordingly, the offence under section 9 (3) of the Act of 1972 could be established without establishing that the defendant was a person in charge of, or driving, or attempting to drive, a motor vehicle on a road or other public place (post, pp. 91H—92A, F–G, 93F–G, 98H, 101F, H—102B).

Reg. v. *Richardson* (*John*) [1975] 1 W.L.R. 321, C.A. and *Williams* v. *Osborne* [1975] R.T.R. 181, D.C. considered.

Per curiam. (1) In construing a consolidation Act where the actual words are clear and unambiguous it is not permissible to have recourse to corresponding provisions in the earlier statute repealed by the consolidation Act and to treat any difference in wording as capable of casting doubt upon what is clear and unambiguous language in the consolidation Act (post, pp. 90H—91A, 101D–E, H, 103H—104A, 105C–D).

(2) Where it is not shown that the defendant was a person in actual charge of, or driving, or attempting to drive, a motor vehicle on a road or other public place the only punishments which may be imposed are disqualification, which lies within the discretion of the court, and endorsement, which is obligatory. It seems likely that the omission to provide for a power to impose a fine in such cases was due to inadvertence. The result can hardly be regarded as satisfactory (post, pp. 93H—94A, 99E–F, 101E–F, H, 102B–C, 104E–F, 105D–H).

Per Lord Hailsham of St. Marylebone, Lord Salmon and Lord Edmund-Davies. The provisions in question call for the early attention of the legislature (post, pp. 101E–F, 105B–C, H).

Decision of the Court of Appeal (Criminal Division) [1975] 1 W.L.R. 876; [1975] 2 All E.R. 1045 affirmed.

The following cases are referred to in their Lordships' opinions:

Foulkes v. *Baker* [1975] 1 W.L.R. 1551; [1975] 3 All E.R. 651, H.L.(E.).

Inland Revenue Commissioners v. *Joiner* [1975] 1 W.L.R. 1701; [1975] 3 All E.R. 1050, H.L.(E.).

Reg. v. *John* [1974] 1 W.L.R. 624; [1974] 2 All E.R. 561, C.A.

Reg. v. *Lennard* [1973] 1 W.L.R. 483; [1973] 2 All E.R. 831, C.A.

Reg. v. *Richardson* (*John*) [1975] 1 W.L.R. 321; [1975] 1 All E.R. 905, C.A.

Williams v. *Osborne* [1975] R.T.R. 181, D.C.

Wiltshire v. *Barrett* [1966] 1 Q.B. 312; [1965] 2 W.L.R. 1195; [1965] 2 All E.R. 271, C.A.

A The following additional cases were cited in argument:

Reg. v. *Sakhuja* [1973] A.C. 152; [1972] 2 W.L.R. 1116; [1972] 2 All E.R. 311, H.L.(E.).

Rex v. *Morris* [1951] 1 K.B. 394; [1950] 2 All E.R. 965, C.C.A.

Rowlands v. *Hamilton* [1971] 1 W.L.R. 647; [1971] 1 All E.R. 1089, H.L.(E.).

B APPEAL from the Court of Appeal (Criminal Division).

The appellant, John Curran, appealed by leave of the Court of Appeal (Lord Widgery C.J., James L.J. and Ashworth J.) from their decision on May 8, 1975, dismissing an appeal by the appellant against his conviction at Middlesex Crown Court (Judge Marven Everett Q.C.) on October 25, 1974, on a count of failing to provide a specimen for a laboratory test,
C contrary to section 9 (3) of the Road Traffic Act 1972. The Court of Appeal certified the point of law of general public importance involved in their decision as being:

"Whether the offence of failing without reasonable excuse to provide a specimen for a laboratory test contrary to section 9 (3) of the Road Traffic Act 1972 can be established without establishing that the defendant was a person in charge of, or driving, or attempting to drive,
D a motor vehicle on a road or public place."

The facts are set out in the opinion of Lord Diplock and Lord Hailsham of St. Marylebone.

Neil Taylor Q.C. and *David Mills* for the appellant.

Donald Farquharson Q.C. and *Ann Goddard* for the Crown.

E

Their Lordships took time for consideration.

December 17. LORD DIPLOCK. My Lords, the appellant was found by a police constable sitting in a stationary car in a street. The ignition key was in the car with him and he was very drunk. In the reasonable
F belief that the appellant had committed an offence under section 5 (2) of the Road Traffic Act 1972 of being a person in charge of a motor vehicle, which was on a road, when he was unfit to drive through drink, the constable arrested him and took him to a police station. After being given an opportunity to provide a specimen of breath for a breath test while at the police station, the appellant was required to provide a specimen of blood or urine. He refused to do so.

G

It should be said at the outset that there are three matters that are not in dispute: (1) that, since the constable had reasonable grounds for his belief that the appellant had committed an offence under section 5 (2), the arrest was lawful under section 5 (5) (see *Wiltshire* v. *Barrett* [1966] 1 Q.B. 312); (2) that the requirement to provide a specimen of blood or urine for a laboratory test was lawfully made under section 9 (1); and
H (3) that the appellant's failure to provide it was "without reasonable excuse" within the meaning of that expression in section 9 (3), since he was neither physically nor mentally unable to provide a specimen nor would the provision of the specimen have entailed a substantial risk to his health (see *Reg.* v. *Lennard* [1973] 1 W.L.R. 483; *Reg.* v. *John* [1974] 1 W.L.R. 624; *Williams* v. *Osborne* [1975] R.T.R. 181).

So there would appear to be an undefended case of an offence under section 9 (3) of the Act which provides that:

> "A person who, without reasonable excuse, fails to provide a specimen for a laboratory test in pursuance of a requirement imposed under this section shall be guilty of an offence." A

The appellant was duly charged at Middlesex Crown Court on an indictment which contained two counts. The first was for an offence under section 5 (2); the second for an offence under section 9 (3). Upon his arraignment and in the absence of the jury a submission was made B on his behalf to the judge. It was indicated that the appellant did not dispute that at the material time he was unfit to drive through drink and that in substance his defence to the charge under section 5 (2) would be based on section 5 (3) of the Act which provides:

> "For the purposes of subsection (2) above a person shall be deemed not to have been in charge of a motor vehicle if he proves that at the material time the circumstances were such that there was no C likelihood of his driving it so long as he remained unfit to drive through drink or drugs."

It was submitted that, upon the true construction of the Act, if the appellant were to be acquitted of the offence under section 5 (2) upon the ground that at the material time he was not in charge or was to be deemed not to have been in charge of the motor vehicle, he was in law D entitled also to be acquitted of the offence under section 9 (3) of failing to provide a specimen for a laboratory test.

The judge rejected this submission. The trial proceeded upon both counts. The jury brought in a verdict of not guilty of the offence charged under section 5 (2) and, in accordance with the ruling that he had previously given, the judge directed the jury to find the appellant E guilty of the offence charged under section 9 (3). For this offence the appellant was sentenced to be fined £10, to be disqualified from driving for 12 months and to have his driving licence endorsed.

Against his conviction, though not against his sentence, the appellant appealed to the Court of Appeal upon a point of law raised by the judge's ruling. The Court of Appeal dismissed the appeal but granted the appellant leave to appeal to your Lordships' House. The point of law F involved was certified as being:

> "Whether the offence of failing without reasonable excuse to provide a specimen for a laboratory test contrary to section 9 (3) of the Road Traffic Act 1972 can be established without establishing that the defendant was a person in charge of, or driving, or attempting to drive, a motor vehicle on a road or other public place." G

My Lords, the answer to this question depends upon the true construction of the Road Traffic Act 1972. It is primarily a consolidation Act, and, while it incorporates certain amendments to give effect to recommendations of the Law Commission and the Scottish Law Commission, none of these amendments relates to any of the provisions of the Act that are relevant to the question of construction which is H involved in the instant case. As has been recently emphasised by this House in *Inland Revenue Commissioners* v. *Joiner* [1975] 1 W.L.R. 1701 it is the consolidation Act that your Lordships have to construe and if you find, as I do in the instant case, that the actual words are clear and unambiguous in their meaning it is not permissible to have recourse to the corresponding provisions in the earlier statute repealed by the consolidation Act and to treat any difference in their wording as capable

A of casting doubt upon what is clear and unambiguous language in the consolidation Act itself.

I start with a general observation about the content and structure of the Road Traffic Act 1972. It creates more than 100 different statutory offences. The ingredients of each offence are stated in the particular section of the Act by which the offence is created. The mode of prosecution of each offence (viz., summarily or on indictment or both) is not
B dealt with in the particular section by which it is created, nor is the type of punishment that may be imposed upon conviction for that offence. These matters are left to be dealt with by Part I of Schedule 4 to the Act, which by section 177 is made applicable to each of the offences created by those provisions of the Act that are specified in column 1 of that Part of the Schedule. That Part of the Schedule is in convenient
C tabular form. It sets out against the number of the particular section or subsection by which the offence is created the mode of trial and the punishment that may be imposed upon a person convicted of that offence. It provides for four different types of punishment for offences with which it deals, viz., imprisonment, fine, disqualification from holding or obtaining a driving licence, and endorsement of the conviction on the offender's driving licence. Column 4 shows the maximum punish-
D ment by way of fine or imprisonment. Column 5 shows whether or not the court is obliged, or empowered at its discretion, to order disqualification from holding or obtaining a driving licence; and column 6 shows whether or not the court is obliged to order endorsement of the offender's driving licence. The reference in section 177 (1) to "prosecution and punishment" as being the subject matter of Part I of Schedule 4 makes
E it clear that disqualification and endorsement as well as fine and imprisonment are to be classified as "punishment" for the purposes of the Act—as indeed they are as a matter of common sense, and always have been for the purposes of the right of appeal against sentence under the Criminal Appeal Act 1907.

My second observation is that sections 8 and 9 of the Act create obligations upon the citizens of an unusual kind which had no precedent
F in English penal law when they were first introduced by the Road Safety Act 1967. What these sections provide is a procedure by which a person who is reasonably suspected by a policeman of having committed an offence under section 5 or section 6 can be required to provide material evidence in the form of a specimen of his blood or urine which may be used against him at his trial for an offence under either section,
G and without which, in the case of an offence under section 6, no prosecution could ever be brought against him. So the procedure under sections 8 and 9 applies to persons when they are suspects only. They may not in fact have committed the offence under section 5 or section 6 of which they are suspected; but, if they have, their refusal to provide a specimen of blood or urine would prevent their being prosecuted for any offence under section 6 and would enhance their prospects of escaping conviction
H for an offence under section 5. If the procedure is to achieve its evident purpose it is essential that a refusal without reasonable excuse to provide a specimen of blood or urine should attract penal sanctions irrespective of whether or not it is ultimately proved that the person refusing to provide the specimen had been guilty of the offence of which he was suspected.

In my opinion this is what section 9 (3) quite plainly does. The language of the subsection is simple, clear and unambiguous and in my view not fairly capable of any other meaning. There is nothing in that A language to suggest that the offence thereby created is in any way connected with the suspect's guilt or innocence of the offence which he was suspected of having committed when he was arrested.

The argument for placing a strained construction upon the words of section 9 (3) is based upon the wording of the entry in column 4 of Part I of Schedule 4 relating to the offence created by that subsection. As already mentioned this entry shows "... the maximum punishment B by way of fine or imprisonment which may be imposed on a person convicted of the offence ... [section 177 (2) (*b*)]." It is convenient to set out the relevant part of that entry alongside the corresponding entries relating to disqualification and endorsement. I omit words relating only to second offences. C

4 Punishment	5 Disqualification	6 Endorsement
(i) Where it is shown that at the relevant time ... the offender was driving or attempting to drive a motor vehicle on a road or other public place, four months or £100 or both; ... (ii) Where in any other case it is shown that at that time the offender was in charge of a motor vehicle on a road or other public place, four months or £100 or both.	(*a*) Obligatory if it is shown as mentioned in paragraph (i) of column 4. (*b*) Discretionary if it is not so shown.	Obligatory.

D E

My Lords, columns 4, 5 and 6 do not deal with whether a defendant is guilty or innocent of the offence referred to in column 1. They deal with punishment alone and do not come into operation unless and until there has been a finding of guilt, that is, in a case tried on indictment, after the jury has returned a verdict of guilty. The instructions which F these columns contain are addressed to those responsible for determining what sentence should be imposed and not to those responsible for determining guilt. The instructions to the latter are contained in the section of the Act which is referred to in column 1.

It is true that, in the case of an offence under section 9 (3), column 4 contains no provision for a maximum punishment *by way of fine or* G *imprisonment* which may be imposed upon a first offender guilty of an offence under section 9 (3) of whom it is not shown, to the satisfaction of the sentencer, that he was a person who was either driving or attempting to drive a motor vehicle on a road or other public place or was a person who was in *actual* charge of such a vehicle. It is to be observed that being shown to have been in actual charge of a motor vehicle is sufficient to attract the punishment by way of fine or imprisonment prescribed in H column 4, despite the absence of any likelihood that the person in actual charge would drive it while he remained unfit to drive through drink or drugs. The "deeming" provision in section 5 (3) applies only where the charge is of an offence under section 5 (2). It has no application to an offence under section 9 (3).

If fine and imprisonment were the only kinds of punishment available for an offence under section 9 (3) there would be some force in the

A argument that the existence of a punitive sanction is an essential
characteristic of every criminal offence and that the absence of any
specific provision for the punishment of that offence where neither of
the matters referred to in column 4 were shown gave rise to an implied
limitation upon the definition of the offence to be found in section 9 (3).
The alternative conclusion would be that Parliament, though it had
fixed relatively low maximum penalties for the offence when aggravating
B circumstances were shown, had nevertheless intended that in the absence
of any of those aggravating circumstances the offence should attract the
penalties appropriate to a misdemeanour at common law, viz., fine or
imprisonment unlimited by any maxima. This is an inference that, for
my part, I should be hesitant to draw in construing modern statutes.

Fine and imprisonment, however, are not the only punishments
C available for an offence under section 9 (3). In addition to column 4 of
Part I of Schedule 4 there are columns 5 and 6. The entry in column 5
relating to disqualification from holding or obtaining a driving licence
is couched in terms that are significantly different from those of column 4.
It divides offences under section 9 (3) into two categories, dealt with in
paragraphs *(a)* and *(b)* respectively, according to whether disqualification
is obligatory or discretionary. Paragraph *(a)*, which makes it obligatory,
D applies only where it is shown that at the relevant time the offender was
driving or attempting to drive a motor vehicle on a road or other public
place. It deals with offences committed in the circumstances referred
to in the first part of paragraph (i) in column 4. Paragraph *(b)* on the
other hand which makes disqualification discretionary deals with offences
committed in *any* other circumstances. The change in language in
E paragraph *(b)* of column 5 is in significant contrast not only to the
language of paragraph *(a)* but also to the language of paragraph (ii) of
column 4. If the draftsman had intended to restrict the discretionary
punishment of disqualification to cases where it was shown that the
offender had been in charge of a motor vehicle at the relevant time the
appropriate words in which to do so would have been before his very eyes
as he was laying out the table in Part I of Schedule 4. Column 6 in its
F turn makes the punishment of endorsement of the offender's driving
licence obligatory without any such qualification as is to be found in
relation to fine and imprisonment in column 4.

The existence of these other punishments which may be imposed for
offences under section 9 (3), where it is not shown that the offender at
the relevant time was driving or attempting to drive or was in actual
G charge of a motor vehicle on a road or other public place, destroys the
foundation for the implication sought to be drawn by counsel for the
appellant from the absence of any provision in column 4 for a maximum
fine or period of imprisonment for offenders where this is not shown.
It also negatives any inference that Parliament intended such offences
to attract the penalties of a misdemeanour at common law.

I would accordingly answer the certified question in the affirmative;
H but would add that where it is not shown that the defendant was a person
in *actual* charge of, or driving or attempting to drive, a motor vehicle
on a road or other public place the only punishments which may be
imposed are disqualification, which lies within the discretion of the court,
and endorsement, which is obligatory.

The result, as is so often the case with these ill drafted statutory
provisions dealing with drink offences in connection with motor vehicles,
can hardly be regarded as satisfactory. A fine would in many cases

appear to be the most appropriate penalty for a refusal to provide a A
specimen of blood or urine by a person who was not in actual charge of, or driving or attempting to drive, a motor vehicle though he was reasonably suspected of it. It seems likely that the omission to provide for a power to impose a fine in such cases was due to inadvertence of the draftsman of the provision in section 3 (3) of the Road Safety Act 1967 part of which is reproduced in section 9 (3) and part reflected in the entry in column 4
of Part I of Schedule 4 to the consolidation Act of 1972. He appears to B
have overlooked the possibility that a person who was lawfully required to provide a specimen of blood or urine because he was reasonably suspected of having committed a drink offence in connection with a motor vehicle might turn out later not to have been in charge of, or driving or attempting to drive, the vehicle. There was little excuse for this
lacuna since *Wiltshire* v. *Barrett* [1966] 1 Q.B. 312, from which the C
possibility arises, had been decided in 1965, and there was no corresponding lacuna in the language used in section 5 (2) of the Road Safety Act 1967 which is reflected in the entry in column 5 of Part I of Schedule 4 to the consolidation Act of 1972.

Shortly before the decision of the Court of Appeal in the instant case there had been two decisions of that court that were in conflict upon the
same point of law as is involved in the instant case. They were *Williams* D
v. *Osborne* [1975] R.T.R. 181 and *Reg.* v. *Richardson* (*John*) [1975] 1 W.L.R. 321. In *Williams* v. *Osborne,* which the Court of Appeal preferred and followed in the instant case, the court had not been referred to Part I of Schedule 4 to the Road Traffic Act 1972 at all. In *Reg.* v. *Richardson,* so far as can be gathered from the judgment, the court
was referred to the entry in column 4 of Part I of Schedule 4, but not E
to the entries in columns 5 and 6. The court did not give any further consideration to the construction of the Act of 1972, which was the only statute governing the offence, but concentrated its attention on the construction of section 3 (3) of the Road Safety Act 1967. It found the wording of this subsection of the repealed statute to be ambiguous and the court's attention was never drawn to section 5 (2) of the same statute
as an aid in resolving the ambiguity. F

The judgment of the Court of Appeal in *Reg.* v. *Richardson* (*John*) [1975] 1 W.L.R. 321 illustrates the danger of going behind the actual language used in a consolidation Act when its meaning read in the context of that Act itself is clear and unambiguous. The presumption that a consolidation Act was not intended to alter the previous statute law which it
repeals and replaces is a legitimate aid to its interpretation where its G
language is fairly and equally capable of bearing more than one meaning; but one of the purposes of a consolidation Act is to resolve possible ambiguities in the language of the statutes which it repeals—not to perpetuate them or to add to the obscurity of the law. The language of those provisions of the Road Safety Act 1967 which dealt with the offence of refusing to provide a specimen of blood or urine for a laboratory
test may not have been so clear as the language of those provisions which H
replaced them in the Road Traffic Act 1972; but this is the worst possible reason for resorting to the repealed statute in order to discover some ambiguity which is not apparent in the language of the provisions of the consolidation Act itself.

There remains to be considered the actual disposition of the instant appeal. It is an appeal against conviction only upon the point of law raised in the certified question. Since that question is to be answered in

A the affirmative the appeal against conviction must be dismissed. There was no appeal against sentence, and in the light of the answer given to the certified question the sentence of disqualification and endorsement was a sentence that the judge was in any event empowered to pass upon the appellant's conviction of the offence under section 9 (3). Whether the judge was empowered to impose a fine as well depends upon whether he was satisfied that the appellant was in actual charge of the motor
B vehicle in which he was found at the time of his arrest. The verdict of the jury on the first count of the indictment for the offence under section 5 (2) throws no light on this, for, of itself, it is consistent with their having found either that the prosecution had not established that the appellant was in actual charge of the vehicle or that, notwithstanding that the prosecution had established this, the defendant had established
C the defence available to him under section 5 (3) under which he was to be *deemed* not to have been in charge of the vehicle for the purposes of that offence—a defence that was not available to him upon the charge in the second count of an offence under section 9 (3). Nevertheless it is a reasonable inference from the way in which the appellant's case was adumbrated in the original submission of law made to the judge and from the judge's summation of the evidence to the jury that the defence
D under section 5 (3) was the real issue of fact determined by the verdict of the jury; and there is no sufficient ground for doubting that the judge was satisfied that the appellant was in actual charge of the motor vehicle at the time of his arrest, although there may have been no likelihood of his driving it before he sobered up.

I would dismiss the appeal.

E

LORD HAILSHAM OF ST. MARYLEBONE. My Lords, for the reasons which follow I am of the opinion that this appeal should be dismissed.

On October 24, 1974, the appellant was arraigned at the Middlesex Crown Court in St. James' Square on an indictment containing two counts, each relating to events which had taken place on May 8, 1974.

The two counts were: (1) A count charging the appellant under
F section 5 (2) of the Road Traffic Act 1972 (being unfit to drive through drink when in charge of a motor vehicle on a road). (2) A count charging the appellant under section 9 (3) of the Road Traffic Act 1972 with failing without reasonable excuse to provide the required specimen of blood or urine for the prescribed laboratory test.

In the event, the appellant was acquitted of the first and convicted
G on the second count. He was fined £10, and disqualified for 12 months (discretionary for this offence when not driving or attempting to drive) and his licence endorsed (obligatory for this offence).

He appealed without leave on a pure point of law to the Court of Appeal (Criminal Division), and his appeal was dismissed. The court certified a question of general public importance (of which more later) and gave leave to appeal to your Lordships' House. There was, and is,
H no appeal against sentence, and no leave to appeal against the summing up was sought.

The appellant's contention has been throughout that the two verdicts are inconsistent, and, in particular, that the verdict of conviction on the second count is inconsistent with the verdict of acquittal on the first.

He has maintained this position throughout. It was raised first before his actual arraignment by agreement between counsel, when it was argued in advance of the trial that the two counts stood or fell together.

When the decision went against him his counsel expressly admitted that, if the appellant were convicted on the first count, he could have no separate argument on the second, and when he was acquitted on the first count he immediately appealed on the ground, to quote Lord Widgery C.J. [1975] 1 W.L.R. 876, 878, that:

> ". . . a conviction of the 'sample' offence, . . ." (section 9 (3)) "is inconsistent with acquittal on the offence of being in charge of the car when unfit through drink" (section 5 (2)).

One ground of the appellant's argument was the same throughout, though it is not identical with the reasons given by the Court of Appeal, nor with the question certified to your Lordships as of general public importance.

The appellant argued that he was entitled on both charges to avail himself of the special defence available to him under section 5 (3) of the Act, of which the burden, on the balance of probabilities, rests on the defendant, to the effect that a person accused under section 5 (2) of the Road Traffic Act 1972 shall be deemed not to have been in charge of a motor vehicle if he proves that at the material time the circumstances were such that there was no likelihood of his driving the vehicle so long as he remained unfit to drive. The defence was clearly available to him on the first count, but the appellant's contention was that this special defence was available to him on the second count as well. That this was his contention of law appears manifestly from the transcript of the preliminary argument before the trial, and, on the second count, and on a fair reading of the transcript, it was, I believe, his main and pehaps his only contention in the event of a conviction on the first count.

In so far as this was the appellant's only contention it was, in my opinion, plainly wrong. The deeming provision of section 5 (3) is expressly limited in application to section 5 (2), and even in section 5 (2), to which it is admittedly applicable, the expression "in charge" is clearly used in the first sentence in a sense free from the application of the deeming provision, since the burden of proof that a defendant was in physical charge of the car under the section must clearly rest on the prosecution throughout, whereas, in order to invoke and apply the deeming provision under section 5 (3), the burden of proof expressly rests on the defence. When the court has to apply punishment after conviction in accordance with the provisions of section 177 and Schedule 4 to the Act the expression "in charge," where it occurs, is manifestly free of any application of the deeming provision of section 5 (3), both on the words and on the sense of the statute.

When the case came to be left to the jury, in addition to the special defence under section 5 (3), the circuit judge made reference to evidence given by the accused to the effect that he was, in any event, not in physical charge of the relevant vehicle at all. I need not summarise this evidence, because I believe that a fair reading of the transcript supports the view that Lord Widgery C.J. [1975] 1 W.L.R. 876, 879 was right in describing the section 5 (3) defence as ". . . really the only live point on the first count . . . ," and that in bringing in the verdict they did there can be little doubt that ". . . it was on section 5 (3) that the jury acquitted the appellant of the offence of being in charge when unfit."

If this is right, and I think it is, it is clear that the two verdicts are not incompatible. As I understand it, where it is alleged that general verdicts of the same jury on successive counts are incompatible with one another, since, in the nature of the case, no reasons are given by the jury, an appellate court can only upset the verdict of conviction, in the absence of any complaint about the summing up (of which none is made here), if there is no logical path by which they can be reconciled. Here there is a path by which the two verdicts can be reconciled, and that one which almost certainly reflects the view actually taken by the jury, and it follows that they are not inconsistent with one another and the appeal fails.

Unfortunately, this is not by any means the end of the matters in dispute. But before I proceed to these, and whatever the merits of the foregoing, I am quite clear from what had passed that the circuit judge then proceeded to pass sentence on the footing that it had been shown to his satisfaction that the appellant was in actual physical charge of the vehicle at the time of the offence. Subject to one serious question of law (to which I will return), this is quite enough to justify the imposition of a sentence, as was imposed, of a fine of £10 under column 4 of paragraph 5 of Schedule 4 to the Act, and a sentence of disqualification, discretionary but not obligatory, under column 5 of the same paragraph. As there was no appeal against sentence, my view, therefore, is that, subject to the point of law, which I will discuss in a moment, the sentence must stand, though I add with whatever emphasis I can command that I would not myself have thought that, in the light of the relative mildness of the fine, disqualification was appropriate to the case. I add, however, further, that I say this only on the short transcript available to your Lordships, and that there may have been factors unknown to me which would change my assessment of the matter.

I now turn to the substantive points which occupied most of the attention of the Appellate Committee, and to which, as I shall endeavour to show, no wholly satisfactory solution presents itself. The question certified by the Court of Appeal as of general public importance was in the following terms:

> " Whether the offence of failing without reasonable excuse to provide a specimen for a laboratory test contrary to section 9 (3) of the Road Traffic Act 1972 can be established without establishing that the defendant was a person in charge of, or driving, or attempting to drive, a motor vehicle on a road or other public place."

To this question so formulated a qualified affirmative answer can now be given on the limited and narrow ground that, where a defendant escapes conviction under section 5 (2) by availing himself of the defence afforded by section 5 (3) of the Act but was physically in charge at the time of his arrest, it is not necessary to prove more than that he was physically in charge of the vehicle.

But is it necessary to prove as much? The Court of Appeal thought not, and in doing so in effect decided that the decision in *Reg.* v. *Richardson* (*John*) [1975] 1 W.L.R. 321 was wrong and should not be followed. The decision of the Court of Appeal was based on the general proposition that, contrary to this decision, a person may be found guilty under section 9 (3) notwithstanding the fact that he was never at the relevant time in charge of the relevant or indeed any motor vehicle at all. The court came to this conclusion because they found *Reg.* v. *Richardson* (*John*) to be inconsistent with the decision in *Williams* v. *Osborne* [1975] R.T.R. 181, in which it was held by the Divisional Court that for a suspect to refuse to give the required sample on the grounds that the suspect had not at the relevant time been actually in charge of the vehicle was not a " reasonable excuse " for declining to give a sample so as to be a defence to a charge under

section 9 (3). Whether or not the Court of Appeal was entitled to follow A
Williams v. *Osborne* in the face of *Reg.* v. *Richardson* (*John*) is a question
I will not canvass further. *Williams* v. *Osborne* was decided on January
22, 1975. *Reg.* v. *Richardson* (*John*), which was not brought to the attention
of the Divisional Court, had been decided on December 10, 1974. *Williams*
v. Osborne was a "reasonable excuse" case and based on the line of
authority of which *Reg.* v. *Lennard* [1973] 1 W.L.R. 483 (Court of Appeal)
is an example. *Reg.* v. *Richardson* (*John*) was a case about the essential B
ingredients of an offence under section 9 (3) and it would follow that, if
Reg v. *Richardson* (*John*) were right, no question of "reasonable excuse"
would arise, as the offence under section 9 (3) would not be proved because
of the failure of an essential ingredient. I am not, at present, prepared
to say more about *Williams* v. *Osborne* than that the Court of Appeal were
clearly right in thinking that the approach to the Act of each of the two C
cases is inconsistent with the other and requires to be reconciled.

In order to decide the matter it is, however, necessary to go rather
deeper into the construction of the Act of 1972. In the instant appeal, the
appellant was arrested under section 5 (5) of the consolidating Act, and was
offered, and accepted, an opportunity to take a breath test under section 9
of the Act. The breath test, when taken, proved positive, and that was what
entitled the police officer to require, as he did, the appellant to provide the D
prescribed blood or urine specimen which he refused to do, thus giving
rise to the second count in the indictment.

If one looks at the words of section 5 (5), the arrest is authorised, on the
grammatical construction of the words, only on the ground that an offence
has, in fact, been committed. But it has long been established, at least since
Wiltshire v. *Barrett* [1966] 1 Q.B. 312, and, in truth, long before that, that E
when such words are used in connection with one of these offences requiring
in the interests of safety the removal of a suspected driver from the road
the effect is to enable the officer to arrest him when, on reasonable grounds,
he forms the view that the suspect has been committing the offence even
though it may subsequently turn out that he was not guilty. In view of
the verdict on the first count, the arrest in this case must be justified on the
basis of the doctrine in *Wiltshire* v. *Barrett* and not on the basis that an F
offence under section 5 had actually been committed. The requirement of
a blood specimen is, accordingly, on this view, to be justified on the basis
of an arrest effected not because an offence had actually been committed,
but because it had apparently been committed. We must now, therefore,
consider whether a refusal to provide the required laboratory specimen,
made in such circumstances without reasonable excuse, gives rise of itself G
to an offence under section 9 (3) of the Act. If it does, it is because it is
not necessary for the prosecution to establish, if the fact be challenged,
to the satisfaction of the jury that the suspect was at the time of the alleged
offence in actual physical charge of the vehicle in question. The question
of reasonable excuse hardly arises in this connection. If being in charge
is an essential ingredient of the offence, no reasonable excuse is required.
The prosecution fails because it has failed to prove what is necessary. If H
it succeeds, it is because the essential ingredients do not include that the
accused should actually have been in charge.

The words of section 9 (3) do not include any reference to a necessity
that the accused should actually have been driving or attempting to drive
the relevant vehicle or actually have been in charge of it. Viewed gram-
matically the only tests of the offence are the failure to comply with the
requirement, and the absence of reasonable excuse.

Nevertheless, *Reg.* v. *Richardson* (*John*) [1975] 1 W.L.R. 321 is authority for the proposition that it is an essential ingredient of an offence under section 9 (3) that the accused should have been either driving or attempting to drive or else in actual charge of the relevant vehicle at the relevant time.

The decision in *Reg.* v. *Richardson* (*John*) is based on the proposition that a distinction is to be drawn between what must be proved in order to establish that a requirement under section 9 is lawful (for which only a valid arrest is required) and what must be proved in order to prove that an offence under section 9 (3) of the Act has been committed. In the latter case, where the fact is challenged, *Reg.* v. *Richardson* (*John*) is authority for the proposition that, in addition to the lawfulness of the requirement, and the fact of the unreasonable refusal, it must be proved that the accused was either (*a*) driving or attempting to drive, or (*b*) in charge of the relevant vehicle at the relevant time.

This conclusion is arrived at by looking at section 177 and Schedule 4 to the Act, in addition to section 9 (3) and in conjunction with it. At first sight this would seem to be impermissible, since it is section 9 (3) which defines and constitutes the offence, whereas section 177 and the Schedule only deal with the method of prosecution (summary trial or indictment) and the maximum punishments available.

Nevertheless, it must be said that a refusal to read the Act in the way proposed by James L.J. in *Reg.* v. *Richardson* (*John*) [1975] 1 W.L.R. 321 leads to some bizarre, inappropriate, and even some unjust, consequences. Column 4 of the Schedule is headed " punishment " and provides for a " punishment " under that column only " where it is shown " that the offender was either driving or attempting to drive (in which case the maxima are higher) or when he was in charge (in which case lower maxima are provided), and this is so whether the case is triable summarily or on indictment, though the particular penalties appropriate for the former method of trial were altered in 1974. The result is that, at any rate so far as regards section 177 and the Schedule, where a man is lawfully arrested solely under the doctrine of *Wiltshire* v. *Barrett*, and lawfully required to produce a specimen, no penalty appears to be available by way of fine and imprisonment since in such a case the defendant will not have been driving, attempting to drive or in charge. This means, for instance, that in a case where a defendant was not proved to be in charge, though guilty of an offence, he may not be fined or imprisoned, unless a common law penalty is available. This result is so unacceptable that James L.J. felt constrained, notwithstanding the absence of any cross reference between the section constituting the offence and section 177 and the Schedule, to draw the inference that no offence was committed at all in these circumstances. The words of section 177 are sufficiently plain to exclude the possibility of treating the case as one of common law misdemeanour with undefined penalties of fine and imprisonment attached, and, if the grammatical meaning of section 9 (3) is to be accepted, it will therefore follow inexorably that a road traffic offence is intended in which neither fine nor imprisonment is available, as a penalty. If so, the offence is unique, and the result undesirable, so undesirable, in fact, that James L.J. felt constrained to hold that such could not have been the intention of the legislature.

Even odder consequences follow if one next looks on to column 5, which deals with disqualification. This presents no difficulty so far as regards drivers driving or attempting to drive. Reasonably enough, the draftsman prescribes by express reference to column 4 that in such a case disqualification is obligatory, as it does in the corresponding case where there is an offence under section 5. But, instead of following the language of column 4 (ii), which one would have thought was staring him in the face when he drafted column 5, the draftsman provides that disqualification is available but discretionary " if it is not . . . shown " that the driver was driving or attempting to drive instead of prescribing that the driver should have been " in charge." In other words, and simply pursuing grammatical meanings, if section 9 (3) means what it says and no more, the man who was not in charge but was rightly arrested under *Wiltshire* v. *Barrett* [1966] 1 Q.B. 312 and lawfully required thereafter under section 9 (1) to provide a specimen but fails to do so without reasonable excuse (*a*) has committed an offence, but (*b*) can even on indictment neither be fined nor imprisoned, yet (*c*) may be disqualified under column (5) and must have his licence endorsed under column (6) even though he had nothing to do with the car in question and may never have held a driving licence. This seems a fantastic result. The particular combination of penalties available would be not only unique, but uniquely inappropriate and unjust, uniquely inappropriate because a person who was neither in charge nor driving or attempting to drive, but who nevertheless was misguided enough to withhold a specimen when lawfully required could most appropriately be dealt with by fine and not disqualification, and unjust because disqualification is a penalty to which, if he holds a licence, such an offender should not usually be subjected to in the circumstances, and, if he does not hold a licence, disqualification is ineffective as well as inappropriate, and ridiculous because the offence could properly and far better be dealt with by a fine.

There are, however, also solid grounds for preferring the contrary view, namely that we must take this ill-drafted Act exactly as we find it where we can, and apply the results no matter what odd consequences appear to follow. Since many of the other consequences of the Act appear equally strange, it may be that this is the greater wisdom. The reasons of policy which make it less unacceptable to do so in the present case were well presented to us by counsel for the respondent. These were that section 9 is not primarily concerned with driving or motoring offences at all, but with the provision of evidence in the form of specimens by certain categories of persons appropriately to be described as suspects, namely those who have been lawfully arrested under section 5 or section 8 of the Act and provided with an opportunity to undergo a breath test. The result of the test of the laboratory specimen is the only method of proving an offence under section 6, and a most useful piece of evidence in support either of the prosecution or of the defence in charges under section 5 by reason of the provisions of section 7. According to this argument, there is not sufficient reason for disregarding the apparently unambiguous language of section 9 (3) as to definition and the apparently unambiguous consequences as to penalty provided by columns 4, 5 and 6 of Schedule 4, however inappropriate these may seem in the rare casus omissus postulated above. This view implies that *Reg.* v. *Richardson* (*John*) [1975] 1 W.L.R. 321 was wrongly decided and, since it has commended itself to a majority of my noble and learned friends as the least unattractive of a number of unattractive options, I am prepared to accept it as such with great reluctance and even greater misgivings. Where the balance of absurdity is so nicely adjusted it may be that the grammatical meaning of the statutory words is to be preferred.

But, lest anyone should think that I am being unreasonable in constantly pillorying the drafting of this part of this statute, in addition to the consequences I have set out in discussing *Reg.* v. *Richardson* (*John*) [1975] 1 W.L.R. 321, let me briefly add the following reflection based on considerations of textual criticism rather than the legal canons of construction which hitherto I have conscientiously sought to apply.

I regard it as wholly incredible that either Parliament or the draftsman should have seriously and subjectively intended the legal consequences I have now hesitantly and reluctantly decided to be the law.

The fact appears to be that, when the draftsman was considering what are now sections 9 (3), 177 and the relevant parts of Schedule 4 in the Act of 1972, he had wholly forgotten, at least until he came to the entry in column 5, and probably even then, that he should provide an express penalty to fit the case of a man who had been lawfully arrested under section 5 by reason of the doctrine of *Wiltshire* v. *Barrett* [1966] 1 Q.B. 312 and lawfully required to provide a specimen of blood or urine, but who unreasonably failed to supply that specimen, and who, nonetheless, had neither been driving, attempting to drive, nor been in charge of the relevant motor vehicle at the relevant time. This, no doubt, was because the decision in *Wiltshire* v. *Barrett* represents so called judge made law putting a gloss on the defective draftsmanship of what is now section 5 (5) which does not in terms incorporate the doctrine. When he went on to draft column 5, the draftsman was using as his model the comparable section 3 (3) of the Road Safety Act 1967 (where the penalties were in the section and not in a Schedule), and was not concerned to draft it in conformity with the comparable entry in column 4, which stems from a different source (section 1 (2) ff. in the Road Safety Act 1967). In construing a consolidation Act which itself is unambiguous, we are, of course, bound to consider its terms rather than the terms of any antecedent statutes. If this were not so, the whole benefit of consolidation might be lost and, as I have said, I am prepared to accept that the terms of the Act of 1972 are unambiguous even if the consequences are absurd. But it is to be hoped that Parliament may take an early opportunity of revising this group of sections which have provided so much litigation, with so little merit, at so much public expense. In their present state they do little credit to British law, cost an immensity of money, and occupy a great deal of time in argument about the meaning of clauses which an amending statute could easily frame in a form free from doubt.

In the meantime, and for the reasons described in the earlier part of this speech, I would dismiss this appeal on the narrow ground that the two verdicts are not incompatible and that that is the only question which strictly we are bound to decide. It follows, moreover, from what I have said about the decision in *Reg.* v. *Richardson* (*John*) [1975] 1 W.L.R. 321 that I agree with the opinion expressed by my noble and learned friends to the effect that, on a charge under section 9 (3), the matters of fact on which the decision as to penalty under columns 4 and 5 of Schedule 4 depend are matters of fact for the court after verdict and not matters of fact for the jury at the trial. With the reluctance and the misgivings already expressed I give an affirmative answer to the question certified.

LORD KILBRANDON. My Lords, I have had the advantage of reading the speech prepared by my noble and learned friend Lord Diplock. For the reasons given by him, I would dismiss this appeal.

LORD SALMON. My Lords, I need not repeat the relevant facts which are so lucidly set out in the judgments of my noble and learned friends.

Lord Diplock and Lord Hailsham of St. Marylebone. I have no doubt at A
all that on the strict literal and grammatical meaning of section 9 (1) and (3) of the Road Traffic Act 1972, looked at in isolation, any person arrested under section 5 (5) of that Act and required by a constable whilst at a police station to provide a specimen of his blood or urine for a laboratory test is guilty of an offence if he fails to provide such a specimen, even if he has in fact never driven, or attempted to drive, or been in charge of any car at any time. B

There is, however, no power under the Act to punish such a person by fine or imprisonment; but there is a power to punish him by disqualifying him from driving and an obligation to punish him by endorsing his licence. I entirely agree with my noble and learned friend, Lord Hailsham of St. Marylebone, that, for the reasons which he gives, the literal and grammatical meaning of section 9 (1) and (3) together with Part 1 of Schedule 4, to which C
I shall presently refer, produce unique, bizarre, inappropriate, absurd and unjust results which I am sure that Parliament can never have intended. In my view, it is reasonably plain that the real purpose of the legislation relating to breath tests and laboratory specimens first introduced by the Road Safety Act 1967 was designed to obtain evidence about the alcohol intake only of persons driving or attempting to drive a motor vehicle or in charge of a motor vehicle when the police had grounds for thinking that D
they had drunk too much.

I am sure that the legislation was not designed to give the police the right to require a specimen in order to measure the alcoholic intake of any individual save in relation to his driving or being in charge of a motor vehicle. Accordingly I do not believe that Parliament can ever have realised that any person could be found guilty of an offence under section E
3 (1) and (3) of the Act of 1967 supposedly reproduced by section 9 (1) and (3) of and Schedule 4 to the Act of 1972 unless he was shown to have been driving or in charge of a motor vehicle at the relevant time.

It is necessary for me to set out so far as relevant section 5 of the Act of 1972:

> "(1) A person who, when driving or attempting to drive a motor F
> vehicle on a road . . . , is unfit to drive through drink . . . shall be guilty of an offence. (2) . . . a person who, when in charge of a motor vehicle which is on a road . . . , is unfit to drive through drink . . . shall be guilty of an offence. (3) For the purposes of subsection (2) above a person shall be deemed not to have been in charge of a motor vehicle if he proves that at the material time . . . there was G
> no likelihood of his driving it so long as he remained unfit to drive through drink . . . (5) A constable may arrest without warrant a person committing an offence under this section."

Any ordinary legislator reading that section in the Bill before it became an Act would have naturally concluded that, unless anyone was driving, H
attempting to drive or in charge of a motor vehicle, he could not properly be arrested under section 5 (5) and therefore could not be guilty of an offence under section 9. And on the literal and natural and ordinary meaning of section 5 (5), the legislator would have been right.

Section 5 (1) and (5) of the Act of 1972, however, derive from and are in virtually the same words as section 6 (1) and (4) of the Road Traffic Act 1960 when the obligation of motorists, in certain circumstances, to

A submit to breath tests and furnish specimens of blood or urine were unknown in our law.

In *Wiltshire* v. *Barrett* [1966] 1 Q.B. 312 the Court of Appeal decided that section 6 (4) of the Act of 1960 could not be given its literal meaning but should be construed as if it read: "a constable may arrest a person *apparently* committing an offence under this section." This was because if any person driving or in charge of a motor car who appears to a police-
B man to be unfit to drive through drink is not immediately stopped from driving there is an obviously grave risk that innocent members of the public may be maimed or killed. The only practical way for the policeman to stop a person from driving would be to arrest him; and it should be his duty to do so. If, however, a policeman were liable to pay damages for arresting a driver whom he had reason to suspect was incapable of driving
C through drink but who in the end was acquitted of being so incapacitated, even the most conscientious policeman might hesitate to do his duty. I ventured to say, at p. 333:

> "It is a pity that the draftsman of section 6 (4) [of the Act of 1960] did not state expressly the intention of Parliament in plain and unambiguous language.... I can only respectfully express the hope that
> D in any further statute in which a power of arrest on reasonable suspicion without warrant may be given, the intention of Parliament will be expressed in plain terms."

These words seem to have fallen on stony ground for a year later when the Act of 1967 (which certainly was not a consolidating Act) was passed, the misleading language of section 6 (4) of the Act of 1960 was reintroduced
E verbatim into the new Act giving a police constable power to arrest without warrant.

Section 3 (3) of the Act of 1967 was in the same terms as section 9 (3) of the Act of 1972 but had the following most important words added to it:

> "... and—(*a*) if it is shown that at the relevant time he was driving or attempting to drive a motor vehicle on a road ..., he shall be
> F liable to be proceeded against and punished as if the offence charged were an offence under section 1 (1) of this Act; and (*b*) in any other case, if it is shown that at that time he was in charge of a motor vehicle on a road ... he shall be liable to be proceeded against and punished as if the offence charged were an offence under section 1 (2) of this Act."

G I agree with the view expressed in the judgment of the Court of Appeal delivered by James L.J. in *Reg.* v. *Richardson* (*John*) [1975] 1 W.L.R. 321 that these words in the Act of 1967, although not free from ambiguity, mean that the person referred to in section 3 (3) must be a person who falls within either (*a*) or (*b*) and that therefore no one can be convicted under that subsection who is not shown to have been driving or attempting to
H drive or to have been in charge of a motor vehicle at the relevant time. This construction at least makes sense, is manifestly just, and is almost certainly what the legislators intended. Accordingly, if the present prosecution had been brought under the Act of 1967, I should have decided the appeal in favour of the appellant. This prosecution, however, is brought under the Act of 1972—a consolidating Act which, amongst other things, is supposed to clear up any ambiguities in the preceding legislation. However ridiculous and unjust the results of the consolidating Act may be, and

this one produces peculiarly ridiculous and unjust results, it has been enacted A
by Parliament and it is our duty to enforce it. And I fear there is no doubt as to what it says, although there is equally little doubt that it says it inadvertently.

Section 9 of the Act (as I have already pointed out) looked at in isolation is unambiguous. It makes it an absolute offence for a person to refuse a specimen when a specimen is duly required after having been arrested under
section 5 (5). Section 177 and Part 1 of Schedule 4 to the Act do not in B
my view mitigate; they only reinforce the plain meaning of section 9. Column 1 is headed "Provision creating offence." In this column we find at the relevant place "9 (3)." Column 2 is headed "General nature of offence" which is "Failing to provide a specimen of blood or urine for a laboratory test." Column 3 is headed "Mode of prosecution" which is
described "(*a*) Summarily. (*b*) On indictment." Then come the three C
important columns headed respectively "Punishment," "Disqualification" and "Endorsement." Column 4 deals with maximum fines and imprisonment and columns 5 and 6 deal respectively with disqualification and endorsement which are also generally recognised as punishment. Indeed, disqualification is often regarded as a much more severe punishment than a fine:

> "*Column 4* (i) Where it is shown that at the relevant time (as defined D
> in Part V of this Schedule) the offender was driving or attempting to drive a motor vehicle on a road or other public place, four months or £100 or both; . . . (ii) Where in any other case it is shown that at that time the offender was in charge of a motor vehicle on a road or other public place, four months or £100 or both. *Column 5* (*a*)
> Obligatory if it is shown as mentioned in paragraph (i) of column 4. E
> (*b*) Discretionary if it is not so shown. *Column 6* Obligatory."

It is clear that, even if a defendant has not been shown to be driving or in charge of a motor vehicle, he commits an offence if he fails to give a specimen of his blood or urine when duly required to do so after arrest because it is clearly stated in columns 5 and 6 of the Schedule that when
he is not shown to have done either of these things he may nevertheless be F
disqualified and his licence must be endorsed. He cannot, however, be fined or imprisoned. There is no other possible construction to put upon the Schedule. In my view, the words "in charge" in paragraph 2 of column 4 of the Schedule bear the same meaning as they bear in the section under which the accused is arrested.

I reach these conclusions on the questions posed by this appeal with the G
greatest reluctance because I feel that they make the law enacted by Parliament look absurd. This is the only statute creating a motoring offence for which you cannot be fined. It is made all the more incongruous by the fact that you may nevertheless be disqualified and must have your licence endorsed if found guilty of such an offence. I find no consolation
in the fact that if a man who has not been driving or in charge of a motor H
vehicle refuses to provide a specimen of his blood or urine he cannot be convicted under section 6 and it may not be so easy to convict him under section 5. He could not in any event be convicted under either of sections 5 or 6 if he was not driving or in charge at the relevant time. If a man could be convicted under section 9 only when he was driving or in charge of a motor vehicle he would be liable to exactly the same penalties as he

A would have been if convicted under sections 5 or 6. Surely section 9 cannot be designed to punish the person who has neither been driving nor been in charge of a motor vehicle for being difficult enough to stand on what some may regard as his ordinary rights.

My Lords, this appeal is against conviction only and for the reasons stated I have reluctantly come to the conclusion that the appeal should be dismissed. I am normally chary of venturing to suggest any alteration by B the legislature in this branch of the law. I fear, as I indicated in *Foulkes* v. *Baker* [1975] 1 W.L.R. 1551, 1558, that its last state may be even worse than its first. The alteration to which I have referred of the Road Safety Act 1967 by the Road Traffic Act 1972 is a vivid illustration of how this sometimes happens. Nevertheless, the Act of 1972 produces such exceptionally grotesque results that I certainly hope that section 9 and the C references to it in the Schedule will be radically redrafted so as to remove the glaring anomalies which they now contain.

LORD EDMUND-DAVIES. My Lords, I am in entire agreement that, for the reasons appearing in the speech of my noble and learned friend, Lord Diplock, the question raised by the point of law of general public importance certified by the Court of Appeal (Criminal Division) calls D for an affirmative answer. It follows that the appeal must be dismissed, and I desire to add only a few observations.

It should be said that, though concurring in holding that *Reg.* v. *Richardson* (*John*) [1975] 1 W.L.R. 321 was wrongly decided, I have great sympathy with James L.J. in his grappling with a problem of construction of the Road Traffic Act 1972, which ought never to have E arisen and which may still give rise to injustice. I say that for this reason: in the instant case I think that this House is entitled to take it that the learned trial judge formed the view that the defendant was in reality in charge of the vehicle at the relevant time and, that being his view, the conclusion of the jury that the defendant must be acquitted on the first count by reason of the "deeming" provision contained in F section 5 (3) left unimpaired his power to impose a term of imprisonment not exceeding four months, or a fine up to £100, or both. On the other hand, had the trial judge considered that the defendant had in reality not been in charge of the vehicle, his powers of punishment would have been limited to imposing a period of disqualification and to ordering the endorsement of the defendant's licence. This illogical and irrational G restriction on the court's powers could well lead to the imposition of disqualification in circumstances not warranting it, for the simple reason that no other course seems open to the court.

The effect would be to destroy, for practical purposes, the discretionary nature of the power to disqualify in all cases not falling within paragraph (i) of column 4 of Schedule 4 to the Act of 1972. Nothing could be H more calculated to arouse a rankling feeling of injustice than to impose the severe punishment of disqualification in circumstances which do not warrant it.

Accordingly, despite the fears expressed by my noble and learned friend, Lord Salmon, in *Foulkes* v. *Baker* [1975] 1 W.L.R. 1551, 1558 that legislation to amend the Act of 1972 might well not improve the present situation, I take the view that Schedule 4 is one of the several parts of the Act which cry out for the speedy attention of the legislature.

However that may be, as far as the instant case is concerned, I concur A
with my Lords in holding that the Court of Appeal (Criminal Division) arrived at the right conclusion. The appeal therefore must accordingly be dismissed.

Appeal dismissed.

Solicitors: *Anthony & Co.; Solicitor, Metropolitan Police.*

B

M. G.

[COURT OF APPEAL]

* REGINA *v.* ANNESLEY C

1975 Nov. 17; 21 Bridge L.J., Bristow and Boreham JJ.

*Crown Court—Jurisdiction—Committal for sentence for motoring offences—No driving licence available—Imposition of sub-
stantive sentence with warning that further sentence to be* D
imposed if totting up provisions applied—Disqualification ordered more than 28 days later—Whether inherent power at common law to postpone passing whole or part of sentence—Courts Act 1971 (*c.* 23), *s.* 11 (2)

The appellant, who pleaded guilty to road traffic offences involving disqualification from driving, was committed to the
Crown Court for sentence where he was sentenced to imprison- E
ment and ordered to be disqualified for a period under section 93 of the Road Traffic Act 1972. His driving licence being unavailable, the court could not immediately determine whether further disqualification by "totting-up" under section 93 (3) was applicable and he was informed that, if his licence was found and the totting-up provisions applied, he would be brought back, the sentence not being deferred under section 1
of the Powers of Criminal Courts Act 1973. By reference to F
the central computer his record was found to contain qualifying convictions, he was brought back later than the 28 days limited for variation of a sentence under section 11 (2) of the Courts Act 1971,[1] and additional disqualification for six months consecutive was ordered.

On appeal against the additional disqualification on the ground that it was imposed out of time and therefore without
jurisdiction since the court's power to defer or vary a sentence G
was limited to the provisions in the Acts of 1971 and 1973:—

Held, dismissing the appeal, that the Crown Court had jurisdiction at common law to postpone passing the whole or part of a sentence if circumstances made it necessary; that the circumstances made it desirable to deal with the substantive sentence at once and postpone what might have to be done in addition, rather than to postpone the whole of the sentence
until all the necessary material was available and, accordingly, H
the Crown Court had jurisdiction and had correctly exercised its discretion to postpone part of the sentence (post, pp. 109G—110B).

Reg. v. *Ingle* [1974] 3 All E.R. 811, C.A. applied.

Reg. v. *Fairhead* [1975] 2 All E.R. 737, C.A. and *Reg.* v. *Talgarth Justices, Ex parte Bithell* [1973] 1 W.L.R. 1327, D.C. distinguished.

[1] Courts Act 1971, s. 11 (2): see post, p. 108H.

A The following cases are referred to in the judgment:

Reg. v. *Fairhead* [1975] 2 All E.R. 737, C.A.
Reg. v. *Ingle* [1974] 3 All E.R. 811; 59 Cr.App.R. 306, C.A.
Reg. v. *Talgarth Justices, Ex parte Bithell* [1973] 1 W.L.R. 1327; [1973] 2 All E.R. 717, D.C.

The following additional case was cited in argument:

B *Reg.* v. *Northampton Justices, Ex parte Nicholson* [1974] R.T.R. 97, D.C.

Appeal against sentence.

On April 18, 1975, at Manchester Crown Court (Judge B. H. Gerrard)
the appellant, Kevin Annesley, appeared on committal in custody for
sentence in respect of offences on December 20, 1974, for which he was
C sentenced as follows: (1) taking a motor vehicle without consent, contrary
to section 12 (1) of the Theft Act 1968—two years' imprisonment and an
order for licence endorsement under section 101 of, and paragraph 2 of
Part III of Schedule 4 to, the Road Traffic Act 1972; (2) driving contrary
to section 6 (1) of the Act of 1972—three months' imprisonment con-
current, and orders for disqualification for three years and licence
endorsement under sections 93 (1) and 101 (1); (3) using a motor vehicle
D contrary to section 143—seven days' imprisonment concurrent and an
order for licence endorsement under section 93 (1). The appellant's
driving licence was not before the court and, in the absence of informa-
tion as to the applicability of section 93 (3), he was informed that, if it
was found that section 93 (3) was applicable, he would be brought back.
On May 13, 1975, he applied for leave to appeal against the severity of
E the sentence. On June 6, 1975, he was brought before the Crown Court
and an order was made under section 93 (3) and (5) for him to be
disqualified for six months consecutive to the three years ordered on
April 18; no similar order was made in respect of the other offences.
The grounds of appeal were, in relation to the sentence of imprisonment
and three years' disqualification, that they were harsh and excessive in
view of the circumstances and wrong in principle, and, in relation to the
F consecutive six months' disqualification, inter alia, that the judge was
wrong in refusing an application that the court had no power on June 6
to "vary" the sentence imposed on him by the same court on April 18,
more than 28 days having elapsed, since the powers of the court to vary
were limited to "within 28 days" by section 11 (2) of the Courts Act
1971, a period which for the relevant purposes was absolute; and, in the
G alternative, the judge was wrong in refusing the appellant's application
that dealing with another sentence in respect of another matter, namely,
"totting-up," seven weeks after sentencing in respect of all other matters,
was in contravention of the recognised practice in postponing sentence,
and was wrong in adding to his sentences on April 18, the words "It
may be if your driving licence is found and totted up that I may have to
have you brought back in respect of that totting-up. If I have to, you
H will be brought back" the onus being on the prosecution to have available
to the court all matters readily available to them in respect of the
appellant's record and, in any event, a time limit of within 28 days should
have been added. On September 1, 1975, the appeal was before the court
(Geoffrey Lane L.J., Eveleigh and May JJ.) when only the appellant
was represented (J. V. Williamson for him), the appeal against severity of
sentence was allowed, a period of six months' imprisonment and two
years' disqualification were substituted, and the point raised on the six

months' consecutive disqualification was adjourned for hearing with the A
Crown represented. Only the appeal on the totting-up disqualification calls for report. The appeal was argued on November 17, 1975, when Bridge L.J. stated that the appeal would be dismissed and the reasons would be put into writing.

The facts are stated in the judgment.

Francis Coles for the appellant. B
Leslie Portnoy for the Crown.

Cur. adv. vult.

November 21. BRISTOW J. read the following judgment of the court. On February 3, 1975, the appellant, Kevin Annesley, then aged 23, pleaded guilty at Manchester City magistrates' court to the following offences: C
(1) taking away a motor vehicle without the owner's consent; (2) driving with blood-alcohol concentration above the prescribed limit; (3) driving without insurance. On March 25, 1975, he was committed for sentence to the Crown Court, and on April 18 was sentenced by Judge Gerrard as follows: (1) two years' imprisonment, licence endorsed; (2) three months' imprisonment concurrent and a three year disqualification, licence endorsed;
(3) seven days' imprisonment concurrent, licence endorsed. D

At the hearing in the Crown Court, the appellant's driving licence was missing, and the judge was not in a position to deal with the problem of further disqualification under the "totting-up" provisions of section 93 (3) of the Road Traffic Act 1972. Having delivered the substantive sentences for the three offences, the judge addressed the appellant in the following terms: E

> "It may be if your driving licence is found and totted up that I will have to have you brought back in respect of that totting-up. If I have to, you will be brought back."

On June 6, 1975, more than 28 days later, the appellant was brought back. His driving licence was still missing, as indeed it is now, but his previous record with the assistance of the computer had been found to F
contain two previous convictions which caused the totting-up provisions of section 93 (3) to bite. Judge Gerrard accordingly imposed a further period of disqualification of six months.

On September 1, before another division of this court, the appellant's appeal against sentence was heard, and the period of two years for the first offence was reduced to six months. The period of disqualification of three years for driving with excess alcohol in the blood was reduced to G
two years. The court adjourned consideration of the question raised in respect of the further disqualification of six months under section 93 (3), granted the appellant legal aid to cover the adjourned hearing, and directed that the Crown should be represented on the adjourned hearing. It is accordingly only this aspect of the matter which has been argued before us. H

The appellant's point, vigorously argued by Mr. Coles on his behalf, is this. Section 11 (2) of the Courts Act 1971, which set up the Crown Court in place of courts of assize and quarter sessions, provides:

> ". . . a sentence imposed, or other order made, by the Crown Court when dealing with an offender may be varied or rescinded by the Crown Court within the period of 28 days beginning with the day on which the sentence or other order was imposed or made . . ."

Mr. Coles submits that this express provision involves the consequence that the Crown Court does not enjoy the common law jurisdiction enjoyed by courts of assize and quarter sessions to adjourn sentence. He submits that the Crown Court can only put off sentence either in pursuance of the power conferred by section 11 (2), or under the power conferred by section 1 of the Powers of Criminal Courts Act 1973. It is clear that the judge was not exercising his power under section 1 for this requires the consent of the offender, and he did not invite the appellant to consent. Therefore, because more than 28 days elapsed between April 18 and June 6, there was no jurisdiction to add the six months' disqualification under section 93 of the Road Traffic Act 1972, and that part of the sentence, says Mr. Coles, must be quashed.

Mr. Coles relied on the decision of this court in *Reg.* v. *Fairhead* [1975] 2 All E.R. 737. In that case the trial judge disqualified the offender on the spot but deferred passing sentence under the statutory powers given by section 1 of the Act of 1973. On appeal this court held that to " split " the order of the court in this way was not only bad practice, but also contrary to the statutory power conferred by the section. This court stressed the importance of care being taken to make clear what course the court was following: see the judgment of James L.J. at p. 739. It is to be noted that in *Fairhead's* case sentence was put off for much longer than 28 days. But it was not argued that, if the postponement was not under the powers conferred by section 1 of the Act of 1973, section 11 (2) of the Act of 1971 would have deprived the court of jurisdiction to pass sentence after more than 28 days.

Reference was also made to *Reg.* v. *Talgarth Justices, Ex parte Bithell* [1973] 1 W.L.R. 1327. In that case the Divisional Court held that there was no power under section 14 (3) of the Magistrates' Courts Act 1952 for justices to adjourn after conviction and before sentence for more than four weeks or to adjourn part of a sentence. Lord Widgery C.J. observed, at p. 1329, that it is " in any event . . . bad sentencing practice to deal on different occasions with different elements in the disposal of a single case." But he also said, at p. 1329, that the court would not have quashed the justices' decision on certiorari merely because it was not in accordance with good sentencing practice.

Mr. Portnoy for the Crown submits that the fallacy underlying the argument for the appellant is to suppose that the only powers under which sentence can be put off by the Crown Court are those under section 11 of the Courts Act 1971 or section 1 of the Powers of Criminal Courts Act 1973. He points to section 1 (7) of the Act of 1973 and section 8 of, and Schedule 1 to, the Act of 1971, as showing that the common law power vested in superior courts of putting off sentences or some part of a sentence has not been removed. *Reg.* v. *Ingle* [1974] 3 All E.R. 811 is an authority to this effect: see the judgment of Roskill L.J., at p. 815.

In the judgment of this court it is clear from these authorities and statutory provisions that the Crown Court still enjoys the common law jurisdiction vested in its predecessors to put off passing the whole of a sentence, or indeed part of a sentence, if the circumstances make it necessary. While accepting the proposition that to take two bites at the sentencing cherry is bad practice, there may be circumstances in which it may be very desirable, when all the material necessary to complete all elements of a sentencing problem is not immediately available, to deal with the substantive sentence at once and postpone

what may have to be done in addition, rather than postpone the whole A
of the sentence till all the material is to hand.

So here. This court thinks it would have been unnecessarily cruel to keep the appellant in the dark as to whether, and if so for how long, he was to receive a custodial sentence, simply because the material necessary for dealing with "totting-up" under section 93 (3) was not immediately available, and must take some time to obtain, up to three weeks in the ordinary way. It took longer than 28 days to obtain in this case, B
because the appellant did his motoring under more than one name. We think that the judge had jurisdiction to do what he did, and that in the circumstances of this case it was not bad practice for him to do it.

The appeal against the additional six months' disqualification accordingly fails.

Appeal dismissed. C

Solicitors: *Pariser & Co., Manchester; D. S. Gandy, Manchester.*

L. N. W.

D

[COURT OF APPEAL]

* REGINA v. CATO

REGINA v. MORRIS

REGINA v. DUDLEY

E

1975 Oct. 13, 14, 15 — Lord Widgery C.J., O'Connor and Jupp JJ.

Crime — Homicide — Manslaughter — Victim dying after being injected with heroin—Whether heroin caused or contributed to death—Consent of victim to injections—Whether unlawful and malicious administration of "noxious thing"—Offences against the Person Act 1861 (24 & 25 *Vict., c.* 100), *s.* 23 F

The appellant with three friends, M, D and F, went from a public house after closing time to the house that they shared. F produced a bag containing heroin and some syringes and invited the others to have a "fix." They injected each other a number of times until M and D went to bed. The appellant G
and F continued, each taking his own syringe and filling it with a mixture of heroin and water to his own requirements, then giving the other the syringe to inject him. The following morning the appellant and F were found apparently asleep but subsequently it became clear that they were having difficulty in breathing. The appellant was revived by first aid but F died, the cause of death being that his respiratory system ceased to function as a result of intoxication from H
drugs. The appellant was charged with manslaughter and with administering a noxious thing contrary to section 23 of the Offences against the Person Act 1861.[1] Medical evidence was given at the trial that there was no evidence of disease causing death; that there was a quantity of morphine in F's body which was consistent with the injection of heroin but which was not sufficient to have been the sole cause of

[1] Offences against the Person Act 1861, s. 23: see post, p. 119E–F.

A death; that there was no morphine in F's blood but that the
symptoms before death and the appearance of his body were
consistent with death resulting from injections of heroin. M
and D gave evidence that they thought that the symptoms
shown by the appellant and F had been caused by heroin
poisoning. The judge directed the jury to consider whether the
injection of heroin caused, contributed to or accelerated F's
death but did not direct them that the cause or contribution
B should be substantial. He also directed that F's consent to
the injections of heroin was irrelevant to the charge of man-
slaughter. The appellant was convicted on both counts and
was sentenced to four years' imprisonment concurrent on each
count.

On appeal against conviction on the grounds, inter alia, that
the judge had misdirected the jury on the issue of causation
and on whether F's consent was relevant, and that the require-
C ments of section 23 of the Offences against the Person Act
1861 that the substance administered must be " noxious " and
administered " maliciously " were not satisfied:—

Held, dismissing the appeal, (1) that the prosecution had to
prove that the injection of heroin was a cause of death and
not merely de minimis; that, although the judge had not
expressly directed the jury that the injection of heroin had to
be a substantial cause of death, the jury must have realised that
D something more than a de minimis contribution was necessary
and, accordingly, they had not been misled when considering
the question of causation and there was ample evidence to
support their verdict of manslaughter (post, p. 117C–D).

(2) That although F's consent to the injection of heroin
might be relevant to consideration of whether the appellant
had acted with recklessness or gross negligence, the victim's
consent was not generally a defence to a charge of man-
E slaughter and in the circumstances of the present case the
judge's direction to the jury that consent was irrelevant was not
misleading and did not render the conviction unsafe or un-
satisfactory (post, pp. 117F–G, 118B–C).

Per curiam. Injecting a person with a mixture of heroin and
water, which at the time of the injection and for the purposes
of the injection the accused had unlawfully taken into his
possession, was an unlawful act in relation to a charge of
F manslaughter (post, p. 118G–H).

(3) That the use of heroin was potentially harmful and,
therefore, it was a " noxious " thing for the purposes of section
23 of the Offences against the Person Act 1861; that proof of
foresight of consequence was not required for a finding that the
noxious substance was administered " maliciously " where the
act was a direct one and accordingly, since the appellant had
deliberately inserted a syringe directly into F's body knowing
G that it contained a noxious substance, his conviction for admin-
istering a noxious thing contrary to section 23 would be
upheld (post, pp. 119H, 120H).

Reg. v. *Cunningham* [1957] 2 Q.B. 396, C.C.A. distinguished.

The following case is referred to in the judgment of the court:

Reg. v. *Cunningham* [1957] 2 Q.B. 396; [1957] 3 W.L.R. 76; [1957] 2 All E.R.
H 412, C.C.A.

The following additional cases were cited in argument:

Reg. v. *Blaue* [1975] 1 W.L.R. 1411; [1975] 3 All E.R. 446, C.A.

Reg. v. *Harris (Janet)* [1968] 1 W.L.R. 769; [1968] 2 All E.R. 49, C.A.

Reg. v. *Hennah* (1877) 13 Cox C.C. 547.

Reg. v. *Instan* [1893] 1 Q.B. 450

Reg. v. *Lamb* [1967] 2 Q.B. 981; [1967] 3 W.L.R. 888; [1967] 2 All E.R. 1282, C.A.

Reg. v. *Smith* [1959] 2 Q.B. 35; [1959] 2 W.L.R. 623; [1959] 2 All E.R. 193, Ct.-M.A.C. A
Rex v. *Donovan* [1934] 2 K.B. 498, C.C.A.
Rex v. *Dyson* [1908] 2 K.B. 454, C.C.A.

APPEAL against conviction.

In June 1975 at St. Albans Crown Court (Thesiger J.) the appellant, Ronald Philip Cato, was convicted of the manslaughter of Anthony Farmer B
and of administering a noxious thing to him contrary to section 23 of the Offences against the Person Act 1861. He was sentenced to four years' imprisonment concurrent on both counts. The applicants, Neil Adrian Morris and Melvin Dudley, were convicted of assisting an offender contrary to section 4 (1) of the Criminal Law Act 1967. The applicant Morris was sentenced to Borstal training and Dudley was sentenced to two years' imprisonment. They applied for leave to appeal against sentence and C
conviction on the ground that their convictions should be quashed if the appellant was not guilty of the offences charged.

The appellant appealed against his convictions on the grounds, inter alia, that the judge had misdirected the jury on the issue of causation and on the relevance or otherwise of Anthony Farmer's consent to the injections of heroin; that heroin was not a "noxious" thing within section 23 of the D
Offences against the Person Act 1861 and that the judge had failed to direct the jury that "maliciously" in section 23 included foresight of consequences. He also applied for leave to appeal against sentence.

The facts are stated in the judgment of the court.

Louis Blom-Cooper Q.C. and *Geoffrey Robertson* for the appellant.
Anthony Ansell for the applicants. E
David Jeffreys for the Crown.

LORD WIDGERY C.J. Following a trial at St. Albans Crown Court in June 1975 the following sentences were imposed upon the appellant, Ronald Philip Cato, and the applicants, Neil Adrian Morris, and Melvin Dudley, in respect of counts in the indictment. The appellant was sentenced F
to four years' imprisonment on count 1 for manslaughter of Anthony Farmer. He was also sentenced to four years concurrent on a charge under section 23 of the Offences against the Person Act 1861 of administering a noxious thing. The two applicants were not concerned with the manslaughter charge directly. Their offences were of assisting the appellant in what might be described as a "cover-up" of the death of Farmer. In respect of those offences the applicant Morris was sentenced to Borstal G
training and the applicant Dudley to two years' imprisonment, but in respect of each of them a condition precedent to it was the conviction of the appellant on the manslaughter charge or the charge under section 23. Unless that could be established, then the offences charged against the applicants did not arise. Equally, it is accepted by their counsel that if the appellant's conviction for manslaughter or administering a noxious thing is upheld, H
then the applicants have nothing further to say in regard to their conviction in this case. Thus, nearly everything in regard to guilt or innocence revolves around the appellant's conviction for manslaughter.

The victim was a young man called Anthony Farmer. The events leading up to his death occurred on July 25, 1974. On that day the appellant and Farmer had been in each other's company for most of the day. The evidence suggests certain intervals when they were apart, but by and large

A they seem to have been together all that day, and they spent much of the
day with the applicants as well. All four of them at that time were living at
a house, 34, Russell Street, and on July 25 their activities brought them
to the Crown public house where they were until closing time, and after
closing time they went back to 34, Russell Street.

There were others living in the house. They went to bed, and the four
(that is to say the appellant, the applicants and Farmer) remained down-
B stairs for a time. The moment came when Farmer produced a bag of white
powder and some syringes and invited the others to have a " fix " with him;
and so they did. The white powder was put in its bag on the mantelpiece,
the syringes were distributed amongst the four who were to participate, and
the procedure which they adopted (which may or may not be a common
one) was to pair off so that each could do the actual act of injection into
C the other half of his pair. Following this procedure the applicants paired
off together and so did the appellant and Farmer. All four had a number
of injections following this procedure, but the time came when the applicants
went to bed, leaving the appellant and Farmer downstairs in the sitting room.
The appellant and Farmer continued to give each other these injections from
time to time right through the night.

The actual method, which I have probably described sufficiently already,
D may deserve a moment's repetition because so much hinges upon it. The
method, as I have already indicated, was that each would take his own
syringe. He would fill it to his own taste with whatever mixture of powder
and water he thought proper. He would then give his syringe to the other
half of his pair (in this case Farmer would give his syringe to the appellant)
and the other half of the pair would conduct the actual act of injection. It
E is important to notice that the strength of the mixture to be used was
entirely dictated by the person who was to receive it because he prepared his
own syringe; but it is also to be noticed that the actual act of injection was
done by the other half of the pair, which of course has a very important
influence on this case when one comes to causation.

When the following morning came Farmer and the appellant were still
F downstairs. They were apparently fast asleep, although everybody thought
they were well enough at 8 o'clock in the morning when they were seen.
But as the next hour or two passed it became apparent that they were both
in difficulties. The appellant indeed was having difficulty in breathing, and
probably his life was saved only because somebody gave him some rudi-
mentary first aid. No one was able to do the same for Farmer, and by
11 o'clock Farmer was dead, and the cause of death was that his respiratory
G system ceased to function consequent upon intoxication from drugs.

When it was discovered Farmer was dead steps were taken to try and
cover up by the two applicants and I need not deal with them in detail at
this stage. But in the end the full story came out and the charges to which
I have already referred were brought against these three men in consequence
of those actions.

H At the trial there was quite a volume of expert evidence. First, there
was a pathologist who conducted the elementary, if I may say so, and
preliminary examination of the body and discovered there was insufficient
evidence of natural disease to account for death and that an autopsy would
be necessary. Then there was other further and detailed investigation of
specimens of various parts of the body which showed (I am condensing this
quite a lot) a quantity of morphine in the body consistent with the injections
of heroin which had been taken, according to their confessions, through

the night. But it was noteworthy, so the expert said, that there was no morphine in the blood—a pointer, as we understand it, to a longer interval between the injection and the death than would have appeared to have occurred having regard to the recital of the facts that I have given. Furthermore, Dr. Robinson, who was called on behalf of the defence, strongly made the point that there was not enough morphine visibly present in the samples to account for death because it was not a fatal dose. She had not seen the samples or worked on them herself because she had come into the case later than that, but she clearly took the view that although there was morphine in the body, and although the morphine may have contributed to the death, it was not exclusively responsible for it because there was, as she said, a missing factor; and she concluded that there was a missing factor because in her view the size of the dose received by the deceased Farmer was insufficient to cause death.

The judge left the manslaughter charge to the jury on the two alternative bases which the Crown had suggested, and it will be appreciated at once what they were. The first alternative was that the death was caused by the injection and the consequent intrusion of morphine into the body, and that was an unlawful act so that the killing was the result of an unlawful act and manslaughter on that footing. Alternatively, it was said that a verdict of guilty would be justified on the footing that there had been no unlawful act, but that the injection of heroin had been done with recklessness or gross negligence, which of course would be sufficient to sustain the conviction of manslaughter.

The judge in his summing up put it this way:

> " Now, manslaughter in law is causing or contributing to the causing or accelerating (that is the hastening on) the death of a human being quite inadvertently by doing an unlawful and dangerous act, or alternatively, by doing a lawful act with gross negligence, that is to say, recklessly." He gets the alternatives there perfectly well. " The consent of the victim is quite immaterial, quite irrelevant, just as it is in the not uncommon case of manslaughter, such as in the next case I have to try. . . . The prosecution say here that this was manslaughter in either of two ways, that is to say, either death was caused, although quite inadvertently, by an unlawful and dangerous act, or, alternatively, by doing an act with gross negligence, recklessly."

In amplification of that direction, which is repeated more than once, the judge quite early in the course of his summing up handed to the jury six questions which he had written out for their consideration, and he told the jury that they should ask themselves these six questions, and that if they answered " yes " to all of them, then the verdict should be guilty. These were the questions in their original version:

> " (1) Did [the appellant] take possession of some heroin in a syringe and then inject the contents of the syringe into Anthony Farmer? (2) Did such injection by [the appellant] endanger the life of Anthony Farmer? (3) Did the injection of heroin by [the appellant] contribute to or accelerate the death of Anthony Farmer? (4) Was the heroin so injected likely to do harm to Anthony Farmer, although not necessarily serious harm? (5) Did [the appellant] realise (a) that it was unlawful for him or Farmer to be in possession of heroin; (b) that heroin was likely, if injected, to do some harm to the deceased Anthony Farmer? "

A The sixth question was introduced by a statement of the judge that this was a slightly fresh question because it dealt with the other approach to the case suggested by the prosecution:

> "Was the conduct of [the appellant], in respect of the injection, grossly negligent or, in other words, reckless?"

Consequent upon some argument later in the course of the hearing the
B judge made two amendments to those questions. For question (1) he substituted:

> "Did he"—that is the appellant—"take into his hand, so as to control and carry out the injection, a syringe which contained heroin and also water which was mixed and then supplied the dose by injection to Tony Farmer?"

C In question (3) he amended the phraseology in this way. He inserted the word "cause" so that the question read: "Did such injection of heroin by [the appellant] cause, contribute to or accelerate the death of Anthony Farmer?" The previous version, it will be remembered, did not contain the word "cause."

So those six questions were delivered to the jury for them to consider,
D not, as it turned out, to produce a special verdict, but for them to consider with an instruction from the judge that if they could answer them all "yes," they must convict of manslaughter, and that if they could not answer them all "yes," they should come back and ask for further guidance. Of course that last direction of the judge is obviously important. The jury did not come back and ask for further guidance, and if they were following the letter of his instruction, and there is really no reason to suggest they did not on
E this point, the fact that they did not come back must mean that they were able to answer all the six questions in the affirmative. So much for a broad outline of the circumstances in which these charges were brought and the developments at the trial.

We can now turn to look more precisely at Mr. Blom-Cooper's submissions in supporting the appeal against conviction. We have had a long
F and very helpful argument from Mr. Blom-Cooper in which all the features of this difficult, and in some respects intriguing, case have been considered. It seems to us that the first and most important single factor to which he directed our attention was concerned with causation, that is to say with the link alleged to exist between the injection of heroin and the death of Farmer.

G First of all, he invited us to look at the evidence of causation, and he pointed out that the medical evidence did not at any point say "This morphine killed Farmer"; the actual link of that kind was not present. The witnesses were hesitant to express such a view and often recoiled from it, saying it was not for them to state the cause of death. It is perfectly true, as Mr. Blom-Cooper says, that the expert evidence did not in positive terms provide a link, but it was never intended to. The expert witnesses
H here spoke to factual situations, and the conclusions and deductions therefrom were for the jury. The first question was: was there sufficient evidence upon which the jury could conclude, as they must have concluded, that adequate causation was present?

When one looks at the evidence it is important to realise that no other cause of Farmer's death was supplied. Dr. Robinson thought that there might have been another drug, and she said at one stage it might have been cocaine, but there was never any cocaine found in the body. The only cause of death actually supplied by the evidence was morphine. No A natural disease was present and no other drug was identified. Furthermore, the symptoms and the external appearance of the body, and the nature of the final terminal cause, was consistent with poison by the administration of heroin in the way which was described. Further, when the people who lived in the house were giving their evidence about the death of Farmer, it was, as the judge pointed out, quite clear that they thought there was no doubt about what the cause had been. It may be of course that young people B living in those circumstances know a great deal about the symptoms of heroin poisoning; I know not.

The judge in the summing up said:

> "Members of the jury, it seems to me that that evidence about the condition of the appellant when he was senseless on the floor and was put to bed, what he looked like and so forth is quite material in regard C to the cause of Tony Farmer's death because [the appellant] and he had both been dosing themselves with the same sort of thing, in the same sort of way, in the same sort of number of times, and that is clear evidence in this particular case. The opinions of the people in the house is of course not medical opinion but everybody there seemed to draw the conclusion that probably the heroin injections had caused both of them to be in the condition they were in." D

That is an important and proper conclusion, if the jury thought fit to adopt it, because the fact that the appellant very nearly suffered the same fate as Farmer, and showed the same kind of symptoms following the same kind of injections, is a pointer to indicate that the cause of Farmer's condition was the heroin which he had taken; and, furthermore, the jury were entitled, if E they thought fit, to be influenced by the fact that the non-medical evidence from the residents was of the kind which the judge related.

Of course behind this whole question of the sufficiency of evidence of causation is the fact that it was not necessary for the prosecution to prove that the heroin was the only cause. As a matter of law, it was sufficient if the prosecution could establish that it was *a* cause, provided it was a cause outside the de minimis range, and effectively bearing upon the acceleration of F the moment of the victim's death. When one has that in mind it is, we think, really possible to say that if the jury had been directed to look for heroin as a cause, not de minimis but a cause of substance, and they came back with a verdict of not guilty, the verdict could really be described as a perverse one. The whole background of the evidence was the other way and there certainly was ample evidence, given a proper direction, upon which a charge G of manslaughter could be supported.

But what about the proper direction? It will be noted that in none of the versions which I have quoted of the judge's direction on this point, nor in any of those which I have not quoted which appear in the summing up, is there any reference to it being necessary for the cause to be a substantial one. It is said in clear terms in one of the six questions that the jury can consider whether the administration of the heroin was a cause or contributed H to or accelerated the death, and in precise terms the word "contributed" is not qualified to show that a substantial contribution is required.

Mr. Blom-Cooper, whose eagle eye misses nothing, sees here, and seeks to exploit here, what is a misdirection on the part of the judge. In other words, taking the judge's words literally it would be possible for the jury to bring in a verdict of guilty of manslaughter even though the contribution was not of substance.

A Before pursuing that, it is worth reminding oneself that some of the more recent dicta in the textbooks about this point do not support as strongly as was once the case the theory that the contribution must be substantial. In *Smith and Hogan Criminal Law*, 3rd ed. (1973), p. 217 there is this rather interesting extract:

> "It is commonly said by judges and writers that, while the accused's
> B act need not be the sole cause of the death, it must be a substantial cause. This appears to mean only that a minute contribution to the cause of death will not entail responsibility. It may therefore be misleading to direct a jury that D is not liable unless his conduct was a 'substantial' cause. Killing is merely an acceleration of death and factors which produce a very trivial acceleration will be ignored."

C Whether that be so or not, and we do not propose to give that passage the court's blessing today at all events, if one looks at the circumstances of the present case with any real sense of reality, we think there can be no doubt that when the judge was talking about contribution the jury knew perfectly well that he was talking about something more than the mere de minimis contribution. We have given this point particular care in our consideration of the case because it worried us to some extent originally, but we do feel in
D the end, having looked at all the circumstances, that there could not have been any question in this case of the jury making the mistake of thinking that the contribution would suffice if it were de minimis. Therefore in our judgment there is no substance in Mr. Blom-Cooper's attack on the basis of causation, whether it be an attack on the available evidence or upon the judge's treatment of that evidence.

E The next main point with which the court would wish to deal is the fact that the judge on more than one occasion, as the extracts which I have read show, told the jury that Farmer's consent was quite irrelevant. Occasionally he says the consent of Farmer is no defence to the charge, but more often he says the consent of Farmer is quite irrelevant. Mr. Blom-Cooper says that that was a misdirection because he says there are two factors, two aspects of this case, which have to be considered separately.
F It may be that if one asks oneself whether the consent of the victim could provide a defence to a charge of manslaughter, the answer should be a vivid "no." In general, as a simple proposition, where this kind of injury is done by one person to another the consent of the person injured is not a defence. On the other hand, one of the matters which the jury at some stage had to consider in the present case was whether the appellant had
G acted with recklessness or gross negligence, and Mr. Blom-Cooper says, and we think rightly, that when considering that aspect of the case the consent of Farmer is something which could not be wholly excluded.

In those circumstances we have tried to look at these two aspects of the matter separately. We think that the judge, when saying so positively that the consent of Farmer was irrelevant or was no defence, was antici-
H pating a question in the jury's mind that they might have been uncertain as to whether it would be a defence or not. One has to realise that laymen will often think that a person who dies in Farmer's circumstances will not produce a charge of manslaughter against his friend if in fact he consented to what was being done to him and the friend did not attempt to do more than that. We think it could very well have been the case that the jury might have asked the judge directly "Is consent a defence?," and if they had, he would have had to say "no," and his saying "no" in the course

of his summing up appears to be an anticipation of that kind of question A
in the jury's mind.

But of course in a perfect world the judge, when faced with this question, would have dealt with both aspects of the matter in contrast. He would have said "It is not a defence in the sense that merely by proving Farmer's permission the matter is at an end; but when you come to consider the questions of gross negligence or recklessness of course you must take it into
account." Whether he would have gone further we very much doubt. If a B
persistent juror had said "Well, what do you mean by 'take into account'? What have we got to do?," it may very well be that the judge would be stumped at that point and really could not do any more than say "You must take it into account." Lawyers understand what it means, but jurors very often do not, and although I have taken more time to discuss this point
than perhaps it really requires, we have come to the conclusion that there is C
not here any matter which gives us cause to think that the conviction may be unsafe or unsatisfactory. We support the judge in dealing head-on with the question of whether consent was a defence or not, and we do not think that he could usefully have said much more in regard to gross negligence or recklessness in order to avoid any possible confusion at that end of the scale.

The next matter, I think, is the unlawful act. Of course on the first
approach to manslaughter in this case it was necessary for the prosecution D
to prove that Farmer had been killed in the course of an unlawful act. Strangely enough, or it may seem strange to most of us, although the possession or supply of heroin is an offence, it is not an offence to take it, and although supplying it is an offence, it is not an offence to administer it. At least it is not made to be an offence, and so Mr. Blom-Cooper says there
was no unlawful act here. That which the appellant did, namely taking E
Farmer's syringe already charged and injecting the mixture into Farmer as directed, is not an unlawful act, says Mr. Blom-Cooper, because there is nothing there which is an offence against the Misuse of Drugs Act 1971, and when he shows us the terms of the section it seems that that is absolutely right.

Of course if the conviction on count 2 remains (that is the charge under F
section 23 of the Offences against the Person Act 1861 of administering a noxious thing), then that in itself would be an unlawful act. The prohibition in that statute would be enough in itself, and it is probably right to say that as we are going to uphold the conviction on count 2, as will appear presently, that really answers the problem and destroys the basis of Mr. Blom-Cooper's argument.

But since he went to such trouble with the argument, and in respect for G
it, we think we ought to say that had it not been possible to rely on the charge under section 23 of the Offences against the Person Act 1861, we think there would have been an unlawful act here, and we think the unlawful act would be described as injecting the deceased Farmer with a mixture of heroin and water which at the time of the injection and for the
purposes of the injection the accused had unlawfully taken into his posses- H
sion. As I say, it is not really necessary to rely on that because of our views on the other count, but we would not wish it to be thought that we had felt that Mr. Blom-Cooper's argument on this point would have succeeded had it been effectively open to him. So much then for the unlawful act.

Lastly, on the first count is the question of recklessness. Of course if the jury convicted on the second approach, the reckless approach, they

A must have considered whether there was recklessness. They were indeed instructed so to do. Mr. Blom-Cooper makes the complaint that the judge has not dealt sufficiently with this aspect of the case to give the jury a proper, fair and adequate direction about it. Of course he recognises, he is far too experienced, if I may say so, not to recognise, that he cannot expect every judge in the hurly-burly of every case to sum up with the polished perfection which counsel can produce in this court some months
B later. But even so, making all allowances for that, the complaint is made that the judge did not do anything to help the jury as to the meaning of recklessness, and in particular that the judge did not refer to one aspect of the appellant's evidence which might have proved of some importance.

The appellant when pressed as to his knowledge of the potentiality of heroin when injected, said that he knew that it might give rise to addiction,
C but he had no idea that it could give rise to death or serious bodily harm. Of course in deciding whether the appellant had himself acted recklessly one would have to have regard to the fact, if it was accepted, that he did not know about the potentiality of the drug. It is said that this was not really sufficiently provided for in the summing up.

We think it was. After all, recklessness is a perfectly simple English word. Its meaning is well known and it is in common use. There is a
D limit to the extent to which the judge in the summing up is expected to teach the jury the use of ordinary English words. Although we have listened to Mr. Blom-Cooper on this point, with respect, we do not find that criticism justifies our concluding that the manslaughter verdict was in any measure unsafe or unsatisfactory, so we shall dismiss the appeal so far as that conviction is concerned.

E I have already given away the fact that a similar consequence will follow in respect of the offence under section 23 of the Offences against the Person Act 1861, but I must just go back and look at the reasons for it. The offence under section 23 of the Offences against the Person Act 1861 is in these terms:

> "Whosoever shall unlawfully and maliciously administer to or cause to be administered to or taken by any other person any poison or
> F other destructive or noxious thing, so as thereby to endanger the life of such person, or so as thereby to inflict upon such person any grievous bodily harm, shall be guilty of an offence. . . ."

Thus, a number of things have to be proved in order to establish the offence, and the two which are relevant to Mr. Blom-Cooper's argument are "maliciously" and "noxious." The thing must be a "noxious thing"
G and it must be administered "maliciously." What is a noxious thing, and in particular is heroin a noxious thing? The authorities show that an article is not to be described as noxious for present purposes merely because it has a potentiality for harm if taken in an overdose. There are many articles of value in common use which may be harmful in overdose, and it is clear on the authorities when looking at them that one cannot describe
H an article as noxious merely because it has that aptitude. On the other hand, if an article is liable to injure in common use, not when an overdose in the sense of an accidental excess is used but is liable to cause injury in common use, should it then not be regarded as a noxious thing for present purposes?

When one has regard to the potentiality of heroin in the circumstances which we read and hear about in our courts today we have no hesitation in saying that heroin is a noxious thing and we do not think that arguments are open to an accused person in a case such as the present, whereby he may say "Well, the deceased was experienced in taking heroin; his tolerance was high," and generally to indicate that the heroin was unlikely to do any particular harm in a particular circumstance. We think there can be no doubt, and it should be said clearly, that heroin is a noxious thing for the purposes of section 23 of the Act of 1861.

"What about maliciously"? Mr. Blom-Cooper says that "maliciously" requires some foresight into the consequences, and he has referred us to *Reg.* v. *Cunningham* [1957] 2 Q.B. 396 as authority for that proposition. It was a rather unusual case. The prisoner had stolen a gas meter and its contents from the cellar of a house, the contents no doubt having been money in a slot machine. He did it in a rough and unskilled way and left an escape of gas from the position which the meter had occupied. The gas percolated up into the higher reaches of the house, and eventually got into the bedroom of an elderly lady who was subjected to considerable exposure to coal gas as a result of what had happened. When the prisoner was charged with an offence under section 23 the question arose as to whether the requirement of malice had been satisfied. Byrne J., giving the judgment of the Court of Criminal Appeal, said, at p. 399:

> "Mr. Brodie argued, first, that mens rea of some kind is necessary. Secondly, that the nature of the mens rea required is that the appellant must intend to do the particular kind of harm that was done, or, alternatively, that he must foresee that that harm may occur yet nevertheless continue recklessly to do the act. Thirdly, that the judge misdirected the jury as to the meaning of the word 'maliciously' . . . We have considered those cases, and we have also considered, in the light of those cases, the following principle which was propounded by the late Professor C. S. Kenny in the first edition of his Outlines of Criminal Law published in 1902 and repeated at p. 186 of the 16th edition edited by Mr. J. W. Cecil Turner and published in 1952: 'In any statutory definition of a crime, malice must be taken not in the old vague sense of wickedness in general but as requiring either (1) An actual intention to do the particular kind of harm that in fact was done; or (2) recklessness as to whether such harm should occur or not (i.e., the accused has foreseen that the particular kind of harm might be done and yet has gone on to take the risk of it). It is neither limited to nor does it indeed require any ill will towards the person injured . . .' We think that this is an accurate statement of the law."

No doubt this is correct in the *Cunningham* type of case where the injury to the victim was done indirectly: done, as it was in that case, by the escape of gas making itself felt in a wholly different part of the house. No doubt if the injury to the victim is indirect, then the element of foresight arises and the element of foresight will be taken from the words of Byrne J. in the *Cunningham* case. But these problems do not arise when the act complained of is done directly to the person of the victim, as it was in this case. We think in this case where the act was entirely a direct one that the requirement of malice is satisfied if the syringe was deliberately inserted into the body of Farmer, as it undoubtedly was, and if the appellant at a time when he so inserted the syringe knew that the syringe contained a noxious substance. That is enough, we think, in this type of direct injury case to satisfy the requirement of maliciousness.

A I am conscious of the fact that I have not done justice to Mr. Blom-Cooper's argument, but those are the reasons why we conclude that the convictions against the appellant must stand and as a consequence, for the reasons I have described, so must the convictions against the applicants.

[Counsel then addressed the court on the applications for leave to appeal against sentence. His Lordship continued:]

Having listened to counsel's argument we are of the opinion that all
B these sentences are what one might describe as on the high side. On the other hand, we do not find it possible to deal with any one of these three otherwise than in terms of a custodial sentence. Having decided those two matters of principle, we have then had to try and produce the most sensible answer we can out of the powers available to this court and having particular regard to the limitation on the sentences which are available for
C those under 21. Doing our best in those circumstances, we shall allow the appeals and substitute sentences as follows, first of all, in the case of the appellant, Cato, we think that had we a free hand we should have sentenced him to prison for something of the order of 18 months to two years. We cannot do that because of his age. We substitute the only possible alternative having regard to his age, which is borstal training on both counts concurrent.

D So far as Morris and Dudley are concerned, Morris is subject to the same type of limitation as Cato, being under 21 at the relevant time; Dudley is not. We think that Morris and Dudley should be treated alike and that in place of the sentences imposed upon them they will each serve a sentence of six months' imprisonment concurrent on each count.

E *Appeals against conviction dismissed.*
Appeals against sentence allowed and sentences varied.

November 7. The court certified, under section 33 (2) of the Criminal Appeal Act 1968, that a point of law of general public importance was
F involved in the decision to dismiss the appeals against convictions, namely, "where the defendant has injected another person by syringe with an unmeasured quantity of heroin with the other's consent (the quantity being selected and prepared by that other person) (i) in relation to a charge of manslaughter (where death results) (a) is that other person's consent a defence? (b) Is the injection an unlawful act? (ii) In relation to a charge under section 23 of the Offences against the Person Act 1861
G (a) is that person's consent a defence? (b) Is heroin a noxious thing? (c) Is proof of foresight of the consequences of the injection required to show that the heroin was administered maliciously?"

Leave to appeal refused.

H Solicitors: *Simons, Muirhead & Allan, Ian Sheratte & Co.; Director of Public Prosecutions.*

J. W.

December 10, 1975. The Appeal Committee of the House of Lords (Viscount Dilhorne, Lord Salmon and Lord Fraser of Tullybelton) dismissed a petition by the appellant for leave to appeal.

[QUEEN'S BENCH DIVISION]

* PRACTICE DIRECTION (CRIME: SENTENCE)

1975 Dec. 19 — Lord Widgery C.J. and May J.

Crime — Sentence — Parole — Offence committed after release on licence—Considerations on sentencing—Criminal Justice Act 1967 (*c.* 80), *ss.* 60, 62 (7)

LORD WIDGERY C.J., at the sitting of the Divisional Court, read the following practice direction.

1. When a prisoner who has been released on licence on the recommendation of the parole board under section 60 of the Criminal Justice Act 1967 is convicted of a further offence during the currency of the licence the conviction does not automatically revoke his licence.

2. Section 62 (7) of the Act, however, provides that if such a person appears before the Crown Court that court may revoke his licence in the circumstances there set out.

3. In such cases the Crown Court should consider all the facts and decide whether the offender should be returned to custody for a term of not less than the remaining effective period of his licence. If so, the court should revoke his licence. The court should then consider whether any sentence of imprisonment passed in respect of the offence committed during the currency of his licence should be concurrent or consecutive to the sentence for the offence in respect of which the court has revoked the licence.

4. The effect of revoking a licence is ordinarily that the offender will be required to serve the time remaining from the date of revocation to the end of the sentence (with remission) or 30 days whichever is the greater. If the offender was on licence in respect of an extended sentence, or was a young prisoner, the effect of revocation is that he will again be required to serve the remainder of the original sentence, with remission not exceeding one-third of that part of his sentence unexpired at the time of recall.

5. If the Crown Court passes a sentence of imprisonment for an offence committed whilst on licence but does not revoke that licence, any subsequent revocation under section 62 (1) or section 62 (2) of the Act cannot make the new sentence consecutive to the original sentence. For this reason it is important that the Crown Court should consider in each case what is the appropriate action to take.

L. N. W.

A

[CHANCERY DIVISION]

* *In re* HELLENIC & GENERAL TRUST LTD.

[No. 00962 of 1975]

B 1975 June 26, 27;
July 1

Templeman J.

Company—Scheme of arrangement—Class meeting—Meeting of ordinary shareholders including wholly owned subsidiary of intended purchasers—Resolution approving scheme carried by subsidiary's votes—Whether agreement of appropriate class—
C *Companies Act* 1948 (11 & 12 *Geo.* 6, *c.* 38), *s.* 206

By a proposed scheme of arrangement, under section 206 of the Companies Act 1948,[1] all the 15 million issued and fully paid ordinary shares of 10p each of a company were to be cancelled and new ordinary shares of the same amount and value were to be issued credited as fully paid to H, which would pay the ordinary shareholders 48p per share for the loss of their shares. H, through its wholly owned subsidiary already
D owned 53·01 per cent. of the ordinary shares. At a separate meeting of the ordinary shareholders summoned to consider, and if thought fit, approve the scheme, approximately 91 per cent. of the shareholders by value attended and voted, and 84·67 per cent. in value, including the votes of the wholly owned subsidiary voted in favour of the arrangement. A minority shareholder, holding 13·95 per cent. in value, voted against the arrangement.

E On the company's petition for the court's sanction of the arrangement, the minority shareholder objecting:—

Held, dismissing the petition, that the interests of a wholly owned subsidiary of an intended purchaser of shares under a scheme of arrangement were different from those of the other ordinary shareholders and different considerations applied in deciding whether to approve the scheme; that, therefore, the purchasers' wholly owned subsidiary was in a different class
F from the other ordinary shareholders and, since the meeting had not been properly constituted, the necessary approval under section 206 of the Act had not been obtained and the court had no jurisdiction to sanction the scheme (post, pp. 125H—126A, E–H).

Sovereign Life Assurance Co. v. *Dodd* [1892] 2 Q.B. 573, C.A. applied.

Per curiam. If the scheme were sanctioned by the court,
G the objectors would be liable to capital gains tax in Greece. In the circumstances of the present case, it would be unfair to deprive the objectors of shares which they were entitled to assume safe from compulsory purchase and which would have the effect of putting on the objectors a swingeing fiscal impost which, if the matter had proceeded under section 209 of the Companies Act 1948, they could have avoided simply and quite properly by refusing to join in approving the scheme under the
H section (post, p. 131A–C).

[Reported by MRS. F. ALLEN MCLEAN, Barrister-at-Law]

[1] Companies Act 1948, s. 206: "(2) If a majority in number representing three fourths in value of the . . . members or class of members, . . . present and voting either in person or by proxy at the meeting, agree to any . . . arrangement, the . . . arrangement shall, if sanctioned by the court, be binding on all . . . the members or class of members, . . ."

The following cases are referred to in the judgment:

Anglo-Continental Supply Co. Ltd., In re [1922] 2 Ch. 723.
Bugle Press Ltd., In re [1961] Ch. 270; [1960] 3 W.L.R. 956; [1960] 3 All E.R. 791, C.A.
General Motor Cab Co. Ltd., In re [1913] 1 Ch. 377, C.A.
Grierson, Oldham & Adams Ltd., In re [1968] Ch. 17; [1967] 1 W.L.R. 385; [1967] 1 All E.R. 192.
Holders Investment Trust Ltd., In re [1971] 1 W.L.R. 583; [1971] 2 All E.R. 289.
Holdsworth (Harold) & Co. (Wakefield) Ltd. v. *Caddies* [1955] 1 W.L.R. 352; [1955] 1 All E.R. 725, H.L.(Sc.).
National Bank Ltd., In re [1966] 1 W.L.R. 819; [1966] 1 All E.R. 1006.
Practice Note [1934] W.N. 142.
Sovereign Life Assurance Co. v. *Dodd* [1892] 2 Q.B. 573, C.A.
United Provident Assurance Co. Ltd., In re [1910] 2 Ch. 477.

No additional case was cited in argument.

PETITION

In May 1975 a separate meeting of the ordinary shareholders of Hellenic & General Trust Ltd., an investment trust company, was held to consider and, if thought fit, to approve a scheme of arrangement under section 206 of the Companies Act 1948 whereby the 15 million issued and fully paid 10p ordinary shares should be cancelled and Hambros Ltd. should be issued with 15 million new ordinary fully paid shares and should pay the holders of the cancelled shares 48p per share. Merchandise & Investment Trust Ltd., a wholly owned subsidiary of Hambros Ltd., owned 53·01 per cent. of the ordinary shares and voted at the meeting in favour of the scheme. The National Bank of Greece, which held 13·95 per cent. of the ordinary shares had voted against the scheme. When the company petitioned the court to sanction the scheme the National Bank of Greece opposed it.

The facts are stated in the judgment.

Allan Heyman Q.C. and *R. Sykes* for the petitioners.
R. Wright Q.C. and *L. J. M. Smith* for the objectors.

TEMPLEMAN J. This is an opposed petition for the sanction by the court under section 206 of the Companies Act 1948 of an arrangement relating to the ordinary shares of the company, Hellenic & General Trust Ltd.

The company carries on business as an investment trust. The ordinary shares of the company are held as to 53·01 per cent. by Merchandise and Investment Trust Ltd. (known as M.I.T.). All the shares of M.I.T. are held by Hambros Ltd. and therefore M.I.T. is a wholly owned subsidiary of Hambros. The objectors, National Bank of Greece S.A., hold 13·95 per cent. of the ordinary shares of the company proposed to be dealt with by the arrangement. By the arrangement the ordinary shares of the company will be cancelled. New ordinary shares will be issued to Hambros and the company will thus become, like M.I.T., a wholly owned subsidiary of Hambros. The former shareholders of the company will be paid by Hambros 48p per share for the loss of their former shares. The result is equivalent to a purchase by Hambros of the ordinary shares of the company at 48p per share.

Section 206 of the Companies Act 1948 provides, so far as material, that where an arrangement is proposed between a company and a class of its creditors or members the court may order a meeting of the class. Then

A if a majority in number representing three-fourths in value of the class
present and voting at the meeting agree to the arangement the arrangement
shall, if sanctioned by the court, be binding on all the members of the class.
Thus, in the present case if there was a proper class meeting which agreed to
the arrangement by the requisite majorities, and if this court sanctions the
arrangement, then the objectors will lose their shares in the company and
will receive 48p per share from Hambros instead. The objectors do not wish
B this to happen.

In the present case the court, on the petition of the company, summoned
a meeting of all the ordinary shareholders. A resolution agreeing to the
arrangement was carried, some 91 per cent. of the shareholders by value
attending and voting. M.I.T., holding 53·01 per cent., voted in favour of the
arrangement. The National Bank of Greece, the objectors, holding 13·95 per
C cent. of the ordinary shares, voted against the arrangement. The arrange-
ment was approved by 86·61 per cent. in number and 84·67 per cent. in
value of those who attended and voted. The votes of M.I.T. were vital. If
they had not attended and voted the requisite majority could not have been
achieved against the opposition of the objectors. The objectors now pursue
their opposition to the arrangement in this court. On their behalf Mr.
D Wright puts forward four objections. The first objection goes to jurisdiction,
and the other three concern the discretion of the court in sanctioning an
arrangement and the proper principles for the exercise of that discretion.

The first objection put forward is that the necessary agreement by the
appropriate class of members has not been obtained. The shareholders
who were summoned to the meeting consisted, it is submitted, of two
classes. First there were the outside shareholders, that is to say the
E shareholders other than M.I.T.: and secondly M.I.T., a subsidiary of
Hambros. M.I.T. were a separate class and should have been excluded
from the meeting of outside shareholders. Although section 206 provides
that the court may order meetings, it is the responsibility of the petitioners
to see that the class meetings are properly constituted, and if they fail
then the necessary agreement is not obtained and the court has no juris-
diction to sanction the arrangement. Thus in *In re United Provident*
F *Assurance Company Ltd.* [1910] 2 Ch. 477 the court held that the holders
of partly paid shares formed a different class from holders of fully paid
shares. The objection was taken that there should have been separate
meetings of the two classes, and Swinfen Eady J. upheld the objection, say-
ing, at p. 481: "... the objection that there have not been proper class
meetings is fatal, and I cannot sanction the scheme."

G Similarly Eve J. issued a practice direction, *Practice Note* [1934] W.N.
142, in which he reminded the profession, in dealing with the predecessor of
section 206, that the responsibility for determining what creditors are to be
summoned to any meeting as constituting a class rests with the petitioner,
and if the meetings are incorrectly convened or constituted, or an objection
is taken to the presence of any particular creditors as having interests com-
H peting with the others, the objection must be taken on the hearing of the
petition for sanction and the petitioner must take the risk of having the
petition dismissed. That direction applies equally to meetings of share-
holders.

The question therefore is whether M.I.T., a wholly owned subsidiary of
Hambros, formed part of the same class as the other ordinary shareholders.
What is an appropriate class must depend upon the circumstances but some
general principles are to be found in the authorities. In *Sovereign Life*

Assurance Co. v. *Dodd* [1892] 2 Q.B. 573, the Court of Appeal held that for the purposes of an arrangement affecting the policyholders of an assurance company the holders of policies which had matured were creditors and were a different class from policyholders whose policies had not matured. Lord Esher M.R. said, at p. 580:

> " . . . they must be divided into different classes . . . because the creditors composing the different classes have different interests; and, therefore, if we find a different state of facts existing among different creditors which may differently affect their minds and their judgment, they must be divided into different classes."

Bowen L.J. said, at p. 583:

> " It seems plain that we must give such a meaning to the term 'class' as will prevent the section being so worked as to result in confiscation and injustice, and that it must be confined to those persons whose rights are not so dissimilar as to make it impossible for them to consult together with a view to their common interest."

Vendors consulting together with a view to their common interest in an offer made by a purchaser would look askance at the presence among them of a wholly owned subsidiary of the purchaser.

In the present case on analysis Hambros are acquiring the outside shares for 48p. So far as the M.I.T. shares are concerned it does not matter very much to Hambros whether they are acquired or not. If the shares are acquired a sum of money moves from parent to wholly owned subsidiary and shares move from the subsidiary to the parent. The overall financial position of the parent and the subsidiary remain the same. The shares and the money could remain or be moved to suit Hambros before or after the arrangement. From the point of M.I.T., provided M.I.T. is solvent, the directors of M.I.T. do not have to question whether the price is exactly right. Before and after the arrangement the directors of the parent and the subsidiary could have been made the same persons with the same outlook and the same judgment. Mr. Heyman, on behalf of the petitioners, submitted that since the parent and subsidiary were separate corporations with separate directors, and since M.I.T. were ordinary shareholders in the company, it followed that M.I.T. had the same interests as the other shareholders. The directors of M.I.T. were under a duty to consider whether the arrangement was beneficial to the whole class of ordinary shareholders, and they were capable of forming an independent and unbiased judgment, irrespective of the interests of the parent company. This seems to me to be unreal. Hambros are purchasers making an offer. When the vendors meet to discuss and vote whether or not to accept the offer, it is incongruous that the loudest voice in theory and the most significant vote in practice should come from the wholly owned subsidiary of the purchaser No one can be both a vendor and a purchaser and in my judgment, for the purpose of the class meetings in the present case, M.I.T. were in the camp of the purchaser. Of course this does not mean that M.I.T. should not have considered at a separate class meeting whether to accept the arrangement. But their consideration will be different from the considerations given to the matter by the other shareholders. Only M.I.T. could say, within limits, that what was good for Hambros must be good for M.I.T.

Mr. Heyman submitted that difficulties will arise in practice if every subsidiary or associated company may constitute a separate class. So far as a wholly owned subsidiary is concerned there is no difficulty at all, and in

A most cases it will be sufficient to judge the class composition by reference to the shareholding. In most cases if the parent controls 50 per cent. or more of the shares of the subsidiary company it can be assumed that they have a community of interest for the purposes of section 206, and in most cases a different interest from that of other shareholders. Mr. Heyman relied on *Harold Holdsworth & Co.* (*Wakefield*) *Ltd.* v. *Caddies* [1955] 1 W.L.R. 352. But this only decided that the managing director of a group
B of companies could be obliged to devote his attention to one subsidiary, and Lord Morton of Henryton said, at p. 363:

> " It is true that each company in the group is in law a separate entity, the business whereof is to be carried on by its own directors and managing director, if any; but there is no doubt that the defenders, by taking any necessary formal steps, could make any arrangements they
> C pleased in regard to the management of the business. . . . They owned all the issued capital and the directors were their nominees."

Since that case was directed to management I do not think it is of any great assistance to either party in this case, but it certainly is of no assistance to Mr. Heyman.

D Accordingly I uphold the first objection, which is fatal to the arrangement. But in view of the careful arguments put forward by both sides I will consider the other objections which are raised by Mr. Wright and which are material if the class meeting in the present case, contrary to my view, was properly constituted.

The second objection is founded on the analysis of the arrangement as an offer by Hambros to acquire the ordinary shares for 48p. Section 209
E provides safeguards for minority shareholders in the event of a takeover bid and in a proper case provides machinery for a small minority of shareholders to be obliged to accept a takeover against their wishes. Thus section 209 provides that where a scheme or contract involving the transfer of shares in a company to another company has been approved by the holders of not less than nine-tenths in value of the shares whose transfer
F is involved (other than shares already held at the date of the offer by, or a nominee for, the transferee company or its subsidiary), the transferee company may give notice to any dissenting shareholder; and then, unless on an application made by the dissenting holder the court thinks fit to order otherwise, shall be entitled and bound to acquire those shares on the terms of the takeover bid. If the present arrangement had been carried out under section 209, M.I.T. as a subsidiary of Hambros would have been
G expressly forbidden to join in any approval for the purposes of section 209, and in any event the objectors could not have been obliged to sell because they hold 10 per cent. of the ordinary shares of the company.

The fact that an arrangement under section 206 produces a result which is the same as a takeover under section 209 is not necessarily fatal. It is not always so unfair as to preclude the court from exercising its discretion in
H favour of the scheme. Thus in *In re National Bank Ltd.* [1966] 1 W.L.R. 819, where a similar objection was taken, Plowman J. considered the argument that the scheme in that case ought to be treated as a section 209 case needing a 90 per cent. majority. He said, at p. 829:

> ". . . I cannot accede to that proposition. In the first place, it seems to me to involve imposing a limitation or qualification either on the generality of the word 'arrangement' in section 206 or else on the discretion of the court under that section. The legislature has not

> seen fit to impose any such limitation in terms and I see no reason A
> for implying any. Moreover, the two sections, sections 206 and 209, involve quite different considerations and different approaches. Under section 206 an arrangement can only be sanctioned if the question of its fairness has first of all been submitted to the court. Under section 209, on the other hand, the matter may never come to the court at all. If it does come to the court, then the onus is cast on the dissenting minority to demonstrate the unfairness of the scheme. There B
> are, therefore, good reasons for requiring a smaller majority in favour of a scheme under section 206 than the majority which is required under section 209 if the minority is to be expropriated."

Accepting that, the present proposals nevertheless seem to me to place the petitioners in an inescapable dilemma. They cannot succeed under section 209 because of the express provisions of that section and the size of the C
shareholding of the objectors. They can only succeed under section 206 by using the votes of their own subsidiary company, M.I.T., to secure the necessary majority. In these circumstances I agree with Mr. Wright that the court should not in the exercise of its discretion authorise the acquisition of the shares of the objectors, the National Bank of Greece, against the wishes of the bank. The petitioners cannot succeed at all D
under section 209 and in my judgment they cannot fairly succeed under section 206.

Earlier authority appears to support that proposition. In *In re General Motor Cab Co. Ltd.* [1913] 1 Ch. 377, a company proposed to sell its assets and undertaking to a new company to be formed for that purpose and to compel shareholders to accept shares in the new company instead of their shares in the old company. The creditors were to be taken over by E
the new company. There was no provision for preserving the rights of dissentient shareholders. It was held by the Court of Appeal that the scheme was not a compromise or arrangement which could be sanctioned. That was admittedly a very strong case where the court came to the conclusion that what was being asked was not a compromise or arrangement at all, but it is significant that the court approached the application F
on the basis of it being something which if it had been a takeover bid would have required the rights of dissentient shareholders to be preserved.

Similarly in *In re Anglo-Continental Supply Co. Ltd.* [1922] 2 Ch. 723, the reconstruction of an existing company by winding up and sale of its entire undertaking and assets for shares in a new foreign company outside the scope of a reconstruction under the Companies (Consolidation) G
Act 1908 was effected as an arrangement under section 120 of that Act, the predecessor of the present section 206. But that was only done on terms that the rights of the dissentient minority were preserved in the same way as they would have been under a reconstruction.

Finally in *In re Bugle Press Ltd.* [1961] Ch. 270, where two majority H
shareholders formed a new company and propounded an arrangement simply for the purpose of enabling them to get the requisite majority under section 209, the court refused to have any truck with the proposals put forward. Lord Evershed M.R. said, at p. 285, that the mechanism of the section had been admittedly invoked especially for the purpose and in order to enable the majority shareholders to expropriate the shares of their minority colleague. Counsel had argued that nevertheless

A "... in the result, the case does fall within the strict language of the section and falling within it the consequences must follow. If that argument is right, it would enable by a device of this kind the 90 per cent. majority of the shareholders always to get rid of a minority shareholder whom they did not happen to like. And that, as a matter of principle, would appear to be contrary to a fundamental principle of our law that prima facie, if a man has a legal
B right which is an absolute right, then he can do with it or not do with it what he will."

Whereas in *Bugle Press* the motives of the applicants for the scheme were not particularly praiseworthy I hasten to say that in the present case the motives of the petitioners are entirely different, as will appear when I come to consider the details of the scheme. The petitioners are
C anxious that the ordinary shareholders should be offered the full net asset value of their shares which exceed the value of those shares on the open market. They are persisting with the scheme because they do not consider that it is fair to those shareholders who wish to accept the scheme that they should be frustrated by the opposition of the objectors. But the decision in *In re Bugle Press Ltd.* fortifies me in thinking that
D where one has what is in effect a section 209 scheme then, putting it at its lowest, there must be a very high standard of proof on the part of the petitioner to justify obtaining by section 206 what could not be obtained by section 209, especially when there is the added element that section 206 itself only works with the help of a wholly owned subsidiary of the petitioners.

The third alternative objection raised by Mr. Wright is that the
E arrangement is unfair to all the ordinary shareholders. I am satisfied that it is more than fair. The shares of the company are listed on the Stock Exchange and in common with other investment trust companies normally stand between 20 per cent. and 25 per cent. below the net asset value of the company's assets. Thus the offer price of 48p, if it represents the true net asset value of the shares, is 20 per cent. to 25
F per cent. more than the shareholders can now obtain elsewhere. The assets of the company consist largely of cash and Stock Exchange investments, so that the ordinary shareholders, if they receive 48p, instead of their existing shares, can follow the same outline of investment and will have roughly 48p to invest instead of a share worth on the Stock Exchange 36p. There has been independent advice provided to shareholders and I am quite satisfied that the offer is extremely
G fair.

On behalf of the objectors several reasons were advanced why it could be said that the scheme was unfair to all the ordinary shareholders, but I do not find any of those reasons convincing. It was said that the scheme would involve the ordinary shareholders in a disposal for the purposes of United Kingdom capital gains tax and that
H would not apply to Hambros and M.I.T. On the other hand I was told that in fact the effect will be disadvantageous to Hambros and M.I.T. in that losses will not be allowed to be carried forward. The imposition of capital gains tax is a fate which we must all suffer. It was said that the offer was made at a time when assets value had declined drastically, that there was a belief that share prices in general would go up, that the offer was made at a time when sterling was low, and, although this may sound rather strange at the moment, it was said to be unwise

to sell until sterling had recovered. Finally it was said that the real A value of the investments can only be maintained by holding shares in investment trusts with a substantial portfolio of overseas investments.

Whatever the future of sterling and whatever the future of Stock Exchange investments, since the holding of this particular company consists almost entirely of cash and Stock Exchange investments anyone who holds at the moment a share in the company is relying simply on the present management. I have heard no argument that the objectors B prefer the management of Hambros Ltd. to their own or any other form of management. If a shareholder receives 48p he can back his fancy as regards the future of Stock Exchange investments, the future value of cash and the future value of sterling. He can even, by taking a list of the company's investments, slavishly follow the exact pattern of their investments. The claim that there is some peculiar C advantage in holding shares in the present company because of its portfolio of overseas investments, was based on a misunderstanding. In fact the overseas investments of this company do not amount to more than 9 per cent., and there are other substantial investment trusts which have a far higher proportion of overseas investments if a shareholder thinks that is a good thing. Accordingly I am quite satisfied that the scheme is fair or more than fair to the ordinary shareholders D as a class.

Mr. Heyman says, that being so, I ought to ignore the earlier indications of unfairness, namely, the effect of the section 209 machinery, and the exploitation of the section 206 machinery; and it may be that in some extraordinary case that would be true. But I cannot bring myself to believe that it would be right to exercise a discretion in E favour of the petitioners in the present case. It may be that there is some advantage in hanging on. At any rate the objectors were entitled to say that they purchased more than 10 per cent., they could not be expropriated under section 209, and they object to expropriation, albeit it is said in the best interest of other shareholders, under section 206.

That leaves the final objection; why if the scheme is beneficial is it not acceptable to the objectors? In the first place they themselves F seem to hold the opinion that there is some advantage in retaining their present shareholding. They voice some misgivings as to whether the petitioners themselves are not doing rather better out of the arrangement than appears to be the case. But substantially the objectors' view is coloured by the fact that they will, as the evidence states, although I am not given details, become liable to a swingeing capital G gains tax in Greece. Mr. Heyman says the tax must be ignored because in considering their votes at a meeting under section 206 each shareholder must put himself in the impossible position of deciding what is in the best interests of the class. That appears from the judgment of Megarry J. in *In re Holders Investment Trust Ltd.* [1971] 1 W.L.R. 583, and in particular the passage at p. 586 where Megarry J. refers to a H general principle that a power conferred on a majority of a class to bind minorities, must be exercised for the purpose of benefiting the class as a whole and not merely individual members only. Similarly in *In re Grierson, Oldham & Adams Ltd.* [1968] Ch. 17, under section 209 it was held the test was one of fairness to the body of shareholders and not to individuals and the burden was on the applicants to prove unfairness and not merely that the scheme was open to criticism. Although

A under section 206 the onus is the other way round it is submitted that the test of fairness is exactly the same.

In a good many cases so it would be, but in the present case it seems to me that the individual loss which the objectors will suffer from the scheme is one which should be borne in mind. When one adds together the three objections of Mr. Wright, first of all that it is really a scheme by Hambros to purchase the outside shareholding,
B secondly, that under section 209 the scheme could not have been carried out against the wishes of the objectors, and thirdly, that it could not have been carried out under section 206 save with the votes of M.I.T., the wholly owned subsidiary of Hambros, it seems to me that it is unfair to deprive the objectors of shares which they were entitled to assume were safe from compulsory purchase and with the effect of
C putting on the objectors a swingeing fiscal impost which, if the matter had proceeded under section 209, they could have avoided simply and quite properly by refusing to join in approving the scheme under that section.

Accordingly in the result, both as a matter of jurisdiction and as a matter of discretion, I am not prepared to make any order approving this scheme.
D

Petition dismissed with costs.

Solicitors: *Norton, Rose, Botterell & Roche; Thomas Cooper & Stibbard.*

E

[QUEEN'S BENCH DIVISION]

* KAPUR *v.* SHIELDS

F

1975 July 31 Phillips J.

Industrial Relations—Unfair dismissal—Excluded classes—Housekeeper sole employee at relevant premises—Employer and wife only shareholders in property companies—Whether housekeeper's employment in "undertaking" employing less than four people—Industrial Relations Act 1971 (*c.* 72), *ss.* 22, 27
G (1) (*a*), 167 (1) [1]

The employer was a company director and property owner. He and his wife were the only shareholders in companies owning property and, in another company owning an hotel in Dublin, they were two of the three shareholders. The employer personally owned a property divided into flatlets at which he employed only the employee as a housekeeper. On her em-
H ployment being terminated by the employer, she applied to the industrial tribunal for compensation for unfair dismissal. The employer alleged in his notice of appearance that she had asked him to dismiss her in order to make it easier for her to obtain a council flat. During the hearing, the employer applied to the tribunal to amend his notice of appearance,

[1] Industrial Relations Act 1971, s. 22: see post, p. 135A–B.
S. 27 (1): see post, p. 135 C–F.
S. 167 (1): see post, p. 135F–H.

in order to allege in the alternative that the employee's dis- A missal was due to her inefficiency and neglect of duty. He also contended that the tribunal had no jurisdiction to hear the application because the employee's employment was excluded by section 27 (1) (*a*) of the Industrial Relations Act 1971 [1] as the employee was the only person employed by the employer at the premises. The tribunal refused him leave to amend his notice of appearance and held that it had jurisdiction to hear the application because the employee was employed in the B employer's "undertaking," within the meaning of section 167 of the Act of 1971, which included the premises where she was employed and the other premises where the employer carried on his business as a property owner through his various property companies and, therefore, the employees of those companies could be taken into account for the purposes of section 27 (1) (*a*).

On the employer's appeal:— C

Held, dismissing the appeal, (1) that although proceedings before industrial tribunals were intended to be as simple and informal as possible and matters which a party felt were important were not to be excluded on mere technical grounds provided there was no injustice to the other party, it was impossible to say that in the circumstances the tribunal had erred in law in exercising its discretion to refuse the employer's request to amend his notice of appearance (post, p. 134D–F). D

(2) That, on the true construction of section 27 (1) (*a*) of the Act of 1971, an employment was excluded from the provisions of section 22 of that Act where there were less than four employees employed in the undertaking, irrespective of the identity of the employer, and, therefore, the tribunal had to consider whether the distinct but similar activities of the employer, his wife and the various companies constituted a single undertaking (post, p. 139B, E, F). E

(3) That, once it was established that the employee was employed by the employer, the onus of proving that that employment was excluded by section 27 (1) (*a*) was on the employer; and that, on the facts, the tribunal were justified in ruling that they had jurisdiction to hear the application (post, pp. 140F, G, H—141A).

The following cases are referred to in the judgment of the court: F

Boston v. *Chilton* (unreported), February 5, 1974, N.I.R.C.

Harold Baim Motion Pictures Theatres (Coleford) Ltd. v. *Nunn* (unreported), October 30, 1973, N.I.R.C.

Haque v. *Stitchen & Co. (1937) Ltd.* [1973] I.C.R. 474, N.I.R.C.

Holdsworth (Harold) & Co. (Wakefield) Ltd. v. *Caddies* [1955] 1 W.L.R. 352; [1955] 1 All E.R. 725, H.L.(Sc.).

Mayhew v. *Richard Alexander & Son* [1973] I.C.R. 441; [1973] 3 All G E.R. 39, N.I.R.C.

Reg. v. *Edwards* [1975] Q.B. 27; [1974] 3 W.L.R. 285; [1974] 2 All E.R. 1085, C.A.

Salomon v. *Salomon and Co. Ltd.* [1897] A.C. 22, H.L.(E.).

The following additional case was cited in argument:

Abernethie v. *A. M. & J. Kleiman Ltd.* [1970] 1 Q.B. 10; [1969] 2 W.L.R. H 1364; [1969] 2 All E.R. 790, C.A.

APPEAL from an industrial tribunal sitting in London.

The employer, Sagar Kapur, appealed from a decision of the industrial tribunal, that he had unfairly dismissed his housekeeper, Mrs. Margaret Shields, the employee. The grounds of the appeal were: (1) that the tribunal, on the true construction of section 27 (1) (*a*) of the Industrial

Relations Act 1971, had no jurisdiction to entertain the employee's complaint of unfair dismissal and should have dismissed it accordingly. (2) That, since the employee was the employer's sole employee at the relevant premises at 48 and 49, Evelyn Gardens, London, S.W.7, and since the business carried on at those premises was a separate business conducted by the employer personally, the tribunal should have held that there were less than four employees who had been continuously employed for 13 weeks in that business and that accordingly there was no jurisdiction to entertain the employee's complaint of unfair dismissal. (3) That the tribunal erred in law in holding that they need not look for the purposes of section 27 (1) (*a*) of the Act of 1971 at the person who was the employer of the employee and that they were entitled to consider and aggregate with the employee who alleged unfair dismissal the employees of other persons engaged in other businesses if those other persons were companies in which the employer had an interest. (4) That the tribunal misdirected themselves in law in holding that the employer's business was that of owning property whereas they should have held that the relevant business was that of letting out furnished rooms and misdirected themselves in law in holding that employees of companies in which the employer had an interest could be aggregated with the employee for the purposes of section 27 (1) (*a*) of the Act of 1971. (5) That the tribunal misdirected themselves in law in holding that the relevant undertaking was anything other than the business of a flatlet house carried out at the relevant premises and were wrong in law in aggregating employees of other types of business such as an hotel. (6) Alternatively that if the tribunal had jurisdiction to entertain the employee's complaint of unfair dismissal the tribunal were wrong in law in refusing to allow the employer to amend his notice of appearance to allege that the employee had been inefficient and had misconducted herself between January and June 1974 which would have justified the dismissal.

The facts are stated in the judgment.

Norman Primost for the employer.
Roger Toulson for the employee.

PHILLIPS J. This is an appeal by the employer, from a decision of an industrial tribunal, sitting in London, dated February 16, 1975, finding that he had unfairly dismissed his employee, and ordering him to pay compensation to her in the sum of £706. The appeal raises two points, one of which, concerning the jurisdiction of industrial tribunals, is of general importance.

The employee was employed at a flatlet house owned by the employer at 48 and 49, Evelyn Gardens, London, S.W.7, as a housekeeper. The tribunal found that she had been unfairly dismissed on June 24, 1974. By his appearance, dated August 1, 1974, to the employee's claim, the employer stated the grounds upon which he intended to resist it, as follows:

> "(1) The applicant requested me to give her notice.
> "(2) The applicant is not redundant as she has been replaced by another housekeeper."

Accordingly, apart from certain questions as to jurisdiction, to which I shall return, the issue in the case was whether the employee was dismissed, or whether, as the employer contended, she had asked for notice to be given in order to make it easier for her to obtain a council flat. The case was presented accordingly. During the cross-examination of the employee, counsel for the employer sought to question her about her alleged inefficiency and neglect of duty. A The relevance of this line of cross-examination being doubted, he applied for leave to amend. The course which the case then took is summarised in the notes of evidence as follows:

> "The [employer] applies to amend, by adding the allegation: 'Alternatively if the [employee] was dismissed the reason was inefficiency and misconduct in neglecting to supervise the cleaning of the staircases and the entrances in both houses from January to June 1974 and not B being available at times when the [employer] gave notice and called to collect the money in the period from January to June 1974.' Mr. Plews on behalf of the [employee] strongly opposed the application. It was too late in the day to make the amendment. There had been proceedings for possession, etc. etc. Mr. Primost had nothing further to say. He added that he was instructed that solicitors were instructed C in regard to this in August or September. The ruling was given that the amendment be not allowed."

The first point taken in support of the employer's appeal is that the tribunal was wrong in law in refusing to allow him to amend his notice of appearance to allege that the employee had been inefficient and had misconducted herself between January and June 1974, which would, it was D alleged, have justified the dismissal.

Proceedings before industrial tribunals are intended to be as simple and informal as possible. The parties are often unrepresented and need assistance from the tribunal in presenting their case. There is no system of formal pleadings. In many cases, the applicant and the respondent will fill up the application and the appearance without the benefit of legal advice. E In fact, the employer, though represented at the hearing and having the assistance of a solicitor in August and September 1974, filled up the appearance in this case by himself. Ordinarily, no doubt, tribunals will strive to allow a party to bring before it all the questions and matters which that party feels to be important, in so far as this can be done with justice to the other party, and will as far as possible not shut out matters of complaint or defence on technical grounds. The guiding principle must F be to allow the parties to have their say. But, the circumstances of every case are different, there is only an appeal to this court on a point of law, and it is impossible to say that the tribunal erred in law in this case in exercising its discretion in the way in which it did, having regard particularly to the fact that the question of the employee's alleged inefficiency and neglect of duty was raised for the first time in the course of cross-examination of her by Mr. Primost for the employer. G

The second point taken in support of the employer's appeal concerns the jurisdiction of industrial tribunals in complaints of unfair dismissal and is, as I have said, of general importance. It is not every employee who is entitled to make such a complaint. In particular, as is well known, there is an exclusion in the case of "small organisations." It is impossible to summarise the effect of the exclusion satisfactorily. Complete accuracy H requires a reference to the statute, but it is normally put in some such words as:

> "before an [employee] can come within the unfair dismissal protection there must have been no less than four employees (including the claimant) who, immediately before the effective date of termination, had been continuously employed for 13 weeks or longer": *Harvey, Industrial Relations* (1974), p. 97.

At the material time the relevant statutory provisions were contained in the Industrial Relations Act 1971. That Act has now been repealed, but these provisions have, with one exception, been re-enacted in the Trade Union and Labour Relations Act 1974, Schedule 1, Part II. Section 22 of the Industrial Relations Act 1971 provided:

"(1) In every employment to which this section applies every employee shall have the right not to be unfairly dismissed by his employer; and accordingly, in any such employment, it shall be an unfair industrial practice for an employer to dismiss an employee unfairly. (2) This section applies to every employment except in so far as its application is excluded by or under any of sections 27 to 31 of this Act. (3) In the following provisions of this Part of this Act 'the claimant' means the employee who claims that he has been unfairly dismissed by his employer."

Section 27, under the general heading "Excluded cases," provided:

"(1) Section 22 of this Act does not apply to any of the following, that is to say,—(*a*) any employment in an undertaking in which immediately before the effective date of termination there were in the aggregate (including the claimant) less than four employees who had been continuously employed for a period of not less than 13 weeks, whether they are, or had been, all employed at the same place or are, or had been, employed at different places; (*b*) any employment where the employer is the husband or wife or a close relative of the employee; (*c*) any employment as a registered dock worker, as defined by any scheme for the time being in force under the Dock Workers (Regulation of Employment) Act 1946, not being employment by virtue of which the employee is wholly or mainly engaged in work which is not dock work as defined by the scheme; (*d*) any employment as master or as a member of the crew of a fishing vessel, where the employee is not remunerated otherwise than by a share in the profits or gross earnings of the vessel; (*e*) any employment as a teacher to whom section 85 of the Education (Scotland) Act 1962 (dismissal of teachers) applies; (*f*) any employment under a contract which normally involves employment for less than 21 hours weekly."

Section 167, which was the interpretation section, read:

"(1) In this Act, except in so far as the context otherwise requires, the following expressions have the meanings hereby assigned to them respectively, that is to say—. . . 'employee' (subject to subsection (4) of this section) means an individual who has entered into or works under (or, where the employment has ceased, worked under) a contract of employment; 'employer' (subject to subsection (2) of this section)—(*a*) where the reference is to an employer in relation to an employee, means the person by whom the employee is (or, in a case where the employment has ceased, was) employed, and (*b*) in any other case, means a person regarded in that person's capacity as one for whom one or more workers work or have worked or normally work or seek to work; . . . 'undertaking' includes a business and, in relation to any body of persons (whether corporate or unincorporate) whose activities would not, apart from this provision, be regarded as constituting an undertaking, includes the aggregate of those activities; . . ."

The part of section 167 relating to "employer" and "undertaking" has

not been re-enacted in the Act of 1974, and that relating to "employee" A
has been re-enacted in somewhat different terms.

The employee was the only person employed at 48 and 49, Evelyn
Gardens, and so it was contended on behalf of the employer that, though
employed by him, her employment was excluded by virtue of the provisions
of section 27 (1) (*a*). The tribunal found in favour of the employee on this
preliminary question of jurisdiction and its reasons are set out in para-
graphs 4 and 5 of the decisions, as follows: B

> "4. The next matter which goes to the jurisdiction is section 22
> (1) (*a*). It may be mentioned that none of these matters were raised
> initially in regard to the application of [the employee] for unfair
> dismissal; the number of employees, the matter now to be raised, and
> the hours of duty were raised when in September she brought the other
> application under the Contracts of Employment Act. Section 27 (1) (*a*) C
> provides that the section giving a right to unfair dismissal does not
> apply to: 'any employment in an undertaking in which immediately
> before the effective date of termination there were in the aggregate
> (including the claimant) less than four employees who had been con-
> tinuously employed for a period of less than 13 weeks, whether they
> are, or had been, all employed at the same place or are, or had been, D
> employed at different places.' [The employer] in his evidence said:
> 'I am a company director and property owner. I own 48 and 49
> Evelyn Gardens personally. The Kiwi Court Hotel, S.W.5, is owned
> by Arlovale Ltd. I own shares. It is a family concern. My wife
> and I each have one share. 3 Beaufort Gardens is owned by Southra
> Developments Ltd. My wife and I each have one share. 33 Cranleigh
> Gardens [which was sold after the employee was dismissed] was owned E
> by the Golden Slipper Caterers Ltd., one share belonging to me and
> one to my wife.'
>
> "64 Elm Park Road was owned by the same company and it was
> held until July 1. An hotel in Dublin is owned by the Great Northern
> Hotel Group Ltd. with three shares, one held by the [employer], one
> by his wife, and one by Mr. Khanna. There is no evidence at all as F
> to the number of employees in employment at any one time or for any
> period in these other places. So that if the other places can be regarded
> as part of the undertaking in which the [employee] was employed
> this objection to jurisdiction also would not be valid.
>
> "5. In deciding whether she was employed in any undertaking in
> which there were more than four employees we have to have regard G
> to the definition of 'undertaking' in section 167 (1): 'includes a
> business and, in relation to any body of persons (whether corporate or
> unincorporate) whose activities would not, apart from this provision, be
> regarded as constituting an undertaking, includes the aggregate of those
> activities.'
>
> "Leaving aside for the moment the definition, we think that if a
> person sets up business as a property owner, and decides to conduct H
> that business by operating through a number of companies in which
> he and his wife are the sole shareholders, or in one case the majority
> shareholders, then it can be said that he is carrying on the business of
> a property owner through the agencies of these various companies.
> No doubt the companies are brought into the matter for reasons of
> taxation and ease of disposal of the properties because it is easier to
> dispose of the shares in a company than to dispose of the property

A itself as far as transfer is concerned. It seems to us that if a person does set up to operate, to make money, in this way, then the undertaking in which he is engaged includes those operations which he carries out through the means of using companies as agents to do them. Of course companies are separate persons to the person who may control them; we are not here concerned with whether the employee, or the other employees we have to count, were employees of different persons; B we have to find out whether they were employees in different places of an 'undertaking.' We think that here it must be said that the undertaking of [the employer] was, through these various companies, to carry on the business of being a property owner, with the ability to sell those properties he wished to dispose of. Even if that were wrong there is much to be said, we do not propose to deal further with it, for C the submission on behalf of the [employee] that this may well fall under the second part of the definition of 'undertaking.' The tribunal therefore has jurisdiction to deal with this application. We have to consider whether it was an unfair dismissal."

It is not wholly clear to me what is the precise basis of the decision. But the use of the words " we are not concerned with whether the employee, D or the other employees we have to count, were employees of different persons: we have to find out whether they were employees in different places of an undertaking " seems to suggest that the tribunal assumed, without argument, that, in applying section 27 (1) (*a*), the identity of the employer is irrelevant, so that it is not necessary that the essential four employees should be employed by the same employer. Mr. Primost's first contention to this court has been (and no doubt was to the tribunal) that the employ- E ment must be *in* an undertaking in which not less than four persons are employed by the same employer; and he submits that the paraphrase used by the tribunal—" we have to find out whether they were employees in different places *of* an undertaking "—is inaccurate and misleading. It seems to me that this is the main question in the case: i.e., must the four employees be employed by the same employer?

F However, before turning to the construction of section 27 (1) (*a*) it is useful to consider the second limb of the definition of " undertaking " in section 167:

" . . . and, in relation to any body of persons (whether corporate or unincorporate) whose activities would not, apart from this provision, be regarded as constituting an undertaking, includes the aggregate of G those activities; . . . "

Even with the assistance of counsel, which in this case has been considerable, I have been unable to think of good examples of the kind of case to which the words are aimed. I do not think they can be of direct assistance here for they concern the aggregation of activities (in order to constitute an undertaking) rather than of employments. But a proper H understanding of the words could throw light on the construction of section 27 (1) (*a*). It may be that they are aimed at cases such as co-operatives, or clubs, or partnerships, where individual activities considered alone do not, but considered together do, constitute an undertaking. If it be that in most such cases the employees are employed by individual employers, rather than the group, it would follow that, since the intention must have been that such cases were not to be excluded under section 27 (for otherwise it would not have been necessary to extend the definition of " undertaking " to include them), section 27 (1) (*a*) would be construed accordingly, so as not to require identity of employer. But, being unable to think of convincing examples, I have thought it better not to take this possibility into account. Mr. Toulson, for the employee, founded a subsidiary argument in support of the decision upon this limb of the definition. According to this, the employer and his wife, and the various companies, together constitute a body of persons whose activities, when aggregated, constitute an undertaking; the employee, and the employees of the companies, being employed in that undertaking. I cannot accept this, because it seems to me that the activities of the employer, and the companies, considered singly and apart from this provision, would in each case constitute an undertaking. The tribunal, which seems to have found a similar difficulty over this part of the definition, though inclined to think that it could assist the employee, eventually shied away and put it on one side, too.

In support of his main contention that section 27 (1) (*a*) is dealing with the employees of a single employer, Mr. Primost relies strongly on the fact that the whole Act of 1971 is concerned with the relationship between employer and employee. He draws attention to the definition of "employer" and "employee," and points out that in paragraphs (*b*), (*c*), (*d*), (*e*) and (*f*) of section 27 (1) the attention is directed to the nature of the particular employment. By way of illustration he cited *Mayhew* v. *Richard Alexander & Son* [1973] I.C.R. 441 and *Haque* v. *Stitchen & Co. (1937) Ltd.* [1973] I.C.R. 474 as showing the importance of the particular relationship of employer-employee involved. Reference was also made to the decision of the National Industrial Relations Court in *Harold Baim Motion Pictures Theatres (Coleford) Ltd.* v. *Nunn* (unreported), October 30, 1973, in which this section was considered. But, except inferentially, it does not deal with the question immediately under consideration, but turns more on the circumstances in which two widely separated businesses can be said to constitute a single undertaking. The purpose of section 27 (1) (*a*), submits Mr. Primost, is to exclude from the ambit of the unfair dismissal provisions of the Act small businesses, i.e., small employers, upon whom the burden of compliance would lie too heavily. If the intention is to protect the employer of small means, it is not easy to see why section 27 (1) (*a*) did not do so simply by reference to the number of persons employed by the employer, or why it was necessary to introduce the test of the number of persons employed in an undertaking. Whichever way the section is construed there are difficulties. Construed as Mr. Primost would have it, it would follow that even though an employer employs a thousand employees, two or three may be excluded from the Act if they are all employed in a separate undertaking employing less than four employees; or persons employed in the same undertaking may find that some are, and some are not, excluded; cf., a partnership of architects employing 15 employees, who vest their premises in a service company which employs a liftman and a boilerman. Construed the other way, single employees may be protected provided that they work in an undertaking with at least three others, each of whom may be a single employee. The difficulties only disappear if it can be said that it is impossible to have an undertaking in which there are employed the employees of different employers. I think it is possible. The firm which runs its office administration through the medium of a separate service company is a familiar example.

In these circumstances, I approach the language of the Act without any particular preference or assumption one way or the other. Section 22

A applies to every employment except in so far as its application is excluded. The construction of section 27 (1) (*a*) for which Mr. Primost contends requires certain words to be read into paragraph (*a*). There can be no justification for doing this, unless it can be seen to be clearly necessary in order to make sense of the provision, and clearly seen what addition is necessary. It is difficult to know what the addition should be. For example, is the requirement to be that all employees in an undertaking should be B employed by the same person, or is it sufficient if at least four are employed by one employer? I prefer to take the language as it is, with the result that an employment is excluded under paragraph (*a*) where there are less than four employees employed in the undertaking, irrespective of the identity of the employer. In short, for the purpose of counting the number of employees one is concerned only with whether they are employed in the C undertaking and not with who employs them.

Upon this construction of the section, the remaining question in the appeal concerns the finding by the tribunal that there was here a single undertaking comprising the activities of the employer and his wife and the various companies. In this connection, it is convenient to consider a submission made by Mr. Toulson. The circumstances, he said, justified the tribunal in disregarding the principle in *Salomon* v. *Salomon* [1897] D A.C. 22 and lifting the corporate veil in order to see that the activities of the companies were the activities of the employer. In support of this submission he cited *Harold Holdsworth & Co.* (*Wakefield*) *Ltd.* v. *Caddies* [1955] 1 W.L.R. 352, and passages in *Gower, Modern Company Law*, 3rd ed. (1969), pp. 189, 201. Unless the arrangements made by the employer constituted a sham (of which there is no evidence), I do not think E that the facts found by the tribunal would justify the conclusion that the acts or activities of the companies were those of the employer, or that the employees of the company were, in truth, his employees. But it is not necessary to go so far. The situation was the perfectly ordinary one of a man conducting affairs, partly personally, and partly through the medium of companies of which he and his wife were the only shareholders. It F seems to me that what the tribunal had to ask itself on this question was whether the distinct but somewhat similar activities of a number of persons, i.e., the employer and his wife, and the various companies, could, and did, for the purposes of section 27 (1) (*a*), constitute a single undertaking. I see no reason why they could not. The tribunal found that they did.

The question, then, is whether there was evidence upon which the G tribunal could so find. Mr. Primost submits that there was not. He criticises the description of the employer's business as that of a property owner. He points out that one of the hotels was in Dublin, seeks support from *Harold Baim Motion Pictures Theatres* (*Coleford*) *Ltd.* v. *Nunn* (unreported), October 30, 1973, and says that hotels are very different from flatlet houses. Nor, he says, was there any evidence as to how many persons were employed in each place. There is a good deal with which I would agree in these H criticisms. Furthermore, there is an absence of evidence of a kind which might be expected. Where it is sought to show that the activities of separate persons together constitute an undertaking, it is not necessarily enough to show that the persons are connected and that the separate activities are similar. One would expect some evidence of organisational unity: e.g., common accounting, management, purchasing arrangements, insurance, and so on. There was none of this. Accordingly, it is of importance to see where was the burden of proof. The employee has established that she

came within section 22 of the Act of 1971. Did she have to prove that A
her employment was not excluded under section 27, or did the employer
have to prove that it was? The burden, submits Mr. Toulson, lay on the
employer, and he cited the decision of the National Industrial Relations
Court in *Boston* v. *Chilton* (unreported) February 5, 1974, where it was
said that the burden of proving that an employment was excluded by section
27 (1) (*a*) lay on the employer. The following is an extract from the
judgment of that court, delivered by Sir Hugh Griffiths, in that case: B

> "The first point taken on the appeal concerns an application to adduce
> further evidence to establish that because the employer allegedly
> employed less than four employees at the time of the dismissal, his
> case fell within one of the excluded categories set out in section 27 (1)
> of the Industrial Relations Act 1971. The employer was legally repre-
> sented before the tribunal and called no evidence to establish that he C
> fell within the excluded categories. Accordingly there was no material
> upon the face of the tribunal's decision to suggest that they did not
> have jurisdiction to deal with the application. It is not accepted by
> the respondent that this was a case in which the employer would be
> able to establish that he fell within the excluded categories. This
> court has already said in a number of its judgments that it will not D
> permit a point of law to be raised in this court which could and properly
> should have been taken before a tribunal. The employer, having had
> the advantage of legal representation, was in a position if he wished
> to raise this matter in evidence before the tribunal [to do so]. The
> burden was upon him to seek to establish the exclusion. He did not
> do so. There is no reason why he should not have done so, if so
> minded, and it is not open to him now to raise it before this court. E
> Accordingly this first ground of appeal is rejected."

It is true that the primary matter under consideration in that case was
the propriety or otherwise of raising, for the first time upon an appeal, a
matter in respect of which no evidence had been given before the tribunal.
Nonetheless there is a clear statement by that court upon a matter which
it had necessarily to take into consideration in reaching its decision, to this F
effect (I quote): "The burden was upon him to seek to establish the
exclusion." That case appears to me to offer helpful guidance, and I shall
follow it.

While the formal burden must be on the claimant to establish that the
tribunal has jurisdiction, the framework of the Act by which all employments
qualify, unless excluded by sections 27 to 31, supports the view that once G
employment is proved it is for the employer to prove that it is excluded.
In a different field, *Reg.* v. *Edwards* [1975] Q.B. 27 provides a useful
analogy. It has to be remembered that the typical case of exclusion
under section 27 (1) (*a*) is that of the small shop or business where less
than four people are employed by one employer. There, no difficulty arises.
It is only in unusual cases that difficulties can arise. Where the respondent H
to a claim of unfair dismissal is (with others, or through the medium of
companies) apparently employing four or more persons in a single under-
taking, it is reasonable that the burden of proving that an employment is
excluded under section 27 (1) (*a*) should fall on him, for he alone can know
the facts and raise the point. This being so, though I accept some of the
criticisms of the reasoning of the tribunal on this point, I find that it was
justified in overruling this objection to the jurisdiction raised on behalf

A of the employee. It follows therefore that the decision must stand and the appeal be dismissed.

Appeal dismissed with costs.

Solicitors: *Loxdales; Knapp-Fishers.*

B P. R. K. M.

C [COURT OF APPEAL]

* ROSE *v.* PLENTY AND ANOTHER

[1972 R. No. 167]

D 1975 July 4, 7 Lord Denning M.R., Lawton and Scarman L.JJ.

Vicarious Liability—Master and servant—Course of employment—Milk roundsman assisted by young boy in collecting and delivering milk bottles—Employers' prohibition on young persons assisting roundsmen—Injury to boy—Whether employers vicariously liable for roundsman's negligence

E A milk roundsman paid the plaintiff, aged 13, to help him collect and deliver milk bottles on his round contrary to his employers' prohibition that young persons should not be employed by roundsmen in the performance of their duties. The plaintiff was injured when he fell off a milk float as a result of the roundsman's negligent driving. In the plaintiff's action for damages for personal injuries against both the milk roundsman and the employers, the judge found the plaintiff 25 per cent. to blame for his injuries and the roundsman F 75 per cent. to blame but he dismissed the action against the employers on the ground that the employers could not be held vicariously liable for the action of their employee because the roundsman was acting outside the scope of his employment and that the plaintiff was a trespasser on the milk float.

On appeal by the plaintiff on the ground that the employers were vicariously liable for the milk roundsman's negligent driving:—

G *Held*, allowing the appeal (Lawton L.J. dissenting), that since it was part of the roundsman's duties to collect and deliver milk bottles, the employers' prohibition affected only the conduct of the employment and did not define or limit the scope of those duties; that the milk roundsman's disregard of his employers' instructions was a wrongful performance of his employers' business and not for his own purposes and, accord-H ingly, was not of such a nature as to take his actions outside the scope of his employment and, therefore, the employers were vicariously liable for the plaintiff's injuries.

Limpus v. *London General Omnibus Co.* (1862) 1 H. & C. 526 and *Ilkiw* v. *Samuels* [1963] 1 W.L.R. 991, C.A. followed.

Twine v. *Bean's Express Ltd.* (1946) 62 T.L.R. 458, C.A. and *Conway* v. *George Wimpey & Co. Ltd.* (*No.* 2) [1951] 2 K.B. 266, C.A. distinguished.

Per Lawton L.J. The roundsman, who had taken the plaintiff as a passenger in his vehicle and had sub-contracted his work to the plaintiff contrary to his employers' instructions, was acting outside the scope of his employment and the employers owed the plaintiff no vicarious duty of care (post, pp. 145H—146D). A

Decision of Judge Russell, sitting as an additional judge of the Queen's Bench Division, reversed.

The following cases are referred to in the judgments:

Canadian Pacific Railway Co. v. *Lockhart* [1942] A.C. 591; [1942] 2 All E.R. 464, P.C. B

Conway v. *George Wimpey & Co. Ltd.* (*No.* 2) [1951] 2 K.B. 266; [1951] 1 All E.R. 363, C.A.

Harris v. *Birkenhead Corporation* [1975] 1 W.L.R. 379; [1975] 1 All E.R. 1001.

Hern v. *Nichols* (1700) 1 Salk. 289.

Herrington v. *British Railways Board* [1972] A.C. 877; [1972] 2 W.L.R. 537; [1972] 1 All E.R. 749, H.L.(E.). C

Hilton v. *Thomas Burton* (*Rhodes*) *Ltd.* [1961] 1 W.L.R. 705; [1961] 1 All E.R. 75.

Ilkiw v. *Samuels* [1963] 1 W.L.R. 991; [1963] 2 All E.R. 879, C.A.

Iqbal v. *London Transport Executive* (1973) 16 K.I.R. 329, C.A.

Jones v. *Staveley Iron and Chemical Co. Ltd.* [1955] 1 Q.B. 474; [1955] 2 W.L.R. 69; [1955] 1 All E.R. 6, C.A. D

Limpus v. *London General Omnibus Co.* (1862) 1 H. & C. 526.

Plumb v. *Cobden Flour Mills Co. Ltd.* [1914] A.C. 62, H.L.(E.).

Southern Portland Cement Ltd. v. *Cooper* [1974] A.C. 623; [1974] 2 W.L.R. 152; [1974] 1 All E.R. 87, P.C.

Twine v. *Bean's Express Ltd.* (1946) 62 T.L.R. 458, C.A.

Young v. *Edward Box & Co. Ltd.* [1951] 1 T.L.R. 789, C.A.

The following additional cases were cited in argument: E

Houghton v. *Pilkington* [1912] 3 K.B. 308, D.C.

Stone v. *Taffe* [1974] 1 W.L.R. 1575; [1974] 3 All E.R. 1016, C.A.

APPEAL from Judge Russell sitting as an additional judge of the Queen's Bench Division.

The plaintiff, Leslie Francis Rose, appealed from a judgment of Judge Russell on July 16, 1974, in an action heard in Bristol awarding him £600 F damages against the first defendant, Christopher Plenty, for injuries sustained when he was a passenger on a milk float driven by the first defendant, an employee of the second defendants, Co-operative Retail Services Ltd. who were held not liable for the injuries. He appealed on the ground that the judge ought to have held that in obtaining the plaintiff's assistance in delivering milk the first defendant was doing work which G he was authorised to do in an unauthorised manner so that the second defendants were vicariously liable for the first defendant's negligence.

The facts are stated in the judgment of Lord Denning M.R.

Christopher Rawlins for the plaintiff.
William Barnett for the second defendants.

H

LORD DENNING M.R. Mr. Plenty was a milk roundsman employed at Bristol by the Co-operative Retail Services Ltd. He started working for them at Easter 1970. There were notices up at the depot making it quite clear that the roundsmen were not allowed to take children on the vehicles. One notice said: "Children and young persons *must not in any circumstances be employed by you* in the performance of your duties." Both employers and trade union did their utmost to stop it.

No doubt Mr. Plenty knew it was not allowed. But in spite of all these warnings, the practice still persisted. Boys used to hang about the depot waiting to be taken on and some of the roundsmen used to take them.

Soon after Mr. Plenty started work as a milk roundsman a boy, Leslie Rose, who was just over 13, went up to Mr. Plenty and asked if he could help him. Mr. Plenty agreed to let him do it. The boy described his part in these words:

> "I would jump out of the milk float, grab the milk, whatever had to go into the house, collect the money if there was any there and bring the bottles back."

That is what he did. The milk roundsman paid the boy 6 shillings for the weekends and 4 shillings for the week days. While the boy was going round some houses the roundsman would go to others. On June 21, 1970, unfortunately, there was an accident. After going to one house, the boy jumped on to the milk float. He sat there with one foot dangling down so as to be able to jump off quickly. But at that time the milk roundsman, I am afraid, drove carelessly and negligently. He went too close to the kerb. As the milk float went round the corner, the wheel caught the boy's leg. He tried to get his leg away, but he was dragged out of the milk float. His foot was broken with a compound fracture, but it was mended. So it was not very serious.

Afterwards he, by his father as his next friend, brought an action for damages against the roundsman and against his employers. The judge found that the milk roundsman was negligent, but he felt that the boy was old enough to bear some part of the blame himself. He assessed the responsibility for the accident at 75 per cent. to the milk roundsman and 25 per cent. to the boy. He assessed the total damages at £800. He gave judgment against the milk roundsman for three-quarters of it: £600. But he exempted the employers from any liability. He held that the roundsman was acting outside the scope of his employment and that the boy was a trespasser on the float. The boy, through his father, now appeals to this court. He says the employers are liable for the acts of their milk roundsman.

This raises a nice point on the liability of a master for his servant. I will first take the notices to the roundsmen saying they must not take the boys on. Those do not necessarily exempt the employers from liability. The leading case is *Limpus* v. *London General Omnibus Co.* (1862) 1 H. & C. 526. The drivers of omnibuses were furnished with a card saying they "must not on any account race with or obstruct another omnibus." Nevertheless the driver of one of the defendants' omnibuses did obstruct a rival omnibus and caused an accident in which the plaintiff's horses were injured. Martin B. directed the jury that, if the defendants' driver did it for the purposes of his employer, the defendants were liable, but if it was an act of his own, and in order to effect a purpose of his own, the defendants were not responsible. The jury found for the plaintiff. The Court of Exchequer Chamber held that the direction was correct. It was a very strong court which included Willes J. and Blackburn J. Despite the prohibition, the employers were held liable because the injury resulted from an act done by the driver in the course of his service and for his masters' purposes. The decisive point was that it was *not* done by the servant for his own purposes, but for his masters' purposes.

I will next take the point about a trespasser. The boy was a trespasser on the milk float so far as the employers were concerned. They had not given him any permission to be on the float and had expressly prohibited A the milk roundsman from taking him on. There are two early cases where it was suggested that the employer of a driver is not liable to a person who is a trespasser on the vehicle. They are *Twine* v. *Bean's Express Ltd.* (1946) 62 T.L.R. 458 and *Conway* v. *George Wimpey & Co. Ltd.* (*No.* 2) [1951] 2 K.B. 266. But these cases are to be explained on other grounds and the statements about a trespasser are no longer correct. Those statements were made at a time when it was commonly supposed B that occupiers of premises were under no duty to use care in regard to a trespasser. But that stern rule has now been abandoned, especially when the trespasser is a child: see *Herrington* v. *British Railways Board* [1972] A.C. 877; *Southern Portland Cement Ltd.* v. *Cooper* [1974] A.C. 623 and *Harris* v. *Birkenhead Corporation* [1975] 1 W.L.R. 379. So far as vehicles are concerned, I venture to go back to my own judgment in *Young* v. *Edward Box & Co. Ltd.* [1951] 1 T.L.R. 789, 793, when I said: C

> "In every case where it is sought to make a master liable for the conduct of his servant the first question is to see whether the servant was liable. If the answer is Yes, the second question is to see whether the employer must shoulder the servant's liability."

That way of putting it is, I think, to be preferred to the way I put it later D in *Jones* v. *Staveley Iron and Chemical Co. Ltd.* [1955] 1 Q.B. 474, 480.

Applying the first question in *Young* v. *Edward Box & Co. Ltd.*, it is quite clear that the driver, the milk roundsman, was liable to the boy for his negligent driving of the milk float. He actually invited the boy to ride on it. So the second question arises, whether his employers are liable for the driver's negligence. That does not depend on whether the boy was a trespasser. It depends, as I said in *Young* v. *Edward Box* E *& Co. Ltd.*, on whether the driver, in taking the boy on the milk float, was acting in the course of his employment.

In considering whether a prohibited act was within the course of the employment, it depends very much on the purpose for which it is done. If it is done for his employers' business, it is usually done in the course of his employment, even though it is a prohibited act. That is clear from F *Limpus* v. *London General Omnibus Co.*, 1 H. & C. 526; *Young* v. *Edward Box & Co. Ltd.* [1951] 1 T.L.R. 789 and *Ilkiw* v. *Samuels* [1963] 1 W.L.R. 991. But if it is done for some purpose other than his masters' business, as, for instance, giving a lift to a hitchhiker, such an act, if prohibited, may not be within the course of his employment. Both *Twine* v. *Bean's Express Ltd.* (1946) 62 T.L.R. 458 and *Conway* v. *George* G *Wimpey & Co. Ltd.* (*No.* 2) [1951] 2 K.B. 266 are to be explained on their own facts as cases where a driver had given a lift to someone else, contrary to a prohibition and not for the purposes of the employers. *Iqbal* v. *London Transport Executive* (1973) 16 K.I.R. 329 seems to be out of line and should be regarded as decided on its own special circumstances. In the present case it seems to me that the course of the milk roundsman's employment was to distribute the milk, collect the money H and to bring back the bottles to the van. He got or allowed this young boy to do part of that business which was the employers' business. It seems to me that although prohibited, it was conduct which was within the course of the employment; and on this ground I think the judge was in error. I agree it is a nice point in these cases on which side of the line the case falls; but, as I understand the authorities, this case falls within those in which the prohibition affects only the conduct within

A the sphere of the employment and did not take the conduct outside the sphere altogether. I would hold that the conduct of the roundsman was within the course of his employment and the masters are liable accordingly, and I would allow the appeal.

In parting with the case, it may be interesting to notice that this type of case is unlikely to arise so much in the future, since a vehicle is not to be used on a road unless there is in force an insurance policy covering,
B inter alia, injury to passengers.

LAWTON L.J. Ever since 1946 employers of drivers have been entitled to arrange their affairs on the assumption that if they gave clear and express instructions to their drivers that they were not to carry passengers on the employers' vehicles, the employers would not be liable in law for
C any injury sustained by such passengers. They were entitled to make that assumption because of the decision of this court in *Twine* v. *Bean's Express Ltd.*, 62 T.L.R. 458. No doubt since 1946 employers when negotiating with their insurers have sought to get reductions in premiums and have done so because of the assumption which, so it seems to me, they were entitled to make about freedom from liability to unauthorised passengers. It may well be that the judgment of Lord Greene M.R. at p. 459 is not
D as clear as the judgments of that great judge normally were; but it was the judgment of the Master of the Rolls and it was accepted by the other two members of the court, both judges of very great distinction who were later to go to the House of Lords: Morton L.J. and Tucker L.J. If between 1946 and 1951 any employers had the kind of doubts about *Twine's* case which in more recent years have been expressed by academic
E writers, their minds would have been put at rest by another decision of this court in 1951, namely, *Conway* v. *George Wimpey & Co. Ltd.* (*No.* 2) [1951] 2 K.B. 266. That was a case in which a lorry driver employed by a firm of contractors on a site where many other contractors were working, contrary to his express instructions, gave an employee of another firm of contractors a lift in his lorry. This man was injured while a passenger. The problem for the court was whether the injured man could
F claim against the employers of the lorry driver who had given him a lift. This court, in a unanimous decision, adjudged that the injured man could not claim. The leading judgment was given by Asquith L.J. and he gave his reason for saying that what the lorry driver had done had not been done in the course of his employment. He said, at p. 276:

> "I should hold that taking men not employed by the defendants on
> G to the vehicle was not merely a wrongful mode of performing the act of the class this driver was employed to perform, but was the performance of an act of a class which he was not employed to perform at all."

These two cases have not been overruled by the House of Lords. Insurers have proceeded ever since on the assumption that these cases are properly
H decided. It would I think be most unfortunate if this court departed from clear decisions save on good and clear grounds. What has been submitted is that those two judgments should not be followed because when the driver of the milk float employed the boy to carry bottles for him, he was employing him to do acts which furthered the employers' business interests. In my judgment he was doing nothing of the sort. The driver had been employed to drive the milk float and deliver the milk. He had not been authorised to sub-contract his work. What he was doing was setting the

boy to do the job for which he had been employed and for which he was getting paid. In my judgment in so doing he was acting outside the scope of his employment—just as in the same way as was the driver in *Conway* v. *George Wimpey & Co. Ltd.* (*No.* 2) [1951] 2 K.B. 266.

If a general principle should be relied upon to justify my opinion in this case, I would adopt the same approach as Lord Greene M.R. in *Twine's* case, 62 T.L.R. 458. What duty did the employers owe to the boy? The plaintiff's counsel says: "Oh well, they put the driver with the milk float on the road: they put him into a position to take passengers if he were minded to disobey his instructions and therefore it is socially just that they should be responsible." I do not agree. When they put the driver with his float on the road they put him into a position where he had to take care not to injure those with whom he was reasonably likely to have dealings or to meet, that is all other road users and his customers. They expressly excluded anyone travelling as a passenger on his milk float. He was instructed specifically that he was not to carry passengers. Had he obeyed his instructions, he would not have had a passenger to whom he owes a duty of care. It was his disobedience which brought the injured boy into the class of persons to whom the employers vicariously owed a duty of care. He had not been employed to do anything of the kind. In my judgment, the injured boy has failed to establish that the employers owed him any duty of care.

I appreciate that in *Ilkiw* v. *Samuels* [1963] 1 W.L.R. 991 to which Lord Denning M.R. has already referred, Diplock L.J. did say that a broad approach must be made to this problem. But the broad approach must not be so broad that it obscures the principles of law which are applicable. Therein lies the danger of too broad an approach. That can be illustrated by examining Diplock L.J.'s suggested general question, namely, what was the job on which he, the employee, was engaged for his employer? If that general question is asked without reference to the particular circumstances, the answer in *Twine's* case would have been to make Bean's Express liable for his injuries. The van driver in that case had been employed to drive carefully. He had not been employed to drive negligently. When Twine was injured the driver was doing the job he had been employed to do, namely, to drive. Unless this court is prepared to say that *Twine* v. *Bean's Express Ltd.*, 62 T.L.R. 458 was wrongly decided, for my part I cannot see how that case can be distinguished from this. In the course of the argument an illustrative example was put to Mr. Rawlins, the plaintiff's counsel. He was asked whether if in *Twine's* case the driver had asked the passenger to do some map reading for him in order that he could get more quickly to the place where in the course of his employment he wanted to go, whether that fact would have made the employers liable. Mr. Rawlins said it would. In my judgment fine distinctions of that kind should have no place in our law, particularly in a branch of it which affects so many employers and their insurers. Having regard to what has been decided in the past, in my judgment it would be wrong now, without the authority either of the House of Lords or of Parliament not to follow the 1946 and 1951 cases. I would dismiss the appeal.

SCARMAN L.J. Should there be an attentive visitor from Mars sitting in court at this moment, he might be forgiven for thinking that he was witnessing the exposure of an irreconcilable breach between two lines of authority in the English common law. But in my judgment no such breach has in fact been opened and the two lines of authority that have led Lawton L.J. to differ from the judgment of Lord Denning M.R. are perfectly well capable, when properly analysed, of being reconciled with the principles of the law as asserted, not for the first time, by Lord Denning M.R. in his judgment in this case.

Let me begin with a statement of the general principle of vicarious liability, as I understand it in its application to compensation for accidental damage. In words which have frequently been quoted both in the courts and in the universities, *Salmond on Torts*, 16th ed. (1973), p. 462, refers to the basis of vicarious liability for accidental damage as being one of public policy. That view is supported by quotations (dated no doubt, but still full of life) of a dictum of Lord Brougham and of another, one hundred years or more earlier, of Sir John Holt. That it is "socially convenient and rough justice" to make an employer liable for the torts of his servant in the cases to which the principle applies, was recognised in *Limpus* v. *London General Omnibus Co.*, 1 H. & C. 526; see the judgment of Willes J. at p. 539. I think it important to realise that the principle of vicarious liability is one of public policy. It is not a principle which derives from a critical or refined consideration of other concepts in the common law, for example, the concept of trespass or indeed the concept of agency. No doubt in particular cases it may be relevant to consider whether a particular plaintiff was or was not a trespasser. Similarly, when, as I shall indicate, it is important that one should determine the course of employment of the servant, the law of agency may have some marginal relevance. But basically, as I understand it, the employer is made vicariously liable for the tort of his employee not because the plaintiff is an invitee, nor because of the authority possessed by the servant, but because it is a case in which the employer, having put matters into motion, should be liable if the motion that he has originated leads to damage to another. What is the approach which the cases identify as the correct approach in order to determine this question of public policy? First, as Lord Denning M.R. has already said, one looks to see whether the servant has committed a tort upon the plaintiff. In the present case it is clear that the milk roundsman, the servant of the dairy company, who are the second defendants, by the negligent driving of the milk float, caused injury to the plaintiff, a boy $13\frac{1}{2}$ years old, who was upon the float at his invitation. There was therefore a tort committed by the servant. The next question, as Lord Denning M.R. has said, is whether the employer should shoulder the liability for compensating the person injured by the tort. With all respect to the points developed by Lawton L.J. it does appear to me to be clear, since the decision of *Limpus* v. *London General Omnibus Co.*, 1 H. & C. 526 that that question has to be answered by directing attention to what the servant was employed to do when he committed the tort that has caused damage to the plaintiff. The servant was, of course, employed at the time of the accident to do a whole number of operations. He was certainly not employed to give the boy a lift, and if one confines one's analysis of the facts to the incident of injury to the plaintiff, then no doubt one would say that carrying the boy on the float—giving him a lift—was not in the course of the servant's employment. But in *Ilkiw* v. *Samuels* [1963] 1 W.L.R. 991 Diplock L.J. indicated that the proper approach to the nature of the servant's employment is a broad one. He says, at p. 1004:

> "As each of these nouns implies"—he is referring to the nouns used to describe course of employment, sphere, scope and so forth—"the matter must be looked at broadly, not dissecting the servant's task

> into its component activities—such as driving, loading, sheeting and A the like—by asking: what was the job on which he was engaged for his employer? and answering that question as a jury would."

Applying those words to the employment of this servant, I think it is clear from the evidence that he was employed as a roundsman to drive his float round his round and to deliver milk, to collect empties and to obtain payment. That was his job. He was under an express prohibition—a matter B to which I shall refer later—not to enlist the help of anyone doing that work. And he was also under an express prohibition not to give lifts on the float to anyone. How did he choose to carry out the task which I have analysed. He chose to disregard the prohibition and to enlist the assistance of the plaintiff. As a matter of common sense, that does seem to me to be a mode, albeit a prohibited mode, of doing the job with which he was entrusted. Why was the plaintiff being carried on the float when the C accident occurred? Because it was necessary to take him from point to point so that he could assist in delivering milk, collecting empties and, on occasions, obtaining payment. The plaintiff was there because it was necessary that he should be there in order that he could assist, albeit in a way prohibited by the employers, in the job entrusted to the servant by his employers. D

We have taken a brief look at the historical origins of the doctrine of vicarious liability. One finds in the analysis of the facts which I have just given an echo of words used by Sir John Holt C.J. as long ago as 1700. In *Hern* v. *Nichols* (1700) 1 Salk. 289 he was enunciating, with I think a good deal of prophetic wisdom, the principle of vicarious liability as he saw it. He said, at p. 289—and one notes the factor of public policy in his thinking: E

> "seeing somebody must be a loser by this deceit, it is more reason that he that employs and puts a trust and confidence in the deceiver should be a loser, than a stranger: . . ."

His words have no direct application to the facts of this case, but there is a family relationship. The "deceiver" is the milk roundsman in whom the F dairy company had placed its trust and confidence. It is he who has encouraged the plaintiff (who acted, of course, in ignorance of the prohibition and perfectly reasonably), to accompany him on his float and assist him in doing his employers' business. The plaintiff was a stranger to the employers. When in the course of such assistance, the "stranger" was injured by the servant's negligence, the question which, according to Sir John Holt, one should ask is: should the stranger be without remedy G against the employer who put trust and confidence in the servant merely because he disobeyed instructions not known to the stranger?

It does seem to me that the principle that I have been attempting to describe is to be found in the case law, notably in *Limpus* v. *London General Omnibus Co.*, 1 H. & C. 526; *Hilton* v. *Thomas Burton* (*Rhodes*) *Ltd.* [1961] 1 W.L.R. 705 and *Ilkiw* v. *Samuels* [1963] 1 W.L.R. 991. H Yet it is said that the flow of this current of authority must be dammed and the stream of the law diverted because of the two decisions to which Lawton L.J. has referred: *Twine* v. *Bean's Express Ltd.*, 62 T.L.R. 458 and *Conway* v. *George Wimpey & Co. Ltd.* (*No. 2*) [1951] 2 K.B. 266. Both of those decisions seem to me distinguishable upon their facts. In *Twine's* case Lord Greene M.R. says, at p. 459:

> "The other thing which he [that is the servant] was doing simultane-

A ously was something totally outside the scope of his employment—
namely, giving a lift to a person who had no right whatsoever to be
there."

In that case the conclusion of fact was that the express prohibition upon
giving lifts was not only a prohibition but was also a limiting factor on the
scope of the employment; and, of course, once a prohibition is properly
B to be treated as a defining or limiting factor upon the scope of employment
certain results follow. In *Twine's* case the driver was engaged to drive his
employers' van, his employers having a contract with the Post Office. When
so doing, he gave Mr. Twine a lift from A to B. With deep respect, I
can well understand why the court reached the conclusion that in the
circumstances of that case the driver in giving Mr. Twine a lift was
acting outside the scope of his employment and was not doing improperly
C that which he was employed to do. Similarly when one looks at
Conway's case [1951] 2 K.B. 266, one again sees that upon the facts
of that case the court considered it right so to define the scope of
employment that what was done, namely, giving somebody a lift, was out-
side it and was not a mode of doing that which the servant was employed
to do. That also was a case of lift and the person given a lift was not in
any way engaged, in the course of the lift or indeed otherwise, in doing the
D master's business or in assisting the servant to do the master's business;
and no doubt it was for that reason that Asquith L.J. was able to say that
what was done—that is giving somebody else's employee a lift from the
airport home—was not a mode of performing an act which the driver was
employed to do, but was the performance of an act which he was not
employed to perform.

E In the present case the milk roundsman, the servant, was employed to
deliver milk, to collect empties, to obtain payment from customers. The
plaintiff was there on the float in order to assist the roundsman to do those
jobs. I would have thought, therefore, that whereas *Conway* v. *George
Wimpey & Co. Ltd.* (*No.* 2) [1951] 2 K.B. 266 was absolutely correctly
decided upon its facts, the facts of the present case lead to a very different
conclusion. The dividing factor between the present case and the
F decisions in *Twine* v. *Bean's Express Ltd.* and *Conway* v. *George Wimpey
& Co. Ltd.* is the category into which the court, upon the study of the facts
of the case, puts the express prohibition issued by the employers to their
servant. In *Ilkiw* v. *Samuels* [1963] 1 W.L.R. 991 Diplock L.J., in a
judgment to which I have already referred, dealt with this problem of the
prohibition, and quoted a dictum of Lord Dunedin in *Plumb* v. *Cobden
G Flour Mills Co. Ltd.* [1914] A.C. 62, which itself has been approved in the
Privy Council case of *Canadian Pacific Railway Co.* v. *Lockhart* [1942]
A.C. 591. Lord Dunedin said, at p. 67:

> "there are prohibitions which limit the sphere of employment, and prohibitions which only deal with conduct within the sphere of employment."

H Now those words are in fact an echo of what has long been the law. Much
the same thing but in a different social context was said by Blackburn J.
in *Limpus* v. *London General Omnibus Co.*, 1 H. & C. 526, 542:

> "A footman might think it for the interest of his master to drive the coach, but no one could say that it was within the scope of the footman's employment, and that the master would be liable for damage resulting from the wilful act of the footman in taking charge of the horses."

And, coming right down to today, one finds the same idea being followed and developed by this court in *Iqbal* v. *London Transport Executive* (1973) 16 K.I.R. 329. In that case the Court of Appeal had to consider whether the London Transport Executive was liable for the action of a bus conductor in driving contrary to his express instructions a motor bus a short distance in a garage. Of course, the court had no difficulty at all in distinguishing between the spheres of employment of a driver and a conductor in the London Transport. Accordingly, it treated the prohibition upon conductors acting as drivers of motor buses as a prohibition which defined their sphere of employment. Now there was nothing of that sort in the prohibition in this case. The prohibition is twofold: (1) that the milk roundsman was not to give lifts on his float, and (2) that he was not to employ others to help him in delivering the milk and so forth. There was nothing in those prohibitions which defined or limited the sphere of his employment. The sphere of his employment remained precisely the same after as before the prohibitions were brought to his notice. The sphere was as a milk roundsman to go round the rounds delivering milk, collecting empties and obtaining payment. Contrary to instructions, he chose to do what he was employed to do in an improper way. But the sphere of his employment was in no way affected by his express instructions not to enlist the help of a stranger.

Finally, I think one can see how careful one must be not to introduce into a study of this sort of problem ideas of trespass and agency. It is perfectly possible, upon the principle that I am now considering, that an employer may authorise his servant, if the servant chooses to do it—"permit" is perhaps a better word—to give lifts. But the effect of that permission does not make the employer liable if in the course of recreational or off duty but permitted activity the servant drives the vehicle negligently and injures the passenger. *Hilton* v. *Thomas Burton (Rhodes) Ltd.* [1961] 1 W.L.R. 705 to which I have referred is a case in which the plaintiff failed although the journey was a permitted journey, because he was not able to show that the journey on which he was being carried was a journey which occurred in the course of the servant's employment. Conversely one has the classic case of *Limpus* v. *London General Omnibus Co.*, 1 H. & C. 526, when what the servant was doing was a defiance and disregard of the bus company's instructions. Nevertheless the plaintiff who was injured by those defiant and disobedient acts was entitled to recover against the employer.

It is for those reasons that I agree with Lord Denning M.R.; and if that visitor from Mars is still in court after this long judgment, he will return to his planet conscious that one member of the court sees no irreconcilable difference opening up in the common law.

Appeal allowed.
Judgment for plaintiff against second defendants for £620 *damages plus* £63·90, *with costs.*
Leave to appeal.

Solicitors: *Ryders for Bobbetts, Harvey & Grove, Bristol; Barlow, Lyde & Gilbert for Sansbury, Hill & Co., Bristol.*

J. W.

A [CHANCERY DIVISION]

* CENTRAL ELECTRICITY GENERATING BOARD *v.* CLWYD COUNTY COUNCIL

[1975 C. No. 1281]

B 1975 April 11; May 21, 22 — Goff J.

Common Rights — Provisional registration — "Common land" — Objection by owners — No rights registered within requisite period—Whether land subject to rights of common—Evidence of grazing and other uses—Commons commissioner's decision
C *confirming provisional registration—Whether in accordance with evidence—Commons Registration Act* 1965 (*c.* 64), *ss.* 1 (2) (*b*), 4, 5, 6, 21 (1), 22 (1) [1]

Common Rights—Common land—Registration—No rights registered within statutory time limit—Whether rights extinguished —Commons Registration Act 1965 (*c.* 64), *s.* 1—*Law of Property Act* 1925 (15 & 16 *Geo.* 5, *c.* 19), *ss.* 193, 194 [2]

The owner of a farm near an unenclosed area of saltings
D in the estuary of the River Dee applied under the Commons Registration Act 1965 to register rights of common over the area. The application was out of time and failed, but a provisional registration of the area as common land, which was not out of time, was made by the local registration authority, the Flintshire (now Clwyd) County Council, under section 4 of the Act. The Central Electricity Generating Board, the appellants, who were owners of the greater part of the area,
E objected to the registration and the matter was referred to a Commons Commissioner under section 5 (6). After an inquiry held pursuant to section 6 of the Act, the commissioner confirmed the council's registration of the area as common land. He took the view, after hearing the evidence as to grazing and other uses, that the land was subject to rights of common within the meaning of the definition in section 22, although none had been registered at the date of the council's provisional registra-
F tion of the area as common land, and none were exercisable at the date of the hearing. He held that any rights of common which might have existed when the provisional registration was made had not been extinguished for want of registration.

The appellants appealed by way of case stated under section 18 of the Act:—

Held, allowing the appeal, that since "common land" meant land subject to rights of common, and no rights of
G common over the area had been registered within the period required by section 1 (2) of the Act, any rights which might have existed were no longer exercisable; further, that having regard to sections 193 and 194 of the Law of Property Act 1925, the fact that any such rights of common were no longer exercisable meant that they were extinguished, and therefore the area in question was not common land and the registration should have been refused on the ground that the land was not
H subject to rights of common (post, pp. 154F–G, 155D–F, H—156B, 157C–E).

Held, further that the commissioner's decision that, on the evidence adduced, the area was subject to rights of common

[1] Commons Registration Act 1965, s. 1: see post, p. 154D.
S. 21: see post, p. 155G.
S. 22: see post, p. 155C–D.

[2] Law of Property Act 1925, s. 193: see post, p. 155G–H.
S. 194: see post, p. 155H.

within the statutory definition was wrong, on the grounds; (i) it was too general, since the onus lay on the respondents to formulate some specific right, but none had been registered or adduced at the hearing; further, the decision failed to show the nature of rights found to exist, or their extent, or who claimed to own them or the land to which they might be appendant or appurtenant; (ii) the commissioner had misdirected himself since the findings on which his determination was based ran counter to facts pointing to there being no rights of common, including the fact that no one had registered any claim; that therefore, the commissioner's decision confirming the respondent's provisional registration would be reversed (post, pp. 158E–F, H—159A, 160E–F, H—161B). A B

Dicta of Lord Radcliffe in *Edwards* v. *Bairstow* [1956] A.C. 14, 35, 36, H.L.(E.) applied.

Chinnock v. *Hartley Wintney Rural District Council* (1899) 63 J.P. 327 and *Behrens* v. *Richards* [1905] 2 Ch. 614 considered. C

The following cases are referred to in the judgment:

Behrens v. *Richards* [1905] 2 Ch. 614.

Chinnock v. *Hartley Wintney Rural District Council* (1899) 63 J.P. 327.

Edwards v. *Bairstow* [1956] A.C. 14; [1955] 3 W.L.R. 410; [1955] 3 All E.R. 48, H.L.(E.). D

Symes and Jaywick Associated Properties v. *Essex Rivers Catchment Board* [1937] 1 K.B. 548; [1936] 3 All E.R. 908, C.A.

White v. *Taylor* [1969] 1 Ch. 150; [1967] 3 W.L.R. 1246; [1967] 3 All E.R. 349.

The following additional cases were cited in argument:

Cooke v. *Amey Gravel Co. Ltd.* [1972] 1 W.L.R. 1310; [1972] 3 All E.R. 579. E

Dalton v. *Angus* (1881) 6 App.Cas. 740, H.L.(E.).

New Windsor Corporation v. *Mellor* [1974] 1 W.L.R. 1504; [1974] 2 All E.R. 510.

Wilkes v. *Gee* [1973] 1 W.L.R. 111; [1973] 1 All E.R. 226; [1973] 1 W.L.R. 742; [1973] 2 All E.R. 1214, C.A.

F

CASE STATED

On May 21, 1970, John Winston Thomas, the owner of Pentre Farm, Chester Road, Flint, applied to the registration authority, the Flintshire (now Clwyd) County Council, for registration under the Commons Registration Act 1965 of certain rights of common over an unenclosed area of land near his property, known as Dee Marsh Saltings, in the estuary of the River Dee. The application was out of time, the last date for such an application being January 2, 1970. The local registration authority, the present respondents, being themselves entitled to register land as common land up to July 31, 1970, made a provisional registration of the Saltings as common land on July 17, 1970, under section 4 of the Act of 1965. On November 6, 1970, an objection to the registration by the British Railways Board who owned part of the land was noted in the Commons register. On August 17, 1971, an objection to the registration by the present appellants, the Central Electricity Generating Board, who owned the greater part of the land in question, was noted in the register. The matter was referred to a commons commissioner under section 5 (6) of the Act. On December 11 and 12, 1973, there was a hearing by H. E. Francis Q.C. sitting as a commons commissioner, when the respondents, the British Railways Board and the appellants were repre- G H sented. During the hearing, the respondents withdrew their case for registration so far as it related to the railways' land. Oral evidence was given by J. W. Thomas of Pentre Farm and by T. Fish, an alderman of the County of Flint, who both testified that farmers had for many years grazed the land. Mr. Fish further testified that fishermen used to graze their horses and dry out their nets on the land. Documentary evidence was produced by the appellants of the grant of grazing licences.

On March 14, 1974, the commissioner confirmed the respondents' registration so far as it related to the land owned by the appellants. The appellants appealed by way of case stated under section 18 of the Act, and, on February 10, 1975, gave notice of motion seeking the opinion of the High Court on the following questions of law.

(1) Whether for the purpose of confirming or refusing to confirm, under section 6 of the Act, the provisional registration of Dee Marsh Saltings as common land, the relevant date for deciding whether the land was subject to rights of common was the date of provisional registration of the land or the date of hearing by the commissioner. (2) Whether if on the appropriate date for determining the position no rights of common had been provisionally registered over Dee Marsh Saltings the commissioner could properly confirm such registration on the grounds that the land was common land within the definition of section 22 (1) (*a*) being land subject to rights of common. (3) Whether there was sufficient evidence to justify the finding of the commissioner that the land was on July 17, 1970, land subject to rights of common within the statutory definition. (4) Whether on the facts so found the land was subject on July 17, 1970, to rights of common within the statutory definition. (5) Whether there was sufficient evidence to establish and justify the finding that land acquired by Mr. Thomas had at the date of its acquisition in 1956 ceased to be part of any common land of which the Saltings formed part. (6) Whether on the facts found the said finding was justified in law. (7) Whether the finding that the rights of Mr. Thomas in relation to Pentre Farm were not extinguished by such acquisition.

On April 11, 1975, Goff J. ruled that the land was not common land and he reversed the decision of the commissioner. Subsequently, Goff J. restored the case for further hearing on learning of a letter from the Department of the Environment propounding arguments to the contrary.

Further facts are stated in the judgment of Goff J.

Charles Sparrow Q.C. and *G. A. Lightman* for the appellants.

The respondents, Clwyd County Council, were not represented.

Goff J. This is an appeal by way of case stated from a decision dated March 14, 1974, of Mr. H. E. Francis Q.C., sitting as a special commissioner under the Commons Registration Act 1965 and it lies only on a matter of law.

The subject matter of the proceedings is an area of the Saltings in the estuary of the River Dee. The nature and character of Saltings is well described by Scott L.J. in *Symes and Jaywick Associated Properties* v. *Essex Rivers Catchment Board* [1937] 1 K.B. 548, 563. It is land which by its nature is not fit for agriculture and, one would think, not very suitable for grazing sheep and cattle. All the relevant parts of the area were completely unenclosed. It had at one time been manorial land but, as the commissioner found, it had been taken out of the manor by certain conveyances and it was not manorial land at any relevant time.

The appellants, who are the Central Electricity Generating Board, desired to use part of it for the erection of a power station, which aroused considerable local opposition, and in consequence a local farmer, Mr. John Winston Thomas, the owner of Pentre Farm, wished to register rights of common over the appellants' land in the Saltings, but the statutory date at which the right for anyone to apply to register rights of common expired was January 2, 1970. Unhappily for him, Mr. Thomas failed to make any application until May 14, 1970. He was therefore out of time and his application failed. The Flintshire County Council, however, were in a position to register the land as common land after January 2, 1970, since, under the relevant statutory orders, that could be done down to July 31 in that year. Whether to assist Mr. Thomas, or for their own purposes in defeating the appellants' plans, or for other reasons, the Flintshire County Council did in fact register the appellants' land as common land on July 17, 1970, so they were just in time. Nobody else applied either in time or at all to register rights of common and none were ever registered.

Section 1 (2) of the Act of 1965 provides:

> "After the end of such period, not being less than three years from the commencement of this Act, as the Minister may by order determine . . . (*b*) no rights of common shall be exercisable over any such land unless they are registered either under this Act or under the Land Registration Acts 1925 and 1936."

I should observe that no rights of common were registered under the Land Registration Acts. The period prescribed for that section expired on July 31, 1970.

The appellants objected to the registration and the matter was referred to the commons commissioner under section 5 (6) of the Act The relevant words of that subsection are: ". . . shall refer the matter to a commons commissioner."

Now it will be seen that when the authority registered the land as common land the rights of common over it, if any, were bound within a short time to become non-exercisable by virtue of section 1 (2) (*b*) of the Act, and nothing could save them, although at that time that statutory provision was not yet operative. By the time, however, that the commissioner came to deal with the matter the section had taken full force and effect, and no rights of common having been registered none could thereafter be exercised.

The commissioner held an inquiry on December 11 and 12, 1973, and, as I have said, gave his decision on March 14, 1974. He took the view that for the purpose of deciding whether to confirm or to refuse to confirm the registration he must consider whether the land in question was subjects to rights of common immediately before the registration, that is on July 17, 1970, and he said:

> "The fact that no rights of common had been registered at that date, or the fact that no commoner could after January 2, 1970, apply for the registration of any right of common, appears to me to be irrelevant. The rights of common (if any) over the land had not been extinguished for want of registration on July 17, 1970."

A He then proceeded to hear evidence, as a result of which he found that there was sufficient to establish the fact that the land in question was, on July 17, 1970, land subject to rights of common within the meaning of the statutory definition, and he therefore confirmed the registration. The effect of that decision, subject to this appeal, is that the registration has, by virtue of section 6 (1), become final; and by section 10 it is to be conclusive evidence of the matters registered as at the date of registra-
B tion.

The appellants say that that was wrong and that the commissioner, finding that when he had to deal with the matter, even if there were rights of common, they could no longer be exercised, ought, on that short ground, to have refused to confirm the registration. I should refer to the definition in section 22 which provides:

C "(1) In this Act, unless the context otherwise requires—'common land' means—(*a*) land subject to rights of common (as defined in this Act) whether those rights are exercisable at all times or only during limited periods; (*b*) waste land of a manor not subject to rights of common; but does not include a town or village green or any land which forms part of a highway; 'rights of common' includes cattle-
D gates or beastgates (by whatever name known) and rights of sole or several vesture or herbage, or of sole or several pasture, but does not include rights held for a term of years or from year to year."

It will be observed that section 1 (2) (*b*) of the Act says that no rights of common shall be exercisable over any such land unless duly registered, whereas the interpretation of the section says that common land means
E land subject to rights of common, and, in order to mount his objection, Mr. Sparrow for the appellants must show that the effect of section 1 (2) (*b*) is to extinguish unregistered rights so that thereafter the land is no longer subject to rights of common.

In my judgment, he has discharged that burden. He relies first on the words in section 22 (1) ". . . whether those rights are exercisable at all times or only during limited periods . . ." Those words are all-embracing,
F and when one finds that description of the words "subject to rights of common," and then finds under section 1 (2) (*b*) that no rights of common in the circumstances in the events which have happened are exercisable, it seems clearly to follow that the rights must have been extinguished and the land no longer be subject to rights of common. But it does not rest there because there is a saving clause, section 21 (1), which provides:

G "(1) Section 1 (2) of this Act shall not affect the application to any land registered under this Act of section 193 or section 194 of the Law of Property Act 1925 (rights of access to, and restriction on inclosure of, land over which rights of common are exercisable)."

That section clearly notes therefore that, but for the saving clause, something in the Act would affect those sections. Now section 193 (1) (*d*) of
H the Law of Property Act 1925 is a proviso that "the rights of access shall cease to apply—(i) to any land over which the commonable rights are extinguished under any statutory provision." And section 194 (3) has a proviso that the section "shall cease to apply (*a*) to any land over which the rights of common are extinguished under any statutory provision." It is to those two provisions that the saving in section 21 of the Act of 1965 is clearly directed, and the significance is that whilst section 1 (2) (*b*) of the Act of 1965 refers only to the rights not being exercisable, it is saved

from operating under the provisions in sections 193 and 194 of the Law A of Property Act 1925 which refer to the rights being extinguished; and therefore clearly the legislature was contemplating section 1 (2) (*b*) of the Act of 1965 as working an extinguishment. That is emphasised by the parenthesis in section 21 (1) which reads as a definition of the relevant parts of sections 193 and 194 of the Act of 1925 as follows:

> " rights of access to, and restriction on inclosure of, land over which B rights of common are exercisable."

In my judgment it is plain that in the Commons Registration Act 1965 the legislature was using the expression " cease to be exercisable " as synonymous with " extinguished."

The matter was heard before me a little while ago, and I had reached that conclusion. But shortly afterwards it came to Mr. Sparrow's notice C that the respondents, the Clwyd County Council (as successors to the Flintshire County Council), had in their hands a letter from the Department of the Environment in which arguments to the contrary were propounded. He very properly drew that to my attention and I therefore restored the matter for further hearing, and he has dealt with those arguments, although the respondents themselves have not appeared to support them. D

It appears to be suggested that it was right for the commissioner to look only at the date of registration because, if he confirmed the registration, it could stand notwithstanding the failure to register any rights of common, and could not be amended under section 13 of the Act of 1965 because that could only be applied if there was some change of circumstance or something outside which caused the failure to register rights E of common. I cannot accept that view. It seems to me that if the commissioner were right in looking at that date and therefore confirming the registration, it would become conclusive evidence that the land was common land at the time of registration but nothing more; and accordingly, when the rights ceased to be exercisable, it would cease to be common land and therefore it would lead inevitably to an application, an unanswerable application, to amend the register. F Of course, land may be registered as common land although there are no rights of common over it, because the definition in section 22 (1) includes " waste land of a manor not subject to rights of common," but that is not this case.

In support of that argument the letter from the Department of the Environment drew attention to the provisions of section 6 (3) and section 12 (*b*), and it was said that, if the argument were not correct, one would G expect some similar automatic provision in the Act applying to the case of land ceasing to be common land through the failure to register any rights of common over it. I am satisfied that there is nothing in that argument. Section 6 (3) is dealing with the registration of land as common land being cancelled, and it provides that the registration authority shall also cancel the registration of any person as the owner thereof. H But the cancellation of the registration of the land as common land does not of itself affect any question of ownership, and therefore the provisions of section 6 (3) are required to deal with that situation; also in section 12 (*b*), where it is provided that on notification that the land has been registered under the Land Registration Acts 1925 and 1936 the registration of the ownership under the Act of 1965 shall be deleted. That is of the same character because the registration under the Land Registration

Acts 1925 and 1936 does not of itself affect the registration under the Commons Registration Act 1965, and so an express provision is required.

The letter from the Department of the Environment takes a further point in support of the argument in which reference is made to section 5 (7) of the Act of 1965. That provides:

> "An objection to the registration of any land as common land or as a town or village green shall be treated for the purposes of this Act as being also an objection to any registration (whenever made) under section 4 of this Act of any rights over the land,"

and it is pointed out that there is no converse provision. However, in my judgment, that has no weight. An objection to the registration of any land as common land is a complete attack on its status and must involve objecting to any rights of common registered over it, but the converse is not true; an attack on a right of common registered over land does not necessarily involve attacking the whole status of the land as common land, which it may continue to be because of other rights or as manorial land over which there are no rights.

In my judgment, therefore, at the time when the commissioner heard the matter the land was not subject to rights of common, and on that short ground he ought to have refused to confirm the registration. What is referred to him under section 5 (6) is "the matter," and the matter in my view is whether or not the land is common land. To confirm the registration because at that time it might have been right, when one knows at the hearing that it is wrong, leaving the objector to apply to amend the register, seems to be a wrong course to pursue.

On that short ground therefore, this appeal succeeds and I refuse to confirm the registration.

Mr. Sparrow dealt with other points also. He submitted that the registration was in any event inherently bad because one cannot register land as common land on the ground that it is subject to rights of common unless there is on the register a registration of rights of common, or the authority when registering it as common land itself registers such rights. It is not necessary for me to determine that question in this case. It is I think a difficult one. There is no respondent here to argue the contrary, and it may be important in other cases, and I therefore express no view on that one way or the other.

Mr. Sparrow also attacked the decision—on the assumption that he was wrong on the first point—on the ground that the decision was wrong in law and I ought to deal with that line of argument. Only one person claimed at the hearing a right of common, and that was Mr. Thomas, but the appellants proved that he had bought part of the common and it is clear from *White* v. *Taylor* [1969] 1 Ch. 150, that that had the effect of destroying his right, if it was a right appurtenant The commissioner found that the land purchased by Mr. Thomas was not part of the common. He said:

> "Finally, it appears to me that the rule relied on by Mr. Lightman only operates where the land was part of the common at the date of purchase by the commoner. In this case, as I see it, the 23 acres purchased by Mr. David Thomas in 1956 had long since ceased to be part of the common. It could have ceased to be part of the common by approvement, or under statutory authority. Presumably, it was conveyed by the Crown to one or other of the British Transport

Commission's predecessors in title—e.g. the Chester and Holyhead A Railway Company—although it is not clear to me whether the conveyance dated September 15, 1856, by the Crown in favour of that company included the 23 acres."

It may be that the commissioner was there confusing the position with the fact that, as he had found, this part of the land had ceased to be part of the waste of the manor, and approvement is a manorial term. B If that is what he had in his mind at that stage, it was, in my respectful view, irrelevant. But if he was in truth saying that that land had ceased to be part of the common, there was no evidence of that at all. Therefore, for Mr. Thomas to have any right it would have to be shown that his right was appendant. Counsel for the respondents, however, had put his whole case on the ground that whatever rights there were were appurtenant, C and although the commissioner was not satisfied of the origin of the rights which he found, there was no evidence of any right appendant. All the evidence was evidence of user which, if it supports anything, shows an appurtenant and not an appendant right. In my judgment, therefore, it was clear on the facts found that Mr. Thomas had not and and could not have any rights of common over the land in question. But, as the commissioner found, other persons had enjoyed the land, and D he said:

"In my view, the premise is not well founded, because the evidence satisfied me that not only the owner of Pentre Farm" (that is Mr. Thomas), "but the owners of other neighbouring farms, had common rights of grazing over the land."

E

And he found in addition to that that the land was on July 17, 1970, subject to rights of common within the meaning of the statutory definition.

In my judgment, with all respect to the commissioner, his decision was wrong on one or other or both of two overlapping grounds: first, that it was too general, and secondly, that the evidence was such that in reaching that conclusion the commissioner must be taken to have misdirected F himself within the meaning of the cases explained by Lord Radcliffe in *Edwards* v. *Bairstow* [1956] A.C. 14, 35, 36. The relevant passage is well known and I need not read it fully, but Lord Radcliffe summed up, at p. 36:

"I do not think that it much matters whether this state of affairs is described as one in which there is no evidence to support the determination G or as one in which the evidence is inconsistent with and contradictory of the determination, or as one in which the true and only reasonable conclusion contradicts the determination. Rightly understood, each phrase propounds the same test. For my part, I prefer the last of the three, since I think that it is rather misleading to speak of there being no evidence to support a conclusion when in cases such as these many of the facts are likely to be neutral in H themselves, and only to take their colour from the combination of circumstances in which they are found to occur."

Speaking of generality, in my judgment the onus lay on the respondents when the registration was challenged to allege and prove at least one right of common exercisable over the land. No specific right was formulated, none was registered, and none was adduced or adumbrated

A at the hearing, and the decision fails to specify the nature of the common rights which were found to exist beyond saying that they were rights of grazing; it fails to quantify the extent of the rights, it fails to show the land to which they were appendant or appurtenant, and it fails to show who claimed to own the rights. In my judgment, it is not sufficient to support a registration to say "Well, there has been a lot of user, and therefore one must assume that somebody has got a right." It must be
B much more definite than that. Of course, where one is dealing with a village green, general evidence of user is all that one requires or can expect; but where it is a question of a particular right, though evidence of user is the way of proving it, the right, in my judgment, ought to be properly formulated and properly found.

So far as the other objection which I have mentioned is concerned,
C there was of course evidence of user of the land in question for pasturage of cattle. There was, however, considerable evidence showing that there was no right, and before I mention that in detail, I ought to refer to two authorities on which Mr. Sparrow relied. The first was *Chinnock* v. *Hartley Wintney Rural District Council* (1899) 63 J.P. 327. He relied on this passage, at p. 328:

D "In order to constitute a valid dedication to the public of a highway by the owner of the soil it is clearly settled that there must be an intention to dedicate—there must be an animus dedicandi of which the user by the public is evidence and no more, and a single act of interruption by the owner is of much more weight upon a question of intention than many acts of enjoyment. To this I may add that, in my judgment, user by the public over land belonging to a non-
E resident owner is less cogent evidence of dedication than where the user is necessarily brought to his personal notice; and, further, that the weight to be attached to user must depend somewhat upon the nature of the land itself, whether it is cultivated land or rough and unproductive land."

That is a case of dedication of a highway, but the principles there stated
F are applicable to the type of case with which the commissioner was concerned. The other authority is *Behrens* v. *Richards* [1905] 2 Ch. 614 in which the court refused to grant an injunction to restrain persons from trespassing because the landowner was not injured thereby, and Buckley J. made some pertinent observations about the distinction between matters being done as of right and matters being done by the
G indulgence of the owner when dealing with this kind of property. He said, at p. 619:

"To those who are conversant with the Cornish coast or with many other parts of the coast in this country it will be familiar that there are frequently to be found rough tracks or paths which have in fact been used without objection made by the landowner for very many
H years. From this fact alone it is difficult in surroundings such as there are in this case to infer an intention to dedicate. I cite again, as I did in *Brinckman* v. *Matley* [1904] 2 Ch. 313, Bowen L.J.'s words in *Blount* v. *Layard* [1891] 2 Ch. 681n, 691n, 'that nothing worse can happen in a free country than to force people to be churlish about their rights for fear that their indulgence may be abused, and to drive them to prevent the enjoyment of things which, although they are matters of private property, naturally give pleasure

> to many others besides the owners, under the fear that their good nature may be misunderstood,' and 'that, however continuous, however lengthy, the indulgence may have been, a jury ought to be warned against extracting out of it an inference unfavourable to the person who has granted the indulgence.' In permitting persons to stray along the cliff edge or wander down the cliff face or stroll along the foreshore the owner of the land was permitting that which was no injury to him and whose refusal would have been a churlish and unreasonable act on his part. From such a user nothing, I think, is to be inferred."

Whilst I appreciate that the question is not what I myself would have decided were I dealing with it at first instance but whether the case falls within the principles stated by Lord Radcliffe in *Edwards* v. *Bairstow* [1956] A.C. 14, 35, 36, nevertheless, in looking to see what evidence there was, I think one ought to bear in mind the principles stated in the last two cited cases.

It is clear, and the commissioner found, that a number of facts existed which told heavily against there being any rights of common over the property in question. Part of it had been enclosed without objection; not the part which is the subject matter of this application, nor Mr. Thomas's land, but part of the Saltings. Fishermen, in the days when they had horsecarts to take their catch away, grazed their horses upon it. And most cogently of all, there were cases in which the owners of neighbouring farms, who were enjoying the Saltings, took licences for the purpose.

If the matter stopped there, it might be a case in which one would say, "Well, I would have reached a different conclusion," but still there was evidence on which the commissioner could find as he did but it does not stop there. In addition to those facts there is the most cogent fact to which I have adverted more than once, that nobody registered any claims, and nobody appeared at the hearing to assert any claims other than the respondents and they did not particularise or formulate the claims which they said they were asserting, or state on whose behalf the claims were asserted. At all events, the commissioner found nothing more specific than that the owners of other neighbouring farms had rights, not specifying which farms. More important still, there was clearly no evidence at all to support any rights appendant. The case had to be and was presented on the basis that there were rights appurtenant, but the commissioner was not satisfied that it had been shown that the rights were appurtenant. He said:

> "True, it was referred to by Mr. McCulloch as an appurtenant right, but there was no evidence before me to show whether it was in origin an appurtenant or appendant right. Presumably, no such evidence is now obtainable. But it seems to me that this somewhat technical and arbitrary rule of law . . ." (he was there dealing with the case of other farms) ". . . ought not to be applied in the absence of clear evidence that the right of common in question was in fact an appurtenant right."

There he was dealing with the case of Mr. Thomas, but it is clear that the other persons were in no different or better position. The commissioner there reaches the conclusion that there was no evidence before him to show whether it was in origin an appurtenant or appendant right, and that there

A was no clear evidence that the right in question was in fact an appurtenant right. There being no evidence that it was an appendant right, and the commissioner's view of the evidence whether it was an appurtenant right being as I have stated, it seems to me that the case falls very clearly within the last part of the citation from Lord Radcliffe in *Edwards* v. *Bairstow* [1956] A.C. 14, 35, 36. Many of the facts were neutral in themselves; they might have been enjoyment as of right; they might have been
B indulgence by a more or less or actual absent landowner; but they take their colour from the combination of circumstances in which they are found to occur, and, taking that colour, in my judgment there was no sufficient evidence to support the commissioner's finding that the land was subject to rights of common within the meaning of the statutory definition, even if it was not defective for want of particularity.

C If I am wrong—and I do not think I am—on the premise that the registration should not have been confirmed because the rights had all ceased to exist at the time of the hearing, and that was the relevant time at which to look, nevertheless, in my judgment, for the reasons I have given, it ought not to be confirmed. I therefore with respect reverse the decision of the special commissioner and, in the words of section 6, refuse to confirm the registration.

D *Appeal allowed.*

Solicitor: *A. L. Wright.*

K. N. B.

E

[CHANCERY DIVISION]

* *In re* REYNETTE-JAMES, DECD.

WIGHTMAN *v.* REYNETTE-JAMES AND OTHERS

[1974 R. No. 539]

F

1975 June 5, 6; 24 Templeman J.

Will—Construction—Omission—Clause providing for life interests in residuary estate followed by gifts of capital—Intended gifts of capital to testatrix's son contained in approved draft of clause inadvertently omitted from will—Whether will to be
G *admitted to probate with clause omitted*
Law Reform—Whether necessary—Will—Rectification

Solicitors prepared a draft will in accordance with the testatrix's instructions. She amended the draft and returned it to the solicitors. In typing out the engrossment of the will, words in clause 10 were inadvertently omitted, which contained an absolute gift of the capital of the residue in favour of
H the testatrix's son to take effect after life interests in one moiety each in favour of the testatrix's sister and a friend. The clause thereafter provided for certain reversionary gifts of the capital of the residuary estate in favour of the son's wife and their children equally in the event of the son not surviving either the testatrix's sister or friend. The omission went unnoticed and the testatrix duly executed the will on May 7, 1973. The testatrix died on July 7.

The plaintiff, as executor, asked the court to pronounce in favour of the will with the omission of clause 10 except for the

initial words containing life interests to the testatrix's sister A
and her friend:—

Held, that in the circumstances the will had to be construed before it was possible to consider whether the whole or a part should be admitted to probate; that on its true construction, clause 10 contained a gift of capital to the testatrix's daughter-in-law and the grandchildren upon the death of both the testatrix's sister and her friend, whereas the testatrix, when she executed the will, thought that it contained a gift of capital B
to her son if he survived the testatrix's sister and the friend; that, having regard to the underlying principle that the court should not admit to probate anything which was not known to and approved by the testatrix, the gifts in clause 10, other than the life interests in favour of the testatrix's sister and her friend, had to be omitted despite the fact by so doing the intended ultimate gift of the capital of the residuary estate in favour of the testatrix's daughter-in-law and grandchildren C
could not be preserved.

In the Goods of Sir J. E. Boehm [1891] P. 247 and *In re Morris, decd.* [1971] P. 62 applied.

In re Smith, Veasey v. *Smith* [1948] Ch. 49; *In re Follett, decd., Barclays Bank Ltd.* v. *Dovell* [1955] 1 W.L.R. 429, C.A. and *In re Whitrick, decd., Sutcliffe* v. *Sutcliffe* [1957] 1 W.L.R. 884, C.A. distinguished.

Per curiam. The result is not satisfactory but will perhaps D
encourage a further study of the recommendations which have been made from time to time that rectification of a will should be allowed on the same terms as rectification of other instruments, with perhaps the added safeguard of written contemporaneous evidence supporting the claim to rectification (post, p. 168C).

The following cases are referred to in the judgment: E

Boehm (Sir J. E.), In the Goods of [1891] P. 247.

Follett, decd., In re, Barclays Bank Ltd. v. *Dovell* [1955] 1 W.L.R. 429; [1955] 2 All E.R. 22, C.A.

Horrocks, In re, Taylor v. *Kershaw* [1939] P. 198; [1939] 1 All E.R. 579, C.A.

Morris, decd., In re [1971] P. 62; [1970] 2 W.L.R. 865; [1970] 1 All E.R. 1057. F

Phelan, decd., In re [1972] Fam. 33; [1931] 3 W.L.R. 888; [1971] 2 All E.R. 1256.

Schott (Louis), In the Goods of [1901] P. 190.

Smith, In re, Veasey v. *Smith* [1948] Ch. 49; [1947] 2 All E.R. 708.

Whitrick, decd., In re, Sutcliffe v. *Sutcliffe* [1957] 1 W.L.R. 884; [1957] 2 All E.R. 467, C.A.

G

The following additional cases were cited in argument:

Cory, decd., In re; Cory v. *Morel* [1955] 1 W.L.R. 725; [1955] 2 All E.R. 630.

Fulton v. *Andrew* (1875) L.R. 7 H.L. 448, H.L.(E.).

Guardhouse v. *Blackburn* (1866) L.R. 1 P. & D. 109.

Morony, decd., In the Goods of (1878) L.R. 1 Ir. 483.

H

ACTION

The testatrix, Mrs. Phyllis May Reynette-James, died on July 12, 1973, having made a will dated May 7, 1973, and having marked with a cross a further purported will on the day of her death. By a writ dated February 7, 1974, the plaintiff, David John Wightman, one of the executors named in the will of May 7, asked the court to pronounce in solemn form for the will, but with the omission of a part of clause 10 thereof which contained reversionary gifts of the capital of the testatrix's residuary estate in favour of the testatrix's daughter-in-law, Diana, and her three grandchildren, being the children of the testatrix's son, Michael, and of Diana, his wife. The writ also asked the court to pronounce against the validity of the purported will of July 12, 1973. The first defendant was Diana Marion Reynette-James, the wife of the testatrix's son, Michael Adrian Bernard Reynette-James, who was the fifth defendant. The second, third and fourth defendants were their children, Phillippa Ann, Louise Amanda and Alastair Justin Kingston Reynette-James. The sixth defendant was Christopher Jeremy Kingston Reynette-James, another son of the testatrix.

The facts are stated in the judgment.

John Knox for the plaintiff.
Timothy Lloyd for the second, third and fourth defendants.
R. A. Henderson for the fifth defendant.
The first and sixth defendants were not represented.
The sixth defendant did not enter an appearance.

Cur. adv. vult.

June 24. TEMPLEMAN J. read the following judgment. The plaintiff seeks probate of a will with the omission of part on the grounds that the testatrix did not know and approve of that part.

The testatrix, Mrs. Phyllis May Reynette-James, had two grown-up children, Michael, the fifth defendant, and Christopher, the sixth defendant; and they will share any property which devolves as on the intestacy of the testatrix. She had three infant grandchildren, Phillipa, Louise and Alistair, the second, third and fourth defendants, who are offspring of the testatrix's elder son, Michael, and his wife Diana, the first defendant.

On April 10, 1973, the testatrix called at the offices of a firm of solicitors, saw a clerk, and gave him oral instructions for her will. She came armed with written notes of her wishes, and the clerk took his own notes. She gave instructions that the income of her residue should be equally divided between her sister, Mrs. Wightman, and her friend, Miss Pedley, and that on the death of either of them her share of the income should be paid to Michael, and that when Mrs. Wightman and Miss Pedley died Michael was to receive the capital. The solicitor's clerk drafted a will intended to give effect to those instructions and sent the draft to the testatrix, suggesting that the draft did not dispose of the capital of residue should Michael predecease both Mrs. Wightman and Miss Pedley. The testatrix amended the draft so that if Michael died before Mrs. Wightman or Miss Pedley his share of income would go to Michael's wife Diana, until both Mrs. Wightman and Miss Pedley were dead, when the capital would devolve on Diana and Michael's three children equally. The clerk made further minor amendments to the draft and handed the draft to his secretary for engrossment. In typing the engrossment the secretary accidentally omitted 33 words from clause 10 which dealt with residue. The will as engrossed was read over to the testatrix by the solicitor's clerk in the presence of the secretary. No one noticed the omission from the engrossment and the will was duly signed and witnessed. The plaintiff is one of the executors appointed by the will.

The contemporary documents and the affidavit evidence now available show beyond any doubt that the testatrix thought and intended that the will she signed contained a gift in reversion of the capital of residue to

Michael. If, on its true construction, the will as executed achieves the A intended result, then the whole of the will must be admitted to probate. If however on its true construction the will as executed is not effective to confer on Michael an interest in capital, then it is suggested that those parts of clause 10 which deal with capital must be omitted from probate on the grounds that the testatrix did not know and approve of the gift of capital in that clause to persons other than Michael.

A will is normally admitted to probate and subsequently construed. In B the present peculiar circumstances the will of the testatrix as executed must first be construed before it becomes possible to consider whether the whole or part should be admitted to probate. I am tempted to construe the will in the light of the known intentions of the testatrix, thus giving effect to her wishes and avoiding any question of omitting part of the will from probate. The will must, however, be construed according to its terms. C

Clause 10 of the will as executed, after a trust to pay the income of the residuary estate to Mrs. Wightman and Miss Pedley in equal shares, continues:

> ". . . and I direct that should either the said Ivy Gladys Wightman or Myra Pedley predecease me then upon such death the share which she would have received shall devolve to my said son Michael Adrian Bernard Reynette-James absolutely but in the event of my said son D Michael not surviving either the said Ivy Gladys Wightman or Myra Pedley or bother "—that is how it is written—" of them the interest to which he would have been entitled under this my will shall devolve to Diana (his wife) and upon the death of both the said Ivy Gladys Wightman and Myra Pedley my residuary estate is to be shared equally between my daughter-in-law Diana and my three aforemen- E tioned grandchildren absolutely in equal shares but not to vest in them until they attain the age of 21 years."

Clause 10 contains no express gift of capital save to Diana and the grandchildren. But there is something odd and something wrong about the clause. Michael is given income but only if either Mrs. Wightman or Miss Pedley dies in the lifetime of the testatrix. That is very odd. If F Mrs. Wightman and Miss Pedley both survive the testatrix and then Mrs. Wightman dies, no provision is made for the destination of Mrs. Wightman's half of the income of the residuary estate arising after her death and until the death of Miss Pedley. Similarly if Miss Pedley dies first no express provision is made for her half of the income. This is very odd. One of them must die first. But neither of these oddities with regard to G income sheds light on the disposition of capital.

Finally and most importantly there is expressly given to Diana, in the event of Michael not surviving either Mrs. Wightman or Miss Pedley, *or both of them*, the interest to which Michael would have been entitled. But according to the express terms of clause 10 Michael is not entitled to any interest in the event of his surviving *both* Mrs. Wightman and Miss Pedley because on the death of *both*, the capital is directed H to be shared between Diana and the grandchildren. There must therefore be something wrong with the clause.

There are three possibilities as a matter of construction. First, that Michael takes capital, but only in the event which did not happen, namely, the deaths of both Mrs. Wightman and Miss Pedley in the lifetime of the testatrix. Secondly, that Michael does not take capital in any circumstances, the reference to the interest which Michael would have taken if

A he had survived both Mrs. Wightman and Miss Pedley being a mistake in
a will which is not a masterpiece of drafting. Thirdly, that Michael takes
capital if he survives both Mrs. Wightman and Miss Pedley; but in that
case it must follow that if Michael does not survive both Mrs. Wightman
and Miss Pedley, then Diana will take the capital interest to which he
would have been entitled if he had survived, namely, the whole of the
capital; but the substitutionary gift of the whole of the capital to Diana
B is inconsistent with the express directions of the will which give Diana a
share, and only a share, of capital, together with the grandchildren "upon
the death of both" Mrs. Wightman and Miss Pedley. As a matter of
construction I cannot spell out of the words of the will an implied gift of
capital to Michael, although it is clear that something is odd and wrong
about clause 10 and at least three possible explanations can be canvassed
C and suspected. Of these explanations I find the second most acceptable
as a matter of construction, namely, that the reference to the interest
which Michael would have taken if he had survived both Mrs. Wightman
and Miss Pedley is of no dispositive effect.

In *In re Smith, Veasey* v. *Smith* [1948] Ch. 49 a testatrix made a gift of
residue to certain persons in the event of her husband predeceasing her or
dying within one month of her death. She made no disposition of her
D residue in the event, which happened, of her husband surviving her by one
month or more. Vaisey J. held that there was a necessary implication that
the husband was intended to take residue if he survived the testatrix by
one month or more. In that case there was no contradiction between the
express dispositions in the will and the implied gift to the husband. In the
present case the express gift of capital to Diana and the grandchildren upon
E the death of both Mrs. Wightman and Miss Pedley would appear to be
contradicted by an implified gift to Michael in that event. Moreover, in
In re Smith common sense indicated that the testatrix must have intended
her husband to take if he survived her by one month or more. In the
present case common sense does not assist Michael, granted the rule,
which he may not regard as common sense, that in construing the will the
actual intentions of the testatrix must be forgotten.

F In *In re Follett, decd., Barclays Bank Ltd.* v. *Dovell* [1955] 1 W.L.R.
429 an odd general power of appointment was not construed as a special
power, although there was something wrong with the power as drafted and
it was plausibly suggested that something had been missed out of a pre-
cedent which had the effect of creating a general power of appointment
in place of an intended special power. The Court of Appeal, at pp. 431
G and 437, approved the principle stated in *Jarman on Wills*, 7th ed. (1930)
vol. 1, p. 556 (and accepted by Vaisey J. in *In re Smith* [1948] Ch. 49, 53):

> "Where it is clear on the face of a will that the testator has not
> accurately or completely expressed his meaning by the words he has
> used, and it is also clear what are the words which he has omitted,
> those words may be supplied in order to effectuate the intention, as
> H collected from the context."

In the present case, as in *In re Follett* [1955] 1 W.L.R. 429, 434:

> ". . . the necessary assurance, both as to the nature and wording of
> what has been left out, as well as to the fact of there having been an
> error or omission . . ."

are not to be found: see Sir Raymond Evershed M.R.

In *In re Whitrick, decd., Sutcliffe* v. *Sutcliffe* [1957] 1 W.L.R. 884 a gift to take effect " in the event of my husband . . . and myself both dying at the same time " was held to imply a gift in the event of the husband predeceasing the testatrix. This, like *In re Smith* [1948] Ch. 49 was a case in which the implication was compelling. These authorities do not enable me to imply a gift of capital to Michael in the present case.

On its true construction therefore the will contained a gift of capital to Diana and the grandchildren upon the death of both Mrs. Wightman and Miss Pedley, whereas the testatrix, when she executed the will, thought that the will contained a gift of capital to Michael if he survived Mrs. Wightman and Miss Pedley. That appears from all the documents and the evidence, and in particular from the draft which the secretary attempted to engross. I reproduce from that draft the words of clause 10 after the gift of income to Mrs. Wightman and Miss Pedley in equal shares:

> " And I direct that should either the said Ivy Gladys Wightman or Myra Pedley predecease me then upon such death the share which she would have received shall devolve to my said son Michael Bernard Reynette-James "

and then follow the missing 33 words as follows:

> " and after the deaths of both the said Ivy Gladys Wightman and Myra Pedley my trustees shall stand possessed of my residuary estate in trust for my said son Michael Adrian Bernard Reynette-James "

and that is where the omission ends, and the will as drafted continues,

> " absolutely but in the event of my son Michael not surviving either the said I.G.W. or M.P. or both of them the interest to which he would have been entitled under this my will shall devolve to Diana his wife and upon the death of both the said I.G.W. and M.P. my residuary estate is to be shared equally between my daughter-in-law Diana and my three aforementioned grandchildren absolutely in equal shares but not to vest in them until they attain the age of 21 years."

Any document other than a will could be rectified by inserting the words which the secretary omitted, but in this respect the court is enslaved by the Wills Act 1834. Words may be struck out but no fresh words may be inserted: see *In the Goods of Louis Schott* [1901] P. 190 and *In re Horrocks, Taylor* v. *Kershaw* [1939] P. 198, where Sir Wilfrid Greene M.R. delivering the judgment of the Court of Appeal said, at p. 216:

> " The jurisdiction, where it exists, is admittedly confined to the exclusion of words and does not extend to the insertion of words, since the insertion of words would run counter to the provisions of the Wills Act."

In *In the Goods of Sir J. E. Boehm* [1891] P. 247, a testator intended to settle two legacies of £10,000 on his daughters Georgina and Florence respectively. The name of Georgina appeared in both clauses dealing with these legacies and was inserted in the second clause instead of Florence by an error similar to that which causes the difficulty in the present case. The court in granting probate omitted the name Georgina from the second clause leaving a blank, but was unable to insert the name Florence. As appears from the argument of Bayford Q.C., at p. 248, the omission from probate of the name Georgina from the second clause was made because

A "It is clear that to this extent the testator signed something of which he did not know and approve, and the will as it stands does not carry out his intention."

In the present case I am asked to omit from probate the gift of capital to Diana and the grandchildren because to that extent the testatrix signed something of which she did not know and approve and the will as it
B stands does not carry out her intention. The omission of the gift of capital to Diana and the grandchildren will not effectuate the intention of the testatrix though Michael will inherit part of residue as a result of her partial intestacy. He will not need to survive Mrs. Wightman and Miss Pedley and if he dies in the lifetime of Mrs. Wightman or Miss Pedley, then Diana and the grandchildren will not obtain the interests which the
C testatrix did intend them to have in that event.

In *In the Goods of Sir J. E. Boehm*, Jeune J. alluded at p. 251 to

". . . the difficulty of rejecting words where their rejection alters the sense of those which remain. But I think that the application of the principle of striking out a word clearly inserted in mistake may be safely extended, if it be an extension, to a case where the effect of its rejection may be to render ambiguous, or even insensible, a clause of
D which it formed part. If a person by fraud obtained the substitution of his name for that of another in a will it would be strange if his name could not be struck out, although the rest of the clause in which it occurred became thereby meaningless. It may be that in the present case the effect of striking out the name in question will be, on the construction of the will, as it will then read, to carry out the
E testator's intentions completely. It is not for me to decide that. But even if to strike out a name inserted in error and leave a blank have not the effect of giving full effect to the testator's wishes, I do not see why we should not, so far as we can, though we may not completely, carry out his intentions."

In *In re Morris, decd.* [1971] P. 62, where a codicil by mistake revoked
F a series of gifts in clause 7 of the will instead of the single gift in clause 7 (iv) of the will, Latey J. omitted the numeral "7" from probate of the codicil on the ground that the testatrix did not know and approve of the contents of the codicil so far as it purported to revoke clause 7. Latey J. rejected the submission that a testator must be taken to know and approve of a testamentary document which is read over to him, rejected a sub-
G mission that a testator must be taken to know and approve of what his draftsman puts in front of him for signature, and, at p. 81, deduced from *In re Horrocks* [1939] P. 198:

". . . that the court could exclude words where there was a mere slip, and could do so where the effect was to leave what was left devoid of ascertainable content and thus inoperative (so altering the intention as expressed on the face of the instrument)."

H

In *Boehm's* case [1891] P. 247 and in *In re Morris, decd.* [1971] P. 62 and also in *In re Phelan, decd.* [1972] Fam. 33 the court omitted something which was not intended to be there and used the power of omission from probate to attempt to get nearer to the intentions of the testator, although in *Boehm* and *Morris* there was a danger that when the will as admitted to probate fell to be construed the attempt would fail. In the present case if the power of omission is exercised, the intended

ultimate gift over to Diana and the grandchildren cannot be preserved A
and the resulting partial intestacy will be different from the result intended by the testatrix to benefit Michael, although Michael will receive some compensation for the loss of his reversionary interest inflicted by the inexcusable blunders of the solicitors' firm employed by the testatrix.

Having regard to the possible effects of the omissions in *Boehm* and *Morris* and to the observations of Jeune J. and Latey J. in those cases respectively, and having regard to the underlying principle that the court B
should not admit to probate anything which was not known and approved by the testator, it follows in my judgment that, whatever the result, the gifts in clause 10 of the will, other than the life interests of Mrs. Wightman and Miss Pedley, must be omitted. Counsel for the grandchildren did not argue the contrary.

The result is not satisfactory but will perhaps encourage a further study C
of the recommendations which have been made from time to time that rectification of a will should be allowed on the same terms as rectification of other instruments, with perhaps the added safeguard of written contemporaneous evidence supporting the claim to rectification. There is ample such evidence in the present case, but it does not enable the will to be rectified.

Order accordingly. D

Solicitors: *Waterhouse & Co. for Ford & Warren, Leeds; Sharpe, Pritchard & Co. for Simpson, Curtis & Co., Leeds.*

T. C. C. B.

E

[CHANCERY DIVISION]

* *In re* BATHAMPTON PROPERTIES LTD. F

[No. 003208 of 1974]

1975 Jan. 20, 27; Feb. 17; March 4, 5, 6; April 17; May 20, 21; 23 — Brightman J.

G

Company—Winding up—Costs—Company unjustifiably opposing petition—Benefit accruing to beneficial owner if petition successfully opposed—Order for costs—Companies (Winding up) Rules 1949 (*S.I.* 1949 *No.* 330), *r.* 195

A petition to wind up a company was presented on the H
ground that a loan which it had guaranteed had been called in but not repaid. The petition was opposed by the company and by the beneficial owner of the company as opposing contributory and creditor. It was held that the company had no defence to the claim and it was ordered to be wound up. The company asked for its costs to be taxed and paid out of the

---

[Reported by Mrs. F. Allen McLean, Barrister-at-Law]

A assets of the company under rule 195 of the Companies (Winding up Rules) 1949.[1] The successful petitioner objected to such an order on the ground that the company's costs had been increased by the opposition of a contributory and creditor in order to secure a benefit to himself as shareholder, with the consequence that the assets available for payment of the debts due to the general body of creditors had been decreased.

On the question whether the court had jurisdiction to
B order that either the costs of the company be borne by the sole beneficial owner as opposing contributory and creditor or that no order be made as to the costs of the company:—

Held, (1) that, although the court had power, under section 50 (1) of the Supreme Court of Judicature (Consolidation) Act 1925, to make an order against an opposing contributory and creditor to a petition to wind up a company, the court would not exercise that discretion in the present case since the oppos-
C ing contributory and creditor's representation had been merely technical and his presence in court nominal (post, p. 172D–G).

(2) That, although it would be right for the order of costs to reflect the fact that the company's costs had been increased by its unsuccessful and unjustifiable opposition to the petition, the order should also reflect the invariable practice of the court to allow as costs of the petition the costs of a company appearing to consent to a winding up order (post, p. 172B–D); that,
D therefore, the costs of the company of the petition down to and including the time when it could have consented to the order, namely, the first hearing on January 20, 1975, should be taxed and paid out of the assets of the company and, thereafter, in the exercise of the court's discretion under rule 195 of the Companies (Winding up) Rules 1949, the company's costs were not to be paid out of the assets of the company in priority to the payment in full of all unsecured creditors of the company
E (post, p. 175C–E).

In re Blériot Manufacturing Aircraft Co. Ltd. (1916) 32 T.L.R. 253 applied.

Per curiam. A solicitor, retained on behalf of a potentially insolvent company to oppose a winding up petition, may feel it prudent to seek an indemnity from one or more of the corporators before embarking on his task (post, p. 175F).

F

The following cases are referred to in the judgment:

Blériot Manufacturing Aircraft Co. Ltd., In re (1916) 32 T.L.R. 253.

C.B. & M. (Tailors) Ltd., In re [1932] 1 Ch. 17.

Container Engineering Co. Ltd., In re (unreported), March 23, 1950.

National Savings Bank Association, In re (1866) 1 Ch.App. 547.

Sinclair, In re, Ex parte Payne (1885) 15 Q.B.D. 616.

G *Welsh Brick Industries Ltd., In re* [1946] 2 All E.R. 197.

The following additional cases were cited in argument:

Adler (William) & Co. Ltd., In re [1935] Ch. 138.

Humber Ironworks Co., In re (1866) L.R. 2 Eq. 15.

Practice Note (Winding up Order: Rescission) (No. 2) [1971] 1 W.L.R.
H 757; [1971] 2 All E.R. 700.

[1] Companies (Winding up) Rules 1949, r. 195: "(1) The assets of a company in a winding up by the court remaining after payment of the fees and expenses properly incurred in preserving, realising or getting in the assets, . . . shall, subject to any order of the court, . . . be liable to the following payments, which shall be made in the following order of priority, namely:— . . . First—The taxed costs of the petition, including the taxed costs of any person appearing on the petition whose costs are allowed by the court."

PETITION A

On December 24, 1974, Air Commodore Harold John Granville Ellis (retired) presented a petition for the compulsory winding up of Bathampton Properties Ltd. on the ground that the company was indebted to him in the sum of £14,356 payable by Harrison and Proud Developments Ltd. by guarantee. On May 23, 1975, a compulsory winding up order was made. B

The facts are stated in the judgment.

Mary Arden for the petitioner.

Brian Parker for the company and the opposing contributory and creditor.

Cur. adv. vult. C

May 23. BRIGHTMAN J. read the following judgment. The question before me concerns the incidence of costs incurred by a company in unsuccessfully opposing a winding up petition on the ground that it is based on a disputed debt.

The company has an issued capital of £8,000. All the shares are beneficially owned by Mr. Dunstan Harrison, a chartered accountant. D The directors of the company are Mr. Harrison and his wife. It is not and never has been in dispute that in 1965 the petitioner lent £10,000 to another company, Harrison and Proud Developments Ltd., and that repayment of this loan was guaranteed by the company. The loan was called in but not repaid, and the petitioner accordingly resorted to the guarantee. On November 9, 1974, the petitioner served a statutory demand on the company. On December 24 he presented a petition for E the winding up of the company. The amount claimed is £10,000 plus £4,356 interest. The petitioner claims that interest is running at the rate of 7 per cent. per annum. Mr. Harrison, if I have understood his affidavit correctly, claims that no interest is accruing; or perhaps that the guarantee does not extend to interest.

The company opposed the petition on the ground that the debt was F not presently payable. Mr. Harrison said that there was an arrangement with the petitioner that the loan should not be repayable until the borrowing company could afford to repay it. The return date of the petition was January 20, 1975, but it was adjourned for evidence on that and two later occasions. The hearing of the petition was finally begun on March 4 and concluded on March 6, when the company was ordered to be wound up. It was held that the company had no defence to the claim, G which was not disputed on any substantial ground, and there was therefore no issue which ought to be tried.

According to a statement of affairs dated March 6, 1975, the secured debts amount to about £19,000, and the unsecured debts to about £22,000. Part of the unsecured indebtedness is owed to Mr. Harrison and companies controlled by him, but I do not think that anything turns on this. H

The company owns three freehold properties in Kent and Somerset which are divided into flats of which six are vacant. The directors of the company estimate that, given time, these properties can be sold so as to realise £108,000. There are also minor assets estimated at £1,000. The company's total cash at March 6, was £260, plus £213 book debts. If the £10,000 guarantee is due, and probably even if it is not due, the company is commercially insolvent.

The statement of affairs shows that if the directors' hopes are ultimately fulfilled, there will be a surplus for Mr. Harrison as sole beneficial owner of the shares on a liquidation of the company of some £68,000. In his evidence Mr. Harrison states categorically that the company is not yet in a position to pay the petitioning creditor, although he expects that it soon will be. The inference from his evidence is that the company's freehold properties cannot at the present moment be sold for £41,000, the amount needed to pay off all the secured and unsecured creditors shown in the statement of affairs, but on the other hand, if realisation is delayed, a sum of £108,000 might be realised and, as I have said, £68,000 would in that event be available to Mr. Harrison as sole beneficial owner of the share capital.

The position therefore amounted to this when the petition came on for hearing. If a winding up order were made, as was desired by the petitioner, he might receive a dividend on his debt but perhaps not the full amount. If on the other hand the petition were dismissed, as desired by Mr. Harrison, time would be gained which might enable a sum of £68,000 to become available for Mr. Harrison as shareholder. The attempt, therefore, by Mr. Harrison to defeat a winding up petition was calculated to produce for Mr. Harrison a large profit as the sole shareholder in the company. I do not use the expression "calculated to produce" in any pejorative sense. That profit would be obtained at the expense of the petitioning creditor to the extent that he would for the time being be kept out of his money as an inevitable consequence of the dismissal of the petition, perhaps free of interest or at a low rate of interest.

The company now asks for its costs of unsuccessfully opposing the petition to be taxed and paid out of the assets of the company under rule 195 of the Companies (Winding up) Rules 1949—subject only to the claims of the mortgagees and the costs of preserving, realising and getting in the assets. Under rule 195, and subject to any order of the court, the taxed costs of the petition are a first charge on the net assets.

If there is a surplus of assets in the liquidation, after all costs, expenses and debts have been paid, such an order will ex hypothesi not prejudice the creditors. If, however, there is not a surplus—and no one at this stage can confidently predict a surplus—the result of the order will be to reduce the assets available for creditors. Prima facie there would seem to be a great injustice in permitting the beneficial owner of all the shares in a company to oppose a winding up petition in order to seek to secure a benefit for himself as shareholder and then, having failed in his opposition, to charge the costs of such unsuccessful opposition to the creditors of the company.

In the present case, counsel for the company also appeared for Mr. Harrison as opposing contributory and creditor. An opposing contributory or creditor does not obtain his costs if a winding up order is made, but this is little comfort to the general body of creditors because I understand that in practice all the costs of the opposition are treated as costs incurred by the company, unless the opposing contributory or creditor sought at the hearing to make out a special case differing from that of the company.

If I were able to do so consistently with my jurisdiction and the established practice, I would think it right to deal with the costs on the facts of this particular case in such a way that the costs of the company so far as increased by its unsuccessful and unjustifiable opposition do not reduce the assets available for payment of the debts due to the general body of creditors.

Counsel for the petitioning creditor has submitted that I have jurisdiction to make, and should make, an order for costs on one or other of the following bases: (1) an order that the costs of the petitioning creditor should be paid out of the assets of the company as costs of the petition, and an order that the costs of the company should be borne by Mr. Harrison as opposing contributory and creditor; (2) a like order in relation to the costs of the petitioning creditor, but no order in relation to the costs of the company.

Before discussing these alternatives I should say that I have no doubt that the company should be allowed, as costs of the petition, its costs incurred down to and including the first hearing of the petition. It is the invariable practice to allow as costs of the petition the costs of the company if it appears and consents to a winding up order. It is occasionally useful to have the company represented in court, even if it does not oppose a winding up order, and I would not wish to interfere with a practice which allows the costs of that appearance. It follows, I think, that in the present case the company should be allowed its costs down to the date when the order might first have been made. The costs which merit special consideration are the costs incurred by the company after the first hearing. In discussing, therefore, alternatives (1) and (2) I direct my mind only to the company's costs incurred after the first hearing.

Alternative (*1*). In my judgment I have jurisdiction to make such an order. Section 50 (1) of the Supreme Court of Judicature (Consolidation) Act 1925 empowers the court to determine by whom and to what extent costs are to be paid. Although this would not entitle the court to make an order against a complete stranger to proceedings, I see no reason why it should not entitle the court to make an order for costs against a person who has the right to appear, and does appear, on a winding up petition.

However, despite the existence of the jurisdiction, I reject this submission. The appearance and representation of Mr. Harrison were purely technical and added nothing to the case. His presence in court was nominal. The proceedings would have taken exactly the same course if he had been absent. It would therefore be anomalous if his accidental appearance should result in an order for costs against him, which could not I think have been made if, with no different impact on the case, he had been absent. There is no precedent for such an order so far as I am aware.

Alternative (*2*). There is no doubt as to my jurisdiction to make such an order. This follows directly from the wording of rule 195 of the Companies (Winding up) Rules 1949. The effect of making no order for the company's costs would be that such costs would not rank as costs of the petition within the first paragraph of rule 195 (1).

In dealing with alternative (2), it would not be right to overlook the problem how, in such circumstances, the solicitors acting for the company would recover their costs. If the solicitors had been retained by Mr. Harrison personally in order to act for the company, the solicitors would be entitled to recover their costs from him. Similarly, if the solicitors, wisely, had obtained from Mr. Harrison an indemnity for their costs.

A Similarly, also, if Mr. Harrison, as a man of honour, voluntarily paid such costs since he is in effect the company.

Counsel for the petitioner was, I think, minded to concede that in the last resort the solicitor could prove in the liquidation for his costs pari passu with the unsecured creditors by analogy with *In re C.B. & M. (Tailors) Ltd.* [1932] 1 Ch. 17. However, I am by no means convinced that this would be the case. The point is not directly before me, has not
B been argued, and I express no view.

Counsel for the petitioner referred me to *In re Blériot Manufacturing Aircraft Co. Ltd.* (1916) 32 T.L.R. 253, a decision of Neville J. That was a contributory's petition to wind up the company, which was solvent, on the ground that the substratum had gone and also on the ground that the board was under the control of three directors who were
C misapplying the moneys of the company. The petition was opposed by the company. A winding up order was made. Counsel for the company submitted that there was no ground for departing from the usual order as to costs. Neville J., however, directed that the company should have no costs. This case is a clear authority that the court has jurisdiction to direct that the costs of the company shall not be costs of the petition, and that it should exercise such jurisdiction if the justice of the
D case so requires. In this context it would not seem to be relevant whether the petition is founded on insolvency, as in the instant case, or on just and equitable grounds as in the *Blériot* case. I may add that rule 187 of the Companies (Winding up) Rules 1909, which was in force in 1916, does not differ from rule 195 in any way material for present purposes.

Counsel for the petitioner next referred me to *In re National Savings
E Bank Association* (1866) 1 Ch.App. 547 and *In re Welsh Brick Industries Ltd.* [1946] 2 All E.R. 197. Each was an unsuccessful appeal from a winding up order. In each case the court directed that the costs of the petitioner, but not the costs of the company, of the appeal should be paid out of the assets of the company. As these cases were unsuccessful appeals from winding up orders which had already been made, I think that they raise somewhat different considerations and do not really
F assist me.

Lastly, counsel for the petitioner drew my attention to *In re Container Engineering Co. Ltd.* (unreported), March 23, 1950. This was a winding up petition presented by two judgment creditors. A director and the majority shareholder was a Mr. Franghia. He swore an affidavit on behalf of the company deposing that the petitioners had agreed not to
G enforce their judgment debts in return for a promise by Mr. Franghia of payment at a future date. His evidence was supported by affidavits sworn by a Miss Moss, and a Mrs. Feakes. It appears from the recitals to the order, and from the registrar's note, that after the cross-examination and re-examination of Mr. Franghia and Mrs. Feakes, counsel for the company informed the court that he did not feel justified in continuing to oppose the making of a winding up order. Thereupon leading
H counsel for the petitioners, who was the late Sir Milner Holland, submitted that the costs of the opposition ought not to be paid out of the company's assets. He referred to the well known passage in *Buckley on the Companies Acts*, 12th ed. (1949), p. 472—it is p. 474 in the current 13th ed. (1957)—which so far as material reads:

> "The practice is to give costs to the petitioner and the company if the petition succeeds, and to the company if it fails . . . If the peti-

> tion succeeds, these costs are given out of the company's estate: if A it fails, they are given against the petitioner. This rule has now been followed for many years. It is not an inflexible rule."

Sir Milner also referred to the *Blériot* case 32 T.L.R. 253. According to the registrar's note Roxburgh J. described the case as an abnormal one which justified an abnormal order as to costs. The order as to costs was ultimately made in the following form: B

> "It is ordered that the costs of the company of the said petition, down to and including the hearing of the said petition on November 28, 1949 . . ."—that was the first hearing—" . . . and the costs of the petitioners of the said petition be taxed and paid out of the assets of the said company, and the costs of the company of the said petition incurred after the hearing of the said petition on November 28, 1949, C are not to be paid out of the assets of the company in priority to the unsecured creditors of the company."

Mr. Parker, appearing for the company and Mr. Harrison, accepted, as he was bound to accept, the undoubted jurisdiction of the court to direct that the costs of the company of the petition are not to be paid out of the assets of the company. He submitted, however, that there D was no sufficient reason in the present case for departing from the usual practice that the company receives its costs. He said, quite correctly, that in both the *Blériot* and the *Container Engineering* cases there was fraud on the part of those who controlled the company; this, he submitted, justified a departure from the normal rule. There is no fraud in the present case.

In my opinion the court ought to look critically at costs incurred by E an insolvent company in unsuccessfully opposing a winding up petition on the ground that the debt is disputed, when the advantage and perhaps the purpose of delaying liquidation is a possible surplus for the beneficial owner of the company's capital. I do not charge Mr. Harrison with lack of good faith but why, I ask myself, should the beneficial owner of the company's capital be entitled to finance such litigation at the expense of F the creditors? In the instant case Mr. Harrison had little or nothing to lose and everything to gain by causing the company to dispute the debt. If he failed in that litigation, which he has promoted, no hardship is caused if the solicitors' bill falls to be paid by him personally rather than by the general body of creditors.

I do not intend to make any inroad into the general practice of allowing a company its costs of appearing on and consenting to a winding up G petition. All that I am seeking to do in the present case is to exercise my discretion in such a way as to produce a result which is just and fair as between Mr. Harrison and his alter ego the company on the one hand, and the general body of creditors on the other hand.

I think it is useful to glance at the bankruptcy position. It is said in *Williams on Bankruptcy*, 18th ed. (1968), p. 264: H

> "The debtor who has committed any act of bankruptcy of which his solicitor has notice, or has had a petition presented against him, is nevertheless entitled to put his solicitor in funds for the purpose of defraying the costs of opposing the bankruptcy proceedings, without the risk of the trustees reclaiming the money from the solicitor."

The principal authority cited is *In re Sinclair, Ex parte Payne* (1885) 15

A Q.B.D. 616. That is a very different situation. If a solicitor acting for a person against whom a bankruptcy petition has been presented is in peril for his costs, it may be impossible for the debtor to secure legal advice. That would be deplorable. It is not, however, a situation that necessarily arises in the case of a company against whom a winding up petition is presented. The corporators are not usually bankrupt and they may in fact be far wealthier than the creditor who seeks payment of his B debt. There is nothing to prevent a corporator guaranteeing the cost of opposing a creditor's winding up petition. If the petition fails, the corporator loses nothing. If the petition succeeds, and the company's costs of opposing the petition are not allowed, the assets are effectively preserved for the benefit of the creditors whose claim thereto is superior to that of the corporator's. However, these are only intended as general C observations.

I think that each case must depend on its own facts. On the facts of the case before me, I consider it just that the costs of opposing the petition for the benefit of the sole corporator should not rank in front of the claims of the unsecured creditors. I therefore order that the costs shall be dealt with as follows:

1. The costs of the petitioner of the petition are to be taxed and paid D out of the assets of the company.

2. The costs of the company of the petition down to and including the hearing on January 20, 1975, are also to be taxed and paid out of the assets of the company.

3. The costs of the company of the petition incurred after the hearing E on January 20, 1975, are not to be paid out of the assets of the company in priority to the payment in full of all the unsecured creditors of the company.

The company, if it desires, may apply for an order for taxation of its costs of the petition incurred after the hearing on January 20, and, subject as aforesaid, for payment thereof out of the surplus assets of the company.

The result of this decision, if it is correct, is that a solicitor retained F on behalf of a company, which is potentially insolvent, for the purpose of opposing a winding up petition, may feel it prudent to seek an indemnity from one or more of the corporators before embarking on his task. I think that this would be salutary; it may help to avoid the assets of the company being wasted on hopeless opposition to a winding up order.

G

Order accordingly.

Solicitors: *Simmons & Simmons; Victor Mishcon & Co.*

H

[FAMILY DIVISION]

* DWYER *v.* DWYER

1975 Oct. 29; Nov. 14 — Payne J. sitting with assessors

Costs—Taxation—Application to review—Matrimonial causes—Preparing for trial of cause or matter—Solicitors' costs limited by statute—Whether discretion to exceed statutory maximum—Matrimonial Causes (Costs) Rules 1971 (*S.I.* 1971 *No.* 987 (*L.* 22)), *r.* 6 (1), *Appendix*

Between January and September 1974, a firm of solicitors undertook the preparation of a wife's petition for dissolution of marriage, the hearing of the undefended suit, an application for an interlocutory injunction and undertakings relating to the matrimonial home and family and an application for ancillary relief.

The matters were heard in a divorce county court. Taxation of costs was ordered on a party and party basis against the husband and on a common fund basis against the legal aid fund. Under item 6 (*a*) of the Appendix to the Matrimonial Causes (Costs) Rules 1971 [1] for preparing for trial, the solicitors claimed £10 an hour plus 50 per cent. for care and attention. On taxation the taxing master reduced that figure to £7 an hour plus 50 per cent. for care and attention. The deduction enabled the taxing master to keep the costs within the maximum of £45 allowed by the divorce scale.

On an application by the solicitors for a review of the taxing master's decision:—

Held, that by rule 6 (1) of the Rules of 1971 a taxing master had a discretion to exceed the statutory maximum in an appropriate case; that a wide discretion had to be left to those who had to tax costs to enable them to adjust costs to meet rising overheads and that there was no justification for placing a limit on the exercise of the discretion when considering costs under items with a statutory maximum fee; accordingly the application for review succeeded and, without attempting to fix a rate of general application, the items would be allowed as claimed.

The following case is referred to in the judgment:

Castillejo v. *Castillejo*, The Times, December 12, 1974.

No additional cases were cited in argument.

SUMMONS

In matrimonial proceedings which included the petition for dissolution of marriage by Beryl Dwyer, the hearing of the undefended suit, an application for an interlocutory injunction and undertaking relating to the matrimonial home and family and an application for ancillary relief which

[1] Matrimonial Causes (Costs) Rules 1971, r. 5: "The costs of matrimonial proceedings in a divorce county court shall be on the divorce scale."

R. 6 (1): "Except where the judge has otherwise directed, the registrar may, if he thinks fit, allow on taxation of the costs of matrimonial proceedings in a divorce county court such larger sums as he thinks fit in respect of all or any of the following items in the divorce scale, namely items . . . 6 . . ."

Appendix, item 6: "(*a*) Preparing for trial of cause or matter—Such sum as is fair and reasonable in all the circumstances not exceeding £45 (*b*) Preparing for hearing of ancillary application, such sum as is fair and reasonable."

A was abandoned, costs were awarded on a party and party basis against the husband, Terence Dwyer, and on a common fund basis against the legal aid fund.

On a taxation of those costs on June 4, 1975, Master Martyn, under item 6 (*a*) of the Appendix to rule 5 of the Matrimonial Causes (Costs) Rules 1971 (divorce scale) reduced the claim from £10 an hour plus 50 per cent. for care and attention to £7 an hour plus 50 per cent. for care and attention.
B By summons the solicitors sought an order that the taxation be reviewed by a judge.

The facts are stated in the judgment.

Edward Bailey for the applicants.

Cur. adv. vult.

C

November 14. PAYNE J. read the following judgment. This is an application by solicitors for review of the taxation of costs by one of the taxing officers in a matrimonial cause and I have had the benefit of the advice and assistance of two assessors in this case.

The proceedings covered a petition for dissolution of marriage by the wife petitioner, the hearing of the undefended suit itself, a successful
D application for an interlocutory injunction and undertakings relating to the matrimonial home and family and a subsequent application for ancillary relief, which the petitioner abandoned.

Taxation of costs was ordered on a party and party basis against the respondent and on a common fund basis against the legal aid fund and, as the matter proceeded in the Principal Registry as a divorce court, the
E relevant scale of costs was that prescribed by the Matrimonial Causes (Costs) Rules 1971, namely, the divorce scale. In preparing their bill of costs for taxation, the wife's solicitors presented one figure under items 6 (*a*) "preparing for trial of cause or matter" and 6 (*b*) "preparing for hearing of ancillary application," because some of their work combined preparation for the injunction and preparation for the trial of the suit and they thus avoided duplication. Later in the bill they presented a further
F figure under item 6 (*a*) for the remainder of their work in preparing for trial. The application for injunction was heard a few months prior to the trial of the suit. Under items 6 (*a*) and (*b*) the petitioner's solicitors claimed throughout an allowance for costs at the rate of £10 per hour plus 50 per cent. for care and attention, but the taxing officer allowed £7 per hour plus 50 per cent. and taking into account other subsidiary deductions, to which
G I need not refer in detail, the figure of £167 claimed for preparation of the case was reduced to £115, the sum taxed off being £52. For the item covering the balance of the preparation for trial the taxing officer allowed £10 per hour because he did not feel that any deduction was necessary as the sum involved was so small, although he considered the claim was higher than it should have been. The solicitors, accordingly, ask for a review of the first item and their objection is to this reduction in the rate per hour
H from £10 to £7. The relevant work was done between January and September 1974 and it will be appreciated that a decision on this point is of interest to all solicitors who practise in the Family Division and the divorce county courts.

In deciding what is a fair rate per hour for the work of a solicitor and his staff, both qualified and unqualified, in the preparation of matrimonial proceedings before a hearing in court or in chambers, it is important to reach a proper balance between the necessity of curbing the cost of litigation and preventing it becoming so expensive as to make justice unattainable by many members of the public, and the no less important factor of providing that solicitors and counsel shall be adequately remunerated for their services. It was within the knowledge of the assessors and myself that, under the rates of remuneration sometimes allowed on taxation in recent years, some firms of solicitors, who have a sufficient volume of more remunerative work, have refused to undertake any matrimonial cases, other firms have ceased to undertake such cases under the legal aid scheme and, what is perhaps more disturbing, some solicitors pass matrimonial work to inexperienced and lower paid clerks in their offices, to the detriment of the client, the court and ultimately the administration of justice. There are, of course, firms which have a substantial volume of divorce work and employ sufficient staff of men experienced in this work to run a department profitably on a scale of costs which deters others. It is important on taxation to appreciate the full picture. It is only right that I should make it clear that in the present case much of the work was done by a solicitor who was also a partner.

In an address to the Law Society in 1967, Master Paul Adams the then senior taxing master said:

> "... It is fortunate for the profession that the High Court scale, which its representatives, aided and abetted by myself, have established, is so flexible that in the main it can expand to give effect to changing circumstances. It is most necessary for taxing officers to remember this and give effect to it. This requires their continual vigilance concerning the movement of market rates for solicitors, counsel, experts and others. I hope, however, that when the time does come to revise the High Court scale as far as any of the more rigid items is concerned, some definite information will be available, from proper analysis, and from which it can be said with certainty that the appropriate charge for this or for that is so much in order to show a proper profit for the work done. . . ."

The scales have, of course, been revised since 1967, but the master's observations are as important now as they were at the time, not least because of the general inflation which has occurred in more recent years.

What is a fair rate for solicitors to charge for the time of themselves and their staff requires a detailed study which is not possible within the confines of one case and taxing masters and officers must have regard to what solicitors in fact currently charge their clients and rely upon their own unique experience in comparing the cases which come before them on taxation.

In the present case it is argued that a higher rate than £7 an hour is justified by the urgency with which the claim for an injunction was undertaken, but I am not impressed by this argument and I share the view of the taxing officer who rejected it. In the daily work of a busy solicitor's office, there must always be the problem of selecting the more urgent matters for immediate or early attention, but all the work has to be completed and, in my opinion, one cannot justify claiming against the other party to a piece of litigation or against the legal aid fund a higher hourly rate of cost for those matters to which preference is given. Moreover the claim for an injunction in this case, though urgent and important to the petitioner, was not a matter of unusual complexity to an experienced solicitor.

The substantial objection to the assessment of £7 per hour is the reason advanced by the taxing officer for regarding that sum as the maximum

A which could be justified. The figure in the divorce scale for item 6 (*a*) was last fixed in 1971 and is described as " such sum as is fair and reasonable in all the circumstances not exceeding £45 " and under item 6 (*b*) relating to preparations for hearing of an ancillary application the amount is " such sum as is fair and reasonable." The taxing officer held the view that £45 in 1971 represented an hourly rate of £6 for the average period estimated as proper for the preparation of a matrimonial suit and recognised that by B virtue of rule 6 (1) he had a discretion to exceed that figure in an appropriate case. He also expressed the opinion that although no maximum was prescribed for item 6 (*b*), the figure of £45 in item 6 (*a*) is

> " an amount enacted by Parliament which sets the standard for all divorce county court costs and how that standard is to be applied is a matter for the discretion of the taxing officer."

C There is a note in the appendix under item 6 as follows: " Note 2: Item 6 (*a*) may only be allowed once in the same cause or matter, but item 6 (*b*) may be allowed in respect of each ancillary application." The greater part of the work covered by the combined item in the bill of costs under review related to the ancillary application for an injunction for which no maximum figure is prescribed.

D The taxing officer stated in his reasons:

> " Although the maximum of £45 has not been increased by Parliament continued pressure by solicitors generally has resulted in higher allowances on taxation more appropriate to an hourly rate of £7, but, in my view, no further increase is possible until the maximum in item 6 (*a*) is either increased or removed entirely. In relation to item 6 (*b*) the E discretion to exceed £45 is properly exercised when a solicitor has spent more time than usual in dealing with a particular case. In such circumstances he is entitled to a higher amount because of the extra time involved and not because of a higher rate. If I am right, the same hourly rate must be applied to item 6 (*b*) but a more flexible approach is used when dealing with the care and attention element."

F Under the Matrimonial Causes (Costs) Rules 1968, county court scale 4 applied to the cost of matrimonial causes in a divorce county court and the maximum fee for preparing for trial was £40 subject to a discretion to allow a larger sum. In 1971 item 6 (*a*) of the divorce scale was increased to £45 and it has not been increased since that time. It is impracticable to alter the items in the scale at frequent intervals to keep pace with changes in the relevant circumstances affecting solicitors such as salaries, rents, rates, G travelling expenses, stationery and the like. The availability of the discretion enables taxing masters to adjust costs to meet rising overheads and I cannot find any authority or justification for placing a limit on the exercise of the discretion by reason of the continuance of the statutory maximum of £45. To do this is to deprive the taxing master or taxing officer of one of the most valuable elements of his discretion. Bearing in mind the H inflationary conditions which have persisted in this country in recent years, the restriction upon the use of the discretion which the taxing officer adopted in this case would often result in inadequate remuneration for practising solicitors.

The decision that £7 an hour is not sufficient for run of the mill cases in 1974 leaves this court with the more difficult problem of offering some guidance as to the appropriate figure. A wide discretion must be left to those who have to tax costs all over the country and it is obvious that the

overhead expenses in a solicitor's office in a small town in the country are A
less than those in London or one of the large cities. It is also apparent that some firms in estimating an hourly rate include a percentage for the profit element, whereas others rely upon the percentage addition for care, skill and attention to cover their profit costs. Registrars and taxing masters and officers are familiar with the systems and practices in their areas and use their experience in exercising their discretion. For these reasons no rigid scale can be applied to the discretionary items. B

In *Castillejo* v. *Castillejo*, The Times, December 12, 1974, a matrimonial cause which was not of exceptional difficulty or complexity but was more difficult than the present case, the husband's solicitors had offered for work between 1970 and 1973 £10 per hour plus 50 per cent. for care and attention, and the taxing officer allowed those rates although the hourly rate was more than he himself would have assessed. Much of the work had been done by C
a partner in the firm representing the wife, as in the present case. When *Castillejo's* case came before this court on review, it was stated in the course of the judgment that the sums offered by one party and approved by the taxing officer were reasonably generous and it should not be taken that the court was sanctioning a rate of £10 an hour for divorce county court work in the general run of cases in 1970 to 1972, but that higher rates must be considered in 1974 when the *Castillejo* review of taxation was heard. D
Without therefore attempting to fix a rate of general application, I am satisfied that in the present case for work in 1974 a rate of £10 per hour is fair under items 6 (*a*) and 6 (*b*) in the exercise of the available discretion. This application for review accordingly succeeds and the items under 6 (*a*) and 6 (*b*) on page 4 of the bill of costs are allowed at £167.

I see no reason to interfere with the taxing officer's allowance of 50 per E
cent. for care and attention. In the simplest of cases I understand that 25 per cent. or 33⅓ per cent. is sometimes allowed, but that is essentially a matter for the taxing officer's discretion.

With regard to costs, I understand that the solicitors appearing in this case for the petitioner were allowed legal aid for the application for review. In those circumstances it seems to me that we should order costs against the fund, that is to say, to direct taxation of the petitioner's solicitors' costs F
on a common fund basis under the Legal Aid and Advice Regulations.

Order accordingly.

Solicitors: *Stringer & Smith.*

G

M. B. D.

H

A [COURT OF APPEAL]

* REGINA *v.* MELVILLE

1975 Nov. 6 Lord Widgery C.J., O'Connor and Lawson JJ.

Crime—Court of Appeal—Fresh evidence—Mental health not in
B *issue at trial — Medical reports after conviction revealing abnormality—Whether medical evidence admissible on appeal —Meaning of " on an issue "—Scope of court's function after conviction—Criminal Appeal Act* 1968 (*c.* 19), *s.* 23 (1) (2) (*a*)

The defendant assaulted and killed a man and was charged with murder. Medical reports obtained before his trial stated that although he suffered from some abnormality he was fit to plead and to be tried; that such abnormality did not sub-
C stantially diminish his responsibility and that there was no medical defence to the charge. The sole defence at his trial was provocation; no mental issue was raised and the defendant was convicted of murder. Shortly after his conviction in May 1973 the defendant was examined in prison by two doctors who obtained electroencephalograph readings which disclosed certain abnormalities.

On the defendant's appeal against conviction and on his
D application pursuant to section 23 of the Criminal Appeal Act 1968 [1] to call additional evidence regarding his mental condition with a view to establishing a defence of diminished responsibility: —

Held, dismissing the application and the appeal, (1) that, on their true construction, the words " on an issue " in section 23 (2) (*a*) of the Criminal Appeal Act 1968 meant on an issue which was raised at the trial and which was the subject of
E the appeal, and since the defendant's mental health had not been an issue at the trial the court was not bound to admit the medical evidence under subsection (2) (*a*) (post, p. 185H).

(2) That the court would not exercise its discretion under section 23 (1) of the Act to admit the medical evidence since the evidence showing mental abnormality was not overwhelming, and paying due regard to the proper division of responsibility between the Court of Appeal and the Home Office, where
F evidence was proffered two years after conviction and concerned matters arising since the conviction, it was prima facie for the Home Secretary and not for the court to receive a complaint of a change in circumstances (post, p. 186E–H).

Reg. v. *Dodd* (unreported), June 10, 1971, C.A. applied.

The following case is referred to in the judgment of the court:
G *Reg.* v. *Dodd* (unreported), June 10, 1971, C.A.

The following additional case was cited in argument:
Reg. v. *Clark* [1962] 1 W.L.R. 180; [1962] 1 All E.R. 428, C.C.A.

[1] Criminal Appeal Act 1968, s. 23: " (1) . . . the Court of Appeal may, if they think it necessary or expedient in the interests of justice—(*a*) order the production of any document, exhibit or other thing connected with the proceedings, the production
H of which appears to them necessary for the determination of the case; (*b*) order any witness who would have been a compellable witness in the proceedings from which the appeal lies to attend for examination and be examined before the Court, whether or not he was called in those proceedings; . . . (2) Without prejudice to subsection (1) above, where evidence is tendered to the Court of Appeal thereunder the Court shall, unless they are satisfied that the evidence, if received, would not afford any ground for allowing the appeal, exercise their power of receiving it if—(*a*) it appears to them that the evidence is likely to be credible and would have been admissible in the proceedings from which the appeal lies on an issue which is the subject of the appeal; and (*b*) they are satisfied that it was not adduced in those proceedings but there is a reasonable explanation for the failure to adduce it. . . ."

APPEAL against conviction.

APPLICATION for leave to call fresh evidence. A

The defendant, Alan Brian Melville, appealed against his conviction for murder at Chelmsford Crown Court (Eveleigh J.) on May 4, 1973, on the ground that medical evidence not available at the trial revealed that he was suffering from diminished responsibility at the time of the offence.

The facts are stated in the judgment of the court. B

Sir Harold Cassel Q.C. and *Ronald Trott* for the defendant.
Anthony McCowan Q.C. and *Tim Nash* for the prosecution.

LORD WIDGERY C.J. On May 4, 1973, at Chelmsford Crown Court before Eveleigh J. this defendant was convicted of the murder of Cyril C
Headley and was sentenced to life imprisonment.

He now appeals against his conviction by leave of Lawson J., and he has applied to call additional evidence which was not available before the court below dealing with his mental condition.

It is not necessary to go into the facts in any detail at all. The defendant killed a homosexual with whom he had been associating. He did not use a weapon, but he used very considerable force, using his boots D
and his fists, and there is no doubt that he had entirely lost control of himself for a period at or near the time of the murder. At the trial the only substantial defence which was run was the defence of provocation, and the jury did not accept that, so that on May 4, 1973, a conviction of murder was entered against him. At no time was his mental condition put under question, and the reason for that is because the medical reports E
which were available pre-trial both made it clear that in the opinion of the highly qualified psychiatrists making the reports there was no medical issue which could be raised.

For example, in the case of Dr. Scott, who made a report on March 20, 1973, some months before the trial, he refers to certain abnormalities appertaining to the defendant, but says there is no disorder of mood or thinking and nothing to suggest psychotic illness. He concluded by F
saying:

> " He is fit to plead and stand his trial. There is no disability of mind in the M'Naghten sense. His mental abnormality does not substantially diminish his responsibility. I cannot suggest any medical defence against the charge."

G

Dr. Blair, reporting at the same time, also gives a long and very comprehensive report about this man and reaches the same conclusion. He is not suffering from any psychosis or psychoneurosis, nor has he ever suffered from such illnesses in the past. Then the doctor goes on to consider the pros and cons of whether he is a psychopathic personality, and in the end comes to the conclusion similar to that of Dr. Scott that when the crime was committed the defendant knew what he was doing. H
He says:

> " He attacked him with tempestuous aggression, in a state of temper which momentarily overwhelmed him. . . . I do not consider it would qualify him for diminished responsibility under the Homicide Act 1957."

Small wonder, one may think, that no mental issue was raised at all at the trial, that the question was provocation or not, and the jury found against the defendant.

After he had been convicted he was sent to Wormwood Scrubs and there he came under the care of Dr. Clark and was also seen by Dr. Neville. It is, we think, clear that the main purpose of those examining the defendant's condition at this time was to consider what advice they might give to the Home Secretary in regard to an order being made under section 72 of the Mental Health Act 1959 for his detention in a special hospital; but be that as it may, further investigations of his mental condition took place in the months succeeding his trial.

Although such electroencephalograph readings as were available at the trial had shown nothing of abnormality, the electroencephalograph readings obtainable after the trial began in some instances to show an abnormality. In particular, as a kind of landmark, on September 29, 1973, three months after the trial, Dr. Williams found some abnormalities.

Those abnormalities were pursued and considered by other doctors who considered the case. I have already said that Dr. Neville was involved and also Dr. Williams, who found the initial abnormality on the electroencephalograph. The effect of that abnormality and of others subsequently found is, we find, conveniently summarised in the report of Dr. Blair which is given on April 5, 1975, before the hearing in this court. He explained how he has now had to re-consider his views in the light of the electroencephalograph evidence which has come before him since the trial. In considering how far the evidence of abnormality helps the defendant to prove a state of diminished responsibility, the doctor says this:

> "The difficulty in accepting this statement in itself is that an electroencephalograph tracing on [the defendant] before September 29, 1973, was normal and tracings afterwards showed 'slight abnormality and eventually no abnormality.'"

Thus, one has what seems to a layman a considerable phenomenon of no abnormality at the time of trial, abnormality arising and discovered quite soon afterwards and then going away again, and eventually disappearing altogether. That is the summary of the activities of the defendant's electroencephalograph results throughout the time his case was under consideration.

This is not the first time that this kind of situation has occurred. Nor is it the first time in which a defendant in the position of the present defendant has sought to call fresh evidence on medical grounds. It is quite obvious, and Sir Harold Cassel does not shrink from it, that in order to succeed in this appeal the defendant has got to show that the introduction of the evidence with regard to his electroencephalograph readings is vital—in other words, that that evidence is enough to get him either a dismissal of his conviction or at least a new trial. Nothing else will help him. In order that he may get the evidence of the electroencephalograph readings before the court he has to have leave from this court to call the fresh evidence because under section 23 of the Criminal Appeal Act 1968 fresh evidence is not to be called except with the leave of the court.

I have said that this is not in any sense a novel situation, and indeed there is a very similar case in this court, *Reg.* v. *Dodd* (unreported), June 10, 1971, to which we will make reference now, raising almost exactly the same points but unfortunately never reported. The presiding judge was Fenton Atkinson L.J. and he sat with Stephenson L.J. and Lawton J.

Here again there was a charge of murder, here again there was a defence A of provocation which failed, and here again after the conviction had been entered and the matter had been completed as far as the trial court was concerned evidence came to light which was thought to justify a conclusion that the appellant had suffered from diminished responsibility at the material time. This is what Fenton Atkinson L.J. said about those issues in that case:

> " It is now said that fresh evidence is available to show that in truth B this appellant was suffering from such abnormality of mind at the relevant time as substantially impaired his mental responsibility, in other words a defence of diminished responsibility. That was a defence which the very experienced counsel representing this man never attempted to run at the trial from first to last, and it is very understandable why they did not because they had a medical report C from Dr. Terry, the senior medical officer at Brixton prison where the appellant had been for some three months on remand before that report was made, saying in emphatic terms that there was no sign of mental illness and nothing whatever to suggest diminished responsibility."

This is very much like the present case, as all must admit. He goes on D a little later in the judgment:

> " That was the material available at the time, and those responsible for the defence decided quite deliberately not to attempt to run any defence of diminished responsibility, but to run the case on provocation, and the case was fought on provocation from first to last."

He then goes on to discuss how a distinguished psychiatrist, Dr. Denham, E came into the picture some ten months after the appellant's trial, and how Dr. Denham had reached conclusions about the mental condition of the appellant which the other witnesses had not reached. Fenton Atkinson L.J. goes on to deal with the principle of the matter which is to be applied in those circumstances in these words:

> " In the view of this court, cases must be rare indeed when the F defence have chosen to run at the trial as their only defence the defence of accident or provocation, or a combination of the two, and when that defence has failed can consult and call a psychiatrist, or a psychiatrist seeing the appellant for the first time many months after the event, with a view to getting a re-trial to run a defence of diminished responsibility. It may well be that if subsequent evidence of diminished responsibility was really overwhelming, the court might G well feel moved to substitute a verdict of manslaughter, or to order a new trial. But we have all read and re-read this fresh report from Dr. Denham. It is based, of course, on various fresh matters revealed to him for the first time, we have already stated, some months after the event, and it shows certainly that this young man was subject to extreme fits of anger and that at the relevant time he was so H enraged by the damage to his face that he was out for revenge. But in our view, if received, that evidence would not afford any ground for allowing the appeal, and that is even assuming in the favour of the defence that there was good reason for not adducing the evidence of a further psychiatrist at the trial."

We think that we should follow the decision of this court in *Dodd's* case and apply to this case the principles laid down by Fenton Atkinson

A L.J. to which I have just referred; and in so doing the first question which the court has to ask itself is whether it is under any obligation to receive the evidence now tendered before it, which is the evidence of three of the doctors who saw this defendant at one stage or another in the course of these matters.

Sir Harold Cassel submits that section 23 of the Criminal Appeal Act 1968, properly understood, requires us to hear this evidence, and we must
B look into this matter first. Section 23 (1) in effect provides that this court may in its discretion order the production before it of fresh evidence virtually without limit. It is an extremely wide power, but it is a purely discretionary power. It is a power which the court can exercise however it wants to, but which it is not bound to exercise. The mandatory provisions in regard to letting in fresh evidence are to be found in section
C 23 (2), and that I should read:

> "Without prejudice to subsection (1) above, where evidence is tendered to the Court of Appeal thereunder the court shall, unless they are satisfied that the evidence, if received, would not afford any ground for allowing the appeal, exercise their power of receiving it if—(*a*) it appears to them that the evidence is likely to be credible and would have been admissible in the proceedings from which the
> D appeal lies on an issue which is the subject of the appeal; and (*b*) they are satisfied that it was not adduced in those proceedings but there is a reasonable explanation for the failure to adduce it."

We do not express any opinion in this case on the question whether the evidence of mental disturbance is strong enough so that if received it might afford a ground for allowing the appeal. We leave that matter
E open, finding it unnecessary to reach a conclusion upon it. But we direct our attention to the fact that the duty to admit fresh evidence arises only where the evidence is not only likely to be credible but would have been admissible in the proceedings from which the appeal lies on an issue which is the subject of the appeal.

Argument has centred on the phrase "on an issue" in the last sen-
F tence, and, as I understand it, Sir Harold Cassel argues that any contention which can affect the ultimate outcome of the proceedings is an issue for present purposes. That means that all he has to do in order to create an issue to bring before this court is to assert that certain things are or are not the case. Then he says that means the issue has been raised and the jurisdiction of this court to solve the ultimate problem appears.

We find it quite impossible to reach that conclusion on the meaning
G of subsection (2) (*a*). We think it inconsistent with the whole of the Criminal Appeal Act 1968 and entirely contrary to any possible intention of Parliament that we should be compelled in this court to receive any quantity of evidence which was put before us merely on the assertion of the party putting the material before us that there was an issue in regard to the point dealt with in the material.

H In our judgment the expression "on an issue" in subsection (2) (*a*) means on an issue which was raised below and is the subject of the appeal in this court. Giving the words that meaning, we can say with confidence, as might have been said in *Dodd's* case, that there is no issue which was litigated in the court below and which is now to be argued on the basis of the fresh evidence.

In reaching that conclusion we are impressed by the fact, first, that the alternative construction, as I have endeavoured to demonstrate, would

be totally unworkable, and, secondly, in the knowledge that the discretion- A
ary power in the court to allow fresh evidence under section 23 (1) should be available in all cases to avoid any kind of injustice which might occur. We conclude for those reasons that this is not a case in which we are bound to admit fresh evidence.

The next thing we have to do therefore is to consider whether it ought to be admitted in the exercise of our discretion. In approaching this problem it is also as well to remember that if the evidence is rejected B
at this stage, then the appeal must fail because Sir Harold accepts that he has no other weapons in his armoury if he is refused leave to call fresh evidence. Secondly, we should remember that if we admit the evidence we shall then have to dispose of the appeal finally by one of three orders. The first would be to dismiss the appeal; the second would be to substitute a verdict of manslaughter; and the third would be to order C
a new trial. So we must mentally go through those stages until we reach the answer in this case.

Should we in our discretion allow this evidence to go in? We turn our minds back to what Fenton Atkinson L.J. said in the virtually identical circumstances, and his words were:

> "It may well be that if subsequent evidence of diminished respon- D
> sibility was really overwhelming, the court might well feel moved to substitute a verdict of manslaughter, or to order a new trial."

Thus, if one was faced with evidence which was really overwhelming to show mental deficiency in the defendant at the material time, not only would we admit the evidence, but no doubt we should follow Fenton Atkinson L.J.'s directions and either order a new trial or substitute a E
verdict of manslaughter. Like that case, this defendant lacks the overwhelming evidence to which reference was there made.

Also in deciding whether to exercise the discretion or not regard should be paid, we think, to a proper division of responsibility between this court and the Home Office in matters of this kind. It is to be remembered that the main function of the Court of Appeal is to supervise the operation of the lower courts and to correct their mistakes. It is for that reason F
that we have power to overrule decisions below and substitute new punishments and the like. But it is not the function of the Court of Appeal to maintain continuous supervision over prisoners when they have already been committed to prison, and it certainly is no function of the Court of Appeal to be invited two years after a conviction has been entered to make some wholly different sentence merely because of changes of cir- G
cumstance in the meanwhile. There is of course the kind of twilight area between the functions of the Home Secretary and our functions in which that may be suitable to provide the relief sought, but in the main, if the functions of the appeal have been completed, if all steps which could be taken according to the Criminal Appeal Rules 1968 have either been taken or now cannot be taken owing to lapse of time, then prima facie if anything happens thereafter which is thought to invalidate the H
proceedings, the proper person to receive the complaint is the Home Secretary.

This court is concerned with changes in the circumstances occurring whilst the court is still seized of the case, which would not normally be brought into action on applications for leave being made long out of time merely in respect of developments which have occurred since the hearing and over which it earlier could not have exercised jurisdiction.

A However in this case the question is whether, bearing those factors in mind, we ought to allow the evidence in our discretion, and we have come to the conclusion that we should not. We refuse the application for the calling of fresh evidence, and that, by concession of Sir Harold, means that the appeal must be and is dismissed.

Appeal dismissed.

B

Solicitors: *R. Voss & Son; Director of Public Prosecutions.*

J. W.

C

[QUEEN'S BENCH DIVISION]

* HAGGARD *v.* MASON

1975 Oct. 29 Lord Widgery C.J., O'Connor and Lawson JJ.

D

Crime—Drugs—Offer to supply—Offering controlled drug for sale—Drug not controlled drug—Whether offence committed—Whether order for forfeiture of drug and money from sale valid—Misuse of Drugs Act 1971 (*c.* 38), *ss.* 4 (1) (3) (*a*), 27 (1)

The defendant possessed a substance which he believed to be Lysergide (L.S.D.), a controlled drug within the meaning of the Misuse of Drugs Act 1971. He offered to sell the drug to
E the purchaser and, at the time of the transaction, both believed it to be Lysergide. It was in fact another drug, which was not a controlled drug within the Act. The defendant was convicted of offering to supply a controlled drug, contrary to section 4 (1) and (3) of the Act.[1] The justices imposed a fine and a suspended prison sentence; they also ordered, under section 27 of the Act, forfeiture of the drug and a sum of money in the defendant's possession which was the remainder
F of the proceeds of the sale.

On appeal by the defendant:—

Held, dismissing the appeal, that an offence was committed, under section 4 (1) and (3) (*a*), when the defendant offered to sell a controlled drug to the purchaser and, for the purposes of the section, it was immaterial that the drug was not in fact a controlled drug; that, accordingly, the justices had come to a
G right decision in convicting the defendant but the order for forfeiture of the money would be deleted from their order because the money did not "relate to the offence" within the meaning of section 27 (1) of the Act.

No cases are referred to in the judgments and none were cited in argument.

H [Reported by MRS. RACHEL DAVIES, Barrister-at-Law]

[1] Misuse of Drugs Act 1971, s. 4: "(1) . . . it shall not be lawful for a person— . . . (*b*) to supply or offer to supply a controlled drug to another. . . . (3) . . . it is an offence for a person—(*a*) to supply or offer to supply a controlled drug to another in contravention of subsection (1) above; . . .

S. 27: (1) . . . the court by or before which a person is convicted of an offence under this Act may order anything shown to the satisfaction of the court to relate to the offence, to be forfeited and either destroyed or dealt with in such other manner as the court may order."

CASE STATED by Newcastle-upon-Tyne justices. A

On July 17, 1974, an information was preferred by the prosecutor, Sidney Mason, against the defendant, David Anthony Haggard, that he between May 1, 1974, and June 1, 1974, in the City of Newcastle-upon-Tyne offered to supply Lysergide, a controlled drug of Class A, to Anthony Gerald Heward, in contravention of section 4 (1) of the Misuse of Drugs Act 1971, contrary to section 4 (3) of the Misuse of Drugs Act, 1971. B

The justices heard the information on August 27, 1974, and found the following facts. On May 17 or 24, 1974, the defendant travelled to Leeds University, and for £250 purchased in the form of impregnated blotting paper one thousand " tabs " of a substance which he, at the time, believed to be Lysergide (L.S.D.). Lysergide is a Class A controlled drug within the provisions of the Misuse of Drugs Act 1971. His intention was C to purchase Lysergide or cannabis, and resell it for profit. The defendant approached various acquaintances who were in a position to introduce him to " acid heads " (regular users of Lysergide), with a view to the sale to such persons of the substance he had purchased as Lysergide. As a result of one of those approaches, the defendant was introduced to Anthony Gerald Heward at a meeting which had been arranged for the purpose of the sale of Lysergide by one Eddy Husband. At the meeting D the defendant offered to sell to Heward a quantity of Lysergide, and a sale took place of some of the substance which the defendant had purchased in Leeds. At the time of the transaction both the defendant and Heward believed that the substance sold was Lysergide, a controlled drug. The substance purchased as Lysergide in Leeds and later sold by the defendant to Heward as Lysergide, was in fact 2,5 Dimethoxy 4 Bromoamphetamine E (Bromo S.T.P.). Bromo S.T.P. was an hallucinogenic drug, similar in appearance and effect to L.S.D., but not controlled under the Misuse of Drugs Act 1971, or regulations made thereunder.

It was contended by the defendant that the offence " to offer to supply a controlled drug to another " under section 4 (3) (*a*) of the Misuse of Drugs Act 1971 required that any substance proffered as a controlled drug must in fact be a controlled drug, and that if the substance F actually proffered and subsequently supplied was not a controlled drug, there could be no unlawful offer to supply within the section. Analogy was sought to be drawn with the decision of the House of Lords in *Reg.* v. *Smith* (*Roger*) [1975] A.C. 476 in which it was held that an offence of attempted handling of stolen goods required that the goods to be handled must in fact be in existence and stolen at the time of the G attempt. Thus it was argued that a controlled drug could only be offered for supply if the substance proffered was in fact a controlled drug. It was conceded that the defendant had the necessary intent to commit the offence but, although fortuitous under the circumstances, he was not in a position to supply the controlled drug.

It was contended by the prosecutor that the words " offer to supply a controlled drug to another " must be given their ordinary and apparent H meaning. Thus, it was argued that once an offer had been made unlawfully to supply a controlled drug the offence under section 4 (3) (*a*) was complete. It was the making of the offer which was forbidden by the section, and the existence of the specific controlled drug or the nature of any drug actually supplied in pursuance of the offer was immaterial. Analogy was drawn with *Reg.* v. *McDonough* (1962) 47 Cr.App.Rep. 37 in which the Court of Criminal Appeal held that an incitement to receive stolen goods was complete on the making of the incitement even though the goods might not yet have been stolen, or might not in fact be stolen at all or even in existence. Thus the offence of incitement was committed whether or not the act incited was ever carried out, and the offence of offering to supply controlled drugs under section 4 (3) of the Misuse of Drugs Act 1971 was committed when the offer was made, and whether or not the supply of the controlled drug in question ever took place. *Reg.* v. *McDonough* was cited as an example of such an alternative charge as was alluded to by Lord Hailsham of St. Marylebone L.C. in *Reg.* v. *Smith* (*Roger*) [1975] A.C. 476, 482.

The justices were of opinion that the defendant had offered to supply Lysergide to Heward both through the agency of Eddy Husband and, more specifically, when he visited Heward and the sale took place. They were also of opinion that when the offer was made to Heward the defendant genuinely believed that the substance he would supply should his offer be accepted was Lysergide. They were not referred to any case law directly affecting the penal provision, and in its absence they interpreted the section within what they took to be the spirit and intent of the Misuse of Drugs Act 1971. It was their opinion that section 4 of the Act created a wide-reaching offence prohibiting offers to supply controlled drugs, and that the offence was completed once the offer was made to supply a substance which was a controlled drug, even if that substance was not yet in the possession of the offeror, or if it was later discovered not to be the drug offered, or indeed if it was not a controlled drug at all.

Accordingly the justices convicted the defendant of the offence as charged, passed the following sentence, and made the following orders: fine of £400, to be paid at £10 per week, and sentence of 12 months' imprisonment suspended for two years, no other method of dealing with the defendant other than imprisonment being appropriate owing to the gravity of the offence (section 20 of the Powers of Criminal Courts Act 1973). Order under section 27 of the Misuse of Drugs Act 1971 that seven drops of Bromo S.T.P. be forfeited and destroyed. Order under section 27 of the Misuse of Drugs Act 1971 that £146, being the remaining proceeds of the defendant's illegal dealings, be forfeited and dealt with as a fine.

The defendant appealed. The question for the opinion of the High Court was whether an offence was committed contrary to section 4 (3) (*a*) of the Misuse of Drugs Act 1971, in the following circumstances: where an offer was made, either directly or through an agent, to supply a controlled drug and the substance which the offeror intended to supply and which he in fact supplied transpired not to be a controlled drug.

The facts are stated in the judgment of Lawson J.

Michael Lewis Q.C. for the defendant.
Anthony Hidden for the prosecutor.

LORD WIDGERY C.J. I will ask Lawson J. to give the first judgment.

LAWSON J. This is an appeal by way of case stated from a decision of the justices for the City of Newcastle-upon-Tyne sitting at Market Street in Newcastle on August 27, 1974. On that day they were hearing an information preferred on July 17, 1974, by the prosecutor against the defendant charging that he, between May 1, 1974, and June 1, 1974, in

Newcastle-upon-Tyne, offered to supply Lysergide, a controlled drug of Class A, to Anthony Gerald Heward, in contravention of section 4 (1) of the Misuse of Drugs Act 1971, contrary to section 4 (3) of that Act. A

Section 4 (1) of the Act reads:

> " Subject to any regulations under section 7 of this Act for the time being in force, it shall not be lawful for a person . . . (*b*) to supply or offer to supply a controlled drug to another." B

Subsection (3) provides that it is an offence for a person to supply or offer to supply a controlled drug to another in contravention of section 4 (1).

Lysergide, the subject of the information, was in fact a controlled drug of the Class A set out in Schedule 2 to the Act.

The facts found by the justices are as follows. On a date in May 1974 before May 24, the defendant travelled to Leeds University and for £250 purchased in the form of impregnated blotting paper 1,000 " tabs " of a substance which he at the time believed to be Lysergide (L.S.D.), which is a Class A drug. The defendant's intention was to purchase Lysergide or cannabis and re-sell it for profit. The defendant approached various acquaintances who were in a position to introduce him to " acid heads " (that is regular users of Lysergide) with a view to the sale to such persons of the substance he purchased as Lysergide. As a result of one of these approaches the defendant was introduced to Anthony Gerald Heward at a meeting which had been arranged for the purpose of the sale of Lysergide by one Eddy Husband. At this meeting the defendant offered to sell to Heward a quantity of Lysergide and the sale took place of some of the substance which the defendant had purchased in Leeds. At the time of this transaction both the defendant and Heward believed that the substance sold was Lysergide, a controlled drug. C D E

The substance which in fact the defendant had bought in Leeds as Lysergide, and which he sold to Heward as Lysergide, was a different drug which is known by a short name Bromo S.T.P. At the material time Bromo S.T.P. was not a drug which was controlled under the Act of 1971. F

The short point therefore is this: bearing in mind that the defendant was charged and convicted of the offence of offering to supply a controlled drug, it is the fact that what he in fact did supply, and that which was intended to be the physical subject of his offer to supply, turned out to be something which was not a controlled drug.

In my judgment the offence was completed at the time when, to follow the findings of the justices, the defendant met Heward and offered to sell him a quantity of Lysergide. To my mind that was a clear situation in which the justices were right to find that there was an offer to supply a controlled drug, an offer made by the defendant to Heward. G

It matters not in relation to the offence of offering to supply that what is in fact supplied pursuant to that offer, the offer having been accepted, is not in fact a controlled drug. Of course if the charge had been supplying a controlled drug, it is clear that the fact that a controlled drug was not in fact supplied would mean that that offence could not have been established. H

Having listened to the arguments and contentions made on behalf of the parties before them, the justices concluded that the defendant had offered to supply Lysergide to Heward and therefore convicted him of

A the offence of offering to supply. They sentenced him to a fine. They imposed a sentence of imprisonment which they suspended for two years in the exercise of their powers under section 20 of the Criminal Courts Act 1973. They made an order for the destruction of seven drops of Bromo S.T.P., which were the subject of the transaction between the defendant and Heward (the matter to which the information related) and they finally ordered the forfeiture of a sum of money which was appa-
B rently in the defendant's possession. In making that order of forfeiture the justices purported to act under section 27 of the Misuse of Drugs Act 1971, which provides that the court by or before which a person is convicted of an offence under the Act may order anything shown to the satisfaction of the court to relate to that offence to be forfeited or dealt with in such other manner as the court may order.

C In my judgment the justices had no power to make an order such as they purported to make in this case, and subject to that point this appeal brought by way of case stated should be dismissed, but the justices' order should be varied by deletion of that part of the order which relates to the forfeiture in the sum of £146.

O'CONNOR J. I agree.

D

LORD WIDGERY C.J. I agree also.

Appeal dismissed but justices' order varied by deletion of order for forfeiture of £146.
Prosecution costs to be paid out of
E *central funds.*
Legal aid taxation.

Solicitors: *Bindman & Partners for Allan Henderson, Beecham & Lee, Newcastle-upon-Tyne; Collyer-Bristow & Co. for Prosecuting Solicitor, Northumbria Police Authority.*

F

[HOUSE OF LORDS]

G * INLAND REVENUE COMMISSIONERS . . . APPELLANTS

AND

GOODWIN . . . . RESPONDENT

1975 Nov. 17, 18, 20; Lord Diplock, Lord Morris of Borth-y-Gest,
1976 Jan. 28 Lord Kilbrandon, Lord Salmon and Lord Edmund-Davies

H

Revenue — Tax advantage — Transaction in securities — Issue of shares by private company to avoid estate duty and retain family control — Irredeemable preference shares issued by mistake—Further issue of redeemable preference shares to correct error—Whether transactions for bona fide commercial reason—Finance Act 1960 (8 & 9 *Eliz.* 2, *c.* 44), *s.* 28 (1)

A family business, established in 1883, was formed into a private company in 1935. Until April 2, 1951, all the issued

shares were held by G, his father and his uncle. In order A
to provide protection against the possibility that, in the event of the father and uncle's deaths, money might have to be raised for estate duty by the forced sale of ordinary shares, thereby reducing the family control of the company, two separate measures were adopted. First, the uncle and the father made settlements; under one settlement the uncle settled 890 ordinary shares on B's wife. Secondly, on April 2,
1951, the company's authorised capital was increased by the B
creation of 45,000 £1 redeemable preference shares and a bonus issue of such shares was made by capitalisation of £44,525 from the profit and loss account. G was allotted 13,355 shares of the issue and B's wife was allotted 4,450 shares. In 1958 the company decided to make a public flotation of ordinary shares and it was then discovered that because of a procedural error the 1951 issue of preference shares was
irredeemable. It was decided to leave the 1951 issue as part C
of the permanent capital of the company and to make a new issue of 44,525 £1 redeemable preference shares in its place. On August 18, 1958, 13,355 of these shares were issued to G to replace the 1951 issue and 4,450 shares to B's wife. Redemption of the 1958 issue was postponed until 1963 in order to facilitate the public flotation of ordinary shares. On September 1, 1958, G transferred his holding of
13,355 redeemable preference shares to his wife and on April D
30, 1963, the redeemable preference shares were redeemed for cash at par. In 1969 the Inland Revenue Commissioners served notices on G and B under section 28 of the Finance Act 1960 [1] adjusting their liability to surtax for the year 1963–64 to counteract the tax advantage obtained by them in consequence of the 1958 and 1963 transactions. The special commissioners allowed appeals by G and B against the
notices, holding, inter alia, that the 1958 and 1963 trans- E
actions had been carried out for bona fide commercial reasons. Walton J. allowed appeals by the Crown. The Court of Appeal allowed appeals by G and B and restored the order of the special commissioners.

On appeal by the Crown in G's case:—

Held, dismissing the appeal, that an overriding reason for the 1958 transaction had been the retention of family control
of the company; that the commissioners' findings had been F
to the effect that loss of family control would have had deleterious consequences for the company; that that amounted to a finding that the 1958 transaction had been carried out for bona fide commercial reasons; that the 1963 transaction had been entered into as the final stage in the attainment of bona fide commercial objects, namely, access to the money market coupled with continuance of family management; and
that, accordingly, the commissioners had been entitled to G
conclude that the transactions had been carried out for bona fide commercial reasons and their decision should be upheld (post, pp.193F, 194A–B, 198E–H, 199A–B, E, F, 200C–D).

Semble. Section 25 (4) of the Finance Act 1962 would have applied to the transfer of the shares by G to his wife between allotment and redemption (post, p. 199D–E).

Decision of the Court of Appeal [1975] 1 W.L.R. 640;
[1975] 1 All E.R. 708 affirmed. H

[1] Finance Act 1960, s. 28: "(1) Where— . . . (*b*) in consequence of a transaction in securities . . . , a person . . . has obtained, a tax advantage, then unless he shows that the transaction or transactions were carried out either for bona fide commercial reasons or in the ordinary course of making or managing investments, and that none of them had as their main object, or one of their main objects, to enable tax advantages to be obtained, this section shall apply to him in respect of that transaction or those transactions: . . ."

A The following cases are referred to in their Lordships' opinions:

Edwards v. *Bairstow* [1956] A.C. 14; [1955] 3 W.L.R. 410; [1955] 3 All E.R. 495, C.A.

Hague v. *Inland Revenue Commissioners* [1969] 1 Ch. 393; [1968] 2 W.L.R. 825; [1968] 1 All E.R. 1096; [1969] 1 Ch. 393; [1968] 3 W.L.R. 576; [1968] 2 All E.R. 1252, C.A.

Inland Revenue Commissioners v. *Brebner* [1967] 2 A.C. 18; [1967] 2
B W.L.R. 1001; [1967] 1 All E.R. 779; 43 T.C. 705, H.L.(Sc.).

The following additional cases were cited in argument:

Bulmer v. *Inland Revenue Commissioners* [1967] Ch. 145; [1966] 3 W.L.R. 672; [1966] 3 All E.R. 801; 44 T.C. 1.

Green v. *Inland Revenue Commissioners* (1972) 51 A.T.C. 169.

Inland Revenue Commissioners v. *Parker* [1966] A.C. 141; [1966] 2
C W.L.R. 486; [1966] 1 All E.R. 399, H.L.(E.).

Inland Revenue Commissioners v. *Saxone, Lilley & Skinner* (*Holdings*) *Ltd.* [1967] 1 W.L.R. 501; [1967] 1 All E.R. 756, H.L.(Sc.).

Ransom v. *Higgs* [1973] 1 W.L.R. 1180; [1973] 2 All E.R. 657, C.A.; [1974] 1 W.L.R. 1594; [1974] 3 All E.R. 949, H.L.(E.).

APPEAL from the Court of Appeal.

D This was an appeal by the Inland Revenue Commissioners by leave of the House of Lords granted on March 24, 1975, from the decision of the Court of Appeal (Russell, Stamp and Scarman L.JJ.) on January 29, 1975, allowing appeals by the respondent taxpayer, John Goodwin, and another taxpayer from a decision of Walton J. on July 9, 1973 [1974] 1 W.L.R. 380. By his decision, Walton J. reversed a decision of
E the Commissioners for the Special Purposes of the Income Tax Acts cancelling notices issued to the taxpayers under section 28 of the Finance Act 1960.

The facts are set out in the opinion of Lord Kilbrandon.

D. C. Potter Q.C. and *Brian Davenport* for the Crown.
Michael Nolan Q.C. and *Stephen Oliver* for the respondent.

F

Their Lordships took time for consideration.

January 28. LORD DIPLOCK. My Lords, I have had the advantage of reading in advance the speech to be delivered by my noble and learned friend, Lord Kilbrandon.

G I agree with him and would dismiss the appeal.

LORD MORRIS OF BORTH-Y-GEST. My Lords, before the commissioners it was for the respondent to show that the transactions in question were carried out either for bona fide commercial reasons or in the ordinary course of making or managing investments and further that none of them had as their main object, or one of their main
H objects, to enable tax advantages to be obtained. As to this latter matter the commissioners found that the obtaining of tax advantage was not a main object of any of the transactions. The point of difficulty in the case concerned the question whether in regard to the 1951 transaction (from which the later transactions stemmed and with which they were linked) the conclusion of the commissioners that its object was a bona fide commercial one was a conclusion which ran counter to and was not warranted by their findings of fact. Was the evidence which

was accepted inconsistent with and contradictory of their conclusion? Though a contention to this effect was very forcibly argued and though during our consideration of the appeal I was impressed by the reasoning in the careful judgment of Walton J. [1974] 1 W.L.R. 380, I came in the end, though after hesitation, to the view that the reasoning of the Court of Appeal [1975] 1 W.L.R. 640 was to be preferred and for the reasons given by my noble and learned friend Lord Kilbrandon—whose speech I have had the advantage of reading in advance—I agree that the appeal should be dismissed.

LORD KILBRANDON. My Lords, R. Goodwin & Sons (Engineers) Ltd. ("the company") are incorporated for the purpose of carrying on an engineering business established in the Midlands in 1883. The founders were a Mr. Goodwin and his sons. When the incorporation into a private company took place in 1935, two of old Mr. Goodwin's grandsons, Frank and John, were directors; in 1954 the board was joined by a great-grandson, who is the respondent, and another director. Economic history testifies to the fact that such concerns have been the backbone of English manufacturing prosperity, and this fact may turn out to be important.

The ensuing narrative is derived from the findings in fact made by the special commissioners in circumstances which will become apparent. The narrative is given in skeleton form, so as, so far as possible, to include only the facts which are essential to a decision of the appeal, because there is a full statement to be found in the judgment of the Court of Appeal [1975] 1 W.L.R. 640, and there is no point in repetition. I may say straight away that I agree with the approach adopted by the Court of Appeal, and the conclusion at which the court arrived.

1. In 1951 consideration was given to the company "going public," thus obtaining access to fresh capital for expansion purposes. But the time was deemed unpropitious, because, inter alia, the recent dividend record had not been such as to make public support probable.

2. The shares at that time were held as to 40 per cent. by John Goodwin senior, then aged 55, and by trustees of family settlements made by him, 30 per cent. by Frank Goodwin, then aged 60, and by trustees of family settlements made by him, and 30 per cent. by the respondent. The trust holdings had been constituted so recently as to make the shares aggregable for estate duty with the estates of the settlors on decease. To meet the duty it would probably have become necessary to sell shares, with the danger of family control being lost. The importance of family control will be adverted to later.

3. It was therefore decided, and the company resolved accordingly, to increase the capital of the company by capitalising £44,525 from profit and loss account, to create 6 per cent. preference shares redeemable by the company at three months' notice after 12 months and to issue those shares to the existing shareholders as a five for one bonus issue. Thus, on redemption, resources would have become available to meet the threat to the family control. It is important to emphasize that the commissioners find as a matter of fact that the decision referred to above was taken for the reasons given under heading 2,

> ". . . that the main object of the 1951 preference share issue was a bona fide commercial one, and that the obtaining of a tax advantage was not a main object."

A 4. In 1958 it was decided that the history and prospects of the
company were such as to make the time ripe for a public issue. The
method by which this was to be effected was described by the Court
of Appeal as follows [1975] 1 W.L.R. 640, 644:

> "After a good many varying suggestions, the scheme evolved for
> a public flotation was as follows, accepted by the Goodwin family
> B and trustees of the settlements: (1) acquisition by the company of
> the outstanding 71 per cent. shareholding in a company ('Akron')
> so as to make it a 100 per cent. subsidiary; (2) the 1951 bonus
> issue of preference shares to be made irredeemable for a period
> of some five years to enable expanding trade to replace the substantial
> sum (some £130,000) of working capital required for the
> Akron acquisition; (3) half the ordinary shares in the company to
> C be converted into deferred ordinary shares, the offer to the public
> to be made out of the unconverted ordinary shares: the deferred
> ordinary shares to remain as such until after the redemption of
> the 1951 preference shares."

5. At this stage a crisis arose; it was discovered that the preference
shares had been issued pursuant to an ordinary, not a special, resolution
D of the company, and that therefore the essential quality of redeemability
did not attach to them. The foundation of the scheme was thus
insecure.

6. Although the danger of shares having to be sold to meet death
duties was now less menacing, owing to the efflux of time having released
the settled shares from liability to duty, it was still real. It was related
E now in part to the survivorship of the respondent. Any action which
was to be taken had accordingly still to be effective in the two respects
of securing the family control and enabling the issue to the public.
The obvious thing to do was, by the most convenient means, so to
restructure the capital as to remake the provision which it was thought
had been made in 1951. Again to quote the judgment of the Court
of Appeal [1975] 1 W.L.R. 640, 645:

> F "This was done first by converting the 1951 preference shares into
> deferred ordinary shares. The company then capitalised the sum
> of £171,095 from its general reserve and applied that sum in paying
> up at par: (a) 44,525 out of 45,000 newly created £1 6 per cent.
> redeemable preference shares; (b) 81,095 of previously unissued
> (6,095) and newly created ordinary shares (75,000); (c) 45,475 of
> G previously unissued (475) and newly created (45,000) deferred
> ordinary shares: the 475 representing the converted unissued 1951
> preference shares. The capital structure of the company for the
> purpose of the public flotation was thus: issued ordinary, £90,000,
> of which a proportion (£54,000) was to be offered to the public:
> issued deferred ordinary shares, 90,000: issued 6 per cent. redeemable
> preference shares, 44,525: unissued redeemable preference
> H shares, 475. The redeemable preference shares were redeemable at
> the company's option after April 30, 1963. The deferred ordinary
> shares were to rank pari passu as one class with the ordinary shares
> only after 12 months from the redemption of the preference shares."

7. As regards this scheme the commissioners observe:

> "We are satisfied on the evidence that the main object of the 1958
> preference share issue was to restore the status quo ante in this

respect. We think that the restoration in itself, and even without regard to the then current intention to embark upon a public flotation of shares in the company, affords a bona fide commercial reason for the 1958 issue of redeemable preference shares, and we find that the obtaining of a tax advantage was not a main object of the 1958 transaction." A

In so far as this passage is a finding of fact, in my opinion the commissioners were well entitled to make it, and so far as it is an inference from facts, I would say that the inference was justifiable if not irresistible. B

8. On August 19, 1958, an offer was made to the public of 540,000 ordinary shares of 2s. each (that is, £54,000 shares of £1 each subdivided). The particulars attached to the offer (signed by John Goodwin senior) contained the following paragraph: C

"Management.—I am 62 years of age and have been actively engaged in the business since the end of the first world war. I have been chairman of directors and managing director of the company since its incorporation in 1935. Mr. Frank Goodwin (my brother) is aged 67 and has spent all his working life with the business. He also has been a director since the incorporation of the company in 1935. Mr. John Goodwin (my son) is 31 years of age and joined the company in August 1946 becoming a director in 1954. He is now vice-chairman and assistant managing director. Mr. Henry Stubbs is aged 47 and has been with the business since June 1927, becoming a director in 1954. We are all actively engaged in the service of the company and have no other business commitments. We have each entered into a service agreement with the company for a minimum period of five years from May 1, 1958 (see contracts numbered (3) to (6) inclusive below). The present management has been responsible for building up the business of the group and I have every confidence in its ability to maintain continued progress." D E

F

9. On April 30, 1963, that is, at the earliest possible date, the company redeemed the preference shares for cash out of the capitalised reserves of the company. The respondent's holding of 13,355 shares had been transferred by him on August 18, 1958, to his wife, to whom, accordingly, the redemption moneys were paid. The commissioners found that the redemption was "... in order ... to implement the bargain made with the public in 1958." This phrase was severely criticised by counsel for the appellants, and for my part I agree that it is not accurate. Such of the public as should subscribe for shares had no interest in the issue or redemption of the preference shares, and no bargain had been with the public relating to them. In my opinion the Court of Appeal [1975] 1 W.L.R. 640, 648 correctly state the nature of the transaction as "... a fulfilment of the expectation of the trustees and other shareholders upon the basis of which the scheme of public flotation went through." It was a sine qua non of the public issue. G H

10. On May 5, 1969, the appellants issued a notice to the respondent under section 28 of the Finance Act 1960, as amended by section 25 (4) of the Finance Act 1962, claiming to make adjustments to his liability to surtax for the year 1963–64 in respect of the following transactions:

> A “1. the special resolution of R. Goodwin & Sons (Engineers) Ltd. (hereinafter called ‘the company’) on August 18, 1958, to capitalise the sum of £171,095, part of the company's general reserve, and, inter alia, to apply part of that sum to paying up in full 44,525 6 per cent. redeemable cumulative preference shares of £1 each, such shares (a) to be distributed amongst the holders of the ordinary shares in the company in the proportions specified in the resolution
> B and (b) to carry rights including the company's right, on giving due notice, to redeem them on or at any time after April 30, 1963; 2. the issue to you, on or about August 18, 1958, pursuant to the aforesaid special resolution, of 13,355 of the aforesaid redeemable preference shares and the transfer of those shares from you to your wife, Mrs. Patricia H. Goodwin, on or about September 1, 1958; 3.
> C the receipt by your wife on or about April 30, 1963, of £13,355 by way of redemption of her holding of 13,355 of the aforesaid redeemable preference shares.”

It is necessary at this stage to quote only a portion of section 28, as follows:—

> “(1) Where—(*a*) in any such circumstances as are mentioned in the
> D next following subsection, and (*b*) in consequence of a transaction in securities or of the combined effect of two or more such transactions, a person is in a position to obtain, or has obtained, a tax advantage, then unless he shows that the transaction or transactions were carried out either for bona fide commercial reasons or in the ordinary course of making or managing investments, and
> E that none of them had as their main object, or one of their main objects, to enable tax advantages to be obtained, this section shall apply to him in respect of that transaction or those transactions: . . . (2) . . . (*c*) the person in question receives, in consequence of a transaction whereby any other person—(i) subsequently receives, or has received, an abnormal amount by way of dividend; or (ii) subsequently becomes entitled, or has become entitled, to a deduction
> F as mentioned in paragraph (*b*) of this subsection, a consideration which either is, or represents the value of, assets which are (or apart from anything done by the company in question would have been) available for distribution by way of dividend, or is received in respect of future receipts of the company or is, or represents the value of, trading stock of the company, and the said person so
> G receives the consideration that he does not pay or bear tax on it as income; or (*d*) in connection with the distribution of profits of a company to which this paragraph applies, the person in question so receives as is mentioned in paragraph (*c*) of this subsection such a consideration as is therein mentioned. . . .”

The arrangements for counteracting tax advantages, and for the con-
H sequent procedures, follow but need not be quoted.

As affecting the respondent personally, there is a special point arising out of the transfer by him to his wife. I will therefore summarise the situation arising on the section in this appeal as it affects the shareholder in general. First, it is conceded that the shareholder is a person who received, within the meaning of section 28 (2) (*c*) and (*d*), assets of the company which were or would have been available for distribution by way of dividend in such a way that he did not bear tax on them as income, and received them in consequence of a transaction or transactions in securities. A He therefore obtained a tax advantage within the meaning of section 28 (1). The section will apply to him, that is to say, the appellants will be entitled to make an adjustment to his liability for surtax, unless he can exempt himself in one of the ways set out in the section. It is further conceded that neither of the transactions referred to in the notice had as its main object to enable the tax advantage to be obtained. The questions therefore are, has he B shown that the transactions were carried out either (a) for bona fide commercial reasons, or (b) in the ordinary course of making or managing investments? It is with (a) that this appeal is mainly concerned.

Although only the 1958 and 1963 transactions figure in the notice, I believe it is generally agreed that those transactions, although they must be considered independently, cannot be evaluated for the purpose of (a) C above, or even intelligibly described, save under colour of the transaction of 1951. The scene was set in 1951, and what followed, in the history of the company over the ensuing 12 years, was the working out of the policies which at that time satisfied the company as being in its best commercial interests. There is an unchallengeable finding in fact by the commissioners that the 1951 transaction was carried out for bona fide commercial reasons. While the onus remains on the respondent to D show that the same is true of the subsequent transactions, it will, I apprehend, not be difficult to do that if the essentially homogeneous character of the successive transactions, and the "reasons" for them, can be established. This will be again largely a question of fact; one of the main difficulties I have found in this appeal is to discern a question of law, upon which alone your Lordships would be justified in E overruling the decision of the commissioners.

An overriding reason for the 1958 transaction—being, besides and apart from the motive of facilitating access to the public money market, as true of 1958 as it was of 1951—was the retention of family control of the company. It was conceded in argument by counsel for the appellants that, if the commissioners had specifically and in so many words found that the loss of family control would have had deleterious com- F mercial consequences to the company, that finding would have amounted to a finding that a transaction entered into for the purpose of protecting that control had been carried out for bona fide commercial reasons. There is no such explicit finding, but the whole tenor of the findings is to that effect, and the substance of the matter seems to be clear and indisputable when the management paragraph in the particulars, already G quoted, is properly taken into account. The public, whose support was being solicited, were being invited to regard the continuity of family management as part of the invisible commercial assets of the company, and that appears to me to go the whole way to finding a commercial reason for the securing of that management.

As regards the 1963 transaction, it was submitted by the appellants that, the only finding in fact justifying its classification as a bona fide H commercial transaction, namely, that it was entered into ". . . in order . . . to implement the bargain made with the public in 1958," having been shown to be erroneous, there were no facts upon which the commissioners were entitled to arrive at their conclusion. My Lords, I have already pointed out that, as the Court of Appeal decided, this is a verbal rather than a substantial criticism. What was implemented in 1963 was an agreement between the company and the shareholders,

A some of whom were under a fiduciary duty to protect rights under settlements, as to the terms upon which the issue of ordinary shares was to be made to the public. The transaction, which the commissioners found did not have as a main object the obtaining of a tax advantage, was entered into as the final stage in the attainment of bona fide commercial objects, namely, access to the money market coupled with continuance of family management, with the advantages to the company to which
B I have referred.

It was also submitted for the respondents that the transactions escaped the consequences which ensue under section 28 on the grounds that they were carried out ". . . in the ordinary course of making or managing investments, . . ." It is not necessary to express any opinion on that, and I refrain from doing so.

C The special position of the respondent is that he had transferred his shares to his wife after allotment and before redemption. On the terms of section 28, accordingly, he could have claimed that not he, but his wife, had received the consideration referred to in section 28 (2) (*c*)—see *Hague* v. *Inland Revenue Commissioners* [1969] 1 Ch. 393—and that thus he had obtained no tax advantage. The legislature sought to alter this situation by section 25 (4) of the Finance Act 1962,
D which provides that in such circumstances section 28 applies to a husband

> ". . . as it would apply if any property, rights or liabilities of the wife were his property, rights or liabilities in relation to which she had acted only as nominee for him, . . ."

E I am bound to say, my Lords, that it appears to me that that amendment covers the present case, but since it is not necessary to decide the point, I would not do so.

My Lords, since in my opinion the findings in fact of the commissioners amount to this, that the transactions referred to in the notice were carried out for bona fide commercial reasons and that neither of them had as a main object to enable a tax advantage to be obtained, I
F would dismiss this appeal.

Lord Salmon. My Lords, I have had the advantage of reading the speech prepared by my noble and learned friend, Lord Kilbrandon. For the reasons given by him, I would dismiss this appeal.

Lord Edmund-Davies. My Lords, I cannot help thinking that the
G special commissioners might well have arrived at different findings of fact on the material available to them in this case than those they in fact made, and that had they done so those different findings would have been unassailable. I am, nevertheless, in agreement that, for the reasons appearing in the speech of my noble and learned friend, Lord Kilbrandon, this appeal should be dismissed. Why this should be so
H was explained in *Edwards* v. *Bairstow* [1956] A.C. 14 by Lord Radcliffe, who said, at p. 38:

> ". . . , the reason why the courts do not interfere with commissioners' findings or determinations when they really do involve nothing but questions of fact is not any supposed advantage in the commissioners of greater experience in matters of business or any other matters. The reason is simply that by the system that has been set up the commissioners are the first tribunal to try an appeal,

and in the interests of the efficient administration of justice their decisions can only be upset on appeal if they have been positively wrong in law. The court is not a second opinion, where there is reasonable ground for the first. . . . Their duty is no more than to examine those facts with a decent respect for the tribunal appealed from and if they think that the *only* reasonable conclusion on the facts found is inconsistent with the determination come to, to say so without more ado."

Looming over all the details of this case is the crucial question: Was the obtaining of a tax advantage the main object, or one of the main objects, of the transactions of 1951, 1958, and 1963, or any of them, to which the respondent was a party? As Russell L.J. said in the Court of Appeal [1975] 1 W.L.R. 640, 648: "This is essentially a matter of subjective fact, . . ." and the conclusion thereon depended on the evidence, both oral and documentary, which was adduced. There are certain features of that evidence which leave me personally unconvinced that I should have arrived at the same findings of fact, subjective as well as objective, as those formed by the special commissioners.

But that is not the test. Accordingly, while I am not prepared to hold that there was here that "ample evidence" which in, for example, *Inland Revenue Commissioners* v. *Brebner* [1967] 2 A.C. 18 led this House to refuse to interfere with the finding of fact at which the special commissioners there arrived, yet since, at the same time, I find it impossible to say that the *only* reasonable conclusion on the facts found is inconsistent with the determination come to in the instant case, I concur in holding that the appeal should be dismissed.

Appeal dismissed with costs.

Solicitors: *Solicitor of Inland Revenue; Waltons & Co. for Pinsent & Co., Birmingham.*

M. G.

[HOUSE OF LORDS]

* RAVENSEFT PROPERTIES LTD. . . . . . RESPONDENTS

AND

NEWHAM LONDON BOROUGH COUNCIL . . PETITIONERS

1975 Dec. 10 — Viscount Dilhorne, Lord Salmon and Lord Fraser of Tullybelton

Petition by the defendants for leave to appeal to the House of Lords from the decision of the Court of Appeal in *Ravenseft Properties Ltd.* v. *Newham London Borough Council* [1976] 2 W.L.R. 131.

The Appeal Committee dismissed the petition.

F. C.

[CHANCERY DIVISION]

* PRACTICE DIRECTION (CHANCERY: ORIGINATING SUMMONS) (No. 2)

[No. 34 of 1976]

Practice — Chancery Division — Originating summons — Grant of new business tenancy—Summons issued with date of hearing to be fixed—Summons for determination of interim rent—Landlord and Tenant Act 1954 (2 & 3 *Eliz.* 2, *c.* 56), *s.* 24A (*as amended by Law of Property Act* 1969 (*c.* 59), *s.* 3 (1))

1. Much time is wasted by first appointments for the hearing of originating summonses for new business tenancies under the Landlord and Tenant Act 1954 because both landlord and tenant wish to negotiate a new tenancy and merely ask the master, by letter or otherwise, to adjourn. This results from the prescribed form of originating summons requiring a date for the first hearing to be inserted in the summons itself, which has to be issued within a strict time limit.

2. In future, where the parties are in negotiation and neither side wishes to press on with the proceedings the tenant may, in issuing his originating summons in Form 10 in Appendix A to the Rules of the Supreme Court, delete the words "on   day, the   day of 19 , at   o'clock" and insert in their place the words "on a day to be fixed." Either party may at any time thereafter issue a notice of appointment to hear the originating summons in Form 12 in Appendix A.

3. It is of the greatest importance that the landlord should be informed promptly of the issue of the originating summons, which must be served strictly within one calendar month from the date of its issue. It is not to be assumed that the time will necessarily be extended if this requirement is not complied with.

4. If the landlord wishes the court to determine an interim rent under section 24A of the Landlord and Tenant Act 1954 but is content that the determination should await the determination of the application for a new lease, and in reliance on the procedure specified above the originating summons has not been brought on for hearing, he may likewise issue a general summons for the determination of the interim rent which states the hearing as being for a day to be fixed instead of for a date and time. Such a summons must be served promptly, and it may be brought on for hearing by either party on a date to be fixed by the court on not less than two days' notice to the opposing party.

5. Chancery practice direction No. 22 of 1974, *Practice Direction (Chancery: Originating Summons)* [1974] 1 W.L.R. 708, is to be read subject to the above; it is still not permissible to issue an originating summons with the provision for a date of hearing left blank and not replaced in accordance with paragraph 2 above.

By direction of the Vice-Chancellor.

R. E. Ball
Chief Master.

January 30, 1976.

[HOUSE OF LORDS] A

*** DERBY & CO. LTD.** . . . . . . APPELLANTS

AND

LARSSON . . . . RESPONDENT

1975 Dec. 15 B
1976 Jan. 28

Viscount Dilhorne, Lord Simon of Glaisdale, Lord Salmon, Lord Fraser of Tullybelton and Lord Russell of Killowen

Practice — Writ — Service out of jurisdiction — Counterclaim — "Properly brought against a person duly served within the jurisdiction"—Meaning—R.S.C., Ord. 11, *r.* 1 (1) (*j*)

By R.S.C., Ord. 11, r. 1 (1): C

> ". . . service of a writ, or notice of a writ, out of the jurisdiction is permissible with the leave of the court in the following cases, that is to say . . . (*j*) if the action begun by the writ being properly brought against a person duly served within the jurisdiction, a person out of the jurisdiction is a necessary or proper party thereto; . . ." D

The plaintiffs, a Swedish company, who had had commercial dealings with the defendants, an English company, trading as commodity brokers, issued a writ againt them claiming a declaration that they were not entitled to debit their account with losses made in certain transactions in zinc. The defendants defended the action and counterclaimed for moneys due on the basis that S. L., who resided in Sweden, E was the plaintiffs' agent for those transactions, the defence and counterclaim being duly served at the plaintiffs' solicitors' office in London. The defendants also sought to join him as defendant to the counterclaim, asserting in the alternative his breach of warranty of authority and personal liability.

On an ex parte application Ackner J. gave the defendants leave to serve the counterclaim on S. L. out of the jurisdiction under Ord. 11, which by virtue of Ord. 15, r. 3 (5) applies to F a counterclaim in the same way as to a writ. On an application to set aside his order, Donaldson J. held that service had been properly allowed. The Court of Appeal reversed his decision.

On appeal by the defendants: —

Held, that the plaintiffs by bringing the action and thereby setting in motion the rules of court had submitted themselves to the risk of a counterclaim and accordingly the counterclaim was " properly brought against a person duly served within G the jurisdiction " and falling within the terms of Ord. 11, r. 1 (1) (*j*), so that the court had jurisdiction to give leave for service on S. L. out of the jurisdiction.

John Russell and Co. Ltd. v. *Cayzer, Irvine and Co. Ltd.* [1916] 2 A.C. 298, H.L.(E.) distinguished.

Decision of the Court of Appeal reversed.

The following cases were referred to in their Lordships' opinions: H

Evans v. *Bartlam* [1937] A.C. 473; [1937] 2 All E.R. 646, H.L.(E.).

Osenton (*Charles*) *and Co.* v. *Johnston* [1942] A.C. 130; [1941] 2 All E.R. 245, H.L.(E.).

Russell (*John*) *and Co. Ltd.* v. *Cayzer, Irvine and Co. Ltd.* [1916] 2 A.C. 298, H.L.(E.).

Tyne Improvement Commissioners v. *Armement Anversois S.A.* [1949] A.C. 326; [1949] 1 All E.R. 294, H.L.(E.).

A The following additional case was referred to in argument:
Lewin v. *Trimming* (1888) 21 Q.B.D. 230.

APPEAL from the Court of Appeal.

This was an appeal from a judgment of the Court of Appeal (Cairns, Roskill and Browne L.JJ.) dated February 26, 1975, whereby the court B ordered that service of points of defence and counterclaim served or effected by the appellants, Derby & Co. Ltd., on the respondent, Stig Larsson, outside the jurisdiction be set aside. In so doing the court rescinded an order made by Donaldson J. on November 22, 1974, whereby he dismissed with costs in cause the application of the respondent to set aside an order obtained ex parte by the appellants from Ackner J. on July 10, 1974, giving leave to serve the points of defence and counterclaim C on the respondent outside the jurisdiction.

The facts are set out in the opinion of Lord Russell of Killowen.

N. A. Phillips for the appellants.
The respondent Larsson did not appear and was not represented.

D Their Lordships took time for consideration.

January 28, 1976. VISCOUNT DILHORNE. My Lords, I have had the advantage of reading in draft the speech of my noble and learned friend, Lord Russell of Killowen. I agree with it and with his conclusions and I wish only to add a few observations.

E When a court is required to consider whether an action begun by a writ or a counterclaim has been "properly brought," I doubt very much whether the court has to consider whether or not the claim or counterclaim is made bona fide or for some improper purpose. For a court to do that appears to be likely to involve something of the nature of a trial before the trial of the action. I am inclined to think that "properly brought" in Ord. 11, r. 1 (1) (*j*) means no more than brought in accordance with the F rules of court. But it is not necessary to decide as to that in this appeal for there is no question as to the genuineness of the appellants' counterclaim against the Swedish company which is suing them.

LORD SIMON OF GLAISDALE. My Lords, I have had the advantage of reading in draft the speech prepared by my noble and learned friend, Lord Russell of Killowen. I agree with it, and I would therefore allow the appeal.

G R.S.C., Ord. 11, r. 1 (1) (*j*) represents a concern to hold in balance two considerations which are liable to conflict. On the one hand there is the principle of international law that the courts of this country will not as a general rule seek to exercise jurisdiction over persons resident outside the territorial limits of their jurisdiction. On the other hand there is the desirability that, in legal proceedings in this country, all such persons H should be before the court as are required for justice to be done.

Ord. 11, r. 1 (1) (*j*) holds the balance between these two considerations by certain requirements which must be met for the court at all to have jurisdiction under it, and by a residual discretion even if these requirements are met. Two of the requirements which must be met are contained in the rule itself. First, the action (which includes a counterclaim in an action: Ord. 15, r. 3 (1) and (5)) must be properly brought against a party within the jurisdiction—i.e., it must be so brought in accordance with law, in particular the procedural code set out in the Rules of the Supreme Court (*John Russell and Co. Ltd.* v. *Cayzer, Irvine and Co. Ltd.* [1916] 2 A.C. 298). Secondly, the writ (or, as the case may be, the counterclaim) in the action must be duly served (i.e., in accordance with law, particularly the Rules of the Supreme Court) on such party within the jurisdiction. A

These two requirements generally involve a third limitation; namely, that jurisdiction under paragraph (1) (*j*) cannot be founded on service made by virtue of another paragraph of Ord. 15, r. 1 (1)—i.e., it is independent of the other heads, not cumulative. B

But, even when these stipulated limitations (available to a party outside the jurisdiction ex debito justitiae) are satisfied, the judge in chambers still has a discretion whether or not to allow service out of the jurisdiction by virtue of paragraph (*j*). He will exercise this discretion, mindful that Ord. 15, r. 1 constitutes an invasion of general principles of international law (see Lord Porter in *Tyne Improvement Commissioners* v. *Armement Anversois S.A.* [1949] A.C. 326, 338), in such a way as to conduce to justice and convenience. It is only in exceptional circumstances that the exercise of such a discretion should be displaced by an appellate court: cf. *Evans* v. *Bartlam* [1937] A.C. 473, 486; *Charles Osenton and Co.* v. *Johnston* [1942] A.C. 130, 138. C

I agree with my noble and learned friend, Lord Russell of Killowen, that the counterclaim here was properly brought against a party (S-M) who was in the circumstances within the jurisdiction and who was duly served with it within the jurisdiction. So far as that party (S-M) is concerned there was no need to rely on any other head of Ord. 15, r. 1 (1). The learned judge in chambers exercised his discretion to allow service of that counterclaim against the respondent (Larsson) outside the jurisdiction. The Court of Appeal set the order aside, not because they considered that the discretion had been wrongly exercised, but because they thought that the authority of *John Russell and Co. Ltd.* v. *Cayzer, Irvine and Co. Ltd.* [1916] 2 A.C. 298 compelled them to hold that one or other or both of the two inwritten limitations on the operation of the rule had not been satisfied. For the reasons given by my noble and learned friend, Lord *Russell of Killowen*, I do not think that *John Russell and Co. Ltd.* v. *Cayzer, Irvine and Co. Ltd.* did have that effect. D E F

LORD SALMON. My Lords, I have had the advantage of reading in draft the speech of my noble and learned friend, Lord Russell of Killowen. I agree with it and I agree that this appeal should be allowed.

LORD FRASER OF TULLYBELTON. My Lords, I have had the benefit of reading in draft the speech prepared by my noble and learned friend, Lord Russell of Killowen. I agree with it, and for the reasons stated in it I would allow the appeal. G

LORD RUSSELL OF KILLOWEN. My Lords, the question in this appeal is whether the facts are such as to confer jurisdiction to give leave to serve a counterclaim out of the jurisdiction. Ackner J. on an application ex parte by the present appellants gave leave: Donaldson J. on an application by the respondent Larsson declined to set aside that order: the Court of Appeal (Cairns, Roskill and Browne L.JJ.) reversed that decision, holding that the authority of *John Russell and Co. Ltd.* v. *Cayzer, Irvine and Co. Ltd.* [1916] 2 A.C. 298 in this House forbade such leave in the circumstances of this case. H

A The question turns on the provisions of R.S.C., Ord. 11, r. 1 (1). So far as now material this provides that " service of a writ, or notice of a writ, out of the jurisdiction is permissible with the leave of the court in the following cases, that is to say . . ." There follow a number of sets of circumstances, none of which apply to the instant case, unless it be " (*j*) if the action begun by the writ being properly brought against a person duly served within the jurisdiction, a person out of the jurisdiction is a
B necessary or proper party thereto." As will be seen we are not here concerned with service of a writ but with service of a counterclaim. However, Ord. 15, r. 3 (1) and (5) provide for the event, such as arose in the present case, of a defendant counterclaiming against the plaintiff joining another person (whether or not a party) as a party against whom the counterclaim is made; and in that event the provisions of Ord. 11 to
C which reference has been made apply in relation to the counterclaim as if the counterclaim were a writ. For present purposes therefore the inquiry under paragraph (*j*) is whether we have a case of " a counterclaim being properly brought against a party served within the jurisdiction, a person out of the jurisdiction is a necessary or proper party thereto."

The facts may for present purposes be very briefly stated. The appellants, London commodity brokers, had dealings in metals with the
D plaintiff S-M, a Swedish company resident in Sweden. On one view of the scope of those dealings the appellants owed a sum to S-M. On the other view S-M owed a sum to the appellants. The difference in view depended upon whether S-M was a party to certain dealings in zinc which showed substantial loss. The appellants contend that S-M was a party through their alleged agent the respondent Larsson: S-M deny any such agency.
E S-M issued a writ endorsed with a statement of claim claiming against the appellants moneys due, on the basis of their contention that the zinc dealings were not their concern. The appellants defended and counterclaimed against S-M moneys due from S-M on the basis of their contention that the respondent Larsson was the agent of S-M for these zinc dealings. The appellants wish to join the respondent Larsson to the counterclaim in the alternative asserting his breach of warranty of authority or personal
F liability. The respondent however is also resident in Sweden, and service of the counterclaim on him out of the jurisdiction is therefore necessary.

My Lords, it was not doubted by the Court of Appeal that such a counterclaim is within Ord. 15, r. 3 (1): nor that within paragraph (*j*) the respondent is a proper party thereto: and had the Court of Appeal thought that they had jurisdiction it is clear that they would have supported
G the exercise of discretion in favour of the appellants. I see no reason to disagree under any of these heads. The question is therefore whether the counterclaim was " properly brought against a person duly served within the jurisdiction." Leaving aside authority it appears to me that it was plainly so. In so far as propriety relates to some lack of genuineness, or by-purpose, there is no such suggestion here. In so far as propriety relates
H to compliance with the rules of court there was no failure in such compliance. If a person chooses to commence proceedings in this jurisdiction he lays himself open to the possibility of a counterclaim by the defendant as well as to a defence. The rules of court permit it subject to compliance with time requirements. Further there can, in my opinion, be no doubt that the plaintiff S-M was duly served with the defence and counterclaim within the jurisdiction. Ord. 6, r. 5 requires in a case such as this that the writ be endorsed with the name and address of the solicitor by whom

A the plaintiff sues and provides that that is the plaintiff's address for service. This was done, and the defence and counterclaim were duly served at the plaintiffs' solicitors' address in Essex Street, London.

But, my Lords, are those conclusions inconsistent with the decision of your Lordships' House in *John Russell and Co. Ltd.* v. *Cayzer, Irvine and Co. Ltd.* [1916] 2 A.C. 298; as the Court of Appeal thought? In my opinion they are not.

B In that case a writ was issued claiming damages against two defendants both resident out of the jurisdiction, as appeared from their addresses on the writ, which was marked "not for service out of the jurisdiction." One defendant by its London solicitor accepted service on its behalf. The question was whether under the then equivalent of paragraph (*j*) there was jurisdiction to give leave to serve out of the jurisdiction on the other defendant, and it was held that there was not. It was the unanimous C opinion in this House (and also in the Court of Appeal) that the action was not "properly brought" because at the time of the issue of the writ, both defendants being resident out of the jurisdiction, there was no jurisdiction to authorise its service on either defendant: and the fact that one defendant subsequently deprived itself of the ability effectively to contend that it was not properly brought by voluntarily entering an appearance D did not deprive the other defendant of that ability. In the concluding words of the speech of Lord Wrenbury, at p. 306:

> "... 'properly brought' means an action brought by a plaintiff against a defendant by virtue of the user of the process of the court—not by user of the process with the addition of a voluntary submission by the defendant to the jurisdiction of the court."

E As I understand them each judgment in the Court of Appeal proceeds upon this basis: that the bringing of proceedings by writ in this jurisdiction is to be regarded as a voluntary submission by S-M to the jurisdiction of the court: that that voluntary submission according to the ratio in *John Russell and Co. Ltd.* v. *Cayzer, Irvine and Co. Ltd.* [1916] 2 A.C. 298 cannot prejudice Larsson: and therefore the counterclaim is not within F the language, properly understood, of paragraph (*j*). My Lords, in my opinion this approach extracts from the speeches in *John Russell and Co. Ltd.* v. *Cayzer, Irvine and Co. Ltd.* a general principle which they do not support. There appears to me to be a radical distinction between the circumstances in which in this House reference was made to voluntary submission, i.e., in the sense of waiver by a person of his right to assert G non-compliance with the rules of the court, and the circumstances of the present case, in which the plaintiff S-M by setting in motion the rules of court (by bringing an action that perhaps it could not bring elsewhere) subjects itself, in a sense involuntarily, to the risk of a counterclaim.

In this appeal your Lordships were invited if necessary to reconsider the decision in *John Russell and Co. Ltd.* v. *Cayzer, Irvine and Co. Ltd.* Had your Lordships thought it necessary on this occasion so to do the Treasury H Solicitor would have been invited to instruct counsel as amicus curiae, Larsson not having appeared at the hearing.

In summary, my Lords, I am of opinion that the facts of this case come squarely within the language of paragraph (*j*), and that nothing to the contrary is to be found in the speeches or decision in this House in *John Russell and Co. Ltd.* v. *Cayzer, Irvine and Co. Ltd.*

I would accordingly allow the appeal, restore the orders of Ackner J. (dated July 10, 1974) and Donaldson J. (dated November 22, 1974), and

A order the respondent to pay the costs of the appellants both in the Court of Appeal and of this appeal, including in the latter the costs of the petition for leave to appeal.

Appeal allowed.

Solicitor: *Coward Chance.*

B F. C.

[QUEEN'S BENCH DIVISION]

C

* REYNOLDS *v.* HOYLE

1975 July 8 — Lord Widgery C.J., Milmo and Wien JJ.

Solicitor—Unqualified person—Conveyance—Draftsman preparing instruments for transfer of land for members of association—
D *Members paying fees to association's transfer agents—Draftsman receiving no fees—Whether draftsman preparing instruments for fee, gain or reward—Solicitors Act* 1957 (5 & 6 *Eliz.* 2, *c.* 27), *s.* 20 (1)

The defendant, who was not a qualified person for the purposes of the Solicitors Act 1957, was described as the "chairman and honorary conveyancer" of an association formed for the purpose of reducing the cost of property
E transfer. He prepared for members of the association instruments for the transfer of property and other instruments relating to real estate to which section 20 (1) (*a*) and (*b*) of the Act [1] applied. The defendant was neither a member of the association nor did he receive any fee or other remuneration for preparing the instruments but the association's transfer agents received a fee for the preliminary work, searches and inquiries prior to the instrument being drafted and, thereafter, the
F work involved in completing the transaction. The defendant was charged with offences, under section 20 (1) of the Act, in that, being unqualified, he prepared instruments for the transfer of property under the Land Registration Acts 1925 to 1966 and conveyances. The justices held that the defendant, when he drafted the conveyances or transfers, knew that the transfer agents would receive a fee and therefore he had not established the defence, under the subsection, that the acts were not done
G for or in the expectation of any fee, gain or reward and they convicted the defendant.

On appeal by the defendant:—

Held, dismissing the appeal, that provided a fee, gain or reward was received by someone for the preparation of an instrument to which section 20 (1) of the Act applied, it was immaterial that the person actually preparing the instrument received no such fee, gain or reward and, accordingly, the
H defendant had been properly convicted of the offences under the subsection.

Beeston and Stapleford Urban District Council v. *Smith* [1949] 1 K.B. 656, D.C. applied.

In re Crowley (1899) 20 N.S.W.L.R. 150 not applied.

[Reported by MRS. RACHEL DAVIES, Barrister-at-Law]

[1] Solicitors Act 1957, s. 20 (1): see post, p. 212F–G.

The following cases are referred to in the judgment of Lord Widgery C.J.: A

Beeston and Stapleford Urban District Council v. *Smith* [1949] 1 K.B. 656; [1949] 1 All E.R. 394, D.C.

Crowley, In re (1899) 20 N.S.W.L.R. 150.

No additional cases were cited in argument.

CASE STATED by Worcester justices. B

On March 20, 1974, and May 9, 1974, eight informations were preferred
by the prosecutor, John Duncan Michael Hoyle, against the defendant,
Francis Reynolds, alleging that the defendant had committed offences con-
trary to section 20 (1) of the Solicitors Act 1957. Four informations alleged
that the defendant, not being a person qualified under the Act, had
prepared an instrument of transfer or an instrument relating to real estate. C
The remaining four informations were in the alternative and relating to
the same transactions, alleged that the defendant had drawn such instru-
ments. The eight informations were therefore effectively in pairs and
alleged that the defendant: (1) on a date unknown between February 26,
1973, and June 1, 1973, at 242, Hylton Road, Worcester, being an unquali-
fied person, prepared an instrument of transfer for the purposes of the Land
Registration Acts 1925 to 1966, namely a transfer of land known as no. 127 D
Frimley Green Road, and land at the back of nos. 123, 125 and 127,
Frimley Green Road, Frimley, Surrey, contrary to section 20 (1) (*a*) of the
Solicitors Act 1957; (2) on the same date and at the same place, being an
unqualified person, drew that instrument, contrary to the same enactment;
(3) on a date unknown between October 31, 1973, and December 4, 1973, at
242, Hylton Road, Worcester, being an unqualified person, prepared an E
instrument relating to real estate, namely a conveyance of land adjoining
the property known as "Hillview," no. 19, Backwell Common, Backwell,
Somerset, contrary to section 20 (1) (*b*) of the Solicitors Act 1957; (4) on
the same date and at the same place, being an unqualified person, drew
that instrument, contrary to the same enactment; (5) on a date unknown
between June 19, 1973, and August 24, 1973, at 242, Hylton Road, Worcester,
being an unqualified person, prepared an instrument relating to real estate, F
namely a conveyance, of land known as no. 31, Wayside Avenue, Horn-
church, Essex, contrary to section 20 (1) (*b*) of the Solicitors Act 1957; (6)
on the same date and at the same place, being an unqualified person, drew
that instrument, contrary to the same enactment; (7) on a date un-
known between May 21, 1973, and August 20, 1973, at 242, Hylton Road,
Worcester, being an unqualified person, prepared an instrument of transfer G
for the purposes of the Land Registration Acts 1925 to 1966, namely a
transfer of land known as no. 18, Old Park Road, Plumstead, S.E.18, in
Greater London, contrary to section 20 (1) (*a*) of the Solicitors Act 1957;
(8) on the same date and at the same time, being an unqualified person,
drew that instrument, contrary to the same enactment.

The justices heard the eight informations over a period of three days
on June 4, 5 and 6, 1974. (There were similar informations against Mrs. H
Doris Green and David Ashford—with the consent of all defendants, all
the informations were tried together.) At the conclusion of the hearing
on June 6, 1974, the justices reserved their decision which they subsequently
delivered in writing on June 25, 1974. They found the following facts.
The Property Transfer Association ("the association") was formed at the
beginning of September 1972 by the defendant and, amongst others, his
co-defendants Mrs. Doris Green and David Ashford for the purpose of

enabling conveyancing to be carried out without contravening the provisions of section 20 of the Solicitors Act 1957. A written constitution was prepared which described the association as a "non-profit making organisation acting for members only and operating on the fees and contributions of members." This constitution provided that the main objects of the association were (a) to encourage the owner-occupation of property by contributing to the reduction of the unnecessarily high cost of acquisition and transfer; (b) to represent the interests of, and to exploit any benefit for, the owner-occupiers of property; (c) to give compassionate help to members whenever needed. Upon the formation of the association the defendant became the chairman and honorary conveyancer. After a few weeks he ceased to be a member so that it might not be said that he received any benefit for the purposes of section 20 (1). He remained for a while as chairman until succeeded by Mr. Edwards, Mrs. Green's son-in-law, although he was still described as "chairman and honorary conveyancer" in association literature distributed to prospective members in February 1974. Mrs. Green was said to do the association's secretarial work, and her husband was described as the treasurer and book-keeper, and they operated the association's bank account. The management committee included the defendant, Mr. and Mrs. Green, David Ashford, Mrs. Edwards (who was Mrs. Green's daughter) and her husband Mr. Edwards. The prime movers of the association included the defendant, Mr. Reynolds, and the agents, Mrs. Green and David Ashford. The association had three transfer agents who conducted the conveyancing transactions—Mrs. Green, David Ashford and Mrs. Edwards—who were not employees of the association. Persons wishing to buy or sell property through the services of the association had first to become members of that association and would fill in an application form and return it to the association's head office with a remittance. One of the three transfer agents would be allocated to act on behalf of the new member. The fee charged was a fixed sum to cover the transaction and was scaled in accordance with the value of the property involved. The transfer agent would conduct the transaction on behalf of the member, carrying out all necessary preliminary and preparatory work, searches and inquiries, until in the case of a purchase it became necessary to draft the transfer or conveyance for submission to the vendor's solicitors for approval. At this stage the agent would write to the defendant at his home address, 242, Hylton Road, Worcester, requesting him to prepare the necessary draft and send it to the vendor's solicitors. With this letter the agent would send the documents necessary to enable the defendant to prepare the draft. The defendant would then draft the necessary transfer or conveyance and send it direct to the vendor's solicitors with a standard letter containing the following request:

> "If you approve the document without amendment, or with minor amendments, please return one copy to the office with which you have previously communicated. In the event of substantial amendments being made to the draft, please return *one* copy to me for approval."

The defendant returned the remaining documents to the particular transfer agent dealing with the transaction who would then carry the transaction through to completion. The association was set up with a view to conducting a conveyancing and transfer business, and the agents did make a business out of the transactions for the buying and selling of houses and/or land by anyone who was prepared to join the association and to pay for and use their services. The agents were not employees of the association but self-employed agents. The control of the association was not in the hands of the members, but in the hands of the agents and chairman. The eight informations preferred against the defendant covered four conveyancing transactions in which the association acted for a purchaser of property in accordance with the general system described above. There was nothing to indicate that the conduct of those transactions differed from the general system. At the appropriate stage in the transaction the defendant drafted the necessary transfer or conveyance, as the case might be, at the request of the transfer agent who was conducting the transaction, that was to say Mrs. Green in the case of 127, Frimley Green Road and 19, Backwell Common, and David Ashford in the case of 31, Wayside Avenue and 18, Old Park Road, and sent the draft to the vendor's solicitors. Subsequently the instrument of transfer or conveyance, as the case might be, was executed. Specifically the defendant drafted and thereby prepared the instrument relating to real estate, namely, conveyances, which were specified in informations (3) and (4), and (5) and (6); and the instruments of transfer for the purpose of the Land Registration Acts 1925 to 1966, which were specified in informations (1) and (2), and (7) and (8).

The defendant was not a qualified person within the meaning of the Solicitors Act 1957. The defendant did not dispute that he had drafted and prepared the instruments relating to real estate specified in informations (3), (4), (5) and (6); the instruments of transfer specified in informations (1), (2), (7) and (8) and that he was not a qualified solicitor.

The defendant did not receive or expect to receive any fee, gain or reward for the work which he had carried out in drafting and preparing the two transfers and two conveyances specified in the eight informations. All the work involved in each of the four transactions conducted on behalf of the purchaser was done by the transfer agent, namely, Mrs. Green in two cases and David Ashford in two cases, except the drafting of the transfer or conveyance as the case may be, which was done by the defendant. Neither Mrs. Green nor David Ashford was a qualified person within the meaning of the Solicitors Act 1957; although both had at one time had considerable experience in a solicitors' office. In respect of each of the four transactions the transfer agent expected to receive and did receive a fee, gain or reward. The defendant drafted the transfer or conveyance, as the case might be, in each of the four cases in the knowledge that the transfer agent would expect to receive and would in fact receive a fee, gain or reward. Although Mrs. Edwards gave evidence that no part of the charge made by the association for the work done related to any work done by the defendant, the justices did not accept that. In an advertising leaflet distributed by the association which described how the association could act for a member in his house sale or purchase, in exactly the same way as a solicitor did, it was stated:

> "We employ highly skilled conveyancing managers with years of practical experience to their credit. Each one is a specialist in conveyancing although they are not solicitors. Conveyancing managers of P.T.A. are bonded and we are insured against negligence, under a professional indemnity policy."

On the back of the leaflet underneath the address of the head office there appears: "Chairman & Hon. Conveyancer: Councillor F. Reynolds LL.B. (HONS) London."

It was contended on behalf of the defendant that although he admitted that he was unqualified and had prepared the documents, he relied upon

A the statutory defence under section 20 (1). In order to establish that, it was only necessary for him to prove that he personally had neither received nor expected to receive any fee, gain or reward for the work which he had carried out in preparing the instruments of transfer or conveyance. That was the correct construction of section 20 (1). The decision in *In re Crowley* (1899) 20 N.S.W.L.R. 150 on a similar enactment should be followed. Observations by Lord Goddard C.J. in *Beeston and Stapleford*
B *Urban District Council* v. *Smith* [1949] 1 K.B. 656, 664 were obiter and wrong. The actual decision in that case was justified by the fact that the council were a corporation who had both received the charge and employed the clerk who carried out the work charged for. That case was therefore no authority for the contention advanced by the prosecutor. In the present case the defendant was not an employee or officer of the
C association. The standard required to discharge the onus of proof on the defendant was, as in a civil case, on the balance of probabilities. That the prosecutor accepted. On the evidence the defendant had discharged that onus. If, contrary to his principal contention, it was necessary for the defendant to show that no fee, gain or reward had been received or expected to be received by anybody for his work of preparing the instruments of transfer or conveyances, he had discharged that onus inasmuch as he had
D shown, by the evidence of Mrs. Edwards, that in calculating the flat scale fee charged by the association for acting for a member in the purchase of a property no charge was included for his work.

It was contended on behalf of the prosecutor that the informations alleging "drawing" were alternative to those alleging "preparing." The production by the defendant of the draft transfers in two cases and
E of the draft conveyances in two cases constituted both preparing and drawing, whether those terms were synonymous or whether the preparation of an instrument of transfer or conveyance involved every act which was preparatory to the production of the instrument of transfer or conveyance, of which the production of the draft transfer or conveyance was but one act. Accordingly the prosecutor invited convictions only on the four informations alleging "preparing." In order to establish
F the statutory defence it was not enough for the defendant to show that he personally had not received or expected to receive any fee, gain or reward for the work which he carried out in preparing the instruments of transfer or conveyances. He had to show that no one had received or expected to receive any fee, gain or reward for that work. *Beeston and Stapleford Urban District Council* v. *Smith* was authority for that conten-
G tion. If the court accepted that the defendant had not personally received or expected to receive any fee, gain or reward for the work which he had carried out in preparing the instruments of transfer or conveyances, the defendant had failed to show that no one had received or expected to receive any fee, gain or reward for that work since, even if the evidence of Mrs. Edwards were accepted, the facts in reality were that (a) while the
H association professed itself to be in form a members' association it was in reality a business carried on by persons, including Mrs. Green, Mrs. Edwards and Mr. Ashford, who for gain acted on behalf of purchasers and vendors of property in carrying through the legal transactions necessary for the transfer or conveyance of the property which they had agreed to buy or sell—in short a conveyancing business. For that service the purchaser or vendor paid a fee most or all of which went to the person who acted in the conveyancing transaction on his behalf. (b) In the case of a purchase

of property, preparation of the instrument of transfer or conveyance was an A
essential step in the completion of the sale and therefore of the conveyancing transaction which was conducted on behalf of the purchaser and in respect of which he paid a fee. (c) In reality therefore the purchaser in each of the four transactions, the subject of the four pairs of information preferred against the defendant, paid for the preparation of the instrument of transfer or conveyance, as the case might be, including the work carried
out by the defendant. B

The justices were of the opinion that the association was set up with a view to conducting a conveyancing and transfer business for the personal gain and reward of the agents of the association, who were acting for themselves and not for the benefit of the association. The " members " of the association were in reality the customer/clients, and the control of the asso-
ciation was not in the hands of the members, but in the hands of the agents C
and chairman. The defendant when he drafted the conveyance or transfer knew that the agent would receive a fee, gain or reward. The defendant had not, therefore, established the statutory defence. The justices accordingly convicted the defendant on each of the four informations alleging " preparing " and imposed a fine of £25 in respect of each offence. They made no order as to the costs and ordered that the four remaining
informations should remain on the court file. D

The defendant appealed. The question for the opinion of the High Court was whether on the above facts the justices came to a correct decision in law.

The defendant appeared in person.
Lionel Read Q.C. and *Alastair Hill* for the prosecutor. E

LORD WIDGERY C.J. This is an appeal by case stated from justices for the City of Worcester acting for the Petty Sessional Division of Worcester in respect of their adjudication as a magistrates' court on June 4, 5 and 6, 1974. On that occasion they convicted the defendant of four charges of preparing a document. Four further charges of drawing such a document
were ordered to be left on the court file. F
The prosecution was brought under section 20 of the Solicitors Act 1957, and the allegation was that, contrary to that section, the defendant had prepared in each case an instrument of transfer or an instrument relating to real estate.

The section, so far as relevant, reads as follows:

> " (1) Any unqualified person who either directly or indirectly—(*a*)
> draws or prepares any instrument of transfer or charge for the purposes G
> of the Land Registration Act 1925, or makes any application or lodges any document for registration under that Act at the registry; or (*b*) draws or prepares any other instrument relating to real or personal estate, or any legal proceeding, shall, unless he proves that the act was not done for or in expectation of any fee, gain or reward, be liable on summary conviction to a fine not exceeding £50: . . ."

H

The section then goes on to exempt certain people from its obligations, notably a barrister or a public officer who is drawing instruments in the course of his duty. The section goes on further to provide certain exemptions in the form of documents to which it does not apply, including amongst other things a will or other testamentary instrument. But the important part of the section for present purposes is that which creates an offence if the act is done by an unqualified person—for practical purposes,

A if a person is not a solicitor—if the act in question is the drawing or preparation of any instrument of transfer or other document of the kind defined by the section, and the defendant cannot prove that the act was not done for or in expectation of fee, gain or reward—the obligation being clearly placed upon him to establish that defence, if he can, under the terms of the section.

B The case is stated very clearly, but at somewhat more length than is strictly necessary. One finds that in Worcester and Hereford, which is where the defendant operates, there has been formed an association of which the defendant is the chairman and honorary conveyancer. The association is called the Property Transfer Association, and it was formed as long ago as September 1972, the defendant being a leading spirit at that time as were his co-defendants in the proceedings, Mrs. Green, and one David
C Ashford. The justices go on meticulously and at some length to explain the fashion in which the association operated. It had three transfer agents who conducted the conveyancing transactions. They were Mrs. Green, David Ashford and Mrs. Edwards—not be it noted, the defendant.

Persons wishing to buy or sell property through the services of the association had first to become members of that association and would fill in an application form and return it to the association's head office
D with a remittance. One of the three transfer agents would be allocated to act on behalf of the new member. There was a fee charged, which was a fixed sum, to cover the transaction scaled in accordance with the value of the property. The transfer agent would conduct the transaction on behalf of the member, carrying out all the usual necessary preliminaries, searches, inquiries and the like, until it became necessary to draft the transfer or
E conveyance for submission to the vendor for approval. At this stage the agent would write to the defendant at his home address at Worcester, requesting him to prepare the necessary draft and send it to the vendor's solicitors. That indeed, as the case finds, was the activity which was attributed to the defendant in this association. He did the drafting. Other people raised the requisitions and conducted the other inquiries, but when the moment came for a draft conveyance or transfer to be prepared, the
F defendant did it and sent his work direct to the vendor's solicitors.

The defendant was not a qualified person, as the justices find, and he did not dispute that in the case of the instruments charged in these informations he drafted, and thereby prepared, instruments of transfer specified in charges 3, 4, 5 and 6, and four others in 1, 2, 7 and 8. He did not receive or expect to receive any fee, gain or reward for the work
G which he carried out in drafting and preparing the two transfers and two conveyances specified in the eight informations. That is an exceedingly important finding, and it is really upon that finding, that the whole argument has revolved. I repeat it: "The defendant did not receive or expect to receive any fee, gain or reward for the work which he had carried out."

H All the work involved in each of the four transactions conducted on behalf of the buyer was done by the transfer agent, except the drafting of the transfer or conveyance, which was done by the defendant.

In respect of each of the four transactions the transfer agent expected to receive and did receive a fee, gain or reward. This again should be underlined. Not only do the justices find that the defendant did not expect to receive a fee, gain or reward, but they find that the transfer agents did, and it is to them that any fee charged was to be paid.

A The final finding of fact, which is material, is that although Mrs. Edwards gave evidence that no part of the charge made by the association for the work done related to any work done by the defendant, the justices did not accept this, and so they evidently took the view that in some respect, or to some extent, the charge made by the agents was in respect of work which was done by the defendant.

B The contentions were brief, and can be put compactly. The defendant contended that he sustained the special statutory defence under section 20 (1) if he proved that he did the act without any expectation of fee, gain or reward. He said that the fact that the agents might receive a fee, gain or reward was of no relevance. If he showed that he was not receiving anything by way of fee, gain or reward, that was enough, according to his argument, to bring it within the special statutory exemption.

C The prosecution, naturally enough, took the opposite view on the same point, and contended that if a fee, gain or reward was obtained in respect of the work by someone, it was not necessary to prove that that someone was the defendant.

D It is a very short point, and to a very large extent one feels it must be a matter of impression. I confess that when I first looked at the section it did not seem to me that it was particularly forceful in indicating that the identity of the person who was given the fee was unimportant. But it is not only a matter of first impression, and having looked into the case more fully with the assistance of the defendant and of counsel, I have come to the conclusion that the offence was proved here and that the justices were right.

E I base that consideration principally on *Beeston and Stapleford Urban District Council* v. *Smith* [1949] 1 K.B. 656, which is a decision of this court. It concerned a charge similar to the charges in the present case, save that it arose under section 47 of the Solicitors Act 1932, which for present purposes is identical to section 20 of the Solicitors Act 1957. It concerned a local authority lending money on mortgage, which decided that it would prepare its own mortgage documents and charge the mortgagor a fee for that being done. Accordingly the clerk to the council, who was not an authorised person to conduct the conveyancing business, drafted these mortgages. The council used them in the sense that they employed them to record the transaction which the council entered into, and the mortgagor paid the fee, which went into the general rate fund of the council.

F

G In due course the council and the clerk were prosecuted, and the clerk put forward a somewhat similar argument to that put forward by the defendant in the present case, except that he added reliance upon a proviso which exempted any public officer drawing or preparing instruments or applications in the course of his duty. In the *Beeston* case there was considerable argument about whether the clerk came within that exemption.

H Suffice it to say that the court held that the clerk was guilty of the offence. He did not come within that exception. It is not altogether easy to find out what Lord Goddard C.J.'s reasons were for holding that the clerk was guilty, and indeed they are to be found not in his judgment proper but in an interjection, where he says, at p. 660:

"The council make a charge, therefore the preparation and drawing of the deed cannot be gratuitous. The council may pay the fee into the rate fund, but that is in fact their banking account. The real question is whether the clerk is a 'public officer'."

A Evidently, Lord Goddard C.J. took the view that if a fee was paid, then that was good enough, regardless of the identity of the person to whom it was paid. But, as I say, it is only in the interjection one finds any guidance of what he had to say.

The really significant factor in my judgment is this, that following upon *Beeston's* case Parliament has re-enacted this provision without any amendment at all, and in accordance with ordinary principles it must be
B assumed that when the Act of 1957, as it was until recently, was being considered in Parliament, Parliament was aware of the meaning given to section 20 in the *Beeston* case, approved of that meaning and therefore enacted the provision in the same way as it did before.

I find all those arguments most compelling in deciding the view which one must take on this point, and I take the view adverse to the defendant,
C notwithstanding the fact that we have been shown a report of a case in New South Wales, *In re Crowley* (1899) 20 N.S.W.L.R. 150, where, under a provision difficult to distinguish from section 20 of the Act of 1957, a divisional court by a majority of two to one held that no offence was committed if the person drafting or preparing the instrument did not personally receive any benefit or fee for it. It is an authority in favour of the defendant and against the view which I have formed.

D But on the whole it seems to me, particularly for the reasons I have already given, that we are bound by the *Beeston* case and should follow it, and it follows from that that the convictions were properly entered and that this appeal should fail.

MILMO J. I agree and there is nothing I can usefully add.

E

WIEN J. I agree also.

Appeal dismissed.
No application for costs.

July 30. The court refused to certify, under section 1 (2) of the Administration of Justice Act 1960, that a point of law of general public
F importance was involved in the decision.

Solicitors: *Richards, Butler & Co.*

G

[CHANCERY DIVISION]

* DIXON (INSPECTOR OF TAXES) *v.* FITCH'S GARAGE LTD.

1975 June 18, 19 Brightman J.

H

Revenue — Corporation tax — Capital allowances — Machinery or plant—Erection of canopy over forecourt of petrol-filling station—Whether canopy "plant"—Finance Act 1971 (*c.* 68), *ss.* 41, 42 (*as amended*)

The taxpayer company, the leasehold owner of garage premises, decided to change to a self-service system. The

---

[Reported by PETER IRWIN-CLARK, ESQ., Barrister-at-Law]

decision involved complete redevelopment of the forecourt A
including the provision of new pumps and storage tanks, an office with a computer console and the erection of a canopy to provide adequate lighting and protection from the weather for the pumps and customers. Capital allowances were made to the company on the cost of self-service pumps and electric lighting, but a first-year allowance was refused on the cost of the canopy. The general commissioners, allowing the company's appeal, held that the canopy was an integral part B
of the petrol-pump complex and, therefore, was "plant" within the meaning of section 41 of the Finance Act 1971.[1]

On appeal by the Crown:—

Held, allowing the appeal, that the proper test was whether the canopy had a functional purpose to enable the company to perform the activity of supplying petrol to motor vehicles; and that, as the petrol-pumps would deliver petrol whether or not there was a canopy overhead, the canopy did not have C
such a purpose and, accordingly, was not "plant" and did not qualify for a first-year capital allowance under section 41 of the Finance Act 1971 (post, p. 220F–G).

Inland Revenue Commissioners v. *Barclay, Curle & Co. Ltd.* [1969] 1 W.L.R. 675, H.L.(Sc.) applied.

Per curiam. In considering whether an item is "plant," it is not permissible to apply the test whether the item is commercially desirable or necessary to enable the taxpayer to D
sell his petrol to the best advantage (post, p. 221A).

The following cases are referred to in the judgment:

Cooke v. *Beach Station Caravans Ltd.* [1974] 1 W.L.R. 1398; [1974] 3 All E.R. 159.

Inland Revenue Commissioners v. *Barclay, Curle & Co. Ltd.* [1969] 1 W.L.R. 675; [1969] 1 All E.R. 732; 45 T.C. 221, H.L.(Sc.). E

Jarrold v. *John Good & Sons Ltd.* [1963] 1 W.L.R. 214; [1963] 1 All E.R. 141; 40 T.C. 681, C.A.

St. John's School v. *Ward* [1974] S.T.C. 69; [1975] S.T.C. 7, C.A.

Schofield v. *R. & H. Hall Ltd.* [1975] S.T.C. 353.

Yarmouth v. *France* (1887) 19 Q.B.D. 647, D.C.

The following additional cases were cited in argument: F

Edwards v. *Bairstow* [1956] A.C. 14; [1955] 3 W.L.R. 410; [1955] 3 All E.R. 48; 36 T.C. 207, H.L.(E.).

Lyons (J.) & Co. Ltd. v. *Attorney-General* [1944] Ch. 281; [1944] 1 All E.R. 477.

Margrett v. *Lowestoft Water & Gas Co.* (1935) 19 T.C. 481.

CASE STATED by the Commissioners for the General Purposes of the G
Income Tax.

The taxpayer company, Fitch's Garage Ltd., leased garage premises in Amersham Road, Chesham, and had installed and owned all the plant, fixtures and fittings on the site. When a garage opposite to the taxpayer company's premises had changed to self-service pumps and had erected

H

[1] Finance Act 1971, s. 41: "(1) Subject to the provisions of this Chapter, where —(*a*) a person carrying on a trade incurs capital expenditure on the provision of machinery or plant for the purposes of the trade, and (*b*) in consequence of his incurring the expenditure, the machinery or plant belongs to him at some time during the chargeable period related to the incurring of the expenditure, there shall be made to him for that period an allowance (in this Chapter referred to as 'a first-year allowance') which shall be of an amount determined in accordance with section 42 below: . . ."

S. 42 (as amended): "(1) . . . a first-year allowance shall be of an amount equal to the whole of the expenditure in respect of which it is made . . ."

A a canopy over their pumps, the taxpayer company decided to do likewise. The changeover involved a complete redevelopment of the forecourt including the provision of new pumps and storage tanks, an office with a computer console and the erection of a canopy to provide adequate lighting and protection from the weather for the pumps and customers. The work was done in the year ended October 31, 1971, at a total cost of £20,959 and the taxpayer company's sales increased in consequence. The original B canopy, which was just large enough to cover the pumps themselves, had been erected in 1966 at a cost of £851 on which a claim for capital allowance had been accepted. The inspector of taxes was prepared to allow £599 on the cost of the self-service pumps and £390 on the cost of electric lighting attached to the canopy but refused first-year allowance of £3,311 on the cost of the canopy itself. The taxpayer company's appeal C was allowed on the basis that the canopy and its fascia were an integral part of the petrol-pump complex and should, therefore, be considered " plant " within the meaning of sections 41 and 42 of the Finance Act 1971.

The Crown appealed.

Brian Davenport for the Crown.

D *J. R. Gardiner* for the taxpayer company.

BRIGHTMAN J. The issue on this appeal is whether a canopy erected over the forecourt of a petrol filling station is " plant for the purposes of the trade " within the meaning of section 41 of the Finance Act 1971. I include within the description " canopy " the fascia fixed thereto except where it is necessary to differentiate between the canopy proper E and the fascia.

On October 9, 1973, the general commissioners decided this issue in favour of the taxpayer. They gave as their reason for that decision " that the canopy and fascia were an integral part of the petrol pump complex and should therefore be considered 'plant.' " They did not elaborate on their reasons. The Crown now appeals from that decision. F An " integral part " is, I apprehend, something which is necessary to the completeness of the whole. A " complex " is, I think, modern jargon for something which is capable of being regarded as an integer or unit though composed of independent or semi-independent parts. My understanding of the reasoning of the general commissioners is that they took the view that the canopy was a part of a unit of which the petrol pumps were the principal components, and that as the petrol pumps were clearly G plant (with which I agree) the canopy, as an integrated component, was also plant.

The facts are lucidly set out in the case stated. They may be summarised as follows. In 1961 the taxpayer company had a garage and petrol station at Chesham. It consisted of a building which looked like a two-storey dwelling house with the ground floor converted for use H as garage premises offering sales and servicing. In front of the building was a forecourt. In the middle of the forecourt was an island upon which were sited petrol pumps. Over the petrol pumps was a small V-shaped covering supported by a pillar at each end. Ten years later, to meet competition from a petrol station on the other side of the road, the company redeveloped the forecourt so that it became a self-service filling station. New petrol pumps and storage tanks were installed, connected to what is known as a computer console in the main building. The console records the amount of petrol drawn by the motorist and the money due from him. Over the forecourt a flat, rectangular canopy or roof was erected, supported on four pillars and extending from front to back of the forecourt. The canopy meets the elevation of the original building without, I understand, being actually bonded into it. The four pillars are, of course, let into the concrete of the forecourt. The provision of the new pumps and the canopy was planned, and the work was executed, as a single improvement. The canopy, according to the facts found by the general commissioners, was designed and built to the company's requirements to cover the whole service area with the object of (1) providing shelter against the elements for the pumps, the employees and customers, and (2) accommodating adequate lighting for the service area. The fascia of the canopy is designed to carry advertisements although it seems at present to advertise only the name of the establishment and the fact that trading stamps are issued. Strip-lighting is fixed to the inside of the perimeter of the fascia, and the underside of the canopy has a reflective capacity that intensifies the illumination over the service area. The company's sales have increased as a result of the work carried out. Although not so stated in the case, it may well be that the protection against the elements that is afforded by the canopy has contributed to the increased sales. The average motorist, I have no doubt, prefers not to fill his car with petrol at an exposed filling station on a rainy day if he has any choice in the matter.

The classic starting point of a consideration of the meaning of "plant" is the familiar wording of Lindley L.J. in *Yarmouth* v. *France* (1887) 19 Q.B.D. 647 where a horse was held to qualify for that fiscal accolade. There have been five cases in recent years which have considered the meaning of "plant," and I think it will be quite sufficient for present purposes if I confine myself to a consideration of those authorities.

The first in point of time is *Jarrold* v. *John Good & Sons Ltd.* [1963] 1 W.L.R. 214, decided by the Court of Appeal. In that case it was held that special movable partitioning required for the conduct of the business of a shipping agent was plant. Pearson L.J. gave this helpful guideline, at p. 225:

> ". . . the short question . . . is whether the partitioning is part of the premises in which the business is carried on or part of the plant with which the business is carried on."

The partitioning fell into the latter category and was therefore plant.

Inland Revenue Commissioners v. *Barclay, Curle & Co. Ltd.* [1969] 1 W.L.R. 675, was a majority decision of the House of Lords in 1969. Barclay, Curle & Co. Ltd., the well known Scottish shipbuilders, had constructed a dry dock. It cost the company £186,000 to excavate the land. It cost them half a million pounds to line the dock with 100,000 tons of concrete. Ancillary equipment, such as the operating machinery, pier installations, keel blocks and shores, and so forth, cost another quarter of a million pounds. The inspector of taxes conceded that the cost of the ancillary equipment was expenditure on plant and machinery, but he denied that status to the cost of the excavation and the concreting. The special commissioners went half-way and allowed the cost of the concreting but not of the excavation. The Court of Session allowed the cost of both, as also did the House of Lords by a majority. Lord Reid delivered the first speech. He said, at p. 679:

A "It seems to me that every part of this dry dock plays an essential part in getting large vessels into a position where work on the outside of the hull can begin, and that it is wrong to regard either the concrete or any other part of the dock as a mere setting or part of the premises in which this operation takes place. The whole dock is, I think, the means by which, or plant with which, the operation is performed."

B

He approved the statement which I have read from the judgment of Pearson L.J. in the *Jarrold* case [1963] 1 W.L.R. 214, 225. So Lord Reid considered that the cost of both excavation and concreting was expenditure on plant. Lord Guest, who was with the majority, described *Yarmouth* v. *France,* 19 Q.B.D. 647 as placing the emphasis on "an apparatus used for carrying on business." He said [1969] 1 W.L.R. 675, C 685 that in order to decide whether a particular subject is an "apparatus" one must enquire what operation it performs. This demands a functional test as a preliminary. The dry dock performed the functional test of lifting the ship from water to land and holding her in position while she was inspected and repaired. So viewed, the whole cost was expenditure on plant. Lord Donovan, at p. 691, also adopted the functional test. The D dry dock was a unit to accommodate a ship and to expose it for repair and then return it to its proper element.

In *St. John's School* v. *Ward* [1974] S.T.C. 69 Templeman J. had to consider a claim that pre-fabricated components of buildings purchased to accommodate a chemical laboratory and a gymnasium at a school were plant. The components when erected became enclosed structures resting on the ground or on a concrete base. He held that they were E buildings or premises in which the educational activities were carried on and not apparatus used for carrying on educational activities. They had no function to perform, he said, except to shelter the pupils. This conclusion was accepted by the Court of Appeal [1975] S.T.C. 7 without calling upon the Crown.

In *Cooke* v. *Beach Station Caravans Ltd.* [1974] 1 W.L.R. 1398, F Megarry J. had to consider expenditure incurred by the proprietor of a caravan park on excavating and lining two bathing pools and paving the surrounding area. The pools were constructed with a heating, filtration and purifying system. The Crown conceded that the ancillaries, such as that system, were machinery or plant, but challenged the cost of the pool excavation and construction and the terracing. In deciding that the pools as a whole constituted plant so as to allow the cost of excavation, G construction and terracing, the judge said, at p. 1403:

"Nobody could suggest that the principal function of the pool was merely to protect the occupants from the elements. If I may use a relatively modern slang expression, the pools are not merely 'where it's at': they are part of the apparatus used by the taxpayer company for carrying on its business as caravan park operators. The pools are H part of the means whereby the trade is carried on, and not merely the place at which it is carried on: . . ."

He referred to the passage which I have read from the *Jarrold* case [1963] 1 W.L.R. 214, 224.

Finally, in *Schofield* v. *R. & H. Hall Ltd.* [1975] S.T.C. 353, the Court of Appeal in Northern Ireland had to consider whether a silo, as distinct from the machinery and other equipment enclosed by the silo, was used by the taxpayer in carrying on its trade of grain importing, or whether the silo was merely part of the setting in which the trade was carried on. The former was held to be the correct view on the ground that the walls of the silo, and the machinery therein housed, constituted a unit with the function of receiving, distributing, cooling, turning over and, if necessary, fumigating the grain which was in transit.

Counsel for the taxpayer submitted that the mere fact that something is a building or structure does not prevent it being plant. With that I agree. The silo in question in *Schofield* v. *R. & H. Hall Ltd.* is an example. A windmill might be another example. Also, counsel submitted, the mere fact that the thing in question plays a passive and not an active role does not preclude it being classified as plant. I also agree with that, but I share with others a difficulty in drawing any rational line between a passive and an active role. On any basis the role of the canopy in the present case is passive, but that alone would not, in my judgment, rule it out as plant. Counsel also submitted that the court is not entitled to adopt a piecemeal approach in deciding what is plant. One must look, he said, quite rightly, to the thing as a whole—to the dock plus its operating machinery, the pools plus their heating and cleansing systems, the top and sides of the silo plus the machinery and other equipment housed inside. With that also I agree. Counsel then submitted that in the case before me the canopy was an essential commercial attribute of a modern self-service filling station necessary to enable petrol to be received by the motorist in the most efficient manner. Petrol, he said, is not delivered in the most efficient manner if the pumps are exposed to the elements and the forecourt is not adequately lighted. The canopy, therefore, performs an essential function in the operation of a self-service petrol station. He did not seek to say that the canopy considered in isolation would be plant. It was, however, plant in this case because it was an integral part of the apparatus for the delivery of the petrol. On that ground he sought to support the reasoning and conclusion of the general commissioners.

In my judgment, the general commissioners applied the wrong test and reached the wrong conclusion. The proper test is whether the canopy had a functional purpose to enable the taxpayer to perform the activity of supplying petrol to motor vehicles. I ask myself, " Does the canopy help to supply petrol, or is it merely part of the setting where petrol is supplied? " To use the words of Lord Reid in *Inland Revenue Commissioners* v. *Barclay, Curle & Co. Ltd.* [1969] 1 W.L.R. 675, 679, which I have already read, is the canopy part of the means by which the operation of supplying petrol is performed? In my judgment, this question admits only of a negative answer. The petrol pumps would deliver petrol to vehicles whether or not there was a canopy overhead. The canopy merely makes the business of supplying petrol more comfortable for motorists and the staff of the petrol station. It does not help to deliver the petrol. It is not part of the means by which it is supplied. This is not like the dock case, where the dock was useless without its operating machinery and vice versa; or the silo case, where the silo and its contents were totally interdependent.

Further, there is a clear thread running through the recent cases, including two Australian cases referred to in the *Schofield* case, showing that a structure is not plant if its only purpose is to provide shelter and if it plays no part in what may be termed " the commercial process." That

A conclusion is, I think, an inevitable result of the application of the functional test. In this difficult area of the law it is, in my view, important to stick to the established tests. In his submissions to me the taxpayer's counsel sought to introduce a new test: whether the item in question is commercially desirable or necessary to enable the taxpayer to sell his petrol to the best advantage. That, to my mind, is an amenity test as distinct from a functional test, and is not a permissible test. The right
B test is the functional test. In my judgment, this appeal should be allowed.

Appeal allowed with costs.

Solicitors: *Solicitor of Inland Revenue; J. D. Langton & Passmore.*

C

D

NOTE

[COURT OF APPEAL]

* CHAUDHRY *v.* CHAUDHRY

1975 Nov. 13 — Stamp and Orr L.JJ. and Sir John Pennycuick

E

Husband and Wife—Property—Practice—Polygamous marriage —Talaq divorce—Application for declaration of interest in matrimonial home—Whether wife entitled to relief

APPEAL from Dunn J. [1975] 3 W.L.R. 559.

The parties married in Pakistan under Islamic law on June 28, 1959.
F On July 2, 1972, the husband, Abdur Rehman Chaudhry, obtained a talaq divorce in the Pakistani Embassy, London, which became final on October 2, 1972. On February 22, 1974, the wife, Kishwar Sultana Chaudhry, issued a summons under section 17 of the Married Women's Property Act 1882 by which she asked for a declaration that she was entitled to an interest in the former matrimonial home, 9, Prothero Road,
G London S.W.6. On July 11, 1974, Mr. Registrar Tickle transferred the application to the High Court for the determination of a preliminary point of law whether the wife was entitled to proceed under the Act of 1882. Dunn J. held that parties to a polygamous or potentially polygamous union married according to the law of their domicile were "husband and wife" within the meaning of section 17 of the Act of 1882 and that
H the court had jurisdiction to hear the wife's application.

The husband appealed on the grounds that the judge misdirected himself in that he held that the applicant was a wife within the meaning of the Married Women's Property Act 1882, and that she was entitled to proceed under the provisions of the Married Women's Property Act 1882; that he

---

[Reported by EMMANUEL C. ABARAONYE, ESQ., Barrister-at-Law]

misdirected himself in holding that a wife of a polygamous or potentially polygamous union was able to make application under the Matrimonial Causes Act 1973 in relation to property; and that he failed to consider the fact that the talaq pronounced by the respondent was not a decree granted by the English court.

The facts are stated in the judgment of Orr L.J.

Jonathan Sofer for the wife.
A. M. Abbas for the husband.

No cases are referred to in the judgment.

The following cases were cited in argument.

Alhaji Mohamed v. *Knott* [1969] 1 Q.B. 1; [1968] 2 W.L.R. 1446; [1968] 2 All E.R. 563, D.C.
Ali v. *Ali* [1968] P. 564; [1966] 2 W.L.R. 620; [1966] 1 All E.R. 664.
Baindail (*orse. Lawson*) v. *Baindail* [1946] P. 122; [1946] 1 All E.R. 342, C.A.
Hyde v. *Hyde and Woodmansee* (1866) L.R. 1 P. & D. 130.
Imam Din v. *National Assistance Board* [1967] 2 Q.B. 213; [1967] 2 W.L.R. 257; [1967] 1 All E.R. 750, D.C.
Shahnaz v. *Rizwan* [1965] 1 Q.B. 390; [1964] 3 W.L.R. 759; [1964] 2 All E.R. 993.

STAMP L.J. I will ask Orr L.J. to give the first judgment.

ORR L.J. The parties to this appeal are Muslims who were born in Pakistan and were married there in 1959 under Islamic rites with the consequence that the marriage was potentially polygamous. Some years later, two children having been born to them, they came to England and made their home here. In 1972 the husband pronounced in the Pakistan Embassy in London a talaq divorce which became final on October 2, 1972, and under English law as it stood at that time validly dissolved the marriage. In consequence divorce proceedings which the wife had previously begun in England were stayed or dismissed, and thereafter in February 1974 she issued a summons entitled "In the Divorce Registry," and also, "In the matter of the Married Women's Property Act, 1882," for a declaration that the last matrimonial home, a house in Fulham, is owned by the parties in equal shares, and for sale of that property. On July 11, 1974, this application was transferred by order of a registrar of the Family Division to the High Court for determination of a preliminary point of law, namely, whether the wife, having been party to a potentially polygamous marriage, was entitled in the circumstances to apply to the court under section 17 of the Act of 1882. On June 12, 1975, Dunn J. gave judgment holding that she was so entitled, and also expressing, obiter, certain conclusions as to the effect of section 47 of the Matrimonial Causes Act 1973, in such a case. From that judgment the husband has now appealed with leave of the judge to this court.

So far as the matter has proceeded I for my part have formed no view as to its likely outcome, but it is an unfortunate feature of the case that if the appeal were to be allowed it would be necessary for the wife to commence fresh proceedings for such relief as may be due to her otherwise

A than in her capacity as a wife for the purposes of section 17, whereas if the summons had not been entitled " In the Divorce Registry " and " In the matter of the Married Women's Property Act, 1882 " it would have been open to the court to grant her whatever relief in respect of the house is due to her, whether in the capacity of a wife under section 17 or otherwise. This matter was raised by Stamp L.J. at the beginning of the hearing yesterday afternoon.

B An alternative course with regard to the form of the summons would be that the headings to which I have referred should be left, but that a note be added at the foot of the summons that the relief sought is sought under section 17 of the Married Women's Property Act and also under the inherent jurisdiction of the court. In my judgment the proper course for this court to take is to order that the summons be amended by the addition
C of such a note, that amendment being permissible under R.S.C., Ord. 2, r. 3. To proceed with the present appeal would in my judgment be potentially wasteful in costs and could delay the final ascertainment of the wife's rights, and in any event I cannot consider it right that we should be required to decide as a preliminary question one which may well never arise.

For these reasons I would make the order which I have indicated and dismiss the appeal.

D

SIR JOHN PENNYCUICK. I suppose it may conceivably be necessary upon the hearing of this summons under the inherent jurisdiction for the court to decide whether for some relevant purpose the appellant is or is not the husband of the respondent. If so, the court on hearing the summons will then decide that question. But it seems to me that it would be altogether
E inappropriate for this court to decide as a preliminary point a question which in all probability will never arise.

STAMP L.J. I agree.

Appeal dismissed.
F *Summons to be amended to read that relief sought is sought under section 17 of the Married Women's Property Act and also under the inherent jurisdiction of the court.*
No order as to costs save legal aid taxation.
G *Leave to appeal refused.*

Solicitors: *Myers, Ebner & Deaner; A. S. Cohen & Co.*

H

A

[FAMILY DIVISION]

* ROSS *v.* PEARSON (FORMERLY ROSS)

1975 Nov. 3 — Sir George Baker P. and Latey J.

B

Husband and Wife—Justices—Maintenance—Remission of arrears —Arrears accruing over period of years—Practice of enforcing only those accruing within 12 *months of complaint—Justices declining to remit—Whether proper exercise of discretion— Magistrates' Courts Act* 1952 (15 & 16 *Geo.* 6 & 1 *Eliz.* 2, *c.* 55), *s.* 76

The justices made an order in 1964, under the Matrimonial C Proceedings (Magistrates' Courts) Act 1960, that the husband should pay £5 a week to the wife and £1 a week for each of the four dependent children of the marriage. Following divorce proceedings, the wife remarried in April 1969. Arrears under the order amounted to £839 when, in September 1969, the justices varied the order by discharging that part relating to the wife, discharging the arrears in respect of payments to her which had accumulated since her remarriage, and discharged D the order in respect of the eldest child who had reached the age of 16. They ordered the husband to continue to pay a £1 a week for each of the three boys who were still under the age of 16 and to pay the balance of the arrears at the rate of 10 shillings a week. In 1970, the justices made an attachment of earnings order to enforce payment of the maintenance.

In September 1973, the youngest child attained the age of E 16. In July 1974, the wife complained to the justices that the husband was £770·54 in arrears under the order. The justices refused to exercise their discretion, under section 76 of the Magistrates' Courts Act 1952 [1] to remit the arrears and ordered the husband to pay them by instalments of £2 a week.

On appeal by the husband:—

Held, allowing the appeal, that justices, in the exercise of their discretion under section 76 of the Magistrates' Courts F Act 1952, should usually follow the practice of the Family Division and enforce only arrears under a maintenance order which had accrued within the year before the complaint was made; that, since the justices had not considered the authorities relevant to that practice and the wife had done nothing between 1970 and July 1974 to enforce payment of the arrears of maintenance, it could not be said that the justices had properly exercised their discretion in refusing to remit any of G the arrears and, accordingly, the court would order the husband to pay £50 and remit the remainder of the arrears.

Pilcher v. *Pilcher* (No. 2) [1956] 1 W.L.R. 298, D.C. applied.

The following cases are referred to in the judgment:

Freeman-Thomas v. *Freeman-Thomas* [1963] P. 157; [1963] 2 W.L.R. H 107; [1963] 1 All E.R. 17.

Luscombe v. *Luscombe* [1962] 1 W.L.R. 313; [1962] 1 All E.R. 668, C.A.

Pilcher v. *Pilcher* (*No.* 2) [1956] 1 W.L.R. 298; [1956] 1 All E.R. 463, D.C.

[1] Magistrates' Courts Act 1952, s. 76: " On the hearing of a complaint for the enforcement, revocation, revival, variation or discharge of an affiliation order or an order enforceable as an affiliation order, the court may remit the whole or any part of the sum due under the order."

A The following additional case was cited in argument:
Grimshaw v. *Dunbar* [1953] 1 Q.B. 408; [1953] 2 W.L.R. 332; [1953] 1 All E.R. 350, C.A.

CASE STATED by Cleveland justices sitting at Hartlepool.

On July 24, 1974, a complaint was preferred in accordance with section 74 of the Magistrates' Courts Act 1952, as amended, against the former
B husband, John Gibson Ross, in respect of arrears of £770·54 due under a maintenance order. The husband sought to have all the arrears remitted in accordance with section 76 of the Magistrates' Courts Act 1952.

The justices heard the evidence in support of the complaint on August 13, 1974, and found the following facts. An order was made under the authority of the Matrimonial Proceedings (Magistrates' Courts) Act 1960
C by the West Hartlepool justices on August 12, 1964. The husband was ordered to pay to the wife, Olga Pearson, through the office of the clerk to the justices the total weekly sum of £9, namely, £5 in respect of the wife and £1 in respect of each of the four children while under the age of 16 years. Complaint was made in respect of arrears under the order amounting to £837 on September 3, 1969, to the Hartlepool magistrates' court. The wife had obtained a decree of divorce and she had remarried on
D April 29, 1969, and the court varied the order by discharging the payment in respect of the wife and also discharged the arrears under the order in respect of her that had accrued since the date of remarriage. The court also ordered that the balance of the arrears be paid at the rate of 10 shillings a week and reduced the total order to £3 a week as the eldest child was over 16. On May 18, 1970, the Fylde magistrates' court made an attach-
E ment of earnings order with a normal deduction rate of £3 a week. The youngest child attained the age of 16 years on September 11, 1973, thus terminating the obligation to make weekly payments and thus leaving only the arrears. The arrears on that date were £774·54 and it was impossible to record what amounts were owed respectively for the wife and for the children of the family. The wife went to South Africa in July 1972 for a three months holiday. The clerk to the justices was not informed.
F Due to the prolonged illness of the wife's present husband, who became ill in October 1972, the wife remained in South Africa until returning to this country in July 1973. The youngest child went to join the wife in South Africa in November 1972. Maintenance payments paid by the husband were received by the wife's mother and paid into the joint bank account in England of the wife and her mother.

G On March 6, 1973, the clerk to the justices wrote to the husband informing him that the wife was in South Africa but that no settled address was available, also that maintenance payments were being paid into a joint bank account in England of the wife and her mother. The husband was advised to take legal advice. The husband was unemployed for about 10 months in 1966 after well paid employment came to an end and he was unemployed from August 21, 1972, to September 23, 1972; from
H October 20, 1972, to November 7, 1972; from November 15, 1972, to January 13, 1973; and from April 2, 1973, to June 2, 1973. The justices were unable on the evidence before them to reach a finding as to unemployment or periods of sickness which the husband might have suffered between 1967 and 1971. The husband had remarried and there were two children of that marriage. After absence of work through illness he was in regular employment. His weekly net wage varied between £18 and £25. His second wife was an unstable diabetic and unable to work.

It was contended by the wife that the husband had always been in arrears under the order and availed himself of any excuse not to pay. Although she had taken the youngest child out of the country without her husband's permission, it should be kept in mind that he had not seen any of the children for 12 years and the maintenance payment for the child was only £1 a week. There was nothing wrong with having the maintenance paid into the joint bank account with her mother. The money was properly used for the benefit of the child. The greater part of the arrears were in respect of herself and the other children and she had been deprived of that income when bringing them up. The wife felt that the husband should not be allowed to discard his responsibilities and payment of the arrears should be made in full.

It was contended by the husband that the wife should not have taken the youngest child out of the country without his permission, thus denying him access, and by doing so she forfeited her right to maintenance; that the payment of maintenance into the joint bank account by the wife's mother was open to suspicion as there was no evidence that the money was being used for the proper purpose; that the periods of unemployment and sickness were such that he had been unable to fulfil his obligations to the full and the serious accumulation of the arrears had occurred for that reason; and that having regard to the circumstances it would be a proper course if the justices remitted all or a substantial part of the arrears and they were invited to come to that decision.

The justices were of the opinion that the husband was now well able to pay the arrears in full as he was in good employment. The wife had no doubt gone short of many things because of the husband's failure to pay in the past. She had not slept on her rights and suddenly decided to claim arrears. On the contrary her whole conduct over the years had been such that the husband must have been, at all times, fully aware that she would expect him to pay every penny of the arrears. They considered that attitude to be understandable as a substantial part of the arrears must have accrued during the husband's earlier days of well paid employment. Having regard to the fact that the wife had doubtless often had to go on short commons prior to her remarriage, the justices felt unable to remit the whole of the arrears and, having regard to the fact that he had quite clearly not paid when he could, the justices felt unable, for the present at least, to remit part. They therefore ordered the husband to pay at £2 a week. They did not see fit to enforce that order by way of attachment of earnings order or any suspended committal to prison in default of payment.

The husband appealed. The question for the opinion of the High Court was whether the refusal of the court to remit all or any substantial part of the £770·54 arrears owed by the husband was a conclusion which any reasonable bench of justices could reach on proper consideration of the facts as found and whether such refusal constituted a proper exercise of judicial discretion.

J. J. Hodgson for the husband.

The wife did not appear and was not represented.

Sir George Baker P. This is an appeal by way of case stated from what was, in effect, the refusal of the Hartlepool justices, on August 13, 1974, to remit all or any of the sum of £770·54 arrears owed by the husband on a maintenance order.

A The relevant background facts are that the West Hartlepool justices, on August 12, 1964, made an order under the Matrimonial Proceedings (Magistrates' Courts) Act 1960, that the husband should pay through the office of the clerk to the justices the total weekly sum of £9, being £5 for his wife and £1 in respect of each of the four children of the marriage under the age of 16 years.

The matter again came before the court on September 3, 1969 (that
B is over five years later), when the arrears amounted to £839. By that time, the wife, had obtained a divorce and had remarried on April 29, 1969. Presumably nothing had been done in the divorce about the children's order; so, the court varied the 1964 order by discharging the payment in respect of the wife, discharging arrears under the order in respect of the wife which had accrued since her remarriage on April 29, 1969, and
C ordered that the balance of the arrears should be paid at 10 shillings a week. One of the boys had reached the age of 16 so the court reduced the total order to £3 a week, that is £1 in respect of each of the relevant children, and, of course, to that was added the 10 shillings a week arrears.

Then on May 18, 1970, the Fylde justices made an attachment of earnings order, with a normal deduction rate of £3 a week. Whether any application was then made in respect of the arrears, or whether it was
D only in respect of the £3 a week order, we do not know. The matter has not been argued, but it seems to me, without going into detail, that by reason of the definition of "maintenance order" in section 2 (*a*) of the Attachment of Earnings Order Act 1971, the arrears could have been the subject of an attachment of earnings order, if that had been requested, and if the man's earnings had justified the making of an order of £3·50
E instead of £3.

The next action that was taken, so far as we know, was a complaint on June 24, 1974, by Mr. Shaw, the clerk to the justices, on behalf of the wife, who is now Mrs. Pearson, in respect of the arrears which then amounted to £770·54, that is to say the arrears in respect of the children had actually increased since September 1969, whereas they should have decreased by 10 shillings a week. Obviously, some sum was in arrears
F in respect of the existing order, as well as the pre-existing arrears.

The mathematics of the matter have been analysed by Mr. Hodgson and, if I may say so, very helpfully. He concludes that £16 must be the amount which has accumulated by reason of non-payment of the orders, as distinct from non-payment of arrears. By September 1973, all the children had attained the age of 16 and, therefore, from that date, only
G the question of arrears remained. The calculations are based on that fact.

In July 1972 the wife went to South Africa. She took the younger boy with her. Neither of these matters seems to me to have any bearing on this particular case, nor is it material that the maintenance payments were made into a joint bank account in England held in the name of the wife and her mother. The ex-husband seems to have had periods of unemployment between 1972 and 1973 amounting to six months out of 10.
H He is now remarried, and we are told that he had a gross wage of between £23 and £30 a week. His wife is unable to work because of ill health.

The wife, the respondent to this appeal, does not appear and is not represented. Consequently we have not had the advantage of argument in respect of what could be difficult points. The essence of the case put by the husband is that it was the practice in the Probate, Divorce and Admiralty Division, carried through to the Family Division, not to enforce arrears

for more than a year backwards. In *Pilcher* v. *Pilcher* (*No.* 2) [1956] A
1 W.L.R. 298, 302 Lord Merriman P. said:

"There is another consideration which I think should apply, and that is that, not, I think, as a matter of law but as a matter of practice, it is usually considered by courts which are asked to enforce orders of this sort, and it certainly is the practice in this division when men are brought up before its courts for committal in respect of mainten- B
ance orders, that there should be a time-limit retrospectively. The custom in this division is not to enforce arrears for more than a year backwards."

Note the word "usually." In *Freeman-Thomas* v. *Freeman-Thomas* [1963] P. 157, 159, Scarman J. referred to *Pilcher* v. *Pilcher* (*No.* 2) 1 W.L.R. 298 in these words: C

"It is pertinent to observe that, had these [school] fees been the subject of a maintenance order made by this court, it is extremely unlikely that in 1962, some three years after the last of them and eight years since the first, the court would have tolerated enforcement of the order: see *Pilcher* v. *Pilcher* (*No.* 2)."

Finally, in *Luscombe* v. *Luscombe* [1962] 1 W.L.R. 313, 315, Ormerod L.J. D
referred, with approval, to *Pilcher* v. *Pilcher* (*No.* 2) in these terms:

"It is true that Lord Merriman P., in that judgment, was referring to the form of enforcement which may result in a committal to prison; and that in a later paragraph, in his judgment, he gave as one of the reasons, if not the reason, for the existence of this rule that it is pointless to make an order committing a man to prison for so large a E
sum that the man would go to prison rather than pay. That, of course, does not apply in this case because here clearly there is no question of committal of the husband to prison; it is an application for a garnishee order in respect of funds which are in the possession of the bank as garnishee, but at the disposal of the husband, and therefore, the consideration may be different. But there would appear to F
be no doubt that that practice of enforcing arrears in the Divorce Division for one year only is a practice which is commonly adopted in that division; and it may well be that the registrar, in considering this order, had in mind that such was the practice."

Note that he uses the words "for one year only." This has raised the question whether in a case like the present, where several years have passed G
since the substantial part of the arrears came into being, the court should enforce only one year of the outstanding arrears, or should remit all the arrears as having been incurred more than one year ago, or more than one year, at any rate, before the complaint. Some guidance on that may be derived from the provision of section 13 (5) of the Matrimonial Proceedings (Magistrates' Courts) Act 1960, which was added to that Act by section 32 H
of the Matrimonial Proceedings and Property Act 1970. Section 13 (5) is in the following terms:

"A person shall not be entitled to enforce through the High Court or any county court the payment of any arrears due under an order made by virtue of this Act without the leave of that court if those arrears became due more than 12 months before proceedings to enforce the payment of them are begun."

A It seems to me that Lord Merriman P. in the words that he used, namely, not to enforce arrears for more than a year backwards was, in fact, saying once the year has passed from the time when the arrears accumulated then there should be no enforcement. But that, unfortunately, does not quite deal with the present case, because it is almost impossible to see when the arrears have accumulated; one can only approach the problem in a very rough and ready way, and remember that at 10 shillings a week—
B the order still being current—payment of the arrears will be £26 in the last year. There is also £16 attributable to non-payment of the children's order, although the last child became 16 in September 1973 which was almost a year before the complaint was made on June 24, 1974.

This is not a matter for which there is a rule of law; it is a rule of practice which is " usually " followed. The court can consider whether
C in the circumstances of any given case it is right to follow the practice either in whole or in part. One question which has been discussed, although we have not had an argument the other way, is whether, this being a matter of discretion for the justices, and there being no rule of law, it can be said that they have failed to exercise their discretion properly when they have disregarded the practice. I think, the answer is twofold. First of all, neither *Pilcher* v. *Pilcher* (*No.* 2) [1956] 1 W.L.R. 298 nor the other
D two cases that I have referred to were mentioned to the magistrate; they do not seem to have had them in mind. Secondly, in *Pilcher's* case, this court came to the conclusion that action should be taken to remit arrears, and, of course, could not have done that unless it was considered that the metropolitan magistrate came to a wrong decision in the exercise of his discretion, that he was wrongly exercising his discretion; that he pro-
E ceeded on a wrong principle, or that he did not have information before him which he should have had, and which would have been relevant to the exercise of his discretion. It seems to me, therefore, that the justices, if they had exercised their discretion with all the matters before them including the decision in *Pilcher's* case, must have come to a different decision.

They referred to the fact that the wife had not slept on her rights
F and suddenly decided to claim arrears, but the fact is, as I have indicated, that nothing, so far as we know, had been done between 1970 and July 24, 1974. I, for my part, would therefore answer the question which they have asked, namely, whether the refusal of the court to remit all or a substantial part of the arrears was a conclusion which any reasonable bench of justices could reach upon proper consideration of the facts as found and whether
G such refusal constituted a proper exercise of the judicial discretion in the negative. In saying that, I do not wish to criticise the justices, because, I think, if *Pilcher* v. *Pilcher* (*No.* 2) [1956] 1 W.L.R. 298 or the other cases had been brought to their attention with section 13 (5) of the Act of 1960, they would probably have come to a very different conclusion.

What can we do? I think that the only course we can take is a
H practical one, and I would, remit all the arrears except for £50. The £50 is made up by taking the nearest round figure of £26 (arrears at 10 shillings a week) plus the arrears of £16. That is £42 so £50 is, I think, near enough. That will be substituted for the justices' order. We are told that the husband has already paid £50. We were told that after we had already reached this solution; so he will not have to pay any more if he has, in fact, paid. Therefore, having answered the question as above I would substitute the order I have indicated, as we are entitled to do under the

provisions of the Summary Jurisdiction Act 1857, as amended: see *Stone's Justices' Manual*, 107 ed. (1975), vol. 1, p. 154. A

LATEY J. I agree, and I wish only to say for myself what Sir George Baker P. has already said on three points. One, it is unfortunate that the justices did not have their attention drawn to the decision in *Pilcher*, that being, together with the other cases cited, the lynchpin of the argument which has been addressed to us by counsel on behalf of the husband B on the hearing of this case stated. The second is that, as Sir George Baker P. has said, more than one point of substantial difficulty and possible importance has been raised during the argument. We have not had the advantage of argument the other way, which is not, of course, in any way to suggest that Mr. Hodgson has not done his best to refer us to any authorities or statutory enactments which apply. The third point is C that, as Sir George Baker P. has pointed out, in *Pilcher* v. *Pilcher* (*No.* 2) [1956] 1 W.L.R. 298, 302 Lord Merriman P., in his judgment, uses the word "usually." Again, in the enactment which applies to the High Court and to the county court there is power for leave to be given for more arrears than one year's to be enforced. So that, speaking for myself, I would not want this decision to be taken by magistrates' courts as an indication that there is a universal absolute rule that justices should never D go back further than the last year's arrears. In that respect, also, I would wish very much to echo what Sir George Baker P. has said. I agree with the order proposed.

Order accordingly.

Solicitors: *Houghton, Craven, Dicksons & Co., Preston.* E

M. B. D.

[COURT OF APPEAL] F

* HORROCKS AND ANOTHER *v.* FORRAY

1975 Nov. 6, 7 Megaw, Scarman and Bridge L.JJ.

Licence or Tenancy — Implied licence — Occupation of house — House purchased as home for mistress and child—Nature of licence—Whether contractual licence to be inferred—Whether licence terminated by death of purchaser G

The defendant was the mistress of S and in 1961 bore him a daughter. Thereafter S wholly maintained and supported the defendant and the daughter providing living accommodation, clothing, holidays and all day to day expenses. In 1973 S bought a house. He told the solicitor that he was buying H it for the defendant and her daughter, but he did not ask for it to be conveyed to her, although he installed them in it. After completion he inquired about transferring the property to the defendant but on learning there would be fiscal charges he decided not to do so. In 1974, S was killed in a motor accident. By his will S left all his estate to his wife. Neither

---

[Reported by A. G. B. HELM, ESQ., Barrister-at-Law]

A she nor the plaintiffs, S's executors, knew of his association with the defendant or of the purchase of the house. The plaintiffs brought an action in the county court for possession of the premises on the ground that the defendant's licence to occupy the house terminated on S's death. The defendant contended that she had a contractual licence whereby she was entitled to live in the house for her life or while her daughter was of school age. The judge held that she could B not infer such an agreement and he made an order for possession.

On appeal by the defendant:—

Held, dismissing the appeal, that the fact that S intended to provide some security for the defendant was not sufficient to bring into existence a binding contract in the nature of a licence and in all the circumstances there was no evidence justifying the inference that the defendant had a contractual C licence to live in the same house (post, pp. 238H—239A).

Tanner v. *Tanner* [1975] 1 W.L.R. 1346, C.A. distinguished.

The following cases are referred to in the judgments:

Tanner v. *Tanner* [1975] 1 W.L.R. 1346; [1975] 3 All E.R. 776, C.A.
Ward v. *Byham* [1956] 1 W.L.R. 496; [1956] 2 All E.R. 318, C.A.

D The following additional case was cited in argument:

Binions v. *Evans* [1972] Ch. 359; [1972] 2 W.L.R. 729; [1972] 2 All E.R. 70, C.A.

APPEAL from Judge McDonnell sitting at West London County Court.

By particulars of claim dated March 21, 1975, the plaintiffs, executors E of the will dated August 15, 1963, of William Charles Ayshford Sanford, the testator, who died on April 6, 1974, the owner of a freehold dwelling-house at 7, Farm Place, London, W.8, which the defendant, Maxine Forray, had occupied since about May 1973, pursuant to the leave and licence of the plaintiffs, claimed that the licence terminated with the death of the testator or, alternatively, was determined by the plaintiffs' letter of August 2, 1974, calling for the defendant to vacate the dwellinghouse by F November 30, 1974, and sought an order for possession of the dwelling-house and payment of mesne profits from December 1, 1974, until possession.

By her re-amended defence and counterclaim the defendant contended that the licence was a contractual licence entitling her to remain in the house for life or for so long as her daughter was of school age or either G of them required the accommodation. The judge found that the testator was under no contractual obligation not to revoke the licence during his lifetime and gave judgment for the plaintiffs. The defendant appealed on the ground that the licence bound both the testator and the plaintiffs.

The facts are stated in the judgment of Megaw L.J.

Simon Goldblatt Q.C. and *John Laws* for the defendant.
H *Walter Blum* for the plaintiffs.

MEGAW L.J. On April 6, 1974, Mr. William Charles Ayshford Sanford was killed in a motor accident. He was 68. He had been married twice. His second marriage was in 1951. There was one child of that marriage, a son, born in 1952. By his will, Mr. Sanford appointed Mr. Arthur Edward Leslie Horrocks and Mr. John Stephen Lloyd as his executors. They, in their capacity as executors, are the plaintiffs in the action out of which this appeal arises. The defendant in the action is Mrs. Maxine Forray. A She had been Mr. Sanford's mistress for, it is said, some 17 years, and had so continued up to the time of his death. It would seem that he first met her when she was 15 years old. Though there was evidence, given by the defendant herself, as to the circumstances in which she met Mr. Sanford and became his mistress, I do not think that that evidence—or indeed a good deal of the rest of the evidence relating to her subsequent life and activities—is of relevance to the issue which this court has to B decide. The evidence has been carefully reviewed by Judge McDonnell, who heard the action out of which this appeal arises in the West London County Court on July 7, 1975. He delivered his judgment on July 18. There has been no substantial criticism of the judge's findings of fact, based upon the evidence of the witnesses whom he saw and heard giving evidence. I shall refer hereafter to such of the facts found by him as C appear to me to be relevant to the issues now before this court: issues which are substantially more limited in scope than those which the judge had to consider on the basis of the much more wide-ranging arguments which were presented before him on behalf of the defendant.

The claim by the plaintiffs is a claim for possession of a house, 7, Farm Place, Kensington, W.8. That house is, and has since about May 1973, been occupied by the defendant and, as I understand it, two children D of hers. One of those children, a girl born in July 1961, is the child of the late Mr. Sanford. The other, a boy born in July 1968, is the son of another man, a Mr. Forray, whom the defendant married in September 1966. As I understand it, that marriage ended in divorce. But during its continuance, the defendant continued to be the late Mr. Sanford's mistress. She has also had not infrequent sexual intercourse with another E man, apparently a great friend of the late Mr. Sanford, and apparently with his knowledge. She has sometimes been known by the name of that other man.

Mrs. Sanford, the widow of Mr. Sanford, had no knowledge or inkling of her husband's relationship with the defendant, whom she never met. Mrs. Sanford, as the judge records, throughout her marriage regarded her husband as a "marvellous husband." It was only after his death that F his widow came to know of the defendant and of this relationship which had in fact existed, concealed from her by her husband, for many years. It was only after his death that she or the plaintiffs became aware of his ownership of 7, Farm Place, which the late Mr. Sanford had bought and which had been conveyed to him in his own name in May 1973, and which, since then, had been the residence of the defendant and her G children. He had paid £36,500 for it in May 1973.

Mr. Sanford had at one time been a wealthy man, but he had lived extravagantly for many years. At the time of his death he was, as the judge says, "coming to the end of his financial tether." If the plaintiffs are unable to sell 7, Farm Place with vacant possession, it is probable that the estate will be insolvent. The widow, to whom Mr. Sanford by his will H left all his estate for life with a gift over on her death to their son, would in those circumstances receive nothing from the estate. She, like the defendant's daughter, the late Mr. Sanford's illegitimate child, may recover compensation under the Fatal Accidents Acts as being dependants of Mr. Sanford, if negligence resulting in his death is proved as against the driver of the car, who was understood to be his brother. But so far as anything from Mr. Sanford's own estate is concerned, the widow, if the defendant is permitted by the law to remain in possession of 7, Farm Place, is likely to be left with nothing.

If, on the other hand, 7, Farm Place can be sold with vacant possession—that is, if this claim against the defendant for possession succeeds—the estate is likely to be, at least, solvent. The widow will get something. As to the defendant's daughter, she may be entitled to damages under the Fatal Accidents Acts as being a dependant of the late Mr. Sanford. She would also be entitled to claim against the estate—should the estate have anything to make such a claim fruitful—under the Inheritance (Family Provision) Act 1938, as amended. In the county court proceedings it was thought that there might be a conflict of interest between the defendant and her daughter, so the Official Solicitor became guardian ad litem of the daughter. We are given to understand that he does not think that there is a conflict which requires any intervention on his part.

It is in those circumstances that the plaintiffs, as executors, started the proceedings which have led to this appeal. By their particulars of claim, which are dated March 21, 1975, they set out the late Mr. Sanford's ownership of 7, Farm Place. This is not challenged. They aver that the defendant, since about May 1973, has occupied the house pursuant to licence of the plaintiffs. That is not challenged; indeed, it is asserted on behalf of the defendant. The plaintiffs, in their particulars of claim, assert that the licence terminated with the death of Mr. Sanford or was determined by a letter dated August 2, 1974. By that letter the plaintiffs' solicitors wrote to the solicitor who was then acting for the defendant, in these terms:

> "With reference to 7, Farm Place, London, W.8, this property clearly falls into the estate and we shall be obliged if you will let us have the deeds of the property as soon as possible. The executors require vacant possession of the house but think it reasonable that Mrs. Forray and her daughter should be given a reasonable period in which to make arrangements for alternative accommodation. We would therefor suggest that Mrs. Forray make arrangements to vacate the premises by November 30, 1974."

The defence and counterclaim, which was originally delivered on April 28, 1975, has been amended and re-amended, the re-amendment being by leave of the court at the trial in the county court. It is a formidable document, but as events have turned out a substantial part of it is not now relevant. The defence "admits and avers" that the defendant and her daughter had a licence from the late Mr. Sanford to occupy 7, Farm Place. There was then an allegation, which is no longer pursued in this court, that the property was held in trust for the defendant or her daughter or for both. There was also a defence that the defendant had acquired a beneficial interest in the property as a result of contribution made by her to expenditure. It was also said that the plaintiffs were estopped from disputing the beneficial ownership of the house by the defendant or her daughter or both; and various particulars were given which are said to give rise to that estoppel. We in this court need not trouble about those defences because they are no longer pursued. It is not now, in this court, contended for the defendant that she has any proprietary right to—any right of ownership in—7, Farm Place. Her claim is solely that she is entitled to remain in occupation by reason of a licence—in ordinary language, by reason of permission to occupy—given to her by the late Mr. Sanford.

So the defence which, having been pleaded by amendment, still remains is, in substance and effect, that the licence for the occupation of the premises—and both parties agree that there was a licence—was and is a contractual licence, the contractual terms of which were binding on Mr. Sanford and remain binding on his executors after his death. Those terms were pleaded, or at least are now put forward on behalf of the defendant perhaps not in precisely the form in which they were pleaded, as involving three possible alternatives. Those alternatives are (a) that the licence was to be for the lifetime of the defendant, so that no one could turn her out as long as she lived; or (b) that the licence was to continue so long as the daughter should be undergoing full-time education; or (c) that it was to continue so long as either or both of them—the defendant and her daughter—reasonably needed the accommodation. In amplification of those terms which are put forward as alternatives, I think it became clear from the argument presented by Mr. Goldblatt in this court on behalf of the defendant that so far as each of them was concerned he would say that it was an implied term that, though the defendant was entitled to continue to live in the house for one or other of those periods, she was not obliged to live there for one moment longer than she herself wished so to do.

Then the pleading sets out, by reference to later and earlier parts of the pleading, various matters on which the defendant would rely in support of this assertion in the amended pleading of a contractual licence. Thus, by reference to earlier particulars in the pleading, there was included reliance upon the assertion that the defendant and Mr. Sanford had, as it is put, " cohabited " for some 17 years prior to his, the testator's death, and from and since the birth of the daughter he wholly maintained and supported the defendant and the daughter and provided living accommodation for them, as well as clothes and holidays and all their day-to-day living expenses.

I shall not refer to the other points that were indicated in the pleadings because they seem to me to be appropriate to the now abandoned allegations of trust or acquisition of a beneficial interest in the property, rather than to the only point now maintained—that is, a contractual licence. It is perhaps desirable, however, to refer to the pleading which appears in sub-paragraph (iii) of the particulars given under paragraph 3 of the defence, as to the consideration which is alleged to exist as giving legal force to the alleged contractual licence. What is said is:

> " Further, so far as necessary the defendant will say that she had offered and given consideration for the licence (a) by relinquishing her possession or occupation of her previous dwelling-house and (b) by reason of the facts and matters pleaded in paragraph 5 of this defence "—those are matters pleaded in relation to estoppel—" and further (c) " (and this was added by re-amendment at the trial) " by her agreement and acceptance that the testator "—that is Mr. Sanford—" should fulfil his legal obligation to support [the daughter] principally by the provision of accommodation and accordingly by her withholding any action or process to enforce such obligation, by seeking an affiliation order or otherwise. In the premises the said licence is not determinable at the behest of the plaintiffs in these proceedings."

So much for the pleadings. The way in which this defence to the claim for possession is now presented on behalf of the defendant is as follows.

A There is authority of this court, particularly the decision in *Tanner* v. *Tanner* [1975] 1 W.L.R. 1346, that a woman who had been a man's mistress was entitled to remain in occupation of a house which had been provided for her and her child by the man whose mistress she had been. The facts of that case are accurately, though briefly, summarised in the headnote which says this.

B "In November 1969 the defendant, a spinster, gave birth to twin daughters of whom the plaintiff was the father. In early 1970 the plaintiff and the defendant decided that a house should be purchased to provide a home for the defendant and her baby daughters. In July 1970 the plaintiff bought a house on mortgage, and the defendant left her rent controlled flat and moved with the babies into the house. Three years later the plaintiff offered the defendant £4,000 to move C out of the house. The defendant refused on the ground that the house was hers and the children's until the latter left school. The plaintiff's solicitor wrote to the defendant purporting to terminate her licence to live in the house and asking her to leave. When she did not do so the plaintiff brought possession proceedings in the county court. The defendant counterclaimed for a declaration that she was entitled to a D beneficial interest in the house. The county court judge rejected the defendant's contentions and made an order for possession, in pursuance of which the defendant and her children were rehoused by the local authority."

The defendant appealed and this court allowed the appeal. There was a complication there which does not arise in the present case, that as, by E order of the county court, the defendant had gone out of possession, there was not any order by the court restoring her to possession of the house; but she was in lieu of that given damages because what had been done at the instance of the plaintiff had been inconsistent with her contractual rights. Continuing with the headnote:

"*Held*, allowing the appeal, (1) that the inference to be drawn from all the circumstances was that the defendant had a contractual licence F to have accommodation in the house for herself and the children so long as the children were of school age and reasonably required the accommodation; and that, accordingly, the order for possession ought not to have been made."

That is a decision of this court which any other division of the court would, of course, follow. We have got to ascertain, as that is the case principally G relied upon in support of the defendant's contention, what *Tanner* v. *Tanner* [1975] 1 W.L.R. 1346 decided, and then apply that to the facts of this case.

What was decided in *Tanner* v. *Tanner* was really very simple. It was decided that on the evidence that had been adduced in that case there was a fair inference to be drawn that the man and his mistress had entered into a contract by which the man had agreed, for consideration, that the H house which was being bought by him for the occupation of the woman and her children should remain available to her, with a continuing licence for her to occupy it so long, at any rate, as the children were of school age, or unless some other circumstances arose meanwhile which would make it reasonable for the possession to cease. It was, therefore, a decision on the facts of that case that there was a contract. There was not an express contract: that is to say, there was no evidence that one had said to the other "I promise that I will do so-and-so." But of course this court is

entitled to infer a contract, even though it is clear that words have not A
been spoken expressly stating a contractual promise or an offer and
acceptance in express words. The court is entitled to infer the existence
of a contract. In the circumstances of that case, this court inferred that
there was a contract such as I have mentioned.

There is really no doubt about what was the basis of the decision there.
It may be that the bringing in of the conception of contract into situations
of this sort does give rise to difficulties. It may be that some other approach B
to situations of this sort would be preferable. But that is not a matter for
us. We have got to take the law as it is and to apply it as it stands. The
law as it stands does involve that the defendant can only succeed in this
case, on the submission now made on her behalf, if she shows that it is
proper to infer the existence of a contract which permitted her to remain in
this house for one or other of the three alternative periods which have been C
put forward and which I have already mentioned. And, of course, she has
to establish that that is a contract which, properly viewed and in accordance
with the terms which have to be applied, was one which continued to exist
as a matter of law after the death of the late Mr. Sanford.

Now, in order to establish a contract, whether it be express or implied
by law, there has to be shown a meeting of the minds of the parties with
a definition of the contractual terms reasonably clearly made out and with D
an intention to affect the legal relationship, that is, that the agreement that
is made is one which is properly to be regarded as being enforceable by
the court if one or the other fails to comply with it; and it still remains a
part of the law of this country, though many people think that it is time
that it was changed to some other criterion, that there must be consideration
moving in order to establish a contract. All those elements, on the facts in E
Tanner v. *Tanner* [1975] 1 W.L.R. 1346, and on the evidence accepted by
the court, were present. Are they present in this case? The county court
judge thought not, and therefore he held that there was no contract and,
therefore, no contractual licence, and the question did not fall to be con-
sidered whether, if there was a contract, its terms were alternative (a) or
alternative (b) or alternative (c), as to the length of the period for which
the defendant was to be entitled to remain in this house. F

The basis of the assertion that there existed here a contractual licence
is really this: that there was evidence that over a period of a good many
years, beginning at any rate soon after the birth of the daughter, the late
Mr. Sanford had continuously provided accommodation for the defendant
and her daughter. That accommodation had, I think we were told, involved
about nine different addresses at one time or another. In addition to G
continuing to provide accommodation for the defendant, the late Mr.
Sanford had expended a very great deal of money, either by way of buying
things for the defendant and her child or children, or by way of providing
her with money with which she could herself buy things; and it is apparent
that she was provided with what one could fairly describe as a reasonably
luxurious existence. Her own evidence, as summarised by the judge H
in his judgment, was that the deceased had expended on her and her
children something of the order of £4,000 or £5,000 a year. That was, as I
understand it, in addition to the provision of accommodation.

There was also evidence that the late Mr. Sanford had at some earlier
time indicated to a solicitor a desire to make some provision for the
defendant. But the principal matter which is put forward as supporting
the existence of a contract is what happened in relation to the purchase

A of 7, Farm Place itself. That is summarised, and as I think quite fairly and lucidly summarised, by the judge. He said:

> "In 1973 the deceased"—that is Mr. Sanford—"decided to buy the house at 7, Farm Place, the subject matter of this action. He did not instruct the first-named plaintiff, who was his family solicitor, but a Mr. Signy to whom the defendant had introduced him. He told Mr. B Signy that he was buying it for the defendant and her child so that they should have some security if anything happened to him but he did not ask for the house to be conveyed to the defendant. Completion of the purchase took place on May 10, 1973, and the deceased was registered as the owner of the freehold on May 24, 1973. After completion the deceased consulted Mr. Signy about transferring the property to the defendant. When he was told that there might be a C liability to capital gains tax and that ad valorem stamp duty would be payable, he decided against doing so. On a later occasion he suggested to Mr. Signy that a trust should be created for the benefit of his child and was advised that ad valorem stamp duty would still be payable and so he took the matter no further. He later asked Mr. Signy to draft a codicil to his will leaving the house in trust for the child; D Mr. Signy said he would like to see the will itself before doing so and the matter proceeded no further."

Pausing at that point in the judge's judgment, it may well be said that those facts, which were not really in dispute, at any rate indicated that the late Mr. Sanford, however anxious he was to make provision for the defendant, baulked at the financial responsibility that he was told would be involved E by way of tax and stamp duty if this step were to be taken to transfer this house to the defendant. That he was not prepared to do. Nor, apparently, having thought about the completely different idea of leaving the house by his will in trust for the child, had he done anything about that at the time of his death. Of course, all those things do not make it impossible that he also had agreed with the defendant, or was minded to agree thereafter with the defendant, that she should, without obtaining F any ownership of the property, nevertheless have a right to continue to live there under one or other of the three alternatives which have been put forward.

The judge then goes on:

> "The defendant said in evidence that for 16 years the deceased had said that he would eventually get her a house and I accept that he may G well have expressed such an intention in general terms from time to time. When No. 7, Farm Place was purchased she may well have believed that it would become her property but I do not believe that the deceased ever expressly told her so. . . ."

Then the judge, having reviewed the evidence and having dealt with various other issues, which no longer arise in this court because they have been H decided against the defendant and are not the subject of appeal, went on to deal with *Tanner* v. *Tanner* [1975] 1 W.L.R. 1346. He analysed that decision, as I think entirely correctly, and went on to say:

> "In the present case I can find no circumstances whatsoever from which to infer an agreement that the defendant was entitled to live in the house for her life or whilst the daughter was of school age. There is a strong moral obligation on a man to provide and care for

his illegitimate child and an additional obligation for the deep wrong he has done to that child by inflicting illegitimacy on her: *In re T.B.* [1967] Ch. 247. At common law there was no obligation on the father to provide for his illegitimate child—*Seaborne* v. *Maddy* (1840) 9 C. & P. 497—but he may be ordered to provide weekly payments unlimited in amount under an affiliation order at the suit of the mother, the Supplementary Benefits Commission or a local authority under the Affiliation Proceedings Act 1957, as amended. It is also well settled that a putative father may make a binding contract with the mother to contribute to the child's maintenance for which her undertaking to care for the child affords the consideration."

Then the judge referred to *Ward* v. *Byham* [1956] 1 W.L.R. 496. He said:

"In the present case there was no such contract because the deceased provided handsomely for the maintenance of the child during his lifetime. Where an affiliation order has been made the death of the putative father puts an end to the order and arrears are not recoverable from his estate . . . I therefore hold that the right of the child or its mother to maintenance from the putative father continues only during the latter's lifetime."

Then the judge referred to the provisions of the Inheritance (Family Provision) Act 1938, to which I have referred, which would enable this daughter to present a claim against the estate, if there was anything in the estate from which a claim could be met.

The judge, in substance, as I see it, was saying that on the facts of this case, as contrasted with the facts that emerged in *Tanner* v. *Tanner* [1975] 1 W.L.R. 1346, he was unable to hold that there were shown any events or facts from which the inference could fairly be drawn, on the balance of probability, that there was a contract such as is suggested giving this defendant a legal right to remain in possession of the house for any of the periods suggested.

Mr. Goldblatt in this court summarised his submission to the contrary in this way. He submitted that, on the facts, over a period of years the defendant was, at the request and the instance of the late Mr. Sanford, subordinating her mode of life, or her "life-style," and her choice of residence to his directions on the "understanding" that he, Mr. Sanford, would generously maintain the defendant and her family in the meanwhile and would, when circumstances permitted, provide her with a permanent home. Then Mr. Goldblatt, as I understand it, submitted that the contract was made long before the purchase of 7, Farm Place, but soon after the birth of the daughter. But, said Mr. Goldblatt, that contract, made earlier and being in existence earlier, was varied when 7, Farm Place was bought, and was varied so that the home that was to be given to the defendant on these terms was now no longer left uncertain, but was now defined as being 7, Farm Place. The "understanding" which is referred to in that summary of the position was amplified by Mr. Goldblatt as involving that a promise—a contractually binding promise—had been given by the late Mr. Sanford, and that it related to the occupation of 7, Farm Place.

With great respect to Mr. Goldblatt's argument, I am quite unable to see, on the facts and circumstances of this case, that there was here any conceivable basis for an implication that any such binding promise had been made by Mr. Sanford as is suggested. The fact that he had it in mind to seek to provide some security for the defendant in the event of his

A death certainly does not go anything like far enough to bring into existence what is necessary to show a binding contract of this nature. There was here, in my judgment, simply nothing on the evidence that would have entitled the judge to come to the conclusion that there was any such contractual licence. I say that without going on to consider what I think might well be an extremely difficult further barrier in the way of the defendant. Supposing that she had established something which otherwise
B could be regarded as being a contract, where is the consideration for that contract to be found? In *Tanner* v. *Tanner* [1975] 1 W.L.R. 1346 the consideration was perfectly clear: the lady had given up her rent-controlled flat as a part of the bargain that she would move into the other accommodation. There is no such consideration here. However, I do not wish to decide this case, as far as I am concerned, on any question relating to
C absence of consideration. But I am satisfied that the judge was completely right in his view that the defendant had wholly failed to show the existence of a contractual licence. I would accordingly dismiss the appeal.

SCARMAN L.J. So fully do I agree with the judgment of Megaw L.J. that I wish to add only a few comments. When an illegitimate child has been born, there is certainly nothing contrary to public policy in the parents
D coming to an agreement, which they intend to be binding in law, for the maintenance of the child and the mother. Parents of an illegitimate child have obligations towards the child. So far from its being contrary to public policy that those obligations should be regulated by contract, I would have thought it was in the public interest that they should be so. Certainly it seems to me far better that parents in such a situation should seek to
E regulate their position by contract than that they should have to resort to the court under the Affiliation Proceedings Act 1957.

But it does not follow that, because there exists a relationship which can be regulated by contract, the proper inference is that the parties in their particular circumstances have so regulated their relationship. In the present case there is no express contract.

Mr. Goldblatt, for the defendant, has sought to persuade the court that
F a contract is to be inferred from a course of conduct, from the development of the relationship between the parties and its course over a period of years. This submission is, as a matter of law, open to him. That has been clearly decided, as I understand it, in two cases in the Court of Appeal to which he has referred us, *Ward* v. *Byham* [1956] 1 W.L.R. 496 and *Tanner* v. *Tanner* [1975] 1 W.L.R. 1346. In each of those cases, however, the
G relationship of man and mistress was either broken or on the point of collapse. The parties to the relationship, the man and the woman, had to consider what best should be done for the innocent product of their relationship, the illegitimate children. In a very real sense, both in *Ward* v. *Byham* and in *Tanner* v. *Tanner*, the man and the woman were making arrangements for the future at arm's-length. The woman was concerned
H for herself and her children, the man was concerned to limit and define his financial responsibilities towards the woman and the children. Here is a fertile area for the growth of an inference of a legally binding contract; and for myself I do not find it surprising, when I look at the facts in *Ward* v. *Byham* or *Tanner* v. *Tanner*, that the court came to the conclusion that a contract was to be inferred from the conduct of the parties. But how different is this case. Right up to the death of the man there was a continuing, warm relationship of man and mistress. He was maintaining his

mistress in luxurious, even, so the judge thought, extravagant style, and, A we now know, in a style beyond his means: his estate is now at risk of being insolvent.

Mr. Goldblatt has tried to tempt us to draw an inference of contract by dangling in front of our eyes various contracts that might be inferred. It one looks at that sort of fishing exercise with a dispassionate lawyer's eye, one begins to wonder whether he is not in difficulty in finding in the relationship any one, certain, contract. Since he is saying that three or four B possibilities arise (Megaw L.J. has analysed them), one wonders whether these parties, in fact, entered into a legally binding agreement or intended to create legal relations upon the basis of terms sufficiently formulated to be clear and certain. But his real difficulty is that, whatever relationship did exist between these two, it could as well be referable to the continuance of natural love and affection as to an intention to enter into an agreement C which they intended to have legal effect. In the other two cases, that relationship had ended and it was necessary to tie up the bits. In the present case the relationship was continuing until the unhappy and unexpected death of the man. Therefore Mr. Goldblatt is in difficulty with the facts of the case.

Fortunately for this court, the facts have been subjected to a most careful and detailed analysis by the trial judge, who, as Megaw L.J. has D already commented, directed himself absolutely correctly on the question of law, that is to say, the effect and scope of *Tanner* v. *Tanner* [1975] 1 W.L.R. 1346.

In the course of his analysis of the facts, the judge commented that the deceased had said, according to the defendant in evidence, that he would eventually get her a house, and the judge accepted that the deceased may E well have expressed such an intention in general terms from time to time. But then the judge went on to find as follows:

> "When No. 7 Farm Place was purchased she may well have believed that it would become her property but I do not believe that the deceased ever expressly told her so."

The judge later commented on the luxurious provision that this man chose F to make for his mistress and their child (the relevance of that I have already mentioned); and then at the very end of his judgment, when he came to consider the effect of his findings, he said—rightly, in my judgment—

> "It is well settled that a putative father may make a binding contract with the mother to contribute to the child's maintenance for which her undertaking to care for the child affords the consideration." G

Then he said:

> "In the present case there was no such contract because the deceased provided handsomely for the maintenance of the child during his lifetime."

When I first read those words I was puzzled. But now that I have had the H benefit of Mr. Goldblatt's argument on behalf of the defendant, I see exactly what the judge was saying. Here was a generous provision made for a woman who was still the mistress and for the child of that relationship. It was generous beyond what one would reasonably expect the man to accept a legally binding obligation to provide. It was generous, not because he was bound or was binding himself, to be generous, but because he chose to be generous to the woman for whom there was a big place in his heart.

A Once one reaches that situation, one can see how the judge inferred that this was a case where there was no contract and where really it was unreasonable to infer a contract.

For those reasons, as well as for the reasons developed by Megaw L.J., I think this appeal should be dismissed.

B BRIDGE L.J. I agree with both the judgments in this court, and indeed with the careful, reserved judgment of the judge who tried the case in the county court. I have nothing of my own to add.

Appeal dismissed with costs.
Order for vacant possession in 28 days.

C

Solicitors: *Rendall & Co.; Frere, Cholmeley & Co.*

D

[INNER LONDON CROWN COURT]

* REGINA *v.* TULLETT

1975 Sept. 26;
E Dec. 23;
1976 Jan. 8 Judge Rubin

Crime—Costs—Legal aid—Crown Court—Application for legal aid made at conclusion of trial—Court's power to grant order—Effect of order—Legal Aid Act 1974 (*c.* 4), *ss.* 28 (7), 37 (2) [1]

F The defendant was committed for trial to the Crown Court on an indictment containing two counts of driving while disqualified. No order for legal aid was made in the magistrates' court. He completed an application form for legal aid but due to a mistake the form was not submitted to the Crown Court. He pleaded guilty at the Crown Court and was granted an absolute discharge.

On the defendant's application for legal aid for the trial made at the conclusion of his trial:—

G *Held*, granting the application, that, under section 28 (7) of the Legal Aid Act 1974, the power of the Crown Court to grant legal aid was exercisable until the final conclusion of the trial and the court had a discretion to order that the application for legal aid and all fees and disbursements incurred before the date of granting legal aid should be included in the order provided that they were payable in connection with the proceedings to which the order related.

H

No cases are referred to in the judgment and none were cited in argument.

[Reported by MRS. RACHEL DAVIES, Barrister-at-Law]

[1] Legal Aid Act 1974, s. 28 (7): see post, p. 245D–E.
S. 37 (2): see post, p. 245E–F.

APPLICATION A

The defendant, George William Tullett, was committed for trial at the Inner London Crown Court on an indictment containing two counts of driving while disqualified. The matter came before the Crown Court for trial on September 26, 1975. The defendant pleaded guilty and was granted an absolute discharge on both counts. At the conclusion of the trial he applied for an order granting him legal aid for the trial. The Metropolitan Police Solicitor instructed counsel to argue the case for B
protecting the public fund.

The facts are stated in the judgment.

John Foy for the defendant.
Roland Watt for the prosecution.

Cur. adv. vult. C

January 8. JUDGE RUBIN read the following judgment. This is an application by the defendant for an order granting him legal aid. In July 1975 he was committed to this court for trial on an indictment containing two counts of driving whilst disqualified. He was not granted legal aid by the magistrates' court. He duly completed a form of application for legal aid, but due to a mistake in his solicitor's office the form D
was never submitted to this court.

The matter came before me for trial on September 26, 1975. Before the trial started the defendant's solicitors went to the appropriate office in this building to seek legal aid but were told to apply to the trial judge.

On the defendant being arraigned he pleaded guilty to both counts. It appeared that after the expiration of three months of his disqualifica- E
tion for three years the defendant had been informed by the new licensing centre at Swansea that he was entitled to apply for a new licence and that such licence had been granted to him. I thought it proper to grant him an absolute discharge on both counts.

At the conclusion of the trial Mr. Foy, who appeared for the defendant, asked for an order granting the defendant legal aid for his trial. I had some doubts whether I had power to make such an order at the F
conclusion of the trial. Accordingly, I adjourned the application for further argument.

Although the defendant, on advice, pleaded guilty in this court, in my judgment the unusual background to the offences fully justified the committal for trial and the employment of solicitors and counsel to investigate the consequences of the grant to the defendant of a new G
licence while he was in fact disqualified. Had an application been made to me before or at the start of the trial I would have granted an order for legal aid subject to an assessment of the defendant's means.

When I adjourned the matter for argument I directed that the application be brought to the notice of the Treasury Solicitor so that the Attorney-General could have an opportunity to instruct counsel to H
argue in protection of the public purse that there was no jurisdiction to make the order sought by the defendant. The Attorney-General did not wish to take advantage of this opportunity. Fortunately, the Metropolitan Police Solicitor was persuaded to instruct Mr. Watt of counsel to lay before the court the case for protecting the fund. In cases involving legal aid in the civil jurisdiction the Law Society instructs counsel to protect that fund. In criminal cases there appears to be no one who

A accepts the duty of protecting the fund and I am therefore grateful for the assistance of Mr. Watt and the Metropolitan Police Solicitor.

The powers of the court are now regulated by the Legal Aid Act 1974, and the regulations made under or adopted by that Act. It was not suggested during the argument that I could obtain any assistance from earlier legislation.

In the case of legal aid for civil litigation, in my judgment, aid starts
B with the grant of the certificate and not before, but there are provisions for the grant of emergency certificates. However, the provisions of the civil scheme administered by the Law Society are so different from the scheme applicable to criminal cases administered by the courts that little assistance can be found in Part I of the Act.

Legal aid under Part II of the Act is granted not by way of certificate
C but by an order. Such an order can be made by the judge orally in open court. It can also be made by the appropriate officer of the court without a hearing in open court: see regulation 2 of the Legal Aid in Criminal Proceedings (General) Regulations 1968 as amended.

Section 28 of the Act contains a long list of proceedings for which legal aid may be granted and specifies the court or courts having power to make the order. In my judgment the theme which runs through that
D section is that the power vested in a court to make an order for legal aid arises when the court becomes seized of the proceeding and continues so long as it remains so seized. It was argued before me that power ceases to exist once the proceedings have been commenced. For example, in the case of a trial on indictment, once the trial has started by the defendant being put in charge of the jury the power ceases to be exer-
E cisable. Section 28 (2), (3) and (4), deal with proceedings before magistrates' courts and juvenile courts. In subsection (2) the power arises where a person is charged with an offence before a magistrates' court or appears or is brought before a magistrates' court to be dealt with. The words used prescribe the events upon which the power to make an order arises, but it seems to me that a person who " is charged . . . before a magistrates' court " remains a person who " is charged " until that charge is finally
F disposed of by that court either by decision or committal to another court.

Subsections (5) and (6) deal with appeals to the Crown Court. The qualification is a person who " desires to appeal to the Crown Court." The magistrates' court is given power to make the order on the basis, in my view, that it is treated as remaining seized of the proceedings for the purpose of the grant of legal aid, notwithstanding that it would otherwise
G have disposed of the matter. The more interesting question under the subsection is: when does the Crown Court power to make the order arise? For the reasons which will appear when I deal with the like powers granted to the Court of Appeal by subsections (8) and (9) the power would not appear to arise until the appeal jurisdiction has been invoked by the service of notice of appeal or an application for leave to
H appeal.

Subsections (8) and (9) deal with appeals to the Court of Appeal from the Crown Court and from a court-martial respectively. In neither case is the court below given a power to grant legal aid, but in each case the Court of Appeal is given the power where a person " desires to appeal." If I am right in the view that under these subsections the power would only arise on the Court of Appeal becoming seized of the matter by application for leave to appeal or the service of a notice to appeal, there

would be no court which could grant legal aid to advise on the merit of A
a proposed appeal or to assist in the preparation of the preliminary
documents.

In section 30 (8) and (9), the draftsman has incorporated express
powers to cover the period up to the lodgement of the application for
leave to appeal or the notice of appeal. These additional powers fill the
gap, if my construction of section 28 (8) and (9) is correct, but would be
unnecessary if the Court of Appeal power to grant legal aid arose under B
section 28 (8) and (9), at the conclusion of the trial below.

I have dealt with these provisions at some length because it has been
suggested, not by Mr. Watt, that the very existence of section 30 (8) and
(9), establishes conclusively that, save under these subsections, a court
can have no power to make an order for legal aid which might in part
cover work already done. I cannot accept that argument. Section 30 (8) C
merely gives the Court of Appeal a power which it would not have under
section 29 to grant legal aid at a time before it would otherwise become
seized of the proceedings and therefore for a time during which no court
would have any power to grant legal aid. Section 30 (9), it is true, gives
the Court of Appeal power to include work already done in an order
made under section 28 (8) and (9), but it is work done which would never
have been covered by an order made under section 28 (8) or (9), even if D
that order had been made at the first possible moment.

I now turn to the subsection with which I am primarily concerned.
Section 28 (7) reads:

> "Where a person is committed to or appears before the Crown
> Court for trial or sentence, or appears or is brought before the
> Crown Court to be dealt with, the court which commits him or the E
> Crown Court may order that he shall be given legal aid for the
> purpose of the trial or other proceedings before the Crown Court."

It has been argued for the Crown that the power given to the Crown
Court by that subsection, if it is to be exercised at all, must be exercised
before the proceeding to which it relates has been commenced. In the
case of a trial, Mr. Watt argues, the power is only exercisable before F
arraignment. Where it is a committal for sentence it is not so easy to
pick a convenient starting-point to the proceeding beyond which the
power ceases to exist. I find it difficult, on the language of the sub-
section, to justify such a limitation on the power. Clearly in most cases
legal aid will be sought and granted before the commencement of the
effective hearing. But that is not necessarily always the case. It is not G
unknown for a defendant in the course of a trial to find himself in
financial trouble and then seek aid. It is also not uncommon for a
defendant to conduct his own defence until conviction. At that stage, if
the court is contemplating a custodial sentence, assistance of counsel may
be most desirable. If Mr. Watt is right, in neither of these cases could
legal aid be granted in the Crown Court. H

In the course of the argument I raised the case of a trial continuing,
after the discharge of a jury, before a new jury. Mr. Watt treated this
as a new trial for which legal aid could be granted before it started. I
doubted this. Though such a trial is often described as a new trial, I
think it would be more accurate to describe it as a continuation of the
original trial which commenced with the arraignment and continues until
verdict, however many juries are discharged on the way. In my judg-

A ment, the term " new trial " is more apt to describe a re-trial following an appeal for which provision is made for legal aid under section 28 (11).

Further, under section 29 (1), which is a section dealing with the circumstances in which legal aid may be ordered, the power is to be exercised " where it appears to the court desirable to do so in the interests of justice." It may only so appear to a trial judge after the commencement of the trial. Finally, section 29 (6) requires that where a doubt
B arises as to whether a legal aid order should be made that doubt should be resolved in the defendant's favour.

For these reasons I am unable to accept that the power is so limited and, in my judgment, it remains exercisable in the case of a committal for trial until the final conclusion of that trial. Further, in my judgment, where an application for legal aid is made before or during a trial or
C proceeding, that trial or proceeding remains before the court and ought not to be treated as concluded for the purposes of the Act of 1974 until that application has been determined by the making or refusal of an order. Under regulation 2 of the General Regulations an order cannot be made until the judge or the proper officer has considered the statement of means of the applicant. It is not normally either convenient or practical for the applicant to make or for the judge to consider such a state-
D ment of means in the middle of a trial on indictment and, accordingly, the practice has arisen of making an order conditional upon the statement of means being considered by the proper officer which may well not happen until the trial is otherwise concluded.

I still have to consider the effect of an order made after the start of a trial. In my judgment section 28 is drafted on the basis that an order
E when made is an order in respect of a " proceeding," whether that proceeding be a trial, a committal for sentence, an appeal or some other proceeding. This conclusion receives support from section 37 and, in particular, section 37 (2), which provides that subject to the regulations:

> " the costs . . . shall include sums on account of the fees payable to any counsel or solicitor assigned to him and any disbursements reasonably incurred by any such solicitor for or in connection with
> F those proceedings."

These are wide words but as far as fees for solicitor and counsel are concerned they are qualified by the word " payable " which, in my view, means that they must remain payable at the time of taxation. Accordingly, in a case where a defendant has been able to pay the fees of his own counsel and solicitor for part of the trial, those fees so paid by
G him would not be payable again out of the legal aid fund. Further, a disbursement incurred by the solicitor would have to retain that character at the time of taxation and, in my judgment, it would cease to be a disbursement if the solicitor had recovered the sum disbursed from his own client or from someone else before taxation.

Once the order is made, what is payable under the order has to be
H determined by the proper officer of the court or the taxing master, but, in my judgment, they have no power to allow, under section 37 (2), any sums on account of fees which have been paid or in respect of discharged disbursements, but I can see no reason why fees which became payable before the order and disbursements incurred before that date should not be allowed so long as they were payable or incurred for or in connection with the proceedings to which the order relates.

Under section 29, in the cases of committal for trial on a charge of murder and appeals by prosecutors to the Court of Appeal, the court is bound to make a legal aid order. In all other cases the order should be made where it appears to the court desirable to do so in the interests of justice. Where an application is made late in the day and, in particular, where the delay is due to some neglect on the part of the defendant's solicitor to make the application in due time that may be a factor which the court can and ought properly to take into account in the exercise of the discretion. How much weight should be given to this factor in any particular case must depend on the circumstances of that case. In the present case I do not propose to give much weight to that factor.

In the circumstances which I mentioned earlier in this judgment, in my view, I ought in the exercise of the discretion to make the order which is sought, subject however to the statement of the defendant's means being considered by the proper officer.

When the bill comes to be taxed it will be a matter for the proper officer or the taxing master to determine what fees and disbursements to allow, but, in my judgment, it would be proper to allow the fees referable to the hearing of the present application on the basis that this application is part of the trial which will not come to an end until the final disposal of the application.

Application allowed.

Solicitors: *Hudgell, Yeates & Co.; Metropolitan Police Solicitor.*

[QUEEN'S BENCH DIVISION]

* PRACTICE DIRECTION

(JUDGE IN CHAMBERS: OUTSIDE LONDON) (No. 3)

1976 Feb. 13 — Lord Widgery C.J., Kilner Brown and Watkins JJ.

Practice — Chambers applications — Queen's Bench Division — Application to judge outside London — Summons issued in district registry — Bail applications

Lord Widgery C.J., at the sitting of the Divisional Court, read the following practice direction:

1. To the extent that the business of the courts permit, and subject to the provisions of this direction, judges of the Queen's Bench Division will sit in chambers at any place where sittings of the High Court are held, as well as in London, to deal with any business which may be dealt with by a judge of the Queen's Bench Division in chambers except any business which may from time to time be notified.

[Reported by CORNELIUS SMITH, ESQ., Barrister-at-Law]

2. Where a party desires that a matter be heard before a judge in chambers outside London the notice of an appeal or summons shall bear the title of the district registry in which the action is proceeding but shall be issued in the district registry at the place at which it is to be heard.

3. Before a party issues a judge's summons or a notice of appeal in a district registry, he should inquire at the registry whether the state of business will permit the matter to be heard there, and it is proper to be so heard.

4. A judge's summons or notice of appeal issued in a district registry may be transferred for hearing to a judge in chambers sitting in London or at another place outside London on the application of a party made to the judge or by the court of its own motion, and such a summons or notice issued in the Central Office may similarly be transferred for hearing to a place outside London. Before a transfer to a place outside London is ordered, the court will require to be informed, from inquiries made by the parties or the court officers, whether the matter can conveniently be taken there.

5. In cases not specifically provided for, the practice of the Central Office as to district registry appeals shall be followed as nearly as circumstances permit.

6. Applications for bail under R.S.C., Ord. 79 to a judge in chambers may, and should wherever possible, be made to a judge of the Queen's Bench Division at any place where sittings of the High Court or of the Crown Court are held, being the place nearest to the court where the applicant has appeared: provided that such applications made through the Official Solicitor may in any case be made in London. Outside London the summons should be issued in the district registry at the place where the application can be heard, and the order drawn up and perfected in that registry.

This direction supersedes the directions dated December 10, 1971 [*Practice Direction* (*Judge in Chambers*: *Outside London*) [1972] 1 W.L.R. 4] and December 11, 1972 [*Practice Direction* (*Judge in Chambers*: *Outside London*) (*No.* 2) [1973] 1 W.L.R. 45].

A

[COURT OF APPEAL]

* REGINA *v.* CHARLES

1975 Nov. 18

Bridge L.J., Bristow and Borehan JJ.

B

Crime — Fraud — Obtaining pecuniary advantage by deception — Cheque card used to back cheques—Amounts drawn in excess of money credited to bank account—Whether representation of authority to draw on account—Theft Act 1968 (*c.* 60), *s.* 16

A bank granted the defendant overdraft facilities of £100 on his bank account and issued him with a cheque card permitting him to issue cheques up to £30, which the bank C guaranteed to honour on presentation. Between December 28 and 31, 1972, the defendant used the cheque card to back 18 cheques each for £30. On January 2, four of the cheques were presented for payment with the result that the defendant's account was overdrawn in excess of £100 but a cheque for £500 had been presented at another branch of the bank and was due to be credited to the defendant's account. Later that day, the manager of the branch, at which the defendant had D his bank account, had an interview with the defendant and told him that he should not use the cheque card more than once on the same day in any one transaction or to obtain cash from a bank. The defendant did not tell the manager that there were a further 14 cheques to be presented and the manager gained the impression that the defendant no longer required overdraft facilities. At the end of the interview, the defendant requested and was given a new cheque book. That E night the defendant used the cheque card to back all 25 cheques in the cheque book for £30 each to obtain gaming chips at a gaming club.

The defendant was convicted of obtaining property by deception, namely, the cheque book, contrary to section 15 of the Theft Act 1968 and two offences, relating to two of the cheques issued at the gaming club, of obtaining a pecuniary advantage by deception, contrary to section 16 of the Act. F

On the defendant's appeal against conviction:—

Held, (1) that there was insufficient evidence of any representation by words or conduct by the defendant of such a half truth that his non-disclosure to the manager that a further 14 cheques were outstanding amounted to a false representation as to the true state of his bank account and, accordingly, the conviction under section 15 of the Act would be quashed (post, p. 253C–E). G

(2) That, although the payee of a cheque backed by a cheque card had no interest in whether the drawer had authority to draw on his account for the amount of the cheque since the bank guaranteed payment, previous authority of the court should be followed, albeit, the decision had been decided without argument, that the defendant, when he issued the cheques backed by the cheque card, represented to the gaming club that he had authority to draw on his account and, accord- H ingly, the appeal against the convictions of obtaining a pecuniary advantage by deception would be dismissed (post, pp. 254A–D, 258F—259A).

Reg. v. *Kovacs* [1974] 1 W.L.R. 370, C.A. followed.

Reg. v. *Page* (*Note*) [1971] 2 Q.B. 330, C.A. applied.

[Reported by S. O. OSUNKOYA, ESQ., Barrister-at-Law]

A The following cases are referred to in the judgment:

Reg. v. *Gould* [1968] 2 Q.B. 65; [1968] 2 W.L.R. 643; [1968] 1 All E.R. 849, C.A.

Reg. v. *Kovacs* [1974] 1 W.L.R. 370; [1974] 1 All E.R. 1236, C.A.

Reg. v. *Newsome* [1970] 2 Q.B. 711; [1970] 3 W.L.R. 586; [1970] 3 All E.R. 455, C.A.

Reg. v. *Page* (*Note*) [1971] 2 Q.B. 330; [1971] 2 W.L.R. 1308; [1971] 2 All
B E.R. 870, C.A.

Rex v. *Ettridge* [1909] 2 K.B. 24, C.C.A.

Rex v. *Norman* [1924] 2 K.B. 315, C.C.A.

The following additional cases were cited in argument:

Reg. v. *Scott* [1974] Q.B. 733; [1974] 2 W.L.R. 379; [1974] 2 All E.R. 204, C.A.; [1975] A.C. 819; [1974] 3 W.L.R. 741; [1974] 3 All E.R. 1032,
C H.L.(E.).

Reg. v. *Terry* [1961] 2 Q.B. 314; [1961] 2 W.L.R. 961; [1961] 2 All E.R. 569, C.C.A.

APPEAL against conviction.

On December 6, 1974, the defendant, Derek Michael Charles, was
D convicted at the Inner London Crown Court on count 3 of an indictment of obtaining property by deception, namely, a cheque book and, on counts 9 and 10, of obtaining a pecuniary advantage by deception. The latter offences related to cheques dated January 2 and 3, 1973, each for £30, issued by the defendant and backed by a cheque card at the Golden Nugget Club for gaming chips. Judge Finestein deferred sentence until June 6, 1975, and, on that date, the defendant was fined £150.

E The defendant appealed against conviction on the grounds, inter alia, that the use of a cheque card when drawing a cheque was not a separate representation from the legal representations of the cheque form itself, but merely guaranteed the representations that the cheque would be met by the bank when it was presented by the payee for payment; that there was no evidence that the defendant ab initio was not entitled and
F authorised to use the cheque card, nor was the use by the defendant expressly subject to any conditions other than those printed on the back of the card itself; that the prosecution case was that a normally authorised use of a cheque card became an unauthorised use if the account on which the cheque was drawn was not sufficiently in credit when it was presented; and that the bank had not withdrawn the cheque card or requested its return and therefore it was wrong to infer a misrepresen-
G tation by breach of an implied condition.

The facts are stated in the judgment.

Eldred Tabachnik for the defendant.

Michael Worsley and *Colin Hart* for the Crown.

H BRIDGE L.J. gave the judgment of the court. On December 6, 1974, at the Inner London Crown Court, after the retrial lasting six days the defendant was convicted of one offence of obtaining property by deception and two offences of obtaining a pecuniary advantage by deception. Sentence was deferred until June 6, 1975, when a fine of £150 was imposed. The defendant appeals against his convictions by leave of the single judge.

The history of the transactions out of which this prosecution arose was as follows. On October 31, 1972, the defendant opened a current bank account at the Peckham Rye branch of the National Westminster Bank. On November 23, he went to see the manager, Mr. Mason, asked for, and was granted, authority to overdraw on his account for a period of one month up to a limit of £100. He went to see Mr. Mason again shortly before Christmas and asked that the overdraft up to a limit of £100 should be extended for a further month. That request was granted. He further indicated to Mr. Mason that he was having certain difficulties, having regard to where his business activities took him, in cashing cheques when he wished to do so. It was at Mr. Mason's suggestion that he was issued with a cheque card. The cheque card was in what is now, no doubt, a common and very familiar form but since important questions arise in the case as to the implications of a transaction in which a cheque is presented, backed by a cheque card, it is appropriate to set out in full the terms of the card which was issued to the defendant in this case. It bore on its front the legend "National Westminster Bank £30 for conditions see over." On the back is written:

> "The issuing banks undertake that any cheque *not exceeding* £30 will be honoured subject to the following conditions: a. The cheque must be signed in the presence of the payee. b. The signature on the cheque must correspond with the specimen signature on this card. c. The cheque must be drawn on a bank cheque form bearing the code number shown on this card."

I interpose to observe that the code number on the card was of course the code number of the defendant's account with the bank.

> "d. The cheque must be drawn before the expiry date of this card. e. The card number must be written on the reverse of the cheque by the payee."

Between December 28 and 31, the defendant issued a total of 18 cheques backed by this cheque card, each for £30, amounting, therefore, in total to £540. The issue of those cheques for that aggregate amount was going to have the consequence, in the events which happened and which, as the jury must be taken to have found, must have been foreseeable by the defendant, of putting his account with the bank into debit to an amount substantially in excess of the £100 authorised overdraft. Some of the 18 cheques issued in the period before the end of the year had, we understand, been presented at banks for encashment. The bulk of them, however, had been paid for the purchase of gambling chips to a gambling club resorted to by the defendant known as the Golden Nugget Club.

On January 2 the first four of those 18 cheques including, it would seem, at least two which had been cashed on the same day at different banks, reached the Peckham Rye branch of the National Westminster Bank. They immediately caused Mr. Mason concern, partly because of the two cheques that had been cashed on the same day at different banks and partly because the immediate state of the defendant's account was then such that the four cheques for £30 each would, themselves, put the account in debit to an amount of £120. There had, however, been paid into another branch of another bank on that same day a cheque for £500 to the defendant's credit of which Mr. Mason was aware; but that cheque had not at that time been cleared and therefore had not been credited to the defendant's account. It was in those circumstances

A that Mr. Mason got in touch with the defendant and asked him to call at the bank, which the defendant did later on January 2. There was a discussion between the defendant and Mr. Mason to which further reference will have to be made hereafter. At the end of the interview the defendant asked for a new cheque book and was supplied with one containing 25 cheques. That evening the defendant went to the Golden Nugget Club again. Perhaps it is not an unreasonable inference that B he was hoping to redeem his fortunes at the gaming tables but, as so often happens in such a situation, instead of saving the day he plunged still further into disaster and in the course of the night's gambling he used all 25 cheques from his new cheque book; paying them out to the manager of the Golden Nugget Club, £30 at a time, each cheque backed by the cheque card and duly completed in accordance with the conditions C on the cheque card. The 25 cheques amounted, in the aggregate, to £750 and on their presentation to the defendant's bank, put his account into debit far beyond the limit of his authorised overdraft.

The three counts, in an indictment originally containing 10 counts, of which the defendant was eventually convicted, were as follows: count 3 charged him with dishonestly obtaining the cheque book which had been issued to him following his interview with Mr. Mason, on D January 2, by deception, namely, by falsely representing the true state of his bank account. Counts 9 and 10 of the indictment related to two of the cheques he had issued on the night of January 2–3, the last one dated the 2nd and the first one dated the 3rd, each for £30. The charge in each count was dishonestly obtaining a pecuniary advantage for himself, namely, increased borrowing by way of ovedraft from the National E Westminster Bank by deception, namely, by deliberately or recklessly representing that he was entitled and authorised to use his cheque card when issuing the cheque in question.

It is important to observe at the outset that, since these counts were laid under sections 15 and 16 of the Theft Act 1968, it was an essential ingredient in each of the offences charged which the prosecution had to establish, that the defendant had, by words or conduct, been guilty of a F deception and that in each case that deception had operated on the mind of the party deceived to induce him to do that which enabled the defendant to obtain in the case of count 3 goods—the cheque book—and in the case of counts 9 and 10 a pecuniary advantage—the illegitimate increase of his overdraft with the bank.

The central point which arises in the appeal, albeit it arises in a G different form in relation to count 3 on the one hand and counts 9 and 10 on the other, is whether on the evidence led by the Crown there was prima facie evidence proper to be left to the jury of the relevant deception alleged to have been practised by the defendant and that that deception operated to induce the party deceived to act as he did.

It is necessary to go back now to examine in more detail the sub-H stance of the interview between Mr. Mason and the defendant on the afternoon of January 2, which had the result, as one of its consequences, of the issue to the defendant of the new cheque book he requested.

First Mr. Mason pointed out to the defendant that of the four cheques, which by that time had arrived back at the Peckham Rye branch, more than one had been cashed at a bank on the same day and, although this had not been explained to the defendant by Mr. Mason when the cheque card had originally been issued to him before Christmas, Mr. Mason now told the defendant that it was one of the bank's rules, which A customers holding cheque cards should observe, that they were not available for cashing more than one cheque for £30 at any bank or banks on any one day. These transactions, it should be pointed out, occurred before it became the common practice of the banks to stamp on the back of the drawer's cheque book a record of his cashing a cheque backed by his cheque card on any day.

B

Mr. Mason further said to the defendant that apart from cashing cheques at banks the cheque card should not be used to issue any cheques for more than £30 in relation to any one transaction. He further pointed out to the defendant that as the £500 cheque paid in that day had not yet been cleared, the four cheques received would create an overdraft in the defendant's account in excess of the permitted limit of £100. The defendant's reply to this was first that he had drawn the four C cheques in question innocently, not knowing the bank's restriction on the number of cheques to be drawn on the strength of the card on any single day, secondly he said that he was surprised that the £500 cheque had not been paid in earlier and he said further that he had paid the four cheques on two days, December 28 and 29, because he had been moving house and had extra expenses.

D

There was undoubtedly a general discussion between Mr. Mason and the defendant regarding the state of the defendant's account. At the end of the interview, Mr. Mason said, he was quite happy. He also said that had he known that in addition to the four cheques, which had reached the Peckham Rye branch on January 2, the defendant, between December 28 and 31, had issued another 14 cheques each for £30 he certainly would not have issued him with a further cheque book; but E at no time did Mr. Mason ask the defendant whether any other cheques were outstanding. Mr. Mason, at one point in his evidence, did say that his impression was that the defendant was indicating he would not require an overdraft any further. If that impression was directly given by something said by the defendant and was unqualified, it would certainly have been a half truth involving a deception in not revealing that the further 14 cheques were outstanding.

F

At the end of the day, after he had been cross-examined about this, Mr. Mason's evidence was vague in the extreme as to precisely what had been said regarding the future of the overdraft. The crux of the whole matter really turns upon a passage in the course of Mr. Mason's cross-examination on behalf of the defendant by Mr. Tabachnik:

G

"Q. . . . Now going back to this interview of January 2 did the defendant say to you explicitly that he no longer required an overdraft? Or was that your general impression? A. I cannot recall. Certainly by the end of the time he went out I had made up my mind he would not want any. Whether it was specifically raised or not I would not like to say. But certainly this was the impression, H because to the best of my recollection the conversation went along the lines that he'd got £500 in now and everything was looking all right for him. Q. Yes. So certainly the question of the cancellation of an overdraft was something that had not really been specifically discussed between you? A. Not to my recollection. Q. Because you see Mr. Charles was under the impression that his overdraft was still continuing until January 19: might that be reasonable in your

A view? A. The overdraft limit of £100? Q. Yes? A. I think that is a reasonable supposition, yes."

Really the high water mark of the argument on behalf of the Crown that there was here sufficient evidence of half truths being represented by the defendant to Mr. Mason, such as to make the non-disclosure of the outstanding cheques a suggestio falsi, has to be extracted, if anywhere,
B from the last part of his answer in the passage just quoted:

> "But certainly this was the impression, because to the best of my recollection the conversation went along the lines that he'd got £500 in now and everything was looking all right for him."

That has to be considered in the context that Mr. Mason also said in terms, with reference to the cheques that had come in:

C

> "It was my impression that those were the only four. My impression was not based on anything that the defendant said to the best of my recollection. My impression was not based on anything that the defendant did."

Having given this aspect of the matter careful consideration all three
D members of this court have reached the conclusion that there was here insufficient evidence of any representation by words or conduct by the defendant of such a half truth as would enable the Crown properly to invite the jury to say that the non-disclosure to Mr. Mason by the defendant of the fact that a further 14 cheques, each for £30, were outstanding was a false representation as to the true state of his bank account. We think that the evidence was too tenuous for that. In
E essence we think that this was a simple failure to disclose something which, so far as the criminal law is concerned at all events, the defendant was under no duty to disclose.

Accordingly we take the view that this count should not have been left to the jury and that the conviction on count three must be quashed.

Turning now to counts 9 to 10, the point in the appeal in respect of
F these counts is one of very much wider, indeed of considerable, general importance. It is a point which raises the whole issue as to what are the implications of the common form of transaction, so familiar in everyday life since the practice of banks to issue cheque cards became common, represented by the presentation of a cheque backed by a cheque card and completed in accordance with the conditions of the cheque card in payment for goods or services or in exchange for cash.

G Before turning to the general point which the arguments have raised, it is again convenient to examine in a little more detail the relevant evidence given by the payee of the cheques which were given by the defendant, in payment for gambling chips, on the night of January 2/3, who was Mr. Cersell, the manager of the Golden Nugget Club. What he said, as recorded in the summing up, was:

H

> ". . . if the club was aware that someone was using his cheque without authority, and without being entitled, . . . they would not accept his cheque or the use of the cheque card" but then he went on: "We accept the cheque card on the basis that we do not know of any reason why not. There was no reason why the club should not accept, or should not have accepted the 25 cheques within a few hours. The club suffered no loss. The only reason we cashed the cheques, was that the cheque card was produced. That is our

policy regarding any customer. What we need is the bank's guarantee of payment to us. So long as the conditions on the back of the card are met, the bank will honour the cheque in relation to which the card is presented, whatever the state of the customer's bank account . . . If a cheque is backed by a cheque card, it is the bank who takes the risk. So if there is the cheque card, we make no inquiries as to his credit-worthiness, or as to the state of his account with the bank. All this is irrelevant unless the club has knowledge that he has no funds, or the club has knowledge that he has no authority to draw." A B

That was the specific evidence of the person who received the cheques and treated them as valid in this case, but it also seems to us to be an eminently common-sense view, which we think most people would take, of the situation arising when a cheque is presented in accordance with conditions on the back of a cheque card. C

The essential question which we have to determine is: what are the implied representations, if any, which the drawer of the cheque, who completes it in accordance with the cheque card and backs it with the authority of the cheque card, makes to the payee?

The convenient starting point is to consider the comparable representations which are implied by the presentation of a cheque which is not backed by a cheque card. In *Reg.* v. *Page* (*Note*) [1971] 2 Q.B. 330, this court considered that matter and in the judgment of the court, delivered by Phillimore L.J., this passage appears on p. 333: D

"What is the law in regard to a cheque? It is set out very conveniently and very clearly in *Kenny's Outlines of Criminal Law,* 15th ed. (1936), p. 284 [now 18th ed. (1962), p. 347] and I am indebted to Geoffrey Lane J. for its assistance. It is put like this: 'Similarly the familiar act of drawing a cheque (a document which on the face of it is only a command of a future act) is held to imply at least three statements about the present: (1) that the drawer has an account with that bank; (2) that he has authority to draw on it for that amount; (3) that the cheque, as drawn, is a valid order for the payment of that amount (i.e. that the present state of affairs is such that, in the ordinary course of events, the cheque will on its future presentment be duly honoured). It may be well to point out, however, that it does not imply any representation that the drawer now has money in his bank to the amount drawn for, inasmuch as he may well have authority to overdraw, or may intend to pay in (before the cheque can be presented) sufficient money to meet it.'" E F G

Is it to be implied that the same representations are made by the conduct of one who presents a cheque completed in accordance with the conditions on such a cheque card as that with which we are here concerned?

Mr. Tabachnik for the defendant, in a cogent submission for which we are most grateful, concedes that the first implied representation of what have been referred to in the argument as the three "*Page*" representations is made, namely, that the drawer has an account with the bank. Closely linked to that, no doubt there is an implied representation in the situation under consideration that the drawer of the cheque is the authorised holder of the cheque card in question. It is immaterial whether there is an implied representation on the lines of the third H

"*Page*" representation because if there is, given that the cheque has been completed in accordance with the cheque card, the representation is true because the cheque will necessarily be a valid order for payment of the amount for which it has been made out.

The whole argument turns on the question whether the second "*Page*" representation should be implied in this situation; namely a representation that the drawer has authority to draw that cheque for that amount, in the sense that he is drawing a cheque for an amount which he has no reason to expect, according to his contractual arrangements with the bank, that the bank would not meet when presented, independently of their pledge to meet it by virtue of the cheque card.

Mr. Tabachnik's submission is that when a cheque card is presented no such representation is to be implied for the simple reason that the payee is not, in the slightest degree, concerned with the question of the drawer's credit-worthiness. The state of the drawer's account at the bank, the state of the contractual relationship between the bank and the drawer is, so the submission runs, a matter of complete indifference to the payee of the cheque; it is a matter to which he never needs to apply his mind.

The necessity for the three "*Page*" representations to be implied in the different circumstances where a cheque is presented in payment for goods or services or in exchange for cash to a stranger without being backed with a cheque card is obvious, says Mr. Tabachnik. Without such representations to rely upon, a person who takes a cheque has nothing to assure him that he can expect payment when the cheque is presented. Accordingly the implication of the three "*Page*" representations, including in particular the second is, in these circumstances, necessary to give the transaction business efficacy.

In the different case where the recipient of the cheque has the bank's express undertaking held out in the form of a cheque card to rely on there is no necessity, in order to give business efficacy to the transaction, that there should be any collateral representation implied on the part of the drawer of the cheque as to the state of his account with the bank or the state of his authority to draw on that account. Still less is there any basis for an inference that any such representation operates on the mind of the recipient of the cheque as an inducement persuading him to accept it. He relies, so runs the submission, and relies exclusively, on the bank's undertaking embodied in the cheque card.

The argument the other way is canvassed in an interesting commentary on *Reg.* v. *Kovacs* [1974] 1 W.L.R. 370 to be found in the *Criminal Law Review* for 1974 at pp. 183 et seq. The commentator points out, as indeed the evidence of Mr. Cersell in this case affirms, that when someone is asked to accept a cheque backed by a cheque card he cannot properly do so and, plainly, if he is honest will not do so, if he has actual knowledge that the cheque is in fact being issued outside the ambit of the drawer's authority to draw upon his account. The reason for that is plain. If the recipient of the cheque is aware that the drawer is already beyond his overdraft limit or is otherwise exceeding his authority as between himself and the bank, and nevertheless accepts the cheque intending to rely on the bank's undertaking embodied in the cheque card that the cheque will be met, he is, in effect, making himself party to a conspiracy to defraud the bank. The argument accordingly is that, at least in a negative sense, the recipient of the cheque backed by the cheque card is concerned to some degree with the question whether or

not the drawer is issuing the cheque within or without the ambit of his A
authority vis-à-vis the bank.

From that premise the inference, it is said, follows that notwithstanding the availability of the cheque card and the bank's undertaking which it embodies, there should also be implied from the transaction a representation by the drawer that he is drawing that cheque within his authority as between himself and the bank, and at least a partial reliance B
upon that representation by the recipient of the cheque.

The point is a difficult one. If it were free of authority, which it is not, all members of the court would be inclined to give effect to Mr. Tabachnik's arguments. That is not to say that the court has reached a concluded view on the matter but our provisional view is that common sense is on the side of Mr. Tabachnik's argument and that the contrary argument based on the premise of the recipient's negative interest, so to C
speak, in the state of affairs as between the bank and the bank's customer is a somewhat tortuous and legalistic one.

Again it is right, we think, to shun the temptation, which sometimes presses on the mind of the judiciary, to suppose that because a particular course of conduct, as was this course of conduct, was anti-social and undesirable, it can necessarily be fitted into some convenient criminal D
pigeon-hole. Before the repeal of section 13 of the Debtor's Act 1869, by the Theft Act 1968, we have no doubt that the present circumstances would have led, and led without difficulty, to a charge of obtaining credit by fraud other than by false pretences. It does not follow from that that there is necessarily a convenient alternative criminal pigeon-hole provided which fits the facts under the provisions of the Theft Act 1968.

However, the point is not res integra. The point arose in this court E
in *Reg.* v. *Kovacs* [1974] 1 W.L.R. 370. In that case the appellant had been convicted of two counts of obtaining a pecuniary advantage by deception when she had presented cheques backed by and in accordance with the conditions of a cheque card, in one instance to a railway booking clerk for purchase of a railway ticket and in another instance to a pet shop owner in purchase of a Pekinese dog. The counts against her F
in respect of her offences alleged as the relevant deception a representation on the part of the appellant that she was in valid possession of, and entitled to use, the cheque card in question.

The judgment of the court given by Lawton L.J. indicates, at p. 372:

> "The prosecution's evidence was that by the end of November 1972 the appellant's account at the Tring branch of the National West- G
> minster Bank Ltd. was overdrawn in the sum of £572. By letter dated November 30, 1972, the bank told her the extent of her indebtedness and that no more cheques drawn by her would be met. Shortly afterwards a bank official named Hedges called on her and asked her for her cheque book and the cheque card referred to in the indictment which had been issued to her. She said they were H
> not in her possession."

The principal argument in the case appears to have been that the conviction for the section 16 offence could not be sustained because the deception had been practised on one party, on the railway clerk and the owner of the pet shop, whereas the pecuniary advantage had been obtained from another party, namely the bank. That appears from the passage, at p. 373:

> "The appellant's counsel accepted that as a result of his client's conduct she had increased her overdraft by the amounts of the two cheques without the consent and contrary to the intentions of the bank, but he submitted that those results had been brought about by the deception of the railway booking clerk and the pet shop owner, not of the bank."

The judgment goes on still, as we read it, summarising the arguments of counsel:

> "The railway booking clerk and the pet shop owner had been deceived because the appellant in presenting the cheque card with her cheque had represented that she was entitled to be in possession of it and to use it."

The court then goes on to reject that argument as not in any way invalidating the convictions on the footing that it is of no moment that the party deceived is a different person from the party from whom the pecuniary advantage is obtained. But the crucial passage with regard to the point with which we are concerned is:

> "The next question is: how did she obtain this pecuniary advantage? On the facts the answer is clear, namely, by inducing the railway booking clerk and the pet shop owner to believe that she was entitled to use the cheque card when she was not."

We have heard much argument on the question whether that is a decision of this court on the very point with which we are concerned this morning and if so whether it is binding on us. Rather half-heartedly, if he will not be offended by our saying so, yesterday Mr. Tabachnik suggested that there might be a ground on which the decision could be distinguished. It does appear on the facts that when the bank official had called on the appellant and demanded the return of the cheque book and the cheque card but not obtained them, because she falsely stated that she had not got them, her authority as holder of the cheque card had been withdrawn and of course part of the deception alleged against her was her representation that she was in valid possession of the card.

In the view we take that is not a solid or sufficient ground on which we can say that the case can be distinguished because equally the case proceeded on the footing that she was making a false representation which deceived the railway booking clerk and the pet shop owner as to her entitlement to use the cheque card.

Mr. Tabachnik realistically does not argue that we can properly treat *Reg.* v. *Kovacs* as a decision which, in relation to this point, was per incuriam, but what he does say is that it was a decision which was reached without argument on the point which we are called on to decide. Certainly the passage quoted, where counsel for the appellant is recorded as submitting that the results were brought about by the deception of the booking clerk and the pet shop owner, would seem to indicate that no argument on the lines addressed to us had been addressed to the court at all.

Our attention has been drawn to the well-known authority of *Reg.* v. *Gould* [1968] 2 Q.B. 65 and *Reg.* v. *Newsome* [1970] 2 Q.B. 711 which certainly indicate that there is a less rigorous adherence to the doctrine of stare decisis in the criminal division of this court than in the civil division. We do not think it helpful to examine those authorities in A detail, nor that they go to the central point which we have to determine. More important, Mr. Tabachnik read us a passage from Professor Cross's book on precedent dealing with the question of the binding authority of cases which appear to have decided a point sub silentio and he specifically drew our attention to cases where the Court of Criminal Appeal assumed jurisdiction to overrule a previous decision of its own basically upon the ground that the previous decision on the point at issue had not been B argued.

The first of these authorities is *Rex* v. *Ettridge* [1909] 2 K.B. 24. The point at issue is of no materiality but it does appear there that the court in which Darling, Walton and Pickford JJ. were sitting together overruled a previous decision of their own, that is to say of the same court similarly constituted the previous week, in which the point in C question had not been argued. Another instance of the same process is to be found in the decision of the Court of Criminal Appeal in *Rex* v. *Norman* [1924] 2 K.B. 315, where, confronted with a previous decision where a point not argued had been decided in a certain way, Lord Hewart C.J. constituted a court of no less than 13 judges to consider the matter and by a majority of 9 to 4 they decided that the earlier decision should D not be followed.

We think there is force in the three submissions made to us on this issue by Mr. Worsley. He submits first that the practice in relation to the question whether it is appropriate for one division of this court to take a different view on a point which has been, even if without argument, apparently decided by another division has changed substantially since the change in the accessibility of the House of Lords as an appellate E tribunal in criminal matters. He says secondly that it is, to some extent, a matter of expediency in the circumstances as to whether this court should, even assuming it has power to do so, depart from a previous decision. He says thirdly, and with great force, that there is a distinction to be made between a point which has been decided sub silentio in circumstances in which the proper inference must be that the point F was never in the mind of the court at all, and a point which has been decided without argument, even perhaps following a tacit concession by counsel, where, nevertheless it is apparent from the judgment that the court must have applied its mind to the point and at least seen no obstacle in the way of the conclusion which it has expressed.

We think that the decision in *Reg.* v. *Kovacs* on the point we are concerned with clearly falls into the second category. Lawton L.J. could G not have said "How did she obtain the pecuniary advantage? On the facts the answer is clear, namely, by inducing the booking clerk and the pet shop owner to believe that she was entitled to use the cheque card" unless the court had thought that it was to be implied from the presentation of a cheque backed by a cheque card that the drawer was representing that she had authority to draw that cheque at that time for that H amount.

In one sense, of course, the question of the implications arising from any particular transaction is a question of fact but the presentation of a cheque backed by a cheque card is such a common form everyday transaction that it must be a question of law for the court to decide what inferences can properly be drawn from such a transaction. We take the expression of opinion in the passage to which reference has been made

A in *Reg.* v. *Kovacs* as indicating the court's view that it could and probably should properly be inferred from such a transaction that the drawer was representing that she had authority as between herself and the bank to draw that cheque for that amount.

However, even if we had felt more strongly than we do in relation to the argument of principle we think it would be undesirable that two divisions of this court should speak with conflicting voices on such an
B important issue. Mr. Tabachnik's powerful arguments deserve the fullest consideration but if they are to be given effect then, in present circumstances, the proper tribunal to give effect to them is not this court but the House of Lords.

Accordingly the appeal against conviction on counts 9 and 10 will be dismissed. £50 of the £150 fine will be remitted. The order will stand
C on the footing that there is a £50 fine on each of counts 9 and 10 on which the convictions still stand. There will be a sentence of three months' imprisonment in default and six months to pay.

Appeal allowed against conviction for obtaining property by deception.
D *Appeal dismissed against convictions for obtaining pecuniary advantage.*
Certificate under section 33 (2) *of the Criminal Appeal Act* 1968 *that point of law of general public importance was involved in decision, namely,* "*When the holder*
E *of a cheque card presents a cheque in accordance with the conditions of the card which is accepted in exchange for goods, services or cash, does this transaction provide evidence of itself from which it can or should be inferred* (*a*) *that*
F *the drawer represented that he then had authority, as between himself and the bank, to draw a cheque for that amount and* (*b*) *that the recipient of the cheque was induced by that representation to accept the cheque.*"
G *Leave to appeal.*
Legal aid including representation by two counsel.

Solicitors: *Registrar of Criminal Appeals; Solicitor, Metropolitan*
H *Police.*

A

[QUEEN'S BENCH DIVISION]

* REGINA *v.* BIRMINGHAM JUSTICES, *Ex parte* WYATT

1975 July 8; 30 — Lord Widgery C.J., Milmo and Wien JJ.

B *Crown Practice—Certiorari—Jurisdiction of inferior tribunals—Justices passing sentence unauthorised by law—Discretion to amend order instead of quashing conviction—Administration of Justice Act* 1960 (8 & 9 *Eliz.* 2, *c.* 65), *s.* 16 (1) [1]

Crown Court — Jurisdiction — Appeal against sentence — Justices imposing unlawful sentence—Jurisdiction of Crown Court in relation to sentence—Courts Act 1971 (*c.* 23), *s.* 9 (4) [2]*—Powers of Criminal Courts Act* 1973 (*c.* 62), *s.* 21 (1) [3] C

The applicant pleaded guilty before the justices to a charge of theft. He had a previous conviction, for which he had received a suspended prison sentence which had not taken effect. He was not legally represented before the justices, and was not informed of his right to legal aid. The justices, mistakenly believing that he had already served a sentence of imprisonment, imposed a six months' prison sentence. He appealed to the Crown Court on the ground that, under D section 21 (1) of the Powers of Criminal Courts Act 1973, the justices had no power to pass a sentence of imprisonment on a person who was unaware of his right to legal aid, was not legally represented, and who had not previously received a prison sentence, which term did not include a suspended sentence. The Crown Court dismissed his appeal, taking the view that, as the applicant was legally represented at the hearing of the appeal, the defects in the justices' decision were E remedied.

On an application for orders of certiorari to quash the applicant's conviction before the justices and the decision of the Crown Court:—

Held, that although the justices had passed a sentence unauthorised by law, being contrary to section 21 of the Powers of Criminal Courts Act 1973, as the applicant's conviction had not been quashed, the Crown Court did have jurisdiction to F hear and determine the appeal against sentence; that the Crown Court had no power, under section 9 (4) of the Courts Act 1971, to pass a sentence greater than that which the particular magistrates' court which had passed the original sentence had power to impose; and that, in all the circumstances, the court would exercise its discretion, under section 16 (1) of the Administration of Justice Act 1960, to amend the conviction, instead of quashing it, by substituting a fine for the G sentence of imprisonment.

The following case is referred to in the judgment of the court:

Rex v. *Willesden Justices, Ex parte Utley* [1948] 1 K.B. 397; [1947] 2 All E.R. 838, D.C.

The following additional cases were cited in argument: H

Dyson v. *Ellison* [1975] 1 W.L.R. 150; [1975] 1 All E.R. 276, D.C.
Harman v. *Official Receiver* [1934] A.C. 248, H.L.(E.).

[Reported by MRS. RACHEL DAVIES, Barrister-at-Law]

[1] Administration of Justice Act 1960, s. 16 (1): see, post, p. 262F–H.
[2] Courts Act 1971, s. 9 (4): see post, p. 263E.
[3] Powers of Criminal Courts Act 1973, s. 21 (1): see post, pp. 261H—262A.

A *Rex* v. *West Kent Quarter Sessions Appeal Committee, Ex parte Files* [1951] 2 All E.R. 728, D.C.

S. (*An Infant*) v. *Recorder of Manchester* [1971] A.C. 481; [1970] 2 W.L.R. 21; [1969] 3 All E.R. 1230, H.L.(E.).

APPLICATION for orders of certiorari.

The applicant, Joseph Michael Wyatt, sought orders of certiorari to
B quash his conviction for theft by Birmingham justices on May 2, 1975, for which he was sentenced to six months' imprisonment, and to quash a decision of the Birmingham Crown Court made on May 22, 1975, dismissing his appeal against that sentence. The ground of the application was that neither the magistrates' court nor the Crown Court had jurisdiction to pass a sentence of imprisonment.

C The facts are stated in the judgment of Wien J.

A. J. Engel for the applicant.

A. J. D. Nicholl for the prosecutor.

Cur. adv. vult.

July 30. MILMO J. In the absence of Lord Widgery C.J., Wien J. will
D read the judgment of the court which has been considered by Lord Widgery C.J. and myself and with which we agree.

WIEN J. In this case counsel moves on behalf of Joseph Michael Wyatt for orders of certiorari to quash (1) a conviction by the Birmingham magistrates, who on May 2, 1975, sentenced the applicant to six months' imprisonment for an offence of theft and (2) a decision of the
E Birmingham Crown Court which on May 22, 1975, dismissed the applicant's appeal against sentence and confirmed the sentence.

The relevant facts are quite short. On May 2, 1975, the applicant appeared at the Birmingham magistrates' court charged with an offence of theft in respect of which he had been arrested the previous day. He pleaded guilty. He was not legally represented. He was not informed
F of his right to apply for legal aid and did not so apply. After learning of his previous convictions for dishonesty the justices sentenced him to six months' imprisonment—the court register states "Record: (Prison before)." In fact he had previously been sentenced to a term of three months' imprisonment by the same court in November 1972, but that sentence had been suspended for a period of two years and the sentence had not taken effect.

G On appeal to the Birmingham Crown Court the applicant was represented by counsel and solicitors. His appeal was presented on the basis that the magistrates' court had no power to pass a sentence of imprisonment by virtue of section 21 (1) (*b*) and (3) (*a*) of the Powers of Criminal Courts Act 1973. The Crown Court took the view that as the appeal was a re-hearing of the case any defect in the proceedings at the
H magistrates' court was cured. The Crown Court accordingly dismissed his appeal against sentence, confirmed the sentence of six months' imprisonment and refused to state a case for the opinion of the High Court on the ground that the application was frivolous.

Section 21 (1) of the Powers of Criminal Courts Act 1973 reads:

"A magistrates' court on summary conviction or the Crown Court on committal for sentence or on conviction on indictment shall not pass a sentence of imprisonment, Borstal training or detention in a

> detention centre on a person who is not legally represented in that court and has not been previously sentenced to that punishment by a court in any part of the United Kingdom, unless . . . (*b*) having been informed of his right to apply for legal aid and had the opportunity to do so, he refused or failed to apply."

This was a case of summary conviction where a sentence of imprisonment could not be passed since the applicant was not legally represented at the magistrates' court and had not been informed of his right to apply for legal aid. He had not been previously sentenced to imprisonment since by section 21 (3) (*a*) a previous sentence of imprisonment which has been suspended and which has not taken effect must be disregarded for the purposes of section 21 (1) (*b*).

It is submitted on behalf of the applicant that the magistrates' court passed a sentence that was not authorised by law and therefore the conviction, albeit on a plea of guilty, was bad on its face and would have entitled the applicant to an order for certiorari to quash the conviction had he applied to this court instead of appealing to the Crown Court.

He relied on *Rex* v. *Willesden Justices, Ex parte Utley* [1948] 1 K.B. 397, 398, where Lord Goddard C.J. said:

> ". . . my opinion remains as it was at the outset, that if a sentence be imposed which is not authorised by law for the offence for which the defendant is convicted, that makes the conviction bad on its face and being a bad conviction, it can be brought up here to be quashed, and when so brought up, must be quashed, for this court has no power, and never has had any power, on certiorari, to amend the conviction. That power could only be exercised if the court was sitting as a court of appeal on magistrates, but the only appellate jurisdiction we have over magistrates is when a special case is stated by them."

We accept counsel's submission as being correct. Prior to 1960 this court could only quash the conviction. However by virtue of section 16 (1) of the Administration of Justice Act 1960 we now have power instead of quashing the conviction to amend it by substituting for the sentence passed any sentence which the magistrates' court had power to impose. Section 16 (1) of the Act of 1960 reads:

> "Where a person who has been sentenced for an offence by a magistrates' court or, on appeal against conviction or sentence, by quarter session applies to the High Court for an order of certiorari to remove the proceedings of the magistrates' court or the court of quarter sessions into the High Court, and the High Court determines that the magistrates' court or court of quarter sessions had no power to pass the sentence, the High Court may, instead of quashing the conviction, amend it by substituting for the sentence passed any sentence which the magistrates' court had power to impose."

Since the applicant appealed to the Crown Court the question arises as to what the powers of that court were on hearing an appeal from the justices. It is submitted on behalf of the applicant (1) that the Crown Court had no jurisdiction to hear the appeal at all and (2) if it did have jurisdiction it had no power in this particular case to pass a sentence of imprisonment.

A As to the first submission we are satisfied that the Crown Court did possess jurisdiction to hear the appeal. Ever since the Criminal Justice Act 1925 there has been a right of appeal to quarter sessions against sentence where there had been a plea of guilty before the magistrates. By section 83 (1) of the Magistrates' Courts Act 1952, as amended, a person convicted by a magistrates' court may appeal to the Crown Court if he pleaded guilty against his sentence. Counsel argues that the con-
B viction by the justices was a nullity. He submits that the word "convicted" in section 83 (1) means a person convicted and validly sentenced and does not include a person whom the justices merely purported to convict. He referred to several cases, but none of these cases was directly in point. In our view the mere fact that the sentence is invalid does not mean that the conviction is a nullity. Unless or until it is
C quashed it remains a conviction entitling the Crown Court to hear the appeal.

As to the second submission we think counsel was on much firmer ground in submitting that the powers of the Crown Court relating to sentencing were restricted to the powers that were possessed by the justices bearing in mind that it was not open to them in this case to pass a sentence of imprisonment by reason of section 21 of the Act of 1973.
D Section 9 (1) of the Courts Act 1971 is not in point since the power of the Crown Court to correct any error or mistake is limited to such error or mistake in the "order or judgment incorporating the decision which is the subject of the appeal." It cannot validate an invalid sentence even though the appeal is by way of re-hearing. Section 9 (4) is very much in point. It reads:

E "If the appeal is against a conviction or a sentence, the preceding provisions of this section shall be construed as including power to award any punishment, whether more or less severe than that awarded by the magistrates' court whose decision is appealed against, if that is a punishment which that magistrates' court might have awarded."

F We underline the words "the" and "that" where they appear as descriptive of magistrates' court. In other words it is "the" magistrates' court whose decision is appealed against and the punishment which "that" magistrates' court might have awarded which govern the powers of the Crown Court on an appeal. If it was intended by Parliament that the Crown Court on appeal should have all the powers of
G sentencing to imprisonment possessed by magistrates' courts in general then quite different language would have been used. Perhaps the concluding words of the subsection would then have read "if that is a punishment which any magistrates' court had power to award." At all events we are of the opinion that the proper construction of section 9 (4) of the Courts Act 1971 leads us to the conclusion that the Crown Court had no power to pass a sentence of imprisonment in the instant case.

H In the result the applicant is now entitled to ask this court to apply the provisions of section 16 (1) of the Administration of Justice Act 1960. We determine that neither the Birmingham magistrates' court nor the Birmingham Crown Court had power to pass a sentence of imprisonment. We do not quash the conviction but substitute a sentence which the Birmingham magistrates' court had power to impose on May 2, 1975, that is a sentence excluding a sentence of imprisonment.

[Counsel for the applicant then addressed the court on sentence.]

MILMO J. The order asked for is an order of certiorari to quash the the proceedings both before the magistrates and before the Crown Court. In the light of the judgment that has been given that would not be appropriate. What we will do is direct that certiorari shall go to quash the sentence and we substitute under section 16 (1) of the Administration of Justice Act a fine of £50, bearing in mind that the applicant has served a term of approximately one month's imprisonment.

Order of certiorari to quash sentence and fine of £50 substituted.
Legal aid taxation.

Solicitors: *Jonas, Grove & Co., Birmingham; I. S. Manson, Birmingham.*

[QUEEN'S BENCH DIVISION]

* LONDON AND HARROGATE SECURITIES LTD. *v.* PITTS

[1975 L. No. 3574]

1975 Oct. 22, 23 — Mocatta J.

Moneylender—Criminal offence—Implication of carrying on banking business—Whether loan recoverable in civil proceedings—Moneylenders Act 1927 (17 & 18 *Geo.* 5, *c.* 21), *s.* 4 (3) [1]

Moneylender — Memorandum — Non-compliance with statutory requirements—Omission of " per annum " after rate of interest — Whether agreement enforceable — Moneylenders Act 1927, *s.* 6 (2)

The plaintiffs who traded under a moneylender's licence lent £16,500 to the first defendant, a property developer. It was agreed that the sum should be repaid with interest at the rate of 23 per cent. per annum, but the memorandum of the loan did not include the words " per annum ". During the course of the loan transaction the plaintiffs posted a letter and a cheque on which they were described as " Merchant Bankers ". The first defendant owned a property which was in the process of being sold, and his solicitor, the second defendant, undertook to hold the title deeds until completion of the sale, whereupon the £16,500 would be repaid to the plaintiffs. The sale fell through, and the first defendant did not repay the principal nor pay the interest on the loan. The second defendant refused to hand over the title deeds to the plaintiffs. On the plaintiffs' claim against the first defendant for repayment of the loan with the agreed interest, and against the second defendant for delivery up of the title deeds: —

Held, giving judgment for the plaintiffs, (1) that although the plaintiffs might be in breach of the prohibition, contained in section 4 (3) of the Moneylenders Act 1927, on the use in a business context of any expression which might imply that

---

[Reported by MRS. RACHEL DAVIES, Barrister-at-Law]

[1] Moneylenders Act 1927, s. 4 (3): see post, p. 269B–D.
S. 6 (2): see post, p. 272A–B.

A they carried on a banking business, and liable thereby to a criminal prosecution, on the principle expressio unius, exclusio alterius it could not be said that section 4 (3) disentitled the plaintiffs to recover the loan (post, p. 271G–H).

(2) That the absence of the words "per annum" from the memorandum of loan did not render the agreement unenforceable by virtue of not containing all the information required by section 6 (2) of the Act, for the terms of the memorandum
B were in themselves unambiguous, and further, the absence was a mere triviality despite which the agreement could be readily understood (post, pp. 272G–H, 273F–H).

In re a Debtor [1938] Ch. 645 applied.

The following cases are referred to in the judgment:

Askinex Ltd. v. *Green* [1969] 1 Q.B. 272; [1967] 2 W.L.R. 820; [1967] 1 All E.R. 65, C.A.
C *Coptic Ltd.* v. *Bailey* [1972] Ch. 446; [1972] 2 W.L.R. 1061; [1972] 1 All E.R. 1242.
Debtor, In re A [1938] Ch. 645; [1938] 2 All E.R. 759, D.C.
Gaskell Ltd. v. *Askwith* (1929) 45 T.L.R. 439, 566, C.A.
Mason and Wood Ltd. v. *Greene* [1936] 2 K.B. 370; [1936] 2 All E.R. 509, C.A.
D *Parkfield Trust Ltd.* v. *Curtis* [1934] 1 K.B. 685, C.A.
Robinson's Settlement, In re, Gant v. *Hobbs* [1912] 1 Ch. 717, C.A.
Temperance Loan Fund Ltd. v. *Rose* [1932] 2 K.B. 522, C.A.

The following additional cases were cited in argument:

Barclay v. *Prospect Mortgages Ltd.* [1974] 1 W.L.R. 837; [1974] 2 All E.R. 672.
E *Burston Finance Ltd.* v. *Speirway Ltd.* [1974] 1 W.L.R. 1648; [1974] 3 All E.R. 735.
Butler v. *Rice* [1910] 2 Ch. 277.
Chetwynd v. *Allen* [1899] 1 Ch. 353.
Collings v. *Charles Bradbury Ltd.* [1936] 3 All E.R. 369.
Diplock, In re, Diplock v. *Wintle* [1948] Ch. 465; [1948] 2 All E.R. 318, C.A.
F *Direct Loans Ltd.* v. *Cracknell, The Times,* April 18, 1975.
Dunn Trust Ltd. v. *Feetham* [1936] 1 K.B. 22, C.A.
Ghana Commercial Bank v. *Chandiram* [1960] A.C. 732; [1960] 3 W.L.R. 328; [1960] 2 All E.R. 865, P.C.
Greendon Investments Ltd. v. *Mills* (1973) 226 E.G. 1957.
Patten v. *Bond* (1889) 37 W.R. 373.
Spector v. *Ageda* [1973] Ch. 30; [1971] 3 W.L.R. 498; [1971] 3 All E.R. 417.
G *United Dominions Corporation (Jamaica) Ltd.* v. *Shoucair* [1969] 1 A.C. 340; [1968] 3 W.L.R. 893; [1968] 2 All E.R. 904, P.C.

ACTION

The plaintiffs, London and Harrogate Securities Ltd., claimed against the first defendant, Clive Berry Pitts, for repayment of £16,500, being
H money lent by the plaintiffs to the first defendant under an agreement in writing, and for payment of interest thereon at the agreed rate of 23 per cent. per annum. The second defendant, Malcolm Brookes, solicitor, in consideration of the loan to the first defendant, agreed in writing to hold to the plaintiffs' order the deeds of a property known as The Old Ropery, which belonged to the first defendant, until completion of the sale thereof, and then immediately to pay to the plaintiffs the sum of £16,500 together with such interest as had accrued in accordance with

the loan agreement. The sale of The Old Ropery was not completed and A the plaintiffs demanded the delivery up of the title deeds by the second defendant. The second defendant refused to deliver up the deeds to the plaintiffs. The plaintiffs claimed against the first defendant payment of the principal with interest at the rate of 23 per cent. per annum, until payment or judgment; against the second defendant, (a) an order requiring him to deliver up the title deeds to the plaintiffs, or alternatively (b) payment of the principal with interest at 23 per cent. per annum until payment or judgment. B

The defendants submitted that, contrary to the provisions of section 4 of the Moneylenders Act 1927, the plaintiffs at all material times held themselves out to the world at large and to the first defendants in particular, as a merchant bank, and the contract was thus rendered illegal and unenforceable. The defendants submitted further and in the alternative that the loan was unenforceable against the first defendant in that the C memorandum of agreement did not express the rate of interest on the loan in terms of a rate per cent. per annum, and so failed to comply with section 6 of the Act.

The facts are stated in the judgment.

J. R. Rylance for the plaintiffs. D

R. A. Payne for the first and second defendants.

MOCATTA J. This is an action brought by the plaintiffs who are a merchant bank and who are also licensed moneylenders. In it they seek to recover £16,500, which they lent the first defendant on May 21, 1974, together with interest thereon at 23 per cent. per annum. This produces a figure down to the date of trial of this action, which began yesterday, E of a further sum of £5,375·38, making a total sum claimed of £21,875·38. They also claim as against the second defendant, who is the solicitor of the first defendant, the delivery up of the title deeds of the property called The Old Ropery, Ropery Road, Hartlepool, Co. Durham.

In answer to the action the defendants raise two defences under the Moneylenders Act 1927. They say that there were breaches of or non- F compliances with section 4 and section 6 (2) of the Act. If they are right on either of those points, the plaintiffs are, they say, unable to enforce their contract of loan and recover from them. The plaintiffs in the alternative, should they prove to be wrong on the two points arising under the Act, claim against both defendants a declaration that they are the equitable assignees of a mortgage of this property on which £3,500 was secured and an order for the sale of the property and the payment of £3,500 and interest G thereon to them out of the proceeds of sale. The parties most usefully reached agreement upon a statement of facts and upon the relevant documents.

The first defendant is, and was at all material times, a property developer. There is a company called Freehold and Leasehold Securities Ltd., in which the first defendant was at all material times a director and had H a controlling interest. That company owned this property near Hartlepool, which I shall call " The Old Ropery ", but in fact it was a site capable of development. I understand that any buildings upon it had been demolished long ago.

This action and the interesting arguments that have arisen in the course of it before me are due to the fact that the first defendant and no doubt his solicitor, the second defendant, and also his company Freehold and

Leasehold Securities Ltd., all hoped at the material time, and had good grounds for hoping, that a contract which they had entered into for the sale of The Old Ropery for £30,000 would go through on the date agreed for completion, which was July 31, 1974. If it had, there would have been none of the difficulties which have given rise to this action. In the expectation that this deal would be completed and in preparation for it, various matters took place.

It was necessary, if the property were to be conveyed to the purchasers for £30,000, to give them a good title, and plainly it would be necessary to rid the property of the encumbrance of a mortgage to Barclays Bank Ltd. for £3,500, which was extant. The first defendant was introduced to the plaintiffs with a view to his borrowing money from them with which he could enable the mortgage to be paid off and also, one assumes, various other debts of the company to be met, the figure in question which it was proposed that he should borrow being £16,500: this was, of course, only slightly over half the sum which it was hoped that the company would receive on July 31 for the sale of The Old Ropery. Negotiations took place through an intermediary with the plaintiffs, and the figure of £16,500 was agreed upon as the principal sum to be lent. The rate of interest on the loan was agreed at 23 per cent. per annum, and as security it was agreed that the first defendant would provide a letter of undertaking from his solicitor, the second defendant, to hold the deeds of the property to the plaintiffs' order until the loan was discharged.

A number of matters took place within a very short space of time. There was a conveyance on May 21, 1974, of the property by Freehold and Leasehold Securities Ltd. to the first defendant, subject to the bank's charge, and there was a deed of trust recording that he would hold the property on trust for his company. The second defendant, the day before those two deeds were entered into, provided the plaintiffs through their solicitors with an undertaking in the following terms:

> "In consideration of your advancing the sum of £16,500 to our client [the first defendant], we undertake to hold the deeds of the above property" that is, The Old Ropery "to your order until completion of its sale and immediately thereupon to pay you the said sum of £16,500 plus interest accrued thereon in accordance with the memorandum of agreement signed by you and by our client."

In fact it was signed the next day.

On May 21, the second defendant wrote to Coward Chance & Co., who were acting on behalf of the plaintiffs, requesting that, of the total sum to be loaned, £3,500 should be paid by way of a draft in favour of Barclays Bank Ltd., so that that bank would release its charge on the property which had been mortgaged to it and so that the second defendant could comply with his undertaking.

The contract of loan made on the same date states that the amount of the advance should be £16,500 and that it should be advanced on that day, May 21, provided that the first defendant should, immediately after the signing of the agreement, deliver to the plaintiffs an undertaking from his solicitor—that is to say, the second defendant—as to repayment of the loan. That undertaking was given. The amount in question was stated to be repayable at the expiry of two months from the date of the agreement—that is to say, on July 21. There would have been a lacuna of some ten days between then and completion date for sale of The Old Ropery for

£30,000, but that presumably would not have presented any particular difficulty. Clause 4 of this agreement read as follows: A

> "Interest shall be calculated at the true rate of 23 per cent. on the balance of the principal sum from time to time outstanding such interest to accrue from day to day to be paid on the day specified in clause 3 hereof provided that if the principal sum or the balance thereof shall be repaid or become repayable earlier all interest accrued shall be immediately payable." B

The first defendant signed a document acknowledging receipt of the principal sum, £16,500. The plaintiffs made out a cheque drawn on the National Westminster Bank Ltd. in favour of Barclays Bank Ltd. for the sum of £3,500. It is to be noticed that that cheque, which was their own printed form, had towards its right-hand top corner the words "Merchant Bankers" after the name of the plaintiffs. Furthermore, on a letter dated May 23, to the second defendant, the letter paper in question, headed in print with the name of the plaintiffs, has again immediately below that name the two words "Merchant Bankers". The letter incidentally, after referring to the memorandum of agreement between the plaintiffs and the first defendant, stated for the information of the second defendant that the amount was lent for two months at an interest rate of 23 per cent. true per annum. It continued: C D

> "According to our calculations the total amount due to us on Monday July 22, 1974 will be £17,132·50 which we look forward to receiving on that day."

On May 22, the second defendant sent to Barclays Bank Ltd. the cheque drawn by the plaintiffs, which I have just mentioned, together with the receipted acknowledgment form for the title deeds and requested the bank to let him hear that the bank's charge had been duly discharged. The bank took a little time over this, but in fact on June 4 it endorsed a receipt on the back of the legal mortgage, pursuant to section 115 of the Law of Property Act 1925, acknowledging on that day the receipt of the balance of the moneys including interest and costs secured by that legal mortgage made between it and Freehold and Leasehold Securities Ltd. on March 13, 1969. The receipt stated that payment had been made by Freehold and Leasehold Securities Ltd. Those words and that printed form stuck onto the back of the mortgage deed were, so to speak, reinforced by the following stamped words appearing upon the deed itself in red: "The within written mortgage has been discharged by the use of adhesive paper attached to this document." No doubt that stamp was put on ex abundanti cautela in case in the course of time the adhesive document containing the receipt should become detached from the actual mortgage deed, and thereby someone might be misled in investigating title unless the stamp had also been attached on the back of the document. E F G

The first defendant has not repaid any part of the loan or interest despite requests from the plaintiffs. Furthermore, the second defendant has refused to deliver up to the plaintiffs the deeds of the property, despite the plaintiffs' request. It is common ground that if the first defendant is entitled to succeed upon the points taken on his behalf under the Moneylenders Act 1927, then the second defendant is entitled to refuse to deliver up the deeds, subject to the alternative claim advanced by the plaintiffs. On the other hand, it is agreed that if the plaintiffs are right upon the two points taken under the Act on behalf of the first defendant, then the H

A second defendant cannot retain the deeds any longer; he must fulfil his undertaking to the plaintiffs.

This case, like a number of other cases under the Moneylenders Act, is one in which there are no merits of any kind whatever on behalf of the first defendant. He has received £16,500 from the plaintiffs; he has not paid back a pennypiece of it; he is submitting through his counsel to the court that he is relieved from so doing by two matters in respect
B of which it is alleged that the plaintiffs have failed to comply with the Act.

The point which has been taken in arguing the first of these two points arises under section 4 of the Moneylenders Act 1927. That section, under the rubric "Names to be stated on documents issued by moneylenders", contains the following in subsection (3):

> "If a moneylender, for the purposes of his business as such, issues
> C or publishes, or causes to be issued or published, any advertisement, circular or document of any kind whatsoever containing expressions which might reasonably be held to imply that he carries on banking business, he shall on summary conviction be liable to a fine not exceeding £100, and on a second or subsequent conviction, in lieu of or in addition to such a fine as aforesaid, to imprisonment for a term not exceeding three months, or, in the case of a second or subsequent
> D conviction of an offender being a company, to a fine not exceeding £500."

It is clear that by using the two words "Merchant Bankers" upon the cheque and the letter which I have mentioned there was an infringement of that provision. No doubt it follows that if the authorities had wished to do so they might have been able to obtain a conviction of the plaintiffs
E under section 4 (3).

That, however, does not determine the matter. The question is whether the breach of section 4 (3) by the plaintiffs disentitles them to recover the loan of £16,500 which they had made to the first defendant. This raises a point of some difficulty, since it is not altogether easy to reconcile the various sections of this statute which may throw light upon the
F particular problem whether, if section 4 (3) is breached, the contract made by the moneylender with a borrower is unenforceable in law. It is plain that the section does not say so. All it says is that the moneylender, if he does any of these things, may be liable to a fine or, in certain circumstances, to imprisonment not exceeding three months. It does not say he cannot get his money back.

G I have been referred by counsel on both sides, however, to various other sections in this statute in order to help me glean from them some light as to the construction that should be put upon section 4 (3) in the sense of its effect on the entitlement of the moneylender to recover the money lent.

Section 1 of the Act is a section of considerable length and clearly of considerable importance, because it deals with licences which have to
H be taken out by moneylenders, unless of course they are bankers, when they may be exempted from the provisions of the Act of 1927 by section 6 of the Moneylenders Act 1900. That important section contains a provision for penalties in the event of someone infringing those provisions, which penalties are the same as those in section 4 (3). It does not, however, say that somebody acting as a moneylender without having a moneylender's certificate is unable to recover money he has lent in a civil action against the borrower. It is, however, admitted by counsel on both sides

that the law is to that effect, although there seems, curiously enough, to be a paucity of authority upon the matter.

There is a case dealing with the earlier statute, namely *In re Robinson's Settlement, Gant* v. *Hobbs* [1912] 1 Ch. 717; the point there being that not only was the debt gone but that a security taken by the unregistered moneylender could be recovered. The section of the Act of 1900 under which that was decided was not in similar words to the section of the Act of 1927. It was more emphatic in its tone and it was easier to derive from it the conclusion that a contract entered into by somebody who ought to have had a moneylender's licence and did not was unenforceable. It does not, however, follow, as it seems to me, that I should necessarily apply the reasoning in that case, which counsel agree is generally assumed to apply to section 1 of the Act of 1927, to section 4 of that Act. Section 1 seems to me to deal with a much more fundamental matter than does section 4 (3).

The problem becomes more interesting and possibly more obscure when one looks at some of the other sections of the Act of 1927. Section 5, which deals with a subject matter not so far removed from section 4—namely, advertisements by moneylenders—after elaborately saying what moneylenders should not do and what they should do in the field of advertising and so forth, contains in subsection (5) a criminal sanction of imprisonment or fine if its provisions are infringed and, and this is the interesting point, in subsection (6) it provides as follows:

> " Where it is shown that a money-lending transaction was brought about by a contravention of any of the provisions of this section, the transaction shall, notwithstanding that the moneylender was duly licensed under this Act, be illegal, unless the moneylender proves that the contravention occurred without his consent or connivance."

So unless the moneylender could prove the latter, if there were a contravention of the advertising provisions of that section the moneylender could not recover in a civil action the money which he had lent, because the contract would have been made illegal.

So there you have in section 5 two provisions, one dealing with the criminal consequences of failing to comply with the section and the other dealing with the consequences at civil law of failing to comply with the section. If that can be done, as it was done in section 5, it is asked rhetorically by Mr. Rylance on behalf of the plaintiffs why the legislature did not have a comparable provision in section 4 if that was its intention.

The matter does not altogether end there, because there are other sections to which I was referred. Section 6 deals with the form of moneylenders' contracts. This is a very important section and has perhaps given rise to more litigation than any other section of this Act. Subsection (1) provides that

> " No contract for the repayment by a borrower of money lent to him or to any agent on his behalf by a moneylender . . . and no security given by the borrower or by any such agent as aforesaid in respect of any such contract shall be enforceable, unless a note or memorandum in writing of the contract be made and signed personally by the borrower . . ."

and so forth. There you have a clear provision as to the effect in civil law, as distinct from criminal law, of failing to comply with a provision of this statute. The same applies to section 7 in relation to the prohibition

A for charging compound interest and, although not completely true of section 8, the same is very nearly true of that section.

Section 8 deals with the obligation of the moneylender to supply information as to the state of the loan to the borrower and copies of documents in relation thereto if asked to produce them. Subsection (3) says:

> "If a moneylender to whom a demand has been made under this
> B section fails without reasonable excuse to comply therewith within one month after the demand has been made, he shall not, so long as the default continues, be entitled to sue for or recover any sum due under the contract on account either of principal or interest, and interest shall not be chargeable in respect of the period of the default . . ."

C So far that subsection is dealing with the consequences in civil law of a failure by a moneylender to comply with its provisions. It then continues, somewhat mysteriously:

> ". . . and if such default is made or continued after proceedings have ceased to lie . . ." which means after civil proceedings have been barred owing to lapse of time by section 13 ". . . in respect
> D of the loan, the moneylender shall be liable on summary conviction to a fine not exceeding £5 for every day on which the default continues."

In other words, section 8 (3) is a mixed one unparalleled in the statute, but the contrast is clear, that the draftsman there directed his mind both to the consequences in civil law and to the consequences in criminal law of an infringement of the provisions of the section.

E Section 10 as well as section 12 have express provisions dealing with the consequences in civil law of failing to comply with certain provisions of the statute.

The point is a short one. There is no direct authority on it. The only well-known textbook on the Moneylenders Act, *Meston on Moneylenders*, 5th ed. (1968), refers to the point very briefly on p. 145 where
F it says:

> "Finally, it will be noted that no civil, but only criminal penalties attach to a moneylender, or moneylending company, who acts in contravention of section 4 of the Act of 1927."

It may be said, as Mr. Payne said, that this is a glimpse of the obvious, but one somehow feels that if the very experienced author of that book
G thought that infringement of section 4 might be argued to invalidate the loan, he would have given in his book some treatment to that subject.

I take the view that there is no reason in law why I should add to the express provisions of section 4 (3), either expressly or otherwise, a consequence that the contract of loan should be unenforceable when the subsection is breached. This can be expressed by the Latin tag, if it is
H desired to use a Latin tag, expressio unius est exclusio alterius. It can perhaps more forcibly be said that section 4 (3) is somewhat on the periphery of the provisions of this statute, inasmuch as it plainly is not in any way as important as section 1. The other matter which points in the same direction, apart from the needs of justice which should not be overlooked in these cases, is the language of section 5 in subsections (5) and (6) which deal separately with the consequences in criminal law and in civil law of a breach of subsections (1) to (4).

I now pass to the second point. This arises in the following way. A
Section 6 (2) of the statute reads:

"The note or memorandum aforesaid shall contain all the terms of the contract, and in particular shall show the date on which the loan is made, the amount of the principal of the loan, and, either the interest charged on the loan expressed in terms of a rate per cent per annum, or the rate per cent per annum represented by the interest B
charged as calculated in accordance with the provisions of Schedule 1 to this Act."

I have read the relevant clause in the loan agreement, and the words at the beginning of the clause are: "Interest shall be calculated at the true rate of 23 per cent on the balance of the principal sum . . ." It will be noted that the words do not include "per annum." It is said that the C
absence of the words "per annum" after "23 per cent" has the consequence that the first defendant can retain £16,500 and snap his fingers at the plaintiffs by reason only of the absence of those two words.

It is true that the courts have in a number of cases had to apply the provisions of section 6 (2) in circumstances in which there have been no merits whatever on the part of the borrower of the money and where the moneylender has acted in a perfectly honest and straightforward way D
and has not infringed any of the other provisions in the statute but has made a slight mistake, for example, in arithmetic. In view of that long line of cases, it may be a matter for rejoicing that the Moneylenders Acts will be repealed when a certain section of the recently passed Consumer Credit Act 1974 comes into effect. For the moment they still remain the law and are applicable to the present case. E

The problem I have to determine is, first of all, whether it can be said that the words in clause 4 of this memorandum of loan fail to comply with section 6 (2); secondly, and alternatively perhaps, if they do, whether I can disregard that non-compliance as falling within what has been called in some of the cases "the doctrine of triviality".

In my opinion, if there were no question of the Act applying here at F
all and someone who had never acted as a moneylender before, and therefore was not within the purview of the Act and did not carry on the business of a moneylender, lent £16,500 to a friend of his on terms as to interest contained in clause 4 of this agreement and his friend did not repay the money, then the lender could bring proceedings under R.S.C. Ord. 14 against his friend for the recovery of the money and there would G
not be the slightest doubt whatever that interest would be calculated on the principal sum at 23 per cent. per annum. In the context in which this phrase appears, ". . . the true rate of 23 per cent. on the balance of the principal sum from time to time outstanding . . ." and so forth, I need not reread the whole of that condition, it seems to me to be unambiguous in its meaning; and if it is unambiguous in its meaning, it means that H
it contains an expression in terms of the rate per cent. of the interest charged on the loan and a rate per cent. per annum of that interest, and I would be prepared to decide this particular matter on that reasoning alone. On the other hand, I may be wrong on that and I think the same conclusion could be arrived at by applying what has been called, rather curiously, "the doctrine of triviality".

In *Temperance Loan Fund Ltd.* v. *Rose* [1932] 2 K.B. 522, 526 Scrutton

A L.J. said that in some of the cases that had come before the courts under the Moneylenders Act the point had arisen whether clerical mistakes in the memorandum of the terms of the contract of loan made it insufficient. He then referred to the headnote in *Gaskell* v. *Askwith* (1929) 45 T.L.R. 439, 566, which said that if the memorandum

> " states the date of the loan incorrectly, the contract is unenforceable,
> B even although the inaccuracy has caused no deception and is due merely to a clerical error."

This, according to Scrutton L.J., did not in his opinion correctly state the effect of the decision in that case. His judgment continues, at p. 526:

> " I find nothing in the judgment of Humphreys J. which supports the latter part of the headnote, nor is there anything in the judgment
> C of this court as reported about a clerical error. The Court of Appeal has apparently no power to amend the memorandum, but I do not wish it to be taken that a clerical error will necessarily invalidate it; in each case it must depend upon the nature of the error."

Then he said that *Gaskell* v. *Askwith* was not a case of clerical error.

The principle, therefore, is clear enough. It was referred to by Farwell J.
D in *In re A Debtor* [1938] Ch. 645. The case was one in which there was a failure to comply literally with the ipsissima verba of section 2 (2) of the Act. Farwell J. said, at p. 651:

> " A large number of authorities have been referred to, the effect of which in my judgment is that an error in a memorandum will not necessarily invalidate it or make it a non-compliance with the Act
> E if it is of such a trivial nature that it does not affect the true obligation or position of the borrower. On the other hand, the provision in the Act for a memorandum was intended for the debtor's protection, to enable him to know exactly what the terms of the loan were: and if the memorandum does not disclose the true terms so that the debtor is in any way prejudiced, then the memorandum is insufficient.
> F If, however, notwithstanding the error, the true terms of the contract can be readily understood from the memorandum, then the error is not sufficient to invalidate it, and the only question here is, is this failure to state the true facts sufficiently serious to prevent the memorandum from being a compliance with the Act?"

In the present case, for reasons which I have given, I do not think when
G one looks at the memorandum that there is any doubt whatever as to the meaning of the true terms of the contract. Quite apart from a matter of common sense and one's familiarity with the English language, I derive some further support for that view from the case which Mr. Rylance referred me to of *Parkfield Trust Ltd.* v. *Curtis* [1934] 1 K.B. 685, and in particular from the judgment of Slesser L.J., at p. 693, where he twice used the phrase " true rate of interest " without adding " per annum,"
H clearly meaning that the reference was to a rate of interest per annum. The same common sense, very familiar, and wholly unambiguous use of the English language is exemplified in a passage from another judgment by Slesser L.J. in *Mason and Wood Ltd.* v. *Greene* [1936] 2 K.B. 370, 377–378. Finally, in a more recent case, *Askinex Ltd.* v. *Green* [1969] 1 Q.B. 272, 281, 282, there are references by Lord Denning M.R. to a similar effect. At the bottom of p. 282 Lord Denning M.R. deals with a specific numerical

rate of interest per cent. but leaves out the words "per annum" because they really went without saying. A

Accordingly, I have reached the conclusion that on each of these points the defendants are wrong and the plaintiffs are right, and the plaintiffs are therefore entitled to recover.

A third point, as I have already mentioned, was advanced in the alternative on behalf of the plaintiffs, should they have proved unsuccessful on the two main points. That third point, if they were right on it, would B enable them to salvage at least £3,500 out of the £16,500 which they lent. The point, however, raises some points of law of considerable difficulty. Moreover, some of those points affect a branch of the law with which I do not claim to have any great familiarity, and I think that it would be a mistake for me to express an opinion upon this aspect of the case when it is unnecessary for me to do so. I can, however, very shortly state what C the point is.

It is claimed, as appears from the amended statement of claim to which I have already made reference, that the plaintiffs claim to be entitled as equitable assignees of the mortgage to Barclays Bank Ltd. I was referred to a long line of authorities dealing with the doctrine of subrogation as applied in this field, where someone discharges a mortgage of another person, either in whole or in part, and thereby steps into the shoes of the D mortgagee. It was argued on behalf of the plaintiffs that that line of authorities covered the case, and I was referred in particular to a very recent example of that line of authorities, namely the decision of Whitford J. in *Coptic Ltd.* v. *Bailey* [1972] Ch. 446. As against this, it was argued very ably by Mr. Payne, with all due respect to Whitford J., that that decision, in so far as it dealt with this matter, was fallacious. The majority E of the judgment in the case dealt with another point, on which the decision has not been followed by Walton J. in a more recent case.*

The point in a nutshell advanced by Mr. Payne is that the mortgage to Barclays Bank Ltd. was a legal mortgage and not an equitable mortgage, and the land was unregistered land. Section 115 (1) of the Law of Property Act 1925 provides that if a receipt is endorsed upon a mortgage for all F the money secured by the mortgage, stating the name of the person paying the money, and this is executed by the chargee, the mortgage is effectively discharged. It has the effect of a re-conveyance to the extent of the interest which is the subject matter of the mortgage to the person who immediately before the execution of the receipt is entitled to the equity of redemption. It is said, therefore, by Mr. Payne, that the plaintiffs could not step into the shoes of Barclays Bank Ltd.; the mortgage had come to an end. G Although in certain circumstances it may be possible for the old cases dealing with persons paying off mortgages in whole or in part becoming equitable assignees of the mortgages in consequence of such payments to apply, that is not possible in a case within the provisions of section 115 (1) of the Law of Property Act. He reinforced this argument by pointing out the difficulties that might arise in the case of subsequent sales of the H property concerned if, despite the production to a would-be purchaser of a mortgage containing a receipt endorsed upon it complying completely with the terms of section 115 (1), there was nevertheless an equitable mortgagee in existence with some claim to the property.

* *Burston Finance Ltd.* v. *Speirway Ltd.* [1974] 1 W.L.R. 1648; [1974] 3 All E.R. 735.

A I do not express, as I have indicated already, any opinion upon this matter. Plainly it raises a subject of considerable and somewhat far-reaching importance and it is best dealt with only if it has to be dealt with as a matter of decision in a case. Accordingly, the plaintiffs are entitled to succeed in this action.

Judgment for the plaintiffs with costs.

B

Solicitors: *Coward Chance; Malcolm Brookes & Co.*

C

[FAMILY DIVISION]

* GENGLER *v.* GENGLER

1975 Nov. 3 — Sir George Baker P. and Latey J.

D

Husband and Wife—Justices—Maintenance—Quantum—Basis of assessment

Justices in considering the amount of maintenance to be paid to a wife, whose marriage had subsisted for more than a short period, should follow the practice of the Family Division and should approach the matter on the basis that the wife should have one third of the parties' joint income but, in
E assessing the joint income, they should take the husband's gross income and the wife's net income. Consideration should also be given to the reduction in the standard of living that the wife had suffered on the breakdown of the marriage and, particularly so, where the wife had to work when she would not reasonably have been expected to do so if the marriage had continued.

Where, therefore, a husband appealed against the refusal of the justices to vary a maintenance order of £6 a week and
F applied for leave to appeal against the original order:—

Held, allowing the appeal and refusing the application, that the maintenance order would be reduced to £3 a week.

Wachtel v. *Wachtel* [1973] Fam. 72, C.A. and *Attwood* v. *Attwood* [1968] P. 591, D.C. applied.

The following cases are referred to in the judgment:

G *Attwood* v. *Attwood* [1968] P. 591; [1968] 3 W.L.R. 338; [1968] 3 All E.R. 385, D.C.

Graves v. *Graves* (1973) 117 S.J. 679, D.C.

Jones v. *Jones* (1929) 142 L.T. 167, D.C.

Wachtel v. *Wachtel* [1973] Fam. 72; [1973] 2 W.L.R. 366; [1973] 1 All E.R. 829, C.A.

Ward v. *Ward* [1948] P. 62; [1947] 2 All E.R. 713, D.C.

H

No additional cases were cited in argument.

APPEAL from West Yorkshire justices sitting at Todmorden.

The parties were married on December 24, 1971. In 1975 the wife, Marilyn Gengler, complained to the justices of the husband's adultery and desertion. On February 10, 1975, the husband, Jeffrey Gengler, admitted the complaints. The justices made an order requiring the husband to pay the weekly sum of £6 for the maintenance of the wife. On June 16, 1975, the justices dismissed the husband's application to vary the order.

The husband appealed on the ground that the justices were wrong in law in assessing the periodical payments of maintenance as high as £6 a week on the grounds that the parties were married on December 24, 1971, and finally parted in December 1974; that there were no children of the family; that the husband was 23 years of age and the wife was 22 years of age and both were in full employment; and that the justices assessed the periodical payments of maintenance by calculating the amounts on the basis of the net earnings of each of the parties and not by reference to the gross earnings. Further the justices failed to consider that the wife was entitled to about one third of the total gross income of the parties.

The facts are stated in the judgment of Sir George Baker P.

David Mitchell for the husband.

The wife did not appear and was not represented.

SIR GEORGE BAKER P. This is another of the many appeals that we have by husbands who seek to reduce the matrimonial order made by justices to a nominal order on the basic ground that it was a short marriage, and on the secondary ground that the wife is working and earning, in relation to the husband, a fairly substantial wage.

These cases vary considerably on their facts and indeed in their results. The parties here were married on December 24, 1971. There is no child. They parted in December 1974. The husband was found to have deserted the wife and he had committed adultery with another woman. So there was a marriage at that point of three years' duration. The justices heard the wife's complaints on February 10, 1975. Desertion and adultery were admitted. The husband was not represented and an order of £6 a week was made.

The husband applied for a variation of that order on June 16, 1975, and that complaint by him was rejected. He now appeals against both the original order of £6 a week and the rejection of his application to vary. Leave is required in respect of the first appeal. It was in my view quite proper to have the matter fully before this court, but I think the simplest way—it is a matter of technicalities—is to refuse leave to appeal against the first order, and deal with this on the rejection of his complaint to vary.

Now, I do not think, for myself, that this can properly be classed as a short marriage. Of course, it was not a very long marriage. I am not seeking to lay down what is short, what is not very short, what is not very long, and what is long; that would be trying to define the length of a piece of string. But it is, I think, to be noted that at the time, or just about the time of the parting, the three years had elapsed within which the wife could not have brought a divorce petition unless on the ground of exceptional depravity or exceptional hardship. So, from the end of 1974 she has been, if she wished, in a position to seek a divorce. As Latey J. has pointed out, there is no compulsion on her to do so. She is entitled to stay as she is, although her husband is living with another woman. But what I think would be unfortunate is, that if she chooses to take that course, she should, by so choosing, be able to keep herself in a better position than she would be if she took divorce proceedings and had to

A rely on periodical payments rather than the justices' order. On all the
facts of this case, it seems to be that in divorce proceedings she would
be unlikely to get more than a small order or possibly only a nominal
order.

Now the approach in divorce proceedings is that which was approved
in *Wachtel* v. *Wachtel* [1973] Fam. 72 by the Court of Appeal, one
starts with the wife having one third of the joint incomes less her own
B earnings. I need not go into the old cases of *Ward* v. *Ward* [1948] P. 62
and *Jones* v. *Jones* (1930) 142 L.T. 167. Social conditions, and the
financial and other status of wives and women have greatly changed since
those days. This court has already said, and I repeat, that there is no
reason, in my opinion, why justices should not start with the one third
approach.

C Mr. Mitchell realistically agrees that the joint income is the husband's
gross income and the wife's net income. That is the correct approach.
One takes the husband's gross income, that is his income before tax
because the maintenance order is deducted from his wage or salary before
tax is calculated, and the wife's net income because that is all she receives
to live on after tax is deducted from her wage or salary. Allowable deduc-
tions from a husband's gross earnings are the statutory insurance
D contributions and travelling expenses to work.

Now, if they had done so in the present case, the result would be as
follows: The husband has £36 a week gross. The wife has £21 or £22
a week net. The joint income is therefore £57. One third of £57 is £19
and, as the wife is taking home £21, she would, on a strict one-third
approach, have only a nominal order. But there are two other factors
E which must, in this type of case, be taken into account. The first is that
where a marriage breaks, and particularly where it breaks in circumstances
other than a consensual parting, the wife will almost inevitably suffer a
reduction in her standard of living. Furthermore, the court need not,
as the justices well realised and accurately said, bring into account all
the wife's earnings. That is the eighth consideration stated in *Attwood* v.
Attwood [1968] P. 591, 596, a decision of this court to which I was a
F party with Sir Jocelyn Simon P. Mr. Mitchell ingenuously argues that this
consideration applies only when a wife has taken up employment in
consequence of the breakdown of the marriage, and inevitably of course
the breakdown must have been brought about by the husband's matri-
monial offence when the wife obtains an order in the magistrates' court.
I do not accept that argument. The ninth consideration in *Attwood* v.
G *Attwood* is as follows:

> "This consideration [that is the ninth] is particularly potent where
> the wife only takes up employment in consequence of the disruption
> of the marriage by the husband, or where she would not reasonably
> be expected to be working if the marriage has not been so disrupted."

It is to be noted that nowhere is it said that if the wife has been working
H during the marriage, as this lady had, the full amount of her earnings
are to be brought into account. The reason, I think, is perfectly clear,
because in any such circumstances where the disruption has been brought
about and the matrimonial offence has been proved, the wife is inevitably,
or almost inevitably, going to suffer loss.

There are cases, (of which the "bread ticket for life" case was one)
in which it is clear that the wife has not suffered in any way, either because
the marriage has been extremely short, or for some other reason so it would

be wrong, unjust to the husband and inequitable, to make anything other A than a nominal order: see *Graves* v. *Graves* (1973) 117 S.J. 679.

In the present case, although the one-third approach would give a nominal order and no more, and although I bear in mind what has been said about the joint expenses given in the figures in the first hearing, I think that the wife here, on her present expenses, which come to £23·25 a week, (that is after deduction of legal aid, which we take it has now been paid) is out of pocket on her own earnings unless something is B brought in by way of maintenance. True her car is £6 a week and that seems high, but there is no finding that it is unnecessarily high, and I think she should be taken as a woman who has to spend £23·25 a week to keep up anything like her standards. So earning £21 to £22, she is nearly a couple of pounds out of pocket. Having regard to the eighth and ninth considerations in *Attwood* v. *Attwood* [1968] P. 591, 596, I C think, trying to approach this matter realistically on the facts of this case, if she were from now on to have £3 a week, she will have had the £6 a week, to date to cover all the disruption of the marriage and her consequent inevitable financial loss, which I do not think can be properly, as we suggested, set against the £1,400 which she has had from the house. That was a special entitlement. I think justice will be done if we reduce the order from today to £3 a week and allow the appeal on the variation D proceedings to that extent.

LATEY J. I entirely agree and will only add something for myself in case it may be of help. The social and economic world which existed in 1947 when *Ward* v. *Ward* [1948] P. 62 was decided was a very different one to that which exists now, from the point of view of nearly all men E and women and husbands and wives. So too was the very limited jurisdiction of the magistrates' courts—limited, that is to say, in its financial powers, which have been very greatly enlarged since.

I entirely and respectfully agree with what Sir George Baker P. has said about the one third calculation being a fair and useful starting point in proceedings in the magistrates' court, as it is in proceedings in this division. It is to be remembered that it is only a starting point. It may, and often F does, end up also as the finishing point. But in many cases it does not. Taking into account the various factors which are enumerated in *Attwood* v. *Attwood* [1958] P. 591 and applying them to the particular facts of a particular case, both the facts and the results are likely to vary one from the other. Approaching this case in that way, on its facts, I entirely agree with the order which Sir George Baker P. has stated. G

Appeal allowed.
No order for costs.

Solicitor: *J. Kendal Lindley, Todmorden.*

H

A [COURT OF APPEAL]

* HARRIS *v.* BIRKENHEAD CORPORATION AND ANOTHER

PASCOE AND ANOTHER THIRD PARTY

B
ALLIANCE ASSURANCE CO. LTD. FOURTH PARTY

[1970 H. No. 278]

1975 Nov. 10, 11, 12 — Megaw, Lawton and Ormrod L.JJ.

C *Occupiers' Liability—Occupation—Compulsory purchase order—Local authority serving notice to treat and notice of entry on owner of house—House vacated and damaged by vandals—Child trespasser injured—Whether local authority or owner in occupation—Right of control—Whether local authority having knowledge of danger—Occupiers' Liability Act* 1957 (5 & 6 *Eliz.* 2, *c.* 31), *s.* 2

A corporation had a programme of slum clearance and,
D between compulsory acquisition of properties and their demolition prior to building new houses, it was their practice to brick up all ground floor openings and cut off the water supply to prevent the properties from being damaged by mischievous children and vandals. In furtherance of that slum clearance programme, the corporation made a compulsory purchase order for an area which included a house owned by the second defendant, managed for her by estate agents
E and occupied by an excellent tenant. On July 31, 1967, the corporation served on the second defendant a notice to treat and a notice of entry. A notice of entry was also served on the tenant. It stated that the corporation would enter the property 14 days from the date of service but it was accompanied by a letter which stated that the corporation required vacant possession and would offer the tenant accommodation. The tenant informed both the corporation
F and the estate agents that she would make her own arrangements and would soon move. She moved from the house by December 23 and, at that time, the property was in good condition.

By March 6, 1968, when the plaintiff, aged 4, wandered from a playground into the house, the corporation had not bricked it up and vandals had broken down the front door and done considerable damage including removing the glass
G from a second floor window. The plaintiff fell 30 feet from that window with the result that she suffered severe brain damage. She brought an action for damages against the corporation and the second defendant claiming that they were in breach of the duty owed to her under the Occupiers' Liability Act 1957. The judge held that the corporation, and not the second defendant, was the occupier for the purpose of the Act and, since the corporation knew of the likelihood
H of empty property in the area being damaged and children playing there and the plaintiff's action was one that a humane person exercising common sense could have expected or prevented, the corporation was liable for the injuries she received.

On appeal by the corporation:—

[Reported by S. O. OSUNKOYA, ESQ., Barrister-at-Law]

Held, dismissing the appeal, (1) that, since the corporation by the notice to treat was asserting its right to enter and control the property after the expiration of 14 days and had continued to assert that right at any time it considered fit, the corporation, having the immediate right of control, became the occupier of the property as soon as it ceased to be physically occupied by the tenant (post, pp. 287E–F, 291C, 292B–C). A

Dictum of Lord Denning in *Wheat* v. *E. Lacon & Co. Ltd.* [1966] A.C. 552, 578, H.L.(E.) applied. B

Per Megaw L.J. There was no duty owed to the corporation by the owner or the tenant of the house to give the corporation notice that they were leaving the house empty for the corporation to enter and control the property (post, p. 287F–G).

(2) That the circumstances were such that if the corporation, as occupier, had known that the house was empty, it was under a duty to protect the infant plaintiff from the danger of trespassing in the property; that, since the tenant had informed an officer of the corporation that at some time she would be moving from the house and other officers, having the duty to secure empty houses in the clearance area against vandals, must have observed that the house was empty, the corporation ought to have known that the house was empty and, accordingly, it had the requisite knowledge to make it liable to the plaintiff for the injuries she had received (post, pp. 289D–F, 290F—291A, H—292B). C D

Herrington v. *British Railways Board* [1972] A.C. 877, H.L.(E.) applied.

Decision of Kilner Brown J. [1975] 1 W.L.R. 379; [1975] 1 All E.R. 1001 affirmed.

The following cases are referred to in the judgments: E

Herrington v. *British Railways Board* [1972] A.C. 877; [1972] 2 W.L.R. 537; [1972] 1 All E.R. 749, H.L.(E.).

Wheat v. *E. Lacon & Co. Ltd.* [1966] A.C. 552; [1966] 2 W.L.R. 581; [1966] 1 All E.R. 582, H.L.(E.).

No additional cases were cited in argument. F

APPEAL from Kilner Brown J.

The infant plaintiff, Julie Harris, brought an action by her next friend against the first defendant, Birkenhead Corporation, and the second defendant, Jessie Kathleen Gledhill, as the occupiers for the purpose of the Occupiers' Liability Act 1957 of a house, 239, Price Street, Birkenhead, for damages for personal injuries she had received at the age of 4½ on March 6, 1968, when she fell from the second floor window of that house. The house was situated in a clearance area and was the subject of a compulsory purchase order made by the corporation. It had been empty since December 1967, when the tenant of the second defendant, the owner of the property, had moved to another house. No steps had been taken by the corporation to brick up the property and it had been damaged by vandals. Third party proceedings were brought against Eric Matthew Pascoe and Douglas McNeill Carson, as partners of a firm of estate agents, Bailey & Neep, who managed the property on behalf of the second defendant. They in turn joined their insurers as fourth party, Alliance Assurance Co. Ltd. G H

Kilner Brown J. heard the action in Liverpool and, on December 16, 1974, gave judgment for the plaintiff against the corporation as occupier

A of the premises. The corporation appealed on the grounds, inter alia, that the judge was wrong to hold that on the date of the accident the property and in particular the upper window thereof amounted to a potentially dangerous situation against which any humane and common sense person would have taken precautions; that the judge was wrong to hold that the corporation had knowledge before the date of the accident
B of facts which ought to have led it to anticipate the occurrence of an accident of the general nature of the accident which in fact occurred; that, if the property amounted to a potentially dangerous situation against which any humane and common sense person would have taken precautions, the judge was wrong to hold that the corporation had notice of the condition of the property before the date of the accident; and that the judge was wrong to hold the corporation was the occupier and in control
C of the property on the date of the accident.

The plaintiff and the second defendant cross-appealed on grounds which only became relevant if the Court of Appeal found that the corporation was not liable to the plaintiff.

The facts are stated in the judgment of Megaw L.J.

D *Michael Morland Q.C.* and *Charles James* for the appellant corporation.
Gerald Crowe Q.C. and *David Clarke* for the plaintiff.
Gerard Wright Q.C. and *Michael Byrne* for the second defendant.

MEGAW L.J. The infant plaintiff, Julie Harris, was $4\frac{1}{2}$ years old when, on March 6, 1968, she fell from a second-storey window of a derelict house, 239, Price Street, Birkenhead. She was very seriously injured.
E She, through her next friend, brought an action against Birkenhead Corporation as the first defendants; and against Mrs. Jessie Kathleen Gledhill as second defendant. Two third parties and a fourth party were added to the proceedings.

The action was tried before Kilner Brown J. at Liverpool. On December 16, 1974, he gave judgment for the plaintiff against the corporation for
F £20,000. That was the amount which had been agreed by all parties concerned to be the proper sum of damages on the assumption that any party was held to be liable. The judge gave judgment for the second defendant against the plaintiff with costs, but he directed that those costs should be paid by the corporation. The judge's formal judgment also contained provisions as to the third party and fourth party proceedings with which we are not concerned.

G The corporation appeal. They contend that the judge was wrong to hold them liable. There is a cross-appeal by the plaintiff, contending that, if the corporation's appeal should succeed, then the plaintiff, contrary to the judge's decision, should have judgment for £20,000 against the second defendant. There is also an amended notice of cross-appeal on behalf of the second defendant to which in the circumstances it is unnecessary to
H refer.

The facts relating to this tragic accident are set out in the judgment of Kilner Brown J. [1975] 1 W.L.R. 379. On one matter of evidence, counsel for the corporation criticises the judge's finding. I shall refer to that point later. In other respects, no criticism is made of the judge's findings; and the facts are substantially undisputed. I shall, however, summarise what appear to me to be the facts which are relevant for the purpose of this appeal.

The plaintiff lived with her mother at 157, Beckwith Street, Birkenhead. A Almost opposite the house was a children's playground, Victoria Court. On the afternoon of March 6, 1968, the little girl's mother took her to the playground. The plaintiff and another small girl wandered away from the playground. They made their way along Moreton Street, which is a designated children's play street. At the end of Moreton Street they entered the house 239, Price Street, the front door of which is in fact in Moreton Street at the corner with Price Street. B The door was open or broken down. The whole house was in a derelict condition, with broken windows. The two little girls made their way up the stairs to a room on the second floor. The plaintiff must have climbed on to the window-sill, which was only about two feet above the floor of the room. The window was open, or the glass broken, or both. The plaintiff fell from the window-sill to the ground below, some 30 feet. These facts are by way of reason- C able reconstruction of what must have happened. No one, so far as I know, noticed the children entering the house. But the fall from the window was seen by a passer-by.

It is accepted on all sides that the plaintiff must, in law, be regarded as a trespasser in the house at the time of her accident. On her behalf it was sought to establish that either the corporation, or the second defendant D Mrs. Gledhill, or both, was or were in law to be treated as the occupier or occupiers of 239, Price Street at the time of the accident; and that, being an occupier, the corporation or Mrs. Gledhill, or both, was or were in breach of a duty owed to the trespassing infant plaintiff.

How had the house come to be in this ruinous condition, unsecured? What was the basis on which it was sought to make the corporation, or Mrs. Gledhill, liable? What was the connection of each of them, respec- E tively, with the ruinous 239, Price Street, which might involve the status of occupier at the time of the accident?

Mrs. Gledhill had become the owner of the house in 1956. She had employed a firm of estate agents, Messrs. Bailey & Neep, to manage the property on her behalf. They were responsible to her, presumably for finding tenants, and for collecting the rents, and having necessary repairs F carried out. For some time—I do not think it matters how long—before July 1969, Mrs. Gledhill's tenant in 239, Price Street had been a Mrs. Redmond. She was a good and careful tenant. Until the end of 1967, when Mrs. Redmond left and the house became empty, 239, Price Street had been kept in very good condition, despite what had been happening to property round about.

G Much of the property in Price Street and neighbouring streets had fallen into decay. In 1966 the corporation decided to make a compulsory purchase order under section 43 of the Housing Act 1957. Section 43 is in Part III of the Act, which is concerned with clearance and redevelopment. The order, made on August 26, 1966, and confirmed by the Minister on May 15, 1967, was known as the County Borough of Birkenhead (Cottage Street Clearance Area) Compulsory Purchase Order 1966. H It covered buildings in a substantial area, including Cottage Street, at least a part of Price Street, and some neighbouring streets and alleys. The Minister's confirmation of the order involved an amendment which took 239, Price Street outside the clearance area. That house was still covered by the order, and was subject to compulsory purchase, but was not on the basis that it itself was unfit for habitation. As I have said, it had been kept in good condition. Nevertheless, with the rest of the neighbourhood,

A it was to be compulsorily purchased so that the whole area might be used for building blocks of flats.

On July 3, 1967, the corporation served on Mrs. Gledhill a notice to treat and, at the same time, a notice of entry in respect of 239, Price Street. On the same date a notice of entry in the same terms was served on Mrs. Redmond, the tenant. A covering letter, in substantially similar terms, was sent to each of these ladies by the corporation. Nothing turns on B the terms of the notice to treat. It was a necessary preliminary step towards the assessment of compensation for the compulsory purchase. The terms of the notice of entry are important. It is headed "The Housing Act 1957." It is further headed "Notice of Intention to Enter." It is addressed to Mrs. Gledhill. A corresponding notice, of the same date, was sent to the tenant: it was addressed to "The occupier." There are C two recitals, the first of which recites the order made on August 26, 1966, and confirmed by the Minister of Housing. (It would seem that the wrong date was given for that confirmation; but nothing turns on that.) The second recital says: "Notice to treat for the said property was served upon the owners of the said property on July 3, 1967." It then said:

> "Now therefore the council in exercise of the power conferred upon D them by paragraph 9 of Part 2 of Schedule 3 to the Housing Act 1957 hereby give you notice that they will upon the expiration of 14 days from the service of this notice upon you enter on and take possession of the said property described in the schedule hereto."

As I have said, that notice was dated and served on July 3, 1967. The schedule referred to 239, Price Street.

E So there was, in the clearest terms, an averment that the corporation would, upon the expiration of 14 days from the service of that notice, which is to be taken as having been served on July 3, enter upon and take possession of 239, Price Street, which, of course, involved an assertion by implication of a legal right in the corporation so to do. The purported statutory authority for this notification, peremptory and unambiguous in F its terms, was paragraph 9 of Part 2 of Schedule 3 to the Housing Act 1957. Paragraph 9 had in fact been repealed by section 39 (4) and Schedule 8 to the Compulsory Purchase Act 1965, the commencement date of which, by section 40 thereof, was January 1, 1966. The purported statutory authority no longer existed. But it has, as I understand it, been agreed between the parties that the misstatement in the notice of entry of the purported statutory authority does not matter. It is not suggested that G the misdescription by the corporation of the statutory power matters, since statutory power did exist. For paragraph 9 had, in effect, been replaced by section 11 of the Compulsory Purchase Act 1965. The relevant part of section 11 provides:

> "(1) If the acquiring authority have served notice to treat in respect of any of the land and have served on the owner, lessee and occupier H of that land not less than 14 days notice, the acquiring authority may enter on and take possession of that land, or of such part of that land as is specified in the notice; and then any compensation agreed or awarded for the land of which possession is taken shall carry interest . . ."

There, then, is the statutory authority which, if the conditions as to notices are fulfilled, gives the acquiring authority the right to enter upon the land

and take possession of it, even though compensation has not yet been A
assessed.

It will be observed that in the present case the corporation's notice of entry prescribed the minimum period of 14 days and affirmatively and unequivocally asserted that it would enter and take possession upon the expiration of the 14 days.

The covering letter, also dated July 3, 1967, to which I have referred
was not consistent with the terms of the notice of entry. It begins by B
saying: "You will find enclosed a notice to treat, claim form in triplicate, and notice of entry." The letter continues, in the second part of the second paragraph:

> "The council need to secure vacant possession of the property and one of their officers will call on the occupiers to make arrangements
> for vacant possession to be given and to offer such other accom- C
> modation as there is available to those who qualify for rehousing. While the property remains occupied the notice of entry does not affect present liabilities for rent etc., and rent should be paid by the occupiers and lessees, and collected by landlords in the usual way. The housing manager will arrange for suitable housing accommodation to be offered to those occupiers who were resident in the area at the
> time of the official count and a member of his department will call D
> upon all occupiers in the course of the next few months to ascertain the needs of the various occupiers. I should perhaps mention that the council have power to enforce the notices when vacant possession cannot be arranged by agreement, or offers of other accommodation are refused. The council are usually able to avoid this final recourse
> to their compulsory powers and I hope that, with your co-operation, E
> this will be possible in your case."

So the one document was saying that the corporation was going to exercise its statutory authority to take possession at the end of 14 days, and the other document appears to say that it was not minded to do so until some unspecified, substantially later, date. The documents can,
I think, only be reconciled (if they have to be reconciled) by the assump- F
tion that the corporation is asserting that it will, indeed, be deemed to have taken possession on the expiry of the 14 days, but that, having thus notionally entered and taken possession, as it asserts in the notice of entry, it will continue to allow the occupier to reside there for as long as the corporation sees fit so to allow.

In other circumstances, the apparent discrepancy between the notice G
of entry and the covering letter might give rise to difficulties. In the circumstances of the present case, I do not think that we need take time in contemplating those potential difficulties or in considering whether the possible reconciliation which I have suggested could be correct. I say that because it is conceded, or, it may be, asserted, on behalf of the corporation that, from the expiry of 14 days after the service of that
notice of July 3, 1967, the corporation, despite the terms of the covering H
letter, had the unqualified right to enter on and take possession of 239, Price Street, at any time. The corporation was not, it is said, obliged to take possession at the end of the 14 days: it was entitled to refrain from actually entering into possession for as long as it chose, stretching into infinity, despite the specific terms of the notice. But it could lawfully enter into possession on July 17, 1967, or on any day thereafter, as of right and without a fresh notice or any amendment of the existing notice.

A The corporation did not enter on or take possession of 239, Price Street, until some days after the accident in March 1968.

I continue with the history, I shall have to return to the question of the effect of that notice. Mrs. Redmond, the tenant, continued to live in 239, Price Street for a further five or six months after July 1967. She did not, in the end, wish to be rehoused by the corporation. She found a new place of abode for herself. She left the house 239, Price Street
B on December 20, or perhaps December 23, 1967. She did not specifically inform the corporation or any official of it of, at any rate, the precise prospective date of her departure; nor, after she had left, of the fact that she had left. She did tell Mr. Harrison, who was a rent-collector employed by Messrs. Bailey & Neep, Mrs. Gledhill's agents who managed the property. On December 13, 1967, she gave him a week's notice. He asked
C her to leave the keys at another house, in Vittoria Street, where Mr. Harrison also collected rents on behalf of Messrs. Bailey & Neep. Mrs. Redmond left the keys in the Vittoria Street house. There is no evidence that Mr. Harrison informed anyone that Mrs. Redmond had left; nor, so far as we have been told, was there any evidence as to what happened to the keys.

D I referred earlier to a criticism which has been made on behalf of the corporation of a finding of fact by Kilner Brown J. That arises on the evidence of Mrs. Redmond; and I can conveniently deal with it at this point in the history. Mrs. Redmond's evidence was given by way of a written statement admitted under the Civil Evidence Act 1968. Having told of her dealings with Mr. Harrison, which I have already summarised, she continued, in the second paragraph of her statement:

E "Some weeks before I left 239, Price Street, I went to see Mr. Rhodes in the legal department of the Birkenhead Corporation to tell him that Mrs. Gledhill was the owner of the house and I would be giving notice to leave to the rent collecter, Mr. Harrison. The point of my going to see this gentleman before I left 239, Price Street was to make it quite clear to him that I did not wish to be rehoused by the corporation as my husband and myself were purchasing our own house."
F

In his judgment, Kilner Brown J. said [1975] 1 W.L.R. 379, 382:

"[Mrs. Redmond] called upon Mr. Rhodes. She informed him and she also informed Mr. Harrison, who was employed by Mr. Pascoe of Bailey & Neep to collect rents, that she did not wish to be rehoused, she preferred to make her own arrangements. She would leave just
G before Christmas 1967 and would leave the keys at a house in nearby Vittoria Street . . ."

Again, the judge said, at p. 384:

"Now although Mrs. Redmond was not a tenant of the [corporation] she was seen by the appropriate officer. She notified the appropriate officer that she was making private arrangements and would be leaving
H before Christmas."

The criticism is that the judge was inaccurate because these passages in his judgment suggest that Mrs. Redmond had said that she had told Mr. Rhodes, an official of the corporation, that she would leave before Christmas 1967, and that she would leave the keys at the house in Vittoria Street; whereas in fact Mrs. Redmond's evidence was that she had said those things to Mr. Harrison, but not to Mr. Rhodes or any other repre-

sentative of the corporation. True, she had indicated to Mr. Rhodes that A
she did not require to be rehoused, and that she was going to move out; but she did not specify to him, so it is said, "before Christmas," or any specific date, nor did she claim to have said anything to him regarding the keys. There might—I say no more than that—be some substance in this criticism, if this had been the sole evidence of the corporation's knowledge before the date of the accident that 239, Price Street had been vacated. But, as will appear, and as is indeed indicated in the judge's judgment B
itself, the knowledge of the corporation was shown apart altogether from any inference which might properly be drawn as to what Mrs. Redmond said in her conversation, or conversations, with Mr. Rhodes.

So, to resume the narrative, Mrs. Redmond moved out shortly before Christmas 1967. The house was left empty. The corporation, who on the evidence were well aware that property left vacant in this area was C
promptly attacked by vandals, broken into and made desolate and ruinous, did nothing. It is said on their behalf that they did not know—or perhaps rather that there was no evidence that they did know—that the house was vacant. It was thus that the plaintiff, on March 6, 1968, with her small companion, was able to enter 239, Price Street through an open and unsecured door, and, having gone up the stairs and climbed on to the window-sill of a smashed or open second floor window, to fall to the D
street below.

So far as concerns the corporation's appeal, two questions arise. First, was the corporation the occupier of 239, Price Street at the relevant time, so as to give rise to the possible existence of a duty towards persons who might be in the house, including trespassing children? Secondly, if the corporation was the occupier in that sense, did it, on the facts which E
appeared on the evidence and the inferences to be drawn therefrom, owe, and fail in the discharge of, a duty owed to the infant plaintiff, by reason of the corporation's failure to take any steps to make the house secure against entry by trespassing children?

I turn to the first question. Was the corporation the occupier? It is well-established law that there may be more than one occupier of property, at the same time, for the purposes of occupier's liability: *Wheat* v. F
E. Lacon & Co. Ltd. [1966] A.C. 552. Therefore this is not a case where it is necessarily "either or" as between the corporation and Mrs. Gledhill. Nevertheless, the corporation's submission does include the contention that Mrs. Gledhill at all relevant times continued to be the occupier for the purposes of the existence of a duty towards persons entering the house. The corporation says that it was not the occupier, G
so that no question of a breach of occupier's duty can arise. The occupier, if any, was Mrs. Gledhill. In law, it is contended, she remained the owner, and the occupier. In law, she could have entered into physical possession after Mrs. Redmond left, or could have put a new tenant into possession. There was nothing in the notice to treat or the notice of entry to prevent her lawfully so doing. By the conduct of Mrs. Gledhill's agent, Mr. Harrison, in asking the tenant, Mrs. Redmond, to hand over the keys, H
not to the corporation, but so as to be collected by him (Mr. Harrison), Mrs. Gledhill has shown, notionally, her intent, or the intent of her agent on her behalf, to retain control of the house, and thus to exclude the corporation from control. The corporation, it is said, on the other hand, though it was entitled to take possession at any time, following upon the expiry of the 14 days after the notice of entry, had not done so, and it is contended on behalf of the corporation that unless and until it did so,

A either by sending some representative there to enter upon the premises with
the intention of taking possession, or by carrying out some symbolic
ceremony such as accepting the proffered keys, if they had been proffered,
the corporation was not an occupier. The mere immediate right which it
had by virtue of the statutory authority created by the steps that it had
taken to serve the notices, to enter and to take possession and to use the
house for any purpose—repair or demolition or anything else—is not
B enough, it is said, to make it an occupier for this purpose. It is put as a
matter of law, and it must be dealt with as such. The proposition is that
the actual taking of possession or some symbolic taking of possession is
necessary before one can become an occupier of property for this purpose.

I do not propose to deal with this as a general proposition of law to
a greater extent than is necessary for the decision of this particular case
C on the facts as they appear before us. It may be, though I certainly
would not like to be taken as suggesting that it would be, that there
might be cases in which one who had the immediate right to enter upon
premises would be held not to have become the occupier of those pre-
mises for purposes of liability to someone who came upon the premises,
unless and until he had actually and physically entered into possession.
But, whatever principle might operate in such cases, it could not, in my
D judgment, extend so far as to apply upon the facts of this case: the
facts being that the corporation has lawfully asserted an immediate right
to enter and control, involving the right at any moment of time to dis-
possess the owner and the person occupying the house when the assertion
is made; and when, as a result of that assertion of legal right, the pre-
existing occupier has moved out and the house is empty.

E I say that by reference to the terms of the notice of entry and the
statutory authority upon which it is based. By that notice of entry the
corporation was asserting its right to control this property after the expiry
of the 14 days. And it was asserting the right to exercise that control
at any time thereafter when it saw fit. In my judgment, such an assertion
of a right of control, even though it has not been followed by an actual
or symbolic, or a "deemed," taking of possession, is sufficient, at any rate
F when, as here happened before Christmas 1967, the property ceases to
be physically occupied by any other person, to make the person who
has that immediate right of control the occupier for these purposes. I
do not see why it should be suggested that as between the corporation
and Mrs. Gledhill or her tenant there should be any duty owed by either
of these ladies to the corporation, after the notice of entry in the terms
G which I have cited had been served on them, to give the corporation
notice that they were leaving the house—leaving it to the corporation
who had, and had continued to assert, the right to enter and control it.
But if there was no such duty as between Mrs. Gledhill and the corpora-
tion, how can the corporation's liability to a third party—the infant
plaintiff—be affected or abrogated by the fact that Mrs. Gledhill had not
told the corporation that she was no longer physically in possession of
H the house, by herself or any tenant?

No authority was cited to us by Mr. Morland, on behalf of the cor-
poration, to support his proposition that one who had complete legal
right of control could not be an occupier unless and until he, by himself
or his servants or agents, had actually moved into the occupation of the
property. It is, therefore, something which has to be put as a matter of
general principle. As a matter of general principle, I do not think that
it can stand, at least with the width of operation suggested. I would

refer to the speech of Lord Denning in *Wheat* v. *E. Lacon & Co. Ltd.* [1966] A.C. 552, 578, where he says:

"In *Salmond on Torts*, 14th ed. (1965), p. 372, it is said that an 'occupier' is 'he who has the immediate supervision and control and the power of permitting or prohibiting the entry of other persons.' This definition was adopted by Roxburgh J. in *Hartwell* v. *Grayson, Rollo and Clover Docks Ltd.* [1947] K.B. 901, 917 and by Diplock L.J. in the present case [1966] 1 Q.B. 335, 368. There is no doubt that a person who fulfills that test is an 'occupier.' He is the person who says 'come in.' But I think that test is too narrow by far. There are other people who are 'occupiers,' even though they do not say 'come in.' If a person has any degree of control over the state of the premises it is enough."

Then Lord Denning goes on to consider what he describes as four groups of cases. Without going through them, it appears to me that when one looks at the cases referred to in those four groups it makes it clear that in law the quality of being in physical possession, or having been in actual physical possession, is not in all cases—and is not in this case—a necessary ingredient of the legal status of occupier for the purposes with which we are concerned.

Accordingly, upon the facts of this case, applied to the law as I understand it to be, I take the view that Kilner Brown J. was entirely right in his conclusion that the corporation was to be treated as occupier for the purpose of consideration of liability towards this trespassing plaintiff.

And so I go on to the second question. The corporation being the occupier for that purpose, was the judge right in holding that it was liable for a breach of duty towards the infant plaintiff? It is here, and not in connection with the first question of "occupier or not," that the question of knowledge of the corporation becomes relevant. Our task in this appeal on this second question has, in my view, been rendered substantially simpler by a concession which was made, and as I think rightly and necessarily made upon the evidence, by Mr. Morland for the corporation. In calling our attention to the leading authority on the question of duty to infant trespassers, *Herrington* v. *British Railways Board* [1972] A.C. 877, Mr. Morland very properly read to us, amongst other passages, a passage from the speech of Lord Morris of Borth-y-Gest at p. 909. It is unnecessary for me to restate the well known facts of *Herrington's* case, in which a small child had been killed by coming into contact with an electric rail. Lord Morris of Borth-y-Gest said, in relation to the facts of that case, at p. 909:

"The duty that lay upon the railways board was a limited one. There was no duty to ensure that no trespasser could enter upon the land. And certainly an occupier owes no duty to make his land fit for trespassers to trespass in. Nor need he make surveys of his land in order to decide whether dangers exist of which he is unaware. The general law remains that one who trespasses does so at his peril. But in the present case there were a number of special circumstances—(a) the place where the fence was faulty was near to a public path and public ground; (b) a child might easily pass through the fence; (c) if a child did pass through and go onto the track he would be in grave danger of death or serious bodily harm; (d) a child might not realise the risk involved in touching the live rail or being in a place where a train might pass at speed. Because of

> A these circumstances (all of them well known and obvious) there was, in my view, a duty which, while not amounting to the duty of care which an occupier owes to a visitor, would be a duty to take such steps as common sense or common humanity would dictate: they would be steps calculated to exclude or to warn or otherwise within reasonable and practicable limits to reduce or avert danger."

B Now, Mr. Morland accepted that, mutatis mutandis, the four special circumstances referred to in that passage under the letters (a) to (d) were present as special circumstances on the evidence in the present case, subject to this (from his point of view) vital qualification: that, as he asserted, the corporation had no knowledge, and had no reason to have knowledge, that this particular house had been vacated and had fallen
C into the derelict condition. But, subject to that reservation, Mr. Morland assented to the proposition that these special circumstances were shown on the evidence in this case. So I translate those special circumstances into the words applicable in the present case: (a) the place where the door of 239, Price Street was was near to a public street; (b) a child might easily pass through the door; (c) if a child did pass through and go into the house, he or she would be in grave danger of death or serious
D bodily harm; (d) a child might not realise the risk involved in going into that house.

On the facts of this case, all those matters were duly established on the evidence. On those facts being duly established, subject to the question of knowledge by the corporation of the emptiness and state of the house, there could, in my judgment, be no doubt that the test as laid down in *Herrington's* case for liability of the occupier would be fulfilled.
E Would a humane person, knowing of those facts, have regarded it as something that ought to be done, to take reasonable steps to prevent children from trespassing into that area of danger? It is not suggested that, if it had been known that the house was unoccupied and in this vandalised condition, there would have been any practical difficulty in steps being taken to secure this house against infant trespassers between
F the date when it fell into this ruinous condition by the end of January 1968, and six weeks later on March 6, 1968, when the accident happened.

So I turn to the question whether or not the corporation had knowledge of the fact that the house was empty and of the fact that the house, being so empty, had been treated by vandals in such a way that it had fallen into a ruinous condition. The question, of course, is whether
G they had knowledge by such a time that, acting reasonably, they would have been in a position before the accident happened to take steps to secure the house.

In my judgment, the judge was right in the conclusion which, as I understand it, he reached upon the evidence, that the corporation did have knowledge of those facts. After he had referred, in a passage which
H I have already cited, to the evidence of Mrs. Redmond, a passage which is criticised on behalf of the corporation, the judge concluded the paragraph in this way [1975] 1 W.L.R. 379, 384:

> "In my view [the corporation] were not only possessed of information that it would be available for demolition, but their officer who recorded the necessity for bricking up must through his subordinates have noticed, if they had kept their eyes open as they toured the area, that there was yet another house ready for treatment."

The reference in that passage is to documentary evidence which was A
produced at the trial (because no oral evidence was called on behalf of
the corporation) coming from the corporation's records and no doubt
fairly and accurately produced by the corporation as being relevant in this
case, showing the steps taken to secure various houses in this Cottage
Street clearance area. The record runs from February 6, 1967, to
November 29, 1968: that is the part, at any rate, with which we are
concerned. It shows that between December 29, 1967, and February 6, B
1968, four properties in streets adjacent to Price Street had in fact been
attended to in various ways, with the intention of securing them, they
having ceased to be occupied by reason of things that had happened under
this clearance scheme. It is to that that the judge is referring. It is
apparent that there were officials of the corporation who were taking
steps to see that houses were thus secured as and when they became C
vacant. The judge is saying, as I understand it, that it is a reasonable
inference, on balance of probability, that those persons who had that
responsibility and who would have had a responsibility to report back
to their superiors any other house which they saw in need of the same
treatment, must, in the course of their work in this area for that purpose,
have observed in the weeks before March 6, 1968, that this house, 239,
Price Street, being unoccupied, had fallen into this ruinous condition as D
a result of the operation of vandals.

Mr. Crowe, for the plaintiff, referred us to evidence that had been
given by a lady who lived in a house next door to 239, Price Street, a
Mrs. Cameron, which at any rate on one view of it might be treated as
having been affirmative evidence that officials of the corporation had
come to her house during this period between the end of January and E
the beginning of March 1968. But, for myself, I think that, on the
examination of that evidence made in reply by Mr. Morland this morning,
it would have been unwise for the judge to have placed any substantial
reliance upon that evidence—not because Mrs. Cameron was seeking to
say anything untruthful, but because it was apparent that her state of
memory (not surprisingly) was defective. Nevertheless, there is the infer-
ence to be drawn from the known facts as to what officials of the corpora- F
tion were doing in that area; and, as I see it, there was a further inference
on which the judge was entitled to act from the evidence which had been
given by Mrs. Redmond, to which I have already referred. When that
evidence is taken in its literal terms, it does show (and there was no
contradiction of this) that Mrs. Redmond had, some weeks before Christ-
mas 1967, gone to see an official of the corporation and had told him G
that she did not require corporation rehousing but that she was going to
move out herself. The corporation were therefore put on notice that
this was something that was likely to happen; and I do not think that
it is an unfair inference that what must have been said by Mrs. Redmond
was that it was going to happen somewhere in the very near future. In
those circumstances, again, it would seem that the corporation must have
been put upon the alert with regard to this house. H

Taking the whole of the material, I would find it impossible to say
that the judge was wrong in the conclusion to which he came that the
corporation did know. But even if that were wrong, I should take the
view that the circumstances show that the corporation ought to have
known; and, as I understand the law, in a case of this sort that is
sufficient to create the existence of liability.

So I would reject the contention on behalf of the corporation that they did not know of the facts which would give rise to the existence of this danger. As I say, knowing those facts, there is nothing that has been put forward that would have prevented the taking of precautions which, if they had been taken, would in all human probability have prevented this accident; and the circumstances were such that if the facts were known, as they either were known or ought to have been known, common humanity required that such measures should have been taken.

The only remaining point, as I understand it, put forward by Mr. Morland on behalf of the corporation is that a young child, unsupervised, may always fall out of a window into a street and therefore there is, as it were, no real causative connection here between any failure to board up this particular house and the fact of this child's accident. It is not an argument which I regard, with all respect to Mr. Morland, as being a possible argument. I think that causation here was plainly shown. I would dismiss this appeal.

LAWTON L.J. I agree with the judgment which has just been delivered by Megaw L.J., and have only one short comment to add. In the course of his submissions, Mr. Morland invited the court's attention to a passage in the speech of Lord Diplock in *Herrington* v. *British Railways Board* [1972] A.C. 877, 941, where he said:

> " The duty "—that is, the duty to child trespassers—" does not arise until the occupier has actual knowledge either of the presence of the trespasser upon his land or of facts which make it likely that the trespasser will come on to his land; and has also actual knowledge of facts as to the condition of his land or of activities carried out upon it which are likely to cause personal injury to a trespasser who is unaware of the danger."

In his submissions, Mr. Morland construed the words " actual knowledge " as meaning positive knowledge. For my part, I doubt whether Lord Diplock did intend " actual knowledge " to mean what Mr. Morland submitted it did mean; and for this reason. In many branches of the law, plaintiffs and prosecutors have to prove knowledge. It has long been accepted that a man cannot claim he has no knowledge when he has shut his eyes to the obvious. Nor can he claim that he has no knowledge when he has knowledge of what are sometimes called primary facts and has not drawn the inferences which can reasonably be drawn from those primary facts.

Now, if my understanding of Lord Diplock's words " actual knowledge " is right, then the corporation were in this situation. 239, Price Street, Birkenhead, was in a clearance area. No less than 27 houses in that street and many more houses in adjoining streets were covered by the County Borough of Birkenhead (Cottage Street Clearance Area) Compulsory Purchase Order 1966. Magistrates and judges all over the United Kingdom know that once houses in clearance areas are left unoccupied, vandals, vagrants and other socially difficult persons move in and put those premises into a dangerous condition. It was accepted by Mr. Morland that the Birkenhead Corporation knew what tends to happen in clearance areas. The only point made was that they had no positive knowledge that 239, Price Street had been vacated. But, as Megaw L.J. has pointed out, the evidence established that their officials, charged with safeguarding derelict premises, were moving about this area during the period between the time when it was left unoccupied by Mrs. Redmond and when the infant plaintiff sustained her injuries. Had they looked at all, they would have seen that these premises were empty and derelict and that they required some attention to safeguard children from entering and possibly injuring themselves. It seems to me, therefore, that the knowledge which the corporation were proved to have was the kind of "actual knowledge" which Lord Diplock was envisaging in *Herrington* v. *British Railways Board.* A

B

ORMROD L.J. I agree; and would wish to add very little indeed. The only question on the first part of this case is whether the corporation are properly regarded in law as a person occupying or in control of the premises in which the accident happened. For the reasons which have been given by Megaw L.J. and Lawton L.J., there is, in my judgment, only one possible answer to that question. C They were at all material times the persons with the right to control that property. It would have been almost absurd to suggest that, in the circumstances of this case, the owner, Mrs. Gledhill, could have been expected by the law to go to expense in securing these premises against the damage which was inevitable and was bound to happen to them immediately or very soon after the tenant vacated them. In those circumstances it would be a disastrous injustice to her to hold her liable for this appalling accident; D and I am glad to be able to agree with the judgments which have just been given that this appeal should be dismissed.

Appeal and cross-appeals dismissed with costs, payable by first defendants. E
Legal aid taxation of plaintiff's costs.
Leave to appeal refused.

Solicitors: *Berrymans for Weightmans, Liverpool; Wm. Easton & Sons for Percy Hughes & Roberts, Birkenhead; Byrne, Frodsham & Co., Widnes.*

F

[CHANCERY DIVISION]

* *In re* J. LESLIE ENGINEERS CO. LTD. (IN LIQUIDATION)

G

[No. 001601 of 1970]

1975 Nov. 4, 5; 13 Oliver J.

Company—Winding up—Disposition of property—Cheque cashed by director from company's bank account—Purchase of money orders to pay part of business debt—Remainder paid by cheque H *from director's private bank account—Company's moneys paid into private account without creditors' knowledge—Whether "disposition" of "property of the company"—Companies Act* 1948 (11 & 12 *Geo.* 6, *c.* 38), *s.* 227

A petition to wind up the company was presented on September 14, 1970, and a winding up order was made on December 15. The respondents had done some work for the company in the summer of 1970. Their charges came to

A £1,050, and, without knowing about the presentation of the petition, they were pressing the company for payment. On October 2 the controlling director H made out a "cash" cheque for £250 on the company's bank account. He obtained the cash and bought five money orders of £50 each and sent them to the respondents. On November 5, H sent to the respondents a cheque for £800 drawn on the joint account of himself and his wife at the same bank. The joint account was overdrawn. B H paid a cheque from the company's account to cover the overdraft and the £800 cheque and other cheques which he had issued on the joint account. The respondents presented the cheque without knowing that the company's moneys had been paid into the joint account to create a credit balance so as to meet the cheques. The respondents thought that the cheque was being paid by H and his wife from their own resources. On November 20 the cheque was cashed.

C On a summons by the liquidator for a declaration that the payment of £1,050, having been made since the commencement of the winding up of the company, was void under section 227 of the Companies Act 1948,[1] and for an order that the respondents should pay the £1,050 to the liquidator:—

Held, (1) that, on the true construction of section 227 of the Act of 1948, the term "dispositions" included dispositions of a company's property whether made by the company or D by a third party or whether made directly or indirectly; that the payment of £250 was a void disposition within the section because the bank notes received from the bank were as much the company's property, and identifiable as such, as were the moneys in the account and they were throughout clearly identifiable as the company's property which passed directly from the company's hands into the respondents'; and that it was immaterial that the director took the bank notes E and converted them into money orders (post, p. 297F–H).

(2) That for the purposes of the section "the property of the company" was not the credit balance in the joint account but was the sum total of the rights of the company created by the transactions leading up to the creation of that balance; and that, accordingly, the payment by the bank of the cheque in favour of the respondents was not a disposition of the company's property avoided by the section (post, p. 299D–E).

F (3) That once it was accepted that the respondents were innocent recipients without notice that the account from which they were paid had been fed by a payment of the company's moneys wrongfully procured by its controlling director, there was no principle on which they could be called on to repay (post, p. 299 E–F); that the respondents were not volunteers and the evidence gave rise to an inference that they had used the moneys to pay their own creditors; and that, accordingly, G although the company might be able to trace its funds in the joint account, those funds could not be traced in the hands of the respondents (post, p. 300B–D).

In re Hallett's Estate (1880) 13 Ch.D. 696, C.A. and *In re Diplock* [1948] Ch. 465, C.A. considered.

(4) The invalidation of a disposition of the company's property under section 227 and the recovery of the property disposed of, were two distinct matters (post, p. 298B), that the H section said nothing about recovery, it merely avoided dispositions, gave discretionary power to the court to validate such dispositions and its object was that the creditors should be paid pari passu (post, pp. 298C–D, 304C); that since the payment of the £250 was clearly a preferential payment to validate it simply because the creditor preferred did not know he was being preferred would be to defeat the whole purpose of the section; and that, accordingly, the liquidator was entitled to

[1] Companies Act 1948, s. 227: see post, p. 298B–C.

the declaration sought in respect of the £250 and an order for repayment of that amount (post, p. 304E–G). A

In re Civil Service and General Store Ltd. (1887) 58 L.T. 220 applied.

In re T. W. Construction Ltd. [1954] 1 W.L.R. 540 considered.

The following cases are referred to in the judgment:

Civil Service and General Store Ltd., In re (1887) 58 L.T. 220. B

Diplock, In re [1948] Ch. 465; [1948] 2 All E.R. 318, C.A.

Hallett's Estate, In re (1880) 13 Ch.D. 696, C.A.

London, Hamburg, and Continental Exchange Bank, In re (1866) L.R. 2 Eq. 231.

Taylor v. *Plumer* (1815) 3 M. & S. 562.

T. W. Construction Ltd., In re [1954] 1 W.L.R. 540; [1954] 1 All E.R. 744.

C

The following additional case was cited in argument:

Dalton (A Bankrupt), In re [1963] Ch. 336; [1962] 3 W.L.R. 140; [1962] 2 All E.R. 499.

European Arbitration, In re, National Bank Case (1873) European Arbitration, L.T. 92.

Steane's (Bournemouth) Ltd., In re [1949] W.N. 490; [1950] 1 All E.R. 21.

Wiltshire Iron Co., In re, Ex parte Pearson (1868) 3 Ch.App. 443. D

SUMMONS

On September 14, 1970, a petition to wind up the company, J. Leslie Engineers Co. Ltd., was presented and a winding up order was made on December 15. The liquidator issued a summons against the respondents, C. & D. Greaves & Sons (a firm), seeking a declaration that the payment E to them of £1,050, of which £250 was paid on October 2, 1970, and £800 on November 20, was void under section 227 of the Companies Act 1948.

The summons further sought an order that the respondents should pay to the liquidator the £1,050.

The facts are sufficiently stated in the judgment.

E. C. Evans Lombe for the liquidator. F

Robin Potts for the respondents.

Cur. adv. vult.

November 13. OLIVER J. read the following judgment. This is a liquidator's summons for a declaration that two payments totalling £1,050 paid to the respondents after the commencement of the winding up of the G company were void under the provisions of section 227 of the Companies Act 1948, and for an order for the recovery of those sums from the respondents. The company, J. Leslie Engineers Ltd., was incorporated in 1969 and was at all material times controlled by a Mr. Hadrys, who was a director. On September 14, 1970, a creditor presented a petition to wind up, and that was advertised on September 25. In October 1970 the Inland Revenue Commissioners were substituted as petitioners, the H original petitioner's debt having been paid, and a winding up order was made on December 15, 1970.

The present summons concerns two cheques which were drawn on the company's bank account at Lloyds Bank, Leigh-on-Sea, the first payable to cash for £250 on October 2, 1970, and the second for £800 drawn in favour of Mr. Hadrys on November 17, 1970, and paid into a joint personal account of Mr. Hadrys and his wife at the same bank. Although, as I

A have said, the petition was presented and advertised in September, both
these cheques were, rather surprisingly, honoured by the bank, but I am
not concerned here with any claims against the bank to which this fact
may have given rise. The first cheque was dated October 2, was made out
by Mr. Hadrys to "cash," was signed by him "for J. Leslie Engineers
Co. Ltd." and was encashed on the same day. He seems to have taken
the cash thus obtained straight to the post office and to have purchased
B with it five telegraphic money orders for £50 each in favour of Mr. Dennis
Reginald Greaves. As I understand it, the reason for sending five orders
instead of one was that this minimises the poundage charged by the post
office on the transaction.

The circumstances in which the second cheque was negotiated were
these: Mr. Hadrys and his wife maintained a joint bank account at the
C same bank as that at which the company's account was kept. At the
beginning of November 1970 it was overdrawn. On November 5 Mr. Hadrys
drew a cheque on the joint account in favour of the respondents (named
in the cheque as "C. and D. Grieves (sic) & Son") for £800. Mr. Dennis
Greaves, who gave evidence before me, told me that after this cheque had
been posted to him he received a telephone call from Mr. Hadrys
who told him that it might not be met and instructed him, if that
D occurred, to re-present it. Well, that prediction proved correct. The cheque
was presented on November 11 but was returned "refer to drawer, please
re-present," and the entries in the joint bank statement of Mr. and Mrs.
Hadrys of that date, shows a payment of £800 and a contra entry of the
same amount. The account continued to be overdrawn until November 16
on which date the overdraft was £183 11s. 10d. On the following day
E there were paid into the account cheques to a total value of £1,135 8s. 2d.
and it is clear that this figure included the cheque for £800 drawn on the
company's account to which I have referred. This resulted in a credit
balance of £951 16s. 4d. against which were drawn cheques totalling £115,
so that on November 20 there was a credit balance of £836 16s. 4d. On
that date the bank honoured three further cheques, one for £15 17s. 1d.,
one for £20 15s. 0d., and the third, the re-presented cheque for £800 in
F favour of the respondents, thus leaving a credit balance of 4s. 3d.

Those are the facts immediately surrounding the payment of the sums
now claimed by the liquidator but I ought, I think, to say something of
the background which has formed the basis of some of the submissions
made.

It seems that Mr. Hadrys, before setting up the company, had been
G employed by a company which did business with the Tully Engineering
Co., an organisation by which, until April 1970, Mr. Dennis Greaves
was employed. They thus became acquainted. After Mr. Hadrys had
left his employment and set up the company in 1969, Mr. Greaves left
Tullys and started an engineering business of his own in partnership with
his brother, and it seems that in the early stages a good deal of the work
done by them was done for Tullys. In the summer of 1970, Mr. Hadrys
H called at Tullys in order to get them to do some sub-contract work for
him at a colliery controlled by the National Coal Board. Tullys were not
able to accept the work because of the holiday period, but Mr. Greaves
told me that their manager telephoned to him, told him that Mr. Hadrys
was with him and wanted this work done, and asked him whether he
and his brother could help out. They agreed to do so and, as a result,
Mr. Hadrys came straight over to their workshop and instructed them
on the job. A few days later, he called and said he was going into

hospital and asked them to deal with his foreman, a Mr. Irvine, who A
lived in the neighbourhood. Mr. Greaves' evidence was that he did not know anything about the structure of Mr. Hadrys' business, but got the address to which to send invoices from Mr. Irvine.

The work was carried out, and on July 28, 1970, an invoice for £1,050 was sent to "J. Leslie Engineering, 18, Rigg Approach, Leytonstone, E.10." Mr. Greaves' evidence was that invoices were prepared by him in long-
hand and then typed by his sister-in-law, who did the office work for the B
business, which was then running on very slender resources. Normally they expected payment within a month, but none came and at the beginning of September a statement was sent. Mr. Greaves says that he does not think that he wrote this out but it was, of course, a long time ago. That statement was addressed this time to J. Leslie Engineering Ltd. and
is dated, "As at August 31, 1970." It set out the figure and the date of C
the invoice, and concludes, "This account is now due for payment and we would appreciate your cheque or your reason for non-payment within the next seven days."

Mr. Greaves said he telephoned several times to press for payment, and this is borne out by a letter of September 16 in which he protested at the continued non-payment and asked for prompt settlement. That
letter, like the invoice, was addressed to "J. Leslie Engineering." Before D
the sum of £250 arrived at the beginning of October, Mr. Hadrys telephoned to say that it was on the way and Mr. Greaves' evidence is that he also telephoned before the cheque for £800 was sent, as well as telephoning afterwards to say that the cheque might not be met. Despite the reference in the statement of August 31 to J. Leslie Engineering Ltd., Mr. Greaves
says that neither he nor his brother had any idea that they were dealing E
with a limited company, and, indeed, that the first intimation that a company existed was when in May 1971, he received an undated letter from Mr. Hadrys in which he said, "As you will know, the company went into liquidation." The reference to J. Leslie Engineering Ltd. in the statement of August 31 to which I have referred, is explained, I think a little speciously, by saying that his sister-in-law thought this "more
businesslike." There is no evidence from Mrs. Greaves herself. F

I have seen extracts from the ledger sheets of the respondents, which were kept by her, and which indicate that the word "limited" was not consistently used in making entries relating to debtors or creditors which were limited companies—sometimes it appears, sometimes it does not, so I derive very little assistance from this. In cross-examination, however,
Mr. Greaves said that he and his brother were not surprised to receive the G
money in October. They thought, he said, that Mr. Hadrys and his wife were "directors of the company." Furthermore, in a letter written by the respondents' solicitors in June 1973 I find this statement:

> "It has been our client's contention all along that they were not in fact paid by the company but by Mr. Hadrys personally, and certainly the cheque for £800 did not come from the company. We gather that
> Mr. Hadrys had promised to pay our clients himself if necessary." H

The clear implication of this is that the liability was known to be a company liability which was being guaranteed by Mr. Hadrys. Nor does the matter end there, because in August and September 1971, the liquidator wrote to the respondents pointing out that the company was in liquidation and asking for "a statement of the account of J. Leslie Engineers Co. Ltd. with yourselves showing transactions effected during 1970." In response,

A there were sent three invoices for goods and services all dated September 4, 1970, and addressed to J. Leslie Engineering, a statement similarly addressed dated October 9, 1970, and showing a balance outstanding of £894 15s. 11d. (subsequently corrected in ink to show the £800 received) and a letter dated January 8, 1970, pressing for the outstanding balance of £94 15s. 11d. and addressed to " J. Leslie Engineering Co." These were accompanied by a compliment slip upon which is written:

B

> " Your letters dated 12/8 and 9/9, I enclose copies of most of our correspondence with J. Leslie Engineering. You will see from this that our total invoices to the firm amounted to £1,144 16s. 11d., of which we are still owed £94 15s. 11d. If you require any further information, please do not hesitate to contact us. (signed) J. E. Greaves."

C

I am bound to say that I find myself unable to accept Mr. Greaves' evidence that he did not appreciate that he was dealing with a limited company. Quite apart from the indicia to which I have already referred, his evidence was that in 1970 he had known Mr. Hadrys for five or six years. It is evident both from Mr. Greaves' own evidence and from the documents that the respondents were having the very greatest difficulty in D extracting payment for the work done. If Mr. Greaves had really believed that he was dealing with Mr. Hadrys personally, I find it quite incredible that he did not address a single letter to him personally asking for payment, and equally incredible that, when approached by the liquidator, he did not at once say that he had no knowledge of the company and had had no dealings with it. I am sure that Mr. Greaves was not, in his evidence, deliberately seeking to mislead me and was doing his best to reconstruct E events which, after all, took place some five years ago. But I am driven to the conclusion, on the material before me, that at the material time he knew that there was a company and believed Mr. Hadrys to be a director of it and that it was for that entity that the work carried out in the summer of 1970 was undertaken.

It is submitted by Mr. Potts, on behalf of the respondents, that the F " dispositions " which were avoided by section 227 do not include such dispositions as are constituted by the payments to the respondents in this case; that " the dispositions " at which the section is aimed are the initial dispositions only—that is to say the encashments of the two cheques—and that it is against Mr. Hadrys alone that any claim will lie. I cannot think that as a general proposition that can be right. It seems to me to be wholly immaterial, so long as one is dealing with the company's property, G whether the purported disposition is made by the company or by a third party, or whether it is made directly or indirectly.

I feel, therefore, no difficulty—and, I may add, no doubt—about the initial payment of £250. The bank notes received from the bank were as much the company's property, and identifiable as such, as were the moneys in the account, and it seems to me to make not the slightest difference that H Mr. Hadrys took the bank notes and converted them into money orders payable to Mr. Greaves. There was, throughout, a clearly identifiable property of the company which passed directly from the company's hands (in the person of Mr. Hadrys, its controlling director) to those of the respondents: see for instance, *Taylor* v. *Plumer* (1815) 3 M. & S. 562. That disposition was, in my judgment, quite clearly invalidated by the section unless and until this court otherwise orders.

The second payment, however, creates to my mind, very much greater difficulty. The disposition which Mr. Evans Lombe, on behalf of the liquidator, attacks, is not the drawing of the cheque to Mr. Greaves or the sending to him of that cheque, and it is not—or it is not alone—drawing by Mr. Hadrys of the cheque on the company's account. It is the application by the bank of the funds in the joint account to meet Mr. Greaves' cheque when it was re-presented. That, says Mr. Evans Lombe, was the disposition of the company's property which is avoided and which gives the liquidator the right to recover the sum claimed from the respondents. Now, it must be remembered that the invalidation of a disposition of the company's property and the recovery of the property disposed of, are two logically distinct matters. Section 227 says nothing about recovery; it merely avoids dispositions and is in these terms: A B

> "In a winding up by the court, any disposition of the property of the company, including things in action, and any transfer of shares, or alteration in the status of members of the company, made after the commencement of the winding up, shall, unless the court otherwise orders, be void." C

What is the appropriate remedy in respect of the invalidated disposition is a matter not regulated by the statute and that has to be determined by the general law. In order to succeed against the respondents, the liquidator does not necessarily have to demonstrate a transaction invalidated by section 227 for there may be claims to recover moneys paid on other grounds. He does, however, have to show a right of recovery, and it is Mr. Evans Lombe's contention that he does that if he demonstrates that the transaction is one which is bitten by section 227 and persuades the court that it ought not to validate it. I think that I should say straight away that although, as I have said, I cannot accept that the respondents were not aware that they were contracting with a limited company, I cannot on the evidence before me find any indication that when the £800 payment was made, or indeed at any material time, the respondents knew or had reason to suspect that the funds to meet it had been provided by the company. I cannot, therefore, treat the case as one of a collusive payment, and I think that I must accept that, so far as the respondents were concerned, they thought that the moneys were being paid by Mr. Hadrys or his wife out of their own resources. D E F

Looking at the transaction in stages, there was clearly no disposition of any property of the company when the cheque in favour of the respondents was first sent and presented. When the cheque on the company's account was drawn and presented there quite clearly was a disposition of the company's property, and one which is, unless validated, avoided by section 227. But that cheque was paid in with a number of other cheques and, after allowing for the overdraft, the moneys represented by the cheque became mixed with Mr. Hadrys' own moneys throwing up a credit balance of some £950. That transaction gave rise, of course, to a number of claims against Mr. Hadrys. First, he was clearly in breach of his fiduciary duty as a director and liable to replace the money taken out of the company's account in misfeasance proceedings. Secondly, the company had claims against him for conversion and for money had and received. But at law, at least, it is difficult to see how the money could be said to be any longer "the property of the company" for it had ceased to be identifiable and the common law doctrine of tracing had ceased to be applicable when the money was mixed with the other moneys in the account. The company's cheque had lost its identity in a new chose of action, that is to say G H

A the debt owed by the bank to Mr. and Mrs. Hadrys on the credit balance in the joint account. It would, in my judgment, be a misuse of language to describe that chose in action as "the property of the company." The fact that the disposition constituted by the payment in of the company's cheque is described by section 227 to be "void" does not mean that it never took place, and even if it did, I do not see how that would help the liquidator in his claim against the respondents, for it would simply mean
B that the bank had paid the cheque in their favour out of funds which did not in fact exist. Nor does it mean that the company has some special remedy—and this is really what Mr. Evans Lombe suggests—which enables it to proceed with a claim against the respondents for money had and received in circumstances where, had the disposition been invalid on some other ground than the section, no such remedy would have lain.

C The position immediately after the payment of the company's cheque into the joint account was that the company had against Mr. Hadrys (among other remedies) the remedies which any beneficiary has against a fiduciary who has misappropriated the trust fund, that is to say a claim in personam for replacement and the right to trace the trust funds in equity.

D "The property of the company" for the purposes of the section was, as it seems to me, not the credit balance in the account owed by the bank to Mr. and Mrs. Hadrys, but the sum total of the rights of the company created by the transactions leading up to the creation of that balance. I do not think that the meeting, out of the credit balance held by the bank to the order of Mr. and Mrs. Hadrys, of the re-presented cheque in favour of the respondents was a disposition of the property of
E the company simply because the company could, by appropriate proceedings, have obtained a declaration of charge on that credit balance. Accordingly, in my judgment, the liquidator's claim to a declaration under paragraph 1 of the summons in respect of the cheque to the respondents must fail.

That, however, is not necessarily the end of the matter, because the mere fact that a payment to the respondents is not avoided by section
F 227 does not mean necessarily that they are not liable to repay. I cannot, however, see upon what principle they could be made liable in the present case if one once postulates—as, in my judgment, one must—that they were innocent recipients without notice that the account from which they were paid had been fed by a payment of the company's moneys wrongfully procured by its controlling director. Any claim
G against them personally for money had and received would, so far as I can see, fail for want of privity between them and the company in relation to the payment which would enable such a claim to be sustained.

As regards any personal claim in equity on the analogy of a claim against an overpaid beneficiary, there appear to me to be two objections. In the first place, I do not think that it can be right to treat the respon-
H dents as volunteers who have received trust moneys, for they gave consideration in as much as it must have been implicit in the transaction that they received the payment in discharge of the debt due to them from the company. But even if they could be regarded as volunteers, *In re Diplock* [1948] Ch. 465 indicates a fatal objection, namely that the exertion of the personal remedy by the beneficiary (the company) against the innocent but wrongly paid recipient, is dependent upon the beneficiary first exhausting his remedies against the persons primarily responsible.

In the instant case, the liquidator, for reasons which have not been explained, has not sought to proceed either against Mr. Hadrys, who was the person directly responsible, nor against the bank without whose co-operation (procured, no doubt, in ignorance of the petition) the payment could not have been made.

Clearly, Mr. Hadrys was a trustee of the company's moneys and could himself have had no defence to an equitable claim by the company to trace its funds in the joint account. Equally clearly, applying the rule in *In re Hallett's Estate* (1880) 13 Ch.D. 696 to the payments out of the account, substantially the whole of the sum of £800 paid to the respondents could have been traced. But for a tracing claim to succeed against the respondents it would have to be established (a) that they were volunteers and (b) that the money was still capable of being followed in their hands. If the innocent recipient has, for instance, used it to discharge debts owing by him, it ceases to be traceable: see *In re Diplock* [1948] Ch. 465, 521, 548, 549. Even, therefore, if the respondents could properly be treated as volunteers, the liquidator has not sought to adduce any evidence that the money is traceable into any assets of the respondents and, having regard to Mr. Greaves' evidence that the business had only been going a few months and was at the time running on extremely slender resources, it may, I think, safely be inferred that the respondents used the money to pay their own creditors. Accordingly, the liquidator's claim to the sum of £800 must, in my judgment, fail.

There remains, however, the question of whether, in the exercise of the discretion conferred on the court by section 227, I ought to make an order validating the payment of £250. Mr. Potts has submitted that I should, because he says: (1) The respondents regarded themselves as dealing with Mr. Hadrys and not with the company; (2) they did not know when the payments were made that a winding up petition had been presented, nor that the money originated from the company; (3) the liquidator has delayed for a long time in making the claim; and (4) it is unfair to proceed against them without first proceeding against Mr. Hadrys, the person really responsible.

I have already rejected the first of Mr. Potts' grounds as a matter of fact. As to the second, Mr. Potts says that there is no reported case that he has been able to find where, in the case of a recipient who did not know that a petition had been presented, the payment has not been validated. He refers me to *In re Civil Service and General Store Ltd.* (1887) 58 L.T. 220, where the repayment was ordered, but points to the express finding that the recipient knew of the petition and to the importance attached to that. In his judgment in that case Chitty J. said, at p. 221:

> "But to affirm a transaction of that kind under the discretion conferred upon the court by section 153,"—which of course, was the forerunner of the present section 227—"would be to exercise such discretion upon a totally erroneous principle. To allow the respondents to retain £175 would be to act in the very teeth of the Act of Parliament, the object of which is that creditors should be paid pari passu. Moreover, the respondents, at the least, knew at the date of the agreement that the company was in embarrassed circumstances, although they do not seem then to have had knowledge of the presentation of the petition. When, however, they actually

A received the two payments of £100 and £75, they were, in my judgment, aware of a petition having been presented, and I can only treat the transaction as an attempt to get a preference over other creditors. The proposition that payment by a company, after the commencement of a winding up, of a bona fide debt previously incurred will be affirmed by the court under section 153 is wholly untenable. I therefore hold that the respondents must repay the
B £175. The payment, however, of the £13 for goods supplied is one which can properly be affirmed."

But it does not, of course, follow (as Mr. Potts recognises) from the fact that knowledge was considered important in a case where the court declined to exercise its discretion that the court will exercise its discretion where there is no knowledge, and Mr. Evans Lombe says that that pro-
C position is simply not correct as a matter of law. All the cases, he suggests, where payments have been sanctioned have either been salvage cases where the creditor receiving payment has put up moneys or supplied goods and services to keep the company going, or cases where there would be some manifest injustice in declining to validate the payment.

D He refers to *In re T. W. Construction Ltd.* [1954] 1 W.L.R. 540, where the principles are set out by Wynn-Parry J. After reading the section, Wynn-Parry J. said, at pp. 542–544:

"Certain authorities have been referred to. It may be convenient if I turn in the first place to the recent case, *In re Steane's* (*Bournemouth*) *Ltd.* [1949] W.N. 490 a decision of Vaisey J. In the course
E of his judgment in that case, Vaisey J. said: 'The legislature, by omitting to indicate any particular principle which should govern the exercise of the discretion vested in the court, must be deemed to have left it at large, and controlled only by those general principles which applied to every kind of judicial discretion. I have reviewed the facts of the present case somewhat at length because I think that such a review must usually be necessary whenever a case of
F this nature falls to be decided.' In the older case of *In re Répertoire Opera Co.* (1895) 2 Manson 314, 316 Vaughan Williams J. said 'I have an absolute discretion to validate this transaction or not. If the transaction is one which would be valid under the protective sections of the Bankruptcy Act, that would be a very strong reason for validating it here. That is what Lord Cairns means in *Ex parte Pearson, In re Wiltshire Iron Co.* (1868) 3 Ch.App. 443.' With that
G statement I respectfully entirely agree. Vaughan Williams J. continued: 'The cases on section 153,'—which was the corresponding section to section 227—'are an adoption by the court of the principle of the protective sections in bankruptcy. It would be very unfortunate if the principles of administration in bankruptcy and in the winding up of companies were not, so far as possible, the same.'
H I have some difficulty in following the reasoning in those two sentences because the protective section in the present Bankruptcy Act 1914, section 45, confers no discretion on the court. A transaction to be protected under that section must fulfil the conditions laid down in the section, otherwise it does not obtain the protection; whereas, as Vaughan Williams J. himself recognised, there was under the section corresponding to section 227 of the present Companies Act an absolute discretion, as was clearly stated by Vaisey J. in the

passage in his judgment in the *Bournemouth* case [1949] W.N. 490, A
to which I have just referred. The facts in *In re Wiltshire Iron Co.*,
3 Ch.App. 443, 446, the case to which Vaughan Williams J. refers,
can be simply stated by reading a sentence from the headnote:
'Where a customer of a trading company had bona fide ordered
and paid for goods, and the company had loaded the goods on a
railway to his address, and sent him the invoices, after the presenting
of the petition but before the winding-up order: *Held*, that the B
disposition of the property was complete before the winding-up
order, and the goods ordered to be delivered to the customer.' In
the course of his judgment, Lord Cairns said: 'Section 153 no doubt
provides that all dispositions of the property and effects of the com-
pany made between the commencement of the winding up (that is
the presentation of the petition) and the order for winding up, shall, C
unless the court otherwise orders, be void. This is a wholesome
and necessary provision, to prevent, during the period which must
elapse before a petition can be heard, the improper alienation and
dissipation of the property of a company in extremis. But where a
company actually trading, which it is the interest of everyone to
preserve, and ultimately to sell, as a going concern, is made the
object of a winding-up petition, which may fail or may succeed, if D
it were to be supposed that transactions in the ordinary course of
its current trade, bona fide entered into and completed, would be
avoided, and would not, in the discretion given to the court, be
maintained, the result would be that the presentation of a petition,
groundless or well-founded, would ipso facto, paralyse the trade of
the company, and great injury, without any counter balance of E
advantage, would be done to those interested in the assets of the
company.' In the later case, *In re Park Ward & Co. Ltd.* [1926]
Ch. 828, 831 Romer J. applied *In re Wiltshire Iron Co.*, 3 Ch.App.
443. After quoting a passage from the judgment of Lord Cairns
which I have myself quoted, he says, at p. 831: 'If I were to adopt
the view put forward by Mr. Clayton, a company would in very few
cases be able to obtain the assistance necessary to enable it to F
carry on business as a going concern. Lord Cairns evidently
regarded the power given to the court by the section as one given
for the benefit and in the interests of the company, so as to ensure
that a company which is made the subject of a winding-up petition
may nevertheless obtain money necessary for carrying on its business
and so avoid its business being paralysed. If, therefore, I were to G
hold that no one who knows of the presentation of a petition can
safely enter into any arrangement with the company, I think I
should be depriving the company of the benefit which, according to
Lord Cairns, the provision of the section was intended to secure to
it.'"

After reviewing the facts of that case, Wynn-Parry J. said, at p. 544: H

". . . it is clear from the evidence, and to my mind it is the only possible inference from the facts, that the accommodation arranged was arranged for a limited period for the express purpose of enabling the company to continue to carry on its business. Therefore, to use the language of Romer J., it was a transaction for the benefit of and in the interests of the company. In the case before Vaisey J., *In re Steane's* (*Bournemouth*) *Ltd.* [1949] W.N. 490, a debenture was

> A issued to secure moneys which were advanced for the purpose, as stated by Vaisey J. in his judgment, of keeping the company going or of keeping things going generally. Those three authorities appear to me to govern this case and to bring it within the benefit of the section."

Then he referred to *In re Liverpool Civil Service Association* (1874)
B 9 Ch.App. 511 and *In re Civil Service and General Store Ltd.*, 58 L.T. 220, the decision of Chitty J. to which I have referred, and he said about that last case:

> "Apart from the circumstance that the *Wiltshire Iron Co.* case, 3 Ch.App. 443, was not cited, it appears to me that that case is clearly distinguishable from the present case."

C And having reviewed the facts, he says, at p. 545:

> "Then in the next sentence there is a circumstance stated which would of itself, I think, be sufficient to distinguish that case from the present case,"

and he quotes from the judgment which I have already read the passage where Chitty J. emphasises that when the payments were actually received,
D the recipients were aware of the petition, and he concludes, at p. 546:

> "Therefore it seems to me that these two cases do not in any sense govern the present case or stand in the way of the disposition in question being validated. It appears to me, viewing the evidence as a whole and drawing the inference that I do, that this was a transaction which is directly within the passage from the judgment
> E of Lord Cairns, . . ."

Now, although Wynn-Parry J. refers to a disposition as being for the benefit of and in the interests of the company, I do not read his judgment as indicating that the mere fact that the payment is made in respect of some past transaction from which the company may have derived a benefit is sufficient to justify the exercise of the court's discretion.

F I accept that when the respondents received the £250, they did not positively know (as was the fact) that it was money of the company. But it was money which was paid to them by a director of the company in response to pressure applied by them to the company in respect of a transaction taking place before the presentation of the petition, and finding myself unable to accept that they did not regard the transaction
G themselves as a dealing with a limited company, I think that the natural inference that they would have drawn if they thought about it at all, would have been that it was the company's money. Certainly there was nothing, as there was in the case of the subsequent payment out of the private account of Mr. and Mrs. Hadrys, to suggest that it was not. There is, however, nothing in the circumstances of the instant case which would lead me to believe that the respondents knew at that time that a petition
H had been presented. They deny it, and I accept that.

If, therefore, one adopts the analogy of section 45 of the Bankruptcy Act 1914 (as is suggested in the passage from Vaughan Williams L.J. in *In re Répertoire Opera Co.*, 2 Manson 314, 316, referred to by Wynn-Parry J. in *In re T. W. Construction Ltd.* [1954] 1 W.L.R. 540) this would be in favour of Mr. Potts' proposition. But I do not think that the matter can be resolved so simply. As Wynn-Parry J. pointed out, section 45 lays down specific conditions as regards payments by the bankrupt and confers no discretion, and I am bound to say that I do not think that the two sections are really comparable. For instance, a very common exercise of the discretion under section 227 is the sanctioning in advance of payments in the ordinary course of business where everybody knows that a petition has been presented. Again, the advertisement of the petition is notice to all the world of its presentation (see *In re London, Hamburg, and Continental Exchange Bank* (1866) L.R. 2 Eq. 231) and there is no real or necessary parallel between that public act and the available act of bankruptcy to which a receiving order relates back. Whilst obviously the absence of any actual knowledge in the recipient of a payment that a petition is in being is a factor—indeed a very powerful factor—to be considered in relation to the exercise of discretion, I do not think that, by itself, it can be conclusive and, indeed, Mr. Potts does not so contend. I think that in exercising discretion the court must keep in view the evident purpose of the section which, as Chitty J. said *In re Civil Service and General Store Ltd.*, 58 L.T. 220, 221, is to ensure that the creditors are paid pari passu. Obviously there are circumstances where this cannot in fairness be the sole criterion in cases where, for instance, the creditor concerned has since the presentation of the petition helped to keep the company afloat, or has otherwise swollen the company's assets, salvage cases and that sort of thing.

But I can see no considerations in the present case, nor do I think that the matter is affected by Mr. Potts' point that it is unfair to proceed against the respondents (a) because no proceedings have been taken against Mr. Hadrys or (b) because there has been long delay in proceeding. As to the first, I cannot think that the existence of an alternative remedy against somebody else can be a good reason for validating a transaction. And, as to the second, there has, it is true, been a delay, but I cannot see that in fact it has prejudiced the respondents who were clearly notified in September 1971, that proceedings were to be brought.

In the circumstances, I do not see my way to exercising my discretion to sanction what was clearly a preferential payment made with the company's money—a payment furthermore which, so far as the available evidence goes, seems clearly to have been intended by Mr. Hadrys to be preferential. It seems to me that to allow payments made in these circumstances to stand simply because the creditor preferred does not know that he is being preferred, would be to defeat the whole purpose of the section.

I have very considerable sympathy for the respondents who laboured long and hard for a reward which in the event has proved at least in part illusory. But I regretfully feel that I must in relation to the sum of £250 make the declaration sought and order its repayment as asked by the liquidator.

In the result, therefore, the liquidator's claim to the £800 fails, but there will be a declaration and order as sought in relation to the payment of the £250.

Order accordingly.
No order as to costs.

Solicitors: *Goldingham, Wellington & Co.; Hodgson, Fox & Co., Newark-on-Trent.*

A. R.

A [QUEEN'S BENCH DIVISION: CARDIFF]

* REGAN *v.* WILLIAMSON

[1974 R. No. 273]

B 1975 Feb. 10, 11; 17 Watkins J.

Fatal Accidents Acts—Damages—Infant dependants—Husband's claim for family's loss of wife's services — Housekeeper employed—Value of wife's services

The plaintiff, the father of four children, was sitting in a stationary motor car with his wife when the defendant, driving
C another car, veered off the road and collided into the plaintiff's car. The plaintiff suffered injuries and his wife was killed. In a claim under the Fatal Accidents Acts 1846 to 1959, the plaintiff sought damages, inter alia, for the cost of employing a housekeeper to look after the children.

On the question of the damages to be recovered for the loss of the wife's services:—

D *Held*, that in determining the pecuniary value to be put on the services rendered by the deceased for the purposes of the Fatal Accidents Acts, acknowledgment should be given to the constant attendance of a mother on her children; that the value placed upon such services should not be limited to a mere computation of the cost of the services of a housekeeper minus an estimate of the cost of maintaining the deceased wife (post, pp. 308B–C, 309C–D).

E

The following case is referred to in the judgment:

Hay v. *Hughes* [1975] Q.B. 790; [1975] 2 W.L.R. 34; [1975] 1 All E.R. 257, C.A.

The following additional cases were cited in argument:

Berry v. *Humm & Co.* [1915] 1 K.B. 627.

F *Burgess* v. *Florence Nightingale Hospital for Gentlewomen* [1955] 1 Q.B. 349; [1955] 2 W.L.R. 533; [1955] 1 All E.R. 511.

Hurt v. *Murphy* [1971] R.T.R. 186.

Jeffery v. *Smith* [1970] R.T.R. 279, C.A.

Pevec v. *Brown* (1964) 108 S.J. 219.

Preston v. *Hunting Air Transport Ltd.* [1956] 1 Q.B. 454; [1956] 2 W.L.R. 526; [1956] 1 All E.R. 443.

G

ACTION

The plaintiff, James Regan, claimed damages on his own behalf and as administrator of the estate of his deceased wife, Maureen Regan, from the defendant, Galon Williamson, under the Fatal Accidents Acts 1846 to 1959 and the Law Reform (Miscellaneous Provisions) Act 1934.
H The defendant admitted liability. The case was heard by Watkins J. in Cardiff and is reported only on the question of the extent of damages under the claim under the Fatal Accidents Acts.

Esyr Lewis Q.C. and *Malcolm Pill* for the plaintiff.

Barry Chedlow Q.C., *Hugh Williams* and *John Prosser* for the defendant.

Cur. adv. vult.

February 17. WATKINS J. read the following judgment. On October 10, 1973, at about 10.45 p.m., the plaintiff, James Regan, was sitting in his stationary motor car chatting to his wife who was in the front passenger seat. The car was parked in a lay-by at the side of the road upon the mountain which separates Cardiff from Caerphilly. Suddenly another motor car, which was driven by the defendant, Galon Williamson, veered off that road and into collision with the plaintiff's car. The primary cause of the collision was the fact that the defendant was under the influence of drink. On his own confession, he was convicted, at the Crown Court on January 14, 1974, of causing death by dangerous driving and with driving with an excess of alcohol in his blood. One dreadful consequence of the collision was that the plaintiff, as soon as he recovered from a brief period of unconsciousness, experienced the awful shock of realising that his wife law dead alongside him in the badly damaged car and, although this was of small account to him beside the tragedy of the loss of his wife, he quite soon realised that he was, himself, injured in many parts of his body.

The late Mrs. Regan, 37 years of age at her death, left a hitherto happy family circle which had consisted of herself, the plaintiff and their four boys. Her loss is a serious blow to them. The result entitles them to be compensated in damages under the Fatal Accidents Acts 1846 to 1959. The deceased's estate is, under the Law Reform (Miscellaneous Provisions) Act 1934, entitled to damages because she lost, by her untimely death, her normal expectation of life. The plaintiff himself has also to be compensated for the various effects upon him of the injuries he sustained. The defendant, not surprisingly, has admitted liability.

My task, which I shall begin by looking at the plaintiff's personal injuries claim, is to assess the scale of the damages. [His Lordship assessed the damages on the plaintiff's claim for personal injuries at £2,250 for pain, suffering, discomfort and such future disability as there might be. He added £500 under the Law Reform (Miscellaneous Provisions) Act 1934.]

Finally, I come to the claim under the Fatal Accidents Acts 1846 to 1959. This affects the plaintiff, of course, and the four boys who are now 14¼ years, 11 years and 10 months, 8 years and 10 months and 3¼ years, respectively. The two eldest boys attend the local state Roman Catholic grammar or comprehensive school; the youngest two boys attend fee-paying Roman Catholic schools. At the time of the death of the deceased, the plaintiff was earning £32 per week, in addition to which he was allowed the use of a company car and, of course, for business purposes, free petrol. These earnings provided for the whole family and paid for the mortgage of the family home in Rhiwbina, which is a suburb of Cardiff. At the present day the mortgage repayments amount to £50 per month and rates. The deceased was a smart, attractive woman. She was a good wife and mother and a good manager of the family income. It seems to me that she needed to be, having regard to the liabilities which faced her of clothing, feeding and so on a fairly large family. The plaintiff estimated that the deceased cost him £10 per week to clothe and feed. If he is wrong in this estimate, I feel sure it is by over-estimation and not otherwise.

At the outset of the marriage, she worked, I think, as a secretary. The first child then arrived and she did not work again until 1970. In that year she worked as a clerical assistant with the Department of the

A Environment and with the Inland Revenue. She and the plaintiff both
wanted a daughter. She gave up work to this end, but she produced
another son. She and the plaintiff were thinking of sending the boys, or
some of them, to Roman Catholic public schools. I think it is likely that
this ambition would have been thwarted merely by economics although,
of course, I cannot be sure of this since the plaintiff may advance appre-
ciably in his employment, and, had she lived, the deceased, as I believe
B probable, would have returned to work and earned something in the
region of £1,250 per annum. I believed the plaintiff when he told me, in
effect, that it was firmly within their contemplation that the deceased would
take up employment again. So many wives nowadays do work in order
to inflate the family income once the quiver of children is full. This may
not have been the case with the deceased but, at 37 years of age, I dare
C say she was nearing a conclusion that ambition for further pregnancy was
over. So for this once united and happy family, the picture of life has
changed.

These are the outlines of the changes. The plaintiff earns £2,750 per
annum now and expects an increase soon through ordinary increment or
promotion, or both. He has no present intention of remarriage, the thought
of it is repugnant to him. He has replaced the deceased, to a certain
D extent, by employing her aunt, Mrs. Gosnell, who is 61 years of age, as
a housekeeper. Mrs. Gosnell had helped to bring up the deceased. She
worked as a dressmaker for the Welsh Hospital Board. She willingly
gave this work up in order to look after the plaintiff and the boys. Some
queries arose in the course of evidence and speeches about how much
Mrs. Gosnell is, in fact, paid. In my judgment, those queries, properly
E pursued, left the plaintiff's bona fides untarnished. I accept that he now
pays Mrs. Gosnell £16 per week. He provides her, in addition, with two
meals a day at a cost which I put at about £2·50 per week. He felt
unable, himself, to provide a precise figure. He also pays her national
insurance stamp of £1·50 per week. It costs him something like £2·50
per week in petrol to bring Mrs. Gosnell to his home daily by car and
take her back to her home in Rumney, another suburb of Cardiff. He
F has no alternative but to provide this shuttle service for Mrs. Gosnell since
use of public transport between Rhiwbina and Rumney is out of the
question. So his total expenditure for Mrs. Gosnell is £22·50 per week.

What has he obtained in return? The answer is that he and the boys
receive the services of Mrs. Gosnell for five days a week, from a time just
before the plaintiff goes to work, having fetched Mrs. Gosnell from her
G home, to about half past six in the evening, when he returns her to her
home. She cleans the family home, provides two meals a day, looks after
the youngest boy, who is in school for only half a day. In holiday times,
of course, her burdens are increased. Occasionally she spends a night
at their home. The plaintiff, himself, puts the youngest boy to bed. It is
suggested that the plaintiff could have got help more cheaply through
H making inquiries at various agencies and the like. I think that the plaintiff
is acting entirely reasonably in bringing to his home someone whom he
knows, who knows the boys and who has a personal attachment to them
all, and that the sums of money which he pays her are equally reasonable.

The weekend care of the plaintiff and the boys remains a problem
which has not been satisfactorily solved. The plaintiff's relatives help him
to a certain extent, especially on Saturday afternoons. But I formed the
clear impression that the plaintiff is often, at weekends, sorely tried in

trying to be an effective substitute for the deceased. The problem could, A
to some extent, be cured by engaging another woman, possibly to do duty
at the weekend, but finding such a person is no simple matter. I think
the plaintiff has not made extensive inquiries in this regard. Possibly
the expense involved in getting more help is a factor which has deterred
him. Whatever be the reason, the plain fact is that the deceased's services
at the weekend have not been replaced. They are lost to the plaintiff and
to the boys. B

Upon looking at the established facts, I suppose I ought, according to
precedent, to do a simple arithmetical sum in searching for the overall figure
of dependency for the plaintiff and the boys by deducting £10, that is
the cost of keeping the deceased, from the £22·50 which is the overall sum
Mrs. Gosnell's services cost the plaintiff. This would result in a dependency
figure of £12·50 per week or £600 per annum, to which a suitable multiplier C
of years should be applied. The simplicity of such an exercise would in
my opinion, work an injustice upon the deceased's dependants which I
think the average member of the public would describe as quite monstrous.

It is, of course, the present law that dependants are to be compensated
only for the value of the services lost to them by the death of a wife and
mother. A wife's companionship is to be ignored, likewise the grief and D
misery caused by her departure and, so too, a mother's love, guidance
and influence in bringing up children. Very recently Lord Edmund-Davies,
in *Hay* v. *Hughes* [1975] Q.B. 790, 802 said of what, to many, may seem
a harsh law:

> "In *Pevec* v. *Brown* (1964) 108 S.J. 219 a widower claimed on behalf
> of himself and his infant son damages in respect of his wife's death,
> and contended that compensation should be awarded for loss, not of E
> a mother's love, but for the disadvantage of the care which the child
> would receive from the nanny whom the father had engaged as com-
> pared with that which he would have received from his mother had
> she survived. The report is a very short one, but it appears that, in
> rejecting this submission, Megaw J. adverted to the irrecoverability of
> compensation for the father's loss of the companionship of his wife F
> and, saying that there was no distinction in principle in relation to the
> child, held that no damages should be awarded in respect of any
> element of the child receiving less care than he would have done had
> his mother survived. Were it now necessary to decide the point, I
> am not at present convinced that I should take the same view, and it
> is to be noted that in *Burgess* v. *Florence Nightingale Hospital for* G
> *Gentlewomen* [1955] 1 All E.R. 511, 513 Devlin J. expressed the
> view that damages should be awarded ' for what the child lost by the
> wife's death, both in respect of the school fees and of what she might
> have done for the child.' While it is undoubtedly established that
> damages can be awarded under the Fatal Accidents Acts only in
> respect of pecuniary loss and not as a solatium for injured feelings
> (see *Taff Vale Railway Co.* v. *Jenkins* [1913] A.C. 1, 4, *per* Viscount H
> Haldane L.C. and *Davies* v. *Powell Duffryn Associated Collieries Ltd.*
> [1942] A.C. 601, 617), so that these two children could recover nothing
> for the deprivation of their mother's love, yet it may sometime have
> to be considered whether Mr. McGregor is not right in saying
> (*McGregor on Damages,* 13th ed. (1972), para. 1232): ' . . . it may
> be argued that the benefit of a mother's personal attention to a child's
> upbringing, morals, education and psychology, which the services of

a housekeeper, nurse or governess could never provide, has in the long run a financial value for the child, difficult as it is to assess.'"

I have been referred to a number of cases in which judges have felt compelled to look upon the task of assessing damages in cases involving the death of a wife and mother with strict disregard to those features of the life of a woman beyond her so-called services, that is to say, to keep house, to cook the food, to buy the clothes, to wash them and so forth. In more than one case, an attempt has been made to calculate the actual number of hours it would take a woman to perform such services and to compensate dependants upon that basis at so much an hour and so relegate the wife or mother, so it seems to me, to the position of a housekeeper.

While I think that the law inhibits me from, much as I should like to, going all the way along the path to which Lord Edmund-Davies pointed, I am, with due respect to the other judges to whom I have been referred, of the view that the word "services" has been too narrowly construed. It should, at least, include an acknowledgment that a wife and mother does not work to set hours and, still less, to rule. She is in constant attendance, save for those hours when she is, if that is the fact, at work. During some of those hours she may well give the children instruction on essential matters to do with their upbringing and, possibly, with such things as their homework. This sort of attention seems to be as much of a service, and probably more valuable to them, than the other kinds of service conventionally so regarded.

So I begin the calculation of the figure of dependency with the sum of £12·50 per week. This, however, covers but a part of the loss of services. What about all those hours in the evening and during the weekends when no substitute service is available? In my judgment, they require to be taken into account. In so doing I recognise the difficulty of reaching conclusions without the assistance of clear guidelines. I am aware that there are good and bad mothers. It so happens that I am concerned in the present case with a woman who was a good wife and mother. I propose, for the foregoing reasons, to raise the dependency figure to £20 a week.

There remains the question of the deceased's financial contribution to the home, had she lived, by going out to work. Some account must be taken of that, although outside employment necessarily reduces the amount of hours spent in the home and to some extent, therefore, the total sum of services rendered to all who live there. Accordingly, I raise the dependency figure yet further to £21·50 per week.

All that remains is the question of the multiplier which it is appropriate to apply. This involves a number of considerations, including the average number of years during which the boys would require the deceased's services, the possibility of her death through natural causes at some later age than the age at which she was killed, and so on. Furthermore, I have to take into account the possibility of the plaintiff remarrying, despite his present firm disinclination so to do.

The claims which widows bring nowadays for damages under the Fatal Accidents Acts must not involve a consideration of this nature. This is because Parliament determined by passing the Law Reform (Miscellaneous Provisions) Act 1971 that, in claims by widows for damages arising out of the death of their husbands, no account should be taken of the prospects of remarriage. But widowers must still, by reason of a distinction which I am unable to comprehend, go through the embarrassing process of being asked questions in the witness box about the possibility of remarrying. Thus the law obliges me to take account of such a possibility. In so doing, I bear in mind that the plaintiff has a comparatively large brood of boys. He may not find it easy, however much he later on becomes inclined to remarry, to find a woman to marry and to undertake the burden of caring for so many children who are not hers. The youngest boy is not yet 4 years of age. The plaintiff, as I have said, is now 43 years old. I think that the proper multiplier in all the circumstances, is 11 years. That means that his claim under the Fatal Accidents Acts amounts to £12,298. The award of £500 to the deceased's estate will, as usual, merge into that figure. I was informed by counsel for the plaintiff, that, at the outset of this case, agreement had been reached upon the special damage claim in the sum of £414·62 which represents loss of wages and is to be added to the personal injuries claim, which I have already assessed at £2,250.

Finally, there remains the question of interest. Upon the award of £2,250, the plaintiff will receive interest at the rate of 8 per cent. Upon the special damage figure of £414·62, he will receive interest at the rate of 4 per cent. from the date of the accident. As to the sum of £12,298, which is the figure I have awarded the dependants under the Fatal Accidents Acts, there will be interest at the rate of 8 per cent. from the date of the service of the writ.

[His Lordship after consultation with counsel adjourned for a short time. He then settled the apportionment of the £12,298 and granted a stay in so far as his award exceeded the sum paid into court.]

Order accordingly.

Solicitors: *Dolmans, Cardiff; Barkers, Cardiff.*

H. J.

[COURT OF APPEAL]

* LORD CHETWODE *v.* INLAND REVENUE COMMISSIONERS

1975 Dec. 5, 8, 9, 10, 11

Buckley and James L.JJ. and Sir John Pennycuick

Revenue—Income tax—Transfer of assets abroad—Taxpayer's "power to enjoy" "income" of trust fund invested in foreign non-trading company—Whether management expenses of company deductible from gross receipts in computing income—Company making short-term capital gains—Taxpayer's liability to pay tax thereon—Method of computation of gains—Income Tax Act 1952 (15 & 16 *Geo.* 6 & 1 *Eliz.* 2, *c.* 10), *s.* 412 (1) [1]*—Finance Act* 1962 (10 & 11 *Eliz.* 2, *c.* 44), *s.* 13 (1), *Sch.* 10 [2]*—Finance Act* 1965 (*c.* 25), *s.* 82 (2) [3]

[Reported by MRS. HARRIET DUTTON, Barrister-at-Law]

[1] Income Tax Act 1952, s 412 (1): see post, p. 313F–H.
[2] Finance Act 1962, s. 10 (1): see post, p. 322C–D.
S. 13 (1): see post, p. 322E–F.
Sch. 10: see post, p. 322G–H.
[3] Finance Act 1965, s. 82 (2): see post, p. 323A–B.

A In 1967 the taxpayer executed a deed of settlement whereby a company incorporated in the Bahama Islands was to hold property as the sole trustee for the benefit of the taxpayer's children but to pay the income of the trust fund to the taxpayer during his life. A total of £167,018 was transferred to the trustee company during 1967. Following the establishment of the settlement, the trustee company acquired all the share capital of Attleborough, a non-trading investment company
B also incorporated in the Bahama Islands. The trustee company transferred the assets of the trust fund to Attleborough which then acquired land and securities with it. Attleborough incurred expenditure during 1967 and 1968 in acquiring, managing and selling its stock. The taxpayer was assessed to income tax for the relevant years on the basis that as he had "power to enjoy" the income of Attleborough it should be deemed to be his income, by virtue of section 412 (1) of the Income Tax
C Act 1952. He appealed against the assessments, contending that the expenses and charges incurred by Attleborough should be deducted in computing the income which was attributable to him. He further contended that he was not liable to pay income tax on short-term gains or that if such tax was payable then the amount should be computed by reference to the difference between the sale price and the market value of the assets at the time of their disposal. The special commissioners
D dismissed the appeal, holding that it was the receipts or gross income of Attleborough that should be regarded as the taxpayer's income. They further held that the short-term gains made by Attleborough should be deemed income of the taxpayer and should be computed in accordance with Schedule 10 to the Finance Act 1962. Megarry J. dismissed the taxpayer's appeal, holding that the references in section 412 (1) to "income" should be construed as referring to gross income.
E He further held that the amount of income tax payable on the short-term gains had been correctly computed.

On appeal by the taxpayer:—

Held, allowing the appeal in part, (1) that the word "income" in section 412 (1) denoted "profits" and that since the taxpayer had "power to enjoy" the income of Attleborough only after deduction of management expenses and charges the deductions claimed in respect of those expenses so far as they
F could be shown properly to be charged to the revenue account were allowable (post, pp. 317G–H, 326D–E, H—327B, 328F—329A, F–H).

Lord Howard de Walden v. *Inland Revenue Commissioners* [1942] 1 K.B. 389, C.A. considered.

But (2) that section 82 (2) of the Finance Act 1965 could not operate to take Attleborough out of the charge to short-term capital gains tax as it had never been within it so that the
G taxpayer was accountable for income tax on short-term capital gains by virtue of section 412 of the Income Tax Act 1952 and that the gains accruing had been correctly computed in accordance with the general provisions of section 13 (1) of the Finance Act 1962 (post, pp. 324H—325A, G).

Sharkey v. *Wernher* [1956] A.C. 58, H.L.(E.) distinguished.

Decision of Megarry J. [1975] 1 W.L.R. 34; [1974] 3 All E.R. 625 reversed in part.
H

The following cases are cited in the judgments:

Congreve v. *Inland Revenue Commissioners* [1948] 1 All E.R. 948; 30 T.C. 163, H.L.(E.).

Howard de Walden (Lord) v. *Inland Revenue Commissioners* [1942] 1 K.B. 389; [1942] 1 All E.R. 287; 25 T.C. 121, C.A.

Latilla v. *Inland Revenue Commissioners* [1943] A.C. 377; [1943] 1 All E.R. 265; 25 T.C. 107, H.L.(E.).

Mangin v. *Inland Revenue Commissioner* [1971] A.C. 739; [1971] 2 W.L.R. 39; [1971] 1 All E.R. 179, P.C.

Mapp v. *Oram* [1969] 1 Ch. 293; [1968] 3 W.L.R. 442; [1968] 3 All E.R. 1, C.A.; [1970] A.C. 362; [1969] 3 W.L.R. 557; [1969] 3 All E.R. 215; 45 T.C. 651, H.L.(E.).

Philippi v. *Inland Revenue Commissioners* [1971] 1 W.L.R. 1272; [1971] 3 All E.R. 70; 47 T.C. 75, C.A.

Sharkey v. *Wernher* [1956] A.C. 58; [1955] 3 W.L.R. 671; [1955] 3 All E.R. 493; 36 T.C. 275, H.L.(E.).

Simpson v. *Grange Trust Ltd.* [1935] A.C. 422; 19 T.C. 231, H.L.(E.).

The following additional cases were cited in argument:

Fattorini (Thomas) (Lancashire) Ltd. v. *Inland Revenue Commissioners* [1942] A.C. 643; [1942] 1 All E.R. 619; 24 T.C. 328, H.L.(E.).

Inland Revenue Commissioners v. *Wood Brothers (Birkenhead) Ltd.* [1959] A.C. 487; [1959] 2 W.L.R. 47; [1959] 1 All E.R. 52; 38 T.C. 275, H.L.(E.).

Taylor v. *Good* [1974] 1 W.L.R. 556; [1974] 1 All E.R. 1137; 49 T.C. 277, C.A.

APPEAL from Megarry J.

The taxpayer, Lord Chetwode, a resident of the United Kingdom, was entitled to the income of a trust fund, the sole trustee being the Trust Corporation of Bahamas Ltd. During 1967 the taxpayer transferred a total of £167,018 13s. 6d. to the trustee company which sum was used to acquire the entire share capital of Attleborough Investment Co. Ltd., a company incorporated under the laws of the Bahama Islands. The taxpayer unsuccessfully appealed to the special commissioners against assessment to income tax for the years 1967–68 in the sum of £2,143 and 1968–69 in the sum of £3,670. Megarry J. dismissed the taxpayer's appeal holding that by virtue of section 412 (1) of the Income Tax Act 1952 the taxpayer should be liable to income tax on the gross receipts of Attleborough without deduction of management expenses and charges. He further confirmed the commissioners' decision that the taxpayer was liable to pay income tax on certain short-term capital gains made by Attleborough and that the amount of such tax had been correctly calculated.

The taxpayer appealed on the grounds (1) that "income" within the meaning of section 412 of the Income Tax Act 1952 formed the measure of assessment only upon an individual ordinarily resident in the United Kingdom having power to enjoy that income; (2) that in the absence of any statutory rules governing its computation, that income must necessarily be ascertained in accordance with the normal principles of commercial accounting; (3) that the judge was therefore wrong (a) in holding that the determination of income within the meaning of section 412 was a question of law; and (b) in rejecting the evidence tendered to the special commissioners of the principles of commercial accounting to be applied in the instant case, with their result; (4) that the preamble to section 412 established that the intention of the section was to restore, inasmuch as what was to be nullified was the avoidance of United Kingdom taxation; (5) that since the section was only activated by a transfer of assets, the true comparison was between what in fact was done and the like transaction if carried through in the United Kingdom, when determining what tax was avoided; (6) that since section 82 of the Finance Act 1965 totally recalled the short term gains tax charged under Case VII of Schedule

A D upon companies resident in the United Kingdom, the judge was wrong in holding: (a) that that recall had no bearing on Case VII of Schedule D where applied to companies for the purposes of section 412, and (b) that the comparison required was to assume that no transfer by the taxpayer had been made and that the income of Attleborough had accrued to the taxpayer personally; (7) that the judge was wrong in holding that there was no basis for an application of the principle
B established by *Sharkey* v. *Wernher* [1956] A.C. 58, since by so doing he gave no proper effect to: (a) the express terms in which Case VII of Schedule D was applied for the purposes of section 412 by section 16 of the Finance Act 1962 and Schedule 10 to that Act, and (b) the special commissioners' finding that the stocks sold by Attleborough had been acquired by, and were held by Attleborough by way of investment.

C

Desmond Miller Q.C., *P. G. Whiteman* and *I. Richards* for the taxpayer.

Leonard Bromley Q.C. and *B. J. Davenport* for the Crown.

BUCKLEY L.J. I will ask Sir John Pennycuick to deliver the first
D judgment.

SIR JOHN PENNYCUICK. This is an appeal from an order of Megarry J. made on July 18, 1974. The taxpayer is Lord Chetwode; the respondents are the commissioners of Inland Revenue. Summarily, the principal question is whether, in computing the income of a foreign company for the purpose of section 412 of the Income Tax Act 1952, it is proper to
E take expenses of management into account. There is a secondary question relating to capital gains tax, with which I will deal altogether separately after the first question.

Dealing then with the first question I will, in order to make it intelligible, read the preamble and the first subsection to section 412:

> "For the purpose of preventing the avoiding by individuals ordinarily
> F resident in the United Kingdom of liability to income tax by means of transfers of assets by virtue or in consequence whereof, either alone or in conjunction with associated operations, income becomes payable to persons resident or domiciled out of the United Kingdom, it is hereby enacted as follows:—(1) Where such an individual has by means of any such transfer, either alone or in conjunction with
> G associated operations, acquired any rights by virtue of which he has, within the meaning of this section, power to enjoy, whether forthwith or in the future, any income of a person resident or domiciled out of the United Kingdom which, if it were income of that individual received by him in the United Kingdom, would be chargeable to income tax by deduction or otherwise, that income shall, whether it would or would not have been chargeable to income tax
> H apart from the provisions of this section, be deemed to be income of that individual for all the purposes of this Act."

The only other relevant subsection in section 412 is subsection (5), which defines and expands the scope of the expression "deemed to have power to enjoy income." I will come back to that subsection at a later stage.

The facts of the case are set out in the case stated by the special commissioners and are relatively simple. On May 9, 1967, the taxpayer, that is Lord Chetwode, who at all material times was ordinarily resident in the United Kingdom executed a deed of settlement. By the settlement the Trust Corporation of Bahamas Ltd., a company incorporated and existing under the law of the Bahama Islands, was appointed the first trustee. By the terms of the settlement the trustees were to pay the income of the trust fund to the taxpayer during his life and subject to a power of appointment in favour of a surviving widow the capital and income of the trust fund was to be held for the benefit of the taxpayer's issue. The settlement contained a proviso that, notwithstanding anything to the contrary, the taxpayer should have power to revest in himself title to all or any part of the capital and unpaid income. The amount of the fund transferred by the taxpayer to the trustee was some £167,000. Immediately after the establishment of the settlement the trustee acquired the entire share capital of Attleborough. Attleborough was a company incorporated on March 21, 1967, under the laws of the Bahama Islands. All the assets of the trust fund were transferred by the trustee to Attleborough, part in payment for the share capital and the remainder upon interest-free loans, and were used by Attleborough to acquire land and securities. Attleborough was at all material times an investment company and did not at any such time carry on a trade. It was common ground that the taxpayer had power to enjoy the income of Attleborough within the meaning of section 412 (1) of the Income Tax Act 1952. Attleborough invested the sums transferred to it by the trustee in the purchase of United States stock and land in the Bahamas. A schedule of the stocks was exhibited to the case stated. In connection with the acquisition and management of its portfolio and purchases and sales of stocks, Attleborough incurred expenses and charges. The case stated then set out, under the two respective years with which the appeal is concerned, namely, 1967 and 1968, the expenses and charges incurred by Attleborough. Those consisted of an investment advisory fee, management fees, safekeeping charges, security handling fees and bank charges, registered office and executive office fees. The largest items were, in each year, the investment advisory fee and the management fees. The total sterling equivalent of the expenses and charges was £878 for 1967 and £1,243 for 1968. I mention in passing that certain other expenses were included in the accounts of Attleborough, but those items have, I think by agreement between the parties, been omitted from the expenses in respect of which deduction is sought. The case stated also sets out a trifling sum in each year representing collection costs.

The case stated then refers to evidence of accountancy practice given by Mr. Hobson on behalf of the taxpayer; Mr. Hobson being a partner in the firm of Messrs. Cooper & Lybrand, chartered accountants; and by Mr. Lawson on behalf of the Crown. The special commissioners said:

> "We took the view that the questions we had to decide were questions of law and not of accountancy practice. We accordingly made no findings with regard to their evidence."

They however set out the evidence in an appendix. I agree that this appeal turns wholly on questions of law, and that accountancy evidence takes the matter no further, except possibly on a matter of detail to which I will refer right at the end of this judgment.

A The commissioners then referred to a considerable number of cases which were cited before them, and proceeded to set out the contentions of the parties. It was contended on behalf of the taxpayer that (a) the accounts of Attleborough were prepared in accordance with the normal principles of commercial accountancy; (b) Attleborough's income was the balance shown by the receipts and expenditure account; and (c) section 412 did not authorise any attribution to the taxpayer of sums in excess
B of that balance. It was contended on behalf of the Crown that (a) the income of Attleborough which by section 412 was deemed to be the taxpayer's was the investment income which he would have received if the investment income actually received by Attleborough had instead been received by him; (b) the "income of a person resident . . . out of the United Kingdom" referred to in section 412 (1) was, in these appeals, the
C dividends and interest received by Attleborough undiminished by any of the "expenses and charges" referred to, and diminished only by the conceded costs of collection; (c) Attleborough did not carry on a trade and accordingly for tax purposes it had no profit consisting of the balance of receipts over expenditure. If it had been a United Kingdom investment company, Attleborough would have been taxable by deduction on its receipts. Any claim for relief in respect of "expenses of management,"
D as which some or all of the expenses itemised might qualify, would require a computation for the purposes only of section 57 (1) of the Finance Act 1965: but for the purposes of section 412 of the Income Tax Act 1952 they were irrelevant; and (d) the taxpayer was therefore in exactly the same position, vis-à-vis expenses, as if Attleborough's role had been played by an individual instead of a company. The special commissioners gave their decision as follows:

E

"It is common ground that section 412 of the Income Tax Act 1952 applies to the transactions in question and accordingly that income of Attleborough is deemed to be income of the [taxpayer]. Dealing first with the submission on behalf of the [taxpayer] that the income deemed to be his is the 'net' income of Attleborough (i.e. receipts less expenses), we think that a distinction is to be made between the
F income of an investment company and the profits of a trading company. The receipts of the latter are normally not 'pure' income, whereas the receipts of the former usually are. Section 412 (1) deems income 'which would be chargeable to income tax by deduction or otherwise' to be income of the individual concerned. Section 413 (2) gives him the same reliefs as if the income deemed to be his had
G actually been received by him. Read in conjunction with the preamble to section 412, and taking Chapter IV of Part 18 as a whole, the language appears to us to be apt to treat the 'pure' income of the non-resident person as income of the individual. We are fortified in this conclusion by a similar view expressed by our colleagues in *Philippi* v. *Inland Revenue Commissioners* [1971] 1 W.L.R. 1272. Accordingly we reject the submission."

H

The taxpayer appealed to the High Court. The case was heard by Megarry J., who gave a full judgment upholding the decision of the commissioners [1975] 1 W.L.R. 34. I will cite a few passages from this judgment, confining myself to those which seem to me to set out the reasoning on which the judge came to his conclusion. He said, at p. 37:

"At the centre of the dispute are the words 'income' that appear in section 412 (1), and in particular, 'any income of a person resident or

domiciled out of the United Kingdom,' here, Attleborough: for it is A
that income which under the subsection is to be deemed the taxpayer's
income. On behalf of the taxpayer, Mr. Miller contended that since
Attleborough is admittedly an investment company, it is impossible
to ascertain what is the 'income of' Attleborough until one has set
Attleborough's management expenses against Attleborough's receipts,
and struck a balance: and Attleborough's income is that balance. On
the other hand, Mr. Bromley, for the Crown, contended that although B
this would be appropriate if Attleborough were carrying on a trade,
it would be quite wrong to do so in the present case, where Attle-
borough has been found not to be trading. 'Income,' he said, meant
'income arising,' or 'income as it arises.' In the case of dividends
from investments the income arising consisted of the whole of the
dividends, with no deduction save for the cost of collection. Apart C
from the cost of collection, Attleborough's income consisted of the
dividends as they arrived on Attleborough's threshold. If Attle-
borough *had* been trading, its income as it arose would have been the
profits emerging on taking the proper accounts. I propose to refer
to Mr. Miller's construction of 'income' as 'net income' and Mr.
Bromley's as 'gross income,' for although neither expression is parti-
cularly explicit or accurate, each is sufficiently indicative of the meaning D
and has the great merit of brevity."

He then referred to the authorities put before him by Mr. Miller,
and read the preamble to section 412. He said, at pp. 38–39:

"The preamble is of assistance here because it states the purpose
of the section as being to prevent individuals resident in the United
Kingdom from avoiding liability to income tax by transferring assets E
whereby 'income becomes payable to' persons resident or domiciled
outside the United Kingdom. That is a phrase which seems to me
to be compatible with 'income' meaning 'gross income' rather than
with 'income' meaning 'net income.' I shall discuss this further
in due course . . ."

"The initial phrase 'income becomes payable to' a person is not, F
of course, verbally identical with the expressions 'income of' a
person, or 'income' simpliciter, which occur later in the subsection.
The question then arises whether the verbal contrast indicates a
difference in meaning. I do not think that it does. For one thing,
I find it difficult to imagine that a draftsman who had any intention
that the meanings of the expressions should differ would entrust his G
intention to so frail a craft as this. For another thing, when the
subsection is stripped down to its essentials, it sufficiently appears
that there is at least identity of nature between the various mentions
of 'income' in the subsection."

Megarry J. illustrated this by a simplified example, and continued, at
p. 39: H

"The question, of course, is whether the words 'income of' a
foreigner under (c) [in the example] can mean net income while the
phrase the 'income becomes payable to' foreigners in (b) is referring
to gross income. It would, I think, be very remarkable if it could,
for both are linked to the self-same transfer by A: it is by virtue
or in consequence of that transfer that income becomes payable to
foreigners under (b), and it is by means of that transfer that A

A has acquired rights by virtue of which he has power to enjoy any income of a foreigner under (c). That is not all. I accept to the full that great care must be exercised in relying on statements made by judges, however great, in cases in which a point did not arise and so the judges' minds may well have not been directed to that point. But I cannot regard it as wholly irrelevant that in [*Congreve* v. *Inland Revenue Commissioners* (1948) 30 T.C. 163] Lord Simonds
B (with whose speech the other Law Lords simply concurred) set out the section and then referred repeatedly (see 30 T.C. 163, 202, 203, 207) to 'income payable to' certain companies resident outside the United Kingdom, rather than, in the statutory phrase, the 'income of' those companies. In my judgment, therefore, the various references in section 412 (1) to 'income' are all to be
C construed as referring to gross income and not net income, in the sense in which I am using these expressions in this judgment; and I do not think that this construction is affected by any of the authorities cited by Mr. Miller on the meaning of 'income' in the taxing statutes generally."

Megarry J. then dealt with an argument by Mr. Miller that section
D 412 was fiscally "restorative" in its effect, restoring the fiscal state by making the taxpayer liable in the same way as if he had not made the transfer. I do not think I need refer separately to that argument, because the question turns on the construction of the section read in its context. Then Megarry J. said, at pp. 40–41: "A further question that arose was that of accountancy practice. . . . I think that the special commissioners were right in their view . . ." Then he referred to *Latilla* v. *Inland*
E *Revenue Commissioners* [1943] A.C. 377 and to one or two other cases, and at greater length to *Lord Howard de Walden* v. *Inland Revenue Commissioners* [1942] 1 K.B. 389, 397 and quoted the words of Lord Greene M.R.: "It scarcely lies in the mouth of the taxpayer who plays with fire to complain of burnt fingers." Megarry J. concluded, at p. 42: "In the result, therefore, I think that the special commissioners were
F right on this branch of the case, and that the appeal on this accordingly fails."

The grounds of appeal perhaps slightly mask the true issue in this case. The relevant ground is: "That in the absence of any statutory rules governing its computation, that income must necessarily be ascertained in accordance with the normal principles of commercial accounting." The question, as was not in dispute, is whether "income" in section 412
G denotes profits in the sense of the balance of receipts over outgoings, or simply dividends and interest. I have reached a different conclusion on this question from that of the commissioners and Megarry J. It seems to me that upon the natural construction of section 412 (1), read in conjunction with the preamble, the word "income" should be treated as denoting profit, i.e. the excess of receipts over outgoings. That means,
H of course, receipts and outgoings properly attributable to revenue account.

I observe first, for what it is worth, that the subject matter of the charge to income tax under the Income Tax Act is profits or gains: see sections 1, 122 and 123, which latter sections impose the charge under Schedule D. The income of an investment company, in the true sense, consists of profit; that is to say, the excess of receipts over outgoings. That is none the less so because in the case of a United Kingdom company dividends and interest are charged separately as such, the expenses being set off by way of allowance against the tax chargeable in respect of the A dividends and interest, normally tax charged by deduction: see on this point, the Income Tax Act 1952, section 425, which I need not read, and *Simpson* v. *Grange Trust Ltd.* [1935] A.C. 422. But, as a matter of reality and substance, it seems to me clear that the income of an investment company is profit in the sense of excess of receipts over outgoings.

My conclusion is supported by a number of considerations. (i) The income attributed to an individual under section 412 indisputably includes B trading income as well as investment income: see *Latilla* v. *Inland Revenue Commissioners* [1943] A.C. 377. Trading income is admittedly ascertained by reference to profit over a period of account. One might expect investment income to be treated in the same way. I doubt whether there is much weight in this point by itself, but it leads up to what I think is a very important point, to which I will refer below. (ii) Where the foreign C company concerned is subject to foreign tax, or where it has liabilities of a revenue character, for instance, mortgage interest, it is quite impossible to determine its income for any period without taking these into account. Mr. Bromley sought to meet this point by referring to section 413 (2) of the Act, which reads as follows:

> "In computing the liability to income tax of an individual chargeable D by virtue of the provisions of the last preceding section, the same deductions and reliefs shall be allowed as would have been allowed if the income deemed to be his by virtue of that section had actually been received by him."

That section, however, does not fit the position; for if indeed the income deemed to be his by virtue of the section, i.e. the income of Attleborough, E had actually been received by the taxpayer, he would not have been entitled to any relief by reference to the liabilities of Attleborough in respect of foreign tax or mortgage interest. We were told that, by way of concession, that subsection is treated as permitting of an allowance from the tax payable under section 412 of these liabilities of the foreign company. That concession is not relevant on the construction of the section. (iii) Those considerations to which I have been referring lead up to this F consideration, which seems to me to be of very great importance. Section 412 applies to persons resident or domiciled out of the United Kingdom; that is to say, persons resident or domiciled anywhere in the world other than in the United Kingdom. I mention in passing that the word "persons" of course includes individuals or partnerships as well as companies; but it is convenient to refer to foreign companies. Now if, G as must be the fact, the tax structure of many foreign countries is different from that of the United Kingdom, it is extremely difficult to see how, in computing the income of a company in such a country, one could apply the United Kingdom tax structure. If, for instance, one takes an investment company in any foreign country—say Ruritania—the tax law of which is entirely different from that of this country, then it seems to me that there is no justification for treating the income of that company as what it would H be if, contrary to the fact, the English tax structure were applicable. It seems to me that one can only compute the income of the Ruritanian company by reference to the law of Ruritania. (iv) Finally, the result seems to me to be fair. I cannot myself see any reason why it should be just to charge an individual resident in this country with a notional income greater than the income which in fact arises in favour of the foreign resident to whom he has transferred his assets. I appreciate that this section has

A been described as a penal section; but I do not think that is any reason, so far as fairness is concerned, for attributing to the English resident income which he never in any sense of the word had power to enjoy.

I should at this stage refer to section 412 (5). That subsection reads as follows:

> " An individual shall, for the purposes of this section, be deemed to
> B have power to enjoy income of a person resident or domiciled out of the United Kingdom if—(*a*) the income is in fact so dealt with by any person as to be calculated, at some point of time, and whether in the form of income or not, to enure for the benefit of the individual; or (*b*) the receipt or accrual of the income operates to increase the value to the individual of any assets held by him or for his benefit; or (*c*) the individual receives or is entitled to receive, at any time, any
> C benefit provided or to be provided out of that income or out of moneys which are or will be available for the purpose by reason of the effect or successive effects of the associated operations on that income and on any assets which directly or indirectly represent that income; or (*d*) the individual has power, by means of the exercise of any power of appointment or power of revocation or otherwise, to obtain for himself, whether with or without the consent of any other
> D person, the beneficial enjoyment of the income, or may, in the event of the exercise of any power vested in any other person, become entitled to the beneficial enjoyment of the income; or (*e*) the individual is able in any manner whatsoever, and whether directly or indirectly, to control the application of the income."

That subsection defines by way of enlargement the meaning of the
E expression " power to enjoy income." The subsection is in a form familiar in deeming provisions in taxing Acts, the effect being that the words " power to enjoy income " have a much wider scope than would be covered by the words in their unexpanded sense. I do not think, however, that subsection (5) has any bearing upon what is meant by the expression " income " in the preamble and subsection (1). Subsection (5)
F is concerned only with the circumstances in which someone is deemed to have power to enjoy income when that income has been ascertained.

Mr. Bromley for the Crown stressed the purpose of section 412 as set out in the preamble. He contended that one should construe the operative provision, subsection (1), so as to give effect to the purpose set out in the preamble. I agree with that contention so far as the terms of the operative provision permit. But it is not, I think, legitimate to distort the natural
G meaning of the operative provision in order to achieve this result.

We were referred to a statement of principle upon construction by Lord Donovan in *Mangin* v. *Inland Revenue Commissioner* [1971] A.C. 739, which appears to me to be exactly in point here. Lord Donovan said, at p. 746:

> "These contentions pose the question of the true construction of
> H section 108. . . . it may be useful to recall at the outset some of the rules of interpretation which fall to be applied. First, the words are to be given their ordinary meaning. They are not to be given some other meaning simply because their object is to frustrate legitimate tax avoidance devices. . . . Secondly, ' . . . one has to look merely at what is clearly said. There is no room for any intendment. There is no equity about a tax. There is no presumption as to tax. Nothing is to be read in, nothing is to be implied. One can only look fairly at

> the language used': *per* Rowlatt J. in *Cape Brandy Syndicate* v. *Inland Revenue Commissioners* [1921] 1 K.B. 64, 71. . . . Thirdly, the object of the construction of a statute being to ascertain the will of the legislature it may be presumed that neither injustice nor absurdity was intended. If therefore a literal interpretation would produce such a result, and the language admits of an interpretation which would avoid it, then such an interpretation may be adopted. Fourthly, the history of an enactment and the reasons which led to its being passed may be used as an aid to its construction."

So here one must certainly, in so far as it is possible to do so, construe the operative provision in section 412 (1) so as to give effect to the intention declared by the preamble; but one cannot go outside the natural meaning of the words contained in subsection (1).

Upon the question of construction, Mr. Bromley contended that the expression "income becomes payable" in the preamble, and the expression "income of" in section 412 (1) bear the same meaning. I agree with that contention, as I have already indicated. Mr. Bromley then contended that the expression "income becomes payable" in the preamble indicates immediate payability of dividends and interest as they arise, and that the expression "income of" in subsection (1) must bear the same meaning. It seems to me, however, that it is impossible to put that construction upon the expression "income becomes payable to" in the preamble without more ado, because the words so construed are wholly inapplicable to the income of a trade, which is likewise covered by the preamble and subsection (1). One is left with two expressions differently worded but bearing the same meaning, namely, "income becomes payable to" and "any income of." The problem is to determine their scope in their context. For the reasons I have given, I think that in both expressions the word "income" should be construed as meaning "profit."

Mr. Bromley summarised his contentions under ten heads. It will be convenient to deal with his contentions under those heads, which, if I may say so, clearly and admirably express the purport of his argument. (i) The time to ascertain income from investment is the time when the income arises. That is to say, upon his contention, the relevant time is from day to day as the dividend or interest is payable. I agree that the relevant time is when the income arises, in the sense that one must ascertain the income from year to year in the same way as one ascertains the income from a trade. I do not agree that the proper time is from day to day. (ii) The words "income of" in section 412 (1) bear the same sense as "income becomes payable to" in the preamble. I agree with this point; but, as I have already said, it seems to me that in both expressions the word "income" means "profit" and it is not possible to construe the word "income" in relation to a company which has trading income as well as investment income as income arising from day to day. (iii) The purpose of section 412 is to prevent the avoidance by an individual resident in the United Kingdom of liability to income tax by means of transfers abroad. With that I agree. (iv) This purpose fails if deductions are permitted which would not be available to the individual. I do not know whether it can be truly said that, by allowing deductions to a foreign company which would not be available to a United Kingdom individual, the purpose of section 412 can be said to fail. However that may be, the purpose of the section is effectuated, so far as it is effectuated, by the operative provision and if that provision fails in any respect to effectuate

A the purpose, then I think it must be accepted that to that extent the section
has misfired, and one must not distort the operative provision. (v) The
Income Tax Act 1952 requires the balancing of receipts and expenditure
in relation to a trade but not in relation to the holding of investments.
(vi) Section 425 recognises a limited balancing in the case of an investment
company. Generally speaking on these two points, it is true that the
scheme of the Income Tax Act is to charge investment income as such,
B leaving expenses in the case of a company to be repaid by way of
allowance. But here one is concerned with the meaning of "income"
in relation to a foreign resident. It seems to me, as I have already
indicated, that different considerations must apply. (vii) Section 412
does not affect the foreign recipient. Indeed, it does not do so; but one
has to measure the income of the foreign recipient. (viii) Dividends are
C "income" for the purpose of the Income Tax Act 1952. That, I think, is
the same point as under head (v) above. (ix) On the taxpayer's construction,
"power to enjoy" under section 412 (5) has a limited operation
defeating the purpose of the preamble. It seems to me that the construction
of "income" as meaning "profit" does not of itself in any way limit
the operation of subsection (5). That subsection is concerned only with
the circumstances in which the income is deemed to be enjoyed, and not
D with the ascertainment of the income. (x) Section 413 (1) does not apply
to earned surplus, but does apply to dividends. I have not read section
413 (1) which is in these terms:

> "Tax at the standard rate shall not be charged by virtue of the last
> preceding section in respect of income which has borne tax at the
> standard rate by deduction or otherwise but, save as aforesaid, tax
> E chargeable at the standard rate by virtue of that section shall be
> charged under Case VI of Schedule D and all assessments in respect
> thereof shall be made by the special commissioners."

With great respect, I do not follow the bearing of this point. So far as
I can see, section 413 (1) saves from double taxation United Kingdom
income received by the foreign resident which has already borne English
F tax, e.g. a dividend, and goes on to provide that with this exception the
income chargeable upon the United Kingdom taxpayer by reference to
the income of the foreign resident shall be chargeable under Case VI.

We were referred to a number of cases of high authority, including
Latilla v. *Inland Revenue Commissioners* [1943] A.C. 377, *Lord Howard
de Walden* v. *Inland Revenue Commissioners* [1942] 1 K.B. 389, *Congreve*
G v. *Inland Revenue Commissioners* [1948] 1 All E.R. 948 and *Mapp* v.
Oram [1970] A.C. 362. In none of these cases did the present point arise
for decision, and I think it unlikely that it was in the mind of any of those
who gave the judgments in those cases. I have not myself found any help
from reference to occasional words or phrases used in those cases in
connection with some quite different issue. That comment applies in
particular to the words or expressions used by Lord Simonds in the
H *Congreve* case. I do not think it would be useful to go through the judgments
or speeches in those cases in order to show that they do not throw
any light on the issue in the present case. I observe in passing that the
decision of this court in the *Lord Howard de Walden* case seems to me
a strikingly harsh one and, although we are bound, of course, to apply it
in proper circumstances, I do not find it a very easy decision.

I should perhaps mention *Philippi* v. *Inland Revenue Commissioners*
[1971] 1 W.L.R. 1272. In that case, the present point arose before the

special commissioners, and they gave a decision to the same effect as the special commissioners and Megarry J. did in the present case. The case went to the High Court and the Court of Appeal; but, for some good reason, this particular point was not pursued, and the judgments in the High Court and the Court of Appeal throw no light upon the point. A

I conclude that on this first question the appeal should be allowed.

I turn to the second question, which can be much more shortly dealt with. There, summarily, the question is whether the taxpayer is liable in respect of short-term capital gains made by Attleborough. Turning back to the case stated, the following facts are set out. In 1967 and 1968 Attleborough sold some securities. The case stated then sets out particulars showing in respect of two securities a gain, and in respect of the other a loss. I will next read, in order that the point may be intelligible, the relevant statutory provision dealing with this point. The Finance Act 1962 imposed a charge in respect of gains from acquisition and disposal of assets. Sections 10, 13 (1) and 16 (8) provide as follows: B C

> "10 (1) Without prejudice to any other provision of the Income Tax Acts directing income tax to be charged under Schedule D, tax under that Schedule for the year 1962–63 or any subsequent year of assessment shall be charged, subject to and in accordance with the rules contained in this Chapter, in respect of all gains accruing to any person resident and ordinarily resident for the year in the United Kingdom from his acquisition and disposal of any chargeable assets, not being gains which accrue as profits of a trade . . . (3) Tax charged under Schedule D by virtue of this section shall be charged under a new Case VII of that Schedule . . . D
>
> "13 (1) Subject to the provisions of this Chapter the gain accruing to a person from his acquisition and disposal of any asset shall be computed for purposes of Case VII in the like manner as it would fall to be computed for purposes of Case I of Schedule D if the acquisition and disposal (together with anything done by him to or in relation to the asset in connection with the acquisition and disposal or with a view to the disposal) had been an adventure in the nature of trade . . . E F
>
> "16 (8) . . . the enactments mentioned in the first column in Schedule 10 to this Act shall, for the purpose of adapting or applying them in relation to the provisions of this Chapter, have effect subject to and in accordance with the provision made in respect thereto in the second column in that Schedule."

Then, turning to Schedule 10 one finds it is headed "Modification of Enactments for Case VII of Schedule D." Then, in the left-hand column: "*Enactment and subject-matter*. . . . Chapter IV of Part XVIII (Avoidance of tax by transfers of income to persons abroad)." That is section 412 of the Income Tax Act 1952. Then, in the right-hand column: G

> "*Adaptation*. . . . References to income shall apply in the case of gains accruing from the acquisition and disposal of chargeable assets as they would apply if the gains were profits from a trade of dealing in the assets, and any such gains shall be treated as payable in the first instance to the person to whom they accrue." H

Pausing there, the effect of the Schedule is that where the foreign company makes a gain accruing from the acquisition or disposal of chargeable assets, that gain is treated as payable in the first instance to the

A foreign company, and then by virtue of section 412 it is to be treated as an element in computing the income which is deemed to be the income of the United Kingdom resident.

Section 82 (2) of the Finance Act 1965 provides:

> "Income tax shall not be charged by virtue of section 10 or section 14 of the Finance Act 1962 (short-term gains) in respect of an acqui-
> B sition and disposal of any chargeable assets by a company . . ."

That provision is part of a code of new provisions relating to the charge of income tax upon companies. The Finance Act 1965 did not repeal of Schedule 10 to the Finance Act 1962.

In that state of affairs and on the facts of the present case, the following contentions were advanced on behalf of the taxpayer. By reason of
C the partial recall of short-term gains by section 82 of the Finance Act 1965, Attleborough was not liable to tax under Case VII on its short-term gains. Schedule 10 to the Finance Act 1962, provided that short-term gains should be treated as payable in the first instance to the person to whom they accrued. In the present case, that person was Attleborough, which was never liable to tax on short-term gains. Accord-
D ingly the taxpayer was not taxable in respect of Attleborough's short-term gains. Then there was an alternative contention: tax on short-term gains should be computed by reference to the difference between the sale price and the open market value of the asset disposed of at the time of disposal on the principle of *Sharkey* v. *Wernher* [1956] A.C. 58. The contention on this point of the Crown was that by section 16 (8) of and Schedule 10 to the Finance Act 1962, references to income in section 412
E included short-term gains. The abolition of tax on a company's short-term gains by section 82 (2) of the Finance Act 1965 did not affect Attleborough which being a foreign company had never, whether before or after the enactment of the Finance Act 1965, been liable to United Kingdom tax on short-term gains. The principle in *Sharkey* v. *Wernher* did not apply to the deeming provisions referred to. The commissioners
F dealt with this point as follows:

> "The next question is whether the short-term gains of Attleborough are deemed to be the [taxpayer's] income, and, if so, the amount thereof. In our view the answer turns on the effect of Schedule 10 to the Finance Act 1962, whereby references to income in Chapter IV apply to short-term gains as if the gains were trading profits.
> G We do not think that the impact of this provision is affected by section 82 of the Finance Act 1965 (or the subsequent amendments thereof), which abolished a company's liability to short-term gains tax. Those gains were never chargeable in the hands of Attleborough, and, as we have indicated above, it is the trading and investment income of Attleborough, as the case may be, which is deemed to be the [taxpayer's] income. The [taxpayer] sought to
> H apply the principle in *Sharkey* v. *Wernher* to the computation of the gains. The gains to which Schedule 10 refers are the gains accruing from an acquisition and disposal of an asset and, in our view, such acquisition and disposal fall to be taken together and there is no room for the substitution of the market value for the price."

Megarry J. [1975] 1 W.L.R. 34 came to the same conclusion, his reasoning being expressed, at p. 43:

"Now the contention of Mr. Miller was, in brief, that section 82 A removed the foundation on which rested any liability of the taxpayer to short-term capital gains tax. Since under section 82 (2) the charge of tax under Case VII of Schedule D ceased to apply to any company, there could thereafter be no avoidance of such tax, and so no basis for applying section 412 to chargeable gains. Alternatively, he said, as the expressed object of section 16 (8) of the Finance Act 1962 was to apply section 412 for the purposes of Case B VII of Schedule D, the repeal of that tax as respected any company involved that application ceasing to have effect in the case of any company. If these contentions failed, Mr. Miller had an alternative contention based on *Sharkey* v. *Wernher* [1956] A.C. 58 to which I shall turn in due course. . . . The short answer to Mr. Miller's contentions seems to me to be that, as Mr. Bromley pointed out, the C charge to short-term capital gains tax is imposed by section 10 (1) of the Finance Act 1962 only on those resident and ordinarily resident in the United Kingdom. Others such as Attleborough were never within the charge. There was thus never any question of section 82 of the Finance Act 1965 taking Attleborough out of the charge, for Attleborough was never within it, and so the section did nothing that is relevant to this case. . . . The *Sharkey* v. *Wernher* D [1956] A.C. 58 point is this. On the footing that Case VII of Schedule D still applied, Mr. Miller said that its application involved a deemed or notional trade of dealing with the assets from which the gain or surplus arose. As the transactions consisted of dealings in shares, the value to be attributed to them, and to be set against the sale price, was the open market value at the date when the E relevant decision to deal in them was taken and implemented. In effect that, I think, meant that the open market value would be taken at the time of disposal, and so there would be no profit on the transaction. Mr. Bromley, on the other hand, said that there was nothing to support any concept of deemed or notional trading, and that the gain was to be computed in accordance with the general provisions of section 13 of the Finance Act 1962. For the purposes F of section 412 of the Income Tax Act 1952, references to income, by virtue of Schedule 10 to the Finance Act 1962, apply in the case of gains 'as they would apply if the gains were profits from a trade of dealing in the assets'; but that does not seem to me to introduce any concept of notional trading in computing the gains. What section 412 says about income is to apply to gains, computed G in accordance with the general provisions of the Act, in the same way as it would apply to profits from a trade: but that is very far from saying that the gains are to be computed in the same way as profits, or that there is to be any deemed trading. I can therefore see no basis for any application of the *Sharkey* v. *Wernher* principle."

H

On this question I am in complete agreement with what was said by the special commissioners and by Megarry J. and really there is nothing which can usefully be added. So far as the first part of the question is concerned, Attleborough is a foreign company to which the charge under the Act of 1962 has never applied. It is concerned only with the ascertainment of Attleborough's income for the purpose of making a charge on the United Kingdom resident. That was dealt with by Schedule 10

A to the Act of 1962. The position of Attleborough itself is in no way affected by the Act of 1965. The provision in Schedule 10 to the Act of 1962 stands unaffected, and there is no reason why by implication one should treat that provision as having been in some way superseded by the Act of 1965. So far as the *Sharkey* v. *Wernher* [1956] A.C. 58 point is concerned, it is quite clear that the effect of the Act of 1962 is not that the person concerned (including, as regards Schedule 10, the foreign company) is B deemed to be carrying on a trade, but that the gains are to be ascertained as if it were carrying on a trade. The principle of *Sharkey* v. *Wernher* has no application in such a case. I would only add that if this argument were well founded, it would, as far as I can see, knock the bottom out of the whole of the capital gains provisions except possibly in respect of somebody who was in truth carrying on a trade. So, on this question, C I would dismiss the appeal.

There is only one further matter which I should mention. I referred to it earlier in this judgment and said I would come back to it. The expenses shown by the accounts of Attleborough include an investment advisory fee and management fee as the two largest expenses. There was a finding by the commissioners that Attleborough incurred those expenses. There was no finding that the expenses were properly attribut- D able to revenue account. This matter was left in the air. Evidence was given by the accountants on either side concerning these items. Mr. Hobson, the accountant called on behalf of the taxpayer, said he did not know to whom and for what purpose the investment advisory fee had been paid, and he had not seen a breakdown of the expenses in the accounts. Mr. Lawson, for the Crown, said that he would require an E explanation of the item "Investment Advisory Fee" before approving it; he would also require to know what services the management fee covered, and for what purpose the "Registered Office and Executive Offices Fees" were included.

As I have said, the commissioners made no finding on this point. So it remains open to the Crown, if it is so minded, to challenge these two items of expenditure in the account, not on the ground that they were not F incurred, because we have the commissioners' finding on that, but on the ground that they are not properly chargeable to revenue. We can perhaps come back to this point after the judgments. So far as I can see, the case must, if necessary, be remitted to the commissioners on this particular point.

G JAMES L.J. I do not wish to add anything to what has been said in the judgment just delivered upon the short-term gains point, save to say I find myself in agreement with the judge and with the special commissioners, whose conclusions are set out in the case stated.

The question whether the amount of income deemed by section 412 of the Income Tax Act 1952, to be the taxpayer's income is the investment H income of Attleborough without deduction save for minor expense of collection, or that investment income less deductions of management and other expenses incurred by Attleborough, is one which, to one coming from a less sophisticated field in the common law, can I think be answered upon a narrow basis. The answer surely must depend in the end on the construction of the word "income" in the expression "that income shall . . . be deemed to be income of that individual" in section 412 (1). I apply, I hope correctly, the principles of construction stated by Lord Donovan in

Mangin v. *Inland Revenue Commissioner* [1971] A.C. 739, 746. There is no definition of " income " in the Act itself. There is a presumption that where a section of a statute uses the same word in different places, then, unless the context clearly indicates the contrary, that word shall be given the same meaning in each place it is used. The preamble to section 412 includes the words " income becomes payable to persons." In the operative part of the section there are some 24 references to " income," and I find nothing in the context in which the word is used in those places to indicate that it should not be given the same meaning wherever it is used. Contrast the position in section 413, a section dealing with double taxation, where the words appear " income which has borne tax at the standard rate by deduction or otherwise," where a particular type of income is by the context defined, namely, that income which has so borne that tax. The words " payable to " in the preamble to section 412, and the words " income arising from any such assets " in section 412 (4), upon which some reliance has been placed in the course of the argument, do not in my judgment help to define the word " income." They merely describe respectively for the purposes of the preamble and subsection (4) the destination of and the source of the income that is there referred to. In the absence of any definition of " income," I think it is right, as we have been invited to do, to have regard to the charging provisions of the Act, and there in section 1 and again in section 123 one finds the reference to profits or gains as the basis for the liability to tax. In the absence of any authority compelling a different construction to be placed on the word " income " in section 412, in my judgment that word should be given the meaning of " profit " in accordance with the meaning, as I see it, to be derived by way of assistance from the charging provisions.

I find some support for this construction of the word " income " in the association of that word with the expression " power to enjoy." I agree with what has already been said, that section 412 (5) provides for the circumstances in which a person shall be deemed to have the power to enjoy, and does not in any way define the word " income " in subsection (1). Nevertheless, the argument addressed to us by Mr. Whiteman for the taxpayer upon the wording of subsection (5), stressing the aspect of income in the sense of something capable of enjoyment, was a powerful one. If the construction for which the Crown contended is adopted, it follows in my judgment that a taxpayer may be taxed upon something which could never be his to enjoy. To adopt that construction would be to use the section for a purpose beyond the undoubted purpose of the section, of preventing the avoidance of liability to pay tax.

I have so far dealt with the question, I will not say untrammelled by authority, but without such assistance as can be derived from authority. In the numerous cases which have been cited in the course of argument, I find no principle which leads me to a different conclusion. It is difficult, and often dangerous I think, to seek to derive help from isolated passages in the speeches or judgments in other cases in which the present point was not in issue. But I do find some support for the views I have formed, in particular in *Mapp* v. *Oram* [1969] 1 Ch. 293, in the opening words of the judgment of Salmon L.J. at p. 312, and in the passage in the speech of Lord Upjohn in the House of Lords [1970] A.C. 362, 376. Lord Upjohn was considering a different section, section 212, but his words " It "—that is, the income—" cannot mean gross receipts, for every person earning an income has expenses " are telling words, and I think they are relevant to a consideration of section 412.

A I agree with the reasoning and the conclusion expressed in the judg-
ment delivered and, for those reasons, I would allow the appeal on that
one point.

Before parting with it, may I add my feeling of unease at the decision
in *Lord Howard de Walden* v. *Inland Revenue Commissioners* [1942]
1 K.B. 389, which decision is of course binding upon us and to which one
must loyally adhere, although it makes no difference to my reasoning in
B the present case.

BUCKLEY L.J. I agree with both the judgments which have been
delivered, and I do not propose to cover the general ground again.
But I would say something about *Lord Howard de Walden* v. *Inland
Revenue Commissioners* [1942] 1 K.B. 389, which was relied upon
C strenuously by Mr. Bromley in support of his contention that the relevant
income here was the income of Attleborough consisting of the dividends
and interest received by Attleborough from the investments held by that
company without deduction for expenses incurred in the management of
the company. Lord Howard de Walden had transferred assets of very
considerable value to four Canadian companies. The Canadian companies
D had no other assets. At the relevant time the only relevant interests of
Lord Howard de Walden in the Canadian companies consisted of a life
interest in certain promissory notes of the companies, a share of certain
sums of money on deposit with the companies payable on demand, a very
small number of shares in the Canadian companies, and certain annuities
payable by one or other of those companies. He had divested himself
of all other interests in the companies. The transfers in question were
E admittedly within the terms of the preamble to section 18 of the Finance
Act 1936, which was the precursor of section 412 of the Income Tax Act
1952. Lord Howard de Walden was assessed on the basis that the whole
income of the Canadian companies would be chargeable to income tax
as if it were his income received by him in the United Kingdom. The
argument presented on behalf of Lord Howard de Walden was to the
F effect that he could only be taxed under section 18 on so much of the income
of the Canadian companies as he had power to enjoy or should be deemed
to have power to enjoy. Accordingly, it was contended, only so much
of the Canadian companies' income as should remain after giving effect
to all other rights in those companies should be taxed. I base this short
statement of the argument on the report at p. 389. Lord Greene M.R.,
delivering the judgment of this court, said that the only question was
G whether the assessment should be based on that part only of the Canadian
companies' income which Lord Howard de Walden was actually in a
position to enjoy, a very small part of the companies' income, or on
the whole income. The grounds relied on in that case for saying that
Lord Howard de Walden had power to enjoy income for the purposes of
the section were paragraphs (*b*) and (*c*) of section 18 (3), now replaced
H by paragraphs (*b*) and (*c*) of section 412 (5) of the Income Tax Act 1952.
Because the receipt by each company of its income was regarded as
operating to increase the value of the notes in which Lord Howard de
Walden had a life interest and to enhance the value of the debts due
to him on account of the deposits, and because the payments made in
respect of these obligations and the annuities out of the companies'
income were benefits received by Lord Howard de Walden out of that
income, all of that income was held to be deemed to be Lord Howard

de Walden's income for the purposes of the charge under the section. A Lord Greene M.R. said that an examination of the language of section 18 (3), in conjunction with section 18 (1), made it clear that the power to enjoy income with which section 18 (1) dealt need not by any means necessarily extend to the whole of the income of the non-resident person, but that the court was unable to accept the argument that the income which was caught by subsection (1) was limited to the income which the taxpayer was in fact entitled or able to receive. B Lord Howard de Walden had in that case no reserve powers enabling him to undo the transactions and to recover the Canadian companies' assets into his own possession as the taxpayer has in the present case. His interest in the Canadian companies was irrevocably confined to the limits I have stated. The rival arguments were that, on the true construction of the section, (a) the extent to which he should be treated as having a power to enjoy income of the Canadian com- C panies should be ascertained by reference to the limited extent of his actual interest in the companies, and (b) that the extent to which he should be treated as having such a power should be treated as extending to the whole of the income of the companies. No question appears to have been raised or debated as to what constituted the whole income of the companies for this purpose. No one could, I think, deny that the consequence of the decision of this court in that case was extremely harsh. D The court justified this on the ground that the section is a penal section. To tax a taxpayer on income he does not in fact receive may perhaps properly be described as penal; but I am sure that none of the distinguished members of that court would have considered that the fact that a statutory provision is of a penal character could justify adopting a harsher construction than the language requires. One cannot tell from the report how far and in what way E the question of construction was developed, but I can see no sign in either the report of the argument or in the judgment that certain considerations which seem to me to arise on the language of the section were taken into account. In any case, however, I do not think that that decision can be treated as authority for the proposition that where the non-resident recipient of income is a non-trading company the gross receipts of that company must be treated as the income of a United Kingdom resident who has or F is to be treated as having power to enjoy the income of that company.

Section 412 of the Income Tax Act 1952, stated shortly, provides that where a United Kingdom resident has, by means of a transfer of assets whereby income becomes payable to a non-resident, acquired any rights by virtue of which he has power to enjoy any income of a non-resident which, if it were his income received in the United Kingdom, would be chargeable G to income tax, *that* income (and I italicise the word "that") shall be deemed to be his income. The relevant income is, in my judgment, any income of the non-resident which the United Kingdom resident had, within the meaning of the section, power to enjoy. One must then turn to subsection (5) to discover what amounts to a power to enjoy within the meaning of the section. I will not read the subsection again. The paragraph directly H applicable here is paragraph (*d*). Of what income of Attleborough had the taxpayer at the relevant date, which I will discuss in a moment, power to obtain for himself the beneficial enjoyment? Clearly he could not obtain the beneficial enjoyment of any income which before the relevant date had been properly spent by Attleborough; nor, in my opinion, could he be properly regarded as having power to obtain the beneficial enjoyment of any income which on proper accounting principles Attleborough ought to set aside to provide for any expenditure properly chargeable against revenue already incurred before the relevant date but not then yet discharged.

What, then, is the relevant date for this purpose? I apprehend that, as a practical matter at any rate, the earliest date would be the end of the fiscal year or other period in respect of which the assessment is made. Until that date, the total income of the company for that period could not be known and no assessment could be raised. By that date the company's expenditure for that period would all have been incurred, if not actually paid. Mr. Bromley submitted that the date at which it must be determined whether section 412 applies is the date when the income becomes payable to the non-resident party. He relied on *Congreve* v. *Inland Revenue Commissioners* [1948] 1 All E.R. 948, and in particular on what was said by Cohen L.J. delivering the judgment of the court, at the foot of p. 197. Cohen L.J. considered the date at which it must be shown that the person to whom income becomes payable in consequence of a transfer of assets and associated operations is a non-resident. The answer to that question must be the date when the income becomes payable, for if the recipient is not then a non-resident, the transfer is not, so far as that income is concerned, a transfer such as is described in the preamble to the section. The question when it must be determined whether a United Kingdom resident has " power to enjoy " is a different question. In the case of a trading company, this obviously could not be the date at which each trade receipt occurs, for such a receipt is not income and the company's income for the period cannot be ascertained until the end of the accounting period, when there might turn out to have been no profit and so no income. I can see no good reason why in this respect a non-trading company should be treated differently from a trading company. It might, I think, be suggested that the date for determining the existence or want of a " power to enjoy " is the date of assessment; but whether this date or the end of the relevant accounting period be selected the consequence is, I think, the same. The United Kingdom resident could not, by the exercise of any such powers as are referred to in section 412 (5) (*d*), obtain for himself the beneficial enjoyment of any income of the non-resident company which had then been expended or incurred for any such purpose that it is proper to be charged against the company's revenue account.

Mr. Bromley suggested that paragraphs (*a*) and (*b*) of section 412 (5) might also apply in this case. But, upon the construction which I, in common with my brethren, think should be put upon the word " income," expenditure on the management of the company's affairs would not be an application of income; and therefore it seems to me that those paragraphs cannot apply. In any case, for my part, I think that I should feel great difficulty in agreeing to the proposition that income spent by Attleborough on ordinary management expenses, or it may be in paying foreign taxes relative to the dividends or interest received by the company, could properly be described as being so dealt with as to be calculated to enure to the taxpayer's benefit within the meaning of paragraph (*a*), or that the receipt or accrual of income which is so spent could be properly said to operate to increase the value of any asset held by the taxpayer or for his benefit within the meaning of paragraph (*b*). These considerations reinforce me in the view that Attleborough's income for any year for the purpose of section 412 consists of its receipts of an income character, less the amount of any expenditure properly chargeable against its revenue account.

For these reasons, and for those which have been developed in the

judgments delivered by my brethren, I agree that this appeal should be A
allowed on the first and perhaps major point, but should be dismissed as regards that part of it which relates to short-term capital gains.

Appeal allowed in part.
Taxpayer to have three-quarters of his costs in Court of Appeal and below.
Case remitted to special commissioners to B
determine Attleborough's income.
Leave to appeal on terms as to taxpayer's costs.

Solicitors: *Withers; Solicitor of Inland Revenue.*

C

[PRIVY COUNCIL]

* PETER ZIDERMAN . . . . APPELLANT D

AND

GENERAL DENTAL COUNCIL . . . . RESPONDENT

[ON APPEAL FROM THE GENERAL DENTAL COUNCIL]

1975 Oct. 28; Dec. 8 — Lord Diplock, Lord Kilbrandon and Lord Russell of Killowen E

Dentist—Discipline—Erasure from register following conviction—Shoplifting—Gravity of offence for which convicted—Relevance of previous convictions—Dentists Act 1957 (5 & 6 *Eliz.* 2, *c.* 28), *s.* 25 (2) (*a*)

Section 25 of the Dentists Act 1957 provides: F

"(1) A registered dentist who . . . (*a*) has been convicted . . . of an offence which, if committed in England, would be a felony or misdemeanour . . . shall be liable to have his name erased from the register. (2) A person's name shall not be erased under this section—(*a*) on account of conviction for an offence which does not, either from
the trivial nature of the offence or from the circumstances G
under which it was committed, disqualify a person for practising dentistry . . ."

The appellant, who was a registered dentist, had been convicted of 10 offences of obtaining money by false pretences in 1970 and, as a result of those convictions, his name was erased from the Dentists' Register in June 1971. His name was
restored to the register in November 1972. On December 31, H
1974, he was convicted of the theft of articles from a shop to the value of £3·40. The Disciplinary Committee of the General Dental Council, acting under section 25 of the Dentists Act 1957, ordered that the appellant's name be erased from the register in respect of that offence of shoplifting.

On appeal to the Judicial Committee, the appellant contended that the legal assessor had failed to advise the committee that they could not consider his previous convictions in deciding, under section 25 (2) (*a*), whether the triviality of the offence

A or the circumstances under which it was committed were such that he should not be disqualified from practising dentistry:—

Held, dismissing the appeal, that section 25 (2) (*a*) of the Act stated in negative form the positive duty of the committee to be satisfied under subsection (1) (*a*) that the offence of shoplifting was of so grave a character that the appellant was unfit to practice his profession; that, in assessing the gravity of the offence for the purpose of considering the imposition of
B the penalty of erasing the appellant's name from the register, previous convictions were relevant and, since the weight to be attached to those convictions was a matter for the committee, the legal assessor was not required to give elaborate advice on the committee's legal duty in exercising their sentencing power and had correctly not advised them that the previous convictions were irrelevant in considering the gravity of the offence.

C *Per curiam.* Since the committee has a discretion whether to erase a name from the register, the conduct of a dentist after conviction is a relevant factor for the committee's consideration and they may properly, in an appropriate case, postpone sentence for a period during which the dentist would have an opportunity to show that he has rehabilitated himself (post, p. 333F–G).

D No case is referred to in the judgment.

The following case was cited in argument:

Pickup v. *Dental Board of the United Kingdom* [1928] 2 K.B. 459, D.C.

APPEAL (No. 19 of 1975) by the appellant, Peter Ziderman, from a
E determination (May 14, 1975) by the Disciplinary Committee of the General Dental Council that by reason of a conviction (December 31, 1974) for theft found proved against him his name should be erased from the Dentists' Register.

The grounds of appeal were that on a true construction of section 25 (2) (*a*) of the Dentists Act 1957 (1) it was the duty of the committee first to consider whether the offence of theft was one which, either
F because of its trivial nature or because of the circumstances under which it was committed, fell within a category of offences which did not show him to be unfitted to continue in practice as a dentist; and (2) in considering whether the offence fell within that category the committee were not entitled to take into account the appellant's previous convictions. Only if the committee were satisfied that the offence
G did not fall within that category were they entitled to take the appellant's previous convictions into account.

The facts are stated in the judgment of their Lordships.

Anthony Hidden for the appellant.
Richard Du Cann Q.C. and *Angela Durand* for the respondent.

H *Cur. adv. vult.*

December 8. The judgment of their Lordships was delivered by LORD DIPLOCK.

The appellant is a registered dentist. On December 31, 1974, he was convicted at the Marlborough Street magistrates' court on a charge of theft, viz. shoplifting. He had stolen a tie and a car leather, worth £3·40, at Selfridges on the previous day. To this offence he pleaded guilty. He was fined £250 and ordered to pay £50 costs. This was not his first conviction for an offence of dishonesty. In July 1970, he had been convicted of 10 offences of obtaining money by false pretences from the Executive Council of the National Health Service committed over a period ending in January 1969. On the occasion of that conviction he had asked for 62 other similar offences to be taken into consideration. Those convictions had been the subject of disciplinary proceedings before the Disciplinary Committee of the General Dental Council as a result of which his name was erased from the Dentists' Register on June 12, 1971. In November 1972, his name was restored to the register.

Disciplinary proceedings were brought against him in respect of the shoplifting conviction of December 31, 1974. They were heard by the committee on May 14, 1975, who again ordered that his name be erased from the register. From that order he now appeals to this Board.

The relevant provisions of section 25 of the Dentists Act 1957 under which the order was made are:

> "(1) A registered dentist who either before or after registration —(*a*) has been convicted either in Her Majesty's dominions or elsewhere of an offence which, if committed in England, would be a felony or misdemeanour . . . shall be liable to have his name erased from the register. (2) A person's name shall not be erased under this section—(*a*) on account of conviction for an offence which does not, either from the trivial nature of the offence or from the circumstances under which it was committed, disqualify a person for practising dentistry . . ."

The only ground upon which this appeal is brought is that the legal assessor gave to the committee advice as to the effect of section 25 (2) (*a*) that was wrong in law.

It was contended on behalf of the appellant that, upon the true construction of section 25 (2) (*a*): (1) It was the duty of the committee first to consider whether the offence of shoplifting for which he had been convicted on December 31, 1974, was one which, either because of its trivial nature or because of the circumstances under which it was committed, fell within a category of offences which did not show him to be the kind of person who was unfitted to continue in practice as a member of the dental profession. (2) In considering whether the offence fell within this category the committee were not entitled to take into consideration his previous convictions for offences of dishonesty committed in the period prior to February 1969. If they were satisfied that the offence of which he had been convicted on December 31, 1974, did not fall into this category, then, but only then, were they entitled to take into consideration those previous convictions in deciding whether or not to impose the penalty of erasing the appellant's name from the register. The legal assessor did not advise the committee to this effect. Indeed the only indication of the advice that he gave which is to be found in the transcript of the proceedings suggests that he advised them to the contrary. He is reported as saying:

> ". . . I propose to advise the committee, if I am asked, that they are entitled to take into account the previous history but, of course, similarity of the offences is very important."

Their Lordships do not doubt that before the committee decide to erase the name of a dentist from the register on the ground that he has been

A convicted of a criminal offence they must be satisfied that the offence which he committed was one that showed him to be unfitted to continue in practice as a member of the dental profession. The committee have no power to reprimand a dentist or to suspend him from practice temporarily. The only order they have power to make is for the erasure of his name from the register; and this prevents him from continuing to practise his profession. The purpose of disciplinary proceedings against a dentist who B has been convicted of a criminal offence by a court of law is not to punish him a second time for the same offence but to protect the public who may come to him as patients and to maintain the high standards and good reputation of an honourable profession. So, quite apart from section 25 (2) (*a*) of the Dentists Act 1957, it would be the duty of the committee, before deciding to inflict the only and draconian penalty which lies within C their power, to satisfy themselves that the offence of which the dentist had been convicted was of so grave a character as to show that he was unfitted to continue to practise his profession.

Section 25 (2) (*a*) does no more than to state expressly and in negative form the obverse of the positive duty of the committee that is implicit in the nature of their disciplinary jurisdiction and the consequences of the only penalty that they have power to impose. The retention of section D 25 (2) (*a*) in the Dentists Act 1957 (a consolidating Act) is due to the survival of a clause in similar terms which had its historical origin in section 13 of the Dentists Act 1878. It there appeared as a proviso to a general provision which made erasure the mandatory penalty for conviction of a criminal offence and gave to the General Council of Medical Education and Registration of the United Kingdom no discretion to refrain from E imposing it. The reference to "the trivial nature" of the offence and "the circumstances under which it was committed" is wide enough to cover, with one exception, all those matters, which the committee ought to take into consideration in deciding whether his committing the offence justified the conclusion that the dentist was unfitted to continue in practice as a member of the dental profession. The one exception is his conduct after the conviction. This may show that he has so rehabilitated himself F by the time the committee pronounces sentence that he has ceased to be unfitted to continue in practice as a dentist. It may be that under the Dentists Act 1878 this was strictly not a matter which the General Council could take into consideration in deciding whether or not to erase the name of a convicted dentist from the register; but once the body exercising disciplinary functions was granted a discretion whether or not to impose G the penalty in each individual case (as it was by the Dentists Act 1921), this matter too may be a relevant consideration. This justifies the current practice of the committee, in appropriate cases, of postponing sentence for a period during which the dentist has an opportunity to show that he has rehabilitated himself.

Convictions previous to that on which the charge before the committee is based do not fall within the category of subsequent conduct. In their H Lordships' view, the previous convictions of a person charged with an offence are relevant matters to be taken into account by a sentencing tribunal in assessing the gravity of the offence with which he is charged. They are thus relevant in determining whether or not it is an offence of too trivial a nature to justify the infliction of a particular penalty, particularly where that penalty is severe. Justice requires that the gravity of an offence should be reflected in the severity of the sentence imposed; and, as is manifest not only from the universal sentencing practice of judges but also

A from statutory provisions limiting the severity of penalties that may be imposed upon first offenders, the national sense of what constitutes justice in the field of sentencing recognises that an offence which is committed by a person who has offended before is graver than a similar offence committed by a person who offends for the first time. Indeed in Scotland, to which the Dentists Act 1957 also applies, an indictment contains a final paragraph (not disclosed to the jury) setting out the previous convictions of the accused as constituting an "aggravation" of the offence with which he B is charged.

The weight to be attached to previous convictions in assessing the gravity (or the trivial nature) of the offence charged is a matter for the tribunal charged with the duty of determining what the penalty shall be. No doubt previous convictions for technical offences which involve no moral turpitude will be given little weight in the assessment of the appropriate C penalty for an offence which does. The weight to be attached to previous convictions for offences which involve some moral turpitude, such as dishonesty, will no doubt vary with their similarity or otherwise to the offence charged and with the interval of time that has elapsed since they were committed. But questions of weight are not questions of law on which the legal assessor to the committee is required or entitled to advise them. They are left to the collective good judgment of the members of the D committee in whom the sentencing function is vested by the Dentists Act 1957.

In their Lordships' view there was no need for the legal assessor to give to the committee any elaborate advice upon their legal duty in exercising their sentencing power in the instant case; and, in particular, he would have been wrong had he advised them as a matter of law that they were E not entitled to take into account the appellant's previous convictions for offences of dishonesty in determining whether the offence of shoplifting, which he had committed and which was the subject of the charge before them, was in all the circumstances so grave as to justify the conclusion that the appellant was unfitted to continue in practice as a member of the dental profession. What weight was to be attached to those previous convictions was a question for the members of the committee themselves—not for their F legal assessor.

For these reasons their Lordships will humbly advise Her Majesty that this appeal should be dismissed.

Solicitors: *Hempsons; Waterhouse & Co.*

T. J. M. G

H

A

[QUEEN'S BENCH DIVISION]

* REGINA *v.* GUILDHALL JUSTICES, *Ex parte* MARSHALL

1976 Jan. 28 — Lord Widgery C.J., Kilner Brown and Watkins JJ.

B
Crime—Practice—Legal aid—Hybrid offence—Summary trial—Application for extension of legal aid to cover counsel—Whether hybrid offence an "indictable offence"—Legal Aid Act 1974 (*c.* 4), *s.* 30 (2) (*a*)

The applicant, who was being tried summarily for an offence which could be tried summarily or on indictment (a
C "hybrid offence"), was granted legal aid to cover representation by a solicitor only. The prosecution was represented by leading and junior counsel, and the matter was extremely complex. The applicant asked the magistrates for an extension of the legal aid order, to cover representation by counsel. They refused on the ground that under section 30 (2) (*a*) of the Legal Aid Act 1974,[1] legal aid granted in proceedings before a magistrates' court could only include representation
D by counsel where the offence was indictable; because the case was being tried summarily, the offence could not be said to be indictable.

On an application for an order of certiorari to quash the magistrates' decision:—

Held, granting the application, that any offence for which an indictment lay was an indictable offence; hence a hybrid offence was an indictable offence for present purposes and
E legal aid could be extended to cover representation by counsel if the other requirement of section 30 (2) (*a*), namely, that the case was unusually grave or difficult, was met.

Hastings & Folkestone Glassworks Ltd. v. *Kalson* [1949] 1 K.B. 214, C.A. applied.

The following case is referred to in the judgment of Lord Widgery C.J.
F *Hastings & Folkestone Glassworks Ltd.* v. *Kalson* [1949] 1 K.B. 214; [1948] 2 All E.R. 1013, C.A.

No additional cases were cited in argument.

APPLICATION for order of certiorari.

G The applicant, William Marshall, sought an order of certiorari to quash the refusal by the Guildhall justices to extend legal aid to cover representation by counsel on December 18, 1975. The grounds on which the relief was sought were as follows. The applicant was summoned under five informations laid under paragraph 1 (1) of Part II of Schedule 5 to the Exchange Control Act 1947 alleging that he conspired with others to contravene sections 17 (2), 9 (2), 2 (1), 7 (1) and 24 (1) of the
H Exchange Control Act 1947. The matters were extremely complex and unusually difficult. The documents in the case could not easily be numbered but together stood 12 inches high. The Crown was represented by leading and junior counsel and was supported by a number of experts

[Reported by RACHEL DAVIES, Barrister-at-Law]

[1] Legal Aid Act 1974, s. 30 (2) (*a*): see post, p. 337E–F.

from the Treasury. Twenty working days were allocated on random A dates within the next seven weeks. The applicant was granted legal aid under an order of the court dated December 11, 1975, for representation by a solicitor only. An application was made to the justices by counsel appearing on behalf of the applicant for legal aid to be extended to cover representation by counsel on December 17, 1975. The application was supported by leading counsel for the Crown. The justices, while indicating that they believed the offences were unusually grave or difficult, were B not sure that they were "indictable" as required by section 30 (2) (*a*) of the Legal Aid Act 1974 and left the matter open for the Law Society to state their views. On December 18, 1975, counsel for the applicant renewed the application and the justices said that if a letter, said to be forthcoming, was provided to their clerk indicating that the Law Society would accept an extension of legal aid to cover counsel then they would C mandate their clerk so to extend it. A letter was produced to the clerk saying that the Law Society would accept an amended legal aid order and was in the hands of the court. The clerk refused to extend the legal aid. The grounds upon which the clerk refused an extension were that the offences were summary offences only, notwithstanding the court's power under paragraph 1 (3) of Part II of Schedule 5 to the Exchange Control Act 1967 to commit the applicant for trial on indict- D ment, and consequently were not "indictable" as required by the Legal Aid Act 1974.

William Glossop for the applicant.
George Cheyne for the justices.
David Jeffreys for the Director of Public Prosecutions. E

LORD WIDGERY C.J. In these proceedings Mr. Glossop moves on behalf of one William Marshall for an order of certiorari to bring up and quash a refusal by the Guildhall justices of an extension of legal aid to cover representation of the applicant by counsel on December 18, 1975, in respect of certain proceedings to which I must return in a F moment. It seems to me just possible that mandamus would have been a more effective approach, but the point has not been raised in argument, and no doubt certiorari will serve if the substance of the applicant's case is a good one.

The applicant is at present being tried by the machinery of summary trial under five informations, all of which allege that he conspired with others to contravene sections 17, 9, 2, 7 and 24 of the Exchange Control G Act 1947. The matters are extremely complex and unusually difficult. The pile of documents stands 12 inches high. The Crown is represented by leading and junior counsel and has a number of experts in support, and some 20 working days have been allotted in the future for a continuation of this complicated summary trial.

The applicant was granted legal aid under an order of the court H dated December 11, 1975, but for representation by a solicitor only. An application was made to the justices by counsel on behalf of the applicant asking for legal aid to be extended to cover representation by counsel, and the justices indicated that they were sympathetic towards the application but believed that they were unable to do so because the circumstances of the case deprived them in their view of making a legal aid order which included representation by counsel. The matter is

A accordingly brought into this court so that we may determine the legal
question: are the justices in this case prohibited as a matter of law
from extending legal aid to counsel on behalf of the applicant?

The offences under the Exchange Control Act 1947 are governed so
far as penalty is concerned by paragraph 1 (3) of Part II of Schedule 5
to the Act, and that shows that these offences are what are commonly
called "hybrid offences," that is to say they can be proceeded against
B either summarily or by trial on indictment. Paragraph 1 (3) of Part II
of Schedule 5 states that:

> "Any person who commits an offence punishable under this Part of
> this Schedule shall be liable—(a) on summary conviction, to imprisonment for not more than three months or to a fine or both; (b) on
> conviction on indictment, to imprisonment for not more than two
> C years or to a fine or to both; . . ."

—a classic example of the so-called hybrid offence where provision is
specifically made for it to be tried by a magistrates' court or on indictment. The difficulty arises in this way. Section 30 of the Legal Aid
Act 1974 first requires that there shall generally be representation under
legal aid in the form of solicitor and counsel. I read subsection (1):

> D "For the purposes of this Part of this Act legal aid, in relation to
> any proceedings to which a person is a party, shall be taken, subject
> to the following provisions of this section, as consisting of representation by a solicitor and counsel assigned by the court, including
> advice on the preparation of that person's case for those proceedings."

E So we start with the proposition that legal aid normally means solicitor
and counsel. Section 30 (2) provides:

> "Notwithstanding anything in subsection (1) above, legal aid ordered
> to be given for the purposes of any proceedings before a magistrates' court shall not include representation by counsel except—(*a*)
> in the case of any indictable offence, where the court is of the
> F opinion that, because of circumstances which make the case unusually grave or difficult, representation by both solicitor and counsel
> would be desirable; . . ."

The magistrates in the present case, as I understand it, have taken
the view that these offences are not indictable offences within section
30 (2) (*a*), and they have taken that view because of the method of trial
G being employed in connection with these offences, which is summary
trial, as I have already described. We have to decide whether that
restricted view is right, or whether the terms permitting representation
by counsel in a magistrates' court are not in fact much wider in their
application.

The critical word is "indictable." The legal aid order may extend
to counsel in the case of an indictable offence subject to the conditions
H stated in the section. The word "indictable" has appeared in innumerable statutes. Very often, probably more often than not, the statute
has contained a definition section which makes clear what an indictable
offence means in that statute, but it is of course of very little value to
look at such statutes unless closely related to the present one for assistance. I think the proper approach to this problem is to go straight to
the word "indictable" and ask oneself what it means in ordinary
common use. I think the answer to that is that you speak of an offence

as being "an indictable offence" when it is an offence for which an indictment lies. In other words, it includes offences like murder, which must be tried on indictment and also hybrid offences. That is my view of the ordinary, straightforward meaning of the word, and if that is so, the present offences were indictable offences because they were capable of being tried on indictment, even though not so tried. A

I am supported in the view I have expressed by, I think, the only authority at which we have been invited to look, and that is *Hastings & Folkestone Glassworks Ltd.* v. *Kalson* [1949] 1 K.B. 214. The question arose in this way. The company's articles provided that a director convicted of an indictable offence should vacate his office. A director of a company pleaded guilty before a court of summary jurisdiction to a charge under the Defence Regulations and was convicted and fined. The offence was a hybrid offence like the present offence. It could have been tried on indictment or summarily. In fact it was tried summarily. The Court of Appeal held that, whether or not an offence was "indictable" within the meaning of the company's articles depended on the nature and quality of the offence when committed, irrespective of the procedural manner in which it might subsequently be dealt with, and, therefore, as the offence of which the defendant was convicted was one which could be dealt with on indictment, he was "convicted of an indictable offence" within the meaning of the articles, and the company was entitled to the declaration asked for. B C D

I am further reinforced in my view as to what is the correct approach to this problem by a word or two of Harman J., who was the junior member of the Court of Appeal in question. He said, at p. 222:

> "Articles in this form though not favoured in the best models have been a familiar feature of such things for many years, and I cannot bring myself to think that disqualification can depend on whether the offence in question is to be found in the schedule to an Act of 1925, or on the method by which the authorities choose to bring it home to the offender. In my judgment, [the argument of counsel for the defendant] lays too much stress on the word 'convicted.' Of course it is a condition precedent to disqualification that there should have been a conviction; mere accusation may be wholly unjustified; but once a conviction has been recorded the test is the nature of the offence. Not every offence brings the sanction into effect; it must have been 'indictable,' and that in plain English means 'for which an indictment lies.' This offence satisfies that test, and the defendant's disqualification in my judgment follows." E F G

I would follow Harman J. by saying that the word "indictable" in plain English means "for which an indictment lies," and consequently the hybrid offences to which I have referred, amongst others, are indictable offences for present purposes. This no doubt means that it will be open to the justices to extend the legal aid order in the instant case, and maybe to grant extended legal aid orders in a number of cases which are to follow. Those who are concerned with the possible burden on the taxpayer may perhaps take some comfort from a reminder that in order to employ counsel under legal aid in the magistrates' court it is not enough just to show that the offence is an indictable offence. It has to be an indictable offence and to be considered unusually grave or difficult. I would stress the importance when extended applications for H

A legal aid are made in the future, as they will be made, of the court considering both points before granting the order, namely, considering whether the offence is an indictable offence as defined here this afternoon, and, if it is, to consider whether the case is so unusually grave or difficult as to make representation by counsel desirable.

In the event in my judgment the order should go quashing the refusal of the magistrates to grant the extended order for legal aid, and thus
B leaving them in a position to make that order if they are so minded, having regard to the other features to which I have referred.

KILNER BROWN J. I agree.

WATKINS J. I agree.

C

Order of certiorari granted.
Costs out of central funds.

Solicitors: *Herbert & Gowers & Co.; Comptroller, City Solicitors; Director of Public Prosecutions.*

D

[COURT OF APPEAL]

E * THE ESCHERSHEIM

THE JADE

ERKOWIT (OWNERS) *v.* SALUS (OWNERS) (FORMERLY ROTESAND) AND OTHERS

F ERKOWIT (OWNERS OF CARGO LATELY LADEN ON BOARD) *v.* ESCHERSHEIM (OWNERS)

1975 June 9, 10, 11, 12, 13; July 22 — Cairns and Scarman L.JJ. and Sir Gordon Willmer

Admiralty—Jurisdiction—Action in rem—Claims arising out of
G *salvage operation for loss of ship and cargo—Claim that cargo washed overboard causing pollution—Court's jurisdiction to hear and determine claims brought against salvors by ship and cargo owners—Administration of Justice Act* 1956 (4 & 5 *Eliz.* 2, *c.* 46), *ss.* 1 (1) (*d*) (*e*) (*g*) (*h*) (*j*), 3 (1) (4)

Arbitration—Arbitration clause in contract—Ambit—Salvage agreement—Allegations of negligence on part of salvors—Whether to be referred to arbitration under contract—Discretion of
H *court to stay actions—Arbitration Act* 1950 (14 & 15 *Geo.* 6, *c.* 27), *s.* 4 (1)

Ships' Names—Dortmund—Erkowit—Eschersheim—Jade—Salus (formerly Rotesand)

Section 1 (1) of the Administration of Justice Act 1956 provides:

[Reported by EMMANUEL C. ABARAONYE, ESQ., Barrister-at-Law]

A "The Admiralty jurisdiction of the High Court shall be as follows, that is to say, jurisdiction to hear and determine any of the following questions or claims—. . . (*d*) any claim for damage done by the ship; (*e*) any claim for damage received by a ship; . . . (*g*) any claim for loss of or damage to goods carried in a ship; (*h*) any claim arising out of any agreement relating to the carriage of goods in a ship or to the use or hire of a ship; (*j*) any claim in the nature of salvage . . ."

B As a result of a collision at sea between the *Erkowit* and the *Dortmund*, the engine room of the *Erkowit* was holed and became flooded. The *Rotesand*, a salvage tug, went to the aid of the *Erkowit* and the masters of the two ships signed a Lloyd's open form salvage agreement on behalf of the salvors, the owners of the *Erkowit* and the owners of her cargo. Under the agreement, the salvors agreed to use their best endeavours C to salve the *Erkowit* and the parties agreed that differences arising out of the agreement would be referred to arbitration in London. The *Rotesand* then took the *Erkowit* in tow and beached her off the Spanish coast. All attempts to patch and refloat the *Erkowit* failed and she became a total loss. Most of the personal belongings of her master and crew were lost. Most of the cargo was lost or damaged and a cargo of insecticide was washed out to sea causing pollution and consequential D interference to fishing in the area. The Spanish government brought proceedings on behalf of fishermen affected by the pollution in the Spanish courts for damages against the owners of the *Erkowit* and the salvors. Two actions in rem were brought in the English courts against the *Dortmund* for damage caused by the collision; the first action by the owners, master and crew of the *Erkowit* and the second by the owners of her cargo.

E Two further actions in rem were brought against sister ships of the *Rotesand*. The first, "ship's action for negligent salvage" included claims by the owners of the *Erkowit* for damages for the loss of the ship and an indemnity against their potential liability in Spain for pollution and by the master and crew for loss of personal effects. The second, "cargo action for negligent salvage" consisted of claims for loss of cargo by the cargo owners. The salvors applied to the court for the F writs in the two actions to be struck out or set aside on the ground that the court had no jurisdiction, under section 1 (1) of the Administration of Justice Act 1956, to hear and determine the claims, and for an order that the actions, in so far as they were not struck out or set aside, be stayed under section 4 of the Arbitration Act 1950 on the ground that, under the salvage agreement, the claims were to be referred to arbitration.

G Brandon J. struck out the claims of the master and crew on the ground that they did not come within section 1 (1) of the Act of 1956 but otherwise dismissed both applications.

On appeal by the salvors:—

Held, dismissing the appeals, (1) that damage which resulted from the salvors' negligence after the *Erkowit* was beached was not damage done by a ship within section 1 (1) (*d*) of the Act but, if damage was caused by the negligent beaching of the H *Erkowit*, it was damage done by those in charge of the *Rotesand* and that ship was the "instrument of mischief" or the "noxious instrument" of the damage and, therefore, both the ship and cargo owners could bring an action in rem within paragraph (*d*) based on the negligent beaching of the vessel (post, pp. 349E–F, 352G, 355A, 359H—360A); that, accordingly, the ship owners could also claim an indemnity from the salvors for any liability in the proceedings brought by the Spanish Government (post, pp. 350C–D, 361H).

Dicta of Brett M.R. and Bowen L.J. in *The Vera Cruz*

A (*No.* 2) (1884) 9 P.D. 96, 99, 101, C.A. and Lord Halsbury L.C. and Lord Watson in *Currie* v. *M'Knight* [1897] A.C. 97, 101, 106, H.L.(Sc.) applied.

(2) That the contract made between the masters of the *Erkowit* and the *Rotesand* for the *Erkowit* to be taken to a place of safety was an agreement for the use or hire of a ship and, accordingly, actions in rem were properly brought under paragraph (*h*) (post, pp. 348G–H, 354H, 360D–E).

B *The Isca* (1886) 12 P.D. 34, D.C. approved.

(3) (Cairns L.J. dubitante) that, on the true construction of section 3 (4) of the Act, the ship in connection with the plaintiffs' claim was the ship that received the damage, namely, the *Erkowit;* that the person liable in an action in personam would be the salvors but they had no possession and control of the *Erkowit* to found an action in rem under the subsection and, therefore, the ship owners' claim under section 1 (1) (*e*) and the
C cargo owners' claim under paragraph (*g*) failed (post, pp. 349G—350A, 354D–G, 358A–B, D–E).

Per Cairns L.J. A more natural meaning of section 3 (4) is that the ship referred to throughout the subsection is a ship not belonging to the plaintiff but having some connection with the damage (not necessarily such as to make the ship the " instrument of mischief ") (post, p. 350B).

(4) (*Per* Scarman L.J. and Sir Gordon Willmer) that " any
D claim in the nature of salvage " in paragraph (*j*) could only arise against the owners of the property salved and, therefore, the ship owners and cargo owners could not bring an action in rem based on a claim under paragraph (*j*) (post, pp. 352G, 359C).

Per Cairns L.J. The words " in the nature of salvage " in section 1 (1) (*j*) could not be construed to include damage done in the course of salvage (post, p. 346E).

E (5) That the judge in exercising his discretion to refuse to stay the actions correctly placed emphasis on the avoidance of a multiplicity of actions; that, although in the circumstances a court or arbitrators might exercise their discretion, under the proviso to section 8 of the Maritime Convention Act 1911, in favour of the plaintiffs and extend the time limit for referring the dispute to arbitration, the judge, in the absence of authority, had not erred in considering it very doubtful that
F the time limit would be extended and the refusal of a stay was a proper exercise of the judge's discretion (post, pp. 350H—351C, 352A–F, 355H—356A).

W. Bruce Ltd. v. *J. Strong* [1951] 2 K.B. 447, C.A. and *The Alnwick* [1965] P. 357, C.A. considered.

Decision of Brandon J. [1975] 1 W.L.R. 83; [1974] 3 All E.R. 304 affirmed but grounds varied.

G The following cases are referred to in the judgments:

Alina, The (1880) 5 Ex.D. 227, C.A.

Alnwick, The [1965] P. 357; [1965] 3 W.L.R. 118; [1965] 1 All E.R. 423; [1965] 2 All E.R. 569, Hewson J. and C.A.

Andrea Ursula, The [1973] Q.B. 265; [1971] 2 W.L.R. 681; [1971] 1 All E.R. 821.

H *Banco, The* [1971] P. 137; [1971] 2 W.L.R. 335; [1971] 1 All E.R. 524, C.A.

Beldis, The [1936] P. 51, C.A.

Bruce (W.) Ltd. v. *J. Strong* [1951] 2 K.B. 447; [1951] 1 All E.R. 1021, C.A.

Cairnbahn, The [1914] P. 25, C.A.

Circe, The [1906] P. 1.

Conoco Britannia, The [1972] 2 Q.B. 543; [1972] 2 W.L.R. 1352; [1972] 2 All E.R. 238.

Currie v. *M'Knight* [1897] A.C. 97, H.L.(Sc.).
Frankland, The [1901] P. 161.
Greaves v. *Tofield* (1880) 14 Ch.D. 563, C.A.
Isca, The (1886) 12 P.D. 34; 6 Asp.M.L.C. 63, D.C.
Molière, The [1925] P. 27.
Pine Hill, The [1958] 2 Lloyd's Rep. 146.
Queen of the South, The [1968] P. 449; [1968] 2 W.L.R. 973; [1968] 1 All E.R. 1163.
Reg. v. *Judge of the City of London Court* [1892] 1 Q.B. 273, C.A.
Taunton-Collins v. *Cromie* [1964] 1 W.L.R. 633; [1964] 2 All E.R. 332, C.A.
Theta, The [1894] P. 280.
Vera Cruz, The (No. 2) (1884) 9 P.D. 96, C.A.
Zeus, The (1888) 13 P.D. 188, D.C.

The following additional cases were cited in argument:

Lister v. *Romford Ice & Cold Storage Co. Ltd.* [1957] A.C. 555; [1957] 2 W.L.R. 158; [1957] 1 All E.R. 125, H.L.(E.).
Merak, The [1965] P. 223; [1965] 2 W.L.R. 250; [1964] 3 All E.R. 638; [1965] 1 All E.R. 230, Scarman J. and C.A.
Mersey Docks and Harbours Board v. *Turner, The Zeta* [1893] A.C. 468, H.L.(E.).
Paterson v. *Chadwick* [1974] 1 W.L.R. 890; [1974] 2 All E.R. 772.
Sobieski, The [1949] P. 313; [1949] 1 All E.R. 701, C.A.

INTERLOCUTORY APPEALS from Brandon J.

By a writ dated June 19, 1972, the owners, the master and crew of the *Erkowit*, a Sudanese ship, brought an action in rem (1972 folio 269) against the *Dortmund*, a West German ship, for damage caused by a collision between the two ships on October 30, 1970, in the Bay of Biscay (the "ship's collision action"). By a writ dated July 3, 1972, the owners of the *Erkowit's* cargo brought an action in rem (1972 folio 290) against the *Dortmund* for damage caused by the collision between the two ships (the "cargo's collision action"). By a writ dated October 23, 1972 (1972 folio 451), the owners, the master and crew of the *Erkowit* commenced an action in rem against the *Jade*, a sister ship of the salvage tug, the *Salus* (formerly the *Rotesand*), for damages for loss and damage caused to the *Erkowit* and consequential loss and expense caused by the salvors' breaches of a contract made on October 30, 1970, on the terms of Lloyd's open form of salvage agreement and/or negligence by the salvors, their servants or agents, in the course of their operations to salve the *Erkowit* and her cargo off La Coruna, Spain, on or after October 31, 1970, following a collision between the *Erkowit* and the *Dortmund* (the "ship's action for negligent salvage"). By a writ dated October 27, 1972, the owners of the cargo on board the *Erkowit* at the time when she collided with the *Dortmund*, began an action against the *Eschersheim*, also a sister ship of the *Salus* (1972 folio 460), for damages for negligence and/or breach of duty and/or breach of contract in the course of the salvage operations (cargo's action for negligent salvage).

By notices of motion dated October 31, 1973, the salvors applied for orders that the writ of summons in the ship's and cargo's actions for negligent salvage be set aside or struck out, on the ground, inter alia, that the Admiralty Court had no jurisdiction in rem in respect of those claims, and for an order that, in so far as those actions had not been set aside or struck out, those actions be stayed under section 4 of the

A Arbitration Act 1950 on the ground that under the contract of salvage the parties agreed to submit all differences arising out of the contract to arbitration and that the claims related in their entirety to differences arising out of the salvage contract.

On June 10, 1974, Brandon J. dismissed the applications holding, inter alia, that (1) an allegation of negligence in the conduct of salvage operation was not a claim "for damage done by a ship" within section 1 (1) (*d*) B of the Administration of Justice Act 1956; (2) "claim for damage" in paragraph (*e*) of the subsection was to be construed as "claim arising out of damage" received by the ship and included both direct and consequential loss; (3) the claim of the cargo owners for loss and damage to the cargo was within paragraph (*g*); (4) the agreement between the masters of the ship and the salvage tug was an agreement for the use of the ship C within paragraph (h); (4) the plaintiffs' claims were to be referred to arbitration and in considering whether the court should order a stay of the proceedings under section 4 (1) of the Arbitration Act 1950, the decisive factor was the need to avoid duplication of proceedings in England.

The defendant, the salvors, appealed inter alia on the grounds that (i) the judge failed to attach any or sufficient weight to the fact that in refusing a stay he was depriving the defendants of their right to raise D in arbitration the defence that the plaintiffs' claim was time-barred under section 8 of the Maritime Conventions Act 1911. In particular: (a) the judge was in error in expressing considerable doubts as to the validity of the defence of time-bar; (b) the judge failed to take into account the fact that the plaintiffs did not serve their writ of summons on the defendants until the two year time limit imposed by section 8 had expired, E notwithstanding that the solicitors acting for the defendants had given notice before the time limit expired, of the contention of the defendants that the plaintiffs' claim should be arbitrated. Further or alternatively it is wrong in principle that by issuing their writ before but serving it after the relevant time limit had expired the plaintiffs should be able both to avoid their contractual obligation to arbitrate and to deprive the defendants of a potential defence; (ii) the judge failed to have any F or sufficient regard to the defendants' legitimate wish to avoid being party to public litigation in England because of the potential consequences of participating in such litigation on their position in Spain; (iii) the judge attached excessive weight to the importance of avoiding multiplicity of proceedings, having particular regard to the facts: (a) that there would in any event be separate proceedings in England and Spain G involving common issues of fact, some of which, would not be disposed of for several years; (b) that until the determination of the proceedings in Spain it would not be possible finally to dispose of the defendants' counterclaim or potential counterclaim against the owners of the *Erkowit* and (c) that costs might be wasted in pursuing claims which the outcome of the Spanish proceedings might render unnecessary; (iv) in the premises, the judge erred in principle in the exercise of his dis- H cretion in refusing a stay.

In their respondents' notice, the plaintiffs, the owners of the *Erkowit* and the cargo owners, gave notice that they intended to argue the grounds that (i) the judge was wrong in holding that the plaintiffs' claim was referred to arbitration by the terms of Lloyd's Standard Form of Salvage Agreement; he ought to have held either (a) that since the provisions of clause 4 and the succeeding clauses of the agreement were inappropriate to claims by the owner of salved property against the contractor for negligence, it was impossible for such claims to be referred to arbitration " in the same way " A within the meaning of clause 1; or, alternatively (b) that such claims were only referred to arbitration when raised as counterclaims or cross-claims to a claim by the contractor for salvage remuneration; (ii) alternatively that the judge was wrong to hold that the refusal of a stay would deprive the defendants of a potential defence under section 8 of the Maritime Conventions Act 1911; he ought to have held either (a) that section 8 of the Act of 1911 had no application to the plaintiffs' claim or (b) that it B would be a proper case for an extension of the period provided by the section.

J. Franklin Willmer Q.C. and *Nicholas Phillips* for the defendant salvors.

Michael Thomas Q.C. and *Anthony Clarke* for the plaintiff owners C of the *Erkowit*.

David Steel for the plaintiff cargo owners.

Cur. adv. vult.

July 22. The following judgments were read. D

CAIRNS L.J. This is an appeal from an interlocutory decision of Brandon J. in two actions in rem for damage caused to the ship *Erkowit* and her cargo in the course of salvage operations in which the defendants' tug *Rotesand* was engaged. The *Jade* and the *Eschersheim* were two sister ships of the *Rotesand*. The owners of the *Erkowit* proceeded against the *Jade* and the owners of the cargo against the *Eschersheim*. (The ship- E owners also proceeded against the *Rotesand*, which had been sold and renamed *Salus* but the action against that ship was discontinued and there is no need to make further reference to it.) In the ship's action the master and crew were joined to claim for loss of their effects. The defendants applied to the judge to strike out the writs or parts thereof, alternatively to stay the actions under section 4 of the Arbitration Act 1950. He struck F out the claim of the master and crew and from that part of his decision there is no appeal. Otherwise he dismissed the defendants' applications and they appeal. There are respondents' notices supporting the judge's decision on alternative grounds.

The facts are set out with the greatest care and clarity in the judgment of Brandon J. [1975] 1 W.L.R. 83 and I shall give only a brief summary of them. On October 30, 1970, a collision took place in the Bay of Biscay G between the *Erkowit* and the *Dortmund*. The *Erkowit* was holed and the *Rotesand* went to her assistance. A salvage agreement in Lloyd's open form was signed on behalf of both plaintiffs and of the defendants. The *Rotesand* towed the *Erkowit* to La Coruna and beached her. The defendants' servants then carried out operations, which were not effective, to save the *Erkowit* or her cargo and both (except perhaps for some small H part of the cargo) became total losses. The cargo included a quantity of insecticide, partly in drums on deck and partly in holds, which was washed into the sea. The Spanish government alleges on behalf of fishermen that the pollution of the sea caused great damage to their interests and claims heavy damages against the owners of the *Erkowit* and against the salvors. There is likely to be much delay before those claims are dealt with.

In this country actions in rem have been brought by both the present plaintiffs against the *Dortmund* and have not yet come to trial. In those actions the owners of the *Dortmund* by their defence contend, inter alia, that the loss of the *Erkowit* and her cargo and the pollution were caused by the negligence of the salvors.

Because the plaintiffs apprehended that such allegations would be made on behalf of the *Dortmund* they started the actions to which this appeal relates, the claims being made in tort or alternatively for the breach of the salvage agreement. The negligence alleged, as appears from an affidavit sworn on behalf of the plaintiffs, is (1) beaching the *Erkowit* in an exposed place; (2) patching her with wood and canvas instead of with steel; (3) delay in carrying out the operations. The damages claimed in the shipowners' action include an indemnity against any liability to the Spanish government.

In their application to the judge the defendants sought to strike out the plaintiff shipowners' claim for indemnity on the ground that the court had no jurisdiction in rem in respect of such a claim. In the course of the hearing of the appeal leave was given to the defendants to amend their notice of appeal and to contend that the whole of the writ should be set aside on the ground that the court had no jurisdiction in rem in respect of any part of the claim. Further, leave was given to the defendants to amend their notice of appeal in the cargo owners' case to raise a similar contention.

In both actions the judge refused a stay under the Arbitration Act 1950 because, although he held that the disputes were within the arbitration clause of the salvage agreement, he exercised his discretion by refusing a stay.

In the respondents' notice in the shipowners' case those plaintiffs sought to found jurisdiction on a basis on which the judge had held against them, as an alternative to the bases on which he had held in their favour. As to stay, they contended that the judge was wrong in holding that the dispute was within the arbitration clause and advanced reasons, additional to those on which the judge based his decision, why the discretion should be exercised against a stay. By amendments for which leave was given during the hearing of the appeal they put forward, in relation to the application to strike out, further alternative bases of jurisdiction.

In the cargo owners' case the original respondents' notice dealt only with the application to stay on broadly similar lines to the shipowners' notice. By supplementary respondents' notice, for which leave was given during the hearing of the appeal, they, like the shipowners, put forward in relation to the application to strike out alternative bases of jurisdiction.

The jurisdiction of the High Court in Admiralty matters is now defined by section 1 (1) of the Administration of Justice Act 1956 in terms which so far as relevant to the present appeal are as follows:

> "The Admiralty jurisdiction of the High Court shall be as follows, that is to say, jurisdiction to hear and determine any of the following questions or claims . . . (*d*) any claim for damage done by a ship; (*e*) any claim for damage received by a ship; . . . (*g*) any claim for loss of or damage to goods carried in a ship; (*h*) any claim arising out of any agreement relating to the carriage of goods in a ship or to the use or hire of a ship; (*j*) any claim in the nature of salvage (including any claim arising by virtue of the application, by or under section 51 of the Civil Aviation Act 1949 of the law relating to salvage to aircraft and their apparel and cargo); . . ."

The mode of exercise of such Admiralty jurisdiction is prescribed by section 3 of the Act, the relevant provisions of which are as follows:

"(1) Subject to the provisions of the next following section, the A
Admiralty jurisdiction of the High Court, the Liverpool Court of Passage and any county court may in all cases be invoked by an action in personam. . . . (4) In the case of any such claim as is mentioned in paragraphs (*d*) to (*r*) of subsection (1) of section 1 of this Act, being a claim arising in connection with a ship, where the person who would be liable on the claim in an action in personam
B
was, when the cause of action arose, the owner or charterer of, or in possession or in control of, the ship, the Admiralty jurisdiction of the High Court and (where there is such jurisdiction) the Admiralty jurisdiction of the Liverpool Court of Passage or any county court may (whether the claim gives rise to a maritime lien on the ship or not) be invoked by an action in rem against—(*a*) that ship, if at the time when the action is brought it is beneficially owned as respects all the C
shares therein by that person; or (*b*) any other ship which, at the time when the action is brought, is beneficially owned as aforesaid."

The plaintiff shipowners contended on the appeal that their claim fell within paragraphs (*d*), (*e*), (*h*) and possibly (*g*) and (*j*) of section 1 (1). Damage, they claim, was done to the *Erkowit* by the *Rotesand*, by beaching the *Erkowit* in an unsafe place; clearly damage was received by the *Erkowit*; D
the claim in contract arises out of the salvage agreement, which was an agreement for the use or hire of the *Rotesand*. As to (*g*), the suggestion is that the claim for indemnity in respect of the pollution may in a broad sense be said to be a claim for the loss of goods carried in a ship; and as to (*j*) it was submitted that a liberal interpretation of the words "in the nature of salvage" would enable a claim for damage done in the course
E
of salvage to be included. I do not consider that either (*g*) or (*j*) is capable of the meaning sought to be attached to it and if the shipowners are to establish jurisdiction at all it must in my view be under (*d*), (*e*) or (*h*).

The cargo owners' contentions were similar except that their main reliance was on (*d*), (*g*) and (*h*). Their attempts to apply (*e*) and (*j*) to the cargo involved as strained a construction of the paragraphs as that suggested by the shipowners in relation to (*g*) and (*j*). So in my opinion F
the cargo owners must look to (*d*), (*g*) or (*h*) if they are to found jurisdiction. Their case under those paragraphs corresponds exactly with that of the shipowners under (*d*), (*e*) and (*h*).

The defendants' case under (*d*) is that neither the *Erkowit* nor her cargo was damaged by the *Rotesand*; that there is no allegation of bad navigation of the salvage tug, the place of beaching may have been chosen
G
by a salvage officer and not by the master or any officer of the *Rotesand*; and any later negligence, even if any of the crew participated in it, cannot be attributed to the tug.

As to (*e*) and (*g*) there is no doubt that the *Erkowit* and her cargo received damage and in the court below it was not argued that either plaintiff was unable to found jurisdiction under the relevant one of those paragraphs. What was contended in relation to the shipowners was that their claim to H
indemnity was not a claim for damage received by a ship. It appeared to us that whatever might be said about jurisdiction under section 1, jurisdiction in rem might not be conferred by section 3 (4) in the case of damage received by a ship, or by goods carried in a ship, if not done by a ship. It was for this reason that the defendants were given leave to amend their notice of appeal.

As to (*h*), the defendants contended that the salvage agreement was not

A an agreement for the use or hire of a ship. It provided for the defendants to use their best endeavours to salve the *Erkowit* and her cargo and take them to a place the name of which was left blank. But it made no reference to the use of the *Rotesand* or any other vessel for this purpose.

The judge did not have to consider whether the cargo claim was within the jurisdiction and, as to the ship, he had only to decide whether the claim to indemnity was within one of the paragraphs relied on. He rejected the B plaintiffs' case under (*d*), holding that no damage was done by the *Rotesand*, but he considered that the salvage agreement was an agreement for the use or hire of a ship, so that the claim was within (*h*) and, as to (*e*), he held that any liability of the owners of the *Erkowit* towards the Spanish government was covered by the words "damage received by a ship."

The Administration of Justice Act 1956 was passed following the C adherence of the United Kingdom to the International Convention Relating to the Arrest of Seagoing Ships made at Brussels on May 10, 1952. Both sides made some reference to the Convention for the purpose of assisting the construction of the Act, as was done by this court in *The Banco* [1971] P. 137. Admittedly in relation to jurisdiction the Act's provisions are in some ways wider than the Convention provides for (for example the Convention has no reference to "damage received by D a ship") and in other ways narrower (for example the Convention does not confine the right of proceeding in rem to a ship owned by the person who might be sued in personam). In these circumstances I do not consider that reference to the Convention throws such light on the meaning of the relevant provisions of the Act as to afford any assistance to the court.

Reference was also made to Part V of the Act, the only part of it E which applies to Scotland, as an aid to the construction of the sections applicable to England. On the one hand it was said that because the maritime law of Scotland is the same as that of England (*Currie* v. *M'Knight* [1897] A.C. 97) the jurisdiction of the English court must be as wide as that of the Scottish court and therefore section 47, which deals with the right of arrest in relation to the Scottish court, can be looked at to assist a liberal interpretation of words in section 1. On the other hand it was F contended that where the words of corresponding provisions differ, Parliament must have intended to differentiate between the two countries. I do not find either argument convincing. The proposition that the maritime law of Scotland is the same as that of England cannot involve that any statutory provision enacted in that field for one country must also apply to the other, while differences in language may be explicable on historical G grounds. I therefore do not derive assistance from looking at the provisions for Scotland.

Some help is to be derived from earlier decisions of the courts on sections in earlier Acts corresponding with parts of section 1 of the Act of 1956. We were referred to a considerable number of authorities but I shall confine my citations to those which are most relevant to our problems.

I start with paragraph (*h*) because it is under that paragraph that in my H opinion the plaintiffs' case is strongest. There was a sharp conflict of opinion in the latter part of the 19th century as to the meaning of the words "any agreement made in relation to the use or hire of a ship," then to be found in section 2 of the County Courts (Admiralty Jurisdiction) Act 1869. In *The Alina* (1880) 5 Ex. D. 227, a Court of Appeal presided over by Sir George Jessel M.R. considered that the words clearly covered a charterparty. In *Reg.* v. *Judge of the City of London Court* [1892] 1 Q.B. 273, a Court of Appeal presided over by Lord Esher M.R. thought that the decision in *The Alina* was wrong and, while feeling bound to "obey" it, A refused to extend it, to quote the language of Lord Esher M.R., at p. 290, "one particle beyond what it actually decides and determines." There was at that time an understandable reluctance of some judges to give other than the narrowest possible meaning to the words, seeing that they conferred a jurisdiction which was not enjoyed by the High Court. It must however be observed that after such jurisdiction was given to the High Court by section 5 of the Administration of Justice Act 1920, Sir Boyd Merriman P. B presiding in the Court of Appeal in *The Beldis* [1936] P. 51 held that the court was still bound by the decision in *Reg.* v. *Judge of the City of London Court*. The actual decision in *The Beldis* was however simply that an action on an award made under an agreement was not an action arising out of the agreement. It is therefore not of direct assistance on the question of what agreements are within the words. In *The Isca* (1886) 12 P.D. 34 C (see also 6 Asp. M.L.C. 63, where the facts are more fully stated) an agreement for towage by a named vessel was held by a Divisional Court to be an agreement for the use or hire of it. In *The Zeus* (1888) 13 P.D. 188 an agreement to load a ship was held by a Divisional Court not to be an agreement for the use or hire of it. Both of these decisions appear to me to be plainly right. In *The Queen of the South* [1968] P. 449 Brandon J. himself held that contracts for mooring services by watermen using motor D boats for the purpose were within the words of (*h*). Counsel for the defendants invite us to overrule that decision. They submit that only a charterparty or an agreement closely akin to a charterparty is covered.

In my opinion there is no good reason for excluding from the expression "an agreement for the use or hire of a ship" any agreement which an ordinary business man would regard as being within it. If A and B E make an agreement for A's ship to be used for carrying out any operation for B, I consider that the agreement is one for the use, if not for the hire, of the ship. Thus an agreement for a ship to be employed for dredging, towing, cable-laying or salvage would be an agreement for the use of the ship. But is an agreement for dredging, or towage or cable-laying or salvage an agreement for the use of a ship if there is no express reference in the agreement to any such use? If the operations can only be carried F out by means of a ship I consider that the agreement must be one for the use or hire of a ship. A towage agreement would therefore always come within the words. Dredging or cable-laying could conceivably be performed by other means but in the great majority of cases it would be so obvious that the use of a ship must be intended that this would be implied. For salvage, every case must depend on the circumstances but G where, as here, the contract is made on board a salvage tug which is in attendance near the casualty and is made between the two masters and provides for the damaged vessel to be "taken to a place of safety" it is in my opinion an agreement for the use or hire of a ship. I therefore agree with Brandon J. that the actions in rem are properly brought under paragraph (*h*).

H

This makes it unnecessary for me to deal at much length with the issues arising under the other paragraphs but in deference to the arguments of counsel I will state my views upon them. As to (*d*), the expression "damage done by a ship" was considered in the Court of Appeal in *The Vera Cruz* (*No.* 2) (1884) 9 P.D. 96. Brett M.R. said, at p. 99, that the words applied to a case in which "a ship was the active cause, the damage being physically caused by the ship." Bowen

A L.J. said, at p. 101: "'Done by a ship' means done by those in charge of a ship, with the ship as the noxious instrument." In *Currie* v. *M'Knight* [1897] A.C. 97, the issue was whether the cutting by the crew of one ship of the moorings of another was to be regarded as the act or fault of the first ship so as to make it liable to a maritime lien. It was held that it was not. In the course of the speeches Lord Halsbury L.C. said, at p. 101:

B "the phrase that it must be the fault of the ship itself is not a mere figurative expresssion, but it imports, in my opinion, that the ship against which a maritime lien for damages is claimed is the instrument of mischief, and that in order to establish the liability of the ship itself to the maritime lien claimed some act of navigation of the ship itself should either mediately or immediately be the cause of

C the damage."

Lord Watson said, at p. 106:

"I think it is of the essence of the rule that the damage in respect of which a maritime lien is admitted must be either the direct result or the natural consequence of a wrongful act or manoeuvre of the ship to which it attaches. Such an act or manoeuvre is

D necessarily due to the want of skill or negligence of the persons by whom the vessel is navigated; but it is, in the language of maritime law, attributed to the ship because the ship in their negligent or unskilful hands is the instrument which causes the damage."

In the present case it was accepted on both sides that the issue in

E *Currie* v. *M'Knight* was in substance the same as the issue whether the damage was "damage done by a ship." On the basis of the dicta I have cited I can see that any damage resulting from the negligence of the crew of the *Rotesand,* or of any other servants of the defendants, after the *Erkowit* was beached, was probably not to be regarded as done by the *Rotesand.* But the plaintiffs claim that damage flowed from the actual beaching and that it was negligent to beach in that place. There

F is no doubt that the *Erkowit* was put on the beach by the *Rotesand.* If that beaching caused damage to the *Erkowit* and its cargo then the *Rotesand* was the "active cause of the damage," the "noxious instrument," the "instrument of mischief." That is sufficient to enable both the plaintiffs to rely on paragraph (*d*) as a foundation for an action in rem.

Paragraph (*e*) gives rise to the most difficult questions that were

G debated before us. To start with, if damage received by a ship can enable the owner of that ship to proceed in rem, against what ship can he proceed? Counsel on both sides agreed that for the purpose of (*e*) the ship referred to throughout section 3 (4) except in paragraph (*b*) at the end, is the ship which has received the damage. If that is so then an action in rem can be brought if the person who is liable in personam was in possession or control of the ship which received the damage at the

H time when the damage was done. Counsel for the plaintiffs contended that that condition was fulfilled here because at that time when the damage was done the *Erkowit* was so much disabled that the salvors had control, and perhaps possession, of her. Counsel for the defendants contended that "possession or control" here means something akin to ownership and that the defendants were in no such relation to the ship, whose master could have dispensed with the services of the salvors at any time, though this might have been a breach of contract. Without

attempting to define exactly what is meant by " possession or control " A
in this context, it is sufficient for me to say that I am not satisfied that on
the facts it was established here.

I am however by no means convinced that the interpretation of
section 3 (4) favoured by both counsel is correct. It seems to me that a
more natural meaning of it is that the ship referred to throughout the
subsection is a ship not belonging to the plaintiff but having some con-
nection with the damage (not necessarily such as to make that ship the B
" instrument of mischief "), otherwise it is difficult to see why claims
under paragraph (*e*) were included in section 3 (4) at all. This would I
think afford a possible basis of jurisdiction in this case but as counsel for
the plaintiff did not in the end rely on it I should prefer not to express
a concluded opinion on it.

Exactly the same considerations apply to paragraph (*g*) in relation to C
the cargo owners' claim. If jurisdiction can be established by the ship
owners under (*e*), can the " damage received " include any liability to the
Spanish government? Counsel for the defendants relies on the fact that
under paragraph (*e*) only a claim for damage received by a ship is covered,
as contrasted with other paragraphs such as (*h*) where the wording is
" any claim arising out of any agreement." It is, however, conceded that
" damage " must include the cost of repairing the damage and any loss D
caused by detention of the ship during repair. I can see no logical
reason why any other consequential loss should be excluded.

Coming then to the defendants' application for a stay under section 4
of the Arbitration Act 1950, the first issue is whether the plaintiffs' claims
are within the arbitration provisions of the salvage agreement. Those
provisions are contained in clause 1 of the agreement which, after E
specifying the services to be rendered by the salvors, and providing for the
amount of their remuneration to be fixed, in certain events, by arbitra-
tion " in the manner hereinafter prescribed " goes on " and any other
difference arising out of this agreement or the operations thereunder
shall be referred to arbitration in the same way." Clauses 4 to 9 of the
agreement contained detailed provision as to the manner of arbitration, F
many of those details being appropriate only to a claim for remuneration.
The plaintiffs contended that as the claims here could not be dealt with
" in the manner prescribed " the terms as to arbitration could not apply
to such claims, or at least could only apply if the claims were made by
way of counterclaim to a claim for remuneration. The judge rejected
that argument and on the face of it it seems to me that he was right to do G
so, because if accepted it would appear to nullify the effect of the
provision for arbitration of " any other differences." However, we did
not hear any argument from counsel for the plaintiffs on this issue so I
say no more about it and, on the assumption that the claims are within
the arbitration clause, go on to consider whether the judge's decision
to refuse a stay is one which this court can and should reverse. H

The grounds put forward by the plaintiffs for resisting a stay were:
first, the avoidance of multiplicity of proceedings; and secondly that
difficult questions of law, or of mixed fact and law, were involved.
The judge considered that the avoidance of duplication of proceedings in
England was the decisive factor. I do not consider that this court should
interfere with his exercise of discretion unless it could be shown either
that he was under some misapprehension about such duplication or

that he failed to give sufficient weight to countervailing considerations on the other side.

It is said on behalf of the defendants that multiplicity of proceedings is unavoidable because the Spanish government is suing in Spain while the claims of the *Erkowit* and her cargo, whether wholly in court or partly by way of arbitration, will of course be pursued in England. The fact that some multiplicity is inevitable does not mean that it is not desirable to limit it as much as possible. There are a number of issues that fall to be tried both as between the plaintiffs and the *Dortmund* and as between the plaintiffs and the salvors. If the four English actions continue they can be heard by the same judge at the same time, costs will be saved and the risk of conflicting decisions will be avoided. The prevention of duplication is not a conclusive ground for refusing a stay: see *W. Bruce Ltd.* v. *J. Strong* [1951] 2 K.B. 447, but it is an important consideration and has often been the main ground on which a stay has been refused: see *The Pine Hill* [1958] 2 Lloyd's Rep. 146, McNair J. and *Taunton-Collins* v. *Cromie* [1964] 1 W.L.R. 633, C.A.

The defendants raise two points in connection with the Spanish proceedings—that they will wish to counterclaim against the owners of the *Erkowit* for indemnity or contribution in respect of any damages that may be found due from them to the Spanish government, which counterclaim could not be formulated till after the conclusion of the Spanish proceedings; and that if the claims against them in England are heard in open court before the Spanish action is heard the publicity (which would be avoided by arbitration) might be detrimental to them. As to the first of these points I think it would be quite wrong that the decision on the plaintiffs' claims, whether pursued in court or before an arbitrator, should be deferred for what might be a period of years pending the decision in Spain. As Brandon J. said, once the facts have been decided by the court there would be nothing to prevent the salvors from raising a claim to contribution or indemnity at a later stage if necessary. As to publicity, the question whether the salvors were negligent is an issue in the collision actions and the investigation of that issue in the actions against the salvors will not substantially add to the publicity.

The contention on the defendants' side which most impressed the judge was this: section 8 of the Maritime Conventions Act 1911 prescribes a time limit of two years for, inter alia, proceedings "in respect of any salvage service." Under section 27 (1) of the Limitation Act 1939, that time limit applies also to arbitrations. If the actions were stayed and an arbitration were commenced, the salvors would be able to rely on the time bar as a defence. If the actions proceed the salvors are deprived of that defence because the actions were started within the two-year period. It is to my mind an unattractive argument for a party to seek to insist on an arbitration so as to enable him to contend that he can render the arbitration ineffective. The authority relied on in support of the argument is *W. Bruce Ltd.* v. *J. Strong* [1951] 2 K.B. 447, where it was held that the fact that an arbitration would be out of time was not a good reason for refusing a stay. That however was a case where the arbitration agreement provided for a special time limit, shorter than the statutory one, so that if a stay had been granted the plaintiff would have been able to escape from the obligation to bring his proceedings within the agreed time. Here no such consideration arises; the plaintiffs have brought their proceedings within the time which is the same for an arbitration as for an action.

This matter was dealt with in the judgment below on the basis that the A
only relevant way in which the plaintiffs' claims could be regarded was as claims in respect of salvage. The judge considered it very doubtful whether they could be so regarded and I agree with him. If, however, I am right in thinking that the plaintiffs' claims can be described, at least in part, as claims for damage done by a ship, then such claims would be subject to the two-year time bar. There is however the further point that the proviso
to section 8 enables any court having jurisdiction (and the same must apply B
to an arbitrator) to extend the period to such extent and on such conditions as it thinks fit. The judge considered it very doubtful whether or not, if the claims were held to fall within section 8, the time would be extended. It was submitted for the defendants that it was clear that the time would not be extended. The only authority on the proviso to which we were referred
was *The Alnwick* [1965] P. 357, where time was extended by the Court of C
Appeal, Willmer L.J. dissenting. The majority considered that the time should be extended because the failure to take proceedings in time was not blameworthy. In the absence of any authority on the question of whether time should be extended where proceedings have been brought within the time limit but the defendants have succeeded in getting those proceedings stayed so as to compel the plaintiffs to proceed by arbitration outside the
time limit, I do not consider that the judge was wrong in regarding that D
as a question to which the answer was very doubtful.

Although I have differed from the judge on one point which he took into account in exercising his discretion I do not consider that that was of sufficient weight to lead to the conclusion that his exercise of discretion should be disregarded. I would add, however, that even if I took the view
that the limitation defence if raised would be bound to succeed, and that E
for that reason this court should exercise a fresh discretion in the matter, I should be of opinion that the stay should be refused because I regard the avoidance of unnecessary multiplicity as a strong ground for letting the actions proceed and, while *W. Bruce Ltd.* v. *J. Strong* establishes that the expiration of the time for arbitration is not a ground for refusing a stay, I do not consider that in the circumstances of this case the deprivation
of the salvors of the opportunity of setting up the defence of limitation is F
a positive reason in favour of a stay.

In the result I would dismiss the appeals.

SCARMAN L.J. I have had the advantage of reading the judgments of the other members of the court. I agree that the appeals should be dismissed.
I do not wish to add to what Cairns L.J. has already said upon the arbitra- G
tion clause. I agree with the construction put by Sir Gordon Willmer upon section 1 (1) of the Administration of Justice Act 1956 and wish to make only a few general observations as to the approach to the interpretation of the subsection.

But, since I think that the crux of the two appeals is the construction
of section 3 (4) of the Act, I propose to consider that subsection at greater H
length.

Part I of the Act deals with the Admiralty jurisdiction of the courts of England and Wales, and Part V with the Admiralty jurisdiction of the courts of Scotland. I would not expect to find any substantial difference between the two jurisdictions, though there are (and, no doubt, will continue to be) differences attributable to the need to fit the law of the sea (which is the same in England, Wales and Scotland: *Currie* v. *M'Knight* [1897]

A A.C. 97) into the two different legal systems. Subject to that one reservation, I think it right to construe Part I of the Act consistently with Part V, upon the basis that the substance of the maritime law is the same in both jurisdictions; and no doubt Scots lawyers will construe Part V, subject to the same reservation, in a way consistent with Part I.

More especially must this approach be correct when interpreting section 3 (4) and section 47 (1) which are the subsections that introduce into the B law of England and Wales and the law of Scotland respectively the provisions of the international convention relating to the arrest of seagoing ships signed at Brussels in 1952 and ratified by the United Kingdom in 1959.

Section 1 (1) of the Act specifies the questions and claims which are the subject of the Admiralty jurisdiction of the High Court (and, within the limits imposed by section 2, of the county courts as well). The section C is the current statutory statement of the extent of the jurisdiction. It is, for the time being, the last of a series of such statements originating with the Act of 1840 which settled in favour of the Admiralty the ancient strife between the courts of the common law and the Admiralty court as to the jurisdiction of the latter over disputes relating to ships within the body of a county, that is to say within internal waters. The price paid for this victory was that the Admiralty jurisdiction was limited to the questions D and claims specified by the Act—at least so far as internal waters were concerned.

The jurisdiction has been enlarged since 1840 in some respects (for example the addition of claims arising out of agreements relating to the use or hire of a ship): but the principle of the list and, subject to some amendment (for instance the Act of 1956 has dropped specific reference to E the body of a county), the descriptions of the claims have remained intact from statute to statute. It is safe, therefore, to infer, according to an accepted principle of statutory interpretation (see *Greaves* v. *Tofield* (1880) 14 Ch.D. 563, 571), that claims specified by the Act of 1956 in language the same as that of previous statutes should be given the same meaning. The extent of the Admiralty jurisdiction is thus the subject of a considerable case law interpreting statutory provisions that over the years have become F well known.

But the mode of its exercise was not the subject of comprehensive enactment until, following the Brussels convention, section 3 was enacted. Case law on the section (save as to its application to " sister ships ") is almost non-existent. The section makes clear that Admiralty jurisdiction may exist and be exercisable by action in personam without an action in G rem being available. The action in rem may be invoked only in the cases mentioned in subsections (2) to (5). One of the reasons for thus limiting the availability of the action in rem is, I have no doubt, that the Brussels Convention provides by article 2, that a ship of a contracting state may not be arrested save in respect of one of the maritime claims set out in article 1. Put briefly, the convention permits the arrest of ships (and, therefore, in the Latin language of the English law the institution of an Admiralty action H in rem) in respect of the maritime claims specified in article 1, " but in respect of no other claims ": article 2. It further permits the arrest of a " sister ship " when the ship in respect of which the claim arises has passed out of the ownership of the defendant: article 3. While some of the maritime claims in respect of which a ship may be arrested do not give rise to maritime lien, each one of them is concerned with either services rendered to a ship or damage arising from the use of a ship, or with problems concerned with rights of ownership, possession or mortgage of a ship. I

The convention does not include amongst its maritime claims a claim A for " damage received by a ship "—although it is a claim that under English law gives rise to Admiralty jurisdiction. In every case covered by the convention there is a clearly defined link between the claim and the ship sought to be arrested—a link such as makes it just and reasonable that the claimant should be permitted to look to the ship (or in a proper case its " sister ship ") as security for the satisfaction of his claim. So far as accidental damage is concerned, the convention identifies the claims that B justify arrest by reference not to ships that receive or suffer damage but to ships that cause damage.

Section 3 (4) is to be presumed to give effect to the Convention and should be construed accordingly. The subsection deals with claims of damage or for services rendered, i.e. those mentioned in paragraphs (*d*) to (*r*) of section 1 (1) of the Act. It declares the circumstances in which C such a claim, " being a claim arising in connection with a ship," may be pursued by an action in rem against that ship (or its " sister ship "). No action in rem is available unless the claim is shown to be a claim against a ship. To establish, therefore, the availability of an action in rem it is not enough merely to ascertain whether the claim is one of those mentioned in paragraphs (*d*) to (*r*) of section 1 (1) of the Act of 1956. It is also necessary that the claim should relate to a ship which has caused damage D or in respect of which services have been rendered or money disbursed. It does not follow that because there is Admiralty jurisdiction to entertain a claim, an action in rem may be invoked to enforce it. The existence of jurisdiction depends upon section 1 of the Act, but the availability of an action in rem depends upon section 3. When the subsection provides that an action in rem can be invoked only if the claim is " a claim arising E in connection with a ship," it is referring, in my judgment, to a ship in respect of which a maritime claim as specified in the convention arises. Section 47 (1) is clearly so limited: and I would not expect any difference in this matter between English and Scots law.

If the shipowners' claim is put solely under paragraph (*e*) of section 1 (1), it has to be regarded as a claim arising in connection with the *Erkowit*, the ship which suffered or " received " the damage. In respect of such F a claim the subsection does not permit an action in rem, for it is not the *Erkowit* in respect of which a convention maritime claim arises. The convention and the subsection contemplate as the " res " which may be arrested: (i) in a damage claim, not the victim but the wrong-doing ship and (ii) in a claim for services rendered, the ship to which the services were rendered. G

The same reasoning would non-suit the cargo owners if they had to rely on paragraph (*g*) alone.

But in truth neither the shipowners nor the cargo owners are so confined. They can establish jurisdiction under paragraph (*d*) by showing, as Sir Gordon Willmer explains, that their claim is for damage done by a ship, that is to say, the defendant's tug *Rotesand*, in which case they are enabled under the subsection to bring their action in rem against the *Rotesand*, or, H as they have done, a sister ship of the *Rotesand*. I think also, though it is unnecessary to decide the point, that they can show a claim under paragraph (*h*). Both the shipowners and the cargo owners have, in my opinion, a claim arising out of an agreement relating to the use of the *Rotesand*, that is to say, the salvage agreement, in which case they may also institute actions in rem against the *Rotesand* or a sister ship. Taking the view that I do of the scope of section 3 (4), I think these appeals should be dismissed.

A Each plaintiff may invoke the jurisdiction by action in rem, for each of them, shipowner and cargo owner, can formulate a claim under paragraph (*d*) or (*h*), citing the *Rotesand* as the ship in connection with which the claim arises.

Sir Gordon Willmer. At the conclusion of his argument against the adoption of an excessively restrictive approach to the Admiralty jurisdiction
B of the court Mr. Thomas remarked that if there is any case that ought to come within the Admiralty jurisdiction in rem, this is it. Mr. Willmer, on the other hand, advocating a more restricted approach, concluded his final address by reminding us, quite properly, that this is a jurisdiction which affects foreigners, and therefore the statute conferring it should be strictly construed. But it is fair to observe that in the present case not
C only are the proposed defendants foreign, but so also are the plaintiffs who invoke the jurisdiction of the court, no doubt in the hope that the court's approach to their claims will not be wholly unsympathetic. However this may be, it is plain to me that the judge whose task it is to navigate in these difficult waters must take care to shape a course which will keep him clear, on the one hand, of the Scylla of excessive restriction and, on the other hand, of the Charybdis of too much liberality . For my
D part I shall do my best to keep in mid-channel.

The relevant facts have already been summarised in the judgment delivered by Cairns L.J., and it is unnecessary for me to repeat them; nor do I need to set out again the relevant statutory provisions, which have already been quoted. It is sufficient to say that the plaintiffs in each of the two actions before us seek to bring themselves within one or more of the
E following paragraphs of section 1 (1) of the Administration of Justice Act 1956, that is to say:

> " (*d*) any claim for damage done by a ship; (*e*) any claim for damage received by a ship; . . . (*g*) any claim for loss of or damage to goods carried in a ship; (*h*) any claim arising out of any agreement relating to the carriage of goods in a ship or to the use or hire of a ship; (*j*) any claim in the nature of salvage "

F

In the case of both actions the claim sought to be enforced in rem is a claim for the total loss of the plaintiffs' property, that is to say, of the *Erkowit* herself and the cargo laden on board her. In the case of the shipowners' action there is a further claim, which it is also sought to enforce in rem, for an indemnity against possible claims, asserted against the owners
G of the *Erkowit* by the Spanish government on behalf of local fishermen, in respect of pollution caused by the escape from the wreck of the *Erkowit* of a number of drums containing a noxious chemical. A further question arises in relation to both actions, namely, whether, assuming the assertion of Admiralty jurisdiction in rem to be well founded, the respective actions ought to be stayed in pursuance of section 4 of the Arbitration Act 1950 on the ground that the damage and loss complained of arose in the course of
H salvage operations being carried on by the tug *Rotesand* in pursuance of a salvage agreement on Lloyd's Form signed on behalf of ship and cargo by the master of the *Erkowit*. As is well known, this form of salvage agreement makes provisions for the reference to arbitration of disputes between salvors and those interested in the property to be salved. So far as this question is concerned I agree, for the reasons already stated by Cairns L.J. that this is not a proper case for granting a stay, and I see no reason for saying that Brandon J. wrongly exercised his discretion in refusing it.

I do not find it necessary to add any further observations of my own with regard to this aspect of the case. A

I confine myself, therefore, to the two questions relating to the Admiralty jurisdiction in rem, namely, (1) whether there is jurisdiction in rem against the *Rotesand* or one of her sister ships in respect of the plaintiffs' claims for the total loss of the *Erkowit* and her cargo, and (2) whether, if so, the owners of the *Erkowit* can include in their claim a declaration that they are entitled to be indemnified, either wholly or in part, against their possible B liability to the Spanish government in respect of the pollution caused by the escape from the wreck of the drums of noxious chemical.

The greater part of section 1 (1) of the Act of 1956 consists of a re-enactment of similar provisions contained in earlier statutes. I agree with Brandon J. in thinking that where expressions used are the same as those used in earlier statutes, they should prima facie be construed as having C the same meaning as may have been assigned to them by prior judicial decision. I also agree that, since Part I of the Act of 1956 was passed for the purpose of giving effect to the Brussels Convention of 1952 relating to the Arrest of Seagoing Ships, it is permissible to look at the terms of the Convention where phrases used in the Act are thought to be capable of more than one meaning. This arises particularly in relation to section 3 of the Act, which governs rights of arrest and is presumably intended to give D effect to article 3 of the Convention.

In construing the five paragraphs of section 1 (1) of the Act of 1956, which have been invoked in this case, I think it is important to start by considering in relation to each what is "the ship" which is referred to. In the case of paragraph (*d*), "damage done by a ship," the ship referred to can only be the alleged wrongdoer, that is to say, the ship whose faulty E navigation is said to be the cause of the damage. In the context of this case that ship would be the tug *Rotesand*. As to paragraph (*e*) "damage received by a ship," the ship referred to must clearly be the ship alleged to have been damaged, which in the context of this case would be the *Erkowit*. So much appears to be plain beyond difficulty.

In the case of paragraph (*g*), "loss of or damage to goods carried in a ship," the answer is perhaps not so immediately obvious. But construing F the words used in their natural and ordinary sense, I conclude that the ship referred to must be the carrying ship. The paragraph must be designed to cover the claim of a cargo owner against the ship to which he has entrusted his cargo. The words do not appear to be apt to cover a claim against some other ship. If it is alleged that goods carried in ship A were damaged in consequence of fault on the part of ship B, it seems to me that G the plaintiffs would have their remedy under paragraph (*d*), on the basis that the damage was done by such other ship, and that they would have no need to invoke paragraph (*g*), the wording of which is at best equivocal. In the context of this case, therefore, I would hold that the only ship to which paragraph (*g*) could apply is the *Erkowit*.

Paragraph (*h*) to my mind also presents some difficulty—for it is directed to two separate eventualities. In so far as it is concerned with a claim H arising out of an agreement relating to the carriage of goods in a ship, the ship referred to must be the ship in which the goods are carried (or to be carried) in pursuance of the agreement. Nothing arises in this case in relation to this part of the paragraph. But the latter part of the paragraph refers to a claim arising out of an agreement relating to the use or hire of a ship. Such a claim does not necessarily have anything to do with the carriage of goods—for a ship can well be hired or used for other purposes.

A It seems to me that the ship referred to in relation to any such claim must be the ship alleged to have been used or hired. In the context of this case that ship is alleged to be the tug *Rotesand*.

In relation to paragraph (*j*), " any claim in the nature of salvage," it appears to me that the only ship in respect of which such a claim could be asserted would be the ship alleged to have been salved. A claim for damage alleged to have been caused to salved property by fault on the part of the B salvors would not be a claim in the nature of salvage. If the damage is alleged to have been caused by fault on the part of a salving ship, such a claim could well fall within paragraph (*d*), but I have difficulty in seeing how it could possibly be caught by paragraph (*j*).

In the present case Brandon J. held that neither the shipowners' nor the cargo owners' claim came within paragraphs (*d*) or (*j*). He held that C the shipowners' claim did come within paragraphs (*e*) and (*h*), and that the cargo owners' claim came within paragraphs (*g*) and (*h*). It was conceded before him by the defendants that the shipowners' claim was within paragraph (*e*) so far as concerned the loss of the *Erkowit*, and the only question argued before him in relation to this paragraph was whether the alleged consequential damage, that is to say, the potential liability for pollution at the suit of the Spanish government, came within the paragraph. D It was also conceded by the defendants before Brandon J. that the cargo owners' claim for the loss of their cargo came within paragraph (*g*).

In the course of the argument before us the case underwent a number of kaleidoscopic changes. Having regard to the manner in which the argument developed we thought it right to grant leave to counsel for the defendants to withdraw the concessions which he made in the court below E in relation to paragraphs (*e*) and (*g*). This necessitated granting leave to amend the notice of appeal in the two actions. We also thought it right in the circumstances to grant leave to amend the respondents' notice in the shipowners' action, by adding submissions that the damage alleged fell within paragraphs (*g*) and (*j*), as well as within paragraph (*d*). In the result we have to consider all five of the relevant paragraphs.

In relation to paragraph (*e*) it is plain that there is Admiralty jurisdiction F in respect of damage received by a ship, and there can be no doubt that such a claim can be enforced by an action in personam: see section 3 (1) of the Act of 1956. But the question is whether any right in rem can be asserted, and if so, against what ship. It is noteworthy that the Convention of 1952, which is concerned only with rights of arrest, makes no mention of the case of " damage received by a ship." It is to be implied that those G responsible for drafting the Convention recognised that in the case of damage received by a ship there would normally be no question of arrest. If the damage were caused by the fault of another ship there could be a right to arrest such other ship, because it would be a case of damage done by that ship and thus within paragraph (*d*). If the damage received were caused otherwise than by a ship, for instance, by fault on the part of a dock or harbour authority, there would be no res capable of being arrested. It was H conceded by counsel for the defendants that there might be one possible case for asserting a right in rem in respect of damage received by a ship. That might arise in the event of the ship receiving the damage being subject to a demise charter. If the damage were caused by the fault of the demise charterers then it could be said that under paragraph (*b*) of section 3 (4) of the Act of 1956 it might be possible to arrest a sister ship beneficially owned by the demise charterers. But that is not this case.

The question must ultimately turn on the true construction of section 3

(4) of the Act. As I read that section, giving the words used their ordinary A and natural meaning, the ship in connection with which the plaintiffs' claim arises is the *Erkowit*, the ship which received the damage. The persons who would be liable in an action in personam would be the salvors, the owners of the *Rotesand*. I do not see how it is possible to extract from the subsequent wording of the subsection any right to arrest the *Rotesand* (or a sister ship of the *Rotesand*). Only the ship in connection with which the claim arises (or a sister ship thereof) can be arrested. I think this view B receives support from the terms of article 3 (1) of the Convention, whereby it is provided:

> " a claimant may arrest either the particular ship in respect of which the maritime claim arose, or any other ship which is owned by the person who was, at the time when the maritime claim arose, the owner of the particular ship." C

Mr. Thomas in his argument on behalf of the plaintiffs put forward two possible alternative ways of construing section 3 (4). In the first place he suggested that at the material time the salvors, the owners of the *Rotesand*, were in possession and control of the *Erkowit*. They were thus virtually in the position of demise charterers, and accordingly it would be possible under paragraph (*b*) of the subsection to arrest another ship beneficially D owned by them. This is an ingenious suggestion, but in my judgment it fails on the facts. Those in charge of the *Rotesand* may have been in physical control of the *Erkowit*, in the sense that, in the absence of any crew on board, her movements were entirely dictated by the action of the *Rotesand*. But in my view Mr. Willmer was well founded when he submitted that in the context of section 3 (4) of the Act the words " possession " E and " control " mean something much more than this, as was held by Brandon J. in *The Andrea Ursula* [1973] Q.B. 265.

The other alternative suggested was to construe the words " being a claim arising in connection with a ship " as meaning a claim arising in connection with the *Rotesand*. For my part, I find this suggestion difficult to accept. It strikes me as involving a strained construction, by no means in accord with the scheme of the Act. It does not fit very easily with F article 3 (1) of the Convention, which I have already quoted. It overlooks the fact that what we are dealing with here is damage received by the *Erkowit*. Moreover, if all that is contended is that jurisdiction existed to arrest the *Rotesand* (or a sister ship thereof) because the *Rotesand* by her faulty navigation caused the damage complained of, the plaintiffs could have their remedy in rem under paragraph (*d*) of section 1 (1), and they do G not need to invoke paragraph (*e*).

In these circumstances I am satisfied that the concession made before Brandon J. below was wrongly made, with the result that, through no fault of his own, he arrived at a wrong conclusion in holding that there was jurisdiction in rem under paragraph (*e*) against the *Rotesand* or a sister ship thereof. In my judgment the defendants are entitled to succeed on this issue. H

Much the same applies in relation to the claim of the cargo owners to assert a right in rem against the *Rotesand* or her sister ship under paragraph (*g*). Had the claim been against the *Erkowit* as the carrying ship, I entertain no doubt that this would have given rise to a right in rem against that vessel. The *Erkowit*, and not the *Rotesand*, was the ship in connection with which the claim arose. Here again I think it is helpful to look at the terms of article 3 (1) of the Convention. If the cargo owners make good their allegation that the loss of their goods was caused by the fault of the *Rotesand*, it seems to me that they may have their remedy in rem against the *Rotesand* (or a sister ship) under paragraph (*d*), as being damage done by the *Rotesand*, and that they have no need to invoke paragraph (*g*). This also in my judgment applies in relation to the contention in the shipowners' action, first put forward by way of amendment in this court, that they too are entitled, as bailees of the cargo, to assert a right in rem under paragraph (*g*) against the *Rotesand* or her sister ship. In relation to this paragraph also the defendants are in my judgment entitled to succeed.

I have already, I think, sufficiently indicated my view as to the claim, put forward both by the shipowners and by the cargo owners, to invoke paragraph (*j*). To be fair to the plaintiffs, this point was not very enthusiastically argued on their behalf either before Brandon J. or in this court. Suffice it to say that I am unable to perceive how a claim in respect of damage caused by negligent salvage can possibly be brought within the words "any claim in the nature of salvage." A claim in the nature of salvage could in my judgment only arise against the owners of the property salved. On this issue too my judgment is in favour of the defendants.

That leaves only the claims put forward by both shipowners and cargo owners under paragraphs (*d*) and (*h*). With regard to paragraph (*d*) the principal authority relied on by both sides was the decision of the House of Lords in *Currie* v. *M'Knight* [1897] A.C. 97. This was a Scottish appeal, but it was expressly held that the Admiralty jurisdiction in Scotland was the same as that in England. It is true that the decision was not directed to the construction of the words "damage done by a ship." The question at issue, however, was the related question whether in the events which occurred a maritime lien attached to the alleged wrongdoing ship, so as to entitle the owners of the damaged ship to assert a right in rem against her. What happened was that the pursuer's ship was alleged to have been damaged by the action of members of the crew of the defender's ship in wrongfully interfering with the moorings of the former. The crew members of the defender's ship were not on board their ship at the time, and it was held that accordingly their alleged wrongful action did not give rise to a maritime lien against the ship. Lord Halsbury L.C. expressed the view, at p. 101, that the ship against which a maritime lien for damages is claimed must be "the instrument of mischief." Similarly, Lord Watson, at p. 106, said that the damage must be either the direct result or the natural consequence of a wrongful act or manoeuvre of the ship to which it attaches. This echoes the dictum of Bowen L.J. in the earlier case of *The Vera Cruz*, 9 P.D. 96 where the question was whether at that date the phrase "damage done by a ship" was apt to confer Admiralty jurisdiction in rem in relation to life claims arising from alleged negligence on the part of a colliding ship. Bowen L.J. said, at p. 101: "damage . . . 'done by a ship' means done by those in charge of a ship, with the ship as the noxious instrument": see also *The Theta* [1894] P. 280 where this dictum was applied in relation to a claim for personal injury.

In the present case what is alleged by the plaintiffs in both actions, that is to say, the owners of both ship and cargo, is that the *Rotesand*, while towing the *Erkowit*, negligently beached her in an exposed position, with the result that with the advent of adverse weather she broke up, and both ship and cargo were totally lost. Assuming that the plaintiffs are able to substantiate these allegations, it seems to me that if ever there was a case where the defendants' vessel was "the noxious instrument" this was it.

On this point I find myself unable to agree with Brandon J. I would hold A that the plaintiffs' claim plainly falls within paragraph (*d*), and that they are entitled in both actions to assert a right in rem on this ground.

This is sufficient to render it impossible to strike out in limine the plaintiffs' claims in respect of the loss of the *Erkowit* and her cargo. It is strictly unnecessary, therefore, to consider the alternative ground under paragraph (*h*), on which the plaintiffs in both actions also rely. But as B this point was fully argued before us I think it is only right to express my views upon it. The plaintiffs assert, and the defendants deny, that the salvage agreement entered into by the master of the *Rotesand* on behalf of the salvors, and by the master of the *Erkowit* on behalf of the ship and cargo, constituted in effect an agreement for the use of the *Rotesand*. It is true that there was no express agreement to this effect. But what was provided was that the contractor, as represented by the *Rotesand* (the only C salvage instrument upon the scene), agreed to use his best endeavours to salve the *Erkowit* and her cargo and take them into a place to be thereafter agreed with the master. Since the *Erkowit* was in a totally disabled condition, some 50 miles or so from land in the Bay of Biscay, what the contractor agreed to do necessarily involved the *Rotesand* taking the *Erkowit* in tow for the purpose of taking her to a place of safety, with or without D further assistance. I think it is necessary to take a realistic view and to construe the terms of the agreement in the light of these surrounding circumstances. Although the *Rotesand* was not actually named as the towing instrument, in order to give business efficacy to the agreement it must at least be implied that she was to be used for the purpose of the necessary towage. In the circumstances I find it impossible to resist the conclusion that the salvage agreement constituted an agreement, inter alia, E for the use of the *Rotesand*. As such it fell within paragraph (*h*), and in my view would entitle the plaintiffs to assert a claim in rem in respect of alleged negligence in the performance of the agreement.

For my part I do not think that much assistance is to be derived from the numerous cases cited to us, whereby in the last century the court sought to apply a restrictive construction to the words of the County Court F (Admiralty Jurisdiction) Amendment Act 1869, by which this class of claim was first brought within the Admiralty jurisdiction, albeit at that time only in the county court. Of the other cases cited, it seems to me that *The Isca* (1886) 12 P.D. 34 (also reported in 6 Asp.M.L.C. 63) is very much in point. It is true that that case arose out of an agreement for the use of a specifically named tug, and on that ground it was sought on behalf of the defendants to distinguish it. But for reasons already adumbrated I do not think that G this is a valid point of distinction. I have found more difficulty with *The Queen of the South* [1968] P. 499 and *The Conoco Britannia* [1972] 2 Q.B. 543, both of which were decisions of Brandon J. In the former case the claim was by watermen, as owners of motor boats, against the ship for whose assistance they were used. In the latter case the claim was by the owners of a tug engaged to assist a ship under a towage contract. In both H cases the use alleged was a use of the plaintiffs' own vessels, that is to say, in both cases these were the vessels " in connection with which " the claim arose. I find it difficult to see how under section 3 (4) of the Act of 1956 jurisdiction in rem could properly be asserted against the ship which the plaintiffs' vessels were assisting. In this connection again I bear in mind the provisions of article 3 (1) of the Convention, to which I have already referred. No point, however, appears to have been taken in either case that there could be no right of arrest as against the defendants' ship. It seems to me that it may be necessary, if and when the point arises again, to reconsider these two decisions. For the purposes of the present case it does not seem necessary to rely on them in support of the plaintiffs' assertion of jurisdiction in rem under paragraph (*h*) against the *Rotesand* or one of her sister ships.

For these reasons, so far as concerns the claims for the loss of the *Erkowit* and her cargo, I am satisfied that the plaintiffs in both actions are entitled to assert a right in rem against the *Rotesand*, whether under paragraph (*d*) or paragraph (*h*), and in aid thereof to arrest the respective sister ships. Thus I agree with the conclusion at which Brandon J. arrived, albeit for rather different reasons.

This leaves for consideration the contention of the plaintiffs in the shipowners' action that they are entitled to include a claim for indemnity (which would presumably include a claim for contribution) in respect of any sum for which they may be found liable in the Spanish proceedings, arising from the alleged pollution caused by the escape of a noxious chemical from the wreck of the *Erkowit*. This is put forward as a claim for consequential loss following upon the alleged negligence of those in charge of the *Rotesand* in beaching the *Erkowit* in an exposed position. It is further alleged that subsequent to the beaching the salvors, the owners of the *Rotesand*, were guilty of further acts of negligence in (a) fitting only a wood and canvas patch, instead of a steel patch, over the hole in the side of the *Erkowit*, and (b) failing to carry out their salvage operations with reasonable expedition. For the defendants it is contended that no part of this claim for consequential loss is capable of forming any ground for asserting a right in rem against the *Rotesand*. In so far as it may be found that the pollution was caused by the alleged negligence of the salvors in carrying out their operations subsequent to the beaching of the *Erkowit*, I am of the opinion that the contention of the defendants is well founded. But in so far as the pollution may have resulted from the earlier alleged negligence of those in charge of the *Rotesand* in beaching the *Erkowit* in an exposed position, it seems to me that different considerations apply. If the plaintiffs succeed in proving that the beaching of the *Erkowit* constituted damage done by the *Rotesand*, so as to confer a right in rem within paragraph (*d*) of section 1 (1) of the Act of 1956, I do not see why they should not be entitled to include in their damage claim a claim for consequential loss. It is well known that a claim for consequential loss of earnings during the period while a damaged ship is laid up for repair is commonly included as a legitimate head of claim. Not infrequently a claim in respect of liabilities incurred towards third parties is also included. As was said by Lord Sumner in *The Cairnbahn* [1914] P. 25, 33:

> "The word 'loss' is wide enough to include that form of pecuniary prejudice which consists in compensating third parties for wrong done to them by the fault of persons for whose misconduct the party prejudiced must answer."

If in the Spanish proceedings the owners of the *Erkowit* were held to be answerable for the alleged pollution, this might well give rise to a good claim for indemnity or contribution as against the owners of the *Rotesand*, whether or not in those proceedings the owners of the *Rotesand* were also held to be answerable.

The difficulty at the present stage is to know exactly what form the claim of the Spanish government in respect of the pollution may take. If the government's claim is framed in tort, and their action is successful on the basis of fault, whether on the part of the *Erkowit* or of the *Rotesand* or both, I do not see any reason why the plaintiffs should not be entitled to include in their claim against the defendants a claim for indemnity or contribution in respect of the damages which they may be adjudged liable to pay: see *The Frankland* [1901] P. 161 and *The Cairnbahn.* But the situation would be different if the Spanish government's claim is based on some provision of Spanish law entitling them to recover compensation in respect of the pollution irrespective of fault. In such case any compensation which the plaintiffs might have to pay could well be held to result solely from the provision of Spanish law, so that it could not properly be included in the plaintiffs' claim against the defendants as part of the damage done by the *Rotesand*: see *The Circe* [1906] P. 1 and *The Molière* [1925] P. 27. Since it is impossible at the present stage to foresee whether or not the plaintiffs' claim for an indemnity or contribution in respect of the alleged consequential loss will be sustainable in law, it seems to me that it would be quite wrong to strike it out in limine. In my judgment the present application to do so is premature.

For these reasons I have come to the conclusion, in agreement with Cairns and Scarman L.JJ. that the appeals in both actions should be dismissed.

Appeals in both actions dismissed with costs.
Leave to appeal refused.

Solicitors: *Richards, Butler & Co.; Ince & Co.; Waltons & Co.*

October 16, 1975. The Appeal Committee of the House of Lords (Lord Diplock, Viscount Dilhorne and Lord Kilbrandon) allowed a petition by the defendants for leave to appeal.

The House of Lords heard argument on January 28 and 29 and February 2, 1976, and reserved their reasons on February 2, 1976.

[COURT OF APPEAL]

* REGINA *v.* BLOOMSBURY AND MARYLEBONE COUNTY COURT, *Ex parte* VILLERWEST LTD.

1975 Nov. 21

Lord Denning M.R., Roskill and Geoffrey Lane L.JJ.

County Court—Jurisdiction—Variation of order—Judgment given in absence of defendant—Judgment set aside on terms with time limit — Terms not complied with — Further application to extend time for compliance with terms—Whether jurisdiction to vary order—County Courts Act 1959 (7 & 8 *Eliz.* 2, *c.* 22), *s.* 103 [1]*—R.S.C., Ord.* 3, *r.* 5 (1) [2]

In an action in the county court the landlords claimed possession of a flat against the defendants, the tenant and

[1] County Courts Act 1959, s. 103: see post, p. 365A.
[2] R.S.C., Ord. 3, r. 5 (1): see post, p. 365B–C.

A sub-tenant respectively. On April 30, 1974, Judge Llewellyn ordered both defendants to give up possession of the flat by May 28, 1974, and the first defendant to pay £890 for rent, mesne profits and costs. On July 8, 1974, the same judge, on the defendants' application, set aside the judgment on condition that £890 was paid into court by the first defendant by July 22, 1974. The £890 was not paid in by that date. On July 24 the defendants gave notice of intention to apply for
B an extension of time for the payment into court. On July 31 Judge Figgis ordered that, if £325 was paid into court on July 31 and the balance of the amount due by August 14, the order setting aside the judgment would stand. The defendants complied with the conditions.

On the landlords' application for an order of certiorari to quash the order made by Judge Figgis, the Divisional Court held that he had had no power on July 31 to vary the earlier
C order and granted the application.

On appeal by the second defendant:—

Held, allowing the appeal, that a judge in the county court had inherent jurisdiction to enlarge the time for complying with such an order as made by Judge Figgis whether the application for such an extension was made before or after the time originally limited for compliance with it had expired (post, pp. 365E–G, 366H—367A, C).

D Dicta of Farwell L.J. in *Keymer* v. *Reddy* [1912] 1 K.B. 215, 221, C.A. applied.

Quaere. Whether R.S.C., Ord. 3, r. 5 (1) is a general principle of practice in the High Court which by virtue of section 103 of the County Courts Act 1959 applies in the county court (post, pp. 365D–E, 367A–B, C).

Decision of Divisional Court of the Queen's Bench Division
E [1975] 1 W.L.R. 1175; [1975] 2 All E.R. 652 reversed.

The following cases are referred to in the judgments:

Keymer v. *Reddy* [1912] 1 K.B. 215, C.A.

Manley Estates Ltd. v. *Benedek* [1941] 1 All E.R. 248, C.A.

Whistler v. *Hancock* (1878) 3 Q.B.D. 83.

F The following additional cases were cited in argument:

Collinson v. *Jeffery* [1896] 1 Ch. 644.

Harris v. *Monro*, December 15, 1972; Bar Library Transcript, No. 387 of 1972, C.A.

Reg. v. *Worthington-Evans, Ex parte Madan* [1959] 2 Q.B. 145; [1959] 2 W.L.R. 908; [1959] 2 All E.R. 457, D.C.

G *Robinson* v. *Fawcett & Firth* [1901] 2 K.B. 325.

APPEAL from Divisional Court.

On February 19, 1975, the Divisional Court (Lord Widgery C.J., Ashworth and Bridge JJ.) [1975] 1 W.L.R. 1175, on the application for an order of certiorari of the plaintiff landlords, Villerwest Ltd., ordered that the order of Judge Figgis at the Bloomsbury and Marylebone County Court
H on July 31, 1974, on the application of the defendants, Maxine McGregor and Joel Gumede, that, if £325 were paid into court on July 31, 1974, and the balance on or before August 14, the order made on July 8 setting aside a judgment for the landlords of April 30 should stand, be removed into the High Court and quashed.

The second defendant, Joel Gumede, appealed on the grounds, inter alia, that Judge Figgis had jurisdiction to vary the terms of the order of

July 8 and that the Divisional Court erred in law in holding that the order A of Judge Figgis had been made without jurisdiction.

The facts are stated in the judgment of Lord Denning M.R.

Richard Perkoff for the second defendant.
Peter Ralls for the landlords.

LORD DENNING M.R. Villerwest Ltd., the plaintiff, let a flat at 22, B Clifton Gardens, W.9. to a tenant. They served notice to quit and issued proceedings in the county court against the tenant and sub-tenant. They sued for possession and arrears of rent. On April 30, 1974, the tenant (the first defendant) did not appear but the sub-tenant (the second defendant) did. The judge ordered both defendants to give possession on May 28, 1974. He ordered that the plaintiffs should recover against the first C defendant £864·50 for rent and for mesne profits, and £25·50 for costs, making £890.

Both defendants applied to set aside that judgment. On July 8, 1974, the county court judge ordered that it be set aside conditional upon the first defendant paying into court on or before July 22, 1974, the judgment debt and costs of £890. The order contains this special direction:

> "Failing compliance with payment of all such money payments as have D been ordered to be paid on or before July 22, 1974, judgment of April 30, 1974, to stand."

The first defendant did not pay in that sum by July 22, 1974. She had gone to South Africa and there was difficulty in getting hold of her. Two days later, namely, on July 24, the defendants gave notice that they E intended to apply to the court to vary the order so as to extend the time for the payment until August 14, 1974. That application came before Judge Figgis on July 31, 1974. Counsel then appeared for the landlords and submitted that the judge had no jurisdiction to extend the time. We are told that the judge was amused to hear this suggestion. He rejected it courteously. He had done it so often that he could not doubt that he had jurisdiction. So he granted an extension of time. He made an order that F provided £325 was paid forthwith into court and the remaining balance by August 14, 1974, the order setting aside would stand. The defendants duly complied with these conditions by August 14, 1974. So under the order the judgment was set aside.

The plaintiffs went to the Divisional Court and applied to quash the judge's order. The Divisional Court [1975] 1 W.L.R. 1175 held that the G county court had no jurisdiction to extend the time as it did. The result was that, although the defendants had paid all the money into court they were not allowed to defend the case. The defendants appeal to this court.

In the County Court Rules 1936 there is only one rule which deals with extension of time. It is Ord. 13, r. 5. It says:

> "Subject to the provisions of these rules, any of the times fixed by H these rules for—(*a*) taking any step in any proceedings; or (*b*) filing any document; or (*c*) giving any notice; may be enlarged or abridged by consent of all parties or by the court on the application of any party."

The Divisional Court held, at p. 1179, that the rule did not apply because the time for paying this money was not "fixed by these rules." It was a time fixed by the order of the judge which he made on July 8, 1974.

A The defendants next sought to rely on the High Court Rules which
they said were imported into the county court powers by section 103 of
the County Courts Act 1959. It says:

> "In any case not expressly provided for by or in pursuance of this
> Act, the general principles of practice in the High Court may be
> adopted and applied to proceedings in a county court."

B The defendants submitted that that section imports the Rules of the
High Court so as to make them applicable in the county court. In
particular R.S.C., Ord. 3, r. 5 (1):

> "(1) The court may, on such terms as it thinks just, by order extend or
> abridge the period within which a person is required or authorised
> by these rules, or by any judgment, order or direction, to do any act
> C in any proceedings. (2) The court may extend any such period as
> is referred to in paragraph (1) although the application for extension is
> not made until after the expiration of that period."

The Divisional Court held, at p. 1180, that that rule was not brought
into the county court practice. They thought it was not a "general
principle of practice in the High Court" within section 103; and that
D section 103 only brought in matters which were not dealt with in the
County Court Rules.

I am afraid that I cannot agree with the Divisional Court. I think
that R.S.C., Ord. 3, r. 5 is a general principle of practice which comes well
within section 103. In dozens of cases in this court we have applied
section 103. Wherever we find a situation for which the County Court
E Rules do not make provision, we turn to the High Court Rules and apply
them without any hesitation.

If this be wrong nevertheless there is a very wide inherent jurisdiction,
both in the High Court and in the county court, to enlarge any time which
a judge has ordered. In *Keymer* v. *Reddy* [1912] 1 K.B. 215, 221, Farwell
L.J. said—and his words seem very appropriate here:

> "It is said . . . that because the master is acting without statutory
> F authority the court has no power to enlarge the time. The argument
> is that the court cannot enlarge the time because the rule as to enlarg-
> ing time . . . applies only to a case where the time is fixed under the
> rules of the court. That seems to me to be a fatal argument. It is
> inconceivable that the court should allow itself to be hampered in
> that way."

G Equally I say that it is inconceivable that the county court should be
hampered in the way that is suggested here. The court obviously has
power to enlarge the time when the application is made within the time
originally fixed. So also when it is made after the time has elapsed.
Instances were suggested in argument. Suppose a man is on his way to
the court in time with the money in his pocket. Then he is run down in
H an accident, or he is robbed of it. Or suppose that his cheque has been
held up in the bank for a short time. Has the court no power to enlarge
the time in such a case? Every court has inherent power to control its
own procedure, even though there is nothing in the rules about it.

There is a decision which supports this view. It is *Manley Estates Ltd.*
v. *Benedek* [1941] 1 All E.R. 248. In that case the plaintiff signed judg-
ment in default of appearance. The master set it aside provided that the
defendant paid the money into court within seven days. He failed to pay

the money within the time and after the seven days had elapsed, applied for an extension. This court held that there was jurisdiction to extend the time. The Divisional Court seem to have thought that that decision was erroneous. I think that it was a perfectly correct decision.

I have one further observation to make. It is about *Whistler* v. *Hancock* (1878) 3 Q.B.D. 83. It seems there to be suggested that if a condition is not fulfilled the action ceases to exist, as though no extension of time can be granted. I do not agree with that line of reasoning. Even though the action may be said to cease to exist, the courts has always power to bring it to life again, by extending the time.

In my opinion the judge had ample jurisdiction to make the order he did.

I would allow the appeal accordingly.

ROSKILL L.J. I confess I have found this a more difficult case than I think Lord Denning M.R. has done, because in certain respects there is much to be said, if I may say so, for the view which the Divisional Court took, particularly upon the interaction of the Rules of the Supreme Court and the County Court Rules by reason of section 103 of the County Courts Act 1959.

I ventured to ask Mr. Ralls in the course of his admirable argument what he would say if the application which was made for an extension of time after the time originally limited for making the payment into court had expired had been made between the date of the original order and its expiry. Consistently as I think with the rest of his argument he said that the county court judge would even at that time have had no jurisdiction to extend the order. But is it right? It seems to me that it would be the most astonishing limitation upon the powers of county court judges with the multitude of Rent Act, landlord and tenant and other possession cases which come before them if we held that when a county court judge says there shall be no order for possession provided that certain conditions for payment of arrears of rent are complied with within a limited time, and an application is then made to him within the time so limited for the purpose of extending that time, he had automatically to send the applicant away from his court. So to hold would, in my judgment, upset the practice which has led to the making of many thousands of such orders which county court judges must have made.

If one rejects that submission of Mr. Ralls it is difficult to see in logic why the position should be different according to whether the application is made before the time runs out or after the time has run out, unless a different answer is compelled by the language of the relevant rules. There seems no doubt that the relevant language of Ord. 13, r. 5 of the County Court Rules is more limited than the language of the comparable R.S.C., Ord. 3, r. 5. But the powers of the court are by no means always limited to what is expressly stated in the rules of practice applicable to that court. The High Court, and indeed the Supreme Court, has an inherent jurisdiction, and so, in my judgment, has the county court. A good illustration of the inherent jurisdiction of the court is afforded by what Farwell L.J. said in *Keymer* v. *Reddy* [1912] 1 K.B. 215, 221, in the passage to which Lord Denning M.R. has already referred. I do not doubt that a county court judge has an inherent jurisdiction, for it is necessary for him to possess it in order to do justice between the parties, to extend the time, whether before or after it has expired for complying with such an order

A as paying into court arrears of rent or the like, within the time originally limited.

As I have already indicated I feel much more difficulty, with great respect to Lord Denning M.R., in saying that we can, as it were, write R.S.C., Ord. 3, r. 5 into the County Court Rules. I venture to think there is much to be said in favour of the view which Lord Widgery C.J. expressed [1975] 1 W.L.R. 1175, 1180. But, however that may be, and
B whether the view that the Divisional Court took on that point is correct or not, or whether the view which Lord Denning M.R. prefers is correct, I agee that there is for the reasons I have already given inherent jurisdiction in a county court judge to make the order which the tenants sought in this case.

Accordingly for that reason I would allow the appeal and say that the
C orders of certiorari and prohibition which the Divisional Court ordered to issue should not issue.

GEOFFREY LANE L.J. I also agree. Judge Figgis had an inherent jurisdiction to make the order which he did, regardless of the provisions of section 103 of the County Courts Act 1959 and regardless of whether under that provision or not the relevant provisions of the Rules of the
D Supreme Court could be imported into the County Court Rules.

For those reasons this appeal should be allowed.

Appeal allowed with costs in Divisional Court and Court of Appeal.

E Solicitors: *Ian Sherrate & Co.; Kaufman, Kramer & Shebson.*

A. H. B.

F

G

H

A

[COURT OF APPEAL]

* REGINA *v.* O'CONNOR

1976 Jan. 16; Feb. 12

Scarman L.J., Phillips and Mais JJ.

B

Justices—Crown Court—Committal for sentence—Offences connected with motor vehicles—Whether jurisdiction to sentence to borstal training and to disqualify from driving—Criminal Justice Act 1948 (11 & 12 *Geo.* 6, *c.* 58), *s.* 20—*Magistrates' Courts Act* 1952 (15 & 16 *Geo.* 6 & 1 *Eliz.* 2, *c.* 55), *s.* 28—*Criminal Justice Act* 1967 (*c.* 80), *s.* 56 (2) (5) (6)

The defendant pleaded guilty before justices to a number C of offences connected with motor cars and was committed, under section 28 of the Magistrates' Courts Act 1952, to the Crown Court for sentence with a view to borstal training. The Crown Court sentenced the defendant to borstal training and imposed a disqualification from driving. The defendant appealed against sentence.

On the question whether section 56 of the Criminal Justice Act 1967 [1] affected the interpretation placed on the provisions D of section 20 (5) of the Criminal Justice Act 1948 [2] that a court imposing a sentence of borstal training had no power to disqualify a defendant from driving:—

Held, dismissing the appeal, that section 56 (1) and (2) read in the context of the section made it clear that subsections (5) and (6) applied to committals for sentence both under section 56 (1) of the Act of 1967 and under section 28 of the Magistrates' Courts Act 1952; that, accordingly, the E Crown Court had power both to sentence the defendant to borstal training and to impose a disqualification from driving.

Reg. v. *Dangerfield* [1960] 1 W.L.R. 268, C.C.A. overruled.

The following case is referred to in the judgment of the court:

Reg. v. *Dangerfield* [1960] 1 W.L.R. 268; [1959] 3 All E.R. 88, C.C.A.

F

The following additional case was cited in argument:

Reg. v. *Gould* [1968] 2 Q.B. 65; [1968] 2 W.L.R. 643; [1968] 1 All E.R. 849, C.A.

[1] Criminal Justice Act 1967, s. 56: "(1) Where a magistrates' court—(*a*) has convicted a person of an offence punishable with imprisonment or of an offence in respect of which the court has a power or duty to order him to be disqualified under section 5 of the Road Traffic Act 1962 . . . and (*b*) commits that person . . . to G a court of assize or quarter sessions under any enactment to which this section applies to be sentenced . . . the magistrates' court may commit him . . . to be dealt with in respect of the offence mentioned in paragraph (*a*) of this subsection. (2) The enactments to which this section applies are . . . sections 28 and 29 of the Magistrates' Courts Act 1952. . . . (5) Where under subsection (1) of this section a magistrates' court commits a person to be dealt with by a court of assize or quarter sessions . . . the latter court may . . . deal with him in any way in which the magistrates' court might have dealt with him, and, without prejudice to the foregoing provision, where under that subsection or any enactment to which this H section applies a magistrates' court so commits a person, any duty or power which, apart from this subsection, would fall to be discharged or exercised by the magistrates' court shall not be discharged or exercised by that court but shall instead be discharged or may instead be exercised by the court of assize or quarter sessions. (6) Any duty imposed or power conferred by virtue of the last foregoing subsection on a court of quarter sessions, in a case where an offender has been committed to the court under section 28 of the Magistrates' Courts Act 1952, shall be discharged or may be exercised by the court notwithstanding that it sentences him to Borstal training . . . .

[2] Criminal Justice Act 1948, s. 20 (5): see post, pp. 369H—370A.

APPEAL against sentence.

The defendant, Oliver Mary O'Connor, appealed against a sentence of two years' disqualification from driving and a period of borstal training imposed for a number of offences connected with motor cars at Manchester Crown Court (Judge Wood) on September 5, 1975. He appealed on the ground that the judge had no jurisdiction to disqualify him from driving in addition to sentencing him to borstal training.

The facts are stated in the judgment of the court.

Nigel Ley for the defendant.
Simon Westbrook for the Crown.

Cur. adv. vult.

February 12. SCARMAN L.J. read the judgment of the court. This is an appeal against sentence by the defendant, Oliver Mary O'Connor, who on September 5, 1975, was sentenced by Judge Wood at the Manchester Crown Court to borstal training, a fine of £4 and a period of two years' disqualification from driving for a number of offences connected with motor cars: taking a motor vehicle without the owner's consent, theft, driving without insurance and driving under age. Counsel for the defendant takes only one point—that, the defendant having been committed by justices for sentence with a view to borstal training pursuant to section 28 of the Magistrates' Courts Act 1952, the Crown Court had no power to impose disqualification: and he relies on *Reg.* v. *Dangerfield* [1960] 1 W.L.R. 268.

The case reached the Crown Court in this way. On May 2, 1975, the defendant pleaded guilty to four offences at the Manchester juvenile court: on June 30 he pleaded guilty to another four offences at the same court: he was remanded for reports and on July 25 the justices committed him for sentence as follows: on charges of taking a motor vehicle without consent and stealing ignition keys under section 28 of the Act of 1952; on charges of driving under age and driving without insurance under section 56 of the Criminal Justice Act 1967. Three days before this committal, on July 22, he pleaded guilty at the Ashton-under-Lyme juvenile court to a charge of attempted theft and was committed to the Crown Court under section 28.

There is, and could be, no challenge to the sentence of borstal training. It is, however, submitted that upon a committal under section 28 it is not open to the Crown Court to impose a disqualification. Section 28 of the Act of 1952 provides that, where a person of the specified age is convicted by a magistrates' court of an offence punishable on summary conviction with imprisonment, and it is considered expedient that he should undergo a period of training in a borstal institution, the court may commit him "for sentence in accordance with the provisions of section 20 of the Criminal Justice Act 1948." That section empowers the Crown Court, in circumstances which the section specifies, to pass a sentence of borstal training "in lieu of any other sentence." Section 20 (5) provides that where an offender is committed by a court of summary jurisdiction for sentence with a view to borstal training, the Crown Court

"... may—(i) ... sentence him to borstal training; or (ii) in any case, deal with him in any manner in which the court of summary jurisdiction might have dealt with him: . . ."

The Court of Criminal Appeal in *Reg.* v. *Dangerfield* [1960] 1 W.L.R. 268 held that these two sub-paragraphs of the subsection are true alternatives. Accordingly it was then decided that " sessions cannot at one and the same time sentence a man to borstal training and disqualify him ": *per* Lord Parker C.J., at p. 270.

The Crown however submits that the decision in *Reg.* v. *Dangerfield* has been overruled by subsequent enactment. The point is one of construction of section 56 of the Criminal Justice Act 1967. It is submitted that committals under section 28 are committals under an enactment to which section 56 applies, and that the combined effect of section 56 (5) and (6) is to overrule *Reg.* v. *Dangerfield*. It is submitted that the effect of section 56 upon section 28 committals is to empower the Crown Court to impose a disqualification in addition to a sentence of borstal training and to remove from the magistrates' court the power to disqualify in any case in which they commit under section 28.

Counsel for the defendant however submits that section 56 (5) and (6) apply only to what he calls " section 56 committals," i.e. committals under section 56 (1), and that a section 28 committal is not a section 56 committal. He recognises that if a section 28 committal is within the section, the combined effect of subsections (5) and (6) is to overrule *Reg.* v. *Dangerfield*.

In our judgment section 56 does cover section 28 committals. This is the effect, we think, of section 56 (2) read in the context of the section as a whole.

Section 56 (2) specifies section 28 of the Magistrates' Courts Act 1952 as one of the enactments to which section 56 applies. Subsection (5) makes assurance doubly sure in that it makes provision not only for cases " Where under subsection (1) . . . a magistrates' court commits," but also:

> " without prejudice to the foregoing provision, where under that subsection or any enactment to which this section applies a magistrates' court so commits . . ."

Finally subsection (6) expressly provides that any duty imposed or power conferred by subsection (5) on the Crown Court, in a case where an offender has been committed to the court under section 28 shall be discharged or may be exercised by the court notwithstanding that it sentences him to borstal training and (as provided by subsection (5)) shall not be discharged or exercised by the magistrates' court.

We have no doubt that Parliament intended in section 56 of the Criminal Justice Act 1967 to correct the anomaly that had arisen as a result of the interpretation placed by the court in *Reg.* v. *Dangerfield* [1960] 1 W.L.R. 268 on section 20 (5) of the Criminal Justice Act 1948. Read as a whole, section 56 effects that intention in the course of a general clarification of the law relating to committals for sentence. The law is now no longer as declared in *Dangerfield's* case. Where an offender is committed (in custody or on bail) under section 28, the law now is that the justices have no power to sentence or otherwise to deal with him: their powers and duties are vested in the Crown Court, which in an appropriate case may impose a disqualification in addition to a sentence of borstal

A training. Disqualification for a period of two years was appropriate in this case. The appeal is therefore dismissed.

Appeal dismissed.
Certificate granted under section 33 (2) of the Criminal Appeal Act 1968 that a point of law of general
B *public importance was involved, namely: "Whether, upon the true construction of section 56 of the Criminal Justice Act 1967, where a person has been committed by a magistrates' court to the Crown*
C *Court under section 28 of the Magistrates' Courts Act 1952, the Crown Court has power both to order him to undergo borstal training and in respect of the same offence also to order him to be disqualified from holding or obtaining*
D *a driving licence."*
Leave to appeal refused.

Solicitors: *Registrar of Criminal Appeals; D. S. Gandy, Manchester.*

J. W.

E

March 9, 1976. The Appeal Committee of the House of Lords (Viscount Dilhorne, Lord Edmund-Davies and Lord Russell of Killowen) dismissed a petition by the defendant for leave to appeal.

F

[QUEEN'S BENCH DIVISION]

* ROBERTON v. SECRETARY OF STATE FOR THE ENVIRONMENT AND ANOTHER

G

1975 Dec. 9 Phillips J.

Highway—Public path—Diversion order—Footpath across Chequers Estate—Proximity to manor house—Need to protect occupants —Whether diversion of footpath for securing "efficient use" of "land"—Whether Public Trustee proper person to apply
H *for diversion order—Chequers Estate Act* 1917 (7 & 8 *Geo.* 5, *c.* 55), *s.* 1—*Highways Act* 1959 (7 & 8 *Eliz.* 2, *c.* 25), *s.* 111

The Chequers Estate was given to the nation in 1917 under a deed of settlement as the official country residence of the Prime Minister of the day. The deed was confirmed by the Chequers Estate Act 1917.[1] A public footpath ran across the estate within 500 yards of the mansion house. From the path

[1] Chequers Estate Act 1917, s. 1: see post, p. 375F.

there was a clear view of the house and terrace and anyone on the terrace would be within the range of a skilled marks- A
man on the footpath. In view of acts of terrorism in recent years and in the interests of the safety of the occupants of the house, the Public Trustee, as custodian trustee of the estate, applied for an order diverting the footpath away from the house. The local authority made the order under section 111 of the Highways Act 1959 [2] which enabled a diversion order to be made, subject to the approval of the Secretary of B
State, for the purpose of "securing the efficient use of the land or of other land held therewith." Following a public inquiry, the Secretary of State confirmed the order stating that it was made "for the purpose of securing the efficient use of land held with that crossed by the existing path, such land being occupied by the house, Chequers Court."

On an application by a local resident to quash the order on the grounds that the Public Trustee was disqualified by C
section 1 of the Chequers Estate Act 1917 from applying for a diversion order and that the object of the order, which was to protect the Prime Minister and his guests, was not within the powers conferred by section 111 of the Act of 1959:—

Held, dismissing the motion, (1) that notwithstanding the preservation of the interests of persons not parties to the deed of settlement by section 1 of the Chequers Estate Act 1917, the Public Trustee as custodian trustee of the estate was a proper D
person to apply for an order diverting the footpath (post, p. 376A–B).

(2) That the term "land" in section 111 (1) of the Highways Act 1959 included land and buildings, and the expression "securing the efficient use of the land" in that section had to be construed in the light of contemporary circumstances, the criterion being whether the "land" was used to the best advantage according to the purpose for which it was occupied (post, E
p. 378C–D, E–F).

(3) That the diversion of the footpath reduced the risk of assassination to a sensible degree and accordingly helped to ensure that the mansion house was put to the most advantageous use and the diversion was therefore within the powers conferred by section 111 (post, p. 379C–D).

No cases are referred to in the judgment. F

The following case was cited in argument:

Kennedy v. *Glasgow and South Western Railway Co.* (1905) 8 F. (Ct. of Sess.) 13; 43 S.L.R. 31.

MOTION G

On October 23, 1974, the respondent local authority Wycombe District Council made a footpath diversion order relating to a footpath which crossed the Chequers Estate. Following a local inquiry on May 6, 1975, the Secretary of State for the Environment confirmed the order on August 13, 1975. By motion dated October 1, 1975, Kenneth Bantock Roberton, a resident of Buckinghamshire applied for an order to quash the decision of the Secretary of State on the grounds that the Public Trustee H
was disqualified by section 1 of the Chequers Estate Act 1917 from making the diversion order application to Wycombe District Council; (2) that the purposes of the application which were to secure the safety of the Prime Minister and his guests and to undertake the efficient operation of security measures on the land were outside the provisions of the Highways

[2] Highways Act 1959, s. 111: see post, p. 376F–G.

A Act 1959; (3) that there was no evidence that the mansion house was held with the land; and (4) the order made and confirmed by the respondents gravely altered the meaning and purpose of the Act of 1959 and substantially reduced the protection of public rights of way.

The facts are stated in the judgment.

B The applicant, Kenneth Roberton, in person.

Harry Woolf for the Secretary of State.

The local authority did not appear and was not represented.

PHILLIPS J. This case concerns the Chequers Estate. Across the the front of the mansion house at a distance of between 400 and 500 yards there runs a public footpath. It has been used by the public for C very many years; for upwards of one hundred years or more. That user has continued since the mansion house became a residence available to the Prime Minister. As far as I can tell from the evidence, after that date the footpath continued to be so used with satisfaction both to members of the public who liked to use it partly in order to think that they were still going across the grounds of a mansion that was used by the Prime Minister, and also to successive Prime Ministers because it was D felt that such user could continue without undue interference with their occupation, and that it was a fine thing that members of the public used it as well as they.

But we live in changing times and we have to adapt to them. The particular thing that has happened in this connection is the sad increase in assassination, terrorism and violence, and this has led to a fear on the E part of the police, who are responsible for the safety of the occupants of Chequers, that the ready availability of the footpath at such a distance from the mansion house, from which the terrace and the persons on the terrace can be seen, will end unfortunately unless that user is restricted in future. This has led to the making of the Wycombe District Council (Footpath No. 28, Chequers Estate, Ellesborough) Public Path Diversion Order under section 111 of the Highways Act 1959. It was made on F October 23, 1974. There had been a public inquiry on May 6, 1975 (because the order had to be confirmed by the Secretary of State). The order was confirmed on August 13, 1975.

The grounds on which the order was made are described in paragraph 2 of the Secretary of State's letter confirming it:

> "The order was made for the purpose of securing the efficient use G of land held with that crossed by the existing path, such land being occupied by the house, Chequers Court. The present route of the path was thought to constitute a security risk to the occupants of the house, being within easy range of possible terrorist activities."

By this motion, Mr. Roberton, who appeared in person and argued with great skill and moderation, seeks to quash the order. He has H approached his task, and the decision whether to take these proceedings, very carefully and without undue haste. He told me that before starting he asked himself three questions. First of all, should a public right be reduced except by express statutory provision? To that he gave me the answer, "No." Secondly, is it wise to make permanent changes in long-established practices on account of what one may hope are merely transient dangers? In effect, he says that this path has been there for 150 years and has seen many troubles in the past, and will no doubt see many troubles in the future. It is not right or wise to abolish it merely because of the difficulties that we are, as he hopes, temporarily enduring. So he would say, "No, it is not wise." Thirdly, he asks himself, will the proposed diversion achieve its intended object? Again, he gives a negative answer. So in effect, although as anxious as anybody for the safety of the occupants of Chequers, whoever from time to time they may be, he feels that other considerations outweigh that, and that he is right to make this application. And so it is with a full sense of responsibility that he has done so. In paragraph 1 of his affidavit he says:

> "In moving this application . . . my sole desire is to draw attention to its possible serious effect on the protection of public rights. It is no part of my purpose to minimise the dangers which have been said to exist although I consider that these must be judged in the balance of public rights and private amenity and safety common in all such situations."

So he recognises the need for protection, but is full of apprehension as to the precedents that the order in this case may have set in other cases where the risk is even less great than he thinks it is in this case. For my part I fully accept the genuineness of his approach and the sincerity of his motives.

Before getting down to the substance of the grounds on which he makes the application it is right to mention one other matter. In order to make the application he has to be a party aggrieved, and it may be that some argument could have been advanced by Mr. Woolf to the effect that technically he is not a party aggrieved. Mr. Woolf for the Secretary of State does not take that point, and I only mention it because it is not desired that his failure to take it should be regarded as a concession in other cases.

The first thing which I ought to say is that the powers of the court in a case of this kind are strictly limited; I think that this is generally understood but perhaps not always as thoroughly as it might be. Some people think, not knowing very much about it, and perhaps it is rather a flattering thought, that the court is a law unto itself and can do what it likes; in other words, it can exercise a discretion which has been entrusted to it by the people. That is not the case, and the power of the court in this case is to be found in Schedule 2 to the Highways Act 1959, which is the Act under which this order purports to have been made. Paragraph 2 of Schedule 2 provides:

> "If a person aggrieved by a scheme or order to which this Schedule applies desires to question the validity thereof . . . on the ground that it is not within the powers of this Act or on the ground that any requirement of this Act . . . has not been complied with . . . he may . . . make an application for the purpose to the High Court."

Paragraph 3 (*b*) provides that:

> "the court—if satisfied that the . . . order . . . is not within the powers of this Act or that the interests of the applicant have been substantially prejudiced by failure to comply with any such requirement . . . may quash . . . the order."

So the powers are limited, and to be able to quash the order I have to be satisfied that it is not within the powers of the Highways Act 1959, or that the making of the order or the order itself fails to comply with

A the requirements laid down by the Act. To all intents and purposes, as the argument has developed here, it is a question of powers. That is the main point. On a fair construction, and on a reasonable view of the Act, was there power to make this order? I repeat that there is no appeal on what is called the merits. Indeed, Mr. Roberton, I think, recognises that fact and has tried to channel his argument into submissions which would fall within Schedule 2 to the Highways Act 1959.

B The first point which he takes is that the land and the mansion house are subject to the provisions of the Chequers Estate Act 1917, as amended. It is not necessary for the purposes of this case to go through it in detail, but the Act is entitled "An Act to confirm and give effect to a deed of settlement relating to the Chequers Estate and other property for purposes connected therewith." There is annexed to the Act a Schedule which is C the settlement by Sir Arthur Hamilton Lee of Chequers, who gave his house and land for the purpose of its being used for occupation by successive Prime Ministers, or, in the event that they declined to occupy it, by other named persons.

It was necessary for there to be an Act of Parliament for a number of reasons, one of which at least is that the settlement would have offended the rule against perpetuities because it is intended to endure forever. The D Schedule in its beginning sets out the objects of the gift, and I will return to that later.

Mr. Roberton's first point is that under section 111 of the Highways Act 1959 the application for a diversion must be made by the owner, lessee or occupier of land crossed by a footpath. In this case the application was made by the Public Trustee, and by virtue of the Chequers Estate Act 1917 E and the Chequers Estate Act 1958 the Public Trustee is what is described as the "custodian trustee of the Chequers Estate." There is no doubt that the land and all of it is vested in him; to put it in ordinary language, he is the owner of it. So all other things being equal, he would be a proper person to make the application, which indeed he did, but Mr. Roberton draws attention to section 1 of the Chequers Estate Act 1917 which provides:

F

> "The said deed of settlement is hereby confirmed, and shall have effect as if enacted in this Act, but nothing in this Act shall prejudice or affect the right, title, or interest, if any, of any person in or to the Chequers Estate other than the right, title, or interest of the parties to the said deed of the first, second, and third parts."

G Mr. Roberton says that the ownership as custodian trustee is of an unusual kind, being an encumbered ownership, the land being held in trust for the nation in that by virtue of section 1 of the Chequers Estate Act 1917 the Public Trustee is restrained from taking action disturbing the rights of the public in and to the estate.

I do not think there is anything in this point. Ordinarily where there is a conveyance of property or a settlement it can only affect immediately H the parties to it, although of course other persons may acquire rights under it, but it cannot affect other persons' rights except to the extent that the settlor or the transferor enjoyed those rights. Because it was necessary for the reason I have given, and I think other reasons, that the settlement should be given effect to by Act of Parliament, it was also necessary in the Act of Parliament to insert a section preserving the rights of third parties. That I think is the effect of section 1 of the Chequers Estate Act 1917. So whereas before the passing of the Act or the execution of the settlement members of the public had rights as members of the public over the rights of way and on the public footpaths over the estate, nothing in the settlement or the Act of 1917 interfered with those rights in the public. They continued unabated, so far as this footpath is concerned, until the making of the order in 1974. There is nothing in section 1 of the Chequers Estate Act 1917, as I read it, to prevent the Public Trustee as owner, if he thought fit and he did here, albeit reluctantly, from making an application to divert a footpath. If it were not so it would be impossible to manage the estate at all, because it is a fairly extensive estate, and if on some other part of it it were necessary in the interests, say, of husbandry, to have a footpath diverted there would be no power in him to make an application to that end. So I find nothing in this first point.

The second point is a combination of two points and is that interference of this kind in public rights ought only to be allowed where it is expressly authorised by a particular Act of Parliament. Allied to that point, it is said that there was an earlier unsuccessful application to divert this footpath on different grounds which properly failed, and that it must have been known by those responsible for that application at the time they made it that it was possible to apply under section 111 of the Highways Act 1959. The reason they did not do so, it is said, was because they thought at that time that it was inappropriate to the case. In my judgment these two arguments take the matter no further. Either there is power to do what has been done under section 111 of the Act of 1959, or there is not. If there is not, then the argument is superfluous; but if there is, then it is of no assistance. I do not think that the fact that some earlier application was made can help. The fact that there is no particular Act of Parliament dealing with this particular footpath is really nothing to the point if section 111 of the Act of 1959 confers the power which purports to have been used in this particular case.

The third point, which in my judgment has more substance in it, relates to section 111 (1) which provides:

> "Where an owner, lessee or occupier of land crossed by a footpath or bridleway (not being a trunk road or a special road) satisfies the local authority in whose area the land is situated that for securing the efficient use of the land or of other land held therewith or providing a shorter or more commodious path or way it is expedient that the line of the path or way across his land, or part of that line, should be diverted . . . the authority may by order . . . made by them and submitted to and confirmed by the [Secretary of State] . . ."

do various things, and do what they have done in this case, which, if one looks at the schedule to the order which has a plan attached to it, is to extinguish a footpath running near to the mansion house and to create a new right of way which runs further away, starting and ending at the points between which the old footpath is extinguished. So the footpath will run in a loop with the effect of taking pedestrians further away from the mansion house. Section 111 (5) of the Highways Act 1959 provides that the Secretary of State shall not confirm an order unless he is satisfied that it is expedient and that the path or way will not be substantially less convenient to the public; and there are various other matters mentioned over which I need not take time. So going back to section 111 (1) of the Act of 1959, one sees that first of all there must be land crossed by a footpath which there is in this case. Then the applicant, here the Public

A Trustee, must satisfy the local authority that it is expedient, and these are
the important words, "for securing the efficient use of the land or of
other land held therewith . . . that the line of the path . . . should be
diverted."

It is desirable to get out of the way certain preliminary points. The
application here was made and granted on the ground that, for securing
the efficient use of "other land" held with the land, it was expedient,
B and so on; the "other land" being the land which the mansion house
constituted. It is not wholly clear on a construction of section 111 what
is meant by "the land." I read the words again: "Where an owner . . .
of land crossed by a footpath . . . satisfies the local authority . . . that
for securing the efficient use of the land." I do not think that "the land"
can be restricted merely to the soil over which the footpath itself runs.
C It can obviously be open to argument in different cases what is the extent
of the land which has to be taken into consideration in determining
whether the proposal is necessary for securing the efficient use of it. For
example, suppose a house and a garden of one acre with a footpath
across it, and an application by the owner of the house and garden: is the
land the efficient use of which is being secured the whole of the house
and garden or only part of it? While it must be a matter of argument
D in every case, I see no reason why the words "the land" should not
extend to the holding in question or what in rating parlance would be
called the hereditament. There are well-understood rules there for deter-
mining what is a single hereditament. So it seems to me that it might well
have been arguable here that the mansion house itself was part of the
land, and that really it was not necessary to make use of the words "other
E land held therewith." I only say this in passing because the case has been
argued and decided on the footing that the mansion house was "other
land held therewith," and it is right, I think, for me to deal with it on
that footing too. I did not wish to leave the point unnoticed in case the
judgment in this case should come up for consideration in other cases.

In paragraph 5 of his affidavit Mr. Roberton deposed:

> "The interpretation of the words 'the efficient use of . . . other land
> F held therewith' to mean in this context the private enjoyment of a
> house raises fundamental questions about the nature of nuisances
> which can be said to reduce the efficiency of use and the extent of
> other land held therewith. It is admitted that a footpath across a
> domestic lawn might properly be the subject of a diversion appli-
> cation, but this need not be true of a footpath separated from the
> G lawn by a hedge or, as the present case may imply, of any footpath
> on the estate of a mansion however distant from the house."

He goes on to say that there is nothing in the Highways Act 1959 or
section 111 of the Act about security provisions, or fear of assassination
or terrorism or anything of that kind, and that no one at the date of the
passing of the Act, although I think he would say even today, could say
H that the prevention of terrorism has got anything to do with securing
the efficient use of the land.

There are, I think, two separate points involved here. One is that
Mr. Roberton is very much afraid that this application will be the thin
end of the wedge for all sorts of other applications in all sorts of different
circumstances and will spell disaster for those who have at heart the
preservation of public rights of way in the countryside. Of course I can
only deal with the case before me, but I would certainly deprecate this

case being used as any kind of charter in other dissimilar cases. Indeed A
it has to be noted, I think, that an order cannot be made under section 111 unless it secures the approval of the local authority which has to be satisfied not merely that the facts are made out but that it is expedient. It then has to be confirmed by the Secretary of State who will usually hold an open inquiry and test local opinion, and who is not empowered to confirm it unless the matters set out in section 111 (5) of the Act of 1959 for the protection of the public are satisfied. But that aspect of B
the matter has nothing to do with me. I am concerned with the second point which arises in this connection, and that is: is this order a legitimate exercise of the powers granted by section 111 of the Highways Act 1959, and, in particular, can the order be said to secure the efficient use of the land when the purpose has nothing whatever to do with husbandry or the use of the land as land, but is really designed to C
protect the safety from assassination of the occupants of a dwelling house? That is an important point which merits and has received serious arguments on both sides.

It is clear in the first place that the word "land" here includes land and buildings. There is therefore no doubt that the mansion house, whether considered as part of the land or whether considered as being held with the land, is itself land. It seems to me that in applying those D
words, by which I mean "securing the efficient use of the land," one has to take account of circumstances as they exist at the date of the application or of the inquiry if there is one. Thus, whereas it may well be that when the Act was passed as recently as 1959, so quickly have things changed, no-one would have thought of the dangers of terrorism or assassination, that does not mean that they must necessarily be E
excluded from consideration in deciding whether it has or has not been made out to the satisfaction of the local authority that the diversion is necessary to secure the efficient use of the land. What the words seem to mean is, that one has to look to see whether the diversion is necessary in order to enable the land to be used to its best advantage according to the purpose for which it is occupied. Land, of course, can be occupied for all sorts of purposes. In the case of houses it can be used for private F
occupation. In the case of land thought of as land it can be used for husbandry and agriculture, and so on. Buildings themselves can be used for different purposes, not only as private residences but as old people's homes, offices, shops and so on. It seems to me that what is necessary to secure the efficient use of land will differ in different cases at different times and in different ages according to the circumstances as they obtain G
from time to time.

This mansion house although of an unusual character is used as a dwelling house, and the only differences between it and any other dwelling house are its size and its splendour, its situation and the importance of the persons to whose use it is devoted. It is quite clear, I think, from the objects of the gift referred to in the Schedule to the Chequers Estate H
Act 1917 that the whole intention is that Prime Ministers from time to time, particularly if they are what is described as "city-bred man," should have a periodic contact with this most typical rural life which will enable them to preserve a just sense of proportion between the claims of town and country. It goes on:

"To the revolutionary statesman the antiquity and calm tenacity of Chequers and its annals might suggest some saving virtues in the

> A continuity of English history and exercise a check upon too hasty
> upheavals, whilst even the most reactionary could scarcely be in-
> sensible to the spirit of human freedom which permeates the country-
> side of Hampden Burke and Milton."

And it ends:

> "The main features of this scheme are therefore designed not
> B merely to make Chequers available as the official country residence
> of the Prime Minister of the day, but to tempt him to visit it
> regularly and to make it possible for him to live there, even though
> his income should be limited to his salary."

One of the attributes that one looks for in any dwelling house,
particularly one of this kind I suppose, is that there should be peace and
C quiet, and I would have thought that if there is any real risk of dis-
turbance by terrorists or any likelihood of assassination that would be
inclined to make the occupation of the dwelling house disadvantageous.
If the diversion of the footpath will reduce that risk to a sensible degree,
then in my judgment it will help to secure that the dwelling house is
put to the best possible and most advantageous use. I think that giving
D fair weight to the words of section 111 of the Highways Act 1959 it could
be said that what is being done is to secure the efficient use of the
dwelling house, which is within the word "land" in the section. So I
reach the conclusion that upon a fair reading of the words of the section
the object which was in mind in this application and in the making of
the order was one within the contemplation of the Act of 1959. I am
unable to find that what was done here was beyond the powers conferred
E by section 111 of the Highways Act 1959.

There are certain other matters raised in argument. It is said that there
was no evidence that the use by the public of the path in the past had
resulted in a diminution in the use of the estate by the Prime Minister.
That may be so, but of course if there is a real apprehended risk that
the continued use of the footpath by the public in the future may lead
F to assassination, then what has happened in the past, although not
irrelevant, is by no means conclusive. As the state of terrorism and
violence mounts no doubt there would come a time, or might come a
time, when those whose duty it is to advise Prime Ministers might advise
them that they could no longer safely stay at Chequers, or if they could
that they ought not to go upon those parts of the ground visible from
that footpath.

G Another matter is this. It is said that there is no evidence here,
beyond evidence of opinion, upon which it was possible to conclude
either that there was a danger, or, if there was a danger that the diversion
of the footpath was going to reduce it. That is a question of evidence.
I only have jurisdiction to interfere if something has gone wrong in
point of law, and I can only really look at the facts if it can be said
H that there is no evidence to justify the conclusions of fact come to by
the inspector. I agree that the conclusions here are based substantially
upon the opinions of the police authorities. I accept readily that those
opinions ought not to be accepted conclusively just because they say so,
but I do not think that is what the inspector did. Everybody's opinion
was given; the inspector listened to everybody's opinion and recorded it.
He reached this conclusion: "On the question of security the police
evidence is quite clear and positive and I conclude that their expert view

must be accepted." I do not read that as accepting it just because that A is what they said. It is quite clear, I think, that he looked into it and heard what everybody else said, and he was satisfied that their evidence was evidence which ought to be accepted. It is noteworthy here that part of the police evidence was to the particular effect that just to the west of the drive there is a clear view of the terrace from the old path at a range of not more than 475 yards. "Any skilled marksman using modern, easily portable firearms would have no difficulty in hitting a B person or group of persons on the terrace at that range." So there was evidence upon which the view that the inspector and the Secretary of State reached could be based, and it is not for me or within my jurisdiction to say that it is wrong. So this point, I think, is not really something that I can go into beyond the extent that I have. Lastly, it is said that there is no real evidence that the new footpath would be any safer C than the old footpath. Again, that is a matter of opinion. It is perfectly true that the police would have preferred quite a different solution, and this solution is a compromise. Nonetheless, it was their view that half a loaf is better than no bread, and that it would be safer but not the ideal solution which they would have preferred. Again that is a matter of fact, and it is not something that I can interfere with.

D So none of the grounds that have been carefully and persuasively argued by the applicant in my judgment justifies an interference by the court. Accordingly the application must be refused.

Application dismissed with costs.

Solicitor: *Treasury Solicitor.*

M. B. D. E

[CHANCERY DIVISION]

* MARX AND OTHERS *v.* ESTATES AND GENERAL INVESTMENTS LTD. F

[1975 M. No. 5017]

1975 Oct. 3, 22, 23, 27, 28; 29 Brightman J.

Company—Meeting—Vote—Proxy—Resolution to approve merger —Unstamped proxy forms distributed by dissentients—Poll— G *Unstamped forms accepted—Whether proxy votes valid*

Revenue—Stamp duty—Proxy vote—Form of proxy enabling proxy to vote at company meeting—Votes accepted at meeting —Subsequent objection that forms not stamped—Decision by Controller of Stamps that stamping not required—Whether duty chargeable—Effect of controller's decision—Stamp Act 1891 (54 & 55 *Vict., c.* 39), *s.* 12, *Sch.* 1 (*as amended by Finance Act* 1949 (12 & 13 *Geo.* 6, *c.* 47), *s.* 35, *Sch.* 8, H *para.* 18)

Costs—Taxation—Common fund basis—Shareholders objecting to company merger—Use of proxy votes to defeat motion— Subsequent objection by company to forms of proxy—Action by shareholders—Validity of proxy votes confirmed—Order for costs on common fund basis—R.S.C., Ord. 62, *r.* 28 (3)

[Reported by MRS. F. ALLEN McLEAN, Barrister-at-Law]

A merger agreement between C. Ltd. and the defendant
A company was entered into, whereby the defendant company should acquire the shares of the former in return for approximately 5,500,000 new ordinary stock units in the defendant company. The agreement was conditional on a resolution being passed by a general meeting of the defendant company approving the merger and increasing the authorised capital. A meeting was convened for June 12, 1975, for that purpose but, as a substantial number of shareholders objected to the
B merger, the meeting was adjourned. The dissentients distributed unstamped forms of proxy providing for the appointment of a proxy to vote "at the adjourned extraordinary general meeting of the company . . . or any further adjournment or adjournments thereof or at any new extraordinary general meeting of the company during 1975" dealing with the matter. The meeting was reconvened for July 16 and was adjourned to July 30. At that meeting the resolution approving
C the merger was defeated on a show of hands and a poll was demanded. The chairman accepted the votes tendered, appointed scrutineers and adjourned the meeting until the result of the poll could be declared. Article 66 of the company's articles provided that no objection should be raised as to the admissibility of any vote except at the meeting at which it was tendered and "every vote not disallowed at such meeting shall be valid for all purposes."

D On August 4, when the count was almost concluded, objections were raised as to the validity of the proxy forms on the ground that as they related to more than one meeting they should have been stamped 50p. in accordance with the Stamp Act 1891.[1] The validity of the votes cast by the proxies appointed on the unstamped forms determined whether the resolution had been passed. The opinion of the Controller of Stamps was obtained that the forms of proxy were not
E chargeable.

On a motion, treated as the trial of the action, by the dissentient shareholders to restrain the defendant company from treating the resolution as having been passed:—

Held, giving judgment for the plaintiffs, that since the proxy forms were capable of being used to vote not only at adjournments of the meeting of June 12 but at any new extraordinary general meeting in 1975, even though they might have
F been intended only for use at one meeting, they were liable to a 50p. stamp and the chairman would have been entitled to reject them at any time at or before the July 30 meeting, but he was entitled to accept the votes of a proxy because the unstamped proxy votes were not void and were valid authorities capable of being stamped; and, accordingly, since the company had accepted them without objection at the meeting the votes cast by the proxies were valid (post, pp. 386H—387A,
G 388A–B, C–D, 391D–E); and that in all the circumstances the dissentient shareholders were entitled to their costs on a common fund basis under R.S.C., Ord. 62, r. 28 (3) (post, pp. 392D–F, H—393A).

Held, further, that by virtue of article 66 the objection taken several days after the meeting at which the votes were tendered was made too late to invalidate them (post, pp. 389H—390A).

Per curiam. (1) Adjudication by the Controller of Stamps
H does not prejudice rights asserted and relied upon prior to adjudication (post, pp. 387H—388A).

Prudential Mutual Assurance Investment and Loan Association v. *Curzon* (1852) 8 Exch. 97 considered.

(2) There is much to commend an article in a company's articles of association to the effect that an objection to the admissibility of a vote should only be raised at the meeting at which it is tendered (post, p. 390A–E).

[1] Stamp Act 1891, Sch. 1, as amended; see post, p. 385B.

The following cases are referred to in the judgment of October 28: A

Colonial Gold Reef Ltd. v. *Free State Rand Ltd.* [1914] 1 Ch. 382.

Peel v. *London and North Western Railway Co.* [1907] 1 Ch. 5, C.A.

Prudential Mutual Assurance Investment and Loan Association v. *Curzon* (1852) 8 Exch. 97.

Reg. v. *Kelk* (1840) 12 Ad. & El. 559.

Rex v. *Fulham, Hammersmith and Kensington Rent Tribunal, Ex parte Zerek* [1951] 2 K.B. 1; [1951] 1 All E.R. 482, D.C. B

Wall v. *Exchange Investment Corporation Ltd.* [1926] Ch. 143, C.A.

Wall v. *London and Northern Assets Corporation* [1899] 1 Ch. 550.

The following additional cases were cited in argument:

Browne v. *Savage* (1859) 7 W.R. 571.

Doe d. Morgan v. *Amos* (1828) 2 Man. & Ry. 180. C

English, Scottish and Australian Chartered Bank, In re, [1893] 3 Ch. 385, C.A.

Harben v. *Phillips* (1883) 23 Ch.D. 14, Chitty J. and C.A.

Indo-China Steam Navigation Co., In re [1917] 2 Ch. 100.

Maynard v. *Consolidated Kent Collieries Corporation Ltd.* [1903] 2 K.B. 121, C.A. D

Narayana Chettiar v. *Kaleeswarar Mills Ltd.* [1952] A.I.R.Mad. 515.

Oughtred v. *Inland Revenue Comrs.* [1960] A.C. 206; [1959] 3 W.L.R. 898; [1959] 3 All E.R. 623, H.L.(E.).

Phillips v. *Morrison* (1844) 12 M. & W. 740.

Vallance v. *Forbes* (1879) 6 R. (Ct. of Sess.) 1099.

The following case is referred to in the judgment of October 29: E

Wallersteiner v. *Moir (No. 2)* [1975] Q.B. 373; [1975] 2 W.L.R. 389; [1975] 1 All E.R. 849, C.A.; (Note) [1975] Q.B. 508, C.A.

MOTION

The seven shareholders of County and Suburban Holdings Ltd. agreed to sell their shares to the defendant company, Estates and General Investments Ltd., F which had an issued capital of more than 9,700,000 ordinary stock units, for five and a half million new ordinary stock units. A substantial body of stock holders in the defendant company objected to the proposed resolution approving the agreement and sent out their own forms of proxy. At a meeting of the defendant company held on July 30, 1975, the resolution was defeated on a show of hands, and a poll was demanded by the chairman. G The poll count was almost complete on August 4 when objection was raised by one of the chief shareholders of County and Suburban Holdings Ltd. that the dissentient's proxy forms should have been stamped. A writ was issued by the dissentient stockholders seeking a declaration that the merger resolution had been defeated. The Controller of Stamps adjudicated that the proxy forms did not require to be stamped. H

The plaintiffs moved for an order that the defendant company be restrained from declaring or publishing that the resolution had been passed. The trial of the motion was treated as the trial of the action.

Further facts are stated in the judgment.

S. E. Brodie Q.C. and *Elizabeth Gloster* for the plaintiffs.

P. J. Millett Q.C. and *T. M. Stockdale* for the defendants.

BRIGHTMAN J. This motion seeks to restrain the defendant company from treating a resolution in favour of a merger as duly passed at a meeting of the ordinary stockholders. It has been agreed that the motion shall be treated as trial of the action.

The resolution in question was to approve a merger of the defendant company, Estates and General Investment Ltd., with another company called County and Suburban Holdings Ltd. The defendant company has an issued capital in excess of 9,700,000 ordinary stock units and a small amount of preference stock. It was formed under the name of Paquin Ltd. 80 years ago to acquire the business of the famous Paris couturiers Paquin et Cie. In 1969 it adopted the less romantic name of Estates and General Investments Ltd. and interested itself in property rather than the fashion world of the Rue de la Paix.

On May 14, 1975, an agreement was made between the seven shareholders of County and Suburban Holdings Ltd. and the defendant company whereby the County and Suburban shareholders, who included a Mr. Prowting, agreed to sell their shares to the defendant company in return for about $5\frac{1}{2}$ million new ordinary stock units in the defendant company. The merger agreement was conditional upon a resolution being passed by the defendant company in general meeting before a specified date approving the acquisition of the share capital of County and Suburban and increasing the authorised share capital of the defendant company. The specified date was later extended to October 31, 1975.

On May 16 the defendant company issued a circular to its ordinary stockholders, to which was attached a formal notice of a meeting convened for June 12, to consider two resolutions. Resolution 1 was the approval of the merger agreement and the creation of five million new ordinary shares. Resolution 2 was a special resolution adopting a new "objects" clause. At that time the chairman of the defendant company was Sir Leonard Dyer. The other two directors were Mrs. Davidson and Mr. Prowting.

The merger proposal did not commend itself to a substantial body of the stockholders of the defendant company. The meeting originally summoned for June 12, was adjourned sine die in order to give the dissentient stockholders an opportunity to present their case to the members of the defendant company. There followed a spirited cross fire of circulars. The meeting was ultimately re-convened for July 16. In the meantime Sir Leonard Dyer unexpectedly died and a Mr. Laurence, who is a professional accountant, became chairman on June 26, 1975.

On July 16, the meeting was again adjourned, on this occasion to July 30. The adjournment was to give the defendant company an opportunity to reply to the last salvo from the dissentient camp. The occasion was taken to improve, in some measure, the terms of the offer from the point of view of those interested in the defendant company. At the meeting held on July 30 the resolution for the merger and increase of capital was proposed first. It was defeated on a show of hands. A poll was demanded by the chairman, Mr. Laurence, and article 59 therefore came into play. This reads in part:

> "If a poll is required, it shall be taken in such manner (including the use of ballot or voting papers or tickets) as the chairman of the meeting may direct, and the result of the poll shall be deemed to be the resolution of the meeting at which the poll was demanded. The

> chairman of the meeting may (and if so directed by the meeting A
> shall) appoint scrutineers and may adjourn the meeting to some place
> and time fixed by him for the purpose of declaring the result of the
> poll."

The chairman appointed Messrs. Touche Ross & Co., accountants, to be
scrutineers, and adjourned the meeting to 12.30 on August 1, for the
purpose of declaring the result of the poll. However, on August 1, the B
chairman announced that the result of the poll could not be declared at
that time because of the closeness of the poll and a number of difficult
legal questions with which he felt himself faced.

The questions to which the chairman alluded had been raised by the
registrars, the National Westminster Bank Ltd., and by the scrutineers in
a letter dated July 31. They asked the company's solicitors for advice on
seven questions. The first question was the combined effect of three C
proxy forms all lodged by the same stockholder, one in time, two out of
time, referring to the identical holding. The second question was the
authority of a proxy to vote 1,000 stock units out of the 44,000 held,
having regard to the fact that the form of proxy related specifically only
to 43,000 stock units. The third problem was the effect of a telephone
message from a stockholder to the chairman on the morning of the meet- D
ing seeking to alter the authority of his proxy. Then there were two
questions which concerned the effect of an earlier proxy form as a result
of a later proxy form lodged out of time. The sixth question raised the
somewhat simple problem what was to happen if the first named proxy
did not vote but the second named proxy did. Then lastly there was the
case of a trust company which sent its representative along to vote and
unfortunately there was a minor error in the technical description of the E
meeting and the date thereof. The solicitors gave their own advice on
five of these questions and told the registrars that they were referring
the other two questions to counsel. Counsel's opinion commendably
arrived within 24 hours, on the afternoon of August 1.

Three days later the company's solicitors again consulted counsel, this
time on the question whether proxy forms distributed from the dissentient F
camp ought to have been stamped for the benefit of the revenue and as
to the effect of the absence of a stamp. It is clear from the evidence that
that advice was not sought at the request of the chairman, or the
registrars, or the scrutineers. What happened was not explained in the
evidence, but it emerged during the hearing, and plainly took the defen-
dant's counsel by surprise. The facts are these. County and Suburban
is controlled by Mr. Prowting. He and his family have a very large G
stake indeed in the company. As I have already mentioned, he is also
a director and shareholder of the defendant company. He was very
anxious indeed that the merger should go through. The stamp duty point
did not occur to Mr. Prowting at the meeting of July 30. It occurred to
him later. So he got his solicitors to raise the objection with the com-
pany's solicitors on August 4. The stamp duty objection was upheld by H
counsel. The chairman came into possession of counsel's advice on
August 5 and passed it on to the scrutineers accordingly. What the
chairman, Mr. Laurence, says in the first of his two affidavits is:

> " As regards the relevant forms " those are the proxy forms in respect
> of which the stamp duty point arises " I decided that I ought to
> reject the votes in question, and I have instructed the registrars
> accordingly. I decided also that I ought to inform the plaintiffs and

> A afford them an opportunity of challenging the rejection. I hope that this can conveniently be done in these proceedings."

I turn to the Stamp Act 1891 as amended by the Finance Act 1949, section 35, and Schedule 8, Part 1. The Stamp Act 1891 in Schedule 1 dealing with the details of duty payable on instruments, shows this, under the heading "*Letter or Power of Attorney*":

> B "Letter or Power of Attorney, and Commission, Factory, Mandate, or other instrument in the nature thereof: (1) For the sole purpose of appointing or authorising a proxy to vote at any one meeting at which votes may be given by proxy, whether the number of persons named in such instrument be one or more—[exempt]. . . . (6) Of any kind whatsoever not hereinbefore described—10s."

C The form of proxy sent out by the dissentient camp reads as follows (I abbreviate slightly):

> "Estates and General Investments Limited. Form of proxy. Extraordinary general meeting. I, being a member of the above named company, hereby appoint so-and-so as my proxy to vote for me on my behalf as indicated below at the adjourned extraordinary general D meeting of the company originally called for Thursday, June 12, 1975, or at any further adjournment or adjournments thereof or at any new extraordinary general meeting of the company during 1975 dealing with any of the matters referred to in the circular to shareholders dated May 16, 1975. Ordinary resolution No. 1. for/against. Special resolution No. 2. for/against."

E There is then a space for a date and the signature. There is a number of notes. I shall not read the notes. Although they refer to a "meeting" in the singular, they have no decisive effect on the construction of that form of proxy.

It is common ground that a form of proxy does not require a 50p stamp merely because it authorises the proxy to vote at one meeting, or any F adjournment thereof. An adjourned meeting is for this purpose regarded as the continuation of the previous meeting. It is however said by those supporting the merger—whose case has been well argued by Mr. Millett —that the form of proxy emanating from the dissentient camp authorises the proxy to vote both at any adjournment of the meeting of June 12 and also at any new extraordinary general meeting during 1975 dealing with any of the matters that the meeting of June 12 was convened to G consider. Therefore, it is said, it ought to have been stamped. As all such proxy forms were unstamped, the votes cast by such proxies should be rejected, so it is argued. This is now the only point in the case, because the validity or invalidity of votes cast by such proxies will be decisive as to whether ordinary resolution 1 was or was not passed, without troubling about interesting minor problems arising out of the lodging H of inconsistent proxy forms and other aberrations.

On August 4, 1975, the writ was issued in this action seeking a declaration that the merger resolution was lost. On August 12, after the issue of the writ, Mr. David Blank, one of the leaders of the dissentients, explained the form of proxy in his affidavit in this way:

> "I was personally responsible for preparing the proxy cards described by Mr. Laurence as the 'relevant forms.' They were prepared between June 20 and June 25, 1975, and at the time I did not know

> the date of the adjourned meeting. When the extraordinary general meeting was held on June 12, 1975, it was adjourned sine die. I had been requested to be informed of the new date but my request had been refused on two occasions. I also had to consider the possibility that the original extraordinary general meeting might have been abandoned by a formal resolution, and that a new extraordinary general meeting might have been requisitioned to approve the proposed merger. It was for this reason that I prepared the relevant forms in the shape of an alternative, i.e. giving the proxy the right to vote at one or other of the meetings. It was not intended that these proxy cards should or could be used at more than one meeting and in my respectful submission the phraseology of the relevant forms did not give the proxy any such authority. An appointment of a proxy to vote at any one meeting is exempt from stamp duty and in my respectful submission these words are applicable to a proxy for voting at any one of two or more meetings."

On August 18 Mr. Blank submitted to the Controller of Stamps for adjudication a completed form of proxy in the form drawn by him. This particular proxy form had not been lodged, which was why it remained in his possession and was available for submission by him. On September 9 the Controller of Stamps expressed the opinion that that form of proxy was not chargeable with any stamp duty. On September 29 the controller stated that all other proxies in identical terms would be similarly adjudged. On October 9 the company's solicitors wrote to the controller urging that such proxy forms were liable to stamp duty and should not be treated as finally adjudged not liable to duty.

Mr. Laurence is an independent chairman of the defendant company, who was brought onto the board in an emergency as a result of the sudden death of Sir Leonard Dyer, the previous chairman. There is I think no reason to attack his impartiality in the way that some of the evidence of the plaintiffs seems to do. On the other hand, I have little doubt that Mr. Prowting, who is vitally affected by the merger, is most anxious to see that it shall go through and is willing to resort to any lawful tactics in order to silence the voice of the dissentient majority. This is no reflection on the attitude or submissions of Mr. Millett.

The first question is whether the proxy form emanating from the dissentient camp, which I will call the disputed proxy form, is liable to stamp duty. This depends on whether it was for the purpose of appointing or authorising a proxy to vote only at a single meeting, including adjournments, or to vote at more than one meeting. There is no doubt that the disputed proxy form relates to more than one meeting. The disputed proxy form relates not only to adjournments of the meeting of June 12. It also relates to any new meeting in 1975, convened to deal with any of the matters referred to in the circular letter of May 16. The two matters referred to were the merger and the alteration to the objects clause. It was theoretically possible, for example, that the objects clause resolution would be moved but the merger resolution would not be moved at an adjournment of the June 12 meeting. The merger resolution might then have been brought before the shareholders at a wholly new extraordinary general meeting in 1975. In my judgment the disputed proxy form would inevitably cover both meetings. There are other equally unlikely possibilities. Although the stamp duty point is

A highly technical and unrealistic, I feel driven to the view that it is a valid point and that the disputed proxy form was liable to a 50p. stamp.

Counsel for the plaintiffs urged on me that no one ever envisaged that the two resolutions would be moved at two wholly different meetings or that the disputed proxy form would ever come to be used more than once. I think that is so. But the real question surely is whether the disputed proxy form was capable of being used at more than one meeting. B If in the events which happened only the non-controversial objects clause resolution had been proposed at the adjourned meeting of June 12, and for some reason or other it had been decided to send out a new notice convening a new extraordinary general meeting to consider the merger resolution, it is difficult to suppose that the disputed proxy form could have been construed so as to confer no right on the proxy to vote at that C new meeting. After all, the draftsman of the disputed proxy form expressly contemplated that a new extraordinary general meeting might be held to consider the merger resolution. There was nothing to prevent the uncontroversial objects clause resolution being got out of the way at an adjournment of the June 12 meeting. I have not overlooked the fact that the Stamp Act is a taxing statute and that the point at issue is whether a tax ought to have been paid. I agree that the court does not D go out of its way to find that an instrument is liable to stamp duty, but I think that I must judge the status of the disputed proxy form for stamp duty purposes by reference to the authority which it truly confers on the proxy and not by reference to the expectations of the parties as to the extent to which that authority would in practice be invoked. So I decide this primary question against the plaintiffs.

E The second question is the effect of the opinion of the Controller of Stamps that a proxy in the disputed form is not liable to duty. Was that an adjudication, and if so what is the effect of such adjudication? This depends on the wording of section 12 of the Act of 1891. Under subsection (1) the commissioners may be required by any person to express their opinion whether an executed instrument is chargeable with any duty. This they have done. The commissioners through the controller have F expressed the opinion that the disputed proxy forms are not chargeable to duty. Accordingly, under subsection (3), the proxy forms may be stamped with a particular stamp denoting that they are not chargeable with any duty. Under subsection (5) when so stamped they will "be admissible in evidence, and available for all purposes notwithstanding any objection relating to duty." I think it may well be that the Controller of G Stamps, if so requested, is now bound to impress on the disputed proxy forms denoting stamps that they are not liable to duty, but I do not think that this will resolve the case before me. To take a simple example, which I put to the plaintiffs' counsel in argument. Suppose a vendor of land requires the purchaser to accept a title deed which is not properly stamped. The purchaser declines. The vendor serves a notice to complete. H The purchaser does not complete. The vendor forfeits the deposit. Suppose that the purchaser was right in law in his assessment of the stamp duty liability. It would be absurd to suppose in that case that the purchaser loses his deposit merely because the vendor between rescission and trial succeeds in getting the instrument in question erroneously adjudicated as not liable to duty. Adjudication does not in my view prejudice rights that have been asserted and relied upon prior to adjudication. This conclusion seems to me to be consistent with *Prudential*

Mutual Assurance Investment and Loan Association v. *Curzon* (1852) 8 Exch. 97.

The third question is whether the chairman was entitled or bound to reject votes cast by proxies in reliance on proxy forms which ought to have been stamped and were not stamped, leaving aside for the moment any special provisions of the articles. In my judgment the chairman would have been entitled at or before the meeting of July 30, at which the votes were cast, to reject the authority of any proxy who purported or desired to act by virtue of a proxy form which ought to have been stamped but was not stamped. Section 14 (4) of the Stamp Act 1891 provides:

> " Save as aforesaid, an instrument executed in any part of the United Kingdom . . . shall not, except in criminal proceedings, be given in evidence, or be available for any purpose whatever, unless it is duly stamped in accordance with the law in force at the time when it was first executed."

" Available for any purpose whatever " must in my judgment mean that one person cannot compel another person to rely upon and accept an instrument which is not at the time of presentation properly stamped. On the other hand, the chairman was entitled to accept the votes of a proxy notwithstanding that the proxy form ought to have been but was not stamped. This follows from the fact that the proxy form, though unstamped, was not void. The words " available for any purpose whatever " cannot be given their strictest meaning where they appear in the Act. That I think is generally accepted by all courts. It is exemplified in *Rex* v. *Fulham, Hammersmith and Kensington Rent Tribunal, Ex parte Zerek* [1951] 2 K.B. 1: see the remarks of Lord Goddard C.J. at p. 7. As I have said, the proxy forms were not void. They were capable of being stamped. There was no attempt at evasion of stamp duty or of the provisions of the articles. In the highly improbable event of the company desiring to prove the authority of the proxy in legal proceedings, and the judge, arbitrator or referee taking objection to the absence of the stamp, the company would have been entitled as of right to stamp under such penalty, if any, as might be demanded.

I was referred to *Reg.* v. *Kelk* (1840) 12 Ad. & El. 559. There, votes at an election of a new drainage commissioner under a special Act of Parliament were rejected because the voting authority given to an agent of a group of proprietors was not properly stamped. Lord Denman C.J. said, at p. 565:

> " As, therefore, Mr. Burnaby " (the agent) " was by the instrument in question substituted for the proprietors signing, and appointed to act for them, we do not see how it is possible to deny that the writing by which he was so appointed is either a letter of attorney or an instrument of procuration: and, however unwilling to yield to an objection of the sort, we feel ourselves bound to hold that the authority was bad, and the vote bad."

That case was decided on the Stamp Act 1815, read with an earlier Stamp Act. But the case, I feel, is not adequately reported. It is not clear what actually occurred at the meeting of the proprietors. It does not really assist me in the present case. I certainly would not regard it as an authority that a proxy voting in reliance upon one of the disputed proxy forms was acting without authority and that his vote was inevitably bad.

It was suggested by the plaintiffs' counsel in argument that if the chairman was entitled to reject, and did reject, proxies which ought to have been stamped, or more accurately votes cast by proxies acting in reliance on such unstamped forms, the chairman ought to have given either the shareholder or the proxy an opportunity to have the disputed proxy forms stamped. That might well be a fair course to adopt in a particular case. But in my judgment the chairman, Mr. Laurence, did not act improperly or unlawfully by failing to give that opportunity. An opposite conclusion, apart from other possible objections, might lead to delays and uncertainties that would be quite unacceptable to the business world.

The next point is whether article 66 precludes the objection based in this case on the absence of a stamp. The present articles were adopted in May 1973. Article 66 reads as follows:

> "No objection shall be raised as to the admissibility of any vote except at the meeting or adjourned meeting at which the vote objected to is or may be given or tendered and every vote not disallowed at such meeting shall be valid for all purposes. Any such objection shall be referred to the chairman of the meeting whose decision shall be final and conclusive."

This article is substantially the same as article 66 of Table A in Schedule 1 to the Companies Act 1948 except that table A refers to "the qualification of any voter" instead of to "the admissibility of any vote." In table A "the qualification of any voter" clearly includes the qualification of the proxy where the vote is tendered by a proxy. "Voter" is not used in table A as synonymous with "member." In my judgment article 66 in the present case includes an objection to the qualification of a person purporting to be a proxy just as article 66 of table A likewise embraces any such objection.

In the case before me it is to the qualification of the proxy that objection is taken. It is said that the proxy was not duly qualified to vote on behalf of the member who had purported to appoint him because the disputed proxy forms ought to have been stamped but were not. That objection was not raised at the adjourned meeting at which the vote was tendered. The vote was tendered at the meeting of July 30, and the objection was not made until August 4 or possibly August 5, and was made by Mr. Prowting after the count had started. This is clear from the evidence of Mr. Laurence, the chairman, in his affidavit of October 3. He knew nothing about a possible stamp duty objection at the meeting, or when he wrote on August 4 to the registrars. He first knew of it when the company's solicitors informed him of counsel's opinion, received on the afternoon of August 5, as a result of Mr. Prowting's objection. The letter of August 4 from Mr. Laurence indicates that not only had the count started by that date but a first count had in fact been concluded, because the letter refers to the closeness of the voting on August 1, necessitating a "recount." The letter of August 4, in its final paragraph, suggests that the count had been concluded subject only to the advice which the registrars and scrutineers had sought on the two questions they had raised and which had been referred to counsel and answered by that date.

So it comes to this, that someone other than the chairman had objected four or five days after the meeting at which the dissentient votes were tendered, and after the count had started and had been virtually concluded, to the absence of any qualification on the part of voters A purporting to vote pursuant to the disputed proxy forms. It seems to me that such an objection must be too late on any fair reading of article 66. It is outside the scope of this judgment, and I certainly do not presume to attempt the task, to define the precise limits of article 66.

I would only add this. It seems to me that there is much sense in an article like article 66 notwithstanding the word of warning in *Buckley on the Companies Acts*, 13th ed. (1957). The editors say, at p. 846: B

> "An article in the above terms may be undesirable in view of the possibility that a chairman or other members present might at the time of the meeting be ignorant of circumstances which in fact would render a substantial vote invalid."

But if an objection can be taken to a vote, cast in pursuance of a proxy C form to which an objection is raised after the close of the meeting at which it is tendered, an injustice may be wrought. A company has plenty of time prior to the meeting, at least under these articles, to examine proxy forms. They have to be lodged 48 hours in advance. If a vote is received but objected to at a later stage what opportunity, I ask myself, does the voter have to answer the objection? Is the chairman under a duty to seek out the voter or the proxy and put the objection to him? D How does he do this? Does the company maintain a record of telephone numbers of members and their proxies? Of course not. Does the chairman have to rely on the postal system and await a reply by letter? Or does the chairman hear the objector, but not the voter against whom the objection is made? If an objection is raised to the form of proxy, there may be an explanation if only it can be heard. What is more sensible E than to provide that an objection must be voiced at the meeting where the vote is to be cast so that there is at least the opportunity for it to be answered?

I was referred to three cases on articles comparable with article 66. Two of them were brought by an enthusiastic objector by the name of Wall, who had two cases in these courts, separated by 27 years, in which he sought to object to votes. The first was *Wall* v. *London and Northern* F *Assets Corporation* [1899] 1 Ch. 550. The second was *Wall* v. *Exchange Investment Corporation Ltd.* [1926] Ch. 143. I think they are only of limited assistance to me in the present case. The articles there were differently worded in relation to the timing of an objection, and furthermore the decisions appear to have turned more on the fact that the chairman's ruling in favour of a vote objected to was prima facie con- G clusive. *Colonial Gold Reef Ltd.* v. *Free State Rand Ltd.* [1914] 1 Ch. 382 is perhaps more to the point. Articles of association provided that no person should be appointed a proxy who was not a member of the company, and by article 73 that no objection should be made to the validity of any vote except at the meeting or poll at which such vote should be tendered, and every vote not disallowed at such meeting or H poll, and whether given personally or by proxy, should be deemed valid for all purposes whatsoever. Proxies had been given to A, who was not a member of the company, and failing him to B, who was a member. A voted under these proxies and no objection was taken at the time. Sargant J. dealing with I think a total of three objections said, at p. 387:

> "With regard to the votes given by Lord Churston as proxy, under the articles of association of the defendant company no one is

> A entitled to act as proxy for other shareholders unless he is himself a shareholder, which Lord Churston was not. It is said, however, that the votes were rightly admitted since no objection on the ground that Lord Churston was not a member of the defendant company was taken at the time of the meeting at which the poll was held, and it appears in fact that the shareholders in question had by the proxies appointed as substitute in lieu of Lord Churston another
> B person who was a member of the defendant company and who could properly have voted as a proxy had objection been taken at the time to Lord Churston. Under these circumstances I think that article 73 of the defendant company's articles applies . . . I hold, therefore, that the objection founded on the admission of these votes cannot be sustained."

C However, I do not think that I need authority to guide me in the present case. This objection was not raised in time. It was raised after the meeting, after the count had started and was almost concluded. The chairman, whose only duty at that stage was to have the votes counted, ought not to have listened to the objection.

There is in my view another answer, quite apart from article 66. As
D was correctly urged in argument again and again, the disputed proxy forms were valid. They conferred a valid authority upon the proxy to vote. The proxy forms were received by the company without objection. They were not waste paper but valid authorities signed by persons entitled to vote in favour of persons entitled to act as proxies. It was not ultra vires for the company to accept such proxies unstamped, nor for the
E chairman to have failed to raise objection to them. The company did accept them, and distributed voting cards to all persons present at the meeting who purported to be proxies. Votes were cast by such proxies. In casting their votes these proxies were acting upon valid authorities which had been deposited with the company in due time. The proxies therefore were, in my opinion, casting valid votes. It does not lie in the mouth of the company to reject such instruments of authority five days
F later because taxes had not been paid to the revenue. If the company is really concerned at its ability to produce them in evidence before a judge, arbitrator or referee—of course it has not in fact the slightest anxiety on that score—it can cause them to be stamped. Such expenditure would not be ultra vires the company since the company's only bona fide concern is to ascertain the wishes of the majority of the corporators
G entitled to vote: see *Peel* v. *London and North Western Railway Co.* [1907] 1 Ch. 5. On this ground also I think that the plaintiffs are entitled to succeed.

I am conscious of the fact that I have not in this judgment covered every point which has been raised by Mr. Brodie for the plaintiffs, and in particular I have not mentioned cases which his industry brought to
H light during the course of his reply, but I think I have dealt with a sufficient part of the arguments presented to me.

Order accordingly.

October 29. BRIGHTMAN J. after hearing argument on behalf of the plaintiffs that, relying on *Wallersteiner* v. *Moir* (*No.* 2) [1975] Q.B. 373, they should receive taxation on the trustee basis, distinguished the present

case from *Wallerstein* v. *Moir* and said: Upon turning to the Rules of A
the Supreme Court, one sees that a trustee basis of taxation is only
appropriate if the matter can be brought within Ord. 62, r. 31 or r. 28 (5).
Under r. 31 (1):

> " This rule applies to every taxation of the costs which a person who
> is or has been a party to any proceedings in the capacity of trustee
> or personal representative. . . ." B

Now it cannot be said that the plaintiffs in the present case sustained the
role of trustees or personal representatives. Ord. 62, r. 28 (5) says:

> " The court in awarding costs to which this rule applies to any person
> may if it thinks fit and if—(*a*) the costs are to be paid out of a fund;
> or (*b*) the person to whom the costs are to be paid is or was a party
> to the proceedings in the capacity of trustee or personal represen- C
> tative, order or direct that the costs shall be taxed as if that person
> were a trustee of the fund or as if the costs were to be paid out of a
> fund held by that person, . . ."

Again the plaintiffs are not trustees or personal representatives, nor do
I think that the assets of the defendant company are a fund within the
meaning of that rule. However, under Ord. 62, r. 28 (3), there is juris- D
diction in any action to direct that costs shall be taxed on the common
fund basis. That is not disputed by Mr. Millett. So I think that the
only question left for me to consider is whether this is a case where the
plaintiffs' costs should be directed to be taxed on that basis.

So far as I am aware the only usual instances in which costs are
directed to be taxed on the common fund basis are the construction or E
administration of a will or settlement, the probate of a will of doubtful
due execution, and committal proceedings. But Ord. 62, r. 28 (3) is not
in terms confined to those specific cases. I accept that a judge should be
careful before he departs from well trodden paths in case he lands him-
self in an unsuspected thicket. Nevertheless I believe I am bound to look
at the realities of this case and see whether it would on this occasion be
just to depart from the common order for taxation. F

Now as I have said, the real issue in this litigation was whether or
not Mr. Prowting and his associates should be permitted to sell their
shares in County and Suburban to the defendant company. Mr. Prowting
was most anxious that the sale should take place. In the end he lost
his cause. Admittedly Estates and General Investments Ltd. are the
nominal defendants to the action, but the persons vitally concerned G
are Mr. Prowting and his associates. He will not need to put his hand
in his pocket at all. Not even his company, County and Suburban will
have had to bear any costs of the action. All the costs of unsuccessfully
defending this action are going to be paid by Estates and General Invest-
ments Ltd. In other words, the cost of unsuccessfully seeking to support
the sale by Mr. Prowting will be paid by Estates and General Investments H
Ltd.

Now I think it is right to regard the plaintiffs as having done a great
service to the members of the company because they have prevented a
purchase taking place which, in accordance with my decision, was against
the will of the majority of those members voting upon it. In such
circumstances I think that it would be just for me to exercise my
discretion by awarding the plaintiffs their costs on the common fund

A basis, which I am entitled to do under R.S.C., Ord. 62, r. 28 (3), so as to alleviate the financial burden upon the plaintiffs. I shall direct taxation accordingly.

Order accordingly.

Solicitors: *Manches & Co. for David Blank & Co., Manchester; Berwin Leighton.*

B

[QUEEN'S BENCH DIVISION]

C

* W. DEVIS & SONS LTD. *v.* ATKINS

1975 Nov. 13, 14 — Phillips J.

Industrial Relations—Unfair dismissal—Reasonableness of dismissal—Employee's misconduct during employment discovered after dismissal—Whether defence to complaint of unfair dismissal—Trade Union and Labour Relations Act 1974 (c. 52), *Sch.* 1,
D *para.* 6 (8) [1]

As the manager of an abattoir, the employee purchased the bulk of the cattle through dealers. His employers ordered that the practice should stop, not for any loss suffered but because it might jeopardise the goodwill of the farmers. When it continued, the employee was dismissed, and the employers offered him compensation for loss of office. Subsequently, however, they withdrew the offer and claimed a right to dismiss the employee
E summarily, on the ground of the employee's gross misconduct during his term of employment, although the alleged misconduct was not discovered before his dismissal. At the hearing of the employee's complaint of unfair dismissal, the industrial tribunal ruled that in determining whether the dismissal was unfair within paragraph 6 (8) of Schedule 1 to the Trade Union and Labour Relations Act 1974,[1] it was not prepared to admit evidence of facts not within the knowledge of the employers
F at the time of the dismissal. The tribunal found that the employee was unfairly dismissed.

On appeal by the employers:—

Held, dismissing the appeal, that on a complaint of unfair dismissal under the Act of 1974, the tribunal was not concerned with the contractual relationship at common law between employer and employee but only with the bare fact of the dismissal; that, in determining for the purposes of paragraph
G 6 (8) of Schedule 1 to that Act whether the employer could satisfy the tribunal that he acted reasonably in dismissing his employee, the tribunal had to confine itself to such facts as were within the knowledge of the employer at the time he formulated his reason for dismissing the employee and, therefore, the information about the employee's conduct which came to the attention of the employers after he had been dismissed was not relevant to the question whether the dismissal was unfair
H (post, pp. 400A–B, 401C–D, 402C–D).

Earl v. *Slater & Wheeler (Airlyne) Ltd.* [1973] 1 W.L.R. 51, N.I.R.C. and *Merseyside and North Wales Electricity Board* v. *Taylor* [1975] I.C.R. 185 applied.

[Reported by BERNARD O. AGYEMAN, ESQ., Barrister-at-Law]

[1] Trade Union and Labour Relations Act 1974, Sch. 1, para. 6 (8): post, p. 397C–D.

Cyril Leonard & Co. v. *Simo Securities Trust Ltd.* [1972] A
1 W.L.R. 80, C.A. and *Boston Deep Sea Fishing and Ice Co.* v. *Ansell* (1888) 39 Ch.D. 339, C.A. distinguished.

Per curiam. It would not be true to say that in no circumstances can evidence of what happened subsequent to the dismissal ever be relevant and admissible for the purposes of paragraph 6 (8) of Schedule 1 to the Act of 1974. Evidence of subsequent events might be admissible in order to prove the accuracy or otherwise of evidence given in relation to a date B
before the dismissal (post, p. 401G).

The following cases are referred to in the judgment:

Boston Deep Sea Fishing and Ice Co. v. *Ansell* (1888) 39 Ch.D. 339, C.A.

Earl v. *Slater & Wheeler (Airlyne) Ltd.* [1973] 1 W.L.R. 51; [1972] I.C.R. 508; [1973] 1 All E.R. 145, N.I.R.C.

Leonard (Cyril) & Co. v. *Simo Securities Trust Ltd.* [1972] 1 W.L.R. 80; C
[1971] 3 All E.R. 1313, C.A.

Maris v. *Rotherham Corporation* [1974] I.C.R. 435; [1974] 2 All E.R. 776, N.I.R.C.

Merseyside and North Wales Electricity Board v. *Taylor* [1975] I.C.R. 185.

No additional cases were cited in argument.

APPEAL from an industrial tribunal sitting at Manchester. D

The employee, Rowland Augustus Atkins, was dismissed as manager of an abattoir on October 22, 1974. The employers, W. Devis & Sons Ltd., having offered to pay the employee six weeks' salary in lieu of notice and £6,000 compensation for loss of office, rescinded the offer on November 1, 1974, on the ground of the employee's misconduct during his term of employment which was discovered after his dismissal. The employee E
made a complaint to an industrial tribunal, which found that the dismissal was unfair.

The employers appealed against the tribunal's decision on the grounds that the tribunal erred in law in refusing to allow the solicitor for the employers to call evidence of gross misconduct by the employee on the ground that such gross misconduct was unknown to the employers on October 22, 1974, when they dismissed him for other reasons, namely, his F
incompetence and inefficiency in the discharge of his duties; that the tribunal should have allowed the evidence to be called and if the evidence had been called the tribunal could not reasonably have found that the dismissal was unfair; and that the tribunal erred in law in disregarding entirely the well-established principle at common law that an employer was entitled summarily to dismiss an employee for gross misconduct of G
which he was unaware at the date of his dismissal but of which within a reasonable time thereafter he became aware.

The facts are stated in the judgment.

Fenton Bresler for the employers.

The employee did not appear and was not represented.

H

PHILLIPS J. This is an appeal by W. Devis & Sons Ltd. from a decision of an industrial tribunal, sitting at Manchester on January 9, 1975, that the employee, Mr. Atkins, was unfairly dismissed. The tribunal said:

"In the absence of adequate information upon which to assess the compensation, both parties undertake to seek a settlement between themselves as to the proper amount, with liberty to apply to the tribunal in case of difficulty or dispute."

A It is convenient to summarise the facts by reading paragraphs 2 to 5 of the
tribunal's reasons:

> "2. It was not in dispute that the [employee], who was born on
> October 31, 1923, was employed by the [employers] from February
> 1962 until he was dismissed on October 22, 1974, when his basic salary
> was £4,224 per annum. 3. Before calling their evidence, the solicitor
> B for the [employers] informed the tribunal that although at the time
> of the dismissal the [employers] offered the [employee] six weeks'
> salary in lieu of notice and a further £6,000 as compensation for loss
> of office, this offer was rescinded early in November when facts came
> to the knowledge of the [employers] which indicated that the [em-
> ployee], prior to his dismissal, had been guilty of gross misconduct.
> Thereupon the [employers] changed the [employee's] termination of
> C employment to one of summary dismissal. 4. The chairman indicated
> that at this stage of the hearing the tribunal was not concerned with
> facts discovered by the [employers] after the dismissal, though they
> could become relevant if subsequently the tribunal found the dismissal
> to have been unfair. The [employers'] solicitor submitted that the
> [employers] were entitled to adduce evidence as to these facts as being
> D relevant to the fairness of the dismissal, and relied on the authority
> in *Boston Deep Sea Fishing and Ice Co.* v. *Ansell* (1888) 39 Ch.D.
> 339 which had been applied in *Cyril Leonard & Co.* v. *Simo Securities
> Trust Ltd.* [1972] 1 W.L.R. 80. He asked the tribunal to rule on his
> submission. 5. After consideration, the tribunal ruled that at the present
> stage it was not prepared to accept in evidence facts not within the
> knowledge of the [employers] at the time of the dismissal on October
> E 22, 1974. As the [employers] admitted the dismissal, the present
> questions which the tribunal had to decide upon were whether the
> [employers] could satisfy the tribunal as to the reason for the dismissal,
> and then further whether they had established that in the circumstances
> they had acted reasonably in treating the reason shown as a sufficient
> reason for dismissing the [employee] as required by Schedule 1,
> F paragraph 6 of the Act. The tribunal based its decision on the judg-
> ment in *Earl* v. *Slater & Wheeler* (*Airlyne*) *Ltd.* [1973] 1 W.L.R.
> 51. . . ."

It is important to note "the reason" as found by the tribunal, and that is
set out in paragraph 6:

> G "The [employee] was appointed manager at the Preston abattoir in
> 1971. Mr. Kneale, the [employers'] northern regional manager, the
> [employee's] immediate superior, became increasingly dissatisfied with
> the [employee's] disregard of directives sent to him by Mr. Kneale.
> The principal cause for this related to the buying of cattle. The bulk
> of the cattle obtained by the [employee] were purchased through
> dealers, a method disapproved of by Mr. Kneale and Mr. Hodginson,
> H the general manager, if used extensively as liable to jeopardise the
> goodwill of the farmers. The tribunal was satisfied that the [employee]
> was made well aware of this, but nevertheless continued to do so."

The tribunal went on to consider various minor matters, but it is plain that
what I have read from paragraph 6 represents its view as to what was the
substantial reason upon which the employers acted in dismissing the
employee.

The evidence which the employers desired to call, but were not allowed to call, was evidence of which they became aware at a later, though not very much later, date and was principally the evidence of two security officers. Inasmuch as that evidence has never been given and, further, the employee does not appear and is not represented, it is probably desirable that I say as little about it as possible, because at the moment, of course, the allegations which it supports are unproved. But the nature of it is to be seen in a letter, one of the documents in the case, from the employers to the employee, dated November 1, 1974, which reads:

> "Dear Mr. Atkins,
> I refer to my letter of October 23, 1974, confirming the termination of your contract of employment with W. Devis & Sons Ltd., and outlining the financial offer which we were prepared to make, in the circumstances as we then knew them. Since that date, information has come to us as you are aware, to the effect that during your term of employment you handled certain commercial transactions in a manner which we can only regard as gross misconduct. This being so, I have to advise you that we are no longer prepared to sustain the offer made and since you have not returned the signed copy of our letter of October 23 to us as requested signifying your acceptance, we will now regard you as having been summarily dismissed on October 22."

In effect, what was alleged was that the employee was in gross breach of his duty of confidence to the employers and had taken secret commissions. I stress that none of that has been proved, but it is necessary to describe it to that extent, as otherwise what the employers sought to put before the tribunal would not be intelligible. For present purposes I ought to assume that the evidence of the two security officers, which I have not seen, is at least of a character that could potentially lead to the establishment of gross misconduct on the part of the employee.

Against that background, the first submission by Mr. Bresler, on behalf of the employers, is that the tribunal was in error of law in rejecting this evidence. The matter was put thus in paragraph 1 of the grounds in the notice of appeal:

> ". . . The tribunal erred in law in refusing to allow the solicitor for the [employers] to call evidence of gross misconduct by the [employee] on the ground that such gross misconduct was unknown to the [employers] on October 22, 1974, when they dismissed him for other reasons, namely, his incompetence and inefficiency in the discharge of his duties."

That submission raises a matter of considerable importance, not merely in this case but generally in the administration of this part of what is now the Trade Union and Labour Relations Act 1974; previously it was the Industrial Relations Act Act 1971. Paragraph 4 of Schedule 1 to the Act of 1974, under the heading "Unfair dismissal, right of employee not to be unfairly dismissed" provides:

> "(1) In every employment to which this paragraph applies every employee shall have the right not to be unfairly dismissed by his employer, and the remedy of an employee so dismissed for breach of that right shall be by way of complaint to an industrial tribunal under Part III of this Schedule, and not otherwise. (2) This paragraph applies to every employment except in so far as its application is excluded by or under any provision of this Schedule."

A Paragraph 5 deals with the definition of "dismissal." Paragraph 6, which relates to "Fair and unfair dismissal," and corresponds to section 24 of the Industrial Relations Act 1971, provides:

> "(1) In determining for the purposes of this Schedule whether the dismissal of an employee was fair or unfair, it shall be for the employer to show—(*a*) what was the reason (or, if there was more than one, the
> B principal reason) for the dismissal, . . ."

I do not think it is necessary to read the rest of sub-paragraph (1), except to say that it is then necessary for the employer to show that "the reason" was one of a certain number of specified categories of reason, because otherwise, although the Act does not expressly say so, the dismissal is taken to be unfair. But assuming that he shows the reason for the dismissal, and
C shows that it falls within one of the specified categories set out in sub-paragraph (2), then the final test, and this is the vital provision for the purposes of this case, is to be found in sub-paragraph (8):

> "Subject to sub-paragraphs (4) to (7) above, the determination of the question whether the dismissal was fair or unfair, having regard to the reason shown by the employer, shall depend on whether the employer
> D can satisfy the tribunal that in the circumstances (having regard to equity and the substantial merits of the case) he acted reasonably in treating it as a sufficient reason for dismissing the employee."

So, that really involves four principal matters. First, was there a dismissal and, if so, when and what was its nature? Secondly, what was the reason for it? Thirdly, what were the circumstances? Fourthly, has the employer
E satisfied the tribunal that in those circumstances he acted reasonably in treating that reason as a sufficient reason for dismissing the employee?

Mr. Bresler, in his argument, relies strongly on the common law in relation to contracts of employment and cites *Cyril Leonard & Co.* v. *Simo Securities Trust Ltd.* [1972] 1 W.L.R. 80. It is not necessary to take time by reading the headnote. That case went to the Court of Appeal, and in the judgment of Sachs L.J. the matter is compendiously put, so far
F as relevant, at p. 87:

> ". . . there has been put before us on behalf of the plaintiffs a full and, as is to be expected from [counsel for the plaintiffs,] an attractively presented submission that we should not follow *Boston Deep Sea Fishing and Ice Co.* v. *Ansell* (1888) 39 Ch.D. 339 in relation to those parts of the judgments that are relevant to the present case. In that
> G case, which in principle applies equally to contracts of service and to contracts for services, it was held (see the judgments of Cotton L.J. at p. 352 and Bowen L.J. at p. 364) that where an employee has in fact been guilty of uncondoned misconduct so grave that it justifies instant dismissal, the employer can rely on that misconduct in defence of any action for wrongful dismissal even if at the date of the dismissal the action was not known to him."

H

What Mr. Bresler says in this case, in an argument which, if I may say so, has been presented as attractively as the argument was in that case, is that the principle in *Boston Deep Sea Fishing and Ice Co.* v. *Ansell* (1888) 39 Ch.D. 339 and *Cyril Leonard & Co.* v. *Simo Securities Trust Ltd.* [1972] 1 W.L.R. 80 applies equally to a complaint of unfair dismissal. He goes on to submit that it is ridiculous that somebody can be said to have been unfairly dismissed, if the circumstances are that at the time of his dismissal,

or before it, he had been guilty of gross misconduct which would have A
justified his dismissal, albeit his employer at that time did not know of it. He cites these words from the judgment of Sachs L.J., at p. 88, and submits that the words are of equal relevance in the context of unfair dismissal:

> "Anyway, that ruling seems to me to embody a thoroughly sensible principle. It would be absurd that an employee who has been guilty of grave but undiscovered misconduct should be in the position of B
> being able to put in a claim for damages for wrongful dismissal. Instances of the absurdities which could flow from a contrary conclusion naturally abound."

That seems to me on the merits to be a very persuasive argument. The difficulty lies partly in the language of paragraph 6 (8) of Schedule 1 to the Act of 1974, and partly in the decided cases. Mr. Bresler recognised C
this difficulty from the outset. In *Earl* v. *Slater & Wheeler* (*Airlyne*) *Ltd.* [1973] 1 W.L.R. 51, Sir John Donaldson, President, sitting with other appointed members in the National Industrial Relations Court, said, at p. 57:

> "With respect to the tribunal, we think that it erred in holding that an unfair procedure which led to no injustice is incapable of rendering unfair a dismissal which would otherwise be fair. The question in D
> every case is whether the employer acted reasonably or unreasonably in treating the reason as sufficient for dismissing the employee and it has to be answered with reference to the circumstances known to the employer at the moment of dismissal." He continued, by way of illustration: "If an employer thinks that his accountant may be taking the firm's money, but has no real grounds for so thinking and dismisses him E
> for this reason, he acts wholly unreasonably and commits the unfair industrial practice of unfair dismissal, notwithstanding that it is later proved that the accountant had in fact been guilty of embezzlement. Proof of the embezzlement affects the amount of the compensation, but not the issue of fair or unfair dismissal."

The court came to the conclusion that the complainant was not entitled to F
any compensation. The reasoning, but not the conclusion, there is now out of date since the later decision in *Maris* v. *Rotherham Corporation* [1974] I.C.R. 435. But he went on to say, and I do not think this part of the judgment is affected by *Maris*, at p. 58.

> "We do not think that there is any room in this field for the award of nominal compensation and in the light of the tribunal's finding that the employee suffered 'no conceivable injustice' they must, even if they G
> had found unfair dismissal, have assessed the compensation at 'nil.'
>
> "It follows that for reasons which differ slightly from those given by the tribunal, we consider that the employee's claim for compensation was rightly dismissed."

Mr. Bresler submits that the observations in that case, at p. 57, which of course posed a considerable difficulty in his path, are obiter dicta; and I H
think, on an analysis of the case, that that is right. But the matter does not end there, because that case has been followed, and not merely followed but applied by O'Connor J., sitting in this court, in *Merseyside and North Wales Electricity Board* v. *Taylor* [1975] I.C.R. 185. After considering section 24 of the Industrial Relations Act 1971, which is the precursor of paragraph 6 of Schedule 1 to the Act of 1974, and in respect of which there is now a change in relation to the burden of proof, he said, at p. 189:

A " But, subject to that, it is for the tribunal itself to look at the circum-
stances and to make up its mind objectively as to whether the employer
has acted reasonably or unreasonably in treating ' the reason ' which
they have proved as a sufficient reason for dismissing the employee.
It is quite plain from the wording of subsection (6) that ' the circum-
stances ' there referred to are those applying at or prior to the date
of dismissal. What happened subsequent to the date of dismissal
B cannot be relevant in considering whether the employer acted reason-
ably or unreasonably in treating the reason as sufficient for dismissing
the employee. That was stated by Sir John Donaldson in *Earl* v.
Slater & Wheeler (*Airlyne*) *Ltd.* [1973] 1 W.L.R. 51 and I have no
doubt that that is a correct construction of section 24 (6) of the Act of
1971. I pause to say that the question of burden of proof has been
C changed by the Trade Union and Labour Relations Act 1974."

So, O'Connor J. not merely followed *Earl* v. *Slater & Wheeler* (*Airlyne*)
Ltd. [1973] 1 W.L.R. 51 but found it to be correct.

It can be said, and has been said by Mr. Bresler, of that judgment that,
in fact, the circumstances with which it dealt were somewhat different from
those involved in the present case. But there is no doubt that the trend of
D those two decisions is very much contrary to his basic submission and is
very much in favour of the proposition that, whatever the nature of the case,
paragraph 6 (8) has to be applied by the tribunal confining itself to such
facts as were within the knowledge of the employer at the time he formulated
his reason for dismissing the employee, and, similarly, that the circum-
stances against which that has to be judged are the circumstances as they
then existed. It is right, I think, to note (and I am not sure that the cases
E are, perhaps, with respect, sufficiently distinguished) the fact that it is
possible to have at least two (maybe more, but certainly at least two)
quite different types of case. First of all, there may be the case where a
man is dismissed for a reason, say drunkenness, which, on the facts known
to the employer at the date of dismissal he was not in a position to establish;
and therefore he might well have been found to have been behaving un-
F reasonably in dismissing the employee for that reason, albeit later it turns
out that for facts not then known to him but relating to an earlier time
he was entirely justified in thinking that the employee had often been
drunk. That is an example of one type of case. Another type of case,
which is really this case, is that a man is dismissed for a particular reason,
for example, general disobedience and incompetence as here, but at a later
date it is discovered that before the dismissal he had been guilty of some
G quite different, serious and gross misconduct. It may be that the two
authorities do not deal with this second type of case specifically. For
example, what Sir John Donaldson was talking about in *Earl* v. *Slater &
Wheeler* (*Airlyne*) *Ltd.* [1973] 1 W.L.R. 51, 57 is really the first case, that
is to say, the employer who thinks that the accountant is putting his hand
into the till, but has no real reason for thinking it, and so dismisses him;
H and in so doing acts wholly unreasonably, although it is later proved that
he was absolutely right. It can, I think, be said that the present case is
rather a different case. But, in a way, I think it is a more difficult case in
which to sustain Mr. Bresler's argument, if, and this really is the foundation
of the judgments in those two cases, the language of paragraph 6 (8) ties
one down to facts known at the date of dismissal.

Naturally, in developing his submissions, Mr. Bresler has pressed me
strongly with the cases of *Boston Deep Sea Fishing and Ice Co.* v. *Ansell*

(1888) 39 Ch.D. 339 and *Cyril Leonard & Co.* v. *Simo Securities Trust Ltd.* A [1972] 1 W.L.R. 80. But, quite apart from the two cases under the Industrial Relations Act 1971, which I cited, it has to be borne in mind, I think, that there is a considerable difference between the position at common law and the position under the Industrial Relations Act 1971 and, now, under the Trade Union and Labour Relations Act 1974. The common law is concerned merely with the contractual relationship between the parties, whereas a complaint of unfair dismissal under the Act of 1974 is B concerned with the statutory right of an employee not to be unfairly dismissed. It is important to note, I think, that the expression " unfair dismissal " is in no sense a common sense expression capable of being understood by the man in the street, which at first sight one would think it is. In fact, under the Act, it is narrowly and, to some extent, arbitrarily defined. And so the concept of unfair dismissal is not really a common sense concept; C it is a form of words which could be translated as being equivalent to dismissal " contrary to the statute " and to which the label " unfair dismissal " has been given.

The tribunal plainly proceeded on the basis (and on the right basis, I think, if it were right in excluding this other evidence at this stage) that if it found a prima facie case of unfair dismissal, and if the question of compensation was not agreed, so that there was a later hearing to determine D the amount of compensation, this excluded evidence would be admissible at that stage. Prima facie I should have thought that was right. I say no more about it because the employee has not appeared and is not represented and may wish, if and when the matter goes back before the tribunal, to present arguments upon it. But as the matter now appears to me, and with the benefit of such argument as I have heard, I would have thought E that this is evidence which would be properly admissible when coming to determine the amount of compensation.

It may well be, therefore, as indeed was the case in *Earl* v. *Slater & Wheeler (Airlyne) Ltd.* [1973] 1 W.L.R. 51, that in the result the compensation will be found to be nil; and I will say something about that in a moment. Having regard to that possibility, at first sight it might seem that it does not matter very much to an employer whether the evidence is F called at the stage where he wished to call it or later on in the hearing when the amount of compensation comes to be determined. But, on reflection, that is not the case; it does matter a good deal, for this reason: if the evidence is excluded at the earlier stage, it is going to result, as it has in this case, in an interim decision to the effect that the employee has been unfairly dismissed. Responsible employers object very much to being told that they G have been " guilty " (that is the way in which they look at it) of unfair dismissal. If what was said was that they had dismissed somebody contrary to the statute, I do not suppose they would mind very much. There is no doubt that in the mind of the ordinary, responsible, decent employer there is the idea that some stigma attaches, if it is said of him that he has unfairly dismissed his employee. And so, as I say, it is a matter of consequence. One can see that difficulty may well arise in cases of this kind, because H if, as in this case, when a case goes back the allegations of gross misconduct are proved, most people would say it was an affront to common sense to say that somebody had been guilty of unfair dismissal in dismissing an employee who had been guilty (I am not speaking of this case) perhaps of a criminal offence, merely because the employer, at the time he dismissed the employee, was not aware of those facts, although he was aware of other facts which seemed to him to justify dismissal. I do not think anybody,

A whether employer, employee, employers' association, trade union or whatever, would think it reasonable in those circumstances to say that the employer had been guilty of unfair dismissal. And that really is an echo of the words that I have cited from the judgment of Sachs L.J. in *Cyril Leonard & Co.* v. *Simo Securities Trust Ltd.* [1972] 1 W.L.R. 80. But there is no doubt that that is the consequence of the cases. The question is whether they are authorities that I ought to follow.

B At the end of the day the matter, I think, turns, as it did before Sir John Donaldson and O'Connor J., on the words of paragraph 6 (8) of Schedule 1 to the Act of 1974, which are very tightly drawn. The word "reason" there plainly refers back to paragraph 6 (1), that is to say, ". . . it shall be for the employer to show . . . what was the reason . . . for the dismissal, . . ." Of course, the tribunal is not bound by what the employer says was the reason,
C because he may put forward a spurious reason. The tribunal has to determine what was the real reason. Of necessity that must be something which existed at the date of dismissal, and so what the tribunal has under consideration is whether the employer acted reasonably, in all the circumstances, in treating that reason as a sufficient reason for dismissing the employee. It is quite clear that the whole matter under consideration is the reasonableness of the behaviour of the employer at and leading up to the time of
D dismissal. In those circumstances it seems to me that there is an extremely powerful, almost an irresistible, argument in favour of holding, as indeed was held in those two cases, that the circumstances also are the circumstances as they existed at that time. So, I think that I ought to follow those two cases. And, although they do not in terms, perhaps, absolutely cover this case, it is quite plain that the reasoning upon which they are based does.
E I follow them for two reasons: first, because in this field it is particularly desirable that there should be a general consensus as to the meaning of particular provisions (because if there are different views expressed it is bound to cause doubt and inconvenience), and secondly, because it seems to me that the language of paragraph 6 (8) supports the conclusions which they reached. If I may put it negatively, on a fair construction of paragraph 6 (8) I have not been able to find a way round the difficulty; though I
F think it follows that, if I had been able to find a way round it, consistent with that language, and without introducing confusion into what ought as far as possible to be kept a simple operation, I should have been happy to do so. Accordingly, I find that this first submission which has been put before me fails.

I would only add one other matter about this part of the case. I think
G that even in following those two cases, as I do, there is one qualification which can usefully be made. I do not think that they lead to the conclusion that in no circumstances whatever can evidence of what happened subsequent to the dismissal ever be relevant and admissible when considering paragraph 6 (8). I would have thought that evidence of subsequent events might be admissible in order to prove the accuracy or otherwise of
H evidence given in relation to a date before the dismissal. This is best illustrated by way of example. Suppose an employee is dismissed on the ground of drunkenness, that being the reason within paragraph 6 (1) and therefore within sub-paragraph (8); and suppose the employer gives and calls evidence to show that on a number of occasions the employee was drunk in the course of his duties. If, before the tribunal, it should be in issue as to whether such evidence was accurate, then I would have thought that evidence of later drunkenness would be admissible in order to establish the accuracy

of the evidence of earlier drunkenness, but not as evidence of later drunken- A
ness in order to constitute a subsequent reason.

The second ground on which Mr. Bresler sought, in perhaps a rather
desperate effort, to get round this difficulty was to say that the dismissal
took place not on October 22 but on November 1 when, after the truth
had come to light, the letter was written saying that the earlier offer of
ex gratia compensation was being withdrawn. It is plain from that letter
that what was affirmed was the dismissal on October 22. The decision of B
the tribunal proceeds on that basis and I do not think that it is possible
to go behind it. Reliance is placed on the form of application for com-
pensation for unfair dismissal, paragraph 4 of which reads: "I do not
agree that there was any sufficient ground for my dismissal without com-
pensation." That, no doubt, is how it appeared to the employee and, no
doubt, if the offer of £6,000 originally made had stood, nothing would have C
been heard of this case. But it is quite plain, I think, and now well estab-
lished, that what is under consideration on a complaint of unfair dismissal
is the bare fact of dismissal. Under paragraph 6 (8), one is concerned with
whether the employer has satisfied the tribunal that he acted reasonably
in treating the reason as a sufficient reason for dismissal—not for dismissing
him peremptorily, or with such-and-such notice, or with or without com-
pensation. So I am afraid that that argument, too, does not really assist D
the employers. Accordingly, the result must be that this appeal is dismissed.

I would mention only one other matter and, in the absence of argument
for the employee, this can only be a preliminary view. It would seem to
me that in a case where a complaint of unfair dismissal has been found by
the tribunal to be made out, but the tribunal find that owing to the employee's
misconduct he is entitled to no compensation, the tribunal could properly E
record their decision in the form, "complaint of unfair dismissal rejected,"
which would prevent, to some extent, the absurdity of an employee being
able to say "I have been unfairly dismissed" in a case where before he
was dismissed he was guilty of gross misconduct and, indeed, possibly
(I am not saying it is this case) of criminal behaviour. But that is a matter
on which I think, without further argument, it would not be possible to
express a concluded view. F

For the reasons I have given the appeal must be dismissed.

Appeal dismissed.
No order as to costs.

Solicitors: *R. A. Roberts.* G

H

A [COURT OF APPEAL]

* CAMPBELL *v.* EDWARDS

[1974 C. No. 4750]

B 1975 Nov. 27 — Lord Denning M.R. and Geoffrey Lane L.J.

Landlord and Tenant—Surrender of lease—Agreement to surrender—Contractual term that lessee surrender at price fixed by agreed valuer—Honest valuation by agreed valuer—Lessor obtaining lower valuations seeking equitable relief after entering into possession—Whether valuation binding on both parties

C By a lease made in June 1973 the plaintiff landlord demised
a second floor flat for consideration to the defendant tenant
for seven years. No rent was payable but clause 3 (11) (b)
provided that if the tenant wished to assign the premises she
should first offer to surrender the lease to the landlord at a
price to be fixed by a chartered surveyor agreed between them.
On January 17, 1974, the tenant offered to surrender the
D residue of the term on March 25; the landlord accepted; and
the parties agreed that a well known firm of surveyors should
be jointly instructed to fix the price. On March 21 the sur-
veyors wrote a letter stating that they had received the
instructions to inspect the premises in order to assess the
proper price, had read the lease carefully, taken its terms into
account, and were of opinion that the proper price was £10,000.
The tenant went out of possession and the landlord entered
E on about June 12; but in the interval he obtained two other
valuations for the residue from two other reputable firms—
£3,500 and £1,250 respectively. On June 17 he issued a writ
claiming that the valuation was incorrect in that the true
surrender value was under £4,000, and asking for a declaration
that he was not bound by the valuation and an order that the
tenant should concur with him in obtaining a new valuation.

The tenant claimed that the valuation was correct and
F binding and counterclaimed for the £10,000; and she applied
to have the statement of claim struck out as disclosing no
cause of action, the landlord having taken possession and the
surrender being completed. The master granted the application
and dismissed the action; and May J. on appeal affirmed that
order.

On appeal by the landlord when he also sought leave to
amend the statement of claim by adding the surveyors as
G defendants:—

Held, dismissing the appeal, that the parties were con-
tractually bound by the honest valuation fixed by the agreed
valuer, which had been acted on by both parties, and there
was therefore no room for any equitable remedy based on
nothing more than the fact that other valuers had subsequently
produced lower valuations.

Per Lord Denning M.R. It is now settled that a valuer
H owes a duty to both vendor and purchaser to make a valuation
with reasonable care and skill so that if he makes it negligently
he may be liable in damages at the suit of a party injured
by his wrong valuation. But an arbitrator is in a different
position. He cannot be sued by either party. The only
remedy against the award of an arbitrator who is negligent
or mistaken in law is that provided by the established procedure
for setting it aside (post, p. 408B–C).

Per Geoffrey Lane L.J. It would be wrong to allow an
amendment to enable the landlord to join the valuer as defen-

dant and allege that he acted negligently, with the effect of giving the landlord discovery of the papers relating to the inspection of the premises to use against the tenant. It is undesirable that valuers undertaking this type of duty should be subject to that additional peril (post, pp. 408H—409A). A

Arenson v. *Arenson* [1975] 3 W.L.R. 815, H.L.(E.) considered.

Decision of May J. affirmed.

The following cases are referred to in the judgments: B

Arenson v. *Arenson* [1973] Ch. 346; [1973] 2 W.L.R. 553; [1973] 2 All E.R. 235, C.A.; [1975] 3 W.L.R. 815; [1975] 3 All E.R. 901, H.L.(E.).

Dean v. *Prince* [1954] Ch. 409; [1954] 2 W.L.R. 538; [1954] 1 All E.R. 749, C.A.

Sutcliffe v. *Thackrah* [1974] A.C. 747; [1974] 2 W.L.R. 295; [1974] 1 All E.R. 319, H.L.(E.). C

The following additional cases were cited in argument:

Collier v. *Mason* (1858) 25 Beav. 200.

Emery v. *Wase* (1801) 5 Ves.Jun. 846.

Jenkins v. *Betham* (1855) 15 C.B. 168.

Pappa v. *Rose* (1871) L.R. 7 C.P. 32; (1872) L.R. 7 C.P. 525. D

Wright (*Frank H.*) (*Constructions*) *Ltd.* v. *Frodoor Ltd.* [1967] 1 W.L.R. 506; [1967] 1 All E.R. 433.

INTERLOCUTORY APPEAL from May J.

The plaintiff, John Colin Campbell, issued a writ indorsed with his statement of claim against the defendant, Miss Irene Donalda Edwards, E former lessee of premises at 2A, Trebeck Street, London, W.1. By a lease dated June 27, 1973, the plaintiff had for consideration demised the premises to her for a period of seven years and two months commencing on June 27, 1973; and, by clause 3 (11) (b) of the lease, the defendant had covenanted not to assign the premises without the previous written consent of the plaintiff provided that she had first offered to surrender the lease to him at a price fixed by a chartered surveyor to be agreed on by the F plaintiff and the defendant and in default of such agreement, the chartered surveyor to be nominated by the President for the time being of the Royal Institution of Chartered Surveyors. It had been further agreed that the plaintiff could accept the surrender within 21 days of the offer of surrender and that if he failed to do so, the offer would be deemed to have been rejected. G

It was claimed that by a letter dated January 17, 1974, and addressed to the plaintiff, the defendant's solicitors offered to surrender the lease on March 25, pursuant to clause 3 (11) of the lease; and that by a letter dated January 24 the plaintiff's solicitors accepted the offer of surrender. It was further claimed that, in about March, Chestertons were appointed as surveyors charged with the duty of assessing the proper price that H should be paid for the surrender of the lease; that by a letter dated March 21, Chestertons had stated that the proper price for the plaintiff to pay for the surrender of the lease as at the specified date would be £10,000; that the valuation was incorrect in that the true surrender value at March 25 was under £4,000; and that in the circumstances Chestertons must be presumed to have assessed the price in an incorrect manner and that their valuation was therefore vitiated.

A The plaintiff claimed (a) a declaration that he was not bound by the valuation of Chestertons; and (b) an order that the defendant should concur with him in obtaining a new valuation of the surrender value of the premises as at March 25, 1974, in accordance with the provisions of clause 3 (11) of the lease.

By her defence the defendant claimed that, in consequence of the agreement that Chestertons should be the chartered surveyor for the pur-
B poses of clause 3 (11) of the lease and by virtue of the valuation made and the price fixed, she was at all times after March 21 until completion of the surrender bound to make and the plaintiff was bound to take a surrender of the residue of the term at the price of £10,000. She denied that the true surrender value was under £4,000 and that Chestertons' valuation was incorrect; and she claimed that the surrender was completed
C on or before June 12, 1974, by the plaintiff entering on the premises and taking possession thereof. She claimed that in the circumstances the plaintiff was not entitled to the relief asked for. By a counterclaim she claimed payment of the price of £10,000 together with interest thereon from June 12, 1974, at such rate as to the court might seem fit.

By a summons in July 1974 the defendant applied for an order under R.S.C., Ord. 18, r. 19 (1) (*a*) that the statement of claim be struck out
D on the ground that it disclosed no reasonable cause of action and that the plaintiff's claim be dismissed with costs; and she asked for judgment on her counterclaim. Master Warren on November 21, 1974, ordered that the statement of claim be struck out, that the action be dismissed and that judgment be entered for the defendant on her counterclaim.

On the plaintiff's appeal against that order May J. on March 26, 1975,
E dismissed the appeal. The plaintiff appealed on the grounds that the judge erred in law in that (a) he failed to hold that at common law and/or in equity, the court was entitled to refuse to uphold an award of a valuer if the figure fixed by the valuer was so extravagantly large that the only conclusion was that the valuer must have made a mistake even though the court could not point to the actual error and/or no express reasons were given for the valuation, and/or the agreement had been completed;
F (b) he held that equity could not intervene if an agreement had been executed before the time of issue of proceedings; (c) he held that at common law and/or in equity, a valuation would be enforced where no reasons had been given by the valuer and in absence of proof of fraud or dishonesty on the valuer's part; and (d) he failed to hold that the facts before the valuer were not reasonably capable of supporting the valuation and
G accordingly the valuation should not be enforced by the courts.

Andrew Bateson Q.C. and *Stephen Silber* for the plaintiff.
John Chadwick for the defendant.

LORD DENNING M.R. We are concerned here with a house in Trebeck
H Street in the very centre of Mayfair. It was built about 200 years ago as a private house. But it is now converted to other uses. On the ground floor there is a restaurant. On the first floor there are offices. On the second floor there is a residential flat. It has its own entrance from the street: and has three rooms, kitchen and bathroom.

On June 28, 1973, the landlords let this second floor flat to Miss Edwards for seven years and two months free of rent. The tenant was liable to do repairs and there was a prohibition against underletting.

The lease contained a special provision that if the tenant desired to assign the premises she had first to offer to surrender them to the landlord, and the price was to be fixed by a surveyor to be agreed upon by the parties. It is clause 3 (11) (b) which says, in the material part:

> ". . . if the tenant desires to assign the whole of the premises as aforesaid she shall first by notice in writing to the landlord offer to surrender this lease . . . at a price fixed by a chartered surveyor to be agreed by the landlord and the tenant or failing agreement to be nominated by the President for the time being of the Royal Institution of Chartered Surveyors and the landlord may within 21 days of the service of such notice upon him accept such offer the acceptance to be in writing."

Six months after the lease was made Miss Edwards desired to assign the lease. Under that clause she had to offer to surrender it to the landlord. By a letter dated January 17, 1974, her solicitors offered to surrender it "at a price to be fixed in the manner provided by the lease." By a letter of January 24, 1974, the landlord accepted the offer. Some names of surveyors were suggested but these were not agreed. Eventually, however, both sides did agree on a very eminent firm of surveyors, Chestertons, a firm who were recognised by both to be quite unimpeachable.

On March 6, 1974, the solicitors for each side signed jointly and sent a letter to Chestertons. It referred to the lease and said:

> "It has been agreed between the parties to instruct yourselves to assess the proper price for the surrender in accordance with the provisions of the lease . . ."

Chestertons duly inspected the premises. On March 21 they wrote this important letter, assessing the price at £10,000:

> "We confirm with thanks, receipt of your letter of March 6, 1974, giving your two firms' instructions to us to inspect the above premises in order to assess the proper price to be paid by the landlord to the tenant for the surrender of the residue of the term of the lease dated June 27, 1973. . . . We have read the lease carefully and have taken into account in assessing the price to be paid, those matters set out in clause 3 (11) (c). After carefully considering the matter, we are of the opinion that the proper price for the landlord to pay to the tenant for the surrender of the lease as at March 25, 1974, is the sum of £10,000 (ten thousand pounds)."

Following that assessment, the tenant went out of possession and the landlord went into possession of the flat. There was some dispute about fixtures and fittings but undoubtedly there was a surrender by operation of law. The landlord then turned round and disputed the assessment of the price. He got new valuations for the value of the surrender of the lease. He got them from two other surveyors. Mann Winkworth & Co. made a valuation dated April 18, 1974, putting the value as £3,500. Hinton & Co., on June 18, 1974, put it at £1,250. I must say that, even to a layman, that seems a remarkably low assessment, especially when you remember that there were over six years to run of this lease and that no rent was payable under it.

Having got those two new valuations the landlord challenged Chestertons' valuation of £10,000. On June 17, 1974, he issued a writ claiming that he was not bound by it. In the statement of claim he said:

A "The valuation was incorrect in that the true surrender value of the lease at the specified date was under £4,000. In the circumstances, Messrs. Chestertons must be presumed to have assessed the price in an incorrect manner and their valuation is therefore vitiated."

He claimed: "(a) a declaration that he is not bound by the valuation," and (b) "an order that the defendant" (Miss Edwards) "concurs with
B the plaintiff in obtaining a new valuation."

Miss Edwards, by her solicitors, put in a defence and counterclaim, relying on Chestertons' price, and counterclaiming £10,000. They sought judgment for the £10,000, and they applied to strike out that statement of claim of the landlord, as disclosing no cause of action. The summons came before Master Warren and before the judge. Both held that the claim by the landlord disclosed no reasonable cause of action. They
C struck it out and gave Miss Edwards judgment for £10,000. The landlord appeals to this court. The appeal was stood over pending the decision of the House of Lords in *Arenson* v. *Arenson* [1975] 3 W.L.R. 815. It was decided only two weeks ago.

The law on this subject has been transformed by two cases in the House of Lords: *Sutcliffe* v. *Thackrah* [1974] A.C. 747 about architects,
D and *Arenson* v. *Arenson* about valuers. Previously, for over 100 years, it was thought that when vendor and purchaser agreed that the price was to be fixed by a valuer, then the valuer was in the position of a quasi-arbitrator and could not be sued for negligence. It is now clear that he owes a duty to both parties to act with reasonable care and skill in making his valuation. If he makes a mistake owing to want of care and skill he may be liable in damages. If he negligently gives a figure which is too
E high, he may be sued by the purchaser. If it is too low he may be sued by the vendor. If he wants to avoid such a responsibility he must put in a special clause exempting him when he accepts the appointment. Unless he stipulates for exemption, he is liable for negligence.

In former times (when it was thought that the valuer was not liable for negligence) the courts used to look for some way of upsetting a valuation
F which was shown to be wholly erroneous. They used to say that it could be upset, not only for fraud or collusion, but also on the ground of mistake: see for instance what I said in *Dean* v. *Prince* [1954] Ch. 409, 427. But those cases have to be reconsidered now. I did reconsider them in the *Arenson* case in this court: [1973] Ch. 346, 363. I stand by what I there said. It is simply the law of contract. If two persons agree that the price of property should be fixed by a valuer on whom they agree,
G and he gives that valuation honestly and in good faith, they are bound by it. Even if he has made a mistake they are still bound by it. The reason is because they have agreed to be bound by it. If there were fraud or collusion, of course, it would be very different. Fraud or collusion unravels everything.

It may be that if a valuer gives a speaking valuation—if he gives his
H reasons or his calculations—and you can show on the face of them that they are wrong it might be upset. But this is not such a case. Chestertons simply gave the figure. Having given it honestly, it is binding on the parties. It is no good for either party to say that it is incorrect. But even if the valuation could be upset for mistake, there is no room for it in this case. The premises have been surrendered to the landlord. He has entered into occupation of them. Months have passed. There cannot be restitutio in integrum.

I may add that Mr. Chadwick put forward an additional argument. He said: " If this valuation is set aside, what is to take its place? " The answer is: Nothing. The only surveyors on whom the parties have agreed are Chestertons. The parties are unlikely to agree on any other surveyors. And Chestertons cannot reasonably be asked to make another valuation. So there would be nothing to take the place of this valuation.

In my opinion, therefore, the landlord is bound by this valuation of £10,000. I would just like to add this. The position of a valuer is very different from that of an arbitrator. If a valuer is negligent in making a valuation, he may be sued by the party—vendor or purchaser—who is injured by his wrong valuation. But an arbitrator is different. In my opinion he cannot be sued by either party to the dispute, even if he is negligent. The only remedy of the party is to set aside the award: and then only if it comes within the accepted grounds for setting it aside. If an arbitrator is guilty of misconduct, his award can be set aside. If he has gone wrong on a point of law, which appears on the face of it, it can be corrected by the court. But the arbitrator himself is not liable to be sued. I say this because I should be sorry if any doubt should be felt about it.

This case is just a postscript to *Arenson* v. *Arenson* [1975] 3 W.L.R. 815. The valuation is binding on the parties. The master and the judge were right and we dismiss the appeal.

GEOFFREY LANE L.J. I agree. The parties here had agreed upon a valuer. They had agreed as to the terms on which the valuer was to value the property and on which he was to be instructed. The valuation took place, it was acted on, and the tenant surrendered the lease. It is a common law situation in which there is no room for an equitable remedy. The most up-to-date and accurate statement of the law in the circumstances is in a passage of Lord Denning M.R.'s judgment in *Arenson* v. *Arenson* in this court [1973] Ch. 346, 363, which states:

> " At common law—as distinct from equity—the parties are undoubtedly bound by the figure fixed by the valuer. Just as the parties to a building contract are bound by the architect's certificate, so the parties are bound by the valuer's valuation. Even if he makes a mistake in his calculations, or makes the valuation on what one or other considers to be a wrong basis, still they are bound by their agreement to accept it."

In this case Mr. Bateson has argued that there is sufficient discrepancy between the valuers' report and the subsequent valuations obtained by his client to indicate that the valuers, Chestertons, must have acted on a wrong principle. He says, despite the fact that this is not a speaking report, that that wide discrepancy is sufficient to cast that doubt upon the valuation. I disagree. There is nothing to suggest that the valuer here did not take into consideration all the matters which he should have taken into consideration; and where the only basis of criticism is that another valuer has subsequently produced a valuation a third of the original one it does not afford, in my view, any ground for saying that Chestertons' valuation must have been or may have been wrong.

The other matter which perhaps I should mention is this. Mr. Bateson asked for leave to amend the statement of claim in order to join the valuer as a defendant as well as the tenant, alleging that the valuer had acted negligently in his work. This would have had the effect, desirable from

A Mr. Bateson's point of view, of permitting him to obtain discovery, no doubt, of the valuer's (Chestertons') papers relating to their inspection of the premises, and so on, and then to use that information by way of attack against the tenant so that the valuation could be set aside vis-à-vis the tenant.

It seems to me that it is undesirable that valuers undertaking this type of duty should be subject to this additional peril. It is not only technically B undesirable; it produces, as I see it, an anomalous situation, for this reason. If the discovery shows that there was no negligence on the part of the valuer, then the action against the valuer will, of course, fail. If on the other hand the discovery shows that there was negligence on the part of the valuer, then that means it would be possible, on Mr. Bateson's argument, to set aside the valuation vis-à-vis the tenant, in which case no C damage would have been suffered by the landlord, and likewise the valuers would not be liable in negligence.

When that sort of anomalous situation is produced, it cannot be right that this sort of amendment should be allowed. For the reasons I have already indicated and those adumbrated by Lord Denning M.R. I agree that there is no fault in the reasoning or conclusion of the judge and that this appeal accordingly should be dismissed.

D

Appeal dismissed with costs.
Stay of execution refused.

Solicitors: *Roney & Co.; Jaques & Co.*

M. M. H.

E

[COURT OF APPEAL]

* PRACTICE DIRECTION (CRIME: INDICTMENT)

1976 March 9 — Lord Widgery C.J., James L.J.,
F Kilner Brown, Griffiths and Watkins JJ.

Crime — Indictment — Joinder of charges — Permissibility of two indictments against defendant for same offence and founded on same facts—Joinder of counts founded on separate committals to indictment already signed against another defendant

The following practice direction was issued as revised by the court on G March 9:

There is no rule of law or practice which prohibits two indictments being in existence at the same time for the same offence against the same person on the same facts. But the court will not allow the prosecution to proceed on both such indictments. They cannot in law be tried together and the court will insist that the prosecution elect the one on H which the trial shall proceed. Where different persons have been separately committed for trial for offences which can lawfully be charged in the same indictment it is permissible to join in one indictment the counts founded upon the separate committals despite the fact that an indictment in respect of any one of those committals has already been signed.

[Reported by A. G. B. HELM, ESQ., Barrister-at-Law]

[CHANCERY DIVISION] A

* MUNBY *v.* FURLONG (INSPECTOR OF TAXES)

1975 Nov. 10, 11, 12; Dec. 19 — Fox J.

Revenue—Income tax—Machinery or plant—Plant—Expenditure by barrister on legal books and law reports—Whether books "plant" qualifying for capital allowance—Finance Act 1971 (*c.* 68), *ss.* 41 (1) (*a*), 47 B

The taxpayer, a barrister, started to practise in chambers in 1972. During the first year he spent over £200 on legal text books and law reports which he required in order to carry on his profession. None of the books were renewals and most C
of the text books were likely to be replaced by new editions within a period of six to nine years. When being assessed to income tax for the relevant periods, the inspector of taxes refused to allow the taxpayer deductions in respect of the expenditure incurred by him in purchasing the books. The taxpayer appealed against the assessments on the ground that the books were "plant" qualifying for capital allowances under Chapter I of Part III of the Finance Act 1971. D
The general commissioners dismissed his appeal holding that they felt unable to extend the meaning of the word "plant" to include books.

On the taxpayer's appeal:—

Held, dismissing the appeal, that, although the books were part of the apparatus used by the taxpayer in carrying on his profession and as such appeared to fall within the accepted definition of "plant," there was well-established authority that E
they were not within that definition and, accordingly, the revenue had correctly refused to make the deductions in respect of the expenditure on the books.

Daphne v. *Shaw* (1926) 11 T.C. 256 followed.

Dictum of Cross J. in *McVeigh* v. *Arthur Sanderson & Sons Ltd.* [1969] 1 W.L.R. 1143, 1154 applied.

The following cases are cited in the judgment: F

Daphne v. *Shaw* (1926) 11 T.C. 256.

Hinton v. *Maden & Ireland Ltd.* [1959] 1 W.L.R. 875; [1959] 3 All E.R. 356, H.L.(E.).

Inland Revenue Commissioners v. *Barclay, Curle & Co. Ltd.* [1969] 1 W.L.R. 675; [1969] 1 All E.R. 732; 45 T.C. 221, H.L.(Sc.).

Jarrold v. *John Good & Sons Ltd.* [1962] 1 W.L.R. 1101; [1962] 2 All E.R. 971; [1963] 1 W.L.R. 214; [1965] 1 All E.R. 141, C.A. G

Lyons (J.) & Co. Ltd. v. *Attorney-General* [1944] Ch. 281; [1944] 1 All E.R. 477.

McVeigh v. *Arthur Sanderson & Sons Ltd.* [1969] 1 W.L.R. 1143; [1969] 2 All E.R. 771; 45 T.C. 273.

Rose & Co. (Wallpaper & Paints) Ltd. v. *Campbell* [1968] 1 W.L.R. 346; [1968] 1 All E.R. 405; 44 T.C. 500.

Yarmouth v. *France* (1887) 19 Q.B.D. 647. H

The following additional cases were cited in argument:

Blake v. *Shaw* (1860) John. 732.

Cooke v. *Beach Station Caravans Ltd.* [1974] 1 W.L.R. 1398; [1974] 3 All E.R. 159.

[Reported by MRS. HARRIET DUTTON, Barrister-at-Law]

A *Dixon* v. *Fitch's Garage Ltd.* [1976] 1 W.L.R. 215; [1975] 3 All E.R. 455.
St. John's School (Mountford and Knibbs) v. *Ward* [1974] S.T.C. 69.

CASE STATED by the Commissioners for the General Purposes of the Income Tax.

The taxpayer, James Lawrence Munby, a practising barrister,
B purchased legal text books and law reports during 1972 and 1973 at a total cost of £213·94. He appealed against assessments under Schedule D Case II of £407 for 1972–73 and £762 for 1973–74 on the ground that the expenditure on the books qualified for capital allowances and should be deductible. The general commissioners held that they should follow the decision in *Daphne* v. *Shaw* (1926) 11 T.C. 256 when a solicitor's law library was held not to be "plant" qualifying for a capital allowance
C and dismissed the appeal. The taxpayer appealed.

The facts are stated in the judgment.

The taxpayer in person.
Brian Davenport for the Crown.

Cur. adv. vult.

D

December 19. FOX J. read the following judgment. The taxpayer is a barrister in practice at the Chancery Bar. He started practice on September 1, 1972. During the period from September 1, 1972, to August 31, 1973, the taxpayer purchased certain text books and law reports (none of them renewals) for the purpose of setting up practice. The majority of the books are likely to be replaced by new editions in the future. The frequency of
E the new editions varies with different books, but none of the books would normally be replaced by a new edition in less than four years and in many cases an average period of six to nine years would be normal.

The issue is whether the purchase by the taxpayer of these books was capital expenditure qualifying for a capital allowance under Chapter I of Part III of the Finance Act 1971. The taxpayer is entitled to this allowance
F if the expenditure was "capital expenditure on the provision of machinery or plant" for the purposes of the profession: see section 41 (1) (*a*) and section 47 of the Finance Act 1971. The revenue conceded that the expenditure was "capital expenditure." The sole question is whether the books and reports are "plant" (which is not defined in the statute).

The commissioners, following, with reluctance, the decision of Rowlatt J. in *Daphne* v. *Shaw* (1926) 11 T.C. 256, held that they are not plant.
G In *Daphne* v. *Shaw* it was held that a solicitor's law library was not "plant" for the purposes of rules 6 and 7 of Cases I and II of Schedule D, which gave allowances in respect of wear and tear of machinery or plant and expenses incurred on replacing obsolete machinery or plant. Rowlatt J. said:

> "I cannot bring myself to say that such books . . . are 'plant.' It
> H is impossible to define what is meant by 'plant and machinery.' It conjures up before the mind something clear in the outline, at any rate; it means apparatus, alive or dead, stationary or movable, to achieve the operations which a person wants to achieve in his vocation. But the books which he consults, on his shelves, and which he does not use as 'implements,' really, in the direct sense of the word, at all, I cannot believe are included in it. . . . The extension of the allowance to professions, employments, vocations or offices, that is to say, to all

the Schedules and all parts of them, I do not think involves an extension of the ordinary, common sense meaning of the word 'plant,' because . . . undoubtedly there are many professions and vocations where machinery and plant is used, but still machinery and plant of the sort that was understood before." A

Daphne v. *Shaw* is therefore a direct decision on the point before me. The taxpayer contended, however, that it is wrong in law and, in particular, is inconsistent with later decisions of higher courts and should not be followed. The basis of the taxpayer's case is that the correct meaning of "plant" is that stated by Lindley L.J. in *Yarmouth* v. *France* (1887) 19 Q.B.D. 647, and that this meaning is now firmly established by decisions of the House of Lords. B

Yarmouth v. *France* was an action to recover compensation under the Employers' Liability Act 1880. The plaintiff was in the employment of the defendant, who was a wharfinger. The plaintiff drove carts for the defendant, and loaded and unloaded the goods that were carried in them. The plaintiff was injured by one of the cart-horses, and the question was whether the horse was "plant" within section 1 (1) of the Act. Lindley L.J. said, at p. 658: C

"There is no definition of plant in the Act: but, in its ordinary sense, it includes whatever apparatus is used by a business man for carrying on his business,—not his stock-in-trade which he buys or makes for sale; but all goods and chattels, fixed or movable, live or dead, which he keeps for permanent employment in his business." D

The taxpayer said that the books in the present case (by which I mean both the text books and the reports) fall squarely within the definition. E

I turn now to the later authorities. In *J. Lyons & Co. Ltd.* v. *Attorney-General* [1944] Ch. 281, a Lyons teashop was damaged by enemy action in 1941. Lyons claimed a cost-of-works payment under the War Damage Act 1943, which included the cost of replacing electric lamps used for lighting the premises, and fittings annexed to the lamps, as being "plant or machinery" on the hereditament within section 103 (5) of the Act. Uthwatt J., at p. 286, said that he did not think that the use of the word "plant" as part of the phrase "plant or machinery" had the effect of confining the word to such plant as is used for mechanical operations or processes. Also, after saying that he did not think it necessary to attempt a general definition of the word "plant," he continued, at p. 286: F

"No definition of 'plant' would include the lamps and fitments here under consideration, if they were found in a private house supplied with electricity by public suppliers. If these articles are plant, it can only be by reason that they are found on premises exclusively devoted to trade purposes. Trade plant alone need be considered. Confining my attention to trade plant, I am content to accept the general description in *Yarmouth* v. *France* that 'plant' includes whatever apparatus or instruments are used by a business man in carrying on his business. The term does not include stock-in-trade, nor does it include the place in which the business is carried on. Whether any particular article more properly falls within 'plant' as thus understood or in some other category depends on all the circumstances of the case." G H

The next case is a decision of the House of Lords, *Hinton* v. *Maden & Ireland Ltd.* [1959] 1 W.L.R. 875. In that case the taxpayer carried

A on the business of shoe and slipper manufacturers. It used machines which could only function when furnished with knives or lasts. The question was whether expenditure on new knives and lasts was expenditure on " plant or machinery " for the purposes of section 16 (3) of the Finance Act 1954 (dealing with investment allowances). It was held that it was. Lord Reid said, at p. 889:

> B " It is not disputed that plant is also used in the Act as an ordinary English word. It is not altogether an easy word to construe: it may have a more or less extensive meaning according to its context. As a general statement of its meaning I would adopt the words of Lindley L.J. in *Yarmouth* v. *France*."

Lord Reid then cited the passage which I have set out above. He also
C referred, as I read it, with approval, to the passage which I have set out above from the judgment of Uthwatt J. in *J. Lyons & Co. Ltd.* v. *Attorney-General*. Lord Tucker agreed with Lord Reid as to the meaning of " plant." Lord Keith of Avonholm and Lord Denning did not deal in any detail with the meaning of the word. Lord Jenkins said, at p. 898:

> " I have no doubt that the knives and lasts were ' plant.' On this point I am for the present purpose, content to accept as a sufficient
> D statement of the ordinary meaning of the expression ' plant ' the words of Lindley L.J. in *Yarmouth* v. *France*."

Jarrold v. *John Good & Sons Ltd.* [1963] 1 W.L.R. 214 was a decision of the Court of Appeal. A company's office accommodation consisted of a large open floor space in which partitions could be erected so as to subdivide the floor space into any number of rooms of any size. The partitions
E were screwed to the floor and ceiling only, and could easily be moved if it was desired to alter the size or number of the rooms. The question was whether the partitions were " plant " within the meaning of section 279 of the Income Tax Act 1952, which gave certain allowances in respect of expenditure on " machinery or plant." It was held that the partitions were plant. The case is of significance in a number of respects. First, the
F Crown contended that as the partitions played a purely passive role they were not plant. Donovan L.J. rejected this. He said, at p. 223:

> " I do not understand this division of assets vis-à-vis the accomplishment of the trading purpose, into ' passive ' and ' active,' followed by the argument that there can be no ' plant ' among the passive assets. The heating installation of a building may be passive in the sense that it involves no moving machinery, but few would deny it the name of
> G ' plant '."

Ormerod L.J. said, at p. 221:

> " But it may well be going much too far to say that it [plant] cannot refer to such part of the building, or to such part of the equipment of the building, as performs anything other than a merely passive
> H role."

Secondly, the case contains a consideration by Donovan L.J., at pp. 223 and 224, of what is not plant (at any rate for the tax purposes with which I am concerned in this case). Thus, there are excluded (a) buildings; (b) machinery (since in the statute with which the court was concerned there, and here, the word is used in contra-distinction to machinery); (c) utensils (the cost of which is allowable by other provisions of the Income Tax Acts); and (d) stock-in-trade. Donovan L.J. added, at p. 224:

> "When all these things have been excluded from the scope of the word 'plant,' there will still be some chattels left, the character of which may be debatable. In the present case we have these partitions. The definition given of 'plant' by Lindley L.J. in *Yarmouth* v. *France* clearly embraces them . . . These partitions *are* required by the nature of the company's trade, as the lamps in *J. Lyons & Co. Ltd.* v. *Attorney-General* were not. I can therefore discover no good reason for excluding these partitions from Lindley L.J.'s definition of 'plant'."

Thirdly, Donovan L.J., at p. 224, expressed some surprise at coming to the conclusion that such things as the partitions could be plant, but he added "no more than, I expect, some people were surprised by finding that a horse is also 'plant'." It may be, therefore, that one must be cautious of any approach to this problem based on what a layman would normally understand by "plant." Fourthly, the case contains, at p. 225, Pearson L.J.'s aphorism, "the short question in this case in whether the partitioning is part of the premises in which the business is carried on or part of the plant with which the business is carried on."

In *Rose & Co.* (*Wallpaper & Paints*) *Ltd.* v. *Campbell* [1968] 1 W.L.R. 346, the company was a retailer of wallpapers. It purchased samples of wallpaper from a manufacturer and had them printed and bound as pattern books which were either distributed free of charge to decorating contractors (while remaining the property of the company) or kept for use at the company's branches. The books had a minimum useful life of about two years. The company claimed to be entitled to investment allowances under section 16 (3) of the Finance Act 1954, in respect of expenditure on the pattern books on the ground that the expenditure was capital expenditure on "plant." The commissioners held that the expenditure was not capital expenditure and the books were not plant. Pennycuick J. on appeal concluded that the expenditure was not capital expenditure. The question whether the books were "plant" did not therefore arise, but he expressed the view, at p. 352, that the commissioners' decision that the books were not plant was reasonable. As I read it, however, the judgment on this point proceeds primarily on the question of whether the books possessed sufficient durability to fall within the word "permanent" in the *Yarmouth* v. *France* definition. No similar question arises in the present case. It is not suggested that the books in the present case lack whatever degree of permanence may be necessary to constitute plant.

The taxpayer referred me to the statement by Pennycuick J., at p. 351, that if expenditure on a chattel is capital expenditure the chattel is "well on its way to being plant." That may well be so. But Pennycuick J. was there indicating only a broad approach to the matter. In the borderline cases and the grey areas such a test would in most cases be insufficiently precise to determine the matter, more particularly in cases such as the present, where the expenditure must be capital expenditure before it can qualify at all for the allowance.

The next case, *Inland Revenue Commissioners* v. *Barclay, Curle & Co. Ltd.* [1969] 1 W.L.R. 675, is a decision of the House of Lords. It again raised the question whether expenditure qualified for an allowance under section 279 (1) of the Income Tax Act 1952 as being expenditure for the provision of machinery or plant. The case concerned a dry dock which the company built for use in its trade as shipbuilders and repairers. The expenditure in issue was the cost of excavating a new basin and

A lining the excavation with concrete. The House of Lords, by a majority of three to two, decided that the dock was "plant." Although Lord Hodson and Lord Upjohn dissented, I do not think there was much difference in the basic approach. Lord Hodson said, at p. 681:

> "The word 'plant' though difficult of precise definition is an ordinary English word which has received judicial consideration on
> B a number of occasions. What was said by Lindley L.J. in construing the word as it appears in the Employers' Liability Act 1880 has been long accepted as good guidance."

Lord Hodson also referred to the *Yarmouth* v. *France* definition as having been adopted as "a general test" in *Hinton* v. *Maden & Ireland Ltd.* Lord Guest, at p. 685, described the *Yarmouth* v. *France* test as the
C "locus classicus." Lord Upjohn, at p. 688, also referred to *Yarmouth* v. *France* as the locus classicus, but said that Lindley L.J. was dealing with plant of such a different nature—a horse—that his words could not safely be bent to the circumstances of the *Barclay, Curle* case. Lord Upjohn, at p. 689, again emphasised that "plant" is an ordinary English word. Lord Donovan, after saying that there was no statutory definition of "plant" and that the courts had been left to formulate the test, said,
D at p. 691:

> "Lindley L.J. did it in *Yarmouth* v. *France* . . . in language which despite the great technological advances since his day is still of great help. Uthwatt J. . . . said in *J. Lyons & Co. Ltd.* v. *Attorney-General* . . . that plant did not include the place where the business was carried on: and my noble and learned friend, Lord Pearson,
> E when sitting in the Court of Appeal in *Jarrold* v. *John Good & Sons Ltd.* . . . spoke of plant being that with which the trade is carried on, as opposed to the place where it was carried on. All these definitions are helpful, but in the nature of things they cannot be exact, and so provide an answer incapable of reasonable dispute in every case."

Later Lord Donovan said:

> F "At the end of the day I find the functional test propounded by Lindley L.J. and by Lord Pearson to be as good as any, though, as was said in *Jarrold* v. *John Good & Sons Ltd.*, some plant may perform its function passively and not actively."

From these authorities I think that the following propositions emerge. (i) "Plant" is an ordinary English word which is not very easy to construe.
G Lindley L.J.'s definition in *Yarmouth* v. *France*, 19 Q.B.D. 647, is a good general definition. (ii) Lindley L.J.'s definition is not to be treated as exact. (iii) For present purposes, buildings, utensils, machinery and stock-in-trade are not plant (though they, or some of them, might come within Lindley L.J.'s definition). But it is not correct to say that, after excluding these items, anything left within Lindley L.J.'s definition is plant. As
H Donovan L.J. said in *Jarrold* v. *John Good & Sons Ltd.* [1969] 1 W.L.R. 214, 224, when all these things have been excluded from the scope of the word "plant" there will still be some chattels left the character of which may be debatable. (iv) Plant is not limited to (a) chattels involving mechanical operations or processes or, probably, (b) active as opposed to passive articles (though as to (b) Lord Guest took the contrary view in *Inland Revenue Commissioners* v. *Barclay, Curle & Co. Ltd.* [1969] 1 W.L.R. 675). (v) The test of what the ordinary person would understand by

plant may not be reliable. While, however, it may be surprising that a horse should be described as "plant," a wharfinger's horse in 1887 represented motive power.

It seems to me that one thing which is clear from all the cases is that the meaning of "plant" is purely a matter of construction to be determined according to ordinary principles of construction and taking into account all the circumstances of the individual case. The modern cases clearly establish Lindley L.J.'s definition as a valuable general guide, and they clarify various other matters. But they do not attempt to lay down a hard and fast meaning or to delineate boundaries with precision. The matter is as it always was, one of construction. If I were free to determine that question of construction in the present case I would take the view that the taxpayer is right and that these books are plant. It seems to me that they do fall within Lindley L.J.'s definition. Put more generally, they are part of the apparatus used by a professional man for carrying on his profession. They do not fall within any of the exceptions so far classified. And as a matter of principle, I do not see good ground for excluding them if as a matter of construction they could properly be included in plant.

But if I depart from *Daphne* v. *Shaw*, 11 T.C. 256, I am merely substituting my view of a question of construction for that of Rowlatt J. in an uncertain and difficult area of the law. It does not seem to me that Rowlatt J. in *Daphne* v. *Shaw*, seriously misdirected himself. He said that plant "means apparatus, alive or dead, stationary or movable, to achieve the operations which a person wants to achieve in his vocation." That, for practical purposes, is the same as the definition of Lindley L.J. Rowlatt J. used "stationary" instead of "fixed"; he omitted the word "permanent," and he did not exclude stock-in-trade. But as a working definition it seems to be substantially the same as Lindley L.J.'s; it is no less wide.

Rowlatt J. said that the extension of the allowance to professions (which was effected by section 16 of the Finance Act 1925) did not extend the meaning of the word "plant." That is, I think, correct; the word merely has to be applied to different circumstances. Rowlatt J. may have gone too far in applying the test of what ninety-nine people out of a hundred would understand by plant. But "plant" is, as the authorities emphasise, an ordinary English word, and I think it must be admitted that to describe books as "plant" is going well beyond the everyday usage of the term. Rowlatt J.'s interpretation is, at the least, a perfectly possible one, and although the modern cases make it easier to come to the opposite conclusion I do not think that, recognising as they do that the matter is one of construction on the facts of the individual case, they are necessarily inconsistent with *Daphne* v. *Shaw*. In these circumstances, the decision having stood for nearly 50 years, I would, in any event, have felt some hesitation at departing from it.

But the matter does not end there. In *McVeigh* v. *Arthur Sanderson & Sons Ltd.* [1969] 1 W.L.R. 1143, the question of the correctness of *Daphne* v. *Shaw* was raised before Cross J. In that case the taxpayer company was the well known manufacturer of wallpaper and fabrics. The designs which it used were in part acquired by the company from free-lance artists and in part produced in its own studios. In order to have a wide field of choice, the company acquired far more designs than it needed. All the designs were filed and kept for at least six years so that a design not used immediately might be used later. The company maintained, therefore, a library of designs. The question was whether the expenditure on the designs was expenditure on "new machinery or plant" within section 16 (3) of the Finance Act 1954. Cross J. after quoting Lindley L.J.'s definition of plant, said that the revenue submitted that to fall within the definition the chattel in question must be nothing more than a material object. The designs in question, according to that submission, were no doubt in one sense pieces of paper filed in the company's library, but the paper was only the material vehicle through which the concept of the artist was conveyed to the eye and lacked, said the revenue, the gross materiality necessary to qualify it as plant. The revenue relied on *Daphne* v. *Shaw*, 11 T.C. 256. Cross J., after quoting from the judgment in *Daphne* v. *Shaw*, said, at p. 1154:

> "If I thought that I was free to do so, I am not sure that I would accept the limitation which the Crown's argument imposes on the meaning of 'plant.' If a barrister has to buy a new edition of a text book in order to help him to write his opinions, I cannot see as a matter of principle why the book should not be regarded as a tool of his trade just as much as the typewriter on which his opinions are typed. Similarly, the designs, which are the tools of the trade of the styling committee and many of which are scrapped after a few years, might, I should have thought, qualify as 'plant' just as fully as the hand blocks, silk screens and rollers, many of which are periodically scrapped. But, having regard to the decision in *Daphne* v. *Shaw*, I think that if any extension of the meaning of the word 'plant' beyond a purely physical object is to be made, it ought to be made by a higher court. So I will proceed on the footing that these designs are not 'plant'."

Inland Revenue Commissioners v. *Barclay, Curle Co. Ltd.* [1969] 1 W.L.R. 675 had not been decided at the time of this decision, but both *Hinton* v. *Maden & Ireland Ltd.* [1959] 1 W.L.R. 675 and *Jarrold* v. *John Good & Sons Ltd.* [1962] 1 W.L.R. 1101 were cited to Cross J.

The position therefore is this, that *Daphne* v. *Shaw*, 11 T.C. 256 has now stood for nearly 50 years, and as recently as 1968 Cross J. came to the conclusion that he could not depart from it. In the circumstances, I think I must follow *Daphne* v. *Shaw* and hold that the books are not plant. I therefore dismiss the appeal.

Appeal dismissed with costs.

Solicitor: *Solicitor of Inland Revenue.*

A

[CHANCERY AND FAMILY DIVISIONS]

* PRACTICE NOTE (INHERITANCE: FAMILY PROVISION)

Family Provision—Practice—Act of 1975—Assignment of proceedings to Chancery Division and Family Division—Transitional arrangements—Extension of time for making application— B
Inheritance (Provision for Family and Dependants) Act 1975 (c. 63), s. 4—R.S.C., Ord. 99, *rr.* 3, 5 (2) (*d*), 8 (*as amended by Rules of the Supreme Court (Amendment)* 1976 (*S.I.* 1976 *No.* 337 (*L.* 6)), *r.* 19)

1. The Inheritance (Provision for Family and Dependants) Act 1975 comes into force on April 1, 1976. In respect of deaths occurring on or
after that date the Act repeals and replaces and enlarges the scope of C
the existing legislation relating to family provision as contained in the Inheritance (Family Provision) Act 1938 (as amended) and applications for maintenance out of the estate of a deceased former spouse under section 26 of the Matrimonial Causes Act 1965 (as amended).

Assignment and commencement of proceedings D

2. The new R.S.C., Ord. 99, introduced by the Rules of the Supreme Court 1976 (S.I. 1976 No. 337), assigns applications in the High Court under the Act to the Chancery Division or Family Division and provides a code of procedure common to both divisions. Application is to be made by general form of originating summons (Form No. 10 in Appendix A to the Rules of the Supreme Court which has been slightly amended) E
and may be commenced either in London (in the Central Office or the Principal Registry of the Family Division) or any district registry of the High Court. The applicant must lodge with the court an affidavit in support of the originating summons and serve a copy with the summons.

3. Where an applicant wishes the court to exercise its discretion under section 4 of the Act by extending the time for making an application for
an order, such relief should be expressly asked for in the originating sum- F
mons and the grounds on which the court's leave to entertain the application is sought should be included in the supporting affidavit.

4. Although new Ord. 99 does not prescribe the contents of the applicant's affidavit in support, the attention of practitioners is drawn to the importance of setting out in it particulars of any known previous proceed-
ings relevant to the application. Such proceedings will often be material G
to the question whether the application ought to be transferred from the Family Division to the Chancery Division or vice versa under R.S.C., Ord. 4, r. 3. Transfer of the proceedings might also be appropriate in other instances, for example, on sufficient grounds being shown by the parties or where the application involves the taking of complicated accounts, for which special facilities exist in the Chancery Division. H

5. Ord. 99, r. 5 (2) (*d*) makes it clear that it is only facts known to the deponent which have to be stated in the affidavit of a personal representative. He is obviously not obliged to make inquiries and investigations in order to ascertain or confirm other matters within the 21 days after service of the summons. Nor is he required to set out facts (possibly distasteful) which are not necessarily relevant at that stage; if they become relevant later he may lodge a further affidavit.

Jurisdiction

6. Under new Ord. 99, r. 8 masters, registrars of the Principal Registry of the Family Division and district registrars may hear applications and make final orders disposing of proceedings under the Act, subject to the directions of the judges.

While at the present time it is not proposed to make any formal directions under R.S.C., Ord. 32, r. 14 (1), and masters, registrars of the Family Division and district registrars may therefore deal with either contested or uncontested applications, it is envisaged that they will exercise their discretion so as to refer to a judge any case which is likely to involve a long or complex issue of fact or law or a question of jurisdiction, unless the amount of the estate in the case is small.

Transitional arrangements

7. The procedure under new Ord. 99 will only apply to an application made under the Act of 1975 in respect of a death occurring on or after April 1, 1976. An application for family provision or maintenance out of the estate of a deceased former spouse in respect of a death occurring before April 1, 1976, will continue to be governed by the procedure under the present R.S.C., Ord. 99 or rule 103 of the Matrimonial Causes Rules 1973, as appropriate, until the period within which applications may be made under the Inheritance (Family Provision) Act 1938 (as amended) or section 26 of the Matrimonial Causes Act 1965 (as amended) has expired.

This note is issued with the concurrence of the President of the Family Division and by the direction of the Vice-Chancellor.

R. E. BALL
Chief Chancery Master

R. L. BAYNE-POWELL
Senior Registrar, Family Division

March 26, 1976.

[HOUSE OF LORDS]

* ISMAIL . . . . PETITIONER

AND

POLISH OCEAN LINES . . . . RESPONDENTS

1976 March 25 — Lord Simon of Glaisdale, Lord Fraser of Tullybelton and Lord Russell of Killowen.

Petition by the claimant charterer for leave to appeal to the House of Lords from the decision of the Court of Appeal in *Ismail* v. *Polish Ocean Lines* [1976] 2 W.L.R. 477.

The Appeal Committee dismissed the petition.

J. A. G.

[QUEEN'S BENCH DIVISION]

* REGINA *v.* NEWHAM EAST JUSTICES, *Ex parte* HUNT

REGINA *v.* OXTED JUSTICES, *Ex parte* FRANKLIN

1976 Jan. 28, 29 — Lord Widgery C.J., Kilner Brown and Watkins JJ.

Public Health—Nuisance—Complaint by tenant—Criminal or civil proceedings—Whether need to serve abatement notice—Public Health Act 1936 (26 *Geo.* 5 & 1 *Edw.* 8, *c.* 49), *ss.* 94, 99 [1]

By information and summons, the applicant H applied to the justices, under section 99 of the Public Health Act 1936, for a nuisance order to be made against a local authority as his landlords. The justices dismissed the summons on the ground that the proceedings were civil and should have been begun by complaint. The applicant F, who was in occupation of premises belonging to another local authority, applied by complaint, under section 99, to the justices for a nuisance order to be made against that local authority. The justices held that there was no case to answer as the applicant had not served an abatement notice on the local authority.

On applications for orders of mandamus to direct the justices to hear and determine the summonses:—

Held, granting the applications, that section 99 of the Public Health Act 1936 gave an individual the right to bring proceedings by information in a magistrates' court and thereby invoke against a local authority the penal provisions of section 94 of the Act; that the service of an abatement notice was not a prerequisite for criminal proceedings to be brought under section 99 and, accordingly, the justices had jurisdiction to hear and determine the proceedings begun by information and, in the circumstances, the justices should treat the other proceedings as if they had been begun by information.

The following cases are referred to in the judgment of Kilner Brown J:

Cocker v. *Cardwell* (1869) L.R. 5 Q.B. 15.

Northern Ireland Trailers Ltd. v. *Preston Corporation* [1972] 1 W.L.R. 203; [1972] 1 All E.R. 260, D.C.

Nottingham City District Council v. *Newton* [1974] 1 W.L.R. 923; [1974] 2 All E.R. 760, D.C.

Reg. v. *Hughes* (1879) 4 Q.B.D. 614.

Salford City Council v. *McNally* [1975] 1 W.L.R. 365; [1975] 1 All E.R. 597, D.C.; [1975] 3 W.L.R. 87; [1975] 2 All E.R. 860, H.L.(E.).

The following additional cases were cited in argument:

Coventry City Council v. *Cartwright* [1975] 1 W.L.R. 845; [1975] 2 All E.R. 99, D.C.

Rex v. *Epping* (*Waltham Abbey*) *Justices, Ex parte Burlinson* [1948] 1 K.B. 79; [1947] 2 All E.R. 537, D.C.

[1] Public Health Act 1936, s. 94: see post, pp. 422F—423A.
S. 99: see post, pp. 423H—424A.

A APPLICATIONS for orders of mandamus

The applicant, David Leslie Hunt of 22, Queensland House, Rymill Street, London E.C.6, a tenant of the respondents, Greater London Council, applied by information and summons, under section 99 of the Public Health Act 1936, in the Newham East Magistrates' Court against that local authority and alleging that, as landlords, they were in default by reason of a nuisance in the premises. On November 27, 1975, the justices refused to
B hear the summons. The applicant applied for an order of mandamus directed to the justices to hear and determine the summons on the grounds, inter alia, that the justices erred in law in determining that the proceedings should have been commenced by complaint and in dismissing the summons accordingly; and that they erred in law in holding that the proceedings under section 99 of the Act of 1936 were civil and not criminal proceedings.

C The applicant, Bertram Frederick Franklin, who was in occupation of Jenner, The Old Vicarage, Vicarage Road, Lingfield, Surrey, served a "notice" in respect of a nuisance in those premises on the respondents, Tandridge District Council. He then by complaint and summons in the Oxted Magistrates' Court sought an order, under section 99 of the Act, against the local authority. On December 11, 1975, the justices held that there was no case to answer and dismissed the summons on the ground that
D the applicant had not validly served an abatement notice in accordance with Part III of the Act. He applied for an order of mandamus directing the justices to hear and determine the summons. He also applied for an order of certiorari to quash the justices' decision that there was no case to answer but that application was not proceeded with. Relief was sought on the ground, inter alia, that the court erred in law in holding that an
E abatement notice should have been served by the applicant as a prerequisite to proceedings under section 99 of the Act.

The facts are stated in the judgment of Kilner Brown J.

Stephen Sedley for the applicants.
J. R. T. Rylance for the Greater London Council.
Anthony Thompson for the Tandridge District Council.

F

LORD WIDGERY C.J. It is convenient that judgment will be given in both these cases together and I will ask Kilner Brown J. to give the first judgment in each case.

G KILNER BROWN J. In the first matter counsel moves on behalf of David Leslie Hunt for an order of mandamus directing the Newham East justices to hear and determine a summons brought under section 99 of the Public Health Act 1936. In the second matter counsel moves on behalf of Bertram Frederick Franklin for orders of certiorari to remove a decision of the Oxted justices and of mandamus to continue the hearing of a summons, as in the first matter, brought under section 99 of the
H Public Health Act 1936.

By common consent, the two matters have been taken together because both involved the interpretation and effect of section 99 of that Act. This section has recently been considered in two cases which have become generally known as the *Nottingham* case and the *Salford* case. The *Nottingham* case was a decision of this court under the name of *Nottingham City District Council* v. *Newton* [1974] 1 W.L.R. 923. The *Salford* case

is reported under the name of *Salford City Council* v. *McNally* [1975] 1 A
W.L.R. 365. It was a decision of this court which was affirmed in the House of Lords: see [1975] 3 W.L.R. 87.

By way of preamble it is appropriate to observe that sections 42, 43 and 44 of the Magistrates' Court Act 1952 make it plain that questions of civil jurisdiction should be initiated by complaint and questions of criminal jurisdiction should be initiated by information and summons. It
is also clear on the authority of *Northern Ireland Trailers Ltd.* v. *Preston* B
Corporation [1972] 1 W.L.R. 203 that the effect of section 94 (2) of the Public Health Act 1936 is to invoke the possibility of a fine and therefore has to be considered as a penal section of the Act. If this subsection is called into being, it should therefore be initiated by information and summons. So much therefore for questions which are beyond argument.

In the first of these two cases the justices were dealing with an infor- C
mation laid under section 99 of the Public Health Act 1936 alleging that the Greater London Council as landlords of premises at 22, Queensland House, Rymill Street, were in default by reason of nuisance at the said premises as defined by section 92 of the Public Health Act 1936.

Section 92, which is headed with the title " Statutory nuisances," reads:

> " (1) Without prejudice to the exercise by a local authority of any D
> other powers vested in them by or under this Act, the following matters may, subject to the provisions of this Part of this Act, be dealt with summarily, and are in this Part of this Act referred to as ' statutory nuisances,' that is to say:—(*a*) any premises in such a state as to be prejudicial to health or a nuisance; . . ."

That is all that is necessary to read from section 92. Section 93 deals with E
the service of an abatement notice. It reads:

> " Where a local authority are satisfied of the existence of a statutory nuisance, they shall serve a notice (hereafter in this Act referred to as ' an abatement notice ') on the person by whose act, default or sufferance the nuisance arises or continues, . . ."

F

Turning then to section 94, that deals with the power of the court to make a nuisance order if an abatement notice is disregarded. It provides:

> " (1) If the person on whom an abatement notice has been served makes default in complying with any of the requirements of the notice, or if the nuisance, although abated since the service of the notice, is, in the opinion of the local authority, likely to recur on the same G
> premises, the authority shall cause a complaint to be made to a justice of the peace, and the justice shall thereupon issue a summons requiring the person on whom the notice was served to appear before a court of summary jurisdiction. (2) If on the hearing of the complaint it is proved that the alleged nuisance exists, or that although abated it is likely to recur on the same premises, then, subject to the pro- H
> visions of subsections (4) and (5) of this section the court shall make an order (hereafter in this Act referred to as ' a nuisance order ') for either, or both, of the following purposes—(*a*) requiring the defendant to comply with all or any of the requirements of the abatement notice, or otherwise to abate the nuisance, within a time specified in the order, and to execute any works necessary for that purpose; (*b*) prohibiting a recurrence of the nuisance, and requiring the defendant,

A within a time specified in the order, to execute any works necessary to prevent a recurrence; and may also impose on the defendant a fine not exceeding £5."

That sum is now increased to £200.

It is clear from the reading of those sections that where a local authority wishes to abate a nuisance caused by the owner or occupier of premises
B there are two stages of process. There has first to be a service of an abatement notice. If that is not effective, the authority may then bring the defaulter before the court under section 94. They may then obtain an order requiring abatement and an order prohibiting recurrence and, if appropriate, also request the imposition of a fine.

The short point in this case, and, as will appear, in the other case also,
C is whether section 99 gives to the individual the right to invoke section 94 in all its powers without the prior service of a notice of abatement and if so whether process under section 99 has to be initiated by complaint or by way of information.

The Newham justices heard a summons by the applicant on November 27, 1975. They went to a great deal of trouble, as their most admirably clear affidavit reveals. They found it a difficult matter. This is not
D surprising in view of the extent or argument deployed before this court with a wealth of forensic talent, and I intend no discourtesy to counsel if I deal with the arguments shortly.

Mr. Sedley, for the applicant Mr. Hunt, submits that section 99 is comprehensive and gives to the individual the right to apply for the orders available under section 94. As this is a penal section, process should be
E initiated by way of information. That is what the applicant did, and it is submitted that the justices were wrong in deciding that he should have applied by way of complaint and were wrong in holding that section 99 invoked civil and not criminal jurisdiction.

Mr. Rylance sought to uphold the justices' decision. He argued that the words of section 99 should not be extended to the criminal aspect of
F section 94 (2). It is said that the legislature could not have contemplated giving to the individual the privilege of short-circuiting a prior warning by means of notice. Section 99 does not lead directly to the power to fine set out in section 94 (2). It refers to the making of orders but not to the imposition of a fine. There ought to be a severance of section 94 (2) and the penal consequences should be excluded. Once the power to fine is
G excluded, section 99 ceases to cover the criminal process envisaged by section 94 (2). The process, it is said, remains civil. If so, proceedings may be by way of complaint and the justices were right in dismissing the information.

The court was invited to consider by analogy reference to the history of the various Public Health Acts and to matters in similarity such as Acts
H dealing with pollution. The words of section 99 read:

"Complaint of the existence of a statutory nuisance under this Act may be made to a justice of the peace by any person aggrieved by the nuisance, and thereupon the like proceedings shall be had, with the like incidents and consequences as to the making of orders, penalties for disobedience of orders and otherwise, as in the case of a complaint by the local authority, but any order made in such proceedings may, if the court after giving the local authority an opportunity of being heard thinks fit, direct the authority to abate the nuisance." A

It seems to me that the words "the like proceedings shall be had, with the like incidents and consequences as to the making of orders, penalties for disobedience of orders and otherwise, as in the case of a complaint by the local authority" can be construed, and should be construed, to give to the B individual the right to go to the justices by way of information and summons and to take the justices straight to section 94. It is to be observed that the word "procedure" is not used in this section. It refers to "proceedings." It refers in terms to the making of orders, penalties for disobedience of orders and otherwise.

In my opinion the mere fact that there is no mention of the word C "fine" in section 99 does not mean that section 94 cannot be invoked. Starting with section 92, the Act deals with the position of a local authority. It sets out preliminary steps. It moves on in section 94 to deal with powers of enforcement and punishment. Then in section 99 it sets out in general and comprehensive terms that an individual may resort to the court so that like proceedings shall be had with like incidents and consequences as to the making of orders, penalties for disobedience of orders D and so forth.

It is to be observed that the precise point in this instant case was not before this court in *Nottingham City District Council* v. *Newton* [1974] 1 W.L.R. 923, nor in *Salford City Council* v. *McNally* [1975] 1 W.L.R. 365; nor when it reached the House of Lords was it a question which their Lordships had to consider: see [1975] 3 W.L.R. 87.

In my judgment the proper interpretation of this section leads to the E conclusion that the individual can by information invoke section 94. Whereas in the past it has, as it was in both the *Nottingham* and *Salford* cases, been done by complaint, once the question calls for decision, as it does now, by this court it seems to me that the justices were wrong to hold that this was a civil process.

The court has been informed that local authorities fear all sorts of F untoward consequences if this be the case. I would have thought that these fears are more imagined than real. To begin with, as the Newham East justices in the affidavit of one of their number properly recognised, there is a heavier burden of proof when recourse is made to process by way of information and summons. Secondly I am confident that the justices will bear in mind the words used by Lord Wilberforce in his speech G in *Salford City Council* v. *McNally* [1975] 3 W.L.R. 87, 92:

> "This aspect of the matter was well explained by the Divisional Court in *Nottingham City District Council* v. *Newton* [1974] 1 W.L.R. 923, the keynote of which is the need, in making abatement notices, to use discretion and common sense."

The words of Lord Widgery C.J. in the *Salford* case [1975] 1 W.L.R. H 365, 371, when referring to *Nottingham City District Council* v. *Newton*, were cited with approval by Lord Edmund-Davies in his speech in the *Salford* case [1975] 3 W.L.R. 87, 98. Lord Widgery C.J. said:

> "This court made it perfectly clear that justices faced with this situation, although bound to make an order under the Act, can use their common sense and are entitled to take into account all the

A circumstances, and thus avoid the expenditure of public money unnecessarily in a case where the house is likely to be pulled down shortly in any event."

True both those cases were dealing with a somewhat different situation where the individual was complaining in respect of houses which were subject to demolition orders. In my view the words are equally applicable
B in circumstances such as this. For the reasons I have given I am of the opinion that the justices came to a wrong decision and the applicant has made out his case for the order which he seeks.

I turn now to the case involving the decision of the Oxted justices. In this case the applicant Mr. Franklin purported to serve a notice on the Tandridge District Council calling upon them to abate a nuisance, namely, defects displayed in a report made upon the inspection of the property
C known as "Jenners," Old Vicarage, Vicarage Road, Lingfield, Surrey.

On November 14, 1975, he issued a summons pursuant to section 99 of the Public Health Act 1936. It was heard on December 11, 1975, when the justices dismissed the summons, holding that there was no case to answer for the reason that the abatement notice had not been properly served. It is common ground that the notice was not served upon the
D proper officer and therefore did not comply with the provisions of section 285 (*d*) of the Public Health Act 1936. That of course deals only with the situation in which it is necessary and incumbent upon any person to serve a notice.

The applicant now seeks to have the matter heard to its conclusion upon the relevant issue in accordance with the provisions of section 94 of
E the Act. It is said that the justices' decision implied that no process was open to the applicant under sections 94 and 99 unless an abatement notice had been served under section 93.

Mr. Sedley submitted that the applicant did not need to serve a notice. He repeated his arguments in general as to the effect of section 99. He referred to two authorities *Cocker* v. *Cardwell* (1869) L.R. 5 Q.B. 15, in which it was held under the old Act in the mid-Victorian period (the pre-
F decessor of the present Act) that notice was not a pre-requisite. He referred also to *Reg.* v. *Hughes* (1879) 4 Q.B.D. 614, which is authority for saying that the presence of the party in court, that is to say the magistrates' court, gives jurisdiction to try the issue.

Mr. Thompson relied on and adopted the general argument used by Mr. Rylance as to the effect of section 99, and he went on to take the
G further point, which was this. The applicant based his case on an abatement notice aand the justices were right because they held on the facts that the applicant had not made out his case, which was that there was a failure to comply with a notice. But the real substance of his complaint was that there was a nuisance in existence in fact.

In my judgment, it would have been wrong to refuse relief on that
H narrow ground. Everybody in this case, and both sides, initially proceeded on the wrong basis. In my opinion, there was no need for a notice and the whole thing, as it was developed before the justices, turned on an irrelevancy.

For the reasons given in the previous case the applicant, in my view, was entitled to rely on section 99 and call upon the justices to invoke section 94 if he made out his case. He has of course to shoulder the burden imposed by invoking a penal section. In all such cases in future the initiation process should be by way of information. I would say that this applicant succeeds on this motion and the justices should hear the case on the merits as if it were brought by way of information.

WATKINS J. I agree.

LORD WIDGERY C.J. I also agree.

Applications for orders of mandamus granted with costs against local authorities.
Certificate that point of law of general public importance refused.

Solicitors: *Hilary Fassnidge, Newham Rights Centre; Hilary Fassnidge for Turner, Garrett & Co., Weybridge; A. G. Gardner, Greater London Council; R. C. Wilson, Tandridge District Council.*

H. J.

[COURT OF APPEAL]

* REGINA *v.* JOHNSON (HARRY)

1975 Dec. 8; 1976 Jan. 16 — Lawton L.J., Croom-Johnson and Peter Pain JJ.

Crime — Sentence — Extended sentence — Offence committed more than three years after previous conviction and before final release from prison — Whether extended sentence valid — Criminal Justice Act 1967 (*c.* 80), *s.* 37 (4) (*a*)

In 1964 the defendant was sentenced to five years' imprisonment. In 1969 he absconded from a prison hostel during the last few weeks of the sentence, committed robbery and was sentenced to 12 years' imprisonment, which was certified to be an extended sentence under the provisions of section 37 of the Criminal Justice Act 1967.

On a reference by the Secretary of State to determine whether the court had power to impose an extended sentence under section 37 (4) (*a*) of the Act [1] since the offence had been committed more than three years after the defendant's last conviction and before his final release from prison for the sentence of imprisonment then imposed:—

Held, that, on the true construction of section 37 (4) (*a*) of the Act, an offender, who was otherwise liable to be sentenced to an extended term of imprisonment for an offence,

---

[Reported by MISS EIRA CARYL-THOMAS, Barrister-at-Law]

[1] Criminal Justice Act 1967, s. 37: "(4) The conditions [for imposing an extended term of imprisonment] are:—(*a*) the offence was committed before the expiration of three years from a previous conviction of an offence punishable on indictment with imprisonment for a term of two years or more or from his final release from prison after serving a sentence of imprisonment, . . . passed on such a conviction; . . ."

A was not liable to serve such a term if, during the three years prior to the commission of that offence, he had neither committed an offence nor served a term of imprisonment; that, since the defendant had during the three years prior to the offence of robbery served a prison sentence, he was liable and had been correctly sentenced to an extended term of imprisonment.

B The following cases are referred to in the judgment:

Reg. v. *Clark* (unreported) July 3, 1970, C.A.
Reg. v. *Gillingham* (unreported) November 24, 1970, C.A.
Rex v. *Ettridge* [1909] 2 K.B. 24, C.C.A.
Rex v. *Norman* [1924] 2 K.B. 315; 18 Cr.App.R. 81, C.C.A.

C The following additional cases were cited in argument:

Kennedy v. *Spratt* [1972] A.C. 83; [1971] 2 W.L.R. 667; [1971] 1 All E.R. 805, H.L.(N.I.).
Reg. v. *Merriman* [1973] A.C. 584; [1972] 3 W.L.R. 545; [1972] 3 All E.R. 42, H.L.(E.).
Reg. v. *Ottewell* [1969] 1 Q.B. 27; [1968] 2 W.L.R. 1536; [1968] 2 All E.R. 593, C.A.; [1970] A.C. 642; [1968] 3 W.L.R. 621; [1968] 3 All E.R. 153, H.L.(E.).

D REFERENCE by the Secretary of State.

On July 31, 1964, the defendant, Harry Johnson, was sentenced at Nottingham Quarter Sessions to two concurrent sentences of five years' imprisonment. Having lost remission of his sentence by his behaviour, he absconded from prison in February 1969 and, on March 4, 1969, com-
E mitted robbery. On May 6, 1969, at Derby Assizes, he pleaded guilty to the robbery and was sentenced by Talbot J., under section 37 of the Criminal Justice Act 1967, to an extended sentence of 12 years' imprisonment. On July 21, 1969, he applied for an extension of time in which to apply for leave to appeal against sentence. After refusal by the single judge, he applied to the full court and, on November 24, 1969,
F that application was refused.

On June 4, 1974, he was convicted of wounding with intent another prisoner. He was sentenced to three years' imprisonment to run consecutively to the extended sentence imposed in 1969. Th Secretary of State referred the case to the Court of Appeal, under section 17 of the Criminal Appeal Act 1968, for determination of the question whether, in the light of the judgment in *Reg.* v. *Clark* (unreported) July 3, 1970, there
G was power to impose an extended sentence prior to the defendant's final release from prison for the offence committed in 1964.

The facts are stated in the judgment of the court.

Alistair Troup for the defendant.

Maurice Drake Q.C., *Douglas Hogg* and *R. A. D. Payne* for the
H Crown.

Cur. adv. vult.

January 16, 1976. LAWTON L.J. read the judgment of the court. On May 6, 1969, at Derby Assizes the defendant was convicted of robbery and was sentenced to 12 years' imprisonment. This sentence was certified to be an extended one under the provisions of section 37 of the Criminal Justice Act 1967. These provisions have been re-enacted as sections 28

and 29 of the Powers of Criminal Courts Act 1973. On July 21, 1969, A
the defendant applied for an extension of time in which to appeal against sentence. After his application had been refused by a single judge he renewed it to the full court, which dismissed it on November 24, 1969. His case comes back to this court as a reference by the Secretary of State pursuant to section 17 of the Criminal Appeal Act 1968.

In 1974, while serving his sentence, he attacked another prisoner and
on June 26, 1974, he was sentenced to three years' imprisonment to run B
consecutively to the extended sentence imposed in 1969. By 1974 there had been two cases in this court, *Reg.* v. *Clark* (unreported), July 3, 1970, and *Reg.* v. *Gillingham* (unreported), November 24, 1970, which seemed to support a submission made by the defendant's solicitor to the Secretary of State that the extended sentence had been made without jurisdiction.
The reference has been made to determine this submission. The doubt C
about the validity of the extended sentence arises because the offence in respect of which it was imposed was committed while the defendant was still serving the last few weeks of a five year sentence. He had been living in a prison hostel from which he had absconded. He had not been finally released from prison within the meaning of sections 37 and 38 of the Criminal Justice Act 1967.

Section 37 provides for the punishment of persistent offenders. Sub- D
section (1) abolished the forms of punishment for such offenders which had been established by the Criminal Justice Act 1948. The difference between the conditions precedent for the new form of punishment and the old is important for the purposes of this appeal. Subsection (2) enacted that, subject to conditions specified in subsection (4), the courts
may impose extended terms of imprisonment if satisfied that by reason E
of the offender's previous conduct and of the likelihood of his committing further offences, it is expedient to protect the public from him for a substantial time. The defendant is such an offender. Subsection (4) sets out the conditions in three paragraphs lettered (*a*), (*b*) and (*c*). The conditions in (*b*) and (*c*) were complied with. The query arises about (*a*) which is in these terms:

F

> "(*a*) the offence was committed before the expiration of three years from a previous conviction of an offence punishable on indictment with imprisonment for a term of two years or more or from his final release from prison after serving a sentence of imprisonment, corrective training or preventive detention passed on such a conviction; . . ."

How is this condition to be construed? There are two possibilities. G
The first would envisage two qualifying periods of three years, the second of them having as a starting point for the running of time final release from prison. The other construction requires the court to look back for three years and to find out what the offender had been doing during that period.

If the first construction be right, the defendant would not have been H
liable for an extended sentence because the robbery for which he was sentenced in 1969 was committed after the expiration of three years from July 31, 1964, the date of his conviction for the offence which had put him into prison for five years. A second qualifying period would not have started because he had not been finally released from prison when he committed the robbery. In both *Reg.* v. *Clark* and *Reg.* v. *Gillingham* this court followed this construction. In both these cases, being appeals

against sentence only, the prosecution had not been represented. No alternative construction was considered.

In this appeal the prosecution has been represented. Mr. Drake has submitted that on its true construction, condition (*a*), when read in its context in the Act of 1967 and against the background of its legislative history, provides an offender, whose convictions qualify him for an extended sentence, with an opportunity of avoiding one if he has kept away from crime for the specified period.

Penal legislation has often had to provide additional punishments for persistent offenders. Section 21 (2) of the Criminal Justice Act 1948 introduced the concept of preventive detention for persistent offenders about whom the court was satisfied that it was expedient for the protection of the public that they should be detained in custody for a substantial time. A person qualified for preventive detention who was not less than 30 years of age and had been convicted at least four times on indictment for offences punishable with imprisonment for a term of two years or more. Once a person had become liable to be sentenced to preventive detention he remained liable for the rest of his life, no matter what efforts he had made to rehabilitate himself, between the conviction for which he was being sentenced and the conviction immediately preceding it.

Section 37 (1) of the Act of 1967 abolished preventive detention and substituted the concept of extended sentences. Subsection (2) sets out what the court had to be satisfied about before imposing an extended sentence, namely, his previous conduct and the likelihood of his committing further offences. This was in addition to being satisfied about the conditions specified in subsection (4). Mr. Drake submitted that subsection (2) of the Act of 1967 envisaged a more flexible approach to the circumstances in which an extended sentence could be imposed than section 21 (2) of the Act of 1948 had done in relation to preventive detention. Condition (*a*) introduced another flexible factor. No longer was a persistent offender always to be such. Extended sentences could only be imposed for offences committed within a specified period of three years. This period, said Mr. Drake, was defined by condition (*a*). A court which was considering imposing an extended sentence, he submitted, had to decide what had happened in the three years before the present offence was committed. If the offender had been in prison during that period, he continued to be liable for an extended sentence; but if he had not been and he had been free of convictions for that period he was not liable. The key words in condition (*a*) were "before" and "after serving a sentence of imprisonment." If one writes out the two conditions set out in subsection (4) (*a*) in their entirety, the subsection would read as follows:

> "(*a*) the offence was committed before the expiration of three years from a previous conviction of an offence punishable on indictment with imprisonment for a term of two years or more
>
> or
>
> the offence was committed before the expiration of three years from his final release from prison after serving a sentence of imprisonment . . . passed on a conviction of an offence punishable on indictment with imprisonment for a term of two years or more."

If it was the intention of the Act of 1967 to free an offender from liability to an extended sentence in specified circumstances (as we find it was) Mr. Drake's suggested construction fits in with both the grammar A and the intention of the Act. It makes more sense than the construction followed in *Reg.* v. *Clark* and *Reg.* v. *Gillingham.* It gets rid of the absurdity which this reference has revealed. The defendant is a dangerous criminal from whom the public should be protected. Had he been serving a three year sentence instead of one of five years when he committed the robbery after absconding from the prison hostel, or had he committed it the day after his final release from prison after completing B his sentence, he could have been given an extended sentence. But as he committed it in between times, if the *Reg.* v. *Clark* and *Reg.* v. *Gillingham* construction is right, the public must be deprived of the protection against him which Parliament envisaged.

We are satisfied that Mr. Drake's suggested construction is the right one. As the court in *Reg.* v. *Clark* and *Reg.* v. *Gillingham* did not have C the benefit of full argument, we need not follow those decisions: see *Rex* v. *Ettridge* [1909] 2 K.B. 24 and *Rex* v. *Norman* [1924] 2 K.B. 315.

The Secretary of State having referred the whole of the case to this court for determination in respect of sentence, pursuant to section 17 (1) (*a*) of the Criminal Appeal Act 1968 we treat the reference as an appeal against sentence and dismiss it.

Appeal dismissed. D

Solicitors: *Registrar of Criminal Appeals; Director of Public Prosecutions.*

[HOUSE OF LORDS] E

* THE ESCHERSHEIM
THE JADE

ERKOWIT (OWNERS) . . . . RESPONDENTS

AND F

JADE (OWNERS) . . . . APPELLANTS

ERKOWIT (OWNERS OF CARGO LATELY LADEN ON BOARD) . . . . RESPONDENTS

AND

ESCHERSHEIM (OWNERS) . . . . . . APPELLANTS G

[CONSOLIDATED APPEALS]

1976 Jan. 28, 29; Feb. 2; March 31 — Lord Diplock, Lord Simon of Glaisdale, Lord Kilbrandon, Lord Salmon and Lord Edmund-Davies H

Admiralty—Jurisdiction—Action in rem—Claims arising out of salvage operation for loss of ship and cargo—Claim that cargo washed overboard causing pollution—Court's jurisdiction to hear and determine claims brought against salvors by ship and cargo owners—Administration of Justice Act 1956 (4 & 5 *Eliz.* 2, *c.* 46), *ss.* 1 (1) (*d*) (*e*) (*g*) (*h*) (*j*), 3 (1) (4)

Ships' Names—Dortmund—Erkowit—Eschersheim—Jade—Salus (formerly Rotesand)

A Section 1 (1) of the Administration of Justice Act 1956 provides:

"The Admiralty jurisdiction of the High Court shall be as follows, that is to say, jurisdiction to hear and determine any of the following questions or claims—. . . (*d*) any claim for damage done by a ship; (*e*) any claim for damage received by a ship; . . . (*g*) any claim for loss of or damage to goods carried in a ship; (*h*) any claim arising
B out of any agreement relating to the carriage of goods in a ship or to the use or hire of a ship; (*j*) any claim in the nature of salvage . . ."

As a result of a collision at sea between the *Erkowit* and the *Dortmund*, the engine room of the *Erkowit* was holed and became flooded. The *Rotesand*, a salvage tug, went to the aid of the *Erkowit* and the masters of the two ships signed a Lloyd's open form salvage agreement on behalf of the salvors,
C the owners of the *Erkowit* and the owners of her cargo. Under the agreement, the salvors agreed to use their best endeavours to salve the *Erkowit* and the parties agreed that differences arising out of the agreement would be referred to arbitration in London. The *Rotesand* then took the *Erkowit* in tow and beached her off the Spanish coast. All attempts to patch and refloat the *Erkowit* failed and she became a total loss. Most of the personal belongings of her master and crew were lost.
D Most of the cargo was lost or damaged and a cargo of insecticide was washed out to sea causing pollution and consequential interference to fishing in the area. The Spanish government brought proceedings on behalf of fishermen affected by the pollution in the Spanish courts for damages against the owners of the *Erkowit* and the salvors. The actions in rem were brought in the English courts against the *Dortmund* for damage caused by the collision; the first action by the owners, master and
E crew of the *Erkowit* and the second by the owners of her cargo.

Two further actions in rem were brought against sister ships of the *Rotesand*. The first, "ship's action for negligent salvage" included claims by the owners of the *Erkowit* for damages for the loss of the ship and an indemnity against their potential liability in Spain for pollution and by the master and crew for loss of personal effects. The second, "cargo action for negligent salvage" consisted of claims for
F loss of cargo by the cargo owners. The salvors applied to the court for the writs in the two actions to be struck out or set aside on the ground that the court had no jurisdiction, under section 1 (1) of the Administration of Justice Act 1956, to hear and determine the claims, and for an order that the actions, in so far as they were not struck out or set aside, be stayed under section 4 of the Arbitration Act 1950 on the ground that, under the salvage agreement, the claims were to
G be referred to arbitration.

Brandon J. struck out the claims of the master and crew on the ground that they did not come within section 1 (1) of the Act of 1956 but otherwise dismissed both applications. On appeal by the salvors, the Court of Appeal dismissed the appeal.

On the salvors' appeal on the issue of jurisdiction:—

H *Held*, dismissing the appeals, (1) that on the true construction of section 3 (4) of the Act the right of arrest conferred thereby was confined to the ship in connection with which the claim in the action arose (or a sister ship) (post, pp. 436H—437A, 439E).

(2) That in their context the words in section 1 (1) (*h*) "any agreement relating . . . to the use or hire of a ship" bore their ordinary wide meaning and since in any ordinary meaning of those words the salvage agreement was an "agreement relating to the use of a ship," namely, the *Rotesand*, for the

purpose of salving the *Erkowit* and her cargo and bringing A
them to a place of safety, the claims of both shipowners and cargo owners fell within paragraph (*h*) of section 1 (1); that they were claims in connection with the *Rotesand* and that they were enforceable under section 3 (4) by an action in rem against the *Rotesand* or any of her sister ships (post, pp. 437G, 438C–E).

Reg. v. *City of London Court Judge* [1892] 1 Q.B. 273,
C.A. distinguished. B

(3) That damage which resulted from the salvors' negligence after the *Erkowit* was beached was not damage done by a ship within section 1 (1) (*d*) of the Act but, if damage was caused by the negligent beaching of the *Erkowit*, it was damage done by those in charge of the *Rotesand* and that ship was the actual instrument of the damage and, therefore, both the ship and cargo owners could bring an action in rem
within paragraph (*d*) based on the negligent beaching of the C
vessel (post, p. 439A–C).

(4) That by virtue of the language of section 3 (4) limiting the right of arrest to the ship in connection with which the claim arose (or a sister ship) the shipowners' claim could not be brought under paragraph (*e*) nor the claims of the cargo owners under paragraph (*g*) of section 1 (1) (post, pp. 439D–G, 440B).

Decision of the Court of Appeal [1976] 1 W.L.R. 339; D
[1976] 1 All E.R. 441 affirmed.

The following cases are referred to in the opinion of Lord Diplock:

Alina, The (1880) 5 Ex.D. 227, C.A.
Bilbao, The (1860) Lush. 149.
Currie v. *M'Knight* [1897] A.C. 97, H.L.(Sc.).
Post Office v. *Estuary Radio Ltd.* [1968] 2 Q.B. 740; [1967] 1 W.L.R. E
1396; [1967] 3 All E.R. 679, C.A.
Reg. v. *City of London Court Judge* [1892] 1 Q.B. 273, C.A.
Salomon v. *Customs and Excise Commissioners* [1967] 2 Q.B. 116; [1966] 3 W.L.R. 1223; [1966] 3 All E.R. 871, C.A.
Vera Cruz, The (*No.* 2) (1884) 9 P.D. 96, C.A.

The following additional cases were cited in argument: F

Beldis, The [1936] P. 51, C.A.
Circe, The [1906] P. 1.
Conoco Britannia, The [1972] 2 Q.B. 543; [1972] 2 W.L.R. 1352; [1972] 2 All E.R. 238.
Isca, The (1886) 12 P.D. 34; 6 Asp.M.L.C. 63, D.C.
Molière, The [1925] P. 27.
Pugsley & Co. v. *Ropkins & Co. Ltd.* [1892] 2 Q.B. 184, C.A. G
Queen of the South, The [1968] P. 449; [1968] 2 W.L.R. 973; [1968] 1 All E.R. 1163.
Riverstone Meat Co. Pty. Ltd. v. *Lancashire Shipping Co. Ltd.* [1961] A.C. 807; [1961] 2 W.L.R. 269; [1961] 1 All E.R. 495, H.L.(E.).
Valsesia, The [1927] P. 115.
Zeus, The (1888) 13 P.D. 188, D.C.

H

APPEALS from the Court of Appeal.

These were appeals from two orders of the Court of Appeal (Cairns and Scarman L.JJ. and Sir Gordon Willmer) both dated July 22, 1975, dismissing appeals from two orders of Brandon J., both dated June 10, 1974. By his orders Brandon J., inter alia, refused to set aside the writ or strike out the whole or any part of the claim of the respondents, the owners of the motor vessel *Erkowit*, in action 1972 folio 451 or to set aside the

A writ or strike out the whole or any part of the claim of the respondents, the owners of cargo lately on board the *Erkowit*, in action 1972 folio 461.

The actions arose out of the loss of the *Erkowit* and her cargo off La Coruña on the Spanish coast in November 1970. On October 30, 1970, the *Erkowit* had been involved in a collision with another vessel, the *Dortmund*, as a result of which her engine room had been holed and her engine room flooded. The appellants entered into a contract in the terms
B of Lloyd's Open Form of Salvage Agreement to use their best endeavours to salve the *Erkowit* and her cargo. Their tug *Rotesand* took the *Erkowit* in tow and on October 31 beached her in a sinking condition. There followed an attempt to patch, pump and refloat the *Erkowit* but it was unsuccessful and on November 9 was abandoned. Part of the cargo consisting of drums of insecticide was washed off the deck and out of the
C holds of the vessel and was alleged to have caused widespread pollution. Claims had been brought in Spain on behalf of numerous Spanish fishermen against both the appellants and the respondent shipowners for very substantial damages.

By their writ in action 1972 folio 451 the respondent shipowners claimed from the appellants damages for loss and damage to the *Erkowit* and indemnities in respect of consequential loss and expense (including
D loss caused by any liability to the Spanish claimants). By their writ in action 1972 folio 461 the respondent cargo owners claimed damages in respect of the loss of their cargo. Both these actions were actions in rem brought against other vessels owned by the appellants, allegedly pursuant to section 3 (4) of the Administration of Justice Act 1956. The appellants moved the court to have the writs in both actions set aside or struck out
E on the grounds that the claims brought by the respondents did not fall within the Admiralty jurisdiction of the court or alternatively that such jurisdiction could not properly be exercised in rem on the facts of the case.

Before Brandon J. and the Court of Appeal the appellants sought an alternative order that the actions be stayed pursuant to section 4 (1) of the Arbitration Act 1950, on the ground that under the Lloyd's Open Form the respondents had agreed to submit the matters raised in the
F actions to arbitration. Both Brandon J. and the Court of Appeal held that in the exercise of the court's discretion a stay of the actions should be refused. The appellants did not seek to challenge further that exercise of the discretion of the court and these appeals were confined to the issues concerning the jurisdiction of the court.

The facts are set out in the judgment of Brandon J. [1975] 1 W.L.R. 83.

G *J. Franklin Willmer Q.C.* and *Nicholas Phillips* for the appellant salvors.

Michael Thomas Q.C. and *Anthony Clarke* for the respondent owners of the *Erkowit*.

David Steel for the respondent cargo owners.

Their Lordships took time for consideration.

H March 31, 1976. LORD DIPLOCK. My Lords, in these conjoined appeals the owners of the ship *Jade* seek to set aside writs issued in actions in rem against that vessel, on the ground that by reason of their subject matter the claims in the actions lie outside that part of the jurisdiction of the High Court that may be invoked by an action in rem.

There are two actions: in one of them, the owners of the ship *Erkowit* (" the shipowners ") are the plaintiffs; in the other, the owners of the cargo on the *Erkowit* (" the cargo owners "). The facts that are relevant

to the question of jurisdiction are set out in the judgment of Brandon J. A
and call for no more than a brief summary here.

On October 30, 1970, the *Erkowit,* a vessel on the Sudanese registry, was involved in a collision with a German vessel and was badly holed. This happened in the Bay of Biscay some 50 miles from La Coruña. Some three hours later in response to a summons a salvage tug the *Rotesand* arrived on the scene from La Coruña and a salvage agreement in Lloyd's open form ("the salvage agreement") was entered into by the B
master of the *Erkowit* on behalf of the shipowners and the cargo owners and by the tugmaster on behalf of the appellants in these appeals ("the salvors") who are professional salvors. The salvage agreement was signed on the *Rotesand,* the master and crew of the *Erkowit* having by this time abandoned ship. Pursuant to the salvage agreement the *Rotesand* took the *Erkowit* in tow and made for the port of La Coruña. The tugmaster C
decided to beach the *Erkowit* on an open beach before reaching the entrance to the harbour and to patch the hole in her before proceeding further. The *Erkowit* was accordingly beached by the tug. Subsequently, while she remained on the beach exposed to the weather the salvors attempted to patch her with canvas and wood. The patches proved ineffective; the vessel was broken up by the waves and her cargo swept away. Both the vessel and her cargo became a total loss. Some of the D
cargo consisted of drums of insecticide which is alleged to have caused pollution of the coastal fisheries in the area. In respect of this alleged pollution a suit claiming very substantial damages has been brought in Spain by the Spanish Government against the owners of the *Erkowit.*

The claims of the shipowners and the cargo owners against the salvors are for negligent performance of the salvage agreement. The negligence E
alleged is (1) beaching the *Erkowit* in a place exposed to wind and waves; (2) patching her with wood and canvas instead of with steel and (3) delay in carrying out the operation, sc. after the beaching. The damages claimed by the shipowners include an indemnity against any liability to the Spanish government.

The salvors have no place of business in England where they could be served with a writ in an action in personam. The *Jade* is a vessel F
belonging to the salvors; while within the jurisdiction she was arrested in actions in rem commenced by writs issued in purported pursuance of section 3 (4) of the Administration of Justice Act 1956. The question in these appeals is whether any of the claims of the shipowners and the cargo owners respectively against the salvors are claims in connection with the *Rotesand* which fall within that subsection. If any of them does the High G
Court has jurisdiction to entertain an action in rem against the *Jade* and this appeal must accordingly fail.

The Admiralty jurisdiction of the High Court and the mode in which it can be exercised, i.e. in actions in rem and actions in personam, is regulated by Part I of the Administration of Justice Act 1956. Like Part V, which deals with "Admiralty Jurisdiction and Arrestment of Ships in Scotland" and Schedule II, which contains similar provisions for Northern H
Ireland, Part I of the Act was passed for the purpose, among others, of enabling the United Kingdom to ratify and to comply with the international obligations accepted by States which become parties to the International Convention Relating to the Arrest of Seagoing Ships which had been signed on behalf of the United Kingdom in 1952.

The purpose of that Convention was to provide uniform rules as to the right to arrest seagoing ships by judicial process to secure a maritime

A claim against the owner of the ship. Article 1 defined by reference to their subject matter various classes of maritime claim in respect of which alone a right of arrest was to be exercisable; while articles 2 and 3 granted and confined the right of arrest to either (*a*) the particular ship in respect of which a maritime claim falling within one or more of those classes arose or (*b*) any other ship owned by the person who was, at the time when the maritime claim arose, the owner of the particular ship.

B The provisions of article 3 represented a compromise between the wide powers of arrest available in some of the civil law countries (including for this purpose Scotland) in which jurisdiction to entertain claims against a defendant could be based on the presence within the territorial jurisdiction of any property belonging to him, and the limited powers of arrest available in England and other common law jurisdictions, where the power to
C arrest was exercisable only in respect of claims falling within the Admiralty jurisdiction of the court and based upon a supposed maritime lien over the particular ship in respect of which the claim arose.

The Admiralty jurisdiction of the High Court of England has always been statutory. In 1875 the newly-created High Court of Justice had inherited the jurisdiction previously vested in the High Court of Admiralty. Its Admiralty jurisdiction was subsequently added to piecemeal by statute.
D Immediately before the passing of Part I of the Act of 1956 the claims and questions which fell within Admiralty jurisdiction of the High Court were listed by reference to their subject matter in section 22 of the Supreme Court of Judicature (Consolidation) Act 1925, and by section 33 (2) this jurisdiction was stated to be exercisable "either in proceedings in rem or in proceedings in personam." What distinguished the Admiralty jurisdiction
E from the other civil jurisdiction of the High Court was that it was exercisable in proceedings in rem.

The claims listed as falling within the Admiralty jurisdiction of the High Court under section 22 of the Supreme Court of Judicature (Consolidation) Act 1925 were substantially the same as the maritime claims listed in article 1 of the 1952 Convention, though with some variation in language which is readily accounted for by the fact that the Convention
F was drawn up in the English and French languages, both texts being equally authentic.

The way in which the draftsman of Part I of the Administration of Justice Act 1956 set about his task of bringing the right of arrest of a ship in an action in rem in English courts into conformity with article 3 of the Convention was (*a*) by section 1 of the Act, to substitute a fresh list
G of claims falling within the Admirality jurisdiction of the High Court, and (*b*) by section 3, to regulate the right to bring an action in rem against a ship by reference to the claims so listed. Sections 22 and 33 of the Supreme Court of Judicature (Consolidation) Act was repealed.

Apart from the addition of claims in respect of salvage, towage and pilotage of aircraft (which in any event are not subject to the Convention) there is again no significant difference between what is contained in the
H new list and what was contained in the 1925 list, except that the language is rather more succinct and a little closer to the language of article 1 of the Convention. In contrast to what the English draftsman did, the draftsman of Part V of the Act of 1956, which deals with the Scots courts, was content merely to list in section 47 (2) the claims in respect of which a warrant might be issued for the arrest of a ship; and in doing so he followed much more closely than his English counterpart the language and order of article 1 of the Convention.

One is thus confronted with three lists of claims by reference to which A a right of arrest of a ship in an action in rem may be regulated: (1) the English list in section 1 of the Act; (2) the Scottish list in section 47 of the Act; and (3) the international list in article 1 of the Convention. Except that both English and Scottish lists refer to claims for "damage received by a ship" as well as for damage done by one and the English list includes some services rendered to aircraft, whereas the international list does not, all three lists cover the same ground though with some variations in B language and in order.

As the Act was passed to enable Her Majesty's Government to give effect to the obligations in international law which it would assume on ratifying the Convention to which it was a signatory, the rule of statutory construction laid down in *Salomon* v. *Customs and Excise Commissioners* [1967] 2 Q.B. 116 and *Post Office* v. *Estuary Radio Ltd.* [1968] 2 Q.B. C 740 is applicable. If there be any difference between the language of the statutory provision and that of the corresponding provision of the Convention, the statutory language should be construed in the same sense as that of the Convention if the words of the statute are reasonably capable of bearing that meaning.

In the instant case the obligation assumed by Her Majesty's Government under the Convention was to give effect to it in all three jurisdictions of the D United Kingdom. So there is also a presumption that the Act was intended to have the same consequences as respects the right of arrest of ships in Scotland as it has in England. Accordingly if the language used in the English list is capable of more than one meaning that meaning is to be preferred that is consistent with the language used to describe the corresponding claim in the Scottish list. E

Similar considerations apply to the provisions of the Act and the Convention which provide for the right of arrest of a ship. By article 1 (2) of the Convention "arrest" is defined as "the detention of a ship by judicial process to secure a maritime claim" and by article 2 of the Convention the right is confined to securing those maritime claims only that are listed in article 1. By article 3 the subject of the arrest is "the particular ship in respect of which the maritime claim arose" or one of F its sister ships. The corresponding reference in section 47 (1) of the Act to the subject of the arrest in Scotland is "the ship with which the action is concerned."

In England the matter is governed by section 3 (4) of the Act which reads as follows:

> "In the case of any such claim as is mentioned in paragraphs (*d*) to G (*r*) of subsection (1) of section one of this Act, being a claim arising in connection with a ship, where the person who would be liable on the claim in an action in personam was, when the cause of action arose, the owner or charterer of, or in possession or in control of, the ship, the Admiralty jurisdiction of the High Court . . . may (whether the claim gives rise to a maritime lien on the ship or not) H be invoked by an action in rem against—(*a*) that ship, if at the time when the action is brought it is beneficially owned as respects all the shares therein by that person; or (*b*) any other ship which, at the time when the action is brought, is beneficially owned as aforesaid."

It is clear that to be liable to arrest a ship must not only be the property of the defendant to the action but must also be identifiable as the ship in connection with which the claim made in the action arose (or a sister ship

A of that ship). The nature of the " connection " between the ship and the claim must have been intended to be the same as is expressed in the corresponding phrase in the Convention " the particular ship in respect of which the maritime claim arose." One must therefore look at the description of each of the maritime claims included in the list in order to identify the particular ship in respect of which a claim of that description could arise.

B The claims described in the separate paragraphs in the lists in section 1 (1) and section 47 (2) of the Act and article 1 (1) of the Convention are not mutually exclusive. As article 1 (1) of the Convention explicitly recognises, a claim may well fall under two or more of them. The shipowners have sought to classify their claim under paragraphs (*d*), (*e*) and (*h*) of section 1 (1) of the Act; the cargo owners have relied on (*d*), (*g*)
C and (*h*).

As it is sufficient to dispose of this appeal that the claims should fall within any of these paragraphs, I propose first to deal with (*h*). In the English list in section 1 (1) of the Act this reads: " (*h*) any claim arising out of any agreement relating to the carriage of goods in a ship or to the use or hire of a ship."

The corresponding provision in article 1 (1) of the Convention is split
D into two paragraphs:

> " . . . a claim arising out of . . . (*d*) agreement relating to the use or hire of any ship whether by charterparty or otherwise; (*e*) agreement relating to the carriage of goods in any ship whether by charterparty or otherwise."

The Scottish list in section 47 (2) of the Act follows the same wording
E as the Convention.

My Lords, neither Brandon J. nor any of the members of the Court of Appeal had any doubt that both the shipowners' and the cargo owners' claims fell within paragraph (*h*) as being a claim arising out of an agreement relating to the use of a ship, the *Rotesand*.

The salvage agreement was entered into by the master of the *Erkowit*
F on behalf of the cargo owners as well as the shipowners. The primary contractual obligation of the salvor under the agreement in Lloyd's open form is to use his best endeavours to bring the vessel and her cargo to a place of safety, providing at his own risk, in the time-honoured phrase, " all proper steam and other assistance and labour." The only possible way in which the salvors could perform their contract was by taking the *Erkowit* in tow and using the tug that had been sent to the scene of the
G casualty for that very purpose— the *Rotesand*.

I agree that in any ordinary meaning of those words the salvage agreement was " an agreement relating to the use of a ship," the *Rotesand*, for the purpose of salving the *Erkowit* and her cargo and bringing them to a place of safety, which it was contemplated by the parties would be La Coruña. The shipowners' and cargo owners' claims are claims for damages
H for negligent performance of that agreement and so far as the negligence alleged includes an averment that the *Erkowit* was towed by the *Rotesand* on a course which beached her on a dangerous shore the claim arises out of the negligent performance of that part of the agreement for which a ship was to be used.

On behalf of the salvors it has been submitted that the words " agreement relating to the use or hire of any ship " should be understood in a very restricted meaning. The ground of this submission is that very similar words "any claim arising out of any agreement made in relation to the A use or hire of any ship" appeared in section 2 (1) of the County Courts (Admiralty Jurisdiction) Act (1868) Amendment Act 1869, as one of three subject matters in respect of which that Act conferred upon county courts jurisdiction exercisable in an action in rem. No similar jurisdiction was exercisable in rem at that date by the High Court of Admiralty or after 1875 until 1920 by the High Court of Justice. In *Reg.* v. *City of London Court Judge* [1892] 1 Q.B. 273 Lord Esher M.R. in the Court of Appeal B expressed the view that Parliament should be presumed not to have intended to confer upon a county court a jurisdiction exercisable in rem which was wider than the corresponding jurisdiction in rem of the High Court and that though the court was bound by a previous decision (*The Alina* (1880) 5 Ex.D. 227) to accept that a claim arising out of a charterparty was within the section although it did not give rise to an action C in rem in the High Court, the words should so far as possible be construed so as to confine the jurisdiction of the county court to subject matters in respect of which jurisdiction in an action in rem was exercisable by the High Court.

My Lords, this was not a decision which ascribed a specific and precise meaning to the words "an agreement relating to the use or hire of a ship." The reasons given in the judgment for giving a restricted meaning D to words conferring Admiralty jurisdiction on county courts, in the context in which they appeared in the Act of 1869, have no application in the context of Part I of the Administration of Justice Act 1956, which is dealing with the jurisdiction of the High Court itself. I see no reason in that context for not giving to them their ordinary wide meaning. That would include the salvage agreement in the instant case. E

I would therefore hold that the claims of both shipowners and cargo owners fall within paragraph (*h*) of section 1 (1); that they are claims in connection with the *Rotesand*; and that they are enforceable under section 3 (4) by an action in rem against the *Rotesand* or any of her sister ships.

Strictly speaking this makes it unnecessary to decide whether the shipowners' and cargo owners' claims also came within paragraph (*d*), viz. "damage done by a ship" or, as it is phrased in article 1 of the Conven- F tion "damage caused by any ship either in collision or otherwise"; but as this was a matter on which the Court of Appeal differed from Brandon J. I will express my views upon it briefly. The figurative phrase "damage done by a ship" is a term of art in maritime law whose meaning is well settled by authority. (*The Vera Cruz* (*No. 2*) (1884) 9 P.D. 96; *Currie* v. *M'Knight* [1897] A.C. 97.) To fall within the phrase not only must the G damage be the direct result or natural consequence of something done by those engaged in the navigation of the ship but the ship itself must be the actual instrument by which the damage was done. The commonest case is that of collision, which is specifically mentioned in the Convention: but physical contact between the ship and whatever object sustains the damage is not essential—a ship may negligently cause a wash by which some other H vessel or some property on shore is damaged.

In the instant case the act of casting off the *Erkowit* in such a way as to beach her upon an exposed shore was something done by those engaged in the navigation of the *Rotesand*, as a result of which the *Erkowit* and her cargo were left exposed to the risk of being damaged by wind and wave if the weather worsened before she could be removed to a more sheltered position.

I do not understand it to be claimed that the actual beaching caused any physical damage to ship or cargo, but for the purposes of this appeal it must be assumed that the chain of causation is unbroken between the beaching of the *Erkowit* and her subsequent breaking-up by wind and wave. Had the damage been caused by the beaching, there could in my view have been no question but that the *Rotesand* could properly be regarded as the actual instrument by which that damage was done. Although for my part I find this a borderline case, I do not think that the intervening failure of the appellants to take steps to avert the risk of damage, which forms the subject of the alternative grounds of negligence, prevents the *Rotesand* from remaining the actual instrument by which the damage subsequent to the beaching was done. I accordingly agree with the Court of Appeal that the shipowners' and cargo owners' claims also fall under paragraph (*d*) of section 1 (1).

Before concluding I should deal with the suggestions (i) that the cargo owners' claims fell also under paragraph (*g*) of section 1 (1) as being a "claim for loss or damage to goods carried in a ship," and (ii) that the shipowners' claim fell also under paragraph (*e*) as being a claim for "damage received by a ship." These were both matters of concession by the salvors before Brandon J. where the argument was confined to the exclusion from paragraph (*e*) of so much of the shipowners' claim as related to an indemnity in respect of any liability of the shipowners to the Spanish Government for pollution of the fisheries. The concessions were, however, withdrawn when the case reached the Court of Appeal.

The cargo owners' claim clearly falls within the description in paragraph (*g*) which reproduces in terms that are practically identical paragraph (*f*) of article 1 (1) of the Convention: but, as I have already pointed out, the right of arrest conferred by section 3 (4) is confined to the ship in connection with which the claim arose (or a sister ship). The claims to which the right of arrest is confined are those mentioned in paragraphs (*d*) to (*r*) of section 1 (1). With three exceptions, each of those paragraphs contains an express reference to "a ship." The ship referred to in each of these paragraphs is the ship in connection with which a claim under that paragraph arises. The three exceptions relate to claims in respect of salvage, general average and bottomry where there can be no doubt as to the ship in connection with which claims of that nature arise. Paragraph (*g*) therefore permits the arrest of the ship in which the goods which have been lost or damaged were carried, in an action in rem by cargo owners against the owner of the carrying vessel. It does not authorise the arrest of any other ship: authority for that must be found under some other paragraph. So the arrest of the *Rotesand* as security for the cargo owners' claim was not authorised under paragraph (*g*) of section 1 (1).

Paragraph (*e*) has no counterpart in article 1 (1) of the Convention. "Damage received by a ship" if it gives rise to any claim against a ship at all gives rise to a claim against the ship that caused the damage and not the ship that received it. So any right of arrest under the Convention could not arise in respect of a claim of this description. In so far as section 1 (1) of the Act defines the Admiralty jurisdiction of the High Court, by reference to which a similar jurisdiction is by section 2 conferred upon the Liverpool Court of Passage and county courts, the inclusion of paragraph (*e*) is not inappropriate. "Damage received by [a] ship" is a time-honoured phrase that was first used in section 6 of the Admiralty Court Act 1840 to extend the jurisdiction of the High Court of Admiralty to claims for damage received by a ship when within the body of a country. Such jurisdiction had been previously confined to damage received by a ship while on the high seas. This section was narrowly construed by Dr. Lushington in *The Bilbao* (1860) Lush. 149 so as to exclude damage done *by* a ship—a lacuna that was promptly filled by section 7 of the Admiralty Court Act 1861. These two sections regulated the Admiralty jurisdiction of the High Court until 1925, when the expressions "damage received by a ship" and "damage done by a ship" were reproduced in section 22 of the Supreme Court of Judicature (Consolidation) Act 1925 to describe a part of its Admiralty jurisdiction.

The description "any claim for any damage received by a ship" describes a claim arising "in connection with" the ship that receives the damage. In such a claim the owners of the ship that receives the damage would be plaintiffs. They cannot invoke the Admiralty jurisdiction by an action in rem against their own ship; and any claim to arrest some other ship must be founded upon some paragraph other than (*e*). Had the draftsman of section 3 (4) been meticulous he would have omitted any reference to paragraph (*e*) of section 1 (1); but the other requirements of the subsection prevent any right of arrest arising under that paragraph.

I would dismiss this appeal.

Lord Simon of Glaisdale. My Lords, I have had the advantage of reading in draft the speech prepared by my noble and learned friend, Lord Diplock. I agree with it, and I would therefore dismiss the appeal.

Lord Kilbrandon. My Lords, I have had the advantage of reading the speech prepared by my noble and learned friend, Lord Diplock. I agree with it and I too would dismiss this appeal.

Lord Salmon. My Lords, I have had the advantage of reading the speech prepared by my noble and learned friend Lord Diplock.

For the reasons given by him, I would dismiss this appeal.

Lord Edmund-Davies. My Lords, for the reasons appearing in the printed speech of my noble and learned friend, Lord Diplock, I concur in holding that the appeal should be dismissed.

Appeal dismissed.

Solicitors: *Richards, Butler & Co.; Ince & Co.*

J. A. G.

A

[CHANCERY DIVISION]

* PRACTICE DIRECTION (CHANCERY DIVISION: MOTIONS)

1976 April 13 Megarry V.-C.

B *Practice — Chancery Division — Motion — Agreed adjournment— Procedure*

MEGARRY V.-C. read the following statement in court. With a view to effecting a saving of time and costs, the judges of the Chancery Division have decided that the following optional procedure for the agreed adjournment of motions should come into effect forthwith.

C 1. If all parties to a motion agree to do so, and no undertakings to the court are to be given, a motion can be adjourned for not more than 14 days by counsel or solicitors for all parties, or for any party, attending before the registrar in chambers between 2 p.m. and 4 p.m. on the day before the motion day, or between 10 a.m. and 11.30 a.m. on the motion day, and producing a consent or consents, signed by counsel or solicitors D representing all parties, agreeing to the adjournment. If a litigant in person is a party, he must attend before the registrar as well as signing a consent.

2. Not more than three successive adjournments may be made under this procedure, and no adjournment under it may be made to the last two motion days of any sittings.

E 3. The procedure is purely optional, and adjournments may continue to be made in court in the usual way, even in cases to which this procedure is applicable. In particular, an application for an adjournment must continue to be made in court in any case in which the parties are not in complete agreement as to the adjournment, or in which any undertaking to the court is to be given. The procedure may, however, be used where undertakings are to be given not to the court but to one or more F of the parties.

4. This procedure will in the first instance be applicable for a trial period until the end of 1976. Towards the end of that period the judges of the division will reconsider the procedure in relation (inter alia) to the extent to which it appears to have contributed towards a saving of time and costs, and to whether the procedure can properly be extended to cases G in which undertakings to the court are to be given.

A. R.

H

A

[CHANCERY DIVISION]

* CARRADINE PROPERTIES LTD. *v.* ASLAM

[1975 C. No. 3380]

1975 Nov. 6 — Goulding J. B

Landlord and Tenant—Notice to quit—Error in notice—Break clause in 21 year lease providing for earlier determination—Landlord's notice giving past date for termination—Whether notice valid

Clause 5 of a lease for a 21 year term from September 27, 1968, provided for its earlier determination by either party C to the lease at the end of the first 7 or 14 years on 12 months' previous notice in writing. A notice by the landlords dated September 6, 1974, served on the tenant stated: ". . . we hereby give you notice that we intend to determine the term created by the lease on September 27, 1973, and that we require you to quit and deliver up possession . . . on that date." The date named in the notice should have been September 27, 1975. D

On the question whether the notice to quit was invalidated by the giving of an incorrect date for determination of the lease:—

Held, that applying legal principles to the landlords' notice and adopting a benevolent approach, the court would treat the giving of a date past for termination of the lease as a slip which would be obvious to a reasonable tenant reading the notice and knowing the terms of the lease; that therefore E the notice would be interpreted as an intention on the part of the landlords to determine the lease on September 27, 1975, and accordingly, subject to Part II of the Landlord and Tenant Act, 1954, the notice to quit was valid.

Doe d. Duke of Bedford v. *Kightley* (1796) 7 Term Rep. 63 applied.

Hankey v. *Clavering* [1942] 2 K.B. 326, C.A. distinguished. F

The following cases are referred to in the judgment:

Cadby v. *Martinez* (1840) 11 Ad. & El. 720.

Doe d. Lord Huntingtower v. *Culliford* (1824) 4 Dow. & Ry. 248.

Doe d. Duke of Bedford v. *Kightley* (1796) 7 Term Rep. 63.

Doe d. Spicer v. *Lea* (1809) 11 East 312.

Doe d. Richmond Corporation v. *Morphett* (1845) 7 Q.B. 577. G

Doe d. Williams v. *Smith* (1836) 5 Ad. & El. 350.

Hankey v. *Clavering* [1942] 2 K.B. 326; [1942] 2 All E.R. 311, C.A.

Wride v. *Dyer* [1900] 1 Q.B. 23.

No additional cases were cited in argument.

ADJOURNED SUMMONS. H

The plaintiff landlords, Carradine Properties Ltd., by their summons dated April 8, 1975, sought a declaration that a notice to quit premises on the ground floor of 5 Lancelot Parade, Wembley, served by them on the defendant, Miam Mohammed Aslam, on September 11, 1974, operated so as validly to determine the defendant's tenancy of the premises on September 27, 1975, in accordance with the terms of a lease of September

A 27, 1968, whereunder the defendant held the premises as tenant and subject to the provisions of the Landlord and Tenant Act 1954.

The facts are stated in the judgment of Goulding J.

R. J. Moshi for the landlords.
T. R. F. Jennings for the tenant.

B GOULDING J. This case concerns a short construction point which is not concluded by authority nor entirely easy to decide.

By a lease dated September 27, 1968, a company called Hazell & Co. (Publicity) Ltd., a predecessor of the plaintiff company, demised certain small business premises at 5 Lancelot Parade, Wembley, to Muhammad Shakil, a predecessor of the defendant, at a rent of £1,200 per annum for
C a term of 21 years less three days from September 27, 1968. The reversion is now vested in the plaintiff company and the defendant is the assignee of the lease.

Clause 5 of the lease contains a provision in a not unusual form for its earlier determination at the end of the first 7 or 14 years of the term on the giving of 12 months' previous notice by either party. Clause 5 is as follows:

D "Provided always and it is hereby agreed if either party shall desire to determine the present demise at the expiration of the first seven or 14 years of the said term and shall give 12 months previous notice in writing of such its or his desire and (in the case of determination by the lessee) if the lessee shall up to the time of such determination pay the rent and perform and observe the covenants on his part herein-
E before contained then immediately on the expiration of such seven or 14 years as the case may be the present demise and everything herein contained shall cease without prejudice to the remedies of either party against the other in respect of any antecedent claim or breach of covenant."

It is common ground that the correct date for termination at the end of
F the first seven years would be September 27, 1975, and the case has been argued throughout on that footing. A notice dated September 6, 1974, was on that day (or very shortly thereafter in course of post) served by the plaintiff company's solicitors. It read as follows:

"In pursuance of the proviso contained in a lease dated September 27, 1968, and made between Hazell & Co. (Publicity) Ltd. of the one
G part and Muhammad Shakil of the other part we hereby give you notice that we intend to determine the term created by the lease on September 17, 1973, and that we require you to quit and deliver up possession of the premises comprised in the said lease on that date."

It is clear that a clerical error occurred and that 1973, already passed, was typed instead of 1975, the correct year. The question is whether that
H invalidates the notice for the purpose of the lease. At the outset, it appeared to me that even were the notice correct, it would have been ineffectual by reason of section 24 of the Landlord and Tenant Act 1954, but I have been assured by both counsel that it does have some effect because it clears the ground, as it were, for a shorter notice under the statute, so I will say no more on that.

Mr. Moshi for the plaintiff company cited a number of cases. I will first refer to *Doe d. Duke of Bedford* v. *Kightley* (1796) 7 Term Rep. 63, which somewhat resembles the present case, and will read the essential A facts and the judgment:

> " On the trial of this ejectment at the last assizes before Lord Chief Justice Eyre, the defendant, who was a tenant to the lessor of the plaintiff, objected to the notice to quit, which was served just before Michaelmas 1795 and was to quit ' at Lady-Day, which will be in the year 1795.' " Lord Kenyon C.J., giving judgment, said " the B time when the notice was given and the words in it ' which will be ' manifestly showed that this was a notice to quit at the then next Lady-Day; and the conduct of the parties also showed that they so considered it. Then the year 1795 in the notice may be rejected as an impossible year."

It does not appear from the report what the conduct of the parties was. C All that appears is some indication of a conversation prior to service of the notice.

Mr. Moshi cited other cases on notices to quit: *Doe d. Lord Huntingtower* v. *Culliford* (1824) 4 Dow. & Ry. 248; *Doe d. Williams* v. *Smith* (1836) 5 Ad. & El. 350; *Doe d. Richmond Corporation* v. *Morphett* (1845) 7 Q.B. 577; *Wride* v. *Dyer* [1900] 1 Q.B. 23. The only relevance of those cases, it seems to me, is that one can see a general principle in them D that the court allows common sense to enter into the interpretation of an inaccurate notice to quit. I will cite two passages. In *Doe d. Williams* v. *Smith*, 5 Ad. & El. 350, Patteson J. said, at p. 353: " It is not required that a notice should be worded with the accuracy of a plea. This is not drawn with strict precision; but I think it is sufficiently clear." Then in the latest of the cases, *Wride* v. *Dyer* [1900] 1 Q.B. 23, Ridley J. said, E at p. 25:

> " I agree, however, with the rule laid down . . . that we must look at the intention of the landlord, and that when language is used which leaves the effect of the notice open to doubt, the rule of construction is to make it sensible and not insensible."

Darling J. agreed, at p. 26: F

> " But what is the rule of construction of such documents as this? It is laid down, I think, by Bayley J. in *Doe d. Lord Huntingtower* v. *Culliford* (1824) 4 D. & R. 248 and it was well expressed by Sir John Jervis in arguing the case of *Doe d. Williams* v. *Smith*, 5 A. & E. 350. ' The court ' he says, ' will give an interpretation to the notice consistent with the intention of the party serving it, if clear.' " G

I would put the test generally applicable as being this: " Is the notice quite clear to a reasonable tenant reading it? Is it plain that he cannot be misled by it? " Applying that test, if applicable, to the present case, I think the notice would be saved because the tenant receiving that notice and knowing the terms of the lease must have seen there was a mistake, H as it would not say " 1973 " in 1974. Once that is accepted, it is obvious that the notice is for 1975 and not 1973. In no ordinary circumstances would a reasonable tenant knowing the terms of the lease take the notice as being other than for 1975. It therefore seems to me that if one applies the test I have mentioned, then the notice would be saved. However, there is a case of a later date and higher authority than those I have referred to which Mr. Jennings for the defendant says would lead

A to a different result. It is *Hankey* v. *Clavering* [1942] 2 K.B. 326. The headnote reads as follows:

> "Under the terms of a lease for 21 years from December 25, 1934, either party could determine the tenancy at the end of seven years on giving six months' notice. The landlord gave to the tenant's solicitors a notice as from June 21, 1941, which purported to determine the B lease on December 21, 1941. The solicitors subsequently acknowledged the receipt of this notice, saying that it had been properly served on them:—*Held*, that the notice, although the mistake as to date was obviously due to a slip on the part of the landlord, was invalid, and that the acceptance of its service by the solicitors did not cure the defect."

C Lord Greene M.R. said, at p. 328:

> "By his letter of January 15, 1940, the plaintiff, on the face of it, was purporting to determine the lease by notice on December 21, 1941. The whole thing was obviously a slip on his part, and there is a natural temptation to put a strained construction on language in aid of people who have been unfortunate enough to make slips. That, however, is a temptation which must be resisted, because documents are not to D be strained and principles of construction are not to be outraged in order to do what may appear to be fair in an individual case. . . ."

and, at p. 329:

> "That takes me back to the real point, namely, whether or not the notice was good, in the sense that it had the effect of terminating the E lease on December 25, 1941. Notices of this kind are documents of a technical nature, technical because they are not consensual documents, but, if they are in proper form, they have of their own force without any assent by the recipient the effect of bringing the demise to an end. They must on their face and on a fair and reasonable construction do what the lease provides that they are to do. It is perfectly true that in construing such a document, as in construing all documents, F the court in a case of ambiguity will lean in favour of reading the document in such a way as to give it validity, but I dissent entirely from the proposition that, where a document is clear and specific, but inaccurate on some matter, such as that of date, it is possible to ignore the inaccuracy and substitute the correct date or other particular because it appears that the error was inserted by a slip. By the clear G wording of this notice the plaintiff purported to bring the lease to an end on December 21, 1941. In so doing he was attempting to do something which he had no power to do, and, however much the recipient might guess, or however certain he might be, that it was a mere slip, that would not cure the defect because the document was never capable on its face of producing the necessary legal consequence."

H

Then Lord Greene M.R. pointed out that he was following *Cadby* v. *Martinez* (1840) 11 Ad. & El. 720. I have been referred to that case also and to *Doe d. Spicer* v. *Lea* (1809) 11 East 312. It is to be noted that most of the cases Mr. Moshi has cited to me were referred to by counsel in *Hankey* v. *Clavering* [1942] 2 K.B. 326 but neither Lord Greene M.R. nor Lord Clauson commented on them. They did not say they were wrong nor in terms distinguish them. Mr. Jennings suggests that that was because of a fundamental distinction between an ordinary notice to quit, terminating a yearly or periodic tenancy, and a break clause in a demise for a fixed term such as that in the present case and in *Hankey* v. *Clavering.* That is not explicitly mentioned by the Court of Appeal as a distinction of importance, and I think it must not be pressed too far. I suppose a break clause can be said to be more in the nature of an option conferring a benefit than a clause providing for a notice to quit in a periodic tenancy, but the latter like the former is a unilateral document which has to be sufficient in form and contents. It acts by its own force to release a given party from an obligation otherwise lying on him. Lord Greene M.R. said, at p. 329: "Notices of this kind are documents of a technical nature, technical because they are not consensual documents." That description fits a notice to quit under a periodic tenancy as well as one under a break clause so that, while recognising the distinction, I must not take it too far. Further, I am not persuaded that the distinction is of so much importance for the present case as Mr. Jennings submitted. In an option clause the requirement is that a party must strictly comply with the condition for its exercise. If the condition includes the giving of a particular notice, it seems to me that the logical first approach is to interpret the notice, looking at the words and applying legal principles to their construction, and then ask whether it complies with the strict requirements as to exercise of the option. If that is right, I think a benevolent approach could be applied in this case, as in the *Duke of Bedford's* case (1796) 7 Term Rep. 63, because reasonably read by a reasonable tenant the mistake is obvious on the face of it, and there is no doubt what the mistake was. Therefore one interprets the notice as asserting an intention to determine in 1975. It is true that if whoever made the mistake had typed 1976 instead of 1973, the error would probably have been incurable because although the tenant might suspect there was a slip, it might be that the landlord did intend 1976, not knowing or understanding his rights under the lease. In such a case the tenant would be entitled to disregard the notice but because a past date was given in the notice it is insensible and therefore an authority such as the *Duke of Bedford's* case is in point.

I will make a declaration in favour of the plaintiff company that, on the true construction of the notice to quit, it is a valid notice, subject to the provisions of Part II of the Landlord and Tenant Act 1954, to determine the demise at the expiration of the first seven years in accordance with clause 5 of the lease.

Declaration accordingly.
No order as to costs.

Solicitors: *D. J. Freeman & Co.; Child & Child.*

K. N. B.

A

[CHANCERY DIVISION]

* POLICYHOLDERS PROTECTION BOARD *v.* OFFICIAL RECEIVER

B [1976 T. No. 279]

1976 Jan. 26, 27, 28 — Brightman J.

Company—Winding up—Liquidator—Indemnity—Insurance company's insolvency—Power of liquidator to make interim payments to policyholders—Indemnity of liquidator by Policy- C *holders Protection Board—Whether personal indemnity only—Policyholders Protection Act* 1975 (*c.* 75), *s.* 15 (3) (*b*) [1]

On July 28, 1975, the official receiver was appointed provisional liquidator of an insurance company, pending the hearing of a petition for the compulsory winding up presented by the Secretary of State for Trade. Subsequently the provisional liquidator and the Policyholders Protection Board, D established by the Policyholders Protection Act 1975, entered into negotiations to agree an arrangement for making interim payments to certain policyholders. It was proposed that the board should give the provisional liquidator an indemnity in order to secure that interim payments were made by him out of the assets of the company under his control. To that end the provisional liquidator caused to be prepared alternative draft deeds of indemnity. The first contained an undertaking E by the board to indemnify the provisional liquidator against any *personal* liability resulting from his making interim payments. The second made the same provision for such interim payments and personally indemnified the liquidator but also contained a direct covenant by the board that if the company was liquidated, it would make good any shortfall of assets resulting from the interim payments.

On a summons to determine whether under section F 15 (3) (*b*) of the Policyholders Protection Act 1975 the board had power to enter into the second form of indemnity:—

Held, that a narrow construction of section 15 (3) (*b*) of the Policyholders Protection Act would largely stultify the intention of the paragraph, and that on its true construction it enabled the board to give an indemnity to a liquidator not only in his personal capacity but in his capacity as guardian of the assets of the company so as to protect it against loss.

G

The following cases are referred in the judgment:

Jackson (*Francis*) *Developments Ltd.* v. *Hall* [1951] 2 K.B. 488; [1951] 2 All E.R. 74, C.A.

Seaford Court Estates Ltd. v. *Asher* [1949] 2 K.B. 481; [1949] 2 All E.R. 155, C.A.

H The following additional cases were cited in argument:

Attorney-General v. *Lockwood* (1842) 9 M. & W. 378.

Knowles v. *Scott* [1891] 1 Ch. 717.

[Reported by MRS. F. ALLEN MCLEAN, Barrister-at-Law]

[1] Policyholders Protection Act 1975, s. 15 (3): see post, p. 449D.

ORIGINATING SUMMONS

On January 23, 1976, the official receiver issued an ex parte summons for directions as to the indemnity he would require to make interim payments to certain policy holders of Fidelity Life Assurance Ltd. for which he had been appointed provisional liquidator on July 28, 1975. In order that the court could decide the construction of section 15 (3) (*b*) of the Policyholders Protection Act 1975, the Policyholders Protection Board issued a summons on January 27, 1976, to determine its powers, the official receiver, as provisional liquidator, being the only defendant. The Secretary of State for Trade, although not a party, appeared by counsel, and was given leave to address the court. The company and its parent company, Fidelity Corporation Inc., although not parties, were also represented.

The facts are stated in the judgment.

D. J. Nicholls Q.C. and *David Oliver* for the plaintiffs.

J. R. Sykes for the official receiver.

J. M. Chadwick and *Elizabeth Gloster* for the Secretary of State for Trade.

E. W. Hamilton for the company and Fidelity Corporation Inc.

BRIGHTMAN J. This originating summons to which the official receiver is the defendant was issued yesterday by the Policyholders Protection Board. It seeks the determination of a question of construction arising on the wording of the Policyholders Protection Act 1975.

Previously I had before me a petition presented in the companies court by the Secretary of State for Trade for the compulsory winding up of a company known as Fidelity Life Assurance Ltd. There was also a summons issued by the official receiver in his capacity as provisional liquidator. That summons was designed to clarify the powers and duties of the Policyholders Protection Board under section 15 of the Act, but it has not been proceeded with for the time being for reasons which I will mention.

The company was incorporated in 1966 to carry on the business of life assurance. In 1974 the company came under observation by the Secretary of State. In January 1975 the company undertook not to effect further contracts of insurance. On July 28, 1975, the Secretary of State presented a petition for the winding up of the company. The petition asserts that it is expedient for the company to be wound up. It also asserts that the company is insolvent. On the same day the official receiver was appointed provisional liquidator pending the hearing of the petition.

The Policyholders Protection Board was established as a body corporate by the Act of 1975. The principal functions of the board are to assist policyholders who may be prejudiced as a result of the inability of an insurance company to meet its liabilities under policies; also to impose levies on insurance companies for the purpose of financing the board's expenditure. The general scheme of the Act is that the board will, in the event of the voluntary or compulsory liquidation of an insurance company that falls within the ambit of the Act, secure that most of the policyholders are paid all, or a high percentage of, the benefits due to them under their policies. I refer to " most " policyholders, because certain types of policies are excluded from the Act. The board also have power to secure that interim payments are made to policyholders so that they do not suffer hardship during the interval which is bound to elapse between the time

A when an insurance company gets into difficulties and the time when some appropriate rescue operation is organised by the board. The carrying out of the scheme of the Act naturally involves money, and that money comes from the imposition of the levy which I have mentioned. In addition, the board have a limited power to borrow money.

In the case with which I am concerned, as I have already mentioned, the petition for a compulsory winding up order has been presented and
B the official receiver is in the saddle as provisional liquidator. No winding up order has been made and no rescue operation has been finalised. The provisional liquidator and the board are currently in negotiation with the object of agreeing an arrangement which will enable interim payments to be made to policyholders, some of whom claim that they are suffering hardship because of non-payment of annuities, death benefits and so on.

C I turn to the provisions of the Act which enable interim payments to be made to policyholders. They are to be found in section 15. Subsections (1) and (2) provide that interim payments are appropriate to be made in the case of certain classes of policy where the company is in compulsory or voluntary liquidation or has had a provisional liquidator appointed in anticipation of a compulsory order.

D Subsection (3):

> " In any case where it appears to the board to be desirable to do so, the board may—(*a*) make payments to or on behalf of policy holders who are eligible for assistance under this section, on such terms (including any terms requiring repayment, in whole or in part) and on such conditions as the board may think fit; or (*b*) secure that payments are made to or on behalf of any such policyholders by the
> E liquidator or the provisional liquidator by giving him an indemnity covering any such payments or any class or description of such payments."

Paragraph (*a*) is not directly relevant. It is not in this case proposed that the board themselves should make any payment to policyholders. What is proposed is that the board should give the provisional liquidator
F an indemnity in order to secure that interim payments are made by him out of the assets of the company under his control.

The solicitors retained by the provisional liquidator have prepared draft forms of indemnity in alternative forms. However, a difficulty has arisen on the construction of section 15 (3) (*b*), as a result of which counsel acting for the board felt unable to give an unqualified opinion to the
G board that they would be acting within their statutory powers if they entered into a deed of indemnity in the form desired by the provisional liquidator.

The two alternative draft deeds are in evidence. One draft, which I will call the two-party deed, is expressed to be made between the board of the one part and the official receiver as provisional liquidator of the
H other part. By this deed the provisional liquidator would undertake in broad effect to procure that the company should make certain interim payments to policyholders until a winding up order is made, or until a scheme approved by the board comes into operation. The board, for their part, would undertake to indemnify the provisional liquidator against any *personal* liability arising from the fact that he permits such payments to be made and thereby reduces the assets available for distribution in a winding up. For example, the interim payments may prove to be in excess

of the funds to which the recipients are ultimately shown to be entitled in A
the liquidation.

The other draft I will call the three-party deed. This is expressed to be made between the board of the first part, the company of the second part and the provisional liquidator of the third part. The deed makes the same provision for interim payments but would contain a direct covenant by the board that if the company is liquidated the board will make good to the company any shortfall in assets available for distribution as B
a result of such interim payments being made.

The principal difference between the two drafts is that, under the two-party deed, the board only provide a *personal* indemnity for the liquidator in case he is sued because the assets have been reduced as a result of the interim payments and thereby creditors have been prejudiced; under the three-party deed, the board actually makes good any such shortfall for C
the benefit of all who thereby suffer.

It is necessary to descend into a little more detail. I take the two-party deed first. Clause 1 provides that the provisional liquidator shall procure that the company shall make the interim payments to policyholders which are specified in the first schedule, such payments to be treated as payments to the policyholders on account. The obligation of the provisional liquidator to procure the company to make such payments D
is to cease in certain events, notably when the company is wound up or a scheme approved by the board comes into operation or the end of this current year. Under clause 2 the board are to indemnify the liquidator against all liability which he may incur *personally* as a result of such interim payments. In particular, the indemnity is to cover his liability by reason of any diminution in the assets available for distribution in a E
winding up, due to the interim payments proving to have been excessive, or increased taxation as a result of the making of such interim payments, or loss of interest resulting from the premature distribution of the company's assets, or the extra administrative expenses involved.

The three-party deed is similar, except that it contains a provision, which is the substantive part of subclause (2) (b), as follows:

> ". . . the board hereby undertakes to the provisional liquidator and F
> to [the company] that it shall, so soon as there has been conclusively determined (pursuant to subclause (g) below) the amount of any reduction of the assets available for distribution in any winding up of [the company] as a result of the payments provided for in clause 1 above being made, pay to [the company] in full in cash the amount of such reduction." G

It also contains a personal indemnity for the protection of the provisional liquidator.

The matter came before me in the first instance in the form of an ex parte summons by the provisional liquidator seeking directions in relation to the proposed resumption of payments to the policyholders and in relation to the form of indemnity which the provisional liquidator should require H
from the board to enable such payments to be made. Although the board are not respondents formally to the summons, they were given notice of it and appeared by counsel. When that summons was opened, the provisional liquidator intimated that he merely sought directions from the court, while the board intimated that they were content to act in whatever way the court decided was proper. This did not seem to me to be a satisfactory way of resolving what was presented as a question of construction

A of section 15 (3). In the upshot, counsel for the board agreed, in order to
enable the question of construction to be decided by the court, to present
to the court the arguments in favour of the narrow construction of paragraph
(*b*), leaving counsel for the provisional liquidator to argue in favour of the
wider powers of the board.

Counsel for the board made it abundantly clear that he would argue
in favour of the narrow construction of section 15, not because the board
B favoured that construction, but so that I should hear arguments on both
sides. I am indebted to him for his assistance and I may say that the
circumstances in which he has been constrained to wear this somewhat
unwelcome mantle have not in any way inhibited the cogency of his sub-
missions.

The position now is that an originating summons has been issued by
C the board under the ordinary procedure of the Chancery Division for the
determination of the question whether upon the true construction of
section 15 (3) (*b*), the board have power in law to enter into a deed in the
form of the three-party deed. The official receiver, as the provisional
liquidator, is the only defendant to that summons. However, the Secretary
of State for Trade, though not a party, has appeared before me, by counsel,
and was given leave to address the court. The Secretary of State has a
D statutory duty under the Policyholders Protection Act 1975 to nominate
the members of the board and he also has the right to give policy directions
to the board. He is therefore intimately concerned with the extent of the
powers of the board and he has joined forces in argument with the pro-
visional liquidator.

The issue before me is the short one whether the powers of the board
E under section 15 (3) (*b*) are confined to affording a liquidator or provisional
liquidator an indemnity against any *personal* liability resulting from interim
payments, or whether the board are authorised to give to the company
itself an undertaking to make good any shortfall of assets resulting there-
from. The principal arguments in favour of construing paragraph (*b*) as
authorising only the giving of *personal* protection to the liquidator are
shortly these. The paragraph refers to "giving him an indemnity"—that is
F to say, giving to *the liquidator or provisional liquidator* an indemnity. If
an instrument contains a provision for giving to a fiduciary an indemnity
in respect of a certain act to be done by him, one would normally read that
provision as referring only to an indemnity to protect the fiduciary against
personal liability. The provision would not, prima facie, be taken to mean
compensation for the benefit of those to whom the fiduciary is answerable.

G So, it is said, that is the construction which I ought to place upon
paragraph (*b*). It is supported, it is submitted, by a comparison between
section 15 (3) and section 13 (2). Section 13 (2) relates to distributions which
do not partake of the character of interim payments. In such a case the
Act provides that the board may secure the payment of any sums to
policyholders, either: "(*a*) by themselves making payments in respect of
H the sum in question," corresponding to paragraph (a) in the other section,
or "(*b*) by securing by any measures appearing to them to be appropriate
that such payments are made by any other person." "Appropriate"
measures are amplified by paragraph 7 (3) of Schedule 1 to the Act. They
include:

> "(*a*) the making of payments to any person, on such terms (including
> terms requiring repayment, in whole or in part) and on such conditions
> as the board think fit; (*b*) the giving of guarantees or indemnities to

or in favour of any person; and (*c*) the making of any other agreement or arrangement with or for the benefit of any person."

Paragraph (*b*) in section 13 can appropriately be contrasted with paragraph (*b*) in section 15. In so doing, one is struck by the great width of section 13 (2) (*b*) by comparison with the prima facie narrow meaning of section 15 (3) (*b*). The inference is, it was submitted, that paragraph (*b*) of section 15 (3) was not intended to have the comprehensive effect of paragraph (*b*) of section 13 (2).

I turn to the principal arguments in favour of the wider construction of section 15. The only difficulty, it is said, in the way of the wider construction of section 15 (3) is the incursion into paragraph (*b*) of the pronoun " him." In the absence of that word the way would be clear for an indemnity in favour of the company whereby the total loss to the company resulting from an interim distribution can be recouped to the company by the board. The word " indemnity " is not confined to protection against a loss resulting from a claim by a third party against the person indemnified. It can also cover compensation or loss directly suffered by the party indemnified without the existence of any claim by a third party. For example, a policy of insurance against fire can properly be described as a policy which indemnifies the policyholder against the loss suffered by him as a result of a fire. Apart from the requirement in paragraph (*b*) that the indemnity is to be given to the liquidator, there would be no argument that the indemnity thereby envisaged is necessarily confined to the personal protection of the liquidator against the claims of others.

I have to choose between those two possible meanings of an indemnity. If the paragraph is confined to the personal protection of the liquidator, difficulties will arise in this case and will arise in many other cases. The provisional liquidator was appointed by an order of July 28, 1975. The order contains:

> " And the court doth hereby limit and restrict the powers of the said provisional liquidator to the following acts: (1) To take possession of and protect the assets of the company but not to distribute or part with the same until further order."

I need not deal with the other paragraphs. If interim payments are to be made in the case before me, the first step must clearly be to vary that order; otherwise the provisional liquidator can make no interim distribution because he has been commanded not to. In varying the order, the court might either authorise specific interim payments, or it might authorise such payments in general terms, leaving the liquidator responsible for calculating the amounts. If the court in varying the order authorises specific interim payments to be made, it must follow that an indemnity to the provisional liquidator will be unnecessary and, in fact, nugatory; in causing the company to make the interim payments, the liquidator will be acting in pursuance of the court's order, and therefore he can incur no liability personally; consequently nothing could ever become due under such an indemnity.

If, per contra, the court does not authorise specific interim payments, but only interim payments in general terms, leaving the liquidator responsible for the amount of such payments, then the liquidator will be personally at risk if such payments produce a loss to the company's assets which causes the other creditors to go short of their just entitlement, at any rate, if the loss is occasioned by the size of the interim payments.

A That would also be the case if the liquidator were acting out of court, for example, in a voluntary winding up. It is difficult to suppose that any liquidator would be prepared to run the risk of personal liability for a wrongful distribution of the assets under his control, unless he is provided from some source with an indemnity which is perfect. The board are not in a position to offer a perfect indemnity. The adequacy of the board's assets is not guaranteed by the government. Any shortfall is
B not charged on the Consolidated Fund. Whether their assets are sufficient to meet a particular indemnity will depend on the amount of all other indemnities which may happen to be outstanding from time to time. Furthermore, section 13 (3) envisages that circumstances may arise in which the funds of the board are not adequate to enable it to meet all their proposed expenditure in carrying out their statutory duties or
C exercising their statutory powers:

> "Nothing in any provision of sections 6 to 11 above shall be construed as requiring the board to make any payment or to incur any other expenditure thereunder at a time when it appears to the board that the funds available to them for expenditure under that provision, together with any funds they may raise by means of a levy under
> D section 19 or 21 below which might be applied on such expenditure, fall short of what they may require; and accordingly the board may—(*a*) postpone making any payment, or any part of any payment, they propose to make under any such provision; and (*b*) postpone taking any measures under any such provision involving expenditure on their part; from time to time, until it appears to them that their funds are adequate to meet the expenditure they propose to incur under
> E the provision in question."

I appreciate that that subsection is not dealing with liabilities under section 15 (3) (*b*), but it does indicate that circumstances may arise in which the board's funds are somewhat straitened.

In the result it does seem to me that the narrow construction of paragraph (*b*) in section 15 (3) will largely stultify the obvious intention
F of the paragraph. Either a liquidator will act under the directions of the court so that the indemnity is not required and produces nothing for the persons who may be prejudiced by the interim payment; or, if the liquidator is not protected by a court order, he may find himself at personal risk.

I do not think it is necessary to adopt the narrow construction of
G paragraph (*b*) in section 15 (3). It is permissible to read the paragraph as contemplating an indemnity which is given to a liquidator or provisional liquidator in his capacity as such for the purpose of safeguarding the assets of the company and not merely for the purpose of safeguarding the liquidator or provisional liquidator in his personal capacity.

In my judgment the indemnity which the board may give the liquidator or provisional liquidator under paragraph (*b*) includes an indemnity given
H to him for the benefit of the company with the object of protecting the company against loss, and not merely protecting the liquidator personally.

I do not think that this construction involves any violence to the language of the Policyholders Protection Act 1975. I find it unnecessary to rely, as I was invited to do in argument, on the principle which can be adopted in an extreme case to rectify a manifest mistake in statutory expression. I am referring to what was said by Denning L.J. in *Seaford Court Estates Ltd.* v. *Asher* [1949] 2 K.B. 481 and followed by the Court

of Appeal in *Francis Jackson Developments Ltd.* v. *Hall* [1951] 2 K.B. A
488. The wide construction can be adopted without any straining of the use of language.

If the board have available funds and so choose, they clearly have power under paragraph (*a*) of section 15 (3) to make direct payments to policyholders. Paragraph (*b*) proceeds on the basis that the company has available funds for the like purpose. It would to my mind be extra-
ordinary if the board had power in such a case to make direct payments B
to policyholders under (*a*), but no power to underwrite the making of like payments out of the company's own funds under (*b*). If the company has available funds, the preferred course may often be to use those funds for interim payments, rather than the board's funds. It seems to me only consistent with the board's powers under (*a*), that it can underwrite the
payments if the scheme of (*b*) is adopted. C

In the result, I decide that the board do have power under paragraph (*b*) of section 15 (3) to give the undertaking on the lines set out in clause 2 (b) of the three-party deed.

I do not think it is appropriate for me to decide anything in relation to the precise formulation which is set out in subclause (c) by way of definition of the expression D

> " reduction of the assets available for distribution in any winding up of [the company] as a result of the payments provided for in clause 1 above being made "

because no particular question on those paragraphs has been argued before me. Nor do I think it appropriate for me to make any declaration in
relation to the powers of the board to execute a deed containing the other E
provisions which are to be found in the three-party deed for the like reason.

I will, however, add this: clause 2 (a) of the three-party deed provides that the board shall indemnify and hold harmless the provisional liquidator from all liabilities resulting from the interim payments. That does not seem to me, for reasons which I think I have sufficiently indicated in my judgment, to be very satisfactory from the point of view of the liquidator.
It seems to me better that he should apply to the court under the summons F
which he issued in the company proceedings for liberty to make the specific interim payments which are contemplated. There will then be no possible personal liability on him and no reason to include the form of indemnity which is contained in clause 2 (a) of the three-party deed, even if it were right to say, having regard to the terms of my judgment, that the board have power to give any such indemnity. G

When the provisional liquidator applies for that approval under the summons which he has issued, it will be necessary for evidence to be filed by a member of the board to the effect that the board are satisfied that the proposed interim payments are proper to be made, having regard to the circumstances, and a like affidavit by the provisional liquidator. The summons in the company proceedings will be restored to chambers to
consider the evidence with a view to an order sanctioning the proposed H
interim payments, thus relieving the provisional liquidator of any possible personal liability.

Order accordingly.

Solicitors: *Hervert Smith & Co.; Treasury Solicitor; Polden, Bishop & Gale.*

[COURT OF APPEAL]

* REGINA v. URBANOWSKI

1976 Jan. 20 — Scarman L.J., Willis and Mais JJ.

Crime—Practice—Time limits—Trial on indictment—Time limit for commencement—Whether directory or mandatory—Date for preferment of bills of indictment—Courts Act 1971 (*c.* 23), *s.* 7 (4)

Section 7 (4) of the Court Act 1971 provides:

> "The trial of a person committed by a magistrates' court—. . . (*b*) shall, unless the Crown Court has otherwise ordered, begin not later than the expiration of the prescribed period beginning with the date of his committal."

Rule 19 of the Crown Court Rules 1971 prescribes the period of 56 days for the purposes of subsection (4) (*b*).

On April 7, 1975, the defendant was committed for trial on two charges. On May 9 the case was listed but was taken out of the list at the request of the defendant's counsel; and an application for extension of time was granted on August 11. The case was relisted on September 22, when the defendant's counsel pleaded to the jurisdiction of the court and moved to quash the indictment on the ground that section 7 of the Courts Act 1971 had not been complied with. The judge, rejecting the submission, made a further extension order. The trial began within that extended period and the defendant was convicted.

On appeal against conviction:—

Held, dismissing the appeal, that section 7 (4) (*b*) of the Courts Act 1971 was primarily addressed to the Crown Court and its officials to ensure that proceedings were begun within the prescribed period beginning with the date of committal, and, accordingly, was directory only and not mandatory; that therefore the Crown Court had jurisdiction to grant an extension of time after the expiration of the prescribed period (post, p. 458B).

Observations on the administration of the provision of section 7 (4) (*b*) of the Courts Act 1971 (post, p. 458F–H).

Per curiam. The court would expect that the time limit dealing with the date for the preferment of a bill of indictment under rule 5 of the Indictment (Procedure) Rules 1971 would be construed as directory (post, p. 459A).

The following cases are referred to in the judgment:

Caldow v. *Pixell* (1877) 2 C.P. 562.
Hughes v. *Wavertree Local Board* (1894) 10 T.L.R. 357, D.C.
Moore v. *Hewitt* [1947] K.B. 831; [1947] 2 All E.R. 270, D.C.
Reg. v. *Edwards* (unreported), April 18, 1975, C.A.

The following additional cases were cited in argument:

Reg. v. *Harper* (unreported), October 29, 1975.
Reg. v. *Stentiforth* (unreported), October 6, 1975.

[Reported by MISS EIRA CARYL-THOMAS, Barrister-at-Law]

APPEAL against conviction. A

On April 7, 1975, the defendant, Peter John Urbanowski, was committed for trial by the Runcorn Magistrates' Court on the charges of wounding with intent, contrary to section 18 of the Offences against the Person Act 1861 and wounding, contrary to section 20 of the Act of 1861. On May 9, the case was listed but taken out at the request of defence counsel, and on August 11 an application for extension of time was granted. When the case was relisted on September 22 at Chester Crown Court B (Judge Robin David) defence counsel moved to quash the indictment on the ground that the requirement in section 7 (4) of the Courts Act 1971 that the trial should begin not later than the expiration of the prescribed time of 56 days beginning with the date of committal had not been complied with. Judge David rejected the application. On September 30 the trial commenced and on October 1 the defendant was convicted. He C appealed on the ground that the judge was wrong in rejecting the application made on September 22.

The facts are stated in the judgment.

R. H. Montgomery for the defendant.
R. G. Waterhouse Q.C. and *Elgan Edwards* for the Crown.

D

SCARMAN L.J. gave the judgment of the court. This appeal raises a short point of construction of section 7 (4) of the Courts Act 1971. The subsection provides, so far as material:

> "The trial of a person committed by a magistrates' court— . . . (*b*) shall, unless the Crown Court has otherwise ordered, begin not later than the expiration of the prescribed period beginning with the date E of his committal . . ."

Rules have prescribed a period of 56 days or, otherwise expressed, eight weeks. In the present case by an administrative oversight, and I shall have to give the details later, the trial of this defendant did not begin until 117 days after the expiration of the prescribed period.

He was arraigned on two counts: one of wounding with intent to which F he pleaded not guilty and the other of wounding to which he pleaded guilty. He was convicted of the unlawful wounding and he was sentenced to a total of two years' imprisonment.

The point is now taken that the trial was a nullity because the language of section 7 (4) of the Courts Act 1971 is mandatory and not directory, and the provision in the subsection that the Crown Court may order an G extension of the time is a provision that has to be activated before the expiration of the prescribed period, and not after.

The submission for the Crown is a simple one, that in all the circumstances and in the context the subsection is directory only.

Before I come to consider the question of construction and to give the judgment of the court upon it, I will outline the course of the proceedings. The defendant was committed for trial by the Runcorn Magistrates' Court H on April 7, 1975, on the two charges of wounding with intent and wounding. The prescribed time (that is to say the period prescribed under the Crown Court Rules 1971) expired on June 2. The case was listed for hearing on May 9 before Mars-Jones J., but was taken out of the list at the request of the defence, counsel being in difficulties. The case was released to Judge David on May 20. Thereafter there occurred some administrative confusion in the office of the Crown Court. As a result of this confusion the case was not listed within the prescribed period and the failure not to list was not noticed until shortly before an application was made on August 11 for an extension of time. This application was heard by Judge David—I think, in chambers. He granted an extension of 28 days, saying that no further extension would be granted.

After that the case was listed for hearing on September 1. Again the office must have overlooked the fact that that was more than 28 days after the date at which the extension of time had been granted. Even so, it was then taken out of the list because a long trial of some other case was occupying the time of the court. Ultimately it was re-listed for hearing on September 22, no further application having been made for an extension of time and no order having been made by the Crown Court judge extending the time.

When on September 22 the case came before the Crown Court judge, counsel for the defence pleaded to the jurisdiction of the court and moved to quash the indictment on the ground that section 7 (4) of the Courts Act 1971 had not been complied with. The response (if I may say so in passing, the very sensible response) of Judge David was not only to reject the submission but to make there and then a further extension order.

It is now, as I have already indicated in the introductory passage of the judgment, the case for the defence that the judge had no power to make that extension order and that the proceedings which then ensued were a nullity. It is to be observed that the failure to bring on this case within the time prescribed by the rules, or within any extension of that time ordered by the Crown Court, arose from the administrative error or errors of a public official.

Mr. Waterhouse, for the Crown, accordingly submits that it would be in accordance with principle to construe the subsection as directory only. He has referred us to the analogous law dealing with the time limit for stating cases to the Divisional Court, and he has referred us to authority which offers guidance as to when the court should hold statutory words to be directory, and when mandatory.

We find considerable assistance in the interpretation of this subsection from a consideration of the law relating to the time limit for a case stated and I will indicate very shortly why. Rule 67 of the Magistrates' Court Rules 1968 provides that the time within which justices shall state a case shall be three months after the application for the case to be stated. The rule contains no provision expressly authorising extension of that period.

This rule has been in the law for a very long time, and the leading authority as to its construction is to be found in *Hughes* v. *Wavertree Local Board* (1894) 10 T.L.R. 357. In that case a Divisional Court of the Queen's Bench Division, considering the rules then in force under the Summary Jurisdiction Act 1879 as to time limits, said as follows, and I quote from the judgment of Cave J., at p. 358:

> "The rule in question provides that on an application to the court of summary jurisdiction under that Act at any time within seven clear days a case shall be stated in three months after the date of the application and after the recognizances are entered into. It is contended that the whole of the rule is a condition precedent, and that it is not merely directory. It may be so as far as relates to acts to be done by the appellant, but not so far as it relates to the magistrates; as to their act it is only directory."

The judgment elaborates that point.

In *Moore* v. *Hewitt* [1947] K.B. 831 the Divisional Court attached A
importance to the decision in *Hughes* v. *Wavertree Local Board*, and in giving the judgment of the court Lord Goddard C.J. emphasised that it was important to observe whether the statute was dealing with what was required of a public official or of a party: see also *Caldow* v. *Pixell* (1877) 2 C.P. 562, 566.

It seems to us plain that this subsection is primarily addressed to the Crown Court, and obliges the court to take steps to ensure that cases are B
begun within the prescribed period. Accordingly in our view this provision, being addressed to the court and its officials, is directory and not mandatory; and it follows from that view of the subsection that it is open to the Crown Court to grant an extension of time if it thinks fit after the expiration of the prescribed period.

Mr. Montgomery, for the defendant has urged that such a construction C
puts altogether too much power in the hands of the Crown Court judge and that the statute must be construed as mandatory and as conferring no more power upon the Crown Court judge than a power to grant an extension of time before the expiration of the prescribed period.

We see absolutely no reason why the Crown Court should not have the more extended power, and we see nothing in the statute, once granted that it is directory in character, abridging the power of the Crown Court. D
It is as well to remember that the Crown Court, established by the Act of 1971, is part of the Supreme Court of Judicature, and its judges will of course act judicially. One need have no fear, I should have thought, that there is any risk of abuse of the power conferred to grant an extension of time.

We are reinforced in our view of the subsection by a decision of this E
court, *Reg.* v. *Edwards* (unreported), April 18, 1975. That was an application dealt with by two judges, and the same point was taken on that application, though it had not been taken in the court below, and in the course of giving the judgment of this court Talbot J. said, shortly but plainly, that in the view of the court the subsection was directory only.

In our view therefore the appeal must fail upon the short point of construction. F

We have been urged by counsel to give some directions or some guidance as to the appropriate way in which to administer this provision. This of course is very much a matter for the Crown Court judges, but it would appear to us as a convenient course for the court or the court office to notify parties, both the Crown and the defence, when it is necessary to make an application for an extension of time. If the parties are perfectly G
happy for the extension of time to be granted, there is no need for either of them to go to the expense of attending the court upon the hearing of the application. If either party wishes to object or to make submissions, then they must have their opportunity at the hearing of the application.

We have been told that in some circuits these applications are dealt with in chambers, whereas in other circuits—and, we believe, in the Central Criminal Court—they are dealt with by the judge in open court. H
There is no need to give any direction as to which is the better course. Plainly if a point of importance falls to be argued the court would be wise to adjourn the matter into court so that there may be a public hearing and a public decision.

We have also been urged to consider the time limit dealing with the date for the preferment of a bill of indictment under the Indictment (Procedure) Rules 1971. That period is one of 28 days from the date of

A committal and, though the language is different, there is also a provision for extension of time: Indictment (Procedure Rules) 1971, rule 5.

Nothing that we have said upon the true construction of the Courts Act 1971 can be directly binding when considering the construction, if the point ever arises, of the Indictment Rules. Nevertheless it may be of some assistance if we say that we would expect this time limit to be construed in a directory way—just as the court has now construed the Courts Act
B 1971, and as in the past the courts have construed the rules relating to the time limit for a case stated. There are differences between the preferring of a bill of indictment and the listing of a case for hearing, but we do not think that the differences are such as to require the courts to construe the relevant indictment rule as mandatory: we think it is directory only.

C For those reasons the appeal is dismissed.

Appeal dismissed.
Costs of prosecution out of central funds.

Solicitors: *Registrar of Criminal Appeals; E. C. Woodcock, Chester.*

D

[COURT OF APPEAL]

E

* LAZENBY GARAGES LTD. *v.* WRIGHT

[Plaint No. 74 51360]

1976 Jan. 22 Lord Denning M.R., Lawton and Bridge L.JJ.

F *Damages—Sale of goods—Refusal to accept goods—Secondhand car—Resale to another purchaser at higher price—Whether dealer entitled to damages for loss of sale where goods unique and no "available market"—Measure of damages—Sale of Goods Act* 1893 (56 & 57 *Vict. c.* 71), *s.* 50 (2) (3) [1]

The plaintiffs, dealers in new and secondhand quality cars, bought a secondhand BMW 2002 motor car on February 14,
G 1974, for £1,325. On February 19 the defendant agreed in writing to buy it from them for £1,670 and to take delivery on March 1, but on February 20 he told the dealers that he did not wish to proceed with the purchase and refused to accept delivery. Some six weeks later the dealers sold the same car to someone else for £1,770. Despite that more profitable sale they claimed damages from the defendant for "loss of profit," namely, £345, being the difference between the £1,325
H they had paid and the £1,670 agreed with the defendant. His

[1] Sale of Goods Act, 1893, s. 50: "(1) Where the buyer wrongfully neglects or refuses to accept and pay for the goods, the seller may maintain an action against him for damages for non-acceptance. (2) The measure of damages is the estimated loss directly and naturally resulting, in the ordinary course of events, from the buyer's breach of contract. (3) Where there is an available market for the goods in question the measure of damages is prima facie to be ascertained by the difference between the contract price and the market or current price at the time or times when the goods ought to have been accepted, or, if no time was fixed for acceptance, then at the time of the refusal to accept."

defence was that the dealers had not suffered any loss by his non-acceptance. A

The judge, having held that there was at the material time no "available market" within section 50 (3) of the Sale of Goods Act 1893, found that the dealers had lost a sale to the defendant; and that if they had sold the car to him there was a 50–50 chance that they would have sold an additional similar car to someone else at a profit; and he awarded the dealers £172·50, half the sum claimed, taking as the measure of damages "the estimated loss directly and naturally resulting, B in the ordinary course of events, from the buyer's breach of contract" under section 50 (2).

On appeal by the defendant:—

Held, allowing the appeal, that where the subject matter of a repudiated sale was a unique article like a secondhand car for which there was no available market within the terms of section 50 (3) of the Act of 1893, the sellers could recover C as damages only the particular loss sustained on the transaction, and nothing more; and as the sellers had resold the very car at a higher price they had suffered no loss and could not recover any damages.

W. L. Thompson Ltd. v. *Robinson* (*Gunmakers*) *Ltd.* [1955] Ch. 177 distinguished.

The following cases are referred to in the judgments: D

Cameron v. *Campbell & Worthington Ltd.* [1930] S.A.S.R. 402.
Hadley v. *Baxendale* (1854) 9 Exch. 341.
Mason & Risch Ltd. v. *Christner* (1920) 54 D.L.R. 653.
Stewart v. *Hansen* (1923) 218 P. 959.
Thompson (*W. L.*) *Ltd.* v. *Robinson* (*Gunmakers*) *Ltd.* [1955] Ch. 177; [1955] 2 W.L.R. 185; [1955] 1 All E.R. 154.
Torkomian v. *Russell* (1916) 97 Atlantic Reporter 760. E

The following additional case was cited in argument:

Hill & Sons v. *Edwin Showell & Sons Ltd.* (1918) 87 L.J.K.B. 1106, H.L.(E.).

APPEAL from Judge Irvine sitting at Leicester County Court.

The plaintiffs, Lazenby Garages Ltd., dealers in secondhand quality F cars, claimed against the defendant, Alan Wright, that by an agreement in writing on February 19, 1974, he had agreed to buy and accept from the plaintiffs on March 1 a BMW 2002 motor car for the sum of £1,670, but that orally on March 1 he had refused to accept the motor car or to pay for it, as a result of which they had suffered £345 loss of profit on the agreement for sale; and they claimed that sum as damages. The defendant G admitted the agreement of February 19 but claimed that he had told the plaintiffs on February 20 that he did not wish to proceed with the purchase, and that subsequently the plaintiffs had sold the same motor car to another purchaser at a price not less than £1,670 so that in the premises the plaintiffs had not suffered any damage or loss.

Judge Irvine on December 16, 1974, gave judgment for the plaintiffs for the sum of £172·50, one half of the sum claimed, and their costs. H

The defendant appealed on the grounds (1) that the judge misdirected himself in law in that, having found as a fact that there was on the evidence no more than a 50–50 chance of the plaintiffs' selling another secondhand car at a profit if the defendant had accepted the car they sold to him, he failed to direct himself that the plaintiffs had not succeeded in proving any loss on balance of probabilities; (2) that he had misdirected himself in law in holding that the measure of damages was not to be

A determined by reference to section 50 (3) of the Sale of Goods Act 1893; (3) that he was wrong in fact in failing to find on the evidence that there was at the material time an available market within the meaning of section 50 (3) of the Act; (4) that he was wrong in fact and in law in failing to hold on the evidence that by reason of the application of section 50 (3), the plaintiffs, having resold the car at a greater profit than they would have gained from selling it to the defendant, had failed to prove any loss
B at all; (5) that he was wrong in fact in failing to find that any other secondhand car which the plaintiffs might have been able to sell, had the defendant accepted the car they sold to him, was as likely to have been sold at no profit or at a loss as at a profit; and that if such other car had been sold at a profit there was no evidence before him of what such profit would have been; (6) that he was wrong in fact and law in holding that
C because there was an equal chance of the plaintiffs selling or not selling an additional secondhand car, he should award them half the actual profit they would have earned on the sale of the car to the defendant; (7) that he was wrong in fact in failing to find that no two secondhand cars which the plaintiffs had for sale were alike in saleability; and that there was no evidence that at the time of resale of the car the plaintiffs had, or could have had, a comparable one which they might have sold to the eventual
D purchaser of the car had the defendant in fact accepted it; and (8) that he was wrong in fact and law in failing to find that the plaintiffs, being under a duty to mitigate any loss arising from breach of contract by the defendant, in fact mitigated any such loss completely by reselling the car at a greater profit.

By a respondents' notice the plaintiffs asked that the judgment be varied
E by setting aside the award of £172·50 and substituting the figure of £345. Their grounds were that (1) the judge erred in fact in finding on the evidence that there was no more than a 50–50 chance of the plaintiffs selling another secondhand car at a profit; and (2) that the judge, having found that there was no available market, misdirected himself in holding that the plaintiffs' loss was half the profit which they would have made if the defendant had accepted the car, and that he should have directed
F himself that their loss was the loss of their bargain—the full amount of the profit they would have made if the defendant had accepted the car.

David Lee for the defendant.
John Scannell for the plaintiff dealers.

G Lord Denning M.R. Mr. Wright works on the land. On February 19, 1974, he went to the showrooms of motor dealers called Lazenby Garages Ltd. He saw some secondhand cars there. He agreed to buy a BMW 2002. He signed a contract to pay £1,670 for it. It was to be delivered to him on March 1, 1974. He went back home to his wife and told her about it. She persuaded him not to buy it. So next day he went
H back to the garage and said he would not have it after all. They kept it there offering it for re-sale. Two months later on April 23, 1974, they re-sold it for £1,770, that is, for £100 more than Mr. Wright was going to pay.

Notwithstanding this advantageous re-sale, the garage sued Mr. Wright for damages. They produced evidence that they had themselves bought the car secondhand on February 14, 1974, that is, five days before Mr. Wright had come in and agreed to buy it. They said that they had bought it for £1,325. He had agreed to buy it from them for £1,670. So they had lost £345 and they claimed that sum as damages. A

In answer Mr. Wright said "You haven't lost anything; you've sold it for a higher price." The garage people said that they were dealers in secondhand cars; that they had had a number of cars of this sort of age and type, BMW 2002s; and they had lost the sale of another car. They said that if Mr. Wright had taken this car, they would have been able to sell one of those other cars to the purchaser. So they had sold one car less and were entitled to profit accordingly. B

The judge thought that they had not proved that they had sold one car less, but that there was a 50–50 chance that they would have sold an extra car. So he gave them damages for half the sum claimed. Instead of £345 he gave them £172·50.

Now there is an appeal to this court. The cases show that if there are a number of new cars, all exactly of the same kind, available for sale, and the dealers can prove that they sold one car less than they otherwise would have done, they would be entitled to damages amounting to their loss of profit on the one car: see the judgment of Upjohn J. in *W. L. Thompson Ltd.* v. *Robinson (Gunmakers) Ltd.* [1955] Ch. 177. The same has been held in the United States: *Torkomian* v. *Russell* (1916) 97 Atlantic Reporter 760 and *Stewart* v. *Hansen* (1923) 218 P. 959; in Canada, *Mason & Risch Ltd.* v. *Christner* (1920) 54 D.L.R. 653; and in Australia, *Cameron* v. *Campbell & Worthington Ltd.* [1930] S.A.S.R. 402. C D

But it is entirely different in the case of a secondhand car. Each secondhand car is different from the next, even though it is the same make. The sales manager of the plaintiffs admitted in evidence that some secondhand cars, of the same make, even of the same year, may sell better than others of the same year. Some may sell quickly, others may be sluggish. You simply cannot tell why. But they are all different. E

In the circumstances the cases about new cars do not apply. We have simply to apply to section 50 of the Sale of Goods Act 1893. There is no "available market" for secondhand cars. So it is not subsection (3) but subsection (2). The measure of damages is the estimated loss resulting directly and naturally in the ordinary course of events from the buyer's breach of contract. That throws us back to the test of what could reasonably be expected to be in the contemplation of the parties as a natural consequence of the breach. The buyer in this case could not have contemplated that the dealer would sell one car less. At most he would contemplate that, if they resold this very car at a lower price, they would suffer by reason of that lower price and should recover the difference. But if they resold this very car at a higher price, they would suffer no loss. F G

Seeing that these plaintiffs resold this very car for £100 more than the sale to Mr. Wright, they clearly suffered no damage at all. In my opinion the appeal should be allowed and judgment entered for the defendant.

LAWTON L.J. In the course of argument Mr. Scannell, on behalf of the plaintiffs, accepted that if a dealer is selling an article which is unique —for example, if a secondhand car dealer was selling a vintage car, or if an antique dealer was selling a picture—then, if there were a repudiation by a buyer of a contract entered into, the damages would be the particular loss which was sustained on that transaction, and nothing more. H

As Lord Denning M.R. has pointed out, when the goods are not unique, but are mass-produced, different considerations may apply from those which apply when an article is unique.

A The problem in this case is whether a secondhand car of the type with
which we are concerned, namely, a BMW 2002, petrol-injected, was a
unique article. The evidence from the plaintiffs' own sales manager shows
that it was; he put the matter in this way: "No one can say what makes
a secondhand car sellable. It is same with new cars. Cars vary as to
date, mileage, sound of engine, wear and tear, upholstery etc." Then, a
few answers later, he said: "In secondhand showroom each car is
B different." In other words, he was saying that secondhand cars are, from
their very nature, unique. In those circumstances it seems to me that the
Thompson type of case [*W. L. Thompson Ltd.* v. *Robinson* (*Gunmakers*)
Ltd. [1955] Ch. 177] has no application to the circumstances of this
particular case. I agree that the appeal should be allowed.

C BRIDGE L.J. I agree with both judgments that have been delivered
and I will only add a few words.

With respect to him, it seems to me that the judge fell into error in
thinking that he could estimate what effect would have been caused to
the plaintiffs' dealing in secondhand cars if the car which was the subject
of the contract had been taken by the defendant in accordance with his
contractual obligation, and not sold on to another buyer. He sought
D to estimate the prospects in those circumstances of the other buyer having
purchased another secondhand car from the plaintiffs. To my mind there
was no basis for any proper inference as to what effect on the plaintiffs'
trade would have been felt if the car in question had been sold and
delivered to Mr. Wright, instead of to the buyer who in fact eventually
bought it. Any consideration of that subject matter would in my judg-
E ment be pure speculation and certainly far too remote to be the subject of
an estimate of loss in accordance with section 50 (2) of the Sale of Goods
Act, that is, an estimate of loss directly and naturally resulting, in the
ordinary course of events, from the buyer's breach of contract; or
alternatively, far too remote to have been considered as being within the
contemplation of the parties at the time of the contract so as to be
recoverable damages under the second rule of *Hadley* v. *Baxendale* (1854)
F 9 Exch. 341.

I agree that the appeal should be allowed.

Appeal allowed, with costs in Court of Appeal and below.
Judgment below set aside and judgment for defendant in lieu.
G *Payment out to defendant of fund in court.*

Solicitors: *Turner, Peacock for R. G. Frisby & Small, Leicester; C. Norman Astill & Sons, Leicester.*

M. M. H.

H

[PRIVY COUNCIL] A

* EUROPA OIL (N.Z.) LTD. . . . . . . APPELLANT

AND

INLAND REVENUE COMMISSIONER . . . . . RESPONDENT B

[ON APPEAL FROM THE COURT OF APPEAL OF NEW ZEALAND]

1975 July 14, 15, 16, 17, 21, 22, 23, 24;
1976 Jan. 13

Lord Wilberforce, Viscount Dilhorne, Lord Diplock, Lord Edmund-Davies and Sir Garfield Barwick

New Zealand—Revenue—Income tax—Assessable income—Claim for expenditure in purchasing trading stock—Oil—Whether profits earned by subsidiary through arrangements connected with sale of oil to be included in expenditure—Whether arrangements void as having purpose and effect of altering incidence of income tax—Land and Income Tax Act 1954 (No. 67 of 1954), *ss.* 108, 111 C

The taxpayer company marketed gasoline in New Zealand. To obtain its supplies of oil it negotiated two series of contracts D with Gulf. The first series covered the period from 1956 to 1964, the second that from 1964 to 1971. One of the objects of the contracts was to obtain for the taxpayer company a reduction below posted prices for its supplies. Of the first series of contracts the organisation contract between Gulf and the taxpayer company provided for the incorporation in the Bahama Islands of Pan Eastern, a company subscribed by E Gulf and A.M.P. (a subsidiary of the taxpayer company) in equal shares. Under the second series of contracts, the taxpayer company obtained supplies of partially refined oil from Europa Refining under successive contracts entered into with Europa Refining for cargo lots at posted prices as required. Both the taxpayer company and Europa Refining were under the same effective management but neither was a subsidiary of the other nor of the same parent company. The tax- F payer company obtained all its supplies from Europa Refining but, after 1964, was not contractually bound to do so. Europa Refining obtained its supplies from a subsidiary of Gulf at posted prices under the supply contract. In order that the cost to the taxpayer company should be 2.5c. per gallon less than the posted price, Gulf arranged in 1964, under the new processing contract, to sell to Pan Eastern at posted prices sufficient crude oil to produce the semi-refined oil required by G Europa Refining under the supply contract. That crude oil was processed by Gulf for Pan Eastern for a fee and the semi-refined oil repurchased by Gulf at prices which ensured that Pan Eastern made a profit equivalent to 5c. per gallon on the oil eventually purchased by the taxpayer company. That arrangement resulted in half the profit earned by Pan Eastern being passed to the taxpayer company in the form of dividend on the shares in Pan Eastern held by A.M.P. Unlike the H arrangements made under the first series of contracts, Gulf did not enter into a covenant with the taxpayer company to perform its obligations under the new processing contract to Pan Eastern.

In assessiing the taxpayer company for income tax for the years ending March 31, 1966 to 1971 the Commissioner of Inland Revenue contended that the expenditure incurred by the taxpayer company under its successive contracts with Europa Refining was not expenditure exclusively incurred in

A the production of assessable income through the marketing of
gasoline but was incurred in part for the purpose of producing
the return through Pan Eastern which part was non-deductible
under section 111 of the Land and Income Tax Act 1954.[1]
The commissioner assessed the taxpayer company accordingly
and, on an objection, referred by case stated to the Supreme
Court the question whether he had acted incorrectly in making
the assessment. He further contended that under section 108
B of the Land and Income Tax Act 1954 he was entitled to
treat as void the successive contracts with Europa Refining,
the organisation contract, the supply contract and the new
processing contract. The Supreme Court affirmed the assessment.
On appeal the Court of Appeal allowed the appeal in
part.

On appeal by both parties to the Judicial Committee:—

Held (Lord Wilberforce dissenting), (1) that where the
C purchase price for goods delivered was claimed to be deducted
under section 111 as being incurred exclusively for the purchase
of trading stock the test was whether the contract of
sale gave rise to legally enforceable rights other than to
delivery of the goods; since on each successive contract between
the taxpayer company and Europa Refining the only legally
enforceable right acquired by the taxpayer company against
anyone was the right to the delivery of oil by Europa Refining,
D the expenditure thereby incurred by the taxpayer company
could only be characterised as the purchase price of its trading
stock and accordingly was deductible in full by virtue of
section 111 (post, pp. 472H—473A, 474F–H).

(2) That section 108 was not a charging section and before
it could be applied there had to be some existing, identifiable
income of the taxpayer company which would have been
chargeable to New Zealand tax if none of the contracts, agree-
E ments or arrangements avoided by the section had been
entered into and that, accordingly: (*a*) since the organisation
contract created a new source of income which was not chargeable
to New Zealand income tax it was not liable to avoidance
under the section; (*b*) even if section 108 entitled the commissioner
to treat as void a contract to which the taxpayer company
was not a party, avoidance of the supply contract would
have no effect on the income of taxpayer company and hence
F that contract was not avoidable under the section; (*c*) the legal
character of the dividend paid by Pan Eastern to the taxpayer
company would not be affected by avoidance of the new
processing contract between Gulf and Pan Eastern and
accordingly that contract was not avoidable under the section
(post, pp. 475B–F, 476D–H).

(3) That it was not for the court or the commissioner to
say from whom the taxpayer company should purchase its
G trading stock and that the finding that the purchase price paid
by the taxpayer company to Europa Refining for the supply of
oil under the successive contracts was deductible by virtue of
section 111 was incompatible with their avoidance under
section 108 (post, pp. 475H—476A).

Per curiam. The reference to "reality" in *Inland Revenue
Commissioner* v. *Europa Oil (N.Z.) Ltd.* [1971] A.C. 760,
772 was directed only to the legal character of the payment
H made pursuant to the provisions of a contract and not to its
economic consequences (post, pp. 472E, 478C–D).

Inland Revenue Commissioner v. *Europa Oil (N.Z.) Ltd.*
[1971] A.C. 760, P.C. considered.

Decision of the Court of Appeal (New Zealand) (1974)
4 A.T.R. 455; (1975) 1 T.R.N.Z. 1 set aside.

[1] Land and Income Tax Act 1954, s. 111: see post, p. 471E–F.
S. 108: see post, p. 475A.

The following cases are referred to in the judgments of their Lordships: A

Ashton v. *Inland Revenue Commissioner* [1975] 1 W.L.R. 1615; [1975] 3 All E.R. 225, P.C.

Cecil Bros. Pty. Ltd. v. *Federal Commissioner of Taxation* (1964) 111 C.L.R. 430.

Hallstroms Pty. Ltd. v. *Federal Commissioner of Taxation* (1946) 72 C.L.R. 634.

Inland Revenue Commissioner v. *Duke of Westminster* [1936] A.C. 1, B H.L.(E.).

Inland Revenue Commissioner v. *Europa Oil (N.Z.) Ltd.* [1971] A.C. 760; [1971] 2 W.L.R. 55, P.C.

Mangin v. *Inland Revenue Commissioner* [1971] A.C. 739; [1971] 2 W.L.R. 39; [1971] 1 All E.R. 179, P.C.

Newton v. *Commissioner of Taxation of the Commonwealth of Australia* [1958] A.C. 450; [1958] 3 W.L.R. 195; [1958] 2 All E.R. 759, P.C. C

Ronpibon Tin No Liability v. *Federal Commissioner of Taxation* (1949) 78 C.L.R. 47.

The following additional cases were cited in argument:

Colquhoun v. *Heddon* (1890) 25 Q.B.D. 129, C.A.

Craddock v. *Zevo Finance Co. Ltd.* (1946) 27 T.C. 267, H.L.(E.).

Federal Commissioner of Taxation v. *Snowden & Willson Pty. Ltd.* (1958) D 99 C.L.R. 431; 7 A.I.T.R. 308.

Hansen v. *Inland Revenue Commissioner* [1973] 1 N.Z.L.R. 483.

Inland Revenue Commissioner (N.Z.) v. *Castle* (1971) 2 A.T.R. 481.

John Fairfax and Sons Pty. Ltd. v. *Federal Commissioner of Taxation* (1959) 101 C.L.R. 30.

Mobil Oil Australia Ltd. v. *Commissioner of Taxation of the Commonwealth of Australia* [1966] A.C. 275; [1965] 3 W.L.R. 269; [1965] E 3 All E.R. 225, P.C.

Moriarty v. *Evans Medical Supplies Ltd.* [1958] 1 W.L.R. 66; [1957] 3 All E.R. 718, H.L.(E.).

Peate v. *Commissioner of Taxation* [1967] 1 A.C. 308; [1966] 3 W.L.R. 246; [1966] 2 All E.R. 766, P.C.

Tout v. *Inland Revenue Commissioner (N.Z.)* (1970) 1 A.T.R. 705.

War Assets Pty. Ltd. v. *Federal Commissioner of Taxation* (1954) 91 F C.L.R. 53.

Wisheart v. *Commissioner of Inland Revenue* (1970) 1 A.T.R. 434.

APPEAL (No. 13 of 1975) by Europa Oil (N.Z.) Ltd. (the taxpayer company) and cross appeal by the Commissioner of Inland Revenue from the judgments and order (June 12, 1974, (1974) 4 A.T.R. 455, November 19, G 1974, (1975) 1 T.R.N.Z. 1) of the Court of Appeal of New Zealand (McCarthy P., Richmond and Beattie JJ.) partly allowing the appeal by the taxpayer company from a judgment (March 22, 1973) of the Supreme Court (McMullin J.) on a case stated under section 32 (5) (*b*) of the Land and Income Tax Act 1954. The question referred to the Supreme Court by the case stated was whether the commissioner had acted incorrectly in making an assessment of income earned by the taxpayer company from H the years ending March 31, 1966 to 1971 inclusive and if he did act incorrectly which assessment should be amended and in what respect. The Supreme Court affirmed the assessment.

The Court of Appeal held, inter alia, (1) that there was too extensive an integration of the taxpayer company's successive orders for oil from Europa Refining with the arrangements between Europa Refining and Gulf and between Gulf and Pan Eastern to permit the separation of the

A successive contracts from the entitlement of the taxpayer company to the Pan Eastern dividend; (2) that an advantage not identifiable with expenditure incurred in the production of assessable income was obtained by the taxpayer company through Pan Eastern; (3) that the price paid by the taxpayer company on the successive contracts with Europa Refining could be apportioned as being paid partly for stock in trade and partly for the Pan Eastern dividend; and (4) that section 108 of the Land and Income
B Tax Act 1954 did not apply.

The facts are stated in the judgment of the majority of their Lordships.

G. P. Barton and *R. F. Pethig* (both of the New Zealand Bar) for the taxpayer company.

R. C. Savage Q.C. (Solicitor-General, New Zealand), *I. L. M. Richardson*
C and *G. Cain* (both of the New Zealand Bar) for the Commissioner of Inland Revenue.

Cur. adv. vult.

January 13. The majority judgment of their Lordships was delivered by LORD DIPLOCK.

This is the second time within the last five years that the Judicial
D Committee of the Privy Council has been called upon to examine the fiscal consequences of a complex set of contracts connected with the purchase by Europa Oil (N.Z.) Ltd. ("the taxpayer company") of its stock in trade. There have been two different sets of contracts. The first set ("the 1956 contracts") covered the period from 1956 to 1964; the second ("the 1964 contracts") covered the period from 1964 to 1971. The economic effect
E of the two sets of contracts and the business reasons for entering into them are similar and can be stated briefly.

The taxpayer company is one of a group of associated companies which it is convenient to refer to as "the Todd group." The effective management of all the companies in the group is exercised by Mr. Bryan Todd. The principal business of the taxpayer company is the marketing in New Zealand of petroleum products from the light end of refining;
F predominantly motor gasoline but including some gas oil. Its principal competitors in New Zealand are companies controlled by or associated with one or other of the major international oil companies which have interests in oilfields and refineries in the Middle East or elsewhere east of Suez from which their requirements of light end products can be obtained. In contrast to its competitors the Todd group has no interests
G in any oilfield and during the period covered by the first set of contracts it had no interest in any refinery. It had to purchase its stock in trade in bulk from one or other of the major international oil companies in the fully refined form in which it was marketed in New Zealand.

Gulf Oil Corporation ("Gulf"), an American company, is one of the major international oil companies. By itself or through its subsidiary companies ("the Gulf group") it had interests in oilfields in the Middle
H East and access to refinery capacity there. The Gulf group had ample outlets east of Suez for the heavy end products of refining crude oil from its oilfields, but an inadequate market for the light end products, and no outlet for these products in New Zealand. So the petroleum products of which it had a surplus to dispose of were those of which the Todd group needed an assured source of supply. In this respect the business interests of the two groups were complementary.

The prices at which bulk supplies of crude oil and refined products were bought and sold on the world market were, at the relevant periods, tightly A controlled by the major international oil companies. Sales were at "posted prices," the posted price for a refined product being greater than the posted price for crude oil by an amount equivalent to the cost of refining with the addition of a refiner's profit. In order to secure an assured outlet for the surplus light ends of the crude oil that it refined in the Middle East it was in the business interests of the Gulf group to forgo some part of the refiner's profit included in the posted prices applicable to those B refined products which it supplied to the Todd group. The amount to be forgone was the subject of hard bargaining between the two groups in 1956. It was ultimately fixed at 2·5c. per gallon of gasoline or gas oil supplied to the taxpayer company. The Gulf group, however, was for business reasons unwilling to depart from the established system of posted prices by making this concession in the form of a reduction in the price C at which it sold the refined products to the taxpayer company. So the benefit of the concession of 2·5c. per gallon had to be given by the Gulf group to the Todd group in some other form. For the period from 1956 to 1964 this was done under the 1956 contracts.

In 1964 a refinery at Whangarei, the first to be constructed in New Zealand, came on full stream. It was, in effect, a co-operative venture in which the Todd group and its principal competitors in the New Zealand D market for refined products each had an interest. Since there is a relatively small demand in New Zealand for the heavy end products of refining crude oil, the refinery was designed to deal not only with crude oil but also, and mainly, with feedstocks in the form of semi-refined products from which the heavy ends had already been extracted by previous refining. When the facilities of the Whangarei refinery became available to the E taxpayer company there was no longer any need for it to purchase its stock in trade in the form of fully-refined products; and it was the policy of the New Zealand government to discourage this. What was now required by the taxpayer company was feedstocks for the Whangarei refinery in the form of semi-refined products. The business reasons for which it was in the mutual interests of the Todd group and the Gulf group that the latter should be the source of supply of the taxpayer company's F requirements for fully-refined light end products applied with equal force to its requirements for semi-refined light end products as feedstocks for the Whangarei refinery. So the Gulf group continued to forgo in favour of the Todd group part of the refiner's profit included in the posted prices of those semi-refined products which were supplied to the Todd group and to give the benefit of this concession to the Todd group indirectly and not G in the form of a reduction in the purchase price. This change in the nature of the petroleum products supplied by the Gulf group to the Todd group would in any event have necessitated some alteration in the contractual relations between the two groups. This took place in 1964 when the 1964 contracts were substituted for the 1956 contracts. The economic effect of the two sets of contracts is similar, but there are major differences in their terms and in the parties to them. H

In particular, under the 1956 contracts the taxpayer company bought its requirements of fully-refined products directly from the Gulf group under a long term contract ("the products contract") expiring on December 31, 1966, whereby it undertook to purchase at posted prices the whole of its requirements of motor gasoline and was granted the option to purchase at posted prices gas oil up to certain limits in quantity. Under the 1964 contracts the taxpayer company did not itself purchase

A any feedstocks directly from the Gulf group. It purchased them from another company in the Todd group, Europa Refining Co. Ltd. ("Europa Refining") which in turn purchased them from the Gulf group under a long term contract ("the supply contract") expiring on December 31, 1973, whereby it undertook to purchase at posted prices all the feedstocks charged by it to the refinery at Whangarei for the purpose of producing the fully-refined products needed to meet the requirements of Europa Refining
B or of the taxpayer company for marketing in New Zealand. Europa Refining is not a subsidiary of the taxpayer company nor are both companies subsidiaries or sub-subsidiaries of the same parent company in the Todd group. The taxpayer company was under no contractual obligation to anyone to purchase any of its own requirements of feedstocks from Europa Refining. In practice it did so but under separate contracts
C entered into with Europa Refining for cargo lots of feedstocks as they were required.

Common to both sets of contracts, however, was the form in which the Todd group obtained the benefit of that part of the refiner's profit included in the posted prices that the Gulf group was willing to forgo in order to obtain an outlet for its light end products. For this purpose the two groups in 1956 caused to be incorporated in the Bahamas a com-
D pany, Pan Eastern Refining Co. Ltd. ("Pan Eastern"), of which one half of the share capital was held by a wholly-owned subsidiary of the taxpayer company, Associated Motorists Petrol Co. Ltd. ("A.M.P."), and the other half by a company in the Gulf group. The 1956 contracts included a contract between Gulf and Pan Eastern ("the processing contract") under which it was agreed that Pan Eastern should purchase from Gulf and Gulf should sell to Pan Eastern at posted prices the quantity of crude
E oil needed to provide the finished products to be purchased by the taxpayer company under the products contract. Gulf undertook to refine the crude oil on behalf of Pan Eastern for a processing fee and to purchase from Pan Eastern the resulting finished products at prices fixed in such a way as to ensure that Pan Eastern should make a profit out of the processing contract equivalent to approximately 5c. per gallon on the finished products
F purchased by the taxpayer company from the Gulf group under the products contract of which A.M.P.'s share by way of dividend would be 2·5 c. per gallon. In 1964, a contract in similar terms ("the new processing contract") was entered into between Gulf and Pan Eastern relating to the feedstocks to be purchased by Europa Refining under the supply contract and the crude oil needed to provide those feedstocks.

Pan Eastern itself did no refining. Under the processing contract and
G the new processing contract this was done exclusively by the Gulf group. What the contracts did was to provide the means by which a share of the refiner's profit on finished products and feedstocks sold by the Gulf group to the Todd group would be obtained by the Todd group in the form of dividends on the shares in Pan Eastern held by A.M.P.

In the instant appeal, as in the previous appeal, their Lordships are
H concerned only with the liability of the taxpayer company for New Zealand income tax; not with the liability of any other members of the Todd group. It is common ground that the dividends receivable by A.M.P. from Pan Eastern or by the taxpayer company from A.M.P. do not, as such, form part of the assessable income of the taxpayer company. Although he relies also on section 108 of the Land and Income Tax Act 1954, the main ground on which the Commissioner of Inland Revenue has sought to recover tax upon them indirectly is by

attacking the claim of the taxpayer company under section 111 to deduct as expenditure incurred in the production of its assessable income from its business of marketing petroleum products in New Zealand, so much of the price paid by the taxpayer company for the motor gasoline and gas oil under the 1956 contracts or for the feedstocks under the 1964 contracts as is equivalent to A.M.P.'s share of the profits made by Pan Eastern under the processing contract or the new processing contract. He contends that upon a true analysis of the legal nature of both sets of contracts the sums which were described in the relevant contracts as being the price of the product sold to the taxpayer company, were paid for a compound consideration consisting partly of goods sold and delivered and partly of other advantages to be received, i.e. profits to be derived by the taxpayer company through Pan Eastern and A.M.P.

The previous appeal was in respect of assessments to income tax made on the taxpayer company for the years ended March 31, 1960 to March 31, 1965 inclusive. In the first five of these years of assessment all the purchases by the taxpayer company were of motor gasoline and gas oil under the 1956 contracts; but in the last year there were also some purchases of feedstocks under the 1964 contracts. The evidence at the hearing in the Supreme Court was directed mainly to the 1956 contracts and the arguments of the parties there, in the Court of Appeal and before this Board, were confined to the legal effect of these contracts. No point was taken in relation to the last year of assessment that the 1964 contracts in connection with the purchases of feedstocks by the taxpayer company might have different legal characteristics.

The consequence of this was that it was the 1956 contracts that were the subject of detailed examination and analysis in both the majority and the minority judgments of this Board in *Inland Revenue Commissioner* v. *Europa Oil (N.Z.) Ltd.* [1971] A.C. 760. That the case under those contracts was a borderline one is apparent from the conflict of judicial opinion that it caused. The majority of this Board, in agreement with McGregor J. in the Supreme Court, upheld the commissioner's contention under section 111. The minority, in agreement with the Court of Appeal, would have rejected it. The majority, however, while recording that it was not disputed that the 1964 contracts bore the same legal character as the 1956 contracts, did go on to consider the 1964 contracts upon such material relating to them as was to be found in the evidence given at the hearing in the Supreme Court. That evidence did not, in the view of the majority of the Board, disclose any difference in legal character between the taxpayer company's expenditure on feedstocks under the 1964 contracts and its expenditure on motor gasoline and gas oil under the 1956 contracts. As stated in the judgment no point had been taken in the appeal that the purchases of feedstocks under the 1964 supply contract were made in the name of Europa Refining instead of that of the taxpayer company. Consequently no evidence at the hearing in the Supreme Court had been specifically directed to the corporate or, what is more important, the contractual relationship between Europa Refining and the taxpayer company in respect of feedstocks purchased by the latter. The Board, in the majority judgment, dealt with the matter on the footing that the taxpayer company was to be treated as the undisclosed principal on whose behalf Europa Refining had entered into the 1964 contracts.

These lacunae in the evidence relating to the 1964 contracts have now been filled by evidence adduced in the instant appeal which is concerned with the assessments to income tax made on the taxpayer company for

A the years ending March 31, 1966 to March 31, 1971 inclusive. During each of these years of assessment the expenditure of the taxpayer company which is in dispute was in respect of feedstocks purchased by it from Europa Refining under the 1964 contracts. The taxpayer company contends that the additional evidence now before the Board makes it manifest that the legal character of this expenditure is different from its former expenditure upon motor gasoline and gas oil under the 1956 contracts
B and that the whole of the price paid by it to Europa Refining for feedstocks supplied under the 1964 contracts is deductible under section 111.

During the six years of assessment that were the subject of the previous appeal section 111 of the Land and Income Tax Act 1954 was in the following terms:

"Expenditure or loss exclusively incurred in production of assessable
C income—(1) In calculating the assessable income of any person deriving assessable income from one source only, any expenditure or loss exclusively incurred in the production of the assessable income for any income year may, except as otherwise provided in this Act, be deducted from the total income derived for that year. (2) In calculating the assessable income of any person deriving assessable income from two or more sources, any expenditure or loss exclusively incurred
D in the production of assessable income for any income year may, except as otherwise provided in this Act, be deducted from the total income derived by the taxpayer for that year from all such sources as aforesaid."

It remained in the same form for the first two years of assessment that
E are the subject of the instant appeal; but in 1968 it was amended [by section 12 of the Land and Income Tax Amendment Act 1968] to read:

"Expenditure or loss incurred in production of assessable income—In calculating the assessable income of any taxpayer, any expenditure or loss to the extent to which it—(*a*) Is incurred in gaining or producing the assessable income for any income year; or (*b*) Is necessarily incurred in carrying on a business for the purpose of gaining or
F producing the assessable income for any income year—may, except as otherwise provided in this Act, be deducted from the total income derived by the taxpayer in the income year in which the expenditure or loss is incurred."

In the last four years of assessment the taxpayer company's claim to the deduction is made under paragraph (*a*) of the amended section. In their
G Lordships' view the amendment to the section in 1968 makes no difference for the purposes of the instant appeal.

The actual language of section 111, both before and after the 1968 amendment, is simple enough. It does not, in their Lordships' view, need any detailed exegesis. The general principles of construction of a taxing statute are well established. Those of particular relevance to section 111
H are referred to in the majority judgment of this Board in the previous appeal where there are cited with approval two leading decisions of the High Court of Australia on the corresponding section in the Australian taxing statute: *Ronpibon Tin No Liability* v. *Federal Commissioner of Taxation* (1949) 78 C.L.R. 47 and *Cecil Bros. Pty. Ltd.* v. *Federal Commissioner of Taxation* (1964) 111 C.L.R. 430. Their Lordships do not find it necessary to repeat them here; they content themselves with emphasising that it is not the economic results sought to be obtained by

making the expenditure that is determinative of whether the expenditure A is deductible or not; it is the legal rights enforceable by the taxpayer that he acquires in return for making it. The difficulty to which the section gives rise is not one of interpretation of the words it uses, but of the application of those words to particular transactions which may be entered into in the course of business where those contractual arrangements are complicated and involve a multiplicity of parties.

In the majority judgment in the previous appeal, however, one thing B was said in connection with the need to analyse the legal character of the contractual arrangements, that would appear to have given rise to some misunderstanding in the instant appeal. It was stated in *Inland Revenue Commissioner* v. *Europa Oil (N.Z.) Ltd.* [1971] A.C. 760, 772:

> ". . . the Crown is not bound by the taxpayer's statement of account, or by the heading under which expenditure is placed. It is entitled to C ascertain for what the expenditure was in reality incurred."

Taken in isolation this might be thought to suggest that the court was entitled to look behind the legal character of a payment made pursuant to the provisions of a contract and to take into account economic benefits which would in fact accrue to the taxpayer otherwise than as a matter of contractual right. Any such suggestion had, however, already been D emphatically repudiated in a preceding paragraph in which *Inland Revenue Commissioners* v. *Duke of Westminster* [1936] A.C. 1 had been referred to as authority; and the repudiation was repeated in the same paragraph as that in which the passage which their Lordships have just cited appears. Its concluding sentence is: "Taxation by end result, or by economic equivalence, is not what the section achieves." Read in this context it E becomes clear that the reference to "reality" was directed only to the legal character of the payment and not to its economic consequences. All that was meant was that the court was not bound by the description, such as "price of goods," attached to it in the taxpayer's own accounts or in a particular contract, if upon an analysis of the contractual arrangements taken as a whole under which the payment was made it appeared that its true legal character did not accord with that description. F

In this appeal, as in the previous appeal, the particular expenditure claimed to be deductible under the section consists of moneys paid by the taxpayer company under contracts for the sale of goods whereby the property in the goods was transferred by the seller to the taxpayer company. The moneys so paid were stated in those contracts to be the price at which the goods were sold; and since the goods were acquired by the G taxpayer company as stock in trade for its business of marketing petroleum products in New Zealand, there is no question that, if those contracts had stood alone, the whole of the moneys payable under them would be expenditure by the taxpayer company that was deductible under section 111. Those contracts, however, did not stand alone. They formed part of a complex of interrelated contracts entered into by various companies that were members of the Todd group or the Gulf group in connection H with the same goods. The question in both appeals can accordingly be stated thus: is the legal effect, as distinct from the economic consequences, of the provisions of the relevant interrelated contracts such that when the taxpayer company orders goods under the contract of sale and accepts the obligation to pay the sum stipulated in that contract as the purchase price, the taxpayer company by the performance of that obligation acquires a legally enforceable right not only to delivery of the goods but also to have some other act performed which confers a benefit in money or in money's worth upon the taxpayer company or some other beneficiary? If the answer is "No," the full amount of the sum stipulated as the purchase price is deductible under section 111. If the answer is "Yes," the sum stipulated as the purchase price falls to be apportioned as to part to expenditure incurred in purchasing the goods and as to the remainder to expenditure incurred in obtaining performance of the other act, which in the instant case would not be deductible.

In their Lordships' view there is a difference that is crucial to the answer to this question in the legal character of payments made by the taxpayer company when it purchased motor gasoline and gas oil under the 1956 contracts and those made when it purchased feedstocks under the 1964 contracts. The provisions of the 1956 contracts are summarised and analysed in the majority judgment of this Board in the previous appeal. For present purposes it is only necessary to draw attention to two respects in which the legally enforceable rights of the taxpayer company under them differed from its legally enforceable rights under the 1964 contracts. (1) All purchases by the taxpayer company of motor gasoline and gas oil were made under a single contract of sale, the products contract, providing for the delivery by periodic instalments of the taxpayer company's requirements for those products over a period of 10 years. The parties were the taxpayer company as buyer and Gulf Iran Company ("Gulfiran"), a subsidiary of Gulf. (2) The nature of the processing contact has already been described. It imposed upon the parties to it, Gulf and Pan Eastern, mutual rights and obligations with respect to the purchase by Pan Eastern from Gulf of the crude oil necessary to provide the requirements of the taxpayer company for motor gasoline and gas oil under the products contract, the processing of the crude oil and the resale of the refined products by Pan Eastern to Gulf at such prices as would ensure to Pan Eastern a profit of approximately 5c. per gallon of motor gasoline or gas oil supplied to the taxpayer company under the products contract. Although the parties to the processing contract itself were Gulf and Pan Eastern, a separate organisation contract to which the parties were Gulf and the taxpayer company incorporated a covenant by Gulf that it would perform its obligations to Pan Eastern under the processing contract and promptly pay to Pan Eastern any moneys due to it thereunder.

The majority of the Board in the previous appeal concluded that the combined effect of these three contracts was that whenever the taxpayer company placed an order with Gulfiran for delivery of an instalment of goods under the products contract and accepted an obligation to pay the sum stipulated in that contract as the purchase price, it acquired by virtue of the placing of that order an enforceable right to have payments made by Gulf to Pan Eastern under the processing contract in such amount as would ensure to Pan Eastern a profit of 5c. per gallon of goods ordered.

In contrast to the position under the 1956 contracts, the taxpayer company was not a party to any of the 1964 contracts entered into with companies that were members of the Gulf group. All its purchases of feedstocks during the years of assessment with which the instant appeal is concerned were made from Europa Refining under contracts of sale for one or more cargo lots of feedstocks entered into from time to time during the years of assessment. These contracts of sale were not in writing. Their terms are a matter of inference from the voluminous evidence as to what was done; and, given the identity of management of the two companies, this has presented the courts below with a difficult task. It has not been rendered easier by the fact that it was apparently the original intention that the sales by Europa Refining to the taxpayer company should be of refined products into which the feedstocks had been converted by treatment in the refinery at Whangarei; but government regulations in New Zealand created obstacles to this. A careful analysis of the evidence by both the Supreme Court and the Court of Appeal has resulted in concurrent findings that the taxpayer company purchased feedstocks and not refined products from Europa Refining.

The taxpayer company was under no pre-existing or continuing contractual obligation to purchase its requirements of feedstocks from Europa Refining. Contractually it was free to buy them wherever it chose. Its liability to pay Europa Refining the sums stipulated as the purchase price arose only as and when the individual contracts for the sale of particular cargo lots were entered into. All the feedstocks sold on by Europa Refining to the taxpayer company had in fact been purchased by Europa Refining from Gulf Exploration Co. ("Gulfex," a member of the Gulf group) under the 1964 supply contract to which the only parties were Europa Refining and Gulfex. As already mentioned, apart from the difference in parties this was in similar terms to the 1956 products contract except that the mutual obligations of the parties as to the quantities of feedstocks to be purchased and delivered were so defined as to be limited, as events turned out, to the quantities actually sold on by Europa Refining to the taxpayer company. Any feedstocks that the taxpayer company might buy from other sources were not within the supply contract.

The 1964 new processing contract relating to feedstocks was also in similar terms to the 1954 processing contract relating to motor gasoline and gas oil which it replaced. The parties were the same, Gulf, and Pan Eastern; but whereas in the 1956 organisation contract Gulf had covenanted with the taxpayer company that it would perform its obligations to Pan Eastern under the 1956 processing contract, it entered into no corresponding covenant with the taxpayer company with respect to its obligations to Pan Eastern under the 1964 new processing contract. A covenant by Gulf to perform its obligations to Pan Eastern under the new processing contract was contained in a 1964 reorganisation contract but the only parties to this contract were Gulf and Todd Participants Ltd., the parent company of Europa Refining but not of the taxpayer company.

It follows that whenever the taxpayer company entered into a contract with Europa Refining for the sale and delivery of one or more cargo lots of feedstocks and thereby accepted an obligation to pay the sum stipulated in that contract as the purchase price, the only right that it thereby acquired which was legally enforceable against anyone was the right to delivery of the feedstocks by Europa Refining.

In their Lordships' view the result upon the commissioner's claim under section 111 is that it must fail. The true legal character of the whole of the expenditure claimed to be deductible is that of the purchase price of stock in trade for the taxpayer company's business of marketing petroleum products and nothing else. As such it is deductible in full in calculating the taxpayer company's assessable income from that business.

Their Lordships must accordingly now turn to the alternative claim by the commissioner under section 108 of the Land and Income Tax Act 1954. During the years of assessment that are in issue in the instant appeal it was substantially in the following terms, which, however, incorporate a minor amendment made in 1968 that does not affect the issue in the instant appeal:

"... Every contract, agreement, or arrangement made or entered into, whether before or after the commencement of this Act, shall be absolutely void as against the Commissioner for income tax purposes in so far as, directly or indirectly, it has or purports to have the purpose or effect of in any way altering the incidence of income tax, or relieving any person from his liability to pay income tax."

There are several things to be noted in connection with the application of this section. First, it is not a charging section; all it does is to entitle the commisioner when assessing the liability of the taxpayer to income tax to treat any contract, agreement or arrangement which falls within the description in the section as if it had never been made. Any liability of the taxpayer to pay income tax must be found elsewhere in the Act. There must be some identifiable income of the taxpayer which would have been liable to be taxed if none of the contracts, agreements or arrangements avoided by the section had been made.

Secondly, the description of the contracts, agreements and arrangements which are liable to avoidance presupposes the continued receipt by the taxpayer of income from an existing source in respect of which his liability to pay tax would be altered or relieved if legal effect were given to the contract, agreement or arrangement sought to be avoided as against the commissioner. The section does not strike at new sources of income or restrict the right of the taxpayer to arrange his affairs in relation to income from a new source in such a way as to attract the least possible liability to tax. Nor does it prevent the taxpayer from parting with a source of income.

Thirdly, the references in the section to "the incidence of income tax" and "liability to pay income tax" are references to New Zealand income tax. The section is not concerned with the fiscal consequences of the impugned contracts, agreements or arrangements in any other jurisdiction. In the instant case it would have made no difference if Pan Eastern, instead of being established in a tax haven, had been established in the United Kingdom and incurred liability to pay corporation tax there upon its profits under the new processing contract.

Fourthly, the section in any case does not strike down transactions which do not have as their main purpose or one of their main purposes tax avoidance. It does not strike down ordinary business or commercial transactions which incidentally result in some saving of tax. There may be different ways of carrying out such transactions. They will not be struck down if the method chosen for carrying them out involves the payment of less tax than would be payable if another method was followed. In such cases the avoidance of tax will be incidental to and not the main purpose of the transaction or transactions which will be the achievement of some business or commercial object: *Newton* v. *Commissioner of Taxation of the Commonwealth of Australia* [1958] A.C. 450, 465; *Mangin* v. *Inland Revenue Commissioner* [1971] A.C. 739 and *Ashton* v. *Inland Revenue Commissioner* [1975] 1 W.L.R. 1615.

Their Lordships' finding that the moneys paid by the taxpayer company to Europa Refining are deductible under section 111 as being the actual price paid by the taxpayer company for its stock in trade under contracts for the sale of goods entered into with Europa Refining, is incompatible with those contracts being liable to avoidance under section 108. In order to carry on its business of marketing refined petroleum products in New Zealand the taxpayer company had to purchase feedstocks from someone.

In respect of these contracts the case is on all fours with *Cecil Bros. Pty. Ltd.* v. *Federal Commissioner of Taxation* (1964) 111 C.L.R. 430) in which it was said by the High Court of Australia, at p. 434: "it is not for the court or the commissioner to say how much a taxpayer ought to spend in obtaining his income"; to which their Lordships would add: it is not for the court or commissioner to say from whom the taxpayer should purchase the stock in trade acquired by him for the purpose of obtaining his income.

The commissioner must therefore be able to point to some other of the 1964 contracts the avoidance of which would have the legal effect of making the profits earned by Pan Eastern under the new processing contract, or the dividends payable out of the these profits to A.M.P. part of the assessable income of the taxpayer company.

He seeks first to avoid the original 1956 organisation contract pursuant to which Pan Eastern was incorporated in the Bahamas. As was held by the Court of Appeal in the previous appeal, there were good commercial reasons, unconnected with the liability of the taxpayer company to New Zealand income tax, for incorporating Pan Eastern and for selecting the Bahamas as its seat. Furthermore the 1956 organisation contract created a new source of income for the taxpayer company which did not exist before the 1956 processing contract came into force. The taxpayer company was perfectly entitled to make arrangements whereby the income from that source was received by it in the form of dividends upon the shares of its wholly-owned subsidiary A.M.P. paid out of A.M.P.'s share of profits earned by Pan Eastern. In their Lordships' view there is no ground upon which the original 1956 organisation contract could be treated as void under section 108.

The commissioner next seeks to avoid the 1964 supply contract and the 1964 new processing contract. To neither of these was the taxpayer company a party. Whatever effect the avoidance of the supply contract might have upon the mutual liabilities of Europa Refining and Gulfex it could not have any effect upon the income of the taxpayer company. The effect of avoidance of the 1964 processing contract is easier to discern. The property in the feedstocks supplied by Gulfex to Europa Refining under the supply contract would never have passed to Pan Eastern but would have remained vested in the Gulf group until sold to Europa Refining; and the payments made by Gulf to Pan Eastern could accordingly have been treated by the commissioner as having been made without consideration. But this would have been of no avail to him. Pan Eastern did in fact receive the payments; it did in fact pay dividends out of the proceeds; what it paid out to its own shareholders does not lose the legal character of a dividend because the profits out of which the dividend was paid must be deemed to have been derived from gratuitous payments. A fortiori this cannot affect the legal character of the dividends upon its own shares payable by Europa Refining to the taxpayer company.

So even if section 108 entitles the commissioner to treat as void for income tax purposes contracts to which the taxpayer himself is not a party and which do not give rise to any beneficial interest in him (a question which it is not necessary to decide for the purposes of the instant appeal) there is, in their Lordships' view, no ground upon which the commissioner's claim can be justified under that section.

Their Lordships will humbly advise Her Majesty that the appeal should be allowed, the orders of the Court of Appeal and the Supreme Court set aside and the matter remitted to the Supreme Court with a direction

A that it answer in the affirmative the question posed in the case stated by the Commissioner of Inland Revenue on October 24, 1972, and amend the assessments accordingly. A cross-appeal by the commissioner concerned questions which do not arise in view of their Lordships' advice on the appeal and they will humbly advise Her Majesty that it be dismissed. The commissioner must pay the costs of the appeal and the cross-appeal to their Lordships' Board.

B

LORD WILBERFORCE delivered the following dissenting judgment. There are three main points for consideration in this appeal, each of which may involve subsidiary questions. 1. Whether section 111 of the Land and Income Tax Act 1954, as it stood in 1968, applied so as to permit the taxpayer company to make certain deductions for the purpose C of calculating its assessable income in the years of assessment 1966, 1967 and 1968; and correspondingly whether section 111 as amended in 1968 applied so as to permit similar deductions to be made as regards the years of assessment 1969, 1970 and 1971. 2. Whether, if the whole of the claimed expenditure in any year was not deductible, an apportionment should be made as between deductible and non-deductible expenditure, and if so what the basis of such deduction should be. 3. Whether sec- D tion 108 of the Act applies so as to avoid all or some of the contracts, agreements or arrangements entered into by the appellant, or otherwise relevant in the case, and if so with what consequences as regards the liability of the appellant company for income tax.

The previous appeal to this Board, *Inland Revenue Commissioner* v. *Europa Oil* (*N.Z.*) *Ltd.* [1971] A.C. 760, involved consideration of an E elaborate series of contracts entered into in 1956. The effect of those contracts, very summarily, was to provide the taxpayer company with a supply of petroleum products by the Gulf Oil Corporation at Middle East posted prices. At the same time, by virtue of the establishment in the Bahamas of Pan Eastern, a company owned as to 50 per cent. by Gulf and as to 50 per cent. by a wholly owned subsidiary of the taxpayer company, a benefit, intended to be the equivalent of 2·5c. per gallon supplied F to the taxpayer company by Gulf, became available to the taxpayer company. It was held by this Board that the consideration paid by the taxpayer company under its supply contract with Gulf was not expenditure exclusively incurred in the production of the assessable income but was in part incurred in order to obtain the benefit through Pan Eastern, and that to that extent it was not deductible.

G The 1971 appeal was concerned mainly with the assessments made in years to which the 1956 contracts applied, but there was also a short period covered by fresh contracts of a similar but not identical character made in 1964. These are the contracts involved in the present appeal.

Their Lordships, on the materials then available, made some examination of the 1964 contracts, and concluded that for income tax purposes they had no different effect from the contracts of 1956. In the present H proceedings, which are wholly concerned with the 1964 contracts (including in that expression certain documents later than 1964), the taxpayer company has contended, as it has every right to do, that there are important and indeed vital differences between the 1956 contracts and the 1964 contracts, so that a different taxation result should follow. This question, as the trial judge and the Court of Appeal found, is not an easy one to answer, so complicated are the arrangements and transactions relevant in the period. Although the 1956 contracts and the judgment of this Board in 1971 have

been fully analysed both in the courts of New Zealand and in the majority A
judgment in this appeal I think it necessary to explain shortly what, as I understand it, was the basis of the 1971 judgment. That judgment took as its starting point the terms of section 111 in its pre-1968 form. For convenience, I repeat it:

> "111. Expenditure or loss exclusively incurred in production of assessable income—(1) In calculating the assessable income of any B
> person deriving assessable income from one source only, any expenditure or loss exclusively incurred in the production of the assessable income for any income year may, except as otherwise provided in this Act, be deducted from the total income derived for that year."

It is seen that the critical words are "expenditure . . . exclusively incurred C
in the production of the assessable income."

It was in the course of examining these words that the judgment used the words "[the Crown] is entitled to ascertain for what the expenditure was in reality incurred." As is explained in the majority judgment in this appeal, the context makes plain that this was not an endorsement of taxation by economic equivalence or end result; indeed any suggestion to that effect was repudiated by the Board's judgment. What the passage was D
saying, and there is nothing new in this, is that it is not sufficient, or decisive, for the taxpayer to call or label his expenditure the purchase price for his trading stock, if in fact the transaction was something different, e.g. if the money was in part paid as the price of his trading stock, in part paid in order to obtain some other benefit. Concretely, in relation to the facts of the case, it was not sufficient for the taxpayer E
company to point to the products contract (see *Inland Revenue Commissioner* v. *Europa Oil (N.Z.) Ltd.* [1971] A.C. 760, 772) under which the taxpayer company agreed to buy gasoline from Gulf at posted prices and to say that the posted price automatically became deductible expenditure. That was the view of the minority in that appeal; they considered that the relevant payments made by the taxpayer company to Gulf under the products contract were simply made as payment for F
trading stock (as in the Australian case of *Cecil Bros. Pty. Ltd.* v. *Federal Commissioner of Taxation* (1964) 111 C.L.R. 430) and that the Pan Eastern benefit was something "collateral" or was simply an inducement to pay posted prices. But that was not the view of the majority, which held that the expenditure was made in part in order to obtain the Pan Eastern benefit; and for that benefit. The decision of the majority thus G
involved an interpretation of section 111 and in particular of the words "incurred in the production of the assessable income" which required the court to examine and analyse the benefit or benefits gained by the expenditure. If what was gained was trading stock and nothing else, the expenditure is wholly deductible. If what is intended to be gained, and what is in fact gained, is some other advantage, the expenditure is not wholly deductible and a problem of apportionment arises. H
The minority judgment took a narrower view, holding as I understand it, that it is not legitimate to look beyond the contract between the buyer and the seller, and that if the contract is nothing but a contract of sale, then (following the *Cecil Bros.* case) the expenditure is wholly deductible.

In my respectful opinion the present case ought to be decided on the basis of the interpretation adopted by the Board in the 1971 appeal,

A as the courts in New Zealand have considered. This brings me to the
question of legal enforceability which perhaps lies at or near the centre of
this appeal. The taxpayer company's argument is that if some other
benefit (in this case the Pan Eastern benefit) is to be considered as something
for which the expenditure was partly incurred, that other benefit
must be contractually enforceable by the person making the expenditure.
It then continues by pointing out that, whereas in 1956 Gulf was under a
B direct contractual obligation to the taxpayer company to secure to Pan
Eastern the Pan Eastern benefit, there was no such direct obligation in
1966. Therefore, it says, the vital element of contractual obligation is
missing. I understand this argument to be accepted by the majority
opinion.

Before I attempt to deal with it, I must mention the other important
C difference between the facts in this appeal and those considered in 1971.
This is that the contracting party with "Gulf" is not the taxpayer company
but Europa Refining. The existence of Europa Refining was made
known in the 1971 appeal but, as the judgment states (*Inland Revenue
Commissioner* v. *Europa Oil* (*N.Z*) *Ltd*. [1971] A.C. 760, 776) no point
had been made by the taxpayer company concerning the use of Europa
Refining instead of the taxpayer company; it was understood, moreover,
D that Europa Refining was a wholly owned subsidiary of the taxpayer
company.

Evidence in the present case now establishes that the latter understanding
was incorrect. Europa Refining is not a subsidiary of the taxpayer
company, nor are both companies subsidiaries of the same parent. Each
is wholly owned by a distinct company in the Todd group, each of which
E companies is controlled by the same shareholder. No doubt if one is
having regard to economic reality there is no substance in the use of one
company or the other. Europa Refining was a paper company with no
staff and a minimum organisation: it took no risks and made no profits.
The reasons for its creation had mainly to do with requirements of New
Zealand law. They are set out fully in the judgment of McCarthy P.:
see *Europa Oil* (*N.Z.*) *Ltd*. v. *Inland Revenue Commissioner* (*N.Z.*) (1974)
F 4 A.T.R. 455, 477. But the taxpayer company is perfectly entitled to
point to the distinct corporate entities, and in a taxation case to rely upon
the distinction. It still remains to see what part Europa Refining played.

In the present case it was Europa Refining which on March 10, 1964,
entered into the supply contract with Gulf. On the same day Gulf entered
into a processing agreement with Pan Eastern, which, as in 1956, would
G ensure for Pan Eastern a "profit" related to the gallonage of oil and
products supplied by Gulf. The taxpayer company had no supply contract
with Gulf, and had no long-term contract with Europa Refining. It simply
placed a series of individual orders with Europa Refining for its requirements,
as needed, these orders being informal, as between closely associated
companies. Each order was then automatically followed by a corresponding
H order by Europa Refining from Gulf. It appears indeed from the
terms of the supply contract of March 10, 1964, that Europa Refining
was under an obligation to Gulf to do this and this was so held by the
Court of Appeal: see (1974) 4 A.T.R. 455, 480. These orders in turn
automatically produced, in due course, as the result of contractual obligations,
the Pan Eastern benefit. It is right to point out that this benefit
was very large; according to a table appearing in the judgment of McMullin
J. it amounted to about 25 per cent. of Europa Refining's (in fact

the taxpayer company's) f.o.b. payments, or U.S. $9·5 million over the six years. A

It is difficult to believe that the taxpayer company, which was going to receive this benefit, did not frame its purchasing arrangements, and accept to pay a price, which would enable it to do so. As the Court of Appeal found, Europa Refining (and so also the taxpayer company) would not have agreed to pay posted prices for crude oil but for the fact that the processing agreement (between Gulf and Pan Eastern) gave Pan Eastern B a profit of 15 per cent. on the posted prices of crude oil so long as no discounts were arranged under the supply contract ((1974) 4 A.T.R. 455, 491). And as and when prices under the supply contract were altered, so automatically were the prices under the processing contract. The taxpayer company's interest in the matter is underlined by letter agreements, contemporaneous with the 1964 contracts, by which Gulf under- C took with the taxpayer company not to require the winding up of Pan Eastern because of the termination of the 1956 processing contract.

There are a number of other differences, real or alleged, between the 1956 situation and that of 1964 which have been painstakingly examined by the Court of Appeal, and which have been covered by unanimous findings. I accept these findings, but since they reinforce rather than weaken the court's ultimate conclusions I need not repeat them. D

The question can now be faced whether the differences above mentioned should lead to a different result in this appeal from that reached in 1971. Such difficulty as there is in answering this question arises because it is first necessary to decide which of the elements relied upon, or referred to, in 1971 in support of the conclusion then reached were necessary to it. Facts which may be relevant to a given conclusion and which may E support it, are not ipso facto necessary for that conclusion. The case relating to the 1956 contracts was, in the view of the 1971 majority, a strong one, particularly because of the explicit undertaking by Gulf to the taxpayer company to perform the processing contract and to secure for Pan Eastern the benefit provided for by that contract. But, in my opinion, it would be to take too narrow a view of the majority judgment, and of section 111, to confine the decision to a case where the benefit F obtained by the expenditure is contractually secured in the sense that as part of the purchasing contract, or even as a part of a separate but integrated contract, the seller agreed with the buyer to pay it. The words of the section "expenditure . . . . exclusively incurred in the production of the assessable income" by contrast point to the disallowance of expenditure not so exclusively incurred, and it is this wording which gave rise to the test of "reality." What was the expenditure for? What was it G intended to gain? What did it gain? What elements entered into the fixing and acceptance of it? These are the questions to be asked. To rephrase this so as to ask, "What did the other party legally bind himself to pay or do"? is to confine the cases where no deduction is allowed to one special case; to substitute a legalistic test for a commercial test. I think in this context of the often quoted words of Dixon J. where he said H in a different but analogous context that what is an outgoing of capital and what is an outgoing on account of revenue depends on

> "what the expenditure is calculated to effect from a practical and business point of view, rather than upon the juristic classification of the legal rights, if any, secured . . . in the process": *Hallstroms Pty. Ltd.* v. *Federal Commissioner of Taxation* (1946) 72 C.L.R. 634, 648.

The words " in the production of the assessable income " are wide words, wider than " in order to obtain trading stock," wider than " in consideration of something which the other party agrees to provide." This was recognised by the 1971 judgment and reflected in its wording.

If then the test is reality (in the sense described), what was the expenditure really for? How does it fit the facts? The simple approach, for which the taxpayer company contends, is to say that the taxpayer company only entered into one contract, or series of contracts from time to time, with Europa Refining and this was simply to buy products. But I find this far too simple. There was Europa Refining with a supply contract with Gulfex under which Europa Refining was obliged to buy from Gulfex all products needed to meet the taxpayer company's New Zealand marketing requirements. There was Gulf with a simultaneous contract with Pan Eastern, a contract in which it was recited that Gulf had agreed to guarantee the performance of Gulfex's obligations, and had agreed to enter into a contract with Pan Eastern in order to obtain the benefits of the contract with the taxpayer company. Under this contract a substantial benefit was contractually secured for the taxpayer company through its subsidiary A.M.P.

The taxpayer company knew all about this (in the words of the Court of Appeal it was " privy " to these arrangements); it knew and contemplated that the moment it placed an order with Europa Refining, Europa Refining would order from Gulfex and that in due course a benefit—very large—would arise for Pan Eastern and so ultimately for itself. If, at the time when the taxpayer company placed orders with Europa Refining, it was not possible to quantify exactly what the amount of this benefit would be because of possible movements in posted prices, the amount could be calculated with reasonable accuracy. I agree with the conclusion of McCarthy P. that it is the circumstance, that the taxpayer company was in a position to expect a substantial profit viz. through Pan Eastern) when incurring the obligation to pay, which is of importance, and the fact that the quantum of that profit was not always determinable in advance is relatively unimportant ((1974) 4 A.T.R. 455, 481). The taxpayer company would never have agreed to pay posted prices for the products had it not known that, related to these prices, for every gallon ordered, a benefit would arise for Pan Eastern. In my opinion it cannot be said, in these circumstances, that the taxpayer company's payments were for products and nothing else. This was the view of the judges in the Court of Appeal.

McCarthy P. considered that if he was to follow the route which he believed was directed by the Privy Council the inquiry should be whether at the time when the stock, whatever it was, was ordered, the taxpayer company knew as a result of the process which it thus put in train that it was to receive, pursuant to the existing machinery, an identifiable advantage: ((1974) 4 A.T.R. 455, 493). Richmond J. summed up his conclusions in the following illuminating passage which I quote in full because I respectfully agree wholly with it:

> " When [the taxpayer company] in subsequent years, in the closest possible co-operation with Europa Refining, initiated the ordering of feedstocks, it was not just initiating orders by Europa Refining for feedstocks from any source. The orders were for feedstocks from Gulfex under the 1964 supply contract and a portion of the moneys advanced by [the taxpayer company] to Europa Refining was for the specific purpose of meeting payments under invoices rendered under

that contract. There was no profit in these transactions from the A
point of view of Europa Refining, apart from the opportunity to
invest funds held in London and possibly, the right to retain the
alternate freight differential. When one reverts to the basic question—
for what was this expenditure in reality incurred—the answer can only
be that it was to obtain both the feedstocks and the Pan Eastern
benefit. Put in a slightly different way, the consideration for [the
taxpayer company's] expenditure was not just the feedstocks but B
also the ordering of those feedstocks from Gulfex. The arrange-
ments between [the taxpayer company] and Europa Refining under
which [the taxpayer company] acquired feedstocks cannot therefore
be isolated from the 1964 series of contracts and were sufficiently
integrated with those contracts to satisfy their Lordships' test."

Richmond J. there refers to the fact that as orders were placed by the tax- C
payer company with Europa Refining, the taxpayer company made its
money available to Europa Refining so as to meet invoices when due.
He also refers to the fact that Europa Refining made no profit on orders.
These, and other factual details, carefully found by the court, fully support
his argument; the contract between the taxpayer company and Europa
Refining was not a normal contract of purchase and sale at all; the D
interested party was the taxpayer company; the benefit to be gained was
the taxpayer company's; part of the benefit was the Pan Eastern benefit.
Beattie J., after stating his initial inclination to follow, in effect, the path
taken by the majority in this appeal, continued, at p. 497:

"However, I am now persuaded by what the President has said in
his judgment when discussing their Lordships' expression, 'as part E
of the contractual relationship' that the contractual arrangement here
was not simply the agreement between [the taxpayer company] and
Europa Refining. By isolating that agreement and ignoring the inter-
relationship of [the taxpayer company] with the Europa Refining-
Gulf-Pan Eastern arrangements, means discarding the 'in reality'
approach adopted by the majority of the Judicial Committee. Clearly,
[the taxpayer company] benefited from the arrangements with Pan F
Eastern when it made payments or advances to Europa Refining.
I say this because, in my opinion, when [the taxpayer company]
arranged its orders with Europa Refining, that company had no
alternative because of the terms of the 1964 feedstock supply contract,
but to pass on those orders to Gulf. At the same time [the taxpayer
company] must have anticipated the benefit that ultimately would
accrue to it through Pan Eastern." G

For these reasons, which the judgments in the Court of Appeal amplify
through a number of factual findings, I would support their conclusions
and hold that the deduction was not allowable under the former sec-
tion 111. I agree further with their conclusions, as I think does the
majority, that the revision of section 111 in removing "exclusively" does H
not lead to a different result. As regards the new limb (*b*) of section 111
introduced in 1968, which introduces the words "necessarily incurred,"
there was some difference of view expressed in the Court of Appeal. As
this is a comparatively recent section in New Zealand, though the subject
of judicial interpretation in Australia, I prefer to express no opinion
upon it.

As to the question of apportionment I do not think that there is any

A doubt that, if total deduction is prohibited by section 111, some apportionment of expenditure is required. That this may be a difficult matter in individual cases does not, in my respectful opinion, indicate that the case is not one for apportionment at all; the courts must do their best as on an issue of fact. In the 1971 case it was assumed that if, as was held, expenditure was to be disallowed, it must be on a pound for pound basis; i.e. for every £1 of benefit secured, £1 of expenditure should be disallowed.
B This assumption has been questioned in the present case, in my opinion with some force. It may well be that some more scientific attempt should be made to ascertain how much of the expenditure was incurred in obtaining the benefit, and this has been attempted by the courts in New Zealand. Neither side is satisfied with the result and each side appeals. Since my view as to the necessity for apportionment does not prevail it
C would be unhelpful to enter into this difficult matter.

As to section 108, on my view of the case this does not arise and I express no view whether it could be applied to the present facts.

Solicitors: *MacFarlanes; Allen & Overy.*

T. J. M.

D

[COURT OF APPEAL]

E * STEVENSON *v.* BEVERLEY BENTINCK LTD.

[1974] S. No. 2905]

1976 Feb. 3 Lord Denning M.R., Roskill and Browne L.JJ.

Hire-Purchase—Owner's right to possession—" Trade or finance
F *purchaser "—Part-time trader purchasing car for own use without notice of hire-purchase agreement—Whether purchaser obtaining good title under statutory protection for " private purchaser "—Hire-Purchase Act* 1964 (*c.* 53), *ss.* 27 (2) (6), 29 (2) [1]

The plaintiff, a tool inspector, who had for some 18 months bought and sold motor vehicles on a modest scale in
G his own time in the evenings and at week-ends, bought a secondhand Jaguar car from a man in January 1974 for his own use for £1,550, without inquiring as to whether or not it was subject to any hire-purchase agreement. He had work done on

[1] Hire-Purchase Act 1964, s. 27: " (1) The provisions of this section shall have effect where a motor vehicle has been let under a hire-purchase agreement . . . and, at a time before the property in the vehicle has become vested in the hirer or buyer, he disposes of the vehicle to another person. (2) Where the disposition referred to
H in the preceding subsection is to a private purchaser, and he is a purchaser of the motor vehicle in good faith and without notice of the hire-purchase agreement or conditional sale agreement, that disposition shall have effect as if the title of the owner or seller to the vehicle has been vested in the hirer or buyer immediately before that disposition."

S. 29: " (2) In this Part of this Act ' trade or finance purchaser ' means a purchaser who, at the time of the disposition made to him, carries on a business which consists, wholly or partly,—(*a*) of purchasing motor vehicles for the purpose of offering or exposing them for sale . . . and ' private purchaser ' means a purchaser who, at the time of the disposition made to him, does not carry on any such business."

it to put it into repair. On March 4, the defendants, a hire-purchase finance company, seized the car as being their property under a hire-purchase agreement made with the defaulting hirer in February 1973. A

On the plaintiff's claim for the return of the car or its value, or damages for conversion and detinue, Bridge J. held that the plaintiff was not entitled to rely on the title given by section 27 (2) of the Hire-Purchase Act 1964 to a private purchaser who purchased in good faith and without notice of a hire-purchase agreement, because at the material time the plaintiff was carrying on a business of the kind which brought him within the definition of "trade or finance purchaser" in section 29 (2) and he gave judgment for the defendants. B

On appeal by the plaintiff: —

Held, dismissing the appeal, that although the plaintiff had bought the particular car for his own use he was at the time of the disposition to him carrying on part-time the business of purchasing motor vehicles within the definition of "trade or finance purchaser" in section 29 (2) of the Act of 1964 which in terms put such a purchaser and a "private purchaser" in mutually exclusive categories. The Act was concerned not with the capacity in which a particular transaction was carried out but with the status of the person carrying it out, giving protection to the "private purchaser" but (*per* Lord Denning M.R.) leaving the "trade or finance purchaser" to protect himself against purchases of vehicles subject to hire-purchase agreements. C D

Decision of Bridge J. affirmed.

The following case is referred to in the judgments:

Moorgate Mercantile Co. Ltd. v. *Twitchings* [1976] Q.B. 255; [1975] 3 W.L.R. 286; [1975] 3 All E.R. 314, C.A. E

The following additional cases were cited in argument:

Astley Industrial Trust Ltd. v. *Miller* [1968] 2 All E.R. 36.

Staffs Motor Guarantee Ltd. v. *British Wagon Co. Ltd.* [1934] 2 K.B. 305.

APPEAL from Bridge J. sitting at Manchester.

The plaintiff, James Stevenson, issued a writ claiming against a finance company, Beverley Bentinck Ltd. (now British Credit Trust Ltd.) an order for the delivery of a Jaguar motor car XJ6 4.2 registration number NUM 555 H or payment of its value as at March 4, 1974, and damages for conversion and/or detinue. By his statement of claim he claimed that he was the owner of the car, having purchased it from one Alan Roberts on January 14, 1974 for £1,550; that he had thereafter caused various repairs, improvements and servicing to be carried out on the car; but that on or about March 4 the company by their servants or agents wrongfully seized and took possession of the car with the intention of permanently depriving him of it and thereby wrongfully converted the car to their own use; and that by letter of March 5 he had through his solicitors demanded the return of the car but that the company had wrongfully failed to return it. F G

By their defence the company denied that the plaintiff was the owner of or was entitled to the possession of the motor car; they admitted that they had taken possession from the plaintiff of the car but claimed that they were the owners of it and on February 16, 1973 had hired it to one Alan Roberts in accordance with the terms of a hire-purchase contract of that date, the total hire-purchase price being £3,000·98; that at all material times the plaintiff was a dealer engaged in the purchase and sale of motor cars and obtained possession of the car when he knew or ought to have known that H

A it was the property of the company; and that for those reasons the plaintiff was not a bona fide private purchaser for value without notice of the company's interest and acquired no title in the car by operation of statute or otherwise; and they denied that he was entitled to the order for delivery or payment or damages as claimed or at all.

Bridge J. on February 13, 1975, gave judgment for the company, finding that when the plaintiff purchased the car he was not purchasing it
B in the course of, or for the purpose of his part-time business as a motor trader and that he bought it in good faith and without notice; but despite those findings he held that the plaintiff was not entitled to rely on the protection of section 27 of the Hire-Purchase Act 1964.

The plaintiff appealed on the ground that on the judge's findings he was wrong in his interpretation of section 27.

C

D. P. Draycott Q.C. and *F. B. Carter* for the plaintiff.
Christopher Rose Q.C. and *Oliver Wilkinson* for the finance company.

LORD DENNING M.R. In February 1973 Mr. Roberts got a secondhand Jaguar on hire-purchase. The finance company was Beverley Bentinck
D Ltd. He did not keep up the monthly instalments. Then in January 1974 he purported to sell the car to Mr. Stevenson for £1,550. Mr. Stevenson paid Mr. Roberts the £1,550 in cash. He paid it in complete good faith, not knowing that Mr. Roberts only had it on hire-purchase. Mr. Stevenson put it into a garage and had some work done on it. Then, a couple of months later, on March 4, 1974, the finance company seized the car. They retook it because Roberts had defaulted. They claimed that they were
E entitled to possession.

At common law Mr. Stevenson would not have got a good title, because the true owner was the hire-purchase company and they could claim it. But Mr. Stevenson relies on the Hire-Purchase Act 1964. Section 27 (2) protects a private purchaser so long as he has bought it in good faith, and without notice of the hire-purchase agreement. But it does not protect a trade or
F finance purchaser. Section 27 (6) says that in a case where the hirer disposes of the motor vehicle to a trade or finance purchaser, nothing in this section shall exonerate the trade or finance purchaser.

So we have to look at the definitions of "trade or finance purchaser" and "private purchaser." These are defined in section 29 (2). It defines "trade or finance purchaser" as:

G "... a purchaser who, at the time of the disposition made to him, carries on a business which consists, wholly or partly,—(*a*) of purchasing motor vehicles for the purpose of offering or exposing them for sale ..."; and it says: "'private purchaser' means a purchaser who, at the time of the disposition made to him, does not carry on any such business."

H So far as Mr. Stevenson is concerned, the judge has found that he did carry on partly (not wholly) the business of purchasing motor vehicles for the purpose of offering them or exposing them for sale. It appears that he had had in the last 18 months or so some 37 dealings in cars, some on his own account and some on account of a principal. His ordinary full time job was as a tool room inspector in a manufacturing company. But he also had this part-time activity, which occupied him most evenings and weekends. Undoubtedly he was carrying on a business which consisted partly of purchasing these vehicles. So he does prima facie come within the A definition of a " trade or finance purchaser."

The judge found, however, that on this occasion Mr. Stevenson did not buy this Jaguar in the course of or for the purpose of his motor trade or business. He bought it for his own use. He was getting rid of his own private Sunbeam and he wanted a Jaguar. He was on the look-out for a good secondhand Jaguar. So he purchased it for his own use, intending to run the Jaguar as his own car. The question is whether he can in B these circumstances claim the protection of the Act as a private purchaser.

He has in his favour a statement by Professor Goode in his book on *Hire-Purchase Law and Practice*, 2nd ed. (1970), p. 622:

> " . . . even a person carrying on a business as a dealer or financier qualifies as a private purchaser if, in relation to the transaction in question, he purchases in his private capacity and not in the course C of his business."

The judge did not agree with the professor. Nor do I. This statute does not contain any words such as " in the course of his business." It simply says that if the purchaser is a trade or finance purchaser and is carrying on that business at the time of the disposition, he has not got the protection of this statute. D

Mr. Draycott for Mr. Stevenson placed stress on the words " at the time of the disposition." He submitted that they meant that, at the very moment of the disposition, Mr. Stevenson must have been carrying on the business of a trade or finance purchaser: and that at the moment when he entered into a private transaction, he was not carrying it on. But I do not feel able to accept that submission. If he was, over the same space of time, be it a E week or a month, carrying on the business of purchasing and offering vehicles for sale, he cannot claim the protection of the statute.

It may be asked: why was no protection given to trade or finance purchasers? No doubt because Parliament thought they were well able to take care of themselves. There is available to them the Hire-Purchase Information Service. Whenever a car is offered to a trade purchaser or motor dealer for sale, he at once wants to know whether it is on hire- F purchase or not. If it is on hire-purchase, then he is not going to buy it until the title is clear. So it is a regular practice in the trade to telephone HPI and ask: " Is this vehicle on hire-purchase or not? " He then gets an answer on which he can safely act: see *Moorgate Mercantile Co. Ltd.* v. *Twitchings* [1976] Q.B. 225, 235–236.

It is unfortunate that Mr. Stevenson does not seem to have been aware G of the service which is provided by HPI. Seeing that he had done 37 transactions, he ought to have been aware of it. He ought to have protected himself by telephoning HPI. He did not do so, and must take the consequences. He was carrying on business partly as a trade purchaser, and therefore he is not within the protection given to private purchasers. I think the judge was right, and I would dismiss the appeal.

H

ROSKILL L.J. I agree that this appeal should be dismissed. My reasons are those given by the judge and by Lord Denning M.R. I would only add a very few words, in deference to the two careful arguments to which we have had the advantage of listening.

Ever since hire-purchase was invented, round about the turn of the century, there have been hire-purchase frauds, and the books are full of examples of such frauds, which have caused loss to innocent parties. Again

A and again—and the present case is yet another example—courts have to decide where, as between two wholly innocent parties, that loss should fall. This is particularly so in the case of motor cars, because persons who hire motor cars under hire-purchase agreements persist in selling them or purporting to sell them, to innocent purchasers when as persons in possession they have no right whatever to sell.

The common law had a plain answer in those cases. It said that the
B true owner was never divested of his title; but as things have progressed through this century (if " progress " is the right word) Parliament thought it necessary to alter the common law position and to give limited protection to those who bought vehicles or other goods in such circumstances.

There was nothing new in that concept. The Factors Acts go back to the early part of the last century, and came to rest, after a number of
C amendments, in 1889. The Act of 1889 is still on the statute book. Section 25 (2) of the Sale of Goods Act 1893 is another example of the statutory protection of an innocent purchaser of goods. Now under section 27 and section 29 of the Hire-Purchase Act 1964 we have yet further though limited protection given to an innocent purchaser of a car on hire-purchase whose hirer has purported to convey a title to that car which at common law he cannot give. The sole question, to my mind, is whether the
D appellant, the present plaintiff, can bring himself within that protection. The argument advanced by Mr. Draycott (I think it was in substance the argument which Mr. Carter advanced in the court below, and which failed) was this: The appellant did not acquire this Jaguar in his capacity as a part time motor trader. He acquired it in his private capacity. Therefore, it is said, he is within the protection given to a " private purchaser " under
E sections 27 and 29.

If it were relevant to look at the capacity in which he bought the car, that would be a very attractive argument; and if this were a case under the Factors Acts that might well be the position; but this is not a case under the Factors Act 1889. As I ventured to point out to Mr. Draycott, the Factors Act is entirely different, both in concept and in expression, from the language of sections 27 and 29 of the Act of 1964. The Factors Act in the
F type of case to which Mr. Draycott referred unquestionably requires the court to look both at the status of the person said to be a mercantile agent, and also at the capacity in which he has dealt with the particular goods in question.

Mr. Rose, if I may say so, put the point in a succinct sentence, when he said that under the present statute the court is concerned not with capacity,
G but only with status. I think that is right. I think Parliament created a clear dichotomy. It may work hardly in some cases. In the present case it seems to work hardly upon the appellant as an innocent purchaser, but we cannot stretch the construction of section 27 and the definitions in section 29 merely to meet a hard case. When one looks at the sections, there is, as Bridge J. put it, a clear dichotomy between a " trade or finance pur-
H chaser " on the one hand and a " private purchaser " on the other. A " private purchaser " does not mean a person who buys a car otherwise than in his capacity as a " trade or finance purchaser." It means someone who does not at the material time carry on any such business as is defined as being the business of a " trade or finance purchaser."

So one has to resolve the question by asking oneself, as did the judge: at the time when the disposition in question was effected, was the purchaser carrying on wholly or partly the business of a " trade or finance purchaser? "

The judge, by a slip of the tongue, used the word "date" instead of "time." That question in this case seems to me to be susceptible of only one answer. The purchaser—the appellant—was at the time of the disposition carrying on in part the business of a motor dealer—a "trade or finance purchaser"—and that disentitles him to the statutory protection given to a "private purchaser" under section 27. I would, therefore, dismiss this appeal. It follows that I am afraid that I am unable to agree with the passage in *Goode, Hire-Purchase Law and Practice*, p. 622, upon which Mr. Draycott relies.

BROWNE L.J. I agree that this appeal should be dismissed for the reasons given by my Lords and by Bridge J. I feel considerable sympathy with this appellant, but in spite of Mr. Draycott's attractive argument I find it impossible to come to any other conclusion.

Mr. Draycott's argument in substance, as I understand it, was that you should look at the capacity in which the appellant, or anyone else, carried out a particular transaction, and not more generally at the business which is being carried on by him, but it seems to me that the words of the Hire-Purchase Act 1964 are too clear to make it possible to accept this argument. As Bridge J. said, and as Roskill L.J. has said, section 29 (2) of the Hire-Purchase Act establishes a dichotomy between trade or finance purchasers and private purchasers. Mr. Rose submitted that this was a dichotomy based on the status of the purchaser and not on the circumstances of a particular transaction. I agree. In other words, the distinction is between categories of persons, not between categories of transactions.

In my view, those categories are mutually exclusive. A "trade or finance purchaser" is defined as somebody who "carries on a business which consists, wholly or partly" (among other things) "of purchasing motor vehicles for the purpose of offering or exposing them for sale." On the other hand, "a private purchaser" means a purchaser who does not carry on any such business.

It was conceded, inevitably, in this case that the appellant did come within the definition of section 29 (2) (*a*) of a trade or finance purchaser which I have just read. In my judgment, that is the end of the matter. I find it impossible to construe this section as introducing any further considerations about whether a particular transaction was in the course of that business, or about the capacity in which the appellant bought this car.

I agree with Mr. Rose that the words "at the time of" are not surplusage in the section. They are put in, I think, as he said, to indicate in a broad way the point of time at which one has to look. If they had been left out, there would have been room for argument that one might look at various other times, for example, the time of the original hire-purchase agreement, or the time of the trial, or possibly other dates. Accordingly, I agree that this appeal must be dismissed.

Appeal dismissed.
No order as to costs.

Solicitors: *Simpson, Silvertown & Co. for Betesh & Co., Manchester; Hall, Brydon & Co., Manchester.*

M. M. H.

[QUEEN'S BENCH DIVISION]

* PRACTICE DIRECTION (Q.B.D.: POSTAL FACILITIES)

Practice—Postal facilities—Queen's Bench Division—Extension of class of business which may be conducted by post—R.S.C., Ord. 1, *r.* 10

Introductory

1. With a view to the despatch of business with greater expedition, economy and convenience, it has been decided, with the approval of the Lord Chancellor, to authorise the use of postal facilities for the conduct of the following classes of business in the Queen's Bench Division, namely:

(1) Entry of judgment in default of appearance in actions for debts or liquidated demands or unliquidated damages.
(2) Issue of masters' summonses.
(3) Drawing up of masters' orders.
(4) Issue of notices of appeal and applications to the judge in chambers.
(5) Drawing up of judges' orders.
(6) Issue of third party notices and similar proceedings.
(7) Consent orders.
(8) Uncontested orders for directions.
(9) Special appointments before masters.
(10) Ex parte applications to masters.

2. In addition, these directions deal with the practice relating to the entry of appearance by post which is already authorised by R.S.C., Ord. 12, r. 1: see paragraph 24 below.

3. The proper use and operation of these postal facilities should avoid unnecessary personal attendances at the court offices and should consequently enable solicitors to utilise their staff more effectively, to smooth the process of their litigation practice, and above all, to save time, effort, costs and expenses. Great care has been taken in spelling out clearly and explicitly the precise conditions for the proper conduct of these classes of business by post, and it is therefore the responsibility of the solicitor or the party concerned to ensure due compliance with these conditions when making use of these postal facilities.

4. Any non-compliance with any of these conditions will be self-defeating and will add to the delay, cost and inconvenience in conducting any business with the court through the medium of the post, and it is therefore the duty of the party employing this method to exercise all due care, attention and diligence in complying with these conditions.

5. The use of these postal facilities is at the risk of the solicitor or party concerned. Where time for any reason is material, important or crucial, particularly having regard to any period of limitation which may be involved, solicitors and parties must be particularly careful in making use of the post for conducting any of the classes of business mentioned in these directions. Wherever the use of these postal facilities may create difficulties as regards any time-factor in the conduct of the litigation, the solicitor or the party concerned should carefully consider whether it would not be better and safer to conduct his business by personal attendance at the court offices.

6. It will not be possible for the Action Department or any part of the Central Office of the Supreme Court to enter into any correspondence or

telephonic communication in respect of any business in relation to which a party has chosen to use the postal facilities dealt with in these directions; nor can the Central Office or any part thereof accept any responsibility for any defect, error or omission in any document sent to it by post, though for the convenience and the assistance of the parties any mere *formal* defect, error or omission may be corrected or supplied by the Central Office. Any queries on such matters may require personal attendance at the appropriate department of the Central Office.

7. Nothing in these directions will preclude personal attendance at the Central Office for the conduct of any business or classes of business.

General provisions

8. *Application by letter*

In relation to each class of business dealt with by these directions, application for the conduct of such business by post must be made by a letter signed by or on behalf of the solicitor for a party or by the party if he is acting in person: (a) specifying precisely what the court is being required to do, (b) enclosing the requisite documents as prescribed below in relation to each class of business, and (c) enclosing, as part of such requisite documents, an envelope of adequate size which must be properly addressed to the sender for the return of the relevant documents to him.

9. *Address for application*

The letter of application, together with the requisite documents, must be posted in a pre-paid envelope properly addressed to:

The Action Department
Postal Section
Central Office
Royal Courts of Justice
Strand
London WC2A 2LL.

10. *Date of application*

Such an application will be treated as having been made at the date and time of the actual receipt of the requisite documents in the Central Office, and for this purpose the date and time of despatch of the requisite documents will be wholly disregarded.

11. *Receipt of requisite documents*

On receiving the requisite documents the proper officer of the Central Office will affix to the application an official stamp showing the date and time on which he received the requisite documents and will then proceed to deal with the application.

12. *Rejection of application by post*

If the requisite documents for any reason appear to the proper officer of the Central Office or the master not to comply with the requirements laid down by these directions or if the master should decline to accede to the application being dealt with by post, the application will not be granted but the relevant documents will all be returned by post to the party making the application in the envelope sent by him for this purpose. It will then be the

A duty of the party to conduct the particular business in question by personal attendance at the Central Office in the ordinary way.

13. *Application to district registries*

Pursuant to R.S.C., Ord. 63, r. 17, the practice of the Central Office as regulated by these directions will be followed in the district registries, with
B such variations as the circumstances may require.

Provisions relating to particular classes of business

14. *Entry of judgment in default of appearance by post in actions for debts or liquidated demands or for unliquidated damages*

(1) Subject to the provisions of this paragraph, in actions for debts or
C liquidated demands or for unliquidated damages under R.S.C., Ord. 13, rr. 1 and 2, the plaintiff may apply by post to the Central Office for the entry of judgment in default of appearance, instead of by personal attendance at such office.

(2) The requisite documents which must accompany the letter of application are the following: (a) the original writ in the action which must
D contain the indorsement of service of the writ within the jurisdiction duly completed. (b) The original affidavit of service of the writ in due and proper form, showing that the writ has been duly served within the jurisdiction or the defendant's solicitor's indorsement of acceptance of service. (c) Two duplicate copies (*not* carbon copies) of the proposed judgment duly completed on proper paper (see Ord. 66, r. 1) stating: (i) that the defendant, or if there is more than one, the defendant against whom
E judgment is requested to be entered, is in default of appearance; (ii) the amount for which judgment is requested to be entered, and the amount, if any, which has been received since the issue of the writ, or in the case of unliquidated damages, that judgment be entered for damages to be assessed; (iii) the amount of the appropriate costs.

(3) If the requisite documents are in proper form and order, the proper
F officer of the Central Office will make a search for appearance of the defendant or if there is more than one, the defendant against whom judgment is requested to be entered, and if no appearance has been entered, he will seal the judgment form with a "non appearance seal" specifying the time when he does so and the officer will then enter judgment as requested and will seal and return one of the duplicate copies of the judgment and retain the other duplicate copy for filing.

G

15. *Issue of masters' summonses by post*

(1) Subject to the provisions of this paragraph, a party may apply to the Central Office for the issue of a master's summons by post for hearing in chambers instead of by personal attendance at such office. Special arrangements apply to special appointments before masters (see paragraph
H 22 below).

(2) The requisite documents which must accompany the letter of application are the following: (a) the proposed summons which must be duly, fully and accurately completed, containing all the necessary particulars relating to the summons, including: (i) the full title of the action and action number; (ii) the name of the master, if any, to whom the action has already been assigned; (iii) the precise nature of the relief or remedy or order sought by the summons; and (iv) the name of the party by or on whose behalf the

summons is being issued; (v) the party or parties to whom the summons is A addressed. (b) In the case of a summons for summary judgment under R.S.C., Ord. 14, a certificate that the defendant has duly entered an appearance.

(3) If the requisite documents are in proper form and order, the proper officer of the Central Office will allocate an appropriate return date for the hearing of the summons and will seal the summons and return it by post to the party making the application in the envelope sent by him for this B purpose.

(4) It is the duty of the party issuing the summons to serve it promptly on the other party or parties together with copies of any supporting affidavits and exhibits in sufficient time before the return date, otherwise he may have to bear the costs of any consequent adjournment. C

16. *Drawing up of masters' orders by post*

(1) Subject to the provisions of this paragraph, a party may apply to the Central Office by post for the drawing up of an order made by a master, instead of by personal attendance at such office.

(2) The requisite documents which must accompany the letter of application are the following: (a) the original summons containing the actual in- D dorsement of his order made by the master duly initialled and dated by him. (b) The engrossed copy of the proposed order in duplicate (*not* carbon copies) stating fully and accurately the terms of the order made by the master, and setting out fully and accurately the following particulars and recitals, namely: (i) the name of the master who made the order; (ii) the date on which the order was made; (iii) the parties who actually appeared before the master and by whom, whether by counsel, solicitors, or in person; E (iv) the affidavits (if any) that were actually read or referred to at the hearing of the summons, and if there were any such affidavits, stating the name of the deponents to each such affidavit and the date of its jurat and certifying on the back-sheet of both copies of the order that all such affidavits have already been duly filed.

(3) In the case of an order requiring the transmission of money from the F High Court to the county court or requiring money to be paid into a county court, the requirements of the Queen's Bench Masters' Practice Directions, Direction No. 19 (4) must be complied with.

(4) The application must be made within the time specified by the master for the order to be drawn up or if no such time has been specified within 21 days of the making of an order, otherwise the leave of the master G must be obtained for drawing up the order out of time, as required by the Queen's Bench Masters' Practice Directions, Direction 19 (1). If the application for drawing up the order by post is made out of time, the application must also enclose the leave of the master to do so which is usually indorsed on the summons upon which the order was indorsed: see paragraph 23 (4) below.

(5) If the requisite documents are in proper form and order, the proper H officer of the Central Office will pass and draw up the order by sealing the order with the seal of the court and return it by post to the party making the application in the envelope sent by him for this purpose but will retain the summons containing the indorsement of the master and the duplicate copy of the order drawn up for filing.

(6) This paragraph will not apply to orders of a master which require a Part II schedule.

A 17. *Issue of notices of appeal and applications to the judge in chambers by post*

(1) Subject to the provisions of this paragraph, a party may apply to the Central Office for the issue by post, instead of by personal attendance at such office of: (a) a notice of appeal to the judge in chambers from the order of a master or district registrar made in chambers; (b) an original
B summons or application to the judge in chambers.

(2) The requisite documents which must accompany the letter of application are the following:

(A) *In the case of a notice of appeal to the judge in chambers*: (a) Two duplicate copies (*not* carbon copies) of the notice of appeal in accordance with the Practice Form, Form No. P.7, 114 (B.56) duly completed and containing all the necessary particulars, including: (i) the name of the
C master or district registrar against whose decision the appeal is brought; (ii) the relevant terms of the order appealed against including the date on which the order was made; (iii) an application for an extension of time in which to appeal, wherever this is necessary; (iv) the full terms of the order or other relief or remedy sought to be obtained on the appeal; (v) the name and address of the party issuing the notice of appeal; (vi) the name and address of each party to whom the notice of appeal is addressed; (vii)
D in the case of an appeal from a district registry, a certificate as to the availability or otherwise of a High Court judge to hear the appeal at the nearest trial centre to the district registry. (b) One of the duplicate copies of the notice of appeal must be duly signed by or on behalf of the solicitor acting for the party issuing the notice or by the party if he is acting in person. (c) A cheque which must be drawn by the solicitor acting for the party
E issuing the notice of appeal or a postal or money order crossed and made payable to H.M. Paymaster-General for the proper amount of the court fee payable on the issue of such a notice, which at present is £5. A cheque not drawn by the solicitor will not be accepted. (d) A certificate stating as accurately as possible what is the estimated time for the hearing of the appeal.

(B) *In the case of an original summons or application to the judge in*
F *chambers*: (a) Two duplicate copies (*not* carbon copies) of the summons or application to the judge in chambers duly completed and containing all the necessary particulars including: (i) the full terms of the order or of the relief or remedy sought to be obtained; (ii) the name and address of the party issuing the summons or application; (ii) the name and address of each of the parties to whom the summons or application is addressed. (b) One of
G the duplicate copies of the summons or application must be duly signed on behalf of the solicitor acting for the party issuing the summons or application or by the party if he is acting in person. (c) A certificate stating as accurately as possible what is the estimated time for the hearing of the summons or application.

(C) *In the case of an originating summons*: (a) The original originating summons and a copy thereof (*not* carbon copy). (b) A certificate stating as
H accurately as possible what is the estimated time for the hearing of the application.

(3) If the requisite documents are in proper form and order, the proper officer of the Central Office will allocate an appropriate return date for the hearing of the appeal or summons or application as the case may be, and will seal it with the seal of the court and issue it and return it by post to the party making the application in the envelope sent by him for this purpose but will retain the duplicate copy.

18. *Drawing up the judges' orders by post*

(1) Subject to the provisions of this paragraph, a party may apply by post to the Central Office for the drawing up of an order made by the judge in chambers, instead of by personal attendance at such office.

(2) The requisite documents which must accompany the letter of application are the following: (a) The original notice of appeal, summons or application containing the actual indorsement of the order made by the judge in chambers duly initialled and dated by him. (b) The engrossed copy of the proposed order in duplicate (*not* carbon copies) stating where applicable the order appealed against and, stating fully and accurately the terms of the order made by the judge, and setting out fully and accurately the following particulars and recitals, namely: (i) the name of the judge who made the order; (ii) the date on which the order was made; (iii) the parties who actually appeared before the judge and by whom, whether by counsel, solicitors or in person; (iv) the affidavits (if any) that were actually read or referred to at the hearing before the judge, and if there were any such affidavits, stating the name of the deponents to each such affidavit and the date of its jurat and certifying on the back-sheet of both copies of the order that all such affidavits have already been duly filed; (v) in the case of an appeal from a district registrar, an extra copy of the engrossed order.

(3) The application must be made within the time specified by the judge for the order to be drawn up or if no such time has been specified within 21 days of the making of the order, otherwise leave must be obtained for drawing up the order out of time. If the application for drawing up the order by post is made out of time, the reasons for the delay must be indorsed on the summons containing the actual indorsement initialled by the judge.

(4) If the requisite documents are in proper form and order, the proper officer of the Central Office will pass and draw up the order by sealing the order with the seal of the court and return it by post to the party making the application in the envelope sent by him for this purpose but will return the original notice of appeal, summons or application containing the indorsement of the judge and the duplicate copy of the order drawn up for filing, and in the case of an appeal from a district registrar he will send the extra engrossed copy of the order to the appropriate registry.

19. *Issue of third party notices and similar proceedings by post*

(1) Subject to the provisions of this paragraph, a party may apply to the Central Office for the issue by post of a third party notice or other similar proceedings, instead of by personal attendance at such office.

(2) The requisite documents, which must accompany the letter of application, are the following: (a) Two duplicate copies (*not* carbon copies) of the proposed third party notice in the prescribed form duly completed and containing all the necessary indorsements and particulars properly completed; and must be duly signed by or on behalf of the solicitor for the defendant or by the defendant if he is acting in person. (b) A certificate that the defence of the defendant by or on whose behalf the third party notice is to be issued has not yet been served *or* a copy of the order of the court granting leave for the issue of the third party notice.

(3) If the requisite documents are in proper form and order, the proper officer of the Central Office will seal one of the duplicate copies of the third party notice with the seal of the court and will return it by post to the party making the application in the envelope sent by him for this purpose but retain the other duplicate copy for filing.

(4) This paragraph will apply, with such variations as the circumstances may require, to the following proceedings: (a) a third party notice or contribution notice as between co-defendants; (c) fourth and subsequent party notices; and (c) a counterclaim against an added party under R.S.C., Ord. 15, r. 3.

20. *Consent orders by post*

(1) Subject to the provisions of this paragraph, a party may apply to the Central Office by post for a consent order to be made by a master and for such order to be drawn up, instead of by personal attendance at such office.

(2) The requisite documents, which must accompany the letter of application, are the following: (a) The summons setting out fully and accurately the precise terms agreed upon by all the parties. (b) The written consent of all the parties to the action, including any third party (if the consent summons relates to him as well) signed and dated by the solicitors for each party and expressly stating that each party consents to the terms agreed as set out in the summons. (c) If it is also desired that the consent order should be drawn up, an engrossed copy of the proposed order in duplicate (*not* carbon copies) stating fully and accurately the terms of the agreed order made by the master and setting out fully and accurately the following particulars, namely: (i) the name of the master assigned to the action, if known; (ii) the fact that the order was made by consent; (iii) the fact that the consent order was made on the application of the parties.

(3) (a) If the requisite documents are in proper form and order, the proper officer of the Central Office will place the proposed consent order before the practice master for his consideration, who, if he thinks fit, will make the order accordingly. (b) If the practice master makes the consent order, the proper officer of the Central Office will then pass the requisite documents to the appropriate section of the Action Department for the order to be duly passed and drawn up. (c) If the requisite documents are in proper form and order, the proper officer of the appropriate section of the Action Department will pass and draw up the order by sealing the order with the seal of the court and will return it by post to the party making the application in the envelope sent by him for this purpose but will retain the original order made by the master and the duplicate copy order as drawn up for filing. He will insert the date on which the order was made and the name of the master who made the order and, if necessary, he will add the particulars set out under sub-paragraph (2) (c) hereof.

21. *Uncontested orders for directions by post*

(1) Subject to the provisions of this paragraph, a party may apply to the Central Office by post for an order for directions, where such an order has been agreed or is uncontested as between the parties, to be made by the master and for such an order to be drawn up, instead of by personal attendance at such office.

(2) The requisite documents which must accompany the letter of application are the following: (a) The original or restored summons for directions issued for hearing before the master, together with the following documents which must be bound up in proper chronological order, namely: (i) the writ; (ii) the pleadings (including any affidavits ordered to stand as pleadings), any request or order for particulars and the particulars served in response

thereto; (iii) any orders for directions already made. (b) A certificate that, if it be the fact, the parties have already exchanged their respective lists of documents or have dispensed with discovery of documents, as the case may be. (c) The proposed order for directions which it is requested the master should make, setting out fully and accurately the precise terms which have been agreed or are uncontested by all the parties and enclosing the request if any for further and better particulars of any pleading *or* any proposed amendment of the pleading. (d) The written consent of all the parties to the action signed and dated by the solicitors for each party and expressly stating that each party agrees to or does not contest the terms as set out in the proposed order. (e) If it is also desired that the uncontested order for directions should be drawn up, an engrossed copy of the proposed order in duplicate (*not* carbon copies) stating fully and accurately the terms of the agreed or uncontested order to be made by the master.

(3) The master will consider all the relevant documents placed before him in the light of the duty of the court under R.S.C., Ord. 25, rr. 2, 3, 4 and 6, and if he is satisfied that the proposed agreed or uncontested order for directions is in proper form and order, the master will make the order accordingly, but if he is not so satisfied the master may either: (a) make any such order or give any such directions as to the future course of the action as he may think necessary or proper, e.g. amend the listing grade of the action as may be necessary and so forth; or (b) decline to make the order or require the attendance of the parties before him or direct that the summons be restored to the list for hearing in the ordinary way.

(4) If the requisite documents are in proper form and order and the master has approved and made the order accordingly, whether as originally submitted or as amended by him, the proper officer of the appropriate section of the Action Department will pass and draw up the order by sealing it with the seal of the court and will return the order together with all the other accompanying documents by post to the party making the application in the envelope sent by him for this purpose but he will retain the original order made by the master and the duplicate copy order as drawn up for filing.

(5) This paragraph applies also to uncontested orders for directions in third party proceedings.

22. *Applications by post for special appointment before masters*

(1) Subject to the provisions of this paragraph, a party may apply to the Central Office by post for obtaining a special appointment for the hearing of a summons or for the hearing of the assessment of damages before the master, instead of by personal attendance at such office.

(2) The requisite documents which must accompany the letter of application are the following: (a) In the case of an application for the hearing of a summons, the original summons which should set out fully and accurately the precise relief or remedy or order sought thereby and setting out the other particulars specified in sub-paragraph (2) of paragraph 15 hereof. (b) In the case of an application for the assessment of damages, an office copy of the judgment and the current appropriate fee for the hearing of the assessment of damages which must be paid by cheque drawn by the solicitor or by a postal or money order crossed and made payable to H.M. Paymaster-General by the solicitor for the party or by the party acting in person. A cheque not drawn by the solicitor will not be accepted. (c) The following form duly and accurately completed:

APPLICATION FOR APPOINTMENT BEFORE A MASTER

MASTER ....

PARTIES IN ACTION ....

TYPE OF SUMMONS (or, if assessment of damages, nature of claim)

....

ESTIMATED LENGTH OF HEARING ....

DATES CONVENIENT TO ALL PARTIES ....

....

DATES TO BE AVOIDED ....

....

ARE COUNSEL ATTENDING? ....

NAMES OF COUNSEL (IF KNOWN) ....

....

DATE APPLICATION MADE ....

SOLICITOR MAKING THE APPLICATION ....

(3) (a) If the requisite documents are in proper form and order the proper officer of the Central Office will place the application for a special appointment before the assigned master for his consideration. (b) If the master considers the requisite documents are in proper form and order he will fix the date, time and place of the appointment. (c) If the master so fixes the date, time and place of the appointment, the proper officer of the Central Office will return the summons or the office copy of the judgment, as the case may be, to the party making the application in the envelope sent by him for this purpose.

23. *Ex parte applications to masters by post*

(1) Subject to the provisions of this paragraph, a party may apply to the Central Office by post for the making of an ex parte application to the court and if so desired for the drawing up of an order made on such ex parte application, instead of by personal attendance at such office.

(2) The requisite documents which must accompany the letter of application are the following: (a) the affidavit supporting the ex parte application duly completed and stating clearly what order is being sought, and containing the necessary jurat, together with any exhibits referred to therein. (b) If it is desired that the ex parte order should be drawn up, the engrossed copy of the proposed order in duplicate (*not* carbon copies) stating fully and accurately the terms of the order made by the master (save for the matters which will necessarily have to be indorsed by the master on making his order, e.g. the amount for which a garnishee order nisi should be drawn up).

(3) (a) If the requisite documents are in proper form and order, the proper officer of the Central Office will place the affidavit supporting the ex parte application before the practice master for his consideration, together with any exhibits thereto. (b) If the proposed ex parte application is in proper form and order, the practice master will make his order accordingly. (c) If the practice master makes his order on the ex parte application, the proper officer of the Central Office will then pass the requisite documents to the appropriate section of the Action Department for the order to be passed and drawn up. (d) If the requisite documents are in proper form and order, the proper officer of the appropriate section of the Action Department will complete the engrossed copy in duplicate by reference to the actual order made by the master, e.g. he will insert the name of the master by whom the order was made and will insert, so far as possible, the terms of the order made by the master, e.g. the amount for which the garnishee order nisi has been made or the address to which a writ of summons may be served by way of substituted service, or as the case may be, and will pass and draw up the order by sealing it with the seal of the court and will return the engrossed order by post to the party making the application in the envelope sent by him for this purpose, but will retain the original affidavit on which the master made his order and the duplicate copy of the order as drawn up for filing.

(4) This paragraph will apply also to an application for the leave of the master to extend the time for drawing up an order after the date specified or if no date is specified after 21 days from the making of the order. The original order of the master indorsed on the summons, must accompany any such application, and a full explanation as to why the order was not drawn up within the requisite time must be given by the applicant.

24. *Entry of appearance by post*

(1) In addition to the above directions governing the classes of business authorised thereby to be conducted by post, the following practice will apply in relation to the entry of appearance by post which is already authorised by R.S.C., Ord 12, r. 1.

(2) If the requisite documents as prescribed by R.S.C., Ord. 12, r. 3 are sent by post to the appropriate office, they should be accompanied by: (a) an envelope duly addressed to the plaintiff's solicitors or to the plaintiff if he is acting in person, as the case may be, at the plaintiff's address for service; and (b) an envelope duly addressed to the defendant's solicitors or to the defendant if he is acting in person, as the case may be, at the defendant's address for service.

25. *Commencement date*

These directions will come into operation on June 8, 1976.

I. H. Jacob,

Senior Master of the Supreme Court.

April 14, 1976.

[COURT OF APPEAL]

* ELLIOTT AND OTHERS *v.* SOUTHWARK LONDON BOROUGH COUNCIL

[1976 E. No. 171]

1976 Feb. 16, 17; 24 — Megaw, James and Geoffrey Lane L.JJ.

Housing—Unfit for human habitation—Rehabilitation order—Houses scheduled for demolition under compulsory purchase order—Requests for rehabilitation orders made under new Act—Refusal on ground that properties to be demolished and sites used for erection of new housing—Whether requests properly considered—Whether reason adequate and intelligible to recipients in circumstances—Housing Act 1974 (*c.* 44) (*as amended by Housing Rents and Subsidies Act* 1975 (*c.* 6), *Sch.* 5), *s.* 114 (1) (2) (4) (5), *Sch.* 10, *para.* 3 (2) [1]

The plaintiffs were owner-occupiers of houses in a clearance area which had been classified as unfit for human habitation and scheduled for demolition under a compulsory purchase order confirmed by the Secretary of State on December 2, 1974, after a public inquiry at which the plaintiffs had appeared as objectors. In May 1975, they applied to the London borough council in whose area their houses were situated pursuant to section 114 of and Schedule 10 to the Housing Act 1974 which, as amended by the Housing Rents and Subsidies Act 1975, had come into force on March 31, 1975, for rehabilitation orders to be made in respect of their houses. The requests were considered first by a sub-committee of the housing committee, and then by the housing committee which recommended to the council that the requests be refused. The council resolved so to do and, by letter of July 21, informed each plaintiff that the request had been refused " for the reason that the properties should be demolished and the sites used for the erection of new housing accommodation."

The plaintiffs issued an originating summons seeking declarations that the council had failed to carry out their statutory duties under the Act of 1974 to consider, determine and give reasons for their refusal to make the rehabilitation orders and an injunction directing the council to consider and determine the requests according to law. Willis J. held that the requests had been properly considered, that the letter of refusal gave a sufficiently clear indication why the request could not be acceded to and was adequate and sufficient, and intelligible to the recipient, bearing in mind the inquiry which had gone before. He accordingly refused the relief sought.

On appeal by four of the plaintiffs:—

Held, dismissing the appeal, (1) that, in considering the requests, the council were entitled to take into consideration what had transpired at the inquiry for, although the arguments thereat were not, and could not at that time have been directed to the making of rehabilitation orders, the objectors were in fact contending for the same result as could be achieved by such an order after the Housing Act 1974 was passed; that there was no evidence that the council had failed to take into account changes in the law and in housing policy which had taken place since the inquiry took place; that there had been no impropriety, and in the face of the evidence of the com-

[1] Housing Act 1974 (as amended), s. 114 (1) (2) (4) (5): see post, p. 502E–H. Sch. 10, para. 3 (2): see post, p. 503B.

mittee procedure which had been followed, it was impossible to infer that the council had not taken into consideration factors relevant at the time the requests were made, or to hold that the requests had not been properly considered (post, pp. 507F—508A). A

Associated Provincial Picture Houses Ltd. v. *Wednesbury Corporation* [1948] 1 K.B. 223, C.A. and *Padfield* v. *Minister of Agriculture, Fisheries and Food* [1968] A.C. 997, H.L.(E.) considered. B

(2) That in considering the requests for rehabilitation orders the council was acting in an administrative and not in a judicial capacity and it was open to them to arrive at a "policy" decision for refusing to accede to the requests therefor; that against the background of the inquiry the appellants and those other house owners to whom the letter of refusal was sent were fully informed by its terms that the request had been refused because it could not be granted C consistently with the policy of the council as housing authority to demolish the existing houses and erect new accommodation; that the letter thus stated the salient reason why the house in question could not be retained and, in the circumstances of the present case, gave a reason for refusal which was sufficient and intelligible (post, pp. 509G—510C).

In re Poyser and Mills' Arbitration [1964] 2 Q.B. 467; and *Mountview Court Properties Ltd.* v. *Devlin* (1970) 21 D P. & C.R. 689, D.C. applied.

Hanks v. *Minister of Housing and Local Government* [1963] 1 Q.B. 999 considered.

Per curiam. This decision does not govern what may be different circumstances in other cases. The wording used for the giving of reasons in this case passes the test, the same wording in another case may fail to do so. The duty to give reasons pursuant to the statute is a responsible one and E cannot be discharged by the use of vague general words which are not sufficient to bring to the mind of the recipient a clear understanding of why his request for a rehabilitation order is being refused (post, p. 510C, D).

Decision of Willis J. affirmed.

The following cases are referred to in the judgment: F

Anisminic Ltd. v. *Foreign Compensation Commission* [1969] 2 A.C. 147; [1969] 2 W.L.R. 163; [1969] 1 All E.R. 208, H.L.(E.).

Associated Provincial Picture Houses Ltd. v. *Wednesbury Corporation* [1948] 1 K.B. 223; [1947] 2 All E.R. 680, C.A.

Givaudan & Co. Ltd. v. *Minister of Housing and Local Government* [1967] 1 W.L.R. 250; [1966] 3 All E.R. 696.

Hanks v. *Minister of Housing and Local Government* [1963] 1 Q.B. 999; G [1962] 3 W.L.R. 1482; [1963] 1 All E.R. 47.

Iveagh (Earl of) v. *Minister of Housing and Local Government* [1964] 1 Q.B. 395; [1963] 3 W.L.R. 974; [1963] 3 All E.R. 817, C.A.

Johnson (B.) & Co. (Builders) Ltd. v. *Ministry of Health* [1947] 2 All E.R. 395, C.A.

Mountview Court Properties Ltd. v. *Devlin* (1970) 21 P. & C.R. 689, D.C.

Padfield v. *Minister of Agriculture, Fisheries and Food* [1968] A.C. 997; H [1968] 2 W.L.R. 924; [1968] 1 All E.R. 694, C.A. and H.L.(E.).

Poyser and Mills' Arbitration, In re [1964] 2 Q.B. 467; [1963] 2 W.L.R. 1309; [1963] 1 All E.R. 612.

The following additional case was cited in argument:

Sovmots v. *Secretary of State for the Environment* [1976] 2 W.L.R. 73; [1976] 1 All E.R. 178.

A APPEAL from Willis J.

The plaintiffs, Mr. Alpheus Elliott, and nine other persons, were owner-occupiers of houses in Cuthill Road, Daneville Road, Kerfield Place and Kerfield Crescent, situate within an area declared to be a clearance area by Southwark London Borough Council. All the houses had been classified as unfit for human habitation and were scheduled for demolition under the London Borough of Southwark (Selborne Road) No. 1 Com-
B pulsory Purchase Order 1973 made by the council and confirmed by the Secretary of State for the Environment on December 2, 1975, and which became operative on March 7, 1975.

By letters dated May 8 and 9, 1975, all the plaintiffs applied to the council, pursuant to section 114 of and Schedule 10 to the Housing Act 1974, as amended by the Housing Rents and Subsidies Act 1975, to make
C rehabilitation orders in respect of their houses. By identical letters dated July 21, 1975, the council, by their deputy town clerk, informed each plaintiff that the council had resolved to refuse the application "for the reason that the properties should be demolished and the sites used for the erection of new housing accommodation."

On January 22, 1976, the plaintiffs issued an originating summons
D seeking (1) a declaration that the council had failed to carry out their statutory duties under the Housing Act 1974 to consider, determine and give reasons for their decision upon the requests made for rehabilitation orders; (2) a declaration that the council's decision to refuse their requests to make rehabilitation orders was invalid; (3) an injunction ordering the council to reconsider and determine the requests for rehabilitation orders according to law; and (4) an injunction restraining the council, their
E servants, agents or otherwise from demolishing and/or damaging any of the houses in certain streets all being subject to demolition under the Selborne Road (No. 1) Compulsory Purchase Order until they had dealt with the rehabilitation order requests according to law.

The council, by their director of housing, filed an affidavit asking, inter alia, for the hearing of the action to be expedited and it was heard
F by Willis J. on February 2, 1976. He held that the council had given proper consideration to the requests for rehabilitation orders, and that, in the circumstances of the case, having regard to what had gone before, the letter of July 21 gave a reason for refusal which was adequate and intelligible and he accordingly dismissed the plaintiffs' claims.

Mr. Elliott and three other plaintiffs, Mrs. Kathleen Louise Iwegbu, Mr. Willie Sydney Davidson and Mrs. Lunette Hunte, appealed, asking
G that the judgment be set aside on the grounds (1) that the judge had misdirected himself on the facts and was wrong in law in concluding (a) that the council had given reasons for their decision to refuse the requests for rehabilitation orders and that the reasons were adequate and intelligible; (b) that the issues material to the requests had been fully considered and determined at the public inquiry in January 1974 and
H in the decision letter of the Secretary of State relating thereto in such a way as to reduce the council's obligation to give explicit reasons for their decision; and (c) that the council gave sufficient and adequate consideration to each of the individual requests for rehabilitation orders. (2) That the judge misdirected himself on the facts and erred in law in (a) failing to take due account of the substantial changes of law and of national, social and economic policy which had occurred since the public inquiry; (b) failing to conclude that the council were in breach of their

duty under section 114 of and Schedule 10, paragraph 3 (2) to the Housing A
Act 1974 (as amended) to give reasons for their decision; and (c) to conclude that the council had failed properly to consider and determine the requests and grant the relief sought.

The facts are stated in the judgment of the court.

Peter Boydell Q.C., Desmond Keane and *Patrick Crawford* for the appellants. B

Gerald Moriarty Q.C. and *Viscount Colville of Culross* for the council.

Cur. adv. vult.

February 24. MEGAW L.J. The judgment which James L.J. is about to deliver is the judgment of the court. C

JAMES L.J. This is an appeal expedited by order of the court from the judgment of Willis J. of February 2, 1976, made on the hearing of an originating summons taken out on January 22, 1976. In that summons 10 plaintiffs claimed declarations and injunctions against the defendants, the Southwark London Borough Council. Four of those plaintiffs are the appellants in this appeal. They are Mr. A. Elliott, Mrs. K. L. D
Iwegbu, Mr. W. S. Davidson and Mrs. Lunette Hunte.

The background to the appeal is the introduction by legislation in 1974 of the concept of the rehabilitation of houses as an alternative to demolition, clearance and redevelopment. The relevant statutory provisions are the Housing Act 1974, section 114, and Schedule 10 to that Act as amended by the Housing Rents and Subsidies Act 1975. The E
Act of 1974 received the Royal Assent on July 31, 1974. Section 114 and Schedule 10 in the unamended form came into force on December 2, 1974, and as amended on March 11, 1975. It is the amended form which is relevant to this appeal.

Subsection (1) of section 114 provides that the section shall apply to houses comprised in a clearance area under Part III of the Housing Act 1957 which fall into any one of three categories. The categories F
are widely defined and are likely to include many houses comprised in clearance areas.

Subsection (2) is in these terms:

> "Where any house to which this section applies—(*a*) was included in the clearance area by reason of its being unfit for human habitation, and (*b*) in the opinion of the local authority is capable of being, and G
> ought to be, improved to the full standard, the local authority may make and submit to the Secretary of State an order (in this section and Schedule 10 below referred to as a 'rehabilitation order') in relation to that house."

Subsection (3) provides that a rehabilitation order "may, if the local authority think fit" apply to any other Part III land. H

Subsection (4) provides that Schedule 10 to the Act shall have effect in relation to rehabilitation orders.

By subsection (5) the local authority is relieved of a duty to demolish or secure the demolition of buildings as from the date on which a rehabilitation order becomes operative. By subsection (6), when the local authority is relieved of the duty to demolish a house included in a clearance area, being unfit for human habitation, "the authority shall take

A such steps as are necessary" to bring or secure that the house is brought up to "the full standard" for the purposes of the Act.

For the purposes of the present appeal it is necessary to refer only to paragraph 3 (2) of Schedule 10. That subparagraph reads:

> "Where the owner of a house to which section 114 above applies and which was included in the clearance area by reason of its being
> B unfit for human habitation requests the local authority to make a rehabilitation order in respect of the house, and the authority refuse to make an order, they shall give him in writing their reasons for so refusing."

The council declared in April 1968 a development area known as "Selborne Road Development Area." In March 1973 they made a
C clearance order under Part III of the Housing Act 1957 in respect of that area and in May 1973 resolved to effect the clearance by the exercise of the compulsory purchase powers. On October 12 that year the council submitted a compulsory purchase order to the Secretary of State for confirmation. At that date there were 157 dwelling houses within the area. Of those, 72 had already been purchased by the council by agreement with the owners. Of the other 85 dwelling houses, 70 were included
D in the proposed order on the ground that they were unfit for human habitation. The four appellants are owner-occupiers of four of those 70 houses. They and many other owners and occupiers of houses to which the order applied objected to the making of the order. Some disputed the alleged unfitness of the house. Many urged that defects could be remedied and improvements made so that the house would con-
E form to the required standard. Many had done work of maintenance and repair. None wanted to leave. All wanted to preserve the existing community. Whatever compensation is payable, many suffer considerable distress when their homes are taken from them by compulsory purchase and they are forced to leave familiar surroundings and start afresh in a strange and sometimes less convenient area. This was expressly recognised in the White Paper "Better Homes, The Next Priorities," presented
F to Parliament in 1973 (1973, Cmnd. 5339). We feel great sympathy with persons who find themselves in the position of the appellants and the other occupiers of houses within the order. The Secretary of State directed that a local public inquiry be held. The inquiry extended over the period of two days in January 1974 and the inspector reported to the Secretary of State on April 22, 1974. The inspector recommended that
G with certain modifications, not relevant for present purposes, the compulsory purchase order be confirmed. On December 2, 1974, the Secretary of State wrote his letter of decision confirming the order which is known as The London Borough of Southwark (Selborne Road) (No. 1) Compulsory Purchase Order 1973. That was the same day as that on which section 114 of the Act of 1974 came into effect. On March 17, 1975, the council served notices to treat. On May 8 and 9 many of
H those who had objected to the making of the order and who had advanced their objections at the public local inquiry wrote to the council letters making application for "a rehabilitation order to be made in respect of houses which are the subject of the above-mentioned order" (the order in question in this appeal). It may perhaps be worth noting that this request is for an order to be made in respect of "houses," in the plural. The letters were all in the same terms and expressly suggested that the appropriate reply to the application "is either to accept it or

give reason for refusing it." Each letter referred to the property or A
properties in which the signatory had the necessary interest as owner.
The applications were considered by a subcommittee of the housing com-
mittee and the housing committee of the council. The recommendation
of those committees was accepted by the council, who resolved on July
16, 1975, to refuse the application. On July 21 by their deputy town
clerk the council wrote to each applicant in these terms (the only variant
being that "property," in the singular, was substituted for "properties" B
in the plural, where appropriate):

> "With reference to your application dated May 8, 1975, for the
> council to make rehabilitation orders in respect of the above
> properties, in accordance with the provisions of section 114 and
> Schedule 10 of the Housing Act 1974, I write to inform you that the
> council, at their meeting on July 16, resolved to refuse the applica- C
> tion for the reason that the properties should be demolished and
> the sites used for the erection of new housing accommodation."

It is the wording of that letter which is the nub of this appeal.

On January 12, 1976, demolition pursuant to the order commenced.
Discussions and negotiations had not succeeded in bringing about any
compromise or modification save to the extent that a number of occu- D
piers of houses had left and been rehoused. Those who remained were
constant in their desire to save their homes and to save the existing
community. The council remained unshaken in the opinion that their
duty lay in the implementation of the order and the clearance of the area
by demolition in order to facilitate redevelopment. So the appellants
and six others joined as plaintiffs in the originating summons in which E
the following relief was sought against the council. [His Lordship read
the declarations and injunctions sought as set out above, and continued]:
On January 17 the plaintiffs in the proposed proceedings obtained an
interim injunction. On February 2 the matter was heard by Willis J.
who refused to grant the relief sought. It is from his judgment that four
of the plaintiffs appeal. The appellants are said to represent the interests
of all the owners of houses affected by the decision of the judge. F

It is desirable to say something as to the function of the courts in a
case such as this. It is not for the court to determine issues which by
statute fall to be decided by a body such as a local housing authority.
Thus, for example, it is no part of the court's function to arrive at a
view, or a decision, even if it had the material necessary to do so, on such
questions as whether or not a particular house or the houses in a parti- G
cular area should be rehabilitated, or should be demolished in order that
new housing may be built. Its function is not to substitute its own view
or opinion or decision on matters which Parliament has left to the judg-
ment of the local housing authority, without provision for appeal. Its
function is, where such issues are raised, in proceedings of this nature, to
decide whether the local authority in reaching their decision have acted
in accordance with the statutory provisions by which Parliament has H
defined the authority's powers, duties and procedure.

The appellants invite the court to say that the council did not comply
with their statutory duty under section 114 (2) and Schedule 10, para-
graph 3 (2), of the Act of 1974 (as amended). They say that the council
were under a duty to consider the applications for a rehabilitation order
and to consider them individually and, having discharged that duty, were
under the further duty to give to each appellant in writing the reasons for

A refusing. They say that the material before the court shows, at least by way of inference, that the council did not apply their minds to those considerations which were relevant to the applications, either individually or at all, and that the letter of July 21, 1975, did not give any or any sufficient reasons for the refusal. The council's case is a denial of these assertions.

B The judge said little in his judgment upon the question whether the council had given consideration to the applications. In the state of the evidence there was no need for him to say more than he did. There was no evidence of any impropriety. There was evidence that the applications had been before a subcommittee of the housing committee, the housing committee itself and, finally, had been the subject matter of a resolution of the council. In those circumstances the judge accepted the submission of counsel that to hold that proper consideration had not been
C given would be "an outrageous thing for a court to do." Upon the question whether the council had properly discharged the duty to give the reason for the refusal, the judge said:

> "It seems to me that it must be right that [paragraph] 3 (2) should be looked at in the context of this legislation, and that in the particular circumstances of the case which is being considered it must appear to
> D the satisfaction of any court which is being asked to review the reasons that the recipient should fairly understand why it is that the housing authority is not able in this case to accede to the request. The question here is whether in the circumstances of this case those reasons do pass that test."

He construed the letter of July 21 as stating:

> E "We cannot accede to the request for a rehabilitation order for the reasons that the whole of the area has got to be demolished and the sites used for housing purposes"; and continued: "That seems to me to be a sufficiently clear indication by the local authority, although not specifically [giving] details of the individual's house, of reasons which cannot be said to either inadequate or insufficient and in the
> F circumstances of the case, bearing in mind what had gone before, intelligible to the recipient of the refusal."

The words "bearing in mind what had gone before" in that passage are one of a number of references which the judge made to the fact that the plaintiffs' contentions had been advanced at the local public inquiry in January 1974. Mr. Boydell, who argued the case for the appellants in
G this court, emphasised the prominence given to this feature in the judgment and argued that the judge was in error in his interpretation of what had taken place at the inquiry. The judge used the expressions "plainly canvassed and dealt with in evidence on both sides," "fully ventilated and dealt with in her report by the inspector" and "thoroughly thrashed out" in relation to the issue of rehabilitation in so far as it was raised at the inquiry. We are inclined to the view that the words "fully ventilated"
H and "thoroughly thrashed out" are something of an overstatement, but this is a matter of minor criticism of the judgment.

In the argument before this court much attention was devoted to the proposition advanced on behalf of the appellants by Mr. Boydell that section 114 of the Act of 1974 not only conveyed a power but imposed a duty upon the local authority to consider making a rehabilitation order, irrespective of a request to do so made by an owner of property which qualifies for consideration. For the council, Mr. Moriarty disputed the proposition and supported his argument by a detailed analysis of the relevant statutory provisions. We find it unnecessary to come to any conclusion on this issue because it is common ground between the parties that once a request has been made pursuant to Schedule 10, paragraph 3 (2), the local authority are under the duty to consider the matters relevant to the application and to give reasons for a refusal. A

It being conceded that in the present case a duty arose to consider the request for a rehabilitation order to be made, Mr. Boydell's next proposition was that in the discharge of the duty the local authority should pay regard to relevant and disregard irrelevant matters. It is not necessary to cite authority in support of that proposition. Mr. Moriarty did not challenge it. Mr. Boydell did however refer, helpfully, to the words of Lord Greene M.R. in *Associated Provincial Picture Houses Ltd.* v. *Wednesbury Corporation* [1948] 1 K.B. 223, 228, in the passage which commences "The exercise of such a discretion must be a real exercise of the discretion." Lord Greene M.R. continued: B C

> "If, in the statute conferring the discretion, there is to be found expressly or by implication matters which the authority exercising the discretion ought to have regard to, then in exercising the discretion it must have regard to those matters. Conversely, if the nature of the subject-matter and the general interpretation of the Act make it clear that certain matters would not be germane to the matter in quesion, the authority must disregard those irrelevant collateral matters." D

Mr. Boydell also cited from the speech of Lord Upjohn in *Padfield* v. *Minister of Agriculture, Fisheries and Food* [1968] A.C. 997, 1058:

> "My Lords, upon the basic principles of law to be applied there was no real difference of opinion, the great question being how they should be applied to this case. The Minister in exercising his powers and duties, conferred upon him by statute, can only be controlled by a prerogative writ which will only issue if he acts unlawfully. Unlawful behaviour by the Minister may be stated with sufficient accuracy for the purposes of the present appeal (and here I adopt the classification of Lord Parker in the Divisional Court): (a) by an outright refusal to consider the relevant matter, or (b) by misdirecting himself in point of law, or (c) by taking into account some wholly irrelevant or extraneous consideration, or (d) by wholly omitting to take into account a relevant consideration." E F

Mr. Boydell's next proposition was that if a statute imposing a duty to consider expressly defines the relevant factors to be considered, the person on whom the duty lies must consider those factors, and if and in so far as the statute does not define the relevant considerations it is for the court to construe the statute and determine what relevant considerations are to be implied. For this proposition Mr. Boydell cites, again, *Padfield's* case in the speech of Lord Reid, at p. 1030: G

> "Parliament must have conferred the discretion with the intention that it should be used to promote the policy and objects of the Act; the policy and objects of the Act must be determined by construing the Act as a whole and construction is always a matter of law for the court." H

The next proposition was that in relation to a request to make a rehabilitation order the local authority must consider two initial questions

A which are prescribed in the Act: (a) is the particular house capable of being improved to the full standard; and (b) if so, ought it to be so improved?

It was argued that consideration of whether the house ought to be improved involves the consideration of other factors. These are the factors which, it was said, the court should imply as necessary to proper consideration by the local authority in order to comply with the spirit and B to fulfil the purpose of the Act. Mr. Boydell expressed them compendiously as the matters involved in balancing the difficulty and expense of improving a particular house and the alternative of demolishing that house and redeveloping the site. Again there was no challenge to Mr. Boydell's proposition that the words of the Act require consideration of the two initial factors, capability of being improved and, if capable, C ought the house to be improved. Also, it is common ground that when considering "ought" the local authority can, and should, take into consideration the area in which the house is situate and neighbouring properties. It is clear that the matters which the local authority should consider when deciding whether a house capable of improvement to the full standard ought to be improved under the provisions of a rehabilitation order rather than be demolished, and the weight which should be given to D one or another factor will vary from case to case. It is not for the court to prescribe a list of matters which must always be considered or to prescribe which factors should be given more weight than others. It is worth repeating that the function of the court, where such issues are raised, is not to substitute its own opinion or decision on matters which Parliament has left to the judgment of the local authority but to decide whether the E local authority in reaching its decision has acted in accordance with the statutory provisions.

The complaint that matters were wrongly considered rested upon the contention that the council relied on the evidence and arguments in the course of the public local inquiry and the findings of the inspector. The complaint that the council failed to consider relevant matters was that they took no account or no sufficient account of changes since January 1974, F in respect of the law, housing policy, economic conditions and costings. In our judgment the council were entitled to take into consideration what had transpired at the public local inquiry. If they had chosen to do so they could have included in the reasons for refusal an express reference to evidence given at the inquiry and to the findings of the inspector: see *Givaudan & Co. Ltd.* v. *Minister of Housing and Local Government* [1967] G 1 W.L.R. 250, 259. Although it is true that the evidence and arguments adduced and advanced in the course of the inquiry were not, and could not be, directed to the making of a rehabilitation order, for at that date no such order could be made, there can be no doubt that the objectors at the inquiry were contending for the same result as can, since the Act of 1974, be achieved by a rehabilitation order. That the arguments ranged around the merits of demolition as against rehabilitation is clear from a study of H the inspector's report: see in particular paragraphs 20, 70, 80 to 84, and the case for the Camberwell Society. Thus there was material fit to be taken into consideration when the requests for rehabilitation orders were received. We can find no evidence indicating that the council failed to consider what, if any, changes had taken place since January 1974. It was suggested that the inadequacy of the purported reason for refusal gave rise to the inference of failure. We do not take that view and we share the view of the judge that, in the face of the evidence of the elaborate com-

mittee procedure followed by the respondents, it is impossible to infer that A
the respondents did not take into consideration the factors relevant at the
time of the request.

We turn to consider the next, and only other, complaint, namely, that
there was a failure to give reasons or adequate reasons. At one stage of
the argument it was suggested on behalf of the appellants that the giving
of reasons had relevance to the basis upon which compensation for com-
pulsory purchase was payable. In the end, however, it became clear that B
the difference, if any, in respect of the basis of compensation was not a
material factor and the point was not pressed by Mr. Boydell.

The first proposition on behalf of the appellants in relation to this
complaint was that where a statute expresses a duty to give reasons the
court should imply a condition that reasons given in discharge of that duty
should be adequate and intelligible. For this Mr. Boydell cited *Earl of* C
Iveagh v. *Minister of Housing and Local Government* [1964] 1 Q.B. 395.
That case was concerned with the duty to give reasons imposed by the
Tribunals and Inquiries Act 1958. Lord Denning M.R. said, at p. 410:

> " The whole purpose of the enactment is to enable the parties and the
> courts to see what matters he has taken into consideration and what
> view he has reached on the points of fact and law which arise. If he
> does not deal with the points that arise, he fails in his duty: and the D
> court can order him to make good the omission."

There is no need to refer in this judgment to a multiplicity of authority
for a proposition which is well established and is not challenged. Mr.
Boydell referred to and relied upon *In re Poyser and Mills' Arbitration*
[1964] 2 Q.B. 467; *Givaudan & Co. Ltd.* v. *Minister of Housing and Local*
Government [1967] 1 W.L.R. 250 and *Mountview Court Properties Ltd.* E
v. *Devlin* (1970) 21 P. & C.R. 689. In the last-mentioned case Lord
Parker C.J. said, at p. 692:

> " What reasons are sufficient in any particular case must, of course,
> depend upon the facts of the case. I approach the matter in this
> way: that reasons are deficient merely because every process of
> reasoning is not set out. I further think that reasons are not F
> insufficient merely because they fail to deal with every point raised
> before the committee at the hearing. Indeed, I would adopt the
> words used by Megaw J. in *In re Poyser and Mills' Arbitration*."

Lord Parker C.J. then cited from the judgment of Megaw J. [1964]
2 Q.B. 467 the passage of the report of that case which concludes with
the words, at p. 478: G

> " Parliament provided that reasons shall be given, and in my view
> that must be read as meaning that proper, adequate reasons must
> be given. The reasons that are set out must be reasons which will
> not only be intelligible, but which deal with the substantial points
> that have been raised."

H

Mr. Boydell argued that the reasons, if any, given by the council in this
case do not pass that test.

The second proposition for the appellants was that if a body under
a statutory duty to give reasons fails to do so then (a) (which it is
conceded does not apply in the present case) if the relevant statute
prescribes the sanction of quashing the order or decision the court should
quash the order or decision; and (b) in other cases, if the failure to give

A reasons is sufficiently serious in the circumstances of the case the court ought to quash the order or decision but, if the court does not quash the order or decision, the court should make an order requiring reasons to be given.

In the present case Mr. Boydell, on behalf of the appellants, invited us to take the course of requiring reasons to be given and remitting the matter to the council for that purpose. Just how far that course would be
B of service to the appellants is very doubtful, unless the court at the same time required the council to give fresh consideration to matters relevant to the request. Such a requirement is not appropriate where the court finds, as we have found in this case, no breach of the duty to consider the relevant factors.

In the light of these propositions Mr. Boydell submitted that the pur-
C ported reasons given in the letter of July 21, 1975, were inadequate and did not convey to those who requested the making of rehabilitation orders why it was that the local authority were refusing the requests. He propounded five points: (1) The request was that a rehabilitation order should be made instead of dealing with the house by demolition. To reply in terms "the property should be demolished and the site used for the erection of new housing accommodation" was, it is said, to state a conclusion and
D not to give a reason; (2) the whole purpose behind the provisions of section 114 of the Act of 1974 is to establish machinery for a review of the question should a house be demolished or rehabilitated in circumstances where a compulsory purchase order has recently been made? Therefore it is particularly inappropriate, in a "review" situation, for the local authority to seek to rely on a case put forward at an inquiry held 18 months
E earlier. This point is emphasised in the light of the facts that, in the 18-months interval, the Act of 1974 had introduced rehabilitation orders, the policy in relation to preserving houses by improvement up to a required standard in preference to demolition had shifted, the economic situation in the country had changed, and it had become recognised that cost was a relevant factor when considering compulsory purchase; (3) the terms of the purported reason did not distinguish between individual houses but stated
F a general conclusion applicable to all; (4) nothing is stated as to whether the house in question is capable of being improved to the full standard; and (5) there is no explanation of why, if a house is capable of improvement, it is not thought right that it should be retained and not demolished.

For the council Mr. Moriarty and Lord Colville argued that the duty to consider and the duty to give reasons for a refusal after consideration
G should be regarded as entirely separate. In the present case they meet in the letter of July 21 which served the dual purpose of communicating the result of the consideration given by the local authority and of giving reasons for the decision. They submitted, and we think rightly, that there was no evidence that the respondents took into account irrelevant matters or failed to take into account relevant matters. The duty imposed by the statute was a duty to act in an administrative not a judicial capacity and it was
H argued that it was open to the respondents to arrive at a policy decision: see *Padfield's* case [1968] A.C. 997, in the words of Lord Upjohn, at p. 1058: "He may have good reasons for refusing an investigation; he may have, indeed, good policy reasons for refusing it." Mr. Moriarty also relied upon *B. Johnson & Co. (Builders) Ltd.* v. *Ministry of Health* [1947] 2 All E.R. 395 and *Hanks* v. *Minister of Housing and Local Government* [1963] 1 Q.B. 999. It was submitted for the council that the purported reason was adequate and intelligible. Against the back-

ground of the inquiry, the inspector's report, and the Secretary of State's A
decision letter, the appellants, and those owners of houses to whom similar letters were sent, were fully informed by the terms of the letter of July 21 that the request for a rehabilitation order was refused because it could not be granted consistently with the policy of the housing authority to demolish the existing and erect new housing accommodation. We think that this submission is correct. The letter was more than a mere statement of conclusion; it did state the salient reason why the house in B
question could not be retained. In the circumstances of the present case we do not think it was necessary to include in the reason given any reference to the cost of demolition as against the cost of improvement, or any reference to the practicability of the house being improved to full standard. There certainly was no need to refer to the various matters of detail which we must assume in the absence of evidence to the contrary C
had been taken into account when considering whether the house ought to be improved to the full standard. To those who received the letters the reason for the refusal was intelligible and sufficient without the inclusion of those details.

It follows that this appeal fails. It should be understood, however, that this decision does not govern what may be different circumstances in other cases. The wording used for the giving of reasons in the present D
case passes the test, the same wording in another case may fail to do so. The duty to give reasons pursuant to statute is a responsible one and cannot be discharged by the use of vague general words which are not sufficient to bring to the mind of the recipient a clear understanding of why his request for a rehabilitation order is being refused.

E

Appeal dismissed.
Injunction discharged.
Legal aid taxation of appellants' costs; certificate for two counsel.
Leave to appeal refused.

Solicitors: *Jeffrey Gordon & Co.; A. J. Allen, Deputy Town Clerk,* F
Southwark London Borough Council.

E. M. W.

G

H

A

[QUEEN'S BENCH DIVISION]

* REGINA *v.* HORSEFERRY ROAD STIPENDIARY MAGISTRATE, *Ex parte* PEARSON

B 1976 March 23, 24 — Lord Widgery C.J., Thompson and Kenneth Jones JJ.

Justices—Bail—Estreatment of recognizances—Surety's serious attempt to discharge obligation lawfully—Forfeiture of full amount of recognizance—Whether proper exercise of discretion

The applicant attended at a police station and entered into a recognizance of £2,000 as a surety for the appearance of
C her brother to answer a charge. Two days before he was due to appear she feared that he would abscond and she went again to the police station where she sought in writing to be released from her obligation as surety. The brother absconded and she was summoned to show cause why she should not suffer forfeiture of the £2,000. She was unrepresented and the magistrate explained that, had she wished effectively to withdraw as surety, she should have produced her brother and
D handed him over to custody; no reference was made to her being able to invoke police assistance for delivering him into custody under section 23 of the Criminal Justice Act 1967.[1] The magistrate considered that the applicant had not carried out her duties as a surety and, as she had the means to pay, he ordered forfeiture of the £2,000.

On her application for an order of certiorari to quash the order of forfeiture:—
E *Held*, granting the application, that the proper approach to considering whether to forfeit a surety's recognizance was that the surety had entered into a serious obligation and ought to pay the amount promised unless circumstances relating to means or culpability made it fair and just for the surety to pay a smaller sum; that, regarding the circumstances fairly, the magistrate should have recognized, or at least considered, the payment of a smaller sum because the applicant had made a
F serious effort to discharge her obligation lawfully, albeit she had not discharged it properly; and that, since he had given her no credit for her effort and had not considered or reached a conclusion on it, the order for forfeiture would be quashed.

Reg. v. *Southampton Justices, Ex parte Green* [1976] Q.B. 11, C.A. applied.

G The following case is referred to in the judgment:

Reg. v. *Southampton Justices, Ex parte Green* [1976] Q.B. 11; [1975] 3 W.L.R. 277; [1975] 2 All E.R. 1073, C.A.

No additional cases were cited in argument.

APPLICATION for an order of certiorari.

H The applicant, Liane June Rita Pearson, a self-employed person engaged in the business of selling furniture and electrical goods, applied for an order

[1] Criminal Justice Act 1967, s. 23: "(1) A constable may arrest without warrant any person who has been admitted to bail—(*a*) if the constable has reasonable grounds for believing that that person is likely to break the condition that he will appear at the time and place required or any other condition on which he was admitted to bail . . . or (*b*) on being notified in writing by any surety for that person that the surety believes that that person is likely to break the first-mentioned condition and for that reason the surety wishes to be relieved of his obligations as a surety . . ."

of certiorari to quash an order made by the metropolitan stipendiary A magistrate, Mr. R. J. A. Romain, at Horseferry Road magistrates' court on December 10, 1975, that she pay a sum of £2,000 on one summons within 21 days. The grounds on which the relief was sought were (i) that the order was in excess of the court's jurisdiction by reason of failure to inquire adequately or at all into all the circumstances of the case and/or by reason of refusal to grant the applicant's application for an adjournment and/or the fact that the applicant was no longer a surety on December B 10, 1975; (ii) that the order was contrary to natural justice by reason of the court's failure to inquire adequately or at all into all the circumstances of the case and/or refusal to grant the application for an adjournment; (iii) that the court failed to exercise discretion judicially in deciding whether or not the applicant should forfeit all or part or any of the £2,000; and (iv) that the record of the court disclosed an error of law, namely, C the matters referred to in (i) to (iii) above.

The facts are stated in the judgment of Lord Widgery C.J.

P. J. Sutton for the applicant.

The respondent did not appear and was not represented.

LORD WIDGERY C.J. In these proceedings Mr. Sutton moves on behalf D of the applicant, Liane June Rita Pearson for an order of certiorari to bring up and quash an order of the metropolitan stipendiary magistrate sitting at Horseferry Road on December 10, 1975, by which order the magistrate determined that the applicant should forfeit £2,000 being a recognizance which she had entered into to secure the attendance of her brother at the Horseferry Road magistrates' court on a date in November E 1975.

The background to the case is as I have recited it. The brother of the applicant was due to appear at the Horseferry Road magistrates' court on November 14, 1975, to answer a charge, the nature of which is not important for present purposes. He had been released on bail and the applicant, his sister, had entered into a recognizance to secure his attendance for £2,000. He did not attend, and the only matter of interest in F the history of the proceedings between her entering into her recognizance and the order by the magistrate is that, according to her evidence, which no one is minded to dispute, she had somehow sensed on November 12, 1975, that her brother might not appear two days later as required, and in consequence of that she went to the police station where she had entered her recognizance and sought to withdraw her suretyship.

G The picture is a very simple one to see. She is not wholly irresponsible about this. She realised her responsibility. She sees a danger of her brother not appearing and, wishing to protect herself, she goes to the police station and asks in writing to be released from her obligations as surety. Her worst fears are proved right. Her brother fails to attend on the day in question and in due course she is summoned to appear before the magistrate to show cause why she should not suffer a forfeiture of the £2,000. H

The magistrate's affidavit, which is the one to which one must refer for present purposes, shows that she put forward the following reasons: first, that she had entered into a recognizance, which is obvious and not really a reason at all; secondly, that on or about November 12, when she became doubtful that she could ensure the brother's attendance at court, she made a written statement to a police officer and had then attended at Canning Circus police station to withdraw as a surety; and, thirdly, that

A the brother did not attend on November 14. All that is a long way of
saying what I have already mentioned, namely, that she did make an
effort on November 12 to put an end to her obligations, and we know
the explanation of that. She told the magistrate that she lived in Nottingham
and that her brother lived in Wales, and the purpose of that was to show
the difficulty which she had in controlling or observing his movements.
She said that she realised that she was responsible for his attendance.
B She told the magistrate that she owned her own business and was worth
some £2,000.

The magistrate said that he explained to her that, if she wanted to
withdraw her obligation as surety, she should have gone to the police
station with her brother and handed him over to custody. He went on
to say:

C "Having heard the applicant's grounds for seeking to be relieved from
forfeiture of her recognizance I considered that she had not carried
out her duties as a surety and that she had the means to pay the sum
of £2,000."

Accordingly he ordered that the sum of £2,000 be forfeited.

I think it unlikely that this case would have seen the light of day but
D for the recent decision of the Court of Appeal in *Reg.* v. *Southampton
Justices, Ex parte Green* [1976] Q.B. 11. In many respects it was a similar
case. The matter was taken to this court initially where leave was refused,
and later to the Court of Appeal on an application for certiorari to quash
the magistrates' order forfeiting the recognizance.

What is to be taken from the *Southampton Justices'* case in my judg-
E ment is as follows. First of all it shows, and with respect entirely rightly
shows, that an application by certiorari in these circumstances is proper
provided it is made on the footing that the complaint is a complaint of
excess of jurisdiction. The excess of jurisdiction complained of is failure
to take into account certain matters which ought to have been taken into
account having regard to the nature of the application. I mention that
F because, put that way, it is not necessary to show an error of law on the
face of the record, no such error being apparent in this case.

What is said here, as was said in the *Southampton Justices'* case, is
that the magistrate failed to take into account certain important factors
and thus exceeded his jurisdiction. Those important factors were two in
number. The first was the means of the surety and the second was his
G or her culpability.

I need not deal in any detail with the question of means because it
seems to me that the applicant made no complaint at all before the
magistrate in regard to her means in this connection. She said that she
was worth £2,000 and had her own business, and that is all that passed
between them, and I cannot see that the magistrate can be criticised for
not having pursued the means question any further.

H But the culpability question is more important. Lord Denning M.R.
said, at p. 19:

"By what principles are the justices to be guided? They ought, I
think, to consider to what extent the surety was at fault. If he or
she connived at the disappearance of the accused man, or aided it
or abetted it, it would be proper to forfeit the whole of the sum. If
he or she was wanting in due diligence to secure his appearance,

> it might be proper to forfeit the whole or a substantial part of it, depending on the degree of fault. If he or she was guilty of no want of diligence and used every effort to secure the appearance of the accused man, it might be proper to remit it entirely." A

Then Lord Denning M.R. goes on to say that in that case the surety had done all that a wife could do, and accordingly the order forfeiting her recognizance was set aside. B

I find it difficult, with all respect to Lord Denning M.R., entirely to follow the passage that I have read because the forfeiture of recognizance is in no way a penalty imposed on the surety for misconduct. I do not doubt that the magistrate, before forfeiting the recognizance, must consider among other things the conduct of the surety and see whether it was open to criticism or not. But one must, I think, start all these problems on the C footing that the surety has seriously entered into a serious obligation and ought to pay the amount which he or she has promised unless there are circumstances in the case, either relating to her means or her culpability, which make it fair and just to pay a smaller sum. Looked at from that point of view, the *Southampton Justices'* case is a helpful authority in the present instance and I would apply it accordingly. D

For the reasons I have already given I do not propose to say any more about the applicant's means. There is no reason why the magistrate should go any further, and I would like to reject totally the proposition which, as I understand it, is put before us by Mr. Sutton that there is an obligation on the magistrate in these cases to indulge in an inquiry of his own, to send for the police and make them ring up the police station where the accused person lives, and so on. That seems to me to be totally wrong and quite E unworkable. The magistrate must proceed on the basis of the evidence before him. True where the applicant is not represented he must help her as the court will always help an unrepresented person, ask questions on her behalf and do things of that kind, but that there is any obligation to investigate the situation beyond that I reject straight away.

So I look at this case as the magistrate should have looked at it by F saying to myself, on the face of it this lady is due to forfeit £2,000. Is there anything in the background which would make that unjust and which indicates a lesser sum to be appropriate?

The only thing that I can find in the background is the fact that she did go to the police on November 12 and made a serious effort to get something done about her apprehension that her brother was going to G abscond. In common law her obligation was to take her brother physically to the police and hand him over—an operation which might not prove altogether easy. The common law has been supplemented in this respect by section 23 of the Criminal Justice Act 1967 whereby the assistance of the police can be invoked by a surety who wants to deliver his accused person into custody. H

I think, looking at this matter fairly, that one ought at least to recognise, at least to consider, the suggestion that some part of the sum in question might be restored to or left in the hands of the surety because she had made a serious effort to discharge her obligation lawfully in the manner described. True she failed to do it properly, but she did make an effort, and for my part I think that the magistrate gave her no credit for that, and I think that it was a matter which he ought to have considered and reached

A a conclusion upon. Therefore, I think that on that last ground this case is one where certiorari should go and I would quash the order accordingly.

THOMPSON J. I agree.

KENNETH JONES J. I agree.

B

Application granted.

Solicitors: *Montague, Gardner & Co.*

L. N. W.

C

[CHANCERY DIVISION]

D * PRACTICE NOTE (WINDING UP: APPEARANCE)

1976 April 12 Brightman J.

Company—Winding up—Notice of appearance—Application by creditor or contributory to be added to list made out of time—Undertaking as to costs—Companies (Winding-up) Rules 1949
E (*S.I.* 1949 *No.* 330 (*L.* 4)), *r.* 34 (*as amended*)

BRIGHTMAN J., at the sitting of the Companies Court, read the following statement.

Rule 34 of the Companies (Winding-up) Rules 1949, as amended, requires a person who intends to appear on the hearing of a winding up
F petition to give the prescribed notice by 4 p.m. on the previous Friday, failing which he cannot appear without the special leave of the court. I am authorised by the Vice-Chancellor, who has consulted the other judges of the Companies Court, to make the following statement:

An application by a creditor or contributory to be added to the list out of time will in normal circumstances be granted as a matter of course, provided that the applicant undertakes not to seek an order for the payment
G of his costs of appearing on the petition. When the petition is ultimately granted or dismissed, an applicant so added to the list may apply to be discharged from his undertaking. In appropriate circumstances he will be discharged from his undertaking.

This procedure is designed to expedite and simplify the work in the Companies Court. It will take effect from the first petition day of next term. It indicates the manner in which the discretion given to the judge by rule
H 34 is likely in future to be exercised, but it in no way impairs that discretion.

[Reported by MRS. F. ALLEN MCLEAN, Barrister-at-Law]

[QUEEN'S BENCH DIVISION]

* PRACTICE DIRECTION (ADMIRALTY: POSTAL FACILITIES)

Admiralty—Practice—Postal facilities—Extension of class of business which may be conducted by post—R.S.C., Ord. 1, *r.* 10

(1) *Practice Direction* (*Q.B.D.: Postal Facilities*) [1976] 1 W.L.R. 489) dated April 14, 1976, and issued by the Senior Master will be followed in the Admiralty Registry subject to the following and any other necessary modifications.

(2) Applications together with the requisite documents must be posted to:

The Admiralty Registry,
Royal Courts of Justice,
Strand,
London,
WC2A 2LL.

(3) Paragraph 22 ("Applications by post for special appointments before masters") shall not apply to applications for the appointment of a date for a reference.

(4) The practice set out below will be followed in connection with the posting of orders drawn up in the Admiralty Registry. (a) When an ex parte application is made by post any order drawn up will be posted to the applicant. (b) If the letter applying for the issue of a summons or the making of a consent order by post includes a request that the order when drawn up be posted to the applicant a copy of any order drawn up will be posted to him. (c) In other cases a copy of any order made by the registrar will be posted to the applicant for the order if an application by letter signed by or on behalf of the solicitor for him (or by the party if he is acting in person) and an envelope, properly addressed to the applicant is lodged in, or received through the post in, the registry.

(5) This direction will come into operation on June 8, 1976.

JAMES ROCHFORD
Admiralty Registrar

May 5, 1976.

A [QUEEN'S BENCH DIVISION]

* REGINA *v.* NEWCASTLE-UPON-TYNE JUSTICES, *Ex parte* JOHN BRYCE (CONTRACTORS) LTD.

B 1975 Dec. 18 — Lord Widgery C.J., Park and May JJ.

Justices—Information—Amendment—Prosecutor's application to amend by alleging different offence more than six months after commission—No injustice to defence—Whether justices having power to allow amendment—Magistrates' Courts Act 1952 (15 & 16 *Geo.* 6 & 1 *Eliz.* 2, *c.* 55), *ss.* 100, 104

C The defendants, a limited company, appeared to answer a charge that they permitted the use on a road of a motor vehicle not complying with regulations, contrary to section 40 (5) of the Road Traffic Act 1972. To comply with section 104 of the Magistrates' Courts Act 1952 the prosecutor had laid the information within six months of the offence, and he served with the summons a notice of facts. The hearing took place more than six months after the offence, and the prosecutor D applied for leave to amend the information to allege a different offence by deleting the allegation of permitting unlawful use, thereby making the charge that the defendants used the vehicle unlawfully. The defendants, who had a possible defence to the original charge, objected but the justices permitted the information to be amended and convicted the defendants.

On the defendants' applications for orders to quash the conviction and prohibit the amendment on the grounds that it E was an expedient to circumvent the six months' limit in section 104 and was not within the justices' power under section 100 of the Act of 1952[1]:—

Held, refusing the applications, that the power of justices to permit an information to be amended under section 100 was to be exercised judicially and so as to do justice between the parties in the context of section 104 by ensuring that there was to be no unnecessary delay in the disposal of summary F offences; that, where justices could exercise the power of permitting amendment without injustice to the defence, an information could be amended to allege a different offence after the expiry of six months from its commission; and that, accordingly, the facts of the offence having been set out in the notice served with the summons and the prosecutor not having sought to depart from them in any material way, the justices were entitled in their discretion to allow the amendment G and determine the amended information against the defendants.

Dictum of Lord Widgery C.J. in *Garfield* v. *Maddocks* [1974] Q.B. 7, 12, D.C. applied.

Ross Hillman Ltd. v. *Bond* [1974] Q.B. 435, D.C. considered.

Per Lord Widgery C.J. Prosecuting authorities are not to think that any licence is available to them to disregard the rules and hope that their troubles may be corrected at the H hearing (post, p. 521A).

The following cases are referred to in the judgment of May J.:

Garfield v. *Maddocks* [1974] Q.B. 7; [1973] 2 W.L.R. 888; [1973] 2 All E.R. 303, D.C.

Ross Hillman Ltd. v. *Bond* [1974] Q.B. 435; [1974] 2 W.L.R. 436; [1974] 2 All E.R. 274, D.C.

[1] Magistrates' Courts Act 1952, s. 100: see post, pp. 519H—520A.

The following additional case was cited in argument: A

Reg. v. *Fairford Justices, Ex parte Brewster* [1975] 3 W.L.R. 59; [1975] 2 All E.R. 757, D.C.

APPLICATIONS for an order of certiorari and, or alternatively, an order of prohibition.

The applicants, John Bryce (Contractors) Ltd., carrying on business as road hauliers in Edinburgh, applied for an order of certiorari to quash an B
order of Newcastle-upon-Tyne justices made on January 21, 1975, convicting the applicants of an offence contrary to regulation 142 (1) (*b*) of the Motor Vehicles (Construction and Use) Regulations 1973 and section 40 (5) of the Road Traffic Act 1972 and, or alternatively, an order prohibiting the justices from allowing an application by the prosecutor, Percy Charles Cooper, senior traffic examiner of the Northern Traffic Area, to C
amend the charge against the applicants at the hearing, thereby causing them to have to meet a substantially different charge. The grounds on which the relief was sought were that (a) the provisions of section 104 of the Magistrates' Courts Act 1952 should not be circumvented by the expedient of amendment applied for by the prosecutor and granted by the justices on a date which was outside the period of limitation in section 104; (b) in the absence of any express provisions to the contrary the justices D
had no power or discretion to grant the application made by the prosecutor and should have refused it; and (c) to allow the expedient to circumvent the provisions of section 104 of the Act of 1952 was unconscionable and contrary to natural justice and ought to be remedied by the court.

The facts are stated in the judgment of May J.

R. A. Percy for the applicants. E

Neither the justices nor the prosecutor appeared or were represented.

LORD WIDGERY C.J. I will ask May J. to give the first judgment.

MAY J. In this case Mr. Percy moves on behalf of the applicants, a limited company, for an order of certiorari to remove into this court for F
the purpose of its being quashed their conviction by Newcastle-upon-Tyne justices on January 21, 1975, of an offence contrary to a particular provision of the Motor Vehicles (Construction and Use) Regulations 1973 and section 40 (5) of the Road Traffic Act 1972, and also for an order of prohibition seeking to prohibit those justices from allowing the prosecution's application to amend in circumstances which will become apparent shortly.

The circumstances are these. The applicants are the owners of a motor G
lorry, and it was alleged that on May 14, 1974, that lorry was being used on a road in an overloaded condition, to put it shortly, contrary to regulation 142 (1) (*b*) of the Regulations of 1973 and section 40 (5) of the Act of 1972. The information, and one has here to be precise, alleged that the applicants *permitted* the driver, their employee, unlawfully to use that vehicle on that road. There is no doubt on the facts, as I understand it, H
that in truth the lorry was overloaded contrary to the provisions of the Regulations.

Section 40 (1) of the Road Traffic Act 1972 gives to the Secretary of State power to make regulations, and it was under that power that the Regulations of 1973 were made. Section 40 (5) provides:

"Subject to the provisions of this section and sections 41 and 42 of this Act, a person—. . . (*b*) who uses on a road a motor vehicle or

A trailer which does not comply with any such regulations or causes or permits a vehicle to be so used, shall be guilty of an offence."

In *Ross Hillman Ltd.* v. *Bond* [1974] Q.B. 435, this court made it clear that that provision of the Act of 1972 creates three separate offences: the offence of *using* a vehicle contrary to the Regulations; the offence of *causing* a vehicle to be used; and, thirdly, the offence of *permitting* a vehicle
B to be used contrary to the Regulations. As I said in that case, at p. 446, prosecutors must be careful to choose the right offence to lay in an information and, if they are in doubt, they should lay the information in the alternative. Had the prosecution adopted that course in the present case, it would never have come before this court.

As I have indicated, however, the prosecution in the present case chose to allege in the information merely that the driver had been *permitted*
C by the applicants unlawfully to use the vehicle on the road. That information was laid on November 13, 1974, just within the six months' period from May 14, 1974, when the offence was alleged to have been committed. Accordingly, it was within the provisions of section 104 of the Magistrates' Courts Act 1952, which provides:

"Except as otherwise expressly provided by any enactment, a magi-
D strates' court shall not try an information or hear a complaint unless the information was laid, or the complaint made, within six months from the time when the offence was commited, or the matter of complaint arose: . . ."

The information then came to be heard by the justices on January 21, 1975. In the course of that hearing, the prosecutor apparently took the view,
E having regard to the nature of the defence which it appeared the applicants were putting forward, that he might be unable to satisfy the justices that in law the applicants had "permitted" the unlawful use of the vehicle. The prosecutor, accordingly, sought leave from the justices to amend the information to charge the applicants, not with the original offence of permitting the unlawful use, but with the offence of using the
F motor vehicle on the road contrary to the Regulations, an offence to which on the facts I do not think Mr. Percy would dispute that the applicants had no defence.

It is contended by Mr. Percy, however, that to permit the amendment of the information on January 21, 1975, outside the six months' period of limitation laid down in section 104 of the Magistrates' Courts Act 1952, to allege a different offence from that originally charged in the information
G ought not to have been allowed. He relies on the provisions of section 104 and submits to this court that, notwithstanding the wide powers of amendment that there may be in magistrates' courts, those powers should not be exercised to permit the amendment of an information after the expiry of six months from the date of the alleged commission of the offence so as to charge a different offence not originally alleged in that information.
H Section 100 of the Act of 1952 provides:

"(1) No objection shall be allowed to any information or complaint, or to any summons or warrant to procure the presence of the defendant, for any defect in it in substance or in form, or for any variance between it and the evidence adduced on behalf of the prosecutor or complainant at the hearing of the information or complaint. (2) If it appears to a magistrates' court that any variance between a summons

> or warrant and the evidence adduced on behalf of the prosecutor or complainant is such that the defendant has been misled by the variance, the court shall, on the application of the defendant, adjourn the hearing."

A

Those provisions were referred to by Lord Widgery C.J. in *Garfield* v. *Maddocks* [1974] Q.B. 7. The facts and circumstances of that case were very different from those of the present case but, referring to section 100 (1), he said, at p. 12:

B

> "Those extremely wide words, which on their face seem to legalise almost any discrepancy between the evidence and the information, have in fact always been given a more restricted meaning, and in modern times the section is construed in this way, that if the variance between the evidence and the information is slight and does no injustice to the defence, the information may be allowed to stand notwithstanding the variance which occurred. On the other hand, if the variance is so substantial that it is unjust to the defendant to allow it to be adopted without a proper amendment of the information, then the practice is for the court to require the prosecution to amend in order to bring their information into line. Once they do that, of course, there is provision in section 100 (2) whereby an adjournment can be ordered in the interests of the defence if the amendment requires him to seek an adjournment."

C

D

In my view the six months' limitation provision in section 104 of the Magistrates' Court Act 1952 is to ensure that summary offences are charged and tried as soon as reasonably possible after their alleged commission, so that the recollection of witnesses may still be reasonably clear, and so that there shall be no unnecessary delay in the disposal by magistrates' courts throughout the country of the summary offences brought before them to be tried. It is in this context that their power to permit the amendment of an information under section 100 referred to by Lord Widgery C.J. in *Garfield* v. *Maddocks* [1974] Q.B. 7, 12 is to be exercised. It must be exercised judicially. It must be exercised so as to do justice between the parties. But where it can be so exercised, where an information can be amended, even to allege a different offence, so that no injustice is done to the defence, I for my part can see no reason why the justices should not so exercise it even though the amendment is allowed after the expiry of the six months' period from the commission of the alleged offence.

E

F

In the present case the facts of the alleged offence were set out in a notice of facts served with the summons charging the original offence of permitting the unlawful user. The prosecutor sought in no material way to depart from those facts. He merely realised, having failed to heed the advice which this court gave in *Ross Hillman Ltd.* v. *Bond* [1974] Q.B. 435, 446 that, whereas those facts substantiated the offence of actual unlawful user, they might not prove the type of offence originally charged. In those circumstances I think that the justices were entitled, within the exercise of their discretion, to allow the amendment sought, as they did, and that accordingly they were entitled to continue thereafter to hear and determine the amended information against the applicants.

G

H

In the circumstances I think that these applications should be refused.

PARK J. I agree.

A LORD WIDGERY C.J. I also agree and would only like to add this. I would not wish prosecuting authorities to think that any licence is available to them to disregard the rules and hope that their troubles may be corrected by amendment at the hearing. On the other hand, in this instance the facts of the two competing offences are really identical, and it seems to me that the justices could hardly have reasonably come to any conclusion other than that the amendment here should be permitted. I agree with the order
B proposed.

Applications refused.

Solicitors: *Sharpe, Pritchard & Co. for Watson Burton, Newcastle-upon-Tyne.*

C L. N. W.

D [COURT OF APPEAL]

* *In re* W. J. KING & SONS LTD.'s APPLICATION

[1975 W. No. 2329]

1976 Jan. 20, 21, 22, 23;
E Feb. 13

Buckley and Orr L.JJ. and Sir John Pennycuick

Mines—Working facilities—Statutory grant of—Interim order—Owner's refusal to grant new lease to company to work land—Application for statutory grant of rights—Whether inherent jurisdiction in court to grant such rights in interlocutory proceedings—Mines (Working Facilities and Support) Act 1966 (c. 4), s. 1 (as amended by Mines (Working Facilities and
F *Support) Act 1974 (c. 36), s. 1), ss. 3, 5*

By a lease dated February 1, 1947, the lessor demised some 12 acres to a company for a term of 26 years for the purposes of quarrying hardstone. By an express provision in the lease the company were entitled during the six months following the expiration of the lease on December 5, 1974, to sell any of the hardstone mined on the land during the term and to
G enter upon the land for the purposes of removing their plant. The lessor died in 1952 and his wife, who became the tenant for life, died in 1971, whereupon his son became beneficially entitled to the reversion. The company applied to the reversioner for a renewal of the lease but he refused on the ground that he wished to mine the land himself. The company applied, under the Mines (Working Facilities and Support) Acts of 1966 and 1974,[1] to the Secretary of State for the Environment
H for the grant to them of mining rights in the demised land and in adjoining land. The Secretary of State referred the application to the court under section 4 of the Act of 1966. On May 16, 1975, the company issued an originating summons applying for the grant of the statutory rights to search and work the land for hardstone and made an interlocutory

[1] Mines (Working Facilities and Support) Act 1966, s. 1, Table, para. 1 (2), as amended: see post, p. 524F–G.
Ss. 3, 4, 5: see post, pp. 524H—525G.

application for an order for the right to continue to mine the land during the interim period before the hearing of the summons. Whitford J. granted the relief sought on the ground that he had an inherent jurisdiction to make an interim order.

On appeal by the reversioner:—

Held, allowing the appeal, that in the absence of any provision conferring jurisdiction to grant interim orders in the Act of 1966, the Judicature Act of 1925 or in the rules thereunder, the power to grant such orders for the purpose of preserving the status quo must be found if at all in the previous practice of the court; that there was no inherent power in the court, by way of interim order to override private rights or to anticipate rights which might or might not be granted in the future and which if granted would have no retrospective effect and, therefore, the interim order would be quashed (post, pp. 531D–G, 532A–B).

F. Hoffmann-La Roche & Co. A.G. v. *Inter-Continental Pharmaceuticals Ltd.* [1965] Ch. 795, C.A. and *Manchester Corporation* v. *Connolly* [1970] Ch. 420, C.A. applied.

Ex parte National Coal Board [1958] 1 W.L.R. 599 doubted.

Per curiam. R.S.C., Ord. 29 contains rules for the preservation or disposal of property pending trial, which are limited provisions and do not entitle the court to infer a wider principle on the basis of preserving the status quo (post, p. 531G–H).

Decision of Whitford J. reversed.

The following cases are referred to in the judgment:

Heathstar Properties Ltd., In re [1966] 1 W.L.R. 993; [1966] 1 All E.R. 628.
Hoffmann-La Roche (F.) & Co. A.G. v. *Inter-Continental Pharmaceuticals Ltd.* [1965] Ch. 795; [1965] 2 W.L.R. 1045; [1965] 2 All E.R. 15, C.A.
Manchester Corporation v. *Connolly* [1970] Ch. 420; [1970] 2 W.L.R. 746; [1970] 1 All E.R. 961, C.A.
National Coal Board, Ex parte [1958] 1 W.L.R. 599; [1958] 2 All E.R. 351.
Russell (Archibald) Ltd. v. *Nether Pollok Ltd.*, 1938 S.C. 1.

The following additional cases were cited in argument:

Glassbrook Bros. Ltd. v. *Leyson* [1933] 2 K.B. 91, C.A.
Henry Lowson Ltd., In re (1931) 144 L.T. 128.
Townend v. *Askern Coal and Iron Co.* [1934] Ch. 463.

APPEAL from Whitford J.

The late W. J. King of Somerset leased to a company, W. J. King & Sons Ltd., of Vale Road, Tonbridge, Kent, 12 acres of land known as Triscombe Quarry, West Bagborough, Somerset, for a term of 28 years from December 25, 1946, for the purpose of quarrying hardstone. The appellant, the lessor's son, William Geoffrey King, Tatham House, Bishops Lydeard, Taunton became entitled to the reversion in 1971 on the death of his mother, the tenant for life. The appellant was managing director of W. J. King & Sons Ltd. and, in April 1948, that company became a wholly-owned subsidiary of Anglo-American Asphalt Co. Ltd. On July 8, 1970, the appellant, following differences between him and the directors of Anglo-American, ceased to be managing director. The company, on the expiration of the term on December 25, 1974, applied to the appellant for a new lease but he refused on the ground that he wished to quarry the land himself. By virtue of section 1 of the Mines (Working Facilities and Support) Act 1966, as amended by the Act of 1974, the company applied

A to the Secretary of State of the Environment for the grant to them of statutory rights to mine the land and adjoining land and the Secretary of State referred the application to the court under section 4 of the Act of 1966.

On May 16, 1975, the company issued an originating summons for an order granting them the rights and on June 4, 1975, made an interlocutory application for the right to search for and work hardstone during the B interim period. On October 3, 1975, Whitford J. granted the relief sought.

The appellant appealed on the grounds (1) that the court had no jurisdiction to make any order for the grant of rights under the Acts of 1966 and 1974 unless the court was satisfied on the evidence before it that the conditions stated in section 3 of the Act of 1966 were satisfied. Accordingly, the judge acted without jurisdiction in making such an order since he was C not and could not be satisfied that the conditions or either of them were satisfied. (2) That the judge misdirected himself in law in relying on the court's jurisdiction to make interlocutory orders for the preservation of property and in holding that the court had inherent jurisdiction to make an interim order for the grant of rights under the Acts, notwithstanding that the conditions prescribed by section 3 were not satisfied. (3) The judge misdirected himself in law in relying on *Ex parte National Coal Board* D [1958] 1 W.L.R. 599 because in that case the court was satisfied as to the aforesaid statutory conditions. Alternatively, if the court was not or should not have been so satisfied the decision was wrong in law. (4) The judge misdirected himself in law in placing reliance on the fact that the Secretary of State thought the application fit to be referred to the court under section 4 of the Act of 1966.

E In the respondents' notice, the company gave notice that the judgment should be affirmed on the additional grounds (1) that the judge ought to have accepted the applicants' submission and ruled that upon the evidence before the court the condition stated in section 3 of the Mines (Working Facilities and Support) Act 1966 had been satisfied, namely, that (a) it was in the national interest that rights be granted to the applicants pending F the hearing of the substantive application and (b) that the appellant had unreasonably refused to grant to the applicants such rights.

The facts are stated in the judgment.

Richard Scott Q.C. and *Timothy Lloyd* for the appellant.

Jeremiah Harman Q.C. and *Elizabeth Appleby* for the respondent G company.

Cur. adv. vult.

February 13. ORR L.J. read the following judgment of the court. Mr. W. G. King, the effective appellant in this case (and whom we shall call "the appellant") is the son of the late Mr. W. J. King, who by a H lease dated February 1, 1947, demised to the respondent company, W. J. King & Sons Ltd., for the purposes of their business of quarrying hardstone, some 12 acres of land, part of an area known as the Triscombe Quarry at West Bagborough in Somerset, for a term of 28 years from December 25, 1946, but subject to an express provision that the respondents should be at liberty during the six months following the expiry of the lease on December 25, 1974, to make merchantable on the demised land any material gotten by them during the term and also to remove their plant. By the

combined effect of the Mines (Working Facilities and Support) Acts 1966 A
and 1974 the respondents became entitled as from July 31, 1974 (the date of enactment of the Act of 1974), to apply to the appropriate Minister (now the Secretary of State for the Environment) for the grant to them of rights to search for and work hardstone in the demised land and also in adjoining land, and by a letter dated November 18, 1974, they made application to the Minister for such rights within an area of some 34 acres B
comprising the demised land, a three-acre site known as the Parish Quarry to which we shall later refer, and certain land adjoining the demised land in respect of which planning permission had been obtained for stone quarrying; and by a subsequent letter of December 16, 1974, they extended the application to include a further area of adjoining land comprising some 32 acres which was the subject of a pending planning application for C
such development, giving as their reason for this amendment that, whereas they had previously estimated that there were four to five years' supply of stone in the 34 acres, they now had reason to believe that the supply might be as little as two years. The Minister having referred the application to the court under section 4 of the Act of 1966, the respondents on May 16, 1975, issued an originating summons in the Chancery Division for the grant D
of such rights, and thereafter on June 4, 1975, made an interlocutory application for the right to search for and work hardstone during the interim period before the hearing of the originating summons, but only, as the application was presented to the court, over the smaller area of 34 acres. This interlocutory application came before Whitford J. on October 3, 1975, who granted the relief sought, and it is in respect of this order that the E
appellant now appeals and the respondents by a cross-notice seek to support the judge's decision on grounds other than those relied on by him.

The relevant provisions of the Acts of 1966 and 1974, so far as material for the present purposes, may be summarised as follows. Section 1 of the Act of 1966 provides that the court may, subject to and in accordance with the Act, confer any rights described in the Table thereto. Paragraph 1 (1) F
of the Table, as originally enacted, specified certain minerals not including hardstone, but by the Act of 1974 a new paragraph 1 (1) was substituted which includes hardstone. Paragraph 1 (2) of the Table provided:

> "A right to search for or work any minerals to which this paragraph applies may be conferred on any person (exercisable either by himself G
> or through a lessee)."

Paragraph 5 of the Table empowers the court to confer ancillary rights as defined in section 2 of the Act of 1966 on a person on whom the right to work minerals is conferred under the Act and the remaining sections of the Act provide, so far as material:

> "3. (1) No right shall be granted under section 1 of this Act unless H
> the court is satisfied that the grant is expedient in the national interest. (2) No right shall be granted under section 1 of this Act unless it is shown that it is not reasonably practicable to obtain the right by private arrangement for any of the following reasons—(*a*) that the persons with power to grant the right are numerous or have conflicting interests; (*b*) that the persons with power to grant the right, or any of them,

A cannot be ascertained or cannot be found; (*c*) that the persons from whom the right must be obtained, or any of them, have not the necessary powers of disposition, whether by reason of defect in title, legal disability or otherwise; (*d*) that the person with power to grant the right unreasonably refuses to grant it or demands terms which, having regard to the circumstances, are unreasonable."

B "4. (1) An application for the grant of a right under section 1 of this Act shall be sent to the Minister, and the applicant for an ancillary right for the purpose of or in connection with working any minerals may be a person either having or applying for the right to work those minerals. (2) The application shall set out the circumstances alleged to justify the grant of the right, and shall be in such form and accompanied by such information verified in such manner as the
C Minister may direct. (3) The Minister shall consider the application, and shall, unless after communication with such other parties interested (if any) as he may think fit, he is of opinion that a prima facie case is not made out, refer the matter to the court: Provided that, where it is alleged that the right in question cannot be obtained by reason
D of any person not having the necessary powers of disposition, or having unreasonably refused to grant it, or having demanded terms which are unreasonable, the Minister shall not refer the application to the court without first having communicated with that person."

"5. (1) Where a matter is referred to the court under the last foregoing section, the court, if satisfied that the requirements of this
E Act are complied with in the case of the applicant, may, by order, grant the right on such terms and subject to such conditions, and for such period, as the court may think fit, and upon such an order being made, the right specified in the order shall, subject to the following provisions of this Act, vest in the applicant. (2) Where a right is granted, such compensation or consideration as in default of agreement
F may be determined by the court shall be paid or given by the applicant in respect of the acquisition of the right to such persons as the court may determine to be entitled thereto."

"10. A right granted under this Act shall not confer on the person to whom it is granted any greater or other power than if the right had been granted by a person legally entitled to grant the right, or relieve
G the grantee from any obligation or liability to which he would have been subject had the right been granted by such a person."

Section 15 of the Act repealed certain provisions as to the grant of working facilities contained in, inter alia, the Mines (Working Facilities and Support) Acts 1923 and 1925 and the Mines (Working Facilities) Act 1938.

H At the hearing the following matters were not in dispute. In February 1936, Mr. W. J. King, the father of the appellant, incorporated the respondent company for the purpose, inter alia, of acquiring the business of a quarry proprietor previously carried on by him, and he and the appellant became at that time directors of the company, and the latter in December 1936 managing director, which office he held until July 1970. In May 1945, Mr. W. J. King bought the Bagborough House estate which embraces the Triscombe Quarry and the land adjoining it and, in January 1947, he granted to the respondents the lease in question. Surrounded, save on one side, by the demised land is an area called the Parish Quarry from which the parishioners claim the right to take stone, and in respect of this area Mr. W. J. King held a licence to quarry stone, granted to him in 1932 by the West Bagborough Parish Council, the benefit of which, and of other quarrying licences held by him, he undertook by an agreement dated February 15, 1936, to hold on behalf of the respondents. In 1952 Mr. W. J. King died, leaving the income of the Triscombe Quarry to his wife, who died in 1971, for her life, and the freehold reversion on the lease to the appellant, with the result that it is now held in trust for the appellant absolutely and will be vested in him as soon as certain estate duty questions have been resolved.

In April 1948, the respondents became a wholly-owned subsidiary of Anglo-American Asphalt Co. Ltd. (which we will call "Anglo-American") and have since been under common management with that company and others in the same group. On July 8, 1970, following differences of opinion which had arisen between him and the directors of Anglo-American, the appellant ceased to be managing director of the respondents, and thereafter in an action brought in the Queen's Bench Division made claims for compensation against Anglo-American, who in their defence pleaded serious allegations against him, but that action has now been settled by a payment of money made by Anglo-American to the appellant. On April 1, 1974, the Bagborough Parish Council granted a 28-year lease, the validity of which is disputed by the appellant, of the Parish Quarry to Anglo-American, but it is common ground that there is no workable stone left in that area and the respondents use it, because it is conveniently level, as a site for most of their plant and also for stocking of processed stone. During the period of the 1947 lease the respondents extended their quarrying operations beyond the boundary of the demise up to an approximate line coloured red on a sketch plan, and in an action for trespass brought by the appellant in the Chancery Division have alleged that on various alternative grounds they had a right to do so, but the appellant has challenged these claims. The respondents have also recently obtained in the county court new leases of two areas of land of which they previously held tenancies from the Bagborough estate and which they use as a washing plant and a transport yard. Finally, it is not in dispute that since the expiry of the 1947 lease on December 25, 1974, the respondents contrary to legal advice given to them, have continued to extract stone from the quarry.

On the hearing of the interlocutory applications no witnesses were called and the evidence before the judge consisted of three affidavits sworn by Mr. Lawrence, general manager of the relevant division of Anglo-American, and one sworn by the appellant, and the exhibits thereto; Mr. Lawrence's evidence being directed to establishing that the two conditions imposed by section 3 of the Act of 1966 on the grant of rights are satisfied in that (i) the grant is expedient in the national interest, and (ii) it is not reasonably practicable for the respondents to obtain the rights by private arrangement because the appellant has unreasonably refused to grant them or has demanded unreasonable terms; and the appellant's affidavit being directed to showing that no detriment to the national interest is involved if the rights are refused, since he can himself undertake the quarrying of the stone within a comparatively short time, and that he has not unreasonably refused to grant the rights or demanded unreasonable terms. On the national interest issue, the evidence in Mr. Lawrence's first two affidavits may be summarised as follows: (i) As to the quality of stone, it is known in the trade as "premium stone" and in the 1974 report of the Transport and Road Research Laboratory, which refers to tests carried out since 1962 on premium stone, it is described as "one of the best stones in the country for road surfaces, particularly in respect of its non-skid and abrasive qualities," and it is further stated that on these tests the Triscombe aggregate gave the best overall performance. (ii) As to demand for the stone, that in 1973 the total (including by-products) produced and sold was 198,800 tons of the value of some £373,000, of which some 69,000 tons (excluding by-products gravel and scalpings) went to the Somerset County Council and various tonnages up to 5,000 tons to other county councils as far afield as Kent, Sussex and Surrey. For 1974 the tonnage produced was substantially lower but was affected by the three-day week, and the demand for the stone is continuing. (iii) As to the provision of employment as a factor of the national interest, that the respondents employ 25 men on working and treating the stone and a further 24 on transport, apart from haulage contractors. (iv) As to the practicability of the appellant taking over the working of the stone, that in order to do so he would, because of the respondents' lease of the Parish Quarry, have to find another level site of sufficient size to accommodate his fixed plant, which it was claimed that he would be unable to do, and also provide a new entrance to the site and find sites for a washing plant and transport yard, and in addition acquire the requisite plant; and it was claimed that even if these difficulties could be overcome, it is unlikely that the appellant would be able to begin operations until after the hearing of the substantive application, with the result that Triscombe stone would not be available during that period.

In answer to this evidence the appellant claimed in his affidavit that there is an area within the demised land of sufficient size, and level enough, to accommodate the plant; that he could construct a new entrance and find on his own land sites for a washing plant and transport yard; and could himself provide some of the necessary plant and acquire without any serious delay such major items of plant as he would have to buy.

In an affidavit in reply, Mr. Lawrence estimated that the cost, if they are bought new, of the major items of plant which the appellant cannot himself provide would be £250,000 and that there would be a delay of 6 to 12 months before delivery could be obtained; and in an affidavit sworn on January 13, 1976, which we admitted by way of fresh evidence in the appeal, Mr. Gaymer, secretary and a director of Anglo-American, disputes the availability of any level area of sufficient size, other than the Parish Quarry, to accommodate the plant and estimates that the major items of plant required could not be obtained new in less than 6 to 12 months or secondhand in less than 9 months.

As to the issue of unreasonable refusal, the respondents relied on a bundle of correspondence between the respective solicitors extending from July 1970 to May 1975, as to which it is, for the present purposes, sufficient to say that on January 24, 1975, by which time the interim position was under discussion, the appellant's solicitors accepted that their client had impliedly, if not expressly, refused to grant any rights after the expiry of the lease, and that the final letter in May 1975, conveys an outright refusal by the appellant of any licence for the interim period and requires the respondents to make an immediate application to the court which it is said will be strongly contested. The appellant's case on this issue, as outlined in his affidavit, is that the land and the stone are his, that he has been concerned in stone-quarrying all his working life, and wishes to quarry the stone in question; and that in these circumstances his refusal is not unreasonable.

These being in summary the facts of the case, and before turning to the issues which arose on the hearing and to the judgment of Whitford J. it should be recorded that before this court, and as we understand before the judge, counsel on both sides were agreed that, having regard to the present state of the lists in the Chancery Division, the parties to this case would be fortunate if the substantive application on the originating summons is heard before the end of this year. Since we reserved judgment, an announcement has been made that additional judges are to be allocated to the Chancery Division, but it can only be a matter of speculation whether a substantially earlier hearing can in fact be obtained.

Before the judge the first issue in the case was whether he had any power to grant the interim rights sought by the respondents, and the second issue was whether, if he had such power, it should be exercised in all the circumstances of the case. As to the first issue, it was accepted by counsel on both sides that in the absence of oral evidence, tested by cross-examination, and on the material before him, it was not open to the judge to come to a conclusion whether, for the purposes of the substantive application, the requirements of section 3 of the Act of 1966 as to the national interest and as to unreasonable refusal had on a balance of probabilities been satisfied, but it was argued by Mr. Harman for the respondents (although this fact does not clearly emerge from the judgment) that it was open to the judge to decide that such requirements had been satisfied as respects the interim period before the substantive application would be heard.

On the first issue, the judge made no finding that the conditions imposed by section 3 had been satisfied either in the long term or as respects the interim period, and as to the law accepted that section 3, like section 101 of the Companies Act 1948, with which Buckley J. was concerned in *In re Heathstar Properties Ltd.* [1966] 1 W.L.R. 993, confers jurisdiction on the court only when satisfied that the specified conditions have been fulfilled; and he also accepted on the authority of the judgment of Lord Diplock (with whom the other members of the court agreed) in *Manchester Corporation* v. *Connolly* [1970] Ch. 420, 428, that jurisdiction to make the order sought must, in the absence of any provision conferring jurisdiction contained in the Act of 1966 itself, be found "either in the Supreme Court of Judicature (Consolidation) Act of 1925, or in the rules made thereunder, or in the previous practice of the court." In these circumstances, it being common ground that there was no relevant

A provision either in the Judicature Act or in the Rules of the Supreme Court, he considered that the matter must turn on the previous practice of the court, as to which he came to the conclusion that there is both a principle whereby the court on an interim application may make such an order as will ensure that if the applicant ultimately succeeds his victory will not be a hollow one, and also a principle whereby the court may make such an order as will preserve the status quo as it existed at the commencement B of the proceedings, and he found some support for this conclusion in the provisions of R.S.C., Ord. 29, r. 2 with reference to the detention and preservation of the subject matter of a cause or matter pending trial and also in the judgment of Roxburgh J. in *Ex parte National Coal Board* [1958] 1 W.L.R. 599.

C Early in his judgment Whitford J. referred to the requirement contained in section 4 (3) of the Act of 1966 that

> "The Minister shall consider the application, and shall, unless after communication with such other parties (if any) as he may think fit, he is of opinion that a prima facie case is not made out, refer the matter to the court . . ."

D and said that he must proceed on the assumption that the Secretary of State had come to a conclusion that a prima facie case had been made out, for otherwise he would not under the statute have directed the reference to the court, and at the end of his judgment he referred to the fact of the reference having been made as a matter to which he had had regard.

The appellant's grounds of appeal against the judge's decision are that E he had no jurisdiction to make the order he did and was wrong in thinking that *Ex parte National Coal Board* [1958] 1 W.L.R. 599 supported his conclusion that he had inherent jurisdiction, and that he also misdirected himself in placing reliance on the fact that the Secretary of State had referred the matter to the court. By a respondents' notice it is claimed that the judge should have held on the evidence that the conditions specified in F section 3 had been satisfied as respects the interim period, and on the hearing of the appeal Mr. Harman on behalf of the respondents offered undertakings that they will confine any interim quarrying to an area of 2½ acres and will also, if they should ultimately fail on the substantive application, render a full account of their interim operations and pay to the appellant compensation to the extent that their net profit from such G operations exceeds the royalties already paid in respect of the stone.

It will be convenient to deal first with the ground of appeal contained in the respondents' notice, which turns on the evidence in the case; thereafter with the appellant's second ground of appeal; and finally with the issue of law as to jurisdiction. On the first of these issues, Mr. Harman's submission was that the judge ought to have been satisfied, on the evidence H contained in Mr. Lawrence's affidavits as to the qualities of the Triscombe stone and its value for road-making, particularly from the aspect of road safety, that there would be a detriment to the public interest if the stone were not quarried during the interim period, and that taking this detriment into account the appellant's refusal to grant rights was unreasonable; but, with great respect to this submission, we are unable to accept it. The evidence as to the quality of the stone amounted to no more than that it is one of the best stones for road surfacing, particularly in respect of its non-skid and abrasive qualities, and that Triscombe aggregate had on certain tests given the best overall performance; and as to the demand for the stone that a very substantial tonnage of it had been supplied to the Somerset County Council and smaller quantities to other county councils. It is, however, in our judgment, an important feature of the case that if Triscombe stone were not worked for a period of months it would not be denied altogether to the councils concerned but would merely be delivered later and there was no evidence that this would involve any detriment to the public interest. In particular there was no evidence as to the requirements of, or stocks held by, the councils, or as to any difficulty in obtaining, during the period in question, other comparable stone of which the Road Research Laboratory report admitted the existence in the words "one of the best stones," or as to the degree of inferiority of further stone outside that category. Equally, in the absence of any evidence as to local employment conditions, there was no evidence of any detriment to the public interest which might arise from the respondents having to dismiss their employees. For these reasons, in our judgment, the evidence fell far short of establishing even a prima facie case of detriment to the public interest if the interim rights are refused, and in the absence of proof of detriment to the public interest we do not see any ground on which the refusal of the rights, which has to be considered in relation to any detriment to the public interest (see *Archibald Russell Ltd.* v. *Nether Pollok Ltd.*, 1938 S.C. 1) could be held unreasonable.

As to the appellant's second ground of appeal, it is clear that the judge did not treat the fact of the reference having been made by the Minister as itself establishing the existence of a prima facie case on the interim application, but it appears from his second reference to this matter that he took it into consideration as a matter lending some support to the respondents' case. In this, with great respect, we think that he was wrong. It is to be noted, in the first place, that the Minister is not required as a condition of referring the matter to the court to make a positive finding that a prima facie case has been made out, but if he is of opinion that a prima facie case has not been made out the reference is not to be made, and there is, it seems to us, an important difference between a negative finding that no prima facie case has been made out, which may amount to no more than that the claim is frivolous, and a positive finding that a prima facie case has been established. But in any event the inquiry which section 4 (3) requires the Minister to make is not in any sense a judicial inquiry embracing examination and cross-examination of witnesses. It consists merely of considering written representations the contents of which have not been disclosed to other persons interested, and it is left entirely to the Minister's discretion with what other persons he will communicate. For these reasons, we think that the judge was wrong in treating the fact of the reference having been made as a matter which could lend support to the respondents' case. It was no more than a step in the proceedings, which had resulted in the matter coming before the court and could not, in our judgment, be treated as reinforcing the respondents' case. What weight the judge gave to it can only be a matter of speculation. He may well have given it very little weight, and having regard to the conclusion

A we have reached on the issue of jurisdiction, we do not find it necessary
to decide whether, if this matter stood alone, it would be sufficient ground
for allowing the appeal.

The remaining and very important issue is that of jurisdiction. There
is no doubt that in certain respects it would be convenient that the court
should have power to make an interim order in such a case as this, for it
B is obvious that if the respondents have to discontinue their operations it
may not be economically possible to resume them in the event of their
being granted rights on the substantive hearing. Mr. Harman also argued
that, if there is no power to grant interim relief, applicants under the Act
may be put in great difficulty because a lessor who is asked to grant rights
may refuse to give a definite answer, with the result that the application
C under the Act is postponed and cannot be heard until after the expiry of
the lease. In the present case, however, the special difficulty which arose
was that the respondents were not in law entitled to apply for rights until
the enactment of the Act of 1974, some five months before the expiry of the
lease. In future cases, if the lessor persistently refuses to give a definite
answer, the lessee's remedy, in our judgment, is to make his substantive
D application in sufficient time for it to be heard before the lease expires.
The present issue is, however, one of law.

It was argued by Mr. Harman that on the true construction of the Act
of 1966 the rights to which it refers may be granted retrospectively and
may also be granted by way of interim order; but we are unable to accept
either part of this argument. In our judgment, if it was intended to confer
E such powers they would have been conferred by clear and specific language,
and we derive some support for that conclusion in the view adopted by
this court in *F. Hoffmann-La Roche & Co. A.G.* v. *Inter-Continental
Pharmaceuticals Ltd.* [1965] Ch. 795, which concerned section 41 of the
Patents Act 1949.

It follows, in our judgment, on the authority of Lord Diplock's judgment
F in *Manchester Corporation* v. *Connolly* [1970] Ch. 420 and in the absence
of any relevant provision either in the Judicature Act or in the Rules of
the Supreme Court, that the jurisdiction claimed must be found, if at all,
in the previous practice of the court, as to which the judge based his
conclusion in part on the provisions of R.S.C., Ord. 29, which he thought
indicated the existence of a wider principle, in part on a basis of preserving
G the status quo, and in part on the judgment of Roxburgh J. in *Ex parte
National Coal Board* [1958] 1 W.L.R. 599 but, with respect, we are
unable to accept any of these grounds for his conclusion. R.S.C., Ord. 29
contains rules for the preservation or disposal of property with the object,
inter alia, of transferring a plaintiff's title from goods themselves to the
proceeds of their sale, but we do not consider that it is possible to infer
H from these very limited provisions the existence of some much wider
principle not to be found in the Rules.

As to preservation of the status quo, the courts frequently make an
interim order which will secure that object, and Mr. Harman claimed that
the order under appeal has that effect, in that it enables the respondents
to continue working the stone as they had been doing before the order.
But another aspect of the matter is that after the expiry of the lease they

were working without any right to do so, and unlawfully, and that the A
continuation of the working will not preserve the status quo as regards the stone, which belongs to the appellant and will be progressively reduced by the operations. In these circumstances it was argued for the appellant that the court has no inherent power, by way of interim order, to override private rights or to anticipate rights that may or may not be granted in the future and, when granted, would have no retrospective effect. In our B
judgment, this argument is well-founded and we consider that it derives some support from the judgment in the *Hoffmann-La Roche* case which seems to us closely analogous.

There remains the judgment of Roxburgh J. in *Ex parte National Coal Board,* where the applicant, whose workings were approaching areas in which they were doubtful whether they had any rights to work, had made C
a substantive application under the Mines (Working Facilities and Support) Act 1923 to work such areas, and, because that application could not be heard for some time, made an interim application for leave to continue their operations. On the substantive application there were a large number of objectors, but only as to method of working and compensation, who were given until May 9 to file evidence. The master ordered service of D
the interim application on seven persons who it was thought might be affected by the workings, and on the hearing of that application on May 6 six of these had replied that they did not object and the seventh had not replied. Roxburgh J. in granting the relief sought, took the view that the seventh had acquiesced, but added that even if that view was wrong he would have granted the application. His judgment does not clearly indicate E
whether he considered that he had jurisdiction under the statute to make the order or relied on an inherent jurisdiction. It is possible that he had jurisdiction under the statute; but if he based the order on inherent jurisdiction, we consider, with respect, that the decision was wrong for the reasons already indicated.

For these reasons, we allow the appeal and quash the order of F
Whitford J.

Appeal allowed with costs.
Leave to appeal refused.

Solicitors: *Kenneth Brown, Baker & Baker; Iliffe & Edwards.*

G

L. G. S.

H

A [HOUSE OF LORDS]

* SEWING MACHINES RENTALS LTD. . . . . . RESPONDENTS

AND

WILSON . . . . PETITIONER

B WILSON . . . . PETITIONER

AND

SEWING MACHINES RENTALS LTD. . . . . . RESPONDENTS

SEWING MACHINES RENTALS LTD. . . . . . RESPONDENTS

AND

C UDEALA . . . . PETITIONER

MORLEN INVESTMENTS LTD. . . . . RESPONDENTS

AND

WILSON AND ANOTHER . . . . PETITIONERS

D 1976 May 12 — Lord Simon of Glaisdale, Lord Edmund-Davies and Lord Russell of Killowen.

Petitions by the defendants for leave to appeal to the House of Lords from the decisions in *Sewing Machines Rentals Ltd.* v. *Wilson; Same* v. *Udeala; Morlen Investments Ltd.* v. *Wilson* [1976] 1 W.L.R. 37; [1975] 3
E All E.R. 553.

The Appeal Committee dismissed the petition.

F. C.

F [COURT OF APPEAL]

* MORRISONS HOLDINGS LTD. *v.* MANDERS PROPERTY (WOLVERHAMPTON) LTD.

[Plaint No. 74 51996]

G

1975 Dec. 12, 15, 17 — Stephenson and Scarman L.JJ. and Sir Gordon Willmer

Landlord and Tenant—Business premises (security of tenure)—Occupation for purposes of tenants' business—Fire occurring and trading ceasing—Fixtures and fittings on premises—
H *Tenants maintaining right to occupy—Landlords purporting to determine tenancy and demolishing premises—Whether tenants "occupied" premises—Locus standi to apply for new lease—Landlord and Tenant Act* 1954 (2 & 3 *Eliz.* 2, *c.* 56), *s.* 23 (1)

The tenants held the ground floor shop and basement of premises known as no. 31, Dudley Street, Wolverhampton, under an underlease from March 25, 1972 to December 24,

---

[Reported by EMMANUEL C. ABARAONYE, ESQ., Barrister-at-Law]

1977. The premises formed part of a larger structure, the A Central Arcade, which comprised several shops and the tenancy was one to which Part II of the Landlord and Tenant Act 1954 applied. By clause 6 (4) of the underlease, the landlords could terminate the tenancy by notice should the arcade be substantially damaged by fire and rendered economically incapable of reinstatement. On May 20, 1974, a devastating fire occurred in the arcade and burnt it down. No. 31, Dudley Street, was not wholly destroyed but considerable damage was B done to the roof and upper storeys as a result of which the tenants' premises became unfit for occupation for purposes of their business. On May 21, they wrote to the landlords suggesting that the premises be made weatherproof and suitable for their occupation and generally expressing their desire to resume trading there. They subsequently re-asserted their claim to occupation; they never gave up possession of the keys to the premises, and they left some fixtures and fittings C on the premises after salvaging their stock. On May 22, the landlords purported to determine the tenancy under clause 6 (4) of the underlease by serving notice on the tenants. On June 17, the landlords demolished the premises to which the tenants had not returned. On July 1, the landlords gave notice to terminate the tenancy under section 25 of the Act of 1954. On October 17, the tenants applied for a new tenancy under Part II of the Act of 1954. The landlords opposed the D application on the ground that they intended to demolish and reconstruct the premises.

On a preliminary issue whether the tenants had locus standi to apply for a new tenancy since prior to their application they had ceased to occupy the premises for the purpose of their business in accordance with section 23 (1) of the Act of 1954 [1], Judge Davison held that they had no locus standi to make the application since the devastating nature of the E fire at the premises justified the inference that the tenants' absence from the premises was permanent.

On appeal by the tenants:—

Held, allowing the appeal, that in order to have locus standi to apply for a new tenancy under Part II of the Act of 1954, the tenants had to show either that they were in physical occupation of the premises for the purposes of a business carried on by them or, if events beyond their control F had led to their absence from the premises, that they continued to assert their right to occupancy; that despite the demolition of the premises, which was unlawful and could not be said to destroy the tenants' locus standi, the tenants had remained in occupation by maintaining their intention and right to occupy up to the date of the order of court and that accordingly they had locus standi to apply for a new tenancy of the premises (post, pp. 540A, B, 541B, C, F, G, 542G—543A).

Caplan (I. & H.) Ltd. v. *Caplan (No. 2)* [1963] 1 W.L.R. G 1247 approved.

The following case is referred to in the judgments:

Caplan (I. & H.) Ltd. v. *Caplan (No. 2)* [1963] 1 W.L.R. 1247; [1963] 2 All E.R. 930.

H

The following additional cases were cited in argument:

Denman v. *Brise* [1949] 1 K.B. 22; [1948] 2 All E.R. 141, C.A.

Ellis & Sons Amalgamated Properties Ltd. v. *Sisman* [1948] 1 K.B. 653; [1948] 1 All E.R. 44, C.A.

Morleys (Birmingham) Ltd. v. *Slater* [1950] 1 K.B. 506; [1950] 1 All E.R. 331, C.A.

---

[1] Landlord and Tenant Act 1954, s. 23 (1): see, post, p. 539D, E.

A APPEAL from Judge Davison sitting at Wolverhampton County Court.

Morrisons Holdings Ltd., who were business tenants of premises known as no. 31, Dudley Street, Wolverhampton, of which Manders Property (Wolverhampton) Ltd. were the landlords, appealed from the order of Judge Davison made on February 6, 1975, dismissing their application for a new tenancy. The grounds of appeal were that (1) the judge misdirected himself in holding on the facts that the tenants did not occupy
B the premises within the meaning of section 23 of the Landlord and Tenant Act 1954 at the date, June 17, 1974, when the landlords entered the premises and destroyed them; (2) if the judge inferred that the tenants' holding on the ground floor of 31, Dudley Street, was incapable of being restored after the fire on May 20 that inference was unsupported by the evidence or his own findings that (i) the Central Arcade of which the
C building formed a part was as a whole economically incapable of being rebuilt or reinstated, but (ii) no part of the holding was actually burned although the structure of the building of which it formed part was affected by water and smoke, and (iii) although the holding was unfit for occupation after the fire, it remained standing, and (iv) the uncontradicted evidence of the chief building surveyor of the local authority given on behalf of the landlords that he would have recommended, in the interest of safety,
D removal only of that part of the building which was above the first floor; (3) the judge misdirected himself in holding that a tenant who (i) retained possession of his holding which he has vacated only by reason of fire, (ii) intended at the date of such vacation that his vacation should be temporary only, and (iii) maintained a desire to return in order to carry on his business, lost the protection of Part II of the Act of 1954 when he ceased
E to be in physical occupation of the holding.

The facts are stated in the judgment of Scarman L.J.

G. M. Godfrey Q.C. and *M. Rich* for the tenants.
J. W. Mills Q.C. and *D. A. McConville* for the landlords.

STEPHENSON L.J. I will ask Scarman L.J. to deliver the first judgment.

F

SCARMAN L.J. This is an appeal by the tenants, Morrisons Holdings Ltd., against a refusal by the county court judge to allow them to continue with their application for a new tenancy under Part II of the Landlord and Tenant Act 1954. The appeal raises a short question which may be put in this way: did the tenants have a locus standi to make an appli-
G cation for a new tenancy under Part II of the Act?

The circumstances are these. The tenants applied for a new tenancy by an application dated October 17, 1974. The landlords, Manders Property (Wolverhampton) Ltd., filed an answer in which they first set out their ground for opposing the grant of a new tenancy, namely, that they intended to demolish and reconstruct the premises which were the subject matter of the application. That issue has not yet been considered
H by the county court judge because, at the invitation of the parties, he directed his attention to a preliminary point which is set out in the landlords' answer. The landlords allege that the tenants are "not entitled to the grant of a new tenancy, since prior to the issue of their application they had vacated the whole of the said premises and were no longer in occupation of the whole or any part thereof." Other matters were also alleged in the answer, but they do not call for consideration upon this appeal.

The proceedings took a strange and, one would hope, an unusual A
course before the judge in the Wolverhampton County Court. Two
preliminary points were raised and dealt with by the judge. The first
preliminary point was dealt with by him on January 31, 1975, when (I put
it quite shortly) he held that the landlords were within their rights in
serving a notice under clause 6 (4) of the lease. That point is no longer
the subject of litigation, and I merely mention that there is no challenge to
the finding of the judge that, in so far as the contract of tenancy was B
concerned, the landlords were entitled to serve their notice. The judge,
of course, did not consider on that preliminary point the implications of
the Landlord and Tenant Act 1954. The second preliminary point is the
point upon which the tenants have come to this court. The judge found
that they were not in occupation of the premises the subject matter of
the tenancy and that, therefore, they had no locus standi to apply for a C
new tenancy under the Act of 1954.

The history of the matter is as follows. The tenants were tenants
pursuant to an underlease dated July 6, 1972, under which they held a
tenancy running from March 25, 1972, until December 24, 1977, at a rent
of £4,750 a year of shop premises, no. 31, Dudley Street, Wolverhampton.
Those premises consisted of a shop on the ground floor and a basement,
and they were part of a larger building which has been compendiously D
described as the Central Arcade. The Central Arcade was a large structure
consisting of shops, four of them facing Dudley Street, and I think some
11 of them facing an arcade which lay to the west of Dudley Street going
from Dudley Street towards the rear of the landlords' other property
known as the Manders' Centre. It was a business tenancy, in that the
underlease contemplated the tenants carrying on the business of clothiers, E
a retail business; and it was one which would normally fall within the
provisions of Part II of the Landlord and Tenant Act 1954.

The landlords own a large area, we are told some four acres, of land
in the centre of Wolverhampton, including this arcade. They had in mind
a large redevelopment scheme for this land, and were working to it at the
time of the events which the court has to consider. They had redeveloped
a good deal of the area behind the Central Arcade and were reaching in F
their demolition and redevelopment programme that part of their land
which included the Central Arcade; that is to say, they were working
towards Dudley Street, and, therefore, also towards no. 31, Dudley Street.

Undoubtedly it was because the landlords had in mind their redevelop-
ment programme and their desire at some time to recover possession of
their Dudley Street frontage, including no. 31, that the lease was framed G
in the way that it was. I have already mentioned that the tenancy was to run
until December 24, 1977, but it included a break clause. That break clause
enabled the landlords to give notice determining the tenancy on December
25, 1975, or at any time thereafter. The lease also contained some not
very unusual clauses in regard to insurance against certain risks, including
fire, and the obligation of the landlords to apply the proceeds of any H
policy of insurance to reinstatement of the premises if damaged by the
occurrence of the risk. But there was a clause, not frequently found,
which clearly was dictated by the particular situation in which, as I have
said, the landlords found themselves. That clause, which has featured
largely in this appeal, is clause 6 (4) which, I have already mentioned, was
the subject of the first preliminary point with which this court is not
concerned. Clause 6 (4) reads as follows:

A " If the demised premises or any part thereof shall at any time during the term hereby created be destroyed or damaged by fire or any other insured risk so as to become unfit for occupation or use and the policy or policies of insurance effected by the [landlords] shall not have been vitiated or payment of the policy monies refused in whole or in part in consequence of any act or default of the [tenants] the rent hereby reserved or a fair proportion thereof according to the
B nature and extent of the damage sustained shall be suspended until the demised premises shall again be rendered fit for occupation. . . . Provided that in the event of the said Central Arcade being so substantially damaged by fire or other insured risks as to render it in the opinion of the [landlords'] architects economically incapable of rebuilding or reinstatement in its existing form and lay-out the [land-
C lords] may at any time following such damage give to the [tenants] notice in writing forthwith terminating this demise whereupon this lease shall immediately be cancelled and all obligations by either party brought to an end."

It will be observed that the landlords were thinking all the time of their policy of redevelopment of this area, including the Central Arcade and, of
D course, no. 31, Dudley Street, which, as Mr. Mills correctly submitted, upon the terms of the lease is itself part of the Central Arcade, although it fronts upon Dudley Street and not upon the internal arcade. Such was the lease creating a business tenancy enjoyed by the tenants and subject to determination in the ways that I have mentioned.

The story of events is as follows. The landlords by May 19, 1974, had got their demolition contractors right up to the back of these premises
E and were intending to demolish the area immediately in the rear of no. 31, Dudley Street, but not, of course, no. 31, Dudley Street, which was then in the occupation of the tenants for business purposes. On May 20 (the next day, or night) the fire took place. The judge described it as a " devastating fire." Mr. Mills has, I think equally correctly, used different epithets which are important to his argument; he has described it as a
F " catastrophic fire " and a " disastrous fire." All three epithets, I think, are fair epithets to describe at any rate the consequences of the fire. The fire burnt down the arcade itself, that is to say, the central passageway which was the central feature of the arcade and the shops on either side. It did not wholly destroy no. 31, Dudley Street, but it did considerable damage to the roof and to the upper storeys, which were not in possession
G of the tenants and not included in the demise.

I do not think I can do better than use the judge's words to describe the effects of the fire upon no. 31, Dudley Street. He said that he was

" satisfied from the evidence that no actual part occupied by the [tenants] was actually burned by fire. Nevertheless, though not burned by fire, I am satisfied the structure of the whole building was affected
H by fire. The walls were affected also by water, perhaps by the activities of the fire brigade. . . . They were also affected by smoke." He found " that the building was rendered wholly and completely unfit for occupation as business premises on May 20, 1974," that is, the day of the fire. " It was quite impossible for the tenants to carry on the business in the premises at that date."

He added as a further factor that the services, that is to say, the drains

and electrical supply, had been destroyed in the fire, and he described A
it briefly in the phrase " all services had completely gone."

The landlords had to consider the situation, and so did the tenants. We have the advantage of contemporary documents which indicate the attitude that each took to the disaster of the fire. On the day after the fire, May 21, the tenants wrote to the landlords a short letter, dated May 21, 1974, which I will quote in full. They said: B

> " We have been in receipt of information from our local supervisor, who informs us that though the roof and upper floors were virtually destroyed by the unfortunate fire which occurred on Monday, May 20, 1974, it would seem that though our premises on the ground floor and basement were damaged by water, used in quenching the fire, it would be possible to make these weatherproof and suitable for reoccupation for the remainder of our lease. Naturally we wish to get back into C
> trade as soon as possible and we would be glad of your early comments as to the time this work is likely to take to complete."

It is clear, in my judgment, from that letter that the attitude of the tenants was that they insisted on retaining their right to occupation, recognising that for the time being physical occupation for business purposes was not possible, and invited the landlords to act under the lease to D
reinstate the premises so that they could resume trading. Their subsequent actions, which are carefully described by the judge, are consistent with the interpretation that I have just put upon their letter of May 21.

The judge found that the tenants never gave up possession of the keys to the premises, and that they left some fixtures and fittings in the premises even after they had arranged for the stock to be extracted by a salvage E
company. He found that they sent someone into the premises and saved what they could of the stock, but they then left the premises and did not return to them certainly at any time before June 17, a date on which, on one view in this case, the landlords took the law into their own hands by demolishing what was left of no. 31, Dudley Street. So much for the attitude at that time of the tenants.

F
The attitude of the landlords is equally clear. As the judge found on the first preliminary point, they received an honest and competent report from their architects upon which they acted perfectly bona fide under clause 6 (4) of the underlease, which I have already read, and gave an immediate notice terminating the contract under that clause. As it so happens, the letter that I have read from the tenants dated May 21 and the notice under clause 6 (4), which the landlords gave on May 22, G
crossed in the post, and this led to some confusion. But in the course of the confusion both parties reiterated and emphasised their respective attitudes. The landlords insisted that their notice was sufficient to terminate the contract of tenancy; the tenants insisted upon their right to have the premises reinstated and upon their right of occupancy. During this period the premises were boarded up and made reasonably safe so far as passers-by H
were concerned, and they were unoccupied.

On June 17 the landlords went into no. 31, Dudley Street, with their bulldozers and knocked the premises down, and since that date no. 31, Dudley Street, even to the extent that it was left by the fire, has disappeared save for the land upon which the premises were built. We were told, although I do not think this is in evidence, that there has been rebuilding on the site to a plan quite different from the no. 31, Dudley

A Street which was the subject matter of the demise. The judge never considered the merits of the substantive plea by the landlords that they required the premises for demolition and reconstruction, and that, therefore, a new tenancy should not be granted. That issue remains, with all its difficulties in the situation I have outlined, to be considered if the tenants are successful in this appeal and are found to have a locus standi to make their application.

B The point turns on the construction of sections 23 and 24 of the Landlord and Tenant Act 1954 and upon the proper inference to be drawn as to the relationship of the tenants towards the property after the devastating fire of May 20. I will deal first with the point of construction. Section 24 (1) of the Act of 1954 provides:

> " A tenancy to which this Part of this Act applies shall not come to C an end unless terminated in accordance with the provisions of this Part of this Act, and subject to the provisions of section 29 of this Act the tenant under such a tenancy may apply to the court for a new tenancy."

The question, therefore, arises whether the tenants are tenants under a tenancy to which Part II of the Act of 1954 applies. Section 23 defines D the tenancies to which Part II of the Act applies, and subsection (1) provides:

> " Subject to the provisions of this Act, this Part of this Act applies to any tenancy where the property comprised in the tenancy is or includes premises which are occupied by the tenant and are so occupied for the purposes of a business carried on by him or for those or other E purposes."

Mr. Mills, for the landlords, submits that from the date of the devastating fire the tenants were not tenants under a tenancy to which the Act applies, because they no longer occupied the premises, and certainly no longer occupied them for the purposes of a business carried on by them. The point of construction with which this court is concerned was con-F sidered by Cross J. in *Caplan (I. & H.) Ltd.* v. *Caplan (No. 2)* [1963] 1 W.L.R. 1247. In the course of his judgment Cross J. addressed his mind to the point of construction and said, at p. 1254:

> " The only sort of tenant who is given by section 24 (1) a right to apply for a new tenancy is a tenant under a tenancy to which the Act applies. And if the tenant ceased to occupy the property for business G purposes after the service by the landlords of a statutory notice but before he himself issued his summons asking for a new tenancy, then, as it seems to me, the landlord could clearly apply to have the summons dismissed on the ground that the tenant had no locus standi to apply to the court."

Later, he returned to the point of construction and, after dealing with the H facts, asked himself, at p. 1260: " . . . what is the legal conclusion? " He then went on to say:

> " I think it is quite clear that a tenant does not lose the protection of this Act simply by ceasing physically to occupy the premises. They may well continue to be occupied for the purposes of the business although they are de facto empty for some period of time. One rather obvious example would be if there was a need for urgent

structural repairs and the tenant had to go out of physical occupation in order to enable them to be effected." A

I respectfully agree with the view of the law expressed by Cross J. in the two passages to which I have referred. I would put it in my own words as follows: in order to apply for a new tenancy under the Act a tenant must show either that he is continuing in occupation of the premises for the purposes of a business carried on by him, or, if events over which B he has no control have led him to absent himself from the premises, if he continues to exert and claim his right to occupancy. This is a question which did not arise in terms in *Caplan (I. & H.) Ltd.* v. *Caplan (No. 2)*, where there was a temporary absence of the tenant which the judge held did not interrupt the continuity of his occupation in the circumstances of that case. However, the temporary absence in *Caplan (I. & H.) Ltd.* v. *Caplan (No. 2)* which did not destroy the continuity of occupation was C absence at the volition of the tenant. In the present case the absenting by the tenants of themselves from the premises after the devastating fire was not their choice, but was brought about by the state of the premises created by the fire, which was none of the tenants' making. Nevertheless, they exhibited immediately after the fire, and continued to exhibit, an intention to retain and to claim their right of occupancy, and reminded D the landlords from time to time of what they thought were the landlords' obligations to reinstate.

The judge was so impressed with the devastating nature of the fire that he was not prepared to draw the inference that the absence of the tenants from the property was temporary. He thought that the reality of the situation was that the tenants had gone for ever. Mr. Mills submits that this was an inference which he was right to draw because of the E catastrophic nature of the fire.

It seems to me that, when events such as I have detailed arise and a tenant is faced with the difficulties of occupation that these tenants were, it must be a question of fact to determine whether the tenant intended to cease occupation or whether he was not only, as the judge found these tenants were, cherishing the hope of return, but also making quite clear that F he intended to maintain his right of occupancy and to resume physical occupation as soon as the landlords reinstated. This sort of approach, says Mr. Mills, is quite unrealistic, because these landlords had immediately following the fire given a notice under section 6 (4), indicating that the Central Arcade was economically incapable of being reinstated to the old design, and terminating the tenancy. But one has to look at the matter as the tenants then looked at it. They had premises which had not been G destroyed. The judge, right at the end of his judgment, expressly found that the part of the premises held by the tenants still stood. He said: "It is not disputed."

The tenants also must be assumed to have appreciated their position under the Landlord and Tenant Act 1954, whereby the landlords could not bring the tenancy to an end save by taking the steps detailed in Part H II of the Act. In particular, the landlords could not bring the tenancy to an end merely by serving a notice under clause 6 (4). Of course, if the tenants were out of occupation or had abandoned their right of occupation at the time that the notice was served, it would determine the contract of tenancy, since the tenancy would no longer be one to which Part II of the Act applied. But if the tenants still either occupied or claimed their right of occupation at the time that the notice was served, then the notice would not avail because in terms it was not a notice as required by the Act. These difficulties create no technical problem for the landlords in this case, because at a later date, on July 1, realising that there might be argument as to the effectiveness of the clause 6 (4) notice, they served an appropriate notice under section 25 of the Act.

That leads me to a further question which arises on this appeal. As Cross J. recognised in *Caplan (I. & H.) Ltd.* v. *Caplan (No. 2)* [1963] 1 W.L.R. 1247, an applicant for a new tenancy has to continue in occupation, by which I mean continue in occupation or maintain his intention, and maintain his right, to occupy, right up to the date of the order made by the court. The question, therefore, arises: were the tenants still occupiers, as I have defined the term, after the demolition in June, and at the time, some fortnight later, when the section 25 notice was served? I would find it surprising if action, which, upon the view of the case that I have formed, was action not lawfully open to the landlords, but, nevertheless, was taken by them, could be said to destroy an applicant's locus standi to apply under Part II of the Landlord and Tenant Act 1954. I do not think that the court is driven to such an unjust conclusion. I think it is clear that right up to today's date the tenants have been saying: "We have a right of occupancy. We want to go back. We are out of occupation only as a result of events over which we have no control. We are still claiming our right of occupation, and that is a right to occupy for the purposes of the underlease and these are plainly business premises." I think, therefore, that, when one considers the full facts, and when one construes the two sections as Cross J. did, it is plain that the cesser of occupation in this case is not to be regarded as an abandonment of occupation by the tenants. They are out because of the events which I have described, but they have at all times indicated not only their hope, but their intention, to go back as soon as the premises are fit for occupation.

Of course, nothing that I have said bears at all on the substantive ground to which I have made reference in the landlords' answer, namely, that they require these premises for reconstruction. It may be that they have a strong case. All that this court is concerned to determine is whether the tenants have a right to apply to the court. For the reasons that I have given, I can find nothing in the facts of this case, and nothing in the statute, to bar them from pursuing their application. I, therefore, would allow the appeal and remit the application to the county court judge.

SIR GORDON WILLMER. I have come to the same conclusion, and I hope that I can be quite brief in explaining the way in which I see this case. As Scarman L.J. has already pointed out, the serving of the notice under clause 6 (4) of the lease, on May 22, 1974, shortly following the fire, did nothing towards getting rid of whatever right the tenants had under the Landlord and Tenant Act 1954. By section 24 of that Act the tenancy which they enjoyed was continued, and would have gone on being continued until such subsequent steps were taken as laid down by the statute to determine it. That was the position at the date of the fire and immediately following the fire.

The tenants enjoyed in pursuance of their underlease the right to occupy the premises in question, namely, no. 31, Dudley Street. They retained, as I see it, after the fire their right under the continuing tenancy to remain in occupation. The question is whether they have shown such continuing occupation as to give them a locus standi to assert any rights A under the Act of 1954. That question, as I think counsel rightly observed, is a mixed question of fact and law.

So far as the law is concerned, I think it can be taken as axiomatic that in order to be in occupation one does not have to be physically present every second of every minute of every hour of every day. All of us remain in occupation, for instance, of our houses even while we are away doing our day's work. It follows, therefore, that occupation neces- B sarily must include an element of intention as well as a physical element. If I leave my premises and emigrate to the United States of America with no intention of returning, it can well be said that I no longer remain in occupation. But if as a shopkeeper I close my shop for a fortnight in the summer to enable my staff to have a holiday, I apprehend that no one would contend that during that fortnight I ceased to be in occupation of C my shop.

It is in the light of those considerations that I think one must look at the facts of this particular case. After the fire the tenants, as tenants, enjoyed the same right to occupy the premises as they enjoyed before. The premises, although damaged, were still in existence, and, as I understand the evidence, the tenants exercised during the first day or two following the fire their rights by going into the premises in order to save D such stores and equipment as they could. If the tenants did not remain in occupation, then one might well ask the question: who did? The answer, I think, having regard to the argument in this case, would have to be that immediately following the fire the tenants ceased to be in occupation and the landlords themselves resumed occupation. But the landlords would be faced with the same difficult question as the tenants E are faced with here, that they were not physically on the premises. For my part, I cannot accept that view of the case. It seems to me that the tenants, who had been in continuous occupation up to the fire and immediately after the fire, and who retained the intention to occupy, remained both in fact and in law the occupiers of the premises at the relevant time. They are consequently entitled to prosecute whatever remedy they may have in pursuance of the Landlord and Tenant Act 1954. F

I omitted to observe, although Scarman L.J. mentioned it, that the tenants retained the keys of the premises. They were thus in a position to exclude the public from the premises, or to open the door and invite the public to come in. If some person was invited to come in, I apprehend that the tenants would have had some difficulty in escaping their liabilities under the Occupiers' Liability Act 1957.

G

However one looks at it, it seems to me that one cannot disregard the tenants' continuing occupation of these premises, notwithstanding the somewhat devastating effects of the fire that took place. I am glad to find that the view which I have been expressing is in accord with that of Cross J. in *Caplan* (*I. & H.*) *Ltd.* v. *Caplan* (*No.* 2), [1963] 1 W.L.R. 1247. I need not read again the passage at p. 1260 of the report to which Scarman L.J. has referred. I only need to say that, for my part, I fully concur with H it. It only remains to add that, assuming I am right so far, I do not see how the subsequent demolition of the building at the instance of the landlords, which took place on June 17, can possibly have affected one way or the other such rights as the tenants had.

My conclusion, therefore, in agreement with Scarman L.J. is that these tenants do have a perfectly good locus standi to pursue their remedy under the Act of 1954.

A STEPHENSON L.J. I agree with both judgments which have been delivered and have nothing to add.

Appeal allowed with costs.
Tenants entitled to apply for a new tenancy; case remitted to county court.

B

Solicitors: *Paisner & Co., Manby & Steward, Wolverhampton.*

C [QUEEN'S BENCH DIVISION]

* NATIONAL COAL BOARD *v.* THORNE

1976 Feb. 24 — Lord Widgery C.J., Kilner Brown and Watkins JJ.

D *Public Health—Nuisance—Abatement notice—Property in disrepair—Owners charged with failure to comply with notice—No evidence of interference with use of neighbouring property—No injury to health—Whether statutory nuisance—Public Health Act* 1936 (26 *Geo.* 5 & 1 *Edw.* 8, *c.* 49), *s.* 92 (1) (*a*)

An information was preferred against the defendant board, the owners of premises which had fallen into disrepair,
E charging them with failing to comply with an abatement notice which required them to carry out repairs to defective windows and gutters. The justices found that although there was no evidence of injury to health or interference with the enjoyment or use of neighbouring property the defects were such as to interfere with the personal comfort of the occupier; that a nuisance existed within the meaning of section 92 (1) (*a*) of the Public Health Act 1936 [1] and that a nuisance order should
F be made.

On appeal by the board:—

Held, allowing the appeal, that "nuisance" in section 92 (1) (*a*) of the Public Health Act 1936 had the same meaning as public or private nuisance at common law and did not arise if the acts complained of affected only the persons occupying the premises where the nuisance allegedly took place.

Quaere. Whether the acts complained of must be directed
G to the health of the person affected to constitute a nuisance within section 92 (1) (*a*) (post, p. 548B–E).

Dicta of Lord Wilberforce and Lord Edmund-Davies in *Salford City Council* v. *McNally* [1975] 3 W.L.R. 87, 91, 95, H.L.(E.), applied.

Betts v. *Penge Urban District Council* [1942] 2 K.B. 154, D.C. disapproved.

H The following cases are referred to in the judgment of Watkins J.:

Betts v. *Penge Urban District Council* [1942] 2 K.B. 154; [1942] 2 All E.R. 61, D.C.

Coventry City Council v. *Cartwright* [1975] 1 W.L.R. 845; [1975] 2 All E.R. 99, D.C.

[1] Public Health Act 1936, s. 92 (1): ". . . the following matters may . . . be dealt with summarily, and are . . . referred to as 'statutory nuisances' . . . (*a*) any premises in such a state as to be prejudicial to health or a nuisance; . . ."

Salford City Council v. *McNally* [1975] 3 W.L.R. 87; [1975] 2 All E.R. A 860, H.L.(E.).

The following additional cases were cited in argument:

Bishop Auckland Local Board v. *Bishop Auckland Iron and Steel Co. Ltd.* (1882) 10 Q.B.D. 138, D.C.

Great Western Railway Co. v. *Bishop* (1872) L.R. 7 Q.B. 550, D.C.

Malton Board of Health v. *Malton Manure Co.* (1879) 4 Ex.D. 302. B

Springett v. *Harold* [1954] 1 W.L.R. 521; [1954] 1 All E.R. 568.

Warman v. *Tibbatts* (1922) 128 L.T. 477, D.C.

CASE STATED by Neath justices.

On March 7, 1975, an information was preferred by the prosecutor, Mr. Harold Kelland Thorne, clerk and chief officer of Neath Borough C Council, the local authority, against the National Coal Board, that the board, being the owners of certain premises at 38, Roman Road, Banwen, on whom the local authority had served an abatement notice dated January 9, 1975, requiring them to abate the nuisance by carrying out repairs to a defective window in the back addition room on the ground floor; a defective window in the back room on the first floor; to provide a stop end for the rain water gutter in the back addition extension on the ground floor; D to repair a defective skirting board in the passage back room on the ground floor; to replace defective woodwork in the window, and leave in proper working order in the back addition room on the ground floor; to provide a stop end for the rain water gutter in the back addition extension on the ground floor; to repair defective and rotted skirting board in the passage back room on the ground floor; as particularised in the abatement notice, E had failed to comply with the requirements of the abatement notice, contrary to section 94 of the Public Health Act 1936.

The justices heard the information on April 4, 1975, and found the following facts. The defects mentioned in the information were present in the premises at 38, Roman Road, Banwen, Neath, and the presence of those defects was not disputed by the board. An abatement notice was served on the board on January 9, 1975, by recorded delivery post on that F day. The requirements of the abatement notice had not been complied with by the board.

The board contended that the defects stated in the information did not constitute a state of affairs which was prejudicial to health as required by section 92 (1) (*a*) of the Public Health Act 1936 and that therefore the defects had to constitute a nuisance as required by the section and that the G meaning of nuisance in that context was the ordinary common law meaning. Further, a nuisance in that context was an interference with the use or enjoyment of neighbouring property and that in the case before the justices the board had not used the property in question so as to interfere with any neighbouring property and that therefore a statutory nuisance could not be said to exist.

H

The prosecutor contended that the board should have appealed against the terms of the abatement notice at the time the notice was received, as provided for in section 290 of the Public Health Act 1936; that there had been ample time for that having regard to the date on which the notice was served, and that the hearing of the information was not the proper time to dispute the existence of a nuisance. The prosecutor did not claim that the defects at 38, Roman Road, Banwen, constituted a state of affairs pre-

A judicial to health but that a statutory nuisance existed when premises were in such a state as to interfere with the personal comfort of the occupier.

The justices were of opinion that they were not in agreement with the prosecutor that the time to dispute the existence of the nuisance was the time the abatement notice was served as it had been held that if there was any dispute between the parties about that, the proper time for hearing the dispute was at the trial of the information for failure to comply with
B the notice. Although the justices were of opinion that "nuisance" in that context should have the ordinary common law meaning, and if not prejudicial to health (and the prosecutor had not shown the defects to be injurious to health) would have to be such as to affect the use of enjoyment of neighbouring property, nevertheless interference with personal comfort as stated to be the criterion in *Betts* v. *Penge Urban District Council* [1942]
C 2 K.B. 154 must have some relevance to public health and the justices were unanimous in agreeing that one of the defects, namely the absence of a stop end for the rain water gutter, and possibly even the defective window might affect the health of an occupant. That was supported by Stephen J. in *Malton Board of Health* v. *Malton Manure Co.* (1879) 4 Ex.D. 302. The justices were unanimous in deciding that these defects were an interference with the personal comfort of the occupier and that the criteria to
D apply in such cases as the present were ones which should apply in the light of present standards and not those which would have applied in earlier years. Accordingly the justices made the nuisance order.

The board appealed. The question for the opinion of the High Court was whether the justices had arrived at the correct definition of the word "nuisance" as used in section 92 (1) (*a*) of the Public Health Act 1936 and
E accordingly were correct in making the nuisance order; whether two defective windows, a missing stop end for a rain water gutter and a defective skirting board in a dwelling-house, in the absence of any evidence that those matters were prejudicial to the health of the occupants of the dwelling-house or of any other person, were within the ambit of section 92 (1) (*a*) of the Public Health Act 1936; and whether there was any evidence on which the justices could conclude that the premises were in such a state as to be
F a nuisance within the meaning of section 92 (1) (*a*) of the Public Health Act 1936.

John Roch for the board.
Alan Fletcher for the prosecutor.

G WATKINS J. The National Coal Board, the "board," own premises known as 38, Roman Road, in the village of Banwen in South Wales. That village, for local government purposes, lies within the jurisdiction of the Neath Borough Council, the local authority. The local authority have the duty under section 91 of the Public Health Act 1936 to inspect from time to time property within their area for the detection of matters requiring to
H be dealt with under the provisions of Part III of the Act as statutory nuisances.

At some time or other an officer of the local authority inspected 38, Roman Road, Banwen, and found the place to be in a state of disrepair in that there were two defective windows, there was no stop end for a rain water gutter, and there was a defective skirting board. Those were matters reported to the local authority. They determined that a nuisance was present in the premises and, using the power which they have under section

93 of the Act, they served upon the board a notice to abate the nuisance, a notice which one supposes set out in terms the precise things which the board had to do in order to bring about an effective abatement. The board did nothing to abate the so-called nuisance so an information was laid before the local justices. A hearing followed, the result of which was that on April 4, 1975, the justices found that an abatement notice had been served on the board on January 9, 1975, by recorded delivery and the requirements of the abatement notice had not been complied with by the board. So they decided that, having regard to those findings and the state of the law as they understood it to be, they had no alternative but to issue a nuisance order. The effect of issuing a nuisance order is to compel the person upon whom it is served to comply with its terms under penalty. The penalty is laid down in the Act; it amounts to the maximum sum of £50.

Before however, the board could be expected to carry out the terms of the nuisance order, they appealed. The appeal comes to this court by way of case stated.

The justices had addressed to them argument affecting the meaning to be attached to the word " nuisance " as it appears in section 92 (1) of the Act. Nothing was said at that hearing suggestive of the fact that there had been any injury or anticipated injury to the health of persons residing either in the premises or in any premises adjoining them. The information itself was laid simply upon the basis that there was a nuisance present at the material time at the premises.

The short point, therefore, arising in this appeal is what is the meaning to be attached to the word " nuisance." *Betts* v. *Penge Urban District Council* [1942] 2 K.B. 154 has been referred to. What happened in that case was that the landlord of a flat, of which the rent was in arrears, made no application for possession but removed the front door and some of the window sashes thereby interfering with the personal comfort of the occupier. It was held that there was a distinction between public and private nuisance which was material to the question whether a statutory nuisance under section 92 (1) of the Public Health Act 1936 existed on the premises, and that it was sufficient in order to sustain a conviction of the appellant for permitting a statutory nuisance on the premises to prove that by his act or default they were in such a state as to interfere with the personal comfort of the occupiers, without necessarily being injurious to health. If the law is accurately stated in that case, then the justices in the present case, it seems to me, cannot be criticised for issuing a nuisance order, since I see no basis for assuming that they came to conclusions of fact which were not properly founded upon the evidence which came before them, and upon their findings of fact they were entitled, assuming the law is corrected stated in *Betts'* case, to proceed to make the nuisance order.

In his very able argument Mr. Roch appearing for the board says that the word " nuisance " cannot have and should not be understood to have the meaning attached to it by *Betts'* case, and that the word " nuisance " as used in section 92 (1) must be understood to equate with the same word as that is understood at common law in relation to nuisances, public or private. A public nuisance at common law has been expressed to be an act or omission which materially affects the material comfort and quality of life of a class of Her Majesty's subjects. A private nuisance has often been defined in this way: private nuisances, at least in the vast majority of cases, are interferences for a substantial length of time by owners or occupiers

A of property with the use or enjoyment of neighbouring property. The distinction which immediately springs to mind therefore between a private nuisance at common law and a nuisance of the kind as found by the justices in the present case is that the justices, feeling compelled to follow the decision in *Betts'* case, found that a nuisance could exist in a dwelling-house in relation to the occupier of it, whereas that notion is obviously alien to the concept of a common law private nuisance.

B When the justices reached their conclusion in April 1975 *Salford City Council* v. *McNally* [1975] 3 W.L.R. 87 had not been decided. Accordingly, they had not the advantage of knowing what I now propose to quote from the speeches made in that case. Lord Wilberforce said, at p. 91:

> "In dealing with each Act it is better to use its own terminology. A similar confusion occurs in some of the cases through the use of
> C the words 'personal comfort.' These words are appropriate enough in the context of what is a 'nuisance' for the purposes of the Public Health Act (see as to this the clear judgment of Stephen J. in *Bishop Auckland Local Board* v. *Bishop Auckland Iron and Steel Co. Ltd.* (1882) 10 Q.B.D. 138), but they are quite inappropriate in relation to the other limb 'prejudicial to health.' Health is not the same as
> D comfort and interference with the latter does not bring a case within the 'health' limb of the Public Health Act. In my opinion *Betts* v. *Penge Urban District Council* [1942] 2 K.B. 154 is guilty of this confusion and was wrongly decided. It was simply a case of what is now called 'harassment,' and not, in my view, under the Act at all. I express no opinion upon *Coventry City Council* v. *Cartwright* [1975] 1 W.L.R. 845, which was reported after argument had been closed in
> E the present case."

Lord Simon of Glaisdale expressly agreed with Lord Wilberforce. Lord Edmund-Davies, at p. 95, said of *Betts'* case:

> "Be that as it may, no. 20 Johnson Street being at the material time undoubtedly a 'statutory nuisance,' i.e. injurious to the health of
> F the occupier, this House is not presently called upon to determine the correctness of the decision in *Betts* v. *Penge Urban District Council* [1942] 2 K.B. 154 that, in order to sustain a conviction for permitting a statutory nuisance, it is sufficient to prove that premises were in such a state as to interfere with the *personal comfort* of the occupiers, without being injurious to their health, though for my part I think it desirable to make clear that I respectfully think it was wrongly
> G decided."

Lord Cross of Chelsea and Lord Fraser of Tullybelton agreed with Lord Edmund-Davies.

Mr. Fletcher, in common with Mr. Roch, submits that the effect of these speeches is such as to cause this court to pronounce that in its opinion *Betts'*
H case was in fact wrongly decided and does not represent the true law upon the crucial matter of the meaning of the word "nuisance" in section 92 (1) of the Public Health Act 1936. I welcome the opportunity of saying that what Lord Wilberforce said in the *Salford* case leads me to the conclusion that *Betts* unquestionably does not express the proper law upon this question. Speaking for myself, I would adopt the words of Lord Wilberforce so as to state that a nuisance cannot arise if what has taken place affects only the person or persons occupying the premises where the nuisance is

said to have taken place. A nuisance coming within the meaning of the Public Health Act 1936 must be either a private or public nuisance as understood by common law.

For that reason, it seems to me that the proper course is to direct that the order of the justices should be quashed.

Before parting with this case I ought in deference to the further interesting argument which has been addressed to us to make some reference to it. It is to this effect. Not only must a statutory nuisance be either of a private or public kind at common law, but the act of nuisance itself must be such as comes within the spirit of the Public Health Act 1936, by which I assume Mr. Roch to be saying that whatever is complained about must in some way be directed to the question of the health of the person who claims to be or who has been affected by the nuisance. I find that proposition to be an attractive one although I foresee difficulties, assuming it to be right, in the application of it in certain circumstances. However, since today we are not called upon to determine that particular question it seems to me that it is better left for resolution upon another day and in circumstances where the facts of the particular case demand that the question be answered.

KILNER BROWN J. I agree.

LORD WIDGERY C.J. I also agree and would only refer to a few words of my own in *Coventry City Council* v. *Cartwright* [1975] 1 W.L.R. 845, 849. We were concerned with the construction of the same statutory provisions although the phrase was "prejudicial to health" rather than "nuisance" but I said:

> "The words are obviously very wide, and one should hesitate, in construing the section in proceedings such as the present, to lay down boundaries which may in another case prove to be unsuitable. But I think that the underlying conception of the section is that that which it struck at is an accumulation of something which produces a threat to health in the sense of a threat of disease, vermin or the like."

I agree with the order proposed.

Appeal allowed.
No order for costs.

Solicitors: *R. Cowles; Sharpe, Pritchard & Co. for H. K. Thorne, Neath.*

A

[HOUSE OF LORDS]

* PRACTICE DIRECTION
(HOUSE OF LORDS: PETITIONS FOR LEAVE TO APPEAL)

B *House of Lords—Leave to appeal—Petition—Incompetent—Certified as such—Fitness for oral hearing—Petitions not referred for oral hearing certified accordingly*

As from October 1, 1976, petitions for leave to appeal to the House of Lords will be referred to an Appeal Committee consisting of three Lords of Appeal, who will consider whether the petition appears to be competent to be received by the House and if so whether it should be referred for an
C oral hearing. Petitions are incompetent if they fall under one of the following heads:

(a) Criminal petitions for leave to appeal to the House of Lords in respect of which no certificate has been granted by the court below under section 1 (2) of the Administration of Justice Act 1960 or section 33 (2) of the Criminal Appeal Act 1968.

D (b) Petitions for leave to appeal to the House of Lords against a refusal of the Court of Appeal to grant leave to appeal to that court from a judgment of a lower court.

(c) Petitions for leave to appeal to the House of Lords barred by section 108 (2) (*b*) of the Bankruptcy Act 1914.

(d) Petitions for leave to appeal to the House of Lords barred by para-
E graph 4 of Schedule 4 to the Housing Act 1957.

(e) Petitions for leave to appeal to the House of Lords brought by a petitioner in respect of whom the High Court has made an order under section 51 of the Supreme Court of Judicature (Consolidation) Act 1925, as amended by the Supreme Court of Judicature (Amendment) Act 1959, unless leave to present such a petition has
F been granted by the High Court or a judge thereof pursuant to that section.

(f) Petitions for leave to appeal to the House of Lords barred by section 27 (2) of the Supreme Court of Judicature (Consolidation) Act 1925.

Petitions will be referred for an oral hearing if any of the three Lords
G of Appeal—(i) considers that the petition is competent or expresses doubts as to whether it is incompetent; and (ii) considers that it is fit for an oral hearing. Petitions not referred for an oral hearing will be certified accordingly by the three Lords of Appeal and the Clerk of the Parliaments will notify the parties that the petition is dismissed.

PETER HENDERSON,
H *Clerk of the Parliaments.*

May 18, 1976.

A

[COURT OF APPEAL]

* REGINA *v.* GREATER LONDON COUNCIL
Ex parte BLACKBURN AND ANOTHER

1976 March 29, 30, 31; April 14 — **Lord Denning M.R., Stephenson and Bridge L.JJ.** B

Licensing—Films—Censorship—County council delegating powers of censorship to unincorporated board with power to review —Whether delegation ultra vires—Council rule incorporating statutory test for obscene publications—Whether proper test—Obscene Publications Act 1959 (7 & 8 *Eliz.* 2, *c.* 66), *s.* 1 (1) [1] *Cinematograph Act* 1909 (9 *Edw.* 7, *c.* 30), *s.* 2 (1) [2]—*Cinematograph Act* 1952 (15 & 16 *Geo.* 6 & 1 *Eliz.* 2, *c.* 68), *s.* 3 (1) [3] C

Crown Practice — Prohibition — Film licensing authority — Application to prohibit local council exercising their powers — Whether sufficient locus standi as ratepayer and parent

The Greater London Council, the licensing authority under the Cinematograph Acts 1909 and 1952 for licensing premises for the public exhibition of films, exercised their powers under D rules, rule 116 of which provided that: "No film shall be exhibited at the premises . . . (2) the effect of which is, if taken as a whole, such as to tend to deprave and corrupt persons who are likely to see it," that being in terms the test of obscenity laid down in section 1 (1) of the Obscene Publications Act 1959 in relation to "articles." The council had for many years delegated their power to censor films to the E British Board of Film Censors, an unincorporated body of persons, which, though connected with the trade, had been recognised by judicial decision since 1925 and by Parliament in section 3 (1) of the Cinematograph Act 1952 as a proper body for performing that function, subject to the council retaining the final power to review any decision by the board.

In 1973 the board refused a certificate for the public exhibition of a particular film, but, on appeal by the exhibitors, F the council, applying the test in their rule 116 (2), licensed its public exhibition. Later, following a complaint to the Metropolitan Police Commissioner by the applicants, residents and ratepayers in the council's area, the exhibitors of that film were prosecuted and convicted by a jury in June 1975 for the common law offence of showing in public a grossly indecent film.

The applicants applied to the Divisional Court of the G Queen's Bench Division for an order of prohibition directed to the council to prevent them from (a) exercising their censorship powers in accordance with a test which was bad in law, namely, the statutory test of obscenity, instead of the common law test of gross indecency applicable to the public exhibition of films; and (b) acting in excess of their powers in delegating those powers to the board, a body having no legal existence, or authorising it to act as their agent, without retaining the H

[1] Obscene Publications Act 1959, s. 1: "(1) For the purposes of this Act an article shall be deemed to be obscene if its effect or (where the article comprises two or more distinct items) the effect of any one of its items is, if taken as a whole, such as to tend to deprave and corrupt persons who are likely, having regard to all relevant circumstances, to read, see or hear the matter contained or embodied in it."

[2] Cinematograph Act 1909 (as amended by Cinematograph Act 1952), s. 2 (1): see post, p. 553G–H.

[3] Cinematograph Act 1952, s. 3 (1): see post, p. 561D–E.

right to revoke the board's decisions to grant certificates and
A acting in such manner that their right of review was normally inoperative.

The Divisional Court refused the applications, holding, inter alia, that the delegation of the council's authority to the board was lawful, that rule 116 (2) was reasonable, and that it supplemented the common law criteria for public exhibition.

On appeal by the applicants:—

B *Held*, allowing the appeal, (1) that the council were acting unlawfully in exercising their licensing powers by reference to a rule which applied the statutory test of obscenity applicable to publications and which was so limited as to permit the public exhibition of grossly indecent films, contrary to the general common law applicable to the licensing of films; that the court could therefore exercise its discretion to issue an order of prohibition to stop the council from misusing their powers;
C but that the order should not issue until the council had had time to repeal or waive rule 116 (2) and to comply with the requirements of the common law or to abandon the censorship of films save in relation to children, leaving it to Parliament to reform the law.

Per Bridge L.J. Though the court's conclusions on the law are inescapable as the law stands, I cannot feel any enthusiasm for the result. The statutory test of obscenity has been much criticised, and with good reason. The law in its
D present state is so full of anomalies and operates so uncertainly and unevenly that some rationalisation is urgently needed (post, p. 567E–G).

(2) That the applicants, as citizens, ratepayers and parents within the council's jurisdiction, had sufficient locus standi to apply for a prerogative order to prohibit a public authority from acting unlawfully.

E But (3) that the council were not acting in excess of their powers by delegating to the British Board of Film Censors the task of censoring films for public exhibition so long as they retained their power to review the board's decisions; for though the board was not a legal entity it had been recognised both by the courts and by Parliament as a proper body to carry out in practice the task of censoring and certifying films for public exhibition, subject to review by the licensing authority
F in whom the statutory discretion was vested.

Dicta in *Reg.* v. *Knuller* (*Publishing, Printing and Promotions*) *Ltd.* [1973] A.C. 435, 458, 493, H.L.(E.) and *Rex* v. *London County Council, Ex parte Entertainments Protection Association Ltd.* [1931] 2 K.B. 215, C.A. applied.

Ellis v. *Dubowski* [1921] 3 K.B. 621, D.C.; *Mills* v. *London County Council* [1925] 1 K.B. 213, D.C. and *Reg.* v. *Stanley* [1965] 2 Q.B. 327, C.C.A. approved.

G Decision of the Divisional Court of the Queen's Bench Division reversed in part.

The following cases are referred to in the judgments:

Attorney-General ex rel. McWhirter v. *Independent Broadcasting Authority* [1973] Q. B. 629; [1973] 2 W.L.R. 344; [1973] 1 All E.R. 689, C.A.

Bradbury v. *Enfield London Borough Council* [1967] 1 W.L.R. 1311;
H [1967] 3 All E.R. 434, C.A.

Dyson v. *Attorney-General* [1911] 1 K.B. 410, C.A.

Ellis v. *Dubowski* [1921] 3 K.B. 621, D.C.

London County Council v. *Bermondsey Bioscope Co. Ltd.* [1911] 1 K.B. 445, D.C.

Mills v. *London County Council* [1925] 1 K.B. 213, D.C.

Prescott v. *Birmingham Corporation* [1955] Ch. 210; [1954] 3 W.L.R. 990; [1954] 3 All E.R. 698, C.A.

Reg. v. *Commissioner of Police of the Metropolis, Ex parte Blackburn* [1968] 2 Q.B. 118; [1968] 2 W.L.R. 893; [1968] 1 All E.R. 763, C.A. A

Reg. v. *Commissioner of Police of the Metropolis, Ex parte Blackburn (No.* 3) [1973] Q.B. 241; [1973] 2 W.L.R. 43; [1973] 1 All E.R. 324, C.A.

Reg. v. *Hereford Corporation, Ex parte Harrower* [1970] 1 W.L.R. 1424; [1970] 3 All E.R. 460, D.C.

Reg. v. *Hicklin* (1868) L.R. 3 Q.B. 360. B

Reg. v. *Knuller (Publishing, Printing and Promotions) Ltd.* [1973] A.C. 435; [1972] 3 W.L.R. 143; [1972] 2 All E.R. 898, H.L.(E.).

Reg. v. *Paddington Valuation Officer, Ex parte Peachey Property Corporation Ltd.* [1966] 1 Q.B. 380; [1965] 3 W.L.R. 426; [1965] 2 All E.R. 836, C.A.

Reg. v. *Saunders* (1875) 1 Q.B.D. 15.

Reg. v. *Staniforth* [1976] 2 W.L.R. 849, C.A. C

Reg. v. *Stanley* [1965] 2 Q.B. 327; [1965] 2 W.L.R. 917; [1965] 1 All E.R. 1035, C.C.A.

Reg. v. *Thames Magistrates' Court, Ex parte Greenbaum* (1957) 55 L.G.R. 129, C.A.

Rex v. *Burnley Justices* (1916) 32 T.L.R. 695, D.C.

Rex v. *London County Council, Ex parte Entertainments Protection Association Ltd.* [1931] 2 K.B. 215, C.A. D

Thorson v. *Attorney-General of Canada* (1975) 1 S.C.R. 138.

The following additional cases were cited in argument:

Director of Public Prosecutions v. *Whyte* [1972] A.C. 849; [1972] 3 W.L.R. 410; [1972] 3 All E.R. 12, H.L.(E.).

Stott, Ex parte [1916] 1 K.B. 7, D.C. E

APPEAL from the Divisional Court of the Queen's Bench Division.

The applicants, Albert Raymond Blackburn, and his wife, Tessa Marion Blackburn, residing in Homefield Road, Chiswick, London W.4, within the area of the Greater London Council, applied for and obtained leave from the Divisional Court to apply for an order of prohibition to issue against the council to prevent them (a) from exercising their censorship F powers over the public exhibition of cinematograph films in accordance with a test of obscenity which was bad in law, namely, whether the effect of a film submitted for censorship was, if taken as a whole, such as to tend to corrupt and deprave persons likely to see it, instead of applying the common law which governed the exhibition of films; (b) from acting ultra vires or invalidly in law in delegating or purporting to delegate their censorship powers to the British Board of Film Censors, because the board G had no legal existence and/or denied its legal existence, and from authorising the board to act as their agent for the censorship of films; (c) from delegating their powers of film censorship to the board or authorising the board to act as their agent for such censorship without retaining a right to revoke the decisions of the board when granting certificates for the exhibition of films; and (d) from delegating their powers of film censorship H or authorising the board to act as their agent without ever exercising or considering whether they should exercise their power to revoke the decisions of the board to pass films for exhibition in public.

The court (Lord Widgery C.J., Kilner Brown and Watkins JJ.) on February 5, 1976, refused the order and dismissed the motion with costs to the respondent council.

The applicants appealed on the grounds that the Divisional Court had been wrong in law in holding that the council were entitled to apply the statutory test of obscenity laid down by the Act of 1959 instead of the common law test of gross indecency; that it was wrong in law in deciding that the council could delegate their powers of censorship to the British Board of Film Censors, a body which did not exist in law and claimed not to exist in law; and that as the Court of Appeal was not bound by *Mills* v. *London County Council* [1925] 1 K.B. 213, as the Divisional Court had been, it should issue the order of prohibition which would ensure the establishment of an effective right of review by the council and enable them to ban a film passed by the board for public exhibition.

The hearing of the appeal was expedited.

The applicants in person.

John Davies Q.C., *Gordon Langley* and *Peter Barber* for the Greater London Council.

Cur. adv. vult.

April 14. The following judgments were read.

LORD DENNING M.R. Mr. Raymond Blackburn comes before us once again. This time he draws to our attention the pornographic films which are being shown openly in cinemas in London, and elsewhere. They are grossly indecent. They are an offence against the common law of England. Yet the Greater London Council, the licensing authority, are doing nothing to stop them. On the contrary, he says, they are virtually permitting them. The rules of the Greater London Council are framed in such limited terms that films get through which are grossly indecent. He gives a striking instance. Last year they gave their consent to a film called "More about the Language of Love." Afterwards the exhibitors were prosecuted on the ground that it was an outrage to public decency. The jury convicted the exhibitors. They had no doubt about it, retiring only for 20 minutes. The judge said to them: "Thank you in the name of the public." The case raises important questions on the censorship of films.

1. *The powers of the Greater London Council*

There are only two statutes which give the council control over cinemas. The first is the Cinematograph Act 1909. It was passed in the early days and was concerned with the safety in cinemas, not with censorship. The title states that it is "An Act to make better provision for securing safety." It gave the county councils the power to grant licences—no doubt with a view to safety—but this power was expressed in such wide terms that it was afterwards interpreted so as to give a power of censorship. It says in section 2 (1):

> "A county council may grant licences to such persons as they think fit to use the premises . . . on such terms and conditions and under such restrictions as, . . . the council may by the respective licences determine."

Although the Act was concerned with safety, nevertheless the courts two years later held that a county council could impose conditions which related to other matters, so long as they were not unreasonable. So in 1911 the courts held that a condition saying that the premises should not be opened on Sundays was valid: see *London County Council* v.

Bermondsey Bioscope Co. Ltd. [1911] 1 K.B. 445. Soon afterwards the county councils began to insert a condition that no film shown should be of a licentious or indecent character. Such a condition was accepted as valid, but it did not permit any censorship beforehand. Next, the county council tried to insert a power of censorship by delegating it to three justices. This was held to be invalid: see *Rex* v. *Burnley Justices* (1916) 32 T.L.R. 695. Once again they tried. They sought to hand over all power of censorship to the British Board of Film Censors: but this was held invalid because the county councils were not allowed to delegate their powers: see *Ellis* v. *Dubowski* [1921] 3 K.B. 621. But in 1924 there was a breakthrough. The courts gave a decision which allowed censorship by the British Board of Film Censors provided that that body did not have the final say, but was subject to review by the county council itself: see *Mills* v. *London County Council* [1925] 1 K.B. 213. That decision has held the field since that time and must, I think, be accepted as good law. It was recognised as such by Parliament itself in 1952 when it made it compulsory for conditions to be imposed for the protection of children: see section 3 of the Cinematograph Act 1952. Under that section the county council are under a duty to impose conditions so as to ensure that, if a film is designated as unsuitable for children, then children are not to be admitted to see it. Such designation is to be done "by the licensing authority or such other body as may be specified in the licence." In speaking of "such other body" Parliament no doubt had in mind the British Board of Film Censors. To that extent, therefore, the board has Parliamentary approval.

2. *The British Board of Film Censors*

The British Board of Film Censors is not a legal entity. It has no existence known to the law. It is but a name given to the activities of a few persons, but it goes back for 60 years. There is a president, at present Lord Harlech, who is responsible for broad policy. There is a secretary, Mr. James Ferman, who makes executive decisions. There are four film examiners, who work full-time. These work in pairs, viewing films on three days each week. They put films into four categories, according to their suitability for various age groups: U, A, AA and X. U for everyone. X for those over 18. They sometimes require cuts before giving a certificate. The examiners are recruited from outside the film industry. They are paid salaries. The money is provided by the manufacturers of films through the Incorporated Association of Kinematograph Manufacturers.

The extent of their work is shown by what they did last year—1975. They saw 417 feature films. They passed 400 and refused 17. But of those 17, they passed five after cuts had been made. They passed 73 documentary films.

Although the board is not a body known to the law, it is, I think, a "body" within section 3 (1) of the Act of 1952. I do not think the county councils can delegate the whole of their responsibilities to the board: see section 5 of the Act of 1909 (repealed in 1972) and *Ellis* v. *Dubowski* [1921] 3 K.B. 621, 625: but they can treat the board as an advisory body whose views they can accept or reject; provided that the final decision—aye or nay—rests with the county council. If the exhibitor—or any member of the public—brings the film up before the county council, they ought themselves to review the decision of the British Board of Film Censors and exercise their own judgment on it. That is, I think, the right way to interpret *Mills* v. *London County Council* [1925] 1 K.B. 213. When the board issues a certificate permitting the exhibition of a film—and the county council takes no objection to it—that is equivalent to a permission by the county council itself. When the board refuses a certificate, the exhibitor can appeal to the county council. The county council can then give their consent to the exhibition, and from their decision there is no appeal.

The upshot of it all is this. The county council are in law the body which have the power to censor films for exhibition in cinemas: but in practice it is the British Board of Film Censors which carries out the censorship, subject to review by the county council.

3. *The tests to be applied*

The next question is: what tests are the county council to apply when they exercise censorship powers? Are they to apply the tests laid down in the Obscene Publications Act 1959? Or the tests laid down by the common law?

(i) *The Obscene Publications Act 1959*

In 1959 Parliament passed the Obscene Publications Act 1959. I remember it well. I attended the debates, and took part. Its object was to strengthen the law against pornography. It contained a test of obscenity which was to be applied to publications. An article was to be deemed obscene if its effect, taken as a whole, was " such as to tend to deprave and corrupt persons " likely to read it. Unfortunately that legislation misfired. I explained the reasons in *Reg.* v. *Commissioner of Police of the Metropolis, Ex parte Blackburn* (*No.* 3) [1973] Q.B. 241. One reason was because of the inadequacy of the definition of obscenity. It did not stop gross indecency. An article might be so indecent as to shock the readers: but yet it might not tend to deprave and corrupt them. Another reason was because of the defence of public good. The courts used to allow so-called experts to come forward and say that pornography is good for those who take pleasure in it. Fortunately this court, only a week or two ago, held that the evidence on those lines was inadmissible: see *Reg.* v. *Staniforth* [1976] 2 W.L.R. 849. But still the fact remains that the test itself is inadequate.

(ii) *The common law test*

It has been established for centuries that it is an offence at common law to show in public an indecent exhibition. There was a case 100 years ago in which two showmen kept on Epsom Downs a booth in which a grossly indecent exhibition took place. The Court for Crown Cases Reserved held that " those facts are abundant to prove a common law offence ": see *Reg.* v. *Saunders* (1875) 1 Q.B.D. 15, 19.

This common law offence was clearly recognised by the House of Lords in *Reg.* v. *Knuller* (*Publishing, Printing and Promotions*) *Ltd.* [1973] A.C. 435. Lord Reid said, at p. 458, in this context that indecency " includes anything which an ordinary decent man or woman would find to be shocking, disgusting and revolting ": and Lord Simon of Glaisdale said, at p. 493, that " the authorities establish a common law offence of conduct which outrages public decency."

This common law offence has proved to be a far better stop upon pornography than the Act of 1959. For this simple reason: pornography shocks and disgusts decent people, but it does not tend to deprave or

corrupt them. They revolt from it and turn away from it. If asked, they A
will be quite ready to say that it is grossly indecent, but far less ready to say that it tends to deprave or corrupt.

The proof of the pudding is in the eating. The customs authorities and Post Office apply the simple test: "Is this indecent?" They have no difficulty in condemning millions of magazines on that account, without their decisions being questioned. But when jurors are asked to apply the
test: "Does this tend to deprave or corrupt?," they have been known B
to allow the most indecent articles to get into circulation.

I notice that the Law Commission in its Report *Criminal Law: Report on Conspiracy and Criminal Law Reform* (Law Com. No. 76), March 17, 1976, recommends that the common law offence (where the test is gross indecency) should be abolished (see paragraph 3.138, p. 120); and that
instead the statutory offence (where the test is to tend to deprave or corrupt) C
should be made to apply to films (see paragraph 3.150 (*a*), p. 123). I hope that Parliament will look closely into this recommendation before it is adopted and made law. Some may think that the common law offence is capable of being far more effective in stopping pornography—and is much easier for juries to understand and apply—than the statutory offence.

D

(iii) *Cinematograph films*

Parliament expressly said that the provisions of the Act of 1959 were not to apply to cinematograph films shown in public. It did so by the proviso to section 1 (3) (*b*). Why did Parliament do this? I propose to look at *Hansard* to find out. I know that we are not supposed to do this. But the Law Commission looked at *Hansard*: see their Report, paragraph
3.46, p. 88. So did Lord Diplock in *Knuller's* case [1973] A.C. 435, 480. E
So I have looked at *Hansard* to refresh my memory. In the Lords Viscount Kilmuir L.C. referred to the four forms of publication which were excepted from the Bill. First, the live performance of stage plays; secondly, the cinema; thirdly, television; and fourthly, broadcasting. He said that the promoters of the Bill—it was a private member's Bill—desired to leave
those four out of the Bill and to allow the common law to apply to them. F
The government were content that this should be so. The Lord Chancellor said that they "have in practice not been prosecuted in the past and . . . are most unlikely, so far as can be contemplated, to be prosecuted in the future": see *Hansard* (House of Lords), June 22, 1959, vol. 217, col. 74. In the Commons the Solicitor-General added that those four forms "are subject, in fact, to censorship either by public authority or internal control
by the Lord Chamberlain, the Board of Film Censors, or whatever it may G
be": see *Hansard* (House of Commons), July 22, 1959, vol. 609, col. 1446.

So we have the reason why cinematograph films were omitted. It was because they could be left to the common law and the existing means of censorship.

No doubt those reasons seemed sufficient in 1959. But they are no H
longer valid today. During the last two or three years pornographic films have been imported from Sweden, I believe, in large numbers—and no doubt at much expense. They have been exhibited in cinemas in London to the shame of its decent citizens. The existing censorship has proved totally ineffective to stop it. This was brought vividlly into the open by *Reg.* v. *Jacey* (*London*) *Ltd.* decided at the Central Criminal Court on June 5, 1975, and reported as news in "The Times," June 6, 1975. A

A film called "More about the Language of Love" was refused a certificate
by the British Board of Film Censors: but the exhibitors appealed to the
Greater London Council. The council granted consent to it being shown.
It was shown at a public cinema. The redoubtable Mr. Blackburn brought
it to the notice of Sir Robert Mark, the Commissioner of Police. A
prosecution was brought on the ground that it offended against common law.
The owners and manager of the cinema were charged with showing a film
B which was grossly indecent. The jury found them guilty. The judge
fined the two companies £500 apiece and the manager £50.

Why did the Greater London Council grant their consent to the showing
of that film—which was found by the jury to be grossly indecent—and
which was, therefore, unlawful? The answer is because they have been
applying the wrong test. They have applied the test of "tendency to
C deprave or corrupt" under the Act of 1959, instead of the test of "in-
decency" under the common law.

The tests laid down by the Greater London Council

The Greater London Council at present accept their responsibilities as
censor of films to be shown in London. They have laid down rules
[*Greater London: Rules of Management for Places of Entertainment*]
D which are incorporated as conditions of every licence issued by the council.
These are the material rules:

> "108. No film shall be exhibited at the premises unless—(*a*) it is a
> 'flash' or current news-reel; (*b*) it has been passed by the British
> Board of Film Censors as a U, A, AA, or X film; or (*c*) the council
> has expressly consented to the exhibition of the film.
>
> E "111. If the council does not agree with the category in which
> any film passed by the British Board of Film Censors is placed it shall
> if it thinks fit alter such category and . . . the film thereafter shall be
> treated as having been placed in the altered category. . . .
>
> "112. Any special conditions which the council may impose in
> respect of the exhibition of any film shall, after notice thereof by the
> F council to the licensee, be complied with.
>
> "116"—quite an important one—"No film shall be exhibited at the
> premises—(1) which is likely —(*a*) to encourage or to incite to crime;
> or (*b*) to lead to disorder; or (*c*) to stir up hatred against any section
> of the public in Great Britain on grounds of colour, race or ethnic
> or national origins; or (2) the effect of which is, if taken as a whole,
> G such as to tend to deprave and corrupt persons who are likely to see it.
>
> "If the licensee is notified by the council in writing that it objects
> to the exhibition of a film on any of the grounds, such film shall not
> be exhibited."

It is to be noticed that, so far as obscenity is concerned, those rules,
in rule 116 (2) adopt the test laid down by section 1 of the Obscene Pub-
H lications Act 1959, which I may abbreviate as "tendency to deprave and
corrupt." And there is overwhelming evidence to show that that is the
test which the county council themselves apply when their viewing com-
mittee exercises their power of censorship. For instance, the chairman of
their film viewing board gave an interview which was published in "Cinema
T.V. Today" on March 1, 1975. He was described as "Phil Bassett,
now GLC censor" and reported as saying: "We just have to ask ourselves
the question of whether the films are likely to deprave or corrupt anyone."

On July 16, 1975, the Arts Committee, in a report to the council, set out A
rule 116, containing the " tendency to deprave and corrupt " and said: " This condition . . . has provided the council's film censorship criteria since [1965]." On October 23, 1975, the solicitor to the Greater London Council said in an affidavit:

> " Since the enactment of the Obscene Publications Act in 1959, it is, I submit, appropriate for the council to consider whether the effect of B
> a film taken as a whole as to tend to deprave and corrupt persons who are likely to see it. The test . . . is, I submit, the very test which Parliament in 1959 expected and hoped cinematograph licensing authorities would apply."

Much further evidence was also put before us by Mr. Blackburn. It shows conclusively that the council apply the test in the Act of 1959, and not the C
common law test.

4. *The validity of the G.L.C. rules*

Those rules made by the G.L.C. prohibit a film which is such as to " tend to deprave and corrupt ": but they do not prohibit a film which is grossly indecent. Test it this way: if the British Board of Film Censors *pass* a film which is grossly indecent, the G.L.C. cannot stop it being shown. D
There is nothing in their rules which enables them to do so. If the British Board of Film Censors *reject* a film which is grossly indecent, the licensee can apply to the G.L.C. for their consent to the exhibition of the film: and they will give their consent (as they did in the *Jacey* case) so long as it does not tend to deprave or corrupt.

By making these rules and so applying them, it follows that a film which E
is unlawful (as being grossly indecent) may, nevertheless, be shown in London cinemas with the sanction of the Greater London Council, as happened in the *Jacey* case. In other words, the Greater London Council, have made rules which permit films to be shown, even though their exhibition is contrary to law. This is, to my mind, a misuse of the licensing power which they have assumed. It is wrong for a licensing authority to give their consent to that which is unlawful. That is shown by *Rex* v. *London* F
County Council, Ex parte Entertainments Protection Association Ltd. [1931] 2 K.B. 215. The L.C.C. there made a condition that a cinema should not be opened on Sundays, but announced that they would take no action if £35 was paid to charity for each Sunday opening. Now Sunday opening was a plain breach of the Sunday Observance Act 1780. This court held that the L.C.C. had acted illegally. They had purported G
to sanction the doing of something which was contrary to law—to dispense with the law—a thing which cannot be done by anyone, not even by the London County Council.

5. *Locus standi*

It was suggested that Mr. Blackburn has no sufficient interest to bring these proceedings against the G.L.C. It is a point which was taken against H
him by the Commissioner of Police: see *Reg.* v. *Commissioner of Police of the Metropolis, Ex parte Blackburn* [1968] 2 Q.B. 118, 137, 149: and against the late Mr. McWhirter of courageous memory by the Independent Broadcasting Authority: see *Attorney-General ex rel. McWhirter* v. *Independent Broadcasting Authority* [1973] Q.B. 629, 648–649. On this point, I would ask: Who then can bring proceedings when a public authority is guilty of a misuse of power? Mr. Blackburn is a citizen of London.

A His wife is a ratepayer. He has children who may be harmed by the exhibition of pornographic films. If he has no sufficient interest, no other citizen has. I think he comes within the principle which I stated in *McWhirter's* case [1973] Q.B. 629, 649, which I would recast today so as to read:

> "I regard it as a matter of high constitutional principle that if there is good ground for supposing that a government department or a
> B public authority is transgressing the law, or is about to transgress it, in a way which offends or injures thousands of Her Majesty's subjects, then any one of those offended or injured can draw it to the attention of the courts of law and seek to have the law enforced, and the courts in their discretion can grant whatever remedy is appropriate."

The applications by Mr. Blackburn and Mr. McWhirter did much good.
C They show how desirable such a principle is. One remedy which is always open, by leave of the court, is to apply for a prerogative writ, such as certiorari, mandamus or prohibition. These provide a discretionary remedy and the discretion of the court extends to permitting an application to be made by any member of the public: see *Reg.* v. *Thames Magistrates' Court, Ex parte Greenbaum* (1957) 55 L.G.R. 129, and especially what was
D said by Parker L.J.; and *Reg.* v. *Hereford Corporation, Ex parte Harrower* [1970] 1 W.L.R. 1424; though it will refuse it to a mere busybody who is interfering in things which do not concern him: see *Reg.* v. *Paddington Valuation Officer, Ex parte Peachey Property Corporation Ltd.* [1966] 1 Q.B. 380, 401. Another remedy open likewise is by asking for a declaration: see *Dyson* v. *Attorney-General* [1911] 1 K.B. 410; *Prescott* v. *Birmingham Corporation* [1955] Ch. 210 and *Thorson* v. *Attorney-General of Canada*
E (1975) 1 S.C.R. 138, where Laskin C.J. and his colleagues notably expanded the scope of the remedy. Also by injunction, as in *Bradbury* v. *Enfield London Borough Council* [1967] 1 W.L.R. 1311.

The remedy

There is nothing in the statute which compels the G.L.C. to exercise
F powers of censorship over films to be shown to adults. They are under a duty to censor films which are unsuitable for children (under the Act of 1952), but not those for adults. If the G.L.C. think it right no longer to act as censors for adults, there is nothing to stop them. But they would have to amend their existing rules before they could do so. Alternatively, they could amend their rules so as to make sure that they prohibit the exhibition of any film which is grossly indecent contrary to the common
G law. Unless they do one or other of these things, I think that this court has power to prohibit them from continuing their present procedure, and should do so. The prerogative writ of prohibition has, in the past, usually been exercised so as to prohibit judicial tribunals from exceeding their jurisdiction. But just as the scope of certiorari has been extended to administrative authorities, so also with prohibition. It is available to prohibit
H administrative authorities from exceeding their powers, or misusing them. In particular, it can prohibit a licensing authority from making rules or granting licences which permit conduct that is contrary to law.

Conclusion

In my opinion, therefore, Mr. Blackburn has made out his case. He has shown that the G.L.C. have been exercising their censorship powers in a manner which is unlawful: because they have been applying a test which is bad in law. If they continue with their present wrong test and in consequence give their consent to films which are grossly indecent, they may be said to be aiding and abetting a criminal offence. In these circumstances this court can and should issue an order of prohibition to stop them. But I do not think we should issue the order today. We should give the Greater London Council time to mend their ways either by applying the proper test or no longer exercising censorship. They have already suspended their viewing of films. They suspended it on July 22, 1975, after the decision in the *Reg.* v. *Jacey*, "The Times," June 6, 1975, case. It may be that, as a result of our decision today, they will discontinue film viewing altogether and give up any responsibility for the censorship of films save in regard to children. If they should do this, it will be imperative for Parliament itself to take action: so as to place the censorship of films on a proper footing.

I would allow the appeal so as to award Mr. Blackburn his costs here and below, and give him leave to apply later if necessary for prohibition.

STEPHENSON L.J. This appeal arises out of the power conferred on county councils, including now the respondent council, by section 2 (1) of the Cinematograph Act 1909 as amended by the Schedule to the Cinematograph Act 1952 to

> "grant licences to such persons as they think fit to use the premises specified in the licence for the purpose of cinematograph exhibitions (as defined in the Cinematograph Act 1952) on such terms and conditions and under such restrictions as, subject to regulations of the Secretary of State, the council may by the respective licences determine."

Although the Secretary of State has exercised his power to make regulations for such premises only to secure safety (except in the case of children), councils have used the power to impose conditions more widely, for example to prohibit opening on Sundays (*London County Council* v. *Bermondsey Bioscope Co. Ltd.* [1911] 1 K.B. 445) and to prohibit certain kinds of film, as the council now do by rule 108 and more particularly by rule 116, which Lord Denning M.R. has read.

There is no question that this power to censor by the imposition of conditions is within the powers conferred upon councils by the statute. Any reasonable conditions—or rather any conditions which are not plainly unreasonable—will if challenged be upheld by the courts (*London County Council* v. *Bermondsey Bioscope Co. Ltd.*, at p. 451; *Mills* v. *London County Council* [1925] 1 K.B. 213, 220), provided always that they are not ultra vires. It is this proviso which in this case the Divisional Court has ignored but I think must be applied.

In the latter case the Divisional Court agreed with a previous decision of the same court in *Ellis* v. *Dubowski* [1921] 3 K.B. 621, that it was beyond the council's statutory powers to impose conditions which in effect transferred or delegated the exercise of the council's statutory powers to the British Board of Film Censors and thereby made the decision of an extraneous body final and unappealable, but that it was within their powers to do so provided that they retained the right to review and revoke the board's decisions by adopting the condition suggested by Sankey J. in *Ellis*' case at p. 624 that no film not certified by the board was to be shown without the express sanction of the council's licensing committee.

Mr. Blackburn, on behalf of the applicants, does not contend that the council have acted unlawfully in delegating their power of censorship to

A the film viewing sub-committee of their Arts and Recreation Committee;
but he submits that rule 108 is ultra vires because it purports to delegate
the council's censorship power to the board and authorises the board to
act as their agent for the censorship of films; and he asks the court to
prohibit the council from so acting. I agree with the judgment of Lord
Widgery C.J. on this point that the decision in *Mills*' case [1925] 1 K.B.
213 is a complete answer to it. That decision is not binding upon us, but
B in my judgment it was right and should be followed.

It is true that in *Mills*' case a point which Mr. Blackburn makes was not taken, namely, that the board, as its solicitors admitted in their letter of March 12, 1973, " is not a formal legal entity." But in *Ellis*' case [1921] 3 K.B. 621, 622, it was stated to be

> " an unofficial body appointed by firms engaged in letting out films
> C on hire, to act as censors of films and so to protect the interests of
> the trade."

It is a body, unincorporated it is true and unable to be sued, which since
it came into existence in 1912 has not only received judicial notice but
has been recognised both by the Home Office in their circulars on the
Cinematograph Acts, and by Parliament. For it was eventually conceded,
D in my opinion rightly, that it was in the mind of the legislature when it
provided by section 3 (1) of the Cinematograph Act 1952:

> " It shall be the duty of the licensing authority, in granting a licence
> under the Act of 1909 as respects any premises,—(*a*) to impose con-
> ditions or restrictions prohibiting the admission of children to cine-
> matograph exhibitions involving the showing of works designated, by
> E the licensing authority or such other body as may be specified in the
> licence, as works unsuitable for children; and (*b*) to consider what (if
> any) conditions or restrictions should be imposed as to the admission
> of children to other cinematograph exhibitions involving the showing
> of works designated by the authority or such other body as afore-
> said as of such other description as may be specified in the licence."

F I agree with the statement put before the council on October 18, 1966, that:

> " The reference in the section to ' such other body as may be specified
> in the licence ' makes it possible for licensing authorities to refer in
> the conditions attached to licences to the system of certification of
> films by the British Board of Film Censors, while preserving the right
> of licensing authorities to act independently of the board's decisions if
> G they see fit to do so."

It is also true, and acknowledged by the council, that they have never
banned a film which has been passed by the board. But rule 116 preserves
the council's power to ban a film passed by the board, though only on the
grounds specified in the rule, and rule 108 (*c*) in effect repeats Sankey J.'s
condition giving them power to permit or ban a film which the board has
H not passed. I agree with the Divisional Court that the powers referred to
in those two rules prevent the council's use of the board from being an
abuse of their power, and this ground of appeal fails.

I cannot, however, follow the Divisional Court in dismissing Mr. Blackburn's other submission that the council have in rule 116 been applying the wrong test and ought to be prohibited from so doing. That rule is clearly intended to enforce the law. In forbidding by rule 116 (1) (*c*) the exhibition of any film which is likely " to stir up hatred against any section of the public in Great Britain on grounds of colour, race or ethnic or national origins" it enforces the Race Relations Acts 1965 and 1968. But in forbidding by rule 116 (2) the exhibition of any film "the effect of which is, if taken as a whole, such as to tend to deprave and corrupt persons who are likely to see it" it enforces the law against obscenity which Parliament derived from *Reg.* v. *Hicklin* (1868) L.R. 3 Q.B. 360, 371, and applied to reading matter and other "articles" by the Obscene Publications Act 1959 and to stage plays by section 2 of the Theatres Act 1968 but did not apply to cinematograph exhibitions, which were left to the common law that makes indecent exhibitions in public unlawful. The miscellaneous authorities which establish this, including *Reg.* v. *Saunders* (1875) 1 Q.B.D. 15 (to which Lord Denning M.R. referred) are collected in paragraphs 3.27 and 3.28 of the Law Commission's Report No. 76 of March 17, 1976 on *Conspiracy and Criminal Law Reform* at p. 81 and in the speech of Lord Simon of Glaisdale in *Reg.* v. *Knuller (Publishing, Printing and Promotions) Ltd.* [1973] A.C. 435, 492–493. The offence seems to be the exposure or exhibition in public of indecent things or acts: *per* Lord Reid at p. 458; and of the offences of which the defendant Saunders was convicted only one was for publishing words and six others were for exhibiting performances, practices and representations, though Lord Simon of Glaisdale mentions that case as dealing with indecent words only.

The Law Commission have in the same report recommended that this well known and much criticised obscenity test should be made applicable to the exhibition of films by amending the Act of 1959; paragraphs 3.86 at p. 103, 3.138 at p. 120 and 3.150 (*a*) at p. 123; see also p. 186. But unless and until Parliament enacts that recommendation the common law against indecency applies to them, and the test of indecency is a different test.

We are told by Mr. Davies for the council that the test of indecency at common law is the test which the board always applies; and that may explain why they refused to pass the film "More about the Language of Love" which the council then passed. On Mr. Blackburn's initiative those who had exhibited it with a notice under rule 114 that it had been passed by the council were prosecuted to conviction for an indecent exhibition contrary to common law. He is now engaged in prosecuting the exhibitors of its predecessor "The Language of Love" and asks the court to enforce the right law by prohibiting them from applying the wrong test.

Indecency and obscenity are alike difficult to define, but they are not the same thing in the natural meaning of the words or in the eyes of the law. The submission that they meant the same thing was rejected by the Court of Criminal Appeal in *Reg.* v. *Stanley* [1965] 2 Q.B. 327. The jury had there convicted the appellant of sending postal packets which enclosed "indecent or obscene" cinematograph films (and a booklet) contrary to section 11 of the Post Office Act 1953. The jury found the articles indecent but not obscene, and the Court of Criminal Appeal upheld the convictions, Lord Parker C.J. saying, at pp. 333, 334:

> "The words 'indecent or obscene' convey one idea, namely, offending against the recognised standards of propriety, indecent being at the lower end of the scale and obscene at the upper end of the scale . . . an indecent article is not necessarily obscene, whereas an obscene article almost certainly must be indecent."

If that is right—and it seems to me common sense—the council are by the express terms of rule 116 (2) forbidding the exhibition of films which are at the upper end of the scale instead of forbidding the exhibition of

A films which are anywhere on the scale, whether at its upper or its lower end or in between. In so doing they are using their power of censorship according to the wrong law and by necessary implication consenting to the exhibition of films at the lower end of the scale which are nevertheless indecent at common law and so unlawful.

It is true, but not, in my judgment, relevant, that there is no duty on the council to impose any censorship conditions at all on films for adults.
B But if the council choose to impose such conditions, they must be lawful conditions. If authority for that were needed, it is to be found in the decision of this court in *Rex* v. *London County Council, Ex parte Entertainments Protection Association Ltd.* [1931] 2 K.B. 215. There certiorari issued to quash an order or decision which in effect waived compliance with the Sunday Observance Act 1780 because it informed a licensee that
C the council would take no action against him for the present if he exhibited films on Sundays. This court there said that it was the duty of the council to obey the law, not to dispense with it.

It may be said that there is a necessity for a council to impose conditions as to days of showing whereas there is no necessity to impose conditions of censorship. But if a council "enter the field" whether by prescribing days or kinds of film for exhibition, they must, in my judgment,
D impose conditions which enforce the law applicable in that field and do not depart from it. It may be said, furthermore, that what the council have done here is not to waive or break the law but to enforce it only to a limited extent, and that by so acting they are not acting contrary to law as was the L.C.C. in the matter of Sunday opening. By doing too little they are not acting ultra vires. Acting ultra vires is doing too much, not
E too little. This line of argument ignores, I think, the implication and effect of prescribing too permissive a test. The implication of rule 116 (2) is that a film, however indecent, may be exhibited, and the council will not object to its exhibition, unless it is also obscene as the law defines obscenity; and the effect of rule 116 (2) is that an indecent film, such as the jury found "More about the Language of Love" to be, will be passed by the council and exhibited. A rule with that implication and that effect may not be
F unreasonable but is ultra vires because that is its implication and its effect. It may be reasonable to apply a test which Parliament has applied to words and public performances of plays, but it involves an excess of jurisdiction in authorising what is illegal. Contrast condition 10 of the Model Licensing Conditions recommended by the Home Office in circulars on the Cinematograph Acts, but not adopted by the council, as an example
G of a condition which prescribes a test that is not too permissive but too exacting:

> "Where the licensing authority have given notice in writing to the licensee of the premises prohibiting the exihibition of a film on the ground that it contains matter which, if exhibited, would offend against good taste or decency or would be likely to encourage or incite to crime or to lead to disorder or to be offensive to public feeling, that film
> H shall not be exhibited in the premises except with the consent in writing of the licensing authority."

(Compare section 3 (1) (*a*) of the Television Act 1964.)

Not every exhibition offending against good taste or offensive to public feeling is an offence against the common law. Such a condition does too much, not too little; yet it could not be successfully contended that it was ultra vires because it went further than the law required. I cannot therefore accept, as Lord Widgery C.J. accepted, the council's last-minute contention, put forward in their solicitor's affidavit of October 23, 1975, that their condition of censorship simply supplemented the common law by adding an additional test.

This opinion of the council's duties does not turn the council's power to impose conditions into a duty, or compel them to impose conditions which Parliament has not required them to impose. It declares that if the council do exercise their power to impose conditions which cover activities restricted by the general law, whether by statute or by the common law, they must cover them correctly in a manner which does not permit infringement of the law, whether directly as in *Rex* v. *London County Council, Ex parte Entertainments Protection Association Ltd.* [1931] 2 K.B. 215 or indirectly as in this case. The council are in my judgment under no duty to impose censorship conditions except on the exhibition of films to children. If our decision in this case leads the council to repeal or waive rule 116 (2), I would not regard them as failing in any legal duty. What they cannot, I think, do is to continue to leave censorship of films, which their licensees exhibit, to the board alone, because that would be to make the board's ipse dixit final, which was what *Ellis'* case [1921] 3 K.B. 621 rightly decided they could not do. If the council give up their power of censoring films, then Parliament, which has relied so long on the existing co-operation between councils and the board to censor films, may have to come to the rescue, perhaps by making a certificate of the board a statutory requirement for exhibition of any film to adults, or by applying the Obscene Publications Act 1959 to cinematograph exhibitions to adults, as the Law Commission recommends, or by re-activating parts of the Cinematograph and Indecent Displays Bill of 1973.* Indeed it is to be hoped that this case may lead to early legislation to improve and clarify the law, which in this notoriously difficult and controversial field of human activity by common consent works badly.

In the present unsatisfactory state of the law, rule 116 (2) is, in my opinion, one which the council have no power to make; it does not supplement the common law but contradicts it and the council should be prohibited from acting upon it.

If that is right, I see no reason why the applicants should not apply for prohibition. They live in the council's jurisdiction and have locus standi, Mrs. Blackburn as a ratepayer. But I agree that we should not in the exercise of the court's discretion, make an order of prohibition yet. I assume that the council grant licences which are in force for one year: section 2 (2) of the Act of 1909; and they must have time to consider our judgments and whether they will amend rule 116 (2) or abolish it altogether before notifying their licensees.

I agree with the order which Lord Denning M.R. proposes.

BRIDGE L.J. The Cinematograph Act 1909 required cinemas to be licensed by local authorities and empowered the grant of licences "on such terms and conditions and under such restrictions as . . . the council may by the respective licences determine." It is odd, as Lord Widgery C.J. said, that this power should have come to be used for a purpose for which it was not originally intended, namely, as a means of censoring the contents of films. It is, perhaps, odder still that the censoring function should in practice have come to be exercised mainly by the British Board of Film Censors. The board is an informal, unofficial and unincorporated

* *Note*: See Hansard for March 24, 1976, vol. 369, no. 51, cols. 645 et seq.

organisation originally set up by the film industry to provide a form of voluntary censorship. In *Ellis* v. *Dubowski* [1921] 3 K.B. 621, a licence condition that no film be shown unless certified for public exhibition by the board, was held ultra vires on the ground that it amounted to an unauthorised delegation of the licensing authority's statutory discretion, there being in that case no provision for the licensee to have recourse to the authority by way of review of any decision by the board. However, as the judges suggested in *Ellis*'s case, and as the court later held in *Mills* v. *London County Council* [1925] 1 K.B. 213, delegation of censorship to the board was unobjectionable provided the licensing authority reserved to itself the power to override the board's decision on appeal by the licensee. In both those cases the court was concerned with the reasonableness of the censorship conditions from the point of view of the licensee. A condition which subjects the licensee, in the matter of censorship, to the arbitrary decision of a third party is obviously unreasonable, in the sense in which that term is used in relation to the exercise of a statutory discretion. But any such unreasonableness is cured by reserving the last word to the authority in whom the statutory discretion is vested.

The Act of 1909 conferred a power of censorship but clearly imposed no duty of censorship on licensing authorities. Such a duty was imposed for the first time, and then only in relation to children under 16, by the Cinematograph Act 1952, section 3 (1), which required that licence conditions should prohibit the admission of children to films "designated by the licensing authority or such other body as may be specified in the licence, as works unsuitable for children." This looks like a legislative recognition of the established practice of delegation to the board. It authorises an out and out delegation of the power to censor children's films, but leaves the previous position, as established in the cases of *Ellis* and *Mills*, unaffected in regard to the censorship of films for adults.

The decision in the *Mills* case [1925] 1 K.B. 213, that a licensee cannot object to a delegation of censorship to the board provided he has a right of appeal to the licensing authority against the board's decision to withhold approval in any particular case, was in my judgment clearly right. By parity of reasoning I think there is no objection from the public point of view to such a delegation to the board, provided again that the licensing authority reserves to itself the right to override any decision of the board approving a film for exhibition and to nullify the effect of that approval. Mr. Blackburn's complaints directed against delegation to the board are, in my judgment, without substance.

The important question raised by this appeal is whether the Greater London Council act lawfully in respect of the criterion which they apply when any decision of the board is challenged. By rule 116 (2) of their standard rules, subject to which licences are granted, the Greater London Council prescribe that no film shall be exhibited: "the effect of which is, if taken as a whole, such as to tend to deprave and corrupt persons who are likely to see it." The rule was adopted by the G.L.C. in 1966. Its language is clearly derived from the statutory test of obscenity in section 1 (1) of the Obscene Publications Act 1959. The G.L.C. must have felt that their wisdom was confirmed when the Theatres Act 1968 abolished theatre censorship by the Lord Chamberlain and applied the same test of obscenity to stage plays. But whereas the Act of 1968 gave to the stage a complete immunity from liability to prosecution for any common law offence of which the essence was that a performance was "obscene, indecent, offensive, disgusting or injurious to morality," the screen remains, on account of its exclusion from the ambit of the Obscene Publications Act 1959 subject to the full rigours of the common law.

The issue was thrown into high relief when the exhibitors of a film called " More about the Language of Love," which was refused a certificate by the board but passed by the G.L.C. in March 1974, were convicted in June 1975 of the common law offence of showing a film which depicted grossly indecent performances, thereby outraging public decency. Following that conviction and the issue of the present proceedings by Mr. and Mrs. Blackburn, the G.L.C. decided for the time being to suspend their activities in viewing films by way of review of any decision of the board. I well understand their reasons for doing so. But this abdication of function has the effect, so long as it continues, of reproducing the situation which was successfully challenged as unlawful in *Ellis* v. *Dubowski* [1921] 3 K.B. 621. It ought to be remedied without delay.

In the Divisional Court Lord Widgery C.J. tested the legality of the G.L.C.'s rule 116 (2) by asking whether it was reasonable. If that is the correct test, I should unhesitatingly agree with him that it is reasonable. It would be absurd to suggest that the test of obscenity adopted by Parliament in the Acts of 1959 and 1968 is unreasonable if applied to films. But, with respect, I do not think the test of reasonableness is here in point. We are not here concerned with whether the rule imposes an unreasonable restriction on the licensee. The question is whether the effect of judging films by the criterion of rule 116 (2) alone is calculated to result in the G.L.C. giving apparent authority for the exhibition of films in contravention of the general law. The Divisional Court was not referred to *Rex* v. *London County Council, Ex parte Entertainments Protection Association Ltd.* [1931] 2 K.B. 215. If they had been, I think they would have decided this case differently. In that case the L.C.C. had exercised their licensing function in such a way as to purport to authorise film performances on Sunday, notwithstanding that such performances were then prohibited under the general law by the Sunday Observance Act 1780. The court held that the council had exceeded its jurisdiction. The principle to be derived from the case is that it is an excess of jurisdiction for a licensing authority to exercise its power in such a way that it appears to sanction that which is contrary to the general law. The fact that a criminal offence has been apparently authorised by the licensing authority does not, of course, give any immunity from prosecution. But this does not prevent such a purported exercise of the licensing authority's power being challenged by way of one of the prerogative orders.

The existence of the common law offence of publicly exhibiting indecent acts or things is beyond doubt: *Reg.* v. *Knuller (Publishing, Printing and Promotions) Ltd.* [1973] A.C. 435. Lord Reid said, at p. 458, that it " includes anything which an ordinary decent man or woman would find to be shocking, disgusting and revolting." It is clear that by this test a film might well be judged unfit for public exhibition which fell short of any tendency to deprave and corrupt.

Lord Widgery C.J. held that the effect of rule 116 (2) was to " supplement the common law by adding additional tests which a film must satisfy if it is to be shown in the G.L.C. area." Again, with respect, I cannot agree. The criteria of indecency and obscenity relate to the same subject matter. Lord Parker C.J. summed the matter up in *Reg.* v. *Stanley* [1965] 2 Q.B. 327, 333–334, when he said:

> " The words ' indecent or obscene ' convey one idea, namely, offending against the recognised standards of propriety, indecent being at the

A lower end of the scale and obscene at the upper end of the scale. . . . As it seems to this court, an indecent article is not necessarily obscene, whereas an obscene article almost certainly must be indecent."

So long as the G.L.C. direct themselves by reference to the statutory test of obscenity and ignore the common law test of indecency, the probable result must be that they will appear to authorise public exhibition of films
B which will offend against the common law. It has been said by Mr. Davies for the G.L.C., that whatever test they apply they cannot ensure that the exhibitor of a film they have approved will not be prosecuted and convicted by the verdict of a jury. This proposition is correct, but it affords no argument for the adoption of a test which does not conform to the general law. If the single criterion relevant to any issue of obscenity or indecency by which the G.L.C. direct themselves in exercising censorship is calculated
C to permit what the common law prohibits, their jurisdiction is not lawfully exercised.

I agree that Mrs. Blackburn has sufficient locus standi, as a ratepayer, to apply for an order of prohibition and that it is in our discretion to make the order. I should be very reluctant to take that ultimate step, which might create many difficulties for the G.L.C., without first giving them a
D reasonable time to put their house in order. This they can do in one of two ways. They can exclude from their licence conditions any provision relating to the films that may be shown save such as is necessary to implement the authority's obligations under section 3 (1) of the Cinematograph Act 1952. Alternatively they can introduce for the censorship of films for adults a criterion directed to prevent the showing of any film which would be an indecent public exhibition.

E Although the conclusions I have reached on the questions of law involved in this appeal seem to me inescapable as the law stands, I cannot say I feel any enthusiasm for the result. The statutory test of obscenity has been much criticised, and with good reason. But I don't know how many people today would accept as an appropriate test of criminality what is "shocking, disgusting and revolting." There are profound differences of opinion as to what are the appropriate standards in relation to such matters
F which the law ought to be designed to maintain. Some want the law to move one way, some another, but surely no one can be content for it to stand still. The one proposition which I imagine nearly everybody would assent to is that the law in its present state is so full of anomalies and operates so uncertainly and unevenly that some rationalisation is urgently needed. If our decision has the result, as seems probable, that many
G authorities will abandon altogether the thankless task of censoring films for adults, perhaps that may emphasise the urgency of some reforming legislation.

I agree with my Lords that the appeal should be allowed to the extent indicated by Lord Denning M.R.

H

Appeal allowed with costs in Court of Appeal and Divisional Court.
Liberty to apply for order of prohibition.
Leave to appeal refused.

Solicitors: *A. G. Gardner, Greater London Council.*

M. M. H.

[CHANCERY DIVISION] A

* UNIVERSAL CITY STUDIOS INC. AND OTHERS v. MUKHTAR & SONS LTD.

[1976 U. No. 714]

1976 March 23, 24 — Templeman J. B

Copyright—Infringement—Ex parte motion—Action for infringement of copyright—Suspicion of likelihood of infringing articles disappearing—Interim injunction and order for custody of infringing articles—Application ex parte for order without notice to other side

The plaintiffs acquired, at a substantial cost, copyright in C
a drawing of a shark's mouth and the accompanying slogan " Jaws." They exploited the rights, inter alia, by making and selling " Jaws T-shirts " which bore the drawing and slogan. They heard that wholesalers, H, were infringing their copyrights by selling unlicensed Jaws T-shirts. On being challenged, H claimed to be innocent, apologised and stopped selling the infringing T-shirts. They explained that they had sold very few T-shirts and could not supply the names of customers. D
The plaintiffs took no further action. Some time later they found similar infringing T-shirts being sold by two other wholesalers, M and the defendants. M gave an explanation similar to that given by H and withdrew their stock. M's stock of infringing T-shirts disappeared but the defendants' stock appeared to increase. The plaintiffs issued a writ seeking various injunctions. They moved, ex parte, without giving the defendants notice of the proposed action, because they E
suspected that the infringing T-shirts might disappear. They sought an order that the defendants should forthwith place all the infringing T-shirts in the custody of the person serving the order (who would be a solicitor or patent agent):—

Held, that although it was impossible to decide whether the plaintiffs' fears were justified there was a possibility that their fears would be realised if litigation took its normal course; that whether the defendants were wholly ignorant of the plaintiffs' F
rights or not, the T-shirts which they sold infringed those rights and, in view of the history of the matter, the plaintiffs were entitled to ensure that the infringing T-shirts were placed in safe custody, and, accordingly, the case was an exceptional one, in which it was proper to grant the ex parte relief sought.

Anton Piller KG v. *Manufacturing Processes Ltd.* [1976] 2 W.L.R. 162, C.A. applied.

G

The following case is referred to in the judgment:

Anton Piller KG v. *Manufacturing Processes Ltd.* [1976] 2 W.L.R. 162; [1976] 1 All E.R. 779, C.A.

No additional cases were cited in argument.

H

EX PARTE MOTION

The plaintiffs, Universal City Studios Inc., MCA Inc., Merchandising Corporation of America Inc. and MacYoung Ltd., by their writ, claimed various injunctions restraining the defendants, Mukhtar & Sons Ltd. from, inter alia, infringing the copyright in a drawing of a shark's mouth with a slogan " Jaws " and converting to their own use infringing copies of the copyright, and from passing off clothing, described as " Jaws T-shirts," not

A being the clothing of the plaintiffs or being in any way connected with the plaintiffs, by the use on them of the whole or a part of a shark and by the use of the word "Jaws." The plaintiffs sought delivery up to them of all articles, documents or things the retention or use of which would constitute a breach of the injunction.

The plaintiffs suspected that if the defendants became aware of the proposed action by them the stock of the infringing shirts might disappear
B from the defendants' premises. They moved ex parte, without notice to the defendants, seeking an order that the defendants should forthwith place in the custody of the person who would serve the order at the premises of the defendants on the manager or other person appearing to be in charge all the Jaws T-shirts.

The facts are stated in the judgment.

C

Hugh Laddie for the plaintiffs.

TEMPLEMAN J. The plaintiffs have spent and are still spending substantial sums of money on acquiring and exploiting copyright, trade mark and other rights in connection with a pictorial representation of the business end of a shark and the accompanying slogan "Jaws." The rights of the
D plaintiffs are valuable and ephemeral, depending as they do on the current blood-curdling success of a book and a film whence they are derived. One device, which happily combines advertisement and exploitation of the plaintiffs' insignia, consists of the manufacture under licence of T-shirts, the present juvenile uniform, bearing on their bosoms prints of the Jaws picture and slogan. Jaws T-shirts, as they are called, display in a manner
E which would appeal to Tom Sawyer at once the wide knowledge and innate ferocity of the wearers. But wearers of T-shirts are notoriously fickle. At any moment, for example, their appetites, satiated with sharks, may demand a pictorial representation of our next Prime Minister or of one of Her Majesty's judges. It behoves the plaintiffs in these circumstances to be vigilant in protecting their rights by preventing the sale of unlicensed Jaws T-shirts.

F The plaintiffs first heard of an infringement of their rights by a wholesale company, H. & A. Hosiery Ltd., which were selling unlicensed Jaws T-shirts. When challenged that company protested their innocence, apologised, ceased to sell the infringing articles, and explained that they had sold very few of the offending articles and could not supply the names of customers. The plaintiffs were not wholly convinced by this explanation,
G but the company being a small company the plaintiffs took no action against them. Shortly thereafter the plaintiffs discovered infringing T-shirts on sale in two other wholesale establishments, M. Comar & Sons Ltd. and the defendants. Rightly or wrongly, the plaintiffs suspected that, if M. Comar & Sons Ltd. and the defendants were challenged and given the chance to dispose of their stocks, the same thing would happen as they feared had happened in the case of H. & A. Hosiery Ltd. and that the
H infringing articles would eventually find their way into the hands of the public to the considerable and unprovable damage of the plaintiffs through untraceable sources. To obtain some check on their suspicions the plaintiffs challenged M. Comar & Sons Ltd., but not the defendants, having first ascertained, according to the plaintiffs' sworn evidence that on the shelves of M. Comar & Sons Ltd. there were some 800 to 1,000 infringing articles and that a similar number were on sale by the defendants. M. Comar & Sons Ltd., when challenged, wrote a letter very much on the same lines

as that written by H. & A. Hosiery Ltd., protesting their innocence, saying A
that they had sold very few and were unable to give the names of their
customers. The stocks which had been known to be on M. Comar & Sons
Ltd.'s shelves disappeared and, possibly by coincidence or possibly not,
the stocks held by the defendants appeared to increase.

The plaintiffs issued a writ against the defendants and appeared yester-
day ex parte to obtain relief against them. The plaintiffs wished to take
effective action to prevent the disappearance, which rightly or wrongly B
they fear, of the offending articles if the defendants were given notice of any
proposed action.

So far as any evidence can be satisfactory in the absence of the party
concerned to challenge it, I am satisfied that the defendants are selling
articles which infringe the plaintiffs' rights. I am unable to tell whether
the plaintiffs' fears for the future are justified or not, but there is a C
possibility that their fears will be realised if litigation takes its normal
course. But even if the defendants are wholly ignorant of the plaintiffs'
rights or are unaware that they are selling unlicensed articles in breach
of the plaintiffs' rights, the T-shirts which the defendants are now selling
do, as the present evidence appears to show beyond a peradventure, infringe
the plaintiffs' rights and ought not to be sold. The defendants, when
apprised of this situation, should not therefore object to handing over the D
infringing articles for safe custody.

In view of the circumstances and the history of this matter I reached
the conclusion that the plaintiffs were entitled to make sure that the
infringing articles held by the defendants will be placed in safe custody
whatever the state of knowledge of the defendants may be. As to that, I
make no finding and form no view. E

Mr. Laddie, who appeared for the plaintiffs, sought part of the relief
which was granted by the Court of Appeal in *Anton Piller KG* v. *Manu-
facturing Processes Ltd.* [1976] 2 W.L.R. 162. In that case the court made
an order ex parte ordering the defendants to allow the plaintiffs' represen-
tatives to enter the defendants' premises and to remove infringing objects
and documents necessary to enable the plaintiffs to succeed in their action
and to prevent further infringement of their rights. In that case it was plain F
that the defendants were not acting in good faith. In the present case there
is mere, albeit plausible, suspicion. Bad faith on the part of the defendants
has not been proved and cannot be assumed.

The order which I was asked to make by the present plaintiffs is a
strong order, albeit less stringent than that ordered in *Anton Piller KG* v.
Manufacturing Processes Ltd. by the Court of Appeal. It does not involve G
entry on the defendants' premises, but that the defendants should hand over
the infringing articles for safe custody. It is a form of relief which the
court will grant with great reluctance and which should seldom be sought
and more seldom granted. That appears from the three judgments of
the Court of Appeal and the headnote, which reads as follows:

> "*Held*, ... that in most exceptional circumstances, where plaintiffs H
> had a very strong prima facie case, actual or potential damage to them
> was very serious and there was clear evidence that defendants
> possessed vital material which they might destroy or dispose of so as
> to defeat the ends of justice before any application inter partes could
> be made, the court had inherent jurisdiction to order defendants to
> 'permit' plaintiffs' representatives to enter defendants' premises to
> inspect and remove such material ..."

A The present circumstances fall within the principles of that case and justify putting infringing articles in safe custody. This result can be achieved without doing damage to the defendants or their goodwill. The result may well not be secured if notice is given to the defendants. In my judgment this is a proper and exceptional case for ex parte relief on the lines claimed.

It is vital that any relief should preserve the defendants' rights and that B the order should be served by some responsible person well aware of the extent and limitation of the legal remedy and the need to protect the defendants. The order must also make clear what the defendants must do, and prevent any doubt about the validity of the order or about the identity of the person to whom the infringing articles are to be confided. To that end I yesterday made this order. First of all, the plaintiffs undertook to C serve the order by a solicitor or patent agent; secondly, that any articles obtained as a result of the order would be retained by the solicitors for the plaintiffs in safe custody; thirdly, there was the usual cross-undertaking in damages. Then the body of the order required the defendants forthwith to place in the custody of the person who shall serve the order at the premises of the defendants, on the manager or other person appearing to be in charge of the premises, all T-shirts held at the premises or elsewhere which articles D bore the representation in which the plaintiffs have shown that they have the rights. That will mean that a responsible person, either a solicitor or a patent agent, will turn up at the warehouse with the order, which he will serve on the manager, and, so far as the manager and other customers are concerned, there will not to all outward appearance, be any difference between what will happen as a result of the order and what would happen E if a customer placed an order for a large number of T-shirts. It seems to me that will adequately protect the rights of the defendants in any event and will remove articles which, whatever the state of the knowledge of the defendants, are, as it seems to me, infringing articles and articles which ought not to be sold.

The order was made yesterday and is being given effect to this morning.

F

Order accordingly.

March 26. On an inter partes motion the defendants, having complied with the ex parte order, gave undertakings not to sell infringing articles and to furnish the names of their suppliers and customers.

G Solicitors: *Bartlett & Gluckstein.*

A. R.

H

NOTE A

[COURT OF APPEAL]

* BECK AND OTHERS *v.* VALUE CAPITAL LTD. AND OTHERS (No. 2)

1976 Jan. 12, 13, 14, 15; Feb. 16 — Buckley and Orr L.JJ. and Sir John Pennycuick B

Practice—Writ—Amendment—Writ served on foreign companies outside jurisdiction by leave—Application to amend writ by adding new claims to relief—Foreign disputants with funds in English banks—Court's discretion—Proper court to exercise jurisdiction—R.S.C., Ord. 20, *r.* 5 (1) C

The following cases are referred to in the judgment of Buckley L.J. on the question of discretion:

Baker (*G. L.*) *Ltd.* v. *Medway Building and Supplies Ltd.* [1958] 1 W.L.R. 1216; [1958] 3 All E.R. 540, C.A.
Evans v. *Bartlam* [1937] A.C. 473; [1937] 2 All E.R. 646, H.L.(E.).
O. (*Infants*), *In re* [1971] Ch. 748; [1971] 2 W.L.R. 784; [1971] 2 All E.R. 744, C.A. D
Thornley, decd., In re [1969] 1 W.L.R. 1037; [1969] 3 All E.R. 31, C.A.

APPEAL from Goulding J. [1975] 1 W.L.R. 6; [1974] 3 All E.R. 442.

By two agreements (collectively referred to as "the bargain") in June 1972 certain assets of Value Capital Ltd. (VCL), a company incorporated in the Bahamas, and Investment Properties International Ltd. (IPI), a company incorporated in Canada, were acquired by Property Resources E Ltd. (PRL), a company incorporated in the Bahamas, in consideration, inter alia, of the issue to the transferor companies of shares in PRL which thereby came under the control of VCL.

In April 1973 two individual shareholders in IPI, Mr. Kuno Beck and Dr. Rolf Fetscher, issued a writ against VCL, PRL, IPI, various directors of those companies and three banks, claiming declarations and injunctions F to protect monetary assets of PRL in London. Leave was given to serve the writ out of the jurisdiction. In October 1973 an order was made in Canada for the compulsory winding up of IPI, and by orders made in February 1974 IPI became the sole plaintiff in the action. On February 19, 1974, IPI issued a summons seeking leave to amend the writ under R.S.C., Ord. 20, r. 5 to seek rescission of the bargain and consequential orders aimed at restoring the parties to the position in which they would G be had the bargain never been made. On May 13, 1974, Goulding J. refused leave to amend the writ.

The plaintiff company appealed.

The full judgment of the Court of Appeal dismissing the appeal does not call for report. H

John Wilmers Q.C. and *T. M. Stockdale* for IPI.
Brian Neill Q.C. and *J. Leckie* for VCL.
H. M. Harrod for PRL.

Cur. adv. vult.

February 16. BUCKLEY L.J. read a judgment in which he stated the history of the proceedings and continued: Upon the summons Goulding J.

A refused to allow the amendment of the writ. In so doing he proceeded upon one ground which he considered to be paramount and conclusive. He said [1975] 1 W.L.R. 6, 16:

> " It will be remembered that the plaintiffs there ask the court to rescind both the sale agreements of June 1972, to work out the consequences of rescission by accounts and inquiries, and to give effect to the result
> B by enforcing the restitution of assets. The programme is one which it is impossible, in my view, for the English court to carry out. The assets in question and the documents required to elucidate their history are in many jurisdictions. The only court that can hope to wield effectively the equitable panoply invoked by the amendment is one that can act in personam on PRL and VCL and compel the use of their names and seals where necessary."

C

This is, I think, a cardinal point in the case, for if the judge was right in the view which he expressed in that passage, the other points raised by the appellant appear to me to answer themselves in the respondent's favour.

The application for leave to amend the writ was made under R.S.C., Ord. 20, r. 5, which confers a wide discretionary power upon the court
D to permit amendment. We were referred to what was said by Davies L.J. in *In re O. (Infants)* [1971] Ch. 748, 754 and 755. Davies L.J. stated the law relating to an appeal from an exercise of a judicial discretion as follows, at p. 755:

> " In my considered opinion the law now is that if an appellate court is satisfied that the decision of the court below is wrong, it is its
> E duty to say so and to act accordingly."

Counsel are sometimes inclined, it seems to me, to treat this as meaning that, where a discretionary jurisdiction is involved, an appellate court is entitled to substitute its own exercise of the discretion for that of the judge of first instance, unfettered by any regard for the view he took, and that if, so exercising its discretion, the appellate court arrives at a
F conclusion differing in some respects from the conclusion of the trial judge, the appellate court is entitled to treat the trial judge as having been wrong to that extent and to vary his order accordingly. In my opinion, this is an erroneous view and one which is likely to encourage unmeritorious appeals. Davies L.J. was founding his statement of the law upon a consideration of what had been said by Lord Wright in *Evans*
G v. *Bartlam* [1937] A.C. 473, 486, and what Harman L.J. had said in *In re Thornley, decd.* [1969] 1 W.L.R. 1037, 1040. Lord Wright had said, [1937] A.C. 473, 486:

> " It is clear that the Court of Appeal should not interfere with the discretion of a judge acting within his jurisdiction unless the court is
> H clearly satisfied that he was wrong."

Harman L.J. had said [1969] 1 W.L.R. 1037, 1040:

> " But although I quite agree that the court would never interfere if it merely thought there was some slight excess or deficiency, if it comes to the conclusion that the judge was quite wrong in the view that he took and that it ought to have been much more or much less, then I think the court is entitled to interfere . . ."

In such a case it is not necessary for an appellant to be able to point to some matter which the judge ought to have taken into account and failed to take into account, or to something which he did take into account but should not have taken into account, or to some other error in principle. It is sufficient if the appellate court is satisfied that the judge, having taken all the proper circumstances into consideration, has arrived at a decision that is so clearly wrong that he must have misappreciated the weight to be given to some aspect or aspects of the case.

In *G. L. Baker Ltd.* v. *Medway Building and Supplies Ltd.* [1958] 1 W.L.R. 1216, on an appeal from a refusal of leave to amend a defence, Jenkins L.J. said, at p. 1231:

> "I should next make some reference to the principle to be followed in granting or refusing leave to amend, and I start by saying that there is no doubt whatever that the granting or refusal of an application for such leave is eminently a matter for the discretion of the judge with which this court should not in ordinary circumstances interfere unless satisfied that the judge has applied a wrong principle or can be said to have reached a conclusion which would work a manifest injustice between the parties."

The Court of Appeal in that case held that the judge of first instance had in fact erred in principle in refusing to grant leave to amend. I do not think that Davies L.J. in *In re O.* (*Infants*) [1971] Ch. 748, 755 was intending to lay down a different test. Where a trial judge is not shown to have erred in principle his exercise of a discretionary power should not be interfered with unless the appellate court is of opinion that his conclusion is one that involves injustice or, to use the language of Lord Wright, the appellate court is clearly satisfied that the judge of first instance was wrong.

I therefore proceed to consider whether the conclusion reached by Goulding J. in the passage which I have read from his judgment was a reasonable conclusion or was so clearly mistaken that we ought to interfere with it. [His Lordship reviewed the facts and submissions and concluded:] In my judgment, the judge had ample material at his disposal to justify him in taking the view which he did that an English court would, as a practical matter, be incapable of resolving the difficulties and problems which must result from setting aside the bargain. Indeed, I agree with him in that view. Mr. Wilmers has suggested that, since IPI and VCL are now both in liquidation, the difficulty of working out a restitution of assets under an English decree setting aside the bargain has disappeared. The liquidators, he says, would obviously obey the orders of an English court. Assuming this to be correct, the difficulty, which is mainly one of machinery of investigation and inquiry, does not seem to me to disappear.

It consequently appears to me that there are no grounds upon which we could reach the conclusion that the judge was wrong in the way in which he exercised his discretion under R.S.C., Ord. 20, r. 5. This makes it unnecessary for me to consider the argument which was presented to us about the effect, on the application for leave to amend, of the writ having been served out of the jurisdiction.

I would dismiss the appeal. I have the authority of Orr L.J., who is unable to be here this morning, for saying that he agrees with the judgment I have delivered.

SIR JOHN PENNYCUICK. I also agree with the judgment delivered by Buckley L.J.

Appeal dismissed with costs.

Solicitors: *Lovell, White & King; Richards, Butler & Co.; Courts & Co.*

C. N.

[QUEEN'S BENCH DIVISION]

* GREEN AND ANOTHER *v.* HOYLE

1976 March 9, 10 — Lord Widgery C.J., O'Connor and Goff JJ.

Solicitors — Unqualified person — Conveyance — Transfer agents undertaking legal work for property transactions—Instrument of transfer prepared by another unqualified person—Whether transfer agent directly or indirectly "draws or prepares" instruments—Solicitors Act 1957 (5 & 6 *Eliz.* 2, *c.* 27), *s.* 20 (1)

An association, which was formed with the object of reducing the high cost of conveyancing, undertook for its members, on payment of a fee, the general conduct of the members' property transactions. The association retained £2·50 of a fee paid and passed the remainder to one of its transfer agents, who undertook all the work involved in the transaction except drafting the instrument of transfer or conveyance. The draft was prepared by R, who was not a person qualified for the purposes of section 20 of the Solicitors Act 1957,[1] and for that work R received no remuneration. The defendants, who acted as transfer agents for the association and were also unqualified for the purposes of the section, were found by the justices to have directly or indirectly prepared such instruments and they were convicted of offences, contrary to section 20 (1) of the Act.

On the defendants' appeal against conviction:—

Held, allowing the appeal, that "directly or indirectly" in section 20 (1) of the Act related to the words "draws or prepares" and the offence created by the subsection was the drawing or preparing, whether directly or indirectly, of an instrument that was prohibited by the section from being so drawn by an unqualified person (post, pp. 582B–D, 583B, H—584A); that (*per* Lord Widgery C.J. and O'Connor J.) the concept of "draws and prepares" was the use of the intellect to compose the document by the selection of the correct words and to place them in the right sequence so that the document expressed the intention of the parties and, therefore, since the defendants had not drawn or prepared the documents within the meaning of the section, they had committed no offence (post, pp. 581F–G, 583B).

Per Goff J. If an unqualified person does any of the relevant acts, either himself or through another, he commits an offence under section 20 of the Act. The question whether the defendants did a prohibited act through R depended on whether they assumed responsibility for the particular act to

[1] Solicitors Act 1957, s. 20 (1): see post, p. 580B–C.

the lay client. Having regard to all the facts, it was R who alone assumed responsibility to the client (post, p. 584A–C).

The following cases are referred to in the judgment:

Beeston and Stapleford Urban District Council v. *Smith* [1949] 1 K.B. 656; [1949] 1 All E.R. 394, D.C.

Reynolds v. *Hoyle* [1976] 1 W.L.R. 207; [1975] 3 All E.R. 934, D.C.

The following additional cases were cited in argument:

Carter v. *Butcher* [1966] 1 Q.B. 526; [1965] 2 W.L.R. 1073; [1965] 1 All E.R. 994, D.C.

Crowley, In re (1899) 20 N.S.W.L.R. 150.

Kushner v. *Law Society* [1952] 1 K.B. 264; [1952] 1 All E.R. 404, D.C.

Taylor v. *Crowland Gas & Coke Co.* (1854) 10 Exch. 293.

CASE STATED by Worcester justices.

On March 20, 1974, eight informations were preferred by the prosecutor, John Michael Duncan Hoyle, against the defendants, Doris Green and David Ashford, and both of them alleging that they had committed offences contrary to section 20 (1) of the Solicitors Act 1957. The informations preferred were (i) that the defendant Green on a date unknown between February 26, 1973, and June 1, 1973, at 1, Osborne Mews, St. Leonards Road, Windsor, being an unqualified person prepared an instrument of transfer for the purposes of the Land Registration Acts 1925 to 1966, namely, a transfer of land known as number 127, Frimley Green Road and land at the back of numbers 123, 125 and 127, Frimley Green Road, Frimley, Surrey, contrary to section 20 (1) (*a*) of the Solicitors Act 1957. [(ii) An information in respect of the same property alleging that she being an unqualified person drew an instrument of transfer for the purposes of the Land Registration Acts 1925 to 1966, contrary to section 20 (1) (*a*) of the Solicitors Act 1957.] (iii) That the defendant Green on a date unknown between October 31, 1973, and December 4, 1973, at 5, Wymers Close, Burnham, Buckinghamshire, being an unqualified person prepared an instrument relating to real estate namely a conveyance of the land adjoining the property known as Hillview, 19, Backwell Common, Backwell, Somerset, contrary to section 20 (1) (*b*) of the Solicitors Act 1957. (iv) That the defendant Green on a date unknown between October 31, 1973, and December 4, 1973, at 5, Wymers Close, Burnham, Buckinghamshire, being an unqualified person drew an instrument relating to real estate namely a conveyance of land adjoining the property known as Hillview, 19, Backwell Common, Backwell, Somerset, contrary to section 20 (1) (*b*) of the Solicitors Act 1957.

Four similar informations were preferred against the defendant Ashford in respect of a conveyance of land known as 31, Wayside Avenue, Hornchurch, Essex, and an instrument of transfer of land known as 18, Old Park Road, Plumstead, London S.E.18.

The justices heard the informations on June 4, 5, 6, 1974. There were similar informations against Mr. Francis Reynolds and with the consent of all the defendants the informations were heard together. The justices gave their decision on June 25, 1974. The defendants made certain admissions of facts, which were exhibited to the case stated.

The justices found that in the beginning of September 1972 an association was formed under the name and style of the "Property Transfer Association." At the material times the defendant Green did secretarial work for the association and the defendant Ashford was a member of the management committee of the same. The published aims of the association were, inter alia, to "reduce the high cost of conveyancing." The association further represented that it could act for members in the sale or purchase of houses and other real property. Persons who wished to avail themselves of the services of the association had first to become members of that association. On becoming a member of the association the general conduct of that member's transaction—other than the drafting of the relevant instrument—was allocated to persons designated as "agents" of the association. At all material times the defendants acted as "transfer agents" of the association. They were not "qualified persons" within the meaning of section 1 of the Solicitors Act 1957. In respect of the services performed by the defendants, they were in receipt of remuneration. The remuneration was paid as follows. A member of the Property Transfer Association whose transaction was being conducted by the association would pay to that association a fee. The association would deduct from the fee a sum of £2·50 and would then remit the balance to the "agent" who had charge of the transaction. In each of the cases before the court where the association was acting for a member on the acquisition of a property the draft form of the land register transfer (in the case of registered land) and the draft deed of conveyance (in the case of unregistered land) was drafted by Mr. Francis Reynolds, who was not a "qualified person" within the meaning of section 1 of the Solicitors Act 1957. In respect of the services provided by Mr. Reynolds in the relevant informations he did not himself receive any fee, gain or reward and did not perform the services for or in the expectation of any personal fee, gain or reward.

In respect of the property known as 127, Frimley Green Road, together with the land at the back of numbers 123, 125 and 127, Frimley Green Road, Frimley, Surrey, and in respect of the land adjoining Hillview, 19, Backwell Common, Backwell, Somerset, the defendant Green acted for the purchasers of both those properties, the purchasers being members of the Property Transfer Association. Save as is set out below she conducted the transaction for the purchasers. In particular she conducted correspondence with the vendors or their solicitors, she negotiated and exchanged the contracts of sale, she made searches on the properties, she delivered on the vendors "enquiries before contract" and "requisitions on title." In respect of the services performed by her, she received moneys from the Property Transfer Association. Those moneys amounted to the fees paid by the purchasers to the association less a deduction of £2·50 made by the association. In the instance of 127, Frimley Green Road, Frimley, Surrey, together with the land at the back of 123, 125 and 127, Frimley Green Road, Frimley, Surrey, the draft form of the land registry transfer was drafted and produced by Mr. Reynolds. He drafted and produced and was enabled to draft and produce the draft form of the land registry transfer from documents supplied to him by the defendant Green. In relation to the land adjoining Hillview, 19, Backwell Common, Backwell,

Somerset, the draft conveyance was drafted and produced by Mr. Reynolds. A He produced and drafted and was enabled to produce and draft the draft form of conveyance from documents supplied to him by the defendant Green. In respect of property known as 31, Wayside Avenue, Hornchurch, Essex, and in respect of the property known as 18, Old Park Road, Plumstead, Essex, the defendant Ashcroft acted for the purchasers who were members of the Property Transfer Association. Save as is set out below, he conducted the transactions on behalf of the purchasers of the B properties. In particular he conducted correspondence with the vendors of the properties or their solicitors, negotiated the contracts of sale, made searches in respect of the properties and delivered upon the vendors "enquiries before contract" and "requisitions on title." He received remuneration being the balance of the fees paid by the purchasers to the Property Transfer Association after that association deducted from those C fees the sum of £2·50. In the instance of 31, Wayside Avenue, Hornchurch, Essex, the draft form of conveyance was drafted and produced by Mr. Reynolds. Mr. Reynolds produced and drafted and was enabled to produce and draft the draft form of conveyance from documents supplied to him by the defendant Ashford. The justices made no findings of fact as to where, when or by whom the draft form of conveyance was engrossed. D In the instance of 18, Old Park Road, Plumstead, Essex, the draft form of the land registry transfer was produced and drafted by Mr. Reynolds. He produced and drafted and was enabled to produce and draft the draft form of the land registry transfer from documents supplied to him by the defendant Ashford.

On the formation of the association, Mr. Francis Reynolds became E the chairman and the honorary conveyancer. He remained for a while as chairman until succeeded by the defendant Green's son-in-law, Mr. Edwards. The defendant Green was secretary of the association; her husband was the treasurer and book-keeper and they operated the association's bank account. The management committee included the defendant Green, the defendant Ashford, Mr. Reynolds, Mr. Green, Mr. Edwards F and Mrs. Edwards (Mrs. Green's daughter). The prime movers of the association included the defendant Green, the defendant Ashford and Mr. Reynolds. The defendants were in reality conducting a business for the transfer of housing and land. In a period of 14 months the defendant Green received £8,197 and the defendant Ashford received £5,724 for the services which they had performed in that business.

It was contended on behalf of the defendants that no fee, gain or reward G was paid by any members of the association in respect of the actual production of the relevant instrument of transfer; that section 20 of the Solicitors Act 1957 was penal in character and should be construed strictly; that the words "to prepare" were not wide enough to embrace the preliminary work admitted to have been done by the defendants; that H the words "to prepare" should be narrowly confined to the actual production of the instrument of transfer; that the words "indirectly" were confined to master-servant relationships and analogous situations and did not have a wider application. Consequently a person who simply did the preliminary work admitted to have been done by the defendants could not be guilty of the offence of either directly or indirectly preparing an instrument.

A It was contended on behalf of the prosecutor that the informations alleging "drawing" were alternative to those alleging "preparing." "Preparing" an instrument was either synonymous with or included "drawing" an instrument. Accordingly the prosecutor invited convictions only on the informations alleging "preparing." The defendants had directly or indirectly prepared the instruments specified in the informations
B preferred against them inasmuch as (a) they were responsible for the preparation by Mr. Reynolds of the instruments and had thereby indirectly prepared them; and/or (b) they themselves had directly prepared the instruments. Preparation involved every act which was preparatory to the production of the instrument. The work carried out by the defendants amounted to the preparation of the instruments. A number of persons
C could combine in the preparation of an instrument, and each defendant could combine and had combined with Mr. Reynolds in the preparation of the instruments. The defendants had received or expected to receive fee, gain or reward for their preparation of the instruments. In deciding whether the defendants had directly or indirectly prepared the instruments in the manner aforesaid and had received or expected to receive fee, gain
D or reward for indirectly preparing them, the court should have regard to the reality of the matter, which was that (a) while the association professed itself to be in form a members' association, it was in reality a business carried on by persons, including the defendants, who for gain acted on behalf of purchasers and vendors of property in carrying through the legal transactions necessary for the transfer or conveyance of the property which
E they had agreed to buy or sell—in short a conveyancing business. For that service the purchaser or vendor paid a fee most or all of which went to the person who acted in the conveyancing transaction on his behalf. (b) In the case of a purchase of property, preparation of the instrument of transfer or conveyance was an essential step in the completion of the sale and therefore of the conveyancing transaction which was conducted
F on behalf of the purchaser and in respect of which he paid a fee. (c) The work carried out by the defendants was essential to the part played by Mr. Reynolds in the preparation of the instruments. (d) The purchaser in each of the four transactions the subject of the informations paid for the preparation of the instrument of transfer or conveyance, as the case may be, including the work carried out by the defendants and
G Mr. Reynolds.

The justices were of the opinion that the defendants were "unqualified" and had directly and indirectly prepared the relevant instruments of transfer. They accordingly, convicted both defendants of "preparing an instrument" and fined them £50 on each of the informations. They directed that the informations which contained the words "to draw" should not be
H separately determined but should be kept on the file.

The defendants appealed. The question for the opinion of the High Court was whether on the above facts the justices came to a correct decision in law.

A. J. Balcombe Q.C. and *D. M. Hogg* for the defendant Ashford.
The defendant Green in person.
Lionel Read Q.C. and *A. M. Hill* for the prosecutor.

LORD WIDGERY C.J. This is an appeal by case stated by the city of A Worcester justices in respect of their adjudication as a magistrates' court at Worcester on June 4, 5 and 6, 1974. On that occasion the justices convicted the two defendants on a number of informations each of which alleged that an offence had been committed contrary to section 20 of the Solicitors Act 1957 in that it was contended that the defendants had either drawn or prepared an instrument of the kind referred to in the section B without themselves being qualified persons; that is to say without being admitted as solicitors.

Section 20, so far as relevant, reads:

> "(1) Any unqualified person who either directly or indirectly—(*a*) draws or prepares any instrument of transfer or charge for the purposes of the Land Registration Act 1925 or makes any application or C lodges any document for registration under that Act at the registry; or (*b*) draws or prepares any other instrument relating to real or personal estate, or any legal proceeding, shall, unless he proves that the act was not done for or in expectation of any fee, gain or reward, be liable on summary conviction to a fine not exceeding £50: . . ."

D

Thereafter follows a list of persons who are exempt from this restriction, such as barristers, and a number of instruments which are exempt from the restriction such as wills or other testamentary documents; but we are concerned with none of those. We are concerned with the defendants, who have no legal professional qualifications and who were convicted by the justices of either drawing or preparing one of the instruments to which E section 20 applies, namely, an instrument of transfer or other instrument relating to real or personal estate.

The background to the case is just this. The two defendants, together with a Mr. Reynolds and a number of other people whose names are unknown to us, formed, in 1972, an unincorporated association which they called the Property Transfer Association. The purpose of this association F was to bring down the level of costs charged by solicitors for the work of transferring property and to set up a system whereby those who were desirous of taking advantage of the offer made by the defendants and Mr. Reynolds could get their conveyancing done at a price considerably lower than the ruling prices amongst solicitors.

But of course section 20 was an obstacle to this in that none of them G was a qualified person within the meaning of the section. So they hit upon an ingenious device (I use the word "device" not in any sense designed to be offensive) which they put forward as enabling them to carry on this activity without committing an offence under the section.

The basis of it was just this. The section creates an offence (in the broadest terms) if an unqualified person draws or prepares a prohibited H document for fee or reward. The device was simply to separate the receipt of the fee from the preparation or drawing of the document.

The section, it will be observed, does not make the rest of the conveyancing work illegal if done by persons other than a solicitor; and that, no doubt, is because until quite recently the supreme piece of effort involved in conveyancing was the preparation of the deed itself. Years ago, when people prided themselves on their use of legal English and

A perhaps were paid by the folio as well, conveyances were lengthy documents constructed with the greatest care. Now it may be that they are easier to prepare and their drafting is less important, but even so it is the instrument of transfer which is struck at by section 20.

The device hit upon by these people was that all the work, other than preparing or drawing the instrument of transfer, should be done by people like the defendants, who were called transfer agents. They would do the B entire conveyancing work, save that they would not draw or prepare the instrument of transfer itself. The transfer agents charged a fee. We do not know what it was; but they charged a fee for their services; but they were not within the scope of section 20 (or so they thought) because they were not drawing the prohibited document, hence the fact that they received a fee was of no consequence.

C Mr. Reynolds, on the other hand, was the person who did all the drafting. Whenever the time came for the preparation or the drafting of an instrument of transfer, the essential papers were sent to Mr. Reynolds. He prepared the document and, as I understand the evidence, sent it back to the vendors' solicitors, but he made no charge and so it was thought that he escaped the possibility of committing an offence under D section 20 because although he prepared or drew the prohibited document, he did not charge for it; and that appeared to give him, as it were, a let-out.

The first occasion on which the matter came before this court was on July 8, 1975, when Mr. Reynolds, having been convicted by the justices, appealed against his conviction: see *Reynolds* v. *Hoyle* [1976] 1 W.L.R. 207. It is not necessary to go into this matter in detail. Suffice it to say E that it was basic to Mr. Reynolds' argument that no fee or reward was charged for his services; and following authority, we held in this court that the fee or reward taken by the transfer agents was enough for present purposes to remove the protection on Mr. Reynolds; therefore Mr. Reynolds lost his appeal and that was the end of the matter as far as he was concerned.

F Today we are deciding appeals arising against the same background in respect of the transfer agents. The argument here is, and must be, not that they acted for nothing because they acted for fees, but that they did not do the prohibited work. In other words, they did not directly or indirectly draw or prepare the instrument of transfer.

The conception of "draw or prepare" in this context seems to me to G mean the use of the intellect to compose the document, the use of the brain to select the correct words, put them in the correct sequence so that the document expresses the intention of the parties. That, to my mind, is the ordinary meaning of "draw or prepare an instrument" in a context such as this. No doubt the draftsman in drawing or preparing a conveyance will normally sit with paper in front of him and will put on paper the words H which he selects as the preparation of the document goes ahead. No doubt if the document is prepared in that way, it is a perfectly sensible thing to say that it was directly drawn or prepared by its author; and for my part I do not think the word "directly" would add very much to that situation, but it is, no doubt, quite sensible and proper to describe this as the drawing or preparation of an instrument directly as opposed to indirectly.

The conception of preparing an instrument indirectly is one which I have found extremely difficult throughout the argument in this case. Of course the person responsible for composing the document may not use his own hand to write it out. He could dictate it to a typist. It may be, and I do not propose to decide it this morning, that to draft through the medium of a typist is " indirectly " drawing or preparing for the purposes of the section. Nowadays people drawing conveyances may, for all I know, use recording machines, and it may be, although I would not decide it, that that again is an instance which amounts to indirect preparation of a document.

But what I feel quite convinced about, having listened to the argument and thought about it a great deal overnight, is that however wide the expression " directly or indirectly " is held to be, it cannot be so wide as to take the operation outside the words " draw or prepare " altogether. That which is being struck at is the drawing or preparation of the document; and, by saying that the prohibition extends to that act, whether done directly or indirectly, it cannot mean that the offence can be committed when that which is being done is not the drawing and preparation of a document at all.

In my judgment, as I have already said, the meaning of " draw or prepare " in this context is to compose, to use the mind to select the words; and it is abundantly clear that neither defendant ever did that. The preparation of the document in that sense was exclusively the function of Mr. Reynolds. It was not done by the defendant Mrs. Green; it was not done by the defendant Mr. Ashford. In my judgment when those people did not, in any sense, prepare or compose the document, it cannot be said that they come within the phrase " directly or indirectly draw or prepare any instrument."

For those reasons I would allow this appeal and I would quash the several convictions of the defendants.

Before I leave the case I would like to make two other points. First of all, I do not regard today as the appropriate moment to consider the situation which may arise in a solicitor's office where the solicitor, having a number of experienced managing clerks, allows the managing clerks to do conveyancing work and draw or prepare instruments without the solicitor having himself applied his mind to the problem at all.

We are told that such a case may be on its way to this court for decision. That is one reason for not prejudicing the matter today. But I can well see, without waiting for the argument, that special circumstances can well arise within the office of a solicitor in the situation in which the actual drafting is done by an unqualified person; albeit under the general supervision of the solicitor himself.

The other point which I would make today before parting with the case entirely is this. I do not think this morning the appropriate time to consider the situation which can arise where a limited company, namely, a corporate body is charged with having drawn or prepared instruments. There was of course one decision in which a corporate body was convicted under the equivalent legislation to that with which we are now concerned: see *Beeston and Stapleford Urban District Council* v. *Smith* [1949] 1 K.B. 656. I mention the authority to show that we have not ignored it, and it may well be that further consideration has to be given to the situation which arises when the defendant has no mind being a corporate body, and when the mind of its servants are arguably to be substituted for its own mind. That again I should leave for consideration on another day.

But I would allow these appeals, as I have said, and quash the relevant convictions on the footing that neither defendant ever applied their intellect to the composition of these documents either in whole or in part.

O'CONNOR J. I agree with the judgment of Lord Widgery C.J. that these appeals should be allowed and the convictions quashed, and I agree with the reasons which he has given. I particularly wish to add that I agree with the reservations that he has made in the latter part of his judgment. As I have arrived at the same conclusion by approximately the same route I will take a minute to state my own reasons for thinking that no offence had been committed here in this case.

Section 20 of the Solicitors Act 1957 makes it an offence for any unqualified person who either directly or indirectly draws or prepares any instrument of transfer. The concept of drawing or preparing a document involves both the use of the pen and the mind that guides the pen. It is the latter element which is paramount. The addition of the words "directly or indirectly" in the section, in my judgment, are declaratory of the two elements. It seems to me that a man who dictates a document to a typist can properly be said to be drawing it or preparing it and that the typist does not either draw or prepare the document. It would be an abuse of English to suggest that the typist did.

That being the case, it may well be that Parliament has repeated in the section the words "directly or indirectly" to avoid any confusion in construing the section. The words making it clear that it is the mind that makes the document that is the true drawer or preparer of the document as opposed to the pen that may physically write it down. A person who furnishes the material from which a document is drawn does not draw the document at all. I do not think it matters that the information is furnished in the course of a business. For those reasons it seems to me that the documents in the present case were drawn or prepared by Mr. Reynolds and were not drawn or prepared by the defendants.

I would only add this: that the fact that, in the present case, it seems to me to be clear that none of these documents were drawn at all by the defendants does not mean that situations may not arise where the business is so organised that it could properly be said that the mind which directed the preparation of the document was in truth and in fact the mind of the person who was drawing or preparing the document. It must depend upon the individual facts of the situations in which the scheme of things is cast. But for the present case I am in no doubt that these convictions were wrong and the appeals should be allowed.

GOFF J. I agree; but I must confess that my conclusion has been reached by a rather different route from that followed by Lord Widgery C.J. and O'Connor J.

I accept Mr. Read's submission as to the meaning of the words "directly or indirectly" in section 20 (1) of the Act. As I read the section, the words "directly or indirectly" govern a number of acts which are

prohibited if carried out by an unqualified person, including the act of A
drawing or preparing certain instruments. I accept Mr. Read's submission that directly means doing the relevant act yourself and indirectly means doing the relevant act through another person. It follows that if an unqualified person does any of the relevant acts, either himself or through another, then he commits an offence under section 20.

But there remains the difficult question whether or not in this particular B
case the defendants did a prohibited act through Mr. Reynolds. I have come to the conclusion that that is a question of responsibility, as Mr. Read himself submits; the question is whether the defendants assumed responsibility for the particular act to the lay client, or whether it was Mr. Reynolds alone who did so. Mr. Reynolds was given the task of drawing and preparing the transfers and conveyances, and indeed Mr. Reynolds C
has in consequence already been convicted of an offence under the section. I have come to the conclusion, having regard to all the facts found by the justices in the case, that it was Mr. Reynolds who alone assumed responsibility to the lay client for the drawing and preparation of the transfers and conveyances. It follows that neither of the defendants did a prohibited act either directy or indirectly, and for these reasons I too would allow D
the appeal.

Appeal allowed with costs in Divisional Court and magistrates' court.

Solicitors: *B. M. Birnberg & Co.; Richard Butler & Co.* E

H. J.

F

G

H

A

[COURT OF APPEAL]

* REGINA v. CHANDLER

1975 Dec. 11; 1976 Jan. 20 — Lawton L.J., Talbot and Pain JJ.

B

Crime—Summing up—Direction to jury—Defendant's silence when questioned by police—Inference to be drawn from defendant's silence

During an interview with a police officer in connection with the activities of a gang which had obtained television sets dishonestly, the defendant, who was suspected of being a
C member of the gang, both before and after he was cautioned, answered some questions but in relation to others either remained silent or refused to answer them. At his trial on a charge of conspiracy to defraud, the judge in his summing up said that a person who had been cautioned had a right to remain silent, but it was for the jury to decide whether the defendant remained silent before caution in the exercise of his common law right to remain silent or whether he remained
D silent because he might have thought, if he had answered, he would have incriminated himself. The defendant was convicted.

On appeal against conviction:—

Held, allowing the appeal, that the issue for the jury was whether, since the defendant and the officer had been speaking on equal terms, the defendant's silence before he had been cautioned could amount to an acceptance by him of what
E the officer had said and, if it did, whether his guilt could reasonably be inferred from that acceptance; that, therefore, the judge's comments were not justified and could have led the jury to a wrong conclusion but, even if the jury, on a proper direction, had found that the defendant had accepted what the officer had said, that acceptance would not have been a safe foundation for the inference that the defendant was a member of the conspiracy.

Rex v. *Christie* [1914] A.C. 545, 554, H.L.(E.) and *Reg.* v.
F *Mitchell* (1892) 17 Cox C.C. 503, 505 applied.

Dictum of Lord Diplock in *Hall* v. *The Queen* [1971] 1 W.L.R. 298, 301, P.C. not applied.

Per curiam. Reading passages from law reports to juries is becoming a forensic practice which is likely to confuse rather than help and should cease (post, p. 587F).

G The following cases are referred to in the judgment:

Bessela v. *Stern* (1877) 2 C.P.D. 265, C.A.
Hall v. *The Queen* [1971] 1 W.L.R. 298; [1971] 1 All E.R. 322, P.C.
Reg. v. *Mann* (1972) 56 Cr.App.R. 750, C.A.
Reg. v. *Mitchell* (1892) 17 Cox C.C. 503.
Reg. v. *Ryan* (1964) 50 Cr.App.R. 144, C.C.A.
Rex v. *Christie* [1914] A.C. 545, H.L.(E.).

H

The following additional cases were cited in argument:

Reg. v. *Davis* (1959) 43 Cr.App.R. 215, C.C.A.
Reg. v. *Foster* [1974] Crim.L.R. 544, C.A.
Rex v. *Gerard* (1948) 32 Cr.App.R. 132, C.C.A.
Rex v. *Tune* (1944) 29 Cr.App.R. 162, C.C.A.

[Reported by BERNARD O. AGYEMAN, ESQ., Barrister-at-Law]

APPEAL against conviction. A

On January 24, 1975, the defendant, Roy Frank Chandler, was convicted at the Central Criminal Court of conspiracy to cheat and defraud and was sentenced by Judge King-Hamilton to three years' imprisonment.

By notice of appeal dated February 10, 1975, the defendant appealed against conviction on the grounds that the judge was wrong in not withdrawing the conspiracy count from the jury when a submission was made at the close of the prosecution's case that there was no case to answer B and, accordingly, since the evidence given on behalf of the other defendants did not materially strengthen the prosecution's case, the verdict was unsafe and unsatisfactory; and that the judge misdirected the jury as to the effect of the defendant's refusal to answer questions put to him before the investigating officer had administered the caution. The defendant also appealed against sentence on the ground, inter alia, that the sentence of C three years' imprisonment was excessive and harsh.

On December 11, 1975, the court allowed the defendant's appeal against conviction, quashed the conviction, ordered that the defendant be released and stated that it would give its reasons later.

The facts are stated in the judgment of the court.

Justin Philips for the defendant. D
Colin Hart-Leverton for the Crown.

Cur. adv. vult.

January 20, 1976. LAWTON L.J. read the following judgment of the court. On January 24, 1975, at the Central Criminal Court, the defendant was convicted of conspiracy to defraud (count 24). He was sentenced to E three years' imprisonment by Judge King-Hamilton. Charged with him in this count of the indictment were two other men named Joy and Apicella. Both pleaded not guilty and no verdict was taken in their cases. Apicella pleaded guilty to a number of other offences charged in the indictment. Joy was found guilty on seven counts charging obtaining property by deception. The defendant's wife was also charged in the indictment with dishonestly assisting in the retention of stolen goods; she was acquitted. The defendant F now appeals against his conviction by leave of the court.

Although the trial lasted many days, the facts relevant to this appeal can be stated shortly. The prosecution's case against the defendant was that he was a member of a gang which had been formed to obtain colour television sets dishonestly. Joy and Apicella called on television hire shops giving false names, and dishonestly entered into hiring agreements G without having any intention of paying the hire charges once they had obtained possession of a set. They got possession of a number and paid nothing. Sets were delivered to various addresses, including a house in which the defendant's wife was living. Thereafter the sets disappeared. The defendant had been living apart from his wife at the material times. There was some shadowy evidence that the defendant had helped the gang to remove a dishonestly acquired television set which had H been sold to a dissatisfied customer. Before this court Mr. Hart-Leverton, for the prosecution, accepted that this evidence could not support the conviction. The only other evidence against the defendant came from a detective sergeant who spoke of an interview which he had had with him on November 23, 1973, at North Woolwich police station. The defendant's solicitor was present. It is necessary to set out part of this interview. The questions were put by the detective sergeant:

A " (Q) I am investigating the theft of a number of colour televisions. Some of these were delivered to 27, Eighth Avenue, a house of which you are part owner. I understand that you have not been residing there. When did you leave? (A) March. (Q) Have you visited? (A) No, not until the trouble my wife's in. I came back to take some control. (Q) You are actually saying you've never visited till . . . (A) About three weeks ago. (Q) You know there are some alterations
B being done in the house by a firm you're working for? (A) Yes. (Q) Have you done any work in the house? (A) No. (Q) I'm going to show you a hire purchase agreement in the name of Ward dated July 27 for the hire of a Spectra 26-inch colour television. It was delivered to 27, Eighth Avenue, on July 27, 1973. Certain identification details were seen by the firm, namely, a rent book
C in the name of R. C. Chandler of 116, Windsor Road, E.7; also a driving licence number. Can you tell me how these particulars got onto this agreement? (A) Not prepared to say anything on that. (Q) Do you know a man by the name of Laurie Apicella? (A) No comment. (Q) Could this man have got hold of a driving licence or rent book in your name? (A) Don't wish to comment. (Q) Do you know a man by the name of Bernard Joy? (A) No. (Q) Could
D this man have got hold of a driving licence or rent book in your name? (A) I don't know whether he could or not. (Q) Do you know him? (A) No. In view of the circumstances, I suspect you may be concerned with these people I have mentioned in assisting them to steal rental televisions."

At this stage the defendant was cautioned. The questioning continued.
E The defendant answered some questions and refused to make any comment when asked others.

In his summing up the trial judge commented on this interview. The defendant's counsel submitted that he was not entitled to make the comments he did. Counsel in his final speech to the jury had read to them passages from two decisions, one of the House of Lords, *Rex* v.
F *Christie* [1914] A.C. 545, and the other of the Privy Council, *Hall* v. *The Queen* [1971] 1 W.L.R. 298. Reading passages from law reports to juries is becoming a forensic practice which would have been stopped by an earlier generation of judges. It is likely to confuse rather than help; and if, as in this case, the reading does not go as far as the judge thinks it should, he then has to read some more with a likelihood of making the confusion greater. The practice should stop. Having read the jury the
G well known passage in the speech of Lord Atkinson in *Rex* v. *Christie* [1914] A.C. 545, 554, the judge commented as follows:

" So although it is absolutely true that even if a person has not been cautioned, if an accusation is made against him and he either says nothing at all or makes a comment to that effect, like ' no comment,' or ' I am not saying,' you must not automatically say that that means
H he is guilty. That would be quite wrong. Nevertheless, it is for you—not for me or anybody else—to decide whether you think a series of answers like that do indicate in your view his guilt or innocence, or neither the one or the other but are completely neutral. In considering that of course you must bear in mind two matters: that where a man has been cautioned—which means being told that he need not say anything unless he wishes to do so, and if he does it will be taken down in writing and may be given in

evidence—and thereafter he remains silent, that is absolutely within his right and he cannot be adversely criticised for so doing, because he accepts that part of the invitation in the caution to remain silent. Even if he is not cautioned, as Mr. Philips rightly said, it is part of what is known as his common law right to decline to answer questions. In those circumstances you must ask yourselves whether he did so in the knowledge that he was exercising his common law right to remain silent, or whether he remained silent because he might have thought if he had answered he would in some way have incriminated himself."

Later, when reminding the jury of the detail of the detective sergeant's evidence about the interview, the judge interrupted the narrative with this comment:

> "From now on until a few answers later it is important to bear in mind, according to the prosecution, that no caution had been administered. According to Mr. Philips that is not important because, as he emphasised quite rightly, there is the common law right to refuse to answer questions. According to me, and basing my decision on *Rex* v. *Christie,* it is a matter for you to determine, if you can, whether the refusal to answer questions was merely being evasive to protect his wife, evasive to protect himself, evasive because he did not know the answers, or evasive because he knew he was entitled to exercise his rights and not answer whether he knew the answer or not and was taking that stand upon the matter."

Counsel submitted that these comments should not have been made because of the decisions in a long line of cases, the most recent being *Reg.* v. *Ryan* (1964) 50 Cr.App.R. 144 and *Reg.* v. *Mann* (1972) 56 Cr. App.R. 750. It is unnecessary for us to review these cases. They were all cases in which it is clear that a caution had been given or the circumstances were such that this court is entitled to infer that one had been given. When this was pointed out to counsel, he invited our attention to what Lord Diplock said in *Hall* v. *The Queen* [1971] 1 W.L.R. 298, 301:

> "In their Lordships' view the distinction sought to be made"—that is that no caution had been given—is not a valid one . . . The caution merely serves to remind the accused of a right which he already possesses at common law. The fact that in a particular case he has not been reminded of it is no ground for inferring that his silence was not in exercise of that right, but was an acknowledgment of the truth of the accusation."

Earlier he had said, at p. 301:

> "It is a clear and widely known principle of the common law in Jamaica, as in England, that a person is entitled to refrain from answering a question put to him for the purpose of discovering whether he has committed a criminal offence. . . . It may be that in very exceptional circumstances an inference may be drawn from a failure to give an explanation or a disclaimer, but in their Lordships' view silence alone on being informed by a police officer that someone else has made an accusation against him cannot give rise to an inference that the person to whom this information is communicated accepts the truth of the accusation."

We have reservations about these two statements of law because they seem to conflict with *Rex* v. *Christie* [1914] A.C. 545 and with earlier cases and authorities. For reasons which will appear later in this judgment, it is not necessary in this case to review the law relating to the so-called right of silence. The law has long accepted that an accused person is not bound to incriminate himself; but it does not follow that a failure to answer an accusation or question when an answer could reasonably be expected may not provide some evidence in support of an accusation. Whether it does will depend upon the circumstances. We could not improve on what Lord Atkinson said in *Rex* v. *Christie,* at p. 554:

> ". . . the rule of law undoubtedly is that a statement made in the presence of an accused person, even upon an occasion which should be expected reasonably to call for some explanation or denial from him, is not evidence against him of the facts stated save so far as he accepts the statement, so as to make it, in effect, his own. . . . He may accept the statement by word or conduct, action or demeanour, and it is the function of the jury which tries the case to determine whether his words, action, conduct, or demeanour at the time when a statement was made amounts to an acceptance of it in whole or in part. It by no means follows, I think, that a mere denial by the accused of the facts mentioned in the statement necessarily renders the statement inadmissible, because he may deny the statement in such a manner and under such circumstances as may lead a jury to disbelieve him, and constitute evidence from which an acknowledgment may be inferred by them."

This statement of the law reflected legal opinion in the 19th century. Thus in *Phillips & Arnold on the Law of Evidence*, 10th ed. (1852), vol. 1, p. 334, the law is stated as follows:

> "In some cases, it is allowable to give evidence of written or verbal statements made, or of acts done, by others, and then to show how the party who heard or read the statements, or saw the acts done, was affected by them,—for the purpose of using his conduct, expressions or demeanour as evidence against him by way of admission. The evidence in such cases is altogether presumptive in its quality and character. . . . This species of evidence is very commonly used in criminal cases, although it appears to be somewhat inconsistent to hold, that the prisoner's silence on hearing an accusation is evidence against him, when his denial of the charge upon such an occasion would not be evidence for him."

This principle was applied in *Bessela* v. *Stern* (1877) 2 C.P.D. 265. In that case, which was an action for breach of promise of marriage, evidence from the plaintiff's sister was accepted as corroboration for the purpose of the statute 32 & 33 Vict. c. 68. This evidence was to the effect that the defendant had made no denial when the plaintiff had upbraided him for having promised to marry her and failing to do so. In *Reg.* v. *Mitchell* (1892) 17 Cox C.C. 503, 508, Cave J. said:

> "Undoubtedly, when persons are speaking on even terms, and a charge is made, and the person charged says nothing, and expresses no indignation, and does nothing to repel the charge, that is some evidence to show that he admits the charge to be true."

As Professor Sir Rupert Cross commented in his book, *Evidence*, 4th ed., p. 189, in reference to *Reg.* v. *Mitchell,* this " is a broad principle of common sense." Indeed it is. It should not be forgotten that the law of evidence developed in the 18th century and the early part of the 19th century as a result of the search by the judges for rules which could be applied during a trial to obtain reliable testimony and to ensure a fair trial for the accused. The search had been made necessary by the disquiet and concern which had arisen after the perjury of Oates, Bedloe, Dugdale, Dangerfield and Turberville in the Popist Plot trials became known. Appeals such as Lord Diplock made in *Hall* v. *The Queen* to the common law for support for a proposition in the law of evidence means seeking, at the earliest, an 18th century precedent. Between 1554 and 1640 a criminal trial bore little resemblance to a modern trial; indeed the examination of the accused in court by counsel for the Crown " was the very essence of the trial ": see *Stephen, History of the Criminal Law in England* (1883), vol. 1, p. 326. This went on until the beginning of the 18th century: see J. H. Wigmore, *Evidence in Trials at Common Law,* 2nd ed. (1923), vol. 1, p. 604. It would be unfortunate if the law of evidence was allowed to develop in a way which was not in accordance with the common sense of ordinary folk. We are bound by *Rex* v. *Christie,* not by *Hall* v. *The Queen. Rex* v. *Christie,* in our judgment, does accord with common sense.

When the judge's comments are examined against the principles enunciated in both *Reg.* v. *Mitchell* and *Rex* v. *Christie* we are of the opinion that the defendant and the detective sergeant were speaking on equal terms since the former had his solicitor present to give him any advice he might have wanted and to testify, if needed, as to what had been said. We do not accept that a police officer always has an advantage over someone he is questioning. Everything depends upon the circumstances. A young detective questioning a local dignitary in the course of an inquiry into alleged local government corruption may be very much at a disadvantage. This kind of situation is to be contrasted with that of a tearful housewife accused of shoplifting or of a parent being questioned about the suspected wrongdoing of his son. Some comment on the defendant's lack of frankness before he was cautioned was justified provided the jury's attention was directed to the right issue, which was whether in the circumstances the defendant's silence amounted to an acceptance by him of what the detective sergeant had said. If he accepted what had been said, then the next question should have been whether guilt could reasonably be inferred from what he had accepted. To suggest, as the judge did, that the defendant's silence could indicate guilt was to short-circuit the intellectual process which has to be followed. Phillips in *A Treatise on the Law of Evidence* pointed out this very error, at p. 334:

> " It very commonly happens, that evidence of the description referred to has the effect of misleading juries, who are frequently influenced by it . . . and are unable, notwithstanding any directions from a judge, to regard it solely as exhibiting demeanour and conduct. In many instances, especially where no observation has been made by the party on hearing it, the evidence is particularly liable to produce erroneous conclusions. An acquiescence in the truth of the statement is frequently inferred, though the inference may, from a variety of causes, be incorrect. Thus the evidence is not only

A > fallacious with reference to its object, but in its collateral effect is prejudicial to the investigation of truth."

The same kind of error is seen in the comment which the judge made as to whether the defendant had been evasive in order to protect himself. He may have been; but that was not what the jury had to decide. It follows, in our judgment, that the comments made were not justified and B could have led the jury to a wrong conclusion.

This is no legalistic quibble. We have looked closely at the evidence provided by the interview. There was no other as the defendant did not give any. Even if the comments had been made in accordance with *Rex* v. *Christie,* we should have quashed the conviction as being unsafe. The defendant, for example, refused to say anything about the fact that his name and driving licence number had got onto a hire-purchase docu- C ment. This could not amount to anything more than the acceptance by him that these particulars were where the detective sergeant said they were. Further, he made no comment when asked if he knew Apicella; at the most this could only amount to some evidence that he did know him. He lied when he said he did not know Joy; but proof that he lied did not amount to proof of any fact other than that he had lied. It is D unnecessary to examine the interview in any more detail. It suffices to say that it did not provide a safe foundation for an inference that the appellant had been a member of the conspiracy alleged.

It was for these reasons that we allowed the appeal.

Appeal allowed.

E

Solicitors: *Registrar of Criminal Appeals; Solicitor, Metropolitan Police.*

F

[COURT OF APPEAL]

* BUSHWALL PROPERTIES LTD. *v.* VORTEX PROPERTIES LTD.

SAME *v.* SAME

[1969 B. No. 4041]

G

[1971 B. No. 2257]

1976 Jan. 23, 27, 28, 29

Buckley and Orr L.JJ. and Sir John Pennycuick

Contract—Formation—Consensus ad idem—Uncertainty—Agreement to purchase land—Purchase price to be paid in stages— H *"Proportionate part" of land to be conveyed on each occasion—No agreement as to selection of land to be so conveyed—Whether contract void for uncertainty*

In June 1968 it was agreed between the parties in an exchange of letters that the plaintiff would purchase land from the defendant in three phases, a certain amount of the purchase price being paid and a "proportionate part" of the land being released on each phase. Following an attempt on behalf of the defendant to alter the terms of the agreement

the plaintiff on July 7, 1969, issued a writ claiming specific A
performance and damages. On July 24, 1969, the defendant conveyed the land to a subsidiary company of the defendant's parent company. During subsequent negotiations between the parties the defendant's solicitors wrote in June 1970 offering the plaintiff "in a final effort to dispose of this matter" one conveyance of the whole land for the full purchase price. The plaintiff accepted the offer and in November 1970 the land was conveyed accordingly. In May 1971 the plaintiff com- B
menced the second action, later consolidated with the earlier action, claiming damages from the defendant for breach of the contract made in June 1968. Oliver J., ordering an inquiry as to the loss sustained by the plaintiff, rejected the defendant's contention that the contract purported to have been made in 1968 failed by reason of uncertainty in that there was no allocation of the power to select the land to be released at each phase, holding that the plaintiff, as owner of the land C
in equity, had the right to select. The judge further found that the plaintiff had not accepted the conveyance in 1970 in settlement of the first action.

On appeal by the defendant: —

Held, allowing the appeal, (1) that in a contract for the sale of land with completion in phases the power to select the land to be included in each phase represented an element which if left uncertain would render the contract as a whole D
uncertain and for that reason unenforceable (post, p. 599C–D); that there was no ground on which, as a matter of law, the power to select the land where no provision had been made had to be regarded as vested in the purchaser (post, p. 599A–B); that, accordingly, the contract purported to have been made in June 1968 was unenforceable by reason of uncertainty (post, pp. 600A, 604D–E, 605C–F).

(2) That, further, as a matter of construction, the E
defendant's solicitors' offer and its acceptance by the plaintiff in 1970 had disposed by way of compromise of the plaintiff's claim for damages (post, pp. 602A–D, 604D–E, 606D–F).

Decision of Oliver J. [1975] 1 W.L.R. 1649; [1975] 2 All E.R. 214 reversed.

The following cases are referred to in the judgments: F

Abdulla v. *Shah* [1959] A.C. 124; [1959] 2 W.L.R. 12, P.C.

Foley v. *Classique Coaches Ltd.* [1934] 2 K.B. 1, C.A.

Hussey v. *Horne-Payne* (1879) 4 App.Cas. 311, H.L.(E.).

Miller (James) & Partners Ltd. v. *Whitworth Street Estates (Manchester) Ltd.* [1970] A.C. 583; [1970] 2 W.L.R. 728; [1970] 1 All E.R. 796, H.L.(E.).

Wickman Machine Tool Sales Ltd. v. *L. Schuler A.G.* [1974] A.C. 235; G
[1973] 2 W.L.R. 683; [1973] 2 All E.R. 39, H.L.(E.).

The following additional cases were cited in argument:

Asten v. *Asten* [1894] 3 Ch. 260.

Brown v. *Gould* [1972] Ch. 53; [1971] 3 W.L.R. 334; [1971] 2 All E.R. 1505.

Clark v. *May* (1852) 16 Beav. 273. H

Clarke v. *Ramuz* [1891] 2 Q.B. 456, C.A.

Cottrill v. *Steyning and Littlehampton Building Society* [1966] 1 W.L.R. 753; [1966] 2 All E.R. 295.

Courtney & Fairbairn Ltd. v. *Tolaini Brothers (Hotels) Ltd.* [1975] 1 W.L.R. 297; [1975] 1 All E.R. 716, C.A.

Egmont (Earl) v. *Smith* (1877) 6 Ch.D. 469.

Jones v. *Lipman* [1962] 1 W.L.R. 832; [1962] 1 All E.R. 442.

A *London School Board and Foster, In re* (1903) 87 L.T. 700, C.A.

Marks v. *Lilley* [1959] 1 W.L.R. 749; [1959] 2 All E.R. 647.

May and Butcher Ltd. v. *The King* (*Note*) [1934] 2 K.B. 17, H.L.(E.).

Payzu Ltd. v. *Saunders* [1919] 2 K.B. 581, C.A.

Pilkington v. *Wood* [1953] Ch. 770; [1953] 3 W.L.R. 522; [1953] 2 All E.R. 810.

Serff v. *Acton Local Board* (1886) 21 Ch.D. 679.

B *Talbot* v. *Talbot* [1968] Ch. 1; [1967] 3 W.L.R. 438; [1967] 2 All E.R. 920, C.A.

Thorpe v. *Fasey* [1949] Ch. 649; [1949] 2 All E.R. 393.

Wright v. *Dean* [1948] Ch. 686; [1948] 2 All E.R. 415.

APPEAL from Oliver J.

By writ dated July 7, 1969, the plaintiff, Bushwall Properties Ltd.,
C claimed specific performance of an agreement constituted by letters dated June 20, 1968, for sale by the defendant, Vortex Properties Ltd., to the plaintiff of 51½ acres of land in Fareham, Hampshire, at the price of £500,000; and damages in addition to specific performance.

By a second writ dated May 14, 1971, the plaintiff claimed damages for breach of the contract referred to in the first writ broken by the defendant's selling and conveying of the land to Medina Estates Ltd.
D on July 24, 1969.

By order dated August 2, 1971, the actions were consolidated. By a defence dated August 30, 1971, the defendant alleged, inter alia, that the letters of June 1968 did not constitute a binding contract; that the first action had been settled between the parties by letters in June 1970; and that the plaintiff was not entitled to continue with either action since the
E subject matter of both was the subject of a binding compromise. On December 9, 1974, Oliver J., rejecting the defendant's contentions, ordered an inquiry as to what loss the plaintiff had suffered by reason of the defendant's failure to perform the agreement of June 1968.

By notice of appeal dated February 24, 1975, the defendant appealed on the grounds, inter alia, that the judge was wrong in law in holding (1) that the letters in June 1970 did not constitute a binding settlement
F of the first action; (2) that the arrangement made in letters in June 1968 was sufficiently certain to constitute a contract enforceable in law for the sale of the land; and (3) that a term was to be implied into that arrangement either by law or by the custom of conveyancers to the effect that the plaintiff as purchaser was to be entitled to select what area of land was to be conveyed on each of the phased completions contemplated by
G the arrangement. By a respondent's notice dated June 9, 1975, the plaintiff gave notice of an intention to contend that the judgment on the issue of the compromise of the first action should be affirmed on additional grounds.

The facts are stated in the judgment of Sir John Pennycuick.

A. J. Balcombe Q.C. and *Michael Barnes* for the defendant.

G. B. H. Dillon Q.C. and *D. M. Burton* for the plaintiff.

H

BUCKLEY L.J. I will ask Sir John Pennycuick to deliver the first judgment in this case.

SIR JOHN PENNYCUICK. We have before us an appeal from an order made by Oliver J. on December 9, 1974. The appeal raises two issues, namely, (1) did certain letters exchanged in June 1968 have contractual effect, or was the contract purported to be made void for uncertainty?

(2) Was the plaintiff's claim for damages for breach by the defendant of that contract disposed of by way of compromise under letters exchanged in June 1970? If those two questions are answered in favour of the plaintiff, as they were answered by Oliver J., a further question as to measure of damages and duty to mitigate arises. A

The facts are set out fully and accurately by Oliver J. in his judgment, and I will summarise them fairly briefly but I hope sufficiently for the purpose of this appeal. B In June 1968 the defendant was the freehold owner of some 51½ acres of land at Fareham in Hampshire. This land was ripe for building development. The defendant was then a subsidiary of a company known as Three Mile Developments Ltd. The plaintiff was anxious to acquire and develop the land. An interview took place on June 20, 1968, between one Duggan, a partner in the firm of Duggan, Turk & Co., as agent for the defendant, and one Crompton, the managing C director of the plaintiff. Mr. Duggan and Mr. Crompton came to terms there and then, and a letter was typed and signed by Mr. Crompton. I will read that letter in full:

"Dear Sirs, Re: Land west of Peak Lane, Fareham: approximately 51½ acres. We hereby confirm our agreement to purchase the whole of the above mentioned land in your ownership at the price of £500,000 D upon the following conditions:— 1. The purchase price to be phased as to £250,000 upon first completion, as to £125,000 12 months thereafter and as to the balance of £125,000 a further 12 months thereafter. 2. On the occasion of each completion a proportionate part of the land shall be released forthwith to us. 3. Upon your making a good and marketable title to the property. 4. Upon outline planning permission being granted for the whole of the property. 5. That a section E 37 agreement affecting the land shall be made at a density of not less than 12 units per acre and with a period of not more than seven years. 6. That detailed planning permission for the first approximate 50 units shall be granted. 7. That upon formal exchange of contracts we shall be let into possession of the land to enable us to commence such operations as we may think fit. 8. The fulfilment of conditions 2–7 F above shall be carried out in conjunction with the purchaser's architects who shall henceforth join in all negotiations and arrangements in connection therewith for the purpose of agreeing and approving the same on our behalf. 9. That the date of first completion shall be eight weeks from the fulfilment of the conditions 1–7 above. Will you please let us have an identical letter to this signed by your solicitor, Mr. David A. J. Duggan, as your authorised agent." G

Mr. Duggan indeed did sign a letter accepting those terms on June 20, 1968.

A number of matters are not in dispute. Mr. Crompton had authority to bind the plaintiff. Mr. Duggan had authority to bind the defendant. Both parties had a contractual intent. The reference to a proportionate part of the land in condition 2 refers to acreage and not to value. Conditions 3, 4, 5 and 6, which I think are the only true conditions H amongst the conditions so described in the letter, have all been fulfilled, the last of the fulfilments being that of condition 5. A section 37 agreement was signed with the county council on April 10, 1969.

The contention of the defendant is that condition 2 is uncertain in that the contract does not provide who is to have the power of selection of the proportionate part of land to be released.

Immediately after that exchange of letters, the plaintiff's solicitors registered an estate contract. Shortly afterwards, a company known as Town and Commercial Properties Ltd. took over the control of Three Mile Developments Ltd. and with it the control of the defendant which had been a subsidiary of Three Mile Developments Ltd. Three Mile Developments Ltd. had another subsidiary company which comes into this story known as Medina Estates Ltd. The control of Medina Estates Ltd. likewise passed to Town and Commercial Properties Ltd. About the same time Linklaters & Paines took over as solicitors for the defendant and also Medina Estates Ltd., and I think they also act for their parent company, Town and Commercial Properties Ltd.

There followed correspondence between Linklaters & Paines and Coffin, Mew & Clover for the plaintiff. That correspondence was in the first place concerned with the preparation of a formal contract pursuant to the provision contained in condition 7 of the letter of June 20. But it soon became apparent in the correspondence that Linklaters & Paines wanted to recast the terms contained in that letter, first by substituting Medina Estates Ltd. for the defendant as the vendor company, and also by converting the sale into a single one-phase completion instead of a completion in three phases. The plaintiff would not have objected to having Medina Estates Ltd. substituted as its vendor, but was not willing to accept the contract on the proposed new terms with a single completion. In the course of correspondence Linklaters & Paines advanced several untenable grounds for their contention that no contract had been made by the letters of June 1968 such as that one or other condition had not been fulfilled or that the letter must be treated as "subject to contract." I need not pursue those contentions. They did, however, take another and altogether more serious point at a later date, March 3, 1970, quite a long time afterwards, namely, that the contract purported to be made by the letters of June 1968 was too uncertain to be enforced.

In due course Linklaters & Paines tendered a draft contract on the proposed new terms. That was on June 26, 1969. Then, on July 4, Coffin, Mew & Clover replied refusing to accept a contract in those terms, and they concluded their letter with a paragraph in these terms:

> "My clients do not wish to be rigid about the personality of the actual vendor"—that refers to Medina Estates Ltd. instead of the defendant —"if for tax reasons your clients wish to reorganise the matter but, unless and until some other binding agreement is reached, my clients will insist on their contract with Vortex Properties Ltd."

From that position they did not resile.

On July 7, 1969, a writ was issued in an action intituled "1969 B. No. 4041," by which the plaintiff claimed specific performance of the agreement purported to have been constituted by the letters of June 1968, with damages in addition to specific performance. On July 31, 1969, the statement of claim in that action was delivered. I need not, I think, refer to that statement of claim. So far, no defence has been delivered. Between the date of the writ and the date of the statement of claim, namely, on July 24, 1969, the defendant conveyed the property to Medina Estates Ltd.

It is accepted by Mr. Balcombe on behalf of the defendant that that was a breach by the defendant of the contract constituted by the letters of June 1968, assuming that there was a binding contract. He says that the breach was only a technical one, bearing in mind that the defendant and Medina Estates Ltd. were both subsidiaries of a single company; but he accepts that it was a breach. At that stage the plaintiff could have joined

Medina Estates Ltd. as a defendant in the action and continued its claim A
for specific performance; but the plaintiff did not elect to take that course.

Shortly afterwards, on July 29, Linklaters & Paines submitted another draft contract, this time substantially in terms of the letters of June 1968, except that the vendor was Medina Estates Ltd. Further correspondence then ensued, the plaintiff through its solicitors at this stage raising a number of difficulties over the selection of the land to be comprised in the first phase. There was considerable delay, much of which I think it is right to B
say was occasioned by the plaintiff's solicitors, and at this stage Linklaters & Paines were pressing for the matter to be got on with.

Then came the next two critical letters in this action. Linklaters & Paines wrote to Coffin, Mew & Clover a letter dated June 5, 1970, in these terms:

> "Dear Sirs, Re: Bushwall v. Vortex. In a final effort to dispose of this C
> matter we are instructed to make the following open offer. Our clients are prepared to dispense with any formal contract and offer to convey the whole of the land in one conveyance for £500,000, completion to take place within a reasonable time, which we would suggest is two months from today's date. You have already satisfied yourselves as to our clients' title. May we please hear from you?" D

To that Coffin, Mew & Clover replied in a letter dated June 12, 1970:

> "Dear Sirs, Bushwall Properties Ltd. v. Vortex Properties Ltd. On behalf of our clients we accept the offer by your clients contained in your letter dated June 5, 1970, to convey the whole of the land in one conveyance for £500,000, completion to take place within a reasonable time. You are in error, however, in supposing that we have satisfied E
> ourselves as to your clients' title. We enclose a list of the documents you have supplied to us relating thereto and request that you complete the abstract as soon as possible. We will contact you in due course with regard to your suggestion as to a date for completion, which must anyway depend on how soon you deduce your clients' title."

Certain further correspondence followed, to which I will refer at a later F
stage. The purchase was in fact completed by a conveyance from Medina Estates Ltd. to the plaintiff on November 27, 1970. Subsequently, the plaintiff commenced a second action against the defendant by a writ dated May 14, 1971. That action is intituled "1971 B. No. 2257." The claim is for damages for breach of the contract made by the letters of June 1968, the breach asserted being the defendant's selling and conveying the land to G
Medina Estates Ltd. Again there was a statement of claim. Again I do not think the statement of claim takes the matter any further. The statement of claim was, however, amended and by the amended statement of claim particulars of damage are given. Those should be looked at, but I will not read them. They refer to mitigation of damages. There was a defence and amended defence to that action. The critical paragraphs in the amended defence run as follows: H

> "7. The writ in action 1969 B. No. 4041 was issued on July 7, 1969. Both prior to and after the said date the defendant through its solicitors asserted and continued to assert that the said letters of July 20, 1968, did not constitute a binding contract between the parties. The plaintiff asserted the contrary. By a letter dated June 5, 1970, to the plaintiff's solicitors the defendant finally offered to settle the action 1969 B. No. 4041 on terms that the whole of the land was conveyed for £500,000,

A completion to take place within a reasonable time. By a letter dated June 12, 1970, the plaintiff's solicitors accepted the said offer of settlement. The defendant has conveyed the land as aforesaid. 8. By reason of the matters pleaded in paragraph 7 hereof action 1969 B. No. 4041 was settled between the parties on the terms as aforesaid. In the premises the plaintiff is not entitled to continue with that action or with action 1971 B. No. 2257. . . ."

B

In that state of affairs, the action came before Oliver J. in late 1974. Evidence was given on both sides; but in the event no question of fact now arises and both parties I think are content to accept the judge's full and clear statement of the facts. The judge dealt with the two issues in the reverse order, for no doubt good reasons. I think, however, it will be convenient to deal with the two issues in the chronological order in which C I have stated them. The issues were argued in that order by counsel before us.

The first issue is whether the contract purported to be made by the letters exchanged in June 1968 fails by reason of uncertainty, the uncertainty going to the power of selection of the land to be allocated upon each phase. The general approach of the court to that question is D not in dispute. The court will uphold a contract if it is possible to do so. On the other hand, as Maugham L.J. said in *Foley* v. *Classique Coaches Ltd.* [1934] 2 K.B. 1, 13:

> "It is indisputable that unless all the material terms of the contract are agreed there is no binding obligation. An agreement to agree in the future is not a contract; nor is there a contract if a material term E is neither settled nor implied by law and the document contains no machinery for ascertaining it."

I must now read that part of the judgment in which the judge dealt with that matter. He first of all disposes of a number of points concerning uncertainty which are not now in issue and goes on [1975] 1 W.L.R. 1649, 1656–1657:

> F "As to the selection of the area to be conveyed, I feel no particular difficulty, nor do I think that it is necessary to imply any term beyond what is implied into an agreement for sale of land by law or the custom of conveyancers in any event. From the date of the contract the vendor is a qualified trustee of the whole of the lands of the purchaser, and the purchaser, subject to paying the purchase money, G is the owner in equity. A recent example of the operation of this is to be found in the decision of Walton J. in *Lake* v. *Bayliss* [1974] 1 W.L.R. 1073 to which Mr. Burton has referred me previously. In the instant case it was an express condition of the contract that the purchaser was to be put into possession of the whole of the land on exchange of formal contracts. Further, the preparation of the conveyance of the land is, in all contracts for sale of land, in the absence H of an express stipulation to the contrary, a duty to be assumed by the purchaser. He can if he wishes insist upon the conveyance to a nominee, and he may, where the nature of the land renders it desirable, insist, within limits, upon taking separate conveyances of different parts and upon apportioning the purchase money between them: see *Dart on Vendor and Purchaser*, 8th ed. (1929), vol. 1, p. 461. He cannot of course insist upon a conveyance until he pays the purchase money, unless the contract otherwise specifies, but in the instant

case the contract does so specify. It provides that an area shall be released proportionate to the amount of purchase price paid, and it seems to me implicit in the relationship arising between vendor and purchaser on a contract of sale that where there is a provision in these terms, with no reservation to the vendor of any right to select the area and no other machinery provided for determining it, that the purchaser, as the owner in equity, has the right to select the land to be included in the draft conveyance which he sends to the vendor for approval, subject only to the overriding limitation that it must not exceed a proportionate part. Mr. Barnes points to the hardship of this from the vendor's point of view, and he takes the perhaps rather fanciful case of a purchaser directing conveyance of innumerable small lots in various parts of the estate. I am not impressed by this. The underlying assumption in all commercial contracts is that the parties are going to behave as reasonable men of business. In any event, if the vendor wishes to protect himself from such risks, then he must stipulate some machinery for selection. I did ask Mr. Barnes whether, if these clauses had been contained in an option conferred by a will, the court could be forced to hold the provision void. He did not feel able so to contend and he referred me to the decision of Romer J. in *Asten* v. *Asten* [1894] 3 Ch. 260, but he submitted that whilst the giving of a right of selection to a legatee is one thing—for, after all, one is there looking only for a unilateral intention; that of the testator —the same cannot be applied to a bilateral transaction where one is seeking to find the common intention. To an extent this is no doubt true, but one has, of course, to look for that common intention against the background of the legal rights and duties which are implicit in the relationship created by the particular type of transaction into which the parties have entered. Certainly the passage which I have quoted from the judgment of Megarry J. in *Brown* v. *Gould* [1972] Ch. 53, 56, indicates that the approach of the courts to problems of uncertainty is the same regardless of the type of document under consideration. I am therefore unimpressed by the points taken on the pleadings. The point of uncertainty, which is one of law, emerged with clarity only upon the service of the particulars of the defence. I suppose that it would technically have been possible then to have served a reply, but it seems to me unnecessary.

"The conclusion at which I arrive derives not from an implied term such as is required to give business efficacy to the contract, but from the marrying of the provisions of clauses 1 and 2 with the rights and duties arising as a matter of law from the contract for the sale and purchase of land."

It will be observed that the judge rests his judgment on the general law, including the terms to be implied under the general law into an agreement for sale of land. He expressly disclaims the implication of any term into the express contract purported to have been made by the parties.

Mr. Dillon, for the plaintiff, likewise expressly disclaimed the implication of a term. The way he put it was: "I rely on the effect of the general law as emphasised and underlined by the terms of the particular contract." That, I think, really means the general law as applied to the express terms of the particular contract. He too disclaimed any implication of a term into the contract on what may be called in shorthand "the officious bystander principle." Having regard to that disclaimer, it is unnecessary

A to express any view as to whether a term as to selection could be implied from the conditions contained in the letter, in particular from conditions 2 and 7 read together.

Leaving aside the implication of a term, I see no ground upon which, under the general law as applied to contracts of the sale of land, where an intending vendor and an intending purchaser enter into a binding contract for sale with completion in phases, the power of selection as to
B what part of the land is to be included in each phase must be regarded as vested in the purchaser. It will be observed that this is no mere matter of machinery. Should the power of selection be vested in the purchaser, the vendor might be severely prejudiced by the manner in which that power is exercised. The point of course would arise if the purchaser, having completed the first phase, were then to make default in the next phase,
C leaving part but not the whole of the land with the vendor, the latter having over it the ordinary rights of a vendor where the purchaser has failed to complete. It is possible that in such circumstances the land left with the vendor might not be appropriate for advantageous development, and one can think of extreme instances such as a landlocked corner of land or pieces of land separated by the part taken by the purchaser. It seems to me that this is a point of substance and not a mere matter of
D machinery. It represents an element in a contract which if left uncertain would render the contract as a whole uncertain and for that reason unenforceable.

The suggestion was made, but not pursued, that the court in such circumstances might leave it to a third party to determine which land should be selected at each phase. The court might, for instance, direct
E an inquiry in chambers. The court would no doubt do that if one were concerned with a mere matter of machinery. For instance, if the contract was for the sale of land at the market price but the parties were unable to agree upon the market price and there was no provision in the contract for reference to some outside party, then I think the court might well direct an inquiry in chambers. Here, however, this is not a mere matter of machinery, and I do not think that course would be open to the court.
F The judge and also Mr. Dillon and Mr. Burton on the present appeal based their argument on the well-recognised principle that the vendor under a contract of which specific performance would be granted is a trustee (although a qualified trustee having regard to his rights with regard to unpaid purchase money) of the land for the purchaser. That is established beyond all question. We were referred to cases in which it
G was held that the vendor as such trustee is bound to protect the purchaser's interests and to comply with the purchaser's wishes in such matters as the grant of a new lease: see, for instance, *Abdulla* v. *Shah* [1959] A.C. 124, in the Privy Council, for a recent instance. It seems to me, however, that this argument begs the question. It proceeds upon the assumption that there is a binding and enforceable contract and affords no help in deciding whether the uncertainty as to selection precludes the creation
H of a binding and enforceable contract.

The same observation applies to the argument advanced by Mr. Burton to the effect that under a contract for sale of land it is for the purchaser to submit and decide on the form of the conveyance or, if he is so minded, a number of conveyances of separate parts of the land. That argument presupposes that there is indeed a binding and enforceable contract. No authorities have been cited to us which bear on the question of whether uncertainty as to the power of selection prevents the formation of a contract.

For the reasons which I have given, I conclude that the contract A
purported to be made by the letters of June 1968 was indeed unenforceable by reason of uncertainty; in other words, it was not an effective contract.

I turn now to the other point, namely, the effect of the letters exchanged in July 1970. Again, I think, in deference to the judge and to the arguments of counsel, I should read the part of his judgment in which he sets out his reasons on this issue. He says: B

"I find difficulty in accepting these submissions. If I am to construe this offer according to its terms, it is simply an offer by Medina Estates Ltd. to sell the land in respect of which it is, at the moment, under no direct contractual obligation to the plaintiff, for a lump sum of £500,000 payable in one sum on completion. No additional consideration is referred to, nor even suggested, in the letter. No reference is made to a surrender of the plaintiff's outstanding rights C
under the original contract with the defendant. No reference is made to the plaintiff's outstanding claim for costs in the proceedings. No reference is made to the plaintiff's obligation to discontinue or otherwise dispose of the action and to cancel the registered land charges. Furthermore there is no clear indication of the person on whose behalf the offer is being advanced. The expression 'our clients' D
had been used by Linklaters & Paines in the past correspondence sometimes to refer to Medina Estates Ltd. who, of course, was not a party to the action. The writer's 'clients' were prepared to dispense with any formal contract, but the only formal contract discussed between the parties since July 1968 was a contract between Medina Estates Ltd. and the plaintiff. 'You have,' says the letter, 'already satisfied yourself as to our clients' title.' But the only clients who E
had any title were Medina Estates Ltd. So that on any analysis the letter was written on behalf of Medina and the only offer being advanced was an offer by Medina. If then it is to be said that the letter was also written on behalf of the defendant and contained an offer by that company, one is left wondering what consideration the defendant was providing for the obligation which it is said the F
plaintiff was being invited to assume of foregoing its rights under the original contract and in the pending action and where the defendant's offer is to be found. On the face of it, the opening words of the letter do not form part of the offer at all; they merely indicate the writer's motive in writing the letter: up to date his clients had been prepared to entertain various proposals for making the conveyance, but this was to be their last work on the subject. I do not G
think that a contract to compromise a pending action can be inferred from a vague and general expression, such as a desire to dispose of the matter, the more so when such desire itself forms no part of the terms offered and such terms themselves contain no reference at all, even inferentially, to any such compromise.

"The suggestion now made is that, in addition to the consideration H
payable to Medina for the land, the plaintiff was being asked to agree to the provision of an additional consideration for the defendant in the form of a release of all rights under the subsisting agreements and all claims in the pending action to which no defence had been served. It is, as it seems to me, making these introductory words, 'In a final effort to dispose of the matter,' perform a heavier duty than they will bear to attribute to them the force which is so suggested.

It is not a meaning which, in my judgment, a reasonable reader would be likely to attribute to them in the circumstances in which the letter was received. The plaintiff had, after a good many difficulties, executed its part of the contract with Medina and had put forward suggestions for division, after threats had been made to strike out the proceedings. It appeared on the face of it that Medina were being as obstructive as possible in agreeing the areas to be transferred on the completion date, whether or not such appearance arose from a misunderstanding. There then arrives a letter from Medina's solicitors, headed in the matter of the action, it is true, and propounding what is called an 'open offer,' that is to say one which is intended to be admissible in evidence on the hearing of the action, and this is stated in effect to be Medina's last word. The motive for writing the letter is stated to be 'a final effort to dispose of this matter.' There has been no previous effort to settle the action, so that the reference to a 'final effort' is hardly appropriate, if that is the matter referred to. But there had been many efforts to dispose of the matter of the phased completions, and that was the matter which up to that point had been troubling the parties, which Mr. Crompton in his letter of May 12, 1970, had invited Mr. Hines"—he is the managing director of Town and Commercial Properties Ltd.—"to consider and on which Linklaters & Paines had stated in their letter of May 22 that they were seeking their clients' instructions. Whilst therefore it might seem at first curious that in their next letter they adopt a new title by referring to 'Bushwall v. Vortex,' instead of, as heretofore, 'Land west of Peak Lane, Fareham,' the letter itself contains a clue to this. It is an open offer, that is to say one which it is intended to refer to in the action. In the light of what had gone before, I do not read 'this matter' as being more than 'the matter which has been troubling us both for the past few months.' The inference in my view is that here is a reasonable proposal being made for getting rid of the problem of division and giving the plaintiff the land which it claims and thus mitigating its damages and that, if this is refused, such refusal will be referred to by the defendant in the action in support of a suggestion that the plaintiff was not behaving reasonably. As Mr. Burton has pointed out, a party to litigation concerning a commercial bargain is obliged to mitigate his damage, if reasonably possible, and such mitigation may in appropriate circumstances include the acceptance of a new offer made by the party in default, as it did in *Payzu Ltd.* v. *Saunders* [1919] 2 K.B. 581. I do not consider that in these circumstances a letter couched in these terms can legitimately be construed as an unequivocal offer to give the plaintiffs a conveyance for some additional consideration on their part by way of settlement of the action which is nowhere expressed."

I regret that on this issue likewise I take a different view from that of the judge. The circumstances prevailing at the date of the letters of July 1970 were these. In June 1968 the defendant and the plaintiff or their representatives had exchanged letters which were intended to be contractual. The defendant's solicitors were denying that any binding contract had been made. The plaintiff had issued a writ and delivered a statement of claim seeking specific performance, the title of that action being of course "Bushwall v. Vortex." Linklaters & Paines were the solicitors to the defendant in the action and were undoubtedly in the present context solicitors both for the defendant and for Medina Estates Ltd. Both sides A were anxious to clinch the deal; and indeed the plaintiff was willing to accept Medina Estates Ltd. as its vendor, but negotiations had broken down.

Then one comes to look at the actual terms of the letter of June 5, 1970. The letter is headed "Bushwall v. Vortex," and even more explicitly the reply of June 12 is headed "Bushwall Properties Ltd. v. Vortex Properties Ltd." That heading is a plain reference to the first action which was then B on foot. Then the letter begins: "In a final effort to dispose of this matter." On the natural meaning of those words, "this matter" is the action of Bushwall v. Vortex. Then they say: "we are instructed to make the following open offer." Then they go on to make the proposal for the conveyance by Medina Estates Ltd. to the plaintiff with a single completion at the same price. It seems to me that on the natural meaning of that C letter it is a letter written by Linklaters & Paines as solicitors for the defendant and for Medina Estates Ltd. containing an offer on behalf of both those companies. The offer is this: "As regards Vortex, we will settle the action to which Vortex is currently the defendant, though Medina could certainly have been joined as an additional defendant. As regards Medina, we offer to convey with a single completion at £500,000." That seems to me the natural meaning of that letter, and I so construe it. The D acceptance was in the terms of the letter. For myself, I find it impossible to construe the letter of June 5 as referring only to the conveyance by Medina Estates Ltd. and not having any but an indirect reference to the action. I say "indirect reference" because it is suggested that it might have had relevance to the action in the sense that the letter could be read in open court and might go to the issue of mitigation of damages. I regard it as an E offer to settle all matters in dispute between the three companies once and for all.

It is not suggested that the expression "within a reasonable time" is too uncertain for the letters to constitute a binding agreement. What follows in the letter of June 5 is the suggestion that a reasonable time would be two months. Then in the letter of June 12 the plaintiff's solicitors repeat the same expression, "within a reasonable time," but make other suggestions F as to what would be a reasonable time. There is, I think, nothing in that which deprives the two letters of certainty. To take an instance similar to one which I gave earlier in this judgment, if there had been an offer to sell at market price, followed by a suggestion "We think the market price is £10,000," and the reply had been an agreement to purchase at market price, followed by a statement "We think the market price is £12,000," G that would certainly not have prevented the letters constituting a binding contract.

It was not, I think, suggested that the agreement could not be binding on the plaintiff as against the defendant on the ground that there was no consideration moving to the plaintiff. That was plainly not so. The compromise of the action, with the removal of a possible liability for costs, is H of itself clearly a good consideration. It was I think suggested that such an agreement would be so unfavourable to the plaintiff that the plaintiff would be unlikely to make it. But I do not think that is by any means clear. The action would not necessarily succeed, nor would the damages necessarily be substantial.

Only one further point remains. There took place certain subsequent correspondence between the solicitors, and I will refer to three letters in

A that subsequent correspondence. The correspondence runs from a letter dated June 16, 1970, from Linklaters & Paines to Coffin, Mew & Clover. I read these shortly. They have a certain significance upon an argument which is adduced. Linklaters & Paines say:

> "We are in receipt of your letter of June 12 and would state that the abstract of title which was prepared a little while ago is being rechecked, and we should be in a position to forward this to you not
> B later than Friday, June 19. We shall therefore require completion to take place within two months . . ."

Then, on June 18, 1970: ". . . we enclose the abstract of title . . . we expect to hear from you fairly soon . . ." There was an acknowledgment. On July 2 there were requisitions; on July 3 the registration of a land
C charge; then on July 13 requisitions and the land charge. July 14, 16 and 17 are not, I think, material. Then on July 23, 1970, Coffin, Mew & Clover write: "Our clients have now given us their instructions concerning the reasonable date for completion of their purchase of the . . . land." The fourth paragraph is important:

> "Finally, we think it necessary to draw your attention to the damage suffered by our clients by virtue of the conveyance of the land by
> D Vortex Properties Ltd. to Medina Estates Ltd. and the creation of the present contract in addition to the other registered contract."

So there is a plain affirmation by Coffin, Mew & Clover that the plaintiff has suffered damage by virtue of the conveyance by the defendant to Medina Estates Ltd., and I think that clearly imports the statement that they still have a claim in damages.

E The next few letters are not material; but on August 6 Linklaters & Paines write, dealing with other matters concerning completion and concluding:

> ". . . our clients for record purposes categorically repudiate your clients' claim that damage has been suffered by your clients by virtue of the conveyance from Vortex Properties Ltd. to Medina Estates
> F Ltd."

The significance of that is that Linklaters & Paines deny that damage has been suffered, but do not set up the answer that any claim for damage has been disposed of by the earlier letters.

Mr. Dillon took the point that where a contract is alleged to have been constituted by correspondence it is legitimate to look at the whole
G correspondence including subsequent letters, in order to determine whether by these letters alleged to constitute the contract the parties really intended at that stage to make themselves contractually liable. That principle is well established: see *Hussey* v. *Horne-Payne* (1879) 4 App.Cas. 311. So, Mr. Dillon says, when you read all of those letters up to and including the letter of August 6, then the proper conclusion is that the two letters
H of June 5 and 12 should not be held to be contractual in intention. I find it impossible to accept that contention. It seems to me that upon a proper reading of the two letters, whatever their construction may be, it is perfectly clear that by the letter of June 5 Linklaters & Paines were making an offer intended to be rendered contractual by acceptance, and that by the letter of June 12 Coffin, Mew & Clover intended to make that offer contractual by their acceptance.

Once it is established that a contract has been concluded at any stage, then subsequent matters cannot be taken into account in the construction of the letters. That applies in particular to anything which may have been said in the subsequent correspondence: see, for instance, the recent affirmation of that principle in *James Miller & Partners Ltd.* v. *Whitworth Street Estates (Manchester) Ltd.* [1970] A.C. 583. I will cite a single sentence. All their Lordships agreed. Lord Reid said, at p. 603: A

> "I must say that I had thought that it is now well settled that it is not legitimate to use as an aid in the construction of the contract anything which the parties said or did after it was made." B

The same principle was affirmed by the House of Lords in *Wickman Machine Tool Sales Ltd.* v. *L. Schuler A.G.* [1974] A.C. 235. I will only add this. Even if one could take the subsequent letters into account upon the construction of the earlier letters, I think that they go only a little way to supporting the construction of the earlier letters put upon them by the judge and Mr. Dillon. C

I conclude then that on both the two issues the appeal should be allowed. It would have been sufficient to dispose of the appeal to determine on the first issue that there was no binding contract. I have, however, felt it right to deal fully with the second issue. If I had reached a different conclusion I would then have had to consider the issue of the measure of damages and mitigation. That issue, however, does not arise, and I do not think it is necessary to express a view upon it. D

I would allow this appeal.

ORR L.J. I agree with the judgment delivered by Sir John Pennycuick; and, for the reasons given by him, I too would allow the appeal. E

BUCKLEY L.J. I also agree with the judgment which has been delivered, and I only add a few short observations out of courtesy to the judge from whom we are differing.

On the first subject matter discussed by Sir John Pennycuick in his judgment, relating to the enforceability of the contract alleged to have been made by the letters of June 1968, the judge twice in the course of the passage read by Sir John Pennycuick affirmed that he was not relying upon any implied term, and that course has been followed also by the plaintiff's counsel in this court. What is relied upon is the fiduciary obligation which arises between the vendor and purchaser of land when a contract of sale is entered into between them which, it is said, in the circumstances of this case has the effect of putting the purchaser into the position of being able to dictate what parcels shall be conveyed to him upon each of the three successive completions contemplated by the contract. That fiduciary relationship is very clearly set out and dealt with in *Megarry and Wade, The Law of Real Property*, 3rd ed. (1966), pp. 582–584. It is there stated with much more elaboration than I propose to adopt that if a purchaser is potentially entitled to specific performance, he obtains an immediate equitable interest in the property contracted to be sold; the contract creates a relationship of trustee and beneficiary, the vendor being said to be trustee for the purchaser and the purchaser to be the beneficial owner of the land. But the authors then go on to point out that the vendor's trusteeship is of a peculiar kind because he has interests of his own in the land as an unpaid vendor under an uncompleted contract for sale, and finally they point out that all these consequences flow from the fact that the contract is a specifically enforceable one, equity F G H proceeding upon the footing that that which ought to be done has been done or will be done when the due time for it to be done arrives. Those principles, it seems to me, cannot operate where there is not a specifically enforceable contract.

The first question therefore must be whether the contract contained in the letters of June 1968 is on the face of it a specifically enforceable contract, which involves consideration of the question whether the parties can be seen to have agreed all the essential terms of the bargain. I do not read the terms of the letter again, but it will be remembered that it provides for payment of the purchase price by three instalments at yearly intervals, and that on the occasion of each payment of an instalment there shall be a conveyance of a proportionate part of the land sold. No machinery is expressly provided for identifying the part of the land to be conveyed on any of those three completions. I fully accept that the court should be reluctant to hold any contract void for uncertainty if that consequence can be avoided; but, on the other hand, it is not the function of the court to make or to perfect contracts entered into between members of the public. In the present case, the contract does not provide any means of ascertaining with certainty what land should be conveyed on any of the three occasions when a partial completion is to be carried out; and, for reasons that have already been indicated by Sir John Pennycuick, I agree that that is an important term of this contract, for the interests of the vendor are liable to be very substantially affected by the choice of the parcels to be conveyed. The contract (so to call it) itself does not provide any machinery for ascertaining the answer to that question, from which, in my judgment, it must follow that this contract is not one of which the court would decree specific performance. If the contract is not one of which the court would decree specific performance, the principles of law relied upon for supplying the defect in the contract cannot apply to the case, and so it is impossible by that means to arrive at the conclusion that the purchaser ought to be regarded as the person having the power to decree what parcels should be included upon each of the occasions when completions are to take place. For that reason, it seems to me to be unavoidable that one must conclude that this is not a contract capable of being specifically performed and is not an enforceable contract.

On the second point, which turns upon the meaning and effect of the letters of June 1970 which are relied upon for saying that there was a settlement of all matters in dispute between the plaintiff and the defendant and Medina Estates Ltd. at that stage, Mr. Dillon sought to rely upon subsequent letters, to which Sir John Pennycuick has referred in his judgment, for showing that there was not any concluded agreement in the two letters of June 5 and 12, 1970. Those subsequent letters all relate to conveyancing matters concerned with the completion of the sale by Medina to the plaintiff, more particularly the time when that transaction should be completed.

Now, it is to be observed that in the letter of June 5, 1970, what is called an "open offer" is made to dispense with a formal contract and "to convey the whole of the land in one conveyance for £500,000, completion to take place within a reasonable time." As I read the letter, that is the offer, and it is an offer made in order finally to dispose of whatever is described as "this matter." The writer then goes on to say: "We would suggest that two months from today's date would be a reasonable time." The two months to completion is not, as I read the letter, part of the offer that is made, but is merely a comment upon the offer and

an expression of the writer's opinion as to how the offer will operate. A
The offer is an offer made for the purpose of disposing of "this matter." As Sir John Pennycuick has pointed out, the letter is given a subject heading "Bushwall v. Vortex," and I can feel no doubt whatever that "this matter" means the first action between the plaintiff and the defendant which was then pending and, of course, the dispute which underlay that action.

As I construe this letter, contrary to the view taken by the judge, this B
was an offer made for the purpose of disposing of the action and if the offer was accepted, all those matters in dispute in the action and in the dispute which underlay the action were to be treated as disposed of. The offer was accepted in unequivocal terms by the letter of June 12, 1970. In fact, the writer restates the nature of the offer:

> "We accept the offer by your clients contained in your letter dated C
> June 5, 1970, to convey the whole of the land in one conveyance for £500,000, completion to take place within a reasonable time."

That is the offer which they are accepting. It was the offer which was made. Nothing is said there about the two months' period for completion, or anything of that kind. There is a comment in the final paragraph of that letter in which Coffin, Mew & Clover say: D

> "We will contact you in due course with regard to your suggestion as to a date for completion, which must anyway depend on how soon you deduce your clients' title."

In my opinion, those letters contain what one might call a clear offer and a clear acceptance. It is clear what one party is offering, and it is clear that the other party is accepting what is offered; and what is con- E
tained in the later letters does not, in my judgment, in any way conflict with the view that a concluded bargain was then reached. For the reasons I have endeavoured to express shortly, I cannot regard the reference in the letter of June 5 to "a final effort to dispose of this matter" as a mere recital of the motive for making the offer. It is, in my judgment, part and parcel of the offer. For these reasons, I also reach the conclusion F
that on June 12, 1970, the parties did arrive at a concluded contract to dispose of all matters in dispute in the first action and underlying that action upon the terms there set out.

For these reasons, as well as for those more elaborately developed by Sir John Pennycuick in his judgment, I agree that this appeal should succeed.

Appeal allowed with costs. G
Leave to appeal refused.

Solicitors: *Linklaters & Paines; Blyth, Dutton, Robins, Hay.*

C. N.

H

A [CHANCERY DIVISION]

* LARTER (INSPECTOR OF TAXES) v. SKONE JAMES

1976 Feb. 26 Walton J.

Revenue—Capital gains tax—Time limit for making assessment—
Deemed disposal of assets " on the death "—Assessment made
B *on executor after expiration of three-year period—Whether*
disposal to be deemed to take place before death—Whether
assessment made within appropriate time limit—Finance Act
1965 (*c.* 25), *s.* 24 (1)—*Taxes Management Act* 1970 (*c.* 9),
ss. 34 (1), 40 (1)

The taxpayer was appointed an executor of the will of
his mother who died in August 1968. Chargeable gains on
C her assets accruing at her death amounted to £12,701. In
April 1974 the taxpayer, as executor, was assessed to capital
gains tax for the year 1968–69 in respect of those gains. He
appealed to the general commissioners contending that the
assessment was out of time as section 40 (1) of the Taxes
Management Act 1970 [1] enacted that the time limit for making
an assessment was the end of the third year following the year
of assessment in which the death occurred because section
D 24 (1) of the Finance Act 1965 [2] deemed the assets to have
been disposed of before the death of the testator. The
commissioners allowed the appeal rejecting the contention of
the inspector of taxes that a six-year time limit was applicable
by virtue of section 34 (1) of the Taxes Management Act 1970.[3]

On the Crown's appeal:—

Held, allowing the appeal, that although the words " on
the death " might, according to context, refer to before, simul-
E taneously with, or after, the death, where, as in section 24 (1)
of the Finance Act 1965, it was the actual death that produced
the deemed disposition, the phrase must refer to the moment
immediately after the death so that the three-year limitation
imposed by section 40 (1) of the Taxes Management Act 1970
did not apply and accordingly the assessment was within the
appropriate time limit (post, pp. 609F–G, 610A–B, 613C–D).

F The following cases are referred to in the judgment:

Inland Revenue Commissioners v. *Graham's Trustees*, 1971 S.L.T. 46, H.L.(Sc.).
Paynter v. *James* (1867) L.R. 2 C.P. 348.
Reg. v. *Arkwright* (1848) 12 Q.B. 960.

The following additional cases were cited in argument:

G *Magan, In re* (*Note*) [1922] 2 I.R. 208.
Smith, decd., In re [1951] Ch. 360; [1951] 1 All E.R. 146.

CASE STATED by the Commissioners for the General Purposes of the Income Tax.

The taxpayer, Edmund Purcell Skone James, was appointed an executor

H

[Reported by MRS. HARRIET DUTTON, Barrister-at-Law]

[1] Taxes Management Act 1970, s. 40 (1): see post, p. 608H.
[2] Finance Act 1965, s. 24 (1): see post, p. 608F–G.
[3] Taxes Management Act 1970, s. 34: " (1) Subject to the following provisions of this Act, and to any other provisions of the Taxes Acts allowing a longer period in any particular class of case, an assessment to tax may be made at any time not later than six years after the end of the chargeable period to which the assessment relates."

and trustee of the will of his mother, Mrs. Kate Eve Skone James, who A died on August 20, 1968. Chargeable gains accruing in consequence of the deemed disposal of her assets on her death amounted to £12,701. The taxpayer appealed against an assessment made on him as executor to capital gains tax in respect of those gains which was dated April 16, 1974, contending that the assessment was made out of time. The general commissioners allowed his appeal and discharged the assessment. B

The Crown appealed.

The facts are set out in the judgment.

Brian Davenport for the Crown.

David Braham for the taxpayer.

WALTON J. This is an appeal by way of case stated from the general C commissioners for the division of Bromley, in the county of Kent. Mrs. Kate Eve Skone James, by clause 1 of her will dated August 23, 1966, appointed the taxpayer, Mr. Edmund Purcell Skone James, and Mr. R. C. Beecher Bryant to be the executors and trustees of her will; and she died on August 20, 1968. The chargeable gains which accrued in consequence of the disposal of all her assets, which was deemed to have been made D by section 24 of the Finance Act 1965 consequent upon her death, amounted to the sum of £12,701. No other chargeable gains accrued to her in the year of assessment in which she died, namely, 1968–69.

On March 6, 1969, probate of her will was granted out of the Principal Probate Registry to the executors therein named. On April 16, 1974 (that is, more than three years after the termination of the year of assessment in which she died), the inspector of taxes raised an assessment to capital E gains tax for that very year of assessment, 1968–69, on the taxpayer as her executor, in that sum of £12,701. The short but extremely difficult question which arises is whether that assessment was in time or was not in time, the two possible periods being three years and six years respectively.

At the end of the day the matter depends upon the true construction of two sections of revenue acts. The first one is section 24 (1) of the Finance F Act 1965, which provides as follows:

> "On the death of an individual all the assets of which he was competent to dispose shall for the purposes of this Part of this Act"— and, pausing there, the Finance Act 1965 was the one which introduced capital gains tax, and "this Part of this Act," is the Part of the Act dealing with capital gains tax—"be deemed to be disposed of by him G at the date of death, and acquired by the personal representatives or other person on whom they devolve, for a consideration equal to their market value at that date."

The other provision to which I have to refer is section 40 (1) of the Taxes Management Act 1970:

> "For the purpose of the charge of tax on the executors or admin- H istrators of a deceased person in respect of the income, or chargeable gains, which arose or accrued to him before his death, the time allowed by section 34, 35 or 36 above shall in no case extend beyond the end of the third year next following the year of assessment in which the deceased died."

Mr. Davenport submitted that there is an extraordinarily short answer to the question "what is the length of the period?" because section 24,

A whatever its true interpretation, says that it takes effect "on the death" and section 40 (1) deals with chargeable gains which arose or accrued to the deceased "before his death." He said that, whatever the comparison of those periods may yield, "before his death" must be prior to "on the death," and that therefore I do not really have to go beyond those two sections to decide that section 40 (1) is inapplicable. I see the force of that, but I should very much hate to decide a case of this nature merely
B on that comparatively narrow ground.

The general commissioners upheld the contention of the taxpayer that section 24 of the Act was looking to a period which was, as it were, the instant before death. The contentions, which are recited in the case, are: "Section 24 of the Finance Act 1965 provided that 'on the death of an individual' the relevant assets were 'deemed to be disposed of by him'"
C —those being the exact words of the subsection—"which, on a literal construction means before his death"; there is nothing else in the Acts which invalidates that construction; and, therefore, in section 24 one is dealing with an instant before the death. That, I think, was basically the reasoning which was adopted by the commissioners themselves.

They said in their case that they "observed that section 24 (1) of the
D Finance Act 1965 did not deem the assets to be disposed of by the individual to his personal representatives." That, I suppose, up to a point, is true, because all it says is "shall . . . be deemed to be disposed of by him at the date of death, and acquired by the personal representatives." They go on to say: "We concluded, therefore, that for the purposes of the assessment under appeal the deemed disposal and the deemed acquisition were not coincident." Mr. Braham, arguing for the taxpayer,
E has said that that cannot be upheld as it stands, but that if one adds the word "necessarily" before the word "coincident" then it can be upheld and it is right. They then went on to say:

> "It seemed to us that deeming the disposal to be by the individual postulated her personal closing of her final capital gains account, which indicated accord between the intention of the legislature and the literal
> F construction of the section. We therefore concluded that the assessment had been made out of time and accordingly we discharged it."

There is, I think, no doubt at all that such words as "on the death" or "at the date of the death" may, according to the context, mean either before the death, or simultaneously with the death, or immediately after the death; and for that proposition Mr. Braham cited to me *Reg.* v. *Arkwright*
G (1848) 12 Q.B. 960 and *Paynter* v. *James* (1867) L.R. 2 C.P. 348. I entirely accept that that is in fact the law. There is no one meaning which can ever be postulated as being the only true and proper meaning of the phrase "on the death." But, in the context of section 24 (1), capital gains tax is used in part as a mutation duty; that is to say, a duty exigible upon the change of ownership, in this case on death. With regard to that
H sort of duty, Lord Donovan, in *Inland Revenue Commissioners* v. *Graham's Trustees*, 1971 S.L.T. 46, a case from Scotland under the provisions of the Finance Act 1894, said, at p. 52:

> "The argument was that the farm passed under section 1 of the Finance Act 1894, and that, in order to ascertain its value for the purposes of estate duty, section 7 (5), upon its true construction, required that the valuer must look at the property as though the deceased was still alive though no doubt on the point of death."

That is precisely, mutatis mutandis, what Mr. Braham, for the taxpayer, has urged me to do with section 24 (1): to look at it as if, the moment before the death, the deceased disposed of his assets. Lord Donovan went on: "As applied to a mutation duty such as estate duty which is intended as a tax to be levied upon a change of ownership, this contention at least has the merit of novelty." Having regard to the contention having been made in that case, I cannot say that Mr. Braham's contention has the merit of novelty, but in my judgment it is unsound. One is here looking at death as producing a particular result, namely, a deemed disposition and a deemed acquisition. Under those circumstances it appears to me to follow as night follows day that death must, in contemplation of law, precede the disposition and acquisition. It is only in that way, I think, that one can make reasonable sense of the subsection.

It was argued by Mr. Braham that there could very easily here be a gap, as it were, between the disposition by the deceased and the acquisition by her personal representatives: of course, she would have no personal representatives until she was dead, nor would the assets devolve on any other person unless and until she had died, so a gap between the disposition and the acquisition is essential to his argument. He said that that is highlighted by the fact that the word "immediately" is not in the subsection. For example, one finds the word "immediately" in section 25 (3) and (4), and in section 23 (4). It seems to me, however, that the reason why the word "immediately" is not in section 24 (1) is that quite clearly the draftsman envisaged that the disposition and the acquisition were but different sides of the same coin; there is not intended to be any gap whatsoever.

Of course, the reason why one has the word "immediately" in the subsections to which Mr. Braham has referred me is because there you are dealing with something utterly notional; for example, in section 25 (3), the disposition of assets by a trustee and his re-acquisition of them in his capacity as a trustee. If one merely put that in, that being so completely notional, one might very well wonder, since there is the same hand to give and the same hand to acquire, whether it was immediate, whether it could be left outstanding or what one was to assume about it at all. But where, as in section 24 (1), the assets are deemed to be disposed of and acquired, the deeming of the disposal and the deeming of the acquisition obviously take place at the same time. It seems to me that that point of time is the death or the moment immediately after the death, and that that is highlighted by the fact that it is not merely the personal representatives, who, if they were administrators, might not be there, but "or other person on whom they devolve."

Now there is plenty of authority in the ordinary estate duty cases under the Finance Act 1894 to show that the death precedes the passing of the property. The very case of *Inland Revenue Commissioners* v. *Graham's Trustees*, 1971 S.L.T. 46, is such a case. It would appear to me to be pessimi exempli if one had to make an entirely different approach when one came to the relevant part of the Finance Act 1965, especially when it quite clearly borrows concepts from the ordinary estate duty legislation. For example, it will have been noted that in section 24 (1) one deals with the concept of "competent to dispose," which is dealt with in subsection (9) in terms which quite clearly are borrowed from section 22 of the Finance Act 1894.

Now, what are the arguments which are urged upon me to reach a

A contrary conclusion? Mr. Braham urged upon me that the essential point
of difference between the capital gains tax and the estate duty was that in
estate duty one was dealing, at any rate in part—that is to say, as regards
property which passes under section 1 of the Act of 1894, as distinct from
property deemed to pass under section 2—with a real event, whereas in
section 24 (1) one was dealing with an event which took place purely in
law and was a deemed event. But, of course, similarly, the passing which
B takes place under section 1 of the Act of 1894 is equally devoid, in most
cases, of real actuality. It has legal effect, but the broad acres remain
exactly where they were, tenanted by the same people; the family silver
remains in the bank; and the family chattels remain in the house. There is
no magic wand whereby a fairy suddenly comes along and presents the
executors with cartloads of assets. It is all completely notional and com-
C pletely taking place in law. It is all utterly unreal until one gets down to
the question of taxes or the distribution of assets.

The second point urged upon me by Mr. Braham was that the phrase
in section 24 (1) "at the date of death" is repeated in subsection (6) of that
section in a context which shows quite clearly that it means the instant
before death. Subsection (6) says:

D "In relation to property forming part of the estate of a deceased person
the personal representatives shall for the purposes of this Part of this
Act be treated as being a single and continuing body of persons . . . , and
that body shall be treated as having the deceased's residence, ordinary
residence, and domicile at the date of death."

I do not think I would get anything out of that anyway. It seems to me
E that one does have a residence, ordinary residence and domicile at the
moment at which one dies, and that it expires with one's own expiry. But
the fact that there, in conformity with the cases quoted to me by Mr.
Braham and to which I have already referred, one might have to take "at
the date of death" in that subsection as being the instant before death
rather than, as in subsection (1), the instant after does not ring my withers
in the slightest. Moreover, Mr. Davenport has pointed out to me that any
F other formula would be very difficult to work, because one has to deal
with the case of the person who, as soon as he sets foot in the country,
will acquire a domicile there—a domicile of origin will revive, or something
of that nature—and, the moment he sets foot in the country, overcome with
pleasurable emotions he immediately surrenders up the ghost. One has to
cater for that case as well as anything else; so I do not think I get anything
G out of that.

Mr. Braham also submitted to me that Parliament had, in the terms of
the amendments which have been made to the scheme of the Act of 1965
in the Finance Act 1969, demonstrated that its view was that the three-year
period applied to such gains as we are considering, and not the six-year
period, because in section 24A, at the end of subsection (5), it is provided:
"An assessment made in pursuance of this subsection shall not be out of
H time if made within six years from the end of the year of assessment in
which the deceased died." I would hesitate long in any event before con-
struing an earlier Act indirectly by the provisions of a subsequent Act. I
am far from saying that it can never be done, but one would have to hesitate
a very long time before doing it. But I do not think that the question really
arises, because the words I have read out show that what is being dealt
with is a particular subsection—subsection (5), in fact—and on any con-
struction that subsection demanded special treatment because capital gains,

which undoubtedly would have attracted only the three-year period (because they are those made "for the year of assessment in which the deceased died," and thus would include capital gains made by the deceased himself), are dealt with in that subsection, and therefore this quite clearly represents an alteration of the law in regard to those capital gains, if in regard to no other. I therefore cannot get any help or assistance from that provision, however I look at it.

Furthermore, Mr. Braham referred me to paragraph 12 of Schedule 10 to the Finance Act 1965. This is in a part of the Schedule headed "Provisions for Capital Gains Tax and Corporation Tax." His submission was that the only differences between an individual and a person who is not an individual as regards capital gains tax lie in a very narrow field. First of all, an individual may escape tax altogether (for example, in relation to property which forms his dwelling house); an individual may, under section 21, be able to pay, if it suits him so to do, part of the capital gains tax as income tax and thus, if he is lucky, may attract rather less tax; and, finally, there is the three-year period which is applicable in the circumstances I have already indicated, which would not be applicable, of course, unless one was dealing with an individual who had died.

With that preface, he said that paragraph 12 (2) shows, when taken in conjunction with paragraph 12 (3), that one is dealing with the three-year period. Paragraph 12 (2) provides:

> "Subject to section 22 (5) of this Act, chargeable gains accruing to the trustees of a settlement or to the personal representatives of a deceased person, and capital gains tax chargeable on or in the name of such trustees or personal representatives, shall not be regarded for the purposes of this Part of this Act as accruing to, or chargeable on, any other person, nor shall any trustee or personal representative be regarded for the purposes of this Part of this Act as an individual, but the provisions of Part XV of the Income Tax Act 1952 as applied by this Schedule shall not affect the question of who is the person to whom chargeable gains accrue, or who is chargeable to capital gains tax, so far as that question is relevant for the purposes of any exemption or of any provision determining the rate at which capital gains tax is chargeable."

Paragraph 12 (3) provides:

> "Chargeable gains which accrue to an individual on the disposal of assets deemed to be made by him on his death shall be regarded for the purposes of this Part of this Act as accruing to an individual notwithstanding that capital gains tax in respect of the gains is chargeable and assessable on his personal representatives."

Now Mr. Braham's point, as I followed him, was that unless paragraph 12 (3) was dealing with the time limits it was completely otiose because the substance of it had already been dealt with in paragraph 12 (2). I regret that I cannot accept that submission in the slightest, for two reasons. First of all, paragraph 12 (3) says nothing at all about time limits, and does not appear to me to be in any way directed to time limits. Secondly, the provisions of Part XV of the Income Tax Act 1952 are dealing with "Bodies of persons, incapacitated persons, trustees and agents, personal representatives and receivers," and one of the relevant sections granting relief to individuals which is not available to people who are not individuals is section 21 of the Finance Act 1965, which is not in terms referred to anywhere in paragraph 12 (2). It therefore appears to me that what paragraph 12 (3) is dealing with is an entirely different subject matter—namely, such matters as section 21 of that very Act itself, and the provisions giving relief to individuals in respect of assets such as their place of residence—and that the reference to Part XV of the Income Tax Act 1952 in paragraph 12 (2) is directed to an entirely different subject matter altogether. There is therefore, in my judgment, no overlap between paragraph 12 (2) and paragraph 12 (3), and I cannot accept Mr. Braham's submissions accordingly.

I have already dealt with Mr. Braham's submissions so far as the estate duty cases are concerned. The short point really is that, like estate duty, section 24 (1) is providing a mutation duty, and in a mutation duty the event precedes the effects. The cause, the death, must of necessity precede what happens on or after the death.

Finally, Mr. Braham submitted that there were merits on his side. I have considerable sympathy with that. Any taxpayer, I think, must have the greatest possible sympathy with any other taxpayer who is trying to avoid the clutches of the Inland Revenue. But I am afraid that there is no such thing as an equity in a taxing statute; one either falls within or, unfortunately, without the scope of any particular provision. In the circumstances, I have no doubt whatsoever that, properly construed, section 40 (1) of the Taxes Management Act 1970 does not apply to the facts of this case for the simple reason that the gains here in question did not arise to Mrs. Skone James before her death; they arose the moment after her death. That being so, the six-year period, the ordinary period, is applicable; the assessment was made in time; and, there being no challenge otherwise to its propriety or amount, I am bound to uphold it.

Appeal allowed with costs.
Assessment restored in the sum of £12,701.

Solicitors: *Solicitor of Inland Revenue; Wilberforce Allen.*

[CHANCERY DIVISION]

* LONDON HOSPITAL MEDICAL COLLEGE *v.* INLAND REVENUE COMMISSIONERS AND ANOTHER

[1973 T. No. 3263]

1976 Jan. 21, 22, 23, 27, 28; Feb. 25 — Brightman J.

Charity—Education—Students' union—Union of clubs for students of medical college—Objects of union to promote social, cultural and athletic activities and comfort of students—Whether charitable purposes

In 1893 a union was founded of the athletic and other clubs formed by the students of the London Hospital, a teaching hospital, and the medical college attached to it. The

---

[Reported by MRS. F. ALLEN McLEAN, Barrister-at-Law]

current rules, which were those adopted in 1970, defined the objects of the clubs' union as being "To promote, encourage and co-ordinate social, cultural and athletic activities amongst the members and to add to the comfort and enjoyment of the students of the London Hospital Medical College." The union was under, and regarded itself as being under, the control of the medical college, an educational charity, which provided substantial assistance of a financial and material nature. Most members using the facilities of the union were medical students, but newly qualified doctors and dentists also used the facilities, and trainee nurses and physiotherapists were admitted to associate membership. In 1972 the Inland Revenue Commissioners informed the medical college that they no longer regarded the objects of the union as exclusively charitable since, they claimed, it existed for the benefit of its members. Registration under section 4 of the Charities Act 1960 was refused. A B C

On a summons by the medical college to determine whether the union was a charity: —

Held, that the union was established and existed for the sole object of assisting the medical college in its charitable purpose of teaching medicine by providing those physical, cultural and social outlets for the students of the college which were needed, or were at any rate highly desirable, if the college was efficiently to perform its charitable purpose and, therefore, the union was itself a charity and entitled to be registered under section 4 of the Charities Act 1960 (post, pp. 620H, 622E, 623G—624A). D

In re Mariette [1915] 2 Ch. 284; *In re Coxen* [1948] Ch. 747 and *Neville Estates Ltd.* v. *Madden* [1962] Ch. 832 applied.

Inland Revenue Commissioners v. *City of Glasgow Police Athletic Association* [1953] A.C. 380, H.L.(Sc.) distinguished.

E

The following cases are referred to in the judgment:

Baldry v. *Feintuck* [1972] 1 W.L.R. 552; [1972] 2 All E.R. 81.

Coxen, In re [1948] Ch. 747; [1948] 2 All E.R. 492.

Inland Revenue Commissioners v. *City of Glasgow Police Athletic Association* [1953] A.C. 380; [1953] 2 W.L.R. 625; [1953] 1 All E.R. 747, H.L.(Sc.).

Inland Revenue Commissioners v. *Yorkshire Agricultural Society* [1928] 1 K.B. 611, C.A. F

Mariette, In re [1915] 2 Ch. 284.

Neville Estates Ltd. v. *Madden* [1962] Ch. 832; [1961] 3 W.L.R. 999; [1961] 3 All E.R. 769.

The following additional cases were cited in argument:

Belfast City Young Men's Christian Association Trustees v. *Valuation Commissioner* [1969] N.I. 3. G

Inland Revenue Commissioners v. *Baddeley* [1955] A.C. 572; [1955] 2 W.L.R. 552; [1955] 1 All E.R. 525, H.L.(E.).

Kearins v. *Kearins* [1957] S.R.(N.S.W.) 286.

Mellody, In re [1918] 1 Ch. 228.

National Deposit Friendly Society Trustees v. *Skegness Urban District Council* [1959] A.C. 293; [1958] 3 W.L.R. 172; [1958] 2 All E.R. 601, H.L.(E.). H

Oppenheim v. *Tobacco Securities Trust Co.* [1951] A.C. 297; [1951] 1 All E.R. 31, H.L.(E.).

Shaw's Will Trusts, In re [1952] Ch. 163; [1952] 1 All E.R. 49.

White's Will Trusts, In re [1951] W.N. 152; [1951] 1 All E.R. 528.

Wynn v. *Skegness Urban District Council* [1967] 1 W.L.R. 52; [1966] 3 All E.R. 336.

SUMMONS

By an originating summons dated October 18, 1973, the London Hospital Medical College sought a declaration that the funds of the London Hospital Clubs Union were held upon valid charitable trusts, that the union constituted a valid charitable trust and that it was entitled to register under section 4 of the Charities Act 1960. The first defendants to the summons were the Inland Revenue Commissioners and the second defendant was the Attorney-General, who supported the plaintiffs' claim. The Charity Commissioners, responsible for the registration of educational charities, although not parties to the summons, had agreed to be bound by the court's decision.

The facts are stated in the judgment.

Gavin Lightman for the medical college.
D. K. Rattee for the commissioners.
Andrew Morritt for the Attorney-General.

Cur. adv. vult.

February 25. BRIGHTMAN J. read the following judgment. The question raised by this summons is whether the London Hospital Clubs Union, which is a students' union, is a charity. The issue arises in the context of a claim for tax relief. The case has, however, implications which lie outside the field of taxation. If the union's purposes are within the law's somewhat eccentric definition of charity, favourable tax consequences, and perhaps also favourable rating consequences, will follow. But it will also follow that the property and money of the union are not at the absolute disposition of the members of the union to deal with as they please, but are subject to the controls imposed by law on funds impressed with a charitable trust, and the union may have a statutory obligation to register under the Charities Act 1960. These controls were enforced by the High Court in *Baldry* v. *Feintuck* [1972] 1 W.L.R. 552, to which I shall have occasion to refer later in this judgment

The London Hospital is a teaching hospital. Attached to it is a medical college which forms part of the University of London. The hospital and college, together with a students' hostel, occupy a large site adjoining the Whitechapel and Commercial Roads in the East End of London. The London Hospital Medical College became a corporate body in 1948. Previously it was an unincorporated general medical school of the university associated with the London Hospital. Its constitution is set out in a scheme pursuant to section 15 of the National Health Service Act 1946.

The London Hospital Clubs Union was founded as long ago as 1893. In May and June of that year circular letters were sent out by the medical college inviting subscriptions and donations to the union. The union was described as having been recently formed. It was designed to embrace all the athletic and other clubs formed by the students of the hospital and college. There were two forms of circular letter, one in print dated May 1, 1893, and the other in manuscript dated June 27, 1893. The printed version was signed by Mr. Gilbart Smith, described as chairman of the amalgamated committee of staff and students, whatever that may have been. The manuscript version was signed by the president of the college, by Mr. Gilbart Smith, there described as the treasurer of the college, and by the financial secretary of the college.

The printed and manuscript versions are for all practical purposes

identical in wording. They constitute the only surviving documentary A
evidence of how the union came to be formed and what were its purposes. One of the manuscript letters which fortuitously survived from the last century was the letter sent to Sir Andrew Clark, the eminent physician, and returned by him to the college with his donation. I will read the printed circular of May 1, 1893:

> " Dear Sir, It will interest you as one who has worked at ' The London B
> Hospital ' to know that at the unanimous desire of the students, a clubs' union has recently been formed which will embrace all the athletic and other clubs formed by the students of the hospital and college. The staff being anxious to encourage athletics and add to the comfort and enjoyment of the students have agreed to subscribe a large sum annually towards the expenses of supporting the union. Owing to this action of the staff, a field for cricket, football, etc., has C
> been leased at Lower Edmonton, and for the first time the students of ' The London ' will have their own ground, which, it is trusted, will prove a great boon to all of them.
>
> " When discussing the arrangements for the clubs' union it was felt that in all probability past students would like to show an interest in the welfare of those following in their footsteps, and accordingly it was decided that any gentleman now in practice, who was formerly at D
> either hospital or college, should be permitted to become a life member on payment of a fee of one guinea. The subscription will confer all the privileges of the clubs' union, including the use of the dining room, the Athenaeum, the Medical Society, etc. It is hoped that many old ' London ' students will respond to this suggestion and that the result will be a closer union between past and present students. Subscriptions E
> can be sent to " [so and so].

There is no evidence as to what happened in the affairs of the union over the next 40-odd years. In May 1937 a set of rules or new rules came into being in circumstances not now known. Rule 2, under the heading " Constitution," stated that the union should consist of certain clubs and societies. There were then described 21 clubs mainly, but not exclusively, of an F
athletic nature. There were five societies, four of which were medical, and the fifth was a dramatic society. The general committee had power to admit new clubs and societies. Any student could become a member of the union on paying an annual subscription of £5. He then became entitled to the privileges of membership of all the component clubs and societies. If a student taking the full medical or dental course paid his subscription from entry to the hospital until he qualified, he was automatically entitled G
to life membership. Honorary members might also be elected. A student who was not a member of the union was not entitled to be a member of any of the component clubs and societies. There was a provision enabling the rules to be altered.

The 1937 rules seem to have remained in force until 1962. In November 1961 the secretary of the medical college reported to a meeting of the H
standing committee of the Council of Governors of the Medical College on the effect of the Licensing Act 1961. One of the purposes of the Act was to curb the activities of bogus or drinking clubs. Section 25 prohibited the serving of drinks to the members of a club unless the club either was registered under the Act or held a justices' licence. A club qualified for registration if, put shortly, it was a bona fide club. A club was presumed to be bona fide if its rules conformed with the provisions set out in Schedule

5 to the Act. One of these provisions is that the members of the club should become such by election. The standing committee resolved that a justices' licence would be unsuitable and that the secretary be instructed to communicate with solicitors and arrange for the drawing up of appropriate rules to meet the requirements of a club licence. On May 8, 1962, an extraordinary general meeting of the union was held which adopted new rules, and these were approved by the medical council of the college.

A feature of the 1962 rules which is not to be found in the 1937 rules is that there is an objects clause. It reads as follows:

> "2. Objects. To promote, encourage and co-ordinate social, cultural and athletic activities amongst the members so as to add to the comfort and enjoyment of the students of the London Hospital Medical College."

The objects so set out may be compared with the second sentence of the circular letter of May 1, 1893. The 1893 circular indicated that the desire of the college staff was "to encourage athletics *and* add to the comfort and enjoyment of the students." The 1962 rules described the objects as being "to encourage and co-ordinate social, cultural and athletic activities amongst the members *so as* to add to the comfort and enjoyment of the students."

Thus, social and cultural activities were added to athletics, and the comfort and enjoyment of students was expressed as the purpose of the social, cultural and athletic activities so described. To comply with the Licensing Act, members were to be elected by the General Committee of the Union. The procedure was to be this. When a student was admitted to the medical college he was to be treated as ipso facto nominated for membership of the union. No act on his part or on anyone else's part was needed. Subsequently his nomination came before the General Committee of the Union, which was required to meet not less than once each term. In the meantime, the candidate for election would enjoy all the privileges of membership. It is clear that the provision for election was merely the result of the Licensing Act. Mr. Laird, who has been the secretary of the medical college for 30 years and for a like time has been responsible for the financial affairs of the union, told me that no potential candidate for membership had ever failed to be elected. I have no doubt that the electoral requirement, though not a sham, in fact made no real difference to the membership. The 1962 rules also enabled qualified staff of the hospital and the medical college to be elected as members though, ex hypothesi, they were not students. In other words, the union ceased to consist exclusively of students, ex-students and honorary members, although the welfare of students remained the governing factor.

The current rules were adopted in 1970. They repeat the objects of the union as defined in the 1962 rules with one small alteration in wording. The 1893 circulars, after spelling out the encouragement of athletics, added the formula "*and* add to the comfort and enjoyment of the students." The 1962 rules, after spelling out the promotion, encouragement and co-ordination of social, cultural and athletic activities, added the formula "*so as* to add to the comfort and enjoyment of the students." The 1970 rules reverted to the 1893 wording saying "*and* to add to the comfort and enjoyment of the students." Something was sought to be made of this change of wording by counsel challenging the charitable status of the union. It was submitted that the 1970 rules established two categories of purpose, one being social, cultural and athletic and the other being, put shortly, sybaritic. I reject that submission. I do not think that the A objects of an association of this sort are to be construed as if they were drawn with the precision to be found in a legal document drafted by a skilled conveyancer. A latitude of language is to be expected and is permissible. In my judgment the words "and to add to the comfort," etc. add nothing to the clause except to emphasise that the union exists for the students.

Under the 1970 rules a further class of person became elegible for B membership; namely, the members of the London Hospital Social Society. They could be elected to associate membership. They consist of student nurses and trainee physiotherapists attached to the hospital. The number of component clubs and societies was also increased by the new rules.

Under the 1970 rules, some of which can be traced back to 1962 or 1937, the affairs of the union are regulated as follows. There are 19 officers C of the union, 14 of whom are drawn from the staff of the hospital or medical college. The president of the union is either a university-appointed teacher attached to the medical college or a consultant of the London Hospital. The affairs of the union are managed by eight committees. The principal committee is the general committee, which controls the policy and finances of the union save so far as delegated to the union council. The general committee has 53 members, of whom 11 are staff of the D hospital or college. The chairman of the general committee is the president of the union, who, as I have said, is a member of the staff. There is then the union council, which has a very limited authority. It is chaired by a past-president of the union. There is a finance committee consisting of three staff and seven student members. It is chaired by the treasurer of the medical college. The remaining committees are principally concerned E with the day-to-day running of the union and consist exclusively or mainly of students. The annual general meetings and extraordinary general meetings of the union are chaired by the president of the union; i.e., a member of the staff.

The accounts of the union are to be audited annually by auditors appointed by the governors of the medical college. The medical college is required to provide a clerk who acts as the accountant of the union and F provides clerical assistance under the supervision of the secretary of the medical college, who is honorary financial secretary of the union.

When the 1970 rules were adopted, it was agreed by the General Committee of the Union and by the extraordinary general meeting to which the rules were submitted that the following rubric should appear before and as a preface to the rules: G

> "Legal responsibility: Inasmuch as the London Hospital Clubs Union is part of, incidental to, and under control of the medical college, any resolution by the union affecting management of its affairs or altering or adding to these rules shall be submitted to the Council of Governors of the London Hospital Medical College for their information and confirmation." H

The precise effect of this statement as a matter of law may be doubtful. The fact that the statement appears at all is, however, of some significance because it shows that the union regards itself as part of and incidental to and under the control of the medical college.

Although I have referred to the 1937 and 1962 rules, only the 1970 rules are directly relevant now. Members inevitably join the union on the

A basis of the 1970 rules, and the earlier rules have no more than historical importance.

The medical college owns the freehold of the sports ground used by the component clubs of the union. The college maintains, at its own expense, the perimeter of the ground and the fabric of the pavilion. The staff of the sports ground are employed by the college although paid (except for the head-groundsman) out of union funds. The medical college
B provides within its precincts, for the benefit of the union, free of charge, a common room with catering facilities and pays for porters and cleaners, and it also discharges the rates. The college also provides, free of charge, a games room and squash courts. The college provides, free of charge, the use of a cottage at Burnham-on-Crouch to promote the activities of the union's sailing club. It maintains the fabric of the cottage and pays
C certain of the running expenses. Directly and indirectly the college makes substantial contributions to the union in cash or kind. I have no doubt that Mr. Laird was right when he told me in his evidence that the union would not be a viable proposition without the financial, material and other assistance which it receives from the college. The subscriptions and other receipts of the union from members would not be anywhere near sufficient to finance the union's activities. The predominant users of the union's
D facilities are undergraduates, who number about 800. Newly qualified doctors and dentists also make substantial use of the facilities. The associate members number about 150 ladies.

Until 1971 the Inland Revenue Commissioners treated the activities of the union as charitable. However, in that year and 1972 the inspector of taxes wrote letters to the medical college (not, be it observed, to the union) stating that the objects of the union were no longer considered exclusively
E charitable. The union, it was claimed, existed for the benefit of its members. Registration under section 4 of the Charities Act 1960 was refused. The Department of Education and Science, as the body then concerned with the registration of educational charities under section 4 of the Act of 1960, concurred. The medical college then issued an originating summons, to which the Inland Revenue Commissioners and the Attorney-General are
F defendants. The medical college claims that the purposes of the union are exclusively charitable. This claim is supported by the Attorney-General. No point was taken before me by the commissioners that the General Committee of the Union ought to have been the plaintiffs, as would be appropriate if the union were an independent club and not a dependency of the college. The Charity Commissioners, who are now responsible for the registration of educational charities, though not parties to the summons,
G have agreed to be bound by the court's decision.

Mr. Lightman, for the medical college, submitted, in the first place, that the union was a charity either because it formed an integral part of the medical college, itself a charity, or because its purposes were ancillary to those of the college. A convenient starting point is *In re Mariette* [1915] 2 Ch. 284. A testator gave a legacy to Aldenham School to build fives
H courts. Counsel for the school argued that it was a good charitable bequest because it tended to the beneficial carrying on of a charitable institution—namely, the school—and the gift therefore furthered education. This argument was accepted. The reasoning which appealed to Eve J. sufficiently appears from one sentence in his judgment, at p. 288:

> "It is necessary . . . in any satisfactory system of education to provide for both mental and bodily occupation, mental occupation by means of the classics and those other less inviting studies to which a portion of

> the day is devoted, and bodily occupation by means of regular and organised games."

The provision of fives courts for the benefit of the public or a section of the public may well not be a charitable purpose under the general law. The maintenance of schools of learning, free schools and scholars of universities is to be found in the preamble to the Charitable Uses Act 1601 and is therefore a charitable purpose. Aldenham School was a school of learning which existed for the benefit of the community, and was therefore charitable. The provision of fives courts advanced that purpose, and the gift was therefore a charitable gift.

The London Hospital Medical College is a school of learning existing for the benefit of the community. It is therefore charitable. A club which provides athletic and social activities for its members is not, per se, charitable. Therefore, the union, standing alone, is not charitable under the general law. But if the union exists solely to further, and does further, the educational purposes of the medical college, then in my judgment it is clearly charitable. *In re Coxen* [1948] Ch. 747 was decided on this principle. The provision of attendance money and a dinner for the Court of Aldermen of the City of London was not per se a charitable purpose. But the trust established by the testator for that purpose was a valid charitable trust because it was established for the better administration of the principal trust (a trust for orthopaedic hospitals) and not for the personal benefit of the recipients. If, put shortly, the union exists for the benefit of the college, it would be immaterial that the union also provided a personal benefit for the individual students who were elected members of the union and chose to make use of its facilities. I would suppose that most schools of learning confer a personal benefit on the individual scholars who are admitted thereto. X, an individual scholar, is not per se an object of charity. The school of learning that X attends is nevertheless charitable if the school exists for the benefit of the community. The fact that X receives a personal benefit is incidental to the implementation of the purposes of the charity. In the present case, if the union exists to further and does further the educational purposes of the medical college, the union is charitable notwithstanding the personal benefit conferred on the union members. Whether the union exists in order to further and whether it does further the educational purposes of the medical college are questions of fact.

Neville Estates Ltd. v. *Madden* [1962] Ch. 832 proceeded on this analysis of the law. In 1937 certain persons of the Jewish faith who lived at Catford banded together to form a congregation or synagogue. A building fund was launched for "the erection of a synagogue with or without appurtenant buildings for religious education and social purposes." Cross J. held that the social activities were merely ancillary to the strictly religious activities of the synagogue and did not therefore preclude his holding that the purposes of the building fund were exclusively charitable.

On the evidence before me I find as a fact that the union exists solely to further and does further the educational purposes of the medical college. There are many indications which point that way. For example, the 1893 appeal was made by the medical college. The union functions almost entirely on premises provided and largely maintained by the college. The important committees of the union are chaired and partly manned by members of the staff of the hospital and college. The college provides, through the union, athletic and social and kindred amenities which would

A otherwise not be available to students living in this area of London. No one who has heard the oral evidence and studied the documentary evidence could seriously doubt that the union is heavily dependent upon the college and is fostered and sponsored by the college just because the college realises the importance of the union to the success of its own educational activities.

Mr. Rattee, in a powerful submission on behalf of the commissioners B submitted that the union was merely a "self-regarding" organisation for the benefit of its elected members. That is not my reading of the situation. If the London Hospital and the medical college moved away from the Commercial Road to another part of the country, the union would go too, and the medical college would certainly speed it on its way. If the medical college withdrew its support from the union, which in present circumstances C is unthinkable, the union would not survive for long. Nor, I think, would it wish to do so. If, for any reason, the union as at present constituted came to an end and its activities ceased, I have no doubt that the medical college would replace it by another similar institution as a matter of high priority. It is patently obvious, in my view, that a medical college, particularly one in a somewhat remote part of London, is bound to provide in one way or another for its pre-clinical and clinical students precisely those D facilities which are provided by the union if it is to have a hard-working and contented student body. I do not accept that the union is a society which exists for the benefit of its members as distinct from a society which exists to further the educational purposes of the college.

Mr. Rattee made the point that the union was only open to those students who were elected to it. There is nothing in this point. It may E often happen that a particular amenity attached to an educational establishment is only open to selected students. That does not prevent the amenity being a charitable activity if it would otherwise qualify as such. A procedure for selection may be necessary to keep down numbers to manageable limits or to maintain standards, or for other reasons wholly consistent with educational purposes.

The mainstay of Mr. Rattee's argument was the decision of the House F of Lords in *Inland Revenue Commissioners* v. *City of Glasgow Police Athletic Association* [1953] A.C. 380, which does bear certain superficial similarities with the present case. It related, as its name implies, to a police athletic association. Membership of the association was restricted to officers and former officers of the Glasgow City Police Force. The chief constable was the president, and assistant chief constables and superintendents were vice-presidents of the association. The executive committee G was chaired by the chief constable. Until 1947 membership was a condition of service. The association was regarded by the authorities as an essential part of the police organisation because it played a valuable part in maintaining the health and morale of the police force. The hours of police duty made it almost essential that some special provision should be made for the recreation of the police. The special commissioners found as a fact H that the association increased the efficiency of the force and thereby directly benefited the public.

It was urged by the Crown in argument that to find the association charitable one would have to discern a charitable purpose and not merely a charitable consequence. I think that proposition was clearly accepted by the House of Lords. It was submitted by the Crown that one has to look at the purpose by interpreting the rules in the light of all the facts. The argument of the Crown prevailed notwithstanding that all their Lordships

held the view that a gift exclusively for the purpose of promoting the A
efficiency of the police force and the preservation of public order would be charitable by analogy with a gift for promoting the efficiency of the Armed Forces. Not unnaturally, Mr. Rattee asked: what was the essential difference between the athletic association in that case and the students' union in this case? Both were clubs which were said to further a charitable purpose, in the one case the maintenance of public order and in the other case the advancement of education. B

In the *Athletic Association* case, the question to be answered was posed thus by Lord Normand, at p. 396:

> ". . . what are the purposes for which the association is established, as shown by the rules, its activities and its relation to the police force and the public."

He considered that the private advantage of the members of the association C
was a purpose for which the association was established. Therefore, he said, it could not be held that it was an association established for a public charitable purpose only. Nevertheless, he quoted, at p. 396, with evident approval this passage from the judgment of Atkin L.J. in *Inland Revenue Commissioners* v. *Yorkshire Agricultural Society* [1928] 1 K.B. 611, 631:

> ". . . if the benefit given to its members is only given to them with a D
> view of giving encouragement and carrying out the main purpose which is a charitable purpose, then I think the mere fact that the members are benefited in the course of promoting the charitable purpose would not prevent the society being established for charitable purposes only."

Applying the last mentioned test I take the view that the benefit given to E
the members of the union by that organisation is only given to them with a view to giving encouragement to and carrying out the main purpose of the medical college, which is a charitable purpose. These benefits, to a very large extent, stem from the college both in cash and kind, and the union is not, in my opinion, "self-regarding" merely because it is, to the extent of its members' subscriptions and certain other payments, self-supporting. F

Lord Morton of Henryton put the matter in this way [1953] A.C. 380, 399:

> "The members pay their subscriptions and get certain benefits in return; they make a profit by running the annual amateur sports meeting already mentioned, and that profit is applied to carrying out the purpose which I have just stated. So far, the association would G
> not appear to be any more a charity than is any other athletic or social association or club established for the like purpose." Then, at p. 400: "Even if I were satisfied that there exists some other purpose for which the association was or is established, for instance, the purpose of maintaining the strength and efficiency of the police force, I should find it impossible to say that the *sole* purpose of the associa- H
> tion is a purpose which is nowhere even mentioned in the constitution and general rules, and that the purpose which emerges so clearly in the rules, and upon which the income of the association appears to have been expended ever since it came into existence, is either non-existent or merely incidental."

In this connection I may observe that the objects of the association were expressed solely as follows: "The objects of the association shall be to

A encourage and promote all forms of athletic sports and general pastimes."
There was nothing, therefore, which expressly linked the purposes of the
association with the efficiency of the police force. In the case with which I
am dealing there is an express link in the objects clause between the
social, cultural and athletic activities which are mentioned and the student
life of the medical college.

Lord Reid said, at p. 402:

B
> "... it is not enough that one of the purposes of a body of persons is
> charitable: the Act requires that it must be established for charitable
> purposes only. This does not mean that the sole effect of the activities
> of the body must be to promote charitable purposes, but it does mean
> that that must be its predominant object and that any benefits to its
> individual members of a non-charitable character which result from
> C its activities must be of a subsidiary or incidental character. . . . The
> peculiarity of this case is that the same activities have a double result.
> They are beneficial to the public by increasing the efficiency of the
> force and they are beneficial to the members themselves in affording
> to them recreation and enjoyment: and all the relevant facts appear
> to me to indicate that the purpose was to produce this double result.
> D It may well be that considerations of public interest were the primary
> cause of the association being established and maintained: but I think
> that it is clear that all or most of the activities of the association are
> designed in the first place to confer benefits on its members by afford-
> ing to them recreation and enjoyment. It is only as a result of these
> benefits that the purpose of increasing the efficiency of the force is
> achieved. In some cases where the end is a charitable purpose the
> E fact that the means to the end confer non-charitable benefits may not
> matter; but in the present case I have come to the conclusion that
> conferring such benefits on its members bulks so largely in the
> purposes and activities of this association that it cannot properly be
> said to be established for charitable purposes only."

Lord Cohen spoke to the same effect, at p. 407:

F
> "... I am unable to draw from the evidence the conclusion that the
> benefits to the members were given with a view only to giving
> encouragement to the maintenance of the strength and efficiency of
> the Glasgow police force. These benefits were and could be given
> to the members and to no one else. Reading the case stated and the
> documents annexed thereto I am forced to the conclusion that the
> G conferment of those benefits was a substantial part of the objects of
> the association."

In the end it seems to me that the question is to some extent a matter of
degree. I must ask myself: What is the object for which the union is
established? Is the predominant object of the union the furtherance of
the purposes of the medical college as a school of learning, or is its object,
H or one of its objects, the private and personal benefit of those students
who are members of the union? I do not think, looking at the origins of
the union and its constitution, that it has any raison d'être except to
further the educational purposes of the medical college. The union does
not, of course, itself teach medicine, but what it does do, and what it is
intended to do, and was established to do, is to assist the teaching of
medicine by providing those physical and cultural and social outlets which
are needed, or are at any rate highly desirable, if the art of teaching is

to be efficiently performed at the college. I think that most people would say that the facilities of the union are a practical necessity in these days if the medical college is to function efficiently. A

I therefore come to the conclusion that the purposes of the union are charitable and that it is entitled to registration under section 4 of the Charities Act 1960. In these circumstances, it is not necessary for me to deal with the alternative submission made by the medical college that the union is a charity by virtue of the Recreational Charities Act 1958. B

In conclusion, I think it is desirable that I should make a brief reference to *Baldry* v. *Feintuck* [1972] 1 W.L.R. 552. Counsel for the medical college sought to rely on that case for the proposition that a students' union is prima facie charitable. It is true that the motion proceeded on the footing that the students' union in that case was a charity. The contrary, however, was never argued. The point went by concession. C
I accepted the concession because I thought it correct. But a case which proceeds on the basis of a proposition which is not tested by argument is not of much value as an authority for the validity of that proposition. *Baldry* v. *Feintuck* has not, therefore, assisted me in reaching my conclusion in the present case.

Declaration that funds of London Hospital Clubs Union were held upon valid charitable trusts. D
Union's party and party costs to be paid by commissioners.
Costs of Attorney-General to be paid by commissioners.

E

Solicitors: *Parker, Garrett & Co.; Solicitor of Inland Revenue; Treasury Solicitor.*

F

[COURT OF APPEAL]

* POST OFFICE *v.* NOTTINGHAM CITY COUNCIL

1976 March 24, 25 — Cairns and Browne L.JJ. and Sir Gordon Willmer

G

Rating — Rateable occupation — Unoccupied hereditament — New telephone exchange—Completion notice served before installation of telephone equipment — Whether building "completed" without necessary equipment for use as telephone exchange—General Rate Act 1967 (*c.* 9), *s.* 17 (1), *Sch.* 1, *paras.* 8, 9

H The appellant ratepayers started the erection of a purpose-built telephone exchange in February 1973. On January 27, 1975, the respondent rating authority served a completion notice on them stating, inter alia, that the building would be

[Reported by EMMANUEL C. ABARAONYE, ESQ., Barrister-at-Law]

[1] General Rate Act 1967, Sch. 1, para. 8 (1): see post, pp. 630H—631A.
Para. 9: see post, p. 631C–D.

treated for the purposes of Schedule 1 to the General Rate Act 1967 as completed on February 28, 1975. The ratepayers appealed to the county court. Judge Heald after taking into account time required for the completion of electrical wiring, supply of a transformer which was necessary for the supply of electricity and the partition of the building, but without taking into account time required to install the telephone equipment, held that the building could reasonably be expected to be completed on August 1, 1975.

On the ratepayers' appeal:—

Held, dismissing the appeal, that the test to be applied in determining the date on which a building would be completed for the purposes of Schedule 1 to the General Rate Act 1967 was the date when the building, as a building, would be ready for occupation, or capable of occupation for the purpose for which it was intended; that, since that test did not include the period between the date when the building was ready for occupation and the date when the necessary equipment or furniture was installed for the use of the building as a telephone exchange, the judge had correctly excluded the time necessary for the installation of the telephone equipment in determining the date when the building could reasonably be expected to be complete as a telephone exchange for the purposes of the Act (post, pp. 635A–B, 636B–D, F–G, 637A–C).

Ravenseft Properties Ltd. v. *Newham London Borough Council* [1976] Q.B. 464, C.A. applied.

The following cases are referred to in the judgments:

Arbuckle Smith & Co. Ltd. v. *Greenock Corporation* [1960] A.C. 813; [1960] 2 W.L.R. 435; [1960] 1 All E.R. 568, H.L.(Sc.).

Easiwork Homes Ltd. v. *Redbridge London Borough Council* [1970] 2 Q.B. 406; [1970] 2 W.L.R. 1199; [1970] 2 All E.R. 653, D.C.

Jarrold v. *John Good & Sons Ltd.* [1962] 1 W.L.R. 1101; [1962] 2 All E.R. 971; [1963] 1 W.L.R. 214; [1963] 1 All E.R. 141, C.A.

Kirby v. *Hunslet Union Assessment Committee* [1906] A.C. 43, H.L.(E.).

Ravenseft Properties Ltd. v. *Newham London Borough Council* [1976] Q.B. 464; [1976] 2 W.L.R. 131; [1976] 1 All E.R. 580, C.A.

Watford Borough Council v. *Parcourt Property Investment Co. Ltd.* (1971) 17 R.R.C. 19.

The following additional case was cited in argument:

Townley Mill Co. (1919) Ltd. v. *Oldham Assessment Committee* [1937] A.C. 419; [1937] 1 All E.R. 11, H.L.(E.).

APPEAL from Judge Heald sitting at Nottingham County Court.

In February 1973, the appellant ratepayers, the Post Office, started the erection of a purpose-built telephone exchange in Nottingham. In January 1975, the respondent rating authority, Nottingham City Council, served a completion notice on them under the General Rate Act 1967 and Schedule 1 to the Act stating, inter alia, that the authority was of the opinion that the erection of the building was to be treated for the purposes of the Schedule as completed on February 28, 1975, and directed the attention of the ratepayers to the provisions of paragraph 8 of the Schedule. In December 1975, the ratepayers appealed to the county court and Judge Heald, after taking into account time required for the completion of electrical wiring, supply of the transformer which was necessary for electricity supply and the partition of the building, allowed the appeal and held that the building could reasonably be expected to be completed on August 1, 1975. The judge however considered that time required to install the telephone equipment should A not be taken into account in determining the time by which the building could reasonably be expected to be completed for the purposes of the Schedule. The ratepayers appealed contending, inter alia, that time required for installing the equipment ought to be taken into account.

The grounds of the appeal were that the judge rightly asked himself, as a preliminary to deciding the question of the date by which the building would be completed, the date by which the building would be B comprised in a relevant hereditament but that he erred in law in concluding that the building would be comprised in a relevant hereditament for the purposes of Schedule 1 at the date when it would be comprised in a technical hereditament; the judge failed to ask himself by what date the relevant hereditament, namely, a telephone exchange, would come into being; he failed to apply correctly the provisions of paragraph C 9 of Schedule 1 to the General Rate Act 1967 in that he did not regard the provision of the telephone equipment as customarily done to a building of the type in question after the erection of the building has been substantially completed; he failed to consider whether prior to the completion of at least the first stage in the equipping of the exchange the building was capable of being rateably occupied; (i) the judge wrongly distinguished between building work and work on plant D and equipment. In particular he failed to take into account that plant could form part of a hereditament although it might not be rateable plant and that some plant might be rateable. In consequence he failed to ask himself whether any of the plant and equipment to be installed in the building in question fell into either of those categories. (ii) Alternatively the judge asked himself the question in (i) above but wrongly E concluded that none of the plant or equipment in question fell into either category.

The facts are stated in the judgment of Browne L.J.

W. J. Glover Q.C. and *Matthew Horton* for the ratepayers.
Geoffrey Rippon Q.C. and *F. A. Amies* for the rating authority.

F

CAIRNS L.J. I will ask Browne L.J. to deliver the first judgment.

BROWNE L.J. This is an appeal by the Post Office from a decision of Judge Heald given at the Nottingham County Court on June 17, 1975. The case relates to the application to a new telephone exchange in Nottingham of the provisions as to the rating of unoccupied property G which were first introduced by the Local Government Act 1966 and are now contained in the General Rate Act 1967, which was a consolidation Act. Section 17 of the Act of 1967 provides, so far as relevant:

> "(1) A rating authority may resolve that the provisions of Schedule 1 to this Act with respect to the rating of unoccupied property—(*a*) shall apply . . . to their area, and in that case those provisions H shall come into operation . . . in that area on such day as may be specified in the resolution."

On February 4, 1974, the Nottingham City Council passed a resolution that those provisions should apply to their area from April 1, 1974. Paragraph 8 (1) of Schedule 1 to the Act of 1967 gives the rating authority power to serve what is described as "a completion notice"; and paragraph 8 (4) gives a right of appeal to the county court. I shall have to come back later to those provisions, and I only mention them at this stage to make the history intelligible.

In February 1973, the Post Office started the erection of a building in Nottingham for use as a telephone exchange. This was a new exchange which was to be known as the Crusader Exchange. The work was to be done under four contracts. First, a contract to erect the building, and this was to be done by an outside contractor. Secondly, the electrical work, which was to be done by the Post Office engineers. This was electricity both for the operational purposes of the exchange and for what Mr. Glover calls the domestic purposes of the building. Thirdly, a contract for ventilation, which was to be done by an outside contractor. Fourthly, the contract for the telephone equipment itself, part of the installation of which was to be done by the Post Office engineers and part by the suppliers of the equipment. Mr. Glover told us that this division of labour was arranged so that the building could be brought into operation as soon as possible.

On January 27, 1975, the Nottingham City Council served a completion notice in respect of this building. Paragraph 1 of the completion notice recites the resolution under section 17 and Schedule 1 to the General Rate Act 1967. Paragraphs 2 and 3 say:

> "2. The rating authority is of the opinion that the work remaining to be done in the building at the corner of Thurland Street and Lincoln Street (hereinafter called 'the building') is such that the erection of the building can reasonably be expected to be completed within three months and that the building when completed will be comprised in a relevant hereditament. 3. The rating authority therefore serve upon you as owner of the building this completion notice stating that the erection of the building is to be treated for the purposes of Schedule 1 to the General Rate Act 1967 as completed on February 28, 1975."

The notice then calls the attention of the person upon whom it is served to the right of appeal.

The Post Office appealed to the county court; the hearing took place on April 17, 18 and May 27, and judgment was given on June 17, 1975.

Mr. Amies, for the rating authority, submitted to the circuit judge that he, the judge, should decide this case by putting himself in the position of the rating authority as at January 27, 1975, when the completion notice was given, and, I gather, decide when the building could then reasonably have been expected to be completed. The judge rejected this approach. He said:

> "The court has to decide on the facts as it knows them and not on an assumed position which it knows to be wrong. In my opinion I have to take into account the supervening events which occurred after January 27, 1975, and in particular the difficulties over the heating system and the tiling sub-contract which meant that for a period of almost two months the electricians were off the site. In my opinion if I come to the conclusion that the rating authority have given a date for the building to be treated as completed, which is in fact earlier than it could be reasonably expected to be completed, then I have to look at the matter afresh on the facts as I know them and have to determine a date which has to be treated as the date of completion."

In my judgment, the judge was right in his approach; anyhow, there is no cross-appeal.

The judge found the following facts. First, he said:

> "The building is purpose-built as a telephone exchange. It could doubtless be adapted to other uses with difficulty, but there are facilities incorporated in it which are only suitable for a telephone exchange. For instance there are a number of fan rooms for ventilation equipment. There is an engine room which is capable of supplying alternative electric power for the whole building, there are battery rooms and cable chambers. This is not a case of a developer not completing a building because he has no tenant to put in it. It is the very reverse. It is the desire of the Post Office to bring the building into operation as soon as possible. Everything they have done has been designed to speed that end and possibly they have laid themselves open to a liability for rates at an earlier point in time than might otherwise be the case."

Secondly, the judge said:

> "In January 1975 the building contract was coming to its end. There was a site meeting on January 27, 1975, between the representatives of the contractor and the Post Office and the Department of the Environment, at which no representative of the rating authority was present, when it was expected that the building would be ready to be handed over very shortly and a tentative handover date of February 17, 1975, was agreed on. However, immediately after that meeting problems with the heating system arose and it became apparent that the tiling would not be complete by February 17. The problem with the heating system became serious and it was clear the building could not be handed over by the contractor until those problems had been cleared up and in fact the building was not handed over until April 17 and 18, which strangely enough were the two days on which this case was first heard."

Thirdly, the judge found that the work remaining at the time of the hearing to be done was as follows: (a) electric wiring; (b) a transformer had to be installed—until that was done there was no permanent or satisfactory supply of electricity to the building; (c) the installation of the ventilation system; (d) the installation of the kitchen equipment; (e) the installation of three or four partitions; and (f) the installation of the telephone equipment itself. The judge said:

> "Lastly, we come to the question of the telephone equipment. This is obviously very complicated and very expensive. All the cables will have to come through the main cable tunnel from the Castle Exchange and then through the main distribution frame. In the building there are going to be a number of different aspects of telephone work. The exchange is being built to cover future expansion as well, so it may be 10 or 15 years before the space is fully utilised. It is intended that the Repair Service Centre (RSC) should be transferred to the building from the Castle Exchange in February 1976. It is intended that the directory enquiry facilities should be moved to the exchange from the Castle Exchange and other outside accommodation in June/July 1976 and it is intended that automatic telephone equipment should be installed in the exchange in June

1977. If these dates are achieved the Post Office is to be congratulated on the speed at which it gets the new exchange equipped."

The judge sets out the argument of Mr. Horton, and then says:

> "It may be that the draftsman did not intend to bring about the situation which has arisen in this case, but I have come to the conclusion that when the building is completed it will be comprised in a relevant hereditament, albeit only a technical one, and therefore it is within the Schedule and rateable. In effect I prefer Mr. Amies' more literal approach. I take the view that I have to decide what time is reasonably required to complete the building, or perhaps more accurately is required to complete the work remaining to be done which is customarily done in the case of the Post Office after the building has been substantially completed. I take into account the completion of the electrical wiring which will take two to three months. I take into account the supply of the transformer, because until that transformer is supplied there will be no permanent supply of electricity and there will not be sufficient power for instance to work the lifts and other electrical appliances at the same time, and I also take into account the time required to do the partitioning. I ignore the provision of the ventilation equipment, the kitchen equipment and the telephone equipment. The period starts to run from April 18, 1975. Work on the various matters can proceed at the same time, but reasonably some time must be allowed for contingencies, difficulties in delivery, failure of equipment to work. I think all this work can be completed in something over three months and therefore for the purposes of Schedule 1 to the General Rate Act 1967 I decide that the building the subject of the appeal shall be treated as being completed on August 1, 1975."

The question in this appeal is about the telephone equipment.

The relevant statutory provisions are all contained in the General Rate Act 1967. I have already referred to section 17. I do not think I need refer to the somewhat cryptic, if not circular, definition of "hereditament" in section 115 (1). I turn, therefore, to Schedule 1 to the Act. Paragraph 1 (1) of Schedule 1 provides:

> "Where, in the case of any rating area in which, by virtue of a resolution under section 17 of this Act, this Schedule is in operation, any relevant hereditament in that area is unoccupied for a continuous period exceeding three months, the owner shall, subject to the provisions of this Schedule, be rated in respect of that hereditament for any relevant period of vacancy; and the provisions of this Act shall apply accordingly as if the hereditament were occupied during that relevant period of vacancy by the owner."

The definitions of "relevant hereditament" and "relevant period of vacancy" are contained in paragraph 15 in these terms:

> "'relevant hereditament' means any hereditament consisting of, or of part of, a house, shop, office, factory, mill or other building whatsoever, together with any garden, yard, court or other land ordinarily used or intended for use for the purposes of the building or part; 'relevant period of vacancy,' in relation to any relevant hereditament, means, subject to paragraph 1 (4) of this Schedule" —and I pause to say that that sub-paragraph has no reference to

> this case and only deals with dwelling houses—" any period beginning A
> with the day following the end of a period of three months during
> which the hereditament has been continuously unoccupied and
> ending with the day preceding that on which the hereditament
> becomes or next becomes occupied or ceases to exist; . . ."

At first sight these provisions look rather involved, but the effect is that
if a building remains unoccupied continuously for more than three B
months it becomes rateable after that period of three months. I think
it is probably convenient while looking at paragraph 15 of Schedule 1
to read the rest of it:

> " and references to a newly erected building or dwelling house include
> references to a building or dwelling house produced by the structural
> alteration of a building included in a relevant hereditament which C
> by virtue of paragraph 10 of this Schedule has ceased or will
> cease to exist on the completion of the structural alteration and,
> in relation to a building or dwelling house so produced, references
> to erection of a building shall be construed as references to the
> structural alteration producing it."

In this case, of course, we are only concerned with a newly erected D
building and not with structural alterations, but as some reliance was
placed on the term " structural alteration " I felt obliged to read that
part of the paragraph.

Going back to the beginning of the Schedule, paragraph 5 (1)
provides:

> " Subject to the provisions of this Schedule, the rateable value of a E
> hereditament for the purposes of paragraph 1 thereof shall be the
> rateable value ascribed to it in the valuation list in force for the
> area in which the hereditament is situated or, if the hereditament
> is not included in that list, the first rateable value subsequently
> ascribed to the hereditament in a valuation list in force for that
> area."

Paragraph 7 provides: F

> " For the purposes of paragraph 1 of this Schedule, a newly erected
> building which is not occupied on the date determined under the
> subsequent provisions of this Schedule as the date on which the
> erection of the building is completed shall be deemed to become
> unoccupied on that date." G

At first sight that looks like an odd use of a " deeming " provision.
However, it becomes intelligible when one realises that the word
" unoccupied " there is used in the technical sense in which it is used
in the rest of the Schedule, particularly paragraph 1 (1).

The vital provisions for the purposes of this appeal are paragraphs 8
and 9. Paragraph 8 provides: H

> " (1) Where a rating authority are of opinion—(*a*) that the erection
> of a building within their area has been completed; or (*b*) that the
> work remaining to be done on a building within their area is such
> that the erection of the building can reasonably be expected to be
> completed within three months, and that the building is, or when
> completed will be, comprised in a relevant hereditament, the
> authority may serve on the owner of the building a notice (hereafter

> A in this paragraph referred to as 'a completion notice') stating that the erection of the building is to be treated for the purposes of this Schedule as completed on the date of service of the notice or on such later date as may be specified by the notice. . . . (4) A person on whom a completion notice is served may, during the period of 21 days beginning with the date of service of the notice, appeal to the county court against the notice on the ground that the erection
> B of the building to which the notice relates has not been or, as the case may be, cannot reasonably be expected to be completed by the date specified by the notice."

Sub-paragraph (5) provides that if an appeal is brought to the county court "the erection of the building shall be treated for those purposes" —that is, the purposes of the Schedule—"as completed on such date as
C the court shall determine." Paragraph 9 provides:

> "In the case of a building to which work remains to be done of a kind which is customarily done to a building of the type in question after the erection of the building has been substantially completed, it shall be assumed for the purposes of paragraph 8 of this Schedule that the erection of the building has been or can reasonably be
> D expected to be completed at the expiration of such period beginning with the date of its completion apart from the work as is reasonably required for carrying out the work"—that is, the work remaining to be done.

Paragraph 10 deals with structural alterations, and provides:

> E "Where by reason of the structural alteration of any building a relevant hereditament becomes or becomes part of a different hereditament or different hereditaments, the relevant hereditament shall be deemed for the purposes of this Schedule to have ceased to exist on the date (as determined in pursuance of the foregoing provisions of this Schedule) of the completion of the structural alteration and, in particular, to have been omitted on that date
> F from any valuation list in which it is then included; but nothing in this paragraph shall be construed as affecting any liability for rates under paragraph 1 of this Schedule in respect of the hereditament for any period before that date."

Mr. Glover relies strongly on *Ravenseft Properties Ltd.* v. *Newham London Borough Council* [1976] Q.B. 464. In that case the rating
G authority served completion notices alleging that the buildings there in question, two new office blocks, had been completed on the day specified in the notice. Lord Denning M.R. stated the facts as follows, at p. 473:

> "This dispute depends on the state of the buildings. It has been agreed between the parties and we have photographs to show it. A big block, A, has 14 storeys of reinforced concrete construction.
> H The whole of the structure, as a structure, is no doubt completed. There are large floors all the way up the 14 storeys. On each of these floors at each end toilets are installed. Central heating and airconditioning systems are installed. These vast floors have not been divided into rooms or offices. There are no partitions in. Each of the 14 floors covers a rectangular space of 8,385 square feet with nothing there except 10 structural columns in a line. There is a fuse box on each floor with wiring for a power circuit. But

no points have been installed for any outlets. There was no wiring for any lighting system. There was no telephone system. No Post Office cables had been installed. No main distribution frame had been installed. Application had been made for a telephone line in different places. But it would be nine months before the telephone can be installed. The main contest is as to these floors. As I say, they are enormous floors with columns down the middle but no divisions whatsoever into rooms or into individual offices. It seems to me that they could not be occupied or ready for occupation until they had been divided up by partitions and rooms and so forth."

A

B

In that case, Ravenseft had appealed to the county court, the appeal had been allowed, and on appeal by the rating authority to this court the appeals were dismissed. Lord Denning M.R. said, at p. 473:

C

"So there we have the contest. Newham London Borough say they were complete because they were structurally complete. Ravenseft Properties Ltd. say No, they are not complete until they are ready for occupation, and they are not ready."

He said again, after quoting paragraph 8 (1) of Schedule 1 to the Act, at p. 474:

D

"It seems to me that the Schedule uses the word 'completed' there as something different from 'structural alteration' in paragraphs 10 and 15, and from the words 'substantially completed' in paragraph 9; and I am impressed by the reference to paragraph 6 to which we were referred. The word 'completed' in paragraph 8 (1) seems to me to mean completed in the sense of being ready for occupation. The test in this case is that the building should be ready for occupation. Once it is completely ready for occupation, there is a free period of three months during which rates are not payable, but after three months rates are payable. That applies not only to a new building but it applies if there is an alteration to an old building."

E

Lord Denning M.R. said, at p. 475:

F

"We had considerable discussion about the telephone cables and the electric wiring, and how far an office building could be said to be complete if the electric wiring had not been completed and the telephones were not installed. I think that may give rise to difficult questions on which I should like to have further evidence as to the condition of a particular building before giving any ruling on that matter."

G

At first sight that seems to me to suggest that Lord Denning M.R. was leaving open the question whether or not the absence of electric wiring, and so on, could mean that the building was not completed, and, for reasons which will appear later, that does seem to me to be what he may have been saying. But Mr. Glover told us that he had consulted counsel who were concerned in that case and had been informed that that statement was in fact directed to a different point and, therefore, we should not attach too great weight to it.

H

James and Bridge L.JJ. agreed that the appeal should be dismissed. James L.J. said, at p. 475:

"It seems to me that the appeal raises two short points, the first being the meaning to be given to the words 'completed' and 'com-

A pletion' where they appear in relation to hereditaments in Schedule 1 to the General Rate Act 1967. It is a Schedule that is not free from difficulty in construction; and, if I may say so, not absolutely clear in places. But I see no warrant whatsoever for importing the word 'structural' into paragraph 8 of that Schedule merely because that word appears in paragraph 10, and there should be the same test for completion in respect of newly erected buildings as for heredita-
B ments which have already been on the valuation list and are subjected to structural alteration, so that they become different or different parts of hereditaments. It seems to me that to adopt that construction, which is the basis of Mr. Fay's argument, strains the meaning of the statutory words. On the other hand, if one looks at the provisions set out below, one finds there strong indications
C all pointing to the test for which the ratepayers contend in this case, namely, that the test of completion is capability of occupation and that is the test to be applied to a newly erected hereditament."

James L.J. then referred to a number of statutory provisions and said, at p. 477:

"One looks forward at the time, in considering a newly erected
D hereditament, to the type of hereditament which is being required and sees whether at the date of the notice there is anything lacking which ought to be there in order to satisfy the nature of that hereditament. If there is something lacking and that which is lacking would, when done, fall to be part of the hereditament and taken into account for the purposes of the valuation, then there is no completion in the sense of capability of occupation."
E

Bridge L.J. said, at p. 478:

"The essential question for decision is what is the appropriate test to be applied under paragraph 8 of Schedule 1 to the Act as to when a building is properly regarded as completed. The key phrase in the paragraph, in my judgment, is the phrase 'and that the building is,
F or when completed will be, comprised in a relevant hereditament.'"

He then read the definition of "relevant hereditament" in paragraph 15 of Schedule 1, and continued:

"Bearing in mind that, under the law as it stood for centuries before unoccupied property became capable of rating, occupation was always
G the test of liability, I should, if I were construing this provision without having regard to its wider context, say without hesitation that what was contemplated was that the building should be completed so as to be capable of occupation for the appropriate purposes of the particular hereditament, that is, as a house, shop, office etc. If the building lacks features which before it can be occupied will have
H to be provided and when provided will form part of the occupied hereditament and form the basis of the valuation of that hereditament, then I would take the view, unless constrained to the contrary, that that building was not within the meaning of the relevant provision a completed building."

Bridge L.J. then referred to Mr. Fay's argument, Mr. Fay appearing for the rating authority in that case, and said, at p. 479:

"In the light of these considerations I come to the conclusion that capability of occupation is the test of completion which should be applicable both under paragraph 8 to a new building and under paragraph 10 to a new hereditament which comes into existence by structural alteration of an old building."

Mr. Glover submits that the hereditament with which we are concerned will not be capable of or ready for occupation for the purposes of this particular hereditament—that is, as a telephone exchange—until it is capable of being occupied for at least some or one of the purposes of a telephone exchange, and this will not be until at least some of the telephone equipment has been installed. He asks us to reject the qualification made by James and Bridge L.JJ. which I have read, namely, that what has to be done would fall to be part of a hereditament and taken into account for the purposes of valuation. He submits that the test is not whether or not the equipment to be installed is part of the hereditament or is rateable plant or equipment within what are now section 21 of and Schedule 3 to the Act of 1967 and the current Plant and Machinery (Rating) Order, but whether they are essential to the operation of the building as a telephone exchange. He submits that until this equipment had been installed neither paragraph 8 nor paragraph 9 of Schedule 1 applies. He says, rightly, that until the legislation of 1925 a factory was valued for rating as it stood, including all the plant and machinery in it (see *Kirby* v. *Hunslet Union Assessment Committee* [1906] A.C. 43), and submits that the subsequent legislation is concerned only with the value of plant and machinery and not with the definition of the hereditament. He further submits that the mischief with which Schedule 1 was intended to deal was the leaving unoccupied by their owners of buildings which are capable of immediate occupation (in the old rating sense), and that this case is not within that mischief.

Mr. Rippon relies on what James and Bridge L.JJ. said in *Ravenseft Properties Ltd.* v. *Newham London Borough Council* [1976] Q.B. 464, and says that the real distinction is between the work remaining to be done on the building itself and work to be done on plant and equipment or the installation of furniture. He stresses the references to "building" throughout Schedule 1.

It may well be that under the law as it was before 1966 the Post Office were not on August 1, 1975, or for some time thereafter, in rateable occupation of this building: see, for example, *Arbuckle Smith & Co. Ltd.* v. *Greenock Corporation* [1960] A.C. 813. But it is clear that the 1966 legislation, now re-enacted in the Act of 1967, was intended to make a fundamental change in the law. I think one is driven back to the wording of Schedule 1. I say at once that I cannot find in that wording any indication that the effect of the Schedule is intended to be limited to the mischief suggested by Mr. Glover: and this argument was in effect rejected by the Divisional Court in *Easiwork Homes Ltd.* v. *Redbridge London Borough Council* [1970] 2 Q.B. 406.

Paragraph 8 (1), (4) and (5) all refer to the date when "the erection of a [or 'the'] building will be completed." Paragraph 8 (1) (*b*) refers to "the work remaining to be done *on* a building . . . such that the erection of the building can reasonably be expected to be completed. . . ." The second requirement of paragraph 8 is that "the building is, or when completed will be, comprised in a relevant hereditament"; the definition of "relevant hereditament" in paragraph 15 is confined to buildings.

A Paragraph 9 also refers throughout to "a building," and to "a building
to which work remains to be done of a kind which is customarily done *to*
a building of the type in question after the erection of the building has
been substantially completed, . . ." The emphasis throughout is on "a"
or "the" building, and on work to be done "on" or "to" it.

In my judgment, the effect of these provisions, as interpreted by this
court in *Ravenseft's* case, is that the question is whether the building,
B *as a building*, is so far completed as to be capable of occupation or ready
for occupation for the purposes for which it is intended—as a house,
shop, office, factory or, in this case, a telephone exchange. In *Ravenseft's*
case this court held that the building there in question was not capable
of occupation or ready for occupation as offices mainly, as I understand
it, because the partitions had not been installed. They clearly did not
C hold that the building would not be completed—in the sense of being
capable of being occupied as offices—until all the furniture and equip-
ment necessary for their actual occupation and use as offices had been
installed. When that stage is reached, the offices would be in rateable
occupation in the pre-1966 sense, and if they are not "completed" for
the purposes of Schedule 1 until then, there would be no scope for the
provision as to the rating of unoccupied buildings. The position would
D be the same as to this telephone exchange if Mr. Glover is right.

I am very reluctant to introduce into the questions to be decided under
Schedule 1 the extremely difficult and complicated questions which arise
under the legislation as to the rating of plant and machinery. In my judg-
ment, those provisions are not relevant under Schedule 1; they were enacted
in a quite different context to deal only with valuation problems. James
E and Bridge L.JJ. in *Ravenseft's* case did not refer to this legislation; nor
did Bridge J. in the earlier case of *Watford Borough Council* v. *Parcourt
Property Investment Co. Ltd.* (1971) 17 R.R.C. 19: in that case he decided
that the building was not completed because the partitions were not com-
pleted, and left open the question whether the lack of electrical fittings
and fixtures rendered it incomplete: see p. 27. Partitions may in some
cases be "plant" (see, for example, *Jarrold* v. *John Good & Sons Ltd.*
F [1963] 1 W.L.R. 214), and, if so, they are non-rateable plant; electrical
fixtures and fittings, I think, would normally be non-rateable plant or
equipment. If in either of those cases the court had thought that the
provisions as to the rating of plant or machinery were relevant, they
would have had to consider the status of the partitions, the electrical
wiring, fixtures and fittings, and the telephone equipment under those
G provisions, and as they did not do so I think they must have thought
those provisions irrelevant. On the facts of *Ravenseft's* case it must have
been held, or assumed, that under the general law at least the partitions
would when completed be part of the hereditament and taken into account
in the valuation. If what was said by James and Bridge L.JJ. was
intended to go further than what was necessary for the facts of that
H particular case and lay down any wider general principle, I think, with
respect, that it was obiter. Nor do I think it necessary to introduce
into this context the highly technical problems of when articles brought
on to land do or do not become part of the freehold.

In my judgment, in deciding under Schedule 1 whether a building
is, or will be, completed on some date a broader and common sense test
must be applied. I think the test is: as a matter of fact and degree, is,
or will the building, as a building, be ready for occupation, or capable

of occupation, for the purpose for which it is intended? For example, A
I think that in the present case the judge was entitled to find that the building would not be completed until the transformer and the electric wiring had been installed, whether those items in themselves are or are not rateable plant or machinery, because until these had been installed the building, as a building, was not ready for occupation. I should myself be inclined to think (without deciding) that the same would apply to the ventilation system, but this is of no practical importance in this B
case, because the judge found that its installation would be completed by about August 1, 1975. The vital distinction, I think, is between the time when the building is ready for occupation as a building, and the subsequent installation in it of equipment or furniture which is necessary for its use for the purpose for which it is intended.

The judge did not have the advantage of knowing the decision in C
Ravenseft, but, in my view, he applied in substance the same test as that laid down by this court in that case. I think that his findings of fact amount to a finding that on August 1, 1975, this building, as a building, would be capable of occupation or ready for occupation as a telephone exchange, even though it could not actually be used as a telephone exchange until further equipment had been installed, and that this finding is fully justified by the evidence. I would dismiss this appeal. D

CAIRNS L.J. I agree that this appeal should be dismissed for the reasons which have been given by Browne L.J. I will express my own conclusions briefly in my own words.

The whole issue is whether a building intended to be occupied as a telephone exchange is complete within the meaning of Schedule 1 to E
the General Rate Act 1967 only when it is equipped for use as a telephone exchange, or whether it can be so complete at an earlier stage. I see no reason for giving to the word "complete" where it is used in this Schedule any other meaning than it would bear when used, in ordinary speech, of a building.

Since there might be some uncertainty as to whether a building F
could be said to be complete when it is substantially complete or only when additional work which would customarily be done to it after it is substantially complete has been done, paragraph 9 makes it clear that the latter meaning is to be adopted. Paragraph 9 refers to work *to* the building, not work *in* the building.

I cannot accept the proposition that a building intended for a telephone exchange is only complete when it is capable of immediate G
use as a telephone exchange. If that were the test, a house could not be said to be complete until it had been furnished, or a factory until the necessary tools for use in it were available.

When Lord Denning M.R. in the *Ravenseft* case [1976] Q.B. 464, 473 and 474 referred to the building being "ready for occupation," I am sure that he did not mean that it must be so equipped that use H
for the intended purpose could be begun immediately. The same applies to the phrase "capable of occupation" used by James and Bridge L.JJ. If the building is, in the ordinary sense, complete, so that it is ready to be equipped for the intended purpose by introducing some equipment which is not to be part of the building, then, in my opinion, the building is ready for occupation for that purpose. When James L.J. referred at p. 477 to "something lacking . . . which when done, would fall to be

part of the hereditament," I do not think he intended to include something which might be deemed to be part of the hereditament for the purpose of valuation. This is perhaps still clearer in the judgment of Bridge L.J. at p. 478, where he used the words "If the building lacks features which before it can be occupied will have to be provided . . ."

I am satisfied that the judge was right in regarding at least the kitchen equipment and telephone equipment as not being work which was reasonably required to be done to complete the building or work which remained to be done to the building. Unless he erred as to these matters, it cannot be said that he arrived at any wrong conclusion about the time of completion.

SIR GORDON WILLMER. I agree with both the judgments which have been delivered, and I do not seek to add anything of my own except to express, I hope without causing offence, some sense of regret that it has been found necessary for two public corporations to incur the expense of ventilating this dispute in court, the costs of which will no doubt have to come out of public funds, whether by way of rates or taxes.

Appeal dismissed with costs.
Leave to appeal refused.

Solicitors: *Saul Rothstein; Marcus Wakely, Nottingham.*

[CHANCERY DIVISION]

* PRACTICE DIRECTION
(CHANCERY: MASTERS' POWERS) (No. 3)

Practice—Chancery Division—Master—Power to hear matters in chambers—Leasehold reform—Leasehold Reform Act 1967 (*c.* 88), *s.* 27

Paragraph 3 of the memorandum on the powers of the Chancery Masters dated December 18, 1974 (*Practice Direction* (*Chancery*: *Masters' Powers*) [1975] 1 W.L.R. 129), as amended on February 21, 1975 (*Practice Direction* (*Chancery*: *Masters' Powers*) (*No.* 2) [1975] 1 W.L.R. 405), is further amended, by the decision of the judges of the Chancery Division, by the addition of the following item:

"(w) Exercising the powers of the court under section 27 of the Leasehold Reform Act 1967 (enfranchisement where landlord cannot be found)."

R. E. BALL
Chief Master
Chancery Division.

May 24, 1976.

[HOUSE OF LORDS]

* PRACTICE DIRECTION
(HOUSE OF LORDS: PETITIONS FOR LEAVE TO APPEAL) (No. 2)

House of Lords — Leave to appeal — Petition — Incompetent — Certified as such — Fitness for oral hearing — Petitions not referred for oral hearing certified accordingly

By virtue of a further Practice Direction dated May 20, 1976, there are to be substituted for the last paragraph of the Practice Direction dated May 18, 1976 [1976] 1 W.L.R. 549, the following paragraphs:

2. Petitions for leave to appeal will be referred for an oral hearing if any member of the Appeal Committee—
(i) considers that the petition is competent or expresses doubts as to whether it is incompetent; and
(ii) considers that it is fit for an oral hearing.

3. Where a petition is not considered fit for an oral hearing, the Clerk of the Parliaments will notify the parties that the petition is dismissed.

4. This Practice Direction supersedes the previous Practice Directions on petitions for leave to appeal.

[QUEEN'S BENCH DIVISION]

* COX v. PHILIPS INDUSTRIES LTD.

[1971 C. No. 3765]

1975 Oct. 13, 14, 15 Lawson J.

Damages—Contract—Breach—Mental distress—Employee relegated to position of lesser responsibility in breach of contract—Whether damages for vexation, frustration and distress suffered by employee in inferior position recoverable

The plaintiff received an attractive offer of employment from a rival company. His employers, who were anxious to retain his services, offered him a better position with greater responsibility and an increase in salary. The plaintiff accepted the offer and, although not a term of the contract, the parties contemplated that he would receive annual increments of salary. He received an increment of £70 at Christmas 1963 and fulfilled the post satisfactorily until December 1964, when he wrote a letter protesting that the increment of £30 for the following years was too small. As a result of that letter, his employers removed him without notice to a position of less responsibility but at the same salary. His duties were vague and he was not told what he had to do. He became depressed, anxious, frustrated and ill. During his illness, he

---

[Reported by B. O. AGYEMAN, ESQ., Barrister-at-Law]

A received a number of letters from his employers telling him that if he could not fill the position, there were no other posts within the company so that the alternatives were either that his name be forwarded to the associated companies or that he be made redundant. Eventually on July 1, 1965, he signed a letter of resignation written by the employers, his employment was immediately terminated and he was paid five months' salary in lieu of notice.

B On the plaintiff's claim against the defendants as part owners of his employers' company for damages for breach of contract and for tort:—

Held, giving judgment for the plaintiff, (1) that, although the plaintiff was induced to sign a letter of resignation, the situation on July 1, 1965, was that the plaintiff was wrongfully dismissed but, since he had been paid the appropriate compensation under the terms of the contract of employment, he
C could not recover damages for the dismissal.

Addis v. *Gramophone Co. Ltd.* [1909] A.C. 488, H.L.(E.) applied.

(2) That the relegation of the plaintiff to a position of lesser responsibility was in breach of contract; and that, since it must have been in the contemplation of the parties that the breach, without reasonable notice, would expose the plaintiff to the vexation, frustration and distress which he had suffered,
D the plaintiff was entitled to damages of £500.

Jarvis v. *Swan Tours Ltd.* [1973] Q.B. 233, C.A. considered.

The following cases are referred to in the judgment:

Addis v. *Gramophone Co. Ltd.* [1909] A.C. 488, H.L.(E.).

Davis & Co. (*Wines*) *Ltd.* v. *Afa-Minerva* (*E.M.I.*) *Ltd.* [1974] 2 Lloyd's Rep. 27.

E *Jarvis* v. *Swans Tours Ltd.* [1973] Q.B. 233; [1972] 3 W.L.R. 954; [1973] 1 All E.R. 71, C.A.

No additional cases were cited in argument.

ACTION

The plaintiff, Glyn Cox, was an industrial metallurgical engineer and,
F between 1946 and 1965, he had been employed by Intertherm Ltd., a company partly owned by the defendants, Philips Industries Ltd. By specially endorsed writ, the plaintiff claimed from the defendants damages for breach of contract and tort while in the employ of Intertherm Ltd. in the sum of £18,000. By an amended statement of claim, he alleged that, having been given a better position in the company, that position was wrongfully taken
G away in December 1964 and that, on July 1, 1965, he was coerced into leaving the company. By further and better particulars, the plaintiff claimed damages for loss of salary equivalent to £1,000 a year for 17 years, £17,000; loss of appreciation in value of the house which he claimed he would have bought but for the defendants' failure to implement the contract by aiding him in buying a house, £4,500; loss of employer's contribution to pension scheme over 19 years, £825; legal fees deducted
H from salary, £13·77½; and interest on loss of the £1,000 a year over a period of six years, £800.

By their defence, the defendants denied that they or Intertherm Ltd. were in breach of contract or that the plaintiff had suffered damage.

The facts are stated in the judgment.

The plaintiff in person.

David Eady for the defendants.

LAWSON J. In this action, the plaintiff, who has conducted this case A in person and done so, if I may say so, with great moderation and common sense, is claiming damages against the defendants, Philips Industries Ltd., for breach of the terms of a contractual arrangement which he alleges he made with the representatives of his then employers, a company called Intertherm Ltd., which was a company partly owned by Philips Industries Ltd., in relation to certain terms and conditions of his employment.

By his writ issued on June 21, 1971, he claims damages for breach B of a contract or contractual terms in the following respects. He alleges that there was a contractual term, and the defendants by their defence admit there was a contractual term, that he should as from the time when this arrangement was made be given a better position within Intertherm Ltd. He alleges, and again it is admitted, that there was a contractual term to the effect that he should be given an immediate increase in salary. It is C admitted that that was part of the contractual arrangements reached at the end of July 1963, and it is common ground that as a result of those contractual arrangements he was in fact given an immediate salary increase bringing his salary to £1,600 per annum with effect from August 1, 1963.

He alleges, but it is denied by the defence, in effect, that it was also a contractual term of those arrangements that he should be given substantial increases of salary at Christmas 1963 and Christmas 1964. I am not D satisfied that there was any such term in the contractual arrangements made in July 1963. I am satisfied that it was in the contemplation of the parties at that time that, as had happened in the normal course of events over earlier years of the plaintiff's employment with this company, he would receive annual increases of salary. But I do not think the parties were in a position to or did agree what precise increases should be given at E Christmas 1963 and Christmas 1964. It is a fact that at Christmas 1963 he was given an increase of salary at the rate of £70 per annum thus bringing his annual salary for the year 1964 up to a figure of £1,670. He does not complain about that. It is a fact that in December 1964 he was given, with effect from January 1, 1965, an increase of salary of the order of £30 a year thus bringing his annual salary to the rate of £1,700 a year as at January 1, 1965. F

By certain further and better particulars the plaintiff has put a gloss on this particular term, the gloss being that it was part of the contractual arrangements made in July 1963 that by January 1965 he would be earning at the rate of £1,750 per annum. I am quite confident that there was a discussion of the probable amount of his earnings in January 1965, but I am not satisfied that there was any firm contractual agreement to the G effect that that would be his salary in January 1965. I am not satisfied about this for two reasons. First, Mr. Savage, who was a very important figure in these July 1963 negotiations, says, and I accept it, that had he believed that a firm commitment for a salary at that rate in January 1965 had been agreed between the parties he would certainly have put this into writing: such an arrangement was never put into writing. The second reason is that whereas the plaintiff in his evidence (and I have not the H slightest doubt that he all the time has been doing his best to give me an accurate account of his recollection) said that Mr. Savage had specifically stated that the January 1965 salary would be at the rate that I mentioned, when the crunch of the matter occurred in December 1963, that is the time at which the plaintiff was informed by letter, undated but certainly before December 10, 1964, that he had been awarded an increase of £30, he wrote a letter of protest about that matter, a letter which I find quite reasonable

A and moderate in its terms and language, protesting about the meagreness of that increase but he did not in that letter say anything to the effect that there was a firm commitment to bring his salary up to the level I have indicated by January 1965.

The plaintiff further alleges that there was a contractual term—it is expressed in rather vague language, but I do not think there is any real issue between the parties about this matter—that he should have the use of B the Philips Housing Scheme, including a bridging loan-cum-gift, to assist him in the purchase of a house. The defence puts the matter in this way. It is agreed that they would give the plaintiff the use of the Philips Housing Scheme to assist the plaintiff in the purchase of a house. There is therefore no question to my mind that there was a contractual term to that effect agreed between the parties in July 1963. The question is whether that term C was broken. [His Lordship considered a further claim for £13·77½ in respect of legal fees relating to an abortive house purchase and concluded that there was really no issue between the parties and that the defendants were prepared to pay that amount. His Lordship considered the facts in relation to the availability of financial assistance in the purchase of a house and was satisfied that the defendants were not in breach of the contractual arrangement in that respect and continued:]

D The other matter which I have to determine arises in relation to the first term of these contractual arrangements. It is necessary for one moment to put these contractual arrangements in their context, against their proper background, and this can very conveniently be done by reference to a memorandum compiled by Mr. Savage on January 23, 1964 (Mr. Savage having taken part in the negotiations which led to contractual E terms in July 1963) in which Mr. Savage, inter alia, says:

> "Mr. Cox is a long serving employee of Intertherm Philips. He is a very valuable member of the staff. A few months ago he had received a substantial offer from Raydyne"—that is a rival company—"which would have given him a salary increase plus substantial housing assistance. The exact nature of the housing assistance is F not known but it is believed to have been in the form of a loan with repayments from annual bonuses to be paid to Mr. Cox. If Raydyne were prepared to make such an offer it was obvious that Intertherm would have to match the offer. If Mr. Cox left it would be a gain to Raydyne and a double loss to Intertherm. Intertherm made an offer of a new position of greater responsibility; a considerable increase in salary was given (the figure was given to G Mr. Gunn)"—that was the increase of £214—"and in addition a promise of housing assistance to match Raydyne's offer was given. . . . Mr. Cox has good growth potential in his new job. . . . The house that Mr. Cox was interested in was a modest one and in line with the type expected of a man in his position. Mr. Cox has a deposit available of £550."

H That gives the background to these contractual arrangements. What happened in fact was that the position of greater responsibility—and this was a genuine position of greater responsibility with the company, not merely a face saving operation to provide him with a higher salary so that he could get housing assistance, as was suggested at a later stage—was the position of what was called "product leader motor generators." This position he occupied, and occupied to everybody's satisfaction, until December 1964, when he wrote what in the event seems to have been a

highly unfortunate letter protesting about the meagreness of his rise in A
salary of £30 for the next financial year.

The effect of this was somewhat dramatic. It is recorded, so far as one can place reliance on these records, in a memorandum made by Mrs. Henshaw, now Mrs. Calthrop, who was some kind of personnel officer employed by the defendant company. The relevant part of the note reads:

> "Mr. Geary called a meeting of Mr. Ashton, Mr. Rupp and Mr. B
> Pinkney, to discuss a letter he had received from Mr. Cox and with particular reference to Cox's future with the company."

So by writing this letter what the plaintiff did in fact achieve, unwittingly no doubt, so far as he was concerned, was to procure the then managing
director to consider his future with the company. A man who writes a C
letter of protest is a man whose future has got to be decided upon. Mr. Geary, as I indicated, is hopelessly at sea about dates. This is not a criticism because he ceased to be connected with this company or its group many years ago. He has got no records. He has had no opportunity to refresh his memory, and he himself quite frankly confessed to me, when I showed him or referred him to this particular memorandum, that he
might have been a year out. Anyhow, what happened was, and I find, D
that, as a result of this meeting which took place between these gentlemen and in which the plaintiff was not at that stage participating, he was removed to a position of lesser responsibility. It so happens that the defendant company keeps record cards and when one looks at the record card showing what his position was as from January 1, 1965, it is demons-
trably different from and changed from the position which he is shown E
occupying on that card in the preceding October. That was in my judgment a breach of contract. Where there is a conflict of evidence between Mr. Geary and the plaintiff about that matter, I entirely accept the evidence of the plaintiff that he was relegated to a lower position of responsibility and I reject the evidence of Mr. Geary. Just concluding the history, from the time this relegation of his position occurred at the end of December
1964, although his salary remained unaffected at the rate for 1965 of F
£1,700 per year, his duties were extremely vague. He did not really know what he was supposed to do and nobody ever really told him what he was supposed to do. This could have been by accident, or on the other hand it could well have been by design. The result of this was that the plaintiff became very depressed, extremely anxious, and very frustrated. He began to have periods of sickness and depression. In the course of these he was
referred to the company doctor, Dr. Greenberg, who saw him and wrote a G
record following an examination of him on March 24, 1965: "I suspect that an important factor in this man's illness is an inimical working environment," that is, his relegation to a position of lower responsibility. "Full recovery will depend on the adjustment of the man and/or his work environment."

Things went on with him in his position of lesser responsibility so far H
as he was able to work, and then he became the object of a series of ultimata delivered by those responsible for the control of the company. These ultimata start with a letter of April 5, 1965, which says in effect: if you cannot do what you are supposed to be doing now, fill this post of lesser responsibility, then there are only two alternatives, either to find you another position, and there is no other position in this company you can fill, but we can forward your name to associated companies, or declare

A you redundant. Then there is a declaration that he would be given as
generous a treatment as possible. At the time when he received this letter
the plaintiff was still under medical attention; he was going to have a
medical examination at the end of April, and he said he would let them
know at the end of April when he had had his medical examination what
he proposed to do. So on April 21, 1965, he wrote to Mr. Sharp following
his medical examination, saying that he had elected for redundancy. He
B gave the reasons, and he asked for generous assistance.

A number of events occurred, but the next step in the matter was that
Mrs. Henshaw, apparently, prepared a letter on May 25. This is again
what I have described as an ultimatum: "1. Your appointment with the
company is in the induction heating department." This is a confirmation
of the reduced position of responsibility. So is 2:

C "You are to report to, and carry out instructions from Mr. Rupp,
the head of the department. 3. In the event of your not carrying out
your duties to the entire satisfaction of Mr. Rupp and the management
your appointment will be terminated. 4. In this event there
will be no question of extended leave, redundancy or any other concession
by the company. I hope the situation is now much clearer
D in your mind and that you will now settle down again."

I am bound to say that whenever there is a conflict of evidence between
the plaintiff and Mrs. Cox on the one hand, and Mrs. Henshaw, now Mrs.
Calthrop, on the other, I have no hesitation at all in accepting the evidence
of Mr. and Mrs. Cox. I have watched Mrs. Calthrop giving her evidence,
I have listened very carefully to her answers, I have read her documents
E and her memoranda, I am not satisfied that she was telling the truth. This
brings me to a particular matter which I find disturbing.

On July 1, 1965, there is no doubt that the plaintiff signed a letter of
that date, a letter which quite clearly is typed on an electric typewriter.
Mr. Cox does not type and had no access to an electric typewriter. There
was however one in the office of the managing director. The letter bears
on its top right hand corner Mr. Cox's address, typed but incorrectly typed:
F he does not live at the address which is stated on that letter. The letter
says, "Dear Mrs. Henshaw, as from today, July 1, 1965, I am resigning
my position with Intertherm Ltd." I have not the slightest doubt that that
letter was prepared in the offices of the defendants, not with the knowledge
of the plaintiff, and that that letter was handed to the plaintiff to sign—
the final ultimatum—and was handed to him at the same time as he was
G given the letter of July 1, 1965, acknowledging receipt of his letter of
July 1 tendering his resignation. It is also fair to say that on July 1 he
was handed an envelope, and in that envelope there was a cheque for five
months' salary in lieu of notice.

Really the situation which was reached on July 1 was a situation in
which the plaintiff was wrongfully dismissed, although he was induced in
H some way or another to sign this letter of resignation. But, unfortunately
for him, he was given and paid the appropriate compensation for wrongful
dismissal because at the material time it was a term of his employment
that, as he had served 16 but under 20 years with the company, the period
of notice to which he was entitled was five months. So that is what he got.
Of course had he brought an action for damages for wrongful dismissal,
having regard to that fact, and to the decision in *Addis* v. *Gramophone Co.
Ltd.* [1909] A.C. 488, he would have recovered nothing at all.

That is the history. I now come back to this question of the breach of the contractual term which I find took place when he was relegated to a position of lesser responsibility. I have already said his salary remained the same but there is not the slightest doubt in my mind that the result of this relegation in breach of contract, contrary to the promise that the defendants had made, did expose him to a good deal of depression, vexation and frustration and indeed lead to ill health. The question is: can I give him damages in respect of those matters for that breach of contract? I have considered *Jarvis* v. *Swans Tours Ltd.* [1973] Q.B. 233, which is referred to but, I think, not particularly helpfully in the later case of *Davis & Co.* (*Wines*) *Ltd.* v. *Afa-Minerva* (*E.M.I.*) *Ltd.* [1974] 2 Lloyd's Rep. 27.

In my judgment this is a case where it was in the contemplation of the parties in all the circumstances that, if that promise of a position of better responsibility without reasonable notice was breached, then the effect of that breach would be to expose the plaintiff to the degree of vexation, frustration and distress which he in fact underwent.

I have had very helpful submissions from Mr. Eady on this matter suggesting that damages for this kind of loss are really only appropriate when you lose a relative and the funeral procession does not turn up at the right time, or you acquire a wife and the photographer does not turn up at the right time, or you do not have the holiday you are promised. But I can see no reason in principle why, if a situation arises which within the contemplation of the parties would have given rise to vexation, distress and general disappointment and frustration, the person who is injured by a contractual breach should not be compensated in damages for that breach. Doing the best I can, because money can never really make up for mental distress and vexation—this is a common problem of course in personal injury cases—I think the right sum to award the plaintiff under that head is the sum of £500.

The plaintiff's claims, and this is not of course surprising where a layman is presenting his own case, are pitched very, very high indeed. I am quite satisfied that the claims which the plaintiff is making in relation to the loss of the appreciation in value of a house do not lie in this case because there was no breach of contract in respect of the promise to give housing assistance. I am quite satisfied that his claims for loss of the pension contribution and his claim for loss of salary equivalent to £1,000 a year, do not lie, first of all, because there was no breach in respect of the termination of his services on which he can rely, and even had there been the amount of damages he would have been able to recover for that would be limited in the way that I previously indicated.

I know that the plaintiff is going to be disappointed by my award but nevertheless I cannot see my way in justice to both parties to deal with the matter in any different way from that in which I have dealt with it.

Judgment for plaintiff for £500 with costs.

Solicitors: *Bird & Bird.*

A

[COURT OF APPEAL]

* STRINGFELLOW *v.* STRINGFELLOW

1976 Feb. 25 — Stamp and Ormrod L.JJ. and Cusack J.

B *Husband and Wife—Divorce—Respondent's behaviour—Test to be applied—Husband's intolerable behaviour for short period prior to desertion—Whether wife entitled to rely on husband's behaviour as ground for divorce—Matrimonial Causes Act* 1973 (*c.* 18), *s.* 1 (2) (*b*) (*c*)

The parties were married in 1969 and had two children. In January 1975, the husband's attitude towards the wife changed
C suddenly: he ceased to show any affection towards her, he refused to have sexual intercourse and he would not take her out because he had no feelings for her and could not stand her being near to him. In March he told the wife to go to her parents for a week so that he could sort out his feelings as he no longer loved her. Although upset by his rejection of her, she went to her parents but, on her return, he insisted on parting from her. On March 23, 1975, he left the
D matrimonial home. On June 12, 1975, the wife petitioned for divorce under section 1 (2) (*b*) of the Matrimonial Causes Act 1973.[1] The judge took the view that the wife could not reasonably be expected to have tolerated the husband's behaviour if it had been persisted in for a long time but, since the behaviour was over a short period and the husband might be suffering from a temporary medical condition, it could not be said that there was no possibility of a reconciliation. He
E held that the marriage had not irretrievably broken down and dismissed the petition.

On appeal by the wife:—

Held, dismissing the appeal, that, since the behaviour of a respondent in desertion was such that a deserted spouse could not reasonably be expected to live with the respondent, section 1 (2) (*b*) of the Matrimonial Causes Act 1973 had to be read
F so that effect could also be given to paragraph (*c*) and behaviour within that paragraph was to be excluded from behaviour within paragraph (*b*); that, accordingly, behaviour in paragraph (*b*) meant conduct other than desertion or behaviour leading up to desertion and since the husband's behaviour amounted only to desertion and conduct leading to desertion, the wife had failed to prove that the husband's behaviour came within paragraph (*b*) and, accordingly, the
G judge had correctly dismissed the petition.

Per curiam. If the only question in the case had been whether the marriage had irretrievably broken down, the better course would have been to adjourn the case under section 6 (2) of the Act for a period of, say, six months so that the court could see whether the parties resumed cohabitation during the interval (post, p. 649C).

H [Reported by EMMANUEL C. ABARAONYE, ESQ., Barrister-at-Law]

[1] Matrimonial Causes Act 1973, s. 1: "(2) The court hearing a petition for divorce shall not hold the marriage to have broken down irretrievably unless the petitioner satisfies the court of one or more of the following facts, that is to say— . . . (*b*) that the respondent has behaved in such a way that the petitioner cannot reasonably be expected to live with the respondent; (*c*) that the respondent has deserted the petitioner for a continuous period of at least two years immediately preceding the presentation of the petition; . . ."

The following case is referred to in the judgment of Ormrod L.J.:

Evans v. *Evans,* February 10, 1976; Bar Library Transcript No. 56 of 1976, C.A.

No additional cases were cited in argument.

APPEAL from Judge Hutchinson sitting at Great Grimsby County Court.

The parties were married in February 1969. There were two children of the marriage: two daughters born in March 1970 and October 1971 respectively. In January 1975, as a result of a sudden change of attitude towards the wife by the husband, married life ceased between the spouses and in March 1975 the husband left the matrimonial home. In June 1975, the wife petitioned for divorce alleging that the husband had behaved in such a way that she could not reasonably be expected to live with him. In September 1975 Judge Hutchinson, although he found that the husband's behaviour was such that if persisted in over a long period the wife could not reasonably be expected to live with him, held that the marriage had not irretrievably broken down because the behaviour complained of was over a period of three months only and the surrounding circumstances indicated that it might have been caused by illness or depression.

The wife appealed on the grounds, inter alia, that the judge erred in law (if he so held) in holding that the conduct as between the wife and the husband was not such that the husband had behaved in such a way that the wife could not reasonably be expected to live with him; that the judge erred in law in failing to give any due weight to the evidence of the wife as to the husband's behaviour and attitude during the period between March 23, 1975, and September 3, 1975; that the finding of the judge that the behaviour of the husband might be temporary was unsupported by the evidence; and that the judge erred in law in holding that the marriage had not irretrievably broken down.

The facts are stated in the judgment of Ormrod L.J.

John Milmo for the wife.

The husband did not appear and was not represented.

STAMP L.J. I will ask Ormrod L.J. to give the first judgment.

ORMROD L.J. This is an appeal from a judgment of Judge Hutchinson given at the Great Grimsby county court on September 3, 1975, when he dismissed the appellant wife's undefended petition for divorce. She had presented a petition for divorce under section 1 (2) (*b*) of the Matrimonial Causes Act 1973, namely, that she averred that her husband had behaved in such a way that she could not reasonably be expected to live with him. The judge clearly dealt with the matter carefully and, unlike the earlier case of *Evans* v. *Evans,* February 10, 1976; Bar Library Transcript No. 56 of 1976, in this case counsel who appeared did make a note of the judgment in accordance with what should be the normal practice; and we have the advantage of a full note of the obviously short judgment together with the comments of the judge himself on that note, which he accepted substantially. There was no note recorded of the actual evidence given by the petitioner wife because there was no shorthand writer, but in this case that does not present any particular difficulty because it is not suggested for a moment by Mr. Milmo, who said everything that could be said in this case on her behalf, that the evidence went outside the particulars set out

A under paragraph 9 of the petition. So this court may safely, in my judgment, take the allegations set out under paragraph 9 as being the sum total of the evidence which the wife gave with one small exception, that it appears from the judge's own comment in his judgment that the wife did refer to the possibility at least that the husband's behaviour had been caused by illness or depression, so there was that possible explanation of his behaviour in the evidence.

B The allegations which are said to constitute behaviour within the limits of section 1 (2) (*b*) are simply these, that having been married since 1969, having had two children, and having been, I assume, reasonably happy together, the situation between them changed in January 1975 when the respondent husband, to quote the words of the petition:

> "(a) . . . ceased to show any interest in keeping the said marriage C alive and has failed and refused to show any affection towards the petitioner. (b) . . . has refused to have sexual intercourse with the petitioner and has rejected all approaches made by the petitioner saying that he was not in the mood or that he was feeling depressed. (c) . . . has regularly gone out in the evenings but has failed to take the petitioner out saying that he had no feelings for her. (d) . . . has told the petitioner that he could not stand her being near to him. D (e) . . . is interested in sport and puts his sporting activities before the petitioner and the said children as a result whereof the said children have had no family life. (f) [He] told the petitioner to go to her parents for a week so that he could sort out his feelings saying that he no longer loved the petitioner and that he wanted his freedom which he had lost by marrying her at the age of 19."

E The wife went to her parents, and returned after a week, but the husband insisted that he wished to part from her; and it is said, naturally enough, that his rejection of her upset her. And finally on March 23, 1975, he left and has lived apart from her ever since.

The judge in his judgment accepted the evidence of the wife. He pointed out that the differences had not lasted very long. He summarised F the matters alleged as I have done, and said:

> "The [wife] tried to persuade the [husband] to see the marriage guidance council and the doctor—he rejected these approaches. The position would be different if the [husband's] behaviour had been prolonged over a long time. The [wife] could not be expected to tolerate his behaviour but his actual conduct was only over a period G of three months and they have been apart for a further six months. I find it difficult to believe that this marriage could not be rehabilitated. I cannot be satisfied that this marriage has irretrievably broken down. There was a sudden change of attitude by the [husband]. Therefore this petition is dismissed."

Apparently during argument the judge had said that he thought there H might have been a temporary medical problem and that during that period of two or three months the husband had behaved in such a way that the wife could not reasonably have been expected to live with him during that short period, although he could not see that the marriage had irretrievably broken down. In his short note of the judgment the judge did not add very much to it, but he made his views clear. He said:

> "My finding was that the behaviour of the respondent was such that if it had been persisted in over a long period the petitioner could not

have been reasonably expected to live with him. However the period A
in this case was very short—three months from January to March 1975 followed by desertion. Further, the surrounding circumstances testified to by the petitioner—in particular her belief that the respondent's behaviour was or might be caused by illness or depression brought on by overwork—indicated that the behaviour might be temporary. I was therefore not satisfied that the conduct actually proved came within section 1 (2) (*b*) of the Act of 1973. I considered B
there was some possibility of reconciliation here, and found therefore that the marriage had not irretrievably broken down."

There are in effect two points in this case. Mr. Milmo submits, first, that the judge found that the husband's conduct fell within the terms of section 1 (2) (*b*), but dismissed the petition on the ground that he was not satisfied that the marriage had irretrievably broken down. Mr. Milmo drew C
our attention, first of all, to section 1 (4) of the Act of 1973, which provides:

"If the court is satisfied on the evidence of any such fact as is mentioned in subsection (2) above, then, unless it is satisfied on all the evidence that the marriage has not broken down irretrievably, it shall, subject to sections 3 (3) and 5 below, grant a decree of divorce."

D
Mr. Milmo also drew our attention to section 6 (2), which provides:

"If at any stage of proceedings for divorce it appears to the court that there is a reasonable possibility of a reconciliation between the parties to the marriage, the court may adjourn the proceedings for such period as it thinks fit to enable attempts to be made to effect such a reconciliation."

E
Mr. Milmo suggests that in this case the judge should have used the power given to him by that subsection. The case, however, does raise a different and quite a difficult question, and that is what is the relationship between the two grounds (*b*) and (*c*) set out in section 1 (2) of the Act of 1973? Ground (*c*) of course is desertion; and, if one reads (*b*) literally, it would be easy to conclude that no spouse could reasonably be expected to live with a spouse who had deserted him or her. In other words, ground (*b*) has to be F
given some meaning which is not quite its literal grammatical one if it is to co-exist with (*c*) because it is clear to me that if (*b*) is to be read literally there will not in fact be any case coming before the court on the ground of desertion because every deserted spouse could maintain that the deserter had behaved in such a way that he or she could not be expected to live with him. So it cannot mean that; it must mean something G
more than that; and, in my judgment, it means some conduct other than the desertion or the behaviour leading up to the desertion. It means something which justifies the court in finding that the marriage had irretrievably broken down before the period of two years had elapsed after the separation. So there must be some conduct on the part of the respondent spouse which goes beyond mere desertion or the steps leading up to mere desertion. H

This case on the evidence seems to me to be a classic case of desertion simpliciter, if I may put it that way. The whole married life came quickly to an end following a change in the husband which took place in January 1975. No complaint is made about his behaviour prior to that at all. In that month either he was ill or something happened to him which altered his attitude completely towards his wife. He did no more as far as I can see than indicate to her that his attitude had changed. His attitude having changed, he could not display affection to her, he could not have sexual intercourse with her or would be very reluctant to do so, and inevitably during those weeks between January and his departure in March this relationship was breaking down. But I do not see any allegation in the petition which goes beyond describing the basic facts of a relationship between husband and wife which has for one reason or another broken down, and I cannot see any behaviour on his part outside the limits of that situation. So for my part I would certainly hold that the wife here failed to show that the husband had behaved in such a way that she could not reasonably be expected to live with him within ground (*b*). She certainly has a case on desertion, but under the statute in its present form she has to wait two years.

On the question of whether or not the judge was satisfied that the marriage had irretrievably broken down, I take Mr. Milmo's point that if that was the only difficulty which the judge saw in the wife's way then it would have been better to adjourn the mattter for, say, six months in order that the court could see what would happen in that interval—whether the parties were going to live together again or not. But in view of the nature of the behaviour complained of in this case in my judgment the judge was right to dismiss this petition, and I would therefore dismiss this appeal.

CUSACK L.J. I agree with the judgment of Ormrod L.J. and I have nothing to add.

STAMP J. I also agree.

Appeal dismissed.
No order for costs save legal aid taxation.

Solicitors: *Beetenson & Gibbon, Grimsby.*

[COURT OF APPEAL]

* MUNTON *v.* GREATER LONDON COUNCIL AND ANOTHER

[Ref. 43/1974]

1976 Feb. 4, 5

Lord Denning M.R., Scarman and Goff L.JJ.

Compulsory Purchase — Compensation — Agreement "subject to contract" — Rise in house values before date of entry into possession — Whether memorandum in writing required on compulsory acquisition — Whether "subject to contract" effective to postpone ascertainment of price—Whether price for land and compensation for disturbance separable—Land Compensation Act 1961 (9 & 10 *Eliz.* 2, *c.* 33), *s.* 5 (6) [1]

In September 1969 the acquiring authority served notice to treat on the claimant owner of a house in an area scheduled

[1] Land Compensation Act 1961, s. 5 (6): see post, p. 653E–F.

for slum clearance. Negotiations were conducted on the basis
of the district valuer's figure of £3,400, all the letters containing A
the words "subject to contract" and stressing the necessity
for the claimant and his family to be rehoused. On March
28, 1972, the claimant's solicitors wrote to say that he had
found alternative accommodation and the sale could proceed
at £3,400 "subject to contract" and settlement of any claim
for disturbance. The completion date was fixed for April 27;
but the alternative accommodation did not materialise. On
December 6 the acquiring authority took possession of the B
property following notice of entry. By that date property
values had risen considerably and the claimant's solicitors said
that he would not accept the original price. The district valuer
revalued the property at £5,100, under all heads of claim, and
the claimant was prepared to accept that sum; but the acquiring
authority then claimed that there had been a binding agree-
ment on March 28 for £3,400 plus disturbance to be agreed.

On a reference as a preliminary point of law on the C
question whether or not the price had been agreed at £3,400
the Lands Tribunal determined that the compensation to be
paid under the Land Compensation Act 1961 was £5,100, find-
ing that at no time had £3,400 been unreservedly agreed. The
Lands Tribunal expressed the views (a) that the acquiring
authority could only succeed if there had been by March 28
a memorandum sufficient to satisfy section 40 of the Law of
Property Act 1925; (b) that even if section 40 did not apply D
the words "subject to contract" could have no lesser effect
on a compulsory purchase than they had in an ordinary
contract for the sale of land; and he also indicated (c) that
the settlement of a claim for disturbance after the price for
the land had been agreed might be ultra vires.

On appeal by the acquiring authority:—

Held, dismissing the appeal, that though (a) the statutory
agreement for compensation on a compulsory purchase neither E
required a memorandum in writing complying with the require-
ments of section 40 of the Law of Property Act 1925 nor in
the normal case involved a contract in writing prior to com-
pletion, and (b) compensation for the land could be assessed
separately from compensation for disturbance (as section 5 (2)
and (6) of the Land Compensation Act 1961 itself made clear),
nevertheless the words "subject to contract" introduced into F
the negotiations for the price were effective to prevent an
agreement binding on the parties at any date before the
acquiring authority entered into possession; and accordingly
the value at that date was the price payable.

Per Goff L.J. Nothing said in the very special circum-
stances of *Michael Richards Properties Ltd.* v. *St. Saviour's
Parish, Southwark, Corporation of Wardens* [1975] 3 All E.R.
416, 424, was intended to throw any doubt on the well
established and well settled sanctity of the words "subject to G
contract" (post, p. 656F–H).

The following cases are cited in the judgments:

Cary-Elwes' Contract, In re [1906] 2 Ch. 143.

Chillingworth v. *Esche* [1924] 1 Ch. 97, C.A.

Harding v. *Metropolitan Railway Co.* (1872) 7 Ch.App. 154. H

Harvey v. *Crawley Development Corporation* [1957] 1 Q.B. 485; [1957] 2 W.L.R. 332; [1957] 1 All E.R. 504, C.A.

Horn v. *Sunderland Corporation* [1941] 2 K.B. 26; [1941] 1 All E.R. 480, C.A.

Inland Revenue Commissioners v. *Glasgow and South Western Railway Co.* (1887) 12 App.Cas. 315, H.L.(Sc.).

Lee v. *Minister of Transport* [1966] 1 Q.B. 111; [1965] 3 W.L.R. 553; [1965] 2 All E.R. 986, C.A.

A *Mercer* v. *Liverpool, St. Helen's and South Lancashire Railway Co.* [1903] 1 K.B. 652, C.A.; [1904] A.C. 461, H.L.(E.).

Pollard v. *Middlesex County Council* (1906) 95 L.T. 870.

Richards (Michael) Properties Ltd. v. *St. Saviour's Parish, Southwark, Corporation of Wardens* [1975] 3 All E.R. 416.

Tiverton Estates Ltd. v. *Wearwell Ltd.* [1975] Ch. 146; [1974] 2 W.L.R. 176; [1974] 1 All E.R. 209, C.A.

B *West Midland Baptist (Trust) Association (Inc.)* v. *Birmingham Corporation* [1970] A.C. 874; [1969] 3 W.L.R. 389; [1969] 3 All E.R. 172, H.L.(E.).

The following additional cases were cited in argument:

Filby v. *Hounsell* [1896] 2 Ch. 737.

C *Nicolene Ltd.* v. *Simmonds* [1953] 1 Q.B. 543; [1953] 2 W.L.R. 717; [1953] 1 All E.R. 822, C.A.

Watts v. *Watts* (1873) L.R. 17 Eq. 217.

APPEAL from the Lands Tribunal.

The London Borough of Newham (the acquiring authority) appealed from the decision of the Lands Tribunal (Mr. Douglas Frank Q.C.,
D president) on July 22, 1974, on a reference of the preliminary point of law whether or not the price for the compulsory purchase of a dwelling house and garden, No. 9, Winton Road, London, E.16, had been agreed between the claimant, Thomas Munton, and the acquiring authority at £3,400 plus surveyors' fees of £63 and legal costs. The Lands Tribunal had determined that the amount of compensation to be paid to the claimant should be
E £5,100, the value placed on the property by the district valuer at the date when the acquiring authority took possession. The question for the court was whether the tribunal erred in law in determining that the price for the compulsory purchase of the premises had at no time before notice of entry been unreservedly agreed at £3,400 plus surveyors' fees and legal costs.

The grounds of appeal were (1) that the Lands Tribunal erred in hold-
F ing that the price for the compulsory purchase of the subject land had not been agreed between the claimant and the acquiring authority at £3,400 plus surveyors' fees of £63 and legal costs, and he should have held that it had been so agreed; (2) that on the evidence and in the circumstances the tribunal should have held that the relationship of vendor and purchaser existed because (a) the words "subject to contract" did not
G preclude an agreement because the parties had reached agreement as to the only matters requiring their agreement; (b) in view of their agreement as to compensation alternatively as to that part of the compensation relating to the price of the land, the addition of the words "subject to contract" were of no effect; (c) alternatively, if they had significance at the time when they were written, subsequent correspondence showed that such significance was waived by the parties' agreement or waiver to
H abandon any further contract and their agreement and intention to complete; (3) that the tribunal erred in holding that the effect of the words "subject to contract" remained extant throughout the correspondence between the parties and their advisers; (4) that section 40 of the Law of Property Act 1925 did not apply so as to make it necessary, before finding there had been an agreement as to the price for the compulsory purchase, that there should be a sufficient memorandum to satisfy the requirements of that section; (5) alternatively if section 40 of the Act of 1925 did apply

to an agreement as to the price of the compulsory purchase, the provisions A
of that section were satisfied.

Lionel Swift Q.C. for the acquiring authority.
Jeremy Sullivan for the claimant.

LORD DENNING M.R. In 1969 there were 1,000 houses in the London
Borough of Newham which were slums. The borough made a compulsory B
purchase order which was confirmed by the Minister. It entitled the borough to acquire the houses, paying the owners the value. One of the houses, No. 9, Winton Road, London, E.16, was owned by a lorry driver, Thomas Munton. He lived there with his wife and three children. On September 12, 1969, the borough served notice to treat. But the borough
did no more at that time because they had not made arrangements to C
rehouse the occupants. Meanwhile the district valuer set to work valuing the houses. In the spring of 1971 he assessed the value of Mr. Munton's house at £3,400. In addition there would be expected to be added about £100 compensation for disturbance. Even then, however, the borough were not ready to occupy. They did not enter into occupation until December 1972. By that time the value had increased so much that the
district valuer put the then value of the house at £5,100, including dis- D
turbance. So in 18 months the value had nearly doubled. But in the next few months the property market collapsed. We have no valuation for this house but I should not be surprised if in the middle of 1973 the value of the house was only £3,000.

The question has arisen as to what is the proper compensation to be
paid to Mr. Munton. The borough say that it is only the £3,400 assessed E
by the district valuer in 1971: whereas Mr. Munton claims that it is the £5,100 which was the value when the borough went into occupation. The president of the Lands Tribunal has held that it is £5,100. The borough appeal to this court.

Before I deal with the facts of the case, I will consider two points of law which were discussed before us. The first is whether, in order to be
binding, there must be a memorandum in writing sufficient to satisfy F
section 40 of the Law of Property Act 1925. Now on this point a compulsory purchase differs from an ordinary contract of sale and purchase. Two propositions are settled. First, when a notice to treat is given, it binds the acquiring authority to purchase and the owner to sell at a price to be ascertained: see *Mercer* v. *Liverpool, St. Helen's and South Lanca-*
shire Railway Co. [1903] 1 K.B. 652, 664, approved by the House of G
Lords [1904] A.C. 461, 463. Second, when there is an unconditional agreement fixing the price—whether in writing or by word of mouth—it is the equivalent of a binding contract between the parties: see *Harding* v. *Metropolitan Railway Co.* (1872) 7 Ch.App. 154. Lord Hatherley L.C. said, at p. 158:

> "... when the price is ascertained ... you have then all the elements H
> of a complete agreement, and, in truth, it becomes a bargain made under legislative enactment between the railway company and those over whom they were authorised to exercise their power."

In *Dart on Vendors and Purchasers*, 8th ed. (1929), vol. I, p. 256, it is said: "Where, however, the price is ascertained ... the contract is complete, and may be specifically enforced by or against the company." Similar statements will be found in *In re Cary-Elwes' Contract* [1906] 2

Ch. 143 and *Halsbury's Laws of England*, 4th ed., vol. 8 (1974), para. 136. Once therefore a notice to treat has been served and there is an agreement on the price, a binding obligation is created which is equivalent to a contract between the parties. But I do not think this obligation is a contract such as to require the observance of section 40 of the Law of Property Act 1925. It is not an ordinary contract but a statutory contract which is not within the Act of 1925. That appears from *Pollard* v. *Middlesex County Council* (1906) 95 L.T. 870 when Parker J. said, at p. 871:

> "It is quite true that statutory agreements arising out of notices to treat are not within the Statute of Frauds, and that oral evidence of them may therefore be admitted; . . ."

This is followed in practice. Very rarely do the parties enter into an actual contract in writing. The local authority serves a notice to treat. There is agreement on the price. Then the matter is completed by the conveyance and payment of the money.

The second point of law is whether, in order to be binding, there has to be one entire sum agreed that comprises not only the value of the property itself but also the compensation for disturbance. Under the Act of 1845 the inquiry was only as to the "value of the land," and it was held that in that sum there was to be included the compensation for disturbance. So that only one sum was to be awarded. That seems to be the effect of *Inland Revenue Commissioners* v. *Glasgow and South Western Railway Co.* (1887) 12 App.Cas. 315, and *Horn* v. *Sunderland Corporation* [1941] 2 K.B. 26. But although only one sum is awarded, it is very proper, in assessing it, to divide it into two parts: (1) the land itself and (2) disturbance. Starting with the Acquisition of Land Act 1919, and repeated in the Land Compensation Act 1961, Parliament itself has made a division between the two. In section 5 (6) it says:

> "The provisions of rule (2)"—that is, about the value of the land—"shall not affect the assessment of compensation for disturbance or any other matter not directly based on the value of land."

Since those Acts, the practice always has been for the compensation for disturbance to be assessed separately from the value of the land. That is as it should be. The value of the land can be assessed while the owner is still in occupation. The compensation for disturbance cannot be properly assessed until he goes out. It is only then that he can tell how much it has cost him to move, such as to get extra premises or to move his furniture. The practice is warranted by two cases in this court: *Harvey* v. *Crawley Development Corporation* [1957] 1 Q.B. 485 and *Lee* v. *Minister of Transport* [1966] 1 Q.B. 111.

In my opinion it is quite proper for the acquiring authority to agree in the first place with the owner on the value of the house itself, and to leave till later the compensation for disturbance. That can be assessed later when the acquiring authority go into occupation and the house owner moves.

There is one other point I must mention. It is the effect of *West Midland Baptist (Trust) Association (Inc.)* v. *Birmingham Corporation* [1970] A.C. 874. Previously for over 100 years the value was taken at the date of the notice to treat. But when inflation came upon us, the House of Lords altered that old rule. They held that in the absence

of agreement, the valuation is to be taken at the date when the acquiring A
authority enters into possession of the property. But if there has been a binding agreement beforehand as to the value, that would no doubt prevail.

Now I turn to the facts. The borough say that there was firm agreement on the price of £3,400; whereas for Mr. Munton it is said that there was no firm agreement, because it was "subject to contract." B
It depends on the correspondence. The borough served notice to treat in 1969. In February 1971 the surveyors for Mr. Munton put in a claim for £3,500 subject to contract and with vacant possession on completion, plus surveyors' fees, legal costs and disbursements. It was referred to the district valuer. On May 19, 1971, he wrote to Mr. Munton's surveyors:

> "I have considered the matter and I am prepared to recommend C
> for the approval of the acquiring authority and government departments concerned, payment of £3,400 . . . in settlement of compensation."

He added that costs would be paid. Also:

> "Any claim for disturbance, if admissible, will be dealt with when D
> removal takes place. On hearing that your client is willing to accept this sum, I will make my recommendation to the acquiring authority concerned."

In reply Mr. Munton's surveyors wrote on December 8, 1971: ". . . we understand that this offer is now acceptable to the vendor subject to contract." On December 14, 1971, his solicitors wrote to E
the town clerk: "We understand that the price agreed, subject to contract, is £3,400." In a letter of January 5, 1972, his surveyors say that the price has been agreed "subject to contract." Newham London Borough replied, saying that the price was agreed and that the conveyancing work was ready to be started. Nevertheless it was not started then, because the arrangements for rehousing were not completed. On F
March 28, 1972, Mr. Munton's solicitors wrote to the town clerk:

> ". . . our client now tells us that he has found alternative accommodation for his wife and family and that the sale of the property to the council can proceed at the price of £3,400 subject to contract. Vacant possession will be given on completion. We understand that there is a disturbance claim pending and completion will of course be subject to this. Will you please let us know when you will be G
> able to complete so that we can ask our client to arrange his removals."

The town clerk replied:

> "I acknowledge receipt of your letter of March 28 and await hearing from you with a full ten days notice of the appointment to H
> complete which should if possible take place on a Monday or a Thursday."

The solicitors replied on April 12:

> "Thank you for your letter of April 6. We enclose a statement for completion on April 27 and we trust that this will be a convenient date so far as the council is concerned."

A They enclosed a completion statement which gives the figures based on the purchase price of £3,400.

That proposal was not fulfilled because the alternative accommodation did not materialise. Seven months later, on November 17, 1972, the council served a notice of entry saying that they would enter into possession in December 1972. In reply Mr. Munton's solicitors wrote:

B "... our client now tells us that he is not prepared to accept the price originally negotiated with the council and the estate agents are re-negotiating with the district valuer."

They did in fact re-negotiate. The district valuer then said the figure should be £5,100 for the property including disturbance.

There the position rests. Mr. Munton says that he is not bound by
C the figure of £3,400 set out in the earlier correspondence and that he is entitled to £5,100 as from the date of entering into possession.

The one question is: Was there a firm agreement on the price before the borough entered into possession? Throughout this correspondence the solicitors and surveyors for the house owner put into their letters the words "subject to contract." In my opinion those words have a decisive effect. They mean: "Although this figure is there and
D we agree it, it is not to be regarded as binding. It is only a provisional figure subject to further negotiation. It is not binding." The principle was discussed recently in *Tiverton Estates Ltd.* v. *Wearwell Ltd.* [1975] Ch. 146. It is of the greatest importance that no doubt should be thrown on the effect of those words. We were referred to *Michael Richards Properties Ltd.* v. *St. Saviour's Parish, Southwark, Corporation*
E *of Wardens* [1975] 3 All E.R. 416, which was decided by Goff J. Goff L.J. will deal with it. It is to my mind a very special case on its own facts. I know that in these cases of compulsory purchase there is no contract prepared or signed, but only a conveyance. So the words "subject to contract" have no real application. But nevertheless they have, I think, the effect of preventing there being any firm agreement on the price. In my view the words used so constantly, "subject to
F contract," mean that the figure of £3,400 was not agreed so as to be binding. It was only a provisional figure.

Apart from this there are letters of February 28 and May 6, 1972, in which the house owner was saying: "Please rehouse me quickly before other people," and the borough were saying to him:

"If we are going to rehouse you prematurely there will have to be
G some reduction in the figure which we were going to pay and it will have to be renegotiated."

Those letters show me that the figure was not regarded as fixed and binding.

In this respect therefore on the effect of the words "subject to contract" I agree with the president of the Lands Tribunal. There was
H nothing equivalent to a contract for a price binding on the parties before the acquiring authority entered into possession. So the ordinary law applies. The value is to be taken as at the date of entering into possession, £5,100. I think the president was right and I would dismiss the appeal accordingly.

SCARMAN L.J. I agree with the judgment delivered by Lord Denning M.R.

GOFF L.J. I agree with the judgment of Lord Denning M.R. and would myself add nothing but for the fact that I think I ought to say a few words about my own decision in *Michael Richards Properties Ltd.* v. *St. Saviour's Parish, Southwark, Corporation of Wardens* [1975] 3 All E.R. 416. That case superficially bears a somewhat attractive similarity to the present case, and Mr. Swift relied strongly upon it, particularly the passage where I said, at p. 424:

> "This was a sale by tender. Nothing remained to be negotiated, there was no need or scope for any further formal contract, and it is difficult to see how it would be drawn. Nobody ever thought there was. The vendors did not submit a draft contract, nor were they asked to do so, and the matter proceeded with the steps necessary not to negotiate or finalise a contract, or even put it into further form or shape, but with the steps required for completion. In the context of a tender document which sets out all the terms of the contract, and which is required to be annexed to the tender offer, it seems to me that the words 'subject to contract' in the acceptance are meaningless, and that I ought to apply the principle of *Nicolene Ltd.* v. *Simmonds* [1953] 1 Q.B. 543."

I pointed out in that judgment that the case turned on the particular facts. I said, at p. 424: "I hope this judgment will not ring warning bells in solicitors' offices. . . . My decision is on the particular facts of this case"—and I desire to emphasise that that was the position.

In *Chillingworth* v. *Esche* [1924] 1 Ch. 97, 114 Sargant L.J. said, at p. 114:

> "The phrase is a perfectly familiar one in the mouths of estate agents and other persons accustomed to deal with land; and I can quite understand a solicitor saying to a client about to negotiate for the sale of his land: 'Be sure that to protect yourself you introduce into any preliminary contract you may think of making the words "subject to contract."' I do not say that the phrase makes the contract containing it necessarily and whatever the context a conditional contract. But they are words appropriate for introducing a condition, and it would require a very strong and exceptional case for this clear prima facie meaning to be displaced."

In my view the facts of the *Michael Richards* case [1975] 3 All E.R. 416 were very strong and exceptional. There may be other cases—I do not know—in which the facts might again be so strong and exceptional as to require the court to treat the words "subject to contract" as meaningless. If there be any such other cases, they must indeed be rare; and although I see no reason to think on the facts of that particular case that I decided it wrongly, I would like to make it clear, as I thought I had made it clear at the time, that the case did not throw any doubt upon the well established and well settled sanctity of the words "subject to contract."

The peculiarity of the facts in that case were, first, that the plaintiffs by their tender made an unqualified offer to purchase the property, and the conditions upon which it was put up for tender required the tender documents to be annexed to that offer, and they were. Those documents contained all the terms of a fully worked out formal contract, including the incorporation of the National Conditions of Sale, and thereby fixed the time for completion; and they specifically provided that the person

A whose tender was accepted should be the purchaser. The tender was accepted; and that, in my judgment, was the end of the matter. The wholly inapposite condition under the signature of the letter informing the plaintiffs that their tender had been accepted did not affect the position at all.

In the present case, of course, the facts are entirely different. There there was a mistake; here there was none. Here the claimant's surveyors
B and solicitors made it clear from the start that the agreement was subject to contract, and they reiterated that in the critical letter of March 28, 1972; the borough did not object to those words or in any way maintain that there was to be a final agreement; the price agreed was closely bound up with the date of completion and, although the parties were contemplating a certain time for completion, there was in
C fact no agreement in the present case as to the time for completion of the alleged final agreement.

I say, therefore, simply this, that my case must be regarded, as I always considered it to be, as a very special case and should not be applied to any other case without very mature thought as to whether the facts of it do come within the ruling of a strong and exceptional case sufficient to oust the well established protection of the words "subject
D to contract."

Appeal dismissed with costs.

Solicitors: *J. J. Warren, Town Hall, East Ham; Prestons & Kerlys.*

M. M. H.

E

[CHANCERY DIVISION]

F

* WILLINGALE (INSPECTOR OF TAXES) *v.* INTERNATIONAL COMMERCIAL BANK LTD.

1976 March 8, 12 **Walton J.**

Revenue — Corporation tax — Profits, assessment of — Anticipated profits from bills and promissory notes discounted or purchased by bank—Whether tax payable on fractional part of
G *anticipated profits from bills—Income and Corporation Taxes Act* 1970 (*c.* 10), *ss.* 108, 109, 129, 238

The taxpayer bank was incorporated in 1967 to provide medium-term finance to commercial companies throughout the world. Its business was not that of a clearing bank but included the purchasing or discounting of bills issued by
H borrowers for periods of less than 10 years. Its normal practice was to hold the bills until they reached maturity but on occasions it sold them prior to maturity. Some of the bills carried interest at a fixed rate and others did not. A fractional part of the anticipated profits from such bills had they been held until maturity were included in the taxpayer bank's annual accounts which were drawn up in the form customary for

---

[Reported by MRS. HARRIET DUTTON, Barrister-at-Law]

clearing banks. It was assessed to corporation tax for the A years from its incorporation to December 1970 on the basis that its annual profits were as set out in its accounts, and included a fractional part of the anticipated profits from the bills. The general commissioners allowed the taxpayer bank's appeal against the assessments, upholding its contention that no part of the anticipated profits from the bills fell to be included in the taxpayer bank's profits for the purposes of corporation tax.

On appeal by the Crown:— B

Held, dismissing the appeal, that profits were not assessable to tax until such time as they were realised; that as the bills were merely the embodiment of an obligation to pay a fixed sum at a future date, no profit could be said to accrue from them until they were either sold or reached maturity, so that no amounts representing a fractional part of the anticipated profits fell to be included in the computation of taxable profits.

Dicta of Lord Morris of Borth-y-Gest, Lord Reid and C Viscount Dilhorne in *B.S.C. Footwear Ltd.* v. *Ridgway* [1972] A.C. 544, 554, 555, 560, 566, H.L.(E.) applied.

Quaere. Whether the bills constituted stock-in-trade of the taxpayer bank and should be treated as such in computing the taxable profits of its trade (post, p. 664B–D).

The following cases are referred to in the judgment:

D

B.S.C. Footwear Ltd. v. *Ridgway* [1972] A.C. 544; [1971] 2 W.L.R. 1313; [1971] 2 All E.R. 534; 47 T.C. 495, H.L.(E.).

Gardner, Mountain and D'Ambrumenil Ltd. v. *Inland Revenue Commissioners* [1947] 1 All E.R. 650; 29 T.C. 90, H.L.(E.).

Harrison v. *John Cronk and Sons Ltd.* [1937] A.C. 185; [1936] 3 All E.R. 747; 20 T.C. 638, H.L.(E.).

Newcastle Breweries Ltd. v. *Inland Revenue Commissioners* (1927) 12 E T.C. 927, H.L.(E.).

Southern Railway of Peru Ltd. v. *Owen* [1957] A.C. 334; [1956] 3 W.L.R. 389; [1956] 2 All E.R. 728; 36 T.C. 602, H.L.(E.).

Sun Insurance Office v. *Clark* [1912] A.C. 443; 6 T.C. 59, H.L.(E.).

No aditional cases were cited in argument.

F

CASE STATED by the Commissioners for the General Purposes of the Income Tax.

The taxpayer bank, International Commercial Bank Ltd., was incorporated in 1967 to provide world-wide medium-term finance to commercial companies. It was assessed to corporation tax for the six-month period to December 31, 1967, in the sum of £170,000; for the year ended G December 31, 1968, in the sum of £880,000; for the year ended December 31, 1969, in the sum of £1,400,000; and for the year ended December 31, 1970, in the sum of £2,000,000. The taxpayer bank appealed against the assessments contending that no sums representing a proportionate part of the expected profits to be made on the maturity or sale of bills issued by borrowers and purchased by the taxpayer bank fell to be H included in the computation of assessable profits for those periods within Case I of Schedule D to the Income and Corporation Taxes Act 1970. The commissioners allowed the appeals and reduced the assessment for the six-month period ended December 31, 1967, to £266,529; for the year ended December 31, 1968, to £615,080; for the year ended December 31, 1969, to £812,478; and for the year ended December 31, 1970, to £434,395.

A The Crown appealed.
The facts are stated in the judgment.

Michael Nolan Q.C. and *Brian Davenport* for the Crown.
F. Heyworth Talbot Q.C. and *J. R. Gardiner* for the taxpayer bank.

Cur. adv. vult.

B

March 12. WALTON J. read the following judgment. I take the follow-
ing facts from the case stated in this matter. The taxpayer bank was
incorporated on July 19, 1967, by a consortium of five major national
banks, namely, National Westminster Bank, First National Bank of
Chicago, Irving Trust Co. of New York, Commerz Bank of Dusseldorf,
C and Hongkong & Shanghai Banking Corporation. It was formed to
provide medium-term finance in world markets to commercial companies
by way of loans running from two to seven years. Later the period of
the loans was in some instances extended to ten years. Apart from
subscribed share capital it had received considerable sums on deposit
and current accounts, the deposit accounts consisting mainly of deposits
made by banks on behalf of customers. The current accounts were
D opened and maintained by customers in respect of medium-term loans.
In 1967 clearing banks did not transact the kind of business the taxpayer
bank was formed to do otherwise than through fully owned subsidiary
companies. The business carried on by the taxpayer bank was not
that of a clearing bank, though as it had a small number of customers'
current accounts it qualified for bank status.

E At all material times the taxpayer bank's business included the dis-
counting or purchase of bills and similar obligations issued by borrowers
(for periods between one year and ten years) all over the world—with an
overall limit, fixed internally by the taxpayer bank, for each country for
loans to companies or individuals resident there. These bills were often
issued in sets of six or twelve, maturing at regular intervals. Some carried
a fixed rate of interest, others carried none. Although the taxpayer bank
F usually held such bills to maturity, on many occasions it sold them prior
to maturity, and also bought them, in the recognised international market
in what was called "medium-term paper." Such sales were normally
effected when new business offered itself in a country already at its limit;
rather than refuse such new business, the taxpayer bank sold old bills of
that country before purchasing fresh bills, thus staying within its limit.
G Sales and purchases of bills also occurred in the market from time to time
when the taxpayer bank considered them advantageous.

There was a large market with a very considerable turnover available
to the taxpayer bank for the buying and discounting of bills which might
be sold before maturity or allowed to run to maturity. Current prices of
discounted bills are affected by the risk involved in rates of interest which
are subject to wide fluctuations. The amount of profit a purchaser or
H discounter of a bill may make is not ascertainable before the bill (a) is
sold or (b) reaches maturity. The present case concerns the correct tax
treatment of the profits earned by the taxpayer bank upon these bills or
promissory notes ("bills") consequent upon the indicated course of
dealings.

Clearing banks do not apparently normally deal in "medium-term
paper," but only in "short-term paper"—90 to 180 days—and the evidence
quite clearly was that there is a recognised method of treatment of the

profits made upon such paper for tax purposes. If a bill has been held for any period of time prior to an accounting date, then there is taken into the profit and loss account the appropriate portion down to that date of the profit which the clearing bank will make if the bill is held to maturity. Looking at the matter very broadly one can easily see why the accountancy profession should consider that this is a suitable method of treatment for the purposes of the " true and fair view " required by the provisions of the Companies Act 1948, for otherwise the clearing bank is taking no credit for the opportunity income value of the moneys expended in purchasing the bills in the first place. Since this lost value is in fact replaced by an increase in the value of the bills, from an economic point of view it is obviously right to set one off against the other.

The taxpayer bank has in fact prepared its accounts in precisely the same manner as the clearing banks, but it now urges that, although this may be the appropriate method of presentation of its accounts from the point of view of company law, from the point of view of tax law this treatment is not correct. In brief, assessments to corporation tax were made upon it for the accounting periods for the years ended December 31, 1967, to December 31, 1970, in various amounts based on its published accounts. It appealed to the general commissioners for the City division of London, and they allowed its appeal. From the general commissioners the Crown has now appealed to this court.

It would of course be highly convenient if the requirements of company and tax law were the same on these matters, particularly bearing in mind the fact that from one point of view what is profit is a pure question of fact, and of fact to be ascertained by the tests applied in ordinary business: see *Sun Insurance Office* v. *Clark* [1912] A.C. 443, 455 *per* Viscount Haldane. Nevertheless it is, I think, unfortunately quite clear from the evidence given before the general commissioners, and not challenged in any way, that there is no such coincidence. Mr. A. D. Wardle, a partner in the distinguished firm of Touche Ross & Co., chartered accountants, gave evidence to the following effect:

> " He had a number of banks among his clients. Between the accounting procedures adopted by banks in accordance with recommendations made in 1969 by Sir Ronald Leach and Sir William Lawson and the requirements of tax law in the computation of bankers' profits there was considerable divergence. In particular (a) the investment income of banks is brought to account on an accrual basis but it is taxed on a receipts basis (b) income accrued on a purchased investment is debited and income accrued on a sold investment is credited to profit and loss, whereas for tax purposes such items are treated as part of the cost or part of the sale proceeds respectively, with consequential adjustments to tax computations of profits and loss on sales of investments; and (c) profits and losses on investments are taken to profit and loss account on the basis of a five years' average, whereas for tax purposes they are attributed wholly to the several years in which the realisations occur."

To this evidence one may usefully add Lord Radcliffe's remark in *Southern Railway of Peru Ltd.* v. *Owen* [1957] A.C. 334, 360:

> ". . . references to an auditor's duty under the Companies Act take us into a field that is not exactly the same as that in which the annual profits of trade should be ascertained for the purposes of income tax."

A Mr. Wardle's partner, Mr. J. F. Taylor, who was actually the partner responsible for the audit of the taxpayer bank's accounts, deposed that he would have been prepared to sign its accounts, prepared in the manner in which the taxpayer bank was now arguing that they should have been prepared, without qualification, but subject to a note setting out the procedure which had been used. In his view, he would have been fully justified in so doing because the taxpayer bank's business differed materially B from that of a conventional clearing bank.

Now the method which the taxpayer bank successfully urged before the general commissioners ought to have been used in computing its profits was that nothing should have been included in respect of the bills unless and until they were either sold or redeemed. Its submissions were, first: " it is a cardinal principle of income tax law that in ascertaining the C assessable profit a profit is not to be taxed until it has been realised." This formulation was taken from the speech of Lord Morris of Borth-y-Gest in *B.S.C. Footwear Ltd.* v. *Ridgway* [1972] A.C. 544, 560. In the light of the submissions which have been made to me, I think it is clear that " realised " here does not imply that the proceeds of realisation have in fact been received by the person whose profit it is. Mr. Nolan, for the Crown, thought that " earned " would be a better word to employ. Subject D to this understanding, which was common ground, this proposition was accepted by both parties. The second submission was: " in ascertaining the assessable profit neither profit nor loss may be anticipated, save as regards a fall in the market value of stock." This again was taken from the speech of Lord Reid in the same case, at pp. 554, 555, and is, I think, once again broadly accepted by both parties. The third submission E was: " in commercial accounting the anticipation of profits should be avoided but that account should be taken of and provision made for expected losses." This is taken from the speech of Viscount Dilhorne in the same case at p. 566, and once again was, I think, not disputed. Nor was the fourth submission, which was: " neither the way in which accounts are made up nor the principle nor the practices of commercial accounting have validity for the purpose of arriving at the profits assessable to tax if F such principles or practices conflict with the principles of income tax law."

This remarkable unanimity as regards the principles applicable breaks down when one comes to apply them to the facts of the present case. The taxpayer bank's fifth proposition was that no part of any unrealised profit on maturity of bills should be anticipated by being included in the computation of the taxpayer bank's profits for corporation tax purposes for G the accounting periods in question. There was also a sixth submission, to which I shall have to turn later, but the nub of this submission is the question of " anticipation."

The Crown's contrary submissions were: (i) the taxpayer bank's accounts for the accounting periods in question had been prepared according to uniform and accepted bank accounting practice and correctly showed the H amount of its assessable profit for corporation tax purposes for the years in question; (ii) there was no distinction in principle whether in law or general accountancy practice or bank accounting practice between earning interest throughout a period and earning discount throughout a period; (iii) in respect of neither is it proper to complain that profit has been anticipated. In the present case if the complaint were well-founded the accounts would not give a true and fair view of the taxpayer bank's affairs so as properly to show the full amount of the profits.

The reasons for the decision of the general commissioners in favour of the taxpayer bank's submissions are as follows:

> "We have considered the cases cited to us and accept the contention on behalf of the bank that the principle to be followed for taxation purposes is that profits are not to be taxed until realised and that if in ascertaining profits on a true and fair view the principles or practices of commercial accountancy conflict with this principle, they are not to be followed. We find on the evidence before us that it was not possible for the bank to realise before maturity the discount on the discounted bills and notes otherwise than by sale on the market. We are of the opinion that it is not open to us to disregard the nature of the discounted bills and notes, and we reach the conclusion that the inclusion by the bank in its accounts of the unrealised appreciation in the value of bills and promissory notes is not in aaccordance with the principles of income tax law for the computation of profits and that no part of the anticipated profits on maturity falls to be included in the computation of the profits of the bank for corporation tax purposes for the years of assessment before us. We leave the figures for the assessments under appeal to be agreed between the parties, following our decision in principle, or in the event of the parties being unable to agree, the figures to be determined by us."

The figures have in fact subsequently been agreed, and these show in some cases quite startling reductions in the assessments. Of course, over a period of time the whole of the profits on any particular bill must be caught in one way or the other for tax purposes; but by postponing liability (if they are in fact entitled so to do) the taxpayer bank obviously improves very considerably its cash flow, and that is what this case is all about. I do not think that there are any special provisions of either the Income and Corporation Taxes Act 1970, or of the earlier Acts replaced by that Act and which were in force at the commencement of the periods here under review, which have any direct bearing on anything I have to decide. This is basically a straightforward Schedule D, Case I situation.

Now it appears to me that the crux of the matter lies in the Crown's second submission, namely, that there is no distinction in principle, whether in law, in general accountancy practice or in bank accounting practice, between earning interest throughout a period and earning discount throughout a period. This is the foundation of their submission that the taxpayer bank is not being required to "anticipate" its profits. However, it appears to me at the end of the day that there is a great deal of difference. A bill is the embodiment of an obligation on the part of X to pay a sum of £Y at a future date. If, of course, the bill carries interest, then that interest will be dealt with in the normal manner, on an accruals basis, and so may for present purposes be left entirely out of account. Now, that obligation is one which remains the same the whole time; it does not in any way change, or have anything added thereto, or produce any fruit. All that happens is that, as the years roll by, its value becomes closer and closer to the full amount of £Y. In the summary of the taxpayer bank's balance sheets which was an exhibit to the case stated, the Crown have labelled one section "Bills included above (with accrued discount)." But this appears to me to be a complete misconception. Discount does not in any way accrue. What happens is that the value of the bill increases by reason of the closer approach of the maturity date; the discount diminishes. If it is an accrual at all, it is a negative accrual.

I do not think there can be any doubt but that if the subject matter of the taxpayer bank's purchases were anything else but bills, were something which did not embody an obligation which would ultimately be satisfied by a sum of money, there would be no possible way in which the taxpayer bank could be asked to bring the increasing value of the item into its profit and loss account year by year. The Crown however said through Mr. Nolan that the fact that what is in issue is a monetary obligation makes all the difference. He said—and said with some force—that it is a remarkable contention for a bank which has prepared its accounts on the usual conventional basis of a clearing bank, to put forward the submission that what those accounts have done is to anticipate its profits.

I am, however, not persuaded by this at all. In my view, this is indeed precisely what accounts prepared on the conventional basis, for the best of reasons, in fact do. Accounts so prepared are much better economic indicators than corporation tax accounts would be as to whether a bank is or is not doing what it ought to be doing, that is to say, steadily making an economic profit for its shareholders. Like the flywheel in a motor car, they help to transmit the violent but irregular profit explosions into a steady forward motion. But if one seeks, as a pure matter of fact, when the taxpayer bank does make a profit out of the purchase of a bill, I cannot see any other answer than that it makes such a profit when the bill is either sold or is held to maturity. Like the general commissioners, I do not think it is open to the Crown to disregard the nature of the discounted bills, and like them I reach the conclusion that no part of the anticipated profit on maturity falls to be included in the profits of the taxpayer bank for corporation tax purposes for the year of assessment in question.

I ought perhaps to say one word on the authorities cited to me. They all deal, apart from the *B.S.C. Footwear Ltd.* case [1972] A.C. 544, with the situation where a trader has disposed of a trading asset in a particular accounting period and all profit arising out of the disposal is referred back to that period. This was, for example, the case in *Newcastle Breweries Ltd.* v. *Inland Revenue Commissioners* (1927) 12 T.C. 927, where there was merely a delay in ascertaining the amount to be paid. Again, in *Harrison* v. *John Cronk and Sons Ltd.* [1937] A.C. 185, the difficulty was in valuing the receipt for the sale price of a house. There was no doubt that if it could be valued it had to be brought in at the moment of sale. The House of Lords somewhat surprisingly decided that, if it could not be valued, the part that could not be valued had to be brought in when it was actually released to the vendor and in that year: one would have expected it to have been then carried back to the original year of sale. But the facts of that case were somewhat special, and it may well be that the House took the view that the moneys might well be released at such a remote date that any additional assessment would be impracticable.

Gardner, Mountain and D'Ambrumenil Ltd. v. *Inland Revenue Commissioners* [1947] 1 All E.R. 650 turned upon the construction of the relevant agreement as to when the profits had been earned. Once that was decided, there was really no question but that they fell into that year, although ascertained much later. *Southern Railway of Peru Ltd.* v. *Owen* [1957] A.C. 334, concerned the making of a provision for contingent liabilities. The House of Lords held that such a provision could be made but that it must be made on proper principles. As the claim actually made by the company was excessive, it could not be

allowed. *B.S.C. Footwear Ltd.* v. *Ridgway* [1972] A.C. 544, though A
containing valuable statements of principle, is a decision on the proper treatment of stock-in-trade.

This brings me to the last, alternative submission for the taxpayer bank. It was that the bills constituted stock-in-trade of the taxpayer bank and should be treated as such in the computation of the taxable profits of the trade of the taxpayer bank; with the contrary submissions of the Crown being as follows: the taxpayer bank is not a trader in bills, it was and is a B
bank. Banks (and others) who periodically adjust their portfolios of bills and securities do not ipso facto qualify as traders; the bills and notes did not constitute stock-in-trade of the taxpayer bank and did not fall to be treated as such in computing the taxable profits of the taxpayer. As to this, although the matter was squarely urged upon them, the commissioners made no findings that the bills were stock-in-trade. In C
spite of a vigorous submission by Mr. Heyworth Talbot, based upon the definition of stock-in-trade in section 137 (4) (the " discontinuance " section), of the Income and Corporation Taxes Act 1970, which definition has been adopted in other contexts such as capital gains tax and tax avoidance, to the effect that the bills here in question were undoubtedly stock-in-trade, I do not find myself able to come to that conclusion. I think that this is primarily a matter of fact upon which, before I can found anything on it D
one way or the other, I ought to have the guidance of the general commissioners. If, therefore, this point had been material, I should have remitted the matter to the general commissioners for them to determine not only whether the bills were stock-in-trade but, if so, whether such bills ought to receive any different accounting treatment from the treatment afforded to ordinary stock-in-trade of an ordinary trader in his accounts. E
Both parties agreed that, if I had made such a remit, that is the form which it should have taken.

However, for the reasons I have already indicated I answer the question of law posed by the general commissioners—namely, " whether upon the facts admitted and found by us as herein set out, there was evidence upon which we could properly arrive at our decision and whether upon such facts our decision was correct in law "—in the affirmative, and dismiss F
this appeal.

Appeal dismissed with costs.

Solicitors: *Solicitor of Inland Revenue; Travers Smith, Braithwaite & Co.*

G

H

A

[CHANCERY DIVISION]

* TERRAPIN INTERNATIONAL LTD. *v.* INLAND REVENUE COMMISSIONERS

B 1976 March 2 Walton J.

Revenue—Stamp duty—Deed of exchange as escrow—Exchange completed after fulfilment of conditions—Rate of stamp duty increased before completion date—Whether document "first executed" when delivered as escrow—Date when stamp duty payable—Stamp Act 1891 (54 & 55 *Vict. c.* 39), *s.* 14 (4) [1]

C A company entered into an agreement in 1974 with a local corporation for the exchange of certain freehold properties and for equality money of £177,500 to be paid by the company to the corporation. A document which was to become the deed of exchange was drawn up and delivered in escrow by the parties stating, inter alia, that subject to satisfactory land searches being obtained by the corporation, the exchange would take place on April 30, 1974. There was a
D delay in obtaining Land Registry certificates of search and completion did not take place until May 8, 1974. The rate of stamp duty was doubled after April 30, 1974. On the deed being submitted for adjudication as to the amount of ad valorem stamp duty payable, the Commissioners of Inland Revenue, rejecting the company's contention that the effective date of the deed was April 30, 1974, assessed the amount of duty payable at the increased rate on the basis that the document did not effect an exchange until May 8, 1974.

E On appeal by the company:—

Held, dismissing the appeal, that notwithstanding that a document intending to take effect as a deed on fulfilment of conditions could be executed as an escrow, it was not executed as an effective deed until all the conditions were fulfilled and that, accordingly, stamp duty did not become payable until the deed was first executed by being unconditionally delivered on
F May 8, 1974 (post, pp. 669G–H, 670H—671A).

The following cases are referred to in the judgment:

Byrne v. *Revenue Commissioners* [1935] I.R. 664.

Clarke v. *Roche* (1877) 3 Q.B.D. 170.

Cory (*Wm.*) *& Son Ltd.* v. *Inland Revenue Commissioners* [1964] 1 W.L.R. 1332; [1964] 3 All E.R. 66, C.A.; [1965] A.C. 1088; [1965] 2 W.L.R.
G 924; [1965] 1 All E.R. 917, H.L.(E.).

Hare v. *Horton* (1833) 5 B. & Ad. 715.

Thompson v. *McCullough* [1947] K.B. 447; [1947] 1 All E.R. 265, C.A.

The following additional cases were cited in argument:

Crane Fruehauf Ltd. v. *Inland Revenue Commissioners* [1974] 1 All E.R.
H 811; [1975] 1 All E.R. 429, C.A.

Kingston v. *Ambrian Investment Co. Ltd.* [1975] 1 W.L.R. 161; [1975] 1 All E.R. 120, C.A.

Suffield (*Lord*) v. *Inland Revenue Commissioners* [1908] 1 K.B. 865.

[Reported by MRS. HARRIET DUTTON, Barrister-at-Law]

[1] Stamp Act 1891, s. 14 (4): see post, p. 667H.

CASE STATED by the Inland Revenue Commissioners.

Terrapin International Ltd. entered into an agreement on April 16, 1974, for the exchange of freehold properties with Milton Keynes Development Corporation and for the payment of equality money of £177,500 by the taxpayer company to the corporation. The document which subsequently became the deed of exchange was delivered in escrow prior to April 30, 1974, and completion took place on May 8, 1974. On the submission of the deed to the Inland Revenue Commissioners for adjudication under section 12 of the Stamp Act 1891, the commissioners assessed the ad valorem stamp duty payable at the rate prescribed by section 49 and paragraph 3 of Schedule 11 to the Finance Act 1974, which came into effect after April 30, 1974. The company appealed.

The facts are stated in the judgment.

Leonard Hoffmann for the company.
Peter Millett Q.C. and *Peter Gibson* for the Crown.

WALTON J. This case raises the question, which is apparently not one which has ever been previously decided, at any rate by an English court, as to the correct rate of stamp duty payable upon a document originally delivered as an escrow. Is it, as maintained by Mr. Hoffman for the company, the rate in force at the date when the document was first signed, sealed and conditionally delivered, either by the first party to do so or by the last of the two parties in the present case, or is it, as maintained by Mr. Millett for the Crown, the rate in force at the date when the document became unconditional? The document here in question is a deed of exchange dated May 8, 1974, and made between Milton Keynes Development Corporation ("the corporation") of the one part and the company of the other part. By the deed, in consideration of the conveyance of certain freehold property by and the covenants on the part of the company thereinafter contained, and of the sum of £177,500 paid by the company to the corporation by way of equality of exchange, the corporation, as beneficial owner, conveyed to the company certain freehold property at Bletchley, Milton Keynes, in the county of Buckingham.

The circumstances in which the deed was made are set out with admirable economy in the case stated as follows:

"(i) On April 16, 1974, the corporation entered into an agreement in writing with the [company] for the exchange of their . . . respective freehold properties. It was provided that the exchange was to be completed and the . . . equality money paid on May 1, 1974. . . . (ii) On April 23, 1974, the chief legal officer of the corporation sent off to the Land Charges Registry a requisition for four official searches against the land which was to be conveyed by the [company]. (iii) On April 26, 1974, in response to correspondence from the solicitors to the [company], the corporation wrote to the [company's] solicitors saying that it would do all it could to assist towards completion on April 30, 1974 (a day earlier than that agreed in the agreement) but that this was subject to the receipt of satisfactory land charges and company searches. . . . (iv) Between April 26 and April 30, 1974, the instrument which was to become the deed and a duplicate thereof were sealed and delivered in escrow by the corporation and the [company] respectively in the expectation that the exchange would take place on April 30, 1974. The conditions of the corporation's escrow were that the corporation should receive clear or otherwise satisfactory official certificates of search relating to the land to be conveyed by the [company], that the equality money should be paid to it by the [company] and that there should be an exchange of the deed and the duplicate thereof. The condition of the [company's] escrow was that there should be such exchange as aforesaid. (v) The official certificates of search had not been received by the corporation on or before April 30, 1974, and neither payment of the equality money nor the exchange of the deed and the duplicate thereof had taken place on or before that date, but on that date the [company] and the corporation respectively assumed physical possession of the respective properties which they respectively were to receive on completion. (vi) The last of the official certificates of search was received by the corporation on May 6, 1974. All the searches were clear and satisfactory to the corporation and completion took place on May 8, 1974, when the deed and the duplicate thereof were exchanged and the equality money was duly paid.

"The deed was submitted to the Commissioners of Inland Revenue for adjudication under section 12 of the Stamp Act 1891. . . . The [company] contended that the effective date of the deed was April 30, 1974, and that the deed was therefore liable to stamp duty as a deed of exchange at the rate of 50p for every £50 of the equality money as prescribed by section 32 of and paragraph 10 of Schedule 7 to the Finance Act 1970 which were in force on that date. The commissioners were of the opinion that the instrument did not effect an exchange on April 30, 1974, and could not therefore attract stamp duty as such until May 8, 1974, when the conditions subject to which the instrument was delivered in escrow were satisfied.

"The commissioners accordingly assessed the duty in accordance with the law in force on May 8, 1974, under the head of charge 'Exchange or Excambion' in Schedule I to the Stamp Act 1891, section 73 of that Act and other relevant statutory provisions as follows: On the sum paid for equality namely £177,500 with the same ad valorem duty as a conveyance on sale for the said sum at the rate prescribed by section 49 and paragraph 3 of Schedule II to the Finance Act 1974," that is to say, "£1 for every £50 of the equality money."

From that assessment the company, having paid the duty in accordance therewith, appeals to the High Court, and the commissioners have accordingly stated and signed the case from which I have been reading.

Mr. Hoffmann submitted, first of all, that the governing section of the Stamp Act 1891 for present purposes is section 14 (4), which reads as follows:

> "Save as aforesaid" and that is dealing with terms upon which instruments not duly stamped may be received in evidence "an instrument executed in any part of the United Kingdom . . . shall not, except in criminal proceedings, be given in evidence, or be available for any purpose whatever, unless it is duly stamped in accordance with the law in force at the time when it was first executed."

While this subsection is in a section ostensibly dealing with the terms A upon which instruments not duly stamped may be received in evidence, it is of course inconceivable that payment of anything less than the proper measure of stamp duty would render the instrument receivable in evidence. If further support for this was required, Mr. Hoffmann submitted that *Clarke* v. *Roche* (1877) 3 Q.B.D. 170, clearly showed that the instrument must bear the stamps which were were required at the time it was "first executed." Mr. Hoffman then went on to ask what was the B meaning of "first executed," and submitted that this meant when the document was executed by the first party to execute it; and he relied for driving this submission home upon a number of references to be found in the Stamp Act 1891 to "first executed" and also to "last executed" (see sections 22, 49 and 50). He admitted that this might well result in the necessity for stamping a document before it took legal effect, but he sub- C mitted that this was in comformity with the original conception of the Stamp Acts, which was that they required all documents to be written on paper which had been already stamped. Although this practice had been much altered when duties became in the main ad valorem, and a period of 30 days' grace was given for the purposes of stamping the document, nevertheless this was, as it were, a gloss upon the original conception of the Stamp Acts. He therefore submitted that the concept of "first execu- D tion" was used for the twofold purpose of fixing (i) per section 14 (4), the date when the current rate of duty had to be fixed; and (ii) per section 15 (2) (*a*), the date from which the normal 30 day period of grace ran. In the first alternative, he submitted that even if the correct moment in time at which to look was the date when the deed became complete, this was the date when it had been executed by both parties at the latest, and E this was, in the present case, prior to the change in the rates of duty.

Mr. Millett's approach was completely different. He pointed out that, as one was dealing with a claim relating to stamp duty, one must first of all read section 1, imposing the charge to duty upon the instruments set out in Schedule 1; then go to that Schedule, which imposed a duty on instruments effecting an exchange (for such is the nature of the instrument here in question) and that took one back to section 73, which laid down F that what was to be so charged was "the principal or only instrument whereby the exchange . . . is effected."

He codified his further submissions in four propositions: (i) "executed" in section 14 (4) means when the document in question has first been executed by every person whose execution is required to make the instrument effective as a chargeable instrument of the kind mentioned; (ii) G execution is not a single instantaneous matter when one is dealing with a deed, but a process involving signature, sealing and delivery; (iii) the process of execution of a deed is not complete until it has been signed, sealed and unconditionally delivered; (iv) where an instrument is originally delivered as an escrow, until the relevant conditions were satisfied (a) it was not a deed but a mere writing, (b) it transferred no estate, (c) it bound H the parties, but only in the sense that they could not recall it—it had no other legal effect, (d) if the conditions were not satisfied, the document was entirely inoperative. And, by way of contrast, it was only when the conditions had been fulfilled that the process of execution of the deed—as distinct from the escrow—was complete. Hence, execution in the present case post-dated the alteration in the rates of duty.

A In reply to all this, Mr. Hoffmann submitted as a third alternative argument that even if it was the case that an escrow did not become stampable until the conditions had been fulfilled, nevertheless the escrow had been executed when it was signed, sealed and delivered conditionally, and that one was once again thrown back on the terms of section 14 (4). He emphasised that this must be the correct moment upon which to focus as otherwise one would run into the difficulty that, although it is undoubted B law that an escrow will take effect as a deed if the conditions are fulfilled even if the grantor has died in the meantime, who could possibly be said to execute the deed in those circumstances?

In my judgment, it is essential to go back to first principles. There are, unfortunately, a large number of dicta to be found in the books which are clearly not consistent with first principles, including one notable C one by Lord Reid in *Wm. Cory & Son Ltd.* v. *Inland Revenue Commissioners* [1965] A.C. 1088, where he said, at p. 1108:

> "Then Lord Denning instanced an executed conveyance delivered in escrow. In my understanding there would then be nothing binding: both parties would have locus poenitentiae. So long as that position continued I do not see that there would be any obligation to stamp the instrument."

D This is, quite clearly, a total misunderstanding of the doctrine of an escrow.

The true position, in my judgment, is accurately stated in *Preston's Abstracts*, 2nd ed., vol. III (1824), p. 65, where that work of authority states the law as follows:

> E "The rules respecting escrows are, 1st, The writing will not operate as a deed till the second delivery. 2ndly, The party deputed to make the second delivery, cannot give effect to the writing by delivering the same before the conditions are performed. 3rdly, On the second delivery of the writing, it will have relation, for the purposes of title, and not for the purpose of giving a right to the intermediate rents, &c. from the delivery. 4thly, So as the conditions be performed, and the F deed delivered a second time, the deed will be good, notwithstanding the death of both or either of the parties before the second delivery."

The matter is dealt with at greater length, but with as great accuracy, in *Halsbury's Laws of England*, 4th ed., vol. 12 (1975), in paragraphs 1332 to 1334.

I think that there can really be no dispute as to the law. A document G which is intended to take effect as a deed when certain conditions have been fulfilled may be executed as an escrow: that is to say, with all the formalities of a deed save that the vital unconditional delivery, which is essential for the proper execution of a true deed, is missing; it is replaced by a conditional delivery, usually express, but capable of being assumed. At this stage, the document is not a deed; and although of course it con- H tains within itself the possibility of becoming an effective deed, a deed rising phoenix-like from the ashes of the escrow, at the stage before the condition is fulfilled it is of no effect whatsoever. Thus, even in a case where the condition is subsequently fulfilled the grantee of land under an escrow would never be entitled to the intermediate rents: see, for example, *Thompson* v. *McCullough* [1947] K.B. 447. When the condition is fulfilled, under the old strict practice there would undoubtedly have been, for the first time, an unconditional delivery of the instrument, which would then become, again for the first time, a deed effecting the purpose therein stated. A The theory of the old law was that an escrow had to be delivered to a third party—not to the person intended to take thereunder because, if so, he took immediately under the deed—and, on the fulfilment of the condition, the third party would deliver it to the person intended to take thereunder. Indeed, so obvious was this that mere possession of the escrow by such party was taken to be prima facie evidence of the fulfilment of the condition: see *Hare* v. *Horton* (1833) 5 B. & Ad. 715, 728, 730. B

Now all this has been changed. The grantor may himself keep possession of the escrow, or it may initially be delivered to the grantee, who in such a case will be restrained by equity from acting upon it until the condition has in fact been fulfilled. But none of this detracts from the reality of the position that until the condition has in fact been fulfilled the escrow is not a deed and is not effective for any purpose. Fulfilment C of the condition is now no longer followed by actual unconditional delivery, but the situation in law is the same; that is to say, it is not until the condition has been fulfilled that the document becomes, for the first time, a deed effective for its purpose.

I have already noted Mr. Hoffmann's searching question: if the grantor be dead, who executes the escrow so that it becomes a deed? The answer is, of course, that Mr. Millett was perfectly correct in his submission that D execution of a deed is a process rather than a single matter at a single instant of time. It consists of signature, sealing and unconditional delivery. Obviously, a live grantor must sign and seal; but he may entrust the resultant document to others, including his personal representatives, to deliver unconditionally. And if he has himself first delivered it conditionally, he may not himself withhold, nor can his personal representatives E on his behalf withhold, the unconditional delivery to the grantee if the condition be fulfilled. It matters not by whose hand that unconditional delivery may take place.

The foregoing analysis is, I think, substantially the same as that made with much greater economy of words by Diplock L.J. in *Wm. Cory & Son Ltd.* v. *Inland Revenue Commissioners* [1964] 1 W.L.R. 1332, in the Court of Appeal. He said, at p. 1346: F

> "A deed delivered as an escrow, which is no more than an old word for scroll, does not, I respectfully and regretfully think, provide an example of an exception to this principle. So long as it remains an escrow it is not yet executed as a deed; for delivery again as a deed is required before it becomes one. While an escrow it conveys nothing, it transfers nothing. It attracts no liability to stamp duty G any more than an unsigned contract. Such liability is attracted when and only when it is delivered again—that is, executed as a deed. It is then that it effects a conveyance or transfer. It is only then that it attracts liability to stamp duty: see Sheppard's *Touchstone*, 58 and 59 and *Xenos* v. *Wickham* (1866) L.R. 2 H.L. 296, 323 and the two cases cited by Lord Denning."

H

If I may repeat the crucial passage: "So long as it remains an escrow it is not yet executed as a deed; for delivery again as a deed is required before it becomes one." It follows, in my judgment, that within the meaning of section 14 (4) the first date on which the deed of exchange which is the subject matter of the present appeal was executed was on the day on which the conditions were fulfilled and it was in the eye of the law for the first time delivered unconditionally, and thus for the first time delivered

A as a deed; namely, on May 8, 1974—that is to say, after the rates of stamp duty had been doubled.

I think that my decision is fully in line with the Irish case of *Byrne* v. *Revenue Commissioners* [1935] I.R. 664, 668, where Johnston J. said, at p. 669:

> "That letter was accepted by the stamp officer as good evidence that the deed had been delivered to the grantors' solicitors to hold as an
> B escrow and that it had not been delivered as a deed until the condition was fulfilled by the payment of the purchase money on May 19. The deed was then marked with an office stamp setting out the name of the commissioners, the date (May 31) and the word 'Escrow' as the explanation why no penalty was or could be imposed."

C I also think it is fully consistent with what Lord Reid himself said in *Wm. Cory & Son Ltd.* v. *Inland Revenue Commissioners* [1965] A.C. 1088, 1108 just after the passage I have already quoted, namely:

> "It seems to me that the respondents were right in admitting that the rule is universally applicable and that every instrument, if stampable at all, must be stamped as soon as it has any legal effect subject to the statutory provisions as to after-stamping with or without
> D penalty."

I think that, in order to pinpoint the matter exactly, one ought to read the words "under the relevant head of charge" between the words "legal effect" and "subject"; but this is, in my opinion, the sense of Lord Reid's statement even as it stands.

Of course, at the end of the day everything depends upon the particular
E provisions of the Stamp Act 1891, but looking at the matter more broadly it would appear a somewhat startling conclusion that a document which as it stood did nothing—albeit capable of doing many things in the future—should at once attract duty under some head or other of the Act, since the one thing which could at that date be postulated would be that the document was not one of whatever class of document it was sought to tax
F it as. Similarly, it would appear an equally startling doctrine that when that document had, by the fulfilment of the condition, been galvanized into life it should be stamped by reference to the rates of duty current at a time when it, like Sleeping Beauty, was wholly dormant and had not yet received the kiss of life in the shape of the fulfilment of the conditions. Taking one's stand strictly on the ipsissima verba of the Stamp Act 1891, the only instrument whereby the exchange in the present case was effected
G was the deed of exchange dated May 8, 1974; a deed which, prior to that date, did not, in the contemplation of the law, exist. For these reasons I shall dismiss this appeal.

Appeal dismissed with costs.

H Solicitors: *Jansons; Solicitor of Inland Revenue.*

A

[COURT OF APPEAL]

* REGINA v. JONES (JOHN)

REGINA v. SMITH (CHRISTOPHER)

1976 March 9 — James and Geoffrey Lane L.JJ. and Cobb J. B

Crime—Burglary—Entry of building "as a trespasser"—General permission to enter—Son entering father's house and stealing goods—Whether entry as trespasser—Theft Act 1968 (*c.* 60), *s.* 9 (1) (*b*)

Section 9 (1) of the Theft Act 1968 provides: C

"A person is guilty of burglary if— . . . (*b*) having entered any building or part of a building as a trespasser he steals or attempts to steal anything in the building . . ."

During the night, the defendants S and J entered a bungalow belonging to S's father and removed two television sets. Later that night, the father reported to the police that his bungalow had been broken into and the sets stolen and the defendants were arrested after being seen by a police constable D driving a car containing the television sets. They were charged and convicted of burglary, contrary to section 9 (1) (*b*) of the Theft Act 1968. The defendants appealed.

On the question whether a person with a general permission to enter premises can be a trespasser for the purposes of section 9 (1) (*b*):—

Held, dismissing the appeal, that for the purposes of section 9 (1) (*b*) of the Theft Act 1968 a person was a E trespasser if he entered the premises of another knowing that, or being reckless whether, he was entering in excess of any permission that had been given to him to enter (post, p. 675D–E).

Hillen and Pettigrew v. *I.C.I.* (*Alkali*) *Ltd.* [1936] A.C. 65, H.L.(E.) and *Reg.* v. *Collins* [1973] Q.B. 100, C.A. applied.

Byrne v. *Kinematograph Renters Society Ltd.* [1958] 1 W.L.R. 762 distinguished.

F

The following cases are referred to in the judgment:

Byrne v. *Kinematograph Renters Society Ltd.* [1958] 1 W.L.R. 762; [1958] 2 All E.R. 579.

Hillen and Pettigrew v. *I.C.I.* (*Alkali*) *Ltd.* [1936] A.C. 65, H.L.(E.).

Reg. v. *Boyle* [1954] 2 Q.B. 292; [1954] 3 W.L.R. 364; [1954] 2 All E.R. 721, C.C.A.

Reg. v. *Collins* [1973] Q.B. 100; [1972] 3 W.L.R. 243; [1972] 2 All E.R. 1105, C.A. G

No additional cases were cited in argument.

APPEALS against conviction.

During a night in May 1975 the defendants, John Jones and Christopher H Smith, entered a bungalow belonging to Smith's father and took away two television sets. Smith's father reported to the police that his bungalow had been broken into and two television sets stolen. In September 1975 at Winchester Crown Court (Mr. Recorder E. H. Laughton-Scott Q.C.) the defendants were indicted on a charge of burglary, contrary to section

---

[Reported by MISS EIRA CARYL-THOMAS, Barrister-at-Law]

A 9 (1) (*b*) of the Theft Act 1968. The defendants were convicted, and each was sentenced to 12 months' imprisonment.

The defendants appealed against their convictions on the ground, inter alia, that the recorder misdirected the jury in his summing up by ruling that if the two defendants had a dishonest frame of mind when entering the house they would be trespassers within the meaning of section 9 (1) (*b*) of the Theft Act 1968; the facts proved at the trial were that the
B defendant Smith was the son of the owner of the house, Alfred William Smith, and that he had a general permission from his father to enter the house at any time as he pleased and, accordingly, neither the defendant Smith nor the defendant Jones could in law be trespassers as alleged and could not be convicted of burglary under section 9 (1) (*b*). The case only calls for report on that one ground of appeal.

C The facts are stated in the judgment of the court.

Graham H. Rose for the defendants.
Christopher Clark for the Crown.

JAMES L.J. delivered the judgment of the court. On September 22,
D 1975, at Winchester Crown Court the defendants were convicted of burglary contrary to section 9 (1) (*b*) of the Theft Act 1968. By leave of the single judge each appeals against his conviction. Strictly speaking one of the grounds upon which the appeal has been argued relates to a point of law and leave was not necessary.

The facts of the matter which gave rise to the charge of burglary were these. Christopher Smith's father, Alfred Smith, lived at 72 Chapel Lane,
E Farnborough. He was in the course of negotiating a move from that house to other premises. At the material time, in May 1975, in that house were two television sets, one owned by Mr. Alfred Smith, the other owned by another person but lawfully in the possession of Mr. Alfred Smith. The defendant Christopher Smith lived with his own family at Aberfield. The defendant Jones lived in the opposite direction from Chapel Lane,
F Farnborough to Aberfield, namely in Lakeside Road, Ashvale.

In the early hours of May 10, 1975, a police officer in Ashvale saw a motor car with the two defendants inside and a television set protruding from the boot of the car. Having regard to that which he saw and the time of the morning he followed the car which turned into a side road where eventually it was stopped by a gate being in its way. The officer called for further officers to attend and when another officer went to the
G car he saw the defendant Jones sitting on the back seat with a second television set beside him. In the front of the car was Smith. They were told that the police believed that the television sets were stolen and that they were being arrested. Smith responded with the question: "Are they bent?" and Jones made the observation: "You cannot arrest me for just having a ride in a car."

H When, at the police station, they were searched, Jones was found to have in his possession a pair of pliers. Another police officer, D. S. Tarrant, who gave evidence for the Crown, had received a report from Mr. Smith (senior) and, as a result, had gone to 72, Chapel Lane where Mr. Smith had pointed out a window in the front bedroom, which window had a hole in it due to an old breakage. The window had been secured with what appeared to be cleanly cut cable tied between the handles of the window. In the living room of the house the officer found a further quantity of cable which had also been cut and the ends of the cut were A clean. That cable was subsequently ascertained to have come from the two television sets that had been in the room. The television sets that had been in the room were the same television sets that were in the car in which the defendants were found and there was no dispute about that. [His Lordship considered a ground of appeal not relevant to the present report and continued:] The next ground of appeal relied on by Mr. Rose in his argument is that which is put forward in the first of each of the B defendants' grounds. It is the point upon which Mr. Rose had laid the greatest stress in the course of his argument. The argument is based upon the wording of the Theft Act 1968, section 9 (1) (*b*) which is this:

> "(1) A person is guilty of burglary if— . . . (*b*) having entered any building or part of a building as a trespasser he steals or attempts to steal anything in the building or that part of it or inflicts or attempts C to inflict on any person therein any grievous bodily harm."

The important words from the point of view of the arguments in this appeal are "having entered any building . . . as a trespasser." This is a section of an Act of Parliament which introduced a novel concept. Entry as a trespasser was new in 1968 in relation to criminal offences of burglary. It was introduced in substitution for, as an improvement upon, the old law D which required considerations of breaking and entering and involved distinctions of nicety which had bedevilled the law for some time.

Mr. Rose argues that a person who had a general permission to enter premises of another person cannot be a trespasser. His submission is as short and as simple as that. Related to this case he says that a son to whom a father has given permission generally to enter the father's house E cannot be a trespasser if he enters it even though he had decided in his mind before making the entry to commit a criminal offence of theft against the father once he had got into the house and had entered that house solely for the purpose of committing that theft. It is a bold submission. Mr. Rose frankly accepts that there has been no decision of the court since this statute was passed which governs this particular point. He has reminded us of *Byrne* v. *Kinematograph Renters Society Ltd.* [1958] F 1 W.L.R. 762, which he prays in aid of his argument. In that case persons had entered a cinema by producing tickets not for the purpose of seeing the show, but for an ulterior purpose. It was held in the action, which sought to show that they entered as trespassers pursuant to a conspiracy to trespass, that in fact they were not trespassers. The important words in the judgment are at p. 776: "They did nothing they were not G invited to do, . . ." That provides a distinction between that case and what we consider the position to be in this case.

Mr. Rose has also referred us to one of the trickery cases, *Reg.* v. *Boyle* [1954] 2 Q.B. 292, and in particular the passage at p. 295. He accepts that the trickery cases can be distinguished from such a case as the present because in the trickery cases it can be said that that which would otherwise have been consent to enter was negatived by the fact that consent H was obtained by a trick. We do not gain any help in the particular case from that decision. We were also referred to *Reg.* v. *Collins* [1973] Q.B. 100 and in particular to the long passage, commencing at p. 104 where Edmund Davies L.J. commenced the consideration of what is involved by the words "the entry must be 'as a trespasser.'" It is unnecessary to cite the passage in full; suffice it to say that this court on that occasion at p. 104 expressly approved the view expressed in Professor Smith's book,

The Law of Theft, 1st ed. (1968), and also the view of Professor Griew in his publication, *The Theft Act 1968*, upon this aspect of what is involved in being a trespasser.

In our view the passage there referred to is consonant with the passage in the well-known case, *Hillen and Pettigrew* v. *I.C.I.* (*Alkali*) *Ltd.* [1936] A.C. 65, 69, where Lord Atkin said:

> "My Lords, in my opinion this duty to an invitee only extends so long as and so far as the invitee is making what can reasonably be contemplated as an ordinary and reasonable use of the premises by the invitee for the purposes for which he has been invited. He is not invited to use any part of the premises for purposes which he knows are wrongfully dangerous and constitute an improper use. As Scrutton L.J. has pointedly said: 'When you invite a person into your house to use the staircase you do not invite him to slide down the banisters.'"

That case, of course, was a civil case in which it was sought to make the defendant liable for a tort.

The decision in *Reg.* v. *Collins* [1973] Q.B. 100 in this court, a decision upon the criminal law, added to the concept of trespass as a civil wrong only the mental element of mens rea, which is essential to the criminal offence. Taking the law as expressed in *Hillen and Pettigrew* v. *I.C.I.* (*Alkali*) *Ltd.* and in *Reg.* v. *Collins* it is our view that a person is a trespasser for the purpose of section 9 (1) (*b*) of the Theft Act 1968 if he enters premises of another knowing that he is entering in excess of the permission that has been given to him, or being reckless as to whether he is entering in excess of the permission that has been given to him to enter. Provided the facts are known to the accused which enable him to realise that he is acting in excess of the permission given or that he is acting recklessly as to whether he exceeds that permission, then that is sufficient for the jury to decide that he is in fact a trespasser.

In this particular case it was a matter for the jury to consider whether, on all the facts, it was shown by the prosecution that the defendants entered with the knowledge that entry was being effected against the consent or in excess of the consent that had been given by Mr. Smith senior to his son, the defendant Smith. The jury were, by their verdict satisfied of that. It was a novel argument that we heard, interesting but one without, in our view, any foundation.

Appeals dismissed.
Application to certify a point of law of general public importance refused.

Solicitors: *Registrar of Criminal Appeals; P. K. L. Danks, Winchester.*

A

[COURT OF APPEAL]

* ALUMINIUM INDUSTRIE VAASSEN B.V. *v.* ROMALPA ALUMINIUM LTD.

[1974 A. No. 5671] B

1975 Feb. 3, 4, 5, 6, 7; 11 — Mocatta J.

1976 Jan. 13, 14, 15, 16 — Megaw, Roskill and Goff L.JJ.

Sale of Goods—Implied term—Obligation to account—Conditions of sale containing reservation of ownership clause—Property not to pass to buyers until all outstanding debts paid—Goods C *sold to sub-purchasers—Buyers in liquidation—Proceeds of sub-sales held in receiver's account—Whether sellers entitled to trace and recover*

Between September 1973 and October 1974 the plaintiffs, a Dutch company, sold to the defendants, an English company, aluminium foil, some of which the defendants re-sold to third parties. D The plaintiffs' general selling terms and conditions, which the court found applied to all transactions between the parties, stipulated by clause 13 that "the ownership of the material to be delivered . . . will only be transferred to the purchaser when he has met all that is owing to" the plaintiffs. The clause went on to refer to articles manufactured by the defendants from material supplied by the plaintiffs and provided that ownership of such articles would be given to the plaintiffs as E "surety" of full payment of what the defendants owed them, that the defendants would keep such articles in their capacity of fiduciary owners, but they were given power to sell such articles to third parties in the normal course of their business. The defendants went into liquidation owing the plaintiffs over £122,000, and the receiver certified that £35,152 was held in an account in his name with the defendants' bankers, representing the proceeds of sale of aluminium foil supplied by the plaintiffs F which the defendants had sold to third parties.

The plaintiffs claimed, inter alia, a declaration that they were entitled to a charge on the money held in the receiver's account and to trace the proceeds of sub-sales of their property in that account. The defendants conceded that the effect of clause 13 was to make them bailees of the material supplied by the plaintiffs until all debts were paid, but contended G that once they had re-sold the material to bona fide purchasers the relationship between them and the plaintiffs was purely that of debtor and creditor and that, in the absence of an express or constructive trust, the plaintiffs were not entitled to avail themselves of the equitable remedy of tracing the money. Mocatta J. held that clause 13 showed an intention to create a fiduciary relationship between the parties and that the plaintiffs were entitled to follow the proceeds of the sub-sales. H

On appeal by the defendants:—

Held, dismissing the appeal, that the obvious purpose of clause 13, in the context of the general conditions, was to secure the plaintiffs as far as possible, in the event of insolvency, against the risk of non-payment after they had parted with possession of but not the legal title to the material delivered, whether or not that material retained its identity before payment was received, and that, in order to give effect

A to that purpose, there had to be implied into the first part of the clause, in addition to the undoubted power to sell the material to sub-purchasers, an obligation on the defendants to account in accordance with the normal fiduciary relationship of principal and agent, bailor and bailee, as expressly contemplated in the second part of the clause; and accordingly the plaintiffs were entitled to trace the proceeds of the sub-sales, and to recover them and the judge had correctly so
B held (post, pp. 668B–C, 690A–B, E–F, 692A–C, 693B–C, 694A–B).

In re Hallett's Estate (1880) 13 Ch.D. 696, C.A. applied.

Decision of Mocatta J., post, pp. 678E et seq.; affirmed.

The following case is referred to in the judgment of the Court of Appeal:

Hallett's Estate, In re [1976] 2 All E.R. 552 (1880) 13 Ch.D. 696, C.A.

C

No additional cases were cited in argument.

The following cases are referred to in the judgment of Mocatta J.:

Diplock, In re [1948] Ch. 465, C.A.

Hallett's Estate, In re (1880) 13 Ch.D. 696, C.A.

Henry v. *Hammond* [1913] 2 K.B. 515, D.C.

D *King* v. *Hutton* [1900] 2 Q.B. 504, C.A.

The following additional cases were cited in argument before Mocatta J.:

Alison (J. Gordon) and Co. Ltd. v. *Wallsend Slipway and Engineering Co. Ltd.* (1927) 43 T.L.R. 323, C.A.

Bolton (H. L.) Engineering Co. Ltd. v. *T. J. Graham & Sons Ltd.* [1957]
E 1 Q.B. 159; [1956] 3 W.L.R. 804; [1956] 3 All E.R. 624, C.A.

Curtis v. *Chemical Cleaning and Dyeing Co. Ltd.* [1951] 1 K.B. 805; [1951] 1 All E.R. 631, C.A.

Hardwick Game Farm v. *Suffolk Agricultural Poultry Producers Association* [1969] 2 A.C. 31; [1968] 3 W.L.R. 110; [1968] 2 All E.R. 444, H.L.(E.).

Ladenburg & Co. v. *Goodwin, Ferreira & Co. Ltd.* [1912] 3 K.B. 275.

McCutcheon v. *David Macbrayne Ltd.* [1964] 1 W.L.R. 125; [1964] 1
F All E.R. 430, H.L.(Sc.).

McEntire v. *Crossley Brothers Ltd.* [1895] 1 A.C. 457, H.L.(I.).

Thornton v. *Shoe Lane Parking Ltd.* [1971] 2 Q.B. 163; [1971] 2 W.L.R. 585; [1971] 1 All E.R. 686, C.A.

Tunstall v. *Steigmann* [1962] 2 Q.B. 593; [1962] 2 W.L.R. 1045; [1962] 2 All E.R. 517, C.A.

Underwood (A. L.) Ltd. v. *Bank of Liverpool and Martins* [1924] 1 K.B.
G 775, C.A.

ACTION

By a specially indorsed writ dated October 30, 1974, and re-amended points of claim dated January 24, 1975, the plaintiffs, Aluminium Industrie Vaassen B.V., a company incorporated under the laws of the
H Kingdom of Holland and carrying on business as manufacturers and suppliers of aluminium goods, claimed, inter alia, a declaration that all goods at any time supplied by them to the defendants, Romalpa Aluminium Ltd., an English company, were the property of the plaintiffs, except in so far as title to the goods might have passed pursuant to section 25 of the Sale of Goods Act 1893 to bona fide purchasers for value from the defendants; an order that the defendants deliver up to the plaintiffs all goods supplied by the plaintiffs and in the actual or

constructive possession or control of the defendants; an order restraining A
the defendants from parting with possession of such goods; a declaration
that the plaintiffs had a charge to the extent of £35,152·66 over the
account of the defendants' receiver/manager with the defendants'
bankers, Hume Corporation Ltd., and an order that such sum be paid
over to the plaintiffs; the price of goods supplied to the defendants but
not paid, namely, £122,239.

They relied on General Selling Terms and Conditions for Foil B
Aluminium which they alleged applied to every transaction between
themselves and the defendants and in particular on clause 13 which
provided:

> "The ownership of the material to be delivered by [the plaintiffs]
> will only be transferred to the purchaser when he has met all that
> is owing to [the plaintiffs], no matter on what grounds . . ." C

By their amended defence the defendants, inter alia, denied that
the general selling terms and conditions applied to the transactions
between them and the plaintiffs, or that the plaintiffs remained the owners
of the goods other than those sold to bona fide purchasers for value or
that the plaintiffs were entitled to any of the relief sought in the writ
and the prayer in the re-amended points of claim. D

The facts relevant to this report are stated in the judgment of
Mocatta J. and of Roskill L.J.

Anthony Lincoln Q.C. and *David Donaldson* for the plaintiffs.
M. A. Pickering for the defendants.

Cur. adv. vult. E

February 11, 1975. MOCATTA J. read the following judgment. The
plaintiffs are a Dutch company making, amongst other things, aluminium
foil. The defendants are an English company in respect of which its
bankers, Hume Corporation Ltd., on November 1, 1974, appointed a
receiver pursuant to powers granted by the defendants under a debenture F
dated January 10, 1974. On October 30, 1974, just before the appoint-
ment of the receiver, a writ had been issued in this action by the
plaintiffs, and an interlocutory injunction was obtained on October 30
from Cusack J. in relation to goods supplied by the plaintiffs to the
defendants and still in the possession of the defendants.

There is no doubt that on November 1, 1974, the defendants owed the
plaintiffs Hfl. 757,886, or £122,239·74 at the rate of exchange of Hfl. 6.20 G
[Dutch Florins] to the £, in respect of a large number of invoices in
relation to sales of aluminium foil to the defendants from August 1,
1974. After his appointment, the receiver certified that £35,152·66 was
held in an account in his name as receiver-manager of the defendants
with the Hume Corporation, and that amount represented the proceeds
of sale of aluminium foil supplied by the plaintiffs to the defendants and H
then sold by the latter to third parties. In this action the plaintiffs now
seek to establish by declaration their right to a charge on this sum,
basing their claim on a right to trace on the principle established in *In
re Hallett's Estate* (1880) 13 Ch.D. 696.

Secondly, the receiver has certified that aluminium foil to a value
alleged to be £50,235 is held by him, having originated in deliveries to
the defendants by the plaintiffs. The plaintiffs seek a second relief,

A namely, a declaration that this quantity of foil is theirs, and an order for its delivery up. Very much as a third string to their claim and only if they should fail on their first and second claims to relief, the plaintiffs sought judgment for the price.

The first major issue in this case turns on whether clause 13, in what the plaintiffs say are their general selling terms and conditions for aluminium foil, applied to the transactions done between the plaintiffs
B and the defendants, in respect of which £122,239 is owing. That clause began with this important reservation of title. The first sentence of the clause reads as follows:

> "The ownership of the material to be delivered by A.I.V." (that is the plaintiffs) "will only be transferred to purchaser when he has met all that is owing to A.I.V., no matter on what grounds."

C I read the remainder of the clause in view of its somewhat elaborate nature and of subsequent issues arising:

> "Until the date of payment, purchaser, if A.I.V. so desires, is required to store this material in such a way that it is clearly the property of A.I.V. A.I.V. and purchaser agree that, if purchaser should make (a) new object(s) from the material, mix this material
> D with (an)other object(s) or if this material in any way whatsoever becomes a constituent of (an)other object(s) A.I.V. will be given the ownership of this (these) new objects(s) as surety of the full payment of what purchaser owes A.I.V. To this end A.I.V. and purchaser now agree that the ownership of the article(s) in question, whether finished or not, are to be transferred to A.I.V. and that this
> E transfer of ownership will be considered to have taken place through and at the moment of the single operation or event by which the material is converted into (a) new object(s), or is mixed with or becomes a constituent of (an)other object(s). Until the moment of full payment of what purchaser owes A.I.V. purchaser shall keep the object(s) in question for A.I.V. in his capacity of fiduciary owner and, if required, shall store this (these) object(s) in such a way that
> F it (they) can be recognized as such. Nevertheless, purchaser will be entitled to sell these objects to a third party within the framework of the normal carrying on of his business and to deliver them on condition that—if A.I.V. so requires—purchaser, as long as he has not fully discharged his debt to A.I.V. shall hand over to A.I.V. the claims he has against his buyer emanating from this transaction."

G If the plaintiffs can establish that clause 13 does apply, as between themselves and the defendants, they are admittedly entitled to succeed on their second claim, the goods in question in the possession of the defendants still being their property. But their first claim, namely, the right to trace, is disputed. I must therefore deal first with the hotly contested point whether clause 13 did apply between the plaintiffs and
H the defendants. The plaintiffs say it did, expressly, or impliedly. The defendants say that it did apply admittedly to trade that had been carried on between the plaintiffs and a firm called Romalpa Aluminium, prior to the plaintiffs beginning to do business with the defendants on September 1, 1973. They deny, however, that the clause applied to business done between the plaintiffs and the defendants from that date onwards.

[His Lordship narrated the course of dealing between the plaintiffs and the partnership and referred to the agreement by the two partners,

A Mr. Rodbard and Mr. Malyon, that the plaintiffs' general selling terms and conditions, which had been deposited in all the district courts of the Netherlands, should apply to all transactions between the plaintiffs and the partnership, including the ownership clause, clause 13. He said that after the defendants acquired the business of the partnership in September 1973 and the two partners became directors, orders were placed as before, and confirmations and acknowledgments were given to the defendants as B before and on exactly the same printed forms as had been in use between the plaintiffs and the partnership since 1971. In his Lordship's judgment it followed from the facts that the full deposited terms, including clause 13, did apply to every order placed by the defendants with the plaintiffs; that there was an express incorporation of clause 13 in the various contracts made between the parties. If there were any doubt about that, C the full terms, including clause 13, were impliedly agreed to apply to each order. His Lordship continued:]

Having decided that clause 13 did apply to the many transactions between the plaintiffs and defendants after September 1, 1973, when the defendants took over the aluminium foil business that the partnership had previously conducted with the plaintiffs, I now have to deal with the consequences of that decision as applying to the claims in the action.

D In the first place, it is admitted that the plaintiffs are the owners of the remaining unsold aluminium foil held by the receiver, and that they are entitled to an order for its delivery up to them. The real contest arose in relation to the plaintiffs' right to a charge on the receiver's account with the Hume Corporation to the extent of £35,152·66 representing, as certified by the receiver, the sum recovered by him from E customers of the defendants as a result of A.I.V. materials supplied to the defendants by the plaintiffs. This right the plaintiffs claim on the basis of the principle established in *In re Hallett's Estate*, 13 Ch.D. 696 entitling them to trace the proceeds of the sale of their property sold by the plaintiffs into the receiver's bank account. It is common ground that the effect of clause 13 is that, while money was owing by the defendants to the plaintiffs, any aluminium foil delivered by the plaintiffs F to the defendants, while still in their possession, was held by them as bailees.

It is further common ground that the clause must be read subject to the necessary implication that the defendants were entitled to sell the foil to sub-purchasers. It is curious that this is not said about sales of unmixed foil whilst it is said in the last sentence of the clause about foil G mixed with other material. In respect of this, it is to be noted that the defendants were, if required, to assign to the plaintiffs their rights against sub-purchasers in respect of the mixed materials sold to them. Notwithstanding the generally far-reaching and somewhat elaborate provisions in clause 13, reserving the plaintiff's right of ownership in the goods until nothing was owing from the purchasers, and the admission that the H clause had the effect of making the defendants bailees of the goods while in their possession until all money owing had been paid, the argument for the defendants was that once foil had been sold to bona fide purchasers, the relationship between the plaintiffs and the defendants was purely one of debtor and creditor. As against this, the plaintiffs argued that a fiduciary relationship stemming from the bailment continued after sales to third parties, and that in consequence equitable remedies applied, including the right to trace proceeds of the sub-sales. It was not

A necessary, said the plaintiffs, to find as a prerequisite to the right to trace an express or constructive trust. The equitable proprietary remedy followed as a consequence of the finding that the defendants were bailees.

Having indicated the general nature of the competing arguments, I can go straight to the judgment of Sir George Jessel M.R. in *In re Hallett's Estate*, 13 Ch.D. 696. Although in that case there had been breaches of express trust, it is clear from the passages I am about to read
B that the reasoning was not founded on this, and that the principle stated applied to much wider circumstances. It is necessary to make certain fairly extensive quotations. Sir George Jessel M.R. said, at p. 708:

> " The modern doctrine of equity as regards property disposed of by persons in a fiduciary position is a very clear and well-established doctrine. You can, if the sale was rightful, take the proceeds of the
> C sale, if you can identify them. If the sale was wrongful, you can still take the proceeds of the sale, in a sense adopting the sale for the purpose of taking the proceeds, if you can identify them. There is no distinction, therefore, between a rightful and a wrongful disposition of the property, so far as regards the right of the beneficial owner to follow the proceeds. . . . "

D
Pausing there for a moment, it is not, of course, suggested here that there was a wrongful disposition of the plaintiff's property when the defendants sold the foil to bona fide sub-purchasers. The latter would get a good title pursuant to section 25 of the Sale of Goods Act 1893. As between the plaintiffs and defendants, however, property had never passed to the defendants. I continue with the quotation, at p. 709:

E
> " But it very often happens that you cannot identify the proceeds. The proceeds may have been invested together with money belonging to the person in a fiduciary position, in a purchase. He may have bought land with it, for instance, or he may have bought chattels with it. Now, what is the position of the beneficial owner as regards such purchases? I will, first of all, take his position when
> F the purchase is clearly made with what I will call, for shortness, the trust money, although it is not confined, as I will shew presently, to express trusts. In that case, according to the now well-established doctrine of equity, the beneficial owner has a right to elect either to take the property purchased, or to hold it as a security for the amount of the trust money laid out in the purchase; or, as we generally
> G express it, he is entitled at his election either to take the property, or to have a charge on the property for the amount of the trust money. But in the second case, where a trustee has mixed the money with his own, there is this distinction, that the cestui que trust, or beneficial owner, can no longer elect to take the property, because it is no longer bought with the trust money simply and purely, but with a mixed fund. He is, however, still entitled to a charge on
> H the property purchased, for the amount of the trust money laid out in the purchase; and that charge is quite independent of the fact of the amount laid out by the trustee. The moment you get a substantial portion of it furnished by the trustee, using the word 'trustee' in the sense I have mentioned, as including all persons in a fiduciary relation, the right to the charge follows. That is the modern doctrine of equity . . ."

There then follows this passage showing the width of the application of A
the principle:

> "Has it ever been suggested, until very recently, that there is any
> distinction between an express trustee, or an agent, or a bailee, or
> a collector of rents, or anybody else in a fiduciary position? I have
> never heard, until quite recently, such a distinction suggested. It
> cannot, as far as I am aware (and since this court sat last to hear B
> this case, I have taken the trouble to look for authority), be found
> in any reported case even suggested, except in the recent decision
> of Fry J. [*Ex parte Dale & Co.* (1879) 11 Ch.D. 772,] to which I shall
> draw attention presently. It can have no foundation in principle,
> because the beneficial ownership is the same, wherever the legal
> ownership may be."

C

There is the following short passage, at p. 710:

> "Now that being the established doctrine of equity on this point,
> I will take the case of the pure bailee. If the bailee sells the goods
> bailed, the bailor can in equity follow the proceeds, and can follow
> the proceeds wherever they can be distinguished, either being
> actually kept separate, or being mixed up with other moneys." D

Finally, this sentence, at p. 711:

> "Therefore, there is no difficulty in following out the rules of
> equity and deciding that in a case of a mere bailee, as Fry J. has
> decided, you can follow the money."

These passages are clearly most apposite, since they refer to the position E
of a mere bailee, and were strongly relied upon by Mr. Lincoln. Mr.
Pickering sought to avoid them by saying that they were obiter or had
in some way been modified in *In re Diplock* [1948] Ch. 465 and that it
was necessary that there should be some express or constructive trust
before the equitable doctrine could apply. My attention was not drawn
to any passage in *In re Diplock* criticising or modifying, in any way, F
the statements of principle which I have quoted. Although I fully
recognise that in considering this problem I find myself in a most un-
familiar field, I feel it my duty to follow and apply those statements.
Mr. Pickering drew my attention to two authorities as illustrating the
simple debtor/creditor relationship, namely, *King* v. *Hutton* [1900] 2
Q.B. 504 and *Henry* v. *Hammond* [1913] 2 K.B. 515. It is unnecessary
to refer to these in detail, save to say that the former makes it clear G
that the special facts of each case are crucial in determining whether
there is a simple debtor/creditor relationship, although the intention of
the parties as ascertained from the terms of their contract shows that
some kind of fiduciary relationship exists. The preservation of owner-
ship clause contains unusual and fairly elaborate provisions departing
substantially from the debtor/creditor relationship and shows, in my H
view, the intention to create a fiduciary relationship to which the
principle stated in *In re Hallett's Estate*, 13 Ch.D. 696 applies. A further
point made by Mr. Pickering was that if the plaintiffs were to succeed
in their tracing claim this would, in effect, be a method available against
a liquidator to a creditor of avoiding the provisions establishing the
need to register charges on book debts: see section 95 (1) (2) (*e*) of
the Companies Act 1948. He used this only as an argument against the

effect of clause 13 contended for by Mr. Lincoln. As to this, I think Mr. Lincoln's answer was well founded, namely, that if property in the foil never passed to the defendants with the result that the proceeds of sub-sales belonged in equity to the plaintiffs, section 95 (1) had no application.

The plaintiffs accordingly succeed and are entitled to the reliefs sought in paragraph 1 of the prayer, to the reliefs sought in paragraphs 2 and 3 of the prayer; and also to a declaration that they have a charge to the extent of £35,152·66 over the account of the receiver-manager of the defendants, with Hume Corporation Ltd., and an order that he pay over that sum to the plaintiffs' solicitors. Their claim for the price of goods sold is adjourned sine die with liberty to apply. It will only become relevant in the event of my decision being reversed in a higher court.

Judgment for plaintiffs with costs.

Solicitors: *Woodham Smith, Greenwood & Holland; Theodore Goddard & Co.*

The defendants appealed on the grounds, inter alia, that the judge had erred in fact or in law or in principle: (1) in holding that clause 13 of the General Selling Terms and Conditions applied to or were incorporated in contracts for the sale of aluminium foil made between the plaintiffs and the defendants; (2) in holding that the plaintiffs were entitled at law to trace sums of money received by the defendants as proceeds of sale for aluminium foil; and (3) in failing to formulate and apply correctly the relevant ratio decidendi in *In re Hallett's Estate*, 13 Ch.D. 696 and other cases to the facts of the present case.

Their Lordships dismissed the appeal on the first ground which does not call for report.

Leolin Price Q.C. and *M. A. Pickering* for the defendants.
Anthony Lincoln Q.C. and *David Donaldson* for the plaintiffs.

MEGAW L.J. I shall ask Roskill L.J. to deliver the first judgment.

ROSKILL L.J. This appeal, from a judgment of Mocatta J. dated February 11, 1975, arises out of a dispute between the plaintiffs, a Dutch company, who amongst other things manufacture aluminium foil in Holland, and the defendants, an English limited company, regarding entitlement, first to certain quantities of aluminium foil admitted to be physically in the defendants' possession and secondly to certain proceeds of sale of other aluminium foil delivered to the defendants by the plaintiffs and sold by the defendants to sub-purchasers in this country for which those sub-purchasers had paid the defendants but for which the defendants had not paid the plaintiffs by the time the defendants—whose business has been in the hands of a receiver since November 1, 1974—got into the serious financial difficulties which led to that receiver being so appointed. At that date the defendants were indebted to the plaintiffs for over £122,000.

The value of the foil concerned in the first head of claim is said to be just over £50,000. The sum involved in the second head of claim is just over £35,000. The present action is thus an attempt by the plaintiffs to reduce that very substantial loss which they have suffered in their trading operations with the defendants, albeit at the expense of the debenture holders by whom the receiver was appointed and to whom the defendants remain very heavily indebted in respect of two advances of £100,000 each made to the defendants by the debenture holders.

The business which has led to these heavy losses was not always conducted between the defendants and the plaintiffs. Before September 1973, it had been conducted by the plaintiffs with a partnership called Romalpa Aluminium (for brevity I shall call it " the partnership ") the two partners in which became the two principal directors of the defendants, the third director of the defendants being a nominee of the debenture holders who first of all financed the defendants in return initially for the issue of unsecured loan stock and later in return for the debentures which the defendants issued to them.

There is no doubt what the express terms were upon which the plaintiffs did business with the partnership. They did their business upon certain general selling terms and conditions dated February 1971, which were deposited or registered with all district or county courts in Holland. The significance of such deposit, in Dutch law, was not the subject of any evidence; nor does it matter, though it would have been interesting to have known what the position was under Dutch law, as indeed it would have been interesting to know how a Dutch lawyer would have construed some of those express terms. Those conditions were in Dutch, but there was what one might describe as an authentic and specially prepared, though not perhaps very well expressed, English translation of the Dutch conditions. On April 4, 1972, the plaintiffs obtained from the partnership the signature of the two partners on a copy of that English translation. The conditions were expressed to be subject to Dutch law, the Amsterdam court being given exclusive jurisdiction by clause 30.

The relevant conditions for present purposes were clauses 13, 22, 25 and 26. I shall read parts of those later. Thereafter, and until the defendants took over the business with the plaintiffs previously done by the plaintiffs with the partnership, there can be no doubt that that business was done, inter alia, upon those express conditions. Individual invoices covered specific transactions incorporated both in Dutch and in English what was described as an " epitome " of the plaintiffs' general conditions to which I have just referred. One hesitates to criticise such a document, for one knows the difficulties of translation of this type of document from one language to another; but it cannot be said that the English translation is happy. Clause 13 is not referred to in the epitome at all—an omission upon which the defendants placed considerable reliance in connection with their submission that though the general conditions had governed the relationship of the plaintiffs with the partnership, they never governed the plaintiffs' relationship with the defendants, notwithstanding that exactly the same printed form of invoice was used for business both with the partnership and with the defendants.

It was argued by Mr. Price for the defendants that since the same procedure had not been gone through with the defendants as with the partnership, that is to say, by obtaining the signatures of the defendants' directors on a copy of the conditions, those general conditions did not apply to the transactions between the defendants and the plaintiffs; and

A he went on to argue that the knowledge of the partnership was not the
knowledge of the defendants even though those two partners were the
defendants' two principal directors.

The avowed purpose of this argument was to enable the defendants,
if they could, to escape, in particular, from the bonds of clause 13 of
the general conditions. For, if the defendants were not bound by those
B conditions, and in particular by clause 13, the whole of the plaintiffs'
claim must fail and Mocatta J.'s judgment would be manifestly wrong.
If, however, the defendants were bound by clause 13, it was admitted
that, as indeed Mocatta J. held, the plaintiffs must succeed on their first
head of claim, though it was strenuously contended on their behalf that,
even so, clause 13 did not enable them to succeed on their second head
of claim. Indeed before us the major part of the argument was directed
C to this latter question which the judge also decided in the plaintiffs'
favour. Indeed Mr. Price, if he will forgive my saying so, for reasons
which I can well understand and indeed sympathise with, argued the
second point first.

The opening sentences of clause 13 read:

> "The ownership of the material to be delivered by A.I.V."—those
> D initials, I should interpose, stand for the plaintiffs—"will only be
> transferred to purchaser when he has met all that is owing to A.I.V.,
> no matter on what grounds. Until the date of payment, purchaser,
> if A.I.V. so desires, is required to store this material in such a way
> that it is clearly the property of A.I.V."

In argument those first two sentences in clause 13 were referred to
E for convenience as the first part of that clause. Following those first
two sentences, which only occupy just over four lines of typescript, there
are some 20 further lines of small print dealing with, and as I think only
with, what were called in argument mixed or manufactured goods, that
is to say goods manufactured from the material supplied by the plaintiffs,
so that that material thus lost its original identity.

F At one stage in his argument Mr. Price submitted that the second
part of clause 13 also applied to unmanufactured goods—by which I
mean goods which remained in the state in which they were delivered to
the defendants; but ultimately he did not press this part of his argument
—rightly, as I think; for it seems to me plain that the two parts of this
clause are dealing with separate subject matters, the first part with
unmanufactured goods and the second with mixed or manufactured
G goods. The second part is, however, relevant, especially in light of the
argument which Mr. Price sought and obtained leave yesterday to
advance by virtue of his amendment to the notice of appeal which we
allowed, for in determining what implication is to be made in the first
part of the clause—which is the all-important issue in this appeal—it
is clearly right to look at clause 13 as a whole and not merely at one part
H of it. The second part reads:

> "A.I.V. and purchaser agree that, if purchaser should make (a)
> new object(s) from the material, mixes this material with (an)other
> object(s) or if this material in any way whatsoever becomes a con-
> stituent of (an)other object(s) A.I.V. will be given the ownership of
> this (these) new object(s) as surety of the full payment of what
> purchaser owes A.I.V. To this end A.I.V. and purchaser now agree
> that the ownership of the article(s) in question, whether finished or

> not, are to be transferred to A.I.V. and that this transfer of owner- A
> ship will be considered to have taken place through and at the moment of the single operation or event by which the material is converted into (a) new object(s), or is mixed with or becomes a constituent of (an)other object(s). Until the moment of full payment of what purchaser owes A.I.V., purchaser shall keep the object(s) in question for A.I.V. in his capacity of fiduciary owner and, if required, shall store this (these) object(s) in such a way that it (they) B
> can be recognised as such. Nevertheless, purchaser will be entitled to sell these objects to a third party within the framework of the normal carrying on of his business and to deliver them on condition that—if A.I.V. so requires—purchaser, as long as he has not fully discharged his debt to A.I.V. shall hand over to A.I.V. the claims he has against his buyer emanating from this transaction." C

Clause 22 reads:

> "Payment has to be made nett cash by purchaser not later than 14 days after the date of invoice, preferably by payment by transfer to the postal giro or banking account of A.I.V. If required a bill of exchange can be drawn. The place of payment for all deliveries is Vaassen." That was where the plaintiffs carried on their business. D
> "This also holds good when a bill is returned unpaid. In spite of any complaints about flaws in the material delivered, purchaser is obliged to pay the purchase price at the time laid down."

The provision regarding 14 days was varied (assuming for the moment that the general conditions applied) in that 75 days' grace was allowed to the defendants and not the 14 days for which clause 22 alone provided. E
While, as I think, one must deal with the question of construction and implication upon the footing that the credit allowed was 75 days, I do not think that that question can be answered differently according to whether the credit period was 14 or 75 days or some other period. Clause 13 appears in the general conditions with clause 22 unvaried. Clause 25 reads: F

> "Should purchaser remain in default of any payment for which he is liable to A.I.V.—which would be the case in exceeding the time within which purchaser should have paid—then A.I.V. is entitled to stop all deliveries, irrespective of which contract with purchaser they spring from, and to rescind the contract in question without judicial interposition, all this without prejudicing their right to full G
> compensation and without prejudicing their right to take back at once from purchaser the material [which], by virtue of what is laid down under 13, is still their property."

It is to be noted that the rights given by clause 25 (again assuming that the general conditions apply) are not limited to non-payment of individual debts due under each individual contract evidenced by individual invoices H
but apply in the case of default "of *any* payment" for which the purchaser (that is to say the defendants) is liable to the plaintiffs—a fact which I regard as of great importance. Clause 26 gives the plaintiffs an additional right to interest on outstanding invoice debts.

I shall deal first (as did the judge) with the question of the alleged incorporation of the general conditions into the transactions with the defendants, it being conceded that those general conditions applied to

A the antecedent transactions with the partnership. The judge had no
difficulty in holding that the business done with the defendants was done
on exactly the same terms as the antecedent business with the partner-
ship. [His Lordship said he entirely agreed with Mocatta J.'s conclusion
on that matter, and that it was obvious that the defendants' directors,
the two ex-partners, knew precisely what the terms of business had been
before the defendants came on the scene as a contracting party with the
B plaintiffs, and what those terms were going to be thereafter, and in fact
were at all material times; and that their knowledge, to his Lordship's
mind, was manifestly the knowledge of the defendants. He accordingly
held that the foil physically held by the receiver was the plaintiffs' foil,
to which they were now entitled, and the appeal against that part of
Mocatta J.'s judgment must clearly fail. His Lordship continued:]

C I turn to the second part, which Mr. Price argued first. Are the
plaintiffs entitled to the proceeds of sales to sub-purchasers now held
by the receiver? We were told both by Mr. Price and by Mr. Lincoln
that the receiver received these moneys after he had entered into his
receivership from sales made by the defendants to sub-purchasers before
that date. The receiver, properly if I may say so, kept those moneys
separate; and we were told that there is no complication arising of those
D moneys having become mixed with other moneys, because they were
always kept separate. There was no suggestion that the sub-sales in
question were other than authorised by the plaintiffs or that the sub-
purchasers concerned did not acquire a valid title to the several quantities
of foil which each of them bought. The sole question is whether, on
the facts and on the true construction of the bargain, including the
E general conditions, between the plaintiffs and the defendants, the plaintiffs
are entitled to trace and recover those proceeds of the sub-sales, upon
the well-known principles laid down in the judgment of Sir George
Jessel M.R. in *In re Hallett's Estate* (1880) 13 Ch.D. 696. Those princi-
ples are so well known that it is not necessary to quote the Master of the
Rolls' famous judgment or from the various restatements of principle in
the several textbooks to which Mr. Price has referred. The most relevant
F passages from that judgment will be found in Mocatta J.'s judgment
(ante, pp. 681A–B et seq.).

The critical question is whether there was a fiduciary relationship
between the plaintiffs and the defendants which entitles the plaintiffs
successfully to claim these moneys in the way and upon the footing
which I have just described. Mr. Price strenuously argued that the
G bargain between the parties was a perfectly ordinary bargain, creating
the ordinary contractual relationship of seller and buyer, with the con-
sequence that if the buyers—that is to say the defendants—became
insolvent before payment for the goods was made by them to the sellers,
—that is, the plaintiffs—the sellers were left with their ordinary con-
tractual or, as he put it, personal remedy as unsecured creditors of the
H buyers, and that there was no additional proprietary remedy (again to
borrow his language) available to them justifying their seeking to trace
and recover the proceeds of the sub-sales which had come from the
sub-purchasers into the hands of the receiver.

It seems to me clear that, but for the provisions of clause 13—which
have to be read in conjunction with the other relevant clauses I have
mentioned—this would be the position. The individual contracts were
for delivery ex the plaintiffs' works in Holland, and, apart from special

provisions, in English law at least—as already stated, there is no evidence A
of Dutch law and therefore we must apply English law to these contracts—both property and risk would have passed to the defendants upon such delivery.

But clause 13 plainly provides otherwise. The defendants as sellers were to retain the property in the goods until all—and I underline "*all*"—that was owing to them had been paid. It is a curious fact that the B
first part of clause 13 is so short while the second part is so long and detailed. But, as Mr. Lincoln said, the problems with which the second part had to deal were infinitely more complex than those with which the first part had to deal. It is obvious, to my mind, that the business purpose of the whole of this clause, read in its context in the general conditions, was to secure the plaintiffs, so far as possible, against the risks of non-payment after they had parted with possession of the goods C
delivered, whether or not those goods retained their identity after delivery. I unhesitatingly accept that part of Mr. Lincoln's submission. In the case of unmanufactured goods this was to be achieved by the plaintiffs retaining the property until all payments due had been made, to which were added the special rights given by clause 25. In the case of mixed or manufactured goods, more elaborate provisions were made D
and indeed were obviously required if the avowed object of clause 13 were to be achieved in the case of the latter class of goods. The plaintiffs were to be given the ownership of these mixed or manufactured goods as "surety" for "full payment." "Surety" I think in this context must mean, as Mr. Lincoln contended yesterday, "security." This is as between the defendants and the plaintiffs, and it is not necessary to consider how far this provision would protect the plaintiffs against E
adverse claims, at any rate in this country, by third parties. Further, the clause later provides that until "full payment" is made the defendants shall keep the mixed goods for the plaintiffs as "fiduciary owners"—not perhaps the happiest of phrases but one which suggests, at least to an English lawyer, that in relation to mixed or manufactured goods there was produced what in English law would be called a fiduciary F
relationship in this respect. The clause goes on to give to the defendants an express power of sale of such goods, and the right to deliver them; and adds an obligation upon the defendants, if required by the plaintiffs so to do, to assign (to use English legal language) to the plaintiffs the benefit of any claim against a sub-purchaser so long as the defendants have not fully discharged all their indebtedness to the plaintiffs.

For my part I accept that this last-mentioned provision is not itself G
an equitable assignment in English law. But I think that Mr. Lincoln is right in his general approach to the construction of the second part of clause 13. Like the first part, it contemplates the resale by the defendants of goods which at the time of such resale were to be the property of the plaintiffs and not of the defendants. The second part of clause 13 clearly contemplates the creation of a fiduciary relationship H
in relation to mixed goods; and the assignment provisions are, as I think, clearly designed to give the plaintiffs, if they so require, an additional security to recover debts otherwise payable to the defendants but not paid to them by the sub-purchasers, if the defendants have failed to discharge all or any of their current indebtedness to the plaintiffs.

The burden of Mr. Lincoln's argument was, first, that all goods dealt with in pursuance of clause 13 were, until *all* debts were discharged, the plaintiffs' goods which the defendants were authorised to sell on the plaintiffs' behalf and for the plaintiffs' account but only within the framework of clause 13. Since the goods were the plaintiffs', the defendants remained accountable to the plaintiffs for them or for their proceeds of sale, so long as any indebtedness whatever remained outstanding from the defendants to the plaintiffs. Hence the creation of the fiduciary relationship upon which Mr. Lincoln sought to rely. The burden of Mr. Price's argument was, as already stated, that the clause created in the first part no more than the ordinary debtor/creditor, buyer/seller, relationship, and that nothing in the second part justified placing additional fiduciary obligations upon the defendants in respect of unmanufactured goods, referred to in the first part of the clause.

It was common ground at the trial and during argument in this court that some implication had to be made into the first part of clause 13; since otherwise the defendants could not lawfully sell the unmanufactured goods in their possession, at least until they were paid for—for, as already pointed out, they were the plaintiffs' and not the defendants' goods. To hold otherwise, as I think both parties accepted, would be to stultify the whole business purpose of these transactions. What (if any) implication is to be made beyond that? The first part of clause 13 is silent not only as to the power of sale but as to the dealing with any proceeds of the goods lawfully so sold by the defendants. Is the admitted power of sale (if I may respectfully borrow Goff L.J.'s phrase during the argument) fettered or unfettered? If it is fettered, is the fetter that, so long as any indebtedness remained outstanding in any respect from the defendants to the plaintiffs, the defendants after a sub-sale remained accountable to the plaintiffs for all proceeds of sub-sales—not even, as Mr. Price pointed out in argument, being able to retain for themselves the profit upon any such sales?

Mr. Price relied much upon the 75-days' credit—though, as I have already ventured to point out, the problem is the same whatever the length of the credit. But the longer the period it can fairly be said the greater the business, if not the legal, force of this part of Mr. Price's argument. If the plaintiffs were right, Mr. Price argued, then whenever sub-purchasers paid the defendants before the 75 days' credit had expired the defendants could not use those proceeds in their business for any purposes whatever save for paying their creditors, the plaintiffs: they must always retain those proceeds specifically for the plaintiffs' account and pay them over to the plaintiffs unless and until the entirety of outstanding indebtedness was discharged. This, he said, would deprive the defendants of all day-to-day finance and, so far from according with business efficacy, would produce precisely the opposite result, for it would cause acute cash-flow problems and make conduct of the defendants' business impossible. This is a formidable argument if one looks at the matter solely from the point of view of the defendants. But this matter has to be regarded in the light of the contractual provisions agreed upon by both parties, and the question of business efficacy, in relation to which there are here obvious competing business considerations, must be answered in the light of what both parties expressly agreed upon and therefore must be taken also impliedly to have agreed upon, and not unilaterally from the point of view of one party only.

Now, the crucial facts to my mind are two: first, that the defendants were selling goods which the plaintiffs owned at all material times; and secondly, that clause 13 as a whole is obviously designed to protect the A plaintiffs, in the event of later insolvency, against the consequences of having parted with possession of, though not with legal title to, these goods before payment was received, 75 days' credit being allowed. When, therefore, one is considering what, if any, additional implication has to be made to the undoubted implied power of sale in the first part of clause 13, one must ask what, if any, additional implication is necessary to make effective the obvious purpose of giving the requisite security to B the plaintiffs? One is, I think, entitled to look at the second part of clause 13 to answer this; for it would be strange if the first part were to afford no relevant security when the second part is (as I think) elaborately drawn to give such security in relation to manufactured or mixed goods.

I see no difficulty in the contractual concept that, as between the defendants and their sub-purchasers, the defendants sold as principals, but C that, as between themselves and the plaintiffs, those goods which they were selling as principals within their implied authority from the plaintiffs were the plaintiffs' goods which they were selling as agents for the plaintiffs to whom they remained fully accountable. If an agent lawfully sells his principal's goods, he stands in a fiduciary relationship to his principal and remains accountable to his principal for those goods and their proceeds. A bailee is in like position in relation to his bailor's D goods. What, then, is there here to relieve the defendants from their obligation to account to the plaintiffs for those goods of the plaintiffs which they lawfully sell to sub-purchasers? The fact that they so sold them as principals does not, as I think, affect their relationship with the plaintiffs; nor (as at present advised) do I think—contrary to Mr. Price's argument—that the sub-purchasers could on this analysis have sued the E plaintiffs upon the sub-contracts as undisclosed principals for, say, breach of warranty of quality.

It seems to me clear (and so far from helping Mr. Price I think the second part of clause 13, properly construed, helps Mr. Lincoln) that to give effect to what I regard as the obvious purpose of clause 13 one must imply into the first part of the clause not only the power to sell F but also the obligation to account in accordance with the normal fiduciary relationship of principal and agent, bailor and bailee. Accordingly, like the judge I find no difficulty in holding that the principles in *Hallett's* case, 13 Ch.D. 696 are of immediate application, and I think that the plaintiffs are entitled to trace these proceeds of sale and to recover them, as Mocatta J. has held by his judgment.

Mr. Price relied upon the conduct of the parties after the defendants G took over from the partnership, pointing out (as was the fact) that the defendants were never required to account to the plaintiffs in the way I think, as a matter of law, the plaintiffs were entitled to require them to account. As a matter of business I would not have expected the plaintiffs so to have required the defendants to account. But, as Mr. Lincoln forcefully replied on this point, clause 13 is directed to a state of H insolvency, not to what he described as to the halcyon days of solvency; and it is only upon insolvency that the question of what the powers are under clause 13 comes into play.

On the view which I have formed of this case it is not necessary to discuss some of the other interesting points on which we had the benefit of argument from counsel on both sides, and I refrain from doing so.

A For the reasons I have given, for my part I would unhesitatingly uphold Mocatta J.'s judgment and dismiss this appeal.

GOFF L.J. I need not repeat any general statement of the facts. They have been fully set out in the judgment just delivered by Roskill L.J.

The first question which arises for determination is whether clause 13 of the general selling terms and conditions applied to the contracts
B made between the plaintiffs and the defendants or only to those made whilst the business was still being carried on by the partnership. If it did apply to the defendants, then it follows that the plaintiffs are entitled to recover the unsold stock and the appeal must fail as to that item. There is, however, then a second question whether, even so, the judgment is right in allowing the plaintiffs to recover the £35,000 odd proceeds of
C sale. I turn to the first of these questions. [His Lordship said that there was in his view no doubt at all that, the partners having accepted and signed the translation of the general terms and conditions, the whole of those terms, including clause 13, applied to the contracts made by them and he agreed with Roskill L.J. that the reasoning of Mocatta J. on that part of the case was quite unchallengeable. His Lordship
D continued:]

In my judgment the second part of the case comes down to a short question of construction. It is common ground that a power of sale during the period that any money remains owing to the plaintiffs must be implied; but the question is upon what terms.

I do not think it is necessary to go into the cases cited before Mocatta J., since it is clear to me, and was for a long time during the argument,
E that the plaintiffs must, on the principle of *In re Hallett's Estate*, 13 Ch.D. 696, be entitled to trace their aluminium into the proceeds of sale so as to enable them to take the £35,000, and to take that sum in priority to the general body of the defendants' creditors and in priority to the secured creditor Hume, unless, as the defendants contend, one ought to imply a power to sell and apply the proceeds of sale for their own purposes,
F or, as they put it, to sell for their own account. In the end this was accepted by both counsel, and nothing short of that will serve the defendants' purpose.

The plaintiffs say that the power should be qualified so as to maintain for them the security which they gave themselves by providing that property in the aluminium should not pass so long as any money remains owing to them, and accordingly it could only be exercised for their benefit
G in this sense, that the proceeds of sale must be held in trust for them until all the defendants' indebtedness to them on any contract be discharged.

In considering this problem, one may at the outset dispose of one point. The provisions in the latter part of clause 13 dealing with cases where there has been admixture cannot, in my judgment, as a matter of
H construction apply to the type of case with which we are concerned where there has been no admixture. Those provisions are, however, as Roskill L.J. has said, relevant in so far as they throw light upon what the implication in the earlier part should be; and indeed in an alternative submission, introduced by amendment, to which I must return later, the defendants submit that the power of sale to be implied is the same as that expressly provided in that latter part of clause 13.

In considering what should be implied in a contract the court has to consider what is required to give it business efficacy; but I agree with Roskill L.J. that there are two distinct and opposing approaches to "business efficacy." The one, looking at the matter from the point of view of the defendants, suggests that an unqualified power is required, because they would need to use the money in carrying on their business, and indeed, so it is suggested, anything else would largely stultify the agreement that they should have 75 days' credit. The other is, from the standpoint of the plaintiffs, that the power should not be so wide as to frustrate the whole purpose of clause 13, which it is submitted, and in my judgment rightly submitted, discloses a manifest intention to preserve the vendors from being left in the position of unsecured creditors.

In the end, in my judgment, the question is which of these ought to prevail; and I have come to a clear conclusion that the plaintiffs' contention should be preferred.

There is no doubt force in Mr. Price's argument that this as a matter of strict law destroys the benefit of the 75 days' credit. I would observe, as Roskill L.J. has pointed out, that the General Selling Terms and Conditions as originally accepted by the partners provided for 14 days' credit only, and it may well be that in considering what should be implied one should disregard the later extension of time, in which case the point would be much weakened, although not altogether destroyed. I will assume, however, that the court ought to consider the matter in the light of that extension. Even so, in my judgment this is not enough to require, or entitle, the court to imply a term plainly and utterly inconsistent with the clear intention of the clause into which it is to be implied.

The difficulty arises largely because the general conditions tie the passing of the property not to the particular contract but to all indebtedness. But for that, the qualified power would not prevent the defendants from enjoying reasonable advantages from the 75 days' credit. No doubt in practice, so long as all went well the plaintiffs would allow the defendants to use the proceeds of sale in their business, as I understand they did; but things ceased to go well, and now one has to determine the strict rights of the parties, and in my judgment the difficulty so imported is not enough to drive one to imply a term defeating the whole object of clause 13.

I turn to the alternative argument which I have already mentioned. I do not myself think it is a correct approach simply to imply in the first part of clause 13 the same power as is expressed in the latter part and which as a matter of construction does not apply to the first part and which is dealing with a different state of affairs. Even, however, if one does, it does not in my view help the defendants.

The argument is that under that clause there is no equitable assignment of the book debts until the plaintiffs require the defendants, in the words of the translation before us, to "hand over to A.I.V. the claims he has against his buyer," and, further, that as no such requirement was made before the security crystallised by the appointment of the receiver any equitable assignment resulting therefrom could only be subject to the security created by the debentures.

I accept that as far as it goes, but it still leaves the question whether one should then construe the power as entitling the defendants to sell and use the proceeds as and when received for their own benefit unless

A and until required to assign the debt, or whether on the contrary, as the plaintiffs contend, it is implicit that the proceeds of sale when received are received on their account and the right to call for an assignment is ancillary only. In my judgment that would be the right view, even if one simply implied a power in precisely the same terms as expressed concerning mixed cases.

In short, my conclusion is that the power of sale to be implied where
B none has been expressed must be so qualified as not to defeat the intention clearly shown by clause 13 as a whole, including the latter part, which only emphasises this. It follows that there was, as Roskill L.J. says, a sufficient fiduciary relationship between the parties, and this is indeed expressly contemplated in the reference to a fiduciary owner in the second part of clause 13. The implied power must, therefore, in my
C judgment be a power to sell, not for the defendants' own account, but for the account of the plaintiffs unless and until all moneys owing be paid.

For these reasons, I agree that this appeal fails as to both parts and should be dismissed.

MEGAW L.J. Ground (1) of the notice of appeal raises the question
D whether Mocatta J. was wrong in holding that the terms of clause 13 of the plaintiffs' General Selling Terms and Conditions (I quote from the notice of appeal) "applied to and were incorporated in contracts for the sale of aluminium foil made between the plaintiff and the defendant"? If the defendants were right on this issue, they would succeed on the whole appeal—each part of it. If they are wrong on this issue, they
E would fail in their appeal as regards the part of the claim by the plaintiffs which relates to the aluminium foil still in the possession of the defendants, or the receiver. They would still have their further argument that, even so, the plaintiffs are not entitled to recover the moneys held by the receiver as moneys received from customers of the defendants. [His Lordship said that in his judgment the judge was clearly right to hold as he did on that first issue, for the reasons given by him. He agreed
F with that part of Mr. Price's submission in which he had contended that more might be required to establish that a contracting party was to be treated as bound by a particular intended term, of the contents of which he was in fact unaware, when that term was an unusual one, than was required when the term was a usual one. He adhered to the view which he had expressed on that point in *Thornton* v. *Shoe Lane Parking*
G *Ltd.* [1971] 2 Q.B. 163, 172. But in the present case the defendants were not unaware of the contents of the particular term. His Lordship continued:]

As regards the other ground put forward on behalf of the defendants, relating to the moneys in the hands of the receiver deriving from material which had been delivered by the plaintiffs to the defendants, the point
H is I think indeed, as it ultimately was defined in this court, a short one, though, I would agree, by no means an easy one. It is a question of the true construction of clause 13 of the general selling terms and conditions. It is accepted by both parties that in the first part of the clause, dealing with, as it is called, "the material"—that is, aluminium foil not made up with other constituents into a "new object"—some further term must be implied. There must be implied a right on the part of the defendants to arrange sales of the material. But are those sales to be

made, as the defendants contend, on their own account; or are they to be made on account of the plaintiffs? A

For the reasons given by Roskill L.J. and Goff L.J., I agree that the submissions made in this court on behalf of the plaintiffs are correct. The power of sale to be implied in the first part of clause 13, where none has been expressed, must be such as not to defeat the intention shown by clause 13. It is not a power to sell for the defendants' own account, but it is a power to sell for the account of the plaintiffs. B

I agree that the appeal should be dismissed.

Appeal dismissed with costs.
Leave to appeal refused.

Solicitors: *Theodore Goddard & Co.; Woodham Smith, Greenwood & Holland.* C

E. M. W.

D

[QUEEN'S BENCH DIVISION]

* STOCK *v.* FRANK JONES (TIPTON) LTD.

1976 March 5 Phillips J. E

Industrial Relations—Unfair dismissal—Strike—Employees on strike as result of dismissals—Two employees returning to work—Remainder of striking employees dismissed—Whether dismissal unfair—Trade Union and Labour Relations Act 1974 (*c.* 52), *Sch.* 1, *para.* 8 (2) (*a*)

The employee worked for a curtain manufacturing company which employed over 60 employees, 53 of whom joined a union. Following a dispute over union recognition between the employers and the union two employees were dismissed as a result of which a number of others, including the employee, went on strike. Two of the strikers returned to work but the other employees did not and were dismissed. The employee's claim for compensation for unfair dismissal was refused by an industrial tribunal which held that paragraph 8 (2) (*a*) of Schedule 1 to the Trade Union and Labour Relations Act 1974[1] referred only to employees who were taking part in a strike at the date of another employee's dismissal, so that the fact that two employees who had been on strike but who had returned to work before the employee's dismissal, were not dismissed did not render the dismissal unfair. F G

On the employee's appeal:—

Held, allowing the appeal, that the tribunal had erred in departing from the ordinary and literal meaning of paragraph 8 (2) (*a*) of Schedule 1 to the Act of 1974; that the two employees who had returned to work before the employee's dismissal were employees "who also took part in" the strike within paragraph 8 and since they had not been dismissed, the employee's dismissal was unfair. H

[1] Trade Union and Labour Relations Act 1974, Sch. 1, para. 8 (2): see post, p. 696E–G.

A The following cases are referred to in the judgment:

Heath v. *J. F. Longman* (*Meat Salesmen*) *Ltd.* [1973] I.C.R. 407, N.I.R.C.

Post Office v. *Crouch* [1974] I.C.R. 378; [1974] 1 W.L.R. 89; [1974] 1 All E.R. 229, H.L.(E.).

No additional cases were cited in argument.

B APPEAL from an industrial tribunal sitting at Birmingham.

The employee, Miss C. Stock, appealed from the dismissal by the industrial tribunal of her complaint of unfair dismissal against her employers, Frank Jones (Tipton) Ltd., on the ground that the tribunal had erred in its construction of paragraph 8 (2) (*a*) of Schedule 1 to the Trade Union and Labour Relations Act 1974 and in holding that the employee
C had not been unfairly dismissed when two other employees who had taken part in the strike had not been dismissed.

The facts are stated in the judgment.

James Mitchell for the employee.
John Fletcher for the employers.

D PHILLIPS J. This is an appeal by Miss Stock, the employee, from a decision of an industrial tribunal, sitting in Birmingham on April 29 and 30, 1975, which dismissed her complaint of unfair dismissal. From that decision she now appeals and the employers, Frank Jones (Tipton) Ltd., have filed a respondents' notice supporting the decision on other grounds.

The background to the matters in contention arose out of an industrial
E dispute and, indeed, a strike. The employers carry on business as manufacturers of curtains, employing something over 60 ladies in making them. In November 1974, 53 of them joined the Transport and General Workers' Union (the union). There followed some correspondence between the employers and an official of the union. It is not necessary for the purposes of this judgment to read that correspondence, but the general effect of it was that the district officer of the union, having got 90 per cent. of the em-
F ployees as members of the union, wanted a discussion on official union recognition; and the employers, while not refusing, adopted what appear to have been delaying tactics. Two of the employees who had been very forward in this affair on behalf of the union were Mrs. Bradley and Mrs. Price, and on November 29, 1974, they were dismissed. In due course, the following year, they made a claim on the ground of unfair dismissal,
G which was not opposed by the employers. Not being opposed, we do not know precisely what was taken to be admitted or not admitted.

But, before the hearing and after the dismissal, a number of the employees went on strike, seeking the reinstatement of Mrs. Bradley and Mrs. Price. That strike took place on December 9. There followed another exchange of correspondence. The employers, on January 6, said that the factory would be open on January 13 and that, if the strikers did not
H present themselves for work at the normal starting time on that day, the employers would assume that they wished to terminate their employment. The strikers' reply was sent on January 7, prepared by the union, pointing out that this was an official trade dispute, and giving as the reason "the dismissal of two of our colleagues." It will be noticed that that does not refer to the question of union recognition. On the other hand, the "two colleagues" were Mrs. Bradley and Mrs. Price who, as I have said, were forward in the matter of union recognition. The letter goes on: "Should

this dispute be terminated satisfactorily, then I do wish to continue my A
employment with you."

The employee and the others did not turn up for work and, although it was not conceded before the tribunal, it is now conceded that, in the circumstances of this case as they are, she and they are taken to have been dismissed on January 13.

The argument about whether they had been dismissed occupied a considerable part of the hearing; and the remaining part of the decision (which B
is the only part with which I am now concerned) is fairly short. But, on that state of facts, it was agreed between the parties, and rightly agreed, that the case fell to be determined in accordance with paragraph 8 of Schedule 1 to the Trade Union and Labour Relations Act 1974—a paragraph on which there is very little authority. The cross-heading is "Dismissal in connection with a strike or other industrial action." Paragraph C
8 (1) reads:

> "The provisions of this paragraph shall have effect in relation to an employee who claims that he has been unfairly dismissed by his employer, where on the date of dismissal he was taking part in a strike or other industrial action."

It is common ground that the facts of this case fall within paragraph 8 (1). D
Paragraph 8 (2) goes on to specify the circumstances in which the dismissal shall not be regarded as unfair; they are all couched negatively. The situation, as I understand it, is that had it not been for paragraph 8 the matter would have fallen to be determined in accordance with paragraph 6 (2) and (8) of Schedule 1. But, as the case falls within paragraph 8, it appears that the provisions of that paragraph supplant the provisions of E
paragraph 6. Paragraph 8 (2) provides:

> "If the reason or principal reason for the dismissal was that the employee took part in the strike or other industrial action"—and it was, so that is satisfied—"the dismissal shall not be regarded as unfair unless it is shown"—and, assuming that it is the employee who has to show it, then what he has to show is—"(*a*) that one or more employees of the same employer . . . who also took part in that action, F
> were not dismissed for taking part in it, or (*b*) that one or more such employees, who were dismissed for taking part in it, were offered re-engagement on the termination of the industrial action and that the employee was not offered such re-engagement, and that the reason (or, if more than one, the principal reason) for which the employee was selected for dismissal or not offered re-engagement was an inadmissible G
> reason."

So the employee here had to show (because (*b*) is not appropriate) that one or more employees of the same employer who also took part in that action were not dismissed for taking part in it. In that she failed before the tribunal. And she had to establish that the reason for it, that is to say, the reason for which the employee was selected for dismissal or not offered re-engagement, was an inadmissible reason; and that is a reference to para- H
graph 6 (4) and (6). In that she succeeded, and it is that which is the subject of the respondents' notice.

The other material facts which it is necessary to state in this connection are these: there were two other ladies, Mrs. Gill and Mrs. Chung, who took part in the strike. The tribunal took a view of the evidence which satisfied them that that was the case and that the two ladies had been seen on the picket line. The tribunal continued:

> A "However, Mrs. Gill and Mrs. Chung decided to cease to participate in the strike and both of them returned to work and continued in their employment before the [employee] was dismissed"

that is, before January 13. There was a little doubt about one of them, but the tribunal was in no doubt at all that there was at least one employee who did take part in the strike and who was not dismissed.

B So, the contention on behalf of the employee was that, in terms of paragraph 8 (2) (*a*), at least one employee of the employers who took part in that action was not dismissed for taking part in it. And, on the facts and a literal reading of paragraph 8 (2) (*a*), that is made good. But the tribunal rejected that view, in deference to the argument presented to them. They accepted, as I have just said, that on a literal reading of 8 (2) (*a*) it was satisfied. They continued:

> C "However, in our unanimous view the paragraph must be construed as a whole. Neither party was able to point to any authority which might assist us in this case. However we consider that some assistance can be gained from the judgment of the National Industrial Relations Court in the case of *Heath* v. *J. F. Longman (Meat Salesmen) Ltd.* [1973] I.C.R. 407."

D They then made a comment which I need not read, and they cited the following extract from that case, from the judgment of the court delivered by Sir Hugh Griffiths, at p. 410:

> "It appears to this court that the manifest overall purpose of section 26"—that is, the predecessor of paragraph 8 (1) and (2)—"is to give a measure of protection to an employer if his business is faced with ruin
> E by a strike. It enables him in those circumstances, if he cannot carry on the business without a labour force, to dismiss the labour force on strike; to take on another labour force without the stigma of its being an unfair dismissal. That being the overall purpose, it would appear to be manifestly wrong, when an employer has been told that strike action has been called off, that he should nevertheless still be free
> F to dismiss those who took part in the strike, without any risk of a finding that he was acting unfairly."

Mr. Fletcher, for the employers, relies not only on that passage, but also on the fact that in that case the Industrial Court gave what might be considered to be a somewhat special or benevolent interpretation to the word "date" where it occurred in section 26 (1) (now paragraph 8 (1)). What
G he invites the court to do here (which he invited the tribunal to do, and they did) is to give a rather special interpretation to paragraph 8 (2) (*a*): in effect, not to read it literally. The effect of reading it in the way in which he would have it read is that it would refer, really, rather than to "who also took part in that action," to "who were also taking part in that action at the time of" a dismissal. In other words, it is clear that although Mrs. Chung, for example, was an employee of the same employer who
H did take part in that action, she was not taking part in that action, i.e. the strike, at the date that this employee was dismissed. What he says is that, unless that is done, it can be seen that paragraph 8 (2) (*a*) would apply to circumstances to which it cannot have been intended to apply; for example, it is said, suppose there was a strike of 50 employees of a firm for some trivial cause and very soon after it started, and before everybody had been dismissed, six of them returned to work feeling they had behaved rather foolishly, then it would be impossible for the employer to dismiss the ones

who remained out on strike, while retaining those who had taken the sensible A
course and returned to work, because, if that were done, those dismissed would have a claim for compensation for unfair dismissal. Reliance is placed on the words of Lord Reid in his speech in *Post Office* v. *Crouch* [1974] I.C.R. 378. Speaking of the Industrial Relations Act 1971, he said, at p. 399:

> "This, in my judgment, shows that the Act must be construed in a B
> broad and reasonable way so that legal technicalities shall not prevail against industrial realities and common sense. An unreasonable employer who tried to insist on his strict legal rights will get no comfort from the Act."

Of course, I accept that approach; but what I am not satisfied about is
that the construction sought by the employers and accepted by the tribunal, C
does produce a more workable result. For example, if adopted, it seems to me that it would result in the situation that, where a number of persons went on strike, the employers would be able safely, without fear of a claim for compensation for unfair dismissal, to dismiss some but not dismiss others, if those others had returned to work before the dismissal of the ones who had remained out. In a process where that may take place in several
instalments, it could obviously lead to considerable hardship, or, if not D
hardship, considerable feelings of resentment and victimisation. There is obviously behind paragraph 8 of Schedule 1 a question of industrial policy. There is not sufficient material in the decision of the tribunal, nor in the decided cases on this paragraph, nor available by way of judicial notice or otherwise, to form a view, it seems to me, which would justify departing
from the plain meaning of the language. The plain meaning of the language E
would result in the employee's claim succeeding, subject to the respondents' notice. That is not reading it in any very technical, restricted or tortured sense; it is just reading it in its ordinary, straightforward sense. Although a court can depart from the plain meaning of a statute where circumstances warrant it, particularly in a case of this kind, in order to enable that to be done it must be shown that, unless it is done, there is
going to be a substantial balance of inconvenience caused, in the sense F
that results are going to be achieved which could hardly be said to have been intended. But I am not at all satisfied that that is the position here. There is little or nothing in the decision of the tribunal to lead me to that conclusion. I am not satisfied that it is a conclusion that I ought to reach. Therefore I prefer to accept the language as it is, which means
that, with respect to the tribunal, I do not think they were justified in G
departing from the words of the statute, which I think they realised that they were doing.

Accordingly, subject to the point taken in the respondents' notice, this appeal succeeds.

The point taken in the respondents' notice is in these terms:

> "that the industrial tribunal ought to have held that there was no or H
> no sufficient evidence upon which it could properly conclude that the [employers'] reason or principal reason for dismissing the [employee] was an inadmissible reason."

That, as I say, relates to the concluding words of paragraph 8 (2); that is, the final matter which the employee has to show in order to establish a claim for unfair dismissal in these circumstances. The tribunal state in their reasons:

A " Let it be said that we consider that the reason for dismissal in this case was an inadmissible reason in that certainly the principal reason for it was that the [employee] was a member of an independent trade union, or had taken, or had proposed to take, part in the activities of an independent trade union."

Those, of course, are inadmissible reasons under paragraph 6 (4). Mr.
B Fletcher draws attention to the disjunctive " or " and says that it shows that the tribunal were not very firm in the view which they were reaching; that they were approaching it in a rather wishy-washy sort of way. He has referred me to the notes of evidence and says that those notes do not contain material justifying the conclusion which the tribunal reached. I am afraid I cannot agree with that. It is true that there are passages which, taken in isolation, might support that submission. The notes of the em-
C ployee's evidence record at one point:

" There was no question of union recognition then "—that is, in December—" I felt I could not continue my employment with the [employers] in the absence of union recognition. From the time of dismissal the question of union recognition was in my mind. There was no question of union recognition at the time of dismissal."

D That seems to me to be ambiguous—not necessarily meaning that she did not have it in her mind, but possibly and probably meaning that there was no question of the employers granting union recognition at the time. But she goes on:

" From January I was determined not to return because the union was not recognised. I would not have gone back even if the women
E were reinstated without union recognition. I had made this decision when I returned. . . . The strike was started for the reinstatement of Mrs. Price and Mrs. Bradley. As time went on union recognition became more important."

She said that in re-examination. But, when it is recognised that Mrs. Bradley and Mrs. Price were the leaders of the claim for recognition, and
F really it was because of that, perhaps, that they were dismissed, in my judgment it is clear that there was ample evidence here upon which the tribunal could reach the decision which they did, if that was what they thought the right decision was. I do not say they were obliged to reach it; that is not within my province. Questions of fact are for them to decide. I think there was material upon which they could decide as they did.

G Mr. Fletcher relies very much on the fact that, in evidence, evidence was given on behalf of the employers to the effect that their reasons were, they said, quite different. So be it. The tribunal does not have to accept that, nor is what one side or the other says about anything conclusive. It is for the tribunal to weigh it all up, and reach their own conclusion. That is what they did in this case, and I am satisfied that there was material on which they could have done so.

H It follows that the appeal is allowed, and the employee is declared to have been unfairly dismissed. The application will be remitted to the tribunal to assess the compensation.

Appeal allowed.

Solicitors: *Pattinson & Brewer; Allan Jay & Co.* for *William F. Hatton & Co., Dudley.*

J. W.

A

[FAMILY DIVISION]

* PRACTICE DIRECTION (MATRIMONIAL PROCEEDINGS: COSTS)

Husband and Wife—Divorce—Costs—Fixed costs—Alterations in respect of costs taxed or fixed—Matrimonial Causes (Costs) Rules 1971 (*S.I.* 1971 *No.* 987 (*L.* 22)), *rr.* 5, 7—*Matrimonial Causes* (*Costs*) (*Amendment*) *Rules* 1976 (*S.I.* 1976 *No.* 606 (*L.* 10)), *rr.* 2, 4 B

This practice note is issued by the President with the concurrence of the Lord Chancellor.

1. The Matrimonial Causes (Costs) Rules 1971 originally provided, C
inter alia, that (i) the costs of matrimonial proceedings in a county court should be taxed on a divorce scale (rule 5: the scale is contained in the appendix to the Rules); and (ii) where in an undefended cause for divorce, judicial separation or nullity of marriage the petitioner was granted a decree with costs, the costs should, if the solicitor so elected, be fixed in accordance with the provisions of the Rules in lieu of taxation (rule 7). D

2. The Matrimonial Causes (Costs) (Amendment) Rules 1976 (S.I. 1976 No. 606) make certain important alterations in respect of costs taxed or fixed on or after June 1, 1976, as follows: (i) the amounts to be allowed in respect of fixed costs have been substantially revised and increased, where appropriate, so as to bring them up to the level of the average amounts currently allowed on taxation, and some new E
allowances have been introduced; (ii) the current allowance for the filing of a reconciliation certificate has been absorbed into the increased fixed costs; (iii) there is additional provision for fixed costs in respect of certain ancillary applications; (iv) fixed costs are no longer available in respect of undefended causes for nullity of marriage; (v) the distinction between higher rate and lower rate cases is abolished; (vi) a F
new provision is made (as an amendment to rule 5) in respect of those causes in which it is now possible to elect for fixed costs (namely, a cause for divorce or judicial separation which has proceeded throughout in a divorce county court, including the Divorce Registry). On a taxation in such a cause the amount to be allowed in respect of certain items in the divorce scale is not to differ from a figure now prescribed in the scale unless the registrar or taxing officer is satisfied in the exercise G
of his discretion that the circumstances of the particular case justify the allowance of an amount different from the *average* for a cause under the same provision of the Matrimonial Causes Act 1973 i.e. based on adultery, unreasonable behaviour, desertion, etc.

3. The amended figures prescribed for fixed costs and the new average figures have been based on the average amounts currently H
allowed throughout the country in respect of causes for divorce or judicial separation which have proceeded in the divorce county court. It follows that on a taxation on or after June 1, 1976, in such a cause the registrar or taxing officer may allow more or less for the item than the average figure prescribed in the scale only where he is specifically satisfied in the particular case that a departure from the norm is justified. The occasions for such departure should be rare,

A because the average figures relate to the prosecution of an undefended cause for divorce or judicial separation and circumstances to justify a departure can only arise from, for example, the nature and complexity of the particular matter, the interest of the parties or the general conduct of the proceedings (C.C.R., Ord. 47, r. 16). The result will inevitably be that in some parts of the country the amounts currently allowed on taxation will have to be reduced, while in other parts they will be
B increased, but overall the level of remuneration should remain the same.

4. It is intended that the fixed costs figures and the average figures should be reviewed periodically at intervals of between one and two years.

5. The right to elect either for the increased fixed costs or to proceed
C to taxation remains. In exercising this right a solicitor will no doubt wish to take into account that (i) unless there are exceptional circumstances which would justify the registrar or taxing officer allowing more than the average figures prescribed in the scale, there will be very little difference between the amount to be obtained from a taxation of his costs and the figure for fixed costs, apart from the cost of the taxation
D itself; and (ii) an election to take fixed costs in such circumstances would save time and avoid the additional expense (particularly to the Legal Aid Fund in legally-aided cases) incurred by a taxation.

6. The new average figures (prescribed by new rule 5 (2)) do not apply to the costs of ancillary proceedings. These can still be taxed even though fixed costs are accepted in respect of the costs of the
E petition. It is, however, anticipated that the wider range of fixed costs for ancillary applications should reduce the need for taxation in many instances.

7. To assist practitioners who elect to take fixed costs, a standard form of election itemising those costs is being printed and, in due course, may be obtained from the Divorce Registry or the appropriate divorce county court office.

F R. L. BAYNE-POWELL
Senior Registrar.

May 18, 1976.

G [COURT OF APPEAL]

* TEMPLE *v.* TEMPLE

[1975 T. No. 3440]

1976 April 2 **Cairns and Orr L.JJ.**

H

Husband and Wife—Practice—Summary procedure under Order **14** ***—Action in Queen's Bench Division—Wife alleging breach of maintenance agreement—Application for summary judgment —Divorce proceedings pending in Family Division—Whether Queen's Bench or Family Divison appropriate forum for trial of wife's action***

[Reported by MISS HENRIETTA STEINBERG Barrister-at-Law]

A The wife issued a writ in the Queen's Bench Division and applied, under R.S.C., Ord. 14, for summary judgment in respect of arrears payable under an alleged maintenance agreement. The husband's proceedings for divorce and ancillary financial matters were then pending in the Family Division. The master ordered the wife's proceedings to be transferred to the Family Division. On the wife's appeal, the judge held that there was no equivalent procedure to Order 14 in the Family Division and, on the basis that the action was essentially in contract, ordered that it should proceed in the Queen's Bench Division. B

On the husband's appeal:—

Held, dismissing the appeal, that although there was jurisdiction for proceedings issued in the Queen's Bench Division to be transferred to the Family Division, the wife's action should continue in the Queen's Bench Division, as she ought not to be deprived of the opportunity of obtaining summary judgment (post, p. 704C–F). C

Decision of Cusack J. affirmed.

No case is referred to in the judgment.

The following case was cited in argument:

Goodinson v. *Goodinson* [1954] 2 Q.B. 118; [1954] 2 W.L.R. 1121; [1954] 2 All E.R. 255, C.A. D

APPEAL from Cusack J.

The husband, George Jack Temple, who had been living apart from his wife, Sheila Miriam Temple, since June 15, 1974, began proceedings in the Family Division on August 6, 1974, petitioning for divorce and he also sought an order under section 17 of the Married Women's Property Act 1882 in respect of a freehold property and of certain money in the wife's bank account. On October 15, 1975, the wife, issuing a writ in the Queen's Bench Division, alleged by her statement of claim that £2,725 was due to her as the arrears payable by the husband under a maintenance agreement made orally on July 9, 1974, and evidenced by or contained in a written agreement of July 15, 1974. When the wife applied for summary judgment under R.S.C., Ord. 14 on December 18, 1975, Master Elton ordered that the action be transferred to the Family Division. The wife appealed. On January 20, 1976, Cusack J. held that the Family Division had no procedure equivalent to an Order 14 summons or for enforcing a judgment for money due under a contract. He accepted that all judges of the Supreme Court had equal jurisdiction but held that, on balance, it would be inappropriate for the action, which was essentially for breach of contract, to be tried in the Family Division and, therefore, he allowed the wife's appeal. E F G

The husband appealed on the grounds that (1) the parties' financial resources had already been placed in issue in the Family Division; (2) the judge was wrong in holding that the action could properly be heard by different judges in different divisions of the High Court when the alleged agreement was one of inter-related issues already before the Family Division; (3) the judge wrongly held that the alleged maintenance agreement, if found to be valid, could not be enforced in the Family Division; (4) it would be inconvenient and expensive to try substantially the same issues H

A in separate proceedings; and that (5) the judge should have found that the only appropriate forum for the action was the Family Division.

The facts are stated in the judgment of Cairns L.J.

Margaret Puxon for the husband.

Peter Singer for the wife.

B CAIRNS L.J. This is an appeal from an order made by Cusack J. on an appeal from an order of Master Elton. The appeal to this court is brought by leave of the judge. It is an unusual point on which there appears to be no direct authority, and I am bound to say that, despite the industry of counsel, they have not been able to produce to the court even an indirect authority which is of any material assistance to us.

C The action is an action between husband and wife. The wife's claim, as appears from the statement of claim endorsed on her writ, is for a sum of £2,725, being, she says, arrears payable to her under a maintenance agreement between herself and her husband made orally on July 9, 1974, and evidenced by, or alternatively comprised in, a written agreement of July 15, 1974.

The writ having been issued, application was made on behalf of the wife D for summary judgment under R.S.C., Ord. 14. At the hearing of that application before Master Elton an application was made, or was intended to be made, on behalf of the husband for an adjournment to enable him to file an affidavit. According to the instructions of Mrs. Puxon for the husband that affidavit would have set up the defence that he never entered into the alleged maintenance agreement or alternatively, if he did so, it E was done under such pressure as invalidated the agreement. However, the point of considering that defence on the husband's part was never reached, because the master spontaneously said that he thought that this action ought to be transferred to the Family Division. The basis upon which he did so is, no doubt, that he was made aware that there were divorce proceedings on foot in the Family Division, the husband having presented a petition on August 6, 1974, for divorce on the ground of F conduct, the wife having by her answer of November 22, 1974, denied the conduct alleged against her, but not having cross-prayed. There are or will be applications for financial relief in that suit.

In addition to the divorce suit the husband had started proceedings under section 17 of the Married Women's Property Act 1882 in respect of money in the wife's bank account and in respect of a freehold property G which stands in the name of the wife, but which, according to the husband, was purchased with his money. The master must have taken the view that, having regard to those other financial disputes between the husband and wife in the Family Division, it was convenient that this further dispute as to the maintenance agreement and the alleged arrears thereunder should be tried in the Family Division.

However, on the wife's appeal to Cusack J. that decision was reversed. H The judge gave reasons for his decision, of which I am glad to say in this case a very helpful note was made by counsel or solicitors. The judge pointed out that the Family Division has no procedure equivalent to an Order 14 summons. It is agreed in this court that that is a correct statement. Cusack J. went on to say: "If the Family Division gave judgment for a money sum due under a contract, there are no facilities for enforcing that judgment." It is common ground in this court that that was a misunderstanding on the part of the judge. It is not argued that there are no such facilities and it is accepted that by means of fieri facias or otherwise A the Family Division could enforce an order for payment of a money sum. The judge went on to accept that all judges of the Supreme Court have equal powers, and he said that if these different matters had to be considered in the Family Division they would have to be taken in order, not all at one time. He accepted that, if judgment were given in the Queen's Bench Division action, it might be considered appropriate that there should be a stay pending a decision in the Family Division on other aspects of the B final relationship of the parties. But he considered that it would be inappropriate that this action, which is essentially in the nature of an ordinary Queen's Bench Division action in a matter of contract, should be transferred to the Family Division.

Unless one can say that the decision of the judge is dependent upon some error of law or wrong approach to the matter, this court ought not C to interfere with the exercise of his discretion. I have indicated that I think that there was one error in the judge's approach in taking the view that there were no facilities in the Family Division for enforcing the judgment. But I do not think that that is really fundamental to his decision and I have reached the conclusion after a great deal of doubt, that on balance and as a matter of convenience, it is right that the Queen's Bench Division action should continue in the Queen's Bench Division and not be transferred to D the Family Division.

I take that view for these reasons. It is accepted that proceedings for summary judgment would not be appropriate to the Family Division. I think that the wife ought not to be deprived of the opportunity of obtaining summary judgment. I do not regard this issue as to the validity of the maintenance agreement as being one which is so intermingled with other E issues which will arise on financial matters that they ought all to be tried together. If, indeed, the wife gets judgment summarily, then that part of the dispute between the parties will have been dealt with and the other financial matters can be considered in the light of it, including among other things the question of whether at this stage, if that maintenance agreement has been held to be a valid agreement, it should be varied. It is quite a separate issue from the question of enforcement of arrears under it. F

It is said by Mrs. Puxon on behalf of the husband that it would be liable to be an embarrassment to a judge of the Family Division hearing the other financial issues if the issue as to the validity of this agreement was already res judicata. I see no reason for that being an embarrassment to him: it would save him part of the work which he would otherwise have to do. Really this part of Mrs. Puxon's case depends on the underlying assumption G that the wife's credit might be destroyed by questions about other matters that would be relevant in the Family Division, but not in the Queen's Bench Division action, which might lead to a different conclusion as to the validity of the agreement. But, of course, it is not an uncommon experience for there to be two actions or two sets of proceedings between particular parties which are quite separate. Sometimes it is convenient to have them tried together; sometimes it is convenient to have them tried separately. But I H do not think that it is ever right to say that they ought to be tried together in order to enable matters to be used by way of testing the credit of a party. Anything which can properly be brought up by way of testing credit can be used when the wife is in the witness-box (if she gets there) in the Queen's Bench Division action.

As I have said, it is a question on which there is no direct authority: and authority is not really likely to be very helpful because it is ultimately

A a question of discretion. I am quite satisfied that there would be jurisdiction for the Queen's Bench Division action to be transferred to the Family Division and that a judge of that division would have jurisdiction to hear it, either separately or along with the other proceedings. But, for the reasons which I have given, I think as a matter of convenience the judge did come to the right conclusion. I would dismiss the appeal.

B ORR L.J. I agree.

Appeal dismissed with costs.

Solicitors: *Israel, Joslin & Co.; Philip Kossoff & Co.*

C

[QUEEN'S BENCH DIVISION]

* GARTHWAITE AND ANOTHER *v.* SHERWOOD

[1970 G. No. 1329]

D

1976 Feb. 25 — Kerr J. sitting with assessors

Legal Aid—Costs—Taxation—Solicitor's decision not to instruct London agents for hearing of appeal — Solicitor's travelling expenses to attend hearing—Whether "proper" costs to allow on taxation—R.S.C., Ord. 62, *r.* 28 (2) (4)

E The plaintiff, who had been granted legal aid, was awarded £32,500 general damages for pain and suffering in her action against the defendant for injuries received in a motor accident. The defendant appealed against the amount of damages awarded, which at that time was a record sum for the type of injury suffered by the plaintiff. The plaintiff's solicitor, who practiced in Bournemouth, decided that he should attend the hearing of the appeal in London rather than instruct F London agents because, as he had had the conduct of the case over the past five years and knew all the circumstances, he might be needed if there was a last-minute offer to settle the matter. He also took into account the fact that the plaintiff would not be attending the hearing of the appeal but was arranging to be easily contacted by telephone and that she relied heavily on his personal advice and moral support. In attending the court, the solicitor incurred £28 travelling G expenses. The taxing master decided that there were no circumstances which made it either necessary, reasonable or desirable for the solicitor to attend personally and, therefore, in the exercise of his discretion under R.S.C., Ord. 62, r. 28,[1] he disallowed the travelling expenses.

On appeal from the taxation of costs:—

Held, allowing the appeal, that, under R.S.C., Ord. 62, r. 28 (2) and (4), the travelling expenses of a solicitor himself H attending court instead of employing an agent were to be allowed on a legal aid taxation if it was "necessary or proper" for him personally to attend the hearing; that it was a wrong exercise of the discretion in deciding whether to allow such costs to place emphasis on whether it was "necessary"

[Reported by RACHEL DAVIES, Barrister-at-Law]

[1] R.S.C., Ord. 62, r. 28 (2): see post, p. 707B–C.

for equal emphasis was to be placed on both "necessary" and "proper" and, therefore, since it was proper for the solicitor to attend the hearing of the appeal personally, the travelling costs would be allowed. A

In re Foster (1878) 8 Ch.D. 598 applied.

Per curiam. There should be no rule of practice that such expenses are only to be allowed in exceptional cases. The correct practice should be for the taxing master to ask himself in each case, what was or would have been the proper course for the solicitor to adopt in the particular circumstances (post, p. 708E). B

The following cases are referred to in the judgment:

Foster, In re (1878) 8 Ch.D. 598.

Francis v. *Francis and Dickerson* [1956] P. 87; [1955] 3 W.L.R. 973; [1955] 3 All E.R. 836. C

Perry & Co. Ltd. v. *Hessin & Co.* (1913) 30 R.P.C. 193.

The following additional cases were cited in argument:

Bradshaw v. *Bradshaw* (*Note*) [1956] P. 274; [1955] 3 W.L.R. 965, D.C.

Marshall (*W. F.*) *Ltd.* v. *Barnes & Fitzpatrick* [1953] 1 W.L.R. 639; [1953] 1 All E.R. 970.

Raybould v. *Raybould* [1968] 1 W.L.R. 366; [1968] 1 All E.R. 608. D

Theocharides v. *Joannu* [1955] 1 W.L.R. 296; [1955] 1 All E.R. 615.

Warman v. *Barclays Bank Ltd.* [1954] 1 W.L.R. 191; [1953] 2 All E.R. 1575.

APPEAL from Master Horne.

On March 17, 1969, the second plaintiff (referred to as "the plaintiff"), Mary Elizabeth Garthwaite, was involved in a motor accident in which E she suffered grave injuries. She obtained legal aid and brought an action against the defendant, John Joseph Sherwood. The action, in which liability was admitted, was heard at Winchester and on December 11, 1973, Rees J. awarded the plaintiff £32,500 general damages. The defendant's appeal against the amount of the award came before the Court of Appeal on July 22, 1974. The plaintiff's solicitor, who practised in Bournemouth F and had had continuous charge of the case for over five years, did not instruct London agents for the purpose of the appeal, but attended the Court of Appeal personally. His travelling expenses were £28. The court dismissed the appeal and ordered the defendant to pay the plaintiff's costs of the appeal to be taxed in accordance with the provisions of Schedule 2 to the Legal Aid Act 1974. The plaintiff's bill of costs was taxed on December 4, 1974, and the solicitor's expenses of £28 were not allowed. G The plaintiff lodged objections and, on February 19, 1975, Master Horne heard and disallowed the objections.

The plaintiff appealed.

The facts are stated in the judgment.

N. H. Lowe, solicitor for the plaintiffs. H

Dennis Mellor, solicitor for the defendant.

KERR J. This is an appeal from a taxation of the costs in a personal injury action. I am giving judgment in open court, because I recognise, as do the assessors sitting with me, that it raises a point of some general importance. The question is: what should nowadays be the general practice in allowing or disallowing the costs of a country solicitor coming

A to London for a trial or, as in the present case, for the purpose of an appeal to the Court of Appeal, in an action in which he is professionally engaged? The same question arises if a London solicitor is engaged in a case tried outside London.

The taxing master has disallowed these costs, and overruled the objections to their disallowance, both in the legal aid taxation, where the common fund basis of taxation applies under Ord. 62, r. 28 (4), as well
B as in the party and party taxation under r. 28 (2). I must set out the material parts of these provisions:

> "(2) Subject to the following provisions of this rule, costs to which this rule applies shall be taxed on the party and party basis, and on a taxation on that basis there shall be allowed all such costs as were necessary or proper for the attainment of justice or for enforcing or
> C defending the rights of the party whose costs are being taxed. . . . (4) On a taxation on the common fund basis, being a more generous basis than that provided for by paragraph (2), there shall be allowed a reasonable amount in respect of all costs reasonably incurred, and paragraph (2) shall not apply; . . ."

The effect of the taxing master's decision was therefore that on both bases
D of taxation the only necessary, proper or reasonable course, to use the operative words of the rule, was for the solicitor to employ London agents.

In his answers to the solicitor's objections the master referred to a number of authorities which are collected in *The Supreme Court Practice* (1976), vol. 1, p. 976, note 62/28/10 under the heading: "Attendance of country solicitor." He did not, however, refer to the first of the authorities
E there mentioned, perhaps because the reference is wrongly stated. That case, *In re Foster* (1878) 8 Ch.D. 598, is summarised in the note as follows:

> "A country solicitor personally attending an appeal instead of employing his London agent may in a proper case on taxation as between party and party be allowed the additional charges and expenses thereby occasioned."

F

I do not propose to go through the authorities which are cited in that lengthy note. Having however looked at them, it seems to me that they show two things in connection with taxations on a party and party basis. The first is that of the words, "all such costs as were necessary or proper for the attainment of justice," which are now to be found in paragraph
G (2), the word "necessary" has on the whole been given much greater emphasis than the word "proper." Secondly, and perhaps because of this, it was stated in a number of cases that the expense of a country solicitor attending a court in London should only be allowed in exceptional cases, or, indeed, as the note says in reference to one case in 1913, "in very exceptional cases": see *Perry & Co. Ltd.* v. *Hessin & Co.* (1913) 30 R.P.C. 193. However, after referring to these cases, the note ends as
H follows:

> "The charges and expenses of a country solicitor attending a hearing in London, or vice versa are in practice disallowed less frequently than hitherto."

I think that this sentence may reflect what is well known to solicitors, and of course also to the taxing masters, that conditions concerning the employment of London or local agents have changed in recent times.

Many firms which used to be willing to act as agents are nowadays unwilling or reluctant to do so, because this work is regarded as uneconomic. A
It follows that there may now be many more cases than in the past in which it would at least be "proper" for a country solicitor to attend in London or for a London solicitor to attend for a hearing in the provinces than to employ local agents.

Notwithstanding the dicta to be found in some of the cases, it is clear that the only words which govern the correct exercise of a taxing master's B
discretion are the words in paragraph (2) or (4), as the case may be, which I have read. Dealing with party and party costs for the moment, it therefore follows that the only consideration should be whether or not the personal attendance of the solicitor in question was proper, or perhaps even necessary, in all the circumstances of the particular case.

In this connection it is helpful to remind oneself of what was said by C
Sachs J. in *Francis* v. *Francis and Dickerson* [1956] P. 87, 95. The passage in question is conveniently cited in *Cordery on Solicitors*, 6th ed. (1968), p. 311 which says: "'Proper' includes costs not strictly necessary but reasonably incurred for the purpose of the proceedings . . ." It then quotes the following passage from this judgment:

> "When considering whether or not an item in a bill of costs is D
> 'proper' the correct viewpoint to be adopted by a taxing officer is that of a sensible solicitor sitting in his chair and considering what in the light of his then knowledge is reasonable in the interests of his lay client . . . [He] should be deemed a man of means adequate to bear the expense of the litigation out of his own pocket—and by 'adequate' I mean neither 'barely adequate' nor 'super-abundant.'"

E

In my judgment there should accordingly be no rule of practice that such expenses are only to be allowed in exceptional cases. The correct practice should be for the taxing master to ask himself in each case, on the basis of the passages which I have read, what was or would have been the proper course for the solicitor to adopt in the particular circumstances. Furthermore, although *In re Foster*, 8 Ch.D. 598 was F
concerned with the hearing of an appeal, as is this case, the principle should be precisely the same whether the solicitor is attending for the purposes of a trial or for the purposes of an appeal. The question is always: was the expense of the solicitor's personal attendance, instead of appointing local agents, necessary or proper in the circumstances?

I now turn to the facts of the present case against this background. The second plaintiff (to whom I refer as the plaintiff for present purposes) G
suffered very grave injuries in a motor accident on March 17, 1969. She obtained legal aid and brought an action against the person responsible for the accident. The case came on for trial at Winchester on December 11, 1973, the only issue being as to quantum. She was awarded £32,500 for general damages for pain and suffering. I have been told by her solicitor, who appeared on the present appeal, that this was at that time H
a record sum for damages of this nature. Prior to the trial the defendant had made a payment into court of £20,000.

The plaintiff's solicitor carries on his practice in Bournemouth. He has been personally concerned with this case for a period of over five years, between March 1969, when the accident occurred, and July 1974 when the case came before the Court of Appeal to which I will turn in a moment, and he attended the trial at Winchester. He has explained,

A and I accept, that during this time the plaintiff relied heavily on his
personal advice and moral support and that he was very considerably
involved in the case.

Before the trial leading and junior counsel instructed on behalf of
the plaintiff had expressed the view that the general damages likely to
be awarded would be of the order of £27,000, that is to say some £5,000
less than the sum which was ultimately recovered. However, their
B expectation was also that the damages would substantially exceed the
sum of £20,000 in court, and this is why the trial proceeded. The sum
awarded to the plaintiff was of vital importance to her, because her
injuries were such that she has been unable to resume any employment
since the accident.

After this heavy award of damages the defendant, i.e. his insurers,
C gave notice of appeal. Not surprisingly, the insurance company treated
the case as a very serious one, and I have been told that at the hearing
before the Court of Appeal the senior partner of the firm of solicitors
instructed on behalf of the defendant was present at the request of the
insurers.

Junior counsel for the plaintiff advised that it was unnecessary for
D the plaintiff or her husband (who had also been involved in the accident
and was deeply involved in its consequences to his wife) to be present on
the hearing of the appeal. However, the plaintiff's father was present,
and junior counsel had also advised that the plaintiff and her husband
should be available on the telephone in case there were any last-minute
developments.

It had occurred to the plaintiff's solicitor that there was at any rate
E some possibility of a last-minute offer, before the hearing of the appeal,
somewhere between the sum of £20,000, which had been paid into court,
and the sum of £32,500 which had been awarded. If such an offer had
been made, this would have required a speedy and by no means easy
decision. There was nothing to indicate that such an offer was going to
be made; in fact it was not made; but it might have been made. This
F was the position when the matter came up before the Court of Appeal,
and although the appeal only took some 2½ hours, it was obviously a
crucial day of decision in the plaintiff's life. In the event the appeal was
unsuccessful.

Now, in all these circumstances, what should the plaintiff's solicitor
have done? Was he to instruct London agents for the purpose of the
appeal, who would know nothing about the case and would have some
G difficulty in familiarising themselves with it, and who would naturally
have charged an appropriate fee which would have been considerably
higher than the cost of the solicitor's travel and attendance? Or should
he in these circumstances himself travel up from Bournemouth for the
hearing of the appeal? He decided on the latter course and in doing
so incurred expenses totalling some £28 on account of fares and other
H disbursements. The taxing master allowed £15 on a party and party
basis for attending court, but he disallowed the £28 entirely, both on a
party and party basis in the inter-party taxation and on the common
fund basis in the legal aid taxation.

I have no doubt (and this view is shared by the Chief Taxing Master
and an experienced solicitor sitting with me as assessors) that in all these
circumstances it was entirely "proper" for the plaintiff's solicitor to
attend himself. He was the person who had had the continuous charge

of this case over a period of many years. He could be of far greater assistance to the plaintiff and to the Court of Appeal than any representative of a firm of London agents. In saying this I am virtually repeating word for word what Bacon C.J. said in similar circumstances in *In re Foster* in 1878. Moreover, by attending himself the total costs were substantially lower than if he had appointed London agents. A

In my view, these expenses should have been allowed on a party and party basis under Ord. 62, r. 28 (2) as having been properly incurred. A fortiori they should have been allowed in the legal aid taxation on the common fund basis under Ord. 62, r. 28 (4). B

In the last paragraph of his answers to the plaintiff's objection the master said:

> "I can find no fact or circumstance in relation to the appeal to show that it was either necessary, reasonable or desirable for the country solicitor to attend the hearing in London. Accordingly, there is no basis on which I can exercise my discretion to avoid the general rule either on a party and party or a legal aid basis of taxation." C

I am bound to say that this court takes precisely the opposite view, at any rate so far as the word "proper" is concerned, but it is clear from other passages in his answers that the master was strongly influenced by the references to "exceptional circumstances" and similar phrases in some of the cases. This is why he referred to "the general rule." I have already dealt with this point, and in the result the appeal succeeds and the solicitor's taxed-off expenses are allowed. D

Appeal allowed with costs. E

Solicitors: *Mooring, Aldridge & Haydon, Bournemouth; Stevensons.*

F

[COURT OF APPEAL]

* ATTORNEY-GENERAL'S REFERENCE (No. 2 of 1975)

1976 March 3; 11 — James and Geoffrey Lane L.JJ. and Cobb J.

G

Crime—Obscene libel—Publication—Cinematograph film—Hire for gain of film for purpose of cinematograph exhibition—Whether "publication" of obscene article—Whether offence—Obscene Publications Act 1959 (7 & 8 *Eliz.* 2, *c.* 66), *ss.* 1 (1) (3) (*b*), 2 (1) (6)—*Obscene Publications Act* 1964 (*c.* 74), *s.* 1 (3) (*b*)

Section 1 of the Obscene Publications Act 1959 provides: "(1) For the purposes of this Act an article shall be deemed to be obscene if its effect . . . is, if taken as a whole, such as to tend to deprave and corrupt persons who are likely, having regard to all relevant circumstances, to read, see or hear the matter contained or embodied in it. . . . (3) For the purposes of this Act a person publishes H

[Reported by R. C. Habesch, Esq., Barrister-at-Law]

> A an article who—(*a*) distributes, circulates, sells, lets on hire, gives or lends it, . . . or (*b*) in the case of an article containing or embodying matter to be looked at or a record, shows, plays or projects it: Provided that paragraph (*b*) of this subsection shall not apply to anything done in the course of a cinematograph exhibition (within the meaning of the Cinematograph Act 1952) . . ."

A company for gain hired to a licensee of a cinema a film,
B which was alleged to be obscene within the meaning of section 1 of the Obscene Publications Act 1959. The company contemplated that the licensee, who was not a person whom the matter would tend to deprave or corrupt within the meaning of the Obscene Publications Acts 1959 and 1964, would show the film, as he did, to audiences at the cinema. The showing of the film at the cinema was a cinematograph exhibition within the meaning of the Cinematograph Act 1952.
C The company was charged by count 1 of an indictment with having an obscene article for publication for gain, contrary to section 2 (1) of the Act of 1959 [1] as amended by section 1 of the Act of 1964 [2]; and by count 2 of publishing an obscene article contrary to section 2 (1) of the Act of 1959. The judge ruled that the question whether an article was obscene for the purposes of the Acts was dependent on whether there had been a publication within the meaning of section 1 (3) of
D the Act of 1959 to persons likely to read, see or hear the matter contained in the article and, since cinema audiences were not persons to whom the film was published, there was insufficient evidence to found a conviction on either count.

On a reference by the Attorney-General for the court's opinion on the true construction of the Act:—

Held, that the Act of 1959 was concerned only with obscene articles that were published or intended or kept for publication;
E that whether an obscene article within the meaning of section 1 (1) of the Act had been published contrary to section 2 (1) of the Act was to be determined not by applying the abstract test of whether the article was obscene but by whether the article was obscene by reference to its publication and by reference only to a publication within the meaning of section 1 (3); that, therefore, since the relationship between the subsections dealing with indirect publication, namely,
F section 2 (6) of the Act of 1959 and section 1 (3) (*b*) of the Act of 1964, and section 1 (1) and (3) of the Act of 1959 was that the subsections had to be read together, it followed that the persons likely to "read, see or hear," referred to in section 1 (1), were persons who read, saw or heard as a result of a direct or indirect publication as defined by the Acts (post, pp. 717H—718D, E–F, H—719C).

Per curiam. The proviso to section 1 (3) of the Act
G of 1959 applies only to a publication within paragraph (*b*) and not to paragraph (*a*) (post, p. 718G–H).

No cases are referred to in the opinion of the court.

The following cases were cited in argument:

H *Attorney-General's Reference* (*No.* 1 *of* 1975) [1975] Q.B. 773; [1975] 3 W.L.R. 11; [1975] 2 All E.R. 684, C.A.

Morgan v. *Bowker* [1964] 1 Q.B. 507; [1963] 2 W.L.R. 860; [1963] 1 All E.R. 691, D.C.

Reg. v. *Barker* [1962] 1 W.L.R. 349; [1962] 1 All E.R. 748, C.C.A.

Reg. v. *Clayton and Halsey* [1963] 1 Q.B. 163; [1962] 3 W.L.R. 815; [1962] 3 All E.R. 500, C.C.A.

[1] Obscene Publications Act 1959, s. 2 (1) (6): see post, p. 715E–F.
[2] Obscene Publications Act 1964, s. 1 (3) (*b*): see post, p. 715G–H.

REFERENCE by the Attorney-General.

The Attorney-General referred, under section 36 of the Criminal Justice Act 1972, the following point of law for the opinion of the Court of Appeal: whether, for the purposes of section 2 (1) of the Obscene Publications Act 1959, as amended by section 1 (1) of the Obscene Publications Act 1964, in relation to offences of having an obscene article for publication for gain and publishing an obscene article, the "persons who are likely, having regard to all the relevant circumstances, to read, see or hear the matter contained or embodied in" (section 1 (1) of the Obscene Publications Act 1959) an article alleged to be obscene were to be or could be defined by reference to their opportunity to read, see or hear the matter contained or embodied in the article otherwise than as a result of a publication of the article within the terms of section 1 (3) of the Obscene Publications Act 1959; and whether and if so, to what extent section 2 (6) of that Act and section 1 (3) (*b*) of the Obscene Publications Act 1964 affected either the definition of the potential audience of the allegedly obscene article, within section 1 (1) or the publication of the article within section 1 (3) of the Act of 1959.

The relevant facts of the case were that (a) on days prior to and on March 5, 1973, the defendant company had copies of a sound film for publication for gain; (b) on a date before March 3, 1973, the company agreed to let a copy of the film on hire to the licensee of a cinema; (c) on March 5, 1973, the copy was delivered to the licensee in a sealed container by an employee of the company; (d) the licensee was not a person whom the matter contained or embodied in the film would tend to deprave and corrupt; (e) the company contemplated and could have expected reasonably that the licensee would show, play or project the film only to audiences attending the cinema in circumstances such that the showing, playing or projecting would amount to a cinematograph exhibition within the meaning of the Cinematograph Act 1952, not being an exhibition in a private house to which the public would not be admitted; (f) on March 5, 1973, and subsequently, the licensee did so show, play or project the film to such audiences.

The facts are stated in the opinion of the court.

Sir Thomas Williams Q.C. and *Michael Hill* for the Attorney-General.

Jeremy Hutchinson Q.C., *Richard du Cann Q.C.* and *David Whitehouse* for the company.

Robert Harman Q.C., *Nigel Mylne* and *P. Cooper* as amici curiae.

Cur. adv. vult.

March 11. JAMES L.J. read the following opinion of the court. This opinion of the court is given upon a reference by the Attorney-General under section 36 of the Criminal Justice Act 1972. The respondent to the reference is United Artists Corporation Ltd., which company has consented to the disclosure of its name. The point of law arose in proceedings against the company for offences under the Obscene Publications Acts 1959 and 1964. The reference had the unusual feature that, on behalf of the Attorney-General, it was not sought to question the ruling of the trial judge on which he directed the acquittal of the respondent company. On the contrary, Sir Thomas Williams, appearing on behalf of the Attorney-General, unreservedly supported the decision of the trial judge, Kenneth Jones J. The only reason why in these circumstances the

A reference was made is to be found in the history of the proceedings. It is necessary to give a brief account of that history.

In late 1973, a Mr. Shackleton commenced a private prosecution of United Artists Corporation Ltd. The offence charged was publishing an obscene article, namely, a copy of the film "Last Tango in Paris," by letting it on hire contrary to section 2 (1) of the Obscene Publications Act 1959. The company elected to be tried upon indictment. The
B magistrate, Mr. John Phipps, rejected a submission by counsel on behalf of the company that in the state of the evidence there should be no committal for trial because no offence was disclosed in law. Apparently he took the view that, on the basis that the submission accurately stated the law, there was still an issue of fact which should be left to a jury to decide. He committed the respondent company for trial.

C On May 21, 1974, the case was listed at the Central Criminal Court before Lord Widgery C.J. The indictment contained four counts. Count 1 charged the offence of having an obscene article for publication for gain contrary to section 2 (1) of the Act of 1959, as amended by section 1 of the Act of 1964. Count 2 charged the offence of publishing an obscene article contrary to section 2 (1) of the Act of 1959. The remaining counts
D are not relevant for present purposes. Suffice it to say that the respondent company were acquitted on those counts upon a different point in the course of the trial.

Mr. Hutchinson, on behalf of the respondent company, moved to quash the indictment. The argument was directed to the alleged failure of the magistrate to have regard to all the evidence and the fact that the evidence was not in dispute. It was submitted that had the magistrate
E paid proper regard to the undisputed character of the evidence he would not, upon his view of the law, have committed the respondent company for trial. The motion was refused. Lord Widgery C.J. ruled that upon a proper construction of the Act of 1959 the magistrate was bound to have committed upon the material before him. The ruling inevitably involved the expression of a view as to the construction of the provisions of section 1 (1) and (3) of the Act of 1959. At the conclusion of the
F ruling Lord Widgery C.J. said that he hoped that the trial judge would not feel bound to apply the same construction if he took a different view. In the event, Kenneth Jones J., having heard argument directed specifically to the point of construction and in greater detail than that put before Lord Widgery C.J., did take a different view. It was the expression of two different views on the construction of the statutory provisions which
G led Mr. Shackleton to urge the Attorney-General to exercise his power under section 36 to refer the point for the opinion of the court.

So it has come about that the reference has been made although the Attorney-General and the respondent company are at one in support of the ruling of the judge. In these circumstances the court invited the assistance of counsel as amicus to present the argument in favour of a contrary construction. The point of law was referred to us in these
H terms:

> "Whether for the purposes of section 2 (1) of the Obscene Publications Act 1959, as amended by section 1 (1) of the Obscene Publications Act 1964, in relation to offences of having an obscene article for publication for gain and publishing an obscene article, the 'persons who are likely, having regard to all the relevant circumstances, to read, see or hear the matter contained or embodied in' (sec-

tion 1 (1) of the Obscene Publications Act 1959) an article alleged A
to be obscene, are to be or can be defined by reference to their opportunity to read, see or hear the matter contained or embodied in the article otherwise than as a result of a publication of the article within the terms of section 1 (3) of the Obscene Publications Act 1959, and whether and if so, to what extent section 2 (6) of that Act and section 1 (3) (*b*) of the Obscene Publications Act
1964 affect either the definition of the potential audience of the B
allegedly obscene article, within section 1 (1) or the publication of the article within section 1 (3) of the Act of 1959."

It is the same point which is raised, although the relevant statutory provisions are not in precisely the same terms, in relation to the charge of having an obscene article for publication for gain and the charge of
publishing an obscene article. Kenneth Jones J. described the point as C
the core of Mr. Hutchinson's submissions and expressed the question to be decided in these words:

"Are these words ('persons who are likely, having regard to all the relevant circumstances, to read see or hear the matter') to be given their ordinary meaning or are they to be construed by the court as
meaning persons who are likely, having regard to all the relevant D
circumstances, to have the matter contained or embodied in the film published to them? Are they to be construed as meaning persons who are likely to see the matter contained in the film as a result of a publication to them?"

A reference of a point of law under section 36 of the Act of 1972
is not a reference in the abstract but is in relation to the case in which E
the point has arisen. The relevant facts of the case in which this point arose are these. At the relevant time United Artists Corporation Ltd. had copies of "Last Tango in Paris" for publication for gain to licensees of cinemas for use in "cinematograph exhibitions" within the meaning of the Cinematograph Act 1952, and agreed to let a copy on hire to the
licensee of a cinema. On March 5, 1973, the copy film was delivered in a F
sealed container by a servant of the company to the licensee who was not a person whom the matter would tend to deprave and corrupt. The company contemplated and could reasonably have expected that the licensee would show the film only to audiences attending the cinema in circumstances in which the showing of the film would amount to a cinematograph exhibition within the Cinematograph Act 1952, not being
an exhibition in a private house to which the public would not be G
admitted. The licensee did show the film to such audiences.

Kenneth Jones J. held that the question whether an article is obscene for the purposes of the Acts of 1959 and 1964 is dependent upon publication to persons who are likely, having regard to all the relevant circumstances, to read, see or hear the matter contained or embodied in it,
and that the only relevant publication for this purpose is publication as H
defined by section 1 (3) of the Act of 1959. He held, upon the facts of the case, that although the cinema audience was composed of persons who were intended to and did see the film shown to them in the ordinary meaning of "see" and "shown," they were not persons to whom the film was published within the provision of section 1 (3). There being no evidence of publication or intended publication to any other person whom the matter would tend to deprave and corrupt, he held that the evidence

was insufficient to found a conviction upon count 1 or count 2 of the indictment.

Section 1 of the Obscene Publications Act 1959 reads:

> "(1) For the purposes of this Act an article shall be deemed to be obscene if its effect or (where the article comprises two or more distinct items) the effect of any one of its items is, if taken as a whole, such as to tend to deprave and corrupt persons who are likely, having regard to all relevant circumstances, to read, see or hear the matter contained or embodied in it."

Subsection (2) need not be read: a film is an "article."

> "(3) For the purposes of this Act a person publishes an article who—(*a*) distributes, circulates, sells, lets on hire, gives, or lends it, or who offers it for sale or for letting on hire; or (*b*) in the case of an article containing or embodying matter to be looked at or a record, shows, plays or projects it: Provided that paragraph (*b*) of this subsection shall not apply to anything done in the course of a cinematograph exhibition (within the meaning of the Cinematograph Act 1952), other than one excluded from the Cinematograph Act 1909 by section 7 (4) of that Act (which relates to exhibitions in private houses to which the public are not admitted), or to anything done in the course of television or sound broadcasting."

Mr. Hutchinson made the point that the inclusion of television and sound broadcasting resulted in the point of law under consideration being of importance beyond the film industry. Section 2 of the Act of 1959 reads: "(1) Subject as hereinafter provided, any person who, whether for gain or not, publishes an obscene article shall be liable . . ." then the maximum penalty on summary conviction and conviction on indictment are set out. Section 2 (6) is applicable in relation to the offence of publishing for gain under section 2 (1). It reads:

> "In any proceedings against a person under this section the question whether an article is obscene shall be determined without regard to any publication by another person unless it could reasonably have been expected that the publication by the other person would follow from publication by the person charged."

By section 1 (1) of the Obscene Publications Act 1964, the words "or who has an obscene article for publication for gain (whether gain to himself or to another)" were added to section 2 (1) of the Act of 1959. Section 1 (3) of the Act of 1964 provided that in proceedings brought against a person for that offence the following provisions should apply in place of section 2 (6) of the Act of 1959. Section 1 (3) (*b*) of the Act of 1964 reads:

> "the question whether the article is obscene shall be determined by reference to such publication for gain of the article as in the circumstances it may reasonably be inferred he had in contemplation and to any further publication that could reasonably be expected to follow from it, but not to any other publication."

It is convenient at this point to refer to other provisions of the Act of 1959 relied upon by Mr. Hutchinson in the course of the argument. Under section 3 provision is made for search and seizure in relation to obscene articles "kept for publication for gain." Section 3 (7) provides:

"For the purposes of this section the question whether an article is obscene shall be determined on the assumption that copies of it would be published in any manner likely having regard to the circumstances in which it was found, but in no other manner."

By section 4 a defence to charges of offences against section 2 of the Act is made available if it is proved that "publication . . . is justified as being for the public good."

Mr. Harman, who conducted the prosecution of the respondent company, advanced as amicus in this court the same arguments as he advanced at the trial. The arguments can be summarised in this way. First the words of section 1 (1) of the Act of 1959 should be construed as bearing their ordinary meaning unless, which he submitted was not the case, the result would be a plain absurdity. Secondly, that there is no necessity to look at section 1 (3) in order to ascertain the meaning of the words in subsection (1), and it is wrong to construe the words "read, see or hear" in subsection (1) as limited, by reason of subsection (3), to what is likely to be read, seen or heard as the result of publication. Thirdly, the words "having regard to all the relevant circumstances" in subsection (1) make it clear that the Act is not concerned with the means whereby persons are likely to read, see or hear. Therefore an article may be deemed to be obscene under the terms of subsection (1) although there is no evidence that the person charged with an offence under section 2 (1) had published or had the article for publication within the meaning of section 1 (3). Fourthly, the judge was right in his ruling that the exception contained in the proviso in section 1 (3) extended only to those publications referred to at (*b*) of that subsection, namely the showing, playing or projection of an article containing or embodying matter to be looked at or a record. Therefore, in respect of a film shown or intended to be shown only in the course of a cinematograph exhibition within the meaning of the Cinematograph Act 1952, there would be no "publication" to the cinema audience, but the distribution, letting or hire and other activities particularised in section 1 (3) (*a*) would be publications of the film. Fifthly, that the absurd consequences which were said by Mr. Hutchinson to flow from the construction of "read, see or hear" otherwise than limited to read, see or hear as a result of publication within the meaning of section 1 (3), were not true absurdities and were not consequences which justified departure from the principle that the words should be given their plain, ordinary meaning. Sixthly, the purpose of section 2 (6) of the Act of 1959 and section 1 (3) (*b*) of the Act of 1964 was not to define obscenity by reference to publication, but was to provide limits to criminal responsibility in relation to offences contrary to section 2 (1).

Finally, Mr. Harman argued that the Cinematograph Acts 1909 and 1952 vested in local authorities only limited powers of control over the showing of films, that the imposition of conditions upon the grant of a licence is discretionary, not obligatory, and that it is through the Obscene Publications Acts that the safeguard of public morals is provided. Mr. Harman said that the effect of the judgment is to exempt the distributors and those who conduct the business activities which precede the showing of a film from the consequences, either at common law or pursuant to statute, of the matter contained in the film tending to deprave and corrupt persons who, in common parlance, are likely to see it. That result, said Mr. Harman, is contrary to the spirit and purpose of the Acts.

The argument of Mr. Hutchinson, supported on behalf of the Attorney-General, was this. The Act of 1959 did not provide that an article is per se obscene. It provided a method whereby the obscenity of an article shall be decided. That method involves the identification of persons likely to read, see or hear the matter contained or embodied in the article. The Act is directed against the publication of obscene matter and, for the purposes of the Act, only those persons who are likely to read, see or hear as a result of publication are relevant to the question of obscenity. The Act defines in section 1 (3) what is publishing for the purposes of the Act. The same meaning should be attached to the word " publishes " and derivatives of that word wherever the word appears in the Act. Section 2 (6) of the Act of 1959 and section 1 (3) (*b*) of the Act of 1964 respectively require obscenity to be tested by reference to publication. The showing of the film to the cinema audience was, by reason of the proviso to section 1 (3) of the Act of 1959, not a publication for the purposes of the Acts. It was to be disregarded for the purposes of the conduct particularised at (*a*) as well as at (*b*) of the subsection. There being no other publication within the meaning of section 1 (3) of the Act of 1959 to a person whom the matter would tend to deprave and corrupt, there was no identifiable person or persons by reference to whom the question of obscenity could be decided.

Mr. Hutchinson further argued that the construction for which Mr. Harman contended would result in the denial of the defence afforded by section 4 of the Act of 1964, and produce consequences which he characterised as absurd. We do not find it necessary to deal with the arguments as to absurdity in any detail. Mr. Hutchinson relied on the three examples which he had submitted to the trial judge: (i) the situation in which a person could be guilty of publishing an obscene article by letting on hire a film although the only purpose of the hiring was to enable a lawful showing of the film to take place; (ii) the situation in which an exhibitor of a film commits no offence by showing the film to the public but yet might be subject to prosecution as a party to the publication of the film to him; (iii) the postulated difficulty facing a magistrate who is called upon to adjudicate upon the prosecution of a person who lets on hire a film for lawful public exhibition and who, or a colleague of whom, exercising powers delegated by the county council, has previously said that the film is fit for public exhibition.

Mr. Harman's answers, taking them shortly, were these: (i) that the proviso to section 1 (3) (*b*) of the Act of 1959 did not make the exhibition a lawful one but excluded the exhibition from publication for the purposes of the Act; (ii) under the present law the hirer could properly be tried as a principal in respect of one publication of the article, although excused by the Act in respect of what would otherwise have been another publication; (iii) that the provision of the Local Government Acts 1963 and 1972 ensure that the postulated difficulty of the magistrate will not now arise.

We do not stay to consider the respective merits of the arguments on each side on this aspect of the reference, because consideration of the consequences flowing from a particular construction is necessary only if there is room for more than one construction.

We are of the opinion that the meaning of the relevant statutory provisions is plain. We think that the starting point is the section which creates the offence charged, section 2 (1) of the Act of 1959. In relation to count 1 of the indictment the essence of the offence is having an obscene article for publication. Two questions arise—what is obscene? and, what is publication? The question whether the article is obscene is to be answered not in the abstract but by reference to publication of the article: see section 1 (3) (*b*) of the Act of 1964 which prescribes the kind of publication which is relevant for this purpose. So one looks for what is meant by publication. The Act of 1959 defines "publication" indirectly by providing in section 1 (3) (*b*) that, for the purposes of the Act, a person publishes an article who acts in one or another of the ways specified. In relation to count 2 of the indictment the same questions arise as to obscenity and publication. In this instance the offence postulates a publication by the defendant and the subsection brings into the determination of the question whether the article is obscene the publication by another person in certain circumstances. Again it is necessary to turn to section 1 (3) of the Act of 1959 to ascertain what is publication.

The terms of that subsection necessarily contemplate the person who publishes, offers for publication or has an article for publication, and a person, or persons in general, to whom publication is made or offered in any of the ways prescribed, or whom the person having the article may be reasonably inferred to have in contemplation, as the recipient or recipients of the publication. It is with reference to those persons who may be described as the recipients or, as the case may be, the contemplated recipients of the publication that the question of obscenity has to be determined for the purposes of an offence under section 2 (1).

The question remains, how is an article determined to be obscene by reference to publication, or contemplated publication, to those people? The answer is provided by section 1 (1). By this subsection the Act deems to be obscene an article according to its effect upon persons who are described as "likely having regard to all relevant circumstances to read, see or hear the matter contained or embodied in the article." These words must bear their ordinary meaning in the context of the Act read as a whole. The Act is not concerned with the obscenity of articles which are not published or intended or kept for publication. In a general sense to read, to see and to hear involve the publication of what is read, seen or heard to the person who reads, sees or hears. It is not a departure from the ordinary meaning of the words in subsection (1) to construe them as "read, see or hear as a result of publications within the meaning of subsection (3)." Such construction applies the ordinary meaning of the words to the subject matter of the Act.

Before turning again to the terms in which the reference was made we must say a word upon the argument, not strongly pressed, that the proviso to section 1 (3) of the Act of 1959 excepts things done in the course of a cinematograph exhibition (within the meaning of the Cinematograph Act 1952) other than one excluded from the Cinematograph Act 1909 by section 7 (4) of that Act, and anything done in the course of television or sound broadcasting not only from being a publication under (*b*) but also under (*a*) of section 1 (3). The trial judge rejected the submission that the proviso applied to publications under (*a*). We are of the opinion that he was right. The words of the proviso itself confine its application to publications within (*b*). Although this is not a case, there may be cases the facts of which exclude the showing, playing or projection in the course of a cinematograph exhibition from being a publication under (*b*) nevertheless involve a publication within (*a*).

The answers to the questions posed by the terms in which the point

A of law was referred are: (i) the words "read, see or hear" in section 1
(1) of the Obscene Publications Act 1959 are to be defined as "read, see
or hear as a result of a publication by a person who publishes within the
meaning of section 1 (3) of that Act and not otherwise." (ii) the relation-
ship between section 2 (6) of the Obscene Publications Act 1959 and
section 1 (3) (*b*) of the Obscene Publications Act 1964 respectively to
section 1 (1) and (3) of the Act of 1959 is that the sections must be read
B together as part of the whole Act of 1959. The effect is (a) that the
publication referred to in section 2 (6) and section 1 (3) (*b*) is a publica-
tion resulting from publishing within the meaning of section 1 (3) of the
Act of 1959 and (b) that the requirement that the court should have regard
to the publication, or contemplated publication, for the purpose of deter-
mining obscenity restricts the persons referred to in section 1 (1) as
C "likely to read, see or hear" to those who read, see or hear as the result
of such a publication.

Opinion accordingly.

Solicitors: *Director of Public Prosecutions; Richards, Butler & Co.; Treasury Solicitor.*

D

[COURT OF APPEAL]

* BURSTON FINANCE LTD. *v.* GODFREY AND OTHERS

E

[1974 B. No. 8938]

1976 March 23, 24; April 13 — Megaw, Scarman and Shaw L.JJ.

Execution—Charging order nisi—Order absolute—Bankruptcy
F *of judgment debtor after order nisi—Order made absolute—*
Whether bankruptcy relevant to decision whether or not to
make order absolute—Discretion of court—R.S.C., Ord. 50,
r. 1

In December 1974, the plaintiffs, bankers, signed judg-
ment in default of defence in the sum of £462,932 against
the defendants, who had been sued as guarantors of the
G indebtedness of a property company. The judgment was not
satisfied. On February 5, 1975, the plaintiffs applied, pursuant
to R.S.C., Ord. 50, r. 1,[1] for a charging order on land owned
by the defendants and for the appointment of a receiver. The
master made an order nisi and fixed the date on which any
sufficient cause to the contrary was to be shown as February 20.
On February 19, the defendants presented bankruptcy petitions
in a county court, receiving orders were made against them
H and both were adjudged bankrupt. The official receiver was
made trustee in bankruptcy of their estates. The official
receiver was not aware of the proceedings to make the
charging order absolute and was not represented on February
20 when Master Bickford-Smith, who was not informed of the
adjudications of February 19, ordered that the charging order
should be made absolute and that the appointment of the
receiver should be continued. Subsequently, another trustee

[1] R.S.C., Ord. 50, r. 1 (2) (6) (7): see post, p. 725B–F.

in bankruptcy of the defendants' estates was appointed in A
place of the official receiver and added as a third defendant to the plaintiffs' action.

On appeal by the trustee against the master's order:—

Held, dismissing the appeal, (1) (Shaw L.J. dissenting) that when the court was considering under R.S.C., Ord. 50, r. 1 whether to make or refuse to make a charging order absolute, it was entitled to consider, as matters which might affect the exercise of its discretion, events which had occurred subsequent B
to the date of the order nisi, and accordingly the trustee in bankruptcy was entitled to prove the receiving orders and adjudications of February 19 (post, pp. 730A–D, H—731A, 734E, G—735A).

Hudson's Concrete Products Ltd. v. *D. B. Evans (Bilston) Ltd.* (1961) 105 S.J. 281, C.A.; *D. Wilson (Birmingham) Ltd.* v. *Metropolitan Property Developments Ltd.* [1975] 2 All E.R. 814, C.A. and *Rainbow* v. *Moorgate Properties Ltd.* C
[1975] 1 W.L.R. 788, C.A. applied.

Dictum of Page Wood L.J. in *Haly* v. *Barry* (1868) L.R. 3 Ch.App. 452, 456 disapproved.

(2) That the court's discretion whether to make or refuse to make the order absolute had to be exercised in the light of all relevant circumstances shown in evidence, which might include events occurring both before and after the order nisi, and the order would not be made absolute if it would be D
inequitable so to do; that, on the relevant facts, which included the making of the receiving orders and the adjudications of February 19, the trustee in bankruptcy had failed to show that it would be inequitable for the charging order to be made absolute, so that sufficient cause to the contrary had not been shown and the order must stand; and since that order was justified, the continuance of the appointment of the receiver was also justified (post, pp. 732D–F, 733C–E, 734G—735A, 736H, E
737C).

The following cases are referred to in the judgments:

Brereton v. *Edwards* (1888) 21 Q.B.D. 488, C.A.

Glass (Cardiff) Ltd. v. *Jardean Properties Ltd.* (1976) 120 S.J. 167; Bar Library Transcript No. 35 of 1976, C.A.

Haly v. *Barry* (1868) L.R. 3 Ch.App. 452. F

Hudson's Concrete Products Ltd. v. *D. B. Evans (Bilston) Ltd.* (1961) 105 S.J. 281; Bar Library Transcript No. 110 of 1961, C.A.

Lee (George) & Sons (Builders) Ltd. v. *Olink* [1972] 1 W.L.R. 214; [1972] 1 All E.R. 359, C.A.

Overseas Aviation Engineering (G.B.) Ltd., In re [1963] Ch. 24; [1962] 3 W.L.R. 594; [1962] 3 All E.R. 12, C.A.

Prichard v. *Westminster Bank Ltd.* [1969] 1 W.L.R. 547; [1969] 1 All G
E.R. 999, C.A.

Rainbow v. *Moorgate Properties Ltd.* [1975] 1 W.L.R. 788; [1975] 2 All E.R. 821, C.A.

Stewart v. *Rhodes* [1900] 1 Ch. 386, C.A.

Wicks v. *Shanks* (1892) 67 L.T. 609, C.A.

Wilson (D.) Birmingham Ltd. v. *Metropolitan Property Developments Ltd.* [1975] 2 All E.R. 814, C.A. H

The following additional cases were cited in argument:

Barclays Bank Ltd. v. *Moore* [1967] 1 W.L.R. 1201; [1967] 3 All E.R. 34, C.A.

Bibby (James) Ltd. v. *Woods (Howard, Garnishee)* [1949] 2 K.B. 499; [1949] 2 All E.R. 1, D.C.

Crompton & Co. Ltd., In re [1914] 1 Ch. 954.

A APPEAL from Master Bickford Smith.

On December 20, 1974, the plaintiffs, Burston Finance Ltd., bankers, signed judgment against the first and second defendants, William Jack Godfrey and his wife, Ann Evelyn Godfrey, for £462,902·82 in default of defence in an action brought against them as guarantors of the indebtedness of Pinewood Homes Ltd., a company of which they were directors. B The judgment was not satisfied.

On February 5, 1975, on the application of the plaintiffs, made ex parte pursuant to R.S.C., Ord. 50, r. 1, Master Jacob made a charging order nisi on the interest of Mrs. Godfrey in a flat in Hambledon Court, Arundel Way, Highcliffe, Hampshire, and on the interest of both defendants in Pankridge Farm, High Wycombe, Buckinghamshire. The date for further consideration was fixed for February 20. On February 19, both defendants C presented their own petitions in bankruptcy at Bournemouth County Court, receiving orders were made against each of them and each was adjudicated bankrupt. The official receiver was appointed receiver of their respective estates. He did not appear at the proceedings to make the charging order absolute on February 20 because he was unaware that they were to take place. Master Bickford Smith, who was not told that the defendants D had been adjudicated bankrupt, ordered that the charging order should be made absolute and the appointment of the receiver continued.

Subsequently, George Albert Auger became the trustee in bankruptcy for the estates of Mr. and Mrs. Godfrey, in succession to the official receiver, and he applied to the master, pursuant to R.S.C., Ord. 15, r. 7, to be added as third defendant to the plaintiffs' action. On July 3, 1975, E the master so ordered.

On July 22, the trustee in bankruptcy appealed to the Court of Appeal against the order of Master Bickford Smith making the charging order absolute and continuing the appointment of the receiver, and asked that the order should be discharged on the grounds (1) that receiving orders and orders of adjudication in bankruptcy having been made against Mr. F and Mrs. Godfrey on February 19, no order ought to have been made on the application on February 20 in the absence of the official receiver, alternatively, without giving the official receiver an adequate opportunity to appear and make representations on the application; (2) that, in the light of the receiving orders and orders of adjudication and of the insolvency of Mr. and Mrs. Godfrey the order absolute ought not as a matter G of discretion to have been made; and (3) in the circumstances the order was wrongly made and was a nullity.

They also applied for leave to adduce further evidence by way of affidavits sworn by Philip George Kaye, a director of the plaintiffs, on February 23, 1975, and by Eric Michael Garston, solicitor to the plaintiffs, sworn on March 2, 1975.

H The facts are stated in the judgment of Megaw L.J.

Leonard Bromley Q.C. and *E. C. Evans Lombe* for the trustee in bankruptcy.

Donald Nicholls Q.C. and *Alan Steinfeld* for the plaintiffs.

Cur. adv. vult.

April 13. The following judgments were read.

MEGAW L.J. The circumstances in which this appeal comes before this court are unusual and in some respects unfortunate. The plaintiffs, Burston Finance Ltd., having obtained judgment in default of defence on December 20, 1974, in the sum of £462,932 against Mr. William Jack Godfrey and Mrs. Ann Evelyn Godfrey, applied ex parte on February 5, 1975, under R.S.C., Ord. 50, r. 1, for a charging order on land owned by Mr. Godfrey, Mrs. Godfrey, or both, and for the appointment of a receiver. The order, as asked, was made by Master Jacob on February 5. The date for further consideration—the date on which any "sufficient cause to the contrary" was to be shown—was fixed by the order as February 20, 1975. On February 19 Mr. and Mrs. Godfrey presented their own petitions in bankruptcy at Bournemouth County Court. On the same day receiving orders were made in respect of both of them and they were both adjudged bankrupt. I shall refer to them hereafter as "the bankrupts." The estimated deficiencies, as appear from the statements of affairs, are over £10,000,000 as regards Mr. Godfrey and over £5,000,000 as regards Mrs. Godfrey. A large part of their debts, including the debts for which the plaintiffs recovered judgment, arise out of guarantees given by the bankrupts in respect of advances made by bankers and others to a property company, Pinewood Homes Ltd., which appears to have dealt extensively in the property market. A receiver for the company had been appointed on July 3, 1974.

On February 20, 1975, the day following the petitions and adjudications in the county court, the proceedings to make absolute the charging order, and to have the receivership in connection therewith continued, came before Master Bickford Smith in London. The plaintiffs were represented by a solicitor; the bankrupts were represented by counsel. The official receiver was not represented. He was unaware that those proceedings were to take place on that day in that court. The master was not told of the receiving orders nor of the bankruptcy adjudications of the previous day. It is unfortunate that that was so. I accept that no blame is to be attributed to the solicitor for the plaintiffs. He knew of the receiving orders but not of the adjudications. He thought, erroneously, that counsel who appeared for the bankrupts also represented the official receiver. Counsel for the bankrupts, it appears, simply stated that he could not show cause why the charging order should not be made absolute. We do not know what information or instructions, if any, he had about the previous day's proceedings. Master Bickford Smith made the order absolute, including an order that the receiver appointed on February 5 should continue to act.

On March 20, 1975, the present trustee in bankruptcy, Mr. George Albert Auger, was appointed. He applied on June 13, 1975, to Master Bickford Smith under R.S.C., Ord. 15, r. 7, that he should be added as a defendant to the action (that is, the action between the plaintiffs and the bankrupts in which the judgment had been given in respect of which the charging order had been obtained) and that the action should be carried on accordingly. The application was supported by an affidavit sworn by the solicitors for the trustee in bankruptcy. We have not seen that affidavit; but the basis of the application was, presumably, that the official receiver, the trustee's predecessor in title, ought to have been made a party to the action when the bankruptcy adjudications had been

A made. He ought to have had the opportunity, as such a party, to be represented at the hearing on February 20, but he had not been given that opportunity. Master Bickford Smith heard the application inter partes on July 13, 1975. It would seem that it was not opposed. At any rate the order, as asked, was made on that day. The trustee in bankruptcy was added to the action as third defendant.

I assume that the order was properly asked for and made. But what
B the effect of it was upon the proceedings which had taken place on February 20 and upon what had purported to be done on that date appears to me to be obscure. I should have thought that it would have been procedurally correct, and for practical reasons preferable, that, such an order having been made in such circumstances, the matter should have been heard afresh by the master, with the trustee in bankruptcy represented
C at the fresh hearing, in substitution for the hearing, or purported hearing, of February 20. The unsuccessful party could then, if so desired, have appealed to this court. (I assume in the absence of submission to the contrary that an appeal lies to this court, as a final appeal, from a master's order under R.S.C., Ord. 50, r. 1.) On an appeal thus brought this court would have had the advantage, which it does not now have, of the decision of, and perhaps the exercise of discretion by, the master; and if any
D issues of fact arose on any relevant matter the evidence which would then have been adduced on affidavit before the master could, if necessary, have been tested by cross-examination before the master. But a different course has been followed. The trustee in bankruptcy has appealed to this court, in his capacity as third defendant, against the order which originated, at that stage properly, in ex parte proceedings on February 5,
E 1975, and which was, or was purported to be, made absolute in supposedly inter partes proceedings on February 20. A notice of appeal was served accordingly, and both parties, the plaintiffs and the trustee in bankruptcy (the bankrupts take no further interest in the matter) have asked for leave to adduce affidavit evidence, being evidence which, inevitably in the circumstances, was not before, or considered by, the master. I have felt doubt whether we ought to allow the matter to proceed in this way.
F But as the parties have urged us to do so, in order to save the time and expense of going back to the master, with a probable appeal thereafter to this court, and as both parties are content that we shall deal with the matter on the basis of the affidavit evidence now before us, drawing any proper inferences therefrom, I think we ought to accept the invitation to determine the appeal as asked; though I am conscious of the possible
G existence of hidden pitfalls in the path of those who take a procedural short cut in such poorly mapped territory with its complicated topography of fact, procedure, statute and case law. So far as the exercise of discretion is concerned, the discretion which would have been the master's discretion thus becomes ours to exercise, as though we were the court of first instance, on the material which would have been before the master.

The first issue is one of law. It does not require any further statement
H of facts than I have already set forth. The essential facts for this issue are simply that the order nisi (I think it is convenient so to refer to it) was made on February 5, 1975; the receiving orders and adjudications in bankruptcy on the bankrupts' petitions were made on February 19, 1975; the consideration whether the charging order should be made absolute was on February 20.

Section 40 (1) and (2) of the Bankruptcy Act 1914, as amended, are as follows:

> "(1) Where a creditor has issued execution against the goods or lands of a debtor, or has attached any debt due to him, he shall not be entitled to retain the benefit of the execution or attachment against the trustee in bankruptcy of the debtor, unless he has completed the execution or attachment before the date of the receiving order, and before notice of the presentation of any bankruptcy petition by or against the debtor, or of the commission of any available act of bankruptcy by the debtor. (2) For the purposes of this Act, an execution against goods is completed by seizure and sale; an attachment of a debt is completed by receipt of the debt; and an execution against land is completed by seizure, or by the appointment of a receiver."

The decision of the majority of the court in *In re Overseas Aviation Engineering* (*G.B.*) *Ltd.* [1963] Ch. 24 has been subjected to criticism, but it is binding on us. The effect of it, so far as is relevant for present purposes, is that a charging order on land under sections 34 to 36 of the Administration of Justice Act 1956 is "execution" for the purposes of section 325 of the Companies Act 1948, and therefore (where, as here, the relevant person is an individual, not a company) is also "execution" for the purposes of section 40 (2) of the Bankruptcy Act 1914; and that execution is not complete until a receiver has been appointed. For the purpose of the decision of this first issue, I leave out the question of the appointment of a receiver. I shall come to that later, as the third issue. So, on the facts which I have stated, had the execution been completed before the date of the receiving orders in respect of the bankrupts? If the charging order was properly made absolute on February 20, the answer to that question is "yes," despite the fact that the receiving orders had been made on February 19: for when the order is made absolute it relates back to the date of the making of the order nisi, which was February 5. If the order nisi should not have been made absolute, but should have been discharged at the hearing of February 20, then the plaintiffs have not become secured creditors. There is no charging order. The issue of law then is: in considering whether the charging order nisi should be made absolute is the court entitled to take into consideration the fact that a receiving order and an adjudication of bankruptcy have been made since the date of the order nisi? The plaintiffs say no. The trustee in bankruptcy says yes. He does not, however, contend that, if the answer is yes, the result is that in such circumstances the order nisi cannot be made absolute. He contends that the making absolute is a matter of discretion, and that, if it be proved or admitted that there has been a receiving order or an adjudication or both, or indeed any other event which can properly be regarded as relevant, between the date of the order nisi and the date of the further hearing, such facts are facts which can and should be taken into account in the decision how to exercise the discretion. I have used the phrase "any other event which can properly be regarded as relevant." This begs the question. The real question is: what matters, if any, occurring after the date of the order nisi may in law be regarded as relevant to the decision whether or not to make the order absolute?

I do not propose to burden this judgment with any lengthy disquisition on historical matters nor with a detailed comparison of the wording of R.S.C., Ord. 50, r. 1, prescribing the procedure for obtaining an order imposing a charge on land, with the similar, though not identical, provisions of R.S.C., Ord. 49 relating to garnishee orders. The relevance of the latter is that this court (Buckley and Ormrod L.JJ.) in *Rainbow* v.

A *Moorgate Properties Ltd.* [1975] 1 W.L.R. 788, has held that the same considerations apply to the question whether the discretion should or should not be exercised to make absolute a charging order as apply to the same question in respect of a garnishee order. Thus this court in *Rainbow* treated as applicable in a charging order case the principles which had been laid down two months previously by this court (Buckley L.J. and Thompson J.) in *D. Wilson (Birmingham) Ltd.* v. *Metropolitan Property*
B *Developments Ltd.* [1975] 2 All E.R. 814, which was concerned with a garnishee order. I shall have to return to those cases later.

Under R.S.C., Ord. 50, r. 1 the application is initially made ex parte. This, as appears from past history including the Judgments Act 1838 (1 & 2 Vict., c. 110) sections 13 and 15, is so provided at least partly in order to preclude or reduce the risk that a judgment debtor, on receiving
C advance notice of an intended application for a charging order, may seek to render himself "judgment-proof" by disposing of, or concealing, his assets. So the judgment debtor has no opportunity to contest the making of the order nisi. He cannot at that stage even say that there is no judgment, or that he is not the person named in the judgment, or that he has satisfied the judgment. The order is made on the plaintiff's application asserting the matters set out in R.S.C., Ord. 50, r. 1 (4). The order nisi
D operates immediately to bind the judgment debtor until the date specified in the order for "further consideration of the matter." The order (r. 1 (2)) "shall in the first instance be an order to show cause." Then paragraphs (6) and (7) of the rule provide what is to happen on that "further consideration":

> "(6) On the further consideration of the matter the court shall, unless
> E it appears (whether on the representation of the judgment debtor or otherwise) that there is sufficient cause to the contrary, make the order absolute with or without modifications. (7) Where on the further consideration of the matter it appears to the court that the order should not be made absolute, it shall discharge the order."

As I understand it, the words "or otherwise" in parenthesis in
F paragraph (6)—"(whether on the representation of the judgment debtor or otherwise)"—enable the court, as would seem to be appropriate where the justice of the case so requires, to hear representations by a person interested, other than the judgment debtor: in the present case, the official receiver.

The plaintiffs stress the words in paragraph (6) "shall" and "unless
G it appears that there is sufficient cause." The onus is clearly on the person opposing the making of the order absolute to show cause. If he fails to do so, the court must make the order absolute. But that does not mean that the court does not have a discretion to exercise, if material is put before it which is, in law, relevant to the question of "cause."

As I have already said, there is no doubt that, if the order is made
H absolute, its effective date is the date of the order nisi. It is also clear, and the plaintiffs say that this is a relevant factor on this issue, that even if the charging order is made absolute the trustee in bankruptcy has still available to him in the bankruptcy proceedings means of preventing the plaintiffs from receiving the benefit of a charging order if it has been unfairly obtained: such, for example, as by showing that the plaintiff had notice of a prior act of bankruptcy, or the doctrine of "relation back." There is, therefore, it is said, no injustice to the other creditors if such matters are

not required or allowed to be fully investigated when the charging order is made absolute.

The plaintiffs' contention is that both on principle and on authority the receiving order and the adjudication subsequent to the order nisi should be excluded from consideration. It is not properly "cause" which can be shown. The principle is that a judgment creditor should not be prejudiced by anything that may be done—particularly anything that may be done on the initiative of the judgment debtor—after the date when the judgment creditor has obtained the order nisi. If, as is the law, the order when made absolute is treated as having been effectively made, not merely for interim purposes, when the order nisi was made, why should anything subsequent to the date of the order nisi be regarded as relevant? The debtor, at any rate, should not be allowed by his own act after learning of the order nisi to destroy the effect of that order. Even where, as here, that which intervenes is an order of the court, not merely something done by the debtor, the same consideration applies. For it was the judgment debtor's initiative, from whatever motive, which brought about the receiving order and the adjudication; and in the circumstances the county court's action in making those orders does not really represent a considered opinion by that court.

So we must consider some of the authorities which have been examined and analysed at length in argument.

The plaintiffs rely primarily on *Haly* v. *Barry* (1868) L.R. 3 Ch.App. 452, a decision of this court (Page Wood and Selwyn L.JJ.). The headnote is as follows:

> "A creditor" (plaintiff) "recovered judgment against his debtor and issued a fi. fa. Shortly afterwards the debtor died. The creditor entered a suggestion on the record, entitling him to have execution against the executrix, and obtained a charging order nisi upon shares belonging to the debtor. After the order nisi had been obtained, but on the same day, a decree was made for administration of the debtor's estate. The order nisi not having been made absolute, the plaintiff in the administration suit applied for an injunction to restrain further proceedings by the judgment creditor: —*Held* (affirming the decision of Malins V.-C.) that an injunction ought not to be granted. A charging order, when made absolute, operates from the making of the order nisi. *Warburton* v. *Hill* (1854) Kay 470 explained."

Page Wood L.J., at p. 456, refers to sections 14 and 15 of the Judgments Act 1838, and stresses that (as is now the case under R.S.C., Ord. 50, r. 1) there is only one order—not separate orders nisi and absolute. Page Wood L.J. then says:

> "Ought then a creditor to be interfered with who has pursued his remedies with such diligence. He has obtained a charging order, subject only to this, that cause may be shewn against making it absolute. I think that, consistently with the scope and spirit of the Act, we must hold that it is liable to be defeated only by something prior to it, shewing that it ought not to have been made, and not by anything subsequent to it."

The proposition in the last sentence in its literal terms is too wide. No one could suggest that all subsequent events are irrelevant. For example, surely the order should not be made absolute if it appeared that, subsequent to the date of the order nisi, the judgment creditor had been paid his judgment debt whether by the judgment debtor or by someone else (for example, where the judgment debt was that of a guarantor by virtue of a guarantee, payment by the principal debtor); or that the judgment debtor had procured the setting aside of the judgment since the date of the order nisi; or perhaps that he had started proceedings for that purpose. Nevertheless, although the dictum in its literal terms may be too widely expressed, the essence of the actual decision appears to have been that an order of the court, in that case the decree of administration, made after the date of the order nisi could not operate to prevent the making of the order absolute. It is, I think, "could not" as a matter of principle, rather than merely "should not in the circumstances of the case" as a matter of discretion. I believe the principle which the court in *Haly* v. *Barry*, L.R. 3 Ch.App. 452 intended to enunciate was that nothing which happens subsequent to the date of the order nisi is relevant, other than events which operate to affect what may be described as the judgment creditor's "title" to the judgment debt: which events could include, as an example, a payment of the judgment debt.

It is true that, as counsel for the trustee in bankruptcy stressed, the actual decision in *Haly* v. *Barry* was the refusal of an injunction; so that strictly and technically it may not be a decision as to the law applicable when the court is considering the substantive question whether the charging order should be made absolute. But there is no indication that the court regarded its decision on the principle as being in any way affected by the fact that it was dealing with an application for an injunction.

Haly v. *Barry* has not, so far as I am aware, been adversely criticised in any relevant respect. (*Stewart* v. *Rhodes* [1900] 1 Ch. 386 does not, I think relate to a relevant respect). It has continued to be cited in standard works such as *Halsbury's Laws of England*, 3rd ed. (1956), vol. 16, p. 96, *Seton's Judgments and Orders*, 7th ed. (1912), vol. I, p. 414 and the *Supreme Court Practice* (1976), vol. 1, p. 767. It was considered in *Brereton* v. *Edwards* (1888) 21 Q.B.D. 488, in which the court consisted of Lord Esher M.R. Lindley and Bowen L.JJ. Certainly no disapproval of *Haly* v. *Barry* was expressed. On the contrary, it was treated as good authority. But I think counsel for the trustee in bankruptcy is right in his submission that the only aspect of *Haly* v. *Barry* with which the court was concerned in *Brereton* v. *Edwards* was as to the effective date of the charging order, when it had been made absolute, being the date of the order nisi; a matter about which there is no dispute in this appeal. As I understand it, it was a question of priority only, and no question arose, or could have arisen, whether the order should have been made absolute.

But *Haly* v. *Barry*, L.R. 3 Ch.App. 452 interpreted as the plaintiffs claim it should be interpreted, is in my judgment inconsistent, and irreconcilable, with at least three recent decisions of this court. In none of them, it would seem, most unfortunately, was *Haly* v. *Barry* cited. That, however, regrettable though it is—particularly as in one of the cases a litigant in person was involved, in whose favour *Haly* v. *Barry* might, if it be good law, have operated—does not mean that the recent decisions have to be disregarded as having been arrived at, in the curious phrase, "per incuriam." It is a factor to be taken into account in deciding which decision or line of decisions this court ought to follow. Would the courts which decided the subsequent cases have been bound, or would they have been likely, to have decided differently, or to have taken a different course as to matters which should be treated as relevant, if *Haly* v. *Barry* had been brought to their attention? *Haly* v. *Barry* was a decision of a court consisting of two Lords Justices dealing with an interlocutory matter.

Hudson's Concrete Products Ltd. v. *D. B. Evans* (*Bilston*) *Ltd.* is reported only in (1961) 105 S.J. 281. Judgment was given on March 14, 1961. The court consisted of Willmer and Donovan L.JJ. We have had the advantage of seeing the full transcript of the judgments. They are, if I may say so, succinct and unambiguous. I assume in favour of the plaintiffs in this appeal that *Haly* v. *Barry* was not cited. It is not referred to in either judgment. The case was concerned with a garnishee order which had been made absolute by the district registrar. The court allowed the appeal and discharged the order. The facts were that the judgment creditor obtained its judgment on December 14, 1960. In November the judgment debtor had convened a meeting of creditors, putting forward proposals which appeared to meet with a favourable response. On December 20 the judgment creditor obtained a garnishee order nisi. On January 16, 1961, two events happened: the judgment debtor took out a summons under section 206 of the Companies Act 1948 for the sanctioning of a scheme of arrangement; and another creditor filed a petition for the winding up of the company. On the following day, January 17, the garnishee order was made absolute. There is no doubt that the court regarded these two events, which had happened after the date of the order nisi, as being relevant to be taken into account in the exercise of the discretion which had to be exercised in the decision whether to make the order absolute. There were other factors as well which the court considered—events preceding the order nisi. But the events which had happened after the order nisi were taken into account; and it cannot be said that they are not relevant in the ascertainment of the ratio decidendi. It cannot be said that the court would have reached the same decision without taking them into acount. As I have said earlier, it has since been decided by this court, in *Rainbow* v. *Moorgate Properties Ltd.* [1975] 1 W.L.R. 788 that for this purpose there is no relevant distinction between the factors relevant to the making absolute of, on the one hand, a garnishee order nisi and, on the other hand, a charging order nisi.

Hudson's Concrete Products Ltd. v. *D. B. Evans* (*Bilston*) *Ltd.*, 105 S.J. 281 was referred to and followed in *D. Wilson* (*Birmingham*) *Ltd.* v. *Metropolitan Property Developments Ltd.* [1975] 2 All E.R. 814 which was, again, a garnishee order case. Again, *Haly* v. *Barry*, L.R. 3 Ch.App. 452 was not cited to the court. Again, there were many events prior to the order nisi which the court took into account in coming to the decision that the registrar, in the exercise of his discretion, should not have made the order absolute. In particular, the court was clearly impressed by the fact that before the two garnishee orders nisi were obtained a very large number of creditors of the group of companies to which the judgment debtor belonged had agreed upon a moratorium of all debts of the companies in the group, and that active preparations had been undertaken for a scheme of arrangement under section 206 of the Companies Act 1948. For the plaintiffs in the present appeal, it is contended that the essence of the decision in *Wilson* is to be found in the judgment of Buckley L.J. in the following passage, at p. 819:

> " The position is, I think, that a court in considering whether or not to exercise its discretion to make absolute a garnishee order in circumstances such as this, must bear in mind not only the position of the judgment creditor, the judgment debtor and the garnishee,

> A but the position of the other creditors of the judgment debtor and must have regard to the fact that proceedings are on foot, and were on foot at the time the garnishee proceedings were launched, for ensuring the distribution of the available assets of the judgment debtor company among the creditors pari passu."

Counsel for the plaintiffs lays much stress on the words in that
B passage: ". . . and were on foot at the time the garnishee proceedings were launched. . . ." Counsel for the trustee in bankruptcy retorts by reference to the preceding words "are on foot," which, he says, shows beyond doubt that the court took into account as a factor at least the negative evidence relating to the period subsequent to the order nisi: that nothing had happened to prevent that which was previously "on foot" from continuing to be on the march.

C I think that the true basis of the decision can be ascertained from an earlier passage in Buckley L.J.'s judgment at p. 818 where he refers, as I think with clearly implied approval, to submissions made in that case by counsel for the judgment debtor, as follows:

> "Counsel for the judgment debtor draws attention to the fact that under the terms of R.S.C., Ord. 49 the making of a garnishee order
> D is a discretionary matter, and that it is not disputed by the judgment creditor. He has further submitted that the court will not, consequently, make such an order if so to do would be inequitable, and that also is not disputed. Counsel for the judgment debtor went on to say that it would be inequitable to make an order in such a case as the present because its effect would be to confer a preference on
> E the creditor and that, a fortiori, the court ought not to make such an order which would have such an effect where a winding-up petition has already been presented for winding up the company."

It is to be noted that the winding up petition on which counsel relied was presented on October 22, 1974, the two garnishee orders nisi having been made on September 12, 1974. Again, I regard this as a decision of
F the court which involved the consideration, as being a consideration proper in law in the exercise of the discretion, of events, not merely related to the title of the judgment creditor, subsequent to the date of the orders nisi. If *Haly* v. *Barry* had been in the mind of counsel as an authority to the contrary, he ought to have brought that case to the notice of the court.

Rainbow v. *Moorgate Properties* Ltd. [1975] 1 W.L.R. 788, decided
G that the principles did not differ in respect of charging orders and garnishee orders; and the court expressly followed both *Hudson*, 105 S.J. 281 and *Wilson* [1975] 2 All E.R. 814. In *Rainbow's* case the judgment creditor appeared in person. I assume again that *Haly* v. *Barry*, L.R. 3 Ch.App. 452 was not in the mind of counsel. Otherwise it certainly ought to have been brought to the notice of the court.

H There has been a yet more recent decision of this court [*Glass (Cardiff) Ltd.* v. *Jardean Properties Ltd.* (1976) 120 S.J. 167] (Lord Denning, M.R., Lawton and Bridge L.JJ.) in which a registrar's decision that a charging order should be made absolute was upheld. But, with all respect and without in any way querying the correctness of the decision, it does not, as I read it, affect the question of principle here involved. There is no suggestion, as I read the judgments, that the court, when considering whether to make a charging order absolute, is not entitled to take into consideration, as relevant to its discretion, events subsequent to the order nisi.

If there be a conflict between *Haly* v. *Barry*, L.R. 3 Ch.App. 452 and the recent decisions of this court, in my judgment we ought to follow those recent decisions. If the plaintiffs are right in their analysis of the ratio decidendi of *Haly* v. *Barry*, there is, I believe, such a conflict. We ought to hold that, when the court under R.S.C., Ord. 50, r. 1, is considering whether or not to make absolute a charging order, it is entitled to consider, as matters which may affect the exercise of its discretion, events subsequent to the date of the order nisi. Thus, in my judgment, *Haly* v. *Barry* is good law in so far as it lays down the principle that when a charging order is made absolute it is to be treated as an order which has been effective since the date of the order nisi. But if *Haly* v. *Barry* decides that a court in considering whether to make the order absolute is debarred from taking into account facts subsequent to the date of the order nisi, or can take into account only those subsequent facts which can be said to affect the judgment creditor's "title" to the judgment debt, I would hold that in that respect *Haly* v. *Barry* is no longer good law. Thus, in this case the trustee in bankruptcy would have been entitled, and is now entitled, to prove the receiving orders and adjudications of February 19. The fact that they are subsequent to the date of the charging order nisi does not make the evidence inadmissible or the facts irrelevant, even though the order, if made absolute, would date back to a date earlier than those events. But it does not follow that those facts are conclusive. They are essential elements in the trustee in bankruptcy's case, but they do not necessarily establish that case. The court has a discretion, which it has to exercise in the light of all the relevant circumstances shown in evidence, which may include circumstances arising after, as well as before, the date of the order nisi.

Curiously, one of the facts which would tend in favour of the plaintiffs is an event which happened after the date of the order nisi: the subsequent granting or purported granting by the judgment debtors to another creditor, Quenby Price Ltd., of a legal charge over the same land as that in respect of which the plaintiffs' charging order had been obtained. For the plaintiffs to have sought in this appeal to rely upon that fact as a material fact would have involved the cutting by them of their anchor cable: the anchor being *Haly* v. *Barry* as construed by them. But—and this perhaps illustrates the curious situation which would exist if the plaintiffs were right on this issue—the plaintiffs sought to suggest that they could rely on that evidence (if I understood the intellectual subtlety correctly), not as evidence of an existing fact, but as an illustration of the sort of thing which might reasonably have been in contemplation at the date of the order nisi as likely to occur thereafter so as to prejudice the plaintiffs' position for the benefit of another creditor. We were told that the trustee in bankruptcy is attacking or is minded to attack this purported legal charge to Quenby Price Ltd. We, of course, can express no view on it. But, if I am right on the first issue, we are entitled to take into account, as a relevant fact, the making or purported making of this legal charge.

So I came to the second issue. On the relevant facts, which, if I am right on the first issue, include the facts of the making of the receiving orders and the adjudications of bankruptcy on February 19,

A 1975, had or had not sufficient cause been shown to require the exercise of the court's discretion to refuse to make the order absolute? That is a mixed question of fact and law: the law consisting of any guiding principle which can properly be formulated to govern the exercise of the discretion.

It is necessary now to state some further facts as they appear either directly in, or as proper inferences to be drawn from, the evidence
B before us. I am left in no doubt that counsel for the trustee in bankruptcy is right in his submission, only faintly if at all challenged by counsel for the plaintiffs, that well before the charging order nisi was sought it was obvious to the plaintiffs that the bankrupts were insolvent and that, to use the phrase used in argument, the insolvency was "massive." Whether it was known that it ran into eight figures does
C not matter. It is also obvious, as counsel for the plaintiffs stresses, that the bankrupts' creditors had not taken any steps to arrange a moratorium, or to collaborate in any way so as to seek to agree upon some scheme which would be likely to put the creditors on something like an equal footing with one another. There was nothing on foot here to correspond with preparation, in the case of an insolvent company, of a scheme for approval under section 206 of the Companies Act 1948.
D There is no evidence of any positive attempt at collaboration between any or all of the creditors of the bankrupts with a view to a sort of mutual self-denying ordinance—a holding back of action for the common benefit. On the other hand, there had been a telephone discussion just before Christmas 1974 between the solicitor for the plaintiffs and the solicitor for the bankrupts (the defendants, as they then were), in which
E much information was given by the latter to the former as to his clients' financial position and the non-existence at that stage of any threats of bankruptcy proceedings or of the levying of execution by any of the creditors. There was also evidence as to the Quenby Price Ltd. purported legal charge.

[His Lordship referred to an affidavit of Philip George Kaye, a director
F of the plaintiffs at the relevant time sworn on February 23, 1976, who stated that although he had a meeting with Mr. Godfrey on November 2, 1974, in the company of a member of the staff of Pinewood Homes, Ltd., Mr. Godfrey did not then suggest to him that there was any possibility of his presenting his own bankruptcy petition nor that any other creditors of his were about to or intending to present any bankruptcy petition or otherwise take any steps to execute any judgment
G which they had obtained over his assets, and that he first learnt of the grant of a mortgage in favour of Quenby Price Ltd. over Pankridge Farm, and that there was any intention by Mr. and Mrs. Godfrey to present petitions in their own bankruptcy, at a meeting at the plaintiffs' solicitor's office on February 18, 1975. His Lordship also referred to an affidavit sworn on July 24, 1975, by Philip Craven, the solicitor who
H had acted for the defendants, who stated that in a telephone conversation with the plaintiffs' solicitor at the end of December 1974, he had mentioned the potential personal liability of Mr. and Mrs. Godfrey as guarantors of loans to Pinewood Homes Ltd. and, lastly, to an affidavit by the plaintiffs' solicitor, Eric Michael Garston, sworn on March 2, 1975, in which he admitted that in that telephone conversation, Mr. Craven had given him full information as regards the various judgments which had been obtained against Mr. and Mrs. Godfrey, but stated that

he had specifically asked whether there were any threats of bankruptcy proceedings or the levying of execution on any of the judgments and was specifically told that there were none. His Lordship continued:] Mr. Garston produces a contemporary note which is, as one would expect, consistent with what he deposes. The note includes the words "No threats of bankruptcies or sheriffs."

Counsel for the plaintiffs contends that a principle can be deduced from the authorities, more particularly *Hudson*, 105 S.J. 281, *Wilson* [1975] 2 All E.R. 814, *Rainbow* [1975] 1 W.L.R. 788, and *Glass*, 120 S.J. 167. That principle counsel defined in the following words: "The court will not decline to make an order absolute unless (a) the debtor is insolvent; and (b) there is already on foot some process, formal or informal, by which the available assets are in the course of being held for an equal distribution."

I find this altogether too obscure to provide a satisfactory, or indeed a workable, criterion or statement of principle. The true principle, I think, as emerges from the recent authorities, cannot be more precisely stated than as it was put by counsel, as recorded in the judgment of Buckley L.J. in *Wilson* [1975] 2 All E.R. 814, 818 (part of the passage I have already read), where the Lord Justice says: "He" (i.e. counsel) "has further submitted that the court will not, consequently, make such an order if so to do would be inequitable, and that also is not disputed."

That principle, as a general principle, is affirmed by dicta in other cases, two of which, *Prichard* v. *Westminster Bank Ltd.* [1969] 1 W.L.R. 547, 549 *per* Lord Denning M.R. and *George Lee & Sons* (*Builders*) *Ltd.* v. *Olink* [1972] 1 W.L.R. 214, 216, *per* Russell L.J., were referred to by Buckley L.J. at p. 818 in his judgment in *Wilson.* True, as counsel for the plaintiffs stresses, those two cases involved different statutory provisions; but that, in my judgment, does not affect the degree of support which they offer to the statement of general principle.

Applying that principle here, this is, I think, on the facts before us, a marginal case. In the end, after hesitation, I have reached the conclusion that the trustee in bankruptcy has failed to show that it would be inequitable in the circumstances that the order should be made absolute. So sufficient cause is not shown and the charging order should stand. I reach that conclusion mainly because there was here, so far as the evidence goes, no understanding nor any indication of any attempt to reach an understanding among the creditors of the bankrupts, or among any of them, as to common forbearance from pressing individual remedies, in the interests of all. Nor is there any evidence that the plaintiffs exercised undue haste to obtain a preferred position for themselves as compared with the general body of creditors; nor that they took, or sought to take, unfair advantage of any knowledge which they had acquired of any other matter or circumstance which was unknown to the other creditors. It is perhaps ironic, in view of the plaintiffs' submission on the first issue, which, if right, would have excluded consideration of the evidence as to the purported legal charge granted by the bankrupts to Quenby Price Ltd., that that evidence should operate in the plaintiffs' favour on this second issue. But I regard it as a relevant factor in their favour, as showing, if nothing more, that there was an absence of any common front among the creditors. Whether that purported legal charge turns out to be good or bad does not matter for this purpose. At any rate we cannot decide it. But it

A would perhaps be hard to regard the discharge of the plaintiffs' charging
order as being equitable if, on the facts as they presently appear, another
creditor were by this transaction to have obtained a valid charge on the
selfsame property of the bankrupts. When one adds to these matters
the further consideration that the plaintiffs' advantage arising from the
charging order being made absolute is subject to review and possible
invalidation in certain events in the bankruptcy proceedings, I have
B come to the conclusion, already stated, that sufficient cause has not been
shown in these proceedings why the charging order should not be made
absolute.

There remains the third issue. Counsel for the trustee in bankruptcy
contended that, even if the charging order itself could properly have
been made absolute, different considerations would apply to the order
C for the continuance of the receivership, originally created by the order
nisi of February 5, 1975. If the receivership ought not to have been
continued, then, on the majority decision in *In re Overesas Aviation*
Engineering (G.B.) Ltd. [1963] Ch. 24, to which I referred at the outset
of this judgment, the plaintiffs would not have completed the execution, so
they would have no effective charge on the land. I shall express my view
D in one sentence, with all respect to the intricate and learned arguments
adduced. If the making absolute of the charging order itself is justified,
as I think it is, I see no good reason why the continuance of the appoint-
ment of the receiver is not also justified.

I would dismiss the appeal. The result would be that the charging
order absolute made on February 20, 1975, would stand, including the
continuance of the receiver's appointment. If there should be any
E difficulty as to the form of the order, we shall be willing to hear counsel
thereon.

After I had written this judgment, I saw Report No. 74 of the Law
Commission, on Charging Orders, which has been published since the
conclusion of the hearing before us. (Cmnd. 6412, March 1976). As a
matter of interest, I find no reference in that report to *Haly* v. *Barry*, L.R.
F 3 Ch.App. 452. I believe that recommendation (2) in paragraph 104 of
of the report, which is reflected in clause 1 (3) of the draft Bill annexed
to the report, in no way conflicts with the view which I have expressed
in this judgment, in my conclusion on the first issue, as being the existing
law. The recommendation reads, at p. 32:

> " It should be made clear that the court has a full discretion whether
> G or not to accede to an application for a charging order; and that in
> exercising this discretion the court should take into account any
> evidence before it not only about the personal circumstances of the
> debtor but also about any other creditors of his who might be
> unfairly prejudiced if the charging order were granted."

H Scarman L.J. I have had the advantage of reading the judgments
of Megaw and Shaw L.JJ. Although they are agreed upon their con-
clusion, they reach it by different routes. I have followed the route
taken by Megaw L.J.; I propose in a very few words to explain why.

There is a conflict between the view of the law expressed by Page
Wood L.J. in *Haly* v. *Barry*, L.R. 3 Ch.App. 452 and the decisions of this
court in *Hudson's Concrete Products Ltd.* v. *D. B. Evans (Bilston) Ltd.*,
105 S.J. 281, *D. Wilson (Birmingham) Ltd.* v. *Metropolitan Develop-*

ments Ltd. [1975] 2 All E.R. 814 and *Rainbow* v. *Moorgate Properties Ltd.* [1975] 1 W.L.R. 788. Most surprisingly, *Haly* v. *Barry* appears not to have been drawn to the attention of the court in the three later cases: it certainly could have assisted Mr. Rainbow, a litigant in person, though I do not think it would have persuaded the court to reach a decision other than that which they did reach. A

How is the conflict to be resolved? The nature of the conflict is this. In *Haly* v. *Barry* Page Wood L.J. said, at p. 456: B

> " He "—that is, the creditor—" has obtained a charging order, subject only to this, that cause may be shewn against making it absolute. I think that, consistently with the scope and spirit of the Act "—that is, the Judgments Act 1838—" we must hold that it is liable to be defeated only by something prior to it, shewing that it ought not to have been made, and not by anything subsequent to it." C

In the three later cases (in *Hudson's* case, and also *Wilson's* case, a garnishee order, in *Rainbow's* case a charging order) events subsequent to the making of the order nisi were taken into consideration and it was held that the court had a discretion to be exercised in the light of all the circumstances existing at the time when the endeavour to show cause against the order nisi was before the court. In my opinion the view expressed by Page Wood L.J. in *Haly* v. *Barry* went further than was strictly needed for a decision in that case. I read the case as deciding at most two issues: (1) whether an order made absolute relates back to the order nisi, so that in law there is only one order; (2) whether " a subsequent decree for administration (of the debtor's estate) is a sufficient cause " against making the order absolute: see p. 457 of the report. The court decided that the order, when made absolute, operated from the making of the order nisi and that the administration decree was not a sufficient cause. When Page Wood L.J. said that the charging order was not liable to be defeated " by *anything* subsequent " to the order nisi, he was stating the law more broadly than was necessary for his decision. D E F

I cannot conceive how the mere making of a decree for administration of the debtor's estate without further evidence as to the debtor's estate could be a sufficient cause for refusing to make the order absolute. I would not, therefore, doubt the correctness of the decision in *Haly* v. *Barry*. Similarly, the mere fact of a receiving order, or even an adjudication of bankruptcy, subsequent to the order nisi, would not necessarily suffice: if, however, there were other circumstances, such as a scheme of arrangement, formal or informal, agreed or being negotiated amongst creditors, the court might well think it equitable to refuse to make the order absolute. And I do not think the decision in *Haly* v. *Barry*, as distinct from the dictum of Page Wood L.J., at p. 456, precludes the court from exercising such a discretion. If, however, I am wrong in my analysis of *Haly* v. *Barry*, there is a conflict between the decisions of this court. It would be absurd to treat the later decisions as per incuriam merely because *Haly* v. *Barry* was not cited: and I unhesitatingly prefer the reasoning of the later cases, and would resolve the conflict in favour of them. G H

In my judgment, on an application to show cause against the order nisi, the court does have a discretion, which is to be exercised in all the circumstances then obtaining, to make, or refuse to make, absolute

A the order. And I think the later decisions offer valuable guidance as to the matters to be considered in the exercise of the discretion. Nevertheless, for the reasons given by Megaw L.J., I think in this case the order should be made absolute. I would dismiss the appeal.

SHAW L.J. I have arrived at the same conclusion as that which has been stated in the preceding judgments. I have, however, followed a B somewhat different road and I therefore add a few observations of my own.

In regard to the first ground of appeal I am of the view that the law was correctly stated in *Haly* v. *Barry*, L.R. 3 Ch.App. 452. In his judgment Page Wood L.J. says, at p. 456, after a reference to sections 14 and 15 of the Judgments Act 1838,

C "It is obvious that throughout these sections one order only is spoken of, which is at first to be an order nisi, and is afterwards to be made absolute. Ought then a creditor to be interfered with who has pursued his remedies with such diligence. He has obtained a charging order, subject only to this, that cause may be shewn against making it absolute. I think that, consistently with the scope D and spirit of the Act, we must hold that it is liable to be defeated only by something prior to it, shewing that it ought not to have been made, and not by anything subsequent to it."

Selwyn L.J. who was the only other member of the court, concisely but cogently supports that view in these terms, at p. 457:

"The question turns upon this, whether the charging order is to be E considered as one or two. It has been urged that there are two orders, and that the first goes for nothing unless followed by the other. The language of the Act appears to me quite opposed to this view, it speaks of one order which is at first an order nisi, and is afterwards made absolute."

I see no reason for any qualification of these statements, certainly not F in the light of principle. Unless the enforcement of just claims by due process of law is to be stultified or aborted, a judgment creditor must be enabled, as well as entitled, to gather the fruits of the judgment he has obtained. For this reason he has a legal right to proceed to execution, a right which the law protects and supports by recognising that as soon as the process of execution has been set in motion the judgment creditor is regarded as having a vested interest in the subject matter of that G process to the extent necessary to satisfy his judgment. Sections 14 and 15 of the Judgments Act 1838 make provision to protect that interest from the time that the judgment creditor first applies to the court for, and obtains, a charging order. It is generally referred to as, in the first instance, an order nisi, but, as Page Wood L.J. pointed out, it is the same order which survives the hearing inter partes if no cause be H then shown to set it aside. In deciding whether the order should be made absolute or whether it should be discharged, only those circumstances which obtain when the order was first made are material, or relevant. It may be that some intervening event will serve to establish what those circumstances were. Thus, if the judgment has in the interval been set aside, this fact will demonstrate that the judgment creditor had no title to his judgment at the time the order nisi was made. If, on the other hand, between the making of the order nisi and the hearing inter partes the judgment has been satisfied, this will have the effect of depriving the judgment creditor of any claim to the benefit of the charge. It will operate ipso facto as a discharge of the judgment debt and of the charge which purports to secure it. There will be nothing left to consider at the hearing inter partes and the judicial discharge of the order is mere formality. A

I see no reason not to regard the judgment in *Haly's* case as still good law despite some modern decisions which are in conflict with it but which were arrived at without the earlier case being cited in argument or otherwise referred to. In *Brereton* v. *Edwards* (1888) 21 Q.B.D. 488, where *Haly* was considered, it survived the scrutiny of a court which consisted of Lord Esher M.R., Lindley and Bowen L.JJ. without provoking any criticism or expression of doubt. That tacit approbation of the view of the law as stated in *Haly* is not to be disregarded, albeit the question then under consideration was different from (though not unrelated to) the issue in *Haly's* case. B C

If I am correct in preferring the principle as stated by Page Wood L.J. to that which emerges from some recent cases, this appeal must fail.

However, on the assumption that the law is now to be regarded as different from *Haly* and settled by such decisions as in *Rainbow* v. *Moorgate Properties Ltd.* [1975] 1 W.L.R. 788, and *D. Wilson* (*Birmingham*) *Ltd.* v. *Metropolitan Property Developments Ltd.* [1975] 2 All E.R. 814, it becomes necessary to consider the question of the exercise of the court's discretion in deciding whether to make a charging order absolute or to discharge it. There is much to be said in favour of the view that the legal rights to pursue a judgment to execution and an execution to satisfaction can only be eroded or encroached upon by some statutory provision. The Bankruptcy Acts provide an elaborate code to ensure the equitable distribution of an insolvent debtor's property among competing creditors. Voluntary settlements, fraudulent preferences and transactions caught by the doctrine of " relation back " are void or voidable as against the trustee in bankruptcy. Executions which are not completed in conformity with section 40 of the Bankruptcy Act 1914, or section 325 of the Companies Act 1948, are rendered ineffectual to serve the interest of the execution creditor. Where the legislature has been at pains to ensure that particular creditors in particular circumstances do not obtain or shall not retain an undue advantage over the general body of creditors, it is, as I see it, both unnecessary and unjustified to add a gloss of unfettered judicial discretion which may make a further inroad into the legal rights of a creditor beyond that which the relevant statutes have designed. Support for this view may be derived from the judgment of Lord Denning M.R. given on January 30, 1976, in the unreported case of *Glass* (*Cardiff*) *Ltd.* v. *Jardean Properties Ltd.* [120 S.J. 167] where the making of a garnishee order absolute was upheld notwithstanding the insolvency of the judgment debtor. D E F G

However, it has long been settled that the language of sections 14 and 15 of the Judgments Act 1838 conferred a discretion on the court in deciding whether to grant or to refuse a charging order absolute: see *Wicks* v. *Shanks* (1892) 67 L.T. 609. H

Nonetheless it would seem that where a judgment creditor has a good title to his judgment and has not acted unfairly in relation to the other creditors he should not be refused an order absolute. Of course, where the circumstances are such that the subject matter of the charging order

A nisi would be valueless to the judgment creditor so that it would be pointless to make the order absolute, refusal would be justified. In such a case the creditor is deprived of nothing which will advantage him in seeking satisfaction of his judgment.

Another class of case where refusal to make an order absolute might be justified is where a creditor of an apparently insolvent debtor has so acted as to suggest or indicate that he is prepared, in common with the
B general or a substantial body of the creditors of that debtor, to forgo the active and immediate pursuit of a claim. To go back on such an indication by seeking an order absolute would be conduct so inequitable as to forfeit the right of the creditor to ask that his interest should be supported or furthered by a judicial order. On this basis some of the recent cases can be understood and explained.

C In the present case, if the master had had before him all the information which has been made available to this court, I consider that he would have exercised his discretion rightly by coming to the conclusion that he did, namely, that the order should be made absolute.

On this aspect of the appeal as well as the remaining question as to the appointment of a receiver I respectfully adopt the reasoning and agree with the conclusions of Megaw L.J.

D I would dismiss the appeal.

Appeal dismissed with costs.
Leave to appeal refused.

Solicitors: *Booth & Blackwell; Michael Garston & Co.*

E E. M. W.

[COURT OF APPEAL]

F

* ATTORNEY-GENERAL'S REFERENCE (No. 3 of 1975)

1976 April 1; 7 Lord Widgery C.J., Lawton L.J. and Thompson J.

Revenue—Customs and excise—Untrue declarations—Causing document untrue in material particular to be delivered to commissioners—If committed knowingly or recklessly offence
G *indictable—Whether two separate offences—Whether jurisdiction in Crown Court if element of knowledge or recklessness absent—Customs and Excise Act* 1952 (15 & 16 *Geo.* 6 & 1 *Eliz.* 2, *c.* 44), *ss.* 283 (2), 301 [1]

Seven counts of an indictment alleged that the defendants had caused a document which was untrue in a material particular to be delivered to the Customs and Excise Commissioners,
H contrary to section 301 of the Customs and Excise Act 1952.[1] The judge ruled that the trial could not proceed in the Crown Court on those counts unless they were amended to allege that the defendants had " recklessly " caused such a document to

---

[Reported by Rachel Davies, Barrister-at-Law]

[1] Customs and Excise Act 1952, s. 283 (2): see post, p. 740E–F.
S. 301: see post, pp. 739G—740A.

be delivered to the commissioners. Although the defendants A were willing to plead guilty " but without recklessness " to the counts, they finally changed their pleas to not guilty and were acquitted on five of the seven counts.

On a reference by the Attorney-General for the court's opinion on whether section 301 created a single offence or two separate offences and whether the Crown Court had jurisdiction to convict an accused person of committing an offence contrary to the section without the elements of knowledge or recklessness B where the indictment alleged that he had committed the offence with knowledge or recklessly:—

Held, that subsections (3) and (4) of section 301 of the Customs and Excise Act 1952 were not concerned solely with penalties but by virtue of section 283 (2) went to the jurisdiction; that the section created two separate offences, namely, the indictable offence under subsection (3) of knowingly or recklessly making, signing, delivering or causing to be delivered C a document containing an untrue statement and the summary and absolute offence under subsection (4) of causing to be delivered such a document; and that, therefore, the Crown Court had no power to convict a defendant unless it was shown that he either had been reckless or had knowledge of the false statement contained in the document.

The following case is referred to in the opinion of the court: D

Parker v. *Pexton* [1962] Crim.L.R. 101, D.C.

The following additional case was cited in argument:

Reg. v. *Lindsay* (unreported), June 17, 1974.

REFERENCE by the Attorney-General.

E

The Attorney-General referred, under section 36 of the Criminal Justice Act 1972, points of law for the opinion of the Court of Appeal in the following terms:

" 1. Whether section 301 of the Customs and Excise Act 1952, creates one single offence or two separate offences. 2. Whether a Crown Court has jurisdiction to convict an accused person of committing an offence contrary to section 301 of the Customs and F Excise Act 1952 without the elements of knowledge or recklessness, where the indictment charges that person with having committed an offence contrary to section 301 either knowingly or recklessly. 3. If a Crown Court does have jurisdiction to convict of an offence contrary to section 301 of the Customs and Excise Act 1952 without the elements of knowledge or recklessness, whether that Crown G Court has jurisdiction to sentence the convicted person having regard to the provisions of section 283 of the said Act."

The relevant facts of the case were that a company and its managing director were jointly indicted for seven offences of causing an untrue document to be delivered to the Commissioners of Customs and Excise contrary to section 301. The counts in the indictment did not contain H any allegation that the act had been done recklessly or knowingly. Those seven counts in the indictment were alternatives to seven further counts for making false returns contrary to paragraph 15 of Schedule 1 to the Betting and Gaming Duties Act 1972, which did contain an allegation that the acts had been done recklessly. At the hearing of the case a Crown Court judge ruled that he could not proceed with the counts under section 301 of the Customs and Excise Act 1952, unless they

A were amended by adding an allegation of recklessness, and that was done. The defendants were arraigned and pleaded not guilty to all seven counts under the Betting and Gaming Duties Act, and guilty to the seven counts under section 301 of the Customs and Excise Act 1952, "but without recklessness." The Crown Court judge adjourned the hearing for further argument. At a further hearing before a second Crown Court judge, the defendants withdrew their pleas of guilty without
B recklessness to the counts under section 301, and pleaded not guilty to all counts in the indictment. The judge rejected submissions made on behalf of the prosecution that the jury were entitled to find the accused guilty of having committed the offence without being reckless. The jury convicted the defendants on two counts under the Betting and Gaming Duties Act 1972, and on the two corresponding counts under
C section 301 of the Act of 1952, and acquitted the defendants on all remaining 10 counts.

Sir Michael Havers Q.C. and *J. M. T. Rogers* for the Attorney-General.

Andrew Rankin Q.C. and *E. G. Goldrein* for the defendants.

D

Cur. adv. vult.

April 7. LORD WIDGERY C.J. read the following opinion of the court. This matter comes before the court in the form of a reference by the Attorney-General under section 36 of the Criminal Justice Act 1972.

According to the facts disclosed by the reference, the defendants
E were convicted before the Crown Court of two offences contrary to section 301 of the Customs and Excise Act 1952, of which charges the following is a specimen:

> "Recklessly causing a document which was untrue in a material particular to be delivered to the Commissioners of Customs and Excise contrary to section 301 of the Customs and Excise Act 1952."

F

The defendants were acquitted on a number of other similar charges.

A stage was reached in the proceedings when the defendants were prepared to plead guilty to all the relevant charges, if they could do so with a reservation that they had acted "without recklessness." The significance of this lies in the fact that section 301 imposes more severe penalties in the event of the conduct of the accused being knowing or
G reckless.

Section 301, so far as material, reads as follows:

> "(1) If any person—(*a*) makes or signs, or causes to be made or signed, or delivers or causes to be delivered to the commissioners or an officer, any declaration, notice, certificate or other document whatsoever . . . being a document or statement produced or made
> H for any purpose of any assigned matter which is untrue in any material particular, he shall be guilty of an offence under this section. . . . (3) Without prejudice to the last foregoing subsection, where any person who commits an offence under this section does so either knowingly or recklessly, he shall be liable to a penalty of £500 or to imprisonment for a term not exceeding two years or to both and may be detained; and any goods in relation to which the document or statement was made shall be liable to forfeiture. (4)

> Without prejudice to subsection (2) of this section, where any person A
> commits an offence under this section in such circumstances that he is not liable under the last foregoing subsection, he shall be liable to a penalty of £300."

The judge at the trial appears to have been of the opinion that section 301 (1) created a single offence, and that subsections (3) and (4) went only to penalties. He accordingly held that a plea of guilty "with- B
out recklessness" was not a plea which he could accept, and the trial continued. The point is, however, one which has given trouble elsewhere, and the Attorney-General has referred the matter to the court for the court to answer the following questions:

> "1. Whether section 301 of the Customs and Excise Act 1952 creates one single offence or two separate offences. C
>
> "2. Whether a Crown Court has jurisdiction to convict an accused person of committing an offence contrary to section 301 of the Customs and Excise Act 1952 without the elements of knowledge or recklessness where the indictment charges that person with having committed an offence contrary to section 301 either knowingly or recklessly.
>
> D
> "3. If a Crown Court does have jurisdiction to convict of an offence contrary to section 301 of the Customs and Excise Act 1952 without the elements of knowledge or recklessness, whether that Crown Court has jurisdiction to sentence the convicted person having regard to the provisions of section 283 of the said Act."

The distinction between subsections (3) and (4) does not relate solely E
to penalty. It goes to jurisdiction also by virtue of section 283 (2) which provides:

> "Subject to any express provision made by the enactment in question, any offence under the customs or excise Acts—(*a*) where it is punishable with imprisonment for a term of two years, with or without a pecuniary penalty, shall be punishable either on F
> summary conviction or on conviction on indictment; (*b*) in any other case, shall be punishable on summary conviction: . . ."

Hence it would appear that the Crown Court has no jurisdiction in these matters unless an offence charged includes the elements of recklessness or knowledge sufficient to bring it within section 301 (3) of the Act of 1952.

G
Until 1961 it was the practice to regard section 301 as creating two separate offences, one requiring proof of knowledge or recklessness, and the other not. In December 1961, and in an unreported part of the case of *Parker* v. *Pexton* [1962] Crim.L.R. 101, Lord Parker C.J., in an observation which was clearly obiter suggested that there was in fact only one offence which would attract different penalties according to whether the requirements of subsection (3) were or were not present. H
Slade J. in the same case (and also obiter) seemed to favour the theory that there were two distinct offences. We are told that these dicta have given rise to uncertainty, and that on this account the Attorney-General would welcome a considered view of the questions set out in the reference.

Looking at the language of section 301 there is much to be said for the single offence theory, and if subsections (3) and (4) were concerned

A solely with penalty, we might have accepted Lord Parker C.J.'s view. In fact, our problem is to construe section 301 against the background of the Act, and particularly the provisions as to jurisdiction contained in section 283.

If there is here a single offence its essentials are to be found in section 301 (1), and there seems to be no reason why the information should allege that the act complained of was done recklessly or know- B ingly. The result will be that a defendant will not know what penalty he faces, and the magistrates will not know whether to treat the case as one for which a defendant can require trial by jury. Indeed, in the uncertainty which will prevail a defendant may be able to insist on a jury even though the prosecution disclaims any intention of leading evidence as to knowledge or recklessness. If a defendant is committed to the Crown C Court the judge may take the view taken at one stage in the present case that he has no jurisdiction unless knowledge or recklessness is expressly pleaded. We need not express a view on this hypothetical situation, but it is, no doubt, a fruitful source of doubts. Further doubts may arise as to the functions of judge and jury respectively on the question of knowledge or recklessness, and jurisdiction may remain in doubt until after the jury has brought in a verdict. All these and many D other problems disappear if section 301 is construed as creating two offences, and we think it should be so construed in order to make the terms of section 283 workable.

The court's answers to the specific questions posed are as follows: (1) The section creates two separate offences. (2) The Crown Court cannot convict the accused if he is not shown to have had knowledge E or to have been reckless. No further proceedings against him are possible unless a separate information charging the absolute offence under subsection (4) is still available in the magistrates' court. (3) This question does not arise.

Opinion accordingly.
Defendants' costs to be paid out of
F *central funds.*

Solicitors: *Solicitor, Customs and Excise; Berkson & Berkson, Birkenhead.*

G

[COURT OF APPEAL]

* REGINA *v.* BELFON

H 1976 March 11; 19 — Stephenson L.J., Wien and Forbes JJ.

Crime—Assault—Mens rea—Wounding with intent to do grievous bodily harm—Whether recklessness as to consequences of acts sufficient intent—"Intent"—Offences against the Person Act 1861 (24 & 25 *Vict. c.* 100), *s.* 18

The defendant was charged with wounding with intent to do grievous bodily harm contrary to section 18 of the Offences against the Person Act 1861.[1] At his trial the judge directed the jury that the necessary intention in section 18 was proved if the jury found that the defendant desired the consequences of his act in that he wished to cause serious injury or if he foresaw the likely consequences of his act, namely, serious injury, but nevertheless committed the act recklessly.

On the defendant's appeal against conviction on the ground that the judge had misdirected the jury since recklessness could not amount to the specific intent required by section 18:—

Held, allowing the appeal, that a specific intention to cause grievous bodily harm must be proved to establish an offence under section 18 of the Offences against the Person Act 1861 and it was not sufficient to prove that the defendant foresaw that serious injury was likely to result from his act and committed the act recklessly; that the judge had accordingly misdirected the jury and the conviction would be quashed.

Reg. v. *Hyam* [1975] A.C. 55, H.L.(E.) distinguished.

The following cases are referred to in the judgment of the court:

Director of Public Prosecutions for Northern Ireland v. *Lynch* [1975] A.C. 653; [1975] 2 W.L.R. 641; [1975] 1 All E.R. 913, H.L.(N.I.).
Reg. v. *Hyam* [1975] A.C. 55; [1974] 2 W.L.R. 607; [1974] 2 All E.R. 41, H.L.(E.).
Reg. v. *Mohan* [1976] Q.B. 1; [1975] 2 W.L.R. 859; [1975] 2 All E.R. 193.
Reg. v. *Mowatt* [1968] 1 Q.B. 421; [1967] 3 W.L.R. 1192; [1967] 3 All E.R. 47, C.A.

The following additional cases were cited in argument:

Hardy v. *Motor Insurers' Bureau* [1964] 2 Q.B. 745; [1964] 3 W.L.R. 433; [1964] 2 All E.R. 742, C.A.
Reg. v. *Ward* (1872) L.R. 1 C.C.R. 356.
Rex v. *Bourdon* (1847) 2 Car. & Kir. 366.
Rex v. *Steane* [1947] K.B. 997; [1947] 1 All E.R. 813, C.C.A.

APPEAL against conviction.

The defendant, Horace Adrian Belfon, appealed against his conviction on August 7, 1975, at the Central Criminal Court (Judge Hines) of wounding with intent to do grievous bodily harm contrary to section 18 of the Offences against the Person Act 1861, on the ground that the judge had misdirected the jury that recklessness was sufficient to constitute an intent to do grievous bodily harm.

On March 11, 1976, the Court of Appeal allowed the appeal and quashed the defendant's conviction but reserved the reasons for their decision.

The facts are stated in the judgment of the court.

Andrew Collins for the defendant.
Nicholas Purnell for the Crown.

Cur. adv. vult.

March 19. WIEN J. read the judgment of the court. For over a century judges have almost daily directed juries as to the essential elements required to constitute the offence of wounding with intent to do grievous

[1] Offences against the Person Act 1861, s. 18: "Whosoever shall unlawfully and maliciously by any means whatsoever wound or cause any grievous bodily harm to any person . . . with intent . . . to maim, disfigure, or disable any person . . . shall be guilty of felony."

A bodily harm contrary to section 18 of the Offences against the Person Act 1861. The adjective "grievous" is outmoded. Therefore the words "really serious" have been properly and sensibly used to describe the nature of the bodily harm that must be intended. There has never been any need to explain what "intent" means since the specific intent is defined in the section. Juries do not seem to have experienced any difficulty in understanding the word "intent" without further explanation and
B convictions under this section are frequent.

In the present case the judge directed the jury in the following terms:

> "The law about intent is this . . . A person intends the consequences of his voluntary act in each of two quite separate cases; first when he desires those consequences and secondly when he foresees that they are likely to follow from his act but he commits the act recklessly
> C irrespective of appreciating that those results will follow."

This appeal raises the question whether that direction with yet a further elaboration was correct. The elaboration was as follows:

> "Let us apply that particular general principle in the case of wounding. A man who in fact wounds another man is guilty of doing so with intent to cause him serious injury if either he wishes to cause
> D him serious injury and that is therefore why he does what he does, or alternatively he foresees that serious injury is likely to result from his using whatever implement he does use in the way that he does and he nevertheless does that injury recklessly, notwithstanding his foresight that serious injury is likely to result. So what you have to ask yourselves when you have to decide what a defendant did in a
> E particular case is this. Did he do it either intending in the sense of wishing that serious injuries should result or even if not that, did he at the time as a matter of fact foresee that serious injury was probably going to result and yet went on and did the act recklessly, ignoring his foresight that really serious injury was a likely consequence of what he was doing? If either of those matters be the case then he is guilty of the necessary intent but unless it is proved that one or other
> F of those matters is true of the case then the necessary intent is lacking."

On August 4, 1975, at the Central Criminal Court the defendant pleaded not guilty to count 3 of an indictment that charged him and another man with wounding Ernest Horne on October 7, 1974, with intent to do him grievous bodily harm. He pleaded guilty to an alternative
G charge (count 4) of maliciously wounding Ernest Horne on the same date, contrary to section 20 of the Offences against the Person Act 1861. The prosecution wished to proceed with the graver charge. The plea of guilty to the lesser charge was withdrawn by order of the court and a trial followed before Judge Hines and a jury. On August 7, 1975, the jury convicted the defendant and the other man on count 3.

H The relevant facts relating to count 3 were simple and not exceptional. Shortly after midnight on October 7, 1974, in Holloway the defendant and another man set upon a group of people who had come out of a public house and had gone to protect a girl who was pushed to the ground by the defendant. Mr. Horne's son Paul was the first to be attacked by the other man. The defendant slashed Mr. Horne with an open razor causing severe injuries to his forehead and wounds to his chin and lower chest, as photographs show. The attack was quite unprovoked. After initial denials by the defendant that he was ever at the scene at all he eventually A admitted his presence. The jury were informed of his plea of guilty to count 4.

Whether the language used by the judge in his directions was liable to confuse the jury or was desirable was not the point of this appeal. Counsel for the Crown submitted that the direction was correct in that foreseeability of the consequences that are likely to follow from a voluntary act is of general application in considering the mens rea required to establish B an offence. He conceded that recklessness by itself was insufficient but argued (a) that being reckless was equivalent to a disregard of the consequences, which it unquestionably is, and (b) that "recklessly" in the context of the direction was an additional element to foreseeability. He said that the jury's verdict was so interpreted by the judge who in imposing sentence said: C

> "... the basis on which the jury have convicted you both of causing those wounds to Ernest Horne with intent must have been based not on an actual desire to do him serious injury but upon a realisation that there was a likelihood that you would cause serious injury and recklessly going on and doing what you did."

Counsel for the defendant submitted that the direction was plainly D wrong. "Recklessness" will not suffice to establish the specific intent required to cause grievous bodily harm though it might be sufficient to establish malice aforethought in a case of murder. In this respect he says that the law is accurately and succinctly stated by the editors of *Smith and Hogan, Criminal Law,* 3rd ed. (1973), p. 47, where it is stated:

> "attention should be drawn to the fact that, where an ulterior intent is E required, recklessness is not enough. On a charge of wounding with intent to cause grievous bodily harm, proof that D was reckless whether he caused grievous bodily harm will not suffice. Yet, paradoxically, if death resulted from the wound, D's recklessness would probably be enough to found liability for murder."

We agree that recklessness cannot amount to the specific intent required F by the section, for the reasons shortly to be stated. Counsel for the defendant further submitted that while foreseeability of serious physical injury that will probably flow from a deliberate act is a relevant factor in cases of murder, it has no application to a case of wounding with intent because the nature of the particular intent is defined in section 18 and no further definition is permissible, let alone desirable.

Prior to *Reg.* v. *Hyam* [1975] A.C. 55, one ventures to think that it G would never have occurred to a judge to explain what "intent" meant when directing a jury in a case of wounding with intent. He would have told the jury that what has to be proved is (1) a wounding of a person concerned, (2) that the wounding was deliberate and without justification, that is, that it was not by way of accident or self-defence, (3) that the wounding was committed with intent to do really serious bodily harm and H (4) that the necessary intent must have been in the mind of the accused, that is, the intent of a reasonable or sensible man is irrelevant, for the test is a subjective one, and not objective. Nothing more than this was ever called for except in certain cases where an explanation of "wounding" was desirable.

Why then did this judge depart from the usual practice? The court can only assume that he has been influenced by certain opinions expressed by their Lordships in *Reg.* v. *Hyam.* Before one turns to the various passages that might be relevant it must be emphasised that *Hyam's* case was concerned with the mens rea necessary to establish murder. Murder is unlawful homicide with malice aforethought. Malice aforethought means

> "(a) An intention to cause the death of, or grievous bodily harm to, any person, whether such person is the person actually killed or not; (b) knowledge that the act which causes death will probably cause the death of, or grievous bodily harm to, some person, whether such person is the person actually killed or not, although such knowledge is accompanied by indifference whether death or grievous bodily harm is caused or not, or by a wish that it may not be caused; . . .": see *Stephen's Digest of the Criminal Law,* 9th ed. (1950), art. 264.

Lord Cross of Chelsea in *Reg.* v. *Hyam* [1975] A.C. 55, 95 accepted that Stephen had correctly stated the law, although he referred to the original edition of 1877 where the same words are used in article 223.

In cases of wounding with intent it has never been considered that recklessness was to be equated with the particular intention that is required in order to constitute an offence described in section 18 of the Act of 1861.

In *Reg.* v. *Mowatt* [1968] 1 Q.B. 421, 425–426, Diplock L.J. said:

> "In the words of the court, 'maliciously in a statutory crime postulates foresight of consequence,' and upon this proposition we do not wish to cast any doubt. But the court in that case"—he was referring to *Reg.* v. *Cunningham* [1957] 2 Q.B. 396—"also expressed approval obiter of a more general statement by Professor Kenny [*Kenny's Outlines of Criminal Law,* 18th ed. (1962), p. 202], which runs as follows: 'in any statutory definition of a crime, "malice" must be taken not in the old vague sense of wickedness in general, but as requiring either (1) an actual intention to do the particular kind of harm that in fact was done, or (2) recklessness as to whether such harm should occur or not (i.e. the accused has foreseen that the particular kind of harm might be done, and yet has gone on to take the risk of it). It is neither limited to, nor does it indeed require, and, in my view, it is not foresight but intention which constitutes the
>
> "This generalisation is not, in our view, appropriate to the specific alternative statutory offences described in sections 18 and 20 of the Offences against the Person Act, 1861, and section 5 of the Prevention of Offences Act, 1851, and if used in that form in the summing-up is liable to bemuse the jury. In section 18 the word 'maliciously' adds nothing. The intent expressly required by that section is more specific than such element of foresight of consequences as is implicit in the word 'maliciously' and in directing a jury about an offence under this section the word 'maliciously' is best ignored.
>
> "In the offence under section 20, and in the alternative verdict which may be given on a charge under section 18, for neither of which is any specific intent required, the word 'maliciously' does import upon the part of the person who unlawfully inflicts the wound or other grievous bodily harm an awareness that his act may have the consequence of causing some physical harm to some other person. That is what is meant by 'the particular kind of harm' in the citation from Professor Kenny. It is quite unnecessary that the accused should have foreseen that his unlawful act might cause physical harm of the gravity described in the section, i.e., a wound or serious physical injury. It is

> enough that he should have foreseen that some physical harm to some person, albeit of a minor character, might result."

It may be different in cases of assault, about which we do not propose to express any considered opinion.

One may now turn to the question of foreseeability not in relation to section 20 of the Act of 1861 where, because no specific intent is required, the word "maliciously" of itself imports an awareness or the foreseeability that some minor harm might result, but in relation to section 18. Some comments by their Lordships in *Hyam's* case [1975] A.C. 55 might give credence to the view that foreseeability of the risk of serious injury can indeed be equated with an intention to cause grievous bodily harm.

Lord Diplock said in a dissenting speech, at p. 86:

> "This appeal raises two separate questions. The first is common to all crimes of this class. It is: what is the attitude of mind of the accused towards the particular evil consequence of his physical act that must be proved in order to constitute the offence? The second is special to the crime of murder. It is: what is the relevant evil consequence of his physical act which causes death, towards which the attitude of mind of the accused must be determined on a charge of murder?
>
> "Upon the first question I do not desire to say more than that I agree with those of your Lordships who take the uncomplicated view that in crimes of this class no distinction is to be drawn in English law between the state of mind of one who does an act because he desires it to produce a particular evil consequence, and the state of mind of one who does the act knowing full well that it is likely to produce that consequence although it may not be the object he was seeking to achieve by doing the act. What is common to both these states of mind is willingness to produce the particular evil consequence: and this, in my view, is the mens rea needed to satisfy a requirement, whether imposed by statute or existing at common law, that in order to constitute the offence with which the accused is charged he must have acted with 'intent' to produce a particular evil consequence or, in the ancient phrase which still survives in crimes of homicide, with 'malice aforethought'."

It might well be said that Lord Diplock was speaking in general terms for he was adverting to what he regarded as the first of two questions raised by the appeal, namely: what is the attitude of mind of the accused towards the particular evil consequence of his physical act that must be proved in order to constitute the offence? He was clearly not dealing with the crime of murder since that was the second question he considered and he treated the first question as common to all crimes in which the mental element includes that attitude of mind. But he did not indicate that he was revising the views he expressed in *Mowatt's* case [1968] 1 Q.B. 421 and no reference seems to have been made to that case.

Viscount Dilhorne said that he inclined to the view that the judge's ruling (based on the passage already quoted from *Stephen's Digest*) was correct and gave the following reason for doing so, at p. 82:

> "A man may do an act with a number of intentions. If he does it deliberately and intentionally, knowing when he does it that it is highly probable that grievous bodily harm will result, I think most people would say and be justified in saying that whatever other

> A intentions he may have had as well, he at least intended grievous bodily harm."

A perusal of the whole of Viscount Dilhorne's speech does not lead one to the conclusion that, except in that tentative opinion, he was dealing with any proposition other than that knowledge that it is highly probable that grievous bodily harm will result from a deliberate and intentional act B amounts to malice aforethought. This court had certified that the following point of law was of general public importance:

> "Is malice aforethought in the crime of murder established by proof beyond reasonable doubt that when doing the act which led to the death of another the accused knew that it was highly probable that that act would result in death or serious bodily harm?"

C Viscount Dilhorne said, at p. 80:

> "The question certified asked whether it constituted malice aforethought. If it did, it does not follow that it established an intent to do grievous bodily harm."

So knowledge of a consequence was treated by him as something different D from intent.

Lord Hailsham of St. Marylebone L.C. clearly distinguished "foresight" from "intention." He said, at p. 77:

> "For the reasons I have given, I do not think that foresight as such of a high degree of probability is at all the same thing as intention, and, in my view, it is not foresight but intention which constitutes the E mental element in murder."

Other passages in his speech indicate that throughout he was dealing with malice aforethought which after all was the question raised in the appeal and little help is to be gained from quoting sentences out of context. For example, we were referred to what he said at pp. 77–78:

> "In the field of guilty knowledge it has long been accepted both for F the purposes of criminal and civil law that '. . . a man who deliberately shuts his eyes to the truth will not be heard to say that he did not know it' (See *per* Lord Reid in *Southern Portland Cement Ltd.* v. *Cooper* [1974] A.C. 623, 638). Cannot the same be said of the state of intention of a man who, with actual appreciation of the risks and without lawful excuse, wilfully decides to expose potential victims to G the risk of death or really serious injury regardless of whether the consequences take place or not? This seems to me to be the truth underlying the statement of the law in *Stephen's Digest*, the summing up of Cockburn C.J. in *Reg.* v. *Desmond*, The Times, April 28, 1868, and of Avory J. in *Rex* v. *Lumley*, 22 Cox C.C. 635 and of those phrases in *Smith* [1961] A.C. 290 in which it seems to be said that a rational man must be taken to intend the consequences of his acts. H It is not a revival of the doctrine of constructive malice or the substitution of an objective for a subjective test of knowledge or intention. It is the man's actual state of knowledge and intent which, as in all other cases, determines his criminal responsibility. Nor, for the like reason, does this set up an irrebuttable presumption. It simply proclaims the moral truth that if a man, in full knowledge of the danger involved, and without lawful excuse, deliberately does that which exposes a victim to the risk of the probable grievous bodily

> harm (in the sense explained) or death, and the victim dies, the A perpetrator of the crime is guilty of murder and not manslaughter to the same extent as if he had actually intended the consequence to follow, and irrespective of whether he wishes it."

However, we read that passage as being confined to the crime of murder. It may be anomalous that to establish the crime of murder it need be necessary only to show that the accused foresaw that his deliberate B acts were likely to expose his victim to the risk of grievous bodily harm whereas to establish an offence under section 18 of the Act of 1861 it must be proved that there was an intent to cause grievous bodily harm. It is not the first time that this court has been faced with an anomalous situation. Such a situation can arise where the offence charged is an attempt to commit a crime. To prove attempted murder nothing less than an intent to kill will do. C To prove an attempt to commit any crime the prosecution has to prove a specific intent. It is not sufficient to establish that the accused knew or foresaw that the consequences of his act would be likely to result in the commission of the complete offence. In *Reg.* v. *Mohan* [1976] Q.B. 1, James L.J. in giving the judgment of the court said, at p. 10:

> "We do not find in the speeches of their Lordships in *Reg.* v. *Hyam* D [1975] A.C. 55 anything which binds us to hold that mens rea in the offence of attempt is proved by establishing beyond reasonable doubt that the accused knew or correctly foresaw that the consequences of his act unless interrupted would 'as a high degree of probability,' or would be 'likely' to, be the commission of the complete offence." E

Counsel for the Crown, in the present case, derives support for his contention (though he does not seek it) from what was said by Lord Simon of Glaisdale in *Director of Public Prosecutions for Northern Ireland* v. *Lynch* [1975] A.C. 653, which concerned a defence of duress on a charge of murder by a person accused as a principal in the second degree. In reference to the second certified question, which in part dealt with willing- F ness to participate in the crime of murder he said, at p. 698:

> "An example is wounding with intent to do grievous bodily harm. The actus reus is the wounding; and the prosecution must start by proving a corresponding mens rea—namely, that the accused foresaw the wounding as a likely consequence of his act. But this crime is defined in such a way that its mens rea goes beyond foresight of the G actus reus; so that the prosecution must in addition prove that the accused foresaw that the victim would, as a result of the act, probably be wounded in such a way as to result in serious physical injury to him."

Perhaps this passage played a part in the formulation of Judge Hine's directions to the jury. This court attaches considerable weight to the H opinion of Lord Simon. Nevertheless his remarks were obiter. They were expressed in a dissenting speech and so far as one can tell no argument was addressed to him, for it was not necessary to do so, as to whether one was entitled to enlarge on the intent necessary in the offence of wounding with intent to do grievous bodily harm. At any rate we do not find in that speech or in any of the speeches of their Lordships in *Hyam's* case anything which obliges us to hold that the "intent" in

A wounding with intent is proved by foresight that serious injury is likely to result from a deliberate act. There is certainly no authority that recklessness can constitute an intent to do grievous bodily harm. Adding the concept of recklessness to foresight not only does not assist but will inevitably confuse a jury. Foresight and recklessness are evidence from which intent may be inferred but they cannot be equated either separately or in conjunction with intent to do grievous bodily harm.

B We consider that the directions given by the judge in this case were wrong in law. Had he refrained from elaborating on the meaning of intent he would have given a quite adequate direction. It is unnecessary in such a case as this to do anything different from what has been done for many years.

It is for the reasons given that on March 11, 1976, the court allowed
C the appeal, quashed the conviction on count 3, substituted a conviction of unlawful wounding and reduced the sentence on this count from three years' imprisonment to two years' imprisonment. The sentence of 12 months' imprisonment concurrent on count 2 stands, and so does the consecutive sentence of 12 months' imprisonment on count 6. The total sentence is thus three years' imprisonment instead of four years.

D

Appeal allowed.

Solicitors: *Registrar of Criminial Appeals; Solicitor, Metropolitan Police.*

J. W.

E

[CHANCERY DIVISION]

* EMMERSON (INSPECTOR OF TAXES) *v.* COMPUTER TIME INTERNATIONAL LTD.

F

1975 Nov. 17, 18, 19;
Dec. 18

Fox J.

Revenue—Corporation tax—Computation of chargeable gains—Company in voluntary liquidation—Assignments of leaseholds by liquidator—Payment of arrears of rent to obtain landlord's consent to assignments—Whether payment of arrears
G *expenditure on "enhancing" value of asset, "preserving" title to, asset—Whether payment of arrears capital or revenue expenditure—Finance Act* 1965 (*c.* 25), *Sch.* 6, *paras.* 4 (1) (*b*), 5 (2)

The taxpayer company was incorporated in 1969 to carry on the business of hiring out computer time. It was the
H tenant of premises, occupying the first floor of those premises under an agreement for a 21-year lease at an agreed annual rent of £16,000, and the second floor by virtue of an underlease at an annual rent of £19,000. It spent a considerable sum on building improvements and electrical equipment to convert the premises for the purposes of its business but it was not a success and the taxpayer company went into

---

[Reported by MRS. HARRIET DUTTON, Barrister-at-Law]

voluntary liquidation in April 1970. At that time it was A
in arrears with the payments of rent. On condition that those arrears would be paid by the liquidator, the landlord agreed to the assignments to new tenants of the leasehold interests in the premises. By June 1970 the assignments were completed and the liquidator received consideration totalling £93,155 from the new tenants and paid to the landlord arrears of rent amounting to £14,689. Of that sum, £6,131 was attributable
to rent and services in respect of the period after the date B
of the liquidation. The special commissioners allowed an appeal by the company in liquidation against an assessment to corporation tax for the period April 1970 to April 1971 on the grounds that the sum of £6,131 was money paid wholly and exclusively for the purposes of enhancing an asset thereby qualifying as an allowable deduction under paragraph 4 (1) (*b*) of Schedule 6 to the Finance Act 1965 [1] and that it was not
a revenue payment expressly excluded by paragraph 5 (2) of C
that Schedule.

On appeal by the Crown:—

Held, allowing the appeal, that although the landlord could not have sued for the arrears but merely proved in the liquidation, the payment was nevertheless a payment of rent; that it was not apt to describe the payment of arrears of rent as expenditure for "enhancing the value of an asset"
but, even if the payment came within the description of D
"preserving" title to the assets in paragraph 4 (1) (*b*) of Schedule 6 to the Finance Act 1965, it was a payment that would have been deductible in computing the taxpayer company's profits and losses and, therefore, was expressly excluded from the allowable deductions in paragraph 4 (1) by paragraph 5 (2) of Schedule 6.

The following cases are referred to in the judgment: E

Downer Enterprises Ltd., In re [1974] 1 W.L.R. 1460; [1974] 2 All E.R. 1074.

Inland Revenue Commissioners v. *Land Securities Investment Trust Ltd.* [1969] 1 W.L.R. 604; [1969] 2 All E.R. 430; 45 T.C. 495, H.L.(E.).

Law Shipping Co. Ltd. v. *Inland Revenue Commissioners*, 1924 S.C. 74; 12 T.C. 621.

Littlewoods Mail Order Stores Ltd. v. *McGregor* [1969] 1 W.L.R. 1241; F
[1969] 3 All E.R. 855; 45 T.C. 519, C.A.

Silkstone and Dodworth Coal and Iron Co. Ltd. In re (1881) 17 Ch.D. 158.

The following additional cases were cited in argument:

Campbell v. *Inland Revenue Commissioners* [1970] A.C. 77; [1968] 3 W.L.R. 1025; [1968] 3 All E.R. 588; 45 T.C. 427, H.L.(E.).

Hyett v. *Lennard* [1940] 2 K.B. 180; [1940] 3 All E.R. 133; 23 T.C. 346. G

Inland Revenue Commissioners v. *Church Commissioners for England* [1975] 1 W.L.R. 1383; [1975] 3 All E.R. 614, C.A.

Inland Revenue Commissioners v. *Falkirk Iron Co. Ltd.*, 1933 S.C. 546; 17 T.C. 625.

Inland Revenue Commissioners v. *Richards' Executors* [1971] 1 W.L.R.
571; [1971] 1 All E.R. 785; 46 T.C. 626, H.L.(Sc.). H

Odeon Associated Theatres Ltd. v. *Jones* [1973] Ch. 288; [1972] 2 W.L.R. 331; [1972] 1 All E.R. 681; 48 T.C. 257, C.A.

CASE STATED by the Commissioners for the Special Purposes of the Income Tax.

[1] Finance Act 1965, Sch. 6, para. 4 (1): see post, p. 753C–E.
Para. 5: see post, p. 753E–H.

The taxpayer company, Computer Time International Ltd., was incorporated in February 1969 to carry on the business of hiring computer time. It rented premises at 214, Oxford Street, London, at an agreed total rental of £35,000 per annum. It went into voluntary liquidation in April 1970 at a time when it was in arrears with the payment of rent. The landlord consented to the liquidator assigning the premises to new tenants on condition that the arrears of rent were met in full. The liquidator paid a total of £14,689 to the landlord in respect of the arrears and on a time apportionment basis £6,131 of those arrears were attributable to a period after the liquidation date. The special commissioners allowed an appeal by the taxpayer company in liquidation against an assessment to corporation tax for the period April 1970 to April 1971 in the sum of £22,352 on the ground that the sum of £6,131 was money paid wholly and exclusively for the purposes of enhancing an asset thus qualifying as an allowable deduction under paragraph 4 (1) (*b*) of Schedule 6 to the Finance Act 1965, and that it was not a revenue payment that would have been excluded by paragraph 5 (2) of that schedule.

The Crown appealed.

The facts are stated in the judgment.

Peter Gibson for the Crown.

Peter Whiteman for the taxpayer company.

Cur. adv. vult.

December 18. FOX J. read the following judgment. This is an appeal by the Crown from a decision of the special commissioners that certain payments made by the taxpayer company in liquidation are deductible in computing chargeable gains arising on a disposal of certain leaseholds of the taxpayer company. The taxpayer company was incorporated in 1969 and carried on the business of hiring computer time. The business was not successful, and on April 24, 1970, the taxpayer company went into voluntary liquidation. Trading ceased on that date.

The taxpayer company was the tenant of premises in Oxford Street, London. These consisted of suites of rooms on the first and second floors. The taxpayer company had entered into occupation of the first floor suites, and agreed to pay rent of £16,000 a year, as from March 8, 1970, for a 21-year term. No formal lease had been granted before the taxpayer company went into liquidation, but it had, with the consent of the landlord, spent considerable sums in making alterations to the premises. The taxpayer company became the tenant of the second floor suites by an underlease of June 23, 1969, for a term of 21 years from March 25, 1969, at the yearly rent of £19,000 payable quarterly in advance with certain additional rents in respect of the costs of insurance, the heating of the premises and the provision of services. The underlease contained a covenant by the taxpayer company not to assign the premises without the consent in writing of the landlord. The underlease also reserved to the landlord a right of re-entry if the taxpayer company should enter into liquidation, whether voluntary or compulsory, except for the purpose of amalgamation or reconstruction, or if the rent should be in arrear for 21 days, whether legally demanded or not.

It was agreed between the Crown and the taxpayer company that, notwithstanding the absence of any formal lease of the first floor premises, for the purpose of this litigation no distinction should be made between the first and second floors as regards the taxpayer company's rights and liabilities. The case has proceeded on the basis that payments made by the taxpayer company in respect of the first floor fall to be treated for the purposes of this appeal in the same way as payments in respect of the second floor lease.

The statement of affairs of the taxpayer company, as at March 31, 1970, shows unsecured creditors with debts amounting to about £144,000 and an estimated surplus available for unsecured creditors of only about £53,000. Accordingly, there was a deficiency so far as unsecured creditors were concerned, and the landlord would therefore be entitled only to a dividend in the liquidation. The rents due (in advance) to the landlord on March 25, 1970, had not been paid when the taxpayer company went into liquidation.

On April 30, 1970, the liquidator wrote to the landlord and asked for a licence to assign the taxpayer company's premises on both the first and second floors. The liquidator expected to be able to obtain about £90,000 on a sale of these premises. The landlord replied on May 4, 1970, in the following terms:

> "Thank you for your letter dated the 30th ultimo and I must first point out that all negotiations for Computer Time's proposed tenancy of the first floor suites were subject to completion of a formal lease. They were allowed to enter the premises to carry out works entirely at their own risk, and subject to reinstatement of the premises, should the lease not be completed. Thus we contend that Computer Time International Ltd., have no interest whatsoever, in the first floor suites. Having said this however we must hasten to assure you that we do not seek to profit by the misfortunes of this company and intend only to avoid any loss to ourselves as a result thereof. We would thus be quite prepared to grant a lease of the first floor suites to a sound tenant nominated by you on exactly the same terms negotiated with Computer Time with of course the same rent commencement date. Similarly we would be prepared to agree an assignment of the second floor lease, to either the same party or another approved assignee, subject to all outstanding arrears being discharged. In this respect we have recently taken a licence from our lessors, permitting alterations to the second floor suites, by Computer Time for which we have paid costs and disbursements amounting to £45 15s. This amount, together with any of our own solicitors' costs for necessary licences, must be reimbursed."

In consequence of this letter it was agreed that an underlease of the first floor suites should be made direct by the landlord to the purchaser (Diners Club Ltd.) found by the liquidator at a rent of £16,000 a year for a term of 21 years from March 25, 1969. Diners Club Ltd. agreed to pay to the liquidator £22,000 on completion of the grant of the underlease to it. The landlord stipulated as a condition of the agreement with the liquidator that, under the provisions of the underlease, the rent must be payable as from March 8, 1970. The transaction was completed on July 3, 1970, when the liquidator received £22,000 from Diners Club Ltd. On the same date he paid to the landlord rent, insurance, heating and service charges amounting in all to £5,548-odd in respect of the period from March 8, 1970, to July 3, 1970.

A As regards the lease of the second floor suites, the liquidator negotiated an assignment to British Oxygen Ltd. of the taxpayer company's underlease and some fixtures and fittings for the price of £71,155. The landlord gave a written consent to this assignment. The transaction was completed on June 24, 1970, when the liquidator received the consideration of £71,155 and paid to the landlord rent, insurance, heating and service charges amounting to £9,140 19s. 4d., being the appor- B tioned part of the rent of £19,000 per year from March 25, 1970, plus the taxpayer company's share of insurance, heating and service charges.

Thus, the total paid by the liquidator to the landlord was £14,689 11s. 5d. Of this, the sum of £6,131 was attributable to rent and other charges for the period from April 24, 1970 (the date of liquidation), to the dates of the disposals of the first and second floor premises. The C taxpayer company claimed to deduct that sum of £6,131 in the computation of its capital gains arising out of the disposal of the underlease and its rights in the first floor premises.

The enactments which I have to construe are contained in Schedule 6 to the Finance Act 1965, and are as follows: paragraph 4 (1):

> "Subject to the following provisions of this Schedule, the sums D allowable as a deduction from the consideration in the computation under this Schedule of the gain accruing to a person on the disposal of an asset shall be restricted to— . . . (*b*) the amount of any expenditure wholly and exclusively incurred on the asset by him or on his behalf for the purpose of enhancing the value of the asset, being expenditure reflected in the state or nature of the asset at the time of the disposal, and any expenditure wholly and exclusively E incurred by him in establishing preserving or defending his title to, or to a right over, the asset, . . ."

Paragraph 5 of Schedule 6 is in the following terms:

> "(1) There shall be excluded from the sums allowable under the last foregoing paragraph as a deduction in the computation under this F Schedule any expenditure allowable as a deduction in computing the profits or gains or losses of a trade, profession or vocation for the purposes of income tax or allowable as a deduction in computing any other income or profits or gains or losses for the purposes of the Income Tax Acts and any expenditure which, although not so allowable as a deduction in computing any losses, would be so G allowable but for an insufficiency of income or profits or gains; and this sub-paragraph applies irrespective of whether effect is or would be given to the deduction in computing the amount of tax chargeable or by discharge of repayment of tax or in any other way. (2) Without prejudice to the provisions of sub-paragraph (1) above there shall be excluded from the sums allowable under the last foregoing H paragraph as a deduction in the computation under this Schedule any expenditure which, if the assets, or all the assets to which the computation relates, were, and had at all times been, held or used as part of the fixed capital of a trade the profits or gains of which were (irrespective of whether the person making the disposal is a company or not) chargeable to income tax would be allowable as a deduction in computing the profits or gains or losses of the trade for the purposes of income tax."

The commissioners held that the liquidator's purpose in agreeing with A the landlord to pay the arrears was to obtain the right to assign the lease freed from the threat of re-entry, and that this benefit enhanced the value of the lease. Accordingly, the commissioners held that the deduction claimed was allowable under paragraph 4 (1) (*b*) of Schedule 6. The question then was whether the exclusion provisions of paragraph 5 (2) of the Schedule applied. The commissioners held that they did not. The view of the commissioners was that the payment enhanced the B value of the lease and was a capital payment, and therefore was not disallowed by paragraph 5 (2).

The Crown made, in effect, the following submissions. First, that, although the landlord could not have sued for the arrears of rent (but could only prove in the liquidation and obtain a dividend), the payment of the £6,131 was expenditure which the liquidator could and did properly C pay as rent. Secondly, that rent is not aptly described as expenditure "wholly and exclusively incurred . . . for the purpose of enhancing the value of the asset" or, in the circumstances of this case, as expenditure "wholly and exclusively incurred . . . in establishing preserving or defending" the taxpayer company's "title to, or to a right over, the asset." Thirdly, if the second submission was wrong, the Crown said that the payment, being a payment of rent, would on the hypothesis D stated in paragraph 5 (2) of Schedule 6 be allowable as a deduction in computing the profits of the hypothetical trade referred to in paragraph 5 (2), and was therefore not allowable in computing the gain on the disposal of the assets in the present case.

As regards the first of the Crown's submissions, the rent in question (I deal with the second floor lease) was payable in advance and was E due prior to the commencement of the liquidation. Accordingly, the Crown accepted at any rate in this court, that the landlord could not, as of right, recover the full amount of the arrears but could only prove in the liquidation and obtain a dividend. In particular, the Crown accepted that the line of cases of which *In re Downer Enterprises Ltd.* [1974] 1 W.L.R. 1460 is an example, and under which, if a company for its own purposes and with a view to the realisation of its property to F better advantage remains in possession of the property, the court in its discretion would direct that the landlord be paid rent as an expense of the administration, applies only to rent becoming due after the commencement of the liquidation. The Crown said, however, that the payment made to the landlord was properly made, and that it was made as rent. I think that is correct. The lease was a valuable asset; it was plainly G the duty of the liquidator to realise it to the best advantage, and he obviously retained it for that purpose. If the risk of re-entry and forfeiture for non-payment of rent was to be removed, the arrears had to be paid in full, as indeed the commissioners found. It seems to me, therefore, that it must have been perfectly proper for the liquidator to agree to pay the arrears in order to realise the asset. If he had felt it H necessary to apply to the court on the matter he would, I apprehend, certainly have obtained leave to make the payment.

Further, in my view, the payment was a payment of rent. What the landlord required was payment of "all outstanding arrears": see the landlord's letter of May 4, 1970. The computations of the actual amounts to be paid are by reference to "rent": see the letters of June 5, 1970, and June 24, 1970. Service, heating and insurance charges are also

A specifically referred to, but under the lease they are payable as additional
rent. It seems to me that what was being discharged was a liability
arising from the covenant in the lease to pay rent (including additional
rents). It is true that the full operation of that covenant was restricted
in consequence of the liquidation, but the covenant had not ceased to
exist. If the landlord had sought leave to commence proceedings for
forfeiture for non-payment of rent, it seems to me that such leave would
B have been given and the taxpayer company would only have obtained
relief against forfeiture upon terms of paying the arrears in full. The
fact that the taxpayer company would be obliged to pay in full derives
from the basic obligation in the lease to pay rent. Nothing was being
asked for in respect of arrears over and above that obligation. The
obligation was not discharged because of the liquidation, but there were
C restrictions on enforcing it. In giving relief in forfeiture proceedings the
court would, it seems to me, recognise the obligation and require it to be
discharged in full if the taxpayer company wanted to keep the lease in
order to realise its value. The liquidator, in agreeing to pay the rent in
full, was merely acknowledging that situation. The landlord was in a
rather similar position to the landlords in *In re Silkstone and Dodworth
Coal and Iron Co. Ltd.* (1881) 17 Ch.D. 158. The landlord did not merely
D have a money claim against the taxpayer company: he had, in the
language of Fry J., at p. 161, "the power to render less valuable an
asset of the company." The *Silkstone* case shows that such a landlord
may be in a privileged position as regards payment of rent.

I turn to the construction of paragraph 4 (1) (*b*) of Schedule 6. I do
not think that it is an apt use of language to describe the payment of the
E arrears as expenditure incurred for the purpose of "enhancing the value
of the asset." No doubt in order to realise the full market value of the
lease the taxpayer company had to pay off the arrears of rent, but I do
not think that such a payment is accurately described as being made for
the purpose of "enhancing" the value of the asset. It is simply a
liability inherent in the asset itself, and is one of the factors which has
to be taken into account in determining what the value of the asset is.

F In my view, however, it is probably correct that the payment was
incurred in "preserving" the taxpayer company's title to the asset. It is
true that there was no immediate threat of forfeiture proceedings by the
landlord, but by reason of the arrears the landlord was in a position to
obtain leave to take proceedings, and the payment removed that possi-
bility and could be said to preserve the title. I will assume that that is so
G and that accordingly the taxpayer company could bring itself within the
provisions of paragraph 4 (1) (*b*) of Schedule 6.

There remains the question of the effect of paragraph 5 (2) of
Schedule 6. That provision requires me to assume: (i) that the lease
was and had at all times been held or used as part of the fixed capital
of a trade, and (ii) that the profits and gains of such trade were (irrespec-
tive of whether the person making the disposal is a company or not)
H chargeable to income tax. The question is whether, if assumptions (i) and
(ii) are made, the expenditure "would be allowable as a deduction in
computing the profits or gains . . . of the trade for the purposes of
income tax."

If a lease is part of the fixed capital of a trade, a periodic payment of
rent on the due date in accordance with the covenants in the lease is,
I think, clearly allowable as a deduction in computing the profits or

gains of the trade for tax purposes. The position, it seems to me, would not be different if the trader got into arrears with his rent and then, in order either to prevent forfeiture proceedings or as a term upon which relief in forfeiture proceedings is granted, paid off the arrears. The payment is no doubt made in order to protect his capital asset, but it is still simply a payment of rent and, it seems to me, deductible expenditure in computing the profits of the trade.

In the present case the situation is more complex. The payment was made with a view to selling the asset and in circumstances when the full amount of the arrears could not have been recovered from the taxpayer company by action on the covenant. The taxpayer company contended that where a payment which would otherwise be regarded as a revenue payment is effectively the purchase price of a capital interest, that payment may itself acquire a capital quality and, therefore, would not be deductible in a trading computation. I was referred to *Littlewoods Mail Order Stores Ltd.* v. *McGregor* [1969] 1 W.L.R. 1241 and *Inland Revenue Commissioners* v. *Land Securities Investment Trust Ltd.* [1969] 1 W.L.R. 604. These, however, were cases of the acquisition of a new capital asset. Here, no new asset was acquired by the taxpayer company. Throughout, until sale, the taxpayer company owned the same lease. That lease was subject to an obligation to pay rent. In the particular circumstances, the landlord was able to ensure, notwithstanding the liquidation, that the covenant was complied with. It does not seem to me that these circumstances turn the payment into a capital payment. It was said that there was here a very close connection between the payment of the arrears and the acquisition of capital sums from Diners Club Ltd. and British Oxygen Ltd. That is quite true, but the capital sums were merely the proceeds of sale of the existing capital asset—the lease.

I was also referred to *Law Shipping Co. Ltd.* v. *Inland Revenue Commissioners,* 1924 S.C. 74. Mr. Whiteman, for the taxpayer company, said that this case is another example of what appears to be revenue expenditure being in fact capital. He sought, I think, to assimilate the rent paid by the taxpayer company here to the repairs paid for in the *Law Shipping Co.* case. The decision in the *Law Shipping Co.* case (in which a company purchased a ship on which repairs were long overdue) was that only the cost of repairs attributable to the period of ownership of the purchasing company was deductible. But in that case the purchaser was a distinct entity from the company which had allowed the ship to get into disrepair. In the present case, the relevant asset was owned by the taxpayer company throughout.

I am required by the statute to assume that the lease was part of the fixed capital of a trade. As I have indicated above, it seems to me that the payment made by the liquidator was a payment of rent in respect of that lease. Prima facie it seems to me that a payment of rent in respect of a lease which is part of the fixed capital of a trade is allowable as a deduction in computing the profits of that trade. The only circumstances which would lead to a different conclusion here are those which I have already mentioned. First, the landlord could not have recovered the arrears by action. But that does not, it seems to me, alter the fact that what is paid is rent. The necessity to pay it derived from the obligation in the lease to pay rent. If a company covenants to pay rent and actually pays it in circumstances when the covenant has not ceased to exist (though there may be restrictions on its enforcement), I do not

A think that the character of the payment is other than a payment of rent. Secondly, the payment was made with a view to selling the lease. But, by virtue of the statutory hypothesis in paragraph 5 (2), the lease at the time it was sold was part of the fixed capital of a trade. What the liquidator undertook, therefore, was to pay arrears of rent of property forming part of the fixed capital of a trade. The consequent payment was, in my view, a payment of rent in respect of the fixed asset of a
B trade and deductible in computing the profits or gains.

Mr. Whiteman contended that the purpose of the concluding words of paragraph 5 (2) are to ensure that a taxpayer would get a deduction either for capital gains tax purposes or income tax purposes, but not both. That intention would be frustrated in circumstances such as the present if the taxpayer was not entitled to the deduction now claimed,
C since as there were no trading receipts there would be no question of any deduction of the payment for tax purposes. I do not think that is correct. Where one is dealing with a non-trader, there may be deductions which are not available either for capital gains tax purposes or for income tax purposes.

In the circumstances, I take the view that this payment falls within the exclusion specified in paragraph 5 (2) of Schedule 6, and is therefore
D not allowable as a deduction on the disposal. Accordingly, I allow the appeal.

Appeal allowed.
By agreement, the Crown to pay taxpayer company's costs.

E Solicitors: *Solicitor of Inland Revenue; Kingsley, Napley & Co.*

[CHANCERY DIVISION]

F

* *In re* DYNAMICS CORPORATION OF AMERICA (IN LIQUIDATION)

[No. 001 753 of 1972]

1975 Dec. 17, 18 **Oliver J.**

G

Company—Winding up—Foreign corporation—Foreign and English debts—Liquidation abroad—Subsequent compulsory winding up in England—Scheme of arrangement with foreign creditors abroad entitling them to dividends in English liquidation—Date for conversion of claims into sterling

The company which was incorporated in New York on
H March 31, 1924, carried on business both in the U.S.A. and the U.K. and had creditors in both countries. In August 1972 a petition for its winding up was presented in the courts of New York. On October 2, 1972, a creditor of the company presented a petition in this country, under section 399 of the Companies Act 1948, for its compulsory winding up. An order was made on that petition on May 23, 1973. Under the Federal Bankruptcy Code, which contained a provision broadly similar to section 206 of the Act of 1948, a scheme of arrangement was entered into with creditors and on November 29, 1974, was

approved in New York. The scheme provided for each creditor to be paid 28·5 per cent. of his debt, to receive two shares of the common stock of the company, and, in addition, such dividend as might be paid in the English liquidation. A

On a summons by the English liquidator to determine, before any arrangements were made with the dollar creditors, the date or dates on which the company's debts and other liabilities should be converted into sterling:—

Held, that in a winding up the court sought to ascertain the liabilities of the company at a particular date and to distribute the available assets as at that date pro rata according to the amounts of those liabilities; that in practice the process could not be immediate but notionally it was, although subsequent events could be taken into account in quantifying the liabilities at the relevant date; that, in the context of a liquidation the relevant date to ascertain the amount of liability was the notional date of discharge of that liability and that date had to be the same for all creditors and was "the date of payment" for the purposes of any judgment which had been entered for the sterling equivalent at the date of payment of a sum expressed in foreign currency (post, pp. 774G—775A), and that, accordingly, the date of the winding up order, namely, May 23, 1973, was the date at which the conversion should be made (post, p. 775E). B C

Dicta of Lord Wilberforce and Lord Cross of Chelsea in *Miliangos* v. *George Frank (Textiles) Ltd.* [1976] A.C. 443, 467, 497, H.L.(E.) not applied. D

The following cases are referred to in the judgment:

British American Continental Bank Ltd., In re [1922] 2 Ch. 575, P. O. Lawrence J. and C.A.

British Eagle International Airlines Ltd. v. *Compagnie Nationale Air France* [1975] 1 W.L.R. 758; [1975] 2 All E.R. 390, H.L.(E.). E

City Equitable Fire Insurance Co. Ltd. (*No.* 2), *In re* [1930] 2 Ch. 293, C.A.

City Life Assurance Co. Ltd., In re [1926] Ch. 191, C.A.

Daintrey, In re [1900] 1 Q.B. 546, C.A.

Davidson (Charles R.) and Co. v. *M'Robb* [1918] A.C. 304, H.L.(Sc.).

Dodds, In re (1890) 25 Q.B.D. 529. F

Ellis and Co.'s Trustee v. *Dixon-Johnson* [1924] 1 Ch. 342.

European Assurance Society Arbitration, In re (*Wallberg's* case) (1872) 17 S.J. 69.

Holloway v. *York* (1877) 25 W.R. 627.

Humber Ironwork and Shipbuilding Co., In re (1869) L.R. 4 Ch.App. 643.

Institute of Patent Agents v. *Lockwood* [1894] A.C. 347, H.L.(Sc.). G

Law Car and General Insurance Corporation, In re [1913] 2 Ch. 103, C.A.

Miliangos v. *George Frank (Textiles) Ltd.* [1976] A.C. 443; [1975] 3 W.L.R. 758; [1975] 3 All E.R. 801, H.L.(E.).

National Benefit Assurance Co. Ltd., In re [1924] 2 Ch. 339.

Northern Counties of England Fire Insurance Co., In re (1880) 17 Ch.D. 337.

Parana Plantations Ltd., In re [1946] 2 All E.R. 214, C.A. H

Russian Commercial and Industrial Bank, In re [1955] Ch. 148; [1955] 2 W.L.R. 62; [1955] 1 All E.R. 75.

Savin, In re (1872) L.R. 7 Ch.App. 760.

Schorsch Meier G.m.b.H. v. *Hennin* [1975] Q.B. 416; [1974] 3 W.L.R. 823; [1975] 1 All E.R. 152, C.A.

United Railways of Havana and Regla Warehouses Ltd., In re [1961] A.C. 1007; [1960] 2 W.L.R. 969; [1960] 2 All E.R. 332, H.L.(E.).

A The following additional cases were cited in argument:

Bates, Ex parte (1879) 11 Ch.D. 914, C.A.
Browne (A Bankrupt), In re [1960] 1 W.L.R. 692; [1960] 2 All E.R. 625.
Cummings v. *London Bullion Co. Ltd.* [1952] 1 K.B. 327; [1952] 1 All E.R. 383, C.A.
Dawson, In re (1966) 84 W.N.(N.S.W.) 339.
Hawkins, decd., In re [1972] Ch. 714; [1972] 3 W.L.R. 265; [1972] 3
B All E.R. 386.
Montreal Trust Co. v. *Abitibi Power & Paper Co.* [1944] 3 D.L.R. 505.
Parana Plantations Ltd., In re [1948] 1 All E.R. 742.
Ruffle, Ex parte (1873) L.R. 8 Ch.App. 997.
Searle, Hoare and Co., In re [1924] 2 Ch. 325.

SUMMONS

C On September 9, 1975, the liquidator in England of the company, Dynamics Corporation of America, issued a summons against the respondents, Westinghouse Electric Corporation, of Park Avenue, New York City, U.S.A., a creditor of the company in respect of whose debt the monetary unit of account was the U.S. dollar, and Electronic Visuals Ltd., of High Road, Byfleet, Surrey, a creditor of the company in respect
D of whose debt the monetary unit of account was the pound sterling. The summons, as amended, sought to determine whether the liquidator should convert into sterling (a) debts arising from contracts, (b) liabilities for damages for breach of contract, and (c) any other liabilities which were provable and were payable in a monetary unit of account other than the pound sterling, at the rate of exchange prevailing on (i) the date such debt became due, such breach occurred or such other liability
E accrued due, or (ii) the date of the commencement of the winding up of the company, or (iii) the date of the order to wind up the company, or (iv) the date on which the proof for each such debt or liability was admitted, or (v) the date or dates on which distributions were to be made to creditors.

The facts are stated in the judgment.

F

Andrew Morritt for the liquidator.
S. D. Graham for the first respondents.
Robin Potts for the second respondents.

OLIVER J. The Dynamics Corporation of America is a company which was incorporated in the State of New York on March 31, 1924,
G and has at all material times carried on business both in the U.S.A. and in the U.K. Up to 1969 it conducted its business in the United Kingdom through a subsidiary company, Dynamco Ltd., but in that year that company ceased to trade and thereafter the company itself traded here, through its United Kingdom division. It thus acquired dollar creditors in the United States and sterling creditors in this country. The company
H got into difficulties and in August 1972 a petition was issued in the courts of New York under which a scheme of arrangement was proposed with creditors pursuant to the Federal Bankruptcy Code which contains a provision broadly similar to section 206 of the Companies Act 1948. On October 2, 1972, a creditor of the company issued a petition in this court under section 399 of that Act, for the compulsory winding up of the company as an unregistered company, and an order was duly made on that petition on May 23, 1973.

The arrangement proposed was approved in New York on November 29, 1974. It is, I think, unnecessary for present purposes to consider its detailed provisions, but, in broad outline, each creditor was to be paid 28·5 per cent. of his debt, to receive two shares of the common stock of the company, and to receive in addition such dividend as might be paid in the English liquidation. The contemplation then was that there would also be a scheme of arrangement in the liquidation here, but that has not yet been formulated—and, indeed, cannot yet be formulated—because certain questions have arisen, and, in particular, the question which I am called upon to answer on the present summons which relates to the date at which the sterling value of claims in the liquidation is to be ascertained. Creditors of the company outside the United Kingdom, in respect of whose debts the monetary unit of account is the U.S. dollar, amount to $48,875,855, and, for convenience, I will refer to those creditors by the shorthand description of "dollar creditors." Creditors in respect of whose debts the monetary unit of account is the pound sterling amount to approximately £8·9 m. The amount of the available assets in the United Kingdom is not capable of being ascertained with complete accuracy at the moment. It depends, I am told, upon the outcome of certain litigation at present in progress, but it is thought to be between £400,000 and £900,000.

At the date when the petition was presented in this country the rate of exchange was $2.42 to the pound; at the date of the winding up order it was $2.56 to the pound. It has since fluctuated widely. For instance, in February 1974 it was $2.27; in September 1974 it was $2.31; in March this year it was $2.43, and at the beginning of last month it was $2.07. It thus makes a critical difference, not only to the different classes of creditors (dollar or United Kingdom) but also, on one view, to the individual dollar creditors, what date is selected as that upon which, for the purposes of distribution of the United Kingdom assets, the dollar creditors' claims are to be treated as converted into sterling, the money of the forum. For instance, on the basis of the rule thought to represent the law, until the decision of the Court of Appeal in *Schorsch Meier G.m.b.H.* v. *Hennin* [1975] Q.B. 416 namely, that the relevant date for conversion was the date when payment fell due—often referred to as "the breach date"—and on the assumption of a divisible fund of £900,000, the dollar creditors would receive 67·67 per cent. of the fund and the United Kingdom creditors 32·22 per cent. If, on the other hand, the relevant date is the date of winding up order, the dollar creditors would do better. They would receive 68·09 per cent. and the United Kingdom creditors 31·91 per cent. If, again, the date to be taken is the date when the liquidator admits the proofs of creditors, then assuming for the sake of example that he did this in the latter part of September 1976, when the rate of exchange was $2.06, the dollar creditors would collect 73·04 per cent. and the United Kingdom creditors 26·96 per cent. The liquidator has not yet adjudicated on claims of the dollar creditors, and, indeed, one of the questions raised by this summons (which I am not asked to decide at the moment) is whether he needs to do so having regard to the fact that these claims have been adjudicated and admitted in the New York proceedings.

By this summons, as originally framed, the first question asked (and which was raised as a result of the *Schorsch Meier* case) was whether debts or liabilities the monetary unit of account of which was a currency other than sterling ought to be converted as at the breach date, the date of the winding up order, the date of distribution, or some other date. In the light, however, of the subsequent case, *Miliangos* v. *George Frank* (*Textiles*) *Ltd.* [1976] A.C. 443, that question has been amended to distinguish between (a) debts arising under contracts, (b) liabilities for damages for breach of contract (and in each case distinguishing between contracts the proper law of which is English and other contracts) and (c) other liabilities. The range of available dates has also had to be expanded to include the date of the commencement of the winding up and the date on which each proof of debt is admitted.

At present there is no evidence that there are any claims of which the monetary unit of account is a currency other than sterling, which do not fall within the first category raised by the amended summons, that is to say debts arising under contracts the proper law of which is of a country other than the United Kingdom, and in what follows I confine my remarks to that category.

Until recently this problem would not have given rise to very much difficulty. It is, of course, necessary in a liquidation, if a proportionate distribution among creditors of the available assets is to be achieved, that the claims of all creditors be reduced at some stage to a common unit of account, and the point of time at which that should be done had been concluded by a series of cases which established that the conversion must be made at the date when payment became due, so that the sterling amount of any claim was ascertainable either before, or at latest upon, the commencement of the winding up; for instance, see *In re Russian Commercial and Industrial Bank* [1955] Ch. 148. This may not have been a rule which operated fairly in all cases but at least it had the merit of being relatively easy to apply. The wind of change, however, bloweth where it listeth and the recent decisions of the Court of Appeal in *Schorsch Meier G.m.b.H.* v. *Hennin* [1975] Q.B. 416, which I have referred to already, and of the House of Lords in *Miliangos* v. *George Frank* (*Textiles*) *Ltd.* [1976] A.C. 443, have established a different rule, namely, that at least in the cases of a debt payable in a foreign currency, as opposed to damages for breach of contract or trust, judgment may be given by an English court in the appropriate currency and that, for the purpose of enforcement, the conversion is to be made at the date of the swearing of the affidavit leading to execution.

What, now, is the position when such a debt, in respect of which no judgment has been obtained, or, indeed, of such a debt where judgment has been obtained but has not yet been enforced, is owed by a company which is wound up in England? I take it to be well established that the purpose of both the Bankruptcy Act 1914 and its predecessors, and of the winding up provisions of the Companies Act 1948 and its predecessors, was to ascertain the liabilities of the bankrupt or of the company, as the case may be, as at the date of the bankruptcy or liquidation, and to secure the division of the debtor's property among the claimants pro rata according to the value of their claims at that date. It is, I apprehend, for this reason that the Limitation Act 1939 ceases to run at the date of the winding up order, and that a creditor claiming in respect of an interest bearing debt due and payable before the bankruptcy or winding up, cannot, in general, claim interest beyond the date of the bankruptcy or winding up.

In the case of bankruptcy the rule is stated in *In re Savin* (1872) L.R. 7 Ch.App. 760, in two short passages from the judgment of James L.J. where he says, at p. 764:

> "There is a general rule in bankruptcy—whether a right and a reasonable rule or not—that there is to be no proof in bankruptcy for interest subsequent to the bankruptcy . . . I believe, however, that if the question now arose for the first time I should agree with the rule, seeing that the theory in bankruptcy is to stop all things at the date of the bankruptcy, and to divide the wreck of the man's property as it stood at that time."

Exactly the same principle was expressed with regard to the liquidation of a company by Selwyn L.J. in *In re Humber Ironworks and Shipbuilding Co.* (1869) L.R. 4 Ch.App. 643. The whole passage is, I think, worth reading because it sets out in a simple, and, at the same time, a compelling way the theory behind the rule, that is to say that the liquidation and the distribution are to be treated as notionally simultaneous. Selwyn L.J. says, at p. 646:

> "There remains the question when the estate is insolvent. Now, it has been very properly admitted, on the part of the appellant, that there can be no question as to any interest due at the time of the winding up. Suppose, at the date of the winding up there is a creditor having £1,000 due to him for principal, and £100 due to him for interest. He would prove for £1,100; and if a dividend of 10s. in the pound were declared, he would be entitled to receive £550, because his interest due at the date of the winding up is just as much a debt as the principal. Suppose, at the same time, there was a creditor with a debt of £1,000, which, like that of the respondents in the present case, carried interest but had no interest due upon it at the time, and a dividend of 10s. in the pound were paid, he would, in my judgment, receive £500. That would be obviously the case if the court were able to do what it would wish to do, namely, to realize all the assets immediately, and distribute them amongst the creditors. It is very difficult to conceive a case in which the assets of a company could be thus immediately realized and divided; but suppose they had a simple account at a bank, which could be paid the next day, that would be the course of proceeding. Justice, I think, requires that that course of proceeding should be followed, and that no person should be prejudiced by the accidental delay which, in consequence of the necessary forms and proceedings of the court, actually takes place in realizing the assets; but that, in the case of an insolvent estate, all the money being realized as speedily as possible, should be applied equally and rateably in payment of the debts as they existed at the date of the winding up. I, therefore, think that nothing should be allowed for interest after that date. . . . I think the tree must lie as it falls; that it must be ascertained what are the debts as they exist at the date of the winding up, and that all dividends in the case of an insolvent estate must be declared in respect of the debts so ascertained. Of course, it will be understood that we are laying down this rule as applicable to all cases under the recent Act where creditors' actions are stayed."

A Giffard L.J. says much the same thing, at p. 647:

> "As to the rule which my learned brother has laid down, it is the rule in bankruptcy. That rule was, as has been said, judge-made law; but it was made after great consideration, and no doubt because it works with equality and fairness between the parties; and if we are to consider convenience, it is quite clear that, where an estate is insolvent, convenience is in favour of stopping all the
> B computations at the date of the winding up. For these reasons I am of opinion that dividends ought to be paid on the debts as they stand at the date of the winding up; for when the estate is insolvent this rule distributes the assets in the fairest way; . . ."

My attention has been drawn also to *In re European Assurance*
C *Society Arbitration* (*Wallberg's* case) (1872) 17 S.J. 69 where Lord Westbury, talking about the valuation of debts in a winding up, says, at p. 70:

> ". . . then where does the necessity for this valuation arise? It arises immediately on the property of the company, the debtor, being directed to be equally distributed. But when is the property of the debtor company subjected to equal distribution among the
> D creditors? At the date of the winding up order. Then, and not till then, is the company divested of its property. In effect, the property is handed over to the official liquidator to be broken up and distributed in proportionate parts among the creditor claimants who are entitled. Well, then, it follows immediately that the valuation must be made when the necessity for a valuation arises. The
> E necessity arises, as I have said, when the order to wind up is made; and that, therefore, becomes necessarily the date of valuation."

And, having referred to section 158 of the Companies Act 1862, which is broadly equivalent to section 316 of the Companies Act 1949, he says:

> "Well, but the right to be admitted as a creditor must be considered as arising immediately that the property is handed over to the
> F creditors, and no longer remains in the hands or under the administration of the debtor company. That is again at the date of the order to wind up."

More recently this was expressed in the well known case, *In re British American Continental Bank Ltd.* [1922] 2 Ch. 575, first of all by P. O. Lawrence J. where he says, at p. 582:

> G "In a winding up, this court has to ascertain all the liabilities of the company being wound up for the purpose of effecting the proper distribution of its assets amongst its creditors. A date has necessarily to be fixed on which all debts and other liabilities are to be treated as definitely ascertained, both for the purpose of placing all creditors on an equality and for the purpose of properly
> H conducting the winding up of the affairs of the company. According to the rules and practice now prevailing, the date so fixed is the date of the winding up order. One effect of fixing that date is to compel those creditors whose claims do not consist of debts or of liquidated demands ascertained and payable before that date to estimate and assess the amounts which they claim to be due to them on that date. Another effect of fixing that date is that when a claim is disputed this court will decide the dispute as though it

> were being determined on the day when the winding up order was A
> made. Accordingly, in a case where a creditor has an unsatisfied
> claim against the company for damages for breach of contract, and
> the amount of those damages is in dispute, this court will ascertain
> the correct amount as if it were sitting on the day of the winding up
> order and was then trying an action for damages for the breach
> of that contract."

And Warrington L.J., having referred to the argument of the claimants B
in the case, said, at p. 587:

> "They also rely on an argument of the same nature upon the form
> of proof, which is as follows: That the company was at the date
> of the order for the winding up of the same—namely, on such and
> such a day—justly and truly indebted to the claimants in so many C
> pounds, shillings and pence. But in my opinion all that these pro-
> visions, the section of the Act and the form of proof and so forth,
> lay down is that if you have to ascertain, and you must do it
> actually after the date of the winding up, when you ascertain you
> are treated as having dealt with the matter on the date of the winding
> up, but no more than that;"

This finds, I think, expression in section 257 (1) of the Act of 1948, which D
provides "As soon as may be after making a winding up order,
the court . . . shall cause the assets of the company to be collected, and
applied in discharge of its liabilities: . . ." The provisions of both the
Companies Act 1948 and the Bankruptcy Act 1914 with regard to the
submission of proof are I think all directed to this end, that is to say,
to ascertaining what, at the relevant date, were the liabilities of the E
company or the bankrupt as the case may be, in order to determine what
at that date is the denominator in the fraction of which the numerator
will be the net realised value of the property available for distribution.
It is only in this way that a rateable, or pari passu, distribution of the
available property can be achieved, and it is, as I see it, axiomatic that
the claims of the creditors amongst whom the division is to be effected F
must all be crystallised at the same date, even though the actual ascer-
tainment may not be possible at that date, for otherwise one is not
comparing like with like; and, indeed, this, as it seems to me, is
implicit in the provisions of section 302 of the Act of 1948, which
provides: "Subject to the provisions of this Act as to preferential pay-
ments, the property of a company shall, on its winding up, be applied
in satisfaction of its liabilities pari passu, . . ." In the notes to this G
section in *Buckley on the Companies Acts*, 13th ed., (1957), p. 601 it is
said:

> "Distribution of assets pari passu is a prominent feature in the
> scheme of the Act; in sections which deal with administration of
> the assets, no construction which would lead to a distribution other
> than pari passu has ever been entertained with favour," H

and this has received a very striking reiteration recently in the speech of
Lord Cross in *British Eagle International Airlines Ltd.* v. *Compagnie
Nationale Air France* [1975] 1 W.L.R. 758.

Now the moment that you start introducing into this scheme of things
different dates for the ascertainment of the value of the claims of
individual creditors or classes of creditors, you introduce, as it seems to

A me, potential inequalities and thus the possibility of that which the Act impliedly prohibits, that is to say a distribution of the property of the company otherwise than pari passu. Not only section 302 itself but the winding up rules and the statutory forms referentially incorporated in them point entirely the other way, and these rules, it must be remembered, are produced under statutory authority and their validity is not open to question: see *Institute of Patent Agents* v. *Lock-*
B *wood* [1894] A.C. 347, and they were clearly framed on the basis that the appropriate date at which claims fell to be ascertained for the purposes of a liquidation was the date of the winding up order. That, indeed, had been established for many years. I have already referred to *Wallberg's* case, 17 S.J. 69, and one can refer also to *In re Law Car and General Insurance Corporation* [1913] 2 Ch. 103, 135, and the judgment
C of Lord Greene M.R. in *In re Parana Plantations Ltd.* [1946] 2 All E.R. 214, 218, 219.

Rule 3 of the Companies (Winding-up) Rules 1949 provides that the forms in the appendix shall be used where applicable, and, where they are not applicable, forms of the like character with such variations as circumstances may require shall be used. Rule 91 imposes on a creditor the obligation in a winding up by the court to prove his debt, and rule
D 92 specifies the mode of proof, that is to say by an affidavit verifying the debt. The form of affidavit is Form 59 in the appendix, and it provides, as one would expect, for proof of the sterling amount. The creditor or an authorised deponent must swear

> "That the above-named company was, at the date of the order for winding up the same, viz:—the day of 19 , and still is
E justly and truly indebted to in the sum of £ . . ."

So the statutory form indicates that the proof must be for a sterling sum and that it must relate to the quantum of indebtedness in sterling at the date of the winding up order.

In the light of the decline in the value of sterling as against the
F U.S. dollar it is in the interests of those creditors who assert claims payable in U.S. dollars to argue for a conversion at the latest possible date, and Mr. Graham, on their behalf, has forcefully argued that this not only has the support of the authority of the House of Lords in *Miliangos* v. *George Frank* (*Textiles*) *Ltd.* [1976] A.C. 443 but that it is inconsistent neither with the scheme of the provisions of the Act of 1948 relating to liquidations nor with the rules made under them.
G Logically, he says, the date of distribution is the appropriate date having regard to the recent decision of the House of Lords, *Miliangos* v. *George Frank* (*Textiles*) *Ltd.*, but the law has to be practical and the liquidator must know before he distributes the amounts which he is going to have to pay. This points to the date upon which the proof of the creditor is admitted as the appropriate date, and that is the date which is indicated
H in at least some of the speeches of their Lordships in *Miliangos* v. *George Frank* (*Textiles*) *Ltd.* There is, Mr. Graham submits, no real difficulty about proving a debt of this sort. Of course it has to be expressed in sterling, because that is the unit of account, and the unit of payment in the liquidation, but there is nothing in the Act or the rules which compulsively points to an ascertainment either at the date of the winding up order, or, indeed, the date when the proof is lodged. Rule 3 of the Rules of 1949, itself, contemplates that there may be circumstances in

which the statutory forms may not be wholly appropriate and may have A
to be adapted, and the position created by the *Miliangos* case can be met, says Mr. Graham, within the framework of the Act and of the rules by the statutory forms as they now stand. He refers me to section 316 of the Act, which is in these terms:

> "In every winding up (subject, in the case of insolvent companies, to the application in accordance with the provisions of this Act of B
> the law of bankruptcy) all debts payable on a contingency, and all claims against the company, present or future, certain or contingent, ascertained or sounding only in damages, shall be admissible to proof against the company, a just estimate being made, so far as possible, of the value of such debts or claims as may be subject to any contingency or sound only in damages, or for some other reason do not bear a certain value," C

and there is a similar provision in section 30 (4) of the Bankruptcy Act 1914 as regards the estimation of provable debts in the bankruptcy.

The claims of the dollar creditors, says Mr. Graham, are claims which do not bear a certain value because they are claims the sterling value of which is, by reason of the principles now enshrined in the D
Miliangos decision, made to depend upon the applicable rate of exchange at some future date. The creditor, therefore, in submitting his proof, has to make the best estimate of what the rate is likely to be at some future time—at which he can only guess—and he must submit his proof for an amount ascertained by the application to his debt of that rate. It will then be for the liquidator to make an adjustment according to the rate applicable at the date when he comes to consider the E
rejection or admission of the proof. An alternative approach might, I suppose, be to estimate the claim on the basis of the rate prevailing at the date of the winding up order, and for subsequent adjustments to be made. It is the trustee's duty, Mr. Graham points out, in relation to the bankruptcy provisions, to make the estimate, and he says "Well, there is really no difficulty about making any adjustments to reflect what is F
the actuality at the date when the proof comes to be adjudicated"; and he points out that rules 109 and 110 of the Rules of 1949, and the equivalent bankruptcy rules, 24 and 25, give power to expunge or vary proofs. Thus, for instance, in the analogous case of the contingent claim there is no difficulty about adjusting a proof where, for instance, the contingency occurs after the date of the proof; subject only to this, that prior dividends cannot be disturbed. He refers me to *In re Northern* G
Counties of England Fire Insurance Co. (1880) 17 Ch.D. 337, and *Ellis and Co.'s Trustee* v. *Dixon-Johnson* [1924] 1 Ch. 342, 357.

There seems to me to be a number of difficulties about this approach. In the first place, the claims of the dollar creditors are clearly not contingent claims, nor do they sound only in damages. But equally, as it seems to me, they are not claims which for any other reason do not H
bear a certain value. There is nothing in the least bit uncertain about a straight claim for, say, $1,000. This is really the crux of Mr. Graham's submission. He says that the claim is not simply a claim for $1,000. The creditor's right at the date of the winding up order is, as a result of *Miliangos* v. *George Frank* (*Textiles*) *Ltd.* [1976] A.C. 443, a right to receive $1,000, or whatever is the sterling equivalent of $1,000 when payment is received. A liquidation is not a payment. Therefore,

A what falls to be valued is not simply $1,000 but the right to receive the sterling equivalent of $1,000 at the time in the future when payment is received, and he quotes, among other cases, *In re Dodds* (1890) 25 Q.B.D. 529, to show that the valuation should take place at the latest possible moment. I do not feel that I can accept this, principally because it seems to me to be a misreading of the *Miliangos* decision. That case was not concerned, I think, with defining specifically the B creditor's substantive rights under his contract, which were not in doubt in fact, but with the procedural question of how, by an English judgment, effect could be given to the rights as nearly as possible, and the concept of the right as a right to damages was decisively rejected. But equally it seems to me implicit in the decision that the right is not treated as a right to $1,000 or its sterling equivalent at the date of C payment; that is merely the form of a judgment which the English court will deliver if called upon to give effect to the right. The right is the right to receive $1,000, and Lord Wilberforce, particularly, was at pains to point out that the creditor is not concerned with sterling fluctuations or with the value of sterling. What he wants is the sum expressed in the foreign currency, and when the winding up order is made the creditor has this right, and there is nothing, as I see it, uncertain about D it, and it is that right which, so it seems to me, is the right which falls to be valued.

Secondly, even if these rights could be considered as of uncertain value, one has, I think, to inquire what it is that the creditor is seeking to do when he lodges his proof. What he is directed to do by the form of proof (and what all the previous authorities direct him to do) E is to indicate the value of the claim at the date of the winding up order. It seems to me that Mr. Graham's submissions lead to a dilemma. If the purpose of the dollar creditor in submitting his proof is to estimate the value of his claim at some other time than that of the winding up order, then he is doing something which involves (a) not merely a variation of, but a radical departure from, the statutory F form of proof, and (b) the assertion of a basis for valuation which not only is not available to any other creditor but which contradicts the whole line of authorities going back over a hundred years, upon which both the winding up rules and the bankruptcy rules have been based. If, on the other hand, what he is seeking to do is, indeed, to value his claim at the date of the winding up order, then the only appropriate value can, as I see it, be the rate of exchange prevailing at that date, G for that is the value which it actually would have if it were then paid. But, then, to bring the distribution into line with Mr. Graham's submission, there has, on the basis of a fluctuating exchange rate, to be a subsequent adjustment of the proof to reflect the actuality. It is, however, I think important to grasp just what such an adjustment means. It is, as Mr. Graham has pointed out, perfectly true that in the case H of contingent claims the court adjusts the proof if the contingency occurs between the date of the proof and the date of the distribution. A most striking example of that is, I think, *In re Northern Counties of England Fire Insurance Co.*, 17 Ch.D. 337, which Mr. Graham referred to, where the claimant was permitted to prove for the full amount due under a fire insurance policy in respect of a fire which occurred after the date of the winding up order. But the reasoning behind this is that the occurrence of the contingency is the best evidence of the value

of the claim at the relevant date, that is the date of the winding up order, and the rule as stated by P. O. Lawrence J. in *Ellis and Co.'s Trustee* A
v. *Dixon-Johnson* [1924] 1 Ch. 342 (and this has been stated as the rule in bankruptcy in successive editions of *Williams on Bankruptcy* to the present day) was expressed in these terms, at pp. 356–357:

> "... there is no doubt that a contingent claim for unliquidated damages is a provable debt and its amount has to be estimated as B
> at the date of the receiving order. That, however, does not mean that the effect of the receiving order is to accelerate the happening of the contingency, so as to fix the amount of the defendants' claim on the basis of the contingency having happened on the day of the receiving order.... The claim must be stated as on the day of the receiving order: if, when the proof is lodged, the contingency has not happened, the amount of the claim must be C
> estimated as accurately as possible; if the contingency happens before the proof is lodged, that fact is pro tanto evidence of the true value of the claim as at the date of the receiving order, and there will, as a rule, be no difficulty in arriving at the amount of the claim; ..."

But the adjustment for which Mr. Graham contends is, in my view, D
something quite different. There is, as I see it, no doubt about what the obligation of the company is at the date of the winding up order: it is not an obligation to pay to the dollar creditor whatever may be the sterling equivalent of his debt at some time, possibly a year or more hence, when the liquidator has time to consider and adjudicate the proof of debt. It is an obligation to pay whatever is the sterling equivalent at E
that date; and to adjust it subsequently to reflect an altered rate of exchange, whether up or down at the time when the proof falls to be adjudicated is not simply the ascertainment of what was the debt at the date of the winding up order but the substitution for the ascertained (or at least readily ascertainable) value at that date of a new and quite different value ascertained at a different date. Either way, therefore, F
Mr. Graham has to say, I think, that *Miliangos* v. *George Frank* (*Textiles*) *Ltd.* [1976] A.C. 443 has the effect of either creating a special class of dollar creditors, for whom the rules applicable to other creditors do not apply, or that it affects the substantive right of the creditor under his contract and entitles him to receive the amount in foreign currency or the equivalent at the date of payment. But, as I have pointed out, Lord Wilberforce was at pains to point out that the foreign creditor is G
not concerned with fluctuations in sterling. He said, at p. 466:

> "The creditor has no concern with pounds sterling; for him what matters is that a Swiss franc for good or ill should remain a Swiss franc.... The relevant certainty which the rule ought to achieve is that which gives the creditor neither more nor less than he bargained for. He bargained for" so many "Swiss francs; whatever H
> this means in (unstipulated) foreign currencies, whichever way the exchange into those currencies may go, he should get" so many "Swiss francs or as nearly as can be brought about."

What the House of Lords was, as I read it, concerned with in the *Miliangos* case was how the English court, in delivering judgment, should give effect to the right which the foreign creditor has to the delivery of a certain quantity of foreign currency. But I certainly do not read

A the decision as entitling the creditor to an uncertain amount, and there does not appear to me to be at the date of the liquidation any uncertainty in the claim which would justify the claim being estimated under section 316. Of course if the *Miliangos* case had the effect for which Mr. Graham contends, I am bound to apply it, but if that case does compulsively lead to this conclusion it does seem to me, I must say, to accord very ill with the provisions of both the winding up and the
B bankruptcy rules, and to cut right across the principle of pari passu distribution which is enshrined in section 302 of the Act of 1948, and this must be so, I think, not only as between dollar creditors and sterling creditors but between the dollar creditors inter se. The liquidator in this case has to deal with proofs from numerous dollar creditors whose total debts, as I have said, amount to over $48m., and as a practical
C matter it would be quite impossible to adjudicate on all proofs on the same day, but the rate of exchange alters daily, or almost daily, and sometimes alters very materially. I have been furnished with a draft which shows the rate of exchange to the nearest cent of lower rate between January 1972 and October 1975, and it is obvious that within even relatively short periods there have been drastic rises and falls. To take only two examples, in the first half of March 1974 the rate rose
D from approximately $2.29 to approximately $2.35 and in the first 10 days of May 1975 it dropped from approximately $2.35 to approximately $2.30; so even assuming a continuous process of adjudication over either of these two periods, the amount for which substantial creditors for exactly the same dollar amounts would be admitted to proof would vary significantly according to the unlucky, or lucky, accident of the date
E upon which the liquidator actually considered their respective claims. Nor do the anomalies end there: section 317 of the Act introduces into the winding up the same rules with respect to the respective rights of secured and unsecured creditors and to debts provable as are in force for the time being under the law of bankruptcy, and this includes, inter alia, the mutual credit and set off provisions of section 31 of the Act of 1914. Section 31 is directory. It provides for an account to be taken
F of what is due from one party to the other, and states in terms that the "balance of the account, and no more, shall be claimed or paid on either side respectively." As regards the availability of the set off, the relevant date is, of course, the date of the commencement of the winding up (see, for instance, *In re Daintrey* [1900] 1 Q.B. 546 and *In re City Equitable Fire Insurance Co. Ltd.* (*No.* 2) [1930] 2 Ch. 293) but it is
G very difficult to see how the set off provisions could be sensibly made to accord with Mr. Graham's suggested date for conversion. Take, for instance, the hypothetical case of this company having, on October 2, 1972, at the commencement of the winding up, a claim against it for $24,200, and having at the same time a cross claim against that creditor for £10,000, arising out of their mutual dealings. At that date the rate
H of exchange was $2.42 to the pound, so that if the account is taken, as directed by section 31, there is really nothing due either way, and nothing, therefore, to prove for in the liquidation. But by May 23, 1972, when the order was made, the rate had risen to $2.56, so that even if that be the right date for ascertaining the quantum of set off there would be a balance in the company's favour. On neither view would the dollar creditor have anything to prove for in the liquidation.

If Mr. Graham's submission is correct, however, the moment the exchange rate fell below $2.40 the dollar creditor could come in and prove, and whether his proof was ever admitted by the liquidator would depend upon the rate at the time when the liquidator came to consider it. If, for instance, it was considered on March 1, 1975, the proof would be rejected. The exchange rate was then $2.43 and there would be a balance due from the dollar creditor. If, on the other hand, it was considered on September 1, when the exchange rate was $2.04, it would be admitted for a sum of £1,860 odd. Again, if I accept Mr. Graham's submissions, there are, as Mr. Potts points out, difficulties with regard to the application of the provisions of rules 134, 140 and 141, although I think that the difficulties are perhaps less formidable than Mr. Potts contended, and Mr. Graham has drawn my attention, in some detail, to the provisions for the valuation of creditors' claims in relation to voting at creditors' meetings. Finally, Mr. Graham's submissions appear to me to create even greater difficulties when it is sought to apply them to a voluntary liquidation, when, after all, the date for conversion must be the same as in a compulsory liquidation. It has to be remembered, I think, that the necessity for proving a debt arises only in winding up by the court. In a voluntary winding up the liquidator may call for formal proof of a debt if he is in any doubt, but in the ordinary way he will accept as valid a debt entered in the company's books without any formal admission, and when, in such a case, is the conversion to take place? Is it at the time when the liquidator makes a mental note (if he ever does) that he is not going to challenge the debt, or is it at the time when he calculates the total indebtedness of the company for the purposes of making his first distribution?

For all these reasons I feel a strong disinclination to accept Mr. Graham's submissions, and, if I am free to do so, I would be minded to declare the date for conversion in the instant case to be the date which seems to me to be more in accord with the scheme of the Act, and with those authorities which govern the question of the appropriate date for the valuation of claims in a liquidation. Mr. Graham, however, contends that I am not free, and that, whether it be convenient or no, the matter is concluded by *Miliangos* v. *George Frank* (*Textiles*) *Ltd.* [1976] A.C. 443. In particular he refers me to the speeches of Lord Wilberforce and Lord Cross. Lord Wilberforce defines the money obligations to which his observations relate in these terms, at p. 467:

> "I would confine my approval at the present time of a change in the breach-date rule to claims such as those with which we are here concerned, i.e., to foreign money obligations, sc. obligations of a money character to pay foreign currency arising under a contract whose proper law is that of a foreign country and where the money of account and payment is that of that country, or possibly of some other country but not of the United Kingdom . . . As regards foreign money obligations (defined above), it is first necessary to establish the form of the claim to be made. In my opinion acceptance of the argument already made requires that the claim must be specifically for the foreign currency—as in this case for a sum stated in Swiss francs. To this may be added the alternative 'or the sterling equivalent at the date of' . . . (see below). As regards the conversion date to be inserted in the claim or in the judgment of the court, the choice, as pointed out in the *Havana Railways* case [1961] A.C. 1007, is between (i) the date of action brought, (ii) the

date of judgment, (iii) the date of payment. Each has its advantages, and it is to be noticed that the Court of Appeal in *Schorsch Meier* [1975] Q.B. 416 and in the present case chose the date of payment meaning, as I understand it, the date when the court authorises enforcement of the judgment in terms of sterling. . . So I would favour the payment date, in the sense I have mentioned. In the case of a company in liquidation, the corresponding date for conversion would be the date when the creditor's claim in terms of sterling is admitted by the liquidator."

And Lord Cross of Chelsea says, at p. 497:

"I ask myself, therefore, whether there has been any change of circumstances since 1961 sufficiently great to justify us in saying that the rule which in the *Havana* case [1961] A.C. 1007 was accepted on all sides without question and which formed an essential foundation for the judgments delivered ought now to be considered to be no longer an existing rule of our law. I agree with my noble and learned friend, Lord Wilberforce, that the change which has come over the 'foreign exchange' situation generally and the position of sterling in particular in the course of the last 15 years justifies us in answering that question in the affirmative. In this connection I am particularly impressed by the fact that awards in commercial arbitrations are now often made in a foreign currency and that the Court of Appeal has held in the *Jugoslavenska* case [1974] Q.B. 292 that such awards can be enforced as judgments under section 26 of the Arbitration Act 1950. It would be most unfortunate for this House to cast any doubt on the correctness of that decision; but, as my noble and learned friend points out, it would be absurd to have one rule with regard to arbitrations on debts expressed in a foreign currency and another with regard to actions brought on similar debts. Like him, however, I would go no further on this occasion than to say that the court has power to give judgment for payment of money in a foreign currency and that one case in which such a judgment should be given is where the action is brought to enforce a foreign money obligation. In that case if the defendant fails to deliver the foreign currency the date for its conversion into sterling should be the date when the plaintiff is given leave to levy execution for a sum expressed in sterling. I say nothing one way or the other as to the date for conversion into sterling of sums ascertained in foreign currency for damages for breach of contract or tort. Further, I agree with my noble and learned friend that where the foreign money obligation is the subject of a proof in bankruptcy or liquidation the date for conversion into sterling should be the date of the admission of the proof."

These are undoubtedly very strong expressions of opinion in carefully considered speeches in a case dealing directly with the appropriateness of giving judgment for a sum of foreign currency, although not dealing directly with the effect of a foreign money claim, whether by an ordinary creditor or a judgment creditor, in a liquidation, and Mr. Graham says that they are part of the ratio decidendi, and so binding upon me; but he also says that, whether binding or no, they are dicta of the highest weight and persuasive authority and that—although I think he avoided putting it so baldly—a puisne judge should consider hard and long before arriving at a different conclusion. That, of course, I accept, subject to the reservation,

first, that dicta of individual members of the House of Lords, although of A
the greatest weight are not—as Lord Dunedin put it in *Charles R. David-*
son and Co. v. *M'Robb* [1918] A.C. 304, 322—to be accepted against
one's own individual opinion unless they can be shown to express a legal
proposition which is a necessary step to the judgment which the House
pronounces in the case, and, secondly, that they cannot, of course, be
followed if to do so would conflict with the provisions of statute.

I turn, therefore, to consider whether the observations of Lord B
Wilberforce and Lord Cross—which I have quoted above—constitute
part of the ratio decidendi of the case and thus amount to a binding
decision upon the application to the position of foreign creditors of the
provisions of the Act of 1948, the Act of 1914, and the rules made
under them respectively. Prior to *Schorsch Meier G.m.b.H.* v. *Hennin*
[1975] Q.B. 416 and *Miliangos* v. *George Frank* (*Textiles*) *Ltd.* [1976] C
A.C. 443 the position of the foreign claimant had been exhaustively
considered by their Lordships in *In re United Railways of Havana and*
Regla Warehouses Ltd. [1961] A.C. 1007. That was a case which con-
cerned a liquidation in which the respondents had claimed to quantify
their debts by reference to the exchanges rates prevailing at the date of
the winding up. The House of Lords rejected that and held that the
correct dates for conversion into sterling of the sums claimed were D
the dates upon which those sums respectively fell due and were not
paid, and not the date of the winding up, and the basis for this decision
was threefold: first, that it was axiomatic that a judgment could only
be obtained in England for a sum in sterling; secondly, that any action
in England for the recovery of a foreign debt was an action for damages
for their failure to pay it; thirdly, that convenience and authority had E
settled that in any action for damages the conversion took place at the
date of the breach or the act, that is to say, in the case of a foreign
debt, the failure to pay it when it fell due. It was to these three steps
that the principal burden of Lord Wilberforce's speech in the *Miliangos*
case was directed, and first, and fundamentally, to the underlying
assumption that judgment could not be entered for anything but a
sterling sum. After considering the authorities he rejected the assump- F
tion in these terms, at p. 467:

> "In *Beswick* v. *Beswick* [1968] A.C. 58 this House laid down that
> in a suitable case specific performance may be ordered of an
> agreement to pay a sum of money of the United Kingdom. Lord
> Pearce, at p. 89, quoted from *Hart* v. *Hart* (1881) 18 Ch.D. 670,
> 685, the words: '". . . when an agreement for valuable consider- G
> ation . . . has been partially performed, the court ought to do its
> utmost to carry out that agreement by a decree for specific perfor-
> mance".' If this is so as regards money of this country, I can see
> no reason why it should not be so as regards foreign money: indeed,
> the latter seems to have a more 'specific' character than the
> former." H

This, as it seems to me, is the first ratio of the decision. The question
before the House which had been directly raised on the appeal was
whether judgment could be given for a sum expressed otherwise than in
sterling, and, that having been answered affirmatively, Lord Wilberforce
went on to consider the form of the claim. It followed from his
reference to specific performance that the claim must be specifically for

A a foreign currency sum, and, indeed, he so states. Since, however, it
might not be practicable to discharge the claim in the foreign currency
specified, and since in any event the judgment would have to be so
framed as to be capable of being executed in England if it became
necessary to enforce it, provision would have to be made for conversion
of the sum for which the judgment was entered into sterling, and Lord
Wilberforce considers how that is to be done. He says, at p. 468: "To
B this" ("this" being the stated sum of foreign currency) "may be added
the alternative 'or the sterling equivalent at the date of . . .' (see below)"
and he goes on then to consider what is to be inserted in the blank
represented by the words "see below," and concludes that it is the date
of payment interpreted as meaning the date when the court authorises
enforcement of the judgment in terms of sterling. So this is the second
C part of the decision: where judgment is entered for a sum expressed in
foreign currency, what is the date to be inserted in the judgment as
the appropriate date for conversion of that sum into sterling? And it
is in this context that Lord Wilberforce refers to the case of a company
in liquidation. It is, I think, obvious, that he was not suggesting for a
moment that there should be inserted in the judgment the words "when
the court authorises enforcement of this judgment in terms of sterling."
D He was merely indicating, I think (as had already been said in the Court
of Appeal in the *Schorsch Meier* case [1975] Q.B. 416) the court's inter-
pretation of what, in the case of a judgment which had to be enforced
by execution, the date of payment would, as a matter of practice,
mean. The following words, "in the case of a company in liquidation,
the corresponding date for conversion would be the date when the
E creditor's claim in terms of sterling is admitted by the liquidator" could
have no possible relevance to what was to be inserted in the judgment,
and can, I think, have been intended as no more than an afterthought,
and as an indication of what Lord Wilberforce considered would in
practice be the date for conversion if a judgment was entered in these
terms but the company went into liquidation before enforcement. It
was not in any sense, I think, a necessary step in the conclusion at
F which his Lordship had already arrived, and was, I think, intended as
nothing more than an illustration of how he considered that conclusion
would work in a particular hypothetical situation, which had not arisen
in the case before the House and with the consideration of which the
House was not concerned. The essence of the decision is that judgment
may be entered for a sum in foreign currency or the sterling equivalent
G at the date of payment. How that would operate in the hypothetical
situation of a company in liquidation was not, as far as I can gather,
argued and was certainly not a matter which was before the House for
its decision. Lord Cross did no more than agree with Lord Wilberforce
on the point. The other two noble and learned Lords who concurred
in the decision do not advert to the point at all, nor does it form any
H part of the reasoning upon which their decisions were based.

I must, therefore, I think, reject Mr. Graham's submission that
Miliangos v. *George Frank* (*Textiles*) *Ltd.* [1976] A.C. 443 decides
the point which falls for decision in this case. At highest, the passages
upon which he relies are obiter dicta—very powerful and persuasive dicta
no doubt, having regard to their source, but I think, nevertheless, dicta.
If I could see my way to follow them, I would feel bound loyally to do
so, but, for the reasons which I have already outlined, I find myself

unable to do so consistently with what I conceive to be the weight of A
precedent and the plain interpretation of the relative statutory pro-
visions. Furthermore, the very reasoning of the *Miliangos* decision
seems to me to militate against the applicability of what I will refer to
as " the proof date " in a liquidation. Essentially the fundamental
basis of the change from the breach date to the payment date is the
destruction of the assumption upon which the *Havana Railways* decision
was based, that a judgment could only be given in sterling, but that B
destruction rests—as the passage which I have cited shows—upon the
ability of the court to decree specific performance. Of course, specific
performance of existing contracts for the sale of land can be decreed
against the liquidator or a trustee in bankruptcy of the vendor, but
that is based upon the existence of the equitable proprietary interest
created by the contract for sale. That is, however, a peculiar case. In C
the ordinary way the court does not, I think, decree specific performance
against a trustee in bankruptcy or a liquidator where the obligation is
simply to pay money, as, for instance, in the case of the insolvent
purchaser of land: see *Holloway* v. *York* (1877) 25 W.R. 627. The
reason is not, I think, far to seek. The effect would be in fact that the
other party to the contract would be receiving payment otherwise than
pari passu with the other creditors. I do not for one moment suppose D
that any of their Lordships who were parties to the decision in *Miliangos*
v. *George Frank* (*Textiles*) *Ltd.* intended to create some special category
of creditor who, in a winding up or bankruptcy, would be treated
differently from other creditors, nor can they, I think, have conceived
that that would be the result of their decision. I cannot think that it is.
The effect of the *Miliangos* case, so far at any rate as debts are con- E
cerned, is to negative the breach date as the appropriate date for
conversion and to give the foreign creditor the right to receive whatever
is the appropriate sterling equivalent at the date when he enforces his
judgment. The illustration given by Lord Wilberforce and by the Court
of Appeal of how that would work in practice if the judgment creditor
had to resort to the ultimate sanction of enforcement by execution is
not, I feel sure, intended in any way either to add to or to qualify the F
judgment creditor's rights. For instance, if he levied execution, was
not paid out and then petitioned to wind up the debtor company, I
cannot conceive that the House of Lords or the Court of Appeal, or
anyone else, would consider that his proof in the subsequent liquidation
would have to be limited to the amount calculated at the rate of
exchange prevailing at the date when he swore the affidavit leading to G
the unsuccessful execution, whilst every other foreign creditor would
prove for a higher amount based upon a subsequent and lower rate of
exchange. What the court is seeking to do in a winding up is to ascertain
the liabilities of the company at a particular date and to distribute the
available assets as at that date pro rata according to the amounts of
those liabilities. In practice the process cannot be immediate, but H
notionally I think it is, and, as it seems to me, it has to be treated as
if it were, although subsequent events can be taken into account in
quantifying what the liabilities were at the relevant date. In the context
of a liquidation, therefore, the relevant date for the ascertainment of
the amount of liability is the notional date of discharge of that liability,
and, despite what was said by Lord Wilberforce and Lord Cross by
way of illustration, that date must, in my judgment, be the same for all

creditors and it must be "the date of payment" for the purposes of any judgment which has been entered for the sterling equivalent at the date of payment of a sum expressed in foreign currency.

Two candidates have been suggested as appropriate in the case of a compulsory winding up, the date of the winding up order and the date of the commencement of the winding up—that is the date of the presentation of the petition. The latter has been suggested because it is said that this would be consistent with the set off cases, but I do not think that is right. It is, of course, perfectly true that the question of the availability of set off has to be ascertained at the commencement of the winding up, but that date does not, as I see it, govern the valuation of the claim set off; so, for instance, in *In re National Benefit Assurance Co. Ltd.* [1924] 2 Ch. 339, Eve J. stated, at p. 345:

> "... in order to bring the mutual dealings section into operation it is not necessary that there should be mutual debts existing at the date of the winding up—that being, according to *In re Daintrey* [1900] 1 Q.B. 546, the material date; it is sufficient if there are contractual obligations the breach of which may give rise to a claim for damages provable in the winding up,"

and that decision was approved by the Court of Appeal in *In re City Life Assurance Co. Ltd.* [1926] Ch. 191. There is nothing that I can find in the set off cases which compels a quantification of the amount of the set off as at the commencement of the winding up and, although in this particular case it would pay the dollar creditors if that date were adjudged the appropriate date for conversion, to ascertain their claims then, would, I think, be anomalous when all other claims fall to be ascertained at the date of the winding up order. In my judgment, the latter date is the date at which such conversion should be made, and I will declare accordingly.

Declaration accordingly.

Solicitor: *Clifford-Turner; Denton, Hall & Burgin; Turner, Garrett & Co., Byfleet.*

A. R.

[COURT OF APPEAL]

* METROBARN LTD. *v.* GEHRING AND ANOTHER

1976 May 13 — Cairns, Lawton and Shaw L.JJ.

Landlord and Tenant—Rent restriction—Furnished letting—Effect of imposition of protection—Furnished letting subsisting at date when protection imposed—Prior registration of fair rent in relation to unfurnished letting of premises—Whether fair rent applicable to protected furnished letting—Rent Act 1974 (*c.* 51), *ss.* 1, 5 (1)

In 1973, a rent officer registered under Part IV of the Rent Act 1968 the fair rent of a flat leased by the landlords on an unfurnished tenancy at £400 a year. In June 1974, the husband took furnished tenancy of the premises at a rent of £20 a week, for six months. In August 1974, the Rent Act 1974 came into operation and the furnished tenancy became protected under section 1 of that Act.[1] When the term expired the husband remained in occupation as a statutory tenant with his wife. In January 1975, the marriage broke down, the husband left the premises and the wife remained in occupation with her child under the Matrimonial Homes Act 1967. In the landlords' action in the county court for possession, arrears of rent and mesne profits, Judge MacDonnell held that the registration of the fair rent under Part IV of the Act of 1968 could not fix the rent for a furnished tenancy and gave judgment against the husband for £954 arrears of rent and against husband and wife for possession, the order for poossession being suspended in the event of the arrears being paid by instalments on specified dates.

On appeal by the wife on the ground, inter alia, that the only rent recoverable was the £400 a year registered fair rent:—

Held, dismissing the appeal, that a registration under Part IV of the Act of 1968 effected in relation to an unfurnished letting did not apply to a furnished letting and that, if Parliament had intended otherwise, much clearer words than the general terms of section 1 of the Rent Act 1974 would have been used to give effect to that intention (post, pp. 780B–C, 781F–G, 782E–F).

The following case is referred to in the judgment of Shaw L.J.:

Signy v. *Abbey National Building Society* [1944] K.B. 449; [1944] 1 All E.R. 448, C.A.

No additional cases were cited in argument.

APPEAL from Judge MacDonnell sitting at Lambeth County Court.

By their particulars of claim dated September 19, 1975, the landlords, Metrobarn Ltd., the owners of a dwelling-house known as Flat 63, Benhurst Court, Leigham Court Road, Streatham, London S.W.16, which had been let by them to the first defendant, John Gehring, at a rent of £20 a week for six months from June 1, 1974, claimed forfeiture, possession and arrears of rent of £579·96, unpaid from March 1, 1975, by the first defendant as statutory tenant, and mesne profits of £20 a week from

---

[Reported by A. G. B. HELM, ESQ., Barrister-at-Law]

[1] Rent Act 1974, s. 1 (1) (2): see post, p. 779D–G.

A September 22, 1975, until possession. By their defence and counterclaim the first defendant and his wife, Celia Gertrude Gehring, the second defendant, pleaded that, inter alia, by letter dated March 7, 1975, the husband notified the landlords that, having ceased to occupy the premises since January 28, 1975, the agreement was terminated; that in so far as he occupied the premises after November 30, 1974, he did so as a statutory tenant and was not liable to the landlords for any rent in respect of any
B period after January 28 or, alternatively, March 7, 1975, and that the rent was not in arrears; that in February 1973 a rent officer registered a fair rent of £400 a year for the premises; that the total rent chargeable from June 1, 1974, until November 8, 1975, was or would have been £576·92; that as after June 1, 1974, the husband had paid the landlords £779·94, he had overpaid £203·02 and was entitled to restitution of the excess under
C section 33 of the Rent Act 1968.

The wife, estranged from the husband, counterclaimed relief from forfeiture; that the landlords were in breach of Part III of the Rent Act 1968 and sought a declaration that she was entitled to deduct from future payments of rent made by her as agent for the husband and by her right of occupation under section 1 (5) of the Matrimonial Homes Act 1967, the sum of £203·02. The landlords contended that the rent registration of
D £400 a year in 1973 was for an unfurnished letting, which did not apply to the present furnished letting.

On February 18, 1976, Judge MacDonnell held that the landlords were entitled to recover possession of the premises and £954·40 arrears of rent. The order for possession was suspended if and for so long as either the husband or the wife paid the current rent of £20 a week as it fell due,
E paid instalments of the arrears of £23 on March 18 and April 18, and paid the balance of the arrears, £908·40, on or before May 18, 1976.

The wife alone appealed on the grounds (1) that the judge erred in law in holding that Case I of Schedule III of the Rent Act 1968 applied to the tenancy on the ground that the recoverable rent under the tenancy was £20 a week, when in law it was £400 a year, the fair rent registered under Part IV of the Rent Act 1968 in respect of a previous tenancy of
F the same premises with effect from November 16, 1972, so that the rent was not in arrears; (2) that, in particular, the judge erred in his construction of the Rent Act 1974 in its effect on the rent recoverable under the present tenancy; alternatively (3) if the recoverable rent were £20 a week, the judge erred fundamentally in the exercise of his discretion by making the payment of the balance of the arrears of rent payable on or before May
G 18, 1976, a term of the suspension of the order for possession.

Stephen Sedley and *Ernest Bano* for the wife.
Paul Collins for the landlords.

CAIRNS L.J. This is an appeal from a judgment of Judge MacDonnell given at the Lambeth County Court on February 18, 1976. It was given in
H an action for possession of a flat No. 63, Benhurst Court, Streatham, and for arrears of rent. The first defendant was the tenant, and at the outset he was the only defendant. The second defendant is his wife, and she asked to be joined because the marriage had broken up, the husband had left her, and she is now living in this flat with the child of the marriage.

The tenancy was at the time of the proceedings a protected tenancy under the Rent Acts 1968 and 1974. The result of the action was judgment against the husband for £954 arrears of rent, and judgment for possession

of the flat, suspended if the current rent were paid and the arrears were A
paid off as to £23 on March 18, £23 on April 18 and the balance of £908·40 by May 18. The wife appeals, contending that by the operation of the Rent Acts and the events which have happened there are no arrears; alternatively that, if the judgment stands, the requirement as a condition of suspension of the possession order that so large a sum as £908 should be paid by May 18 is wrong in principle.

The history of the matter is as follows. In February 1973, at a time B
before the defendants came on the scene and when only unfurnished tenancies were protected under the Rent Act 1968, the rent officer registered the rent of this flat at the sum of £400 a year. On June 1, 1974, the husband took a six months' tenancy of the flat, with furniture, at a rent of £20 a week. There was an option for renewal, but it was not exercised. There was at the outset of the hearing in the county court an issue whether C
the furniture was sufficiently substantial to make the tenancy a furnished tenancy under the Act of 1968; but before judgment was given, after an adjournment, it was accepted that the furniture was sufficiently substantial for that purpose. On August 14, 1974, during the currency of the six months' tenancy, the Rent Act 1974 came into operation and the tenancy then became a protected one under section 1 of that Act. After November
30, 1974, the husband and wife continued in occupation, and it is now D
common ground that the husband became a statutory tenant. In January 1975 the husband left, and it is agreed that since then he has continued to be the statutory tenant, the wife occupying the flat by reason of her rights under the Matrimonial Homes Act 1967.

The issue with regard to the rent arises in this way. The wife says that the rent recoverable is the registered rent and that more than this has E
already been paid. The landlords say that the registered rent was registered under Part IV of the Act of 1968, which deals only with unfurnished tenancies, and that rent for a furnished tenancy is now the contractual rent of £20 a week.

Section 5 (1) of the Rent Act 1974 reads as follows:

> " In any case where—(*a*) immediately before the commencement date," F
> that was August 14, 1974, " a dwelling is subject to a furnished letting and a rent is registered for that dwelling under the relevant Part of the Rent Act, and (*b*) on the commencement date that furnished letting becomes a protected tenancy by virtue of section 1 above, the amount which is so registered under the relevant Part of the Rent Act shall be deemed to be registered under Part IV of that Act as the rent for the dwelling-house which is let on that tenancy, and that G
> registration shall be deemed to take effect on the commencement date."

Section 15 of the Rent Act 1974 defines, for the purposes of the Act, the expression " the relevant Part of the Rent Act " as being " Part VI of the Rent Act 1968."

The judge held that a registration under Part IV of the Act of 1968 H
could not fix the rent payable for a furnished tenancy. He said that it would be absurd if, after a good deal of furniture had been put in the premises, the fair rent fixed for an unfurnished tenancy should continue to apply.

Mr. Sedley, who has presented a very interesting argument to the court on behalf of the wife, who is the only appellant, seeks to refute the argument as to absurdity by saying that the landlords could immediately

A apply for the registration of an increased rent. He has drawn our attention to section 44 (3) of the Act of 1968, which provides:

> "Where a rent for a dwelling-house has been registered under this Act no application by the tenant alone or by the landlord alone for the registration of a different rent for that dwelling-house shall be entertained before the expiry of three years from the relevant date B (as defined in subsection (4) below) except on the ground that, since that date, there has been such a change in the condition of the dwelling-house (including the making of any improvement therein), the terms of the tenancy or any other circumstances taken into consideration when the rent was registered or confirmed as to make the registered rent no longer a fair rent."

C And, says Mr. Sedley, the presence or the absence of furniture would be a circumstance taken into account in registering a fair rent: see section 21 (2) (*c*) and section 24 (1) (*b*) of the Act of 1968.

It remains true that, if Mr. Sedley's argument is right, the effect of the Act of 1974 would be to displace the rent which was a lawful rent up to August 14, 1974, in favour of a rent which would be manifestly inappropriate, and to place on the landlords the onus of getting it changed. Mr. D Sedley says that this is the necessary result of section 1 of the Act of 1974. Subsections (1) and (2) of section 1 provide as follows:

> "(1) On and after the commencement date,—(*a*) a tenancy of a dwelling-house shall no longer be prevented from being a protected tenancy for the purposes of the Rent Act by reason only that, under the tenancy, the dwelling-house is bona fide let at a rent which includes E payments in respect of the use of furniture; and (*b*) subject to the following provisions of this Act, references in the Rent Act (and in any other enactment or instrument in which those expressions have the same meaning as in that Act) to a protected tenancy, a statutory tenancy or a regulated tenancy shall be construed accordingly. (2) Any reference in this Act or the Rent Act to a protected furnished tenancy, F a statutory furnished tenancy or a regulated furnished tenancy is a reference to a protected tenancy, . . . or a regulated tenancy, as the case may be, under which the rent for the dwelling-house concerned includes such payments in respect of the use of furniture as, apart from subsection (1) above, subsection (4) (*a*) below and the repeals effected by this Act, would prevent a tenancy of the dwelling-house at that rent from being a protected tenancy."

G

Mr. Sedley says that, once a furnished tenancy becomes a protected tenancy, it becomes subject to all the incidents attached by the Act of 1968 to protected tenancies, one of which is that once a rent has been registered under Part IV of the Act of 1968 no higher rent (with immaterial exceptions) can be recovered until such higher rent has been registered. That H is the result of section 20 of the Act of 1968, subsections (1) and (2) of which provide:

> "(1) Where the rent payable for any contractual period of a regulated tenancy of a dwelling-house would exceed the limit specified in the following provisions of this section (in this Part of this Act referred to as 'the contractual rent limit'), the amount of the excess shall, notwithstanding anything in any agreement, be irrecoverable from the tenant. (2) Where a rent for the dwelling-house is registered under

Part IV of this Act, then, subject to section 47 (3) of this Act, the contractual rent limit is the rent so registered." A

Similar provisions are made by section 22 of the Act of 1968 in respect of statutory periods, that is to say, periods after the contractual tenancy has come to an end and the tenant is there as a statutory tenant.

When Part IV of the Act of 1968 was passed it applied only to tenancies of premises without furniture or with an insubstantial amount B of furniture. Furnished lettings were quite differently dealt with in Part VI of that Act. I see no reason to interpret section 1 of the Rent Act 1974 as carrying the implication that a Part IV registration effected in relation to unfurnished lettings should have effect in relation to a furnished letting. What had to be registered under Part IV was a fair rent: see section 45 (1). What would be a fair rent for an unfurnished letting would not be a fair rent for a substantially furnished letting. If the registration C under Part IV was to apply to furnished tenancies, in my judgment, much clearer words than the general words of section 1 of the Act of 1974 would be required to bring about that result.

I therefore agree with the judge as to what was the recoverable rent from these premises, and, accordingly, agree that his judgment as to the rent to be recovered and as to possession of the premises must stand. D

Then as to the question of the terms of suspension of the operation of the order for possession, Mr. Sedley asked us to look at section 11 of the Act of 1968, which provides:

"(1) Subject to subsection (5) below, a court may adjourn, for such period or periods as it thinks fit, proceedings for possession of a dwelling-house which is let on a protected tenancy or subject to a E statutory tenancy. (2) On the making of an order for possession of such a dwelling-house, or at any time before the execution of such an order (whether made before or after the commencement of this Act), the court, subject to subsection (5) below, may—(*a*) stay or suspend execution of the order, or (*b*) postpone the date of possession, for such period or periods as the court thinks fit."

F

It is not necessary to refer to subsection (5).

Mr. Sedley goes so far as to say that the judge was wrong in law, because having purported to grant a suspension under section 11 (2) of the Act of 1968, he granted what was not really an effective suspension at all, because the £900 odd was something which it was plainly impossible for either the husband or the wife to pay. That argument seems to me to be quite unsustainable. What is given by section 11 of the Act of 1968 is G a discretion to the judge to suspend. It cannot be said that a suspension for three months, when there must be payment in the meanwhile and a large payment at the end of it, is not a suspension. It clearly is.

The only way, it seems to me, in which it would be possible to make any sort of attack on the order made by the judge in this respect was by convincing this court that the exercise of his discretion was plainly wrong. H I am by no means satisfied that it was. In deciding whether to grant a suspension, and if so to what extent, the interests of the landlords as well as those of the tenants have to be taken into account. The wife was given three months to pay this admittedly large sum, because neither she nor her husband is a person of means. She might be able with the assistance of her husband or with the assistance of friends to provide it; there is really no evidence whether she could or not. But it seems to me that it

A could not be said that it was unreasonable that if she could not provide it the landlords should be entitled to possession.

Judge MacDonnell is a very experienced judge, with great knowledge of the Rent Acts and of the local conditions. I should hesitate long before reaching the conclusion that a decision which he made in a matter of discretion of this kind was unsustainable. I am certainly not satisfied of it in this case, and I would accordingly dismiss that part of the appeal.

B

LAWTON L.J. I agree with the judgment delivered by Cairns L.J. and I have only two short comments to make. The first relates to the effect of the Rent Act 1974 on the tenancy which the wife enjoyed. Ever since 1920 Parliament has sought to control the tenancies of dwelling-houses. The subject matter of the legislation can perhaps be described as the C genus. Under that legislation some species and sub-species have been identified. Under the Rent Act 1968 Parliament identified and defined a number of species and sub-species. All I need refer to are two, the protected tenancy defined by section 1 of the Act of 1968, and those tenancies which were not protected tenancies which were defined by section 2. The species were dealt with separately in the Act of 1968. The legal consequences of belonging to one or the other of the species D were different.

In 1974, Parliament decided to get rid of the distinctions between the protected tenancy and the furnished tenancy which was not a protected tenancy under the Act of 1968. The opening words of section 1 of the Act of 1974 show, in my judgment, that Parliament was looking to the future. Those opening words are:

E
> "On and after the commencement date,—(*a*) a tenancy of a dwelling-house shall no longer be prevented from being a protected tenancy for the purposes of the Rent Act . . ."

On the day before the commencement date, which was August 14, 1974, protected tenancies had particular characteristics, as did furnished tenancies.

There had to be some transitional provisions to deal with the abolition F of the difference between the two species. Those transitional provisions are to be found in section 5 of the Rent Act 1974. Parliament appreciated that there might have to be a carry-over of attributes from one species to another. By section 5 Parliament made a special provision for the carry-over of a registered rent under Part VI of the Rent Act 1968 into the new situation created by the Act of 1974. Parliament did not see fit to make G any special provision for a carry-over from a fair rent for a protected tenancy under Part IV of the Act of 1968 into the new protected furnished tenancy created by the Act of 1974. I would infer that Parliament had not intended that the fair rent provision in the Act of 1968 in relation to unfurnished tenancies should apply automatically to the furnished tenancies which were brought within the Act of 1974.

So far as suspension is concerned, as Cairns L.J. has pointed out, H section 11 of the Act of 1968 gave the county court judge a discretion. It was a discretion which he had to exercise judicially. He had to do justice to both parties. He had to make an order which had some reality about it. An order would not have any reality if the effect of any order for suspension and the payment of arrears, was that the tenant would probably not be able to pay off the arrears without beggaring herself over a long period. In my judgment, this order fits the case admirably. It gives the wife an opportunity to try and raise the money, perhaps from

her family or friends, to pay off the arrears. It realistically faces the fact A
that her own financial resources are very limited indeed. On the other
hand, it gives the landlords the prospect of getting the arrears of rent, if
they are to get them at all, paid to them within the near future: if they
are not paid, they can have possession.

I can see nothing wrong with the order which was made. I would not
interfere with it. I agree that the appeal should be dismissed. B

SHAW L.J. I agree with both judgments. I need only add a reference
to a decision of this court in *Signy* v. *Abbey National Building Society*
[1944] K.B. 449 where a not wholly dissimilar question fell for consider-
ation under the old Rent Restrictions Acts. What had happened there
was that the first letting of a house was a furnished letting, and when
that tenancy had expired the landlords re-let to a different tenant, but C
this time unfurnished, at a rent which was less advantageous to the tenant
than the furnished rent. The tenant sought an order, which he obtained
from the county court, to the effect that the first letting under a furnished
tenancy was the criterion for determining the standard rent. This court
reversed the county court judge, and in giving the judgment of the court
Luxmoore L.J. said, at p. 454: D

> "A careful consideration of the Acts, including especially the pro-
> visions of sections 9 and 10 and proviso (i) to section 12 (2), seems to
> us to impose a restricted meaning on the word 'rent,' for otherwise the
> standard rent of an unfurnished house to which alone the Acts apply
> would be fixed if the first letting at the material date should happen
> to be of that house furnished, with reference to the rent of a furnished
> house to which the Acts have no application. For these reasons we E
> hold that the first letting material to be considered in the present case
> is the letting to the plaintiffs of the house unfurnished . . ."

The same considerations apply to the present case, namely, that a Part IV
registration under the Rent Act 1968 had no relevance to a furnished
letting and cannot, therefore, become the criterion by which a proper rent
thereafter was to be determined. F

So far as the question of suspension is concerned, in my view, the
judge in the county court extended indulgence to the wife so far as was
practicable in all the circumstances of the case. Quite obviously it would
have suited the wife better if she had been given an even greater indul-
gence, but it seems to me that that is not the way in which a judge should
look at the matter. The landlords also have to be considered. I should G
like to pay a tribute to the clarity of the judgment of Judge MacDonnell
and to the careful way in which he dealt with all the issues which were
raised. I would dismiss the appeal.

Appeal dismissed with costs up to amount of security in court.
Leave to appeal refused. H
Stay for 28 days pending application to House of Lords; if leave granted, stay to continue conditional on payment of £23 each month off arrears and payment of current rent.

Solicitors: *J. K. Woolley; Cowan, Lipson & Rumney.*

A

[CHANCERY DIVISION]

* *In re* HERBERT BERRY ASSOCIATES LTD. (IN LIQUIDATION)

[No. 001532 of 1975]

B 1976 May 19, 20; 28 — Templeman J.

Company—Winding up—Preferential debt—Unpaid taxes—Distress by collector of taxes under statutory powers before winding up—Resolution to wind up within three months of distress but before sale of distrained goods—Whether distress void as against liquidator—Property in distrained goods—Companies C *Act* 1948 (11 & 12 *Geo.* 6, *c.* 38), *s.* 319 (7)

On January 29, 1975, the collector of taxes, pursuant to section 61 of the Taxes Management Act 1970, distrained on the goods of the company, at its premises, for unpaid P.A.Y.E. tax and national insurance graduated contributions which under section 319 of the Companies Act 1948 were preferential debts in a company's winding up. On March 3, the company sent out notices under section 293 of the Act of 1948 con- D vening meetings of creditors with a view to going into creditors' voluntary liquidation. A resolution to wind up the company was passed on March 20. In accordance with the collector's prior arrangements, and by agreement with the liquidator, the collector sold the distrained goods on March 27.

On a summons by the liquidator seeking an order that all the proceedings on the distress be stayed on the ground that section 319 (7) [1] avoided the distress as against the liquidator, E and a declaration that the distrained goods were the property of the company available for distribution by the liquidator among the creditors:—

Held, (1) that the court had a duty to allow a creditor to complete distress unless there were special circumstances relating to the conduct of the person seeking to complete distress which rendered such a course inequitable; since the collector, relying on his statutory rights of distress, had taken F possession prior to the date of winding up he was entitled to complete distress by sale and the fact that he would obtain priority over the other preferential creditors was not sufficient to justify the court's interference (post, pp. 786A–B, 787F–G).

In re Roundwood Colliery Co. [1897] 1 Ch. 373 applied.

Food Controller v. *Cork* [1923] A.C. 647, H.L.(E.) distinguished.

(2) That the property of a company directed by section 302 G of the Companies Act 1948 to be applied for the benefit of the creditors, subject to preferential payments, was the property subject to such rights as were exercised prior to the date of the winding up; and that, in the present case, at the date of the winding up the distrained goods were in possession of the collector of taxes and he had power to sell them in order to discharge unpaid taxes and that, accordingly, the property of the company at the date of the winding up consisted only of H its right to any surplus realised on the sale (post, p. 787C–D).

The following cases are referred to in the judgment:

Food Controller v. *Cork* [1923] A.C. 647, H.L.(E.).
Great Ship Co. Ltd., In re (1863) 4 De G.J. & S. 63.
MacGregor v. *Clamp & Son* [1914] 1 K.B. 288, D.C.

[1] Companies Act 1948, s. 319 (7): see post, p. 786C–D.

Roundwood Colliery Co., In re [1897] 1 Ch. 373, Stirling J. and C.A. A
Venner's Electrical Cooking and Heating Appliances Ltd. v. *Thorpe* [1915] 2 Ch. 404, C.A.
Winterbottom (G.) (Leeds) Ltd., In re [1937] 2 All E.R. 232.

The following additional cases were cited in argument:

Bywaters (Margot) Ltd., In re [1942] Ch. 121; [1941] 3 All E.R. 471.
Caidan, In re [1942] Ch. 90; [1941] 3 All E.R. 491. B
Centrebind Ltd., In re [1967] 1 W.L.R. 377; [1966] 3 All E.R. 889.
Eros Films Ltd., In re [1963] Ch. 565; [1963] 2 W.L.R. 496; [1963] 1 All E.R. 383.
Murray v. *Epsom Local Board* [1897] 1 Ch. 35.
Overseas Aviation Engineering (G.B.) Ltd., In re [1963] Ch. 24; [1962] 3 W.L.R. 594; [1962] 3 All E.R. 12, C.A.
Westbury v. *Twigg & Co. Ltd.* [1892] 1 Q.B. 77. C

ORIGINATING SUMMONS

On May 5, 1975, the liquidator of the company, Herbert Berry Associates Ltd., in creditors' voluntary liquidation, issued a summons against the Inland Revenue Commissioners, seeking an order to stay all further proceedings on a distress levied by the Crown on January 29, 1975, D on certain property and chattels of the company. The summons also sought a declaration that the property and chattels were the property of the company available for distribution by its liquidator among the creditors of the company in accordance with the provisions of the Companies Act 1948.

The facts are stated in the judgment. E

Allan Heyman Q.C. and *Michael Crystal* for the liquidator.
Peter Gibson for the Crown.

Cur. adv. vult.

May 28. TEMPLEMAN J. By section 61 of the Taxes Management Act 1970 a collector of taxes is entitled to distrain on the goods of a taxpayer F and to sell the goods in satisfaction of the unpaid taxes. By section 319 (1) and (5) of the Companies Act 1948 certain debts, including unpaid taxes, are designated preferential debts, and on the liquidation of a company all those preferential debts must be paid in full and pari passu before any payment is made to any other unsecured creditor. The question in the present case is whether the collector, and thus the Crown, can retain the G benefit of a distress which was levied but not completed by sale before the date when the company, Herbert Berry Associates Ltd., went into creditors' voluntary winding up.

On January 29, 1975, the Crown distrained on the goods of the company, at the company's premises, for about £9,500 of unpaid taxes—P.A.Y.E. and national insurance graduated contributions. On the same day, the company entered into what is known as a "walking possession" H agreement with the Crown whereby, for the personal convenience of the company, and in consideration of the Crown not leaving a man in possession of the goods upon which the Crown had distrained, the company agreed, first, that by not leaving a man in possession the Crown had not abandoned the distraint and, secondly, that the company would not, without the written authority of the Crown, remove or allow to be removed from the premises the goods which had been distrained. The company

A also agreed, although I do not think it matters in the present case, that it would tell anybody else who visited the premises that the goods were already in the possession of the Crown, and that it would warn the Crown of any such visit.

On March 3, 1975, the company sent out notices under section 293 of the Act of 1948 convening meetings of creditors with a view to going into creditors' voluntary liquidation. The statement of affairs as at March
B 18, 1975, showed an overall deficiency of £91,000, and that there were preferential creditors of £31,000 and assets of £25,000, including the distrained goods, which have since been sold for £10,500. Accordingly, if the Crown is entitled to the proceeds of sale of the distrained goods, the unpaid taxes will be paid in full and the other preferential creditors will receive a dividend of only roughly 70p in the pound. If the Crown
C cannot claim the proceeds of sale of the distrained goods so that they are thrown into the pool to provide for all the preferential debts, including the unpaid taxes pari passu, then all the preferential creditors, including the Crown in respect of the unpaid taxes, will receive a dividend of about 80p in the pound.

Before the company went into creditors' voluntary winding up on March 20, 1975, the Crown had arranged for the distrained goods to be
D sold on March 27, 1975. The distrained goods were subsequently and sensibly sold by agreement between the liquidator and the Crown without prejudice to the legal rights of the parties. So this is a case where the remedy of distress was exercised on January 29, 1975, and, without any undue delay or other prejudicial omission or action by the Crown, the company went into creditors' voluntary winding up on March 20, before
E the distrained goods had been sold and the distress completed.

In *In re Roundwood Colliery Co.* [1897] 1 Ch. 373, Stirling J. referred to the judgment of Turner L.J. in *In re Great Ship Co. Ltd.* (1863) 4 De G.J. & S. 63, 69, which was a case dealing with execution, and continued, at p. 381:

> "The result, as I understand it, is this: that a creditor who has issued execution, or a landlord who has levied a distress, before the
> F commencement of the winding up will be allowed to proceed to sale unless there is established the existence of special reasons rendering it inequitable that he should be permitted to do so."

Mr. Heyman, who appeared for the liquidator in the present case, sought to distinguish *In re Roundwood Colliery Co.* on the grounds that
G the Crown in the present case, unlike a landlord, is distraining for preferential debts. He submitted that the Crown cannot, by distraining, obtain priority over the other preferential creditors because by section 319 (5) of the Act of 1948 all the preferential debts are required to be treated pari passu and, if necessary, to abate pari passu. He referred to *Food Controller* v. *Cork* [1923] A.C. 647. In that case, the Crown was not allowed to assert a right under the Crown prerogative to require payment in full
H of a debt owed to the Crown, but was bound by the predecessor of section 319 to accept payment pari passu with the other preferential creditors, and by the predecessor of section 302, which provided for all other unsecured debts to be paid pari passu. Similarly, says Mr. Heyman, the Crown cannot in the present instance assert its right to distrain in order to secure payment in full, but is bound by section 319, which provides for unpaid taxes to be dealt with pari passu with other preferential debts.

In my judgment, all that *Food Controller* v. *Cork* decided was that the Crown surrendered its prerogative rights to require payment in full when it accepted the provisions of the Companies Act which gave the Crown limited, specified priority rights. In the present case the Crown is relying on the rights of distress conferred on the collector of taxes by section 61 of the Taxes Management Act 1970. Those rights have never been surrendered. *In re Roundwood Colliery Co.* [1897] 1 Ch. 373 demonstrates that the Crown is entitled to complete distress by sale provided it has asserted its statutory right to distrain by taking possession prior to the date of the winding up. In this respect there is no distinction between distraint by a landlord and distraint by the Crown. The fact that the unpaid taxes, if not recovered in full by distress, rank as a preferential debt under section 319 is not in itself, it seems to me, a special circumstance which renders it inequitable for the distress to be completed.

Mr. Heyman then submitted that *In re Roundwood Colliery Co.* was wrong because in that case, and in all cases which followed, the provisions of what is now section 319 (7) were overlooked. Section 319 (7) provides:

> "In the event of a landlord or other person distraining or having distrained on any goods . . . within three months next before the date of a winding up order," the preferential debts "shall be a first charge on the goods . . . so distrained on, or the proceeds of the sale thereof . . ."

Mr. Heyman submitted that on its true construction section 319 (7) applies not only to a compulsory winding up where a winding up order is made by the court but also to a voluntary winding up when a resolution for winding up is passed by the company. It would be perverse, he submitted, to have one rule for a compulsory winding up and another rule for a creditors' voluntary winding up.

I see the force of that argument, but section 319 (8) (*d*), and other sections of the Act—for example, section 326 (1)—show that the draftsman was well aware of the distinction between the two kinds of winding up. Section 319 (7) is expressly limited to a company ordered to be wound up compulsorily. The section can be extended to a company wound up by resolution only by Parliamentary or judicial legislation. Both types of legislation are beyond my ken.

Mr. Heyman further submitted that there is a distinction between distress by a landlord and distress by the Crown. Distress by a landlord, he submitted, is a form of execution, and by section 325 of the Act of 1948, it is provided:

> "(1) Where a creditor has issued execution . . . or has attached any debt due to the company, and the company is subsequently wound up, he shall not be entitled to retain the benefit of the execution or attachment against the liquidator in the winding up . . . unless he has completed the execution or attachment before the commencement of the winding up . . ."

Mr. Heyman relied on the statement in *MacGregor* v. *Clamp & Son* [1914] 1 K.B. 288 where Bray J., following Lord Mansfield C.J. in *Hutchins* v. *Chambers* (1758) 1 Burr. 579, said, at p. 291, that a distress was really in the nature of execution and that, in particular, "the right of distress by the Crown for taxes was really by way of execution." In *MacGregor* v. *Clamp & Son* the court was deciding only that implements of trade could not be seized under a distress for rent, but that limitation did not apply

A to a distress for unpaid taxes, which was, as it was put, "really by way of execution."

The Act of 1948 distinguishes between distress, whether by a landlord or the Crown, and execution. Thus, section 228 refers to the four remedies of attachment, sequestration, distress and execution. Section 319 (7) deals with distress by landlords or other persons, and section 325 deals with execution or attachment. In my judgment, it is not possible to extract
B distress by the Crown from distress in general in section 319 and include it somehow or other in section 325, which is not dealing with distress.

Finally, Mr. Heyman argued that the Crown had abandoned or prejudiced its right of distress by accepting the "walking possession" agreement. In my judgment the express terms of that agreement are inconsistent with the submission. The agreement was freely entered into by the company
C for its own benefit before the date of the winding up, and both the company and the liquidator, and the other creditors, are bound thereby. In my judgment, the property of a company, which is directed by section 302 to be applied for the benefit of the creditors subject to preferential payments, is the property subject to such rights as were exercised prior to the date of the winding up. At the date of the winding up in the present case
D the goods in question were in the possession of the Crown, and it had power to sell them in order to discharge unpaid taxes. The property of the company at the date of the winding up consisted only of its right to any surplus realised on that sale.

Mr. Gibson, who appeared for the Crown, accepted that the Crown's right to sell and complete the distraint was subject to the power of the court, by injunction, to prevent the exercise of that right in special circum-
E stances; that is to say, if it was inequitable to allow the distress to be completed. In *In re Great Ship Co. Ltd.* (1863) 4 De G.J. & S. 63, Turner L.J. said, at p. 69, that the then Companies Act did not give the general creditors any right to have their interests consulted in preference to the interests of the particular creditor whose case may come before the court. In that case it was a creditor seeking to complete execution. Similarly,
F in the present case the Act of 1948 does not give the preferential creditors any right to have their interests consulted in preference to the interests of the particular preferential creditor who is now seeking to complete distress. In *In re Roundwood Colliery Co.* [1897] 1 Ch. 373 Stirling J. stated that it was the duty of the court to allow a creditor to complete distress unless there were special circumstances which rendered such a course inequitable. Similarly, here, it seems to me, the court is under an obligation to allow
G the creditor to complete distress unless there are special reasons.

In *Venner's Electrical Cooking and Heating Appliances Ltd.* v. *Thorpe* [1915] 2 Ch. 404 the court held that it was not inequitable to allow a landlord to complete a distress for rent payable in advance. Lord Cozens-Hardy M.R., at p. 408, in giving illustrations of the circumstances in which the court would refuse to allow a distress to be completed, instanced
H fraud or unfair dealing as possible grounds for depriving a landlord of the right to complete the distress he had begun. In *In re G. Winterbottom (Leeds) Ltd.* [1937] 2 All E.R. 232 Simonds J. restrained landlords from completing a distress for rent which was five and a quarter years in arrears because the landlords were also the directors of the company and should not have postponed collecting their money or exercising their remedies for such a long time while allowing the company to incur further debts from unsecured creditors.

These cases seem to show that there must be some inequitable conduct on the part of the person seeking to complete distress if the court is to interfere with his rights. The mere fact, in the present case, that the Crown will obtain priority over the other preferential creditors is no more relevant, it seems to me, than the fact that a landlord who is allowed to complete distress thereby obtains priority over all the unsecured creditors in the liquidation.

Mr. Heyman rightly points out the anomalies and different results which are achieved by the exercise of the power of distress if the company goes into voluntary winding up, or by the exercise of the power of distress if the company is compulsorily wound up by the court so that section 319 applies, or by the exercise of the power of execution or attachment so that section 325 applies. It is not possible for me to clear up these anomalies or difficulties. It may be that the Law Commission can be encouraged to give further consideration to these matters, and perhaps even to recommend the abolition of execution, distress, attachment and sequestration against a company, provided the Companies Court gives up the pretence of not allowing a winding up petition to be employed to enforce the payment of a debt. If winding up were the proper remedy, then either the creditor would be paid in full if the company were solvent or the company would be wound up and all the preferential and other rights of creditors would be maintained pari passu and would apply, whatever the reason for the winding up or the steps by which the winding up was achieved.

Summons dismissed with costs.
Leave to appeal.

Solicitors: *A. Kramer & Co.; Solicitor of Inland Revenue.*

A. R.

[QUEEN'S BENCH DIVISION]

* B.P. EXPLORATION CO. (LIBYA) LTD. *v.* HUNT

[1975 B. No. 4490]

1975 Oct. 13, 14, 15, 16, 31; Nov. 4 — Kerr J.

Practice—Writ—Service out of jurisdiction—Claim for declaration that contract governed by English law frustrated and consequential relief—Whether claims which "affect" contract—Whether jurisdiction to order service of notice of writ out of jurisdiction—Law Reform (Frustrated Contracts) Act 1943 (6 & 7 *Geo.* 6, *c.* 40), *ss.* 1 (1), 2 (3)—*R.S.C., Ord.* 11, *r.* 1 *(f)*

The defendant was granted a concession by the Libyan government for the search and exploitation of oil. He entered into an agreement signed in London with the plaintiffs, an oil company, for the development and joint exploitation of that

---

[Reported by Rachel Davies, Barrister-at-Law]

A concession, each party to receive half the beneficial interest
deriving from the concession. In return for the plaintiffs' pay-
ing the defendant's expenses and costs until exports from the
concession began, the defendant agreed that he should deliver to
the company three-eighths of his half share of the petroleum,
until the whole of the company's outlay was repaid. In 1971
the plaintiffs' assets and activities relating to the concession
were nationalised by the Libyan government. The defendant's
interests were nationalised in 1973 and he ceased to deliver
B petroleum to the plaintiffs. The plaintiffs issued a writ for
a declaration that the agreements had been frustrated by
nationalisation, and claimed, inter alia, sums in respect of
valuable benefits obtained by the defendant under the agree-
ments, pursuant to the Law Reform (Frustrated Contracts) Act
1943.[1] The defendant, who was resident in Dallas, Texas,
refused to accept service of the writ in this country through
C agents or solicitors, and the company obtained leave under
R.S.C., Ord. 11, r. 1 (*f*),[2] to serve notice of the writ on him
by post in Dallas. The defendant applied to set aside service
of notice of the writ and all subsequent proceedings.

On the question whether the court had jurisdiction under
R.S.C., Ord. 11, r. 1 (*f*), to order service of notice of the writ
outside the jurisdiction:—

Held, that a claim for a declaration that a contract had
D become discharged as a result of frustration was a claim that
affected the contract in question and therefore was a claim
within the meaning of "or otherwise affect a contract" in
R.S.C., Ord. 11, r. 1 (*f*) (post, p. 795D); that, since section
1 (3) of the Law Reform (Frustrated Contracts) Act 1943 had
effect in relation to frustrated contracts governed by English
law, the plaintiffs' claim for relief under the Act was one that
affected the contract within the meaning of Ord. 11, r. 1 (*f*)
E (post, p. 796H); and that, accordingly, since the contract was
governed by English law and England was the forum con-
veniens, leave to serve notice of the writ outside the jurisdiction
had been properly granted (post, pp. 797G, 798F, 799B).

The following cases are referred to in the judgment:

Bonython v. *Commonwealth of Australia* [1951] A.C. 201, P.C.
Bowling v. *Cox* [1926] A.C. 751, P.C.
F *Entores Ltd.* v. *Miles Far East Corporation* [1955] 2 Q.B. 327; [1955] 3 W.L.R. 48; [1955] 2 All E.R. 493, C.A.
G.A.F. Corporation v. *Amchem Products Inc.* [1975] 1 Lloyd's Rep. 601, C.A.
Hagen, The [1908] P. 189, C.A.
Italian, The [1969] 1 Lloyd's Rep. 11.
Johnson v. *Taylor Brothers & Co. Ltd.* [1920] A.C. 144, H.L.(E.).
G *Kernot* (*An Infant*), *In re* [1965] Ch. 217; [1964] 3 W.L.R. 1210; [1964] 3 All E.R. 339.
Macaulay (*A.*) (*Tweeds*) *Ltd.* v. *Independent Harris Tweed Producers Ltd.* [1961] R.P.C. 184.
Rein v. *Stein* [1892] 1 Q.B. 753, C.A.
Rousou's Trustee v. *Rousou* [1955] 1 W.L.R. 545; [1955] 2 All E.R. 169; [1955] 3 All E.R. 486.
H *Tyne Improvement Commissioners* v. *Armement Anversois S.A.* (*The Brabo*) [1949] A.C. 326; [1949] 1 All E.R. 294, H.L.(E.).

The following additional cases were cited in argument:

Appleby v. *Myers* (1867) L.R. 2 C.P. 651.

[1] Law Reform (Frustrated Contracts) Act 1943, s. 1 (1): see post, p. 795G.
S. 2 (3): see post, p. 796C–D.
[2] R.S.C., Ord. 11, r. 1 (*f*): see post, p. 795B.

Assunzione, The [1954] P. 150; [1954] 2 W.L.R. 234; [1954] 1 All E.R. 278, C.A. A

Buttes Gas & Oil Co. v. *Hammer* [1971] 3 All E.R. 1025, C.A.

Coast Lines Ltd. v. *Hudig & Veder Chartering N.V.* [1972] 2 Q.B. 34; [1972] 2 W.L.R. 280; [1972] 1 All E.R. 451, C.A.

Compagnie Tunisienne de Navigation S.A. v. *Compagnie d'Armement Maritime S.A.* [1971] A.C. 572; [1970] 3 W.L.R. 389; [1970] 3 All E.R. 71, H.L.(E.). B

Ellinger v. *Guiness, Mahon & Co.* [1939] 4 All E.R. 16.

Fibrosa Spolka Akcyjna v. *Fairbairn Lawson Combe Barbour Ltd.* [1943] A.C. 32; [1942] 2 All E.R. 122, H.L.(E.).

Hamlyn & Co. v. *Talisker Distillery* [1894] A.C. 202, H.L.(Sc.).

Hemelryck v. *Lyall Shipbuilding Co. Ltd.* [1921] 1 A.C. 698, P.C.

Lazard Brothers & Co. v. *Midland Bank Ltd.* [1933] A.C. 289, H.L.(E.).

Massey v. *Heynes & Co.* (1888) 21 Q.B.D. 330, C.A. C

Monro (George) Ltd. v. *American Cyanamid and Chemical Corporation* [1944] K.B. 432; [1944] 1 All E.R. 386, C.A.

Paradine v. *Jane* (1647) Aleyn 26.

Republic of Peru v. *Dreyfus Brothers & Co.* (1888) 38 Ch.D. 348.

Robey & Co. v. *Snaefell Mining Co. Ltd.* (1887) 20 Q.B.D. 152, D.C.

Russell (John) & Co. Ltd. v. *Cayzer, Irvine & Co.* [1916] 2 A.C. 298, H.L.(E.). D

Sayers v. *International Drilling Co. N.V.* [1971] 1 W.L.R. 1176; [1971] 3 All E.R. 163, C.A.

Schintz, In re [1926] Ch. 710, C.A.

Sinclair v. *Brougham* [1914] A.C. 398, H.L.(E.).

Société Générale de Paris v. *Dreyfus Brothers* (1887) 37 Ch.D. 215, C.A.

United Railways of Havana and Regla Warehouses Ltd., In re [1960] Ch. 52; [1959] 2 W.L.R. 251; [1959] 1 All E.R. 214, C.A. E

SUMMONS

The defendant, Nelson Bunker Hunt, a private citizen domiciled and resident in Dallas, Texas, U.S.A., applied for an order against the plaintiff company, B.P. Exploration Co. (Libya) Ltd., to set aside an order dated May 1, 1975, a writ of summons issued pursuant to that order, and service of notice of the writ by post in Dallas, and all subsequent proceedings, on the grounds, inter alia, that it was not a proper case for service out of the jurisdiction; that the proper law of the contract was either Libyan or Texan law rather than English law; and that the convenient forum for the trial of the dispute was the United States District Court for the Northern District of Texas in Dallas, Texas. F

The facts are stated in the judgment. G

Sir John Foster Q.C., *Gordon Slynn Q.C.* and *Nicholas Lyell* for the defendant.

Anthony Lloyd Q.C. and *Kenneth Rokinson* for the plaintiff company.

Cur. adv. vult. H

November 4. KERR J. read the following judgment. This is an application by the defendant, Mr. Hunt, to set aside service of notice of the writ and of all subsequent proceedings, leave to serve him by post in Dallas, Texas, having been granted to the plaintiffs ex parte by Donaldson J. on June 19, 1975. Mr. Hunt submits on numerous grounds that this is not a proper case for service out of the jurisdiction. The

A application raises issues of some importance in relation to R.S.C., Ord. 11, and the action involves very large sums of money.

Background

At some time during the fifties Mr. Hunt had been granted a concession known as "concession 65" by the then government of Libya
B for the search and exploration for oil. On June 24, 1960, he concluded an agreement with the plaintiffs, a subsidiary of British Petroleum Co. Ltd. with its registered office at the same address in London, for the development and joint exploitation of this concession. I will refer to the parties for convenience generally as "B.P." and "Mr. Hunt." The agreement consisted primarily of a letter from B.P. to Mr. Hunt at an address in Dallas, but it is common ground that this letter was not in
C fact sent, but signed by both parties in London. I will refer to this as the "letter agreement." It incorporated and annexed a lengthy "operating agreement" with several exhibits; this was never signed, but it is common ground that it became contractually binding at the same time. I will refer to these documents compendiously as "the 1960 agreement" and it is admitted that the 1960 agreement was made in
D London and therefore within the jurisdiction.

I must shortly refer to the effect and some of the terms of the 1960 agreement. By clause 1 of the letter agreement, B.P. agreed to pay the sum of $2 million to Mr. Hunt, and did so within a few days. Mr. Hunt agreed to hold concession 65 "subject to the one-half beneficial interest of B.P. therein in such manner and to such extent as is com-
E patible with the law of Libya," and agreed to execute an assignment of this beneficial interest. However, by clause 14, the letter agreement also provided that if the Libyan authorities should refuse consent to the assignment or withhold approval of it, Mr. Hunt would nevertheless continue to hold concession 65 subject to B.P.'s interest as to one-half, and that the parties would in that event consult together and take any necessary steps to ensure that the same financial result would still be
F achieved between them. The last part of clause 18 of the letter agreement provided:

> "Should any term or provision of this letter or of the operating agreement or assignment be construed under Libyan laws to operate as a forfeiture or breach of concession 65, then such term or provision shall be void and of no force or effect at the time of
> G agreement or any time thereafter."

Next I must refer to certain provisions of clause 9 of the operating agreement. Their main effect was as follows. Under clause 9 (3), B.P. was to advance and pay for Mr. Hunt's account his share of all costs and expenses incurred until exports of petroleum from the concession began.
H It must be borne in mind that in 1960 the commercial prospects of the concession were still uncertain and that nothing had yet been done or installed to extract any oil or to bring it to the Libyan seaboard. Under clause 9 (a), B.P. was to be reimbursed for all its costs incurred in this connection by the delivery f.o.b. Libyan seaboard of three-eighths of Mr. Hunt's share of the oil production from concession 65 until B.P. should have received a quantity of crude oil equal to the following, and I quote:

> "(1) A quantity equal in value to 125 per cent. of all costs and expenses advanced by B.P. for Hunt's account on exploration development or any other work performed in or in connection with the concession. (2) A quantity equal in value to $2,500,000. (3) 5 million barrels."

These quantities were therefore intended to repay the whole of B.P.'s outlay, including the initial $2 million, together with increments presumably intended to compensate B.P. for the interest on the money laid out and for the risks which they were taking about the commercial viability of concession 65.

Clause 6 of the letter agreement is important and I must set it out in full:

> "It is specifically understood and agreed that Hunt shall have no personal liability to repay the sums required in the operating agreement and this letter agreement to be advanced by B.P. for Hunt's account or paid to Hunt, but B.P.'s right to recover any such sums which B.P. is required to pay or advance for Hunt's account shall be limited to recovery solely out of three-eighths of Hunt's half of the production and in the manner specified under clause 9 of the operating agreement if, as and when produced, saved and delivered at the Libyan sea terminal."

I must also set out clause 27 of the operating agreement headed "Force majeure":

> "If any party is rendered unable wholly or in part by force majeure to carry out its obligations under this agreement other than the obligation to make money payments, that party shall give to all other parties prompt written notice of the force majeure with reasonably full particulars concerning it. Thereupon the obligations of the party giving the notice, so far as they are affected by the force majeure, shall be suspended during, but no longer than, the continuance of the force majeure. The affected party shall use all possible diligence to remove the force majeure as quickly as possible. The requirement that any force majeure should be remedied with all reasonable despatch shall not require the settlement of strikes, lock-outs, or other labour difficulty by the party involved contrary to its wishes. How all such difficulties shall be handled shall be entirely within the discretion of the party concerned. The term 'force majeure' as here employed shall mean an act of God, strike, lock-out or other industrial disturbance, act of a public enemy, war, blockade, public riot, lightning, fire, storm and flood, explosion, governmental restraint, unavailability of equipment and any other cause, whether of a kind specifically enumerated above or otherwise, which is not reasonably within the control of the party claiming suspension."

The Libyan authorities consented to the assignment of 50 per cent. of Mr. Hunt's interest to B.P. and this was executed in November 1960. B.P. thereafter proceeded with the development and exploitation of concession 65 as agreed. The concession ultimately proved successful and profitable to both sides for some time.

The next relevant event is that the 1960 agreement was amended in 1967. This was done by a memorandum of agreement dated June 30,

1967, which was initialled on behalf of both parties in Dallas, but which also provided that it was:

> "subject to the premise that such memorandum was only binding if confirmed by each party to the other in writing or by cable not later than the close of business on July 7, 1967."

This was done by Telexes from London and Dallas with certain very minor modifications. I will refer to these documents compendiously as "the 1967 amendment." The nature and extent of the amendments of the 1960 agreement by the 1967 amendment need not be referred to in detail. Among the most important were substantial amendments to clause 9 (3) of the operating agreement so as to produce a revised quantification of the "reimbursement oil" and to provide a rate at which this was to be delivered to B.P. f.o.b. Libyan seaboard. There were also a number of other substantial amendments. The overall position is that the 1967 amendment cannot stand on its own without the 1960 agreement, but that thereafter the full contractual terms between the parties, to which I will refer simply as "the contract," were contained in a combination of the 1960 agreement and the 1967 amendment.

The next relevant event is that by a Libyan nationalisation law of December 7, 1971, the activities and assets of B.P. relating to concession 65 were nationalised with certain provisions for compensation. I must set out article 1 of this Law:

> "The activities of B.P. Exploration Co. (Libya) Ltd. in Oil Concession No. 65 shall be nationalised. Ownership of all properties, rights, assets and shares relating to the above-mentioned activities shall revert to the state, including specifically the installations and facilities for exploration, drilling, production of crude oil and natural gas, transportation, utilisation, refining, storage and export, and other assets and rights relating to such activities."

Thereafter Mr. Hunt was evidently able to continue to exploit concession 65 for his own account until his interests were also nationalised some time in 1973. Meanwhile, disputes had arisen between B.P. and the government of Libya about the amount of B.P.'s compensation, but these were ultimately settled on November 20, 1974, in an agreed amount.

I then turn to the present action. The writ was issued on May 2, 1975, whereby B.P. claimed the following relief:

> "(1) A declaration that the letter agreement contained in or evidenced by a letter from the plaintiffs to the defendant dated June 24, 1960, a copy whereof was signed by the defendant, and/or the operating agreement, the terms of which were attached to the said letter in schedule 'B' thereto, as well as all subsequent agreements supplementary to the said agreements and/or varying the terms thereof, such agreements all relating to concession 65, were frustrated by the nationalisation or purported nationalisation by the Libyan government of the plaintiffs' activities and interests in concession 65 in December 1971 and/or the measures taken pursuant thereto. (2) Such sum or sums as the court considered just in respect of valuable benefits obtained by the defendant under the said agreements pursuant to the Law Reform (Frustrated Contracts) Act 1943. Further or alternatively: (3) Sums due and owing by the

defendant to the plaintiffs under the said agreements before the A frustration thereof. Further or alternatively: (4) Damages for breach thereof. (5) Interest. (6) Such further or other relief as the court may consider just and expedient."

Mr. Hunt declined to accept service of the writ through agents or solicitors in this country, and attempts to serve him personally during a short visit here proved unsuccessful. On June 19, 1975, B.P. then B obtained leave to serve notice of this writ on Mr. Hunt by post in Dallas as already mentioned. However, on June 10, 1975, Mr. Hunt had meanwhile himself instituted proceedings against B.P. in the Northern District Court of Texas for a declaration that he was under no liability to B.P. Mr. Hunt therefore brought his proceedings in Texas after B.P. had brought this action in England; he did so before service of the C English proceedings was effected upon him but after he had become aware that they had been brought. His summons to set aside the service of notice of the writ and all subsequent proceedings, which is now before me, was then issued on July 23, 1975. It did not prove possible to hear this summons before the long vacation because both parties wished to file considerable evidence. This has now been done, and the hearing before me included an adjournment to enable Mr. Hunt to file further D evidence in reply. B.P. disputes the jurisdiction of the Texan court on various grounds, and I am therefore now giving judgment while that decision is still pending. However, one court or the other has to give judgment first, and it has not been suggested that the decision of this court can depend upon whatever may be the decision of the Texan court, which I am in any event unable to foresee. E

Contentions in support of the application to set aside

Leave to serve outside the jurisdiction was given on the basis of an affidavit by Mr. John Gauntlett of the plaintiffs' solicitors, his contention being that the court had jurisdiction under Ord. 11, r. 1 (*f*) (i) and/or (iii), viz. that the 1962 agreement had been made within the jurisdiction F and/or was by implication governed by English law. On behalf of Mr. Hunt a large number of contentions were put forward by Sir John Foster in support of the present application. These can conveniently be grouped as follows: (1) the court has no jurisdiction because the case does not fall within Ord. 11, r. 1. (2) Even if there is jurisdiction, the service should be set aside because the plaintiffs' claim is bound to fail in any event. (3) The case is not a proper one for service outside the G jurisdiction, as required by Ord. 11, r. 4 (2), because London is not the forum conveniens. (4) The service should in any event be set aside because Mr. Gauntlett's affidavit failed to give a sufficiently full and fair account of the position as required by the rule.

I will accordingly deal with these contentions in turn. In doing so I bear in mind the three well known criteria relating to the exercise of H this jurisdiction as summarised by Farwell L.J. in *The Hagen* [1908] P. 189, 201 and often re-stated since, viz., that the jurisdiction is to be exercised with caution; that any doubts should be resolved in favour of the foreigner, bearing in mind that the case must not only fall within the letter but also within the spirit of the sub-rules; and that an insufficiently full and fair disclosure of the material circumstances in B.P.'s affidavit in support of the ex parte application would justify the discharge

A of the order granting leave even though B.P. may be in a position to make another application.

Jurisdiction under Ord. 11, *r.* 1 (*f*)

Sir John Foster took two points which logically precede the question whether the contract was made in London and whether the proper law
B was English under sub-rule (*f*). He submitted that the relief claimed by B.P. under paragraphs (1) and (2) of the writ did not fall within rule 1 at all, because this is not an "action begun . . . to enforce, rescind, dissolve, annul or otherwise affect a contract . . ."

In relation to the claim for a declaration under paragraph (1) of the writ that the contract had become frustrated, it was accepted by Mr. Lloyd that B.P. could only rely on the words of sub-rule (*f*) "or otherwise
C affect the contract." However, Sir John Foster submitted that a claim for a declaration that a contract has been discharged by frustration—and indeed any claim relating to an allegedly frustrated contract—cannot fall even within these words, since ex hypothesi there no longer is any contract, because on the plaintiffs' case it has been discharged by frustration. He said, in effect, that on the plaintiffs' own contention the court is dealing
D with an ex-contract, a corpse, and that there is therefore no longer any contract which can be "affected." I cannot accept this contention. The words "or otherwise affect" are very wide; indeed, almost as wide as they can be. A claim for a declaration that a contract has become discharged, whether as the result of frustration, repudiation, or otherwise, is in my view a claim which affects the contract in question. The contrary construction would have serious and highly inconvenient consequences.
E For instance, a contract might be entirely English, made here, governed by English law, and broken here, but on this submission our courts would nevertheless be obliged to decline jurisdiction and to leave it to a foreign court to declare whether according to English law the contract had for some reason become discharged. I think that the wide words "or otherwise affect" were deliberately included to prevent a result such as this, and
F I therefore reject this contention.

In my view, similar considerations equally apply to Sir John Foster's second point under this head, viz. that the claim under paragraph (2) of the writ for relief under the Law Reform (Frustrated Contracts) Act 1943 is not within any of the sub-rules of rule 1. In this connection I must first set out certain provisions of this Act. Section 1 (1):

G "Where a contract governed by English law has become impossible of performance or been otherwise frustrated, and the parties thereto have for that reason been discharged from the further performance of the contract, the following provisions of this section shall, subject to the provisions of section 2 of this Act, have effect in relation thereto."

H The Act therefore only applies to contracts governed by English law. I have to deal with the question of the proper law hereafter, but for present purposes I will assume that this requirement is satisfied, since otherwise cadit questio. I need not read any of the other provisions of section 1 save to state that the plaintiffs' claim under paragraph (2) of the writ which I have quoted is founded on subsection (3), the provision dealing with pre-frustration benefits conferred by one party upon the other. The alleged benefits in question, as I understand, are all the installations and

activities by means whereof Mr. Hunt's concession 65 was exploited, and A
the oil in the ground converted into marketable oil delivered at the Libyan seaboard.

Subsections (1), (2) and (3) of section 2 of the Act each refer to "contracts" to which the Act applies, notwithstanding that the Act only applies "Where a contract . . . has become impossible of performance or been otherwise frustrated." This is of some relevance to Sir John Foster's first argument with which I have already dealt, since it shows that the Act B
itself is drafted on the basis that contracts, albeit frustrated, are to be affected by the provisions of the Act. I set out in this connection section 2 (3), since this is also material to another point on which Sir John Foster relies and to which I turn hereafter:

> "Where any contract to which this Act applies contains any provision which, upon the true construction of the contract, is intended to have C
> effect in the event of circumstances arising which operate, or would but for the said provisions operate, to frustrate the contract, or is intended to have effect whether such circumstances arise or not, the court shall give effect to the said provision and shall only give effect to the foregoing section of this Act to such extent, if any, as appears to the court to be consistent with the said provision." D

If one then asks oneself: "Is a claim under the Act one which 'affects' a contract which has been (allegedly) frustrated?" it seems to me that the answer must be in the affirmative as a matter of ordinary English, and indeed on the basis of the language of the Act itself. The dictionary meaning of the verb "to affect" in this context is "to produce a material effect" on something. It seems to me that this is precisely what the Act E
is doing in relation to a frustrated contract governed by English law. Section 1 (1) provides that as regards such a contract "the following provisions of this section . . . shall have effect in relation thereto." The word "thereto" can in my view only relate to the frustrated contract, in the same way as the word "thereto" a little earlier in the same sentence. It follows that the Act provides that section 1 (3) is to have effect in relation to a frustrated contract governed by English law. In these circum- F
stances it appears to me that a claim under this subsection is clearly one which "affects" such a contract. Here again, the contrary construction would produce undesirable results, which I do not think can have been intended. The consequence would be that an English court would have jurisdiction to give leave to serve a defendant out of the jurisdiction where the plaintiff claims that a contract governed by English law has become G
frustrated, but, if this issue is decided in favour of the plaintiff, that the English court would then have to leave it to a foreign court to decide the consequences between the parties which flow from the Act of 1943.

I think that this is the short answer to Sir John Foster's point on the relief claimed under paragraph (2) of the writ and that it really stands or falls with his point on paragraph (1). In my view the court's powers to H
determine the issues which "affect" a contract falling within sub-rule *(f)* do not cease by reason of the frustration of the contract, and they include the application of the Act of 1943 to the extent that its provisions have effect in relation to the contract. I therefore also reject this contention.

However, in case I am wrong about this, and for the sake of completeness, I must also shortly deal with a different point raised by Mr. Lloyd as his main submission in answer to the second contention. He

A submitted that the relief provided by section 1 (3) of the Act is of a quasi-contractual nature, albeit provided by statute and not available at common law (which was indeed the reason for the passing of the statute), and that obligations under a quasi-contract governed by English law (or arising within the jurisdiction) are within sub-rule (*f*) and can be " enforced " in proceedings served out of the jurisdiction. For the proposition that quasi-contractual obligations can fall within sub-rule (*f*) he relied on the
B decision of the Privy Council in *Bowling* v. *Cox* [1926] A.C. 751 and on the decisions of Danckwerts J. in *Rousou's Trustee* v. *Rousou* [1955] 1 W.L.R. 545 and *Rousou's Trustee* v. *Rousou* [1955] 3 All E.R. 486 which followed *Bowling* v. *Cox*. He pointed out that in *Rousou's* case Danckwerts J. accepted this reasoning although the primary relief sought by the plaintiff arose by statute, in particular under the Bankruptcy Act
C 1914, though it is also clear from p. 491 of the second report that the judge was basing his decision solely upon the quasi-contractual right of recovery at common law and in no way on the statutory position. Mr. Lloyd submitted, however, that it was only a short further step to hold that the same result follows if the relief of a quasi-contractual nature is only conferred by statute, and not at common law, as in the present case. This reasoning is attractive, because it is obviously desirable, if possible,
D to conclude that an English court should have jurisdiction under Order 11 where an English statute creates rights of a quasi-contractual nature which are governed by English law. But on balance I think that this argument is too artificial, at any rate in the present context, to fall within sub-rule (*f*), though I must not be taken to express any view on the position under other statutes. In the present context the argument involves
E no more than a fiction, viz. to hold that after the original contract is discharged by frustration there comes into being a new statutory quasi-contract in the terms of whichever subsection of section 1 of the Act is relied upon, in this case subsection (3). But this is not at all the reality. The reality is that there is only one contract, the original contract which has become frustrated, but that the statute engrafts upon this contract certain post-frustration rights and obligations which in the view of the
F legislature the justice between the parties requires. I therefore consider that from start to finish one is only dealing with one contract, but one which is " affected " by the provisions of the Act, and that for this reason, though not for any other, a claim under the Act can fall within sub-rule (*f*) if the requirements of the sub-rule and of the Act are otherwise met.

I now turn to the remaining questions under sub-rule (*f*), viz. whether
G the contract was made within the jurisdiction or impliedly governed by English law. [His Lordship considered the evidence, referred to *Bonython* v. *Commonwealth of Australia* [1951] A.C. 201, 219 *per* Lord Simonds, and continued:] In all these circumstances I conclude that the proper law of the contract is English law, with the consequence that the case falls within Ord. 11, r. 1 (*f*) (iii).

H However, in case I am wrong about this I must also shortly deal with Mr. Lloyd's alternative contention, which he put in the forefront of his argument, that the contract was made within the jurisdiction and therefore also falls within sub-rule (*f*) (i). During the argument it seemed to me that the answer to this contention was that the contract includes the 1967 amendment, that this was made in Dallas (though remaining to be mutually confirmed by Telex), and that the contract sued upon as a whole was therefore made partly in London and partly in Dallas and accordingly not within the jurisdiction. On further consideration, however, I have come to the conclusion that it is not the right approach. I think that the correct analysis is that the contract was made in London and amended in Dallas; not that it was made partly in London and partly in Dallas, or elsewhere. The 1967 amendment could not stand alone; it merely amended certain provisions of the 1960 agreement. The position would, of course, have been different if the 1967 amendment had operated as a discharge of the 1960 agreement and substituted a fresh agreement. The foregoing analysis is also in accord with what Denning L.J. appears to have thought in *Entores Ltd.* v. *Miles Far East Corporation* [1955] 2 Q.B. 327, 334, where he preferred the view that an agreement made in one country and amended in another should be regarded as not having been made in the latter country. Secondly, even if this analysis be wrong, I think that it is sufficient for the purposes of the rule if the contract which is the subject matter of the action was *substantially* made within the jurisdiction. Otherwise the effect of the rule could be avoided by some very minor subsequent amendment or addendum executed abroad. This analysis is consonant with what was the position relating to successive contractual breaches outside and within the jurisdiction before the adoption of the present wording of sub-rule (*g*), i.e. before the addition of the words " irrespective of the fact . . . that the breach was preceded or accompanied by a breach committed out of the jurisdiction. . . ." In relation to the earlier wording of the corresponding sub-rule it was held sufficient to attract jurisdiction if a substantial part of the contract had to be performed within the jurisdiction and if there was a breach of that part: see *Rein* v. *Stein* [1892] 1 Q.B. 753. As I read the decision of the House of Lords in *Johnson* v. *Taylor Brothers & Co. Ltd.* [1920] A.C. 144 this also approved the principle that a sufficient ground to found jurisdiction existed under the former wording if a substantial breach had occurred within the jurisdiction, though not if this merely resulted inevitably in consequence of a breach outside. I accordingly hold that leave to serve out of the jurisdiction was also justified on the basis of sub-rule (*f*) (i) because the contract was made within the jurisdiction.

[His Lordship then considered the defendant's submissions that the plaintiffs' claims were bound to fail and that London was not the forum conveniens, referred to *Tyne Improvement Commissioners* v. *Armement Anversois S.A.* [1949] A.C. 326; *The Italian* [1969] 1 Lloyd's Rep. 11 and *In re Kernot* (*An Infant*) [1965] Ch. 217. His Lordship held that the plaintiffs' claims were not bound to fail and that, between England and Texas, the English courts were the forum conveniens.]

Alleged defectiveness of Mr. Gauntlett's affidavit

While Sir John Foster made it clear, rightly in my view, that he was in no way imputing to Mr. Gauntlett any intention to mislead the court, he submitted that the affidavit on the basis of which leave was granted did not contain a full and fair disclosure of all the material facts in a number of respects, with the result that the service on Mr. Hunt should be set aside. [His Lordship considered the defendant's submissions, referred to *G.A.F. Corporation* v. *Amchem Products Inc.* [1975] 1 Lloyd's Rep. 601 and *A. Macaulay* (*Tweeds*) *Ltd.* v. *Independent Harris Tweed Producers Ltd.* [1961] R.P.C. 184 and continued:] The primary question should be whether in all the circumstances the effect of the affidavit is such as to mislead the court in any material respect concerning its

A jurisdiction and the discretion under the rule. The alleged deficiencies in the present affidavit do not in my view have this effect or even approach it, and any deliberate attempt to mislead was expressly disclaimed. I therefore also reject this contention.

Conclusion

B For all the foregoing reasons I conclude that leave to serve out of the jurisdiction was properly given in this case, with the result that the application fails.

Application refused.

Solicitors: *Franks, Charlesley & Co.; Linklaters & Paines.*

C

[COURT OF APPEAL]

* PRACTICE DIRECTION (JUDGE: MODE OF ADDRESS)

D 1976 July 26 Lord Widgery C.J., Melford Stevenson and Caulfield JJ.

Judge—Circuit judge—Deputy—Mode of address and listing

LORD WIDGERY C.J., at the sitting of the court, read the following practice direction.

1. A deputy circuit judge (including a retired judge sitting as a deputy)
E when sitting in court should be addressed as "Sir" or "Madam," as the case may be.

2. When a case is listed for hearing before a deputy circuit judge, the court list should refer to him or her as "Mr. (Mrs. or Miss or other title) A.B., sitting as a deputy circuit judge."

L. N. W.

F

[COURT OF APPEAL]

* PRACTICE DIRECTION (CRIME: INCONSISTENT DECISIONS)

G 1976 July 26 Lord Widgery C.J., Melford Stevenson and Caulfield JJ.

Crime—Plea—Guilty—Not guilty plea entered—Counsel advising change of plea after conversation with judge—Principle to be followed

LORD WIDGERY C.J., at the sitting of the court, read the following
H practice direction.

The decision in *Reg.* v. *Cain*, The Times, February 23, 1976, has been subject to further consideration by the Court of Appeal.

In so far as it is inconsistent with *Reg.* v. *Turner* [1970] 2 Q.B. 321; [1970] 2 W.L.R. 1093, C.A. the latter decision should prevail.

L. N. W.

A

[QUEEN'S BENCH DIVISION]

* CORNER *v.* CLAYTON

1976 May 5 Lord Widgery C.J., Donaldson and Boreham JJ.

Aircraft—Public transport—Hire or reward—Flying club aircraft B *used to transport passengers—Aircraft flown by club member —Payment to club of normal fee for member's use—Whether "hire or reward" for carriage of passengers—Air Navigation Order* 1974 (*S.I.* 1974 *No.* 1114), *art.* 91 (1) (6) (*a*) (i)

The defendant, who held a private pilot's licence not qualifying him to fly an aircraft used for the purpose of public transport within article 19 (1) of the Air Navigation C Order 1974,[1] was a member of a flying club owning aircraft for which members paid £9 an hour for flying. W., who was not a member of the club, asked V., a member, whether it was possible for him or any available pilot using a club aircraft to fly W. and his family from Exeter to Jersey and back to attend a wedding. The defendant and an aircraft being available, V. made the arrangements and W. paid £27 to the club through V. The payment, which involved no profit D element to the club, covered a member's cost of use of the aircraft for the flight, and no payment was made to the defendant. Four informations were preferred against him charging him with acting as pilot on a flight for the purpose of public transport without an appropriate licence, in contravention of the Order of 1974. All the informations involved consideration of the definition in article 91 (1) of "public transport" and its deemed meaning in article 91 (6) (*a*) (i). The justices, who were of E opinion that payment for use of the aircraft could not constitute hire or reward within article 91 (6) (*a*) (i) in the absence of any profit element in the payment, dismissed the informations.

On appeal by the prosecutor:—

Held, allowing the appeal, that hire meant engaging the services of a person or the use of a chattel for payment, and a profit element in the charge for hiring was immaterial; that F the question to be asked was, for what the payment or hire was being made, given or promised; and that, since the offer accepted by W. was for the carriage of himself and his family from Exeter to Jersey and back for payment of £27, there was a hiring of the aircraft for the carriage of passengers; so that the aircraft was carrying passengers on each flight in pursuance of that hiring; and that, accordingly, the case would be remitted to the justices with a direction to convict on the G four informations.

The following case is referred to in the judgment of Boreham J.:

Albert v. *Motor Insurers' Bureau* [1972] A.C. 301; [1971] 3 W.L.R. 291; [1971] 2 All E.R. 1345, H.L.(E.).

No additional cases were cited in argument. H

CASE STATED by Devon justices sitting at Exeter.

On May 4, 1975, four informations were preferred by the prosecutor, Michael Richmond Corner on behalf of the Civil Aviation Authority,

[1] Air Navigation Order 1974, art. 19 (1): see post, p. 803G, H.
Art. 91 (1): see post, p. 804A.

A against the defendant, John Clayton, as follows: (a) that he on October 12, 1974, being the commander of an aircraft bearing the registration letters G-BAOE did act as pilot in command of the aircraft on a flight for the purpose of public transport from Exeter Airport to Jersey Airport without being the holder of an appropriate licence entitling him so to act, in contravention of article 19 (1) of the Air Navigation Order 1974; (b) that he did fly the aircraft over water on a flight for the purpose of public transport
B from Exeter Airport to Jersey Airport below such altitude as would enable the aircraft in the event of failure of its engine to reach a place at which it could safely land at a height sufficient to enable it to do so, in contravention of articles 28 (3) and 85 of the Order of 1974; (c) that he did act as pilot in command of the aircraft on a flight for the purpose of public transport from Jersey Airport to Exeter Airport without being the holder of an
C appropriate licence entitling him so to act, in contravention of article 19 (1) of the Order of 1974; and (d) that he did fly the aircraft over water on a flight for the purpose of public transport from Jersey Airport to Exeter Airport below such altitude as would enable the aircraft in the event of the failure of its engine to reach a place at which it could safely land at a height sufficient to enable it to do so, in contravention of articles 28 (3) and 85 of the Order of 1974.

D The justices heard the informations together on August 22, 1975, and found the following facts. The defendant, a member of the Dunkeswell Flying Club near Exeter held a private pilot's licence issued on September 25, 1973, and valid until September 24, 1978. The licence was subject to the conditions laid down in Part A of Schedule 9 to the Air Navigation Order 1974 including, inter alia, a condition "he shall not
E fly such an aeroplane for the purpose of public transport . . ." About October 5, 1974, Gerald Raymond Weatherall, who was not a member of the club, received an invitation to a wedding to take place in Jersey on October 12, 1974. Mr. Weatherall requested a Mr. John Vicary, the holder of a private pilot's licence and a member of the club, to inquire whether it was possible to arrange for Mr. and Mrs. Weatherall and their baby to be flown from Exeter to Jersey and back on October 12, 1974,
F either by himself or by any other available pilot, using an aircraft belonging to the club. There being an aircraft available and a pilot willing to make the flight, Mr. Vicary made those arrangements. In consideration of the flight Mr. Weatherall paid £27 to the club by way of Mr. John Vicary. The charge was for three hours' flying at £9 an hour. That was the standard charge which would be payable by a member of the club if he
G wished to use the aircraft. The payment covered the cost of the use of the aircraft for that flight without gain or any element of profit to the club. On October 12, 1974, the defendant met the Weatherall family at Exeter Airport and flew them at an altitude of approximately 2,000 feet from Exeter to Jersey subsequently returning the same day at a similar altitude. The aircraft flown by the defendant was a single engined Socata Rallye MS 880B aircraft. On both journeys it was flown over
H water at a height of 2,000 feet or thereabouts, other than when taking off or landing. Had the flight been for the purpose of public transport the aircraft should have been flown over water at a minimum height of 14,750 feet, other than when taking off or landing to comply with articles 28 (3) and 85 of the Air Navigation Order 1974. The defendant received no payment for flying the aircraft. He paid the £1 landing fee at Jersey Airport out of his own pocket. The defendant was an enthusiastic pilot who was accumulating flying hours to enable him to apply for a commercial

pilot's licence. The flying hours on the journey contributed towards such accumulation. On the Thursday afternoon preceding October 12, 1974, the defendant would, had he not undertaken the flight to Jersey, have been flying an aircraft for the benefit of members of a parachuting club subject to weather conditions. Had that taken place he could have been flying from 3.00 p.m. to 9.30 p.m. and the hours then flown would have counted towards the flying hours for his commercial pilot's licence.

It was contended by the prosecutor that the defendant was flying for the purpose of public transport as defined by article 91 of the Air Navigation Order 1974 on the basis that if the court was satisfied (a) that the payment of £27 to the club was hire or reward, or (b) that the benefit, enjoyment, experience and the accumulation of flying hours was reward, then the defendant was flying for the purpose of public transport and was guilty of the offences alleged on the basis of article 91 (6) (*a*) (1) of the Air Navigation Order 1974.

It was contended on behalf of the defendant that the payment of the £27 could not constitute hire or reward within the ordinary sense of those words in the absence of any profit element in the charge of £27; further, because the defendant had not piloted members of the parachuting club but had flown to Jersey, there could be no question of reward as he had flown fewer hours by undertaking the trip to Jersey than he would have had he been engaged by the parachuting club.

The justices were of the opinion that the prosecutor had not proved his case since payment of the £27 for the use of aircraft could not constitute hire or reward in the absence of any profit element in the payment. Payment was to cover operating costs of the aircraft only. The justices further found, in relation to the question of hire or reward, that an isolated occasion was insufficient to constitute that within the meaning of the Order of 1974 and they referred to the judgment of Lord Donovan in *Albert* v. *Motor Insurers' Bureau* [1972] A.C. 301, 319; they further felt that the flying experience gained by the defendant on October 12, 1974, did not constitute hire or reward within the context of the Order. They therefore, dismissed the summonses.

The prosecutor appealed. The question for the opinion of the court was whether the justices were wrong in holding on the facts that the flight in question was not for the purposes of public transport.

Roger Toulson for the prosecutor.
Julian Sandys for the defendant.

LORD WIDGERY C.J. I will ask Boreham J. to give the first judgment.

BOREHAM J. This is an appeal by way of case stated from the decision of Devon justices sitting at Exeter on August 22, 1975.

On that date the defendant appeared to answer four informations which had been preferred by the prosecutor. Those informations all related to a flight from Exeter to Jersey and the return flight from Jersey to Exeter on October 12, 1974. In the first information he was charged with being the commander of an aircraft on a flight for the purpose of public transport from Exeter to Jersey without being the holder of the appropriate licence. In the second information he was charged as a commander of that same aircraft on a flight for the purpose of public transport from Exeter to Jersey flying at an inadequate height. The other two informations

A are in exactly the same form and relate to the return journey from Jersey to Exeter.

There is, therefore, common to each of those four informations, and an essential ingredient in the proof of each of the offences charged against the defendant, that he was in command of an aircraft, and these are the important words, "on a flight for the purpose of public transport" from one aerodrome to another.

B From the facts found by the justices it appears that the defendant was a member of a local flying club near Exeter, that he held at the time of the flights a private pilot's licence which was valid until September 24, 1978, and that that licence was subject to the important condition that he should not fly an aeroplane for the purpose of public transport.

It is also apparent from the facts found by the justices that he was an
C enthusiastic pilot, keen on accumulating flying hours in order to enable him to apply ultimately for a commercial pilot's licence. They found that the flying hours completed on those particular journeys contributed towards that accumulation.

The offences arose in this manner. On October 5, 1974, a Mr. Weatherall, who had been invited to a wedding in Jersey on October 12, approached one of the members of the defendant's flying club, a
D Mr. Vicary and asked:

> "whether it was possible to arrange for Mr. and Mrs. Weatherall and their baby to be flown from Exeter to Jersey and back on October 12, 1974, either by himself"—that is, Mr. Vicary—"or by any other available pilot, using an aircraft belonging to the club."

There being an aircraft available and a pilot willing to make the flight,
E Mr. Vicary made the arrangements. The case continues:

> "In consideration of the flight Mr. Weatherall paid £27 to the club by way of Mr. John Vicary. The charge was for three hours' flying at £9 an hour. That was the standard charge which would be payable by a member of the club if he wished to use the aircraft. The payment covered the cost of the use of the aircraft for that flight
> F without gain or any element of profit to the club. On October 12, 1974, the defendant met the Weatherall family at Exeter Airport and flew them at an altitude of approximately 2,000 feet from Exeter to Jersey subsequently returning the same day at a similar altitude."

Had the flight been for the purpose of public transport the aircraft should have been flown over water at a minimum height of 14,750 feet.

G The justices find that the defendant himself received no payment for flying the aeroplane; indeed, he paid £1 landing fee out of his own pocket at Jersey Airport. Those, in my judgment at any rate, are the material facts which are found by the justices.

The statutory provisions on which the informations were based are to be found in the Air Navigation Order 1974. Article 19 (1) provides:

> H "Subject to the provisions of this article, a person shall not act as a member of the flight crew of an aircraft registered in the United Kingdom unless he is the holder of an appropriate licence granted or rendered valid under this order: . . ."

By article 20 and Part A of Schedule 9 it is clear (and I need say no more about it because there is no argument to the contrary) that the pilot's licence which was held by the defendant did not qualify him to fly an aircraft which was being used for the purpose of public transport.

The definition of "public transport" is to be found in article 91, A which provides:

> "(1) . . . 'Public transport' has the meaning assigned to it by paragraph (6) of this article; . . . (6) (*a*) Subject to the provisions of this paragraph, an aircraft in flight shall for the purposes of this Order be deemed to fly for the purpose of pubic transport—(i) if hire or reward is given or promised for the carriage of passengers or cargo in B the aircraft on that flight; . . ."

It is to the words of article 91 (6) (*a*) (i) that the argument has been directed. It is pertinent perhaps to observe that article 91 (6) gives no indication as to whom the hire or reward is to be paid if the aircraft is to be deemed to be flying for the purpose of public transport.

Before turning to the contentions which are raised in this case on this C appeal, let me return to the case stated by the justices and to the findings that they have made and the conclusions which they have reached on the question whether hire or reward was given or promised. I quote from the case:

> "We were of the opinion that the prosecutor had not proved his case since payment of the £27 for the use of the aircraft could not D constitute hire or reward in the absence of any profit element in the payment. Payment was to cover operating costs of the aircraft only. We further found, in relation to the question of hire or reward, that an isolated occasion is insufficient to constitute this within the meaning of the Order of 1974."

Then they quote, in the latter connection, *Albert* v. *Motor Insurers' Bureau* E [1972] A.C. 301.

I deal with the latter conclusion first, namely, that an isolated occasion is insufficient to constitute hire or reward. It is contended on behalf of the prosecutor here that in that respect the justices misdirected themselves, and that *Albert's* case had really nothing to do with the problem which they, and now this court, had to resolve, namely, the construction of article 91 (6) (*a*). F

It is now conceded, as I understand it, by Mr. Sandys on behalf of the defendant that the decision in *Albert's* case has no bearing on the problem that we have to resolve. In this I agree with him. Furthermore, he does not rely on the fact that this was an isolated incident as a valid reason for holding that this was not a flight for the purpose of public transport. Here again I agree with him. It seems to me that in respect G of each flight the question must be asked: was hire or reward given or promised for the carriage of passengers?

As to the justices' first conclusion, namely, that the payment of £27 for the use of the aircraft could not constitute hire or reward in the absence of any profit element in the payment, as I understand Mr. Sandys he does not entirely relinquish that point. The prosecutor, through H Mr. Toulson, contends that profit is an irrelevant consideration; he points to the difficulty that would arise in deciding cases if courts had first to decide whether or not there could properly be said to be a profit element.

It is enough to say in this regard that, in my judgment, hire means engaging the services of a person or the use of a chattel for payment, and it is immaterial, as I see it, whether or not there is in the hiring charge a profit element. In these circumstances, I have come to the conclusion

A that the justices did misdirect themselves on the two matters which I have briefly outlined and, I hope, adequately dealt with.

The question at the end of the day is this: what do the words "if hire or reward is given or promised for the carriage of passengers or cargo in the aircraft on that flight" in article 91 (6) (*a*) (i) of the Air Navigation Order 1974 mean?

Mr. Sandys on behalf of the defendant contends, first, that those are
B words which are apt to denote, and to denote only, a transaction which is commercial in its character rather than of a purely social nature; he contends that here the facts disclose what is essentially a social transaction.

I do not accept that the words hire or reward should be given anything other than their normal, ordinary, sensible meaning whatever other label may be attached to the transaction in question.

C Mr. Sandys' second contention is this; if the aircraft is to be deemed to be flying for the purpose of public transport, then it must be shown that hire or reward is given or promised for the carriage of passengers and not merely for the use of the aircraft. He argues that in this case there was merely a procuring of the use of the aircraft.

It seems to me that in each case one has to ask the question: for what was the payment or the hire being made, given or promised? It may well
D be more or less correct to say that it was given for the use of the aircraft, but that may not be a complete answer. It may be that the complete answer is that it was given for the use of the aircraft to carry passengers.

The complete answer in the present case is clear from the facts found by the justices, and I remind myself of them. Mr. Weatherall's inquiry was "whether it was possible to arrange for Mr. and Mrs. Weatherall and
E their baby to be flown from Exeter to Jersey and back" using an aircraft belonging to the club. The answer to that inquiry was yes; yes, on payment of a certain sum—£27. That was the offer that Mr. Weatherall accepted.

It seems to me that, on those facts, there is but one conclusion that could be reached, namely, that here was a hiring for carriage of Mr. Weatherall and his family by this particular aircraft. If I am right in that, then it seems to me that that is conclusive of this case. There was a hiring
F for the carriage of passengers and it is clear that it was in pursuance of that hiring that the aircraft was carrying passengers on the relevant flights.

In those circumstances I have come to the conclusion that the justices misdirected themselves so far as the law was concerned; they applied too restricted a construction to article 91 (6) (*a*). There being only one conclusion that could be reached on the facts as they have found them in this case I would allow this appeal and order that the case be returned to
G the justices with a direction that they convict on each of the four informations.

DONALDSON J. I entirely agree with the order proposed by Boreham J. I will only add that this was a difficult problem for the justices, and I have every sympathy with them in the difficulties which confronted them.

H

LORD WIDGERY C.J. I also agree with the order proposed and I also will add a word or two in deference to the helpful argument in this court and the trouble which the justices have clearly taken over this matter themselves. The case is admirably stated.

Of course much of the trouble is due to the draftsman here. The phrase "fly for the purpose of public transport," if one is allowed to give the words their normal meaning, is a fairly simple phrase to apply. But not so. There is a specific definition of "public transport" which produces A an effect to my mind quite different from that which the natural meaning of the words would have. This is a perfect formula for confusing justices. It is a pity it has to be employed.

I at one time was troubled by Mr. Sandys' argument in which he stressed, and I think rightly stressed, that one must always watch in these cases to make sure that the payment put forward as hire or reward is not paid for the aircraft rather than for the carriage of passengers or cargo. B Whether or not one particular case falls into one category or the other is primarily a question of fact.

In the end it was for the justices, correctly directing themselves in law, to decide that ultimate question of fact in this case. But, as Boreham J. has pointed out, the facts of this case are such that I think it unnecessary to send the matter back to the justices because a conclusion that in this C case the offence was committed is, I think, inescapable.

I accordingly agree with the order proposed.

Appeal allowed.
Case remitted to justices with direction to convict on the four informations.
Prosecutor's costs out of central funds. D

Solicitors: *Ashford, Penny & Harward, Exeter; Peter J. Bartlett, South Molton.*

L. N. W.

E

[CHANCERY DIVISION]

* *In re* ROBINSON'S SETTLEMENT TRUSTS

[1975 No. R. 5247] F

1976 March 3, 17 Templeman J.

Trusts—Variation—Tax liability—Capital transfer tax—Family arrangement—Division of trust fund between life tenant and remaindermen—Infant remainderman's share liable to shortfall by incidence of capital transfer tax on life tenant's premature death—Insurance to provide for shortfall—Form of policy G

By a settlement dated November 1, 1952, the settlor settled certain property on the plaintiff, his daughter, on protective trusts for life, giving her a power to appoint among her children and remoter issue and, in default of appointment, in trust for such of the plaintiff's children as attained the age of 21 years, and if more than one, in equal shares. By his will dated November 2, 1952, the settlor settled certain property on H trusts similar to the trusts of the settlement. The plaintiff, at the date of these proceedings, was 55, and had three children, two of them, the first two defendants, being over 21 years and one, the third defendant, an infant. In order to save capital transfer tax expected to be levied on the plaintiff's death and to spread the wealth of the trust fund among those members of the family beneficially entitled to it, an arrangement was proposed whereby the trust fund was to be divided so that the plaintiff took 52 per cent. and the children took 48 per cent.,

A the capital gains tax incurred by the division to be borne proportionately and the plaintiff to pay one sixth of the capital transfer tax incurred on the children's share. The plaintiff proposed to effect and pay for a three year insurance policy protecting the children against the risk of capital transfer tax being payable at the death rate if the plaintiff died within three years of the proposed division.

The plaintiff issued a summons for the court's approval of
B the arrangement under section 1 of the Variation of Trusts Act 1958. The figures before the court showed that the third defendant's share was worth some £58,000 gross, which, if capital transfer tax was payable, was likely to be reduced by about £14,000. If an insurance was taken out by the plaintiff to provide for payment of that tax it was thought that the premium for that policy might also attract the tax. Templeman J. adjourned the hearing for the parties to reconsider insurance
C proposals so as to overcome that reduction in the infant's share. On amendment of the arrangement to provide a life with profits policy on the plaintiff's life, the payment of the premiums to be paid out of the third defendant's income from her own share:—

Held, that it could not be assumed that the plaintiff would live so long that the arrangement, viewed as a whole, would benefit the third defendant; that the court had to be satisfied that the arrangement was beneficial; that the arrangement could
D be approved provided that, although it was anomalous, the third defendant's income was to a certain extent made available for insurance so as to protect her own share against loss caused by the premature death of the plaintiff; and that, accordingly, a policy for £8,000, which with profits would yield over £11,000 in 10 years and more thereafter, and costing about £400 a year would be, having regard to the income at present, a proper
E policy to take out.

The following cases are referred to in the judgment:

Cohen's Settlement Trusts, In re [1965] 1 W.L.R. 1229; [1965] 3 All E.R. 139.

Cohen's Will Trusts, In re [1959] 1 W.L.R. 865; [1965] 3 All E.R. 523.

F No additional case was cited in argument.

ORIGINATING SUMMONS.

By a settlement dated November 1, 1952, and made between Gordon Hope Robinson, of the one part ("the settlor"), and the settlor, Edward Marrow, Frederick Thomas Brockes and Walter Brown Chapman of the other part, 1,252 fully paid shares of £1 each in Fairplay Publications Ltd.
G were settled on the following trusts (a) that the income was to be held on the statutory protective trust for the benefit of the settlor's daughter, the plaintiff, Margaret Hope Heard, during her life; and (b) from and after the plaintiff's death capital and income were to be held in trust for her children and remoter issue as she, by deed revocable or irrevocable, or by will or codicil, might appoint; and (c) in default of appointment, capital
H and income were to be held in trust for all or any of the plaintiff's children, or child, who attained the age of 21 years, and if more than one in equal shares, subject to a hotchpot.

By his will dated November 3, 1952, the settlor bequeathed all his shares and other interests in Fairplay Publications Ltd. to his trustees on trust to pay the income to his wife during her life and from and after her death on the same beneficial and other trusts and subject to the same powers and provisions as were declared in the settlement. The settlor died on

March 20, 1953. His estate had long since been fully administered without recourse to his shares in Fairplay Publications Ltd. The third to fifth defendants, Walter Brown Chapman, Frederick Thomas Brockes and Malcolm Claude Faircliff, were the present trustees of both the settlement and the settlor's will. The trust fund was now worth about £368,000. The plaintiff was 55 years. She had three children. Two of them, namely the first defendant, David Robert Heard who had been adopted, and the second defendant, Margaret Jane Heard, were over 21 years. The third defendant, Nicola Margaret Heard, was 17 years. None of them had yet married.

In order to reduce the burden of capital transfer tax expected to be levied on the plaintiff's death and with a view to spreading the wealth of the trust fund among the members of her family interested in it, an arrangement was entered into as follows. It was proposed to divide the trust fund, the plaintiff taking 52 per cent. and the children, as a class, 48 per cent.; the capital gains tax incurred by the partition was to be borne proportionately; the plaintiff was to pay one-sixth of capital transfer tax, if any, incurred on the children's share. It was further proposed that the plaintiff would effect and pay for a three year insurance policy protecting the children against the risk of capital transfer tax being payable at the "death" rate in case the plaintiff died within three years of the partition.

The plaintiff issued a summons under the Variations of Trusts Act 1958 seeking the court's approval of the proposed arrangement on behalf of the third defendant and any future children and remoter issue of the plaintiff and of all persons who might be or might become entitled to any discretionary interest arising on a forfeiture of the plaintiff's life interest.

On March 3, 1976, when the summons came before Templeman J., he was not satisfied that the proposed insurance was sufficiently beneficial to the third defendant. He adjourned the summons for the parties to reconsider those proposals and to amend the arrangement. The following proposal was subsequently added: if the court thought fit, the plaintiff was to effect a whole life with profits insurance policy on her own life for the third defendant's absolute benefit. The premiums on the policy were to be paid out of the income of the third defendant's share.

Lynton A. Tucker for the plaintiff.

J. O. Taylor for the first and second defendants, the plaintiff's adult children.

Mark Cockle for the third defendant, the infant daughter of the plaintiff.

T. M. Shelford for the fourth, fifth and sixth defendants, the trustees of the settlement and the settlor's will.

TEMPLEMAN J. This is an application under the Variation of Trusts Act 1958 which involves the division of a trust fund between life tenant and remaindermen. One of the remaindermen is an infant of about 17.

Under what might be termed the old fashioned calculations for estate duty, such a division was comparatively simple. The rates of estate duty were such that the amount which a remainderman stood to inherit if nothing was done was usually very small. In most schemes it was possible to make a division whereby the remainderman took more in any event than he would otherwise take on the death of the life tenant.

Into that simple form of division complications were introduced by the abolition of estate duty and its replacement by capital transfer tax. Evidence in these proceedings demonstrates that the old calculations simply do not fit the new tax. For example, whereas in the old days a tax was

A payable on death and so all one had to do was to find out what would be left on death after deduction of estate duty, now capital transfer tax is payable on the coming into operation of the division effected by the arrangement.

For that and for other reasons it is very difficult to provide for every possible contingency. The impact of the tax has also this quirk, that the actuarial value of the interest of the life tenant is much reduced. In the B present instance, figures have been produced which show, for example, that if nothing is done and capital transfer tax is paid on the death of the life tenant, the plaintiff, then the share of the infant remainderman, the third defendant, will be somewhere between £58,000 and £60,000, if no alterations in the law are made in the meantime. Under the proposed arrangement, produced as a result of the independent advice of actuaries, the share which C the third defendant gets is of a gross value of £58,000, and if capital transfer tax is payable—as to which there is a doubt in the present instance —the tax will reduce the share by something like £11,000 or £14,000. This entails a serious possibility of a loss accruing to the third defendant. I was much pressed by all counsel, including counsel for the third defendant, with the observations of Stamp J. and Danckwerts J. in *In re Cohen's Settlement Trusts* [1965] 1 W.L.R. 1229 and in *In re Cohen's Will Trusts* D [1959] 1 W.L.R. 865 respectively, to the effect that a reasonable view of a bargain must be taken. It is not necessary to insist that in all possible circumstances the infant is bound to benefit. It is said that capital transfer tax may not be payable and if it is then even taking into account the possible shortfall of £14,000, there will be acceleration of the income of the share which the third defendant is to take, and her mother, the plaintiff, E is only about 55 years old, and so, in the normal course of events, acceleration will catch up with the shortfall.

Acceleration of income, at present rates of taxation on income, will take a good deal of catching up to compensate for a shortfall of £14,000. I cannot assume that the plaintiff will live long enough to procure that the arrangement viewed as a whole will benefit the third defendant. I must be satisfied that the arrangement is beneficial.

F I expressed doubts and sent the parties away to consider insurance. In the old days of estate duty insurance could be effected by the life tenant to make good any shortfall so far as the reversion was concerned. Capital transfer tax introduces a new complication in that an insurance policy effected and kept up by the plaintiff may itself be liable to capital transfer tax with disastrous consequences. Although it is slightly anomalous, if G the third defendant is to be protected against the possibility of shortfall, that protection can only be, to some extent, at the expense of the third defendant in that a policy must be kept up out of income.

I am quite satisfied that it would not be sensible to leave matters entirely as they are. There are other people interested besides the third defendant, and to preserve the present trusts with present, and future, rates of income and capital taxation does not seem sensible. I am satisfied H that the plaintiff will only receive under the arrangement a reasonable and fair proportion having regard to the value of her life interest in her present situation.

In these circumstances I think I can accept the arrangement, provided that the third defendant's income is to a certain extent made available for insurance in order to protect the third defendant's own share against loss caused by the premature death of the plaintiff. A quotation has been obtained, and it would appear that to insure a shortfall of £14,000 would cost about £800 a year. Having regard to the amount of the income that seems to me to be weighing too much on the future and not enough on the present. A policy for £8,000, which with profits will yield something over £11,000 in 10 years and more thereafter, will only cost about £400 a year. That will still leave a substantial income for the third defendant to receive straight away.

It seems to me if insurance of £8,000 with profits is effected, I can, relying on the observations of Stamp J. in *In re Cohen's Settlement Trusts* [1965] 1 W.L.R. 1229 and Danckwerts J. in *In re Cohen's Will Trusts* [1959] 1 W.L.R. 865, approve this arrangement, although I still think it is a borderline case. Great powers of advocacy were used to persuade me that capital transfer tax has made such a change that the possible result of a death must be disregarded, the actuarial division accepted and a risk taken. I do not take that view. I start with the principle that all these schemes should, if possible, prove that an infant is not going to be materially worse off. There are difficulties with capital transfer tax, and borderline cases, and one may then have to take a broad view, but not a galloping, gambling view.

In my judgment, taking a reasonably prudent view, insurance of £8,000 in the present instance will be sufficient, and I am prepared to sanction the arrangement thus amended.

Scheme sanctioned.

Solicitors: *Roche, Son & Neale.*

A. R.

[COURT OF APPEAL]

* WARD *v.* TESCO STORES LTD.

[Plaint No. 7406072]

1975 Nov. 13 — Megaw, Lawton and Ormrod L.JJ.

Negligence—Burden of proof—Spillage—Customer slipping on spillage on floor of supermarket—Owners' system of dealing with spillage—Burden of proving whether owners' system adequate

While shopping in the defendants' supermarket, the plaintiff slipped and fell when she trod on some yoghurt that had been spilt on the floor. In her action against the defendants for damages for negligence, she gave no evidence of how long the yoghurt had been on the floor but stated that about three weeks later she had been in the supermarket and noticed some orange squash spilt on the floor and, during a period of about 15 minutes, no member of staff had dealt with that spillage. The defendants denied negligence and gave evidence of their system for keeping the floor clean including brushing it five to six times a day; that spillage occurred about 10 times a week and that the staff were instructed that if they saw spillage on the floor, and there was usually a member of staff in the vicinity, they were to stay by it and call another member of staff to clean it up. The judge held that the plaintiff had proved a prima facie case of negligence. The defendants appealed.

On the question whether the plaintiff had proved a prima

A facie case without proving that the spillage had been on the floor for a sufficient time for the defendants to have dealt with it:—

Held, dismissing the appeal (Ormrod L.J. dissenting), that in the circumstances, the plaintiff having proved that the defendants knew or ought to have known of the likelihood of spillage on the floor and the danger to customers if that spillage was not dealt with quickly, it was for the defendants
B to show on the balance of probabilities that the plaintiff would have slipped on the yoghurt despite a proper system designed to give reasonable protection to customers against spillage (post, pp. 814A–C, 816C).

Dicta of Erle C.J. in *Scott* v. *London and St. Katherine Docks Co.* (1865) 3 H. & C. 596, 601 and Lord Goddard C.J. in *Turner* v. *Arding & Hobbs Ltd.* [1949] 2 All E.R. 911, 912 applied.

C *Richards* v. *W. F. White & Co.* [1957] 1 Lloyd's Rep. 367 distinguished.

Per Ormrod L.J. There was no prima facie case against the defendants without evidence of when the yoghurt was spilt (post, p. 815C).

The following cases are referred to in the judgments:

Richards v. *W. F. White & Co.* [1957] 1 Lloyd's Rep. 367.
D *Scott* v. *London and St. Katherine Docks Co.* (1865) 3 H. & C. 596.
Turner v. *Arding & Hobbs Ltd.* [1949] 2 All E.R. 911.

The following additional cases were cited in argument:

Byrne v. *Boadle* (1863) 2 H. & C. 722.
Dollman v. *A. and C. Hillman Ltd.* [1941] 1 All E.R. 355, C.A.
Stowell v. *Railway Executive* [1949] 2 K.B. 519; [1949] 2 All E.R. 193.
E

APPEAL from Judge Nance sitting at Liverpool County Court.

The plaintiff, May Ward, claimed damages against the defendants, Tesco Stores Ltd., for the injury she received when she slipped on some yoghurt spilt on the floor of the defendants' supermarket at Smithdown Road, Liverpool. On February 21, 1975, Judge Nance, finding that the
F plaintiff had proved a prima facie case of negligence, gave judgment for the plaintiff. The defendants appealed on the grounds, inter alia, that the judge, having found as facts (a) that the yoghurt on which the plaintiff slipped had more probably than not been spilled by a customer and not by a servant or agent of the defendants and (b) that the yoghurt might have been spilled only seconds before the plaintiff slipped on it, was wrong in law in holding that the defendants had been negligent; and that the
G judge was wrong in law in holding that the onus was on the defendants to prove how long the yoghurt had been on the floor.

The facts are stated in the judgment of Lawton L.J.

David Owen for the defendants.
Norbury Dugdale for the plaintiff.

H

MEGAW L.J. I shall ask Lawton L.J. to deliver the first judgment.

LAWTON L.J. This is an appeal by the defendants from a judgment of Judge Nance given in the Liverpool County Court on February 21, 1975, whereby he adjudged that the plaintiff should recover against the defendants £178·50 damages and her costs on scale 2, for personal injuries said to have been caused by the negligence of the defendants in the maintenance of the floor in their supermarket at Smithdown Road, Liverpool. By A consent the sum awarded has been reduced to £137·10. The higher figure was due to an arithmetical error.

At about midday in June 1974, the plaintiff went to the defendants' supermarket. It is a large one and is carried on in premises which used to be a cinema. Inside the premises were laid out in the way which is usual nowadays in supermarkets. On duty there was a total of about 30 to 35 staff; but in the middle of the day that number was reduced B because staff had to be relieved in order to enable them to get their midday meals.

The plaintiff went round the store, carrying a wire basket, as shoppers are expected to do in supermarkets. She was doing her shopping at the back of the store when she felt herself slipping. She appreciated that she was slipping on something which was sticky. She fell to the ground, and C sustained minor injuries. She had not seen what had caused her to slip. It was not suggested, either at the trial or in this court, that she had in any way been negligent in failing to notice what was on the floor as she walked along doing her shopping. When she was picking herself up she appreciated that she had slipped on some pink substance which looked to her like yoghurt. It was yoghurt. Later, somebody on the defendants' staff found a carton of yoghurt in the vicinity which was two-thirds D empty.

A member of the staff helped to pick the plaintiff up. The manager was called. The plaintiff was taken to his office. She was dealt with there in a kindly and considerate way. The defendants offered to, and did, arrange for such of her clothes as had been soiled by the fall to be cleaned. E

That was all the plaintiff was able to prove, save for one additional fact. About three weeks later when she was shopping in the same store she noticed that some orange squash had been spilt on the floor. She kept an eye on the spillage for about a quarter of an hour. During that time nobody came to clear it up.

The judge was of the opinion that the facts which I have related F constituted a prima facie case against the defendants. I infer that this case, which involves only a small amount of damages, has been brought to this court because the defendants are disturbed that any judge should find that a prima facie case is established merely by a shopper proving that she slipped on a supermarket floor.

At the trial the defendants called some evidence. Their manager spoke about the store and how many staff were employed. He went on G to say that the staff had the following instruction about spillages: "Stay where the spill has taken place and call someone else." He said that usually in a store of this kind and size there was to be found some member of the staff near where the spillage had occurred. He went on to say that the store had a system for keeping the floor clean. Contractors came in every night to give it a general clean-up. Twice a week those H contractors carried out "buffing"—which in the South of England would be called "polishing." The manager said that every day while the store was open the floor was brushed five or six times. The defendants did not call any evidence as to when the store floor had last been brushed before the plaintiff's accident. It follows that there was no evidence before the court as to whether the floor had been brushed a few moments before the accident, or an hour, or possibly an hour and a half. The

A court was left without any information on what may have been an important matter.

The manager in cross-examination said that spillages did occur from time to time; he thought there were about 10 breakages a week, but most of them came from the breaking of squash bottles.

It follows that those in charge of the store knew that during the course of a working week there was a likelihood of spillages occurring B from time to time. It was accepted at the trial that shoppers, intent on looking to see what is on offer, cannot be expected to look where they are putting their feet. The management should have appreciated that if there are patches of slippery substances on the floor people are liable to step into them and that, if they do, they may slip. It follows too that if those are the conditions to be expected in the store there must be some C reasonably effective system for getting rid of the dangers which may from time to time exist. The only precautions which were taken were, first, the system of having the floor brushed five or six times during the working day, and secondly, giving instructions to the staff that if they saw any spillage on the floor they were to stay where the spill had taken place and call somebody to clean it up.

The main complaint of the defendants in this case has been that the D judge should never have taken the view that the plaintiff had proved a prima facie case. It was submitted before this court that it was for the plaintiff to show that the spillage had been on the floor for an unduly long time and that there had been opportunities for the management to clean it up which they had not taken. In support of that proposition, Mr. Owen, on behalf of the defendants, invited our attention to *Richards* v. E *W. F. White & Co.* [1957] 1 Lloyd's Rep. 367. It is necessary to say something about the facts of that case because, as in all cases of negligence, the facts are important. A dock labourer who was working on a ship in dock which was being unloaded slipped on a patch of oil and injured himself. At the material time between 300 and 400 men in various trades were working on the ship. In the course of his judgment Devlin J. said, at p. 369:

F

> "If there had been evidence which showed that there was some danger, not perhaps of oil but some other danger, which was being left on the ship for two or three days, or anything of that sort, which the shipowners were doing nothing about, a prima facie case of negligence would be made out; but to make out a prima facie case of negligence in a case of this sort, there must, I think, be some evidence to show G how long the oil had been there, some evidence from which it can be inferred that a prudent shipowner, who had a reasonable system of inspection for the purpose of seeing that dangers of this sort were not created, ought to have noticed it."

That case was decided on its own facts. I doubt whether Devlin J. intended to make any general statement of principle. If he did, I would H not agree with what he said. This case, too, has to be decided on its own facts, to which established principles must be applied. The relevant principles were enunciated in the classical judgment of Erle C.J. in *Scott* v. *London and St. Katherine Docks Co.* (1865) 3 H. & C. 596, 601:

> "where the thing is shown to be under the management of the defendant or his servants, and the accident is such as in the ordinary course of things does not happen if those who have the management use

> proper care, it affords reasonable evidence, in the absence of expla- A
> nation by the defendants that the accident arose from want of care."

Now, in this case the floor of this supermarket was under the manage-
ment of the defendants and their servants. The accident was such as in
the ordinary course of things does not happen if floors are kept clean
and spillages are dealt with as soon as they occur. If an accident does
happen because the floors are covered with spillage, then in my judgment B
some explanation should be forthcoming from the defendants to show that
the accident did not arise from any want of care on their part; and in
the absence of any explanation the judge may give judgment for the plain-
tiff. Such burden of proof as there is on defendants in such circumstances
is evidential, not probative. The judge thought that prima facie this
accident would not have happened had the defendants taken reasonable
care. In my judgment he was justified in taking that view because the C
probabilities were that the spillage had been on the floor long enough
for it to have been cleaned up by a member of the staff.

The next question is whether the defendants by their evidence gave
any explanation to show that they had taken all reasonable care. The
only explanation which they gave was that to which I have already referred.
The judge weighed the evidence and decided as a matter of fact from which D
in this case there can be no appeal that the precautions taken were not
enough, and that the plaintiff in consequence had proved her case. In
coming to that conclusion he followed the judgment of Lord Goddard C.J.
in *Turner* v. *Arding & Hobbs Ltd.* [1949] 2 All E.R. 911. Lord
Goddard said, at p. 912:

> "The duty of the shopkeeper in this class of case is well-established. E
> It may be said to be a duty to use reasonable care to see that the
> shop floor, on which people are invited, is kept reasonably safe, and
> if an unusual danger is present of which the injured person is
> unaware, and the danger is one which would not be expected and
> ought not to be present, the onus of proof is on the defendants to
> explain how it was that the accident happened."

F

It is clear from a later passage in his judgment that Lord Goddard C.J.,
in referring to the burden of proof, was not saying that the defendants
had to disprove negligence. What he had intended to say is apparent
from what he said later on the same page:

> "Here, however, I think that there is a burden thrown on the defen-
> dants either of explaining how this thing got to the floor or giving G
> me far more evidence than they have as to the state of the floor and
> the watch that was kept on it immediately before the accident."

The judge had that passage in mind when he decided as he did. In
my judgment he was right; and accordingly I would dismiss this appeal.

ORMROD L.J. I have the misfortune to disagree with the judgment H
of Lawton L.J. Starting from the beginning, I do not think that it was
established that this accident was caused by any want of care on the part
of the defendants. The accident described by the plaintiff—and she did
no more than describe the accident, namely, that she slipped on some
yoghurt which was on the floor of the supermarket—could clearly have
happened no matter what degree of care these defendants had taken. The
crucial question is how long before the accident the yoghurt had been

A on the floor. Had some customer knocked it off the shelf a few moments before, then no reasonable system which the defendants could be expected to operate would have prevented this accident. So I think that the plaintiff fails at the outset.

So far as concerns the proposition which Lawton L.J. has cited from Erle C.J., all I would say is that, since this accident could quite easily have happened without any want of care on the part of the defendants,
B I do not think that that broad proposition is applicable.

I for my part am unable to distinguish this case in any material respect from the judgment of Devlin J. in *Richards* v. *W. F. White & Co.* [1957] 1 Lloyd's Rep. 367. Devlin J. put the matter in the clearest possible terms at the bottom of p. 369 in the passage which Lawton L.J. has read. I cannot improve upon that statement of the law, and would not attempt
C to. It seems to me quite clear that unless there is some evidence as to when the yoghurt got on to this floor no prima facie case can be made against these defendants. I would only add that to hold otherwise would seem to me to put upon the defendants a wholly unreasonable burden, not only of care, but also of proof. I ask myself what evidence could they have called? It would have been fortunate, perhaps, if they had been able to show that their sweeper had passed over this bit of the floor five
D minutes before the accident. But it would not have shown that their system was either better or worse than if the sweeper had gone by that bit of the floor an hour earlier. I cannot think that the case would have been carried any further by calling evidence from such employees as may or may not have been about. This is a supermarket, not a place with counters and assistants behind the counters. I cannot imagine what
E evidence they could give except to say that they had not noticed the spill; and the matter would have been taken no further.

For those reasons, in my judgment Mr. Owen's submission is right, and I would allow the appeal.

MEGAW L.J. I agree with the conclusion expressed by Lawton L.J.,
F and with the reasons given by him for that conclusion. But as unfortunately the court is not unanimous I feel that it is desirable that I should add a few words of my own, not, I believe, in any way departing from the reasons given by Lawton L.J.

It seems to me that the essence of the argument put forward on behalf of the defendants in this appeal is this: never mind whether the defendants had any system of any sort to protect their customers against the risk of
G slipping on the floor of the supermarket as a result of breakages or spillages—which on their own evidence happened about 10 times a week: even if they had no system of any sort to guard against such a risk to their customers, nevertheless, when an accident happens such as the accident in this case, a lady customer who undoubtedly slips, through no fault of her own, on such a spillage on the floor, she cannot recover against
H the defendants. And why can she not recover? Because she is unable to prove that the spillage did not take place within a matter of a few seconds before she slipped and fell on it. So that, however perfect a system the defendants had had, it would not have enabled them to prevent this particular accident.

With great respect to those who support that proposition, it appears to me to be contrary to the law as I understand it to be. It is for the plaintiff to show that there has occurred an event which is unusual and

which, in the absence of explanation, is more consistent with fault on the A
part of the defendants than the absence of fault; and to my mind the judge was right in taking that view of the presence of this slippery liquid on the floor of the supermarket in the circumstances of this case: that is, that the defendants knew or should have known that it was a not uncommon occurrence; and that if it should happen, and should not be promptly attended to, it created a serious risk that customers would fall and injure themselves. When the plaintiff has established that, the defen- B
dants can still escape from liability. They could escape from liability if they could show that the accident must have happened, or even on balance of probability would have been likely to have happened, even if there had been in existence a proper and adequate system, in relation to the circumstances, to provide for the safety of customers. But if the defendants wish to put forward such a case, it is for them to show that, on balance C
of probability, either by evidence or by inference from the evidence that is given or is not given, this accident would have been at least equally likely to have happened despite a proper system designed to give reasonable protection to customers. That, in this case, they wholly failed to do. Really the essence of Mr. Owen's argument—and he did not shrink from it—was: "Never mind whether we had no system at all: still, as the plaintiff has failed to show that the yoghurt was spilt within a few seconds D
before the accident, she must fail." As I have said, in the circumstances of this case, I do not think that the plaintiff, to succeed, had to prove how long it was since the defendants' floor had become slippery.

I take the view that the decision of the judge in this case is fully in line with the decision of Lord Goddard C.J. in *Turner* v. *Arding & Hobbs Ltd.* [1949] 2 All E.R. 911, which has been cited by Lawton L.J. E
Indeed, I am unable to see how, consistently with that decision, on the facts and the evidence here the judge could have reached any other conclusion.

As regards the decision of Devlin J. in *Richards* v. *W. F. White & Co.* [1957] 1 Lloyd's Rep. 367, to which Lawton L.J. and Ormrod L.J. have referred, I agree with Lawton L.J. that that case has to be looked at in relation to its very special facts. When Devlin J. said, at p. 369: F

> "but to make out a prima facie case of negligence in a case of this sort, there must, I think, be some evidence to show how long the oil had been there, . . ."

I am confident that he did not intend to lay down any general principle. It is, to my mind, not a part of the law, as I have said, that in this case G
the plaintiff must fail merely because she is unable to disprove that the yoghurt fell on the floor within a few seconds of the time that she trod on it.

I agree that the appeal should be dismissed.

Appeal dismissed with costs.

H

Solicitors: *Willey, Hargrave & Co. for A. W. Mawer & Co., Liverpool; Sharpe, Pritchard & Co. for E. Rex Makin & Co., Liverpool.*

H. J.

A

[COURT OF APPEAL]

* MILFORD HAVEN CONSERVANCY BOARD *v.* INLAND REVENUE COMMISSIONERS AND OTHERS

B

SAME *v.* SAME

[1972 M. No. 3453]

[1974 M. No. 3104]

1976 March 8, 9, 10; 26 — Cairns and Scarman L.JJ. C and Sir Gordon Willmer

Rating—Rateable value—Assessment of—Statutory undertaking—Harbour board's income derived from sources other than occupancy of hereditaments—Statutory orders providing for rateable value to be assessed on " relevant receipts "—Assessment based on annual receipts of harbour dues, property outside rating area, and rent from property—Whether orders D *ultra vires—General Rate Act* 1967 (*c.* 9), *s.* 35 (1) (6)[1]*—Docks and Harbours* (*Valuation*) *Order* 1971 (*S.I.* 1971 *No.* 561), *arts.* 2, 3 (2)*—Docks and Harbours* (*Valuation*) (*Amendment*) *Order* 1973 (*S.I.* 1973 *No.* 654), *art.* 4[2]

The plaintiff board was established by the Milford Haven Conservancy Act 1958 to " maintain, improve, protect and regulate the navigation " in the haven. The bed of the haven E was vested in the Crown while the board occupied two hereditaments only consisting of a jetty with its offices and premises and a small wireless telegraphy station. The board's income, which included charges for pilots' services and the rent of a cottage that was separately rated, came principally from dues levied on vessels entering and leaving the haven which arose independently of its occupation of the hereditaments. In 1973 the rateable value of the board's hereditaments was F assessed in accordance with the provisions of the Docks and Harbours (Valuation) Order 1971, on the basis that its " relevant receipts " within the meaning of article 4 of the Docks and Harbours (Valuation) (Amendment) Order 1973 consisted of all its sources of income including the dues levied on vessels and the rent from the cottage. The board, by consolidated actions sought, inter alia, declarations that the Orders of 1971 and 1973 were ultra vires on the ground that G the delegated legislative power in section 35 (1) of the General Rate Act 1967 to modify the method of valuation for certain hereditaments had to be exercised within existing principles of valuation in rating law and that the Orders were contrary to the basic principles that, in assessing the rateable value of a hereditament, no account should be taken of receipts arising independently of the occupancy of the hereditament nor of property outside the rating district and disallowing H double assessment of rent. The judge refused the declarations on the ground that the wide language of section 35 (1) and (6) of the Act of 1967 gave the Secretary of State an unfettered

---

[Reported by MISS HENRIETTA STEINBERG, Barrister-at-Law]

[1] General Rate Act 1967, s. 35: see post, pp. 820G—821C.

[2] Docks and Harbours (Valuation) (Amendment) Order 1973, art. 4: see post, p. 822A–D.

power to provide whatever code he thought appropriate for valuing the hereditaments falling within section 35 (2), with subsections (4), (5) and (7) providing sufficient safeguards against unfair or unreasonable exercise of the power. A

On the board's appeal:—

Held, dismissing the appeals, that the clear and unambiguous language of section 35 (1) and (6) of the Act of 1967 empowered the Secretary of State to prescribe any method of valuation for hereditaments falling within B section 35 (2), however far such a method departed from previously established principles of valuation; that the Orders of 1971 and 1973 only provided a method of valuation of the hereditaments for rating purposes and did not seek to impose liability to rates on the haven or on the board's dues, income or rents received, and, accordingly, they were within the powers conferred on the Secretary of State by section 35 (post, pp. 824F, G, 827D, 829B, C). C

Per Scarman L.J. and Sir Gordon Willmer. The Secretary of State's power under section 35 was not an "unfettered" power (post, pp. 827F, 829E).

Decision of Bridge J. affirmed.

The following cases are referred to in the judgment of Cairns L.J.:

Doncaster Union Assessment Committee v. *Manchester, Sheffield and Lincolnshire Railway Co.* [1895] A.C. 133n.; 71 L.T. 585, H.L.(E.). D

Kingston Union Assessment Committee v. *Metropolitan Water Board* [1926] A.C. 331, H.L.(E.).

Reg. v. *Musson* (1858) 8 E. & B. 900.

Smith & Son v. *Lambeth Assessment Committee* (1882) 10 Q.B.D. 327, C.A.

Swansea Union Assessment Committee v. *Swansea Harbour Trustees* (1907) 97 L.T. 585. E

Westminster Corporation v. *Southern Railway Co. Assessment Authority* [1936] A.C. 511; [1936] 2 All E.R. 322, H.L.(E.).

The following additional case was cited in argument:

Attorney-General v. *Prince Ernest Augustus of Hanover* [1957] A.C. 436; [1957] 2 W.L.R. 1; [1957] 1 All E.R. 49, H.L.(E.). F

APPEALS from Bridge J.

The plaintiffs, Milford Haven Conservancy Board, brought actions by originating summons against the Inland Revenue Commissioners, Ronald Eli Jones, a valuation officer, and the rating authorities, Preseli District Council and South Pembrokeshire District Council, for declarations that (1) the Docks and Harbours (Valuation) Order 1971 was ultra vires and G void; (2) the commissioners were not empowered to calculate in accordance with the provisions of that Order the rateable values of the hereditaments occupied by the plaintiff board as dock and harbour undertakers; and (3) the valuation officer was not empowered to alter the valuation list in accordance with the provisions of the Order in respect of the hereditaments occupied by the board. The board also sought similar declarations in H respect of the Docks and Harbours (Valuation) (Amendment) Order 1973.

Bridge J. refused the declarations, holding that the wide ambit of section 35 (1) and (6) of the General Rate Act 1967 empowered the Minister to provide whatever code he thought proper for the valuation of the hereditaments falling within the section.

The plaintiff board appealed from the judge's decision on the grounds that the judge had erred in construing section 35 as conferring a power

A to make an order which would bring into rateable liability property which was not otherwise rateable; that the judge was wrong in holding that section 35 (4), (5) and (7) supported his construction of the powers contained in section 35; and that the judge erred in relying on sections 31 to 34 as supporting his construction of section 35 of the Act.

The facts are stated in the judgment of Cairns L.J.

B

David Widdicombe Q.C. and *Anthony Anderson* for the plaintiff board.

Geoffrey Rippon Q.C. and *Alan Fletcher* for the Inland Revenue Commissioners and the valuation officer.

Gerald Moriarty Q.C. and *Charles Fay* for the rating authorities.

Cur. adv. vult.

C

March 26. The following judgments were read.

CAIRNS L.J. This is an appeal from a judgment of Bridge J. in two consolidated actions. The subject matter of the actions was the method of valuation for rating of the hereditaments of the plaintiff board at D Milford Haven. Section 35 of the General Rate Act 1967 authorised the Minister of Housing and Local Government (now the Secretary of State for the Environment) to prescribe methods of valuation for four categories of hereditament one of which was (to put it shortly) any hereditament of a statutory dock or harbour undertaking. The Docks and Harbours (Valuation) Order was made in 1971, in purported pursuance of section 35, prescribing a method of valuation of such hereditaments. An E amending order was made in 1973. The plaintiff board is a harbour undertaking within the section. In the first action the board claimed a declaration that the Order of 1971 was ultra vires and void. In the second action the board claimed a similar declaration about the Order of 1973.

Bridge J. dismissed the the actions. The board appeals.

The board's case is that the Orders are contrary to certain fundamental F principles of rating valuation law and, under the guise of prescribing a method of valuation, impose a form of tax which Parliament cannot have intended to authorise. The Orders base the valuation on receipts of the board not limited to receipts derived from the occupation of the hereditaments in question and this, say the board, is not a method of valuation of the hereditaments at all. The defendants are the Inland Revenue Commissioners, the valuation officer and two rating authorities. There have G been changes in the identity of the rating authorities since the action was started, but it is unnecessary to go into that. The defendants all say that the Orders are within the wide powers conferred by section 35 of the Act which include power to repeal or amend enactments relating to valuation. Bridge J. accepted the contentions of the defendants and rejected the contentions of the board.

H The general provisions for the ascertainment of rateable value are now contained in section 19 of the Act of 1967. Section 19 (1) reads:

> "Subject to the provisions of this Part of this Act and of any scheme for the time being in force such as is mentioned in section 117 (7) of this Act, the rateable value of a hereditament shall be taken to be the net annual value of that hereditament ascertained in accordance with subsections (2) to (4) of this section."

Subsection (2) relates to houses and other non-industrial buildings. Subsection (3) reads: A

> "The net annual value of any other hereditament shall be an amount equal to the rent at which it is estimated the hereditament might reasonably be expected to let from year to year if the tenant undertook to pay all usual tenant's rates and taxes and to bear the cost of the repairs and insurance and the other expenses, if any, necessary to B maintain the hereditament in a state to command that rent."

It is well known that the sections of earlier Acts which contain similar provisions gave rise to difficulties with regard to various types of hereditaments which are not normally the subject of letting. Various methods of assessment such as the contractor's basis and the profits basis were adopted by rating surveyors and came to be recognised by the courts as appropriate to different kinds of hereditament. C In relation to public utilities with hereditaments in more than one rating district it was decided by the House of Lords in *Kingston Union Assessment Committee* v. *Metropolitan Water Board* [1926] A.C. 331 that the profits basis was the *only* proper basis of valuation in the absence of special circumstances: see *per* Lord Cave L.C. at pp. 338–340 and 345. But in the course of time this basis was not found always to produce satisfactory results and accordingly D special provisions were enacted from time to time for various sorts of undertaking. Such provisions were made for railway and canal undertakings and for electricity boards in 1948, for gas undertakings in 1955, for water undertakings, mines and docks, and harbours in 1961 and for the National Coal Board in 1963.

In the General Rate Act 1967, a consolidating Act, provisions for the E valuation of water undertakings are contained in section 31; for railways and canal undertakings in section 32; for gas authorities in section 33; for electricity boards in section 34; and for four types of undertakings, including docks and harbours, in section 35. Under sections 31, 33 and 34 the methods of assessment are set out in detail in Schedules 4, 6 and 7 respectively. Railways and canals, unlike all the others, are largely taken outside of rating altogether and provision is made for stated sums to be paid F in lieu of rates: see section 32 and Schedule 5.

Section 35 has no attached Schedule, but provides for each type of undertaking covered by it that the Secretary of State may prescribe by order the method of valuation. The provisions of section 35, so far as material, are as follows:

> "(1) The Minister may by order make provision for determining the G rateable value of hereditaments to which this section applies, or any class or description of such hereditaments specified in the order, by such method as may be so specified. (2) This section applies to—(*a*) any hereditament occupied by the National Coal Board; (*b*) any other hereditament which consists of or includes a mine or quarry . . . (*c*) any hereditament occupied by the persons carrying on, under authority H conferred by or under any enactment, a dock or harbour undertaking; and (*d*) any hereditament occupied by the persons carrying on an undertaking for the diffusion by wire of sound or television programmes; . . . (4) Before making any order under this section the Minister shall consult with such associations of local authorities or of persons carrying on undertakings as appear to him to be concerned and with any local authority or person carrying on an undertaking

with whom consultation appears to him to be desirable. (5) In the year following the coming into force of the second valuation lists for the purposes of which any order under this section has or has had effect the Minister shall, in consultation with such associations, local authorities and persons as aforesaid, cause investigations to be made into the effect of the operation of the order; and the Minister shall cause to be laid before Parliament a report on any investigations made under this subsection and their result. (6) An order under this section may repeal or amend any enactment so far as that enactment relates to the valuation of hereditaments to which the order relates, may as regards such hereditaments apply, restrict or modify the provisions of this Act relating to proposals for alterations of valuation lists and to appeals in connection with such lists and to the withholding of rates where proposals are pending, and shall have effect notwithstanding anything in any of those provisions. (7) No order under this section shall have effect unless approved by a resolution of each House of Parliament."

Orders have been made under section 35 (2) (*a*), (*b*) and (*c*) and those with which we are concerned, made under paragraph (*c*), are the Docks and Harbours (Valuation) Order 1971 and the Docks and Harbours (Valuation) (Amendment) Order 1973.

The Order of 1971 contains the following provisions. Article 2 provides:

> "(1) Subject to paragraphs (2) and (3), this order shall apply, in respect of the rate periods beginning on April 1, 1971, and subsequent rate periods, to any hereditament which comprises (wholly or partly) a dock or harbour undertaking and is occupied by the persons carrying on such undertaking under authority conferred by or under any enactment."

Article 3 is the "interpretation" article and in paragraph (2) it contains the definition of "relevant receipts" in these terms:

> ". . . 'relevant receipts,' in relation to any dock or harbour undertaking, means all receipts, other than receipts in respect of cargo handling, by way of revenue"—including the rents of parts of the dock or harbour let notwithstanding that such parts as let are separately rated —" included or to be included in the accounts of the undertaking, whether derived from the operations carried on under the authority referred to in article 2 (1) or otherwise, and includes such receipts from all ancillary land and buildings occupied by the persons carrying on the undertaking in connection with the dock or harbour; . . ."

Article 4 provides:

> "Subject to articles 8 and 9, for any year, the rateable value of any hereditament to which this order applies shall—(*a*) where the dock or harbour undertaking is wholly comprised in one hereditament, be 4 per cent. of the relevant receipts of the dock or harbour undertaking in the year; (*b*) where the dock or harbour undertaking extends to two or more hereditaments, be the portion of 4 per cent. of the relevant receipts of the dock or harbour undertaking allocated to the hereditament under article 5 (2)."

The relevant provisions of the Order of 1973 are in articles 4 and 5. Article 4 reads:

"For the definition of 'relevant receipts' in article 3 (2) (interpretation) of the 1971 order there shall be substituted the following definition: '"relevant receipts," in relation to any dock or harbour undertaking, means all receipts by way of revenue included or to be included in the accounts of the undertaking, whether derived from the operations carried on under the authority referred to in article 2 (1) or otherwise, and includes such receipts from all ancillary land and buildings occupied by the person carrying on the undertaking in connection with the dock or harbour, but shall exclude—(*a*) receipts in respect of cargo handling; (*b*) receipts in respect of pilotage; (*c*) investment income from—(i) investments required to be shown in the accounts of the undertaking (other than investments in subsidiary companies); (ii) loans or deposits made for a period of 60 calendar months or less; (iii) investments in companies engaged wholly or mainly in cargo handling and not falling within either of the two preceding items; (*d*) the rents of parts of the dock or harbour undertaking let, notwithstanding that such parts as let are separately rated, except in so far as those rents exceed 10 per cent. of the sum arrived at after deducting the excluded items (*a*), (*b*) and (*c*) above from all receipts of the undertaking.'"

Article 5 of that order amends the percentage from 4 per cent. to 6 per cent. subject to some details to which I need not refer.

Now what is said by the board is that these Orders, unlike any of the Schedules under sections 31 to 34 of the Act of 1967 and unlike any other orders made under section 35, purport to rate receipts which are not the product of the hereditament, to rate property outside the rating district and, in relation to rents, to produce double rating. In all these respects, says the board, the Orders are ultra vires.

Now as the attack is on the provisions of the Orders and not on their application to the board, the facts relating to the board's undertaking are only useful as an illustration of how the Orders may operate. The board's rights and duties are laid down in a local Act, the Milford Haven Conservancy Act 1958. These are its relevant provisions. Section 1 (1):

"There shall be a Milford Haven Conservancy Board (in this Act referred to as 'the board') who shall be charged with the duty of taking such steps as the board may from time to time consider necessary or expedient to maintain, improve, protect and regulate the navigation, and in particular the deep-water facilities, in the area bounded by—(*a*) a straight line drawn from the south-western extremity of St. Anne's Head to the southern extremity of Studdock Point; and (*b*) high water mark on the shores of Milford Haven and the approaches thereto within the straight line aforesaid, including all bays, creeks, pools, inlets and rivers, as far as the tide flows, which area is in this Act referred to as 'the haven.'"

Section 4 (1):

"The board may construct, whether within or outside the haven, any works required for the purposes of their functions under this Act, including any moorings, and from time to time alter or extend any such works: . . ."

Then there is a proviso which I need not read. Section 5 (1):

"The board may from time to time deepen, dredge, scour and improve the bed and foreshore of the haven and the bed of the sea in or near

A any approach to the haven, and blast any rock within the haven and any rock in the sea in or near any approach to the haven, and any material taken up or collected in the course of any such operations shall be the property of the board and may be used, sold, removed, deposited, or otherwise disposed of as the board may think fit: . . ."

Again there is a proviso which I need not read. Section 9 (1):

B "The board may from time to time by byelaws confirmed by the Minister make provision for any matter falling within their duty under section 1 of this Act and in particular, but without prejudice to the generality of their power, provision—(*a*) for regulating the use of the haven, including the movement of vessels therein and the time, manner and condition in which vessels shall enter or leave the haven C or any installation therein, the speed of vessels within the haven, and the laying down of moorings and the anchoring, mooring, unmooring and placing of vessels in the haven; . . ."

and below there are a number of other provisions in paragraphs from (*b*) to (*j*) which I do not find it necessary to refer to. Section 11 (1):

"The board may demand and take in respect of every vessel entering D and in respect of every vessel departing from the haven dues at such rate not exceeding the appropriate rate specified in Schedule 3 to this Act as the board may from time to time determine, being, subject to section 85 of the Merchant Shipping Act 1894, dues calculated by reference to the vessel's tonnage: . . ."

The only other provision of the Act to which I need refer is section 23 (2):

E "Nothing in the provisions of this Act or any instrument made thereunder shall prejudice any estate, right, power, privilege or exemption of the Crown, and in particular no such provision shall authorise the board without the prior consent in writing of the Crown Estate commissioners to take, use or in any manner interfere with any portion of the shore or bed of the sea or of the haven or any property F or rights of whatsoever description belonging to Her Majesty in right of Her Crown and under the management of the said commissioners."

The only rateable hereditaments which the board occupies are a jetty, a small block of offices, a wooden building in temporary use as an office and a small wireless telegraphy station. The board's "relevant receipts" include dues levied on vessels entering and leaving the haven; rent of a G pilots' waiting room in the office block; rent of a cottage which is separately rated; and income for the boarding and landing services of pilots carried out by the board as agents for Trinity House. It was estimated that if the formula contained in the Orders were applied the rateable values would rise from about £23,322 in 1971 to £55,000 in 1976 as against the valuation of £4,602 which previously applied.

H Now the board relies on certain well-established propositions in the law of rating and about these as general propositions, and disregarding for the moment the effect of section 35, there is no dispute. I can therefore deal with them briefly.

"Tolls in gross" are not rateable; that is to say, receipts not dependent on the exclusive occupation of a hereditament cannot be taken into account in valuing the hereditament: *Swansea Union Assessment Committee* v. *Swansea Harbour Trustees* (1907) 97 L.T. 585.

If a body has rights and duties in respect of a waterway this does not A constitute exclusive occupation unless the body owns the bed of the waterway: *Swansea* case and *Doncaster Union Assessment Committee* v. *Manchester, Sheffield and Lincolnshire Railway Company* [1895] A.C. 133n.; 71 L.T. 585.

Land which is "extra-parochial," that is, not within any rating district, is not rateable. Any land which is outside low water mark is extra-parochial and any land which is outside high water mark is prima facie B extra-parochial: *Reg.* v. *Musson* (1858) 8 E. & B. 900.

Double assessment is not permitted. So where a tenant is assessed to rates, the landlord is not to be assessed too: *Smith & Son* v. *Lambeth Assessment Committee* (1882) 10 Q.B.D. 327, 330 and *Westminster* v. *Southern Railway Assessment Committee* [1936] A.C. 511, 563.

Now it is clear that dues levied on vessels entering or leaving the C haven are not dependent on the board's occupation of the rateable hereditaments nor is the board's investment income; that the board's right to dredge the haven does not give the exclusive occupation of it; that the haven is extra-parochial; and that the cottage which is separately let is double assessed if the board is rated in respect of it. These facts show how great a departure from the classical rules about rating is involved in the Order complained of. It is true that the Order of 1973 in articles D 4 and 5 goes some way towards reducing the extent of that departure, inasmuch as most investment income and some income from rents is excepted from "relevant receipts," but the departure is not entirely removed.

It is, of course, clear that Parliament can by statute override in whole or in part any existing rule of rating law, whether statutory or established E by the courts. Thus tolls in gross are rated under section 29 of the Act of 1967 (sporting rights) and section 4 (4) of the board's local Act of 1958 makes rateable works which are outside any parish—thus making the pier rateable. But it is contended that Parliament cannot have intended to give power to the Secretary of State to make such fundamental amendments of the law by his orders, and it is further contended that by the Orders of 1971 and 1973 the Secretary of State has purported to repeal F not only sections dealing with valuation, but sections dealing with liability to rates.

In my view, the language of both subsections (1) and (6) of section 35 is sufficiently clear to entitle the Secretary of State to prescribe any method of valuation, however far it departs from previously established principles. I cannot find in the words of the section any such ambiguity as the court G could be asked to resolve in favour of the ratepayer. Nor does it appear to me that the Orders deal in any respect with liability to rates as distinct from valuation for rates. It cannot be said that the Orders seek to impose rates on the haven or on the dues, investment income or rents received. When the profits basis of valuation is adopted it is not the profits which are being rated, but the hereditaments, and the rule that tolls in gross are H not to be taken into account is a rule of valuation.

But is the method prescribed by the Orders a method of valuation at all? If what was required by section 35 to be assessed were the net annual value I should be inclined to say that the Orders could not fairly be considered to be directed to ascertaining that value. But rateable value, whenever it departs from net annual value, either by being related to net annual value in some specific way or by being assessed without reference

A to net annual value, is an artificial concept. The profits basis of valuation was a means of estimating the rent that the hypothetical tenant would pay: see the *Kingston* case [1926] A.C. 331, 339. But none of the methods of assessment under sections 31 to 35 have that character. Water, gas and electricity undertakings are dealt with on the basis of supply. Mines and quarries (other than National Coal Board properties) are given a rateable value ascertained by applying a fraction, at first three-quarters and later
B a half, to the rateable value previously assessed. No complaint is made by the board of the method of applying a percentage to receipts, so long as the definition of relevant receipts is not too wide.

Bridge J. expressed the view that, if the board's contentions were accepted, the effect of section 35 would be only to confer on the Minister "a power to tidy up a few technical anomalies," whereas the provisions
C for consultation, affirmative resolution of both Houses of Parliament and report to Parliament after the first year's operations of an Order showed that Parliament intended to confer on the Minister powers "of far-reaching consequence." Mr. Widdicombe, for the board, contended that this was not a proper approach to the construction of an Act of Parliament. I do not agree with that criticism: if the words of one section are ambiguous and one construction would make the provisions of great importance,
D whereas another would reduce them to triviality, I consider it legitimate to look at other sections or subsections as throwing light on how much importance Parliament attached to the matter. I should not, however, with great respect to the judge, consider that section 35 (1) and (6) on Mr. Widdicombe's interpretation would only be tidying up anomalies. Presumably the Secretary of State could by order prescribe methods at
E least as far-reaching as those prescribed for other types of undertaking in Schedules 4, 6 and 7. I do not, however, find it necessary to rely on any extraneous means of discovering the intention of Parliament, because to my mind subsections (1) and (6) are clear and unambiguous and do confer on the Secretary of State power to make the orders in question.

I would also reject Mr. Widdicombe's argument that Parliament cannot have intended to permit a basis of assessment which would give heredita-
F ments five or ten times the rateable value that they formerly had. It may be that the board's earlier rateable values were much too low. If it were found that an Order operated unfairly, either in relation to docks and harbours as a whole or as between one undertaking and another, that would be eminently a matter for investigation and report under section 35 (5) of the Act.

G I do not find in the Orders of 1971 and 1973 anything which conflicts with provisions in the Act of 1967 other than those dealing with valuation. Mr. Widdicombe, for the board, contends that they conflict with section 1 (2) which provides:

> "Every rating authority shall have power in accordance with this Act to make and levy rates on the basis of an assessment in respect
> H of the yearly value of property in their rating area for the purpose of applying the proceeds thereof to local purposes of a public nature.",

and with section 16 which provides:

> "Subject to the provisions of this Act, every occupier of property of any of the following descriptions, namely—(*a*) lands; (*b*) houses; (*c*) coal mines; (*d*) mines of any other description, other than a mine of which the royalty or dues are for the time being wholly reserved in

kind; (*e*) any right of sporting (that is to say, any right of fowling, of shooting, or taking or killing game or rabbits, or of fishing) when severed from the occupation of the land on which the right is exercisable, shall be liable to be assessed to rates in respect of the hereditament or hereditaments comprising that property according to the rateable value or respective rateable values of that hereditament or those hereditaments determined in accordance with the provisions of this Act."

Linking those two provisions together, what they provide is that rates are to be levied on the basis of a rateable value which is to be determined in accordance with the provisions of the Act of 1967. The method of determination is for most hereditaments under section 19, but for docks and harbours a special method of determination is provided in accordance with Orders. The Orders do not purport to rate anything which is not rateable under section 1 (2) and section 16 of the Act.

I would dismiss the appeal.

SCARMAN L.J. I agree. The point is a short one. Does section 35 (1) of the General Rate Act 1967 empower the Secretary of State to make an order the effect of which is that the rateable value of the hereditaments of a dock or harbour undertaking is to be determined not by reference to the rent which a hypothetical tenant would pay, but by reference to the receipts of the undertaking as a whole? The Minister's Order, the Docks and Harbours (Valuation) (Amendment) Order 1973, though it excludes certain receipts from valuation, stands or falls with the earlier Order of 1971. Mr. Widdicombe for the board submits that the Secretary of State has exceeded his powers. He argues that under the guise of specifying a method of valuation the Secretary of State by his order has, in truth, altered the basis of rating so far as docks and harbour undertakings are concerned. He points out—and it is conceded by the Inland Revenue Commissioners and the rating authorities—that by valuing the board's modest shore establishment, which consists only of a small jetty and harbour, offices, signal and wireless telegraphy stations, by reference to the undertaking as a whole, receipts from activities carried on elsewhere than upon the hereditament are used to calculate the rateable value of the hereditament. The result, Mr. Widdicombe submits, is contrary to the general principles of rating law. And so it all is. But the history of rating has shown that there are special cases which require special solutions. The so-called "statutory formulae" which are to be found in sections 26 to 36 of the Act of 1967 bear witness to the truth that the general principles of rating law are ineffectual to deal with the hereditaments of certain undertakings. Section 35, which is one of these sections, leaves it to the Secretary of State to determine how the rateable value of the hereditaments to which it applies is to be determined. The only limitation upon the power conferred upon him is that the Order he makes must be one which "makes provision for determining the rateable value" of the hereditaments to which it applies. Rates have to be based on an assessment of the yearly value of property: see section 1 (2) of the Act. Provided, therefore, that the Order is concerned with the assessment of the yearly value of the hereditament, the method of assessment is left to the Minister in the cases covered by section 35. The Secretary of State, in the two Orders challenged, has abandoned the traditional methods of valuation in

A favour of an assessment of value by reference to the receipts of the under-
taking as a whole. In doing so, has he gone beyond the assessing of a
yearly value to be put upon the hereditament? The plausibility of Mr.
Widdicombe's argument, that he has gone beyond his powers, derives not
only from the history of rating, of which Mr. Widdicombe gave the court
a sketch (for which I will ever be grateful), but from the inescapable fact
that, by requiring the board's modest shore establishment to be valued by
B reference to its receipts, the Secretary of State has required to be brought
into the calculation (i) receipts from activities on the waters of the
haven which are in no way dependent upon the occupation of the land
and (ii) receipts by way of rent from properties, the tenants of which also
pay rates. Once, however, it is recognised, as the General Rate Act 1967
recognises, that there are special cases for which valuation by reference
C to a hypothetical rent (the ordinary principle of valuation: see section 19)
provides no appropriate solution, is it so strange that in such a case a
hereditament should be valued for the purpose of rating by reference to the
use to which the occupier chooses to put it? The board finds it con-
venient to use this hereditament for the purposes of its statutory activities.
Common sense suggests that they find a shore establishment indispensable
—though theoretically it might be possible for the board to do without
D one. If, therefore, the Secretary of State makes an order which requires
a body such as the board to pay rates upon a valuation of its land by
reference to the undertaking as a whole, can it be said that the Secretary
of State is doing anything other than prescribing a method of valuing the
hereditament? I think not. I think, therefore, that the two Orders are
within the power conferred upon the Secretary of State by the section.

E I confess that I am less happy on the question of "double rating,"
though the amounts in question are not large. It appears wrong that rates
should be paid twice—once by the tenant and secondly by the landlord.
But this wrong—if it be a wrong— does not avail the board if, upon their
true construction, the two Orders of the Secretary of State are, as I think
they are, concerned only with method of valuation. It is a wrong which
the Secretary of State can, if he thinks fit, remedy by further order: it
F goes to the fairness of the method, not the power of the Minister.

For these reasons, as well as for those given by Cairns L.J., I would
dismiss the appeal. But I think the judge went too far in two respects.
He said that section 35 gave the Secretary of State, in effect, an unfettered
power with respect to the valuation of hereditaments to which it applies.
This is not really so. The Secretary of State's power is limited to specify-
G ing by his order a method for determining rateable value: see section 35
(1) of the Act. Had Mr. Widdicombe persuaded me that the two Orders
under challenge dealt with matters other than specifying a method of
valuation, I would have accepted his submission that they were ultra vires.
Secondly, the judge appears to have attached some importance to the
safeguards of consultation (section 35 (4)) and Parliamentary Affirmative
H Resolution procedure (section 35 (7)) when construing the ambit of the
rule-making power conferred by the section. No doubt these safeguards
find place in the section because of the width of the rule-making power
and the possibility of very serious financial consequences following upon
its exercise: but I think it would be contrary to principle to allow the
existence of these safeguards to influence one's view as to the extent of
the power conferred. That is a question of construction of the language
used which confers the power.

SIR GORDON WILLMER. I have much enjoyed this excursion into the A esoteric field of inquiry concerning methods of rating—a subject with which I had not hitherto acquired any noteworthy degree of familiarity. Applying what I hope is a fresh mind to the subject, and having read, and since the conclusion of the argument having carefully re-read, the judgment of Bridge J., I have come to the same conclusion as Cairns and Scarman L.JJ. and find myself quite unable to say that the judge's decision was wrong. In the circumstances, I have but little to add to what Cairns and B Scarman L.JJ. have already said and I shall not attempt to do more than touch briefly on some of the points which have been argued before us.

The hereditaments in the occupation of the board are, as stated by the judge, quite modest in extent, comprising only a small jetty and boat harbour, a small block of offices, with a signal station adjacent thereto, as well as a very small hereditament comprising a wireless telegraphy station. C These hereditaments had, prior to the coming into force of the Docks and Harbours (Valuation) Order 1971, been valued on what has been called the "profits basis," that is to say, the basis which is now enshrined in section 19 (3) of the Act of 1967. The board is not in occupation of the bed of the haven, although under the Milford Haven Conservancy Act 1958 it exercises various statutory powers over the haven, notably in relation to the construction of moorings, dredging, disposal of wrecks, D lighting and buoying, together with power to make byelaws regulating, inter alia, the navigation of vessels within the haven.

I can well understand the indignation of the board when it was discovered that the Order of 1971 completely revolutionised the system under which their hereditaments had previously been rated. No longer were they rated on the basis of the rent at which their modest hereditaments E might reasonably be expected to let from year to year. Under the new Order the rateable value of their hereditaments was to be based on "relevant receipts," which meant all receipts by way of revenue included, or to be included, in the accounts of their undertaking as a whole, including all the harbour dues collected from vessels entering and leaving the haven, boarding and landing fees charged in respect of pilots, mooring agency F fees, investment income, as well as rents received in respect of properties let, notwithstanding that such properties had already been subject to rating in the hands of their tenants. It was contended on behalf of the board, and readily admitted on behalf of the Inland Revenue Commissioners and the valuation officer, that this involved valuing the board's modest hereditaments by reference to the value of the undertaking as a whole. It was further admitted that this involved departure from the old- G established principles against rating in respect of what are called "tolls in gross," extra-parochial activities and investment income, as well as against the prohibition of double assessment.

The question, and the only question, before the court is whether this revolutionary departure from the old-established principles of rating was within the powers conferred on the Secretary of State by section 35 of the H Act of 1967. The relevant provisions are contained in sections 35 (1) and (6) which, subject to the safeguards provided by subsections (4), (5) and (7), undoubtedly confer extremely wide powers on the Secretary of State. I need not read again the words of sections 35 (1) and (6). I note, however, that subsection (1) makes provision for determining the rateable value, as opposed to the net annual value, of the relevant hereditaments. Moreover, the power to repeal or amend any enactment contained in sub-

A section (6) must be construed as including power to repeal or amend other provisions of the enabling Act itself, for instance, section 16 (relating to the types of hereditament liable to be rated) and section 19 (3) (relating to valuation by reference to the " hypothetical tenant ").

It appears to me, as it appeared to the judge, that it is highly significant that section 35 of the Act immediately follows four sections making specific provisions for the rating of other types of public utility undertakings.
B Section 31 relates to water undertakings, section 32 to railways and canals, section 33 to gas boards and section 34 to electricity boards. In each case the previous methods of rating in respect of such undertakings have been completely revolutionised and a wholly new system adopted, bearing little or no relation to previously accepted principles. It is reasonable to assume that Parliament intended by section 35 of the Act to confer on the Secretary
C of State power to make corresponding revolutionary innovations in relation to the rating of hereditaments occupied by the Coal Board, mines and quarries, as well as dock and harbour undertakings, without regard to previously accepted principles and subject only to the safeguards contained in subsections (4), (5) and (7).

The judge concluded:

D " . . . that there really is no warrant in the statutory context in which one finds section 35 for restricting the extremely wide ambit of the language of section 35 (1) and (6). By subsection (6) the Minister is given, in effect, an unfettered power to provide whatever code, whatever principles, he thinks appropriate with respect to the valuation of hereditaments of a class falling within subsection (2)."

E As I have said, I have read and re-read the judge's judgment and have carefully considered the reasoning whereby he reached his conclusion. Subject to possible criticism of the use of the word " unfettered " in the passage that I have just read, I can find no fault with it. On the contrary, I consider that he came to the only possible conclusion. I, therefore, agree with Cairns and Scarman L.JJ. that this appeal should be dismissed.

F *Appeal dismissed with costs.*
Leave to appeal refused.

Solicitors: *Norton, Rose, Botterell & Roche; Solicitor of Inland Revenue; Rutland & Crauford.*

G

H

[COURT OF APPEAL] A

* REGINA v. NOWAZ

1976 April 13 James L.J., Michael Davies and Jupp JJ.

Crime—Evidence—Secondary evidence—Document in possession of consul—Consul claiming diplomatic immunity from giving evidence and producing document—Whether evidence of content of document admissible B

The applicant was charged with making a false declaration, contrary to section 5 (*a*) of the Perjury Act 1911, namely, that he made a false statement as to his name in an application for registration as a citizen of the United Kingdom and Colonies. At the trial the prosecution sought to adduce evidence which included oral evidence of a police officer relating to a photograph, which was produced, and to the contents of a passport application which had been submitted to a Pakistani consulate. The consul, who had shown the documents and given one photograph to the police officer, claimed diplomatic immunity from attending the trial to give evidence and from producing the documents. The evidence was admitted and the applicant was convicted. C D

On an application for leave to appeal against conviction:—

Held, refusing the application, that the rule of evidence which permits secondary evidence in the form of copies of documents or oral evidence as to the contents of documents to be adduced in civil proceedings when original documents are not produced because the person in whose custody they are cannot be compelled to produce them applies also to criminal proceedings (post, pp. 832D, E, 833D, E); that, accordingly, the claim of diplomatic immunity having precluded the prosecution from producing the best evidence, the evidence of the police officer was rightly admitted. E

No cases are referred to in the judgment.

The following case was cited in argument: F

Reg. v. *Collins* (1960) 44 Cr.App.R. 170, C.C.A.

APPLICATION for leave to appeal against conviction.

On February 10, 1976, the applicant, Gul Nowaz, was charged at Derby Crown Court (Judge Heald) with making a false declaration contrary to section 5 (*a*) of the Perjury Act 1911, namely that in an application for registration as a citizen of the United Kingdom and Colonies under the British Nationality Act 1948 he made the false statement that he was Abdul Karim. At the trial evidence of a police officer relating to a photograph and to the contents of a passport application was admitted in the absence of the original documents, after a Pakistani consul claimed diplomatic immunity from attending the court to give evidence and to produce the documents. On February 26, 1976, the applicant was convicted and sentenced to six months' imprisonment with a recommendation for deportation. The applicant applied for leave to appeal against conviction on the ground, inter alia, that the judge had erred in overruling the defendant's submission that the officer was not entitled to give secondary G H

[Reported by MISS EIRA CARYL-THOMAS, Barrister-at-Law]

A evidence of the documents or statement made to the police by the witness who had claimed diplomatic immunity.

The facts are stated in the judgment of the court.

Ghulam Yazdani for the applicant.
D. J. Farrer for the Crown.

B JAMES L.J. delivered the judgment of the court. This is an application for leave to appeal against conviction. It is somewhat unusual in that it has been brought on for hearing before a transcript of the proceedings and in particular of the argument, made on a submission by counsel, has been made available to the court. The reason for that is that on February 26, 1976, at Derby Crown Court the applicant, Gul Nowaz, who also calls
C himself Abdul Karim, was convicted of making a false declaration contrary to section 5 (*a*) of the Perjury Act 1911 and was sentenced to six months' imprisonment. If we waited for the transcript to be received by the court, having regard to the difficulties in transcribing long cases—and this was a long case, the sentence would have been fully served and, in the particular circumstances of this case, there would be difficulties in relation to any application for bail meanwhile. Fortunately, however, the
D application is based upon what is a short point as to the admissibility of certain evidence, and we have had the advantage of having the argument put before us by Mr. Yazdani, who was at the trial conducting the defence for the applicant.

The charge preferred against the applicant, of which he was convicted, was that on May 6, 1974, he wilfully made a false statement in an application for registration as a citizen of the United Kingdom and
E Colonies under the British Nationality Act 1948. The defence put forward by the applicant was that the statement he made, which he admitted he had made, was not false. The statement which was alleged to be false was that he was the person Abdul Karim. His defence was "I am Abdul Karim."

The prosecution sought to establish the charge that had been preferred
F by evidence of different sorts. There was some fingerprint evidence on a document; there was evidence of a person in a managerial capacity at a place of employment in Derby where, it was said by the applicant, he had previously been employed, who said, "that is not the man"; there was evidence given by a police officer, a detective constable, in relation to a document that was produced, namely a photograph, and in addition the contents of an application for a passport which had been submitted to
G the Pakistani Consulate at Bradford.

It is in respect of that last-mentioned type of evidence that was put before the jury that the point has been taken in this application. It is common ground between the applicant and the Crown that if the evidence of the police officer was wrongly admitted—was inadmissible evidence—then this conviction cannot stand. If, on the other hand, it was admissible
H evidence then there is no irregularity, misdirection as to law or any aspect rendering the verdict of the jury unsafe or unsatisfactory that can be relied upon by the applicant as a ground for quashing the conviction.

The position was this. On April 23, 1975, D.C. Kilbane visited the Pakistani consul at Bradford, Mr. Ahmad, and was shown two photographs attached to an application form which was made out in the name of Abdul Karim. One of those photographs was handed to him. The officer also gave evidence of the fact that he had returned to the office

of Mr. Ahmad on February 4, 1976, and at that time Mr. Ahmad pro- A
duced to him the passport application form. He also saw attached to it a photograph which he identified as being identical to the photograph that he had received the previous April. The officer gave evidence that the application form that he saw contained the name Abdul Karim, the address 98, Rosehill Street, Derby, the fact that Abdul Karim was the son of Imam Din, the date of birth January 2, 1931, the place of birth Mirpur,
Kashmir. B

That evidence was admitted in the trial because, when it came to it, Mr. Ahmad claimed diplomatic immunity from attending the court to give evidence himself and to produce the documents. Statements had been taken from him. It was the intention of the Crown to call Mr. Ahmad to produce these documents. Had he been called he would have given the evidence, which the police officer gave, and produced the docu- C
ments. The point, then, is a short one. Were the photograph and the contents of the application form wrongly or rightly admitted in evidence? Had the original application form and the photograph been produced there can be no doubt that they would have been admissible. Mr. Yazdani submits that the admission of the secondary evidence, in the absence of the original document, in the form of oral evidence of the police officer was wrong, and that, in those circumstances, in a criminal D
case the Crown were not entitled to adduce evidence of this type.

It appears that there is a dearth of authority in relation to the reports on criminal proceedings upon this particular topic. There are cases, which we have not found it necessary to consider in detail, which involved the civil law and evidence admissible in civil proceedings which clearly show that in circumstances such as these where a document is not pro- E
duced because it cannot be produced—because the person in whose custody it is cannot be compelled to produce it—then the secondary evidence is admissible.

A general statement of the law can best be summarised, we think, in a passage to which our attention was invited in Professor Cross' book on *Evidence*, 4th ed. (1974), p. 524, under the heading "Stranger's lawful refusal to produce document," which reads: F

> "When the original of a document is in the possession of a stranger to the litigation, the proper course for the party desiring to prove the contents of the document is to serve the stranger with a subpoena duces tecum. The stranger may, however, be able to establish a claim to privilege in respect of the document when secondary evidence of its contents becomes admissible." G

Relating that to criminal proceedings, the subpoena duces tecum referred to is the equivalent of a witness summons requiring the attendance of a witness and production by the witness of the documents. That was complied with in this case we are told. The passage goes on: "The governing principle is the same as that which covers the next two exceptions . . ." I interpolate, those are the exceptions of a lost document H
and production of the original document being impossible. Returning to the text:

> "it is impossible to compel production of the document, and it will apply in cases in which the person in possession of the original is beyond the jurisdiction of the court; . . ."

I need read no further. A person who rightly claims diplomatic immunity

A is a person beyond the jurisdiction of the court. Therefore that statement applies to this case.

The one point which has given us some cause for thought is whether the same principles apply to the criminal law as to civil. Passages to the same effect as that which I have just read appear in *Archbold Criminal Pleading Evidence & Practice*, 38th ed. (1973), para. 1001 and succeeding paragraphs. Similar passages are to be found in the standard work of
B *Phipson on Evidence* and we need not recite them. In none of those passages is there any distinction drawn between civil and criminal proceedings. In *Cross on Evidence*, p. 3, the statement is made, after referring to the departures that would be made between the law of evidence in criminal proceedings and the law of evidence in civil proceedings if and when the recommendations in the 11th report of the Criminal Law Revision
C Committee were implemented, Professor Cross states:

> "It is still formally true to say that, subject to exceptions, the rules of evidence are the same in each instance, but the number of exceptions, coupled with the all important fact that the rules are applied with much greater rigour in criminal proceedings, renders the statement somewhat unreal."

D In a footnote the professor lists the principal distinguishing features of criminal cases, which listed features do not include the matter of when secondary evidence is admissible. That secondary evidence can take one of different forms; it may be a copy of a document, it may be oral evidence as to the contents of the document.

We are satisfied in the event, despite Mr. Yazdani's persuasive argu-
E ment, that in all the circumstances of this case Mr. Ahmad, the consul who claimed diplomatic immunity, precluded the prosecution from producing the best evidence in the form of the original document. In those circumstances the law of evidence relating to criminal proceedings did permit the prosecution to produce the secondary evidence of D.C. Kilbane. That evidence was rightly admitted. As I have already indicated, there were no other irregularities, misdirections or other features that would
F render the verdict of the jury unsafe and unsatisfactory and therefore the application must be, and is, refused.

Application refused.

Solicitors: *Fox, Hayes & Co., Leeds; D. R. K. Seddon, Derby.*

G

H

[EMPLOYMENT APPEAL TRIBUNAL] A

* COULSON *v.* CITY OF LONDON POLYTECHNIC

1976 May 5; 19 — Phillips J. and Mr. A. C. Blyghton

Industrial Relations—Unfair dismissal—Continuous employment—Computation of 26-week period of employment—Whether to include whole of weeks in which employee engaged and dismissed—Trade Union and Labour Relations Act 1974 (*c.* 52), *Sch.* 1, *paras.* 10, 30—*Contracts of Employment Act* 1972 (*c.* 53), *Sch.* 1, *paras.* 4, 11 B

Between Tuesday, October 1, 1974, and Monday, March 24, 1975, when he was dismissed, the employee worked for the C employers as an assistant librarian. His application for compensation for unfair dismissal was refused by an industrial tribunal which, calculating the length of his employment on a calendar basis, being 24 weeks, held that since he had not been "continuously employed for a period of not less than 26 weeks" as required by paragraph 10 (*a*) of Schedule 1 to the Trade Union and Labour Relations Act 1974,[1] they had no jurisdiction to hear his claim. D

On the employee's appeal on the ground that by reason of paragraph 30 of Schedule 1 to the Act of 1974, the tribunal ought to have had regard to Schedule 1 to the Contracts of Employment Act 1972 [2] when calculating the number of weeks he had worked:—

Held, allowing the appeal, that paragraph 10 of Schedule 1 to the Trade Union and Labour Relations Act 1974 enabled the final day of the period of employment to be determined, E but by reason of paragraph 30 of Schedule 1, the provisions of Schedule 1 to the Contracts of Employment Act 1972 applied when calculating the number of weeks in the period of employment; that since "week" in paragraph 4 meant a week ending with Saturday and since the whole of the week in which the employment started and the whole of the week in which the employment was terminated were weeks during the whole or part of which the employee's relations with the employer were F governed by a contract of employment within the meaning of paragraph 4, those weeks were to be included in calculating the qualifying period of employment with the result that the employee had been continuously employed for 26 weeks and was entitled to claim compensation for unfair dismissal.

Per curiam. A similar method should be applied when computing the period of continuous employment for the requisite period for the purposes of section 8 (2) of the Redundancy G Payments Act 1965 (post, p. 838H).

The following cases are referred to in the judgment:

Dean v. *Polytechnic of North London* [1973] I.C.R. 490, N.I.R.C.
Dixon v. *Stenor Ltd.* [1973] I.C.R. 157, N.I.R.C.
Pearson v. *Williames Transport* (*Scotland*) *Ltd.* [1976] I.R.L.R. 43.
Parkes Classic Confectionery Ltd. v. *Ashcroft* (1973) 8 I.T.R. 43, D.C. H

[1] Trade Union and Labour Relations Act 1974, Sch. 1, para. 10: see post, pp. 835H—836A.
Para. 30: see post, p. 836C.

[2] Contracts of Employment Act 1972, Sch. 1, para. 4: "Any week during the whole or part of which the employee's relations with the employer are governed by a contract of employment which normally involves employment for 21 hours or more weekly and shall count in computing a period of employment."
Para. 11: "'week' means a week ending with Saturday."

The following additional case was cited in argument:

Mabey v. *B.R.T. Industries Ltd.* (unreported), April 11, 1975.

APPEAL from an industrial tribunal sitting in London.

The employee, Robert Coulson, appealed from a decision of the industrial tribunal on July 17, 1975, that they had no jurisdiction to hear his application for compensation for unfair dismissal from his employers, City of London Polytechnic, on the ground that the tribunal had erred in holding that he had not been continuously employed for 26 weeks as required by paragraph 10 of Schedule 1 to the Trade Union and Labour Relations Act 1974.

The appeal was transferred from the Queen's Bench Division of the High Court to the Employment Appeal Tribunal under paragraph 9 of Schedule 17 to the Employment Protection Act 1975. On May 5, 1976, the Employment Appeal Tribunal allowed the appeal but reserved their reasons.

The facts are stated in the judgment.

Margaret Rae for the employee.

D. Mackie, solicitor, for the employers.

Cur. adv. vult.

May 19. PHILLIPS J. read the following judgment of the appeal tribunal. The question which arises in this appeal is how to calculate the qualifying period of employment which will entitle an employee who has been dismissed to make a claim for compensation for unfair dismissal. It is a question which has been considered by industrial tribunals on numerous occasions. Unfortunately, the answers which they have given are not in agreement. Consequently the appeal is of some importance. Furthermore, the answer will apply equally to the similar question which arises under the Redundancy Payments Act 1965 in relation to a claim for a redundancy payment.

The appeal is by Mr. Coulson, the employee, against a decision of an industrial tribunal sitting in London on July 17, 1975, which decided that they had no jurisdiction to entertain his claim for compensation for unfair dismissal. The tribunal found that the employee had not been continuously employed for the period necessary to entitle him to make such a claim. It should be said that the City of London Polytechnic, the employers, did not wish to take the point, and on the hearing of the appeal, that position has been re-stated, although the solicitor for the employers has argued the case most helpfully. The industrial tribunal took the point for themselves, as they were obliged to do if it seemed that there was doubt as to their jurisdiction to entertain the claim.

The employee's employment began on October 1, 1974. It is common ground that the date of termination of his employment was March 24, 1975. October 1, 1974, was a Tuesday; March 24, 1975, was a Monday. The employee's normal hours of work were 36¾ hours a week. 26 weeks from October 1, 1975, calculated on a calendar basis, did not expire until March 31, 1975.

Paragraph 10 of Schedule 1 to the Trade Union and Labour Relations Act 1974 provides:

"Subject to paragraph 11 below"—dismissal for an inadmissible

> reason—" paragraph 4 above "—the right not to be unfairly dismissed A —" does not apply to the dismissal of an employee from any employment if the employee—(*a*) was not continuously employed for a period of not less than 26 weeks ending with the effective date of termination, . . ."

Accordingly, if the matter falls to be determined in accordance with that paragraph alone, it can be seen that the employee had not been B continuously employed for a period of not less than 26 weeks ending with the agreed " effective date of termination," i.e., March 24, 1975, in accordance with paragraph 5 (5) (*b*).

However, Miss Rae, for the employee, relies on the provisions of paragraph 30 (1) of Schedule 1 to the Act of 1974, which provides:

> " The provisions of Schedule 1 to the Contracts of Employment C Act 1972 (computation of period of employment), and the provisions of any order for the time being in force under section 10 of that Act in so far as it modifies that Schedule, shall have effect for the purposes of this Act in determining for what period an employee has been continuously employed."

According to this submission, the period of not less than 26 weeks D must be calculated in accordance with the provisions of Schedule 1 to the Contracts of Employment Act 1972. The argument then proceeds as follows: during his first week of employment, the employee worked on Tuesday, Wednesday, Thursday and Friday. In accordance with the provisions of paragraph 4 of Schedule 1 that counts as one week. For the purpose of the computation of periods of employment, a " week " means a week ending with Saturday (paragraph 11 of Schedule 1). E Between the Saturday at the end of the first week of his employment and the Saturday preceding the Monday on which he was dismissed, the employee was employed for 24 weeks. Until then, therefore, he had been employed for a total of 25 weeks. He was dismissed on Monday, March 24 but continued to be employed during that day. Thus, in accordance with paragraph 4 of Schedule 1, the week commencing on the F Saturday preceding his dismissal was a week during part of which his relations with his employers were governed by a contract of employment which normally involved employment for 21 hours or more weekly, and therefore counted in computing the period of his employment. That week added to the 25 weeks expiring on the previous Saturday gave him the necessary total of 26 weeks.

G

In our judgment, this conclusion follows as a matter of calculation, if it is correct to calculate the period of employment in accordance with the provisions of Schedule 1 to the Contracts of Employment Act 1972. The question which arises in the appeal, and which has been the subject of the numerous decisions of industrial tribunals referred to above, is whether this is the correct approach to the matter. It will be seen that it involves praying in aid, in order to reach a total of 26 weeks, a period H of employment subsequent to the effective date of termination of the employee's employment which was March 24, 1975. The question is whether that is legitimate having regard to the words in paragraph 10 (*a*): " *ending with* the effective date of termination."

The difficulty arises from the fact that paragraph 10 (*a*) and paragraph 30 (1) do not mesh together easily. The former seems to be dealing with periods of weeks ending on a particular day (which may be any day of

A the week, leading to the conclusion that the calculation is to be done on
a calendar basis, rather in the manner of determining the proper date of
expiry of a notice to quit or of a notice of dismissal in accordance with
the terms of a contract), whereas the latter, by bringing in Schedule 1 to
the Contracts of Employment Act 1972, is dealing in weeks ending with
a Saturday, of a notional character determined in accordance with the
provisions of that Schedule.

B It is not out of disrespect to the various decisions of industrial
tribunals mentioned above that we do not examine them in detail but it is
merely for simplicity. We have, in fact, received considerable help from
an examination of the reasoning which led them to reach such differing
conclusions. Perhaps the most elaborate, and closely reasoned, is the
decision of a tribunal sitting in Scotland in *Pearson* v. *Williames Trans-*
C *port (Scotland) Ltd.* [1976] I.R.L.R. 43. The tribunal in that case
accepted that regard must be had to the provisions of Schedule 1 to the
Contracts of Employment Act 1972 for the purpose of determining the
number of weeks which a claimant has been employed. However, they
went on to decide, out of deference to the words in paragraph 10 (*a*) of
Schedule 1 to the Act of 1974, "ending with the effective date of
termination," that no regard should be had to events occurring after that
D date. Since, in counting weeks, they must be taken to end with a Satur-
day, the tribunal further found that where an employee is dismissed in
the middle of a week he can only count weeks up to and including the
Saturday before the week in which he was dismissed. The broken week
which follows dismissal cannot be taken into account because it is not
itself a complete week, and can only be treated as one by taking into
E account events following the effective date of termination. This result
is logical, but unsatisfactory, as it prevents an employee from counting
for the purpose of establishing how many weeks he has been employed
days which he has actually served. None of the cases decided in the
National Industrial Relations Court, or in the Divisional Court (and there
are no others in the superior courts), expressly decides this point. *Dean*
v. *Polytechnic of North London* [1973] I.C.R. 490 and *Dixon* v. *Stenor*
F *Ltd.* [1973] I.C.R. 157 touch upon it, but the question was not directly
in issue; nor is any reference made to the Contracts of Employment Act
1972. In *Parkes Classic Confectionery Ltd.* v. *Ashcroft* (1973) 8 I.T.R.
43, 44, Lord Widgery C.J. said, of the somewhat similar provisions in
section 8 (1) and (2) of the Redundancy Payments Act 1965:

> "So we have the requisite period being 104 weeks, and a reference
> G to the Act of 1963 to determine whether employment has been for
> these purposes in force during that period."

Those observations somewhat support the employee's argument in this
case, but only marginally, for the matter does not appear to have been
fully canvassed, nor did the specific question in issue in this appeal arise
there.

H Miss Rae submits that there is ambiguity, or conflict between para-
graph 10 and paragraph 30 of Schedule 1 to the Act of 1974, and that
the application of Schedule 1 to the Contracts of Employment Act 1972
produces certainty of calculation which would otherwise be lacking.

Mr. Mackie, for the employers, submits that paragraph 10 means
what it says, and he places particular reliance upon the word "with" in
the expression "ending with the effective date of termination" as show-
ing quite clearly that the period of employment to be counted ends at

that date and no other. The effect of this way of looking at it would be that reference to the Contracts of Employment Act 1972 is only necessary for the purpose of determining whether employment has been continuous, and not for determining the length of employment. He concedes that for the former purpose it is necessary to refer to the Act of 1972.

We are impressed by the fact that ever since the Contracts of Employment Act 1963 (predecessor of the Act of 1972) it has been familiar law, in conformity with industrial practice, that periods of employment should be calculated on the lines laid down in Schedule 1 to the Act of 1972. It seems inherently probable, therefore, that when the Redundancy Payments Act 1965 (which in section 8 provides a somewhat similar test to justify the making of a claim for a redundancy payment) and section 28 of the Industrial Relations Act 1971 (predecessor of paragraph 10 of Schedule 1 to the Act of 1974) were enacted, the intention was to apply a similar system for the computation of periods of employment. Furthermore, we are impresed by the need for a clear and, as far as possible, uniform method of calculating such periods. Even on the submission put forward by Mr. Mackie, or on somewhat similar submissions which have been accepted in some of the cases before industrial tribunals (e.g., *Pearson* v. *Williames Transport* (*Scotland*) *Ltd.* [1976] I.R.L.R. 43) it would be necessary to refer to Schedule 1 to the Act of 1972 for some purposes including determining continuity, even if not for all. This seems to us to be most inconvenient and a likely source of confusion.

Accordingly, unless the language of the Act of 1974 compels us to hold otherwise, it seems to us that the meaning of paragraph 10 of Schedule 1, read together with paragraph 30, is that the computation of the period of continuous employment ending with the effective date of termination is to be made in accordance with the provisions of Schedule 1 to the Act of 1972. We do not think that we are so compelled. It seems to us that the answer to the difficulty caused by the words " period . . . ending with the effective date of termination " is this: they enable one to identify the last day of the period of employment to be taken into account, but it is the Contracts of Employment Act 1972 which provides the measure by which one computes the number of weeks which that period contains. By taking into account, for the purpose of such computation, days subsequent to the effective date of termination, one is not extending the period, but merely determining that a period so ending, when computed in accordance with the provisions of the Act of 1972, contains a certain number of weeks.

Accordingly, in our judgment, the steps to be taken in calculating the period of continuous employment for the purpose of paragraph 10 (*a*) of Schedule 1 to the Act of 1974 are these: decide upon what day the employment began; decide the effective date of termination, and calculate how many weeks of continuous employment that period contains when computed in accordance with the provisions of Schedule 1 to the Act of 1972.

Similar results will follow when computing the period of continuous employment for the requisite period for the purpose of section 8 of the Redundancy Payments Act 1965. It seems to us that the general sense of the language of section 8 (2) of that Act is the same as that of paragraph 30 (1) of Schedule 1 to the Act of 1974. We have noted the point made by the tribunal in *Pearson* v. *Williames Transport* (*Scotland*) *Ltd.*

[1976] I.R.L.R. 43 that if Schedule 1 to the Contracts of Employment Act 1972 applies for all purposes it might be thought that paragraph 8 of Schedule 1 to the Redundancy Payments Act 1965 was superfluous or, at the least, that some similar provision would have been incorporated in section 8. However, if we are right in our analysis of paragraph 10 and paragraph 30 of Schedule 1 to the Act of 1974 (and similarly of section 8 of the Redundancy Payments Act 1965) there is no reason why the days leading up to the relevant date occurring before the end of a week should not, when computed in accordance with Schedule 1 to the Contracts of Employment Act 1972, constitute a week—paragraph 4. The amount of the redundancy payment in accordance with Schedule 1 to the Redundancy Payments Act 1965 is calculated by reckoning backwards from the end of the period of employment. Were it not for the provisions of paragraph 8 of Schedule 1 to the Act of 1965, in a case where that date was in the course of a week, a result would be produced which would be inconsistent with the broken week in which that date fell being treated as a week of employment.

In our judgment the appeal must be allowed, and the case remitted to the tribunal to hear the complaint of unfair dismissal.

Appeal allowed.
Case remitted to tribunal.
No order as to costs.

Solicitors: *Nicholas Carter; Allen & Overy.*

J. W.

[COURT OF APPEAL] A

* REGINA *v.* OWEN

1976 May 17 — Lawton and Browne L.JJ. and Willis J.

Crime — Embracery — Sentence — Whether immediate custodial B
sentence appropriate

The defendant's brother-in-law was charged with murdering
his wife, the defendant's sister. At the outset of the trial the
judge in open court gave the jury the usual warning about not
speaking to anyone or allowing anyone to speak to them
about matters bearing on the trial. On the second day, a
woman juror reported to the police that the defendant had C
spoken to her while she was walking near the court during
the luncheon adjournment, saying that the accused was guilty
and had stabbed someone previously. The trial judge was
informed and the jury was discharged. The defendant was
later charged with embracery, convicted, and sentenced to nine
months' imprisonment and ordered to pay £350 towards the
costs of his defence.

On appeal against sentence:— D

Held, allowing the appeal, that an immediate custodial
sentence was the only appropriate sentence to be imposed on
offenders who interfered with the administration of justice,
unless the circumstances were wholly exceptional (post, p. 843G);
that on the facts of the present case, a sentence of nine months'
imprisonment was too long and, accordingly, a sentence would
be substituted which would have been appropriate had the
defendant been released by the court on the date when he was E
given leave to appeal and released on bail.

The following case is referred to in the judgment:

Balogh v. *St. Albans Crown Court* [1975] Q.B. 73; [1974] 3 W.L.R. 314; [1974] 3 All E.R. 283, C.A.

No additional cases were cited in argument. F

APPEAL against sentence.

On November 5, 1975, at the Crown Court, Caernarvon, the defen-
dant, Norman Owen, was convicted of embracery and sentenced by
Cobb J. to nine months' imprisonment and ordered to pay £350 towards
the cost of his defence. On November 19 the single judge granted him
leave to appeal against conviction and sentence and released him on G
bail. Notice of abandonment of appeal against conviction was served,
and the defendant appealed against the sentence on the ground that it
was too severe.

The facts are stated in the judgment.

Peter Weitzman Q.C. and *J. M. T. Rogers* for the defendant. H

LAWTON L.J. On November 5, 1975, before the Crown Court at Caernarvon the defendant was convicted of embracery. He was sentenced by Cobb J. to nine months' imprisonment and ordered to pay

---

[Reported by MISS EIRA CARYL-THOMAS, Barrister-at-Law]

A £350 towards the costs of his defence. He applied for leave to appeal against both his conviction and sentence. The single judge granted leave to appeal against both and on November 19, 1975, released him on bail.

The defendant has had the advantage of being represented by Mr. Weitzman. Mr. Weitzman, reading the transcript of the summing up, came to the conclusion that it could not be criticised. Accordingly he
B advised his client to serve notice of abandonment of his appeal against conviction. The defendant wisely accepted Mr. Weitzman's advice and a notice of abandonment was served. It follows that the only appeal now before the court is against sentence.

The charge is a very rare one these days. *Archbold Criminal Pleading Evidence & Practice*, 38th ed. 1973, p. 1321, para. 3447, defines embracery
C in these terms:

> "Embracery is an offence indictable at common law, punishable by fine and imprisonment, and consists in any attempt to corrupt or influence or instruct a jury, or any attempt to incline them to be more favourable to the one side than to the other, by money, promises, letters, threats or persuasions, whether the jurors on
> D whom such an attempt is made give any verdict or not, or whether the verdict given be true or false."

The editors of *Archbold* then set out a number of references to support that definition of embracery. Most of them are 18th-century references. There are two references to cases on the files of the Central Criminal Court. Counsel has industriously turned up the file relating to the later
E of the two cases in the Central Criminal Court. That was a case at the end of the 19th century. There does not appear to have been any reported case since.

In our judgment the reason for this offence becoming obsolescent is probably that in modern times the kind of conduct envisaged by the offence of embracery has been dealt with in one of two ways. If more than one person had been involved, the charge was likely to have been
F conspiracy to pervert the course of justice. If only one person was involved, then the charge was likely to have been contempt of court. As this sort of incident arises during the progress of the trial, the contempt could be, and in the past probably has normally been, dealt with by the judge exercising his summary jurisdiction to deal with the contempt forthwith.

G It is relevant to point out that in *Balogh* v. *St. Albans Crown Court* [1975] Q.B. 73, the court reviewed the circumstances in which a judge should exercise his summary jurisdiction and it seems to us that this case could have been dealt with summarily. If I may refer to my own judgment I said, at p. 92:

> "In my judgment this summary and draconian jurisdiction should only be used for the purpose of ensuring that a trial in progress or
> H about to start can be brought to a proper and dignified end without disturbance and with a fair chance of a just verdict or judgment. Contempts which are not likely to disturb the trial or affect the verdict or judgment can be dealt with by a motion to commit under R.S.C., Ord. 52, or even by indictment."

As I shall be recounting in a moment, this was just the kind of case which I had in mind when I made the comment which I did and to which I have just referred. Stephenson L.J., who had had the draft of my judgment before I delivered it, said, at p. 91:

> "It must be left to the common sense of judges of the High Court and the Crown Court to decide when they must resort to this power to deal with such contempts as are listed in the judgment which Lawton L.J. is about to deliver."

In our judgment, this is just the sort of case in which it would have been better to proceed summarily for contempt, rather than by reviving the obsolescent offence of embracery.

The circumstances in which the charge came to be made are these. At the end of the Michaelmas Term 1974 at Caernarvon Crown Court, a trial for murder was going on before Mars-Jones J. The accused was a man called Robert Selwyn Davies. He was charged with murdering his wife, who was the sister of this defendant. The defendant and other members of his family were in court to hear the trial. Not unnaturally, feelings ran high amongst the members of the family who were present. The jury was duly empanelled and amongst the jurors was a lady called Mrs. Gwendoline Mary Owen. At the beginning of the trial the trial judge gave the jury in open court the usual warning about not speaking to anyone or allowing anyone to speak to them about any matter bearing on the trial. On the second day of the trial, namely December 18, 1974, at the mid-day adjournment, Mrs. Owen, before leaving the court building, went to the lavatory. When she came out her fellow jurors had all left. She decided to take her mid-day refreshment at a nearby café. As she walked along a road near the court, she saw ahead of her a group of people whom she had seen in court that morning and she inferred, and rightly inferred, that they were connected with the deceased woman's family. Mrs. Owen, who kept in mind the judge's admonition to the jury about not talking to any one about the case, was very keen not to be drawn into conversation with anybody. As a result she slowed down so as not to catch up with the people ahead. As she walked, however, she saw the defendant coming up behind her. The defendant said to her in a normal voice "Guilty. He's guilty you know. He's already stabbed somebody before."

She said at the trial that the words which the defendant had used to her were said in such a way that she doubted whether other members of the family group could have heard them. That matter was the sole issue at the trial, because it was the defendant's case that he did not speak to the juror consciously at all, that his remarks had been directed solely to the other members of the family in whose company he had been.

As a result of what had happened, Mrs. Owen was somewhat disturbed. She rightly drew away from the defendant and went into the café. Whilst she was there two police officers came in. Mrs. Owen, very wisely, told them what had happened. They reported what they had heard to the appropriate officer of the court. That officer reported the matter to the judge when he returned to court after the mid-day adjournment. The judge, as was inevitable in the circumstances, decided to discharge the jury. Another jury had to be empanelled and the trial had to start all over again.

Those are the facts out of which this appeal arises. With hindsight this court can see that it would have been better for Mars-Jones J. to have dealt with the matter summarily. Had he done so and imposed a short sentence of imprisonment, this defendant would have had little

A chance of succeeding on an appeal to the civil division of this court, which
is the court to which appeals from judges exercising summary jurisdiction
for contempt go.

The judge not having taken that course, police inquiries started. It is
only fair to the defendant to record that when he learned that police
inquiries had started, he went round to the police station to present him-
self there for questioning. When he did so, he was told why the police
B were making inquiries, and he said at once that he had not consciously
spoken to Mrs. Owen at all, and that his remarks had been directed to
the family group. Maybe it was because he had denied at the time that
he had consciously spoken to Mrs. Owen that it was decided to proceed
by way of the common law offence of embracery rather than by the
summary procedure for contempt. Be that as it may, most unfortunately
C the proceedings on the charge of embracery have dragged on over a
period now of nearly 18 months. The defendant was not arrested. He was
served with a summons. We do not know the date upon which he was
served, but we do know that the preliminary inquiry before the justices
took place on July 17, 1975, some six months after the event leading to
the charge. The defendant was then committed for trial to the Crown
D Court at Caernarvon. The trial took place at the beginning of November
1975. As I have already recounted, the defendant was convicted and
sentenced.

Cobb J. when sentencing the defendant said:

> ". . . it is thankfully a relatively rare occurrence for anyone to inter-
> fere with the machinery of the administration of justice. It is in my
> E experience even more, almost unique, for anyone to interfere with
> or to approach the most important, the most sensitive, and the most
> vulnerable part of that machinery, a juror when empanelled in a trial.
> When, however, that does occur, condign punishment must follow for
> the quality of justice must be as perfect as mankind can make it, and
> no attempt to corrupt it will be countenanced by the courts. Jurors
> must be free and feel free to reach their conclusions without any
> F outside pressure or influences."

Then he referred to the defendant's background and ended his sentencing
in these terms:

> "I have a distasteful task to perform, but I must perform it. The
> sentence of the court is that you be imprisoned for nine calendar
> G months. You will also pay £350 out of substantial capital resources
> which you have, towards the costs of your own defence."

In our judgment the approach of the judge was right. Those who do
interfere with the administration of justice must expect to go to prison
and any prison sentence should take immediate effect. We cannot envisage
any other kind of sentence being appropriate unless the circumstances are
H wholly exceptional.

What then should have been the length of sentence? This defendant
is a hard-working man. He has never been in any kind of trouble before.
He supports a wife and a number of young children. There is every
reason to think that he is held in high esteem by those who know him.
This court accepts that when he was in the court room where his brother-
in-law was being tried for the murder of his sister, feelings were bound
to run high. All the same he was present when the judge gave the

warning to the jurors. He must have known that he was acting in breach A of the judge's order and that by trying to influence a juror he was doing something which was wrong and which called for punishment. In our judgment the punishment would have been adequate if he had gone to prison for a short time. We do not think it was necessary, on the facts of this particular case, to impose a sentence as long as nine months.

Mr. Weitzman called our attention to the possibility that the sentence could have been suspended. B We do not accept that. Suspended sentences are inappropriate for this kind of behaviour. Had we been trying this case, all three of us are of the opinion that we would have passed a sentence of three months' imprisonment taking immediate effect. We are not trying this case. We are reviewing it in the light of what happened.

One of the facts which we have got to bear in mind (and it is unfortunate that we have to) is that justice has been long delayed. It seems C to us wrong that after such a long interval as 18 months, this man should have to go back to prison to serve what would have been a short remnant of his sentence if we had reduced the sentence from nine months to three months. Perhaps it was unfortunate that he was released on bail in the circumstances in which he was. It might have been better if the single judge had said that he was to remain in custody and had requested the registrar to expedite the hearing of the appeal. D The judge released him on bail on November 19. He returned to his family and to his work. In our judgment it would be unduly harsh to make him go back to prison some six months later.

Accordingly we allow the appeal. We quash the sentence of nine months' imprisonment and substitute the sentence which would have been appropriate had he been released by this court on November 19, 1975. E To that extent the appeal is allowed.

Appeal allowed.

Solicitor: *Registrar of Criminal Appeals.*

F

G

H

A

[COURT OF APPEAL]

* RICHARD CLARKE & CO. LTD. *v.* WIDNALL

1976 May 20; 27 Megaw and Orr L.JJ. and Milmo J.

B *Landlord and Tenant—Forfeiture of lease—Relief from forefeiture —Non-payment of rent—Lease giving landlords right of immediate re-entry or after period of notice—Landlords electing to give notice—Tenant paying arrears of rent—Whether forfeiture of lease—Whether tenant entitled to relief from forfeiture*

The landlords, a firm of brewers, granted a tenancy of
C licensed premises to the tenant, determinable by 12 months' notice by either party, at a rent of £480 per annum payable quarterly. Clause 13 (4) of the tenancy agreement provided that, if the tenant committed, inter alia, a breach of the covenant to pay rent, the landlords would be entitled under sub-paragraph (i) to obtain possession of the premises or, alternatively, by sub-paragraph (ii) to give the tenant three months' notice in writing to determine the tenancy, provided
D that the alleged breach was specified in the notice. The tenant failed to pay rent on the quarter days in June, September and December 1974. On February 26, 1975, the landlords served a three months' notice to quit on the tenant, expressed to be "in accordance with clause 13 (4) of the agreement" for breach of the covenant to pay rent. The tenant, having paid the whole of the outstanding rent, remained in occupation of the premises after May 25, the date when the three months'
E notice expired. The landlords brought proceedings in the county court for possession and mesne profits and the tenant counterclaimed for relief from forfeiture. On September 15 the judge, holding that forfeiture arose only under sub-paragraph (i) of clause 13 (4), granted the landlords possession and mesne profits on the basis that, as they had exercised their right under sub-paragraph (ii) to terminate the tenancy on short notice, the tenant was not entitled to relief from forfeiture.

F On the tenant's appeal: —

Held, allowing the appeal, that the immediate right of re-entry in clause 13 (4) (i) was to be regarded as merely security for the payment of rent and, if the landlords had elected to act under sub-paragraph (i), the tenant would be entitled to relief from forfeiture; that the fact that the right of re-entry under sub-paragraph (ii) was only effective after the period of notice had expired did not alter the character
G and legal consequences of that right and, therefore, since it was immaterial that the period of notice under sub-paragraph (ii) was less than the period of notice for either party to terminate the agreement, the tenant was entitled to relief against forfeiture.

Dictum of Lord Greene M.R. in *Chandless-Chandless* v. *Nicholson* [1942] 2 K.B. 321, 323, C.A. applied.

H

The following cases are referred to in the judgment of Megaw L.J.:

Canas Property Co. Ltd. v. *K.L. Television Services Ltd.* [1970] 2 Q.B. 433; [1970] 2 W.L.R. 1133; [1970] 2 All E.R. 795, C.A.

Chandless-Chandless v. *Nicholson* [1942] 2 K.B. 321; [1942] 2 All E.R. 315, C.A.

[Reported by MISS HENRIETTA STEINBERG, Barrister-at-Law]

The following additional cases were cited in argument: A

Barton Thompson & Co. Ltd. v. *Stapling Machines Co.* [1966] Ch. 499; [1966] 2 W.L.R. 1429; [1966] 2 All E.R. 222.

Central Estates (Belgravia) Ltd. v. *Woolgar (No.* 2) [1972] 1 W.L.R. 1048; [1972] 3 All E.R. 610, C.A.

Clarke v. *Grant* [1950] 1 K.B. 104; [1949] 1 All E.R. 768, C.A.

Shiloh Spinners Ltd. v. *Harding* [1973] A.C. 691; [1973] 2 W.L.R. 28;
[1973] 1 All E.R. 90, H.L.(E.). B

APPEAL from Deputy Judge Woolley sitting at Macclesfield County Court.

The landlords, Richard Clarke & Co. Ltd., a firm of brewers, granted
a tenancy by an agreement of April 3, 1974, to the tenant, Frederick Edward
Widnall, in respect of licensed premises known as Stag's Head Hotel, Mill
Lane, Great Warford, Cheshire, at a rent of £480 a year and determinable C
by either party by 12 months' notice in writing. The tenant was in default
of payment of rent due in June, September and December 1974. The
landlords served a notice to quit on February 26, 1975, giving three months'
notice to determine the tenancy in accordance with clause 13 (4) of the
agreement for breach of covenant to pay rent. On the following day, the
tenant paid £186 towards the outstanding rent. On March 21 the landlords D
made a demand for rent due on June 24, 1975. On March 27 the tenant
paid £294 to cover the arrears of rent, including the amount for the period
ending on June 24. The tenant continued to occupy the premises after
May 25, the date on which the three months' notice expired. On June 10
on the landlords' claim for possession and mesne profits from May 26, the
tenant denied the landlords' right to possession and by his counterclaim
sought relief from forfeiture. On June 13 the landlords sent the tenant a E
refund of £38·13, being the rent from May 26 to June 24.

On September 15, the judge found that the landlords, by proceeding
under clause 13 (4) (ii) of the agreement, had elected to give the tenant
short notice to quit, without invoking the provision for forfeiture contained
in clause 13 (4) (i), and that the notice had not been waived by their
acceptance of rent. Accordingly, he granted the landlords possession of the F
premises and mesne profits of £150·35 to the date of the judgment continuing until possession, with stay of execution pending appeal.

The tenant appealed on the grounds that the judge was wrong in holding
that clause 13 (4) (ii) was not a forfeiture clause; that he had erred in
holding that there had been no waiver and that he should have exercised
his jurisdiction to relieve the tenant from forfeiture. G

P. W. Watkins for the tenant.
A. W. Simpson for the landlords.

Cur. adv. vult.

May 27. MEGAW L.J. read the following judgment. The landlords,
Richard Clarke & Co. Ltd., the plaintiffs in the action out of which this H
appeal arises, are brewers. They are the freehold owners of licensed
premises, Stag's Head Hotel, Mill Lane, Great Warford, Cheshire. The
defendant, Frederick Edward Widnall, who is the appellant in this court,
became the tenant of Stag's Head Hotel by a tenancy agreement dated
April 3, 1974, granted by the landlords. By a notice to quit dated February
25, 1975, served the following day, the landlords gave the tenant three
months' notice to determine the tenancy:

> A " in accordance with clause 13 (4) or your agreement . . . dated April 3, 1974, by reason of your non-observance of clause 2 (1) (to pay rent) of the same agreement."

The tenant was substantially in default in payment of rent when the notice was served. Under the agreement the rent was £480 per annum, payable quarterly. The tenant had failed to pay the rent due on the quarter days
B in June, September and December 1974. On February 27, 1975, the tenant paid £186 towards the outstanding rent. On March 21, 1975, the landlords made a demand on the tenant for the quarter's rent due on June 24, 1975. Such a demand was inconsistent with the intended effect of the notice to terminate: for the notice, if effective, would have put an end to any obligation on the part of the tenant to pay any rent in respect of any
C period after May 25, 1975. It is conceded, however, that the landlords did not intend by this demand, so far as their intention may be relevant, to create a new tenancy, assuming that the notice to terminate was effective. On March 27, 1975, the tenant paid the landlords £294, which covered both the arrears of rent and the whole rent for the quarter ending June 24, 1975. After May 26, 1975, the tenant continued in occupation of the premises. On June 10, 1975, the landlords began proceedings in the Maccles-
D field County Court, claiming possession against the tenant and also mesne profits from May 26, 1975. On June 13, 1975, the landlords sent the tenant a cheque for £38·13, being a refund of rent for the period from May 26, to June 24, 1975. By his defence in the action the tenant denied that the plaintiffs were entitled to possession, for reasons which will appear after the relevant provisions of the tenancy agreement have been cited.

E At the county court hearing on September 15, 1975, there was no material dispute as to the facts, as stated above. Deputy Judge Woolley gave judgment for the landlords for possession and for mesne profits of £150·35 to the date of judgment, continuing until possession should be obtained. He granted a stay of execution pending an appeal. The tenant now appeals to this court.

The tenancy agreement of April 3, 1974, provided by clause 1 for the
F letting of the premises to the tenant from April 11, 1974, at the rent already mentioned. Clause 2 (1) provided that the tenant should pay rent "at the times and in manner aforesaid". Then follow numerous provisions which are not relevant in this appeal. Part V of the agreement, comprising clauses 13 and 14, is headed "Termination". The provision which is primarily of importance in the issue before us is a part of clause 13 (4).

G Clause 13 (1) contains a provision enabling either the landlords or the tenant to determine the tenancy by giving 12 months' notice in writing, at any time after the first 6 months have expired. Clause 13 (2) makes special provision in the event of the death of the tenant. It is not necessary to set it out in detail. Its broad effect is to enable the landlords to determine the tenancy by 14 days' notice, presumably to the deceased tenant's personal representatives; but there is special provision enabling the tenant's
H widow, if she wishes and if she obtains a transfer of the licence to herself, to require a new agreement with her on the same terms. It is desirable to set out sub-clauses (3) and (4) in full, lengthy though they are. Clause 13 (3) reads:

> "If the tenant shall either:— (a) fail to observe and perform or commit any breach of any one or more of the agreements contained in clauses 2 (2) (to repair inside), 2 (3) (not to make alterations or

> additions), 2 (4) (to insure plate glass and third party risks), 2 (5) (not to increase fire risks), 2 (8) (not to use except as licensed premises), 2 (9) (not to cause a nuisance), 6 (to purchase goods from landlords), 7 (not to dispose of fixtures, etc.), 9 (1) (to allow landlords to enter), 9 (2) (to allow prospective tenants to view), 9 (6) (to permit inspection and sampling), 9 (8) (not to give undertakings), 9 (9) (not to permit slate clubs), or 12 (1) (to keep premises and utensils clean to supply food, to observe public bar prices and to reside on the premises) hereof; or (b) after due complaint commit any further breach of the agreements contained in clause 12 (2) (reasonable prices and courtesy) hereof; or (c) be convicted of a misdemeanour involving in the opinion of the landlords his suitability as a licensee the tenancy may be determined by the landlords giving to the tenant three calendar months' notice in writing expiring at any time as well during the first as during any subsequent year and either at or at any time earlier than the end of such first year or any subsequent year thereafter provided that such notice shall specify the clause (if any) of this agreement alleged to have been broken or not to have been observed and performed."

Clause 13 (4) has a marginal side-note "Forfeiture"; it reads:

> "(4) If the tenant shall either:— (a) fail to observe and perform or commit any breach of any one or more of the agreements contained in clauses 2 (1) (to pay rent, etc.) 2 (7) (not to assign), or 12 (3) (not to transfer or surrender licence to comply with the law to renew licences to perform undertakings to keep open not to alter not to apply for conditions not to give bills of sale and not to allow acquisition of easements) hereof; or (b) become bankrupt or compound with his creditors or suffer his goods or any of them to be taken in execution or depart out of the country; or (c) be convicted of any offence specified in section 10 (3) of the Licensing Act 1964 notwithstanding the provisions of the Criminal Justice Act 1948 with regard to felonies committed by a licensee; it shall be lawful either:— (i) for the landlords or any person duly authorised by them into or upon the said premises or any part thereof in the name of the whole to re-enter and the said premises peacefully to hold and enjoy thenceforth as if this letting or agreement had not taken place but without prejudice to any action or remedy of the landlords for any arrears of rent or in respect of any antecedent breach (if any) of the agreements by the tenant herein contained; or (ii) for the landlords to give to the tenant three calendar months' notice in writing expiring at any time as well during the first as during any subsequent year and either at or at any time earlier than the end of such first year or any subsequent year thereafter determining the tenancy hereby granted provided that such notice shall specify the clause (if any) of this agreement alleged to have been broken or not to have been observed and performed."

Clause 14 reads:

> "The provisions of section 146 of the Law of Property Act 1925 with regard to restrictions on and relief against forfeiture of this agreement shall apply but the landlords shall be entitled to apply to the court for the appointment of a receiver and manager before any notice has been given to the tenant under the said section if the tenant has committed a breach of covenant which entitles the landlords to re-enter the said premises and endangers the licence."

A Clause 15 (Part VI of the agreement) provides for arbitration. It begins:

> " In the event of three months' notice of termination being served by the landlords under clause 13 (3) or 13 (4) hereof and of the tenant denying that any ground for service of the notice had arisen the tenant shall within seven days of the receipt of the notice notify the landlords of such denial whereupon the dispute shall be referred to
> B the local panel. . ."

The three months' notice to terminate which the landlords served on the tenant, as quoted at the beginning of this judgment, was served " in accordance with clause 13 (4) " and was expressly based on the breach of the covenant to pay rent. Clause 13 (4), in the event of such a breach, gave the landlords the choice of acting under sub-paragraph (i) or sub-
C paragraph (ii). If they had acted under sub-paragraph (i), there is no doubt that this would have constituted a " forfeiture " within the meaning of that word as it is ordinarily understood in the law of landlord and tenant. As a matter of long-established law, the tenant would then have had the right to claim, in proceedings against him for possession, relief against forfeiture. There is no doubt that, in that event, in the circumstances of this case relief would inevitably have been granted, because payment of all arrears
D had been made before proceedings for possession had been initiated. Section 191 (1) of the County Courts Act 1959 may, perhaps, technically not cover this case, since payment of the arrears had been made before the action was begun. But clearly this is an a fortiori case. It may be, as Mr. Watkins for the tenant submitted, that section 212 of the Common Law Procedure Act 1852, provides direct statutory authority.

E However, the landlords did not choose to act under the provisions of sub-paragraph (i) of clause 13 (4). They chose to proceed under sub-paragraph (ii). The consequence, the landlords say and the judge in the court below accepted, is that no question of relief against forfeiture arises because sub-paragraph (ii) does not involve forfeiture. It involves an ordinary contractual right to terminate on the expiry of a contractually
F provided period of notice, which notice was duly given. There is no forfeiture; there is no right of relief against forfeiture; and also the tenant cannot rely on waiver consisting of the demand for, and acceptance of, rent.

The question raised is simply stated. Does a notice to terminate given under clause 13 (4) (ii) by reason of a breach of the covenant to pay rent constitute, or have the same effect in law as, a forfeiture? If the answer is " Yes ", the tenant succeeds in this appeal; he is entitled to relief. If
G the answer is " No ", then the landlords are entitled, as the judge has held, to possession on the expiry of three months' notice.

For the landlords it is submitted that the essence of a forfeiture, in the law of landlord and tenant, is that it takes effect immediately: not immediately upon the breach of covenant occurring, but immediately upon the landlord's giving an unequivocal indication, by words or conduct, to the
H tenant of the landlord's intention to treat the breach as a forfeiture of the tenant's right to continuing possession: see, for example, *Canas Property Co. Ltd.* v. *K.L. Television Services Ltd.* [1970] 2 Q.B. 433, where it was held that the service on the tenant of proceedings for possession effected a forfeiture. But there is no case in which it has been held that there is a forfeiture where the date of the termination of the lease specified by the landlord is a date which follows the running of a period of notice. So, it is submitted for the landlords, if the contractual term, as

here, provides for the giving of a period of notice, it is not a forfeiture, A
even though the event which gives rise to the contractual right on the part of the landlord to terminate the lease is a breach of a covenant; in particular, as here, a breach of a covenant to pay rent. There is no reason, the landlords submit, why the parties should not validly agree by their contract to give to the landlord a right to terminate by notice on the happening of a certain event. There is no reason why that should not be a shorter period of notice, as here, than the general period of notice B
available to either party; in this case clause 13 (1). The whole of the indication, it is submitted, from the context of this tenancy agreement is that the parties intended that clause 13 (4) (ii) should not be regarded as giving rise to forfeiture. The very fact that the landlords were given the option as between sub-paragraph (i) and sub-paragraph (ii) shows this. There are also indications to the same effect elsewhere in the tenancy C
agreement: for example, by reference to the contrasting provisions of clause 14 and clause 15.

For the tenant it is conceded that no case can be found in which it has been clearly held that a contractual provision giving the landlord a right to terminate for non-payment of rent by shorter notice than the notice otherwise available to either party constitutes, or has the same legal effect as, D
a forfeiture: that is, that there is a right in the tenant to apply for relief. But equally, it is contended, there is no authority which either expressly or by implication indicates the contrary.

The doctrine of relief against forfeiture for breach of covenant to pay rent is a long-established doctrine in the law. The reasons for its existence are not in doubt. In *Chandless-Chandless* v. *Nicholson* [1942] 2 K.B. 321, Lord Greene M.R. said, at p. 323: E

> "The court, in exercising its jurisdiction to grant relief in cases of non-payment of rent is, of course, proceeding on the old principles of the court of equity which always regarded the condition of re-entry as being merely security for payment of the rent and gave relief if the landlord could get his rent."

F
So the "condition of re-entry" in clause 13 (4) (i) is "regarded . . . as being merely security for payment of the rent"; and therefore the tenant would have his right of relief. Is there any reason, first, in logic why the "condition of re-entry" in clause 13 (4) (ii) should be regarded as something essentially different in character and legal consequence, merely because there is a contractual provision for a period of notice before the landlord's right to re-enter is to be effected? In my judgment, there is no G
such logical reason.

Is there, then, secondly, any practical reason why different legal consequences should be attributed to clause 13 (4) (ii), as contrasted with clause 13 (4) (i), affecting the tenant's right to claim relief? Again, I can see no practical reason. On the contrary, I think there are strong practical reasons why no distinction should be drawn in respect of the right to relief H
as between sub-paragraph (i) and sub-paragraph (ii). If the landlords were right, it would mean that both (in a case such as the present) the long-established doctrine of equity as to relief against forfeiture and also (in cases falling within section 146 of the Law of Property Act 1925) the statutory requirement as to relief from forfeiture, could be evaded by the mere insertion in the tenancy agreement of a provision for short notice—perhaps one day's notice—in the event of a breach of covenant. That

A cannot be right. The answer suggested by Mr. Simpson for the landlords is that the court could, perhaps, disregard the provision for a short period of notice if in the view of the court it was, as it was put, "illusory" or "merely a sham." It would then become a question of degree, to be decided on the basis of some undefined and, I suspect, undefinable criterion; unless, indeed, the criterion were to be whether the motive for the insertion of the clause was to enable the landlord to avoid the B possibility that the tenant might be entitled to relief in respect of a breach of covenant. If that were the criterion, could the present provision of clause 13 (4) (ii) escape the category of "illusory"? I think not.

I would hold that, whether or not technically clause 13 (4) (ii) is to be described as a "forfeiture clause," its effect in law, as regards the tenant's right of relief for breach of covenant to pay rent, is no different from the C effect of a clause which provides for forfeiture operating immediately upon the landlord indicating his intention to act on it. The inclusion of a period of notice before the lease terminates, being a period unilateral to the landlord and less than the general period of notice available to either party, does not deprive the tenant of his right to claim relief where, as here, the event on which the landlord relies as giving rise to his right to terminate is a breach by the tenant of his covenant to pay rent.

D Accordingly, I would allow the appeal as regards the order for possession. What may be the proper order as regards the money judgment is a matter on which counsel will no doubt wish to address us.

ORR L.J. I agree.

E MILMO J. I agree.

Appeal allowed in respect of possession order, with costs in Court of Appeal and below.
Judgment for tenant on counter-claim.
F *Payment out of court to landlords' solicitors of £150·35 by way of rent.*
Order as to mesne profits discharged.
Leave to appeal conditional on landlords' undertaking not to seek to disturb order as to costs in Court of Appeal, not to seek costs in G *House of Lords and to pay tenant's costs in House of Lords in any event.*

Solicitors: *Barlow, Lyde & Gilbert for Foysters, Manchester; Cobbetts, Manchester.*

H

A

[HOUSE OF LORDS]

* METROBARN LTD. . . . . RESPONDENTS

AND

GEHRING AND ANOTHER . . . . PETITIONERS

1976 July 26 — Lord Diplock, Lord Morris of Borth-y-Gest and Lord Hailsham of St. Marylebone B

Petition by the wife for leave to appeal to the House of Lords from the decision of the Court of Appeal [1976] 1 W.L.R. 776.

The Appeal Committee dismissed the petition.

M. G. C

[COURT OF APPEAL]

* D.H.N. FOOD DISTRIBUTORS LTD. *v.* TOWER HAMLETS LONDON BOROUGH COUNCIL D

BRONZE INVESTMENTS LTD. *v.* SAME

D.H.N. FOOD TRANSPORT LTD. *v.* SAME

1976 March 2, 3, 4 — Lord Denning M.R., Goff and Shaw L.JJ. E

Compulsory Purchase—Compensation—Disturbance, for—Extinguishment of business—Group of associated companies—Trading company providing money for purchase of trading premises—Freehold title in wholly owned subsidiary—Whether trading company having irrevocable licence to occupy or acquiring equitable interest in premises—Whether companies to be treated as single economic entity for purposes of compensation—Land Compensation Act 1961 (9 & 10 *Eliz.* 2, *c.* 33), *s.* 5 (2) (6) F

The claimants were a group of three limited companies associated in a wholesale grocery business. In 1963 the parent company, D.H.N., agreed with a bank that the bank would provide £115,000 to purchase properties in the acquiring authority's area, from which D.H.N. could carry on the existing business; the freehold title was to be conveyed to Bronze Ltd., then a wholly owned subsidiary of the bank: and Bronze contracted to sell the properties for £120,000 to D.H.N. within a year of completion. D.H.N. entered into occupation and traded from the premises. D.H.N. negotiated a mortgage advance with a finance company; but in February 1966 the plan was varied by a further agreement, by which the bank sold all the shares in Bronze to D.H.N. which in turn undertook that on completion of the shares sale Bronze would pay the bank a sum which, together with the price for the shares, would total £120,000. The loan and mortgage were negotiated by D.H.N., with Bronze joined as a necessary party. Thereafter Bronze was a wholly owned subsidiary of D.H.N.; it had the same directors, it carried on no operations, and its only asset was the freehold properties. In 1968 the third claimant company (the transport company) was registered, its G H shares all being owned by D.H.N., its directors being the same, its only assets being vehicles used in the grocery trade; and it too carried on no operations.

In 1969 the acquiring authority made a compulsory purchase order which included the properties scheduled for demolition. Compensation for " the value of the land " under rule (2) of section 5 of the Land Compensation Act 1961 was agreed at £360,000, which was paid to Bronze as the legal owners. As no suitable alternative premises could be found the business came to an end, and the three companies went into voluntary liquidation.

On a reference to the Lands Tribunal of the preliminary question of law whether D.H.N. and the transport company were entitled to compensation for disturbance the tribunal determined that the only compensation for disturbance to which D.H.N. was entitled was the value of the unexpired interest of a yearly tenant.

On appeals by the claimant companies:—

Held, allowing the appeals, (1) that where the question at issue was the entitlement of the owner of a business to be compensated for its extinguishment and on the facts the trading company was in a position to control the subsidiary companies in every respect, the court could pierce the corporate veil which regarded limited companies as separate legal entities and treat the group as a single economic entity for the purpose of awarding compensation for disturbance.

Harold Holdsworth & Co. (*Wakefield*) *Ltd.* v. *Caddies* [1955] 1 W.L.R. 352, H.L.(Sc.) applied.

(2) That if the companies had to be treated as separate entities, there was a necessary implication from the business association between the trading company D.H.N. and the legal owners, Bronze, and the facts that D.H.N. had paid all the purchase money for the premises and held all the shares in Bronze, that D.H.N. had by agreement an irrevocable licence to occupy and remain in the premises for as long as they wished to remain; and that that gave D.H.N. a sufficient interest in the land to justify payment of compensation for disturbance.

Binions v. *Evans* [1972] Ch. 359, C.A. applied.

(3) (*Per* Goff and Shaw L.JJ.) that an analysis of the transactions from 1963 onwards showed that at the start the legal title was held by Bronze in trust for the bank as equitable owner of the premises and, after D.H.N. had paid the purchase money to the bank and taken over all the shares in Bronze, Bronze held the legal title in trust for D.H.N. which thereby acquired the bank's equitable interest in the premises; and that that interest was also sufficient to entitle D.H.N. to compensation for disturbance.

The following cases are referred to in the judgments:

Bannister v. *Bannister* [1948] 2 All E.R. 133, C.A.

Binions v. *Evans* [1972] Ch. 359; [1972] 2 W.L.R. 729; [1972] 2 All E.R. 70, C.A.

Holdsworth (*Harold*) *& Co.* (*Wakefield*) *Ltd.* v. *Caddies* [1955] 1 W.L.R. 352; [1955] 1 All E.R. 725, H.L.(Sc.).

Horn v. *Sunderland Corporation* [1941] 2 K.B. 26; [1941] 1 All E.R. 480, C.A.

Merchandise Transport Ltd. v. *British Transport Commission* [1962] 2 Q.B. 173; [1961] 3 W.L.R. 1358; [1961] 3 All E.R. 495, C.A.

Scottish Co-operative Wholesale Society Ltd. v. *Meyer* [1959] A.C. 324; [1958] 3 W.L.R. 404; [1958] 3 All E.R. 66, H.L.(Sc.).

Siew Soon Wah v. *Yong Tong Hong* [1973] A.C. 836; [1973] 2 W.L.R. 713, P.C.

The following additional cases were cited in argument:

Abbey, Malvern Wells, The v. *Ministry of Local Government and Planning* [1951] Ch. 728; [1951] 2 All E.R. 154.

Apthorpe v. *Peter Schoenhofen Brewing Co. Ltd.* (1899) 4 T.C. 41, C.A.

Beatty v. *Gughenheim Exploration Co.* (1919) 225 N.Y. 380.

Gissing v. *Gissing* [1971] A.C. 886; [1970] 3 W.L.R. 255; [1970] 2 All E.R. 780, H.L.(E.).

Gravesend Corporation v. *Kent County Council* [1935] 1 K.B. 339.

Newham London Borough Council v. *Benjamin* [1968] 1 W.L.R. 694; [1968] 1 All E.R. 1195, C.A.

Pointe Gourde Quarrying and Transport Co. Ltd. v. *Sub-Intendent of Crown Lands* [1947] A.C. 565, P.C.

Smith, Stone and Knight Ltd. v. *Birmingham Corporation* [1939] 4 All E.R. 116.

Tull's Personal Representatives v. *Secretary of State for Air* [1957] 1 Q.B. 523; [1957] 2 W.L.R. 346; [1957] 1 All E.R. 480, C.A.

Tunstall v. *Steigmann* [1962] 2 Q.B. 593; [1962] 2 W.L.R. 1045; [1962] 2 All E.R. 417, C.A.

APPEAL from the Lands Tribunal.

The claimants, D.H.N. Food Distributors Ltd., Bronze Investments Ltd. and D.H.N. Food Transport Ltd., all in voluntary liquidation at the relevant time applied to the Lands Tribunal (Mr. Douglas Frank Q.C., President) for determination of preliminary points of law involving the issue whether the first and third claimant companies (" D.H.N." and " Transport ") were entitled to compensation for disturbance (amounting to extinguishment of their businesses) as a result of the compulsory acquisition by the acquiring authority, Tower Hamlets London Borough Council, of premises in Malmesbury Road, Bow, Tower Hamlets, included in the Tower Hamlets Malmesbury Road Area (No. 1) Compulsory Purchase Order 1968 made by the council on March 6, 1969, under Part V of the Housing Act 1957 and confirmed with modifications on October 12, 1970, by the then Minister of Housing and Local Government.

The preliminary points were determined on a schedule of agreed facts, which included the following: The reference properties were 27, Malmesbury Road, a house and shop. 51, Malmesbury Road, used as warehouses, stores, offices, loading bay, workshop for repair of vehicles, fuel pumps, storage tanks and yard. Nos. 53 to 69A all used solely as residential accommodation. Possession of the properties was taken by the acquiring authority on March 17, 1971; and the freehold interest was transferred to the acquiring authority on May 10, 1971, the consideration for the transfer being £360,000, which, it was agreed, represented the value of the freehold interests transferred but did not include any sum in respect of disturbance or any other claim under section 5, rule (6) of the Land Compensation Act 1961. It was further agreed that any claims in respect of disturbance by any parties should be left over to be settled by negotiation or, in default of agreement, by reference to the Lands Tribunal.

In 1963 premises were sought to house the business of D.H.N. It was decided to acquire the reference properties for the purpose. It was necessary for the company to obtain finance for that acquisition. Towards the end of 1963 it was agreed between D.H.N. and the Palestine British Bank that the bank would provide finance on a short term basis for the acquisition of the properties. That agreement was concluded by a letter dated December 2, 1963, written by I. H. Solomons on behalf of D.H.N.

to H. Landy on behalf of the bank and an endorsement on that letter by H. Landy on December 3, 1963.

The essential terms of the agreement were as follows:—(a) the bank were to pay for the acquisition of the properties, which were to be sold by the vendors at a price of £115,000; (b) the properties were to be transferred to a company known as Bronze Investments Ltd. (" Bronze "), which was then a company controlled by the bank, its shares being wholly owned by the bank; (c) Bronze was to enter into a contract to sell the properties to D.H.N. at a price of £120,000. Completion under that contract was to be one year after the completion of the purchase by Bronze. £20,000 of the purchase price was to be paid on exchange of contracts and the balance of £100,000 on completion; (d) D.H.N. were to pay interest at 12 per cent. per annum on the balance of £100,000; (e) the bank were to have an option to acquire a 12½ per cent. equity interest in D.H.N. for cash consideration at par on the completion date; (f) D.H.N. were to be entitled to full occupation of the properties as from the date of acquisition by Bronze.

The freehold interest in the properties was tranferred to Bronze on January 6, 1964, for a consideration of £115,000. D.H.N. entered into occupation of the premises on or about that date, and after completion of alterations and works commenced to trade from 51, Malmesbury Road from about July 1964.

A contract dated May 27, 1964, was entered into between Bronze (as vendors) and D.H.N. (as purchasers) whereby D.H.N. were to purchase the properties at a price of £120,000 with completion to take place on or before January 6, 1965. The contract was subject to the National Conditions of Sale (17th ed.) and special conditions A to K endorsed thereon. There were two further agreements of May 27, 1964, one of which conferred on H. Landy an option to purchase 12½ per cent. of the equity of D.H.N. and one being a guarantee by H. Landy that Bronze would carry out its obligation to sell the properties to D.H.N. The option to purchase the shares in D.H.N. was never exercised.

On December 14, 1964, a further agreement was entered into between D.H.N. and Bronze whereby Bronze granted to D.H.N. the right to postpone completion of the sale of the properties for a further year, viz., until on or before January 6, 1966, in consideration of the sum of £1,150. D.H.N. were permitted to continue in occupation of the properties on the terms and conditions of special condition K contained in the agreement dated May 27, 1964, as provided in clause 2 of the agreement of December 14, 1964. Interest due under the agreements, though paid by D.H.N. to the bank, was charged to the accounts of Bronze. During 1965 D.H.N. negotiated a loan of £110,000 from Credit for Industry Ltd., a subsidiary of United Dominions Trust. The loan was to be secured by a mortgage of the reference properties.

By an agreement dated February 8, 1966, made between Israel British Bank Ltd. (successors to the Palestine British Bank) and D.H.N., the latter company agreed to purchase the shares in Bronze owned by the bank at a price of £3,597 5s. By clause 6 of that agreement D.H.N. undertook that on completion it would procure that Bronze would pay to the bank the sum of £116,402 15s. being the balance of £120,000. The shares in Bronze were acquired by D.H.N. pursuant to that agreement. A deed of mortgage was entered into on February 8, 1966, whereby Credit for Industry Ltd. loaned £110.000 to D.H.N. and Bronze and D.H.N. charged the reference properties and their interest therein in favour of Credit for A Industry Ltd.

On February 22, 1966, a caution in favour of D.H.N. in respect of the reference properties (registered at H.M. Land Registry under Title No. LN 7726) was removed from the register.

At all times from February 8, 1966, until the voluntary winding up of the companies, D.H.N. owned the whole of the issued share capital of Bronze. The directors of the two companies were at all times the same. B Bronze had no employees; Bronze had no bank account; Bronze carried out no trading or other operations. The only asset of Bronze was its legal ownership of the freehold of the reference properties. All interest due under the mortgage was paid by D.H.N. Rent in respect of the reference properties which were subject to leases was collected by agents on behalf of D.H.N. and paid by the agents to D.H.N. C

At all times from January 6, 1964, until May 10, 1971, Bronze was the registered proprietor of the freehold interest in all the properties. The accounts for Bronze from January 7, 1964, showed rent receivable of £28,150 in respect of the period from January 7, 1964, to July 31, 1966, and thereafter at the rate of £13,500 per annum, which was charged as an expense in the accounts of D.H.N. By an agreement dated April 7, 1971, Bronze agreed to sell the properties to D.H.N. at a price of £117,685. D

The Transport company was registered on April 10, 1968, as a company carrying on business as haulage and transport contractors. D.H.N. owned at all times the whole of the issued share capital of Transport. The directors of the two companies were at all times the same. Transport had no bank account. It owned vehicles which were used wholly and exclusively in connection with the business carried on by D.H.N. and did E no work for any other person and carried on no other business or activity. On October 1, 1971, the shareholders of D.H.N. passed a resolution for the voluntary winding up of that company. This was followed by similar action on the part of the shareholders of Transport on January 18, 1972 and Bronze on January 19, 1972.

The hearing before the Lands Tribunal was on December 16 and 17, 1974, and the President gave his decision on January 30, 1975, and F determined that the answers to the two questions of law were "yes" in both cases, with the effect that (1) D.H.N. and the Transport company were confined to such compensation for disturbance as could be allowed under section 20 of the Compulsory Purchase Act 1965, and (2) their compensation for loss or injury under section 20 had to be assessed on the basis that they could expect to remain in occupation of the subject land G for only such period as would extend from March 17, 1971, the date when the council took possession, to the earliest date on which their tenancy could have been determined by a notice to quit served on that date.

The claimants appealed on the grounds that on the facts as agreed or proved before the Lands Tribunal (1) Bronze in law held the freehold interest in the reference properties at all material times as agents for and on behalf of D.H.N.; (2) alternatively, Bronze in law H held the freehold interest in the reference properties at all material times as trustees on trust for D.H.N. either: (a) as a consequence of a resulting trust, or (b) as a consequence of an uncompleted contract of sale dated May 27, 1964: (3) alternatively, that in assessing the compensation due to D.H.N. under section 20 of the Compulsory Purchase Act 1965 for any loss or injury sustained by them (as opposed to the value of any unexpired term or interest in the land) it did not have to be assumed as

A a matter of law that any periodic tenancy of the reference properties vested in them would be terminated on the earliest date on which such a tenancy was capable of being terminated by a notice to quit served on the date on which possession of the properties was required to be given up but rather that it should for the purpose be considered as a question of fact whether and when that periodic tenancy was likely to determine.

B

George Dobry Q.C. and *Michael Barnes* for the claimants.
Graham Eyre Q.C. and *A. D. Dinkin* for the acquiring authority.

Lord Denning M.R. This case might be called the "Three in one." Three companies in one. Alternatively, the "One in three." One group
C of three companies. For the moment I will speak of it as "the firm." In 1963 at Bow in the east end of London there was a firm of grocery and provision merchants. It imported groceries and provisions and distributed them to shopkeepers. It had a warehouse in Malmesbury Road. The firm had lorries which collected goods from the docks: and distributed them to shopkeepers. Soon afterwards the firm developed a "cash and carry" business. Private individuals came by car. They bought sub-
D stantial quantities wholesale. They paid for them in cash and carried them away.

Six years later in 1969 Tower Hamlets London Borough Council made a compulsory purchase order. They wanted to acquire the property of the firm, to demolish the warehouse, and to build houses on the site. In February 1970 there was a local inquiry. The firm made strong objection.
E They said that if the property was taken, it would mean the end of their business. The acquiring authority realised that the firm would lose its business, but they said that the housing requirements took priority and that the firm would receive compensation for any loss.

The inspector accepted the view of the acquiring authority. He said in his report:

F "Whatever the cost may be (of acquisition) it must be seen against the gain in housing accommodation which would result from the residential development of the application site."

So he recommended the implementation of the compulsory purchase order. It was confirmed by the Minister in his decision letter of October 12, 1970. The acquiring authority acted quickly. On October 30, 1970, they gave a notice to treat and a notice of entry. The firm tried to find other accom-
G modation so as to move their business there, but, finding none, the business had to be closed down.

Now comes the point. It is about compensation. Compensation under the statute is to be made for the value of the land and also compensation for disturbance of the business: see section 5 (2) and (6) of the Land Compensation Act 1961.

H If the firm and its property had all been in one ownership, it would have been entitled to compensation under those two heads: first, the value of the land, which has been assessed in excess of £360,000. Second, compensation for disturbance in having its business closed down. The figure has not yet been assessed. But the firm and its property were not in one ownership. It was owned by three companies. The business was owned by the parent company, D.H.N. Food Distributors Ltd. The land was owned at the time of acquisition by a subsidiary, called Bronze

Investments Ltd. The vehicles were owned by another subsidiary, D.H.N. Food Transport Ltd. The parent company D.H.N. held all the shares both in the Bronze company and in the Transport company. The directors were the same in all three companies. As the result of the business having to be closed down, all the three companies are in liquidation. A

The question is: what is the effect of the firm being in truth the three companies? The acquiring authority say that the owners of the land were Bronze Investments Ltd., and that company are entitled to the value of the land £360,000. They have actually been paid it. But the acquiring authority say that that company are not entitled to compensation for disturbance because they were not disturbed at all. The authority admit that D.H.N. (who ran the business) and the Transport subsidiary (who owned the vehicles) were greatly disturbed in their business. But the acquiring authority say that those two companies are not entitled to any compensation at all, not even for disturbance, because they had no interest in the land, legal or equitable. They say that in 1970 D.H.N. were only licensees of Bronze, the subsidiary which owned the land: and D.H.N. being licensees only, with no interest in the land, their only claim was under section 20 (1) of the Compulsory Purchase Act 1965. That section says that if a person has no greater interest than a tenant from year to year in the land, then he is only entitled to compensation for that lesser interest. Seeing that a licensee can be turned out on short notice, the compensation payable to D.H.N. would be negligible. B C D

The strange thing about the case is this, that the acquiring authority admit that at any time from February 1970, during the local inquiry and afterwards (right up to the time in October 1970 when the council gave notice to treat) the people running these three companies could have put their house in order so as to make the claim impregnable. All they had to do was to take a very simple step. Being in control of all three companies, they could have arranged for Bronze to convey the land to D.H.N. No stamp duty would be payable because it would be exempt under section 42 of the Finance Act 1930. And D.H.N., being the owners, could also claim compensation for disturbance. So at any time up to October 30, 1970, this group of three companies could have put themselves in an unassailable position to claim not only the value of the land but also compensation for disturbance. But that was not done. The acquiring authority say that, by failing to do it, the group have missed the boat. They are left behind on the quay because of the technical provisions of our company law whereby each of the three companies is in law a separate person. Each of its interests must be considered separately. D.H.N. had no interest in the land. It was only a licensee. So it cannot claim compensation for disturbance. E F G

The President of the Lands Tribunal was asked to determine preliminary points of law. He held that D.H.N. had no interest in the land such as to entitle them to any compensation for disturbance beyond the amount allowed by section 20 of the Act of 1965, which is negligible. D.H.N. appeal to this court. H

We were told by Mr. Eyre, who argued the case for Tower Hamlets, that a similar contention has succeeded in other cases before the Lands Tribunal. So much so that, in order to overcome the technical point, it seems that it is the regular thing for the legal advisers of a group of companies to do the necessary conveyancing before the notice to treat. But that in this case the group did not put their house in order in time. And so, he submits, there is no claim for disturbance.

A Mr. Dobry, for D.H.N., took three points before us: first, that they
had an equitable interest in the land; second and alternatively, that they
had an irrevocable licence; third, that we should lift the corporate veil
and treat D.H.N. as the owners. And that, in one or other of these three
capacities, they were entitled to compensation for disturbance.

First, equitable interest. This depends on the conveyancing transactions
by which the land was acquired. They were very complicated. In 1963
B the vendors of the factory and warehouse agreed to sell it to the group
for £115,000. The group had not the money to pay the price. So they
got the help of the Palestine British Bank. This bank provided the
£115,000. In 1964 the conveyance was made to Bronze Investments Ltd.
which was a wholly owned subsidiary of the bank. Two years later, in
1966, D.H.N. (having borrowed money elsewhere) acquired all the shares
C in Bronze (so that Bronze then became a wholly owned subsidiary of
D.H.N.) and D.H.N. repaid the £115,000 provided by the bank. So the
legal title remained in Bronze, but D.H.N. had the benefit of the property.
D.H.N. occupied the premises from the time when they were first acquired
in 1964 until the local authority entered under their compulsory powers.

It is said that, on those facts, in the first place Bronze held the legal
title on a resulting trust for the bank (which provided the purchase money):
D and that afterwards, when D.H.N. repaid the purchase money to the bank,
D.H.N. acquired the equitable interest of the bank. That may be right,
but the President of the Lands Tribunal rejected it, and I am not prepared
to say that he was wrong.

Second, irrevocable licence. It may be that, on those facts, the bank
lent the £115,000 to Bronze with which Bronze bought the property. If
E so, the bank would not have acquired any equitable interest. They would
only be creditors of Bronze. But when D.H.N. repaid the £115,000 to the
bank, they simply stood in the shoes of the bank as creditors of Bronze.
In that case Mr. Eyre submits that D.H.N. have no legal or equitable
interest in the property but are only licensees.

Now I am prepared to allow that D.H.N. were licensees of Bronze.
Mr. Eyre suggested that they were bare licensees, but I do not think so.
F Bronze was a wholly owned subsidiary of D.H.N. Both companies had
common directors running the companies. It is plain to me that there-
after Bronze could not determine the licence so as to ruin D.H.N. The
directors of Bronze could not turn out themselves as directors of D.H.N.
They would be in breach of their duties to both companies if they did so:
see *Scottish Co-operative Wholesale Society Ltd.* v. *Meyer* [1959] A.C.
G 324, 366–367. In the circumstances, I think the licence was virtually an
irrevocable licence. D.H.N. was the parent company holding all the shares
in Bronze. In those circumstances D.H.N. were in a position to carry on
their business on these premises unless and until, in their own interests,
D.H.N. no longer wished to continue to stay there. It was equivalent to
a contract between the two companies whereby Bronze granted an
irrevocable licence to D.H.N. to carry on their business on the premises.
H In this situation Mr. Dobry cited to us *Binions* v. *Evans* [1972] Ch. 359,
to which I would add *Bannister* v. *Bannister* [1948] 2 All E.R. 133 and
Siew Soon Wah v. *Yong Tong Hong* [1973] A.C. 836. Those cases show
that a contractual licence (under which a person has the right to occupy
premises indefinitely) gives rise to a constructive trust, under which the
legal owner is not allowed to turn out the licensee. So, here. This
irrevocable licence gave to D.H.N. a sufficient interest in the land to
qualify them for compensation for disturbance.

Third, lifting the corporate veil. A further very interesting point was raised by Mr. Dobry on company law. We all know that in many respects a group of companies are treated together for the purpose of general accounts, balance sheet, and profit and loss account. They are treated as one concern. Professor Gower in *Modern Company Law*, 3rd ed. (1969), p. 216 says:

> " there is evidence of a general tendency to ignore the separate legal entities of various companies within a group, and to look instead at the economic entity of the whole group."

This is especially the case when a parent company owns all the shares of the subsidiaries—so much so that it can control every movement of the subsidiaries. These subsidiaries are bound hand and foot to the parent company and must do just what the parent company says. A striking instance is the decision of the House of Lords in *Harold Holdsworth & Co. (Wakefield) Ltd.* v. *Caddies* [1955] 1 W.L.R. 352. So here. This group is virtually the same as a partnership in which all the three companies are partners. They should not be treated separately so as to be defeated on a technical point. They should not be deprived of the compensation which should justly be payable for disturbance. The three companies should, for present purposes, be treated as one, and the parent company D.H.N. should be treated as that one. So D.H.N. are entitled to claim compensation accordingly. It was not necessary for them to go through a conveyancing device to get it.

I realise that the President of the Lands Tribunal, in view of previous cases, felt it necessary to decide as he did. But now that the matter has been fully discussed in this court, we must decide differently from him. These companies as a group are entitled to compensation not only for the value of the land, but also compensation for disturbance. I would allow the appeal accordingly.

GOFF L.J. I agree. The book-keeping adopted by the claimants was in many respects unhappy and in some, in my view, wholly inaccurate. The result is that this case has come to appear complicated and difficult, whereas in truth, in my view, it is simple and straightforward.

In my judgment the appeal succeeds on each of three entirely separate grounds. First, assuming, contrary to the view which I hold, that D.H.N. were licensees only, and that subject thereto the whole legal and equitable interest in the business premises was vested in Bronze, still it seems to me that one must imply, from the business association between these three companies and the fact (which is uncontroverted) that D.H.N. paid all the money that was paid, that there was an agreement that that licence should not be revoked during the continuation of the business. In my judgment, therefore, compensation for disturbance must be assessed on the basis that D.H.N. had an irrevocable or indefinite licence.

Mr. Eyre, who argued this case with great skill on behalf of the acquiring authority, relied on *Horn* v. *Sunderland Corporation* [1941] 2 K.B. 26, and he said that compensation for disturbance is only part of the price which is being paid for the land compulsorily acquired, and you cannot acquire a licence even though it be an irrevocable one.

But it seems to me that that is answered, if not by section 5 (2) of the Compulsory Purchase Act 1965 then certainly by *Binions* v. *Evans* [1972] Ch. 359, in this court, and I cite from the judgment of Lord Denning M.R., at p. 367:

A " Seeing that the defendant has no legal estate or interest in the land, the question is what right has she? At any rate, she has a contractual right to reside in the house for the remainder of her life or as long as she pleases to stay. I know that in the agreement it is described as a tenancy: but that does not matter. The question is: What is it in reality? To my mind it is a licence, and no tenancy. It is a privilege which is personal to her. On all the modern cases, which
B are legion, it ranks as a contractual licence, and not a tenancy.

" What is the status of such a licence as this? There are a number of cases in the books in which a similar right has been given. They show that a right to occupy for life, arising by contract, gives to the occupier an equitable interest in the land: just as it does when it arises under a settlement: see *In re Carne's Settled Estates* [1899]
C 1 Ch. 324 and *in Re Boyer's Settled Estates* [1916] 2 Ch. 404. The courts of equity will not allow the landlord to turn the occupier out in breach of the contract: see *Foster* v. *Robinson* [1951] 1 K.B. 149, 156; nor will they allow a purchaser to turn her out if he bought with knowledge of her right . . ."

Secondly, on the footing that that is not in itself sufficient, still, in my
D judgment, this is a case in which one is entitled to look at the realities of the situation and to pierce the corporate veil. I wish to safeguard myself by saying that so far as this ground is concerned, I am relying on the facts of this particular case. I would not at this juncture accept that in every case where one has a group of companies one is entitled to pierce the veil, but in this case the two subsidiaries were both wholly owned; further, they had no separate business operations whatsoever; thirdly, in
E my judgment, the nature of the question involved is highly relevant, namely, whether the owners of this business have been disturbed in their possession and enjoyment of it.

I find support for this view in a number of cases from which I would make a few brief citations, first from *Harold Holdsworth & Co.* (*Wakefield*) *Ltd.* v. *Caddies* [1955] 1 W.L.R. 352, where Lord Reid said, at p. 367:

F " It was argued that the subsidiary companies were separate legal entities each under the control of its own board of directors, that in law the board of the appellant company could not assign any duties to anyone in relation to the management of the subsidiary companies and that therefore the agreement cannot be construed as entitling them to assign any such duties to the respondent.

G " My Lords, in my judgment this is too technical an argument. This is an agreement in re mercatoria and it must be construed in light of the facts and realities of the situation. The appellant company owned the whole share capital of British Textile Manufacturing Co. Ltd. and under the agreement of 1947 the directors of this company were to be the nominees of the appellants. So, in fact,
H the appellants could control the internal management of their subsidiary companies, and, in the unlikely event of there being any difficulty, it was only necessary to go through formal procedure in order to make the decision of the appellants' board fully effective."

That particular passage is, I think, especially cogent having regard to the fact that Mr. Eyre was constrained to admit that in this case, if they had thought of it soon enough, D.H.N. could, as it were, by moving the

pieces on their chess board, have put themselves in a position in which A
the question would have been wholly unarguable.

I also refer to *Scottish Co-operative Wholesale Society Ltd.* v. *Meyer* [1959] A.C. 324. That was a case under section 210 of the Companies Act 1948, and Viscount Simonds said, at p. 343.

> " I do not think that my own views could be stated better than in the late Lord President Cooper's words on the first hearing in this case. B
> 'In my view,' he said, 'the section warrants the court in looking at the business realities of a situation and does not confine them to a narrow legalistic view.' "

My third citation is from the judgment of Danckwerts L.J. in *Merchandise Transport Ltd.* v. *British Transport Commission* [1962] 2 Q.B. 173, 206–207 where he said: C

> " [the cases] show that where the character of a company, or the nature of the persons who control it, is a relevant feature the court will go behind the mere status of the company as a legal entity, and will consider who are the persons as shareholders or even as agents who direct and control the activities of a company which is incapable of doing anything without human assistance." D

The third ground, which I place last because it is longest, but perhaps ought to come first, is that in my judgment, in truth, D.H.N. were the equitable owners of the property. In order to resolve this matter, it will be necessary for me to refer in some detail to the facts.

When the three original companies had amalgamated by causing D.H.N. to be incorporated and assigning their businesses to that company, E
it was necessary to obtain outside financial assistance so that suitable new premises could be acquired. Short-term finance was arranged with the Palestine British Bank (later called the Israel British Bank), and the terms of the arrangements which were made are set out in a letter dated December 2, 1963. It was written by D.H.N.'s accountants to the managing director of the bank and confirmed by him by endorsed written note the next day. It is headed in the matter of the three original companies, but F
I think it is clear it must be treated as embodying an agreement between the bank and D.H.N.

It provided that the bank should buy the property and sell it to the group, meaning, as I have said, D.H.N., for £120,000, of which £20,000 was to be paid on exchange of contracts between the bank and the group. The group was to have one year after completion of the bank's purchase G
in which to complete the subcontract and were to pay interest on the balance of the purchase money £100,000, in the meantime at 12 per cent. There was also a provision giving the bank an option to acquire an equity interest in the group, but nothing turns on that as it was not exercised. Finally, the letter said:

> " It is understood that the group will be permitted full and exclusive use and enjoyment of the said property as from the date of your H
> own completion with the vendors."

The premises were bought for £115,000 and transferred to Bronze, a then wholly owned and inactive subsidiary of the bank. Bronze were duly registered at Her Majesty's Land Registry on March 12, 1964, as proprietors of the freehold interest. On May 27, 1964, they entered into a contract (which I will call the resale contract) whereby they agreed to

A sell to D.H.N. for £120,000, and D.H.N. duly paid £20,000 as a deposit to the bank as stakeholders.

Pursuant to the original agreement, the resale contract provided for completion on January 6, 1965, being in fact one year after the transfer to Bronze. A caution to protect the resale contract was duly entered on the register, and D.H.N. were at once let into possession and began to carry on their new business, which flourished extremely well. So far, all
B in accordance with the letter of December 2.

It seems that D.H.N. needed more time to arrange permanent finance, and, therefore, by a further agreement of December 14, 1964, made between Bronze and D.H.N., in consideration of a further payment of £1,150 which D.H.N. made to Bronze, the date for completion of the resale contract was postponed to January 6, 1966, and interest was reduced
C from 12 per cent to 10 per cent.

By December 1965 D.H.N. had managed to borrow £110,000 from Credit for Industry Ltd., but at this stage, possibly taking up a suggestion which the bank itself had made on December 6, 1963, it was decided that in order to save a second lot of stamp duty on the conveyance by Bronze to D.H.N., the latter should buy the shares in Bronze from the bank.

Those proposals were set out in a letter dated December 17, 1965, from
D D.H.N.'s solicitors to D.H.N.'s accountants. That letter reads as follows:

> "Bronze Investments Ltd. bought the property in January 1964 for the sum of £115,000. D.H.N. entered into a contract to buy the property from Bronze Investments Ltd. for £120,000. It is now intended that, in order to obviate stamp duties so far as possible, D.H.N. should buy the issued share capital of Bronze Investments
> E Ltd. and the shareholders of Bronze Investments Ltd. are agreeable in principle.
>
> "They have suggested that since Bronze Investments Ltd. is selling for £5,000 more than it paid, the consideration for the shares of Bronze Investments Ltd. should be £5,000. They state that Bronze Investments Ltd. is indebted to Israel British Bank Ltd. for the amount
> F of the purchase money, namely £115,000.
>
> "D.H.N. have paid a deposit of £20,000 and are, as you know, obtaining a mortgage advance of £100,000 from Credit for Industry Ltd. It is suggested, therefore, that of the £20,000 deposit now held by Israel British Bank Ltd., £5,000 should be applied towards the purchase of the shares of Bronze Investments Ltd. and the balance towards discharging the indebtedness of that company to Israel British
> G Bank Ltd. The mortgage advance coming from Credit for Industry Ltd. would then be applied entirely towards discharging the remaining part of the moneys due from Bronze Investments Ltd."

Then on February 8, 1966, there was a further agreement between the bank and D.H.N. under which, first, the bank agreed to sell the shares in Bronze to D.H.N., not for £5,000, but for £3,597 5s. How this particular
H figure was arrived at I do not know, but no matter. Secondly, D.H.N. undertook that on completion, Bronze would pay £116,402 15s. to the bank, making a total, with the £3,597 5s., of £120,000. The sum of £116,402 15s. was, in clause 6 of the agreement, described as "being the amount loaned to the company"—that is Bronze—"by the vendor"—that is, the bank. The bank warranted and declared that on receipt of the sum, it would have no further claim against the company or the purchaser on any account whatsoever.

On the same day, February 8, 1966, D.H.N. borrowed the £110,000 A
from Credit for Industry Ltd., and D.H.N. and Bronze concurred to
mortgage the freehold to secure repayment. It is clear from that mortgage,
and is the fact, that D.H.N., not Bronze, borrowed this money, and it was
utilised to pay the bank for the shares and the £116,400 odd, less credit
for the £20,000, already held by the bank.

Mr. Eyre, for the acquiring authority, takes his stand on that agreement
of February 8, 1966. He says it is the only, or at any rate, the most B
cogent, evidence of what the relevant transaction was, and he says:
"There we have the bank and D.H.N. solemnly declaring and agreeing
that what happened was that the bank lent the money to Bronze to enable
it to purchase for its own benefit; that the relationship between the bank
and Bronze was simply that of creditor and debtor; and when D.H.N.
paid off the Bronze liability of £116,400 odd, that was either a voluntary C
payment, which gave it no rights—but that did not matter because it also
bought all the shares—or was a payment which subrogated D.H.N. to
the bank's rights against Bronze as a creditor." If this was an action on
that agreement, there might well be an estoppel, but it is not, and I do not
see anything to prevent D.H.N. asserting, and this court accepting, if it be
satisfied, that the agreement of February 8, 1966, and the letter of

In my judgment, that agreement and letter are not the only, or even D
December 17, 1965, both misstated the position.
the most cogent, evidence of the original transaction, since we have the
letter of December 2, 1963, which I have read, which is the fons et origo
of the whole matter, and that clearly provided that the bank were going to
be the purchasers.

Then the letter four days later is not without interest. In that letter the E
bank itself proposed an entirely different arrangement, namely, that
D.H.N. should form a new company and mortgage the shares to the
bank. That was never implemented in any shape or form, but the bank
there referred to "our nominee company," clearly Bronze, and suggested
that the security should be taken in its name, plainly as nominee. That
stamps the character of Bronze.

Pausing there, I would have thought the clear inference was that when F
the property was purchased, the bank was carrying out the original agree-
ment of December 2/3, save only that, as it had the right to do, it caused
the property to be conveyed to a nominee. If so, there was clearly a
resulting trust situation and Bronze held in trust for the bank. I do not
think it would be a correct inference that Bronze borrowed the money
from the bank and bought the property for its own use and benefit. G

Then it was argued that, if that were so, Bronze could not have entered
into the resale contract because the bank would have been a necessary
party, but I do not agree. There was nothing to prevent Bronze entering
into that contract with the approval of its beneficiary, which it clearly
had, because that was the original agreement. As in all the circumstances
D.H.N. would have constructive notice of the trust, the bank would no H
doubt have been a necessary party to the conveyance had the contract
not been rescinded; but that is purely a conveyancing matter.

Then came the admittedly important letter of December 17, and the
contract of February 8, 1966, but it is to be observed that the contract
is in any event inaccurate, because it did not provide what was to happen
to the £20,000 which was held by the bank as stakeholders. That sum,
of course, became repayable to D.H.N. when the contract was rescinded,

A and was no doubt used towards paying the total of £120,000, but the
contract should have dealt with this.

Much more seriously, however, on Mr. Eyre's hypothesis, that contract
was wrong in substance. If Bronze had borrowed the money to buy the
property, it borrowed £115,000 and no more, and that was the sum which
fell to be repaid, not £116,402 15s. Even if the bank had chosen for some
reason or other to give credit against the loan for the purchase price of
B the shares, the £3,597 5s. would have fallen to be deducted from £115,000,
not £120,000.

It is clear that what the parties were seeking to do was to give effect
to the original agreement in a substituted form. The bank was to have
the £120,000, which it would have got under the resale contract, in return
for which, instead of conveying the property, it was to transfer the shares
C and release its equitable interest. The way in which the contract of
February 8, 1966, was drawn was, of course, inconsistent with any original
resulting trust in favour of the bank, but the substance of the transaction
was entirely consistent with it. It went wrong at this stage, as I think,
because the solicitors and accountants in the letter of December 17, 1965,
failed to appreciate the true position.

D Mr. Eyre argued that if D.H.N. had intended to get in an outstanding
equitable interest, it would have been easy to say so. Of course it would,
and, but for the mistake, no doubt that is what would have been done,
but if Bronze borrowed the money, it borrowed £115,000. Why then did
D.H.N. pay £120,000? I understand Mr. Eyre conceded that if one could
go behind the letter of December 17, 1965, and the agreement of February
8, 1966, and if one found, as I do, an initial relationship between Bronze
E and the bank of trustee and cestui que trust, not debtor and creditor, the
result would be that D.H.N. acquired the bank's equitable interest. Even
if not conceded, it seems to me to follow. True, there was no writing,
such as is required under section 53 of the Law of Property Act 1925 for
the assignment of an equitable interest in land, but this was not a gift.
D.H.N. were purchasers. On my hypothesis, they paid the £120,000 to
F acquire the whole of the bank's interest in the property, and the bank
intended to dispose of it. Then D.H.N. would be entitled to call for a
proper written assignment, and that would be enough, just as if they had
been purchasers under an uncompleted contract to purchase the property
itself. Even if clause 6 of the agreement of February 8, 1966, operated as
a release to Bronze of the bank's equitable interest, it would not merge
because the price had been paid by D.H.N., and Bronze would hold it on a
G resulting trust for D.H.N.

In my judgment, therefore, for those reasons, the claimants are right
in saying that in truth Bronze held the premises in trust for D.H.N. In
my judgment, therefore, the appeal succeeds on each of these three grounds.

SHAW L.J. I agree with both judgments and I add a few observations
H because it seems to me that the facts of this matter are of an exceptional
and unusual character. When D.H.N. were minded in 1963 to acquire the
land in question, they sought the assistance of an institution then called
the Palestine British Bank, and later the Israel British Bank. The original
plan was that the bank should buy the land concerned and then sell it to
the group (as the consortium represented by D.H.N. Food Distributors
Ltd. describe themselves in a letter dated December 2, 1963, which
initiated the proposals for the acquisition of the land). The date of com-

pletion on the resale was to be a year after the date when the bank itself A completed. The bank was thus to be the first purchaser from the then owners. No doubt in order to keep this transaction separate from their ordinary banking business, the bank took a conveyance to a shell company called Bronze Investments Ltd., which was their wholly owned subsidiary. Only the subscribers' shares (two of 2s. each) had been issued and the company had not carried on any business, though its principal object was stated to be property investment. B

The introduction of the Bronze company to the scene was, so far as D.H.N. were concerned, both fortuitous and superfluous. So the purchase money for the payment of the original vendors had to come from the bank, who duly paid it.

In this situation, before the onset of variations and complications, it can hardly be in question that while the legal title was vested in Bronze, C there was a resulting trust of the beneficial interest in favour of the bank. As such a trust arises by operation of law, its existence is independent of the intention of the parties, and their knowledge or ignorance of its existence is irrelevant and immaterial, save in so far as ignorance may throw light on the later conduct of those concerned.

In May 1964 Bronze entered into a contract to sell the properties to D D.H.N. The date for completion was January 6, 1965, but a supplemental agreement postponed completion for a year. In the interval D.H.N. procured a loan of £110,000 from a company called Credit for Industry Ltd., secured by a mortgage on the reference properties. To that mortgage Bronze was, of course, a necessary party as the titular owner. The advance was to enable D.H.N. to pay the bank, for the objective was still that D.H.N. should become the owners. They had established themselves in E the property and used the warehouse premises comprised in it for their business.

But in February 1966 a change of method was proposed and adopted. Instead of taking a conveyance from Bronze, D.H.N. were to buy from the bank their entire shareholding in that company. The value of the shares was adjusted so as to account for the £20,000 which had been paid as a F deposit under the contract of sale made in May 1964. There was little, if anything, of advantage to D.H.N. or anyone else in this elaboration of what was meant to be a simple purchase of the reference properties for the purposes of the group's business. The role of Bronze was throughout entirely negative. It had no business, no capital and no function.

What was in the minds of D.H.N.'s professional advisers in adopting this tortuous mode of proceeding it is difficult to fathom. Their new and G more complicated procedure was proposed and documented in a letter dated December 17, 1965, and an agreement made on February 8, 1966. The outcome of it was that D.H.N. became the owners of all the shares in Bronze while that wholly redundant legal persona retained the bare legal title to the land.

According to clause 6 of the agreement, D.H.N. undertook that it H would, on completion of the purchase of the shares, procure that Bronze should pay to the vendor the sum of £116,000, " being the amount loaned " to that company by the vendor. Goff L.J. has already pointed out the inaccuracy inherent in that introductory passage. As Bronze had no funds and had never had any, it was manifest that the moneys they were to be procured to pay must have their source in D.H.N., who nonetheless had no direct overt title to the properties concerned. The moneys to be

A paid were expressed to be "the amount loaned to Bronze by the bank."
This was the method adopted for whatever reason of describing the result
of the bank having paid the initial purchase price and taken the con-
veyance in the name of their then subsidiary. In the light of the history,
that language was not only inaccurate but inept. It seems to me that the
true position was that the resulting trust in favour of the bank which
came into existence in 1963 still hovered about the parties in 1966. When
B D.H.N. in their turn paid the bank, that equitable interest settled upon
them. Thus they were entitled to call for the execution in due form of an
assignment of that equitable interest by the bank. On this basis, D.H.N.
would have a sufficient interest in the land, as was properly conceded by
Mr. Eyre, to make their claim for compensation for disturbance both
competent and proper.

C Even if this were not right, there is the further argument advanced
on behalf of the claimants that there was so complete an identity of the
different companies comprised in the so-called group that they ought to
be regarded for this purpose as a single entity. The completeness of that
identity manifested itself in various ways. The directors of D.H.N. were
the same as the directors of Bronze; the shareholders of Bronze were the
same as in D.H.N., the parent company, and they had a common interest
D in maintaining on the property concerned the business of the group. If
anything were necessary to reinforce the complete identity of commercial
interest and personality, clause 6, to which I have referred already,
demonstrates it, for D.H.N. undertook the obligation to procure their
subsidiary company to make the payment which the bank required to
be made.

E If each member of the group is regarded as a company in isolation,
nobody at all could have claimed compensation in a case which plainly
calls for it. Bronze would have had the land but no business to disturb;
D.H.N. would have had the business but no interest in the land.

In this utter identity and community of interest between D.H.N. and
Bronze there was no flaw at all. As Bronze did not trade and carried on
no business, it had no actual or potential creditors other than its own
F parent, D.H.N. The directors of that company could at any time they
chose have procured the transfer of the legal title from Bronze to itself.
Mr. Eyre again conceded that if they had gone through that formal
operation the day before the notice to treat was served on October 12,
1970, they would have had a secure claim for compensation for
disturbance. Accordingly, they could in law have sought and obtained
G whatever advantages were derived up to that date from a separation of
title and interest between the two companies and still quite legitimately
have re-disposed matters right up till October 1970 so as to qualify for
compensation. They could not have been criticised, still less prevented,
if they had chosen to do so. Yet if the decision of the Lands Tribunal be
right, it made all the difference that they had not. Thus no abuse is
H precluded by disregarding the bonds which bundled D.H.N. and Bronze
together in a close and, so far as Bronze was concerned, indissoluble
relationship.

Why then should this relationship be ignored in a situation in which
to do so does not prevent abuse but would on the contrary result in what
appears to be a denial of justice? If the strict legal differentiation between
the two entities of parent and subsidiary must, even on the special facts
of this case, be observed, the common factors in their identities must at

A the lowest demonstrate that the occupation of D.H.N. would and could never be determined without the consent of D.H.N. itself. If it was a licence at will, it was at the will of the licensee, D.H.N., that the licence subsisted. Accordingly, it could have gone on for an indeterminate time; that is to say, so long as the relationship of parent and subsidiary continued, which means for practical purposes for as long as D.H.N. wished to remain in the property for the purposes of its business.

B The President of the Lands Tribunal took a strict legalistic view of the respective positions of the companies concerned. It appears to me that it was too strict in its application to the facts of this case, which are, as I have said, of a very special character, for it ignored the realities of the respective roles which the companies filled. I would allow the appeal.

C *Appeal allowed.*

Solicitors: *Asher Fishman & Co.; H. D. Cook, Tower Hamlets London Borough Council.*

M. M. H.

D

[QUEEN'S BENCH DIVISION]

* TRENDTEX TRADING CORPORATION *v.* CENTRAL BANK OF NIGERIA

E [1975 T. No. 3663]

1976 March 16, 17, 18, 19; 26 — Donaldson J.

Conflict of Laws—Sovereign immunity—Bank—Commercial transaction for supply of cement to Nigerian state—Central Bank of Nigeria issuing irrevocable letter of credit—Action to enforce payment—Status of bank—Whether department of state—Whether claim involved impleading foreign state F

Early in 1975 the federal government and state agencies of Nigeria contracted with suppliers throughout the world, including the plaintiffs, for the purchase of 20 million tons of cement, delivery to be over a period of 12 months. All the contracts incorporated an irrevocable letter of credit issued G by the Central Bank of Nigeria, which was a separate legal entity but whose functions included state business, for the purchase price of the cement and demurrage incurred on discharge. A new military administration took over the government in July 1975, by which time there was serious congestion of shipping in the ports of Nigeria to which the cement had been consigned. The new federal government dealt with the situation, inter alia, by the introduction of import controls H for cement and instructed the Central Bank to refuse payment for unauthorised consignments. The Central Bank accordingly did not honour its obligations under various letters of credit and the claims against it totalled nearly $50,000,000. The plaintiffs, who were among the claimants, brought proceedings against the Central Bank for the moneys due and

---

[Reported by MRS. RACHEL DAVIES, Barrister-at-Law]

A obtained an injunction requiring the Central Bank to retain funds in the United Kingdom sufficient to meet their claim.

On an application by the Central Bank for an order to set aside the writs and statement of claim and that all further proceedings be stayed on the ground that it was a department of state immune from proceedings in the United Kingdom:—

Held, allowing the application, (1) that, although the Central Bank was incorporated by statute as a separate legal
B entity and there were no express provisions declaring it to be a department of state, its main functions were to issue and control the national currency, to operate the machinery of exchange control and to act as the state treasury; that those functions were essential functions of the state and, although the bank had certain limited private banking functions and had a certain discretion in the conduct of its affairs, its discretion had to be exercised on behalf of and in the interests
C of the state; that in fact the Central Bank's affairs were state business and it was an emanation, an alter ego and a department of the state and, therefore, the principle of sovereign immunity applied (post, pp. 876B; 876E–877A).

Dictum of Lord Cross of Chelsea in *The Philippine Admiral* [1976] 2 W.L.R. 214, 232, P.C. applied.

Tamlin v. *Hannaford* [1950] 1 K.B. 18, C.A. considered.

(2) That, since it was claimed that all moneys deposited in
D the United Kingdom in the name of the Central Bank were funds held on deposit for or on behalf of the Nigerian state, the investigation of that claim would involve impleading the state of Nigeria and, as neither the Central Bank nor the state of Nigeria were estopped from relying on their sovereign immunity, the action would be stayed (post, pp. 877D–E; 878E–H).

Per curiam. When the Lomé Convention comes into force on April 1, 1976, it will not prohibit discrimination between
E litigants on grounds other than nationality. Nor will it require the courts of the E.E.C. members to harmonise their policies on sovereign immunity, provided that those policies are not discriminatory on grounds of nationality (post, p. 879C).

The following cases are referred to in the judgment:

Baccus S.R.L. v. *Servicio National del Trigo* [1957] 1 Q.B. 438; [1956] 3
F W.L.R. 948; [1956] 3 All E.R. 715, C.A.

Fox v. *Government of Newfoundland* [1898] A.C. 667, P.C.

Gilbert v. *Trinity House Corporation* (1886) 17 Q.B.D. 795, D.C.

Juan Ysmael & Co. Inc. v. *Government of the Republic of Indonesia* [1955] A.C. 72; [1954] 3 W.L.R. 531; [1954] 3 All E.R. 236, P.C.

Krajina v. *Tass Agency* [1949] 2 All E.R. 274, C.A.

Larivière v. *Morgan* (1872) L.R. 7 Ch.App. 550.

G *Mighell* v. *Sultan of Johore* [1894] 1 Q.B. 149, C.A.

Rahimtoola v. *Nizam of Hyderabad* [1958] A.C. 379; [1957] 3 W.L.R. 884; [1957] 3 All E.R. 441, H.L.(E.).

Philippine Admiral, The [1976] 2 W.L.R. 214; [1976] 1 All E.R. 78, P.C.

Tamlin v. *Hannaford* [1950] 1 K.B. 18; [1949] 2 All E.R. 327, C.A.

United States of America and Republic of France v. *Dollfus Mieg et Cie. S.A. and Bank of England* [1952] A.C. 582; [1952] 1 All E.R. 572,
H H.L.(E.).

The following additional cases were cited in argument:

Application des Gaz S.A. v. *Falks Veritas Ltd.* [1974] Ch. 381; [1974] 3 W.L.R. 235; [1974] 3 All E.R. 51, C.A.

Bank voor Handel en Scheepvaart N.V. v. *Administrator of Hungarian Property* [1954] A.C. 584; [1954] 2 W.L.R. 867; [1954] 1 All E.R. 969, H.L.(E.).

Bank voor Handel en Scheepvaart N.V. v. *Slatford* [1953] 1 Q.B. 248; [1951] 2 All E.R. 779. A

Bulmer (H.P.) Ltd. v. *J. Bollinger S.A.* [1974] Ch. 401; [1974] 3 W.L.R. 202; [1974] 2 All E.R. 1226, C.A.

Charkieh, The (1873) L.R. 4 A. & E. 59.

Compania Mercantil Argentina v. *United States Shipping Board* (1924) 93 L.J.K.B. 816, C.A.

Compania Naviera Vascongada v. *S.S. Cristina (The Cristina)* [1938] A.C. 485; [1938] 1 All E.R. 719, H.L.(E.). B

Costa v. *ENEL* [1964] C.M.L.R. 425.

Duff Development Co. v. *Government of Kelantan* [1924] A.C. 797, H.L.(E.).

Dollfus Mieg et Cie. S.A. v. *Bank of England* [1949] Ch. 369; [1949] 1 All E.R. 946.

Government of Congo v. *Venne* (1971) 22 D.L.R. (3d) 669.

Mellenger v. *New Brunswick Development Corporation* [1971] 1 W.L.R. 604; [1971] 2 All E.R. 593, C.A. C

Merricks v. *Heathcote-Amory and Minister of Agriculture Fisheries and Food* [1955] Ch. 567; [1955] 3 W.L.R. 56; [1955] 2 All E.R. 453.

Metropolitan Meat Industry Board v. *Sheedy* [1927] A.C. 899, P.C.

Minister of Supply v. *British Thomson-Houston Co. Ltd.* [1943] K.B. 478; [1943] 1 All E.R. 615, C.A.

Morgan v. *Larivière* (1875) L.R. 7 H.L. 423, H.L.(E.). D

Parlement Belge, The (1880) 5 P.D. 197.

Swiss-Israel Trade Bank v. *Government of Salta* [1972] 1 Lloyd's Rep. 497.

Thai-Europe Tapioca Service Ltd. v. *Government of Pakistan, Directorate of Agricultural Supplies* [1975] 1 W.L.R. 1485; [1975] 3 All E.R. 961, C.A.

Victorian Railways Commissioners v. *Herbert* [1949] V.L.R. 211. E

Woodhouse A.C. Israel Cocoa Ltd. S.A. v. *Nigerian Produce Marketing Co. Ltd.* [1972] A.C. 741; [1972] 2 W.L.R. 1090; [1972] 2 All E.R. 271, H.L.(E.).

SUMMONS

On November 4, 1975, the plaintiffs, Trendtex Trading Corporation, F issued a writ against the Central Bank of Nigeria in respect of payments due to the plaintiffs from the Central Bank under a letter of credit dated July 24, 1975, relating to a contract of the same date for the purchase of cement from the plaintiffs by Pan-African Export Import Co. Ltd. Mocatta J. ordered that the plaintiffs should have leave to issue a concurrent writ of summons against the Central Bank and to serve notice of that writ by post on the Central Bank at its registered office in Nigeria, G and he granted an injunction that the Central Bank should retain within the jurisdiction $13,968,190 or the equivalent in sterling, against the plaintiffs' claim until after the hearing of a summons returnable on November 11, 1975. On November 11 Mocatta J. ordered that the injunction be continued until December 9, 1975, and on that date he ordered that it be continued until trial of the action or further order. H

By a summons dated December 16, 1975, the Central Bank applied for an order that the writ of summons, the concurrent writ of summons and the statement of claim be set aside and all further proceedings be stayed on the ground that the Central Bank was a department of the Federal Republic of Nigeria and thereby immune from suit and/or that the action impleaded the Government of the Federal Republic of Nigeria and/or, that relief claimed in the action sought to interfere with the right or interest

A in property of the government, and that the government declined to sanction the institution of the proceedings.

F. P. Neill Q.C., *M. A. Pickering* and *D. P. O'Connell* for the plaintiffs.
T. H. Bingham Q.C. and *A. G. Guest* for the Central Bank.

B *Cur. adv. vult.*

March 26. DONALDSON J. read the following judgment. The plaintiffs in these actions claim damages from the Central Bank of Nigeria for failing to honour its obligations under various irrevocable letters of credit. The claims are considerable—nearly U.S. $50 million. But let it be said at once that the solvency of the Central Bank is not in question. The
C reason why it has not paid the plaintiffs is that the government of Nigeria has instructed it not to do so.

The plaintiffs have obtained an injunction requiring the Central Bank to retain funds in this country which would be sufficient to meet the plaintiffs' claims. These funds are in fact held by the Midland Bank Ltd. in London. The Central Bank now seeks an order discharging the injunction
D and setting the proceedings aside on the ground that they infringe the sovereign immunity of the Federal Republic of Nigeria.

The background to the proceedings is the Nigerian cement problem. This is well known to those engaged in the cement and shipping trades. In early 1975 the then federal government and its agencies placed contracts with 80 suppliers throughout the world for 20 million tons of cement valued at about $1,200,000,000. Delivery was to be over a period of 12
E months. The reason for this action is obscure. The normal annual rate of importing cement was 2 million tons and it was physically impossible to handle the discharge of 20 million tons within a 12-month period even if no other commodity was carried to Nigeria by sea.

A new military administration took over the federal government in July 1975 and found itself faced with serious congestion of shipping
F throughout the ports of Nigeria, and, in particular, in the Lagos port complex, to which the cement with which these actions are concerned, was consigned. It, therefore, sought to devote an increased proportion of the port's facilities to the import of cement, to extend those facilities and to take measures to prevent or discourage the arrival of vessels until such time as their cement cargoes could be discharged. As part of these measures, the federal government introduced a system of import controls
G for cement and instructed the Central Bank to refuse payment for consignments which were not authorised under those controls.

It is not for me to form or express any view on whether the Central Bank was entitled in law to refuse payment under the letters of credit. The sole issue before me is whether the established doctrine of sovereign immunity under English law requires me to set the proceedings aside and
H to discharge the injunctions. That issue is one of considerable public importance and I have been asked to give judgment in open court.

The various legal issues have been argued most fully and ably by Mr. Bingham, for the Central Bank, and Mr. Neill, for the plaintiffs. I am most grateful to both for their assistance and hope that they will forgive me if I do not set out their respective arguments in full.

The onus of establishing this immunity is upon the Central Bank. Mr. Bingham puts the argument in two different ways. First, he submits that the Central Bank is sufficiently a part of the federal government of Nigeria for any proceedings against it in personam to infringe the sovereign immunity of the state of Nigeria. Second, he submits that, in any event, the assets to which the injunctions relate are part of the external reserves of Nigeria and are controlled by the federal government. Accordingly, any order which affects the power of the federal government to deal with these assets infringes the sovereign immunity of Nigeria.

Mr. Neill, for the plaintiffs, submits that the Central Bank is a legal entity which is independent of the federal government and that the assets held by the Midland Bank Ltd. are not owned or sufficiently controlled by the Central Bank for any right of sovereign immunity to be infringed by these proceedings or by the injunctions. Alternatively, he submits that the subject matter of the actions are ordinary commercial transactions to which a right of sovereign immunity does not apply. In the further alternative, he submits that the funds held by the Midland Bank Ltd. constitute a trust in favour of the plaintiffs and that proceedings in respect of such funds within the jurisdiction are an exception to the general rule. In case these arguments fail, Mr. Neill also submits that the federal government has waived or is estopped from asserting any right based upon sovereign immunity. Finally, he submits that under the legislation of the European Economic Community and, in particular, under the Lomé Convention, which was promulgated on January 30, 1976, and comes into force on April 1, 1976, the English courts cannot grant an immunity to the Central Bank which would not be granted by some or all of the courts of the other member nations of the E.E.C.

These arguments can be considered under five heads: (1) The personality issue. Is the Central Bank so much a part of the machinery of government of the state of Nigeria that impleading it impleads that state? Is it material whether the transaction in dispute was undertaken as an act of state (jure imperii) or as an act of commerce (jure gestionis)? (2) The property issue. Has the federal government a sufficient interest in the funds affected by the injunctions for those injunctions to infringe the Nigerian state's right of sovereign immunity? (3) The trust issue. Are these assets affected by a trust in favour of the plaintiffs and, if so, is the court entitled to adjudicate upon the plaintiffs' right to those assets? (4) The waiver and estoppel issues. (5) The E.E.C. issue.

The personality issue

I can dispose at once of the suggestion that it matters whether the opening of the letter of credit was an act of state or an ordinary commercial transaction. The factual position may not be clear in that the letters of credit were opened in favour of non-governmental purchasers from the plaintiffs, but called for shipped bills of lading drawn to the order of the Nigerian Ministry of Defence. However, any doubt about the legal position, at least at first instance, is removed by the recent opinion of the Judicial Committee of the Privy Council in *The Philippine Admiral* [1976] 2 W.L.R. 214. Lord Cross of Chelsea delivered the opinion of the Board and said, at pp. 232–233:

> "The rule that no action in personam can be brought against a foreign sovereign state on a commercial contract has been regularly accepted by the Court of Appeal in England and was assumed to be the law even by Lord Maugham in *The Cristina* [1938] A.C. 485. It is no

doubt open to the House of Lords to decide otherwise but it may fairly be said to be at the least unlikely that it would do so, and counsel for the respondents did not suggest that the Board should cast any doubt on the rule."

The remaining part of this issue involves more complex considerations. What has to be decided is whether the Central Bank is an arm, an organ, an alter ego, a part or an agency of the Nigerian government. When I use the word 'agency,' I intend to indicate not an agent but a body which is part of the machinery of the state. The state can claim immunity from suit for any agency but not for a simple agent, that being too remote from the machinery of government to qualify. In the case of an agent, the sovereign's right is to claim immunity for assets which he alleges to be controlled by him and which are in the hands of the agent. Effect can sometimes be given to this right—and could be given in this case—by allowing the action to proceed against the agent while excluding the assets concerned from the effects of any judgment or order.

It is, therefore, necessary to examine the juridical status and practical working of the Central Bank. This is a matter of evidence. During the argument it was suggested by Mr. Bingham that the judgments of Tucker L.J. in *Krajinar* v. *Tass Agency* [1949] 2 All E.R. 274, 281 and of Parker L.J. in *Baccus S.R.L.* v. *Servicio Nacional del Trigo* [1957] 1 Q.B. 438, 471 establish the proposition that the best evidence is that of the ambassador concerned. I think that this is an overstatement. Clearly the best evidence of the existence of the claim to sovereign immunity is that of the ambassador. Indeed, it is difficult to see how it could succeed if it were not supported by him. His may also be the best evidence of the practical workings of the machinery of government in the country which he represents. But I see no reason why his evidence of the law of his country should have some special persuasive power.

Fortunately, in the present case I have had the advantage of affidavit evidence from the High Commissioner, the Acting High Commissioner, the Solicitor-General, the Governor of the Central Bank and its Chief of Banking Operations. The High Commissioner states that the Central Bank is a department of the Nigerian state and claims sovereign immunity for it. The Acting High Commissioner states that all funds held or deposited in the United Kingdom in the name of the Central Bank are funds held or deposited for or on behalf of the Federal Government of Nigeria. The Solicitor-General deals in detail with the relevant Nigerian law and the practical exercise by the government of its legal powers in relation to the Central Bank. The two bankers explain the history and work of the bank. In addition, I have read affidavit evidence from Mr. Gerstein, formerly Deputy General Counsel to the International Monetary Fund, on his view of the degree of autonomy enjoyed by the Central Bank of Nigeria as compared with the position of other central banks.

From the plaintiffs' side, I have been assisted by affidavit evidence from Professor Read, the University of London, Professor of Comparative Public Law with special reference to Africa, and from Mr. Cotram, a lecturer in African law at that University's School of Oriental and African Studies. Both express the view that the Central Bank is not to be regarded as a department of the federal government. In addition, I have evidence from Mr. Kennedy, the general manager of Trendtex Trading Corporation, one of the plaintiffs, on the background of their claim.

The Central Bank is a legal entity, which was incorporated in 1958 by A
the Central Bank of Nigeria Act. This Act has been amended inter alia,
in 1962 and 1969. The Act neither originally nor as amended declared
the Central Bank to be a department of state. The principal objects of
the Central Bank are stated in section 4 of the Act to be:

> ". . . to issue legal tender currency in Nigeria, to maintain external
> reserves in order to safeguard the international value of that currency, B
> to promote monetary stability and a sound financial structure in
> Nigeria and to act as banker and financial adviser to the federal
> government."

The powers and functions of the Central Bank can be summarised as
follows. (*a*) It has power to require information from persons having
such information relating to, or touching or concerning matters affecting, C
the national economy of Nigeria, and a refusal to furnish this information
constitutes a criminal offence: section 29A. (*b*) It has the exclusive right
to finance the operations of the state marketing boards: Central Bank of
Nigeria Act (Amendment) (No. 3) Decree 1968 (Decree No. 50 of 1968).
(*c*) Subject to immaterial exceptions, the Central Bank is forbidden to: (i)
engage in trade or to have a direct interest in any commercial, agricultural,
industrial or other undertaking, save only an undertaking set up with the D
approval or under the authority of the federal government and then only
with the approval of the Commissioner of Finance (the equivalent of the
Chancellor of the Exchequer), (ii) invest in property, (iii) draw or accept
bills payable otherwise than on demand, (iv) give time to the drawees of
bills of exchange discounted by the Central Bank, save to a limited extent
and for limited amounts, (v) pay interest on deposits, (vi) open accounts E
for anyone other than (A) the federal government, the state governments
and their respective funds, institutions and corporations, banks and other
credit institutions, an international or foreign national central bank or
monetary authority or (B) but only with the prior approval of the com-
missioner, other persons in Nigeria: sections 29 and 30. (*d*) The Central
Bank is entrusted with the federal government's banking and foreign
exchange transactions both in Nigeria and abroad: section 32. (*e*) The F
Central Bank is obliged to receive and disburse federal government
moneys and keep account thereof without remuneration: section 32. (*f*)
the Central Bank is entrusted with the issue and management of Federal
Government loans: section 35. (*g*) The Central Bank has power to give
directions to other Nigerian banks in relation to cash reserves, liquidity
ratios and special deposits and can enforce these directions by levying
fines and prohibiting the bank concerned from extending new loans or G
undertaking new investments. (*h*) Under a decree of February 7, 1969
(Banking Decree 1969 (No. 1 of 1969) the Central Bank has extensive
supervisory powers over all registered banks and is entitled to compound
offences by the acceptance of sums in lieu of fines, such sums to be credited
to the Consolidated Revenue Fund of the Federation. (*i*) Under the same
decree both the Central Bank and its officers are protected from adverse H
claims in respect of all acts or omissions in good faith in pursuance or execu-
tion or intended execution of any statutory power. (*j*) The Central Bank
prints, mints and issues the whole of the currency of Nigeria. It also holds
all the external gold and currency reserves of the Nigerian state and other
assets which, together with part of the external assets, provides backing
for the currency: see the Central Bank's balance sheet and the governor's
evidence. (*k*) The Central Bank is responsible for the management of

A the Exchange Control machinery of the country: Exchange Control Act
1962 and various exchange control memoranda. (*l*) Subject to the approval
of the Federal Executive Council (the Nigerian Cabinet) the Central Bank
is empowered to vary the gold parity of the Nigerian pound: section 2
of the Central Bank of Nigeria (Amendment) Act 1962. (*m*) The Central
Bank may act generally as agent for the federal government or for a
state government, but only where it can do so appropriately and con-
B sistently with its duties and functions as a central bank: section 37. (*n*)
The Central Bank is under a duty to organise a clearing house: section 42.

The relationship between the Central Bank and the Federal Govern-
ment, and the degree of control and supervision exercised by the latter,
is illustrated by the following matters in addition to those which have
already been mentioned. (A) The Central Bank is, and has always been,
C wholly owned by the Nigerian state which takes all the profits other than
such as are placed to reserve: sections 6 (3) and 7 (3). (B) The Governor,
Deputy Governor and directors of the Central Bank are appointed by the
head of the Federal Military Government (sections 9 (1) and 10 (1)), but
they are not officers in the public service and have considerable security
of tenure. (C) The salaries of employees are to be related to those payable
to the staffs of statutory corporations and their allowances and benefits are
D the same as the allowances and benefits of those who are in the
public service of the federation: section 14 of the Act of 1958 and
section 5 of Central Bank of Nigeria (Amendment) Decree (No. 40
of 1970). (D) The departmental responsibility of the Commissioner
for Finance includes: banks and banking, including matters concern-
ing the Central Bank and the following matters which also concern
E the Central Bank, namely currency coinage and legal tender exchange
control, external borrowing, federal accounts and budgetary control, in-
ternal borrowing, monetary policy and relations with international financial
institutions: Official Gazette 1967 and 1975. (E) The Commissioner for
Finance is the link between the federal government and the Central Bank.
The following matters are either his responsibility, acting on the board's
recommendation, or ultra vires the bank, unless the approval or consent
F of the commissioner is obtained. (i) Entering into contracts for movable
or immovable property to a value of £50,000 or more; section 2 of Central
Bank of Nigeria (Amendment) Decree 1970. (ii) Opening branches or
appointing agents and correspondents: section 3 of the Central Bank
of Nigeria (Amendment) Decree 1970. (iii) Determining the pro-
portion of the Central Bank's capital which shall be paid up or increasing
G that capital: section 6. (iv) A decision on the denominations of the
Nigerian currency, the form and design of bank notes and the weight and
composition of the coinage: section 20. (v) The regulation of advances
to indigenous persons: section 2 of Central Bank of Nigeria Act
(Amendment) (No. 3) Decree 1968 (No. 50 of 1968). (vi) Making
by-laws for the good order and management of the Central Bank: section
H 48. (F) Although the monetary and banking policy of the Central Bank
is by statute the responsibility of the bank subject only to the right of the
commissioner to be kept informed and, if he disagrees, to refer it to the
Federal Executive Council which has power to issue directions, in practice
the Commissioner for Finance informs the Central Bank of the federal
government's general policies and formulates guidelines for the Central
Bank's policy and the bank is obliged to conform. Furthermore, where
the commissioner's consent or approval is required, this is no formality.

(G) The governor is responsible to the board for the day to day management of the Central Bank (section 8 (3)), and the Central Bank is, in this respect, independent of the federal government, provided that it and the governor are acting consistently with the Central Bank's banking and monetary policy over which the federal government has control. (H) The Central Bank is exempt from certain provisions of the Income Tax Act (section 49) and from stamp duty on its notes issued as currency: section 24.

In this case the plaintiffs are entitled to rely, and do rely, upon the fact that the Central Bank has been incorporated as a separate legal entity and that nowhere is it stated that the bank is a department of state. But this is not conclusive: see the judgment of Jenkins L.J. in *Baccus S.R.L.* v. *Servicio Nacional del Trigo* [1957] 1 Q.B. 438, 467.

Mr. Neill relied heavily on *Tamlin* v. *Hannaford* [1950] 1 K.B. 18. There the body concerned was the British Transport Commission. Its board, like that of the Central Bank, was appointed by the government. It, like the Central Bank, was subject to directions from the Minister. It, like the Central Bank, was a public authority and its purposes were public purposes. A similar analogy can be drawn with the National Oil Corporation of Nigeria. But it should not be overlooked that the British Transport Commission was held not to be an emanation of the Crown in spite of, rather than because of, these attributes. The reason is clear. The commission is a successor in title to the old private railway companies. The running of railways is not an essential function of the state any more than is the provision of lighthouses: see *Gilbert* v. *Trinity House Corporation* (1886) 17 Q.B.D. 795; or the provision of education: see *Fox* v. *Government of Newfoundland* [1898] A.C. 667.

The position of the Central Bank is quite different. Its prime functions are to issue and control the national currency of Nigeria, to operate the machinery of exchange control and to act as the treasury, in the literal sense of the word, of the state of Nigeria. These are essential functions of the state and could not be performed by any other body. In addition, the Central Bank is charged with the supervision and regulation of the banking industry which again is essentially a function of the state. Its power to act as banker to the provincial (state) governments is one which could be performed by a private banker but is much more appropriate to an arm of the federal government. Similarly, its advisory function could be discharged by a private individual but is more appropriately undertaken by a state official or body. It is only when one comes to the Central Bank's ancillary functions, such as issuing letters of credit in a commercial transaction, that one leaves the area of operations which is properly that of the state. Even then it is necessary to bear in mind that the Central Bank's power to have "private" customers is severely limited and that it is forbidden to pay interest on deposits. It therefore lacks the most important powers of an ordinary bank.

I accept that the Central Bank has been so incorporated as to occupy what Mr. Neill described as a "stand-off" position. The reason for this I do not know. It may have been in order to encourage the provincial (state) governments to use its services. There may have been other reasons. I also accept that the Central Bank has a measure of discretion in deciding how to conduct its affairs. However, that discretion has to be exercised on behalf and in the interests of the state and not of the Central Bank. Its business is, in truth, the state's business. Accordingly,

A I have no doubt that looking at the matter as a whole, the Central Bank of Nigeria is an emanation, an arm, an alter ego and a department of the state of Nigeria.

The property issue

In *Juan Ysmael & Co. Inc.* v. *Government of the Republic of Indonesia* B [1955] A.C. 72, 89 Earl Jowitt, delivering the opinion of the Judicial Committee, said:

> ". . . a foreign government claiming that its interest in property will be affected by the judgment in an action to which it is not a party, is not bound as a condition of obtaining immunity to prove its title to the interest claimed, but it must produce evidence to satisfy the court that its claim is not merely illusory, nor founded on a title C manifestly defective. The court must be satisfied that conflicting rights have to be decided in relation to the foreign government's claim. When the court reaches that point it must decline to decide the rights and must stay the action, but it ought not to stay the action before that point is reached."

In the present case the Acting High Commissioner has sworn that all D funds held or deposited in the United Kingdom in the name of the Central Bank are funds held or deposited for and on behalf of the Nigerian state and form part of that state's strategic monetary reserves. This is a clear claim to a beneficial interest in, or at least control over, the funds within the jurisdiction. It may be that the claim can be defeated on full investigation, but it is not merely illusory or manifestly E defective. Further investigation would, therefore, involve impleading the state of Nigeria.

The trust issue

It is well settled that where property, which is within the jurisdiction, is impressed with a trust, the courts will supervise the administration of F that trust, notwithstanding that a foreign sovereign may assert an interest in the property: see *Larivière* v. *Morgan* (1872) L.R. 7 Ch.App. 550; *United States of America and Republic of France* v. *Dollfus Mieg et Cie. S.A. and Bank of England* [1952] A.C. 582, 617–618 and *Rahimtoola* v. *Nizam of Hyderabad* [1958] A.C. 379, 397–398, 401, 408 and 420.

But unfortunately for the plaintiffs there is no evidence of any trust in their favour. The facts are simply that the Central Bank has funds G standing to its credit with the Midland Bank Ltd. It authorised that bank to make payments in accordance with the letters of credit, but before the moment for payment arose it countermanded those instructions. Merely authorising an agent to make payments to a third party, even if the authority is communicated to the third party, does not create a trust unless a specific fund is earmarked for this purpose. There was no such ear-H marking. The Central Bank remained free at all times to withdraw all or any part of the funds standing to its credit with the Midland Bank, although a total withdrawal might well have led to the Midland Bank refusing to exercise its authority to pay the plaintiffs.

The waiver and estoppel issues

Mr. Neill concedes that in the light of the authorities I am not free to find that there has been any waiver of the right to claim sovereign immunity. However, he hopes that the House of Lords may feel free to re-examine the whole position and with this in mind, wishes to reserve argument on the waiver issue. This is obviously a sensible course to take.

However, Mr. Neill submits that nothing in the authorities prevents me holding that the bank is estopped from alleging that it is in a position to claim sovereign immunity. This estoppel is said to arise out of a letter dated April 28, 1975, addressed by the Central Bank to Credit Suisse of Lausanne concerning a letter of credit in favour of Lonlag Impex & Co. For this purpose I will assume that if the letter contains representations, they are representations to the plaintiffs and that the plaintiffs acted to their detriment on the faith of them. The letter is in these terms:

> "I write to inform you that no confirmation is required for credits opened by us direct with our correspondent banks, of which the Midland Bank Ltd., London, is one. We are irrevocably committed to honour our engagements under this credit. Moreover, our correspondent, the Midland Bank Ltd., has our authority to pay the beneficiary the full value of this letter of credit through your bank on presentation of relevant shipping documents to them in London, provided the documents are in order. (See our letter of authority dated March 11, 1975, to our correspondent bank attached.) As a government bank and a prime bank, no supplier should have any cause to doubt our ability to pay our bills promptly. The question of our correspondents confirming our letters of credit should, therefore, not arise. We are sending a copy of this letter to our correspondent bank, the Midland Bank Ltd., London, and you may wish to contact them for any further information you may require about us."

There seem to me to be two formidable difficulties in the way of this plea. The first is that the letter does not represent that the Central Bank is not in a position to claim sovereign immunity. It represents that (*a*) the Central Bank is irrevocably committed to honouring its obligations under the letter of credit, (*b*) the Central Bank is a government bank, (*c*) the Central Bank is a prime bank and (*d*) the Central Bank had not then, and would not in the future, be unable to meet its obligations. All these representations were then true and remain true to this day. A commitment is no less irrevocable, because it is not honoured in the event. "Irrevocable" means at most that the commitment cannot be revoked without a breach of contract. None of them is inconsistent with a claim to sovereign immunity. Indeed, the representation that the Central Bank was a government bank might well have forewarned the plaintiffs.

The second difficulty arises out of the fact that the estoppel, to be effective, must bind the state of Nigeria as distinct from the Central Bank. An estoppel is a procedural rule preventing a party to proceedings from leading evidence or putting forward a claim which is inconsistent with a binding representation. But the state of Nigeria is not before the court. What has happened is that the court has been put on notice that these proceedings may implead that state. It has thereupon become its duty to consider this possibility. But this would have been its duty however the point came to its notice: see *per* Kay L.J. in *Mighell* v. *Sultan of Johore* [1894] 1 Q.B. 149, 162.

Accordingly, in my judgment the estoppel plea fails.

A *The E.E.C. issue*

It appears that in December 1975 the Provincial Court of Frankfurt, 8th Chamber for Commercial Matters, refused to give effect to a plea for sovereign immunity in proceedings similar to the present, in which a Liechtenstein company sued the bank on a letter of credit. From these small beginnings an interesting and educational edifice has been constructed,
B but I fear that it is not weight bearing. I probably do it an injustice, although I do not so intend, if I say that it amounts to a submission that if these proceedings had been begun after April 1, 1976, or perhaps even if I delayed judgment until after that date, I should be in breach of community law in giving effect to the plea for sovereign immunity.

The first answer is that it is still March. The second answer is that when the Convention of Lomé comes into force and takes its place in
C community law and thus in English law, it may prohibit discrimination between citizens of the E.E.C. states, on the one hand, and those of the A.C.P. (African, Caribbean and Pacific) states, on the other. It will not however, prohibit discrimination between litigants on grounds other than nationality. Nor will it require the courts of the E.E.C. members to harmonise their policies on sovereign immunity, provided that those policies are not discriminatory on grounds of nationality. The third answer is that
D article 62 of the Convention, which is the article relied upon, relates to "matters of establishment and provision of services" which have nothing to do with sovereign immunity: see chapters 2 and 3 of the E.E.C. Treaty.

For these reasons the injunctions will be discharged, the proceedings set aside and all further proceedings will be stayed.

E *Order accordingly.*

Solicitors: *Theodore Goddard & Co.; Hedleys, Botterell, Roche & Temperley.*

F [EMPLOYMENT APPEAL TRIBUNAL]

* BARREL PLATING & PHOSPHATING CO. LTD. *v.* DANKS

1976 June 14 — Cumming-Bruce J., Mr. W. Sirs and Mrs. M. Sunderland

G *Industrial Relations—Unfair dismissal—Compensation—Dismissal of employee in year preceding sixtieth birthday—Compensation assessed on basis that employee but for dismissal would have continued to work after retirement age—Whether compensation payable for period after retirement age—Trade Union and Labour Relations Act* 1974 (*c.* 52), *Sch.* 1, *paras.* 10 (*b*), 19 (2) [1]

H The employee, who was aged 59, was unfairly dismissed by her employers. On her complaint of unfair dismissal, an industrial tribunal found that but for her dismissal she would have continued in her employment for another two years, which included a period of several months beyond the normal

[1] Trade Union and Labour Relations Act 1974, Sch. 1, para. 10 (*b*): see post, p. 881A-B.
Para. 19 (2): see post, p. 881H.

retiring age of 60. The tribunal assessed the compensation A to be awarded to the employee, in accordance with paragraph 19 (2) of Schedule 1 to the Trade Union and Labour Relations Act 1974, on the basis that she had lost the benefit of wages for the two-year period.

On appeal by the employers on the ground that having regard to paragraph 10 (*b*) of Schedule 1 to the Act of 1974, the industrial tribunal had erred in assessing compensation beyond the employee's sixtieth birthday:— B

Held, dismissing the appeal, that the restriction on the right of an employee to claim compensation for unfair dismissal after reaching the age of retirement imposed by paragraph 10 (*b*) of Schedule 1 to the Trade Union and Labour Relations Act 1974, did not affect the assessment of compensation payable to an employee who had been unfairly dismissed before that date; and that accordingly the employee was entitled to compensation for the two years' loss of wages C she would have received but for her dismissal.

No cases are referred to in the judgment or were cited in argument.

APPEAL from an industrial tribunal sitting at Birmingham.

The employers, Barrel Plating & Phosphating Co. Ltd., appealed from a decision of the industrial tribunal on December 29, 1975, awarding the D employee, Miss M. Danks, £1,354·80 compensation for unfair dismissal, on the ground, inter alia, that the tribunal erred in assessing compensation so as to include a period beyond her sixtieth birthday.

The appeal was transferred from the Queen's Bench Division of the High Court to the Employment Appeal Tribunal under paragraph 9 of Schedule 17 to the Employment Protection Act 1975. E

The facts are stated in the judgment.

Nicholas Webb for the employers.
Graham Platford for the employee.

CUMMING-BRUCE J. delivered the following judgment of the appeal tribunal. This is an appeal against the decision of an industrial tribunal F sitting at Birmingham, given on December 29, 1975, whereby the tribunal decided that the employee had been unfairly dismissed and was entitled to £1,354·80 compensation. The employers seek an order that the application for unfair dismissal be retried; alternatively for an order that the matter be remitted to the tribunal for a review of their decision and, alternative to that variation, an order for the reduction of compensation. G [His Lordship considered the first ground of appeal and, having concluded that it was no ground for interfering with the decision of the industrial tribunal in relation to the employee's unfair dismissal, continued:] The second point is more interesting. In the notice of appeal it is expressed: "That the tribunal erred in law in assessing compensation for the [employee] beyond her sixtieth birthday."

The case under that head is put by the employers in two ways: first, H that as a matter of statutory construction of the Industrial Relations Act 1971, as re-enacted in subsequent legislation, it was the intention of the legislature, when giving a right to a person unfairly dismissed to come to an industrial tribunal for compensation, to bring down the guillotine upon the benefit which the employee might reasonably be expected to have had but for the dismissal, at normal retiring age or, in the case of a man the age of 65, and in the case of a woman the age of 60. The way

A in which it is put is this: the legislation (and I take for this purpose
paragraph 10 of Schedule 1 to the Trade Union and Labour Relations
Act 1974) provides that the right to apply for compensation on the ground
of unfair dismissal does not apply to the dismissal of an employee from
any employment if the employee:

> " (*b*) on or before the effective date of termination attained the age
> B which, in the undertaking in which he was employed, was the normal
> retiring age for an employee holding the position which he held, or,
> if a man, attained the age of 65, or, if a woman, attained the age of
> 60."

So it is quite clear, on the scheme of legislation under successive Acts,
that the right to come to an industrial tribunal to seek compensation for
C unfair dismissal is a right which the class of persons who can enjoy the
remedy and claim the right is restricted so as to exclude the classes of
person set out in paragraph 10 of Schedule 1 to the Act of 1974. Thus
it is said, and in our view said rightly, that if the employee had stayed
in her employment with the employers until her sixtieth birthday, and if
they had then dismissed her unfairly, in a situation in which she could
reasonably have expected otherwise to continue in their employment for
D a year or so, she would not have had any right at all to apply to an
industrial tribunal for compensation. Then it is said that if that is so,
there is an extraordinary anomaly in the Act of 1974 which cannot have
been intended, if the fact is, on a proper construction, that if the employee
was dismissed one day before her sixtieth birthday she could have
claimed a remedy for unfair dismissal quantified in accordance with the
E statute as the benefit that she might reasonably have expected to have
had for the next two years, if that was the period for which she might
reasonably have expected to continue working, although, if she had been
sacked on the next day she would have had no right at all. It is submitted
by Mr. Webb that Parliament cannot have intended such an anomaly.
He goes further and says there is no anomaly, because the right approach
to the construction of section 116 (2) (*b*) of the Act of 1971, as re-enacted
F in the Trade Union and Labour Relations Act 1974, is that Parliament
contemplated that compensation for unfair dismissal would terminate at
normal retiring age, or, in the case of a man, at the age of 65, or, if a
woman, at the age of 60. He says that that is quite natural because, in
that situation, the party unfairly dismissed, from the date of normal
retiring age, or 65 or 60 as the case might be, could look to a retirement
G pension which pro tanto reduces or removes the necessity for giving the
employee a statutory right to claim compensation in the amount of wages
that he or she might have earned if he or she had stayed in employment
after the age of 65 or 60 as the case might be.

The difficulty about the submission, which has been put elegantly
by Mr. Webb, is that it involves the appeal tribunal reading into the words
of the statute words that are not there and which give rise in themselves
H to no sort of drafting problem. Paragraph 19 (2) of Schedule 1 to the
Act of 1974 provides:

> " The said loss shall be taken to include—(*a*) [expenses] and (*b*) loss
> of any benefit which he might reasonably be expected to have had
> but for those matters, . . ."

On the finding of fact of the industrial tribunal, with which I will
deal in a moment, the employee, Miss Danks, at the date of her dismissal,

could reasonably have looked forward to employment as far ahead as A
February 1977, which is some six months after her sixtieth birthday.
According to the plain words of the section, on those facts the benefit
which the employee might reasonably be expected to have had but for
the dismissal means the wages that she would have earned with the
employers up to February 1977, subject to mitigation of damage or the
other statutory deductions which fall to be taken into account.

Mr. Webb's submission is that when one looks at the scheme of the B
legislation it cannot have been the intention of Parliament to do anything
so arbitrary as to confer a right for compensation, which might be quanti-
fied in terms of wages for three or four or more years ahead, in the case
of an application for compensation brought by somebody who was dis-
missed at the age of 59 years and 364 days, and then, if the employee was
dismissed only one day later, to deprive the employee of any right to C
compensation at all. And the way that anomaly can be removed, which
Mr. Webb submits must have been the intention of Parliament, is that
underlying the provisions for compensation for unfair dismissal is the same
intention as that which one finds expressly appearing in relation to the
right to make a claim, namely, that compensation rights for unfair dismissal
determine on normal retiring age, 65 or 60, as the case may be. On such
a construction, he submits, there is no anomaly: one would not then find D
the situation of the statutory accident that if you unfairly dismiss some-
one on Tuesday you may find that they have a right to compensation
against you for several years ahead, but that if you dismiss them on
Wednesday they have no rights at all. That, it is submitted, cannot be the
intention; it must be necessary to read into section 116 (2) (*b*) and its
successor paragraph 19 (2) of Schedule 1 to the Act of 1974, some E
limitation, and the limitation must be that when calculating the loss of
benefit which the employee might reasonably be expected to have had,
the tribunal is intended to keep its eye fixed on the normal retiring age of
65 or 60, in the case of a man or a woman respectively, as the guillotine
which falls on the whole of the remedy created by the legislation.

There is certainly a logical attraction in the submission. In our view
it does not, however, succeed. It is true that Parliament, in bringing into F
existence the scheme of legislation, granting the right to apply for a
remedy for unfair dismissal, and giving a right to compensation therefor,
has restricted the classes of person who have the right and can claim
the remedy. The restriction that the legislature has determined is that
there shall be no right, and no remedy, in the case of a person who at
the date of the dismissal is over normal retiring age, 65 or 60. In our G
view it does not follow that Parliament is to be taken to have intended
to have extended that statutory guillotine to the quantum of compensation
in the case of those parties who have a valid claim which under the statute
they are entitled to bring. If it had been intended by the draftsman to
impose upon the industrial tribunals the duty to determine the benefit
which the employee might reasonably be expected to have had but for
the dismissal, but to restrict that determination of benefit accruing or likely H
to accrue before normal retiring age or 65 in the case of a man, or 60
in the case of a woman, the draftsman would have expressly stated that
limitation in the provisions dealing with the calculation of compensation.
It could be said that there is an anomaly in the decision of Parliament to
exclude from the classes of person who may apply for compensation for
unfair dismissal, those classes who reach normal retiring age at 65 or 60.
We see no reason to import into the statute, in the case of those applications

for compensation for unfair dismissal which are properly founded, a restriction of the kind for which Mr. Webb contends. For those reasons, the decision of the appeal tribunal on the question of construction is that there is no such implied limitation, in the exercise which the industrial tribunal has to perform when calculating the loss of benefit which might reasonably flow to an applicant, as is contended by Mr. Webb.

The second ground of appeal taken is that, on the evidence, the industrial tribunal could not reasonably have come to the decision that it did, that the employee was reasonably to be expected to have continued working for the employers up to February 1977. That is founded in this way. The employee herself, in evidence, said: "If not dismissed I would have retired at 60 if asked to. Would have continued if allowed and able." Counsel submits that when one looks at the history of personal relations revealed in the evidence it is as plain as a pikestaff that the employers, from a very early stage indeed, were extremely anxious to end the employee's employment, and it is wildly unlikely that they would have contemplated continuing to employ her beyond the age of 60, which would have meant beyond October 1976. Fortifying that submission is, for example, the discovery by the employers, after the employee had left, that her value added tax returns were in a lamentable degree of arrear, the petty cash discrepancy was upsetting, and so on; and that, if one looks at all the facts, it is wildly unreal, it is submitted, to suppose that this employee would ever have been offered employment by the employers beyond the age of 60. The other view of that is disclosed in the findings of fact of the industrial tribunal:

> "After many years of devoted service to Mr. Cohen much adaptation was required of [the employee]. However, the impression left with us by the evidence was that she was adapting herself and there was no reason why she should not have completed the process, if she had not already done so, by the time of her dismissal. We believe the [employers] could have found that she had a valuable contribution to make. She is an intelligent person with much experience of the business and its customers, and qualified to conduct routine chemical analyses. We do not consider that the [employers] seriously tried to appreciate and utilise her abilities. Her working hours and lunch time arrangements reflected no neglect of the business, and were modified to suit the requirements of Mr. Hunt and Mr. Jones."

They then give certain details. They make a finding that the value added tax returns had deliberately not been sent in to delay the payments which should accompany the returns. I will deal with that when I deal with the third ground of appeal.

On those findings of fact it is implicit that the employee was adapting herself, had a capacity to adapt herself, had a great contribution to make to the business and that provided that the employers had acted properly and reasonably they could have found, and would have found, that she had a valuable contribution to make, in which case the only question really is: having such a useful employee, who is approaching 60, is it likely that she would be able to continue to give the employers valuable service beyond October 1976? On that, the industrial tribunal has made a finding of fact, which is founded on the qualification "if the employers had acted reasonably." In the view of the appeal tribunal the employers cannot, in relation to the employee's future, in their employment, claim a benefit from a probability that they would continue to act unreasonably.

The question of her future employment with the employers must be considered on the assumption, and on the basis, that the employers would themselves act reasonably. On such a basis, the finding of fact of the industrial tribunal cannot be disturbed.

The third ground relied upon is that compensation should be reduced having regard to the fact that the employee contributed to her own loss. [His Lordship having given the appeal tribunal's reasons for rejecting that ground of appeal, continued:] For those reasons there is no ground for contribution in this case and the appeal is dismissed.

Appeal dismissed.

Solicitors: *Allan Jay & Co. for Edge & Ellison, Birmingham; Gamlens for Needham & James, Birmingham.*

J. W.

[CHANCERY DIVISION]

* PRACTICE DIRECTION (VARIATION OF TRUSTS: COUNSEL'S OPINION)

[No. 2 of 1976]

Trusts—Variation—Act of 1958—Infant representation—Arrangement affecting infant or unborn beneficiary—Need for case to counsel and counsel's written opinion

1. Where any infants or unborn beneficiaries will be affected by an arrangement under the Variation of Trusts Act 1958, evidence must normally be before the court which shows that their guardians ad litem or the trustees support the arrangement as being in the interests of the infants or unborn beneficiaries, and exhibits a case to counsel and counsel's written opinion to this effect. In nearly every case such a written opinion is helpful, and in complicated cases it is usually essential to the understanding of the guardian ad litem and the trustees, and to the consideration by the court of the merits and the fiscal consequences of the arrangement.

2. Where the interests of two or more infants, or two or more of the infants and unborn beneficiaries, are similar, a single written case to counsel and opinion will suffice; and no case to counsel or written opinion is required in respect of those who fall within the proviso to section 1 (1) of the Act (discretionary interests under protective trusts). Further, in proper cases the requirement of a case to counsel and a written opinion may at any stage be dispensed with by the master or the judge.

3. The effect of this practice direction is to extend to variations of trusts the long-established practice in the Chancery Division of requiring a case to counsel and counsel's opinion when proceedings in which an infant is interested are compromised: see *The Supreme Court Practice* (1976), vol. 2, para 2073.

By the direction of the Vice-Chancellor.

R. E. BALL,
Chief Master.

July 27, 1976.

A

[COURT OF APPEAL]

* PEXTON (INSPECTOR OF TAXES) *v.* BELL AND ANOTHER

CROWE *v.* APPLEBY (INSPECTOR OF TAXES)

B 1976 March 16, 17, 18, 19 — Buckley and Lawton L.JJ. and Sir John Pennycuick

Revenue—Capital gains tax—Settled property—Death of holders of life interests in part of settled property—Whether deemed disposals by trustees of whole of settled property—"Part"—Whether including fractions or shares of settled property—
C *Finance Act* 1965 (*c.* 25), *s.* 25 (4) (12)

The taxpayers in the first case under appeal were the trustees of a settlement in which R had, until her death in 1969, a life interest in one quarter of the settled property. R's three sisters had equal life interests in the remaining three quarters. On R's death the trustees were assessed to capital gains tax on the basis that there had been a deemed disposal
D of the whole of the settled property by virtue of the provisions of section 25 (4) of the Finance Act 1965.[1] The taxpayers appealed against the assessment to the special commissioners, contending that, as R had a life interest in a fractional part of the settled property, by virtue of section 25 (12) of the Act only that part of the property was chargeable to capital gains tax. The special commissioners allowed their appeal. On appeal by the Crown, Walton J. upheld the commissioners'
E decision on the ground that the word "part" in section 25 (12) of the Act included a fractional share so that section 25 (4) of the Act could not operate to make capital gains tax payable on the whole of the settled property on R's death.

In the second case under appeal, a testator, who died in 1938, gave his residuary estate on trust for the benefit of his five children in stated shares to trustees, one of whom was the taxpayer. The residuary estate consisted solely of certain
F freehold properties in the City of London. One of the children died in 1952 and his share in the trust property devolved absolutely on his only child. On the death in 1968 of a second child, the taxpayer as trustee was assessed to capital gains tax in respect of the residuary estate. In December 1968 the whole estate was sold for £360,000 and a further assessment to capital gains tax was made on the taxpayer. The special commissioners, on the taxpayer's appeal against both assessments,
G upheld the first assessment on the basis that, notwithstanding the provisions of section 25 (12) of the Finance Act 1965, on the death of the second child in 1968 there was a deemed disposal of the whole of the residuary estate by virtue of section 25 (4) of the Act. They also confirmed the second assessment to be correct on the ground that at the date of sale the whole of the residuary estate remained settled property for
H the purposes of calculating capital gains tax. On appeal by the taxpayer, Goff J., following the decision of Walton J. in the first case, allowed the appeal against the first assessment ordering that the amount of tax payable be substantially reduced. He affirmed in principle the second assessment but ordered

---

[Reported by MRS. HARRIET DUTTON, Barrister-at-Law]

[1] Finance Act 1965, s. 25 (4) (12): see post, pp.888H—889A, D-E.

that it be remitted to the special commissioners to be reduced A as a result of the reduction of the first assessment.

On appeal by the Crown, it being conceded that the two appeals raised one common point and that a decision against the Crown in the first appeal would be conclusive against it in the second appeal:—

Held, dismissing the appeals, that the word "part" in section 25 (4) and (12), given its natural meaning, included a fractional or undivided share in settled property and was B not confined to a specific or identifiable asset vested in the trustees; and that accordingly section 25 (4) did not apply to enable capital gains tax to be levied on the whole of the settled property on the death of a life tenant of an undivided share in the settled property (post, pp. 895C-D, 902D-H, 903G-H).

Per Sir John Pennycuick. A disposition of property by a testator to trustees for the benefit of his children for life and with remainders over could not be said to create several C separate settlements but a single settlement with a single trust fund (post, p. 901A-C).

Decisions of Walton J. [1975] 1 W.L.R. 707; [1975] 1 All E.R. 498 and Goff J. [1975] 1 W.L.R. 1539; [1975] 3 All E.R. 529 affirmed.

The following case is referred to in the judgments: D

Lassence v. *Tierney* (1849) 1 Mac. & G. 551.

The following additional cases were cited in argument:

Banff Magistrates v. *Ruthin Castle Ltd.*, 1944 S.C. 36.

Burdett-Coutts v. *Inland Revenue Commissioners* [1960] 1 W.L.R. 1027; [1960] 3 All E.R. 153.

Cape Brandy Syndicate v. *Inland Revenue Commissioners* [1921] 2 K.B. E 403; 12 T.C. 358, C.A.

Fraser v. *Murdock* (1880) 6 App.Cas. 855, H.L.(Sc.).

Kidson v. *Macdonald* [1974] Ch. 339; [1974] 2 W.L.R. 566; [1974] 1 All E.R. 849; 49 T.C. 503.

Ogle's Settled Estates, In re [1927] 1 Ch. 229.

Stephenson v. *Barclays Bank Trust Co. Ltd.* [1975] 1 W.L.R. 882; [1975] 1 All E.R. 625. F

Vestey v. *Inland Revenue Commissioners* [1962] Ch. 861; [1962] 2 W.L.R. 221; [1961] 3 All E.R. 978; 40 T.C. 112.

Wood, In re [1913] 2 Ch. 574, C.A.

PEXTON (INSPECTOR OF TAXES) *v.* BELL AND ANOTHER

APPEAL from Walton J. G

The trustees, William H. C. Bell and Bernard Colbourne, of the James Colbourne Will Trust held, inter alia, property the income from which was paid to the testator's four daughters in equal shares for their lives. In February 1969 one of the daughters, Mrs. Gladys Roberts, died. The trustees were assessed to capital gains tax for the year 1968–69 in the sum of £10,000 on the basis that on the death of Mrs. Roberts the trustees H were deemed by virtue of section 25 (4) of the Finance Act 1965 to have disposed of the whole of the settled fund and not merely of a one quarter share. The special commissioners allowed an appeal by the taxpayers and discharged the assessment. On the Crown's appeal, Walton J. upheld that decision.

The Crown appealed on the grounds set out in the judgment of Sir John Pennycuick: see post, p. 894 A-E.

A CROWE *v.* APPLEBY (INSPECTOR OF TAXES)

APPEAL from Goff J.

The taxpayer, Harold Michael Crowe, as one of four trustees of the Frederic George Bird Will Trust, held property for the benefit of the testator's five children for life with remainders over. In 1952, one of his children, George Robert Bird, died and his 5/30th share devolved on his
B only child absolutely. In 1968 a second child, Constance Lillian Cook, died and her share devolved on her two children as tenants in common in equal shares absolutely. In 1969 the trustees sold the trust property for £360,000. The taxpayer was assessed to capital gains tax for the year 1968–69 in the sum of £31,385 on the basis that on the death of Mrs. Cook in 1968 the trustees were deemed to have disposed of the whole of the trust property. He was further assessed for the year 1969–70 in the sum of £103,763
C as being the chargeable gains accruing on the sale of the property.

Goff J. allowed in part an appeal by the taxpayer from a decision of the special commissioners that had affirmed both assessments, and ordered that the first assessment be reduced to £5,229 and that the second assessment be remitted to the commissioners for determination. The Crown appealed on the grounds that (i) the decision in *Pexton* v. *Bell* which
D Goff J. followed was wrong in law on the grounds that: (a) where there was a life interest in possession in one of two or more shares of settled property and no appropriation had been made of any of the assets forming part of the settled property, the life tenant of that share has an interest in possession in all the assets forming part of the settled property, and (b) for the purposes of section 25 (4) and (12) of the Finance Act 1965 " a part of the settled property " did not mean a fraction of the settled property
E but referred to one or more appropriated or otherwise distinguishable assets comprised in the settled property. (ii) That for the purposes Constance Lillian Cook as life tenant of a share of settled property which consisted of real property and no assets of which had been appropriated had at her death a life interest in possession in all, and not in only part of, the settled property. (iii) That on that death there was a termination of the life
F interest and all the assets forming part of the settled property were deemed to be disposed of under section 25 (4) and that section 25 (12) had no application in relation thereto. (iv) That the chargeable gains for the years 1968–69 and 1969–70 respectively fell to be calculated as set out in paragraph 6 (vi) and (vii) respectively of the case.

D. C. Potter Q.C. and *Peter Gibson* for the Crown.
G *P. W. E. Taylor* for Mr. Bell and Mr. Colbourne.
Peter Millett Q.C. and *J. R. Cherryman* for Mr. Crowe.

BUCKLEY L.J. I will ask Sir John Pennycuick to deliver the first judgment.

H SIR JOHN PENNYCUICK. We have before us two appeals, one entitled *Pexton* v. *Bell*, the other entitled *Crowe* v. *Appleby*. In the first appeal the appellant is the inspector of taxes; the respondents are the taxpayers. In the title to the second appeal the appellant is the taxpayer; the respondent is the inspector of taxes; the reason for this will appear later on.

The two appeals raise one common point which, if decided in favour of the taxpayers on one appeal, will also be admittedly conclusive in favour of the taxpayer on the other appeal. I propose to deal with the first appeal—that is, *Pexton* v. *Bell*—separately in the first instance and, A having expressed my conclusion on that appeal, turn more shortly to the other appeal; that is *Crowe* v. *Appleby.*

The appeal in *Pexton* v. *Bell* is an appeal from an order made by Walton J. on November 28, 1974. The taxpayers are the trustees of a trust created by the will of one James Colbourne. Summarily, the question is whether upon the death of the life tenant of an aliquot share in the trust fund under that trust there was a disposal for the purposes of capital B gains tax of the whole of the trust fund or only of a corresponding aliquot share of the fund. Walton J. affirmed the decision of the special commissioners, deciding that the latter was the correct view.

It will be convenient, before setting out the facts of the present case, to refer to the statutory provisions under which the question arises. Capital gains tax was a novel tax introduced for the first time by Part III of C the Finance Act 1965. In the broadest terms, the tax is charged upon the gain arising from the disposal of assets; that is to say, the excess of the price realised upon the disposal over the real or notional cost of the assets. Sections 19 and 20 create the charge to tax. There are a number of provisions not now in point as to the property subject to the tax and as to how the cost of acquisition and the amount realised on disposal are to be D ascertained. I need not read those. I should refer in passing to section 22 (5) which provides in effect that where assets are held by a person as nominee for another person or as trustee for another person absolutely entitled, the Act is to apply as if the property were vested in the beneficial owner. Section 23 deals with losses; section 24 with death. Then one comes to section 25, which is the critical section for the present purpose. That is a lengthy section dealing with the case of settled property. There E is a definition of "settled property" in section 45 of the Act, but I do not think that definition really takes one much further. "Settled property" is defined as meaning (subject to a qualification not now material) any property held in trust other than property to which section 22 (5) applies; that is, other than property held by a nominee or a trustee for an absolute owner. F

Section 25 (1) provides that the trustees of the settlement are to be treated as a single and continuing body of persons. Then subsection (2):

> "A gift in settlement, whether revocable or irrevocable, is a disposal of the entire property thereby becoming settled property notwithstanding that the donor has some interest as a beneficiary under the settlement . . ." G

Subsection (3) is marginally relevant in the present case:

> "On the occasion when a person becomes absolutely entitled to any settled property as against the trustee all the assets forming part of the settled property to which he becomes so entitled shall be deemed to have been disposed of by the trustee, and immediately reacquired by him in his capacity as a trustee within section 22 (5) of this Act, H for a consideration equal to their market value."

Subsection (4) is one of the crucial subsections for the purpose of this case:

> "On the termination at any time after April 6, 1965, of a life interest in possession in all or any part of settled property, all the assets forming part of the settled property, except any which at that time

cease to be settled property, shall be deemed for the purposes of this Part of this Act at that time to be disposed of and immediately reacquired by the trustee for a consideration equal to their market value."

Subsection (5) is concerned with relief. Subsections (6) and (7) provide, broadly, that there is to be a notional disposition and acquisition every 15 years during the currency of a settlement, with certain relief in respect of what may be called "quick succession" during that 15-year period. I need not read subsections (8), (9) or (10). Subsection (11) again is marginally relevant:

> "For the purposes of this section, where part of the property comprised in a settlement is vested in one trustee or set of trustees and part in another (and in particular where settled land within the meaning of the Settled Land Act 1925 is vested in the tenant for life and investments representing capital money are vested in the trustees of the settlement), they shall be treated as together constituting and, in so far as they act separately, as acting on behalf of a single body of trustees."

Subsection (12) is the other subsection which is of crucial importance in the present case:

> "If there is a life interest in a part of the settled property and, where that is a life interest in income, there is no right of recourse to, or to the income of, the remainder of the settled property, the part of the settled property in which the life interest subsists shall while it subsists be treated for the purposes of subsections (4), (5), (6) and (7) of this section as being settled property under a separate settlement."

I need not read subsection (13).

So the scheme of that section is that, over and above an actual disposition of assets comprised in settled property, there is to be a deemed disposition of either the whole or a part of the settled property upon the death of a life tenant and also at the expiration of every 15-year period, with relief for quick succession. I am expressing that in very broad terms.

Before proceeding to analyse those provisions further, I will set out the facts of the present case so far as they appear from the case stated:

> "1. The special commissioners heard an appeal by the trustees of the Colbourne Will Trust against an assessment to capital gains tax for the year 1968–69. 2. Shortly stated the question for our decision was whether on the death of a person who was entitled under a will to a life interest in a one-fourth share of a settled fund (no appropriation of investments within that fund having been made) the trustees of the will are deemed under section 25 (4) of the Finance Act 1965 to have disposed of the whole of the settled fund or, by virtue of section 25 (12) of the Finance Act 1965, of only a one-fourth share thereof."

Then they set out a number of relevant documents, and in paragraph 4 they come to the admitted facts:

> "(a) James Colbourne died on April 1, 1929. (b) By his will he created a settlement in favour of his nine children. The residuary estate was left to trustees and they were directed to hold the net proceeds thereof in trust for such of his sons as attained the age of

25 and for such of his daughters as attained the age of 21 or married. The share of each of the daughters was directed to be retained by the trustees who were to hold each such share separately in trust to invest it and to pay the daughter the income of it for life." A

Then there is a codicil which settled the share of the son Linser. "(c) The will contains the following provisions" . . . . I need not quote the whole extract from the will. It starts with a direction that the trustees shall: B

"stand possessed of my trust property upon trust for all or such one or more of my nine children now living as shall survive me and being sons have attained or shall live to attain the age of 25 years or being daughters have attained or shall live to attain the age of 21 years or be married."

Then there is a provision for lapse. Then: C

"Nevertheless as to the share of every daughter of mine in my trust property I direct that the same shall not be paid to her but shall be retained by my trustees upon the trusts hereinafter declared concerning the same that is to say:—As to the share of every such daughter separately upon trust to invest the same pursuant to the clause concerning investments hereinafter contained and upon further trust D
to pay the income of such share and the investments thereof for the time being (which are hereinafter referred to as 'the portion of my same daughter') to my same daughter without power of anticipation during her life and from and after her decease as to the capital and future income of the portion of my same daughter upon trust for all or such one or more of the issue of my same daughter including E
grand-children and more remote issue born in her lifetime for such interests and in such shares and subject to such limitations as my same daughter shall by will or codicil appoint and in default of and subject to any such appointment upon trust for her child if only one or for all her children equally as tenants in common if more than one who being a son or sons shall attain the age of 21 years or being a daughter or daughters shall attain that age or be married." Then F
there is a default trust "for the person or persons who at my decease would have been entitled thereto under the trusts hereinbefore contained if my same daughter had died in my lifetime childless."

It will be observed that that trust is in the *Lassence* v. *Tierney* (1849) 1 Mac. & G. 551 form, and the direction is that the share of each daughter which the testator describes as her "portion" shall be invested separately. G
I need not deal with the first codicil. (e) refers to certain charts showing the names of the nine children of the testator—that is Ethel Stiles, Frances Colbourne, James Colbourne, Horace Colbourne, Gladys Roberts, Linser Colbourne, Margaret Bridgman Christine Hudson and Bernard Colbourne —and the names of their marriage partners and issue and the dates of death: H

"(f) On the death of Mrs. Stiles in 1938 one eighth of her share in the settlement went to each of the settled shares of Miss Frances Colbourne, Mrs. Roberts, Mrs. Bridgman, Mrs. Hudson and the son Linser, and the remainder thereof went to the other surviving sons and the personal representatives of a deceased son. Part of Linser's share was transferred to him in his lifetime in exercise of the trustees' powers,"

A and the rest went to each of the other shares by way of accrual. Then:

"(g) Mrs. Bridgman who died in 1962 exercised her power of apointment in her will" in favour of her daughter. "(h) Immediately before Mrs. Roberts' death on February 24, 1969, the daughters' shares were the only funds remaining in settlement, and part of the original trust fund had been appropriated to them collectively (the
B daughters' fund). The sons or their personal representatives had under the relevant trusts and powers become absolutely entitled to the remaining part of the original trust fund and the assets appropriated to this remaining part had been paid or transferred to them. The daughters' fund was a single fund not appropriated into shares. Each daughter's settled share was a one-fourth share of this fund and the net income from the fund was divided and paid to Mrs. Roberts,
C Miss Frances Colbourne, Mrs. Hudson and Pauline May Simonds (the daughter of Mrs. Bridgman) in equal shares. . . . The fund consisted of stocks and shares quoted on the London Stock Exchange, secured loans and a building society deposit. (i) The point at issue in this appeal arose as a result of the death of Mrs. Roberts, and the computations of liability based on the rival contentions are as follows:
D A. On the basis that trustees' contentions are correct. Total gains on securities held on behalf of settled shares of four daughters—as agreed, £8,245. One fourth representing Mrs. Gladys Roberts' share, £2,061. Available relief under sections 24 (2) and 25 (5) of the Finance Act 1965, £4,831. Assessable gains, nil. B. On basis that inspector of taxes' contentions are correct. Total gains as above, £8,245. Available relief as above, £4,831. Assessable gains,
E £3,414."

In other words, there is no division into fourths.

"5. It was contended on behalf of the trustees that: (a) on a proper construction of the relevant provisions of the will and codicil of James Colbourne deceased the late Mrs. Roberts had a life interest
F in a fractional part of the property settled under that will; (b) within the meaning of section 25 (12) that interest was a life interest in income and there was no right of recourse to, or to the income of, the remainder of the settled property, that is to say, the property so settled other than the fractional part in which Mrs. Roberts had a life interest; (c) accordingly for the purposes of section 25 (4) the part of the settled property in which Mrs. Roberts' life interest had
G subsisted should while it subsisted be treated as being settled property under a separate settlement." Then it deals with computation. "6. It was contended on behalf of the [revenue] that: (a) as no appropriation of the daughters' fund had been made before her death, Mrs. Roberts had a life interest in the whole of that fund, that is to say, in each and every asset that formed part thereof; (b) she
H could not be said to have had a life interest in only part of the daughters' fund within the meaning of section 25 (4) and (12) as she had an interest in each and every asset thereof; (c) even if she did have a life interest in part of the daughters' fund within the meaning of the said subsections, subsection (12) could not apply as she had a right of recourse to the income of the remainder thereof; (d) accordingly, on the death of Mrs. Roberts all the assets forming part of the daughters' fund were deemed under section 25 (4) to have

been disposed of and reacquired by the trustees for a consideration equal to their market value. . . . 7. We, the commissioners who heard the appeal, preferred the arguments addressed to us on behalf of the trustees. We therefore allowed the appeal and discharged the assessment before us."

The commissioners did not give any further reasons for their decision.

It will be observed that the trustees were guilty of at least a technical breach of trust in not making an immediate appropriation of assets to meet the settled share of each daughter. However, I do not think anything really turns on that point, and I do not propose to follow it up.

The inspector of taxes appealed by way of case stated to the High Court, and Walton J. upheld the decision of the commissioners [1975] 1 W.L.R. 707. In his judgment he set out the facts. I need not go through that again. He said, at p. 709:

> "The first point made by Mr. Gibson, on behalf of the Crown, is that subsection (12) is a relieving section and that it is therefore for the taxpayers to show clearly that they fall within it. Mr. Taylor, for the taxpayers, says that subsection (12) is not, properly construed, a relieving subsection; it is a subsection which is part of the whole structure of the provisions of section 25. He says that it is not in any sense a relieving subsection; it merely has to be applied in order to see what the effects of the section are. If anything turns on that—and I do not think in fact that anything does—I should have preferred the submissions of the taxpayers."

I interpose to say that nothing much has been made of that point in the appeal before us, and I agree with the judge upon the point.

The judge then proceeded to analyse subsection (12), and he dealt with the words "there is no right of recourse to, or to the income of, the remainder of the settled property." He said, at pp. 709–710:

> "Of course, those words, '. . . there is no right of recourse to, or to the income of, the remainder of the settled property . . .' would more naturally apply to an annuity, and do not apply to a mere income interest. However, Mr. Taylor and I both thought at the same point of time of a possible explanation which would account for there being these words, which at first sight do not appear very appropriate to a life interest. That explanation is this: that one might very well find a type of provision under which somebody who is entitled to a share in the income of a trust fund might nevertheless be entitled to have that income interest made up to a fixed figure, in the event of it falling below that particular fixed figure, out of the income of the remainder of the settled property, and the possibility of that kind of provision would make it sensible to include those words in subsection (12)."

Again, not much has been made of that point in the appeal before us. I agree that the judge has given an adequate reason for the inclusion of those words. He continued, at p. 710:

> "The real point at issue between the parties is, I think, an extremely narrow one. It is whether the word 'part' in the phrase 'in a part of the settled property' in subsection (12) includes a fractional share, in this particular case one quarter, and I really have no hesitation at all in saying that it does. One of the meanings of the word 'part'

> A as given in the *Oxford English Dictionary* is 'fraction,' the full scope of this portion of the definition being: 'A portion, division, section, element, constituent, fraction, fragment, piece.' It appears to me that 'a part' very easily comprises, and in its natural meaning comprises, a fraction."

Indeed, the first definition of all in the *Oxford English Dictionary* runs as
B follows:

> "Portion or division of a whole. That which together with another or others makes up a whole (whether really separate from the rest, or more often only separated in thought)."

To continue the judgment, at p. 710:

> "Indeed, I think that that is in a sense self-evident if one goes back
> C to subsection (4). Subsection (4) starts off: 'On the termination at any time after' the relevant date 'of a life interest in possession in all or any part of settled property . . .' Now, what was the situation here? The situation here was that Mrs. Roberts was certainly not possessed at the time of her death of a life interest in possession in all the settled property. That would be an absurd suggestion. She was entitled to a life interest in possession in part of the settled pro-
> D perty, namely, a one quarter share. So it seems to me that, on the natural meaning of subsection (4), the charging section, which the Crown certainly says charges her 'part,' must include of its very nature a fraction. Therefore, it seems to me that, when one gets to subsection (12), 'part' there also must mean 'fraction.' Really, on that very short ground, I would come to the conclusion that this
> E appeal falls to be dismissed.
>
> "Mr. Gibson, for the Crown, argued that the word 'part' in subsection (12) meant something different from a fraction or a share: it meant either a completely separated out part or a particular bit, for example, a house or a field, or something of that nature, forming part of the settled property. But I am afraid that I think, in spite of the valiant effort by Mr. Gibson to maintain to the contrary, that his
> F argument really proves too much. It seems to me that if by 'part' you mean a separated out part then when you come to apply subsection (4) the settled property in question is the separated out part, or alternatively it is the portion of the trust fund which, though not a fraction, is somehow distinct from it, as a field or house. Thus you do not require the provision relating to a part at all. . . . Mr. Gibson
> G sought to counter that by saying that if you had a partial appropriation so that you had a one quarter share separated out but not the three quarters separated out then the situation would be that, if one of the life tenants of one of the fractions which was not separated out died, one would then have subsection (4) applying so as to make the whole of the three quarters which had not been separated out deemed to be disposed of for the purpose of capital
> H gains tax. It seems to me that that is really a very odd use of these two subsections."

So Walton J. found no difficulty in holding that in subsection (12) the word "part" covers not only a distinct item or parcel of property comprised in the entirety of the settled property, but also an undivided share in the entirety of the settled property; and he applied subsections (4) and (12) accordingly.

The inspector of taxes appealed to this court; and, at the risk of a little repetition, I think I should read the grounds of appeal, which rather amplify the contentions of the inspector of taxes before the commissioners:

> "1. That where there is a life interest in possession in a share of settled property and no appropriation has been made of any of the assets forming part of the settled property, the life tenant has an interest in possession in all the assets forming part of the settled property as there is no identifiable asset or share of any identifiable asset to which his interest is limited. 2. That for the purposes of section 25 (4) and (12) of the Finance Act 1965 'a part of the settled property' does not mean a fraction thereof but refers to one or more appropriated or otherwise identifiable assets comprised in the settled property. 3. That for the said purposes Gladys Roberts as life tenant of a share of settled property no assets of which had been appropriated had at her death a life interest in possession in all, and not in only part of, the settled property. 4. That on that death there was a termination of the said life interest and all the assets forming part of the settled property (except such as at that time ceased to be settled property and were deemed to be disposed of under section 25 (3) were deemed to be disposed of under section 25 (4). 5. That section 25 (12) had no application in relation to the property deemed to be disposed of under section 25 (4) as aforesaid. 6. That the learned judge in affirming the determination of the commissioners wrongly proceeded on the footing that the said Gladys Roberts had a life interest in possession of one fourth of each of the assets forming part of the settled property and that on her death only such one fourth of each of the said assets not ceasing at that time to be settled property was to be deemed to be disposed of under section 25 (4)."

A cross-notice was put in on behalf of the taxpayers in these terms:

> "That the settled property in which, for the purposes of section 25 (4) of the Finance Act 1965, Gladys Roberts had a life interest in possession consisted:—(a) of specific assets, namely, one-fourth as nearly as may be of:—(i) each holding of stock or shares comprised in the daughters' fund, (ii) each secured loan so comprised, and (iii) the building society deposit so comprised; or (b) so far as material for capital gains tax purposes, of specific assets, namely, one-fourth as nearly as may be of each holding of stock or shares so comprised."

I will now return to look more closely at the two subsections on which primarily this appeal turns. Section 25 (4) provides:

> "On the termination . . . of a life interest in possession in all or any part of settled property, all the assets forming part of the settled property, except any which at that time cease to be settled property, shall be deemed for the purposes of this Part of this Act at that time to be disposed of and immediately reacquired by the trustee for a consideration equal to their market value."

So far, whether one treats the word "part" in line 2 of that subsection as denoting only distinct items of property or a share in the entirety of the settled property, the effect of the subsection (unless one can read a great deal into it which is not there) is that on a termination of a life interest in part of the settled property, however small the proportion of the settled property that may be, the whole of the settled property is deemed to have been disposed of, with a consequent liability to charge of capital gains tax. That would be a very remarkable provision. Then one comes to subsection (12): "If there is a life interest in a part of the settled property and, where that is a life interest in income"—pausing there, I think that means simply "where there is a right to the income of part of the settled property for life"—(I need not read again the words about recourse), then:

> "the part of the settled property in which the life interest subsists shall while it subsists be treated for the purposes of subsections (4), (5), (6) and (7) of this section as being settled property under a separate settlement."

It seems to me that, upon the natural construction of the words used in their context, the word "part" in the subsection is apt to denote either a distinct item of property comprised in the entirety of the settled property or an undivided share of the entirety of the settled property. The word "part" is not a legal term of art. The word has a wide scope and is unquestionably appropriate of itself, unless in some way controlled by the context, to denote an undivided share in a single asset as well as a distinct asset. I have already referred to the dictionary definition. I feel no doubt that in its present context the word "part" should be construed as bearing that wide meaning so as to comprise an undivided share.

Then, when one reads subsections (4) and (12) together, the result is that when a life interest in possession in an undivided share of settled property comes to an end on the death of the life tenant, the share in question is to be treated as being settled property under a separate settlement, so that in effect it is only a corresponding proportion of the entire settled fund which is deemed to be disposed of on the death of the life tenant. That seems to me to be the natural construction of the words contained in the section. Moreover, it is a construction which produces a fair and logical result; that is to say, it relates the charge of duty to the property in which the life interest subsisted.

Mr. Potter for the Crown contended, in accordance with the grounds of appeal, that the word "part" in subsections (4) and (12) only denotes a distinct item of property. That would be the position, for example, where specific assets comprised in a settled fund had been appropriated to a particular settled share in that fund. The word "part" does not, upon his contention, apply to an undivided share. As I have said, I do not think that is the natural meaning of the word in the two subsections. The difficulty, I suppose, arises from the curious nature of an undivided share. Where property is held in undivided shares, each tenant in common has an interest in the whole of the property concerned, but his interest is confined to a proportionate share of that property. He has an interest in every asset of the fund, but his co-tenants have equally a concurrent interest in every asset of the fund, and the true result is that each tenant in common is only the beneficial owner of a rateable share of the fund. In the present context it seems to me altogether more natural to look at the true position rather than at refinements of the law of property in this connection.

Mr. Potter contended that the policy of the Act is to tax gains accruing to trustees on real or notional dispositions of assets vested in them, and not to tax gains accruing to beneficiaries on real or notional dispositions of the interests of which they are the owners. However that may be, I cannot see why the policy of the Act should require that a larger proportion of the settled assets should be treated as the subject of a notional disposal on the death of a beneficiary than is fairly referable to the interest of that beneficiary. A B

In the construction of the section, Mr. Potter placed reliance on the use of the word "part" in subsection (11). I agree that in that subsection the word "part," at least primarily if not exclusively, denotes actual assets. The subsection is concerned "in particular" with the position under the Settled Land Act 1925. I do not think that the fact that in this one particular and limited context the content of the word "part" is confined to actual assets goes very far towards cutting down the natural and much wider meaning of the word in other passages in the absence of some indication of such an intention in the context in which it is contained. C

Reference was also made to the use of the word "part" in subsection (3) and in subsection (4) itself, where the expression "all the assets forming part of the settled property" plainly refers to distinct items. On the other hand, the critical words, "all or any part of the settled property" in subsection (3) are equally applicable to distinct assets and to an undivided share. D

Some reliance was placed by Mr. Potter on the difficulties of computation and administration which would arise if this construction is adopted. It may well be that the construction which I have put upon the section would give rise to more complicated computation and administration. At the same time, no suggestion has been made that these difficulties would be in any way insuperable, and I think the difficulties are inherent in the nature of a subject matter such as property held in undivided shares, where, as for example in relation to estate duty, some burden falls on one undivided share and not on the other. I do not think this point really admits of any further elaboration. E F

Mr. Taylor, for the taxpayers in this case, relied on the further point raised in his cross-notice. He expressed this further point (unless I misunderstood him) in these terms: "(1) Pending appropriation Mrs. Roberts' share consisted of one fourth of each specific asset, that is to say, the shares, the mortgage and the money on deposit; and (2) the testator himself expressly created separate settlements." So far as the first of those contentions goes, I do not think it really solves the problem. I will assume that pending appropriation each of the beneficiaries should be treated as entitled to a fourth of each specific asset, in contradistinction to a fourth of the fund as a whole. But, even if one goes down to blocks of shares or single shares, the fact remains that pending appropriation the shares are still held for the four tenants in common in undivided shares and no item of property, not one single share, could be said to belong exclusively to one of the settled shares. G H

I should mention one further difficulty in the way of Mr. Potter's contentions, namely, that it would make the charge of duty depend upon the purely administrative acts of the trustees by way of appropriation or omission to appropriate. Liability for tax frequently follows from the exercise of a discretion of trustees affecting beneficial interests, but the

A court is normally very reluctant to make liability to tax depend on purely administrative acts of trustees.

I would only say in conclusion on this case that if Mr. Potter's contention were correct, it would produce a result so demonstrably illogical and so demonstrably oppressive that it is difficult to ascribe such an intention to Parliament.

B I turn now to the other case; that is, *Crowe* v. *Appleby.* In this case the special commissioners decided in favour of the inspector of taxes and Goff J. before whom the appeal came, decided one point in favour of the inspector of taxes. In this case the appeal is from an order of Goff J. made on June 27, 1975 [1975] 1 W.L.R. 1539. The judge followed the decision of Walton J. in *Pexton* v. *Bell,* but decided another point in favour of the inspector of taxes. That was upon a matter of computation, C which is not now in issue. It was common ground that if the inspector of taxes' appeal in *Pexton* v. *Bell* fails, then the inspector of taxes' in *Crowe* v. *Appleby* must likewise fail. For that reason, I do not go into this case at any great length; but, in deference to the arguments which we have heard, I think I ought to set out the facts of the case and express a provisional view on one contention which has been advanced by Mr. D Millett, who on this appeal appeared for the taxpayer.

I will summarise the facts as they appear in the case stated:

> "1. At a meeting of the special commissioners held on July 29, 1974, Mr. Crowe (the appellant) as trustee of Frederic George Bird, deceased (hereinafter called 'the testator') appealed against the following assessment to capital gains tax: 1968–69, £31,383; 1969–70, E £103,763. Shortly stated the questions for our decision, which turned on the construction of section 25 of the Finance Act 1965, were: (1) whether for the purposes of capital gains tax on the death in 1968 of a life tenant of a 5/30 share of the proceeds of sale of unsold realty comprising the residuary estate of the testator (no appropriation of assets in respect of such share having been made) the trustees of the said estate are deemed to have disposed F of the whole of the assets comprised therein or only a 5/30 share of the proceeds of sale thereof; (2) the amount of the chargeable gain for capital gains tax purposes arising on the sale in 1969 of the said realty having regard to: (i) the death in 1952 of the life tenant of another 5/30 share of the proceeds of sale of the said realty and (ii) the death in 1968 of the life tenant referred to in G sub-paragraph (1) . . ."

> "4. The following facts were admitted between the parties: (1) The appellant was assessed to capital gains tax as one of four trustees of the testator's will (hereinafter called 'the trustees'). (2) The testator died on September 24, 1938. By clauses 7 and 8 of his will he gave the residue of his estate (hereinafter called 'the residue') H to trustees on trust to sell, with power to postpone, and to hold the proceeds in certain shares for his five children. The will contained a proviso that the share of each child should not vest absolutely but should be held on protective trusts for the benefit of such child for life with remainders over. (3) Following the completion (on April 5, 1940) of the administration of the testator's estate, the capital of the residue consisted solely of the freehold property, no. 12, Lime Street and nos. 4 & 5, Beehive Passage in the City of London

(hereinafter called 'the freehold property'). (4) The first to die A
(on August 2, 1952) of the testator's children was George Robert
Bird (hereinafter called 'G. R. Bird'), life tenant of 5/30 of the
residue. His share devolved in events on his son Frederic George
Bird (hereinafter called 'F. G. Bird') absolutely. (5) The second to
die (on May 16, 1968) was Constance Lillian Cook (hereinafter
called 'Mrs. Cook'), life tenant of a further 5/30 of the residue.
Her share devolved in events on her two children as tenants in B
common in equal shares absolutely. (6) At the time of the appeal
proceedings before us the testator's other three children were living
and were life tenants respectively of 9/30, 6/30 and 5/30 of the
residue. (7) The freehold property was of the following values on
the following dates respectively: (a) September 24, 1938 (the
testator's death) £17,000; (b) August 2, 1952 (the death of G. R. Bird) C
£34,000; (c) May 16, 1968 (the death of Mrs. Cook) £250,000. (8)
By contract dated December 11, 1969 (which was completed by
transfer dated December 30, 1969) the trustees sold the freehold
property for £360,000. The net proceeds of that sale were, and the
relevant value for calculating the gain on that disposal for the
purposes of capital gains tax is, £353,763.

"It was contended on behalf of" the taxpayer—I will only read D
the first three of these contentions, because the remaining con-
tentions correspond to those in the *Pexton* case—"(i) that having
regard to the equitable doctrine of conversion the testator's will
created separate trusts of five separate shares in the proceeds of
sale of the freehold property in favour of each of his five children;
(ii) that on the death of G. R. Bird his son F. G. Bird became E
absolutely entitled as against the trustees to his 5/30 share and that
the said share thereupon ceased, by virtue of section 25 (3) of and
paragraph 31 of Schedule 6 to the Finance Act 1965, to be settled
property as defined in section 45 (1) of the said Act; (iii) that the
settled property deemed for the purposes of section 25 (4) of the
Finance Act 1965 to have been disposed of on Mrs. Cook's death
was not the entirety of the freehold property but was 5/30 of the F
proceeds of sale thereof."

Then it goes on to deal with the contentions common to the other case,
and it goes on further to deal with the basis of computation.

"6. It was contended on behalf of the respondent: (i) that it
matters not whether, by virtue of the equitable doctrine of con- G
version, the testator's will created separate trusts in the proceeds of
sale of the settled property in favour of each of his five children;
(ii) that for the purposes of section 25 (3) and (4) of the Finance
Act 1965 the freehold property was 'the assets forming part of the
settled property'; (iii) that on the death of G. R. Bird his son F. G.
Bird did not become, and should not be deemed to have become, H
absolutely entitled to any settled property as against the trustees,
and section 25 (3) of the Finance Act 1965 did not apply and should
not be deemed to have applied by virtue of paragraph 31 of Schedule
6 to that Act; (iv) that on the death of Mrs. Cook her life interest
terminated in part of the settled property (namely the freehold
property) within the meaning of section 25 (4) of the Finance Act
1965 but that asset did not then cease to be settled property."

Then it goes on to deal with the subsection (12) point, and goes on further to deal with computation. In this case the commissioners did give their reasons as follows:

"8. This appeal raises a difficult point, on which lawyers differ among themselves, on the construction of provisions in the Finance Act 1965 relating to the charge to capital gains tax on the death of a life tenant of an undivided share of settled property where no appropriation of the deceased life tenant's share has been made. Despite the carefully reasoned and cogent arguments advanced by counsel on behalf of the appellant, we have come to the same conclusion on the point as we and our colleagues have done in previous cases which have come before the special commissioners. We think that we are required to look at the underlying assets, namely the freehold property in the City of London which comprised the entire residuary estate of the testator, and that that was the settled property in which for the purposes of section 25 (4) of the Finance Act 1965 (before that subsection was amended in 1971) Mrs. Cook must be regarded as having had a life interest. In our view the wording of that subsection, with its reference to 'the assets forming part of the settled property' is more apt to fit the construction for which the respondent contends. Moreover, we think that for capital gains tax purposes there was one settlement only and that there were not separate settlements on each of the five life tenants."

Then they deal with the subsection (12) point.

The case came before Goff J. who gave his judgment on June 27, 1975: [1975] 1 W.L.R. 1539. After setting out the facts, he said, at p. 1541:

"The taxpayer submitted, however, that it should be on 5/30ths only. He based that on two contentions: first, that the relevant settled property was her 5/30ths share, and no more, to which I will return later; and, secondly, on section 25 (12) of the Finance Act 1965 which he submitted applies and, irrespective of his first contention, requires that share to be treated as 'being settled property under a separate settlement'".

He then refers to Walton J.'s decision in *Pexton* v. *Bell* and rightly concludes that he ought to follow that decision. He then went on to deal with the second assessment; that is the assessment made in 1969–70 on the gain arising from the actual sale of the property. He then turned to the arguments addressed to him by Mr. Francis for the taxpayer upon this second assessment. He said, at p. 1541:

"[Mr. Francis] took two points. I am not quite sure whether they are entirely separate or hinge upon each other, but either way I am unable to accept them. He said first the relevant 'settled property' on the death of Mrs. Cook was not the whole fund of realty but her 5/30ths settled share of the proceeds of sale and of the net rents and profits pending sale."

Then he went to Mr. Francis's second point. He continued:

"On the first point, 'settled property' is defined in section 45 (1) of the Act. . . . It seems to me quite clear that the property held in trust was at all material times the land which the trustees held on

> trust for sale, and I do not think that one can segregate a share A
> in notional proceeds of sale of unsold land even in a case such as this, to which the rule in *Lassence* v. *Tierney* (1849) 1 Mac. & G. 551 applies."

In the event, the judge decided the point with regard to the computation upon the second assessment in favour of the inspector of taxes; but the inspector of taxes has now made a new computation on the B
basis that *Pexton* v. *Bell* was rightly decided. That computation is rather more favourable to the taxpayer than his original computation. The taxpayer gladly accepted that revised computation, and no further point arises with regard to the computation, assuming that the decision in *Pexton* v. *Bell was* right, as I have held it to be.

The inspector of taxes stated the grounds of his appeal as follows: C

> "1. That the decision in the case of *Pexton* v. *Bell* was wrong in law"—I need not pursue that. "2. That for the said purposes Constance Lillian Cook as life tenant of a share of settled property which consisted of real property and no assets of which had been appropriated had at her death a life interest in possession in all, and not in only part of, the settled property. 3. That on that death
> there was a termination of the said life interest and all the assets D
> forming part of the settled property were deemed to be disposed of under section 25 (4)."

That is really the same basic contention as was made in the other case.

The taxpayers gave a cross-notice, which I should read:

> "That, for the purposes of section 25 (4) of the Finance Act 1965, E
> the settled property in which the life interest of George Robert Bird terminated on his death on August 2, 1952, and the settled property in which the life interest of Constance Lillian Cook terminated on her death on May 16, 1968, consisted not of the real property comprised in the residuary estate of the testator, but of their respective 5/30ths settled shares of the net proceeds of sale and the net rents
> and profits until sale of such real property. That, on the death of F
> the said George Robert Bird, his son Frederic George Bird became absolutely entitled as against the trustees (within the meaning of sections 22 (5) and 25 (3) of the said Act) to the said George Robert Bird's said settled share which thereupon ceased to be settled property. That on the death of the said Constance Lillian Cook,
> her two children became jointly absolutely entitled as against the G
> trustees (within the meaning of the said statutory provisions) to the said Constance Lillian Cook's said settled share which thereupon ceased to be settled property. That, at the date of the sale by the trustees of the said real property on December 11, 1969, the only remaining settled property consisted of the 20/30ths settled shares of the net proceeds of sale and the net rents and profits until sale
> of the said real property of which the life tenants were the surviving H
> daughters of the testator."

A decision in favour of the taxpayers in *Pexton's* case admittedly concludes this appeal in favour of the taxpayer; but, in deference to Mr. Millett's argument, I will deal shortly with the further argument which he placed first amongst his grounds. What I say, however, is obiter and I am only expressing a provisional view upon it. Mr. Millett

A contended that under a disposition in the present form the settlor creates not a single settlement but several distinct settlements, namely, first, a settlement of the trust fund upon his children as tenants in common absolutely and, secondly, a separate settlement upon each child of the share of that child upon trusts for the child and his children. I do not think this is a correct analysis of the position. It is of course competent for the owner of an undivided share in property to make a B settlement of that share; and I do not doubt that if he does so, that would be a different settlement distinct from the head settlement which creates the undivided share. But where the trusts of each share are declared by the settlor himself, then I think there is a single settlement upon the totality of those trusts and a single trust fund subsisting until it is broken up by payment out or appropriation. Indeed, the settlor C could not achieve his purpose otherwise, since once he had divested himself of the ownership of the fund by settlement upon his children as tenants in common without more ado, it would no longer be open to him to declare trusts of those shares by a separate disposition. I take that view irrespective of whether the settlement is or is not in the *Lassence* v. *Tierney* form. That is my provisional view upon what is D logically the first contention advanced by Mr. Millett. No further point arises before us as to computation.

There is only one further observation which I ought I think to make. By the Finance Act 1971, section 59, and paragraph 7 of Schedule 12, the provisions of section 25 were amended in respect of deaths occurring after March 30, 1971, in the sense in which I have construed section 25. That provision is not retrospective. It was not contended on either E side that it affects one way or the other the construction of section 25 as originally drawn. I have left the amended provision in the Act of 1971 completely out of account in reaching my conclusion.

I would dismiss this appeal.

LAWTON L.J. In the *Pexton* case, Walton J. described the point at F issue between the parties as very simple. The submissions of counsel in this court have spread over four days. We have had cited to us ten cases. We have been referred to three textbooks, including the 1911 edition of *Challis's Law of Real Property.* This has come about, so it seems to me, because counsel on all sides have brought to bear upon the elucidation of the issue, which to Walton J. appeared to be simple, their extensive knowledge of conveyancing and the law relating to trusts. G I have not the advantage of that knowledge. So all that I can bring to the construction of the statute is, I hope, a modicum of literacy, reasonableness and common sense. That modicum has to be used to construe the word "part" as used in section 25 (4) and (12) of the Finance Act 1965. I have asked myself a series of questions; and I will relate them, if I may, to the *Pexton* case. Did Mrs. Roberts have H a life interest in possession of settled property? The answer clearly is: she had. Did she have that interest in all the settled property? By the standards of anyone other than a conveyancer, the answer I am sure would be "No." If she had not got an interest in all the settled property, what had she got an interest in?—and the answer is: a part.

Mr. Potter has submitted that I ought not to answer the question as to whether she had got an interest in all the settled property in the way I have because she undoubtedly had (said Mr. Potter) an interest in an undivided share of the whole of the property. Coming from Mr. Potter, I have to give considerable attention to that submission. I have found comfort in the fact that the language of subsection (4) is not the language of conveyancers. It is language which Parliament intended to be applied in Scotland, Northern Ireland, as well as in England and Wales. I construe this language in the way I think a literate Englishman would construe it. He would not think of Mrs. Roberts having an interest in every item of the assets comprising the settled property.

Once I answer the question as I have, it follows, under subsection (4), unless there is some exception, that all the assets comprised in the settled property are deemed to have been disposed of and immediately reacquired by the trustees for a consideration equal to their market value. Mr. Potter accepted in the course of argument that that might in some cases produce harsh results. Indeed it might, because if Mrs. Roberts had had a far larger share or part of the settled property than the other beneficiaries, as a result of her death the other beneficiaries could well have been deprived of a substantial part of their income under their life interests for the next fifteen years. I find it difficult to conceive that Parliament intended such a result to come about. So I have looked in section 25 to see if Parliament has put in any provision to relieve the harshness which would come about by the application of subsection (4) in the way that Mr. Potter submitted it should. I find the relief in subsection (12), to which Sir John Pennycuick in his judgment has referred. I agree with him that the joint application of subsections (4) and (12) brings about the results for which Mr. Millett and Mr. Taylor have contended.

I too would dismiss these appeals, for the reasons given by Sir John Pennycuick.

BUCKLEY L.J. I also agree that these appeals should be dismissed, for the reasons given by Sir John in the judgment which he has delivered. The crucial question in the *Pexton* case is whether upon the death of Mrs. Roberts, the life tenant of an undivided one fourth of the daughters' settled fund, a life interest in possession in all or any part of settled property terminated. To answer that question, one has to consider precisely what the character of the lady's interest was in the daughter's settled fund. Has a tenant for life of one undivided quarter of a settled fund, no appropriation having been made, a life interest in all the settled property? In my opinion, and with deference to the arguments which have been presented in this case by counsel for the Crown, the answer to that question is an obvious one. The question answers itself, I think, in the negative. A life tenant of an undivided share has a life interest in that undivided share, not in the whole fund. He has an interest no doubt in every individual asset in the fund, but he does not have a life interest in the whole of any of those assets. He has a life interest only in an undivided share of each of those assets. So I find myself in agreement with what was said by Walton J. in the course of his judgment in *Pexton* v. *Bell* [1975] 1 W.L.R. 707, 710 where he said.

> "The situation here was that Mrs. Roberts was certainly not possessed at the time of her death of a life interest in possession in all the settled property. That would be an absurd suggestion. She

A was entitled to a life interest in possession in part of the settled property, namely, a one quarter share."

Now, it has been submitted in this court by counsel for the Crown that " part " in subsection (4), in the expression " part of settled property," and in subsection (12) in the expression " part of the settled property," —those are subsections of section 25—does not extend to and include
B an undivided share in the settled property, but carries the meaning which can be rather neatly conveyed by the synonym " parcel," which was in fact a word used by Mr. Potter in the course of his reply; that is to say, it is said that it is used in a sense indicating an identifiable asset vested in the trustee. But, if that is the sense in which " any part of settled property " is to be construed in subsection (4) of section 25, then in my opinion subsection (4) could not apply at all upon the cesser of a
C life interest in an undivided share, and that would lead to a most extraordinary effect under the section as a whole, as it seems to me.

So I reach the conclusion that in subsection (4) " any part of settled property " must be intended to extend to and include an undivided share of the settled property. That seems to me to be a natural meaning for the words " any part " to bear, and one which in the context of
D that subsection it is, I think, reasonably clear that they are intended to bear. It is quite true that when one turns to subsection (11), one finds a context which indicates that the words " part of the property comprised in a settlement " there refer to identifiable assets the legal ownership of which is vested in particular trustees. But they bear that meaning because the context in that subsection requires them to bear
E it there, whereas in my judgment the context in subsection (4) requires the word " part " to be given a wider meaning capable of including an undivided share. Then, if subsection (4) were to be read alone, the result would be that upon the life tenant's life interest terminating, all the assets forming part of the settled property would be deemed to be disposed of. That would be all the assets comprised in the trust; not the undivided share, but all the physical assets. But, when one looks
F at subsection (12), one finds that that position is rectified, because it provides that if there is a life interest in a part of the settled property, and there is not a right of recourse to other parts of the settled property, then for the purposes of subsection (4), amongst other subsections, the part of the settled property in which the life interest subsists is to be treated as being settled property under a separate settlement; so that, upon the death of a life tenant of an undivided share, that undivided
G share is to be treated as being the subject of a separate settlement, and it is only in respect of that undivided share that the assets comprised in the settlement are to be treated as disposed of and reacquired by the trustees under the operation of subsection (4). This construction seems to me to give both rational and intelligible effect to the section, whereas the alternative construction contended for upon this appeal by the
H Crown in my opinion gives an irrational operation to the section. Therefore, I prefer the one which results in the rational effect.

It has been suggested that to construe the words in this way will result in great complications in the working out of the trust and the working out of the tax position in respect of capital gains tax, upon later events. I am not persuaded myself that those complications are nearly as great as has been suggested, but I think it would be dangerous to try to explain why, because one would almost inevitably choose

examples which would turn out to be ill-chosen; and this, after all, is A
an aspect of the case of wide application. So I do not say more about that.

For these reasons, as well as those elaborated by Sir John Pennycuick, I agree that the appeal in *Pexton* v. *Bell* fails. It follows that the other appeal before us, of *Crowe* v. *Appleby*, also fails on the same ground; and I agree that it is unnecessary to express any concluded view upon
the other question which has been argued in *Crowe* v. *Appleby*, which B
Sir John Pennycuick has referred to in the course of his judgment. So I say nothing further about that part of the case. In the result, both appeals will be dismissed.

Appeals dismissed with costs.

Solicitors: *Solicitor of Inland Revenue; Stanleys & Simpson North* C
for Chapman, Baker & Wilson, Brighton; Hunt & Hunt, Romford.

[COURT OF APPEAL] D

* GILSON *v.* KERRIER DISTRICT COUNCIL

[1969 G. No. 2554]

1976 March 23, 24, 25 — Buckley, Geoffrey Lane and Goff L.JJ. E

Public Health—Water supply—Artificial watercourse—Watercourse constructed by public subscription over farmland to provide water supply for village—Watercourse so constructed as to benefit farm—Cessation of use by village—Whether public supply—Whether vested in local authority—Watercourse rendered inaccessible outside farm—Whether cessation of
public supply—Whether determination of estate vested in local F
authority—Whether farm owner's consent to accumulation of water to be inferred—Public Health Act 1875 (38 & 39 *Vict.* c. 55), *s.* 64 [1]

Rylands v. *Fletcher—Exceptions to rule—Consent to danger—Escape of water from watercourse—Watercourse constructed over farmland to provide public water supply—Watercourse so constructed as to benefit farm—Liability*

G

The plaintiff was the fee simple owner of a tenanted farm across which flowed an artificial watercourse constructed in 1845 by public subscription to provide a supply of water for the inhabitants of a nearby village. The watercourse was constructed in such a way as to provide a supply of water for the farmyard and three fields though no grant of any right to take water was made to the owner of the farm. In 1963,
following the establishment of a main water supply and main H
drainage for the village, the watercourse downstream of the farm was covered over and rendered inaccessible. In 1968, by virtue of the South Cornwall Water Board Order 1967, " the water undertakings " (including waterworks) " of such . . . councils as are . . . supplying water " were transferred to the water board. In 1969 following heavy rain serious flooding occurred on part of the farm and neighbouring land due to

[1] Public Health Act 1875, s. 64: see post, p. 908A–B.

A a blockage in the watercourse. The plaintiff brought an action against the local authority, the rural district council, for a declaration that the council was under a duty to maintain the watercourse or alternatively was liable to take steps to prevent damage from the watercourse arising by reason of its constituting a nuisance or trespass, and damages. Templeman J. dismissed the action.

On appeal by the plaintiff:—

B *Held*, dismissing the appeal, (1) that there was no justification for limiting the vesting provision of section 64 of the Public Health Act 1875 to supplies of water fit for human consumption; that, in any event, the supply of water established in 1845 by means of the watercourse was a supply for all purposes (post, pp. 908D, 914B-D); that the watercourse comprised "conduits aqueducts and works used for the gratuitous supply of water to the inhabitants of the district" within the
C meaning of section 64, its character as a public supply being unaffected by the fact that the occupants of the farm enjoyed benefits not enjoyed by other inhabitants; that, accordingly, the watercourse vested in the council by the operation of section 64 (post, p. 908E–G); and that that vesting extended to all the works of a man-made kind which contributed to making the water available to members of the public in the area (post, p. 908H).

D (2) That on the vesting of the watercourse under section 64 the council acquired an estate in fee simple absolute and not a determinable estate (post, p. 911E); that, accordingly the council would not cease to be liable for the watercourse merely by discontinuing its use as a public supply; and that, in any event, the watercourse did not cease to be a public supply after it was rendered inaccessible downstream of the farm as its use by the farm, which continued thereafter, con-
E stituted the enjoyment of a public supply and not a private right (post, p. 911D).

(3) That in 1968 the watercourse, as an asset then vested in the council in relation to its water undertaking, was transferred to and vested in the South Cornwall Water Board by virtue of the South Cornwall Water Board Order 1967 (post, p. 912E–F); that, accordingly, in 1968 the council ceased to be liable for the watercourse.

F (4) That, in any event, the council would not have been liable to the plaintiff in nuisance or under the rule in *Rylands* v. *Fletcher* as it was proper to infer that the owner of the farm at the time had consented to the construction of the watercourse across his land because of the benefits ensuing to the farm therefrom (post, pp. 912H—913B); and that, further, it was incumbent on the plaintiff, having leased the farm, to prove damage to her reversion which she had not done (post, p. 913E).

G *Carstairs* v. *Taylor* (1871) L.R. 6 Ex. 217 and *A. Prosser & Son Ltd.* v. *Levy* [1955] 1 W.L.R. 1224, C.A. applied.

Decision of Templeman J. affirmed on different grounds.

The following cases are referred to in the judgments:

Buckley (R. H.) & Sons Ltd. v. *N. Buckley & Sons* [1898] 2 Q.B. 608, C.A.

H *Carstairs* v. *Taylor* (1871) L.R. 6 Ex. 217.

Foley's Charity Trustees v. *Dudley Corporation* [1910] 1 K.B. 317, C.A.

Prosser (A.) & Son Ltd. v. *Levy* [1955] 1 W.L.R. 1224; [1955] 3 All E.R. 577, C.A.

Rolls v. *Vestry of St. George the Martyr, Southwark* (1880) 14 Ch.D. 785, C.A.

Tithe Redemption Commission v. *Runcorn Urban District Council* [1954] Ch. 383; [1954] 2 W.L.R. 518; [1954] 1 All E.R. 653, C.A.

Tunbridge Wells Corporation v. *Baird* [1896] A.C. 434, H.L.(E.).

The following additional cases were cited in argument: A

Jones v. *Llanrwst Urban Council* [1911] 1 Ch. 393.

Rust v. *Victoria Graving Dock Co. and London and St. Katharine Dock Co.* (1887) 36 Ch.D. 113, C.A.

Sedleigh-Denfield v. *O'Callaghan* [1940] A.C. 880; [1940] 3 All E.R. 349, H.L.(E.).

Smith v. *Archibald* (1880) 5 App.Cas. 489, H.L.(Sc.).

B

APPEAL from Templeman J.

By writ dated July 16, 1969, and later amended the plaintiff, Mrs. Mary Denise Gilson, the fee simple owner of " Trebarvah," 37 acres of land in Cornwall, claimed a declaration that the defendant, Kerrier District Council (formerly Kerrier Rural District Council), was under a statutory or other or alternatively a common law duty to maintain and C repair a watercourse running through the plaintiff's land or alternatively was liable to take such steps by way of maintenance and repair as were appropriate to prevent damage from the watercourse arising by reason of its constituting a nuisance or trespass; and damages.

By its defence the council denied that the watercourse was or had ever been vested in the council; but that if it had the watercourse was now vested in the South Cornwall Water Board by reason of the South D Cornwall Water Board Order 1967, or alternatively that the watercourse, having ceased to be used as a water supply or for sewerage purposes, had divested from the council and revested in the plaintiff. On February 13, 1975, Templeman J. dismissed the action holding that, although all the works on the plaintiff's land had vested in the council by the operation of section 64 of the Public Health Act 1875, the estate so vested had E determined, the use of the watercourse by the occupiers of the plaintiff's farm being in the nature of a private right.

By notice of appeal dated June 20, 1975, the plaintiff appealed on the grounds that the judgment was wrong and that there was no or insufficient evidence to support the judge's findings that (1) in 1845 it was intended to create or continue a private water supply to the farm F as well as to create a public supply for the village; and (2) the water supply was now used as a water supply for the farm.

The facts are stated in the judgment of Buckley L.J.

J. A. R. Finlay Q.C. and *Patrick Powell* for the plaintiff.

Mervyn Davies Q.C. and *G. C. Raffety* for the defendant council.

G

BUCKLEY L.J. This is an appeal from the dismissal by Templeman J. of this action on February 13, 1975. The subject matter of the dispute is a watercourse traversing a farm called Trebarvah in the parish of Constantine in Cornwall. The farm and the village lay at all material times within the district of the defendant council. The farm lies to the north of the village of Constantine. The plaintiff is the owner of the H fee simple of the farm.

The watercourse is an artificial watercourse carrying water from certain springs situated some four miles to the north or north-west of Trebarvah. It seems that the water from these springs flows eastwards for a short distance in a natural course to a point in or near ordnance survey 830. There, instead of continuing to flow eastwards as it naturally would, it is diverted through an artificial course in a southerly direction

A through a farm called Trewardreva and another called Bosahan to a
point on the boundary of Trebarvah at the north-east corner of ordnance
survey 1039, which is a field called High Castle Rise and which forms
part of Trebarvah farm. The watercourse then makes a right-angled
turn in a westerly direction across High Castle Rise to its north-west
corner, where it passes under a road by means of a culvert and, having
done so, turns immediately south down the western margin of ordnance
B survey 1036, which is another Trebarvah field, called Mowey Field.
Near the southern extremity of that field it again passes by means of
another culvert under the same road in an easterly direction into ordnance
survey 1040, a third Trebarvah field called Lower Castle Rise, and flows
south for a short distance down the western margin of that field, leaving
the farm at the south-west corner of Lower Castle Rise. It then appa-
C rently flows down the verge of the road in a south-easterly direction to
the village of Constantine. It continues down what appears from the
ordnance survey map to have been the main street of the village and
continues on in the same direction until it flows into a stream running
through ordnance survey 2217.

At the point where the watercourse enters High Castle Rise there is
a catchpit or pool of no very great size, and from that point to the
D north-west corner of High Castle Rise the watercourse is carried under-
ground in a culvert or drain. At the point near the southern extremity
of Mowey Field where the watercourse passes for the second time
under the road, a pipe leads out of the watercourse through the farmyard
of Trebarvah and rejoins the watercourse near where it leaves the
farm in the verge of the road. Some means were provided for access
E to the water from this pipe in the farmyard.

The judge held that down to the point at which it enters High Castle
Rise the channel was an ancient one. The judge assumed that at that
point it was diverted to the course downstream from that point which I
have described in the year 1845. That assumption has not been chal-
lenged and indeed has been accepted by Mr. Davies in this court. In
F or about 1845 a public supply of water was brought to the village of
Constantine by public subscription by means of the watercourse as I
have described it. Except where it crosses High Castle Rise and at two
points upstream from there, the watercourse at that time and for many
years afterwards flowed in an open channel.

In 1899 the local authority, the East Kerrier District Council, sued
the then occupant of Trebarvah in the local county court for damages
G for having breached a dam on the watercourse forming part of or
adjoining the catchpit in the north-east corner of High Castle Rise. We
have a fairly full report of the case published in the "Falmouth Packet
and Cornwall Advertiser" on May 13, 1899. The judge inferred from
the 1899 report that the dam was part of the works carried out in 1845,
but I think this must have been a misapprehension on his part, for,
H according to the 1899 report, the particular dam which was the subject
matter of the county court proceedings had been installed by the East
Kerrier District Council. This would not have been until after 1875.
The evidence as recorded indicated that formerly a mud obstruction had
performed the function of the dam at that point. Neither the 1899
report nor any of the evidence in this case establishes what course the
water followed before the works carried out in 1845. But, on the view
which I take of the case, this is of no significance.

Whatever the history may have been, this watercourse was not, where A
it traversed Trebarvah, a natural stream. It was an artificially constructed watercourse used for the supply of water to inhabitants of the village of Constantine and its neighbourhood.

The Public Health Act 1875, section 64, provides as follows:

> "All existing public cisterns pumps wells reservoirs conduits aqueducts and works used for the gratuitous supply of water to the B
> inhabitants of the district of any local authority shall vest in and be under the control of such authority, and such authority may cause the same to be maintained and plentifully supplied with pure and wholesome water . . ."

In the county court proceedings in 1889 the case of the plaintiff council (as it then was) was that the watercourse had vested in the C
council under section 64. In the present proceedings the plaintiff similarly asserts that the watercourse vested in the council under that section, but the defendant council denies this. Mr. Davies has contended that, upon its true construction, section 64 only applies to a supply of water fit for human consumption, and he says that the watercourse did not provide such a supply. It is true that the section empowers a local D
authority to provide a plentiful supply of pure and wholesome water, but I see no justification for limiting the operation of the vesting provision in the way suggested. In any case, the judge found as a fact that the supply of water as established in 1845 was a supply for all purposes, and I see no reason to disturb that finding.

In my judgment, the watercourse with which we are concerned does fall within the words "conduits aqueducts and works" in section 64. E
The supply of water to the inhabitants of the district was gratuitous. It was gratuitous also so far as the occupants of Trebarvah were concerned, and the fact that the occupants of Trebarvah enjoyed benefits in respect of watering their cattle which were not enjoyed by other inhabitants does not seem to me to take the case out of the section. In the sense that this water supply was available to be enjoyed by all who had access to it F
anywhere along its course, it was a public supply; and, indeed, the history of its conception by public subscription and the fact that the public subscription was designed to provide water in the village clearly indicates, in my judgment, that this was a public supply. Accordingly, in my judgment, this watercourse did vest in the defendant council by the operation of section 64, and that was the view of the judge.

It might be convenient to mention at this point that in 1969, due to G
a particularly heavy rainfall and to a blockage in the watercourse at or near the catchpit, serious flooding occurred. The flood water flowed down over Lower Castle Rise and flooded some bungalows situated to the south of that field on land which did not form part of Trebarvah. Thereafter, the plaintiff from time to time urged the council to carry out works of maintenance on the watercourse, but nothing was done and the H
council eventually disclaimed any liability to carry out any such works.

The next question to which I turn is: what was the estate which vested in the council under section 64? In my judgment, what vested extends to all the works of a man-made kind which contributed to making the water available as a public supply to members of the public in the area. This must, in my opinion, embrace all the man-made or man-contrived diversions of the watercourse which resulted in the water

A being accessible to members of the public within the relevant area; and this, I think, must embrace the whole of the watercourse upstream to the point in ordnance survey 830 where it had been first diverted from what would otherwise have been its natural flow.

The judge, in the course of his judgment, said:

> "I accept that section 64 applied, the water in the first instance at
> B any rate being provided for all purposes. I reject Mr. Mervyn Davies' next submission that the catchpit, Cornish drain and culverts"—the reference to the Cornish drain is a reference to where the water passes underground across High Castle Rise—"were not public works within section 64 because the public did not have access to them. It appears from the 1899 report and from the evidence that the council had access to the whole of the watercourse as it
> C flowed through Trebarvah Farm on behalf of the public and for the purpose of maintaining the supply of water to the public in the village, and in my judgment that suffices."

For my part, I think that the vesting operated not only in respect of the works actually on Trebarvah Farm, but also extended to any artificial works upstream to the point where the artificial diversion first operates.

D In or about 1946 the Cornish drain referred to by the judge in that passage was replaced by the defendant council by a pipe. That appears to have been an unsatisfactory job in the first instance, and in 1948 another pipe was substituted for the pipe first installed to replace the Cornish drain. That work was carried out by the defendant council at their own expense.

E The next question, I think, is: what was the nature of the estate which vested in the council under the section? We have been referred, in this connection, to *Tithe Redemption Commission* v. *Runcorn Urban District Council* [1954] Ch. 383. That was a case which related to a highway, and the question was whether there was vested in the highway authority a sufficient interest in the highway to make the authority liable to contribute to the relevant tithe redemption annuity. The section of the
F Public Health Act 1875 dealing with highways is section 149, which provides:

> "All streets, being or which at any time become highways repairable by the inhabitants at large within any urban district, and the pavements stones and other materials thereof, and all buildings implements and other things provided for the purposes thereof,
> G shall vest in and be under the control of the urban authority. . . ."

The question was, as I say, whether whatever estate in the highways was vested in the local authority as highway authority was sufficient to render them liable for payment of tithe redemption annuity. This court came to the conclusion, following certain earlier authorities, that a highway authority which had a highway vested in it under the section
H acquired an estate which was known to the law, namely, a determinable fee simple; and, because that was a legal estate known to the law, the court came to the conclusion that the authority was liable to contribute to the tithe redemption annuity.

The authorities which the court followed were *Rolls* v. *Vestry of St. George the Martyr, Southwark* (1880) 14 Ch.D. 785; *Tunbridge Wells Corporation* v. *Baird* [1896] A.C. 434; and *Foley's Charity Trustees* v. *Dudley Corporation* [1910] 1 K.B. 317. From the first of those cases it appears that the court construed section 149 by reference to its particular language, for in a passage cited in the *Tithe Redemption* case [1954] Ch. 383, 399 James L.J. said, 14 Ch.D. 785, 796:

> "It appears to me that the legitimate construction of the enactment that streets being highways shall vest is that streets if and so long as they are highways shall be vested. . . . So in this case it appears to me that when the thing has ceased to be a highway, when it has ceased to be a street, then it ceases to be vested, because the period for which it was to be vested in the board has come to an end."

He drew a comparison between the estate so vested and the estate given to a lady during widowhood.

That point is brought out perhaps rather more clearly by what was said by Fletcher Moulton L.J. in *Foley's Charity Trustees* v. *Dudley Corporation* [1910] 1 K.B. 317, 324, a passage which is cited in the *Tithe Redemption* case [1954] Ch. 383, 408. What Fletcher Moulton L.J. said was:

> "Therefore the defendants have this property in the land in question. It certainly includes the surface, and it includes so much as is necessary to support the surface as a road. For what period does this last? It is a fee simple subject to this, that if the road should be properly and legally abandoned and cease to be a highway, then the freehold will revert to some other person."

In that case the court was concerned with a different section of the Act of 1875 from the one with which we are concerned, which was couched in different language, and it was concerned with a different kind of subject matter. A highway when it has ceased to be a highway is inert. It may be an awkward piece of property for the person to whose ownership it reverts, but it is unlikely to give rise to nuisance or any acute problems of maintenance. A watercourse, on the other hand, is dynamic. If the watercourse is not kept clean and in repair, the water will be liable to damage not only the property traversed by the watercourse but other neighbouring property as well. It would, in my opinion, be surprising if, by merely discontinuing the use of a watercourse as a public supply, the local authority could shift on to the shoulders of the owners or occupiers of the land through which the watercourse passes, to whom it would revert if there were a reverter, the burden of maintaining it in a state in which it would not be likely to cause trouble. Moreover, a highway can only cease to be a highway if it is formally closed by a closure order under the Highways Act 1959 or by statute or under some statutory authority. There must be some formal legal act putting an end to its existence as a highway. There is no similar procedure for putting an end to a water supply as a public water supply.

In the present case it is suggested that the watercouse with which we are concerned de facto ceased to be used as a public supply in or about 1963 when the part of the watercourse downstream from the point at which it leaves Trebarvah was covered over and rendered inaccessible, following the establishment of a main water supply which was piped to the houses in the village and the establishment at about the same time of main drainage. But the question whether the estate vested in the local authority under section 64 is determinable or not has to be decided in the light not of the facts of the present case, but of the sort of facts which would be likely to occur in other cases as well. I think that in

A a great number of cases it would be very difficult, if not well nigh
impossible, to determine precisely at what point of time what had
previously been a public water supply ceased to be used as a public water
supply.

Indeed, in the present case, has the public supply afforded by this
watercourse wholly ceased to exist? I think not. The judge regarded
the use of the watercourse by the occupiers of Trebarvah as in the nature
B of a private right. I take a different view. In 1845 the subscribers chose
to conduct the new channel which they then constructed across certain
Trebarvah fields as an open watercourse. They did so in a way which
was clearly designed to make water available to animals pastured in the
three Trebarvah fields through which it passed. In doing so they
certainly made water available to Trebarvah Farm. There is no
C evidence of any grant to the owner of Trebarvah of any right to take
water from the watercourse; nor, on the other hand, is there any evidence
of any express grant to anyone of a right to take the watercourse over
the farm. The inference to be drawn is, I think, that by implication
the owner of Trebarvah agreed to the watercourse being taken over his
land in the knowledge that in fact he would in that way get a free
supply of water to three of his fields and to his farmyard. In this way
D he would benefit from the establishment of the gratuitous public supply
which the works were designed to provide. Although Trebarvah's enjoyment of the supply so provided was different in character from the
enjoyment of it by a villager living in the village street, I see no reason
to regard it as other than a form of enjoyment of the gratuitous public
water supply afforded by the works. If this be right, the public supply
E has never wholly ceased.

In my judgment, a highway cannot properly be regarded as analogous
for present purposes to a watercourse, and I would hold that the watercourses vested in the council for an estate in fee simple absolute and
not for a determinable estate. Consequently, I reject the submission
that whatever estate vested in the council under section 64 has determined. I therefore differ from the judge in his conclusion, which I
F understand to have been based upon the contrary view, that on that
ground the council ceased to own the watercourse. But I think that it
has ceased to own the watercourse for another reason.

In 1967 an order was made, called the South Cornwall Water Board
Order 1967, S.I. 1967 No. 1928. It came into operation on December 27,
1967. By paragraph 15 of that Order it was provided:

G

> "(1) Subject to the provisions of this Order, on the day of transfer the transferred undertakings shall by virtue of this Order be transferred to and vest in the board. (2) For the purposes of this Order, any mains, pipes or other works so transferred shall be deemed to have been laid or constructed by the board."

H "The day of transfer" is defined in paragraph 3 (1) as April 1, 1968.
"The transferred undertakings" are defined in the same subparagraph
as meaning "the council's undertakings;" and the expression "the councils'
undertakings" is defined as meaning

> "the water undertakings of such of the constituent councils as are immediately before the day of transfer supplying water in any part of the limits of supply and includes subject to the provisions of this order:—(*a*) all the lands, buildings, waterworks, water, sources of

supply"—and there is a long catalogue of things—"vested in or enjoyed by the transferor councils respectively in relation to their respective water undertakings immediately before the day of transfer and all liabilities and obligations to which they were then subject in relation to those undertakings. . . ." A

Then the definition goes on to include benefits and records, and contains certain exceptions which I do not think I need read. The board referred to is the South Cornwall Water Board. B

Mr. Finlay says that the watercourse with which we are concerned was not part of a water undertaking immediately before the day of transfer. He says that, I think, because he asserts that it was not at that time supplying water in any part of the limits of supply. If I am right in thinking that the estate in this watercourse which vested in the council had not determined by April 1, 1968, this watercourse was, in my judgment, then vested in the council in relation to its water undertaking, such as it was. It may have been an obsolete or an obsolescent asset of that undertaking, but I think that it must have been vested in the council in relation to its water undertaking, unless the council could be said at that time to have had no such undertaking. That it had no such undertaking has certainly not been established; and, having regard to the view which I have expressed about the nature of the enjoyment of the watercourse by the occupants of Trebarvah, I am of opinion that the contrary is the case. We do not know to whom the public supply which was installed in 1963 belongs, or whose undertaking it was. It may have been the undertaking of the local authority; that we do not know. But, on the evidence before the court, it certainly is not established, in my opinion, that the defendant council then had no water undertaking; and, if it had a water undertaking, then I think that this was an asset which was at that time vested in the council in relation to that undertaking. C D E

Consequently, it seems to me—and for the purposes of this appeal I hold—that on April 1, 1968, the watercourse with which we are concerned vested in the South Cornwall Water Board. This decision will, of course, be binding only upon the parties to these proceedings, and not upon the water board. But, for the purposes of this appeal, I proceed upon that footing. F

It follows that the council cannot be liable for any damage suffered by the plaintiff in consequence of the flooding in 1969, subsequent to the date of the vesting of the watercourse in the South Cornwall Water Board. That flooding seems to have been due to a failure to clear away flotsam which had accumulated against a grid over the outflow from the catchpit into the culvert under High Castle Rise. G

We were referred to *Carstairs* v. *Taylor* (1871) L.R. 6 Ex. 217 and *A. Prosser & Son Ltd.* v. *Levy* [1955] 1 W.L.R. 1224 as authority for the proposition that, even if the council was not immune from liability on any of the grounds which I have already discussed, it could not be liable either in nuisance or under the rule in *Rylands* v. *Fletcher* if the works were carried out for the benefit of, amongst other persons, the occupiers of Trebarvah. As I understand those cases, they proceeded upon the basis that anyone who collects a potentially dangerous subject matter such as an accumulation of water on his own property is not liable for damage caused by its escape to another person for whose benefit, at least H

A in part, the accumulation was made and whose consent to the accumu-
lation should consequently be inferred.

In the present case, for reasons already indicated, I consider that
the proper inference from the nature of the works is that the owner of
Trebarvah at that time consented to the watercourse being constructed
across his land because of the benefits he would obtain from being able
to get access to the water. Mr. Finlay says that the plaintiff's predecessor
B in title may have consented to water running over Trebarvah in an
innocuous and properly controlled manner, but did not consent to its
being allowed or caused to accumulate so as to overflow. This would
no doubt be relevant to a claim against the council in negligence, but
not, in my opinion, to a claim in nuisance or under the rule in *Rylands*
v. *Fletcher*, if no negligence is alleged. Negligence was pleaded in the
C present case, but was not pursued in the court below, nor is it mentioned
in the plaintiff's notice of appeal.

Mr. Finlay has urged that no element of joint benefit or of consent
by the owner of Trebarvah was pleaded, but the point that the water-
course was so constructed as to benefit Trebarvah came out clearly in
the evidence and no submission was made to the judge that the point
D was not open on the pleadings. Counsel may perhaps have been some-
what taken by surprise by the emergence of this aspect of the case and
by the reliance placed upon it by the judge, but I think that it is too late
at this stage for the plaintiff to rely upon a pleading point. Accordingly,
even if not immune on any other ground, I think that the council would
be immune on this ground of consent.

Moreover, Trebarvah has been leased by the plaintiff to a tenant
E farmer who is in occupation. So it would be incumbent on the plaintiff,
if she could otherwise succeed in the action, to prove damage to her
reversion; and this, in my opinion, she has not done.

For these reasons, which are not precisely those upon which the
judge reached his conclusion, I come to the conclusion that he was right
in dismissing the action; and, accordingly, I would dismiss this appeal.

F

GEOFFREY LANE L.J. It is unfortunate that this appeal has done so
little to provide any final solution to the problems which face the plaintiff.
It is to be regretted—at least with hindsight—that the South Cornwall
Water Board were not joined as defendants, so that that authority could
have argued their case and been bound by the result. It is also to be
G regretted that the argument before the judge proceeded on the basis of
an allegation of nuisance or *Rylands* v. *Fletcher* type of liability when, as
it now appears, the true cause of action, if one existed at all, was in
negligence.

Be that as it may, I agree that this appeal must be dismissed, for the
reasons already advanced, subject to one very small matter. I would not
H go so far as to hold—nor indeed do I think it is necessary in determining
this appeal so to hold—that any part of the watercourse north of the point
where it enters the land of Trebarvah Farm ever vested in the local
authority under section 64 of the Public Health Act of 1875.

GOFF L.J. I agree that this appeal should be dismissed, for the
reasons which have been given, and I desire only to add a very few
words of my own.

So far as the reach of the watercourse north of Trebarvah is concerned, I respectfully agree with Geoffrey Lane L.J. that it is not necessary to make any finding about it; but, if it were, I would agree with the conclusion reached by Buckley L.J.

So far as the initial vesting under section 64 is concerned, as Buckley L.J. observed, the judge found that the water, in the first instance at any rate, was provided for all purposes, and I agree that there is no occasion to go behind that. Even if one did, however, in my judgment the result would still be the same. Mr. Mervyn Davies argued that the only purpose which the water ever served was to flush the stream where it flowed through the village and where the villagers used to empty slops and because dirt from the road might enter the water. I think that is too narrow a view, because there was evidence in the 1899 proceedings that when the works were done in 1845, taps were provided for the villagers; and, if that be right, those taps must have been at all events for general domestic purposes, if not to provide drinking water. But, even if the matters were as narrow as Mr. Mervyn Davies would have it, section 64 does not require that the water should be provided for drinking purposes; and section 51 refers to " a supply of water proper and sufficient for public and private purposes." In my judgment, therefore, even if the matter were as Mr. Mervyn Davies would have it, the result would still be the same.

The only other point on which I wish to comment is with regard to *Carstairs* v. *Taylor*, L.R. 6 Ex. 217 and *A. Prosser & Son Ltd.* v. *Levy* [1955] 1 W.L.R. 1224. On that aspect of the matter, Mr. Finlay relied on *R. H. Buckley & Sons Ltd.* v. *N. Buckley & Sons* [1898] 2 Q.B. 608. In that case, the owner of a goit and sluice gate, which served his mill and the mill of an adjoining owner, was held liable for damage caused to the property of the adjoining owner through the goit being out of repair. At first sight that might appear strange, because there the goit and sluice gate were used for the benefit of both owners. The explanation and reconciliation of that case is that, when the goit and sluice gate were made, they were made exclusively for the owner of them, and the fact that the adjoining owner later by prescription or grant acquired rights over them did not affect the position.

For the reasons given by my brethren and with these slight additions of my own, I agree that this appeal should be dismissed.

Appeal dismissed with costs.

Solicitors: *E. P. Rugg & Co. for Frank & Caffin, Truro; Balderston, Warren & Co. for Hancock & Lawrence, Helston.*

C. N.

A

[CHANCERY DIVISION]

* THORN AND OTHERS *v.* INLAND REVENUE COMMISSIONERS

1976 March 4, 5 — Walton J.

B *Revenue—Stamp duty—Variation of settlement—"Conveyance or transfer operating as a voluntary disposition"—Beneficiary relinquishing protected life interest in income of trust fund for no consideration—Trust fund thereafter held for unascertained class of beneficiaries—Beneficiary relinquishing reversionary life interest in income and taking discretionary interest—Whether operating as "voluntary disposition" capable of valuation—Whether stamp duty payable—Finance*
C *(1909–1910) Act* 1910 (10 *Edw.* 7 & 1 *Geo.* 5 *c.* 8), *s.* 74 (1) (5)

In 1947 the settlor settled 50,000 5s. shares in his company on trustees to hold the income on protective trusts for his wife for life and thereafter to pay the income from one half of the fund to his son and from the other half to his daughter. After their deaths the two halves were to be held on discretionary trusts for the grandchildren or remoter issue
D as the trustees should appoint. In 1951 the settlor increased the trust fund by £19,375. In 1965 the court approved under the Variation of Trusts Act 1958 an arrangement varying the settlement so as to mitigate the effects of estate duty that would become payable on the death of the settlor's wife. By that arrangement the settlor's wife gave up her life interest in the daughter's share of the fund and the daughter relinquished her life interest in 20 per cent. of her half share and took a
E discretionary interest in the remaining 80 per cent. At the date of the order the trust fund was valued at £3,467,852. On the order being presented to the Commissioners of Inland Revenue for adjudication as to whether stamp duty was payable, the settlor's contentions that stamp duty was not payable because the only property conveyed by the order was (i) his wife's right to receive income until a forfeiture occurred which right had no value and (ii) her discretionary interest
F that would arise on such forfeiture and which had only a nominal value, were rejected by the commissioners. They also rejected a further contention that the settlor's daughter had been compensated under the order for relinquishing part of her life interest so that such disposition was not a voluntary disposition that attracted stamp duty. Accordingly they held that the order was for the purpose of section 74 of the Finance (1909–10) Act 1910[1] a conveyance attracting stamp duty
G which they assessed at £1,880·50.

On appeal against the assessment:—

Held, dismissing the appeal, (1) that the effect of the scheme of variation was to transfer the totality of the income during the life of the settlor's wife and, although the consent of everyone who might conceivably have an interest in that income was requisite, it was the total income which was the
H subject matter transferred and not a collection of separate interests of indeterminate value; accordingly the order operated as a voluntary disposition that was capable of valuation and was liable to stamp duty by virtue of section 74 of the Finance (1909–10) Act 1910 (post, pp. 921C–D, G—922A).

[Reported by MRS. HARRIET DUTTON, Barrister-at-Law]

[1] Finance (1909–10) Act 1910, s. 74 (1) (5): see post, p. 918B–D.

(2) That in ascertaining whether the settlor's daughter's A
disposition was or was not "voluntary," the test to be applied was the objective one of whether a satisfactory bargain had been made and that as that was a family arrangement with no evidence that that was the case the disposition had rightly been held to be "voluntary" and to attract ad valorem stamp duty (post, pp. 923C–D, G—924A).

Attorney-General v. *Kitchin* [1941] 2 All E.R. 735, C.A. distinguished. B

The following cases are referred to in the judgment:

Attorney-General v. *Kitchin* [1941] 2 All E.R. 735, C.A.
Gartside v. *Inland Revenue Commissioners* [1968] A.C. 553; [1968] 2 W.L.R. 277; [1968] 1 All E.R. 121, H.L.(E.).
Inland Revenue Commissioners v. *Crossman* [1935] 1 K.B. 26, C.A.; [1937] A.C. 26; [1936] 1 All E.R. 762, H.L.(E.). C
Letts v. *Inland Revenue Commissioners* [1957] 1 W.L.R. 201; [1956] 3 All E.R. 588.
Nelson, In re (*Note*) [1928] Ch. 920, C.A.

The following additional cases were cited in argument:

Aschrott, In re [1927] 1 Ch. 313.
Baker v. *Inland Revenue Commissioners* [1924] A.C. 270, H.L.(E.). D
Cassel, In re [1927] 2 Ch. 275.
Holmden's Settlement Trusts, In re [1968] A.C. 685; [1968] 2 W.L.R. 300; [1968] 1 All E.R. 148, H.L.(E.).
Lynall decd., In re [1972] A.C. 680; [1971] 3 W.L.R. 759; [1971] 3 All E.R. 914; 47 T.C. 375, H.L.(E.).
Stanyforth v. *Inland Revenue Commissioners* [1930] A.C. 339, H.L.(E.).
Weir's Settlement Trusts, In re [1971] Ch. 145; [1969] 3 W.L.R. 860; E
[1970] 1 All E.R. 297, C.A.

CASE STATED by the Inland Revenue Commissioners.

In 1947, the settlor, Sir Jules Thorn, settled 50,000 5s. shares in Thorn Electrical Industries Ltd. on protective trusts for his wife for life and then for his two children for life and thereafter on discretionary trusts F
for their children or remoter issue. In 1951, a sum of £19,375 was added to the settlement by the settlor. In 1964, by an order of the court made under the Variation of Trusts Acts 1958, the settlement was varied in that the settlor's wife voluntarily relinquished some of her rights under the settlement and the settlor's daughter's rights were altered. At the date of the order the settled property was valued at £3,467,852. The settlor, the trustees, Frederick Maw and Harry Swales, G
and the settlor's daughter, Mrs. Ann Rylands, appealed against an assessment to ad valorem stamp duty of £1,880·50 made on the order when it was presented to the Inland Revenue Commissioners for adjudication under section 12 of the Stamp Act 1891.

The facts are set out in the judgment.

H

J. M. Price for the settlor, his daughter and the trustees.
D. J. Nicholls Q.C. and *Peter Gibson* for the Crown.

WALTON J. By a settlement made on January 31, 1947, the settlor, Sir Jules Thorn, the well-known industrialist and bencher of the Middle Temple, settled 50,000 shares of 5s. each in his company, Thorn Electrical Industries Ltd., upon trusts for the benefit of his wife, son and daughter. The income of the whole of the trust fund was to be held upon protective trusts for the benefit of his wife during her life. Thereafter the trust fund was to be divided into two. One moiety was to be held upon trust to pay the income to his son for life, and after his son's death this half was to be held for his children and remoter issue as the trustees should appoint, and in default of appointment in trust for all his children who if male should attain the age of 21 years or if female should attain that age or marry, and if more than one in equal shares. The other moiety of the trust fund was held upon identical trusts, mutatis mutandis, for the daughter, Mrs. Rylands, and her children and remoter issue. There were also provisions for accruer between the shares, and an ultimate trust for charity if all the trusts concerning both such moieties should fail or determine.

To the funds so settled, the settlor added, on March 22, 1951, a sum of cash of £19,375. His company prospered mightily, and by January 21, 1964, the trust fund was worth some £2·7 million. It had therefore come to represent a sitting target from the point of view of death duties, so the settlor's wife caused an arrangement under the Variation of Trusts Act 1958 to be prepared and presented to the court. The essential features of this scheme, which only applied to the daughter's moiety, were: (i) that the life interest of the settlor's wife was eliminated; (ii) that 20 per cent. of this moiety should forthwith be held as to capital and income for the then present and future children of the settlor's daughter who should attain the age of 21 or being females attain that age or marry, and if more than one in equal shares; and (iii) that 80 per cent. of this moiety should forthwith be held upon trust to pay or apply the income therefrom as it arose to or for the benefit of all or any one or more exclusively of the others or other of the settlor's daughter and her issue as the trustees should think fit. As soon as any child of the settlor's daughter attained the age of 21 (or, if female, married)—thus, of course, eliminating any question of accruer between the two moieties, the daughter's and the son's—there arose a power of appointment over capital and income among the settlor's daughter and her issue exercisable as the trustees in their absolute discretion should think fit in relation to this 80 per cent.

Application was duly made to the court to sanction this scheme, and by the time the scheme was so sanctioned (on April 17, 1964) the trust fund had, I was informed, topped the £3 million mark. The order of April 17, 1964, was not immediately submitted for adjudication as regards stamp duty; the current practice of requiring an undertaking from the plaintiff to present the order for adjudication did not come into effect until two years later. Some question having arisen which required the production of the order to the inspector of taxes, however, the order was ultimately, in August 1966, so presented.

It will be observed that the salient features of the scheme from the point of view of stamp duty were as follows. (i) That whereas the income from the whole of the moiety of the daughter was formerly payable to the settlor's wife on the usual protective trusts during her lifetime, it was now disposed of to the beneficiaries of the 20 per cent. and 80 per cent. slices of the moiety; and that this was, so far as the settlor's wife was concerned, an act of pure bounty on her part. She received no consideration of any nature under the scheme. (ii) That the daughter surrendered the whole of her prospective reversionary life interest in

the income of her moiety after the death of her mother, but this was A
not entirely without recompense so far as she was concerned as she was one of the discretionary beneficiaries of the 80 per cent.

The crucial statutory provisions are those contained in section 74 (1) and (5) of the Finance (1909–10) Act 1910, which, so far as material, read as follows:

> "74 (1) Any conveyance or transfer operating as a voluntary dis- B
> position inter vivos shall be chargeable with the like stamp duty as if it were a conveyance or transfer on sale, with the substitution in each case of the value of the property conveyed or transferred for the amount or value of the consideration for the sale: . . ."

There is a proviso to that which I need not read.

> "(5) Any conveyance or transfer (not being a disposition made in C
> favour of a purchaser or incumbrancer or other person in good faith and for valuable consideration) shall, for the purposes of this section, be deemed to be a conveyance or transfer operating as a voluntary disposition inter vivos, and (except where marriage is the consideration) the consideration for any conveyance or transfer shall not for this purpose be deemed to be valuable consideration where
> the commissioners are of opinion that by reason of the inadequacy D
> of the sum paid as consideration or other circumstances the conveyance or transfer confers a substantial benefit on the person to whom the property is conveyed or transferred."

This section, by virtue of section 96 (5) of the Act of 1910, is to be construed together with the Stamp Act 1891.

There are in fact separate trustees of the 20 per cent. and the 80 E
per cent., and they are all together the appellants. Their contentions with regard to the income of the daughter's moiety during the life of the settlor's wife are set out in the case stated as follows:

> "The appellants contended that in respect of the income of the daughter's moiety during the life of [the settlor's wife], the only
> property conveyed or transferred by virtue of the order was—(i) [the F
> right of the settlor's wife] to receive that income until a forfeiture was incurred by her, which right was not capable of being sold on the open market and accordingly had no value; and (ii) [the interest of the settlor's wife] as an object of the discretionary trust of income to arise on such forfeiture, which interest had only a nominal value."
G

They also gave notice on February 25, 1976, that they would be taking further points as follows:

> "(1) They will contend that the order of April 17, 1964, did not operate as a disposition of the discretionary interests of the persons other than [the settlor's wife] under the protective trusts declared by
> the settlement, because the effect of the order was to extinguish H
> those interests. (2) They will further contend that if the order did operate as disposition of the discretionary interests of those persons, then it was not a voluntary disposition, because the effect of the order, having regard to the exception to the proviso to section 1 (1) of the Variation of Trusts Act 1958, was to expropriate those interests. (3) They will further contend that if the order did operate as a voluntary disposition of the discretionary interests of those

A persons, then it operated as a separate disposition of the interest of each such person and not as a single disposition of the whole of their [and the settlor's wife's] combined interests; that each such disposition should be separately assessed for stamp duty purposes; and that the value of the property transferred by each such disposition was nominal. (4) They will further contend that if the order did operate as a voluntary disposition of the discretionary
B interests of any of those persons, then the only persons on whose part there was any such disposition were those who took no beneficial interest under the trusts declared by the arrangement set forth in the schedule to the order."

Their contentions with regard to the disposition of the daughter's reversionary life interest were as follows:

C "The appellants further contended that the disposition by the daughter of her reversionary life interest in the daughter's moiety contained no element of bounty as she was adequately compensated therefor by the interests which she took under the trusts as varied by the order, and that accordingly such disposition was not a voluntary disposition attracting ad valorem stamp duty."

D The Commissioners of Inland Revenue, on the other hand, were of the opinion that for the purpose of section 74 of the Act of 1910 a conveyance operated as

"(i) a voluntary disposition by [the settlor's wife] and the other persons who in the event of a forfeiture by [the settlor's wife] of her protected life interest would have discretionary interests under the
E protective trusts as expressed in section 33 (1) Trustee Act 1925, such disposition being of the whole of their combined interests in the income of the daughter's moiety of the trust fund during the life of [the settlor's wife]; (ii) a voluntary disposition by the daughter of her reversionary life interest in the daughter's moiety, subject to the interest which she took as an object of the discretionary trust of the
F income of 80 per cent. of that moiety and the possibility of benefiting as an object of the trustees' power of appointment over the capital and income of that 80 per cent."

They therefore assessed the duty payable as follows:

"Ad valorem conveyance on sale duty at 50p per £50 on the transfer of the interests of the income beneficiaries in the daughter's moiety
G during the life of [the settlor's wife] valued at £182,650," stamp duty payable £1,826·50;

"Ad valorem conveyance on sale duty at 50p per £50 on the transfer of the daughter's reversionary life interest valued at £5,400," £54·00; "Total duty on the order—£1,880·50."

There is no dispute as to these figures if the general contentions of the
H commissioners are correct. The settlor, his daughter and the trustees were dissatisfied with the assessment made, so they paid the duty, as they were bound to do, and appealed to this court, requiring the commissioners to state and sign the case from which I have been reading. The case stated concluded:

"The questions for the opinion of the court are: (i) whether the order is liable to duty as assessed by the commissioners; (ii) if not, to what duty it is liable."

Mr. Price, for the settlor, his daughter and the trustees, analysed the A matter as follows. He said that section 74 raised the following questions: (i) was there a conveyance or transfer? (ii) if so, did it operate as a voluntary disposition? (iii) if so, what was the property conveyed or transferred? (iv) what was the value of that property? He accepted that the answer to his first question was in the affirmative in the light of section 62 of the Stamp Act 1891, which reads as follows:

B

> " Every instrument, and every decree or order of any court or of any commissioners, whereby any property on any occasion, except a sale or mortgage, is transferred to or vested in any person, is to be charged with duty as a conveyance or transfer of property."

Then there is a proviso to that which I need not read. He also accepted, in the light of section 74 (5) of the Act of 1910, that it was a voluntary C disposition, because the settlor's wife received no recompense for it.

It was as regards question (iii) that Mr. Price made his stand. He submitted that all that was transferred was the bundle of rights which the settlor's wife had under the original settlement, which were: (a) the right to receive income until a forfeiture occurred; and then (b) the right to receive income as an object of the discretionary trust of income D which then arose under section 33 (1) of the Trustee Act 1925. He further submitted that these interests were basically incapable of valuation; by itself, each individual right was of no ascertainable value, particularly having regard to the fact that the first and the more important of the two rights, so far as the settlor's wife was concerned, was quite incapable of sale, since a sale would destroy the right; and even if one were to follow the analogy of the well known company case of E *Inland Revenue Commissioners* v. *Crossman* [1937] A.C. 26 and were to consider the position of somebody standing in the shoes of the settlor's wife, this would not work, because merely by this kind of switch the essential nature of the interest was completely altered. Whose bankruptcy would now cause the forfeiture?

Mr. Price then faced the fact that the powers of the court, under F section 1 of the Variation of Trusts Act 1958, extend to approving a scheme in the present class of case on behalf of

> " any person in respect of any discretionary interest of his under protective trusts where the interest of the principal beneficiary has not failed or determined . . . Provided that except by virtue of " the very paragraph I have been reading " the court shall not approve an G arrangement on behalf of any person unless the carrying out thereof would be for the benefit of that person "

that being precisely the position in the present case, since the settlor's wife had not, prior to the date of the order, forfeited her life interest.

Here, Mr. Price's submission was that the effect of the consent to the scheme on behalf of each person so interested by the court was, at H the highest, to effect a conveyance by that person of his or her own individual parcel of rights to the beneficiaries benefited thereby. There was, in effect, a number of voluntary dispositions, one by each such person (and, of course, one by the settlor's wife herself). The provisions of section 4 of the Stamp Act 1891, which reads as follows:

> " Except where express provision to the contrary is made by this or any other Act,—(*a*) An instrument containing or relating to several

A distinct matters is to be separately and distinctly charged, as if it
were a separate instrument, with duty in respect of each of the
matters; . . ."

ensured that each of these dispositions should be treated separately, and
separately assessed for stamp duty. However, the rights of each and
every one of these persons were so shadowy, and of so little worth, that
B they had only a nominal value, and therefore no stamp duty whatsoever
was payable in respect of the transaction. And, anticipating the kind
of analysis which he expected Mr. Nicholls, for the Crown, to make of
the situation, Mr. Price submitted that the interests of the discretionary
beneficiaries were competing interests: they were not like joint tenants,
or tenants in common, so that when the totality of discretionary benefi-
C ciaries joined in or consented to the scheme they were not jointly or
severally making a disposition of the whole of the income arising from
the relevant moiety of the trust fund during the life of the settlor's wife,
they were merely dealing with their own separate interests.

Mr. Nicholls, on the other hand, as correctly anticipated by Mr.
Price, submitted that what was being disposed of by the scheme was the
whole of the income during the life of the settlor's wife, and that, although
D in order to effectuate that purpose the consent of every person who
might conceivably have any interest in that income under the trusts
imposed by section 33 of the Trustee Act 1925 was requisite, what they
were by the scheme doing, all of them acting together, was to dispose of
that whole income, and not their own separate interests.

In my opinion, there is no answer to this analysis by Mr. Nicholls.
E Doubtless, it might be possible to frame a scheme which took effect as
a separate assignment of each individual bundle of rights on behalf of
each person who might possibly be an object under the trusts declared
by section 33; but, in view of the fact that it can never, save in
exceptional circumstances, be postulated that all such persons are known
and ascertained at the date of the scheme (and, if they were, the
matter could of course be dealt with entirely out of court), I doubt
F whether this is, in fact, a practical possibility. It would certainly not
be in the present case, where the court has expressly consented to the
scheme on behalf of unborn and unascertained persons. It is quite
ridiculous to think that there has been any attempt to assign the interests
of such persons. What has been done is quite different: the relevant
income has been disposed of as a whole by the process of obtaining the
G consent to such disposition of every single person who has, or who might
hereafter have, any title to such income on any account.

What Mr. Price was in effect attempting to do is to split up the
entirety of the income into individual parcels and to say that, because
the individual parcels cannot be valued, the totality of what has been
disposed of is also valueless. But this is, in fact, patently not the case.
Although no individual right can be valued, the totality of those
H individual rights makes up a single, composite whole; and it is the single,
composite whole which is most plainly being dealt with. In the present
case, the owners of all these interests were simply assenting to a
direction to the trustees to hold the totality of the life interest upon
different trusts. This is not, I think, a point which admits of much
elaboration. It has always been recognised, certainly from *In re Nelson*
(*Note*) [1928] Ch. 920, reported as a note, onwards, if not before, that if
all those who had any conceivable interest all joined together in disposing

of a fund they were entitled so to do although their own particular interests A
might, by themselves, be one and all unquantifiable. As Lord Reid put
it in one of the cases which was quoted to me, the sum of x, y and z
might well be shown to be 100 although neither x, y nor z could be
quantified: *Gartside* v. *Inland Revenue Commissioners* [1968] A.C.
553, 606. In such circumstances, unless the form of the document in
question drives one to the conclusion that the owners of those three
interests are, indeed, disposing of their own separate interests, logic and B
common sense alike indicate that what they are doing is to dispose of the
totality of the interest being dealt with. Moreover, it is interesting to
observe that in *In re Nelson* the Court of Appeal treated the present
kind of case, i.e., a gift of a protected life interest, as being in substance
the gift of the life interest with particular provisions as to the mode of
enjoyment superadded. If this be the right way to look at the matter, C
then the argument that that which the beneficiaries dispose of when
they all join together to effect such a disposition is the whole life interest
and nothing else is immensely strengthened.

Mr. Price did not pursue his alternative submission, set out in the
notice of February 25, 1976, to the effect that the order of April 17,
1964, did not operate as a disposition of the discretionary interests of the
persons other than the settlor's wife, since the effect of the order was to D
extinguish those interests, with any vigour. Of course, that, in one sense,
is the effect of the order, but the extinguishment is not the result of the
destruction of those interests but of their kaleidoscoping together into
the interest actually disposed of. Nor was it in any sense any expropria-
tion of those interests. The court is empowered to consent to the scheme
on behalf of the owners of such interests, and that is just what it did. E
Of course, it may well be that some of such persons are also bene-
ficiaries of the new trusts declared of the 20 per cent. and the 80 per
cent., but I cannot possibly regard this circumstance as being sufficient
to negative the purely voluntary nature of the disposition of the life
interest in income. In respect of that disposition, nobody received any
consideration. F

This is sufficient to deal with the first point which arises. I may add
this out of respect to the arguments which were addressed to me by both
sides in relation to an alternative basis of claim by the commissioners on
the supposition that the settlor's wife's protected life interest had, of
course together with the rights of all other interested parties, been
actually transferred under the scheme, on the basis that this interest G
should then be valued on the same kind of lines as were used in *Inland
Revenue Commissioners* v. *Crossman* [1937] A.C. 26 to value shares
which could not in fact be freely transferred. I would only say that I
remain wholly unconvinced that there is any comparison whatsoever
between the two kinds of cases. If the matter had been material, my
present inclination is to agree with the submissions of Mr. Price to the H
effect that, since a protected life interest is attended by circumstances all
of which are personal to the life tenant, any assumed transferee would
of necessity hold an interest entirely different from that of the transferor.
In my view, if the matter had indeed proceeded as (i) a transfer of the
interests of the settlor's wife, plus (ii) separate transfers of everybody
else's interests, those interests would all have been the same; namely, the
right to receive income as one of the members of the discretionary class,

A the protective trusts having been brought into operation by the very act of the settlor's wife making such a transfer.

I now turn to the second head of claim, that in relation to the disposition of the settlor's daughter's reversionary life interest. Here the contention of the settlor was that his daughter was adequately compensated for the surrender of this interest by the interests which she took under the scheme, albeit discretionary. Mr. Price first of all took the B point that under section 74 (5) of the Act of 1910 it was only where the commissioners were of the opinion that by reason of the inadequacy of the sum paid as consideration or other circumstances the conveyance or transfer conferred a substantial benefit on the person to whom the property was conveyed that that section bit, and that there was in the case stated no such expression of the commissioners' opinion. Mr. C Nicholls retorted that, be that so, there was the clearest possible inference from the case that that was indeed their opinion.

Without deciding this particular point, I will assume in Mr. Price's favour that there is no such express finding against him, and that the matter is therefore, so far as I am concerned, at large. Approaching the matter in this way, I am first of all of opinion that the true test must be, not whether the daughter thought she was in fact making a satisfactory D bargain but whether in fact she did so. In other words, that the test is objective rather than subjective. Mr. Price submitted that *Attorney-General* v. *Kitchin* [1941] 2 All E.R. 735, indicated that the test was subjective and not objective; but in that case what was in issue was the compromise of a claim honestly believed in. It is really impossible to quantify such a claim in monetary terms in any satisfactory manner E whatsoever, and if the parties against whom such a claim is made are prepared, as a pure matter of business, and not of bounty, to compromise it at a figure which others might think was excessive, how can the courts say they are wrong? Many an apparently cast-iron defence has been wrecked before now upon the unpredictability of witnesses' recollections, or a surprise decision of the House of Lords. But where there is no such problem, where there can be no doubt as to the facts of the interest F given up and the interests acquired, then the matter is, I think, purely one of weighing one against the other, as was done by Upjohn J. in *Letts* v. *Inland Revenue Commissioners* [1957] 1 W.L.R. 201. I may add that, even if I had been in favour of Mr. Price in principle on this point, I see not the faintest evidence from which I could properly infer that the daughter was, or thought she was, making a bargain of any description. G The whole initiative for the scheme appears to have emanated from the settlor's wife, who was herself, of course, making the whole thing possible by reason of her own willingness to give up her own very considerable personal benefits for the sake of the family as a whole. And, on the whole, I think that this is precisely what the daughter herself was doing when she gave up her reversionary life interest.

In the context of a family arrangement of this nature, I think the H proper way to regard the actions of a person who gives up a fixed and certain interest in exchange for the somewhat spectral interest of being included in a class of discretionary beneficiaries is that the interest has been given up for the benefit of those who obtain the benefit of it under the scheme, the benefit conferred by the discretionary trust being much more in the nature of a long stop, in case anything should go seriously wrong with the finances of the person giving up the interest thereafter,

rather than as a seriously intended quid pro quo. Mr. Price pointed out A
that this was the only manner in which the settlor's daughter could hope
to obtain any capital out of the trust. This is, of course, in one sense,
completely accurate, but if that was what she wanted she could quite
simply have bargained for some modest slice of capital when the scheme
was on foot. This she quite deliberately did not do; and I do not think
I can objectively regard the prospect of the trustees exercising their
powers in her favour to give her capital as representing, in any real sense, B
any entitlement to capital in her.

For the foregoing reasons, therefore, I propose to dismiss this appeal
on both heads.

Appeal dismissed with costs.

Solicitors: *Swales; Solicitor of Inland Revenue.* C

[CHANCERY DIVISION] D

* *In re* TEBBS, DECD.

REDFERN *v.* TEBBS AND ANOTHER

[1972 T. No. 3034] E

1976 March 16, 17 — Slade J.

Trusts — Trustee — Wilful default — Account — Trustees' admitted act of wilful default in respect of land forming part of estate— Whether order for account to be general or limited to affected land

By his will, the testator appointed his son, the first F
defendant, and the second defendant as executors and trustees
and bequeathed to them his share in three family companies,
which he controlled, to apply such part of the dividends as
might be necessary for the benefit of his wife and then, in
the events that happened, to transfer 80 per cent. of the
shares to the first defendant and the remaining 20 per cent.
to the testator's daughter, the plaintiff. The testator's residuary G
real and personal estate was to be divided equally between
the first defendant and the plaintiff. Clause 7 (*a*) of the will
provided that if practicable and satisfactory terms could be
agreed, the "Wash land" should be sold to one of the three
companies ("the company"). The testator died in 1965 and the
Wash land was included in the Inland Revenue affidavit as
valued at £5,642 and was eventually sold at that figure to the
company in September 1969 despite repeated warnings in H
correspondence from the plaintiff's solicitors that it would
be improper to sell the land except at its fair current market
price. Being dissatisfied with the administration of the estate
and with the accounts and information supplied to her, the
plaintiff issued an originating summons for relief including
a claim for an order for an account of the testator's real
and personal estate to be taken on the basis of the defendants'
wilful default. The first defendant admitted that the sale had
been an act of wilful default and that she was entitled to an

order for an account on the footing of wilful default in respect of the Wash land. He also conceded that she was entitled to a general account in respect of the rest of the estate, but not on the footing of wilful default as she desired.

On the question whether the court's discretion should be exercised to order on account on the footing of wilful default in respect of the whole real and personal estate in view of the one admitted act of wilful default:—

Held, that in determining whether a general account on the footing of wilful default should be ordered on the basis of one or more proved or admitted past breaches of trust, the court had to consider whether the past conduct of the trustees gave rise to a reasonable prima facie inference that other breaches of trust not yet known to the plaintiff or the court had occurred; that frank admissions by a defaulting trustees were merely a factor to be taken into account; in all the circumstances, there was no reasonable prima facie inference that there had been other breaches of trust and, therefore, the order for an account on the footing of wilful default would be restricted to the Wash land, an account being ordered in respect of the rest of the real and personal estate in common form.

Wildes v. *Dudlow* [1870] W.N. 231 considered.

The following case is referred to in the judgment:

Wildes v. *Dudlow* [1870] W.N. 231.

The following case was cited in argument:

Youngs, In re, (1885) 30 Ch.D. 421.

ORIGINATING SUMMONS

By an originating summons dated December 29, 1972, as amended pursuant to the fiat of Master Chamberlain dated July 18, 1974, the plaintiff, Mrs. Sherran Rosemary Redfern, sought against the defendants, Brian Edward Tebbs and William Ramsay Fox, the surviving executors of the will of her late father, Arthur Edward Tebbs, an order for an account of the testator's real and personal estate to be taken on the footing of wilful default.

The facts are stated in the judgment.

Jonathan Parker for the plaintiff.
P. St.J. Langan for the first defendant.
The second defendant did not appear and was not represented.

SLADE J. These proceedings concern the estate of Arthur Edward Tebbs, who died on November 15, 1965. The originating summons, in which the plaintiff is his daughter, Mrs. Sherran Rosemary Redfern, claims a wide variety of relief, including a prayer for the appointment of a judicial trustee and for a general order for administration. But in the event the only paragraph of the originating summons which is before me today is paragraph 5 of the amended pleading, which seeks an order for an account of the real and personal estate of the testator to be taken on the footing of wilful default.

The plaintiff is a beneficiary under the testator's will. The first defendant, Mr. Brian Edward Tebbs, is the principal beneficiary under the will and one of the two surviving executors. The second defendant, Mr. William Ramsey Fox, is the other surviving executor. He has no beneficial interest in the estate. He does not appear before me today but he has A sworn an affidavit in which he admits that the plaintiff is entitled to an account on the footing of wilful default of the real and personal estate of the testator.

Before the testator's death he and his son, the first defendant, had been concerned with running various family companies, which I understand mainly carried on gravel businesses, in which the testator held most of the shares. These three companies were Newark, Peterborough Sand and B Gravel Co. Ltd., William Tebbs and Sons Ltd., and A. E. Tebbs (Farms) Ltd. I will call A. E. Tebbs (Farms) Ltd., which features in this story again, "the company." The testator also owned in his own right the freehold of some 80 acres of land in Stanground Wash, which I will call "the Wash land." From the terms of his will it appears that at the date of his will the Wash land was occupied, or proposed to be occupied, by the C company.

By his will, which was dated October 1, 1965, the testator appointed his son the first defendant, Mr. Fox the second defendant and a Mr. William Henry Cleever as his executors and trustees. After giving certain specific and pecuniary legacies to his wife and his two children he then devised a freehold property to Mr. Cleever, gave a life interest to his D widow in a house called Windyridge and directed that on her death it should fall into his residuary estate. He then bequeathed to his trustees all his shares in the three companies and directed them to hold them upon trust, in effect, for the widow for her life or until her remarriage or the date when the first defendant should attain the age of 40 years, whichever should be the later date, and on such later date he directed his trustees to transfer the shares, in the events which have happened, as to 80 per E cent. to the first defendant and as to 20 per cent. to the plaintiff, Mrs. Redfern, who was then known as Sherran Rosemary Holman. The testator then devised and bequeathed all his residuary estate equally between the first defendant and the plaintiff.

By clause 7 (a) of his will, the testator then conferred on the company what was in effect an option to purchase. It was in these terms F

> "I hereby authorise, empower and direct my trustees (a) if practicable and satisfactory terms can be agreed to sell [the Wash land] and subject to the then existing terms of tenancy or user thereof by [the company] to [the company] at such price as may be agreed between my trustees and the company, failing agreement as shall be assessed by Messrs. Norman Wright and Partners as arbitrators." G

By clause 7 (b), he conferred what was in effect a right of pre-emption on members of his family or the family companies in the following terms:

> "That if any of the members of my family whether trustees or not or any of the family companies be tenants of any of the property passing under this my will the trustees shall before offering such properties for sale by private treaty or public auction if practicable cause H the said properties to be offered firstly to such tenants at a price to be ascertained by Messrs. Norman Wright and Partners on behalf of my trustees according to the then market price."

I think the wording of clauses 7 (a) and (b) is not entirely clear or satisfactory. One particular point which I think could have given rise to confusion is that the formula for ascertaining the price to be paid

A on the exercise of the option, or of the right of pre-emption respectively, is slightly different in each case; while clause 7 (b) contains an express reference to the "then market price" there is no express reference to the "then market price" in clause 7 (a). Nevertheless it is accepted by Mr. Langan, who appears on behalf of the first defendant, I think rightly, that clause 7 (a) did not entitle the trustees to sell the Wash land to the company at less than the full market value at the date of the sale.

B Probate of this will was granted on May 27, 1966, to the three executors. The estate was sworn at some £33,605 gross, and some £18,889 net, because the testator appears to have had some heavy liabilities. Mr. Cleever died about October 1966. In the same year the plaintiff instructed solicitors, Messrs. Roythorne & Co., in her interest. She wanted a speedy administration of the estate. A number of issues arose, most of which are
C not directly relevant to what is now before me. These issues included, for example, a possible set-off of an alleged debt of £400 against the £750 legacy due to the plaintiff under the will. There were also issues concerning valuations of shares in family companies. There were also allegations as to the absence of proper accounts. Eventually, after a number of years, on December 29, 1972, the present originating summons was issued in consequence of these and other issues, in particular the
D Wash land with which today's application is primarily concerned.

The Wash land was included in the Inland Revenue affidavit sworn by the executors at a figure of £5,642, which represented £70 an acre. Acting for the executors at that time were Messrs. Wyman and Abbott, solicitors of Peterborough. At all material times the partner in that firm dealing with the executors' business appears to have been an elderly solicitor,
E the late Mr. Abbott. No valuation was obtained prior to the insertion of this figure in the Inland Revenue affidavit. The first defendant thought it was either the second defendant or Mr. Abbott who supplied the figure.

On October 18, 1966, the district valuer wrote to Messrs. Wyman and Abbott saying that the case had been referred to him by the Estate Duty Office and asking for details of any sales that had taken place or were
F contemplated. After some intermediate correspondence, Messrs. Wyman and Abbott wrote to the district valuer on November 15, 1966, saying that the Wash land had been sold for £5,642. This statement was untrue, because at the time all that had been carried through was some negotiation in regard to the possible sale of the Wash land to the company. In due course I understand that the district valuer accepted this figure of £5,642 as representing the value of the land. It may or may not be that
G he was influenced by the representation that had been made to him by Messrs. Wyman and Abbott. But whether or not he was so influenced, it seems clear that no valuation of the land was ever effected either by the district valuer or by anyone else. He made no valuation of his own so far as appears from the evidence before me.

In the event the company was unable to raise the £5,642 required for
H the projected sale which was under discussion in 1966, and so it went off. But in about April 1969, the project was resurrected and the possibility was again mooted of selling the Wash land to the company at the probate value of £5,642.

Between May and September 1969, Messrs. Roythorne & Co. on behalf of the plaintiff, represented to Messrs. Wyman and Abbott over and over again, both orally and in correspondence, that the Wash land could only properly be sold to the company at its fair current market price

and that it would be improper for the executors to sell at the price of A
£5,642, or any other price without ensuring that it represented a fair current market price. Despite all the warnings which their solicitors had thus received, the executors carried through the sale of the Wash land to the company, about September 1969, at a price of £5,642. This was followed by repeated protests on behalf of the plaintiff by Messrs. Roythorne & Co. over the next year, who reiterated their point as to value and supported it with an extract from counsel's opinion. A wide B
variety of points were taken by Messrs. Wyman and Abbott in answer to these protests, including the suggestions that no valuation was required and that £5,642 was a fair price anyway. I do not propose to summarise these points further. Every one of them was bad.

Finally, in a letter of September 1, 1970, Messrs. Wyman and Abbott went so far as to "confirm" that a binding contract for the sale of the C
property to the company had been concluded by the executors before Mr. Cleever died, a point which like all the other points taken by Messrs. Wyman and Abbott was later abandoned on behalf of the executors.

Looking at the correspondence passing between Messrs. Roythorne & Co. and Messrs. Wyman and Abbott in 1969 and 1970, I am bound to say that I think the attitude taken on behalf of the executors by their then solicitors was consistently wrong headed and unreasonable. With their eyes wide D
open as to the legal position, in view of the warning which they had received from Messrs. Roythorne & Co., they nevertheless allowed the executors improperly to complete the sale to the company in about September 1969, without obtaining the professional advice as to value that plainly should have been taken. And then, after it had been completed, with equal obstinacy they resisted on his behalf any attempts by Messrs. E
Roythorne & Co. to get the position rectified without the need for proceedings. The first defendant told me in the witness box, and I accept, that he naturally relied on the advice of his solicitors, that he never knew of the existence of much of the correspondence that was read in court. His own attitude was, I think, also influenced by the fact that he personally believed that on the true interpretation of the will the executors were entitled to sell at less than the market value, though he now accepts, in F
the light of advice which he has since received, that this interpretation was wrong. Mr. Langan, however, quite rightly in all the circumstances, accepts that the first defendant cannot shelter behind any advice given to him by Messrs. Wyman and Abbott for the purpose of deciding the question whether the sale of the Wash land amounted to an act of wilful default. He accepts that it amounted to an act of wilful default on the G
part of the first defendant, and that the plaintiff is entitled to an account on the footing of wilful default in respect of the Wash land. He also accepts that the plaintiff is entitled to a general account in respect of the estate, but not on the footing of wilful default as claimed by her. This then is the area of dispute between the parties: should an account on the footing of wilful default be ordered merely in regard to the Wash land or in regard to the whole estate? H

One act of wilful default having been proved, it is common ground that the court has jurisdiction to make an order for an account on the footing of wilful default in respect of the whole estate. Mr. Parker, who appears on behalf of the plaintiff, also accepts that I have a discretion either to make this order or to make the more limited order suggested by Mr. Langan. Mr. Langan has relied heavily on the decision of the Court of Appeal in Chancery in *Wildes* v. *Dudlow* [1870] W.N. 231. The

A report is unfortunately extremely short but the facts, as appear from the report, were these:

> "The testator in this case had given a legacy of £5,000 to be paid in priority to any other legacies, and subject thereto he had given legacies to the plaintiffs. The plaintiffs filed a bill against the executors and the principal legatee to have the estate of the testator administered, charging the executors with wilful default. The executors, by their B answer, in effect admitted that they were liable for two sums lost or not received, but said that this was done with the assent of the principal legatee, whose legacy would more than exhaust the estate. The plaintiffs entered into no evidence. The Vice-Chancellor Malins made a decree for an ordinary account. The plaintiffs appealed, on the ground that the decree ought to have included an account of what C the executors might have received but for their wilful neglect and default."

Reading from the report, their Lordships said:

> "that as the executors had in fact admitted that they would be liable for the two sums mentioned, no case of wilful neglect or default was made out against them, and therefore no decree for such an account D could be made. The decree of the Vice-Chancellor was substantially right, and would be affirmed with a variation, that the executors submitted to be charged with the two sums in question."

This case is cited by *Williams & Mortimer, Executors, Administrators and Probate*, 15th ed. (1970), p. 583 as authority for the proposition that E if what is alleged is admitted, the practice is only to make the common decree for administration, adding a submission by the representative to account with respect to the matters so admitted. Mr. Langan on behalf of the first defendant relied on the fact that in an affidavit sworn in the proceedings on June 27, 1975, the first defendant had very properly said as follows:

> "I have been advised by my present solicitors and by my counsel that F I and [the second defendant] were under a fiduciary obligation to obtain the best price reasonably obtainable for Wash land and that if we failed to do so we were liable to make good to the trust estate any loss occasioned by our neglect together with interest."

He also relied on the fact that at the beginning of the hearing before me he expressly conceded on behalf of the first defendant that the plaintiff G was entitled to an account on the footing of wilful default in respect of the Wash land.

I cannot accept *Wildes* v. *Dudlow* [1870] W.N. 231 as constituting authority for the proposition that in any case where one or more acts of wilful default have occurred but these are admitted before or at the trial, the court will *never* make a general order for an account on the H footing of wilful default. First, it is not clear from the report that the court in *Wildes* v. *Dudlow* regarded the loss or failure to receive the two sums in question as having constituted wilful default. Secondly, I cannot believe that the court would decline to make a general order for an account on the footing of wilful default if, on the facts of a particular case, a number of past breaches of trust of a serious nature were admitted by the trustees at or before the hearing. The court would not, in my judgment, regard the admission as rendering any less necessary the roving inquiry to

which an account on the footing of wilful default will give rise. Never- A
theless I accept Mr. Langan's submissions based on *Wildes* v. *Dudlow*
to the extent that a frank admission by a defaulting trustee may be one
factor to which the court should pay regard in deciding on the form of
order it should make. If, in contrast, it has before it a case where a
trustee has persisted in denying the relevant facts or persisted in wrong-
ful assertions as to the legal position, even after it has become plain, the
court may be more inclined to consider that this is a case where the wider B
form of account should be taken, because the wrongful or misguided
persistence of the trustee itself supports the inference that he may have
been guilty of other wrongful or misguided acts in the administration
of the trust.

Counsel have not been able to refer me to any reported case in which
the court has discussed the principles which should be applied in exercising
its discretion as to whether or not a general account on the footing of C
wilful default should be ordered in a case where one or more past
breaches of trust have been proved or admitted. In the absence of such
authority it seems to me that the test should be this: is the past conduct
of the trustees such as to give rise to a reasonable prima facie inference
that other breaches of trust not yet known to the plaintiff or the court
have occurred? D

Mr. Parker, on behalf of the plaintiff, pointed out that the administration
of the estate has gone seriously wrong at least in relation to the Wash land,
and he referred me to a passage in an affidavit sworn by the plaintiff in
which she said:

> "The misconduct of the executors in relation to the sale of the Wash
> land has caused me to feel very considerable anxiety as to the way E
> in which the rest of the estate is being administered."

Mr. Parker pointed out that Mr. Abbott, who was the partner in Messrs.
Wyman and Abbott at all material times advising the first defendant,
had given advice in relation to the Wash land which was not only
incorrect but demonstrably bad advice. Mr. Abbott up to his death in
1971 had personally advised the first defendant and acted for him in F
the administration of the estate. In these circumstances Mr. Parker
submitted that it is not unreasonable for the plaintiff to be apprehensive
as to the other transactions as yet unknown to her which Mr. Abbott
might have advised in the administration of the estate and which might
have been carried out by the executors in reliance on such advice. The
breach of their duty over the Wash land was so serious. Mr. Parker G
submitted, as to lead to strong suspicions that other similar improper
transactions might have occurred, and he pointed to the fact that there
are three family companies involved here controlled by the first defend-
ant, which might increase the suspicions. I think there is some force
in these submissions. I think he is also right in saying that the first
defendant himself cannot be entirely acquitted from any personal blame H
in the sense that not only was he personally a party to the sale in 1969,
but he knew it was being effected at a figure which might well represent
less than its current market value, because that current market value
had never been tested. The first defendant, since he has realised the
true legal position, has told me that he recently obtained a valuation
of the property as at 1969, placing a value of £8,000 on the property.
While he naturally disclaimed any expert knowledge as to the value of

A the property he did not dispute the accuracy of this valuation as at that date.

On the other hand in my judgment the following points can fairly be made in the first defendant's favour, and indeed in favour of both the executors. First, Mr. Parker quite rightly disclaimed any suggestion that the first defendant had acted with any personal dishonesty. There is no evidence whatever that he or his co-executors acted otherwise than in good
B faith. He was at the time of his father's death a young man of 27 or 28 years. Mr. Abbott, he told me, was not only an elderly man but a man of strong personality. Not unnaturally, having sought legal advice from Mr. Abbott, he followed it. It was his misfortune that at least in relation to the Wash land the advice as it turns out, and as the first defendant now frankly admits, was incorrect advice and led to his effecting a sale to the
C company which should never have been effected. Secondly, while vigilant inquiries have been made on behalf of the plaintiff in relation to the administration of this estate by Messrs. Roythorne & Co. between 1966 and 1970, and by her present solicitors since about 1971 when they took over her affairs, they have failed to reveal any further instances of wilful default on the part of the executors. Mr. Parker pointed out in effect that there is an obvious limit to the extent to which inquiries can be effectively
D carried out by solicitors' correspondence, and that one of the purposes of ordering a general account on the footing of wilful default would be to enable the inquiry to be carried further, so that the plaintiff's suspicions could be either confirmed or allayed as the case might be. In the end, however, I am not satisfied that the present evidence—and I emphasise the present evidence—gives rise to a prima facie inference that other
E breaches of trust not yet known to the plaintiff or to the court have taken place.

Bearing in mind that the honesty of the executors is not in question and that the inquiries already made have revealed nothing beyond the Wash land transaction, I do not think I am justified in assuming the probability that other improper transactions may have occurred. In all the
F circumstances, I do not think it would be right at this stage to take the somewhat drastic step of ordering an account of the whole of the estate on the footing of wilful default. I therefore propose to order that an account be taken of the Wash land on the footing of wilful default. and that an account be taken of the rest of the testator's real and personal estate in common form. But I should emphasise, in conclusion, that I am not finally dismissing the plaintiff's claim for an account on the footing of
G wilful default in respect of the rest of the estate. At any subsequent stage of the proceedings it will be open to the court, upon evidence of further default being produced to it, to direct further accounts and inquiries on that footing. If the plaintiff wishes to have express liberty to apply for further accounts and inquiries upon producing such evidence, I shall give her such liberty.

H *Order accordingly.*
Liberty for plaintiff to apply for further accounts and inquiries.

Solicitors: *Wedlake Bell for G. F. Lodder & Sons, Stratford-upon-Avon; Bower, Cotton & Bower.*

T. C. C. B.

A

[QUEEN'S BENCH DIVISION]

* TREWBY AND OTHERS *v.* CUSTOMS AND EXCISE COMMISSIONERS

1976 March 19; April 1 — Geoffrey Lane L.J., Kenneth Jones and Goff JJ. B

Revenue — Value added tax — Exempt supply — Subscription to members' club — Club owning land providing facilities for sport and recreation—Members' beneficial ownership of land —Whether subscription paid for interest in or licence to occupy land — Whether exempt supply — Finance Act 1972 (*c.* 41), *s.* 13 (1), *Sch.* 5, *Group* 1, *item* 1 (*as substituted by Value Added Tax* (*Consolidation*) *Order* 1974 (*S.I.* 1974 *No.* 1146, *Sch.* 2) C

A members' club occupied a club-house and about 40 acres of land on which facilities for various sports were provided. Under the rules of the club a member had the right to enjoy the club facilities and, in the event of the club being dissolved, a share in the assets of the club in proportion to the D amount of the subscription paid. The Customs and Excise Commissioners rejected value added tax returns made on behalf of the club, on the ground that they were incorrect in that they excluded any sum for value added tax on the members' subscriptions and entrance fees and made an assessment which included tax on those items. The appellant, the club secretary, appealed on behalf of the members of the club to the value added tax tribunal against the assessment on the E ground that by the payment of his subscription a member obtained the grant of an interest in, or right over or a licence to occupy land and that such a supply was exempt from tax under section 13 (1) and item 1 of Group 1 of Schedule 5 to the Finance Act 1972.[1] The tribunal dismissed the appeal.

On appeal against the decision of the tribunal: —

Held, dismissing the appeal, that a member of the club paid his subscription for the right to enjoy the facilities pro- F vided by the club for sport and recreation and not for the incidental right of an undivided share in the beneficial ownership and the potential right to share in the proceeds on the club being dissolved (post, p. 937B–C); that such beneficial ownership could neither be described as "any interest in or right over land" within the meaning of item 1 of Group 1 nor a licence to occupy any part of the club's premises and, accordingly, the facilities provided by the club on payment of G the subscription were not an exempt supply within section 13 (1) of the Act (post, pp. 937G–H, 938A–B).

The following cases are referred to in the judgment of the court:

Campbell v. *Thompson* [1953] 1 Q.B. 445; [1953] 2 W.L.R. 656; [1953] 1 All E.R. 831.

Customs and Excise Commissioners v. *Automobile Association* [1974] H 1 W.L.R. 1447; [1974] 1 All E.R. 1257; [1974] 3 All E.R. 337, D.C.

Customs and Excise Commissioners v. *Guy Butler* (*International*) *Ltd.* [1976] Q.B. 106; [1975] 3 W.L.R. 36; [1975] 2 All E.R. 245, D.C.

[Reported by MRS. H. WHICHER, Barrister-at-Law]

[1] Finance Act 1972, s. 13 (1): see post, p. 936B.
Sch. 5, Group 1, item 1: see post, p. 936C–E.

A *Edis's Declaration of Trust, In re* [1972] 1 W.L.R. 1135; [1972] 2 All E.R. 769.

National Provincial Bank Ltd. v. *Hastings Car Mart Ltd.* [1965] A.C. 1175; [1965] 3 W.L.R. 1; [1965] 2 All E.R. 472, H.L.(E.).

The following additional cases were cited in argument:

British Airports Authority v. *Customs and Excise Commissioners* [1975]
B 3 All E.R. 1025, D.C.

Carlton Lodge Club v. *Customs and Excise Commissioners* [1975] 1 W.L.R. 66; [1974] 3 All E.R. 798, D.C.

Customs and Excise Commissioners v. *Glassborow* [1975] Q.B. 465; [1974] 2 W.L.R. 851; [1974] 1 All E.R. 1041, D.C.

Ellenborough Park, In re [1956] Ch. 131; [1955] 3 W.L.R. 892; [1955] 3 All E.R. 667, C.A.

C *Graff* v. *Evans* (1882) 8 Q.B.D. 373, D.C.

Newcastle City Council v. *Royal Newcastle Hospital* [1959] A.C. 248; [1959] 2 W.L.R. 476; [1959] 1 All E.R. 734, P.C.

Rochdale Hornets Football Club Co. v. *Customs and Excise Commissioners* [1975] V.A.T.T.R. 71.

Sick and Funeral Society of St. John's Sunday School, Golcar, In re [1973] Ch. 51; [1972] 2 W.L.R. 962; [1972] 2 All E.R. 439.

D

APPEAL from value added tax tribunal.

The Hurlingham Club, Fulham, London, was required by the Finance Act 1972, to submit returns to the Customs and Excise Commissioners of their assessment of their liability for value added tax from the period November 1, 1973, to January 31, 1974. The return sent in by the club
E was for £219·33. The commissioners rejected that return and assessed the club in the sum of £13,042·26 as tax on the supplies made to the members for their subscriptions and entrance fees. The club appealed to the value added tax tribunal in London.

On August 29, 1975, the tribunal dismissed the appeal of the secretary of the club, David Forsyth Allan Trewby on behalf of himself and all
F the members of the club, against the commissioners' assessment for the period November 1973 to January 1974. There were also two other assessments for the periods February 1 to April 30, 1974, and May 1 to July 31, 1974.

The club appealed on the grounds, inter alia, that since the tribunal had held that the supply by the club to its members was basically the right to use the club's premises and that that was a right over land, the
G tribunal had erred in law in holding that such supply was not an exempt supply as falling within item 1 of Group 1 of Schedule 5 to the Finance Act 1972; and that since the tribunal had held that the members of the club owned the assets of the club and also that the members were the occupiers of its premises, they erred in law in holding that no part of the subscriptions or entrance fees were attributable either to the supply of
H any interest in land or licence to occupy land within the exemptions in Schedule 5, Group 1, item 1.

The facts are stated in the judgment of the court.

Peter Whitworth for the appellant.

Robin Auld Q.C. and *Harry Woolf* for the respondent commissioners.

Cur. adv. vult.

April 1. GEOFFREY LANE L.J. read the following judgment of the A court. This is an appeal by David Forsyth Allan Trewby on behalf of himself and all other members of Hurlingham Club (hereinafter called "the club") from a decision of the value added tax tribunal in London. The respondents are the Customs and Excise Commissioners. The tribunal gave its decision on August 28, 1975, in proceedings under section 40 of the Finance Act 1972. Those proceedings were themselves by way of appeal from the decision of the commissioners whereby they assessed B the club in respect of value added tax at a figure greatly in excess of that which the club deemed lawful or proper.

These are the facts. The club is an unincorporated members' association carrying on its activities in an area of some 40 acres laid out as gardens, tennis courts, croquet lawns and so on. The land lies on the north side of the River Thames near Putney railway bridge. The club C is a "taxable person" under the relevant enactments and was required by Part I of the Finance Act 1972 and regulation 46 (1) of the Value Added Tax (General) Regulations 1972 to furnish not later than February 28, 1974, a return showing the amount of value added tax payable by them in respect of the period November 1973 to January 1974. The club sent in such a return showing the amount of £219·33 as being the sum properly payable. The club made no secret of the fact that in arriving at D that figure it had excluded from the calculation of the net tax payable all receipts for supplies made to members and in particular all members' subscriptions.

The commissioners took the view that that return was incorrect and they made an assessment of the figure which they considered to be correct. Here again, it is only fair to point out that the club gave the com- E missioners every assistance by the provision of figures and information to enable them to arrive at a proper assessment, should the commissioners' reading of the relevant statutory provisions be correct and the club's wrong. This assessment was served on the club secretary. The commissioners' assessment was £13,000-odd.

Two other assessments of a similar nature were made in respect of succeeding periods. Exactly similar problems arise on these. The club F appealed against them as well. The decision on the main point as hereafter appears will serve to determine equally the correctness or otherwise of the other two assessments.

The club has eight categories of member, by far the greatest in number being "ordinary members" who on January 1, 1974, numbered 3,361. The total of all categories of member is some 6,500. In 1973 the ordinary G members paid almost £115,000 by way of annual subscription. The club's contention before the commissioners was that the supplies made in consideration of the subscriptions and other payments made by the members were virtually all exempt supplies under the Finance Act 1972. The tribunal rejected that contention and the club appeals to this court under the provisions of the Tribunals and Inquiries Act 1971.

H

The material rules of the club are as follows:

"2. The object of the club shall be the maintenance of a club house and grounds for the use of the members of the club and their families and friends.

"31. The president and trustees shall be elected by the members in general meeting, and they shall respectively hold office until death or resignation, unless removed from office by a resolution of the

A members in general meeting. The number of trustees shall be not less than two or more than four, and the freehold and leasehold property and the investments of the club shall be placed in their names or under their control as custodian trustees. They shall deal with such property of the club as directed by resolution of the committee . . .

"56. If at any general meeting a resolution for the dissolution of B the club shall be passed by a majority of the members present and such resolution shall at a special general meeting held not less than one month thereafter at which not less than one-half of the members shall be present be confirmed by a resolution passed by a majority of two-thirds of the members voting thereon, the committee shall thereupon, or at such future date as shall be specified in such resolu- C tion, proceed to realise the property of the club and after the discharge of all liabilities shall divide the same rateably in proportion to the amount each member has paid in entrance fee (if any) and subscriptions among all the ordinary, life, country and service members, and upon the completion of such division the club shall be dissolved."

The relevant provisions in the Finance Act 1972 are as follows. D Section 1 (1):

"A tax, to be known as value added tax, shall be charged in accordance with the provisions of this Part of this Act on the supply of goods and services in the United Kingdom (including anything treated as such a supply) and on the importation of goods into the United Kingdom."

E Section 2:

"(1) Except as otherwise provided by this Part of this Act the tax shall be charged and payable as follows. (2) Tax on the supply of goods or services shall be charged only where—(*a*) the supply is a taxable supply; and (*b*) the goods or services are supplied by a taxable person in the course of a business carried on by him; and shall F be payable by the person supplying the goods or services. . . . (4) Any reference in the following provisions of this Part of this Act to the supply by any person of goods or services is a reference to such a supply in the United Kingdom in the course of a business carried on by him."

Then by section 5 it is provided:

G "(1) The following provisions apply for determining for the purposes of this Part of this Act what is a supply of goods or services. (2) Supply of goods includes all forms of supply and, in particular, the letting of goods on hire and the making of a gift or loan of goods; but supply of services does not include anything done otherwise than for a consideration. . . . (8) Subject to the preceding provisions of this H section, anything which is not a supply of goods but is done for a consideration (including, if so done, the granting, assignment or surrender of the whole or part of any right) is a supply of services."

Pausing there, the tax is to be charged on the supply of services in the United Kingdom where the supply is a taxable supply and the services are supplied by a taxable person in the course of a business carried on by him. Anything not a supply of goods if done for a consideration is a supply of services. By section 45 (1) it is provided:

> "In this Part of this Act 'business' includes any trade, profession A or vocation; and— . . . (*b*) the provision by a club or by an association to which this paragraph applies of the facilities available to its members; . . ."

There is no doubt that upon those various sections without any exempting provisions the club would have been liable to tax in respect of the subscriptions from its members. However, exempting provisions are to be B found in section 13 (1) and (2) of the Act as follows:

> "(1) A supply of goods or services is an exempt supply if it is of a description for the time being specified in Schedule 5 to this Act. (2) The Treasury may by order vary that Schedule by adding to or deleting from it any description of supply or by varying any description of supply for the time being specified in it." C

The original Schedule has been so varied [Value Added Tax (Consolidation) Order 1974 (S.I. 1974 No. 1146)]—and at the material times it read as follows as was agreed between the parties. Item 1 of Group 1 of Schedule 5 as amended reads as follows:

> "The grant, assignment or surrender of any interest in or right over land or of any licence to occupy land, other than—(*a*) the provision D of accommodation in a hotel, inn, boarding house or similar establishment or of holiday accommodation in a house, flat, caravan or houseboat; (*b*) the granting of facilities for camping in tents or caravans; (*c*) the granting of facilities for parking a vehicle; (*d*) the granting of any right to take game or fish; (*e*) the granting of any right to fell and remove standing timber; and (*f*) the granting of E facilities for housing, or storage of, an aircraft or for mooring, or storage of, a ship, boat or vessel."

The outcome of this appeal turns on the meaning of those words as applied to the circumstances of this case.

Mr. Whitworth on behalf of the club makes the following submissions: (1) that this being a members' club the beneficial ownership of the club F property and land is in the individual members; bound inter se by the club rules governing its disposal, but free in principle to change such rules: *In re Edis's Declaration of Trust* [1972] 1 W.L.R. 1135, 1141 *per* Goulding J; that whatever else the member gets in return for his subscription he gets that share in the beneficial ownership of the club land; that that is an interest in or a right over land and accordingly what is G supplied to the member in return for the consideration of his subscription is an exempt supply under section 13 (1) of the Act. Mr. Whitworth prays in aid, in support of this part of his submissions, the fact that by rule 56 of the club rules, the terms of which have already been set out, upon dissolution of the club the property has to be realised and the net proceeds divided amongst those who are then members.

If these submissions are correct, it means that members' clubs would H be exempt whereas proprietary clubs would be subject to the tax, since members of the latter have no beneficial share in the land owned by the club. That is perhaps a small point, but the Act does not expressly draw any distinction between the two types of club, see section 45 (1) (*b*).

In our judgment this submission fails. Tax is to be charged only where the relevant services are, inter alia, supplied in the course of a business carried on by the taxable person; see section 2 (2) (*b*). By section 45 (1) (*b*), that part of the club's activities which is deemed to be a business (when apart from the express words of the section it would not be) is "the provision . . . of the facilities available to its members." The acquisition by a member of an undivided share in the beneficial ownership of the land could not, we think, be described as the acquisition of a facility. Thus it is very doubtful whether there is any need to go as far as the exemption clause at all. In so far as the subscription was paid in return for the undivided share it was probably not given for services supplied in the course of a "business" at all and was probably not subject to the tax at all.

That raises the next and more important question, namely, can it be said that the member pays any part of his subscription for his share of beneficial ownership? Looking at the matter realistically, it is plain that the object of becoming a member of the club is to enjoy the grounds and club house, to enjoy the facilities provided there for sport and recreation. The fact that as an adjunct of those matters he also gets an undivided share in the beneficial ownership and the potential right to share in the proceeds on dissolution would plainly not even occur to the average member.

Put in another way, if any prospective member were to be told that his membership would not include any share in the beneficial ownership of the property or in the proceeds on dissolution, would he withdraw his membership application? The answer, obviously, is no. In other words, no part of the entrance fee or subscription can properly be said to be referable to such interest in land as the member obtains. Alternatively the proportion of the subscription which is properly referable to the beneficial interest is so small as to be negligible. The correct approach is to see what in reality the member is getting for his money. What is the appropriate description of the services supplied by the taxable person in return for the member's subscription? See *Customs and Excise Commissioners* v. *Automobile Association* [1974] 1 W.L.R. 1447 and *Customs and Excise Commissioners* v. *Guy Butler (International) Ltd.* [1976] Q.B. 106. The answer here is the privilege of going upon the grounds and enjoying the facilities, not the somewhat recondite enjoyment of his share in the beneficial ownership.

Mr. Whitworth's second submission is as follows. The rights given to members by the rules (and particularly rule 2), that is to say the rights of going upon the gardens and into the club house and of playing or watching the various games, are rights over land or alternatively constitute a licence to occupy land granted to the members and are therefore exempt under the Schedule. It is true that in one sense of the word the member does obtain a "right" but when one considers the words of item 1 of the Schedule as a whole, it is clear that the expression "right over land" must receive a restricted interpretation. If it were given the broad meaning contended for by Mr. Whitworth, the words which follow (that is to say "or of any licence to occupy land") would be otiose. A licence of almost any description would be covered by the words "right over land." In our judgment in order to make sense of this part of Schedule 5, the words "any interest in or right over land" must be confined to a legal or equitable interest in the land in the sense used by Lord Upjohn in *National Provincial Bank Ltd.* v. *Hastings Car Mart Ltd.* [1965] A.C. 1175, 1237. "Interest" and "right" are treated together as practically synonymous. "Licence to occupy" is in a contrasting category.

Mr. Whitworth sought to derive support for his argument on this point from the exceptions to the exemption clause (to which we have already referred) as showing that "right over land" must be given a broad interpretation. We disagree. Each of these exceptions can involve either a right over or an interest in land in the strict sense, or a licence to occupy or something so akin to such a licence that the draftsman was entitled to mention it for the avoidance of doubt.

What the members receive is a licence to go upon the club land and to enjoy the various facilities provided. This is not a "right over land" within the meaning of the Schedule; it is a licence. The only type of licence which will provide exemption is a licence to occupy land. Expressum facit cessare tacitum. Is this such a licence? Mr. Whitworth argues that it is. We disagree. It is impossible to say that the members of the club have a licence to occupy any part of the club's premises. The judgment of Pilcher J. in *Campbell* v. *Thompson* [1953] 1 Q.B. 445 to which we were referred does not assist on this point. The assertion in that case that "club members are technical occupiers" was used by the judge simply to show that all members of the club had a common interest in resisting the plaintiff's claim. It is no authority for the proposition that the members of this club have a licence to occupy any part of the club premises.

The tribunal in their reasons put the matter in this way:

> "For present purposes it is sufficient to say that in our view, the right given to members to use and enjoy the club grounds in accordance with the rules, by wandering about and sitting in the grounds and using, as available, the sports facilities provided by the club during the hours when the club is open, is not, in any ordinary use of language, a licence to occupy those grounds."

We cannot improve upon those words, and we respectfully adopt them as a clear and correct indication of the meaning of the words in question.

In our judgment the tribunal came to the correct conclusion in this case and we accordingly dismiss the appeal.

Appeal dismissed with costs.
Leave to appeal.

Solicitors: *Waterhouse & Co.; Solicitor for Customs and Excise Commissioners.*

A

[CHANCERY DIVISION]

* VAPORMATIC CO. LTD. *v.* SPAREX LTD. AND ANOTHER

PRACTICE NOTE

B [1976 V. No. 1124]

1976 May 12; 18 — Graham J.

Practice—Discovery—Motion for—Ex parte application for order preventing defendants' use or disclosure of confidential
C *information—Necessity for hearing in camera—Service of order—Method—Need for evidence of means*

EX PARTE MOTION

The plaintiffs, Vapormatic Co. Ltd., whose business consisted primarily in the marketing and selling of a wide range of products for the agricultural industry throughout the world, applied ex parte on May 12, 1976, for an
D interlocutory injunction to restrain the first defendants, Sparex Ltd., and the second defendant, Douglas Brian Mitchell, a former employee of the plaintiffs, acting by their servants or agents or otherwise howsoever from doing the following acts or any of them:

> ". . . (i) disclosing, publishing or in any way using without the leave of the plaintiffs the plaintiffs' customer lists, lists of suppliers or confidential costing information, (ii) infringing the copyright in any of
> E the plaintiffs' literary works, (iii) converting to their own use infringing copies of the said literary works."

The motion also sought an order that the defendants give discovery upon oath within four days, or within two days of the service of the order upon them respectively, whichever was the later, of the names and addresses of all persons or companies to whom the defendants had disclosed or sent
F the plaintiffs' customer lists, lists of suppliers, or confidential costing information derived from such lists or information or any of them; such further or other order as should be meet; and such order as to costs as should be appropriate.

Graham J. held that the alleged facts justified his holding that the case fell within the principles of *Anton Piller KG* v. *Manufacturing Processes*
G *Ltd.* [1976] Ch. 55, that the preservation of the plaintiffs' confidential information and its denial to the defendants was urgent. He made the necessary orders but reserved judgment as the case raised points of practice on which it would be useful to give judgment in open court.

Hugh Laddie for the plaintiffs.

Cur. adv. vult.

H

May 18. GRAHAM J. read the following judgment. This is another case where an order is asked for which entitles the plaintiff to enter the premises of the defendant with the latter's permission for the purpose of inspecting documents. Such orders have been described as resembling search warrants.

So far as I know the only recently reported cases in this field are *E.M.I. Ltd.* v. *Pandit* [1975] 1 W.L.R. 302 and *Anton Piller KG* v. *Manufacturing*

Processes Ltd. [1976] Ch. 55. In the former case, Templeman J. made such an order and in the latter the Court of Appeal, reversing Brightman J., also did so and laid down clear principles as to when and subject to what conditions such orders can be made. In addition to the reported cases, the registrar has produced for me copies of similar orders which were made in *Pall Europe Ltd.* v. *Micro Filtrex Ltd.* (1974 P. No. 4640) and *Universal City Studios Inc.* v. *Mukhtar & Sons Ltd.* [since reported [1976] 1 W.L.R. 568].

[His Lordship stated that the facts before the court on the hearing of the ex parte application on May 12, 1976, and the plaintiffs' affidavit evidence showed that there was a strong prima facie case that the defendant Mitchell, who had been employed by the plaintiffs, had taken an unknown quantity of the plaintiffs' confidential information, including lists and evaluation of customers, and given them to the defendant company, and continued:] The plaintiffs have shown that they have a very strong prima facie case, that potential damage to them is very serious and that there is clear evidence that the defendants possess vital information which they might destroy or dispose of so as to defeat the ends of justice before any application inter partes could be made. In short, I was satisfied that the exceptional circumstances specified by the Court of Appeal in *Anton Piller's* case [1976] Ch. 55 as necessary for the exercise of the inherent jurisdiction of the court to make ex parte the strong order asked for by the plaintiffs are present here, and I therefore did so order.

In these cases it is important that counsel should make it clear at the outset, before the hearing starts, that its nature is such that the court should sit in camera. Mr. Laddie did not do this and I raised the point and went into camera as soon as I appreciated what the position was. As it so happened, I do not think that any damage was done, because there did not appear to be any strangers in court at the start of the case. However, there might well have been, and it would be possible for the procedure to be rendered nugatory if the defendants, by some means, learnt of the nature of the proceedings before the order could be executed upon them.

Secondly, in view of the necessity for the actual service and subsequent procedure to be carried out satisfactorily, but at the same time with due circumspection and proper regard for the defendants' rights, as clearly laid down by the Court of Appeal in *Anton Piller's* case (see pp. 61C, 62D and 62E), it is I think highly desirable that the person in charge and who effects service should be a qualified solicitor, who is, as such, an officer of the court. Further if, as he normally will be, this solicitor is accompanied by one or more of the plaintiffs' directors or employees or expert witnesses employed on their behalf, they should, if possible, be named in the order and the order should provide for them to be identified to the defendants by the solicitor effecting service. By such means the court is doing the best it can to ensure that service is proper and effective, that objections as to the identity of those concerned cannot properly be taken by the defendant, and that the proceedings following service are also conducted in an effective but at the same time orderly and correct manner. It will thus be seen that I have been slightly more rigorous in the requirements specified for the persons effecting service and any subsequent search and their identification.

Finally, it is of course a condition of the grant of an ex parte injunction that the plaintiff should give a cross-undertaking in damages or other adequate security. In the *Anton Piller* case the cross-undertaking was supported by a bond for £10,000. It is important that the court should be

A satisfied that the plaintiff is good for any damages which might ultimately
be ordered against him on the cross-undertaking. Normally then, it is only
prudent that a plaintiff, asking for such an injunction ex parte, should pro-
duce specific evidence that he is good for such damages. This was not in
fact done in the present case, but I am satisfied from the evidence as a
whole and, for example, from the turnover figures that the plaintiffs are a
substantial company. As the period before which an inter partes hearing
B takes place is likely to be short I think that it is proper in the present case
to make the order I have made without requiring more detailed evidence on
this point. It is, however, in my judgment normally an important require-
ment that such evidence should be available at the ex parte hearing, since,
for example, it would be quite possible that in the case of a specialised
export business a defendant who obeys an injunction not to export his
C goods, such injunction turning out afterwards to have been wrongly granted,
may literally miss the boat and thereby suffer considerable damage or
possibly penalties for non-delivery on time. This damage he would be
entitled to recover under the cross-undertaking.

*Order stating terms on which solicitor
of firm of McKenna & Co., accom-*
D *panied by R. H. C. Tanner and
W. A. Nicholas, should enter named
premises of defendant company
between 8 a.m. and 9 p.m. (i) to
inspect all documents or articles
relating to plaintiffs' or defendants'*
E *customers, suppliers or costings and
(ii) to remove all documents and/or
articles which wholly or partly repro-
duced or were derived from plain-
tiffs' list of customers, information
relating to plaintiffs' suppliers or
plaintiffs' costing information or*
F *which reasonably appeared to be so
reproduced or derived.*

*Order that defendants do further
disclose to plaintiffs names and
addresses of all persons or com-
panies to whom defendants respec-*
G *tively have disclosed or sent
plaintiffs' lists of customers, infor-
mation relating to plaintiffs' sup-
pliers or confidential costing
information or any information
derived wholly or in part from such
lists or information.*

H

Solicitors: *McKenna & Co.*

T. C. C. B.

[QUEEN'S BENCH DIVISION] A

* EDWARDS v. DDIN

1976 June 18 — Lord Widgery C.J., Croom-Johnson and May JJ.

B

Crime—Theft—Dishonest appropriation—Petrol and oil put into motorist's car at his request—Motorist driving away without paying—Whether sale conditional on payment—Whether appropriation of property belonging to another—Theft Act 1968 (*c.* 60), *ss.* 1 (1), 5 (3) [1]—*Sale of Goods Act* 1893 (56 & 57 *Vict., c.* 71), *s.* 18, *r.* 5 [2]

The defendant drove his car into a garage and requested C the attendant to fill up the tank with petrol and put two pints of oil into the engine. After the attendant had done so, the defendant drove off without paying. He was charged with theft, contrary to section 1 of the Theft Act 1968. The justices dismissed the information holding that the ownership of the petrol and oil had been transferred to the defendant when the attendant put them into his car and, therefore, as the sale was not conditional on payment, the defendant had D not appropriated the property of another when he drove away from the garage premises.

On appeal by the prosecutor:—

Held, dismissing the appeal, that a garage owner selling petrol and oil to a motorist did not retain the right to dispose of the petrol and oil once it had been put in the motorist's car and mixed with the petrol or oil already there; that the delivery of the petrol and oil was an unconditional appropria- E tion of the goods to the contract and, under rule 5 (2) in section 18 of the Sale of Goods Act 1893, the property passed to the defendant when they were placed in his car; that, since section 5 (3) of the Theft Act 1968 did not apply to a case of an outright sale, the property could not be regarded as belonging to the owner of the garage until payment and, accordingly, the defendant had not appropriated the goods of another at the time he drove away from the garage. F

No cases are referred to in the judgment.

The following cases were cited in argument:

Reg. v. *Collis-Smith* [1971] Crim.L.R. 716, C.A.

Reg. v. *Greenberg* [1972] Crim.L.R. 331.

G

CASE STATED by Buckinghamshire justices sitting at Amersham.

On August 24, 1975, an information was preferred by the prosecutor, Mervyn Edwards, against the defendant, Roheim Ddin, that he on Sunday,

---

[Reported by MRS. HEATHER WHICHER, Barrister-at-Law]

H

[1] Theft Act 1968, s. 1: "(1) A person is guilty of theft if he dishonestly appropriates property belonging to another with the intention of permanently depriving the other of it; . . ."

S. 5 (3): see post, p. 945G.

[2] Sale of Goods Act 1893, s. 18: "Unless a different intention appears, the following are rules for ascertaining the intention of the parties as to the time at which the property in the goods is to pass to the buyer. . . . Rule 5 . . . (2) Where, in pursuance of the contract, the seller delivers the goods to the buyer . . . and does not reserve the right of disposal, he is deemed to have unconditionally appropriated the goods to the contract."

A August 24, 1975, at Amersham in the County of Buckingham stole three gallons of petrol and two pints of oil together of the value of £1·77, the property of Mamos Garage, Amersham, contrary to section 1 of the Theft Act 1968.

The justices heard the information on October 30, 1975, and the following was a short statement of the prosecution evidence. At 11.00 a.m. on August 24, 1975, the defendant drove a mini car on to the forecourt
B of Mamos Garage, Amersham and asked the attendant to fill up the tank with petrol. The attendant put in petrol to the value of £1·16. The defendant then asked for a quart of oil to be put into the engine which was done by the same attendant. The attendant then went to the garage to clean her hands. At that time the defendant returned to his car and drove away without paying for either the petrol or the oil, the total value
C of which was £1·77. At no time during the transaction was there any mention of payment either by the attendant or by the defendant. Customers using the garage normally paid by way of cash, cheque or credit card, but none of those means was either requested or tendered on that occasion. The defendant did not ask to be excused payment for the petrol or the oil. The police were called and shortly afterwards the defendant was stopped by a police officer in a police vehicle. The defendant then told
D the police officer that he had paid for the petrol by means of a five pound note, and he denied driving away from the garage without paying. He was subsequently arrested and charged with the offence of theft of the petrol and oil. The justices then heard a submission on behalf of the defendant to the effect of the defendant's contentions set out below. That submission was dismissed. The defendant gave evidence asserting that he
E asked for only one pint of oil; that he paid with a £5 note; that he received change and that he gave the attendant a tip.

The justices found the following facts. That petrol and oil to the value of £1·77 had been placed voluntarily into the defendant's car at his request by the attendant. On ordering the petrol and oil the defendant had impliedly made to the attendant the ordinary representation of an ordinary customer that he had the means and the intention of paying
F for it before he left. The defendant was not asked by the attendant to pay for the petrol or oil. The defendant did not pay for the petrol or the oil before he drove away from the garage, or at any other time, nor did he seek to be excused payment. The petrol and oil which had been placed in the car could not reasonably be recovered by the garage in default of payment. The ownership of the petrol and oil had been trans-
G ferred to the defendant when the attendant put them into his car, since that was his intention at the time of doing so.

It was contended by the prosecutor that by his action in leaving the garage in possession of the petrol and oil but without having paid for either, the defendant had dishonestly appropriated the property of another with the intention of permanently depriving the other of it and was thus
H guilty as charged of the offence of theft.

It was contended by the defendant that when the petrol and oil were placed in his car ownership of the petrol and oil was transferred to him and thus he could not have appropriated the property of another and was therefore not guilty of theft.

The justices were of the opinion that the ownership of the petrol and oil was transferred to the defendant when the garage put them into his car and therefore the defendant had not appropriated the property of

another for the purposes of section 1 of the Theft Act 1968 and they A
therefore dismissed the information.

The prosecutor appealed. The question for the opinion of the High Court was whether a customer had appropriated property belonging to another for the purposes of section 1 of the Theft Act 1968 when petrol and oil had been delivered into his vehicle by a retailer, such delivery being conditional upon payment being made immediately thereafter, and the customer drove off from the retailer's premises without making B
payment.

Anthony Hidden Q.C. for the prosecutor.
Simon Freeman for the defendant.

LORD WIDGERY C.J. I will ask Croom-Johnson J. to give the first C
judgment.

CROOM-JOHNSON J. This is an appeal by way of case stated from the magistrates' court sitting at Amersham in which the defendant had an information preferred against him that he stole three gallons of petrol and two pints of oil together of the value of £1·77, the property of Mamos Garage at Amersham, contrary to section 1 of the Theft Act 1968. D

On the facts as found by the justices the following things happened. The defendant arrived with a motor car and he asked for some petrol and oil to be placed in his car. Petrol and oil to the value as stated, £1·77, was placed into the car at his request by the garage attendant. When he ordered the petrol and oil the defendant impliedly made to the attendant the ordinary representation of an ordinary customer that he E
had the means and the intention of paying for it before he left. He was not in fact asked to pay and he did not in fact pay, but the moment when the garage attendant was doing something else he simply drove away. The justices also found, as one would think was perfectly obvious, that whilst the petrol and oil had been placed in the car, either in the tank or in the sump, it could not reasonably be recovered by the garage in default of payment. F

The questions therefore which have to be resolved in order to satisfy section 1 of the Act were two in number. First of all, was the defendant dishonest? It appears that the justices must have considered that that was so. Secondly, had he appropriated property belonging to another with the intention of permanently depriving the other of it? Upon that point the defence submitted successfully that at the time when the car G
was driven away the petrol and oil which had got into the tank or sump were in fact not the property of the garage any more but were the property of the defendant. On that basis the justices said that that particular essential ingredient of theft under section 1 of the Act had not been fulfilled and dismissed the information.

The whole question therefore was: whose petrol and oil was it when the defendant drove away? Property passes under a contract of sale H
when it is intended to pass. In such transactions as the sale of petrol at a garage forecourt ordinary common sense would say that the garage and the motorist intended the property in the petrol to pass when it is poured into the tank and irretrievably mixed with the other petrol that is in it, and I think that is what the justices decided.

But the prosecutor has appealed and has based his appeal on a consideration of the Sale of Goods Act 1893 and the provisions of that Act,

A and seeks a ruling that transfer of the petrol was conditional only and that therefore until payment the petrol remained the property of the garage.

But if one considers the provisions of the Sale of Goods Act 1893 one comes out at the same answer as common sense would dictate.

The prosecution argument went this way, that when the motorist arrives at the garage and says " will you fill me up, please?" or " will you give me two gallons? ", then there is a contract for the sale of unascer-
B tained goods by description. In such circumstances when does the property in the petrol pass? Nothing will have been said between the motorist and the pump attendant about that, so one is thrown back on section 18 of the Sale of Goods Act 1893 and rules made under it in order to ascertain the intention of the parties.

By pouring the petrol into the tank the goods have been appropriated
C to the contract with the assent of both parties. If that is done unconditionally, then the property in the petrol passes to the motorist: rule 5 (1). The prosecution argument then goes on that, however, there is a condition which is waiting to be fulfilled, namely, payment, and says that under section 19 of the Sale of Goods Act 1893 the garage reserves the right of disposal of the petrol until the payment has been made and that therefore the property has not passed under rule 5 (1).

D It is at this point that the argument breaks down. The garage owner does not reserve the right to dispose of the petrol once it is in the tank, nor is it possible to see how effect could be given to any such condition wherever petrol has been put in and is all mixed up with what other petrol is already there. Consequently one passes back to rule 5 (2) of section 18, which says that where a seller delivers the goods to the buyer
E and does not reserve the right to dispose of them, he is deemed to have unconditionally appropriated the goods to the contract and in those circumstances the property has passed to the buyer in accordance with rule 5 (1).

Reference was also made by the prosecutor to section 5 of the Theft Act 1968 which deals with one of the subsidiary definitions arising under section 1, which is the initial section dealing with theft. Section 5, which
F deals with but is not definitive of the expression " belonging to another," is concerned with all manner of interests in property. It was urged upon us that the motorist is under an implied obligation to retain his car with the petrol in its tank on the garage premises and not to take it away until such time as he has paid for it, and that until that has been done the garage owner retains some proprietary interest in the petrol in the tank.

G The relevant part of section 5, which is in subsection (3), reads:

> " Where a person receives property from or on account of another, and is under an obligation to the other to retain and deal with that property or its proceeds in a particular way, the property or proceeds shall be regarded (as against him) as belonging to the other."

That section in my view is not apt to cover a case such as the present
H where there has been an outright sale of the goods and the property in the goods has passed and the seller is only waiting to be paid. Therefore the provisions of section 5 do not affect the conclusion in the present case.

I do not enter into any discussion for the purposes of this judgment of what might have been the position if the charge had been brought under some other section of the Theft Act 1968, or if the appropriation for the purposes of section 1 had been said to have arisen at an earlier stage of the events which took place. On the facts as found and on the case as it was presented to the magistrates, in my view the magistrates reached a correct conclusion in law and I would dismiss the appeal. A

MAY J. I agree.

LORD WIDGERY. I also agree.

Appeal dismissed with costs. B

Solicitors: *Sharpe, Pritchard & Co. for J. Malcolm Simons, Oxford; Prothero & Prothero.*

C

[COURT OF APPEAL]

* REGINA *v.* BARRETT (GEORGE)

1976 March 22; April 12 — James L.J., Michael Davies and Jupp JJ. D

Crime—Corruption—Agent—Additional superintendent registrar of births, deaths and marriages—Whether serving under Crown—Prevention of Corruption Act 1906 (6 *Edw.* 7, *c.* 34), *s.* 1 [1]

The defendant was appointed an additional superintendent registrar of births, deaths and marriages and, while acting in that capacity, he accepted £4 for arranging a marriage ceremony at an early date. He pleaded not guilty to a count of an indictment alleging that he, being an additional superintendent registrar of births, deaths and marriages and an agent of the Crown within the meaning of the Prevention of Corruption Act 1906, corruptly accepted money as an inducement or reward for doing an act in relation to his principal's affairs. After legal argument the judge ruled that as a matter of law the defendant was, in the performance of his duties, "a servant of the Crown." The defendant thereupon changed his plea to one of guilty. E F

On appeal against conviction on the ground that his plea of guilty resulted from a wrong decision by the judge on a question of law:—

Held, dismissing the appeal, that, since the registration of births, deaths and marriages was a function of central government and the effect of a celebration of marriage on the personal status of the parties to a marriage was of concern to the state, an additional superintendent registrar acted on behalf of the Crown in the performance of his duties and was appointed so to act under the provisions of the Registration Service Act 1953; and that, accordingly, the defendant was serving under the Crown within the meaning of section 1 (3) of the Prevention of Corruption Act 1906 and was thus an agent for the purposes of section 1 (1) of the Act. G H

The following cases are referred to in the judgment:

Attorney-General for New South Wales v. *Perpetual Trustee Co. Ltd.* [1955] A.C. 457; [1955] 2 W.L.R. 707; [1955] 1 All E.R. 846, P.C.

[Reported by MISS EIRA CARYL-THOMAS, Barrister-at-Law]

[1] Prevention of Corruption Act 1906, s. 1: see post, p. 948C–F.

A *Enever* v. *The King* (1906) 3 C.L.R. 969.
Fisher v. *Oldham Corporation* [1930] 2 K.B. 365.
Mersey Docks and Harbour Board Trustees v. *Cameron* (1865) 11 H.L. Cas. 443, H.L.(E.).
Ranaweera v. *Ramachandran* [1970] A.C. 962; [1970] 2 W.L.R. 500, P.C.
Reg. v. *Commissioner of Police of the Metropolis, Ex parte Blackburn* [1968] 2 Q.B. 118; [1968] 2 W.L.R. 893; [1968] 1 All E.R. 763,
B C.A.
Stanbury v. *Exeter Corporation* [1905] 2 K.B. 838.
Tamlin v. *Hannaford* [1950] 1 K.B. 18; [1949] 2 All E.R. 327, C.A.

No additional cases were cited in argument.

C APPEAL against conviction.

On November 4, 1975, at the Middlesex Crown Court the defendant, George Barrett, pleaded not guilty to four counts of an indictment charging him with corruptly accepting for himself sums of money as an inducement or reward for doing an act in relation to his principal's affairs, contrary to section 1 of the Prevention of Corruption Act 1906. Counts 1 and 3 stated that he was an additional superintendent registrar and an
D agent of the Crown; counts 2 and 4 were alternative and stated that, being an additional superintendent registrar, he was an agent of the London Borough of Ealing. After hearing legal argument, Judge Trapnell ruled that as a matter of law the defendant was, in the performance of his duties as additional superintendent registrar, a servant of the Crown. The defendant thereupon changed his plea to one of guilty to the third count, which alleged that he had accepted £4 in addition to the lawful fee of £6 for
E arranging a particular date for a marriage ceremony. The prosecution did not proceed on the other counts. The defendant appealed against his conviction on the ground that the judge had misdirected himself in law in ruling that an additional superintendent registrar was an agent of the Crown within the meaning of section 1 (1) of the Prevention of Corruption. Act 1906.

F

Maurice Drake Q.C. and *Sean Overend* for the defendant.
George Shindler Q.C. and *Paul Purnell* for the Crown.

Cur. adv. vult.

G April 12. JAMES L.J. read the following judgment of the court. The question raised by this appeal is whether an additional superintendent registrar appointed pursuant to the provisions of the Registration Service Act 1953 is, in relation to the performance of the duties of that office, an "agent" within the meaning of section 1 of the Prevention of Corruption Act 1906.

On November 4, 1975, the defendant pleaded not guilty to each of four
H counts of an indictment which charged him with corruptly accepting for himself sums of money as an inducement or reward for doing an act in relation to his principal's affairs. The first and third counts stated that he was an additional superintendent registrar and an agent of the Crown. The second and fourth counts were alternative and stated that being an additional superintendent registrar he was an agent of the London Borough of Ealing. On the following day after hearing legal argument the circuit judge, Judge Trapnell, ruled that as a matter of law the defendant was,

in the performance of his duties as additional superintendent registrar, "a servant of the Crown." The defendant thereupon changed his plea to one of guilty to the third count and the prosecution did not proceed on the other counts.

The defendant appeals against his conviction on the ground that it resulted from a wrong decision of a question of law by the trial judge.

On January 1, 1970, the defendant was appointed an additional superintendent registrar for the Ealing registration district. On November 24, 1973, a Mr. Whitely consulted the defendant in his capacity of additional superintendent registrar with a view to arranging his marriage to a Cypriot lady. In order to comply with a condition of the lady's visa the marriage had to be celebrated before February 19, 1974. The defendant accepted £4 additional to the lawful fee of £6 as an inducement or reward for arranging a date earlier than February 19 for the marriage ceremony. Clearly on the facts there was no defence to the charge to which he pleaded guilty if the defendant acted as an agent in relation to his principal's affairs within the meaning of section 1 of the Prevention of Corruption Act 1906. Section 1 of that Act reads, so far as is material:

> "(1) If any agent corruptly accepts or obtains, or agrees to accept or attempts to obtain, from any person, for himself or for any other person, any gift or consideration as an inducement or reward for doing or forbearing to do, or for having after the passing of this Act done or forborne to do, any act in relation to his principal's affairs or business, or for showing or forbearing to show favour or disfavour to any person in relation to his principal's affairs or business; . . . he shall be guilty of a misdemeanour, . . . (2) For the purposes of this Act the expression 'consideration' includes valuable consideration of any kind; the expression 'agent' includes any person employed by or acting for another; and the expression 'principal' includes an employer. (3) A person serving under the Crown or under any corporation or any municipal, borough, county, or district council, or any board of guardians, is an agent within the meaning of this Act."

For the purposes of the Act a person may be an agent although he does not stand in the relationship of an employee or servant to an employer or master. Similarly the principal in relation to whose affairs the agent acts does not for the purposes of the Act have to be the employer of the agent. Further, by subsection (3), persons "serving under the Crown" are agents for the purposes of the Act.

The argument for the defendant was that he was not the servant of the Crown, nor was he serving under the Crown, but an independent office holder appointed for the purpose of carrying out the prescribed statutory duties assigned to his office. The argument was supported by a detailed analysis of the Registration Service Act 1953. Additional superintendent registrars may be appointed pursuant to a "local scheme" in force in a county or county borough. Section 13 of the Act makes provision for local schemes. A local scheme does not take effect unless and until it is approved by the Minister of Health. Sections 1 to 4 of the Act provide for the appointment of a Registrar General under the Great Seal and for the offices, staff and salaries, receipts and expenses in relation to the Registrar General and persons appointed by him.

For the defendant, Mr. Drake conceded that the Registrar General is

A a person "serving under the Crown" but argued that he was not necessarily an "agent" for the purposes of the Act of 1906. Section 5 of the Act of 1953 provides for the division of counties into districts and subdistricts and for the office of superintendent registrars for each district and registrars for each subdistrict. Section 6 (1) provides for the appointment of superintendent registrars by the council of the county or county borough or, in default, by the Registrar General. Section 6 (3) provides that a
B superintendent registrar shall be paid a salary by the council, shall account to the Registrar General for fees received by or payable to him and pay to the council such sums as the Registrar General directs. Section 6 (4) provides that a superintendent registrar shall hold office during the pleasure of the Registrar General. By section 10 the council has the duty to provide suitable office accommodation. On relinquishing his post a superin-
C tendent registrar is required by section 15 to hand over his register boxes, records and so forth to his successor or, if there is no successor, to the Registrar General's nominee. By section 16 a superintendent registrar is not obliged to comply with any application made to him until he has been paid the appropriate fee, and any fee due is recoverable by him as a debt due to him.

Mr. Drake argued that the statutory provisions, which may be sum-
D marised as stating that a superintendent registrar is not appointed by the Crown, not paid by the Crown, not superannuated by the Crown, not provided for materially nor accommodated by the Crown and not dismissible by the Crown, create an office which is held by a person who does not serve under the Crown in the performance of the duties of that office.

In *Fisher* v. *Oldham Corporation* [1930] 2 K.B. 365, it was held that
E the defendant corporation were not liable civilly for the acts of police officers in the unlawful arrest and detention of the plaintiff. McCardie J. held that the police constables were not servants of the local authority when acting in the course of their police duties although the local authority appointed them, paid them and had the power to dismiss them. He held, at p. 377, that the police officers were "not acting as the servants or agents of the defendants. They were fulfilling their duties as public servants and
F officers of the Crown sworn to 'preserve the peace'..."

Mr. Drake argued that *Fisher's* case is authority for the proposition that a police officer does not act in the course of his duty as a servant or agent of the local authority who appointed him but not for the further proposition that a police officer acts as a servant of the Crown or a person serving under the Crown. The same argument was advanced in relation to
G *Stanbury* v. *Exeter Corporation* [1905] 2 K.B. 838, in which it was held that the local authority were not liable for the acts of an inspector appointed by that authority for the purposes of the Diseases of Animals Act 1894. Mr. Drake argued that the position of the constable acting in the course of his duty was correctly put in *Enever* v. *The King* (1906) 3 C.L.R. 969, 975 by Griffith C.J.:

> H "At common law the office of constable or peace officer was regarded as a public office, and the holder of it as being, in some sense, a servant of the Crown."

In *Attorney-General for New South Wales* v. *Perpetual Trustee Co. Ltd.* [1955] A.C. 457, the New South Wales Government sought to recover damages for the loss of the services of a police officer due to the tortious act of a wrongdoer. It was held that the relationship between the state and the police officer was not one which could support the action per quod

servitium amisit. For the present defendant reliance was placed on the A
words of Viscount Simonds, at p. 489:

> "Their Lordships can now express their final opinion upon the case. They repeat that in their view there is a fundamental difference between the domestic relation of servant and master and that of the holder of a public office and the state which he is said to serve. The constable falls within the latter category. His authority is original, not B
> delegated, and is exercised at his own discretion by virtue of his office: he is a ministerial officer exercising statutory rights independently of contract. The essential difference is recognised in the fact that his relationship to the government is not in ordinary parlance described as that of servant and master."

Reliance was also placed on the passage in the judgment of Lord C
Denning M.R. in *Reg.* v. *Commissioner of Police of the Metropolis, Ex parte Blackburn* [1968] 2 Q.B. 118, 135–136. That was a case in which the constitutional status of the Commissioner of Police fell for consideration. Lord Denning M.R. stressed the aspect of independence of the executive and said, at p. 136: "he is not the servant of anyone, save of the law itself." Likewise, argued Mr. Drake, a superintendent registrar
performs his statutory duties and in doing so serves the law laid down by D
Parliament, but he is an independent authority and serves no one but the law itself.

Finally Mr. Drake referred to *Tamlin* v. *Hannaford* [1950] 1 K.B. 18, a Rent Restrictions Act case in which it was held that the statutory body, British Transport Commission, was not a servant or agent of the Crown administering property to which the Rent Restrictions Act did not apply E
by reason of the property being Crown property. Denning L.J. having referred to the powers exercisable by the Minister of Transport in relation to the commission, said at p. 24:

> ". . . we cannot regard the corporation as being his agent, any more than a company is the agent of the shareholders, or even of a sole shareholder. In the eye of the law, the corporation is its own master
> and is answerable as fully as any other person or corporation." F

The only other authority to which we would refer is *Ranaweera* v. *Ramachandran* [1970] A.C. 962, to which Mr. Shindler invited our attention in the course of his argument for the Crown. The case is a revenue case on appeal from the Supreme Court of Ceylon. The question arose as to whether members of the Board of Review, whose members were G
appointed by the Minister of Finance, were "servants of the Crown" in respect of the Government of Ceylon. The majority of their Lordships reached the conclusion expressed in the judgment of Lord Donovan, at p. 971:

> "Their Lordships must nevertheless still come to a conclusion on the language of the definition; and they have reached the conclusion that
> members of the Board of Review cannot properly be described as H
> 'servants of the Crown' within the meaning of section 3 of the Constitution."

Mr. Shindler invited our attention to the words of Lord Diplock in a dissenting judgment, at p. 973:

> "There may be cases where a function of central government, such as the maintenance of order, is carried out through officers appointed

locally and paid out of local funds. Police constables are a well-known example and there may be room for doubt whether in view of the manner of their appointment and the source of their pay they are strictly 'servants of the Crown' or are, as Blackburn J. put it in *Mersey Docks* v. *Cameron* (1865) 11 H.L.Cas. 443, 464–465, only in consimili casu. This, however, does not arise in the present appeal.

"A member of the Board of Review under the Income Tax Ordinance holds an 'office.' It is so described in section 74 (1). It is a 'paid office,' for section 74 (6) provides for his remuneration which is paid out of the revenues of the central government of Ceylon. In my opinion, the test whether or not he is a 'servant of the Crown' in the sense in which that expression is used in public law is whether or not the functions conferred or imposed by the Income Tax Ordinance upon the Board of Review which he is appointed to perform are under the Constitution of Ceylon functions of central government.

"The assessment and collection of taxes to defray the expenses of the central government of the country is a classic constitutional function of central government itself. The performance of this function must needs be undertaken by natural persons for the purpose of administering the fiscal legislation on the central government's behalf. Those natural persons who so administer it, at any rate if appointed by a Minister of the Crown acting in his official capacity and if paid out of the central revenues of Ceylon, are in my view 'servants of the Crown.'"

In our judgment although some assistance may be derived from the "police officer" cases the question whether the defendant was an agent for the purposes of section 1 of the Prevention of Corruption Act 1906 must be determined by construing the words of that section and by applying the section to the holder of the office of additional superintendent registrar appointed under the Registration Service Act 1953. The registration of births, deaths and marriages is one of the functions of central government. The Registrar General is appointed under the Great Seal. The celebration of marriage affects the status of the parties to the marriage and change of personal status is the concern of the state. The duties of an additional superintendent registrar are performed by him on behalf of the Crown, it being necessary for the Crown to exercise its functions through some human agency.

Parliament provided machinery for the appointment of a person to act on behalf of the Crown in relation to these matters and called him a superintendent registrar. An additional superintendent registrar is in exactly the same position. That being the position of the defendant it is, in our judgment, clear that he is an "agent" for the purposes of the Prevention of Corruption Act 1906. Section 1 (2) provides that a person "acting for another" is included in the expression "agent" for the purposes of the Act. The defendant was acting for the Crown. Section 1 (3), in our judgment is apt, when the wording is given its natural and ordinary meaning, to cover the position of the defendant. The question is not whether he was employed by the Crown or employed by any person or body. The question is whether he was serving under the Crown. In our judgment the defendant in the performance of his duties was serving under the Crown.

Before parting with this appeal we would add in fairness to the defendant that the evidence reveals that before proceedings against him were commenced, he wrote a letter of abject apology to Mr. Whitely and refunded the £4. A

The appeal is dismissed.

Appeal dismissed.

Solicitors: *Registrar of Criminal Appeals; Director of Public Prosecutions.*

B

[CHANCERY DIVISION]

* *In re* A DEBTOR (No. 24 of 1971)

Ex parte MARLEY *v.* TRUSTEE OF THE PROPERTY OF THE DEBTOR C

1976 Jan. 19, 20; 29; May 10 — Foster and Fox JJ.

Bankruptcy—Property passing to trustee—Tenants in common—Legal charge to bank on joint property of father and son to secure loan to son—Father surety for loan—Son made bankrupt—Trustee's claim to son's half-share—Whether bank loan deductible from son's half-share on sale of property D

A father helped his son to get a bank loan by conveying his freehold house into the joint names of himself and his son on trust for sale, the net proceeds of sale to be held for father and son as tenants in common in equal shares. Father and son then charged the house to the bank, the father acting as surety, to secure a loan to the son for the purchase of business premises. The business failed and the son was adjudicated bankrupt. The house was valued at some £10,300. The son owed the bank some £4,289, plus accrued interest of £450 but the bank did not seek to enforce its security. On the application of the trustee in bankruptcy, the county court judge directed that the house be sold and that the net proceeds of sale be divided equally between the trustee and the father. The father appealed. E F

On the question whether the son's debt to the bank should be deducted from the son's half share in the house:—

Held, that an intention should be implied as between father and son that the son's beneficial interest should bear the burden of the loan; that on that basis the son's interest vested in the trustee in bankruptcy, subject to an inchoate right of indemnity if the father as surety was called upon to pay or the debt fell to be discharged; that, therefore, the debt being primarily repayable out of the son's half-share in the house, the trustee in bankruptcy was only entitled to the small sum that was the remainder of the son's half share in the property. G

Gee v. *Liddell* [1913] 2 Ch. 62 applied.

The following cases are referred to in the judgment: H

Cowcher v. *Cowcher* [1972] 1 W.L.R. 425; [1972] 1 All E.R. 943.

Duncan, Fox & Co. v. *North and South Wales Bank* (1880) 6 App.Cas. 1, H.L.(E.).

Gee v. *Liddell* [1913] 2 Ch. 62.

Keily, In re (1857) 6 I.Ch.R. 394.

Solomon, A Bankrupt, In re, Ex parte Trustee of the Property of the Bankrupt v. *Solomon* [1967] Ch. 573; [1967] 2 W.L.R. 172; [1966] 3 All E.R. 255.

A *Turner (A Bankrupt), In re, Ex parte Trustee of the Property of the Bankrupt* v. *Turner (A Bankrupt)* [1974] 1 W.L.R. 1556; [1975] 1 All E.R. 5.

Wright v. *Sandars* (1857) 3 Jur.N.S. 504.

The following additional case was cited in argument:

Rushton (A Bankrupt), In re, Ex parte National Westminster Bank Ltd.
B v. *Official Receiver* [1972] Ch. 197; [1971] 2 W.L.R. 1477; [1971] 2 All E.R. 937, D.C.

APPEAL from Judge Duveen sitting at Reading County Court.

On July 30, 1975, on the application to Reading County Court in bankruptcy of the trustee of the property of Howard James Marley (a
C bankrupt), Judge Duveen ordered that the trustee in bankruptcy be entitled against the appellant, James Marley, the bankrupt's father, and against the bankrupt, to vacant possession of 60, Shirley Avenue, Whitley Wood, Reading, a house conveyed by the father on December 17, 1969, into the joint names of himself and the bankrupt, and that they should concur with the trustee in the sale of the house by auction, conduct of the sale being given to the trustee, and that the net proceeds of sale
D should be divided and paid to the trustee and to the father in equal shares. The father appealed.

The facts are stated in the judgment of Foster J.

Peter Millett Q.C. and *Michael Driscoll* for the appellant.

J. A. R. Finlay Q.C. and *Robert Gray* for the respondent trustee.

E The debtor did not appear and was unrepresented.

Cur. adv. vult.

January 29. FOSTER J. read the following judgment. This is an appeal from the judgment of Judge Duveen who, on July 30, 1975, on the application of the trustee in bankruptcy of Howard James Marley (to whom
F I shall refer to as " the bankrupt ") directed that certain properties should be sold, and that the net proceeds of sale should be divided equally between the trustee in bankruptcy and the bankrupt's father.

The facts. These are not in dispute and can be shortly stated. James Marley, the bankrupt's father, purchased the freehold premises known as 60, Shirley Avenue, Whitley Wood, Reading, Berkshire (which I shall call
G " the property ") in 1937 or 1938, and has lived there ever since with his wife, his daughter and a grandson aged six. He is now some 66 or 67 years old. He is an old age pensioner but also does some part-time work.

The bankrupt in late 1969 was working as a butcher but was wanting to go into business on his own as a purveyor of frozen goods on a cash and carry basis under the style of " H. & J. Marley Meats " and as a supplier of freezers under the style of " Easy freeze." He was married
H and lived at Kentor, 33, Ryeish Green, Reading. In order to start the new business, he wished to raise money in order to purchase a property and provide working capital. He was unable to do this on his own premises—perhaps because it was already mortgaged —so he approached his father and asked him to provide some security on which he could get a loan from his bank, Barclays Bank Ltd. His father was willing to do this and accordingly, on December 17, 1969, the bankrupt's father conveyed the property into the joint names of himself and the bankrupt on trust for sale

and to hold the net proceeds of sale for himself and the bankrupt as A tenants in common in equal shares. On January 29, 1970, the bankrupt's father and the bankrupt executed a legal charge to Barclays Bank Ltd. by which the property was charged to secure to the bank the overdraft of either of them. In fact, the bankrupt's father never had an account with that bank. As a result of that, the bankrupt obtained loan facilities from the bank, and in February 1970 purchased premises at 49/51, Ravensbourne Drive, Woodley, Berkshire, and started business. That business B proved wholly unsuccessful, so that on June 3, 1971, a receiving order was made, the bankrupt was adjudicated bankrupt on June 24, 1971, and the trustee was appointed on July 14, 1971.

Unconscionable bargain. Before Judge Duveen it was submitted that the conveyance of December 17, 1969, should be set aside as an unconscionable bargain. The judge rejected this contention emphatically, and in this C appeal counsel for the bankrupt's father did not seek to upset that finding, so that we must assume that the conveyance and legal charge are valid.

The present position. Before us there was a surveyor's valuation of the property at some £10,300. It is common ground that Barclays Bank Ltd. advanced moneys to the bankrupt alone and never to the father. The amount owing to the bank on July 30, 1975, was some £4,289, with interest accruing thereafter. A dividend of some 20 pence in the pound D was paid to the creditors on January 2, 1975, but the deficiency remains at some £5,000.

The question. The trustee in bankruptcy contends that if the property realises £10,300, he is entitled to half the net proceeds after the bank's secured debt is discharged. That is £10,300, minus £4,300, which equals £6,000, and half of that is £3,000. For the bankrupt's father it E is submitted that the loan from the bank was made to the bankrupt and that he is entitled to have it debited to the bankrupt's share and not to his; that is, half of £10,300, which is £5,150. If one deducts from that the bank's debt of £4,300 plus accrued interest of some £450, together with legal costs, very little equity will remain, if any. The question therefore can be posed in this way: is the bankrupt's father entitled to have the indebtedness to the bank debited to the bankrupt's share of the F property, or is the trustee in bankruptcy entitled to half the net proceeds of sale after the bank's debt has been repaid? If the former is correct, it is submitted that the court should not order a sale as the trustee's interest is minimal and the bankrupt's father should be given an opportunity to purchase the trustee's interest before a sale is ordered.

The effect of the conveyance and legal charge. For the bankrupt's G father it was submitted that the effect of these deeds was that in respect of loans made to the bankrupt, the father was merely a surety. Reliance was placed on *In re Keily* (1857) 6 I.Ch.R. 394; *Wright* v. *Sandars* (1857) 3 Jur.N.S. 504; *Duncan, Fox & Co.* v. *North and South Wales Bank* (1880) 6 App.Cas. 1, and *Gee* v. *Liddell* [1913] 2 Ch. 62. It was submitted that since the bankrupt's father was merely a surety for the loan to the H bankrupt, he was entitled to a charge on the bankrupt's interest to secure recoupment to him of any money which he had to pay. Alternatively it was submitted that this was a trust, and in winding up the trust, equitable principles apply, so that the bank's debt would be marshalled against the bankrupt's interest: see *Cowcher* v. *Cowcher* [1972] 1 W.L.R. 425 and passages in the judgment of Bagnall J. at pp. 432 and 441.

A For the trustee in bankruptcy it was accepted that the father was only a surety but that as a matter of implied contract between the father and the son the latter was bound to indemnify the father against the bank's claim. But it was submitted that when the receiving order was made on June 3, 1971, the bank had not, and still has not, sought to enforce its security, and that the surety is not entitled to any remedy against the creditor unless and until he is called upon to pay and has
B paid something. Until then, it was submitted that no charge can have come into existence, since no payment has been made, and therefore it was said that the father could only prove in the bankruptcy and had no right of property binding on the trustee. It was suggested that it was quite different if the father had paid off the debt to the bank and become entitled to the security which would, of course, amount to
C subrogation.

Conclusion. In my judgment, if there had been no bankruptcy, on a sale of the property the bank's debt would necessarily have been paid off out of the proceeds of sale and the father, as a matter of marshalling, could have insisted upon the debt being discharged out of the bankrupt's share. The general principle of marshalling is that if a beneficiary is disappointed of his benefit through a creditor being paid out of property
D intended for the beneficiary, then to the extent of the disappointment he is entitled to recoup or compensate himself by going against the property which ought to have been used to pay the debt: see *Snell's Principles of Equity*, 27th ed. (1973), p. 321.

As between the father and the bankrupt—and bearing in mind that the father is admittedly only a surety—it should be implied that their
E intention was that the bankrupt's beneficial interest should bear the burden. If that is so, it seems to me that the bankrupt's interest vested in his trustee in bankruptcy, subject to an inchoate right of indemnity, if the surety were called upon to pay, or the debt fell to be discharged, as it would have to be, out of the proceeds of sale of the property. Alternatively, I think that the father could be regarded as having an actual charge on the bankrupt's interest within the principle discussed
F by Warrington J. in *Gee* v. *Liddell* [1913] 2 Ch. 62, 72, where he says:

> "Now there is some authority on the question to which I will presently refer, but I should like first to deal with it as a matter of principle independently of authority. Two persons mortgage in one deed their respective estates to secure an advance made to one of them, and the deed gives to each of them power to redeem, and it
> G appears on the face of the deed that as between the two the estate of the person to whom the money is paid is to be primarily liable. Has not the person who joins in mortgaging his own estate by virtue of that deed itself an interest in the estate of the person to whom the money is advanced? In my opinion he has, and I think that the nature of his interest is a charge upon the estate of the
> H principal debtor by way of indemnity for the purpose of enforcing against that estate the right which he has, as between himself and the principal debtor, to have that estate resorted to first for the payment of the debt. If it were not so, the result would be a startling one."

It is said that the present case can be distinguished from *Gee* v. *Liddell* in the following ways. First, in *Gee* v. *Liddell* the mortgagors expressly charged their separate beneficial interest. Mr. Finlay for the

trustee says that in the present case the father and son charge the A
entirety by way of legal mortgage but it seems to me that the practical
effect of that was to charge the beneficial interest of the father and of
the son. Secondly, Mr. Finlay said that the father paid nothing to the
bank. But Warrington J., at p. 73, dealt with the position of a mere
surety by covenant who had paid nothing. He said that there was a
difference between a person who was joined as a co-mortgagor and a
mere surety by covenant. He said: B

> "In my judgment a person who has joined as co-mortgagor in such a deed as this has from the moment when the deed is executed an interest in the estate of the principal mortgagor."

Thirdly, in that case the deed showed on the face of it that as between
the two mortgagors the estate of the person to whom the money was C
lent was to be primarily liable. There is no such express provision here.
But, as I have said, I think that such a provision must be inferred. It
follows that out of the proceeds of sale of the property, the bank's
indebtedness is, in my judgment, primarily payable out of the bankrupt's
half share, leaving little, if anything, for his trustee.

The order for sale. The trustee applies under both section 30 of
the Law of Property Act 1925 and section 105 of the Bankruptcy Act D
1914. It is well settled that the trustee is not entitled as of right to a
sale of the property. The court has a discretion: see *In re Solomon, A
Bankrupt, Ex parte Trustee of the Property of the Bankrupt* v. *Solomon*
[1967] Ch. 573 and *In re Turner* (*A Bankrupt*), *Ex parte Trustee of the
Property of the Bankrupt* v. *Trustee* (*A Bankrupt*) [1974] 1 W.L.R. 1556.
It would seem that if I am right that the bankrupt's share must be primarily E
liable for the bank's debt, it may be possible for the bankrupt's father
to come to some arrangement with the trustee to purchase his interest.

I propose, therefore, that this application should be adjourned until
a convenient date, and we must then reconsider the position if no agree-
ment has been reached. I should add that I do not think that the father
can be charged anything for his use and occupation of the property,
since he has resided there as one of two co-owners and each is entitled F
to possession.

Fox J. I agree.

*Application adjourned to enable
bankrupt's father and trustee to
agree, if possible, value of trustee's
interest in house.* G

May 10. The court was informed that the value of the trustee's
equity in the house had been agreed at £150 and, that in those circum-
stances, there would be no need for a sale of the property.

Appeal allowed. H
*No order for costs save legal aid
taxation of appellant's costs.*

Solicitors: *Rowberry, Morris & Co., Reading; Blandy & Blandy,
Reading.*

K. N. B.

[FAMILY DIVISION]

* PRACTICE DIRECTION (PROBATE: CAVEAT)

Probate—Practice—Caveat—Extension of period caveat in force—Non-Contentious Probate Rules 1954 (*S.I.* 1954 *No.* 796), *r.* 44 (*as amended by Non-Contentious Probate* (*Amendment*) *Rules* 1976 (*S.I.* 1976 *No.* 1362 (*L.* 23)), *r.* 5 (*a*))

1. Rule 44 of the Non-Contentious Probate Rules 1954 provides that any person who wishes to ensure that no grant of representation is sealed without notice to himself may enter a caveat in the prescribed form either in the Principal Registry or in any district probate registry. A caveat normally remains in force for a period of six months from the date on which it is entered. Under existing rule 44, a caveator cannot directly renew or extend a caveat, although he can usually enter a fresh caveat in the estate.

2. Probate rule 44 is amended, with effect from October 1, 1976 (Non-Contentious Probate (Amendment) Rules 1976: S.I. 1976 No. 1362), so as to provide that a caveator may, on or after that date, apply for an extension of an existing caveat entered by him. New rule 44 (4A) requires the application to be lodged in the registry in which the caveat was entered and further provides that the application must be made within the last month before the caveat to which it relates is due to expire. The extension will be for a further period of six months from the caveat's expiry date; a caveat may be extended more than once. The amending rules also provide that a caveator whose caveat remains in force may not enter a further caveat in that estate except with the leave of a registrar of the Principal Registry.

3. No form of application for the extension of a caveat is prescribed by the amending rules, other than the requirement that it must be in writing. Application may, therefore, be made by the caveator or his solicitor attending personally at the registry in which the caveat was entered and endorsing the relevant caveat with a request for its extension or by sending the application to the registry by post. Where postal application is made the related caveat number should be quoted. In every case where a caveat is extended, the registry will issue a receipt.

4. Fee No. 5 of the Non-Contentious Probate Fees Order 1975 has been amended to provide that the fee for extending a caveat shall be £2 (The Supreme Court (Non-Contentious Probate) Fees (Amendment) Order 1976: (S.I. 1976 No. 1363).

R. L. BAYNE-POWELL
Senior Registrar.

September 15, 1976.

[COURT OF APPEAL] A

* REGINA *v.* GENESE

1976 March 25 — James L.J., Michael Davies and Jupp JJ.

Crime—Sentence—Fine—Fine in addition to suspended sentence— B *Whether appropriate where offender under* 21*—Whether justifiable in principle—Powers of Criminal Courts Act* 1973 (*c.* 62), *s.* 19 (2)

The defendant, who was under the age of 21, pleaded guilty to affray and was sentenced to four months' imprisonment suspended for two years and fined £150.

On his application for leave to appeal against sentence on the ground that the judge had failed to take into account C the restrictions imposed by section 19 (2) of the Powers of Criminal Courts Act 1973 [1] on the court's power to imprison an offender under 21, and that a sentence of imprisonment was inappropriate since an alternative sentence, namely a fine, was available:—

Held, refusing the application, that it was not wrong in principle for a court, once it had decided in accordance with section 19 (2) of the Powers of Criminal Courts Act 1973 that D imprisonment was the only appropriate method of dealing with an offender under the age of 21, to impose a fine in addition to a term of imprisonment, provided that the amount of the fine was reasonable and appropriate and that in the circumstances of the present case an additional penalty by way of a fine was justified.

Reg. v. *Ankers* (1975) 61 Cr.App.R. 170, C.A. explained.

E

The following cases are referred to in the judgment of the court:

Reg. v. *Ankers* (1975) 61 Cr.App.R. 170, C.A.
Reg. v. *Ffoulkes* (unreported), January 16, 1976, C.A.
Reg. v. *Foster* (unreported), February 10, 1976, C.A.
Reg. v. *King* [1970] 1 W.L.R. 1016; [1970] 2 All E.R. 249, C.A.
Reg. v. *Leigh* (1969) 54 Cr.App.R. 169, C.A.

F

No additional cases were cited in argument.

APPLICATION

The defendant, Paul Arthur Genese, applied for leave to appeal against a sentence of four months' imprisonment suspended for two years and a fine of £150 imposed at the Oxford Crown Court (Judge Mynett) on G December 15, 1975, on the ground that the judge had erred in imposing both a fine and a sentence of imprisonment on an offender under the age of 21.

The facts are stated in the judgment of the court.

Alexander Dawson for the defendant.
The Crown was not represented. H

JAMES L.J. The matter before the court raises a point of some general importance. On December 15, 1975, at the Crown Court at Oxford, Paul Arthur Genese the defendant, who was a young man under the age of 21, pleaded guilty to an offence of affray. He was sentenced by the circuit

[1] Powers of Criminal Courts Act 1973, s. 19 (2): see post, p. 960A.

A judge, Judge Mynett, to a term of four months' imprisonment suspended for two years. In addition he was fined the sum of £150 with an alternative of four months' imprisonment in default of payment.

His application for leave to appeal against his sentence has been referred by the registrar to the full court, without it going through the section 31 procedure to the single judge.

B The grounds of appeal were settled by Mr. Dawson who, with the leave of the court, has added a further ground, which became necessary because since the suspended sentence was imposed upon the defendant, he has appeared at the Crown Court at Oxford in January 1976 and again in March and we are informed that a sentence of borstal training was imposed upon him on those occasions. That sentence is not under appeal and the effect of the order of borstal training is to remove the
C liability to serve the suspended sentence by virtue of the provisions of section 22 (5) of the Powers of Criminal Courts Act 1973. So the suspended sentence upon the defendant that was imposed in December has disappeared, but the fine of £150 is not affected by the imposition of the borstal training order.

Little need be said of the facts that gave rise to the suspended sentence
D of imprisonment and the fine. The charge of affray arose out of an incident that occurred on the evening of March 7, 1975, an incident which involved the defendant's parents, his sister Mrs. McCarthy and her husband. It appears that the McCarthys lived next door to a family called Mello. There was trouble between them, which came to a head on that evening, and there was an invasion of the Mellos' territory by the McCarthys.

E The Crown case, a case accepted by the judge as a fact, was that the defendant took part in the physical violence. His case was that he was guilty of affray and pleaded guilty to affray on the basis that he shouted abuse and gave verbal encouragement to those who were inflicting the violence. Those briefly were the facts which gave rise to the charge.

The defendant is a young man who has been before the courts unfortu-
F nately on a number of previous occasions. In 1971 for theft and burglary he was fined; in 1972 for obstructing the police he was fined; in 1974 for an offence of altering a vehicle licence he was fined; in the same year for criminal damage he was fined and ordered to pay compensation; and in 1975 for theft he was placed on probation for 12 months. Those offences of course, as will be seen, were not of the most serious kind on their facts. Otherwise he would have been dealt with differently. They are not
G offences which involve any violence on his part.

No point is taken in relation to the sentence that was imposed by the Crown Court at Oxford except that it was a sentence that was wrong in law. Mr. Dawson puts it this way. In the original grounds of appeal he said that the judge failed to take into account the effect of the provisions of section 19 (2) of the Powers of Criminal Courts Act 1973, which restricts
H the powers of the court to impose imprisonment upon a person under the age of 21; and he contends in his grounds that the judge should not have imposed a sentence of imprisonment at all, whether suspended or not, because there was another way of dealing with the offender.

In the amended grounds the same point is raised but from a different angle, in that it is said that if the judge concluded that there was no appropriate method of dealing with the defendant except by imprisonment, then he was wrong in law in adding a fine.

The argument is to a substantial degree based on the wording of the A
statute and on one case decided in this court, namely *Reg.* v. *Ankers* (1975) 61 Cr.App.R. 170.

I will first read section 19 (2) of the Act of 1973.

> "No court shall impose imprisonment on a person under 21 years of age unless the court is of opinion that no other method of dealing with him is appropriate; . . ." B

The subsection then goes on to specify what the court should do before making a decision as to whether to impose imprisonment upon a person of that age.

The argument of Mr. Dawson is that this court is bound by its previous decision in *Reg.* v. *Ankers,* 61 Cr.App.R. 170, which was heard on May 2,
1975. That was a case in which Ankers, aged 18 years, and two other C
young men, had been involved in taking no less than 12 motor cars without their owners' consent, and the trial judge had imposed a sentence which was contended to be contrary to the provisions of the statute which I have just cited. The report states the appellant's point in this way, at p. 171:

> "[Counsel for the appellant's] point is that this sentence of imprison- D
> ment was wrong in principle, having regard to the appellant's previous good character. He draws attention to the Powers of Criminal Courts Act 1973, section 19 (2)"—and then Park J. cited the subsection, and continued—"In our judgment, the learned judge, having decided in all the circumstances of the case to deal with the appellant by the imposition of fines, was wrong in deciding to impose, in addition, sentences of imprisonment, as it could not be said that no other E
> method of dealing with him was appropriate. For this reason, the suspended sentences of imprisonment will be quashed and the appeal against sentence is allowed to that extent."

Before commenting further upon the judgment, it is pertinent to observe that that case was first reported in the *Criminal Law Review* ([1975] Crim.
L.R. 402) in very brief form. To the report there is appended a commen- F
tary by Mr. David Thomas in which the general principle governing the use of suspended sentences is referred to. At the conclusion of the commentary these words are used, at p. 403:

> "It has been held that a fine may be imposed in conjunction with a suspended sentence of imprisonment (*Reg.* v. *Leigh* (1969) 54
> Cr.App.R. 169), but it is submitted that as a general rule it is inappro- G
> priate to combine these measures unless the case is one where a fine could properly be combined with an immediate sentence of imprisonment (as for instance where the offender has made a substantial profit from his offence). To impose a fine in combination with a suspended sentence of imprisonment tends at best to reinforce the impression that a suspended sentence is a meaningless 'let off,' and at worst
> result in punishing the offender twice over, if he is subsequently H
> ordered to serve the suspended sentence."

With those observations at the end of the commentary this court does not agree. They do not reflect the true sentencing policy of the courts.

The report in the *Criminal Law Review*, and it may be that the very recent report in the Criminal Appeal Reports also, has led to a widespread belief that *Reg.* v. *Ankers* (1975) 61 Cr.App.R. 170 is authority for

A the proposition that it is wrong in principle to impose a fine upon a person who is at the same time being sentenced to a suspended term of imprisonment. That understanding is reflected in *Morrish and McLean, The Crown Court*, 7th ed. (1975), p. 96, where it is said, citing *Reg.* v. *Ankers* as the authority:

> "However, in the case of a young adult offender aged 17 and over B but under 21 years, it is wrong having imposed a suspended sentence of imprisonment also to impose a fine, because it cannot be said that no other method of dealing with that offender is appropriate."

With that statement in that book we also disagree.

We think one has first to consider what the basic principle is. It is that there is no statutory provision at all which forbids a fine being imposed C in addition to a sentence of imprisonment. There is a statement in *Archbold Criminal Pleading Evidence & Practice*, 38th ed. (1973), para. 749, p. 454, which reads:

> "There is nothing wrong in principle when passing a suspended sentence in imposing a fine on the same count, but special care should be taken to see that the fine is well within the defendant's means to D pay:"

and *Reg.* v. *King* [1970] 1 W.L.R. 1016 is cited accurately as authority for that proposition. So we have no statutory provision forbidding it and a decision which says that in the case of suspended sentences of imprisonment a fine can be imposed subject to the qualification that it is appropriate to the means of the offender.

E Then one has the Powers of Criminal Courts Act 1973. Section 30 (1) of that Act provides:

> "Where a person is convicted on indictment of any offence other than an offence for which the sentence is fixed by law, the court, if not precluded from sentencing the offender by its exercise of some other power (such as the power to make a probation order), may impose a fine in lieu of or in addition to dealing with him in any other way in F which the court has power to deal with him, subject however to any enactment limiting the amount of the fine that may be imposed or requiring the offender to be dealt with in a particular way."

Mr. Dawson says that the words at the end of that subsection, "any enactment . . . requiring the offender to be dealt with in a particular way" lead one to section 19 (2) of the Act of 1973 which, he argues, is a section G which requires the offender to be dealt with in a particular way.

We cannot accept that argument. Section 19 (2) does not require the defendant to be dealt with in a particular way. It says that no court shall impose imprisonment on an offender under the age of 21 unless certain conditions are fulfilled. That is a simple provision which is to be construed according to the ordinary natural meaning of the words.

H One goes from the statutory provisions to *Reg.* v. *Leigh* (1969) 54 Cr.App.R. 169 to which I have already referred in citing the commentary of Mr. Thomas in the *Criminal Law Review*. This court decided that a sentence of imprisonment suspended, plus a fine, was an appropriate sentence in that case. It is true that in that case the person concerned was over 21 years of age.

This matter has come before the court on other occasions. In *Reg.* v. *Ffoulkes* (unreported), January 16, 1976, the judgment of Eveleigh J.

includes a reference to *Reg.* v. *Ankers* (1975) 61 Cr.App.R. 170 in these A
terms:

> "The first ground is misconceived, a misconception that is based on *Reg.* v. *Ankers.* That case concerned an accused of 18 years of age where different considerations were applicable. Furthermore it has been decided by this court in *Reg.* v. *Leigh* (1969) 54 Cr.App.R. 169 that such a sentence is permissible." B

In *Reg.* v. *Ffoulkes* this court was distinguishing *Reg.* v. *Ankers* on the ground that Ankers was 18 whereas Ffoulkes was over 21 years of age (he was some 39 years of age) and was also drawing attention to the fact that *Reg.* v. *Ankers* seemed to be in conflict with *Reg.* v. *Leigh.*

Lastly, before coming back to consider *Reg.* v. *Ankers* it is necessary to refer to *Reg.* v. *Foster* (unreported), February 10, 1976, in which the C
court decided to allow the appeals of the three young men concerned against their sentences. Mr. Dawson rightly argues that the reference in that case to *Reg.* v. *Ankers* (1975) 61 Cr.App.R. 170 was not necessary for the purpose of the court's decision, and to that extent can be said to be obiter dictum. But the argument was addressed to the court and the court felt it right to deal with it. *Reg.* v. *Ankers* is referred to in some D
detail as to its facts, and Shaw L.J., giving the judgment, said:

> "If that passage"—the passage which is relied upon by Mr. Dawson in this case from the judgment of Park J. in *Reg.* v. *Ankers*—"was intended to convey that if a fine is imposed the judge who imposed it must be regarded as having come to the conclusion that imprisonment in the circumstances cannot be an appropriate penalty as well, E
> this court would respectfully demur. A sentence of imprisonment is to be regarded as the primary punishment and the decision that a sentence of imprisonment is appropriate must be made before the question of whether a supplemental penalty by way of fines is to be imposed at all."

There is then a sentence which commences "What the judge in *Reg.* v. F
Ankers (1975) 61 Cr.App.R. 170 had done . . . ," which, when one looks at the transcript of the proceedings in *Reg.* v. *Ankers,* is clearly a misconception of what occurred in that case, due to the fact that in *Reg.* v. *Foster* this court did not have the full transcript before them. The judgment concludes:

> "The view there was not that a fine alone was appropriate, but that imprisonment and a fine together were appropriate. This court does G
> not read section 19 (2) of the Act of 1973 as a foundation for the proposition that where a fine is imposed that of itself is an indication on the part of the judge who imposed it that imprisonment is not the appropriate method of dealing with the offender."

One comes back eventually to *Reg.* v. *Ankers* (1975) 61 Cr.App.R. H
170, to see just what was being said in the judgment of this court when Park J. said, at p. 171:

> "the learned judge, having decided in all the circumstances of the case to deal with the appellant by the imposition of fines, was wrong in deciding to impose, in addition, sentences of imprisonment, as it could not be said that no other method of dealing with him was appropriate."

A The recitation of the facts in the judgment of this court in *Reg.* v. *Ankers* does not bring out the salient features of the particular circumstances of that case. The transcript of the proceedings in *Reg.* v. *Ankers* shows that, in the course of his mitigation, counsel appearing for Ankers was at pains to persuade the recorder to impose a financial penalty and he adduced evidence to show that a reasonable level of financial penalty could be imposed and that Ankers would be able to pay the fine. The B transcript also shows that Mr. Higgs, the recorder, was very receptive to the suggestion. Indeed, the terms of the probation officer's report by implication indicated that a fine would be a suitable disposal for the case. Mr. Ankers' father was called to persuade the court that if the court did impose a fine, that fine would come out of Ankers' pocket and not out of his father's pocket. There it was left at the end of the mitigation and C from the transcript it seemed that the recorder and counsel for Ankers were at one, that the proper punishment for the accused was a fine. But when it came to sentencing, addressing the co-accused Avers and Ankers, the recorder said:

> "With considerable hesitation, bearing in mind the number of offences in which you were involved, I have decided not to send either of you D to prison or to any other kind of custodial sentence."

Stopping there the recorder was there saying "I have decided that prison is not the appropriate sentence in this case." Then the recorder goes on to announce the amount of the fines imposed on Avers and Ankers. Then, having announced the amount of the fines and summarised the total, the recorder said:

> E "In addition, you will be sentenced on each of these five charges to six months' imprisonment suspended for a period of two years."

It is quite clearly a case in which the recorder misdirected himself. He had arrived, as Park J. said, at a decision by which the young man Ankers could be dealt with otherwise than by imprisonment, namely by imposition of a fine. Having done that he was quite wrong to say, in effect, "Having F decided that this is an appropriate way of dealing with you, I am also imposing a sentence of imprisonment and suspending it." That was the situation with which this court was dealing on the appeal against sentence by Ankers, and that is the way in which the words of Park J. in *Reg.* v. *Ankers* must be construed. It is not authority, and it must be clearly understood that it is not authority, for the proposition, whether a person is over G the age of 21 or under, that it is wrong in principle to impose a fine when that person is also being sentenced to a term of imprisonment, albeit a suspended term. There is nothing wrong in principle in such a sentence. The court must be careful of course in these circumstances, as in any circumstances when a fine is imposed, to ensure that the fine is one which is reasonable, proper and appropriate to the means of the defendant paying it, but there is nothing wrong at all in coupling that mode of dealing H with an offender with a suspended sentence of imprisonment. There is nothing, in our view, in section 19 (2) of the Act of 1973 which forbids a court taking this course.

The mental processes which a judge has to go through are these. In the case of a young man under the age of 21, the court must consider every way of dealing with him—borstal detention, conditional discharge, probation, fine, anything that is open to the court to do—before deciding that imprisonment is the penalty that he must suffer. If all these matters have been excluded, and if the court decides that there is no other appropriate A method of dealing with the offender than imprisonment and imposes a prison sentence, the court can then, in the appropriate case, go on to consider that the sentence should be suspended. That is what happened in this case. If the court does go on to consider that the sentence should be suspended, or even if it does not do so, in the appropriate case the court can also consider whether an additional penalty by way of a fine is justified in the circumstances. B

Having heard an argument that was advanced by Mr. Dawson with as much force as could be advanced, we find that there is no substance in the ground of appeal, and the application is refused.

Application refused.
Leave to appeal refused. C

Solicitor: *Registrar of Criminal Appeals.*

J. W.

D

[QUEEN'S BENCH DIVISION]

* UNITED OVERSEAS BANK *v.* JIWANI

[1974 U. No. 2005]

E

1976 March 30, 31 MacKenna J.

Restitution—Money credited in error—Claim by bank for repayment—Bank crediting money to customer's account by mistake—Bank confirming credit—Customer transferring sum to third party—Whether customer liable to repay money—Whether bank estopped from claiming restitution F

In 1969 J., a resident in Uganda, opened a bank account with the plaintiffs in Switzerland. In May 1972, J. left Uganda to live in Europe and, at the end of August, his account stood at $10,000. On October 2, he drew a cheque for $20,000 in favour of P., from whom he intended to purchase an hotel. On October 9, $11,000 was credited to J.'s account and a further $11,000 was credited to his account in error on the following day. J. was advised that those amounts had been G credited; he also checked his account by telephone and by a personal visit to the plaintiffs. Thereupon he arranged for the plaintiffs to transfer a further $11,000 to P. On October 17, the cheque for $20,000 was paid; and the $11,000 was transferred on October 20. The latter sum was transferred by the plaintiffs in the belief that J.'s account was in credit; if the $11,000 had not been forthcoming in that way, J. would have been able to raise the extra money for the purchase of the H hotel from other sources, albeit less easily.

On the claim by the plaintiffs for the repayment of the $11,000 and interest which J. contended they were estopped from pursuing:—

Held, giving judgment for the plaintiffs, that even if J. had been misled by the plaintiffs (which he had not), the plaintiffs

---

[Reported by BERNARD O. AGYEMAN, ESQ., Barrister-at-Law]

A would only be estopped from pursuing their remedy if J. could show that he had changed his position as a result of his mistaken belief in such a way that it would be inequitable to require him to repay the money and that J. had failed to establish (post, pp. 968C–D, 970E–F).

Holt v. *Markham* [1923] 1 K.B. 504, C.A. and *Deutsche Bank* (*London Agency*) v. *Beriro and Co. Ltd.* (1895) 1 Com. Cas. 123; 255, C.A. distinguished.

B

The following cases are referred to in the judgment:

Deutsche Bank (*London Agency*) v. *Beriro and Co. Ltd.* (1895) 1 Com.Cas. 123; 255, C.A.

Holt v. *Markham* [1923] 1 K.B. 504, C.A.

Lloyds Bank Ltd. v. *Brooks* (1950) 6 Legal Decisions Affecting Bankers 161.

C *Skyring* v. *Greenwood* (1825) 4 B. & C. 281.

The following additional cases were cited in argument:

Holland v. *Manchester and Liverpool District Banking Co.* (1909) 25 T.L.R. 386.

Jones (*R. E.*) *Ltd.* v. *Waring and Gillow Ltd.* [1926] A.C. 670, H.L.(E.).

D *Larner* v. *London County Council* [1949] 2 K.B. 683; [1949] 1 All E.R. 964, C.A.

ACTION

The plaintiffs, United Overseas Bank, Geneva, by mistake credited the account of the defendant, Shokatali Hassanali Jiwani, who was their customer and resident in London, with a payment of U.S. $11,000. There-
E after, having made a payment out of the account as instructed by the defendant, the plaintiffs discovered the mistake and that the account was overdrawn by $9,892.10. By a writ issued on June 14, 1974, the plaintiffs claimed against the defendant the sum of $9,892.10 as money had and received, together with interest.

By his defence the defendant pleaded, inter alia, that it was the duty
F of the plaintiffs, as his bankers, to keep him correctly informed as to the state of his account and not to over-credit it; and that if the plaintiffs credited his account by mistake with the sum of $11,000 (and the defendant made no admissions as to that) they were estopped from relying upon the mistake and from claiming to recover that sum or any part of it from him.

The facts are stated in the judgment.

G *Henry Brooke* for the plaintiffs.
Paul Norris for the defendant.

MACKENNA J. The plaintiffs, a Swiss bank in Geneva, sue their customer, Mr. Jiwani, for $9,892.10 and interest. As my statement of the facts will make clear, the claim is in substance one for money paid under
H a mistake of fact and the defence one of estoppel by representation.

The facts relating to the payment and to the mistake were proved by the oral evidence of the plaintiffs' sub-manager, M. Cottet, and by the documents in the case. They can be briefly narrated.

Mr. Jiwani opened the account on October 13, 1969. He was then resident in Uganda, being one of the Asian subjects of that state. His object in opening the account was to build up a reserve of assets outside Uganda in case of trouble in the future. There were a few payments into the account

in 1969 and 1970. The first was made shortly after the opening of the A
account. This was a payment of $3,000 described in the credit advice
sent by the bank to Mr. Jiwani on October 20, 1969, as a remittance
received in his favour from Mr. and Mrs. Ghelani. There was another
in September 1970 of $13,343.30 which, again according to the bank's
credit advice, had been provided by a Mr. Alibhai. The third in
December 1970, also provided by Mr. Alibhai, was $29,985. On December
31, 1971, the balance was $34,323. Drawings on the account were made B
by Mr. Jiwani during the summer of 1972 which reduced the balance
to $10,108.50 by the end of August. Some of the money had been drawn
to cover Mr. Jiwani's living expenses in Europe where he had come from
Uganda in May 1972. There was a drawing on August 18 of $12,212 in
favour of a Mr. Pirani, a London businessman with whom Mr. Jiwani had
some complicated business dealings during that summer culminating, in C
November 1972, in the purchase by Mr. Jiwani of an hotel owned by Mr.
Pirani's private company. It is doubtful whether this particular drawing
had anything to do with that purchase. Its effect, at all events, was to
reduce the balance to the figure I have given of $10,108.50.

On October 6, 1972, a telex message from a bank in Zurich informed
the plaintiffs in Geneva that the Zurich bank was crediting them as
from that date with the sum of $11,000 in favour of Mr. Jiwani on the D
instructions of an unnamed client. The plaintiffs were told in the message
that the transfer would be made through the Union of Swiss Banks in
Geneva, which I take to be some sort of clearing house. On the same day,
October 6, the plaintiffs sent Mr. Jiwani in London a credit advice informing
him that the Zurich bank had made this transfer of $11,000 in his
favour, available for him to draw against from October 9. It is apparently E
the practice of Swiss banks, when they receive a sum of money for a
client on one day, to credit it to his account not on that day but on the
next working day which, in this case, was Monday, October 9, as October
6 was a Friday. The statement of Mr. Jiwani's current account contains
a credit entry against the date October 9 of $11,000. The balance was then
$21,108.50. On the same day as it sent the telex message, the Zurich
bank posted to the plaintiffs a written advice of payment stating as follows: F

> "Through Union de Banques Suisses we transferred to you $11,000
> as from October 6, which please utilise by order of one of our clients
> for account of Mr. S. H. Jiwani."

The document bears stamped words in German and French stating that
it is sent in confirmation of a telex message. These words would have been G
put on in Zurich. It was probably received by the plaintiffs on October 9.
The clerk who dealt with it apparently overlooked the stamped words and
treated the document as if it were a new transfer of a second sum of
$11,000. The clerk caused another credit entry to be made in Mr. Jiwani's
statement of account which brought the apparent balance to $32,108.50,
and caused him to be sent a second credit advice informing him that the
Zurich bank had made a transfer of $11,000 in his favour, available for H
him to draw against from October 10.

Mr. Jiwani says that he inquired from the plaintiffs by telephone from
London on or before October 16 about the state of his account and was
given the figure of $32,108.50. He visited the plaintiffs at Geneva on
October 17 when he was again given the figure of $32,108.50. I see no
reason for disbelieving this part of Mr. Jiwani's evidence. The plaintiffs
had not yet discovered their error. Mr. Jiwani had already on October 2

A drawn a cheque in favour of Mr. Pirani for the sum $20,000. He now gave instructions to the plaintiffs to transfer to Ontario another $11,000.60 for Mr. Pirani's credit, which the bank did. The statement of account shows, if I read it correctly, that the $20,000 was paid on October 17 and that the transfer of $11,000.60 was made on October 19. These payments reduced the apparent credit balance to $1,107.90. As the account had been over-credited with $11,000, the account, if it had been correctly stated, B was not in credit but was overdrawn by $9,892.10.

On October 20, 1972, a M. Losi, an employee of the plaintiffs, when making a routine check, discovered their mistake. He informed the lady dealing with Mr. Jiwani's account. She caused a debit advice to be prepared debiting Mr. Jiwani with $11,000 and sent it to him under cover of an explanatory letter dated October 25 asking Mr. Jiwani to cover the C overdraft. I am satisfied that Mr. Jiwani received this letter in October, within a few days of its being posted on the 25th and, at all events, before the purchase of the hotel, to which I have already briefly referred, was completed. Mr. Jiwani did not answer this or a number of other letters. In May 1973, one of the plaintiffs' representatives visited Mr. Jiwani in England and took from him a promissory note for the amount of the overdraft and interest which had accrued in the meantime. The note was D eventually dishonoured and this action was begun.

I have no doubt whatever that the bank transferred the $11,000 to Mr. Pirani on Mr. Jiwani's instructions under a mistake of fact, believing that the Zurich bank had transferred for his credit two sums of $11,000, whereas it had transferred only one. In my opinion, it can make no difference to the right of the plaintiffs to recover this money from Mr. E Jiwani that they made the payments to Mr. Pirani at Mr. Jiwani's request and not to Mr. Jiwani himself. In the circumstances of this case the position is exactly the same as if they had paid the money to Mr. Jiwani and he had transferred it by some other means to Mr. Pirani in Ontario.

Mr. Jiwani has given me some sort of explanation of his dealings with Mr. Pirani and of the value he received in exchange for the transfer of the $11,000. It was a confused explanation. All things considered, F including the want of documents passing between the gentlemen in question, I think it likely that the value given by Mr. Pirani for the $11,000 must have been one or more of the large sums of money paid into Mr. Jiwani's account with Lloyds Bank at Ealing in October 1972, probably the sum of £4,969 credited to that account on October 19.

I have already mentioned that Mr. Jiwani bought an hotel from Mr. G Pirani's private company in November 1972. To be more accurate, he acquired the sub-lease of that hotel, the completion date being November 3. I think it is probable that the transfer to Mr. Pirani of the $11,000, which was the use to which Mr. Jiwani put the overpayment, made it easier for Mr. Jiwani to complete this purchase which he effected by drawing on his account with Lloyds Bank and with the help of a loan from that bank. I H am reasonably sure that if the $11,000 had not been forthcoming in the way it was, that is through the plaintiffs' error, Mr. Jiwani would have found the extra money for his purchase in some other way, either by a larger borrowing from Lloyds Bank or, if they were unwilling to lend, by Mr. Pirani giving him more time to pay. I am equally certain that the purchase of the hotel was for Mr. Jiwani and his family a good investment. If it be a relevant consideration, I find that Mr. Jiwani knew of the plaintiffs' mistake before the date when he completed his contract to buy

the hotel. Lastly, and again if it be a relevant consideration, I believe that A
if he is now required to repay the plaintiffs, he will be able to do so by
borrowing if he has not the cash available. He is a man of property. He
owns, in addition to the hotel, a dwelling house which he acquired at about
the same time as the hotel for some £18,000.

The question remains whether Mr. Jiwani is liable to repay the plaintiffs
the sum with which they credited him in error. In my opinion, which I
base on the statement of the law in *Goff and Jones, The Law of* B
Restitution (1966), pp. 491, 492, he is liable unless he can show that the
plaintiffs are estopped from claiming restitution, and there are three condi-
tions to be satisfied by him if he is to make good this estoppel. First, he
must show that either the plaintiffs were under a duty to give him accurate
information about the state of this account and that in breach of this duty
they gave him inaccurate information, or that in some other way there was C
a misrepresentation made to him about the state of the account for which
the plaintiffs are responsible. Secondly, he must show that this inaccurate
information misled him about the state of the account and caused him to
believe that the plaintiffs were his debtors for a larger sum than was the
case and to make the transfer to Mr. Pirani in that mistaken belief. Thirdly,
he must show that because of his mistaken belief he changed his position in
a way which would make it inequitable to require him to repay the money. D
I have no doubt that the first of these requirements is satisfied. I shall
assume for the moment that he has satisfied the second, returning to that
matter a little later in this judgment. He has, I think, completely failed
to establish the essential third condition.

Mr. Norris, arguing for Mr. Jiwani, contended that if a bank's customer
has spent the money with which he has been mistakenly credited, he E
cannot, in any case whatever, be required to repay it. If he has to show a
detriment making it inequitable to require him to repay, he shows that
detriment, it is argued, by proving that he has spent the money, irrespective
of the purpose for which it was spent or of the effects of the expenditure,
and that he will have to make it good, if at all, out of other moneys. To
test Mr. Norris's proposition I put the case to him of a customer who uses
the overpayment to buy a gilt-edged security which can be immediately F
resold and which rises in value between the date of the purchase and the
date when the mistake is discovered and he is called on to repay. Mr.
Norris did not shrink from accepting the logical consequence of his argu-
ment. He said that in such a case the customer would be under no
obligation to repay; he could treat his acquisition of the security as a
windfall and let the bank whistle for its money. I do not believe that is G
the law.

Undoubtedly there are cases in which the customer who has spent the
money in ignorance that he was being overpaid will not be required to
repay. *Holt* v. *Markham* [1923] 1 K.B. 504 was such a case. *Skyring* v.
Greenwood (1825) 4 B. & C. 281, which *Holt's* case followed, was another.
A third was *Lloyds Bank Ltd.* v. *Brooks* (1950) 6 Legal Decisions Affecting H
Bankers 161. There was reason for believing in each of those cases that
the defendant would have acted differently if he had not mistakenly
believed that he was richer than he was, that because of his mistake, he
had, to use Goff and Jones's words, altered his mode of living. There was
the further fact in *Holt* v. *Markham* [1923] 1 K.B. 504 that the defendant
had invested part of the overpayment in a company which had since gone
into liquidation.

A There is in the present case, as I have already said, no reason for thinking that Mr. Jiwani would have acted differently in the matter of the purchase or in any other way if the extra dollars had not been mistakenly made available to him. He would still have completed the purchase of the hotel by a further borrowing from Lloyds Bank or in some other way. The completion of the purchase, wherever he got the money to do it with, was in itself a benefit and is a continuing benefit, unlike the investment
B in *Holt's* case.

Other cases cited by Mr. Norris are distinguishable in the same way. There was the case of the customer who had paid the money over to a third party which he was not bound to do if the money were not truly his own and who was unable to recover it from the third party on the discovery of the mistake: *Deutsche Bank* (*London Agency*) v. *Beriro and*
C *Co. Ltd.* (1895) 1 Com.Cas. 123 and 255. That the customer in that case was not liable to repay the bank does not help Mr. Norris.

What I have already said is enough to show that there must be judgment in the plaintiffs' favour, but I have something to add on the second of the three requirements, namely, that the bank's misstatement caused Mr. Jiwani to believe that there had in fact been two transfers of $11,000 to the credit of his account. He told me a story which I did not believe about
D the reason why he thought that there had been two transfers. He said that after he had left Uganda in May 1972 he had spoken on the telephone to his brother, who was still living there, and had asked him to arrange with Mr. Alibhai, for the transfer to the plaintiffs for Mr. Jawani's credit of a sum in dollars equivalent to 245,000 Ugandan shillings to be paid in Uganda to Mr. Alibhai along with his commission. The defendant told
E me that it was his understanding and his brother's that the equivalent of this amount of Ugandan currency would be about $24,000. He said that on some date which he could not now remember he had received a telephone call in London from Mr. Alibhai speaking from Uganda who told him that he had transferred, or was going to transfer, $11,000 that day and that either that evening or the next day or after two days he would transfer the balance. After this conversation with Mr. Alibhai the
F defendant expected, so he said, that there would be two transfers made by Mr. Alibhai and that, therefore, when he received the information from the plaintiffs about the supposed second transfer, he believed that it represented the amount of the second expected transfer. Mr. Alibhai, it seems, did not transfer any other money to Mr. Jiwani, who has not heard from him since. He does not know where he is.

G Mr. Jiwani's brother gave evidence supporting him to some extent. He said that he had spoken to Mr. Jiwani on the telephone, that Mr. Jiwani had told him to arrange with Mr. Alibhai for the transfer of $25,000, of which he said the Ugandan equivalent was 175,000 shillings, and that he had made the arrangement.

My reasons for not accepting Mr. Jiwani's story about the two expected
H transfers can be stated very shortly. There is, it seems to me, an improbability in the substance of the supposed telephone conversation with Mr. Alibhai: why the two transfers? Why not a single transfer, made when Mr. Alibhai had the whole amount available, which would be, at the latest, in a day or two, and might even be the day on which he was speaking? That is one reason. Another is the strange coincidence that Mr. Jiwani should have been expecting two transfers at about the same time and of about the same amount from Mr. Alibhai and that the plaintiffs should,

as they undoubtedly did, wrongly mistake the confirmation of the telex A
for a second transfer. The improbability of this coincidence is, it seems
to me, the greater when it is realised that Mr. Alibhai never made any
second transfer. This goes against the view that there was an arrangement
with him that he should send any larger sum than the $11,000 which he
sent in fact, or that he had told Mr. Jiwani on the telephone that he would
be making a second transfer. A third reason can be found in the fact
already mentioned, that on October 2 Mr. Jiwani had drawn a cheque B
on his account with the plaintiffs for $20,000 in favour of Mr. Pirani,
which Mr. Pirani apparently did not present until October 16. On
October 2 the credit balance was $10,108.50. It is not unreasonable to
infer that at the time when he drew the cheque, only a few days before the
plaintiffs received the transfer of $11,000, Mr. Jiwani was expecting the
transfer of a sum which would put him in credit to an amount sufficient C
to meet the cheque. If on October 2 he was both expecting a much larger
transfer than $11,000 and intending to give Mr. Pirani not $20,000 but
$31,000, namely, the amount of the cheque and of the subsequent transfer
to Ontario, why did he not give Mr. Pirani in the first instance a cheque
for the larger amount? If, as I believe, the burden is on Mr. Jiwani of
satisfying me that on October 17, or thereabouts, he honestly believed that
there had been a second transfer made by Mr. Alibhai, he has not dis- D
charged that burden. It seems to me equally possible that he knew or
strongly suspected that the plaintiffs were making a mistake. In saying
this I do not exclude the possibility that Mr. Jiwani, though not expecting
a second transfer from Mr. Alibhai, on hearing from the plaintiffs that
there had been two transfers, may have thought that some arrangement, of
which he had not previously been told, had been made by his brother E
either with Mr. Alibhai or with somebody else for the transfer of this
further sum. But that is not the story told by Mr. Jiwani in the witness
box and I see no reason why I should speculate about this possibility.

For the reasons, first that Mr. Jiwani has not satisfied me that he
honestly believed that the two transfers had been made, and second that
in any event, he has not proved that if he was misled by the plaintiffs he
changed his position in such a way as would make it inequitable to require F
him to repay the money, I hold that this action succeeds.

I have been told that it is agreed between the parties that the correct
amount for which judgment should be given is $13,302.50 and there will be
judgment for that amount.

Judgment for the plaintiffs for $13,302.50
with costs up to date of defendant's G
legal aid certificate.
Costs thereafter adjourned into chambers
for inquiry into defendant's means.

Solicitors: *Simmons & Simmons; Gerard Hales & Co.*

H

A

[QUEEN'S BENCH DIVISION]

* REGINA v. GOVERNOR OF RISLEY REMAND CENTRE, *Ex parte* HASSAN

B 1976 March 23, 24 — Lord Widgery C.J., Thompson and Kenneth Jones JJ.

Habeas corpus—Onus of proof—Entry—Detention of alien—Alien alleged to be " illegal entrant"—Onus on alien of establishing prima facie case of unlawful detention—Unacceptable explanation of lost passport held on entry—Whether onus of proof discharged—Immigration Act 1971 (*c.* 77), *s.* 33 (1), *Sch.* 2,
C *paras.* 8, 9, 16 (2)

The applicant, a Pakistani national, entered the United Kingdom at an airport. Some 11 months later the applicant, who was in possession of a Pakistani passport issued after his entry, was ordered to be detained, as an illegal entrant within section 33 (1) of the Immigration Act 1971,[1] by an immigration officer acting under paragraph 16 (2) of Schedule 2
D to the Act of 1971, and was transferred to custody at a remand centre. He applied for a writ of habeas corpus to secure his release on the ground that he had been given leave to enter and remain for six months on entry so that his detention as an illegal entrant was unlawful. Inconsistent accounts of the loss of his old passport appeared not only in his own affidavits and those in support but also in those of officers who had interrogated him and recorded his answers.
E An affidavit by the governor of the remand centre stated that the applicant was transferred into custody pursuant to the immigration officer's written authority.

On the application for a writ of habeas corpus:—

Held, refusing the application, that the applicant being an alien and his detention being apparently valid in view of the governor's affidavit, the onus was on the applicant to establish a prima facie case that his detention was illegal; and that,
F since his conflicting accounts of the loss of his old passport were unacceptable, he had not discharged the onus on him, and the writ of habeas corpus would not be issued (post, pp. 977G, 978B–C, 979B).

Dictum of Lord Denning M.R. in *Reg.* v. *Governor of Pentonville Prison, Ex parte Azam* [1974] A.C. 18, 31–32, C.A. applied.

Reg. v. *Governor of Brixton Prison, Ex parte Ahsan* [1969] 2 Q.B. 222, D.C. distinguished.

G

The following cases are referred to in the judgment of Lord Widgery C.J.:

Reg. v. *Governor of Brixton Prison, Ex parte Ahsan* [1969] 2 Q.B. 222; [1969] 2 W.L.R. 618; [1969] 2 All E.R. 347, D.C.

Reg. v. *Governor of Pentonville Prison, Ex parte Azam* [1974] A.C. 18; [1973] 2 W.L.R. 949; [1973] 2 All E.R. 741, C.A.

H *Rex.* v. *Halliday* [1917] A.C. 260, H.L.(E.).

Rex v. *Secretary of State for Home Affairs, Ex parte Greene* [1942] 1 K.B. 87; [1941] 3 All E.R. 104, C.A.; [1942] A.C. 284; [1941] 3 All E.R. 388, H.L.(E.).

No additional cases were cited in argument.

[1] Immigration Act 1971, s. 33 (1): see post, p. 973C.
Sch. 2, para. 16 (2): see post, p. 973F–G.

APPLICATION for a writ of habeas corpus. A

The applicant, Wajid Hassan, a Pakistani national, arrived in England and was subsequently detained in custody at Risley remand centre under the authority of an immigration officer. He applied for a writ of habeas corpus to secure his release.

The facts are stated in the judgment of Lord Widgery C.J.

W. R. Rees-Davies Q.C. and *Mukhtar Hussain* for the applicant. B

Harry Woolf for the governor of the remand centre and the Secretary of State for the Home Department.

LORD WIDGERY C.J. In these proceedings Mr. Rees-Davies moves for a writ of habeas corpus on behalf of one Wajid Hassan at present detained in Risley remand centre. C

The applicant, who was a Pakistani national, arrived at Heathrow on April 7, 1975, on a scheduled flight from Karachi. There is no doubt that he was on that aircraft; the passenger list amongst other things shows that he was; and there is no doubt that outside the boundaries of Terminal 3 at Heathrow he was met by his sister and by another relative, a Dr. Ali. D

The applicant, as will appear in more detail in a moment, gives in an affidavit an account of his movements to show that between the time when the aircraft landed on the tarmac and his meeting with his sister and Dr. Ali he passed through immigration in the normal way, and it is his case that, in the course of passing through immigration in the normal way, he was granted leave to enter the country, leave which he required in view of his national status, and furthermore that the leave was to E persist for six months.

Having met his sister and Dr. Ali, and after a slight contretemps about his suitcase (because apparently according to the evidence supplied by him he came out of the terminal without his luggage and Dr. Ali had to go back, armed with the ticket and passport, and recover it for him), he says that they set off, the three of them, for Manchester in a hired car. F

Nothing else of significance then happened in connection with the story until February 26, 1976. On that day the applicant was arrested by officers of the Greater Manchester police force and brought for interview to Manchester airport where he was interrogated by the immigration authorities. We do not know exactly how that came about, but something happened to give the immigration authorities cause to suspect that the applicant had not entered through immigration in the ordinary way G but had come into this country without having been examined by an immigration officer and without obtaining permission so to do.

The theory—and it is not meant to be offensive to put it that way—put forward by the Crown in this case is that, although the applicant was on the aircraft in question, by some device he managed to get through the terminal building without submitting himself to the immigration H authorities and therefore in fact entered this country without permission. That is the theory adopted by the Home Office and the immigration authorities in this case.

Of course the whole problem might be answered by one single document, namely, the passport upon which the applicant travelled when he came to Heathrow, but that passport has not been seen by the court, it being the applicant's case (and again I shall have to go into this in more

A detail in a moment) that the passport was lost after his arrival in this
country, and indeed a new passport was issued to him on May 5, 1975.

Having regard to those views possessed by the immigration officers and after interrogation, an order was made for the detention of the applicant in the Risley remand centre, and he has been there ever since.

He contends that he came into this country lawfully, and, although
he has outstayed his authorised period and might be sent back by the
B use of other machinery, he says that it is illegal to detain him as though
he were an illegal entrant when, according to his case, he was nothing of
the kind.

The Crown case in more specific detail is that the applicant came
through Terminal 3 without being interrogated by an immigration officer
and he is therefore an illegal entrant by virtue of section 33 (1) of the
C Immigration Act 1971, which provides:

> "... 'entrant' means a person entering or seeking to enter the United Kingdom, and 'illegal entrant' means a person unlawfully entering or seeking to enter in breach of a deportation order or of the immigration laws, and includes also a person who has so entered; ..."

D Contending that the applicant comes into that class, the immigration
authorities, or perhaps I should say the Home Office for simplicity and
accuracy, justify their subsequent action by reference to Schedule 2 to
the Act of 1971.

Paragraph 8 of Schedule 2 makes general provision whereby a would-
be entrant who is refused permission can be returned to his home country
E on the aircraft which brought him. I need not look at it in any detail.
Paragraph 9 is important; it provides:

> "Where an illegal entrant is not given leave to enter or remain in the United Kingdom, an immigration officer may give any such directions in respect of him as in a case within paragraph 8 above are authorised by paragraph 8 (1)."

F Thus, if the applicant is an illegal entrant it is lawful for an order to be
made in respect of him upon the lines of paragraph 8, namely, "Go back
on an aeroplane flying to Pakistan on a scheduled flight." In regard to
intermediate custody paragraph 16 (2) of Schedule 2 provides:

> "A person in respect of whom directions may be given under any
> of paragraphs 8 to 14 above may be detained under the authority of
> G an immigration officer pending the giving of directions and pending
> his removal in pursuance of any directions given."

So, if the Home Office is right in its basic contention that the applicant
is, or is to be treated as, an illegal entrant, there is authority for keeping
him and that would justify a refusal of this application. On the other
hand, if he did obtain permission, Mr. Woolf does not seek in these pro-
H ceedings to argue that he is liable to immediate return to Pakistan. What
would happen on that footing is that the matter would then have to be
inquired into because, if the proper conclusion here is that he was not
an illegal entrant, then the order of habeas corpus can go.

I turn now to the evidence. A good deal has been said about the difficulties which this court may suffer when it is faced with a conflict of evidence which it will not as a rule attempt to determine on affidavits, but this is not really a case in which there is a conflict of evidence in that sense. This is rot a case in which there are two witnesses each of whom purports to give first-hand evidence of a particular happening, and the two accounts are in conflict; that is not this case. In this case the applicant is saying "I had leave" and the Home Office is saying "We do not believe you; prove it." This is a matter which can properly be investigated in this court.

So far as the relevant evidence is concerned, I am not going to go in detail through a number of instances in which it is said that the applicant's evidence was inconsistent either with his own evidence or that of his supporters on occasion. There are some quite telling points in the affidavits such as, for example, a statement that on one occasion the applicant described his meeting with his sister as being on the tarmac by the aeroplane. Everybody knows, not having VIP status, the applicant would not be greeted by his sister on the tarmac by the aeroplane. There are a number of instances of that kind, but I accept what Mr. Rees-Davies says about this, that we must be very careful about attaching specific importance to actual language used, when we have a Pakistani whose knowledge of English is not by any means established in these proceedings, and who is being interrogated on those lines.

What I find important, and I shall confine myself substantially to it, are the accounts which the applicant has given of the loss of his passport. This is very important because the passport, if it were available, would answer this question once and for all. It would either contain the immigration officer's stamp or it would not and, if it did not, no one would venture to contend that he passed through immigration. The passport has gone. If the applicant intended to overstay his leave he has thereby lost an encumbrance which might show his true status. On the other hand, if he intended to go home within the period which he says was allotted to him, it is surprising if he did not keep good care of his passport because it would be the one document which proved his status and right to be in this country.

What happened to the passport? There are a number of accounts, and the first one I turn to is one given by an immigration officer, Mr. Everard. He went along to the Pakistani embassy earlier this week to see what he could find out about the grant of a new passport for the applicant. His evidence shows that he was shown a file relating to a new passport which was issued on May 2, 1975, and on the file there was a written application form signed by the applicant requesting the issue of a new passport to him and giving details of the loss of the previous one. The details of the loss of the previous one then given were these: "During travelling on tube train to Hounslow lost briefcase containing papers and passport." So we find on that explanation that he lost his passport on the tube train.

The same file contains photocopies of the first nine pages of the old passport, and it would of course be extremely valuable if we knew precisely how it came about that that photocopy appeared in the files of the Pakistani embassy in London. Precise information about the source of those photographs might again answer this question once and for all, but we have no evidence as to how they got there. We do not know whether they were brought there by the applicant as part of his application for a new passport. We do not know whether the Pakistani embassy cabled Karachi and said "We have an applicant named Wajid

A Hassan. Have you got any record of his old passport?" Any of those things might have happened, but it is right, in referring to the fact that the photo-copies were there, to say, according to Mr. Everard, that the first nine pages, which is all that he could see on photograph, contained no indication of an immigration stamp showing a landing in London. One must hesitate to attach too much finality to that, but I am bound to mention it because Mr. Rees-Davies said that the conduct of Mr. B Everard was dishonest, and I just do not agree with that.

If one looks at a typical Pakistani passport, which we have been given for our consideration, one finds that the first seven pages in accordance with normal international usage are devoted to the personal particulars of the holder, and pages 8 and 9 are the first two of a successive series of pages which are headed "Visas." I expect everybody C who has ever been abroad knows that if a passport is stamped on arrival a neat and tidy immigration officer will put his stamp on page 8 and a slightly more casual and haphazard one will not take it amiss if he puts his stamp on page 12. Therefore it seems to me that little can be drawn from that fact individually, but the suggestion that in some way the immigration officer was being dishonest in his treatment of the matter D is one which I certainly can find no vestige of support for at all. So much for the explanation in the Pakistani embassy file.

The next explanation to refer to is the original explanation given by the applicant himself, and that is in his affidavit, which reads: "That soon after my arrival at Manchester my passport was lost and I obtained a new passport from the Pakistani embassy at London." That does not take us very far, but that is the first thing he said when he was asked E to explain what had happened to his original passport. In his second affidavit he takes the matter a little further where he said:

> "That on my arrival at Manchester when the luggage was being unloaded from the car I noticed that my leather handbag was missing. My passport was in this leather handbag."

So the explanation being given there is that for some reason or another F the bag containing the passport was not loaded at Heathrow and therefore did not arrive at Manchester and was left behind at Heathrow.

His sister, who makes an affidavit dealing with the circumstances in which she went to meet him, deals with that point; she said:

> "That on arrival at Manchester and whilst the baggage was being unloaded it was noticed that my brother's leather hand case was G missing. I understand from my brother that his passport was in that leather handcase."

So she is confirming the second account was given by the applicant.

Then there are other accounts spoken to by immigration officers of explanations given by the applicant to them in the course of their H inquiries. I have already dealt with Mr. Everard's evidence so far as it is valuable. I pass to the evidence of Mr. Cotton, and in his affidavit he said:

> "I then asked him"—that is, the applicant—"about the loss of his passport. He told me that he had placed his passport in his travelling bag but had placed his vaccination certificate, air ticket and other papers in his inside pocket. I asked him why he had separated them from his passport and he said that he did not know why. He

said that he and his sister had sat down on a bench and that when A he came to pick up his small bag which he had placed on the floor at his side he found that it had been stolen. I asked him whether he had taken a photocopy of his passport before it was stolen and he told me that he had not."

That explanation is significantly different from the second one. The second one gives a picture of their driving happily off to Manchester and B not finding the bag is stolen till they get there. This, as I understand it, describes a situation in which they are sitting on a bench at London Airport and discover there and then that the bag is gone, presumably stolen.

Then there is Mr. Cooke, another immigration officer, who also raises this question with the applicant, and he said in his affidavit that the account given by the applicant was: C

"He then said that he sat down on a bench with his sister waiting for someone to come to pick him up and his bag was stolen. I asked him if the bag contained all his papers and he said that it did. I then asked him specifically if it had contained his vaccination certificate and air ticket and after some hesitation he said that they were in his pocket. He said that no copies of his passport had D been made before it was stolen."

Those are the accounts given by him at various times to explain the loss of this vital document, and, as I have already said, the attitude of the Secretary of State is that he does not believe that the applicant came through lawfully in view in particular of that evidence.

What is the position in regard to the law here, because it is quite E clear that the answer that this court provides must depend in large measure in a case of this sort upon where the onus of proof lies and what is the standard of proof required? In connection with that problem there is some interesting modern authority.

I go first to *Reg.* v. *Governor of Brixton Prison, Ex parte Ahsan* [1969] 2 Q.B. 222, not because the actual decision in that case is neces- F sarily the most helpful but because it is a very valuable collection of opinions upon a problem very similar to our own. That case arose in 1968 and was concerned with illegal immigrants who were found with their feet wet and sand in their pockets on the Kent coast, and who claimed to have been entitled to remain in this country, because at that time the law said that an immigrant entering howsoever could escape any proceedings for his return to his native land if he managed to stay G in this country for 24 hours. So the issue in the *Ahsan* case was whether the court should accept the evidence of those men that they had been in the country for more than 24 hours. They said they had been here for 28 hours or something like that. So it raised the same kind of problem that we have here.

The court, consisting of Lord Parker C.J., Ashworth and Blain JJ., H reached widely different opinions in their conclusion. It is noticeable that the fact that the men in question were British subjects in that instance, which is not the case with the applicant, carried a good deal of weight in the opinions expressed, and Blain J. in particular was obviously very reluctant to hold that a British subject in Kent should ever be required to prove (the onus being on him) that he had entered the country lawfully.

A Be that as it may, the case is very useful for a review of the earlier authorities, and in particular it contains a very valuable selection of extracts from *Rex* v. *Secretary of State for Home Affairs, Ex parte Greene* [1942] 1 K.B. 87, and thereafter in the Court of Appeal and the House of Lords. On page 233 of the *Ahsan* report are three extracts from the judgment of Goddard L.J. in the *Greene* case; he said, at p. 113:

B "In my opinion, when once it is shown that he is detained under a warrant or order which the executive has power to make, it is for the applicant for the writ to show that the necessary conditions for its making do not exist."

The onus in other words is on the applicant. A little later there is this extract from the judgment of Goddard L.J. with reference to a C passage from the speech of Lord Wrenbury in *Rex* v. *Halliday* [1917] A.C. 260, 274:

"That in terms puts the onus on the applicant, and I think the conclusion is that the applicant can controvert the return, and if he proves his case, and it is for him to prove it, he will be discharged."

Finally Goddard L.J. said, at p. 116:

D "I am of opinion that where on the return an order or warrant which is valid on its face is produced it is for the prisoner to prove the facts necessary to controvert it, and in the present case this has not been done."

Notwithstanding those powerful extracts of opinion indicative of the E fact that the onus is on the applicant, Lord Parker C.J. came to a different conclusion. He based his different conclusion, as I see it, on the special circumstances of that case, involving as it did British subjects, and an obligation that they had to prove their right to be in this country He also quoted (on p. 235) a passage of the judgment of MacKinnon L.J., in *Greene's* case which again so clearly expresses my own views that I would like to repeat it. MacKinnon L.J. said [1942] 1 K.B. 87, F 108:

"No evidence on the part of the gaoler, or of the Home Secretary, to establish the validity of the order (except proof of its signature if that is disputed) is necessary, unless the applicant has adduced evidence of its invalidity sufficient to discharge and shift the onus of proof which rests primarily on him."

G I do not propose to read further from the judgments in *Ahsan's* case because, as I say, the decision (as I understand it) was based very largely upon the fact that there one was dealing with British subjects, and here one is dealing with an alien who prima facie has no right to be in this country at all. Perhaps I should mention, before leaving that case, that Ashworth J. said, at p. 237:

H "I accept entirely the principle that the custodian is called upon to justify the detention, but he does so by making a return which is valid on the face of it. If such return discloses on its face that the detention is unjustified, there is no more to be said: see *Bushell's* case (1677) Vaugh. 135. But the return may be valid on its face and it is then for the person detained to place evidence before the court showing that what appears to be a valid return is in fact invalid."

I believe that that is the law applicable to the present case. A

Mr. Woolf's submission is that, if one comes to the conclusion that the obligation on the part of the applicant has not been discharged, the proper place to look is section 16 of the Immigration Act 1971, which contains a right of appeal in respect of amongst other things a person who is said to be an illegal entrant, and Mr. Woolf's submission (and I hope I do justice to it) is that the existence of that right of appeal means that in this case a writ of habeas corpus should not go, but instead the B applicant should remain in detention unless and until further steps to remove him are taken.

I do not find myself persuaded that that is the right approach to the present case on the assumption which can now be made that the applicant has not discharged the onus of proof upon him. I make that assumption because I find his conflicting accounts of the loss of his vital document C —the passport—quite unacceptable, and therefore it seems to me that if the law is as I have stated it to be the onus is not discharged and the applicant is to be treated as an illegal entrant. I do not for myself see that the existence of a right of appeal under section 16 has really got anything to do with the matter.

In my judgment the case can be disposed of in a different way, for D which purpose I rely on certain dicta of Lord Denning M.R. in the later case of *Reg.* v. *Governor of Pentonville Prison, Ex parte Azam* [1974] A.C. 18. That was concerned with a very important question of whether or not the provisions of the Act of 1971 with regard to the return of illegal entrants was retrospective, and it was held eventually that they were retrospective. Lord Denning M.R.—and here again he so expresses my own view that I would like to quote it; having dealt with the equi- E valent of Mr. Woolf's argument about section 16 of the Act of 1971—said, at pp.31–32:

"These provisions as to appeal give rise to a question of the first importance. Do they take away a person's right to come to the High Court and seek a writ of habeas corpus? I do not think so. If Parliament is to suspend habeas corpus, it must do so expressly F or by clear implication. Even in the days of the war, when the enemy were at the gate, habeas corpus was not suspended or taken away. When a man was detained under regulation 18B, he was entitled to apply for a writ of habeas corpus if he could show a prima facie case that he was unlawfully detained. During the war, a man called Budd made an application which was successful, G because the prerequisites of a lawful detention had not been complied with. But in his next application he failed, because the Home Secretary had made a return which could not be faulted: see *Rex* v. *Secretary of State for Home Affairs, Ex parte Budd* [1942] 2 K.B. 14. Lord Greene M.R. put an illustration which is appropriate here, at pp. 22–23: 'if, for example, a regulation empowered the Home Secretary to detain any person who was in fact an alien, the H court could inquire into the nationality of the applicant, since, if it transpired that he was not in fact an alien, his detention would be ultra vires.' Under Schedule 2 the power to detain and remove applies in respect to a person who is in truth an illegal entrant. If a man can make a prima facie case that he is not an illegal entrant, he is entitled to a writ of habeas corpus as of right: see *Greene* v. *Home Secretary* [1942] A.C. 284, 302 by Lord Wright. The court

A has no discretion to refuse it. Unlike certiorari or mandamus, a writ of habeas corpus is of right to every man who is unlawfully detained. If a prima facie case is shown that a man is unlawfully detained, it is for the one who detains him to make a return justifying it."

That exactly describes in my view the position in which the applicant
B now finds himself. The gaoler's return is good on the face of it. The gaoler said "I detain this man by virtue of an order under paragraph 16 of Schedule 2 to the Act of 1971." Therefore, it seems to me, the onus is upon the applicant to show a prima facie case that his detention is illegal and for reasons I have already given I am satisfied that that onus is not discharged and therefore the proper course here is to say that habeas corpus should not go and I would refuse the application.

C

THOMPSON J. I agree.

KENNETH JONES J. I also agree.

Application refused.

Solicitors: *Daweck & Co.; Treasury Solicitor.*

D

L. N. W.

E

[COURT OF APPEAL]

* REGINA *v.* CHIEF IMMIGRATION OFFICER, HEATHROW AIRPORT AND ANOTHER, *Ex parte* SALAMAT BIBI

1976 May 10, 11 — Lord Denning M.R., Roskill and
F Geoffrey Lane L.JJ.

Immigration—Refusal of entry—Non-Commonwealth nationals—Settled Commonwealth citizen from Pakistan—Family refused entry after Pakistan leaving Commonwealth—New rules for non-Commonwealth nationals—Whether intra vires—Whether family of settled immigrant required to obtain visas in Pakistan—Effect of European convention on English law—Statement
G *of Change in Immigration Rules for Control on Entry: EEC and Other Non-Commonwealth Nationals* (*October* 16, 1973) (*H.C.* 437)—*Convention for the Protection of Human Rights and Fundamental Freedoms* (1953) (*Cmd.* 8969), *arts.* 8, 25—*Immigration Act* 1971 (*c.* 77), *s.* 1 (5)

The applicant and two young children arrived at London airport from Pakistan on March 11, 1976, carrying affidavits
H and documents stating that she had been married to one BA in Pakistan in 1952, and birth certificates of the children. She told the immigration officer that she had come to visit her husband in the United Kingdom for about two weeks. BA met her at the airport. He had been in the United Kingdom since 1967 and was a Commonwealth national settled here on January 1, 1973, when the Immigration Act 1971 came into force. He told the immigration authorities that she was his wife and that he wished the family to stay here permanently with him if the Home Office would grant permission. The

officer, after making further inquiries, interviewed the family A
again and refused them leave to enter, stating that he was not satisfied that they intended to stay as visitors only for the limited period stated; and they were sent back to Pakistan.

An application on their behalf was made to the Divisional Court for orders of certiorari and mandamus directed to the chief immigration officer and the Home Secretary on the grounds, inter alia, that the immigration officer had erred in
law in dealing with the applicants under the immigration rules B
applicable to non-Commonwealth nationals; and that he ought to have treated them as the wife and children of a person settled here on January 1, 1973, to whom section 1 (5) of the Act of 1971 [1] gave a right to enter and remain indefinitely. The court refused the orders.

On appeal it was submitted, inter alia, that the immigration officer ought to have exercised his discretion in favour of the
family by having regard to article 8 (1) of the European Con- C
vention for the Protection of Human Rights [2]:—

Held, dismissing the appeal, (1) that section 1 (5) of the Act of 1971 was directed only to ensuring that the rules made under that Act (for controlling the entry of families of Commonwealth citizens settled here on January 1, 1973) should not be more restrictive than those applicable to them before that Act came into force and did not confer any right of entry
on such families; that the rules prior to the Act of 1971 and D
those made under it required such families when seeking admission to the United Kingdom to have a current entry clearance certificate so that the rules now in force were intra vires section 1 (5); and that as the applicants did not hold such certificates on their arrival they had no right to enter.

(2) That the immigration officer who interviewed the applicants had correctly dealt with their case under the rules
applicable to non-Commonwealth nationals since they came E
from Pakistan which was no longer in the Commonwealth; that as they had no visas from the British Embassy in Pakistan they had not complied with those rules; and that as the officer was not satisfied that they intended to stay only for the limited period as visitors he had exercised his discretion properly in refusing them entry.

(3) That the immigration officers performed their functions
under the Act in accordance with the rules made by the F
Secretary of State and were not under any further duty to apply the principles laid down in the Convention on Human Rights, for even if it were practicable for them to do so the Convention had not yet been made law by Parliament and was therefore not part of the law of the United Kingdom, though, as the United Kingdom was a party to the Convention, Parliament when enacting a statute or a Minister when making
rules would be presumed to have had regard to its provisions. G

Reg. v. *Secretary of State for the Home Department, Ex parte Bhajan Singh* [1976] Q.B. 198, C.A.; *Reg.* v. *Secretary of State for the Home Department, Ex parte Phansopkar* [1976] Q.B. 606, C.A. and *Pan-American World Airways Inc.* v. *Department of Trade* [1976] 1 Lloyd's Rep. 257, C.A. explained.

Per Roskill L. J. The statements of rules for control on H
entry made under the Act of 1971 and laid before Parliament are as much a part of the law of this country as any other form of rule-making activity or delegated legislation empowered by Act of Parliament (post, p. 985E–F).

Decision of the Divisional Court of the Queen's Bench Division affirmed.

[1] Immigration Act 1971, s. 1 (5): see post, p. 983C–D.

[2] Convention on Human Rights, art. 8 (1) (2): see post, pp. 984D, 988E.

A The following cases are referred to in the judgments:

Pan-American World Airways Inc. v. *Department of Trade* [1976] 1 Lloyd's Rep. 257, C.A.

Reg. v. *Secretary of State for the Home Department, Ex parte Bhajan Singh* [1976] Q.B. 198; [1975] 3 W.L.R. 775; [1975] 2 All E.R. 1081, D.C. and C.A.

Reg. v. *Secretary of State for the Home Department, Ex parte Phan-*
B *sopkar* [1976] Q.B. 606; [1975] 3 W.L.R. 322; [1975] 3 All E.R. 497, D.C. and C.A.

The following additional cases were cited in argument:

Attorney-General for Ontario v. *Attorney-General for Canada* [1947] A.C. 127 [1947] 1 All E.R. 137, P.C.

Broome v. *Cassell & Co. Ltd.* [1972] A.C. 1027; [1972] 2 W.L.R. 645;
C [1972] 1 All E.R. 801, H.L.(E.)

Civilian War Claimants Association Ltd. v. *The King* [1932] A.C. 14, H.L.(E.).

Golder Case, February 21, 1975, European Court of Human Rights.

Reg. v. *Criminal Injuries Compensation Board, Ex parte Lain* [1976] 2 Q.B. 864; [1967] 3 W.L.R. 348; [1967] 2 All E.R. 770, D.C.

Reg. v. *Secretary of State for the Home Department, Ex parte Akhtar*
D [1975] 1 W.L.R. 1717; [1975] 3 All E.R. 1087, D.C.

Wigg v. *Attorney-General of Irish Free State* [1927] A.C. 674, P.C.

APPEAL from the Divisional Court of the Queen's Bench Division.

The applicant, Salamat Bibi, applied on March 17, 1976, on her own behalf and on behalf of her two children, Parvin Akhtar and Pervez
E Barkat, for an order of certiorari to quash the refusal of leave to enter to her and her two children by an immigration officer at Heathrow airport on March 13, 1976, and an order of mandamus directed to the immigration officer and/or the Secretary of State for the Home Department to reconsider the refusal of leave and to admit her and her two children into the United Kingdom. Her grounds were that (a) she was the wife of Mr. Barkat Ali, a citizen of Pakistan, who had been settled in the United
F Kingdom since 1967 and who at the coming into force of the Immigration Act 1971 was a Commonwealth citizen settled in the United Kingdom so that his wife and children also had a right of settlement in the United Kingdom; and (b) the refusal of leave to enter to her and her children was contrary to (i) section 1 (5) of the Immigration Act 1971; (ii) article 8 of the European Convention on Human Rights; and (iii) the rules of
G natural justice.

The Divisional Court on March 19, 1976, granted her leave ex parte to apply for the orders but on the hearing inter partes on April 9, 1976, refused the orders. An appeal on her behalf was filed on the grounds that the Divisional Court wrongly held (1) that there was no error of law on the face of the record because the fact that the immigration officer dealt with the applications under paragraph 13 of the Statement of
H Immigration Rules for Control on Entry: EEC and Other Non-Commonwealth Nationals (1973) (H.C. 81) was such an error; (2) that since section 1 (5) of the Immigration Act 1971 was not the basis on which the applicant and her two children were seeking entry into the United Kingdom, it could not be relied on as an error on the face of the record susceptible to an order of certiorari; and (3) that the court ought to have held that the fact that the immigration officer failed to consider the effect of section 1 (5) of the Act of 1971 as it affected the applicant and her two

children was itself a ground for quashing his decision. By a notice of A
additional grounds she relied further on the grounds that (4) the court
wrongly held that there was no obligation placed on the immigration
officer " to sit down and turn up his pamphlets and decide whether per-
haps a more convincing application might be made "; (5) the immigration
officer in refusing the application to enter exercised his discretion without
taking into account the applicant's right under article 8 of the European
Convention on Human Rights, namely, the right of respect for family life; B
and (6) in the alternative, that article 8 of the convention was directly
enforceable in the English court and had to be read in conjunction with
the provisions of section 1 (2) and (5) of the Act of 1971.

Louis Blom-Cooper Q.C. and *Eugene Cotran* for the applicants.
Harry Woolf for the chief immigration officer and the Home Secretary. C

LORD DENNING M.R. On March 11, 1976, a lady from Pakistan
arrived at Heathrow with two small children. She gave her name as
Salamat Bibi. On the way from Pakistan she had stayed six days at
Mecca and three days at Medina, and she arrived at Heathrow at 9.30 a.m.
She had not got an entry certificate. She could not speak English, but
through an interpreter she said she was coming as a visitor to be with D
her husband for a couple of weeks. She had about $700 in cash on her,
and an open-dated return ticket to take her back to Karachi. She also
produced what purported to be an affidavit made by herself declaring
that she had been married to one Barkat Ali in 1952 in Pakistan. She
produced what purported to be copies of birth certificates showing that
the eldest child—a girl—was born on April 19, 1967; and the younger E
one—a boy—was born on October 12, 1971. They were not in English,
but translated that is the information which they gave.

A Mr. Barkat Ali was at the airport to meet her, together with an
articled clerk of a firm of solicitors. He said that the lady was his wife
and he wanted her to come in with the children and stay with him per-
manently, if the Home Office would grant permission. Mr. Barkat Ali
said that he had been here since 1967. He had come from Pakistan and F
had settled here. He said that he had married the lady in 1955 and was
the father of the children. He was in business in England earning £2,000 a
year and had been claiming tax relief for his wife and children since 1974.

The immigration officer thought it necessary to make further inquiries,
so he gave her temporary admission for 48 hours. Having made these,
he was not satisfied with her story. No doubt because Mr. Barkat Ali G
said he wanted her to stay permanently: and she said she wanted to
stay for a couple of weeks. On March 13, 1976, the immigration officer
issued a notice refusing to give her leave to enter. He said on the official
form:

> " You have asked for leave to enter the United Kingdom as a visitor
> for two weeks but I am not satisfied that you intend to stay only for H
> this limited period. I, therefore, refuse you leave to enter. . . ."

He gave directions for her removal. She eventually went back with her
children.

The solicitors made application for certiorari to quash the refusal of
leave to enter. The application was made on the basis that she could
prove that she was in fact the wife of Barkat Ali, and that the children

A were his. Assuming that she is his wife, it is said that she is in law entitled to enter this country as of right.

The argument ran on these lines. Until 1972 Pakistan was a member of the Commonwealth, but it withdrew from the Commonwealth on January 30, 1972. This was recognised in our law by the Pakistan Act 1973, which came into operation on September 1, 1973. Thereafter, from September 1, 1973, Barkat Ali ceased to be a Commonwealth citizen. He
B became a citizen of a non-Commonwealth country—Pakistan.

Now Mr. Barkat Ali relies on his status eight months earlier, on January 1, 1973, when the Immigration Act 1971 came into force. At that date he was a Commonwealth citizen. He was settled in this country, having been ordinarily resident here ever since 1967. He himself was to be treated as having been given indefinite leave to remain here: see
C section 1 (2) of the Act of 1971.

Such being his position on January 1, 1973, he says that his wife and children are entitled to come here as of right. He relies on section 1 (5) of the Immigration Act 1971, which says of the Immigration Rules:

> ". . . The rules shall be so framed that Commonwealth citizens settled in the United Kingdom at the coming into force of this Act"
> D (that is, on January 1, 1973) "and their wives and children are not, by virtue of anything in the rules, any less free to come into and go from the United Kingdom than if this Act had not been passed."

I do not think that section gives any right to the wife and children to come in without entry clearance. The section is not dealing with rights at all. It is only dealing with the rules which are to be made by the
E Secretary of State. It says that the rules for wives and children who come after January 1, 1973, are not to be any more restrictive than the previous rules. So we have to look at the rules applying before January 1973 and the rules applying afterwards. Before January 1973, the rules were contained in Cmd. 4298. The rule about wives and children is in paragraph 34. That made it clear (as did section 20 of the Immigration
F Appeals Act 1969) that the wife of a Commonwealth citizen was not free to come into this country unless she was in possession of a current entry certificate granted to her. It said: "If she has no entry certificate, she is not to be admitted." After January 1973, the rules relating to Commonwealth citizens were contained in the Statement of Immigration Rules for Control on Entry: Commonwealth Citizens (1973) (H.C. 79). This contains the same restrictions as before. The wife of a Commonwealth citizen
G was not to be admitted unless she had a current entry certificate. Paragraph 40 says: ". . . a passenger seeking admission as a dependant . . . must hold a current entry clearance granted to him for that purpose." So the rules after 1973 contain the same restrictions as before 1973. The wives of Commonwealth citizens were not to be admitted unless they held a current entry clearance. In these circumstances Mr. Blom-Cooper
H has to admit that the rules in H.C. 79 do comply with section 1 (5) of the Act of 1971. But he then turns to the change in the rules made about Pakistan, when that country left the Commonwealth. The change is contained in Statement of Change in Immigration Rules for Control on Entry: EEC and Other Non-Commonwealth Nationals (1973) (H.C. 437) made on October 16, 1973. It provides that thereafter a citizen of Pakistan is to be treated in the same way as any other non-Commonwealth citizen. He or she must get a visa and satisfy the rules relating to non-Commonwealth

citizens. It says: ". . . the entry clearance for which they may apply A
will take the form of a visa." Whereas previously he or she had to get
entry clearance from our High Commissioner: now he or she had to get a
visa from our Embassy. Mr. Blom-Cooper suggested that H.C. 437 was
ultra vires. I see nothing ultra vires at all. It is perfectly valid.

Accordingly, after Pakistan had left the Commonwealth and after
September 1, 1973, anyone coming from Pakistan must comply with the B
rules relating to non-Commonwealth citizens. These are contained in
Statement of Immigration Rules for Control on Entry: EEC and Other
Non-Commonwealth Nationals (1973) (H.C. 81). To comply with them,
this lady, if she came as a visitor, would have to satisfy paragraph 13.
It says that visitors are to be admitted if the immigration officer is satisfied
that no more than a visit is intended and in all cases leave to enter
should be refused if the immigration officer is not so satisfied. In the C
present case the lady came as a visitor. The immigration officer was not
satisfied that she was only going to stay for a short visit. So he quite
rightly refused her entry and she has gone back to Pakistan. If the lady
had come as a wife, she would have had to satisfy paragraphs 34, 35
and 36, and she could not do this, as she held no current entry certificate,
nor a visa or its equivalent.

Then Mr. Blom-Cooper took another point altogether. He said that D
the immigration officer ought to have admitted the lady because of the
European Convention on Human Rights. Article 8 (1) says: "Everyone
has the right to respect for his private and family life, his home and his
correspondence." In sub-paragraph (2), there is a set of exceptions in the
interests of national security, public safety, and the like. We have again
been invited to consider how far this Convention is part of the law of E
this country. Mr. Blom-Cooper drew our attention to some declarations
which have been made by the government of the United Kingdom. This
country has declared, in accordance with article 25 of the Convention,
that the European Commission is competent to receive petitions from
persons who complain that the rights set forth in the Convention have
been violated. If a person has exhausted all remedies available to him in
England, he can apply to the European Commission to get a remedy F
there. Mr. Blom-Cooper submits that, in consequence of those declarations,
every person is given, by article 8, a right which the courts must recognise
and enforce. I cannot accept this submission. I would repeat what
I said in *Reg.* v. *Secretary of State for the Home Department, Ex parte*
Bhajan Singh [1976] Q.B. 198 and in *Pan-American World Airways Inc.*
v. *Department of Trade* [1976] 1 Lloyd's Rep. 257. G

The position as I understand it is that if there is any ambiguity in
our statutes, or uncertainty in our law, then these courts can look to the
Convention as an aid to clear up the ambiguity and uncertainty, seeking
always to bring them into harmony with it. Furthermore, when Parliament
is enacting a statute, or the Secretary of State is framing rules, the
courts will assume that they had regard to the provisions of the Convention, H
and intended to make the enactment accord with the Convention:
and will interpret them accordingly. But I would dispute altogether that
the Convention is part of our law. Treaties and declarations do not
become part of our law until they are made law by Parliament. I desire,
however, to amend one of the statements I made in the *Bhajan Singh* case
[1976] Q.B. 198, 207. I said then that the immigration officers ought to
bear in mind the principles stated in the Convention. I think that would

be asking too much of the immigration officers. They cannot be expected to know or to apply the Convention. They must go simply by the immigration rules laid down by the Secretary of State, and not by the Convention.

I may also add this. The Convention is drafted in a style very different from the way which we are used to in legislation. It contains wide general statements of principle. They are apt to lead to much difficulty in application: because they give rise to much uncertainty. They are not the sort of thing which we can easily digest. Article 8 is an example. It is so wide as to be incapable of practical application. So it is much better for us to stick to our own statutes and principles, and only look to the Convention for guidance in case of doubt.

Coming back to this case, it seems to me that the immigration officers were right to go by the rules: and by the rules, beyond all question, the immigration officer was entirely right to refuse entry to this lady and her children. She had no visa. She had no current entry clearance. She said she was coming as a visitor and he was not satisfied that she was staying for a short period. That is a complete answer to the case. I would dismiss the appeal.

ROSKILL L.J. I entirely agree that the decision of the immigration officer was right and I would dismiss this appeal for the reasons which Lord Denning M.R. has given. I only add a few words on one or two points.

In his reply Mr. Blom-Cooper made what I hope he will forgive me calling a somewhat startling submission, namely, that the rules made by the Secretary of State under section 3 (2) of the Immigration Act 1971 were not "part of the law of this country." He said that they were but departmental circulars laying down no more than good administrative practice. With respect, I profoundly disagree. If one looks at the section which empowers the Secretary of State to make these rules one finds in section 3 (2) that he shall lay before Parliament as soon as may be statements of the rules or any changes in the rules laid down by him. These rules are just as much delegated legislation as any other form of rule-making activity or delegated legislation which is empowered by Act of Parliament. Furthermore these rules are subject to a negative resolution (see the second paragraph of section 3 (2) of the Act of 1971); and it is unheard of that something which is no more than an administrative circular stating what the Home Office conceives to be good administrative practice should be subject to a negative resolution from both Houses of Parliament. These rules to my mind are just as much a part of the law of England as the Act itself.

That leads me to the next point. It is, as I understand it, the plain duty of immigration officers to obey the law. If they go outside the law as laid down in the Act and in the rules, action can be taken against them for exceeding the powers given by the Act or the rules, just as action can be taken against them if they do not properly exercise those powers which are given by the Act or the rules. Accordingly, it seems to me that it was, in relation to this lady, the duty of the immigration officers concerned to consider the matter as they did and to take their decision in accordance with the rules. That, as Lord Denning M.R. has already said, I think they did.

I would only add one word on the argument to which we have listened on the European Convention on Human Rights. Like Lord Denning M.R., A I am of the view that this Convention is not part of the law of England. It is not necessary to go into elaborate reasons why that is so. Suffice it to say that a treaty does not become part of the municipal law of this country unless and until it is the subject of legislation in the ordinary way. That is axiomatic; it has been laid down for many years. What is said is that the immigration officers should, in exercising their powers under the rules, which, as I have already said, are part of the law of this country, take B into account the provisions of the Convention, which is not. With respect I am unable to agree. In *Reg.* v. *Secretary of State for the Home Department, Ex parte Phansopkar* [1976] Q.B. 606 and again in *Pan-American World Airways Inc.* v. *Department of Trade* [1976] 1 Lloyd's Rep. 257, Scarman L.J., who was a member of the court on both occasions, as was Lord Denning M.R. and Lawton L.J., went, if I may most respectfully say C so, rather further in this connection than did the other two members of the court. Scarman L.J., after a reference to Magna Carta, said [1976] Q.B. 606, 626:

> "This hallowed principle of our law is now reinforced by the European Convention on Human Rights to which it is now the duty of our public authorities in administering the law, including the Immigration Act 1971, and of our courts in interpreting and applying the D law, including the Act, to have regard: . . ."

With respect, that dictum was obiter. I venture to think it is somewhat too wide and may call for reconsideration hereafter. In his judgment, to which Lord Denning M.R. has referred, in the *Pan-Am* case [1976] 1 Lloyd's Rep. 257, a few days later, Scarman L.J. dealt with what I might E call the overall position, but then he went on to say very much the same thing as he had said in the *Phansopkar* case [1976] Q.B. 606, 626 in the passage to which I have referred. He said at p. 261:

> "Such a Convention"—and there he was referring to the Convention on Human Rights—"especially a multilateral one, should then be considered by courts even though no statute expressly or impliedly incorporates it into our law." F

There again with great respect I think the matter is somewhat too widely expressed. Lord Denning M.R. has already said that perhaps he too went somewhat too far in the *Bhajan Singh* case in [1976] Q.B. 198, 207. I most respectfully agree with that view.

Accordingly, in my judgment, there are no grounds for imposing on G those who have the difficult task which immigration officers have to perform the additional burden of considering upon every occasion the application of the Convention. Geoffrey Lane L.J. asked Mr. Blom-Cooper this morning whether it was his submission that an immigration officer must obey the provisions of the Convention, even if those provisions were in conflict with the statutory rules; to which Mr. Blom-Cooper, not I thought for a moment without a note of hesitation in his voice, replied: H "Yes, it was." With great respect to that reply I am clearly of the view that an immigration officer is under no such duty. I would dismiss this appeal.

GEOFFREY LANE L.J. I agree. As I see this case, the appellant here never succeeds in getting to the stage where Mr. Blom-Cooper's interesting and novel points need to be decided, although it is only fair to pay tribute

A to the amount of research which he has applied to the matter and to the ingenuity with which he has put forward his arguments. In my judgment both the result and the reasons given for it in the Divisional Court were correct.

This appellant presented herself first of all on March 11 at London Heathrow with a man said to be her husband and a legal executive called Mr. Omar and through them, or with their assistance, put her application
B and story to the immigration officer. Her husband, she said, was already in England and she wished to pay him a visit for a short time, about a fortnight. She said she would see how she liked this country and if it met with her approval she might in due course stay here, applying for leave to that end; or otherwise if it did not suit her she would return to Pakistan.

C The rules governing the immigration officer's decision are those contained in H.C. 81. The matter was adjourned for a time; the officers no doubt considered the rules, and the interview was resumed on March 13, two days later. Having heard what she said, through an interpreter on that occasion, and having heard what her husband said to them, namely, a request that she be given limited leave to enter as a visitor in order to pursue an application for permanent settlement with the Home Office,
D they came to the conclusion that this lady, first of all, was a non-Commonwealth national, and, secondly, that she had not satisfied them that no more than a visit was intended; and accordingly permission was refused. She has now returned to Pakistan.

There was no obligation on the officers to inquire of this lady whether she had disclosed all the reasons for her visit. There was no obligation
E on these officers to suggest to her, if such was the case, that she might have more solid grounds on which to base her application to them, or more persuasive arguments to put forward than those which she did in fact advance. The officers were entitled to assume that she was putting her case forward on the best grounds that were available to her and truthfully. She was in truth a non-Commonwealth national, Pakistan having left the Commonwealth in 1972. She had said in terms that she was quite
F likely to stay for longer than the 14 days or so of her temporary visit which was the basis of her application, and therefore the rules contained in H.C. 81 obliged the immigration officers to act as they did and refuse her application. They had no alternative. The application for prerogative orders therefore fails in limine. Moreover having now left this country she is free to appeal against the decision of the immigration officers. She has
G that alternative remedy open to her which, on its own would, in my judgment, disentitle her to the discretionary remedies which she seeks, particularly so when there is an outstanding issue of fact still to be decided, namely, whether she is indeed the wife of Mr. Barkat Ali, as to which the less said the better.

I wish only to add this. It is submitted by Mr. Blom-Cooper that the rules themselves made by virtue of the Act of 1971 and section 1 (5) thereof
H which requires the rules to be so framed

> "that Commonwealth citizens settled in the United Kingdom at the coming into force of this Act and their wives and children are not, by virtue of anything in the rules, any less free to come into and go from the United Kingdom than if this Act had not been passed"

have been contravened. For the reasons already advanced by Lord Denning M.R. it is quite clear that the rules in fact abide precisely by that injunction. In any event the rules as to visas and entry certificates are the same as they were before, and it is conceded that this applicant did not comply with those rules, and therefore she must inevitably fail on that point.

That leaves Mr. Blom-Cooper's final submission, namely, that the European Convention on Human Rights and Fundamental Freedoms is part of our law. That is what he submits. Moreover, goes on the submission, in so far as there is no rule of the common law and no statute in conflict therewith the rules of the Convention have full effect in the courts of this country. It is perfectly true that that Convention was ratified by this country. It is true that in 1966 and thereafter Her Majesty's Government has declared that article 25 is available to the citizens of this country and of which they may take advantage. Nevertheless, the Convention, not having been enacted by Parliament as a statute, it does not have the effect of law in this country; whatever persuasive force it may have in resolving ambiguities it certainly cannot have the effect of overriding the plain provisions of the Act of 1971 and the rules made thereunder. That is what Mr. Blom-Cooper indeed is suggesting.

Finally it is submitted that the immigration officers had a discretion which they should have exercised in favour of the applicant and in the exercise of which they should have been guided by the provisions of article 8 of the Convention. In my judgment they had no such discretion in this case. Secondly, even if they had, there was no obligation on them to have regard to the terms of the Convention. One only has to read the article in question, article 8 (2), to realise that it would be an impossibility for any immigration officer to apply a discretion based on terms as wide and as vague as those in that sub-article which reads as follows:

> "There shall be no interference by a public authority with the exercise of this right except such as is in accordance with the law and is necessary in a democratic society in the interests of national security, public safety or the economic well-being of the country; for the prevention of disorder or crime, for the protection of health or morals, or for the protection of the rights and freedoms of others."

For those various reasons I agree that this appeal should be dismissed.

Appeal dismissed.
Leave to appeal refused.

Solicitors: *Clifford Watts, Compton & Co.; Treasury Solicitor.*

M. M. H.

A

[HOUSE OF LORDS]

* MURPHY . . . . PETITIONER

AND

CULHANE . . . . RESPONDENT

B 1976 July 26 — Lord Diplock, Lord Morris of Borth-y-Gest and Lord Hailsham of St. Marylebone

Petition by the plaintiff for leave to appeal to the House of Lords from the decision of the Court of Appeal [1976] 3 W.L.R. 458.

The Appeal Committee dismissed the petition.

C M. G.

[HOUSE OF LORDS]

* REARDON SMITH LINE LTD. . . . . . APPELLANTS

D AND

YNGVAR HANSEN-TANGEN (TRADING AS H. E. HANSEN-TANGEN) . . . . APPELLANTS

YNGVAR HANSEN-TANGEN (TRADING AS H. E. HANSEN-TANGEN) . . . . RESPONDENTS

E AND

SANKO STEAMSHIP CO. . . . . RESPONDENTS

[CONJOINED APPEALS]

1976 July 14, 15, 19, 20, 21, 22;
F Oct. 7 — Lord Wilberforce, Viscount Dilhorne, Lord Simon of Glaisdale, Lord Kilbrandon and Lord Russell of Killowen

Shipping—Charterparty—Description of vessel—Time charter of newbuilding motor tank vessel—Identification by owners' declaration of yard and hull number—Yard and hull number confirmed in addendum to charter—Sub-charter on "back-to-back" terms identifying vessel in similar terms—Vessel built
G *at different yard with different hull number—Both charters governed by English law—Construction of charters—Whether charterers entitled to refuse to take delivery of vessel*

In order to help finance the building of a Japanese motor tank vessel of some 88,000 tons it was arranged for the vessel to be chartered on completion even before work on it was started. The two charterparties in question were on the form
H Shelltime 3 and provided, inter alia, that they were to be construed according to English law. The charterparties referred to the vessel as one to be built at Osaka with the yard or hull number 354, but eventually because of its size the vessel was built at Oshima where it bore the yard or hull number Oshima 004 although in all external documents it was "known" as, or "called," Osaka 354. For the purpose of the proceedings it was assumed that the physical attributes of the vessel corresponded with those required under the respective charters. By the time the vessel was ready for delivery in 1974 the mar-

ket had collapsed owing to the oil crisis of that year, and the A charterers sought to escape from their obligation by rejecting the vessel on the ground, by analogy with contracts for the sale of goods, that the vessel tendered did not correspond with the contractual description in that it was Oshima 004 and not Osaka 354. Mocatta J. (in proceedings commenced by originating summons) found against the charterers on the ground that although the vessel tendered did not comply with the description nevertheless in the circumstances the charterers B were not entitled to refuse to take delivery. On appeal, the Court of Appeal, dismissing the appeal, held that the vessel in question did comply with the description set out in the respective charters.

On appeal:—

Held, dismissing the appeal, (1) (*per* Lord Wilberforce, Lord Simon of Glaisdale and Lord Kilbrandon) that the authorities as to "description" in sale of goods cases were not to be C extended, or applied to contracts of the present nature (post, pp. 998C, 1001A–D).

Per Lord Wilberforce, Lord Simon of Glaisdale and Lord Kilbrandon. Some of the cases as to "description" in sale of goods are excessively technical and due for fresh examination in this House (post, pp. 998C–D, 1001A–D).

(2) (*Per* Lord Wilberforce, Lord Simon of Glaisdale and Lord Kilbrandon) that even if a strict and technical view had D to be taken as regards the description of unascertained future goods (e.g. commodities) as to which each detail of the description must be assumed to be vital, it was right to treat other contracts of sale of goods in a similar manner to other contracts generally so as to ask whether a particular item in a description constituted a substantial ingredient of the "identity" of the thing sold, and, only if it did, to treat it as a condition; and that in the present case it was plain that the E hull or yard number of the vessel had no special significance for the parties so as to raise it to a matter of fundamental obligation (post, pp. 998D–F, 1001A–D).

Dictum of Roskill L.J. in *Cehave N.V.* v. *Bremer Handelgesellshaft m.b.H.* [1976] Q.B. 44, 71, C.A. approved.

(3) That in any event the charterers failed to bring the present case within the strictest rules as to "description" since the words "yard 354" were not and were never intended to F be part of the description of the vessel but only a means of identifying it, and that the vessel tendered was the vessel that was contracted for (post, pp. 998H—999D, F. H, 1000D–E, 1001A–D, G–H, 1002C–E).

Observations on the correct approach to the construction of commercial contracts (post, pp. 995D—997D).

Decision of the Court of Appeal [1976] 2 Lloyd's Rep. 60 affirmed. G

The following cases are referred to in their Lordships' opinions:

Behn v. *Burness* (1863) 3 B. & S. 751.

Cargo Ships "El-Yam" Ltd. v. *Invoer-en Transport Onderneming "Invotra" N.V.* [1958] 1 Lloyd's Rep. 39.

Cehave N.V. v. *Bremer Handelgesellschaft m.b.H.* [1976] Q.B. 44; [1975] H 3 W.L.R. 447; [1975] 3 All E.R. 739, C.A.

Charrington & Co. Ltd. v. *Wooder* [1914] A.C. 71, H.L.(E.).

Couchman v. *Hill* [1947] K.B. 554; [1947] 1 All E.R. 103, C.A.

Hongkong Fir Shipping Co. Ltd. v. *Kawasaki Kisen Kaisha Ltd.* [1962] 2 Q.B. 26; [1962] 2 W.L.R. 474; [1962] 1 All E.R. 474, C.A.

Hvalfangerselskapet Polaris Aktieselskap Ltd. v. *Unilever Ltd.* (1933) 39 Com.Cas. 1, H.L.(E.).

Lewis v. *Great Western Railway Co.* (1877) 3 Q.B.D. 195, C.A.

A *Moore and Co. and Landauer and Co., In re* [1921] 2 K.B. 519, C.A.
Prenn v. *Simmonds* [1971] 1 W.L.R. 1381; [1971] 3 All E.R. 237, H.L.(E.).
Utica City National Bank v. *Gunn* (1918) 118 N.E. 607.
Wickman Machine Tool Sales Ltd. v. *L. Schuler A.G.* [1974] A.C. 235; [1973] 2 W.L.R. 683; [1973] 2 All E.R. 39, H.L.(E.).

B The following additional cases were cited in argument:
Andrews Brothers (Bournemouth) Ltd. v. *Singer and Co. Ltd.* [1934] 1 K.B. 17, C.A.
Arcos Ltd. v. *E. A. Ronaasen and Son* [1933] A.C. 470, H.L.(E.).
Astley Industrial Trust Ltd. v. *Grimley* [1963] 1 W.L.R. 584; [1963] 2 All E.R. 33, C.A.
Barker v. *Windle* (1856) 6 E. & B. 675.
C *Bowes* v. *Shand* (1877) 2 App.Cas. 455, H.L.(E.).
Bradford v. *Williams* (1872) L.R. 7 Ex. 259.
Flight v. *Booth* (1834) 1 Bing.N.C. 370.
Hardwick v. *Hardwick* (1873) L.R. 16 Eq. 168.
Hillas (W. N.) & Co. Ltd. v. *Rederi Aktiebolaget Aeolus* (1926) 32 Com. Cas. 69.
Hill (Christopher) Ltd. v. *Ashington Piggeries Ltd.* [1972] A.C. 441; [1971] 2 W.L.R. 1051; [1971] 1 All E.R. 847, H.L.(E.).
D *Madeleine, The* [1967] 2 Lloyd's Rep. 224.
Manbre Saccharine Co. Ltd. v. *Corn Products Co. Ltd.* [1919] 1 K.B. 198.
Rapalli v. *K. L. Take Ltd.* [1958] 2 Lloyd's Rep. 469, C.A.
Smyth (Ross T.) and Co. Ltd. v. *T. D. Bailey, Son and Co.* (1940) 45 Com.Cas. 292, H.L.(E.).
United Dominions Trust (Commercial) Ltd. v. *Eagle Aircraft Services Ltd.* [1968] 1 W.L.R. 74; [1968] 1 All E.R. 104, C.A.
E *Universal Cargo Carriers Corporation* v. *Citati* [1957] 2 Q.B. 401; [1957] 2 W.L.R. 713; [1957] 2 All E.R. 70.
Varley v. *Whipp* [1900] 1 Q.B. 513, D.C.
Whitworth Street Estates (Manchester) Ltd. v. *James Miller and Partners Ltd.* [1970] A.C. 583; [1970] 2 W.L.R. 728; [1970] 1 All E.R. 796, H.L.(E.).

F APPEALS from the Court of Appeal.

These appeals were conjoined appeals by the respective appellants from an order of the Court of Appeal (Lord Denning M.R., Stephenson and Bridge L.JJ.) dated March 29, 1976, dismissing their respective appeals from the judgment of Mocatta J. dated March 15, 1976, whereby it was declared upon the true construction of the relevant charterparties (a) the G appellants in the first appeal, Reardon Smith Line Ltd., were not entitled to refuse to take delivery from the respondents in the first appeal, Yngvar Hansen-Tangen (trading as H. E. Hansen-Tangen); and (b) the appellants in the second appeal, H. E. Hansen-Tangen, were not entitled to refuse to take delivery from the respondents in the second appeal, Sanko Steamship Co., of the tank vessel now known as *Diana Prosperity*.

These appeals arose out of two time charterparties, each in the Shell- H time form, viz.: (a) A charterparty dated August 15, 1972, with addenda thereto dated August 10, 1973, concluded between Sanko (a Japanese company) and Hansen-Tangen (a Norwegian partnership), under which Sanko obliged themselves to deliver to Hansen-Tangen to perform that charter a newbuilding motor tank vessel "to be built by the Osaka Shipbuilding Co. Ltd. and known as Hull No. 354"; (b) a sub-charterparty dated October 12, 1973, concluded between Hansen-Tangen and Reardon Smith (a Cardiff company) for the specific purpose of sub-chartering that vessel, under which Hansen-Tangen obliged themselves to deliver to Reardon Smith to perform that charter a "newbuilding motor tank vessel called Yard No. 354 at Osaka Zosen."

Each of those charterparties (which were, in substance, on "back-to-back" terms save as to hire rate and length of charter term) expressly provided, by clause 40, that it should be construed, and that the relations between the parties should be determined, in accordance with the law of England. The Sanko/Hansen-Tangen charter was referred to in the proceedings as the "intermediate charter," Sanko being in turn charterers under a head charter between themselves and Sculptor Shipping Co. Ltd. The Hansen-Tangen/Reardon Smith charter was referred to as the "sub-charter." It was common ground that the expression "Osaka Zosen," as used in the sub-charter, was equivalent to "Osaka Shipbuilding Co. Ltd.," "Zosen" being the Japanese word for "Shipbuilding."

The matter came before Mocatta J. upon (a) an originating summons taken out on behalf of Reardon Smith and dated November 13, 1975, whereby Reardon Smith requested determination of the question whether, upon the true construction of the sub-charter, Reardon Smith were entitled to refuse to take delivery from Hansen-Tangen of a tank vessel which Sanko proposed to tender upon its completion in early 1976 for delivery to Hansen-Tangen under the intermediate charter; and (b) a third part notice issued on behalf of Hansen-Tangen and dated November 27, 1975, whereby Hansen-Tangen requested determination as between themselves and Sanko of a similar question in relation to the intermediate charter.

The issues (common to both disputes) between the respective parties were: (i) Was it the contractual obligation of the respective disponent owners to deliver a motor tank vessel which had been built by the Osaka Shipbuilding Co. Ltd. ("the Osaka company") at a yard of that company under the yard serial number 354? (ii) If that was the contractual obligation of the respective disponent owners, were the respective charterers entitled to refuse to take delivery of the tendered vessel, being a vessel built by Oshima Shipbuilding Co. Ltd. ("the Oshima company") at the new yard of that company at Oshima?

For the purpose of the proceedings the courts had been invited to assume, and had assumed, that the physical attributes of the vessel in question would correspond with those required under Form B of the respective charters.

Mocatta J. held that, although the first of the foregoing issues had to be decided in favour of the respective charterers (Reardon Smith and Hansen-Tangen), the resulting breach of obligation on the part of the respective disponent owners was not such as to entitle the charterers to refuse delivery of the vessel. He declined accordingly to grant declarations as requested by Reardon Smith and Hansen-Tangen and declared that Reardon Smith and Hansen-Tangen were not entitled to refuse to take delivery of the vessel.

The Court of Appeal upheld the decision of Mocatta J., but upon different grounds. The Court of Appeal unanimously disagreed with the conclusion reached by the judge on the first issue, holding that the vessel which it was proposed to tender complied with the description set out in the respective charters. Lord Denning M.R. further indicated his concurrence with the conclusion at which Mocatta J. had arrived on the second issue. Stephenson and Bridge L.JJ. found it unnecessary to express any view as to the correctness or otherwise of the reasoning on the second issue which had led Mocatta J. to decide the case against the appellants.

A Shortly after the institution of the present proceedings the vessel proposed to be tendered was launched at Oshima, at the shipyard of the Oshima company, and named *Diana Prosperity.* She was due for delivery from that shipyard between April 1–21, 1976, and she was in fact so delivered on April 1. It was agreed between the parties, prior to delivery of the judgments in the Court of Appeal, that the *Diana Prosperity* should, pending the outcome of any appeal to the House of Lords,
B be traded on a without prejudice basis for account of whomsoever might ultimately be concerned; and the vessel was presently being so traded by Reardon Smith.

The facts are set out in the opinion of Lord Wilberforce.

R. A. MacCrindle Q.C., *Basil Eckersley* and *Alan Pardoe* for Reardon
C Smith, appellants in the first appeal.

J. S. Hobhouse Q.C. and *Michael Dean* for Hansen-Tangen, respondents in the first appeal, appellants in the second appeal.

R. S. Alexander Q.C., *Nicholas Phillips* and *Timothy Charlton* for Sanko, respondents in the second appeal.

D Their Lordships took time for consideration.

October 7, 1976. LORD WILBERFORCE. My Lords, these appeals arise out of a charterparty and sub-charterparty both relating to a medium size newbuilding tanker to be constructed in Japan. By the time the tanker was ready for delivery the market had collapsed, owing to the oil crisis of 1974, so that the charterers' interest was to escape from their
E contracts by rejecting the vessel. The ground on which they hoped to do so was that the vessel tendered did not correspond with the contractual description.

Both charterparties were on the well known form Shelltime 3. The result of the appeal depends primarily upon the view taken of the sub-charterparty between the appellants in the first appeal ("Reardon Smith") and
F the respondents in that appeal ("Hansen-Tangen"), but, for the issue to be understood, it is necessary first to state some dates.

In 1972 the respondents in the second appeal ("Sanko"), a Japanese company, formed the "Sanko plan" which was a project for the construction in Japanese yards of some 50 tankers of about 80,000 tons each which would be placed on charter by Sanko. At this time the market was strong. Before any vessels were actually built or even started Sanko
G arranged a number of charters—called "fixtures"—defining the contractual terms of hire, the actual ships covered by each of them to be nominated later by Sanko. One such charter was that between Sanko and Hansen-Tangen (referred to in these proceedings as the "intermediate charter"). It was dated August 15, 1972. Clause 41 contained the following (emphasis supplied):

H "This charter party, subject to what is hereinafter stated, is for a motor tank vessel *to be built at a yard in Japan to be declared by owners (s.c. Sanko) together with the applicable Hull number for the vessel* within June 30, 1973. . . ."

Clause 42 conferred an option (not exercised) to nominate a slightly smaller vessel . . . "owners to declare name of shipyard and Hull number . . . at the time such option . . . is exercised."

The description of the vessel—warranted by the owners—was (as A
provided by clause 24) set out in Form B which is a standard form giving very detailed particulars about the ship, its equipment and performance. It is to be assumed for the purposes of these appeals that the vessel tendered complied in all respects with these requirements, and that therefore the charterers got precisely the kind of ship they wanted of precisely the description stipulated.

On March 28, 1973, by which time progress had been made with the B
plan, Sanko as charterers entered into a charterparty with a Liberian company called Sculptor as "owners" for "the good newbuilding tank vessel called Osaka Shipbuilding Co. Ltd. Hull No. 354 until named." This charterparty also contained a Form B in the same form as in the intermediate charter. Osaka Shipbuilding Co. Ltd. is a substantial and reputable Japanese shipbuilding company with a yard at Osaka, which, C
however, could not build ships exceeding 45,000 tons. (The vessel contracted for was of about 88,000 tons.) So at this point, as the document shows, the vessel to be taken to Sanko, and passed on by Sanko to charterers from Sanko had gained an identity, not a physical identity, since construction had not yet started, but an identity in contracts and in order books.

Following on this, Sanko nominated the vessel to perform the inter- D
mediate charter. This was done by an addendum to that charterparty dated August 10, 1973, which also altered the duration of the intermediate charter and the hire payments to be made under it. The nomination was made in the following terms:

> "With reference to clause[s] 41 and 42 of [the intermediate charter] the vessel to perform this charter is to be built by Osaka Shipbuilding E
> Co. Ltd. and known as Hull No. 354 until named and shall have a deadweight of about 87,600 . . . (other details follow)."

Soon after this, on October 12, 1973, the sub-charter between Hansen-Tangen and Reardon Smith was signed. I set out the preamble having italicised the words which were added to the printed form:

> "It is this day agreed between H. E. Hansen-Tangen of Kristian- F
> sands, Norway (hereinafter referred to as 'Owners') being *disponent* owners of the good *Japanese flag* (*subject to clause* 41) *Newbuilding motor tank vessel called Yard No.* 354 *at Osaka Zosen* [Zosen = shipbuilding] (hereinafter described as 'the vessel') described as per clause 24 hereof and Reardon Smith Line Limited of Cardiff (*Sir William Reardon Smith and Sons Ltd. of Cardiff—Managers*) (here- G
> inafter referred to as 'charterers')."

The charterparty contained a clause 24 and Form B similar to the intermediate charter.

Parallel with these charter agreements were a number of contracts and arrangements concerning the building of the vessel. It is not necessary to specify these in detail. Osaka Shipbuilding Co. Ltd. ("Osaka") was, as H
I have mentioned, unable to build a vessel of 80,000 tons in its Osaka yard so it set about arranging for a new yard to be built at Oshima, which is on the island of Kyushu about 300 miles from Osaka. The method chosen was for Osaka to enter into a joint venture with two companies of the powerful Sumitomo Group followed by the formation of a new company called Oshima Shipbuilding Co. Ltd. ("Oshima") in which Osaka had a 50 per cent. interest and two Sumitomo companies the other 50 per cent.

Oshima took over responsibility for building the new yard. A series of contracts was entered into by which the Liberian company Sculptor ordered the vessel from a Sumitomo company, which agreed to build it by sub-contract with Osaka; the Sumitomo company placed a shipbuilding contract with Osaka; and Osaka placed a shipbuilding (sub-) contract with Oshima. As mentioned above it was Sculptor from whom Sanko chartered the vessel on March 28, 1973. As regards Oshima, a large part of its work force and a preponderant part of its expert managerial staff was provided on secondment from Osaka. The vessel to be constructed was to be numbered 004 in Oshima's books but also 354 in Osaka's books and in export documents. The chain, therefore, was (1) Oshima agreed to construct the vessel under contract with Osaka, (2) Osaka contracted with a Sumitomo company to build and deliver the vessel, (3) the Sumitomo company agreed to build the vessel by Osaka and to sell it to Sculptor, (4) Sculptor agreed to hire it to Sanko, (5) Sanko agreed to hire it to Hansen-Tangen, (6) Hansen-Tangen agreed to hire it to Reardon Smith. In all these contracts the vessel was described as No. 354 in connection with Osaka.

These being the background facts, the whole case, as regards the first appeal, turns, in my opinion, upon the long italicised passage in the sub-charter set out above which, for convenience of reference I repeat:

> "(the good) Japanese flag (subject to Clause 41) Newbuilding motor tank vessel called Yard No. 354 at Osaka Zosen"

I shall refer to this as the "box" since it appears enclosed in a typed box on the document.

The contract is in the English language and (clause 40) is to be construed in accordance with English law. But it has been sought to introduce, as an aid to construction, a considerable amount of evidence as to Japanese usages and practice, some of which was in fact taken into account by the Court of Appeal. To decide how far this is legitimate one must make a distinction. When it comes to ascertaining whether particular words apply to a factual situation or, if one prefers, whether a factual situation comes within particular words, it is undoubtedly proper, and necessary, to take evidence as to the factual situation. Thus once one has decided what is meant by "Yard No. 354," or "to be built at a Yard" it is proper by evidence to establish the characteristics of particular yards, the numbering used at those yards, and the "building" which may have been done, in order to answer, yes or no, the question whether the contractual requirements have been met. There is no difficulty, in law, about this part of the case.

It is less easy to define what evidence may be used in order to enable a term to be construed. To argue that practices adopted in the shipbuilding industry in Japan, for example as to sub-contracting, are relevant in the interpretation of a charterparty contract between two foreign shipping companies, whether or not these practices are known to the parties, is in my opinion to exceed what is permissible. But it does not follow that, renouncing this evidence, one must be confined within the four corners of the document. No contracts are made in a vacuum: there is always a setting in which they have to be placed. The nature of what is legitimate to have regard to is usually described as "the surrounding circumstances" but this phrase is imprecise: it can be illustrated but hardly defined. In a commercial contract it is certainly right that the court should know the commercial purpose of the contract and this in turn presupposes knowledge of the genesis of the transaction, the background, the context, the market in which the parties are operating. I give a few illustrations. In *Utica City National Bank* v. *Gunn* (1918) 118 N.E., 607; 222 N.Y. 204 the New York Court of Appeals had to consider the meaning of "loans and discounts" in a contract of guaranty. The judgment of Cardozo J. contains this passage, at p. 608:

> "The proper legal meaning, however, is not always the meaning of the parties. Surrounding circumstances may stamp upon a contract a popular or looser meaning. The words 'loans and discounts' are not so clear and certain that circumstances may not broaden them to include renewals. They often have that meaning in the language of business life. To take the primary or strict meaning is to make the whole transaction futile. To take the secondary or loose meaning, is to give it efficacy and purpose. In such a situation, the genesis and aim of the transaction may rightly guide our choice. *Wigmore on Evidence*, vol. IV, para. 2470, *Stephen, Digest of Law of Evidence*, art. 91, subds. 5 and 6."

In *Prenn* v. *Simmons* [1971] 1 W.L.R. 1381 it was necessary to construe "profits available for dividend." The judgment in that case, following Cardozo J., relied upon the commercial background of the objective aim of the transaction to give meaning to that phrase.

In *Wickman Machine Tool Sales Ltd.* v. *L. Schuler A.G.* ([1974] A.C. 235) the critical word was "condition." Their Lordships interpreted this word (unusually) in the light of a special business situation.

It is often said that, in order to be admissible in aid of construction, these extrinsic facts must be within the knowledge of both parties to the contract, but this requirement should not be stated in too narrow a sense. When one speaks of the intention of the parties to the contract, one is speaking objectively—the parties cannot themselves give direct evidence of what their intention was—and what must be ascertained is what is to be taken as the intention which reasonable people would have had if placed in the situation of the parties. Similarly when one is speaking of aim, or object, or commercial purpose, one is speaking objectively of what reasonable persons would have in mind in the situation of the parties. It is in this sense and not in the sense of constructive notice or of estopping fact that judges are found using words like "knew or must be taken to have known" (see, for example, the well-known judgment of Brett L.J. in *Lewis* v. *Great Western Railway Co.* (1877) 3 Q.B.D. 195.

This proposition can be illustrated by some authoritative judgments. In *Hvalfangerselskapet Polaris Aktieselskap Ltd.* v. *Unilever Ltd.* (1933) 39 Com.Cas. 1 the different emphasis placed by individual members of this House on knowledge, Lord Atkin not referring to it (p. 3), Lord Russell of Killowen mentioning it as an element (p. 19), Lord Macmillan distinguishing between objective and subjective elements (p. 25), seems to show that mutual knowledge of extrinsic circumstances, while relevant, is not an essential condition of the admissibility of factual evidence.

Particularly interesting are the speeches in *Charrington & Co. Ltd.* v. *Wooder* [1914] A.C. 71, the question being what was meant by "fair market price." Viscount Haldane L.C. uses once more the expression "circumstances which the parties must be taken to have had in view" (p. 77). Lord Kinnear, after explaining that the term had no fixed meaning, said at p. 80 "Words of this kind must vary in their signification with the particular objects to which the language is directed" and continued, at p. 80:

A "... it may be necessary to prove the relation of the document to facts; and I take it to be sound doctrine that for this purpose evidence may be given to prove any fact to which it refers, or may probably refer ..."

And Lord Dunedin, at p. 82:

B "... in order to construe a contract the court is always entitled to be so far instructed by evidence as to be able to place itself in thought in the same position as the parties to the contract were placed, in fact, when they made it—or, as it is sometimes phrased, to be informed as to the surrounding circumstances."

I think that all of their Lordships are saying, in different words, the same
C thing—what the court must do must be to place itself in thought in the same factual matrix as that in which the parties were. All of these opinions seem to me implicitly to recognise that, in the search for the relevant background, there may be facts which form part of the circumstances in which the parties contract in which one, or both, may take no particular interest, their minds being addressed to or concentrated on other facts so that if asked they would assert that they did not have
D these facts in the forefront of their mind, but that will not prevent those facts from forming part of an objective setting in which the contract is to be construed. I shall show that this is so in the present case.

So I ask what was the commercial purpose of these charterparties and what was the factual background against which they were made? The purpose is clear: it was to make available to (1) Hansen-Tangen
E and (2) to Reardon Smith a medium-sized tanker suitable for use as such, this tanker not being in existence, or even under construction at the date of either charter, and, at the date of the intermediate charter not even the subject of contracts made by the supplying company. The vessel was to be constructed in a Japanese yard and made available on charter to Sanko as part of a programme. At the date of the subcharter the vessel was identified in contracts for its construction in Japan
F and had a serial number. In order to ensure that the tanker was suitable for its purpose a detailed specification was drawn up—by way of a warranted description with which of course the vessel must strictly comply.

In addition, since at the time of either charterparty the vessel was not in existence or under construction, some means had to be agreed upon for identifying the particular vessel—one out of a programme—which would
G form the subject matter of the charters. This was indispensable so as to enable those committing themselves to hire the vessel, to sub-hire it, if they wished, and if necessary to arrange finance. This necessary identification was to be effected by nomination, by Sanko in the first place and then by Hansen-Tangen.

The text of the charterparties confirms beyond doubt that this was what was intended and done. The preamble, in the Shelltime 3 form, provides
H for the insertion of a name—"being owners of the good ... tank vessel called. ..." The box insertion in the subcharter was made in this place—"called Yard No. 354 at Osaka Zosen." The intermediate charter, entered into before Sanko had nominated any vessel, provided in its preamble—instead of "called ..." for declaration by the owners together with the Hull number, and the addendum, entered into after Sanko had nominated, provided "to be built by Osaka Shipbuilding Co. Ltd. and known as Hull No. 354 until named." What is vital about each of these insertions

is that they were simple substitutes for a name, serving no purpose but to provide a means whereby the charterers could identify the ship. At the dates when these insertions were made no importance could have been attached to the matters now said to be so significant—they were not a matter of negotiation, but of unilateral declaration. What is now sought is to elevate them into strict contractual terms in the nature of "conditions."

The appellants sought, necessarily, to give to the box and the corresponding provision in the intermediate charter contractual effect. They argued that these words formed part of the "description" of the future goods contracted to be provided, that, by analogy with contracts for the sale of goods, any departure from the description entitled the other party to reject, that there were departures in that the vessel was not built by Osaka Shipbuilding Co. Ltd., and was not Hull No. 354. I shall attempt to deal with each of these contentions.

In the first place, I am not prepared to accept that authorities as to "description" in sale of goods cases are to be extended, or applied, to such a contract as we have here. Some of these cases either in themselves (*In re Moore and Co. and Landauer and Co.* [1921] 2 K.B. 519) or as they have been interpreted (e.g. *Behn* v. *Burness* (1863) 3 B. & S. 751) I find to be excessively technical and due for fresh examination in this House. Even if a strict and technical view must be taken as regards the description of unascertained future goods (e.g., commodities) as to which each detail of the description must be assumed to be vital, it may be, and in my opinion is, right to treat other contracts of sale of goods in a similar manner to other contracts generally so as to ask whether a particular item in a description constitutes a substantial ingredient of the "identity" of the thing sold, and only if it does to treat it as a condition (see *Couchman* v. *Hill* [1947] K.B. 554, 559, *per* Scott L.J.). I would respectfully endorse what was recently said by Roskill L.J. in *Cehave N.V.* v. *Bremer Handelsgesellschaft m.b.H.* [1976] Q.B. 44, 71:

> "In principle it is not easy to see why the law relating to contracts for the sale of goods should be different from the law relating to the performance of other contractual obligations, whether charterparties or other types of contract. Sale of goods law is but one branch of the general law of contract. It is desirable that the same legal principles should apply to the law of contract as a whole and that different legal principles should not apply to different branches of that law,"

and similarly by Devlin J. in *Cargo Ships "El-Yam" Ltd.* v. *Invoer-en Transport Onderneming "Invotra" N.V.* [1958] 1 Lloyd's Rep. 39, 52. The general law of contract has developed, along much more rational lines (e.g., *Hongkong Fir Shipping Co. Ltd.* v. *Kawasaki Kisen Kaisha Ltd.* [1962] 2 Q.B. 26), in attending to the nature and gravity of a breach or departure rather than in accepting rigid categories which do or do not automatically give a right to rescind, and if the choice were between extending cases under the Sale of Goods Act 1893 into other fields, or allowing more modern doctrine to infect those cases, my preference would be clear. The importance of this line of argument is that Mocatta J. and Lord Denning M.R. used it in the present case so as to reject the appellants' argument on "description" and I agree with them. But in case it does not appeal to this House, I am also satisfied that the appellants fail to bring the present case within the strictest rules as to "description."

In my opinion the fatal defect in their argument consists in their use of the words "identity" or "identification" to bridge two meanings. It is one thing to say of given words that their purpose is to state (identify) an essential part of the description of the goods. It is another to say that they provide one party with a specific indication (identification) of the goods so that he can find them and if he wishes sub-dispose of them. The appellants wish to say of words which "identify" the goods in the second sense, that they describe them in the first. I have already given reasons why I can only read the words in the second sense.

The difference is vital. If the words are read in the first sense, then, unless I am right in the legal argument above, each element in them has to be given contractual force. The vessel must, as a matter of contract, and as an essential term, be built by Osaka and must bear their Yard No. 354—if not the description is not complied with and the vessel tendered is not that contracted for.

If in the second sense, the only question is whether the words provide a means of identifying the vessel. If they fairly do this, they have fulfilled their function. It follows that if the second sense is correct, the words used can be construed much more liberally than they would have to be construed if they were providing essential elements of the description.

The two significant elements (whether in the box, or in the intermediate charter) are (i) the Yard No. 354, (ii) the expression "built by Osaka Shipbuilding Co. Ltd." [These words do not appear in the box but I will assume, very much in the appellants' favour, that the box has the same meaning as if the word "built" were used.] The appellants at one time placed great stress on the yard no. provision. They contended that by using it the "owners" assumed an obligation that the vessel should bear a number which would indicate that it would be constructed in the yard, where that number was appropriate, in sequence after vessels bearing earlier yard numbers (350–353). But this argument broke down in face of the fact, certainly known to Sanko which used and introduced the number into the charterparties, that the sequence through 354 was the sequence used at Osaka Shipbuilding Company's yard at Osaka, which yard could not construct the vessel. Thus the use of the yard no. for the contracted vessel must have had some other purpose than indicating construction at a particular yard. This turns the argument against the appellants—for it shows the words to be "labelling" words rather than words creating an obligation.

So the question becomes simply whether, as a matter of fact, it can fairly be said that—as a means of identification—the vessel was Yard No. 354 at Osaka Zosen or "built by Osaka Shipping Co. Ltd. and known as Hull No. 354 until named." To answer this, regard may be had to the actual arrangements for building the vessel and numbering it before named.

My Lords, I have no doubt, for the reasons given by the Court of Appeal, that an affirmative answer must be given. I shall not set out the evidence which clearly makes this good. The fact is that the vessel always was Osaka Hull No. 354—though also Oshima No. 4—and equally it can fairly be said to have been "built" by Osaka Shipbuilding Co. Ltd. as the company which planned, organised and directed the building and contractually engaged with Sculptor to build it, though also it could be said to have been built by Oshima Shipbuilding Co. Ltd. For the purpose of the identificatory clause, the words used are quite sufficient to cover the facts. No other vessel could be referred to: the reference fits the vessel in question.

There are other facts not to be overlooked. (1) So long as the charterers A could identify the nominated vessel they had not the slightest interest in whatever contracting or sub-contracting arrangements were made in the course of the building, a fact which no doubt explains the looseness of the language used in the box. (2) In making the arrangements they did for building the vessel Osaka acted in a perfectly straightforward and open manner. They cannot be said to be substituting one vessel for another; they have not provided any ground upon which the charterers can claim B that their bargain has not been fulfilled. The contracts all down the chain were closely and appropriately knitted into what Osaka did. (3) If the market had risen instead of fallen, it would have been quite impossible for Osaka or Sculptor, or Sanko, to refuse to tender the vessel in accordance with the charters on the ground that it did not correspond with that contracted for. No more on a falling market is there, in my opinion, any C ground on which the charterers can reject the vessel. In the end I find this a simple and clear case.

I would dismiss both appeals. Hansen-Tangen must pay the costs of the second appeal and Reardon Smith must pay the costs of the first appeal including the costs which Hansen-Tangen has to pay to Sanko under the second appeal.

D

VISCOUNT DILHORNE. My Lords, I have had the advantage of reading in advance the speech of my noble and learned friend, Lord Wilberforce and I only desire to add a few observations.

I agree with him in thinking that the appellants have failed to bring the case within the present rules as to " description " in connection with the sale of goods. I think that the material words of the " sub-charter " E and the " intermediate charter " strongly support that conclusion.

The preamble to the sub-charter says

> " the good Japanese flag (subject to clause 41) newbuilding motor tank vessel called Yard No. 354 at Osaka Zosen (hereinafter described as the vessel) described as per clause 24 hereof . . . "

The use of the word " called " followed by the words " described as per F clause 24 " is to my mind a clear indication that the words " Yard No. 354 " were not and were never intended to be part of the description of the vessel but only a means of identifying it.

The intermediate charter also distinguished between the identity of the vessel and its description. It made provision for it to be identified at a later date and separately described the vessel. The addendum to the G policy provided the identification, stating the vessel was " to be built by Osaka Shipbuilding Co. Ltd. and known as Hull No. 354."

Again I regard the use of the word " known " as significant. I, too, do not take the reference to the ship being built by Osaka as involving any contractual obligation but as a part of its identification.

In these circumstances I do not find it necessary to consider whether the present rules as to " description " in relation to the sale of goods H require to be reconsidered and whether they should be treated as applicable to other contracts. Even if they can be, they cannot in my opinion apply to these charters. Strong arguments can no doubt be advanced for not altering rules which have stood for so long and for not now restricting the right of a purchaser of goods to reject goods which do not answer the description of those he agreed to buy. It may be that strong arguments, too, can be advanced for saying that the hirer of an article should have a

A similar right of rejection when the article does not comply with the description given to him and on the basis of which he agreed to hire. But I now express no opinion thereon.

In my opinion these appeals should be dismissed.

LORD SIMON OF GLAISDALE. My Lords, I have had the advantage of reading in draft the speech prepared by my noble and learned friend on the
B Woolsack. I agree with it. It would be odd were the law to elevate a matter obviously immaterial to the parties at the time of contracting into a matter of fundamental obligation. I agree that the cases on the sale of goods may call for reconsideration on this basis.

I would dismiss these appeals.

C LORD KILBRANDON. My Lords, I have had the advantage of reading the draft prepared by my noble and learned friend, Lord Wilberforce. I so entirely agree with it, not only as to the conclusions which have to be drawn from the facts, but also from the consequences which in law ought to follow therefrom, that I have not thought it desirable to add any words of my own. I wish, however, to emphasise my express agreement with his analysis and criticism of the older authorities relating to description, and
D to hope that the more modern tendencies towards a business-like content of that word may in time cover its use in relation to contracts of sale. I would accordingly dismiss these appeals.

LORD RUSSELL OF KILLOWEN. My Lords, in my opinion the question in this appeal is one of identity: was the *Diana Prosperity* when built the
E vessel identified by the sub-charter as its future subject matter? The words, and the only words, of identification in the sub-charter are "Newbuilding motor tank vessel called Yard No. 354 at Osaka Zosen": the sub-charter of course contained a very full specification of the vessel and its equipment and fittings, but without the words quoted there were no means by which it could ever be said of any completed vessel that it was the vessel the subject of the sub-charter.

F There is in my opinion one matter of certainty to be extracted from the short and somewhat obscure quoted phrase; that is that the Osaka Shipbuilding Co. Ltd. had entered into a contract for the building of a relevant tanker and on entering into that contract had allotted in its books to the vessel to be built thereunder the yard or hull No. 354. Find the vessel built pursuant to such contract, and you find the vessel the subject
G of the sub-charter. (We were told by counsel that shipbuilders sometimes build a ship without a contract, hoping to find a purchaser for it when completed: but it was not suggested that this was conceivable in the case of a vessel of this size.)

Once it is concluded, as I conclude, that the essence of the identification of the vessel in the sub-charter lies in necessary assumption of a shipbuilding contract to which Osaka was party there is no difficulty in identify-
H ing the *Diana Prosperity* as the vessel subject to the sub-charter: and it is not necessary to attribute to the sub-charterers Reardon Smith any knowledge of a Japanese practice of 100 per cent. sub-contracting whether by failure to inquire or otherwise. On December 18, 1972, by an Export Building Contract S.S.K. [a member of the Sumitomo Group] (as seller) contracted with Sculptor: the contract contained these words ". . . the seller, sub-contracting with Osaka . . . (hereinafter called 'the builder') agrees to build, launch and complete at the shipyard of the builder or its

sub-contractor hereinafter called 'the shipyard') . . . " the vessel therein specified: in article I it was provided that " The vessel shall have the builder's Hull No. 354." Osaka though not a party thereto subscribed that contract " We . . . undertake the due performance as the builder in accordance with the terms and conditions specified in this contract." The underlining in the first quotation is mine.

On the same date S.S.K. and Osaka entered into the domestic contract: that recited the export contract (calling it the original contract) and that pursuant thereto S.S.K. had placed an order with Osaka for the construction of the vessel the subject of the original contract. Article I of the domestic contract provided that " Osaka shall construct the vessel in accordance with the terms of the original contract . . . ," which as indicated envisaged in terms that that construction might be through a sub-contractor. Article III provided that Osaka should carry out the construction of the vessel at its Oshima Yard under the supervision of S.S.K. and [Sculptor]: and further that the hull number should be No. 354 of Osaka which number should be shown on all documents relating to the vessel that should at any time be submitted to S.S.K. and Sculptor by Osaka.

The vital point, in my opinion, is that under the domestic contract, which was the Osaka contract necessarily referred to as identification in the sub-charter, Osaka was plainly entitled to sub-contract the whole construction of the vessel, and this Osaka did to Oshima when Oshima was formed. The vessel nevertheless remained the vessel identified as that which was the outcome of the proper carrying out of the domestic contract: and the vessel was the *Diana Prosperity*. Accordingly, in my judgment Reardon Smith having sub-chartered a vessel identified as the product of, in the event, the domestic contract, was not entitled to refuse to accept the *Diana Prosperity,* and its appeal against Hansen-Tangen fails. The fall-back appeal of Hansen-Tangen under the intermediate charter becomes in those circumstances in practice irrelevant, for the latter is under no obligation to Reardon Smith to reject the *Diana Prosperity* even if they were entitled to do so, and will naturally not do so, since the sub-charter was on more favourable terms to Hansen-Tangen than the intermediate charter.

Thus far, my Lords, I have construed the sub-charter in isolation, despite evidence that Reardon Smith had previously inspected the intermediate charter and that the sub-charter was intended to be " back to back " with it. I incline to the view that this is the correct approach. But it was argued that the reference in the sub-charter to Hansen-Tangen as " disponent owners " indicates that the latter were themselves charterers of the vessel in question, and so, in search of identity, involved the intermediate charter in the inquiry, with the result (it was argued) that the inquiry thus extended showed that it was a term of the contracts that the vessel should be one built by Osaka, which (at least in a narrower sense) *Diana Prosperity* was not.

The intermediate charter dated August 15, 1972, was by Sanko " being owners or disponent owners to be declared on delivery " to Hansen-Tangen of " newbuilding motor tank vessel (see clauses 41 and 42)." The specifications of the vessel I need not rehearse. Clause 41 provided that the charter was " for a motor tank vessel to be built at a yard in Japan to be declared by [Sanko] together with the applicable hull number within June 30, 1973, . . ." Thus it was a matter of indifference to the intermediate charterers and entirely at the option of Sanko by what shipbuilders and at what yards in Japan the vessel was to be built. On August 10, 1973, there

A was an agreement in part varying the intermediate charter and also identify-
ing the vessel under clause 41: this by addendum No. 1 provided that
"the vessel to perform this charter is to be built by Osaka Shipbuilding
Co. Ltd. and known as Hull No. 354 until named. . . ." It is argued
that here is a contractual obligation that the vessel shall be built by Osaka:
that the *Diana Prosperity* was built by Oshima, which alone was licensed
under Japanese law to build her: and that the phrase which I have quoted
B as the phrase of identification from the sub-charter should therefore be
construed as involving a contractual obligation or requirement of descrip-
tion of the vessel that she be built by Osaka. I observe at once that it is
strange that if that were intended by the parties to the sub-charter they
should have elected to reject the wording of the amended intermediate
charter in favour of the quite different language of the sub-charter. Rather
C does this change suggest to me, particularly in the context that Sanko was
entirely free to nominate the provenance of the vessel, that "to be built by
Osaka" was to be broadly construed and in a manner which would em-
brace that which was already clearly envisaged under the export contract,
the domestic contract and the head charter by Sculptor to Sanko. Indeed,
if the reference in the sub-charter to Hansen-Tangen as disponent owners
in the sub-charter is justification for construing that charter in the light of
D the intermediate charter, so also should the reference in the latter to
Sanko as "owners or disponent owners" be justification for construing
the intermediate charter in the light of what had gone before. On that basis
the whole genesis is opened up, and *Diana Prosperity* is the undoubted
outcome.

I have not rehearsed the details of the formation of Oshima under the
E inspiration of Osaka in partnership with other Japanese interests, nor the
preponderant contribution by Osaka to Oshima of management and other
staff, which may well justify a conclusion that in a broad sense *Diana
Prosperity* was built by Osaka. I do not find it necessary to decide this
appeal on that ground, though it may serve to underline the fact that
Reardon Smith and (by way of fall-back) Hansen-Tangen seek to avoid
the sub-charter and intermediate charter on very technical grounds. I prefer
F to decide the appeal upon the grounds which I have stated, which I trust
are not an over-simplification of the complicated and sometimes tortuous
arguments so lucidly presented to your Lordships' House.

Accordingly, I would dismiss the appeal of Reardon Smith, and the
fall-back appeal of Hansen-Tangen, with the consequence that the former
should pay the costs of the latter and of Sanko of these appeals.

G

Appeals dismissed.

Solicitors: *Norton, Rose, Botterell & Roche; Sinclair, Roche & Temperley; Ince & Co.*

J. A. G.

H

A

[QUEEN'S BENCH DIVISION]

* LIVELY LTD. AND ANOTHER *v.* CITY OF MUNICH

[1975 L. No. 784]

1976 June 14, 15, 16, 17, 18; 30 — Kerr J. B

Currency—Contract—Par value—Redemption of foreign bonds—Commercial objective—Calculation based on par value—Floating currency—Whether par value "in force"

The plaintiffs were the registered holders of City of Munich six per cent. bonds issued by the defendant in 1928. The terms of the bonds provided that they could be redeemed at C the latest by December 1, 1953, either in sterling or in United States dollars, at a fixed rate of $4.86 to the £, that being the value of the gold dollar in terms of sterling at the time. The bonds were not all redeemed by the final date and in 1955 the terms of the bonds were modified to provide that the final redemption date should be extended to December 1, 1973, and that the option to redeem the bonds in dollars should be removed. The amount of the payment to be made was to be D calculated on the basis that the equivalent in dollars of the amounts due at the rate of $4.86 to the £ would be re-converted into sterling at the appropriate rate of exchange, determined in accordance with article 13 of the Agreement on German External Debts dated February 27, 1953, applicable at the date when the respective amount was payable. That agreement provided in article 13 (*a*) that wherever an amount was to be calculated on the basis of a rate of exchange, that E rate should be determined by "the par values of the currencies concerned in force on the appropriate date as agreed with the International Monetary Fund"; article 13 (*b*) provided that if no such par values were in force on the appropriate date, the rate of exchange agreed for current payments in a bilateral payments agreement between the governments concerned or their monetary authorities should apply; article 13 (*c*) provided that if neither par values nor rates in bilateral payments agree- F ments were in force on the appropriate date, the middle rate of exchange generally applicable for transactions ruling for cable transfers in the currency of the country in which payment was to be made on the principal exchange market of the other country on that date, should apply. The United States and the United Kingdom were both members of the International Monetary Fund which was set up in July 1944 by the Articles of Agreement of the International Monetary Fund G (the Bretton Woods Agreement). The par values of their currencies were determined by the fund, and they were obliged, as were all members, to maintain the values of their currencies within margins of 1 per cent. up or down from the par values. By December 1, 1973, however, both the United States and the United Kingdom had ceased to confine their currencies within the defined parity margins, and were allowing them to float freely as against each other and against all other major H currencies. They maintained the par values only for certain purposes such as measuring their countries' obligations to the fund, and in the case of the United Kingdom, for determining the amount to be contributed to the budget of the European Economic Community, and as a statistical measure for the purpose of computing the country's gold and currency reserves.

[Reported by MRS. RACHEL DAVIES, Barrister-at-Law]

A The defendants, taking the view that the par values last determined by the fund remained in force at December 1, 1973, in that there had not been a new determination of par values by agreement between the member countries and the fund, discharged payment at the rate of exchange deriving from the terms of article 13 (*a*) of the agreement.

On a claim by the plaintiffs that payment should be made at the middle rate of exchange as defined in article 13 (*c*) of
B the agreement, on the ground that the par values were no longer in force, and no bilateral pay agreement had been entered into between the countries concerned:—

Held, giving judgment for the plaintiffs, that in construing the words " par values . . . in force . . . as agreed " in article 13 (*a*), as incorporated in the bonds, in accordance with the commercial objects which the bonds were designed to achieve, par values, which might still exist for the purpose of carrying
C out intergovernmental obligations, were not to be construed as " in force " for the purpose of a commercial agreement when dollar and sterling currencies were floating; further, once the margins to the par values of either or both currencies were removed, causing them to float, par values ceased to achieve the intended objective of the agreement which was to ensure equalisation of payment to bondholders in sterling and in dollars; accordingly, the middle market rate as defined
D in article 13 (*c*) was the appropriate rate of exchange (post, pp. 1015F–G, 1016E–F, 1017G).

The following cases are referred to in the judgment:

Gillett v. *Commission of the European Communities* [1975] E.C.R. 463.

Prenn v. *Simmonds* [1971] 1 W.L.R. 1381; [1971] 3 All E.R. 237, H.L.(E.).

River Wear Commissioners v. *Adamson* (1877) 2 App.Cas. 743, H.L.(E.).

E *Seyfang* v. *G. D. Searle & Co.* [1973] Q.B. 148; [1973] 2 W.L.R. 17; [1973] 1 All E.R. 290.

No additional cases were cited in argument.

ACTION

F By a writ dated February 27, 1975, the first plaintiff, Lively Ltd., and the second plaintiff, Control Nominees Ltd., claimed £14,417·70 and £3,021·35 respectively, with interest, being loss or damage suffered by reason of breaches of contract by the defendant, the City of Munich.

The facts are stated in the judgment.

Sir John Foster Q.C. and *Anthony Colman* for the plaintiffs.

G *S. A. Stamler Q.C.*, *Gerald Butler Q.C.* and *Susanna Fitzgerald* for the defendant.

Cur. adv. vult.

June 30. KERR J. read the following judgment. This case raises the question whether par values, as referred to in the Bretton Woods Agree-
H ment which created the International Monetary Fund continued to be in force for sterling and the United States dollar when both these currencies were floating. This issue arises, as I understand, in relation to a number of pre-war bonds which were reissued in modified form after the war.

Introduction

In 1928 the City of Munich raised a loan of £1,625,000 six per cent. sterling bonds under an agreement with Lazard Bros. & Co. Ltd. of London acting on behalf of the bondholders. Although expressed in sterling, the holders were given the option of requiring payment of the interest and of the principal sum on redemption in U.S. dollars at the fixed rate of $4.86 per £, this being then the value of the gold dollar in terms of sterling. This option was in the following terms so far as material:

> "Payment of the principal sum and interest as and when due will be made through Lazard Bros. & Co. Ltd. (hereinafter called 'the bankers') at the option of the holder either in sterling or in United States gold dollars (which expression in this bond and in the conditions endorsed herein means United States gold dollars of the weight and fineness ruling on November 24, 1928) at the fixed rate of exchange of $4.86 to the £ sterling. Principal and interest will be paid by warrants sent through the post to the registered address of the bond holder as appearing in the register of bondholders mentioned in the conditions endorsed hereon and any such warrant will be payable in sterling in London but with the option of the registered holder be exchangeable at the offices of the bankers for a draft on New York for United States gold dollars at the fixed rate of exchange of $4.86 to the £ sterling."

The latest date for the redemption of all outstanding bonds was December 1, 1953, but the loan went into default on the outbreak of war. As the result of an agreement between the City of Munich and Lazard Bros. & Co. Ltd. dated June 14, 1955, the terms of the bonds were modified in a number of respects, the most important for present purposes being the removal of the dollar option and the extension of the final redemption date to December 1, 1973. The removal of the dollar option took into account three important international developments which had taken place after the war. First, the International Monetary Fund (I.M.F.) had been set up in July 1944 and its articles of agreement had come into effect in December 1945. The United Kingdom and the United States were both members of the fund. Secondly, in September 1953, the intergovernmental Agreement on German External Debts had come into force. Thirdly, the value of the pound had greatly depreciated in relation to the dollar since 1928, and the United Kingdom had also introduced exchange control measures which precluded the free convertibility of sterling into dollars. The par value of sterling in terms of the dollar had been $4.03 since December 1946, but sterling was devalued to $2.80 per £ in March 1949, £1 being equivalent to 2·48828 grams of gold.

It is against this background that I must read the relevant modified terms of the re-issued bonds:

> "Payment of principal and interest secured by the within-written bond will be made in accordance with the terms and conditions of a settlement resulting from an offer made by the City of Munich in pursuance of the provisions of Annex 1 to the Agreement on German External Debts dated February 27, 1953. Reference is made to the said offer for its full content and effect, the main features of which are reproduced below, namely: (1) Such principal moneys and interest thereon at 4½ per cent. per annum will be made as and when due through Lazard Bros. & Co. Ltd., in sterling only, and the amount thereof will be calculated on the basis that the equivalent in U.S. dollars of the nominal amounts due at the rate of $4.86 to the £ will be reconverted into sterling at the appropriate rate of exchange (determined

A in accordance with article 12 of the said agreement of February 27, 1953) applicable to the date when the respective amount is payable to Lazard Bros. & Co. Ltd. . . . (3) Unless earlier redeemed, this bond will become payable on December 1, 1973."

I must next set out the material terms of Annex 1 to the Agreement on German External Debts referred to above. Section B deals inter alia
B with external bonds issued by municipalities in the Federal Republic of Germany, and I set out clause 7 (1) (*d*) and (*e*):

> "(*d*) The maturity dates of these loans shall be extended by 20 years from the existing maturity dates; (*e*) in respects other than those indicated above," and no others are relevant for present purposes, "the terms of the original loan contracts shall be maintained unless
> C otherwise agreed by the creditor in special circumstances. . . ."

It was not suggested on behalf of the defendants that any such "special circumstances" existed in the present case.

I then turn to article 13, the most important provision of the agreement for present purposes which provides as follows so far as material:

> "*Rates of exchange.* Wherever it is provided in the present agree-
> D ment and the annexes thereto that an amount shall be calculated on the basis of a rate of exchange, such rate shall . . . be (*a*) determined by the par values of the currencies concerned in force on the appropriate date as agreed with the International Monetary Fund under article IV section 1 of the Articles of Agreement of the International Monetary Fund, or (*b*) if no such par values are or were in force on the appro-
> E priate date, the rate of exchange agreed for current payments in a bilateral payments agreement between the governments concerned or their monetary authorities; or (*c*) if neither par values nor rates in bilateral payments agreements are or were in force on the appropriate date, the middle rate of exchange generally applicable for transactions ruling for cable transfers in the currency of the country in which payment is to be made in the principal exchange market of the other
> F country on that date, or on the last date before that date on which such rate was ruling; or (*d*) if there is or was no rate of exchange as specified under (*a*), (*b*) or (*c*) at the appropriate date, the cross-rate of exchange resulting from the middle rates of exchange ruling for the currencies in question in the principal exchange market of a third country dealing in those currencies on that date or the last date
> G before the said date upon which such rates were ruling."

I must also set out the parts of articles 11 and 12 as follows. Article 11 is headed "Currency of Payment" and paragraph 2 (*b*) provides:

> "If a currency option provides for payment of a fixed amount of an alternative currency, the creditor shall be entitled to receive, in the currency of the country in which the loan was raised or from which
> H credit was advanced, the equivalent, at the rate of exchange current on the date payment shall fall due, of such amount of the alternative currency as would have been payable if the option had been exercised."

Then article 12 is headed "Treatment of Gold Clauses." I read paragraph (*b*):

> "The amount to be paid on a debt which, under the terms of the obligation existing at the time of the settlement, is denominated or

payable in any other non-German currency on a gold basis or with a gold clause, shall be determined as follows:—(i) The equivalent in A
United States dollars of the nominal amount due shall be calculated at the rate of exchange on the date when the obligation was contracted or, in the case of a bonded debt, when the bonds were issued; (ii) the dollar figure so calculated shall be converted into the currency in which the obligation is to be paid in accordance with article 11 at the rate of exchange between the United States dollar and such currency on B
the date when the amount payable is due, except that if such rate of exchange is less favourable for the creditor then the rate of exchange between the United States dollar and such currency on August 1, 1952, the conversion shall be made on the basis of the rate of exchange on August 1, 1952."

The issue in the present case is whether the applicable rate of exchange C
is that provided by article 13 (*a*) or (*c*). It turns on the question whether par values for sterling and the U.S. dollar were in force on December 1, 1973, the date with which I am concerned, when both these currencies were floating, i.e., when neither of them was maintained in relation to gold within fixed margins on either side of their par values. However, in order to follow the implications of this issue it is necessary to set out and consider D
certain articles of the I.M.F. agreement.

The I.M.F. agreement

The purposes of the International Monetary Fund are set out in article I. So far as material, they are to promote international monetary co-operation and exchange stability, to maintain orderly exchange arrange- E
ments among members, to avoid competitive exchange depreciation, and to assist in the establishment of a multilateral system of payments in respect of current transactions between members. Article IV headed "Par Values of Currencies," is important and I must set out most of it.

"Section 1. Expression of par values. (*a*) The par value of the currency of each member shall be expressed in terms of gold as a F
common denominator or in terms of the United States dollar of the weight and fineness in effect on July 1, 1944. (*b*) All computations relating to currencies of members for the purpose of applying the provisions of this agreement shall be on the basis of their par values. Section 2. *Gold purchases based on par values.* The fund shall prescribe a margin above and below par value for transactions in gold by members, and no member shall buy gold at a price above par G
value plus the prescribed margin, or sell gold at a price below par value minus the prescribed margin. Section 3. *Foreign exchange dealings based on parity.* The maximum and the minimum rates for exchange transactions between the currencies of members taking place within their territories shall not differ from parity, (i) in the case of spot exchange transactions, by more than 1 per cent.; and (ii) in the case of H
other exchange transactions, by a margin which exceeds the margin for spot exchange transactions by more than the fund considers reasonable. Section 4. *Obligations regarding exchange stability.* (*a*) Each member undertakes to collaborate with the fund to promote exchange stability, to maintain orderly exchange arrangements with other members, and to avoid competitive exchange alterations. (*b*) Each member undertakes, through appropriate measures consistent with this agreement, to

> A permit within its territories exchange transactions between its currency and the currencies of other members only within the limits prescribed under section 3 of this article. A member whose monetary authorities, for the settlement of international transactions, in fact freely buy and sell gold within the limits prescribed by the fund under section 2 of this article shall be deemed to fulfilling this undertaking. Section 5. *Changes in par values.* (*a*) A member shall not propose a change in B the par value of its currency except to correct a fundamental disequilibrium. (*b*) A change in the par value of a member's currency may be made only on the proposal of the member and only after consultation with the fund . . . Section 6. *Effect of unauthorised changes.* If a member changes the par value of its currency despite the objection of the fund, in cases where the fund is entitled to object, C the member shall be ineligible to use the resources of the fund unless the fund otherwise determines; and if, after the expiration of a reasonable period, the difference between the member and the fund continues, the matter shall be subject to the provisions of article XV, section 2 (*b*). Section 8. *Maintenance of gold value of the fund's assets.* (*a*) The gold value of the fund's assets shall be maintained notwithstanding changes in the par or foreign exchange value of the D currency of any member. (*b*) Whenever (i) the par value of a member's currency is reduced, or (ii) the foreign exchange value of a member currency has, in the opinion of the fund, depreciated to a significant extent within that member's territories, the member shall pay to the fund within a reasonable time an amount of its own currency equal to the reduction in the gold value of its currency held E by the fund. (*c*) Whenever the par value of a member's currency is increased, the fund shall return to such member within a reasonable time an amount in its currency equal to the increase in the gold value of its currency held by the fund."

The initial determination of par values was fixed by article XX, section 4. To prevent speculation on the market, these were based on each original F member's rates of exchange prevailing 60 days before the entry into force of the agreement. Their final determination, as in the case of members acceding later, was then to be agreed with the fund. In the event of any continuing difference between a member and the fund about an agreed re-assessment of the member's par value the member may be required to withdraw from the fund under article XV, section 2 (*b*).

The central provisions of the agreement concerning the maintenance of G rates of exchange, which are also crucial for present purposes, are therefore contained in article IV, and their gist can be summarised as follows. First, the basic yardstick for determining the par value of the currency of each member is gold as a common denominator or the 1944 gold dollar. It was common ground before me that in 1955 no one anticipated any change in the gold dollar, and until August 1971 this expectation was ful- H filled. Indeed, it was because the U.S. dollar was regarded as equivalent to gold when the I.M.F. was set up that article IV, section (1) (*a*), provided for the dollar as an alternative measure of parity. In practice, the par values of most currencies, in particular sterling with which I am concerned, was therefore usually expressed in terms of the dollar.

The second point, also of fundamental importance to this case, is that under sections 3 and 4 of this article all foreign exchange dealings within the territories of any member are to be based on parity, and that the

members are obliged to maintain the stability of their currencies in relation A
to the agreed par values unless and until these are changed in agreement
with the fund. Members are obliged to maintain the value of their cur-
rencies within a range of 1 per cent. up or down from the par value.
This obligation can be performed in different ways by the central banks
or monetary authorities of each member. Under the second sentence of
section 4 of article IV it can be performed by permitting a free market
in gold within the limits prescribed by section 2, and this is how the B
United States performed their obligations under the agreement until August
1971.

The third important factor is that the agreement envisages that these
obligations may nevertheless fail to be complied with by members in two
relevant respects. First, if a member fails to maintain the required mar-
gins on either side of the par value of its currency, as by allowing the C
currency to float, it can be required to pay a compensating amount to the
fund under section 8 (*b*) (ii) of article IV to replenish the fund's holdings
of its currency to the required level. The ultimate issue in this case is
whether, when this happens, the member's par value is nevertheless still
in force for the purposes of article 13 (*a*) of the inter-governmental Agree-
ment on German External Debts. Secondly, section 6 of article IV envi-
sages that a member may change the par value of its currency despite D
objection by the fund, in which case the articles provide that it may be
required to cease to be a member.

I should add that par values are also relevant for certain other pur-
poses with which I deal hereafter.

Changes in par values and parities E

I must now return to the history. Expert evidence was called on both
sides. The plaintiffs called Professor Hirsch who had worked as a senior
adviser to the I.M.F. for a number of years during the relevant period.
The defendants called Mr. Fawcett, a member of the bar who was general
counsel to the fund from 1955 to 1960. As one would expect, their
evidence did not differ on questions of fact but only on the application of F
the articles to the post-1971 situation, though this is ultimately a matter
of law for the court. While I therefore found their evidence of great
assistance, the differences between them cannot in any way be determina-
tive of the issue which I have to decide. For the sake of completeness I
should add that the plaintiffs had previously served a subpoena on an
official of the Bank of England to be available as a witness. On the appli-
cation of the bank I set this aside, not because of the bank's special posi- G
tion, but on the basis that the court has a discretion not to compel an
expert to give evidence against his wishes when he has had no connection
with the facts or the history of the matter in issue: see *Seyfang* v. *Searle
& Co.* [1973] 1 Q.B. 148.

What happened in relation to the I.M.F. agreement can be summarised
as follows. The initial par value of the pound to the dollar having been H
agreed at $4.03 and having been devalued to $2.80 in 1949, sterling was
again devalued in November 1967 to $2.40, or 2·13281 grams of gold.
Financial stability under the I.M.F. agreement had meanwhile been main-
tained, though Canada and Peru had for some years allowed their curren-
cies to float, in an upward direction as I understand, but without any
material international consequences.

The foundation of the whole system was then shaken on August 15,

A 1971, when the U.S. government notified the I.M.F. that it would no longer buy or sell gold for the settlement of international transactions. This had been the manner whereby the United States (under the second sentence of of article IV, section 4 (*b*)) had always complied with their obligations under the I.M.F. agreement until then. The United States did not propose to substitute any other method of performing their obligations under the I.M.F. agreement, such as by official intervention to maintain the dollar
B within its prescribed margins.

This event had profound international financial repercussions throughout the world. For some time all major currencies were allowed to float until a measure of order was restored by an agreement reached in December 1971 at the Smithsonian Institute in Washington between representatives of the major members of the I.M.F. This agreement had two main
C results. First, the United States announced that it proposed to devalue the dollar in relation to gold by 7·89 per cent., which produced a par value relationship of $2.605 to the pound and reduced the value of the dollar from 0·888671 to 0·818513 grams of gold. The legal measures to effect this were completed in May 1972. Secondly, a decision was adopted by the executive board of the I.M.F. (No. 3463 of December 18, 1971) headed "A Temporary Regime, Central Rates and Wider Margins." Its main
D effect for present purposes is that, inconsistently with the obligations prescribed by section 3 of article IV to maintain margins for spot exchange transactions within 1 per cent. of the par values, it sanctioned the widening of these margins by 2¼ per cent. on either side of the par values. In effect, this decision represented the adoption of a modus vivendi without any legal basis under the I.M.F. agreement. The purely pragmatic
E character of this decision is indicated by its preamble and paragraph 1 as follows:

> "*Preamble.* This decision is adopted by the executive directors in order to indicate practices that members may wish to follow in present circumstances consistently with article IV, section 4 (*a*) and Board of Governors Resolution No. 26–9, which called on all members to col-
> F laborate with the fund and with each other in order to maintain a satisfactory structure of exchange rates within appropriate margins. The decision is intended to enable members to observe the purposes of the fund to the maximum extent possible during the temporary period preceding the resumption of effective par values with appropriate margins in accordance with the articles. Paragraph 1. Par values and wider margins. (*a*) A member will be deemed to be act-
> G ing in accordance with article IV, section 4 (*a*) and resolution No. 26–9 if it takes appropriate measures, consistent with the articles, to permit spot exchange transactions between its currency and the currencies of other members taking place within its territories only at rates within 2¼ per cent. from the effective parity relationship among currencies as determined by the fund, provided that these margins may
> H be within 4½ per cent. from the said relationship if they result from the maintenance by the member of rates within margins of 2¼ per cent. from the said relationship for spot exchange transactions between its currency and its intervention currency."

Although the United States were taking no measures after the Smithsonian agreement to maintain the dollar within any prescribed margins, the dollar did not effectively begin to float freely for some time, because other major currencies were maintained within a parity margin of 2½ per cent. on either side of the dollar as sanctioned by the I.M.F. decision. A This was the effect of the so-called "Snake" agreement in April and May 1972 whereby it was agreed between eight European states, including the United Kingdom, that they would maintain this parity margin in relation to the dollar amongst their currencies. However, on June 23, 1972, the United Kingdom left the "Snake," and formally informed the I.M.F. that sterling would be allowed to float "as a temporary measure," and that in consequence the market rate for sterling would not necessarily be confined B within announced limits either in respect of the dollar or in respect of the currencies of other countries of the European Economic Community. This meant that for the time being the United Kingdom was going beyond the temporary expedient of the Smithsonian agreement of wider margins by allowing sterling to float freely on the basis of its value in the international monetary market. This was still the position on December 1, 1973, the C material date for present purposes, and remains the position today.

I must then return to the subsequent history of the dollar. The proposed devaluation announced in December 1971 had become the law of the United States on May 8, 1972, reducing the value of the dollar against gold by 7·89 per cent. The I.M.F. consented to the change, so that the dollar thereafter had a new par value. However, since the United States did nothing to maintain any margins in relation to this par value, not even D the wider margins sanctioned by the Smithsonian agreement, the dollar was in one sense already floating. But, except in relation to the pound, which was clearly floating, the parity of the dollar within the wider margins was effectively being maintained by agreement between most of the other major currency countries, in particular the "Snake" agreement as already mentioned.

E

The position changed again on February 12, 1973, when the United States announced that it would propose a further devaluation of the dollar by 10 per cent. This led to the abandonment of support for the dollar by the other remaining major currencies, so that from about March 1973 the dollar was fully floating. The formal steps concerning this further devaluation were taken on September 22, and October 18, 1973, when the United States Congress approved it, and a new par value was agreed with F the I.M.F. reducing the dollar in terms of gold to 0·7366 grams.

It follows from the foregoing account that on December 1, 1973, the redemption date of the bonds, the two currencies with which the bonds were concerned were floating as against each other and all other major currencies. The only difference between their status was formal, in that the United Kingdom had formally notified the fund that it was allowing G the pound to float, whereas the United States government had not done so as regards the dollar. It was no doubt for this reason that in Table 1.1 to the 1973 Report of the I.M.F. a par value is still shown for the United States but none for the United Kingdom, with a footnote that the latter had notified the fund that its currency was floating.

On November 7, 1973, the executive board published a further decision (No. 4083). It was a revision of that of December 18, 1971, from which H I have already quoted, still sanctioning the wider margins "preceding the resumption of effective par values with the appropriate margins in accordance with the articles." However, the differences between these two decisions are not material for present purposes, and in practice it was not observed, either in relation to the dollar or to the pound, or in relation to many other major currencies which were by then effectively also floating.

In an article by Mr. J. Gold, general counsel to the I.M.F. and head of

A its legal department ("The Legal Structure of the Par Value System,"
Law and Policy in International Business, vol. 5, 1973, p. 190) Mr.
Gold described the state of affairs after 1971 as "a temporary extra-legal
regime." In my view this is an appropriate description of the position,
though by 1976 one wonders how temporary it is going to be.

B *Computation of redemption value of the bonds*

I must now turn to the different ways in which the parties compute this
value by reference to different exchange rates. Their basic position is as
follows. The plaintiffs' claim is founded on article 13 (*c*) of the inter-
governmental Agreement on German External Debts because they say that
article 13 (*a*) does not apply. The defendants contend that article 13 (*a*)
does apply. Adapting the material parts of the wording of paragraph
C (*a*) for present purposes, the issue between them is accordingly whether
or not "par values of the pound and the dollar were in force on December
1, 1973, as agreed with the I.M.F.," when both these currencies were
floating. Since the plaintiffs contend that paragraph (*a*) does not apply,
they contend that by applying paragraph (*c*) the applicable rate of ex-
change was the market rate of the pound to the dollar on December 1,
D 1973. This is agreed to have been $2.34 to the £.

Before explaining the defendants' computation under article 13 (*a*),
it is necessary to note an apparently paradoxical situation which applies on
either view and results from the wording of the bonds. This is that the
appropriate rate of exchange of the dollar to sterling has to be divided into
the fixed rate of $4.86 to the £ for which the bonds provide; this having
been the par value relationship in 1928. Since the appropriate rate of
E exchange is the divisor, the result is that the higher this rate of exchange,
the less sterling the plaintiffs receive. One can see this as follows. For
reasons to which I turn in a moment, as against the market rate of $2.34
taken by the plaintiffs, the defendants contend for a rate of $2.89 which
they then reduce to $2.80, both of these being therefore higher than the
plaintiffs' market rate of exchange. If one divides either of these higher
F rates into $4.86 one gets a lesser number of pounds than if one takes the
lower market rate. But the reason is clear: the modified bonds were
designed to provide that if the pound depreciated against the dollar from
the fixed 1928 rate of $4.86 to the pound, the bondholders were to be
compensated by receiving a correspondingly greater number of pounds.

I now turn to the way in which the defendants arrive at their rate of
exchange. They say that agreed par values were in force on December 1,
G 1973, so that paragraph (*a*) of article 13 applies. They say that once a
par value has been agreed with the I.M.F. it remains in force unless and
until it is changed in agreement with the I.M.F. On this basis they say
that on December 1, 1973, both the pound and the dollar still had an
agreed par value in relation to gold, and that this was still in force. The
par value for the pound is the one which resulted from the last formal
H devaluation in November 1967, i.e. 2·13281 grams of gold per pound,
giving a rate of exchange of $2.40 per £. As regards the dollar they
take the last agreed par value, which was formally sanctioned on October
18, 1973, as the result of the devaluation announced on February 12, 1973,
producing a par value of 0·7366 grams of gold to the pound. The cross-
rate of exchange which can then be calculated by reference to these two
gold values produces a rate of $2.89 to the £. This is a rate which no-
one at the trial before me had ever heard of before. Equally, it bears

no relation to any commercial or market rate of exchange between the A
pound and the dollar which has ever existed.

The defendants then reduce this rate to $2.80 on the basis that this results from the application of article 12 (*b*) (ii) of the Agreement on German External Debts, because this was the rate on August 1, 1952, and because a higher rate of exchange would be less favourable to the bond-holders in the present case due to the effect of increasing the divisor, the
point with which I have already dealt. The plaintiffs agree that if the B
rate of $2.89 is initially correct, then it falls to be reduced to $2.80, and this is the basis on which the plaintiffs have in fact been paid. Their monetary claim in this action results from the difference between taking a rate of $2.34 and $2.80. There was some argument whether, if the defendants are right about the rate of $2.89, they were bound to reduce
this to $2.80, or whether this was a concession, but it was agreed that I C
need not and should not decide this point, since it might affect other cases and was not fully argued before me.

The defendants' contentions

It is convenient to consider the issues in this case by reference to two
contentions which were clearly formulated by Mr. Stamler on behalf of D
the defendants. These were as follows. (1) The words "in force" in article 13 (*a*) add nothing. One is simply dealing with a single concept of "par values . . . in force . . . as agreed . . ." and not with par values which must be (i) in force and (ii) agreed with the I.M.F. To put it another way, all par values agreed with the I.M.F. remain in force unless and until changed in agreement with the I.M.F. (2) If this be wrong, and
if the words "in force" add a requirement which must also be satisfied, E
then the defendants submit that the respective par values already mentioned were in fact still in force for various reasons with which I have not yet dealt. I therefore begin by considering these two submissions.

I cannot accept the first submission for a number of reasons. First, the words "in force" are there in addition to the words "as agreed" and
were presumably intended to have some additional effect. Secondly, F
there is at least one case (apart from the issue which arises here) in which the words "in force" clearly have some additional effect even under the scheme of the I.M.F. articles. Take the case of an unauthorised change in the par value of a currency which is dealt with in article IV, section 6. Suppose that a country changes the agreed par value of its currency despite objection from the fund. What is then "the par value . . . in force . . . as
agreed?" The par value "as agreed" is the original one, but the par G
value "in force" clearly appears to be that which the member has adopted without the authority of the fund. The difficulty which results from the continuing existence of an agreed par value on the one hand, and on the other hand the enforcement of a different par value by a member, appears to be precisely what section 6 envisages. As I understood Mr. Stamler, he
was prepared to concede this, but said that would be a different case. So H
it would be, but it provides a clear illustration of a situation in which an agreed par value would no longer be in force and therefore lends meaning to the words "in force" in article 13 (*a*). Thirdly, I think that this submission fails to give any realistic commercial effect to the circumstances with reference to which the bonds were re-issued in their modified form and the object, appearing from these circumstances, which the parties clearly had in mind. I adapt these words from the speech of Lord Wilberforce

A in *Prenn* v. *Simmonds* [1971] 1 W.L.R. 1381, 1384, quoting from the judgment of Lord Blackburn in *River Wear Commissioners* v. *Adamson* (1877) 2 App.Cas. 743, 763, and also bear in mind the passage at p. 1385 where he refers to the genesis and objective aim of the transaction. However, it is easier to deal with this point by reference to the defendants' second submission.

The second submission, that the par values of the pound and dollar
B which were last agreed with the I.M.F. were still in force on December 1, 1973, although these currencies were floating, was based on the admitted fact that these par values, as well as the par values of all other floating currencies, continue to be used for certain purposes. These purposes are the following. First, under article III of the I.M.F. agreement, which provides for the quotas and subscriptions by each member to the fund,
C the par value of each member's currency was and remains the applicable measure of the obligation by the member to the fund. For instance, each member's minimum subscription is 25 per cent. of its quota in gold and the balance in the member's currency. The amount of currency payable, both initially and when further subscriptions have been required, is determined by the par value of the currency in question. Secondly, the amount which a member may be required to pay to the fund under article IV,
D section 8 (*b*) (ii), whenever its currency depreciates to a significant extent below its par value is equally measured by reference to the last agreed par value. Like section 6 of this article, this provision envisages a situation in which a member may be in breach of his obligations, in this case by failing to maintain the required margin. The member may then be called upon to top up the fund's holdings of the currency in question to restore these in
E relation to the par value. Thirdly, upon the withdrawal of a member from the fund and upon the possible liquidation of the fund, Schedules D and E to the articles provide that all the accounts will be adjusted on the basis of the par values. All these are instances of the application of the par values in dealings between members and the fund and in effect flow from section 1 (*b*) of article IV which I have already set out. The par value of sterling also continues to be used in two other ways so far as the United
F Kingdom is concerned. First, it determines the amount of this country's contribution to the European Economic Community's budget. Secondly, it is used as a statistical measure for the purpose of computing the gold and currency reserves of this country.

The question is whether by reason of any or all of these admitted facts, par values continue to be " in force " for the purposes of article 13 (*a*) of
G the Agreement on German External Debts as incorporated into these bonds, notwithstanding the fact that sterling and the dollar were floating on the relevant date. In my view the answer is " No " when these words are construed in article 13 (*a*) in accordance with the commercial object which these bonds, and indeed the Agreement on German External Debts itself, were designed to achieve.

What was the commercial object of the bonds, both originally and in
H their modified form? It was to secure to the bondholders an equalisation in value between sterling and the dollar. On the evidence before me the assumption in 1928, and still in 1955, was no doubt that the dollar would not be devalued in the foreseeable future and would remain freely convertible into gold. However, I put this on one side, as I put aside evidence of rumours about the future of sterling in 1954 and 1955. Without any extrinsic evidence it is clear that the bonds, both in their original and modified forms, were designed to protect the bondholders against a possible

depreciation of sterling against the dollar. In the original bonds this A
was the reason for taking the 1928 gold dollar of $4.86 to the £ as the
measure of the sterling obligation and for giving to the bondholder the
option of requiring the payment of interest and principal in dollars at this
rate of exchange. Although this option then had to be eliminated in 1955
because sterling was no longer freely convertible, the objective remained
the same; this is why the rate of $4.86 was retained even though the current
parity had by then fallen to $2.80. The fact that this was the object is also B
shown by the statement in the modified bonds that they were issued in
pursuance of the provisions of annex 1 to the Agreement on German
External Debts. I have already quoted the provision from clause 7 (*e*) of
this annex which was applicable to bonds such as these and which shows
that the creditor's position under the original loan was to be maintained
unless otherwise agreed by him in special circumstances. The same C
objective is to be found in article 12 (*b*) (ii) which I have also already
set out.

How then do these considerations apply to the construction of article 13
in a situation in which the currencies in question are floating? In my view
there are two fundamental factors to be borne in mind when one comes
to construe this article in such a situation, and these would apply even apart
from the foregoing considerations. First, the essential commercial character- D
istic of par values being in force for exchange transactions in the territory of
any member is the maintenance of the required margins as provided by
sections 3 and 4 of article IV. If no margins are maintained, then par
values become commercially meaningless; as meaningless as the defen-
dants' rate of exchange of $2.89 to the £ on December 1, 1973, when
the real rate of exchange was $2.34. In an issue concerning the E
applicable rate of exchange between a debtor and creditor under a bond
which incorporates article 13 it is in my judgment essential to construe this
article in a commercially realistic sense. The present issue is concerned
with a rate of exchange applicable to a commercial transaction; it is not
concerned with treaty obligations by governments to the I.M.F. or inter se.
It does not follow from the fact that par values continued to be used for
certain purposes in the latter field that they were in force for the purpose F
of construing these words when article 13 (*a*) is incorporated into a bond.
In that context par values are in my view no longer in force when margins
are no longer being maintained in relation to the currencies in question.
The fact that par values continue to exist does not necessarily mean that
they remain in force.

The second factor, which leads to the same conclusion, is to consider the G
various rates of exchange referred to in article 13. It was common ground
that for this purpose it was also permissible to have regard to articles 11
and 12, in particular 11 (2) (*b*) and 12 (*b*) (ii). The defendants relied in
their pleadings on the latter provision and this in turn refers back to the
former. What is the scheme of all these provisions? In my view it is to
provide various means, as set out in paragraphs (*a*) to (*d*) of article 13,
to arrive at a rate of exchange which represents the value of one currency H
in terms of another at the material date. I do not accept, as submitted
by the defendants, that paragraphs (*a*) and (*b*) merely provide what might
be called conventional rates or formulae which may lead to arbitrary results
without any commercial reality. All four rates are intended, to use the
words of article 11 (2) (*b*), to be rates of exchange "current on the date
payment shall fall due." So long as par values are in force in the sense
of margins being maintained as required by sections 3 and 4 of article IV

A of the I.M.F. agreement, the rate under paragraph (*a*) can only produce a
difference of plus or minus 1 per cent. from the middle market rate provided
for in paragraph (*c*).

Mr. Stamler sought to support his submissions on the meaning of " in
force " in paragraph (*a*) by reference to the same expression in paragraphs
(*b*) and (*c*). I did not get much help from this but would in any event
construe this expression in these provisions in a similar sense. Thus, take
B the words " in force " in paragraph (*b*). Suppose that on the appropriate
date there was a bilateral payments agreement between two countries which
provided for an agreed rate of exchange for current payments. Suppose
then that, without being formally abrogated, this agreement was no longer
observed by either or both countries so that the actual rates of exchange
applied to current payments differed from the agreed rates. In my judg-
C ment the agreed rates would then no longer be in force if paragraph (*b*) had
to be construed in a commercial context. The fact that, from the point of
view of the treaty creating the bilateral payments agreement, both govern-
ments would still be bound by its terms does not appear to me to affect
the true construction of paragraph (*b*) when incorporated into a commercial
contract.

Finally, there is yet another way which points to the same conclusion.
D The terms of the modified bonds provide that the nominal amounts due
at the rate of $4.86 to the £ were to be converted into sterling " at the
appropriate rate of exchange " under article 13. The defendants submit
that this merely means that one goes through the alternative paragraphs (*a*)
to (*d*) in that order and stops at the point at which one of them is applicable
on its true construction. Prima facie this is of course the correct approach.
E But if, contrary to my view, they are correct in their construction of para-
graph (*a*), then the resulting rate of $2.89 cannot by any stretch of the
imagination be described as a rate which is " appropriate." The defen-
dants also say that when this rate is reduced to $2.80 under article 12 (*b*) (ii)
it becomes an appropriate rate because this happened to be the rate which
prevailed in 1955. But this is pure sophistry. On December 1, 1973, a
rate of $2.80 to the £ was no more appropriate than a rate of $2.89,
F except that it was a rate which had once existed. It bore no relation
to the then value of the pound to the dollar, whereas in my judgment the
essential objective was to ensure that for the face value of the bonds the
bondholders would receive an amount in sterling which was either equiv-
alent to U.S. dollars at the rate of $4.86 per £ or which compensated
them for any depreciation of sterling from this rate of exchange. If margins
G had been maintained as required by the I.M.F. agreement, then this object
would have been achieved by the application of article 13 (*a*). Once either
or both of the currencies floated, par values were in my judgment no longer
in force, so that paragraph (*a*) ceased to apply, ceased to be appropriate,
and ceased to achieve the intended objective. It follows that in my view
the plaintiffs are right in submitting that the middle market rate on
December 1, 1973, applies by virtue of article 13 (*c*).

H For the sake of completeness I should refer briefly to one of the
authorities relied on by the defendants, *Gillet* v. *Commission of the
European Communities* [1975] E.C.R. 463, a decision of the European
Court of Justice (Second Chamber) of March 19, 1975. It concerned
article 63 of the Staff Regulations of Officials of the European Com-
munities which provides that an official's remuneration shall be ex-
pressed in Belgian francs but paid in the currency of the country in
which he performs his duties. It then goes on to provide: " Remuner-

ation paid in a currency other than Belgian francs shall be calculated on the basis of the parities accepted by the International Monetary Fund which were in force on January 1, 1965." It seems that this regulation is still in force and now applies to British officials of the European Economic Community. The applicant worked in Italy and was accordingly paid in lire. One of his complaints was that the number of lire which he was paid was computed on the basis of a rate of exchange to Belgian francs established by reference to the par values of these currencies in force on January 1, 1965, although the purchasing power of the lira had substantially depreciated in relation to other currencies in 1974, this being the time when the relevant facts arose. He therefore contended that this regulation infringed article 184 of the European Economic Community Treaty which provides for equality of treatment of officials. This argument was rejected for reasons which are irrelevant to the present case. There was no argument or decision on the meaning of the words "in force" in the regulation. This is not surprising, since neither the Belgian franc nor the lira was floating on January 1, 1965, with the result that the issue in the present case could not arise. It was therefore accepted, as it had to be, that the par values of these currencies were in force on that date and that the conversion had to be made accordingly.

The plaintiffs' claims on the basis of a middle market rate of exchange on December 1, 1973, under article 13 (*c*) of the Agreement on German External Debts are not challenged so far as the figures are concerned. It follows that these claims succeed and that there will be judgment for the sums claimed, that is, £14,417·70 in the case of the first plaintiffs and £3,021·35 in the case of the second plaintiffs.

Judgment for the plaintiffs.

Solicitors: *Herbert Smith & Co.; Slaughter & May.*

[QUEEN'S BENCH DIVISION]

* DEPARTMENT OF HEALTH AND SOCIAL SECURITY *v.* ENVOY FARMERS LTD.

[1974 H. No. 1113]

1976 March 3; 11 Jupp J.

Costs—Incidental proceedings—Inquiry by Secretary of State—Classification of insured person in question—Court referring question to Secretary of State for determination—Whether costs of minister's inquiry "incidental to . . . proceedings in . . . court"—Supreme Court of Judicature (Consolidation) Act 1925 (15 & 16 *Geo.* 5, *c.* 49), *s.* 50 (1) [1]*—National Insurance Act* 1956 (*c.* 51), *s.* 97 (2) [2]

[Reported by BERNARD O. AGYEMAN, ESQ., Barrister-at-Law]

[1] Supreme Court of Judicature (Consolidation) Act 1925, s. 50: "(1) Subject to the provisions of this Act and to rules of court and to the express provisions of any other Act, the costs of and incidental to all proceedings in the Supreme Court . . . shall be in the discretion of the court or judge, and the court or judge shall have full power to determine by whom and to what extent the costs are to be paid."

[2] National Insurance Act 1965, s. 97 (2): see post, p. 1020G.

A The Department of Health and Social Security claimed in an action against a company that national insurance contributions were payable by the company in respect of insured persons alleged to be employees. The company denied liability on the ground that the persons were self-employed. On a reference by the court, under section 97 (2) of the National Insurance Act 1965 for determination of the question whether the company were liable as employers to pay the contributions,
B the Secretary of State for Social Services, after an inquiry, decided that the company were not liable. Thereupon, the master dismissed the action with costs to include the costs of and incidental to the inquiry.

On appeal by the department:—

Held, allowing the appeal, that the costs of the inquiry before the Secretary of State into the question referred by the court were not incidental to the proceedings in court within
C section 50 (1) of the Supreme Court of Judicature (Consolidation) Act 1925; so that the court had no power to make an award of such costs and, accordingly, the order would be amended by deleting the reference to the costs relating to the inquiry.

The following cases are referred to in the judgment:

D *Department of Health and Social Security* v. *Walker Dean Walker Ltd.* [1970] 2 Q.B. 74; [1970] 2 W.L.R. 588; [1970] 1 All E.R. 757.

Strand In re, Ex parte Board of Trade (1884) 13 Q.B.D. 492; 53 L.J.Q.B. 563, D.C.

APPEAL from Master Lubbock.

On November 25, 1975, the plaintiff, the Department of Health and
E Social Security, was ordered by the master to pay the costs of the defendants, Envoy Farmers Ltd., to include the costs of and incidental to an inquiry held pursuant to a reference to the Secretary of State for Social Services of a question for determination. The department appealed. Jupp J. heard the appeal in chambers on March 3, 1976. Judgment was given in open court.

The facts are stated in the judgment.

F

Harry Woolf for the department.
Jonathan Gilman for the company.

Cur. adv. vult.

March 11. JUPP J. read the following judgment. This appeal raises
G a matter of interpretation of the National Insurance Act 1965 and the Supreme Court of Judicature (Consolidation) Act 1925. Similar wording is concerned in the National Insurance (Industrial Injuries) Act 1965, and because it may affect a number of cases I have been asked to give judgment on this appeal, which was heard in chambers, in open court. It is an appeal by the plaintiff department against an order of the master made on summons for judgment under R.S.C., Ord. 14, giving the
H defendant company their costs as parties to an inquiry held by the Secretary of State for Social Services under Part IV of the National Insurance Act 1965.

For the purpose of compulsory insurance under that Act, insured persons are by section 1 of the Act divided into three distinct classes: the employed, the self-employed and the non-employed. The class distinction is important, and Part IV of the Act provides for the determination of claims and questions. If any question arises under the Act as to the class in which a person is to be included, that question must, by section 64 (1) (*c*) A of the Act, be determined by the minister. The same section also provides for the determination of certain other questions in a similar manner, and by subsection (3) the minister may appoint a person to hold an inquiry into the question. Regulations have been made under sections 73 to 75 of the Act providing for the procedure to be followed in the determination of such questions and, subject to the regulations, section 75 (2) enacts that "the Arbitration Act 1950 shall not apply to any proceedings under B sections 64 to 74 of this Act." In section 80, also, the word "proceedings" is used in connection with the determination of questions of the kind here in issue. By that section the minister is empowered to pay travelling and other allowances "to any person required to attend at any proceedings" under Part IV of the Act. The Act gives no power to the minister to award costs as between parties to such proceedings but, if a question of law C arises in connection with the determination of the question, section 65 makes provision for reference or appeal to the High Court and, by subsection (7), the court is given power to order the minister to pay costs of any other person, whether or not he is successful and whether or not the minister appears on the reference or appeal. That, together with section 80 already referred to, shows the draughtsman had the question of costs well in mind. D

In short, the Act institutes a special form of proceedings in which the minister has jurisdiction to determine certain questions, including any question as to the class of insured persons in which a person is to be included. Of course, a question such as the minister might determine in this way could easily arise in other proceedings. It did in the present case where the department claimed by specially endorsed writ in the High Court E that the company owed national insurance contributions payable in respect of certain of their employees over a period of 27 months or so ending in April 1973. The company claimed that the alleged employees were in fact self-employed people.

The department went before the master to obtain summary judgment under R.S.C., Ord. 14. The company had put in a defence alleging in paragraph 4 that a decision as to the class of the people concerned was F necessary to the determination of the court proceedings and that the court had no jurisdiction to entertain the claim; and they asked in the alternative that the proceedings should be stayed. The master was faced with section 97 of the National Insurance Act 1965 which provides:

> "(1) Where in any proceedings . . . (*b*) involving any question as to the payment of contributions under this Act . . . any question G arises such as is mentioned in section 64 (1) (*a*) to (*c*) of this Act, then . . . the decision of the minister shall be conclusive for the purpose of those proceedings. (2) If the decision of any such question is necessary for the determination of the proceedings, and the decision of the minister has not been obtained, . . . the question shall be referred to the minister for determination . . . in accordance . . . with Part IV of this Act." H

This was the section relied upon by the company in their defence. The master, therefore, had no option but to refer the question. In fact, he referred a larger and more all-embracing question, viz., "whether Envoy Farmers Ltd. is liable as employer to pay" the contributions claimed in the action. Thus, the matter was treated as a question under section 64 (1) (*a*), which covers "any questions arising under this Act (*a*) . . . relating

A to a person's contributions." The company's appeal against that order was dismissed by the judge in chambers and in due course the Secretary of State for Social Services, who has now taken the place of "the minister" in the relevant legislation, decided that the company were not liable as employers to pay the contributions claimed in the action. That decision, of course, decided the issue in the action and the company accordingly applied to the master to dismiss the action with costs. That he did and B ordered those costs to include the costs "of and incidental to the inquiry held pursuant to the reference to the Secretary of State for Social Services." It will remove a possible source of confusion if I refer to those costs simply as the company's costs of the inquiry.

The department contend that that part of the order was wrong. They say that the court has no power to make the company's costs of the action C include their costs in the inquiry. In the alternative, they say, if the court has the power, then, as a matter of discretion, it should not award such costs. The master gave leave to appeal.

The court's power in this regard stems from section 50 (1) of the Supreme Court of Judicature (Consolidation) Act 1925, whereby the court or judge is given discretion to award "the costs of and incidental to all proceedings in the Supreme Court." What the company have been awarded D in this order are the costs of proceedings before the Secretary of State. Can it be said that the costs of those proceedings are incidental to the proceedings in this court? I take it that a thing is incidental if it occurs in "subordinate conjunction with something else": see the *Shorter-Oxford English Dictionary*, 3rd ed. (1944), rev. (1965), p. 978.

It is clear from section 97 (2) of the National Insurance Act 1965 that E a decision on the question referred was necessary for the determination of the court proceedings. The costs of the reference were, therefore, incidental to those proceedings. But the reference set in train other proceedings on a matter in which the court had no jurisdiction: *Department of Health and Social Security* v. *Walker Dean Walker Ltd.* [1970] 2 Q.B. 74. The proceedings in court had to await the conclusion of the proceedings before F the Secretary of State and, until those proceedings ended, the court proceedings had to remain in abeyance. Compare *In re Strand, Ex parte Board of Trade* (1884) 13 Q.B.D. 492, 495. Section 97 (3) compels the court to adjourn the proceedings before it until such time as a final decision on the question has been obtained on the proceedings before the Secretary of State. In my judgment, therefore, whilst the costs of getting the matter referred are costs incidental to the court proceedings, the costs of the fresh G proceedings then taken, that is to say, the inquiry before the Secretary of State, are not incidental to the court proceedings. They are, as indeed the order under appeal itself states, incidental to the proceedings before the Secretary of State. Those proceedings were forced upon the parties by the lack of jurisdiction in the court to deal with the matter of contention.

The situation here is different from the situation where the court, as H part of its own jurisdiction, initiates a proceeding to forward the work it has to do. For example, it may order evidence to be taken by examiners, R.S.C., Ord. 39; or damages to be assessed by a special referee, R.S.C., Ord. 37; or some issue to be tried before a special referee, R.S.C., Ord. 36. In such cases the court sets up the necessary machinery, and the proceedings before the examiner or special referee, or as the case may be, are undoubtedly incidental to the proceedings in court. In this case, by contrast, the machinery is set up by Act of Parliament independently of the courts, and the proceedings have to be taken by means of that machinery because the court's jurisdiction is excluded.

For these reasons, the appeal must be allowed and the master's order amended to delete reference to the costs relating to the inquiry.

It is perhaps worth remarking that the company suffer no injustice by this. It is common ground that the Secretary of State had no power to award costs as between the parties at the inquiry. If the department had gone to the Secretary of State in the first place instead of issuing a writ, the company would have won but without costs. The company could properly complain here that that is what the department should have done, although the department take the view that they had no power to refer the matter to the Secretary of State for the decision on their own initiative. As to that, I heard no argument and, therefore, make no further comment. As it is, the action commenced by writ has proved fruitless; but the company have been awarded their costs of that. So they are back to the position which would have obtained had the department done as the company might say they should have done. The company have won but without costs. If it were otherwise, a strange situation would result. By going to the Secretary of State first, the company would get no costs in relation to the inquiry. By going to the Secretary of State in the course of an action in the courts, they would get their costs of the inquiry. That would be an unfortunate anomaly.

The department have not pressed for the costs of this appeal and so I make no order as to costs but simply allow the appeal and order the deletion of reference to the costs relating to the inquiry.

Appeal allowed.
Leave to appeal.
No order as to costs.

Solicitors: *Solicitor, Department of Health and Social Security; Amphlett & Co.*

A

[CHANCERY DIVISION]

* *In re* POULSON (A BANKRUPT), *Ex parte* GRANADA TELEVISION LTD. *v.* MAUDLING AND ANOTHER

B

[No. 1 of 1972]

1976 April 12, 13, 14; May 6 — Foster and Walton JJ.

Bankruptcy — Private examination of witness — " Stop order" — Inspection of file of proceedings for purposes of libel action C *—Refusal by trustee to produce transcripts of private examinations — Validity of " stop order" procedure — Bankruptcy Act* 1914 *(4 & 5 Geo. 5, c. 59), s. 25—Bankruptcy Rules* 1952 *(S.I.* 1952 *No.* 2113 *(L.* 14)), *r.* 15 *(as amended by Bankruptcy (Amendment) Rules* 1962 *(S.I.* 1962 *No.* 295 *(L.* 3)), *r.* 1 *(b)*)

On an application in April 1973 by the Director of Public Prosecutions under rule 15 (2) of the Bankruptcy Rules 1952,[1] D the registrar of the county court sitting in bankruptcy gave special leave to a deputy assistant commissioner of police for the inspection of the file of proceedings in the bankruptcy of P and for copies to be taken of such documents on the file as might be necessary, including copies of all such documents as were or might be subject to a " stop order." In July 1973, on an application by the trustee in bankruptcy under section 25 of the Bankruptcy Act 1914, a private E examination was conducted of M, a director of certain companies in which P was interested. The registrar ordered that certain questions and answers should be left out of the transcript of the bankruptcy proceedings and be recorded and attached only to the court copy, marked " most confidential," and that the transcript itself should not, for the time being, be placed on the file (a " stop order ").

In May 1974, the appellants broadcast a programme about F P's business activities and M's alleged connection therewith to which M took exception. In September 1974 he issued a writ against them for libel. For the purposes of evidence in the action, both parties applied to the trustee in bankruptcy for a sight of documents and transcripts on the trustee's file relating to those business activities, including transcripts of private examinations of persons in the bankruptcy proceedings. The trustee refused to produce the documents without the G direction of the court. In the event the appellants made a formal application to the county court under rule 15 of the Bankruptcy Rules 1952, with M objecting to the release of the transcript of his private examination.

On appeal to the Divisional Court in Bankruptcy from the registrar's refusal to authorise the production of transcripts of private examinations: —

Held, dismissing the appeal, that having regard to the H purpose of the private examination procedure, which was to enable the trustee to obtain information leading to the discovery and recovery of assets, the registrar's " stop order " was justified in the present case and the Divisional Court was not prepared to treat M's deposition as if it were on the file and available for inspection.

In re Standard Gold Mining Co. [1895] 2 Ch. 545 considered.

[1] Bankruptcy Rules, 1952, r. 15, as amended: see post, p. 1028E, F.

Per curiam. The "stop order" procedure ought not to be allowed to rest merely upon practice—however sound that practice is—unregulated by rule. Bankruptcy rule 15 itself ought to be considerably tightened so as to afford the court a real and unappealable discretion, in all cases where inspection is sought, to refuse it to anybody but the trustee. Following a similar kind of complaint by Vaughan Williams J. in *In re Standard Gold Mining Co.* [1895] 2 Ch. 545, 547, a suitable change was made in the company rules (post, p. 1035E–G). A B

The following cases are referred to in the judgment:

Beall, In re, Ex parte Beall [1894] 2 Q.B. 135, C.A. *Learoyd* v. *Halifax Joint Stock Banking Co.* [1893] 1 Ch. 686.

Pratt, Ex parte, In re Hayman (1882) 21 Ch.D. 439, C.A.

Standard Gold Mining Co., In re [1895] 2 Ch. 545. C

The following additional cases were cited in argument:

Conway v. *Rimmer* [1968] A.C. 910; [1968] 2 W.L.R. 998; [1968] 1 All E.R. 874, H.L.(E.).

Debtor, In re A, Ex parte Trustee of the Property of the Bankrupt v. *Clegg* [1968] 1 W.L.R. 788; [1968] 2 All E.R. 725.

Fraser v. *Evans* [1969] 1 Q.B. 349; [1968] 3 W.L.R. 1172; [1969] 1 All E.R. 8, C.A. D

Green (A Bankrupt), In re, Ex parte The Trustee [1958] 1 W.L.R. 405; [1958] 2 All E.R. 57n., C.A.

Grey's Brewery Co., In re (1883) 25 Ch.D. 400.

Kenrick, Ex parte, In re Sleigh (1862) 7 L.T. 287.

Merchants' Fire Office, In re [1899] 1 Ch. 432.

North Australian Territory Co. v. *Goldsborough, Mort and Co.* [1893] 2 Ch. 381, C.A. E

Norwich Equitable Fire Insurance Co., In re (1884) 27 Ch.D. 515, C.A.

Rolls Razor Ltd., In re (No. 2) [1970] Ch. 576; [1970] 2 W.L.R. 100; [1969] 3 All E.R. 1386.

Slim v. *Daily Telegraph Ltd.* [1968] 2 Q.B. 157; [1968] 2 W.L.R. 599; [1968] 1 All E.R. 497, C.A.

The following case was cited when seeking leave to appeal: F

Gilchrist, Ex parte, In re Armstrong (1886) 17 Q.B.D. 521, C.A.

APPEAL from Wakefield County Court sitting in Bankruptcy.

The appellants, Granada Television Ltd., were defendants to a libel action brought by the first respondent, Reginald Maudling M.P., following their broadcast, on May 6, 1974, of a programme entitled "Business in Gozo", which dealt with contracts obtained by J. G. L. Poulson, the bankrupt, and made references to the first respondent's connection therewith to which he took exception. The registrar of the Wakefield County Court had made an order on January 26, 1976, authorising the second respondent, the trustee in bankruptcy, to produce transcripts of public examinations and other documents to the appellants and to the first respondent, but excluding transcripts of private examinations which the appellants sought to be produced. The appellants now appealed to the Divisional Court in Bankruptcy on the grounds inter alia that the consent of the first respondent to the production of his private examination evidence was not necessary and that that transcript should be treated in the same way as the transcripts of the private examinations of other persons. G H

The facts are stated in the judgment of the court.

A *G. B. H. Dillon Q.C.* and *J. R. A. Rampton* for the appellants.
Richard Hartley Q.C. for the first respondent.
Muir Hunter Q.C. and *David Graham* for the second respondent, the trustee in bankruptcy.

Cur. adv. vult.

B May 6. WALTON J. read the following judgment of the court. The bankrupt is an architect, and immediately before his bankruptcy he was carrying on business in partnership with others under the name or style of J.G.L. Poulson, as architects, quantity surveyors and town planners, at 29, Ropergate, Pontefract, Yorkshire. He presented his own petition on January 4, 1972, on which day also both the receiving and adjudication
C orders were made. The trustee in bankruptcy was appointed on March 1, 1972.

It became apparent in the course of the bankruptcy that the bankrupt had on many occasions used the most questionable means of obtaining contracts for his firm and for other firms and companies with which he was associated. So much so that those responsible for the administration of the criminal law became very interested in the matter, and on April 19,
D 1973, the Director of Public Prosecutions applied to the Wakefield County Court in Bankruptcy for the following orders:

> "(1) An order granting the applicant, Deputy Assistant Commissioner James Crane, or such other person or persons as may in writing from time to time be nominated by them or either of them, special leave pursuant to rule 15 (2) of the Bankruptcy Rules 1952 to inspect the
> E file of proceedings herein at all reasonable times and to take copies of such documents upon the said file as may be necessary. (2) An order extending such leave to permit the applicant, Deputy Assistant Commissioner James Crane, or such other person or persons as may in writing from time to time be nominated by them or either of them, to inspect and take copies of all such documents as are or may be subject to a 'stop order.' (3) Such further or other relief as for this honour-
> F able court may seem just or expedient."

This application was supported by an affidavit of the Director of Public Prosecutions, which reads:

> "(1) On July 17, 1972, the solicitor, Department of Trade and Industry, forwarded to me a preliminary report submitted by the official
> G receiver at Leeds concerning the above-named bankrupt. (2) On July 19, 1972, I requested officers of the Metropolitan Police to investigate the circumstances surrounding the bankruptcy, as it appeared that serious criminal offences might have been committed. (3) I am informed that since July 19, 1972, a number of detective officers under the command of Deputy Assistant Commissioner James Crane have been exclusively engaged in these inquiries. (4) The result of their
> H inquiries as so far communicated to me appear to confirm that serious criminal offences may well have been committed, and that evidence may be forthcoming such as to require the institution of criminal proceedings in due course. (5) I am informed and verily believe that both in the public examination of the debtor and the private examination of various persons certain documents have been produced to the court which contain matters of great confidential importance to the said police investigation, and further that all other such documents

are likely to be produced to the court during the continuance of the bankruptcy hearings. (6) It is essential in the interests of the administration of justice that Deputy Assistant Commissioner Crane (or such police officers as he may nominate) should have access to these documents and be permitted to make copies of them."

Consequent on that application the order was made by the registrar substantially in the form asked, as follows:

"(1) The applicant, Deputy Assistant Commissioner James Crane, or such other person or persons as may in writing from time to time be nominated by them or either of them be granted special leave pursuant to rule 15 (2) of the Bankruptcy Rules 1952 to inspect the file of proceedings herein at all reasonable times and to take copies of such documents upon the said file as may be necessary. (2) An order be granted extending such leave to permit the applicant, Deputy Assistant Commissioner James Crane, or such other person or persons as may in writing from time to time be nominated by them or either of them, to inspect and take copies of all such documents as are or may be subject to a 'stop order'."

It will be observed that there is in that application and order a reference to a "stop order" (deliberately placed in inverted commas) and to that concept we shall have to return later.

During the course of the bankruptcy it became apparent that the first respondent, the Right Honourable Reginald Maudling M.P. (Mr. Maudling), the well known politician, had been a director and shareholder in a number of companies in which the bankrupt, or those in his immediate circle, were interested. Mr. Maudling had, by his solicitors, been supplying the trustee with information relating to various matters about which he had been requested to provide it; but the trustee considered that a private examination of Mr. Maudling under section 25 of the Bankruptcy Act 1914 would be of assistance to him, and so an order was obtained for the holding of such an examination, which duly took place on July 19, 1973. Mr. Maudling did not object to the order and volunteered to give evidence. As is usual, a shorthand writer was appointed to take down Mr. Maudling's evidence and to make a transcript thereof. During the course of that examination, for extremely good reasons, the registrar before whom the examination was conducted ordered that certain questions and answers should not be transcribed into the body of the transcript, but that they should be recorded and attached to the court copy transcript only and marked "most confidential."

On May 6, 1974, the appellants in their World in Action programme broadcast an item entitled "Business in Gozo," which was basically critical of two separate although obviously interrelated matters. The first was the decision of the then Maltese Government reached in or about 1967 to erect a hospital on the island of Gozo (a matter which has nothing to do with the bankrupt) and, secondly, the methods adopted by the bankrupt to secure all the contracts relating to the design, erection and furnishing of that hospital. The programme further alleged that as regards the second matter, Mr. Maudling played at times a crucial role in obtaining the necessary contracts for the bankrupt. Mr. Maudling took exception to this broadcast and issued a writ for libel against the appellants on September 18, 1974. The statement of claim sets out in full the script for the broadcast, and then proceeds:

A "The said words which have been underlined, in their natural and ordinary meaning and in the context of the said broadcast as a whole, meant and were understood to mean: (i) that the plaintiff's speeches and interventions in the House of Commons during the period February to October 1967 were part of his role in the pursuit of the Gozo Hospital contract and were thus an abuse of his position both as a Member of Parliament and as opposition front bench spokesman;
B (ii) that the plaintiff was guilty of misconduct as a Member of Parliament in failing to make due disclosure of a direct pecuniary interest in the course of the said speeches and interventions; (iii) that the plaintiff abused his said position by seeking to obtain and, in fact, obtaining a grant of British taxpayers' money to finance the hospital, which said grant would not otherwise have been made; (iv) that the
C plaintiff's actions in connection with the Gozo Hospital contract were part of a corrupt and dishonest scheme, which involved inter alia bribery, to obtain the said contract";

and Mr. Maudling claims damages accordingly.

The defence is (a) that the words complained of neither bear nor were understood to bear any of the meanings attributed to them in the para-
D graph of the statement of claim which we have already read, or indeed any meaning defamatory of Mr. Maudling at all; (b) that the words were true in substance and in fact; (c) that the said words were fair comment upon matters of public interest. There is a reply on behalf of Mr. Maudling, which alleges malice.

It is obvious that there must be some documents in the trustee's files relating to the bankrupt which contain evidence relating to the Gozo
E Hospital project, and so, very sensibly, the solicitors for both the appellants and Mr. Maudling agreed to co-operate in obtaining a sight of the relevant documents, and the solicitor for the trustee made it apparent that he was willing to assist. When the matter came to a head, in January 1976, the proposed scope of the investigation into the bankruptcy documents was extended—and extended with the apparent support of both sets of solicitors
F —to cover transcripts of private examinations. The form of authority which they requested the trustee to sign was in the following terms:

"I . . . trustee in bankruptcy of John Garlick Llewellyn Poulson, hereby authorise and request you to produce to Messrs. Oswald Hickson, Collier & Co. . . . solicitors for the plaintiff herein and Messrs. Goodman Derrick & Co. . . . solicitors for the defendants
G herein all books, files, papers, correspondence, accounts, drafts, minutes, notes, memoranda, indices, statements, transcripts of public and/or private examinations and all other documentary evidence assembled by me for the purpose of the bankruptcy proceedings in respect of the above-named John Garlick Llewellyn Poulson and to supply such copies as each of the parties at their own expense may require and to allow them to take copies of the aforesaid documents."

H

When he appreciated the true position the solicitor for the trustee very properly replied as follows:

"We thank you for your letter . . . There is no doubt in our minds but that the reference to both public and private examinations makes it absolutely vital that this matter be referred to the court for its directions forthwith. Indeed it is our view that the trustee in bankruptcy has absolutely no power to consent to the production of private examinations to any party for any purpose without a direction from the court. We are to see counsel . . . and we understand from the court that our application, which we shall lodge on Monday, could be heard at 3.30 p.m. on Monday, January 26. We are instructed to invite you to attend upon the hearing of our client's application to the court. We must say that in all the circumstances we would expect the court to ask whether the person examined has consented to the request for the production of the transcript."

So, on January 19, 1976, the trustee initiated an application to the court for its directions as to whether he should sign the authority required, the return date being fixed for January 26, 1976. In the meantime, on January 20, 1976, Mr. Maudling's solicitors had discovered that in apparently agreeing to extend the authority to a transcript of Mr. Maudling's own private examination they had acted without authority. They wrote to the appellants' solicitors as follows:

"As we informed you on the telephone yesterday, Mr. Maudling has instructed us that he is not prepared to consent to production of the transcript of his private examination in Mr. J. G. Poulson's bankruptcy. He gave evidence in those proceedings on the basis of confidentiality and considers that that confidentiality should be preserved."

What was originally an application made on behalf of the trustee for directions, the appellants and Mr. Maudling being interested spectators as it were, was finally transformed into a formal application by the appellants. It has been very sensibly accepted by all parties that the matter must be looked at as if it had from the first been a formal application by the appellants under rule 15 of the Bankruptcy Rules 1952, as amended by the Bankruptcy (Amendment) Rules 1962 which reads as follows:

"(1) All proceedings of the court shall be kept and remain of record in the court for such period as the Lord Chancellor may from time to time direct. (2) The trustee, the debtor, and any creditor who has proved, or any person acting on behalf of the trustee, debtor, or creditor, and, by special direction of the judge or registrar, any other person, may at all reasonable times inspect the file of proceedings."

The registrar's decision on the application was given in the following terms:

"The only documents which trouble me are the transcripts of private examinations. Mr. Maudling objects to the release of the transcript of his private examination. It is clear that the trustee must sit on the fence. And as the trustee has not given a copy of the transcript of his private examination to Mr. Maudling, that transcript must be treated in the same way as all other transcripts of private examinations. I feel unhappy about ordering its release. Some of the witnesses examined were very forthcoming; but others put every conceivable obstacle in the way of answering the simplest question. Those who answered frankly could well have done so too, but they knew or thought that their examinations were private and would remain so, and I have heard nothing to make me think that their transcripts should be released. Where Scotland Yard have applied for transcripts, different considerations apply."

Pausing there for one moment, we entirely agree with the registrar: different considerations do indeed apply. Of necessity, public policy

A demands that those who are entrusted with the administration of the
criminal law should have every legitimate source of information open to
their inspection, and that no obstacles should be put in their way in relation
to obtaining it. Such persons are public servants who are accountable to
the public through the proper channels for their actions, and would be
accountable for their use or misuse of such information. The appellants—
and, for that matter, Mr. Maudling himself—have no such public account-
B ability. We only interpose these observations because Mr. Dillon, for the
appellants, made great play with the fact that such leave as he was in fact
seeking for his own client had in fact been given to the Director of Public
Prosecutions. We do not consider that this fact advances his arguments
one whit.

We return then to the judgment of the registrar. He proceeded:

C "But the parties to the libel action are private individuals, and if a
particular transcript is to be produced, a specific application should
be made and the person examined informed. I am not prepared to
allow access to the file of proceedings or index thereof in order that
a list might be made of persons whose consents should be obtained
to disclose the transcripts of their examinations in private. I confirm
that access to all transcripts of Mr. Poulson's examination in public
D is covered by my order and the form of authority attached thereto.
This does not however cover the three occasions when he was ex-
amined in private."

Then details of those are given.

"Mr. Poulson's consent should be obtained. Applications for pro-
E duction of transcripts should be upon notice to the respective private
examinees. I confirm that I have made a ruling that the transcript
of Mr. Maudling's private examination shall not be produced in the
absence of his consent. As regards any appeal, which may be straight
to the Divisional Court, I do not think my leave is needed. I will grant
liberty to apply and I confirm that Granada Television Ltd. are to be
treated as respondents to the application now before me. The produc-
F tion of the documents shall be subject to written undertakings to be
given to the court by the respective solicitors in due course. I confirm
that my order and the form of authority shall be in favour of Mr.
Maudling himself and Granada Television Ltd. itself as the actual
parties and that access will also extend to their solicitors."

So the order actually made read as follows:

G "It is ordered that leave be granted for the trustee in bankruptcy of
the above-named bankrupt to give the authority to his solicitors in the
form attached hereto to produce the documents herein referred to,
such documents to be used solely in respect of the action referred to,
with undertakings to be given by the plaintiff's and the defendants'
solicitors. Liberty to apply."

H The form of authority was in the form that he was to produce:

"all books, files, papers, correspondence, accounts, drafts, minutes,
notes, memoranda, indices, statements, transcripts of public exam-
inations and all other documentary evidence assembled by me for the
purpose of the bankruptcy proceedings in respect of the above-named
John Garlick Llewellyn Poulson, excluding transcripts of private ex-
aminations, and to supply such copies as each of the parties at their

own expense may require and to allow them to take copies of the aforesaid documents, subject at all times to such documents being relevant to the issues in the above action." A

For the sake of completeness we record that undertakings were given to the court by each firm of solicitors that any information so obtained should be used solely in respect of the libel action.

From this order, considered in the light we have already indicated, the appellants have appealed to this court, their notice of appeal being in the following form: B

> "The authority attached to the order of Mr. Registrar Garside dated January 26, 1976, be varied so as to authorise the production to the appellants of the transcript of the first-named respondent's private examination by the insertion of the word 'all' between the existing word 'excluding' and 'transcripts' and of the words 'save that of the plaintiff's private examination' between the existing words 'private examinations,' and 'and.' And further take notice that the grounds of this appeal are: (1) That the learned registrar was wrong in holding that it was a necessary condition of his granting leave for the appellants to inspect the transcript of the first-named respondent's private examination that the first-named respondent should have given his consent to such inspection." C D

Pausing at this point, we do not ourselves think that this was the registrar's real point. We think his point was a different one, namely that if any person who had been privately examined was willing that his transcript should be made available, there was really not much point in refusing to release it as that person could, if he so wished, supply precisely the information, whatever it was, contained in the relevant transcript to anybody else he might wish. Hence in such a case it would be pointless to refuse. E

Coming to the second ground of appeal, which is as follows:

> "(2) That the learned registrar was wrong in holding that the transcript of the first-named respondent's private examination must be treated in the same way as the transcripts of the private examinations of other persons" F

we entirely reject this ground. It must never be forgotten that, judged from the point of view of the bankruptcy court, each and every transcript of a private examination is in precisely the same position. We defer a consideration of this point however to a little later stage. G

Head (3) is closely allied thereto. It reads:

> "That the transcript of the first-named respondent's private examination is in a different category from the transcripts of the private examinations of other persons, in that the first-named respondent has brought an action for damages for libel against the appellants, to the issues in which action the matters contained in or referred to in the said transcript are relevant." H

"Are relevant" is an obvious pitching of the appellants' case too high. Mr. Dillon conceded that it should read "are highly likely to be relevant" or something to that effect. Head (4) is in these terms: "That the refusal of leave for the appellants to inspect the said transcript will or may delay the trial of the said libel action." This we do not accept. We can see no reason at all why the refusal of inspection should delay the trial of

A the action in any way. It will be observed that all the documents which were in the possession of the trustee and on the basis of which he was enabled to cross-examine Mr. Maudling in his private examination will be made available to the appellants; and that they are therefore in a position to ask Mr. Maudling precisely the same questions thereon as the trustee's counsel in fact asked. This consideration led Mr. Dillon to submit that it must follow that Mr. Maudling had two standards of
B truthfulness, one when answering questions in his private examination and one when answering questions in the witness box in the libel action. We consider this a completely unjustified remark, which can only have been based on a profound misconception of the aim and object of a private examination. Once again, however, we defer further consideration of this point to a later time.

C The final ground taken in the notice of appeal is as follows:

> "(5) That the learned registrar was wrong in holding that it was a ground for refusing leave to inspect the transcript of the private examination without the consent of the person examined that other persons privately examined on other occasions might otherwise refrain from giving frank or honest answers to the questions put to them upon their examination."

D

There is no doubt that the registrar did to some extent put his decision on this ground and to the extent that he did so we agree with the appellants that he was wrong to do so. After all, there is no doubt that, sooner or later, all such transcripts must find their way on to the file, and that normally not later than the time when the bankrupt applies for his
E discharge: *see In re Beall, Ex parte Beall* [1894] 2 Q.B. 135, 140 *per* Lopes L.J.

With these preliminary observations, we now approach this appeal on the basis, and exclusively on the basis, of the provisions of rule 15 of the Bankruptcy Rules 1952. Assuming for one moment that any order under rule 15 (2) were to be made in favour of the appellants there is the practical difficulty that the only order which can be made in their
F favour is an order enabling them to inspect the file. It appears that "inspection" under this rule does not include the right to be furnished with a copy: see *Ex parte Pratt, In re Hayman* (1882) 21 Ch.D. 439 but to some extent, in the context of what the appellants are seeking to discover —namely the extent of the business involvement of Mr. Maudling with the bankrupt—this seems a somewhat unreal matter.

G The plain fact however is that certainly the transcript of Mr. Maudling's own private examination and, we understand, the transcripts of other private examinations are not on the file, so that an order for their inspection would benefit the appellants nothing. Mr. Dillon's answer to this is that they ought to be on the file, and that if they are not in fact physically on such file—as they are not—they must nevertheless be treated for such purpose as if they were, following *In re Standard Gold Mining*
H *Co.* [1895] 2 Ch. 545, a case arising under parallel provisions in the Companies Acts. There Vaughan Williams J., having discovered that an irregular practice was being pursued in the Companies Court of keeping the depositions off the file said, at p. 549: "If the depositions ought to be on the ordinary file, I shall treat them as if they were." We agree with Vaughan Williams J. The mere fact that something which ought to be on the file is specifically not on it appears to us to be nihil ad rem.

Nevertheless, for many years now (certainly, according to our own

researches, since the turn of the century and probably long before) the A
practice has been adopted in a case where it is desirable in the interests
of the bankruptcy as a whole that the depositions taken in private examination
should be kept off the file of the registrar making a "stop order."
This practice has no specific statutory warrant. It is referred to as a fact
of life but without any attempt at justification in *Williams on Bankruptcy*:
see, for example, 18th ed. (1968), p. 622 and *Halsbury's Laws of England*
4th ed., vol. 3 (1973), para. 585, note 15. There is no piece of paper B
recording the order; it is merely a direction by the registrar that filing
is not to take place immediately, and it is doubtless intended to be
extremely flexible in its application. Its existence is manifested in practice
by the fact that the document in question is, as a matter of pure fact,
not filed when it would otherwise in the normal course of events have
been so filed. C

Can this practice, without express statutory warrant, be justified? We
turn to consider the objects of a private examination. They are to be
found in section 25 (1) of the Bankruptcy Act 1914:

> "The court may, on the application of the official receiver or trustee,
> at any time after a receiving order has been made against a debtor,
> summon before it the debtor or his wife, or any person known or D
> suspected to have in his possession any of the estate or effects belonging
> to the debtor, or supposed to be indebted to the debtor, or any
> person whom the court may deem capable of giving information
> respecting the debtor, his dealings or property, and the court may
> require any such person to produce any documents in his custody
> or power relating to the debtor, his dealings or property." E

Shortly put, the whole object of such an examination is to enable the
trustee to obtain information which will enable him to discover and recover
assets for the distribution to creditors in the bankruptcy. In other words,
although doubtless the procedure can be used in an accusatorial manner
if that is what will best serve the trustee's overriding purpose, it is also
capable of being used, and frequently is used most fruitfully, in an
inquisitorial manner. And when so used, many answers given by a witness F
who is prepared to be co-operative and prepared to volunteer information
may be of the utmost assistance to the trustee although they might well
not be proper answers, or even admissible answers, in the more normal
proceedings. If a witness so examined says to the trustee "I do not
know where £X went to" the answer may well be a perfectly frank and
truthful answer, and may well be the whole truth. If in the course of an G
ordinary cross-examination the witness were to add "But I did once hear
a rumour—I think via Z—that it had in fact been used to pay a bribe
to R, or some name like that, in South America," no weight would or
could be paid to that circumstance, even assuming he was allowed to
complete the answer unchecked. But in the course of a private examination,
such a clue—for it is no more than that—may well be of immense
assistance to the trustee in tracing assets. It may quite unexpectedly tie H
in with something else, or open up ideas and prospects which had never
even remotely occurred to him. It is not, as Mr. Dillon would have it,
that there are two standards of truth; there are two quite different aims
being served by the ordinary cross-examination in court and the procedure
under a private examination, albeit that the two aims may well in many
places overlap. But the analysis goes much deeper than that. We remind
ourselves again that the object of the examination is to obtain assets to

swell the estate. Suppose, to take a romantic example, the person being examined says "Oh, yes, I know what became of all those Kruggerrands you have been talking about. The debtor went and buried them in a desert island, the one marked on this map at P, and I am certain that they all are still there." Is such a statement to be made available to the debtor, and any creditor who has proved as of right under bankruptcy rule 15? The answer is obviously in the negative; it takes time to gather a ship's company, hire a suitable vessel, and sail off to the South Seas to recover the gold; and if while the trustee is doing all this—possibly having difficulty with the raising of the necessary funds to man the expedition—creditors are entitled as of right to learn precisely when and where the ill-gotten gains are secreted, or in the case of the bankrupt himself that the trustee knew this, the whole purpose of the examination will be self-stultifying. The fact that the treasure is more likely, in modern times, to be buried in a numbered bank account in Switzerland or elsewhere and that the forces which have to be mustered to man the expedition are more likely to be prosaic lawyers and accountants rather than swashbuckling sea captains is nihil ad rem (save that they are likely to be even more expensive). The whole exercise would be self-defeating. This fact was well recognised by Stirling J. in *Learoyd* v. *Halifax Joint Stock Banking Co.* [1893] 1 Ch. 686, 693 where he said:

> "The trustee then takes out a summons, and gets leave to examine certain persons named. His solicitor personally conducts the examination and gets a transcript of the proceedings. That transcript is a private document. It is true that the rules in bankruptcy provide that the evidence so taken is to be filed; but they do not say that it is to be filed immediately. If that was done the main object of the examination might often be defeated. The point has often been considered both by myself and by other judges with reference to depositions taken under section 115 of the Companies Act 1862. The practice under that section in all branches of the court is that the depositions, when taken, shall be returned to the chief clerk for use in the liquidation; but they are not filed until the court is satisfied, through the chief clerk, that no harm can be done by their publication."

"No harm" there, of course, means no harm in the bankruptcy, but we conceive that it is by no means beyond the bounds of possibility that information so obtained might well do other kinds of harm which it would not be in the public interest to allow.

We would incidentally observe that a close reading of the judgments of Lord Esher M.R. and Lopes and Davey L.JJ. in *In re Beall, Ex parte Beall* [1894] 2 Q.B. 135 shows clearly that all three contemplated that filing might well be delayed (albeit not beyond the stage of application for a discharge) and Lord Esher M.R. further contemplated that sealing up of portions of the transcripts—presumably permanently—could, in a proper case, be allowed.

It is, we think, out of the simple proposition that the procedure of private examinations under section 25 of the Bankruptcy Act 1914 must not be allowed to be self-destructive in purpose that the justification for the "stop order" procedure arises. We do not, we think, need to draw examples from other branches of the law, but there are many such, relating to trade secrets and the like, where the normal rules have to be displaced in view of the overriding necessity to produce a just end result.

Mr. Dillon devoted a large part of his address to an attack on the A
" stop order " procedure coupled with any exercise of the court's undoubted discretion under bankruptcy rule 15 not to release the file because the appellants do not fall within the limited class of the trustee, the bankrupt, and creditors who have proved, based on the ground that the underlying basis was that the witness was being protected in order to encourage " confidentiality " in other witnesses. This misconception of the position arose, we think, partly from a misconception of Mr. Maudling himself, B
who apparently believed that he was giving his evidence on a confidential basis. We do not find it necessary to delve into this aspect of the matter further because we think that Mr. Maudling was mistaken, and that ultimately, save in so far as any part of the evidence justifies a permanent stop order being placed on it, the transcript of Mr. Maudling's evidence must all be filed when it can do no harm in the bankruptcy so to file it. C
And we consider that all witnesses who gave evidence in this way, whether they realise it or not, give their evidence on the same basis.

Mr. Dillon urged on us that we ought to read the transcript ourselves to see whether there was anything in it which ought to be protected, and that, subject to any such portions being expunged, his clients ought to be entitled to see the transcript. If the real question at issue was confidentiality we would agree with him, and would undoubtedly have taken D
this course, but it is not. It is, as we see it, purely a question of the non-dissemination of information which may be of use to the trustee in the bankruptcy. As to this, we could not possibly be in anything like as good a position as the registrar who has been in charge of the bankruptcy proceedings all through and is obviously extremely familiar with a whole host of documents and facts of which we have not the faintest conception, E
let alone the intimate and detailed knowledge which would enable us to form any view of any worth as to the possible impact of seemingly harmless pieces of information on the prospects of recovery in the bankruptcy. To take a well known example, the casual reader may see nothing significant in the fact that the dog did not bark in the night, yet that was a clue essential, as it turned out, to solving the mystery.

Hence, looking at the matter purely from the point of view of the F
" stop order " procedure, we are satisfied that the registrar has properly made such an order in the present case, and we are not simply prepared to treat the deposition as if it were on the file and thus available for inspection.

We now approach the matter from the other end. Assuming that the deposition were to be considered to be notionally on the file, would it be G
right to allow the appellants to inspect it and to take copies? They are complete strangers to the bankruptcy, and since the whole purpose of a private examination is to assist the trustee or—if he will not—others in recovering assets in the bankruptcy, we consider that it can only be in the most exceptional circumstances that a person not interested in the bankruptcy would be granted leave to inspect. In this connection we would observe that we do not find the cases in which the deponent H
himself has been allowed to inspect the file as of any real assistance; clearly this is a very special situation, although it is interesting to observe that, even in such cases, inspection is by no means allowed automatically. The words used in bankruptcy rule 15 are " by special direction," and we think that the use of these words, and not the more colourless " by leave," indicates that the direction is one which will be sparingly given. We are fortified in that conclusion by the fact that the Solicitors Act

A 1974, section 83, confers an express power on The Law Society to inspect the file. Most clearly and obviously The Law Society must always be highly concerned professionally with the bankruptcy of a solicitor, and if the words "by special direction" were only equivalent to "by leave" it is we think unlikely that any such special section in the Solicitors Acts would have been required.

Would then the fact that the deponent has brought an action against
B some other party be a sufficiently special circumstance entitling the other party to an inspection of the file? Clearly, we should have thought, not. It must surely at the very least be made out that the deposition has a material and direct bearing on some issue involved in the action before inspection is even discussed. Now of course it is known that the deposition in the present case covers certain aspects of Mr. Maudling's business
C relationships with the bankrupt, and in a very general sense the true nature of these relationships may be said to be in issue in the action, and indeed this has been pressed upon us with great vigour by Mr. Dillon. We would not however think that that was anything like enough. It is here of course that a major difficulty arises. The appellants cannot of course know what the deposition contains, even in outline. It might very well be that contained therein there is some admission by the deponent which would
D be, we will not say vital, but highly material to an issue in the action. If there were, to pitch the matter at its highest, an express admission by the deponent that he had been guilty of one of the matters alleged in the libel, this would be of such materiality that it would doubtless be necessary in the interests of justice to allow inspection of the crucial passages.

It is in the light of this kind of difficulty that we have reluctantly come
E to the conclusion that we ought to consider the transcript ourselves to determine whether there is or is not anything therein which is so obviously relevant to the libel action in the present case that, had the depositions not been subject to a "stop order," it ought to have been disclosed. We have been unable to discover any such material.

In the result this application will be refused. We cannot however part from this case without observing that the "stop order" procedure,
F essential as it is for the very purposes for which private examinations are held at all, ought not to be allowed to rest merely upon practice—however sound that practice is—unregulated by rule. Rule 15 itself ought, in our view, to be very considerably tightened so as to afford the court a real and unappealable discretion, in all cases where inspection is sought, to refuse it to anybody but the trustee. We observe that following a similar
G kind of complaint by Vaughan Williams J. in *In re Standard Gold Mining Co.* [1895] 2 Ch. 545, 547, a suitable change was made in the company rules.

In the court's judgment, we have therefore come to the conclusion that the present appeal should be dismissed.

Order accordingly.

H *Appellants to pay first respondent's costs on party and party basis and second respondent's costs on common fund basis.*

Leave to appeal refused.

Solicitors: *Goodman Derrick & Co.; Oswald Hickson Collier & Co.; R. C. Moorhouse & Co., Leeds.*

K. N. B.

A

[COURT OF APPEAL]

* CUSTOMS AND EXCISE COMMISSIONERS *v.* BRITISH RAILWAYS BOARD

1976 May 10, 11 — Buckley, Orr and Browne L.JJ. B

Revenue—Value added tax—Deduction of input tax—Corporation carrying on business and managing employees' pension fund —Value added tax incurred on fees for professional advice regarding pension fund—Whether corporation to be regarded as two bodies for purpose of tax—Whether corporation entitled to deduct tax as input tax when accounting for tax chargeable on its own services—Finance Act 1972 (*c.* 41), *s.* 3 (1) (*a*) C

The British Railways Board as the trustee of its employees' pension fund paid value added tax in respect of professional services rendered in regard to the management of the fund. The board's claim to be entitled to deduct, as input tax pursuant to section 3 (1) (*a*) of the Finance Act 1972,[1] value added tax so paid from the tax chargeable on services supplied by the board itself in the course of carrying on its railway undertaking was upheld by the value added tax tribunal, and, on D the Customs and Excise Commissioners' appeal therefrom, by the Divisional Court.

On appeal by the commissioners on the ground that the board should be regarded as two separate bodies for the purpose of the tax, a railway operating board and a fiduciary board, and that the professional services, having been rendered to the fiduciary board, were not deductable by the operating board under section 3 (1) (*a*): — E

Held, dismissing the appeal, that on the facts the administration of the pension fund was part of the board's general function as a railway operator and that there was no justification for treating the board acting in its capacity as trustee of the pension fund as a different person from the board in its capacity as a railway operator for the purposes of the tax (post, p. 1041E–G); and that, accordingly, the board was entitled under section 3 (1) (*a*) of the Finance Act 1972 to F deduct as input tax the value added tax paid to the professional advisers.

Decision of the Divisional Court of the Queen's Bench Division [1975] 1 W.L.R. 1431; [1975] 3 All E.R. 451 affirmed.

No cases are referred to in the judgments.

G

The following cases were cited in argument:

Customs and Excise Commissioners v. *Glassborow* [1975] Q.B. 465; [1974] 2 W.L.R. 851; [1974] 1 All E.R. 1041, D.C.

Johnson, In re (1880) 15 Ch. D. 548.

Kelly v. *Rogers* [1935] 2 K.B. 446; 19 T.C. 692, C.A.

Reid's Trustees v. *Inland Revenue Commissioners,* 1929 S.C. 39; 14 T.C. 512. H

APPEAL from the Divisional Court of the Queen's Bench Division.

The Customs and Excise Commissioners appealed from the dismissal on July 18, 1975, by the Divisional Court (Lord Widgery C.J., Milmo and Wien JJ.) of their appeal from the decision of the London value added

[1] Finance Act 1972, s. 3 (1) (*a*): see post, p. 1039E.

A tax tribunal on February 27, 1975, that the British Railways Board were entitled to claim relief under section 3 (1) (*a*) of the Finance Act 1972 in respect of value added tax paid on fees for professional assistance in the administration of the board's employees' pension fund.

The facts are stated in the judgment of Buckley L.J.

Robin Auld Q.C. and *Peter Gibson* for the commissioners.

B *John Gardiner* for the board.

BUCKLEY L.J. This is an appeal from a decision of the Divisional Court of the Queen's Bench Division of July 18, 1975, on an appeal from a decision of the London value added tax tribunal under section 13 of the Tribunals and Inquiries Act 1971 from which there only lies an appeal
C upon questions of law. It raises the question about the position in relation to value added tax of the British Railways Board in respect of the pension fund that exists in the railway undertaking.

The board is a body which was set up under the Transport Act 1962 as a corporation and in which there were vested certain of the assets, rights and liabilities of the former British Transport Commission. The same Act established also the London Transport Board, the British Transport Docks
D Board and the British Waterways Board. Other assets, rights and liabilities of the commission were vested in those boards. The primary duty of the board is laid down by section 3 (1) of that Act in these terms:

> "It shall be the duty of the Railways Board in the exercise of their powers under this Act to provide railway services in Great Britain and, in connection with the provision of railway services, to provide
> E such other services and facilities as appear to the board to be expedient, and to have due regard, as respects all those railway and other services and facilities, to efficiency, economy and safety of operation."

By the Act, as I have said, certain assets, rights and liabilities of the commission were vested in the board. By section 14 (1) certain supplemental provisions were made as to the powers of the board which confer
F upon the board certain specific powers including, in paragraph (*l*), the power "to do all other things which in the opinion of the board are necessary to facilitate the proper carrying on of their business."

Section 73 of the Act empowers the board to pay pensions and enter into obligations under pension schemes to pay the employer's contributions and so forth. Section 74 confers upon the Minister the power to
G make orders with respect to provision of pensions by the board in respect of their employees, and for the establishment and administration of existing or future pension schemes and pension funds for any of those purposes. Under that power, the Minister made the British Transport (Amalgamation of Railways Pensions Funds) (No. 1) Order 1970. The order amalgamated the pension funds which had previously been administered at the time of the transfer from the British Transport Commission to the board by the
H commission and had been inherited from the four independent railway companies that previously existed before the nationalisation of the railways.

First of all, I ought to refer to article 2 of the order, which provided that on the amalgamation date the four existing pension funds should be amalgamated and become one pension fund, referred to as the "amalgamated fund;" and that the amalgamated fund should be vested in the board but should be administered in four sections reflecting the pre-existing separate funds; and that after the amalgamation date the board should,

subject to the provisions of the order, hold all the assets of the existing A
funds as assets of the amalgamated fund.

Article 5 permitted the board to continue investment of the moneys of the fund in deposits that the board itself might use in its railway undertaking, and article 9 provided that the cost of the acquisition or disposal of investments of the amalgamated fund should be borne by the fund except in so far as the board might decide to bear such costs, but all other costs, charges and expenses whatsoever incurred in connection with the B
management of the amalgamated fund should be borne by the board.

In due course, a trust deed was made on August 21, 1970. By that deed, the board declared trusts of the moneys so vested in them. Clause 6 of that trust deed provided:

> "The board shall hold all moneys and investments which may from time to time be in their hands or under their control in respect of the C
> fund upon trust to deal with the same for the absolute benefit of the fund in accordance with the provisions of this deed and of the rules."

The detailed operative trusts are to be found not in the deed itself but in the rules which are attached to it. The trust deed contained in clause 11 provisions as to the costs of management and so forth corresponding to the provisions in that respect in the order. It is in these terms: D

> "All costs charges and expenses whatsoever incurred in or about the management of the fund shall be borne by the board provided that the costs of acquisition and disposal of investments shall be borne by the fund except to such extent (if any) as the board shall determine."

The effect of the order, which has statutory force, is that the board is E
the sole trustee of the amalgamated fund. It is charged with the administration of that fund in accordance with the rules and it is obliged to pay out of its own moneys not forming part of the fund all the management expenses other than the costs and expenses actually attending changes of investment.

Value added tax was established by the Finance Act 1972. Section 1 sets up the tax. Section 2 prescribes the scope of the tax: F

> "(1) Except as otherwise provided by this Part of this Act the tax shall be charged and payable as follows. (2) Tax on the supply of goods or services shall be charged only where—(*a*) the supply is a taxable supply; and (*b*) the goods or services are supplied by a taxable person in the course of a business carried on by him; and shall be payable by the person supplying the goods or services." G

Section 2 (3) deals with imports, which we are not concerned with. Section 2 (4) provides:

> "Any reference in the following provisions of this Part of this Act to the supply by any person of goods or services is a reference to such a supply in the United Kingdom in the course of a business carried on by him." H

So, in order to discover whether a liability to tax arises, one has first of all to ask the question: have goods or services been supplied? Section 5 provides what shall constitute a supply of goods or services. I do not think I need read section 5. We are concerned in the present case with the supply of services. That will appear in a minute.

The second question one has to ask under section 2 (2) is: was the

A supply a taxable supply? To discover what that means, one must look at section 46, which says: " 'taxable supply' means any supply of goods or services in the United Kingdom other than an exempt supply." We are not here concerned with any exempt supply.

The next question is: were the goods or services supplied by a taxable person? To discover who is a taxable person, one goes to section 4, which provides:

> B "(1) A person who makes or intends to make taxable supplies is a taxable person while he is or is required to be registered under this Part of this Act. (2) Schedule 1 to this Act shall have effect with respect to the registration of persons under this Part of this Act."

If one turns to Schedule 1, one finds that the liability to registration
C depends upon the extent of the person's turnover. I need not read that in any detail.

The final question one has to ask under section 2 is whether the goods or services were supplied by the taxable person in the course of a business carried on by him. In the present case, we are concerned with services provided to the board by merchant bankers who gave investment management and advice services to the board in connection with the administration
D of the pension fund and with services provided by actuaries who advised the board and supervised the management of the fund in relation to actuarial matters. The persons who provided those services were taxable persons. The services were provided in the course of their businesses so that value added tax became payable in respect of the supply of the services by those merchant bankers and actuaries. That is called "output tax" in
E the Act in relation to those who supply the services.

I must now turn to what is described in the Act as "input tax." Section 3 deals with that:

> "(1) The following tax (in this Part of this Act referred to as 'input tax'), that is to say—(*a*) tax on the supply to a taxable person of any goods or services for the purpose of a business carried on or to be carried on by him"—(*b*), which deals with imports, I can leave out—
> F "may, at the end of any prescribed accounting period, be deducted by him, so far as not previously deducted and to the extent and subject to the exceptions provided for by or under this section, from the tax chargeable on supplies by him (in this section referred to as 'output tax')."

G The question in the present case is whether the board is entitled to treat the tax which was paid in relation to the services supplied to it by the merchant bankers and actuaries as input tax which can be set against its liability for output tax in relation to services and goods which the board itself supplies to others in the course of carrying on its general railway undertaking? The value added tax tribunal held that it was so entitled and the Divisional Court upheld that decision. The Customs and Excise
H Commissioners appeal from the decision of the Divisional Court.

It has been argued on behalf of the commissioners that where some person or corporate body carries on a business on his or its own behalf and also carries on another business as a trustee, that person or body should be regarded as constituting two persons or bodies for the purpose of the tax. It is said in the present case that the board should be regarded as if it consisted of (a) an operating board conducting the railway undertaking and (b) a fiduciary board administering the trusts of the pension fund, and that for the purposes of registration under the Act and of liability to tax under the Act it should be regarded as constituting two separate persons in that way.

The commissioners concede that if it is not right to regard the board as constituting two separate persons for the relevant purposes, then the services in question were supplied to the board for the purposes of its own business. They further concede that the provision of pension funds is nowadays a normal part of the operation of any large commercial undertaking such as the board conducts in the present case.

The value added tax tribunal, having adumbrated the argument about the dichotomy of the capacities in which the board acts, said in the course of their decision:

> "Before considering this alternative submission further"—that is a reference to the argument about dichotomy—"we will deal with the more factual question of whether the supplies were made for the purposes of a business carried on by the board ignoring for the moment Mr. Dearbergh's alternative submission."—Mr. Dearbergh was appearing for the commissioners—"In our view, on that basis, Mr. Gardner's submission that the supplies were made for the purposes of the board's business as railway operators is clearly right. We think that any other view would be quite unrealistic. Assuming that Mr. Dearbergh is right in saying that the merchant banks and the actuaries were either performing functions on behalf of the board as trustee, e.g. managing the investments of the fund, or providing services to enable the board to perform its function as trustee, e.g. the provision by the actuaries of a comparative survey of the investment performance of the funds, it seems to us that the board's performance of its functions as the trustee of these funds is simply a part of its railway business. It maintains, manages and accounts separately for these funds, not as a professional trustee, but as the employer of the beneficiaries. It acts as a trustee, not for fun or out of philanthropic motives, but because the provision of proper pension arrangements is an integral part of the management of a modern business. Just as it employs Mr. Lewis and his staff of over 70 people in a pensions department, so it engages outside professional advisers as well: in our view the staff is employed and the professional advisers are engaged for the purposes of the railway business."

The tribunal then went on to consider the dichotomy argument and did not accept it. Accordingly, they held that the tax on the services supplied by the merchant bankers and the actuaries to the board in the way referred to was input tax for the purposes of the Act capable of being set off against output tax in respect of goods and services supplied by the board in the course of operating its railway undertaking. That view of the matter was approved by the Divisional Court.

Counsel for the commissioners has pressed upon us a number of considerations indicating, as he says, the difficulties which would arise if a distinction in function between a beneficial owner and a trustee is not recognised in the administration of this tax. He has suggested that it would be surprising if the liability to tax should depend upon the personalities of the trustees, who might change from time to time, and matters of that kind. He suggests that there is a fundamental principle of taxation law that a person who is operating in a fiduciary capacity should be regarded differently from the same person when operating in relation to

A his own personal affairs. For my part, I think that we must consider this
case on its own facts and concentrate upon those facts.

In this case, the board was entrusted by Parliament with the duty of
providing the railway services of this country and had vested in it the
assets of the existing railway undertakings, and provision was made for its
continuing to pay and continuing to contribute to and to participate in the
pension arrangements in relation to those matters. In due course the
B Minister, under Parliamentary authority, saw fit to establish the board as
the sole trustee of the amalgamated pension fund and to lay down that the
board should pay out of its own moneys for the management of those
funds apart from the cost directly incident to changes of investment.

I entirely agree with the view expressed by the value added tax tribunal
in the passage which I have read from their decision that on the true view
C of the facts the contribution to pensions, the management of the pension
fund and generally the execution of the trust—the trust deed of the pension
fund—are matters which are all part of the board's functions as employer
in the railway undertaking.

One must read the statute which imposes the tax and discover whether
on the facts of the case it lays a liability for the tax upon a particular
person; and in the present case, upon the facts of this case, it appears to
D me that the Act does impose a liability upon the board to pay value added
tax in respect of all services provided by it in the course of its undertaking
and it authorises the board to bring into account against that liability as
input tax any tax which has been paid on the supply to the board of goods
or services supplied for the purposes of the business carried on by the
board.

E I see no justification in this statute for saying that the board has got to
be regarded as other than one body in respect of its general undertaking
on the one hand and its administration of the pension fund on the other
hand.

It seems to me upon the facts of this case that the administration of the
pension fund is in fact all part of the conduct of the general undertaking
and upon that rather short reasoning I have come to the conclusion that in
F this case the Divisional Court reached the right conclusion, as indeed did
the value added tax tribunal. I would dismiss this appeal.

ORR L.J. I agree. I, too, take the view that we must consider this case
on its own facts. I have not been persuaded by the argument that there is
anything either in the terms of the Finance Act 1972 or in general legal
G principle which requires or would entitle this court to hold that the British
Railways Board, acting in its capacity as trustee of a pension fund, is to
be treated for the purposes of the Finance Act 1972 as a different person
from the board in its capacity as an operator of railways.

For the reasons given by Buckley L.J. I, too, would dismiss this appeal.

H BROWNE L.J. I agree with all that Buckley L.J. and Orr L.J. have said,
and I do not wish to add anything.

Appeal dismissed with costs.
Leave to appeal refused.

Solicitors: *Solicitor, Customs & Excise; Solicitor, British Railways Board.*

C. N.

[COURT OF APPEAL] A

* TECHNISTUDY LTD. *v.* KELLAND

[1974 T. No. 727]

1976 May 5 — Lord Denning M.R., Roskill and B
Geoffrey Lane L.JJ.

Practice — Summary procedure on admissions of fact — Official referees' business—Order giving leave to enter judgment on admissions of fact—Facts in dispute—Whether appeal interlocutory or final—Need for Rules Committee to clarify position —R.S.C., Ord. 27, *r.* 3 [1] C

The plaintiffs, building contractors, claimed against the defendant owner of a house £1,590, the balance of the price for work done under a contract (which provided that the final instalment of the price did not become payable until all the work had been completed), and interest thereon. The defendant delivered a defence and particulars of work done badly or not completed and counterclaimed as damages for breach of contract the sum claimed in the writ. The circuit judge D
conducting official referees' business ordered that the parties prepare a Scott schedule on the disputed items. The defendant's part of the schedule contained omissions and mistakes in figures.

The contractors applied under R.S.C., Ord. 27, r. 3, for judgment on admissions. Despite the defendant's challenge by his defence, counterclaim, and particulars, the judge gave the contractors leave to sign judgment for the whole sum E
claimed, less one cash item agreed to have been omitted by mistake.

The defendant appealed, asking for the order to be set aside, on the ground, inter alia, that as no admissions had been made, the judge had erred in law in making an order under R.S.C., Ord. 27, r. 3. Questions were raised on the hearing of the appeal whether a judgment on admissions under R.S.C., Ord. 27, r. 3, was interlocutory or final, whether leave F
was required to appeal, and as to the present status of a circuit judge transacting the business of the official referee under the Courts Act 1971:—

Held, allowing the appeal and setting aside the order, (1) that leave to sign judgment on admissions under R.S.C., Ord. 27, r. 3, should only be given if there were either clear express or implied admission; and that as there were no such admissions but a clear challenge (on the pleadings and the Scott G
schedule) to the contractors' claim for the balance of the price under the lump sum form of contract, the judge's order was wrongly made.

(2) That an order for judgment on admissions under R.S.C., Ord. 27, r. 3 was, like a judgment under R.S.C., Ord. 14, interlocutory and not final, but that leave to appeal was not required since a point of law was involved.

Per Roskill L.J. The technical position of the official H
referee in relation to appeals from his orders is unsatisfactory

[1] R.S.C., Ord. 27, r. 3: "Where admissions of fact are made by a party to a cause or matter either by his pleadings or otherwise, any other party to the cause or matter may apply to the court for such judgment or order as upon those admissions he may be entitled to, without waiting for the determination of any other question between the parties, and the court may give such judgment, or make such order, on the application as it thinks just. An application for an order under this rule may be made by motions or summons."

A and it is desirable that it should be referred to the Rules Committee (post, p. 1046B, C).

The following cases are referred to in the judgments:

Attorney-General v. *Great Eastern Railway Co.* (1879) 48 L.J. Ch. 428, C.A.

Salter Rex & Co. v. *Ghosh* [1971] 2 Q.B. 597; [1971] 3 W.L.R. 31;
B [1971] 2 All E.R. 865, C.A.

The following additional cases were cited in argument:

Ellis v. *Allen* [1914] 1 Ch. 904.

Hampden v. *Wallis* (1884) 27 Ch.D. 257.

Standard Discount Co. v. *La Grange* (1877) 3 C.P.D. 67, C.A.

C

INTERLOCUTORY APPEAL from Judge Norman Richards transacting official referees' business.

The plaintiffs, Technistudy Ltd., claimed against the defendant, D. P. Kelland, the sum of £1,883·70, being £1,590·30, the price of building work and labour done and materials supplied on the order and at the request of the defendant, together with interest thereon.

D By his defence, the defendant denied that he was indebted to the plaintiffs in the sum of £1,883·70 as alleged, or at all. He claimed that by contract and specification and drawings made between the parties and dated June 5, 1972, the plaintiffs contracted with him to do certain works at his premises at 23, Stevenage Road, Knebworth, Hertfordshire, in accordance therewith, but that they failed to complete the works in accordance
E with the contract, drawings and specification or to a reasonable standard, whereby he had suffered loss and damage and in order to rectify the defects and complete the work not carried out or properly carried out he had been put to expense at least equal to the amount of the claim for £1,590·30 and interest thereon; and he counterclaimed damages for breach of contract limited to the sum of £1,883·70. Later he served further and better particulars of the defects alleged.

F The plaintiffs by their reply joined issue with the defence save in so far as it consisted of admissions and applied to the circuit judge who ordered that the parties prepare a Scott schedule of the items in dispute. After that had been done, the plaintiffs issued a summons under R.S.C., Ord. 27, r. 3, for leave to sign judgment on alleged admissions. The judge made the order in the sum of £1,182·30 and interest and ordered that the
G costs be the plaintiffs' in any event.

The defendant appealed, asking that the order be set aside on the grounds, inter alia, that (1) the official referee was wrong in law in making an order under R.S.C., Ord. 27, r. 3, when no admissions had been made; (2) he misdirected himself by directing that the Official Referee (Scott) Schedule consisted of a series of admissions on the part of the defendant;
H (3) in making the order, he failed to take into account the defence and counterclaim and the particulars served by the defendant; (4) in making the order, he relied on the Official Referee (Scott) Schedule when it was defective and incomplete, in that at item 3, the sum of £491 was missing; and (5) his order was wrong and should be set aside.

The plaintiffs filed a respondents' notice claiming that the defendant had by letters from his solicitors admitted their claim unequivocally subject only to the alleged set-off in respect of defective work.

Roger Henderson for the defendant.
Colin Reese for the plaintiff contractors.

LORD DENNING M.R. Mr. Kelland owns a house, 23, Stevenage Road, Knebworth. In 1972 he was minded to put an extension on this house. He entered into an agreement with a firm of contractors called Technistudy Ltd. They agreed to do work for the total sum of £2,703·90. There was a complete specification showing what was to be done and showing the quality and standard of the work. Payment was to be made as the work progressed. Ten per cent. on signing the contract, 40 per cent. on completion of the roof, 40 per cent. on completion of the contract, and then the balance, the final 10 per cent. one month after completion. There was a special clause, saying " . . . subject to the performance by the contractor of this contract, the contractor shall receive and be paid . . . the above inclusive sum of £2,703·90 " by those instalments.

The first 10 per cent. and the first 40 per cent. were paid. But Mr. Kelland did not pay the second 40 per cent. or the last 10 per cent. because he was most dissatisfied with the work done. He went to solicitors, who wrote a letter in which they pointed out that the work had not been properly done. They said that if it was not put right, they would advise their client to get other builders to carry out the work and deduct the cost from the contract price. Mr. Kelland acted accordingly. He went to other contractors. The defects were remedied at a cost of £918·00.

The contractors issued a writ on March 8, 1974, for £1,590·30, the whole of the balance that they said was due, together with interest.

A defence was put in by solicitors for Mr. Kelland. They said that the contractors had failed to complete the work in accordance with the contract and that Mr. Kelland owed nothing more than he had already paid.

The matter was referred to Judge Norman Richards, one of the official referees, but now, under the Courts Act 1971, a circuit judge officiating as an official referee. He made an order on November 7, 1975, for a Scott schedule. It is so called because long ago Mr. Scott, an official referee, ordered that the parties should set out in a schedule a list of the defects alleged, the defendant's estimated cost of remedy, the plaintiff's estimate, and the plaintiff's observations.

In this case a Scott schedule was prepared, from which it appeared as though there was a sum of only £408 as the cost of remedying the defects. But that was due to a clerical error. There was an additional £491, which was the cost of strengthening a wall. So the total cost of remedying the defects was £899.

After getting the Scott schedule the contractors applied for judgment under R.S.C., Ord 27, r. 3, which says:

> " Where admissions of fact are made by a party to a cause or matter either by his pleadings or otherwise, any other party to the cause or matter may apply to the court for such judgment or order as upon those admissions he may be entitled to . . . ."

When the application came before the official referee he took the apparent figure of £408 as the cost of remedying the defects. He deducted that £408 from the £1,590 so claimed by the plaintiffs, and gave judgment to the plaintiffs for £1,182·30 and interest.

An order was drawn up accordingly. Leave was given to sign judgment for £1,182 and interest, the costs to be the contractors' in any event. The

A clerical error about the £491 was afterwards pointed out to the official referee. I do not think he succeeded in correcting it, because Mr. Kelland has appealed to the court against the whole judgment.

A question has arisen whether it is a final appeal or an interlocutory appeal. As we have said before in this court (*Salter Rex & Co.* v. *Ghosh* [1971] 2 Q.B. 597) it is impossible to lay down any principles about what is final or what is interlocutory. The only thing to do is to go to the
B practice books and see what has been done in the past. If you look at *The Supreme Court Practice* 1976, under R.S.C., Ord. 59/4/4 (vol. 1, p. 855), you might think an appeal from a judgment on admissions was a final appeal. In support, it refers to *Attorney-General* v. *Great Eastern Railway Co.* (1879) 48 L.J.Ch. 428. I do not think that case supports the statement in the *Supreme Court Practice*. A judgment on admissions
C cannot be distinguished from a judgment under R.S.C., Ord. 14, which we know is always interlocutory. In my opinion, in a case under R.S.C., Ord. 27, r. 3, if leave is given to sign judgment, it is an interlocutory order and an appeal ranks as an interlocutory appeal.

There is another point. It concerns the position of an official referee. Under the Courts Act 1971, section 25 (1) and R.S.C., Ord. 58, r. 5, there is an appeal from him on points of law. It looks as if there is no need to
D obtain leave to appeal. But if there is need, this is certainly a case in which leave would be given.

Coming now to this case itself, it seems to me that there should not be a judgment on admissions. Many points have been canvassed before us. One emerges at the outset. It does not appear distinctly on the pleadings, but can be inferred. This may be said to be a "lump sum contract."
E Payments are only due as and when the work is substantially performed. If there are only small defects or failures, that does not warrant non-payment of price or of an instalment; there is only a deduction of the cost of remedying the defects or failures. But if the work is substantially incomplete, the party is not entitled to his lump sum. It seems to me that the clause I have read—" subject to the performance by the contractor "—
F is an important clause. Having regard to the defects and the extent of the uncompleted work (such as the soakaway), it is clearly a case where it is very arguable that the contractor has not completed the contract so as to entitle him to the last 50 per cent. In any event, there is no clear admission that the contractor is entitled to the balance, or indeed to any specific part of it. If it were under R.S.C., Ord. 14, there might be a case for leave to defend on condition of paying a certain amount into court, but
G this is not an Order 14 case at all. The plaintiffs seek judgment on admissions, I cannot see any clear admission that any specific sum is due which could be ascertained. The issues are so wide open that it seems to me that there should be no judgment on admissions; the order of the official referee should be set aside and the matter remitted to him for hearing.

H

ROSKILL L.J. I entirely agree, and I only add a very few words as we are differing from the official referee before whom this matter came.

It seems to me, with great respect to him, that he made the wrong order. The reason why his order was wrong is that there is no clear admission of any kind, either in the pleadings or in the correspondence, which entitled him to make the order that he did under R.S.C., Ord. 27, r. 3. As the cases show, an order should only be made under that rule if it is plain that there are either clear express, or clear implied, admissions. A I can see no clear express admissions; I can see no clear implied admissions.

Furthermore, there is the point to which Lord Denning M.R. alluded earlier in the proceedings, namely, that under this rather peculiar form of contract the whole of the work had to be completed before the full amount became payable. That is enough to determine this appeal.

I would add only a few words on the question of procedure. Like Lord Denning M.R., I am clearly of the view that this is an interlocutory B appeal. I am also clearly of the view that this being a point of law, leave was not required. I do not feel it necessary to enter the statutory jungle which we have been investigating this afternoon. It is sufficient to say that the technical position is unsatisfactory, and to my mind it is desirable that the matter be referred to the Rules Committee, in order that the position can be placed beyond doubt, and, if it were thought right C so to provide, that interlocutory appeals from an official referee can only be brought with leave, even if they raise a point of law, so that the position can be assimilated with that of an appeal from the county court. I agree that the appeal should be allowed.

GEOFFREY LANE L.J. I also agree that the appeal should be allowed. D

I think that in fairness to the official referee it should be said that very little assistance was given to him, as it now transpires, to help him to come to the correct conclusion. The pleadings are masterpieces of obscurity; the Scott schedule is now admittedly wrong. If he came to the wrong conclusion, as this court thinks he did, it was by no means his fault. It was not, as it emerges, a proper case for judgment under R.S.C., Ord. 27, r. 3, at all, though R.S.C., Ord. 14 procedure might have been appropriate. E

So far as the procedural matters are concerned, I agree that an order under R.S.C., Ord. 27, r. 3, is interlocutory and not final.

I agree further with my brethren that this was a point of law and that leave was not required in those circumstances. I am not prepared to express any opinion on the position of a circuit judge transacting the business of an official referee, vis-à-vis the necessity for leave to appeal F against his judgment.

For the reasons already given by my brethren, and for the short reasons I have given, I agree that this appeal should be allowed.

Appeal allowed.
No order as to costs in the Court of Appeal or below. G
Leave to take out money paid into court.
Leave to remedy notice by which it was paid in.

Solicitors: *Passingham & Hill, Stevenage; Freedman & Co.* H

M. M. H.

[QUEEN'S BENCH DIVISION]

* REGINA *v.* BARNSLEY SUPPLEMENTARY BENEFITS APPEAL TRIBUNAL, *Ex parte* ATKINSON

1976 April 8, 9 — Lord Widgery C.J., Thompson and Kenneth Jones JJ.

Social Security—Supplementary allowance—Calculation—Student receiving minimum educational grant—Element in full grant for maintenance during vacation—Minimum grant less than vacation element—Application for benefit while seeking employment during vacation—Benefit reduced by vacation element—Whether correct in law—Supplementary Benefit Act 1966 (*c.* 20), *Sch.* 2, *para.* 4 (1)

The applicant was a student who was in receipt of the minimum educational grant of £50 because of his father's resources. The full grant was £605 which included a sum of £58 towards the maintenance of the student during the vacation. The applicant applied for, and was granted, supplementary benefit during the summer vacation of 1975. Schedule 2 to the Supplementary Benefit Act 1966 [1] allowed the Supplementary Benefits Commission to calculate the applicant's resources in order to arrive at the correct weekly benefit payable. The commission assumed that the applicant received the full grant from his father and therefore decided that the element for maintenance during the vacation was a resource and the applicant's weekly benefit should be reduced by that amount. The applicant appealed to the supplementary benefits appeal tribunal against that reduction. The tribunal upheld the decision of the commission to reduce the benefit paid to the applicant by the amount of the maintenance element.

On an application for an order of certiorari to quash the decision of the tribunal:—

Held, dismissing the application, that as there was no specific provision in the Supplementary Benefit Act 1966 that dealt with the question of parental contributions and there was no evidence of failure by the applicant's father to maintain him to the extent assumed, the reduction of the benefit was a perfectly valid exercise of the powers of discretion of the commission under the wide terms of paragraph 4 of Schedule 2 to the Act.

Dictum of Lord Denning M.R. in *Reg.* v. *Preston Supplementary Benefits Appeal Tribunal, Ex parte Moore* [1975] 1 W.L.R. 624, 631, C.A. applied.

The following case is referred to in the judgment of Lord Widgery C.J.:

Reg. v. *Preston Supplementary Benefits Appeal Tribunal, Ex parte Moore* [1975] 1 W.L.R. 624; [1975] 2 All E.R. 807, C.A.

The following additional case was cited in argument:

Reg. v. *West London Supplementary Benefits Appeal Tribunal, Ex parte Clarke* [1975] 1 W.L.R. 1396; [1975] 3 All E.R. 513, D.C.

APPLICATION for order of certiorari.

The applicant, Robin Leonard Atkinson, applied for supplementary

[Reported by MRS. H. WHICHER, Barrister-at-Law]

[1] Supplementary Benefit Act 1966, Sch. 2, para. 4 (1): see post, 1050G.

benefit while seeking employment during the summer vacation of 1975. The Supplementary Benefits Commission calculated that the applicant had a resource of £2·63 per week by dividing the vacation maintenance of £58 by 22, the number of weeks of vacation. The commission therefore reduced the single person non-householder benefit of £8·60 to £5·97 for the applicant. That decision was made by the commission on June 23, 1975, and the applicant appealed against it to the Barnsley Supplementary Benefits Appeal Tribunal. On August 14, 1975, the tribunal upheld the decision of the commission. The applicant applied for an order of certiorari to quash the decision on the grounds, inter alia, that in deducting £2·63 per week from the applicant's benefit, the commission had failed to carry out the provisions of the Supplementary Benefit Act 1966 and that there was no evidence that the applicant was in receipt of any allowance from his father, who was under no obligation to maintain him.

The facts are stated in the judgment of Lord Widgery C.J.

The applicant in person.

Harry Woolf for the Supplementary Benefits Commission.

LORD WIDGERY C.J. In these proceedings Mr. Atkinson applies for an order of certiorari to remove into this court for the purpose of its being quashed, a decision of the Barnsley Supplementary Benefits Appeal Tribunal given on August 14, 1975, whereby it was decided that the decision of the Supplementary Benefits Commission of June 23, 1975, be confirmed, namely, that supplementary allowance of £5·97 determined and paid to the applicant weekly from the prescribed pay day in the week commencing June 16, 1975 was correct.

This is a case which requires the court to consider the workings of student grants both under the Education Acts and also under the Supplementary Benefit Act 1966, and it is, I think, convenient to draw attention right at the beginning to what has been said both in this court and the Court of Appeal as to the proper approach to problems arising under this legislation.

The most convenient extract by which to make the point is to cite from the judgment of Lord Denning M.R. in *Reg.* v. *Preston Supplementary Benefits Appeal Tribunal, Ex parte Moore* [1975] 1 W.L.R. 624. Lord Denning said, at p. 631:

> "It is plain that Parliament intended that the Supplementary Benefit Act 1966 should be administered with as little technicality as possible. It should not become the happy hunting ground for lawyers. The courts should hesitate long before interfering by certiorari with the decisions of the appeal tribunals. Otherwise the courts would become engulfed with streams of cases just as they did under the old Workmen's Compensation Acts,"

and then he gives an example. He goes on to say:

> "The courts should not enter into a meticulous discussion of the meaning of this or that word in the Act. They should leave the tribunals to interpret the Act in a broad reasonable way, according to the spirit and not to the letter: especially as Parliament has given them a way of alleviating any hardship. The courts should only interfere when the decision of the tribunal is unreasonable in the sense that no tribunal acquainted with the ordinary use of language could

reasonably reach that decision: see *Cozens* v. *Brutus* [1973] A.C. 854, 861."

I need read no further but merely observe that in deciding this application for certiorari this court must do its best to follow the directions there contained.

What happened was that in the summer of 1975 the applicant, who is a student, registered himself under the appropriate methods prescribed by the Supplementary Benefit Act 1966 as being willing to undertake full-time employment during the period of the vacation. This, one gathers, is not a unique idea of the applicant's and students are quite widely doing this for various reasons into which one need not go. So he registered himself as being available for work during the vacation, not perhaps with any great confidence that he would get work but with some considerable confidence that if he did not get work he would qualify for a supplementary benefit in respect of it.

Sure enough he was given a supplementary benefit calculated in this way. First of all, he was regarded as having a requirement of £8·60. I pause to remind myself that in this legislation the entitlement of a person to benefit normally turns on whether his resources do or do not exceed his requirements; and applying that approach the applicant was found to have a requirement of £8·60.

Then the officer of the commission dealing with the case asked himself whether there were any resources which were to be set against those requirements, and he determined that there was a resource of £2·63 so to be set off, reducing the amount of entitlement to £5·97. The basis upon which that £2·63 was assessed and allowed for in this way is again somewhat complex, but it is this. The applicant was in receipt of a grant under the Education Acts in respect of his studies at a university, and the maximum grant to which his circumstances would have entitled him had his father not been able to contribute would have been £605. The education authorities and the Supplementary Benefits Commission between themselves, as I understand it, have reached the conclusion, which no one really seriously challenges, that of that figure of £605 £58 is fairly attributable to maintenance during the fairly comfortable vacations which the recipient of the benefit would receive. Having taken £58 as being the element of the £605 which is attributable to vacation maintenance, the commission has divided that figure by 22, which is the number of weeks' vacation in the year; the resultant figure is £2·63. That is the figure which has been deducted from the applicant's supplementary benefit, and it is that deduction which is in substance his grievance here.

His grievance is one which certainly appealed to this court when considering his application for leave to move because, although if the applicant's father had been penniless the applicant would have received a grant of £605, since his father has resources he only receives the minimum grant of £50. It does not require any great imagination to realise that he was somewhat surprised, receiving a grant of £50, to be told that the vacation maintenance element therein amounted to £58.

This is not a case where in my judgment this court is expected, or indeed advised, to go in great detail into the arguments which have been placed before it. There obviously was here a point of substance of the kind referred to by Lord Denning M.R. where it was proper and of assistance that the matter should come before this court and that a decision should be reached upon it. But, as Lord Denning M.R. has pointed out, these

arguments have to be dealt with with a comparatively broad brush, and A
what we have to look at is some fundamental error, if such can be discerned, in the proceedings upon which we can properly set aside the decision. On the face of it the fact that the applicant is being charged as it were, £58 for his vacation maintenance, and he only receives a total of £50, suggested to our minds that there was here some fundamental point which it was proper to investigate.

When one has heard argument and has all the material before the court B
the short explanation of the conduct of the Supplementary Benefits Commission in my judgment is just this. The grants under the Education Acts to which I have referred assume that the applicant's father by reason of his resources will contribute £555 a year towards his maintenance; that is to say the amount by which the grant of £50 falls short of the total. There is, as far as I know, no legally enforceable obligation on the father in this C
situation to maintain his son to the tune of £555 or any other sum. But in deciding what part government money should play in the maintenance of students it is assumed that a father who has the resources will provide the parental share which the Acts contemplate.

The explanation of the commission's decision on the applicant as I understand it now, is simply this. When one looks at the applicant's resources at the relevant time one assumes that he is receiving £605 in all— D
£50 from the education authorities and £555 from his father. One assumes that he is in receipt of that sum because the basis of the award of the grants under the Education Acts and the whole scheme of father and child relationships so far as it applies to the Supplementary Benefit Act assumes that the father is providing the measure of financial support which is assumed as down to him for the purposes of the initial calculation. So E
really the only question we have to decide is whether that approach by the commission was wrong or whether there is some legitimate explanation which justifies a father's contribution as being treated as a resource in the hands of the son.

I confess I had confidently expected when Mr. Woolf began his argument that we should be shown a section of an Act or a regulation which precisely dealt with this question of father's contribution, but not so. F
Typical of the very general way in which this legislation is drafted, as Lord Denning M.R. pointed out, is the fact that nowhere is there a section which says that a father's contribution was or was not to be treated in this way.

The commission falls back on paragraph 4 of Schedule 2 to the Supplementary Benefit Act 1966 which provides: G

> "(1) Where there are exceptional circumstances—(*a*) benefit may be awarded at an amount exceeding that (if any) calculated in accordance with the preceding paragraphs; (*b*) a supplementary allowance may be reduced below the amount so calculated or may be withheld; as may be appropriate to take account of those circumstances."

Mr. Woolf on behalf of the commission cites that as his client's authority H
for treating the parental contribution in the way which I have endeavoured to describe.

I am bound to say that wider words could hardly be found than those in paragraph 4. The exceptional circumstances which have to open the door to the use of paragraph 4 are, so it is submitted, the exceptional circumstances affecting students who until quite recently had no motive to register for work in the vacation, and now have, and who have produced

A a highly specialised and unusual situation with which the commission is faced. It is said that these are exceptional circumstances, and accordingly the benefit may be awarded really at such figure as the commission thinks fit, provided it acts reasonably in that sense, as Lord Denning M.R. has said, and does not go outside the conclusions which a reasonable tribunal might conceivably come to.

I do not find it at all attractive to think that the powers of the com-
B mission vis-à-vis the control of the court are as wide as they seem to be; but it quite clearly is so, and it is the will of Parliament, and we must adopt it. It seems to me that we should be going against the directions provided for us in the Court of Appeal if we did not recognise that to treat the parental contribution in this case in the way in which it was treated is a perfectly valid exercise of the powers of the commission under para-
C graph 4. I say " in this case " because one can foresee that there may be different circumstances. We have not heard whether the applicant's father maintains him to the tune of £555 or not, but it would be a bold man to assume that he did not. There may however be a case another day in which the father does not contribute and then I have no doubt other considerations could arise, but it seems to me that the action of the commission in this case is justified by the wide terms of paragraph 4.

D There were other less important points raised in the course of argument. One of them which is of interest, if nothing else, concerns the first £1 of resources which is under general provisions in the Supplementary Benefit Act 1966 to be disregarded for the purposes of the balancing calculation.

In this particular case the commission, having fixed £8·60 as the requirement, then proceeded to calculate the resources by taking £2·63, which it will be remembered is 1/22 part of £58 allocated to the vacation main-
E tenance. The commission has taken this £2·63 and deducted £1 as the statutory disregard under paragraph 25 of Schedule 2 to the Act. But in the next line of the calculation it has added it back again in the exercise of its discretion under paragraph 4. It seems an odd way of making the calculation, and at one time I thought it was open to serious doubt on the footing that there seemed to be a mistake as to whether public funds were
F not being called upon twice for the same obligation. But in the end I am persuaded that this again is a matter which can properly be regarded as coming within the umbrella of paragraph 4 of Schedule 2 and accordingly it seems to me consistent with the decision in *Moore's* case [1975] 1 W.L.R. 624, that we should refuse this application, and I would do that.

G THOMPSON J. I agree.

KENNETH JONES J. I also agree.

Application refused.
No order as to costs.

H Solicitor: *Solicitor, Department of Health and Social Security.*

[COURT OF APPEAL]

* REGINA *v.* BARNSLEY METROPOLITAN BOROUGH COUNCIL, *Ex parte* HOOK

[DC/4/75]

1976 Feb. 20

Lord Denning M.R., Scarman L.J. and Sir John Pennycuick

Market—Right to trade—Termination of licence—Local authority terminating stallholder's licence to trade for trivial misconduct —Officer acting as prosecutor present during appeal hearings by council committee in absence of stallholder—Whether committee acting administratively or judicially—Whether decision void for want of natural justice—Whether prerogative order available to quash decision depriving stallholder of livelihood —Barnsley Corporation Act 1969 (*c. xi*)

In October 1974 the applicant, who was a stallholder in an ancient town market under an oral licence from the borough council, the owners, had his licence terminated by letter from the market manager. His appeals to two council committees were dismissed without any specific reasons being given to him. He applied to the Divisional Court for an order of certiorari to quash the decision on the ground that there had been a denial of natural justice in that he had not been told what, if any, rule or practice of the market he was alleged to have breached; that the committee meetings had been held substantially in his absence; and that neither he nor his representative had had an opportunity to hear or question the evidence, if any, on which the market manager's decision had been confirmed. He set out in his statement the conduct in respect of which the market manager had banned him, namely, that at about 6.30 p.m. after the market had closed and the public lavatories were locked he had been seen urinating in a side street by two council sweepers; that words had been exchanged which had been overheard by a council security officer who had reported the incident to the market manager; and that the next day the market manager by letter terminated his licence at a few days' notice. The market manager's affidavit evidence was that he had done so because of the abuse of his staff and not because of the urinating. The Divisional Court dismissed the application on the ground that the council's decision was administrative and within its powers.

On the applicant's appeal, the court received further evidence, including the Barnsley Corporation Act 1969 and byelaws made under the Act which contained no express provisions about, inter alia, the determination or revocation of a stallholder's licence or the terms on which it was held. The court of its own motion inquired into the common law rights of the public in an ancient market and into the evidence, which showed that the market manager had been present throughout the two appeal proceedings: —

Held, allowing the appeal, that where the council was exercising its discretionary power under the Act of 1969 to regulate the common law public right to buy and sell in a market, it was not merely dealing with the contractual relationship but also with the common law right of a man to earn his living in the market; that in those circumstances it was under a duty to act judicially; and that the appeal hearings had been conducted in breach of the rules of natural justice because on the evidence the market manager, the prosecutor, was present

A throughout the proceedings while the applicant was not; accordingly certiorari was the appropriate remedy to quash the decision, a fortiori where the punishment for trivial misconduct unconnected with the market was excessive.

Decision of Divisional Court of the Queen's Bench Division reversed.

The following cases are referred to in the judgments:

B *Attorney-General* v. *Colchester Corporation* [1952] Ch. 586; [1952] 2 All E.R. 297.

Cooper v. *Wilson* [1937] 2 K.B. 309; [1937] 2 All E.R. 726, C.A.

H. K. (An Infant), In re [1967] 2 Q.B. 617; [1967] 2 W.L.R. 962; [1967] 1 All E.R. 226, D.C.

London Corporation v. *Lyons, Son & Co. (Fruit Brokers) Ltd.* [1936] Ch. 78.

C *Northampton Corporation* v. *Ward* (1795) 2 Str. 1238.

Reg. v. *Gaming Board for Great Britain, Ex parte Benaim and Khaida* [1970] 2 Q.B. 417; [1970] 2 W.L.R. 1009; [1970] 2 All E.R. 528, C.A.

Reg. v. *London County Council, Ex parte Akkersdyk, Ex parte Fermenia* [1892] 1 Q.B. 190, D.C.

Rex v. *Electricity Commissioners, Ex parte London Electricity Joint*
D *Committee Ltd.* [1924] 1 K.B. 177.

Rex v. *Northumberland Compensation Appeal Tribunal, Ex parte Shaw* [1952] 1 K.B. 338; [1952] 1 All E.R. 122, C.A.

Yarmouth Corporation v. *Groom* (1862) 1 H. & C. 102.

The following additional cases were cited in argument:

Rendell v. *Roman* (1893) 9 T.L.R. 192, D.C.

E *Ridge* v. *Baldwin* [1964] A.C. 40; [1963] 2 W.L.R. 935; [1963] 2 All E.R. 66, H.L.(E.).

Winter Garden Theatre (London) Ltd. v. *Millennium Productions Ltd.* [1948] A.C. 173; [1947] 2 All E.R. 331, H.L.(E.).

APPEAL from the Divisional Court of the Queen's Bench Division.

The applicant, Harry Hook, of 9, Mexborough Drive, Leeds, who
F carried on the business of market trader in the Barnsley market, applied to the Divisional Court (Lord Widgery C.J., Park and Stocker JJ.) for an order of certiorari to quash a decision made by the civic amenities committee of Barnsley Metropolitan Borough Council on October 30, 1974, that he be banned from trading in Barnsley market for the rest of his life.

The grounds on which the relief was sought were (i) that there was a
G denial to the applicant of natural justice before the committee in that (a) he was not informed what, if any, rule or practice of the market it was alleged he had breached; (b) the meeting of the committee was convened in the absence of himself and of his representative, and lasted for about one hour before he and his representative were invited to attend; (c) he did not have the opportunity to hear or question the evidence, if any, on which the decision was based; and (d) neither he nor his representative
H were permitted to question members of the committee; and (ii) the committee failed to act judicially in imposing the ban on the applicant in that another trader in the market had recently been reported to the market authorities for the same offence as was alleged against the applicant, that the other trader had committed the same offence some four times in all, but has not been banned from trading in the market; and that the disparity between the two decisions indicated that the market authorities failed to act judicially.

The borough council, as respondents to the application, opposed the motion. They denied that there had been a denial of natural justice to the applicant at the meeting of the indoor services subcommittee of the amenity services committee of the council held on October 30, 1974, in that (a) on October 18, 1974, the council's market manager, Alan Fretwell, interviewed the applicant and informed him that a complaint had been received regarding certain conduct of the applicant on the evening of October 16, 1974; the applicant was given an opportunity of explaining his conduct B
and was subsequently informed by letter dated October 18, that he was no longer considered to be a suitable tenant and that his stalls and pitch would cease to be available to him after October 23; (b) the applicant was granted a right of appeal before the chairman and vice-chairman of the amenity services committee, the amenities and recreation officer, and the market manager on October 24, 1974, when the case was fully discussed with him C
and a union representative; and that the markets manager's decision was confirmed at that meeting; (c) the applicant was granted a further appeal before the indoor services subcommittee on October 30, when he was represented by his legal adviser and the union official, although he himself did not appear before the committee; that at that meeting, as the appeal was an additional item on the agenda of the subcommittee, other business was dealt with to enable the council's legal representative at the committee D
to peruse the papers before the subcommittee dealt with the appeal; a period of one hour elapsed before the applicant and his representatives were invited to appear before the subcommittee; the applicant's representatives were both given the opportunity of speaking on his behalf; the subcommittee discussed the representatives' case but decided to adhere to the original decision. E

With regard to the reference made in the applicant's statement to the conduct of the other trader, the council were unable to obtain sufficient evidence to support the complaints referred to and therefore decided to take no further action with regard to those complaints. They claimed, therefore, that they had acted judicially in both matters. The Divisional Court refused the order on May 14, 1975.

The applicant appealed on the grounds that the court erred in finding F
that the decision of the market manager to terminate the applicant's licence to trade in the Barnsley market was administrative; that the court should have granted the order of certiorari; that the court erred in judging that there had been no breach of the rules of natural justice, and in finding that the applicant had had an opportunity of cross-examining witnesses, and that the evidence was not in issue. G

On the hearing of the appeal the court received additional evidence on affidavit by the applicant's solicitor in which he stated that he understood that the Divisional Court had been much exercised by the absence of information as to (a) whether or not there were regulations or byelaws which would indicate the nature and extent of the market manager's authority or the authority and powers of the council's indoor services sub- H
committee or of the civic amenities committee and (b) whether or not on the quashing of the decision of the indoor services subcommittee as confirmed by the civic amenities committee, the applicant could still be refused the right of trading in the Barnsley market, thereby rendering the decision of the Divisional Court nugatory. In respect of the first matter he exhibited to the affidavit a copy of the Barnsley Corporation Act 1969 and of the byelaws issued by the council and made in exercise of their powers under

section 61 of the Food and Drugs Act 1955 and section 8 of the private Act of 1969 (making further provisions with respect to the market undertaking); and he stated that nowhere was there contained in those byelaws any express power in the market manager or the committees to determine or revoke a market trader's licence; and that he had been informed by a representative of the council's solicitors that there were no other regulations or byelaws pertaining to the administration and regulation of the market.

Further, in respect of the second matter, he had been informed by a representative of the council's solicitors that the licence was an oral one and "continues until determined by the act of either party or revoked by the order of the committee," and that the licence was issued on the payment of a fee, the amount of which he did not know; but he understood that it was payable on a daily or weekly basis. He admitted that evidence of the above matters could have been adduced before the Divisional Court, but submitted that by referring to the new affidavit the Court of Appeal would be assisted in deciding the appeal.

The court received the new evidence, and of its own motion inquired further into the circumstances of the hearings of the applicant's appeals to the two council committees.

John Mullick for the applicant.
Michael Howard for the Barnsley Metropolitan Borough Council.

LORD DENNING M.R. To some this may appear to be a small matter, but to Mr. Harry Hook it is very important. He is a street trader in the Barnsley market. He has been trading there for some six years without any complaint being made against him; but, nevertheless, he has now been banned from trading in the market for life. All because of a trifling incident. On Wednesday, October 16, 1974, the market closed at 5.30. So were all the lavatories, or "toilets" as they are now called. They were locked up. Three-quarters of an hour later, at 6.20, Harry Hook had an urgent call of nature. He wanted to relieve himself. He went into a side street near the market and there made water, or "urinated," as it is now said. No one was about except one or two employees of the council, who were cleaning up. They rebuked him. He said: "I can do it here if I like." They reported him to a security officer who came up. The security officer reprimanded Harry Hook. We are not told the words used by the security officer. I expect they were in language which street traders understand. Harry Hook made an appropriate reply. Again we are not told the actual words, but it is not difficult to guess. I expect it was an emphatic version of "You be off." At any rate, the security officer described them as words of abuse. Touchstone would say the security officer gave the "reproof valiant" and Harry Hook gave the "countercheck quarrelsome": "As You Like It," Act V, Scene IV.

On the Thursday morning the security officer reported the incident. The market manager thought it was a serious matter. So he saw Mr. Hook the next day, Friday, October 18. Mr. Hook admitted it and said he was sorry for what had happened. The market manager was not satisfied to leave it there. He reported the incident to the chairman of the amenity services committee of the council. He says that the chairman agreed "that staff should be protected from such abuse." That very day the market manager wrote a letter to Mr. Hook, banning him from trading in the market. It read:

"H. Hook, Esq., Semi-Open Market, Barnsley. Dear Sir, Further to A
your interview on Friday, October 18, 1974. In confirmation of that interview I have to give you notice that you are no longer considered to be a suitable tenant of this authority. The stalls and pitch at present reserved for you each market day will cease to be available for your use after Wednesday next the 23rd instant. Please arrange to clear stock from your cupboards by this date. Yours faithfully, . . ."

B

So there he was on Friday, October 18, dismissed as from the next Wednesday, banned for life.

He was, however, granted a further hearing. On the next Thursday, October 24, he was allowed to state his case before the chairman of the amenity services committee, the vice-chairman, the amenities officer and the market manager himself. He went there accompanied by the president C
of the Barnsley Market Traders' Union. The matter was discussed. The council people saw no reason to alter the decision, but told Mr. Hook that he could be heard further by the indoor services subcommittee. This met on the following Wednesday, October 30. Mr. Hook went there with a young articled clerk from his solicitors and the trade union representative. The committee met at 10 a.m. but Mr. Hook and his representatives had to wait for an hour before they were allowed in. Then the articled clerk D
and the union representative went in. But Mr. Hook himself did not go in. He stayed outside in the corridor. The articled clerk and the union representative were allowed to address the committee, but they were not given particulars of the charge or of the evidence against Mr. Hook. At that meeting the market manager was present and was in a position to tell the committee his view of the evidence. After Mr. Hook's representatives had been heard, that subcommittee discussed the case (with the market E
manager still present) and decided to adhere to the original decision.

Thereupon Mr. Hook applied to the Divisional Court for leave to apply for a writ of certiorari. The Divisional Court gave leave to make the application, but after hearing both sides, they dismissed his application. Now there is an appeal to us.

There is much more material before us than was before the Divisional F
Court. In particular about the market at Barnsley. The right of having a market at Barnsley was granted as long ago as the year 1249 by a charter by King Henry III to the Prior and Convent of Pontefract. After the dissolution of the monasteries, it became vested in lay hands and eventually in the Dukes of Leeds. In 1861 the market rights were conveyed to the Barnsley Local Board, and thence to the Barnsley Corporation. In 1969 a G
private Act was passed called the Barnsley Corporation Act 1969 which confirmed the title of the Barnsley Corporation and gave them the power to regulate the conduct of the market and to make byelaws.

This right of holding a market is subject to the common law of England. It says that every member of the public is entitled to come into the market place, to bring things there for sale: and others are entitled to come in to buy them. Sellers and buyers can come without let or hindrance, moving H
about and walking to and fro. But a seller has not any right to pitch a stall there unless it has been allocated to him by the owner of the market. When it is so allocated, the owner can charge a fee for it called stallage, which the seller has to pay. It was so stated in 1795 in *Northampton Corporation* v. *Ward* (1795) 2 Stra. 1238 and *Yarmouth Corporation* v. *Groom* (1862) 1 H. & C. 102. It was restated in modern times in the case of the Spitalfields Market, *London Corporation* v. *Lyons Son & Co. (Fruit*

Brokers) *Ltd.* [1936] Ch. 78; and the Colchester Market case, *Attorney-General* v. *Colchester Corporation* [1952] Ch. 586; and *Halsbury's Laws of England,* 3rd ed. (1958), vol. 25, pp. 391–398.

In the Barnsley Corporation Act 1969, there is a section which says that if a stallholder is in arrear with his stallage for his stall and fails to pay within three days of the demand, the corporation can take possession and relet the space. In addition, the Barnsley Corporation have made byelaws which conform to the common law. Byelaw 4 prohibits any person from erecting a stall unless a space has been allocated by the superintendent. Byelaw 5 prohibits any person from erecting a stall without the previous written consent of the superintendent. There are also byelaws for preventing damage and throwing litter about, and the like. For a breach of the byelaws an offender can be taken before the magistrates and fined up to £20.

Such being the legal position, I do not think that the right of a stallholder arises merely under a contract or licence determinable at will. It is a right conferred on him by the common law under which, so long as he pays the stallage, he is entitled to have his stall there: and that right cannot be determined without just cause. I agree that he has to have the permission of the marketholder to start with. But once he has it and has set up his stall there, then so long as he pays the stallage, he has a right to keep it there. It is not to be taken away except for just cause and then only in accordance with the provisions of natural justice. I do not mind whether the marketholder is exercising a judicial or an administrative function. A stallholder counts on this right in order to enable him to earn his living. It is not to be taken away except for just cause and in accord with natural justice.

So it was quite right for the committee to hold the hearings. I will assume that Mr. Hook was given sufficient notice of the charge to be able to deal with it. But, nevertheless, each of the hearings was, to my mind, vitiated by the fact that the market manager was there all the time. He was the one who gave evidence—the only one who did—and hearsay evidence, too. His evidence was given privately to the committee, not in the presence of Mr. Hook or his representatives. Mr. Hook was not himself in the room. His representatives were there, and they were heard. But when the committee discussed the case and came to their decision, the market manager was there all the time. His presence at all their deliberations is enough to vitiate the proceedings. It is contrary to natural justice that one who is in the position of a prosecutor should be present at the deliberations of the adjudicating committee. That is shown by *Reg.* v. *London County Council, Ex parte Akkersdyk, Ex parte Fermenia* [1892] 1 Q.B. 190 and *Cooper* v. *Wilson* [1937] 2 K.B. 309.

But there is one further matter: and that is that the punishment was too severe. It appears that there had been other cases where men had urinated in a side street near the market and no such punishment had been inflicted.

Now there are old cases which show that the court can interfere by certiorari if a punishment is altogether excessive and out of proportion to the occasion. In one case the Commissioners of Sewers imposed an excessive fine: and it was quashed by the Court of King's Bench on the ground that in law their fines ought to be reasonable: see *Rex* v. *Northumberland Compensation Appeal Tribunal, Ex parte Shaw* [1952] 1 K.B. 338, 350. So in this case if Mr. Hook did misbehave, I should have thought the right thing would have been to take him before the magistrates under the

byelaws, when some small fine might have been inflicted. It is quite wrong A
that the Barnsley Corporation should inflict upon him the grave penalty of depriving him of his livelihood. That is a far more serious penalty than anything the magistrates could inflict. He is a man of good character, and ought not to be penalised thus. On that ground alone, apart from the others, the decision of the Barnsley Corporation cannot stand. It is said to be an administrative decision: but even so, the court has jurisdiction to quash it. Certiorari would lie to quash not only judicial decisions, but B
also administrative decisions.

Then Mr. Howard, on behalf of the corporation, said that these two matters (which I have mentioned)—the presence of the market manager and the excessive penalty—were not mentioned in the grounds on which Mr. Hook applied for certiorari to the Divisional Court. That is correct. But I think he should still be able to raise them. It must be remembered C
that, in applications for certiorari, the applicant knows very little of what has happened behind the scenes. He only knows that a decision has been taken which is adverse to him, and he complains of it. His statement of grounds (filed under R.S.C., Ord. 53, r. 1 (2)) should not be treated as rigidly as a pleading in an ordinary civil action. If the Divisional Court give leave (as it did here) the practice is for the respondent to put on affidavits the full facts as known to them. The matter is then considered D
at large upon the affidavits. If there then appear to be other grounds on which certiorari may be granted, the court can inquire into them without being bound by the grounds stated in the original statement. The Divisional Court will always look into the substance of the matter. So here. On the case as it has developed in this court it seems to me that the Barnsley Corporation, in all good faith but erroneously, have taken away E
this man's licence to trade without justification and without having that due inquiry which the law requires.

I think the appeal should be allowed and certiorari go to quash their decision.

SCARMAN L.J. Mr. Hook asks the court to bring up and quash a decision by the Barnsley Corporation given on October 18, 1974, whereby, F
as is conceded, they in effect cancelled his opportunity of trading in the Barnsley market.

This is a serious matter, because what has been done is to revoke an existing licence, a licence which enabled its holder to earn his living. The late Professor S. A. de Smith, in *Judicial Review of Administrative Action*, 3rd ed. (1973), p. 197 described very well the gravity of such a step. He G
said:

> "Non-renewal of an existing licence is usually a more serious matter than refusal to grant a licence in the first place. Unless the licensee has already been given to understand when he was granted the licence that renewal is not to be expected, non-renewal may seriously upset his plans, cause him economic loss and perhaps cast a slur on his H
> reputation. It may therefore be right to imply a duty to hear before a decision not to renew when there is a legitimate expectation of renewal, even though no such duty is implied in the making of the original decision to grant or refuse the licence."

The author is there dealing with non-renewal, but everything that he says about non-renewal applies with even greater force to revocation.

The first question which the court has to decide is whether certiorari

A will lie in the circumstances of this case at all. The Divisional Court,
without the full information we now have, expressed the view that
certiorari would not lie because, as they saw it upon the material before
them, the decision of which Mr. Hook complains was a purely administra-
tive decision. I would have thought that there was some difficulty in
maintaining that view of the character of the decision once Mr. Howard,
for Mr. Hook, conceded, as he did before the Divisional Court, that this
B was a case where it was necessary to determine whether the rules of
natural justice had been adhered to. Like Lord Denning M.R., I think
the concession by Mr. Howard was correctly made, but I do not think it
would be correct to decide the question of jurisdiction merely upon the
concession of counsel arguendo.

Certiorari may issue in the circumstances which were indicated many
C many years ago in the well known judgment of Atkin L.J. in *Rex* v.
*Electricity Commissioners, Ex parte London Electricity Joint Committee
Co.* (*1920*) *Ltd.* [1924] 1 K.B. 171. In the course of his judgment,
Atkin L.J. said, at p. 205:

> "Wherever any body of persons having legal authority to determine
> questions affecting the rights of subjects, and having the duty to act
> judicially, act in excess of their legal authority they are subject to the
> D controlling jurisdiction of the King's Bench Division . . ."

The first question to consider is whether the Barnsley Corporation, in
its administration of this market, is to be considered a body of persons
having legal authority to determine questions affecting the rights of subjects.
Historically, going right back to the beginning of the history of the preroga-
E tive writs of certiorari and prohibition, they were the writs that enabled
the King's justices to control the actions of local authorities. Of course,
in those days, almost invariably, the justices of the peace were the local
authorities charged with administrative as well as judicial duties. There
are, therefore, good, respectable historical antecedents for expecting a local
authority to be a body of persons amenable to control by orders of
certiorari and prohibition. But one has to see whether in the instant case
F the corporation was a body of persons having legal authority to decide
questions affecting the rights of subjects.

Lord Denning M.R. has already pointed out that when one is con-
sidering, as one is here, a market situation, the public have by common law
the right to go to market and there to buy and sell. That right remains
part of the law of England, but is now subject to considerable statutory
G regulation. In the instant case the statutes regulating the conduct of this
market are the private Act, the Barnsley Corporation Act 1969, and
sections 55 to 61 of the Food and Drugs Act 1955. Byelaws have been
made under the private Act, and indeed the Food and Drugs Act contains
enabling provisions which would support the byelaws if for any reason
they might appear to be ultra vires the private Act.

I can take quite shortly what the resulting situation is. The public
H retain their right of going to this market, but the conduct of the market
is regulated by the byelaws issued by the Barnsley Corporation. A trader,
or a member of the public, can only acquire effectively the opportunity
to trade in this market if he can obtain a licence, which no doubt as
between him and the corporation is contractual, to use the facilities or
equipment for trading that are under the Act provided by the corporation
in the market. Although his rights are to that extent contractual, neverthe-
less in granting or withholding them the local authority has the discretion

granted by its private Act of Parliament, and plainly the discretion is a discretion to regulate the exercise of the public's common law right to buy and sell in the market.

Although, therefore, there is a contractual element in this case, there is also an element of public law, viz., the enjoyment of rights conferred upon the subject by the common law. I think, therefore, upon analysis, it is clear that the Barnsley Corporation in its conduct of this market is a body having legal authority to determine questions affecting the rights of subjects. I think also it must follow that it is under a duty to act, in the broadest sense of the term, judicially, because, although the end product of a negotiation between the corporation and a would-be trader is a contractual licence, that licence is available in accordance with the discretion conferred by a statute which regulates a common law right.

I therefore disagree with the view expressed by the Divisional Court that the decision taken here to revoke Mr. Hook's licence was a purely administrative matter. I think it was the exercise of a discretion by a local authority charged with the regulation of common law rights and a discretion which had to be exercised in a manner judicial. Therefore, and for those reasons, I think Mr. Howard was correct to concede before the Divisional Court that we are here dealing with a decision where the local authority was under a duty to act with natural justice.

In my judgment, the local authority was in breach of one rule of natural justice which is so old that it can be put in the Latin language: nemo debet esse judex in causa propria. Before I come to consider that aspect of the matter, it is only fair to Mr. Howard's admirable and tenacious argument to consider his preliminary point that really this point was never taken by Mr. Hook, the applicant. It is true that the point does not appear in the statement of his case which he was under a duty, pursuant to the Rules of the Supreme Court, to lodge when he applied for leave to seek his order. Like Lord Denning M.R., I think it not uncommon that at that stage of the proceedings the applicant is in a state of only partial knowledge as to the matters affecting his rights. He knows what has happened to him and what has been done in his presence, but he knows nothing else. At that stage he does the best that he can with his advisers in putting his material into his statement of case, but, of course, if that material is enough to persuade the Divisional Court to grant leave, then there comes a duty upon the respondent to file evidence, if need be, and in filing evidence to fill up the gaps in the knowledge of the court, bearing in mind that the court is exercising a supervisory jurisdiction: an ancient jurisdiction by which the King's judges have for centuries controlled local authorities when acting judicially.

When the authority came to file its evidence, then it seems to me it did appear that Mr. Fretwell, the market manager, and the chairman of the committee had participated, first, in the decision to revoke the licence; secondly, in the first appeal, which was conducted a week later on October 24; and, lastly, in the final appeal, which was conducted on October 30. There can be no doubt upon the affidavit of Mr. Fretwell himself that he and the chairman were parties to the original decision to revoke the licence. It seems to me an inescapable inference from the way in which Mr. Fretwell has described what was then done. There can be no doubt that the two of them were both members of the first appeal committee. There can be no doubt that one of them, namely, the chairman, was a party to the final appeal, and it is clear from the evidence that, whether or not he participated in the decision, Mr. Fretwell, the market manager, was present with the committee throughout the discussion, hearing, and determination of the final appeal.

This point was not argued, we have been told, before the Divisional Court, but it arises without the need of any further supplementation on the evidence of Mr. Fretwell and Mr. Nettleton, the chairman, and it is covered by the general terms of the notice of appeal, although the specific point is not taken. Mr. Howard has not asked for an adjournment to deal with the point, and I do not think that an adjournment could possibly help him, since he has accepted that the evidence of Mr. Fretwell indicates plainly his presence throughout, his participation in the first appeal, and the participation of the chairman throughout. Even if there was room for ambiguity as to whether it was the chairman who was consulted by Mr. Fretwell before the first decision, there can be no ambiguity or doubt as to his presence at the two appeals. Forensically I have some sympathy with Mr. Howard in having to deal with this point when I am sure that he did not expect it, but he has dealt with it vigorously and effectively, and we have, I am satisfied, the material upon which to consider it.

Mr. Howard relied on *Reg.* v. *Gaming Board for Great Britain, Ex parte Benaim and Khaida* [1970] 2 Q.B. 417, to support the proposition, with which I agree, that the requirements of natural justice have to be considered always in the particular circumstances of the case. I think it is certainly possible to envisage cases in which the presence of somebody like Mr. Fretwell at a hearing might not constitute a breach of natural justice. One has to see what it is that is being considered and what is the subject matter for decision.

The point, if I may say so, with respect, was admirably made by Lord Denning M.R. in *Benaim's* case, at pp. 430–431. There, having quoted the well known words of Lord Parker C.J. in *In re H. K. (An Infant)* [1967] 2 Q.B. 617, 630, Lord Denning M.R. made this comment:

> "Those words seem to me to apply to the Gaming Board. The statute says in terms that in determining whether to grant a certificate, the board 'shall have regard only' to the matters specified. It follows, I think, that the board have a duty to act fairly . . . But I do not think that they need quote chapter and verse against him as if they were dismissing him from an office, as in *Ridge* v. *Baldwin* [1964] A.C. 40; or depriving him of his property, as in *Cooper* v. *Wandsworth Board of Works* (1863) 14 C.B.N.S. 180. After all, they are not charging him with doing anything wrong. They are simply inquiring as to his capability and diligence and are having regard to his character, reputation and financial standing."

That being the nature of the inquiry in *Benaim's* case, it is not surprising that the court was able to reach the conclusion that the Gaming Board was under no duty to disclose its sources of information. In the present case the corporation was considering something very like dismissing a man from his office, very like depriving him of his property, and they were charging him with doing something wrong. It was the revocation of a licence because of misconduct that they had under consideration—not merely the man's fitness or capacity for the grant of a licence. There was, therefore, a situation here in which (using the terms broadly) Mr. Hook was on trial, and on trial for his livelihood. There was a complainant, the market manager. The market manager had a professional interest in the matter since he was concerned to protect his employees, or the employees for whom he was responsible, from abuse and

misconduct by stallholders in the market. Mr. Fretwell was a prosecutor, A
a complainant; Mr. Hook was a man, albeit in an administrative field, who was on trial not for his life but for his livelihood.

If ever there was a case in which it was imperative that the complainant or the prosecutor should not participate in the adjudication, I should have thought it was this one; and that is why I would distinguish it from *Benaim's* case.

There is respectable authority, to which Lord Denning M.R. has B
already referred, which shows that in an appropriate case it is important that the complainant or prosecutor should not participate in a decision or in an appeal from a decision, and should not even appear to participate. The Master of the Rolls has referred to the two cases, and I need not go back to them. In the first of them, *Reg.* v. *London County Council, Ex parte Akkersdyk* [1892] 1 Q.B. 190, the members of the committee, whose C
presence vitiated the decision of that committee, took no part in the final voting; but they were there and had participated in the first decision from which the appeal was being taken.

It all depends, of course, on the nature of the case. In that case it was whether or not a licence should be granted for music and dancing. It was a " renewal " case. In the present case it is whether or not a licence to trade should be revoked. I would have thought, therefore, that this case D
is a more serious one than the *L.C.C.* case, and that, if indeed it was being considered whether or not Mr. Fretwell had been right to revoke Mr. Hook's licence (as it was), then most certainly the rule of nemo debet esse judex in causa propria should have been rigorously observed throughout the whole appellate process.

I place my judgment on that ground and on that ground alone, and it E
is for that reason I agree that this appeal should be allowed.

SIR JOHN PENNYCUICK. I agree that this appeal should be allowed. As we are differing from the Divisional Court and in deference to the argument of counsel, I will state summarily my own reasons for this decision. I will read again the letter dated October 18, 1974, from the market manager to Mr. Hook: F

> " Further to your interview on Friday October 18, 1974. In confirmation of that interview I have to give you notice that you are no longer considered to be a suitable tenant of this authority. The stalls and pitch at present reserved for you each market day will cease to be available for your use after Wednesday next the 23rd instant. Please arrange to clear stock from your cupboards by this date." G

The narrow question raised by that notice is whether it was effective to determine Mr. Hook's contractual licence to occupy his particular stall. That narrow question, however, is part of a wider question, namely, whether the corporation, in exercise of its powers of administering the market, could indirectly deprive Mr. Hook of his common law right to trade in the market and thereby indirectly deprive him of his livelihood. H

The narrow question I think turns upon the ordinary principles of contract in relation to the use of land. The wider question imports a right to a hearing in accordance with the requirements of natural justice and admits the remedy of certiorari. The corporation's power is not, I think, a merely administrative power.

However one poses the question, I would answer it in the negative. It is clear that the council could not determine Mr. Hock's licence on

A five days' notice, and a fortiori could not exclude him from the market, except upon some good cause, and that, I think, was accepted by Mr. Howard. There is no express provision in the Barnsley Corporation Act 1969 which would warrant this step.

Is there then any good cause? If the court is satisfied that the council has acted without good cause, the court must, I think, be bound to interfere. It seems to me that the isolated and trivial incident at the end of a
B working day is manifestly not a good cause justifying the disproportionately drastic step of depriving Mr. Hook of his licence, and indirectly of his livelihood. I would base my judgment in part upon that ground.

I agree with what has been said by Lord Denning M.R. and Scarman L.J. with regard to the failure of the committee of the corporation to comply with the rules of natural justice, and I would also base my
C judgment in part upon that ground. I will not go over this part of the case again. I would then allow this appeal.

Appeal allowed with costs in Court of Appeal but not in Divisional Court.

Solicitors: *White and Leonard for Morrish & Co., Leeds; D. P. Clephan,*
D *Barnsley.*

M. M. H.

E

[COURT OF APPEAL]

* LONDON & HARROGATE SECURITIES LTD. *v.* PITTS

[1974 L. No. 3574]

F 1976 July 8 — Megaw, Browne and Geoffrey Lane L.JJ.

Moneylender—Criminal offence—Implication of carrying on banking business—Whether loan recoverable in civil proceedings—Moneylenders Act 1927 (17 & 18 *Geo.* 5, *c.* 21), *s.* 4 (3) [1]
Moneylender — Memorandum — Non-compliance with statutory requirements—Omission of "per annum" after rate of interest —Whether agreement enforceable—"Per cent."—Meaning—
G *Moneylenders Act* 1927, *s.* 6 (2)

The plaintiffs, licensed moneylenders, lent £16,500 to the first defendant. The sum was to be repaid at the end of two months. The memorandum of agreement stated: "Interest shall be calculated at the true rate of 23 per cent. . . .," without adding "per annum." During the course of the loan transaction the plaintiffs in a letter heading and on a cheque
H referred to themselves as "merchant bankers" when, at that time, they did not have that status. The first defendant did not repay the loan, and the plaintiffs brought an action against him for repayment with the agreed interest. The first defendant by way of defence contended that by virtue of the plaintiffs' breach of section 4 (3) of the Moneylenders Act 1927 by their reference to being "merchant bankers" the

[1] Moneylenders Act 1927, s. 4 (3): see post, pp. 1066H–1067A.
S. 6 (2): see post, p. 1069G.

transaction was tainted with illegality and the plaintiffs were debarred from recovering, and that by virtue of the omission from the memorandum of the words "per annum" section 6 (2) of the Act rendered the contract invalid. Mocatta J. rejected those defences and gave judgment for the plaintiffs.

On appeal: —

Held, dismissing the appeal, (1) that section 4 (3) of the Act of 1927 was concerned only with criminal liability and did not provide a defence in a civil action for repayment of a loan (post, pp. 1069B, C, 1072C, E).

Dictum of Atkin L.J. in *Phillips* v. *Britannia Hygienic Laundry Co. Ltd.* [1923] 2 K.B. 832, 840–841, C.A. applied.

(2) That in the ordinary use of words "per cent.," expressed without any further indication, meant "per cent. per annum"; that there was nothing in the memorandum of agreement in the present case which could reasonably lead to any other meaning; and that, accordingly, although the loan was for a period of two months only the omission of "per annum" did not affect the meaning of the contract or lead to any ambiguity and did not render the contract invalid (post, pp. 1070D–F, G, H, 1072D, E).

Decision of Mocatta J. [1976] 1 W.L.R. 264; [1974] 1 All E.R. 184 affirmed.

The following cases are referred to in the judgment of Megaw L.J.:

McCall v. *Abelesz* [1976] Q.B. 585; [1976] 2 W.L.R. 151; [1976] 1 All E.R. 727, C.A.

Phillips v. *Britannia Hygienic Laundry Co. Ltd.* [1923] 2 K.B. 832, C.A.

Victorian Daylesford Syndicate Ltd. v. *Dott* [1905] 2 Ch. 624; sub nom. *Bonnard* v. *Dott* [1906] 1 Ch. 740, C.A.

The following additional cases were cited in argument:

Askinex Ltd. v. *Green* [1969] 1 Q.B. 272; [1967] 2 W.L.R. 820; [1967] 1 All E.R. 65, C.A.

Direct Loans Ltd. v. *Cracknell*, The Times, April 18, 1975.

Parkfield Trust Ltd. v. *Curtis* [1934] 1 K.B. 685, C.A.

Robinson's Settlement, In re, Gant v. *Hobbs* [1912] 1 Ch. 717, C.A.

APPEAL from Mocatta J.

The plaintiffs, London & Harrogate Securities Ltd., licensed money-lenders, claimed against the first defendant, Clive Berry Pitts, repayment of £16,500 being money lent by them to him on May 21, 1974, and repayable on July 21, 1974, under an agreement in writing made between the plaintiffs and the first defendant dated May 21, 1974, and for payment of interest thereon at the agreed rate of 23 per cent. per annum until repayment or judgment (a total of £17,903·63 at the date of writ). They further alleged that on May 20, 1974, the second defendant, Malcolm Brookes, solicitor, in consideration of their making the loan to the first defendant agreed in writing to hold to their order the deeds of The Old Ropery, Ropery Road, Hartlepool, Co. Durham, until completion of the sale thereof and immediately thereon to pay to them the sum of £16,500 together with all such interest as had accrued thereon in accordance with the loan agreement. The sale of the property had not been completed and, by letter dated October 1, 1974, they, by their solicitors, had demanded the delivery up of the deeds to them by the second defendant. The second defendant had refused to deliver up the deeds and still detained them. The plaintiffs claimed against the second defendant an order requiring him to deliver up the deeds to them, alternatively, £17,903·63 together with interest at the

A rate of 23 per cent. per annum on the sum of £16,500 until payment or judgment.

By way of defence, the first defendant admitted the loan but denied that it was recoverable against him by the plaintiffs, on the grounds (i) that contrary to the provisions of section 6 of the Moneylenders Act 1900 and section 4 (3) of the Moneylenders Act 1927 the plaintiffs had at all material times held themselves out to the world at large and the first
B defendant in particular as a merchant bank, (ii), further and alternatively, that the memorandum of agreement of May 21, 1974, failed to comply with section 6 of the Act of 1927 in that it did not express the rate of interest on the loan in terms of a rate per cent. per annum, or the rate per cent. per annum represented by the interest charged as calculated in accordance with the provisions of Schedule 1 to the Act. The second
C defendant admitted the undertaking alleged, but contended that it had been given as security for the loan to the first defendant and thus by virtue of the matters referred to was unenforceable; he denied that he was under any other liability in respect of the loan.

Mocatta J. on October 23, 1975, rejected the defendants' grounds of defence and gave judgment for the plaintiffs, ordering that they recover against the first defendant £21,875·38, that The Old Ropery be sold and
D that the first defendant pay the plaintiffs' costs, such costs to be added to the charge.

The defendants appealed, contending that the judge had misdirected himself in law in holding that the admitted breach by the plaintiffs of section 4 (3) of the Act of 1927 did not render the contract between the plaintiffs and the first defendant illegal and unenforceable; that the plain-
E tiffs had complied with the requirements of section 6 (2) of the Act; and in the alternative that the omission of the words "per annum" in the plaintiffs' memorandum of agreement was a trivial error which he could disregard.

R. A. Payne for the appellant defendants, Clive Berry Pitts and Malcolm Brookes.

F *J. R. T. Rylance* for the respondent plaintiffs, London & Harrogate Securities Ltd.

MEGAW L.J. This is an appeal from the judgment of Mocatta J. given in the Commercial Court on October 23, 1975. The relevant facts, which sensibly were agreed in the Commercial Court between the parties in an
G agreed statement of facts, are clearly set out in that judgment.

Mr. Pitts, who is the first defendant in the action and the appellant in this court, is a property developer. The company of which he was a director and a majority shareholder was known as Freehold & Leasehold Securities Ltd. That company owned a property called The Old Ropery, in Hartlepool. The company was in process of selling that property, which was subject to a mortgage held by a bank. The contract for sale between
H Freehold & Leasehold Securities Ltd. and the potential buyer had been exchanged. The company, or Mr. Pitts, desired to obtain a loan of money for the purpose of enabling that transaction of sale of the property to be carried through. The company was minded, having bought the property under the intended contract, to resell it, at what no doubt would have been a substantial profit. Unfortunately, before that sale by Freehold & Leasehold Securities Ltd. was completed the potential purchaser went into liquidation, and so that intended sale fell through.

Mr. Pitts, for the purpose of financing those arrangements, took a con- A
veyance from his company, Freehold & Leasehold Securities Ltd., to
himself. He executed a trust deed under which he declared that he was
holding that property on trust for the company Freehold & Leasehold
Securities Ltd. At the same time, Mr. Pitts' solicitor, Mr. Brookes, who
is the second defendant in the action, gave an undertaking to the solicitors
for the plaintiffs, London & Harrogate Securities Ltd., that he would hold
the deeds of the property The Old Ropery to the order of the plaintiffs' B
solicitors as security for the money which it was intended should be
advanced by London & Harrogate Securities Ltd. to Mr. Pitts for the
purpose of this transaction. So, after discussions, or negotiations, a loan
was made by London & Harrogate Securities Ltd. to Mr. Pitts. The total
amount of that loan was £16,500. It was to be paid by way of a cheque
for £3,500 from the plaintiffs to the bank which was concerned in the C
mortgage of the property, to pay off that bank's mortgage; the balance of
the £16,500 to be lent was to be available to Mr. Pitts to draw on, having
been placed to his credit in an account. London & Harrogate Securities
Ltd. are licensed moneylenders.

The memorandum of agreement for the loan was dated May 21, 1974,
being the date on which the loan was made. It showed that the amount
to be advanced was to be £16,500, described as "the principal sum." That D
sum was to be advanced on May 21, 1974, provided certain conditions had
been complied with, which in the event were complied with. Clause 3
provided: "Subject as provided herein the borrower"—that is, Mr. Pitts
—"shall repay the principal sum or the balance outstanding thereof on
the expiry of two months from the date hereof"—two months from
May 21, 1974. Then clause 4 begins with these words: E

> "Interest shall be calculated at the true rate of 23 per cent. on the
> balance of the principal sum from time to time outstanding such
> interest to accrue from day to day to be paid on the day specified in
> clause 3 hereof provided . . ."

and I need not trouble about the proviso.

The loan having been made, it was not repaid at the end of two months, F
or at all, nor was any payment made to the plaintiffs in respect thereof.
The plaintiffs brought their action claiming the repayment of the loan and
interest.

The defence, so far as is now relevant, related to two points, both
depending on the provisions of the Moneylenders Act 1927. The first
issue which the judge had to decide as it was raised by way of defence was
this: that (as was set out in the agreed facts) the plaintiffs had, in two G
documents which came into being on or after May 21, 1974, included a
reference to themselves as "Merchant Bankers." One of those documents
was the cheque for £3,500 made payable to the bank, and the other was
a letter to Mr. Brookes' firm dated May 23. The defendants in their
defence relied on section 4 of the Act of 1927. Section 4 (3) provides:

> "If a moneylender, for the purposes of his business as such, issues or H
> publishes, or causes to be issued or published, any advertisement,
> circular or document of any kind whatsoever containing expressions
> which might reasonably be held to imply that he carries on banking
> business, he shall on summary conviction be liable to a fine not
> exceeding £100, and on a second or subsequent conviction, in lieu of
> or in addition to such a fine as aforesaid, to imprisonment for a
> term not exceeding three months, or, in the case of a second or

A subsequent conviction of an offender being a company, to a fine not
exceeding £500."

As I say, in the two documents to which I have referred, which are
mentioned in the agreed statement of facts, the plaintiffs had applied
to themselves the phrase "Merchant Bankers." They were not at the
time, as I understand it, a bank within the now statutory provisions,
B though I think that I am right in saying that they have subsequently been
given that status. The defendant's contention was that the provisions of
section 4 (3), while they expressly make what was done by the plaintiffs
a criminal offence rendering them liable to punishment in the criminal
courts, also, by necessary implication, having regard to the purpose of the
Act, the public policy of the Act and the true construction of the Act,
involve that an infringement of that subsection gave the defendant civil
C rights, rights in civil proceedings: so that the transaction of the loan
to him was "tainted with illegality" (as it was put by counsel for the
defendant) and, being tainted with illegality, the defendant in this action
was entitled to say "I am not under any obligation in law to repay to
you any part of the principal of the loan or any interest."

Mr. Payne, who has appeared on behalf of the defendant, made it clear
D at the outset of his submissions that (as he put it) there were no merits in
the appeal, but he said that merits were irrelevant. Having regard to the
policy of the legislature in relation to moneylenders as shown in this Act
and an earlier Act, even though there was no suggestion that the defendant
Mr. Pitts had been in any way led or induced into entering into this contract
by virtue of any reference to "Merchant Bankers," nevertheless he was
entitled to repudiate any liability.

E That argument, adduced before Mocatta J., was rejected by him.
Mocatta J. has in his judgment set out, if I may respectfully say so, very
clearly, fully and carefully the relevant statutory provisions and the relevant
considerations, and if it had not been for the attractive argument presented
by Mr. Payne in this court I would have been content to say that I agreed
entirely with everything which Mocatta J. has said on that issue in his
reasoning and in his conclusion. However, having regard to the attractive
F argument which Mr. Payne has presented, I think that it is right that I
should say a little more than merely that Mocatta J. in my view was right
in every word that he said on that issue, especially since the argument as
presented to us by Mr. Payne went a little further than the argument which
he presented to Mocatta J. That is because meanwhile, as a result of his
diligent researches, he has found a further authority which he submits is
G helpful to him and which was not cited to Mocatta J.

That authority is *Victorian Daylesford Syndicate Ltd.* v. *Dott* [1905]
2 Ch. 624, a decision of Buckley J. That decision was approved by this
court under the title *Bonnard* v. *Dott* [1906] 1 Ch. 740. In the *Victorian
Daylesford Syndicate* case the plaintiffs, who had lent money, were not
registered moneylenders under the provisions of the then prevailing relevant
statute, the Moneylenders Act 1900, and in particular section 2 (1) (*c*)
H thereof. Buckley J. in his judgment, which was specifically approved by
this court, expressed the view that the policy of the Moneylenders Act
1900 was for the protection of the public, and said, at p. 630:

> "If I arrive at the conclusion that one of the objects is the protection of the public, then the act is impliedly prohibited by the statute, and is illegal."

That that was the policy of the Act was, as I say, affirmed by this court.

However, I do not think, with great respect to Mr. Payne, that the citation of that authority makes any difference, or would have made any difference to Mocatta J.'s conclusion had it been cited to him. Mocatta J. made it clear that he accepted, even though the authority in that regard was somewhat scanty, that the provisions of section 1 of the Moneylenders Act 1927, the applicable Act in this case, are such that non-compliance with the provisions of that section would, in the view of the law, result in the loan by the moneylenders not being recoverable.

Section 1 of the Act of 1927 is, as Mr. Payne submits, in substance the same, though there are many differences of detail in the provisions, as section 2 of the Act of 1900. Mocatta J. accepted that, but nevertheless he was not prepared to accept that it followed from that, or from any of the other provisions of the Act, or from any principle of statutory construction, that section 4 (3) of the Act of 1927 was similarly to be construed as avoiding a contract which was made where it was shown that there had been an infringement by the moneylenders, the plaintiffs, resulting in the possibility of criminal proceedings being taken against them.

In my judgment the view which Mocatta J. took is right. In particular, it is to my mind clear that section 4 (3) of the Act of 1927, in accordance with the ordinary principles applied in such a case, is not to be treated as giving rise to this additional right—providing a defence in a civil action for the repayment of the loan—when one finds that in the following section of the Act of 1927, section 5, which is dealing with a subject matter comparable to that of section 4, namely, advertising by moneylenders, there is an express provision, by virtue of section 5 (6), that the "transaction" shall be illegal, so that the contract is to be treated in the civil courts as an illegal contract. Section 5 (5) provides for criminal responsibility if the provisions of that section relating to restrictions on moneylending advertisements are infringed. Section 5 (6) provides:

> "Where it is shown that a moneylending transaction was brought about by a contravention of any of the provisions of this section, the transaction shall, notwithstanding that the moneylender was duly licensed under this Act, be illegal, unless the moneylender proves that the contravention occurred without his consent or connivance."

Section 4, on the other hand, while providing by subsection (3) for the criminal sanction, contains no provision whatsoever corresponding to that express provision in section 5 (6).

In my judgment, that is conclusive. Mocatta J. was right in saying that the view which the courts had taken in relation to section 1 was taken because of the essential nature of the provisions of section 1, contrasted with the much less important subject matter of section 4 of the Act.

We were referred to various authorities relating to the general question of the effect on rights in civil proceedings, whether by way of cause of action or by way of defence, where a statute provides for a criminal sanction. I think that the position for present purposes is most clearly set out in the observations made by Atkin L.J. in *Phillips* v. *Britannia Hygienic Laundry Co. Ltd.* [1923] 2 K.B. 832, 840–841. This is a passage which was recently cited in the judgment of Ormrod L.J. in *McCall* v. *Abelesz* [1976] Q.B. 585, 595. Atkin L.J. said:

> "In my opinion, when an Act imposes a duty of commission or omission, the question whether a person aggrieved by a breach of the duty has a right of action depends on the intention of the Act. Was it intended to make the duty one which was owed to the party

> A aggrieved as well as to the state, or was it a public duty only? That depends on the construction of the Act and the circumstances in which it was made and to which it relates. One question to be considered is, Does the Act contain reference to a remedy for breach of it? Prima facie if it does that is the only remedy. But that is not conclusive. The intention as disclosed by its scope and wording must still be regarded, and it may still be that, though the statute
> B creates the duty and provides a penalty, the duty is nevertheless owed to individuals."

The prima facie view, then, is: there being here express provision for a criminal sanction, and no express provision as to any other "remedy" if the provision is infringed, it is to be presumed that there is not a civil remedy. As Atkin L.J. says, however, that is not conclusive. In relation to
C the provisions of section 1 of the Act of 1927, for reasons which no doubt are good and sufficient, those provisions do displace that prima facie presumption, but, in so far as section 4 (3) is concerned, I see no ground for saying that that prima facie presumption falls to be overridden or excluded, particularly having regard, as I say, to the provisions of the analogous and closely related section 5, where Parliament has made express provision for
D the civil "remedy."

I would add this: that, if Mr. Payne were right in his submission in relation to the consequences of section 4 (3), it would—as he frankly accepts—produce this remarkable consequence: that if, for example, a loan were made by a licensed moneylender in 1970 and at that date the moneylender had not described himself in any way in any document as a bank or a banker, but three or four years later, before the loan was repaid, he
E had in some subsequent document described himself as a bank or banker, it would thereupon become open to the person who had borrowed in 1970, and, presumably, all other prior borrowers who had not repaid, to say, "By reason of the provisions of section 4 (3) we are not under an obligation to repay our loan, even though you have only described yourself as a bank subsequent to the date when the loan was made." That is not a consequence
F which I would be prepared to accept, unless the statute made it perfectly clear that it must be so. In that respect also, I think that there is a material difference from section 1.

So much for the first issue. The second issue arises on section 6 of the Moneylenders Act 1927. Section 6 (1) provides that there shall be a note or memorandum of the loan. Subsection (2) reads:

> G "The note or memorandum aforesaid shall contain all the terms of the contract, and in particular shall show the date on which the loan is made, the amount of the principal of the loan, and, either the interest charged on the loan expressed in terms of a rate per cent. per annum, or the rate per cent. per annum represented by the interest charged as calculated in accordance with the provisions of Schedule 1 to this Act."

H

The memorandum in the present case, which I have already read, by clause 4 provided: "Interest shall be calculated at the true rate of 23 per cent. . . ." It did not say, "23 per cent. *per annum*." Mr. Payne submitted before Mocatta J., and submits again in this court, that the absence of the words "per annum" in the memorandum are fatal because, as is shown in the authorities, if there is any failure in the required memorandum to show the things which are required by that statutory provision to be shown in

the memorandum, then the consequence is that the contract is not a valid A
contract and the borrower is not obliged to repay.

The essence of Mr. Payne's argument is that in the present case the
period of the loan, as expressed in clause 3 of the memorandum, was "two
months." He says that, whatever might be the case if there had been
some different provision as to the period of the loan, since it was, as shown
by the memorandum itself, "two months" there is an ambiguity, or a
possible ambiguity, in the words "true rate of 23 per cent." While the B
words might mean 23 per cent. *per annum*, they might, alternatively, mean
a simple arithmetical calculation of 23 per cent. of the capital sum, £16,500,
without any reference to any period of time as a factor in the calculation.
The amount of interest would be payable when the capital sum was due
to be repaid: that is, at the end of two months.

Mocatta J., referring to various authorities, took the view, first, that C
there was here no such ambiguity by reason of the fact that the words
"per annum" were not included. There could be no doubt but that
"true rate of 23 per cent." meant "23 per cent. *per annum*." Mocatta J.
referred to various passages in various judgments of various judges at one
time and another in which the words "per cent." have been used without
the addition thereafter of "per annum" when it is perfectly plain to the
meanest intelligence that what was meant was "per annum." Indeed, it is D
really beyond dispute, I should have thought, that, in the ordinary common
sense use of words, unless there be something in the context to suggest that
there is a possibility of some different meaning attaching, if a rate "per
cent." is expressed without any further indication, that rate means "per
cent. per annum" just as much as if the words "per annum" were written
in. It is, of course, true that there could be a context which would indicate E
either that the percentage was to be something other than "per cent. per
annum" or that it might be so. In the absence of some context which
leads to that possibility, however, I have no doubt that "per cent." would
be taken, by any reasonable, sensible person, as being "per cent. per
annum." I do not think that in the present case the mere fact that this
loan was for a period of two months would give rise to any doubt or
ambiguity in the mind of anybody who reads the document that "interest F
shall be calculated at the true rate of 23 per cent." means "23 per cent.
per annum." Of course, for this purpose one looks at the memorandum,
and the memorandum only. One does not look at evidence of the
negotiations leading up to the making of the loan or any other extraneous
evidence. It would be wrong to take any such extraneous matter into
account in this context, however much it might be permissible to take it
into account in other contexts, in construing the terms of the memorandum. G

Putting out of my mind altogether, as Mocatta J. did, any information
or any indications that arise here from anything outside the document itself,
and simply taking this as it stands on the document itself, I take the view,
as Mocatta J. did, that there is here no ambiguity, nothing on which any
reasonable person could, in this context, have treated the words "true rate
of 23 per cent." as meaning other than "true rate of 23 per cent. per H
annum." That being so, the law does not result in the conclusion that the
mere omission of the words "per annum," since their inclusion would not
have altered the meaning of the document one whit, is relevant so as to
lead to the consequence that the borrower is entitled to escape from liability
to repay.

Again, had it not been for Mr. Payne's attractive argument I would
have been fully content to say that I entirely agreed with the conclusion

A expressed by Mocatta J. on that aspect of the case and with his reasons
for it. True, Mocatta J. went on to say that if he were wrong as to the
meaning of the words "23 per cent." in this context he would have arrived
at the same result in relation to the case by reason of what was referred to
as the doctrine of "triviality," in respect of which various authorities were
referred to. We did not find it necessary to consider that matter or to
B invite Mr. Payne to make submissions about it, since he frankly and pro-
perly conceded that, if we took the view which I have expressed in this
judgment as being my view as to the meaning of the words as they stand,
the doctrine of triviality, even if Mocatta J. was wrong about it, could not
avail him. Indeed, really in substance I think it comes to this: that if
there were any true doubt as to the meaning of the words "rate of 23
per cent." in the memorandum, so that a possible meaning were "23 per
C cent. on the principal payable at the end of two months" and not "23
per cent. per annum," then it would be very difficult to say that such an
ambiguity came within the doctrine of triviality. Because, however, of the
view which I have formed in relation to the earlier part of Mocatta J.'s
reasons on this part of the case, that matter does not arise.

I should add that a further issue was raised before Mocatta J. on
D behalf of the plaintiffs which would become relevant, as I understand it,
only if the defendant were successful on either of the two defences which
I have already discussed. Mocatta J., while setting out at the end of his
judgment what that issue was, did not find it necessary to go into it or to
express any conclusion upon it. The same applies in this court, and in
the circumstances we have not invited argument on that issue.

I would dismiss the appeal.

E

BROWNE L.J. I agree that this appeal should be dismissed, for the reasons given by Megaw L.J. I only add a few words in tribute to the very attractive arguments of Mr. Payne.

As to the first point, that is, the point based on section 4 (3) of the Act
of 1927, Mr. Payne relied on the authorities, to which Megaw L.J. has
F referred, decided on section 2 (1) (*c*) of the Moneylenders Act 1900. He
relied on those authorities in support of his argument that the loan agree-
ment with which we are concerned in this case was made unenforceable
by section 4 (3).

The wording of section 2 (1) (*c*) of the Act of 1900 is very different
from the wording of section 4 (3) of the Act of 1927. That provision of
the Act of 1900 is in these words:

G

> "A moneylender as defined by this Act . . . (*c*) shall not enter into any agreement in the course of his business as a moneylender with respect to the advance and repayment of money, or take any security for money in the course of his business as a moneylender, otherwise than in his registered name."

H So in terms that subsection is saying that a moneylender shall not enter
into any agreement under which he does certain things.

Megaw L.J. has already read section 4 (3) of the Act of 1927, and I need not read it again. It contains no reference to entering into any agreement; still less does it contain anything corresponding to section 5 (6) of the Act of 1927, which is limited to moneylending transactions "brought about by a contravention" of the provisions of that section relating to advertisement.

As Megaw L.J. has said, if the argument of Mr. Payne is right it seems A
that if a moneylender issued any document which contravened section 4 (3)
any loan agreement entered into by him before or after that publication
would be unenforceable. In my judgment, the authorities under section
2 (1) (*c*) of the Act of 1900 have no application to section 4 (3) of the
Act of 1927.

Like Megaw L.J., I think that the conclusive argument in this case is
the contrast between section 4 of the Act of 1927, which provides only B
for a criminal sanction, and other sections of the Act which provide
expressly for a civil sanction. Megaw L.J. has already referred to section
5 (5) and (6). By section 6 (1) it is provided that no contract for the
repayment of money and no security shall be enforceable unless the pro-
visions of that section as to a note or memorandum are complied with.
So that section is giving a civil sanction to the observance of its require- C
ments. So also is section 7, which I need not read in detail. That pro-
vides that certain contracts shall be illegal. Again, section 8 (3) provides
that a contract shall not be illegal but shall not be enforceable so long as
the moneylender is in default under that section.

In my judgment, the contrast between those provisions makes it quite
impossible to say that the effect of section 4 (3) is to make the loan
agreement in this case unenforceable in civil proceedings. D

So far as the second point is concerned—that is, the point under
section 6 (2)—I confess that my mind is not so clear on that as Mocatta J.'s
mind was and as Megaw L.J.'s mind is. I did in fact feel some doubt
in the course of the argument. Having heard the case out and having
read again Mocatta J.'s judgment and having heard Megaw L.J.'s judgment,
however, I have come clearly to the conclusion that this point also fails, E
for the reasons given by Mocatta J. and by Megaw L.J.

Accordingly, I agree that the appeal must be dismissed.

GEOFFREY LANE L.J. I also agree.

Appeal dismissed with costs against first defendant. F

Leave to respondents to file cross-notice out of time; no order as to costs thereof.

Leave to appeal refused.

Solicitors: *Malcolm Brookes & Co.; Coward Chance.* G

M. G.

H

A

[CHANCERY DIVISION]

* SANSOM AND ANOTHER *v.* PEAY (INSPECTOR OF TAXES)

B 1976 June 30 — Brightman J.

Revenue—Capital gains tax—Settled property—Trust fund of discretionary trust used to acquire dwelling house—Beneficiary occupying house as main residence with trustees' consent—Gain arising on sale of house—Whether beneficiary "entitled to occupy" house under terms of settlement—Whether gain exempted from tax—Finance Act 1965 (c. 25), *s.* 29 (9)

C In 1960 £12,000 was settled on trustees upon discretionary trusts for the benefit of the settlor's son and family. In 1966 the trustees, exercising a power conferred on them in the settlement, used trust funds to purchase a house at a cost of £12,566 for the settlor's son to live in. With his family, he lived in the house as a main residence until 1971 when it was disposed of by a deed of exchange. The notional gain that arose on the disposal was £5,450. On appeal by the trustees against
D an assessment to capital gains tax in respect of the disposal of the house, the general commissioners held that the settlor's son and family were not persons who under the settlement were "entitled to occupy" the house and that accordingly the disposal did not fall within the exemption from capital gains tax contained in section 29 (9) of the Finance Act 1965.[1]

On appeal by the trustees:—

Held, allowing the appeal, that although the terms of the
E settlement did not give the beneficiaries a right to occupy the house, the situation was that at the time of the "disposal" of the property they were persons who had been "entitled to occupy" it by consent of the trustees, and that as the purpose of the section was to exempt the gain arising on the sale of a person's home from capital gains tax, the terms of section 29 (9) had been satisfied and the gain accruing to the trustees was exempt (post, p. 1077D–F).

F

The following case is referred to in the judgment:

Muir v. *Muir* [1943] A.C. 468, H.L.(Sc.).

The following additional cases were cited in argument:

Petre's Settlement Trusts, In re [1910] 1 Ch. 290.

G *Truell* v. *Tysson* (1856) 21 Beav. 437.

CASE STATED by the Commissioners for the General Purposes of the Income Tax.

In 1960, Mrs. Catherine Ridge settled £12,000 on Kenneth Howard Sansom and Anthony Bridge, as trustees, on discretionary trusts for the benefit of Ronald Charles Malby and his family. In 1966, the trustees
H purchased a freehold house in Sussex for £12,566 for occupation by the settlor's son and his family. When the house was disposed of in 1971, its value was £20,000 and after deduction of allowable expenses a notional gain of £5,450 accrued. The general commissioners dismissed an appeal

[Reported by MRS. HARRIET DUTTON, Barrister-at-Law]

[1] Finance Act 1965, s. 29 (9): see post, p. 1075F–G.

against an assessment to capital gains tax made on the trustees for the A year 1971–72 in the sum of £5,613 (of which £5,450 related to the notional gain on the disposal of the property) holding that the disposal of the house did not fall within the exemption from capital gains tax contained in section 29 (9) of the Finance Act 1965. The trustees appealed.

The facts are stated in the judgment.

E. F. R. Whitehead for the trustees. B
Peter Gibson for the Crown.

BRIGHTMAN J. This is an appeal from the general commissioners against an assessment to capital gains tax. The gain arose upon the disposal of a dwelling house which was the subject matter of a discretionary trust settlement. Put shortly, the question before me is whether C that gain is exempt from tax pursuant to section 29 (9) of the Finance Act 1965. The subsection exempts a gain from tax where it results from the sale of a dwelling house which is the only or main residence of a person or persons entitled to occupy it under the terms of a settlement.

The settlement was made on January 15, 1960. The settlor was Mrs. Catherine Ridge, and the settlement comprised a sum of money. It was in the usual form of a discretionary trust settlement. The discretionary D beneficiaries were the settlor's son, Mr. Ronald Malby, his wife, Mrs. Stella Malby, his sons Donald and David, who were at that time infants; and future children and remoter issue of Mr. Ronald Malby. Subject to a five-year accumulation period, the trust fund was settled in trust to pay or apply the income thereof at the absolute discretion of the trustees, or to pay or apply the whole or any part of the capital, to or for the benefit of E all or any of the beneficiaries as the trustees should in their absolute discretion think fit. The settlement contained a wide investment clause authorising the trustees to invest money in the purchase of or at interest upon the security of shares, stocks, funds, securities, land or other investments or property of any nature.

Clause 7 contained a power to purchase land with vacant possession for occupation by any one or more of the beneficiaries. Sub-clause (4) of F clause 7 contained:

> "Power to permit any beneficiary to reside in any dwelling house or occupy any property or building which or the proceeds of sale of which may for the time being be subject to the trusts hereof upon such conditions as to payment of rent, rates, taxes and other expenses and outgoings and as to repair and decoration and for such period G and generally upon such terms as the trustees in their discretion shall think fit."

The facts in the case were agreed before the general commissioners. In 1966 the trustees, in exercise of the power which I have read from the settlement, bought a dwelling house known as "Wickwoods" in Sussex at the cost of £12,566 with a view to its occupation by persons who were H beneficiaries under the settlement. The house was conveyed to the trustees on trust for sale. In September 1971 the house was disposed of by the trustees. It was not sold, but exchanged. Its value at that time was £20,000. After taking into account certain allowable expenses, there was a notional gain for capital gains tax purposes of £5,450.

The situation in the meantime was this; Mr. Ronald Malby, the settlor's son, and his two sons Donald and David, together with his wife Stella,

A resided there. Mrs. Stella Malby remained until her marriage to Mr. Ronald Malby was ended by divorce. It was the main residence of the father and the two children, and of Mrs. Malby while she was there. Their occupation was by permission of the trustees pursuant to clause 7 (4) of the settlement. No payment was made or demanded in respect thereof; and, so far as the case discloses, there were no other conditions.

Whether capital gains tax is payable on the notional gain of £5,450 B depends on the true construction of section 29 (9). Section 29 is a section which in certain circumstances exempts from tax a gain which accrues to a person so far as attributable to the disposal of his home. I will read subsection (1) in full:

> "This section applies to a gain accruing to an individual so far as attributable to the disposal of, or of an interest in,—(*a*) a dwelling C house or part of a dwelling-house which is, or has at any time in his period of ownership been, his only or main residence, or (*b*) land which he has for his own occupation and enjoyment with that residence as its garden or grounds up to an area (inclusive of the site of the dwelling-house) of one acre or such larger area as the commissioners concerned may in any particular case determine, on being satisfied that, regard being had to the size and character of the dwelling-D house, the larger area is required for the reasonable enjoyment of it (or of the part in question) as a residence."

Subsection (2) provides:

> "The gain shall not be a chargeable gain if the dwelling-house or part of a dwelling-house has been the individual's only or main residence E throughout the period of ownership, or throughout the period of ownership except for all or any part of the last 12-months of that period."

Subsection (3) contains a formula for apportionment where the house has been the person's only or main residence for part of his period of ownership, and subsection (4) deals with periods of temporary absence.

F I can go straight to subsection (9), which is the subsection that I now have to construe. It reads:

> "This section shall also apply in relation to a gain accruing to a trustee on a disposal of settled property being an asset within subsection (1) of this section where during the period of ownership of the trustee the dwelling-house or part of the dwelling-house mentioned in G that subsection has been the only or main residence of a person entitled to occupy it under the terms of the settlement . . ."

I can stop there without quoting the concluding words of the subsection.

Section 45 defines "settled property," subject to an exception which is not relevant, as meaning: ". . . any property held in trust other than property to which section 22 (5) of this Act applies." I am not con-H cerned with section 22 (5). There is no definition of the expression "the settlement."

For section 29 (9) to apply, certain conditions have to be satisfied. The dwelling house must have been "the only or main residence of a person"; such person must be entitled to occupation; and that entitlement must satisfy the words "under the terms of the settlement." No difficulty arises from the fact that the occupation was by more than one person. The singular includes the plural, and it is not suggested that it makes any

difference in this case that the property was occupied by the father, his A
wife and his two sons, and ultimately by the father and his two sons, rather than by a single individual. Nor is it in dispute that the house was the only or main residence of those individuals.

Mr. Gibson, appearing for the Crown, has made the very fair concession, and I think correct concession, that the expression "under the terms of the settlement" is capable of including "under the exercise of a power conferred by the settlement." That concession is in accordance with the B
general principles which will be found in *Muir* v. *Muir* [1943] A.C. 468. So, in the end, I think the case principally turns on the shade of meaning which the court must give to the words "entitled to occupy it." No doubt the obvious case to which section 29 (9) applies is where a dwelling house is vested in trustees upon trust for sale and to pay the income of the property until sale to X, with a power or direction to let X into occupation C
pending a sale. Possibly also it is directed to the case of a tenant for life under the Settled Land Act 1925 who also would come within the expression "a trustee."

The case before me is quite different. The income is held on discretionary trusts. When the house was first purchased and before any permission to occupy was granted by the trustees, the rents and profits of the house as and when they might accrue (assuming an interval of time D
between a purchase and occupation) would be held on discretionary trusts for the benefit of a number of beneficiaries. I think I am correct in saying that the trustees would not have been in a position, except by creating some sort of sub-settlement, to entitle any individual beneficiary to receive as of right for an indefinite period of time the rents and profits of any such house. The trustees, however, were given a power, which they might E
or might not decide to exercise, to permit a beneficiary or more than one beneficiary, or all the beneficiaries, to reside in the dwelling house so long as the trustees thought fit. They could impose conditions such as the payment of rent or the discharge of outgoings. They could, if acting in the proper exercise of their discretion, turn the beneficiary or beneficiaries out of occupation at will. The question which faces me therefore, is whether in those particular circumstances it is right to say that the bene- F
ficiaries come within the expression "entitled to occupy [the dwelling house] under the terms of the settlement."

Mr. Whitehead, for the trustees, has submitted that the proper approach to this problem is not to place myself in the position of an observer from time to time during the years 1966 to 1971 and to ask myself, at every instant of time, whether it is correct to describe those in occupation as G
then entitled as of right under the terms of the settlement to remain in occupation. My proper course, he said, is to look at the matter at the time of the disposal and then to glance back over my shoulder to see whether it is right to describe the beneficiaries as persons who were, in the events which happened, entitled to occupy the house under the terms of the settlement.

Mr. Gibson, for the Crown, whose duty it was to argue in favour of H
the narrower construction, submitted that "a person entitled to occupy it under the terms of the settlement" means strictly a person who, under the terms of the settlement, always had during the relevant period a right to occupy and to remain in occupation. He submitted that the beneficiaries did not have that absolute right; they were merely in occupation by the licence of the trustees, which licence was revocable at the will of the trustees. It would not, he submitted, be correct to construe entitlement

A to occupation as including persons merely in residence as licensees under a revocable arrangement.

In my view section 29 (9) is capable of bearing either the strict construction for which Mr. Gibson has argued or the broader construction advocated by Mr. Whitehead. Subsection (9) is an exempting subsection, and it is not of course my duty, even in the case of a taxing statute, to try to ensure that the exemption applies. But I think I am permitted to
B take into consideration one factor which must have been present to the mind of Parliament when enacting section 29. The general scheme of section 29 is to exempt from liability to capital gains tax the proceeds of sale of a person's home. That was the broad conception. The justification for the exemption is that when a person sells his home he frequently needs to acquire a new home elsewhere. The evil of inflation was evident
C even in 1965. It must have occurred to the legislature that when a person sells his home to buy another one, he may well make a profit on the sale of one home and lose that profit, in effect, when he buys his new home at the new, inflated price. It would not therefore be surprising if Parliament formed the conclusion that, in such circumstances, it would be right to exempt the profit on the sale of the first home from the incidence of capital gains tax so that there is enough money to buy the new home.
D Nevertheless, it would not be permissible for me to construe section 29 (9) in a manner which I thought was fair or reasonable unless the wording permits that construction. Nor do I intend to travel outside the facts of the particular case before me.

In this case the beneficiaries were in occupation of "Wickwoods" throughout the relevant period as their only or main residence. They were
E in occupation pursuant to the exercise by the trustees of a power expressly conferred by the settlement to permit those beneficiaries to go into occupation and remain in occupation. The trustees exercised that power, and the beneficiaries thereupon became entitled to go into occupation and to continue in occupation until the permission was withdrawn. The trustees never withdrew the permission until they required vacant possession in order to complete the exchange. Therefore, looking at the matter at the
F date of the disposal, the beneficiaries were persons who, in the events which happened, were entitled to occupy the house and did occupy it under the terms of the settlement. That, in my view, is the correct approach to the subsection in dealing with the type of case which is before me, and in those circumstances I reach the view that the terms of section 29 (9) have been satisfied and that the gain is exempt from capital gains tax.

G

Appeal allowed with costs.

Solicitors: *Collyer-Bristow & Co.; Solicitor of Inland Revenue.*

H

[COURT OF APPEAL]

* J. EVANS & SON (PORTSMOUTH) LTD. *v.* ANDREA MERZARIO LTD.

1975 Nov. 11, 12, 13 — Lord Denning M.R., Roskill and Geoffrey Lane L.JJ.

Contract—Condition or warranty—Oral assurance—Printed contract of carriage with exemption clause—Goods customarily carried under deck—Change to container system—Oral promise by forwarding agents to ensure goods in containers to be carried under deck—Subcontractors loading container on deck—Goods lost at sea—Whether oral promise as to future conduct overriding printed exemption from liability—Whether oral promise contractual—Whether enforceable

The plaintiffs, English importers of machines from Italy, had since about 1959 arranged the carriage of the machines to England under contracts with the defendants, forwarding agents. The contracts were in printed standard form and included conditions which gave the forwarding agents complete freedom as to means, route and procedure in handling and transportation of the goods, subject to any express written instructions from the customer; exempted them from liability for loss of or damage to goods unless it occurred while they were in their actual custody and control and by reason of their wilful neglect or default, and limited their liability to £50 per ton. As the plaintiffs' machines were liable to rust the forwarding agents always arranged for their transport to England in crates or trailers which were always shipped under deck while at sea.

In the autumn of 1967 the forwarding agents proposed to change their system to packing and transporting machines in containers. Their general manager in England discussed the proposed change with the plaintiffs' traffic agent. He gave him an oral assurance that for the future machines shipped in containers would be carried under deck; and in reliance on that oral promise the plaintiffs accepted the change and agreed the terms; but they did not include any written provision about carrying goods in containers under deck.

In October 1968 the forwarding agents, through an associated company, loaded one of the plaintiffs' machines, valued at nearly £3,000, packed in a container, with other containers, on deck. Owing to a swell at sea, it fell overboard and was a total loss. The plaintiffs brought an action claiming damages of £2,720. The forwarding agents denied liability, relying on the exemptions in their printed conditions of carriage. Kerr J. held that the oral assurance was not a legally binding warranty such as would operate collaterally to the contract and override the standard conditions, and dismissed the action.

On appeal by the plaintiffs:—

Held, allowing the appeal, (1) that the forwarding agents had given the plaintiffs an enforceable contractual promise that if the plaintiffs agreed that in the future their goods should be shipped in containers those containers like the trailers used previously would be shipped under and not on deck; and that, as the lost container had been shipped on and not under deck and was thereby lost, the forwarding agents were in breach of that promise and were liable to the plaintiffs in damages unless they could rely on the exemption in the standard printed conditions.

A *Per* Lord Denning M.R. It was binding as a collateral warranty (post, p. 1081E–G).

Dick Bentley Productions Ltd. v. *Harold Smith (Motors) Ltd.* [1965] 1 W.L.R. 623, C.A. applied.

Heilbut, Symons & Co. v. *Buckleton* [1913] A.C. 30, H.L.(E.) distinguished.

(2) That the defendants could not rely on the printed conditions to exempt them from liability for breach of the oral
B promise that the container would be carried under deck, for
the printed conditions were repugnant to the oral promise, which therefore overrode the printed conditions.

Mendelssohn v. *Normand Ltd.* [1970] 1 Q.B. 177, C.A. applied.

Decision of Kerr J. [1975] 1 Lloyd's Rep. 162 reversed.

The following cases are referred to in the judgments:

C *Bentley (Dick) Productions Ltd.* v. *Harold Smith (Motors) Ltd.* [1965] 1 W.L.R. 623; [1965] 2 All E.R. 65, C.A.
City and Westminster Properties (1934) Ltd. v. *Mudd* [1959] Ch. 129; [1958] 3 W.L.R. 312; [1958] 2 All E.R. 733.
Couchman v. *Hill* [1947] K.B. 554; [1947] 1 All E.R. 103, C.A.
Firestone Tyre and Rubber Co. Ltd. v. *Vokins & Co. Ltd.* [1951] 1 Lloyd's Rep. 32.
D *Harling* v. *Eddy* [1951] 2 K.B. 739; [1951] 2 All E.R. 212, C.A.
Heilbut, Symons & Co. v. *Buckleton* [1913] A.C. 30, H.L.(E.).
Mendelssohn v. *Normand Ltd.* [1970] 1 Q.B. 177; [1969] 3 W.L.R. 139; [1969] 2 All E.R. 1215, C.A.

The following additional cases were cited in argument:

Curtis v. *Chemical Cleaning and Dyeing Co. Ltd.* [1951] 1 K.B. 805;
E [1951] 1 All E.R. 631, C.A.
De Lassalle v. *Guildford* [1901] 2 K.B. 215, C.A.
Gillespie Brothers & Co. Ltd. v. *Roy Bowles Transport Ltd.* [1973] Q.B. 400; [1972] 3 W.L.R. 1003; [1973] 1 All E.R. 193, C.A.
Kenyon, Son and Craven Ltd. v. *Baxter Hoare & Co. Ltd.* [1971] 1 W.L.R. 519; [1971] 2 All E.R. 708.
Rio Tinto Co. Ltd. v. *Seed Shipping Co. Ltd.* (1926) 24 Ll.L.Rep. 316.
F *Rose (F. E.) (London) Ltd.* v. *W. H. Pim Jnr. & Co.* [1953] 2 Q.B. 450; [1953] 3 W.L.R. 497; [1953] 2 All E.R. 739, C.A.
Shanklin Pier Ltd. v. *Detel Products Ltd.* [1951] 2 K.B. 854; [1951] 2 All E.R. 471.

APPEAL from Kerr J.

G The plaintiffs, J. Evans & Son (Portsmouth) Ltd., importers of Italian
machines, by a writ issued on June 28, 1972, brought an action against
the defendants, Andrea Merzario Ltd., forwarding agents, claiming damages
for breach of a contract, partly written and partly oral and/or duty in and
about the carriage of the plaintiffs' goods from Italy to the United Kingdom.
They claimed that the defendants were in breach of a term of the contract
of carriage between the parties, or of a collateral warranty to the contract,
H that goods in containers would be shipped under deck. The defendants
relied on the printed standard conditions of the Institute of Shipping and
Forwarding Agents which contained clauses exempting them from liability
in certain circumstances. On October 23, 1974, Kerr J. [1975] 1
Lloyd's Rep. 162 gave judgment dismissing the plaintiffs' action on the
grounds that a statement made by the defendants that the plaintiffs' goods
if packed in containers would be carried under deck did not constitute a
binding warranty collateral to the contract of carriage and so did not

override the printed conditions incorporated in the contract of carriage; and that the fact that the container had been carried on deck did not involve the defendants in a fundamental breach of the contract of carriage.

The plaintiffs appealed on the grounds, inter alia, that the judge was wrong in holding that there was no contract collateral to the printed contract consisting in the oral assurance that the goods carried in containers would be carried under deck; alternatively, that the oral warranty as to future conduct had become a term of the contract and either because it was fundamental or as a matter of construction it necessarily overrode the written conditions of the contract.

Roger Buckley for the plaintiffs.
Anthony Hallgarten for the defendant forwarding agents.

LORD DENNING M.R. Strangely enough, this is the first case we have had in this court about container traffic. The motor vessel *The Ruhr* was not purpose-built for containers. It was built as a merchant ship but it had been converted so as to carry containers. On November 3, 1968, *The Ruhr* was going from Rotterdam to Tilbury. Twenty containers were under the deck. Eight containers were on deck. She met with a slight swell. Two containers fell off and went to the bottom of the water. One of them contained a special injection moulding machine of about £3,000 in value. It was completely lost.

No claim lies against the shipowners. They had issued a bill of lading which said: "Shipped on deck at shippers' risk."

The claim we have to consider is by the English importers against the forwarding agents. They claim that the containers ought not to have been carried on deck.

The importers were Evans of Portsmouth. They had bought the machines from an Italian manufacturer in Milan. The English importers employed forwarding agents to make all the transport arrangements. The forwarding agents were a company, Andrea Merzario Ltd. They have an associated company in Holland and also their parent company in Italy. These forwarding agents made arrangements under which the goods were carried by rail from Milan to Rotterdam, then by ship for Tilbury, unloaded at Tilbury, and carried to the destination in England. The forwarding agents had for some years previously arranged for these machines to be imported, but they had been packed in crates and not in containers. The forwarding agents had always arranged that these machines so packed in crates should be carried under deck because they were liable to rust if carried on deck. When it was proposed to change over to packing them in containers, the forwarding agents talked to the English importers about it. Their manager, Mr. Spano, who was visiting Portsmouth, saw Mr. Leonard of the importers. He said that they proposed to use containers in future. Mr. Leonard said: "I have heard about these containers. I am afraid that our machines may get rusty if they are carried on deck. They must not be carried on deck." Mr. Spano assured Mr. Leonard: "If we do use containers, they will not be carried on deck." The judge accepted that that assurance was given. He said [1975] 1 Lloyd's Rep. 162, 164,

> ". . . Mr. Leonard was assured by Mr. Spano that, in so far as goods were subsequently to be transported in containers, these would be carried under deck in the same way as all goods transported by the defendants."

On getting that assurance, Mr. Leonard was content. The forwarding agents gave a quotation for the new charges for carrying in containers. The English importers accepted it. The contract went forward on that basis. Invoices were sent and goods carried on the usual terms and conditions appearing on the form. Nothing was put in writing about being carried under deck.

Unfortunately there was some mistake made somewhere during the forwarding of this consignment from Italy to England. The Dutch company failed to ensure that the containers which contained these machines were loaded under deck at Rotterdam. They allowed them to be shipped on deck and accepted a bill of lading which contained the excepting clause: "Shipped on deck at shippers' risk."

So after these containers fell off the deck into the water, the English importers, through their insurers, claimed damages against the forwarding agents. In reply the forwarding agents said there was no contractual promise that the goods would be carried under deck. Alternatively, if there was, they relied on the printed terms and conditions. The judge held there was no contractual promise that these containers should be carried under deck. He thought that, in order to be binding, the initial conversation ought to be contemporaneous; and that here it was too remote in point of time from the actual transport. Furthermore, that, viewed objectively, it should not be considered binding. The judge quoted largely from the well known case of *Heilbut, Symons & Co.* v. *Buckleton* [1913] A.C. 30, in which it was held that a person is not liable in damages for an innocent misrepresentation; and that the courts should be slow to hold that there was a collateral contract. I must say that much of what was said in that case is entirely out of date. We now have the Misrepresentation Act 1967 under which damages can be obtained for innocent misrepresentation of fact. This Act does not apply here because we are concerned with an assurance as to the future. But even in respect of promises as to the future, we have a different approach nowadays to collateral contracts. When a person gives a promise or an assurance to another, intending that he should act on it by entering into a contract, and he does act on it by entering into the contract, we hold that it is binding: see *Dick Bentley Productions Ltd.* v. *Harold Smith (Motors) Ltd.* [1965] 1 W.L.R. 623. That case was concerned with a representation of fact, but it applies also to promises as to the future. Following this approach, it seems to me plain that Mr. Spano gave an oral promise or assurance that the goods in this new container traffic would be carried under deck. He made the promise in order to induce Mr. Leonard to agree to the goods being carried in containers. On the faith of it, Mr. Leonard accepted the quotations and gave orders for transport. In those circumstances the promise was binding. There was a breach of that promise and the forwarding agents are liable—unless they can rely on the printed conditions.

It is common ground that the course of dealing was on the standard conditions of the forwarding trade. Those conditions were relied upon: condition 4 which gives the company complete freedom in respect of means, route and procedure in the transportation of goods; condition 11 which says that the company will not be liable for loss or damage unless it occurs while in their actual custody and then only if they are guilty of wilful neglect or default; condition 13 which says that their liability shall not exceed the value of the goods or a sum at the rate of £50 per ton of 20 cwt.

The question is whether the company can rely on those exemptions. A
I do not think so. The cases are numerous in which oral promises have
been held binding in spite of written exempting conditions: such as
Couchman v. *Hill* [1947] K.B. 554; *Harling* v. *Eddy* [1951] 2 K.B. 739;
City and Westminster Properties (1934) Ltd. v. *Mudd* [1959] Ch. 129. The
most recent is *Mendelssohn* v. *Normand* [1970] 1 Q.B. 177, 184, where
I said: "The printed condition is rejected because it is repugnant to the
express oral promise or representation." During the argument Roskill L.J. B
put the case of the Hague Rules. If a carrier made a promise that goods
would be shipped under deck, and, contrary to that promise, they were
carried on deck and there was a loss, the carrier could not rely on the
limitation clause. Following these authorities, it seems to me that the
forwarding agents cannot rely on the condition. There was a plain breach
of the oral promise by the forwarding agents. I would allow the appeal. C

Roskill L.J. I agree that this appeal should be allowed for the
reasons which Lord Denning M.R. has given. I venture to add to those
reasons out of respect for Kerr J., from whom in a matter of this kind I
differ with hesitation. But this case has been put before us rather differ-
ently from the way it was put before the judge, though, as Mr. Buckley
said a moment ago, the point on which he succeeds was in fact mentioned D
to the judge, as appears from the judgment.

It is regrettable that this loss happened almost seven years ago. I hope
no one thinks that the ensuing delay is the fault of the courts. Almost
seven years ago this container was lost overboard in Rotterdam harbour.
It is obvious that it was lost overboard because it was shipped on deck and
was not properly stowed. It is also perfectly clear that under the arrange- E
ments that had been made, whatever their legal effect as between the
plaintiffs and the defendants, that container ought not to have been shipped
on deck, and that if it had not been shipped on deck it would not have
been lost. But the plaintiffs were insured; their underwriters paid the
claim and their underwriters now seek by right of subrogation to recover
from the defendants that which they have paid. The defendants are not
carriers: they are forwarding contractors who arranged for the transport F
of goods—in this case from Milan—by rail, no doubt by the Rhine valley
to Rotterdam, and thence by sea to this country. The work which they
do is performed by them through many subcontractors; the particular sub-
contractors who carried this container and allowed it to fall into the sea
were shipowners known as E.U.R. [European Unit Routes Ltd.] The
shipping arrangements were made by the defendants' Dutch associated G
company in Rotterdam, and it would appear to have been common ground
at the trial (and Mr. Hallgarten has very properly accepted it in this
court) that what went wrong was the fault of the defendants' associated
company. But the defendants in effect say: "We are not liable for two
reasons: first, we never promised that these goods would not be shipped
on deck: all we did was to say that it was our policy that container units
should not be shipped on deck; and, secondly, if, contrary to our first H
contention, we ever made such an enforceable promise to the plaintiffs
that the container would not be shipped on deck, our printed exceptions
protect us." That is the view that the judge accepted. Like Lord Denning
M.R., I do not propose to go through all the evidence. This case presented
the striking feature that each of the principal witnesses were ad idem in
their recollection, though, of course, they did not profess six years after
the conversation in question to remember the exact words that they had

A used. It seems to me, as it seems to Lord Denning M.R., absolutely plain that the plaintiffs thought they had got an assurance from the defendants that if the plaintiffs, instead of using the trailers which had hitherto always been shipped under deck, were to allow the defendants to ship the plaintiffs' goods in containers, those containers, like the trailers before them, would be shipped under deck. It is only necessary to refer to though not to read passages from the evidence to see that that is absolutely plain. B The judge said that all the defendants gave was an assurance: they did not give a guarantee. The real question, as I venture to think, is not whether one calls this an assurance or a guarantee, but whether that which was said amounted to an enforceable contractual promise by the defendants to the plaintiffs that any goods thereafter entrusted by the plaintiffs to the defendants for carriage from Milan to the United Kingdom via C Rotterdam and thence by sea to England would be shipped under deck. The matter was apparently argued before the judge on behalf of the plaintiffs on the basis that the defendants' promise (if any) was what the lawyers sometimes call a collateral oral warranty. That phrase is normally only applicable where the original promise was external to the main contract, that main contract being a contract in writing, so that usually parole evidence cannot be given to contradict the terms of the written contract. The D basic rule is clearly stated in paragraph 742 of *Benjamin's Sale of Goods*, 9th ed. (1974) to which I refer but which I will not repeat. But that doctrine, as it seems to me, has little or no application where one is not concerned with a contract in writing (with respect, I cannot accept Mr. Hallgarten's argument that there was here a contract in writing) but with a contract which, as I think, was partly oral, partly in writing, and partly E by conduct. In such a case the court does not require to have recourse to lawyer's devices such as collateral oral warranty in order to seek to adduce evidence which would not otherwise be admissible. The court is entitled to look at and should look at all the evidence from start to finish in order to see what the bargain was that was struck between the parties. That is what we have done in this case and what, with great respect, I think the judge did not do in the course of his judgment. I unreservedly accept F Mr. Hallgarten's submission that one must not look at one or two isolated answers given in evidence; one should look at the totality of the evidence When one does that, one finds, first, as I have already mentioned, that these parties had been doing business in transporting goods from Milan to England for some time before; secondly, that transportation of goods from Milan to England was always done on trailers which were always under G deck; thirdly, that the defendants wanted a change in the practice—they wanted containers used instead of trailers; fourthly, that the plaintiffs were only willing to agree to that change if they were promised by the defendants that those containers would be shipped under deck, and would not have agreed to the change but for that promise. The defendants gave such a promise, which to my mind against this background plainly H amounted to an enforceable contractual promise. In those circumstances it seems to me that the contract was this: "If we continue to give you our business, you will ensure that those goods in containers are shipped under deck"; and the defendants agreed that this would be so. Thus there was a breach of that contract by the defendants when this container was shipped on deck; and it seems to me to be plain that the damage which the plaintiffs suffered resulted from that breach. That being the position, I think that Mr. Hallgarten's first argument fails.

I will deal very briefly with the second point, with which Lord Denning M.R. has already dealt fully. It is suggested that even so these exemption clauses apply. I ventured to ask Mr. Hallgarten what the position would have been if when the defendants' first quotation had come along there had been stamped on the face of that quotation: "No containers to be shipped on deck"; and this container had then been shipped on deck. He bravely said that the exemption clauses would still have applied. With great respect, I think that is an impossible argument. In the words which Devlin J. used in *Firestone Tyre and Rubber Co. Ltd.* v. *Vokins & Co. Ltd.* [1951] 1 Lloyd's Rep. 32, 39, and approved by Lord Denning M.R. in *Mendelssohn* v. *Normand Ltd.* [1970] 1 Q.B. 177, 184, the defendants' promise that the container would be shipped under deck would be wholly illusory. This is not a case of fundamental breach. It is a question of construction. Interpreting the contract as I find it to have been, I feel driven to the conclusion that none of these exemption clauses can be applied, because one has to treat the promise that no container would be shipped on deck as overriding any question of exempting conditions. Otherwise, as I have already said, the promise would be illusory.

There is only one other thing I would mention. There was some discussion in this court—and the judge mentioned the point at the end of his judgment—whether the old law relating to deck cargo is still applicable to modern container traffic. The old law is very familiar and is to be found in article 85 of the current edition of *Scrutton on Charterparties* 18th ed. (1974), p. 163. The judge said that he thought that old law did not apply to container traffic. It is not necessary to express any view whether the judge was right or wrong, though I am far from suggesting that he was wrong. We do not have to decide that question in this case. The question may hereafter arise. When it does, no doubt evidence will be made available whether there is at the present time a custom or practice under which containers may be shipped on deck without express permission from the cargo owners so to do. Whether or not that is so I do not know. I do not think we should express any view about that question in a case in which there is no evidence from shipowners or others what the current customary practice, if any, is.

For those reasons, which I have given at some length out of deference to Kerr J., in addition to those given by Lord Denning M.R., I would allow this appeal and enter judgment for the plaintiffs for the sum claimed.

GEOFFREY LANE L.J. I agree, for the reasons already expressed, that the effect of the conversation between Mr. Spano of the defendants and Mr. Leonard for the plaintiffs in the autumn of 1967 was to produce a binding obligation on the defendants to ensure that the plaintiffs' machinery in containers would be carried under deck between Rotterdam and Tilbury. This was not a collateral contract in the sense of an oral agreement varying the terms of a written contract. It was a new express term which was to be included thereafter in the contracts between the plaintiffs and the defendants for the carriage of machinery from Italy. Given that promise, the question which remains is whether the defendants' printed trading conditions affect that new express term in favour of the defendants. It seems to me that no great matter of principle is involved. There is no dispute that the terms of the printed contract had by the time of this particular incident, by the course of dealings, become a part of each individual contract between the plaintiffs and the defendants in so far as

A they were apposite. There is equally no doubt that if they are to be applied to this new express term and applied literally, they would render that term valueless to the plaintiffs. Condition 4, for example, reads as follows:

> " Subject to express instructions in writing given by the customer, the company reserves to itself complete freedom in respect of means
> B route and procedure to be followed in the handling and transportation of the goods."

If that is applied to this new term, then the new term would be stillborn. The two are logically inconsistent with each other. The express new term must be taken to override the printed condition. Conditions 11 and 12 would have the effect of restricting the defendants' liability for a breach of this term to the circumstances in which such breach was due
C to their wilful default or wilful negligence. Whatever that may mean, the chances of the plaintiffs ever being compensated for breach of the term would be remote in the extreme. Taking the facts of the present case, for example, the undoubted breach of the term when this container was shipped on deck and therefore fell overboard was due to the defendants failing to ensure that their sister company in Rotterdam had insisted on
D under deck stowage. It was careless, it was inefficient, but that would not have been enough to allow the plaintiffs to succeed if conditions 11 and 12 are to be applied. It seems to me that whether the test is an objective or a subjective one, whether one takes the view of the officious invisible bystander, or the view of Mr. Spano or the view of Mr. Leonard himself as to the effect of the meeting in autumn 1967, the answer would be the same. The effect of their agreement was to remove from the new term
E the restrictions or exemptions contained in those trading conditions. Any other conclusion would be to destroy the business efficacy of the new agreement from the day it started. Similarly with condition 13: if applied, it would restrict the defendants' liability to £50 per ton, that is, some £100 all told instead of the £2,700 odd which was the value of the lost machinery. If Mr. Spano or indeed the bystander had been asked whether this term
F was to apply to the agreement, he would have replied unhesitatingly No. For these reasons I agree that this appeal succeeds.

Appeal allowed with costs in court below and in Court of Appeal.
Judgment for plaintiffs for £2,720·90 with interest at 9 per cent. from November
G *1970.*

Solicitors: *Clyde & Co.; Crawley and de Reya.*

M. M. H.

H

[CHANCERY DIVISION]

* DUNMORE v. McGOWAN (INSPECTOR OF TAXES)

1976 June 24, 25 Brightman J.

Revenue — Income tax — " Interest of money " — Bank interest — Deposit of money at bank as condition of guarantee—Deposit and interest repaid at termination of guarantee—Whether taxpayer " receiving or entitled to " interest for years of assessment—Income Tax Act 1952 (15 & 16 *Geo.* 6 & 1 *Eliz.* 2, *c.* 10), *s.* 148

The taxpayer had been involved in property transactions through the media of limited companies. In June 1967 one of the companies acquired a bank loan, that was guaranteed by the taxpayer, to finance its transactions. The bank required the guarantee to be supplemented by the taxpayer depositing with it £28,000. That sum was transferred to a deposit account in the bank's name where it was credited with interest until July 1969. At that time the company repaid the loan to the bank and the deposit was repaid to the taxpayer together with interest of approximately £5,000. Further assessments to income tax under Schedule D, Class III, were made on the taxpayer for the three years, 1967–68, 1968–69 and 1969–1970 of £200 each in respect of the bank interest. The general commissioners, dismissing an appeal by the taxpayer against the assessments, rejected his contention that as it was the bank in a fiduciary capacity who received and was entitled to the interest for the years in question, section 148 of the Income Tax Act 1952 [1] did not apply and he was not assessable to income tax on the accumulated interest.

On appeal by the taxpayer:—

Held, dismissing the appeal, that during the period of the guarantee the taxpayer did not have merely a contingent beneficial interest in the bank interest because no trust had been created either expressly or by implication and therefore the bank did not hold the money as trustee and that although the taxpayer could not have demanded repayment of his deposit during the subsistence of the guarantee, the interest enured to his benefit in any event and accordingly was " received " by him at the times it was credited to the deposit account (post, pp. 1089H, 1090E–G).

Stanley v. *Inland Revenue Commissioners* [1944] K.B. 255, C.A. distinguished.

The following cases are referred to in the judgment:

Foley v. *Hill* (1848) 2 H.L.Cas. 28, H.L.(E.).

Stanley v. *Inland Revenue Commissioners* [1944] K.B. 255; [1944] 1 All E.R. 230; 26 T.C. 16, C.A.

Whitworth Park Coal Co. Ltd. v. *Inland Revenue Comrs.* [1961] A.C. 31; [1959] 3 W.L.R. 842; [1959] 3 All E.R. 703, H.L.(E.); sub nom. *Inland Revenue Commissioners* v. *Whitworth Park Coal Co. Ltd.* [1958] Ch. 792; [1958] 2 W.L.R. 815; [1958] 2 All E.R. 91; 38 T.C. 531, C.A.

[Reported by MRS. HARRIET DUTTON, Barrister-at-Law]

[1] Income Tax Act 1952, s. 148: see post, p. 1089B.

A The following additional cases were cited in argument:

Bulmer v. *Inland Revenue Commissioners* [1967] Ch. 145; [1966] 3 W.L.R. 672; [1966] 3 All E.R. 801; 44 T.C. 1.
Gasgoigne v. *Inland Revenue Commissioners* [1927] 1 K.B. 594, C.A. [1928] A.C. 252; 13 T.C. 573, H.L.(E.).
Hughes v. *Young* (1862) 1 New Rep. 166.
Kayford Ltd., In re [1975] 1 W.L.R. 279; [1975] 1 All E.R. 604.
B *Ransom* v. *Higgs* [1974] 1 W.L.R. 1594; [1974] 3 All E.R. 949; 50 T.C. 1, H.L.(E.).
Waterman's Will Trusts, In re [1952] 2 All E.R. 104.
Williams v. *Singer* [1921] 1 A.C. 65; 7 T.C. 409, H.L.(E.).

CASE STATED by the Commissioners for the General Purposes of the Income Tax Acts.

C The taxpayer, William Sydney Dunmore, carried out property transactions through the media of a limited liability company, Belmound Investments Ltd. As a condition of a bank providing that company with finance the taxpayer by July 1967 had deposited with the bank £28,190. By July 1969 the company repaid its debt to the bank and the taxpayer was credited with £33,010. On appeal by the taxpayer against three further assessments to income tax under Schedule D, Case III, the com-
D missioners held that the interest in respect of the deposit account was properly assessable on the taxpayer for the years in question and determined them in the sums of £1,109 for 1967–68, £2,431 for 1968–69 and £1,540 for 1969–70.

The taxpayer appealed.

The facts are stated in the judgment.

E

Marcus Jones for the taxpayer.
Brian Davenport for the Crown.

BRIGHTMAN J. This is an appeal against further assessments to income tax under Schedule D, Case III, for each of three years, 1967 to 1970, in respect of interest credited to a deposit account at a bank. On September
F 30, 1965, the taxpayer entered into a written guarantee in favour of Lloyds Bank Europe Ltd. He guaranteed to pay on demand all moneys then or thereafter owing to the bank by Belmound Investments Ltd. on any current or other account. The amount recoverable under the guarantee was limited to £50,000 with interest.

On April 1, 1967, the taxpayer opened a deposit account with Lloyds Bank Europe Ltd. with a credit of £2,000. I will call it "the first deposit
G account." There was no information in the case stated as to the circumstances in which that account was opened. The first deposit account was headed, "Lloyds Bank Europe Limited—Re W. S. Dunmore [i.e. the taxpayer]—Deposit Account at 7 days' notice—Interest allowed at half per cent. over bank rate." On April 10, 1967, a further £4,000 was credited to the first deposit account, the payer being described as "Bardimore
H Investments." On May 24, £2,000 was debited to the account in favour of a payee whom I take to be Belmound Investments Ltd. On May 26, £24,000 was paid into the first deposit account by one Chandler, thus producing a credit balance of £28,000.

On June 5, 1967, the taxpayer addressed a letter in the following terms to the bank:

"With reference to my guarantee in favour of the bank on behalf of [Belmound Investments Ltd.] dated September 30, 1965, for the sum of £50,000, I authorise you to transfer to a deposit account in your name the sum of £4,000 plus £25,000 which you will be receiving from the liquidator of Bardimore Investments Ltd., representing my share of the proceeds of sale of Bardimore Investments Plot 4 of the Golden Valley Estate. These sums are to be retained by you whilst I remain under any liability under the aforementioned guarantee. You may at any time apply the amount for the time being standing to the credit of the said deposit account in or towards payment of any monies payable by me to you under the aforementioned guarantee." A B

I will refer to that letter as " the June letter."

It seems probable that the taxpayer was unaware when he signed the June letter of the credits already made to the first deposit account. It would also seem probable that the credits of £4,000 and £24,000 which had already been made to the first deposit account represent the credits of £4,000 and £25,000 described in the June letter as anticipated future receipts. Paragraph 6 (iii) of the stated case described the sums of £4,000 and £24,000 as having been received " Soon after June 5, 1967." This contradicts the page of the first deposit account statement from which I have read. That is an admitted document, and I will treat " Soon after " in that paragraph as a mere slip for " Shortly before." C D

It is perhaps a little odd that the first deposit account statement from which I have read is headed, " Lloyds Bank Europe Limited—Re W. S. Dunmore." Such a heading implies that the account was in the name of Lloyds Bank Europe Ltd. in connection with the affairs of the taxpayer and operable by Lloyds Bank Europe Ltd., because that was the name of the account. The implication might be that it was not operable, when opened, by the taxpayer. Perhaps there was some informal arrangement in effect prior to June 5, 1967, which anticipated the arrangement set out in the June letter. However, that is speculation on my part, and in the absence of any contrary finding by the general commissioners, from whom this appeal comes, I shall proceed on the footing that the first deposit account was in the name of and operable by the taxpayer. That at least accords with the description of the account in paragraph 6 (iii) of the stated case, which sets out the facts admitted or proved before the commissioners. E F

There is one further preliminary matter I must mention. It is common ground between the parties that the interest to accrue on the moneys to be transferred to the new account mentioned in the June letter would be caught by the terms of the June letter, and that it would not be open to the taxpayer to require interest which might be credited on the moneys in the new deposit account to be paid to him. Whether or not I might have reached that interpretation of the letter had it been my function to construe it is neither here nor there. G

On June 20, 1967, interest amounting to £190 (I ignore fractions of a pound throughout this judgment) was credited to the first deposit account. On July 4, 1967, the sum of £28,190, being the sum to the credit of the first deposit account, was transferred to the credit of a new deposit account headed, " Lloyds Bank Europe Limited. Re liability of W. S. Dunmore on behalf of Belmound Investments." That again was a deposit account with Lloyds Bank Europe Ltd. I will call it the " second deposit account." Interest was thereafter periodically credited to this account, the last credit of interest being made on July 31, 1969. On that day, the loan to Belmound Investments Ltd. having then or previously been paid off, the H second deposit account was closed. A sum of £31,500 was withdrawn by the taxpayer, and the balance of £1,510 was placed to the credit of a third deposit account with Lloyds Bank Europe Ltd. in the sole name of the taxpayer. The total interest accumulated in the second deposit account plus the £190 credited to the first deposit account amounted to just over £5,000.

The question in issue is whether the interest attributable to each of the years I have mentioned is assessable to tax as the taxpayer's income. The liability to tax depends on section 148 of the Income Tax Act 1952, which provides:

> "Tax under Schedule D shall be charged on and paid by the persons receiving or entitled to the income in respect of which tax under that Schedule is in this Act directed to be charged."

The problem therefore is whether the taxpayer was a person "receiving or entitled to" the interest in question in the years of assessment that I have mentioned.

The sum of £190 credited to the first deposit account on June 20, 1967, was clearly assessable to tax as the taxpayer's income of that year if the first deposit account was truly in his name and operable by him. The June letter was no more than a mandate authorising the bank to transfer certain moneys into another deposit account in its own name as collateral security. The bank had not made use of that mandate when the £190 was credited. Indeed, much of the interest would seem to have accrued prior to the existence of the mandate. Later interest payments are, however, subject to different considerations.

The taxpayer primarily contended that the bank held the money in the second deposit account as a trustee. The terms of the trust, it was said, were such as to require the bank to re-transfer the money to the taxpayer upon the happening of a contingency, namely, the termination of the guarantee liability. In those circumstances, it was submitted, the taxpayer's interest in the principal and accumulated income was a contingent interest during the period in question; that is to say, down to July, 1969. The case accordingly fell, it was submitted, within the principle of *Stanley* v. *Inland Revenue Commissioners* [1944] K.B. 255. There it was held that interest accumulated under a trust for a beneficiary contingently entitled was not taxable as the income of the beneficiary.

The Crown contended that the money in the second deposit account was not the subject matter of any trust. That submission is in my judgment clearly correct. If a customer places money with a bank on current account or deposit account, no trust is created: the relationship is that of creditor and debtor. The statement of account delivered by a bank to its customer does not indicate money held by the bank in trust for the customer but the balance due under the contract of loan: see *Foley* v. *Hill* (1848) 2 H.L.Cas. 28. The whole system of banking is founded on that conception. The taxpayer naturally does not seek to challenge that as a general proposition, but he submitted that in the particular circumstances of this case a trust was created. In my judgment, it would need an express arrangement to create the relationship of trustee and cestui que trust between banker and customer quoad money paid by a customer into a banking account. No such arrangement is in my view capable of being implied from the primary facts of the present case.

That is not, however, the end of the matter. The taxpayer could not be assessed to tax on these amounts of interest for the years in question

unless it can be shown that the taxpayer received or was entitled to that A
interest. I will take the year 1968/69 as an example. On June 20, interest of £347 was credited to the second deposit account. It was submitted that the taxpayer did not receive and was not entitled to the sum of £347 on June 20. It did not come to his hands on that day, and he could not demand it from the bank on that day because he was not entitled to demand it; he was precluded from so doing by the June letter. In fact, he
might never be entitled to receive or demand it because it might be taken B
by the bank to answer the liability under the guarantee. Interest, it was argued, is not received by a taxpayer, nor is receivable by him at the relevant time, unless he can obtain it: there is no receipt without receivability. Concepts of receipt and receivability and entitlement coincide in the context of this legislation. One cannot have receivability until the particular
sum becomes payable or the taxpayer has entitlement to the relevant pay- C
ment. Such propositions, it was said, were wholly consistent with the language of paragraph (a) of Case III.

The Crown's proposition, it was said, was wholly contrary to a series of well-established authorities which were approved in *Whitworth Park Coal Co. Ltd.* v. *Inland Revenue Commissioners* [1961] A.C. 31. In particular, counsel cited this passage from the speech of Viscount Simonds,
at p. 63: D

> "Traders pay tax on the balance of profits and gains and bring money owed to them into account in striking that balance, but ordinary individuals are not assessable and do not pay tax until they get the money because until then it is not part of their income."

The taxpayer's argument is superficially attractive and was well pre-
sented by Mr. Marcus Jones, but it is not in my judgment correct. The true E
way of analysing the position is, I think, this. I return by way of example to the £347 interest. This was credited to the second deposit account on June 20, 1968. As from June 20, 1968, every penny of that interest enured to the taxpayer's benefit in any event; it swelled the assets of the taxpayer on that day. The reasoning is this. If the guarantee ended without the
interest being resorted to under the terms of the June letter, then the £347 F
would be withdrawable by the taxpayer from the account in due course. If the £347 was resorted to under the terms of the June letter, then it would pro tanto reduce the personal liability of the taxpayer under the guarantee. In either event, every penny of the interest enured immediately to the benefit of the taxpayer and to the full extent of the £347. Admittedly the money was locked up in the deposit account while the guarantee subsisted, but it
was locked up in such a way that it enured to the taxpayer's benefit at G
once, either as money coming to his hands or reducing his liabilities. Whatever might be the ultimate destination of the £347, it was in my judgment received by the taxpayer on the day when it was credited to the second deposit account. On that day it swelled his estate to the extent of £347. I do not think that there is anything in this reasoning which is contrary
to the logic of *Whitworth Park Coal Co. Ltd.* v. *Inland Revenue Com-* H
missioners.

In his reply, I think that Mr. Marcus Jones was perhaps not disposed wholly to challenge this reasoning. He submitted, however, that if it were right then it was not the interest which should be assessed but money's worth, which would involve a different process from that adopted by the inspector in this case. I am afraid that I cannot accept that as a valid criticism of the reasoning. It seems to me that, for the reason which I

A have endeavoured to explain, every penny of the £347 enured to the benefit of the taxpayer on June 20, 1968. In these circumstances, I think that the assessments were made on the correct principle and that the appeal must be dismissed.

Appeal dismissed with costs.

Solicitors: *W. S. Dunmore, Croydon; Solicitor of Inland Revenue.*

B

[CHANCERY DIVISION]

C

* VARTY (INSPECTOR OF TAXES) *v.* LYNES

1976 July 1 Brightman J.

Revenue—Capital gains tax—Disposal of assets—Dwelling house and garden occupied as main residence—Part of garden and
D *house sold — Subsequent sale of remainder of garden with outline planning approval—Whether gain on sale of garden chargeable gain—Finance Act* 1965 (*c.* 25), *s.* 29 (1) (2) [1]

In 1968 the taxpayer purchased a house and garden for £6,920. The total area of the property was less than an acre. He used it as his private residence until June 1971 when he sold the house and part of the garden for £10,000. He obtained outline planning approval for the remainder of the
E garden and sold it in May 1972 for £10,000. The general commissioners allowed his appeal against an assessment to capital gains tax in respect of the gain that accrued on the sale of the garden, holding that the exemption from tax provided for by section 29 (2) of the Finance Act 1965 applied to the disposal of the garden notwithstanding that it was sold at a later time than the house.

On appeal by the Crown:—
F *Held*, allowing the appeal, that on its true construction section 29 (1) (*b*) related only to a situation where at the actual time of disposal the taxpayer had the land for his own occupation with the dwelling house as its garden and, accordingly, the exemption contained in section 29 (2) did not apply where the garden was disposed of after the dwelling house to which it had been attached.

G

No cases are referred to in the judgment or were cited in argument.

CASE STATED by the Commissioners for the General Purposes of the Income Tax.

The taxpayer, John Francis Edward Lynes, purchased a freehold dwelling house at Hailsham, Sussex, in 1968 for £6,920. He sold the
H house and part of the garden in June 1971 for £10,000. The remainder of the garden was sold with outline planning approval in May 1972 for £10,000. On appeal against an assessment to capital gains tax for the year 1972–73 in the sum of £6,930, the general commissioners held that

---

[Reported by MRS. HARRIET DUTTON, Barrister-at-Law]

[1] Finance Act 1965, s. 29 (1) (2): see post, pp. 1092H—1093D.

the exemption contained in section 29 (1) of the Finance Act 1965 applied A
and reduced the assessment to nil. The Crown appealed.

The facts are stated in the judgment.

Brian Davenport for the Crown.
The taxpayer in person.

BRIGHTMAN J. This is an appeal by the Crown from a decision of the B
general commissioners. The short point at issue is the capital gains tax position where the taxpayer is the owner of a dwelling house and a garden, the dwelling house being his only residence; he sells off his dwelling house and a small piece of the garden; then, at a later date, he disposes of the remainder of the garden. Is the gain resulting from the disposal of the remainder of the garden a taxable gain? The question is a short C
one under section 29 of the Finance Act 1965 and is not in my view susceptible of any very satisfactory answer.

Section 19 of the Act of 1965 provided that tax should be charged in respect of chargeable gains accruing to a person on the disposal of assets. All forms of property are assets for this purpose by virtue of section 22. There are a few exceptions from the tax. The exception with which I
am concerned is that which applies under section 29 to certain private D
residences. Before I go to the section in detail, I will recount the brief facts.

The dwelling house was known as "Dalesford," at Hailsham in the county of East Sussex. It was acquired in 1968 by the taxpayer, Mr. Lynes, who appears before me in person. He paid £6,920 for it, including costs. The total area of the property, including the garden, was less E
than an acre. The property was intended for use as a private residence, and was in fact so used by him. In June 1971 he sold the house and a part of the garden at a price of £10,000. Thereupon, of course, it ceased to be his private residence. He retained the remainder of the garden and sold it in May 1972 for a like sum of £10,000. It appears that at the time when he sold off the dwelling house and the small part of the garden he
was informed by the local planning authority that favourable consideration F
would be given to a planning application for the development of the remainder of the garden. He applied for outline planning approval, which he obtained in January 1972, and sold the remainder of the garden a few months later.

On those facts the inspector of taxes assessed the taxpayer to capital gains tax in respect of a chargeable gain which the inspector maintained G
the taxpayer had secured on selling the remainder of the garden. When the matter came before the general commissioners, the taxpayer maintained that section 29 of the Act of 1965, to which I will refer in detail in a moment, did not expressly deal with the case of the disposal of a property in two parts, and that the exemption afforded by that section was equally applicable whether the whole of the property was the subject of a single
disposal or of two separate disposals. H

I will leave the respective contentions of the parties and turn to the statute itself. Section 29 (1) defines the items of property to which section 29 applies. It reads:

"This section applies to a gain accruing to an individual so far as attributable to the disposal of, or of an interest in,—(*a*) a dwelling house or part of a dwelling house which is, or has at any time in his

A period of ownership been, his only or main residence, or (*b*) land which
he has for his own occupation and enjoyment with that residence as
its garden or grounds up to an area (inclusive of the site of the dwelling
house) of one acre or such larger area as the commissioners concerned
may in any particular case determine, on being satisfied that, regard
being had to the size and character of the dwelling house, the larger
area is required for the reasonable enjoyment of it (or of the part in
B question) as a residence. In the case where part of the land occupied
with a residence is and part is not within this subsection, then (up to
the permitted area) that part shall be taken to be within this sub-
section which, if the remainder were separately occupied, would be
the most suitable for occupation and enjoyment with the residence."

Section 29 (2) contains the words of exemption. Section 29 (1) has
C identified the two items which can qualify for exemption; namely, the
dwelling house or what I will shortly describe as "the garden." The word
"or" is used, but clearly it is not intended to be disjunctive. Subsection
(2) reads:

> "The gain"—that means the gain in respect of the dwelling house or
> the gain in respect of the garden—"shall not be a chargeable gain if
> D the dwelling house or part of a dwelling house has been the individual's
> only or main residence throughout the period of ownership, or through-
> out the period of ownership except for all or any part of the last 12
> months of that period."

The qualification for the exemption, which applies to the two items within
section 29, is defined accordingly by reference to one only of those items;
E there is no mention in subsection (2) of the garden. The exception of "all
or any part of the last 12 months of that period" may perhaps have been
inserted in order to take into account the not uncommon case where a
person who is changing his residence buys and enters into occupation of
the new residence before he has been able to sell the previous residence.

Section 29 (3) deals with apportionment in a case where the dwelling
F house was the only or main residence for part only of the period of the
taxpayer's ownership, leaving aside the 12 months period covered by section
29 (2). It reads:

> "Where subsection (2) of this section does not apply a fraction of the
> gain shall not be a chargeable gain, and that fraction shall be—(*a*)
> the length of the part or parts of the period of ownership during which
> G the dwelling house or the part of the dwelling house was the indi-
> vidual's only or main residence, but inclusive of the last 12 months of
> the period of ownership in any event, divided by (*b*) the length of the
> period of ownership."

Section 29 (4) contains a further relaxation. I need not read subsection
(4) in detail, but paragraph (*a*) allows one to disregard a period of absence
H not exceeding three years; paragraph (*b*) a period of absence when the
taxpayer worked outside the United Kingdom; and paragraph (*c*) a period
of absence of up to four years where his employment precluded occupation.
Then there are various other subsections dealing with particular situations,
to which I need not refer.

As I have already said, the contention of the taxpayer was that the
exemption afforded by section 29 was equally applicable whether the house
and garden were sold off in the course of one or two separate transactions.

In particular, he contended that the phrase in section 29 (1) (*b*), “ land A which he has,” did not necessarily imply “ at the date of disposal.” He submitted that the phrase should be interpreted as meaning land which he has while owning the residence. In the instant case, the remainder of the garden was quite clearly land which the taxpayer had for his own occupation and enjoyment with the dwelling house as its garden during the whole period of his ownership of the dwelling house. Therefore, the taxpayer submitted, there is much reason and good sense in saying that it B should fall within the exemption afforded by section 29.

The contention of the inspector before the general commissioners was that the words “ has for his own occupation and enjoyment ” refer only to the moment of disposal. Accordingly, the garden would not be exempt in any case where it was disposed of at a time when the taxpayer no longer owned the dwelling house to which the garden had been attached. It was C contended by the inspector that there was no provision in the section which would allow for an apportionment of the gain on some sort of time basis in relation to the garden comparable with the apportionment which is appropriate in certain circumstances in the case of the dwelling house.

The commissioners expressed themselves very shortly in their decision in favour of the taxpayer. They held:

> “ . . . that the exemption contained in section 29 (2) of the Finance D Act 1965 applied having regard particularly to the words contained in the last part of that subsection. We therefore found in favour of the taxpayer and reduced the assessment to nil.”

The general commissioners, as they said, placed great emphasis on the concluding words of section 29 (2). It will be recalled that subsection (2) E grants exemption where the dwelling house was the taxpayer's only residence throughout his period of ownership but allows one to disregard the last 12 months of that period. To fall within subsection (2), the house must be the “ only or main residence throughout the period of ownership, or throughout the period of ownership except for all or any part of the last 12 months of that period.” I think that the general commissioners must have said to themselves this: “ It was clearly the intention of Parliament F that the dwelling house should be exempt notwithstanding that a few months before sale the taxpayer went out of occupation. If, therefore, we, the general commissioners, do not accede to the taxpayer's argument, we shall in effect be saying that Parliament intended that a garden should not qualify for exemption in a case where the taxpayer goes out of residence a month before he sells; and that,” the commissioners may have said to G themselves, “ would be an absurd construction.”

The point of interpretation is a short one. I think it can be summarised in exactly the way that the taxpayer put it in his contentions before the general commissioners; namely, should the court read the words “ land which he has for his own occupation and enjoyment with that residence as its garden or grounds ” as meaning land which he has at the H date of the disposal or land which he has at any time while owning the residence? The contentions advanced by the taxpayer before me are really exactly the same as the contentions advanced before the general commissioners.

Mr. Davenport, appearing for the Crown, has, I think quite rightly, not regarded it as any part of his duty to seek to justify the anomalies which may be thrown up by the Crown's construction of section 29 (1) (*b*)

A of the Act of 1965; nor, indeed, does he seek to deny that anomalies could be said to exist. The anomaly which I find most striking on the Crown's construction is the anomaly which I think impressed itself on the general commissioners; namely, the disregard for the purposes of section 29 (2) of the last 12 months of the period of ownership in respect of the dwelling house. Why, I ask myself, should that exemption not equally cover the garden? On the construction advanced by the Crown it must follow, I
B am disposed to think, that if the taxpayer goes out of occupation of the dwelling house a month before he sells it, the exemption will be lost in respect of the garden. That, however, is merely my impression, and I do not intend so to decide because it is not a matter for decision before me. A comparable anomaly may arise under section 29 (3), where one has an apportionment on a time basis in relation to the dwelling house.

C On the other hand, there would also seem to be anomalies thrown up by the construction advanced by the taxpayer. The taxpayer, in his short submission to me, did not shrink from conceding that his construction might produce anomalies. Take the case of a taxpayer who buys his dwelling house and garden in 1960, sells off his dwelling house in 1970 and retains the garden for future disposal. That garden is sold off, perhaps, 20 years later as a desirable and extremely valuable building site. In those
D circumstances, is the garden (or the former garden, as perhaps I should describe it) to fall within the exemption?

I accept Mr. Davenport's submission that in these circumstances all that the court can do is to look at the wording adopted by the legislature and decide whether or not the remainder of the garden in the present case falls or does not fall within the description in section 29 (1) (*b*). If it does
E fall within that description, then it qualifies for exemption under section 29 (2): if it falls outside that description, then it does not. It is no good counting up anomalies on one side and the other and twisting the language in order to produce what may seem to be, on balance, the most sensible result, and the one which perhaps Parliament might have preferred if all the various combinations of circumstances had been fully debated. The words are: "This section applies to a gain accruing to an individual so
F far as attributable to the disposal of, or of an interest in, . . . land which he has for his own occupation and enjoyment with that residence" i.e., a dwelling house or part of a dwelling house which is, or has at any time in his period of ownership been, his only or main residence "as its garden or grounds." The difficulty of relating the expression "land which he has for his own occupation and enjoyment with that residence as its
G garden or grounds" to any moment except the actual time of disposal is that section 29 (1) (*a*) is clearly looking both to the present and the past —"a dwelling house or part of a dwelling house which is, or has at any time in his period of ownership been, his only or main residence"—while by contrast section 29 (1) (*b*), as a matter of language, is looking only to the present; namely, "land which he has for his own occupation and
H enjoyment with that residence as its garden." In the face of that comparative wording, it does not seem to me possible, without doing violence to the language of section 29 (1) (*b*), to read it in the manner desired by the taxpayer.

In these circumstances it seems to me that I am bound to accept the argument advanced by the Crown and allow the appeal. I appreciate that this construction can produce anomalies and perhaps injustices. I am slightly comforted by the fact that the alternative construction would have A had its own crop of anomalies. Accordingly, I allow the appeal.

Appeal allowed and assessment restored.
No application for costs.

Solicitor: *Solicitor of Inland Revenue.* B

[HOUSE OF LORDS]

C

* BRUMBY (INSPECTOR OF TAXES) . . . . RESPONDENT

AND

MILNER . . . . APPELLANT

1975 Oct. 4, 5; 27 — Lord Wilberforce, Lord Diplock, Lord Simon of Glaisdale, Lord Kilbrandon D and Lord Edmund-Davies

Revenue—Income tax—Employment—Employees' profit-sharing scheme wound up—Distribution to employees of balance of funds—Whether payments emoluments arising from employment—Schedule E, Case I—Income and Corporation Taxes Act 1970 (*c.* 10), *ss.* 181 (1), 183 (1) [1]

E

Shareholders in a company wished to reduce their shareholdings but were anxious not to dispose of shares to people who might change the running of the company, and the directors of the company wanted to encourage their employees with a share incentive scheme. A profit-sharing scheme, therefore, was set up in 1963 whereby the company lent money to trustees to purchase the shares of those shareholders wishing to sell. A trust deed stated that the scheme's primary object was F that the shares acquired should provide income for division among employees and that on determination of the scheme any balance should be distributed among the employees and former employees in receipt of pensions in such proportions as the trustees should determine. In 1969 the company merged with another company and the administrative difficulties of continuing with the scheme were so great that the board was forced to wind it up. The trustees decided that a standard award G should be made for four years' service with increases for longer service or reductions for less. The amounts were not related to the level of the recipient's remuneration. The taxpayer had served the company since 1962. The appropriate

[1] Income and Corporation Taxes Act 1970, s. 181 (1): "The Schedule referred to as Schedule E is as follows:— Schedule E 1. Tax under this Schedule shall be charged in respect of any office or employment on emoluments therefrom which H fall under one, or more than one, of the following Cases—Case I: where the person holding the office or employment is resident and ordinarily resident in the United Kingdom, and does not perform the duties of the office or employment wholly outside the United Kingdom in the chargeable period (and the emoluments are not excepted as foreign emoluments), any emoluments for the chargeable period; . . ."

S. 183 (1): "Tax under Case I, II or III of Schedule E shall, except as hereinafter mentioned, be chargeable on the full amount of the emoluments falling under that Case, subject to such deductions only as may be authorised by the Tax Acts, and the expression 'emoluments' shall include all salaries, fees, wages, perquisites and profits whatsoever."

A amount in his case was £200·52 of which in the tax year 1971–72 he received £100 on an interim distribution. The special commissioners quashed the assessment to income tax holding that the causa causans of the payment was the decision to wind up the scheme. Walton J. allowed the Crown's appeal, holding that the taxpayer had received the payments in return for being an employee and accordingly income tax was payable under Schedule E. The Court of Appeal affirmed
B his decision.

On appeal by the taxpayer:—

Held, dismissing the appeal, that the capital payments, which could not be distinguished from the annual distributions, were taxable as being emoluments arising from the employment.

Hochstrasser v. *Mayes* [1960] A.C. 376, H.L.(E.) and *Laidler* v. *Perry* [1966] A.C. 16, H.L.(E.) applied.

C Decision of the Court of Appeal [1976] 1 W.L.R. 29; [1975] 3 All E.R. 1004 affirmed.

The following cases are referred to in their Lordships opinions:

Hochstrasser v. *Mayes* [1960] A.C. 376; [1960] 2 W.L.R. 63; [1959] 3 All E.R. 817, H.L.(E.).

Laidler v. *Perry* [1966] A.C. 16; [1965] 2 W.L.R. 1171; [1965] 2 All E.R.
D 121, H.L.(E.).

Pritchard v. *Arundale* [1972] Ch. 229; [1971] 3 W.L.R. 877; [1971] 3 All E.R. 1011.

Smith, Hogg & Co. Ltd. v. *Black Sea and Baltic General Insurance Co. Ltd.* [1940] A.C. 997; [1940] 3 All E.R. 405, H.L.(E.).

The following additional cases were cited in argument:

E *Dewhurst* v. *Hunter* (1932) 146 L.T. 510, H.L.(E.).

Moorhouse v. *Dooland* [1955] Ch. 284; [1955] 2 W.L.R. 96; [1955] 1 All E.R. 93, C.A.

Seymour v. *Reed* [1927] A.C. 554, H.L.(E.).

APPEAL from the Court of Appeal.

This was an appeal, by leave of the Court of Appeal (Russell, Stamp
F and Geoffrey Lane L.JJ.) from an order of that court dated October 3, 1975, which unanimously affirmed an order of the Chancery Division of the High Court of Justice (Walton J.) dated December 19, 1974, allowing an appeal by the present respondent, Michael Brumby (Inspector of Taxes), from a determination of the Commissioners for the Special Purposes of the Income Tax Acts in favour of the present appellant,
G Samuel Milner, and confirming an assessment to income tax as originally made by the respondent on the appellant.

On September 25, 1963, a trust deed was entered into by the directors of William Park & Co. Forgemasters Ltd. The deed was made in order to give employees of the company an incentive by means of a profit sharing scheme, and also to enable those of the shareholders in the company who wished to dispose of some of their shares in the company to
H sell them to the trustees. The company lent money to the trustees to enable them to purchase those shares. The trust deed recited that the primary object of the scheme was that shares in the company should provide income for division between employees. The trustees were to hold the income of the trust fund in trust to divide it between employees in such proportions as they thought fit and failing such decision between the employees equally. The trust could be determined in several ways and on such determination the trustees were bound to distribute any

balance after repayment of the loan between the employees in such proportion as they might determine and in default of determination, equally. In 1969 the company, to merge with another company, formed a holding company and the difficulties in continuing with the scheme were so great that the board was genuinely forced to wind it up. The trustees adopted a formula whereby employees should get a standard award for four years' service, with an increase for additional service or a reduction for less service. The amounts awarded were not related in any way to the level of the recipient's remuneration. Samuel Milner had served the company since 1962. The appropriate amount in his case was £200·52, of which in the tax year 1971–72 he received £100 as an interim distribution on June 23, 1971. The revenue assessed him thereon. On the appeal by the taxpayer to the special commissioners, it was held that the employment was not the causa causans of the payments, but the decision to wind up the scheme, and the assessment was therefore quashed.

Martin Nourse Q.C. and *Joseph Turner* for the appellant.
Peter Rees Q.C. and *Brian Davenport* for the respondent were not called on to argue.

Their Lordships took time for consideration.

October 27. LORD WILBERFORCE. My Lords, in 1963 William Park & Co. Forgemasters Ltd. decided to set up a profit-sharing scheme for the benefit of its employees. A sum of £700,000 was provided on loan to trustees, who were to use it to purchase shares in the company to be held upon the trusts of the scheme. These trusts were declared in a deed dated September 25, 1963. Dividends on the shares were to be used either to pay off the loan or to make payments to employees of the company and the scheme was so operated. Some £111,000 was applied in repayment of the debt, and £108,000 was distributed to employees, who individually received sums from £9 to £14 a year after deduction of tax.

Then in 1969 a change took place. The company became a subsidiary of a holding company which also controlled an allied undertaking, and the directors had to decide what to do with the scheme. They decided that it was impracticable to continue it, and so they used the power, which they had under the trust deed, to terminate the scheme by one year's notice. The trustees, then, realised the trust assets, paid off the balance of the debt and, in accordance with the clause in the trust deed which provided for this situation, they decided to distribute the balance in proportions fixed by them between 1,802 employees and 49 pensioners. Mr. Milner, the appellant, was one of the employees and he became entitled to £200. When the revenue heard about this they decided to assess him to income tax under Schedule E.

The test under Schedule E, now set out in sections 181 (1) and 183 (1) of the Income and Corporation Taxes Act 1970 is whether the sum in question is an emolument from the taxpayer's employment. "Emoluments" include any perquisite or profit. The only question in this, and in the many similar cases which come before the courts relating to such payments as cricketers' or footballers' benefits or for Easter offerings, or housing subsidies, is whether the emolument can be said to

A arise "from" the employment or office. In some instances, as the decisions show, this is not an easy question to answer: here it is plain.

The taxability of the annual distributions under the scheme is not an issue in this appeal but nobody has suggested, or could suggest, that these were not taxable. The only question is whether any ground could be found for distinguishing the capital payments made on the winding up of the scheme. In my opinion, with all respect to the efforts
B of learned counsel for the taxpayer, there is no ground for any such distinction. I shall not attempt to demonstrate this by detailed analysis of the trust deed, or by reference to such authorities as may, possibly, be relevant, since this has been done to my complete satisfaction by the Court of Appeal, affirming Walton J. To restate the argument in words of my own, even if this were to result in a difference of formu-
C lation, would not be productive of advantage, and I am more than content fully to adopt the single judgment of the Court of Appeal delivered by Lord Russell of Killowen.

The appeal can only be dismissed.

Lord Diplock. My Lords, I agree.

D

Lord Simon of Glaisdale. My Lords, the issue in this appeal has, in my respectful opinion, been satisfactorily disposed of in the unanimous judgment of the Court of Appeal delivered by my noble and learned friend, Lord Russell of Killowen. There is, indeed, little that can be added.

As the argument developed before your Lordships, there appeared
E to be some danger that the task of interpretation should be focused, not on the words of the statute, but on various judicial glosses of those words. What Lord Radcliffe said in *Hochstrasser* v. *Mayes* [1960] A.C. 376, 391, is therefore in point:

> "In the past several explanations have been offered by judges of eminence as to the significance of the word 'from' in this context.
> F It has been said that the payment must have been made to the employee 'as such.' It has been said that it must have been made to him 'in his capacity of employee.' It has been said that it is assessable if paid 'by way of remuneration for his services,' and said further that this is what is meant by payment to him 'as such.' These are all glosses, and they are all of value as illustrating the idea which is expressed by the words of the statute. But it is
> G perhaps worth observing that they do not displace those words."

Lord Radcliffe did not include among the glosses which he thus reviewed a distinction between "causa causans" and "causa sine qua non,"; though this distinction has had some eminent users in this context, and the concept was strongly pressed on your Lordships on behalf of the appellant. It was said that the causa causans of the payment was the
H decision to wind up the scheme: the appellant's employment was no more than its causa sine qua non. The distinction between a "causa causans" and a "causa sine qua non" was formerly much used in other branches of the law; but it was found to confuse rather than to illuminate (see Lord Wright in *Smith, Hogg & Co. Ltd.* v. *Black Sea and Baltic General Insurance Co. Ltd.* [1940] A.C. 997, 1003, cited by Megarry J. in *Pritchard* v. *Arundale* [1972] Ch. 229, 237, 238) and it has been generally abandoned. Causation has been debated by meta-

physicians and logicians throughout the recorded history of philosophy: the debate continues, with more sophisticated tools of analysis than the terms "causa causans" and "causa sine qua non." These will rarely if ever assist the law, where they have frequently been used without definition or analysis. "Causa causans" is a tautology. "Causa sine qua non," seems to have been used in two senses: first, to denote a matter which has had no effect on the situation before the court, but has merely provided a setting for a matter which has had such an effect; and, secondly, to denote a matter which has had some effect, but which, other matters having had a more potent effect, it is the policy of the law to disregard. In my respectful submission these terms are of little assistance in solving the problem before your Lordships. But even were I to think that the issue before your Lordships could be determined by outmoded and ambiguous concepts of causation couched in Latin, I would not, with all respect, be prepared to accept the appellant's categorisation.

A far less question-begging test was suggested by Lord Radcliffe in *Hochstrasser* v. *Mayes* [1960] A.C. 376 and by Lord Reid in *Laidler* v. *Perry* [1966] A.C. 16. The former case was concerned with a large employer, many of whose employees (including the taxpayer) were required by their service agreements to be prepared to move to new work locations. Their moves might well involve the sale of their houses at a loss. The employer undertook to make good any such loss. The question was whether such compensatory payment was taxable under Schedule E. Lord Radcliffe said [1960] A.C. 376, 392:

> "The essential point is that what was paid to [the taxpayer] was paid to him in respect of his personal situation as a house-owner."

If the payment to the appellant was not made to him in respect of his personal situation as an employee, in what respect was it paid to him? This question was not answered.

Lord Reid adopted a complementary approach in *Laidler* v. *Perry* [1966] A.C. 16, 30:

> ". . . we must always return to the words in the statute and answer the question—did this profit arise from the employment? The answer will be 'no' if it arose from something else."

It was conceded that payments to the instant taxpayer from the income of the trust fund arose relevantly from the appellant's employment. From what else did the capital payment arise?

I would dismiss the appeal.

LORD KILBRANDON. My Lords, in my opinion the disposing of this appeal does not call for yet another attempt to substitute some exegetical phrase for the simple words of section 183 (1), namely, emoluments from any office or employment. I prefer to adopt the approach taken by Lord Reid in *Laidler* v. *Perry* [1966] A.C. 16, 30:

> "There is a wealth of authority on this matter and various glosses on or paraphrases of the words in the Act appear in judicial opinions, including speeches in this House. No doubt they were helpful in the circumstances of the cases in which they were used, but in the end we must always return to the words in the statute and answer the question—did this profit arise from the employment? The answer will be 'no' if it arose from something else."

Taking that approach, I find myself in entire agreement with the conclusion arrived at by the Court of Appeal, and there is little more that need be said.

It is conceded that the income payments made from the trust fund to employees arose from their several employments and were properly taxable in their hands. It was therefore necessary for the appellant to show that, by contrast, the payment out of capital, to use Lord Reid's words, " arose from something else." It was submitted that the payment arose not from the appellant's employment but from the company's reluctant decision to wind up the profit-sharing scheme. I cannot agree with that. Certainly the money forming the payment became available in consequence of certain events and decisions connected with the structure of the company. But the sole reason for making the payment to the appellant was that he was an employee, and the payment arose from his employment. It arose from nothing else, as it would have done, if for example, it had been made to an employee for some compassionate reason. In such a case, as Lord Reid pointed out in *Laidler* v. *Perry*, at pp. 31–32, " the gift is not made merely because the donee is an employee." There would be another reason personal to the recipient, namely his distress. There is no such other reason here.

I would accordingly dismiss this appeal.

LORD EDMUND-DAVIES. My Lords, I respectfully concur with the judgment of my noble and learned friend on the Woolsack and would accordingly dismiss the appeal.

Appeal dismissed.

Solicitors: *Field, Fisher & Martineau for Arthur Smith & Broadie-Griffith, Wigan; Solicitor of Inland Revenue.*

F. C.

[QUEEN'S BENCH DIVISION]

* REGINA *v.* FENNY STRATFORD JUSTICES, *Ex parte* WATNEY MANN (MIDLANDS) LTD.

1976 Feb. 25, 26 — Lord Widgery C.J., Kilner Brown and Watkins JJ.

Nuisance—Public—Noise abatement—Order to abate nuisance—Noise not to exceed 70 *decibels—Whether jurisdiction to impose term—Whether void for uncertainty—Public Health Act* 1936 (26 *Geo.* 5 & 1 *Edw.* 8, *c.* 49), *s.* 94 (2)

Three local residents made a complaint to justices under the Public Health Act 1936 that music from a juke-box played in a public house was so loud that it created a statutory nuisance. The justices found that the complaint was true and ordered,

---

[Reported by BERNARD O. AGYEMAN, ESQ., Barrister-at-Law]

under section 94 (2) of the Act,[1] that the nuisance be abated A
and that the level of noise in the premises should not exceed
70 decibels. The proprietors of the public house applied for
an order of certiorari to quash that part of the order that
restricted the level of sound to 70 decibels:—

Held, granting the application, (1) that the justices were
not restricted to making an order to abate a nuisance but
had power to impose any additional terms provided that
those terms were practical, couched in language easily under- B
stood by both those who were aggrieved by the nuisance
and those on whom the order was imposed and, where
appropriate, the action which had to be taken to comply
with the terms of the order (post, p. 1106D–E).

(2) That, although the justices had rightly considered
using the modern method of measuring sound to incorporate
into the order a term stating the level of noise in decibels
which it was impermissible to exceed, they had failed to C
state in the order the place where the sound meter was to
be positioned to record the number of decibels and they
had also failed to consider the likelihood of sounds other
than the noise from the juke-box; that, therefore, the term
was so imprecise as to be void for uncertainty (post, pp. 1105H
—1106A, E—1107A, B–E).

Nottingham City District Council v. *Newton* [1974] 1
W.L.R. 923, 929, 930, D.C. and *Salford City Council* v. *Mc-* D
Nally [1976] A.C. 379, H.L.(E.) applied.

The following cases are referred to in the judgment:

McGillivray v. *Stephenson* [1950] 1 All E.R. 942, D.C.
Nottingham City District Council v. *Newton* [1974] 1 W.L.R. 923; [1974] 2 All E.R. 760, D.C.
Reg. v. *Wheatley, Ex parte Cowburn* (1885) 16 Q.B.D. 34, D.C. E
Salford City Council v. *McNally* [1976] A.C. 379; [1975] 3 W.L.R. 87; [1975] 2 All E.R. 860, H.L.(E.).

The following additional cases were cited in argument:

Millard v. *Wastall* [1898] 1 Q.B. 342, D.C.
Tough v. *Hopkins* [1904] 1 K.B. 804, D.C. F

APPLICATION for order of certiorari.

The respondents, Peter Frederick Cartlidge, David John Vicarage
and John Trevor Shawn Coles, were the occupiers of premises near
Fingals public house, 111, Serpentine Court, Bletchley, in the county
of Buckingham. They made a complaint to the justices of a nuisance G
caused by noise from a juke-box played in the public house. The
justices found that a statutory nuisance existed on the premises
and ordered "that the nuisance be abated and that the level of
noise in the said premises known as 'Fingals' shall not exceed
70 dB(A)."

The applicants, Watney Mann (Midlands) Ltd., the proprietors of H
the public house, applied for an order of certiorari to quash that
part of the order requiring that the level of noise at the public house
should not exceed 70 decibels on the ground that the inclusion of those
words constituted an error of law on the face of the record.

The facts are stated in the judgment of Watkins J.

[1] Public Health Act 1936, s. 94 (2): see post, p. 1104C–D.

A *Anthony Scrivener Q.C.* and *Richard Rundell* for the applicants.
Anthony Hidden for the respondents.

LORD WIDGERY C.J. I will ask Watkins J. to give the first judgment.

WATKINS J. The applicants, Watney Mann (Midlands) Ltd., who are well known brewers, move for an order of certiorari, upon the
B grounds set out in a statement which accompanies the motion, to have brought into this court and quashed part of an order made by the justices of the petty sessional division of Fenny Stratford in the county of Buckingham on May 15, 1975, whereby it was ordered that the level of noise in their premises known as Fingals public house, 111, Serpentine Court, Bletchley, should not exceed 70 decibels.

C The public house lies within a large building which contains also a number of flats. Adjoining or nearby this building are other blocks of flats and houses. At one time the applicants had a band on the premises which played music during the evenings for the entertainment of customers. Complaints were made by local residents both within and without the building where the public house is situate
D about the noise which that band was making. It was disturbing their peace and comfort in the enjoyment of their own homes. So the applicants dispensed with the services of the band. They installed in its place a juke-box—an instrument which operates gramophone records automatically upon the insertion of a coin. That instrument had not very long been installed by the applicants before the same people who had been complaining before about the noise of the band, or some of
E them, made a complaint about the noise which was coming into their homes as a result of playing the juke-box. Because they had no satisfaction, so they thought, from complaints made to the managers of the public house, they brought proceedings before the justices, as they were entitled to do by the provisions of section 99 of the Public Health Act 1936 as amended by section 1 (2) (*a*) of the Noise Abatement Act
F 1960. Those sections enable not less than three aggrieved persons to go on complaint to a magistrates' court and seek a nuisance order, which the justices must make if satisfied that the existence of a statutory nuisance has been proved by the evidence before them.

It is well known to anyone who, during his practising days, has been concerned with applications for injunctions in nuisance cases referable to noise, that the terms of such injunctions have, after the
G making of them, given rise to considerable perplexity and difficulty. It is, I think, also well recognised—at any rate it is my opinion—that excessive noise is one of the curses of the modern age. One of the reasons why this is so is that somebody invented the amplifier, which serves at least one purpose, namely, very nearly to blast out the eardrums of anyone within its proximity.

H Returning to the legislation relating to a statutory nuisance, which is what this court is concerned with in this application, I need to refer very briefly to the powers which lie within Part III of the Public Health Act 1936 so far as a local authority is concerned. The authority is enabled to cause to be examined dwelling houses and other places in the area which it governs and to serve, if it thinks fit, having regard to whether or no it considers there is a statutory nuisance within its jurisdiction, an abatement notice. That abatement notice

can impose whatever terms the local authority considers necessary A
to effectively abate the nuisance complained of. If the terms of the notice are not complied with, then the local authority is enabled to make a complaint to the justices. The justices, upon the complaint, can then make a nuisance order. Upon the making of a nuisance order, the person against whom it is made is under a statutory duty to carry out its terms. If he fails to do so, he lays himself open to
a maximum penalty of £5. B

When three aggrieved persons make a complaint, that procedure is not wholly available to them. They do not have to serve an abatement notice. Their first action is to go immediately by complaint to the justices. So I look at the provisions of section 94 of the Act which deals with the power of the court to make a nuisance order.
Section 94 (2) provides: C

> "If on the hearing of the complaint it is proved that the alleged nuisance exists, or that although abated it is likely to recur on the same premises, then, subject to the provisions of subsections (4) and (5) of this section the court shall make an order (hereafter in this Act referred to as 'a nuisance order') for either,
> or both, of the following purposes—(*a*) requiring the defendant D
> to comply with all or any of the requirements of the abatement notice, or otherwise to abate the nuisance, within a time specified in the order, and to execute any works necessary for that purpose; . . ."

Omitting those parts which are referable only to the making of a
complaint by a local authority subsection (2) (*a*) reads: E

> "requiring the defendant . . . to abate the nuisance, within a time specified in the order, and to execute any works necessary for that purpose."

It has been argued before us that while on the evidence before the justices, to which I shall refer in a moment, they were entitled
to make a nuisance order simpliciter, they were disentitled to go on F
in that order to add the words complained of, namely, that the noise in the public house should not exceed 70 decibels.

Mr. Scrivener founds his argument that those words should not have been included upon two bases. First, he contends that the words must be void for uncertainty because no one who has the task of ensuring that the noise limits should not exceed 70 decibels knows precisely where to
go in order to determine what the sound level is at any particular G
time. Secondly, he submits that all that persons aggrieved can achieve by way of a nuisance order at the hands of the justices is one or more of these effects. First, they may have a nuisance order simpliciter, that is to say one without any terms whatsoever added to the simple order to abate. Secondly, the order can contain a time within
which the nuisance is to be abated. Thirdly, where it is necessary in H
order to abate the nuisance for works to be undertaken by the person upon whom the order is imposed, those works should be set out in sufficient particularity for the person concerned to know exactly what it is he has to do to abate the nuisance. Now it is quite clear that justices may simply make a nuisance order without adding any further words to the order. Those affected by it are then left to their own devices to carry out the order as best they think fit. It

A is equally clear that time limits may be imposed upon the person or persons who have to carry out the order, and that a specification of works can be made in the order. But, says Mr. Scrivener, nothing else can be put in the order since the Act makes it plain that those three conditions and no more contain the powers of justices. He referred in support of this argument to a number of cases, including *Reg.* v. *Wheatley, Ex parte Cowburn* (1885) 16 Q.B.D. 34; *McGillivray*
B v. *Stephenson* [1950] 1 All E.R. 942 and *Nottingham City District Council* v. *Newton* [1974] 1 W.L.R. 923.

What is the answer, if answer there be, to these submissions? It seems to me to be abundantly plain from the authorities to which I choose to refer in some detail that there is a complete answer. In the *Nottingham* case Lord Widgery C.J. said, at pp. 929–930:

C "In my view the position of the justices as a matter of law was this: once they were satisfied that the house constituted a statutory nuisance they were bound to make a nuisance order under section 94 but they have within the framework of the section a considerable tolerance as regards the precise terms which the nuisance order shall take. It must be directed, of
D course, to the abatement of the nuisance, that is the purpose of the order, but the section makes it clear that the justices have a discretion as to whether to require the owner to do the whole of that work referred to in the abatement notice as opposed to only part of it. Further the section expressly gives a discretion in regard to the time within which the work has to be done, and in my judgment would certainly enable the justices to divide
E the work into phases or programmes requiring some to be done quickly and others to be done at a later time. If there is real danger to the health of the occupier of the house, the justices of course, within the terms of section 94, can impose a prohibition on the house being lived in until the work is done, a prohibition which might have been unpopular with the tenant, but never-
F theless it was urged by her counsel as one of the factors which might be taken into account.

"In deciding within that wide ambit of detailed discretion just what the terms of the nuisance order should be, I have no doubt it is the duty of the justices, as common sense dictates, to look at the whole circumstances of the case and to try and make an order which is in its terms sensible and just having
G regard to the entire prevailing situation."

In *Salford City Council* v. *McNally* [1976] A.C. 379, 389; [1975] 3 W.L.R. 87, 92 Lord Wilberforce said:

"And the magistrate should find specifically under which limb the case falls. If he answers either question in the affirmative
H he must make an abatement order, and he should, if possible, make this as specific as he can, rather than order in general terms to abate the statutory nuisance."

These two quotations serve, in my opinion, to demonstrate that justices, when a complaint is made to them, be it by a local authority or by three or more aggrieved persons, have a wide discretion as to what terms they include in any nuisance order which they feel enabled to make as a result of evidence provided to them. I think it was

very helpful of the justices in the instant case to attempt to provide A
not only the applicants but also those who had complained with some
specific guidance upon the question of noise, so that this very difficult
problem could be thereby more easily solved.

Modern science enables it to be solved to some extent. Sound
meters have been devised which are capable of measuring the volume
of sound in decibels. It is pertinent to recall that at the first hearing
before the justices one of the matters which seems to have disturbed B
the person called on behalf of the applicants was that he could not
get sufficient assistance from the local public health authority about
precisely what it was he had to do in order to abate the nuisance.
So the justices adjourned the hearing. The adjournment enabled
someone from the health department of the local authority to go to
the premises and to the flats and dwellings outside them to make C
recordings upon a sound meter of the volume of noise flowing into
those premises as a result of the operation of the juke-box inside the
public house. In that way the justices at the second hearing felt
able to determine a level of noise above which it was impermissible,
in their view, for the applicants to permit the juke-box to be operated.

My conclusions about the powers of the justices when making
nuisance orders are that they can add any additional term they D
choose to the simple order to abate, provided that, first, the term is
practical in its effect; secondly, it is couched in such language as to
be easily understood not only by those who claim to have been
aggrieved by the statutory nuisance but also by any person upon
whom the order is imposed; and, thirdly, words are used to specify,
where appropriate, the action which has to be taken by the person E
upon whom the order is imposed to comply with this term.

I agree, however, with Mr. Scrivener that in the instant case it
can properly be said that there was an imprecision in the form of
the term complained of in the order which makes it void for un-
certainty. The sound meter, assuming it to be accurately used and
adjusted, can, according to the order of the justices, be taken to any
part of the public house, and I dare say at any one of different places F
it could produce a different reading. Moreover, the readings which
would be registered upon the sound meter would be affected not only
by the sound coming from the juke-box but also by the number of
people in the public house and the hubbub created by their general
conversation and so forth. The form can be validly criticised upon
the basis that the place for determining whether a nuisance exists G
is not to be ascertained by standing, in the case of noise, in the
premises from which the noise emanates, but by standing in the nearest
of the dwelling places, and listening to the noise flowing into that
place. Thus, if I had been the justices and tempted to make such
an order as this, I would, in yielding to the temptation, have chosen
a spot, after visiting all the relevant premises, at which sound meter H
readings should be taken so as to judge whether the terms of the
nuisance order were being kept or not. For the sole reason that the
justices failed to achieve that result I have come to the conclusion
that this application succeeds.

KILNER BROWN J. I agree.

A LORD WIDGERY C.J. I agree that this order should be set aside on the ground that it is void for uncertainty. That is sufficient to dispose of the matter presently before us, and I have been somewhat perplexed in my own mind as to how far we could usefully go. I think, having regard to what we have been told, it may be helpful if we express some views such as Watkins J. has expressed in regard to the use of decibels and the sound meter in future.

B Of course, the law allows the occupier of premises alleged to be creating a nuisance to abate the nuisance in his own way if no specific works are required. Of course, it is open to those who draft the summons, the order or the notice (which can be relevant under these provisions) to describe the nuisance in general terms as a nuisance and to require its abatement in general terms. This case, however,
C does throw up for the first time the very interesting question of whether the introduction by modern science of the conception of the decibel cannot be used for the purposes of precision in cases such as the present.

I agree with Watkins J. that it can and should. It seems to me that if the justices take the trouble to hear evidence which translates noise into a decibel reading and satisfy themselves that any emanation
D of noise in excess of a certain level is a nuisance, they can as well describe that which is to be done as a reduction of noise volume to below so many decibels instead of using the time-honoured formula of "abate the nuisance." I think that we should try to use the advantages which scientific development gives us rather than to reject them, and I think here there is an opportunity of using a scientific
E approach to what has always previously been a somewhat haphazard assessment.

I agree that the order must be quashed and the basis of my agreement is that it is void for uncertainty.

Application granted with costs.
Part of order set aside and matter
F *remitted to justices for rehearing.*

Solicitors: *Bower, Cotton & Bower for Becke Phipps, Northampton; Sharpe, Pritchard & Co. for S. A. J. Levene, Milton Keynes.*

G

[HOUSE OF LORDS]

* ARSENAL FOOTBALL CLUB LTD. . . . . . PETITIONERS

AND

SMITH AND ANOTHER . . . . RESPONDENTS

H 1976 Oct. 25 — Lord Diplock, Lord Kilbrandon and Lord Russell of Killowen

Petition by the club for leave to appeal to the House of Lords from the decision of the Court of Appeal in *Arsenal Football Club Ltd.* v. *Ende* [1976] 3 W.L.R. 508.

The Appeal Committee allowed the petition.

M. G.

[HOUSE OF LORDS]

* ANNS AND OTHERS . . . . . . RESPONDENTS

AND

MERTON LONDON BOROUGH COUNCIL . . . APPELLANTS

1976 Oct. 21 Lord Wilberforce, Lord Diplock and Lord Kilbrandon

House of Lords—New point raised on appeal—Leave to argue—Action held to be time-barred—Court of Appeal granting leave on limitation point—Leave to argue question of duty

Limitation of Action—Time, computation of—Local authority—Defective premises—Allegation of negligence in approving foundations of dwelling house—Action started more than six years after foundations passed—Action held statute-barred—Subsequent decision holding contrary—Appeal allowed—Leave to argue question of duty on appeal

APPLICATION for leave to argue an additional point.

The respondents, lessees for 999 years of certain maisonettes in a block within the area of the appellant council, sued, inter alia, the council for damages on the ground that there was a cause of action against a local authority which had negligently approved faulty foundations of a house: *Dutton* v. *Bognor Regis Urban District Council* [1972] 1 Q.B. 373; [1972] 2 W.L.R. 299; [1972] 1 All E.R. 462. The appellants denied that such a duty existed and contended that, in any event, any cause of action was time-barred.

The Official Referee (Judge Fay) held that the action was time-barred.

The Court of Appeal [1976] Q.B. 882; [1976] 2 W.L.R. 512 allowed the appeal and, in view of the decision in *Sparham-Souter* v. *Town and Country Developments (Essex) Ltd.* [1976] Q.B. 858; [1976] 2 W.L.R. 493; [1976] 2 All E.R. 65, in relation to limitation of actions, granted leave to appeal to the House of Lords.

The appellants sought leave to argue before the House of Lords not only the question of limitation but also that of duty.

K. F. Goodfellow Q.C. and *John Tackaberry* for the appellants.
Michael Johnson for the respondents.

The Appeal Committee granted leave.

Application granted.

Solicitors: *Barlow, Lyde & Gilbert; W. H. Matthews & Co.*

F. C.

A

[QUEEN'S BENCH DIVISION]

* READER'S DIGEST ASSOCIATION LTD. *v.* WILLIAMS

1976 July 26 — Lord Widgery C.J., Melford Stevenson and Caulfield JJ.

B

Gaming—Lottery—Draw—Promotion of sales—Goods offered for sale with participation in lucky number draw—Chance of prize unaffected by refusal to purchase—Whether lottery

The defendants who were publishers and sellers of magazines, books and records organised a sales promotion whereby
C £30,000 was to be distributed as prize money in a draw. 4,700,000 sets of numbers were allocated names of individuals from the defendants' computer file and out of those 2,103 were selected at random as winning numbers. Each of the 4,700,000 individuals was sent, through the post, an envelope containing an offer to sell some of the defendants' goods together with a list of numbers. If a recipient returned a winning number he was entitled to a prize irrespective of
D whether he agreed to purchase the defendants' goods or not. The number of recipients with winning numbers who had not agreed to purchase goods was estimated at 69 per cent. of the numbers returned. On an information preferred against the defendants, they were convicted by the justices of using premises for purposes connected with the promotion or conduct of a lottery contrary to section 42 (1) (*f*) of the Betting, Gaming and Lotteries Act 1963.

E On appeal by the defendants against conviction:—

Held, allowing the appeal, that the requirements of a lottery were a distribution of prizes, an element of chance in winning a prize and a contribution made by each participant towards his chance of winning a prize (post, p. 1113C–D); that although some of the participants might have contributed towards the defendants' profits by making purchases, eligibility for a prize was not dependent on agreeing to make a purchase,
F and, therefore, since the participants were not obliged to pay for their chance, either directly or indirectly, the defendants were not running a lottery (post, pp. 1113E–F, 1116C–E, 1117C).

Whitbread & Co. Ltd. v. *Bell* [1970] 2 Q.B. 547, D.C. applied.

Willis v. *Young and Stembridge* [1907] 1 K.B. 448, D.C. distinguished.

G

The following cases are referred to in the judgments:

Atkinson v. *Murrell* [1973] A.C. 289; [1972] 3 W.L.R. 465; [1972] 2 All E.R. 1131, H.L.(E.).

McCollom v. *Wrightson* [1968] A.C. 522; [1968] 2 W.L.R. 578; [1968] I All E.R. 514 H.L.(E.).

Whitbread & Co. Ltd. v. *Bell* [1970] 2 Q.B. 547; [1970] 2 W.L.R. 1025; [1970] 2 All E.R. 64, D.C.

H

Willis v. *Young and Stembridge* [1907] 1 K.B. 448, D.C.

The following additional cases were cited in argument:

Barnes v. *Strathern*, 1929 J.C. 41.

Bartlett v. *Parker* [1912] 2 K.B. 497, D.C.

[Reported by RACHEL DAVIES, Barrister-at-Law]

Douglas v. *Valente*, 1968 S.L.T. 85. A
Hall v. *McWilliam* (1901) 85 L.T. 239.
Minty v. *Sylvester* (1915) 84 L.J. K.B. 1982.

CASE STATED by the City of London justices sitting at the Guildhall.

On March 6, 1975, an information was preferred by the prosecutor, Hywel Williams, against the defendants, Reader's Digest Association Ltd. that on September 25, 1974, they used certain premises, namely, 7–10 Old B Bailey, for the purposes connected with the promotion or conduct of a lottery known as the Reader's Digest £30,000 Summer Prize Draw contrary to section 42 (1) (*f*) of the Betting, Gaming and Lotteries Act 1963.

The justices heard the information on July 22 and 23, 1975, and found the following facts which were admitted in court under section 10 of the Criminal Justice Act 1967. They were, in part, contained in an agreed C statement of facts. No other evidence was given. The defendants used the premises 7–10 Old Bailey to conduct the £30,000 Summer Draw on September 25, 1974. The prize money for the Summer Draw was paid out of the defendants' general funds. 4,700,000 sets of numbers were included in the draw. 2,103 of these were winning numbers and were selected by chance. The 4,700,000 sets of numbers were allocated names from a computer file of over 20 million names. Of the computer file D names allocated sets of numbers in the Summer Draw, some 1,300,000 were those of "current customers" (i.e. people who had ordered some product from the defendants during the preceding 12 months or were currently taking a periodical series of products from the defendants), some 2,500,000 were those of "previous customers" (i.e. those who had ordered, but not necessarily bought, some product from the defendants E since 1968, but excluding "current customers"); and some 783,000 were of those who had never before had any dealings with the defendants. The numbers were sent to the computer file names in an envelope containing an invitation either to: (a) subscribe to Reader's Digest at a reduced price or (b) subscribe to Reader's Digest Condensed Books and receive a free book or (c) purchase the Repair Manual at a liberal discount and receive a free gift. F

Prizes were offered to call attention "to a money saving trial subscription offer to Reader's Digest." Those persons who were sent numbers were asked to return them for checking in either the "No" envelope or the "Yes" envelope provided. They were advised that they did not have to order or subscribe to any product to participate in the Summer Draw, that numbers returned would be checked against the list of winning G numbers and that those people who had winning numbers and returned them would, without any further action on their part, be informed of their success. A full list of winners would be prepared and would be available to anyone on request. The number of "Yes" envelopes returned was 856,307. No full record of "No" envelopes returned was kept but the best estimate available was that the number was in excess of 1,589,000. 69 per cent. of those who proved to have winning numbers had used "No" H envelopes. The closing date of the Summer Draw, namely the date by which envelopes had to be returned to the defendants, was October 31, 1974. 132,005 of those readers who returned the "Yes" envelopes placed an order for Reader's Digest magazine. Of the remaining "Yes" recipients, some bought other products and others took products on approval but did not buy. Unclaimed prizes totalling £23,725 were distributed to charity. The defendants' net pre-tax profits to June 1974 were £2,592,203.

A Subject to a wide margin for error the net pre-tax profits of the defendants from the " Yes " answers were very approximately £200,000.

It was contended by the defendants that an essential feature of the case was that participants who did not want the product on its merits did not buy it, and those who bought it did so because they wanted it at the price; that it was a gratuitous scheme; that there was not a sufficient
B contribution, if the participants contributed to the general profits of the promoter out of which prize funds might come, unless such contribution was for the opportunity to obtain a prize; that *Willis* v. *Young and Stembridge* [1907] 1 K.B. 448 was distinguishable from the present case in that a substantial body of participants bought the paper to see if they held a winning medal and thus contributed towards their opportunity of getting a prize and it had been restricted by later authority as depending " entirely
C . . . on its very special facts " an essential one being that many participants paid " not to read it (the paper) but in order to ascertain their winning numbers."

It was contended by the prosecutor that there was a sufficient contribution as the participants contributed to the general profits of the promoters out of which the prize fund came, and that *Willis* v. *Young and Stembridge* did not apply in the present case.
D
The justices were of the opinion that: the Summer Draw was a distribution of money by chance; that it was the defendants' hope and intention that the recipients of the invitations sent would either purchase or subscribe to one of their products, thus contributing to the profits out of which the prizes were paid; and that a sufficient number of participants had paid for their chance by contributing to the funds out of which prizes
E were provided. The justices found the case proved and fined the defendants £50 and ordered them to pay £150 in respect of the costs of the prosecution.

The question for the opinion of the High Court was whether the contribution by some participants to the funds out of which prizes were provided was sufficient payment to establish an unlawful lottery contrary
F to section 41 of the Betting, Gaming and Lotteries Act 1963.

Norman Tapp Q.C. and *Nigel Inglis-Jones* for the defendants.
G. W. Cheyne for the prosecutor.

Lord Widgery C.J. This is an appeal by case stated by justices for the City of London sitting as a magistrates' court at the Guildhall in
G July 1975. On that occasion the justices found the defendants guilty of an offence under the Betting, Gaming and Lotteries Act 1963 in that it was alleged against them, and found to be properly alleged by the justices, that they had used premises 7–10 Old Bailey—a rather odd choice for criminal activity—to conduct the £30.000 Summer Prize Draw on September 25, 1974. The justices found that the use to which the premises
H were put was the promotion of a lottery and convicted.

The defendants appeal to this court, saying that the justices were wrong in law. It is an interesting and important case, and we have been very much assisted in it by the help which we had from counsel.

This is what happened. The defendants ran what is clearly an advertising campaign, and they addressed this campaign to no less than 4,700,000 people in this country whose names and addresses they possessed on magnetic tape obtained by one means or another. Amongst those 4,700,000 people were to be distributed, assuming they were all playing, 2,103 prizes. The way in which it was worked was this.

Each of the 4,700,000 would receive through the post an envelope and letter addressed to him personally. When he opened the envelope he would find that it contained, first of all, an offer to sell some of the defendants' material, their magazine, one of their books, a gramophone record, or something of that kind. Secondly, there was a list of six numbers, but more of that anon. In the cases before me each number contained six digits, but I think that is perhaps coincidental. There were also two envelopes—one marked " Yes please " and the other marked " No, thank you."

Reading the instructions, it appears this is what was to be done. You had to consider whether you wished to take advantage of the sale offer contained in the paper, whatever that might be. If you wished to take advantage of the sale offer, you returned the envelope marked " Yes please "; if you did not wish to take advantage of the offer, you returned the " No, thank you " envelope, and there was no sort of obligation upon you to buy the article in question at all. But whether you returned the " Yes " or " No " envelope, by doing so you made yourself eligible to receive one of the 2,103 prizes to which I have already made reference because if any of your six numbers which you returned in your " Yes " or " No " envelope, as the case may be, proved to be one of the prize numbers, then you had a prize attributable to that number. The numbers were chosen at random before the campaign began, and the numbers were unique in that there was no duplication at all throughout the entire scope of this mammoth enterprise. If therefore 107164, to take an example, happened to be a prize number and you had it in your envelope, then you qualified for the appropriate prize whether you returned the " No " label or the " Yes " label.

It is in my judgment of the utmost importance to bear in mind that the eligibility to secure a prize, and indeed that means the prize appropriate to the numbers which had been sent to you, was in no way dependent upon whether you accepted the purchase offer or not. Whether you sent back the " Yes " envelope or the " No " envelope was exactly the same; you qualified for a prize if you had got the right number. If you had not got the right number, you did not get it.

In deciding how these various offers should be distributed the defendants sent them to three categories of person. 1,300,000 were sent to current customers—customers who had bought from the defendants at least within the last year; 2,500,000 were those of " previous customers " who had bought goods from the defendants in the past but not in the last 12 months, and the remainder—some 783,000—were what are called " new customers," that is to say customers who had never dealt with the defendants before. I do not understand the importance apparently attached to that breakdown or division because it does not seem to me to make any difference to the conclusion.

The results of the Summer Draw are perhaps of some importance. Out of the 4,700,000 envelopes originally sent out the " Yes " envelope was returned by 856,307 people. The " No " envelope at the best estimate was returned by 1,589,000 people so a very marked majority opted for the " No " envelope, who even if they could not be made to pay anything might be lucky enough to get a prize.

One asks oneself what lies behind all this and why it is done. Of course the short answer is that no doubt the defendants are good business people

A and they know their business, and they know this is a sensible thing to do. But, be that as it may, the best estimate of the profit arising from this operation was something of the order of £200,000, so that it obviously was worthwhile putting up a prize fund of about £30,000 in order to launch such a transaction.

But of course all is lost if the arrangement is illegal, and if, as the prosecution say in this case, the whole thing is illegal and a lottery, then
B it has been a failure.

The Act of Parliament relevant to this is the Betting, Gaming and Lotteries Act 1963, section 41 of which provides: "Subject to the provisions of this Act, all lotteries which do not constitute gaming are unlawful."

The question, as I say, has been: is this a lottery as a matter of law?
C A lottery is the distribution of prizes by chance where the persons taking part in the operation, or a substantial number of them, make a payment or consideration in return for obtaining their chance of a prize. There are really three points one must look for in deciding whether a lottery has been established: first of all, the distribution of prizes; secondly, the fact this was to be done by means of a chance; and thirdly, that there must be some actual contribution made by the participants in return for
D their obtaining a chance to take part in the lottery.

It must not be entirely forgotten in the construction of these Acts of Parliament that the evil which the lottery law has sought to prevent was the evil which existed where poor people with only a few pence to feed their children would go and put these few pence into a lottery and lose it, and this sociologically was a bad thing. It is for that reason—the reason
E that that is the mischief aimed at—that the lotteries have always required the third factor to which I have referred, namely, that there should be some contribution from the participant, or from a substantial number of the participants, in return for obtaining a chance.

If one looks at the present case there is absolutely no such contribution that I can see payable in return for obtaining a chance. I need not
F go over the ground again because I hope I have dealt with it adequately, but on the facts which I have outlined the prospect of a prize was exactly the same whether one filled up a "Yes" envelope or "No" envelope. Accordingly there was no actual payment or consideration in my judgment tendered by the participant in order to take part in the prize draw.

One must look briefly at any rate at the previous authorities to see how they deal with the point, and in particular to see whether they
G confirm or contradict what I venture to submit seem to me to be the main principles. It so happens that the first case in point of time is the one which is most heavily relied upon by the prosecution. It is *Willis* v. *Young and Stembridge* [1907] 1 K.B. 448. This was a case very much like the present one. The proprietors of a newspaper caused medals to be distributed gratuitously amongst members of the public. They sent a man
H out with bags of their medals, and they were individually pushed through letter boxes and distributed in that way. Each medal bore a distinctive number. The Weekly Telegraph, which was the paper these people published, carried each week a list of the winning numbers, and the idea was that you would go along and buy your copy of the Weekly Telegraph to see whether the number on your medal was a winning number or not.

But it is here again clear that it was possible to win a prize without actually buying the paper. In other words, if you could persuade a friend

to let you look at his copy, or if you went round to the newspaper office A
and inquired, you could discover whether you had won a prize or not without buying a paper. It was therefore naturally enough contended on behalf of the defendants that this was no true lottery because there was no necessary contribution by the participant. He was not bound to spend money buying the paper. He could find out whether he had won a prize in a different way.

The matter was considered by this court—the Divisional Court—pre- B
sided over by Lord Alverstone C.J. and, about the general principles, he said, at p. 454:

> "Now it has been admitted by the respondents' counsel that if a coupon had been delivered with each medal, and a charge of a penny had been made, the scheme would undoubtedly have been a lottery, but it is contended that the fact that no charge was made for the C
> medal made all the difference. In my opinion this court would be stultifying itself were it to give any effect to the ingenious argument by which this ingenious device was supported. If we look merely at the position of the holder of one of these medals, it is perfectly true that he may not have bought a copy of the newspaper; he may only know by oral information that he has won a prize. But the fact D
> remains, and has been found by the magistrate, that the scheme was devised by the proprietors to induce persons to inspect the paper. I do not know why the learned magistrate uses the word 'inspect,' and not 'buy,' which is obviously what he really meant, but I take the word actually used; under ordinary circumstances inspection of a newspaper would mean getting hold of the paper and reading it. We know the mischief which was aimed at by the Gaming Act 1802 and E
> if we read the preamble to that Act we must ask ourselves how many of the recipients of these medals, who are unable to go into the office and inspect the paper for nothing, would pay a penny for the paper, not for the purpose of reading it in the ordinary way, but in order to see whether the number of their medal is the lucky one."

The judgment goes on to say that the proprietors' hope and intention was F
that the circulation of the paper might thereby go up. Lord Alverstone C.J. said, at p. 455:

> "The persons who receive the medals therefore contribute collectively (though each individual may not contribute) sums of money which constitute the fund from which the profits of the newspaper, and also the money for the prize winners in this competition, come. I adopt G
> the definitions of 'lottery' which have been cited to us in the present case, and, looking at the real substance of the scheme, I think that it falls within the narrowest and most limited definition of a lottery, though it is not necessary for the purpose of our decision to go so far as that. If the scheme had been to deliver a medal with each copy of the paper to the person buying that copy, there could have been no H
> question that it would have been a lottery; in the present case the mischief is really the same, and an inducement is held out to the same class of people to buy copies of the paper . . ."

What Lord Alverstone C.J. is there accepting is that first of all it was possible to find out whether you had won a prize without buying a paper. My understanding of his judgment is that he said that in practice it was exactly the same as though every person participating had to buy a paper.

A He says that in practice they would go and buy it in order to find out whether they had won, and therefore the matter should be treated as though they had to go and buy it, and it is in that way that he supports the view that there was a contribution made collectively by all the participants towards the profits of the newspaper.

Darling J. agreed, but he said, at p. 455:

B "But I wish it to be clearly understood that I am not prepared to hold that an absolutely free and gratuitous distribution of chances, none of which have been paid for, would be a lottery. In the present instance all chances are paid for in the mass by the general body of purchasers of the paper . . ."

It may be that in the very peculiar circumstances of that case that was the
C correct way of looking at it.

For my own part, if I faced this untrammelled by authority, I should be inclined, I think, to say I regard *Willis* v. *Young and Stembridge* as being wrongly decided because I cannot make it square with what I have already stated in my judgment to be the essentials of a true lottery. But there it is at all events, and that is really the high watermark of the case against the defendants, because ever since then—ever since 1907—as Lord
D Parker C.J. was to point out later on in *Whitbread & Co. Ltd.* v. *Bell* [1970] 2 Q.B. 547, the trend has been the other way.

I hope Mr. Tapp will not think me disrespectful to his argument if I do not refer to all the authorities he put before us. I prefer to go on to *Whitbread & Co. Ltd.* v. *Bell* which is a comparatively modern case. Again it is a case very much like the present one. The brewers,
E Whitbreads, set up a scheme whereby people patronising their public houses might be given an envelope, and the envelope contained the facility for obtaining letters and sticking them on and making words—much the same as in the instant case but a slightly different method. There again was the factor that it was not necessary for a person who went to a public house and joined in the scheme to make any money contribution; it was not necessary for him to drink anything; it certainly was not necessary
F for him to buy any drinks for anybody else. Accordingly, it was contended by Whitbreads that, there being no consideration for obtaining the individual chance, the whole scheme was not a lottery.

Lord Parker C.J. dealt with this in two brief passages which I will read. Having referred to the argument of the prosecutor that there was here a lottery for the reasons I have already indicated, Lord Parker C.J. said,
G at p. 555:

". . . I am quite unable to accept that argument. There is, so far as I know, no case of a successful prosecution for running a lottery which has not involved some payment or contribution by the participants, and indeed the trend of authority has all been the other way. There must be some payment or contribution, if not towards the prizes
H themselves, at any rate towards funds, i.e. profits, out of which prizes are provided."

I think, with all respect to Lord Parker C.J., that that last sentence goes too far. I do not think it is sufficient to say that the prize is paid out of funds which are themselves derived from the scheme, and I think his reference to profits out of which prizes are provided is a reference which should not be employed.

But that he approves of the general principles to which I have referred is beyond doubt, and he refers to *Willis* v. *Young and Stembridge* [1907] 1 K.B. 448 as being a case which depended entirely on its very special facts. That is how I would deal with *Willis* v. *Young and Stembridge* also in the absence of being in a position of taking a different view of it.

Then finally one has *Atkinson* v. *Murrell* [1973] A.C. 289. This has many different features from the lottery cases that I have been referring to, but there is in *Atkinson* v. *Murrell* some discussion of the earlier lottery cases to which I have referred, and I would draw attention to the speech of Lord Dilhorne where, referring to *Whitbread & Co. Ltd.* v. *Bell* and Lord Parker C.J.'s reference to profits out of which prizes are provided, he said, at p. 294: "In my opinion, *Whitbread & Co. Ltd.* v. *Bell* . . . decided no more than that for there to be a lottery, the participants must pay for their chances."

It seems to me to be entirely consistent with principle because the law and public morals are not concerned with profits made by the organisers nearly so much as they are by the injury to the participants who are unduly tempted to spend their money, as I have already suggested. It seems to me that the whole matter is summed up by Lord Dilhorne when he says that *Whitbread's* case decided no more than that for there to be a lottery the participants must pay for their chances.

I am confident that that is the law and has been for a very long time, and I think that the justices in this case were misled by paying too much attention to *Willis* v. *Young and Stembridge* [1907] 1 K.B. 448 and not appreciating how little support that case had obtained since 1907 when it was decided.

I would allow this appeal and quash the conviction.

MELFORD STEVENSON J. I entirely agree with the judgment which has just been delivered. I have found myself faced with considerable difficulty by *Willis* v. *Young and Stembridge* [1907] 1 K.B. 448, but I am helped to resolve that difficulty by a sentence in the speech of Lord Hodson in *McCollom* v. *Wrightson* [1968] A.C. 522, where, having referred to *Willis's* case, he said, at p. 528:

> "The decision against the respondents holding that there was a lottery was reached on the basis that the purchasers of the paper contributed towards the prize fund although the individual purchaser"—I think he meant "participant"—"might not be paying for his chance."

Here there were some 783,000 "No" envelopes, and that in my view makes it quite clear that a significant proportion of those who can be described by the word "participants" were paying nothing. They were not contributing. For myself that fact, even if it stood alone, takes this case outside the frontiers of a lottery and for that reason I would allow this appeal.

CAULFIELD J. I agree with the judgment delivered by Lord Widgery C.J., and my approach has been the same. *Willis* v. *Young and Stembridge* [1907] 1 K.B. 448 was one where the informations were laid under the Act of 1802, and Lord Alverstone C.J. in that case referred to the preamble of that Act as showing the mischief that the Act sought to remedy. It is interesting when one reads the preamble to that Act where it is declared that there has been great impoverishment and utter ruin of many families because of those evilly disposed persons who, in premises

A such as public houses, set up lotteries to their great profit. By the Act they were declared vagabonds and rogues, and they were liable to penalties of up to £500. That is the background to the legislation, and that is the approach that I have made.

I have come to the same conclusion as my Lords because it is clear here on the facts that thousands and thousands of participants, whether showing wisdom or not, decided to participate in the draw as they could
B without the slightest detriment to themselves.

I would not like to define a donkey; I would not like to define a lottery. But the fact that I do not define does not prevent me from recognising a donkey or a lottery when I see it. I think the approach to cases of this sort is to examine the facts, and not then to decide whether or not the facts satisfy a particular definition, but whether the court can then declare
C that the facts show a lottery.

The absence of detriment on the part of the participants is in my judgment the critical factor here, and for that reason I would allow this appeal.

Appeal allowed.

D Solicitors: *Bower, Cotton & Bower; Comptroller and City Solicitor.*

E [HOUSE OF LORDS]

* SEAY . . . . RESPONDENT

AND

EASTWOOD AND ANOTHER . . . . APPELLANTS

F 1976 July 5, 6; 28 — Lord Wilberforce, Lord Simon of Glaisdale, Lord Kilbrandon, Lord Salmon and Lord Russell of Killowen

Gaming—Gaming machine—Licensed bookmaker's premises—Bookmaker taking fixed percentage of money inserted in machine on premises—Whether player of machine making bet with bookmaker—Whether bookmaker carrying on business
G *other than "bookmaking"—Betting and Lotteries Act (Northern Ireland)* 1957 (5 & 6 *Eliz.* 2, *c.* 19), *ss.* 13 (1) (*a*), 20

The appellants, a bookmaker and his manager, had installed two gaming machines on premises in respect of which a bookmaking office licence was held pursuant to the Betting and Lotteries Act (Northern Ireland) 1957.[1] The machines were available to customers in the office to operate in the hope of
H personal gain by the insertion of the appropriate coin and the operation of a lever. The mechanism of the machines was so adjusted as to enable the owner of them to retain a fixed percentage of the overall input. The appellants were convicted, respectively, of carrying on a business other than bookmaking on licensed premises contrary to section 13 (1) (*a*) of the Act

[1] Betting and Lotteries Act (Northern Ireland) 1957, s. 13 (1) (*a*): see post, p. 1124C–D.
S. 20: post, p. 1124F.

of 1957, and aiding and abetting the commission of such an A
offence.

The appellants appealed, contending that, when a customer inserted an appropriate coin into the machine he was making a bet with the owner and the owner was receiving a bet from him, and that, accordingly, that was "bookmaking" within the meaning of section 20 of the Act:—

Held, dismissing the appeal, that in the operation of the
machine the essential element necessary for making a bet was B
missing in that the player of the machine played against or with the machine and not with the owner, who in this connection was not carrying on the business of receiving bets but was merely providing his customers with a means of enjoyment in exchange for a fixed percentage of the money inserted in the machine; and that, accordingly, the appellants were rightly convicted (post, pp. 1121G—1122B, 1123D–F, H—1124B, 1125B–C).

Decision of the Court of Appeal in Northern Ireland C
affirmed.

The following cases are referred to in their Lordships' opinions:

Cozens v. *Brutus* [1973] A.C. 854; [1972] 3 W.L.R. 521; [1972] 2 All E.R. 1297, H.L.(E.).

Peers v. *Caldwell* [1916] 1 K.B. 371, D.C.

The following additional cases were cited in argument: D

Attorney-General v. *Casino Amusement Theatres Ltd.* (1957) 91 I.L.T.R. 41.

Attorney-General v. *Luncheon and Sports Club Ltd.* [1929] A.C. 400, H.L.(E.).

Bennett v. *Ewens* [1928] 2 K.B. 510, D.C.

Daniels v. *Pinks* [1931] 1 K.B. 374, D.C. E

Ellesmere (Earl) v. *Wallace* [1929] 2 Ch. 1, C.A.

Fielding v. *Turner* [1903] 1 K.B. 867, D.C.

Keep v. *Stevens* (1909) 100 L.T. 491, D.C.

Payne v. *Bradley* [1962] A.C. 343; [1961] 3 W.L.R. 281; [1961] 2 All E.R. 882, H.L.(E.).

Reg. v. *Stoddart* [1901] 1 K.B. 177.

Rex v. *Brennand* (1930) 22 Cr.App.R. 95, C.C.A. F

Rex v. *Kirby* (1927) 20 Cr.App.R. 12, C.C.A.

Rex v. *Peers* (1917) 33 T.L.R. 231, C.C.A.

Tote Investors Ltd. v. *Smoker* [1968] 1 Q.B. 509; [1967] 3 W.L.R. 1239; [1967] 3 All E.R. 242, C.A.

APPEAL from the Court of Appeal in Northern Ireland. G

This was an appeal by the appellants, Bernard Joseph Eastwood and
William Laverty, from the decision of the Court of Appeal in Northern
Ireland (McGonigal and Gibson L.JJ.) dismissing an appeal by way of
case stated from the decision of the Recorder of Belfast (Judge W. W. B.
Topping Q.C.) affirming the determination of Albert J. Walmsley, the
resident magistrate sitting at the Belfast Magistrates' Court, who on
October 10, 1974, convicted the appellants on complaints laid by the H
respondent, J. H. Seay, a superintendent in the Royal Ulster Constabulary
of, inter alia, carrying on in premises licensed as a bookmaker's office a
business other than that of bookmaking contrary to section 13 (1) (*a*) of
the Betting and Lotteries Act (Northern Ireland) 1957.

The following facts were found by the recorder. Bernard Joseph Eastwood was a licensed bookmaker carrying on business in premises at 431 Ormeau Road, Belfast. The premises were the subject of a certificate

A of suitability issued under the provisions of the Betting and Lotteries Act (Northern Ireland) 1957.

William Laverty was at all material time the manager of the premises.

On the dates alleged in the complaints two slot machines were positioned in the portion of the premises open and available to customers resorting to the premises. The machines were gaming machines and were duly licensed under the provisions of the Finance Act (Northern
B Ireland) 1969. Excise duty had been paid by Eastwood in respect of the licence issued to him authorising the provision of the gaming machines in the premises.

On the said dates customers in the premises placed coins in the gaming machines. The machines were activated by the insertion of a coin in a slot provided thereon. This set drums rotating inside the machine. These
C drums carried certain images or pictures. If certain sequences of images or pictures appeared at apertures visible to the person playing the machine, at the front thereof, the machine would return or pay out money to the player, the amount of which varied in relation to the odds offered by the machine against the different winning sequences. If a winning sequence did not appear, the machine retained the money inserted by the player. If a winning sequence did appear the player had the option of taking his
D winnings from the machine, which he did by pulling a lever, or of gambling those winnings by playing for a jackpot.

The machines were electrically operated and no result either of a single play on the machines, or series of plays was predictable. No element of skill was involved. The operation of the machine was geared to ensure a profit of 27 per cent.; the machine automatically or mechanically yielded a steady fixed profit to its owner. The adjustment of the
E machine to yield such amount was within the control of the owner.

On any single play the player could lose his money or win. One witness, called by the complainant as an expert to explain the working of the machine, did make a profit over a series of plays.

It was conceded that the profits from the machines were included in the earnings and profits of the bookmaking business carried on at 431
F Ormeau Road, Belfast. The machines were located in the interior of the premises, in the portion used for betting by members of the public and were not visible from outside the premises. There were no signs or notices outside the premises indicating that the machines were available for playing inside.

The recorder summarised his decision as follows:

G "Upon the facts I held that by any natural application or interpretation of the words contained in the Betting and Lotteries Act (Northern Ireland) 1957, the operation of the machine could not be a bookmaking transaction. I had no doubt that the proprietor could not properly be described as making a bet and I did not consider that the provision and operation of the machine could be described as making a book. Even if an individual user of the machine could
H be described as making a bet when he put his coin into the machine, which I doubt, I cannot hold that he could be said to be making it with a bookmaker. I held that there were two vital ingredients to a wagering or gambling transaction. First there must be an uncertain or unascertained event. Secondly the parties thereto must lose or gain according to the determination of the event. I cannot hold that this can describe the transactions which are carried out in the slot machine as constructed or adjusted. I held that the ultimate result

of the use of the machine is not in doubt or uncertain in that the owner will make a profit and does not stand to lose. I held that the provision of the said machine in the said premises was not part of the owner's business as a bookmaker, it was therefore a separate business and an offence. It was also an attraction and therefore a further offence. The licence under the Finance Act (Northern Ireland) 1969 did not have the effect of legalising the use of the machine in bookmakers premises."

The convictions and sentences on the appellants were accordingly confirmed.

On November 27, 1975, the Court of Appeal in Northern Ireland dismissed the appellants' appeal and adjourned the appellants' applications, pursuant to section 1 (2) of the Administration of Justice Act 1960, for leave to appeal to the House of Lords. On February 16, 1976, the court granted leave to appeal and certified the following point of law of general public importance:

"Whether for the purpose of the Betting and Lotteries Act (Northern Ireland) 1957 the business of bookmaking may include the provision of a machine in which the player stakes a sum of money on the outcome of an unpredictable event and where, though the machine is so regulated that over a number of operations a profit is ensured to the person who provides the machine, a player may on the outcome of a single operation either win or lose."

J. D. McSparran Q.C., *R. C. Hill Q.C.* and *S. Clayton* (all of the Bar of Northern Ireland) for the appellants.

J. B. E. Hutton Q.C., *J. A. Creaney Q.C.* and *B. F. Kerr* (all of the Bar of Northern Ireland) for the respondent.

Their Lordships took time for consideration.

July 28. LORD WILBERFORCE. My Lords, Mr. Eastwood is a licensed bookmaker carrying on business as such at a licensed office in Belfast; Mr. Laverty manages the business. They installed two fruit machines in the premises for use by their customers. The question is whether in so doing they are carrying on in the premises "any trade, profession or business whatsoever except the business of bookmaking." To do so is made an offence by section 13 (1) (*a*) of the Betting and Lotteries Act (Northern Ireland) 1957. They were convicted by the resident magistrate and the conviction was upheld by the Court of Appeal in Northern Ireland.

The validity of the conviction depends upon what is included in the "business of bookmaking." In section 20 of the Act of 1957 we find the following:

"'bookmaker' means any person who whether on his own account or as servant or agent of any other person, carries on, whether occasionally or regularly, the business of receiving or negotiating bets, or who in any manner holds himself out, or permits himself to be held out in any manner, as a person carrying on such business, and the expression 'bookmaking' shall be construed accordingly; . . ."

There follow certain exclusions relating to pool betting and totalisators. The appellants contend that the operation of the machines is part of their

A business of bookmaking, a proposition which appears implausible unless this result is produced by statutory enactment.

My Lords, before one attempts to apply the so-called definition, it is necessary to establish the climate, or atmosphere in which it has been given birth.

Legislation against, or controlling, gaming, wagering and betting is many centuries old in the United Kingdom. With only moderate success
B Parliament has endeavoured to keep up with the enormous variety of these activities which has arisen from the ingenuity of gamblers and of people who exploit them. It is impossible to frame accurate definitions which can cover every such variety: attempts to do so may indeed be counter-productive, since each added precision merely provides an incentive to devise a variant which eludes it. So the legislation contains a
C number of expressions which are not, or not precisely defined: bet, wager, lottery, gaming, are examples of this. As to these, while sections appear in various Acts saying that a particular activity is, or is deemed to be, within the word, the general meaning is left to be decided by the courts as cases arise under the common law. The process, and I think it a very sound one, is then for magistrates, using their local knowledge, experience of the world and common sense, to give a sensible inter-
D pretation of the expressions used, subject to control of their decision by a court itself experienced in deciding this type of question. When, as should rarely occur, higher appellate courts are required to review these cases, they should, in my opinion, endorse decisions which they can see have been reached and confirmed in this way. Refined analytical tools are not suitable instruments in this context.

E The definition contained in section 20, on the face of it, calls for just such common sense interpretation as I have described. A bookmaker, it says, is a person who makes or negotiates bets—but what in this context are bets? Are they what a man places with a bookmaker or something else? If the former, the definition may be circular, but at least it conforms with popular belief. If the latter, the definition may have more content, but its scope is completely uncertain. I shall revert to this
F point. In the search for a common sense meaning, I look first at the recorder's decision, embodied in the case stated. He describes in some detail the operation of the machines. He points out that a player may win or lose on any single play; that there are odds, according to which the machine is supposed to produce one combination or another, no doubt very unfavourable to the player; that over a period the machine yields a
G steady profit of about 27 per cent., the amount of which can be adjusted. There is no finding or suggestion that the owner of the machine is responsible for paying the player if the machine does not do so. On these facts the learned recorder held that by natural interpretation of the statutory words the operation of the machine could not be a bookmaking transaction. He had no doubt that the proprietor could not properly be described as making a book, and even if a user could be described as
H making a bet when he put his coin into the machine, he could not be said to be making it with a bookmaker.

My Lords, I doubt very much whether, as to this type of legislation, one can carry the argument much further than this. It is possible to take various elements supposed to be essential to a "bet"—an uncertain event, the possibility of loss, the holding of opposite views, an interest in winning or losing—and debate whether all or some of these are present. If I were to follow this process, I would say, for myself, that an essential element necessary for a bet is missing because the player plays against or A with the machine, i.e., the stakes provided by other players. The owner does not stake anything: he may provide some initial capital, but he knows—and the player knows—that the owner will get this back plus a fixed profit. The player merely takes his chance of sharing in the 73 per cent. of the stakes put into the machine. But in the end, the determination is a magistrate's decision, to be upheld unless he has misapplied his mind to the question. So far as I am capable of placing myself in his chair, I B would reach the conclusion that the appellants in installing the machines were not conducting a bookmaking business, that the players were not placing bets—at least not the sort of bets one places with a bookmaker.

There are just three points which an appellate court may properly have regard to in reviewing his decision.

First, I think it is correct to say that, in general, gaming machines have C been treated in law as a separate subject from betting. I do not, for this proposition, rely upon later legislation whether in Northern Ireland or in Great Britain because I doubt whether this can be looked at in order to interpret the Act of 1957. The distinction is clearly made in *Peers* v. *Caldwell* [1916] 1 K.B. 371 and cases which have followed it. All three of the judges in that case seem to have considered that the operation of a gaming machine was not betting in the ordinary sense of the term and D the decision was that it came under the second portion of section 1 of the Betting Act 1853—which omits the word "bet"—rather than under the first portion which includes it. It may be like betting, but not betting properly so called.

Secondly, it is to be noted that the Act of 1957 does not deal with gaming machines at all—leaving them under the Gaming Houses Act 1854. (Later Acts in Northern Ireland provide for licensing gaming machines E and those with which this case is concerned are in fact so licensed.) But if the appellants' argument is right as to the meaning of the definition all operators of gaming machines whether in arcades or elsewhere have to be regarded as bookmakers and are liable to obtain a bookmaker's licence. An interpretation which avoids this and which conforms with ordinary understanding appears to me to be preferred. F

Thirdly, as I have noted, the definition of "bookmaking" in section 20 excludes certain kindred activities which might well be considered to be "betting"—pool betting and totalisator betting. This seems to show that the intention was to confine the business of "bookmaking" within narrow limits, and to prohibit the carrying on in licensed premises of anything outside this narrow range. This, whether sound social policy or not, is at least intelligible and capable of being administered. G

I would dismiss the appeal.

LORD SIMON OF GLAISDALE. My Lords, the first appellant is a licensed bookmaker carrying on business at a licensed betting office in Belfast, and the second appellant is his manager. They installed two gaming machines in the betting office, countenancing their operation and taking H (by a suitable and lawful adjustment) a fixed 27 per cent. of the money inserted in the machines by the players. The ultimate issue in this appeal is whether, in relation to the machines, the appellants were carrying on "the business of receiving or negotiating bets" within the meaning of section 20 of the Betting and Lotteries Act (Northern Ireland) 1957.

The purpose of the Act was evidently to permit facilities for lawful betting, but with safeguards and restrictions. The safeguards were mainly provided by the licensing system and by powers of entry and investigation (section 18). The restrictions are contained in sections 12 to 17. I need not set them out. The impression they make on me is that betting offices, whatever the safeguards, were regarded austerely, to be tolerated as preferable to illegal street betting and bookies' runners, but hardly to be welcomed as intrinsically desirable social institutions. The argument on behalf of the appellants that gaming machines in Northern Ireland were lawful in licensed betting offices but everywhere else unlawful is irreconcilable with the general impression of the Act—that Parliament would certainly not have wished that betting offices could hold out uniquely (or indeed at all) the attraction of gaming machines. Any interpretation supported by such an argument is inherently suspect.

Moreover, the fiscal implications of the appellants' argument were truly fantastic: general betting duty is payable on any bet which is made with a bookmaker in Northern Ireland: section 16 (1) (*a*) of the Miscellaneous Transferred Excise Duties Act (Northern Ireland) 1972. No attempt was made to explain how this could work if every go at one of these machines constituted a bet with the bookmaker.

The language of the statute is about as close to ordinary speech as is to be expected in an Act of Parliament, and "bet" is not a term of art, but an ordinary English word. The appellants were convicted of an offence which involved that the resident magistrate at petty sessions did not consider that the appellants in relation to the gaming machines were carrying on the business of receiving or negotiating bets. On appeal the recorder made the following finding:

> "Upon the facts I held that by any natural application or interpretation of the words contained in the . . . Act . . . the proprietor could not properly be described as making a bet . . . Even if an individual user of the machine could be described as making a bet when he put his coin into the machine, which I doubt, I cannot hold that he could be said to be making it with a bookmaker."

That is really the beginning and the end of the case (cf. *Cozens* v. *Brutus* [1973] A.C. 854). I have quoted the learned recorder (a professional judge) in case it were considered that the linguistic register of the statute was not entirely that of ordinary speech, but has some legal overtone. For what it is worth, my own view coincides entirely with his. Moreover, I derive confidence from the fact that other judicial minds would apparently respond similarly to the meaning of the word "bet" in relation to a gaming machine. In *Peers* v. *Caldwell* [1916] 1 K.B. 371 Ridley J., at p. 378, considered the operation of such machines not to be "betting in the ordinary sense of that term," but to be an offence under other statutory wording not using that term. Avory J., at p. 379, concurring, considered that such other wording was used "in order, apparently, to cover cases as to which there might be a question whether they amounted to betting in the ordinary sense of that term."

Lush J., dissenting, nevertheless said, at p. 380:

> "Here the magistrate has not found that the use of these machines amounted to a betting transaction, nor was there, I think, any evidence on which he could have so found."

I would therefore dismiss the appeal.

LORD KILBRANDON. My Lords, I have had the advantage of reading the speech prepared by my noble and learned friend Lord Russell of

Killowen. I agree with his conclusions. I shall state my own opinion in A a single sentence. When the occupier of premises instals a gaming machine therein for the entertainment of visitors, and recoups himself by arranging that the machine shall reserve to him a percentage of the sums paid by the visitors for the privilege of working the machine—and that is all that the facts in the present appeal disclose—there is no usage of the English language which will permit it to be said that the owner had made or organised bets between himself and the visitors. B

LORD SALMON. My Lords, I have had the advantage of reading in draft the speech prepared by my noble and learned friend, Lord Wilberforce. I entirely agree with the reasons given by him and accordingly I would dismiss the appeal.

C

LORD RUSSELL OF KILLOWEN. My Lords, the first appellant is a licensed bookmaker carrying on his bookmaking business at premises for which he holds a bookmaking office licence under the Betting and Lotteries Act (Northern Ireland) 1957. Section 13 (1) (*a*) provides:

> "A person shall not—(*a*) carry on or permit to be carried on in a licensed office any trade, profession or business whatsoever except the D business of bookmaking . . ."

The appellant was convicted of an offence under that provision, and the question for determination is whether the facts of the case justify that conviction as a matter of law.

At his licensed office the appellant maintained two gaming machines, commonly known as fruit machines or one-armed bandits, available to E customers in the office to operate in the hope of personal gain by the insertion of an appropriate coin and the operation of a lever. As is common with such machines the machinery was adjusted so as to result in the owner of the machine retaining a percentage—in this case 27 per cent.—of the overall input. By section 20 of the Act of 1957 it is provided, so far as presently relevant:

F

> "the expression—'bookmaker' means any person who whether on his own account or as servant or agent of any other person, carries on, whether occasionally or regularly, the business of receiving or negotiating bets, . . . and the expression 'bookmaking' shall be construed accordingly; . . ."

For the appellant it is contended that when a person inserts the appropriate coing into the slot he is making a bet with the owner and the G owner is receiving a bet from him: therefore the provision and operation of the machines are part of a bookmaking business and the conviction was accordingly wrong.

My Lords, I am quite unable to accept that in providing these machines for use by frequenters of his office premises it can fairly be said that the appellant was carrying on the business of receiving bets. It is, of course, H true that the machine bears upon it a statement of the payout to be expected—which can be described as the odds—on varying combinations of objects appearing in the window after the lever has been operated. But when a customer inserts his coin it is a matter of absolute and complete indifference to the owner of the machine whether that customer is lucky or unlucky. It cannot make the slightest difference to the owner, who will get his 27 per cent. of the total input in any event, no more and

A no less. Assuming the insertion of the coin to be in some sense a trans-
action between the customer and the owner, in my opinion a transaction
under which by its very nature one party cannot be affected in any way
by the outcome cannot be properly described as a bet. Of course a
bookmaker in the ordinary course will try to make his book so as to show
a profit in all circumstances: and of course a person who lays £5 to £1
with A against an event and then stakes £1 at the same odds with B on the
B same event is wholly indifferent to the outcome. But this indifference or
relative indifference does not arise from the very nature of any one
transaction whose characteristics as a bet are under scrutiny. In the
present case I would not say that the owner was carrying on the business
of receiving bets: rather was he providing his customers with a means of
gambling in exchange for a percentage of the money inserted in the
C machines.

I would also say that the action of inserting a coin, taken by itself, can-
not properly be described as the making of a bet by the person inserting
it. He is not forecasting an event or series of events: he is not backing
his estimate of any outcome: he is simply hoping that some paying com-
bination may turn up: he is gambling but not in any ordinary sense of the
word betting.

D The argument for the appellant required several rather sweeping pro-
positions. The Finance Act (Northern Ireland) 1966 (since replaced) by
section 9 introduced a duty of excise to be known as the general betting
duty of an amount equal to $2\frac{1}{2}$ per cent. of the amount staked. For the
appellant it was accepted that his contention involved the application of
such duty to each coin inserted in the machines, notwithstanding that the
E same statute by section 10 introduced a duty of excise of a substantial
annual sum on a licence for every machine made available for play on
premises specified in the licence.

It was further contended that the operation of such machines was wholly
illegal everywhere unless it was permitted as part of the bookmaker's busi-
ness at a licensed betting office. If the operation of such machines is indeed
illegal the system of licensing their operation for substantial annual sums
F under section 10 of the Act of 1966, continued in subsequent statutes,
must rank as a legislative confidence trick, leading presumably (on the
appellant's argument) to a substantial group of unlicensed bookmakers
offending also under the Act of 1957: it is not necessary to express an
opinion upon this. I am content to say that the argument that, if the
appellant is right on his main point, the confidence trick is at least not
G played on licensed bookmakers does not persuade me on this main point.

On these grounds, I am of the opinion that the appellants were
rightly convicted, and I would dismiss the appeal.

Appeal dismissed.

Solicitors: *Robin Thompson & Partners for Gerald McClure, Belfast;*
H *Director of Public Prosecutions, for Director of Public Prosecutions,*
Northern Ireland.

J. A. G.

[COURT OF APPEAL] A

* TOWN INVESTMENTS LTD. *v.* DEPARTMENT OF THE ENVIRONMENT

LONDON COUNTY FREEHOLD AND LEASEHOLD PROPERTIES LTD. *v.* SAME

B

MEPC (MAYFAIR PROPERTIES) LTD. *v.* SAME

[1973 T. No. 2823]

[1973 L. No. 3774]

[1974 M. No. 5012]

C

1975 March 11, 12, 13, 14; 21 — Foster J.

1976 March 8, 9, 10, 11; May 10 — Buckley and Lawton L.JJ. and Sir John Pennycuick

Landlord and Tenant—Rent—Counter-inflation—Demise to Secretary of State for Environment—Premises provided and D *serviced by Department of Environment for other government departments—Whether occupied by tenant for purposes of "business" carried on by him—Counter-Inflation (Business Rents) Order* 1972 (*S.I.* 1972 *No.* 1850), *art.* 2 (2) [1]*—Counter-Inflation (Business Rents) Order* 1973 (*S.I.* 1973 *No.* 741), *art.* 2 (2) [1]

Crown—Statute—Application to—Crown not bound by counter-inflation legislation—Whether Crown entitled to take advantage of provisions—Crown Proceedings Act 1947 (10 & 11 E *Geo.* 6, *c.* 44), *s.* 31 (1) [2]

In September 1973 the plaintiffs in the second and third actions granted new underleases of their respective properties at rents much greater than had been payable under the expiring underleases of 1952, the grant in each case being made to "the Secretary of State for the Environment F (hereinafter called 'the tenant' which expression shall where the context so admits include his successors and assigns) for and on behalf of Her Majesty." The premises in the second action were sublet by the defendant department apart from a small area which it fitted out and maintained for use as a job centre by the Department of Employment. The premises in the third action were used by two government departments and a statutory body, all services being provided by the G defendant department which retained two small rooms for its electricians and carpenters to keep tools and materials in. The defendant department refused to pay the new rents claiming that it was not bound to do so because of the Counter-Inflation (Business Rents) Orders 1972 and 1973. The plaintiffs issued originating summonses, later consolidated, to recover the new rents. Foster J., giving judgment for the plaintiffs, held that the defendant department could not take advantage of the H counter-inflation legislation as it did not bind the Crown; and that, in any event, it did not occupy either set of premises for the purposes of any business carried on by it within the meaning of article 2 (2) of the Counter-Inflation (Business Rents) Order 1972.

---

[1] Counter-Inflation (Business Rents) Orders 1972 and 1973, art. 2 (2): see post, p. 1136A–B.

[2] Crown Proceedings Act 1947, s. 31 (1): see post, p. 1142E–F.

A On appeal by the defendant department: —

Held, dismissing the appeal, that the tenant under both underleases was the Secretary of State for the Environment and not the Crown (post, pp. 1143B–D, 1147H); that neither set of premises was occupied by the Secretary of State for the Environment (post, pp. 1137F–G, 1148F—1149A); and that, in any event, the conduct of government business at neither set of premises constituted the carrying on of " a business " within
B the meaning of article 2 (2) of the Counter-Inflation (Business Rents) Orders 1972 and 1973 (post, pp. 1141F, 1150A).

Lee-Verhulst (Investments) Ltd. v. *Harwood Trust* [1973] Q.B. 204, C.A. distinguished.

Per curiam. Although the counter-inflation legislation did not apply to the Crown, the defendant department could have relied on it by way of answer to the claim of the plaintiffs, provided the evidence had been available (post, pp. 1142G,
C 1146D–E).

Cayzer, Irvine & Co. Ltd. v. *Board of Trade* [1927] 1 K.B. 269, C.A. considered.

Decison of Foster J., post, p. 1129H, affirmed.

The following cases are referred to in the judgments of the Court of Appeal:

D *Abernethie* v. *A. M. & J. Kleiman Ltd.* [1970] 1 Q.B. 10; [1969] 2 W.L.R. 1364; [1969] 2 All E.R. 790, C.A.

Addiscombe Garden Estates Ltd. v. *Crabbe* [1958] 1 Q.B. 513; [1957] 3 W.L.R. 980; [1957] 3 All E.R. 563, C.A.

Anon. (1497) Y.B. 12 Hen. VII, 20.

Attorney-General v. *Tomline* (1880) 15 Ch.D. 150, C.A.

Case of a Fine Levied by the King (1606) 7 Co.Rep. 32a.

E *Cayzer, Irvine & Co. Ltd.* v. *Board of Trade* [1927] 1 K.B. 269, C.A.

Cozens v. *Brutus* [1973] A.C. 854; [1972] 3 W.L.R. 521; [1972] 2 All E.R. 1297, H.L. (E.).

Lee-Verhulst (Investments) Ltd. v. *Harwood Trust* [1973] Q.B. 204; [1972] 3 W.L.R. 772; [1972] 3 All E.R. 619, C.A.

Magdalen College Case (1615) 11 Co.Rep. 66b.

Reg. v. *Cruise* (1852) 2 Ir.Ch.R. 65.

Rolls v. *Miller* (1884) 27 Ch.D. 71, C.A.

F *Stonor (William)'s Case* (1497) Y.B. 13 Hen. VII, 7.

The following additional cases were cited in argument in the Court of Appeal:

Bagettes Ltd. v. *G.P. Estates Ltd.* [1956] Ch. 290; [1956] 2 W.L.R. 773; [1956] 1 All E.R. 729, C.A.

G *Hills (Patents) Ltd.* v. *University College Hospital Board of Governors* [1956] 1 Q.B. 90; [1955] 3 W.L.R. 523; [1955] 3 All E.R. 365, C.A.

Horford Investments Ltd. v. *Lambert* [1976] Ch. 39; [1973] 3 W.L.R. 872; [1974] 1 All E.R. 131, C.A.

Kodeeswaran v. *Attorney-General of Ceylon* [1970] A.C. 1111; [1970] 2 W.L.R. 456, P.C.

Nisbet Shipping Co. Ltd. v. *The Queen* [1955] 1 W.L.R. 1031; [1955] 3 All E.R. 161, P.C.

H *Rael-Brook Ltd.* v. *Minister of Housing and Local Government* [1967] 2 Q.B. 65; [1967] 2 W.L.R. 604; [1967] 1 All E.R. 262, D.C.

Rustomjee v. *The Queen* (1876) 1 Q.B.D. 487.

Secretary of State for Social Services v. *Rossetti Lodge Investment Co. Ltd.*, February 18, 1975; Bar Library Transcript No. 83 of 1975, C.A.

Willion v. *Berkley* (1561) 1 Pl. 222a.

Willis v. *Association of Universities of the British Commonwealth* [1965] 1 Q.B. 140; [1964] 2 W.L.R. 946; [1964] 2 All E.R. 39, C.A.

The following cases are referred to in the judgment of Foster J.:

Abernethie v. *A. M. & J. Kleiman Ltd.* [1970] 1 Q.B. 10; [1969] 2 W.L.R. 1364; [1969] 2 All E.R. 790, C.A.

Cayzer, Irvine & Co. Ltd. v. *Board of Trade* [1927] 1 K.B. 269, C.A.

City Permanent Building Society v. *Miller* [1952] Ch. 840; [1952] 2 All E.R. 621, C.A.

Nisbet Shipping Co. Ltd. v. *The Queen* [1955] 1 W.L.R. 1031; [1955] 3 All E.R. 161, P.C.

Sayce v. *Coupe* [1953] 1 Q.B. 1; [1952] 2 All E.R. 715, D.C.

Secretary of State for Social Services v. *Rossetti Lodge Investment Co. Ltd.*, February 18, 1975; Bar Library Transcript No. 83 of 1975, C.A.

Tavistock Developments Ltd. v. *Banks, Wood & Partners* (unreported), May 1, 1974, Shaw J.

The following additional cases were cited in argument before Foster J.:

Addiscombe Garden Estates Ltd. v. *Crabbe* [1958] 1 Q.B. 513; [1957] 3 W.L.R. 980; [1957] 3 All E.R. 563, C.A.

Attorney-General v. *Tomline* (1879) 15 Ch.D. 150.

Barnard Castle Urban District Council v. *Wilson* [1902] 2 Ch. 746, C.A.

Bramwell v. *Lacy* (1879) 10 Ch.D. 691.

Board of Trade v. *Cayzer, Irvine & Co. Ltd.* [1927] A.C. 610, H.L.(E.).

Cafeteria (Keighley) Ltd. v. *Harrison* (1956) 168 E.G. 668.

Cannon Street (No. 20) Ltd. v. *Singer & Friedlander Ltd.* [1974] Ch. 229; [1974] 2 W.L.R. 646; [1974] 2 All E.R. 577.

Doe d. Bish v. *Keeling* (1813) 1 M. & S. 95.

Grace Rymer Investments Ltd. v. *Waite* [1958] Ch. 314, 831; [1958] 2 W.L.R. 200, 3 W.L.R. 337; [1958] 1 All E.R. 138, 2 All E.R. 777, C.A.

Gray v. *Southouse* [1949] 2 All E.R. 1019.

Hills (Patents) Ltd. v. *University College Hospital Board of Governors* [1956] 1 Q.B. 90; [1955] 3 W.L.R. 523; [1955] 3 All E.R. 365, C.A.

Kiriri Cotton Co. v. *Dewani* [1960] A.C. 192; [1960] 2 W.L.R. 127; [1960] 1 All E.R. 177, P.C.

Lee-Verhulst (Investments) Ltd. v. *Harwood Trust* [1973] Q.B. 204; [1972] 3 W.L.R. 772; [1972] 3 All E.R. 619, C.A.

National Magazine Co. Ltd. v. *Department of Trade and Industry*, *The Times*, December 8, 1973.

Rael-Brook Ltd. v. *Minister of Housing and Local Government* [1967] 2 Q.B. 65; [1967] 2 W.L.R. 604; [1967] 1 All E.R. 262, D.C.

Reg. v. *Cruise* (1852) Ir.Ch.R. 65.

Rolls v. *Miller* (1884) 27 Ch.D. 71 C.A.

South-West Suburban Water Co. v. *Guardians of the Poor of St. Marylebone* [1904] 2 K.B. 174.

Wheat v. *E. Lacon & Co. Ltd.* [1966] A.C. 552; [1966] 2 W.L.R. 581; [1966] 1 All E.R. 582, H.L.(E.).

Williams' Will Trusts, In re [1953] Ch. 138; [1953] 2 W.L.R. 418; [1953] 1 All E.R. 536.

Willis v. *Association of Universities of the British Commonwealth* [1965] 1 Q.B. 140; [1964] 2 W.L.R. 946; [1964] 2 All E.R. 39, C.A.

ORIGINATING SUMMONSES

In the first action the plaintiffs, Town Investments Ltd., by originating summons dated November 30, 1973, sought declarations, inter alia, that the Counter-Inflation (Business Rents) Orders 1972 and 1973 did not apply to the tenancy of 11 and 12, Buckingham Gate, London S.W.1, created by a lease dated March 2, 1973, made between the plaintiffs and the Secretary of State for the Environment.

In the second action the plaintiffs, London County Freehold and Leasehold Properties Ltd., by originating summons dated November 30, 1973,

A sought declarations similar to those sought in the first action in relation
to the tenancy of Keysign House, Oxford Street, London W.1, created by
an underlease made on September 14, 1973, between the plaintiffs and the
Secretary of State for the Environment.

In the third action the plaintiffs, MEPC (Mayfair Properties) Ltd., by
originating summons dated November 30, 1973, sought declarations similar
to those sought in the first action in relation to the tenancy of 17, North
B Audley Street, London W.1, created by underlease made on September 28,
1973, between the plaintiffs and the Secretary of State for the Environment.
The three plaintiff companies were all wholly owned subsidiaries of one
company.

On February 21, 1974, the actions were consolidated.

In relation to 11 and 12 Buckingham Gate, Foster J. stated the
C following facts. Town Investments Ltd. owned the freehold of the pro-
perty. By a lease dated March 2, 1951, they leased the property to the
Minister of Works for 21 years from May 15, 1950, at an annual rent of
£4,127. That lease expired on May 15, 1971. On October 28, 1970, the
usual landlord's notice under the Landlord and Tenant Act 1954 was sent
to terminate the tenancy. On December 3, 1970, the defendant department
sent to Town Investments Ltd. the usual counter-notice stating that the
D department was not willing to give up possession of the property at the
date of determination. On February 8, 1971, the department applied to
the High Court for a new tenancy and by agreement that application was
adjourned generally. Negotiations took place and by the end of August
1971 the parties had agreed that the term should be from May 15, 1971
until June 24, 1978, at an annual rent of £63,000. Difficulties occured in
E agreeing the other terms in the lease which was not finally executed until
March 2, 1973. The new rental was paid by the department up to Sept-
ember 29, 1973, when it took the point that it was only liable to pay the
old rent of £4,127 by reason of the various counter-inflation Acts and
Orders and it sought to get back the amount overpaid. At all material
times the Director of Public Prosecutions had used the premises as offices
for himself and his staff. It was common ground that one of the func-
F tions of the defendant department was to provide accommodation and other
ancillary services for government departments and other organisations and
persons in the public service. The Director of Public Prosecutions had no
sort of tenancy or license. The defendant department paid the rent and the
water, gas and electricity charges for the property. It provided and owned
all the furniture and furnishings on the property and, at its own expense,
G decorated and repaired the property, serviced the boiler and the lift and
generally maintained it. It had keys to the main doors and provided a
night custody service. Its staff visited the premises for maintenance pur-
poses every week.

The facts relating to Keysign House and 17, North Audley Street, the
properties concerned in the second and third actions, are stated in the
judgment of Lawton L.J.

H

Roger Parker Q.C. and *Christopher Priday* for the plaintiffs.

C. L. Hawser Q.C. and *Peter Gibson* for the defendant department.

Cur. adv. vult.

March 21. FOSTER J. read the relevant provisions from, inter alia, the
Counter-Inflation (Temporary Provisions) Act 1972, the Counter-Inflation

A (Business Rents) Order 1972, the Counter-Inflation Act 1973 and the Counter-Inflation (Business Rents) Order 1973, stated the facts and continued: The lease of 11–12 Buckingham Gate ended before the Act and Order of 1972 came into effect. In view of two recent decisions, *Tavistock Developments Ltd.* v. *Banks, Wood & Partners,* an unreported decision of Shaw J. on May 1, 1974, and *Secretary of State for Social Services* v. *Rossetti Lodge Investment Co. Ltd.*, Bar Library Transcript B No. 83 of 1975, counsel for the defendant department formally submitted that they were both wrongly decided, to keep the point open in a higher court, but did not ask me to try and distinguish them. They both clearly bind me and cover the case of 11–12, Buckingham Gate. It follows that in this court the plaintiffs succeed in the first of the summonses. In the other two cases, the relevant underleases did not expire until the time when the Act and Order of 1972 were in operation. C

The questions which I have to decide can be formulated as follows. (A) Do the Acts and Orders apply to the defendant department? (B) If so, does the department occupy the premises? (C) If so, is a business carried on there?

(A) For the department, it is submitted that while it is not bound by the provisions of Acts and Orders, so that the rent it could charge a tenant or subtenant would not be frozen, yet it can take advantage of the pro- D visions of the Act and say that it, as a tenant, need not pay its landlord more than the old rent fixed in 1951 which was frozen by the Act and Orders; or, to put it shortly, the Crown, although not bound by a statute, can take advantage of its provisions. I get no assistance from the recent Court of Appeal decision in *Rossetti* on this point, as it was not argued there, either in the Court of Appeal or below. The doctrine is mentioned E in several textbooks. *Chitty's Prerogatives of the Crown* (1820), states at p. 382:

> "The general rule clearly is, that though the King may avail himself of the provisions of any Acts of Parliament, he is not bound by such as do not particularly and expressly mention him."

In *Craies on Statute Law,* 7th ed. (1971), at p. 438, there is a heading: F "Crown may avail itself of statute without being named in it" which reads:

> "Although the Crown may not be prejudiced by the operation of a statute which does not specially name the Crown, and although, as Alderson B. put it in *Attorney-General* v. *Donaldson* (1842) 10 M. & W. 117, 124, 'it is inferred prima facie that the law, made by the Crown with the assent of Lords and Commons, is made for subjects G and not for the Crown,' still, if the King is desirous of performing some act in his natural capacity as an Englishman, and not in his public and royal capacity, it is a general rule that 'the King may take the benefit of any particular Act, although he be not especially named in it.' 1 B.L.Comm. 262. Thus . . . the question was discussed whether the King, being tenant in tail, might, by fine levied bar the estate tail by virtue of the Statute *De Donis*, and it was there stated H by Lord Coke, who was then Attorney-General, that the King could bar an entail; 'for as he claims in respect of his natural capacity as heir of the body of a subject, and not in respect of his public and royal capacity, it would be hard that the King, being issue in tail of a gift made to a subject, should be in a worse condition than if he had not been King.' In 1927 a doubt was expressed as to whether the Crown can take advantage of a statute which is not binding on it."

A The doubt expressed is to be found in the judgment of Scrutton L.J. in *Cayzer, Irvine & Co. Ltd.* v. *Board of Trade* [1927] 1 K.B. 269, 294:

> "The only remaining question, which is one of great historical interest and importance, is whether the Crown can successfully say: 'We are not bound by the statute but we are at liberty to take advantage of it.' At first sight such a statement appears somewhat strange. There is
> B undoubtedly a long series of statements in text-books repeating each other for some centuries; but there is something to be said for the view argued by Sir John Simon that they start with a passage in an unsuccessful argument of a law officer which was not even relevant to the case before the Court, but which has been taken out by a text-writer and repeated for centuries until it was believed that it must have some foundation. Again, I have not heard the Solicitor-
> C General on this point and, therefore, I am not going to say more than this, that it will need careful consideration when that question arises in a case in which it has to be decided, whether there is any foundation for this confidently repeated statement of text-writers except the passage in the *Magdalen College Case,* 11 Co.Rep. 66b and possibly a passage in 7 Rep. 32a, which is not the report of a case decided in the
> D House of Lords, but the case of a private conference between the law officers and the Chief Justices of the Stuart Kings in a case in which the parties, the subjects affected by the decision which was given against them, were not present and were not heard. Which of the two is the more satisfactory foundation for the statement in the text-books I do not quite know, but the history of the story of the text-books will need to be carefully looked at when the question becomes material to be
> E decided. It is not material in this case and, therefore, I say nothing more than there is ample material for considering the question when it has to be decided."

I assume that the defendant department can be considered as the Crown. Section 31 (1) of the Crown Proceedings Act 1947 does not, in my judgment, assist the department in this case, since not only is the Crown named
F in the Act of 1972 but the defence now raised by the Crown could never be raised as between subject and subject. In any event, if one finds in a statute that the position of the Crown is expressly dealt with, the rule and the section has, in my judgment, no relevance: see *Nisbet Shipping Co. Ltd.* v. *The Queen* [1955] 1 W.L.R. 1031, a Privy Council case.

By paragraph 8 (1) of the Schedule to the Act of 1972, it is expressly
G stated that the Act does not bind the Crown. However, if the position was that the Crown could nevertheless take advantage of it, it could freeze the remuneration of its servants. But by paragraph 8 (2), section 3 of the Act which freezes wages is expressly applied to Crown servants, which is totally unnecessary if the Crown could take advantage of its provisions in any event. It was further submitted for the plaintiffs that the court should not adopt a construction which might lead to the position where
H the Crown had committed an offence. In the case of 11–12 Buckingham Gate, if the Crown is bound by the Act it has committed an offence of aiding and abetting the landlord to receive excess rents: see *Sayce* v. *Coupe* [1953] 1 Q.B. 1. For the Crown it was argued that there could not be such an offence committed, as in paragraph 8 of the order of 1972 there is provision for the criminal court to order the excess to be repaid, and it would be curious if the person being repaid was also guilty of an offence. However, a similar position arises under section 2 of the Land-

lord and Tenant (Rent Control) Act 1949. By section 2 (5), provision A
is made for the premium to be recovered, and by section 2 (6) a person
receiving a premium is liable to a fine, and in *City Permanent Building*
Society v. *Miller* [1952] Ch. 840, 856, Hodson L.J. says, in reference to
section 2 of the Act of 1949, "The tenant would be a party to the crime."

In my judgment, the provisions of the Orders of 1972 and 1973 do not
apply to the defendant department (or to the Crown) and it is liable to
pay the full rent under the underlease of September 14, 1973, in regard B
to Keysign House and the underlease of September 28, 1973, in respect
of 17, North Audley Street. That makes it unnecessary for me to consider
the second and third questions, but in deference to the careful arguments
which have been addressed to me and in case my judgment on the first
point is wrong, I will deal with them shortly.

(B) and (C). Does the defendant department occupy the property C
comprised in the tenancy for the purpose of a business carried on by it?
The definition in the Order of 1972 of "business tenancy" is exactly the
same as is to be found in section 23 (1) of the Landlord and Tenant Act
1954 with the addition of the words in the Order "but does not include
a tenancy of or a right to occupy land used for agriculture" since agri-
cultural rents were dealt with in a separate order. The definition of
"business" in the Order of 1972 is taken word for word from section 23 (2) D
of the Act of 1954, so that there can be no doubt that the draftsman of
the Order of 1972 had the provisions of the Act of 1954 well in mind.
Section 56 of the Act of 1954 applies Part II of the Act to the Crown
expressly, but there is no similar provision in the Order of 1972. If then
the draftsman thought that the Order of 1972 should apply to the Crown,
he would have inserted similar provisions as those contained in section 56 E
of the Act of 1954. He did not do so. However, it is submitted for the
department that it does occupy Keysign House and 17, North Audley
Street "for the purposes of a business carried on by him." The only
occupation which the department has itself got are the two small rooms
in North Audley Street amounting to 1·94 per cent. of the whole area,
which I would not have thought is sufficient for it to be said that the
department occupies that building. In the definition of "business" a F
distinction is drawn between "trade, profession or employment" on the
one hand and "an activity carried on," for the latter has to be carried on
by a body of persons whether corporate or unincorporate. This distinc-
tion is recognised by Harman L.J. in *Abernethie* v. *A. M. & J. Kleiman*
Ltd. [1970] 1 Q.B. 10, 17. It is therefore necessary for the department
to bring itself within the words "trade, profession or employment" and G
the only business which it is suggested it carries on is the provision of
accommodation and its upkeep and maintenance for other government
departments and bodies. That might well come within the meaning of
the word "activity" but, in my judgment, it would stretch too far the
ordinary meaning of the word business to say that the department or, if
it be so, the Crown carries on a business on these properties.

For these reasons I think that the various plaintiffs succeed. H

Declarations accordingly.

Solicitors: *Beachcroft, Hyman Isaacs; Treasury Solicitor.*

K. N. B.

A By notice of appeal dated June 5, 1975, the defendant department appealed on the grounds, inter alia, that (1) the judge erred in law in holding that the Counter-Inflation (Business Rents) Orders 1972 and 1973 did not apply to the Secretary of State for the Environment or the Crown; (2) the judge erred in law in holding that the fact that the Crown was referred to in the Acts, pursuant to which the Orders had been made, deprived the Crown of the right, in relation to the Orders, which the
B Crown (including the Secretary of State) had, as confirmed in section 31 (1) of the Crown Proceedings Act 1947, to take advantage of the provisions of an Act of Parliament, including an order made pursuant to such an Act, even though not bound by the Act; (3) the defendant as a department of the Crown had the right under section 31 (1) of the Act of 1947 in any civil proceedings against it to rely on the provisions of any Act (including
C an Order) which could if the proceedings had been between subjects have been relied upon as a defence subject to express provision to the contrary; (4) on the true construction of the Orders of 1972 and 1973 a tenancy where the whole or any part of the property comprised in the tenancy was occupied by the Secretary of State or the Crown as tenant for the purposes of his or its public functions was a business tenancy for the purposes of the orders; (5) on a proper view of the facts the Secretary
D of State as tenant occupied a shop on the ground floor of Keysign House and the whole of 17, North Audley Street, or, alternatively two rooms in the basement, for the purposes of his public functions; and (6) alternatively the Crown as tenant of Keysign House occupied the shop and as tenant of 17, North Audley Street occupied the whole for the purposes of its public functions and, accordingly, had a business tenancy in relation to both
E premises.

On October 14, 1975, the defendant department gave notice of its intention not to proceed with its appeal so far as it related to the first action.

Gordon Slynn Q.C. and *Peter Gibson* for the defendant department.
F *Roger Parker Q.C.* and *Christopher Priday* for the plaintiffs.

Cur. adv. vult.

May 10. The following judgments were read.

LAWTON L.J. These consolidated appeals raise the following questions.
G When the Secretary of State for the Environment, acting "for and on behalf of Her Majesty," in September 1973 entered into as tenant two underleases of properties in the West End of London, was the rent payable that reserved thereunder or that which had been payable under tenancies of the same premises which the Secretary of State acting in the same capacity had held on November 5, 1972? The answer to this question
H depends upon the answers to two more. By whom were the premises occupied under each of these underleases? Were each of the premises occupied for the purposes of a business carried on by either the Secretary of State or the Crown?

These questions arise under the counter-inflation legislation which first came into operation on November 30, 1972, and continued until March 19, 1975. The relevant statutes are the Counter-Inflation (Temporary Provisions) Act 1972 and the Counter-Inflation Act 1973. Both

Acts empowered the appropriate Ministers to make orders restricting A increases in rent. Under the Act of 1972 the Counter-Inflation (Business Rents) Order 1972 froze the rent reserved in respect of business tenancies as from December 1, 1972. Both the Act of 1972 and the Order made under it expired on April 1, 1973, when the Act of 1973 and the Counter-Inflation (Business Rents) Order 1973 came into operation continuing the freezing of business rents until the Act of 1973 itself expired.

If these Acts and Orders applied to the underleases with which these B appeals are concerned, then in respect of one set of premises, namely, 17, North Audley Street, the annual rent payable was £17,500 instead of £190,000, being the annual rent agreed in September 1973, and in respect of the other premises, Keysign House, Oxford Street, the annual rent was £39,690 instead of the agreed annual rent of £369,500. Foster J. held that they did not apply. He gave three reasons: first, because the C defendant department could not take advantage of the counter-inflation legislation; secondly, because the defendant department did not occupy either set of premises; and, thirdly, because even if it did, the premises were not occupied for the purposes of any business carried on by it. The defendant department has submitted that all these three reasons were wrong and the counter-inflation legislation did apply and produced the results to which I have referred. D

For the purposes of this judgment I find it unnecessary to go into the facts in much detail. It suffices to mention that Keysign House had been under government control, partly by lease, partly by requisitioning, since about 1940. By an underlease made on November 25, 1952, the plaintiffs in the second action, London County Freehold and Leasehold Properties Ltd., let to the Minister of Works "for and on behalf of Her E Majesty" most of that building for a term of 21 years expiring on December 25, 1972, at an annual rent of £39,690. The underlease restricted use to offices and for display purposes. A part known as 423, Oxford Street had, however, to be used as a retail shop. Until 1968 this part was used by the Stationery Office for the sale of its publications. From 1969 onwards it had been used as a job centre by the Ministry of Labour F and its successor, the Department of Employment. For most of the period of this underlease the remainder of the building included in it was let to the United States Government. The United States Navy were in occupation at all material times until January 1974. The defendant department, as the Minister of Works' successor, is now getting this accommodation ready for use by the Department of Health and Social Security. It has long maintained the shop part, providing furniture and fittings, paying for G the supply of services, doing repairs, supplying and fixing lighting tubes and bulbs, making improvements and cleaning the windows. Although the superficial area of the shop part is only 1·69 per cent. of the whole, the annual rental value of the shop is about £35,000, which is approximately 9 per cent. of the annual rent reserved by the 1973 underlease.

Towards the end of the term reserved by the 1952 lease the defendant H department, after having applied to the High Court for the grant of a new tenancy under the Landlord and Tenant Act 1954, negotiated with the lessors for the grant of a new underlease. As a result the September 1973 underlease was made. It was for a term of five years from December 25, 1972, at an annual rent of £369,500, the first payment being due on March 25, 1973. The defendant department has refused to pay it, claiming that it is not bound to do so because of the counter-inflation legislation. The

A terms as to the user of Keysign House were substantially the same as under the 1952 underlease.

The history of the letting of 17, North Audley Street is much the same. Between 1952 and 1973 the lessors of these premises changed. By September 1973 they were the plaintiffs in the third action, MEPC (Mayfair Properties) Ltd. The original lessee had been the Minister of Works "for and on behalf of Her Majesty." The original term of 21
B years expired on December 25, 1972. The annual rent reserved was £17,500. The user was to be for office and ancillary purposes. During the period of this underlease the premises had been used by government departments and one statutory body. A new underlease was negotiated with the plaintiffs, MEPC (Mayfair Properties) Ltd., for a term of five years at an annual rent of £190,000. The covenants as to user were
C substantially the same as in the 1952 underlease. At all material times after November 5, 1972, the ground, first and second floors of 17, North Audley Street had been occupied by the Registrar of Friendly Societies, the third floor by the Inland Revenue Commissioners and the fourth and fifth floors by the Customs and Excise Commissioners for VAT tribunals. The defendant department itself used two rooms in the basement for its own staff of electricians and carpenters. They kept their tools and materials
D there. The superficial area of these two rooms was 1·94 per cent. of the whole. The defendant department provided all services; its staff visited the building daily.

On November 30, 1972, Parliament passed the Counter-Inflation (Temporary Provisions) Act 1972. Its long title was "An Act to authorise measures to counter inflation." Counsel for the defendant department told
E us that it had passed through all its stages to the statute book in one day. It was a piece of crisis legislation. The Act was to apply for a limited period: see section 1. Section 2 enabled the appropriate Ministers to freeze prices, pay, dividends and rents. Section 2 (4) provided: "The appropriate Minister may by order provide for preventing increases of rent over rent payable before November 6, 1972." Section 3 enacted that existing contracts of employment should be modified while section 2 was
F in force. Section 8, the interpretation section, contained this provision: "(1) . . . 'business' includes any trade, profession or vocation, and the expression 'in the course of business' shall be construed accordingly. . . ." This definition is different from that in section 23 (2) of the Landlord and Tenant Act 1954. Paragraph 8 of the Schedule to the Act of 1972 has two sub-paragraphs which are of some relevance in deciding whether the
G defendant department is entitled to take advantage of the Act by paying the old rents rather than the new ones. They read:

> "(1) Although this Act does not bind the Crown, an order may be made under this Act so as, without imposing any obligation on the Crown as an employer or otherwise, to apply (either expressly or impliedly) to persons employed by or under the Crown, and section
> H 5 (2) of this Act shall apply accordingly. (2) Section 3 of this Act shall apply, where a person employed by or under the Crown has any enforceable claim to remuneration for that employment, as it applies in the case of an employee of a private person."

The next day, December 1, 1972, the appropriate Minister, being the Secretary of State for the Environment, made the Counter-Inflation (Business Rents) Order 1972. On the same day he made the Counter-Inflation (Rents) (England and Wales) Order 1972 which froze the rents

A of dwelling houses; and the Minister of Agriculture, Fisheries and Food made the Counter-Inflation (Agricultural Rents) Order 1972 which did the same for the rents of agricultural holdings. Article 2 (2) of the Counter-Inflation (Business Rents) Order 1972 contained the following definitions:

> " 'business tenancy' means any tenancy where the property comprised in the tenancy is or includes premises which are occupied by the tenant and are so occupied for the purposes of a business carried on B by him or for those and other purposes but does not include a tenancy of or a right to occupy land used for agriculture; 'business' includes a trade, profession or employment and includes any activity carried on by a body of persons, whether corporate or unincorporate. . . ."

Article 3 froze business rents at the rates and for the period specified in the order. Article 9 provided that, subject to article 8 (which created C offences) any question arising under the order in relation to the rent might be examined by the court and the jurisdiction conferred should be examined in accordance with section 63 of the Landlord and Tenant Act 1954 as if the jurisdiction were conferred by Part II of that Act. Article 11 (2) provided that Part II of the Landlord and Tenant Act 1954 should have effect subject to the provisions of the order. Part II of that Act is headed "Security of Tenure for Business, Professional and Other Tenants." D The definition of "business" in the order was different from that in the Act of 1972 itself. The words "or vocation" in the Act had been changed to "or employment" and the reference to "any activity" had been added. This definition, unlike that in the Act of 1972, was the same as that in section 23 (2) of the Landlord and Tenant Act 1954. It was not suggested by either party that the change of definition was ultra vires. E

The Act and Order of 1972 were replaced as from April 1, 1973, by the Counter-Inflation Act 1973 and the Counter-Inflation (Business Rents) Order 1973. This Act, besides affording powers of control over prices, pay, dividends and rents, established a Price Commission and a Pay Board. The power to freeze rents by order was continued. In the Act of 1973 the definition of "business" was the same as in the Act of 1972 and that F in the Order of 1973 was also the same as in the Order of 1972. There was, however, a change in the definition of "business tenancy." The Order of 1973 excluded a building lease. Paragraph 6 of Schedule 3 to the Act contained a sub-paragraph similar to paragraph 8 (1) of the Schedule to the Act of 1972; but there was no provision in the Act of 1973 similar to paragraph 8 (2).

Foster J. found it convenient to consider whether the counter-inflation G legislation applied (as he put it) to the Department of the Environment before he decided whether there was any occupation of the premises by the tenant under the two underleases for the purposes of a business carried on by him. I find it more convenient to decide first whether there was any relevant occupation. It is only if there was, that the broader question whether the counter-inflation legislation applied to these two underleases H has to be answered.

By whom were the premises occupied?

The North Audley Street lease made a demise to

> "The Secretary of State for the Environment (hereinafter called 'the tenant' which expression shall where the context so admits include his successors and assigns) for and on behalf of Her Majesty."

A In the Keysign House underlease the words of the lease were substantially
the same. We were told by counsel that this wording is that which is used
nowadays when premises are rented for government purposes. In whom
is the term of years vested? In my judgment, it is vested in the Secretary
of State for the Environment as trustee for Her Majesty in right of the
Crown. Any other construction would ignore the opening words of
the underleases. No legal estate became invested in the Department of the
B Environment as such. Mr. Parker developed an interesting argument as to
the constitutional status and powers of the Department of the Environment
under the Ministers of the Crown (Transfer of Functions) Act 1946, the
Ministers of the Crown Act 1964 and the Secretary of State for the
Environment Order 1970. I do not find it necessary to make any findings
on that argument because I am satisfied that for the purposes of this case
C the Secretary of State for the Environment as a trustee for the Crown holds
the terms of years granted by these underleases. Whatever may be the
position in other circumstances, in relation to these two underleases the
Department of the Environment itself is nothing more than an adminis-
trative grouping of persons in the employment of the Crown. These
proceedings are against the Crown. They have been instituted against the
defendant department because it has been specified by the Treasury as
D the authorised department to defend: see section 17 (1) and (3) of the
Crown Proceedings Act 1947. All who work at 17, North Audley Street
and in the job centre at Keysign House are servants of the Crown. Their
duty is to the Crown. It is the Crown who can dismiss them. As a matter
of administration they work in groups, some of which have statutory
functions to perform; but this does not change the nature of their
E employment as servants of the Crown.

Being the tenant of premises is not enough to attract the benefits of the
counter-inflation legislation. Those benefits only accrue in respect of
premises "occupied by the tenant . . . for the purposes of a business." Did
the Secretary of State for the Environment occupy either Keysign House
or 17, North Audley Street? Persons who worked in his department, who
F were not his servants but Crown servants, went to Keysign House for
maintenance and other service purposes connected with the job centre.
This could not be occupation of that property or any part of it by him.
The occupying was being done by Crown servants; and those who were
there from day to day were not even under his control: they were under
that of another minister. At 17, North Audley Street two rooms in the
G basement were used by electricians and carpenters working in his depart-
ment which provided all services there. Once again such occupation as
there was (and it was so tiny as to be de minimis) was occupation by the
Crown, not by the Secretary of State for the Environment. The fact that
the Crown's right to occupy was derived from the two underleases did not
make the Secretary of State for the Environment the occupier.

H On the opinion which I have come to as to occupancy, it is unnecessary
for me to deal with Mr. Slynn's submission that the Department of the
Environment should be adjudged to have been in joint occupation of both
sets of premises with the other government departments. Even if I had
been of the opinion that these government departments as separate entities
from the Crown had occupied the premises, on the evidence I would not
have adjudged that the Department of the Environment had been in joint
occupation with them.

The purposes of a business

In order to succeed in these appeals the defendant department has to establish that the Secretary of State for the Environment's occupation was "for the purposes of a business" which he carried on. Government activities were carried on in both sets of premises. The problem is whether within the meaning of the two Orders such activities can fairly be said to be a business carried on by the Secretary of State for the Environment or by the Crown itself. Article 2 (1) of both Orders does not define "business." The statutory interpretation provision specifies what the word includes. It may have the effect of extending the meaning; but it does not follow that what is stated to be included would be outside the ordinary meaning of the word. It must be construed in its context in these Orders. As a word in ordinary use "business" has a wide meaning. The *Concise Oxford Dictionary* lists ten meanings, only two of which have a commercial connotation. One, "thing needing attention, agenda, dealings with men and matters," is apt to cover government activities in all their aspects. The next step in construction is to consider whether the dictionary meaning has been cut down or extended by its statutory context.

The Order of 1972 was "a measure to counter inflation." The Act of 1973 was one "to afford powers of control over prices, pay, dividends and rents." I infer from the fact that orders were made controlling agricultural and residential rents as well as business rents that there was an intention to freeze a wide range of rents. This is borne out by the use of words in the description of "business" in the Order which cover activities far removed from the concept of "business" as a commercial undertaking.

I turn now to consider the impact upon the meaning of the word "business" in the Landlord and Tenant Act 1954. That there is some impact seems to me to result from the provisions of the Orders themselves. Article 11 (2) of the Order of 1972 and article 15 of the Order of 1973 both stated that Part II of the Act of 1954 should have effect subject to the provisions of the Orders. The Act of 1954 was divided into four parts. Part I was concerned with the security of tenure for residential tenants, Part II with that for business, professional and other tenants, Part III with compensation for improvements, and Part IV which was headed "Miscellaneous and Supplementary." The provisions applying the Act to the Crown came in Part IV. The very first section in Part II was section 23. Its marginal note is "Tenancies to which Part II applies." Section 23 (1) is in the same terms as the definition of business tenancy in the orders of 1972 and 1973, save that the Order of 1972 excluded agricultural leases and the Order of 1973 both agricultural and building leases. Section 23 (2) is in the same terms as the description of "business" in the Orders of 1972 and 1973 save that it is preceded by the words "In this Part of this Act . . ."

It follows, so it seems to me, that the concept of a business tenancy under Part II is one which covers a wide range of activities. Little seems to be excluded other than residential occupation and recreational activities carried on by individuals. Section 23 (4) made provision for the case where a tenant was carrying on a business in breach of a prohibition of use for business purposes. This is a much used form of covenant. I would infer that the draftsman had in mind how this kind of covenant had been construed. An example is provided by *Rolls* v. *Miller* (1884) 27 Ch.D. 71. In that case the running as a charity of a hostel for girls was held to be

A a breach of a covenant against carrying on "any trade or business." Lindley L.J. said, at pp. 88–89:

> "When we look into the dictionaries as to the meaning of the word 'business,' I do not think they throw much light upon it. The word means almost anything which is an occupation as distinguished from a pleasure—anything which is an occupation or duty which
> B requires attention is a business—I do not think we can get much aid from the dictionary. We must look at the words in the ordinary sense, and we must look at the object of the covenant; and, looking at both, I have no hesitation in saying that this is clearly within the words and within the object of the covenant."

The sections immediately following section 23 of the Act of 1954 deal
C with the continuation and renewal of tenancies. Section 30 sets out the grounds upon which a landlord may oppose an application by a tenant for a new tenancy. One ground, section 30 (1) (*g*), is

> ". . . that on the termination of the current tenancy the landlord intends to occupy the holding for the purposes, or partly for the purposes, of a business to be carried on by him therein, or as his
> D residence."

Now the Crown owns a considerable amount of property which it lets. Section 56 (1) applies Part II of the Act "where there is an interest belonging to Her Majesty in right of the Crown . . ." If the Crown cannot exercise the right to oppose given to other landlords by section 30 (1) (*g*) it is at a serious disadvantage. Section 56, however, gave the Crown all
E the rights of landlords, subject to certain modifications. We were informed by Mr. Slynn that since 1954 the Crown, on a number of occasions, has claimed to exercise the right to object given by section 30 (1) (*g*). So far no tenant has challenged its right to do so. This is understandable because section 56 applies the Act to the Crown. It does not follow that without the provisions of that section, to which I shall refer later, running a government department would be adjudged to be a carrying on of a
F business.

Section 37 of the Act of 1954 is of importance because it is connected with section 56 (3) which, Mr. Parker submitted, revealed that "the purposes of a government department" were not "business" within the meaning of Part II. Under section 37 (1) if a tenant fails to obtain a new tenancy because of his landlord's successful opposition under section 30
G (1) (*e*), (*f*) or (*g*) he becomes entitled to compensation in an amount determined in accordance with the remaining subsections; but conditions have to be satisfied. Under section 37 (3) these are:

> "(*a*) that, during the whole of the 14 years immediately preceding the termination of the current tenancy, premises being or comprised in the holding have been occupied for the purposes of a business
> H carried on by the occupier or for those and other purposes; (*b*) that, if during those 14 years there was a change in the occupier of the premises, the person who was the occupier immediately after the change was the successor to the business carried on by the person who was the occupier immediately before the change."

Section 56 (3) applies Part II of the Act "Where a tenancy is held by or on behalf of a government department." These words do not correspond exactly with the words in section 56 (1) which apply Part II to the

Crown's interest in more general terms; but I construe them as meaning that Part II applies to any tenancy "held on behalf of Her Majesty for the purposes of a government department": see the second half of section 56 (1). Section 56 (3) goes on as follows:

> ". . . and the property comprised therein is or includes premises occupied for any purposes of a government department, the tenancy shall be one to which Part II of this Act applies; and for the purposes of any provision of the said Part II or Schedule 9 to this Act which is applicable only if either or both of the following conditions are satisfied, that is to say—(*a*) that any premises have during any period been occupied for the purposes of the tenant's business; (*b*) that on any change of occupier of any premises the new occupier succeeded to the business of the former occupier, the said conditions shall be deemed to be satisfied respectively, in relation to such a tenancy, if during that period or, as the case may be, immediately before and immediately after the change, the premises were occupied for the purposes of a government department."

Mr. Parker's submission was that if the running of a government department amounted to the carrying on of a business within the meaning of section 23 (2) there would have been no need to refer in section 56 (3) to "any purposes of a government department." Still less would there have been any need for a deeming provision to bring into operation section 37 (3). I agree. Had the draftsman thought that the word "business" in Part II covered the activities carried on by government departments, section 56 would have been worded in much simpler terms. Without that section these activities would not have come within the description of business in section 23 (2). The Orders of 1972 and 1973 contained no provision similar to section 56.

It does not follow, however, that the word "business" as used in the Landlord and Tenant Act 1954 has the same meaning as it does in the Orders of 1972 and 1973. The object of the Act of 1954 was to provide security of tenure for many, but not all, tenants. The object of the counter-inflation legislation was to curb an economic evil. The Act of 1954 was expressed to apply to the Crown. The Acts of 1972 and 1973 did not bind the Crown, save to the limited extent set out in paragraph 8 (2) of the Schedule to the Act of 1972. The definition of "business" in the Orders must have been taken from section 23 (2) of the Act of 1954; but it does not follow, submitted Mr. Slynn, that it should be given the same meaning as in that Act, particularly as section 56 had no relevance to counter-inflation legislation. This is so. The question in these appeals is whether under the Orders of 1972 and 1973 the running of a government department can fairly be said to be the occupation of premises for the purposes of *a* business carried on by the Secretary of State as tenant. Nevertheless, what Parliament meant by a business tenancy in Part II of the Act of 1954 is, in my opinion, some guide to what the same words mean in orders which are expressly linked with it.

Mr. Slynn conceded that the Secretary of State for the Environment could not say that the running of a government department involved "activities carried on by a body of persons, whether corporate or unincorporate." As the word "activities" was limited by its descriptive words, it follows that to come within the ambit of the Orders activities by themselves must be of a kind within the ordinary meaning of the word "business." Clearly the Secretary of State for the Environment cannot bring

A himself within the words "trade" or "profession." It is not easy to construe the word "employment" in this context. The word "vocation" in both the Acts of 1972 and 1973 gives some help. I would construe "employment" in both Orders as "a way of earning a living" which was not a profession. The Secretary of State for the Environment cannot, in my judgment, be said to be occupying either 17, North Audley Street or Keysign House as a way of earning a living. It follows that to succeed in
B these appeals the Secretary of State for the Environment must prove that the activities of his department come within the ordinary meaning of the word "business." There is nothing in the Orders, other than the words of inclusion, to show that the word should have a special meaning or that it was used in any unusual sense. This brings into operation, so it seems to me, Lord Reid's statement of principle in *Cozens* v. *Brutus* [1973] A.C.
C 854, 861:

> "The meaning of an ordinary word of the English language is not a question of law. The proper construction of a statute is a question of law. If the context shows that a word is used in an unusual sense the court will determine in other words what that unusual sense is. But here there is in my opinion no question of the word 'insulting'
> D being used in any unusual sense. It appears to me, for reasons which I shall give later, to be intended to have its ordinary meaning. It is for the tribunal which decides the case to consider, not as law but as fact, whether in the whole circumstances the words of the statute do or do not as a matter of ordinary usage of the English language cover or apply to the facts which have been proved."

E In order to decide such a question of fact a judge has to think of himself as the embodiment of a jury. I have tried to do just that. I have reminded myself that in ordinary speech people use phrases such as "the business of government," "the business of the meeting," "minding one's own business" and "sending someone about his business." But in the end I have had to concentrate my attention on the words "for the purpose of *a* business carried on" by the Secretary of State for the Environment.

F In my judgment, in the ordinary usage of the English language no literate person would say that the Secretary of State for the Environment was occupying either set of premises "for the purpose of *a* business carried on by him." Such a person might say that the business of government was being carried on in these premises. That is a different concept altogether. On the evidence in this case he was not occupying either set of premises;
G but even if he was, he was not occupying them for the purpose of *a* business. This finding concludes this appeal in favour of the plaintiffs.

Can the Crown take advantage of the counter-inflation legislation?

Foster J., however, found against the defendant department on the much broader ground that the counter-inflation legislation did not apply
H to the Crown at all and that the Crown could not take advantage of it in any circumstances. As I do not share this opinion and cases could arise in which the evidence established that the Crown were occupying rented premises for the purpose of a business which it carried on (for example, the business of the Stationery Office) I will examine the constitutional position shortly. From the 18th century onwards it has been commonly believed amongst lawyers, first, that a statute did not apply to the Crown unless there was an express provision in it to that effect and, secondly, that the

Crown can take the benefit of any statute although not specifically named in it: see *Blackstone's Commentaries,* 5th ed. (1763), Book 1, p. 261. 19th-century textbook writers followed *Blackstone*: see *Stephen, Commentaries on the Laws of England*, 2nd ed. (1842), vol, 2, p. 519. The courts did the same: see *Reg.* v. *Cruise* (1852) 2 Ir.Ch.R. 65 and *Attorney-General* v. *Tomline* (1880) 15 Ch.D. 150. In *Cayzer, Irvine & Co. Ltd.* v. *Board of Trade* [1927] 1 K.B. 269 Rowlatt J. at first instance had held that the Crown could take advantage of the Limitation Act 1623, but on appeal the Court of Appeal decided the case on another ground so it was unnecessary to decide whether the Crown could take advantage of that Act. The point was, however, argued at length by the appellants. At the end of his judgment Scrutton L.J., at pp. 294–295, queried whether the statement of principle set out in *Blackstone* was well founded.

Mr. Slynn invited our attention to the foundations provided by *Anon.*, Y.B. 12 Hen. VII, 20; *William Stonor's Case* (1497) Y.B. 13 Hen. VII, 7 (see *Select Cases in the Exchequer Chamber*, Selden Society, vol. 2 (1948), p. 161); *Case of a Fine Levied by the King* (1604) 7 Co.Rep. 32a; and the *Magdalen College Case* (1615) 11 Co.Rep. 66b. I find it unnecessary to express any opinion about these foundations. By themselves they may not be of much value; but what has come about since is. First, there is the consensus of weighty legal opinion over two centuries, and, secondly, and more importantly in my judgment, the Crown's rights in this respect have now been recognised by Parliament. This came about under the Crown Proceedings Act 1947, the long title of which describes it as "An Act to amend the law relating to the civil liabilities and *rights* of the Crown. . . ." Section 31 (1) provides:

> "This Act shall not prejudice the right of the Crown to take advantage of the provisions of an Act of Parliament although not named therein; and it is hereby declared that in any civil proceedings against the Crown the provisions of any Act of Parliament which could, if the proceedings were between subjects, be relied upon by the defendant as a defence to the proceedings, whether in whole or in part, or otherwise, may, subject to any express provision to the contrary, be so relied upon by the Crown."

Mr. Parker submitted that the opening words of that subsection should be read as if the words "if any" came after the word "right." This cannot be so. But even if they did the second part of the subsection would apply. Foster J. thought otherwise. This must be wrong. If the underleases in these appeals had been granted to subjects and they had been sued by the plaintiffs for the covenanted rents during the period of the rent freeze the counter-inflation legislation would have provided a defence. In my judgment, provided the evidence had been available, the defendant department could have relied on the counter-inflation legislation by way of answer to the claim by the plaintiffs in their originating summonses.

I would dismiss these appeals.

SIR JOHN PENNYCUICK. I will endeavour to answer the following questions, namely, (1) Who was the tenant of the premises respectively comprised in the two leases? (2) Were the premises or any part of them occupied by the tenant? (3) If so, were the premises or such part of them occupied by the tenant for the purposes of a business carried on by him for those and other purposes? (4) Can the Crown take advantage of the counter-inflation legislation?

A (1) The description of the tenant in the lease dated March 13, 1952, of 17, North Audley Street runs: "The Minister of Works (hereinafter called the 'tenant' which expression shall where the context so admits include his assigns) for and on behalf of Her Majesty."

The description of the lessee in the underlease dated November 25, 1952, of Keysign House runs: "The Minister of Works (hereinafter called 'the lessee' which expression where the context so admits includes his
B successors and assigns) for and on behalf of Her Majesty."

These unhappily worded descriptions are, I think, capable of two interpretations, namely: (a) the lessee is the Minister as principal. This construction fits the inclusion of assigns in the one case and successors and assigns in the other case, but gives no effect to the words "on behalf of Her Majesty." (b) The lessee is the Crown, the grant being to the Minister
C as agent for the Crown. This construction gives effect to the words "on behalf of Her Majesty" but does not fit the inclusion of assigns in the one case and successors and assigns in the other case, since the only relevant assigns, or successors and assigns, could be those, not of the Minister as agent, but of the Crown as principal.

I have with considerable hesitation reached the conclusion that inter-
D pretation (a) is to be preferred. I find it easier to treat the words "on behalf of Her Majesty" as mere surplusage designed to make clear that the Minister is acting as a Minister of the Crown than to do real violence to the reference to assigns in the one case and successors and assigns in the other case. This interpretation is supported by the fact that the lessee's covenants are made simply by "the tenant" in the one case and "the lessee" in the other case and are not expressed to be made "on behalf
E of Her Majesty."

(2) If interpretation (a) is correct, I find it impossible on the facts to say that the defendant department occupied any part of either premises. I do not think the facts would warrant the finding of a joint occupation by the department and the occupiers of the various floors and rooms comparable to that held upon very special facts to exist in *Lee-Verhulst Invest-*
F *ments Ltd.* v. *Harwood Trust* [1973] Q.B. 204. The two small basement rooms in 17, North Audley Street used as storerooms should I think be disregarded as de minimis. I mention in parenthesis that even if one could treat the defendant department as in occupation of part by virtue of the storerooms, the defence would still fail under a variant of the answer given under the next question.

If, however, interpretation (b) were correct then the Crown through
G its various departments must be regarded as the occupier of the whole of 17, North Audley Street and of a significant part of Keysign House, namely, the ground floor shop or office in Keysign House which clearly cannot be disregarded as de minimis. I turn then to the next question on the assumption that, contrary to my own rather hesitant view, interpretation (b) is correct.

H (3) Did the Crown occupy these respective premises for the purposes of a business carried on by it or for those and other purposes? I will consider this question under the Counter-Inflation (Temporary Provisions) Act 1972 and the Counter-Inflation (Business Rents) Order 1972 to which latter I will refer as "the Order." The purpose of the Act, as appears from its long title and the circumstances in which it was passed, was to curb inflation and one would expect it to have a far-reaching and pervasive operation. I approach its construction and that of the Order from that angle.

A The Act itself contains only one subsection which is directly relevant to rents, namely, section 2 (4) which runs as follows: "The appropriate Minister may by order provide for preventing increases of rent over rent payable before November 6, 1972."

The Act contains in section 8 a definition of "business," but the word "business" only occurs in the Act in a different context from that of rents and in any event the definition throws no significant light on the slightly different definition in the order. B

The Act makes it clear that it is not intended to bind the Crown and the contrary has not been contended. This is an important consideration when one comes to the construction of the Order. If the Crown were bound by the Order in its capacity of landlord it is hardly conceivable that it should not be entitled to the benefit of the Order in its capacity as tenant and one might be compelled to strain the provisions of the Order in order to avoid C such an anomaly. But since the Crown is not bound in its capacity as landlord there is at least no anomaly in a construction which excludes it from the benefit of the order in its capacity as tenant and one must give the provisions their natural meaning according to the terms used read as a whole in their context.

The Act, so far as rents are concerned, was effectuated next day by D three Orders, namely, the Order dealing with business rents, and Orders dealing with residential rents and agricultural rents respectively.

Article 2 (2) of the Order contains the two following definitions:

> "'business tenancy' means any tenancy where the property comprised in the tenancy is or includes premises which are occupied by the tenant and are so occupied for the purposes of a business carried on E by him or for those and other purposes but does not include a tenancy of or a right to occupy land used for agriculture; 'business' includes a trade, profession or employment and includes any activity carried on by a body of persons, whether corporate or unincorporate."

The definition of "business tenancy" is a definition in the strict sense prefaced by the word "means." To fall within this definition premises F comprised in the tenancy must be occupied by the tenant and be so occupied "for the purposes of a business carried on by him" or for those and other purposes. I stress the word "a" which seems to me of critical importance.

The definition of "business" in marked contrast is prefaced by the word "includes." The effect of a definition in this form is that it embraces the subject matter of the word defined upon its natural meaning and also G the subject matter of the other words whether or not that subject matter would fall within the word defined without its extension by the other words. I deliberately use the expression "natural meaning" rather than the expression "residual meaning" which was used in argument. One looks first to the word defined and then to the words of inclusion and not vice versa. Many statutory definitions in this form come to mind.

H The word "business," is one of wide and imprecise scope and I should, in the context of the Order, be disposed to hold that the operations of a government department constitute "business" and the occupation of premises on behalf of the Crown by a department for the purpose of these operations an occupation for business purposes. We were referred to cases which make clear that the word "business" has indeed a wide scope and does not necessarily import the concept of profit: see *Rolls* v. *Miller*, 27 Ch.D. 71.

A In order, however, to bring these tenancies within the definition of "business tenancy" it is not sufficient to show that the operations of the defendant department constitute "business." It must be shown that the Crown through the department "carries on a business." I find it impossible so to hold. The expression "a business" conveys upon its ordinary meaning the notion of a distinct enterprise (not necessarily for profit) having distinct objects, distinct management and distinct assets and liabilities. It seems B to me that only upon an impermissibly loose use of the words can one say that the vast and amorphous operations of the Crown or of a single government department, constitute "a business" upon the ordinary meaning of that expression. Are the ships of the Royal Navy really assets of a business carried on by the Crown or the Ministry of Defence?

There is no escape in concentrating one's attention on the operations C carried on upon the particular premises with which one is concerned. These could not be said to constitute of themselves a separate business.

One turns then to the words added by way of inclusion. It is accepted that the operations of the various departments do not constitute a "trade" or "profession," but it is contended that they constitute an "employment." The word "employment" like the word "business" itself is certainly D one of wide and imprecise scope. It seems to me, however, that in the trilogy of "trade, profession or employment" its natural meaning is a source of livelihood comparable to that of a trade or profession though not strictly falling within either expression. Alternatively, it may bear a narrower meaning as denoting employment by another. I do not think that upon any natural use of words the Crown or one of its departments could be said to "carry on an employment."

E Finally, it is accepted that the Crown or one of its departments is not a "body of persons whether corporate or unincorporate."

I conclude that even if these premises are occupied by the Crown they were not so occupied for the purposes of a business carried on by the Crown or for those and other purposes.

Much reliance was placed by counsel for the plaintiffs upon a comparison between the provisions of the Order and those contained in Part II F of the Landlord and Tenant Act 1954. Summarily, that Act applies to the Crown alike in the capacity of landlord and in the capacity of tenant. Section 22 contains definitions of "business tenancy" and "business" in the same terms as those contained in the order. Then, section 56 contains elaborate provisions dealing with the position of the Crown, including subsection (3) which so far as material runs:

G

> ". . . the tenancy shall be one to which Part II of this Act applies; and for the purposes of any provision of the said Part II or Schedule 9 to this Act which is applicable only if either or both of the following conditions are satisfied, that is to say—(*a*) that any premises have during any period been occupied for the purposes of the tenant's business; (*b*) that on any change of occupier of any premises the new H occupier succeeded to the business of the former occupier, the said conditions shall be deemed to be satisfied respectively, in relation to such a tenancy, if during that period or, as the case may be, immediately before and immediately after the change, the premises were occupied for the purposes of a government department."

So there is first a statement that in the circumstances mentioned the tenancy "shall be" one to which Part II of the Act applies; then follow deeming words designed to apply certain provisions of the Act relating to compensation and succession. The contention on behalf of the plaintiffs is that if the Order had been intended to apply to premises occupied by the Crown or its departments the Order would have contained express provisions comparable to those in Part II of the Act of 1954 and that in the absence of such provisions one must construe the definitions in the order as not applicable to premises so occupied. I think there is some force, but only a limited force, in this contention. The presence of express provisions in the Act of 1954 and their absence in the Order affords a valid ground for not putting an extended construction upon the definitions in the Order. It would not afford a valid ground for cutting down the natural meaning of the definitions in the Order.

I need not deal separately with the Act and Order of 1973. The only relevant difference between the two Orders is that in the Order of 1973 the definition of "business" precedes instead of following the definition of "business tenancy." Nothing appears to turn upon this alteration.

I venture to add that the construction of the definitions is in my view a question of law. It is only when one has construed the definitions that one reaches the question of fact whether the particular circumstances of the tenancy bring it within the definitions. Here, where there is no dispute upon the facts, the whole question is, I think, for all practical purposes one of law.

(4) Can the Crown take advantage of the counter-inflation legislation? With all respect to the judge I think it perfectly clear that, not only upon a principle accepted for centuries, but under the express words of section 31 of the Crown Proceedings Act 1947, the Crown is entitled to take advantage of this legislation. The difficulty is that the particular circumstances do not fit the provisions of the legislation.

For the reasons which I have given I conclude that the defendant department has failed to show that the Crown or the department occupies a part of 17, North Audley Street or of Keysign House for the purposes of a business carried on by it, and on this ground I would dismiss the appeal.

BUCKLEY L.J. The primary question for decision in this case is whether the underleases of Keysign House and of 17, North Audley Street which were granted on September 14 and 28, 1973, respectively constitute "business tenancies" within the meaning of the Counter-Inflation (Business Rents) Order 1973. If they do, a second question arises whether the immediately pre-existing subtenancies of these properties were "business tenancies" within the meaning of the Counter-Inflation (Business Rents) Order 1972. These two questions depend upon the construction of the Orders and involve precisely similar considerations. If both are answered in the affirmative, then, if the subtenant were not the Crown, article 5 of the Order of 1973 would restrict the rent payable in respect of the new subtenancies to a standard rent ascertained by reference to the rent payable under the pre-existing subtenancies on November 5, 1972.

The Counter-Inflation Act 1973, under which the Order of 1973 was made, does not bind the Crown; so a third question arises whether, if the Order would have applied, had the subtenant been other than the Crown, the Crown can claim the benefit of the Order and refuse to pay a rent in excess of the standard rent.

Lawton L.J. has already stated the relevant facts and I need not

A repeat them. The first two questions depend upon the meaning of the expression "business tenancy" in the Orders. This is defined in article 2 (2) of the Orders. To constitute a "business tenancy" it is sufficient if part of the premises comprised in the tenancy is occupied by the tenant for the purposes of a business carried on by him: this is the result of the words "or includes."

It will be recalled that at all relevant times the shop part of Keysign B House has been used as a job centre by the Ministry of Labour and the Department of Employment successively, and the remainder of the building has been occupied by the United States Government. If the shop premises have been occupied by the tenant under the underlease of Keysign House for the purposes of a business carried on by such tenant the subtenancy of the whole of Keysign House must constitute a "business tenancy" for C the purposes of the orders.

In the case of Keysign House the new underlease defines the lessee thereunder as

> "the Secretary of State for the Environment (hereinafter called 'the lessee' which expression where the context so admits includes his successors and assigns) for and on behalf of Her Majesty."

D

The demise is to "the lessee" and the covenantor in respect of the tenant's covenants is described as "the lessee." The underlease of 17, North Audley Street is in a corresponding form with what appears to me to be immaterial variations in the language identifying the lessee. Were it not for the words in brackets, I would have thought that the Secretary of State for the Environment was made a party to the underlease merely E as Her Majesty's agent or amanuensis to execute the document on her behalf with the consequence that the legal estate in the term created by the underlease would have vested in Her Majesty in right of the Crown, but the reference to "successors and assigns" seems to me to make this construction untenable. If by the operation of the underlease the term created by it were vested in the Crown, to what could any successor of the F Secretary of State for the Environment succeed or what could the Secretary of State assign? It is his successors and assigns who are referred to within the brackets, not Her Majesty's. It seems to me to be inescapable that the demise is to the Secretary of State for the Environment and his successors and assigns and that the term must have become vested in him in his corporate capacity. What then are the meaning and effect of the words "for and on behalf of Her Majesty?" There seem to me to be two G possibilities here, and I can think of no other: first, that the Secretary of State for the Environment entered into the underlease as a trustee for Her Majesty or, secondly, that the words indicate that he entered into the underlease in his capacity as a Minister of the Crown and in no other capacity. In the former alternative I think he would be a bare trustee of the term for Her Majesty in right of the Crown; in the latter he would, in my H opinion, hold the term for the purposes of those particular executive functions of the Crown, that is to say, of government, which are committed to him by virtue of his office. In either case the Secretary of State for the Environment would in law be the tenant under the underlease and not Her Majesty. Accordingly, I do not think that the Crown is the tenant under either of the subleases: so the question whether the Crown is in occupation of any part of the buildings on account of some other government department being accommodated there does not arise.

It is a function of the Secretary of State for the Environment to provide accommodation for other ministries and for other departments of government and bodies carrying on the manifold activities of the executive, such for instance as the Department of Employment. The defendant department provides, furnishes and maintains the buildings. The other ministries and bodies accommodated in them occupy them. The Department of Employment occupies the shop at Keysign House. That department's occupation may properly be called occupation by the Crown but is not occupation by the Secretary of State for the Environment any more than the occupation of the rest of the building by the United States Government has been.

At 17, North Audley Street the defendant department provides accommodation free of charge for the Registrar of Friendly Societies, the Inland Revenue Commissioners and the Customs and Excise Commissioners. The defendant department furnishes and maintains the building. It retains only two small basement rooms for storing materials, implements and so forth, but the rest of the building is occupied by the bodies accommodated there.

Mr. Slynn, relying on *Lee-Verhulst (Investments) Ltd.* v. *Harwood Trust* [1973] 1 Q.B. 204, has contended that the defendant department occupies the shop and the whole of 17, North Audley Street, apart from the two retained rooms, concurrently with the other occupiers of those parts of the buildings by virtue of its maintenance activities, which involve members of its staff having access to those parts of the buildings and visiting them regularly and frequently. In the *Lee-Verhulst* case this court considered whether the tenant of a house in South Kensington was in occupation of the house for the purposes of a business carried on there by the tenant within section 23 of the Landlord and Tenant Act 1954 which uses language identical with the definitions of business tenancy and business in the Counter-Inflation (Business Rents) Orders 1972 and 1973. The plaintiff company, which was the tenant, carried on the business of letting furnished rooms with services. The sole director of the company lived in the basement and devoted his whole time to the business, supervising and providing the services. He exercised a considerable degree of control over his tenants in respect of their use of their rooms and had access to all parts of the house. This court affirmed the county court judge in his view that on the facts of that case the tenant was in occupation of the whole house for the purposes of its business. Much reliance was placed in the judgments upon the constant and pervasive presence of the director, the nature of the services provided and the degree of control exercised. The case is clearly distinguishable from the present case upon its facts and I am not persuaded that we could properly say, on the facts of this case and giving to the word "occupied" a non-technical, ordinary, natural meaning, that the defendant department was in occupation of any part of either building except the two store rooms at 17, North Audley Street. If this is right, it disposes of the appeal in relation to Keysign House. In case, however, I should be wrong I should deal with the question whether, if the Secretary of State for the Environment ought to be regarded as in occupation of any part of the buildings, he ought to be regarded as being so for the purposes of a business carried on by him.

First let me deal with the two retained rooms at 17, North Audley Street. In terms of relative size these are a very small part of the building. If otherwise their retention and use by the defendant department might constitute the subtenancy of 17, North Audley Street a business tenancy for the purposes of the Orders, I should be strongly tempted to treat them

A as minima; but I do not think that it is a business tenancy. Moreover use and occupation of these rooms by members of the staff of the department, that is by servants of the Crown, does not, in my opinion as at present advised, constitute occupation by the Secretary of State for the Environment in his corporate capacity.

The word "business" has a protean quality which makes it susceptible of many meanings. A glance at *Stroud's Judicial Dictionary* will show this.
B What does it mean in the context of the Counter-Inflation (Business Rents) Orders 1972 and 1973? Mr. Parker has laid great stress on the provisions of Part II of the Landlord and Tenant Act 1954. This deals with business tenancies and uses the same terminology as the Orders. I am reluctant, however, to construe the Orders by reference to an Act dealing with another aspect of the law of landlord and tenant. Although the subject
C matters are related and the draftsman of the Orders seems to have modelled his language on that of the Act, it does not, in my opinion, necessarily follow that we should construe the language of the Orders in precisely the same way as the context of the Act of 1954 may require a court to adopt in construing that Act. I prefer to approach the language of the Orders without regard to the Act of 1954. Paragraph 2 (2) of the Order of 1973 states not what the word "business" means in the Order but what it
D shall include. It may be an extending provision: it cannot be restrictive. It is not suggested that we are concerned in this case with the carrying on of any trade or profession and, like my brethren, I do not think we are concerned with the carrying on of an employment. We have, therefore, to consider what the word "business" in its ordinary connotation means.

It seems easier to say what is not "business" than what is. Purely
E domestic activities are not "business." Purely recreational activities are not in my opinion "business," unless, maybe, when carried on by a body of persons: see *Addiscombe Garden Estates Ltd.* v. *Crabbe* [1958] 1 Q.B. 513. Nor, I think, are purely cultural pursuits, distinct from a business of providing education. A commercial element may not be essential: see *Rolls* v. *Miller*, 27 Ch.D. 71; but on the other hand a philanthropic activity may not constitute a business if it be a gratuitous pursuit of a spare time
F activity: see *Abernethie* v. *A. M. & J. Kleiman Ltd.* [1970] 1 Q.B. 10. But a serious undertaking earnestly pursued for the purpose of fulfilling a social obligation may constitute a business, even if not undertaken for profit. It seems to be to a great extent a question of degree and to depend largely upon the character of the particular activity.

The Queen's government undoubtedly carries on the business of govern-
G ment, and each department or ministry or executive agency of the government can be said without inaccuracy to carry on a part of that business; but it seems to me, as to my brethren, that to carry on some part of the business of government is something different from carrying on "a business." I do not think that in any ordinary sense of the English language the Admiralty or the Treasury or the Home Office or the Foreign Office
H can be said to carry on a business. The same would, I think, be clearly true of many other government departments. There are some, of which perhaps the Department of Health is not a bad example, which might seem in respect of some of their activities to come nearer to carrying on businesses because of the nature of their functions. Some government departments may within their functions carry on commercial or quasi-commercial activities, such as the Stationery Office which sells government publications, and these activities may for some purposes properly be regarded as con-

stituting the carrying on of a business; but generally speaking the conduct A
of a branch of government business should not, in my opinion, be regarded as the carrying on of " a business " within the meaning of the Orders. In my judgment, the provision of the services provided by the Department of the Environment in respect of either Keysign House or 17, North Audley Street does not constitute the carrying on of " a business " by the department within the meaning of the order.

For these reasons, I am of opinion that the present case does not fall B
within the terms of either Order. It follows that the Secretary of State for the Environment on behalf of the Crown cannot claim the benefit of the Order. It is consequently not strictly necessary for me to express an opinion upon the question whether the Crown can claim the benefit of an Act of Parliament although not bound by it. I do not wish to retraverse ground already covered by my brethren. It is sufficient for me to say that I agree C
with what Lawton L.J. has said on the topic. In a case to which the Order would otherwise apply the Crown, if it be the landlord, may be able to assert that the Order cannot bind it; but it by no means follows that if the Crown be the tenant, it cannot assert that it would be contrary to law for the landlord to claim or receive more than a standard rent.

I also would dismiss these appeals.

D

Appeal dismissed with costs.
Leave to appeal on defendant's undertaking to pay costs of appeal.

Solicitors: *Treasury Solicitor; Beachcroft, Hyman Isaacs.*

E

C. N.

[CHANCERY DIVISION] F

* T. & E. HOMES LTD. *v.* ROBINSON (INSPECTOR OF TAXES)

1976 July 9, 12, 13, 14 — Goulding J.

Revenue — Income tax—Rent — Excess rent — Land containing minerals leased at nominal rent—Royalties payable for licence to get and carry away minerals—Whether payments chargeable to income tax as excess rents—Income Tax Act 1952 (15 & 16 *Geo.* 6 & 1 *Eliz.* 2, *c.* 10), *s.* 175 G

In 1957 the taxpayer company purchased land containing sand and gravel and leased it for a period of 21 years to W Ltd. at an annual " rent " of £60. The lease was in the form of an agricultural lease and did not permit the lessee to get H
and carry away minerals from the land. At the same time the taxpayer company granted W Ltd. a licence under seal to get and carry away minerals and to pay four shillings for every cubic yard of sand or gravel taken from it. The lease and the licence though executed contemporaneously were embodied in

[Reported by MRS. HARRIET DUTTON, Barrister-at-Law]

A two separate documents. In 1960 a similar procedure was adopted by the taxpayer company in respect of another area of land that it leased to W Ltd. The taxpayer company appealed against assessments to income tax made under Schedule D, Case VI, for the period from 1957 to 1960. The special commissioners reduced the amounts of the assessments but dismissed the appeal in principle rejecting the taxpayer company's contention that the royalties paid to it by W Ltd. B under the licences did not constitute " rent payable under a lease " within section 175 of the Income Tax Act 1952.[1]

On appeal by the taxpayer company:—

Held, allowing the appeal, that the word " rent " in section 175 of the Income Tax Act 1952 must be given its strict legal meaning of payments issuing out of land and recoverable by distress; that a clear distinction had been made by the parties between the rents payable under the leases and the sums paid C as royalties under the licences and for which the common law remedy of distress would not have been available to a landlord to recover arrears; and that accordingly the payments made under the licences were not to be assessed to income tax under Case VI, Schedule D as excess rents chargeable by virtue of section 175.

Cox v. *Harper* [1910] 1 Ch. 480, C.A.; *Duke of Westminster* v. *Store Properties Ltd.* [1944] Ch. 129 and *Associated* D *London Properties Ltd.* v. *Williams* [1948] 1 All E.R. 442; 30 T.C. 57, C.A. applied.

Reg. v. *Westbrook* (1847) 10 Q.B. 178 and *Tollemache Settled Estates Trustees* v. *Coughtrie* [1961] A.C. 880, H.L.(E.) distinguished.

The following cases are referred to in the judgment:

E *Associated London Properties Ltd.* v. *Williams* [1948] 1 All E.R. 442; 30 T.C. 57, C.A.
Cox v. *Harper* [1910] 1 Ch. 480, C.A.
De Voil v. *Welford Gravels Ltd.* [1963] Ch. 95; [1962] 3 W.L.R. 489; [1962] 2 All E.R. 657, C.A.; [1965] A.C. 34; [1963] 3 W.L.R. 292; [1963] 2 All E.R. 1039; 41 T.C. 172, H.L.(E.).
Earl Fitzwilliam's Collieries Co. v. *Phillips* [1943] A.C. 570, H.L.(E.).
F *Reg.* v. *Westbrook* (1847) 10 Q.B. 178.
Revell v. *Scott* (1895) 3 T.C. 403.
Sutherland (Duke of) v. *Heathcote* [1892] 1 Ch. 475, C.A.
Tollemache Settled Estates Trustees v. *Coughtrie* [1961] A.C. 880; [1961] 2 W.L.R. 318; [1961] 1 All E.R. 593, H.L.(E.).
Westminster (Duke of) v. *Store Properties Ltd.* [1944] Ch. 129; [1944] 1 All E.R. 118.

G The following additional cases were cited in argument:

Brown v. *Peto* [1900] 2 Q.B. 653, C.A.
Campbell v. *Inland Revenue Commissioners* (1879) 1 T.C. 234.
Daniel v. *Gracey* (1844) 6 Q.B. 145.
Greville-Nugent v. *McKenzie* [1900] A.C. 83, H.L.(E.).
Gwyther v. *Boslymon Quarries Ltd.* [1950] 2 K.B. 59; [1950] 1 All
H E.R. 384.
Loughnan v. *Marston's Dolphin Brewery Ltd.* [1936] A.C. 393; [1936] 1 All E.R. 468; 20 T.C. 367, H.L.(E.).

[1] Income Tax Act 1952, s. 175: (1) If, as respects any year of assessment, the immediate lessor of a unit of assessment is entitled in respect of the unit to any rent payable under a lease or leases to which this section applies, he shall be chargeable to tax under Case VI of Schedule D in respect of the excess, if any, of the amount which would have been the amount of the assessment of the unit for the purposes of Schedule A, . . .

Stanley v. *Hayes* (1842) 3 Q.B. 105. A
Ward v. *Day* (1864) 5 B. & S. 359.

CASE STATED by the Commissioners for the Special Purposes of the Income Tax Acts.

On February 22, 1957, the taxpayer company, T. & E. Homes Ltd., purchased 23½ acres of land in Essex containing sand and gravel. On December 31, 1957, the land was leased to Welford Gravels Ltd. for 21 B years at an annual rent of £60. By a licence under seal executed on the same day as the lease the taxpayer company authorised Welford Gravels Ltd. to excavate and to carry away sand, gravel, ballast and other mineral at a cost of four shillings per cubic yard. On April 30, 1960, the taxpayer company leased other land to Welford Gravels Ltd. for 21 years at an annual rent of £50. A similar licence under seal was executed for the C excavation of minerals but at a price of two shillings per cubic yard. The taxpayer company was assessed to Schedule D, Case VI income tax for the year 1957–58 of £14,054; for 1958–59 of £10,608 and for 1959–60 two assessments of £6,279 and £6,865. The special commissioners dismissed in principle the taxpayer company's appeal against the assessment holding that the payments received from Welford Gravels Ltd. under the licences constituted "Rent payable under a lease" within the meaning of D section 175 of the Income Tax Act 1952. They ordered the assessment to be reduced to £11,082 for 1957–58; £8,045 for 1958–59 and £4,218 and £6,023 for 1959–60. The taxpayer company appealed.

The facts are stated in the judgment.

Martin Nourse Q.C. and *Donald Campion* for the taxpayer company. E
Ian Edwards-Jones Q.C. and *Brian Davenport* for the Crown.

GOULDING J. This is an appeal by a company called T. & E. Homes Ltd. from a decision of the special commissioners. The subject matter of assessment is certain money received by the taxpayer company and assessed to income tax under Case VI of Schedule D as excess rents chargeable by virtue of section 175 of the Income Tax Act 1952. The F years of assessment in question are 1957–58 and the two following years. The material legislation is no longer of general interest. It has been greatly altered in respect of the year 1963–64 and all subsequent years. The money in question came to the taxpayer company as owner of two gravel pits, one in Essex and the other in Northamptonshire. Like the special commissioners, I think the differences between the facts affecting G the two pits are not of critical importance, and, like them, I shall direct my observations to the property in Essex.

The special commissioners found that on February 22, 1957, the taxpayer company, which was then named Besbuilt Ltd., had purchased 23½ acres of land at Tillingham, Essex. The land contained sand and gravel, and development permission had been given for its extraction and for the erection of plant and machinery for that purpose. The company bought H the land so that one of its associate companies, called Welford Gravels Ltd., could extract sand and gravel for commercial purposes. Having bought the land, the taxpayer company immediately let Welford Gravels Ltd. into occupation, allowing that company to install plant and machinery and extract sand and gravel. By the end of 1957, up to which point the relevant documents had not yet been executed, Welford Gravels Ltd. had extracted some 56,000 cubic yards of sand and gravel.

A It appears that in framing the arrangement between the taxpayer company and its associated company, Welford Gravels Ltd., the taxpayer company's advisers paid special attention to the revenue law then existing. For a long time it had been believed that the owners of sand and gravel pits should be assessed under Case I of Schedule D on the full amount of the profits made in the preceding year, but a decision of the House of Lords in 1948 had shown that view to be mistaken in law. Thus, in 1957 the
B position was that the owner of a sand or gravel pit was liable to pay income tax, first of all, in the amount of the Schedule A assessment on the land in question and, secondly, under Case VI of Schedule D, on any excess rents chargeable by virtue of section 175 of the Income Tax Act 1952. The advisers of the taxpayer company sought to turn that state of the law to advantage by, if possible, arranging that the larger part of the consideration
C to be paid by Welford Gravels Ltd. for the gravel pit should come to the taxpayer company in a form that would not be excess rents for the purpose of section 175. The question that arises in this appeal is whether that plan was successful.

On December 31, 1957, two documents were executed, both of them under seal and both of them made between the taxpayer company, of the one part, and Welford Gravels Ltd. of the other part. The first was
D described as a lease, and it contains definitions of "landlord" and "tenant" expressed to include their respective successors in title. By clause 1, the landlord demises unto the tenant all that piece of land particularised in the schedule to the lease. The schedule contains a description of 23½ acres by reference to the ordnance survey map, together with certain easements. It does not contain any exception or reservation relating
E to minerals. The demise under clause 1, to which I now return, was for a term of 21 years from March 1, 1957, and the clause of demise ended with the words "Paying therefor yearly during the said term the rent of £60 to be paid without any deduction (save landlord's property tax) by equal quarterly payments on" the four usual quarter days.

The tenant's covenants, which are in clause 3 of the lease, were concise and not in any way unusual. The first was: "To pay the said rent hereby
F reserved on the days and in the manner aforesaid." The second, putting it shortly, was to pay all the rates and other outgoings on the demised premises "or the produce thereof or any buildings machinery or works thereon," and it has been pointed out in argument that that would oblige Welford Gravels Ltd. to pay rates in respect of any buildings or other rateable subjects that it had already affixed to the land in the course of its
G mineral workings. Then there was a covenant to keep buildings in repair. Fourthly, there was a covenant as to fences, which I should read:

> "To make and keep in repair sufficient fences for the protection of man and beast round every quarry pit or other open place made or hereafter during the said term to be made in the said lands and sufficiently to fence off all roads and ways from the adjoining lands and to make gates in such fences where required by the landlord."

H

It will be observed that that language clearly contemplates that quarries or pits in addition to those already existing might be made during the term.

The fifth tenant's covenant was to permit the landlord by its agents to enter and inspect the premises, and to repair on notice, and in default to repay to the landlord the expenses incurred by the landlord in repairing. That covenant ends with the words, "such expenses to be recoverable as

rent in arrear." Then, the last two covenants by the tenant are to deliver A
up at the end of the term, and not to assign, sublet or part with possession without the landlord's consent, not to be unreasonably withheld. There follows the usual covenant for quiet enjoyment, which I shall read, as much turns upon its language. It says:

> "The landlord hereby covenants with the tenant that the tenant paying the rent hereby reserved and observing and performing the several B
> covenants and stipulations herein on their part contained shall peaceably hold and enjoy the premises hereby demised and granted during the said term without any interruption by the landlord or any person rightfully claiming under or in trust for it."

There follow in the last clause in the lease three provisos. The first is a proviso for re-entry, which has effect "if any part of the rent hereby C
reserved shall be unpaid for 30 days . . . or" in the case of insolvency of the tenant, or "if any covenant on the tenant's part herein contained shall not be performed or observed." The second proviso relates to service of notices, and I need not read it. The third proviso is as follows:

> "Nothing in this lease shall be taken to authorise the tenant to get or carry away sand gravel ballast or any other mineral from the said land D
> whether or not from a pit or quarry which is now or was at the commencement of the term hereby granted already open."

The contemporaneous second document is described as a licence, and it starts with a recital of the lease and with two further recitals:

> "(B) The demised land contains sand gravel and ballast and may contain other minerals which Welford is desirous of working and E
> carrying away but the said lease grants Welford no right to do so. (C) Besbuilt" (that, as I have said, was the then name of the taxpayer company) "is desirous of granting such right in manner and subject to the provisions hereinafter contained." Clause 1: "Welford shall during the continuance in force of the said lease have the following liberties: (1) To search for dig work and obtain by excavations F
> and quarryings open to the daylight and not by underground workings in and from the demised land sand gravel ballast and all other minerals which may be found therein and to carry away and dispose of the same for Welford's own benefit. . . . 2: Welford shall during the continuance in force of the said lease pay to Besbuilt on January 1 and July 1 in every year four shillings for every cubic yard of sand gravel or ballast got by them in the half-year ending on such day. G
> 3: Welford shall pay to Besbuilt during the continuance in force of the said lease one equal quarter part (or such other proportion as may from time to time be agreed) of the moneys for which any mineral got under the liberties hereby granted other than sand gravel or ballast (the same having been first dressed and made merchantable where such process is required) shall be sold the said share of sale moneys to be H
> paid within 21 days of sale and before the minerals sold are removed from the demised land."

Then there is a covenant by Welford during the continuance in force of the lease to work the quarries and minerals in a proper and efficient manner, to fence properly, to pay compensation to parties who may be injured by the workings and to keep proper records of the mineral extracted. Next follows a provision that Welford will:

A "Permit Besbuilt by its agents with or without clerks . . . to enter upon inspect and examine the demised quarries and premises and every part thereof for the purpose of ascertaining whether the same are being worked and carried on in a proper manner and are in good and substantial order condition and repair in accordance with the terms of this deed."

B Then there are provisions for repair by Welford or, in default, by the taxpayer company, and further obligations which I need not read.

In clause 5 of the licence there is a provision for the taxpayer company to accept a surrender of the lease on exhaustion of the sand and gravel pits and notice by Welford Gravels Ltd. that that has occurred. It is also a condition of requiring a surrender that:

C "Welford shall up to the time of such surrender pay the rents and royalties and perform and observe the covenants on its part in the said lease and herein contained." Clause 6: "If Welford shall assign the lease aforesaid it shall assign to the assignee of the said lease the benefit of this licence and shall obtain the assumption of such assignee of the burden of the covenants herein contained and on Welford's part to be performed (including this covenant)."

D Such are the two documents executed and a similar course was followed in regard to the gravel pit in Northamptonshire. The differences that one can observe are that in that case the lease was dated April 30, 1960, and the licence was a little later, namely, May 2, 1960. That small interval of time, in my judgment, has no bearing on the construction of the deeds since it is quite clear from the passages I have read that each contemplated E the existence of the other and is to be construed accordingly. Further differences are that in the Northamptonshire licence deed the royalty reserved was two shillings per cubic yard and not four shillings; and the provision for surrender of the lease on exhaustion of the gravel pit—that is, clause 5 in the licence deed—was not included.

Section 175 of the Income Tax Act 1952 applied only to rent payable under a short lease in respect of a Schedule A unit of assessment. No F question arises here as to the length of the lease or as to the unit of assessment. The taxpayer company contends that royalties payable in pursuance of the licence deed are not rent payable under a lease at all. There is powerful encouragement for that argument in an observation of Lord Evershed M.R. Many years ago, the facts of the present case which I have just recounted gave rise to litigation between the revenue authorities and Welford Gravels Ltd. They were in dispute regarding the G ascertainment and amount of that company's liability to income tax under Schedule A as occupier of the gravel pit under the lease of 1957. The case *De Voil* v. *Welford Gravels Ltd.* was finally decided in the House of Lords. On its way there, Lord Evershed M.R., delivering his judgment in the Court of Appeal [1963] Ch. 95, said, at p. 115:

"It is not, I think, in doubt that, were it not for the somewhat unusual H form of the two documents executed on December 31, 1957, the assessment in respect of the gravel pit would almost certainly have been made under Schedule D on the 'excess rents' received by the landlords, as was done in the recent case of *Tollemache Settled Estates Trustees* v. *Coughtrie*. It is clear, however, that the form of the documents of December 1957 is such that it may (at the least) be doubtful whether what is received by Besbuilt Ltd. can rightly be called 'rents' within the meaning of section 175 of the Income Tax Act 1952."

Naturally, Mr. Nourse, appearing for the taxpayer company, relied strongly A
on Lord Evershed M.R.'s obiter dictum. I must not, however, exaggerate its authority, for it does not appear that the question about section 175 needed to be argued, or ever was argued, during the hearing of *De Voil* v. *Welford Gravels Ltd.*

When the present appeal was before the special commissioners, the taxpayer company's main contention was "that the sums in question were not 'rent payable under a lease' within . . . section 175, but were royalties B
paid by virtue of a licence as compensation," and in giving their decision the commissioners said that the question, as the case was argued before them, was whether the four shillings per cubic foot was a rent payable under a lease or, as the taxpayer company contended, a royalty payable under a licence. They went on:

> "In view of the decision in *Tollemache* . . . the company was obliged C
> to concede, before us, that if the four shillings was payable under a lease then it fell to be regarded as rent. To determine the question we have to examine the true nature of the legal relationship between the company and Welford. The parties went out of their way to create, so far as they could, two distinct legal relationships, one being that of landlord and tenant, the other that of licensor and licensee. D
> The arrangement however was part of one bargain. Welford occupied the land, and the relationship of landlord and tenant was created, only to enable Welford to take the minerals; the right to take minerals was co-terminous with and could not (according to its terms) exist apart from the tenancy. Clause 5 (3) of the lease provided that nothing therein should be taken to authorise Welford to take minerals: it was nevertheless intended that Welford should take them and that the E
> company should get its four shillings, and it would be naïve to envisage the company granting the lease if Welford had not intended to execute the licence deed.
>
> "The factual reality is that the lease and licence together formed one transaction, whereby the company leased the land with a right to take minerals, for a rent and royalty. In our opinion, to get at the F
> true nature of the legal relationship we should read the two documents together: if (as we conclude) they were intended to supplement each other, we should read the licence as supplemental to the lease; so reading them, we conclude that Welford took the minerals and paid the four shillings in the capacity of lessee and occupier, and not in any other distinct capacity."

G

Accordingly, they held that the payments of four shillings per cubic foot were rent payable under a lease.

In this court, the taxpayer company's contentions have taken a rather different form. Mr. Nourse did not dispute the finding that the lease and licence together formed one transaction. Indeed, he did not attach any vital importance to the separation of the terms of the transaction into two H
distinct documents. He accepted, I think, and certainly I myself am of opinion, that the same legal situation could have been produced by a single instrument, although its terms would look unusual and somewhat surprising. Mr. Nourse's submissions in this court centred on two propositions. First, he said that the word "rent" in section 175 of the Income Tax Act 1952 has its proper legal sense of payments issuing out of land and recoverable by distress. Secondly, he said that the royalties contracted for by the

A licence deed are not payments of that character. If both the premises are correct it follows that the assessments based on section 175 are ill-founded.

In support of his first proposition, Mr. Nourse pointed to the context of the Income Tax Act 1952. Section 175 occurs in Chapter II of Part VII of the Act, a chapter entitled "Rents and Other Receipts from Land in the United Kingdom." Within that very chapter we find that section 177, which deals with rents under long leases and analogous payments, contains
B an enumeration of subject matter that strongly suggests the draftsman did not rely on the word "rent" beyond the limits of its strict signification. Still in the same chapter is section 180, which taxes mining rents and royalties. That section contains an extended definition of rent limited to the purposes of section 180. Again, in section 181, dealing with the management expenses of owners of mineral rights, Parliament has used the
C expression "rent or royalties." There is therefore a strong inference, said Mr. Nourse, that in section 175 the unadorned word "rent" bears no more than its literal meaning in the law.

This argument would, I think, be irresistible had the Act of 1952 been an original statute, drawn in one piece. It was, however, an Act to consolidate pre-existing laws, and in fact sections 175, 180 and 181 were taken into the Act of 1952 from three different sources. Section 177, like section
D 175, is drawn from the Finance Act 1940, but it is there couched in a referential form that makes the inference less obvious. Mr. Nourse's argument from context was thus somewhat weakened by close examination of legislative history.

He has, however, other arms to deploy in support of his first proposition. Mr. Nourse cited several reported cases where the word "rent"
E in various statutes has been held to bear its technical legal meaning. One of them was a decision of Bennett J. on legislation relating to war damage, namely *Duke of Westminster* v. *Store Properties Ltd.* [1944] Ch. 129. His judgment was referred to in the Court of Appeal, clearly with approval, in *Associated London Properties Ltd.* v. *Williams* [1948] 1 All E.R. 442. Let me quote some observations of Tucker L.J., at p. 447:

F "The second argument for the Crown is that the word 'rent' in this proviso should not be given a strict and technical meaning, but that it should be given the meaning which would be attributed to it by an ordinary business man or the man in the street. I cannot accept that contention either. I think that in a taxing enactment such as section 17 of the [Finance] Act of 1938 the intention is to give the word a technical meaning. The foundation for this assumption is to be found
G in No. 1 of Schedule A where the word 'rent' is used as meaning 'rack-rent.' That, in itself, is a technical term. If it were intended by the legislature that the word 'rent' should mean any benefit which the landlord shall obtain as a result of the erection of an air-raid shelter it would have been perfectly easy to say so, but the legislature chose to use the word 'rent,' and I think it must be given a technical meaning."

H

Mr. Edwards-Jones, for the Crown, suggested that the word "rent" in section 175, notwithstanding those authorities, has a much broader sense. It covers, he said, any return or equivalent adapted to the nature of the subject demised; or, in the words of Lord Denman C.J. in *Reg* v. *Westbrook* (1847) 10 Q.B. 178, 205, "the compensation which the occupier pays the landlord for that species of occupation which the contract between them allows."

Mr. Edwards-Jones's argument ranged over a wide ground, on which A the following peaks stand out. First and foremost, he said, section 175 (or its statutory predecessor in the Finance Act 1940) was enacted to supplement the deficiencies of Schedule A under the conditions prevailing in 1940 by charging the subject's gains from land in excess of the Schedule A valuation. This broad and manifest object of the legislature would be defeated, it is submitted, if a narrowly technical interpretation were applied to the word " rent." The statutory remedy should be co-extensive with the B presumed mischief. Mr. Edwards-Jones pointed to a number of anomalies which could arise in hypothetical situations if a strict construction is applied.

Secondly, just as Mr. Nourse referred to authorities in which the court has applied a strict interpretation to the word " rent," so Mr. Edwards-Jones produced some where a loose or broad construction was adopted. C A good example is the speech of Lord Wright in *Earl Fitzwilliam's Collieries Co.* v. *Phillips* [1943] A.C. 570. Lord Wright said, at p. 581:

> " The Crown's right to tax cannot be affected by the mere words which the parties have chosen to use. The word ' rent ' is itself a word of very wide import, not always correctly employed in ordinary current user, particularly in taxing provisions. ' Rent ' at common law, in its D strict sense, could not properly be applied to denote a rent reserved in a lease of incorporeal hereditaments because rent would not issue out of the premises: *Buszard* v. *Capel* (1828) 8 B. & C. 141, but such payments would ordinarily be called rent. In *Coltness Iron Co.* v. *Black* (1881) 6 App.Cas. 315, 335, Lord Blackburn observes on the use which he says is perhaps not quite accurate of the term ' rent reserved in a mineral lease,' to describe what in one sense is pay- E ment by instalments of the price of minerals forming the land."

His Lordship went on to show that the case before him was governed by the extended (but express) definition of " rent " in what afterwards became section 180 of the Income Tax Act 1952.

Thirdly, Mr. Edwards-Jones pointed out that the technical English meaning of the word " rent " would be inappropriate in Scotch cases, if F only because the landlord's right of distress is in Scotland obsolete, having, as I understand, been superseded almost four centuries ago, in a process of judicial evolution, by a different remedy called hypothec.

There is force in these and the other submissions by Mr. Edwards-Jones, but in the end I ought, in my judgment, to follow the clear lead given in relation to this branch of revenue law by *Duke of Westminster* G v. *Store Properties Ltd.* and *Associated London Properties Ltd.* v. *Williams.* I therefore accept Mr. Nourse's first proposition and must go on to his second proposition. I will say at once that I find it raises a question of great difficulty. Mr. Nourse developed his second proposition in this way. He said, first, that although mineral royalties may often be rent in the true sense, they are not so in the present case, for the question depends on the true construction of the leases and licences, and there is H no objection to the parties agreeing that the royalties will not be rent. Secondly, the leases do not contain any reservation of the royalties as rent, nor any covenant to pay them. Thirdly, the leases contain qualified covenants for quiet enjoyment which are expressed to depend on the tenant " paying the rent hereby reserved and observing and performing the several covenants and stipulations herein on their part contained," but not on payment of the royalties or on the performance of the covenants in the licences. Fourthly, the licences do contain covenants by the tenant to pay the royalties, but there is no reservation of them as rent. Fifthly, the landlord cannot distrain for arrears of royalties unless it can enter lawfully upon the land, but it cannot enter lawfully for that purpose because that would be a breach of the covenant for quiet enjoyment.

In support of the first step in the foregoing argument, Mr. Nourse read *Cox* v. *Harper* [1910] 1 Ch. 480, a case in the Court of Appeal. From the judgments of Lord Cozens-Hardy M.R. and Fletcher Moulton L.J. in that case, I draw these principles of construction. First, contracting parties can by their agreement give or refuse the quality of rent to a particular payment from tenant to landlord. Secondly, a mere label is not enough; you have to look at the character of the sum in question. Thirdly, the court should not strive to defeat the parties' manifest intention in the contract. Let me read a part of Lord Cozens-Hardy's judgment, at p. 487:

> "The public house was expressed to be let 'at the rent of £150 a year for the said premises.' . . . When you find this £150 defined as being the rent for the said premises I cannot see why we should fail to adopt that definition. Then there are these very peculiar words: 'and the additional yearly sum'—it is not called rent—'of £1,250 in lieu of premium for the goodwill of the business and for the use of the fixtures and fittings upon the premises.' There may be a doubt whether the words 'in lieu of premium' ought to be enclosed in brackets, but I pass that over. This sum is not described as rent—a circumstance which I agree is not conclusive—but throughout this document it appears to me that a distinction is drawn between the rent of £150 for the said premises and another sum, not called rent, of £1,250 which is described as in lieu of premium for the goodwill. No doubt in spite of that description the court might conclude upon the construction of this document that both these sums were reserved as rent issuing out of the premises. But when I find that a clear distinction is drawn between rent and yearly sum I am not disposed to give those words any other than their natural meaning. Therefore I think that the landlord had no right to distrain for this additional yearly sum."

Mr. Edwards-Jones maintained, on the contrary, that even if the strict construction of the word "rent" is adopted in interpreting section 175, the royalties nevertheless fall within it. He pointed out, first, that where a mineral lease reserves in one breath a fixed rent and also royalties to be calculated by weight or volume, both together are rent in the legal sense of the word. The leading authority is *Reg.* v. *Westbrook*, which was followed (for the most part without dispute) in all courts in *Tollemache Settled Estates Trustees* v. *Coughtrie* [1961] A.C. 880. If the two documents are read together, as they must be in accordance with the special commissioners' findings, it is argued that that is the true legal situation here.

Then, as to the combination of two documents, Mr. Edwards-Jones has referred to the Scotch case of *Revell* v. *Scott* (1895) 3 T.C. 403, where the annual value of a sheep farm was arrived at (for the purposes of Schedule B) by addition of two rents paid by the occupier to the same landlord, one under a grazing lease and the other under a lease of shooting rights. I hardly need authority to convince me that the payments under the two instruments in the present case can be added for the purposes of section 175 if, but only if, they are both rent in the English legal sense of the word.

Mr. Nourse pointed out that the parties have done all they can to deprive the royalties of the quality of rent. They are nowhere called by that name, A they are not reserved by the common form words of reddendum nor expressed to be recoverable as rent in arrear, and failure to pay them gives no right of re-entry upon the land. Most important, according to Mr. Nourse, an attempt to distrain for arrears of royalties would be a breach of the covenant for quiet enjoyment, which is introduced by the words " paying the rent hereby " (that is, by the lease itself) " reserved."

Mr. Edwards-Jones submitted that since the parties contemporaneously B executed the licence deed, or possibly by reason of their common contemplation that it would be executed immediately after the lease, the covenant for quiet enjoyment must bear a modified construction so that it would not be broken by distress for unpaid royalties. I feel unable to accept that submission. It seems to me to be contrary to the principles I extracted from *Cox* v. *Harper* [1910] 1 Ch. 480. The parties have en- C deavoured to make a real distinction between the two classes of payment, and the court should not be astute to defeat their contractual intention. If I imagine the question arising in a suit between the taxpayer company and Welford Gravels Ltd. or let us say between the taxpayer company and a receiver or liquidator in possession of the assets of Welford Gravels Ltd., I am of opinion that the taxpayer company would fail to convince the court that the royalties are truly rent and recoverable as such. The parties D did too much to produce the contrary result for the court to disregard their intentions, and their writings must bear the same construction in a revenue case as in any other.

By way of an alternative argument, Mr. Edwards-Jones relied on the principle of law that a right to work minerals is something more than a mere licence, namely, a profit à prendre, an incorporeal hereditament lying E in grant: see *Duke of Sutherland* v. *Heathcote* [1892] 1 Ch. 475, 483. Therefore, even if we look only at the licence deed itself, the royalties, he submitted, are fairly described as rent for real property demised for a term. It would be carrying technicality to excess, said Mr. Edwards-Jones, to object that rent for which distress may be made cannot be reserved out of an incorporeal hereditament. As to that objection, see *Coke on Littleton*, 47A, and *Halsbury's Laws of England*, 4th ed. vol. 13, (1975), para. 209. F It is, I think, perfectly good law. Quite apart from the technical point, however, I do not think it can be right, as a matter of construction, in view of the special commissioners' finding of the unity of the bargain and the indications to that effect in the deeds, to defeat the parties' intention by dividing the contract they deliberately brought into being and artificially isolating one part of it. Here again I get guidance from *Cox* v. *Harper* G [1910] 1 Ch. 480.

Mr. Edwards-Jones further argued that Mr. Nourse's contentions open the door to extensive and easy avoidance of tax in a way the legislature can never have intended. I am afraid that submission is too general to affect my conclusion, valuable though it might be in a case where a single question of construction is precisely defined and the language of Parliament leaves the arguments finely balanced. The present case is not to my mind H of that character. It is well known that the system of taxing income from land was by no means perfectly coherent during the 1940s and the 1950s. Accordingly, Mr. Nourse, in my judgment, has made good his second proposition as well as his first, and the taxpayer company must succeed.

As an alternative contention, Mr. Nourse submitted that even if the royalties are rent for the purposes of section 175 of the Income Tax Act 1952, they are not rent payable under a lease or leases. I think it is better,

A as I have decided the appeal on his main argument, that I should not complicate the matter by expressing any views on that alternative. Accordingly, the appeal is allowed.

Appeal allowed with costs.

Solicitors: *Borneo, Martell & Partners, Bedford; Solicitor of Inland*
B *Revenue.*

[CHANCERY DIVISION]

C

* HARRISON (INSPECTOR OF TAXES) *v.* NAIRN WILLIAMSON LTD.

1976 July 16, 19, 20 Goulding J.

D *Revenue—Corporation tax—Disposal of assets—Computation of allowable losses—Acquisition of unissued loan stock—Bargain not made at arm's length—Loss accruing on sale of loan stock—Whether acquisition deemed to be for consideration equal to market value—Whether total amount of loss allowable in computing amount of gains—Finance Act* 1965 (*c.* 25), *s.* 22 (4)

E In 1964 N Ltd., a subsidiary of the taxpayer company, purchased the share capital of T Ltd. for £13,176 and made an interest-free loan to T Ltd. of £95,640. Between 1965 and 1967 N Ltd. lent a further £114,360 to T Ltd. T Ltd.'s business failed to expand as N Ltd. had expected and in consequence in March 1967 the taxpayer company purchased from N Ltd. the share capital of T Ltd. for £13,176. The taxpayer company then subscribed to T Ltd. and was issued with £210,000 of unsecured loan stock that the directors of T Ltd. had resolved to create only a few days before. From
F the proceeds of the sale of loan stock, T Ltd. repaid its debts to N Ltd. In July 1967 the taxpayer company sold its investment holding in T Ltd. for £40,000. The parties agreed that in March 1967 the true value of the shares and loan stock of T Ltd. was only £72,500. The taxpayer company was assessed to corporation tax for the years 1967 and 1968 on the basis that section 22 (4) of the Finance Act 1965 [1] applied to the taxpayer company's acquisition of the share capital and loan stock of
G T Ltd. with the consequence that it was deemed to be for "a consideration equal to the market value at the time," namely £72,500. The special commissioners, allowing an appeal against the assessments, upheld the taxpayer company's contention that section 22 (4) of the Act was concerned only where there was both an "acquisition" and a "disposal of" and that as there had not been a disposal to the taxpayer company by T. Ltd. of the unissued loan stock the consideration money of £210,000
H governed the computation and not the market value of the assets.

On appeal by the Crown:—

Held, allowing the appeal, that as the emphasis throughout section 22 (4) of the Act was on the "acquisition" of assets and

---

[Reported by MRS. HARRIET DUTTON, Barrister-at-Law]

[1] Finance Act 1965, s. 22 (4): see post, p. 1164B, C.

as it would be anomalous to treat for tax purposes the original A subscription for company stock or shares differently from other bargains not made at arm's length, section 22 (4) on its true construction operated where there was an "acquisition" of an asset regardless of whether or not there had been a concomitant "disposal" and accordingly the allowable loss must be calculated according to the market value at the time of acquisition.

B

No cases are referred to in the judgment.

The following cases were cited in argument:

Cleveleys Investment Trust Co. v. *Inland Revenue Commissioners* (1971) 47 T.C. 300.

Inland Revenue Commissioners v. *Europa Oil (N.Z.) Ltd.* [1971] A.C. 760; [1971] 2 W.L.R. 55, P.C. C

Inland Revenue Commissioners v. *Richards' Executors* [1971] 1 W.L.R. 571; [1971] 1 All E.R. 785; 46 T.C. 626, H.L.(Sc.).

Mangin v. *Inland Revenue Commissioners* [1971] A.C. 739; [1971] 2 W.L.R. 39; [1971] 1 All E.R. 179, P.C.

Seramco Ltd. Superannuation Fund Trustees v. *Income Tax Commissioner* [1976] 2 W.L.R. 986; [1976] 2 All E.R. 28, P.C.

D

CASE STATED by the Commissioners for the Special Purposes of the Income Tax Acts.

In March 1967 the taxpayer company, Nairn Williamson Ltd., purchased the share capital of Tercol Ltd. for £13,176 and was issued with £210,000 of loan stock in that company. At that time the value of the shares and loan stock of Tercol Ltd. was only £72,500. In July 1967 the taxpayer company sold its interest in Tercol Ltd. for £40,000 of which E £39,900 related to the loan stock. It was assessed to corporation tax for the accounting period ended December 31, 1967, of £76,366 and for the period ended December 31, 1968, of £1,200,000. The special commissioners allowed an appeal against the assessments holding that in calculating the taxpayer company's allowable losses for those periods, section 22 (4) of the Finance Act 1965 did not apply to cause the allowable losses made F on the transactions to be reduced. The assessments were reduced for the accounting period ended December 31, 1967, to £12,049 and for the period ended December 31, 1968, to £607,142. The Crown appealed.

The facts are stated in the judgment.

Michael Nolan Q.C. and *Brian Davenport* for the Crown.

Stewart Bates Q.C. and *Peter Whiteman* for the taxpayer company. G

GOULDING J. This is an appeal by the Crown from a decision of the special commissioners. The case raises a short point which is said, however, to be of some importance, on the ascertainment of chargeable gains and allowable losses under Part III of the Finance Act 1965. The present question arises on assessments of the taxpayer company, Nairn Williamson H Ltd., to corporation tax for two accounting periods which coincide with the calendar years 1967 and 1968. I will take the facts from the case stated and summarise them, simplifying to a slight extent but, I hope, not distorting the situation disclosed.

The taxpayer company has, or had at the material times, a subsidiary company with a name very similar to its own, which subsidiary has been identified in the case stated by the name Nairn. I shall follow that use

A of the name. Nairn is a trading company resident in the United Kingdom, and in September 1964 it purchased the ordinary share capital of a company later called Tercol Ltd. In connection with and as part of the terms of that purchase, Nairn lent £95,640 to Tercol free of interest to enable Tercol to repay a loan which it owed to the vendor of its share capital. Endeavouring to improve or expand the business of Tercol in the years 1965, 1966 and 1967 Nairn made further loans for business purposes to B Tercol. They, like the original loan, were free of interest and amounted in the aggregate to £114,360, making a total, if you include the money lent on the purchase of the shares of £210,000.

Tercol was a disappointment to Nairn, and early in 1967 the directors of Nairn no longer found it commercially attractive to carry on business through Tercol. Certain steps were then taken which led up to the situa- C tion with which the present litigation is concerned. On March 10, 1967, the directors of Tercol passed a resolution creating £250,000 of 5 per cent. unsecured loan stock of Tercol. It was called "5 per cent. Unsecured Loan Stock 1972," which I take to mean that there was an obligation to repay in that year. On the same day, the taxpayer company purchased from Nairn the share capital of Tercol, and a few days later, on March 16, 1967, the taxpayer company subscribed at par for £210,000 of the new loan D stock. The subscription money was paid by the taxpayer company to Tercol and then passed to Nairn in repayment of the aggregate debt of Tercol to Nairn, the origin of which I have already explained. Somewhat later there was a reorganisation of the capital structure of Tercol wherein the taxpayer company received a holding of preferred shares in Tercol in replacement of the £210,000 of loan stock. That conversion is not of E material importance for the purpose of the present case for it is common ground that it constituted what is known as a "roll-over" situation. Accordingly for the relevant tax purposes the preferred shares can be identified with the pre-existing loan stock. Then in July 1967 a purchaser unconnected, so far as appears, with the taxpayer company or Nairn bought from the taxpayer company the share capital of Tercol, including the preferred shares derived from the loan stock. The consideration paid was in F total £40,000, of which £100 was allocated to the ordinary shares, leaving £39,900 in respect of the holding of preferred shares.

The taxpayer company claimed to have made an allowable loss on that occasion estimated, so far as the loan stock was concerned, by the difference between £210,000, the subscription money when the stock was issued, and £39,900, the price paid by the eventual purchaser. The Crown was G unwilling to concede so large an allowable loss. It was agreed between the parties that the aggregate market value on March 16, 1967, of the ordinary shares of Tercol and the loan stock issued at that time was only £72,500. If, for the purposes of illustration, I treat as negligible the value of the ordinary shares—and it cannot have been great—then, according to the Crown, the allowable loss would be the difference between £72,500 H and the £39,900 obtained on sale. That is the point in dispute as I understand it.

The main argument for the taxpayer company was simply that the consideration it gave for the acquisition of the stock was £210,000 and no less, and there was no dispute as to the consideration obtained on the disposal later on. The answer made by the Crown to that simple analysis was that the amount or value of the consideration given by the taxpayer company for the stock, if computed according to the provisions of the

Finance Act 1965, was a sum equal to its market value—that is, only £72,500 A
or some small amount less.

The question depends on the interpretation of section 22 (4) of the
Finance Act 1965. There was an alternative argument raised by the
Crown which I will mention later, but the main argument has centred on
section 22 (4), which provides:

> "Subject to the provisions of this Part of this Act, a person's acqui-
> sition of an asset and the disposal of it to him shall for the purposes B
> of this Part of this Act be deemed to be for a consideration equal to
> the market value of the asset—(*a*) where he acquires the asset otherwise
> than by way of a bargain made at arm's length and in particular
> where he acquires it by way of gift or by way of distribution from a
> company in respect of shares in the company, or (*b*) where he acquires
> the asset wholly or partly for a consideration that cannot be valued, C
> or in connection with his own or another's loss of office or employ-
> ment or diminution of emoluments, or otherwise in consideration for
> or recognition of his or another's services or past services in any office
> or employment or of any other service rendered or to be rendered by
> him or another, or (*c*) where he acquires the asset as trustee for creditors
> of the person making the disposal."

D

I should mention that paragraph (*c*) has subsequently been repealed,
but the repeal cannot, I think, affect the interpretation of the subsection
as a whole.

The Crown argued that section 22 (4) (*a*) exactly fits this case. Nairn
and the taxpayer company were not parties at arm's length. The bargain
they made between them was by clear inference made to secure the best E
financial consequences for the group of which they both formed a part.
Therefore, the taxpayer company acquired the asset "otherwise than by
way of a bargain made at arm's length," and the final result was that the
acquisition must be deemed to be for a consideration equal to the market
value of the loan stock.

The taxpayer company said that that was an entire misapplication of
section 22 (4). It provides: "a person's acquisition of an asset and the F
disposal of it to him shall . . . be deemed" in certain circumstances "to
be for a consideration equal to the market value of the asset." On those
words, it was submitted, the subsection can apply only when there is an
acquisition and a concomitant disposal. The taxpayer company said that
where a company has unissued stock or shares or debentures there is no
disposal by it on the first issue of the securities. There is certainly an
acquisition by the subscriber, but no concomitant disposal. For that G
reason, said the taxpayer company, section 22 (4) cannot apply to the case
at all and the real consideration money, £210,000, must govern the com-
putation.

In support of that submission Mr. Stewart Bates, for the taxpayer
company, maintained that the whole of these provisions operate on the
occasion of a disposal of assets within the meaning of the Act; that the H
scheme is one for ascertaining a gain or loss on a disposal, and without a
disposal it is not meant to apply at all. He pointed out that at the very
beginning of Part III of the Act, where the charge of tax is introduced—
that is to say, in section 19 (1)—the subject matter of tax is defined as
"chargeable gains computed in accordance with this Act and accruing
to a person on the disposal of assets." Similarly, in section 22 itself, when
you come to the enactment of detailed computation provisions, which are

A set out in the schedules, the subject matter is defined as, " The amount of
the gains accruing on the disposal of assets," and that is to be computed
in accordance with Part I of Schedule 6 and subject to other provisions
in the schedules. Mr. Bates said that against that background the court
should look at the language of section 22 (4) itself, where market value is
to be applied as the deemed consideration for " a person's acquisition
of an asset and the disposal of it to him." On that language and in that
B framework, it was asked, how can the subsection be applied where there is
only an acquisition and no disposal? What is more, in Mr. Bates's sub-
mission, you would not really expect to find in section 22 a rule essentially
relating to allowed deductions on the computation of a gain or loss, because
you find such rules concentrated in another part of the Act, namely,
paragraph 4 of Schedule 6.

C The way I have to approach this pure question of verbal interpretation
is, I think, to give the words used by Parliament their ordinary meaning in
the English language, and if, consistently with the ordinary meaning, there
is a choice between two alternative interpretations then to prefer the con-
struction that maintains a reasonable and consistent scheme of taxation
without distorting the language. I do not think myself that section 22 (4)
is so subordinated to any other subsection in that section that I ought
D to read it otherwise than as a self-contained provision. Conjunctive
language such as that used in subsection (4) must take its colour from
context and scheme. The wording " . . . a person's acquisition of an asset
and the disposal of it to him shall for the purposes of this Part of this Act
be deemed to be for a consideration equal to the market value of the asset "
is, as a mere matter of language, equally capable, to my mind, of being
E applicable or inapplicable where an acquisition occurs without a disposal,
or vice versa. One can imagine a slight modification of language which
made the point perfectly clear one way or the other. For example, the
draftsman might have said, " a person's acquisition of an asset and the
disposal of it to him if any," etc. In that case, the Crown would clearly
be right. On the other hand, there may be a context which leaves no
doubt that the provisions can operate only if both acquisition and disposal
F are present. Without seeking to prejudge any future case, I may say that
it has been argued in this case that that result is obtained further on in
this same Act, namely, in paragraph 17 of Schedule 7 which opens in
subparagraph (1): " This paragraph shall apply where a person acquires
an asset and the person making the disposal is connected with him."
Having regard to the subject matter and the grammar of that sentence, it
G is at least strongly arguable that there must be both an acquisition and a
disposal for paragraph 17 to work.

Paragraph 17 has been relied on by both sides in the present contro-
versy. Mr. Nolan, for the Crown, contrasted it with the neutral language
of section 22 (4) and said that the draftsman knew how to impose the
condition of both acquisition and disposal when he wanted to. Mr.
Stewart Bates, on the other hand, suggested that what is made clear in
H paragraph 17 is really necessarily implied, if it is not expressed, in
section 22 (4), being part of the same general scheme of arriving at a
computation of a gain or loss. On the whole, I think that paragraph 17
favours the Crown rather than the taxpayer company, particularly so since
in paragraph 17 (2) we find the saving words, " Without prejudice to the
generality of section 22 (4) of this Act."

However that may be, I am in the end of opinion that the Crown's contention is right. The emphasis of the subsection is on acquisition. Each of the three paragraphs begins, " where he acquires the asset," paragraph (*a*) being where the acquiring party acquires the asset " otherwise than by way of a bargain made at arm's length "; paragraph (*b*) being, putting it shortly, where he acquires the asset for a consideration that cannot be valued or in consideration of services; and paragraph (*c*) being " where he acquires the asset as trustee for creditors of the person making the disposal." Only in paragraph (*c*) is the disposal an essential element of what is enumerated; paragraphs (*a*) and (*b*) put the emphasis entirely on acquisition, as do the opening words of (*c*). So it seems natural to regard section 22 (4) as intended to operate where there were acqusitions of these various species, without worrying whether there was a disposal or not.

Moreover, as to the general scheme of the Act, it would in my view be anomalous if market value were not applied to this limited class of transactions not at arm's length. I can see no reason why the original subscription for stock or shares issued by a company or a local authority or other body should be differently treated, where the bargain is not at arm's length, from other such bargains, and therefore I would not be disposed to think special treatment was intended unless the language leads to it. In my view the language does not lead to it with any clarity at all. It seems to me that the language is sufficiently satisfied if the words are left to operate as far as they may whenever one of the specified cases, (*a*), (*b*) or (*c*), is in point.

Those considerations are sufficient to dispose of the appeal, the Crown succeeding on its main contentions. I should mention two alternative contentions. One was the submission that the word " disposal " in section 22 (4) was no more than a necessary counterpart to " acquisition "; that is to say, wherever there is an acquisition there is within the language of section 22 (4) a disposal. That is perfectly possible as a matter of ordinary English language, because one can well speak of a company disposing of unissued shares, for example, when it issues them. But it is clear that problems and difficulties would arise if the draftsman were treated as having used in that way the word " disposal," which has a technical meaning in other parts of the Act.

The final argument advanced in the alternative on behalf of the Crown avoids relying on section 22 (4) altogether. Mr. Nolan referred me to paragraph 4 of Schedule 6 to the Act, where sums allowable as deductions from the consideration in the computation of gains or losses under Part III are set out. For the cost of acquisition to be deductible, it has to answer this description: " the amount or value of the consideration, in money or money's worth, given . . . wholly and exclusively for the acquisition of the asset." Mr. Nolan submitted that by necessary inference from the facts of the case the consideration money of £210,000 given for the loan stock, at any rate as regards the excess over market value, cannot have been given wholly and exclusively for the acquisition of the stock; it must have been given equally, or primarily, for the opportunity to acquire an allowable loss when the stock came to be disposed of. Mr. Bates would have said that that is really to confuse consideration with motive, and that the money, in his contention, was given entirely and exclusively for the stock, whatever hopes or ulterior prospects may have been in the taxpayer company's

A mind. It is also a matter for argument how far the facts found by the special commissioners lay the necessary foundation for inferring the full purposes of the taxpayer company in acquiring the loan stock.

Having mentioned those alternative arguments, I think it is undesirable that I should express any view upon their merits, because I intend to allow the appeal simply on the main argument and I do not wish to make
B any observations that in some other case may be thought to have a significance probably not intended. Accordingly, I shall allow the appeal.

Appeal allowed with costs.
Case remitted to special commissioners for assessments to be adjusted.

C Solicitors: *Solicitor of Inland Revenue; Clifford-Turner & Co.*

D [CHANCERY DIVISION]

* FLOOR *v.* DAVIS (INSPECTOR OF TAXES)

1976 July 6, 7 Goulding J.

Revenue—Capital gains tax—Disposal of assets—Scheme to avoid
E *tax on sale of shareholding—Company incorporated to transfer shares to ultimate purchaser and to pass purchase price to overseas company — Taxpayer acquiring shares in new company in exchange for his shareholding — Whether deemed disposal of shares — Finance Act* 1965 (c. 25), *Sch.* 7, *para.* 6 (1) (2) [1]

Revenue — Capital gains tax — Control of company — Company acting so that value passing out of its shares to overseas
F *company — Whether company's action result of shareholders "exercising control" — Whether "person having control" includes plural—Interpretation Act* 1889 (52 & 53 *Vict. c.* 63), *s.* 1 [2]—*Finance Act* 1965, *Sch.* 7, *para.* 15 (2)

In 1969 the taxpayer and his two sons-in-law held the majority of the share capital of IDM. In common with the remaining shareholders they wished to sell all IDM's shares
G to an American company, KDI for £833,333. Before that sale was agreed the taxpayer caused a scheme to be put into effect for the purposes of avoiding or reducing the liability to capital gains tax that would arise on the sale. The scheme involved the incorporation of FNW, a company that had its share capital divided into ordinary and preferred shares. Under its articles of association the ordinary shares carried rights to six-sevenths of its surplus assets on a winding-up. In February 1969 the taxpayer and his family's IDM shares were trans-
H ferred to FNW in exchange for 100,000 of FNW's preferred shares of 1s. each. The taxpayer received 43,954 of those

---

[Reported by MRS. HARRIET DUTTON, Barrister-at-Law]

[1] Finance Act 1965, Sch. 7, paras. 6 (1) (2): see post, p. 1173A–C.
Sch. 7, para. 15 (2): see post, p. 1175D, E.
[2] Interpretation Act 1889, s. 1: see post, p. 1175F, G.

shares. FNW then sold the shares it had acquired in IDM to KDI for £560,889. The next step in the scheme involved an application in March 1969 by D Ltd., a company registered in the Cayman Islands, to purchase 100 preferred shares in FNW for £500. At a board meeting of FNW it was agreed to accept that application and to offer to all preferred shareholders a rights issue of the ordinary shares in the company. The only shareholder to accept the offer of the rights issue was D Ltd. who, in April 1969, was issued with 50 ordinary shares. Shortly thereafter FNW was voluntarily wound up and as a result six-sevenths of its surplus assets passed to D Ltd., being the only holder of its ordinary shares.

In respect of those transactions the taxpayer was assessed to capital gains tax of £235,000. On appeal against the assessment, the special commissioners reduced the amount to £104,655 but dismissed the appeal in principle, holding that when the value went out of the IDM shares and passed into the FNW shares held by D Ltd., there was a deemed 'disposal' for tax purposes by the taxpayer by virtue of the provisions of paragraph 15 (2) of Schedule 7 to the Finance Act 1965.

On appeal by the taxpayer: —

Held, allowing the appeal, (1) that as FNW was concerned in real share transactions not as an agent or nominee but as a principal, it was not possible to look at the transactions as a whole and find a deemed "disposal" for tax purposes by the taxpayer to the ultimate purchaser; that in the absence of an enforceable agreement that FNW acquire the shares in IDM to sell them to the American company, FNW acquired control of IDM and, accordingly, the exemption from tax on the share exchange contained in paragraph 6 of Schedule 7 to the Act applied (post, pp. 1172C–F, 1174F–H).

Campbell v. *Inland Revenue Commissioners* [1970] A.C. 77, H.L.(E.) and *In re Nichols, decd.* [1975] 1 W.L.R. 534, C.A. distinguished.

(2) That there could only be a disposal for the purposes of paragraph 15 (2) of Schedule 7 when the taxpayer's shares diminished in value on D Ltd. acquiring ordinary shares in FNW if the taxpayer and his sons-in-law could be considered together as persons exercising control of FNW so that the value of the shares diminished; that, on the true construction of paragraph 15 (2), the intention was to exclude the construction, under section 1 of the Interpretation Act 1889, that the singular included the plural and, therefore, "a person" could not include a group of people having control; and that, since there was no positive act capable of specific identification as an exercise of control of FNW by its shareholders, there had been no exercise of a person's power of control and, accordingly, there was no deemed disposal, under the subparagraph, of the taxpayer's shares in FNW (post, pp. 1176H—1177A, H—1178A).

The following cases are cited in the judgment:

Campbell v. *Inland Revenue Commissioners* [1970] A.C. 77; [1968] 3 W.L.R. 1025; [1968] 3 All E.R. 588; 45 T.C. 427, H.L.(E.).

Feversham's (Earl of) Contract, In re [1942] Ch. 33; [1941] 3 All E.R. 100

Nichols, decd., In re [1975] 1 W.L.R. 534; [1975] 2 All E.R. 120, C.A.

The following additional cases were cited in argument:

Bailey, Hay & Co. Ltd., In re [1971] 1 W.L.R. 1357; [1971] 3 All E.R. 693.

Inland Revenue Commissioner v. *Europa Oil (N.Z.) Ltd.* [1971] A.C. 760; [1971] 2 W.L.R. 55, P.C.

A *Quistclose Investments Ltd.* v. *Rolls Razor Ltd.* [1970] A.C. 567; [1968] 3 W.L.R. 1097; [1968] 3 All E.R. 651, H.L.(E.).

Ransom v. *Higgs* [1974] 1 W.L.R. 1594; [1974] 3 All E.R. 949; 50 T.C. 1, H.L.(E.).

CASE STATED by the Commissioners for the Special Purposes of the Income Tax.

B The taxpayer, Major Ides Maria Floor, held a large part of the share capital in IDM Electronics Ltd. Together with all the other shareholders, he wished to sell the IDM shares to KDI International Corp. for £833,333. As a result of a scheme devised to avoid or reduce the amount of capital gains tax payable on that sale, a large proportion of the proceeds from the sale of the shares passed to Donmarco Ltd., a company registered in the
C Cayman Islands. In respect of those transactions, the taxpayer was assessed to capital gains tax for the year 1968–69 in the sum of £235,000. On appeal against the assessment, the special commissioners confirmed it in principle on the basis that at the time when the value went out of the IDM shares and passed into shares held by Donmarco Ltd. there was a deemed "disposal" for tax purposes by the taxpayer by virtue of the provisions of Schedule 7, paragraph 15 (2), to the Finance Act 1965. They ordered that
D the assessment be reduced to an agreed amount of £104,655.

The taxpayer appealed. The questions of law for the opinion of the High Court were: (a) whether the special commissioners were right in holding that there was no disposal for capital gains tax purposes when the taxpayer's shares in IDM were exchanged for shares in FNW; (b) whether paragraph 15 (2) of Schedule 7 to the Act applied where a group of persons
E exercised control of a company so that value passed out of the shares owned by them into other shares in the same way as it applied to such an exercise of control by one person only; and (c) whether the transactions relating to FNW constituted the "exercise of control" of that company within the meaning of paragraph 15 (2).

F *C. N. Beattie Q.C.* and *G. R. Aaronson* for the taxpayer.
Peter Millett Q.C. and *Brian Davenport* for the Crown.

GOULDING J. This is an appeal by way of case stated from a decision of the special commissioners on a question of capital gains tax. The taxpayer had a substantial holding of shares in a company known as IDM Electronics Ltd. In common with other shareholders in that company, he
G sold his shares to a company incorporated in the United States of America, or one of them. Desiring to reduce his probable liability to capital gains tax in respect of the gain accruing on the sale of the shares to the American company, the taxpayer, in conjunction with his two sons-in-law, evolved and carried into effect an elaborate scheme of operations. The question in substance is whether that scheme, designed no doubt by
H skilled advisers of the taxpayer, has achieved its object of reducing a liability to capital gains tax at the stages of the transaction where it was likely to arise.

The facts are carefully set out in the case stated by the special commissioners, and I had better narrate them in outline before I try to answer the questions which are asked at the end of the case. I shall follow the special commissioners in using three abbreviations. The company, IDM Electronics Ltd., in which the taxpayer originally held shares, is referred to as "IDM"; the American company which ultimately acquired his shares is referred to as "KDI"; and another company that plays a part, FNW Electronic Holdings Ltd., is referred to as "FNW." A

In February 1969, the taxpayer and his two sons-in-law between them held the majority of the share capital of IDM, although none of the three was by himself able to control IDM. At some date not later than February 27, 1969, it had been agreed, subject to contract, that all the shareholders in IDM should sell their shares to KDI for a cash consideration, the total consideration being £833,333, of which the greater part, though not the whole, would come to the taxpayer and his two sons-in-law. B

At a time when no contract with KDI had yet been entered into but when sale at the price I have mentioned was clearly in contemplation, the first step in the taxpayer's scheme was carried out by incorporating FNW. FNW was incorporated on February 24, 1969. Its memorandum C and articles of association provided for two classes of shares, which had equal voting rights but different financial interests in the company, namely preferred shares and ordinary shares, all of a nominal value of 1s. each. The two subscribers' shares were preferred shares, and one of them was taken by the taxpayer. It was not, I think, originally subscribed for, but it was transferred to the taxpayer. The other came to one of his sons-in-law. D It is convenient at this point to mention what the special commissioners emphasised in their decision; namely, that the sole reason for FNW's existence was to provide a vehicle for the transfer of the shares in IDM to KDI and for the subsequent syphoning off of part of the purchase consideration to a party whom I have not yet mentioned.

FNW having been incorporated and KDI still not having contracted to buy the shares which it wanted, a written agreement was entered into E between the taxpayer and his two sons-in-law, described as "vendors," and FNW, described as "purchaser." That agreement was dated February 27, 1969. It contains common form recitals and clauses providing for the purchase of the vendors' shares in IDM by FNW in exchange for the allotment and issue of 100,000 preferred shares in FNW, to be distributed among the three vendors in proportion to their holdings in IDM.

F

However, that is not all that the agreement contains. It recites that negotiations had been concluded, subject to contract, with KDI for the purchase of the IDM shares, and it recites also that the sale and purchase by the three vendors and FNW was agreed with a view to FNW reselling the shares to KDI. There is also a clause by which the three vendors undertook with FNW to use their best endeavours to procure IDM and all other necessary parties to co-operate in such manner and G generally to do such things as might be requisite to enable a formal agreement for the sale of all the issued share capital of IDM to KDI to be entered into as soon as possible. The wording of that undertaking may not have been entirely apt, since the three vendors were parting with their own shares in IDM and hence, so far as appears, would no longer be in a position directly to influence the acts of IDM. On the H other hand, for all I know, they might well have had influence with the remaining shareholders, whose co-operation was required to carry through the desired sale to KDI. So far as the taxpayer was concerned, he received 43,954 preferred shares in FNW in exchange for 38,075 ordinary shares and a like number of "A" ordinary shares of IDM.

The purchase carried out under the agreement I have just narrated was previously the subject of formal approval by the directors of FNW,

A a Mr. Gibbs and a Mr. Drinkwater, at a meeting held on the same date, February 27. On the same day the shares in IDM were delivered to FNW, and the preferred shares coming to the taxpayer and his two sons-in-law were duly allotted and issued. On the next day, February 28, FNW joined with the other shareholders in IDM to sell the entire share capital of IDM to KDI.

Nearly a month later a further transaction, part of the same scheme, B took place. This involved Donmarco Ltd., a company registered in the Cayman Islands, an archipelago which when I was young provided the material for turtle soup and now contributes to financial haute cuisine. Donmarco Ltd. made an application to the board of FNW for 100 preferred shares of 1s. each, enclosing a cheque for £500 to represent the price of £5 per share. And on the same day the directors of FNW, Mr. C Gibbs and Mr. Drinkwater again, resolved to accept that application. The shares were issued, at the request of Donmarco Ltd., in the name of a bank nominee company, Roycan Nominees Ltd. It was not suggested that that transaction involved any watering of the existing issued capital of FNW. It appears that £5 per preferred share was a reasonable consideration based on the assets then in the hands of FNW. However, the ground was prepared for a further step in the scheme at the same board D meeting at which the application from Donmarco Ltd. was accepted. The directors then determined to offer unissued ordinary shares—and none had as yet been issued—to the holders of preferred shares at the price of 1s., being par for the ordinary shares, and in the quantity of one ordinary share for every two preferred shares held. That rights issue was the subject of letters to the shareholders of FNW, and it allowed them E until April 3, 1969, to accept. Neither the taxpayer nor his sons-in-law saw fit to accept the allotment offered to them, but Donmarco Ltd. did take up its rights and so, being already the holder of 100 preferred shares, became the holder of 50 ordinary shares. Having regard to the rights of the respective classes of shares and the issue at par of the 50 ordinary shares, that transaction represented some dilution of the existing issued preferred shares. So far as the taxpayer was concerned, some value at F that stage flowed out of his preferred shares into the ordinary shares held by Donmarco Ltd.

But more was to come. FNW having, like a mayfly in summer, performed the elegant manoeuvres that were consistent with its nature, its ephemeral life was shortly due to end. An extraordinary general meeting of the members of FNW was held on April 5, 1969—often a convenient G day of the year for business transactions—and a resolution was passed that FNW be voluntarily wound up. The minute of that meeting shows that the persons present were a proxy for one of the taxpayer's two sons-in-law and a proxy for Roycan Nominees Ltd., the nominee holder on behalf of Donmarco Ltd. It does not appear from the minute whether either of them abstained or whether they both voted for the special resolution, but at any rate the special resolution was passed that the company be wound H up voluntarily and that one of the shareholders, one of the two sons-in-law, be appointed liquidator.

The effect of winding up, having regard to the relative rights given to preferred shares and ordinary shares by the memorandum and articles of association of FNW, was to convey the great bulk of the net assets of FNW to Donmarco Ltd. as the only ordinary shareholder. Accordingly, at that stage a very much larger proportion of the value of the taxpayer's preferred shares flowed out of those shares for the benefit of Donmarco

Ltd. What the motive of the taxpayer and his sons-in-law was in wishing A
to benefit Donmarco Ltd. does not appear. It seems not impossible that
it may have had something to do with the benefit of members of the
taxpayer's family, but that is pure conjecture.

The special commissioners have helpfully isolated the three questions
of law on which the court's opinion is desired, and have formulated them
at the end of their stated case. However, a fourth question has here been
raised on behalf of the Crown which was never argued before the special B
commissioners. That new question should logically, I think, come first.
It was put like this by Mr. Millett, on behalf of the Crown. He submitted
that there was a disposal of the taxpayer's shares for the purposes of the
capital gains tax provisions of the Finance Act 1965, direct by the taxpayer
to KDI. FNW, Mr. Millett said, in accordance with what the commis-
sioners found, was only a vehicle; it existed only to be a vehicle for the
desired transaction. Mr. Millett pointed out that there is no exhaustive C
definition of the term "disposal" in the Act of 1965. In such cases as
this, he submitted, the court is entitled to look at the transaction as a whole
and to say that the reality of it was that the taxpayer disposed of his
shares to KDI for cash.

To my mind, it is quite impossible to apply the very detailed code
contained in the relevant sections of and schedules to the Act of 1965 D
in so general a way as that, ignoring the legal and formal steps and simply
placing the start against the finish and saying, "there is a disposal."
Inconsistent and overlapping claims and liabilities might well result. The
documents embodied in the agreed facts are not suggested to be shams.
It is impossible, accordingly, to treat FNW as simply a nominee or agent
for the taxpayer and his two sons-in-law. Once it is accepted, as in my
judgment on the agreed facts it must be, that FNW was concerned as a E
principal, it follows that the taxpayer exchanged his shares in IDM for
preferred shares of FNW. The question arises at once, "was that or was it
not a disposal for the purposes of capital gains tax?" and it has to be
answered at that stage. Then another question arises. When the taxpayer
suffered operations to take place which removed value from his shares and
fed the value into the shares held by Donmarco Ltd., was that a partial F
disposal by him of the shares he then held in FNW? In my judgment,
once it is accepted that the transactions, designed as a single scheme and
carried out formally one by one, are real transactions, it is impossible
simply to look at it in a broad way and say that the taxpayer disposed of
his shares in IDM to KDI. I therefore reject this first and new submission
made by the Crown.

As I have said, the consequence of rejecting that broad approach is G
that one has first to look at the exchange of shares between the taxpayer
and FNW and ask, "Was that, for tax purposes, a disposal of the taxpayer's
original shares in IDM?" That is the first question which the special
commissioners have invited the court to determine. They formulate it as
follows: "whether we were right in holding that there was no disposal for
capital gains tax purposes when the appellant's shares in IDM were H
exchanged for shares in FNW."

It is necessary, in order to answer that question, to look at Schedule
7 to the Finance Act 1965. Apart from special provision, where shares
in one company are exchanged for shares in another company the
shares in the first company are of course disposed of by the owner, but
the code of the capital gains tax makes some artificial alterations in that
use of language. By paragraph 4 of Schedule 7, provision is made for

A cases where a single company's share capital is reorganised or reduced. Subject to a number of requirements and provisions such reorganisation or reduction is not treated as involving any disposal of the original shares or any acquisition of the new holding, but the original shares and the new holding are in general treated as the same asset and taken to have been acquired when the original shares were acquired.

Then, two paragraphs later, in paragraph 6 (1) of Schedule 7, it is B provided that subject to the later subparagraphs in paragraph 6, where there is an exchange of shares in one company for shares in another paragraph 4 shall apply as if the two companies were the same company and the exchange were a reorganisation of share capital. That rule is subject to the requirements of paragraph 6 (2), which says:

> "This paragraph shall apply only where the company issuing the C shares . . . has or in consequence of the exchange will have control of the other company, or where the first mentioned company issues the shares . . . in exchange for shares as the result of a general offer made to members of the other company or any class of them . . . , the offer being made in the first instance on a condition such that if it were satisfied the first mentioned company would have control of D the other company."

I have missed out certain words, but they are immaterial for present purposes. Thus the share exchange did not constitute a "disposal" of the taxpayer's holding in IDM, and the roll-over, as it is popularly called, identifying the new shares with the old, takes effect if and only if FNW, in consequence of the exchange, acquired control of IDM. I will not take E time to read the elaborate definition of "control" contained in the Act of 1965: suffice it to say that it is very widely framed and covers a great variety of cases, some of them rather wider, perhaps, than the unadorned meaning of the word. The conclusion of the special commissioners was that the conditions of paragraph 6 (2) were satisfied. The Crown, on this appeal, said that that was wrong. The Crown submitted that FNW never obtained control of IDM except in a purely nominal sense. In reality, F said Mr. Millett, FNW was not intended to obtain control or exercise control over IDM, its sole function being to sell the shares in IDM to KDI. In fact and reality, it was said, however you look at it, there was no control of IDM by FNW during the brief span of one night and some portions, I suppose, of two days in which FNW held the shares.

The special commissioners put their decision as follows:

> G "We derive no great assistance from figures of speech which identify the circumstances of incorporation with a veil which cloaks a company's transactions. Once it is accepted that the company existed and carried out certain transactions by resolutions being passed and agreements being executed, it seems to us that there is no choice but to observe whether the wide description in paragraph 3 of Schedule H 18 of what constitutes 'control' was satisfied. The only relevant 'control' is 'control' within the meaning of that paragraph. It was no part of the argument before us, and seemingly there was no evidence available to support such an argument, that FNW's acquisition of the IDM shares was subject to a binding condition that the shares would be sold on, or subject to a contract to sell already made with KDI, so that FNW never acquired a beneficial title to the shares. Clearly on that basis the position might have been different."

On the appeal, Mr. Millett submitted that the commissioners were A
wrong there. He did not agree that there was no evidence available to support an argument that FNW was subject to a binding condition that the shares would be sold on to KDI. Indeed, he went so far as to submit that all the evidence before the commissioners pointed to the opposite conclusion. In developing that submission, Mr. Millett compared the situation in the present case with the situation in *In re Nichols, decd.* [1975]
1 W.L.R. 534. That was a case where a father had made over a freehold B
estate to his son by way of gift on the understanding, or at least in the contemplation, of the solicitors acting for both parties, that the son would forthwith make a lease of part of the estate back to the father. In that case, the Court of Appeal took the view that the obligation to grant the lease back was not a mere matter of honour but was an obligation that, if
necessary, could be enforced by the court. C

Another illustration was taken from *Campbell* v. *Inland Revenue Commissioners* [1970] A.C. 77. There, a deed of covenant to pay certain annual sums had been entered into by a company with trustees in the clear contemplation that the trustees would use the money in a particular way, and the conclusion was reached, at any rate in the House of Lords, that that again was not a mere matter of honour, but there
were enforceable obligations resting on the recipients of the annual sums. D
Of course, one cannot get very far by simply comparing the facts of different cases, but Mr. Millett sought to extract from *Campbell's* case a principle stated by Lord Upjohn where he said, at p. 106:

> "When persons enter into a business arrangement, as this certainly was, the presumption is that they intend that their business arrange-
> ments shall be legally enforceable but, of course, the language that E
> the parties have employed, whether oral or written, may show either expressly or as a matter of the proper inference to be drawn from their language and of all the relevant circumstances that they did not intend their arrangements to be legally enforceable."

Accordingly, it was submitted that here the whole scheme was a business
arrangement and it must be presumed that the taxpayer and his sons-in-law F
intended that FNW should be bound by some enforceable contract or other obligation to sell the shares on to KDI should the latter company remain willing to purchase them.

I can see no proof of the existence of any such obligation. To my mind, there is no true analogy between the present case and *Nichols* or
Campbell's case. In those cases, the parties concerned were independent G
beings: father and son in the case of *Nichols*, a company and trustees whom it in no way controlled in the case of *Campbell.* Here there was no need for any obligation to make the business arrangement effective. The taxpayer and his two sons-in-law had brought FNW into being for the purposes of their scheme, and at all times until after the sale of shares to KDI they were the only shareholders in FNW. It was
their creature, and they could compel it to act as they wanted. There was H
no need for FNW, as an artificial person, to be under any contractual or other bond of obligation to the taxpayer and the other two gentlemen. Accordingly, the special commissioners were in my view right when they thought that, for the purposes of the Finance Act 1965, FNW acquired control of IDM by the share exchange.

The point can be put very simply by reference to paragraph 3 of Schedule 18 to the Act, already mentioned in the extract I have read from

A the commissioners' decision, which defines "control" for the relevant purposes. One of the situations in which a person is to be taken to have control of a company is "if he possesses or is entitled to acquire, the greater part of the share capital or voting power in the company." By the exchange of shares with the taxpayer and his two sons-in-law, FNW undoubtedly, once it is accepted that the whole thing is not a sham, acquired the greater part of the share capital of IDM. Accordingly, by
B the statutory definition it acquired control of IDM, whatever the other elements in this case.

The next question formulated by the special commissioners is:

> "whether paragraph 15 (2) of Schedule 7 to the Finance Act 1965 applies where a group of persons exercise control of a company so that value passes out of shares owned by them into other shares in
> C the same way as it applies to such an exercise of control by one person only."

That question relates to a later stage in the scheme. The taxpayer having, without a disposal for tax purposes, got rid of his shares in IDM for shares in FNW, then suffered those shares to lose value in the circumstances I have already mentioned, with a corresponding benefit to shares held by
D Donmarco Ltd. The weapon relied on by the Crown in those circumstances is contained in paragraph 15 (2) of Schedule 7 to the Act of 1965. It reads as follows:

> "If a person having control of a company exercises his control so that value passes out of shares in the company owned by him or a person with whom he is connected, or out of rights over the company exercisable by him or by a person with whom he is connected, and
> E passes into other shares in or rights over the company, that shall be a disposal of the shares or rights out of which the value passes by the person by whom they were owned or exercisable."

The taxpayer was not himself a person having control of FNW. In conjunction with his two sons-in-law, possibly in conjunction with either one of them, he did have control. The special commissioners were of
F opinion that the provisions in the Interpretation Act 1889, applied to paragraph 15 (2) in such a way that the taxpayer, in conjunction with his two sons-in-law, could be treated as the person having control of FNW. Consequently the taxpayer could be taxed on the footing that at the two stages where value passed from his shares into the shares of Donmarco Ltd. there was a part disposal of his shares. The relevant provision of
G the Interpretation Act 1889 is in section 1 of that Act, and is simply that in statutes, unless the contrary intention appears, words in the singular shall include the plural and words in the plural shall include the singular.

Mr. Beattie, for the taxpayer, has submitted that in the context of the Act of 1965 there is a manifestation of a contrary intention that prevents the Act of 1889 from applying to paragraph 15 (2). Mr. Millett, on the other hand, emphasised that the Act of 1889 must operate unless there
H is a clear indication of contrary intention. Mere difficulty or inconsistency in the drafting, he said, is not enough to exclude it; and he referred me to *In re Earl of Feversham's Contract* [1942] Ch. 33, to show how general is the application of the Act of 1889. He further pointed out that if "person" in the singular were confined to a single person in paragraph 15 (2), share operations could be used to avoid capital gains tax in many circumstances where it might be conjectured that the framers of the Act intended to stop such avoidance.

That being the general frame of the arguments, I have to look at paragraph 15 (2) in its context. Quite a cursory examination of the elaborate schedules to the Act of 1965 shows that, according to the necessity of the subject matter and the requirements of clarity, the draftsman has sometimes expressly distinguished the singular number from the plural, and sometimes has left the Interpretation Act 1889 to apply, with a consequent economy of wording. There is no doubt that some problems of construction must arise if the singular includes the plural in paragraph 15 (2). The question is whether they are serious enough and important enough to amount to the manifestation, the appearance, of a contrary intention against the application of the Act of 1889.

Paragraph 15 (2) begins: " If a person having control of a company exercises his control so that value passes out of shares in the company owned by him . . ." Going no further than that, if we rewrite it thus, " If a person or persons having control of a company exercises or exercise his or their control so that value passes out of shares in the company owned by him or them," the question at once arises whether, in the case of a plurality of controllers, " shares owned by them " means shares owned by them in co-ownership or shares owned by them or any of them; and there is nothing in the context that would enable one easily to solve that problem.

Again, going a little further, the shares out of which the value may pass when control is exercised are defined as " shares in the company owned by him "—that is, the controller—" or a person with whom he is connected." If we read " person " as " person or persons " at the beginning, the phrase reads, " shares owned by him or them or a person or persons with whom he or they is or are connected." Here, further problems arise. " Connection," for this purpose, is a relationship artificially defined by paragraph 21 of Schedule 7 to the Act. It is a relationship between one person, either individual or corporate, and another person, either individual or corporate. If a group of persons exercises control of a company in order to devalue the shares of a connected person, must the connected person, for the case to fall within paragraph 15 (2), be connected with every member of the controlling group, or is connection with any one member of the controlling group enough? One can imagine seemingly capricious or surprising results on either construction by inventing fanciful cases of various sorts.

Mr. Millett, as I have said, urged a liberal construction in favour of the Crown. He said that, after all, the purpose of paragraph 15 (2) was to stop people from evading capital gains tax by schemes that drain value out of shares without actually disposing of them in the ordinary sense; and how strange it would be to leave a group free to do what an individual could not do without being liable to taxation. However, subtle devices to avoid or reduce tax are legion in their variety and complexity. If the purpose was really as general as Mr. Millett proposed, I think the framers of the Act might not have confined the subparagraph to shares belonging to the controller or persons connected with him, even given the help provided by paragraph 21 (7) of Schedule 7. I can ascertain the intended scope of the provision only from the language used.

I observe that the draftsman of these schedules was certainly not insensitive to the drafting problems which plurality presents. In particular, the definition of " control " of a company in paragraph 3 of Schedule 18 specially provides for the case of control by two or more persons, so that must have been constantly in mind when the other provisions of the Act were framed or studied. The fact that no indication is given how to

A resolve the problems that I have mentioned, which quite obviously arise if the person first mentioned in paragraph 15 (2) of Schedule 7 may be two or more persons, in my judgment indicates an intention contrary to the application of the Interpretation Act to that subparagraph. So here I differ from the special commissioners with respect and some hesitation, and I hold that the taxpayer is not caught by paragraph 15 (2) because he himself did not have control of FNW.

B Now I come to the third and last of the questions posed by the special commissioners. It is this: "whether the transactions relating to FNW constituted the 'exercise of control' of that company within the meaning of paragraph 15 (2) of Schedule 7" to the Act of 1965. It will be remembered that the shift of value between shares is treated as a disposal only where "a person having control of a company exercises his control
C so that value passes." On this point, as on their second question, the decision of the special commissioners was adverse to the taxpayer. They said in their decision:

> "Throughout its existence the [taxpayer] and his two sons-in-law had control of FNW. Whatever the company did, it did in consequence of their exercise of control. The creation of the preferred and ordinary
> D shares with particular rights, the issue of a small number of preferred shares to Donmarco, the acquisition of ordinary shares by Donmarco in consequence of the rights issue, and the ultimate liquidation of FNW, all occurred in consequence of the three original shareholders' exercise of control. As a result value passed, as it was intended to pass, from the [taxpayer's] shares into Donmarco's."

E The alternative view is that all those matters enumerated by the special commissioners occurred in consequence of the three shareholders' original decision to carry the scheme into effect; but all parties concerned were willing to co-operate in a prearranged plan, and the taxpayer and his two sons-in-law did not need to exercise, and did not exercise, the control of FNW which they undoubtedly possessed. The value passed out of their shares, on this view, in consequence of their decision that the scheme
F should be carried into effect but without any actual exercise of control over FNW.

This is a question of difficulty and of some breadth. Mr. Millett submitted quite generally that to refrain from stopping action by a company which one has power to prevent and with knowledge of the consequences, may in suitable circumstances be an exercise of control of the company.
G Of course, one does not need to have control of a company in any sense to be able in some circumstances to allow a result to happen by abstention. One can think at once of the 30 per cent. holder of voting shares who refrains from blocking a special resolution although he could do so. He certainly exercises no control of the company although his abstention has a certain result. Of course, Mr. Millett intended his formulation to apply only to cases where the person who refrains from acting is one who has
H control in the statutory sense.

I am unable to accept either Mr. Millett's general submission or the assertion of the special commissioners, on the basis of the primary agreed facts, that whatever FNW did throughout its existence it did in consequence of its shareholders' exercise of control. In my judgment, to satisfy the words "exercises . . . control" in paragraph 15 (2) of Schedule 7 some positive act that is capable of specific identification as an exercise of control is required. It is not everyone who has control who exercises it, even though the company controlled may in fact do things that he would like it to do. Accordingly, on this point also I respectfully differ from the special commissioners.

In the end, I answer the questions posed by the special commissioners as follows: (a) yes, (b) no, (c) no; and, relying on my answers to (b) and (c) as alternative grounds for my decision, I allow the appeal and remit the assessment to the special commissioners to adjust or discharge it in accordance with my decision.

Appeal allowed with costs.

Solicitors: *Courts & Co.; Solicitor of Inland Revenue.*

[COURT OF APPEAL]

* INLAND REVENUE COMMISSIONERS *v.* BULLOCK

1976 June 8, 9, 10; 25 — Buckley, Roskill and Goff L.JJ.

Revenue—Income tax—Domicile—Taxpayer born and educated in Canada — Taxpayer living and working in England — Matrimonial home established in England—Intention to return to Canada should taxpayer survive wife—Whether acquisition of English domicile of choice

The taxpayer whose domicile of origin was Canadian lived in Canada until he came to England in 1932 in order to join the Royal Air Force. In 1946, while still serving in the Royal Air Force, he married an English woman. From 1947 to 1961 the taxpayer and his wife visited his family in Canada on a number of occasions. He retired from the Air Force in 1959 and took civilian employment. His father died in Canada in 1960. The money he inherited on his father's death enabled him to retire and he went with his wife to live in Dorset. He wished to return to live in Canada after leaving the Air Force but did not do so because his wife disliked the idea. In 1966 he executed a will that had been prepared in Nova Scotia and which contained a declaration that his domicile continued to be Canadian. By then, in deference to his wife's wishes, he had given up the idea of returning to Canada but he retained Canadian citizenship. However if his wife were to change her mind or predecease him it was his intention to return there immediately. The special commissioners allowed the taxpayer's appeal against the rejection by the Board of Inland Revenue in 1972 of his claim that he had not acquired a domicile of choice in England during the tax years 1971–72 and 1972–73.

On appeal by the Crown, Brightman J., reversing the commissioners' decision, held that as the matrimonial home was permanently established in England, the taxpayer had acquired a domicile of choice in England.

On appeal by the taxpayer:—

Held, allowing the appeal, that although the establishment of a matrimonial home in a new country was an important

---

[Reported by MRS. HARRIET DUTTON, Barrister-at-Law]

factor in deciding whether that new country became the permanent home, it was not conclusive and that, as the taxpayer had maintained a firm intention to return to Canada should he survive his wife which was not merely a vague aspiration but amounted to a real determination, he could not have had the intention of establishing a permanent home in England and accordingly had not acquired a domicile of choice in England (post, pp. 1185F, G, 1186H—1187A).

Decision of Brightman J. [1975] 1 W.L.R. 1436; [1975] 3 All E.R. 541 reversed.

The following cases are referred to in the judgment:

Aikman v. *Aikman* (1861) 4 L.T. 374, H.L.(Sc.).
Anderson v. *Laneuville* (1854) 9 Moo.P.C.C. 325, P.C.
Attorney-General v. *Yule & Mercantile Bank of India* (1931) 145 L.T. 9, C.A.
Bell v. *Kennedy* (1868) L.R. 1 Sc. & Div. 307, H.L.(Sc.).
Buswell v. *Inland Revenue Commissioners* [1974] 1 W.L.R. 1631; [1974] 2 All E.R. 520, C.A.
Doucet v. *Geoghegan* (1878) 9 Ch.D. 441, C.A.
Forbes v. *Forbes* (1854) Kay 341.
Fuld, decd. (No. 3), In the Estate of [1968] P. 675; [1966] 2 W.L.R. 717; [1965] 3 All E.R. 776.
Jopp v. *Wood* (1865) 4 De G.J. & Sm. 616.
Lord v. *Colvin* (1859) 4 Drew. 366 (sub nom. *Moorhouse* v. *Lord*) (1863) 10 H.L.Cas. 272, H.L.(E.).
Platt v. *Attorney-General of New South Wales* (1878) 3 App.Cas. 336, P.C.
Udny v. *Udny* (1869) L.R. 1 Sc. & Div. 441, H.L.(Sc.).
Whicker v. *Hume* (1858) 7 H.L.Cas. 124, H.L.(E.).
Winans v. *Attorney-General* [1904] A.C. 287, H.L.(E.).

The following additional cases were cited in argument:

Aitchison v. *Dixon* (1870) L.R. 10 Eq. 589.
Bruce v. *Bruce* (1790) 2 Bos. & P. 229, H.L.(E.).
Casdagli v. *Casdagli* [1919] A.C. 145, H.L.(E.).
Corbridge v. *Somerville* (1914) 51 Sc. L.R. 406.
Henderson v. *Henderson* [1967] P. 77; [1965] 2 W.L.R. 218; [1965] 1 All E.R. 179.
Qureshi v. *Qureshi* [1972] Fam. 173; [1971] 2 W.L.R. 518; [1971] 1 All E.R. 325.
Ramsay v. *Liverpool Royal Infirmary* [1930] A.C. 588, H.L.(E.).

APPEAL from Brightman J.

The taxpayer, Group Captain Charles Heber Beverley Bullock, was born in Halifax, Nova Scotia, in 1910. He had lived in England since 1932 but, since retirement from the Royal Air Force in 1959, wished to return permanently to Canada. He did not do so because his wife did not wish to live in Canada. He would return immediately should his wife predecease him. By letter dated July 31, 1972, the Board of Inland Revenue rejected his claim that he was not domiciled in the United Kingdom during the years 1971–72 and 1972–73. The special commissioners allowed his appeal holding that he had not acquired a domicile of choice in the United Kingdom.

Brightman J. allowed an appeal by the Crown, holding that, as the matrimonial home was permanently established in England without the foreseeable prospect of its ever being established elsewhere, the taxpayer had acquired a domicile of choice in England.

The taxpayer appealed on the grounds that (1) the judge was wrong in A law in holding that on the facts found by the special commissioners the taxpayer had by the years of assessment 1971–72 and 1972–73 formed the intention of remaining permanently or indefinitely in England so as to acquire a domicile of choice there; (2) in considering the facts found by the special commissioners, the judge misdirected himself in treating the death of the wife of the taxpayer in his lifetime as otherwise than a clearly foreseen and reasonably anticipated contingency and in disregarding the B possibility that he would persuade her during their joint lives to live in Canada; (3) the judge further misdirected himself in treating the findings of fact that by 1966 the taxpayer had given up any idea of returning to Canada to live during the lifetime of his wife and that he thought that he had no option but to defer to her wishes, although if she changed her mind he would pack up fast and take the first available boat, as equivalent to a C finding that the taxpayer intended to reside for the rest of his life in England, unless he survived his wife; (4) the judge further misdirected himself in holding that there was clear evidence that the matrimonial home was permanently established in England without the least foreseeable prospect of it ever being established elsewhere and in inferring therefrom that the taxpayer had the intention of remaining permanently or indefinitely in England; (5) the judge was wrong in law in attaching no or no sufficient D weight to the following facts or any of them (i) the taxpayer's domicile of origin in Nova Scotia, (ii) his deep and permanent ties with Nova Scotia, (iii) his desire to live there, (iv) his intention of returning there to live permanently if his wife should change her mind and consent or if she should predecease him, (v) the fact that the taxpayer had not given up hope of persuading his wife to live in Nova Scotia, (vi) the absence of any real E and substantial link or tie between him and England save his marriage; (6) the judge was wrong in law in applying the dictum of Kindersley V.-C. in *Lord* v. *Colvin* (1859) 4 Drew. 366, 367, in preference to the statements of the law made by Lord Chelmsford in the same case on appeal, *Moorhouse* v. *Lord* (1863) 10 H.L.Cas. 272, 285, 286, or by Lord Westbury in *Udny* v. *Udny* (1869) L.R. 1 Sc. & Div. 441, 458, or by Scarman J. in *In the Estate of Fuld, decd.* (*No.* 3) [1968] P. 675, 684, 685, which was F approved by the Court of Appeal in *Buswell* v. *Inland Revenue Commissioners* [1974] 1 W.L.R. 1631; (7) the judge was wrong in placing reliance upon *Aitchison* v. *Dixon* (1870) L.R. 10 Eq. 589, which was decided upon special facts different in significant respects from those of the present case or upon *Anderson* v. *Laneuville* (1854) 9 Moo.P.C.C. 325, which was based upon a line of cases upon Anglo-Indian domicile decided upon principles G disapproved by the House of Lords in *Casdagli* v. *Casdagli* [1919] A.C. 145; (8) the judgment of the judge was wrong and ought to be set aside.

Leolin Price Q.C. and *D. J. Ritchie* for the taxpayer.
A. J. Balcombe Q.C. and *Brian Davenport* for the Crown.

Cur. adv. vult. H

June 25. Buckley L.J. read the following judgment. This is an appeal from a judgment of Brightman J. delivered on July 10, 1975, when, allowing an appeal from a decision of the special commissioners, the judge declared that the taxpayer, Group Captain Bullock, had acquired an English domicile of choice and was so domiciled for the fiscal years 1971–72 and 1972–73. The facts of the case, as found by the commissioners,

A are set out in the case stated and I need not restate them in full. For the purposes of this judgment I need only mention the salient facts and certain important findings made by the commissioners.

The taxpayer was born in Halifax, Nova Scotia, in August 1910, being one of the third generation born in that province. His domicile of origin was in Nova Scotia. Having been unable to obtain a commission in the Canadian Air Force, the taxpayer joined the Royal Air Force in 1932.
B He served in the Royal Air Force until 1959, when he retired with the rank of Group Captain. In 1946 he married an English wife, whose home was in England. From 1959 to 1961 the taxpayer was in civilian employment in England. When his father died in 1960, the taxpayer inherited sufficient money to enable him to retire, which he did in 1961. Before his marriage it was the taxpayer's intention to resign his commission at the
C end of the war and return to Canada, but his marriage to his English wife altered this. The taxpayer and his wife visited Canada on a number of occasions after their marriage. At first he hoped to persuade her that they should live in Canada after his retirement. Unfortunately she did not care for this prospect. The commissioners found as follows:

> "He gradually realised that she did not take to the idea of living in
> D Canada after his retirement, but he continued to hope that she might change her mind when the time came."

The taxpayer retired in 1961. The commissioners found as follows:

> "Had his wife been willing to do so the [taxpayer] could (and would) then have retired to Canada. Naturally he was not prepared to insist that she should do so and he felt he had no option but to defer to her
> E wishes. . . . By 1966 the [taxpayer] had given up any idea of returning to Canada to live during the lifetime of his wife. He thought that he had no option but to defer to her wishes, although if she changed her mind he would pack up fast and take the first available boat."

In 1961 or 1962, the taxpayer's wife bought a site in Lyme Regis on which she built a bungalow, in which she and the taxpayer have since
F lived. On April 8, 1966, the taxpayer executed a will, prepared in 1960 by a lawyer in Halifax, whereby he appointed a Nova Scotian corporation to be his executor. That will contained a declaration in the following terms:

> "I hereby declare that my domicile is and continues to be the Province of Nova Scotia, Dominion of Canada, where I was born and brought
> G up, to which province I intend to return and remain permanently upon my wife's death."

By that will the taxpayer left his estate to his wife, but if she should predecease him then half was to go to a cousin of his and the other half equally between the University of King's College, Halifax, and the congregation of All Saints' Cathedral, Halifax, to be used partly for establishing one or
H more scholarships and a memorial to the taxpayer's great-grandfather, who had been dean of the diocese of Nova Scotia. The will contained a declaration that it should be read, construed and take effect in accordance with the law of Nova Scotia. The taxpayer had made no English will and all his assets were in Canada. He kept the property which he had inherited upon his father's death invested in Canada. His wife had some means of her own, but their joint means in the United Kingdom, which no doubt included the taxpayer's pension, were not always sufficient for their needs,

and occasionally he drew upon his Canadian capital or income, in A
particular for holidays abroad.

The commissioners accepted the evidence of the taxpayer's wife to the following effect:

> "She had always regarded her husband as Canadian and realised that he wanted desperately to live in Canada. He had not given up hope of persuading her to reside there with him, but the difficulty was that B
> her impression of Canada formed on their visits had been disappointing."

She had made an English will, and also a will governed by the law of Canada.

Notwithstanding several invitations to do so, the taxpayer refused to take part in local government in England, and in fact he never voted in C
local or parliamentary elections, holding the opinion that as a Canadian citizen it would be wrong for him to take part in either local or national affairs. The taxpayer has retained his Canadian passport and has never considered obtaining a United Kingdom one. He maintained contact with his Canadian relatives and friends and was a regular reader of a Toronto newspaper.

The decision of the commissioners contains the following findings: D

> "During the period 1947 to 1961 the [taxpayer] and his wife visited Canada on a number of occasions. [His wife] however did not take to the idea of living in Canada, for the following reasons. First, her parents were still alive, residing in England. Second, she did not relish the prospect of living in the old family house in Halifax while the [taxpayer's] father resided there. Third, she found the Canadian E
> climate too cold in winter. Fourth, she preferred the English scene to the Canadian. The first two objections ceased to obtain after 1961; in 1960 the [taxpayer's] father died, and in 1961 her own father died, her mother having died some years earlier. There remained the last two objections. For a while the [taxpayer] was hopeful of persuading his wife to overcome her objections, but from about 1966 onwards he realised that it was too much to ask of her, and so he deferred to her F
> wishes, having (in his own words) no option. Nevertheless his intention persisted, and should his wife change her mind, or unhappily predecease him, he would (again to use his own words) pack up as fast as he could and get on the first boat to Canada."

The commissioners held that the taxpayer was not domiciled in the G
United Kingdom during the years 1971–72 and 1972–73. On appeal Brightman J. reversed this decision, declaring that the taxpayer had acquired an English domicile of choice and was so domiciled in each of these years. The taxpayer appeals from that decision. Since, in cases of this kind, there is no appeal from the commissioners on findings of fact, the question for decision is whether upon the facts as found the commissioners were right in law in holding as they did or whether upon H
those facts the judge was right in law in holding as he did. The solution depends upon the question whether the taxpayer at any time lost his domicile of origin in Nova Scotia by acquiring a domicile of choice in England.

As long ago as 1865 Turner L.J. said in *Jopp* v. *Wood* (1865) 4 De G.J. & Sm. 616, 621 that nothing was better settled with reference to the law of domicile than that the domicile can be changed only animo et

A facto; that is to say, by intention as well as action. The necessary act is that of taking up residence in some country other than the country of the domicile of origin. There was no dispute in the present case about the taxpayer having taken up residence in England. What his intention was in doing so is a question of fact. What we have to determine is whether that intention was such as to clothe his residence in England with the necessary quality to result in his having adopted a domicile of choice in England.

B The effect upon a man of a change of domicile is to make the law of his new domicile his personal law in place of the law of his previous domicile. The intention which has to be sought, however, is not a conscious intention to achieve this result. I think it would be unusual for anyone who changed his domicile to have done so consciously or primarily for the purpose of subjecting himself to the legal system of his new country.
C The intention which must be sought is an intention on the part of the person concerned to make the new country his permanent home.

In *Whicker* v. *Hume* (1858) 7 H.L.Cas. 124, 160, Lord Cranworth said:

> "By domicile we mean home, the permanent home; and if you do not understand your permanent home, I am afraid that no illustration drawn from foreign writers or foreign languages will very much help
> D you to it."

In *Lord* v. *Colvin* (1859) 4 Drew. 366, 376, Kindersley V.-C. said:

> "I would venture to suggest that the definition of an acquired domicile might stand thus: that place is properly the domicile of a person in which he has voluntarily fixed the habitation of himself and his family, not for a mere special and temporary purpose, but with
> E a present intention of making it his permanent home, unless and until something (which is unexpected or the happening of which is uncertain) shall occur to induce him to adopt some other permanent home."

When that case reached the House of Lords under the name of *Moorhouse* v. *Lord* (1863) 10 H.L.Cas. 272, Lord Chelmsford, at pp. 285–286,
F criticised this passage in the Vice-Chancellor's judgment as follows:

> "Now, this definition," he was referring to a definition propounded by counsel, "and that of the Vice-Chancellor appear to me to be liable to exception, in omitting one important element, namely, a fixed intention of abandoning one domicile and permanently adopting another. The present intention of making a place a person's per-
> G manent home can exist only where he has no other idea than to continue there, without looking forward to any event, certain or uncertain, which might induce him to change his residence. If he has in his contemplation some event upon the happening of which his residence will cease, it is not correct to call this even a present intention of making it a permanent home. It is rather a present intention of making a temporary home, though for a period indefinite
> H and contingent. And even if such residence should continue for years, the same intention to terminate it being continually present to the mind, there is no moment of time at which it can be predicated that there has been the deliberate choice of a permanent home."

At p. 286, Lord Chelmsford referred to what had been said by Lord Wensleydale in *Aikman* v. *Aikman* (1861) 4 L.T. 374 as laying down the rule upon this subject very clearly:

> "Every man's domicile of origin must be presumed to continue until A he has acquired another sole domicile by actual residence, with the intention of abandoning his domicile of origin. This change must be animo et facto and the burden of proof unquestionably lies on the party who asserts that change."

In defence of Kindersley V.-C. it seems to me only fair to remark that, since no man can have more than one domicile at one time, the act of B acquiring a new domicile must necessarily involve the abandonment of the previous domicile. That this was present to the mind of the vice-chancellor is clear from later passages in his judgment in *Lord* v. *Colvin*, for example at p. 422, where he referred to a man intending to abandon an acquired domicile and to resume his domicile of origin or to his abandoning his domicile of origin to acquire a domicile of choice. In truth the C insistence of Lord Chelmsford upon the importance of finding a fixed intention of abandoning one domicile and permanently adopting another is but a method of emphasising the importance of finding that the person in question intends to make his new country his permanent home. The abandonment of the previous home is implicit in the adoption of the new home, if the latter is intended to be exclusive and permanent. A man may have homes in more than one country at one time. In such a case, D for the purpose of determining his domicile, a further inquiry may have to be made to decide which, if any, should be regarded as his principal home. We are not concerned, however, with any considerations of that sort.

I must accordingly consider whether on the facts of this case it has been shown that the taxpayer had the intention of establishing a "permanent home" in England within the meaning of that expression appropriate to E the law of domicile. It is clear in my judgment that the intention does not have to be shown to have been immutable. It would be rarely that a man could be shown to have set up his home in a new country with the intention that his decision to live there and make his home there should be irrevocable. On the other hand, the intention must not be to make a home in the new country merely for a limited time or for some temporary F or special purpose.

We were very properly referred to a considerable number of authorities bearing upon this branch of the law, but it will not, I think, be necessary for me to refer to very many of them. The law of domicile was recently reviewed by Scarman J. in *In the Estate of Fuld, decd. (No. 3)* [1968] P. 675. The judge's judgment at p. 682 contains a very useful restatement of the law which, with one slight correction, was accepted as correct in this G court in *Buswell* v. *Inland Revenue Commissioners* [1974] 1 W.L.R. 1631. Scarman J. said:

> "A domicile of choice is acquired when a man fixes voluntarily his sole or chief residence in a particular place with an intention of continuing to reside there for an unlimited time."

H

I accept that statement, which derives from the speech of Lord Westbury in *Udny* v. *Udny* (1869) L.R. 1 Sc. & Div. 441, 458, with this qualification only, that the expression "unlimited time" requires some further definition. A man might remove to another country because he had obtained employment there without knowing how long that employment would continue but without intending to reside there after he ceased to be so employed. His prospective residence in the foreign country would be indefinite but

A would not be unlimited in the relevant sense. On the other hand, as I have already indicated, I do not think that it is necessary to show that the intention to make a home in the new country is irrevocable or that the person whose intention is under consideration believes that for reasons of health or otherwise he will have no opportunity to change his mind. In my judgment, the true test is whether he intends to make his home in the new country until the end of his days unless and until something happens
B to make him change his mind. Thus in *Winans* v. *Attorney-General* [1904] A.C. 287, 291, Lord Macnaghten, referring to what Lord Cairns had said in *Bell* v. *Kennedy* (1868) L.R. 1 Sc. & Div. 307, 311, said that the question was whether the person whose domicile was in question had "determined" to make, and had in fact made, the alleged domicile of choice "his home with the intention of establishing himself and his family there and ending
C his days in that country."

In the present case the commissioners, adopting the language of Lord Chelmsford in the passage from *Moorhouse* v. *Lord*, 10 H.L.Cas. 272, 285, 286, which I have already cited, expressed the view that the taxpayer had in contemplation some event, that was his wife's change of mind or prior death, upon the happening of which his residence in England would cease. They therefore concluded that he had not acquired a
D domicile of choice in England. The judge on the other hand was very much impressed by the fact that the taxpayer had established his matrimonial home in England and that there was no foreseeable prospect of that matrimonial home ever being established elsewhere. He clearly regarded this as the decisive factor in deciding that the taxpayer had acquired a domicile of choice in England.

E For the purpose of determining the true nature and quality of the taxpayer's intention it is clearly necessary to take into account all relevant circumstances. Domicile is distinct from citizenship. The fact that the taxpayer chose to retain his Canadian citizenship and not to acquire United Kingdom citizenship would not be inconsistent with his having acquired a domicile in the United Kingdom, but his adherence to his Canadian citizenship is, in my opinion, one of the circumstances properly
F to be taken into consideration in deciding whether he acquired a United Kingdom domicile. The declaration as to domicile contained in the taxpayer's will is also a matter to be taken into account, although the weight to be attributed to it must depend on the surrounding circumstances.

Undoubtedly the fact that a man establishes his matrimonial home in a new country is an important consideration in deciding whether he intends
G to make that country his permanent home (see, for example, *Forbes* v. *Forbes* (1854) Kay 341; *Platt* v. *Attorney-General of New South Wales* (1878) 3 App.Cas. 336, 343; *Attorney-General* v. *Yule & Mercantile Bank of India* (1931) 145 L.T. 9, 14) but this is not a conclusive factor. In *Forbes* v. *Forbes*, Page-Wood V.-C. said at p. 366: "The effect of the residence of the wife being, after all, but evidence of intention may be rebutted by stronger evidence of a contrary character."

H The judge disregarded as remote the theoretical possibility that the taxpayer may somehow persuade his wife to live in Canada or that she may change her mind and reconcile herself to life in Canada. I think he was justified in so doing upon the findings made by the commissioners. I am consequently prepared to accept that in the present case the matrimonial home will continue to be in England as long as both the parties to the marriage survive. It is clear, however, from the findings of the commissioners that the taxpayer never abandoned his intention of returning to live in Canada in the event of his surviving his wife. The tax- A payer's wife is some three or four years younger than he is and her health is good. The taxpayer said in his evidence before the commissioners that he would put the possibility of her predeceasing him at no higher than a possibility and considered it an even chance which of them might die first. We must, in my opinion, proceed upon the footing that the possibility of the taxpayer surviving his wife is not unreal and that he is at least almost as likely to survive her as she is to survive him. B

No doubt, if a man who has made his home in a country other than his domicile of origin has expressed an intention to return to his domicile of origin or to remove to some third country upon an event or condition of an indefinite kind; for example, "if I make a fortune" or "when I've had enough of it," it might be hard, if not impossible, to conclude that he retained any real intention of so returning or removing. Such a man, C in the graphic language of James L.J. in *Doucet* v. *Geoghegan* (1878) 9 Ch.D. 441, 457, is like a man who expects to reach the horizon; he finds it at last no nearer than it was at the beginning of his journey. In *Aikman* v. *Aikman* (1861) 4 L.T. 374, 376, Lord Campbell L.C. said that a mere intention to return to a man's native country on a doubtful contingency would not prevent residence in a foreign country putting an end to his domicile of origin. D

In the present case it seems to me impossible not to hold that the taxpayer has always maintained a firm intention to return to Canada in the event of his surviving his wife. Whether that event will or will not occur is of course doubtful. That is the characteristic of a contingency. But there is no doubt about the nature of the contingency, nor will there eventually be any doubt whether the contingency has or has not occurred. E There is nothing embryonic, vague or uncertain about the taxpayer's intention in this respect. Suppose a man to establish his home in a foreign country with the intention of returning to his country of origin when or if he survives the age of 60; or with the intention of returning to his country of origin when he retires; or of doing so if and when he inherits a particular family title. I apprehend that in neither the first nor the second case could it be contended that he had adopted a permanent home in the F foreign country, notwithstanding that the event upon which he proposed to return to his country of origin was one which might never occur. His intention would have been limited to making a temporary home there. The occurrence of the contingency of the man inheriting a family title might well be more uncertain than his surviving the age of 60 or living to retirement; but, if there were a real likelihood of the contingency occurring, I G can see no reason why that man should more readily be treated as having an intention of making a permanent home in the foreign country than the other two examples.

The contingency of the taxpayer surviving his wife seems to me no more remote or unreal than this. *Anderson* v. *Laneuville* (1854) 9 Moo. P.C.C. 325, must be read in the context of the facts of that case, and Dr. Lushington's statement, at p. 334, that it could never be said that residing H in a country until the death of an individual is a residence merely for a temporary purpose, cannot in my opinion be taken as an enunciation of a rule of universal application. The question can perhaps be formulated in this way where the contingency is not itself of a doubtful or indefinite character: is there a sufficiently substantial possibility of the contingency happening to justify regarding the intention to return as a real determination to do so upon the contingency occurring rather than a vague

A hope or aspiration? In the present case in my opinion that question should be answered affirmatively. I feel that that conclusion is reinforced by the consideration that the taxpayer's decision to live in this country, although no doubt it has been his own free choice reached in consequence of a wish to comply with his wife's wishes, has been induced by his wife's unwillingness to live in Canada. In these circumstances I feel myself unable to agree with the conclusion reached by the judge. I would
B allow this appeal.

ROSKILL L.J. I have had the advantage of discussing the draft of the judgment just delivered with Buckley L.J. and with Goff L.J. I entirely agree with it and no reasonable purpose would be served by my delivering a separate judgment. I agree that the appeal should be allowed..

C

GOFF L.J. I have had the like advantage of having discussed the draft with Buckley and Roskill L.JJ. and I entirely agree with the conclusion and the reasons. I have nothing to add, except perhaps to quote some words which figured in certain of the cases cited during the argument and say that I agree *in toto* or *in omnibus.*

D

Appeal allowed with costs.
Leave to appeal refused.

Solicitors: *Turner & Evans, Radlett; Solicitor of Inland Revenue.*

E

[COURT OF APPEAL]

* SHELL U.K. LTD. *v.* LOSTOCK GARAGE LTD.

[1976 S. No. 1777]

F [1976 L. No. 868]

1976 May 17, 18, 19; June 30 — Lord Denning M.R., Ormrod and Bridge L.JJ.

Restraint of Trade—Sale of goods—Restriction on brand of goods —Tied garage—Sales agreement with oil company for supply of petrol—Competitive price war—Temporary support scheme
G *for some but not all tied garages—Whether discrimination rendering solus agreement void or in suspense while operating in unreasonable restraint of trade—Whether equitable relief available to oil company or garage*

In March 1955, the defendants, a small country garage, entered into a 20-year solus agreement with a large oil company on terms that they would sell only petrol supplied by the
H oil company and keep open six and a half days a week. The contract was varied in March 1966 to enable the defendants to terminate it on 12 months' notice after March 1971. The garage operated in competition with four neighbouring garages, two of which were also tied to the same oil company. In 1975, following the oil crisis, when supplies of petrol exceeded demand and independent suppliers were selling petrol to garages at lower prices in a cut-price war, the four neighbouring garages all sold petrol at 70p a gallon, but the defendants, being bound by the terms of their solus agreement, had to

sell at 75p a gallon. Their sales fell so drastically that in January 1976 they informed the oil company that they would have to get their supplies elsewhere and that in any event they considered that the solus contract had come to an end in March 1975. The oil company's manager told them, first, that the agreement as varied in 1966 could be terminated only on a year's notice, and secondly, that the oil company had introduced a temporary price support scheme for the benefit of their tied garages enabling garages whose sales had dropped by 40,000 gallons in 1975 to sell the company's petrol at 70p, the company making good any resulting loss. But that scheme did not apply to the defendants, so they did not benefit from it. They therefore obtained cheaper supplies elsewhere and their trade rapidly improved.

The oil company issued a writ claiming, inter alia, an injunction to restrain the defendants from obtaining or selling motor fuel other than that supplied by them and from acting in breach of the 1955 agreement as varied. The defendants then discovered that the two neighbouring tied garage competitors were enjoying the benefit of the support scheme. By their defence and counterclaim they claimed that the agreement of 1955 and as varied was void and unenforceable as in unreasonable restraint of trade.

Kerr J. held that so long as the support scheme lasted its effect was to inflict an unreasonable and unforeseen degree of hardship on the defendants and that on grounds of public policy the oil company could not enforce the contract so long as that hardship continued; and he awarded the defendants £482 on their counterclaim as the loss suffered during the weeks when they had carried out the terms of the contract without benefit of the support scheme. The scheme was brought to an end for extraneous reasons on April 30.

The defendant garage appealed. The oil company cross-appealed.

On the cross-appeal by the oil company, asking for a judgment that the tie was binding even during the time that the support scheme was in existence:—

Held (Ormrod L.J. dissenting), that the cross-appeal should be dismissed.

Per Lord Denning M.R. Although the solus agreement was not at its inception in unreasonable restraint of trade, it became unreasonable and therefore unenforceable so long as the oil company operated the support scheme to the prejudice of the defendants (post, pp. 1197H, 1198E–G, 1199C).

Per Ormrod L.J. A restraint of trade could not be temporarily suspended because it was temporarily operating oppressively. However although the defendants remained bound by the tie the oil company, in so far as they were seeking equitable relief, were not entitled to an injunction so long as they operated the support scheme to the prejudice of the defendants but should be left to their remedy in damages (post, pp. 1201D, 1202A–B, D–G).

On the appeal by the defendant garage, asking for a declaration that they were relieved altogether from the tie even after the support scheme had ended:—

Held (Bridge L.J. dissenting), that the appeal should be dismissed on the ground that the contract was not unenforceable at its inception as being in unreasonable restraint of trade and there was no implied term such as to enable the defendants to terminate the contract altogether.

Per Bridge L.J. A term must be implied into the contract prohibiting such discrimination by the oil company as would render it commercially impracticable for the defendants to continue to operate their petrol sales business. It is the character of the discrimination at its inception and not its

A duration which determines the legal result, viz. that by reason of the oil company's breach of that implied term the defendants were no longer bound by the contract (post, pp. 1204H, 1205D–E, 1206A).

Liverpool City Council v. *Irwin* [1976] 2 W.L.R. 562, H.L.(E.) considered.

Decision of Kerr J. affirmed on different grounds.

B The following cases are referred to in the judgments:

Chappell v. *Times Newspapers Ltd.* [1975] 1 W.L.R. 482; [1975] I.C.R. 145; [1975] 2 All E.R. 233, Megarry J. and C.A.

Commercial Plastics Ltd. v. *Vincent* [1965] 1 Q.B. 623; [1964] 3 W.L.R. 820; [1964] 3 All E.R. 546, C.A.

Davis Contractors Ltd. v. *Fareham Urban District Council* [1956] A.C. 696; [1956] 3 W.L.R. 37; [1956] 2 All E.R. 145, H.L.(E.).

C *Esso Petroleum Co. Ltd.* v. *Harper's Garage (Stourport) Ltd.* [1966] 2 Q.B. 514; [1965] 3 W.L.R. 469; [1965] 2 All E.R. 933; [1966] 2 Q.B. 514; [1966] 2 W.L.R. 1043; [1966] 1 All E.R. 725, C.A.; [1968] A.C. 269; [1967] 2 W.L.R. 871; [1967] 1 All E.R. 699, H.L.(E.).

Eugenia, The [1964] 2 Q.B. 226; [1964] 2 W.L.R. 114; [1964] 1 All E.R. 161, C.A.

Gillespie Bros. & Co. Ltd. v. *Roy Bowles Transport Ltd.* [1973] Q.B. 400; [1972] 3 W.L.R. 1003; [1973] 1 All E.R. 193, C.A.

D *Gledhow Autoparts Ltd.* v. *Delaney* [1965] 1 W.L.R. 1366; [1965] 3 All E.R. 228, C.A.

Greaves & Co. (Contractors) Ltd. v. *Baynham Meikle & Partners* [1975] 1 W.L.R. 1095; [1975] 3 All E.R. 99, C.A.

Home Counties Dairies Ltd. v. *Skilton* [1970] 1 W.L.R. 526; [1970] 1 All E.R. 1227, C.A.

E *Instone* v. *A. Schroeder Music Publishing Co. Ltd.* [1974] 1 W.L.R. 1308; [1974] 3 All E.R. 616, H.L.(E.).

Lister v. *Romford Ice and Cold Storage Co. Ltd.* [1957] A.C. 555; [1957] 2 W.L.R. 158; [1957] 1 All E.R. 125, H.L.(E.).

Liverpool City Council v. *Irwin* [1976] Q.B. 319; [1975] 3 W.L.R. 663; [1975] 3 All E.R. 658, C.A.; [1976] 2 W.L.R. 562; [1976] 2 All E.R. 39, H.L.(E.).

F *Luxor (Eastbourne) Ltd.* v. *Cooper* [1941] A.C. 108; [1941] 1 All E.R. 33, H.L.(E.)

Measure Brothers Ltd. v. *Measures* [1910] 2 Ch. 248, C.A.

Rex v. *Paddington and St. Marylebone Rent Tribunal, Ex parte Bedrock Investments Ltd.* [1947] K.B. 984; [1947] 2 All E.R. 15, D.C.

Stickney v. *Keeble* [1915] A.C. 386, H.L.(E.).

Williamson v. *John I. Thornycroft & Co. Ltd.* [1940] 2 K.B. 658; [1940] 4 All E.R. 61, C.A.

G

The following additional cases were cited in argument:

Amoco Australia Pty. Ltd. v. *Rocca Bros. Motor Engineering Co. Pty. Ltd.* [1975] A.C. 561; [1975] 2 W.L.R. 779; [1975] 1 All E.R. 968, P.C.

Curwen v. *James* [1963] 1 W.L.R. 748; [1963] 2 All E.R. 619, C.A.

Livock v. *Pearson Brothers* (1928) 33 Com.Cas. 188.

Moorcock, The (1889) 14 P.D. 64, C.A.

H *Nordenfelt* v. *Maxim Nordenfelt Guns & Ammunition Co.* [1894] A.C. 535, H.L.(E.).

APPEAL from Kerr J.

The plaintiffs, Shell U.K. Ltd., suppliers and distributors of Shell petroleum products in the United Kingdom, brought an action against the defendants, Lostock Garage Ltd., which occupied and carried on the business of a filling station at Manchester Road, Lostock Gralam, Northwich,

Cheshire. By their writ, as amended, they claimed that by the terms of a A
written sales agreement dated March 25, 1955, or by a subsequent agreement
or agreements the defendants agreed with their predecessors, Shell Mex
and B.P. Ltd., inter alia, (a) (i) out of the total five pumps then installed
on the premises forthwith to sell from four of such pumps only motor fuel
supplied by Shell-Mex and B.P. Ltd.; (ii) from the remaining pumps . . .
to sell only such motor fuel . . . as Shell-Mex and B.P. Ltd. might . . .
approve . . . (c) . . . to exhibit such . . . signs and advertising matter . . . B
as might be indicated . . . by Shell-Mex and B.P. Ltd. and not to exhibit
any other. . . ."

They claimed that the defendants, since January 28, 1976, had without
their consent in breach of the agreement (i) commenced and continued
to take supplies of motor fuel from Mansfield Petroleum Co. Ltd. ("Mans-
field") and to sell it from all except one pump on the premises; and com- C
menced and continued to replace Shell insignia and advertisements with
those of Mansfield; that the defendants by letter of February 11, 1976, had
wrongfully rejected the agreement and unless enjoined therefrom would
continue to act in breach of it, whereby the plaintiffs had suffered and
would suffer loss and damage.

They claimed against the defendants (i) damages; (ii) an order restrain-
ing them from accepting supplies of or from selling motor fuel except that D
supplied by them, and (iii) an order that they remove from the premises all
motor fuel advertising matter and signs of Mansfield forthwith, or within
such time as the court should determine.

By their defence the garage company admitted the agreement of March
25, 1955, with Shell-Mex and B.P. Ltd., and that the agreement was
purportedly varied by successive agreements including a variation as of E
March 31, 1966, but claimed that the agreement was at all material times
void and unenforceable as being in unreasonable restraint of trade, or that
it had been repudiated and that the defendants had accepted such repu-
diation; alternatively that the plaintiffs were in breach of the agreement
and the defendants had given notice in writing under clause 8 treating it
as having been terminated by such breach; or that it had been frustrated.
Further or alternatively, they claimed that if the agreement was not void F
and unenforceable and had not been repudiated, terminated or frustrated,
the plaintiffs would derive no benefit from enforcing the restriction in
clause 4 (A) of the agreement, as varied, since the sole effect of so doing
would be to prevent the defendants from selling any motor fuel at all from
their pumps installed at the premises, because the specified goods were
and would remain unobtainable; and that the plaintiffs were enforcing or
seeking to enforce the agreement in such manner as unreasonably to G
restrain the defendants' freedom to trade and that it would be contrary to
public policy to enforce it; and that the court should not grant the relief
sought or any relief at all.

They claimed (by paragraph 16) further or alternatively that the agree-
ment contained (by necessary implication of law) the following implied
terms: (1) that Shell-Mex and B.P. Ltd., the plaintiffs' predecessors and H
their successors, Shell U.K. Ltd., or any person should not discriminate
against the defendants in favour of competing and neighbouring retailers
of petroleum products in fixing prices, rebates and/or discounts or in
conferring benefits in respect of petrol supplied by them; and/or (2) that
they should not so discriminate in such a way as to render the defendants'
petrol sales not economically viable; (3) that the restriction contained in
clause 4 (A) of the agreement should not be enforced against the defend-

ants in such manner or in such circumstances as would render their petrol sales not economically viable.

They claimed that in breach of the alleged implied terms the plaintiffs had discriminated against them in favour of, inter alia, Charles Barber Ltd. and the Plumley Filling Station, both of Manchester Road, Northwich, Cheshire (the road on which the defendants' premises were situated) and both of whom were competitors of the defendants, and had enforced the restriction against the defendants thereby rendering their petrol sales not economically viable. They denied that they had repudiated or were in breach of the agreement as alleged or at all.

By their counterclaim the defendants repeated their defence and claimed that from about January 29, 1976, to March 2, 1976, they regularly obtained supplies of petrol from Mansfield Petroleum Co. Ltd.; that by an oral agreement made between them and Mansfield Petroleum on or about March 2, 1976, Mansfield Petroleum agreed to sell and deliver to them on March 5, 1976, 3,000 gallons of petrol; that in breach of that agreement Mansfield had refused to deliver any further petrol to them on March 5 or at all, because by a letter of March 1 from the plaintiffs to Mansfield Petroleum and by other means and on other occasions the plaintiffs had wrongfully caused or procured the breach by Mansfield Petroleum of the agreement with them; that by reason of the plaintiffs' wrongful inducement of breach of contract the defendants had suffered loss and damage in that: (a) they had lost the profit which they would have made on the sale of the 3,000 gallons of petrol, viz. about £90; and (b) they had been compelled to buy petrol from the plaintiffs and, in order to compete with neighbouring petrol retailers, to sell that petrol at a loss of 4p. per gallon.

They asked for (1) a declaration that the agreement was void and unenforceable as being in unreasonable restraint of trade; (2) an injunction restraining the plaintiffs from enforcing or seeking to enforce it against them; (3) an injunction restraining the plaintiffs from causing or procuring or seeking to cause or procure Mansfield Petroleum or any other supplier of petrol not to supply them with petrol in breach of any contract for the supply of petrol made between them and Mansfield Petroleum or any such other supplier; (4) damages; and (5) interest on such damages at such rate and for such period as the court thought just.

Kerr J. on April 14, 1976, held, inter alia that the defendants were not entitled to the declaration or the injunctions sought in their counterclaim, as amended. He awarded them agreed damages of £482, representing the actual loss suffered by them between December 1975 and January 1976 by adhering to the terms of the sales agreement.

The defendants appealed, asking for an order (1) that the Court of Appeal declare that the agreement sought to be enforced by the plaintiffs was void and unenforceable as being in unreasonable restraint of trade; (2) that the plaintiffs be restrained from enforcing or seeking to enforce it; (3) that they be restrained from causing or procuring or seeking to cause or procure Mansfield Petroleum Co. Ltd. or any other supplier of petrol not to supply them with petrol in breach of any contract between the defendants and Mansfield or any such other supplier; and that (4) the defendants should have leave to reamend their amended counterclaim in the terms set out in the document appended to the notice of motion.

The pleaded grounds of appeal (not relevant to the decision) were in substance related to alleged or purported variations or novations of the original agreement all of which were claimed to be void as an unreasonable restraint of trade, but included the ground that there should be implied in the agreement one or more of the terms set out in the document appended to the notice of appeal or alternatively one or more of the terms set out in paragraph 16 of the amended defence and counterclaim; and that the plaintiffs' predecessors Shell-Mex and B.P. Ltd. or, alternatively, the plaintiffs had broken the agreement and that the defendants had given notice under clause 8 of the agreement treating it as terminated by such breach. A B

By a respondent's notice the oil company gave notice of its intention to contend: (1) that so much of the judgment of Kerr J. as adjudged that the plaintiffs' claims be dismissed should be set aside, and that judgment be entered for the plaintiffs with costs, with (i) an order for damages to be assessed, and (ii) an injunction in the terms of paragraph (ii) of the prayer in the consolidated statements of claim; (2) that so much of the judgment as awarded the defendants damages in the sum of £482 on their counterclaim be set aside and that judgment be entered on the counterclaim for the plaintiffs with costs. C

The grounds of the cross-appeal were that: (1) the judge was wrong in law, nor was there any evidence properly to support him in finding that the defendants had committed no breach of the terms of, or were entitled to be relieved from the enforcement against them of the disputed agreement in restraint of trade, whether by an award of damages or by injunction, by reason of the plaintiffs' conduct as found by the judge, and for so long as the conduct, namely a dealers' retail price support scheme, remained in force; (2) the judge was further wrong in law in finding that the plaintiffs had procured the alleged or any breach of contract between the defendants and Mansfield Petroleum; (3) there was no evidence nor any proper grounds in law on which the judge could properly find in any event, as he did, that to enforce the alleged agreement by injunction would inflict excessive hardship on the defendants, or would be a wrong exercise of the discretion of the court, having found, as he did, that the agreement was neither void nor contrary to public policy at the date when it was made. D E

F

David Kemp Q.C., *Derrick Turriff* and *Stephen Richards* for the defendants.

Victor Durand Q.C. and *Michael Kennedy* for the plaintiffs, Shell U.K. Ltd.

Cur. adv. vult.

G

June 30. The following judgments were read.

LORD DENNING M.R. There is quite a small garage in Cheshire called Lostock Garage. It has only three or four petrol pumps in action. It has a workshop for repairs. It also sells cars. Geoffrey Clarke runs it, as his father did before him, as a private company—Lostock Garages Ltd. He employs two men. He keeps open all day, every day, six days a week, and Sunday afternoons. In all 81 hours a week. H

For over 20 years the petrol has been supplied by the Shell company or its associates. The garage has been tied to Shell by a solus agreement for all those years. Their relations were excellent until the oil crisis broke a year or so ago. As a result petrol increased sharply in price. Motorists economised and used less. By December 1975 there was a price war.

Lostock Garage was caught up in it. They had to meet competition
A from four other garages in the neighbourhood. All four within a radius of two miles. Two of them were Shell garages—one being owned by Shell, the other tied to Shell. Two were free of any ties, one selling V.I.P. petrol, the other I.C.I. petrol. In December 1975 these two free garages cut their prices. They sold four star petrol at 70p a gallon, while Lostock were still selling at 75p. The two other Shell garages also cut their prices
B to 70p a gallon, or the equivalent, by giving incentives, such as Green Shield stamps.

Lostock Garage could not afford to cut their prices to 70p in that way: because Shell were still charging them the "pre-war" price. Shell were still charging Lostock 68p a gallon. On top of it, Lostock had to add their own expenses of men, and so forth. They had to charge 75p
C to pay their way.

So Lostock were faced with cut prices all round. To meet the competition, Mr. Clarke decided that he must leave Shell and buy cheaper elsewhere. He thought that the tie to Shell had come to an end. The "solus" tie had been for 20 years from March 1955. If so, it would have ended in March 1975. So he made inquiries of suppliers called Mansfield Petroleum Co. Ltd. This was a company which could undercut
D Shell. At that time there were surplus stocks of petrol at Rotterdam—available cheaply to Mansfield, and others. Mansfield offered to supply Lostock with petrol at low prices. So on Friday, January 24, 1976, Mr. Clarke telephoned to Shell and said to their manager: "Our sales are suffering because of cut-price people, and we intend to take deliveries from Mansfield Petroleum so as to be able to compete." The manager
E replied: "Wait a bit. I am attending a meeting today to hear Shell's plans to combat the cut price people. I will let you know next week."

Mr. Clarke did wait a bit. But on Wednesday, January 28, 1976, Mr. Clarke had his worst day ever. He sold only 35½ gallons during the whole day as against "pre-war" sales of 250 gallons a day. He straightaway ordered deliveries from Mansfields.

On Thursday, January 29, 1976, the Mansfield tanker arrived outside
F the garage. Before it started delivery, the Shell manager arrived. The manager told Mr. Clarke that Shell had a "support scheme" for helping some of the Shell garages, but that it did not apply to the Lostock Garage.

Under this "support scheme" the supported garages were expected to reduce their selling prices to 70p to meet the competition: and Shell guaranteed that they would not lose by so doing: because Shell would
G make up any loss. But this scheme only applied to garages which had suffered a drop in sales of 40,000 gallons in 1975. It did not apply to Lostock because they were only a small garage. They had suffered a drop of 13,000 gallons in that year. It was large for them, but would be small for a big garage.

The Shell manager told Mr. Clarke the scheme in outline. Mr. Clarke replied: "That's not very helpful to me. I think my tie to Shell has
H expired. I am going to get deliveries from Mansfield."

The Shell manager said that he thought that 12 months' notice was necessary to end the tie: and he went off. And Mr. Clarke took action. He asked the Mansfield tanker to deliver. And it did. 3,000 gallons into the Lostock tanks. And Lostock began selling at 70p instead of 75p. The lowering of the price brought a tremendous boost in sales. Whereas in January 1976 Lostock's sales had fallen to 900 gallons a week, by the end of February 1976 they had increased to 3,000 gallons a week.

But there was, as I said, a difference about the tie. To resolve it, the Shell manager went back to his office. He looked up the correspondence and found that, although the original tie was for 20 years from March 1975, nevertheless in 1966 it had been varied by a letter so as to be determinable by 12 months' notice at any time after 1971. So the manager went back to Mr. Clarke and told him so. Mr. Clarke said: "I do not feel bound by any such letter: but, even if I am, the situation calls for drastic action. I must continue to take supplies from Mansfield." He did so.

Both sides went to their lawyers. Shell claimed that the tie was still binding on Lostock: and that Mansfield were inducing a breach of the contract. Faced with the threat of legal proceedings, Mansfield stopped supplying Lostock on March 6, 1976. Lostock then had no option but to take their supplies from Shell, paying them the "pre-war" price of 68p. But to meet the competition, Lostock had to sell it at 70p, thus suffering serious loss because the 2p difference did not cover their expenses. Lostock still claimed that they were not bound by the tie: but, in case they were, they gave 12 months' notice to determine the "solus" agreement—to expire on March 4, 1977.

Legal proceedings took place. During them, Lostock discovered that Shell had been supporting the two Shell garages near to them. The extent of it was not known to Lostock. But it undoubtedly enabled these two Shell garages to reduce prices and to give incentives so as to undercut the Lostock garage. The judge summarised it in this way:

> "Shell contend that they are entitled to continue to enforce the tie against Lostock notwithstanding the inclusion in their price support scheme of the two Shell garages on either side of Lostock. Shell accept—and they could not do otherwise on the evidence—that this has operated harshly on Lostock . . . Lostock must continue to keep their premises open for the sale of petrol at all reasonable times. But so long as the two Shell garages are supported, and Lostock is not, I am satisfied that Lostock must operate at a loss if the agreement is enforced."

The judge held that the effect of the support scheme was "to inflict an unreasonable and unforeseen degree of hardship" on Lostock: and that Shell were not entitled to enforce the tie so long as hardship was caused. Both Lostock and Shell appeal to this court. Lostock say that the tie is gone altogether. Shell say that it remained in being all the time and that they are entitled to an injunction and damages. As it happens, Shell gave up their support scheme at the end of April 1976. The question of principle is: was the tie binding while Shell operated their support scheme?

Before dealing with this question of principle, I must set out the principal provisions of the "solus" agreement.

The "solus" agreement

The original agreement was between Shell-Mex and B.P. Ltd. (the sellers) and Mr. Clarke, senior (the buyers). It was for 20 years, from April 1, 1955, to March 31, 1975. The principal clauses for the present purposes were these:

> Clause 3: "The sellers agree: [A] To supply to the buyers . . . such quantities of those brands of motor fuel supplied by Shell-Mex and B.P. Ltd. . . . as the buyers may reasonably require . . . [B] To allow

> A to the buyers a special rebate of one penny per gallon . . . [D] To
> maintain . . . in good mechanical working condition . . . all those fuel
> pumps." Clause 4: "The buyers . . . agree: . . . [A] . . . to sell from
> four of (their) pumps only motor fuel supplied by Shell-Mex and
> B.P. Ltd.; . . . [E]. To keep the premises in a clean and smart condition
> provide an adequate staff and keep open for the sale of motor
> fuel . . . at all reasonable times and to ensure that a proper and
> B effective service is provided to the public."
> Clause 6: "[A] The buyers agree to make payment at or before the
> time of delivery for motor fuel at a price which shall be the wholesale
> schedule price ruling at that date and place of delivery."

Clause 6 (B) (C): Shell-Mex and B.P. Ltd. were not to be under any
liability to the buyers if there was a shortage of supplies or be under any
C liability to the buyers if delivery was prevented by any event which was
not within the reasonable control of Shell-Mex and B.P. Ltd.: but that,
in those circumstances, the buyers were at liberty to buy from other sources
to make good and sell the same.

Clause 8 said:

> "In the event of any breach whatsoever by either party of any of
> D their obligations hereunder, the other party shall have the right
> (without prejudice to any other right or remedy arising from such
> breach) forthwith upon giving notice in writing to the party in breach
> to treat this agreement as having been terminated by such breach."

In 1966 there was a decision in the courts in which it was said that
a "solus" agreement might be in unreasonable restraint of trade if it
E exceeded five years: see *Esso Petroleum Co. Ltd.* v. *Harper's Garage
(Stourport) Ltd.* [1966] 2 Q.B. 514; [1968] A.C. 269. In consequence, that
"solus" agreement was varied by a letter dated March 31, 1966, from
Shell-Mex and B.P. Ltd. to the garage. It said:

> "The period of the said sales agreement shall be varied so as to
> enable you to terminate such agreement by giving to us twelve
> F calendar months previous notice in writing at any time to take effect
> after the expiration of a period of five years from the date of this
> letter."

There were also various assignments, consents and novations by which
that "solus" agreement was transferred to and became binding on Shell
U.K. Ltd. as suppliers and Lostock Garage Ltd. as buyers. At one time
G Mr. Kemp took some technical points on the validity of the variation
and novations, and so forth. But these technical points disappeared in
the course of the argument. I need say no more about them, except that
I agree entirely with what the judge said about them.

Implied terms

H It was submitted by Mr. Kemp on behalf of the garage that there was
to be implied in the solus agreement a term that Shell, as the supplier,
should not abnormally discriminate against the buyer and/or should
supply petrol to the buyer on terms which did not abnormally discriminate
against him. He said that Shell had broken that implied term by giving
support to the two Shell garages and refusing it to Lostock: that, on that
ground, Shell were in breach of the solus agreement: and that Lostock
were entitled to terminate it.

This submission makes it necessary once again to consider the law as to implied terms. I ventured with some trepidation to suggest that terms implied by law could be brought within one comprehensive category—in which the courts could imply a term such as was just and reasonable in the circumstances: see *Greaves & Co. (Contractors) Ltd.* v. *Baynham Meikle & Partners* [1975] 1 W.L.R. 1095, 1099–1100; *Liverpool City Council* v. *Irwin* [1976] Q.B. 319, 331–332. But, as I feared, the House of Lords in *Liverpool City Council* v. *Irwin* [1976] 2 W.L.R. 562, have rejected it as quite unacceptable. As I read the speeches, there are two broad categories of implied terms. A B

(i) *The first category*

The first category comprehends all those relationships which are of common occurrence. Such as the relationship of seller and buyer, owner and hirer, master and servant, landlord and tenant, carrier by land or by sea, contractor for building works, and so forth. In all those relationships the courts have imposed obligations on one party or the other, saying they are "implied terms." These obligations are not founded on the intention of the parties, actual or presumed, but on more general considerations: see *Luxor (Eastbourne) Ltd.* v. *Cooper* [1941] A.C. 108, 137 by Lord Wright; *Lister* v. *Romford Ice and Cold Storage Co. Ltd.* [1957] A.C. 555, 576 by Viscount Simonds, and at p. 594 by Lord Tucker (both of whom give interesting illustrations); and *Liverpool City Council* v. *Irwin* [1976] 2 W.L.R. 562, 571 by Lord Cross of Chelsea, and at p. 579 by Lord Edmund-Davies. In such relationships the problem is not to be solved by asking what did the parties intend? Or would they have unhesitatingly agreed to it, if asked? It is to be solved by asking: has the law already defined the obligation or the extent of it? If so, let it be followed. If not, look to see what would be reasonable in the general run of such cases: see by Lord Cross of Chelsea at p. 570H: and then say what the obligation shall be. The House in *Liverpool City Council* v. *Irwin* [1976] 2 W.L.R. 562 went through that very process. They examined the existing law of landlord and tenant, in particular that relating to easements, to see if it contained the solution to the problem: and, having found that it did not, they imposed an obligation on the landlord to use reasonable care. In these relationships the parties can exclude or modify the obligation by express words; but unless they do so, the obligation is a legal incident of the relationship which is attached by the law itself and not by reason of any implied term. C D E F

Likewise, in the general law of contract, the legal effect of frustration does not depend on an implied term. It does not depend on the presumed intention of the parties, nor on what they would have answered, if asked: but simply on what the court itself declares to amount to a frustration: see *Davis Contractors Ltd.* v. *Fareham Urban District Council* [1956] A.C. 696, 728 by Lord Radcliffe and *The Eugenia* [1964] 2 Q.B. 226, 238, 239. G

(ii) *The second category* H

The second category comprehends those cases which are not within the first category. These are cases—not of common occurrence—in which from the particular circumstances a term is to be implied. In these cases the implication is based on an intention imputed to the parties from their actual circumstances: see *Luxor (Eastbourne) Ltd.* v. *Cooper* [1941] A.C. 108, 137 by Lord Wright. Such an imputation is only to be made when it is necessary to imply a term to give efficacy to the contract and make it a workable agreement in such manner as the parties would clearly have done if they had applied their mind to the contingency which has arisen. These are the "officious bystander" types of case: see *Lister* v. *Romford Ice and Cold Storage Co. Ltd.* [1957] A.C. 555, 594, by Lord Tucker. In such cases a term is not to be implied on the ground that it would be reasonable: but only when it is necessary and can be formulated with a sufficient degree of precision. This was the test applied by the majority of this court in *Liverpool City Council* v. *Irwin* [1976] Q.B. 319, and they were emphatically upheld by the House on this point: see [1976] 2 W.L.R. 562, 571D–H by Lord Cross of Chelsea; p. 578G–579A by Lord Edmund-Davies.

There is this point to be noted about *Liverpool City Council* v. *Irwin.* In this court the argument was only about an implication in the second category. In the House of Lords that argument was not pursued. It was only the first category.

Into which of the two categories does the present case come? I am tempted to say that a solus agreement between supplier and buyer is of such common occurrence nowadays that it could be put into the first category: so that the law could imply a term based on general considerations. But I do not think this would be found acceptable. Nor do I think the case can be brought within the second category. If the Shell company had been asked at the beginning: "Will you agree not to discriminate abnormally against the buyer?" I think they would have declined. It might be a reasonable term, but it is not a necessary term. Nor can it be formulated with sufficient precision. On this point I agree with Kerr J. It should be noticed that in the *Esso* case Mocatta J. also refused to make such an implication: see [1966] 2 Q.B. 514, 536–541; and there was no appeal from his decision. In the circumstances, I do not think any term can be implied.

Restraint of trade

It is now settled beyond doubt that a solus agreement is a contract in restraint of trade: see *Esso Petroleum Co. Ltd.* v. *Harper's Garage* (*Stourport*) *Ltd.* [1968] A.C. 269. As such, it comes within that special class in which the courts can investigate the terms of the contract, and see whether they are fair and reasonable. If they are unfair or unreasonable, the courts may refuse to enforce them: see *Instone* v. *A. Schroeder Music Publishing Co. Ltd.* [1974] 1 W.L.R. 1308, 1315–1316, where Lord Diplock puts the doctrine in its modern setting.

In the general run of cases the courts consider the reasonableness at the time when the contract is made. If the terms impose a restraint which is unreasonable in the sense that it may work unfairly in circumstances which may reasonably be anticipated, the courts will refuse to enforce the restraint: but it will not hold it to be unenforceable simply because it might work unfairly in certain exceptional circumstances outside the reasonable expectation of the parties at the time of making the agreement: see *Commercial Plastics Ltd.* v. *Vincent* [1965] 1 Q.B. 623, 644 and *Home Counties Dairies Ltd.* v. *Skilton* [1970] 1 W.L.R. 526, 533, 536.

Testing this contract at the time it was made—or rather when it was varied in 1966—there was nothing unreasonable about the tie. It was only for five years, during which it was legitimate for Shell to preserve this outlet by means of a tie. Nothing unreasonable was foreseen. At that time the parties did not anticipate that circumstances would arise in which Shell should subsidise neighbouring garages to such an extent as to force Lostock to trade at a loss. That contingency was so improbable and extravagant that it would not invalidate the tie at the time it was made.

But now that the improbable and unforeseen event has happened, does it mean that the tie can be enforced when it would be most unfair and unreasonable to do so? If such an event had been foreseen as probable, the courts would have held that the restraint was unreasonable and would not have enforced it. Now that it has been proved in practice to be unreasonable, are the courts bound to enforce it? I do not think so. I can, of course, see the argument on the other side. It is said that "a covenant in restraint of trade is invalid ab initio, or valid ab initio. There cannot come a moment at which it passes from the class of invalid into that of valid covenants": see *Gledhow Autoparts Ltd.* v. *Delaney* [1965] 1 W.L.R. 1366, 1377 by Diplock L.J. But there is a fallacy in this argument. It is a mistake to say that a covenant in unreasonable restraint of trade is "invalid" or "void" ab initio. It is nothing of the sort. It is only unenforceable. Lord Reid made this clear in *Esso Petroleum Co. Ltd.* v. *Harper's Garage (Stourport) Ltd.* [1968] A.C. 269, 297, when he said:

> "One must always bear in mind that an agreement in restraint of trade is not generally unlawful if the parties choose to abide by it: it is only unenforceable if a party chooses not to abide by it."

And all the members of the House were careful to use the word "unenforceable" rather than "void" or "invalid": see Lord Morris at p. 304: Lord Hodson at p. 321: Lord Pearce at p. 324: and Lord Wilberforce at p. 333.

Once it is recognised that the covenant itself is not invalid or void, but only unenforceable, the position becomes clear. It operates in two situations. First, when *at the time* of making the contract, it is seen that it may *in the future* operate unfairly or unreasonably, the courts will not enforce it. Secondly, when it is found *afterwards* to operate unreasonably or unfairly—in circumstances which were not envisaged beforehand—the courts will not enforce it. At the time of making the contract, the court has to speculate whether or not the restraint will operate unfairly or unreasonably: but if it afterwards turns out to have operated in fact unfairly or unreasonably, there is no need to speculate. The facts are known. The court never speculates as to what may happen when it knows for certain what has happened: see *Williamson* v. *John L. Thornycroft & Co. Ltd.* [1940] 2 K.B. 658. The court should, therefore, not enforce a covenant in restraint of trade if circumstances afterwards arise in which it would be unreasonable or unfair to enforce it. This reasoning finds its exact parallel in the modern law as to exemption clauses, already in contracts for the sale of goods, and it may be extended to other fields as well. In the sale of goods, a party is not entitled to rely on an exemption clause which is seen at the time of the contract to be unfair or unreasonable. In addition, he is not entitled to rely on an exemption clause which, although superficially reasonable at the time of the contract, nevertheless is prayed in aid in circumstances when it is unfair or unreasonable for him to rely on it: see the Supply of Goods (Implied Terms) Act 1973, bringing a new section 55A into section 55 of the Sale of Goods Act 1893: and the *Second Report of the Law Commission and the Scottish Law Commission on Exemption Clauses* (1975) (Cmnd. 605), in paragraphs 178 to 183, pp.

69–71, which are well worth reading in this context: and my own few words in *Gillespie Bros. & Co. Ltd.* v. *Roy Bowles Transport Ltd.* [1973] Q.B. 400, 415–416.

Applying this test, what do we find here? Shell stipulated in 1966 that the garage owner should be tied to Shell and buy petrol only from Shell for five years at the schedule price (less a rebate) and should keep open the garage all day and every day during that time. That stipulation appeared superficially to be fair and reasonable at the time of the contract in 1966. But at the end of 1975, Shell started to subsidise two neighbouring Shell garages to such an extent that they were able to, and did, undercut Lostock. This meant that customers would flock to the other two Shell garages and not buy from Lostock at all: unless Lostock reduced their prices to a competitive level, and this would cause Lostock serious loss. To insist on the tie in these circumstances—and forcing Lostock to keep open paying wages to men—was most unfair and unreasonable. So much so that I think the courts should decline to enforce it. At any rate, they should not enforce it so long as Shell operated their support scheme to the prejudice of Lostock. This was the view of the judge and I agree with it.

"He who comes to equity"

There is another way of reaching the same result. As I have already said, I do not think there was any implied term that Shell would not abnormally discriminate against Lostock. So there was no breach of contract by Shell. Nevertheless, there was conduct by Shell which was unfair to Lostock. It was not done by Shell deliberately so as to injure Lostock. It was done to avoid the impact of the Price Code—so as not to break the code in the overall conduct of their business. But whatever the reason, the fact is that Shell insisted on maintaining the tie in circumstances where it was unfair and unreasonable for them to do so. To my mind this frees the garage from the tie during the time when the support scheme was operated by Shell to the prejudice of the garage. At any rate no court would grant Shell an injunction against the garage. It is well settled that "he who comes to equity must do equity." I need only refer to such cases as *Stickney* v. *Keeble* [1915] A.C. 386, 419; *Measure Brothers Ltd.* v. *Measures* [1910] 2 Ch. 248 and *Chappell* v. *Times Newspapers Ltd.* [1975] 1 W.L.R. 482, 495. So long as Shell were operating the support scheme to the prejudice of Lostock, a court of equity would not grant Shell any equitable relief by way of injunction or otherwise. And a court of law would not grant Shell any damages, because they could prove no loss, and in any case they were themselves the cause of any loss. If Shell had continued the support scheme for any substantial length of time—so that it struck at the root of the consideration for the tie—Lostock might have been relieved altogether from the tie. But as the support scheme was short-lived, Lostock were only relieved of the tie during its continuance.

Conclusion

Such being the law, I return to the facts. I think that, on discovering the support scheme, Lostock were justified in buying their supplies from Mansfield from January 29, 1976, to March 6, 1976. During that time Lostock suffered no loss. From March 6, 1976, to April 30, 1976, in consequence of pressure exerted by Shell, Lostock bought from Shell at the schedule price but had to sell at a loss in order to keep their customers. A They should be given compensation for this loss. It was agreed at £482. On April 30, 1976, the support scheme was ended. So Lostock suffered no further loss by it. From that time forward they again became bound by the tie. This seems to me to meet the justice of the case. Neither side gets an injunction against the other. The situation reverts to what it was before Shell started the support scheme. The tie remains until the solus agreement comes to an end on March 4 next year. But Lostock B gets £482 compensation. I agree with Kerr J. I would, therefore, dismiss both the appeal and cross-appeal.

ORMROD L.J. I agree with Kerr J. in his conclusion that most of the points raised in the defence and in the course of Mr. Kemp's argument are purely semantic. The court is, or ought to be, primarily concerned to C see that agreements entered into in the course of business are effective in law; it is no part of the court's function to pick such an agreement to pieces with logical tweezers in order to categorise it in such a way as to render it ineffectual. I accordingly reject all Mr. Kemp's arguments directed to showing that the contract of March 1955 was not a valid and binding agreement, at any rate up to the end of 1975, or the introduction by Shell of their so-called competitive price scheme in the area where D Lostock Garage Ltd. carry on business.

The only point of substance in the defence is contained in paragraph 16 of the defence and counterclaim. In its final, reamended form, this alleges that the contract was subject to a number of implied terms which, in summary, amount to (i) an implied term that Shell would not abnormally discriminate against Lostock in such a way as to render their E petrol sales not economically viable; and (ii) that Shell would not seek to enforce the "tie" during any period while abnormally discriminating against Lostock. Mr. Kemp has argued strenuously that in the absence of some such implied term Lostock are at the mercy of Shell who could force them out of the petrol retailing business by subsidising competitors on the one hand, and insisting on the "tie" on the other. F

Kerr J. rejected this submission altogether, saying that the formulation of implied terms for "the mere purpose of dealing ex post facto with unexpected situations should be rejected," on the ground that it is a purely artificial device. With respect, I do not think that this, by itself, is a sufficient reason for excluding the possibility of implying a term or terms in a contract. Nevertheless, Mr. Kemp has two extremely formidable obstacles to surmount. The House of Lords, in *Liverpool City Council* v. G *Irwin* [1976] 2 W.L.R. 562, has recently reviewed the law on this question and has affirmed the principle that where the parties have entered into a carefully drafted written contract containing detailed terms agreed between them, as in this case, the court should only imply a term or terms if it is "necessary" to do so. This necessity test is a stringent one, and, in my judgment, the proposed terms go well beyond the bound of necessity. H Lostock might, perhaps, be able to insist on an implied term that Shell would not deliberately or intentionally use the "tie" to injure it in its petrol retailing business, for example, by opening and subsidising a filling station in its immediate neighbourhood, because, using the "officious bystander" test, while Shell would almost certainly have rejected the suggestion that express terms such as those proposed in the defence should be included in the agreement, they would probably have agreed to give an

A undertaking not to do anything intentionally to injure their customer's business.

The second obstacle is the difficulty in formulating the proposed terms, as demonstrated by the vagueness and the ambiguity inherent in such words as "discriminate" and "abnormality." The suggested term might lead to greater difficulty, especially in relation to Plumleys. This business, which is owned by Shell, might be preferentially treated by Shell in all
B kinds of ways, for example, by capital loans on very advantageous terms or by being deliberately run at a loss for a time or by being overstaffed, not for the purpose of reducing the defendants' sales but to promote the growth of their own business. Would this amount to "abnormal discrimination"? If it does, is it conceivable that Shell would have accepted an express term in the contract to that effect? The proposed terms
C certainly fall foul of Lord Goddard C.J.'s test in *Rex* v. *Paddington and St. Marylebone Rent Tribunal, Ex parte Bedrock Investments Ltd.* [1947] K.B. 984. There is an additional reason for caution in the present case and that lies in clause 8 of the agreement. Under this clause either party may terminate the contract completely and immediately by notice "in the event of any breach whatsoever." So, for an unwitting breach of a term which does not appear on the face of the contract, one party might be
D faced with loss of all his rights under the contract.

Accordingly, I agree with Kerr J., although for different reasons, that Mr. Kemp's submission on this part of the case also fails. The consequence is that in my judgment the defendants are still bound by the agreement of March, 1955, and are in breach of the "tie." I have had an opportunity of reading the judgment which Bridge L.J. is about to
E deliver but regret that I am unable to agree with it, partly because it seems to me to depend upon a point which was not pleaded or argued, partly because it is open, though to a lesser degree, to the same objections which have led me to reject Mr. Kemp's submission.

Without a much closer examination of the facts I would hesitate to conclude that the inclusion of Plumleys and Barbers in the scheme would
F have had more than a marginal and temporary adverse effect on the defendants' business. For these reasons I would dismiss the defendants' appeal and hold that they were, and are, bound by the March 1955 contract.

It remains to deal with the cross-appeal. The plaintiffs seek to enforce the terms of their contract but Kerr J. refused to do so on the grounds of public policy. He said:

G "However reluctant the courts are to grasp the nettle of public policy, I have come to the conclusion that this case presents a situation in which they cannot avoid doing so. The whole of the law concerning agreements in restraint of trade is founded on considerations of the public interest. The law enforces such agreements if the restrictions imposed on the covenantor are not greater than is reasonably necessary
H when balanced against the legitimate interests of the covenantee. Such agreements are therefore only enforced when they strike a balance which is consistent with the public interest. But when unforeseen and unforeseeable acts by the covenantee disturb this balance in his favour, to an extent which renders the covenant harsh and oppressive upon the covenantor, then I think that considerations of public policy should lead the courts to refuse their aid to the enforcement of the covenant, at any rate so long as this imbalance persists."

While sympathising with his wish to relieve Lostock temporarily of their obligation to buy only Shell petrol at an uneconomic price, I do not think that it is possible to achieve this result in this entirely novel way. There is no authority to support it. It would introduce into the law an unprecedented discretion in the court to suspend for a time a term in a contract; the repercussions of this are quite unforeseeable and unmanageable. For example, it would at once alter the approach of the courts to covenants in restraint of trade generally, because, if the restraint could be temporarily suspended when it was operating oppressively, many more covenants would pass the normal test at the time they were entered into. Moreover, neither party will be able to know when a covenant is or is not enforceable, or if temporarily unenforceable, when it becomes enforceable again.

However, a similar, though not identical, result can be achieved in another way. By their writ, Shell claimed (i) damages (ii) an order restraining Lostock from accepting supplies of petrol other than from Shell and (iii) an order that they remove petrol and advertising matter of Mansfield from their premises. This is in effect, though not in form, a claim for specific performance of the covenants contained in clause 4 of the contract. But it is a fundamental principle of equity that relief by way of decree of specific performance (or by injunction) will only be granted when "it is just and equitable so to do": *per* Lord Parker in *Stickney* v. *Keeble* [1915] A.C. 386, 419. "Thus the plaintiff will be left to his remedy at law if a decree of specific performance would inflict a hardship on the defendant . . .": see *Cheshire & Fifoot's Law of Contract*, 9th ed. (1976), p. 613, and the cases there cited. I think that the defendants are in a position to show that the plaintiffs have inflicted hardship on them by making their position more difficult by helping Plumleys and Barbers with their competitive price support scheme and refusing them similar assistance. So it would be reasonable to withhold, in the exercise of the discretion of the court, the remedy of specific performance (or its equivalent by way of injunction) so long as the plaintiffs are operating their scheme and excluding the defendants from it. So I agree to that extent with Kerr J.'s conclusion, although for different reasons. That leaves Shell to their remedy at law, that is, in damages, if they can prove they have suffered any loss. This is by no means certain since Lostock might have decided not to stock any petrol during the emergency; and in any event would have sold little or no petrol after January, 1976, if they could only have afforded to sell it at the normal price, that is, if the terms of the contract had been performed.

I would, therefore, dismiss the defendants' appeal and allow the cross-appeal to the extent of setting aside the judgment of the court below and ordering, if Shell want it, an inquiry as to damages. What effect this conclusion will have on the compromise agreement made on March 23, 1976, may be a matter for argument.

BRIDGE L.J. It was contended for the defendants (Lostock), at the trial and in this court that the solus agreement could not be enforced against them on a number of grounds unrelated to the introduction by the plaintiffs (Shell) of their "competitive price support scheme" ("the scheme"). I agree with the judge in rejecting all these contentions and with the reasons he gave for so doing. Having stated the relevant facts with respect to the introduction of the scheme, the judge continued:

> "What then is the legal position in these circumstances? The authorities clearly show that the reasonableness or otherwise of an agree-

A ment in restraint of trade must be determined once and for all at the time when the agreement is concluded. They also show that in determining this, one must not have regard to improbable and extravagant contingencies which would be outside the reasonable contemplation of the parties at the time when the agreement was made."

Thus far I entirely agree with him. But the judge then concluded that
B the introduction of the scheme had brought about just such an improbable and extravagant contingency as to upset what he called the balance of the agreement and he held that on grounds of public policy this conduct on the part of Shell rendered the contract unenforceable in law for so long as Shell continued to discriminate against Lostock by the operation of the scheme, but no longer. With this view I cannot agree. A principle by the operation of which, according to the conduct of one of the parties,
C a contract may temporarily lose, but subsequently regain, its binding character, on grounds of public policy, or indeed on any other grounds, is, so far as I am aware, a complete novelty in the law. The introduction of such a principle seems to me to be open to formidable theoretical objections. But such a principle can in any event be of little value to the party in whose favour it is to operate. If a situation arises in which
D justice requires that one party to a contract should be relieved of his contractual obligations because of the conduct of the other party, it is of no practical assistance to him to tell him that he is free of the contract so long as the other party's offending conduct continues, but that, as soon as the other party chooses to desist, he will again be contractually bound. This leaves him in a kind of limbo in which he cannot predict whether or when the other party will unilaterally decide to reimpose contractual obliga-
E tions upon him, and makes it commercially impossible for him to plan and organise his affairs on a business-like footing.

I must add, with respect, that I do not find it any easier either to understand or to accept the novel principle after reading the exposition of it in the judgment of Lord Denning M.R. If it would be "most unfair and unreasonable" to hold a covenantor bound by his covenant when the
F covenantee discriminates against him, as Shell did against Lostock, I am concerned that, under the new doctrine, the law can give the covenantor no clear indication at the outset of the extent of the relief to which he is entitled. In this case nobody knew until after the trial how long the discrimination was going to continue. If Lord Denning M.R. is right in his conclusion, then presumably if Lostock had wanted to know at any time up to the end of April (when the scheme in fact ceased to operate) whether
G they were temporarily or permanently free of the tie to Shell, the only answer they could have been given would have been: "Wait and see. It depends whether the scheme continues for any substantial length of time." If they had then asked: "What is a substantial length of time?" I do not know what answer they would have received. All this introduces what is, to my mind, a most unsatisfactory state of uncertainty into the law.

H Whether the introduction by Shell of the scheme had any and, if so, what effect on the parties' contractual rights and obligations must depend, in my judgment, on the following questions: First, what, if any, term can be implied in the contract limiting Shell's freedom to discriminate against Lostock? Secondly, if a term can be implied, was there here a breach of it? Thirdly, if there was a breach, what was its effect?

It is clearly not possible to imply in this agreement a term which would inhibit Shell altogether from discriminating against Lostock. It is recognised that in the course of normal trading oil companies like the plaintiffs do in fact negotiate marginally different rates of rebate with different dealers with whom they enter into solus agreements. In some agreements, we are told, an express term is introduced to the effect that no other buyer shall be given more favourable terms than the contracting party. But it does not follow that in the absence of any such express term the plaintiffs must be at liberty to discriminate against the defendants to any degree. An extreme example will serve to illustrate that such a freedom on the part of the plaintiffs would lead to absurdity. Suppose that an oil company concludes a five-year solus agreement with A at a normal rate of rebate. If on the very next day the company were to conclude two other five-year solus agreements with B and C, A's nearest competitors, giving them in each case a rebate at a rate 10p. per gallon higher than the rate of rebate given to A, this would make it manifestly impossible for A to trade on the terms expressly agreed. To say that in those circumstances A must still be bound by his contract would be an absurdity. Obviously the parties as reasonable men cannot have intended such an absurdity. Accordingly, it seems to me to follow that the necessary foundation for the application of the classic doctrine on which terms are implied in contracts is here present. That doctrine, as I undertsand it, requires that terms should be implied to prevent contractual absurdities which reasonable parties cannot have intended.

The extreme difficulty which this case presents is that of defining appropriately the degree of discrimination which any implied term is to preclude. If one were to say that the plaintiffs must not discriminate abnormally, unfairly, or unreasonably, none of those criteria indicate where the line is to be drawn with any precision. If any term is to be implied, it may be appropriate to define it by reference to the necessary effect of the discrimination on the defendants. If the effect of the discrimination is, so long as it continues, such as to render it commercially impracticable for the defendants to continue to trade on the express contractual terms, then, in my judgment, one could say with confidence that the limitation to be imposed by implication on the plaintiffs' freedom to discriminate has been exceeded.

It is said that lack of precision in the criterion to be embodied in the implied term is fatal to any implication. But it is no novelty in the common law to find that a criterion on which some important question of liability is to depend can only be defined in imprecise terms which leave a difficult question for decision as to how the criterion applies to the facts of a particular case. A clear and distinct line of demarcation may be impossible to draw in abstract terms; yet the court does not shrink from the task of deciding on the facts of any case before it on which side of the line the case falls. This kind of pragmatism is so deeply entrenched in the common law's approach to a multitude of legal problems that I decline to accept that the difficulty of defining with precision what term is to be implied in this case is an insuperable obstacle to the implication of any term limiting the plaintiffs' freedom to discriminate. I am content, in my approach to the further questions arising, to take as the test of the degree of discrimination prohibited by the implied term whether it is such as to render the defendants' commercial operation of their petrol sales business impracticable.

The judge's finding on the all-important question of the effect of the discrimination on the defendants was as follows:

> A "I am satisfied on the evidence that, so long as the scheme lasts, the plaintiffs would be compelling the defendants to trade at a loss so far as their sales of petrol are concerned if the covenants in the agreement are enforceable against them. The defendants must continue to keep their premises open for the sale of petrol at all reasonable times. But so long as Barbers and the Plumley garage are supported and the defendants are not, as is the present position, I am satisfied
> B that the defendants must operate at a loss if the agreement is enforced. The advent of the V.I.P. garage, together with the operations of the I.C.I. and Esso garages, would probably in any event have put the defendants under great pressure and perhaps have forced them into a loss-making situation. This would be a situation which they would have had to accept. But the grant of the plaintiffs' price support
> C scheme to Barbers and Plumleys undoubtedly made their position much worse, and for the time being economically untenable so far as their sales of petrol are concerned."

This finding is amply justified by the evidence. Indeed the figures put before the court by the plaintiffs show that, quite apart from the effect of the sales of petrols other than Shell in the neighbourhood, the sale of Shell
D petrol by Plumleys and Barbers at 70p a gallon was bound to face the defendants with the alternatives of offering petrol at the same price and inevitably trading at a loss, or of offering petrol at the standard price of 75p a gallon and selling virtually no petrol at all. By the operation of the scheme the plaintiffs were in effect giving to Plumleys and Barbers a subsidy of about 5p a gallon which was not available to the defendants. This was, in my judgment, as a matter of fact and degree, a clear breach of the
E term against excessive discrimination to be implied in the solus agreement, however the criterion of excess be defined.

Mr. Durand argued that even if the discrimination would have amounted to a breach of contract by the plaintiffs if continued indefinitely, it did not, on the facts of this case, because of its temporary duration. It was at the end of January 1976 that the defendants had to make, and did make, their
F decision, and it is in the light of the facts as they then appeared that one must judge the parties' legal rights and obligations. I have not overlooked the circumstance that at this time Mr. Clarke erroneously believed that the contract between the plaintiffs and the defendants had expired by effluxion of time. If he believed his conduct to be justified in law on one ground but it was in fact justified on another ground I do not see any reason why his error should prevent him from relying on that other ground
G in these proceedings. The relevant findings of the judge are as follows:

> "By January 23, Mr. Clarke had for the first time heard rumours that the plaintiffs were proposing to introduce their price support scheme in his area. He believed, correctly, that it would be offered to Barbers and Plumleys and that they would no doubt accept it. The remaining question was whether or not it would be offered to
> H him."

The judge goes on to find that, when the plaintiffs' representative saw Mr. Clarke on January 29, he told him that his garage would not be included in the scheme. It was then that Mr. Clarke finally decided to take Mansfield petrol and it is then that one must ask whether he was in breach of contract in doing so. It seems to me that on the facts at that stage there was no means of foretelling how long the situation was to continue in which the

defendants' Shell competitors were to be subsidised but the defendants A
were not. Accordingly, in my judgment, it is the character of the dis-
crimination at its inception which determines the legal result in this case
and not its duration, as it turned out in the event.

This brings me to the final question. What was the effect of the breach?
If there is to be implied in the contract such a term limiting discrimination
as I have sought to indicate, it must be a term which has both a negative
and a positive aspect. Its negative aspect precludes Shell from offering B
to the Lostock's competitors terms which are, to an extent which the
implied term prohibits, more favourable than the terms available to
Lostock. Its positive aspect imposes an obligation on Shell to supply to
Lostock on terms which are not, to the extent which the implied term
prohibits, less favourable to Lostock than the terms on which his com-
petitors are supplied. Thus in its positive aspect the implied term operates C
as a gloss on the express obligation which the contract imposes on Shell
to supply their products to Lostock "at the wholesale scheduled price . . .
ruling at the date and place of delivery."

On this view of the matter it seems to me to follow that Shell, when
their representative told Mr. Clarke that he could only be supplied at
the normal price, notwithstanding the subsidy to his competitors, were
refusing to perform their own essential obligation under the contract and D
thereby were not merely in breach of it but were repudiating it. The case
was argued before us by Mr. Kemp for Lostock on the basis, inter alia,
that there had been such a repudiation by Shell and that Lostock had
accepted it. Lostock rely in their pleadings on a repudiation of the agree-
ment by Shell and also on a breach of an implied term against discrimina-
tion. But by a curious omission, to which attention was not drawn in the E
course of the argument, the alleged breach of the implied term is not, as
a matter of pleading, expressly relied on as a repudiation. For my part, I
do not think that this technical shortcoming in the pleading should prevent
the court from giving effect to the conclusion which I have stated. The
main question which the parties came to this court to have determined was
whether Lostock were or were not bound by the contract after the scheme
ceased to be operated. For the reasons I have sought to explain I think F
they were not.

At the end of the day therefore I find myself in agreement with Lord
Denning M.R. that Shell's cross-appeal should be dismissed, though for
quite different reasons. As I am in a minority in thinking that Lostock's
appeal should be allowed, it is unnecessary to consider what would be the
appropriate relief to give effect to this view if it were to prevail. G

Appeal and cross-appeal dismissed.
Discussion on damages, costs and leave to appeal to House of Lords adjourned.

Solicitors: *Bristows, Cooke & Carpmael; Rowe & Maw.* H

M. M. H.

A [QUEEN'S BENCH DIVISION]

* CAWLEY v. FROST

1976 July 29 — Lord Widgery C.J., Melford Stevenson and Caulfield JJ.

B
Crime—Public order—"Public place"—Football ground—Football pitch surrounded by speedway track—Public having no access to track or pitch—Threatening behaviour on speedway track —Whether "public place"—Public Order Act 1936 (1 *Edw.* 8 & 1 *Geo.* 6, *c.* 6), *s.* 9 (1) (*as substituted by Criminal Justice Act* 1972 (*c.* 71), *s.* 33)

The defendant was a spectator at a football match. The
C football pitch was surrounded by a speedway track about seven
yards wide, where the public were not allowed. The spectators
were separated from the track and the pitch by a fence. At
the conclusion of the match the rival spectators climbed over
the fence and surged on to the pitch, running across the track,
shouting abuse at each other. The defendant was arrested
on the speedway track and was charged with using threatening
behaviour in a public place contrary to section 5 of the Public
D Order Act 1936. He was convicted before the juvenile court.
His appeal to the Crown Court was allowed on the ground
that although he was guilty of threatening behaviour the speed-
way track was not a public place.

On appeal by the prosecutor on the ground that the whole of the football ground was a "public place" within the definition in section 9 (1) of the Act of 1936 [1]:—

Held, allowing the appeal, that, where the public had
E access to premises, those premises should be considered in
their entirety and the fact that the public were denied access
to certain areas of the premises did not exclude those areas
from being part of a "public place" within the meaning of
section 9 of the Act of 1936; that the football ground, in-
cluding all its appurtenances, formed a public place and,
accordingly, the defendant had committed an offence contrary
to section 5 of the Act (post, pp. 1211F–H, 1212C–D, E–H).

F

The following case is referred to in the judgment of Melford Stevenson J.:

Cozens v. *Brutus* [1972] 1 W.L.R. 484; [1972] 2 All E.R. 1, D.C.

The following additional cases were cited in argument:

Cooper v. *Shield* [1971] 2 Q.B. 334; [1971] 2 W.L.R. 1385; [1971] 2
G All E.R. 917, D.C.

Reg. v. *Kane* [1965] 1 All E.R. 705.

Reg. v. *Waters* (1963) 47 Cr.App.R. 149, C.C.A.

Wilson v. *Skeock* (1949) 113 J.P. 294; 47 L.G.R. 499, D.C.

CASE STATED by Bradford Crown Court.

On November 4, 1975, the defendant, John Joseph Cawley, was arrested
H without warrant and charged that he, at the Shay Football Ground,
Halifax on Tuesday November 4, 1975, used threatening, abusive, insulting
words or behaviour whereby a breach of the peace was occasioned or was
likely to be occasioned contrary to section 5 of the Public Order Act 1936.

[Reported by MRS. H. WHICHER, Barrister-at-Law]

[1] Public Order Act 1936, s. 9 (1), as substituted: see post, 1211D.

On November 27, 1975, the Halifax juvenile court heard the charge A
and adjudged that the defendant was guilty as charged and ordered him to pay a fine of £30 within 20 days of the adjudication.

The defendant appealed against the conviction on the ground that the verdict was against the weight of the evidence; that the defendant was not guilty of the offence; that the charge against him did not disclose an offence and further and in the alternative that even if it did disclose an offence the charge was bad for duplicity and/or uncertainty. B

The Bradford Crown Court heard the appeal on March 18, 1976, when evidence was given by witnesses for the defendant of the following facts. The ground of the Halifax Town Association Football Club was at the Shay, Halifax where the football pitch was surrounded by a motorcycle speedway track about seven yards wide. Spectator stands surrounded the speedway track and were separated from it by a hardboard fence four feet C
high. When a football match was played at the Shay, members of the public were admitted on payment to the stands but were not permitted to go onto the speedway track or football pitch. No means of access from the public stands to the track was provided and the football pitch could be reached only by crossing the track. The purpose of the fence was to prevent access by the public to the pitch and track and one of the duties of police officers in attendance at the ground was to keep the public off those D
areas. On the evening of November 4, 1975, Halifax Town played Preston North End at the Shay. The bulk of the Halifax supporters were in the west stand and the bulk of the Preston supporters were diagonally across the ground from them in the east stand and a number of police officers, including P.C. Sharp and P.C. Hume, were stationed on the speedway track in front of the Preston supporters. During the match the rival E
factions shouted aggressive slogans at each other. At one stage the Preston supporters swayed towards the fence and were warned back by P.C. Sharp who feared that they would cross the fence and move towards the Halifax supporters, who were acting in a similar manner on the other side of the ground. At the end of the match about 200 Halifax supporters invaded the pitch and started to cross it diagonally, shouting, jeering and clapping their hands above their heads. P.C. Sharp went onto the pitch with a police F
dog to prevent them reaching the Preston supporters, who had themselves a little earlier been throwing stones at the line of police. Most of the 200 or so Preston supporters then came over the fence and ran towards the advancing Halifax supporters shouting threatening and provocative phrases. It appeared to the police officers that if the rival groups were allowed to meet a fight would be inevitable. The only witness who saw the defendant G
before his arrest was P.C. Hume, who first saw him running with the crowd of Preston supporters across the speedway track. He was stopped by P.C. Hume when he had almost reached the football pitch and when told that he was being arrested for a breach of the peace said, "I was only running across the field." Later at the police station, when asked by the same officer why he had run onto the field he replied, "I was pushed over the fence by the crowd behind me." H

At the close of the case for the defendant the following contentions were advanced on his behalf: that there was no evidence that his behaviour had been threatening, abusive or insulting; that even if the court were to hold that the evidence could support a finding that the defendant had used threatening behaviour whereby a breach of the peace was likely to have been occasioned, the only place in which such behaviour could be said to have taken place was the speedway track; that the speedway track was not a place to which the public had or were permitted to have access within the meaning of section 9 (1) of the Public Order Act 1936, as substituted by section 33 of the Criminal Justice Act 1972. It was accordingly submitted that there was no case for the defendant to answer.

It was contended on behalf of the prosecutor, Kenneth Frost, that there was evidence that the defendant had used threatening behaviour whereby a breach of the peace was likely to be occasioned and that although the public were not permitted to have access to the speedway track the Shay football ground should be regarded as one complete entity and as such was a public place. It was further contended that the case was similar to *Cozens* v. *Brutus* [1972] 1 W.L.R. 484 in which the Divisional Court by implication had decided that the no. 2 court at the All England Lawn Tennis Club, Wimbledon, was an open space to which the public had or were permitted to have access despite a finding of fact in that case that no person was permitted at any time to go onto the playing area of any of the courts or any of the grass immediately adjacent to the playing area other than the players, ballboys or club officials.

The court rejected the first contention made on behalf of the defendant, being of the opinion that there was evidence sufficient to justify a finding that his behaviour was threatening on the basis that he was a willing participant in a threatening display. The court was further of the opinion that the evidence was sufficient to justify a finding that the defendant's behaviour was such that a breach of the peace was likely to be occasioned thereby. Although the court considered that the evidence warranted the inference that the defendant had left the stand voluntarily it accepted the second contention made on his behalf, being of the opinion that any behaviour of his contrary to the statute could be found to have taken place only on the speedway track.

The court was further of the opinion that the speedway track was not a place to which at the material time the public had or were permitted to have access. It distinguished this case from *Cozens* v. *Brutus* [1972] 1 W.L.R. 484 on the ground that the speedway track and football pitch formed a substantial part of the Shay football ground whereas an essential part of the prosecution's contention before the justices in *Cozens* v. *Brutus* was that the area prohibited to the public was a small part of a large complex. It also appeared to the court that although the opinion of the Divisional Court was that no. 2 court was an open space it did not purport to give any guidance on the question whether it was a place to which the public had or were permitted to have access. The court therefore upheld the submission and allowed the appeal.

The prosecutor appealed. The question for the opinion of the High Court was whether or not the court's decision was correct in law, having regard to the evidence given before it.

J. W. Mellor for the prosecutor.
David Gothorp for the defendant.

LORD WIDGERY C.J. I will ask Melford Stevenson J. to give the first judgment.

MELFORD STEVENSON J. This is a prosecutor's appeal from a determination of the Crown Court sitting at Bradford, presided over by Judge Hartley with two justices, who on March 18, 1976, allowed an appeal from a decision of the Halifax juvenile court given on November 27,

1975, in a case where the defendant was charged that he, at the Shay A
Football Ground, Halifax, on Tuesday, November 4, used threatening, abusive, insulting words or behaviour whereby a breach of the peace was likely to be occasioned, that being an offence under section 5 of the Public Order Act 1936. The justices convicted the defendant and imposed a fine of £30.

On appeal to the Bradford Crown Court that conviction was quashed,
and it is against the order quashing that conviction that this prosecutor's B
appeal is brought.

It is desirable I should read the facts quoted from the evidence which are set out at paragraph 4 of the case stated by the judge. He says:

> "The ground of the Halifax Town Association Football Club was at the Shay, Halifax where the football pitch was surrounded by a
> motorcycle speedway track about seven yards wide. Spectator stands C
> surrounded the speedway track and were separated from it by a hardboard fence four feet high. When a football match was played at the Shay, members of the public were admitted on payment to the stands but were not permitted to go onto the speedway track or football pitch. No means of access from the public stands to the
> track was provided and the football pitch could be reached only by D
> crossing the track. The purpose of the fence was to prevent access by the public to the pitch and track and one of the duties of police officers in attendance at the ground was to keep the public off those areas."

A state of affairs with which most of us are familiar. On November 4,
1975, in the evening, Halifax Town played Preston North End at the E
Shay. The case goes on:

> "The bulk of the Halifax supporters were in the West Stand and the bulk of the Preston supporters were diagonally across the ground from them in the East Stand and a number of police officers, including P.C. Sharp and P.C. Hume, were stationed on the speedway track in front of the Preston supporters. During the match the rival
> factions shouted aggressive slogans at each other. At one stage the F
> Preston supporters swayed towards the fence and were warned back by P.C. Sharp who feared that they would cross the fence and move towards the Halifax supporters, who were acting in a similar manner on the other side of the ground. At the end of the match about 200 Halifax supporters invaded the pitch and started to cross it diagonally,
> shouting, jeering and clapping their hands above their heads. P.C. G
> Sharp went onto the pitch with a police dog to prevent them reaching the Preston supporters, who had themselves a little earlier been throwing stones at the line of police. Most of the 200 or so Preston supporters then came over the fence and ran towards the advancing Halifax supporters shouting threatening and provocative
> phrases," H

which are set out in the paragraph and include a great deal of abusive and obscene language. Then the case goes on to state, I think perhaps rather naively,

> "It appeared to the police officers that if the rival groups were allowed to meet a fight would be inevitable. The only witness who saw the defendant before his arrest was P.C. Hume, who first saw him running with the crowd of Preston supporters across the speed-

A way track. He was stopped by P.C. Hume when he had almost reached the football pitch and when told that he was being arrested for a breach of the peace said 'I was only running across the field.' Later at the police station, when asked by the same officer why he had run onto the field he replied 'I was pushed over the fence by the crowd behind me.'"

B It is worth observing perhaps that the justices rejected that statement by the defendant.

We are in this case, I think, concerned only with one question, and that arises out of the contention on behalf of the prosecutor, that the Shay Football Ground should be regarded as one complete entity and as such was a public place.

The Crown Court found that the speedway track—the seven yards C wide track—was not a place to which at the material time the public had or were permitted to have access. They then went on to consider the authority of *Cozens* v. *Brutus* [1972] 1 W.L.R. 484 and to examine what was said in that case about the no. 2 court at Wimbledon.

I do not think we are concerned with that or any similar question in this case. What we are concerned with is the question whether under D section 33 of the Criminal Justice Act 1972, which has substituted the definition of a "public place" which appears in section 9 (1) of the Public Order Act 1936, this speedway track can properly be treated as part of a public place. The substituted definition is in these terms:

> "'Public place' includes any highway and any other premises or place to which at the material time the public have or are permitted to have access, whether on payment or otherwise."

E

I have to consider whether the Crown Court was correct in differentiating the area of the speedway track so as to treat it as losing the character of a public place because it was not a part of the general football ground or general stadium, if that is an appropriate word, which was used for football matches and for motor cycle racing.

Speaking for myself, and looking at the facts which emerge from this F case stated, I cannot escape from the view that the Shay ground including all its appurtenances together formed a public place for the purposes of the Act of 1936, and that the defendant in running onto it in the circumstances I have described on the findings of the court below did commit the offence with which he was originally charged before the Halifax justices.

I fully appreciate that, where you are dealing with what may be G generally described as a stadium or area which is designed for various forms of public entertainment, such an area may well include parts to which the public are not expected to go, and indeed steps may be taken to exclude them from it. A fairly obvious example is a kitchen or restaurant on a race course. It may be some part of the stabling which is normally part of a race course complex. It is an easy but I think not a useful expenditure of time to multiply examples of that kind.

H Every such case must depend on its own facts, but I am left in no doubt on the description of the Shay at Halifax which is set out in the case we are now dealing with that this speedway track was a part of a public place. The fact that there was a fence obviously designed to discourage, if not prevent, members of the public from jumping over it and onto the pitch is fairly obvious. But in my view that makes no difference whatever for the purpose of deciding whether this offence was committed in the kind of public place which this statute contemplates.

I would therefore allow this appeal. I do not find it necessary to refer A
to a large number of authorities which have been cited because I do not think any of them help. This is a question of fact in every case, and I think the facts here should be determined in the way I have indicated. I would therefore allow this appeal and send the matter back to the Crown Court with a direction to continue the hearing.

B

CAULFIELD J. I agree. To support the decision of the Crown Court in this case means that those who are disposed to be hooligans in Halifax during a football match can delight themselves by insulting each other to the annoyance of the public provided they restrict their arguments and their insulting words to the speedway that surrounds the football pitch.

I am of course, in relating the facts in this way, showing or trying to show the absurdity of such a situation from the point of view of common C
sense, but I approach my decision on the interpretation of "public place" as contained in the Act of 1936. The words to which I pay particular attention are the words "premises or place." In any particular case, whether it be the Ascot Race Course, Old Trafford Football Ground or Cricket Ground, or the Shay at Halifax, I think the proper approach is to identify the premises to which the public have access and then to decide whether or not there has been an offence committed in those premises. D

It is plain in my judgment from the facts here that the speedway track surrounding the football pitch was part of the premises. In those circumstances the finding of the Crown Court in my judgment is wrong. I would therefore follow the course that this case should be remitted to continue the hearing.

E

LORD WIDGERY C.J. I agree with both judgments and with the order proposed. It must be remembered, I think, that the Public Order Act 1936 was designed to promote good order in places to which the public have access. That was the purpose of the Act itself. That may have an influence on its proper interpretation.

In my judgment where you have an establishment which is set up to provide for the public, such as the Halifax Town Football Club or Wembley F
Stadium, one ought to approach it on the basis that this is a public place in its entirety. I do not think that one ought to be in any way influenced against that conclusion by the fact that for the convenience of organising the crowds, or otherwise for administrative purposes, certain areas within the stadium have been roped off and are denied to the public by the intervention of the police. The fact that areas of that kind are not in fact to G
be enjoyed by the public on a given occasion does not justify the apportionment of the total establishment into a number of separate parts and the application of a separate judgment to each part. Prima facie you look at the whole establishment and you are not, as I say, deterred from doing that merely by finding that certain portions of the establishment have been denied to the public for one reason or another.

The case therefore will go back for the Bradford Crown Court to H
continue the hearing.

Appeal allowed.
Prosecutor's costs out of central funds.
Legal aid taxation of defendant's costs.

Solicitors: *Hewitt, Woollacott & Chown for M. D. Shaffner, Wakefield; Shuttleworth, Dallas & Crombleholme, Preston.*

A

[COURT OF APPEAL]

* FERGUSON *v.* JOHN DAWSON & PARTNERS (CONTRACTORS) LTD.

B [1973 F. No. 121]

1976 June 21, 22, 23; July 22 — Megaw, Lawton and Browne L.JJ.

Master and Servant—Contract of service—Service, of, or for services—Workman taken on as self-employed labour only sub-contractor—Whether label conclusive—Need to look at reality C *of relationship between parties as found in express and implied terms of contract*

Building—Safety regulations—"Working place"—Plaintiff engaged in throwing down scaffold boards from roof—Fall from roof —No guard-rail—Whether breach of statutory duty—Judge's finding that work would have taken 10 or 15 minutes—Whether appreciable time—Construction (Working Places) Regulations 1966 (*S.I.* 1966 *No.* 94), *reg.* 28 (1)

D

The defendants were contractors who had undertaken building work involving the use of scaffolding on a flat roof. After completion of that part of the work, the scaffolding was taken down, and the plaintiff workman was instructed by the defendants' site agent to remove some scaffold boards from the roof by throwing them down to the ground. While doing so, he fell off the roof and was injured. The roof was more E than six feet six inches above the ground, and was not provided with a guard-rail. The plaintiff claimed damages against the defendants for breach of statutory duty, relying on regulation 28 (1) of the Construction (Working Places) Regulations 1966.[1] The questions for decision at the trial were whether the roof had been a "working place" within regulation 28 (1) and whether the plaintiff had been employed by the defendants or had been an independent contractor. In his evidence, which F the judge accepted, the defendants' site agent said that when the plaintiff had been taken on by the defendants he had told him that "there were no cards, we were purely working as a lump labour force." The defendants did not make deductions in respect of income tax from their weekly payments to the plaintiff, nor any payments in respect of national insurance contributions. The judge found that the job of throwing down the scaffold boards would have taken 10 or 15 minutes, and G held that the flat roof had been the plaintiff's working place within regulation 28 (1). He said that he was satisfied that the plaintiff and the defendants had regarded the plaintiff as "a self-employed labour only subcontractor," but held that the concept of "the lump," in the circumstances of the case, was no more than a device which did not affect the relationship of the parties or the substance of the contract between them. He held that the relationship of master and servant had existed, H and gave judgment for the plaintiff.

On appeal by the defendants:—

Held, dismissing the appeal (Lawton L.J. dissenting), (1) (*per curiam*) that the 10 or 15 minutes required for the plaintiff's intended work had been an appreciable time, and accordingly the roof had been the plaintiff's working place and regulation 28 (1) applied (post, pp. 1217A–C, 1227G–H).

Gill v. *Donald Humberstone & Co. Ltd.* [1963] 1 W.L.R.

[1] Construction (Working Places) Regulations 1966, reg. 28 (1): see post, p. 1216C–D.

929, H.L.(E.); *Kelly* v. *Pierhead Ltd.* [1967] 1 W.L.R. 65, C.A. and *Boynton* v. *Willment Brothers Ltd.* [1971] 1 W.L.R. 1625, C.A. applied. A

(2) (Lawton L.J. dissenting) that, notwithstanding the label which the parties had put on their relationship to the effect that the plaintiff was to be, or was to be deemed to be, "a self-employed labour only subcontractor," there were other terms necessarily to be implied into the contract between them, including, on the evidence, that the defendants' site agent could B dismiss the workmen, including the plaintiff, that he could move men from site to site, that it was for the defendants to provide necessary tools, that it was for the defendants' site agent to tell the workmen, including the plaintiff, what work they were to do and that the men, including the plaintiff, were employed on an hourly basis and the money paid to them was correctly described as "a wage"; and that those terms indicated that the reality of the relationship between the defendants and C the plaintiff had been that of employer and employee (post, pp. 1221F—1222B, 1224D–F, 1229F—1230B).

Ready Mixed Concrete (South East) Ltd. v. *Minister of Pensions and National Insurance* [1968] 2 Q.B. 497 and *Market Investigations Ltd.* v. *Minister of Social Security* [1969] 2 Q.B. 173 approved.

Addiscombe Garden Estates Ltd. v. *Crabbe* [1958] 1 Q.B. 513, C.A. applied.

D

Global Plant Ltd. v. *Secretary of State for Social Services* [1972] 1 Q.B. 139 and *Maurice Graham Ltd.* v. *Brunswick* (1974) 16 K.I.R. 158, D.C. considered.

Decision of Boreham J. affirmed.

The following cases are referred to in the judgments:

Addiscombe Garden Estates Ltd. v. *Crabbe* [1958] 1 Q.B. 513; [1957] 3 W.L.R. 980; [1957] 3 All E.R. 563, C.A. E

Boynton v. *Willment Brothers Ltd.* [1971] 1 W.L.R. 1625; [1971] 3 All E.R. 624, C.A.

Construction Industry Training Board v. *Labour Force Ltd.* [1970] 3 All E.R. 220, D.C.

Facchini v. *Bryson* [1952] 1 T.L.R. 1386, C.A.

Gill v. *Donald Humberstone & Co. Ltd.* [1963] 1 W.L.R. 929; [1963] 3 All E.R. 180, H.L.(E.). F

Global Plant Ltd. v. *Secretary of State for Social Services* [1972] 1 Q.B. 139; [1971] 3 W.L.R. 269; [1971] 3 All E.R. 385.

Graham (Maurice) Ltd. v. *Brunswick* (1974) 16 K.I.R. 158, D.C.

Kelly v. *Pierhead Ltd.* [1967] 1 W.L.R. 65; [1967] 1 All E.R. 657, C.A.

Liverpool City Council v. *Irwin* [1976] 2 W.L.R. 562; [1976] 2 All E.R. 39, H.L.(E.).

Market Investigations Ltd. v. *Minister of Social Security* [1969] 2 Q.B. 173; [1969] 2 W.L.R. 1; [1968] 3 All E.R. 732. G

Ready Mixed Concrete (South East) Ltd. v. *Minister of Pensions and National Insurance* [1968] 2 Q.B. 497; [1968] 2 W.L.R. 775; [1968] 1 All E.R. 433.

Smith v. *George Wimpey & Co. Ltd.* [1972] 2 Q.B. 329; [1972] 2 W.L.R. 1166; [1972] 2 All E.R. 723, C.A.

Whitworth Street Estates (Manchester) Ltd. v. *James Miller & Partners* Ltd. [1970] A.C. 583; [1970] 2 W.L.R. 728; [1970] 1 All E.R. 796, H.L.(E.). H

Wickman Machine Tool Sales Ltd. v. *L. Schuler A.G.* [1974] A.C. 235; [1973] 2 W.L.R. 683; [1973] 2 All E.R. 39, H.L.(E.).

The following additional cases were cited in argument:

Binding v. *Great Yarmouth Port and Haven Commissioners* (1923) 16 B.W.C.C. 28, C.A.

A *Buchmann* v. *May* (1976) 120 S.J. 384; The Times, May 6, 1976, C.A.
Jones v. *Minton Construction Ltd.* (1973) 15 K.I.R. 309.

APPEAL from Boreham J.

The respondent plaintiff, Michael Joseph Ferguson, claimed against the appellant defendants, John Dawson & Partners (Contractors) Ltd., damages for personal injuries sustained by him when he fell from a roof. He alleged B that at all material times he had been employed by the defendants as a labourer and that his accident had been caused by their breach of their statutory duty under regulation 28 (1) of the Construction (Working Places) Regulations 1966. By their defence the defendants alleged that the plaintiff had been working at the place in question as a self-employed labour only subcontractor and denied that they had owed him any duties under C the Regulations of 1966. Boreham J., on July 28, 1975, gave judgment for the plaintiff. The defendants appealed, on the grounds that the judge erred in fact and in law in finding that it was the duty of the defendants to comply with such of the requirements of regulation 28 of the Construction (Working Places) Regulations 1966 as affected the plaintiff; that he erred in fact and in law in finding that the plaintiff was a workman "employed" by the defendants for the purposes of regulation 3 (1) (*a*) of the Regula- D tions of 1966 and not a "contractor"; that, having found that the plaintiff was engaged by the defendants expressly as a "labour only" subcontractor, and that the parties mutually regarded his subsequent status as such, he failed to accord effect in law to such status; that he erred in fact in finding that the roof from which the plaintiff fell was at the material time a working place within the meaning of regulation 28 of the Regulations of 1966; that he erred in fact in finding that the plaintiff had to work on the roof for E an appreciable time; that in any event he erred in fact in finding that (i) there was a considerable amount of rubble and debris distributed about the roof; (ii) the work that the plaintiff was then engaged in would take even 10 to 15 minutes to complete; (iii) the plaintiff had to spend a subsequent and appreciable period of time discharging rubble from the roof; that he erred in taking into account possible subsequent activities of the F plaintiff on the roof when assessing whether he was at the material time engaged in work likely to last an appreciable time; and that, having rejected the plaintiff's account as to the circumstances in which he was engaged by the defendants and having found that he had been a willing and active party to the dishonest evasion of income tax liability, he then accepted his evidence as to, respectively, the state of the roof, his activities thereon and the time that such activities would take in preference to such evidence as G was called on behalf of the defendants.

The facts are stated by Megaw L.J.

Oliver Popplewell Q.C. and *Christopher Holland* for the defendants.
Roy Beldam Q.C. and *Roger Hunt* for the plaintiff.

H *Cur. adv. vult.*

July 22. The following judgments were read.

MEGAW L.J. On April 19, 1972, the plaintiff, Mr. Michael Joseph Ferguson, fell some 15 feet from a flat roof on which he was working. He suffered serious injuries. He claimed damages for breach of statutory duty from the defendants, John Dawson & Partners (Contractors) Ltd.

The action was heard by Boreham J. at Leeds. On July 28, 1975, the judge gave judgment for the plaintiff for £30,387·88, including interest. The defendants appeal on issues as to liability. There is no appeal as to the amount of damages.

The facts of the accident are not in dispute. The defendants were contractors who had undertaken building operations for the extension of a shop building in Walmgate, York. The work had involved the use of scaffolding erected on a flat roof. The scaffolding, after that part of the work had been finished, was taken down. The day after it had been taken down the plaintiff was ordered by Mr. Murray, the defendants' site agent, to remove some 12 or 14 scaffold boards which had been left on the flat roof. There was also some rubble on the roof. The plaintiff was to throw the scaffold boards over the edge of the flat roof to the ground below. He had thrown down two or three boards. When he was engaged in throwing down another board, he stumbled and fell off the flat roof. There was no guard-rail on the flat roof.

Regulation 28 (1) of the Construction (Working Places) Regulations 1966, so far as is relevant, provides:

> "*Guard-rails and toe-boards at working platforms and places.* 28 (1) Every side of a working platform or working place, being a side thereof from which a person is liable to fall a distance of more than six feet six inches, shall, . . . be provided with a suitable guard-rail or guard-rails of adequate strength to a height of between three feet and three feet nine inches above the platform or place . . ."

Regulation 3 (1), so far as is relevant, reads:

> "It shall be the duty of every contractor, and every employer of workmen, who is undertaking any of the operations or works to which these regulations apply—(*a*) to comply with such of the requirements of the following regulations as affect him or any workman employed by him, that is to say, regulations 6 to 23, 25, 30, 31, 32, 36 and 38 and, in so far as they relate to the falling or slipping of persons, regulations 24, 26, 27, 28, 29, 33, 34 and 35: . . ."

The judge held, contrary to the defendants' submissions, (i) that the plaintiff was employed by the defendants so that the defendants owed to him the statutory duty comprised in regulation 28 (1), and (ii) that the place where the plaintiff was working when the accident happened, the flat roof, was a "working place" within regulation 28 (1). The defendants appeal on each of those issues.

I propose to deal first, out of logical order, with the second of those issues. The defendants have at all times conceded that this flat roof in all its characteristics except one would be a working place within the regulation. The one essential characteristic which is said to be missing is the length of time for which the place was going to be used by the plaintiff for the purposes of the work which he had been required to do. The authorities, *Gill* v. *Donald Humberstone & Co. Ltd.* [1963] 1 W.L.R. 929, a decision of the House of Lords, and *Kelly* v. *Pierhead Ltd.* [1967] 1 W.L.R. 65 and *Boynton* v. *Willment Brothers Ltd.* [1971] 1 W.L.R. 1625, decisions of this court, say that a necessary characteristic of a working place is that it is to be used for work for "an appreciable time." The defendants say that the intended use here, namely, the removal from the roof and the throwing to the ground of 12 or 14 scaffold boards, did not involve work at this place, on the flat roof, for "an appreciable time."

A The judge held on the evidence that that work would have taken about 10 or 15 minutes. The judge, in error, thought that the plaintiff's instructions had included also the removal of rubble from the roof. But in my judgment that mistake does not matter. In any ordinary use of the word "appreciable," which word is accepted by both parties as being the relevant adjective, the 10 or 15 minutes required for the plaintiff's intended work was an appreciable time. I do not find it necessary to consider the
B further submission by Mr. Beldam for the plaintiff that the evidence indicates that there must have been a substantial period of time during which work was being carried out, though not by the plaintiff himself, on this flat roof on the previous day and also on the morning of the accident. Mr. Popplewell submits that the plaintiff cannot rely upon such work by other persons to whom no duty may have been owed by the defendants.
C But the 10 or 15 minutes is an appreciable time. The appeal on that issue fails.

I turn to the other issue. Was the plaintiff employed by the defendants? For the plaintiff it is submitted that he was employed by the defendants under a contract of service. For the defendants it is contended that the contract was a contract for services, and that therefore the defendants were not under a statutory duty to him to provide a guard for the
D working place. For if it were a contract for services the plaintiff would not have been "employed" by the defendants, and in the circumstances of this accident regulation 3 (1) (*a*) would not have brought regulation 28 (1) into effect so as to impose on the defendants a duty towards the plaintiff. Regulation 28 (1) is brought into operation only in relation to "... the falling or slipping of persons, ..." (which this accident was) so far as
E the requirements of that regulation "... affect ... any workman employed by him, ..."—"him," here, being the defendants. Regulation 3 (1) (*b*) has a wider scope as regards the persons who are under the duty, but it is confined to "the falling of materials and articles."

It is conceded by the defendants that, if the plaintiff was employed under a contract of service, they were, subject only to the issue as to "appreciable time," under a duty to the plaintiff; they failed to carry out
F that duty, and that failure was the cause of the accident. But, say the defendants, the plaintiff was employed under a contract for services: he was "self-employed": he owed a statutory duty to himself to take the statutory precautions: *Smith* v. *George Wimpey & Co. Ltd.* [1972] 2 Q.B. 329. It was for him, under the regulations, not for the defendants, to ensure that the guard-rail was erected. The defendants were under no
G such duty.

What is the basis for that contention? The judge accepted the evidence given by Mr. Murray, the defendants' site agent, as to the circumstances in which the plaintiff came to work for the defendants in January 1972, some three months before the accident happened. The evidence was simply this: the plaintiff came with four other Irishmen, already working for the defendants, and asked, or perhaps one of his friends asked, if he
H could "come along." Mr. Murray's evidence is: "I said he could start on Monday and that was it. But I did inform him there were no cards, we were purely working as a lump labour force."

Mr. Ferguson gave a false name, Goff. That was the name by which he was known to Mr. Murray. That was the name in which he signed at least some receipts for the moneys paid to him weekly—referred to by Mr. Murray in evidence as "his wages." The evidence showed that, as was no doubt intended as a feature of the so-called "lump," the defendants did not make deductions in respect of income tax from the weekly payments to the plaintiff, nor did they make any payments in respect of national insurance contributions. They did not have his insurance card, nor his tax form, known as P.45. It is fair to the defendants to say that this engagement of the plaintiff, in January 1972, whatever its legal effect, was made some months before the provisions of section 28 of the Finance Act 1971 came into effect. When those provisions came into force on April 1, 1972, the defendants thereafter, up to the time of the accident, deducted 30 per cent. from the sums due to the plaintiff, since he did not have a certificate, as specified in the Act, entitling him to exemption from P.A.Y.E. deductions.

In the circumstances, although neither party has raised, nor wishes to raise, any issue as to possible illegality—arising in particular out of the judge's reference to the plaintiff's use of a false name in conjunction with the facilities afforded by "the lump" as being "a thoroughly dishonest device" for the purpose of evading his tax liabilities—we thought it right to raise the question on our own initiative. However, I think Mr. Beldam is justified in his submission that, however suspicious the facts may appear —and they are indeed gravely suspicious—it would not be right for this court to hold affirmatively that there was here dishonesty which would affect the contract, whatever it was, with illegality. Mr. Beldam stresses that the plaintiff has not been given the opportunity to answer any questions suggesting such dishonesty. He was not cross-examined on that topic. The defendants did not seek to raise it. The judge asked no questions about it. In those circumstances we did not think it necessary to consider further arguments which Mr. Beldam would have wished to present, if the court had held that there was here illegality affecting the contract, to the effect that in the circumstances such illegality of the contract or dishonesty of the plaintiff ought not to affect the plaintiff's right of recovery for a breach of statutory duty by the defendants, even though the defendants were themselves innocent of any complicity in the dishonesty and illegality. Moreover, if dishonesty and illegality were to be an issue, it would have been for consideration whether questions of possible complicity by the defendants might not also have been relevant to any decision as to the legal consequences. That question, again, was not raised with any witness, and it would be wrong, on the material which is available, that the defendants should be held, or assumed, to have been themselves dishonest, or to have connived at dishonesty of the plaintiff.

I return to the question of the plaintiff's status: was he employed under a contract of service or a contract for services? The defendants' argument is largely founded on the passage in Mr. Murray's evidence which I have quoted already, and on the judge's exposition (not based on anything specifically contained in the evidence) of the meaning of that passage. The judge as a result of that evidence, rejecting completely the plaintiff's evidence to a different effect, held that the plaintiff "regarded himself as working on the lump." The judge then says:

> "I am satisfied that the plaintiff and the defendants regarded the plaintiff as 'self-employed labour only subcontractor' and in this there were advantages for each side."

The judge then summarises those advantages, which included, for the defendants, escaping liability for payment of selective employment tax in respect of the plaintiff, and, for the plaintiff, evading, as the judge thought, his liability for income tax.

A The defendants say that the judge has thus held that the contract is to be treated as though it contained an express term by which both parties had agreed that the plaintiff's relationship to the defendants—his status in the work which he would do on the defendants' behalf—would be "a self-employed labour only subcontractor." There are no other contractual terms, the defendants say, or, at least, no admissible evidence of any other contractual terms. That, say the defendants, is the end of this case; it is B the end of any claim by the plaintiff in respect of breach of statutory duty by the defendants, for by agreement between the parties—the only agreement between them—the plaintiff was self-employed. If he was self-employed, say the defendants, he was not employed by the defendants. So regulation 3 (1) (*a*) did not put the defendants under a regulation 28 statutory duty to the plaintiff to see that guard-rails were erected at the C working place. That duty was the plaintiff's own duty.

The judge rejected that argument. He said:

> "For the plaintiff it is contended that I must look at the realities of the situation and not to the form alone, and particularly not alone to the label that was put upon the plaintiff by both plaintiff and defendant, for it is contended that the form may be, and in this case is, a D mere façade; whether or not the plaintiff regarded himself, whether or not the defendants regarded him, as 'self-employed labour only contractor' may be a matter, a serious matter, to be taken into consideration, but it is by no means conclusive, and the question remains whether in reality the relationship of master and servant existed."

The judge then considered various authorities and in particular the judg- E ment of MacKenna J. in *Ready Mixed Concrete (South East) Ltd.* v. *Minister of Pensions and National Insurance* [1968] 2 Q.B. 497. Applying the tests and criteria suggested in that case to the realities of the plaintiff's employment as, in the judge's view, they had emerged in evidence in this case, the judge arrived at the following conclusion:

> "I accept what the parties accept, namely, the label, as a guide and F no more. I regard the concept of 'the lump' in the circumstances of the present case as no more than a device which each side regarded as being capable of being put to his own advantage in a manner that I have attempted to describe earlier in this judgment, but which in reality did not affect the relationship of the parties or the performance of the substance of the contract between them."

G The judge was in my opinion right in his approach and in his conclusion.

Certainly it had not crossed Mr. Murray's mind that by reason of anything he had said he had altered the obligations which the defendants would have had for the safety of workmen on their site, as compared with what those obligations would have been apart from his reference to "the lump." In cross-examination, Mr. Murray seems to have had H no hesitation in accepting that he (on behalf of the defendants) was responsible for providing scaffold guard-rails and toe-boards and that sort of thing for the safety of labourers on the site. But, of course, Mr. Murray may have been mistaken about the legal effect of the words which he used.

The defendants, as I have said, contend that the contract which governed the legal relationship between the plaintiff and the defendants for the three months up to the time of the accident was a single term

A contract. The single term, derived from Mr. Murray's words ". . . I did inform him that there were no cards, we were purely working as a lump labour force," was that the plaintiff's status vis-à-vis the defendants was to be, or was to be deemed to be, "a self-employed labour only sub-contractor."

I shall assume for present purposes, though counsel for the plaintiff was not disposed to accept the assumption, that this is a correct inter-

B pretation of the intended, and understood, meaning of the Delphic words which were spoken by Mr. Murray and tacitly accepted by the plaintiff.

I am not, however, prepared to accept the defendants' further contention that there were no other terms of the contract. Indeed, if there were no other terms the only conclusion in law, I think, would be the absurd conclusion that there was no contract at all during the three months in

C which the plaintiff was working for the defendants. Counsel for the defendants, when this was put to him, was disposed to accept that there must have been a contractual term as to remuneration. There must, as I think, have been many other contractual terms, also necessarily to be implied, even though they were not mentioned in the brief conversation when Mr. Murray and the plaintiff agreed that the plaintiff should start work on the following Monday. This is so whether the contract was a

D contract of service or for services. For example, what sort of work could the defendants require the plaintiff to do? Was he to work in his own time or during stated hours, and, if the latter, what hours? Where could he be required to work? What notice, if any, was required by either side for the termination of the contract? What control could the defendants through Mr. Murray exercise over the order in which the plaintiff did such work as he might be required to do, or the manner of

E doing it?

In my opinion, the law is not so divorced from reality as to assume that the same considerations as to the ascertainment of the relevant contractual terms, if a legal analysis of the terms has to be made for any purpose, apply to a contract of the nature with which we are here concerned, the taking on of a labourer on casual application to a site agent

F on a building site, as apply to commercial contracts between business men, whether made orally after discussion of terms or in writing with elaborate provisions. The terms—even the essential terms—of a contract of the present nature would often not be spoken or written at the time when the workman was taken on. They would be understood by reference to the known circumstances and the existing practices and conventions of a particular trade or a particular contractor or a particular site. Moreover,

G if and in so far as they were not implied, by common knowledge of what the practice was, at the time when the labourer was first taken on—the date when the legal analysis would regard the contract as being made—terms could well be added thereafter as particular questions of the rights and obligations of the parties arose during the progress of the work. Again, to apply legal analysis, such terms would be treated as having been added, or the contract as being varied.

H In this context of the implication of terms, I would refer to what was so helpfully said by Lord Wilberforce in the recent House of Lords case, *Liverpool City Council* v. *Irwin* [1976] 2 W.L.R. 562, 566–567. In the last paragraph of that passage, Lord Wilberforce said:

"The present case, in my opinion, represents a fourth category, or I would rather say a fourth shade on a continuous spectrum. The court here is simply concerned to establish what the contract is, the

A parties not having themselves fully stated the terms. In this sense the court is searching for what must be implied."

So also in this case with which we are concerned.

Accordingly I reject the defendants' contention that on legal analysis there were no contractual terms governing the relationship between the plaintiff and the defendants other than a term " self-employed labour only B subcontractor." There were such other contractual terms. For this purpose it does not matter whether they were originally incorporated by implication when the plaintiff was taken on by Mr. Murray in January 1972 or were added thereafter by the acceptance of the parties by conduct. What the relevant terms were was sufficiently proved by the evidence of Mr. Murray himself in cross-examination. His evidence, except in minor respects, is not, C as the defendants suggest, merely evidence of what was done in performance of the contract. It is evidence of what the contractual rights and obligations were throughout the plaintiff's work for the defendants. True, it is not expressed in the questions and answers as being of agreed terms of a contract. But I have no doubt that Mr. Murray understood, and everyone understood, that what he was being asked about was the relationship between the parties—the rights and obligations of the defendants and the D workmen, including the plaintiff, which were understood and accepted as existing: that is, on legal analysis, the contractual terms.

Whitworth Street Estates (Manchester) Ltd. v. *James Miller & Partners Ltd.* [1970] A.C. 583 and *Wickman Machine Tool Sales Ltd.* v. *L. Schuler A.G.* [1974] A.C. 235, House of Lords authorities relied on by the defendants, are not relevant. They hold that, subject to certain exceptions, E you may not look at what has been done in pursuance of a contract in order to construe that contract. There are a number of other reasons, also, why I think those decisions are not relevant here. But the main reason is that we are here concerned not with construing a contract but with evidence as to what the terms of a contract were—the implication of terms within Lord Wilberforce's fourth category or fourth " shade of the spectrum ": *Liverpool City Council* v. *Irwin* [1976] 2 W.L.R. 562, 567.

F Mr. Murray accepted that he was responsible for " hiring and firing." In other words, as between the defendants and the workmen, including the plaintiff, he could dismiss them. There would be no question of his being able to determine a contract between the defendants and a subcontractor. He could move men from site to site, if he was so minded, and in support of the existence of that contractual right on behalf of the G defendants he gave instances of having done so. If tools were required for the work, it was for the defendants to provide them. Again, as confirmation of that contractual obligation Mr. Murray gave evidence of instances where the plaintiff had required tools for the work which he had been required to do, and the defendants had provided them. It was for Mr. Murray to tell the workmen, including the plaintiff, what particular H work they were to do: " I tell him what to take and what to do." The centurion in St. Matthew's Gospel says to the man under him: " 'Do this,' and he doeth it." The man under him is a servant, not an independent contractor. All these things are in relation to the contractual relationships existing. " I tell him what to do," and he does it on Mr. Murray's instructions because, when legal analysis has to be applied, it is a term of the contract that the plaintiff shall carry out the defendants' instructions what to do when they tell him to do it. The men, including the

plaintiff, were employed on an hourly basis. The money paid to them A
would be correctly described as "a wage."

In my judgment, on the tests laid down in the authorities, all of this indicates beyond doubt that the reality of the relationship was of employer and employee—a contract of service. I do not propose to lengthen this judgment by examining afresh the criteria, so fully discussed in so many cases. The judge, as I have already said, based himself on the judgment
of MacKenna J. in *Ready Mixed Concrete (South East) Ltd.* v. *Minister* B
of Pensions and National Insurance [1968] 2 Q.B. 497. Another judgment which I have found very helpful is that of Cooke J. in *Market Investigations Ltd.* v. *Minister of Social Security* [1969] 2 Q.B. 173.

My own view would have been that a declaration by the parties, even if it were incorporated in the contract, that the workman was to be, or was
to be deemed to be, self-employed, an independent contractor, ought to be C
wholly disregarded—not merely treated as not being conclusive—if the remainder of the contractual terms, governing the realities of the relationship, showed the relationship of employer and employee. The Roman soldier would not have been a self-employed labour only subcontractor because of any verbal exchange between him and the centurion when he enlisted. I find difficulty in accepting that the parties, by a mere expression
of intention as to what the legal relationship should be, can in any way D
influence the conclusion of law as to what the relationship is. I think that it would be contrary to the public interest if that were so, for it would mean that the parties, by their own whim, by the use of a verbal formula, unrelated to the reality of the relationship, could influence the decision on whom the responsibility for the safety of workmen, as imposed by
statutory regulations, should rest. But, as I shall indicate later, I am E
prepared for the purposes of this appeal to accept a less stringent view of the law on this point, and my decision is therefore not based on that view.

I would apply the principle laid down by Jenkins L.J. in *Addiscombe Garden Estates Ltd.* v. *Crabbe* [1958] 1 Q.B. 513. That was a case where the issue was whether the legal relationship between the parties was that of landlord and tenant or licensor and licensee. The relevant contractual
document was clearly and deliberately directed towards emphasising that the F
relationship was that of licensor and licensee. Yet the court held that it was not. Jenkins L.J. quotes from the judgment of Denning L.J. in *Facchini* v. *Bryson* [1952] 1 T.L.R. 1386, 1389 as follows, at pp. 527–528:

> "'The occupation has all the features of a service tenancy, and the parties cannot by the mere words of their contract turn it into something else. Their relationship is determined by the law and not by the G
> label which they choose to put on it' . . . ." Then Denning L.J. cited another authority (*Customs and Excise Commissioners* v. *Pools Finance (1937) Ltd.* [1952] 1 T.L.R. 792) and went on: "'It is not necessary to go so far as to find the document a sham. It is simply a matter of finding the true relationship of the parties. It is most important that we should adhere to this principle, or else we might
> find all landlords granting licences and not tenancies, and we should H
> make a hole in the Rent Acts through which could be driven—I will not in these days say a coach and four, but an articulated vehicle.'"

That is the end of Jenkins L.J.'s quotation from Denning L.J. Jenkins L.J. himself goes on, at p. 528:

> "The present case, of course, has nothing to do with the Rent Acts, but the important statement of principle is that the relationship is

determined by the law, and not by the label which parties choose to put on it, and that it is not necessary to go so far as to find the document a sham. It is simply a matter of ascertaining the true relationship of the parties."

So here. Counsel for the plaintiff does not assert that the reference to "the lump," whatever the words meant, was, or involved, "a sham." But, as the judgment of Jenkins L.J. shows, at least in certain types of case where the law has to decide whether the nature of a contract is A or B, even though the parties' expression of intention is not "a sham," it may still be properly ignored or overridden. If that is the correct approach in a case such as *Addiscombe Garden Estates Ltd.* v. *Crabbe,* surely the present type of case is an even stronger one for the acceptance of that approach. The parties cannot transfer a statute-imposed duty of care for safety of workmen from an employer to the workman himself merely because the parties agree, in effect, that the workman shall be deemed to be self-employed, where the true essence of the contract is, otherwise, of a contract of service.

However, as I have previously indicated, I am content for the purposes of this appeal to accept, in favour of the defendants, the less stringent view which appears hitherto to have found favour in a number of cases, that is, that the expression of the parties' intention may be a relevant factor, though certainly not a conclusive factor, in deciding what is the true nature of the contract. Thus, MacKenna J., in *Ready Mixed Concrete (South East) Ltd.* v. *Minister of Pensions and National Insurance* [1968] 2 Q.B. 497, expressed it, with deliberate circumspection, in these words, at pp. 512–513:

> "It may be stated here that whether the relation between the parties to the contract is that of master and servant or otherwise is a conclusion of law dependent upon the rights conferred and the duties imposed by the contract. If these are such that the relation is that of master and servant, it is irrelevant that the parties have declared it to be something else. I do not say that a declaration of this kind is always necessarily ineffective. If it were doubtful what rights and duties the parties wished to provide for, a declaration of this kind might help in resolving the doubt and fixing them in the sense required to give effect to that intention."

Lord Widgery C.J. in *Global Plant Ltd.* v. *Secretary of State for Social Services* [1972] 1 Q.B. 139, put it more confidently, in these words, at p. 152:

> "One must not overlook that the intention of the parties was that the relationship should be that of an independent contractor, and although the parties cannot by intention make a transaction into something which it is not, yet it is recognised that such intention is a factor for consideration in these cases."

Incidentally, although in that case the court was considering whether or not a decision of the Minister should be quashed, the decision of the court shows that the mere fact that under the contract the workman receives his remuneration without deductions of P.A.Y.E. income tax and without having his insurance card stamped by the other party does not in itself necessarily, at least, involve the conclusion in law that it is not a contract of service. For, despite those factors being present in that case, and despite the fact that the parties clearly intended that the contract should not have

the legal effect of a contract of service, the Minister's decision that it did A
have that legal effect was upheld.

So on this basis, which for the purposes of this appeal I am prepared to assume in favour of the defendants to be correct, the parties' own expressed wish or intention may be a factor in determining what is the nature of the contract and thus in determining on whom the statutory duty is to rest. On that basis, which the judge accepted, how did he deal with B
this issue? He said:

> "There remains the question: What matters are alleged to be inconsistent with the relationship of master and servant? First, there is the fact that the plaintiff and the defendants both regarded, or labelled, him as a 'self-employed labour only contractor.' Secondly, there is the fact, and fact it is, that the plaintiff was supposed to pay his C
> own insurance stamp as a self-employed person; that his wages were paid free of tax and that the obligation was upon him as upon a self-employed person to account to the Inland Revenue properly for tax. But I ask this question: When all the other indicia point to the relationship being that of master and servant, are these inconsistencies which should compel me to a contrary conclusion? It could not, as a true matter of law, be that they should so compel me, . . ." Then the D
> judge makes reference to a case in the Queen's Bench Divisional Court (*Maurice Graham Ltd.* v. *Brunswick* (1974) 16 K.I.R. 158) and goes on: "Nevertheless, should it lead me to that conclusion? I think not."

Then there is a passage which I have already read but will read again:

> "I accept what the parties accept, namely, the label, as a guide and no more. I regard the concept of 'the lump' in the circumstances E
> of the present case as no more than a device which each side regarded as being capable of being put to his own advantage in a manner that I have attempted to describe earlier in this judgment, but which in reality did not affect the relationship of the parties or the performance of the substance of the contract between them. I therefore arrive at the conclusion that this was in reality a contract of service and that the F
> relationship of master and servant existed between the defendants and the plaintiff."

I agree with all the judge says in that passage. I would dismiss the appeal.

LAWTON L.J. For many years past the building trade, and many outside it, have been familiar with phrases such as "working on the lump" or G
"working as a lump labour force." The trade union movement has expressed grave concern about this method of working. Parliament has had to protect the revenue by legislation because of the difficulties which it creates in the collection of income tax, but no attempt has been made so far by statute to forbid it. Indeed, the Finance Act 1971 recognised it as a way of working (see section 29) but put obstacles in the way of getting any fiscal benefits from it. We were told by counsel for the defendants H
that this appeal was the first one, as far as he knew, which called for consideration of the legal consequences to anyone alleged to have been "working as a lump labour force" in relation to any injuries sustained whilst at work and as a result of the builder who had had the benefit of his work (I use a neutral phrase deliberately) failing to use the safeguards which he would have been obliged to use under the statutory regulations for the safety of any workman employed by him. What "working on the

A lump " or "as a lump working force " means must, of course, depend upon the evidence in each case. The judge however, held that both parties in this case regarded the plaintiff as a " self-employed labour only subcontractor." What was the legal effect of " working as a lump working force " when, as in this case, the plaintiff was taken on (again I use a neutral phrase) as a general labourer?

As a matter of law I can see no reason why a general labourer should
B not offer his labour on some such terms as these: " I do not mind what you ask me to do or where and when you ask me to do it but you must understand that I am not going to call you master and I will not be your servant." Many men offer their labour on some such terms as these; the jobbing gardener is familiar to us all, as are self-employed farm workers to East Anglian farmers. When working they allow themselves to be con-
C trolled by those with whom they made a bargain. In most cases when the bargain is made nothing is said about control, but it is accepted by both parties as an implied term that the hirer will exercise control. This does not mean either in fact or, in my opinion, in law that the hired man becomes a servant.

As I understood Mr. Beldam's argument on behalf of the plaintiff, he did not challenge the general proposition which I have set out above. His
D case was that on the evidence the plaintiff did agree to work as the defendants' servant. Mr. Popplewell's argument was that, as the object of both parties to the hiring was to avoid the relationship of master and servant and the only express words of the bargain were to that effect, the implied understandings as to which party was to exercise control did not operate to destroy the object of the bargain and to override the only express
E term of it.

Now one thing is clear about the plaintiff's object in offering his labour to the defendants: he did not like having income tax deducted from his earnings and wanted to avoid, maybe evade, paying any more tax than he had to do. He was no 20th-century John Philpott Curran maintaining eternal vigilance to safeguard the right of individuals to be self-employed. He must have known all about the deduction of income tax from earnings
F and the payment as an employed person of national insurance contributions. For many years he had been employed as a general labourer by builders. The employer he had had for six years before he started with the defendants had deducted tax from his earnings and had stamped his national insurance card. After leaving this employer and returning from a short visit to Ireland the plaintiff was unemployed for about a
G fortnight. Four of his friends were then working " on the lump " for the defendants. They asked their foreman, a Mr. Murray, if he would take on the plaintiff. He said he would. Soon afterwards the plaintiff came along to the defendants to start work. He spoke to Mr. Murray. From the trial judge's findings I infer that he told Mr. Murray that his name was Goff. There can only have been one reason for doing this, namely, to make the task of the Inland Revenue in tracing him more difficult. Had I been sitting
H in another jurisdiction and had the plaintiff been charged before me with some offence concerned with the fraudulent evasion of tax, I should have had no hesitation in adjudging that his giving a false name was strong evidence of intending to evade fraudulently the payment of tax. But, as Mr. Beldam pointed out, the plaintiff has not been charged with the fraudulent evasion of tax, and although the trial judge found that by giving a false name he was " a willing and dishonest party to a device to evade his tax liabilities " that had never been put to him in the witness-box so that

he had never had an opportunity of meeting that allegation. With some A reluctance I felt bound to accept this submission, with the result that I have had to approach the problem presented by this appeal on the basis that the plaintiff intended to order his working relations with those who accepted his offer of work so that the tax attaching to his earnings under the appropriate Acts was less than it otherwise would have been.

There can be no doubt what the defendants' intention was. Mr. Murray, whose evidence seems to have been accepted on this point, and B generally, said: "But I did inform him that there were no cards, we were purely working as a lump labour force." The defendants could properly use independent subcontractors. This is common in the building trade, and when skilled craftsmen are used, in most cases, if not all, there can be no doubt that such men are working as independent contractors. The taking on of genuine independent subcontractors provides builders with a C number of administrative and fiscal advantages. They are spared the task of accounting to the Inland Revenue for tax deducted from earnings and do not have to pay out money for the employer's contribution to national insurance. In addition, when in 1972 the plaintiff was working for them they did not have to pay selective employment tax. Clearly Mr. Murray wanted to get these benefits for the defendants.

It follows that both parties to the labour bargain which was made in D this case wanted to order their affairs so as to avoid the incidence of taxation. They could only succeed in doing so, however, if they avoided bringing into existence the relationship of master and servant. This comes about because of the provisions of section 181 of the Income and Corporation Taxes Act 1970. As is common knowledge, assessment for tax under Schedule D, which applies to the self-employed, gives small tax advantages E which those assessed under Schedule E do not enjoy. It is unnecessary to state what they are; but as every judge who has had experience of the criminal courts knows, and probably most of the public nowadays, it is not these advantages which attract many men who work "on the lump" but the opportunities for the evasion of tax which Schedule D provides. Section 181 (1) of the Act of 1970 is in these terms: ". . . Schedule E. 1. Tax F under this Schedule shall be charged in respect of any office or employment on emoluments therefrom . . ." Section 204 (1) imposes upon any person who makes a payment of income assessable to tax under Schedule E the duty to deduct income tax. Neither the plaintiff nor the defendants wanted these provisions to apply, and they could only legally and effectively bring this about by agreeing that the defendants would not employ the plaintiff. G Assuming, as I must for the purposes of this appeal, that the parties were not conspiring with each other to evade tax fraudulently, this is what they thought they had done. The defendants acted as if they had attained their objective. They did not deduct tax until they were obliged to do so under section 28 of the Finance Act 1972.

If the avoidance of the relationship of master and servant was the prime H object of the bargain, as I find it was from the circumstances in which it was made and the few words used, then I can see nothing in the implied terms which is inconsistent with this object. As I said at the beginning of this judgment, I can see no reason why in law a man cannot sell his labour without becoming another man's servant even though he is willing to accept control as to how, when and where he shall work. If he makes his intention not to be a servant sufficiently clear, the implications which

A would normally arise from implied terms do not override the prime object of the bargain. In my judgment this is just such a case.

I appreciate that there are powerful arguments for thinking that "working on the lump" is socially undesirable and that many men who do so work do not appreciate that they may be depriving themselves of safeguards which statutory regulations enact must be provided for em-
B ployed men, but these considerations are not sufficiently strong to make labour bargains of this kind void as being against public policy. If in a particular case the evidence leaves the court in doubt as to what the parties had agreed, there would, no doubt, be a finding which was more in accordance with public policy than against it. That is not this case. In my judgment there is no doubt what the parties intended and it was that the plaintiff should not be a servant of the defendants. Anyway, public policy
C is an awkward horse for a judge to ride, particularly when it wants to go in more than one direction. Maybe the law should try to save workmen from their folly, but it should not encourage them to change a status which they have freely chosen when it suits them to do so. In my judgment it would be contrary to public policy to allow a man to say that he was self-employed for the purpose of avoiding the incidence of taxation but a servant for the purpose of claiming compensation. For these reasons I
D would allow the appeal.

In coming to this conclusion I have not overlooked the decisions in *Global Plant Ltd.* v. *Secretary of State for Social Services* [1972] 1 Q.B. 139; *Market Investigations Ltd.* v. *Minister of Social Security* [1969] 2 Q.B. 173 and *Construction Industry Training Board* v. *Labour Force Ltd.* [1970] 3 All E.R. 220. The first two were appeals by way of case stated,
E the last from a decision of the industrial tribunal. In all three cases the appellate courts were concerned with deciding whether there had been errors in law. This court has a wider jurisdiction and is entitled to consider all the evidence given in the trial court. That I have done, and to that evidence I have sought to apply the principles which were discussed in these three cases. In the enunciation of principle I found them helpful, but in the application of principle in the special jurisdiction with which
F they were concerned I got no help from them.

As I understand the law there is no single test for deciding whether a man is a servant of another. Various factors have to be considered and weighed. Control of working is one; intention is another; carrying on business on one's own account is a third. The label which the parties attach to a bargain is not to be disregarded but it is far from being
G conclusive. It was after considering and weighing these factors that I adjudged that the parties' intention to avoid the relationship of master and servant was the predominating and all-important factor. I was helped in this decision by Mr. Beldam's acceptance that the bargain which the parties made was not a sham.

I should add that I agree with the judgment of Megaw L.J. on all the
H remaining points in this appeal.

BROWNE L.J. I agree with Megaw L.J. that this appeal should be dismissed. As to the "working place" point, I have nothing to add. If Lawton L.J. did not think differently on the "employment" point, I should be content to say that I agree with Megaw L.J. for the reasons which he has given and for the reasons given by Boreham J. in the passage which Megaw L.J. has read (*ante*, p. 1224B–F), but as it is I think I should state my

own reasons, even though they are really the same as those already given A
by Megaw L.J.

As I understand it Lawton L.J.'s reasons for holding that the relationship of master and servant did not exist between the plaintiff and the defendants are: (a) both parties wanted to order their affairs so as to avoid the incidence of taxation. (b) They could only succeed in doing this if they avoided bringing into existence the relationship of master and B
servant between them (see sections 181 (1) and 204 (1) of the Income and Corporation Taxes Act 1970). (c) The avoidance of the relationship of master and servant was "the prime object of the bargain." (d) If the intention not to create the relationship of master and servant is sufficiently clear from the circumstances and the express words used, implications which would normally arise from implied terms do not override the prime object of the bargain. C

If Lawton L.J.'s view is right, I think it must follow that *Global Plant Ltd.* v. *Secretary of State for Social Services* [1972] 1 Q.B. 139 was wrongly decided. In that case it had been expressly agreed between Global Plant and the man in question (supported by a written document) that he should be a self-employed subcontractor, that tax should not be deducted by Global Plant and that he should stamp his own insurance card: see D
pp. 142 and 148. In spite of that, Lord Widgery C.J. held that the Secretary of State was not wrong in law in holding that, having regard to the other factors in that case, the relationship was that of master and servant: see p. 152, which Megaw L.J. has already quoted, and pp. 152–155. I think it would probably also follow that the decision of the Divisional Court in *Maurice Graham Ltd.* v. *Brunswick*, 16 K.I.R. 158 was wrong, as Mr. Popplewell submitted. These two cases are not binding on this E
court, but in my view they were rightly decided, supported as I think they are by earlier authorities, including *Ready Mixed Concrete (South East) Ltd.* v. *Minister of Pensions and National Insurance* [1968] 2 Q.B. 497 and *Market Investigations Ltd.* v. *Minister of Social Security* [1969] 2 Q.B. 173.

Even if the "prime object of the bargain" between the plaintiff and F
the defendants in the present case was the avoidance of the relationship of master and servant, the question is whether they succeeded in that object. The parties cannot by a label decide the true nature of their relationship: see especially the passage from *Addiscombe Garden Estates* v. *Crabbe* [1958] 1 Q.B. 513 which Megaw L.J. has quoted. But I am afraid that I cannot agree with Lawton L.J. that this was the prime object of the bargain. The prime object, I think, was that the plaintiff should G
work as a general labourer on sites where the defendants were carrying on their business as building contractors. It is true that both parties intended that it was to be a term of the bargain that the defendants should not deduct tax and should not pay for the plaintiff's national insurance stamps, but that was only one term. I agree with Megaw L.J. that there must have been—and were—other terms, and that the court must look H
at the arrangements as a whole to decide what the real relationship was.

On the basis of the single sentence in Mr. Murray's evidence which Megaw L.J. has quoted, Boreham J. found that "the plaintiff and the defendants regarded the plaintiff as 'self-employed labour only subcontractor' . . ." I am not sure that I should have given that sentence such a wide and important effect. The only evidence about what is meant by "being on the lump" was four questions and answers in the cross-exam-

A ination of the plaintiff and three in the re-examination of Mr. Murray. The plaintiff said that it meant that the employer did not deduct tax and the man stamped his own card, and Mr. Murray went no further; I doubt if either of them intended or understood what Mr. Murray said to mean more than that. But, like Megaw L.J., I am prepared to assume that the judge's interpretation is right. Even making this assumption, I agree with Megaw L.J. that this appeal fails, for the following reasons:

B (1) The term as to tax and stamps cannot have been the only term of the contract: as Megaw L.J. has pointed out, there would have been no contract at all unless there were other terms, tacitly understood, or "implied" in the sense explained by Megaw L.J. and by Lord Wilberforce in the speech which Megaw L.J. has quoted: *Liverpool City Council* v. *Irwin* [1976] 2 W.L.R. 562, 566–567.

C (2) *Whitworth Street Estates* (*Manchester*) *Ltd.* v. *James Miller & Partners Ltd.* [1970] A.C. 583 and *Wickman Machine Tool Sales Ltd.* v. *L. Schuler A.G.* [1974] A.C. 235 are irrelevant. Those cases were concerned with the construction of written contracts; the rule that ". . . it is not legitimate to use as an aid in the construction of the contract anything which the parties said or did after it was made" (*per* Lord Reid in *Whitworth Street Estates* (*Manchester*) *Ltd.* v. *James Miller & Partners Ltd.*,
D at p. 603) is only a particular application of

> "the general rule . . . that extrinsic evidence is not admissible for the construction of a written contract; the parties' intentions must be ascertained, on legal principles of construction, from the words they have used" (*per* Lord Wilberforce in *Wickman Machine Tool Sales* v. *L. Schuler A.G.*, at p. 261; on this point he agreed with the other
> E members of the House, though he dissented on another point).

In the present case, the question is not one of construction of the contract, but of what were the terms of an oral and only partially expressed contract. In my opinion, the court can in such a case take into account what was done later as a basis for inferring what was agreed when the contract was made, or as establishing later additions or variations. But I
F do not think that this point arises in the present case, because I agree with Megaw L.J. that Mr. Murray's evidence related to what was understood by both parties at the time when the contract was made. I need not set out that evidence or analyse it again, because I entirely agree with Megaw L.J.'s statement of its effect.

(3) I agree with Megaw L.J. and Boreham J. that on the tests laid down
G by the authorities the evidence establishes beyond doubt that in reality the contract between the plantiff and the defendants was a contract of service and their relationship was that of master and servant. *Market Investigations Ltd.* v. *Minister of Social Security* [1969] 2 Q.B. 173 does not seem to have been cited to Boreham J., but I think that the application of the test suggested by Cooke J. in that case, which I find very helpful, strongly supports his conclusion. After quoting Lord Wright, Denning
H L.J. and the Supreme Court of the United States, Cooke J. said, at p. 184, that these observations

> ". . . suggest that the fundamental test to be applied is this: 'Is the person who has engaged himself to perform these services performing them as a person in business on his own account?' If the answer to that question is 'yes,' then the contract is a contract for services. If the answer is 'no,' then the contract is a contract of service."

On this test, the distinction between the plaintiff in the present case and the jobbing gardener is plain. A

(4) I agree with Megaw L.J. that a declaration by the parties ought to be disregarded if the remainder of the contractual terms show that the reality of the relationship is one of master and servant, but, like him, I am prepared to assume that the less stringent view adopted by the authorities is right, namely, that it is a relevant, but certainly not a conclusive, factor.

(5) In my judgment, Boreham J. directed himself rightly in law, subject B
to the additional test suggested by Cooke J. to which I have referred and to (4) above; the omission of these factors makes the tests which he applied more and not less favourable to the defendants. When the right tests have been applied, the conclusion to be drawn is in my view a question of fact: see *Global Plant Ltd.* v. *Secretary of State for Social Services* [1972] 1 Q.B. 139, 152–155. The defendants have entirely failed to satisfy me that C
Boreham J.'s conclusion was wrong; in my judgment it was right.

As I have said, I would dismiss this appeal.

Appeal dismissed with costs.
Leave to appeal; stay of execution to continue, defendants undertaking, through counsel, to prosecute appeal, if taken, with due diligence. D

Solicitors: *John King & Co., York; Crombie, Wilkinson & Robinson, York.*

M. G. E

[CHANCERY DIVISION]

* NORTHERN DEVELOPMENTS (HOLDINGS) LTD. AND OTHERS *v.* F
U.D.T. SECURITIES LTD. AND OTHERS

[1975 N. No. 710]

1975 March 21, 24; 26 Megarry J.

Land Registration—Land charges register—Pending actions register—Vacation of—Action to set aside sale of land—Allegation of wrongful exercise of power of sale—Registration of caution and "pending land action" by chargor subsequent to issue of proceedings—Purchaser's motion to vacate register—Court's jurisdiction to vacate registration of "pending land action" against unregistered land — Land Charges Act 1972 (*c.* 61), *ss.* 1 (6), 5 (10)[1] G

The plaintiff company and six of its subsidiaries brought an action against the first defendants, U.D.T., to whom they owed over £4 million, claiming damages for wrongful, improper and fraudulent exercise of U.D.T.'s power of sale in respect of certain building sites which had been the subject of legal H

[1] Land Charges Act 1972, s. 1 (6): "Subject to the provisions of this Act, registration may be vacated pursuant to an order of the court."
S. 5 (10): see post, p. 1233A–B.

A charges in favour of U.D.T. as security for the debt. There was also a claim against the third defendants and other companies in their group who had bought the site from U.D.T., for an order setting aside the sales. The plaintiffs entered cautions against dealings and pending land actions in respect of the sites, some of which were registered and others unregistered land, in the appropriate registers.

On a motion by the third defendants for an order vacating B the entries:—

Held, that in the case of the registered land the court, as conceded, had an inherent jurisdiction to make orders vacating the entries; that in the case of the unregistered land the Land Charges Act 1972 had extended to all registers the general power to vacate entries which formerly had applied only to land charges, so that although it was a consolidation Act the presumption against it having changed the law was rebutted; C that in relation to pending actions the general power to vacate entries conferred by section 1 (6) was not ousted by the provisions of section 5 (10), which for pending actions conferred wider powers in narrower circumstances; and that the general power to vacate entries given by section 1 (6) applied to pending actions and ought to be exercised.

Calgary and Edmonton Land Co. Ltd. v. *Dobinson* [1974] Ch. 102 followed.

D *Norman* v. *Hardy* [1974] 1 W.L.R. 1048 not followed.

The following cases are referred to in the judgment as reported:

American Cyanamid Co. v. *Ethicon Ltd.* [1975] A.C. 396; [1975] 2 W.L.R. 316; [1975] 1 All E.R. 504, H.L.(E.).
Calgary and Edmonton Land Co. Ltd. v. *Dobinson* [1974] Ch. 102; [1974] 2 W.L.R. 143; [1974] 1 All E.R. 484.
E *Heywood* v. *B.D.C. Properties Ltd.* (*No. 2*) [1964] 1 W.L.R. 971; [1964] 2 All E.R. 702, C.A.
Norman v. *Hardy* [1974] 1 W.L.R. 1048; [1974] 1 All E.R. 1170.
Strousberg v. *M'Gregor* (1890) 6 T.L.R. 145.
Taylor v. *Taylor* [1968] 1 W.L.R. 378; [1968] 1 All E.R. 843, C.A.

The following additional cases were cited in argument:

F *Hodson* v. *Deans* [1903] 2 Ch. 647.
Seal v. *Gimson* (1914) 110 L.T. 583.

MOTION

On March 13, 1975, the third defendant in this action, Drindle (Properties) Ltd. (now known as Poco Developments Ltd.) (" Poco ") gave G notice of motion seeking an order against the plaintiffs, Northern Developments (Holdings) Ltd. (" N.D. "), J. Kelly Homes (Stoke-on-Trent) Ltd., Daleholme (Estates) Ltd., Woodshaw Industrial Properties (Preston) Ltd., Dealgood Builders Ltd., and G.C.T. Construction Ltd., restraining them from registering cautions or other entries in respect of the pending action, and an order vacating any such entries.

The following facts are confined to those facts which are material to H this report.

In February 1975 N.D. and its subsidiaries, which included all the other plaintiffs, owed the first defendants, U.D.T. Securities Ltd. (" U.D.T. "), some £4,000,000, the debt being secured by legal charges on certain building sites which included both registered and unregistered land. By an agreement dated November 1, 1974, U.D.T. was given the right, on serving notice of no specified length, to exercise any power contained in the charges, which included the power of sale. By a letter dated November

15, U.D.T. demanded payment of the capital sums and interest and gave notice of intention to exercise the power of sale. At the same time U.D.T. commenced negotiations to persuade the plaintiffs to sell the sites which were being developed. When, by January 1975, the negotiations had proved unsuccessful, U.D.T. opened negotiations with Poco and the companies in its group for the sale of the sites to them. On February 25 the sales to Poco and the third defendants were completed and the documents of sale executed. N.D. knew nothing of the sales up to that point. The following day Poco and the third defendants took possession of the sites. Some hours later U.D.T. informed the plaintiffs of the completed sales. On March 5 the plaintiffs issued the writ in this action claiming damages for U.D.T.'s wrongful, improper and fraudulent exercise of the power of sale and their failure to give adequate notice, and an order setting aside the sales; they further claimed an injunction against the second and third defendants restraining them from remaining in occupation of the sites. On March 13 Poco gave notice of motion claiming an order restraining the plaintiffs from registering cautions or other entries in respect of the pending action and an order vacating any such registrations. At the hearing of this motion it was common ground that only the second order was in question, as the plaintiffs had in fact registered pending actions in the Land Charges Register and cautions in the Land Register.

The first and second defendants, U.D.T. Securities Ltd., and Price Bros. (Somerford) Ltd., took no part in the motion.

H. E. Francis Q.C. and *B. C. Maddocks* for Poco.
A. J. Balcombe Q.C. and *Frederic Reynold* for the plaintiffs.

Cur. adv. vult.

March 26. MEGARRY J. stated the facts, read section 104 (2) of the Law of Property Act 1925 and having considered the arguments of counsel on behalf of the plaintiffs held that the sale to Poco was a true sale, that there was no evidence that Poco had notice of any such impropriety in the sale as would justify its being set aside and that, accordingly, Poco had the protection of section 104 (2) of the Law of Property Act 1925 and the defendants had made out a case for vacation of the registrations on motion. His Lordship continued: That brings me to the question of jurisdiction. On this, there is no difficulty about the registered land, for Mr. Balcombe for the plaintiffs concedes that there is an inherent jurisdiction to make orders vacating the cautions. On the other hand, for the unregistered land he contends that the only jurisdiction is that conferred by section 5 (10) of the Land Charges Act 1972 and that this does not apply to the present case. This contention takes me to the latent conflict between two decisions in the Chancery Division, made within a few days of each other, and in ignorance of each other. One is a decision of my own and the other is a decision of Goulding J. The two decisions are *Calgary and Edmonton Land Co. Ltd.* v. *Dobinson* [1974] Ch. 102 and *Norman* v. *Hardy* [1974] 1 W.L.R. 1048. Section 1 (6) of the Act of 1972 provides that "Subject to the provisions of this Act, registration may be vacated pursuant to an order of the court." Section 1 appears under the cross-heading "Preliminary," and there then follow sections 2 to 4 under the cross-heading "Registration in register of land charges" and section 5 to 8 under the cross-heading "Registration in registers of pending actions, writs and orders and deeds of arrangement." Thus far,

A section 1 (6) appears to be a perfectly general provision, applicable to all registers. However, in the case of pending actions, there is section 5 (10). This runs as follows:

"The court, if it thinks fit, may, upon the determination of the proceedings, or during the pendency of the proceedings if satisfied that they are not prosecuted in good faith, make an order vacating a
B registration under this section, and direct the party on whose behalf it was made to pay all or any of the costs and expenses occasioned by the registration and by its vacation."

The question, then, is whether pending actions can be vacated only in accordance with the limited provisions of section 5 (10), or whether the unconfined provisions of section 1 (6) apply, with section 5 (10) as merely
C a particular instance.

In *Calgary and Edmonton Land Co. Ltd.* v. *Dobinson* I held that in circumstances not within section 5 (10) the provisions of section 1 (6) nevertheless empowered the court to vacate the entry of a pending action, for the provisions of section 1 (6) were wide and general in their terms. The precursor of section 1 (6) was section 10 (8) of the Land Charges Act 1925, and this read: "The registration of a land charge may be vacated pur-
D suant to an order of the court or a judge thereof." As a matter of language that applied only to land charges, and not to pending actions and other matters; and this was emphasised by the fact that section 10 appeared in Part V of the Act, headed "Land Charges," and not in Parts I to IV, which were respectively entitled "Pending Actions," "Annuities," "Writs and Orders affecting Land" and "Deeds of Arrangement." The change of
E language and arrangement in the Act of 1972 seemed to me to make it clear that section 1 (6) of the Act of 1972 applied quite generally, and embraced pending actions as well as land charges, despite section 5 (10).

However, in *Norman* v. *Hardy* [1974] 1 W.L.R. 1048 my brother Goulding took a different view. He said, at p. 1055:

"Then my attention is drawn to section 1 (6) of the Land Charges Act
F 1972 which applies to all the registers kept under the Act. It says: 'Subject to the provisions of this Act, registration may be vacated pursuant to an order of the court.' The phrase 'subject to the provisions of this Act' leaves open two possible views: one is that section 1 (6) gives a wide discretionary power in the case of pending actions additional to the more limited power under section 5 (10); the other is that section 5 (10) operates to narrow, as regards pending actions,
G the scope which section 1 (6) has in relation to the other registers. On an examination of the arrangement of the Act and the contents of its predecessor, the Land Charges Act 1925, and having regard to the long title of the Act of 1972, namely, 'An Act to consolidate certain enactments relating to the registration of land charges and other instruments and matters affecting land,' I feel little doubt that the
H second interpretation is the correct one. In other words, I do not think that section 1 (6) in relation to the register of pending actions gives the court any power additional to section 5 (10)."

From this, two points emerge. First, that the Act of 1972 is a consolidation Act and so is presumed not to have changed the law; and second, that as a matter of construction the words "Subject to the provisions of this Act" in section 1 (6), when taken with section 5 (10), operate so as to exclude the effect of section 1 (6) in relation to pending actions,

with the result that the power to vacate the register is quite general for all A
types of entry under the Act except for pending actions, where it is narrowly
confined to the circumstances of section 5 (10), which substantially re-
enacted section 2 (6) of the Act of 1925.

I need hardly say that I regard any decision of Goulding J. with great
respect, and that this respect is enhanced when, as appears to be the case,
he had more ample argument deployed before him than I had had in
Calgary and Edmonton Land Co. Ltd. v. *Dobinson* [1974] Ch. 102. At B
the same time, I should say that the argument before me in the present
case has been advanced with all the advantage that flows from the points
in issue having been sharpened by two reported cases which reached differ-
ent conclusions. Let me take first the well known presumption that a mere
consolidating statute does not change the immediately pre-existing law.
The long title of the Act of 1972 is cited in the judgment of Goulding J. C
in *Norman* v. *Hardy* [1974] 1 W.L.R. 1048, and this plainly shows that
the Act is a consolidating Act, so that the presumption applies. Thus far I
entirely agree with Goulding J. But there then arises the question whether
the presumption is rebutted. To this I think that there can only be one
answer. Under the Act of 1925, there were three categories. First, land
charges were subject to the general and unrestricted provisions for vacation
contained in section 10 (8). Second, pending actions were subject to the D
closely limited provisions for vacation contained in section 2 (6). Third,
the Act contained no express provision for the vacation of entries relating
to annuities, writs and orders affecting land, and deeds of arrangement
affecting land. Under the Act of 1972, it seems manifest that, apart from
the dispute about pending actions, the new general provision, section 1 (6),
applies to all registers. Indeed, in the passage that I have cited Goulding E
J. himself said that section 1 (6) "applies to all the registers kept under
the Act," and he referred to "the scope which section 1 (6) has in relation
to the other registers." The result seems inescapable. I do not see how
the presumption against a consolidating Act changing the law can continue
to apply to a provision which perfectly plainly has changed the law. Once
the conclusion is reached that under the Act of 1972 the general power to
vacate entries in the land charges register alone has been extended to other F
registers, the presumption is rebutted. Thereupon the language of the
later Act in this respect falls to be construed without the presumption.

I turn, then, to the question of construction. Is the statutory jurisdic-
tion to order the vacation of a pending action confined to the circum-
stances set out in section 5 (10)? The jurisdiction given to the court by
that subsection arises in two circumstances, namely, (1) "upon the deter- G
mination of the proceedings" and (2) "during the pendency of the pro-
ceedings if satisfied that they are not prosecuted in good faith." The
powers that the court has in such cases are twofold. First, there is the
power to make an order vacating the registration; and, second, there is
the power to direct the party on whose behalf the registration was made "to
pay all or any of the costs and expenses occasioned by the registration
and by its vacation." In view of the general power of vacation conferred H
by section 1 (6) having been given "Subject to the provisions of this Act,"
what is the effect of section 5 (10) on that general power?

Now three things are plain. First, section 5 (10) is drafted in terms of
conferring the powers that it mentions rather than of restricting other
powers. Second, the powers conferred by section 5 (10) are wider than
those conferred by section 1 (6): powers to order the vacation of a registra-
tion and also to direct the payment of money are wider than a mere power

A to order the vacation of a registration. Third, so far as interlocutory proceedings are concerned, the circumstances in which section 5 (10) can apply are narrower than those in which section 1 (6) can operate: the words "if satisfied that they are not prosecuted in good faith" in section 5 (10) contrast sharply with the absence of any restriction in section 1 (6). Does, then, the conferring of extended powers in narrower circumstances oust the operation of lesser powers in wider circumstances? I must say that at B present I do not see why they should. If section 5 (10) had omitted any power to direct the payment of money, then matters might well have been different; but that power is there. Even if Mr. Francis is wrong in suggesting that the words "Subject to the provisions of this Act" which open section 1 (6) may have been intended to refer to sections 8, 16 or 19 (2), and in truth they refer solely to section 5 (10), they are words which the C draftsman of the Act of 1972 might have added to make it plain that the limited relief which can be given under section 1 (6) did not detract from the wider relief which section 5 (10) authorises in limited circumstances.

Looked at as a matter of substance, I do not see why the only circumstances in which the registration of a pending action can be vacated before judgment should be if the proceedings "are not prosecuted in good D faith." Why should Parliament wish to protect a registration relating to hopeless or vexatious proceedings merely because they are being prosecuted in good faith? Bona fides and reasonableness are far from being the same thing, and sometimes the most unreasonable of men are the most honest and sincere in their unreason. In relation to pending actions, the terms "good faith" and "bona fides," I may say, clearly seem to bear the E meaning of honesty: see *Strousberg* v. *M'Gregor* (1890) 6 T.L.R. 145, *per* Cotton L.J.

Considering the matter as a whole, in my judgment the special provisions of section 5 (10) do not, in relation to pending actions, oust the general powers of the court under section 1 (6). On this point, with the advantage of the argument that I have heard, I would respectfully dissent from the view taken in *Norman* v. *Hardy* [1974] 1 W.L.R. 1048, despite F its cogency; for there seem to be countervailing considerations which were not mentioned in that case. I may add that in his firm but decorous attack on the reasoning in *Calgary and Edmonton Land Co. Ltd.* v. *Dobinson* [1974] Ch. 102, Mr. Balcombe submitted that the result in that case was right because what had been registered had been held not to be a pending action at all, and so the jurisdiction to vacate the entry was not G limited by section 5 (10), which applied only when what was registered was truly a pending action. I would only say that this distinction seems to me to increase the difficulty in holding that section 5 (10) curtails the operation of section 1 (6).

That brings me to the inherent jurisdiction. In *Norman* v. *Hardy* Goulding J. accepted that there was an inherent jurisdiction to vacate the registration as a pending action of something that was not a pending H action at all, as in *Heywood* v. *B.D.C. Properties Ltd.* (*No.* 2) [1964] 1 W.L.R. 971, and, I may add, *Taylor* v. *Taylor* [1968] 1 W.L.R. 378. But where, as here, what is registered as a pending action is truly a pending action, then in the words of Goulding J. in *Norman* v. *Hardy* [1974] 1 W.L.R. 1048, 1055:

> ". . . if I were to assume an inherent jurisdiction to cancel the registration during the pendency of the action in a case not covered

by section 5 (10), I should, in effect, be altering what Parliament has A
provided."

If I may say so, that approach seems to me to emphasise the restrictive effect that is being ascribed to the outwardly facultative language of section 5 (10). If, of course, I am right in the view that I have taken of the effect of sections 1 (6) and 5 (10), when read together, the difficulty does not arise: but if I am wrong, it does. One then reaches the situation B
that if something that is registered as a pending action is not a real pending action at all, the registration can on motion be vacated under the inherent jurisdiction, whereas if it is truly a pending action, then, however insubstantial it is, the registration can be vacated on motion only under the statute and so only if the action is not being prosecuted in good faith. If I may say so, I can see much force in the reasoning of Goulding J., given his premise: but the force of the reasoning accentuates my doubts about C
the premise, particularly when contrasted with registered land. The amplitude of the jurisdiction in respect of registered land leads one to question whether Parliament really intended the protection afforded to registrations relating to pending actions to vary so markedly according to whether the land was registered or unregistered. The point is not easy, but I still think, as I thought in *Calgary and Edmonton Land Co. Ltd.* v. D
Dobinson [1974] Ch. 102, 110, that the true view is that

> "the inherent jurisdiction is there all the time, but that the court, as a matter of discretion, will usually not exercise it if there is a satisfactory statutory jurisdiction, satisfactory, that is, in terms of amplitude, speed, and convenience."

In the result, I hold that I have a statutory jurisdiction to vacate the E
entries under section 1 (6). If necessary, I would also hold that the statute is not inconsistent with the existence of an inherent jurisdiction, though I do not think that I need decide this. In the background there is the consideration that what is sometimes sought in these cases is not an order in the impersonal form for the vacation of the entry but a mandatory order for the defendant to remove his entry: and an application for such F
an order must, I think, be considered on the general principles applicable to mandatory orders. During the argument there were indeed various references to the decision of the House of Lords in *American Cyanamid Co.* v. *Ethicon Ltd.* [1975] A.C. 396 on the exercise of the jurisdiction to grant interlocutory injunctions; and if and so far as the principles there enunciated have any analogy with the jurisdiction that I am asked to exercise, I can see some support for the contention that N.D. should be G
left to its remedy in damages and the registrations vacated. However, the analogy does not seem to me to be at all close, and what is perhaps more in point on any matter of discretion is the present state of affairs on the sites, with rival work-forces on some of them. Whichever side has possession, any building operations are under threat, and purchasers of houses are unable safely to complete their purchases. Unless N.D. raise H
the money to pay off U.D.T., a successful attack on the sale to Poco will still leave U.D.T. free to exercise the power of sale again, and so N.D.'s prospects of retaining the sites and developing them themselves seem relatively slender. On the whole, any discretion that I have in the matter should, I think, be exercised in favour of vacating the registrations.

Both sides seek an order for a speedy trial. I think it highly desirable that there should be as speedy a trial as is possible. With the assistance

A of counsel I shall consider what appropriate directions to that effect can be given. I should also say that N.D. has made an open offer that existing contracts for the sale of houses should be completed and that the proceeds of sale should be placed on deposit in a stakeholders' account. That offer has not been accepted, and one can see obvious difficulties in it, in view of the existing obligations to U.D.T. as to the disposal of the moneys received on dispositions of houses. I can do no more than decide B this case according to the law as I understand it; but I express the hope that those concerned will do all that is possible to avoid hardship to innocent third parties.

For the reasons that I have given, this motion succeeds, and I order the vacation of the entries as prayed in the notice of motion.

C *Order accordingly.*

Solicitors: *Nabarro, Nathanson for Rowlands, Manchester; Ward Bowie for David Blank & Co., Manchester.*

A. R.

D

[COURT OF APPEAL]

* REGINA *v.* CRIMINAL INJURIES COMPENSATION BOARD, E *Ex parte* TONG

1976 June 14 Lord Denning M.R., Orr L.J. and Waller J.

Crime—Criminal Injuries Compensation Board—Date of entitlement—Assessment of compensation—Death of victim before payment—Whether compensation assessed payable to deceased F *victim's estate—Criminal Injuries Compensation Scheme* 1964 (*rev.* 1969), *para.* 21 [1]

The victim of a criminal assault applied to the Criminal Injuries Compensation Board under the Criminal Injuries Compensation Scheme 1964 (1969 revision) for compensation. On February 25, 1973, the "initial decision" under paragraph 21 of the scheme was made by a single member of the board who G determined that the compensation payable on the basis of 20 per cent. disability should be £450. On March 6, before that decision had been communicated to the applicant, he died from causes unconnected with the assault. His widow, as his executrix, was informed that as the applicant had died "before the award could be notified" there was no obligation, in the board's view, to pay the amount to his estate. After a protest made on the widow's behalf, a full board of three members H decided on September 16, 1974, that the award of the single member was an "offer" addressed to the applicant himself and that as he had died before he had accepted it the offer had lapsed.

The widow applied to the Divisional Court for an order of certiorari to quash the board's decision. The court refused the order on the ground that the wholly ex gratia payment

[1] Criminal Injuries Compensation Scheme 1964 (rev. 1969), para. 21: see post, p. 1243B–C.

under the scheme vested in the applicant when the money was paid to him and as it had not been paid while he was alive it was not payable to his estate. A

On appeal by the widow:—

Held, allowing the appeal, that although an award under the scheme was ex gratia and personal to the applicant, and although the scheme did not cover the situation where an applicant died before the initial decision to award him a specific amount had been notified to him, the date on which B the award vested in him was, on the proper interpretation of paragraph 21, the date when the single member made his initial decision; and that the court in its supervisory jurisdiction over the board could quash the decision of September 16, 1974, and order that the amount be paid to his estate.

Per Lord Denning M.R. In accordance with the principle that no one should suffer by reason of the delays of the court or its officers, the widow should not suffer by reason of the C case officer's delay in notifying the applicant of the award (post, p. 1242B–C).

Decision of the Divisional Court of the Queen's Bench Division [1976] 1 W.L.R. 47; [1975] 3 All E.R. 678 reversed.

The following cases are referred to in the judgment of Lord Denning M.R.

D

Reg. v. *Criminal Injuries Compensation Board, Ex parte Ince* [1973] 1 W.L.R. 1334; [1973] 3 All E.R. 808, C.A.

Reg. v. *Criminal Injuries Compensation Board, Ex parte Lain* [1967] 2 Q.B. 864; [1967] 3 W.L.R. 348; [1967] 2 All E.R. 770, D.C.

Reg. v. *Criminal Injuries Compensation Board, Ex parte Lawton* [1972] 1 W.L.R. 1589; [1972] 3 All E.R. 582, D.C.

Reg. v. *Criminal Injuries Compensation Board, Ex parte Schofield* [1971] E 1 W.L.R. 926; [1971] 2 All E.R. 1011, D.C.

No additional cases were cited in argument.

APPEAL from the Divisional Court of the Queen's Bench Division.

The applicant, Ivy Florence Tong, executrix of the will of her husband, William Henry Tong, deceased, applied for an order of certiorari to quash F a decision by the Criminal Injuries Compensation Board on September 16, 1974, that £450, the amount of compensation awarded by a single member of the board (Sir Henry Long) on February 25, 1973, to the deceased was not payable.

The Divisional Court [1976] 1 W.L.R. 47 refused the application holding that under the scheme payments of compensation were entirely G ex gratia and there was no obligation to pay the award made on February 25, 1975, to the deceased's estate because the date on which he became entitled to the ex gratia award was the date when payment was made to him and that as he had died before payment was made the award was not payable to his estate.

The widow appealed on the grounds that the Divisional Court was wrong in law (1) in finding that there was no obligation to pay the sum H awarded to the estate because the victim of the assault had died on March 6, 1973, after the award was made but before it was notified to him; (2) in not finding that the board's contention that the award by the single member of the board constituted "an offer" which was capable of being accepted and that an award only became payable if and when the "offer" was accepted was wrong; (3) in not finding that the board were wrong in holding that the award by the single member did not, without more, constitute a final award and that accordingly the award was not payable; (4) in holding that the payment of compensation by the board was entirely ex gratia; (5) in holding that the stage when a decision was made about an award to a live victim was when payment was made to the victim; (6) in holding that if no payment had been made to a victim there was no entitlement and no right on the part of the victim to the award; (7) in not finding that if the board were correct in holding that notification of the award and/or acceptance were necessary steps before payment could be made the board were themselves at fault in failing to notify the deceased on or immediately after February 25, 1973, of the award, thereby depriving him of the opportunity of accepting it, and that it was inequitable and unjust for the board to be able to rely on their own default; and (8) in not finding that the board were not entitled by virtue of paragraph 21 of the scheme to refer the decision of the single member to three members of the board for hearing on September 16, 1974.

I. E. Jacob for the applicant.
Harry Woolf for the board.

LORD DENNING M.R. Mr. William Tong was a rent collector employed by the London Borough of Ealing. On April 14, 1970, he, with another man, collected rents from tenants. They put the takings in a car ready to leave the rent office. Suddenly a van pulled up in front of them. Four men rushed out and attacked the rent collectors. The men had woollen masks on their faces. They hit the rent collectors with pickaxe handles. They pulled them out of the car. They beat Mr. Tong until he fell into the road unconscious. They took the money and went off. They were never caught. Mr. Tong suffered severe head injury. He went to hospital and was off work for some weeks. He did not lose any wages because his employers paid him while he was off work. But he suffered for a long time from headaches, depression and giddiness. He wanted to get compensation for these ill effects. He could not get it from his assailants. And at common law he could not get it from anyone else. But ever since 1964 the Crown, that is, the executive government, has operated a scheme by which a person like Mr. Tong—who was the victim of criminal violence—can be paid compensation by the state.

It is that scheme which comes up for consideration in this case. I must give an outline of it. The scheme has no statutory sanction. No enactment was passed. No regulations were made. All that happened was that moneys were appropriated by Parliament so as to finance the scheme. The executive government prepared the scheme, made known its provisions, and invited persons like Mr. Tong to apply for compensation. The scheme did not give him, or any one else, a legal right to compensation. Any grant that was made was purely ex gratia. But nevertheless the amount was to be assessed much the same as if he had been injured in a road accident by a negligent driver—instead of by a wicked criminal. He was to get compensation for loss of earnings, pain and suffering, and loss of amenities. If he had been killed by the assailant or died from the injuries, his widow and dependants were to get compensation for their pecuniary loss much as if he had been killed in a road accident.

In order to administer the scheme, the executive government set up a Criminal Injuries Compensation Board. It consisted of a chairman of wide legal experience and eight others, also legally qualified. This board were to receive applications for compensation and determine them in accordance with the provisions of the scheme. But the whole board did not sit on every application. The scheme in paragraph 21 provided that, in the first instance, an application should be considered by a single member of the board. If he considered it a straightforward case, which he could properly determine on his own, he would decide what the compensation should be. His decision was then communicated to the applicant. If that applicant was satisfied with it—and accepted it—that was the end of the matter. If the applicant was not satisfied, his case was heard by three other members of the board: and those three would decide it. However, in any case which the single member did not consider straightforward—so that he could not determine it on his own—the single member could refer it to three other members for a hearing.

To return now to Mr. Tong. He was certainly the victim of a crime of violence. His case was directly covered by the scheme. He ought to receive compensation. The only question was, how much? This depended on the extent of his disability. A provisional assessment was made of 20 per cent. disability. His application was placed before Sir Ronald Long, a single member of the board. He made an interim award of £50 generally on account. That was on April 14, 1971. Mr. Tong was asked to sign a receipt accepting it. He signed the receipt on April 20, 1971, and sent it back and got his £50.

Later on, a final assessment was made of his disability. It was assessed at 20 per cent. The case was then sent back to Sir Ronald Long for final determination. On February 25, 1973, Sir Ronald made his decision. He assessed the final award at £450, that is, £400 extra to the interim award of £50. This award was as compensation for his pain and suffering and loss of amenities. Sir Ronald's decision ought to have been communicated to Mr. Tong. The scheme so provides. But it was not communicated to him at all. The reason was because the case work officer employed by the board did not get down to that simple task. I suppose he was engaged on other things. He took his time over it. Several days passed—from February 25, 1973—and still nothing was done. Then, before the case worker got down to it, Mr. Tong died. He died on March 6, 1973, that is, eight working days after Sir Ronald had made his decision. The case work officer got to know of Mr. Tong's death and asked the secretary what was to be done. The secretary took the view—afterwards confirmed by the board—that no communication should be made because Mr. Tong had died. So nothing was said to his widow at that time. She did not know that Sir Ronald had made the award of £450.

Mr. Tong's union looked into the case from a different angle. They inquired whether Mr. Tong's death was due to the injuries he received in the attack. For, if it had been, the widow and dependants would have a claim under paragraph 12 of the scheme for their pecuniary loss to be assessed similarly to the Fatal Accidents Acts. But that inquiry came to nothing. His death was not due to the injuries in the attack, but to high blood pressure and heart trouble.

But then the board very properly thought that the widow should be told about the award by Sir Ronald Long of £450: so that she could make a claim on that account, if so advised. On August 15, 1974, the secretary of the board wrote to the trade union with this information:

"In Mr. Tong's case a member of the board made an assessment of

A compensation of £450 on February 25, 1973. News of Mr. Tong's death was received before the award could be notified. The board's view is that in these circumstances there is no obligation to pay the award to Mrs. Tong or to the executors of Mr. Tong's estate . . ."

On August 20, 1974, Mrs. Tong's solicitor replied: saying: ". . . This appears to me to be grossly unfair. The whole matter appears to depend
B on how busy your department is at any time. . . ."

Seeing that a point of principle emerged, the board had a special hearing on September 16, 1974, before Sir William Carter Q.C. (the chairman), Mr. Ogden Q.C. and Mr. Law Q.C. After full argument and consideration, they held that:

> "If an applicant dies before he has accepted the amount of compensation offered, the offer lapses since it is an offer to the applicant
> C himself. If an offer has not been accepted by an applicant before his death, the only persons entitled to compensation are those dependants who can apply under paragraph 12 or 13 of the scheme."

Paragraph 12 deals with cases where the victim has died in consequence of the injury. That was not Mr. Tong's case. Paragraph 13 deals with cases where the victim has died otherwise than in consequence of the injury.
D It says that the board may make an award in respect of his loss of wages before his death where hardship to dependants would otherwise result. But Mr. Tong was only off work for a few weeks during which his employer paid his wages. So paragraph 13 did not apply to this case. The award of £450 was for his pain and suffering and loss of amenities. So the board rejected the claim. The widow applied to the Divisional
E Court for an order of certiorari. They rejected the widow's claim also, but on somewhat different grounds from those given by the board. They said that the "cut-off" point was not when the offer was accepted, but when payment was actually made to the victim. They said: "If no payment has been made, then there is no entitlement": see [1976] 1 W.L.R. 47, 50.

To my mind the situation here is one which was not envisaged by the
F framers of the scheme. It is not covered by it. That was pointed out by the Divisional Court, at p. 50F–G. The scheme does not deal with the situation where a single member of the board has made his decision but it so happens that, before the decision is communicated to the applicant (so that he can say whether he is satisfied with it, or not), the applicant dies.

G I do not myself care for the solution adopted by the Divisional Court. It would mean that after a man had accepted an award for his pain and suffering, if he then died, the board would not pay anything. Even if the full board of three, after a hearing, had awarded a sum, if he then died, the board would not pay anything.

Nor do I care for the solution adopted by the board itself. It would mean that if the board's staff were expeditious and despatched the notifi-
H cation at once (before the man died) he could accept the award and his widow get the compensation. But if the board's staff were dilatory—so that he died before he could accept it—his widow would get nothing.

Now it is quite plain that the award of compensation under the scheme is personal to the applicant. In that respect it is like damages for personal injuries at common law before the Law Reform Act 1934. Actio personalis moritur cum persona. It does not survive to his personal representatives. That is, I think, apparent from paragraph 13, which enables a hardship

A award to be made in certain circumstances to his dependants. But although the award is personal, yet there may come a point when it becomes vested in him in his lifetime—so that on his death the benefit of it passes to his widow or personal representatives. In the court below this was called the " cut-off " point. The board held that the award became vested when a single member made it, and the man accepted it. The Divisional Court held that it only became vested when the compensation was paid. For myself, I think it should be regarded as vested in him as B soon as the single member makes his award. In this respect it is rather like the common law which held that a man's damages for personal injuries became vested in him as soon as the verdict was given, even though he died before judgment was entered. I say this also because I do not think that the man or his widow should suffer by reason of the delay of the board's staff. It is a general principle of our law that no one C should suffer by the delay of the court or its officers. The maxim is actus curiae nemini facit injuriam: see notes to *Cumber* v. *Wane* in 1 Smith L.C., 13th ed. (1929), pp. 391–392. So here, the widow should not suffer by the delay of the case officer in notifying Mr. Tong of the award of Sir Ronald Long. If Mr. Tong had been notified on February 26 or 27, 1973, of the award of £450, he would no doubt have accepted it before his death on March 6, 1973: and the board would, on their own showing, D have regarded it as payable to his widow or personal representative. Seeing that she should not suffer by the delay, it should now be paid to her.

There remains, however, the question whether this court can interfere. Can it issue an order of certiorari so as to quash the decision of the board refusing compensation and thus in effect say that compensation should be paid? At one time there would have been much debate about this. The E person who is injured by a crime of violence has no legal right to compensation. Any payment to him is ex gratia. The board's awards have no legal backing. They cannot be enforced by law. They are in truth part and parcel of an administrative system. But now by a series of important decisions it has been held that the High Court has a supervisory jurisdiction over the board which it can exercise by way of certiorari: see *Reg.* v. *Criminal Injuries Compensation Board, Ex parte Lain* [1967] 2 Q.B. 864. F The High Court can interfere if the board makes an error of law, or misinterprets the scheme, or acts contrary to natural justice, or does any other act or thing which calls for the intervention of the court. There are several instances already reported, such as *Reg.* v. *Criminal Injuries Compensation Board, Ex parte Schofield* [1971] 1 W.L.R. 926; *Reg.* v. *Criminal Injuries Compensation Board, Ex parte Lawton* [1972] 1 W.L.R. 1589; *Reg.* v. G *Criminal Injuries Compensation Board, Ex parte Ince* [1973] 1 W.L.R. 1334. The present case presents a question of principle as to how the board should act when an applicant dies. Such a question is, I think, properly determinable by the court in the exercise of its supervisory jurisdiction. I would, therefore, allow the appeal and allow certiorari to issue to quash the decision of the board of September 16, 1974.

H

ORR L.J. I agree.

WALLER J. I also agree. Of the three possibilities as to the date when the entitlement to compensation arises—namely, first, when the single member makes his decision; or, secondly, when the offer is accepted; or, thirdly, when the money is actually paid—acceptance (although adopted by the board) is in my opinion one which cannot stand, because there

A is no such word as "acceptance" in the whole of the scheme. No doubt as a matter of practical politics in the working of the scheme it is convenient for the board to have a notification of acceptance, because that puts out of possibility the fact that the individual is dissatisfied with the award; but, as it is not any part of the scheme, that cannot possibly be the day when entitlement vests.

That leaves two possibilities, namely, the date of decision or the date
B of payment, which was the date adopted by the Divisional Court. We have heard of hard cases which may run from both of those, but the reading of paragraph 21 really compels the earlier date. It reads as follows:

"The initial decision whether the application should be allowed (and, if so, what amount of compensation should be offered) or should be
C rejected will normally be taken by one member of the board, whose decision will be communicated to the applicant; if the applicant is not satisfied with that decision, whether because no compensation is offered or because he considers the amount offered to be inadequate, he will be entitled to a hearing before three other members of the board. . . ."

That means that if he is satisfied with that decision, it is the final decision.
D It is as if in an ordinary court of law when a judgment has been given, and notice of appeal is not given, it becomes final because he does not express his dissatisfaction. In my view that leads to the conclusion that the initial decision becomes the final one when the applicant does not express his dissatisfaction. It then becomes the date on which the entitlement arises.

Appeal allowed with costs.

E

Solicitors: *J. G. Haley; Treasury Solicitor.*

M. M. H.

F

[COURT OF APPEAL]

* REGINA *v.* HAMMERTONS CARS LTD.

1976 May 27, 28; Lawton and Browne L.JJ.
G July 14 and Willis J.

Trade Description—False description—Car—Mileometer recording less than actual mileage—Accuracy of mileometer reading disclaimed during negotiations and in small print in contractual document—Whether sufficient—Whether supply of goods to which false trade description applied—"Supplied"—Trade Descriptions Act 1968 (*c.* 29), *ss.* 1 (1) (*b*), 2 (1) (*j*), 4

H

The appellants, who were dealers in secondhand motor cars, sold two such cars, each with a mileometer recording less than the car's actual mileage. In respect of each car they were charged with contravening section 1 (1) (*b*) of the Trade Descriptions Act 1968,[1] in that, in the course of a trade or business, they supplied goods to which a false trade description was applied. Their defence was that no false trade description

[1] Trade Descriptions Act 1968, s. 1 (1): see post, p. 1245F.

had been applied because their salesman had stated clearly during negotiations for sale that the mileage on the mileometer was not guaranteed and a contractual document, which was handed to the purchaser on delivery, stated in small print that they were "not answerable for the mileage shown on the vehicle's mileometer." The jury, who must have rejected the salesman's evidence, convicted the appellants. A

On appeal against conviction:—

Held, dismissing the appeal, that, on a charge under section 1 (1) (*b*) the question for determination by the court of trial on the evidence considered as a whole was whether the prosecution had proved that the person charged supplied goods to which a false trade description was applied; that a mileometer reading was on the car to be seen and taken into consideration when deciding whether to buy, and dealers who wished a customer to disregard it had to take positive and effective steps to ensure that he understood it to be meaningless; that a court would probably find that a casual remark during oral negotiations or small print in a contractual document was ineffective; and that no reasonable jury could have found that the small print on the appellants' document displaced the inference to be drawn from the false mileometer reading; so that, albeit there had been a misdirection as to the burden of proof and the misdirection had been inadequately retracted, no miscarriage of justice had occurred (post, pp. 1248A, B–C, D, 1250G). B C

Tarleton Engineering Co. Ltd. v. *Nattrass* [1973] 1 W.L.R. 1261, D.C. affirmed. D

Norman v. *Bennett* [1974] 1 W.L.R. 1229, D.C. considered.

Per curiam. In the context of the Act of 1968 "supplied" comprehends more than an act of delivery (post, p. 1248E).

The following cases are referred to in the judgment:

Naish v. *Gore* [1971] 3 All E.R. 737; [1972] R.T.R. 102, D.C. E

Norman v. *Bennett* [1974] 1 W.L.R. 1229; [1974] 3 All E.R. 351, D.C.

Reg. v. *Moon* [1969] 1 W.L.R. 1705; [1969] 3 All E.R. 803, C.A.

Richmond-upon-Thames London Borough Council v. *Motor Sales (Hounslow) Ltd.* [1971] R.T.R. 116, D.C.

Tarleton Engineering Co. Ltd. v. *Nattrass* [1973] 1 W.L.R. 1261; [1973] 3 All E.R. 699, D.C.

F

The following additional cases were cited in argument:

Cottee v. *Douglas Seaton (Used Cars) Ltd.* [1972] 1 W.L.R. 1408; [1972] 3 All E.R. 750, D.C.

Hotchin v. *Hindmarsh* [1891] 2 Q.B. 181, D.C.

McGuire v. *Sittingbourne Co-operative Society Ltd.* [1976] Crim.L.R. 268, D.C.

Preston v. *Albuery* [1964] 2 Q.B. 796; [1964] 2 W.L.R. 218; [1963] 3 All E.R. 897, D.C. G

Rees v. *Munday* [1974] 1 W.L.R. 1284; [1974] 3 All E.R. 506, D.C.

Shulton (Great Britain) Ltd. v. *Slough Borough Council* [1967] 2 Q.B. 471; [1967] 2 W.L.R. 1289; [1967] 2 All E.R. 137, D.C.

Simmons v. *Potter* [1975] R.T.R. 347, D.C.

Taylor v. *Smith* [1974] R.T.R. 190, D.C.

Zawadski v. *Sleigh* [1975] R.T.R. 113, D.C. H

APPEAL against conviction and sentence.

On September 9, 1975, at Snaresbrook Crown Court (Judge Sellers) the appellants, Hammertons Cars Ltd., were convicted on an indictment containing two counts each charging contravention of section 1 of the Trade Descriptions Act 1968. Count 1 charged that they on August 22, 1972, in the course of a trade or business supplied to Dane Structures Ltd. a motor car to which a false trade description was applied by means of an odometer which showed a mileage of about 25,600 miles whereas the actual mileage was about 53,714; count 2 charged a similar supply on the same date to the same company of a different car with an odometer which showed a mileage of about 25,300 where the actual mileage was about 34,000. The appellants were fined £1,000 on count 1 and £500 on count 2. They appealed against conviction on the grounds that a mileometer which at the time of supply gave a false reading could not be a false trade description; that an irrelevant and misleading issue had been left to the jury because of reliance on *Norman* v. *Bennett* [1974] 1 W.L.R. 1229, which had been wrongly decided; and that the judge has misdirected the jury as to the burden of proof. They applied for an extension of time and for leave to appeal also against sentence on the ground that the fines were excessive and the fine on count 1 was inconsistent with that on count 2.

The facts are stated in the judgment of the court.

John Hall Q.C. and *Richard Rains* for the appellants.
Anthony Scrivener Q.C. and *A. Trevelyan Thomas* for the Crown.

Cur. adv. vult.

July 14. Lawton J. read the following judgment of the court. On September 9, 1975, the appellants, who carry on business as dealers in secondhand motor cars, were convicted in the Snaresbrook Crown Court on two counts of supplying a motor car to which a false trade description was applied. They were fined £1,000 upon count 1 and £500 upon count 2 and, in addition, ordered to pay the costs of the prosecution. They now appeal against their convictions on questions of law and apply for leave to appeal on grounds of both questions of fact and of mixed law and fact. This court grants leave to appeal against conviction and with the consent of the appellants' counsel treats the hearing of the application as the hearing of the appeal.

On both counts of the indictment the appellants were charged with offences under section 1 (1) (*b*) of the Trade Descriptions Act 1968, which is in these terms:

> "Any person who, in the course of a trade or business,—(*a*) applies a false trade description to any goods; or (*b*) supplies or offers to supply any goods to which a false trade description is applied; shall, subject to the provisions of this Act, be guilty of an offence."

This subsection creates three offences. That in paragraph (*a*) is one with an element of dishonesty in it. Those in paragraph (*b*) involve proof of an act coupled with proof of the specified condition of the goods.

In the course of their business as motor dealers the appellants had supplied on or about August 22, 1974, two motor cars to a company called Danes Structures Ltd. Both were Jaguars. When supplied the milometer on one showed a figure of 25,600 whereas it had been used over a distance of about 53,714 miles; that on the other showed a figure of 25,300 miles whereas it had been used over a distance of about 34,000 miles. At or about the time of delivery the purchasers were given in respect of both motor cars a printed document headed in large type "Specific guarantee of used motor vehicle." The top half of this document was taken up with particulars of the suppliers, the purchasers, the vehicle and the period covered by the so-called guarantee. These particulars were set out clearly.

Across the middle there was set out in clear type what the suppliers A undertook to do. Underneath there came five paragraphs which were not so clearly set out. Each had a heading which was in larger type than what followed. One heading was "Mileage and date." What followed started with this sentence:

> "Any estimate or opinion of the mileage or date or model or past use of the vehicle which the suppliers may have given to the customer B during negotiations for its purchase or hire-purchase was given according to their best information and belief."

At the end of this paragraph, in brackets, came these words: "The suppliers are not answerable for the mileage shown on the vehicle's mileometer."

At the trial the appellants' salesman, who had carried out the negotiations C for the purchase with the purchasers' representatives, said that he had given them clearly to understand that the mileage as shown on the mileometers was not guaranteed. From the way the trial judge summed up upon the issue as to what was said in the course of negotiations, we feel sure that the jury must have rejected the salesman's evidence on this point.

On these facts Mr. Hall made three submissions on behalf of the D appellants: first, that a mileometer which at the time of supply gives a false reading cannot in law be a false trade description; secondly, that the trial judge's reliance on the decision of the Divisional Court in *Norman* v. *Bennett* [1974] 1 W.L.R. 1229 resulted in an irrelevant and misleading issue being left to the jury since that case had been wrongly decided; and thirdly, that the trial judge had misdirected the jury as to the burden of proof. E

Mr. Hall's first submission was bold but hopeless. Section 2 of the Act defines a trade description as follows: "(1) A trade description is an indication, direct or indirect, and by whatever means given, of any of the following matters with respect to any goods or parts of goods, that is to say . . ." There then follow a number of paragraphs by way of examples covering such matters as quantity, method of manufacture, F fitness for purpose, place and date of manufacture, and person by whom manufactured. The list ends with paragraph (*j*) which is in these terms: "other history, including previous ownership or use."

In our judgment a reading on a mileometer on a motor car is an indication of the use which it has had. It follows that it is a trade description and if the reading is false, as it was on both the motor cars with which this appeal is concerned, it is capable of being a false trade description. G

As the statutory words are so clear it would be pointless to examine the reported cases in detail. When convictions under section 1 (1) (*b*) of the Act first came before the Divisional Court on appeal from justices, counsel for the appellants do not appear to have considered it worthwhile to argue the point taken by Mr. Hall: see *Richmond-upon-Thames London Borough Council* v. *Motor Sales* (*Hounslow*) *Ltd.* [1971] R.T.R. 116 and H *Naish* v. *Gore* [1971] 3 All E.R. 737. The point was argued in *Tarleton Engineering Co. Ltd.* v. *Nattrass* [1973] 1 W.L.R. 1261 and rejected; see the judgment of Wien J. at p. 1268, which was the judgment of the court. We affirm that judgment on this point. In that judgment Wien J. said, at p. 1268:

> "If the description is in fact false because the true mileage is in excess of 40,000 an offence is committed by the seller who applies that

A description to the goods even though he is unaware of the falsity of
the description. He can protect himself by some disclaimer of the
accuracy of the mileometer."

That statement, although accurate, has been misunderstood by motor
traders. Some seem to have thought that provided they made some dis-
claimer, either orally or by means of a clause in a contractual document,
B they could provide themselves with a defence. In *Norman* v. *Bennett*
[1974] 1 W.L.R. 1229, Lord Widgery C.J. made some comments about
this, at pp. 1232, 1233:

> "I think that, where a false trade description is attached to goods, its
> effect can be neutralised by an express disclaimer or contradiction of
> the message contained in the trade description. To be effective any
> C such disclaimer must be as bold, precise and compelling as the trade
> description itself and must be effectively brought to the notice of any
> person to whom the goods may be supplied. In other words, the
> disclaimer must equal the trade description in the extent to which it
> is likely to get home to anyone interested in receiving the goods. To
> be effective as a defence to a charge under section 1 (1) (*b*) of the Act
> of 1968 any such disclaimer must be made before the goods are sup-
> D plied. . . . Can a supplier who has made a sale on the strength of a
> false trade description protect himself by withdrawing the description
> before delivery? He certainly should not be able to do so, and I
> think that the answer to that problem is that the words 'is applied'
> in section 1 (1) (*b*) mean 'is applied at the time of supply or has been
> so applied in the course of negotiations leading to such supply.'"

E Mr. Hall submitted that these observations were wrong in law and
that the trial judge's reliance on them led him to introduce an irrelevant
issue into the case and to give a wrong direction as to the burden of proof.
The proscribed act under section 1 (1) (*b*) is supplying goods to which a
false trade description is applied. Once the prosecution has established
that fact an offence has been proved unless the accused can rely upon the
F statutory defence of accident or mistake, coupled with the taking of all
reasonable precautions and the exercise of all due diligence: see section
24. In this case the appellants did not try to rely upon any statutory
defence. What they tried to do was to submit that a false trade description
had not been applied to all because of what their salesman had said during
the negotiations and what was in the guarantee documents which they
had given to the purchasers.

G Whether a false trade description had been applied was an issue for
the jury to decide on the evidence before them. In our judgment Lord
Widgery C.J. in *Norman* v. *Bennett* [1974] 1 W.L.R. 1229 was not
seeking to introduce a new defence to a charge under section 1 (1) (*b*).
Still less was he seeking to put upon accused persons the burden of nega-
tiving evidence led by the prosecution. We understand his judgment as
H meaning that, when there is clear evidence that a false trade description
has been affixed or annexed to or marked on or incorporated with the
goods (see section 4 (1) (*a*)), then there is a strong inference that that
description has been applied to them unless other evidence shows that what
looks like an indication as to the matters which can constitute a trade
description was not such an indication at all. Common sense says that
such other evidence should be bold, precise and compelling. In our judg-
ment it is unwise and likely to cause confusion as to the burden of proof

to try to divide the evidence into that which establishes that a trade description has been applied and that which is said to be a disclaimer of that description. The evidence must be looked at as a whole. At the end of the case, when all the evidence has been heard, the right question for the court of trial is this: "Have the prosecution proved that this defendant supplied goods to which a false trade description was applied?" If the evidence was positive that at the beginning of the negotiations a false trade description was applied but before they were concluded the defendant made it clear to the purchaser that the trade description should be disregarded, then the answer to the question will be "no"; but if he did not make it clear then the answer will probably be "yes."

Each case must depend upon its own facts; but in most cases of the kind now before the court a mileometer reading is on the motor car for the prospective purchaser to see and to take into consideration when deciding whether to buy. If dealers do not want prospective purchasers to take any notice of mileometer readings they must take positive and effective steps to ensure that the customer understands that the mileometer reading is meaningless. Whether any such steps were taken, and if they were whether they were effective, is always a matter for assessment by the justices in the case of summary proceedings and by the jury when there is a trial on indictment. We should expect both justices and juries to find that a casual remark in the course of oral negotiations or "small print" in a contractual document were not effective.

Mr. Hall also criticised that part of Lord Widgery C.J.'s judgment in which he set out his construction of the words "is applied" in section 1 (1) (*b*). He submitted that the only relevant time to be considered was the moment when the goods were supplied and, if at that moment the dealer told the purchaser that the mileometer reading could not be relied upon, the motor car had not been supplied with a false trade description applied to it. He equated supply with delivery. We do not agree that this is so. The word "supplied" in this Act, in our judgment, comprehends more than an act of delivery. The issue for the court of trial is whether when the purchaser takes possession of the goods he gets them with a false trade description applied to them. What he has seen during the negotiations may have made such an impact upon him that an oral statement made when delivery was given might not be effective to displace the mileometer reading. Whether it had been would be a question of fact. If Lord Widgery C.J.'s judgment on the construction of the words "is applied" amounts to the proposition that a dealer can never disclaim when making a delivery (which it probably does not) we do not agree. A dealer who delays disclaimer as late as this may have difficulty in persuading a court that a false trade description has not been applied; but he may be able to do so.

We turn now to consider how the trial judge dealt with the evidence relating to disclaimer. Early in his summing up he told the jury—and did so correctly—that it was for them to decide whether the mileometer readings could amount to trade descriptions in the light of the evidence before them. He went on to deal with disclaimer and did so in terms which may have led the jury to think that disclaimer was a defence in itself whereas, as we have already said, evidence of disclaimer may lead to the displacing of such inferences as arise from the presence on the motor car of a false mileometer reading.

Juries, unless clearly directed, are liable to think that a defendant has

A to establish a defence. The trial judge himself made this very error. He said:

> "Their defence in this case is that there was some disclaimer. If you think, on the balance of probability, there was a sufficient disclaimer, then you must acquit, because the burden of proof is not as high on the defence as it is on the prosecution, so if you think, 'well, B there was a disclaimer which probably would be sufficient to satisfy a normal purchaser,' then, members of the jury, you must acquit because the prosecution would not have proved their case so that it would be safe for you to convict."

Mr. Scrivener, who appeared for the prosecution at the trial, appreciated that the trial judge had misdirected the jury as to both the nature of the C issue and the burden of proof. In concise and tactful terms he intervened to correct the error. His first attempt was not successful. The judge, thinking that he had understood Mr. Scrivener rightly, put his direction upon the burden of proof in different words but he made the same error again. Then came the midday adjournment. When the court reassembled, the judge directed the jury as follows:

> "Members of the jury, I said to you, I think, just before I rose that D the burden of proof is upon the prosecution. They must prove the case so that you feel sure and I did point out to you that if you think, on the balance of probabilities, there was a disclaimer, you must acquit. When I say 'disclaimer,' I mean not only that words were uttered or written but also that they were sufficient. I must go further than that and say that if you think that may have been the case, then E you must also acquit. You must only convict if you are satisfied that there was a trade description which was false and that there has been no disclaimer, and when I say 'no disclaimer,' I mean there has been no sufficient disclaimer and you are the judges of whether there has been a sufficient disclaimer or not. I hope I have made that clear, members of the jury, because perhaps I did not make it quite clear before. The prosecution must prove its case so that you F are sure that the case has been proved in the way it is alleged in the indictment and that there has been no disclaimer; in other words, that the defendant has not exempted himself from responsibility for the false trade description, if you are satisfied that it is one, by a sufficient disclaimer. If you think he may have done, then you must acquit him. If you think he may have given a sufficient disclaimer, G you must acquit. If, on the other hand, you are satisfied that there was this false trade description as has been alleged and if you are satisfied that it is a material lie—in this case, there is no doubt about it; you may think it is a very material falsity—if you are satisfied about that and if you are satisfied that there was not a sufficient disclaimer, then, members of the jury, it is your duty to convict."

H Mr. Hall criticised this direction on the grounds: first, that having regard to the judge's initial error the retraction of it was inadequate; and, secondly, that the jury were given to understand that the appellants had to exempt themselves in some way from responsibility for the false trade description, whereas the issue was whether, in view of the evidence about a disclaimer, a false trade description had been applied at all.

In support of the first of these criticisms Mr. Hall invited our attention to *Reg.* v. *Moon* [1969] 1 W.L.R. 1705, in which this court adjudged

that a misdirection as to the burden of proof on an issue of self defence A
can be corrected; but the correction must be in the plainest possible terms.
Salmon L.J. said, at p. 1707:

> "It would be necessary for the [trial judge] to repeat the direction
> which he had given, to acknowledge that that direction was quite
> wrong, to tell the jury to put out of their minds all that they had
> heard from him relating to self defence up to that moment about the
> burden of proof and then in clear terms, which would be incapable B
> of being misunderstood, tell them very plainly and simply what the
> law is."

In this case the judge's retraction of his misdirection as to the burden
of proof did not come up to this standard; but that fact by itself would
not make the verdicts unsafe or unsatisfactory. It is, however, a factor C
to be taken into consideration when considering whether the corrected
direction was adequate. The judge does not seem to have appreciated
that the evidence as to disclaimer went solely to the issue as to whether
a false trade description had been applied at all. This is shown by his
reference to "sufficient disclaimer" and his use of the words "the defend-
ant has not exempted himself from responsibility." In our judgment there
was some confusion of thought in this direction. It might have left the D
jury in doubt as to where the probative burden lay. It cannot be approved.

Once the prosecution had proved, however, that the mileometer read-
ings were false, there was, as we have said, a strong inference that false
trade descriptions had been applied and this inference could only be dis-
placed by evidence which had the effect of showing that the appellants
may not have supplied motor cars to which a false trade description was E
applied. On the facts of this case no such evidence came from the prose-
cution's witnesses. If there was to be any, it had to come from the
appellants' witnesses, which means that there was an evidential burden,
but not a probative one, upon the appellants. Although the trial judge's
choice of words was inaccurate and revealed a misconception of the issues,
what he left the jury to decide was whether such evidence as there was
about disclaimer raised a reasonable doubt about the application of a F
false trade description. By their verdict the jury found that they had no
such doubt. This must have meant first that they did not believe the
appellants' salesman and that the "small print" in the so-called guarantees
did not displace the inference to be drawn from the false mileometer
readings. Can we be sure that they would have convicted the appellants
had there been a more accurate direction? In our judgment we can. No G
reasonable jury could have found that the "small print" displaced the
inference to be drawn from the false mileometer readings. There has
been no miscarriage of justice despite the misdirection. The appeal against
conviction is dismissed.

As to sentence, we grant the extension of time. Mr. Hall submitted
that the fines were too heavy and that the one of £1,000 imposed on count
1 was inconsistent with that of £500 on count 2. We do not agree. The H
Trade Descriptions Act 1968 was intended by Parliament to provide
protection for the public against unscrupulous and irresponsible traders.
Section 1 (1) (*a*) deals with those who are proved to have been actively
unscrupulous, as for example, by turning back mileometers; and section
1 (1) (*b*) with those who do not take the trouble to check as best they can
that mileometer readings are genuine. In this case the prosecution did
not allege that the defendants had been actively unscrupulous; but they

for their part did not seek to prove that they had taken all reasonable precautions and exercised all due diligence. In plain English they took a chance that the mileometer readings were genuine. Traders in second-hand motor cars should not take such chances; and if they do and are prosecuted to conviction the courts should discourage them by taking all the profit out of the transaction and a good deal more.

There is nothing whatsoever in the submission that there was any disparity between the fines on counts 1 and 2. The difference between the genuine and bogus mileometer readings on the motor car in count 1 was much greater than on that in count 2.

The application for leave to appeal against sentence is dismissed.

Appeal dismissed.
Order for payment by appellants of costs of appeal to be taxed by registrar.

Solicitors: *H. Montlake & Co., Ilford; L. C. Alexander, Ilford.*

L. N. W.

[PRIVY COUNCIL]

* DONALD PARKES . . . . APPELLANT

AND

THE QUEEN . . . . RESPONDENT

[ON APPEAL FROM THE COURT OF APPEAL OF JAMAICA]

1976 July 20; Oct. 5

Lord Diplock, Lord Morris of Borth-y-Gest, Lord Salmon, Lord Edmund-Davies and Lord Fraser of Tullybelton

Crime — Evidence — Silence — Accusation by victim's mother — Inference to be drawn from silence

The defendant was charged with the murder of a woman who had died from stab wounds. At his trial the dead woman's mother gave evidence that she had found her daughter injured and had gone to the defendant and said "What she do you—why you stab her?"; that she had repeated the question and that the defendant had made no answer and had tried to stab her when she threatened to hold him until the police came. The judge directed the jury that the defendant's failure to reply to the mother's accusation coupled with his conduct immediately afterwards was evidence from which the jury could infer that the defendant had accepted the truth of the accusation. The defendant was convicted and appealed on the ground of misdirection. The appeal was dismissed.

On appeal to the Judicial Committee:—

Held, dismissing the appeal, that, notwithstanding the rule that a person was entitled to refrain from answering a question put to him by a person in authority for the purpose of discovering whether he had committed an offence, where a person was accused of a crime by another speaking to him on even terms his silence in the face of the accusation together

with his conduct might be taken into account by a jury in A
deciding whether he accepted the truth of the accusation; and
that, accordingly, since the mother was speaking on even
terms with the defendant the trial judge's direction was correct
and the defendant's silence and conduct in the face of the
accusation could properly be considered by the jury.

The following cases are referred to in the reasons of their Lordships:

Hall v. *The Queen* [1971] 1 W.L.R. 298; [1971] 1 All E.R. 322, P.C. B
Reg. v. *Mitchell* (1892) 17 Cox C.C. 503.
Rex v. *Christie* [1914] A.C. 545, H.L.(E.).

No additional cases were cited in argument.

APPEAL (No. 40 of 1975) by Donald Parkes from a judgment of the C
Court of Appeal of Jamaica (Luckhoo Ag. P., Swaby J.A. and Robinson
Ag. J.A.) of July 12, 1974, dismissing his application for leave to appeal
against his conviction in the circuit court for the Parish of Kingston,
Jamaica before Smith C.J. and a jury on January 21, 1974, of the murder
on September 14, 1971, of Daphne Graham.

On July 20, 1976, at the close of the hearing of the appeal, Lord
Diplock said that their Lordships would advise Her Majesty that the D
appeal should be dismissed for reasons to be delivered later.

The facts are stated in the reasons of their Lordships.

Berthan Macaulay Q.C. and *Berthan Macaulay Jnr.* (both of the
Jamaica Bar) for the defendant.

J. S. Kerr Q.C. (of the Jamaica Bar) and *Gerald Davies* for the Crown. E

Cur. adv. vult.

October 5. The reasons for the report of their Lordships were delivered
by LORD DIPLOCK.

The defendant was convicted of murdering a young woman, Daphne
Graham. He was tried in the circuit court for the parish of Kingston F
before Smith C.J. and a jury. The evidence against him was circum-
stantial and given mainly by Mrs. Graham, the mother of the deceased.
The defendant and the deceased lived in separate rooms of a house
owned by Mrs. Graham. She lived in the adjoining house. According
to her evidence Mrs. Graham left her house on the morning of September
14, 1971, at about 7.30 a.m. in order to go to work. She then saw G
the deceased standing at her room door. Before she left she had seen the
defendant standing on the verandah on to which the deceased's room
opened. As soon as she had got on to the road outside the house she
was told something which caused her to return. She found her daughter
in her room bleeding from two stab wounds from which she died
three days later. She was assisted to her bed and said something to
her mother as a result of which Mrs. Graham went out of the room to H
the yard which was common to the two houses. There she found the
defendant with a ratchet knife in his hand. The knife was at that time
closed. Mrs. Graham said to the defendant "What she do you—why you
stab her?" The defendant made no reply nor did he reply when she
repeated the question. Mrs. Graham then boxed him twice and seized
him by the waist-band of his trousers saying she would keep him there
until the police came. The defendant then opened the knife and made

A to strike Mrs. Graham with it. She noticed that it had blood stains on the blade. She put up her arm to defend herself and her finger was cut requiring five stitches. A Mr. Jarrett, the uncle-in-law of the defendant, who had by then arrived upon the scene told the defendant to hand over the knife to him. The defendant did so, and Mr. Jarrett subsequently handed over the knife to the police.

The defendant called no evidence. He did not go into the witness box
B himself, but elected to make an unsworn statement from the dock. In the course of the statement he said that he had just woken up and gone out to wash his face in the yard when Mrs. Graham approached him and held him by the waist. In substance, he confirmed Mrs. Graham's account of what was then said and explained that he said nothing in reply because he did not know what she was speaking about. He denied
C that he had stabbed at Mrs. Graham and accounted for the cut on her finger by saying that she had searched his pocket for the knife, had found the knife in it, opened it and said that she was going to stab him with it because he had stabbed her daughter. He took the knife from her and while he was doing so she cut her finger with it. After a long and detailed summing up by the Chief Justice, the jury brought in a verdict of murder against the defendant.

D On appeal to the Court of Appeal of Jamaica, the principal point argued on behalf of the defendant appears to have been that Smith C.J. was wrong in instructing the jury that the failure of the defendant to reply to the accusation twice made against him by Mrs. Graham that he had stabbed her daughter, coupled with his conduct immediately after that accusation had been made, were matters from which the jury could,
E if they thought fit, draw an inference that the defendant accepted the truth of the accusation. Before their Lordships, however, equal reliance was placed on a submission that in his summing up the Chief Justice had mis-stated to the defendant's prejudice the effect of the evidence of Mrs. Graham that she had seen the defendant on her daughter's verandah before she, Mrs. Graham, left the house on the morning of the murder. There was also a general submission that taken as a whole the evidence
F against the defendant was insufficient to justify a conviction.

The Court of Appeal dealt very shortly with the two latter submissions. Their Lordships propose to emulate their brevity. The defendant's contention is that Mrs. Graham's evidence as recorded on the shorthand note was equivocal as to how long it was before she left that she saw the defendant on her daughter's verandah, whereas the judge in remind-
G ing the jury of her evidence had stated unequivocally that she said that she had seen him there when she was actually leaving the premises. In view of the defendant's denial in his statement from the dock that he had been out of his room at all before Mrs. Graham approached him and seized him by the waist-band of his trousers, minutes do not matter. Their Lordships agree with the Court of Appeal that this minor error in the summing up, if it was one, can have had no influence on the jury's
H verdict. The further submission that there was insufficient evidence was based on absence of confirmation by any other witness of Mrs. Graham's evidence that when the defendant opened the flick knife to stab her there were already blood stains on it; but if, as they were entitled to, the jury accepted the evidence of Mrs. Graham on this and the other matters to which she had deposed, the circumstantial evidence against the defendant was overwhelming.

In support of the argument that the defendant's failure to answer Mrs.

Graham's accusation that he had stabbed her daughter was not a matter A from which the jury were entitled to draw any inference that the defendant accepted the truth of the accusation the defendant relied on the following passage in the judgment of this Board in *Hall* v. *The Queen* [1971] 1 W.L.R. 298, 301:

> "It is a clear and widely known principle of the common law in Jamaica, as in England, that a person is entitled to refrain from B answering a question put to him for the purpose of discovering whether he has committed a criminal offence. A fortiori he is under no obligation to comment when he is informed that someone else has accused him of an offence. It may be that in very exceptional circumstances an inference may be drawn from a failure to give an explanation or a disclaimer, but in their Lordships' view silence alone on being informed by a police officer that someone else has made C an accusation against him cannot give rise to an inference that the person to whom this information is communicated accepts the truth of the accusation."

As appears from this passage itself, it was concerned with a case where the person by whom the accusation was communicated to the accused was a police constable whom he knew was engaged in investigating a D drug offence. There was no evidence of the defendant's demeanour or conduct when the accusation was made other than the mere fact that he failed to reply to the constable. The passage cited had been preceded by a quotation from a speech of Lord Atkinson in *Rex* v. *Christie* [1914] A.C. 545, 554, in which it was said that when a statement is made in the presence of an accused person: E

> "He may accept the statement by word or conduct, action or demeanour, and it is the function of the jury which tries the case to determine whether his words, action, conduct or demeanour at the time when the statement was made amount to an acceptance of it in whole or in part."

In the instant case, there is no question of an accusation being made F by or in the presence of a police officer or any other person in authority or charged with the investigation of the crime. It was a spontaneous charge made by a mother about an injury done to her daughter. In circumstances such as these, their Lordships agree with the Court of Appeal of Jamaica that the direction given by Cave J. in *Reg.* v. *Mitchell* (1892) 17 Cox C.C. 503, 508 (to which their Lordships have supplied the emphasis) is applicable: G

> "Now the whole admissibility of statements of this kind rests upon the consideration that if a charge is made against a person in that person's presence it is reasonable to expect that he or she will immediately deny it, and that the absence of such a denial is some evidence of an admission on the part of the person charged, and of the truth of the charge. *Undoubtedly, when persons are speaking* H *on even terms*, and a charge is made, and the person charged says nothing, and expresses no indignation, and does nothing to repel the charge, that is some evidence to show that he admits the charge to be true."

Here Mrs. Graham and the defendant were speaking on even terms. Furthermore, as the Chief Justice pointed out to the jury, the defendant's

A reaction to the twice-repeated accusation was not one of mere silence. He drew a knife and attempted to stab Mrs. Graham in order to escape when she threatened to detain him while the police were sent for. In their Lordships' view, the Chief Justice was perfectly entitled to instruct the jury that the defendant's reactions to the accusations including his silence were matters which they could take into account along with other evidence in deciding whether the defendant in fact committed the act
B with which he was charged. For these reasons their Lordships have humbly advised Her Majesty that the appeal be dismissed.

Solicitors: *Simons, Muirhead & Allan; Charles Russell & Co.*

T. J. M.

C

[HOUSE OF LORDS]

* FAIRMOUNT INVESTMENTS LTD. . . . FIRST RESPONDENTS

D

AND

SECRETARY OF STATE FOR THE ENVIRONMENT . . . . APPELLANT

AND

SOUTHWARK LONDON BOROUGH COUNCIL . . . . SECOND RESPONDENTS

E

1976 May 17, 18, 19, 20; June 24

Lord Diplock, Viscount Dilhorne, Lord Simon of Glaisdale, Lord Edmund-Davies and Lord Russell of Killowen

Housing—Compulsory purchase—Clearance area—Public inquiry —Owners' objection to demolition of dwelling houses—Sug-
F *gested rehabilitation—Site inspection—No reference to settlement of foundations—Confirmation of order recommended on ground of inadequacy of foundations—No opportunity for owners to deal with that ground—Breach of natural justice— Housing Act* 1957 (5 & 6 *Eliz.* 2, *c.* 56), *Sch.* 3, *para.* 3 (3)

Within a clearance area, so declared by the local authority by virtue of section 42 (1) of the Housing Act 1957, a com-
G pany owned several houses in respect of which the local authority made a compulsory purchase order by virtue of section 43 of the Act, requiring them to be demolished as unfit for human habitation. The company objected on the ground that they were not unfit and, alternatively, that they were suitable for rehabilitation. The Secretary of State for the Environment appointed an inspector to hold a public local inquiry under paragraph 3 (3) of Schedule 3 to the Act.
H Before the hearing the local authority published documents setting out the reasons for their proposal and the chief grounds of unfitness, including settlement affecting walls and floors, though there was no suggestion that the settlement was continuing or that the foundations were so defective as to eliminate the possibility of rehabilitation. At the conclusion of the inquiry, at which the state of the foundations was not mentioned, the inspector inspected the premises. His report, recommending the confirmation of the order, stated that the settlement seemed to be due to the foundations not having

been dug deep enough in clay subject to expansion and contraction and that accordingly rehabilitation would not be a financially viable proposition. A

The Secretary of State having confirmed the order, the owners applied to the High Court to quash the order on the ground that, contrary to the rules of natural justice, the inspector had taken into account matters not raised at the inquiry. Cusack J. dismissed the application. The Court of Appeal reversed his decision. B

On appeal by the Secretary of State:—

Held, dismissing the appeal, that it was contrary to natural justice for the Secretary of State to confirm the order on a basis of facts as to the inadequacy of the foundations, which the owners had no opportunity of showing was erroneous, and of an opinion, with which they had no opportunity to deal, that the state of the foundations made rehabilitation impractical (post, pp. 1260C–F, 1265C–D, H—1266A, D–F). C

Decision of the Court of Appeal affirmed.

The following case is referred to in their Lordships' opinions:

Rex v. *Paddington and St. Marylebone Rent Tribunal, Ex parte Bell, London & Provincial Properties Ltd.* [1949] 1 K.B. 666; [1949] 1 All E.R. 720, D.C.

D

The following additional cases were cited in argument:

Anisminic Ltd. v. *Foreign Compensation Commission* [1969] 2 A.C. 147; [1969] 2 W.L.R. 163; [1969] 1 All E.R. 208, H.L.(E.).

Board of Education v. *Rice* [1911] A.C. 179, H.L.(E.).

Burwoods (Caterers) Ltd. v. *Secretary of State for the Environment* (1972) 224 E.G. 2021.

Coleen Properties Ltd. v. *Minister of Housing and Local Government* [1971] 1 W.L.R. 433; [1971] 1 All E.R. 1049, C.A. E

Errington v. *Minister of Health* [1935] 1 K.B. 249, C.A.

Glynn v. *Keele University* [1971] 1 W.L.R. 487; [1971] 2 All E.R. 89.

Gordondale Investments Ltd. v. *Secretary of State for the Environment* (1971) 70 L.G.R. 158; 23 P. & C.R. 334, C.A.

Hibernian Property Co. Ltd. v. *Secretary of State for the Environment* (1973) 72 L.G.R. 350; 27 P. & C.R. 197. F

Lake District Special Planning Board v. *Secretary of State for the Environment* (unreported), February 13, 1975, Kerr J.

Local Government Board v. *Arlidge* [1915] A.C. 120, H.L.(E.).

London-Portsmouth Trunk Road (Surrey) Compulsory Purchase Order (No. 2) 1938, In re [1939] 2 K.B. 515; [1939] 2 All E.R. 464, D.C.

McMeechan v. *Secretary of State for the Environment* (unreported), February 7, 1974, Willis J.

Malloch v. *Aberdeen Corporation* [1971] 1 W.L.R. 1578; [1971] 2 All E.R. 1278, H.L.(Sc.). G

Maxwell v. *Department of Trade and Industry* [1974] Q.B. 523; [1974] 2 W.L.R. 338; [1974] 2 All E.R. 122, C.A.

Reg. v. *Secretary of State for the Environment, Ex parte Ostler* [1976] 3 W.L.R. 288; [1976] 3 All E.R. 90.

Rex v. *Cambridge University* (1723) 1 Stra. 557.

Ridge v. *Baldwin* [1964] A.C. 40; [1963] 2 W.L.R. 935; [1963] 2 All E.R. 66, H.L.(E.). H

Salsbury v. *Woodland* [1970] 1 Q.B. 324; [1969] 3 W.L.R. 29; [1963] 3 All E.R. 863, C.A.

Smith v. *East Elloe Rural District Council* [1956] A.C. 736; [1956] 2 W.L.R. 888; [1956] 1 All E.R. 855, H.L.(E.).

Spackman v. *Plumstead District Board of Works* (1885) 10 App.Cas. 229, H.L.(E.).

A *Wilson* v. *Secretary of State for the Environment* [1973] 1 W.L.R. 1083; [1974] 1 All E.R. 428.

Wiseman v. *Borneman* [1971] A.C. 297; [1969] 3 W.L.R. 706; [1969] 3 All E.R. 275, H.L.(E.).

APPEAL from the Court of Appeal.

This was an appeal from an order of the Court of Appeal (Cairns, B James and Shaw L.JJ.) dated November 5, 1975, whereby the court allowed an appeal by the present first respondents, Fairmount Investments Ltd., against an order of the High Court (Cusack J.) dated March 5, 1975, dismissing the company's motion for an order to quash the London Borough of Southwark (Aldridge Street) (No. 1) Compulsory Purchase Order 1973.

The parties to this appeal were the present appellant, the Secretary of State for the Environment, whose decision to confim the order was called C in question, the first respondents, who owned 64 houses within the area covered by the order, and the second respondents, the London Borough of Southwark, the acquiring authority that made the order in the first instance.

The facts are stated in their Lordships' opinions.

D *Peter Archer Q.C. S.-G.*, *William Glover Q.C.* and *Harry Woolf* for the appellant.

Michael Mann Q.C., *Daniel Robins* and *Christine Gorna* for the respondent company.

Their Lordships took time for consideration.

E June 24. LORD DIPLOCK. My Lords, I have had the advantage of reading in draft the speech prepared by my noble and learned friend, Lord Russell of Killowen. I agree with it and I would therefore dismiss the appeal.

VISCOUNT DILHORNE. My Lords, the first respondents are the owners of 64 out of 68 houses in an area of about 2·94 acres declared by the F Southwark Borough Council to be a clearance area as in their view the houses were unfit for human habitation and the most satisfactory way of dealing with the conditions in the area was to demolish all the houses. On January 9, 1973, they made a compulsory purchase order which, if confirmed by the Secretary of State, would enable them to acquire the respondents' 64 houses on payment of site value.

G The respondents also owned houses within a quarter of a mile which the inspector in his report said were "almost identical . . . in design and condition" but "inferior for rehabilitation purposes." In 1973 the council gave the respondents notice of their intention to acquire those houses to improve them "in order to deal in some measure with their long housing list, put at 8,242 families."

The council sought to acquire the respondents' 64 houses not to provide H homes fit for human habitation for those on their housing list but to make the area an open space.

In June 1970 the respondents' agent had met the council's surveyor and together they had inspected some of the 64 houses which were typical of the rest. Following the inspection the respondents were told that the council would consider an application for improvement grants in respect of five houses, typical of the others. The respondents submitted plans and specifications in relation to two houses showing what they proposed to do to improve them and on August 6, 1970, the council's property surveyor wrote to the respondents saying: "After careful inspection I can see no reason that your scheme should not be adopted and I await your formal applications."

Before formal application was made, the respondents were told that it would be a waste of time for them to proceed further as the council proposed to make the area an open space. On April 6, 1972, the respondents were told by letter that that was the council's intention.

As the respondents objected to the compulsory purchase order and did not withdraw their objection, a public local inquiry was ordered. It was held in September 1973 and lasted two days. After the hearing the inspector inspected the houses. He reported in favour of the compulsory acquisition of the respondents' 64 houses under Part III of the Housing Act 1957, which meant their acquisition for site value. His findings, conclusions and recommendations were generally accepted by the Secretary of State with some modifications immaterial to this case.

The respondents then applied unsuccessfully to the High Court for an order quashing the compulsory purchase order but their appeal to the Court of Appeal (Cairns, James and Shaw L.JJ.) succeeded, all the members of that court being in favour of allowing the appeal. From that decision the Secretary of State now appeals.

The respondents alleged that the requirements of natural justice had not been met and that they had in consequence been substantially prejudiced.

In 1957 the Committee on Administrative Tribunals and Inquiries (1957) (Cmd. 218) (commonly referred to as the Franks Committee) reported. It, inter alia, considered and made recommendations as to the procedure to be followed in relation to inquiries, stressing the need for an authority seeking to acquire land to inform those affected of its reasons for doing so in order that they might be better able to prepare and present their case (paragraphs 280, 281) and that the right of individuals to state their case cannot be effective unless the case of the authority is adequately presented at the inquiry (paragraph 306).

Following their report, the Compulsory Purchase by Local Authorities (Inquiries Procedure) Rules 1962 (S.I. 1962 No. 1424) were made. They do not apply, we were told, to acquisitions under Part III of the Housing Act 1957. They only have legal effect in relation to local inquiries held under the Acquisition of Land (Authorisation Procedure) Act 1946 and no similar rules have been made in relation to acquisitions under Part III. Nevertheless we were told that in practice local authorities seeking to acquire under Part III have regard to them.

They embody certain recommendations of the Franks Committee designed to secure fairness and natural justice. Under them an acquiring authority has to serve on "statutory objectors," who include the owners of the land affected, a written statement of their reasons for making the order (rule 4 (4)) and the inspector appointed to hold the inquiry can allow the reasons stated to be altered and added to "but shall (if necessary by adjourning the inquiry) give every statutory objector an adequate opportunity of considering any fresh reason . . ." (rule 7 (5)).

Similar provisions are contained in the Town and Country Planning (Inquiries Procedures) Rules 1974 (S.I. 1974 No. 419).

Their object clearly was to ensure that the requirements of natural justice were met, and that an objector knew what case he had to meet.

In the present case no criticism can be made of the conduct of the borough council in relation to the inquiry but to decide whether or not there was a failure to comply with the requirements of natural justice, one must consider what was their case and the case the respondents had to meet.

The respondents were served with a summary of the principal grounds on which the council based its opinion that the houses were unfit for human habitation. It included the following.

> "Stability
>
> *External:* Settlement with some bulged and fractured walls
>
> *Internal:* Uneven settlement in floors."

In compliance with paragraph 3 (4) of Schedule 3 to the Housing Act 1957 they were also served with a document in relation to each house in the area, including, it appears, houses which they did not own, stating in detail the defects in the house. All these documents mentioned settlement but only in one, and that not one of the respondents' houses, was there said to be "progressive settlement." In houses of this type built in the 1880's some settlement is perhaps to be expected. From these documents it might be inferred that, save in respect of that one house, it was not suggested that the settlement was continuing and that the case the respondents had to meet was that the settlement which had occurred together with the other defects rendered the houses unfit for habitation and led to the conclusion that the best way of dealing with the area was to demolish them.

What is significant is that in none of these documents was there any reference to foundations. It was not suggested that the foundations were so defective as to rule out any question of rehabilitation. Indeed such a suggestion would have been inconsistent with the council's surveyor's statement that after careful consideration he saw no reason why the respondents' improvement scheme should not be adopted, and inconsistent too, if the foundations of the respondents' other houses "almost identical . . . in design and condition" were similar, with the council's action in seeking to acquire them to improve them.

At the inquiry the respondents put forward two contentions, first that the houses were not unfit, and, secondly, that if they were, their demolition was not the best way of dealing with the conditions in the area as they were capable of rehabilitation. They put forward proposals for that directed to showing that, taking into account improvement grants, rehabilitation was an economic proposition.

A surveyor gave evidence on their behalf at the hearing. He testified that there was no evidence of instability which would constitute a threat to the occupants of any house and that "The existence of settlement did not indicate the probability, nor indeed the slight possibility, of further movement and this was no ground for unfitness."

The foundations of the houses were not referred to at the hearing. If they had been, perhaps the inspector would have thought it desirable, if necessary by adjourning the inquiry, to give the respondents an opportunity of considering their position.

In his report, under the heading of "Stability," he described what he had seen of the settlement and included in it a reference to a "tell-tale" which he had seen in one house and which had sheared through. The document served on the respondents by the council as to that house did not refer to a tell-tale and there was no evidence as to the date when it had been put up and when it had sheared through. If the inspector had not attached importance to this tell-tale, he presumably would not have mentioned A it. He did not state what inference he drew from it but presumably he thought it showed that movement was still continuing.

In his conclusions he said that:

> "The settlement which is evident in all the houses in clearance area No. 1 would appear to be due to the foundations not having been taken deeply enough into the clay so as to avoid that area which is B subject to seasonal expansion and contraction. Because of this and other previously stated defects I am of the opinion that satisfactory rehabilitation would not be a financially viable proposition and that the award of discretionary grants would be unlikely."

I do not think that the inspector can be criticised either for referring to the tell-tale, if, as appears to be the case, he thought that significant, or C for giving his expert opinion on what appeared to him to be the cause of the settlement and to lead to the conclusion that there was seasonal movement. It was his duty to report on what he saw on his inspection.

The respondents' complaint is twofold. They were given no opportunity of showing that what appeared to the inspector to be the case, was not so in fact. No trial holes had been bored which would have established whether or not the foundations were inadequate. They were given no D opportunity of showing that if they were inadequate, that did not make satisfactory rehabilitation not a financially viable proposition.

It was on account of his belief as to the inadequacy of the foundations that the inspector, taking that into account with the other defects, ruled out rehabilitation. So it appears that the inspector attached great weight to a factor which formed no part of the council's case, of which the respondents E had not been given notice and with which they had been given no opportunity of dealing.

In my opinion there is great substance in the respondents' complaints. Just as it would have been contrary to natural justice if the Secretary of State in making his decision had taken into account evidence received by him after an inquiry without an objector having an opportunity to deal with it, so here in my view it was contrary to natural justice for his decision to F confirm the order to be based to a very considerable extent on an opinion, which investigation might have shown to be erroneous, that the foundations were not taken down deep enough, and an opinion, which also might have been shown to be erroneous, that the inadequacy of the foundations showed that rehabilitation was impractical.

By the failure to give the respondents any opportunity to deal with G these matters, they were in my opinion substantially prejudiced and, for the reasons I have given, in my view the Court of Appeal came to the right conclusion and this appeal should be dismissed.

LORD SIMON OF GLAISDALE. My Lords, I have had the advantage of reading in draft the speeches prepared by my noble and learned friends, H Viscount Dilhorne and Lord Russell of Killowen. I agree with them, and for the reasons they give I would dismiss the appeal.

LORD EDMUND-DAVIES. My Lords, for the reasons appearing in the printed speeches of my noble and learned friends, Viscount Dilhorne and Lord Russell of Killowen, which I have had the advantage of reading in draft, I concur in holding that this appeal should be dismissed.

A LORD RUSSELL OF KILLOWEN. My Lords, this appeal by the Secretary of State for the Environment is from an order of the Court of Appeal reversing a decision of Cusack J. and quashing a compulsory purchase order (the London Borough of Southwark (Aldbridge Street) (No. 1) Compulsory Purchase Order 1973) confirmed by the Secretary of State for the Environment after a public inquiry ordered and held by an appointed inspector, an architect, and on the basis of the inspector's report. The
B grounds for quashing the order were: that the inspector formed and expressed an opinion that rehabilitation of buildings belonging to the respondent objector ("Fairmount") on the site the subject of the order was not a financially feasible alternative to their demolition, in part due to the unsatisfactory nature of their foundations: that at the hearing no suggestion was made that the foundations were other than satisfactory: that
C on the contrary the history recited in the report was against such an inference: and that it was contrary to the principles of natural justice that this inference of indequate foundations should have been relied upon against Fairmount without its being given any opportunity to challenge either the inference, or (if the inference were correct) to refute the conclusion that rehabilitation was not financially a feasible alternative to the demolition proposed.

D The local authority resolved on May 2, 1972, that an area containing 68 terraced houses approaching 100 years old, of which 64 in multiple occupation belonged to Fairmount, should be a clearance area under section 42 of the Housing Act 1957. Section 42 (1) provides as follows:

"Where a local authority, upon consideration of an official representation or other information in their possession, are satisfied as respects
E any area in their district—(*a*) that the houses in that area are unfit for human habitation . . . and (*b*) that the most satisfactory method of dealing with the conditions in the area is the demolition of all the buildings in the area; the authority shall cause that area to be defined on a map . . . and shall pass a resolution declaring the area so defined to be a clearance area, that is to say, an area to be cleared of all
F buildings. . . ."

Section 4 (1) of the Act deals with the question of unfitness for human habitation.

"In determining . . . whether a house is unfit for human habitation, regard shall be had to its condition in respect of the following matters, that is to say—(*a*) repair; (*b*) stability; (*c*) freedom from damp; (*cc*)
G internal arrangement; (*d*) natural lighting; (*e*) ventilation; (*f*) water supply; (*g*) drainage and sanitary conveniences; (*h*) facilities for . . . preparation and cooking of food and for the disposal of waste water; and the house shall be deemed to be unfit for human habitation if and only if it is so far defective in one or more of the said matters that it is not reasonably suitable for occupation in that condition."

H Under section 43, following upon a clearance resolution the local authority may either make a clearance order, or make a compulsory purchase order for submission for confirmation to the Secretary of State and carry out the demolition of the buildings themselves. In the present case the authority chose the latter course and made the compulsory purchase order on January 9, 1973: they wanted the area for an open space, and in adopting that course would only have to pay site value.

Schedule 3 to the Act provides for advertisement and notices of the A
compulsory purchase order and for objections. Paragraph 3 (3) provides:

> "If any objection duly made is not withdrawn, the [Secretary of State] shall, before confirming the order, either cause a public local inquiry to be held or afford to [an objector] . . . an opportunity of appearing before and being heard by a person appointed by the [Secretary of State] for the purpose, and, after considering any objection . . . and B the report of the person who held the inquiry or of the person appointed as aforesaid, may subject to the provisions of this Part of this Schedule, confirm the order . . ."

As already indicated a public local inquiry was directed to be held, and it was held on September 18 and 19, 1973. Before that the local authority had promulgated two documents not strictly required by statute C or regulation, but in accordance with practice. One (document No. 14) was a statement of reasons for the compulsory purchase proposal, designed to show that acquisition of the land was the more desirable course having regard to the open space intention. The other (document No. 15) was a summary of the principal grounds of unfitness, making brief comments under nearly all the heads found in section 4 (1): in particular it said:

> "Stability D
>
> *External*: Settlement with some bulged and fractured walls.
>
> *Internal*: Uneven settlement in floors."

On January 26, 1973, Fairmount lodged a notice of grounds of objection to the compulsory purchase order (see the Act, Schedule 3, paragraph 6). E This asserted that (1) the houses were not unfit for human habitation, and (2) the most satisfactory way of dealing with the conditions in the area is not by demolition of all the buildings in the area but by the renovation of the buildings. The second objection is of course directed to section 42 (1) (*b*), and is an alternative ground of objection should the first not to be sustained.

The final pre-inquiry document is Appendix, Part III, of the record, containing in considerable detail in respect of each building in the area F the facts alleged by the local authority as their principal grounds for being satisfied that the building is relevantly unfit: see the Act, Schedule 3, paragraph 4.

At the hearing evidence was called by the local authority and by Fairmount. The latter maintained its opposition on both the grounds mentioned above; G but the inspector having concluded and reported, and the Secretary of State having accepted, that unfitness for human habitation had been established, that is no longer disputed by Fairmount. What is complained of is that for the purposes of section 42 (1) (*b*) the inspector should have arrived at a conclusion (which the Secretary of State accepted) that rehabilitation as a satisfactory alternative to demolition was not financially feasible, having regard in part to an inference that the foundations were inadequate to prevent further settlement, H without giving Fairmount any opportunity to deal with that suggestion.

Before returning to the facts of the case I refer to the statutory provisions under which the matter came before the court. The Act, Schedule 4, paragraph 2, provides that when the order is confirmed, as it was:

> "If any person aggrieved by such an order . . . desires to question the validity thereof on the ground that it is not within the powers of this Act or that any requirement of this Act has not been complied

with, he may, within six weeks after the publication of the notice of confirmation of the order . . . make an application for the purpose to the High Court, and where any such application is duly made the court . . . (ii) if satisfied upon the hearing of the application that the order . . . is not within the powers of this Act or that the interests of the applicant have been substantially prejudiced by any requirement of this Act not having been complied with, may quash the order . . . either generally or in so far as it affects any property of the applicant."

Paragraph 3 of the same Schedule provides comprehensive terms against any other form of challenge to the validity of the confirmed order, and enacts that subject to paragraph 2 the order shall become operative at the expiration of the six-week period.

There was a certain amount of discussion before your Lordships on the significance and applicability of the phrase "may quash" and on the difference between the phrase "not within the powers of this Act" and "the interests of the applicant have been substantially prejudiced by any requirement of this Act not having been complied with." In my view the instant appeal does not require discussion of these points: for I am satisfied that if the true conclusion is that the course which events followed resulted in that degree of unfairness to Fairmount that is commonly referred to as a departure from the principles of natural justice it may equally be said that the order is not within the powers of the Act and that a requirement of the Act has not been complied with. For it is to be implied, unless the contrary appears, that Parliament does not authorise by the Act the exercise of powers in breach of the principles of natural justice, and that Parliament does by the Act require, in the particular procedures, compliance with those principles.

At the hearing before the inspector there was evidence which was not challenged by Fairmount except as a matter of degree that in most if not all of the houses there had been some settlement: this was included in the schedule of particulars of unfitness put in by the local authority, but nowhere in that schedule was it suggested that settlement was other than static in any of the Fairmount houses, or that the foundations were inadequate so as to lead to an inference that settlement might be progressive. Indeed there was a sharp contrast drawn in the particulars of unfitness, Appendix Part III, between the Fairmount houses and one non-Fairmount site house, the former having noted under "Stability" the word "settlement" and the latter (reference p. 17) the words "Progressive settlement" with a note "Progressive structural settlement has been noted in these premises over a period of 5 years." Professional evidence given for Fairmount was summarised by the inspector in his report thus: "The existence of settlement did not indicate the probability, nor indeed the slight possibility, of further movement. . . ." As recently as 1970 Fairmount had been in discussion with the council's surveyor about proposed rehabilitation or improvement of typical examples of Fairmount's houses on the site: the surveyor inspected them: in August 1970 Fairmount submitted informally plans and specifications of its proposals for two of the houses and the surveyor replied: "After careful inspection I can see no reason that your scheme should not be adopted and I await your formal applications." These applications would of course be for improvement grants for rehabilitation under the Housing Act 1969. This matter went no further because of the council's open space scheme. It indicated however that it did not occur to the council's surveyor that rehabilitation of those typical houses

was not a satisfactory and feasible project; and in particular that it did not A
occur to him that the foundations (for which the specifications made no
provision) were or might be inadequate.

At the hearing Fairmount advanced in evidence a simple scheme of
rehabilitation which was criticised by the local authority on the ground
not that it was not financially feasible but on the ground that a maisonette
over a ground floor flat was unsuitable on social grounds, with a reference
to a fire risk, and the need to keep a pram in a 3 feet 3 inch common B
entrance passage.

One other matter was put by Fairmount before the inspector at the
hearing and not sought to be controverted by the local authority: that
the latter had served notice on Fairmount under Part V of the Act to
acquire other houses of Fairmount almost identical in design and con-
dition within a quarter of a mile of the present site for the very purpose C
of improving them for housing.

At the end of the hearing the inspector visited the site and inspected
some of the houses agreed to be typical examples. Such an inspection is a
customary and indeed important part of the functions of such an inspector
leading to his report. He is not only the ears of the minister but also
the eyes. D

The passages in the inspector's report, accepted by the Secretary of
State in his reasons for confirming the compulsory purchase order, of
which Fairmount now complain, are these:

Paragraph 78 (*b*)—which occurs in that part of the report dealing with
the heads of unfitness:

> "There is evidence of settlement in all of these properties which is E
> evidenced in many humped and sloping ground floors, sloping first
> floors, the majority of door heads are out of alignment varying from
> about $\frac{1}{4}$ inch to $1\frac{1}{2}$ inches in the worst cases. Many side back addition
> walls are bulged; some of these walls have been rebuilt owing to war
> damage, but some others appear to have been rebuilt pre-war; this is
> apparent by materials and workmanship. These rebuilt walls are
> generally sound. Most back walls to the back additions appear to be F
> somewhat bulged outwards. This is evidenced by excessive mortar
> filling between the sash window and the wall in the external window
> reveal. The back walls of the three-storeyed blocks appear to be
> bulged outwards at second floor level and this is evidenced by long
> vertical cracks in the staircase partition walls at or near their junctions
> with the back walls. These cracks extend through the partition walls G
> from staircase to bedrooms. <u>A 'tell-tale' has been secured across a
> typical crack in Reference P62 and this has sheared through.</u> A
> number of the lean-to scullery blocks are pulling away from the main
> building at the roof intersection level with the main back addition
> wall and fractured brickwork is frequently evident at this point."

The underlining is mine. H

Paragraph 81 (*c*):

> "The settlement which is evident in all the houses in clearance area
> No. 1 would appear to be due to the foundations not having been
> taken deeply enough into the clay so as to avoid that area which is
> subject to seasonal expansion and contraction. Because of this and
> other previously stated defects I am of the opinion that satisfactory

A rehabilitation would not be a financially viable proposition and that the award of discretionary grants would be unlikely."

Finally in his conclusions the inspector said:

"The properties in the order are largely held by one owner who wishes to rehabilitate and improve his dwellings. Since for reasons already stated, I do not consider this to be a financially viable
B proposition. . ."

It was not disputed by the Secretary of State before your Lordships that the conclusion of the inspector under section 42 (1) (*b*), that the most satisfactory method of dealing with the conditions of unfitness in this area was demolition, was based on his view that rehabilitation was not a financially feasible method, and that that view was based in part upon
C his inference or view that the foundations were inadequate in the respect stated. For Fairmount it is contended that this suggestion of inadequate foundations was truly a bolt from the blue, a suggestion so contrary to everything that had emerged both before and at the hearing that Fairmount has been unfairly deprived of an opportunity, in defending its property in a matter of considerable financial consequence to it, of either
D demonstrating that the inference as to inadequacy of foundations was erroneous or of demonstrating that any inadequacy that exists can be cured within the bounds of financial feasibility.

For the Secretary of State it was in substance submitted that the question of stability and settlement had been raised, and therefore Fairmount should reasonably have anticipated all possible causes by leading evidence directly as to the state of the foundations: consequently it was
E not right to say that Fairmount had been deprived of the opportunity, as would have been the case had the inspector at the hearing cast doubt on the foundations but refused to hear evidence designed to correct his doubt.

This submission for the appellant appears to me to be at the core of this appeal, and, my Lords, I do not, in the circumstances of the case that
F I have rehearsed, accept it. I entirely accept that such an inspector, in a case such as this, is not merely trying an issue or issues between the local authority and the objector owner, and may from his professional experience supply deficiencies in the case as presented by the local authority. I equally accept that he is not bound to accept as established a contention in evidence for the objector owner simply because it is not, or is not adequately, challenged or contested on the part of the acquiring
G authority at the hearing. Part of his function lies in his own knowledge of the subject. Nor would I wish to introduce into procedures such as this—which include, prior to report, his inspection of the site—a rigidity more appropriate to a private issue to be decided by a judge; and in that connection I do not believe that a "view" by a judge is to be equated in any way with such a site inspection by such an inspector, a possibility
H which (it was said) might have been in the mind of the Court of Appeal in the instant case.

But in this case I am unable, consonant with the essential principles of fairness in a dispute, to uphold this compulsory purchase order. All cases in which principles of natural justice are invoked must depend on the particular circumstances of the case. I am unable, my Lords, in the instant case, to generalise. I can only say that in my opinion, in the circumstances I have outlined, Fairmount has not had—in a phrase whose derivation neither I nor your Lordships could trace—a fair crack of the whip. A passage at p. 682 of *Rex* v. *Paddington and St. Marylebone Rent Tribunal, Ex parte Bell, London & Provincial Properties Ltd.* [1949] 1 K.B. 666 on being taken by surprise is of relevance here. A

I would only add two points. The first is the suggestion that the inspector should perhaps have kept silent about his views or inference as to the foundations. With this I wholly disagree: it was not suggested by Fairmount. What he should have done was either to reconvene the hearing, or to invite the department to do so; or, in a relatively straightforward case such as this, have in writing invited views on his provisional conclusions as to the foundations and financial feasibility. There is nothing either in the statute or in any rules to prevent this. B

The second point is the question of the sheared tell-tale. Of course we know nothing of the details of this. For the applicant it was argued that this *fact* should have been known to Fairmount, and so Fairmount should have anticipated a possible conclusion, based upon it, as to progressive settlement, and therefore due, in even these old houses, to foundation inadequacy. I agree that it was reasonable for the inspector to suppose that Fairmount knew of the existence of a "tell-tale," just as in the *Paddington Rent Tribunal* case it might be supposed that the landlord knew that the ceilings were only eight feet; but that is not the same as reasonably anticipating the inference that might be drawn; and we know nothing of the date of the tell-tale, or of its shearing. Its existence does not persuade me that Fairmount was not taken by surprise in a relevantly unfair way by the conclusions of the inspector accepted by the Secretary of State. C D

I do not wish to be thought to impute any moral blame to the inspector by my conclusion that the procedure in this case involved unfairness: no one can be expected to be perfect in all circumstances; and he may take comfort from the fact that one judicial mind thought that he was in no way at fault. E

For these reasons I would uphold the quashing of the confirmed compulsory purchase order by the Court of Appeal and dismiss this appeal. F

Appeal dismissed.

Solicitors: *Treasury Solicitor; Laytons for John Gorna & Co., Manchester.*

F. C. G

H

[FAMILY DIVISION]

* PRACTICE DIRECTION (ADOPTION: APPLICATIONS)

Adoption — Adoption order — Applications — Preliminary examination of jurisdiction—Procedure for applications for removal or return of child to jurisdiction — Adoption (High Court) Rules 1976 (*S.I.* 1976 *No.* 1645 (*L.* 30)), *rr.* 11, 23

Certain provisions of the Children Act 1975 come into force on November 26, 1976, thereby bringing into operation the Adoption (High Court) Rules 1976 (S.I. 1976 No. 1645). These rules replace, with amendments and additions, the Adoption (High Court) Rules 1971.

Rule 11 (Preliminary examination of jurisdiction). The procedure under this rule will be as follows: All applications for adoption in the High Court which appear to be governed by rule 11 will be automatically referred to a judge for his directions once the guardian ad litem has made his report to the court pursuant to rule 13 (2). But if the applicant for the adoption order or the guardian ad litem wishes to apply to have this preliminary issue as to jurisdiction determined at an earlier stage, he may do so by applying ex parte to the registrar.

The registrar will fix a date for the hearing of the preliminary examination by a judge in chambers and notice of the date will be sent by the court to the applicant and the guardian ad litem.

Rule 23 (Applications for removal, return etc., of child). On any application under this rule, the applicant should lodge in the Divorce Registry two copies of the summons (or originating summons), endorsing thereon an estimate of the likely length of the hearing. No date of hearing will be given by the Registry until the summons has been considered by the registrar.

After fixing a date for the hearing of the application by a judge in chambers, the registrar will notify the applicant and serve a copy of the summons on the persons prescribed by the rule.

This direction is issued with the approval of the President of the Family Division.

R. L. BAYNE-POWELL,
Senior Registrar

November 17, 1976.

[MIDDLESEX CROWN COURT]

* PATEL v. SPENCER

1976 Aug. 18 — Judge Solomon

Crime — Compound proceedings — Agreement to — Defendant requesting to be released from agreement — Customs and Excise Commissioners purporting to release defendant from agreement — Whether valid release — Whether subsequent criminal proceedings nullity — Customs and Excise Act 1952 (15 & 16 *Geo.* 6 & 1 *Eliz.* 2, *c.* 44), *s.* 288 (*a*)

The appellant, who at Heathrow airport attempted to avoid paying duty on goods he had brought into the country and thereby committed certain customs offences, was asked by a customs officer if he wished to make a request, under section 288 of the Customs and Excise Act 1952,[1] that the Customs and Excise Commissioners compound the proceedings to be taken for the offences. The appellant did make the request, signed a document to that effect and paid the sum of £31, which was accepted by the commissioners on the basis that the proceedings were compounded. The appellant then began a correspondence with agents of the commissioners in which he stated that he would prefer his case to be heard by a court. The commissioners returned the money to the appellant and proceedings were brought before the justices. The appellant was convicted of the offences and he appealed to the Crown Court.

On the question whether the justices had jurisdiction to entertain proceedings for offences which had been compounded:—

Held, that, since it was in the public interest that a person who had second thoughts concerning an agreement he had entered into with the commissioners to compound proceedings should be released from such an agreement, the commissioners had correctly and fairly released the appellant from the agreement and, therefore, since it was a valid release, the justices had jurisdiction to hear and determine the subsequent proceedings.

Per curiam. It is not in the public interest that the commissioners, having agreed to compound an offence, should ever be allowed to resile from their agreement (post, p. 1271D).

No cases are referred to in the judgment or were cited in argument.

RULING

Proceedings were brought by the respondent, John Spencer, a customs officer, in the Uxbridge Magistrates' Court against the appellant, Ranchobai Purshottam Patel, alleging that the appellant had committed certain customs offences. The appellant was convicted and appealed against conviction and sentence. In his grounds of appeal he stated that the justices had no jurisdiction to try the case as the offences, if any, had been properly and finally compounded.

The facts are stated in the judgment.

V. T. Haridas for the appellant.
John Rogers Q.C. and *John Zieger* for the respondent.

[1] Customs and Excise Act 1952, s. 288: "The commissioners may, as they see fit—(*a*) stay, sist or compound any proceedings for an offence or for the condemnation of any thing as being forfeited under the customs or excise Acts; . . ."

A JUDGE SOLOMON. This appeal of Mr. Patel raises a preliminary point of law. The appellant was convicted by the Uxbridge justices on May 24, 1976, of three offences under the laws relating to Customs and Excise: (1) for an offence of failing to declare certain goods, contrary to section 6 of the Finance Act 1968; (2) for an offence of making false statements to a customs officer, contrary to section 301 of the Customs and Excise Act 1952; and (3) for an offence of being knowingly concerned in the fraudulent B evasion of duty on certain goods, contrary to section 304 of the Customs and Excise Act 1952. He has appealed to this court on three general grounds, namely, against conviction, against sentence and on the jurisdiction of this court and the magistrates' court to hear the case. It is upon this last ground that I give my ruling.

The appellant stated in his grounds of appeal:

C "The magistrates had no jurisdiction to try the case and ignored all pleas by the appellant that all the offences, if any, had been properly and finally compounded, and that he had even paid the penalty under the compromise."

Upon this issue I have now heard argument by counsel for both parties.

The brief facts are that on May 5, 1975, the appellant arrived at D Heathrow airport having in his possession two gold bangles, two gold rings and 13 embroidered saris. He failed to declare those items. He knowingly made a false declaration and he was knowingly concerned in the evasion of duty on those items. He was stopped in the "Green" channel by a customs officer, and after a period of rather less than three hours, he was told that the articles described were to be treated as having E been seized. He was told he had a right of appeal against that seizure. He was asked if he wished to make a request for the criminal offences to be compounded.

The Customs and Excise Commissioners are empowered by Parliament acting under section 288 of the Customs and Excise Act 1952, in their discretion, to compound any proceedings for an offence or for the restoration of anything forfeited.

F The appellant then decided that he did wish to request that the proceedings for the criminal offences be compounded, and accordingly he signed a document, which reads:

"H.M. Customs and Excise
Request for Proceedings to be Compounded
Section 288 (*a*) of the Customs and Excise Act 1952

G "I understand that the law provides substantial penalties for customs offences, and that when a person is proceeded against in court and convicted the amount of penalty is decided by the court.

"I request to be allowed to pay the sum of thirty one pounds (£31·00) as an alternative to proceedings being taken against me for a customs H offence in respect of:—two gold bangles, two gold rings, thirteen embroidered saris seized as liable to forfeiture under the customs laws."

The appellant signed it and wrote his address; it was witnessed by a customs officer. Immediately below those signatures the following notes appear: "Received cheque for £31 travellers cheque number 78538092. Proceedings will be compounded provided cheque is honoured when first presented," and this is signed by a representative of the commissioners.

Almost immediately the appellant opened correspondence with the A
commissioners and/or their agents. It suffices for me to say that in a letter to the Secretary of Customs and Excise on September 3, 1975, he wrote: "I would prefer to have my case heard before a court." That is the clearest indication that the appellant was unhappy that he had agreed to have the proceedings compounded.

On February 5, 1976, the solicitor for the commissioners wrote to the
appellant and said, inter alia: B

> "I should wish to hear from you within the next 14 days if you wish the proceedings to be commenced and I would advise you to seek the advice of a solicitor who will advise you in this matter."

The appellant replied on February 12, 1976, saying: "I hereby again
inform you that I prefer to have my case heard by a court. . . . I do not C
wish to consult a solicitor."

On February 19, 1976, the commissioners wrote to the appellant saying that the money paid by him for compounding the offences in relation to the two gold bangles and two rings would be restored to him; and it was. The letter added that legal proceedings were being ordered against him under section 6 of the Finance Act 1968 and sections 301 and 304
of the Customs and Excise Act 1952. A balance of £6 which was not D
mentioned in that letter had previously been returned because the commissioners on reconsideration had decided that the amount of duty they had calculated in respect of the 13 saris was wrong. At this point the saris disappear from the case.

On May 24, 1976, this matter was heard before the Uxbridge justices
who convicted the appellant of the three offences. It is in these circum- E
stances that he appeals to this court and his appeal raises a preliminary point of law going to the jurisdiction of this court.

It is said on behalf of the appellant that, notwithstanding what he has requested in the correspondence he personally has conducted, the commissioners ought not to have returned any part of the money received from him on May 5 when the criminal offences were compounded. It is
said that, as a matter of law, there are no circumstances in which a F
criminal offence, once compounded by the commissioners, can be re-opened either by the smuggler or by the commissioners. Of course, if that submission is correct in law, then the proceedings before the Uxbridge justices were a nullity and must be set aside and the appeal allowed.

It has been frankly stated on behalf of the commissioners that there
is in fact no decision on this particular point. There is no reported G
decision and Mr. Rogers has said his instructions are that the commissioners are quite certain there is no decision at all on the point. This being so, I have to construe the intention of Parliament and certainly there are no words that the respondent's counsel can point to which, expressly or impliedly, give the commissioners a discretion, in any circum-
stances, to release a smuggler from an agreement to compound. But, says H
counsel, Parliament had in mind the public interest when it vested the commissioners with a discretion to compound any proceedings if they saw fit to do so.

It is clearly in the public interest that such a discretion has been conferred on the commissioners, because once an offence has been detected it is salutary that it should be dealt with there and then if the commissioners think it should be, without recourse to the courts. In so

A way can the exchequer be the loser, there is the payment of the com-
pounded penalty, the goods are seized, and the costs of court proceedings
are avoided.

On the other side of the coin, it seems to me that it is also in the
public interest that if a citizen or a non-resident or an alien who has
entered into an agreement to compound an offence has second thoughts
about the wisdom of what he has done, he should be allowed by the
B commissioners to withdraw his compounding. In other words, it is a
healthy thing that he should be allowed to say "I have really had second
thoughts about what I did by compounding and I would like to be released
from the terms of the agreement and I would like the alleged offence to
be heard before a court of law in this country."

It must be remembered that travellers are often very tired when they
C arrive at any point of entry into this country, they are often anxious to
be on their way, and very often they suffer from language difficulties.
These are some of the matters which have led me to conclude that even
if the smuggler has entered into an agreement under section 288, it is
none the less in the public interest that he has the right to request to be
released from it; and the commissioners ought to grant such a request
unless there is very good reason to the contrary.

D On the other hand, I do not believe that it is in the public interest
that the commissioners, having agreed to compound an offence, should
ever be allowed to resile from their agreement. Different considerations
apply in their case; for one thing, the document which the commissioners
require the traveller or smuggler to sign carry these words: "Proceedings
will be compounded providing the cheque is honoured when first pre-
E sented," and the commissioners should be bound by those words. Even
if the words were not used, it seems to me that when persons in authority
take a decision which has this effect, that criminal proceedings will not
be instituted provided a sum of money is paid, those persons should
always be bound by their decision.

In the circumstances, therefore, it seems to me that the commissioners
correctly and most fairly agreed, on this correspondence, to release the
F appellant from the agreement they had entered into to compound these
offences. That being so, the justices had jurisdiction and so has this court.

Ruling accordingly.

Solicitors: *J. C. Patel, Wembley; Solicitor, Customs and Excise.*

G

H. J.

H

A

[PRIVY COUNCIL]

* OTERI AND ANOTHER . . . . APPELLANTS

AND

THE QUEEN . . . . RESPONDENT

B

[ON APPEAL FROM THE FULL COURT OF THE SUPREME COURT OF WESTERN AUSTRALIA]

1976 July 6, 7; Oct. 4

Lord Diplock, Viscount Dilhorne, Lord Hailsham of St. Marylebone, Lord Edmund-Davies and Lord Fraser of Tullybelton C

Admiralty — Jurisdiction — Crime — Australians charged under English criminal law in court of Western Australia with theft on high seas—Vessel not registered as British ship—Whether offences committed within Admiralty jurisdiction — Whether offences triable in Western Australia

D

The appellants, both Australian citizens residing in Fremantle, were charged on indictment in the district court of Western Australia with two offences of stealing crayfish pots and tackle on January 24, 1974, "on the vessel *Providence* on the high seas approximately 22 miles from the coast of Australia within the jurisdiction of the Admiralty of England." *Providence* was a powered fishing vessel of 24·6 gross tons owned by the first appellant and his wife (also an Australian E citizen) but not registered as a British ship under section 2 of the Merchant Shipping Act 1894. The appellants demurred to the indictment on the grounds that it disclosed no offence because neither the criminal law of Western Australia nor that of the United Kingdom was in force at the place where the offence was alleged to have been committed and that in any event the district court of Western Australia had no jurisdiction to try an offence committed in the place alleged. The F district court reserved the case for the consideration of the Full Court of the Supreme Court which decided that the indictment disclosed an offence triable in the district court by virtue of that court's Admiralty jurisdiction.

On the appellants' appeal to the Judicial Committee:—

Held, dismissing the appeal, (1) that the vessel being owned by British subjects was a British ship by virtue of section 1 of the Merchant Shipping Act 1894; that, although the failure G to register her under section 2 of the Act deprived the vessel of recognition as a British ship, the fact that she was not recognised did not affect the ship's nationality and, accordingly, she was to be treated as a British ship by the law of the sea as administered by the courts of Admiralty for the enforcement of the criminal law (post, p. 1276A–E).

(2) That, under the Offences at Sea Act 1799, which was still in force in Western Australia, a new offence created by H a statute of the United Kingdom became an offence on a British ship on the high seas unless excluded by express words or by necessary implication; that such an implication could not be drawn from the fact that the Theft Act 1968 did not apply to Scotland or Northern Ireland and, accordingly, the appellants had been rightly charged with theft under that Act (post, pp. 1276A–B, H—1277E).

William Holyman & Sons Pty. Ltd. v. *Eyles* [1947] Tas. S.R. 11 approved.

A (3) That by section 1 of the Admiralty Offences (Colonial) Act 1849 the courts of criminal justice in Western Australia were empowered to try all offences committed within the jurisdiction of the Admiralty on the high seas and, accordingly, the offences created by the Theft Act 1968 were triable in the district court of Western Australia in the exercise of its Admiralty jurisdiction (post, pp. 1276A–B, 1277F, H—1278A).

Decision of the Full Court of the Supreme Court of
B Western Australia affirmed.

The following cases are referred to in the judgment of their Lordships:

Chung Chuck v. *The King* [1930] A.C. 244, P.C.

Forbes v. *Cochrane* (1824) 2 B. & C. 448.

Holyman (William) & Sons Pty. Ltd. v. *Eyles* [1947] Tas.S.R. 11.

Reg. v. *Liverpool Justices, Ex parte Molyneux* [1972] 2 Q.B. 384; [1972]
C 2 W.L.R. 1033; [1972] 2 All E.R. 471, D.C.

Rex v. *Gordon-Finlayson, Ex parte An Officer* [1941] 1 K.B. 171, D.C.

The following additional cases were cited in argument:

Bonser v. *La Macchia* (1969) 122 C.L.R. 177.

Chartered Mercantile Bank of India, London and China v. *Netherlands*
D *India Steam Navigation Co. Ltd.* (1882) 10 Q.B.D. 521, C.A.

Commonwealth of Australia v. *District Court of the Metropolitan District Holden at Sydney* (1954) 90 C.L.R. 13.

Reg. v. *Bull* (1974) 131 C.L.R. 203; 48 A.L.J.R. 232.

Reg. v. *Dodd* (1874) 2 N.Z.C.A. 598.

Reg. v. *Keyn* (1876) 2 Ex.D. 63.

Reg. v. *Seberg* (1870) 1 C.C.R. 264.

E *Rex* v. *Amarro (Manuel)* (1814) Russ. & Ry. 286.

Rex v. *Bailey* (1800) Russ. & Ry. 1.

Rex v. *Coombes* (1786) 1 Leach 388.

APPEAL (No. 34 of 1975) by special leave (July 23, 1976) by Santo and Gaetano Oteri from a judgment of the Full Court of the Supreme
F Court of Western Australia (Virtue Ag.C.J., Burt and Wallace JJ.) delivered December 6, 1974, answering points of law reserved for the opinion of the court on November 4, 1974, by Judge O'Connor in the district court of Western Australia. The indictment (October 1, 1974) charged the appellants with two offences of stealing crayfish pots and tackle "on the vessel *Providence* on the high seas approximately 22 miles from the coast of Western Australia within the jurisdiction of the
G Admiralty of England." The appellants were arraigned before Judge O'Connor on October 17, 1974, and demurred to the indictment. The judge acting pursuant to section 49 of the District Court of Western Australia Act 1969–1972 reserved the following points of law for the Full Court: (*a*) does the indictment disclose any offence under the laws of Western Australia or otherwise triable there?; (*b*) if "Yes," has the dis-
H trict court jurisdiction to try the appellants for the offence?; (*c*) if "Yes," is the matter within the ordinary or Admiralty jurisdiction of the court or otherwise cognisable there? The Full Court answered "Yes" to (*a*) and (*b*) and in answer to (*c*) said the offence was within the Admiralty jurisdiction of the district court. The Full Court granted leave to appeal to the Judicial Committee of the Privy Council saying that the matter was of great general and public importance. Before the Judicial Committee

on July 6, 1976, the appellants petitioned for, and their Lordships agreed to advise Her Majesty to grant, special leave to appeal.

The facts are stated in the judgment of their Lordships.

F. M. Robinson and *K. N. Allan* (of the Western Australia Bar) for the appellants.

R. D. Wilson Q.C., Solicitor-General, Western Australia and *K. H. Parker* (of the Western Australia Bar) for the Crown.

Cur. adv. vult.

October 4. The judgment of their Lordships was delivered by LORD DIPLOCK.

The appellants, Santo and Gaetano Oteri, were charged in the district court of Western Australia with two offences of having stolen crayfish pots and tackle "on the vessel *Providence* on the high seas approximately 22 miles from the coast of Australia within the jurisdiction of the Admiralty of England." Both appellants are Australian citizens by naturalisation. So is Santo Oteri's wife. All three usually reside in Fremantle. The *Providence* is a powered fishing vessel of some 24·6 gross tons. She is owned by Santo Oteri and his wife and normally operates out of Fremantle. She is the subject of a boat licence issued to her owners under Division 1 of Part VIII of the Western Australian Marine Act 1948–1973, and a fishing boat licence issued pursuant to regulations made under the Fisheries Act 1905–1973; but she is not registered as a British ship under section 2 of the Merchant Shipping Act 1894 (Imp.) in Fremantle or at any other port in Australia or the United Kingdom. Upon arraignment before the district court, the appellants demurred to the indictment upon the grounds (1) that no offence was disclosed, because neither the criminal law of Western Australia nor that of the United Kingdom was in force at the place where the offences were alleged to have been committed, and (2) in any event the district court of Western Australia had no jurisdiction to try an offence committed in the place alleged.

The district court judge acting pursuant to section 49 of the District Court of Western Australia Act 1969-1972 reserved for the consideration of the Full Court of the Supreme Court of Western Australia the following points of law. In respect of each count in the indictment:

> (*a*) Does the indictment disclose any offence under the laws of Western Australia or otherwise triable in Western Australia? (*b*) If the answer to question (*a*) is "Yes," has the district court of Western Australia jurisdiction to try the accused for the offence? (*c*) If the answer to question (*b*) is "Yes," is the matter—(i) within the ordinary jurisdiction of the court (ii) within the Admiralty jurisdiction of the court (iii) otherwise cognisable by the court?

The Full Court by an order of December 6, 1974, answered questions (*a*) and (*b*): "Yes"; and in answer to question (*c*) said that the offences were within the Admiralty jurisdiction of the district court.

The appellants applied to the Full Court for leave to appeal from this decision to Her Majesty in Council. The application was sought to be founded on rule 2 (*b*) of the Order in Council regulating appeals from the Supreme Court of Western Australia to His Majesty in Council (S.R. & O. 1909 No. 760). It was resisted on behalf of the prosecution on the ground that the order made by the Full Court on the reference was not a decision of the court within the meaning of the Order in Council but was a mere advisory opinion from which no appeal would lie. This contention was rightly rejected by the Full Court. They granted leave to appeal, and expressed their view that the subject was one of great general and public importance:

> "upon which the opinion of the Judicial Committee may properly be considered to be of very great value and importance to this country and also possibly elsewhere."

Unfortunately in concentrating their argument upon whether or not the order of the Full Court of December 6, 1974, was an advisory opinion only, counsel for both parties had overlooked the fact that the matter in which the order was made was a criminal matter and for that reason fell outside rule 2 (*b*) of the Order in Council—as had been decided by this Board in *Chung Chuck* v. *The King* [1930] A.C. 244, under an identical provision in the British Columbia Order in Council of 1911. An appeal to Her Majesty in Council from an order or decision of the Full Court in a criminal matter lies only with the special leave of Her Majesty granted upon the advice of the Judicial Committee itself. The Full Court itself has no power to grant leave.

The procedural defect has, however, been cured by the appellants lodging a petition to Her Majesty in Council for special leave to appeal from the order of the Full Court of December 6, 1974. Although it would not normally be in accordance with the practice of the Board to grant special leave to appeal in a criminal matter from the Supreme Court of a State of Australia, their Lordships have taken into account in the instant case the fact that the questions of law that it raises are common to all the States and Territories of Australia, and they have given weight to the strongly expressed desire of the Full Court itself that those questions should be considered by the Judicial Committee. Accordingly, they humbly advised Her Majesty that special leave to appeal should be granted, and an Order in Council granting such special leave was made on July 23, 1976.

The legislative power of the Commonwealth of Australia does not extend to criminal law. That lies within the competence of the States. It is conceded by the Solicitor-General on behalf of the Crown that the criminal law of Western Australia does not extend beyond the territorial boundaries of the State and accordingly was not applicable in the place, 22 miles from the coast, where the offence was alleged to have been committed. He contends that the law applicable was the criminal law of England and that the offence was properly charged under section 1 of the Theft Act 1968 (Imp.).

It may at first sight seem surprising that despite the passing of the Statute of Westminster 1931, and the creation of separate Australian citizenship by the British Nationality Act 1948 (Imp.) and the Australian Citizenship Act 1948–1973, two naturalised Australian citizens whose home was in Fremantle should find themselves subject to English criminal law upon leaving that port to fish within a few miles of the coast in a vessel owned by Australian citizens; or, put in another way, that Parliament in the United Kingdom when it passes a statute which creates a new criminal offence in English law is also legislating for those Australian passengers who cross Bass Strait by ship from Melbourne to Tasmania.

In the submission of the Solicitor-General, however, the explanation of this apparent oddity is simple. It depends upon four propositions: (1) The *Providence* was a British ship; (2) the criminal law of England extends to all British ships; (3) offences which are committed on British ships are within the criminal jurisdiction of the Admiralty; (4) in Western Australia the district court of Western Australia exercises the criminal jurisdiction of the Admiralty.

In the opinion of their Lordships, which accords with that expressed by the Full Court, each of these propositions is correct.

(1) By the law of the sea administered by the courts of Admiralty as far back as the records go, a ship has been a British (before the Act of Union an English) ship if and only if she is owned by persons, natural or corporate, who are British (formerly English) subjects. Section 1 of the Merchant Shipping Act 1894 (Imp.), which is still in force in Western Australia, takes this for granted. It sets out the qualifications which the owners must possess if a ship is to be a British ship. The relevant qualification in the instant case is "British subjects," an expression which since the passing of the British Nationality Act 1948, section 1, includes persons who are Australian citizens by naturalisation. Section 2 of the Merchant Shipping Act 1894 imposes an obligation to register in the appropriate register of merchant shipping (of which there is one in Fremantle) every British ship, unless it falls within an exempted category. If it is not registered it is not recognised as a British ship; but non-recognition does not deprive the ship of her British nationality: by section 72 it only serves to deprive the unregistered ship of benefits, privileges, advantages and protection usually enjoyed by British ships. So far as concerns offences committed on board the ship or by persons belonging to her, she is to be dealt with in exactly the same way as if she were recognised. The *Providence* was wholly-owned by British subjects: she was accordingly a British ship and, although unregistered, is to be treated as a British ship so far as regards the punishment of offences committed on her.

(2) Again it is trite and ancient law that the criminal law of England extends to British ships upon the "high seas"—an expression which in the context of Admiralty jurisdiction includes in addition to the open sea all waters below low-water mark where great ships can go: see *Reg.* v. *Liverpool Justices, Ex parte Molyneux* [1972] 2 Q.B. 384 and the cases there cited. The explanation sometimes given of this extension of the applicability of English law that "an English ship may be considered as a floating island" (see *Forbes* v. *Cochrane* (1824) 2 B. & C. 448, 464, *per* Holroyd J.) should, however, be understood metaphorically rather than literally. A British ship is not accurately described in law as part of the United Kingdom: *Rex* v. *Gordon-Finlayson, Ex parte An Officer* [1941] 1 K.B. 171, 178–179. A more acceptable rationalisation juristically is that at common law a British ship fell under the protection of the sovereign; those on board her were within the King's peace and subject to the criminal law by which the King's peace was preserved. However this may be, the applicability of English law to "treasons, felonies, robberies, murders and confederacies . . . committed upon the sea" was recognised by a statute of 1536, An Acte for Punysshement of Pyrotes and Robbers of the See. The Offences at Sea Act 1799 was but expository of the common law in providing:

> "that all and every offence and offences, which, after the passing of this Act, shall be committed upon the high seas out of the body of any county of this realm, shall be, and they are hereby declared to be offences . . . liable to the same punishments respectively, as if they had been committed upon the shore."

This is the only part of the Act of 1799 which was left unrepealed by the Criminal Law Act 1967 (Imp.). It is still in force in Western Australia. It is, in their Lordships' view, ambulatory in its effect, with the consequence that when a new offence in English law is created by a statute of the United Kingdom Parliament it ipso facto becomes an offence if it is committed on a British ship unless the extension of the statute to British ships is excluded by express words or by necessary implication. Such an implication cannot, in their Lordships' view, be drawn from the fact that the Theft Act 1968 (Imp.) does not apply to Scotland or Northern Ireland. As with Australia, there is not a single criminal law that is common to the whole of the United Kingdom; and it has always been the criminal law of England that was applied to persons on British ships within the jurisdiction of the Admiralty. Accordingly in their Lordships' view the Theft Act 1968 (Imp.) applied to the appellants when they were on board the *Providence* and that vessel was on the high seas. That this should be so involves no novel concept in Australian jurisprudence. In *William Holyman & Sons Pty. Ltd.* v. *Eyles* [1947] Tas.S.R. 11, Morris C.J., in a judgment which sets out the history of the law upon this topic lucidly and succinctly, treated the Protection of Animals Act 1911 (Imp.) and not the Tasmanian Cruelty to Animals Prevention Act 1925, as applicable to an offence of cruelty to animals on board a ship owned by a company incorporated in Tasmania while it was crossing Bass Strait.

(3) In discussing the first two propositions their Lordships have already said enough to indicate their concurrence with the view of the Full Court that all offences committed on board British ships on the high seas were within the criminal jurisdiction of the Admiralty—though in the United Kingdom the Admiralty criminal jurisdiction during the course of the 19th century became exercisable through the ordinary criminal courts.

(4) In Western Australia, as elsewhere in Australia, the exercise of the jurisdiction is regulated by the Admiralty Offences (Colonial) Act 1849. The effect of section 1 is to empower the courts of criminal justice in Western Australia to try all offences committed within the jurisdiction of the Admiralty upon the high seas. The effect of the Courts (Colonial) Jurisdiction Act 1874 is to supplement this as respects punishment, by providing (by section 3) that in the case of conviction for an offence on the high seas, the punishment shall be the same as if the offence had been committed within the limits of Western Australia or if the offence is not punishable under the law of Western Australia, to award such punishment as would

> "seem to the court most nearly to correspond to the punishment to which such person would have been liable in case such crime or offence had been tried in England."

Their Lordships have done little more than to reiterate the reasons that were given in Full Court by Burt J. and Wallace J. and agreed to by Virtue Ag.C.J. for answering the questions in the manner indicated. Their Lordships are in full agreement with the Full Court in the answers that they have given to the questions. In their view the indictment discloses

an offence against English law for which the district court of Western A
Australia has jurisdiction to try the appellants as being a matter within the Admiralty jurisdiction of the court. They will humbly advise Her Majesty that the appeal be dismissed.

Solicitors: *de Berenger & Coyne; M. L. Moss & Son.*

T. J. M. B

[CHANCERY DIVISION]

C

* MOORE PROPERTIES (ILFORD) LTD. *v.* McKEON AND OTHERS

[1976 M. No. 1378]

1976 March 24; April 13 — Fox J.

D

Landlord and Tenant—Assignment of lease or underletting—Absolute prohibition against underletting—Sub-tenants enter into occupation during tenancy without knowledge or consent of landlord—Payment of rent to tenant—Tenant determines tenancy—Claim for possession—Status of unlawful sub-tenant —Whether R.S.C., Ord. 113, *effective*

Practice — Possession of land — Unlawful sub-tenant — Lawful tenancy with absolute prohibition against underletting—Sub- E
tenants entering into occupation during tenancy without knowledge or consent of landlord—Payment of rent to tenant — Tenant determining tenancy — Whether summary proceedings for possession available—R.S.C., Ord. 113, *r.* 1

The plaintiff, by an agreement in writing dated December 8, 1971, granted the tenancy of a furnished flat to two tenants for one year and thereafter from month to month, the tenancy F
to be terminated by one month's notice on either side. The agreement contained an absolute prohibition against assigning or underletting. From November 1, 1974, one of the tenants was accepted as the sole tenant on the same terms. On November 22, 1975, the tenant informed the plaintiff that he had vacated the flat on September 22, and they treated his letter as notice to determine the tenancy. During December the plaintiff's agent, on inspecting the premises, found the four G
named defendants in occupation. Subsequent inquiries disclosed that there were other, unidentified, persons also in occupation. Three of the named defendants claimed to have been in occupation prior to the tenant's departure and to have paid rent to him. The second named defendant had received a rent book and claimed to be a tenant holding over from the termination of the tenancy.

On the plaintiff's summons for possession under R.S.C., H
Ord. 113:—

Held, that the words in R.S.C., Ord. 113, r. 1 "not being a tenant or tenants holding over after the termination of the tenancy" referred only to persons who could establish that they held over under tenancies binding upon the person claiming possession; and that since the sub-tenancy of the

---

[Reported by MRS. F. ALLEN McLEAN, Barrister-at-Law]

A second defendant had been granted in breach of an absolute prohibition against sub-letting, and without the knowledge or consent of the plaintiff, such sub-tenancy was not binding on the plaintiff who was entitled to possession.

No cases are referred to in the judgment.

B The following cases were cited in argument:

Bristol Corporation v. *Persons Unknown* [1974] 1 W.L.R. 365, 369; [1974] 1 All E.R. 593.

Parker v. *Jones* [1910] 2 K.B. 32.

Works Commissioners v. *Hull* [1922] 1 K.B. 205, D.C.

ORIGINATING SUMMONS

C By an agreement in writing dated December 8, 1971, the plaintiff company let a furnished flat, Flat 1, Alyn Bank, 21 Crescent Road, Crouch End, London N.8, to Nicholas Gaffney and Kate Collingwood for one year from January 1, 1972, and thereafter on a monthly basis. Subsequently Kate Collingwood left and, from November 1, 1974, Nicholas Gaffney became the sole tenant on the same terms, which included an absolute prohibition against sub-letting. Nicholas Gaffney wrote to the D plaintiff on November 22, 1975, to say that he had vacated the premises on September 22. In December the plaintiff's agent found in occupation J. P. McKeon, Evelyn Beury, John Hudson and B. Celleher. Further inquiries in January 1975 revealed that there were also some unidentified persons living there. The first three named defendants claimed to have been there when Nicholas Gaffney had occupied the flat and to have E paid him rent. Evelyn Beury had a rent book; B. Celleher had been in occupation for about six weeks and had paid no rent to Nicholas Gaffney and had not seen him. The plaintiff issued a summons for possession under R.S.C., Ord. 113 against the named defendants and persons unknown.

The facts are stated in the judgment.

F *J. S. Trenhaile* for the plaintiff.

E. H. Bailey for the second defendant.

The other defendants did not appear and were not represented.

Cur. adv. vult.

G April 13. FOX J. read the following judgment. This is a claim for possession of a flat under R.S.C., Ord. 113.

By an agreement in writing of December 8, 1971, the plaintiff let the flat to a Mr. Gaffney and Miss Collingwood for one year from January 1, 1972, and thereafter from month to month, with a proviso that the tenancy could be terminated by either party to the agreement giving to the other one month's notice in writing expiring at the end of the term H or of any subsequent rental period.

Miss Collingwood subsequently terminated her interest in the tenancy and, from November 1, 1974, Mr. Gaffney was accepted by the plaintiff as and became the sole tenant on the terms of the agreement of December 8, 1971. Those terms (by clause 2 (vi)) included an absolute prohibition against assigning, underletting or parting with the possession of the flat or any part thereof.

On November 22, 1975, Mr. Gaffney wrote to the plaintiff saying

that he had vacated the flat on September 22 and apologising for not A
having given adequate notice. The plaintiff, in its evidence in these proceedings, treats this as a notice to determine the tenancy rather than as a surrender. I think that is correct. In my view therefore the tenancy came to an end on December 31, 1975, being the end of the relevant rental period, and any sub-tenancy came to an end with it.

In December 1975, after receiving Mr. Gaffney's letter, the plaintiff
sent an agent to inspect the premises. As a result it was discovered that B
the four named defendants were in occupation of various rooms in the flat and that the first three defendants claimed to have been in occupation since prior to Mr. Gaffney's departure and to have paid him rent. The fourth named defendant had then (mid-December) been in occupation for about six weeks and had paid no rent to Mr. Gaffney, and had not seen
him. All these persons entered into possession without the knowledge or C
consent and remain in possession without the consent of the plaintiff. From subsequent inquiries at the flat, in January 1975, it appears that there are further persons living in the flat whose names cannot be ascertained. On inquiry at the flat, names were refused. Accordingly, this summons was issued against the four named defendants and persons unknown.

D
The second defendant, Miss Beury, has filed evidence from which it appears that she was given a rent book by Mr. Gaffney. The other named defendants have not filed evidence, but the plaintiff's evidence, as far as it goes, is that they had no rent books. I will assume that Miss Beury was, in the circumstances, a sub-tenant of Mr. Gaffney and not merely a licensee. On this basis (that Miss Beury is a tenant) it is asserted
that R.S.C., Ord. 113 has no application to this case, since, so it is said, E
Miss Beury, at least, is a tenant holding over after the termination of the tenancy and is therefore excluded from the scope of the Order. Under Ord. 113, r. 1, the Order applies:

> "Where a person claims possession of land which he alleges is occupied solely by a person or persons (not being a tenant or tenants holding over after the termination of the tenancy) who entered into
> or remained in occupation without his licence or consent or that of F
> any predecessor in title of his . . ."

I do not accept that argument. It seems to me that the words "not being a tenant or tenants holding over after the termination of the tenancy" are directed only to persons who, as against the person claiming possession, can establish that they were holding over under tenancies
binding upon him. There seems no reason of principle why unlawful sub- G
tenants should be treated differently from other unauthorised occupiers for the purpose of the Order in such circumstances as the present. Lawful sub-tenants are different; they may be protected by the Rent Acts.

If the words "not being a tenant or tenants" etc. are treated as extending to any sub-tenancy, whether binding on the person seeking
possession or not, the scope of R.S.C., Ord. 113 could be seriously H
narrowed. If, for example, a tenant near the end of his term chooses to grant, in breach of covenant against sub-letting, sub-tenancies to would-be squatters, Ord. 113 could not be applied. Further, quite apart from the deliberate creation of sub-tenancies in that way, it is at least exceedingly inconvenient that, where, for example, premises are occupied by squatters and unlawful sub-tenants whose sub-tenancy has come to an end, the whole claim for possession cannot be dealt with under Ord. 113.

A The construction which I have adopted does not, it seems to me, prejudice any right which an unlawful sub-tenant may have under the general law or the Rent Acts.

As regards the general law, if there is any issue as to whether the tenancy was binding on the plaintiff that must be tried. As regards the Rent Acts, I was referred to section 18 of the Rent Act 1968, but the protection given by that section is in terms only applicable to lawful B sub-tenancies.

In the present case the sub-tenancy was granted in breach of an absolute prohibition against sub-letting. There is no suggestion at all of any consent by the plaintiff or of any waiver. The plaintiff's evidence, which is not disputed, is that the defendants entered into possession without the knowledge or consent of the plaintiff.

C Accordingly, it seems to me that any sub-tenancy which any of the defendants may have is not and never was binding upon the plaintiff. I should add that in my view the defendants are not in possession with the licence or consent of any predecessor in title of the plaintiff. Mr. Gaffney was not a predecessor in title but a person claiming under the plaintiff.

In the circumstances the plaintiff is in my view entitled to possession D as sought.

Order accordingly with costs.

Solicitors: *Shavin & Co.; Windsor & Co.*

E

[EMPLOYMENT APPEAL TRIBUNAL]

* FOUGÈRE *v.* PHOENIX MOTOR CO. LTD.

F

1976 June 30 Phillips J., Mr. A. C. Blyghton and Mrs. A. L. T. Taylor

Industrial Relations—Unfair dismissal—Compensation—Assessment —Age and health of employee disregarded by tribunal when assessing probable period of unemployment—Whether matters to be taken into account in assessing compensation—Appeal against trifling error in assessing compensation—Trade Union G *and Labour Relations Act* 1974 (c. 52), *Sch.* 1, *para.* 19 (1)

The employee, who was aged 58 and in poor health, was unfairly dismissed by the employers. On his application for compensation for unfair dismissal, an industrial tribunal, assessing the probable length of time the employee would remain unemployed and the loss of wages for that period, in accordance with paragraph 19 (1) of Schedule 1 to the Trade H Union and Labour Relations Act 1974,[1] based their consideration on the likely period of unemployment for a person of average health on the ground that the extended period of unemployment due to the employee's illness was not loss attributable to the employers.

On the employee's appeal against the amount of compensation:—

[1] Trade Union and Labour Relations Act 1974, Sch. 1, para. 19 (1): see post, p. 1285E–F.

Held, allowing the appeal, that paragraph 19 (1) of A
Schedule 1 to the Trade Union and Labour Relations Act 1974 provided for compensation to be awarded to an employee for the loss sustained by him in consequence of his dismissal including a reasonable estimate of his financial loss while he remained unemployed; that the loss due to any additional period of unemployment resulting from the employee's personal characteristics, namely, ill-health, at the time of his dismissal was clearly attributable to action taken by the B
employers within the meaning of paragraph 19 (1), namely his dismissal, and that, accordingly, the tribunal had erred in failing to take into account the employee's ill-health when assessing compensation.

Per curiam. The Employment Appeal Tribunal will not interfere with awards of compensation for unfair dismissal by industrial tribunals unless the error is shown to be more than trifling (post, p. 1283A–B). C

No cases are referred to in the judgment.

The following cases were cited in argument:

Maris v. *Rotherham Corporation* [1974] I.C.R. 435; [1974] 2 All E.R. 776, N.I.R.C.

York Trailer Co. Ltd. v. *Sparkes* [1973] I.C.R. 518, N.I.R.C. D

APPEAL from an industrial tribunal sitting in London.

The employee, Patrick John Fougère, appealed against a decision of the industrial tribunal on August 5, 1975, awarding him compensation of £298·46 for unfair dismissal against his employers, Phoenix Motor Co. Ltd., on the ground, inter alia, that the industrial tribunal ought to have taken E
into account the fact that the employee's ill-health had caused him to remain unemployed for a longer period than usual when assessing compensation.

The appeal was transferred from the Queen's Bench Division of the High Court to the Employment Appeal Tribunal under paragraph 9 of Schedule 17 to the Employment Protection Act 1975.

The facts are stated in the judgment. F

David Barnard for the employee.
Graeme Williams for the employers.

PHILLIPS J. delivered the following judgment of the appeal tribunal. This is an appeal from a decision of an industrial tribunal sitting in London G
on August 5, 1975. The basic facts can be simply stated. Mr. Fougère, the employee and appellant before this tribunal, was 58 years of age; he was in poor health—he suffered from a hernia and also from bronchitis in the winter. It was said of him that he was fit only for light work and at his own pace. On May 9, 1975, he was dismissed with two weeks' notice, so that the effective date of dismissal was May 23, 1975. In the earlier stages of litigation the question of unfair dismissal was in issue, but, by the H
time it reached the industrial tribunal, unfair dismissal had been conceded and the only issue before the industrial tribunal was—subject to something which I will mention in a moment—the question of compensation. Having heard the arguments, each side being represented by counsel, the industrial tribunal assessed the amount of compensation in the sum of £298·46. It is from that decision that the employee now appeals to this appeal tribunal.

Five separate points have been taken in support of the appeal. The

A fifth point was abandoned during the course of the argument, leaving four.
Of the four remaining points there is one which, in our judgment, is a
matter of some substance and importance. Before coming to deal with
that, it is perhaps helpful to say a word about appeals where the only issue
is as to the amount of compensation. There is, of course, only an appeal
to this appeal tribunal on a question of law. Where it can be established
that the industrial tribunal has misdirected itself in assessing compensation,
B that, no doubt, will or may constitute an arguable point of law. Nonetheless,
having said that, and as a matter of practice, it needs to be known that the
appeal tribunal will not interfere with awards of compensation, unless the
error is shown to be something which could be described as more
than trifling. The reason for that is a practical one: industrial tribunals
have to work in practical conditions, and they are obliged to assess the
C amount of compensation quickly—and fairly of course—but they are bound
of necessity to operate in a somewhat rough and ready way, and to paint
the picture with a broad brush. It is in everybody's interest that that
should be the case. It may mean that sometimes an employee will get
a bit less than he might have expected; it may mean that sometimes an
employer will have to pay a little more than he had expected. But, if
the compensation were to be worked out accurately to the very last half-
D penny, it would require prolonged hearings, elaborate interlocutory pro-
cedures and all sorts of refinements which would be wholly out of place
in a procedure which is meant to be quick, open to the unrepresented, and
simple. Of course, if there is a serious error and that can be shown, then
the appeal tribunal will interfere. But it will not do so in respect of
trifling amounts or unimportant errors.

E We turn now to the remaining four points. The first complaint is that
the industrial tribunal not only did not order re-engagement or re-instate-
ment, but never, apparently, applied their minds to it. It is said that as
a matter of law that, before turning to compensation, an industrial tribunal
ought first to consider that question. There may be something in that
point of view; we do not propose to lay down any firm rule about it. It
may often be desirable. It is enough to say that in this case it is quite
F clear, from the very full notes of the chairman of the tribunal, that the
only question seriously argued before the industrial tribunal, each of the
parties being represented by counsel, was the question of compensation
and the matter of re-engagement or re-instatement was never really gone
into. In those circumstances it is not surprising that the industrial tribunal
did not deal with the question and, in our judgment, that is not a matter
G of which complaint can now be made at this stage.

Secondly, it is said that the industrial tribunal should have awarded
compensation for the manner of the dismissal. In particular, it is said
that as a result of the dismissal, or as a result of the answers given by the
employers to questions asked by the Department of Health and Social
Security, the unemployment benefit to which the employee was entitled
H was suspended for five or six weeks. The facts are that the full entitle-
ment was in the end paid. The consequence was that for that period the
employee was out of the money to which he was entitled and so his
benefit was postponed. Mr. Barnard, for the employee, when asked to
quantify that in terms of the present value of the postponement of the
entitlement—as a result of a calculation in which all the assumptions were
the most favourable to his case; no complaint is made of that—arrived at
a figure for the quantification of something in the order of £1·50. That is

far too trifling a sum for us to be troubled with on an appeal to this A tribunal.

In so far as this employee claims compensation for the unpleasantness and the inconvenience of being unemployed, while accepting that it was unpleasant and inconvenient, the answer in our judgment is that that is one of the subjects in respect of which compensation under the Trade Union and Labour Relations Act 1974 is not recoverable. Compensation, broadly speaking, is awarded for the financial loss suffered by the employee. B

Thirdly, it is said that no allowance was made, in the computation of compensation, for the fact, known to the industrial tribunal, that wages were about to increase. The hearing, as I have said, was on August 5, the decision is dated September 22, and we were told that the wages were due to go up sometime in September. The dismissal was effective on May 23. The industrial tribunal assumed a period of unemployment of 26 weeks. C The period, therefore, during which it was right for them to take the prospective increase in wages, if it was right so to do, would have been from sometime in September to the expiry of the 26 weeks in November. The exact period cannot be calculated; it might be 10 or 12 weeks. The gross amount of the proposed increase was £2. We do not know precisely the net amount. But again, making the most favourable assumptions to the employee's case, the figure is too small for this appeal tribunal to D interfere.

Furthermore, there are certain facts which have been assumed in favour of the employee and in regard to which we cannot tell whether the assumption was correctly made or not. It is not known, for example, when the increase of £2 was due to take place. It is not even clear whether or not the industrial tribunal, in fixing the figure of 26 weeks, and the figure of E wages by which to multiply that, did or did not have this sort of point in mind.

It should be repeated that industrial tribunals, although they are required, and it is quite right that they should be required, to give reasons for their decisions and show how the award of compensation is made up, are not to be criticised on appeal merely because the total award is a small amount above or below the figure which should have been arrived at upon precise F and pedantic calculations; so there again, in our judgment, there is nothing in that ground.

The fourth ground is much more difficult and is one which could have potentially far-reaching consequences in other cases, whichever way we were to decide it. What the industrial tribunal did, in deciding—which was a necessary decision to make for the purpose of assessing the amount G of compensation—the length of time that they thought it likely that the employee would be unemployed, was to ignore, not by mistake, but deliberately to ignore, his age, which was 58, and, in particular, the fact that he was was in a poor state of health, and had a somewhat limited capacity. That was in fact the employer's explicit submission to the industrial tribunal, and the tribunal set out in their reasons the arguments upon it and the conclusion which they reached. They say: H

> "The tribunal consider it to be a matter of general knowledge not needing proof that there is a wide field of work open to persons doing similar work to what the [employee] was doing prior to his unfair dismissal, and that it would be likely that at the expiry of 26 weeks he could reasonably be expected to find similar employment. The tribunal awards the [employee] 26 weeks at £25 per week, i.e. £650 under this heading."

A Read in isolation, that passage is unobjectionable; but it is clear, we think, from what the industrial tribunal said before and subsequently in their reasons that, when they say "he could reasonably be expected to find," they are referring to "he" in his notional capacity, that is to say, "he," putting on one side that he was in poor health. This is quite clear from their reasons, where they say:

B "It is the tribunal's view that if the [employee] does not succeed in obtaining employment within 26 weeks from the date of his dismissal (which in the tribunal's view is a reasonable period for a person in his position who is *not suffering from ill health*) that this would be a consequence of his state of ill health and not a consequence of his unfair dismissal."

C The accentuation of the words "not suffering from ill health" is ours. In other words, they are explicitly directing themselves on this point in deference to the submission made to them. They decided that what they had to consider was, not how long would it be before the employee was re-employed, but how long would it be before a man in his position, of average health, was re-employed? The ground of appeal is that, in approaching the matter in that way, the industrial tribunal misdirected
D themselves. In our judgment, if that conclusion is not justified by the terms of the Act of 1974, they did misdirect themselves and there was there an error of law.

The view of the industrial tribunal was based on the submission of Mr. Williams, who appeared for the employers before them, and, in turn, is based by him on the terms of paragraph 19 (1) of Schedule 1 to the
E Trade Union and Labour Relations Act 1974. That paragraph reads:

"Where in any proceedings on a complaint under paragraph 17 above an industrial tribunal makes an award of compensation to be paid by a party to the proceedings (in this paragraph referred to as the party in default) to another party (in this paragraph referred to as the aggrieved party), the amount of the compensation shall, subject
F to paragraph 20 below, be such amount as the tribunal considers just and equitable in all the circumstances, having regard to the loss sustained by the aggrieved party in consequence of the matters to which the complaint relates, in so far as that loss was attributable to action taken by or on behalf of the party in default."

Mr. Williams relies in particular on the concluding words, "in so far
G as that loss was attributable to action taken by or on behalf of the party in default." He submits that those words qualify the extent of the loss which falls to be compensated. At first sight, particularly to those who have been versed in the common law in relation to the award of damages for personal injury, and so on, that seems a strange conclusion, because the courts are accustomed to awarding damages to the party injured, relying on the expression that the defendant is required to take the plaintiff "as he finds
H him." But Mr. Williams says, with a good deal of force (and there is authority for this), that we ought as far as possible to put out of our minds ordinary common law principles; that this is a code separate and apart, and that confusion will be caused if we do otherwise. He draws attention to the fact, as for example in paragraph 19 (2), that where the legislature was minded to bring in the ordinary law in relation to the assessment of damages it explicitly said so. It seems to us there is a great deal of force in that submission and that we ought to approach the con-

struction of paragraph 19—which, of course, has already been construed in the National Industrial Relations Court—as far as possible as a separate code, and that it is better on the whole to make a fresh start, not bringing in common law principles. So far we go along with his submissions. But that, of course, is not conclusive, because it is still necessary to see what paragraph 19 means.

Mr. Williams further draws attention to the fact that if the employers have to pay increased compensation as a result of the poor state of health of their dismissed employee, it will be a disincentive to employers to engage persons of mature years who, if they are unfortunate enough to be unfairly dismissed, will or may have a formidable claim for compensation. We see the force of that argument. Indeed, the position which could result is a slightly odd one, because, if an elderly employee in poor health is lucky enough to be taken on, in circumstances where, if he were on the labour market he would be unlikely for some considerable time to be re-employed, not only has he the quasi-property in his employment which is now conferred on all employees by the legislation, but, in his particular case, it will be a quasi-property of extraordinary value to him. Furthermore, Mr. Williams says, one can see, as indeed those observations show, that compensation for unfair dismissal is a quite different sort of conception from the award of damages for personal injury, or different even from damages for wrongful dismissal. Nonetheless it is important to see that what is being compensated is the loss sustained by the aggrieved party "in consequence of the matters to which the complaint relates." The matter to which the complaint relates is the dismissal with all its attendant circumstances. Common sense would seem to suggest that, if a man has been dismissed, the loss which he has sustained in consequence of the dismissal includes the financial loss during the period when he, and not some notional person, remains unemployed. Accordingly, unless the concluding words of the paragraph lead to some other conclusion, one would have thought, as a matter of ordinary common sense, that the loss sustained by the person dismissed included a reasonable estimate of the financial loss suffered by him during the period when *he* could be expected to remain unemployed.

It is possible to put the matter more vividly by looking at the tribunal's reasons. The industrial tribunal have said that if, in the result, he remained unemployed for longer than might be expected, or anyhow longer than they expected, that would be in consequence of his state of ill-health, and not a consequence of his unfair dismissal. It seems to us that that conclusion is wrong. It would rather, as we would prefer to put it, be a consequence of the dismissal of a man who, at the time of his dismissal, and indeed during his employment, had been in a state of ill-health. In other words, it seems to us, generally speaking at least, that, when looking to see what loss has been sustained in consequence of the dismissal, one does not, as in effect this industrial tribunal has said one does, ignore, or put on one side, the personal characteristics of the dismissed employee. Accordingly, in our judgment, the industrial tribunal came to a wrong conclusion on this point. It came to a wrong conclusion upon it because its members misconstrued paragraph 19 (1) of Schedule 1. That appears to us to be an error of law.

It is necessary to say a word or two more about the construction of paragraph 19 (1). There are three effective limbs which go to the assessment of compensation. Taking it in the order in which it is stated, first of all it must be an amount which is just and equitable. In a way, it would have been better if that had been stated at the end, rather than at

A the beginning, because, as we see it, it is that requirement which entitles
the industrial tribunal, having considered the matter, and all other relevant
circumstances, to moderate the figure to which arithmetic alone might lead
in arriving at a total which in their view is just and equitable. Secondly,
the compensation is to have regard to the loss sustained by the applicant
in consequence of the dismissal. Thirdly, that compensation is to be
limited in as much as no account is to be taken of loss which is not attri-
B butable to action taken by or on behalf of the employer. It is quite clear,
as a matter of construction, that a loss, in order to be considered in terms
of the last phrase of paragraph 19 (1)—that is to say, in order for it to be
considered whether it was attributable to action taken by or on behalf of
the employer—must be a loss sustained by the applicant in consequence of
the dismissal. In other words, paraphrasing it, one does not get to the last
C phrase of paragraph 19 (1) unless one has already fallen within the words
in the preceding phrase. The importance of that seems to us to be this:
the question in this case is not so much, finally, whether the loss here sus-
tained by the employee, namely, his prolonged unemployment, was in
consequence of the dismissal, as quite obviously in our view it was; the
question is whether, although it was, it has to be in whole or in part dis-
regarded as being not attributable to action taken by the employers. It
D seems to us that it *was* attributable to action taken by the employers in as
much as they unfairly dismissed an employee who, at the date of his
dismissal and before, was elderly and in poor health. It seems to us,
without trying in any way to limit the ambit of the last words of paragraph
19 (1), but merely to illustrate it by example, that the words are aimed at
the kind of supervening, unforeseeable event, as illustrated by Mr. Barnard,
E for example, when he suggested that if an employee, who had previously
been in good health, as a result of his dismissal had a nervous breakdown,
and consequently was unemployed for an unforeseeably long period. We
say at once that we are not deciding that case; it will be decided if and when
it arises. But one can see it might well be arguable that, there, it could be
said that the loss, in the sense of the extended period of unemployment,
was not attributable to action taken by or on behalf of the employer.
F Accordingly, in our judgment, the tribunal was in error here on a point
of law.

It remains only to mention two matters, before coming to the form of
the order which we should make. The first is that if, as it follows from
our judgment we believe is the case, it is right, ordinarily at all events,
for the tribunal to take into account the personal characteristics of the
G employee in so far as they existed both before and after the dismissal (in
this case, ill-health), it must be right to bring them into both sides of
the account. From the point of view of the employee, there will be an
extended period of unemployment. From the point of view of the em-
ployers, there will be the possibility that he might in any event have lost
his employment, otherwise than by unfair dismissal, as a result of his
ill-health.

H The second point we would make is this. This case will no doubt be
of importance in other cases. Sometimes, cases are relied on as being
authority for propositions other than that which was intended at the time
the judgment was given. We would say that we mean, by what we have
said, no more than that in our judgment the industrial tribunal, in assess-
ing the compensation, ought to take into account, as one of the circum-
stances, the personal characteristics of the person dismissed, provided they
existed at the date of dismissal, i.e., usually, during the period of employ-

ment; and, we stress this, it is entirely a matter for them, in discharging their function under paragraph 19, to determine what weight should be given to that factor in deciding the amount of compensation which in their judgment is just and equitable in all the circumstances. We should deprecate this judgment being used as authority for the proposition that what we have said authorises, or even enjoins, some particular type of arithmetical calculation. We merely say that these are part of the circumstances which ought to be taken into account under paragraph 19.

It follows that as, in our judgment, there is an error of law on this one point, the appeal must be allowed. It is impossible for us, because we have not the material and we cannot re-hear the case, to assess the compensation. It seems, as at present advised, that all we can do is to order the case to be re-heard on the issue of compensation by, subject to any argument on the point, the same industrial tribunal, if available. We would certainly urge and encourage the parties, if at all possible, to see if they cannot reach agreement. Nothing would be less satisfactory, after this long period of time, than for there to be a long, protracted episode of litigation. It ought to be easy enough, one would have thought, to determine the correct figure. It may also be that some question will arise, if, unhappily, a further hearing is necessary, as to precisely what material is properly to be considered as being in issue before the industrial tribunal—for example, over what period of time are they to range their consideration? If there is any further argument on that, we should be pleased to listen and, if necessary, give directions; or the parties might prefer to work it out for themselves.

Appeal allowed.

Solicitors: *Simpson, Millar; Kenneth Brown, Baker, Baker.*

J. W.

[EMPLOYMENT APPEAL TRIBUNAL]

* DUGDALE AND OTHERS *v.* KRAFT FOODS LTD.

1976 Oct. 11; 28 — Phillips J., Mr. J. G. C. Milligan and Ms. P. Smith

Discrimination—Sex—Equal pay—Differences of practical importance—Women engaged on " broadly similar " work to men save for Sunday and night shift working—Whether " differences . . . of practical importance " in relation to terms and conditions of employment—Equal Pay Act 1970 (*c.* 41), *ss.* 1 (4), 2 (1) (*as amended by Sex Discrimination Act* 1975 (*c.* 65), *s.* 8, *Sch.* 1, *para.* 2)

The appellants, women quality control workers at the employers' food processing factory, earned a lower basic wage than six male quality control inspectors at the same factory. The appellants and the men worked in shifts and were paid a shift allowance but the women did not work the night shift, which was compulsory for the men and for which a greater shift allowance was paid, nor did they work every third Sunday morning as the men were able to do and in fact did so work. On a complaint by the appellants, pursuant to section 2 (1) of

A the Equal Pay Act 1970,[1] claiming equal pay with the men, an industrial tribunal found that, although the men worked in a different department, their work required greater versatility and they were required to do more and heavier lifting than the appellants, those were not differences of practical importance within the meaning of section 1 (4) of the Act of 1970; but that the fact that the male quality control inspectors worked a Sunday morning shift and compulsory night shifts and the B appellants did not were differences such as to negative any alleged similarity between the appellants' work and that of the men. The tribunal held that the appellants were not, therefore, entitled to equal pay with the men.

On appeal:—

Held, allowing the appeal, that having regard to the work done by the appellants and that done by the male quality control inspectors, it was clear that the appellants' work was of C a broadly similar nature to that of the men, within the meaning of section 1 (4) of the Equal Pay Act 1970; that the mere time at which the work was performed should be disregarded when considering whether the differences between the things which the appellants did and the things which the men did were of practical importance in relation to terms and conditions of employment, in accordance with section 1 (4), but that the industrial tribunal ought to have considered the nature of the D work done on Sundays and on night shifts when considering whether the differences were of practical importance; and that therefore the case should be remitted to an industrial tribunal for a rehearing.

Johnson v. *Nottinghamshire Combined Police Authority* [1974] 1 W.L.R. 358, C.A. considered.

Per curiam. It is highly desirable that, in any cases where particular use is made by an industrial tribunal of the know- E ledge or experience of one or more of their members in reaching their decision, that fact should be stated and that particulars of the matter taken into account should be fully disclosed (post, p. 1295B).

The following case is referred to in the judgment:

Johnson v. *Nottinghamshire Combined Police Authority* [1974] 1 W.L.R. 358; [1974] I.C.R. 170; [1974] 1 All E.R. 1082, C.A.

F

No additional cases were cited in argument.

APPEALS from an industrial tribunal sitting at Liverpool.

The appellants, Mrs. Alice Dugdale, Miss Gray, Mrs. Wellens, Mrs. Roache and Mrs. Owen, who were quality control workers, appealed from

G

[1] Equal Pay Act 1970, as amended, s. 1: "(1) If the terms of a contract under which a woman is employed at an establishment in Great Britain do not include . . . an equality clause they shall be deemed to include one. (2) An equality clause is a provision which relates to terms (whether concerned with pay or not) of a contract under which a woman is employed . . . and has the effect that —(*a*) where the woman is employed on like work with a man in the same employment—(i) if (apart from the equality clause) any term of the woman's contract is or becomes less favourable to the woman than a term of a similar kind in the contract under which that man is employed, that term of the woman's contract shall H be treated as so modified as not to be less favourable . . . (4) A woman is to be regarded as employed on like work with men if, but only if, her work and theirs is of the same or a broadly similar nature, and the differences (if any) between the things she does and the things they do are not of practical importance in relation to terms and conditions of employment; and accordingly in comparing her work with theirs regard shall be had to the frequency or otherwise with which any such differences occur in practice as well as to the nature and extent of the differences."

S. 2: "(1) Any claim in respect of the contravention of a term modified or included by virtue of an equality clause, including a claim for arrears of remuneration or damages in respect of the contravention, may be presented by way of a complaint to an industrial tribunal."

a decision of the industrial tribunal on April 20, 1976, dismissing their A
applications under the Equal Pay Act 1970, as amended by the Sex
Discrimination Act 1975, for equal pay with six male quality control
inspectors also employed by the respondents, Kraft Foods Ltd. They
appealed on the ground that the tribunal had misdirected themselves in
holding that the working of Sunday overtime and night shifts by the men
and not by the women was a difference of practical importance within the
meaning of section 1 (4) of the Act of 1970. B

On October 11, 1976, the Employment Appeal Tribunal allowed the
appeals but reserved their reasons.

The facts are stated in the judgment.

John Hand for the appellants.
James Hammond for the employers. C

Cur. adv. vult.

October 28. PHILLIPS J. read the following judgment of the appeal
tribunal. These are five appeals, heard together by consent, from a decision
of an industrial tribunal sitting at Liverpool on April 5, 1976, entered on
April 20, 1976, dismissing applications under the Equal Pay Act 1970, as
amended by the Sex Discrimination Act 1975. On October 11, 1976, we D
allowed the appeals, set aside the decision of the industrial tribunal and
remitted the cases to be reheard by the same industrial tribunal or as
might be directed by the regional chairman of industrial tribunals. We
now give the reasons for our decision.

Each of the appellants was employed in the quality control department
of Kraft Foods Ltd., the employers, and the work which each of them did E
(which was not identical) was typical of that done by a number of other
employees. Mrs. Dugdale was a quality control inspector grade II, Miss
Gray was a senior line-up inspector grade I, Mrs. Wellens was a weight
control assistant grade III, Mrs. Roache was a finished produce laboratory
assistant (or analyst) grade I, and Mrs. Owen was a junior analyst grade
III. For the purposes of their applications the appellants compared the
work done by each of them with the work done by the male quality F
control inspectors, of whom there were six. The industrial tribunal has
set out the reasons for their decision fully and clearly.

Amongst the exhibits put in at the hearing were various job descriptions,
including A. 1 job description—quality control inspector (female), A. 2 job
description—quality control inspector (male) and A. 3 job description—
quality control inspector (male)—night shift. From these job descriptions, G
the other exhibits, and the evidence given, it was easy to see what work
each of the appellants and the six male quality control inspectors did. It
is obvious from the reference in the heading to certain of these job
descriptions, which refer to "male" or "female," that they came into
existence at a time when it was permissible to discriminate in that way.
It might be thought that they thus tend to support the view that the work
(and remuneration) was deliberately arranged in a manner to discriminate H
between men and women. That fact, of course, is not enough to enable
the appellants to succeed; in order to do that they must show that they
come within the provisions of the Act of 1970.

Exhibit R. 1 sets out certain wage scales which were in operation at
the material time. In some respects the details were difficult to follow,
and for this reason we made an exception to our normal practice and
received evidence to explain them. Item 4 of the exhibit, headed "Labora-

A tory," sets out the basic wage rate for male staff and shows that a man aged over 19, employed for two years, received a basic wage of £42·45. Included in this scale were the six male quality control inspectors. The male quality control inspectors were employed on a three-shift system, changing weekly so that each would work a night shift once every three weeks. Item 6 sets out under the heading "Shift Allowances" the remuneration payable in respect of the shift worked. For either the morning or afternoon shift
B £5·80 would be paid, and for the night shift £11·60. Thus a male quality control inspector working the morning or afternoon shift would receive £42·45 plus £5·80. The female staff, including the appellants, employed in the quality control department were employed on a two-shift system, and the details of their remuneration is set out at item 4 under the heading "Laboratory—Shifts (37½ p.w.)." It will be seen that, unlike the male
C quality control inspectors, the female workers in this department were graded into three grades, I, II and III. Thus a grade II female worker would be paid £30·80 after one year. She would receive similar shift allowances—i.e. £5·80 per shift worked. The female workers in the quality control department did not work on the night shift. Thus, at this time, the difference in remuneration between a male quality control inspector and a grade I female worker in the quality control department was £42·45
D minus £32·80, equals £9·65. The male quality control inspectors, unlike the female workers, in the quality control department also worked a Sunday morning shift once every three weeks. Work by the male quality control inspectors on the night shift was compulsory, but work by them on the Sunday morning shift was voluntary, though they all in fact did work on Sundays. It would have been unlawful for the female workers in the
E quality control department to have worked on the night shift or upon the Sunday morning shift: see section 93 of the Factories Act 1961. The employers had not applied for an exemption from this prohibition.

In accordance with the provisions of section 1 (1) of the Equal Pay Act 1970 (as amended) the appellants' contracts of employment are deemed to include an equality clause. The question is whether the equality clause in the circumstances of the case has effect as provided in section 1 (2). It
F was not suggested that this case fell within paragraph (*b*) of that subsection, for there had been no evaluation study. Accordingly, the question was whether the appellants were employed on "like work" with the male quality control inspectors, being men in the same employment, as defined in subsection (6). The answer turns upon the application of section 1 (4) to the facts of the case.

G The first step is to determine whether the work done by the appellants and that done by the male quality control inspectors was of the same or a broadly similar nature. The industrial tribunal did not answer this question in terms, but it seems to us to be clear that the answer, certainly in the case of Mrs. Dugdale, and very probably in the case of the other appellants, is that her work and the men's work was of at least a broadly similar nature. The question then is whether the difference between the things
H which she did and the things which they did are of practical importance in relation to terms and conditions of employment. The industrial tribunal found that they were. It is necessary to look a little carefully at the way in which they reached this conclusion.

The industrial tribunal, in considering the application of section 1 (4), first considered in detail the case of Mrs. Dugdale, being inclined to the view that if she could not succeed nor could the other appellants. In the view of the industrial tribunal the fact that the appellants and the male quality control inspectors worked in different departments was not of much significance, nor did they accept the argument that the work done by the male quality control inspectors required significantly greater versatility. They further regarded as unimportant the fact that the male quality control inspectors did more and heavier lifting than the appellants, and that on the morning shift the male quality control inspectors took the place of the raw material technician and in his absence were responsible for drawing off and testing samples. However, they took a different view of the fact that on the Sunday morning shift the male quality control inspectors did pre-production overtime, carrying out laboratory analysis tests.

It appears, however, from the subsequent paragraphs of the decision that the industrial tribunal were doubtful whether this difference between the work done by the male quality control inspectors and that done by the appellants was by itself alone sufficient to defeat the appellants' claim. But they did say in paragraph 12:

> "We take the view that if there is a difference between the man's job and the woman's job which, even if it occurs relatively infrequently, nevertheless arises from statutory prohibitions, and is in respect of work which is vital to the employer, then it cannot be said to be 'not of practical importance,' and therefore it would negative the alleged broad similarity between their jobs."

Nonetheless it appears that the industrial tribunal would not have found against the appellants—or, at least, might not have done—but for the importance which they attached to the night shift working. They point out in paragraph 13 that the appellants could not do night work. They say that there is only one relatively small production line operating at that time, but add that the night time is used for the absolutely essential cleaning operations. They continue in paragraphs 13 and 14:

> "the fact that the female applicants do not, and as things stand, cannot do night work represents a substantial dissimilarity between their respective work and that of the male quality control inspectors whom they put forward as doing broadly similar work. . . . This night working every third week is, in our view a substantial element of difference which is of practical importance and which negatives any argument that the work of the female and the male quality control inspectors is broadly similar. . . . We find therefore against all the appellants, irrespective of other matters, on the basis that the work of the male quality control inspectors includes, as a normal part of their job, Sunday overtime and night working which are essential to the employers and which the appellants, in the absence of any exemption from statutory prohibitions, cannot do. This of itself is a difference of such practical importance in relation to terms and conditions of employment as to negative any alleged broad similarity between the appellants' work and that of the male quality control inspectors."

To summarise: it seems to us on the admitted facts to be clear that the appellants' work (or certainly Mrs. Dugdale's) and that of the male quality control inspectors was of the same or a broadly similar nature, and that the question, then, was whether the differences between the things which the appellants did and the things which they did were of practical importance in relation to terms and conditions of employment. This involves

A a consideration of two separate matters: (1) the fact that the male quality control inspectors unlike the appellants worked at night and on Sunday morning, and (2) the nature of the work which they did on those occasions. It is not clear to us that the industrial tribunal in reaching its decision distinguished between these two matters.

It appears to us to be necessary to decide, as a matter of the construction of section 1 (4), whether the first of these matters, i.e. the fact of
B doing work at a different time, falls within the words "the things she does and the things they do." To simplify the question by an example: take a factory in which a simple repetitive process of assembly takes place, employing men and women engaged upon identical work. Suppose that the men did, but the women did not, work at night and on a Sunday morning doing the same work. Undoubtedly, the women's work and the
C men's work would be of the same or a broadly similar nature. Prima facie, therefore, they would be employed on "like work." Does the fact that the men work at night and on Sunday morning, and the women do not, constitute a difference between the things which the women do and the things which the men do? It may be that either view is possible. A man, if asked what he does, might reply, "I assemble radio components," or he might reply, "I assemble radio components on the night shift."
D We have come to the conclusion that, in the context of the Equal Pay Act 1970 (as amended), the mere time at which the work is performed should be disregarded when considering the differences between the things which the woman does and the things which the man does. Were it not so, the Act could never apply in cases where it must obviously have been intended to apply, where the men doing the same work are engaged on a night shift.

E Some support for this view is to be obtained from the judgments of the Court of Appeal in *Johnson* v. *Nottinghamshire Combined Police Authority* [1974] 1 W.L.R. 358. That was the case of a claim for a redundancy payment. Women clerks were dismissed because they were, for good reason, unwilling to change from ordinary day work to an alternating shift system. The work which they had done was substantially the same as the work which was done by their replacements. The only difference
F was in the hours worked. In order to succeed it had to be established that the requirement of the employers for employees to carry out work of a particular kind had diminished. The Court of Appeal held that the change in the hours of working, without any change in the tasks performed, did not effect a change in the particular kind of work. Certainly, that case is not directly applicable, and it is true that it depends in part on the
G reference in section 1 of the Redundancy Payments Act 1965 to the place of employment. But it seems to us to be generally in line with our thinking on the subject. In short, in our judgment, in applying section 1 (4) no attention should be paid to the fact that the men work at some different time of the day, if that is the only difference between what the women do and they do.

It does not seem to us that this interpretation of section 1 (4) would
H lead to any unfairness; rather the reverse. Where the work done is the same, and the only difference is the time at which it is done, the men will be compensated for the extra burden of working at night or on Sundays by the shift payment or premium. There seems to be no reason why the women should not have equality of treatment in respect of the basic wage, or in respect of the day shift payment, if any. In a case in which the men are not paid a shift payment or premium for night working or Sunday working, but are paid at an enhanced basic wage to reflect their readiness

to work at nights or on Sundays, there seems to us to be no reason why, A in giving effect to the equality clause in accordance with section 1 (2) (*a*) (i), the terms in the women's contracts as to remuneration should not be so modified as to take account of the fact that the men do, and they do not, work at nights or on Sunday. It should be emphasised that the equality clause is to have effect so as to modify any less favourable term of the women's contracts so as to be not less favourable, i.e. it need not produce equality if, though they are engaged on "like work," the payment to the B men includes remuneration for something affecting the men but not the women, such as working at night.

Turning to the facts of this case, it is thus necessary, in deciding whether the differences between the things which the appellants do and the things which the male quality control inspectors do are of practical importance in relation to terms and conditions of employment, to disregard the fact C that the men do, and the appellants do not, work at nights and on Sunday mornings. In answering the question attention must be confined to the work which they do. It is not clear to us from an examination of the industrial tribunal's reasons what conclusion they would have reached if they had approached the matter in this way, because they have considered the two matters simultaneously; that is, the fact of the men working at a different time from the women and the nature of the work done by the D men on those occasions. Accordingly, in our judgment it is necessary that the case be remitted to the industrial tribunal, or, in the event of difficulty over the availability of the members, to such other industrial tribunal as the regional chairman may determine. We think it desirable that there should be a rehearing.

For clarity, we would add that our decision applies in the case of all E the appeals. Paragraph 16 of the reasons might be read so as to suggest that the industrial tribunal would have rejected the applications other than that of Mrs. Dugdale even if the male quality control inspectors had not done additional work at night and on Sunday mornings; but this view seems to be contradicted by the terms of paragraph 15. In the circumstances, it seems to us that the fair thing is for all the appeals to be reheard. It is desirable in decisions upon applications under the Equal F Pay Act 1970, if different verdicts are given in different cases, for the industrial tribunal in their reasons to summarise separately the relevant facts and considerations applicable to each case.

It is necessary to note this one final matter. At the end of paragraph 10 of the reasons the industrial tribunal say:

> "In this matter, as in many other aspects of our decision, our G unanimous view is reinforced by the invaluable shop floor experience of our lady member who works in a similar food manufacturing industry to that of the [employers]."

It is suggested that this indicates a wrong approach, and that the decision is based on evidence improperly obtained. The members of industrial tribunals are appointed because of their special knowledge and H experience, and we have no doubt that they are entitled to draw upon it in playing their part in assisting the tribunal as a whole to reach a decision. The main use which they will make of this knowledge and experience is for the purpose of explaining and understanding the evidence which they hear. Certainly, they are entitled to use their knowledge and experience to fill gaps in the evidence about matters which will be obvious to them but which might be obscure to a layman. More difficult is the case where

A evidence is given which is contrary to their knowledge and experience. If such an occasion arises, we think that they ought to draw to the attention of the witnesses the experience which seems to them to suggest that the evidence given is wrong, and ought not to prefer their own knowledge or experience without giving the witnesses an opportunity to deal with it. Provided that this opportunity is given there seems to us to be no reason why they should not draw on their own knowledge and experience in this
B way also. But it is highly desirable that in any case where particular use is made by an industrial tribunal of the knowledge or experience of one or more of their members in reaching their decision this fact should be stated, and that particulars of the matter taken into account should be fully disclosed.

Appeal allowed.
C *Case remitted to industrial tribunal for rehearing.*

Solicitors: *Rowleys & Blewitts, Manchester; Walker, Smith & Way, Chester.*

J. W.

D

[COURT OF APPEAL]

* TRELOAR *v.* NUTE

E

1976 June 8, 9; July 7

Stamp and Ormrod L.JJ and Sir John Pennycuick

Limitation of Action—Land, recovery of—Possessory title—Disputed land adjoining defendant's land derelict—Owner not intending to use it for any particular purpose in future—
F *Possession and user of land for* 12 *years—Whether inconvenience to owner necessary requirement of adverse possession —Limitation Act* 1939 (2 & 3 *Geo.* 6, *c.* 21), *s.* 10 (1) [1]

The plaintiff was the freehold owner of land of which the disputed area, amounting to about one-seventh of an acre, formed part. She had previously used it for her farm but by 1961 it was derelict and, apart from a shed, there were no buildings on it. A gully, about 10 feet wide, ran across
G it. In 1961 the defendant's father bought certain land adjacent to the plaintiff's, believing that the disputed land was included in the purchase. It was included in the subsequent conveyance to him in September 1962. Between the date of the purchase in 1961 and the commencement of the limitation period in September 1972 the defendant's father used the land for grazing animals and placed in the gully soil taken from a well dug on his adjoining land. He also used it for storing timber
H and stone and the defendant and his brother rode motor bicycles upon it. In 1963 the defendant's father erected a fence along the western boundary of the land. The plaintiff protested and removed it but the defendant's father re-erected it. In 1965 the defendant's father conveyed the disputed land

---

[Reported by EMMANUEL C. ABARAONYE, ESQ., Barrister-at-Law]

[1] Limitation Act 1939, s. 10 (1): see post, p. 1300C–D.

to the defendant by way of a gift. In 1966 the plaintiff protested at the dumping of earth on the land. In 1974 the defendant, having completely filled up the gully, started erecting a bungalow on the land. In September 1974 the plaintiff brought an action in the county court claiming an injunction restraining the defendant from trespassing on the disputed land; an order that he should remove all deposits of earth and other materials which he had deposited there; damages for trespass and a declaration that she was the owner in fee simple absolute in possession of the disputed land. There was no evidence as to the purpose for which the plaintiff intended to use the land in the future. Judge Chope gave judgment for the plaintiff holding that although the defendant's father took possession of the land in 1961, the acts done by him on it did not inconvenience the plaintiff and were, therefore, not adverse to her possession. A B

On appeal by the defendant:— C

Held, allowing the appeal, that section 10 (1) of the Limitation Act 1939 defined adverse possession as possession of some person in whose favour the period of limitation could run, and it was not permissible to import into that definition a requirement that the owner had to be inconvenienced or otherwise affected by that possession (post, p. 1302C); that, accepting possession before the commencement of the limitation period and the absence of the plaintiff's intention to put the disputed land to a special purpose, time began to run from such taking of possession irrespective of whether the plaintiff suffered inconvenience from the possession (post, p. 1302E–F); and that accordingly, the defendant acquired a possessory title to the land before the plaintiff brought her action. D

Wallis's Cayton Bay Holiday Camp Ltd. v. *Shell-Mex and B.P. Ltd.* [1975] Q.B. 94, C.A. distinguished. E

The following cases are referred to in the judgment:

Leigh v. *Jack* (1879) 5 Ex.D. 264, C.A.

Littledale v. *Liverpool College* [1900] 1 Ch. 19, C.A.

Lord Advocate v. *Lord Lovat* (1880) 5 App.Cas. 273, H.L.(Sc.).

Tecbild Ltd. v. *Chamberlain* (1969) 20 P. & C.R. 633, C.A.

Wallis's Cayton Bay Holiday Camp Ltd. v. *Shell-Mex and B.P. Ltd.* [1975] Q.B. 94; [1974] 3 W.L.R. 387; [1974] 3 All E.R. 575, C.A. F

Williams Brothers Direct Supply Ltd. v. *Raftery* [1958] 1 Q.B. 159; [1957] 3 W.L.R. 931; [1957] 3 All E.R. 593, C.A.

The following additional cases were cited in argument:

Hughes v. *Griffin* [1969] 1 W.L.R. 23; [1969] 1 All E.R. 460, C.A. G

Smith v. *Stocks* (1869) 38 L.J.Q.B. 306.

APPEAL from Judge Chope at Aldershot and Farnham County Court.

The plaintiff, Mrs. Joanna Treloar, brought an action for, inter alia, an injunction restraining the defendant, E. R. Nute, from trespassing on the land at Halwin Wendron in Cornwall, numbered 2817 on the 1906 edition of the ordinance survey map. She also claimed damages and a declaration that she was the owner in fee simple absolute in possession of the land. Judge Chope entered judgment for the plaintiff and held, inter alia, that since the defendant's acts, although long enough, did not inconvenience the plaintiff over the limitation period, they did not amount to adverse possession. H

The defendant appealed on the grounds that the judge misdirected himself in holding that none of the acts of possession done by the defendant

A and members of his family prior to October 1962 was an act of adverse possession and that the judgment was against the weight of the evidence given to the court.

The facts are stated in the judgment of the court.

The appellant defendant in person.

B *Paul Dunkels* for the plaintiff respondent.

Cur. adv. vult.

July 7. SIR JOHN PENNYCUICK read the following judgment of the court. This is an appeal from an order made on August 5, 1975, by Judge Chope in the Penzance County Court. The plaintiff is Mrs. Joanna C Treloar who claims an injunction restraining trespass by the defendant, Mr. E. R. Nute, upon a small plot of land in the parish of Wendron, Cornwall. The defendant sets up a possessory title. The action was commenced on September 5, 1974, so that the 12-year period of limitation must be treated as running from September 5, 1962. I will refer to this period as the "limitation period." The judge held that the defendant had failed to establish the necessary adverse possession over the limitation D period. The defendant appeals from that decision.

I will state summarily the facts as they appear from the notes of evidence and the judgment. This statement must be read in conjunction with one of the plans based on the ordnance survey which have been put in evidence.

In 1961 the plaintiff, who is now a lady of 80, was the freehold owner E of a number of parcels of land at Halwin in the parish of Wendron. These parcels included a plot numbered 2817 containing ·316 acres lying to the east of the junction of two minor roads. There was some question as to whether the plaintiff herself had a paper title or a possessory title to no. 2817 but the question turned out to have no practical importance since under one or other title she indisputably owned the fee simple of no. 2817 in 1961.

F In 1961 the defendant's father purchased a number of parcels lying to the east of the plaintiff's land. It appears that his purchase and the subsequent conveyance dated September 1962 were expressed to include the eastern part of no. 2817, which in fact belonged to the plaintiff. This part contained very approximately half the area of no. 2817, about one-seventh of an acre. I will refer to this part of no. 2817 as "the disputed G land."

In 1961 the disputed land had some sort of shed in its south-west corner. There was no other building upon it. Across the centre in an arc from west to east ran a broad depression or gully, eight to 10 feet in width. The land had previously been used by the plaintiff in connection with her farm but in 1961 was derelict and was not in use for any purpose. At the time of his purchase in 1961 the defendant's father believed the H disputed land to be included in the purchase.

During the period between the purchase and the commencement of the limitation period in September 1962 the defendant's father and members of the family, including the defendant, did certain acts upon the disputed land, namely, as found by the judge; (i) a couple of cows and a yearling were grazed upon it; (ii) spoil taken from a well dug on land of the defendant's father to the south of the disputed land was placed in the gully, thus partially filling it up; (iii) some unspecified work was done upon the northern boundary; (iv) materials such as timber and stone were A stored upon it; (v) the defendant and his brother rode motor bicycles upon it. Between the defendant's father's purchase in 1961 and the commencement of the limitation period the plaintiff did no acts upon the disputed land.

In the summer of 1963, i.e. after the commencement of the limitation period, the defendant's father erected a fence along the western B boundary of the disputed land. The plaintiff protested by letter dated August 14, 1963, and had the fence removed, The defendant's father re-erected it and it remains in position. In 1965 the defendant's father conveyed the disputed land to the defendant by way of gift. Nothing further seems to have happened between 1963 and 1966, when the plaintiff through her solicitors protested at the dumping of earth on the disputed land. A correspondence ensued in the course of which the defendant C claimed to be the owner of the disputed land. Again the matter was allowed to slide until 1974 when the defendant, having by now completely filled up the gully, set about the erection of a bungalow on the disputed land. The plaintiff did no acts upon the disputed land during the limitation period apart from pulling down the fence in 1963.

On September 3, 1974, after some correspondence, the plaintiff com- D menced the present action. The plaintiff claims:

> "(1) An injunction restraining the defendant from trespassing on the plaintiff's said land as aforesaid or at all. (2) An order that the defendant do forthwith remove all deposits of earth and other materials which he has deposited or brought onto the plaintiff's said land. (3) Damages for trespass limited to £750. (4) A declaration that the plaintiff is the owner in fee simple absolute in possession of the said E property."

The defendant originally relied on ownership under a paper title, but by supplemental defence and counterclaim set up a possessory title.

The action was heard by Judge Chope on August 5, 1975. A considerable part of the evidence was concerned with the paper title to the disputed land which is not now a live issue. There was evidence as to F pulling down and re-erection of the fence in 1963; no reliance was placed on these activities in the argument before us. There was no evidence as to any purpose which the plaintiff may have had in mind with regard to the future use of the disputed land. The defendant and his father and brother, also one Tremayne, gave evidence as to the acts upon the disputed land which we have already summarised. G

We turn next to the notes of judgment. After dealing in an eminently sensible way with the question of title, the judge proceeds as follows:

> "The defendant establishes that his father went into possession in 1961 and the condition of the land was derelict and that in 1961 a couple of cows and yearlings were grazed by the defendant on the disputed land and that some work was done by the defendant to the northern boundary and it is also established that when a well was dug H on the defendant's property on the other side of the road some of the spoil was taken and placed upon the disputed land to fill in a gully in the land. The defendant also establishes that the land was used by himself and his brother for riding motor cycles in 1961 but the defendant and the father and his brother all accept the state of the land as it was and no one putting it to any use at all these acts of grazing cattle and riding motor cycles and storing some materials

A prior to October 1962 these acts would clearly not have inconvenienced
the owner [sic]. In other words they were not acts adverse to possession by the plaintiff. They could have been called acts indicating the defendant in possession but not exclusive and not adverse to the plaintiff's title and therefore I find the plaintiff was at that period the true owner whether or not by the paper title or as the person in possession."

B He goes on to deal with the fence and concludes:

"At the end of the day, the plaintiff has established title before the defendant entered into possession in 1961. Because of the derelict way in which the land has been allowed to remain it is for the defendant to prove adverse possession. By the very reason that it was left
C fallow it was much more difficult for the defendant to show that the
acts were adverse to the plaintiff. That is why the defendant's evidence of acts such as the riding of motor cycles, storage of goods, etc. in my judgment do not amount to possession, adverse to the plaintiff, and she scrambles home as a matter of time simply by virtue of the fact that the defendant's most cogent acts of adverse possession were not over a sufficient period of time."

D The findings in the judgment with regard to possession are in one critical respect unclearly expressed. As we understand these passages, what the judge is saying is that the defendant's father did go into possession in 1961 but that because the acts done by him could not have inconvenienced the plaintiff the acts of possession were not adverse to the plaintiff. I quote again three lines from the judgment:

E "... these acts would clearly not have inconvenienced the owner.
In other words, they were not acts adverse to the possession by the plaintiff. They could have been called acts indicating the defendant in possession but not exclusive and not adverse to the plaintiff's title."

There can be no question of non-exclusive possession in any other sense, e.g. concurrent possession. We proceed on the basis that the judge did
F indeed intend to find that the defendant's father went into possession in
1961. If this was his finding, we see no sufficient ground upon which this court would be justified in setting it aside.

The particular acts found by the judge are we think rather on the borderline of what can properly be regarded as constituting possession, always apart from the consideration of adverse possession. Whether or
G not a person has taken possession of land is a question of fact depending
on all the particular circumstances. The test is well put by Lord O'Hagan in *Lord Advocate* v. *Lord Lovat* (1880) 5 App.Cas. 273 (a case not otherwise in point) in the following words, at p. 288:

"As to possession, it must be considered in every case with reference to the peculiar circumstances. The acts, implying possession in one
H case, may be wholly inadequate to prove it in another. The character
and value of the property, the suitable and natural mode of using it, the course of conduct which the proprietor might reasonably be expected to follow with a due regard to his own interests—all these things, greatly varying as they must, under various conditions, are to be taken into account in determining the sufficiency of a possession."

In the present case the disputed land is extremely small, about one-seventh of an acre and admitted of very limited agricultural use, but would be a

convenient site for a small house or bungalow. The defendant's father A
did put it to some small agricultural use by grazing two cows and a
yearling. Much more important, in our view, is the change in the surface
of the land by placing soil in the gully, thereby setting in train the levelling
of the land upon which a bungalow could be built. It seems to us that
these acts were sufficient to support a finding of possession and indeed on
the material before us we would be disposed to reach the same conclusion. B
The other acts relied upon are of very little weight.

We turn then to the law. We will quote from three sections of the
Limitation Act 1939:

> "4 (3) No action shall be brought by any other person to recover
> any land after the expiration of 12 years from the date on which the
> right of action accrued to him or, if it first accrued to some person
> through whom he claims, to that person. 5 (1) Where the person C
> bringing an action to recover land, or some person through whom he
> claims, has been in possession thereof, and has while entitled thereto
> been dispossessed or discontinued his possession, the right of action
> shall be deemed to have accrued on the date of the dispossession or
> discontinuance. . . . 10 (1) No right of action to recover land shall
> be deemed to accrue unless the land is in the possession of some D
> person in whose favour the period of limitation can run (hereafter
> in this section referred to as 'adverse possession'), and where under
> the foregoing provisions of this Act any such right of action is
> deemed to accrue on a certain date and no person is in adverse pos-
> session on that date, the right of action shall not be deemed to accrue
> unless and until adverse possession is taken of the land."

It is not in doubt that under the Act of 1939 as under the previous E
law, the person claiming by possession must show either (1) discontinuance
by the paper owner followed by possession or (2) dispossession (or as it
is sometimes called "ouster") of the paper owner. Clearly, possession
concurrent with the paper owner is insufficient. On the other hand, where
the person claiming by possession establishes possession in the full sense
of exclusive possession, that by itself connotes absence of possession on F
the part of the paper owner and I doubt if there is any real difference
in the concept of taking possession and the concept of dispossession except
in the special type of case where the owner, although not technically in
possession, has some purpose to which he intends to put the land in the
future. We will refer to this special type of case in a moment.

The law, as we understand it, always apart from that special type of G
case, is that if a squatter takes possession of land belonging to another
and remains in possession for 12 years to the exclusion of the owner that
represents adverse possession and accordingly at the end of the 12 years
the owner's title is extinguished. That is the plain meaning of the statutory
provisions which I have quoted and no authority to the contrary has been
quoted to us. The simple question is, "Did the squatter acquire and
remain in exclusive possession?" H

The literal application of the statutory provisions has been adapted
by this court to meet one special type of case. It sometimes happens that
the owner of a piece of land retains it with a view to its utilisation for some
specific purpose in the future and that meanwhile some other person has
physical possession of it. When that state of affairs exists, the owner is
not treated as dispossessed: see *Leigh* v. *Jack* (1879) 5 Ex.D. 264, where
factory materials were placed upon a strip of land intended by the owner

A to be dedicated as a road; in particular *per* Cockburn C.J., at p. 271 and *per* Bramwell L.J., where the latter said, at p. 273:

> ". . . in order to defeat a title by dispossessing the former owner, acts must be done which are inconsistent with his enjoyment of the soil for the purposes for which he intended to use it: that is not the case here, where the intention of the plaintiff and her predecessors in B title was not either to build upon or to cultivate the land, but to devote it at some future time to public purpose."

See also *Williams Brothers Direct Supply Ltd.* v. *Raftery* [1958] 1 Q.B. 159, where a strip of land intended by the owner for development was used during and after the war for growing vegetables and keeping greyhounds.

The principle was restated and applied by the majority of the Court C of Appeal in the recent case, *Wallis's Cayton Bay Holiday Camp Ltd.* v. *Shell-Mex and B.P. Ltd.* [1975] Q.B. 94. In that case a strip of land was intended by the owner to be the site of a garage which would front upon a projected road, which in fact never materialised, and meanwhile was occupied successively as part of a farm and part of a holiday camp. The Court of Appeal held that the owner had not been dispossessed. Lord D Denning M.R. stated the principle in the following terms, at p. 103:

> "There is a fundamental error in that argument. Possession by itself is not enough to give a title. It must be *adverse* possession. The true owner must have discontinued possession or have been dispossessed and another must have taken it adversely to him. There must be something in the nature of an ouster of the true owner by the wrongful possessor. That is shown by a series of cases in this E court which, on their very facts, show this proposition to be true. When the true owner of land intends to use it for a particular purpose in the future, but meanwhile has no immediate use for it, and so leaves it unoccupied, he does not lose his title to it simply because some other person enters on it and uses it for some temporary purpose, like stacking materials; or for some seasonal purpose, like F growing vegetables. Not even if this temporary or seasonal purpose continues year after year for 12 years, or more: see *Leigh* v. *Jack* (1879) 5 Ex.D. 264; *Williams Brothers Direct Supply Ltd.* v. *Raftery* [1958] 1 Q.B. 159; and *Tecbild Ltd.* v. *Chamberlain* (1969) 20 P. & C.R. 633. The reason is not because the user does not amount to actual possession. The line between acts of user and acts of possession is too fine for words."

G

The subsequent passage has clearly no application to the facts of the present case. Stamp L.J. dissented, holding that upon the facts the case could not be brought within the principle of *Leigh* v. *Jack*. Ormrod L.J. in company with Lord Denning M.R. held that applying the principle of *Leigh* v. *Jack* there was upon the facts no dispossession of the owner. He makes a rather broad statement at p. 114. But the theme of purpose, H i.e. the purpose to which the owner intends to put the land in the future, runs throughout his judgment and we do not read him as saying that in the absence of such purpose there can be no dispossession merely by reason that the owner has no present use for the land. We have referred at length to this case because it was much relied upon by counsel for the plaintiff and although the judge does not specifically mention it we think it is clear that he had it in mind in the critical passage where he refers to the defendant's possession as not being adverse.

A It is worth observing that all these cases were concerned with a narrow strip of land of such a character that the acquisition of a possessory title to it would not fall within the ordinary purview of the statute and the court was clearly anxious not to put too literal a construction upon the words of the statute. The same observation applies to *Littledale* v. *Liverpool College* [1900] 1 Ch. 19, a case distinguishable on other grounds.

B A full statement of the law as it stood before *Wallis's Cayton Bay Holiday Camp Ltd.* v. *Shell-Mex and B.P. Ltd.* will be found in *Preston and Newsom's Limitation of Actions*, 3rd ed. (1953), pp. 88 et seq., and in *Halsbury's Laws of England*, 3rd ed., vol. 24 (1958), pp. 251 et seq.

We return then to the present case. The judge found, as we read his judgment, that the defendant's father took possession of the disputed land outside the limitation period but that this possession was not adverse by reason that it caused no inconvenience to the plaintiff. In our judgment C the second part of this finding is contrary to the plain terms of section 10 of the Act of 1939 which in effect defines adverse possession as possession of some person in whose favour the period of limitation can run. It is not permissible to import into this definition a requirement that the owner must be inconvenienced or otherwise affected by that possession. Apart from the cases relating to special purpose no authority has been cited to us which would support the requirement of inconvenience to the D owner and we are not ourselves aware of any such authority. On the contrary, so far as our own experience goes, the typical instance in which a possessory title is treated as having been acquired is that in which a squatter establishes himself upon a piece of land for which the owner has no use. Indeed, if inconvenience to the owner had to be established it would be difficult indeed ever to acquire a possessory title since the E owner if inconvenienced would be likely to take proceedings.

We conclude that, once it is accepted that the judge found, and could properly find, that the defendant's father took possession of the disputed land before the commencement of the limitation period, and in the absence of any evidence of special purpose on the part of the plaintiff, time began to run from such taking of possession, irrespective of whether the plaintiff suffered inconvenience from the possession, and that the defendant must F be treated as having acquired a possessory title before the commencement of this action.

We think it right to mention that upon the hearing of the appeal the defendant appeared in person and was unable to give us any assistance upon the law. Mr. Dunkels for the plaintiff gave us what help he could but we have been at a considerable disadvantage in deciding an important G and difficult question. We would allow the appeal.

Appeal allowed with costs.
Declaration that defendant was owner and entitled to actual possession of disputed land.

H

Solicitors: *Thrall, Llewellyn & Pearce, Truro.*

END OF VOLUME 1